# MAP PAGES

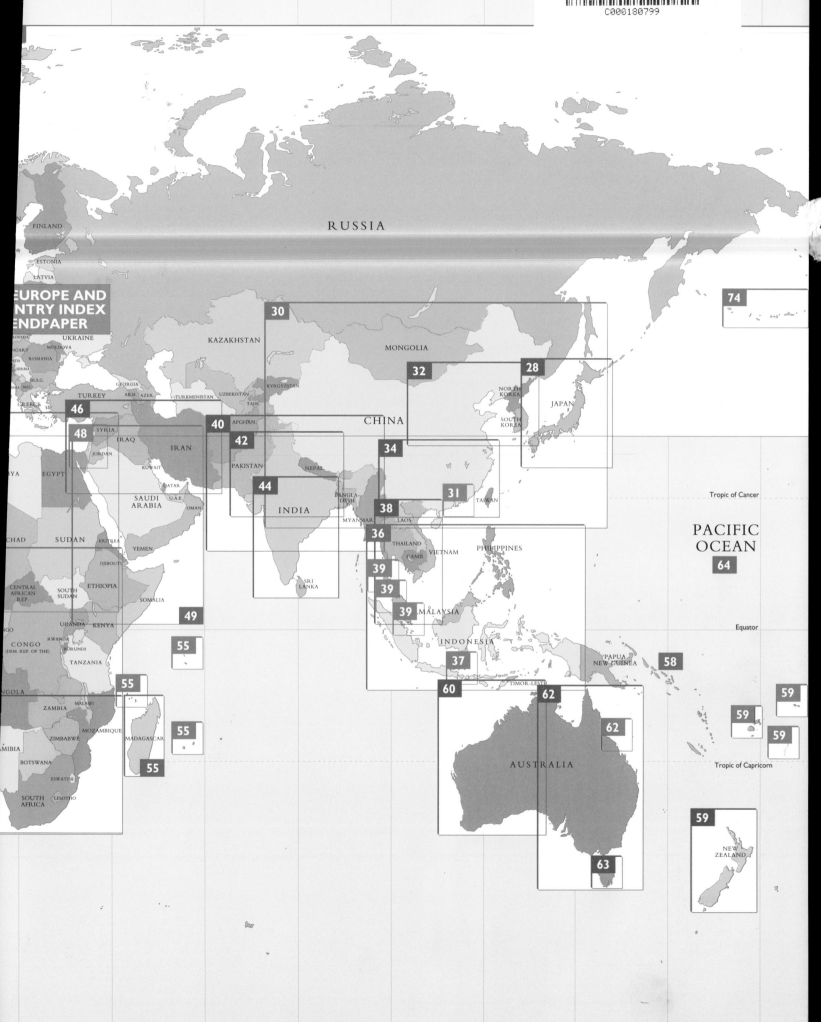

2020 Xmas

To Abbey
with loads of love
from
Grandad + Granny

**PHILIP'S**

# WORLD
# ATLAS

Philip's are grateful to the following for acting as specialist geography consultants on 'The World in Focus' front section:

Professor D. Brunsden, Kings College, University of London, UK
Dr C. Clarke, Oxford University, UK
Dr I. S. Evans, Durham University, UK
Professor P. Haggett, University of Bristol, UK
Professor K. McLachlan, University of London, UK
Professor M. Monmonier, Syracuse University, New York, USA
Professor M-L. Hsu, University of Minnesota, Minnesota, USA
Professor M. J. Tooley, University of St Andrews, UK
Dr T. Unwin, Royal Holloway, University of London, UK

**THE WORLD IN FOCUS**
**Cartography by Philip's**

**Picture Acknowledgements:**
**Cover photography** left, Best View Stock/Alamy Stock Photo; centre, Timothy Hodgkinson/Alamy Stock Photo; right, Siempreverde2/iStock
**Robin Scagell/Galaxy Picture Library** page 3
**Thinkstock**/iStockphoto page 7 (bottom left & bottom right), /Digital Vision page 7 (centre)

**WORLD CITIES**
**Cartography by Philip's**

 Page 11, Edinburgh, and page 15, London:
**This product includes mapping data licensed from Ordnance Survey® with the permission of the Controller of Her Majesty's Stationery Office. © Crown copyright 2019. All rights reserved. Licence number 100011710.**

**All satellite images in this section courtesy of NPA Satellite Mapping, CGG Services (UK) Ltd, Edenbridge, Kent, UK (www.npa.cgg.com).**

Published in Great Britain in 2019 by Philip's,
a division of Octopus Publishing Group Limited
(www.octopusbooks.co.uk)
Carmelite House, 50 Victoria Embankment, London EC4Y 0DZ
An Hachette UK Company (www.hachette.co.uk)

Copyright © 2019 Philip's

Cartography by Philip's

HARDBACK EDITION: ISBN 978–1–84907–517–6
PAPERBACK EDITION: ISBN 978–1–84907–516–9

A CIP catalogue record for this book is available from the British Library.

Printed in Malaysia

Details of other Philip's titles and services can be found on our website at:
**www.philips-maps.co.uk**

**Royal Geographical Society**
with IBG

Advancing geography
and geographical learning

PHILIP'S World Atlases are published in association with THE ROYAL GEOGRAPHICAL SOCIETY (with THE INSTITUTE OF BRITISH GEOGRAPHERS).

The Society was founded in 1830 and given a Royal Charter in 1859 for 'the advancement of geographical science'. It holds historical collections of national and international importance, many of which relate to the Society's association with and support for scientific exploration and research from the 19th century onwards. It was pivotal in establishing geography as a teaching and research discipline in British universities close to the turn of the century, and has played a key role in geographical and environmental education ever since.

Today the Society is a leading world centre for geographical learning – supporting education, teaching, research and expeditions, and promoting public understanding of the subject. The Society welcomes those interested in geography as members. For further information, please visit the website at: **www.rgs.org**

**Royal Geographical Society**
with IBG
Advancing geography
and geographical learning

# Join us!

## Find out more about your world.

Visit our website www.rgs.org/joinus
to join the Society to discover:

● Why is the world changing and what are the consequences?
● Enhance your understanding of the world through Geography
● Be challenged and entertained by great achievers

Royal Geographical Society (with IBG) 1 Kensington Gore London SW7 2AR
☎ +44 (0) 20 7591 3000 📠 +44 (0) 20 7591 3001
Image © NASA

# PHILIP'S

# WORLD ATLAS

**Royal Geographical Society** with IBG

In association with
**The Royal Geographical Society**
with The Institute of British Geographers

# Contents

## World Statistics

| | |
|---|---|
| Countries | vi |
| Physical Dimensions | vii |
| User Guide | viii |

## The World in Focus

| | |
|---|---|
| Planet Earth | 2–3 |
| Restless Earth | 4–5 |
| Landforms | 6–7 |
| Oceans | 8–9 |
| Climate | 10–11 |
| Water and Vegetation | 12–13 |
| Environment | 14–15 |
| Population | 16–17 |
| The Human Family | 18–19 |
| Wealth | 20–21 |
| Quality of Life | 22–23 |
| Energy | 24–25 |
| Production | 26–27 |
| Trade | 28–29 |
| Travel and Tourism | 30–31 |

## World Cities

| | |
|---|---|
| Amsterdam | 2 |
| Athens | 2 |
| Atlanta | 3 |
| Baghdad | 3 |
| Bangkok | 3 |
| Barcelona | 4 |
| Beijing | 4 |
| Berlin | 5 |
| Boston | 6 |
| Brussels | 6 |
| Budapest | 7 |
| Buenos Aires | 7 |
| Cairo | 7 |
| Cape Town | 8 |
| Copenhagen | 8 |
| Chicago | 9 |
| Dallas–Fort Worth | 9 |
| Dubai | 9 |
| Delhi | 10 |
| Edinburgh | 11 |
| Guangzhou (Canton) | 11 |
| Helsinki | 11 |
| Hong Kong | 12 |
| Istanbul | 12 |
| Jakarta | 12 |
| Jerusalem | 13 |
| Johannesburg | 13 |
| Karachi | 13 |
| Kolkata (Calcutta) | 14 |
| Lagos | 14 |
| Las Vegas | 14 |
| Lima | 14 |
| London | 15 |
| Lisbon | 16 |
| Los Angeles | 16 |
| Madrid | 17 |
| Manila | 17 |
| Melbourne | 18 |
| Mexico City | 18 |
| Milan | 18 |
| Miami | 19 |
| Moscow | 19 |
| Montréal | 20 |
| Mumbai (Bombay) | 20 |
| Munich | 21 |
| New Orleans | 21 |
| New York | 22 |
| Orlando | 23 |
| Osaka | 23 |
| Oslo | 23 |
| Paris | 24 |
| Prague | 25 |
| Rio de Janeiro | 25 |
| Rome | 26 |
| San Francisco | 26 |
| St Petersburg | 27 |
| Santiago | 27 |
| São Paulo | 27 |
| Seoul | 27 |
| Shanghai | 28 |
| Singapore | 28 |
| Stockholm | 29 |
| Sydney | 29 |
| Tokyo | 30 |
| Tehran | 31 |
| Toronto | 31 |
| Venice | 32 |
| Vienna | 32 |
| Warsaw | 33 |
| Washington | 33 |
| Index to City Maps | 34–39 |
| World Cities Satellite Images | 40–48 |

## World Maps

| | |
|---|---|
| **Map Symbols** | 1 |
| **The World: Political** 1:95 000 000 | 2–3 |
| **Arctic Ocean** 1:35 000 000 | 4 |
| **Antarctica** 1:35 000 000 | 5 |

## Europe

| | |
|---|---|
| **Europe: Physical** 1:20 000 000 | 6 |
| **Europe: Political** 1:20 000 000 | 7 |
| **Scandinavia** 1:6 000 000 Iceland 1:6 000 000 Færoe Islands 1:6 000 000 | 8–9 |
| **Ireland** 1:2 000 000 | 10 |
| **Scotland** 1:2 000 000 | 11 |
| **England and Wales** 1:2 000 000 | 12–13 |
| **British Isles** 1:5 000 000 | 14 |

| | |
|---|---|
| **Netherlands, Belgium and Luxembourg** 1:2 500 000 | 15 |
| **Central Europe** 1:5 000 000 | 16–17 |
| **Eastern Europe and Turkey** 1:10 000 000 | 18–19 |
| **France** 1:5 000 000 | 20 |
| **Spain and Portugal** 1:5 000 000 | 21 |
| **Italy and the Balkan States** 1:5 000 000 | 22–23 |

## Asia

| | |
|---|---|
| **Asia: Physical** 1:47 000 000 | 24 |
| **Asia: Political** 1:47 000 000 | 25 |
| **Russia and Northern Asia** 1:20 000 000 | 26–27 |
| **Japan** 1:5 000 000 | 28–29 |

| | |
|---|---|
| **China and the Far East** 1:15 000 000 Hong Kong, Macau and Shenzhen 1:1 000 000 | 30–31 |
| **Northern China and Korea** 1:6 000 000 | 32–33 |
| **Southern China** 1:6 000 000 | 34–35 |
| **Indonesia and the Philippines** 1:12 500 000 Java and Madura 1:7 500 000 Bali 1:2 000 000 | 36–37 |
| **Mainland South-east Asia** 1:6 000 000 Ko Phuket 1:1 000 000 Ko Samui 1:1 000 000 Pinang 1:1 000 000 Singapore 1:1 000 000 | 38–39 |
| **South Asia** 1:10 000 000 | 40–41 |
| **Northern India, Pakistan and Nepal** 1:6 000 000 Jammu and Kashmir 1:6 000 000 | 42–43 |

**Southern India and Sri Lanka**
1:6 000 000
Andaman and Nicobar Islands
1:6 000 000

44–45

**The Middle East**
1:7 000 000

46–47

**The Near East**  1:2 500 000

48

**Arabia and the Horn of Africa**  1:15 000 000

49

# Africa

**Africa: Physical**
1:42 000 000                                                50

**Africa: Political**
1:42 000 000                                                51

**Northern Africa**
1:15 000 000
Azores 1:15 000 000
Cape Verde Islands 1:10 000 000

52–53

**Central and Southern Africa**
1:15 000 000
Comoros 1:8 000 000
Seychelles 1:2 500 000
Réunion 1:2 500 000
Mauritius 1:2 500 000
Madagascar 1:15 000 000

54–55

**Southern Africa**
1:8 000 000

56–57

# Australia and Oceania

**Australia and Oceania: Physical and Political**
1:50 000 000                                                58

**New Zealand**  1:6 000 000
Fiji 1:6 000 000
Samoan Islands 1:6 000 000
Tonga 1:6 000 000
Tahiti and Moorea 1:1 000 000

59

**Western Australia**
1:8 000 000

60–61

**Eastern Australia**
1:8 000 000
Torres Strait 1:8 000 000
Whitsunday Islands 1:2 500 000
Tasmania 1:8 000 000

62–63

**Pacific Ocean**
1:54 000 000                                                64–65

# North America

**North America: Physical**
1:35 000 000                                                66

**North America: Political**
1:35 000 000                                                67

**Canada**  1:15 000 000

68–69

**Western Canada**  1:7 000 000

70–71

**Eastern Canada**  1:7 000 000

72–73

**United States**  1:15 000 000
Hawai'i 1:15 000 000
Alaska 1:15 000 000

74–75

**United States – West**
1:6 700 000

76–77

**Central and Southern California and Western Washington**
1:2 500 000

78–79

**United States – Midwest and North-east**
1:6 700 000

80–81

**North-eastern United States**
1:2 500 000

82–83

**United States – South**
1:6 700 000

84–85

**Mexico**  1:8 000 000

86–87

**Central America and the West Indies**  1:8 000 000
Jamaica 1:3 000 000
Guadeloupe 1:2 000 000
Martinique 1:2 000 000
Puerto Rico 1:3 000 000
Virgin Islands 1:2 000 000
St Lucia 1:1 000 000
Barbados 1:1 000 000

88–89

# South America

**South America: Physical**
1:35 000 000                                                90

**South America: Political**
1:35 000 000                                                91

**South America – North**
1:16 000 000
Trinidad and Tobago 1:2 500 000

92–93

**Central South America**
1:8 000 000

94–95

**South America – South**
1:16 000 000

96

# Index to World Maps

97–176

# World Statistics: Countries

This alphabetical list includes the principal countries and territories of the world. If a territory is not completely independent, the country it is associated with is named. The area figures give the total area of land, inland water and ice. The population figures are 2017 estimates where available. The annual income is the Gross Domestic Product per capita (ppp) in US dollars. The figures are the latest available, usually 2017 estimates.

| Country/Territory | Area km² Thousands | Area miles² Thousands | Population Thousands | Capital | Annual Income US $ |
|---|---|---|---|---|---|
| Afghanistan | 652 | 252 | 34,125 | Kabul | 1,900 |
| Albania | 28.7 | 11.1 | 3,048 | Tirana | 12,500 |
| Algeria | 2,382 | 920 | 40,969 | Algiers | 15,100 |
| American Samoa (US) | 0.20 | 0.08 | 52 | Pago Pago | 13,000 |
| Andorra | 0.47 | 0.18 | 86 | Andorra La Vella | 49,900 |
| Angola | 1,247 | 481 | 29,310 | Luanda | 6,800 |
| Anguilla (UK) | 0.10 | 0.04 | 17 | The Valley | 12,200 |
| Antigua & Barbuda | 0.44 | 0.17 | 95 | St John's | 26,300 |
| Argentina | 2,780 | 1,074 | 44,293 | Buenos Aires | 20,700 |
| Armenia | 29.8 | 11.5 | 3,045 | Yerevan | 9,100 |
| Aruba (Netherlands) | 0.19 | 0.07 | 115 | Oranjestad | 25,300 |
| Australia | 7,741 | 2,989 | 23,232 | Canberra | 49,900 |
| Austria | 83.9 | 32.4 | 8,754 | Vienna | 49,200 |
| Azerbaijan | 86.6 | 33.4 | 9,961 | Baku | 17,400 |
| Azores (Portugal) | 2.2 | 0.86 | 246 | Ponta Delgada | 15,197 |
| Bahamas | 13.9 | 5.4 | 330 | Nassau | 25,100 |
| Bahrain | 0.69 | 0.27 | 1,411 | Manama | 51,800 |
| Bangladesh | 144 | 55.6 | 157,827 | Dhaka | 4,200 |
| Barbados | 0.43 | 0.17 | 292 | Bridgetown | 17,500 |
| Belarus | 208 | 80.2 | 9,550 | Minsk | 18,600 |
| Belgium | 30.5 | 11.8 | 11,491 | Brussels | 46,300 |
| Belize | 23.0 | 8.9 | 360 | Belmopan | 8,300 |
| Benin | 113 | 43.5 | 11,039 | Porto-Novo | 2,200 |
| Bermuda (UK) | 0.05 | 0.02 | 71 | Hamilton | 85,700 |
| Bhutan | 47.0 | 18.1 | 758 | Thimphu | 8,700 |
| Bolivia | 1,099 | 424 | 11,138 | La Paz/Sucre | 7,500 |
| Bosnia-Herzegovina | 51.2 | 19.8 | 3,856 | Sarajevo | 11,400 |
| Botswana | 582 | 225 | 2,215 | Gaborone | 18,100 |
| Brazil | 8,514 | 3,287 | 207,353 | Brasília | 15,500 |
| Brunei | 5.8 | 2.2 | 444 | Bandar Seri Begawan | 76,700 |
| Bulgaria | 111 | 42.8 | 7,102 | Sofia | 21,600 |
| Burkina Faso | 274 | 106 | 20,108 | Ouagadougou | 1,900 |
| Burundi | 27.8 | 10.7 | 11,467 | Bujumbura | 800 |
| Cabo Verde | 4.0 | 1.6 | 561 | Praia | 6,900 |
| Cambodia | 181 | 69.9 | 16,204 | Phnom Penh | 4,000 |
| Cameroon | 475 | 184 | 24,995 | Yaoundé | 3,400 |
| Canada | 9,971 | 3,850 | 35,624 | Ottawa | 48,100 |
| Canary Is. (Spain) | 7.2 | 2.8 | 2,105 | Las Palmas/Santa Cruz | 19,900 |
| Cayman Is. (UK) | 0.26 | 0.10 | 58 | George Town | 43,800 |
| Central African Republic | 623 | 241 | 5,625 | Bangui | 700 |
| Chad | 1,284 | 496 | 12,076 | Ndjaména | 2,400 |
| Chile | 757 | 292 | 17,789 | Santiago | 24,600 |
| China | 9,597 | 3,705 | 1,379,303 | Beijing | 16,600 |
| Colombia | 1,139 | 440 | 47,699 | Bogotá | 14,500 |
| Comoros | 2.2 | 0.86 | 808 | Moroni | 1,600 |
| Congo | 342 | 132 | 4,955 | Brazzaville | 6,700 |
| Congo (Dem. Rep. of the) | 2,345 | 905 | 83,301 | Kinshasa | 800 |
| Cook Is. (NZ) | 0.24 | 0.09 | 9 | Avarua | 12,300 |
| Costa Rica | 51.1 | 19.7 | 4,930 | San José | 17,200 |
| Côte d'Ivoire (Ivory Coast) | 322 | 125 | 24,185 | Yamoussoukro | 3,900 |
| Croatia | 56.5 | 21.8 | 4,292 | Zagreb | 24,100 |
| Cuba | 111 | 42.8 | 11,147 | Havana | 11,900 |
| Curaçao (Netherlands) | 0.44 | 0.17 | 150 | Willemstad | 15,000 |
| Cyprus | 9.3 | 3.6 | 1,222 | Nicosia | 36,600 |
| Czechia | 78.9 | 30.5 | 10,675 | Prague | 35,200 |
| Denmark | 43.1 | 16.6 | 5,606 | Copenhagen | 49,600 |
| Djibouti | 23.2 | 9.0 | 865 | Djibouti | 3,600 |
| Dominica | 0.75 | 0.29 | 74 | Roseau | 12,000 |
| Dominican Republic | 48.5 | 18.7 | 10,734 | Santo Domingo | 17,000 |
| Ecuador | 284 | 109 | 16,291 | Quito | 11,000 |
| Egypt | 1,001 | 387 | 97,041 | Cairo | 13,000 |
| El Salvador | 21.0 | 8.1 | 6,172 | San Salvador | 8,900 |
| Equatorial Guinea | 28.1 | 10.8 | 778 | Malabo | 34,900 |
| Eritrea | 118 | 45.4 | 5,919 | Asmara | 1,400 |
| Estonia | 45.1 | 17.4 | 1,252 | Tallinn | 31,500 |
| Eswatini (Swaziland) | 17.4 | 6.7 | 1,467 | Mbabane | 9,900 |
| Ethiopia | 1,104 | 426 | 105,350 | Addis Ababa | 2,100 |
| Falkland Is. (UK) | 12.2 | 4.7 | 3 | Stanley | 96,200 |
| Faroe Is. (Denmark) | 1.4 | 0.54 | 51 | Tórshavn | 40,000 |
| Fiji | 18.3 | 7.1 | 921 | Suva | 9,900 |
| Finland | 338 | 131 | 5,518 | Helsinki | 44,000 |
| France | 552 | 213 | 67,106 | Paris | 43,600 |
| French Guiana (France) | 90.0 | 34.7 | 250 | Cayenne | 8,300 |
| French Polynesia (France) | 4.0 | 1.5 | 281 | Papeete | 17,000 |
| Gabon | 268 | 103 | 1,772 | Libreville | 19,300 |
| Gambia, The | 11.3 | 4.4 | 2,051 | Banjul | 1,700 |
| Georgia | 69.7 | 26.9 | 4,926 | Tbilisi | 10,600 |
| Germany | 357 | 138 | 80,594 | Berlin | 50,200 |
| Ghana | 239 | 92.1 | 27,500 | Accra | 4,600 |
| Gibraltar (UK) | 0.006 | 0.002 | 29 | Gibraltar Town | 61,700 |
| Greece | 132 | 50.9 | 10,768 | Athens | 27,800 |
| Greenland (Denmark) | 2,176 | 840 | 58 | Nuuk | 37,600 |
| Grenada | 0.34 | 0.13 | 112 | St George's | 14,700 |
| Guadeloupe (France) | 1.7 | 0.66 | 402 | Basse-Terre | 7,900 |
| Guam (US) | 0.55 | 0.21 | 167 | Agana | 30,500 |
| Guatemala | 109 | 42.0 | 15,461 | Guatemala City | 8,200 |
| Guinea | 246 | 94.9 | 12,414 | Conakry | 2,000 |
| Guinea-Bissau | 36.1 | 13.9 | 1,792 | Bissau | 1,800 |
| Guyana | 215 | 83.0 | 738 | Georgetown | 8,300 |
| Haiti | 27.8 | 10.7 | 10,647 | Port-au-Prince | 1,800 |
| Honduras | 112 | 43.3 | 9,039 | Tegucigalpa | 5,500 |
| Hungary | 93.0 | 35.9 | 9,851 | Budapest | 28,900 |
| Iceland | 103 | 39.8 | 340 | Reykjavik | 52,100 |
| India | 3,287 | 1,269 | 1,281,936 | New Delhi | 7,200 |
| Indonesia | 1,905 | 735 | 260,581 | Jakarta | 12,400 |
| Iran | 1,648 | 636 | 82,022 | Tehran | 20,000 |
| Iraq | 438 | 169 | 39,192 | Baghdad | 17,000 |
| Ireland | 70.3 | 27.1 | 5,011 | Dublin | 72,600 |
| Israel | 20.6 | 8.0 | 8,300 | Jerusalem | 36,200 |
| Italy | 301 | 116 | 62,138 | Rome | 38,000 |
| Jamaica | 11.0 | 4.2 | 2,991 | Kingston | 9,200 |
| Japan | 378 | 146 | 126,451 | Tokyo | 42,700 |
| Jordan | 89.3 | 34.5 | 10,248 | Amman | 12,500 |
| Kazakhstan | 2,725 | 1,052 | 18,557 | Astana | 26,100 |
| Kenya | 580 | 224 | 47,616 | Nairobi | 3,500 |
| Kiribati | 0.73 | 0.28 | 108 | Tarawa | 1,900 |
| Korea, North | 121 | 46.5 | 25,248 | Pyo'ngyang | 1,700 |
| Korea, South | 99.3 | 38.3 | 51,181 | Seoul | 39,400 |
| Kosovo | 10.9 | 4.2 | 1,895 | Pristina | 10,400 |
| Kuwait | 17.8 | 6.9 | 2,875 | Kuwait City | 69,700 |
| Kyrgyzstan | 200 | 77.2 | 5,789 | Bishkek | 3,700 |
| Laos | 237 | 91.4 | 7,127 | Vientiane | 7,400 |

| Country/Territory | Area km² Thousands | Area miles² Thousands | Population Thousands | Capital | Annual Income US $ |
|---|---|---|---|---|---|
| Latvia | 64.6 | 24.9 | 1,945 | Riga | 27,300 |
| Lebanon | 10.4 | 4.0 | 6,230 | Beirut | 19,500 |
| Lesotho | 30.4 | 11.7 | 1,958 | Maseru | 3,900 |
| Liberia | 111 | 43.0 | 4,689 | Monrovia | 900 |
| Libya | 1,760 | 679 | 6,653 | Tripoli | 9,800 |
| Liechtenstein | 0.16 | 0.06 | 38 | Vaduz | 139,100 |
| Lithuania | 65.2 | 25.2 | 2,824 | Vilnius | 31,900 |
| Luxembourg | 2.6 | 1.0 | 594 | Luxembourg | 109,100 |
| Macedonia (FYROM) | 25.7 | 9.9 | 2,104 | Skopje | 15,200 |
| Madagascar | 587 | 227 | 25,054 | Antananarivo | 1,600 |
| Madeira (Portugal) | 0.78 | 0.30 | 289 | Funchal | 25,800 |
| Malawi | 118 | 45.7 | 19,196 | Lilongwe | 1,200 |
| Malaysia | 330 | 127 | 31,382 | Kuala Lumpur/Putrajaya | 28,900 |
| Maldives | 0.30 | 0.12 | 393 | Malé | 19,200 |
| Mali | 1,240 | 479 | 17,885 | Bamako | 2,200 |
| Malta | 0.32 | 0.12 | 416 | Valletta | 42,500 |
| Marshall Is. | 0.18 | 0.07 | 75 | Majuro | 3,400 |
| Martinique (France) | 1.1 | 0.43 | 371 | Fort-de-France | 14,400 |
| Mauritania | 1,026 | 396 | 3,759 | Nouakchott | 4,500 |
| Mauritius | 2.0 | 0.79 | 1,356 | Port Louis | 21,600 |
| Mayotte (France) | 0.37 | 0.14 | 213 | Mamoudzou | 4,900 |
| Mexico | 1,958 | 756 | 124,575 | Mexico City | 19,500 |
| Micronesia, Fed. States of | 0.70 | 0.27 | 104 | Palikir | 3,400 |
| Moldova | 33.9 | 13.1 | 3,474 | Kishinev | 5,700 |
| Monaco | 0.002 | 0.0008 | 31 | Monaco | 115,700 |
| Mongolia | 1,567 | 605 | 3,068 | Ulan Bator | 12,600 |
| Montenegro | 14.0 | 5.4 | 643 | Podgorica | 17,400 |
| Montserrat (UK) | 0.10 | 0.39 | 5 | Brades | 8,500 |
| Morocco | 447 | 172 | 33,987 | Rabat | 8,600 |
| Mozambique | 802 | 309 | 26,574 | Maputo | 1,300 |
| Myanmar (Burma) | 677 | 261 | 55,124 | Rangoon/Naypyidaw | 6,300 |
| Namibia | 824 | 318 | 2,485 | Windhoek | 11,500 |
| Nauru | 0.02 | 0.008 | 10 | Yaren | 12,200 |
| Nepal | 147 | 56.8 | 29,384 | Katmandu | 2,700 |
| Netherlands | 41.5 | 16.0 | 17,085 | Amsterdam/The Hague | 53,600 |
| New Caledonia (France) | 18.6 | 7.2 | 279 | Nouméa | 31,100 |
| New Zealand | 271 | 104 | 4,510 | Wellington | 38,500 |
| Nicaragua | 130 | 50.2 | 6,026 | Managua | 5,800 |
| Niger | 1,267 | 489 | 19,245 | Niamey | 1,200 |
| Nigeria | 924 | 357 | 190,632 | Abuja | 5,900 |
| Northern Mariana Is. (US) | 0.46 | 0.18 | 52 | Saipan | 13,300 |
| Norway | 324 | 125 | 5,320 | Oslo | 70,600 |
| Oman | 310 | 119 | 3,424 | Muscat | 45,500 |
| Pakistan | 796 | 307 | 204,925 | Islamabad | 5,400 |
| Palau | 0.46 | 0.18 | 21 | Melekeok | 16,700 |
| Panama | 75.5 | 29.2 | 3,753 | Panamá | 24,300 |
| Papua New Guinea | 463 | 179 | 6,910 | Port Moresby | 3,800 |
| Paraguay | 407 | 157 | 6,944 | Asunción | 9,800 |
| Peru | 1,285 | 496 | 31,037 | Lima | 13,300 |
| Philippines | 300 | 116 | 104,256 | Manila | 8,200 |
| Poland | 323 | 125 | 38,476 | Warsaw | 29,300 |
| Portugal | 88.8 | 34.3 | 10,840 | Lisbon | 30,300 |
| Puerto Rico (US) | 8.9 | 3.4 | 3,352 | San Juan | 37,900 |
| Qatar | 11.0 | 4.2 | 2,314 | Doha | 124,900 |
| Réunion (France) | 2.5 | 0.97 | 845 | St-Denis | 6,200 |
| Romania | 238 | 92.0 | 21,530 | Bucharest | 24,000 |
| Russia | 17,075 | 6,593 | 142,258 | Moscow | 27,900 |
| Rwanda | 26.3 | 10.2 | 11,901 | Kigali | 2,100 |
| St Kitts & Nevis | 0.26 | 0.10 | 52 | Basseterre | 26,800 |
| St Lucia | 0.54 | 0.21 | 164 | Castries | 13,500 |
| St Vincent & Grenadines | 0.39 | 0.15 | 102 | Kingstown | 11,600 |
| Samoa | 2.8 | 1.1 | 200 | Apia | 5,700 |
| San Marino | 0.06 | 0.02 | 34 | San Marino | 59,500 |
| São Tomé & Príncipe | 0.96 | 0.37 | 201 | São Tomé | 3,200 |
| Saudi Arabia | 2,150 | 830 | 28,572 | Riyadh | 55,300 |
| Senegal | 197 | 76.0 | 14,669 | Dakar | 2,700 |
| Serbia | 77.5 | 29.9 | 7,111 | Belgrade | 15,200 |
| Seychelles | 0.46 | 0.18 | 94 | Victoria | 28,900 |
| Sierra Leone | 71.7 | 27.7 | 6,163 | Freetown | 1,800 |
| Singapore | 0.68 | 0.26 | 5,889 | Singapore City | 90,500 |
| Slovakia | 49.0 | 18.9 | 5,446 | Bratislava | 32,900 |
| Slovenia | 20.3 | 7.8 | 1,972 | Ljubljana | 34,100 |
| Solomon Is. | 28.9 | 11.2 | 648 | Honiara | 2,100 |
| Somalia | 638 | 246 | 11,031 | Mogadishu | 400 |
| South Africa | 1,221 | 471 | 54,842 | Cape Town/Pretoria | 13,400 |
| Spain | 498 | 192 | 48,958 | Madrid | 38,200 |
| Sri Lanka | 65.6 | 25.3 | 22,409 | Colombo | 13,000 |
| Sudan | 1,886 | 728 | 37,346 | Khartoum | 4,600 |
| Sudan, South | 620 | 239 | 13,026 | Juba | 1,500 |
| Suriname | 163 | 63.0 | 592 | Paramaribo | 13,900 |
| Sweden | 450 | 174 | 9,960 | Stockholm | 51,300 |
| Switzerland | 41.3 | 15.9 | 8,236 | Bern | 61,400 |
| Syria | 185 | 71.5 | 18,029 | Damascus | 2,900 |
| Taiwan | 36.0 | 13.9 | 23,508 | Taipei | 49,800 |
| Tajikistan | 143 | 55.3 | 8,469 | Dushanbe | 3,100 |
| Tanzania | 945 | 365 | 53,951 | Dodoma | 3,300 |
| Thailand | 513 | 198 | 68,414 | Bangkok | 17,800 |
| Timor-Leste | 14.9 | 5.7 | 1,291 | Dili | 5,000 |
| Togo | 56.8 | 21.9 | 7,965 | Lomé | 1,600 |
| Tonga | 0.65 | 0.25 | 106 | Nuku'alofa | 5,600 |
| Trinidad & Tobago | 5.1 | 2.0 | 1,218 | Port of Spain | 31,200 |
| Tunisia | 164 | 63.2 | 11,404 | Tunis | 12,000 |
| Turkey | 775 | 299 | 80,845 | Ankara | 26,500 |
| Turkmenistan | 488 | 188 | 5,351 | Ashkhabad | 18,700 |
| Turks & Caicos Is. (UK) | 0.43 | 0.17 | 53 | Cockburn Town | 29,100 |
| Tuvalu | 0.03 | 0.01 | 11 | Fongafale | 3,800 |
| Uganda | 241 | 93.1 | 39,570 | Kampala | 2,400 |
| Ukraine | 604 | 233 | 44,034 | Kiev | 8,700 |
| United Arab Emirates | 83.6 | 32.3 | 5,927 | Abu Dhabi | 68,200 |
| United Kingdom | 242 | 93.4 | 64,769 | London | 43,600 |
| United States of America | 9,629 | 3,718 | 326,626 | Washington, DC | 59,500 |
| Uruguay | 175 | 67.6 | 3,361 | Montevideo | 22,400 |
| Uzbekistan | 447 | 173 | 29,749 | Tashkent | 7,000 |
| Vanuatu | 12.2 | 4.7 | 283 | Port-Vila | 2,800 |
| Vatican City | 0.0004 | 0.0002 | 1 | Vatican City | |
| Venezuela | 912 | 352 | 31,304 | Caracas | 12,400 |
| Vietnam | 332 | 128 | 96,160 | Hanoi | 6,900 |
| Virgin Is. (UK) | 0.15 | 0.06 | 35 | Road Town | 42,300 |
| Virgin Is. (US) | 0.35 | 0.13 | 107 | Charlotte Amalie | 36,100 |
| Yemen | 528 | 204 | 28,037 | Sana' | 2,300 |
| Zambia | 753 | 291 | 15,972 | Lusaka | 4,000 |
| Zimbabwe | 391 | 151 | 13,805 | Harare | 2,300 |

*OPT 5 Occupied Palestinian Territory

# World Statistics: Physical Dimensions

Each topic list is divided into continents and within a continent the items are listed in order of size. The bottom part of many of the lists is selective in order to give examples from as many different countries as possible. The order of the continents is the same as in the atlas, beginning with Europe and ending with South America. The figures are rounded as appropriate.

## World, Continents, Oceans

| | $km^2$ | $miles^2$ | % |
|---|---|---|---|
| The World | 509,450,000 | 196,672,000 | – |
| Land | 149,450,000 | 57,688,000 | 29.3 |
| Water | 360,000,000 | 138,984,000 | 70.7 |
| | | | |
| Asia | 44,500,000 | 17,177,000 | 29.8 |
| Africa | 30,302,000 | 11,697,000 | 20.3 |
| North America | 24,241,000 | 9,357,000 | 16.2 |
| South America | 17,793,000 | 6,868,000 | 11.9 |
| Antarctica | 14,100,000 | 5,443,000 | 9.4 |
| Europe | 9,957,000 | 3,843,000 | 6.7 |
| Australia & Oceania | 8,557,000 | 3,303,000 | 5.7 |
| | | | |
| Pacific Ocean | 155,557,000 | 60,061,000 | 46.4 |
| Atlantic Ocean | 76,762,000 | 29,638,000 | 22.9 |
| Indian Ocean | 68,556,000 | 26,470,000 | 20.4 |
| Southern Ocean | 20,327,000 | 7,848,000 | 6.1 |
| Arctic Ocean | 14,056,000 | 5,427,000 | 4.2 |

## Ocean Depths

| Atlantic Ocean | m | ft |
|---|---|---|
| Puerto Rico (Milwaukee) Deep | 8,605 | 28,232 |
| Cayman Trench | 7,680 | 25,197 |
| Gulf of Mexico | 5,203 | 17,070 |
| Mediterranean Sea | 5,121 | 16,801 |
| Black Sea | 2,211 | 7,254 |
| North Sea | 660 | 2,165 |

| Indian Ocean | m | ft |
|---|---|---|
| Java Trench | 7,450 | 24,442 |
| Red Sea | 2,635 | 8,454 |

| Pacific Ocean | m | ft |
|---|---|---|
| Mariana Trench | 11,022 | 36,161 |
| Tonga Trench | 10,882 | 35,702 |
| Japan Trench | 10,554 | 34,626 |
| Kuril Trench | 10,542 | 34,587 |

| Arctic Ocean | m | ft |
|---|---|---|
| Molloy Deep | 5,608 | 18,399 |

| Southern Ocean | m | ft |
|---|---|---|
| South Sandwich Trench | 7,235 | 23,737 |

## Mountains

| Europe | | m | ft |
|---|---|---|---|
| Elbrus | *Russia* | 5,642 | 18,510 |
| Dykh-Tau | *Russia* | 5,205 | 17,076 |
| Shkhara | *Russia/Georgia* | 5,201 | 17,064 |
| Koshtan-Tau | *Russia* | 5,152 | 16,903 |
| Kazbek | *Russia/Georgia* | 5,047 | 16,558 |
| Pushkin | *Russia/Georgia* | 5,033 | 16,512 |
| Katyn-Tau | *Russia/Georgia* | 4,979 | 16,335 |
| Shota Rustaveli | *Russia/Georgia* | 4,860 | 15,945 |
| Mont Blanc | *France/Italy* | 4,808 | 15,774 |
| Monte Rosa | *Italy/Switzerland* | 4,634 | 15,203 |
| Dom | *Switzerland* | 4,545 | 14,911 |
| Liskamm | *Switzerland* | 4,527 | 14,852 |
| Weisshorn | *Switzerland* | 4,505 | 14,780 |
| Taschorn | *Switzerland* | 4,490 | 14,730 |
| Matterhorn/Cervino | *Italy/Switzerland* | 4,478 | 14,691 |
| Grossglockner | *Austria* | 3,797 | 12,457 |
| Mulhacén | *Spain* | 3,478 | 11,411 |
| Zugspitze | *Germany* | 2,962 | 9,718 |
| Olympus | *Greece* | 2,917 | 9,570 |
| Galdhøpiggen | *Norway* | 2,469 | 8,100 |
| Ben Nevis | *UK* | 1,345 | 4,411 |

| Asia | | m | ft |
|---|---|---|---|
| Everest | *China/Nepal* | 8,850 | 29,035 |
| K2 (Godwin Austen) | *China/Kashmir* | 8,611 | 28,251 |
| Kanchenjunga | *India/Nepal* | 8,598 | 28,208 |
| Lhotse | *China/Nepal* | 8,516 | 27,939 |
| Makalu | *China/Nepal* | 8,481 | 27,824 |
| Cho Oyu | *China/Nepal* | 8,201 | 26,906 |
| Dhaulagiri | *Nepal* | 8,167 | 26,795 |
| Manaslu | *Nepal* | 8,156 | 26,758 |
| Nanga Parbat | *Kashmir* | 8,126 | 26,660 |
| Annapurna | *Nepal* | 8,078 | 26,502 |
| Gasherbrum | *China/Kashmir* | 8,068 | 26,469 |
| Broad Peak | *China/Kashmir* | 8,051 | 26,414 |
| Xixabangma | *China* | 8,012 | 26,286 |
| Kangbachen | *Nepal* | 7,858 | 25,781 |
| Trivor | *Pakistan* | 7,720 | 25,328 |
| Pik Imeni Ismail Samani | *Tajikistan* | 7,495 | 24,590 |
| Demavend | *Iran* | 5,604 | 18,386 |
| Ararat | *Turkey* | 5,165 | 16,945 |
| Gunong Kinabalu | *Malaysia (Borneo)* | 4,101 | 13,455 |
| Fuji-San | *Japan* | 3,776 | 12,388 |

| Africa | | m | ft |
|---|---|---|---|
| Kilimanjaro | *Tanzania* | 5,895 | 19,340 |
| Mt Kenya | *Kenya* | 5,199 | 17,057 |
| Ruwenzori (Margherita) | *Ug./Congo (D.R.)* | 5,109 | 16,762 |
| Meru | *Tanzania* | 4,565 | 14,977 |
| Ras Dashen | *Ethiopia* | 4,553 | 14,937 |
| Karisimbi | *Rwanda/Congo (D.R.)* | 4,507 | 14,787 |
| Mt Elgon | *Kenya/Uganda* | 4,321 | 14,176 |
| Batu | *Ethiopia* | 4,307 | 14,130 |
| Toubkal | *Morocco* | 4,165 | 13,665 |
| Mt Cameroun | *Cameroon* | 4,070 | 13,353 |

| Oceania | | m | ft |
|---|---|---|---|
| Puncak Jaya | *Indonesia* | 4,884 | 16,024 |
| Puncak Trikora | *Indonesia* | 4,730 | 15,518 |
| Puncak Mandala | *Indonesia* | 4,702 | 15,427 |
| Mt Wilhelm | *Papua New Guinea* | 4,508 | 14,790 |
| Mauna Kea | *USA (Hawai'i)* | 4,205 | 13,796 |
| Mauna Loa | *USA (Hawai'i)* | 4,169 | 13,678 |
| Aoraki Mt Cook | *New Zealand* | 3,724 | 12,218 |
| Mt Kosciuszko | *Australia* | 2,228 | 7,310 |

| North America | | m | ft |
|---|---|---|---|
| Denali (Mt McKinley) | *USA (Alaska)* | 6,168 | 20,237 |
| Mt Logan | *Canada* | 5,959 | 19,551 |
| Pico de Orizaba | *Mexico* | 5,610 | 18,405 |
| Mt St Elias | *USA/Canada* | 5,489 | 18,008 |
| Popocatépetl | *Mexico* | 5,452 | 17,887 |
| Mt Foraker | *USA (Alaska)* | 5,304 | 17,401 |
| Iztaccihuatl | *Mexico* | 5,286 | 17,342 |
| Mt Lucania | *Canada* | 5,226 | 17,146 |
| Mt Steele | *Canada* | 5,073 | 16,644 |
| Mt Bona | *USA (Alaska)* | 5,005 | 16,420 |
| Mt Whitney | *USA* | 4,418 | 14,495 |
| Tajumulco | *Guatemala* | 4,220 | 13,845 |
| Chirripó Grande | *Costa Rica* | 3,837 | 12,589 |
| Pico Duarte | *Dominican Rep.* | 3,175 | 10,417 |

| South America | | m | ft |
|---|---|---|---|
| Aconcagua | *Argentina* | 6,962 | 22,841 |
| Bonete | *Argentina* | 6,872 | 22,546 |
| Ojos del Salado | *Argentina/Chile* | 6,863 | 22,516 |
| Pissis | *Argentina* | 6,779 | 22,241 |
| Mercedario | *Argentina/Chile* | 6,770 | 22,211 |
| Huascarán | *Peru* | 6,768 | 22,204 |
| Llullaillaco | *Argentina/Chile* | 6,723 | 22,057 |
| Nevado de Cachi | *Argentina* | 6,720 | 22,047 |
| Yerupaja | *Peru* | 6,632 | 21,758 |
| Sajama | *Bolivia* | 6,520 | 21,391 |
| Chimborazo | *Ecuador* | 6,267 | 20,561 |
| Pico Cristóbal Colón | *Colombia* | 5,800 | 19,029 |
| Pico Bolivar | *Venezuela* | 5,007 | 16,427 |

| Antarctica | m | ft |
|---|---|---|
| Vinson Massif | 4,897 | 16,066 |
| Mt Kirkpatrick | 4,528 | 14,855 |

## Rivers

| Europe | | km | miles |
|---|---|---|---|
| Volga | *Caspian Sea* | 3,700 | 2,300 |
| Danube | *Black Sea* | 2,850 | 1,770 |
| Ural | *Caspian Sea* | 2,535 | 1,575 |
| Dnieper | *Black Sea* | 2,285 | 1,420 |
| Kama | *Volga* | 2,030 | 1,260 |
| Don | *Black Sea* | 1,990 | 1,240 |
| Petchora | *Arctic Ocean* | 1,790 | 1,110 |
| Oka | *Volga* | 1,480 | 920 |
| Dniester | *Black Sea* | 1,400 | 870 |
| Vyatka | *Kama* | 1,370 | 850 |
| Rhine | *North Sea* | 1,320 | 820 |
| N. Dvina | *Arctic Ocean* | 1,290 | 800 |
| Elbe | *North Sea* | 1,145 | 710 |

| Asia | | km | miles |
|---|---|---|---|
| Yangtse | *Pacific Ocean* | 6,380 | 3,960 |
| Yenisey–Angara | *Arctic Ocean* | 5,550 | 3,445 |
| Huang He | *Pacific Ocean* | 5,464 | 3,395 |
| Ob–Irtysh | *Arctic Ocean* | 5,410 | 3,360 |
| Mekong | *Pacific Ocean* | 4,500 | 2,795 |
| Amur | *Pacific Ocean* | 4,442 | 2,760 |
| Lena | *Arctic Ocean* | 4,402 | 2,735 |
| Irtysh | *Ob* | 4,250 | 2,640 |
| Yenisey | *Arctic Ocean* | 4,090 | 2,540 |
| Ob | *Arctic Ocean* | 3,680 | 2,285 |
| Indus | *Indian Ocean* | 3,100 | 1,925 |
| Brahmaputra | *Indian Ocean* | 2,900 | 1,800 |
| Syrdarya | *Aralkum Desert* | 2,860 | 1,775 |
| Salween | *Indian Ocean* | 2,800 | 1,740 |
| Euphrates | *Indian Ocean* | 2,700 | 1,675 |
| Amudarya | *Aralkum Desert* | 2,540 | 1,575 |

| Africa | | km | miles |
|---|---|---|---|
| Nile | *Mediterranean* | 6,695 | 4,160 |
| Congo | *Atlantic Ocean* | 4,670 | 2,900 |
| Niger | *Atlantic Ocean* | 4,180 | 2,595 |
| Zambezi | *Indian Ocean* | 3,540 | 2,200 |
| Oubangi/Uele | *Congo (D.R.)* | 2,250 | 1,400 |
| Kasai | *Congo (D.R.)* | 1,950 | 1,210 |
| Shaballe | *Indian Ocean* | 1,930 | 1,200 |
| Orange | *Atlantic Ocean* | 1,860 | 1,155 |
| Cubango | *Okavango Delta* | 1,800 | 1,120 |
| Limpopo | *Indian Ocean* | 1,770 | 1,100 |
| Senegal | *Atlantic Ocean* | 1,640 | 1,020 |

| Australia | | km | miles |
|---|---|---|---|
| Murray–Darling | *Southern Ocean* | 3,750 | 2,330 |
| Darling | *Murray* | 3,070 | 1,905 |
| Murray | *Southern Ocean* | 2,575 | 1,600 |
| Murrumbidgee | *Murray* | 1,690 | 1,050 |

| North America | | km | miles |
|---|---|---|---|
| Mississippi–Missouri | *Gulf of Mexico* | 5,971 | 3,710 |
| Mackenzie | *Arctic Ocean* | 4,240 | 2,630 |
| Missouri | *Mississippi* | 4,088 | 2,540 |
| Mississippi | *Gulf of Mexico* | 3,782 | 2,350 |
| Yukon | *Pacific Ocean* | 3,185 | 1,980 |
| Rio Grande | *Gulf of Mexico* | 3,030 | 1,880 |
| Arkansas | *Mississippi* | 2,340 | 1,450 |
| Colorado | *Pacific Ocean* | 2,330 | 1,445 |
| Red | *Mississippi* | 2,040 | 1,270 |
| Columbia | *Pacific Ocean* | 1,950 | 1,210 |
| Saskatchewan | *Lake Winnipeg* | 1,940 | 1,205 |

| South America | | km | miles |
|---|---|---|---|
| Amazon | *Atlantic Ocean* | 6,450 | 4,010 |
| Paraná–Plate | *Atlantic Ocean* | 4,500 | 2,800 |
| Purus | *Amazon* | 3,350 | 2,080 |
| Madeira | *Amazon* | 3,200 | 1,990 |
| São Francisco | *Atlantic Ocean* | 2,900 | 1,800 |
| Paraná | *Plate* | 2,800 | 1,740 |
| Tocantins | *Atlantic Ocean* | 2,750 | 1,710 |
| Orinoco | *Atlantic Ocean* | 2,740 | 1,700 |
| Paraguay | *Paraná* | 2,550 | 1,580 |
| Pilcomayo | *Paraná* | 2,500 | 1,550 |
| Araguaia | *Tocantins* | 2,250 | 1,400 |

## Lakes

| Europe | | $km^2$ | $miles^2$ |
|---|---|---|---|
| Lake Ladoga | *Russia* | 17,700 | 6,800 |
| Lake Onega | *Russia* | 9,700 | 3,700 |
| Saimaa system | *Finland* | 8,000 | 3,100 |
| Vänern | *Sweden* | 5,500 | 2,100 |

| Asia | | $km^2$ | $miles^2$ |
|---|---|---|---|
| Caspian Sea | *Asia* | 371,000 | 143,000 |
| Lake Baikal | *Russia* | 30,500 | 11,780 |
| Tonlé Sap | *Cambodia* | 20,000 | 7,700 |
| Lake Balqash | *Kazakhstan* | 18,500 | 7,100 |
| Aral Sea | *Kazakhstan/Uzbekistan* | 6,800 | 2,620 |

| Africa | | $km^2$ | $miles^2$ |
|---|---|---|---|
| Lake Victoria | *East Africa* | 68,000 | 26,300 |
| Lake Tanganyika | *Central Africa* | 33,000 | 13,000 |
| Lake Malawi/Nyasa | *East Africa* | 29,600 | 11,430 |
| Lake Chad | *Central Africa* | 25,000 | 9,700 |
| Lake Bangweulu | *Zambia* | 9,840 | 3,800 |
| Lake Turkana | *Ethiopia/Kenya* | 8,500 | 3,290 |

| Australia | | $km^2$ | $miles^2$ |
|---|---|---|---|
| Lake Eyre | *Australia* | 8,900 | 3,400 |
| Lake Torrens | *Australia* | 5,800 | 2,200 |
| Lake Gairdner | *Australia* | 4,800 | 1,900 |

| North America | | $km^2$ | $miles^2$ |
|---|---|---|---|
| Lake Superior | *Canada/USA* | 82,350 | 31,800 |
| Lake Huron | *Canada/USA* | 59,600 | 23,010 |
| Lake Michigan | *USA* | 58,000 | 22,400 |
| Great Bear Lake | *Canada* | 31,800 | 12,280 |
| Great Slave Lake | *Canada* | 28,500 | 11,000 |
| Lake Erie | *Canada/USA* | 25,700 | 9,900 |
| Lake Winnipeg | *Canada* | 24,400 | 9,400 |
| Lake Ontario | *Canada/USA* | 19,500 | 7,500 |
| Lake Nicaragua | *Nicaragua* | 8,200 | 3,200 |

| South America | | $km^2$ | $miles^2$ |
|---|---|---|---|
| Lake Titicaca | *Bolivia/Peru* | 8,300 | 3,200 |
| Lake Poopo | *Bolivia* | 2,800 | 1,100 |

## Islands

| Europe | | $km^2$ | $miles^2$ |
|---|---|---|---|
| Great Britain | *UK* | 229,880 | 88,700 |
| Iceland | *Atlantic Ocean* | 103,000 | 39,800 |
| Ireland | *Ireland/UK* | 84,400 | 32,600 |
| Novaya Zemlya (N.) | *Russia* | 48,200 | 18,600 |
| Sicily | *Italy* | 25,500 | 9,800 |
| Corsica | *France* | 8,700 | 3,400 |

| Asia | | $km^2$ | $miles^2$ |
|---|---|---|---|
| Borneo | *Southeast Asia* | 744,360 | 287,400 |
| Sumatra | *Indonesia* | 473,600 | 182,860 |
| Honshu | *Japan* | 230,500 | 88,980 |
| Celebes | *Indonesia* | 189,000 | 73,000 |
| Java | *Indonesia* | 126,700 | 48,900 |
| Luzon | *Philippines* | 104,700 | 40,400 |
| Hokkaido | *Japan* | 78,400 | 30,300 |

| Africa | | $km^2$ | $miles^2$ |
|---|---|---|---|
| Madagascar | *Indian Ocean* | 587,040 | 226,660 |
| Socotra | *Indian Ocean* | 3,600 | 1,400 |
| Réunion | *Indian Ocean* | 2,500 | 965 |

| Oceania | | $km^2$ | $miles^2$ |
|---|---|---|---|
| New Guinea | *Indonesia/Papua NG* | 821,030 | 317,000 |
| New Zealand (S.) | *Pacific Ocean* | 150,500 | 58,100 |
| New Zealand (N.) | *Pacific Ocean* | 114,700 | 44,300 |
| Tasmania | *Australia* | 67,800 | 26,200 |
| Hawai'i | *Pacific Ocean* | 10,450 | 4,000 |

| North America | | $km^2$ | $miles^2$ |
|---|---|---|---|
| Greenland | *Atlantic Ocean* | 2,175,600 | 839,800 |
| Baffin Is. | *Canada* | 508,000 | 196,100 |
| Victoria Is. | *Canada* | 212,200 | 81,900 |
| Ellesmere Is. | *Canada* | 212,000 | 81,800 |
| Cuba | *Caribbean Sea* | 110,860 | 42,800 |
| Hispaniola | *Dominican Rep./Haiti* | 76,200 | 29,400 |
| Jamaica | *Caribbean Sea* | 11,400 | 4,400 |
| Puerto Rico | *Atlantic Ocean* | 8,900 | 3,400 |

| South America | | $km^2$ | $miles^2$ |
|---|---|---|---|
| Tierra del Fuego | *Argentina/Chile* | 47,000 | 18,100 |
| Falkland Is. (E.) | *Atlantic Ocean* | 6,800 | 2,600 |

# User Guide

The reference maps which form the main body of this atlas have been prepared in accordance with the highest standards of international cartography to provide an accurate and detailed representation of the Earth. The scales and projections used have been carefully chosen to give balanced coverage of the world, while emphasizing the most densely populated and economically significant regions. A hallmark of Philip's mapping is the use of hill shading and relief colouring to create a graphic impression of landforms: this makes the maps exceptionally easy to read. However, knowledge of the key features employed in the construction and presentation of the maps will enable the reader to derive the fullest benefit from the atlas.

## Map sequence

The atlas covers the Earth continent by continent: first Europe; then its land neighbour Asia (mapped north before south, in a clockwise sequence), then Africa, Australia and Oceania, North America and South America. This is the classic arrangement adopted by most cartographers since the 16th century. For each continent, there are maps at a variety of scales. First, physical relief and political maps of the whole continent; then a series of larger-scale maps of the regions within the continent, each followed, where required, by still larger-scale maps of the most important or densely populated areas. The governing principle is that by turning the pages of the atlas, the reader moves steadily from north to south through each continent, with each map overlapping its neighbours.

## Map presentation

With very few exceptions (for example, for the Arctic and Antarctica), the maps are drawn with north at the top, regardless of whether they are presented upright or sideways on the page. In the borders will be found the map title; a locator diagram showing the area covered; continuation arrows showing the page numbers for maps of adjacent areas; the scale; the projection used; the degrees of latitude and longitude; and the letters and figures used in the index for locating place names and geographical features. Physical relief maps also have a height reference panel identifying the colours used for each layer of contouring.

## Map symbols

Each map contains a vast amount of detail which can only be conveyed clearly and accurately by the use of symbols. Points and circles of varying sizes locate and identify the relative importance of towns and cities; different styles of type are employed for administrative, geographical and regional place names. A variety of pictorial symbols denote features such as glaciers and marshes, as well as man-made structures including roads, railways, airports and canals.

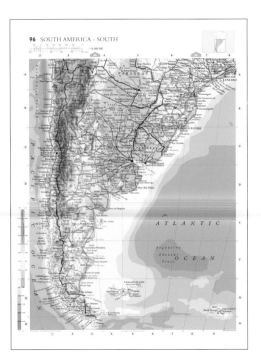

International borders are shown by red lines. Where neighbouring countries are in dispute, for example in the Middle East, the maps show the de facto boundary between nations, regardless of the legal or historical situation. The symbols are explained on the first page of the World Maps section of the atlas.

## Map scales

The scale of each map is given in the numerical form known as the 'representative fraction'. The first figure is always one, signifying one unit of distance on the map; the second figure, usually in millions, is the number by which the map unit must be multiplied to give the equivalent distance on the Earth's surface. Calculations can easily be made in centimetres and kilometres, by dividing the Earth units figure by 100 000 (i.e. deleting the last five 0s). Thus 1:1 000 000 means 1 cm = 10 km. The calculation for inches and miles is more laborious, but 1 000 000 divided by 63 360 (the number of inches in a mile) shows that the ratio 1:1 000 000 means approximately 1 inch = 16 miles. The table below provides distance equivalents for scales down to 1:50 000 000.

| LARGE SCALE | | |
|---|---|---|
| 1:1 000 000 | 1 cm = 10 km | 1 inch = 16 miles |
| 1:2 500 000 | 1 cm = 25 km | 1 inch = 39.5 miles |
| 1:5 000 000 | 1 cm = 50 km | 1 inch = 79 miles |
| 1:6 000 000 | 1 cm = 60 km | 1 inch = 95 miles |
| 1:8 000 000 | 1 cm = 80 km | 1 inch = 126 miles |
| 1:10 000 000 | 1 cm = 100 km | 1 inch = 158 miles |
| 1:15 000 000 | 1 cm = 150 km | 1 inch = 237 miles |
| 1:20 000 000 | 1 cm = 200 km | 1 inch = 316 miles |
| 1:50 000 000 | 1 cm = 500 km | 1 inch = 790 miles |
| SMALL SCALE | | |

## Measuring distances

Although each map is accompanied by a scale bar, distances cannot always be measured with confidence because of the distortions involved in portraying the curved surface of the Earth on a flat page. As a general rule, the larger the map scale (i.e. the lower the number of Earth units in the representative fraction), the more accurate and reliable will be the distance measured. On small-scale maps such as those of the world and of entire continents, measurement may only be accurate along the 'standard parallels', or central axes, and should not be attempted without considering the map projection.

## Latitude and longitude

Accurate positioning of individual points on the Earth's surface is made possible by reference to the geometrical system of latitude and longitude. Latitude *parallels* are drawn west–east around the Earth and numbered by degrees north and south of the Equator, which is designated 0° of latitude. Longitude *meridians* are drawn north–south and numbered by degrees east and west of the *prime meridian*, 0° of longitude, which passes through Greenwich in England. By referring to these co-ordinates and their subdivisions of minutes ($1/60$th of a degree) and seconds ($1/60$th of a minute), any place on Earth can be located to within a few hundred metres. Latitude and longitude are indicated by blue lines on the maps; they are straight or curved according to the projection employed. Reference to these lines is the easiest way of determining the relative positions of places on different maps, and for plotting compass directions.

## Name forms

For ease of reference, both English and local name forms appear in the atlas. Oceans, seas and countries are shown in English throughout the atlas; country names may be abbreviated to their commonly accepted form (for example, Germany, not The Federal Republic of Germany). Conventional English forms are also used for place names on the smaller-scale maps of the continents. However, local name forms are used on all large-scale and regional maps, with the English form given in brackets only for important cities – the large-scale map of Russia and Central Asia thus shows Moskva (Moscow). For countries which do not use a Roman script, place names have been transcribed according to the systems adopted by the British and US Geographic Names Authorities. For China, the Pin Yin system has been used, with some more widely known forms appearing in brackets, as with Beijing (Peking). Both English and local names appear in the index, the English form being cross-referenced to the local form.

# THE WORLD IN FOCUS

| | | | | | |
|---|---|---|---|---|---|
| PLANET EARTH | 2 | WATER AND VEGETATION | 12 | QUALITY OF LIFE | 22 |
| RESTLESS EARTH | 4 | ENVIRONMENT | 14 | ENERGY | 24 |
| LANDFORMS | 6 | POPULATION | 16 | PRODUCTION | 26 |
| OCEANS | 8 | THE HUMAN FAMILY | 18 | TRADE | 28 |
| CLIMATE | 10 | WEALTH | 20 | TRAVEL AND TOURISM | 30 |

# Planet Earth

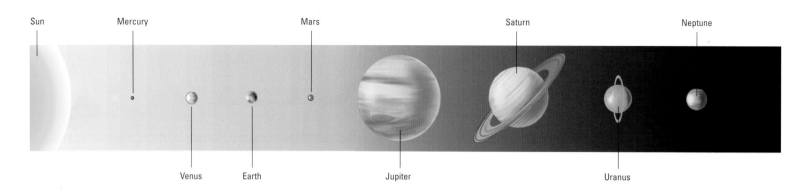

Sun — Mercury — Mars — Saturn — Neptune — Venus — Earth — Jupiter — Uranus

## THE SOLAR SYSTEM

A minute part of one of the billions of galaxies (collections of stars) that populate the Universe, the Solar System lies about 26,000 light-years from the centre of our own Galaxy, the 'Milky Way'. Thought to be about 5 billion years old, it consists of a central Sun with eight planets and their moons revolving around it, attracted by its gravitational pull. The planets orbit the Sun in the same direction – anti-clockwise when viewed from above the Sun's north pole – and almost in the same plane. Their orbital distances, however, vary enormously.

The Sun's diameter is 109 times that of the Earth, and the temperature at its core – caused by continuous thermonuclear fusions of hydrogen into helium – is estimated to be 15 million degrees Celsius. It is the Solar System's source of light and heat.

## PROFILE OF THE PLANETS

|  | Mean distance from Sun (million km) | Mass (Earth = 1) | Period of orbit (Earth days/years) | Period of rotation (Earth days) | Equatorial diameter (km) | Number of known satellites* |
|---|---|---|---|---|---|---|
| Mercury | 57.9 | 0.06 | 87.97 days | 58.65 | 4,879 | 0 |
| Venus | 108.2 | 0.82 | 224.7 days | 243.02 | 12,104 | 0 |
| Earth | 149.6 | 1.00 | 365.3 days | 1.00 | 12,756 | 1 |
| Mars | 227.9 | 0.11 | 687.0 days | 1.029 | 6,792 | 2 |
| Jupiter | 778 | 317.8 | 11.86 years | 0.411 | 142,984 | 67 |
| Saturn | 1,427 | 95.2 | 29.45 years | 0.428 | 120,536 | 62 |
| Uranus | 2,871 | 14.5 | 84.02 years | 0.720 | 51,118 | 27 |
| Neptune | 4,498 | 17.2 | 164.8 years | 0.673 | 49,528 | 14 |

*Number of known satellites at mid-2018*

All planetary orbits are elliptical in form, but only Mercury follows a path that deviates noticeably from a circular one. In 2006, Pluto was demoted from its former status as a planet and is now regarded as a member of the Kuiper Belt of icy bodies at the fringes of the Solar System.

## THE SEASONS

Seasons occur because the Earth's axis is tilted at an angle of approximately 23½°. When the northern hemisphere is tilted to a maximum extent towards the Sun, on 21 June, the Sun is overhead at the Tropic of Cancer (latitude 23½° North). This is midsummer, or the summer solstice, in the northern hemisphere.

On 22 or 23 September, the Sun is overhead at the Equator, and day and night are of equal length throughout the world. This is the autumnal equinox in the northern hemisphere. On 21 or 22 December, the Sun is overhead at the Tropic of Capricorn (23½° South), the winter solstice in the northern hemisphere. The overhead Sun then tracks north until, on 21 March, it is overhead at the Equator. This is the spring (vernal) equinox in the northern hemisphere.

In the southern hemisphere, the seasons are the reverse of those in the north.

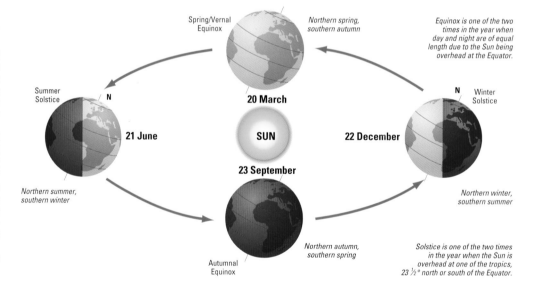

Equinox is one of the two times in the year when day and night are of equal length due to the Sun being overhead at the Equator.

Solstice is one of the two times in the year when the Sun is overhead at one of the tropics, 23 ½° north or south of the Equator.

## DAY AND NIGHT

The Sun appears to rise in the east, reach its highest point at noon, and then set in the west, to be followed by night. In reality, it is not the Sun that is moving but the Earth rotating from west to east. The moment when the Sun's upper limb first appears above the horizon is termed sunrise; the moment when the Sun's upper limb disappears below the horizon is sunset.

At the summer solstice in the northern hemisphere (21 June), the Arctic has total daylight and the Antarctic total darkness. The opposite occurs at the winter solstice (21 or 22 December). At the Equator, the length of day and night are almost equal all year.

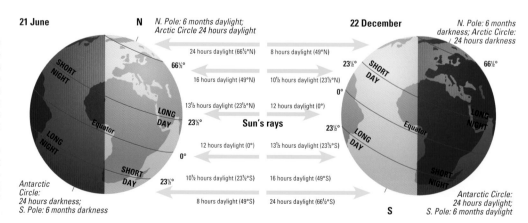

**2**

## TIME

**Year:** The time taken by the Earth to revolve around the Sun, or 365.24 days.

**Leap Year:** A calendar year of 366 days, 29 February being the additional day. It offsets the difference between the calendar and the solar year.

**Month:** The 12 calendar months of the year are approximately equal in length to a lunar month.

**Week:** An artificial period of 7 days, not based on astronomical time.

**Day:** The time taken by the Earth to complete one rotation on its axis.

**Hour:** 24 hours make one day. The day is divided into hours a.m. (ante meridiem or before noon) and p.m. (post meridiem or after noon), although most timetables now use the 24-hour system, from midnight to midnight.

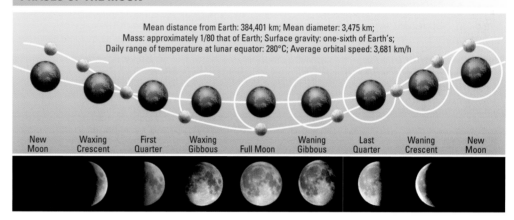

## THE MOON

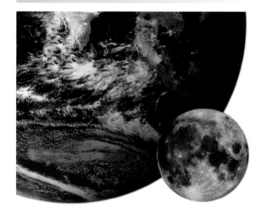

The Moon rotates more slowly than the Earth, taking just over 27 days to make one complete rotation on its axis. This corresponds to the Moon's orbital period around the Earth, and therefore the Moon always presents the same hemisphere towards us; some 41% of the Moon's far side is never visible from the Earth. The interval between one New Moon and the next is 29½ days – this is called a lunation, or lunar month. The Moon shines only by reflected sunlight, and emits no light of its own. During each lunation the Moon displays a complete cycle of phases, caused by the changing angle of illumination from the Sun.

## PHASES OF THE MOON

Mean distance from Earth: 384,401 km; Mean diameter: 3,475 km;
Mass: approximately 1/80 that of Earth; Surface gravity: one-sixth of Earth's;
Daily range of temperature at lunar equator: 280°C; Average orbital speed: 3,681 km/h

| New Moon | Waxing Crescent | First Quarter | Waxing Gibbous | Full Moon | Waning Gibbous | Last Quarter | Waning Crescent | New Moon |
|---|---|---|---|---|---|---|---|---|

## ECLIPSES

When the Moon passes between the Sun and the Earth, the Sun becomes partially eclipsed (1). A partial eclipse becomes a total eclipse if the Moon proceeds to cover the Sun completely (2) and the dark central part of the lunar shadow touches the Earth. The broad geographical zone covered by the Moon's outer shadow (P) has only a very small central area (often less than 100 km wide) that experiences totality. Totality can never last for more than 7½ minutes at maximum, but is usually much briefer than this. Lunar eclipses take place when the Moon moves through the shadow of the Earth, and can be partial or total. Any single location on Earth can experience a maximum of four solar and three lunar eclipses in any single year, while a total solar eclipse occurs an average of once every 360 years for any given location.

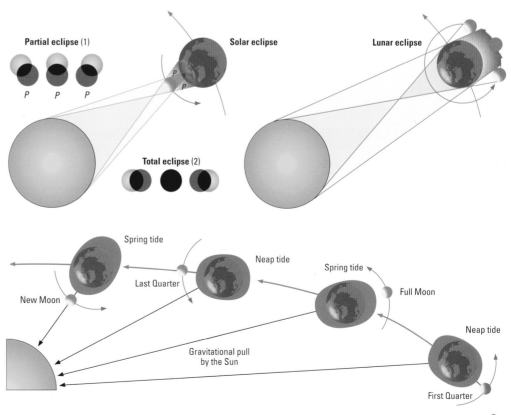

Partial eclipse (1)    Solar eclipse    Lunar eclipse

P    P    P

Total eclipse (2)

## TIDES

The daily rise and fall of the ocean's tides are the result of the gravitational pull of the Moon and that of the Sun, though the effect of the latter is not as strong as that of the Moon. This effect is greatest on the hemisphere facing the Moon and causes a tidal 'bulge'.

Spring tides occur when the Sun, Earth and Moon are aligned; high tides are at their highest, and low tides fall to their lowest. When the Moon and Sun are furthest out of line (near the Moon's First and Last Quarters), neap tides occur, producing the smallest range between high and low tides.

Spring tide
Neap tide
Last Quarter
Spring tide
New Moon
Full Moon
Gravitational pull by the Sun
Neap tide
First Quarter

**3**

# Restless Earth

## THE EARTH'S STRUCTURE

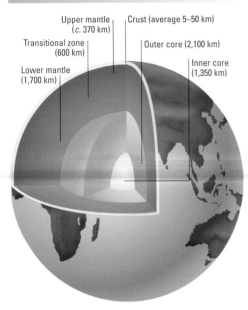

Upper mantle (c. 370 km)
Crust (average 5–50 km)
Transitional zone (600 km)
Outer core (2,100 km)
Lower mantle (1,700 km)
Inner core (1,350 km)

## CONTINENTAL DRIFT

About 200 million years ago the original Pangaea landmass began to split into two continental groups, which further separated over time to produce the present-day configuration.

180 million years ago

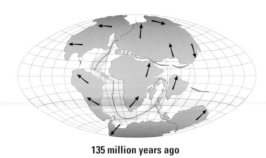

135 million years ago

Present day

——— Trench
——— Rift
New ocean floor
Zones of slippage

## NOTABLE EARTHQUAKES SINCE 1900

| Year | Location | Richter Scale | Deaths |
|---|---|---|---|
| 1906 | San Francisco, USA | 8.3 | 3,000 |
| 1906 | Valparaiso, Chile | 8.6 | 22,000 |
| 1908 | Messina, Italy | 7.5 | 83,000 |
| 1915 | Avezzano, Italy | 7.5 | 30,000 |
| 1920 | Gansu (Kansu), China | 8.6 | 180,000 |
| 1923 | Yokohama, Japan | 8.3 | 143,000 |
| 1927 | Nan Shan, China | 8.3 | 200,000 |
| 1932 | Gansu (Kansu), China | 7.6 | 70,000 |
| 1934 | Bihar, India/Nepal | 8.4 | 10,700 |
| 1935 | Quetta, India (now Pakistan) | 7.5 | 60,000 |
| 1939 | Chillan, Chile | 8.3 | 28,000 |
| 1939 | Erzincan, Turkey | 7.9 | 30,000 |
| 1960 | S. W. Chile | 9.5 | 2,200 |
| 1960 | Agadir, Morocco | 5.8 | 12,000 |
| 1962 | Khorasan, Iran | 7.1 | 12,230 |
| 1964 | Anchorage, USA | 9.2 | 125 |
| 1970 | N. Peru | 7.8 | 70,000 |
| 1972 | Managua, Nicaragua | 6.2 | 5,000 |
| 1976 | Guatemala | 7.5 | 22,500 |
| 1976 | Tangshan, China | 8.2 | 255,000 |
| 1978 | Tabas, Iran | 7.7 | 25,000 |
| 1980 | El Asnam, Algeria | 7.3 | 20,000 |
| 1985 | Mexico City, Mexico | 8.1 | 4,200 |
| 1988 | N.W. Armenia | 6.8 | 55,000 |
| 1990 | N. Iran | 7.7 | 36,000 |
| 1993 | Maharashtra, India | 6.4 | 30,000 |
| 1994 | Los Angeles, USA | 6.6 | 51 |
| 1995 | Kobe, Japan | 7.2 | 5,000 |
| 1998 | Rostaq, Afghanistan | 7.0 | 5,000 |
| 1999 | Izmit, Turkey | 7.4 | 15,000 |
| 2001 | Gujarat, India | 7.7 | 14,000 |
| 2003 | Bam, Iran | 6.6 | 30,000 |
| 2004 | Sumatra, Indonesia | 9.0 | 250,000 |
| 2005 | N. Pakistan | 7.6 | 74,000 |
| 2006 | Java, Indonesia | 6.4 | 6,200 |
| 2008 | Sichuan, China | 7.9 | 70,000 |
| 2010 | Haiti | 7.0 | 230,000 |
| 2011 | Christchurch, New Zealand | 6.3 | 182 |
| 2011 | N. Japan | 9.0 | 20,000 |
| 2015 | Nepal | 7.8 | 8,500 |
| 2016 | Ecuador | 7.8 | 668 |
| 2017 | Chiapas, Mexico | 8.2 | 98 |

## EARTHQUAKES

Earthquake magnitude is usually rated according to either the Richter or the Modified Mercalli scale, both devised by seismologists in the 1930s. The Richter scale measures absolute earthquake power with mathematical precision: each step upwards represents a tenfold increase in shockwave amplitude. Theoretically, there is no upper limit, but most of the largest earthquakes measured have been rated at between 8.8 and 8.9. The 12–point Mercalli scale, based on observed effects, is often more meaningful, ranging from I (earthquakes noticed only by seismographs) to XII (total destruction); intermediate points include V (people awakened at night; unstable objects overturned), VII (collapse of ordinary buildings; chimneys and monuments fall), and IX (conspicuous cracks in ground; serious damage to reservoirs).

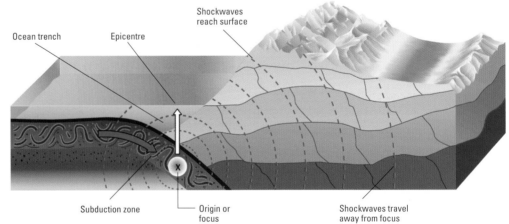

Shockwaves reach surface
Ocean trench
Epicentre
Subduction zone
Origin or focus
Shockwaves travel away from focus

## DISTRIBUTION OF EARTHQUAKES

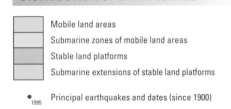

Mobile land areas
Submarine zones of mobile land areas
Stable land platforms
Submarine extensions of stable land platforms

● 1995 Principal earthquakes and dates (since 1900)

Earthquakes are a series of rapid vibrations originating from the slipping or faulting of parts of the Earth's crust when stresses within build up to breaking point. They usually happen at depths varying from 8 km to 30 km. Severe earthquakes cause extensive damage when they take place in populated areas, destroying structures and severing communications. Most initial loss of life occurs due to secondary causes such as falling masonry, fires and flooding.

Projection: Interrupted Mollweide

# PLATE TECTONICS

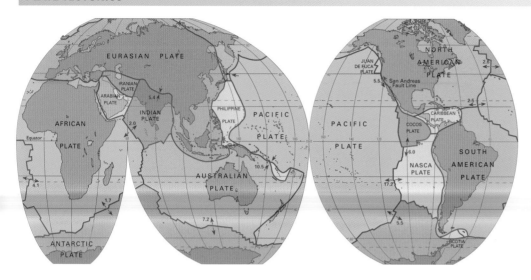

 Plate boundaries

Direction of plate movements and
rate of movement (cm/year)

The drifting of the continents is a feature that is unique to planet Earth. The complementary, almost jigsaw-puzzle fit of the coastlines on each side of the Atlantic Ocean inspired Alfred Wegener's theory of continental drift in 1915. The theory suggested that the ancient supercontinent, which Wegener named Pangaea, incorporated all of the Earth's landmasses and gradually split up to form today's continents.

The original debate about continental drift was a prelude to a more radical idea: plate tectonics. The basic theory is that the Earth's crust is made up of a series of rigid plates which float on a soft layer of the mantle and are moved about by continental convection currents within the Earth's interior. These plates diverge and converge along margins marked by seismic activity. Plates diverge from mid-ocean ridges where molten lava pushes upwards and forces the plates apart at rates of up to 40 mm [1.6 in] a year.

The three diagrams, left, give some examples of plate boundaries from around the world. Diagram (a) shows sea-floor spreading at the Mid-Atlantic Ridge as the American and African plates slowly diverge. The same thing is happening in (b) where sea-floor spreading at the Mid-Indian Ocean Ridge is forcing the Indian plate to collide into the Eurasian plate. In (c) oceanic crust (sima) is being subducted beneath lighter continental crust (sial).

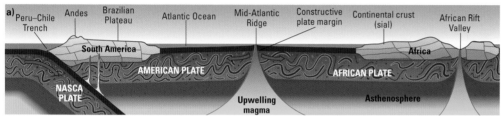

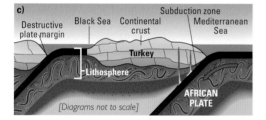

## VOLCANOES

Volcanoes occur when hot liquefied rock beneath the Earth's crust is pushed up by pressure to the surface as molten lava. Some volcanoes erupt in an explosive way, throwing out rocks and ash, whilst others are effusive and lava flows out of the vent. There are volcanoes which are both, such as Mount Fuji. An accumulation of lava and cinders creates cones of variable size and shape. As a result of many eruptions over centuries, Mount Etna in Sicily has a circumference of more than 120 km [75 miles].

Climatologists believe that volcanic ash, if ejected high into the atmosphere, can influence temperature and weather for several years afterwards. The 1991 eruption of Mount Pinatubo in the Philippines ejected more than 20 million tonnes of dust and ash 32 km [20 miles] into the atmosphere and is believed to have accelerated ozone depletion over a large part of the globe.

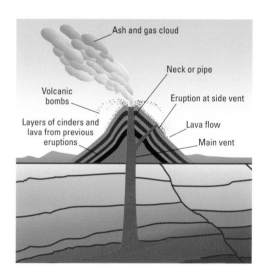

## DISTRIBUTION OF VOLCANOES

Volcanoes today may be the subject of considerable scientific study but they remain both dramatic and unpredictable: in 1991 Mount Pinatubo, 100 km [62 miles] north of the Philippines capital Manila, suddenly burst into life after lying dormant for more than six centuries. Most of the world's active volcanoes occur in a belt around the Pacific Ocean, on the edge of the Pacific plate, called the 'ring of fire'. Indonesia has the greatest concentration with 90 volcanoes, 12 of which are active. The most famous, Krakatoa, erupted in 1883 with such force that the resulting tidal wave killed 36,000 people, and tremors were felt as far away as Australia.

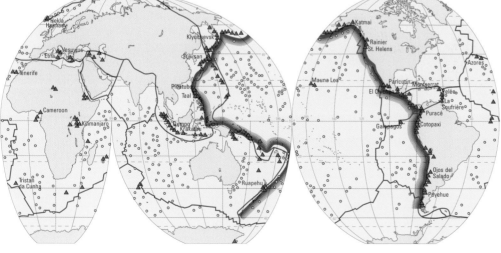

'Ring of Fire'

° Submarine volcanoes

▲ Land volcanoes active since 1700

—— Boundaries of tectonic plates

**5**

# Landforms

## THE ROCK CYCLE

James Hutton first proposed the rock cycle in the late 1700s after he observed the slow but steady effects of erosion.

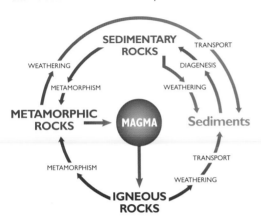

Above and below the surface of the oceans, the features of the Earth's crust are constantly changing. The phenomenal forces generated by convection currents in the molten core of our planet carry the vast segments or 'plates' of the crust across the globe in an endless cycle of creation and destruction. A continent may travel little more than 25 mm [1 in] per year, yet in the vast span of geological time this process throws up giant mountain ranges and creates new land.

Destruction of the landscape, however, begins as soon as it is formed. Wind, water, ice and sea, the main agents of erosion, mount a constant assault that even the most resistant rocks cannot withstand. Mountain peaks may dwindle by as little as a few millimetres each year, but if they are not uplifted by further movements of the crust they will eventually be reduced to rubble and transported away.

Water is the most powerful agent of erosion – it has been estimated that 100 billion tonnes of sediment are washed into the oceans every year.

Three Asian rivers account for 20% of this total: the Huang He, in China, and the Brahmaputra and the Ganges in Bangladesh.

Rivers and glaciers, like the sea itself, generate much of their effect through abrasion – pounding the land with the debris they carry with them. But as well as destroying they also create new landforms, many of them spectacular: vast deltas like those of the Mississippi and the Nile, or the deep fjords cut by glaciers in British Columbia, Norway and New Zealand.

Geologists once considered that landscapes evolved from 'young', newly uplifted mountainous areas, through a 'mature' hilly stage, to an 'old age' stage when the land was reduced to an almost flat plain, or peneplain. This theory, called the 'cycle of erosion', fell into disuse when it became evident that so many factors, including the effects of plate tectonics and climatic change, constantly interrupt the cycle, which takes no account of the highly complex interactions that shape the surface of our planet.

## MOUNTAIN BUILDING

Mountains are formed when pressures on the Earth's crust caused by continental drift become so intense that the surface buckles or cracks. This happens where oceanic crust is subducted by continental crust or, more dramatically, where two tectonic plates collide: the Rockies, Andes, Alps, Urals and Himalayas resulted from such impacts. These are all known as fold mountains because they were formed by the compression of the rocks, forcing the surface to bend and fold like a crumpled rug. The Himalayas were formed from the folded former sediments of the Tethys Sea, which was trapped in the collision zone between the Indian and Eurasian plates.

The other main mountain-building process occurs when the crust fractures to create faults, allowing rock to be forced upwards in large blocks; or when the pressure of magma within the crust forces the surface to bulge into a dome, or erupts to form a volcano. Large mountain ranges may reveal a combination of these features; the Alps, for example, have been compressed so violently that the folds are fragmented by numerous faults and intrusions of molten igneous rock.

Over millions of years, even the greatest mountain ranges can be reduced by the agents of erosion (most notably rivers) to a low rugged landscape known as a peneplain.

**Types of faults:** Faults occur where the crust is being stretched or compressed so violently that the rock strata break in a horizontal or vertical movement. They are classified by the direction in which the blocks of rock have moved. A normal fault results when a vertical movement causes the surface to break apart; compression causes a reverse fault. Horizontal movement causes shearing, known as a strike-slip fault. When the rock breaks in two places, the central block may be pushed up in a horst fault, or sink (creating a rift valley) in a graben fault.

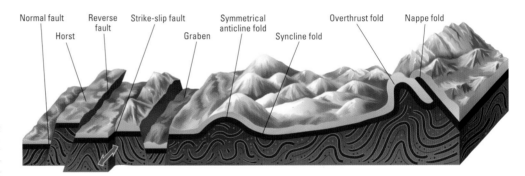

**Types of fold:** Folds occur when rock strata are squeezed and compressed. They are common, therefore, at destructive plate margins and where plates have collided, forcing the rocks to buckle into mountain ranges. Geographers give different names to the degrees of fold that result from continuing pressure on the rock. A simple fold may be symmetric, with even slopes on either side, but as the pressure builds up, one slope becomes steeper and the fold becomes asymmetric. Later, the ridge or 'anticline' at the top of the fold may slide over the lower ground or 'syncline' to form a recumbent fold. Eventually, the rock strata may break under the pressure to form an overthrust and finally a nappe fold.

## CONTINENTAL GLACIATION

Ice sheets were at their greatest extent about 200,000 years ago. The maximum advance of the last Ice Age was about 18,000 years ago, when ice covered virtually all of Canada and reached as far south as the Bristol Channel in Britain.

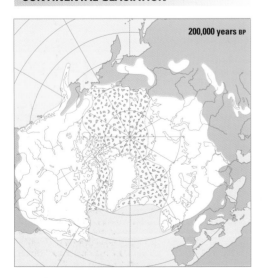

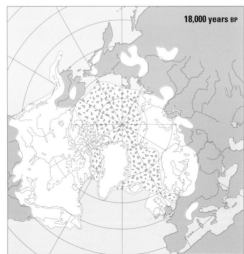

# NATURAL LANDFORMS

A stylized diagram to show some of the major natural landforms found in the mid-latitudes.

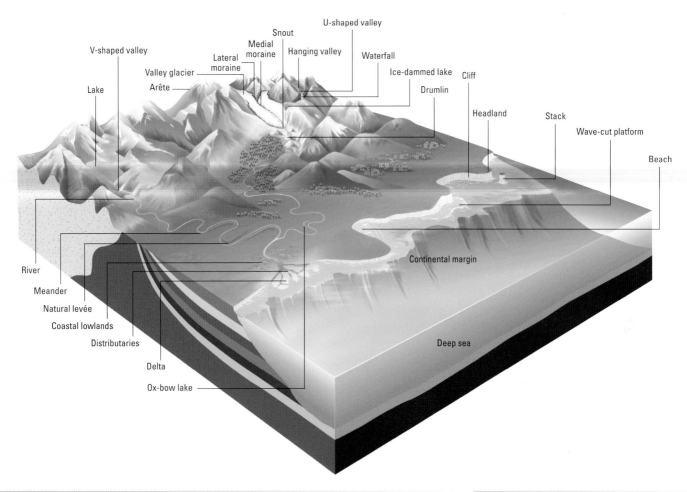

## DESERT LANDSCAPES

The popular image that deserts are all huge expanses of sand is wrong. Despite harsh conditions, deserts contain some of the most varied and interesting landscapes in the world. They are also one of the most extensive environments – the hot and cold deserts together cover almost 40% of the Earth's surface.

The three types of hot desert are known by their Arabic names: sand desert, called *erg*, covers only about one-fifth of the world's desert; the rest is divided between *hammada* (areas of bare rock) and *reg* (broad plains covered by loose gravel or pebbles).

In areas of *erg*, such as the Namib Desert, the shape of the dunes reflects the character of local winds. Where winds are constant in direction, crescent-shaped *barchan* dunes form. In areas of bare rock, wind-blown sand is a major agent of erosion. The erosion is mainly confined to within 2 m [6.5 ft] of the surface, producing characteristic mushroom-shaped rocks.

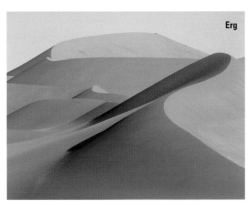

Erg

Hammada

Reg

## SURFACE PROCESSES

Catastrophic changes to natural landforms are periodically caused by such phenomena as avalanches, landslides and volcanic eruptions, but most of the processes that shape the Earth's surface operate extremely slowly in human terms. One estimate, based on a study in the United States, suggested that 1 m [3 ft] of land was removed from the entire surface of the country, on average, every 29,500 years. However, the time-scale varies from 1,300 years to 154,200 years depending on the terrain and climate.

In hot, dry climates, mechanical weathering, a result of rapid temperature changes, causes the outer layers of rock to peel away, while in cold mountainous regions, boulders are prised apart when water freezes in cracks in rocks. Chemical weathering, at its greatest in warm, humid regions, is responsible for hollowing out limestone caves and decomposing granites.

The erosion of soil and rock is greatest on sloping land and the steeper the slope, the greater the tendency for mass wasting – the movement of soil and rock downhill under the influence of gravity. The mechanisms of mass wasting (ranging from very slow to very rapid) vary with the type of material, but the presence of water as a lubricant is usually an important factor.

Running water is the world's leading agent of erosion and transportation. The energy of a river depends on several factors, including its velocity and volume, and its erosive power is at its peak when it is in full flood. Sea waves also exert tremendous erosive power during storms when they hurl pebbles against the shore, undercutting cliffs and hollowing out caves.

Glacier ice forms in mountain hollows and spills out to form valley glaciers, which transport rocks shattered by frost action. As glaciers move, rocks embedded into the ice erode steep-sided, U-shaped valleys. Evidence of glaciation in mountain regions includes cirques, knife-edged ridges, or arêtes, and pyramidal peaks.

# Oceans

## THE GREAT OCEANS

Relative sizes of the world's oceans

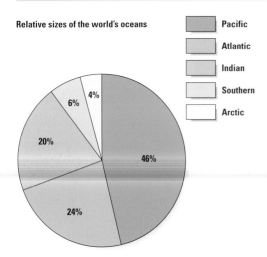

Legend:
- Pacific
- Atlantic
- Indian
- Southern
- Arctic

Pie chart values: 46%, 24%, 20%, 6%, 4%

From ancient times to about the 15th century, the legendary 'Seven Seas' comprised the Red Sea, Mediterranean Sea, Persian Gulf, Black Sea, Adriatic Sea, Caspian Sea and Indian Sea.

The Earth is a watery planet: more than 70% of its surface – over 360,000,000 sq km [140,000,000 sq miles] – is covered by the oceans and seas. The mighty Pacific alone accounts for nearly 36% of the total, and more than 46% of the sea area. Gravity holds in around 1,400 million cubic km [320 million cubic miles] of water, of which over 97% is saline.

The vast underwater world starts in the shallows of the seaside and plunges to depths of more than 11,000 m [36,000 ft]. The continental shelf, part of the landmass, drops gently to around 200 m [650 ft]; here the seabed falls away suddenly at an angle of 3° to 6° – the continental slope. The third stage, called the continental rise, is more gradual with gradients varying from 1 in 100 to 1 in 700. At an average depth of 5,000 m [16,500 ft] there begins the aptly-named abyssal plain – massive submarine depths where sunlight fails to penetrate and few creatures can survive.

From these plains rise volcanoes which, taken from base to top, rival and even surpass the tallest continental mountains in height. Mauna Kea, on Hawai'i, reaches a total of 10,203 m [33,400 ft], some 1,355 m [4,500 ft] higher than Mount Everest, though scarcely 40% is visible above sea level.

In addition, there are underwater mountain chains up to 1,000 km [600 miles] across, whose peaks sometimes appear above sea level as islands, such as Iceland and Tristan da Cunha.

## OCEAN DEPTHS

Average and maximum depths of the world's great oceans, in metres

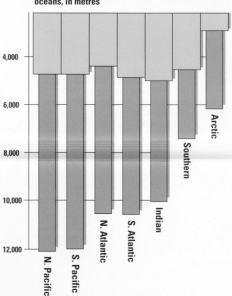

Depth axis labels: 4,000 / 6,000 / 8,000 / 10,000 / 12,000

Ocean labels: N. Pacific, S. Pacific, N. Atlantic, S. Atlantic, Indian, Southern, Arctic

## OCEAN CURRENTS

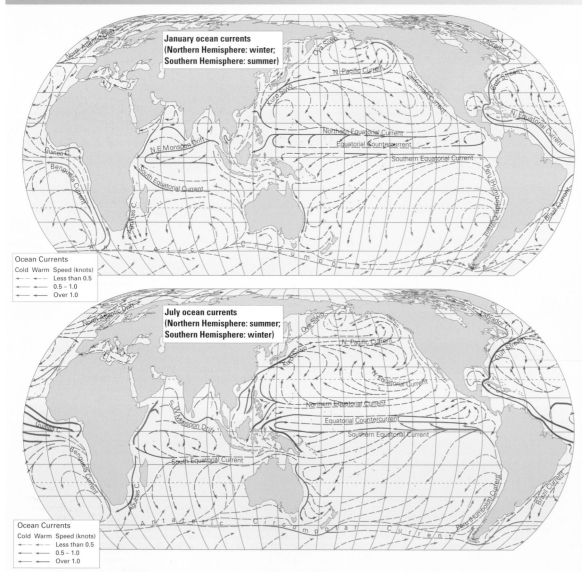

January ocean currents
(Northern Hemisphere: winter; Southern Hemisphere: summer)

Ocean Currents
Cold Warm Speed (knots)
- Less than 0.5
- 0.5 – 1.0
- Over 1.0

July ocean currents
(Northern Hemisphere: summer; Southern Hemisphere: winter)

Ocean Currents
Cold Warm Speed (knots)
- Less than 0.5
- 0.5 – 1.0
- Over 1.0

Moving immense quantities of energy as well as billions of tonnes of water every hour, the ocean currents are a vital part of the great heat engine that drives the Earth's climate. They themselves are produced by a twofold mechanism. At the surface, winds push huge masses of water before them; in the deep ocean, below an abrupt temperature gradient that separates the churning surface waters from the still depths, density variations cause slow vertical movements.

The pattern of circulation of the great surface currents is determined by the displacement known as the Coriolis effect. As the Earth turns beneath a moving object – whether it is a tennis ball or a vast mass of water – it appears to be deflected to one side. The deflection is most obvious near the Equator, where the Earth's surface is spinning eastwards at 1,700 km/h [1,050 mph]; currents moving polewards are curved clockwise in the northern hemisphere and anti-clockwise in the southern.

The result is a system of spinning circles known as 'gyres'. The Coriolis effect piles up water on the left of each gyre, creating a narrow, fast-moving stream that is matched by a slower, broader returning current on the right. North and south of the Equator, the fastest currents are located in the west and in the east respectively. In each case, warm water moves from the Equator and cold water returns to it. Cold currents often bring an upwelling of nutrients with them, supporting the world's most economically important fisheries.

Depending on the prevailing winds, some currents on or near the Equator may reverse their direction in the course of the year – a seasonal variation on which Asian monsoon rains depend, and whose occasional failure can bring disaster to millions of people.

## WORLD FISHING AREAS

Total world fish catch in metric tonnes, inland and marine fishing (2015)

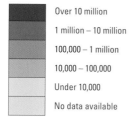

- Over 10 million
- 1 million – 10 million
- 100,000 – 1 million
- 10,000 – 100,000
- Under 10,000
- No data available

Leading fishing nations

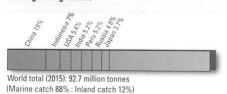

China 19%  Indonesia 7%  USA 5.4%  India 5.2%  Peru 5.2%  Russia 4.8%  Japan 3.7%

World total (2015): 92.7 million tonnes
(Marine catch 88% : Inland catch 12%)

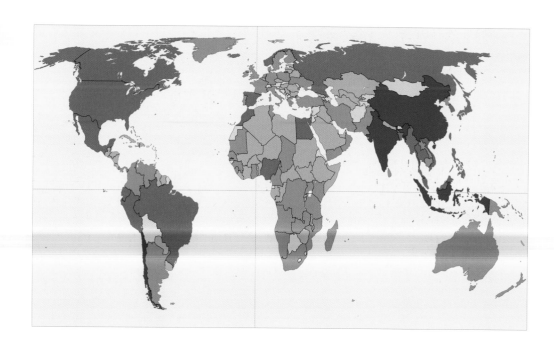

## MARINE POLLUTION

Sources of marine oil pollution

- Tanker operations
- Municipal wastes
- Tanker accidents
- Bilge and fuel oils
- Natural seeps
- Industrial waste
- Urban runoff
- Coastal oil refining
- Offshore oil rigs
- River runoffs
- Other

Pie chart values: 1%, 1.5%, 3%, 3.5%, 6%, 7.5%, 9%, 12.5%, 22%, 22%, 12%

## OIL SPILLS

Major oil spills from tankers and combined carriers

| Year | Vessel | Location | Spill (barrels)* | Cause |
|------|--------|----------|------------------|-------|
| 1979 | Atlantic Empress | West Indies | 1,890,000 | collision |
| 1983 | Castillo de Bellver | South Africa | 1,760,000 | fire |
| 1978 | Amoco Cadiz | France | 1,628,000 | grounding |
| 1991 | Haven | Italy | 1,029,000 | explosion |
| 1988 | Odyssey | Canada | 1,000,000 | fire |
| 1967 | Torrey Canyon | UK | 909,000 | grounding |
| 1972 | Sea Star | Gulf of Oman | 902,250 | collision |
| 1977 | Hawaiian Patriot | Hawaiian Is. | 742,500 | fire |
| 1979 | Independenta | Turkey | 696,350 | collision |
| 1993 | Braer | UK | 625,000 | grounding |
| 1996 | Sea Empress | UK | 515,000 | grounding |
| 2002 | Prestige | Spain | 463,250 | storm |

Other sources of major oil spills

| Year | Vessel | Location | Spill (barrels)* | Cause |
|------|--------|----------|------------------|-------|
| 1983 | Nowruz oilfield | Persian Gulf | 4,250,000[†] | war |
| 1979 | Ixtoc 1 oilwell | Gulf of Mexico | 4,200,000 | blow-out |
| 2010 | Deepwater Horizon | Gulf of Mexico | 3.6 – 4,610,000 | blow-out |

* 1 barrel = 0.136 tonnes/159 lit./35 Imperial gal./42 US gal.  [†] estimated

## RIVER POLLUTION

Sources of river pollution, USA

- Agriculture
- Mining
- Forestry
- Urban runoff
- Hydro-engineering
- Construction
- Land disposal
- Other

Pie chart values: 1%, 2%, 4%, 5%, 6%, 9%, 9%, 64%

## EL NIÑO

El Niño, 'The Little Boy' in Spanish, was originally the name given by local fishermen to the warm current that can appear off the Pacific coast of South America. In a normal year, south-easterly trade winds drive surface waters westwards off the coast of South America, drawing cold, nutrient-rich water up from below. In an El Niño year, warm water from the west Pacific suppresses upwelling in the east, depriving the region of nutrients and driving the fish away. The water is warmed by as much as 7°C, disturbing the tropical atmosphere circulation. During an intense El Niño, the south-east trade winds change direction and become equatorial westerlies, resulting in climatic extremes in many regions of the world, such as drought in parts of Australia and India, and heavy rainfall in south-eastern USA.

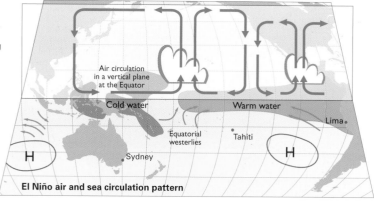

**El Niño air and sea circulation pattern**

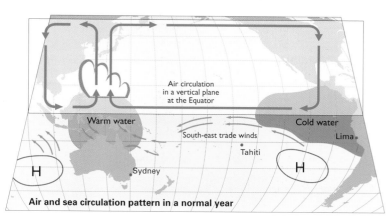

**Air and sea circulation pattern in a normal year**

El Niño events occur about every 4 to 7 years and typically last for around 12 to 18 months. El Niño usually results in reduced rainfall across northern and eastern Australia. This can lead to widespread and severe drought, as well as increased temperatures and bushfire risk. However, each El Niño event is unique in terms of its strength as well as its impact. It is measured by the Southern Oscillation Index (SOI) and the changes in ocean temperatures.

La Niña, or 'The Little Girl', is associated with cooler waters in the central and eastern Pacific. A La Niña year can result in cooler land temperatures across the tropics and subtropics, and more storms in the North Atlantic.

# Climate

## CLIMATE REGIONS

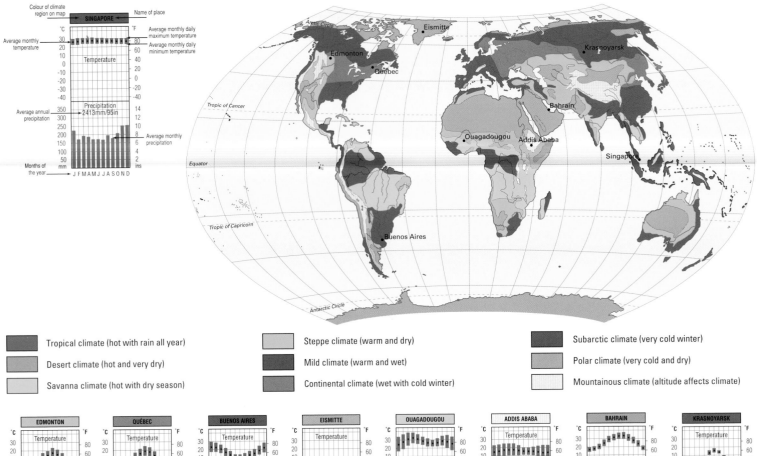

- ■ Tropical climate (hot with rain all year)
- ■ Desert climate (hot and very dry)
- ■ Savanna climate (hot with dry season)
- ■ Steppe climate (warm and dry)
- ■ Mild climate (warm and wet)
- ■ Continental climate (wet with cold winter)
- ■ Subarctic climate (very cold winter)
- ■ Polar climate (very cold and dry)
- ■ Mountainous climate (altitude affects climate)

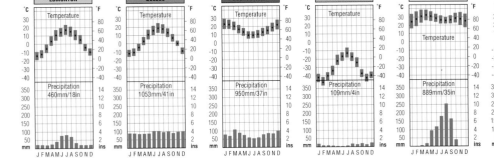

## THE MONSOON

Monthly rainfall

| mm | mm |
|----|----|
| 400 | 50 |
| 200 | 25 |
| 100 | 0 |

→ Wind direction

— ITCZ (intertropical convergence zone)

In early March, which normally marks the end of the subcontinent's cool season and the start of the hot season, winds blow outwards from the mainland. But as the overhead sun and the ITCZ move northwards, the land is intensely heated, and a low-pressure system develops. The south-east trade winds, which are drawn across the Equator, change direction and are sucked into the interior, bringing heavy rain. By November, the overhead sun and the ITCZ have again moved southwards and the wind directions are again reversed. Cool winds blow from the Asian interior to the sea, losing any moisture on the Himalayas before descending to the coast.

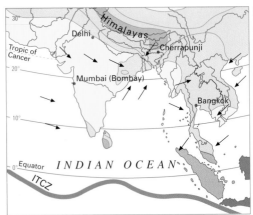

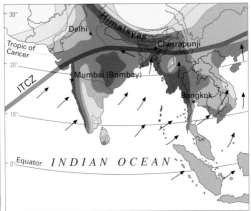

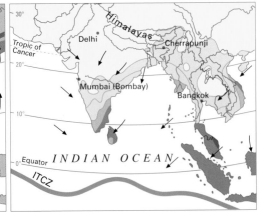

**March** – Start of the hot, dry season, the ITCZ is over the southern Indian Ocean.

**July** – The rainy season, the ITCZ has migrated northwards; winds blow onshore.

**November** – The ITCZ has returned south, the offshore winds are cool and dry.

10

COPYRIGHT PHILIP'S

# CLIMATE

Climate is weather in the long term: the seasonal pattern of hot and cold, wet and dry, averaged over time (usually 30 years). At the simplest level, it is caused by the uneven heating of the Earth. Surplus heat at the Equator passes towards the poles, levelling out the energy differential. Its passage is marked by a ceaseless churning of the atmosphere and the oceans, further agitated by the Earth's diurnal spin and the motion it imparts to moving air and water. The heat's means of transport – by winds and ocean currents, by the continual evaporation and recondensation of water molecules – is the weather itself. There are four basic types of climate, each of which can be further subdivided: tropical, desert (dry), temperate and polar.

## COMPOSITION OF DRY AIR

| | | | |
|---|---|---|---|
| Nitrogen | 78.09% | Sulphur dioxide | trace |
| Oxygen | 20.95% | Nitrogen oxide | trace |
| Argon | 0.93% | Methane | trace |
| Water vapour | 0.2–4.0% | Dust | trace |
| Carbon dioxide | 0.03% | Helium | trace |
| Ozone | 0.00006% | Neon | trace |

## CLIMATE RECORDS

### Temperature
Highest recorded shade temperature: Death Valley, USA, 56.7°C [134.1°F], 10 July 1913.

Highest mean annual temperature: Dallol, Ethiopia, 34.4°C [94°F], 1960–66.

Longest heatwave: Marble Bar, W. Australia, 162 days over 38°C [100°F], 23 October 1923 to 7 April 1924.

Lowest recorded temperature (outside poles): Verkhoyansk, Siberia, –68°C [–93.6°F], 7 February 1982.

Lowest mean annual temperature: Polus Nedostupnosti, Pole of Cold, Antarctica, –57.8°C [–72°F].

### Precipitation
Driest place: Quillagua, Chile, mean annual rainfall 0.5 mm [0.02 in], 1964–2001.

Wettest place (average): Mt Wai-ale-ale, Hawai'i, USA, mean annual rainfall 11,680 mm [459.8 in].

Wettest place (12 months): Cherrapunji, Meghalaya, N. E. India, 26,461 mm [1,042 in], August 1860 to July 1861. Cherrapunji also holds the record for the most rainfall in one month: 2,930 mm [115 in], July 1861.

Wettest place (24 hours): Fac Fac, Réunion, Indian Ocean, 1,825 mm [71.9 in], 15–16 March 1952.

Heaviest hailstones: Gopalganj, Bangladesh, up to 1.02 kg [2.25 lb], 14 April 1986 (killed 92 people).

Heaviest snowfall (continuous): Bessans, Savoie, France, 1,730 mm [68 in] in 19 hours, 5–6 April 1969.

Heaviest snowfall (season/year): Mt Baker, Washington, USA, 28,956 mm [1,140 in], June 1998 to June 1999.

### Pressure and winds
Highest barometric pressure: Agata, Siberia (at 262 m [862 ft] altitude), 1,083.8 mb, 31 December 1968.

Lowest barometric pressure: Typhoon Tip, Guam, Pacific Ocean, 870 mb, 12 October 1979.

Highest recorded wind speed: Bridge Creek, Oklahoma, USA, 512 km/h [318 mph], 3 May 1999. Measured by Doppler radar monitoring a tornado.

Windiest place: Port Martin, Antarctica, where winds of more than 64 km/h [40 mph] occur for not less than 100 days a year.

### Conversions
°C = (°F − 32) × 5/9;  °F = (°C × 9/5) + 32;  0°C = 32°F

1 in = 25.4 mm;  1 mm = 0.0394 in;  100 mm = 3.94 in

# TEMPERATURE

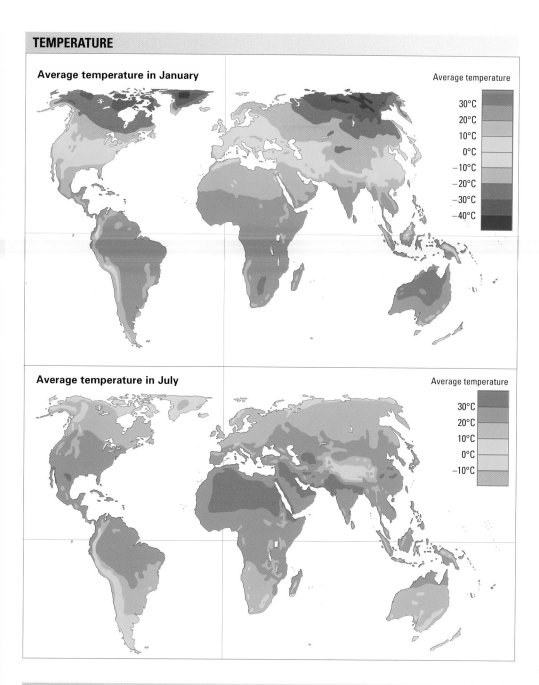

**Average temperature in January**

Average temperature

- 30°C
- 20°C
- 10°C
- 0°C
- −10°C
- −20°C
- −30°C
- −40°C

**Average temperature in July**

Average temperature

- 30°C
- 20°C
- 10°C
- 0°C
- −10°C

# PRECIPITATION (RAINFALL AND SNOW)

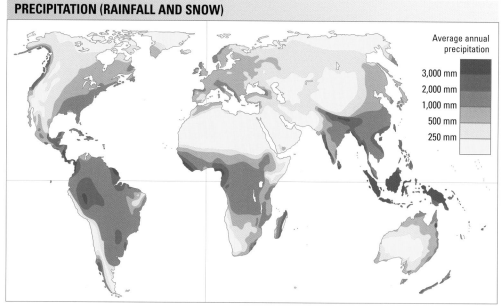

Average annual precipitation

- 3,000 mm
- 2,000 mm
- 1,000 mm
- 500 mm
- 250 mm

# Water and Vegetation

## THE HYDROLOGICAL CYCLE

The world's water balance is regulated by the constant recycling of water between the oceans, atmosphere and land. The movement of water between these three reservoirs is known as the hydrological cycle. The oceans play a vital role in the hydrological cycle: 74% of the total precipitation falls over the oceans and 84% of the total evaporation comes from the oceans.

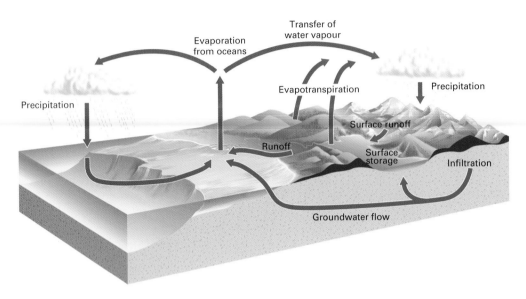

## WATER DISTRIBUTION

The distribution of planetary water, by percentage. Oceans and ice caps together account for more than 99% of the total; the breakdown of the remainder is estimated.

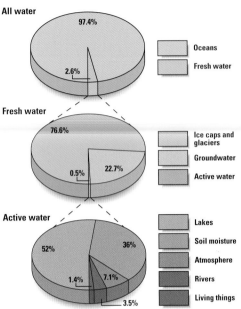

## WATER UTILIZATION

The percentage breakdown of water usage by sector, selected countries

Domestic  Industrial  Agriculture

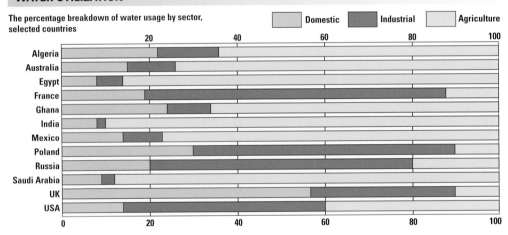

## WATER USAGE

Almost all the world's water is 3,000 million years old, and all of it cycles endlessly through the hydrosphere, though at different rates. Water vapour circulates over days or even hours, deep ocean water circulates over millennia, and ice-cap water remains solid for millions of years.

Fresh water is essential to all terrestrial life. Humans cannot survive more than a few days without it, and even the hardiest desert plants and animals could not exist without some water. Agriculture requires huge quantities of fresh water: without large-scale irrigation most of the world's people would starve. In the USA, agriculture uses 40% and industry 46% of all water withdrawals.

According to the latest figures, the average North American uses 1.5 million litres of water per year. This is more than six times the average African, who uses just 186,000 litres of water each year. Europeans and Australians use 694,000 litres per year.

## WATER SUPPLY

Percentage of total population with access to safe drinking water (2015)

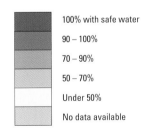

- 100% with safe water
- 90 – 100%
- 70 – 90%
- 50 – 70%
- Under 50%
- No data available

**Least well-provided countries**

| | | | |
|---|---|---|---|
| Somalia | 32% | Mozambique | 51% |
| Papua New Guinea | 40% | Madagascar | 52% |
| Equatorial Guinea | 48% | Congo (Dem. Rep.) | 52% |
| Angola | 49% | Libya | 54% |
| Chad | 51% | Yemen | 55% |

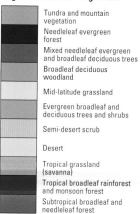

# NATURAL VEGETATION

### Regional variation in vegetation

- Tundra and mountain vegetation
- Needleleaf evergreen forest
- Mixed needleleaf evergreen and broadleaf deciduous trees
- Broadleaf deciduous woodland
- Mid-latitude grassland
- Evergreen broadleaf and deciduous trees and shrubs
- Semi-desert scrub
- Desert
- Tropical grassland (savanna)
- Tropical broadleaf rainforest and monsoon forest
- Subtropical broadleaf and needleleaf forest

The map shows the natural 'climax vegetation' of regions, as dictated by climate and topography. In most cases, however, agricultural activity has drastically altered the vegetation pattern. Western Europe, for example, lost most of its broadleaf forest many centuries ago, while irrigation has turned some natural semi-desert into productive land.

## LAND USE BY CONTINENT

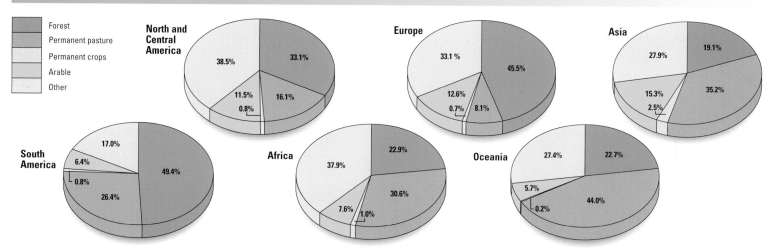

Legend:
- Forest
- Permanent pasture
- Permanent crops
- Arable
- Other

**North and Central America:** 33.1%, 16.1%, 0.8%, 11.5%, 38.5%

**Europe:** 45.5%, 8.1%, 0.7%, 12.6%, 33.1%

**Asia:** 19.1%, 35.2%, 2.5%, 15.3%, 27.9%

**South America:** 49.4%, 26.4%, 0.8%, 6.4%, 17.0%

**Africa:** 22.9%, 30.6%, 1.0%, 7.6%, 37.9%

**Oceania:** 22.7%, 44.0%, 0.2%, 5.7%, 27.4%

## FORESTRY: PRODUCTION

**Fuelwood**
**Top producers (2016)**
(million cubic metres)

| | |
|---|---|
| India | 306 |
| China | 169 |
| Brazil | 112 |
| Ethiopia | 109 |
| Congo, Dem. Rep. | 84 |
| World | 1,863 |

**Industrial roundwood***
**Top producers (2016)**
(million cubic metres)

| | |
|---|---|
| USA | 357 |
| Russia | 198 |
| China | 164 |
| Canada | 158 |
| Brazil | 145 |
| World | 1,874 |

* roundwood is timber as it is felled

**Paper and Board**
**Top producers (2016)**
(million tonnes)

| | |
|---|---|
| China | 113 |
| USA | 72 |
| Japan | 26 |
| Germany | 23 |
| India | 15 |
| World | 409 |

**Top exporters (2016)**
(million tonnes)

| | |
|---|---|
| Germany | 13 |
| USA | 11 |
| Sweden | 10 |
| Finland | 10 |
| China | 8 |

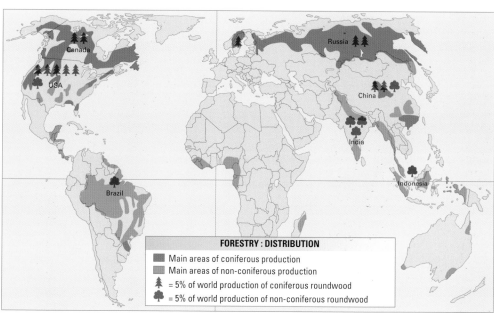

### FORESTRY : DISTRIBUTION

- Main areas of coniferous production
- Main areas of non-coniferous production
- ♠ = 5% of world production of coniferous roundwood
- ♣ = 5% of world production of non-coniferous roundwood

# Environment

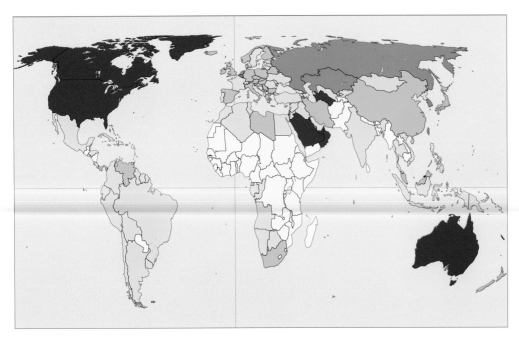

## GLOBAL WARMING

**Carbon dioxide emissions in tonnes per capita (2015)**

- Over 15
- 10 – 15
- 5 – 10
- 1 – 5
- Under 1
- No data available

## CARBON DIOXIDE EMISSIONS

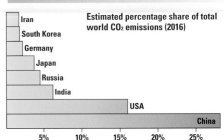

Estimated percentage share of total world CO₂ emissions (2016)

- Iran
- South Korea
- Germany
- Japan
- Russia
- India
- USA
- China

5%   10%   15%   20%   25%

## PREDICTED CHANGE IN PRECIPITATION

The difference between actual annual average precipitation, 1960–1990, and the predicted annual average precipitation, 2070–2100. It should be noted that these predicted annual mean changes mask quite significant seasonal detail.

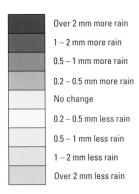

- Over 2 mm more rain
- 1 – 2 mm more rain
- 0.5 – 1 mm more rain
- 0.2 – 0.5 mm more rain
- No change
- 0.2 – 0.5 mm less rain
- 0.5 – 1 mm less rain
- 1 – 2 mm less rain
- Over 2 mm less rain

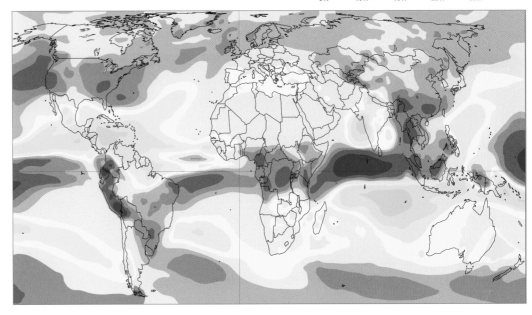

## PREDICTED CHANGE IN TEMPERATURE

The difference between actual annual average surface air temperature, 1960–1990, and the predicted annual average surface air temperature, 2070–2100. This map shows the predicted increase, assuming a 'medium growth' of global economy and assuming that no measures are taken to combat the emission of greenhouse gases.

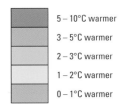

- 5 – 10°C warmer
- 3 – 5°C warmer
- 2 – 3°C warmer
- 1 – 2°C warmer
- 0 – 1°C warmer

*Source: The Hadley Centre of Climate Prediction and Research, The Met. Office*

# GLOBAL WARMING PROJECTIONS

**Projected Change in Global Warming**

⌁ Rise in average temperatures assuming present trends in $CO_2$ emissions continue

⌁ Assuming some cuts are made in emissions

⌁ Assuming drastic cuts are made in emissions

Climate models are used to provide the best scientifically-based estimates of the future global climate. A typical method is to run the models for some decades ahead and then to compare the predicted average with a past 30-year period. A range of climate models are used, run with different scenarios that express the breadth of possibilities of, for example, industrial development and the degree of atmospheric pollution 'clean-up' by industrial nations.

The diagram on the right shows global observed and predicted surface mean temperature change from 1950 to 2070 with three prediction scenarios. The first (red) assumes rapid economic growth and continued population increases. The second (blue) assumes some attempts are made to cut greenhouse gas emissions, while the green line involves the greater use of cleaner technologies, with global population peaking mid-century then declining.

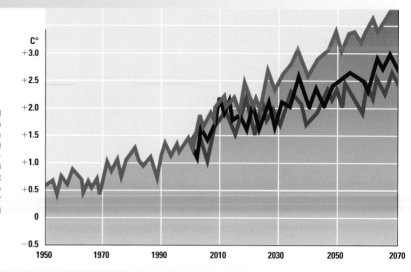

# GREENHOUSE EFFECT

Carbon dioxide is increased by burning fossil fuels and cutting forests

Carbon dioxide

Carbon dioxide and other greenhouse gases trap the heat being reflected from the Earth, although some heat is lost

The warming increases water vapour in the air, leading to even greater absorption of heat

Rising temperatures would melt snow and ice causing oceans to rise

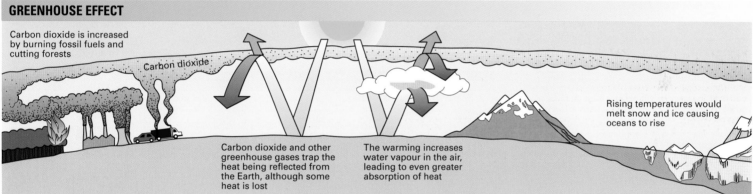

# DEFORESTATION 1990–2015

| | Total forest cover in 1000 sq kms 1990 | Total forest cover in 1000 sq kms 2015 | % change 1990-2015 |
|---|---|---|---|
| Venezuela | 520 | 148 | -71.5 |
| Togo | 7 | 2 | -71.4 |
| Nigeria | 172 | 70 | -59.3 |
| Uganda | 48 | 21 | -56.3 |
| Pakistan | 25 | 15 | -40.0 |
| North Korea | 82 | 50 | -39.0 |
| Sudan | 307 | 192 | -37.5 |
| Zimbabwe | 222 | 141 | -36.5 |
| Nicaragua | 45 | 31 | -31.1 |
| Timor-Leste | 10 | 7 | -30.0 |
| Paraguay | 212 | 153 | -27.8 |
| Myanmar | 392 | 290 | -26.0 |
| Ethiopia | 167 | 125 | -25.1 |
| Nepal | 48 | 36 | -25.0 |
| Indonesia | 1,185 | 910 | -23.2 |
| Somalia | 83 | 64 | -22.9 |
| Cameroon | 243 | 188 | -22.6 |
| Namibia | 88 | 69 | -21.6 |
| Tanzania | 559 | 461 | -17.5 |
| Ecuador | 146 | 125 | -14.4 |
| Bolivia | 628 | 548 | -12.7 |
| Mozambique | 434 | 379 | -12.7 |
| Senegal | 93 | 83 | -10.8 |
| Brazil | 5,467 | 4,935 | -9.7 |
| Madagascar | 137 | 125 | -8.8 |
| Zambia | 528 | 486 | -8.0 |
| Mexico | 698 | 660 | -5.4 |
| Peru | 779 | 740 | -5.0 |
| Australia | 1,285 | 1,248 | -2.9 |
| Congo | 227 | 223 | -1.8 |

# DESERTIFICATION AND DEFORESTATION

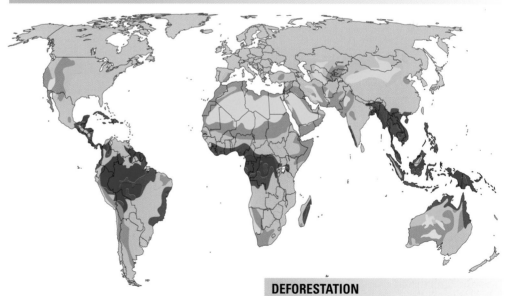

Existing deserts

Areas with a high risk of desertification

Areas with a moderate risk of desertification

Former areas of rainforest

Existing rainforest

# DEFORESTATION

The Earth's remaining forests are under attack from three directions: expanding agriculture, logging, and growing consumption of fuelwood, often in combination. Sometimes deforestation is the direct result of government policy, as in the efforts made to resettle the urban poor in some parts of Brazil; just as often, it comes about despite state attempts at conservation. Loggers, licensed or unlicensed, blaze a trail into virgin forest, often destroying twice as many trees as they harvest. Landless farmers follow, burning away most of what remains to plant their crops, completing the destruction. However, some countries such as Vietnam, Philippines and Costa Rica have successfully implemented reafforestation programmes.

15

# Population

Developed nations such as the UK have populations evenly spread across the age groups and, usually, a growing proportion of elderly people. The great majority of the people in developing nations, however, are in the younger age groups, about to enter their most fertile years. In time, these population profiles should resemble the world profile (even Nigeria has made recent progress by reducing its birth rate), but the transition will come about only after a few more generations of rapid population growth.

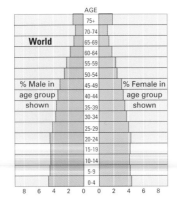

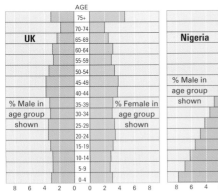

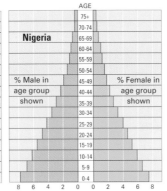

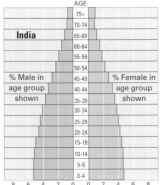

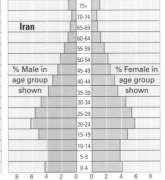

## MOST POPULOUS NATIONS

### Totals in millions (2017 estimates)

| | | | | | |
|---|---|---|---|---|---|
| 1. China | 1,379 | 9. Russia | 142 | 17. Iran | 82 |
| 2. India | 1,282 | 10. Japan | 126 | 18. Turkey | 81 |
| 3. USA | 327 | 11. Mexico | 125 | 19. Germany | 81 |
| 4. Indonesia | 261 | 12. Ethiopia | 105 | 20. Thailand | 68 |
| 5. Brazil | 207 | 13. Philippines | 104 | 21. France | 67 |
| 6. Pakistan | 205 | 14. Egypt | 97 | 22. UK | 65 |
| 7. Nigeria | 191 | 15. Vietnam | 96 | 23. Italy | 62 |
| 8. Bangladesh | 158 | 16. Congo (Dem. Rep.) | 83 | 24. Myanmar (Burma) | 55 |

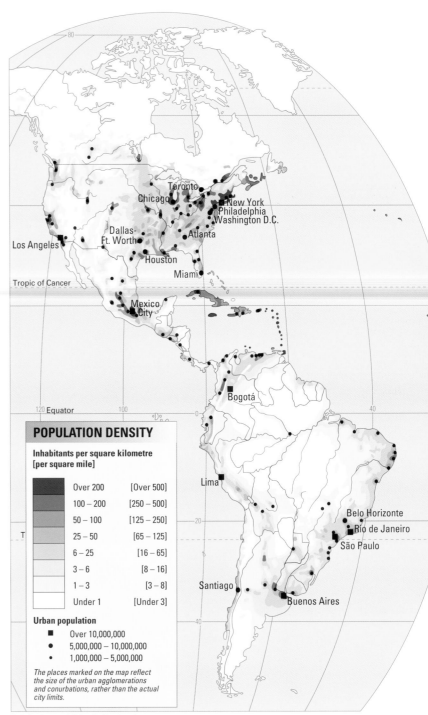

## POPULATION DENSITY

**Inhabitants per square kilometre [per square mile]**

| | | |
|---|---|---|
| | Over 200 | [Over 500] |
| | 100 – 200 | [250 – 500] |
| | 50 – 100 | [125 – 250] |
| | 25 – 50 | [65 – 125] |
| | 6 – 25 | [16 – 65] |
| | 3 – 6 | [8 – 16] |
| | 1 – 3 | [3 – 8] |
| | Under 1 | [Under 3] |

**Urban population**

- ■ Over 10,000,000
- ● 5,000,000 – 10,000,000
- • 1,000,000 – 5,000,000

*The places marked on the map reflect the size of the urban agglomerations and conurbations, rather than the actual city limits.*

Projection: Interrupted Mollweide's Homolographic

## CONTINENTAL COMPARISONS

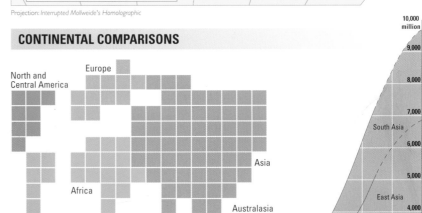

**Each square in the diagram above represents 1% of the total world population.**

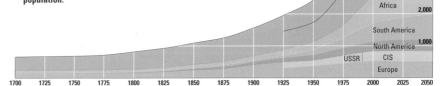

**16**

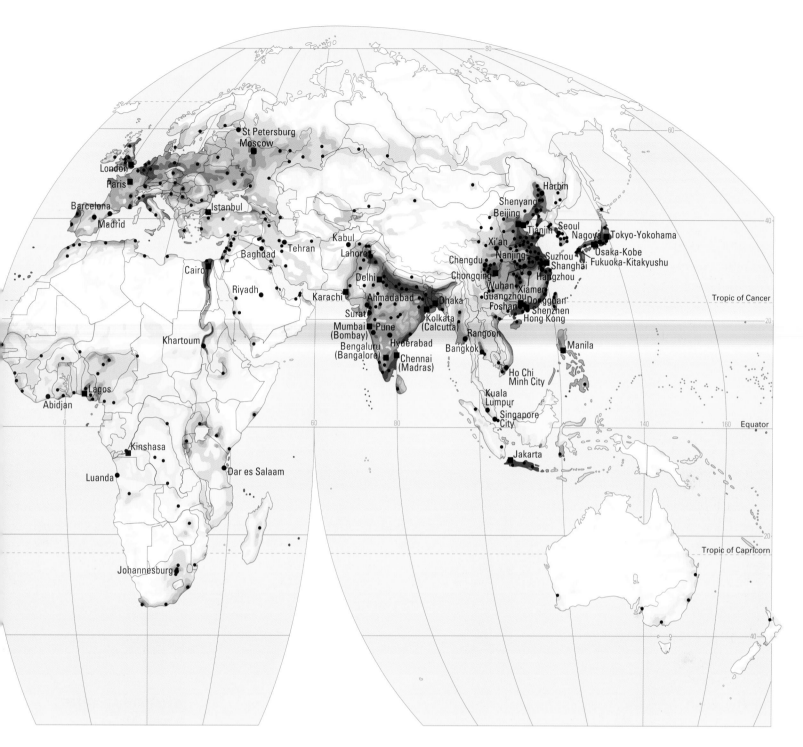

St Petersburg
Moscow
London
Paris
Barcelona
Madrid
Istanbul
Kabul
Baghdad
Tehran
Cairo
Lahore
Riyadh
Delhi
Karachi
Ahmadabad
Khartoum
Surat
Mumbai (Bombay)
Pune
Bengaluru (Bangalore)
Hyderabad
Chennai (Madras)
Kolkata (Calcutta)
Dhaka
Rangoon
Bangkok
Ho Chi Minh City
Kuala Lumpur
Singapore City
Jakarta
Lagos
Abidjan
Kinshasa
Luanda
Dar es Salaam
Johannesburg

Harbin
Shenyang
Beijing
Tianjin
Seoul
Xi'an
Nagoya
Tokyo-Yokohama
Nanjing
Suzhou
Osaka-Kobe
Fukuoka-Kitakyushu
Chengdu
Shanghai
Chongqing
Wuhan
Hangzhou
Xiamen
Guangzhou
Dongguan
Foshan
Shenzhen
Hong Kong
Manila

Tropic of Cancer
Equator
Tropic of Capricorn

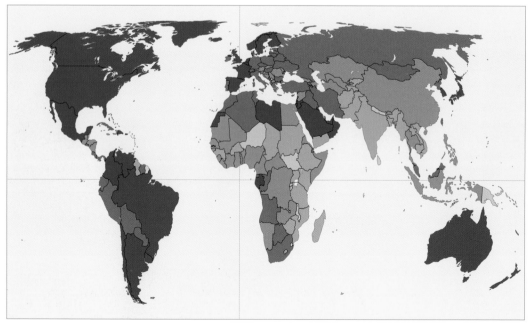

## URBAN POPULATION

**Percentage of total population living in towns and cities (2018)**

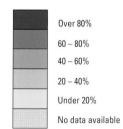

Over 80%

60 – 80%

40 – 60%

20 – 40%

Under 20%

No data available

| Most urbanized | | Least urbanized | |
|---|---|---|---|
| Singapore | 100% | Burundi | 13% |
| Kuwait | 100% | Papua New Guinea | 13% |
| Monaco | 100% | Liechtenstein | 14% |
| Kuwait | 100% | Niger | 16% |
| Qatar | 99% | Malawi | 17% |

# The Human Family

## LANGUAGES OF THE WORLD

Language can be classified by ancestry and structure. For example, the Romance and Germanic groups are both derived from an Indo-European language believed to have been spoken 5,000 years ago.

**First-language speakers, in millions**
Mandarin Chinese 850, Spanish 430, English 340, Hindi 260, Arabic 240, Portuguese 215, Bengali 190, Russian 160, Japanese 130, Javanese 84, French 80, German 78, Wu Chinese 77, Korean 77, Telugu 74, Marathi 72, Tamil 69, Vietnamese 68, Italian 64, Punjabi 63.

### Distribution of Living Languages

The figures refer to the number of languages currently in use in the regions shown

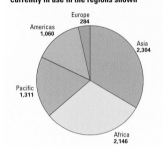

Europe 284
Americas 1,060
Asia 2,304
Pacific 1,311
Africa 2,146

### INDO-EUROPEAN FAMILY

| | |
|---|---|
| 1 | Balto-Slavic group (incl. Russian, Ukrainian) |
| 2 | Germanic group (incl. English, German) |
| 3 | Celtic group |
| 4 | Greek |
| 5 | Albanian |
| 6 | Iranian group |
| 7 | Armenian |
| 8 | Romance group (incl. Spanish, Portuguese, French, Italian) |
| 9 | Indo-Aryan group (incl. Hindi, Bengali, Urdu, Punjabi, Marathi) |
| 10 | CAUCASIAN FAMILY |

### AFRO-ASIATIC FAMILY

| | |
|---|---|
| 11 | Semitic group (incl. Arabic) |
| 12 | Kushitic group |
| 13 | Berber group |
| 14 | KHOISAN FAMILY |
| 15 | NIGER-CONGO FAMILY |
| 16 | NILO-SAHARAN FAMILY |
| 17 | URALIC FAMILY |

### ALTAIC FAMILY

| | |
|---|---|
| 18 | Turkic group (incl. Turkish) |
| 19 | Mongolian group |
| 20 | Tungus-Manchu group |
| 21 | Japanese and Korean |

### SINO-TIBETAN FAMILY

| | |
|---|---|
| 22 | Sinitic (Chinese) languages (incl. Mandarin, Wu, Yue) |
| 23 | Tibetic-Burmic languages |
| 24 | TAI FAMILY |

### AUSTRO-ASIATIC FAMILY

| | |
|---|---|
| 25 | Mon-Khmer group |
| 26 | Munda group |
| 27 | Vietnamese |
| 28 | DRAVIDIAN FAMILY (incl. Telugu, Tamil) |
| 29 | AUSTRONESIAN FAMILY (incl. Malay-Indonesian, Javanese) |
| 30 | OTHER LANGUAGES |

## RELIGIOUS ADHERENTS

**Religious adherents in millions**

| | | | |
|---|---|---|---|
| Christianity | 2,000 | Chinese traditional | 394 |
| *Roman Catholic* | *1,500* | Buddhism | 360 |
| *Orthodox* | *225* | Sikhism | 23 |
| *Anglican* | *70* | Taoism | 20 |
| *Lutheran* | *66* | Judaism | 14 |
| *Methodist* | *8* | Mormonism | 12 |
| Islam | 1,300 | Spiritism | 11 |
| *Sunni* | *940* | Baha'i | 6 |
| *Shi'ite* | *120* | Confucianism | 5 |
| Non-religious | 1,100 | Jainism | 4 |
| Hinduism | 900 | Shintoism | 4 |

| | |
|---|---|
| ▲ | Roman Catholicism |
| | Orthodox and other Eastern Churches |
| • | Protestantism |
| | Sunni Islam |
| | Shi'ite Islam |
| | Buddhism |
| | Hinduism |
| | Confucianism |
| • | Judaism |
| | Shintoism |
| | Tribal Religions |

# UNITED NATIONS

Created in 1945 to promote peace and co-operation, and based in New York, the United Nations is the world's largest international organization, with 193 members and an annual budget of US $5.4 billion (2018-19). Each member of the General Assembly has one vote, while the five permanent members of the 15-nation Security Council – China, France, Russia, the UK and the USA – each hold a veto. The Secretariat is the UN's principal administrative arm. The 54 members of the Economic and Social Council are responsible for economic, social, cultural, educational, health and related matters. The UN has 16 specialized agencies – based in Canada, France, Switzerland and Italy, as well as the USA – which help members in fields such as education (UNESCO), agriculture (FAO), medicine (WHO) and finance (IFC). By the end of 1994, all the original 11 trust territories of the Trusteeship Council had become independent.

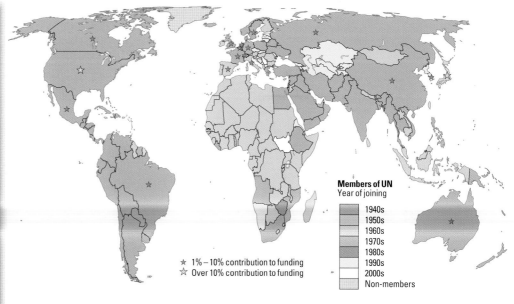

**Members of UN**
Year of joining

- 1940s
- 1950s
- 1960s
- 1970s
- 1980s
- 1990s
- 2000s
- Non-members

★ 1% – 10% contribution to funding
☆ Over 10% contribution to funding

**MEMBERSHIP OF THE UN** From the original 51, membership of the UN has now grown to 193. Recent additions include Switzerland, Montenegro and South Sudan. There are only two independent states which are not members of the UN – Taiwan and the Vatican City. All the successor states of the former USSR had joined by the end of 1992. The official languages of the UN are Chinese, English, French, Russian, Spanish and Arabic.

**FUNDING** The UN budget for 2018-19 was US $5.4 billion. Contributions are assessed by the members' ability to pay, with the maximum 22% of the total (USA's share), and the minimum 0.001%. The 28-member EU pays 35% of the budget.

**PEACEKEEPING** The UN has been involved in 67 peacekeeping operations worldwide since 1948.

# INTERNATIONAL ORGANIZATIONS

**ACP** African-Caribbean-Pacific (formed in 1963). Members have economic ties with the EU.
**APEC** Asia-Pacific Economic Co-operation (formed in 1989). It aims to enhance economic growth and prosperity for the region and to strengthen the Asia-Pacific community. APEC is the only intergovernmental grouping in the world operating on the basis of non-binding commitments, open dialogue, and equal respect for the views of all participants. There are 21 member economies.
**ARAB LEAGUE** (formed in 1945). The League's aim is to promote economic, social, political and military co-operation. There are 22 member nations. Syria's membership was suspended in 2011.
**ASEAN** Association of South-east Asian Nations (formed in 1967). Cambodia joined in 1999.
**AU** The African Union replaced the Organization of African Unity (formed in 1963) in 2002. Its 55 members represent over 94% of Africa's population. Arabic, English, French and Portuguese are recognized as working languages.
**COLOMBO PLAN** (formed in 1951). Its 27 members aim to promote economic and social development in Asia and the Pacific.
**COMMONWEALTH** The Commonwealth of Nations evolved from the British Empire. Pakistan was suspended in 1999, but reinstated in 2004. Zimbabwe was suspended in 2002 and, in response to its continued suspension, Zimbabwe left the Commonwealth in 2003. Fiji was suspended in 2006 following a military coup. Rwanda joined the Commonwealth in 2009, as the 54th member state. The Gambia left in 2013. There are currently 53 members.
**EU** European Union (evolved from the European Community in 1993). Cyprus, Czechia, Estonia, Hungary, Latvia, Lithuania, Malta, Poland, Slovakia and Slovenia joined the EU in May 2004; Bulgaria and Romania joined in 2007; Croatia joined in 2013. The other 15 members of the EU are Austria, Belgium, Denmark, Finland, France, Germany, Greece, Ireland, Italy, Luxembourg, Netherlands, Portugal, Spain, Sweden and the UK. There are currently 28 members: the UK is scheduled to leave the EU in 2019.
**LAIA** Latin American Integration Association (1980). Its aim is to promote freer regional integration.
**NATO** North Atlantic Treaty Organization (formed in 1949). It continues despite the winding-up of the Warsaw Pact in 1991. Bulgaria, Estonia, Latvia, Lithuania, Romania, Slovakia and Slovenia became members in 2004, Albania and Croatia in 2009. Montenegro joined in 2017.

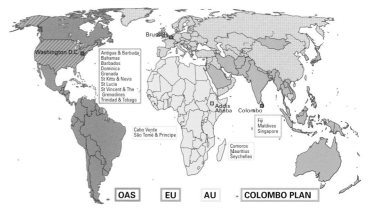

**OAS** Organization of American States (formed in 1948). It aims to promote social and economic co-operation between countries in developed North America and developing Latin America.
**OECD** Organization for Economic Co-operation and Development (formed in 1961). It comprises 35 major free-market economies. Chile, Estonia, Israel and Slovenia joined in 2010. The 'G7' is its 'inner group' of leading industrial nations, comprising Canada, France, Germany, Italy, Japan, the UK and the USA.
**OPEC** Organization of Petroleum Exporting Countries (formed in 1960). It controls about three-quarters of the world's oil supply. Gabon rejoined in 2016.

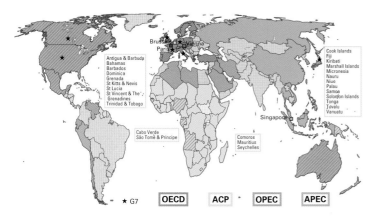

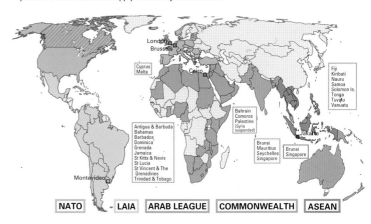

# Wealth

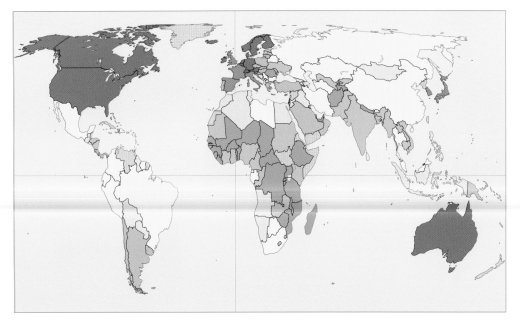

## LEVELS OF INCOME

Gross National Income per capita: the value of total production divided by the population (2017)

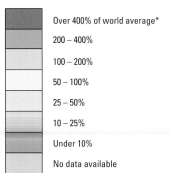

- Over 400% of world average*
- 200 – 400%
- 100 – 200%
- 50 – 100%
- 25 – 50%
- 10 – 25%
- Under 10%
- No data available

*World average = US$ 10,366 (2017)

## WEALTH CREATION

The Gross National Income (GNI) of the world's largest economies, US $ million (2017)

| | | | |
|---|---|---|---|
| 1. USA | 18,980,259 | 21. Argentina | 577,148 |
| 2. China | 12,042,906 | 22. Sweden | 529,460 |
| 3. Japan | 4,888,124 | 23. Poland | 482,526 |
| 4. Germany | 3,596,610 | 24. Belgium | 475,205 |
| 5. UK | 2,675,928 | 25. Iran | 438,368 |
| 6. France | 2,548,257 | 26. Thailand | 411,731 |
| 7. India | 2,430,837 | 27. Norway | 401,390 |
| 8. Italy | 1,878,330 | 28. Austria | 400,263 |
| 9. Brazil | 1,796,487 | 29. Nigeria | 397,525 |
| 10. Canada | 1,573,492 | 30. Philippines | 383,509 |
| 11. South Korea | 1,460,492 | 31. UAE | 367,821 |
| 12. Russia | 1,355,593 | 32. Hong Kong (China) | 342,344 |
| 13. Spain | 1,265,880 | 33. Israel | 324,678 |
| 14. Australia | 1,263,489 | 34. Denmark | 318,623 |
| 15. Mexico | 1,112,530 | 35. Pakistan | 311,667 |
| 16. Indonesia | 934,365 | 36. South Africa | 308,189 |
| 17. Turkey | 882,852 | 37. Singapore | 306,048 |
| 18. Netherlands | 791,270 | 38. Malaysia | 305,051 |
| 19. Switzerland | 682,059 | 39. Egypt | 293,380 |
| 20. Saudi Arabia | 661,495 | 40. Colombia | 286,066 |

## THE WEALTH GAP

The world's richest and poorest countries, by Gross National Income (GNI) per capita in US $ (2017)

| Richest countries | | Poorest countries | |
|---|---|---|---|
| 1. Switzerland | 80,560 | 1. Malawi | 270 |
| 2. Norway | 75,990 | 2. Burundi | 280 |
| 3. Luxembourg | 70,260 | 3. Central African Rep. | 320 |
| 4. Qatar | 61,070 | 4. Congo (Dem. Rep.) | 400 |
| 5. Iceland | 60,830 | 5. Liberia | 410 |
| 6. USA | 58,270 | 6. Niger | 410 |
| 7. Ireland | 55,290 | 7. Madagascar | 440 |
| 8. Denmark | 55,220 | 8. Guinea | 460 |
| 9. Singapore | 54,530 | 9. Ethiopia | 470 |
| 10. Sweden | 52,590 | 10. Eritrea | 490 |
| 11. Australia | 51,360 | 11. Gambia, The | 510 |
| 12. Netherlands | 46,180 | 12. Uganda | 510 |
| 13. Austria | 45,440 | 13. Guinea-Bissau | 520 |
| 14. Finland | 44,580 | 14. Togo | 530 |
| 15. Germany | 43,490 | 15. Mozambique | 590 |
| 16. Canada | 42,870 | 16. Rwanda | 620 |
| 17. Belgium | 41,790 | 17. Tanzania | 630 |
| 18. UK | 40,530 | 18. Burkina Faso | 670 |
| 19. UAE | 39,130 | 19. Mali | 670 |
| 20. Japan | 38,550 | 20. Sierra Leone | 680 |

## CONTINENTAL SHARES

Shares of population and of wealth (GNI) by continent

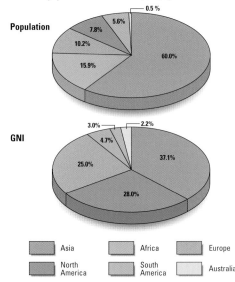

Population

- 0.5 %
- 5.6%
- 7.8%
- 10.2%
- 15.9%
- 60.0%

GNI

- 2.2%
- 3.0%
- 4.7%
- 25.0%
- 37.1%
- 28.0%

- Asia
- Africa
- Europe
- North America
- South America
- Australia

## INFLATION

Average annual rate of inflation (2017)

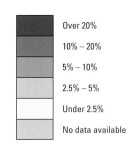

- Over 20%
- 10% – 20%
- 5% – 10%
- 2.5% – 5%
- Under 2.5%
- No data available

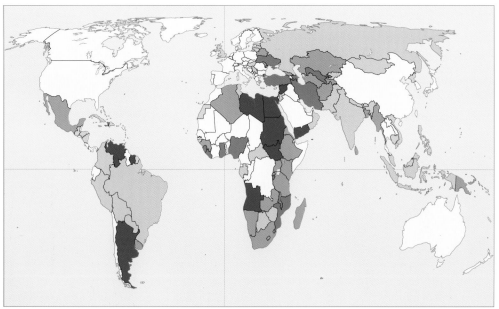

| Highest average inflation | | Lowest average inflation | |
|---|---|---|---|
| Venezuela | 652% | Andorra | -0.9% |
| South Sudan | 182% | Solomon Islands | -0.5% |
| Libya | 33% | Liechtenstein | -0.4% |

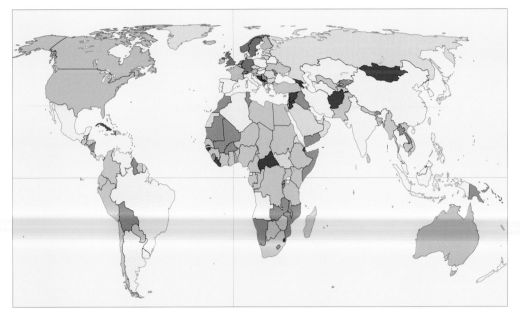

## INTERNATIONAL AID

**Official Development Assistance (ODA) provided and received, per capita (2016)**

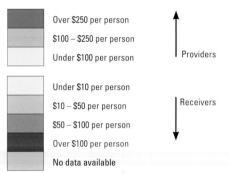

| | |
|---|---|
| Over $250 per person | |
| $100 – $250 per person | Providers |
| Under $100 per person | |
| Under $10 per person | |
| $10 – $50 per person | Receivers |
| $50 – $100 per person | |
| Over $100 per person | |
| No data available | |

## DEBT AND AID

**International debtors and the aid they receive**

Although aid grants make a vital contribution to many of the world's poorer countries, they are usually dwarfed by the burden of debt that the developing economies are expected to repay. It is estimated that the total debt burden of developing countries has increased by 60% between 2014 and 2017. It is now at its highest level since 2004..

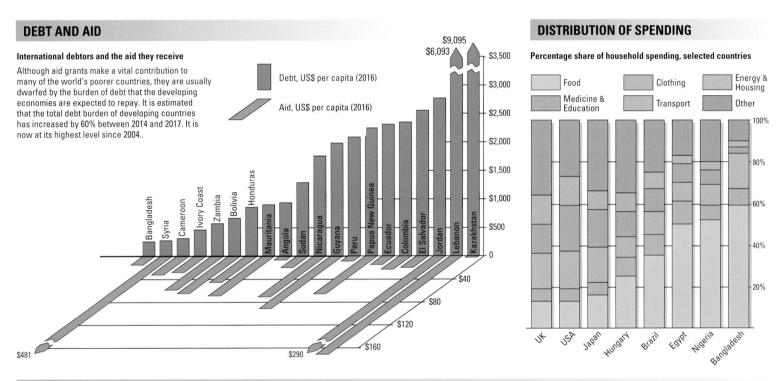

Debt, US$ per capita (2016)

Aid, US$ per capita (2016)

## DISTRIBUTION OF SPENDING

**Percentage share of household spending, selected countries**

| | | |
|---|---|---|
| Food | Clothing | Energy & Housing |
| Medicine & Education | Transport | Other |

## WEALTH INDICATORS

**Number of motor vehicles, Internet users and mobile phones for each 1,000 people, selected countries (2016)**

Motor vehicles    Internet users    Mobile phones

### High Income

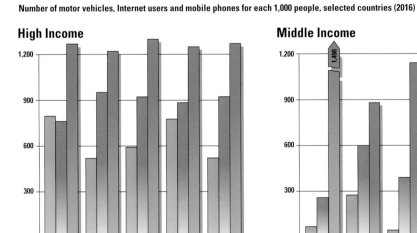

### Middle Income

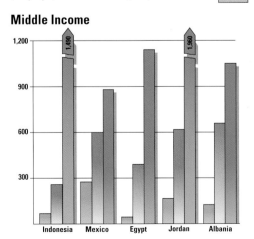

### Low Income

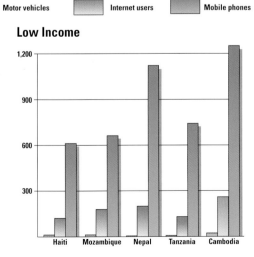

**21**

# Quality of Life

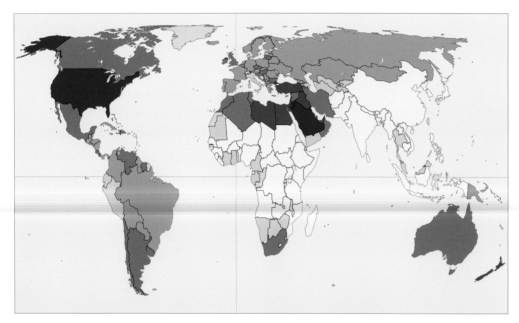

## LEVEL OF OBESITY

Percentage of total adult population considered to be obese (2016)*

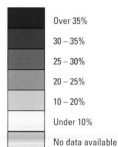

| | |
|---|---|
| | Over 35% |
| | 30 – 35% |
| | 25 – 30% |
| | 20 – 25% |
| | 10 – 20% |
| | Under 10% |
| | No data available |

*Obesity is defined as an adult having a Body Mass Index (BMI) greater than 30.0*

## HOSPITAL CAPACITY

Hospital beds available for each 1,000 people (2015)

| Highest capacity | | Lowest capacity | |
|---|---|---|---|
| Monaco | 13.8 | Mali | 0.1 |
| Japan | 13.4 | Madagascar | 0.2 |
| North Korea | 13.2 | Iran | 0.2 |
| South Korea | 11.5 | Senegal | 0.3 |
| Belarus | 11.0 | Niger | 0.3 |
| Ukraine | 8.8 | Guinea | 0.3 |
| Somalia | 8.7 | Ethiopia | 0.3 |
| Germany | 8.3 | Mauritania | 0.4 |
| Russia | 8.2 | Côte d'Ivoire | 0.4 |
| Austria | 7.6 | Chad | 0.4 |
| Turkmenistan | 7.4 | Burkina Faso | 0.4 |
| Liechtenstein | 7.3 | Uganda | 0.5 |
| Lithuania | 7.3 | Nigeria | 0.5 |
| Hungary | 7.0 | Benin | 0.5 |
| Mongolia | 7.0 | Afghanistan | 0.5 |

Although the ratio of people to hospital beds gives a good approximation of a country's health provision, it is not an absolute indicator. Raw numbers may mask inefficiency and other weaknesses: the high availability of beds in Belarus, for example, has not prevented infant mortality rates over twice as high as in the United States.

## LIFE EXPECTANCY

Years of life expectancy at birth, selected countries (2017)

The chart shows combined data for both sexes. On average, women live longer than men worldwide, even in developing countries with high maternal mortality rates. Overall, life expectancy is steadily rising, though the difference between rich and poor nations remains dramatic.

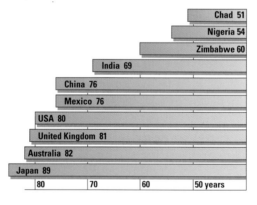

| | |
|---|---|
| Chad | 51 |
| Nigeria | 54 |
| Zimbabwe | 60 |
| India | 69 |
| China | 76 |
| Mexico | 76 |
| USA | 80 |
| United Kingdom | 81 |
| Australia | 82 |
| Japan | 89 |

80    70    60    50 years

## CAUSES OF DEATH

Causes of death for selected countries by percentage

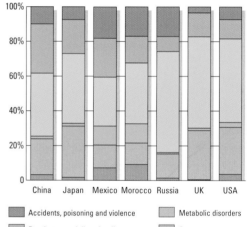

China  Japan  Mexico  Morocco  Russia  UK  USA

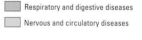 Accidents, poisoning and violence     Metabolic disorders

Respiratory and digestive diseases    Cancers

Nervous and circulatory diseases    Infectious and parasitic diseases

## INFANT MORTALITY

Number of babies who died under the age of one, per 1,000 live births (2017)

| | |
|---|---|
| | Over 75 deaths per 1,000 births |
| | 50 – 75 deaths per 1,000 births |
| | 25 – 50 deaths per 1,000 births |
| | 10 – 25 deaths per 1,000 births |
| | Under 10 deaths per 1,000 births |
| | No data available |

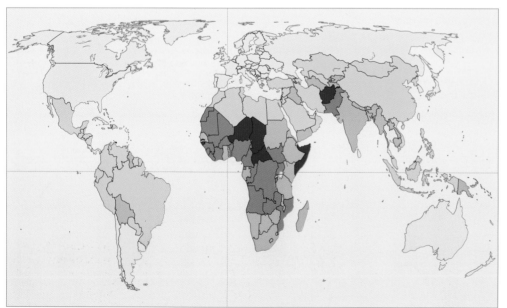

| Highest infant mortality | | Lowest infant mortality | |
|---|---|---|---|
| Afghanistan | 111 deaths | Monaco | 1.8 deaths |
| Somalia | 95 deaths | Japan | 2.0 deaths |
| CAR | 86 deaths | Iceland | 2.1 deaths |

## ILLITERACY

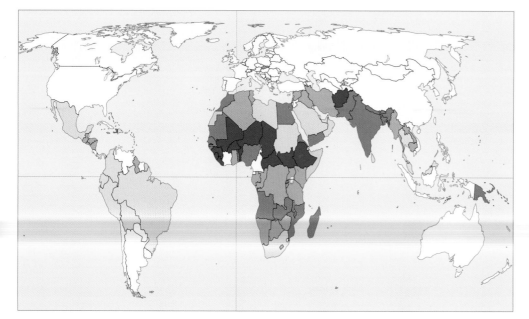

Percentage of the total adult population unable to read or write (2015)

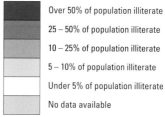

- Over 50% of population illiterate
- 25 – 50% of population illiterate
- 10 – 25% of population illiterate
- 5 – 10% of population illiterate
- Under 5% of population illiterate
- No data available

Countries with the highest illiteracy rates as percentage of population

| | | | |
|---|---|---|---|
| Niger | 81% | Burkina Faso | 64% |
| Chad | 78% | CAR | 63% |
| South Sudan | 73% | Afghanistan | 62% |
| Guinea | 70% | Benin | 62% |
| Mali | 67% | Liberia | 52% |

## FERTILITY AND EDUCATION

Fertility rates compared with female education, selected countries

Percentage of females aged 12–17 in secondary education

Fertility rate: average number of children borne per woman

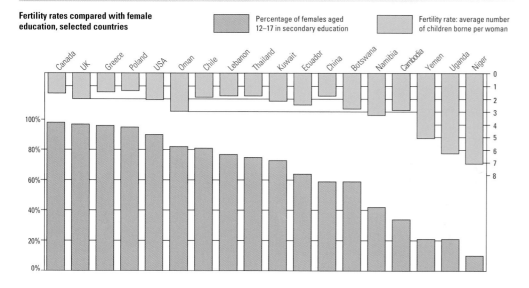

## LIVING STANDARDS

At first sight, most international contrasts in living standards are swamped by differences in wealth. The rich not only have more money, they have more of everything, including years of life. Those with only a little money are obliged to spend most of it on food and clothing, the basic maintenance costs of their existence; air travel and tourism are unlikely to feature on their expenditure lists. However, poverty and wealth are both relative: slum dwellers living on social security payments in an affluent industrial country have far more resources at their disposal than an average African peasant, but feel their own poverty nonetheless. A middle-class Indian lawyer cannot command the earnings of a counterpart living in New York, London or Rome; nevertheless, he rightly sees himself as prosperous.

The rich not only live longer, on average, than the poor, they also die from different causes. Infectious and parasitic diseases, all but eliminated in the developed world, remain a scourge in the developing nations. On the other hand, more than two-thirds of the populations of OECD nations eventually succumb to cancer or circulatory disease.

## HUMAN DEVELOPMENT INDEX

The Human Development Index (HDI), calculated by the UN Development Programme (UNDP), gives a value to countries using indicators of life expectancy, education and standards of living (2015). Higher values show more developed countries.

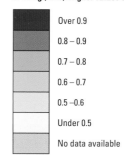

- Over 0.9
- 0.8 – 0.9
- 0.7 – 0.8
- 0.6 – 0.7
- 0.5 – 0.6
- Under 0.5
- No data available

| Highest values | | Lowest values | |
|---|---|---|---|
| Norway | 0.949 | Central African Rep. | 0.352 |
| Australia | 0.939 | Niger | 0.353 |
| Switzerland | 0.939 | Chad | 0.396 |
| Germany | 0.926 | Burkina Faso | 0.402 |
| Denmark | 0.925 | Burundi | 0.404 |

# Energy

## ENERGY PRODUCTION

Each square represents 1% of world primary energy production, by region

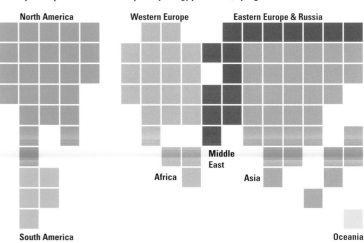

North America
Western Europe
Eastern Europe & Russia
Middle East
Africa
Asia
South America
Oceania

## ENERGY CONSUMPTION

Each square represents 1% of world primary energy production, by region

North America
Western Europe
Eastern Europe & Russia
Middle East
Africa
Asia
South America
Oceania

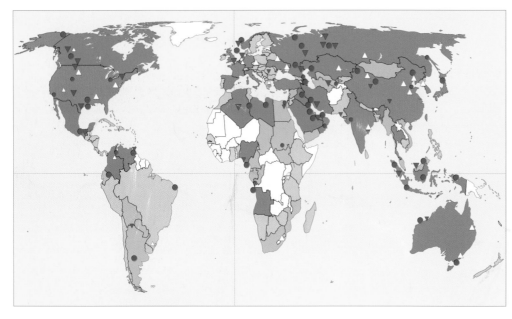

## ENERGY BALANCE

Difference between energy production and consumption in millions of tonnes of oil equivalent (MtOe)

**Energy surplus**

Over 35 MtOe surplus

1 – 35 MtOe surplus

Between 1 deficit – 1 surplus (approx. balance)

1 – 35 MtOe deficit

Over 35 MtOe deficit

No data available

**Energy deficit**

- ● Principal oilfields
- ▼ Principal gasfields
- △ Principal coalfields
- ◤ Secondary oilfields
- ▾ Secondary gasfields
- △ Secondary coalfields

## WORLD ENERGY CONSUMPTION

**Energy consumed by world regions, measured in million tonnes of oil equivalent (2017)**
Total world consumption was 13,513 MtOe. Only energy from oil, natural gas, coal, nuclear and hydroelectric sources are included. Excluded are biomass fuels such as wood, peat and animal waste, and wind, solar and geothermal energy which, though important locally in some countries, are not always reliably documented statistically.

Oil   Gas   Coal   Nuclear   Hydro

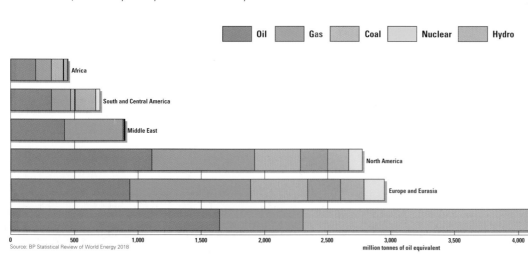

Africa
South and Central America
Middle East
North America
Europe and Eurasia
Asia Pacific

0   500   1,000   1,500   2,000   2,500   3,000   3,500   4,000   4,500   5,000   5,500
million tonnes of oil equivalent

Source: BP Statistical Review of World Energy 2018

**World energy consumption, by source (2017)**

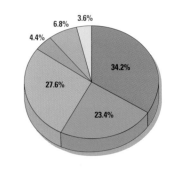

34.2%
27.6%
23.4%
4.4%
6.8%
3.6%

24

## ENERGY

Energy is used to keep us warm or cool, fuel our industries and our transport systems, and even feed us; high-intensity agriculture, with its use of fertilizers, pesticides and machinery, is heavily energy-dependent. Although we live in a high-energy society, there are vast discrepancies between rich and poor; for example, a North American consumes six times as much energy as a Chinese person. But even developing nations have more power at their disposal than was imaginable a century ago.

The distribution of energy supplies, most importantly fossil fuels (coal, oil and natural gas), is very uneven. In addition, the diagrams and map opposite show that the largest producers of energy are not necessarily the largest consumers. The movement of energy supplies around the world is therefore an important component of international trade.

As the finite reserves of fossil fuels are depleted, renewable energy sources, such as solar, hydro-thermal, wind, tidal and biomass, will become increasingly important around the world.

## NUCLEAR POWER

**Major producers by percentage of world total and by percentage of domestic electricity generation (2016)**

| Country | % of world total production | Country | % of nuclear as proportion of domestic electricity |
|---|---|---|---|
| 1. USA | 32.5% | 1. France | 73.3% |
| 2. France | 15.6% | 2. Slovakia | 54.1% |
| 3. China | 8.0% | 3. Ukraine | 52.3% |
| 4. Russia | 7.4% | 4. Belgium | 51.7% |
| 5. South Korea | 6.2% | 5. Hungary | 51.3% |
| 6. Canada | 3.9% | 6. Sweden | 40.0% |
| 7. Germany | 3.2% | 7. Slovenia | 35.2% |
| 8. Ukraine | 3.1% | 8. Bulgaria | 35.9% |
| 9. UK | 2.6% | 9. Switzerland | 34.4% |
| 10. Sweden | 2.4% | 10. Finland | 33.7% |

Although the 1980s were a bad time for the nuclear power industry (fears of long-term environmental damage were heavily reinforced by the 1986 disaster at Chernobyl), the industry picked up in the early 1990s. Despite this, growth has recently been curtailed whilst countries review their energy mix, in light of the March 2011 Japanese earthquake and tsunami which seriously damaged the Fukushima nuclear power station.

## HYDROELECTRICITY

**Major producers by percentage of world total and by percentage of domestic electricity generation (2015)**

| Country | % of world total production | Country | % of hydroelectric as proportion of domestic electricity |
|---|---|---|---|
| 1. China | 28.4% | 1. Albania | 100.0% |
| 2. Brazil | 9.6% | 2. Paraguay | 100.0% |
| 3. Canada | 9.5% | 3. Nepal | 99.7% |
| 4. USA | 6.3% | 4. Tajikistan | 99.7% |
| 5. Russia | 4.0% | 5. Zambia | 99.7% |
| 6. Norway | 3.5% | 6. Congo (Dem. Rep.) | 99.6% |
| 7. India | 3.2% | 7. Mozambique | 97.7% |
| 8. Japan | 2.3% | 8. Norway | 96.0% |
| 9. Venezuela | 2.0% | 9. Ethiopia | 95.6% |
| 10. Sweden | 1.9% | 10. Namibia | 95.6% |

Countries heavily reliant on hydroelectricity are usually small and non-industrial: a high proportion of hydroelectric power more often reflects a modest energy budget than vast hydroelectric resources. The USA, for instance, produces only 6% of its power requirements from hydroelectricity; yet that 6% amounts to almost half the hydropower generated by most of Africa.

## ELECTRICITY PRODUCTION

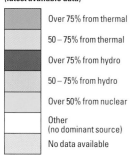

**Percentage of electricity generated by source (latest available data)**

- Over 75% from thermal
- 50 – 75% from thermal
- Over 75% from hydro
- 50 – 75% from hydro
- Over 50% from nuclear
- Other (no dominant source)
- No data available

- ● Selected geothermal plants
- ◆ Selected hydroelectric plants

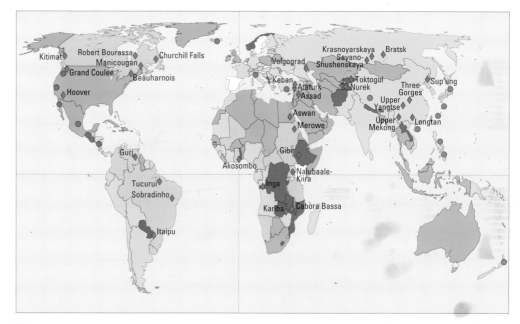

### Conversion Rates

**1 barrel** = 0.136 tonnes or 159 litres or 35 Imperial gallons or 42 US gallons

**1 tonne** = 7.33 barrels or 1,185 litres or 256 Imperial gallons or 261 US gallons

**1 tonne oil** = 1.5 tonnes hard coal or 3.0 tonnes lignite or 12,000 kWh

**1 Imperial gallon** = 1.201 US gallons or 4.546 litres or 277.4 cubic inches

### Measurements
For historical reasons, oil is traded in 'barrels'. The weight and volume equivalents (shown right) are all based on average-density 'Arabian light' crude oil.

The energy equivalents given for a tonne of oil are also somewhat imprecise: oil and coal of different qualities will have varying energy contents, a fact usually reflected in their price on world markets.

## ENERGY RESERVES

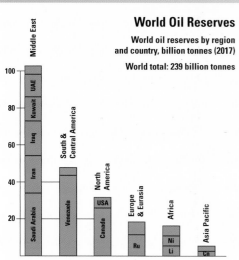

**World Oil Reserves**

World oil reserves by region and country, billion tonnes (2017)

World total: 239 billion tonnes

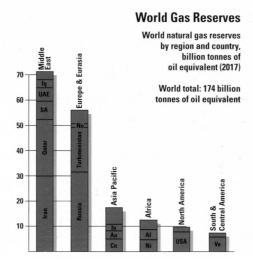

**World Gas Reserves**

World natural gas reserves by region and country, billion tonnes of oil equivalent (2017)

World total: 174 billion tonnes of oil equivalent

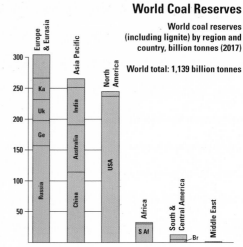

**World Coal Reserves**

World coal reserves (including lignite) by region and country, billion tonnes (2017)

World total: 1,139 billion tonnes

**25**

# Production

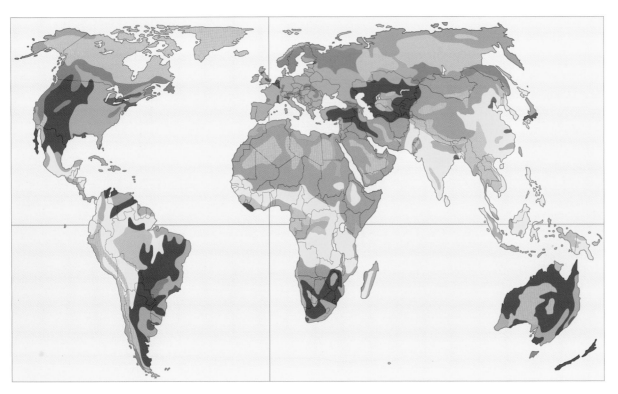

## AGRICULTURE

Predominant type of farming or land use

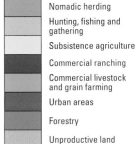

- Nomadic herding
- Hunting, fishing and gathering
- Subsistence agriculture
- Commercial ranching
- Commercial livestock and grain farming
- Urban areas
- Forestry
- Unproductive land

The development of agriculture has transformed human existence more than any other. The whole business of farming is constantly developing: due mainly to the new varieties of rice and wheat, world grain production has more than doubled since 1965. New machinery and modern agricultural techniques enable farmers to produce food for the world's developed economies, but the poorer third world relies very much on subsistence agriculture.

## STAPLE CROPS

### Wheat
China 17.6%
India 12.5%
Russia 9.8%
USA 8.4%
Canada 4.1%
France 3.9%
Ukraine 3.5%

World total (2016): 749,460,077 tonnes

### Maize
USA 36.3%
China 21.9%
Brazil 6.1%

World total (2016): 1,060,107,470 tonnes

### Barley
Russia 12.7%
Germany 7.6%
France 7.3%
Australia 6.4%
Canada 6.2%
Spain 5.6%

World total (2016): 141,277,993 tonnes

### Millet
India 36.3%
Niger 13.7%
China 7.0%
Mali 6.4%
Nigeria 5.2%

World total (2016): 28,357,451 tonnes

### Rice/Paddy
China 28.6%
India 21.2%
Indonesia 9.6%
Bangladesh 6.1%
Vietnam 5.3%
Myanmar (Burma) 4.7%
Thailand 4.6%

World total (2016): 740,961,445 tonnes

### Potatoes
China 26.3%
India 11.6%
Russia 8.3%
Ukraine 5.8%
USA 5.3%

World total (2016): 376,826,967 tonnes

### Soybeans
USA 35.0%
Brazil 28.8%
Argentina 17.6%
India 4.2%

World total (2016): 334,894,085 tonnes

### Cassava
Nigeria 20.6%
Thailand 11.2%
Brazil 7.6%
Indonesia 7.5%
Ghana 6.4%
Congo (D.R.) 5.3%

World total (2016): 277,102,564 tonnes

## SUGARS

### Sugar cane
Brazil 38.2%
India 17.3%
China 12.2%
Thailand 4.3%
Pakistan 3.3%
Mexico 2.8%

World total (2016): 2,013,721,491 tonnes

### Sugar beet
Russia 18.5%
France 12.2%
USA 12.1%
Germany 9.2%
Turkey 7.0%
Ukraine 5.1%
Poland 4.3%
Egypt 4.8%

World total (2016): 277,230,790 tonnes

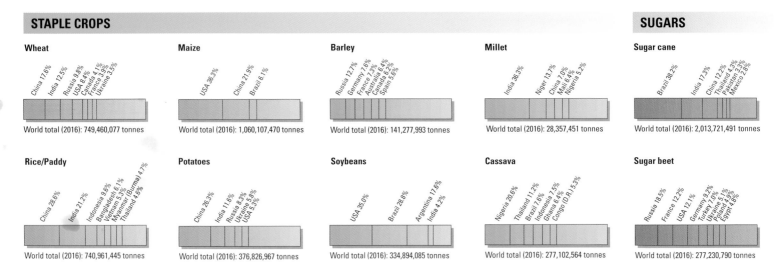

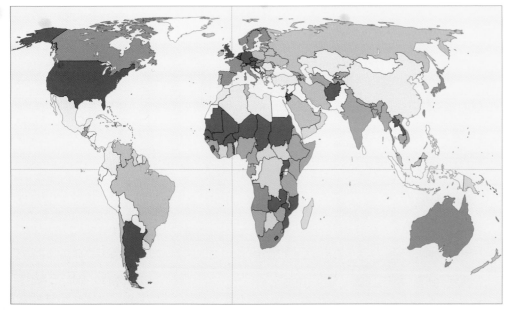

## EMPLOYMENT

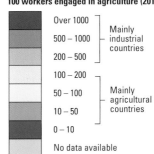

The number of workers employed in industry for every 100 workers engaged in agriculture (2017)

- Over 1000 ⎤
- 500 – 1000 ⎬ Mainly industrial countries
- 200 – 500 ⎦
- 100 – 200
- 50 – 100 ⎤
- 10 – 50 ⎬ Mainly agricultural countries
- 0 – 10 ⎦
- No data available

Countries with the highest number of workers employed in industry per 100 workers engaged in agriculture (2017)

| | | | |
|---|---|---|---|
| 1. Argentina | 4,960 | 6. St Kitts & Nevis | 2,727 |
| 2. Liechtenstein | 4,613 | 7. Luxembourg | 1,818 |
| 3. Austria | 3,614 | 8. Germany | 1,729 |
| 4. Bahrain | 3,200 | 9. Israel | 1,573 |
| 5. USA | 2,900 | 10. Singapore | 1,550 |

# MINERAL PRODUCTION

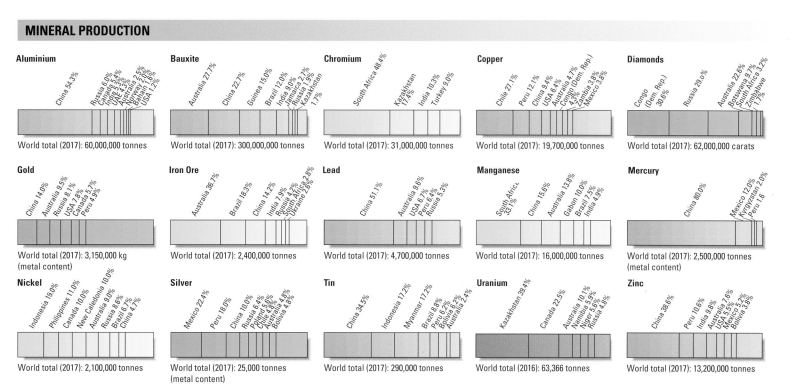

**Aluminium**
China 54.3%, Russia 6.0%, Canada 5.4%, India 4.3%, UAE 4.3%, Australia 2.5%, Norway 2.0%, Bahrain 1.6%, USA 1.2%
World total (2017): 60,000,000 tonnes

**Bauxite**
Australia 27.7%, China 22.7%, Guinea 15.0%, Brazil 12.0%, India 9.0%, Jamaica 2.7%, Russia 1.9%, Kazakhstan 1.7%
World total (2017): 300,000,000 tonnes

**Chromium**
South Africa 48.4%, Kazakhstan 17.4%, India 10.3%, Turkey 9.0%
World total (2017): 31,000,000 tonnes

**Copper**
Chile 27.1%, Peru 12.1%, China 9.4%, USA 6.4%, Australia 4.7%, Congo (Dem. Rep.) 4.3%, Zambia 3.8%, Mexico 3.8%
World total (2017): 19,700,000 tonnes

**Diamonds**
Congo (Dem. Rep.) 30.6%, Russia 29.0%, Australia 22.6%, Botswana 9.7%, South Africa 3.2%, Zimbabwe 1.7%
World total (2017): 62,000,000 carats

**Gold**
China 14.0%, Australia 9.5%, Russia 8.1%, USA 7.8%, Canada 5.7%, Peru 4.9%
World total (2017): 3,150,000 kg (metal content)

**Iron Ore**
Australia 36.7%, Brazil 18.3%, China 14.2%, India 7.9%, Russia 4.2%, South Africa 2.8%, Ukraine 2.0%
World total (2017): 2,400,000 tonnes

**Lead**
China 51.1%, Australia 9.6%, USA 6.7%, Peru 6.4%, Russia 5.3%
World total (2017): 4,700,000 tonnes

**Manganese**
South Africa 33.1%, China 15.6%, Australia 13.8%, Gabon 10.0%, Brazil 7.5%, India 4.9%
World total (2017): 16,000,000 tonnes

**Mercury**
China 80.0%, Mexico 12.0%, Kyrgyzstan 2.0%, Peru 1.6
World total (2017): 2,500,000 tonnes (metal content)

**Nickel**
Indonesia 19.0%, Philippines 11.0%, Canada 10.0%, New Caledonia 10.0%, Australia 9.0%, Russia 8.6%, Brazil 6.7%, China 4.7%
World total (2017): 2,100,000 tonnes

**Silver**
Mexico 22.4%, Peru 18.0%, China 10.0%, Russia 6.4%, Poland 4.8%, Chile 4.8%, Australia 4.8%, Bolivia 4.8%
World total (2017): 25,000 tonnes (metal content)

**Tin**
China 34.5%, Indonesia 17.2%, Myanmar 17.2%, Brazil 8.8%, Peru 6.2%, Bolivia 6.2%, Australia 2.4%
World total (2017): 290,000 tonnes

**Uranium**
Kazakhstan 39.4%, Canada 22.5%, Australia 10.1%, Namibia 5.9%, Niger 5.6%, Russia 4.8%
World total (2016): 63,366 tonnes

**Zinc**
China 38.6%, Peru 10.6%, India 9.8%, USA 7.6%, Australia 5.5%, Mexico 5.2%, Bolivia 3.8%
World total (2017): 13,200,000 tonnes

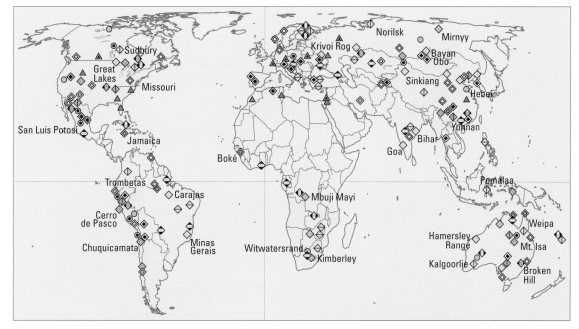

## MINERAL DISTRIBUTION

The map shows the richest sources of the most important minerals

**Precious metals**
◇ Diamonds
○ Gold
◉ Silver

**Iron and ferro-alloys**
◇ Chromium
◈ Cobalt
◇ Iron ore
◇ Manganese
◈ Molybdenum
◇ Nickel ore
◈ Tungsten

**Non-ferrous metals**
◈ Bauxite
  (◈ Aluminium)
◇ Copper
◇ Lead
◈ Mercury
◇ Zinc

**Fertilizers**
▲ Phosphates
▲ Potash

The map does not show undersea deposits, most of which are currently inaccessible.

Map labels: Sudbury, Great Lakes, Missouri, San Luis Potosi, Jamaica, Trombetas, Carajas, Cerro de Pasco, Chuquicamata, Minas Gerais, Boké, Mbuji Mayi, Witwatersrand, Kimberley, Norilsk, Krivoi Rog, Mirnyy, Bayan Obo, Sinkiang, Hebei, Yunnan, Bihar, Goa, Pomalaa, Hamersley Range, Kalgoorlie, Weipa, Mt. Isa, Broken Hill

# INDUSTRIAL PRODUCTION

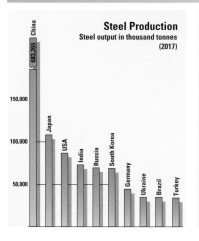

**Steel Production**
Steel output in thousand tonnes (2017)
China 663,265, Japan, USA, India, Russia, South Korea, Germany, Ukraine, Brazil, Turkey

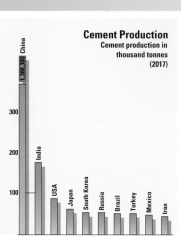

**Cement Production**
Cement production in thousand tonnes (2017)
China 2,388,380, India, USA, Japan, South Korea, Russia, Brazil, Turkey, Mexico, Iran

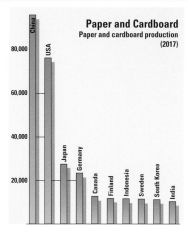

**Paper and Cardboard**
Paper and cardboard production (2017)
China, USA, Japan, Germany, Canada, Finland, Indonesia, Sweden, South Korea, India

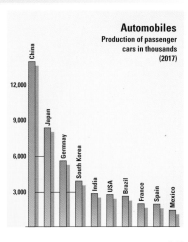

**Automobiles**
Production of passenger cars in thousands (2017)
China, Japan, Germany, South Korea, India, USA, Brazil, France, Spain, Mexico

# Trade

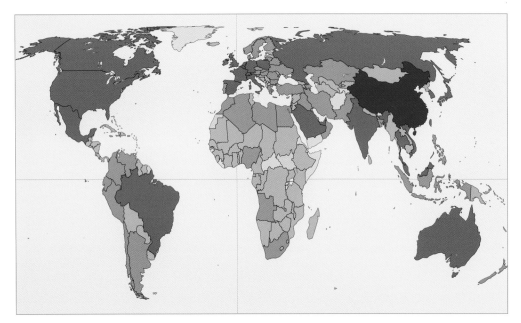

Over 10% of world trade

1 – 10% of world trade

0.1 – 1.0% of world trade

0 – 0.1% of world trade

No world trade

No data available

### Countries with the largest share of world trade (2017)

| | | | |
|---|---|---|---|
| 1. China | 12.4% | 6. France | 3.1% |
| 2. USA | 9.1% | 7. Netherlands | 3.0% |
| 3. Germany | 8.1% | 8. Italy | 2.9% |
| 4. Japan | 3.9% | 9. UK | 2.5% |
| 5. South Korea | 3.2% | 10. Canada | 2.5% |

## THE MAIN TRADING NATIONS

The imports and exports of the top ten trading nations as a percentage of world trade (2016). Each country's trade in manufactured goods is shown in dark blue

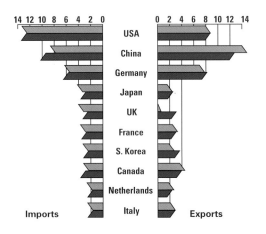

## MAJOR EXPORTS

Leading manufactured items and their exporters

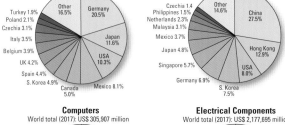

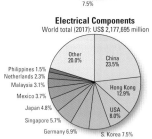

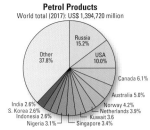

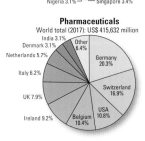

## BALANCE OF TRADE

Value of exports in proportion to the value of imports (2017)

More than 50%

25 – 50%

0 – 25%

0 – 25%

25 – 50%

More than 50%

No data available

Exports exceed imports

Imports exceed exports

The total world trade balance should amount to zero, since exports must equal imports on a global scale. In practice, at least $100 billion in exports go unrecorded, leaving the world with an apparent deficit and many countries in a better position than public accounting reveals. However, a favourable trade balance is not necessarily a sign of prosperity: many poorer countries must maintain a high surplus in order to service debts, and do so by restricting imports below the levels needed to sustain successful economies.

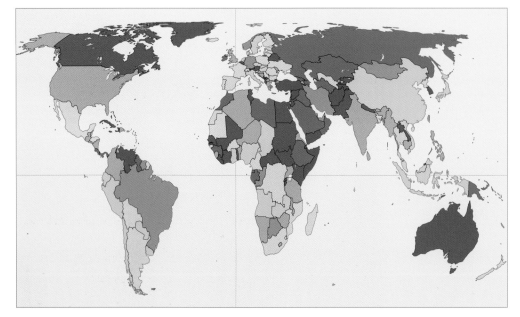

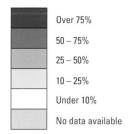

## INDUSTRY AND TRADE

**Manufactured goods as a percentage of total exports (2016))**

- Over 75%
- 50 – 75%
- 25 – 50%
- 10 – 25%
- Under 10%
- No data available

**Countries most dependent on the export of manufactured goods (2016)**

| | | | | | |
|---|---|---|---|---|---|
| 1. Botswana | 94% | 4. Israel | 93% |
| 2. China | 94% | 5. Switzerland | 91% |
| 3. Cambodia | 93% | 6. Czechia | 90% |

## MERCHANT FLEETS

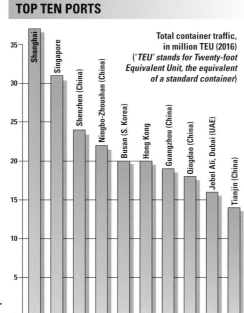

**Merchant fleets by gross register tonnage (millions) (2017).** Although a large number of vessels are registered in Liberia and Panama, they are not part of the national fleet

USA, India, South Korea, Bermuda, Indonesia, United Kingdom, Norway, Italy, Denmark, Cyprus, Japan, Greece, China, Bahamas, Malta, Singapore, Hong Kong, Liberia, Marshall Islands, Panama (216)

0 10 20 30 40 50 60 70 80 90 100 110 120 130 140

## TOP TEN PORTS

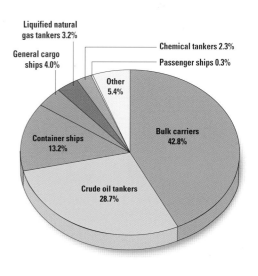

**Total container traffic, in million TEU (2016)** ('*TEU*' stands for Twenty-foot Equivalent Unit, the equivalent of a standard container)

Shanghai, Singapore, Shenzhen (China), Ningbo-Zhoushan (China), Busan (S. Korea), Hong Kong, Guangzhou (China), Qingdao (China), Jebel Ali, Dubai (UAE), Tianjin (China)

## TYPES OF VESSELS

**World fleet by type of vessel (2017)**

- Liquified natural gas tankers 3.2%
- General cargo ships 4.0%
- Chemical tankers 2.3%
- Passenger ships 0.3%
- Other 5.4%
- Container ships 13.2%
- Bulk carriers 42.8%
- Crude oil tankers 28.7%

## IMPORTANCE OF SERVICE SECTOR

**Percentage of total GDP from service sector (2017)**

- Over 70%
- 60 – 70%
- 50 – 60%
- 40 – 50%
- Under 40%
- No data available

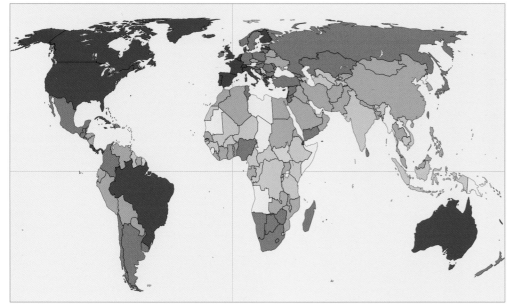

**Countries with the highest and lowest percentage of GDP from services (2017)**

| Highest | | Lowest | |
|---|---|---|---|
| 1. Bahamas | 90% | 1. Timor-Leste | 14% |
| 2. Malta | 88% | 2. Chad | 27% |
| 3. Luxembourg | 88% | 3. Angola | 28% |
| 4. Barbados | 87% | 4. Austria | 31% |
| 5. Cyprus | 87% | 5. Somalia | 33% |

**29**

# Travel and Tourism

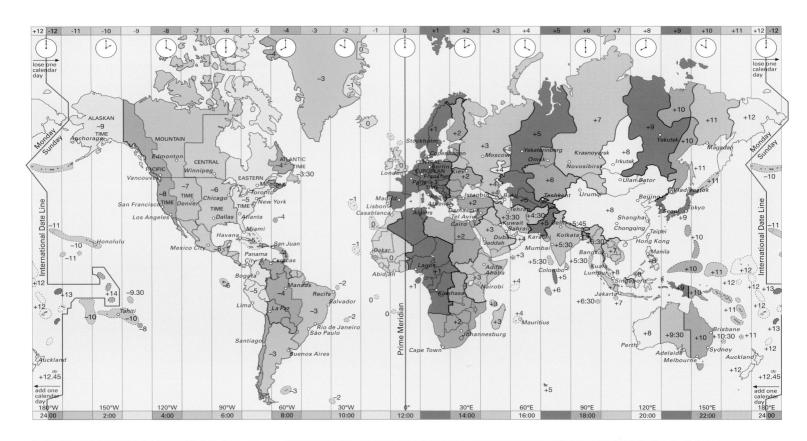

## TIME ZONES

| | |
|---|---|
| ░ Zones using UT (GMT) | ▓ Zones ahead of UT (GMT) |
| ▤ Zones behind UT (GMT) | ▒ Half-hour zones |
| — International boundaries | — Time-zone boundaries |
| **10** Hours fast or slow of UT or Co-ordinated Universal Time | — International Date Line |

Certain time zones are affected by the incidence of daylight saving time in countries where it is adopted.

Actual solar time, when it is noon at Greenwich, is shown along the top of the map.

The world is divided into 24 time zones, each centred on meridians at 15° intervals, which is the longitudinal distance the sun travels every hour. The meridian running through Greenwich, London, passes through the middle of the first zone.

## RAIL AND ROAD: THE LEADING NATIONS

| | Total rail network ('000 km) | | Passenger km per head per year | | Total road network ('000 km) | | Vehicle km per head per year | | Number of vehicles per km of roads |
|---|---|---|---|---|---|---|---|---|---|
| 1. | USA ............... 293.5 | Switzerland ........ 2,430 | | USA ................. 6,586.6 | | Peru ................. 38,553 | | Monaco ............... 388 |
| 2. | China .............. 124.0 | Japan ................. 1,995 | | India ................ 4,699.0 | | USA .................. 34,560 | | Portugal .............. 278 |
| 3. | Russia ............. 87.2 | Denmark ............ 1,329 | | China .............. 4,106.4 | | Tunisia ............... 25,225 | | Hong Kong .......... 271 |
| 4. | Canada ........... 77.9 | France ................ 1,298 | | Brazil ............... 1,580.9 | | Pakistan ............ 25,199 | | UAE .................... 230 |
| 5. | India .............. 68.5 | Austria ............... 1,245 | | Russia ............. 1,282.3 | | Ecuador ............. 23,570 | | Singapore .......... 230 |
| 6. | Germany ......... 43.5 | Russia ................ 1,220 | | Japan .............. 1,218.7 | | Chile ................. 22,671 | | Macau ................ 228 |
| 7. | Australia ......... 37.0 | Ukraine .............. 1,150 | | Canada ............ 1,042.3 | | South Korea ...... 21,763 | | Japan ................. 222 |
| 8. | Argentina ........ 36.9 | Belarus .............. 1,030 | | France ............. 1,028.4 | | Singapore ......... 21,563 | | Kuwait ............... 217 |
| 9. | Brazil .............. 29.9 | Belgium .............. 1,009 | | Australia .......... 832.2 | | Morocco ........... 18,455 | | South Korea ....... 174 |
| 10. | France ............ 29.6 | UK ....................... 981 | | South Africa ...... 737.0 | | Croatia .............. 17,723 | | Bulgaria ............ 157 |
| 11. | Japan ............. 27.3 | Germany ............. 959 | | Spain ............... 683.1 | | Finland .............. 17,639 | | Jordan ............... 152 |
| 12. | Ukraine ........... 21.7 | Netherlands ......... 940 | | Germany .......... 645.0 | | Canada ............. 17,498 | | Israel ................. 138 |
| 13. | South Africa ..... 21.0 | Kazakhstan ......... 880 | | Sweden ............ 579.5 | | Denmark ........... 16,903 | | Bahrain .............. 112 |
| 14. | Italy ............... 20.2 | Italy .................... 780 | | Indonesia ......... 496.6 | | Thailand ........... 16,823 | | Mauritius .......... 107 |
| 15. | Poland ............ 19.2 | India ................... 777 | | Italy ................. 487.6 | | Isreal ............... 16,721 | | Puerto Rico ........ 92 |

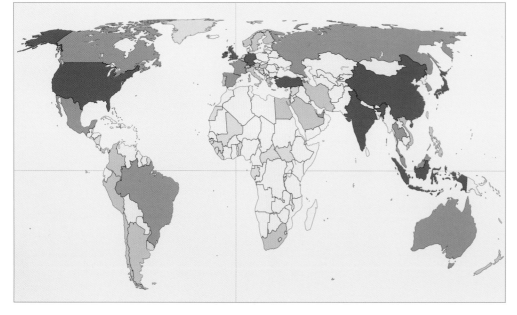

## AIR TRAVEL

**Number of air passengers carried (2016)**

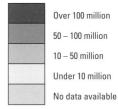

| | |
|---|---|
| ■ | Over 100 million |
| ▓ | 50 – 100 million |
| ▒ | 10 – 50 million |
| ░ | Under 10 million |
| ▫ | No data available |

**World's busiest airports (2017) – total passengers in millions**

1. Atlanta Hartsfield International (ATL) ...................................... 103.9
2. Beijing Capital International (PEK) ............................................ 95.8
3. Dubai International (DXB) ......................................................... 88.2
4. Tokyo Haneda (HND) ............................................................... 85.4
5. Los Angeles International (LAX) ............................................... 84.6
6. Chicago O'Hare International (ORD) ......................................... 79.8
7. London Heathrow (LHR) ........................................................... 78.0
8. Hong Kong International (HKG) ................................................ 72.7
9. Shanghai Pudong International (PVG) ....................................... 70.0
10. Paris Charles de Gaulle (CDG) ............................................... 69.5

## TOURIST CENTRES

- ■ Cultural and historical centres
- ◻ Coastal resorts
- ◻ Ski resorts
- ■ Centres of entertainment
- ■ Places of pilgrimage
- ■ Places of great natural beauty
- ── Popular holiday cruise routes

## VISITORS TO THE USA

**Overseas arrivals to the USA, in thousands (2016)**

| | | |
|---|---|---|
| 1. | Canada | 19,302 |
| 2. | Mexico | 18,730 |
| 3. | UK | 4,574 |
| 4. | Japan | 3,577 |
| 5. | China | 2,972 |
| 6. | Germany | 2,034 |
| 7. | South Korea | 1,973 |
| 8. | Brazil | 1,693 |
| 9. | France | 1,628 |
| 10. | Australia | 1,346 |

## TOURIST SPENDING

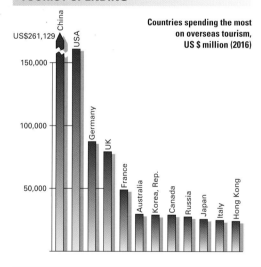

**Countries spending the most on overseas tourism, US $ million (2016)**

US$261,129 (China)

## TOURISTS

**International tourist arrivals**

| | | millions (2016) |
|---|---|---|
| 1. | France | 82.6 |
| 2. | United States of America | 75.6 |
| 3. | Spain | 75.6 |
| 4. | China | 59.3 |
| 5. | Italy | 52.4 |
| 6. | United Kingdom | 35.8 |
| 7. | Germany | 35.6 |
| 8. | Mexico | 35.0 |
| 9. | Thailand | 32.6 |
| 10. | Austria | 28.1 |

The UNWTO (United Nations World Tourism Organization) ranks countries by international tourism receipts (see bar chart right) and international tourist arrivals as table above. France has remained at the top of the list of main destinations for several years, with the USA in second place.

## TOURIST EARNINGS

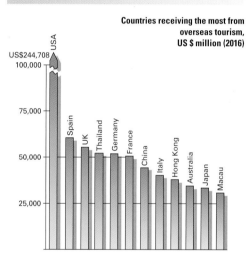

**Countries receiving the most from overseas tourism, US $ million (2016)**

US$244,708 (USA)

## IMPORTANCE OF TOURISM

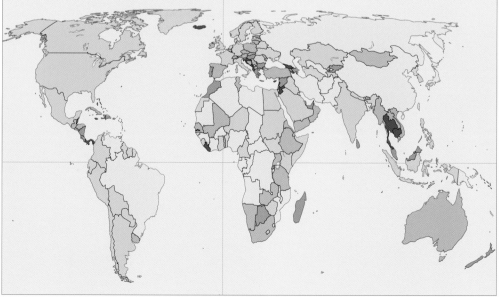

**Tourism receipts as a percentage of Gross National Income (2016)**

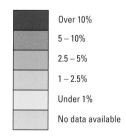

- Over 10%
- 5 – 10%
- 2.5 – 5%
- 1 – 2.5%
- Under 1%
- No data available

**Countries with the highest tourism receipts as % of GNI (2016)**

| | | | | | |
|---|---|---|---|---|---|
| 1. | Palau | 75 | 6. | Vanuatu | 39 |
| 2. | Grenada | 52 | 7. | St Kitts & Nevis | 39 |
| 3. | St Lucia | 52 | 8. | Seychelles | 35 |
| 4. | Antigua & Barbuda | 51 | 9. | St Vincent & Grenadines | 28 |
| 5. | Dominica | 45 | 10. | Bahamas | 25 |

**31**

# WORLD CITIES

| | | | | | | |
|---|---|---|---|---|---|---|
| AMSTERDAM | 2 | GUANGZHOU | 11 | MOSCOW | 19 | SYDNEY | 29 |
| ATHENS | 2 | HELSINKI | 11 | MONTRÉAL | 20 | TOKYO | 30 |
| ATLANTA | 3 | HONG KONG | 12 | MUMBAI | 20 | TEHRAN | 31 |
| BAGHDAD | 3 | ISTANBUL | 12 | MUNICH | 21 | TORONTO | 31 |
| BANGKOK | 3 | JAKARTA | 12 | NEW ORLEANS | 21 | VENICE | 32 |
| BARCELONA | 4 | JERUSALEM | 13 | NEW YORK | 22 | VIENNA | 32 |
| BEIJING | 4 | JOHANNESBURG | 13 | ORLANDO | 23 | WARSAW | 33 |
| BERLIN | 5 | KARACHI | 13 | OSAKA | 23 | WASHINGTON | 33 |
| BOSTON | 6 | KOLKATA | 14 | OSLO | 23 | | |
| BRUSSELS | 6 | LAGOS | 14 | PARIS | 24 | INDEX | 34–39 |
| BUDAPEST | 7 | LAS VEGAS | 14 | PRAGUE | 25 | | |
| BUENOS AIRES | 7 | LIMA | 14 | RIO DE JANEIRO | 25 | | |
| CAIRO | 7 | LONDON | 15 | ROME | 26 | | |
| CAPE TOWN | 8 | LISBON | 16 | SAN FRANCISCO | 26 | | |
| COPENHAGEN | 8 | LOS ANGELES | 16 | ST PETERSBURG | 27 | | |
| CHICAGO | 9 | MADRID | 17 | SANTIAGO | 27 | | |
| DUBAI | 9 | MANILA | 17 | SÃO PAULO | 27 | | |
| DALLAS- | | MELBOURNE | 18 | SEOUL | 27 | | |
| FORT WORTH | 10 | MEXICO CITY | 18 | SHANGHAI | 28 | | |
| DELHI | 10 | MILAN | 18 | SINGAPORE | 28 | | |
| EDINBURGH | 11 | MIAMI | 19 | STOCKHOLM | 29 | | |

## WORLD CITIES SATELLITE IMAGES

| | |
|---|---|
| BANGKOK | 40 |
| BOSTON | 41 |
| ISTANBUL | 42 |
| LAS VEGAS | 43 |
| MELBOURNE | 44 |
| MEXICO CITY | 45 |
| NEW ORLEANS | 46 |
| ROME | 47 |
| ST PETERSBURG | 48 |

## CITY MAPS

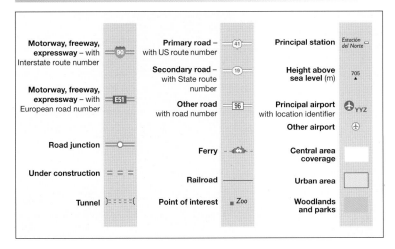

Motorway, freeway, expressway – with Interstate route number

Motorway, freeway, expressway – with European road number

Road junction

Under construction

Tunnel

Primary road – with US route number

Secondary road – with State route number

Other road with road number

Ferry

Railroad

Point of interest

Principal station

Height above sea level (m)

Principal airport with location identifier

Other airport

Central area coverage

Urban area

Woodlands and parks

## CENTRAL AREA MAPS

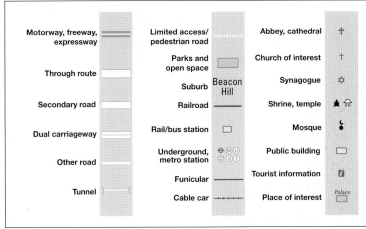

Motorway, freeway, expressway

Through route

Secondary road

Dual carriageway

Other road

Tunnel

Limited access/ pedestrian road

Parks and open space

Suburb

Railroad

Rail/bus station

Underground, metro station

Funicular

Cable car

Abbey, cathedral

Church of interest

Synagogue

Shrine, temple

Mosque

Public building

Tourist information

Place of interest

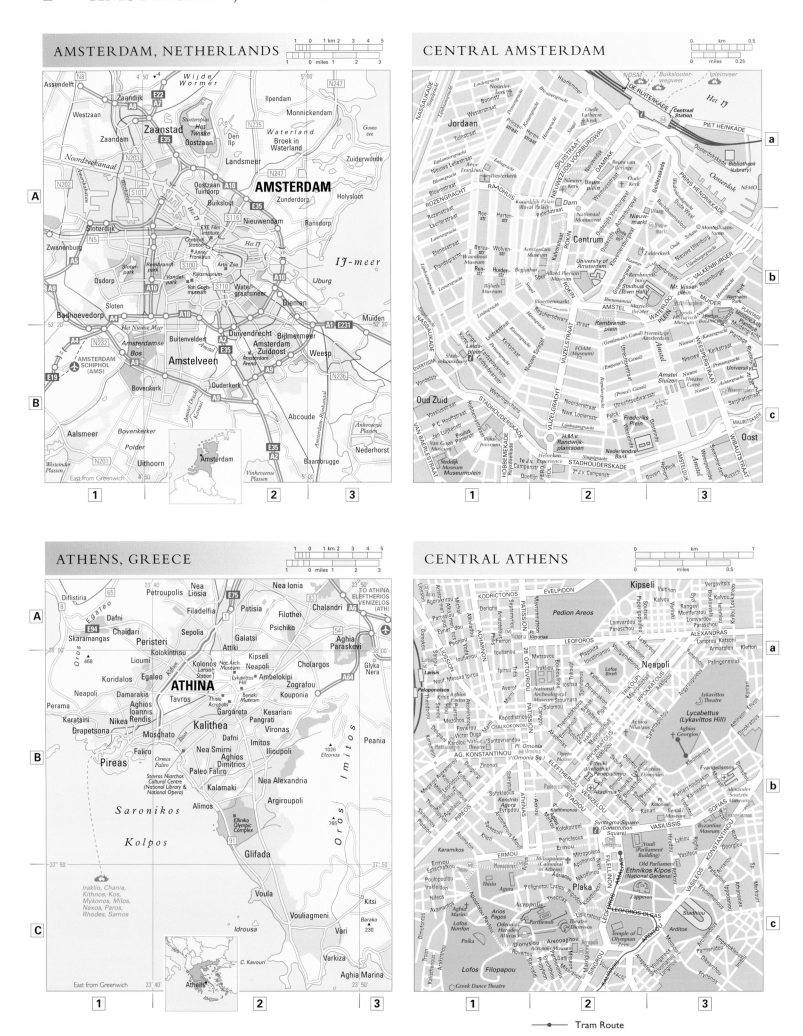

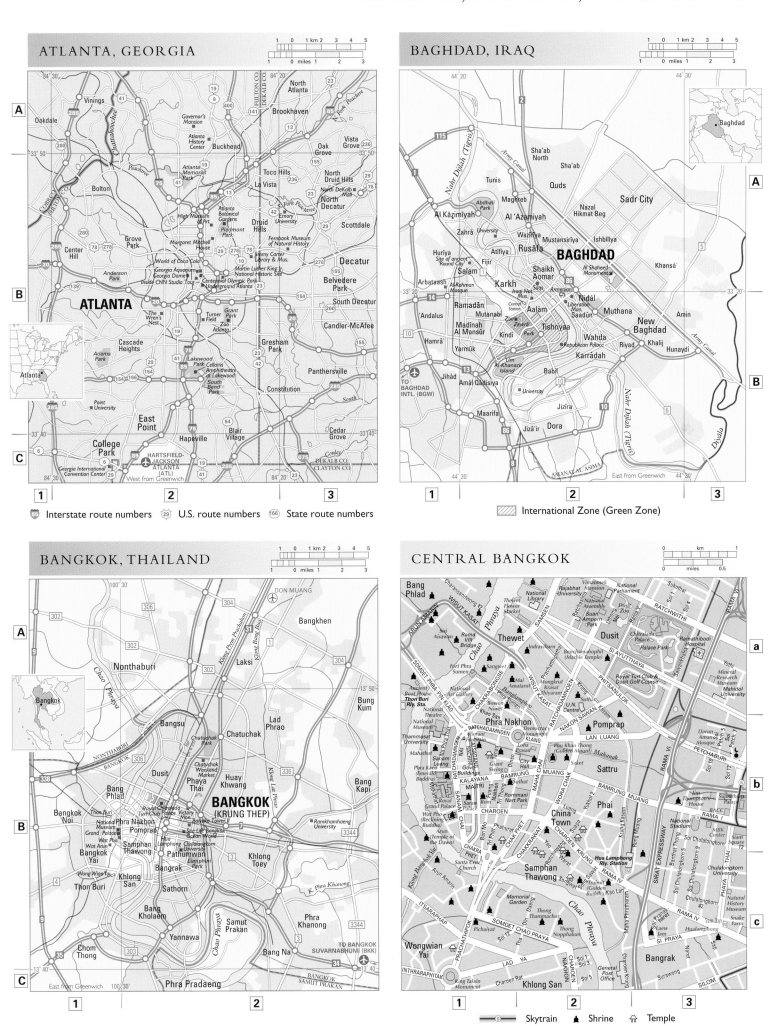

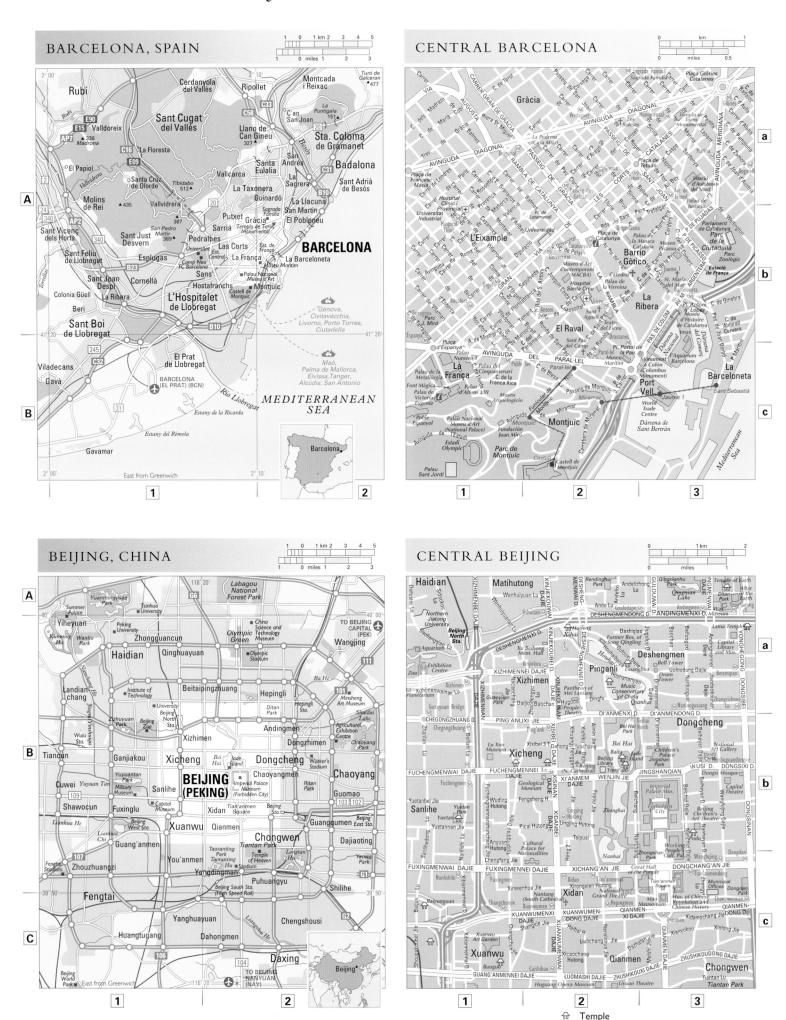

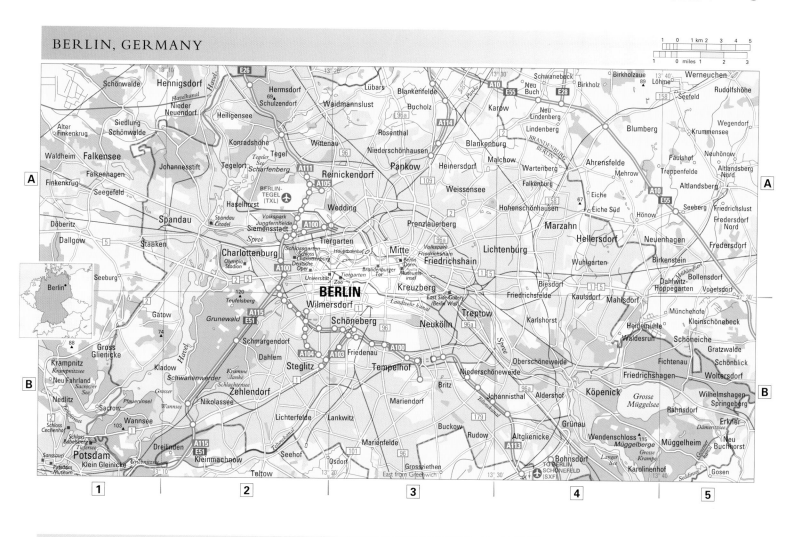

## BERLIN, GERMANY

## CENTRAL BERLIN

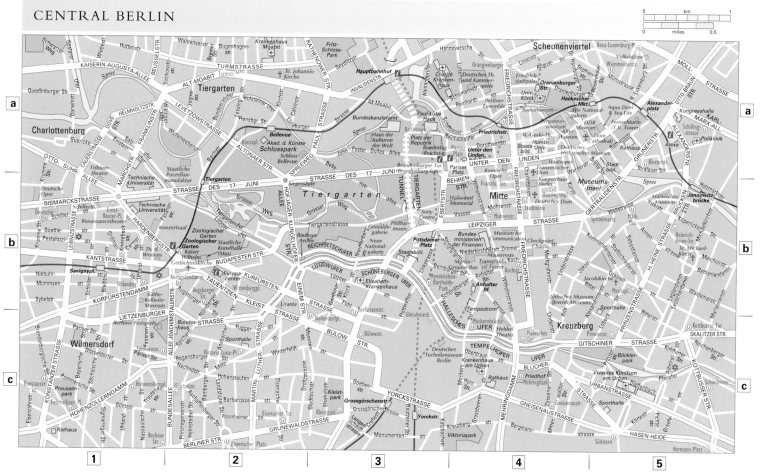

COPYRIGHT PHILIP'S

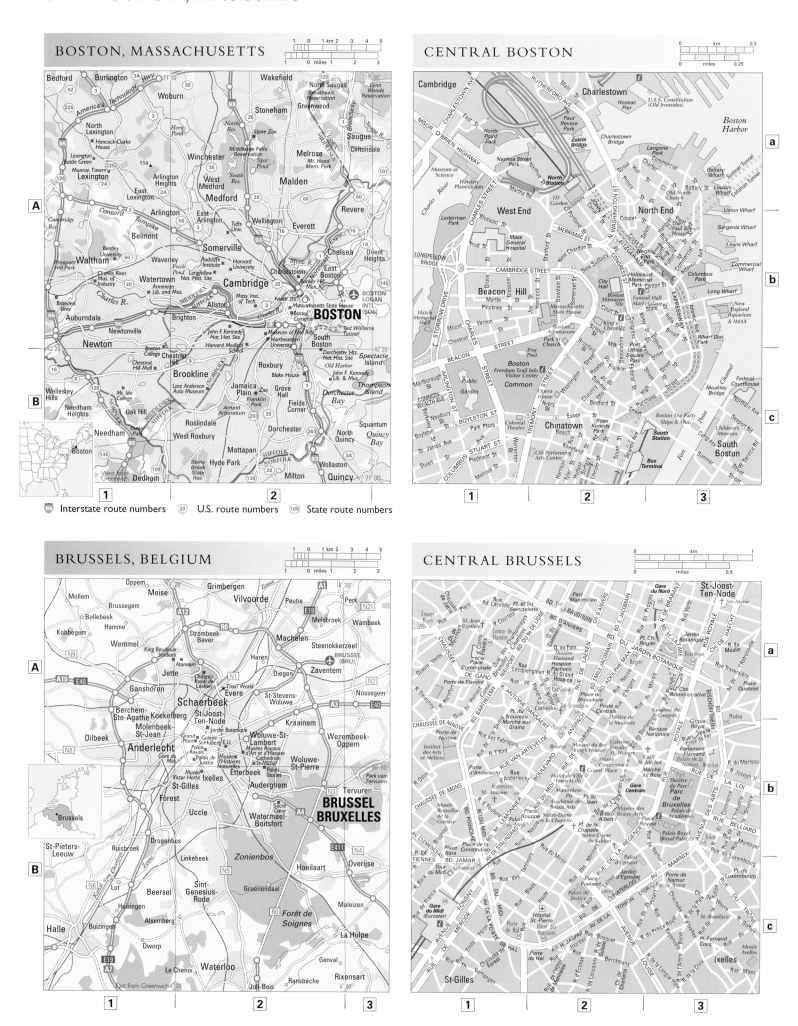

## BOSTON, MASSACHUSETTS

Bedford · Burlington · HWY · Wakefield · North Saugus · Lynn Woods Reservation
62 · America's Technology · Woburn · 129 · Breakheart Reservation
225 · Stoneham · Greenwood
North Lexington · North Res. · Stone Zoo · Saugus
Hancock-Clarke House · Horn Pond · Cliftondale
Lexington Battle Green · Winchester · Middlesex Falls Reservation · Melrose · Mt. Hood Mem. Park
Munroe Tavern · 114 · Arlington Heights · Spot Pond · Malden · 107
Lexington · East Lexington · West Medford · Medford · Revere
Concord Turnpike · Arlington · East Arlington · Wellington
Belmont · Tufts Univ. · Everett · Orient Heights
Cambridge Res. · Somerville · Chelsea · East Boston
Bentley University · Waverley · Fresh Pond · Radcliffe Institute · Harvard University · Charlestown · BOSTON LOGAN INTL. (BOS)
Waltham · Watertown · Longfellow Nat. Hist. Site · Cambridge · Bunker Hill Mon. · North Sta.
Prospect Hill Park · Charles River Mus. of Industry · Armenian Lib. and Mus. · Mass. Inst. of Tech. · Massachusetts State House
Brandeis Univ. · Allston · BOSTON
Auburndale · Brighton · Museum of Fine Arts · Ted Williams Tunnel
Newtonville · John F. Kennedy Nat. Hist. Site · Northeastern University · South Boston
Newton · Harvard Medical School · Dorchester Hts. Nat. Hist. Site · Spectacle Island
Boston College · Chestnut Hill · Roxbury · Old Harbor
Wellesley Hills · Chestnut Hill Mall · Brookline · Blake House · John F. Kennedy Lib. & Mus. · Thompson Island
Mt. Ida College · Larz Anderson Auto Museum · Jamaica Plain · Grove Hall · Dorchester Bay
Needham Heights · Oak Hill · Franklin Park · Fields Corner
Needham · Roslindale · Arnold Arboretum · Dorchester · Squantum · Quincy Bay
West Roxbury · Mattapan · North Quincy · Wollaston
West from Greenwich · Dedham · Stony Brook State Res. · Hyde Park · Milton · Quincy

**1** | **2**

95 Interstate route numbers  20 U.S. route numbers  109 State route numbers

## CENTRAL BOSTON

Cambridge · Charlestown · U.S.S. Constitution (Old Ironsides)
Hoosac Pier · Boston Harbor
MSGR. O'BRIEN HIGHWAY · Paul Revere Park · Zakim Bridge · Charlestown Bridge
West Point Park · Museum of Science · Hayden Planetarium · North Station · North End · Battery Wharf
Charles River · Lederman Park · TD Garden · Old North Church · Union Wharf
West End · MERRIMAC ST. · Sargents Wharf
LONGFELLOW BRIDGE · Fruit St. · Mass General Hospital · New Chardon St. · Lewis Wharf
CAMBRIDGE STREET · City Hall · Faneuil Hall Marketplace · Commercial Wharf
Hatch Memorial Shell · Grove St. · Beacon Hill · Holocaust Memorial Park · Columbus Park · Long Wharf
STORROW DRIVE · Myrtle St. · Boston Athenaeum · King's Chapel · New England Aquarium & IMAX
Mount Vernon St. · Massachusetts State House · Wharf Dist. Park
BEACON STREET · Park St. Church · Post Office Square Park
CHARLES STREET · Boston Common · Freedom Trail Info Visitor Center · Moakley Bridge
Marlborough St. · Public Garden · Opera House · Federal Courthouse
Newbury St. · BOYLSTON ST. · Colonial Theatre · Chinatown · Boston Tea Party Ships & Mus.
COMMONWEALTH AVE. · Berkeley St. · Park Plaza · Rose Kennedy Park · Children's Museum
St. James Ave. · STUART ST. · Beach · South Station · South Boston
Stuart · Columbus Ave · Piedmont St. · Citi Performing Arts Center · Bus Terminal

**1** | **2** | **3**

## BRUSSELS, BELGIUM

Oppem · Grimbergen · A1 · Perk · N21
Mollem · Meise · Vilvoorde · Peutie · E19
Brussegem · A12 · Wambeek
Bollebeek · Strombeek-Bever · Melsbroek
Kobbegem · Hamme · Machelen · Steenokkerzeel
Wemmel · Haren · BRUSSEL (BRU)
N9 · King Baudouin Stadium · Zaventem
Jette · Atomium · Diegem · N2
Château Royal de Laeken · Train World · Evere
Ganshoren · Schaerbeek · St-Stevens-Woluwe · E40
Berchem-Ste-Agathe · Koekelberg · St-Joost-Ten-Node · Kraainem
Molenbeek-St-Jean · Jardin Botanique · Woluwe-St-Lambert · Wezembeek-Oppem
Dilbeek · Anderlecht · Grand Place · Galerie St-Hubert · E.U. · Musées Royaux d'Art et d'Histoire · Cathédrale · Woluwe-St-Pierre
N8 · Gare du Midi · Palais Royale · Musée d'Histoires Naturelles · Palais Stoclet
Musée Victor Horta · Ixelles · Etterbeek · Park van Tervuren
St-Gilles · Auderghem · Tervuren · N3
St-Pieters-Leeuw · Forest · Uccle · Sacré Cœur · BRUSSEL BRUXELLES · A4
Drogenbos · Watermael-Boitsfort · E411 · N4
Ruisbroek · Linkebeek · Overijse
Halle · Buizingen · Zonienbos · Hoeilaart
N6 · Lot · Beersel · N5 · Groenendaal
Sint-Genesius-Rode · Maleizen
Huizingen · Forêt de Soignes · La Hulpe
E19 · Alsemberg · Le Chenoi
A7 · Dworp · Waterloo · Genval · Rixensart
West from Greenwich · Joli-Bois · Ransbèche

**1** | **2** | **3**

## CENTRAL BRUSSELS

St-Joost-Ten-Node · Ste-Marie
Gare du Brabant · RUE DE BRABANT
Parc Maximilien · BD. BAUDOUIN · Jardin Botanique · CH. DE HAECHT
BD. D'ANVERS · Botanique · Rue Traversière
RUE ROYALE · Place Quetelet
BD. ADOLPHE MAX · Cité Administrative · Madou
Théâtre Flamand · Poste Centrale · Colonne du Congrès · Parlement Flamand
Bourse · Galeries St-Hubert · Banque Nationale
BOULEVARD ANSPACH · Maison du Roi King's House · Cath. St. Michel · Marché au Bois
Grand Place · Gare Centrale · Théâtre du Parc · Parc de Bruxelles · Palais des Académies
Manneken-Pis · Musées des Beaux Arts · Palais Royal Royal Palace
Notre-Dame de la Chapelle · Palais des Académies · RUE DE LA LOI
Gare du Midi (Eurostar) · Palais de Justice · WATERLOO · Porte de Namur
Tour du Midi · Hôpital St-Pierre · Porte de Hal · AVENUE LOUISE · Ixelles
St-Gilles · Porte de Hal

**1** | **2** | **3**

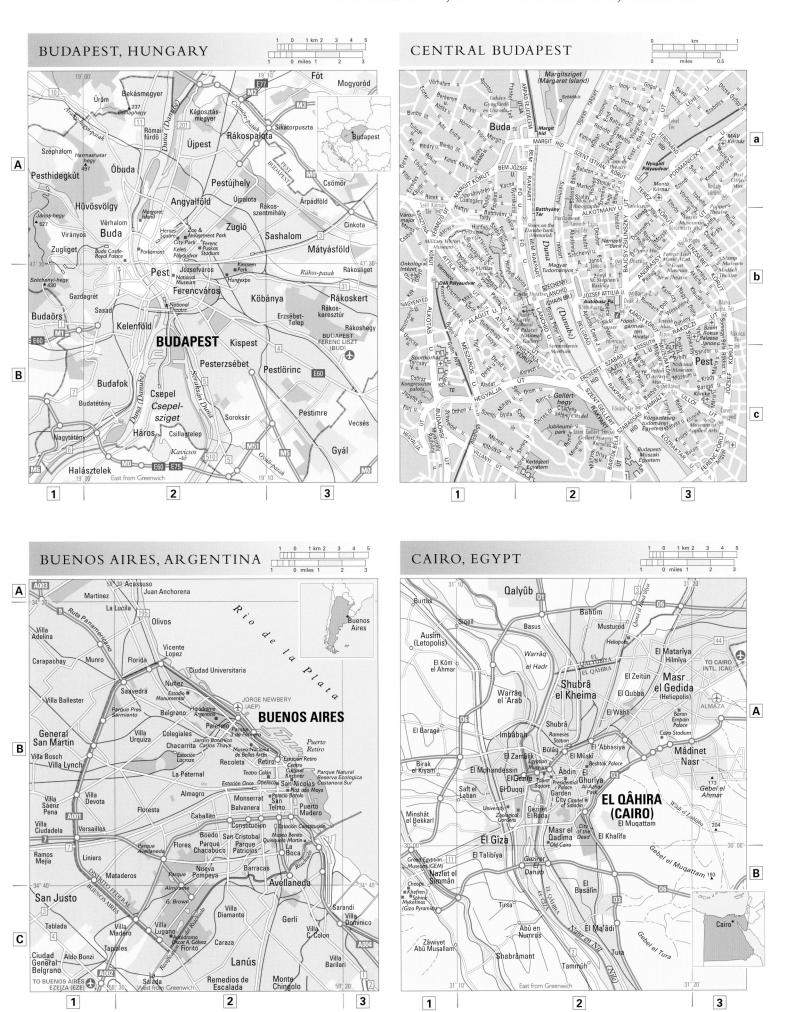

## BUDAPEST, HUNGARY

Üröm • Bekásmegyer
Csillaghegy 237
Aranyhegyi-patak
Római-fürdő • Káposztás-megyer
Széphalom • Harmashatár hegy 497
Óbuda • Rákospalota • Sikátorpuszta
Pesthidegkút • Újpest • Csömör
Hűvösvölgy • Pestújhely • BUDAPEST
János-hegy 527 • Angyalföld • Árpádföld
Vérhalom • Újpalota • Rákosszentmihály
Virányos • Buda • Zugló • Sashalom
Zugliget • Margaret Island • Heroes' Square • Zoo & Amusement Park • City Park • Cinkota
Széchenyi-hegy 430 • Buda Castle-Royal Palace • Ferenc Puskás Stadium • Mátyásföld
Budaörs • Pest • Józsefváros • Kincsem Park • Rákosliget
Gazdagrét • Ferencváros • Rákos-patak • Rákoskert
Sasad • Köbánya • Erzsébet-Telep • Rákoshegy • Rákoskeresztúr
Budafok • Kelenföld • Kispest • BUDAPEST FERENC LISZT (BUD)
Budatétény • Pesterzsébet • Pestlőrinc
Háros • Csepel • Pestimre • Vecsés
Nagytétény • Csepel-sziget • Csillagtelep • Soroksár
Halásztelek • Kavicsos-tó • Gyál
East from Greenwich

## CENTRAL BUDAPEST

Margitsziget (Margaret Island)
Buda • Margit híd • MARGIT HÍD
Nyugati Pályaudvar
Parliament • Danube • Pest
Castle (Royal Palace) • Gellért-hegy • Citadel
Gellért Spa

## BUENOS AIRES, ARGENTINA

Acassuso • Juan Anchorena
Martinez • La Lucila
Villa Adelina • Olivos
Carapachay • Munro • Vicente Lopez • Rio de la Plata
Villa Ballester • Florida
Saavedra • Ciudad Universitaria
Nuñez • JORGE NEWBERY (AEP)
General San Martín • Belgrano • Hipódromo Argentino
Villa Bosch • Villa Lynch • Villa Urquiza • Palermo • Parque de Febrero
Colegiales • BUENOS AIRES
Chacarrita • Jardín Botánico Carlos Thays • Puerto Retiro
Villa Devota • La Paternal • Retiro
Villa Sáenz Pena • Almagro • Museo Nacional de Bellas Artes • Recoleta
Villa Ciudadela • Floresta • Teatro Colón • Parque Natural Reserva Ecologica Costanera Sur
Versailles • Caballito • Estación Once • Obelisco • San Nicolás • Centro Cultural Kirchner
Ramos Mejia • Liniers • Boedo • Monserrat • Balvanera • San Telmo • Puerto Madero
Mataderos • Flores • San Cristobal • Constitución • Estación Constitución • Palacio Barolo
San Justo • Parque Avellaneda • Parque Chacabuco • Parque Patricios • Museo Benito Quinquela Martin • La Boca
Tablada • Villa Madero • Nueva Pompeya • Barracas
Ciudad General Belgrano • Aldo Bonzi • Villa Lugano • Almirante G. Brown • Avellaneda
TO BUENOS AIRES EZEIZA (EZE) • La Salada • Taptales • Oscar A. Gálvez Fiorito • Caraza
West from Greenwich • Lanús • Remedios de Escalada • Monte Chingolo • Gerli • Villa Diamante • Villa C. Colon • Sarandi • Villa Dominico • Villa Barilari

## CAIRO, EGYPT

Qalyûb • Burtus • Siqeil
Ausîm (Letopolis) • Basus • Bahtîm • Musturud
El Kôm el Ahmar • Warrâq el Hadr • Heliopolis
Warrâq el 'Arab • El Qâhira • El Matarîya Hilmiya • TO CAIRO INTL. (CAI)
El Baragil • Shubrâ el Kheima • El Zeitûn • Masr el Gedida (Heliopolis)
Imbâbah • Shubrâ • El Qubba • Baron Empain Palace
Birak el Kiyam • Bûlâq • El Wâhli • ALMÁZA
El Zamâlik • Rameses Station • El Abbasiya • Cairo Stadium
El Mohandessin • El Gezira • El Mûski • Mâdinet Nasr
Saft el Laban • El Duqqi • Abdîn • El Ghuriya • Al-Azhar Park
Minshât el Bekkâri • University • Tahrir Square • Presidential Palace • City • Citadel of Saladin • Gebel el Ahmar 173
Masr el Qadîma Old Cairo • Gezîret el Roda • EL QÂHIRA (CAIRO) • El Muqattam • 204
El Gîza • City of the Dead • El Khalîfa
Grand Egyptian Museum (GEM) • El Talibîya • Gezîret El Dahab • Gebel el Muqattam 193
Nazlet el Simmân • El Basâlîn • Nahr en Nîl
Cheops • Khefren • Sphinx • Mykerinos (Giza Pyramids) • Tirsa • El Ma'âdi • Gebel el Tura
Abû en Numrus • Nahr en Nîl • Tura
Zâwiyet Abû Musallam • Shabrâmant • Tammûh
East from Greenwich

COPYRIGHT PHILIP'S

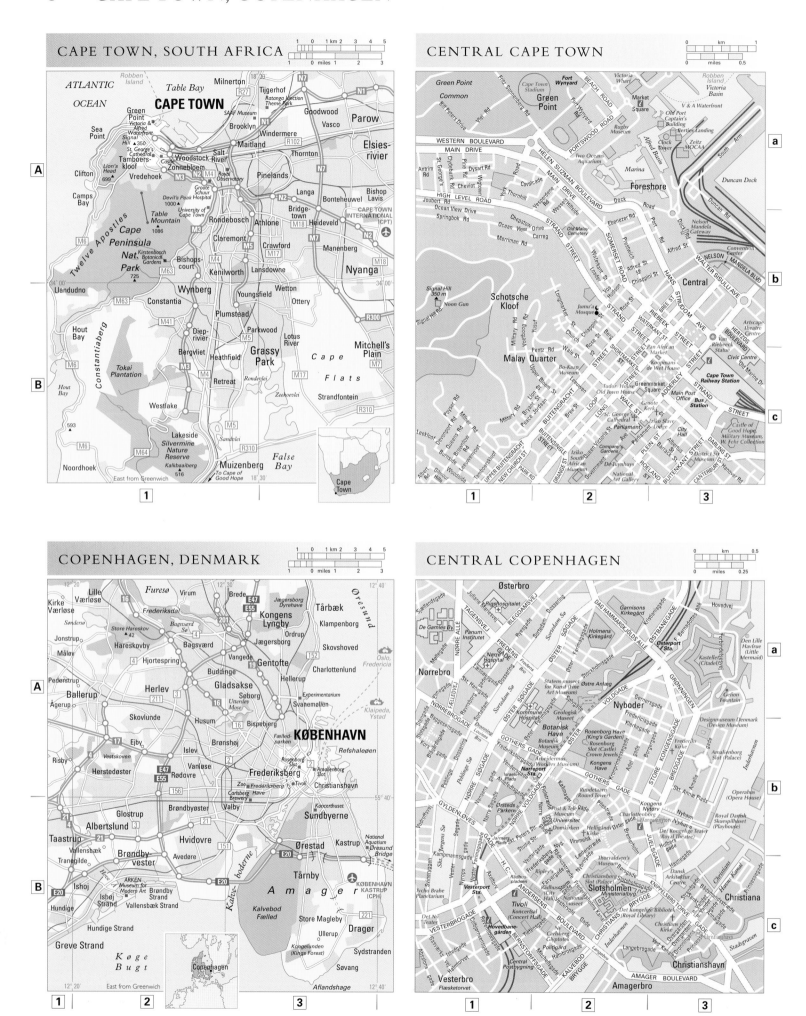

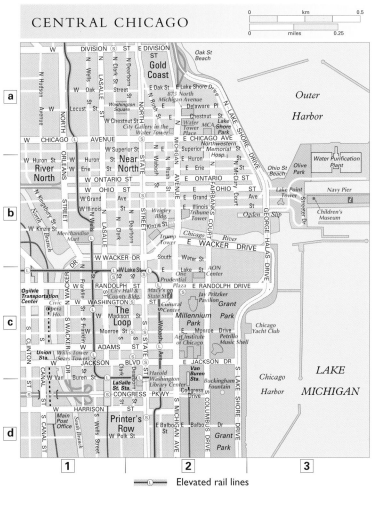

CENTRAL CHICAGO

Elevated rail lines

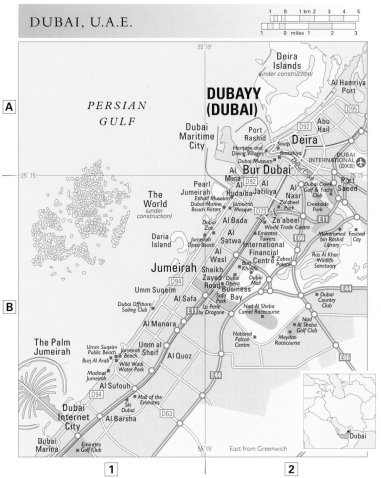

DUBAI, U.A.E.

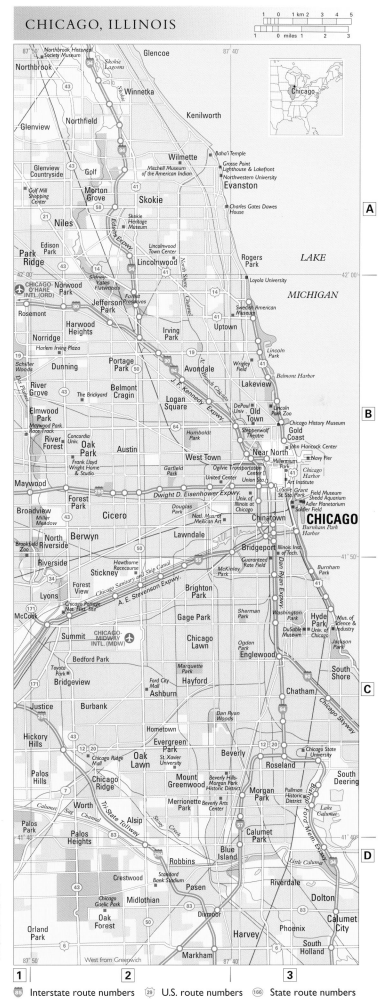

CHICAGO, ILLINOIS

Interstate route numbers　　U.S. route numbers　　State route numbers

COPYRIGHT PHILIP'S

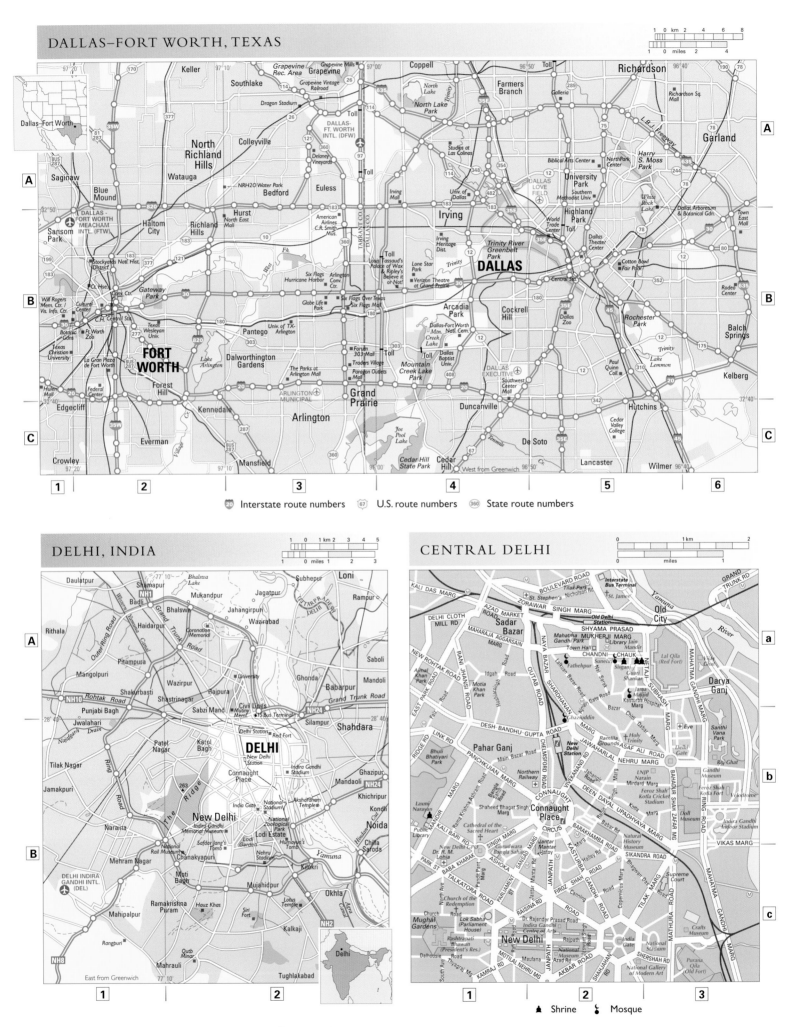

## DALLAS–FORT WORTH, TEXAS

Interstate route numbers    U.S. route numbers    State route numbers

## DELHI, INDIA

## CENTRAL DELHI

▲ Shrine    Mosque

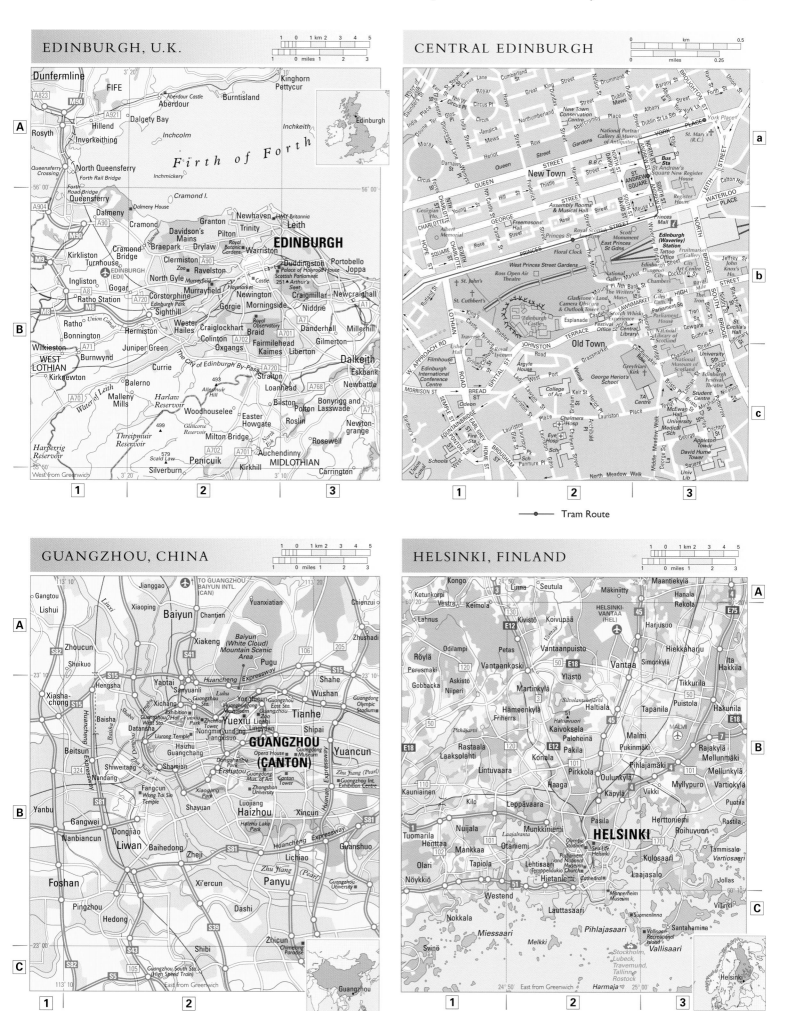

## EDINBURGH, U.K.

## CENTRAL EDINBURGH

●— Tram Route

## GUANGZHOU, CHINA

## HELSINKI, FINLAND

## HONG KONG, CHINA

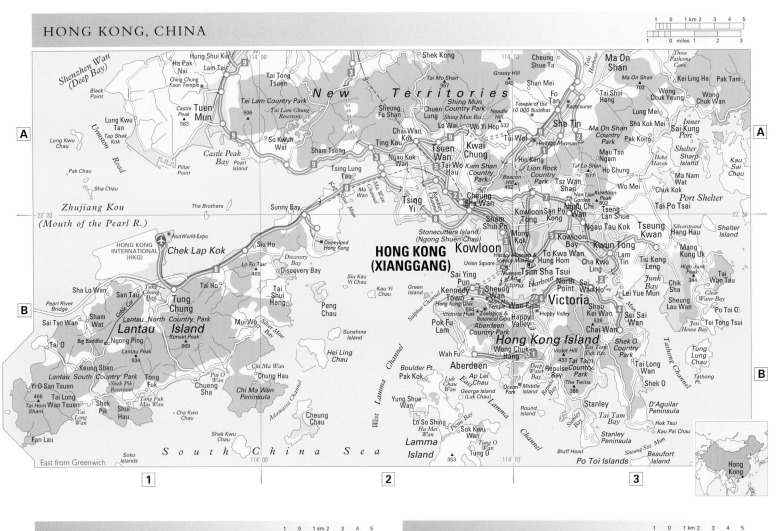

## ISTANBUL, TURKEY

## JAKARTA, INDONESIA

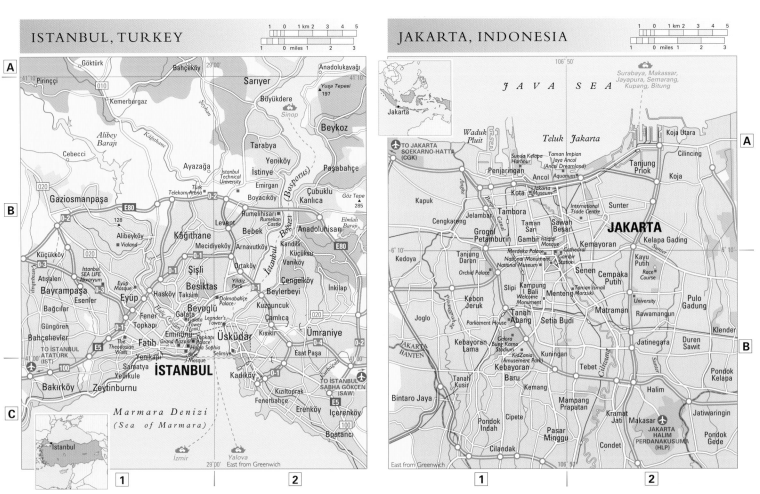

## JERUSALEM, ISRAEL / W. BANK

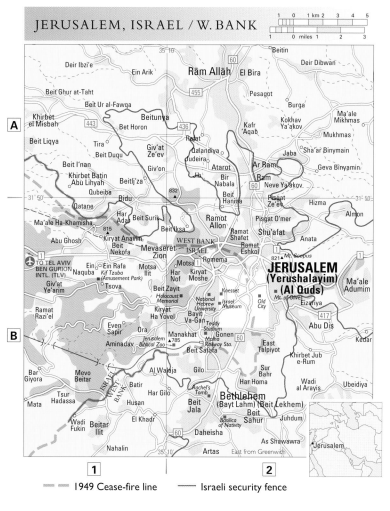

## CENTRAL JERUSALEM

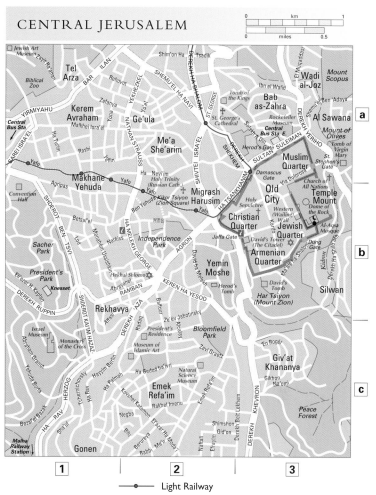

- - - 1949 Cease-fire line    —— Israeli security fence

●—● Light Railway

## JOHANNESBURG, S. AFRICA

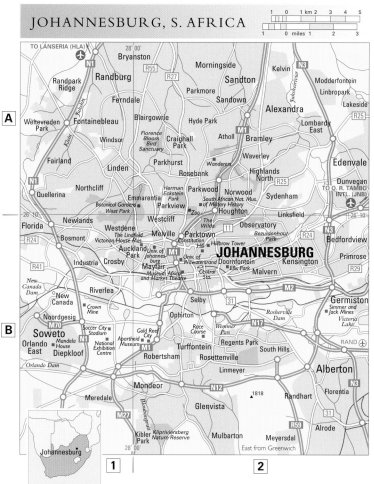

## KARACHI, PAKISTAN

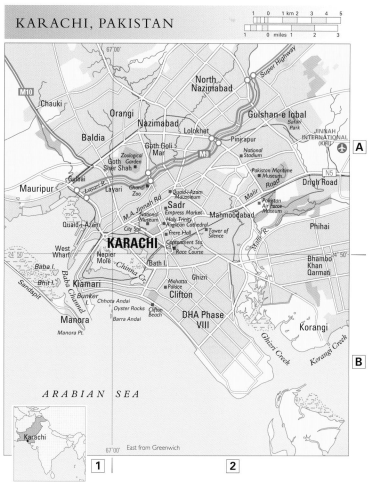

COPYRIGHT PHILIP'S

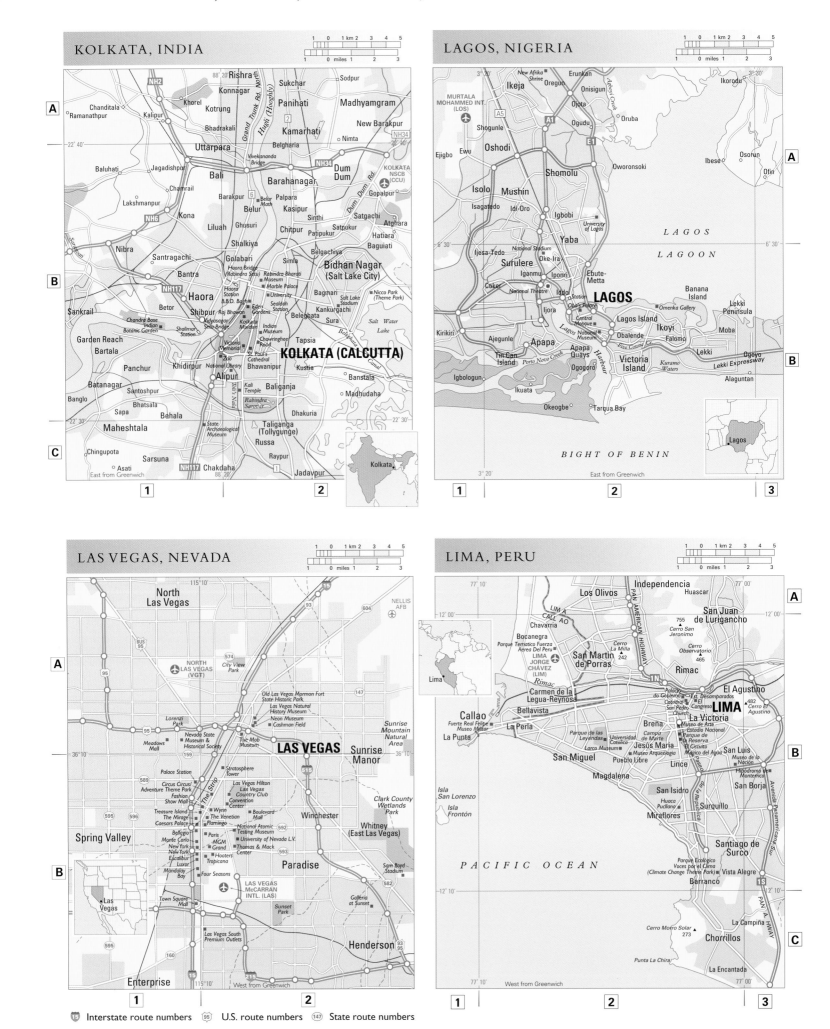

LONDON, U.K.

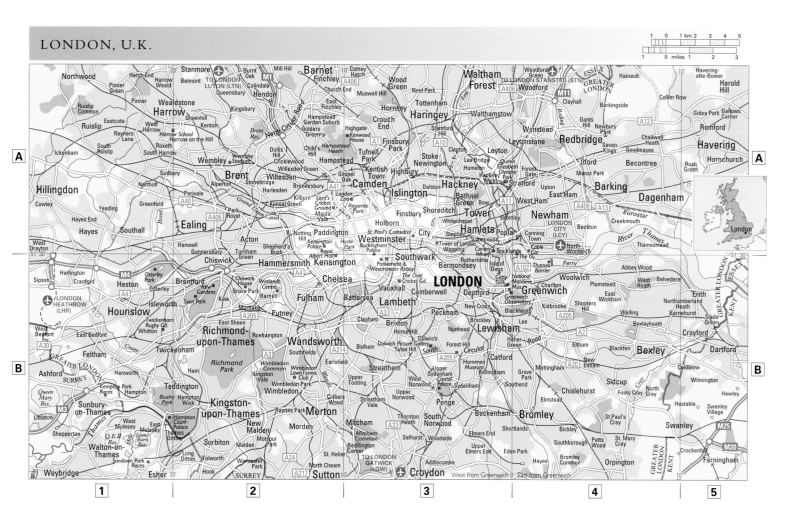

CENTRAL LONDON

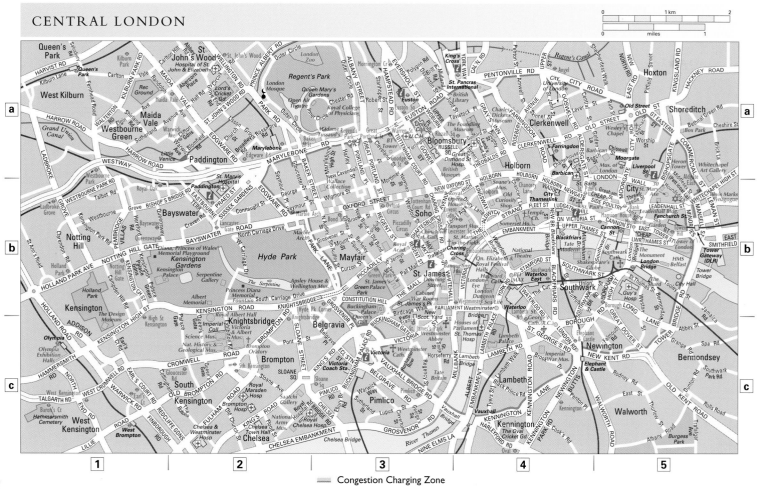

—— Congestion Charging Zone

## LISBON, PORTUGAL

## CENTRAL LISBON

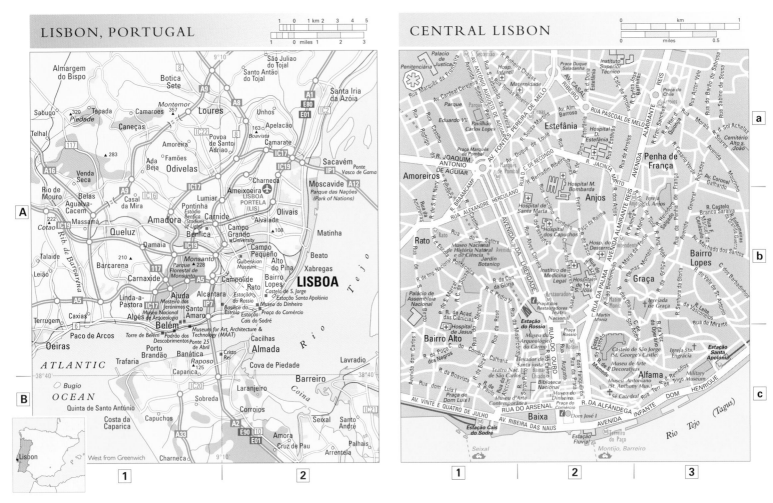

## LOS ANGELES, CALIFORNIA

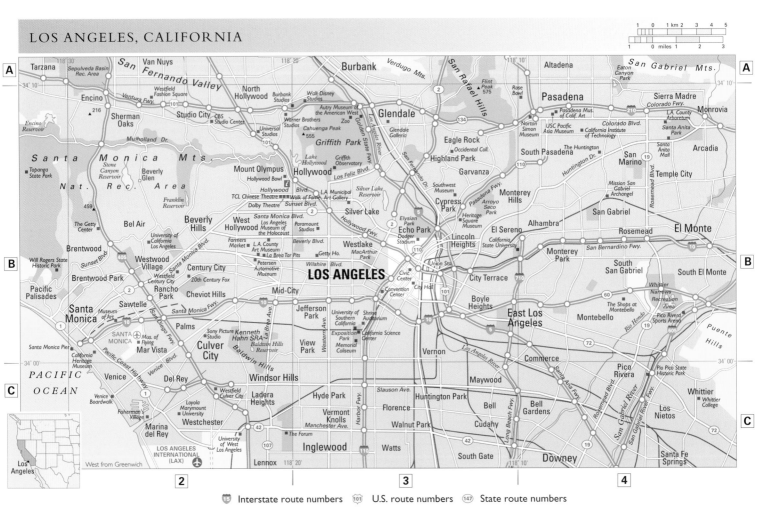

15 Interstate route numbers   101 U.S. route numbers   147 State route numbers

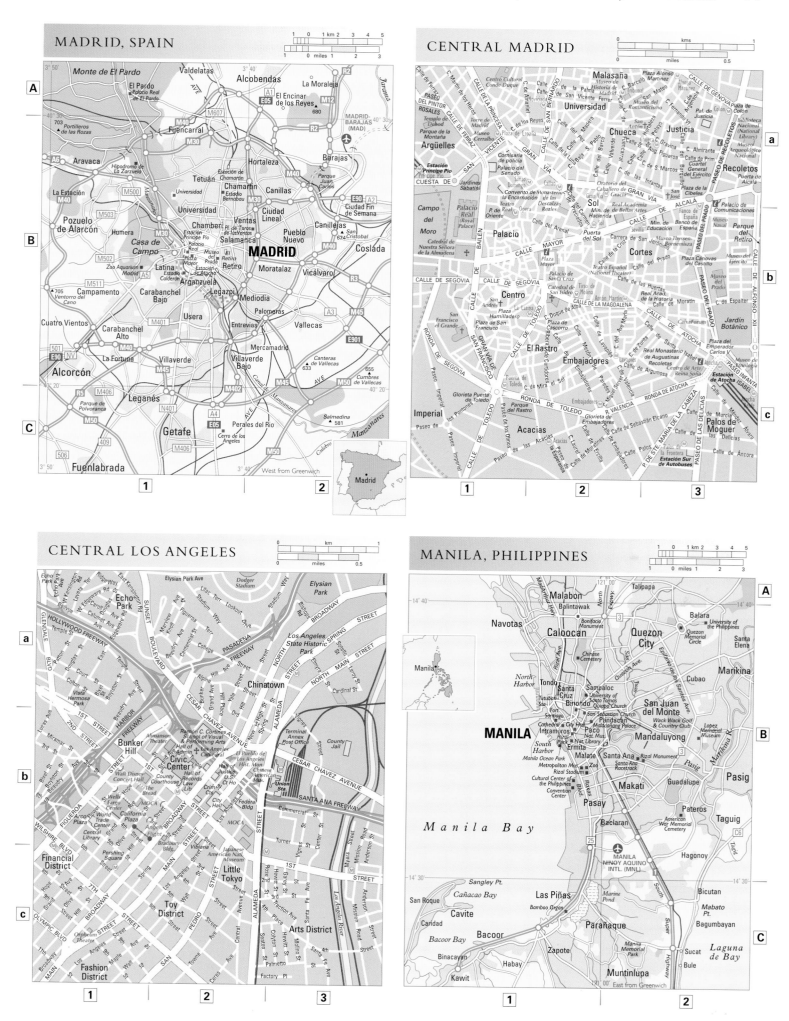

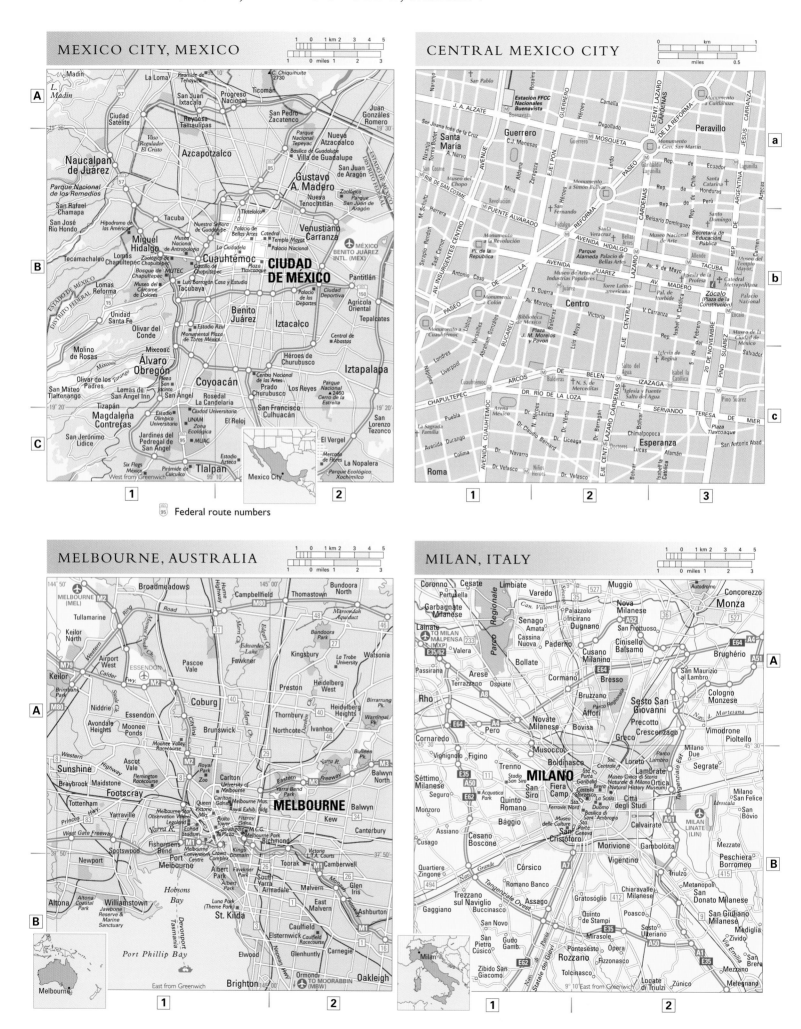

## MEXICO CITY, MEXICO

## CENTRAL MEXICO CITY

95 Federal route numbers

## MELBOURNE, AUSTRALIA

## MILAN, ITALY

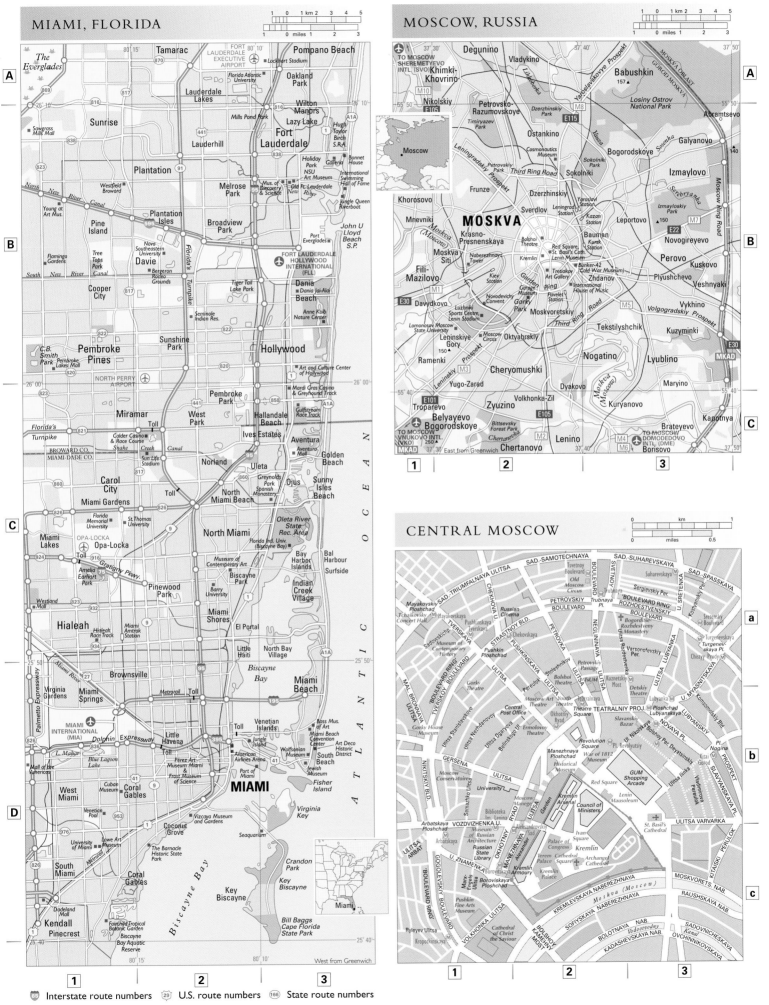

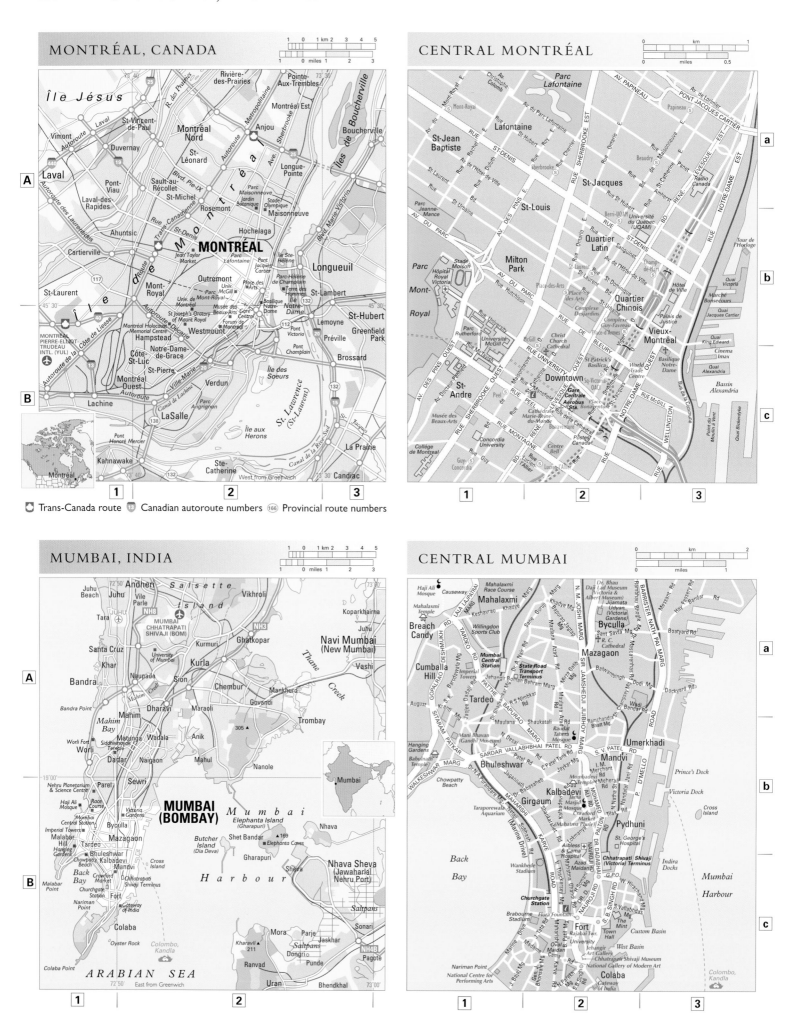

## MUNICH, GERMANY

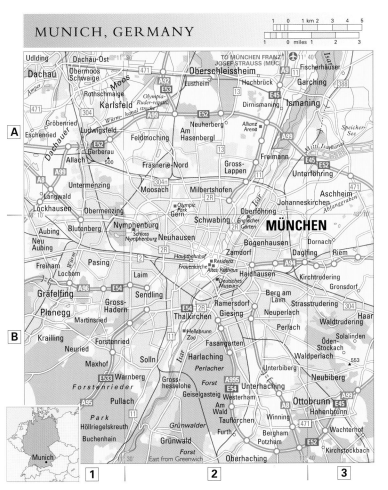

## CENTRAL MUNICH

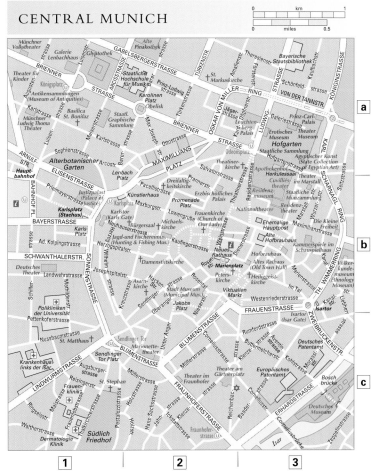

## NEW ORLEANS, LOUISIANA

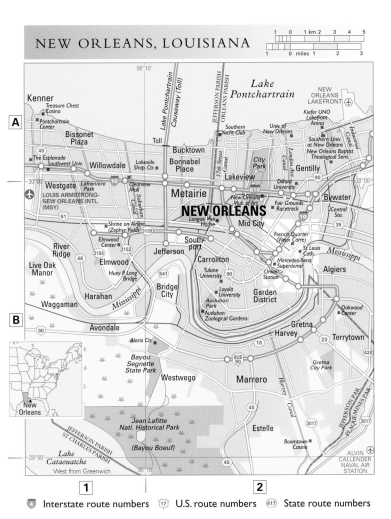

## CENTRAL NEW ORLEANS

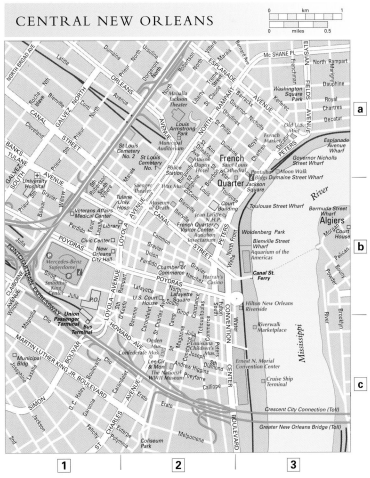

Interstate route numbers    U.S. route numbers    State route numbers

## NEW YORK, NEW YORK

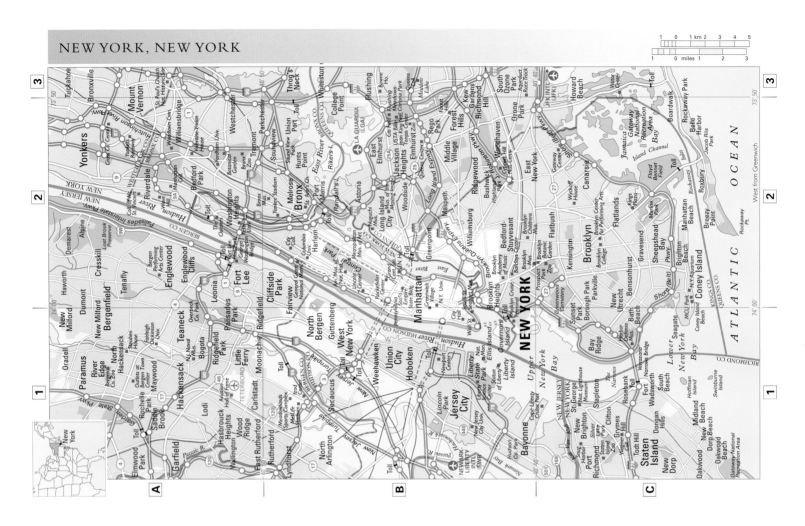

## CENTRAL NEW YORK

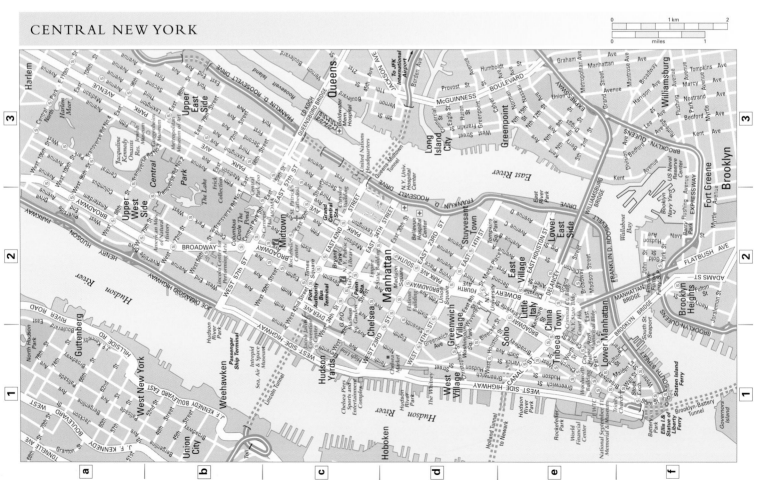

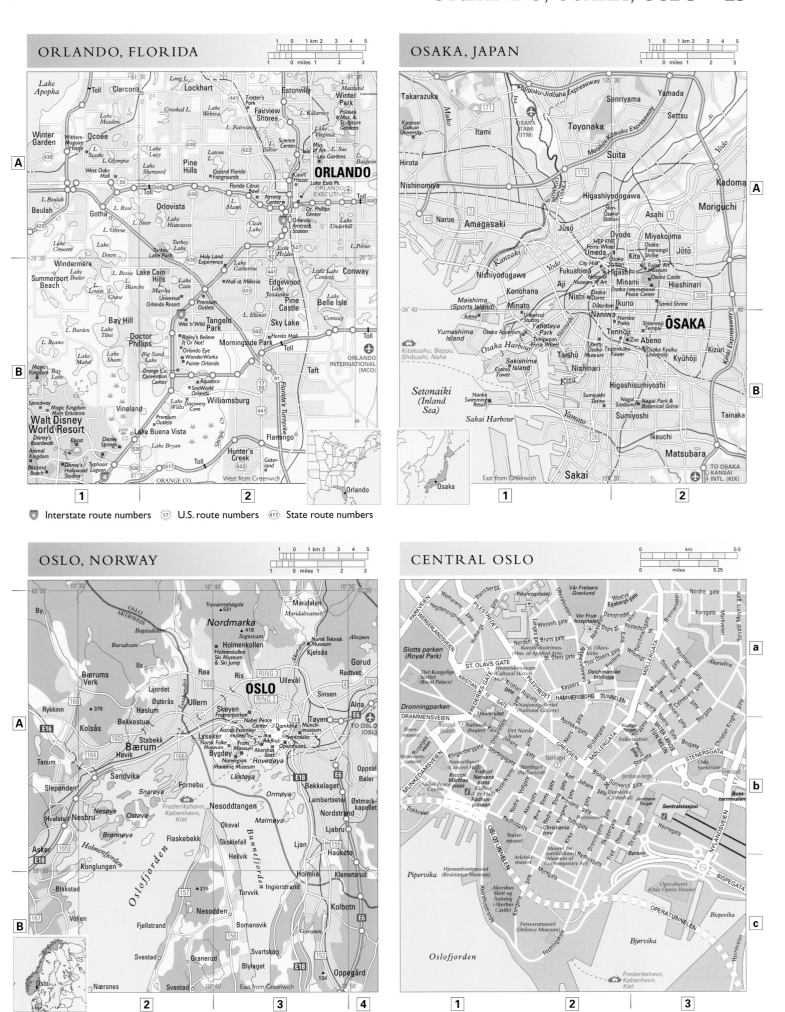

COPYRIGHT PHILIP'S

## PARIS, FRANCE

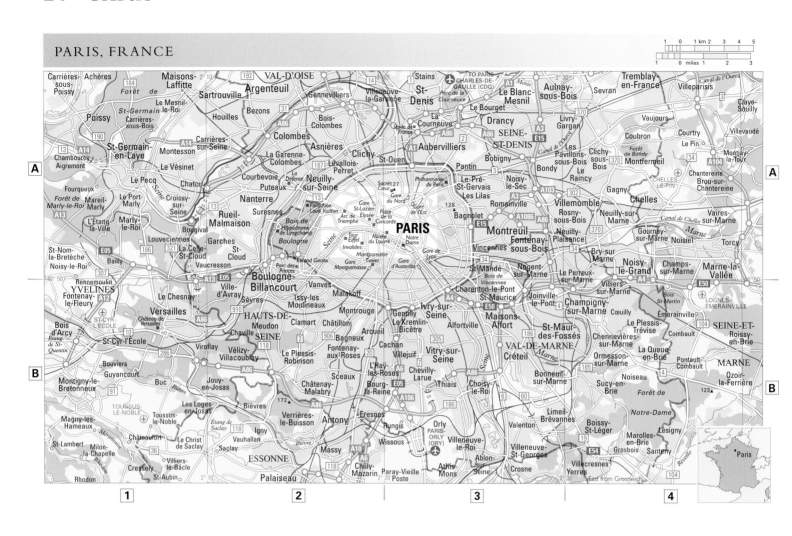

## CENTRAL PARIS

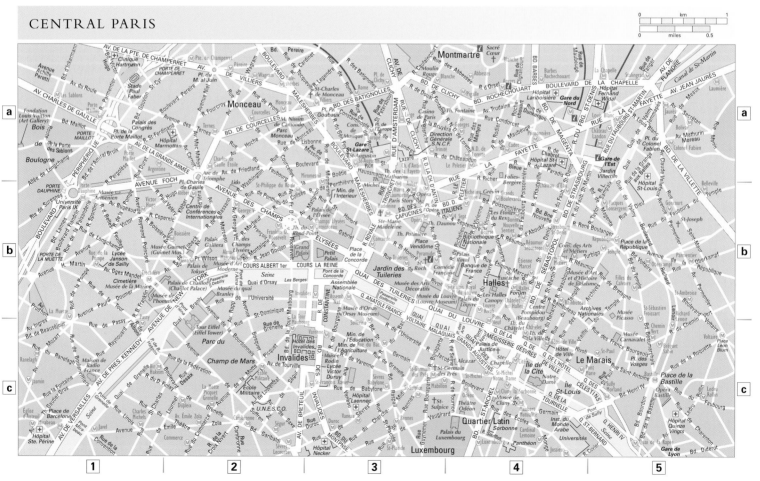

## PRAGUE, CZECHIA

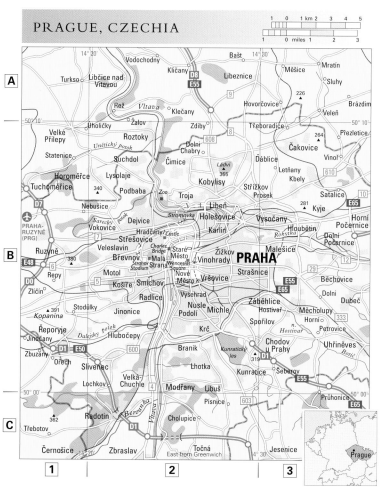

## CENTRAL PRAGUE

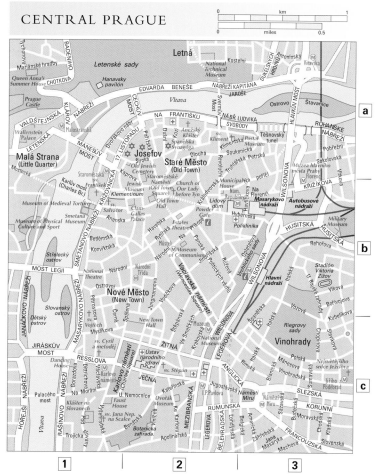

## RIO DE JANEIRO, BRAZIL

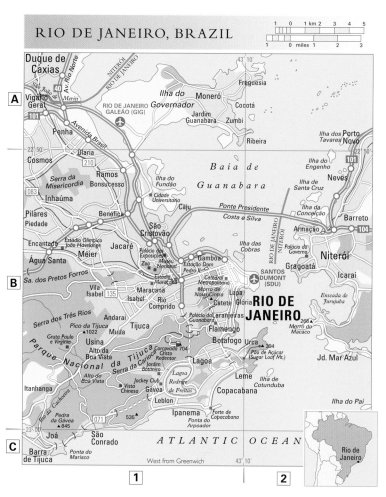

## CENTRAL RIO DE JANEIRO

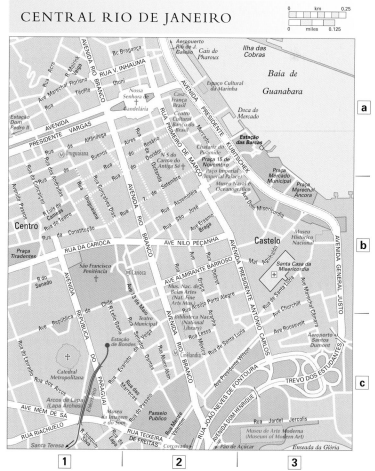

COPYRIGHT PHILIP'S

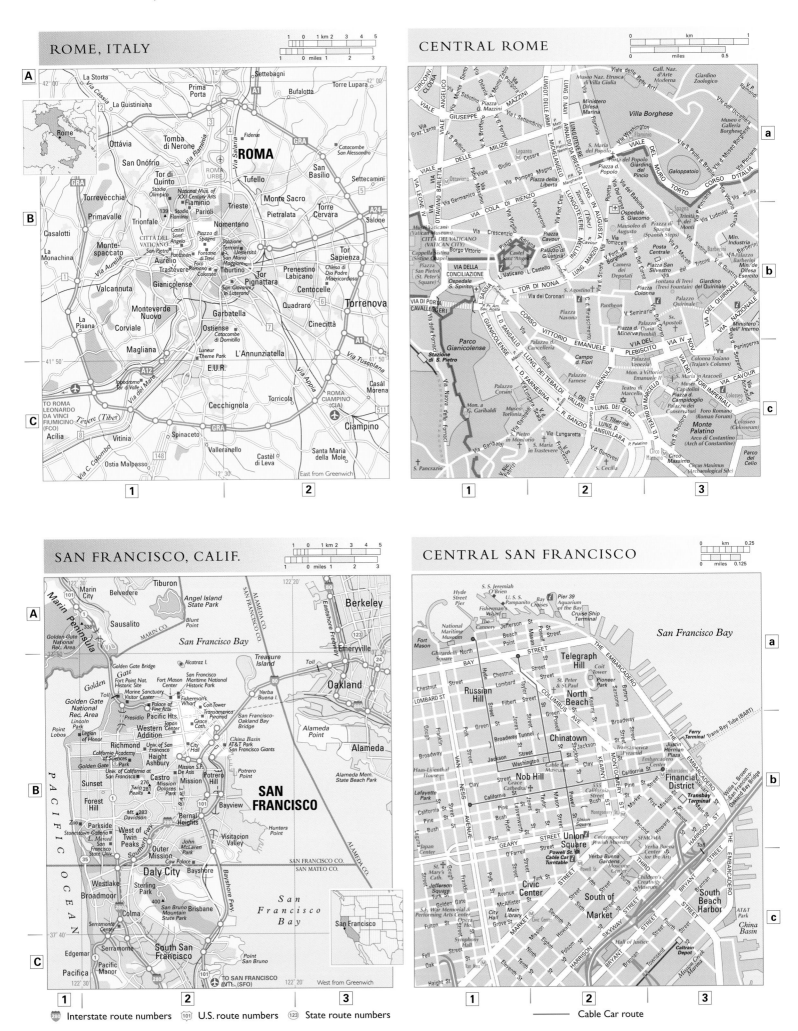

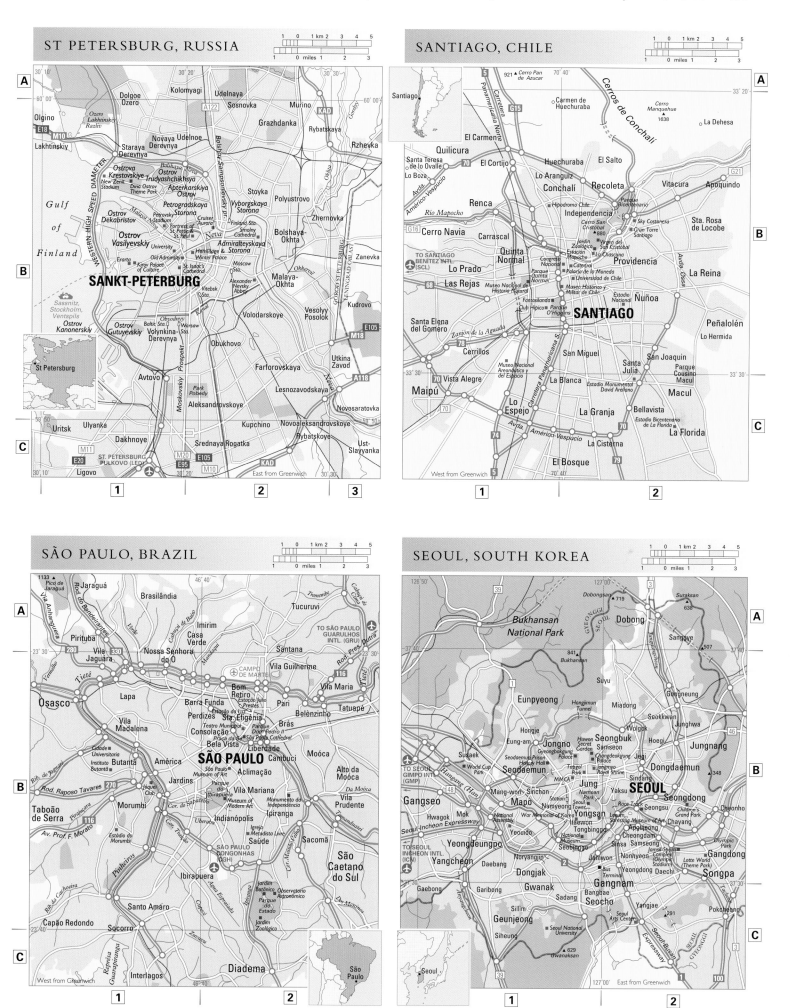

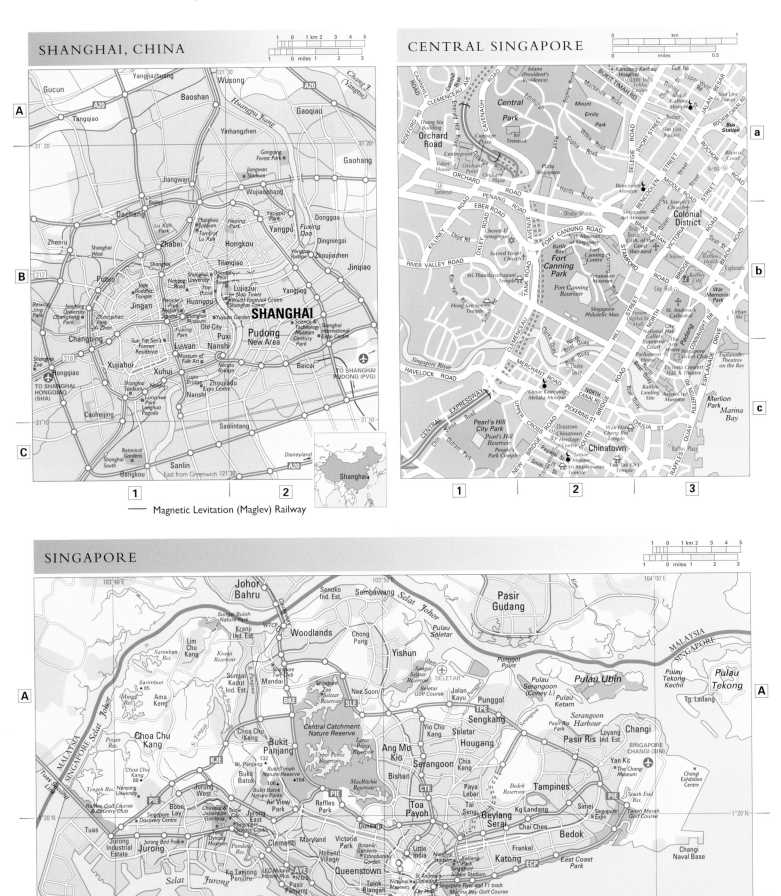

## SHANGHAI, CHINA

## CENTRAL SINGAPORE

— Magnetic Levitation (Maglev) Railway

## SINGAPORE

## STOCKHOLM, SWEDEN

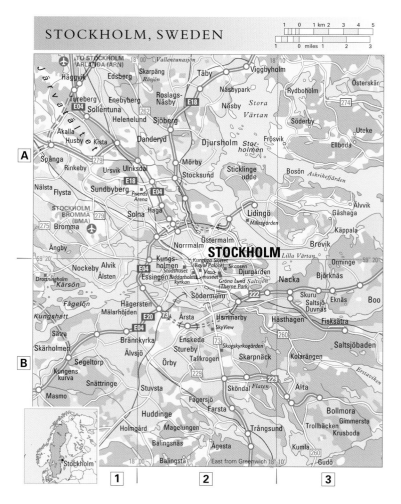

## CENTRAL STOCKHOLM

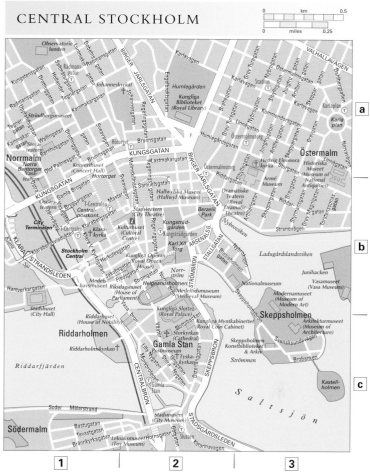

## SYDNEY, AUSTRALIA

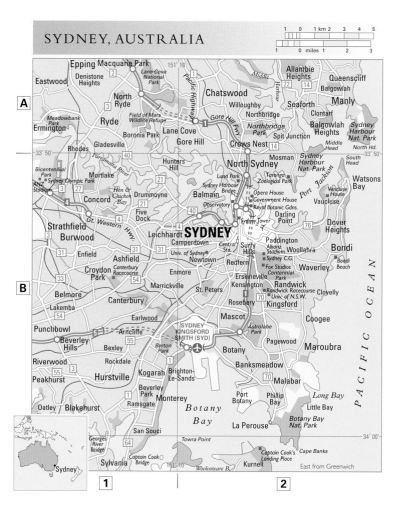

## CENTRAL SYDNEY

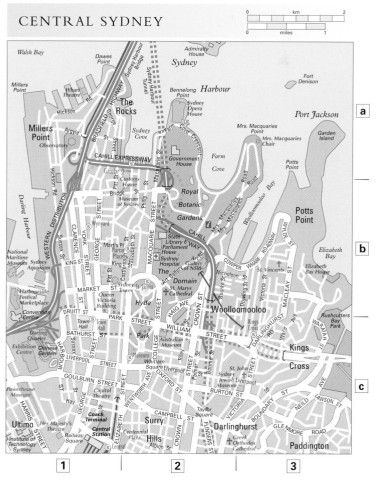

## TOKYO, JAPAN

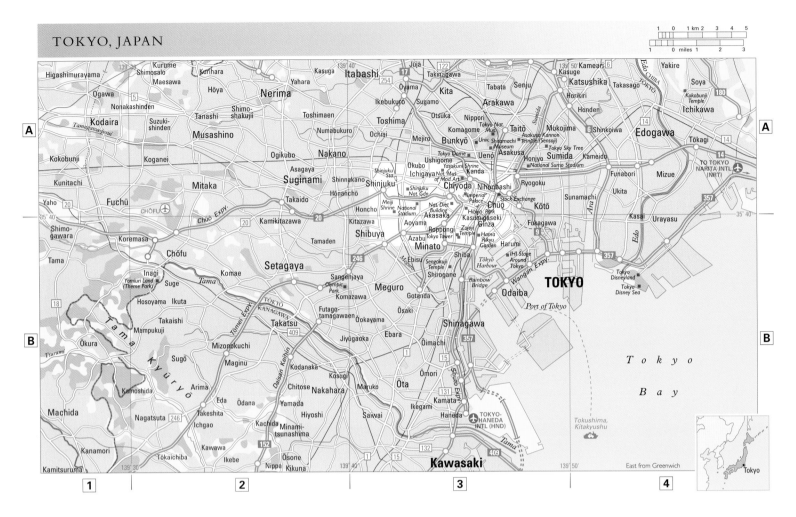

## CENTRAL TOKYO

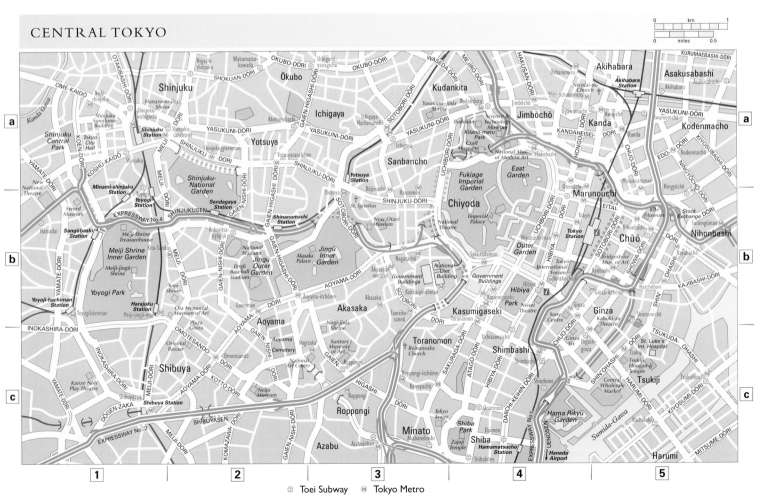

Ⓣ Toei Subway   Ⓜ Tokyo Metro

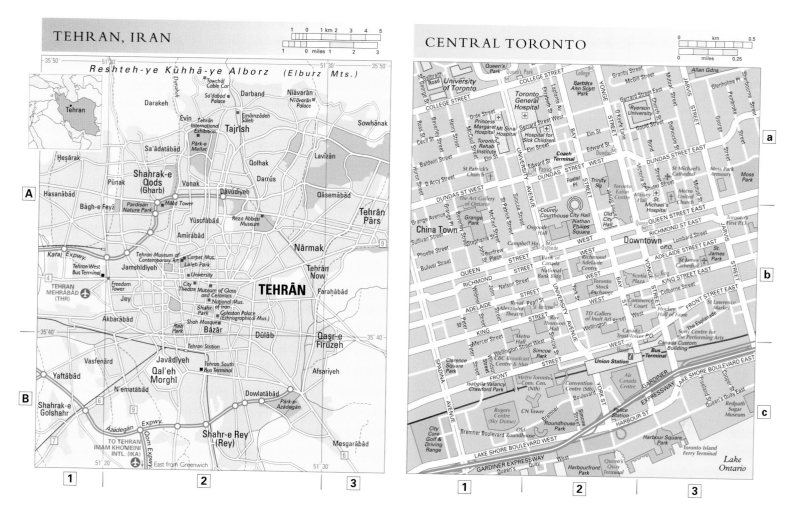

## TEHRAN, IRAN

Reshteh-ye Kūhhā-ye Alborz (Elburz Mts.)

Darakeh
Sa'dābād Palace
Towchāl Cable Car
Darband
Niāvarān Palace
Evīn
Emāmzādeh Sāleh
Niāvarān Sowhānak
Tehran International Exhibition
Tajrīsh
Pārk-e Mellat
Sa'ādatābād
Qolhak
Lavīzān
Hasanābād
Heşārak
Bāgh-e Feyż
Pūnak
Shahrak-e Qods (Gharb)
Pardisan Nature Park
Mīlād Tower
Vanak
Dāvūdīyeh
Qāsemābād
Tehrān Pārs
Yūsofābād
Reza Abbasi Museum
Darrūs
Amīrābād
Karaj Expwy.
Tehran Museum of Contemporary Art
Carpet Mus.
Tehran West Bus Terminal
Jamshīdīyeh
Laleh Park
University
Nārmak
Tehrān Now
TEHRAN MEHRĀBĀD (THR)
Freedom Tower
Jey
City Theatre
Museum of Glass and Ceramics
National Mus.
of Iran
Farahābād
Freedom Tower
Akbarābād
Razi Park
Shahr Park
Golestan Palace (Ethnographical Mus.)
Shah Mosque
Bāzār
Dūlāb
Qaşr-e Fīrūzeh
Vasfenārd
Yaftābād
Javādīyeh
Qal'eh Morghī
Tehran Station
Afsarīyeh
Tehran South Bus Terminal
N'ematābād
Dowlatābād
Pārk-e Āzādegān
Shahrak-e Golshahr
Azādegān Expwy.
Dowlatābād
TO TEHRAN IMAM KHOMEINI INTL. (IKA)
Qom Expwy.
Shahr-e Rey (Rey)
Mesgarābād
East from Greenwich

## CENTRAL TORONTO

## TORONTO, CANADA

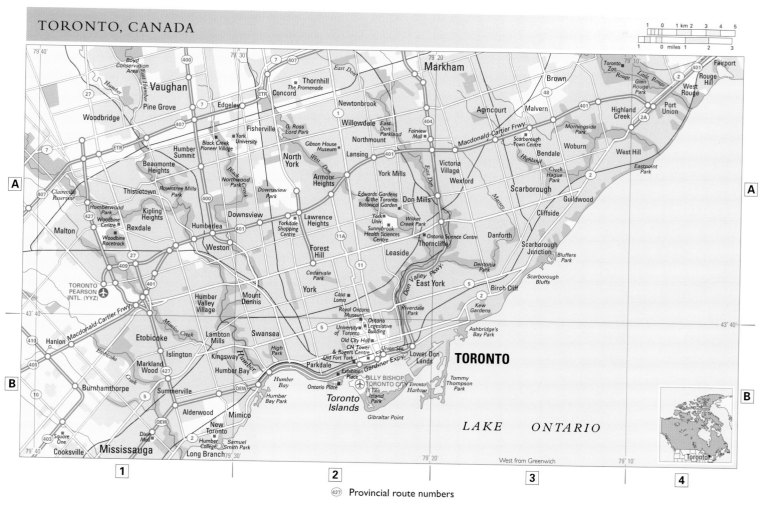

Boyd Conservation Area
Vaughan
Thornhill
Markham
Fairport
Toronto Zoo
Rouge Hill
West Rouge
Woodbridge
Pine Grove
Concord
The Promenade
Newtonbrook
Brown
Port Union
Edgeley
Fisherville
Willowdale
Agincourt
Malvern
Highland Creek
York University
G. Ross Lord Park
East Don Parkland
Fairview Mall
Humber Summit
Black Creek Pioneer Village
North York
Gibson House Museum
Northmount
Lansing
Macdonald-Cartier Frwy.
Morningside Park
Beaumonte Heights
Blacks Northwood Park
Downsview Park
Armour Heights
York Mills
Scarborough Town Centre
Bendale
Woburn
West Hill
Thistletown
Rowntree Mills Park
Victoria Village
Wexford
Clairville Reservoir
Kipling Heights
Downsview
Edwards Gardens & the Toronto Botanical Garden
Don Mills
Scarborough
Guildwood
Humberwood Park
Woodbine Centre
Humberlea
Lawrence Heights
York Univ. Sunnybrook Health Sciences Centre
Wilket Creek Park
Cliffside
Malton
Rexdale
Yorkdale Shopping Centre
Ontario Science Centre
Weston
Forest Hill
Thorncliffe
Scarborough Junction
Bluffers Park
TORONTO PEARSON INTL. (YYZ)
Cedarvale Park
Leaside
Dentonia Park
York
Casa Loma
Don Valley Pkwy.
East York
Birch Cliff
Scarborough Bluffs
Hanlon
Humber Valley Village
Mount Dennis
Royal Ontario Museum
Riverdale Park
Kew Gardens
Etobicoke
Swansea
University of Toronto
Ontario Legislative Building
Old City Hall
Ashbridge's Bay Park
Markland Wood
Lambton Mills
Kingsway
High Park
CN Tower & Rogers Centre
Old Fort York
Lower Don Lands
Islington
Humber Bay
Parkdale
Gardiner Expwy.
Union Sta.
TORONTO
Burnhamthorpe
Summerville
Humber Bay Park
Exhibition Place
BILLY BISHOP TORONTO CITY
Toronto Island Harbour
Tommy Thompson Park
Ontario Place
Alderwood
Mimico
Toronto Islands
Dixie Mall
New Toronto
Humber College
Samuel Smith Park
Gibraltar Point
Cooksville
Mississauga
Long Branch
West from Greenwich
LAKE ONTARIO
Toronto

427 Provincial route numbers

COPYRIGHT PHILIP'S

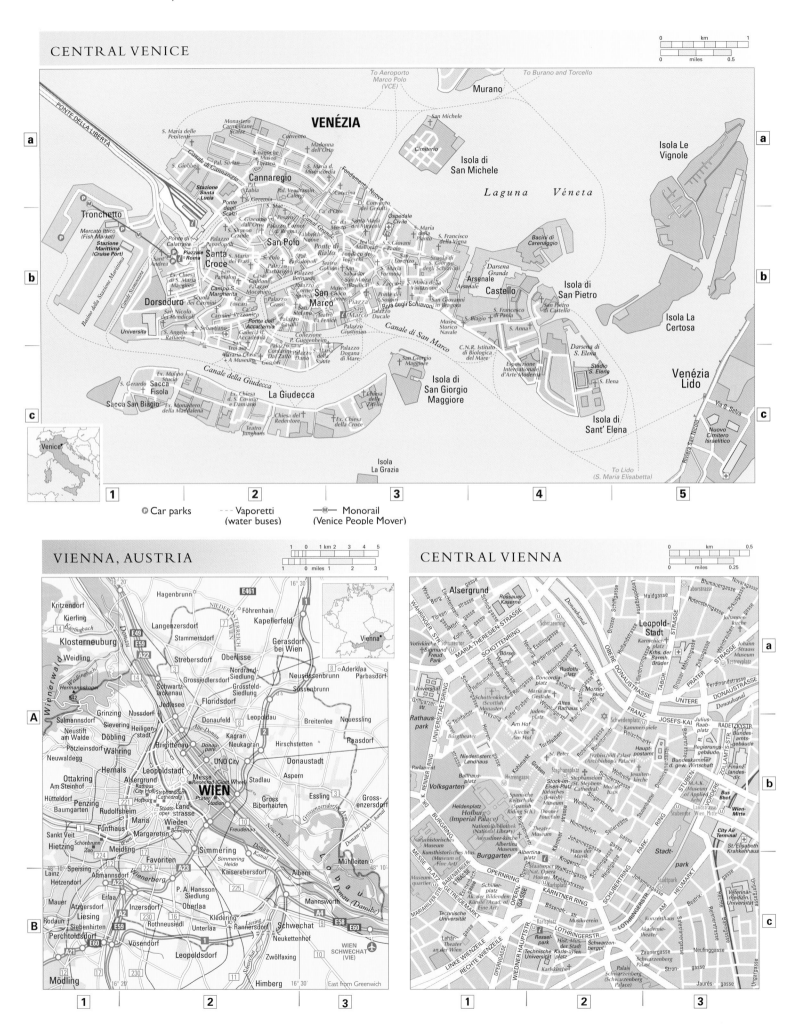

## CENTRAL VENICE

To Aeroporto Marco Polo (VCE)

To Burano and Torcello

Murano

VENÉZIA

Isola Le Vignole

S. Michele
Cimitero
Isola di San Michele

Laguna Véneta

Monastero Carmelitane Scalze
S. Maria delle Penitenti
Convento
Madonna dell'Orto

Sinagoghe Museo Ebraico
Canale di Cannaregio
Pal. Surian
S. Giobbe

Cannaregio
Pal. Labia
Pal. Vendramin Calergi
S. Maria d. Misericordia
Fondamenta Nuove

Stazione Santa Lucia
Ponte degli Scalzi
S. Geremia
Ca' d'Oro
S. Caterina
Convento dei Gesuiti

S. Maria dei Miracoli
Ospedale Civile
S. Maria del Pianto
S. Francisco della Vigna

Bacini di Carenággio

Ponte di Calatrava
S. Giacomo dall'Orio
S. Simeon Grande
Palazzo Pesaro
Canal Grande
Fabbriche Nuove
Teatro Malibran
S.S. Giovani e Paolo
Scuola di S. Giorgio degli Schiavoni

Isola di San Pietro

Tronchetto
Mercato Ittico (Fish Market)
Stazione Marittima (Cruise Port)

San Polo
S. Stae
Palazzo Papadopoli
Pal. Papadopoli
Ponte di Rialto
Fondaco dei Tedeschi
Santa Maria del Miracoli
Teatro Goldoni
S. Salvador
S. Maria Formosa
Arsenale
Darsena Grande
S. Pietro di Castello

Piazzale Roma
Santa Croce
S. Maria Mater Domini
S. Polo
Casa Goldoni
Pal. Barbarigo
Palazzo Mocenigo
S. Maria dei Frari
Campo S. Margherita
Ca' Foscari
Palazzo Grassi
S. Stefano

Castello

Isola di San Pietro

Dorsoduro
Scuola dei Carmini
Carmini
S. Pantalon
S. Barnaba
Ca' Rezzonico
Palazzo Corner
Museo Correr
Piazza San Marco
S. Zaccaria
S. Maria della Visitazione
S. Giovanni in Bragora
S. Biagio
S. Francesco di Paola
S. Anna

Museo Storico Navale

Università
S. Nicolo dei Mendicoli
S. Angelo Raffaele
Ponte dell'Accademia
Teatro La Fenice
Palazzo Ducale
Riva degli Schiavoni

San Marco
Darsena di S. Elena

S. Trovaso
Galleria dell'Accademia
Palazzo Contarini Dal Zaffo
S. Maria della Salute
Canale di San Marco

C.N.R. Istituto di Biologica del Mare
Esposizione Internazionale d'Arte Moderna
Stadio S. Elena

'Squaria Glass + A Museum
Collezione P. Guggenheim
Palazzo Dario
Palazzo Dogana di Mare

S. Elena

Venézia Lido

Sacca Fisola
Ex. Mulino Stucky
S. Gerardo
Canale della Giudecca
S. Giorgio Maggiore
Isola di San Giorgio Maggiore

Via G. Selva

Sacca San Biágio
Ex. Chiesa d. S. Cosimo e Damiano
La Giudecca
Chiesa delle Zitelle

Isola di Sant' Elena

Ex. Monastero della Maddalena
Chiesa del Redentore
Chiesa della Croce
Teatro Junghans

Nuovo Cimitero Israelitico

Isola La Grazia

To Lido (S. Maria Elisabetta)

Venice

| 1 | 2 | 3 | 4 | 5 |

℗ Car parks
--- Vaporetti (water buses)
Ⓜ Monorail (Venice People Mover)

## VIENNA, AUSTRIA

WIEN

Kritzendorf
Kierling
Hagenbrunn
E461
Föhrenhain
Kapellerfeld

Klosterneuburg
Weidling
Langenzersdorf
Stammersdorf
Gerasdorf bei Wien

Salmannsdorf
Schwartzlackenau
Grossjedlersdorf
Grossfeld-Siedlung
Neustessenbrunn
Parbasdorf
Aderklaa

Grinzing
Nussdorf
Jedlesee
Floridsdorf
Sössenbrunn

Neustift am Walde
Sievering
Heiligenstadt
Donaufeld
Kagran
Leopoldau
Breitenlee
Neuessling

Pötzleinsdorf
Döbling
Brigittenau
Donaupark
Neukagran
Hirschstetten
Reasdorf

Währing
UNO City
Donaustadt
Aspern

Ottakring
Am Steinhof
Hernals
Alsergrund
Rathaus (City Hall)
Hofburg
Messe
Riesenrad (Giant Wheel)
Stadlau

WIEN
Prater Stadion
Essling
Grossenzersdorf

Hütteldorf
Penzing
Baumgarten
Rudolfsheim
Stephansdom (Cathedral)
Staats oper
Land strasse
Gross Biberhaufen

Sankt Veit
Schönbrunn Zoo
Fünfhaus
Maria Wieden
Margareten
Belvedere

Hietzing
Meidling
Simmering
Simmering Heide

Lainz
Hetzendorf
Favoriten
Kaiserebersdorf
Albern

Mauer
Atzgersdorf
Erlaa
Inzersdorf
Oberlaa

Rodaun
Liesing
Siebenhirten
Rothneusiedl
Unterlaa
Kledering
Rannersdorf
Schwechat
Neukettenhof

Perchtoldsdorf
Vösendorf
Leopoldsdorf

WIEN SCHWECHAT (VIE)

Mödling
Himberg
Zwölfaxing

East from Greenwich

| 1 | 2 | 3 |

## CENTRAL VIENNA

Alsergrund
Rossauer Kaserne
Leopold-Stadt

Votivkirche
Sigmund Freud Park
Schottenring
Börse
Universität
Schottenkirche (Scottish Monastery)
Altes Rathaus (Museum)
Judenplatz

Rathaus park
Rathaus
Burgtheater
Universität
Parlament
Niederösterr. Landhaus
Am Hof
St. Peter
Stephansplatz
Stephansdom (St. Stephens Cathedral)
Mozarthaus

Volksgarten
Heldenplatz
Hofburg (Imperial Palace)
Spanische Reitschule (Spanish Riding Sch.)
Jüdisches Museum (Jewish Museum)

Nationalbibliothek (National Library)
Augustiner-kirche
Albertina
Theater Museum
Donner Fountain
Haus der Musik

Naturhistorisches Museum
Kunsthistorisches Mus.
Burggarten
Staatsoper (Nat. Opera House)
Karlsplatz

Ak. der Bildenden Künste (Acad. of Fine Art)
Nat. Mus. der Stadt (Museum of the City)
Karlskirche

Technische Universität
Technische Universität
Resselpark
Hist.-Mus. der Stadt Wien
Schwarzenbergpl.

Lehár Theater an der Wien
Veterinärmedizin. Universität

Palais Schwarzenberg (Schwarzenberg Palace)

M.A.K. (Museum of Applied Arts)
Bus Bhof
Wien-Mitte
City Air Terminal
St. Elisabeth Krankenhaus

Stadt-park
Stadtpark

| 1 | 2 | 3 |

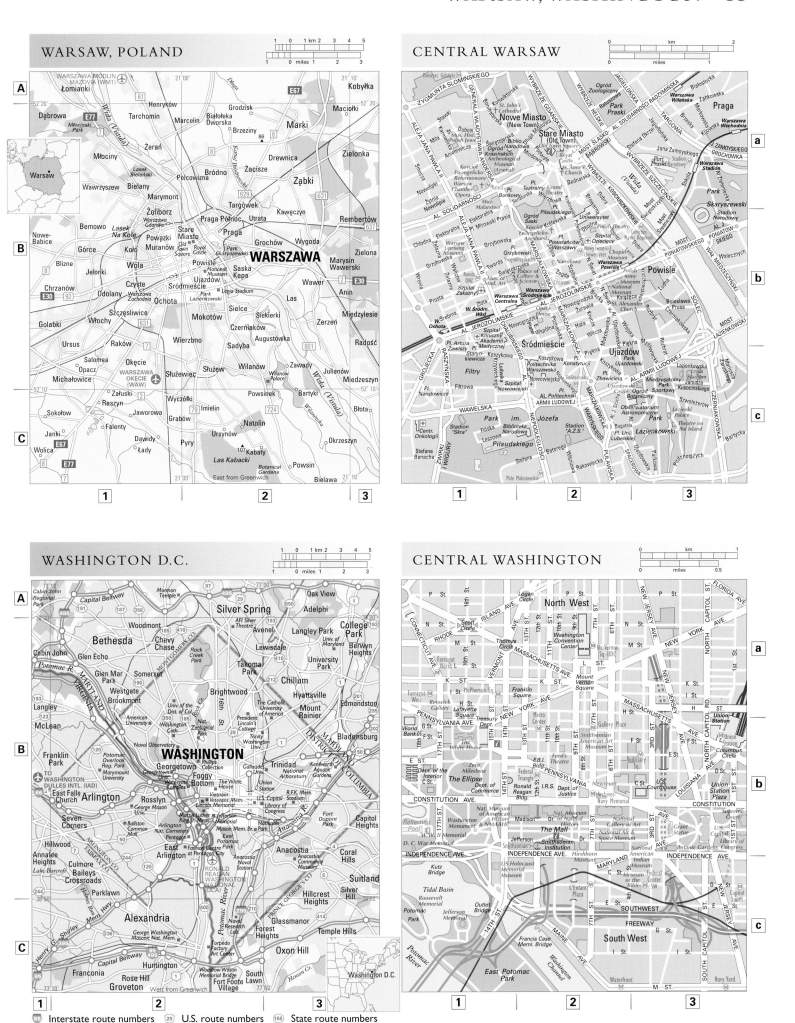

WARSAW, POLAND

CENTRAL WARSAW

WASHINGTON D.C.

CENTRAL WASHINGTON

Interstate route numbers   U.S. route numbers   State route numbers

COPYRIGHT PHILIP'S

# INDEX TO CITY MAPS

The index contains the names of all the principal places and features shown on the City Maps. Each name is followed by an additional entry in italics giving the name of the City Map within which it is located.

The number in bold type which follows each name refers to the number of the City Map page where that feature or place will be found.

The letter and figure which are immediately after the page number give the grid square on the map within which the feature or place is situated.

The letter represents the latitude and the figure the longitude. The full geographic reference is provided in the border of the City Maps.

The location given is the centre of the city, suburb or feature and is not necessarily the name. Rivers, canals and roads are indexed to their name. Rivers carry the symbol ➔ after their name.

An explanation of the alphabetical order rules and a list of the abbreviations used are to be found at the beginning of the World Map Index.

## A

A.N.Z. Stadium *Sydney* **29** B1
Aaläm *Baghdad* **3** B2
Aalsmeer *Amsterdam* **2** B1
Abbey Wood *London* **15** B4
Aboude *Amsterdam* **2** B2
Åbdin *Cairo* **7** A2
Abeno *Osaka* **23** B2
Aberdeen *Hong Kong* **12** B2
Aberdeen Country Park △ *Hong Kong* **12** B2
Aberdour *Edinburgh* **11** A2
Aberdour Castle *Edinburgh* **11** A2
Abfanggraben ➔ *Munich* **21** A3
Ablon-sur-Seine *Paris* **24** B3
Abramtsevo *Moscow* **19** B3
Abu Dis *Jerusalem* **13** B2
Abû en Numrus *Cairo* **7** B2
Abu Ghosh *Jerusalem* **13** B1
Abu Hail *Dubai* **9** A2
Acassuso *Buenos Aires* **7** A2
Achères *Paris* **24** A1
Acilia *Rome* **26** C1
Aclimação *São Paulo* **27** B2
Acropolis *Athens* **2** B2
Acton *London* **15** A2
Açúcar, Pão de *Rio de Janeiro* **25** B2
Ada Beja *Lisbon* **16** A1
Adamasta Channel *Hong Kong* **12** B2
Adams Park *Atlanta* **3** B2
Addiscombe *London* **15** B3
Adelphi *Washington* **33** B3
Aderklaa *Vienna* **32** A3
Adler Planetarium *Chicago* **9** C2
Admiralteyskaya Storona *St. Petersburg* **27** B2
Äffort *Milan* **18** A2
Aflandshage *Copenhagen* **8** B3
Afsariyeh *Tehran* **31** B2
Agboyi Cr. ➔ *Lagos* **14** A2
Ågerup *Copenhagen* **8** A1
Ågesta *Stockholm* **29** B2
Aghia Marina *Athens* **2** C3
Aghia Paraskevi *Athens* **2** B2
Aghios Dimitrios *Athens* **2** B2
Aghios Ioannis Rendis *Athens* **2** B1
Agincourt *Toronto* **31** A3
Agra Canal *Delhi* **10** B2
Agricola Oriental *Mexico City* **18** B2
Água Espraiada ➔ *São Paulo* **27** B2
Agualva-Cacem *Lisbon* **16** A1
Ahrensfelde *Berlin* **5** A4
Ahuntsic *Montreal* **20** A1
Ai ➔ *Osaka* **23** A2
Aigremont *Paris* **24** A1
Air View Park *Singapore* **28** A2
Airport West *Melbourne* **18** A1
Ajegunle *Lagos* **14** B2
Aji *Osaka* **23** A1
Ajuda *Lisbon* **16** A1
Akalla *Stockholm* **29** A1
Akasaka *Tokyo* **30** A3
Akbaräbäd *Tehran* **31** A2
Akershus Slott *Oslo* **23** A3
Al 'Azamiyah *Baghdad* **3** A2
Al Bada *Dubai* **9** A2
Al Barsha *Dubai* **9** B1
Al Hamriya Port *Dubai* **9** A2
Al Hudaiba *Dubai* **9** B2
Al Jafiliya *Dubai* **9** B2
Al Manara *Dubai* **9** B1
Al Mina *Dubai* **9** B2
Al Nasr *Dubai* **9** B2
Al Quds = Jerusalem *Jerusalem* **13** B2
Al Quoz *Dubai* **9** B1
Al Safa *Dubai* **9** B1
Al Satwa *Dubai* **9** B2
Al Sufouh *Dubai* **9** B1
Al Walaja *Jerusalem* **13** B1
Al Wasl *Dubai* **9** B2
Alaguntan *Lagos* **14** B2
Alameda *San Francisco* **26** B3
Alameda Memorial State Beach Park *San Francisco* **26** B3
Albern *Vienna* **32** B2
Albert Park *Melbourne* **18** B1
Alberton *Johannesburg* **13** B2
Albertslund *Copenhagen* **8** B2
Alcantara *Lisbon* **16** A1
Alcatraz I. *San Francisco* **26** B2
Alcobendas *Madrid* **17** A2
Alcorcón *Madrid* **17** B1
Aldershof *Berlin* **5** B4
Alderwood *Toronto* **31** B1
Aldo Bonzi *Buenos Aires* **7** C1
Aleksandrovskoye *St. Petersburg* **27** B2
Alexander Nevsky Abbey *St. Petersburg* **27** B2
Alexandra *Johannesburg* **13** A2
Alexandra *Singapore* **28** B2
Alexandria *Washington* **33** C2
Alfortville *Paris* **24** B3
Algés *Lisbon* **16** A1
Algiers *New Orleans* **21** B2
Alhambra *Los Angeles* **16** B4
Alibey ➔ *Istanbul* **12** B1
Alibey Baraji *Istanbul* **12** B1
Alibeyköy *Istanbul* **12** B1
Alimos *Athens* **2** B2
Alipur *Kolkata* **14** B1
Allach *Munich* **21** A1
Allambie Heights *Sydney* **29** A2
Allermuir Hill *Edinburgh* **11** B2
Allianz Arena *Munich* **21** A2

Allston *Boston* **6** A2
Almada *Lisbon* **16** A2
Almagro *Buenos Aires* **7** B2
Almargem do Bispo *Lisbon* **16** A1
Almirante G. Brown, Parque *Buenos Aires* **7** C2
Almon *Jerusalem* **13** B2
Almond ➔ *Edinburgh* **11** B2
Alna *Oslo* **23** A4
Alnsjoen *Oslo* **23** A4
Alperton *London* **15** A2
Alpine *New York* **22** A2
Alrode *Johannesburg* **13** B2
Alsemberg *Brussels* **6** B2
Alsergrund *Vienna* **32** A2
Alsip *Chicago* **9** C2
Älsta *Stockholm* **29** B3
Alta *Stockholm* **29** B1
Altadena *Los Angeles* **16** A4
Alte-Donau ➔ *Vienna* **32** A2
Alter Finkenkrug *Berlin* **5** A1
Altes Rathaus *Munich* **21** B2
Altglienicke *Berlin* **5** B4
Altlandsberg *Berlin* **5** A5
Altlandsberg Nord *Berlin* **5** A5
Altmannsdorf *Vienna* **32** B1
Alto da Boa Vista *Rio de Janeiro* **25** B1
Alto da Mooca *São Paulo* **27** B2
Alto do Pina *Lisbon* **16** A2
Altona *Melbourne* **18** B1
Alvalade *Lisbon* **16** A2
Alvik *Stockholm* **29** B1
Alvin Callendar Naval Air Station *New Orleans* **21** B2
Älvsjo *Stockholm* **29** B2
Älvvik *Stockholm* **29** A3
Am Hasenbergl *Munich* **21** A2
Am Steinhof *Vienna* **32** A1
Am Wald *Munich* **21** B2
Ama Keng *Singapore* **28** A2
Amadora *Lisbon* **16** A1
Amagasaki *Osaka* **23** A1
Amager *Copenhagen* **8** B3
Amål Qådisiya *Baghdad* **3** A2
Amalienborg Slot *Copenhagen* **8** A3
Amata *Milan* **18** A1
Ambelokipi *Athens* **2** B2
Ameixoeira *Lisbon* **16** A2
Amelia Earhart Park *Miami* **19** C1
América Sul *Rio de Janeiro* **25** B1
American Univ. *Washington* **33** B2
Amin *Baghdad* **3** B2
Aminadav *Jerusalem* **13** B1
Amîråbâd *Tehran* **31** A2
Amora *Lisbon* **16** B2
Amoreira *Lisbon* **16** A1
Amper ➔ *Munich* **21** A1
Amstel-Drecht-Kanaal *Amsterdam* **2** B2
Amstelveen *Amsterdam* **2** B2
Amstelzoom *Amsterdam* **2** A2
Amsterdam ✈ (AMS) *Amsterdam* **2** B1
Amsterdam Arena *Amsterdam* **2** B2
Amsterdam-Rijnkanaal *Amsterdam* **2** B2
Amsterdam Zuidoost *Amsterdam* **2** B2
Amsterdamse Bos *Amsterdam* **2** B1
Anacostia *Washington* **33** B3
Anacostia ➔ *Washington* **33** B3
Anadoluhisarı *Istanbul* **12** B2
Anadolukavağı *Istanbul* **12** A2
Anata *Jerusalem* **13** B2
Ancol *Jakarta* **12** A1
'Andalus *Baghdad* **3** B1
Andarai *Rio de Janeiro* **25** B1
Anderlecht *Brussels* **6** A1
Anderson Park *Atlanta* **3** B2
Andingmen *Beijing* **4** B2
Ang Mo Kio *Singapore* **28** A2
Ängby *Stockholm* **29** A1
Angel I. *San Francisco* **26** A2
Angel Island State Park △ *San Francisco* **26** A2
Angke, Kali ➔ *Jakarta* **12** A1
Angyalföld *Budapest* **7** A2
Anik *Mumbai* **20** A2
Anin *Warsaw* **33** B2
Anjou *Montreal* **20** A2
Annalee Heights *Washington* **33** B1
Anne Frankhuis *Amsterdam* **2** A2
Antonio Carlos Jobim Int. ✈ (GIG) *Rio de Janeiro* **25** A1
Antony *Paris* **24** B2
Aoyama *Tokyo* **30** B3
Ap Lei Chau *Hong Kong* **12** B2
Apapa *Lagos* **14** B2
Apapa Quays *Lagos* **14** B2
Apelacão *Lisbon* **16** A2
Apgujeong *Seoul* **29** B2
Apopka, L. *Orlando* **23** A1
Apoqundo *Santiago* **27** B2
Apterkarskiy Ostrov *St. Petersburg* **27** B2
Ar Kazimiyah *Baghdad* **3** B1
Ar Ram *Jerusalem* **13** A2
Ara ➔ *Tokyo* **30** A4
Arakawa *Tokyo* **30** A3
Arany-hegyi-patak ➔ *Budapest* **7** A2
Aravaca *Madrid* **17** B1
Arbatash *Baghdad* **3** A1
Arc de Triomphe *Paris* **24** A2
Arcadia *Los Angeles* **16** B4
Arcadia Park *Dallas-Fort Worth* **10** B4
Arcueil *Paris* **24** B2
Arese *Milan* **18** A1

Arganzuela *Madrid* **17** B1
Argenteuil *Paris* **24** A2
Argiroupoli *Athens* **2** B2
Arima *Tokyo* **30** B2
Arken *Copenhagen* **8** B2
Arlanda, Stockholm ✈ (ARN) *Stockholm* **29** A1
Arlington *Boston* **6** A1
Arlington *Dallas-Fort Worth* **10** C3
Arlington *Washington* **33** B2
Arlington, L. *Dallas-Fort Worth* **10** B2
Arlington Heights *Boston* **6** A1
Arlington Municipal ✈ (JLH) *Dallas-Fort Worth* **10** B3
Arlington Nat. Cemetery *Washington* **33** B2
Armação *Rio de Janeiro* **25** B2
Armadale *Melbourne* **18** B2
Armour Heights *Toronto* **31** A2
Arncliffe *Sydney* **29** B1
Arnold Arboretum *Boston* **6** B2
Árpádföld *Budapest* **7** A3
Arrentela *Lisbon* **16** B2
Arroyo Seco Park *Los Angeles* **16** B3
Årsta *Stockholm* **29** B2
Artas *Jerusalem* **13** B2
Arthur's Seat *Edinburgh* **11** B3
Arts, Place des *Montreal* **20** A2
As Shawarra *Jerusalem* **13** B2
Asagaya *Tokyo* **30** A2
Asahi *Osaka* **23** A2
Asakusa *Tokyo* **30** A3
Asati *Kolkata* **14** C1
Aschheim *Munich* **21** A3
Ascot Vale *Melbourne* **18** A1
Ashbridge's Bay Park *Toronto* **31** B3
Ashburn *Chicago* **9** C2
Ashburton *Melbourne* **18** B2
Ashfield *Sydney* **29** B1
Ashford *London* **15** B1
AsiaWorld-Expo *Hong Kong* **12** B1
Askisto *Helsinki* **11** B2
Askrikefjärden *Stockholm* **29** A3
Asnières *Paris* **24** A2
Aspern *Vienna* **32** A2
Assago *Milan* **18** B1
Assendelft *Amsterdam* **2** A1
Assiano *Milan* **18** A1
Astoria *New York* **22** B2
Astrolabe Park *Sydney* **29** B2
Atarot *Jerusalem* **13** A2
Atarot ✈ (JRS) *Jerusalem* **13** A2
Atghara *Kolkata* **14** B2
Athens = Athina *Athens* **2** B2
Athina *Athens* **2** B2
Athina ✈ (ATH) *Athens* **2** A3
Athínai = Athina *Athens* **2** B2
Athis-Mons *Paris* **24** B3
Athlone *Cape Town* **8** A2
Atholl *Johannesburg* **13** A2
Atifiya *Baghdad* **3** A2
Atisalen *Istanbul* **12** B1
Atlanta *Atlanta* **3** B2
Atlanta Hartsfield-Jackson Int. ✈ (ATL) *Atlanta* **3** C2
Atlanta History Center *Atlanta* **3** B2
Atlanta Zoo *Atlanta* **3** B2
Atomium *Brussels* **6** A2
Attiki *Athens* **2** A2
Atzgersdorf *Vienna* **32** B1
Aubervilliers *Paris* **24** A3
Aubing *Munich* **21** B1
Auburndale *Boston* **6** A1
Auchenbergy *Edinburgh* **11** B2
Auckland Park *Johannesburg* **13** B2
Auderghem *Brussels* **6** B2
Audubon Park *New Orleans* **21** B2
Augustówka *Warsaw* **33** B2
Aulnay-sous-Bois *Paris* **24** A3
Aurelio *Rome* **26** B1
Ausim *Cairo* **7** A1
Austerlitz, Gare d' *Paris* **24** A3
Austin *Chicago* **9** B2
Autry Museum of the American West *Los Angeles* **16** B3
Avedore *Copenhagen* **8** B2
Avellaneda *Buenos Aires* **7** C2
Avenel *Washington* **33** B1
Aventura *Miami* **19** C3
Avondale *Chicago* **9** B2
Avondale *New Orleans* **21** B1
Avondale Heights *Melbourne* **18** A1
Avtovo *St. Petersburg* **27** B1
Ayazağa *Istanbul* **12** B2
Ayer Chawan, Pulau *Singapore* **28** B2
Ayer Merbau, Pulau *Singapore* **28** B2
Azabu *Tokyo* **30** B3
Azcapotzalco *Mexico City* **18** B1
Azteca, Estadia *Mexico City* **18** C2
Azucar, Cerro Pan de *Santiago* **27** B2

## B

Baambrugge *Amsterdam* **2** B2
Baba Channel *Karachi* **13** A1
Baba I. *Karachi* **13** A1
Babarpur *Delhi* **10** A2
Babushkin *Moscow* **19** A3
Back B. *Mumbai* **20** B1
Baclaran *Manila* **17** B1
Bacoor *Manila* **17** C1
Bacoor B. *Manila* **17** C1

Badalona *Barcelona* **4** A2
Badhoevedorp *Amsterdam* **2** A1
Badli *Delhi* **10** A1
Bærum *Oslo* **23** A2
Bağcılar *Istanbul* **12** B1
Bäggio *Milan* **18** B1
Bâgh-e-Feyz *Tehran* **31** A1
Baghdâd *Baghdad* **3** A2
Baghdad Int. ✈ (BGW) *Baghdad* **3** B1
Bagmari *Kolkata* **14** B2
Bagneux *Paris* **24** B2
Bagnolet *Paris* **24** A3
Bagsværd *Copenhagen* **8** A2
Bagsværd Sø *Copenhagen* **8** A2
Baguiati *Kolkata* **14** B2
Bagumbayan *Manila* **17** C2
Baha'i Temple *Chicago* **9** A2
Bahçeköy *Istanbul* **12** A1
Bahçelievler *Istanbul* **12** B1
Bahtîm *Cairo* **7** A2
Baihedong *Guangzhou* **11** B2
Baileys Crossroads *Washington* **33** B2
Bailly *Paris* **24** A1
Bairro Lopes *Lisbon* **16** A2
Baisha *Guangzhou* **11** B2
Baiyun *Guangzhou* **11** A2
Baiyun Mountain Scenic Area △ *Guangzhou* **11** A2
Bakırköy *Istanbul* **12** C1
Bal Harbor *Miami* **19** C3
Balara *Manila* **17** B2
Balch Springs *Dallas-Fort Worth* **10** B6
Baldia *Karachi* **13** A1
Baldwin, L. *Orlando* **23** A2
Baldwin Hills *Los Angeles* **16** B2
Baldwin Hills Res. *Los Angeles* **16** B2
Balgowlah *Sydney* **29** A2
Balgowlah Heights *Sydney* **29** A2
Balham *London* **15** B3
Bali *Kolkata* **14** B1
Baligania *Kolkata* **14** B2
Balingsnäs *Stockholm* **29** B2
Balingsta *Stockholm* **29** B2
Balintawak *Manila* **17** B1
Ballerup *Copenhagen* **8** A2
Ballygunge *Kolkata* **14** B2
Balmain *Sydney* **29** B2
Baluhati *Kolkata* **14** B1
Balvanera *Buenos Aires* **7** B2
Balwyn *Melbourne* **18** A2
Balwyn North *Melbourne* **18** A2
Banana Island *Lagos* **14** B2
Banática *Lisbon* **16** A1
Bandra *Mumbai* **20** A1
Bandra Pt. *Mumbai* **20** A1
Bang Kapi *Bangkok* **3** B2
Bang Na *Bangkok* **3** B2
Bangbae *Seoul* **27** C1
Bangkhen *Bangkok* **3** A2
Bangkok *Bangkok* **3** B2
Bangkok Don Muang Int. ✈ (BKK) *Bangkok* **3** A2
Bangkok Noi *Bangkok* **3** B1
Bangkok Yai *Bangkok* **3** B1
Banglo *Kolkata* **14** B1
Bangrak *Bangkok* **3** B2
Bangsu *Bangkok* **3** B2
Banks, C. *Sydney* **29** C2
Banksmeadow *Sydney* **29** B2
Banstala *Kolkata* **14** B2
Bantra *Kolkata* **14** B1
Baoshan *Shanghai* **28** A1
Bar Giyora *Jerusalem* **13** B1
Barahanagar *Kolkata* **14** B2
Barajas *Madrid* **17** B2
Barajas, Madrid ✈ (MAD) *Madrid* **17** B2
Barakpur *Kolkata* **14** A2
Barcarena *Lisbon* **16** A1
Barcarena, Rib. de ➔ *Lisbon* **16** A1
Barcelona *Barcelona* **4** A2
Barcelona, El Prat ✈ (BCN) *Barcelona* **4** B1
Barcroft, L. *Washington* **33** B2
Barking *London* **15** A4
Barkingside *London* **15** A4
Barnes *London* **15** B2
Barnet *London* **15** A2
Baron Empain Palace *Cairo* **7** A2
Barra Andai *Karachi* **13** B2
Barra Funda *São Paulo* **27** B2
Barracas *Buenos Aires* **7** B2
Barrackpur = Barakpur *Kolkata* **14** A2
Barranco *Lima* **14** B2
Barreiro *Lisbon* **16** B2
Barretto *Rio de Janeiro* **25** B2
Bartala *Kolkata* **14** B1
Barton Park *Sydney* **29** B1
Bartyki *Warsaw* **33** C2
Basus *Cairo* **7** A2
Batanagar *Kolkata* **14** B1
Bath Beach *New York* **22** C1
Bath I. *Karachi* **13** B2
Batir *Jerusalem* **13** B2
Batok, Bukit *Singapore* **28** A2
Batorri *Rio de Janeiro* **25** B2
Battersea *London* **15** B3
Bauman *Moscow* **19** B3
Baumgarten *Vienna* **32** A1
Bay, L. *Orlando* **23** B1
Bay Harbor Islands *Miami* **19** C3
Bay Hill *Orlando* **23** B1
Bay Ridge *New York* **22** C1
Bayit Va-Gan *Jerusalem* **13** B1
Bayonne *New York* **22** B1
Bayou Boeuf *New Orleans* **21** A2
Bayou Segnette State Park △ *New Orleans* **21** B1
Bayrampaşa *Istanbul* **12** B1

Bayshore *San Francisco* **26** B2
Bayt Lahm *Jerusalem* **13** B2
Bayview *San Francisco* **26** B2
Bäzär *Tehran* **31** A2
Beacon Hill *Hong Kong* **12** A3
Beato *Lisbon* **16** A2
Beaumonte Heights *Toronto* **31** A1
Bebek *Istanbul* **12** B2
Bêchovice *Prague* **25** B3
Beckenham *London* **15** B3
Beckton *London* **15** A4
Becontree *London* **15** A4
Beddington Corner *London* **15** B3
Bedford *Boston* **6** A1
Bedford *Dallas-Fort Worth* **10** A3
Bedford Park *Chicago* **9** C2
Bedford Park *New York* **22** A2
Bedford Stuyvesant *New York* **22** B2
Bedford View *Johannesburg* **13** B2
Bedok *Singapore* **28** B3
Bedok, Res. *Singapore* **28** A3
Beersel *Brussels* **6** B1
Behala *Kolkata* **14** B1
Bei Hai *Beijing* **4** B2
Beicai *Shanghai* **28** B2
Beijing *Beijing* **4** B1
Beit Duqu *Jerusalem* **13** A1
Beit Qur at-Taht *Jerusalem* **13** A1
Beit Ghur el-Fawqa *Jerusalem* **13** A1
Beit Hanina *Jerusalem* **13** A2
Beit Ij'za *Jerusalem* **13** A1
Beit Iksa *Jerusalem* **13** A2
Beit I'nan *Jerusalem* **13** A1
Beit Jala *Jerusalem* **13** B2
Beit Lahm = Bayt Lahm *Jerusalem* **13** B2
Beit Liqya *Jerusalem* **13** B1
Beit Nekofa *Jerusalem* **13** B1
Beit Sofafa *Jerusalem* **13** B2
Beit Surik *Jerusalem* **13** A1
Beit Ur al-Fawqa *Jerusalem* **13** A1
Beit Zayit *Jerusalem* **13** B1
Beitaipingzhuan *Beijing* **4** B1
Beitar Ilit *Jerusalem* **13** B1
Beitin *Jerusalem* **13** A2
Beitsun *Guangzhou* **11** B2
Beitunya *Jerusalem* **13** A2
Beixing Jing Park *Shanghai* **28** B1
Bêkásmegyer *Budapest* **7** A2
Bekkelaget *Oslo* **23** A3
Bekkestua *Oslo* **23** A2
Bel Air *Los Angeles* **16** B2
Bela Vista *São Paulo* **27** B2
Bélanger *Montreal* **20** A1
Belas *Lisbon* **16** A1
Beleghata *Kolkata* **14** B2
Belém *Lisbon* **16** A1
Belém, Torre de *Lisbon* **16** A1
Belênzinho *São Paulo* **27** B2
Belgachia *Kolkata* **14** B2
Belgharia *Kolkata* **14** B2
Belgrano *Buenos Aires* **7** B2
Bell *Los Angeles* **16** C3
Bell Gardens *Los Angeles* **16** C4
Bell Cr. ➔ *Toronto* **31** A2
Bellavista *Lima* **14** B2
Bellavista *Santiago* **27** C2
Belle Harbor *New York* **22** C2
Bellingham *London* **15** B3
Bellmore *London* **15** A2
Belmont *Boston* **6** A1
Belmont *London* **15** A2
Belmont Cragin *Chicago* **9** B2
Belmont Harbor *Chicago* **9** B3
Belmore *Sydney* **29** B1
Belur *Kolkata* **14** B2
Belvedere *London* **15** B4
Belvedere *San Francisco* **26** A2
Belvedere Park *Atlanta* **3** B3
Belyayevo Bogorodskoye *Moscow* **19** C2
Bemowo *Warsaw* **33** B1
Benaki Museum *Athens* **2** B2
Bendale *Toronto* **31** A3
Benefica *Rio de Janeiro* **25** B1
Benfica *Lisbon* **16** A1
Benítez Int. ✈ (SCL) *Santiago* **27** B1
Benito Juárez Int. ✈ (MEX) *Mexico City* **18** B2
Bensonhurst *New York* **22** C2
Berchem-Ste-Agathe *Brussels* **6** A1
Berg am Laim *Munich* **21** B2
Bergenfield *New York* **22** A2
Bergham *Munich* **21** B2
Bergvliet *Cape Town* **8** B1
Beri *Barcelona* **4** A1
Berkeley *San Francisco* **26** A3
Berlin *Berlin* **5** A3
Berlin Brandenburg ✈ (BER) *Berlin* **5** B4
Berlin Dom *Berlin* **5** A3
Berlin Tegel ✈ (TXL) *Berlin* **5** A2
Bermondsey *London* **15** B3
Bernabeu, Estadio *Madrid* **17** B1
Bernal Heights *San Francisco* **26** B2
Berwyn *Chicago* **9** B2
Berwyn Heights *Washington* **33** B3
Besiktas *Istanbul* **12** B2
Besós ➔ *Barcelona* **4** A2
Bessie, L. *Orlando* **23** B1
Bet Horon *Jerusalem* **13** A1
Bethesda *Washington* **33** B2
Bethlehem = Bayt Lahm *Jerusalem* **13** B2
Bethnal Green *London* **15** A3
Betor *Kolkata* **14** B1
Beulah *Orlando* **23** A1
Beulah, L. *Orlando* **23** A1
Beverley Hills *Sydney* **29** B1

Beverley Park *Sydney* **29** B1
Beverly *Chicago* **9** C3
Beverly Arts Center *Chicago* **9** C2
Beverly Glen *Los Angeles* **16** B2
Beverly Hills *Los Angeles* **16** B2
Beverly Hills -Morgan Park Historic District *Chicago* **9** C2
Bexley *Sydney* **29** B1
Bexley □ *London* **15** B4
Bexleyheath *London* **15** B4
Beykoz *Istanbul* **12** B2
Beylerbeyi *Istanbul* **12** B2
Beyoğlu *Istanbul* **12** B1
Bezons *Paris* **24** A2
Bezuidenhout Park *Johannesburg* **13** B2
Bhadrakali *Kolkata* **14** A2
Bhalswa *Delhi* **10** B2
Bhambo Khan Qarmati *Karachi* **13** A1
Bhatsala *Kolkata* **14** B2
Bhawanipur *Kolkata* **14** B2
Bhendkhal *Mumbai* **20** B2
Bhit I. *Jerusalem* **13** B1
Bhuleshwar *Mumbai* **20** B1
Bialoleka Dworska *Warsaw* **33** B2
Bicentennial Park *Sydney* **29** B1
Bickley *London* **15** B4
Bicutan *Manila* **17** C2
Bidhan Nagar *Kolkata* **14** B2
Bidu *Jerusalem* **13** A1
Bielany *Warsaw* **33** B1
Bielawa *Warsaw* **33** C2
Biesdorf *Berlin* **5** A4
Bièvre ➔ *Paris* **24** B1
Bièvres *Paris* **24** B2
Big Buddha *Hong Kong* **12** B1
Big Sand L. *Orlando* **23** B2
Bijlmermeer *Amsterdam* **2** B2
Bill Baggs Cape Florida State Recr. Area △ *Miami* **19** D3
Bilston *Edinburgh* **11** B2
Binacayan *Manila* **17** C1
Binondo *Manila* **17** B1
Bintaro Jaya *Jakarta* **12** B1
Bir Nabala *Jerusalem* **13** A2
Birak el Kiyam *Cairo* **7** A1
Birch Cliff *Toronto* **31** B3
Birkenstein *Berlin* **5** A4
Birkholz *Berlin* **5** A4
Birkholzaue *Berlin* **5** A4
Birrarrung Park *Melbourne* **18** A2
Biscayne Bay Aquatic Reserve *Miami* **19** C2
Biscayne Park *Miami* **19** C2
Bishop Lavis *Cape Town* **8** A2
Bishopscourt *Cape Town* **8** A1
Bispebjerg *Copenhagen* **8** A3
Bissonet Plaza *New Orleans* **21** A1
Bittsevsky Forest Park *Moscow* **19** C2
Björknas *Stockholm* **29** B3
Black Cr. ➔ *Toronto* **31** A2
Black Creek Pioneer Village *Toronto* **31** A1
Blacken *London* **15** B4
Blackheath *London* **15** B3
Bladensburg *Washington* **33** B3
Blair Village *Atlanta* **3** C2
Blairgowrie *Johannesburg* **13** A2
Blake House *Boston* **6** B2
Blakehurst *Sydney* **29** B1
Blakstad *Oslo* **23** B1
Blanche, L. *Orlando* **23** B1
Blankenburg *Berlin* **5** A3
Blankenfelde *Berlin* **5** A3
Blizne *Warsaw* **33** B1
Blota *Warsaw* **33** C2
Blue Island *Chicago* **9** D2
Blue Lagoon L. *Miami* **19** D1
Blue Mosque = Sultanahme Camil *Istanbul* **12** B1
Blue Mound *Dallas-Fort Worth* **10** A2
Bluff Hd. *Hong Kong* **12** B2
Bluffers Park *Toronto* **31** A3
Blumberg *Berlin* **5** A4
Blunt Pt. *San Francisco* **26** A2
Blutenberg *Munich* **21** B1
Blylaget *Oslo* **23** B3
Boa Vista, Alto do *Rio de Janeiro* **25** B1
Boardwalk *New York* **22** C3
Boavista *Lisbon* **16** A2
Bobigny *Paris* **24** A3
Bocanegra *Lima* **14** B2
Boedo *Buenos Aires* **7** B2
Bogenhausen *Munich* **21** B2
Bogorodskoye *Moscow* **19** B3
Bogota *New York* **22** A1
Bogstadvatnet *Oslo* **23** A2
Bohnsdorf *Berlin* **5** B4
Bois-Colombes *Paris* **24** A2
Bois-d'Arcy *Paris* **24** B1
Boissy-St-Léger *Paris* **24** B4
Boldinasco *Milan* **18** B1
Boler *Oslo* **23** A4
Boltate *Milan* **18** A1
Bollebeek *Brussels* **6** A1
Bollendorf *Berlin* **5** A5
Bollmora *Stockholm* **29** B3
Bolshaya Okhta *St. Petersburg* **27** B2
Bolton *Milan* **18** A1
Bom Retiro *São Paulo* **27** B2
Bombay = Mumbai *Mumbai* **20** B2
Bondi *Sydney* **29** B2

Bondy *Paris* **24** A3
Bondy, Forêt de *Paris* **24** A4
Bonifacio Monument *Manila* **17** B1
Bonnabel Place *New Orleans* **21** A2
Bonneuil-sur-Marne *Paris* **24** B3
Bonnington *Edinburgh* **11** B1
Bonnyrigg and Lasswade *Edinburgh* **11** B3
Bonsucesso *Rio de Janeiro* **25** B1
Bontheuwel *Cape Town* **8** A2
Boo *Stockholm* **29** A3
Borisovo *Moscow* **19** C3
Borle *Mumbai* **20** A2
Boronia Park *Sydney* **29** A1
Bosmont *Johannesburg* **13** B1
Bosön *Stockholm* **29** A3
Bosporus = İstanbul Boğazı *Istanbul* **12** B2
Bostanci *Istanbul* **12** C2
Boston *Boston* **6** A2
Boston Common *Boston* **6** A2
Boston Logan Int. ✈ (BOS) *Boston* **6** A2
Botafogo *Rio de Janeiro* **25** B1
Botany *Sydney* **29** B2
Botany B. *Sydney* **29** B2
Botany Bay △ *Sydney* **29** B2
Botiè ➔ *Prague* **25** B3
Botica Sete *Lisbon* **16** A1
Boucherville *Montreal* **20** A3
Boucherville, Is. de *Montreal* **20** A3
Bougival *Paris* **24** A1
Boulder Pt. *Hong Kong* **12** B2
Boulogne, Bois de *Paris* **24** A2
Boulogne-Billancourt *Paris* **24** B2
Bourg-la-Reine *Paris* **24** B2
Bouviers *Paris* **24** B1
Bovenkerk *Amsterdam* **2** B2
Bovenkerker Polder *Amsterdam* **2** B2
Bovisa *Milan* **18** A2
Bow *London* **15** A3
Boyacıköy *Istanbul* **12** B2
Boyd Conservation Area *Toronto* **31** A1
Boyle Heights *Los Angeles* **16** B3
Braepark *Edinburgh* **11** B2
Braid *Edinburgh* **11** B2
Bramley *Johannesburg* **13** A2
Brandeis Univ. *Boston* **6** A1
Brandenburger Tor *Berlin* **5** A3
Brani, Pulau *Singapore* **28** B3
Branik *Prague* **25** B2
Brännkyrka *Stockholm* **29** B2
Brás *São Paulo* **27** B2
Brasilândia *São Paulo* **27** A1
Brateyevo *Moscow* **19** C3
Braybrook *Melbourne* **18** A1
Brázdim *Prague* **25** A3
Breakheart Reservation *Boston* **6** A2
Brede *Copenhagen* **8** A3
Breezy Point *New York* **22** C2
Breitenlee *Vienna* **32** A3
Breña *Lima* **14** B2
Brent □ *London* **15** A2
Brent Res. *London* **15** A2
Brentford *London* **15** B2
Brentwood *Los Angeles* **16** B2
Brentwood Park *Los Angeles* **16** B2
Brera *Milan* **18** B2
Bresso *Milan* **18** A2
Brevik *Stockholm* **29** A3
Břevnov *Prague* **25** B2
Brickyard, The *Chicago* **9** B2
Bridge City *New Orleans* **21** B2
Bridgeport *Chicago* **9** B3
Bridgetown *Cape Town* **8** A2
Bridgeview *Chicago* **9** C2
Brighton *Boston* **6** A2
Brighton *Melbourne* **18** B1
Brighton Beach *New York* **22** C2
Brighton Park *Chicago* **9** C2
Brightwood *Washington* **33** B2
Brigittenau *Vienna* **32** A2
Brimbank Park *Melbourne* **18** A1
Brisbane *San Francisco* **26** B2
Britz *Berlin* **5** B3
Brixton *London* **15** B3
Broadmeadows *Melbourne* **18** A1
Broadmoor *San Francisco* **26** B2
Broadview *Chicago* **9** B1
Broadview Park *Miami* **19** C2
Brockley *London* **15** B3
Bródno *Warsaw* **33** B2
Bródnowski, Kanal *Warsaw* **33** B2
Broek *Amsterdam* **2** A2
Bromley □ *London* **15** B4
Bromley Common *London* **15** B4
Bromma *Stockholm* **29** A1
Bromma ✈ (BMA) *Stockholm* **29** A1
Brøndby Strand *Copenhagen* **8** B2
Brøndbyøster *Copenhagen* **8** B2
Brøndbyvester *Copenhagen* **8** B2
Brondesbury *London* **15** A2
Brønnoya *Oslo* **23** B2
Bronnitsy *Copenhagen* **8** A2
Bronxville *New York* **22** A2
Bronx, The *New York* **22** B2
Brookfield Zoo *Chicago* **9** B1
Brookhaven *Atlanta* **3** A2
Brookline *Boston* **6** A2
Brookline Station *Boston* **6** A1
Brooklyn *Cape Town* **8** A1
Brooklyn *New York* **22** C2
Brooklyn Heights *New York* **22** B2
Brookmont *Washington* **33** B2
Brossard *Montreal* **20** B3
Brothers, The *Hong Kong* **12** B1
Brou-sur-Chanterine *Paris* **24** A4
Brown *Toronto* **31** A3

Brownsville *Miami* **19** D1
Brughério *Milan* **18** A2
Brunswick *Melbourne* **18** A1
Brussegem *Brussels* **6** A1
Brussel *Brussels* **6** A2
Brussel ✈ (BRU) *Brussels* **6** A2
Brussels = Brussel *Brussels* **6** A2
Bruxelles = Brussel *Brussels* **6** A2
Bruzzano *Milan* **18** A2
Bry-sur-Marne *Paris* **24** A4
Bryan, L. *Orlando* **23** B1
Bryanston *Johannesburg* **13** A1
Brzeziny *Warsaw* **33** B2
Bubeneč *Prague* **25** B2
Buc *Paris* **24** B1
Buchenhain *Munich* **21** B1
Buchholz *Berlin* **5** A3
Buckhead *Atlanta* **3** B2
Buckingham Palace *London* **15** A3
Buckow *Berlin* **5** B3
Bucktown *New Orleans* **21** A2
Buda *Budapest* **7** A2
Buda Castle = Budaváripalota *Budapest* **7** A2
Budafok *Budapest* **7** B2
Budaörs *Budapest* **7** B1
Budapest *Budapest* **7** B2
Budapest Ferenc Liszt ✈ (BUD) *Budapest* **7** B3
Budatétény *Budapest* **7** B2
Budaváripalota *Budapest* **7** A2
Buddinge *Copenhagen* **8** A3
Buenos Aires *Buenos Aires* **7** B2
Buenos Aires Ezeiza ✈ (EZE) *Buenos Aires* **7** C1
Bufalotta *Rome* **26** B2
Buiksloot *Amsterdam* **2** A2
Buitenveldert *Amsterdam* **2** B2
Buizingen *Brussels* **6** B1
Bukhansan *Seoul* **27** B1
Bukit Batok *Singapore* **28** A2
Bukit Panjang *Singapore* **28** A2
Bukit Panjang Nature Reserve △ *Singapore* **28** A2
Bukit Timah Nature Reserve △ *Singapore* **28** A2
Bukum, Pulau *Singapore* **28** B2
Bule *Manila* **17** C2
Bullen Park *Melbourne* **18** A2
Bund, The *Shanghai* **28** B1
Bundoora North *Melbourne* **18** A2
Bundoora Park *Melbourne* **18** A2
Bunker Hill Memorial *Boston* **6** A2
Bunker I. *Karachi* **13** B1
Bunkyō *Tokyo* **30** A3
Bunnefjorden *Oslo* **23** A3
Buona Vista Park *Singapore* **28** B2
Bur Dubai *Dubai* **9** A2
Burbank *Chicago* **9** C2
Burbank *Los Angeles* **16** B3
Burden, L. *Orlando* **23** B1
Burj Al Arab *Dubai* **9** B1
Burj Khalifa *Dubai* **9** B2
Burlington *Boston* **6** A1
Burnham Park *Chicago* **9** C3
Burnham Park Harbor *Chicago* **9** B3
Burnhamthorpe *Toronto* **31** B1
Burnt Oak *London* **15** A2
Burntisland *Edinburgh* **11** A2
Burnwynd *Edinburgh* **11** B1
Burqa *Jerusalem* **13** A2
Burtus *Cairo* **7** A1
Burudvatn *Oslo* **23** A2
Burwood *Sydney* **29** B1
Bushwick *New York* **22** B2
Bushy Park *London* **15** B1
Business Bay *Dubai* **9** B2
Butantã *São Paulo* **27** B1
Butcher I. *Mumbai* **20** B2
Butler, L. *Orlando* **23** B1
Büyükdere *Istanbul* **12** B2
Byculla *Mumbai* **20** B2
Bygdoy *Oslo* **23** A3
Bywater *New Orleans* **21** B2

## C

C.B.S. Fox Studios *Los Angeles* **16** B2
C.N. Tower *Toronto* **31** B2
Caballito *Buenos Aires* **7** B2
Cabin John *Washington* **33** B1
Cabin John Regional Park △ *Washington* **33** A1
Cabuçú de Baixo ➔ *São Paulo* **27** A2
Cabuçú de Cima ➔ *São Paulo* **27** A2
Cachan *Paris* **24** B2
Cachoeira, Rib. da ➔ *São Paulo* **27** B2
Cacilhas *Lisbon* **16** A2
Cahuenga Pk. *Los Angeles* **16** B3
Cain, L. *Orlando* **23** B2
Cairo = El Qâhira *Cairo* **7** A2
Cairo Int. ✈ (CAI) *Cairo* **7** A2
Calabasas *Los Angeles* **16** B1
Calcutta = Kolkata *Kolkata* **14** B2
California Institute of Technology *Los Angeles* **16** B4
California Los Angeles, Univ. of *Los Angeles* **16** B2
California State Univ. *Los Angeles* **16** B3
Callao *Lima* **14** B2
Caloocan *Manila* **17** B1

36 Göktürk INDEX TO CITY MAPS


Göktürk Istanbul 12 A1
Golabari Kolkata 14 B2
Golabki Warsaw 33 B1
Gold Coast Chicago 9 B3
Golden Beach Miami 19 C3
Golden Gate San Francisco 26 B2
Golden Gate ⌂ San Francisco 26 A2
Golden Gate Bridge San Francisco 26 B2
Golden Gate Park San Francisco 26 B2
Golden Horn = Haliç Istanbul 12 B1
Golders Green London 15 A2
Golestan Palace Tehran 31 A2
Golf Chicago 9 A2
Gonen Jerusalem 13 B2
Gongneung Seoul 27 B2
Goodmayes London 15 A4
Goodwood Cape Town 8 A2
Gopalpur Kolkata 14 B2
Górce Warsaw 33 B1
Gore Hill Sydney 29 A2
Gorelyy → St. Petersburg 27 A3
Gorgie Edinburgh 11 B2
Gorky Park Moscow 19 B2
Gosen Berlin 5 B5
Gosener kanal Berlin 5 B5
Gospel Oak London 15 A3
Gotanda Tokyo 30 B3
Goth Goli Mar Karachi 13 A2
Goth Sher Shah Karachi 13 A1
Gotha Orlando 23 A1
Gournay-sur-Marne Paris 24 A4
Governador, I. do Rio de Janeiro 25 A1
Governors I. New York 22 B1
Grabów Warsaw 33 C1
Gràcia Barcelona 4 A2
Gräfelfing Munich 21 B1
Gragoatá Rio de Janeiro 25 B2
Grand Bazaar = Kapali Carsi Istanbul 12 B1
Grand Central Station New York 22 B2
Grand Palace Bangkok 3 B1
Grand Place Brussels 6 A2
Grand Prairie Dallas-Fort Worth 10 B3
Grande Place Brussels 6 A2
Grankulla = Kauniainen Helsinki 11 B1
Grant Park Chicago 9 B3
Granton Edinburgh 11 B2
Grapevine Dallas-Fort Worth 10 A3
Grapevine Recr. Area Dallas-Fort Worth 10 A3
Grassy Park Cape Town 8 B2
Gratosóglio Milan 18 B2
Gratzwalde Berlin 5 B5
Gravesend New York 22 C2
Grazhdanka St. Petersburg 27 B2
Greco Milan 18 A2
Green I. Hong Kong 12 B2
Green Point Cape Town 8 A1
Greenfield Park Montreal 20 B3
Greenford London 15 A1
Greenhill London 15 A2
Greenwich □ London 15 B3
Greenwich Observatory London 15 B3
Greenwich Village New York 22 B2
Greenwood Boston 6 A2
Grefsen Oslo 23 A3
Gresham Park Atlanta 3 B2
Gretna New Orleans 21 B2
Gretna City Park New Orleans 21 B2
Greve Strand Copenhagen 8 B1
Greynolds Park Miami 19 C3
Griebnitzsee Berlin 5 B1
Griffith Park Los Angeles 16 B3
Grimbergen Brussels 6 A2
Grinzing Vienna 32 A2
Gröbenried Munich 21 A1
Grochów Warsaw 33 B2
Grodzisk Warsaw 33 B2
Groenendaal Brussels 6 B2
Grogol Petamburin Jakarta 12 A1
Gronsdorf Munich 21 B3
Grorud Oslo 23 A4
Gross Glienicke Berlin 5 B1
Gross-Hadern Munich 21 B1
Gross-Lappen Munich 21 A2
Grosse Krampe Berlin 5 B5
Grosse Müggelsee Berlin 5 B4
Grosse Point Lighthouse Chicago 9 A2
Grossenzersdorf Vienna 32 A3
Grossenzersdorfer Arm → Vienna 32 A3
Grosser Biberhaufen Vienna 32 A2
Grosser Wannsee Berlin 5 B2
Grossfeld-Siedlung Vienna 32 A2
Grosshesselohe Munich 21 B2
Grossjedlersdorf Vienna 32 A2
Grossziethen Berlin 5 B3
Grove Hall Boston 6 B2
Grove Park Atlanta 3 B2
Grove Park London 15 B4
Grove Park London 15 B2
Groveton Washington 33 C2
Grünau Berlin 5 B4
Grunewald Berlin 5 B2
Grünwald Munich 21 B2
Grünwalder Forst Munich 21 B2
Grymes Hill New York 22 C1
Guadalupe Manila 17 B2
Guadalupe, Basilica de Mexico City 18 B2
Guanabara, B. de Rio de Janeiro 25 B1
Guanabara, Jardim Rio de Janeiro 25 A1
Guanabara, Palácio da Rio de Janeiro 25 B1
Guang'anmen Beijing 4 B1
Guangdong Olympic Stadium Guangzhou 11 B3
Guangqumen Beijing 4 B2
Guangzhou Guangzhou 11 B2
Guanshuo Guangzhou 11 B3
Gucun Shanghai 28 A1
Gudö Stockholm 29 B3
Güell, Parque de Barcelona 4 A2
Guildwood Toronto 31 A3
Guinardó Barcelona 4 A2
Gulbai Karachi 13 A1
Gulshan-e Iqbal Jerusalem 13 A2
Güngören Istanbul 12 B1
Gunnersbury London 15 B2
Guomao Beijing 4 B2
Gustavo A. Madero Mexico City 18 B2
Guttenberg New York 22 B1
Gutuyevskiy, Ostrov St. Petersburg 27 B1
Guyancourt Paris 24 B1
Gwanak Seoul 27 C1
Gwanaksan Seoul 27 C1
Gyál Budapest 7 B3
Gyáli-patak → Budapest 7 B2

H

Haaga Helsinki 11 B2
Haar Munich 21 B3
Habay Manila 17 C1
Hackbridge London 15 B3
Hackensack New York 22 A1
Hackensack → New York 22 B1
Hackney □ London 15 A3
Hackney Wick London 15 A3
Hadr, Warrâq el Cairo 7 A2
Haga Stockholm 29 A2
Hagenbrunn Vienna 32 A2
Hägersten Stockholm 29 B1
Häggvik Stockholm 29 A1
Hagonoy Manila 17 B2
Hague Park Toronto 31 A3
Haidari = Chaidari Athens 2 A1
Haidarpur Delhi 10 A1
Haidhausen Munich 21 B2
Haidian Beijing 4 B1
Haight-Ashbury San Francisco 26 B2
Hainault London 15 A4
Haizhou Guangzhou 11 B2
Haizhu Guangchang Guangzhou 11 B2
Hakunila Helsinki 11 B3
Halandri = Chalandri Athens 2 A2
Halásztelek Budapest 7 B1
Haliç Istanbul 12 B1
Halim Perdana Kusuma Int. ✕ (HLP) Jakarta 12 B2
Hallandale Beach Miami 19 C3
Halle Brussels 6 B1
Haltiala Helsinki 11 B2
Haltiavuori Helsinki 11 B2
Haltom City Dallas-Fort Worth 10 B2
Ham London 15 B2
Hämeenkylä Helsinki 11 B1
Hammarby Stockholm 29 B2
Hamme Brussels 6 A1
Hammersmith London 15 B2
Hampstead London 15 A2
Hampstead Montreal 20 B2
Hampstead Garden Suburb London 15 A2
Hampstead Heath London 15 A2
Hampton London 15 B1
Hampton Court Palace London 15 B1
Hampton Wick London 15 B2
Hamrā' Baghdad 3 B1
Hanala Helsinki 11 A3
Haneda Tokyo 30 B3
Haneda, Tōkyō ✕ (HND) Tokyo 30 B3
Hang Hau Hong Kong 12 B3
Hanging Gardens Mumbai 20 B1
Hanlon Toronto 31 B1
Hanwell London 15 A1
Hanworth London 15 B1
Haora Kolkata 14 B1
Hapeville Atlanta 3 C2
Happy Valley Hong Kong 12 B3
Har Adar Jerusalem 13 B1
Har Gilo Jerusalem 13 B2
Har Homa Jerusalem 13 B2
Har Nof Jerusalem 13 B2
Harahan New Orleans 21 B1
Harbour Front Centre Singapore 28 B2
Haren Brussels 6 A2
Hareskovby Copenhagen 8 A2
Haringey □ London 15 A3
Harjusuo Helsinki 11 B3
Harlaching Munich 21 B2
Harlaw Res. Edinburgh 11 B2
Harlem New York 22 B2
Harlesden London 15 A2
Harlington London 15 B1
Harmaja Helsinki 11 C2
Harmashatar hegy Budapest 7 A2
Háros Budapest 7 B2
Harperrig Res. Edinburgh 11 B1
Harrow □ London 15 A1
Harrow on the Hill London 15 A1
Harrow School London 15 A1
Harrow Weald London 15 A1
Harry S. Moss Park Dallas-Fort Worth 10 A5
Hartsfield-Jackson Atlanta Int. ✕ (ATL) Atlanta 3 C2
Harumi Tokyo 30 B3
Harvard Univ. Boston 6 A2
Harvey Chicago 9 D3
Harvey New Orleans 21 B2
Harwood Heights Chicago 9 B2
Hasanābād Tehran 31 A1
Hasbrouck Heights New York 22 A1
Haselhorst Berlin 5 A2
Hasköy Istanbul 12 B1
Hasle Oslo 23 B2
Haslum Oslo 23 A2
Hästhagen Stockholm 29 B2
Hatch End London 15 A1
Hatiara Kolkata 14 B2
Hauketo Oslo 23 A3
Hauz Khas Delhi 10 B2
Havel → Berlin 5 A2
Havelkanal Berlin 5 A2
Havering □ London 15 A5
Havering-atte-Bower London 15 A5
Haworth New York 22 A2
Hawthorne Racecourse Chicago 9 C2
Hayes London 15 B4
Hayes London 15 A1
Hayes End London 15 A1
Hayford Chicago 9 C2
Heathfield Cape Town 8 B1
Heathrow, London ✕ (LHR) London 15 B1
Hebe Haven Hong Kong 12 A3
Hedong Guangzhou 11 B2
Hei Ling Chau Hong Kong 12 B2
Heidelberg Heights Melbourne 18 A2
Heidelberg West Melbourne 18 A2
Heidemühle Berlin 5 B5
Heideveld Cape Town 8 A2
Heiligensee Berlin 5 A2
Heiligenstadt Vienna 32 A2
Heinersdorf Berlin 5 A3
Hélène de Champlain, Parc ⌂ Montreal 20 A2
Helenelund Stockholm 29 A1
Heliopolis = Masr el Gedida Cairo 7 A2
Hellersdorf Berlin 5 A4
Hellerup Copenhagen 8 A3
Helsingfors = Helsinki Helsinki 11 B2
Helsinki Helsinki 11 B2
Helsinki-Vantaa ✕ (HEL) Helsinki 11 B2
Hen and Chicken B. Sydney 29 B1
Henderson Las Vegas 14 B2
Hendon London 15 A2
Hengsha Guangzhou 11 B2
Hennigsdorf Berlin 5 A2
Henryków Warsaw 33 B1
Henson Cr. → Washington 33 C3
Henttaa Helsinki 11 B1
Heping Park Shanghai 28 B2
Hepingli Beijing 4 B2
Herlev Copenhagen 8 A2
Herman Eckstein Park Johannesburg 13 A2
Hermannskogel Vienna 32 A1
Hermiston Edinburgh 11 B2
Hermitage and Winter Palace St. Petersburg 27 B2
Hermsdorf Berlin 5 A2
Hernals Vienna 32 A2
Herne Hill London 15 B3
Héroes de Churubusco Mexico City 18 B2
Herons, Î. aux Montreal 20 B2
Herstedøster Copenhagen 8 A2
Herttoniemi Helsinki 11 B3
Ḩeşārak Tehran 31 A1
Heston London 15 B1
Hetzendorf Vienna 32 B1
Hextable London 15 B5
Hialeah Miami 19 C1
Hialeah Race Track Miami 19 C1
Hiawassa, L. Orlando 23 A2
Hickory Hills Chicago 9 C2
Hiekkaharju Helsinki 11 B3
Hietaniemi Helsinki 11 B2
Hietzing Vienna 32 A1
Higashi Osaka 23 A2
Higashimurayama Tokyo 30 A1
Higashinari Osaka 23 A2
Higashisumiyoshi Osaka 23 B2
Higashiyodogawa Osaka 23 A1
High Junk Pk. Hong Kong 12 B3
High Park Toronto 31 B2
Highbury London 15 A3
Highgate London 15 A3
Highland Cr. → Toronto 31 A3
Highland Creek Toronto 31 A3
Highland Park Dallas-Fort Worth 10 B5
Highland Park Los Angeles 16 B3
Highlands North Johannesburg 13 A2
Hillbrow Tower Johannesburg 13 B2
Hillcrest Heights Washington 33 C3
Hillend Edinburgh 11 A1
Hillingdon □ London 15 A1
Hillwood Washington 33 B2
Hilmiya Cairo 7 A2
Hin Keng Hong Kong 12 A3
Hirota Osaka 23 A1
Hirschstetten Vienna 32 A2
Hither Green London 15 B3
Hiyoshi Tokyo 30 B2
Hizma Jerusalem 13 B2
Hjortekær Copenhagen 8 A3
Hjortespring Copenhagen 8 A2
Hlubočepy Prague 25 B2
Ho Chung Hong Kong 12 A3
Hoboken New York 22 B1
Hobsons B. Melbourne 18 B1
Hochbrück Munich 21 A2
Hochelaga Montreal 20 A2
Hoegi Seoul 27 B2
Hoeilaart Brussels 6 B2
Hofburg Vienna 32 A2
Hoffman I. New York 22 C1
Hohenbrunn Munich 21 B3
Hohenschönhausen Berlin 5 A4
Hok Tsui Hong Kong 12 B3
Holargos = Cholargos Athens 2 B2
Holborn London 15 A3
Holden, L. Orlando 23 B2
Holešovice Prague 25 B2
Holiday Park Miami 19 B3
Holland Village Singapore 28 B2
Höllriegelskreuth Munich 21 B1
Hollywood Los Angeles 16 B3
Hollywood Miami 19 B3
Hollywood Bowl Los Angeles 16 B2
Holmenkollen Oslo 23 A3
Holmgård Stockholm 29 B1
Holmlia Oslo 23 B3
Holocaust Memorial Jerusalem 13 B2
Holyrood House, Palace of Edinburgh 11 B3
Holysloot Amsterdam 2 A3
Homerton London 15 A3
Hometown Chicago 9 C2
Hōnanchō Tokyo 30 A2
Honcho Tokyo 30 A3
Honden Tokyo 30 A4
Hondo, Rio → Los Angeles 16 B4
Hong Kong I. Hong Kong 12 B3
Hong Kong Int. ✕ (HKG) Hong Kong 12 B1
Hong Kong Univ. Hong Kong 12 B2
Hongje Seoul 27 B1
Hongjimun Tunnel Seoul 27 B1
Hongkou Shanghai 28 B1
Hongqiao Shanghai 28 B1
Honjyo Tokyo 30 A3
Honoré Mercier, Pont Montreal 20 B1
Hönow Berlin 5 A4
Hook London 15 B2
Horikiri Tokyo 30 A4
Horn Pond Boston 6 A1
Hornchurch London 15 A5
Horni Prague 25 B3
Horni Počernice Prague 25 B3
Hornsey London 15 A3
Horoměřice Prague 25 B1
Hortaleza Madrid 17 B2
Hosoyama Tokyo 30 B2
Hostafranchs Barcelona 4 A1
Hostivař Prague 25 B3
Houbětin Prague 25 B3
Hougang Singapore 28 A3
Houghton Johannesburg 13 B2
Houilles Paris 24 A2
Hounslow □ London 15 B1
Hout Bay Cape Town 8 B1
Hove Å → Copenhagen 8 B2
Hovedøya Oslo 23 A3
Høvik Oslo 23 A2
Hovorčovice Prague 25 A3
Howard Beach New York 22 C2
Howrah = Haora Kolkata 14 B1
Hōya Tokyo 30 A2
Hradčany Prague 25 B2
Huanghuagang Mausoleum Guangzhou 11 B2
Huangpu Shanghai 28 B2
Huangpu Jiang → Shanghai 28 B1
Huangtugang Beijing 4 C1
Huascar Lima 14 A2
Huay Khwang Bangkok 3 B2
Huddinge Stockholm 29 B2
Huechuraba Santiago 27 B1
Hugh Taylor Birch State Recr. Area ⌂ Miami 19 B3
Huizingen Brussels 6 B1
Humayun's Tomb Delhi 10 B2
Humber → Toronto 31 A1
Humber B. Toronto 31 B2
Humber Bay Toronto 31 B2
Humber Bay Park Toronto 31 B2
Humber College Toronto 31 B1
Humber Summit Toronto 31 A1
Humber Valley Village Toronto 31 A1
Humberlea Toronto 31 A1
Humberwood Park Toronto 31 A1
Humboldt Park Chicago 9 B2
Humera Madrid 17 B1
Hunaydī Baghdad 3 B2
Hundige Copenhagen 8 B1
Hundige Strand Copenhagen 8 B2
Hung Hom Hong Kong 12 B3
Hunters Hill Sydney 29 B1
Hunters Pt. San Francisco 26 B2
Huntington Washington 33 C2
Huntington Park Los Angeles 16 C3
Hurīya Baghdad 3 A1
Hurst Dallas-Fort Worth 10 B3
Hurstville Sydney 29 B1
Husan Jerusalem 13 B1
Husby Stockholm 29 A1
Husum Copenhagen 8 A2
Hutchins Dallas-Fort Worth 10 C5
Hütteldorf Vienna 32 A1
Hüvösvölgy Budapest 7 A2
Huwon Secret Garden Seoul 27 B1
Hvalstad Oslo 23 A1
Hvalstrand Oslo 23 A2
Hvidovre Copenhagen 8 B2
Hwagok Seoul 27 B1
Hyattsville Washington 33 B3
Hyde Park Boston 6 B2
Hyde Park Chicago 9 C3
Hyde Park Johannesburg 13 A2
Hyde Park London 15 A2
Hyde Park Los Angeles 16 C3

I

Ibese Lagos 14 A2
Ibirapuera São Paulo 27 B1
Ibirapuera, Parque do São Paulo 27 B2
Icarai Rio de Janeiro 25 B2
Içerenköy Istanbul 12 C2
Ichgao Tokyo 30 B2
Ichigaya Tokyo 30 A3
Ichikawa Tokyo 30 A4
Ickenham London 15 A1
Iddo Lagos 14 B2
Idi-Oro Lagos 14 A2
Iganmu Lagos 14 B2
Igbobi Lagos 14 A2
Igbologun Lagos 14 B1
Igny Paris 24 B2
IJ, Het → Amsterdam 2 A2
IJ-meer Amsterdam 2 A3
IJburg Amsterdam 2 A3
Ijesa-Tedo Lagos 14 B1
Ijora Lagos 14 B2
Ikebe Tokyo 30 B2
Ikebukuro Tokyo 30 A3
Ikegami Tokyo 30 B3
Ikeja Lagos 14 A2
Ikeuchi Osaka 23 B2
Ikorodu Lagos 14 A2
Ikoyi Lagos 14 B2
Ikuata Lagos 14 B2
Ikuno Osaka 23 A2
Ikuta Tokyo 30 B2
Ila Oslo 23 A2
Ilford London 15 A4
Ilioupoli Athens 2 B2
Illinois at Chicago, Univ. of Chicago 9 B3
Illinois Institute of Technology Chicago 9 B3
Ilpendam Amsterdam 2 A2
Ilsos → Athens 2 B2
Imbâbah Cairo 7 A2
Imbiah Lookout Singapore 28 B2
Imielin Warsaw 33 C2
Imirim São Paulo 27 A2
Imitos Athens 2 B2
Imitos, Oros Athens 2 B2
Imperial Palace Museum Beijing 4 B2
Inagi Tokyo 30 B2
Inchcolm Edinburgh 11 A2
Inchkeith Edinburgh 11 A3
Inchmickery Edinburgh 11 A2
Incirano Milan 18 A1
Independencia Lima 14 A2
Independencia Santiago 27 B2
India Gate Delhi 10 B2
Indian Creek Village Miami 19 C3
Indianópolis São Paulo 27 B2
Indira Gandhi Int. ✕ (DEL) Delhi 10 B1
Indira Gandhi Memorial Museum Delhi 10 B2
Industria Johannesburg 13 B1
Industrial Canal New Orleans 21 A2
Ingierstrand Oslo 23 B3
Inglewood Los Angeles 16 C3
Ingliston Edinburgh 11 B1
Inhaúma Rio de Janeiro 25 B1
Inner Port Shelter Hong Kong 12 A3
Interlagos São Paulo 27 C1
Intramuros Manila 17 B1
Invalides Paris 24 A2
Inverkeithing Edinburgh 11 A1
Inzersdorf Vienna 32 B2
Ipanema Rio de Janeiro 25 B1
Ipiranga São Paulo 27 B2
Ipiranga → São Paulo 27 B2
Iponri Lagos 14 B2
Irving Dallas-Fort Worth 10 B4
Irving Park Chicago 9 B2
Isabel Rio de Janeiro 25 B1
Isagatedo Lagos 14 A1
Isar → Munich 21 A3
Ishbīlīya Baghdad 3 A2
Ishøj Strand Copenhagen 8 B2
Island Park Toronto 31 B2
Islev Copenhagen 8 A2
Isleworth London 15 B2
Islington Toronto 31 B1
Islington □ London 15 A3
Ismā'ilīya, Qanâ el Cairo 7 A2
Ismaning Munich 21 A3
Ismayloskiy Park Moscow 19 B3
Isolo Lagos 14 A1
Issy-les-Moulineaux Paris 24 B2
İstanbul Istanbul 12 C1
İstanbul Boğazı Istanbul 12 B2
İstinye Istanbul 12 B2
Itä Hakkila Helsinki 11 B3
Itaewon Seoul 27 B1
Itami Osaka 23 A1
Itanhanga Rio de Janeiro 25 B1
Ivanhoe Melbourne 18 A2
Ives Estates Miami 19 C2
Ivry-sur-Seine Paris 24 B3
Ixelles Brussels 6 B2
Izmaylovo Moscow 19 B3
Iztacalco Mexico City 18 B2
Iztapalapa Mexico City 18 B2

J

Jaba Jerusalem 13 A2
Jabotabek = Jakarta Jakarta 12 A2
Jacaré Rio de Janeiro 25 B1
Jackson Heights New York 22 B2
Jackson Park Chicago 9 C3
Jacques-Cartier Montreal 20 A3
Jacques-Cartier, Pont Montreal 20 A2
Jadavpur Kolkata 14 C2
Jade Buddha Temple Shanghai 28 B1
Jægersborg Copenhagen 8 A3
Jægersborg Dyrehave Copenhagen 8 A3
Jagadishpur Kolkata 14 B1
Jagatpur Delhi 10 A2
Jaguaré, Rib. do → São Paulo 27 B1
Jahangirpur Delhi 10 A2
Jakarta Jakarta 12 A2
Jakarta, Teluk Jakarta 12 A1
Jakarta Halim Perdana Kusuma Int. ✕ (HLP) Jakarta 12 B2
Jalan Kayu Singapore 28 A3
Jamaica B. New York 22 C3
Jamaica Plain Boston 6 B2
Jamakpuri Delhi 10 B1
Jamshīdīyeh Tehran 31 A2
Jamsil Seoul 27 B2
Jamwon Seoul 27 B2
Janki Warsaw 33 C1
Jaraguá São Paulo 27 A1
Jaraguá, Pico de São Paulo 27 A1
Jardim Paulista São Paulo 27 B1
Järvatältet Stockholm 29 A1
Jaskhar Mumbai 20 B2
Jatinegara Jakarta 12 B2
Javādīyeh Tehran 31 B2
Jawaharlal Nehru Port = Nhava Sheva Mumbai 20 B2
Jaworowa Warsaw 33 C1
Jean Lafitte Nat. Historical Park ⌂ New Orleans 21 B1
Jedlesee Vienna 32 A2
Jefferson New Orleans 21 B2
Jefferson Memorial Washington 33 B2
Jefferson Park Chicago 9 B2
Jefferson Park Los Angeles 16 B3
Jegi Seoul 27 B2
Jelambar Jakarta 12 A1
Jelonki Warsaw 33 B1
Jerónimos, Mosteiro dos Lisbon 16 A1
Jersey City New York 22 B1
Jerusalem Jerusalem 13 B2
Jessamine, L. Orlando 23 B2
Jésus, Î. Montreal 20 A1
Jesús Maria Lima 14 B2
Jette Brussels 6 A1
Jey Tehran 31 B2
Jianggao Guangzhou 11 A2
Jiangwan Shanghai 28 B1
Jib Jerusalem 13 A2
Jihād Baghdad 3 B1
Jingan Shanghai 28 B1
Jinnah Int. ✕ (KHI) Karachi 13 A2
Jinočany Prague 25 B1
Jinonice Prague 25 B2
Jinqiao Shanghai 28 B2
Jiulong = Kowloon Hong Kong 12 B3
Jiyūgaoka Tokyo 30 B3
Jīzā'ir Baghdad 3 B2
Jīzīra Baghdad 3 B2
Joe Pool Lake Dallas-Fort Worth 10 C4
Joglo Jakarta 12 B1
Johannesburg Johannesburg 13 B2
Johannesburg, Univ. of Johannesburg 13 B2
Johanneskirchen Munich 21 A2
Johannesstift Berlin 5 A2
Johannisthal Berlin 5 B4
John F. Kennedy Nat. Historic Site ⌂ Boston 6 A2
John McLaren Park San Francisco 26 B2
John U. Lloyd Beach ⌂ Miami 19 B3
Joinville-le-Pont Paris 24 B3
Joli-Bois Brussels 6 B2
Jollas Helsinki 11 B3
Jongmyo Royal Shrine Seoul 27 B1
Jongno Seoul 27 B1
Jonstrup Copenhagen 8 A2
Joppa Edinburgh 11 B3
Jorge Chavez Int. ✕ (LIM) Lima 14 B2
Jorge Newbery ✕ (AEP) Buenos Aires 7 B2
Józefa Piłsudskiego Park Warsaw 33 B1
Joss House B. Hong Kong 12 B3
Jōtō Osaka 23 A2
Jouy-en-Josas Paris 24 B2
Juan Anchorena Buenos Aires 7 A2
Juan González Romero Mexico City 18 A2
Juárez Int. ✕ (MEX) Mexico City 18 B2
Judeira Jerusalem 13 A2
Juhdum Jerusalem 13 B2
Juhu Mumbai 20 A2
Jūjā Tokyo 30 A3
Jukskeirivier → Johannesburg 13 A2
Julianów Warsaw 33 B2
Jumeirah Dubai 9 B1
Jung Seoul 27 B1
Jungfernheide, Volkspark Berlin 5 A2
Jungfernsee Berlin 5 B1
Junghwa Seoul 27 B2
Jungnang Seoul 27 B2
Jungnangcheon → Seoul 27 B1
Juniper Green Edinburgh 11 B2
Junk B. Hong Kong 12 B3
Jurong Singapore 28 B2
Jurong, Selat Singapore 28 B2
Jurong Industrial Estate Singapore 28 B1
Jurujuba, Enseada de Rio de Janeiro 25 B2
Jūsō Osaka 23 A1
Justice Chicago 9 C2
Jwalahari Delhi 10 B1

K

Kaapstad = Cape Town Cape Town 8 A1
Kabaty Warsaw 33 C2
Kadıköy Istanbul 12 C2
Kadoma Osaka 23 A2
Kafr 'Aqab Jerusalem 13 A2
Kâğıthane Istanbul 12 B1
Kâğıthane → Istanbul 12 B1
Kagran Vienna 32 A2
Kahnawake Montreal 20 B1
Kaimes Edinburgh 11 B2
Kaiserebersdorf Vienna 32 B2
Kaivoksela Helsinki 11 B2
Kalamaki Athens 2 B2
Kalbadevi Mumbai 20 B1
Kalipur Kolkata 14 A1
Kalithea Athens 2 B2
Kalkaji Delhi 10 B2
Kalookan = Caloocan Manila 17 B1
Kalvebod Fælled Copenhagen 8 B3
Kalveboderne Copenhagen 8 B3
Kam Shan Country Park ⌂ Hong Kong 12 A2
Kamarhati Kolkata 14 A2
Kamata Tokyo 30 B3
Kameari Tokyo 30 A4
Kameido Tokyo 30 A4
Kami-Itabashi Tokyo 30 A3
Kamikitazawa Tokyo 30 B2
Kamitsuruma Tokyo 30 B1
Kamoshida Tokyo 30 B2
Kampong Landang Singapore 28 A3
Kampong Tanjong Penjuru Singapore 28 B2
Kampung Bali Jakarta 12 B1
Kanamori Tokyo 30 B1
Kanda Tokyo 30 A3
Kandilli Istanbul 12 B2
Kankurgachi Kolkata 14 B2
Kanlıca Istanbul 12 B2
Kanonerskiy, Ostrov St. Petersburg 27 B1
Kansai Int. ✕ (KIX) Osaka 23 B2
Kanzaki → Osaka 23 A1
Kapali Carsi Istanbul 12 B1
Kapellerfeld Vienna 32 A2
Káposztásmegyer Budapest 7 A2
Kapotnya Moscow 19 C3
Käppala Stockholm 29 A3
Kapuk Jakarta 12 A1
Käpylä Helsinki 11 B2
Karachi Karachi 13 A2
Karkh Baghdad 3 A2
Karlin Prague 25 B2
Karlsfeld Munich 21 A1
Karlshorst Berlin 5 B4
Karlův most Prague 25 B2
Karol Bagh Delhi 10 B2
Karolinenhof Berlin 5 B4
Karow Berlin 5 A3
Karrādah Baghdad 3 B2
Kärsön Stockholm 29 B1
Kasai Tokyo 30 B4
Kasipur Kolkata 14 B2
Kastrup Copenhagen 8 B3
Kastrup, København ✕ (CPH) Copenhagen 8 B3
Kasuga Tokyo 30 A2
Kasuge Tokyo 30 A3
Kasumigaseki Tokyo 30 B3
Katong Singapore 28 B3
Katsushika Tokyo 30 A4
Kau Pai Chau Hong Kong 12 B3
Kau Sai Chau Hong Kong 12 A3
Kau Yi Chau Hong Kong 12 B2
Kaulsdorf Berlin 5 B4
Kauniainen Helsinki 11 B1
Kawasaki Tokyo 30 B3
Kawawa Tokyo 30 B2
Kawęczyn Warsaw 33 B2
Kayu Putih Jakarta 12 B2
Kbely Prague 25 B3
Kebayoran Baru Jakarta 12 B1
Kebayoran Lama Jakarta 12 B1
Kebon Jeruk Jakarta 12 B1
Kedar Jerusalem 13 B2
Kedoya Jakarta 12 B1
Kei Ling Ha Hong Kong 12 A3
Keilor Melbourne 18 A1
Keilor North Melbourne 18 A1
Keimola Helsinki 11 A1
Kelapa Gading Jakarta 12 A2
Kelberg Dallas-Fort Worth 10 B6
Kelenföld Budapest 7 B2
Keller Dallas-Fort Worth 10 A2
Kelvin Johannesburg 13 A2
Kemang Jakarta 12 B1
Kemayoran Jakarta 12 B2
Kemerburgaz Istanbul 12 B1
Kempton Park Races London 15 B1
Kendall Miami 19 D1
Kenilworth Cape Town 8 A1
Kenilworth Chicago 9 A2
Kennedale Dallas-Fort Worth 10 C2
Kennedy Town Hong Kong 12 B2
Kenner New Orleans 21 A1
Kenneth Hahn State Recreation Area ⌂ Los Angeles 16 B2
Kensal Green London 15 A2
Kensington Johannesburg 13 B2
Kensington London 15 B2
Kensington New York 22 C2
Kensington Sydney 29 B2
Kensington Palace London 15 A2
Kentish Town London 15 A3
Kenton London 15 A2
Kenwood House London 15 A3
Kepa Warsaw 33 B2
Keppel Harbour Singapore 28 B2
Kesariani Athens 2 B2
Keung Shan Hong Kong 12 B1
Kew London 15 B2
Kew Melbourne 18 A2
Kew Gardens London 15 B2
Kew Gardens Toronto 31 A3
Key Biscayne Miami 19 D3
Khalīj Baghdad 3 B2
Khansā' Baghdad 3 A2
Kharavli Mumbai 20 B2
Khefren Cairo 7 B1
Khichripur Delhi 10 B2
Khidirpur Kolkata 14 B1
Khimki-Khovrino Moscow 19 A2
Khirbet Batin Abu Lihyah Jerusalem 13 A1
Khirbet el-Misbah Jerusalem 13 A1
Khirbet Jub e-Rum Jerusalem 13 B2
Khlong San Bangkok 3 B2
Khlong Toey Bangkok 3 B2
Khorel Kolkata 14 A1
Khorosovo Moscow 19 B1
Kiamari Karachi 13 B1
Kierling Vienna 32 A1
Kierlingbach → Vienna 32 A1
Kifisos → Athens 2 B2
Kikuna Tokyo 30 B2
Kilburn London 15 A2
Kilo Helsinki 11 B1
Kilokri Delhi 10 B2
Kincsem Park Budapest 7 B2
Kindi Baghdad 3 B2
Kinghorn Edinburgh 11 A2
Kings Domain Melbourne 18 A1
Kings Forest = Kongelunden Copenhagen 8 B3
Kingsbury London 15 A2
Kingsbury Melbourne 18 A2
Kingsford Sydney 29 B2
Kingsford Smith, Sydney ✕ (SYD) Sydney 29 B2
Kingston-upon-Thames □ London 15 B2
Kingston Vale London 15 B2
Kingsway Toronto 31 B1
Kipling Heights Toronto 31 A1
Kipseli Athens 2 B2
Kirchstockbach Munich 21 B3
Kirchtrudering Munich 21 B3
Kirikiri Lagos 14 B1
Kirke Værløse Copenhagen 8 A1
Kirkhill Edinburgh 11 B2
Kirkliston Edinburgh 11 B1
Kirknewton Edinburgh 11 B1
Kirov Palace of Culture St. Petersburg 27 B1
Kiryat Anavim Jerusalem 13 B1
Kiryat Ha Yovel Jerusalem 13 B1
Kısıklı Istanbul 12 B2
Kispest Budapest 7 B2
Kista Stockholm 29 A1
Kita Osaka 23 A2
Kita Tokyo 30 A3
Kitazawa Tokyo 30 B3
Kivistö Helsinki 11 B2
Kiza → Osaka 23 B1
Kızıltoprak Istanbul 12 C2
Kizuri Osaka 23 B2
Kjelsås Oslo 23 A3
Kladow Berlin 5 B1
Klampenborg Copenhagen 8 A3
Klečany Prague 25 A2
Kledering Vienna 32 B2
Klein Jukskei → Johannesburg 13 A1
Kleinmachnow Berlin 5 B2
Kleinschönebeck Berlin 5 B5
Klemetsrud Oslo 23 A4
Klender Jakarta 12 A2
Kličany Prague 25 A2
Klipriviersberg Nature Reserve ⌂ Johannesburg 13 B2
Klosterneuburg Vienna 32 A1
Kőbánya Budapest 7 B2
Kobbegem Brussels 6 A1
København Copenhagen 8 A2
København ✕ (CPH) Copenhagen 8 B3
Kobylisy Prague 25 B2
Kobyłka Warsaw 33 A3
Kodaira Tokyo 30 A1
Kodanaka Tokyo 30 B2
Koekelberg Brussels 6 A1
Koganei Tokyo 30 A2
Kogarah Sydney 29 B1
Koivupää Helsinki 11 B2
Koja Jakarta 12 A2
Koja Utara Jakarta 12 A2
Kokhav Ya'akov Jerusalem 13 A2
Kokobunji Tokyo 30 A1
Kokobunji-Temple Tokyo 30 A4
Kolarängen Stockholm 29 B3
Kolbotn Oslo 23 B3
Kolkata Kolkata 14 B2
Kolkata Maidan Kolkata 14 B1
Kolkata Netaji Subhash Chandra Bose Int. ✕ (CCU) Kolkata 14 B2
Koło Warsaw 33 B1
Kolokinthou Athens 2 B2
Kolomyagi St. Petersburg 27 A1
Kolonos Athens 2 B2
Kolsås Oslo 23 A2
Komae Tokyo 30 B2
Komagome Tokyo 30 A3
Komazawa Tokyo 30 B3
Kona Kolkata 14 B1
Konala Helsinki 11 B2
Kondli Delhi 10 B2
Kongelunden Copenhagen 8 B3
Kongens Lyngby Copenhagen 8 A3
Kongo Helsinki 11 A1
Konnagar Kolkata 14 A2
Konohana Osaka 23 A1
Konradshöhe Berlin 5 A2
Kopanina Prague 25 B1
Koparkhairna Mumbai 20 A2
Köpenick Berlin 5 B4
Korangi Karachi 13 B2
Koremasa Tokyo 30 B1
Koridalos Athens 2 B1
Kosino Moscow 19 B4
Kosugi Tokyo 30 B2
Kota Jakarta 12 A1
Kōtō Tokyo 30 A3
Kotrung Kolkata 14 A2
Kouponia Athens 2 B2
Kowloon Hong Kong 12 B3
Kowloon Peak Hong Kong 12 A3
Kowloon Tong Hong Kong 12 B3
Kraainem Brussels 6 A2
Krailling Munich 21 B1
Krampnitz Berlin 5 B1
Krampnitzsee Berlin 5 B1
Kranji Industrial Estate Singapore 28 A2
Kranji Res. Singapore 28 A2
Krasno-Presnenskaya Moscow 19 B2
Krč Prague 25 B2
Kremlin Moscow 19 B2
Krestovskiye, Ostrov St. Petersburg 27 B1
Kreuzberg Berlin 5 A3
Kritzendorf Vienna 32 A1
Krumme Lanke Berlin 5 B2
Krummensee Berlin 5 A5
Krung Thep = Bangkok Bangkok 3 B2
Krusboda Stockholm 29 B3
Kuangchou = Guangzhou Guangzhou 11 B2
Küçükköy Istanbul 12 B1
Küçüksu Istanbul 12 B2
Kudrovo St. Petersburg 27 B3
Kulosaari Helsinki 11 B3
Kumla Stockholm 29 B3
Kungens kurva Stockholm 29 B1
Kungliga Slottet Stockholm 29 B2
Kungshatt Stockholm 29 B1
Kungsholmen Stockholm 29 A2
Kuningan Jakarta 12 B1
Kunitachi Tokyo 30 A1
Kunming Hu Beijing 4 B1
Kunratice Prague 25 B2
Kupchino St. Petersburg 27 B2
Kuramo Waters Lagos 14 B2
Kurbağalı → Istanbul 12 C2
Kurihara Tokyo 30 A2
Kurla Mumbai 20 A2
Kurmuri Mumbai 20 A2
Kurume Tokyo 30 A2
Kuryanovo Moscow 19 C3
Kuskovo Moscow 19 B3
Kustia Kolkata 14 B2
Kuzguncuk Istanbul 12 B2
Kuzyminki Moscow 19 B3
Kwai Chung Hong Kong 12 A2
Kwangchow = Guangzhou Guangzhou 11 B2
Kwun Tong Hong Kong 12 B3
Kyje Prague 25 B3
Kyūhōji Osaka 23 B2

L

L.A. County Art Museum Los Angeles 16 B2
La Barceloneta Barcelona 4 A2
La Blanca Santiago 27 C2
La Boca Buenos Aires 7 B2
La Bretèche Paris 24 A1
La Campiña Lima 14 C2
La Celle-St-Cloud Paris 24 A1
La Cisterna Santiago 27 C2
La Courneuve Paris 24 A3
La Dehesa Santiago 27 B2
La Encantada Lima 14 C2
La Estación Madrid 17 B1
La Floresta Barcelona 4 A1
La Florida Santiago 27 C2
La Fortuna Madrid 17 B1
La França Barcelona 4 A1
La Garenne-Colombes Paris 24 A2
La Giustiniana Rome 26 B1
La Granja Santiago 27 C2
La Guardia, New York ✕ (LGA) New York 22 B2
La Hulpe Brussels 6 B2
La Llacuna Barcelona 4 A2
La Loma Mexico City 18 A1
La Lucila Buenos Aires 7 B2
La Maladrerie Paris 24 A1
La Milla, Cerro Lima 14 B2
La Monachina Rome 26 B1
La Moraleja Madrid 17 A2
La Nopalera Mexico City 18 C2
La Paternal Buenos Aires 7 B2
La Perla Lima 14 B2
La Perouse Sydney 29 B2
La Pisana Rome 26 B1
La Prairie Montreal 20 B3
La Punta Lima 14 B1
La Puntigala Barcelona 4 A2
La Queue-en-Brie Paris 24 B4
La Reina Santiago 27 B2
La Ribera Barcelona 4 A1
La Sagrera Barcelona 4 A2
La Salada Buenos Aires 7 C2
La Scala Milan 18 B2
La Storta Rome 26 A1
La Taxonera Barcelona 4 A2
La Victoria Lima 14 B2
La Vista Atlanta 3 B2
Laajalahti Helsinki 11 B1
Laajasalo Helsinki 11 B3
Laaksolahti Helsinki 11 B1
Labagou Nat. Forest Park ⌂ Beijing 4 A2
Lablâba, W. el → Cairo 7 A2
Lachine Montreal 20 B1
Lachine, Canal de Montreal 20 B2
Lad Phrao Bangkok 3 B2
Ladera Heights Los Angeles 16 C2
Ládví Prague 25 B2
Łady Warsaw 33 C1
Lafontaine, Parc Montreal 20 A2
Lagoa Rio de Janeiro 25 B1
Lagos Lagos 14 B2
Lagos Harbour Lagos 14 B2
Lagos-Ikeja ✕ (LOS) Lagos 14 A1
Lagos Island Lagos 14 B2
Lagos Lagoon Lagos 14 B2
Laguna de B. Manila 17 C2
Lai Chi Wo Hong Kong 12
Laim Munich 21 B2
Lainate Milan 18 A1
Lainz Vienna 32 B1
Lake Buena Vista Orlando 23 B1
Lake Cain Hills Orlando 23 B2
Lakemba Sydney 29 B1
Lakeside Cape Town 8 B1
Lakeside Johannesburg 13 A2
Lakeview Chicago 9 B3
Lakeview New Orleans 21 A2
Lakewood Park Atlanta 3 B2
Lakhtinskiy St. Petersburg 27 B1
Lakhtinskiy Razliv, Oz. St. Petersburg 27 B1
Lakshmanpur Kolkata 14 B1
Laksi Bangkok 3 A2
Lal Qila Delhi 10 B2
Lam Tin Hong Kong 12 B3
Lambert Oslo 23 A3
Lambeth □ London 15 B3
Lambrate Milan 18 B2
Lambro, Parco Milan 18 B2
Lambton Mills Toronto 31 B1
Lamma I. Hong Kong 12 B2
Lancaster Dallas-Fort Worth 10 C5
Landianchang Beijing 4 B1
Landsmeer Amsterdam 2 A2
Landstrasse Vienna 32 A2
Landwehr kanal Berlin 5 B3
Lane Cove Sydney 29 A1
Lane Cove Nat. Park △ Sydney 29 A1
Langa Cape Town 8 A2
Langenzersdorf Vienna 32 A2
Langer See Berlin 5 B4
Langley Washington 33 B1
Langley Park Washington 33 B3
Langwald Munich 21 A1
Lankwitz Berlin 5 B3
L'Annunziatella Rome 26 C2
Lansdowne Cape Town 8 A2
Lansing Toronto 31 A2
Lantau I. Hong Kong 12 B1
Lantau Pk. Hong Kong 12 B1
Lanus Buenos Aires 7 C2
Lapa Rio de Janeiro 25 B1
Laranjeiras Rio de Janeiro 25 B1
Las Warsaw 33 B2
Las Corts Barcelona 4 A1
Las Kabacki Warsaw 33 C2
Las Pinas Manila 17 C1
Las Rejas Santiago 27 B1
Las Vegas Las Vegas 14 A2
Las Vegas McCarran Int. ✕ (LAS) Las Vegas 14 B2
LaSalle Montreal 20 B2
LaSalle Street Station Chicago 9 B3
Lasek Bielański Warsaw 33 B1
Lasek Na Kole Warsaw 33 B1
Latina Madrid 17 B1
Lauderdale Lakes Miami 19 B1
Lauderhill Miami 19 B2
Lauttasaari Helsinki 11 C2
Laval-des-Rapides Montreal 20 A1
Lavīzān Tehran 31 A2
Lavradio Lisbon 16 A2
Lawndale Chicago 9 B2
Lawne L. Orlando 23 A2
Lawrence Heights Toronto 31 A2
Layari Karachi 13 A2
Layari → Karachi 13 A1
Łazienkowski Park Warsaw 33 B2
Lazy Lake Miami 19 B3
Le Blanc-Mesnil Paris 24 A3
Le Bourget Paris 24 A3
Le Chenoi Brussels 6 B2
Le Chesnay Paris 24 B1
Le Christ de Saclay Paris 24 B2
Le Kremlin-Bicêtre Paris 24 B3
Le Mesnil-le-Roi Paris 24 A1
Le Pecq Paris 24 A1
Le Perreux Paris 24 A3

Le Pin Paris 24 A4
Le Plessis-Robinson Paris 24 B2
Le Plessis-Trévise Paris 24 B4
Le Port-Marly Paris 24 A1
Le Pré-St-Gervais Paris 24 A3
Le Raincy Paris 24 A4
Le Vésinet Paris 24 A1
Lea Bridge London 15 A3
Leaside Toronto 31 A2
Leblon Rio de Janeiro 25 B1
Lee London 15 B4
Leganés Madrid 17 C1
Legazpi Madrid 17 B1
Lehtisaari Helsinki 11 B2
Lei Yue Mun Hong Kong 12 B3
Leião Lisbon 16 A1
Leichhardt Sydney 29 B1
Leith Edinburgh 11 B3
Lekki Lagos 14 B2
Lekki Peninsula Lagos 14 B2
Leme Rio de Janeiro 25 B1
Lemmon, L.
Dallas-Fort Worth 10 B5
Lemoyne Montreal 20 B3
Lenino Moscow 19 C2
Leninskiye Gory Moscow 19 B2
Lennox Los Angeles 16 C2
Leonia New York 22 A2
Leopoldau Vienna 32 A2
Leopoldsdorf Vienna 32 B2
Leopoldstadt Vienna 32 A2
Leportovo Moscow 19 B3
Leppävaara Helsinki 11 B1
Les Lilas Paris 24 A3
Les Loges-en-Josas Paris 24 B1
Les Pavillons-sous-Bois
Paris 24 A4
Lésigny Paris 24 B4
Lesnozavodskaya
St. Petersburg 27 B2
Lester B. Pearson Int.,
Toronto ✕ (YYZ) Toronto 31 A1
L'Étang-la-Ville Paris 24 A1
Letňany Prague 25 B3
Letopolis = Ausîm Cairo 7 A1
Levallois-Perret Paris 24 A2
Levent Istanbul 12 B2
Lewisdale Washington 33 B3
Lewisham □ London 15 B3
Lexington Boston 6 A1
Leyton London 15 A3
Leytonstone London 15 A4
L'Haÿ-les-Roses Paris 24 B3
L'Hospitalet de Llobregat
Barcelona 4 A1
Lhotka Prague 25 B2
Liangshui He → Beijing 4 C2
Lianhua Chi Beijing 4 B1
Lianhua He → Beijing 4 B1
Libčice nad Vitavou Prague 25 A2
Libeň Prague 25 B2
Liberdade São Paulo 27 B2
Liberton Edinburgh 11 B3
Liberty I. New York 22 B1
Liberty Ōsaka Museum
Osaka 23 B1
Liberty State Park ⌂
New York 22 B1
Libeznice Prague 25 A2
Libuš Prague 25 B2
Lichiao Guangzhou 11 B2
Lichtenburg Berlin 5 A4
Lichterfelde Berlin 5 B2
Lidingö Stockholm 29 A2
Lieshi Lingyuan Guangzhou 11 B2
Liesing Vienna 32 B1
Liesing → Vienna 32 B2
Ligovo St. Petersburg 27 C1
Lijordet Oslo 23 A2
Likhoborka → Moscow 19 A2
Lilla Värtan Stockholm 29 A3
Lille Værløse Copenhagen 8 A2
Liluah Kolkata 14 B1
Lim Chu Kang Singapore 28 A2
Lima Lima 14 B2
Lima Jorge Chavez Int. ✕
(LIM) Lima 14 B2
Limbiate Milan 18 A1
Limehouse London 15 A3
Limeil-Brévannes Paris 24 B3
Linate, Milano ✕ (LIN)
Milan 18 B2
Linbropark Johannesburg 13 A2
Lincoln Center for
Performing Arts
New York 22 B2
Lincoln Heights Los Angeles 16 B3
Lincoln Memorial
Washington 33 B2
Lincoln Park Chicago 9 B3
Lincoln Park New York 22 B1
Lincoln Park San Francisco 26 B1
Lincoln Park Zoo Chicago 9 B3
Lincolnwood Chicago 9 A2
Linda-a-Pastora Lisbon 16 A1
Linden Johannesburg 13 A2
Lindenberg Berlin 5 A4
Lindøya Oslo 23 A3
Liniers Buenos Aires 7 B1
Linkebeek Brussels 6 B2
Linksfield Johannesburg 13 A2
Linmeyer Johannesburg 13 B2
Linna Helsinki 11 A2
Lintuvaara Helsinki 11 B1
Lion Rock Country
Park ⌂ Hong Kong 12 A3
Lion's Head Cape Town 8 A1
Lioumi Athens 2 B2
Lisboa Lisbon 16 A2
Lisboa ✕ (LIS) Lisbon 16 A2
Lisbon = Lisboa Lisbon 16 A2
Lishui Guangzhou 11 A1
Little B. Sydney 29 B2
Little Calumet → Chicago 9 D3
Little Ferry New York 22 A1
Little Haiti Miami 19 C2
Little Havana Miami 19 D1
Little India Singapore 28 B3
Little Lake Conway Orlando 23 B2
Little Rouge → Toronto 31 A4
Liuhang Shanghai 28 A1
Liurong Temple Guangzhou 11 B2
Live Oak Manor
New Orleans 21 B1
Livry-Gargan Paris 24 A4
Liwan Guangzhou 11 B2
Ljan Oslo 23 A3
Llano de Can Gineu
Barcelona 4 A2
Lo Aranguiz Santiago 27 B2
Lo Boza Santiago 27 B1
Lo Espejo Santiago 27 C1
Lo Hermida Santiago 27 B2
Lo Prado Santiago 27 B1
Lo So Shing Hong Kong 12 B2
Lo Wai Hong Kong 12 A2
Loanhead Edinburgh 11 B3
Lobau Vienna 32 A3
Lobos, Pt. San Francisco 26 B1
Locham Munich 21 B1
Lochkov Prague 25 B2
Lockhausen Munich 21 A1
Lodi New York 22 A1
Lodi Estate Delhi 10 B2
Logan Int., Boston ✕
(BOS) Boston 6 A2
Logan Square Chicago 9 B2
Lognes-Émerainville ✕
(XLG) Paris 24 B4
Löhme Berlin 5 A5
Lokholet Karachi 13 A2
Lomas Chapultepec
Mexico City 18 B1
Lomas de San Angel Inn
Mexico City 18 B1
Lombardy East Johannesburg 13 A2
Lomianki Warsaw 33 A1
Lomus Reforma Mexico City 18 B1
London London 15 B3
London Avenue Canal
New Orleans 21 A2
London City ✕ (LCY)
London 15 A4
London Heathrow ✕
(LHR) London 15 B1
London Zoo London 15 A3
Long B. Sydney 29 B2
Long Branch Toronto 31 B1
Long Ditton London 15 B2
Long Island City New York 22 B2
Longchamp, Hippodrome
de Paris 24 A2
Longhua Pagoda Shanghai 28 B1
Longhua Park Shanghai 28 B1
Longtan Hu → Beijing 4 B2
Longue-Pointe Montreal 20 A2
Longueuil Montreal 20 A3
Loni Delhi 10 A2
Lord's Cricket Ground
London 15 A2
Loreto Milan 18 B2
Los Angeles Los Angeles 16 B3
Los Angeles Int. ✕ (LAX)
Los Angeles 16 C2
Los Angeles Museum of
the Holocaust Los Angeles 16 B2
Los Cerrillos ✕ (ULC)
Santiago 27 B1
Los Nietos Los Angeles 16 C4
Los Olivos Lima 14 A2
Los Remedios △ Mexico City 18 B1
Los Reyes Mexico City 18 B2
Losiny Ostrov △ Moscow 19 A3
Lot Brussels 6 B1
Lotus River Cape Town 8 B2
Lotus Temple Delhi 10 B2
Louis Armstrong New
Orleans Int. ✕ (MSY)
New Orleans 21 B1
Louise, L. Orlando 23 B1
Louisiana Superdome =
Mercedes-Benz
Superdome New Orleans 21 B2
Loures Lisbon 16 A1
Louveciennes Paris 24 A1
Louvre, Musée du Paris 24 A3
Lower B. New York 22 C1
Lower Don Lands Toronto 31 B2
Lower New York B. =
Lower B. New York 22 C1
Lower Peirce Res. Singapore 28 A2
Loyola Univ. Chicago 9 B3
Lu Xun, Tomb of Shanghai 28 B1
Lu Xun Park Shanghai 28 B1
Lübars Berlin 5 A3
Lucy, L. Orlando 23 A2
Ludwigsfeld Munich 21 A1
Luhu Guangzhou 11 B2
Luk Chau = George I.
Hong Kong 12 B2
Lumiar Lisbon 16 A2
Lundtofte Copenhagen 8 A3
Lung Kwu Chau Hong Kong 12 A1
Lung Kwu Tan Hong Kong 12 A1
Lung Mei Hong Kong 12 A3
Luojiang Guangzhou 11 B2
Lustheim Munich 21 A2
Luwan Shanghai 28 B1
Luz, Estádio da Lisbon 16 A1
Luzhniki Sports Centre
Moscow 19 B2
Lyndhurst New York 22 B1
Lynn Woods Res. Boston 6 A2
Lyon, Gare de Paris 24 A3
Lyons Chicago 9 C2
Lysaker Oslo 23 A2
Lysakerselva → Oslo 23 A2
Lysolaje Prague 25 B2
Lyublino Moscow 19 B3

## M

Ma Nam Wat Hong Kong 12 A3
Ma On Shan Hong Kong 12 A3
Ma On Shan Country
Park ⌂ Hong Kong 12 A3
Ma Wan Hong Kong 12 A2
Ma Wan Channel
Hong Kong 12 A2
Ma'ale Adumim Jerusalem 13 B2
Ma'ale Ha Khamisha
Jerusalem 13 B1
Ma'ale Mikhmas Jerusalem 13 A2
Maantiekylä Helsinki 11 A3
Maarifa Baghdad 3 B2
Mabato Pt. Manila 17 C2
Mabel, L. Orlando 23 B1
Macaco, Morro do
Rio de Janeiro 25 B2
McCarran Int., Las
Vegas ✕ (LAS) Las Vegas 14 B2
McCook Chicago 9 C2
McGill Univ. Montreal 20 A2
Machelen Brussels 6 A2
Machida Tokyo 30 B1
Maciolki Warsaw 33 B2
McKinley Park Chicago 9 C2
McLean Washington 33 B1
Macopocho → Santiago 27 B1
MacRitchie Res. Singapore 28 A2
Macul Santiago 27 C2
Madhudaha Kolkata 14 B2
Madhyamgram Kolkata 14 A2
Madin Mexico City 18 A1
Madin, L. Mexico City 18 A1
Madînah Al Mansûr
Baghdad 3 B2
Mâdinet Nasr Cairo 7 A2
Madrid Madrid 17 B1
Madrid Barajas ✕ (MAD)
Madrid 17 B2
Madrona Barcelona 4 A1
Maesawa Tokyo 30 A2
Magdalena Lima 14 B2
Magdalena Contreras
Mexico City 18 C1
Magelungen Stockholm 29 B2
Maghreb Baghdad 3 A2
Maginu Tokyo 30 B2
Magliana Rome 26 B1
Magny-les-Hameaux Paris 24 B1
Mahar, L. Miami 19 D1
Maheshtala Kolkata 14 C1
Mahim Mumbai 20 A2
Mahim B. Mumbai 20 A1
Mahipalpur Delhi 10 B1
Mahlsdorf Berlin 5 A4
Mahmoodabad Karachi 13 A2
Mahrauli Delhi 10 B2
Mahul Mumbai 20 A2
Maida Vale London 15 A2
Maidstone Melbourne 18 A1
Maipú Santiago 27 C1
Maisonneuve, Parc
Montreal 20 A2
Maisons-Alfort Paris 24 B3
Maisons-Laffitte Paris 24 A1
Maissoneuve Montreal 20 A2
Maitland Cape Town 8 A1
Makasar Jakarta 12 A2
Makati Manila 17 B2
Mäkiniitty Helsinki 11 A2
Malá Strana Prague 25 B2
Malabar Sydney 29 B2
Malabar Hill Mumbai 20 B1
Malabar Pt. Mumbai 20 B1
Malabon Manila 17 B1
Malacañang Palace Manila 17 B1
Malakoff Paris 24 B2
Mälarhöjaen Stockholm 29 B1
Malate Manila 17 B1
Malaya Neva St. Petersburg 27 B1
Malaya Okhta
St. Petersburg 27 B2
Malchow Berlin 5 A3
Malden Boston 6 A2
Malden London 15 B2
Maleizen Brussels 6 B3
Malešice Prague 25 B3
Malir → Karachi 13 B2
Malleny Mills Edinburgh 11 B2
Malmi Helsinki 11 B2
Malmøya Oslo 23 A3
Målov Copenhagen 8 A1
Malpense, Milano ✕
(MXP) Milan 18 A1
Malton Toronto 31 A1
Malvern Johannesburg 13 B2
Malvern Melbourne 18 B2
Malvern Toronto 31 A3
Mampang Prapatan Jakarta 12 B1
Mampukuji Tokyo 30 B2
Man Budrukh Mumbai 20 A2
Man Khurd Mumbai 20 A2
Manakhat Jerusalem 13 B2
Mandai Singapore 28 A2
Mandaluyong Manila 17 B2
Mandaoli Delhi 10 B2
Mandaqui → São Paulo 27 A2
Mandoli Delhi 10 A2
Mandvi Mumbai 20 B2
Manenberg Cape Town 8 A2
Mang Kung Uk Hong Kong 12 B3
Mang-won Seoul 27 B1
Mangolpuri Delhi 10 A1
Manhattan New York 22 B2
Manhattan Beach
New York 22 C2
Manila Manila 17 B1
Manila Ninoy Aquino
Int. ✕ (MNL) Manila 17 B2
Mankkaa Helsinki 11 B1
Manly Sydney 29 A2
Mann, L. Orlando 23 A2
Mannswörth Vienna 32 B3
Manor Park London 15 A4
Manora Karachi 13 B1
Manora Pt. Karachi 13 B1
Manquehue, Cerro Santiago 27 B2
Mansfield Dallas-Fort Worth 10 C3
Manzanares, Canal de
Madrid 17 C2
Mapo Seoul 27 B1
Mar Vista Los Angeles 16 B2
Maracanã, Estádio
Rio de Janeiro 25 B1
Maraoli Mumbai 20 A2
Marcelin Warsaw 33 B1
Mareil-Marly Paris 24 A1
Margaret I. = Margitsziget
Budapest 7 A2
Margareten Vienna 32 A2
Margitsziget Budapest 7 A2
Maria Vienna 32 A2
Maridalen Oslo 23 A3
Maridalsvatnet Oslo 23 A3
Mariendorf Berlin 5 B3
Marienfelde Berlin 5 B3
Marikina Manila 17 B2
Marikina → Manila 17 B2
Marin City San Francisco 26 A1
Marin Pen. San Francisco 26 A1
Marina Bay Sands
Singapore 28 B3
Marina del Rey Los Angeles 16 C2
Marisco, Ponta do
Rio de Janeiro 25 C1
Markham Chicago 9 D2
Markham Toronto 31 A2
Marki Warsaw 33 B2
Markland Wood Toronto 31 B1
Marly, Forêt de Paris 24 A1
Marly-le-Roi Paris 24 A1
Marne-la-Vallée Paris 24 A4
Marolles-en-Brie Paris 24 B4
Maroubra Sydney 29 B2
Marquette Park Chicago 9 C2
Marrero New Orleans 21 B2
Marrickville Sydney 29 B1
Marsfield Sydney 29 A1
Marsha, L. Orlando 23 B2
Marte, Campo de São Paulo 27 B2
Martesana, Naviglio della
Milan 18 A2
Martin Luther King Nat.
Historic Site ⌂ Atlanta 3 B2
Martinez Buenos Aires 7 A1
Martinkylä Helsinki 11 B2
Martinsried Munich 21 B1
Maruko Tokyo 30 B3
Maryino Moscow 19 B3
Maryland Singapore 28 B3
Marymont Warsaw 33 B1
Marysin Wawerski Warsaw 33 B2
Marzahn Berlin 5 A4
Mascot Sydney 29 B2
Masmo Stockholm 29 B1
Maspeth New York 22 B2
Masr el Gedida Cairo 7 A2
Masr el Qadîma Cairo 7 A2
Massachusetts Inst. of
Tech. Boston 6 A2
Massamá Lisbon 16 A1
Massey → Toronto 31 A3
Massy Paris 24 B2
Mata Jerusalem 13 B1
Matinha Lisbon 16 A2
Matraman Jakarta 12 B2
Matsubara Osaka 23 B2
Mattapan Boston 6 B2
Mátyásföld Budapest 7 A3
Mau Tso Ngam Hong Kong 12 A3
Mauer Vienna 32 B1
Mauripur Karachi 13 A1
Maxhof Munich 21 B1
MAXXI National Museum
of 21st Century Arts
Rome 26 B1
Mayfair Johannesburg 13 B2
Maywood Chicago 9 B1
Maywood Los Angeles 16 C3
Maywood New York 22 A1
Maywood Park Race
Track Chicago 9 B1
Mazagaon Mumbai 20 B2
Meadowbank Park Sydney 29 A1
Meadowlands Sports
Complex New York 22 B1
Měcholupy Prague 25 B3
Měčice Prague 25 A3
Mecidiyeköy Istanbul 12 B2
Medford Boston 6 A2
Mediodia Madrid 17 B2
Meguro Tokyo 30 B3
Meguro → Tokyo 30 B3
Mehrābād ✕ (THR) Tehran 31 A1
Mehram Nagar Delhi 10 B1
Mehrow Berlin 5 A4
Meidling Vienna 32 A2
Méier Rio de Janeiro 25 B1
Meiji Shrine Tokyo 30 A3
Meise Brussels 6 A1
Mejiro Tokyo 30 A3
Melbourne Melbourne 18 A1
Melbourne ✕ (MEL)
Melbourne 18 A1
Melkki Helsinki 11 C2
Mellunkylä Helsinki 11 B3
Mellunmäki Helsinki 11 B3
Melrose Boston 6 A2
Melrose New York 22 B2
Melrose Park Miami 19 B3
Melsbroek Brussels 6 A2
Melville Johannesburg 13 B2
Menteng Jakarta 12 B1
Mérantaise → Paris 24 B1
Mercamadrid Madrid 17 B2
Merced, L. San Francisco 26 B2
Mercedes-Benz
Superdome New Orleans 21 B2
Meredale Johannesburg 13 B1
Merlimau, Pulau Singapore 28 B2
Merri Cr. → Melbourne 18 A1
Merrionette Park Chicago 9 C2
Merton □ London 15 B2
Mesgarābād Tehran 31 B3
Messe Vienna 32 A2
Metairie New Orleans 21 A2
Metanópoli Milan 18 B2
MetLife Stadium New York 22 B1
Metro Toronto Zoo Toronto 31 A3
Metropolitan Museum of
Art New York 22 B3
Meudon Paris 24 B2
Mevaseret Zion Jerusalem 13 B1
Mevo Beitar Jerusalem 13 B1
México, Ciudad de
Mexico City 18 B2
Mexico City Int. ✕ (MEX)
Mexico City 18 B2
Meyersdal Johannesburg 13 B2
Mezzate Milan 18 B2
Miadong Seoul 27 B2
Miami Miami 19 D2
Miami → Miami 19 D1
Miami Beach Miami 19 D3
Miami Gardens Miami 19 C1
Miami Int. ✕ (MIA) Miami 19 D1
Miami Lakes Miami 19 C1
Miami Shores Miami 19 C2
Miami Springs Miami 19 D1
Miasto Warsaw 33 B2
Michalowice Warsaw 33 B1
Michle Prague 25 B2
Mid-City Los Angeles 16 B2
Mid City New Orleans 21 B2
Middle Harbour Sydney 29 A2
Middle Hd. Sydney 29 A2
Middle Park Melbourne 18 B1
Middle Village New York 22 B2
Middlesex Fells
Reservation Boston 6 A2
Midland Beach New York 22 C1
Midlothian Chicago 9 D2
Midwood New York 22 C2
Miedzeszyn Warsaw 33 B3
Międzylesie Warsaw 33 B3
Miessaari Helsinki 11 C1
Miguel Hidalgo Mexico City 18 B1
Milan = Milano Milan 18 B1
Milanese, Parco
Regionale ⌂ Milan 18 A1
Milano Milan 18 B1
Milano Due Milan 18 B2
Milano Linate ✕ (LIN)
Milan 18 B2
Milano Malpense ✕
(MXP) Milan 18 A1
Milano San Felice Milan 18 B2
Milbertshofen Munich 21 A2
Mill Hill London 15 A2
Millennium Dome London 15 A4
Miller Meadow Chicago 9 B2
Millerhill Edinburgh 11 B3
Milnerton Cape Town 8 A1
Milon-la-Chapelle Paris 24 B1
Milton Boston 6 B2
Milton Bridge Edinburgh 11 B2
Mimico Toronto 31 B2
Mimico Creek → Toronto 31 B1
Minami Osaka 23 A2
Minamitsunashima Tokyo 30 B2
Minato Osaka 23 B1
Minato Tokyo 30 B3
Minshât el Bekkari Cairo 7 A1
Miraflores Lima 14 B2
Miramar Miami 19 C1
Misericordia, Sa. da
Rio de Janeiro 25 B1
Mission San Francisco 26 B2
Mississauga Toronto 31 B1
Mitaka Tokyo 30 A2
Mitcham London 15 B2
Mitcham Common London 15 B3
Mitchell Museum of the
American Indian Chicago 9 A2
Mitchell's Plain Cape Town 8 B2
Mitte Berlin 5 A3
Mittel Isarkanal → Munich 21 A3
Mixcoac Mexico City 18 B1
Miyakojima Osaka 23 A2
Mizonokuchi Tokyo 30 B2
Mizue Tokyo 30 A4
Mlocinski, Park Warsaw 33 B1
Mlociny Warsaw 33 B1
Mnevniki Moscow 19 B1
Moba Lagos 14 B2
Moczydło Warsaw 33 C2
Modderfontein Johannesburg 13 A2
Modřany Prague 25 B2
Mogyoród Budapest 7 A3
Moinho Velho, Cor. →
São Paulo 27 B2
Mok Seoul 27 B1
Mokotów Warsaw 33 B2
Molenbeek-St-Jean Brussels 6 A1
Molino de Rosas
Mexico City 18 B1
Mollem Brussels 6 A1
Mollins de Rey Barcelona 4 A1
Mondeor Johannesburg 13 B2
Moneda, Palacio de la
Santiago 27 B2
Moneró Rio de Janeiro 25 A1
Mong Kok Hong Kong 12 B3
Monnickendam Amsterdam 2 A3
Monrovia Los Angeles 16 B4
Monsanto Lisbon 16 A1
Monsanto, Parque
Florestal de Lisbon 16 A1
Mont-Royal Montreal 20 A2
Mont-Royal, Parc Montreal 20 A2
Montcada i Reixac Barcelona 4 A2
Monte Chingolo Buenos Aires 7 C2
Montebello Los Angeles 16 B4
Montemor Lisbon 16 A1
Monterey Hills Los Angeles 16 B3
Monterey Park Los Angeles 16 B4
Montespaccato Rome 26 B1
Montesson Paris 24 A1
Monteverde Nuovo Rome 26 B1
Montfermeil Paris 24 A4
Montigny-le-Bretonneux
Paris 24 B1
Montjay-la-Tour Paris 24 A4
Montjuïc Barcelona 4 A2
Montparnasse, Gare Paris 24 A2
Montréal Montreal 20 A2
Montréal, Î. de Montreal 20 A2
Montréal, Univ. de Montreal 20 B2
Montréal Est Montreal 20 A2
Montréal Nord Montreal 20 A2
Montréal Ouest Montreal 20 B1
Montréal Trudeau Int. ✕
(YUL) Montreal 20 B1
Montreuil Paris 24 A3
Montrouge Paris 24 B2
Montserrat Buenos Aires 7 B2
Monza Milan 18 A2
Monzoro Milan 18 B1
Moóca São Paulo 27 B2
Moonachie New York 22 B1
Moonee Ponds Melbourne 18 A1
Moonee Valley
Racecourse Melbourne 18 A1
Moosach Munich 21 A2
Mora Mumbai 20 B2
Moratalaz Madrid 17 B2
Mörby Stockholm 29 A2
Morden London 15 B2
Morée → Paris 24 A3
Morgan Park Chicago 9 C3
Moriguchi Osaka 23 A2
Morivione Milan 18 B2
Morningside Edinburgh 11 B2
Morningside Johannesburg 13 A2
Morningside Park Orlando 23 B2
Morningside Park Toronto 31 A3
Morro Solar, Cerro Lima 14 C2
Mortlake London 15 B2
Mortlake Sydney 29 B1
Morton Grove Chicago 9 A2
Morumbi São Paulo 27 B1
Moscavide Lisbon 16 A2
Moschato Athens 2 B2
Moscow = Moskva Moscow 19 B2
Moscow Sheremetyevo
Int. ✕ (SVO) Moscow 19 A1
Moskva Moscow 19 B2
Moskvoretskiy Moscow 19 B2
Mosman Sydney 29 B2
Moti Bagh Delhi 10 B2
Motol Prague 25 B2
Motsa Jerusalem 13 B2
Motsa Illit Jerusalem 13 B1
Motspur Park London 15 B2
Mottingham London 15 B4
Mount Dennis Toronto 31 A2
Mount Greenwood Chicago 9 C2
Mount Hood Memorial
Park ⌂ Boston 6 A2
Mount Olympus Los Angeles 16 B2
Mount Rainier Washington 33 B3
Mount Vernon New York 22 A3
Mountain Creek L.
Dallas-Fort Worth 10 B4
Mountain Creek Lake
Park Dallas-Fort Worth 10 B4
Müggelberge Berlin 5 B4
Müggelheim Berlin 5 B5
Muggiò Milan 18 A2
Mühleiten Vienna 32 A3
Mühlenfliess → Berlin 5 A5
Mui Wo Hong Kong 12 B1
Muiden Amsterdam 2 A3
Muizenberg Cape Town 8 B1
Mujahidpur Delhi 10 B2
Mukandpur Delhi 10 A2
Mukhmas Jerusalem 13 A2
Muko → Osaka 23 A1
Mukojima Tokyo 30 A3
Mulbarton Johannesburg 13 B2
Mumbai Mumbai 20 B2
Mumbai Chhatrapati
Shivaji Int. ✕ (BOM)
Mumbai 20 A2
Mumbai Harbour Mumbai 20 B2
Munch-museum Oslo 23 A3
Münchehofe Berlin 5 B5
München Munich 21 B2
München Franz Josef
Strauss ✕ (MUC) Munich 21 A2
Munich = München
Munich 21 B2
Munkkiniemi Helsinki 11 B2
Munro Buenos Aires 7 B1
Muntinlupa Manila 17 C2
Murai Res. Singapore 28 A2
Muranów Warsaw 33 B1
Murino St. Petersburg 27 B2
Murrayfield Edinburgh 11 B3
Murtala Mohammed
Int. ✕ (LOS) Lagos 14 A1
Musashino Tokyo 30 A2
Museumsinsel Berlin 5 A3
Mushin Lagos 14 A2
Musocco Milan 18 B1
Mustansiriya Baghdad 3 A2
Musturud Cairo 7 A2
Muswell Hill London 15 A3
Mutanabi Baghdad 3 B2
Muthana Baghdad 3 B2
Myllypuro Helsinki 11 B3
Mystic → Boston 6 A2

## N

N.S.C.B. Int. ✕ (CCU)
Kolkata 14 B2
Naberezhnaya Tower
Moscow 19 B2
Nacka Stockholm 29 B3
Nærsnes Oslo 23 B1
Nagatsuta Tokyo 30 B2
Nagytétény Budapest 7 B1
Nahalin Jerusalem 13 B1
Najafgarh Drain → Delhi 10 B1
Nakahara Tokyo 30 B2
Nakano Tokyo 30 A2
Namsan Park Seoul 27 B1
Namyeong Seoul 27 B1
Nanbiancun Guangzhou 11 B1
Nanchang He → Beijing 4 B1
Nandang Guangzhou 11 B2
Nangal Dewat Delhi 10 B1
Naniwa Osaka 23 B1
Nanole Mumbai 20 A2
Nanpu Bridge Shanghai 28 B2
Nanshi Shanghai 28 B1
Nanterre Paris 24 A2
Napier Mole Karachi 13 B1
Naraina Delhi 10 B1
Nariman Pt. Mumbai 20 B1
Närmak Tehran 31 A2
Naruo Osaka 23 A1
Näsby Stockholm 29 A2
Näsbypark Stockholm 29 A2
National Arboretum
Washington 33 B2
National Atomic Testing
Museum Las Vegas 14 B2
National Maritime
Museum London 15 B3
National University
(N.U.S.) Singapore 28 B2
National Zoological Park
Washington 33 B2
Nationals Park Washington 33 B2
Nativity, Basilica of
Jerusalem 13 B2
Natolin Warsaw 33 C2
Naucalpan de Juárez
Mexico City 18 B1
Naupada Mumbai 20 A2
Navi Mumbai Mumbai 20 A2
Naviglio di Pavia Milan 18 B1
Naviglio Grande Milan 18 B1
Navotas Manila 17 B1
Navy Pier Chicago 9 B3
Nazal Hikmat Beg Baghdad 3 A2
Nazimabad Karachi 13 A2
Nazlet el Simmân Cairo 7 B1
Nea Alexandria Athens 2 B2
Nea Ionia Athens 2 A2
Nea Liosia Athens 2 A2
Nea Smirni Athens 2 B2
Neapoli Athens 2 B2
Near North Chicago 9 B3
Nebušice Prague 25 B1
Nederhorst Amsterdam 2 B3
Nedlitz Berlin 5 B1
Nee Soon Singapore 28 A2
Needham Boston 6 B1
Needham Heights Boston 6 B1
Nellis Air Force Base ✕
(LSV) Las Vegas 14 A2
N'ematābād Tehran 31 B2
Nerima Tokyo 30 A3
Nesodden Oslo 23 B3
Nesoddtangen Oslo 23 A3
Nesøya Oslo 23 A2
Netaji Subhash Chandra
Bose Int. ✕ (CCU) Kolkata 14 B2
Neu Aubing Munich 21 B1
Neu Buch Berlin 5 A4
Neu Buchhorst Berlin 5 B5
Neu Fahrland Berlin 5 B1
Neu Lindenberg Berlin 5 A4
Neubiberg Munich 21 B3
Neuenhagen Berlin 5 A4
Neuessling Vienna 32 A3
Neuhausen Munich 21 B2
Neuherberg Munich 21 A2
Neuhönow Berlin 5 A5
Neuilly-Plaisance Paris 24 A4
Neuilly-sur-Marne Paris 24 A4
Neuilly-sur-Seine Paris 24 A2
Neukagran Vienna 32 A2
Neukettenhof Vienna 32 B2
Neukölln Berlin 5 B3
Neuperlach Munich 21 B2
Neuried Munich 21 B1
Neustift am Walde Vienna 32 A1
Neusüssenbrunn Vienna 32 A2
Neuwaldegg Vienna 32 A1
Neve Ya'akov Jerusalem 13 A2
Neves Rio de Janeiro 25 B2
New Baghdād Baghdad 3 B2
New Barakpur Kolkata 14 A2
New Brighton New York 22 C1
New Canada Johannesburg 13 B1
New Canada Dam
Johannesburg 13 B1
New Cross London 15 B3
New Delhi Delhi 10 B2
New Dorp New York 22 C1
New Dorp Beach New York 22 C1
New Malden London 15 B2
New Milford New York 22 A1
New Mumbai = Navi
Mumbai Mumbai 20 A2
New Orleans New Orleans 21 B2
New Orleans Int. ✕ (MSY)
New Orleans 21 B1
New River → Miami 19 B3
New Territories Hong Kong 12 A2
New Toronto Toronto 31 B1
New Utrecht New York 22 C2
New York New York 22 B2
New York La Guardia ✕
(LGA) New York 22 B2
Newark B. New York 22 B1
Newbattle Edinburgh 11 B3
Newbury Park London 15 A4
Newcraighall Edinburgh 11 B3
Newham □ London 15 A4
Newhaven Edinburgh 11 B2
Newington Edinburgh 11 B2
Newlands Johannesburg 13 B1
Newport Melbourne 18 B1
Newton Boston 6 B1
Newtonbrook Toronto 31 A2
Newtongrange Edinburgh 11 B3
Newtonville Boston 6 A1
Newtown Sydney 29 B2
Ngau Chi Wan Hong Kong 12 A3
Ngau Tau Kok Hong Kong 12 B3
Ngong Ping Hong Kong 12 B1
Ngong Shuen Chau =
Stonecutters I. Hong Kong 12 B2
Ngua Kok Wan Hong Kong 12 A2
Nhava Sheva Mumbai 20 B2
Niāvarān Tehran 31 A2
Nibra Kolkata 14 B1
Nidāl Baghdad 3 B2
Niddrie Edinburgh 11 B3
Niddrie Melbourne 18 A1
Nieder Neuendorf Berlin 5 A2
Niederschöneweide Berlin 5 B3
Niederschönhausen Berlin 5 A3
Niemeyer Rio de Janeiro 25 B1
Nieuwendam Amsterdam 2 A2
Nihonbashi Tokyo 30 A3
Niipperi Helsinki 11 B1
Nikea Athens 2 B1
Nikolassee Berlin 5 B2
Nikolskiy Moscow 19 B1
Niles Chicago 9 A2
Nimta Kolkata 14 A2
Ninoy Aquino Int. ✕
(MNL) Manila 17 B2
Nippa Tokyo 30 B2
Nippori Tokyo 30 A3
Nishi Osaka 23 A1
Nishinari Osaka 23 B1
Nishinomiya Osaka 23 A1
Nishiyodogawa Osaka 23 A1
Niterói Rio de Janeiro 25 B2
Nockeby Stockholm 29 B1
Noel Park London 15 A3
Nogatino Moscow 19 B3
Nogent-sur-Marne Paris 24 A3
Noida Delhi 10 B2
Noiseau Paris 24 B4
Noisiel Paris 24 A4
Noisy-le-Grand Paris 24 A4
Noisy-le-Roi Paris 24 A1
Noisy-le-Sec Paris 24 A3
Nokkala Helsinki 11 C1
Nomentano Rome 26 B2
Nonakashinden Tokyo 30 A2
Nongminyundong
Jiangxisuo Guangzhou 11 B2
Nonhyeon Seoul 27 B2
Nonthaburi Bangkok 3 A1
Noordgesig Johannesburg 13 B1
Noordzeekanaal Amsterdam 2 A1
Nord, Gare du Paris 24 A3
Nordmarka Oslo 23 A3
Nordrand-Siedlung Vienna 32 A2
Nordstrand Oslo 23 A3
Norland Miami 19 C2
Norridge Chicago 9 B2
Norrmalm Stockholm 29 A2
North Arlington New York 22 B1
North Atlanta Atlanta 3 A3
North Bay Village Miami 19 C3
North Bergen New York 22 B1
North Cheam London 15 B2
North Cray London 15 B4
North Decatur Atlanta 3 B3
North Druid Hills Atlanta 3 B3
North Esk → Edinburgh 11 B2
North Gyle Edinburgh 11 B2
North Hackensack
New York 22 A1
North Harbor Manila 17 B1
North Hd. Sydney 29 A2
North Hollywood
Los Angeles 16 B2
North L. Dallas-Fort Worth 10 A4
North Lake Park
Dallas-Fort Worth 10 A4
North Las Vegas Las Vegas 14 A1
North Las Vegas ✕ (VGT)
Las Vegas 14 A1
North Lexington Boston 6 A1
North Miami Miami 19 C2
North Miami Beach Miami 19 C2
North Nazimabad Karachi 13 A2
North Perry ✕ (HWO)
Miami 19 B2
North Point Hong Kong 12 B3
North Queensferry
Edinburgh 11 A1
North Quincy Boston 6 B2
North Res. Boston 6 A2
North Richland Hills
Dallas-Fort Worth 10 A2
North Riverside Chicago 9 B2
North Saugus Boston 6 A2
North Shore Channel →
Chicago 9 B2
North Station Boston 6 A2
North Sydney Sydney 29 B2
North Woolwich London 15 A4
North York Toronto 31 A2
Northbridge Sydney 29 A2
Northbridge Park Sydney 29 A2
Northbrook Chicago 9 A2
Northcliff Johannesburg 13 A1
Northcote Melbourne 18 A2
Northeastern Univ. Boston 6 A2
Northfield Chicago 9 A2
Northmount Toronto 31 A2
Northolt London 15 A1
Northumberland Heath
London 15 B5
Northwestern Univ. Chicago 9 A2
Northwood London 15 A1
Northwood Park Toronto 31 A1
Norwood Johannesburg 13 A2
Norwood Park Chicago 9 B2
Noryangjin Seoul 27 B1
Nossa Senhora do Ó
São Paulo 27 B1
Nossegem Brussels 6 A3
Notre-Dame Paris 24 A3
Notre-Dame, Basilique
Montreal 20 B2
Notre-Dame, Bois Paris 24 B4
Notre-Dame-de-Grace
Montreal 20 B2
Notting Hill London 15 A2
Nova Milanese Milan 18 A2
Novate Milanese Milan 18 A1
Novaya Derevnya
St. Petersburg 27 A1
Nové Město Prague 25 B2
Novoaleksandrovskoye
St. Petersburg 27 B2
Novodevichy Convent
Moscow 19 B2
Novogireyevo Moscow 19 B3
Novosaratovka
St. Petersburg 27 B3
Nowe-Babice Warsaw 33 B1
Nöykkiö Helsinki 11 B1
Nueva Atzacoalco
Mexico City 18 B2
Nueva Pompeya Buenos Aires 7 C2
Nueva Tenochtitlán
Mexico City 18 B2
Nuijala Helsinki 11 B1
Numabukuro Tokyo 30 A2
Nuñez Buenos Aires 7 B2
Nunhead London 15 B3
Ñuñoa Santiago 27 B2
Nusle Prague 25 B2
Nussdorf Vienna 32 A2
Nyanga Cape Town 8 A2
Nymphenburg Munich 21 B2
Nymphenburg, Schloss
Munich 21 B2

## O

Oak Forest Chicago 9 D2
Oak Grove Atlanta 3 A3
Oak Hill Boston 6 B1
Oak Lawn Chicago 9 C2
Oak Park Chicago 9 B2
Oak View Washington 33 A3
Oakdale Atlanta 3 A2
Oakland San Francisco 26 B3
Oakland Park Miami 19 A3
Oaklawn Washington 33 C3
Oakleigh Melbourne 18 B2
Oakwood Beach New York 22 C1
Oatley Sydney 29 B1
Obalende Lagos 14 B2
Oba's Palace Lagos 14 B2
Oberföhring Munich 21 B2
Oberhaching Munich 21 B2
Oberlaa Vienna 32 B2
Oberlisse Vienna 32 A2
Obermenzing Munich 21 A1
Obermoos Schwaige
Munich 21 A1
Oberschleissheim Munich 21 A2
Oberschöneweide Berlin 5 B4
Observatory Johannesburg 13 B2
Óbuda Budapest 7 A2
Obukhovo St. Petersburg 27 B2
Obvodny Kanal
St. Petersburg 27 B1
Ocean Park Hong Kong 12 B3
Ochota Warsaw 33 B1
Ocoee Orlando 23 A1
Odaiba Tokyo 30 B3
Ōdana Tokyo 30 B2
Öden-Stockach Munich 21 B3
Odilampi Helsinki 11 B1
Odivelas Lisbon 16 A1
Odolany Warsaw 33 B1
Oeiras Lisbon 16 A1
Ofin Lagos 14 A3
Ogawa Tokyo 30 A1
Ogden Park Chicago 9 C2
Ogikubo Tokyo 30 A2
Ogilvie Transportation
Center Chicago 9 B3
Ogogoro Lagos 14 B2
Ogoyo Lagos 14 B2
Ogudu Lagos 14 A2
O'Higgins, Parque Santiago 27 B2
Ōimachi Tokyo 30 B3
Ojota Lagos 14 A2
Ojus Miami 19 C3
Oke-Ira Lagos 14 B2
Okęcie Warsaw 33 B1
Okęcie, Warszawa ✕
(WAW) Warsaw 33 B1
Okeogbe Lagos 14 B2
Okhla Delhi 10 B2
Okhta → St. Petersburg 27 B2
Okkervil → St. Petersburg 27 B2
Okrzeszyn Warsaw 33 C2
Oksval Oslo 23 A3
Oktyabrskiy Moscow 19 B2
Ōkubo Tokyo 30 A3
Ōkura Tokyo 30 B1
Olari Helsinki 11 B1
Olaria Rio de Janeiro 25 B1
Old Admiralty St. Petersburg 27 B1
Old City Jerusalem 13 B2
Old City Shanghai 28 B1
Old Fort York Toronto 31 B2
Old Harbor Boston 6 B2
Old Town = Stare Miasto
Warsaw 33 B2
Old Town Chicago 9 B3
Old Town Hall = Altes
Rathaus Munich 21 B2
Oleta River State Rec.
Area Miami 19 C3
Olgino St. Petersburg 27 B1
Olimpico, Estadio
Mexico City 18 C1
Olivais Lisbon 16 A2
Olivar de los Padres
Mexico City 18 B1
Olivar del Conde
Mexico City 18 B1
Olives, Mt. of Jerusalem 13 B2
Olivia, L. Orlando 23 A1
Olivos Buenos Aires 7 B2
Olona → Milan 18 B1
Olympia, L. Orlando 23 A1
Olympic Green Beijing 4 B2
Olympic Stadium =
Turner Field Atlanta 3 B2
Olympic Stadium Beijing 4 B2
Olympic Stadium Helsinki 11 B2
Olympique, Stade Montreal 20 A2
Ōmori Tokyo 30 B3
One World Trade Center
New York 22 B1
Onisigun Lagos 14 A2
Ontario Science Centre
Toronto 31 A2
Ōokayama Tokyo 30 B3
Oostzaan Tuindorp
Amsterdam 2 A2
Opa-Locka Miami 19 C1
Opa-Locka ✕ (OPF) Miami 19 C1
Opacz Warsaw 33 B1
Opera House Sydney 29 B2
Ophirton Johannesburg 13 B2
Oppegård Oslo 23 B3
Oppem Brussels 6 A1
Oppsal Oslo 23 A4
Ora Jerusalem 13 B1
Oradell New York 22 A1
Oradell Res. New York 22 A1
Orangi Karachi 13 A2
Ordrup Copenhagen 8 A3
Ořech Prague 25 B1
Oregun Lagos 14 A2
Ørestad Copenhagen 8 B3
Orient Heights Boston 6 A3
Oriental Pearl Tower
Shanghai 28 B2
Orland Park Chicago 9 D2
Orlando Orlando 23 A2
Orlando Dam Johannesburg 13 B1
Orlando East Johannesburg 13 B1
Orlando Executive ✕
(ORL) Orlando 23 A2
Orlando Int. ✕ (MCO)
Orlando 23 B3
Orlovista Orlando 23 A2
Orly Paris 24 B3
Orly, Paris ✕ (ORY) Paris 24 B3
Ormesson-sur-Marne Paris 24 B4
Ormond Melbourne 18 B2
Ormøya Oslo 23 A3
Orpington London 15 B4
Ortaköy Istanbul 12 B2
Ortica Milan 18 B2
Oruba Lagos 14 A2
Ōsaka Osaka 23 A2
Ōsaka Castle Osaka 23 A2
Ōsaka Harbour Osaka 23 B1
Ōsaka Itami Int. ✕ (ITM)
Osaka 23 A1
Ōsaka Kansai Int. ✕ (KIX)
Osaka 23 B2
Ōsaki Tokyo 30 B3
Osasco São Paulo 27 B1
Osdorf Berlin 5 B3
Osdorp Amsterdam 2 A1
Oshodi Lagos 14 A2
Oslo Oslo 23 A3
Oslo ✕ (OSL) Oslo 23 A4
Osone Tokyo 30 B2
Osorun Lagos 14 A2
Ospiate Milan 18 A1
Ostankino Moscow 19 B2
Osterley London 15 B1
Osterley Park London 15 B1
Östermalm Stockholm 29 A2
Österskär Stockholm 29 A3
Óstia Malpasso Rome 26 C1
Ostiense Rome 26 B1
Østmarkkapellet Oslo 23 A4
Østøya Oslo 23 A2
Ōta Tokyo 30 B3
Otaniemi Helsinki 11 B1
Otsuka Tokyo 30 A3
Ottakring Vienna 32 A1
Ottávia Rome 26 B1
Ottery Cape Town 8 B2
Ottobrunn Munich 21 B3
Ouderkerk Amsterdam 2 B2
Oulunkylä Helsinki 11 B2
Ourcq, Canal de l' Paris 24 A3
Outer Mission San Francisco 26 B2
Outremont Montreal 20 A2
Overijse Brussels 6 B3
Oworonsoki Lagos 14 A2
Oxgangs Edinburgh 11 B2
Oxon Hill Washington 33 C3
Oyodo Osaka 23 A1
Oyster Rock Mumbai 20 B1
Oyster Rocks Karachi 13 B2
Ozoir-la-Ferrière Paris 24 B4
Ozone Park New York 22 B2

## P

Pacific Heights *San Francisco* 26 B2
Pacific Manor *San Francisco* 26 C2
Pacific Palisades *Los Angeles* 16 B1
Pacifica *San Francisco* 26 C2
Paco *Manila* 17 B1
Paco de Arcos *Lisbon* 16 A1
Paddington *London* 15 A2
Paddington *Sydney* 29 B2
Paderno *Milan* 18 A1
Pagewood *Sydney* 29 B2
Pagote *Mumbai* 20 B2
Pai, I. do *Rio de Janeiro* 25 B2
Pak Kok *Hong Kong* 12 B2
Pak Kong *Hong Kong* 12 A3
Pak Tam *Hong Kong* 12 A3
Pakila *Helsinki* 11 B2
Palacio Real *Madrid* 17 B1
Palaiseau *Paris* 24 B2
Palazzolo *Milan* 18 A1
Paleo Faliro *Athens* 2 B2
Palermo *Buenos Aires* 7 B2
Palhais *Lisbon* 16 B2
Palisades Park *New York* 22 A1
Palm Jumeirah, The *Dubai* 9 B1
Palms *Los Angeles* 16 B2
Paloheinä *Helsinki* 11 B2
Palomeras *Madrid* 17 B2
Palos Heights *Chicago* 9 D2
Palos Hills *Chicago* 9 C2
Palos Park *Chicago* 9 C1
Palpara *Kolkata* 14 B2
Panchur *Kolkata* 14 B1
Pandacan *Manila* 17 B2
Pandan, Selat *Singapore* 28 B2
Pandan Res. *Singapore* 28 B2
Pangrati *Athens* 2 B2
Pangsua, Sungei → *Singapore* 28 A2
Panihati *Kolkata* 14 A2
Panjang, Bukit *Singapore* 28 A2
Panke → *Berlin* 5 A3
Pankow *Berlin* 5 A3
Pantego *Dallas-Fort Worth* 10 B3
Pantheon *Rome* 26 B1
Panthersville *Atlanta* 3 B3
Pantin *Paris* 24 A3
Pantitlán *Mexico City* 18 B2
Panyu *Guangzhou* 11 B2
Papiol *Barcelona* 4 A1
Paradise *Las Vegas* 14 B2
Paramount Studios *Los Angeles* 16 B3
Paramus *New York* 22 A1
Paranaque *Manila* 17 B1
Paray-Vieille-Poste *Paris* 24 B3
Parc des Princes *Paris* 24 A2
Pardisān Nature Park *Tehran* 31 A2
Parel *Mumbai* 20 B1
Pari *São Paulo* 27 B2
Parioli *Rome* 26 B1
Paris *Paris* 24 A3
Paris Orly ✈ (ORY) *Paris* 24 B3
Parje *Mumbai* 20 B2
Pārk-e Āzādegān *Tehran* 31 B2
Pārk-e Mellat *Tehran* 31 A2
Park Ridge *Chicago* 9 A1
Park Royal *London* 15 A2
Parkchester *New York* 22 B2
Parkdale *Toronto* 31 B2
Parkhurst *Johannesburg* 13 A2
Parklawn *Washington* 33 B2
Parkmore *Johannesburg* 13 A2
Parkside *San Francisco* 26 B2
Parktown *Johannesburg* 13 B2
Parkview *Johannesburg* 13 A2
Parkville *New York* 22 C2
Parkwood *Cape Town* 8 B1
Parkwood *Johannesburg* 13 A2
Parow *Cape Town* 8 A2
Parque Chacabuco *Buenos Aires* 7 B2
Parque Patricios *Buenos Aires* 7 B2
Parramatta → *Sydney* 29 A1
Paşabahçe *Istanbul* 12 B2
Pasadena *Los Angeles* 16 B4
Pasar Minggu *Jakarta* 12 B1
Pasay *Manila* 17 B1
Pascoe Vale *Melbourne* 18 A1
Pasig *Manila* 17 B2
Pasig → *Manila* 17 B2
Pasila *Helsinki* 11 B2
Pasing *Munich* 21 B1
Pasir Panjang *Singapore* 28 B2
Pasir Ris *Singapore* 28 A3
Passaic *New York* 22 A1
Passaic → *New York* 22 B1
Passirana *Milan* 18 A1
Patel Nagar *Delhi* 10 B1
Pateros *Manila* 17 B2
Pathumwan *Bangkok* 3 B2
Patipukur *Kolkata* 14 B2
Patisia *Athens* 2 A2
Paulo E. Virginia, Gruta *Rio de Janeiro* 25 B1
Paulshof *Berlin* 5 A5
Paya Lebar *Singapore* 28 A3
Peakhurst *Sydney* 29 B1
Peania *Athens* 2 B3
Pearson Int. Toronto ✈ (YYZ) *Toronto* 31 A1
Peckham *London* 15 B3
Pederstrup *Copenhagen* 8 A2
Pedralbes *Barcelona* 4 A1
Pedregal de San Angel, Jardines del *Mexico City* 18 C1
Peip'ing = Beijing *Beijing* 4 B1
Peking = Beijing *Beijing* 4 B1
Pelcowizna *Warsaw* 33 B2
Pembroke Park *Miami* 19 C2
Pembroke Pines *Miami* 19 B1
Peñalolén *Santiago* 27 B2
Peng Chau *Hong Kong* 12 B2
Peng Siang → *Singapore* 28 A2
Penge *London* 15 B3
Penha *Rio de Janeiro* 25 A1
Penicuik *Edinburgh* 11 B2
Penjaringan *Jakarta* 12 A1
Pentagon *Washington* 33 B2
Penzing *Vienna* 32 A1
People's Park *Shanghai* 28 B1
People's Square *Shanghai* 28 B1
Perales del Rio *Madrid* 17 C2
Perchtoldsdorf *Vienna* 32 B1
Perdizes *São Paulo* 27 B2
Peristeri *Athens* 2 A2
Perivale *London* 15 A2
Perk *Brussels* 6 A2
Perlach *Munich* 21 B2
Perlacher Forst *Munich* 21 B2
Pero *Milan* 18 A1
Peropok, Bukit *Singapore* 28 B2
Perovo *Moscow* 19 B3
Pertusella *Milan* 18 A1
Pesagot *Jerusalem* 13 A2
Pesanggrahag, Kali → *Jakarta* 12 B1
Peschiera Borromeo *Milan* 18 B2
Pesek, Pulau *Singapore* 28 B2
Pest *Budapest* 7 B2
Pesterzsébet *Budapest* 7 B2
Pesthidegkút *Budapest* 7 A1
Pestimre *Budapest* 7 B3
Pestlörinc *Budapest* 7 B3
Pestújhely *Budapest* 7 A2
Petas *Helsinki* 11 B2
Petrogradskaya Storona *St. Petersburg* 27 B2
Petroupoli *Athens* 2 A2
Petrovice *Prague* 25 B3
Petrovskiy Park *Moscow* 19 B2
Petrovsko-Razumovskoye *Moscow* 19 B2
Petrovsky Stadium *St. Petersburg* 27 B1
Pettycur *Edinburgh* 11 A2
Peutie *Brussels* 6 A2
Pfaueninsel *Berlin* 5 B1
Phaya Thai *Bangkok* 3 B2
Phihai *Karachi* 13 A2
Phillip B. *Sydney* 29 B2
Phoenix *Chicago* 9 D3
Phra Khanong *Bangkok* 3 B2
Phra Nakhon *Bangkok* 3 B2
Phra Pradaeng *Bangkok* 3 C2
Picnic B. *Hong Kong* 12 B2
Pico Rivera *Los Angeles* 16 C4
Piedade *Lisbon* 16 A1
Piedade *Rio de Janeiro* 25 B1
Piedade, Cova da *Lisbon* 16 A2
Piedmont Park *Atlanta* 3 B2
Pierre Elliott Trudeau Int. ✈ (YUL) *Montreal* 20 B1
Pietralata *Rome* 26 B2
Pihlajamäki *Helsinki* 11 B2
Pihlajasaari *Helsinki* 11 C2
Pilares *Rio de Janeiro* 25 B1
Pilton *Edinburgh* 11 B2
Pine Castle *Orlando* 23 B2
Pine Grove *Toronto* 31 A1
Pine Hills *Orlando* 23 A2
Pine Island *Miami* 19 B1
Pinecrest *Miami* 19 D1
Pinewood Park *Miami* 19 C2
Pingzhou *Guangzhou* 11 B2
Pinheiros → *São Paulo* 27 B1
Pinjrapur *Karachi* 13 A2
Pinner *London* 15 A1
Pinner Green *London* 15 A1
Pioltello *Milan* 18 A2
Piræus = Pireas *Athens* 2 B1
Piraiévs = Pireas *Athens* 2 B1
Pirajuçara → *São Paulo* 27 B1
Pireas *Athens* 2 B1
Pirinçi *Istanbul* 12 B1
Pirituba *São Paulo* 27 A1
Pirkkola *Helsinki* 11 B2
Pisgat O'mer *Jerusalem* 13 B2
Pisgat Ze'ev *Jerusalem* 13 B2
Písnice *Prague* 25 C2
Pitampura *Delhi* 10 A1
Pitkäjärvi *Helsinki* 11 B1
Planegg *Munich* 21 B1
Plantation *Miami* 19 B2
Plantation Isles *Miami* 19 B2
Plaza Mayor *Madrid* 17 B1
Pleasure Island *Orlando* 23 B1
Plumstead *Cape Town* 8 B1
Plumstead *London* 15 B4
Plyushchevo *Moscow* 19 B3
Po Toi Is. *Hong Kong* 12 B3
Po Toi O *Hong Kong* 12 B3
Poasco *Milan* 18 B2
Podbaba *Prague* 25 B2
Podoli *Prague* 25 B2
Pointe-Aux-Trembles *Montreal* 20 A2
Poissy *Paris* 24 A1
Pok Fu Lam *Hong Kong* 12 B2
Pokcheong *Seoul* 27 C2
Polton *Edinburgh* 11 B3
Polvoranca, Parque de *Madrid* 17 C1
Polyustrovo *St. Petersburg* 27 B2
Pompano Beach *Miami* 19 A3
Pomprap *Bangkok* 3 B2
Pondok Gede *Jakarta* 12 A2
Pondok Indah *Jakarta* 12 B1
Pont-Viau *Montreal* 20 A1
Pontault-Combault *Paris* 24 B4
Pontinha *Lisbon* 16 A1
Poplar *London* 15 A3
Port Botany *Sydney* 29 B2
Port Melbourne *Melbourne* 18 B1
Port Rashid *Dubai* 9 A2
Port Richmond *New York* 22 C1
Port Saeed *Dubai* 9 B2
Port Shelter *Hong Kong* 12 A3
Port Union *Toronto* 31 A4
Portage Park *Chicago* 9 B2
Portela, Lisboa ✈ (LIS) *Lisbon* 16 A2
Porter, L. *Orlando* 23 A3
Porto Brandão *Lisbon* 16 A1
Pôrto Novo *Rio de Janeiro* 25 A2
Porto Novo Cr. → *Lagos* 14 B2
Portobello *Edinburgh* 11 B3
Portrero *San Francisco* 26 B3
Posen *Chicago* 9 D2
Potomac Overlook Reg. Park ⌓ *Washington* 33 B2
Potrero Pt. *San Francisco* 26 B2
Potsdam *Berlin* 5 B1
Potzham *Munich* 21 B2
Pötzleinsdorf *Vienna* 32 A1
Póvoa de Santo Adriao *Lisbon* 16 A2
Powązki *Warsaw* 33 B1
Powiśle *Warsaw* 33 B2
Powsin *Warsaw* 33 C2
Powsinek *Warsaw* 33 C2
Poyan Res. *Singapore* 28 A2
Pozuelo de Alarcón *Madrid* 17 B1
Prado, Museo del *Madrid* 17 B1
Prado Churubusco *Mexico City* 18 B2
Praga *Warsaw* 33 B2
Prague = Praha *Prague* 25 B2
Praha *Prague* 25 B2
Praha ✈ (PRG) *Prague* 25 B1
Praires, R. des → *Montreal* 20 A2
Prater *Vienna* 32 A2
Precotto *Milan* 18 A2
Prenestino Labicano *Rome* 26 B2
Prenzlauerberg *Berlin* 5 A3
Preston *Melbourne* 18 A1
Pretos Forros, Sa. dos *Rio de Janeiro* 25 B1
Préville *Montreal* 20 B3
Přezletice *Prague* 25 B3
Prima Porta *Rome* 26 B1
Primavalle *Rome* 26 B1
Primrose *Johannesburg* 13 B2
Progreso Nacional *Mexico City* 18 A2
Prosek *Prague* 25 B3
Prospect Hill Park *Boston* 6 A1
Providencia *Santiago* 27 B2
Průhonice *Prague* 25 C3
Psichiko *Athens* 2 A2
Pudong New Area *Shanghai* 28 B2
Pueblo Libre *Lima* 14 B2
Pueblo Nuevo = El Pobleneu *Barcelona* 4 A2
Pueblo Nuevo *Madrid* 17 B2
Puerto Madero *Buenos Aires* 7 B2
Pugu *Guangzhou* 11 A2
Puhuangyu *Beijing* 4 B2
Pui O Wan *Hong Kong* 12 B1
Puistola *Helsinki* 11 B3
Pukinmäki *Helsinki* 11 B2
Pulkovo Int. ✈ (LED) *St. Petersburg* 27 C1
Pullach *Munich* 21 B1
Pullman Historic District *Chicago* 9 C3
Pulo Gadung *Jakarta* 12 B2
Pūnak *Tehran* 31 A2
Punchbowl *Sydney* 29 B1
Punde *Mumbai* 20 B2
Punggol *Singapore* 28 A3
Punggol, Sungei → *Singapore* 28 A3
Punggol Pt. *Singapore* 28 A3
Punjabi Bagh *Delhi* 10 A1
Puotila *Helsinki* 11 B3
Puteaux *Paris* 24 A2
Putney *London* 15 B2
Putuo *Shanghai* 28 B1
Putxet *Barcelona* 4 A1
Puxi *Shanghai* 28 B1
Pyramids *Cairo* 7 B1
Pyry *Warsaw* 33 C1

## Q

Qalandiya *Jerusalem* 13 A2
Qal'eh Morghī *Tehran* 31 B2
Qāsemābād *Tehran* 31 A3
Qasr-e Fīrūzeh *Tehran* 31 B3
Qatane *Jerusalem* 13 B1
Qianmen *Beijing* 4 B2
Qinghuayuan *Beijing* 4 B1
Qingningsi *Shanghai* 28 B2
Qolhak *Tehran* 31 A2
Quadraro *Rome* 26 B2
Quaid-i-Azam *Karachi* 13 A1
Quartiere Zingone *Milan* 18 B1
Qubeiba *Jerusalem* 13 A1
Quds *Baghdad* 3 A2
Queen Elizabeth Olympic Park *London* 15 A3
Queen Mary Res. *London* 15 B1
Queen Victoria Market *Melbourne* 18 A1
Queensbury *London* 15 A2
Queenscliffe *Sydney* 29 A2
Queensferry *Edinburgh* 11 B1
Queenstown *Singapore* 28 B2
Quellerina *Johannesburg* 13 A1
Queluz *Lisbon* 16 A1
Quezon City *Manila* 17 B2
Quilicura *Santiago* 27 B1
Quincy *Boston* 6 B2
Quincy B. *Boston* 6 B3
Quinta Normal *Santiago* 27 B1
Quinto de Stampi *Milan* 18 B2
Quinto Romano *Milan* 18 B1
Quirinale *Rome* 26 B1
Qutb Minar *Delhi* 10 B2

## R

R.F.K. Memorial Stadium *Washington* 33 B3
Raasdorf *Vienna* 32 A3
Radcliffe College *Boston* 6 A2
Rådhus *Oslo* 23 A3
Radlice *Prague* 25 B2
Radość *Warsaw* 33 B3
Radotin *Prague* 25 C2
Rafat *Jerusalem* 13 A2
Raffles Park *Singapore* 28 B2
Rahnsdorf *Berlin* 5 B5
Rajakylä *Helsinki* 11 B3
Rajpura *Delhi* 10 A2
Rákos-patak → *Budapest* 7 B3
Rákoshegy *Budapest* 7 B3
Rákoskeresztúr *Budapest* 7 B3
Rákoskert *Budapest* 7 B3
Rákosliget *Budapest* 7 B3
Rákospalota *Budapest* 7 A2
Rákosszentmihály *Budapest* 7 A2
Raków *Warsaw* 33 B1
Ram *Jerusalem* 13 A2
Rām Allāh *Jerusalem* 13 A2
Ramadān *Baghdad* 3 B2
Ramakrishna Puram *Delhi* 10 B1
Rāmallāh = Rām Allāh *Jerusalem* 13 A2
Ramanathpur *Kolkata* 14 A1
Ramat Allon *Jerusalem* 13 B2
Ramat Eshkol *Jerusalem* 13 B2
Ramat Razi'el *Jerusalem* 13 B1
Ramat Shafet *Jerusalem* 13 B2
Rambler Channel *Hong Kong* 12 A2
Ramenki *Moscow* 19 B1
Ramersdorf *Munich* 21 B2
Rameses Station *Cairo* 7 A2
Ramos *Rio de Janeiro* 25 B1
Ramos Mejía *Buenos Aires* 7 B1
Ramot *Jerusalem* 13 B2
Rampur *Delhi* 10 A2
Ramsgate *Sydney* 29 B1
Rancho Park *Los Angeles* 16 B2
Rand ✈ (QRA) *Johannesburg* 13 B2
Randalls I. *New York* 22 B2
Randburg *Johannesburg* 13 A1
Randhart *Johannesburg* 13 B2
Randpark Ridge *Johannesburg* 13 A1
Randwick *Sydney* 29 B2
Rangpuri *Delhi* 10 B1
Rannersdorf *Vienna* 32 B2
Ransbèche *Brussels* 6 B2
Ransdorp *Amsterdam* 2 A2
Ranvad *Mumbai* 20 B2
Raposo *Lisbon* 16 A1
Rastaala *Helsinki* 11 B1
Rastila *Helsinki* 11 B3
Raszyn *Warsaw* 33 C1
Ratho *Edinburgh* 11 B1
Ratho Station *Edinburgh* 11 B1
Rato *Lisbon* 16 A2
Ravelston *Edinburgh* 11 B2
Rawamangun *Jakarta* 12 B2
Rayners Lane *London* 15 A1
Raynes Park *London* 15 B2
Raypur *Kolkata* 14 C2
Real Felipe, Fuerte *Lima* 14 B2
Reams, L. *Orlando* 23 B1
Reclining Buddha = Wat Pho *Bangkok* 3 B1
Recoleta *Buenos Aires* 7 B2
Recoleta *Santiago* 27 B2
Red Fort = Lal Qila *Delhi* 10 B2
Red Square *Moscow* 19 B2
Redbridge □ *London* 15 A4
Redfern *Sydney* 29 B2
Refshaleøen *Copenhagen* 8 A3
Regents Park *Johannesburg* 13 B2
Regent's Park *London* 15 A3
Rego Park *New York* 22 B2
Reinickendorf *Berlin* 5 A3
Rekola *Helsinki* 11 B3
Rembertów *Warsaw* 33 B2
Rembrandtpark *Amsterdam* 2 A2
Remedios de Escalada *Buenos Aires* 7 C2
Rémola, Estany del *Barcelona* 4 B1
Renca *Santiago* 27 B1
Rennemoulin *Paris* 24 A1
Řeporyje *Prague* 25 B1
Repulse Bay *Hong Kong* 12 B3
Repy *Prague* 25 B1
Residenz *Munich* 21 B2
Retiro *Buenos Aires* 7 B2
Retiro *Madrid* 17 B1
Retiro, Puerto *Buenos Aires* 7 B2
Retreat *Cape Town* 8 B1
Reutov *Moscow* 19 B4
Réveillon → *Paris* 24 B4
Revere *Boston* 6 A2
Rexdale *Toronto* 31 A1
Reynosa Tamaulipas *Mexico City* 18 A1
Rho *Milan* 18 A1
Rhodes *Sydney* 29 A1
Rhodon *Paris* 24 B1
Rhodon → *Paris* 24 B1
Rialto Towers *Melbourne* 18 A1
Ribeira *Rio de Janeiro* 25 A1
Ricarda, Estany de la *Barcelona* 4 B1
Richardson *Dallas-Fort Worth* 10 A5
Richland Hills *Dallas-Fort Worth* 10 B2
Richmond *Melbourne* 18 A2
Richmond *San Francisco* 26 B2
Richmond Hill *New York* 22 B2
Richmond Park *London* 15 B2
Richmond-upon-Thames □ *London* 15 B2
Ridge, The *Delhi* 10 B2
Ridgefield *New York* 22 B1
Ridgefield Park *New York* 22 A1
Ridgewood *New York* 22 B2
Riem *Munich* 21 B3
Riesenrad *Vienna* 32 A2
Rijksmuseum *Amsterdam* 2 A2
Rikers I. *New York* 22 B2
Rimac *Lima* 14 B2
Rinkeby *Stockholm* 29 A1
Rio Comprido *Rio de Janeiro* 25 B1
Rio de Janeiro *Rio de Janeiro* 25 B1
Rio de Janeiro Galeão ✈ (GIG) *Rio de Janeiro* 25 A1
Rio de Mouro *Lisbon* 16 A1
Ripollet *Barcelona* 4 A1
Ris *Oslo* 23 A3
Risby *Copenhagen* 8 A1
Rishra *Kolkata* 14 A2
Rithala *Delhi* 10 A1
Rive Sud, Canal de la *Montreal* 20 B2
River Edge *New York* 22 A1
River Forest *Chicago* 9 B2
River Grove *Chicago* 9 B1
River Ridge *New Orleans* 21 B1
Riverdale *Chicago* 9 D3
Riverdale *New York* 22 A2
Riverdale *Washington* 33 B3
Riverdale Park *Toronto* 31 A2
Riverlea *Johannesburg* 13 B1
Riverside *Chicago* 9 C2
Riverwood *Sydney* 29 B1
Rivière-des-Praires *Montreal* 20 A2
Rixensart *Brussels* 6 B3
Riyad *Baghdad* 3 B2
Rizal Park *Manila* 17 B1
Rizal Stadium *Manila* 17 B1
Røa *Oslo* 23 A2
Robbins *Chicago* 9 D2
Robertsham *Johannesburg* 13 B2
Rochelle Park *New York* 22 A1
Rochester Park *Dallas-Fort Worth* 10 B5
Rock Cr. → *Washington* 33 B2
Rock Creek Park *Washington* 33 B2
Rockaway Beach *New York* 22 C3
Rockaway Pt. *New York* 22 C2
Rockdale *Sydney* 29 B1
Rockefeller Center *New York* 22 B2
Roda, Gezîret el *Cairo* 7 A2
Roda I. = Roda, Gezîret el *Cairo* 7 A2
Rodaon *Vienna* 32 B1
Rødovre *Copenhagen* 8 A2
Rodrigo de Freitas, L. *Rio de Janeiro* 25 B1
Roehampton *London* 15 B2
Rogers Park *Chicago* 9 A3
Roihuvuori *Helsinki* 11 B3
Roissy-en-Brie *Paris* 24 B4
Rokytka → *Prague* 25 B3
Roland Garros *Paris* 24 A2
Roma *Rome* 26 B1
Roma Urbe ✈ *Rome* 26 B2
Római-Fürdö *Budapest* 7 A2
Romainville *Paris* 24 A3
Roman Forum = Foro Romano *Rome* 26 B1
Romano Banco *Milan* 18 B1
Rome = Roma *Rome* 26 B1
Romema *Jerusalem* 13 B2
Romford *London* 15 A5
Ronald Reagan Nat. Washington ✈ (DCA) *Washington* 33 B2
Rondebosch *Cape Town* 8 A1
Roppongi *Tokyo* 30 B3
Rose, L. *Orlando* 23 A1
Rose Bowl *Los Angeles* 16 B4
Rose Hill *Washington* 33 C2
Rosebank *Johannesburg* 13 A2
Rosebank *New York* 22 C1
Rosebery *Sydney* 29 B2
Rosedal La Candelaria *Mexico City* 18 B2
Roseland *Chicago* 9 C3
Rosemead *Los Angeles* 16 B4
Rosemont *Chicago* 9 B1
Rosemont *Montreal* 20 A2
Rosenborg Slot *Copenhagen* 8 A3
Rosenthal *Berlin* 5 A3
Rosettenville *Johannesburg* 13 B2
Rosewell *Edinburgh* 11 B3
Rosherville Dam *Johannesburg* 13 B2
Rösjön *Stockholm* 29 A2
Roslags-Näsby *Stockholm* 29 A2
Roslin *Edinburgh* 11 B3
Roslindale *Boston* 6 B2
Rosny-sous-Bois *Paris* 24 A4
Rosslyn *Washington* 33 B2
Rosyth *Edinburgh* 11 A1
Rotherhithe *London* 15 B3
Rothneusiedl *Vienna* 32 B2
Rothschmaige *Munich* 21 A1
Rouge Hill *Toronto* 31 A4
Round I. *Hong Kong* 12 B3
Roxbury *Boston* 6 B2
Roxeth *London* 15 A1
Royal Botanic Gardens *Edinburgh* 11 B2
Royal Exhibition Building *Melbourne* 18 A1
Royal Observatory *Edinburgh* 11 B2
Royal Palace = Kungliga Slottet *Stockholm* 29 B2
Royal Palace = Palacio Real *Madrid* 17 B1
Royal Park *Melbourne* 18 A1
Röylä *Helsinki* 11 B1
Rozas, Portilleros de las *Madrid* 17 B1
Roztoky *Prague* 25 B2
Rozzano *Milan* 18 B1
Rubí → *Barcelona* 4 A1
Rudolfsheim *Vienna* 32 A2
Rudolfshöhe *Berlin* 5 A5
Rudow *Berlin* 5 B3
Rueil-Malmaison *Paris* 24 A2
Ruisbroek *Brussels* 6 B1
Ruislip *London* 15 A1
Rumelihisarı *Istanbul* 12 B2
Rungis *Paris* 24 B3
Rusāfa *Baghdad* 3 A2
Rush Green *London* 15 A5
Russa *Kolkata* 14 C2
Rutherford *New York* 22 B1
Ruzyně *Prague* 25 B1
Ruzyně, Praha ✈ (PRG) *Prague* 25 B1
Rybatskaya *St. Petersburg* 27 B2
Rydboholm *Stockholm* 29 A3
Ryde *Sydney* 29 A1
Ryogoku *Tokyo* 30 A3
Rzhevka *St. Petersburg* 27 B3

## S

Sa'ādatābād *Tehran* 31 A2
Saadūn *Baghdad* 3 B2
Saavedra *Buenos Aires* 7 B2
Saboli *Delhi* 10 A2
Sabugo *Lisbon* 16 A1
Sabzi Mand *Delhi* 10 A2
Sacavém *Lisbon* 16 A2
Saclay *Paris* 24 B2
Saclay, Étang de *Paris* 24 B1
Sacomã *São Paulo* 27 B2
Sacré Cœur *Paris* 24 A3
Sacrow *Berlin* 5 B1
Sacrower See *Berlin* 5 B1
Sadang *Seoul* 27 C1
Saddle → *New York* 22 A1
Saddle Brook *New York* 22 A1
Sadr *Karachi* 13 A2
Sadr City *Baghdad* 3 A2
Sadyba *Warsaw* 33 B2
Safdar Jang's Tomb *Delhi* 10 B2
Saft el Laban *Cairo* 7 A2
Sagene *Oslo* 23 A3
Saginaw *Dallas-Fort Worth* 10 A1
Sagrada Família, Templo de *Barcelona* 4 A2
Sahar, Mumbai ✈ (BOM) *Mumbai* 20 A2
Sai Kung *Hong Kong* 12 A3
Sai Tso Wan *Hong Kong* 12 B1
Sai Wan Ho *Hong Kong* 12 B3
Sai Ying Pun *Hong Kong* 12 B2
St-Aubin *Paris* 24 B1
St-Cloud *Paris* 24 A2
St-Cyr-l'École *Paris* 24 B1
St-Cyr-l'École ✈ *Paris* 24 B1
St-Denis *Paris* 24 A3
St-Germain, Forêt de *Paris* 24 A1
St-Germain-en-Laye *Paris* 24 A1
St-Gilles *Brussels* 6 B2
St. Helier *London* 15 B2
St-Hubert *Montreal* 20 B3
St-Hubert, Galeries Royales *Brussels* 6 A2
St. Isaac's Cathedral *St. Petersburg* 27 B1
St-Jacques → *Montreal* 20 B3
St-Joost-Ten-Node *Brussels* 6 A2
St. Kilda *Melbourne* 18 B1
St-Lambert *Montreal* 20 A3
St-Lambert *Paris* 24 B1
St-Laurent *Montreal* 20 A1
St-Léonard *Montreal* 20 A2
St-Mandé *Paris* 24 A3
St-Martin, Bois *Paris* 24 B4
St. Mary Cray *London* 15 B4
St-Maur-des-Fossés *Paris* 24 B3
St-Maurice *Paris* 24 B3
St-Michel *Montreal* 20 A2
St-Ouen *Paris* 24 A3
St. Paul's Cray *London* 15 B4
St. Peters *Sydney* 29 B2
St. Peter's Square = San Pietro, Piazza *Rome* 26 B1
St. Petersburg = Sankt-Peterburg *St. Petersburg* 27 B1
St. Petersburg Pulkovo Int. ✈ (LED) *St. Petersburg* 27 C1
St-Pierre *Montreal* 20 B2
St-Pieters Leew *Brussels* 6 B1
St-Quentin, Étang de *Paris* 24 B1
St. Stephen's Cathedral = Stephansdom *Vienna* 32 A2
St-Stevens-Woluwe *Brussels* 6 A2
St-Vincent-de-Paul *Montreal* 20 A2
St. Xavier Univ. *Chicago* 9 C2
Ste-Catherine *Montreal* 20 B2
Ste-Hélène, Î. *Montreal* 20 A2
Saiwai *Tokyo* 30 B3
Sakai *Osaka* 23 B1
Sakai Harbour *Osaka* 23 B1
Sakra, Pulau *Singapore* 28 B2
Salam *Baghdad* 3 A2
Salamanca *Madrid* 17 B1
Salmannsdorf *Vienna* 32 A1
Salmedina *Madrid* 17 C2
Salomea *Warsaw* 33 B1
Salsette I. *Mumbai* 20 A2
Salt Lake City = Bidhan Nagar *Kolkata* 14 B2
Salt Lake Stadium *Kolkata* 14 B2
Salt River *Cape Town* 8 A1
Salt Water L. *Kolkata* 14 B2
Saltsjö-Duvnäs *Stockholm* 29 B3
Samatya *Istanbul* 12 C1
Sampaloc *Manila* 17 B1
Samphan Thawong *Bangkok* 3 B2
Samseon *Seoul* 27 B2
Samseong *Seoul* 27 B2
Samuel Smith Park *Toronto* 31 B1
Samut Prakan *Bangkok* 3 B2
San Andrés *Barcelona* 4 A2
San Angel *Mexico City* 18 B1
San Basilio *Rome* 26 B2
San Borja *Lima* 14 B3
San Bóvio *Milan* 18 B2
San Bruno, Pt. *San Francisco* 26 C2
San Bruno Mountain State Park ⌓ *San Francisco* 26 B2
San Cristóbal *Buenos Aires* 7 B2
San Cristobal *Madrid* 17 B2
San Cristóbal, Cerro *Santiago* 27 B2
San Cristóbal, Virgen del *Santiago* 27 B2
San Cristoforo *Milan* 18 B1
San Donato Milanese *Milan* 18 B2
San Francisco *San Francisco* 26 B2
San Francisco B. *San Francisco* 26 B3
San Francisco Culhuacán *Mexico City* 18 C2
San Fruttuoso *Milan* 18 A2
San Gabriel *Los Angeles* 16 B4
San Gabriel → *Los Angeles* 16 C4
San Giuliano Milanese *Milan* 18 B2
San Isidro *Lima* 14 B2
San Jerónimo Lidice *Mexico City* 18 C1
San Joaquín *Santiago* 27 B2
San José Río Hondo *Mexico City* 18 B1
San Juan → *Manila* 17 B2
San Juan de Aragón *Mexico City* 18 B2
San Juan de Aragón, Parque *Mexico City* 18 B2
San Juan de Lurigancho *Lima* 14 A2
San Juan del Monte *Manila* 17 B2
San Juan Ixtacala *Mexico City* 18 A1
San Just Desvern *Barcelona* 4 A1
San Justo *Buenos Aires* 7 C1
San Lorenzo Tezonco *Mexico City* 18 C2
San Luis *Lima* 14 B2
San Marino *Los Angeles* 16 B4
San Martín *Barcelona* 4 A2
San Martín de Porras *Lima* 14 B2
San Mateo Tlaltenango *Mexico City* 18 B1
San Miguel *Lima* 14 B2
San Miguel *Santiago* 27 B2
San Nicolás *Buenos Aires* 7 B2
San Onófrio *Rome* 26 B1
San Pedro Mártir *Barcelona* 4 A1
San Pedro Zacatenco *Mexico City* 18 A2
San Pietro, Piazza *Rome* 26 B1
San Po Kong *Hong Kong* 12 B3
San Rafael Chamapa *Mexico City* 18 B1
San Rafael Hills *Los Angeles* 16 A3
San Roque *Manila* 17 B2
San Siro *Milan* 18 B1
San Souci *Sydney* 29 B1
San Tau *Hong Kong* 12 B1
San Telmo *Buenos Aires* 7 B2
San Vicenç dels Horts *Barcelona* 4 A1
Sandown *Johannesburg* 13 A2
Sandown Park Races *London* 15 B1
Sandton *Johannesburg* 13 A2
Sandvika *Oslo* 23 A2
Sangenjaya *Tokyo* 30 B2
Sanggye *Seoul* 27 B2
Sangley Pt. *Manila* 17 C1
Sankrail *Kolkata* 14 B1
Sankt-Peterburg *St. Petersburg* 27 B1
Sankt Veit *Vienna* 32 A1
Sanlihe *Beijing* 4 B1
Sanlin *Shanghai* 28 C1
Sanlintang *Shanghai* 28 C1
Sans *Barcelona* 4 A1
Sansom Park *Dallas-Fort Worth* 10 B1
Sanssouci *Berlin* 5 B1
Sant Ambrogio, Basilica di *Milan* 18 B2
Sant Boi de Llobregat *Barcelona* 4 A1
Sant Cugat *Barcelona* 4 A1
Sant Feliu de Llobregat *Barcelona* 4 A1
Sant Joan Despi *Barcelona* 4 A1
Santa Ana *Manila* 17 B2
Santa Anita Park *Los Angeles* 16 B4
Santa Coloma de Gramenet *Barcelona* 4 A2
Santa Cruz *Manila* 17 B1
Santa Cruz *Mumbai* 20 A1
Santa Cruz, I. de *Rio de Janeiro* 25 B2
Santa Cruz de Olorde *Barcelona* 4 A1
Santa Efigénia *São Paulo* 27 B2
Santa Elena *Manila* 17 B2
Santa Elena del Gomero *Santiago* 27 B1
Santa Eulalia *Barcelona* 4 A2
Santa Fe Springs *Los Angeles* 16 C4
Santa Iria da Azóia *Lisbon* 16 A2
Santa Julia *Santiago* 27 C2
Santa Monica *Los Angeles* 16 B2
Santa Monica Mts. *Los Angeles* 16 B2
Santa Rosa de Locobe *Santiago* 27 B2
Santa Teresa de la Ovalle *Santiago* 27 B1
Santahamina *Helsinki* 11 C3
Santana *São Paulo* 27 A2
Santeny *Paris* 24 B4
Santiago *Santiago* 27 B2
Santiago Benítez Int. ✈ (SCL) *Santiago* 27 B1
Santiago de Surco *Lima* 14 B2
Santo Amaro *Lisbon* 16 A1
Santo Amaro *São Paulo* 27 B1
Santo André *Lisbon* 16 B2
Santo Antão do Tojal *Lisbon* 16 A2
Santo Antônio, Qta. de *Lisbon* 16 B1
Santo Tomas, Univ. of *Manila* 17 B1
Santos Dumont ✈ (SDU) *Rio de Janeiro* 25 B2
Santoshpur *Kolkata* 14 B1
Santragachi *Kolkata* 14 B1
Sanyuanli *Guangzhou* 11 B2
São Caetano do Sul *São Paulo* 27 B2
São Conrado *Rio de Janeiro* 25 B1
São Cristóvão *Rio de Janeiro* 25 B1
São Jorge, Castelo de *Lisbon* 16 A2
São Juliao do Tojal *Lisbon* 16 A2
São Paulo *São Paulo* 27 B2
São Paulo Congonhas ✈ (CGH) *São Paulo* 27 B2
Sapa *Kolkata* 14 B1
Sapateiro, Cor. do → *São Paulo* 27 B1
Sarandi *Buenos Aires* 7 C2
Saraswati → *Kolkata* 14 A1
Sarecky potok → *Prague* 25 B2
Sarimbun *Singapore* 28 A2
Sarimbun Res. *Singapore* 28 A2
Sarıyer *Istanbul* 12 A2
Sarriá *Barcelona* 4 A1
Sarsuna *Kolkata* 14 C1
Sartrouville *Paris* 24 A2
Sasad *Budapest* 7 B2
Sashalom *Budapest* 7 A3
Saska *Warsaw* 33 B2
Satalice *Prague* 25 B3
Satgachi *Kolkata* 14 B2
Satpukur *Kolkata* 14 B2
Sätra *Stockholm* 29 B1
Saúde *São Paulo* 27 B2
Saugus *Boston* 6 A2
Saugus → *Boston* 6 A2
Sault-au-Récollet *Montreal* 20 A2
Sausalito *San Francisco* 26 A2
Sawah Besar *Jakarta* 12 A1
Sawtelle *Los Angeles* 16 B2
Scald Law *Edinburgh* 11 B2
Scarborough *Toronto* 31 A3
Scarborough Bluffs *Toronto* 31 A3
Scarborough Junction *Toronto* 31 A3
Sceaux *Paris* 24 B2
Schaerbeek *Brussels* 6 A2
Scharfenberg *Berlin* 5 A2
Schiller Woods *Chicago* 9 B1
Schiphol, Amsterdam ✈ (AMS) *Amsterdam* 2 B1
Schlachtensee *Berlin* 5 B2
Schlossgarten *Berlin* 5 A2
Schmargendorf *Berlin* 5 B2
Schönblick *Berlin* 5 B5
Schönbrunn *Vienna* 32 A1
Schöneberg *Berlin* 5 B3
Schönefeld *Berlin* 5 B4
Schöneiche *Berlin* 5 B5
Schönwalde *Berlin* 5 A1
Schulzendorf *Berlin* 5 A2
Schwabing *Munich* 21 B2
Schwanebeck *Berlin* 5 A4
Schwanenwerder *Berlin* 5 B2
Schwarzlackenau *Vienna* 32 A2
Schwechat *Vienna* 32 B2
Schwechat, Wien ✈ (VIE) *Vienna* 32 B3
Science and Industry, Museum of *Chicago* 9 C3
Scopus, Mt. *Jerusalem* 13 B2
Scottdale *Atlanta* 3 B3
Scottish Parliament *Edinburgh* 11 B2
Scutari = Üsküdar *Istanbul* 12 B2
Sea Point *Cape Town* 8 A1
Seacliff *San Francisco* 26 B2
Seaforth *Sydney* 29 A2
Seagate *New York* 22 C1
SeaWorld *Orlando* 23 B2
Šeberov *Prague* 25 B3
Secaucus *New York* 22 B1
Seddinsee *Berlin* 5 B5
Seeberg *Berlin* 5 A5
Seeburg *Berlin* 5 A1
Seefeld *Berlin* 5 A5
Seegefeld *Berlin* 5 A1
Seehof *Berlin* 5 B2
Segeltorp *Stockholm* 29 B1
Segrate *Milan* 18 B2
Seguro *Milan* 18 B1
Seixal *Lisbon* 16 B2
Selby *Johannesburg* 13 B2
Seletar *Singapore* 28 A3
Seletar, Pulau *Singapore* 28 A3
Seletar Hills *Singapore* 28 A3
Seletar Res. *Singapore* 28 A2
Selhurst *London* 15 B3
Sembawang *Singapore* 28 A2
Senago *Milan* 18 A1
Senayan Stadium = Gelora Bung Karno Stadium *Jakarta* 12 B1
Sendling *Munich* 21 B2
Senju *Tokyo* 30 A3
Senkang *Singapore* 28 A3
Senriyama *Osaka* 23 A2
Sentosa *Singapore* 28 B2
Seobinggo *Seoul* 27 B1
Seocho *Seoul* 27 C1
Seodaemun *Seoul* 27 B1
Seokkwan *Seoul* 27 B2
Seongbuk *Seoul* 27 B2
Seongdong *Seoul* 27 B2
Seongsu *Seoul* 27 B2
Seoul *Seoul* 27 B2
Seoul Nat. Univ. *Seoul* 27 C1
Seoul Tower *Seoul* 27 B1
Sepolia *Athens* 2 A2
Sepulveda Dam Rec. Area ⌓ *Los Angeles* 16 A2
Serangoon *Singapore* 28 A3
Serangoon, Pulau *Singapore* 28 A3
Serangoon, Sungei → *Singapore* 28 A3
Serangoon Harbour *Singapore* 28 A3
Seraya, Pulau *Singapore* 28 B2
Serebryanka → *Moscow* 19 B3
Serramonte *San Francisco* 26 C2
Sesto San Giovanni *Milan* 18 A2
Sesto Ulteriano *Milan* 18 B2
Setagaya *Tokyo* 30 B2
Seter *Oslo* 23 A3
Setia Budi *Jakarta* 12 B1
Settebagni *Rome* 26 A2
Settecamini *Rome* 26 B2
Séttimo Milanese *Milan* 18 B1
Settsu *Osaka* 23 A2
Seutula *Helsinki* 11 A2
Seven Corners *Washington* 33 B2
Seven Kings *London* 15 A4
Seventeenth Street Canal *New Orleans* 21 A2
Sévesco → *Milan* 18 A1
Sevran *Paris* 24 A4
Sèvres *Paris* 24 B2
Sewri *Mumbai* 20 B2
Sforzesso, Castello *Milan* 18 B2
Sha Chau *Hong Kong* 12 A1
Sha Kok Mei *Hong Kong* 12 A3
Sha Lo Wan *Hong Kong* 12 B1
Sha Tin *Hong Kong* 12 A3
Sha'ab *Baghdad* 3 A2
Sha'ab North *Baghdad* 3 A2
Sha'ar Binyamin *Jerusalem* 13 A2
Shabrâmant *Cairo* 7 B2
Shah Mosque *Tehran* 31 A2
Shahdara *Delhi* 10 A2
Shahe *Guangzhou* 11 B2
Shahr-e Rey *Tehran* 31 B2
Shahrak-e Golshahr *Tehran* 31 B1
Shahrak-e Qods *Tehran* 31 A2
Shaikh Aomar *Baghdad* 3 A2
Shakurbasti *Delhi* 10 A1
Shalkiya *Kolkata* 14 B2
Sham Shui Po *Hong Kong* 12 B2
Sham Tseng *Hong Kong* 12 A2
Sham Wat *Hong Kong* 12 B1
Shamapur *Delhi* 10 A1
Shamian *Guangzhou* 11 B2
Shan Mei *Hong Kong* 12 A3
Shanghai *Shanghai* 28 B2
Shanghai Hongqiao Int. ✈ (SHA) *Shanghai* 28 B1
Shanghai Pudong Int. ✈ (PVG) *Shanghai* 28 B2
Sharp I. *Hong Kong* 12 A3
Shastrinagar *Delhi* 10 A2
Shau Kei Wan *Hong Kong* 12 B3
Shawocun *Beijing* 4 B1
Shayuan *Guangzhou* 11 B2
Sheen, L. *Orlando* 23 B1
Sheepshead Bay *New York* 22 C2
Sheikh Zayed Road *Dubai* 9 B2
Shek Kong *Hong Kong* 12 A2
Shek Kwu Chau *Hong Kong* 12 B1
Shek O *Hong Kong* 12 B3
Shek O Country Park ⌓ *Hong Kong* 12 B3
Shek Pik *Hong Kong* 12 B1
Shek Pik Res. *Hong Kong* 12 B1
Shelter I. *Hong Kong* 12 B3
Shepherds Bush *London* 15 A2
Shepperton *London* 15 B1
Sheremetyevo Int., Moscow ✈ (SVO) *Moscow* 19 A1
Sherman Oaks *Los Angeles* 16 B2
Sherman Park *Chicago* 9 C2
Sherwood, L. *Orlando* 23 A2
Shet Bandar *Mumbai* 20 B2
Sheung Fa Shan *Hong Kong* 12 A2
Sheung Lau Wan *Hong Kong* 12 B3
Sheung Wan *Hong Kong* 12 B2
Sheva *Mumbai* 20 B2
Sheva Nhava *Mumbai* 20 B2
Shiba *Tokyo* 30 B3
Shibpur *Kolkata* 14 B1
Shibuya *Tokyo* 30 B3
Shilihe *Beijing* 4 B2
Shimogawara *Tokyo* 30 B1
Shimosalo *Tokyo* 30 A2
Shimoshakujii *Tokyo* 30 A2
Shinagawa *Tokyo* 30 B3
Shing Mun Country Park ⌓ *Hong Kong* 12 A2
Shing Mun Res. *Hong Kong* 12 A2
Shinjuku *Tokyo* 30 A3
Shinjuku Nat. Garden *Tokyo* 30 A3
Shinkoiwa *Tokyo* 30 A4
Shinnakano *Tokyo* 30 A3
Shipai *Guangzhou* 11 B3
Shirinashi → *Osaka* 23 B1
Shirogane *Tokyo* 30 B3
Shitennoji Temple *Osaka* 23 B2
Shiweitang *Guangzhou* 11 B2
Shogunle *Lagos* 14 A2
Shomolu *Lagos* 14 A2
Shooters Hill *London* 15 B4
Shoreditch *London* 15 A3
Shortlands *London* 15 B4
Shu'afat *Jerusalem* 13 B2
Shubrâ *Cairo* 7 A2
Shubrâ el Kheima *Cairo* 7 A2
Shui Hau *Hong Kong* 12 B1
Shuikuo *Guangzhou* 11 A2
Sidcup *London* 15 B4
Siebenhirten *Vienna* 32 B1
Siedlung *Berlin* 5 A1
Siekierki *Warsaw* 33 B2
Sielce *Warsaw* 33 B2
Siemensstadt *Berlin* 5 A2
Sierra Madre *Los Angeles* 16 B4
Sievering *Vienna* 32 A2
Sighthill *Edinburgh* 11 B2
Signal Hill *Cape Town* 8 A1
Siheung *Seoul* 27 C1
Sikátorpuszta *Budapest* 7 A3
Silampur *Delhi* 10 B2
Sillim *Seoul* 27 C1
Silver, L. *Orlando* 23 A2
Silver Hill *Washington* 33 B3
Silver Lake *Los Angeles* 16 B3
Silver Mine B. *Hong Kong* 12 B2
Silver Spring *Washington* 33 A2
Silvermine Nature Reserve *Cape Town* 8 B1
Silverstrand *Hong Kong* 12 B3
Silvolantekojärvi *Helsinki* 11 B2
Simei *Singapore* 28 A3
Simla *Kolkata* 14 B2
Simmering *Vienna* 32 A2
Simmering Heide *Vienna* 32 A2
Simonkylä *Helsinki* 11 B3
Sinchon *Seoul* 27 B1
Sindang *Seoul* 27 B2
Singapore ■ *Singapore* 28 B3
Singapore Changi ✈ (SIN) *Singapore* 28 A3
Sinki, Selat *Singapore* 28 B2
Sinsa *Seoul* 27 B2
Sint-Genesius-Rode *Brussels* 6 B2
Sion *Mumbai* 20 A2
Sipson *London* 15 B1
Siqeil *Cairo* 7 A1
Şişli *Istanbul* 12 B1
Siu Kau Yi Chau *Hong Kong* 12 B2
Skansen *Stockholm* 29 B2
Skärholmen *Stockholm* 29 B1
Skarpäng *Stockholm* 29 A2
Skarpnäck *Stockholm* 29 B2
Skaryszewski, Park *Warsaw* 33 B2
Skogskyrkogården *Stockholm* 29 B2
Skokie *Chicago* 9 A2
Skokie → *Chicago* 9 A2
Skokie Heritage Museum *Chicago* 9 A2
Skoklefall *Oslo* 23 A3
Sköndal *Stockholm* 29 B2
Skovlunde *Copenhagen* 8 A2
Skovshoved *Copenhagen* 8 A3
Skuru *Stockholm* 29 B3
Sky Lake *Orlando* 23 B2
Slade Green *London* 15 B5
Slependen *Oslo* 23 A2
Slipi *Jakarta* 12 B1
Slivenec *Prague* 25 B2
Sloten *Amsterdam* 2 A1
Sloterdijk *Amsterdam* 2 A1
Sloterpark *Amsterdam* 2 A1
Sluhy *Prague* 25 A3
Służew *Warsaw* 33 B2
Służewiec *Warsaw* 33 B2
Smíchov *Prague* 25 B2
Smith Forest Preserve *Chicago* 9 B2
Smolny *St. Petersburg* 27 B2
Smolny Cathedral *St. Petersburg* 27 B2
Snake Creek Canal *Miami* 19 C2
Snarøya *Oslo* 23 A2
Snättringe *Stockholm* 29 B1
So Kwun Wat *Hong Kong* 12 A2
Søborg *Copenhagen* 8 A2
Sobreda *Lisbon* 16 B1
Soccer City Stadium *Johannesburg* 13 B1
Söderby *Stockholm* 29 A3
Södermalm *Stockholm* 29 B2
Sodpur *Kolkata* 14 A2
Soeurs, Î. des *Montreal* 20 B2
Sognsvatn *Oslo* 23 A3
Soignes, Forêt de *Brussels* 6 B2
Sok Kwu Wan *Hong Kong* 12 B2
Soko Is. *Hong Kong* 12 B1
Sokolniki *Moscow* 19 B3
Sokolniki Park *Moscow* 19 B3
Sokołów *Warsaw* 33 C1
Solalinden *Munich* 21 B3
Sollentuna *Stockholm* 29 A1
Solln *Munich* 21 B2
Solna *Stockholm* 29 A1
Somerset *Washington* 33 B2
Somerville *Boston* 6 A2
Sonari *Mumbai* 20 B2
Søndersø *Copenhagen* 8 A2
Songpa *Seoul* 27 B2

Sony Picture Studio Los Angeles 16 B2
Soroksár Budapest 7 B2
Soroksari Duna → Budapest 7 B2
Sosenka → Moscow 19 B3
Sosnovka St. Petersburg 27 B2
Sŏul = Seoul Seoul 27 B2
Soundview New York 22 B2
South African National Museum of Military History Johannesburg 13 A2
South Beach Miami 19 D3
South Beach New York 22 C1
South Bend Park Atlanta 3 B2
South Boston Boston 6 A2
South Decatur Atlanta 3 B3
South Deering Chicago 9 C3
South El Monte Los Angeles 16 B4
South Gate Los Angeles 16 C3
South Harbor Manila 17 B1
South Harrow London 15 A1
South Hd. Sydney 29 B2
South Hills Johannesburg 13 B2
South Holland Chicago 9 D3
South Lawn Washington 33 C2
South Miami Miami 19 D1
South Norwood London 15 B3
South of Market San Francisco 26 B2
South Ozone Park New York 22 B3
South Pasadena Los Angeles 16 B4
South Res. Boston 6 A2
South Ruislip London 15 A1
South San Francisco San Francisco 26 C2
South San Gabriel Los Angeles 16 B4
South Shore Chicago 9 C3
Southall London 15 A1
Southborough London 15 B4
Southend London 15 B3
Southern California, Univ. of Los Angeles 16 B3
Southfields London 15 B2
Southlake Dallas-Fort Worth 10 A3
Southport New Orleans 21 B2
Southwark □ London 15 B3
Southwest Museum Los Angeles 16 B3
Søvang Copenhagen 8 B3
Soweto Johannesburg 13 B1
Sowhānak Tehran 31 A3
Soya Tokyo 30 A4
Spandau Berlin 5 A1
Spånga Stockholm 29 A1
Spectacle I. Boston 6 A3
Speicher-See Munich 21 A3
Speising Vienna 32 B1
Sphinx Cairo 7 B1
Spinaceto Rome 26 C1
Spit Junction Sydney 29 A2
Spořilov Prague 25 B3
Spot Pond Boston 6 A2
Spotswood Melbourne 18 B1
Spring Valley Las Vegas 14 B1
Springeberg Berlin 5 B5
Springfield Washington 33 C1
Squantum Boston 6 B2
Srednaya Rogatka St. Petersburg 27 C2
Śródmieście Warsaw 33 B2
Staaken Berlin 5 A1
Stabekk Oslo 23 A2
Stade de France Paris 24 A3
Stadlau Vienna 32 A2
Stadshuset Stockholm 29 B2
Stains Paris 24 A3
Stamford Hill London 15 A3
Stammersdorf Vienna 32 A2
Stanley Hong Kong 12 B3
Stanley B. Hong Kong 12 B3
Stanley Pen. Hong Kong 12 B3
Stanmore London 15 A2
Stapleton New York 22 C1
Staraya Derevnya St. Petersburg 27 B1
Staré Město Prague 25 B2
Stare Miasto Warsaw 33 B2
Starke, L. Orlando 23 A1
Staten Island Zoo New York 22 C1
Staten Islands Ferry Terminal New York 22 C1
Statenice Prague 25 B1
Stavros Niarchos Cultural Centre Athens 2 B2
Steele Creek Melbourne 18 A1
Steenokkerzeel Brussels 6 A2
Steer, L. Orlando 23 B2
Steglitz Berlin 5 B2
Stephansdom Vienna 32 A2
Stepney London 15 A3
Sterling Park San Francisco 26 B2
Sticklinge udde Stockholm 29 A2
Stickney Chicago 9 C2
Stockholm Stockholm 29 B2
Stockholm Arlanda ✈ (ARN) Stockholm 29 A1
Stocksund Stockholm 29 A2
Stoclet, Palais Brussels 6 B2
Stodůlky Prague 25 B1
Stoke Newington London 15 A3
Stone Canyon Res. Los Angeles 16 B2
Stone Zoo Boston 6 A2
Stonebridge London 15 A2
Stonecutters I. Hong Kong 12 B2
Stoneham Boston 6 A2
Stony Brook Res. Boston 6 B2
Stony Creek → Chicago 9 C2
Stora Värtan Stockholm 29 A2
Store Hareskov Copenhagen 8 A2
Store Magleby Copenhagen 8 B3
Storholmen Stockholm 29 A2
Stoyka St. Petersburg 27 B2
Straiton Edinburgh 11 B3
Strandfontein Cape Town 8 B2
Strašnice Prague 25 B2
Strasstrudering Munich 21 B3
Stratford London 15 A4
Strathfield Sydney 29 B1
Streatham London 15 B3
Streatham Vale London 15 B3
Strebersdorf Vienna 32 A2
Střešovice Prague 25 B2
Strip, The Las Vegas 14 B2
Střížkov Prague 25 B2
Stromovka Prague 25 B2
Strombeek-Bever Brussels 6 A2
Studio City Los Angeles 16 B2
Stureby Stockholm 29 B2
Stuvsta Stockholm 29 B2
Subhepur Delhi 10 A2
Suburban Canal New Orleans 21 B1
Sucat Manila 17 C2
Suchdol Prague 25 B2
Sucy-en-Brie Paris 24 B4
Sue, L. Orlando 23 A2
Sugamo Tokyo 30 A3
Sugar Loaf Mt. = Açúcar, Pão de Rio de Janeiro 25 B2
Suge Tokyo 30 B2
Suginami Tokyo 30 A2
Sugō Tokyo 30 B2
Sui Sai Wan Hong Kong 12 B3
Suita Osaka 23 A2
Suitland Washington 33 B3
Sukchar Kolkata 14 A2
Sulphur Channel Hong Kong 12 B2
Sultanahme Camil Istanbul 12 B1
Sumida Tokyo 30 A3
Sumida → Tokyo 30 A3
Sumiyoshi Osaka 23 B2
Sumiyoshi Shrine Osaka 23 B1
Summerville Toronto 31 B1
Summit Chicago 9 C2
Sunamachi Tokyo 30 A4
Sunbury-on-Thames London 15 B1
Sundbyberg Stockholm 29 A1
Sundbyerne Copenhagen 8 B3
Sungei Kadut Industrial Estate Singapore 28 A2
Sungei Selatar Res. Singapore 28 A3
Sunny Bay Hong Kong 12 B1
Sunny Isles Beach Miami 19 C3
Sunrise Miami 19 B2
Sunrise Manor Las Vegas 14 A2
Sunrise Mountain Natural Area ⌓ Las Vegas 14 A2
Sunset Park Las Vegas 14 B2
Sunset Park New York 22 C2
Sunset Peak Hong Kong 12 B1
Sunshine I. Hong Kong 12 B1
Sunshine Park Miami 19 B2
Sunter Jakarta 12 A2
Sunter, Kali → Jakarta 12 B2
Suomenlinna Helsinki 11 C2
Sur Bahr Jerusalem 13 B2
Sura Kolkata 14 B2
Suraksan Seoul 27 A2
Surbiton London 15 B2
Suresnes Paris 24 A2
Surfside Miami 19 C3
Surquillo Lima 14 B2
Surrey Hills Sydney 29 B2
Surulere Lagos 14 B2
Susaek Seoul 27 B1
Süssenbrunn Vienna 32 A2
Sutton London 15 B2
Suyu Seoul 27 B2
Suzukishinden Tokyo 30 A2
Svanemøllen Copenhagen 8 A3
Sveaborg = Suomenlinna Helsinki 11 C2
Sverdlov Moscow 19 B2
Svestad Oslo 23 B2
Svinö Helsinki 11 C1
Swanley London 15 B4
Swansea Toronto 31 B2
Swinburne I. New York 22 C1
Sydenham Johannesburg 13 A2
Sydney Sydney 29 B2
Sydney, Univ. of Sydney 29 B2
Sydney Harbour △ Sydney 29 B2
Sydney Harbour Bridge Sydney 29 B2
Sydney Kingsford Smith ✈ (SYD) Sydney 29 B2
Sydstranden Copenhagen 8 B3
Sylvania Sydney 29 C1
Syon Park London 15 B2
Szczęśliwice Warsaw 33 B1
Széchenyi-hegy Budapest 7 B1
Széphalom Budapest 7 A1

T

Taastrup Copenhagen 8 B1
Tabata Tokyo 30 A3
Tablada Buenos Aires 7 C1
Table B. Cape Town 8 A1
Table Mountain △ Cape Town 8 A1
Table Mt. Cape Town 8 A1
Taboão da Serra São Paulo 27 B1
Täby Stockholm 29 A2
Tacuba Mexico City 18 B1
Tacubaya Mexico City 18 B1
Tafelbaai = Table B. Cape Town 8 A1
Taft Orlando 23 B2
Tagig → Manila 17 B2
Taguig Manila 17 B2
Tahrir Square Cairo 7 A2
Tai Ho Hong Kong 12 B1
Tai Lam Chung Res. Hong Kong 12 A2
Tai Lam Country Park ⌓ Hong Kong 12 A2
Tai Lo Shan Hong Kong 12 A3
Tai Long Wan Tsuen Hong Kong 12 B1
Tai Mo Shan Hong Kong 12 A2
Tai O Hong Kong 12 B1
Tai Po Tsai Hong Kong 12 A3
Tai Seng Singapore 28 A3
Tai Shui Hang Hong Kong 12 A3
Tai Tam B. Hong Kong 12 B3
Tai Tam Country Park ⌓ Hong Kong 12 B3
Tai Tam Tuk Res. Hong Kong 12 B3
Tai Wai Hong Kong 12 A3
Tai Wan Tau Hong Kong 12 B3
Tai Wo Hau Hong Kong 12 A2
Tai Yue Shan = Lantau I. Hong Kong 12 B1
Tainaka Osaka 23 B2
Taishō Osaka 23 B1
Tajrīsh Tehran 31 A2
Takaido Tokyo 30 A2
Takaishi Tokyo 30 B2
Takarazuka Osaka 23 A1
Takasago Tokyo 30 A4
Takatsu Tokyo 30 B2
Takeshita Tokyo 30 B2
Takinegawa Tokyo 30 A3
Takoma Park Washington 33 B2
Taksim Istanbul 12 B1
Talaide Lisbon 16 A1
Taliganga Kolkata 14 B2
Talipapa Manila 17 A2
Tallkrogen Stockholm 29 B2
Tama Tokyo 30 B1
Tama → Tokyo 30 B2
Tama Kyūryō Tokyo 30 B2
Tamaden Tokyo 30 B2
Tamagawa-josui → Tokyo 30 A1
Taman Sari Jakarta 12 A1
Tamanduateí → São Paulo 27 B2
Tamarac Miami 19 A1
Tamboerskloof Cape Town 8 A1
Tambora Jakarta 12 A1
Tammisalo Helsinki 11 B3
Tammûh Cairo 7 B2
Tampines Singapore 28 A3
Tanah Abang Jakarta 12 B1
Tanah Kusir Jakarta 12 B1
Tangelo Park Orlando 23 B2
Tanjung Duren Jakarta 12 B1
Tanjung Priok Jakarta 12 A2
Tanum Oslo 23 A1
Tap Shek Kok Hong Kong 12 A1
Tapada Lisbon 16 A1
Tapanila Helsinki 11 B3
Tapiales Buenos Aires 7 C1
Tapiola Helsinki 11 B1
Tapsia Kolkata 14 B2
Tara Mumbai 20 A1
Tarabya Istanbul 12 B2
Tårbæk Copenhagen 8 A3
Tarchomin Warsaw 33 B1
Tardeo Mumbai 20 B1
Targówek Warsaw 33 B2
Tårnby Copenhagen 8 B3
Tarqua Bay Lagos 14 B2
Tathong Channel Hong Kong 12 B3
Tathong Pt. Hong Kong 12 B3
Tatuapé São Paulo 27 B2
Taufkirchen Munich 21 B2
Tavares, I. dos Rio de Janeiro 25 A2
Tavros Athens 2 B2
Teaneck New York 22 A1
Tebet Jakarta 12 B2
Tecamachalco Mexico City 18 B1
Ted Williams Tunnel Boston 6 A2
Teddington London 15 B1
Tegel Berlin 5 A2
Tegel, Berlin ✈ (TXL) Berlin 5 A2
Tegeler See Berlin 5 A2
Tegelort Berlin 5 A2
Teheran = Tehrān Tehran 31 A2
Tehrān Tehran 31 A2
Tehrān Mehrābād ✈ (THR) Tehran 31 A1
Tehrān Pārs Tehran 31 A3
Tei Tong Tsui Hong Kong 12 B3
Tejo, Rio → Lisbon 16 A2
Tekstilyshchik Moscow 19 B3
Telhal Lisbon 16 A1
Telok Blangah Singapore 28 B2
Teltow Berlin 5 B2
Teltow kanal Berlin 5 B3
Tempelhof Berlin 5 B3
Temple City Los Angeles 16 B4
Temple Hills Washington 33 C3
Temple of Heaven Beijing 4 B2
Temppeliaukio Church Helsinki 11 B2
Tenafly New York 22 A2
Tenayuca, Piramide de Mexico City 18 A1
Tengah → Singapore 28 A2
Tennoji Osaka 23 B2
Tepalcates Mexico City 18 B2
Tepeyac △ Mexico City 18 B2
Terrazzano Milan 18 A1
Terre des Hommes Montreal 20 A2
Terrugem Lisbon 16 A1
Terrytown New Orleans 21 B2
Tervuren Brussels 6 B3
Tervuren, Park van Brussels 6 B3
Tetuán Madrid 17 B1
Teufelsberg Berlin 5 B2
Thalkirchen Munich 21 B2
Thames Ditton London 15 B1
Thamesmead London 15 A4
Thana Cr. → Mumbai 20 A2
Thiais Paris 24 B3
Thisio Athens 2 B2
Thistletown Toronto 31 A1
Thomastown Melbourne 18 A2
Thompson I. Boston 6 B3
Thon Buri Bangkok 3 B1
Thornbury Melbourne 18 A2
Thorncliffe Toronto 31 A2
Thornhill Toronto 31 A2
Thornton Cape Town 8 A2
Thornton Heath London 15 B3
Three Fathoms Cove Hong Kong 12 A3
Threipmuir Res. Edinburgh 11 B2
Throg's Neck New York 22 B3
Tian Tan Buddha = Big Buddha Hong Kong 12 B1
Tiancun Beijing 4 B1
Tianhe Guangzhou 11 B2
Tibet, L. Orlando 23 B1
Tibidabo Barcelona 4 A1
Tiburon San Francisco 26 A2
Tiburtino Rome 26 B2
Ticomán Mexico City 18 A2
Tiefersee Berlin 5 B1
Tiergarten Berlin 5 A3
Tijgerhof Cape Town 8 A2
Tijuca Rio de Janeiro 25 B1
Tijuca, Pico da Rio de Janeiro 25 B1
Tijuca △ Rio de Janeiro 25 B1
Tikkurila Helsinki 11 B3
Tilak Nagar Delhi 10 B1
Tilanqiao Shanghai 28 B1
Timah, Bukit Singapore 28 A2
Timiryazev Park Moscow 19 B2
Tin Can I. Lagos 14 B2
Ting Kau Hong Kong 12 A2
Tira Jerusalem 13 A1
Tirsa Cairo 7 B2
Tishrīyaa Baghdad 3 B2
Tiu Keng Leng Hong Kong 12 B3
Tizapán Mexico City 18 C1
Tlalnepantla → Mexico City 18 A1
Tlalpan Mexico City 18 C2
To Kwa Wan Hong Kong 12 B3
Toa Payoh Singapore 28 A3
Točná Prague 25 C2
Toco Hills Atlanta 3 B2
Todt Hill New York 22 C1
Tōkagi Tokyo 30 A4
Tokai Plantation Cape Town 8 B1
Tōkaichiba Tokyo 30 B2
Tōkyō Tokyo 30 B3
Tōkyō B. = Tōkyō-Wan Tokyo 30 B4
Tōkyō Haneda ✈ (HND) Tokyo 30 B3
Tōkyō Harbour Tokyo 30 B3
Tōkyō Sky Tree Tokyo 30 A3
Tōkyō-Wan Tokyo 30 B4
Tollygunge = Taliganga Kolkata 14 B2
Tolo Harbour Hong Kong 12 A3
Tolworth London 15 B2
Tomba di Nerone Rome 26 B1
Tommy Thompson Park Toronto 31 B3
Tondo Manila 17 B1
Tong Fuk Hong Kong 12 B1
Tongbinggo Seoul 27 B1
Tongqiao Shanghai 28 A1
Toorak Melbourne 18 B2
Topanga State Park ⌓ Los Angeles 16 B1
Topkapı Istanbul 12 B1
Topkapı Palace Istanbul 12 B1
Tor di Quinto Rome 26 B1
Tor Pignattara Rome 26 B2
Tor Sapienza Rome 26 B2
Torcy Paris 24 A4
Toronto Toronto 31 B2
Toronto, Univ. of Toronto 31 B2
Toronto City Centre ✈ (YTZ) Toronto 31 B2
Toronto Harbour Toronto 31 B2
Toronto I. Toronto 31 B2
Toronto Lester B. Pearson Int. ✈ (YYZ) Toronto 31 A1
Torre Lupara Rome 26 B2
Torre Nova Rome 26 B2
Torrellas → Barcelona 4 A1
Torrevécchia Rome 26 B1
Toshima Tokyo 30 A3
Toshimaen Tokyo 30 A2
Tottenham London 15 A3
Tottenham Melbourne 18 A1
Toussus-le-Noble Paris 24 B1
Toussus-le-Noble ✈ (TNF) Paris 24 B1
Towchāl Cable Car Tehran 31 A2
Tower Hamlets □ London 15 A3
Tower of London London 15 A3
Towra Pt. Sydney 29 C2
Tøyen Oslo 23 A3
Toyonaka Osaka 23 A1
Trafaria Lisbon 16 A1
Traição, Cor. → São Paulo 27 B2
Trangegilde Copenhagen 8 B2
Trångsund Stockholm 29 B2
Trappenfelde Berlin 5 A4
Trastévere Rome 26 B1
Treasure I. San Francisco 26 B2
Třeboradice Prague 25 B3
Třebotov Prague 25 C1
Tree Tops Park Miami 19 B1
Tremblay-en-France Paris 24 A4
Tremembe → São Paulo 27 A2
Tremont New York 22 A2
Trenno Milan 18 B1
Treptow Berlin 5 B3
Três Rios, Sa. dos Rio de Janeiro 25 B1
Trevi, Fontana di Rome 26 B1
Trezzano sul Naviglio Milan 18 B1
Trieste Rome 26 B2
Trinidad Washington 33 B3
Trinity Edinburgh 11 B2
Trinity River Greenbelt Park Dallas-Fort Worth 10 B4
Trionfale Rome 26 B1
Triulzo Milan 18 B2
Troja Prague 25 B2
Trollbäcken Stockholm 29 B3
Trombay Mumbai 20 A2
Troparevo Moscow 19 C1
Trudeau Int., Montréal ✈ (YUL) Montreal 20 B1
Trudyashchikhsya, Ostrov St. Petersburg 27 B1
Tryvasshøgda Oslo 23 A3
Tseng Lan Shue Hong Kong 12 B3
Tseung Kwan Hong Kong 12 B3
Tsim Sha Tsui Hong Kong 12 B3
Tsing Lung Tau Hong Kong 12 A2
Tsing Yi Hong Kong 12 A2
Tsova Jerusalem 13 B1
Tsuen Wan Hong Kong 12 A2
Tsur Hadassa Jerusalem 13 B1
Tsurumi → Tokyo 30 B3
Tsz Wan Shan Hong Kong 12 A3
Tuas Singapore 28 B1
Tuchoměřice Prague 25 B1
Tuckahoe New York 22 A3
Tucuruvi São Paulo 27 A2
Tuen Mun Hong Kong 12 A1
Tufello Rome 26 B2
Tufnell Park London 15 A3
Tufts Univ. Boston 6 A2
Tughlakabad Delhi 10 B2
Tullamarine Melbourne 18 A1
Tulse Hill London 15 B3
Tung Chung Hong Kong 12 B1
Tung Lung Chau Hong Kong 12 B3
Tung O Hong Kong 12 B2
Tunis Baghdad 3 A2
Tuomarila Helsinki 11 B1
Tureberg Stockholm 29 A1
Turffontein Johannesburg 13 B2
Türk Telekom Arena Istanbul 12 B1
Turkey L. Orlando 23 A2
Turkey Lake Park Orlando 23 A2
Turner Field Atlanta 3 B2
Turnham Green London 15 B2
Turnhouse Edinburgh 11 B1
Tuscolana, Via Rome 26 B2
Twelve Apostles Cape Town 8 A1
Twentieth Century Fox Studios Los Angeles 16 B2
Twickenham London 15 B1
Twickenham Rugby Ground London 15 B1
Twin Peaks San Francisco 26 B2
Twins, The Hong Kong 12 B3

U

U.S. Capitol Washington 33 B2
U.S. Cellular Field Chicago 9 C3
Ubeidiya Jerusalem 13 B2
Uberaba → São Paulo 27 B2
Ubin, Pulau Singapore 28 A3
Uccle Brussels 6 B2
Udelnaya St. Petersburg 27 A2
Udelnoe St. Petersburg 27 B1
Udlding Munich 21 A1
Ueno Tokyo 30 A3
Úholičky Prague 25 B1
Uhříněves Prague 25 B3
Uithoorn Amsterdam 2 B1
Ujazdów Warsaw 33 B2
Újpalota Budapest 7 A2
Újpest Budapest 7 A2
Ukita Tokyo 30 A4
Uleta Miami 19 C2
Ullerup Copenhagen 8 B3
Ullevål Oslo 23 A3
Ulriksdal Stockholm 29 A1
Ulyanka St. Petersburg 27 B1
Um Al Khanazir I. Baghdad 3 B2
Umeda Osaka 23 A1
Umm al Sheif Dubai 9 B1
Umm Suqeim Dubai 9 B1
Ümraniye Istanbul 12 B2
Underground Atlanta Atlanta 3 B2
Underhill, L. Orlando 23 A3
Unětický potok → Prague 25 B2
Unhos Lisbon 16 A2
Unidad Santa Fe Mexico City 18 B1
Union City New York 22 B1
Union Port New York 22 B2
Union Square Hong Kong 12 B2
Union Station Toronto 31 B2
United Center Chicago 9 B2
United Nations Headquarters New York 22 B2
Universal Studios Los Angeles 16 B2
Universal Studios Orlando 23 B2
Universidad Madrid 17 B1
University Park Dallas-Fort Worth 10 A5
University Park Washington 33 B3
Unterbiberg Munich 21 B2
Unterföhring Munich 21 A3
Unterhaching Munich 21 B2
Unterlaa Vienna 32 B2
Untermenzing Munich 21 A1
Upper B. New York 22 C1
Upper Elmers End London 15 B3
Upper New York B. = Upper B. New York 22 C1
Upper Norwood London 15 B3
Upper Peirce Res. Singapore 28 A2
Upper Sydenham London 15 B3
Upper Tooting London 15 B3
Upton London 15 A4
Uptown Chicago 9 B2
Uran Mumbai 20 B2
Urayasu Tokyo 30 B4
Urbe ✈ Rome 26 B2
Urca Rio de Janeiro 25 B2
Uritsk St. Petersburg 27 C1
Urmston Road Hong Kong 12 A1
Üröm Budapest 7 A2
Ursus Warsaw 33 B1
Ursvik Stockholm 29 A1
Usera Madrid 17 B1
Ushigome Tokyo 30 A3
Usina Rio de Janeiro 25 B1
Üsküdar Istanbul 12 B2
Ust-Slavyanka St. Petersburg 27 C3
Uteke Stockholm 29 A3
Utrata Warsaw 33 B2
Uttarpara Kolkata 14 B1
Utterslev Mose Copenhagen 8 A2

V

Vaclavské náměstí Prague 25 B2
Vadaul Mumbai 20 A2
Vaires-sur-Marne Paris 24 A4
Valby Copenhagen 8 B2
Valcannuta Rome 26 B1
Valdelatas Madrid 17 A1
Valenton Paris 24 B3
Valera Milan 18 A1
Vallcarca Barcelona 4 A1
Valldoreix Barcelona 4 A1
Vallecas Madrid 17 B2
Vallecas, Cumbres de Madrid 17 B2
Vallensbæk Copenhagen 8 B2
Vallensbæk Strand Copenhagen 8 B2
Vallentunasjön Stockholm 29 A2
Valleranello Rome 26 C1
Vallisaari Helsinki 11 C3
Vallvidrera Barcelona 4 A1
Valvidrera → Barcelona 4 A1
Van Gogh Museum Amsterdam 2 A2
Vanak Tehran 31 A2
Vanda = Vantaa Helsinki 11 B2
Vangede Copenhagen 8 A3
Vaniköy Istanbul 12 B2
Vanløse Copenhagen 8 A2
Vantaa Helsinki 11 B2
Vantaankoski Helsinki 11 B2
Vantaanpuisto Helsinki 11 B2
Vanves Paris 24 B2
Varedo Milan 18 A1
Varkiza Athens 2 C2
Vartiokylä Helsinki 11 B3
Vartiosaari Helsinki 11 B3
Vasamuseet Stockholm 29 B2
Vasco Cape Town 8 A2
Vasfenārd Tehran 31 B2
Vashi Mumbai 20 A2
Vasilyevskiy, Ostrov St. Petersburg 27 B1
Vatican City ■ Rome 26 B1
Vaucluse Sydney 29 B2
Vaucluse House Sydney 29 B2
Vaucresson Paris 24 A2
Vaughan Toronto 31 A1
Vauhallan Paris 24 B2
Vaujours Paris 24 A4
Vauxhall London 15 B3
Vecsés Budapest 7 B3
Veleň Prague 25 A3
Veleslavín Prague 25 B2
Vélizy-Villacoublay Paris 24 B2
Velka-Chuchle Prague 25 B2
Velké Přílepy Prague 25 A1
Venda Seca Lisbon 16 A1
Venetian Islands Miami 19 D3
Venice Los Angeles 16 C2
Ventas Madrid 17 B1
Ventorro del Cano Madrid 17 B1
Venustiano Carranza Mexico City 18 B2
Verde → São Paulo 27 A1
Verdugo Mts. Los Angeles 16 A2
Verdun Montreal 20 B2
Vérhalom Budapest 7 A2
Vermelho → São Paulo 27 B1
Vermont Knolls Los Angeles 16 C3
Vernon Los Angeles 16 B3
Verrières-le-Buisson Paris 24 B2
Versailles Buenos Aires 7 B1
Versailles Paris 24 B1
Veshnyaki Moscow 19 B3
Vesolyy Posolok St. Petersburg 27 B2
Vestra Helsinki 11 B1
Vestskoven Copenhagen 8 A2
Vicálvaro Madrid 17 B2
Vicente Lopez Buenos Aires 7 B2
Victoria Hong Kong 12 B2
Victoria, Pont Montreal 20 B2
Victoria and Alfred Waterfront Cape Town 8 A1
Victoria Gardens Mumbai 20 B2
Victoria Harbour Hong Kong 12 B3
Victoria Island Lagos 14 B2
Victoria, L. Johannesburg 13 B2
Victoria Lawn Tennis Courts Melbourne 18 B2
Victoria Park Singapore 28 B2
Victoria Peak Hong Kong 12 B2
Victoria Terminus = Chhatrapati Shivaji Terminus Mumbai 20 B2
Victoria Village Toronto 31 A3
Vienna = Wien Vienna 32 A2
Vietnam Veterans Memorial Washington 33 B2
Vieux Carré = French Quarter New Orleans 21 B2
View Park Los Angeles 16 B3
Vigário Geral Rio de Janeiro 25 A1
Vigentino Milan 18 B2
Viggbyholm Stockholm 29 A2
Vighignolo Milan 18 B1
Viikki Helsinki 11 B3
Vikhroli Mumbai 20 A2
Vila Guilherme São Paulo 27 B2
Vila Isabel Rio de Janeiro 25 B1
Vila Jaguára São Paulo 27 B1
Vila Madalena São Paulo 27 B1
Vila Maria São Paulo 27 B2
Vila Mariana São Paulo 27 B2
Vila Prudente São Paulo 27 B2
Viladecans Barcelona 4 B1
Vile Parle Mumbai 20 A2
Villa Adelina Buenos Aires 7 B1
Villa Ballester Buenos Aires 7 B1
Villa Barilari Buenos Aires 7 C2
Villa Bosch Buenos Aires 7 B1
Villa C. Colon Buenos Aires 7 C2
Villa Ciudadela Buenos Aires 7 B1
Villa de Guadalupe Mexico City 18 B2
Villa Devoto Buenos Aires 7 B1
Villa Diamante Buenos Aires 7 C2
Villa Dominico Buenos Aires 7 C3
Villa Lugano Buenos Aires 7 C2
Villa Lynch Buenos Aires 7 B1
Villa Madero Buenos Aires 7 C1
Villa Sáenz Peña Buenos Aires 7 B1
Villa Urquiza Buenos Aires 7 B2
Villaverde Madrid 17 B1
Villaverde Bajo Madrid 17 B1
Ville-d'Avray Paris 24 B2
Villecresnes Paris 24 B4
Villejuif Paris 24 B3
Villemomble Paris 24 A4
Villeneuve-la-Garenne Paris 24 A2
Villeneuve-le-Roi Paris 24 B3
Villeneuve-St-Georges Paris 24 B3
Villeparisis Paris 24 A4
Villevaudé Paris 24 A4
Villiers-le-Bâcle Paris 24 B1
Villiers-sur-Marne Paris 24 B4
Villinki Helsinki 11 C3
Villoresi, Canale Milan 18 A1
Vilvoorde Brussels 6 A2
Vimodrone Milan 18 A2
Vimont Montreal 20 A1
Vincennes Paris 24 A3
Vincennes, Bois de Paris 24 B3
Vineland Orlando 23 B1
Vinings Atlanta 3 A2
Vinohrady Prague 25 B2
Vinoř Prague 25 B3
Violet Hill Hong Kong 12 B3
Virányos Budapest 7 A1
Virginia, L. Orlando 23 A2
Virginia Gardens Miami 19 D1
Virginia Key Miami 19 D3
Viroflay Paris 24 B2
Vironas Athens 2 B2
Virum Copenhagen 8 A2
Visitacion Valley San Francisco 26 B2
Vista Alegre Lima 14 B3
Vista Alegre Santiago 27 C1
Vista Grove Atlanta 3 A3
Vitacura Santiago 27 B2
Vitinia Rome 26 C1
Vitry-sur-Seine Paris 24 B3
Vladykino Moscow 19 A2
Vokovice Prague 25 B2
Vogelsdorf Berlin 5 B5
Volkhonka-Zil Moscow 19 C2
Vollen Oslo 23 B1
Volodarskoye St. Petersburg 27 B2
Volynkina-Derevnya St. Petersburg 27 B1
Vondelpark Amsterdam 2 A2
Vösendorf Vienna 32 B2
Voula Athens 2 C2
Vouliagmeni Athens 2 C2
Vredehoek Cape Town 8 A1
Vršovice Prague 25 B2
Vyborgskaya Storona St. Petersburg 27 B2
Vykhino Moscow 19 B3
Vyšehrad Prague 25 B2

W

Wachterhof Munich 21 B3
Wadala Mumbai 20 A2
Wadi al-Arayis Jerusalem 13 B2
Wadi Fukin Jerusalem 13 B1
Waduk Pluit Jakarta 12 A1
Waggaman New Orleans 21 B1
Wah Fu Hong Kong 12 B2
Wahda Baghdad 3 B2
Währing Vienna 32 A2
Waidmannslust Berlin 5 A3
Wakefield Boston 6 A2
Waldesruh Berlin 5 B4
Waldperlach Munich 21 B3
Waldtrudering Munich 21 B3
Wall Street New York 22 B1
Walt Disney World Resort Orlando 23 B1
Waltham Boston 6 A1
Waltham Forest □ London 15 A3
Walthamstow London 15 A3
Walton-on-Thames London 15 B1
Wambeek Brussels 6 A3
Wan Chai Hong Kong 12 B3
Wandle → London 15 B2
Wandsworth □ London 15 B2
Wangjing Beijing 4 B2
Wannsee Berlin 5 B1
Wansdorf Berlin 5 A1
Wanstead London 15 A4
Wapping London 15 A3
Wards I. New York 22 B2
Warnberg Munich 21 B2
Warner Brothers Studios Los Angeles 16 B2
Warrāq el 'Arab Cairo 7 A2
Warringal Park Melbourne 18 A2
Warriston Edinburgh 11 B2
Warsaw = Warszawa Warsaw 33 B2
Warsaw Chopin ✈ (WAW) Warsaw 33 B1
Warszawa Warsaw 33 B2
Wartenberg Berlin 5 A4
Washington Washington 33 B2
Washington Heights New York 22 A2
Washington Park Chicago 9 C3
Washington Ronald Reagan Nat. ✈ (DCA) Washington 33 B2
Wat Pho Bangkok 3 B1
Watauga Dallas-Fort Worth 10 A2
Water of Leith → Edinburgh 11 B1
Watergraafsmeer Amsterdam 2 A2
Waterland Amsterdam 2 A2
Waterloo Brussels 6 B2
Watermael-Boitsfort Brussels 6 B2
Watertown Boston 6 A1
Watsonia Melbourne 18 A2
Watts Los Angeles 16 C3
Waverley Boston 6 A1
Waverley Johannesburg 13 A2
Waverley Sydney 29 B2
Wawer Warsaw 33 B2
Wawrzyszew Warsaw 33 B1
Wazirabad Delhi 10 A2
Wazīriya Baghdad 3 A2
Wazirpur Delhi 10 A2
Wealdstone London 15 A1
Wedding Berlin 5 A3
Weehawken New York 22 B1
Weesp Amsterdam 2 B3
Weidling Vienna 32 A1
Weidlingbach Vienna 32 A1
Weissensee Berlin 5 A3
Wellesley Hills Boston 6 B1
Welling London 15 B4
Wellington Boston 6 A2
Weltevreden Park Johannesburg 13 A1
Wembley London 15 A2
Wemmel Brussels 6 A1
Wemmer Pan Johannesburg 13 B2
Wenceslas Square = Vaclavské náměstí Prague 25 B2
Wendenschloss Berlin 5 B4
Wennington London 15 A5
Werneuchen Berlin 5 A5
West Don → Toronto 31 A2
West Drayton London 15 A1
West Ham London 15 A4
West Harrow London 15 A1
West Heath London 15 B4
West Hill Toronto 31 A3
West Hollywood Los Angeles 16 B2
West Lamma Channel Hong Kong 12 B2
West Los Angeles, Univ. of Los Angeles 16 C2
West Medford Boston 6 A2
West Miami Miami 19 D1
West Molesey London 15 B1
West New York New York 22 B1
West of Twin Peaks San Francisco 26 B2
West Park Johannesburg 13 A1
West Park Miami 19 C2
West Rouge Toronto 31 A4
West Roxbury Boston 6 B2
West Town Chicago 9 B2
West Wharf Karachi 13 B1
Westchester Los Angeles 16 C2
Westchester New York 22 A2
Westcliff Johannesburg 13 B2
Westdene Johannesburg 13 B1
Westend Helsinki 11 C1
Wester Hailes Edinburgh 11 B2
Westerham Munich 21 B2
Western Addition San Francisco 26 B2
Westgate New Orleans 21 A1
Westgate Washington 33 B2
Westlake Cape Town 8 B1
Westlake Los Angeles 16 B3
Westlake San Francisco 26 B2
Westminster London 15 A3
Westmount Montreal 20 B2
Weston Toronto 31 A1
Westwego New Orleans 21 B2
Westwood Village Los Angeles 16 B2
Westzaan Amsterdam 2 A1
Wetton Cape Town 8 B2
Wexford Toronto 31 A3
Weybridge London 15 B1
Wezembeek-Oppem Brussels 6 A2
White Cloud Hill = Baiyun Mountain Scenic Area ⌓ Guangzhou 11 A2
White House, The Washington 33 B2
White Rock L. Dallas-Fort Worth 10 A5
Whitechapel London 15 A3
Whitney Las Vegas 14 B2
Whittier Los Angeles 16 C4
Whittier Narrows Recreation Area ⌓ Los Angeles 16 B4
Whitton London 15 B1
Wieden Vienna 32 A2
Wien Vienna 32 A2
Wien-Schwechat ✈ (VIE) Vienna 32 B3
Wienerberg Vienna 32 B2
Wierzbno Warsaw 33 B2
Wijde Wormer Amsterdam 2 A2
Wilanów Warsaw 33 B2
Wilanówka → Warsaw 33 C2
Wilds, The Johannesburg 13 B2
Wilhelmshagen Berlin 5 B5
Wilket Creek Park Toronto 31 A2
Wilkieston Edinburgh 11 B1
Will Rogers State Historical Park ⌓ Los Angeles 16 B1
Willesden London 15 A2
Willesden Green London 15 A2
Williamsbridge New York 22 A2
Williamsburg New York 22 B2
Williamsburg Orlando 23 B2
Williamstown Melbourne 18 B1
Willis, L. Orlando 23 B2
Willoughby Sydney 29 A2
Willowdale New Orleans 21 A1
Willowdale Toronto 31 A2
Wilmer Dallas-Fort Worth 10 C5
Wilmersdorf Berlin 5 B2
Wilmette Chicago 9 A2
Wilmington London 15 B5
Wilton Manors Miami 19 B3
Wimbledon London 15 B2
Wimbledon Common London 15 B2
Wimbledon Park London 15 B2
Wimbledon Tennis Ground London 15 B2
Winchester Boston 6 A2
Winchester Las Vegas 14 B2
Windermere Cape Town 8 A2
Windermere Orlando 23 B1
Windsor Johannesburg 13 A1
Windsor, Gare Montreal 20 B2
Windsor Hills Los Angeles 16 C2
Winnetka Chicago 9 A2
Winning Munich 21 B2
Wissous Paris 24 B3
Wittenau Berlin 5 A2
Witwatersrand, Univ. of Johannesburg 13 B2
Włochy Warsaw 33 B1
Wo Mei Hong Kong 12 A3
Wo Yi Hop Hong Kong 12 A2
Woburn Boston 6 A2
Woburn Toronto 31 A3
Wola Warsaw 33 B1
Wolica Warsaw 33 C1
Wollaston Boston 6 B2
Woltersdorf Berlin 5 B5
Woluwe-St-Lambert Brussels 6 A2
Woluwe-St-Pierre Brussels 6 A2
Wong Chuk Hang Hong Kong 12 B3
Wong Chuk Wan Hong Kong 12 A3
Wong Chuk Yeung Hong Kong 12 A3
Wood Green London 15 A3
Wood Ridge New York 22 A1
Woodbine Race Track Toronto 31 A1
Woodbridge Toronto 31 A1
Woodford London 15 A4
Woodford Bridge London 15 A4
Woodford Green London 15 A4
Woodhaven New York 22 B2
Woodhouselee Edinburgh 11 B2
Woodlands Singapore 28 A2
Woodmont Washington 33 B2
Woodside London 15 B3
Woodside New York 22 B2
Woodstock Cape Town 8 A1
Woollahra Sydney 29 B2
Woolooware B. Sydney 29 C1
Woolwich London 15 B4
Worker's Stadium Beijing 4 B2
World Financial Centre Shanghai 28 B2
Worli Mumbai 20 A1
Worth Chicago 9 C2
Wren's Nest Atlanta 3 B2
Wrigley Field Chicago 9 B3
Wuhlgarten Berlin 5 A4
Wujiaochang Shanghai 28 B2
Würm → Munich 21 B1
Würm-kanal Munich 21 A1
Wushan Guangzhou 11 B3
Wusong Shanghai 28 A1
Wyczółki Warsaw 33 C1
Wygoda Warsaw 33 B2
Wynberg Cape Town 8 B1

X

Xabregas Lisbon 16 A2
Xiakeng Guangzhou 11 A2
Xiaogang Park Guangzhou 11 B2
Xiaoping Guangzhou 11 A2
Xiashachong Guangzhou 11 B1
Xichang Guangzhou 11 B2
Xicheng Beijing 4 B1
Xidan Beijing 4 B2
Xi'ercun Guangzhou 11 B2
Xincun Guangzhou 11 B2
Xizhimen Beijing 4 B1
Xochimilco, Parque Ecológico Mexico City 18 C2
Xuanwu Beijing 4 B1
Xuhui Shanghai 28 B1
Xujiahui Shanghai 28 B1

Y

Yaba Lagos 14 A2
Yaftābād Tehran 31 B1
Yahara Tokyo 30 A2
Yaho Tokyo 30 A1
Yakire Tokyo 30 A4
Yaksu Seoul 27 B2
Yamada Osaka 23 A2
Yamada Tokyo 30 B2
Yamato → Osaka 23 B1
Yan Kit Singapore 28 A3
Yanbu Guangzhou 11 B1
Yangcheon Seoul 27 B1
Yanghuayuan Beijing 4 C1
Yangjae Seoul 27 C2
Yangjiazhuang Shanghai 28 A1
Yangjing Shanghai 28 B2
Yangpu Shanghai 28 B2
Yangpu Park Shanghai 28 B2
Yannawa Bangkok 3 B2
Yaotai Guangzhou 11 B2
Yarmūk Baghdad 3 B1
Yarra Bend Park Melbourne 18 A2
Yarraville Melbourne 18 A1
Yauza → Moscow 19 B4
Yeading London 15 A1
Yedikule Istanbul 12 B1
Yenikapı Istanbul 12 B1
Yeniköy Istanbul 12 B2
Yeongdeungpo Seoul 27 B1
Yeongdong Seoul 27 B2
Yeouido Seoul 27 B1
Yerba Buena I. San Francisco 26 B2
Yerres Paris 24 B4
Yerushalayim = Jerusalem Jerusalem 13 B2
Yi O San Tsuen Hong Kong 12 B1
Yiheyuan Beijing 4 B1
Yıldız Park Istanbul 12 B2
Yinhangzhen Shanghai 28 A2
Yishun Singapore 28 A3
Ylästö Helsinki 11 B2
Yodo → Osaka 23 A2
Yongdingmen Beijing 4 B2
Yongfucun Guangzhou 11 B2
Yongsan Seoul 27 B1
Yonkers New York 22 A2
York Toronto 31 A2
York Mills Toronto 31 A2
York Univ. Toronto 31 A1
You'anmen Beijing 4 B1
Youngsfield Cape Town 8 B1
Yuancun Guangzhou 11 B3
Yuanmingyuan Park Beijing 4 A1
Yuanxiatian Guangzhou 11 A2
Yuexiu Guangzhou 11 B2
Yuexiu Park Guangzhou 11 B2
Yugo-Zarad Moscow 19 B2
Yung Shue Wan Hong Kong 12 B2
Yūsofābād Tehran 31 A2

Z

Za'abeel Dubai 9 B2
Zaandam Amsterdam 2 A1
Zaandijk Amsterdam 2 A1
Zaanstad Amsterdam 2 A1
Záběhlice Prague 25 B2
Ząbki Warsaw 33 B2
Żacisze Warsaw 33 B2
Zahrā Baghdad 3 A1
Žalov Prague 25 A2
Załuski Warsaw 33 C1
Zamdorf Munich 21 B2
Zanevka St. Petersburg 27 B3
Zapote Manila 17 C1
Zaventem Brussels 6 A2
Zawady Warsaw 33 B2
Zāwiyet Abū Musallam Cairo 7 B1
Zawrā' Park Baghdad 3 B2
Zbraslav Prague 25 C2
Zbuzany Prague 25 B1
Zdiby Prague 25 B2
Zeekoevlei Cape Town 8 B2
Zehlendorf Berlin 5 B2
Zenne → Brussels 6 A2
Zephyr Field New Orleans 21 B1
Żerań Warsaw 33 B1
Żerzeń Warsaw 33 B2
Zeytinburnu Istanbul 12 C1
Zhabei Shanghai 28 B1
Zhdanov Moscow 19 B3
Zheji Guangzhou 11 B2
Zhenru Shanghai 28 B1
Zhernovka St. Petersburg 27 B2
Zhicun Guangzhou 11 B2
Zhongguancun Beijing 4 B1
Zhongshan Park Shanghai 28 B1
Zhoucun Guangzhou 11 B2
Zhoujiadu Shanghai 28 B1
Zhoujiazhen Shanghai 28 B2
Zhouzhuangzi Beijing 4 B1
Zhulebino Moscow 19 B4
Zhushadi Guangzhou 11 A3
Zielona Warsaw 33 B3
Zielonka Warsaw 33 B2
Zizhuyuan Park Beijing 4 B1
Žižkov Prague 25 B2
Zličín Prague 25 B1
Zografou Athens 2 B2
Żoliborz Warsaw 33 B1
Zonnebloem Cape Town 8 A1
Zugliget Budapest 7 A1
Zugló Budapest 7 A2
Zuiderwoude Amsterdam 2 A3
Zumbi Rio de Janeiro 25 A1
Zunderdorp Amsterdam 2 A2
Zuvuvu → São Paulo 27 C1
Zwanenburg Amsterdam 2 A1
Zwölfaxing Vienna 32 B2

# New Orleans, USA

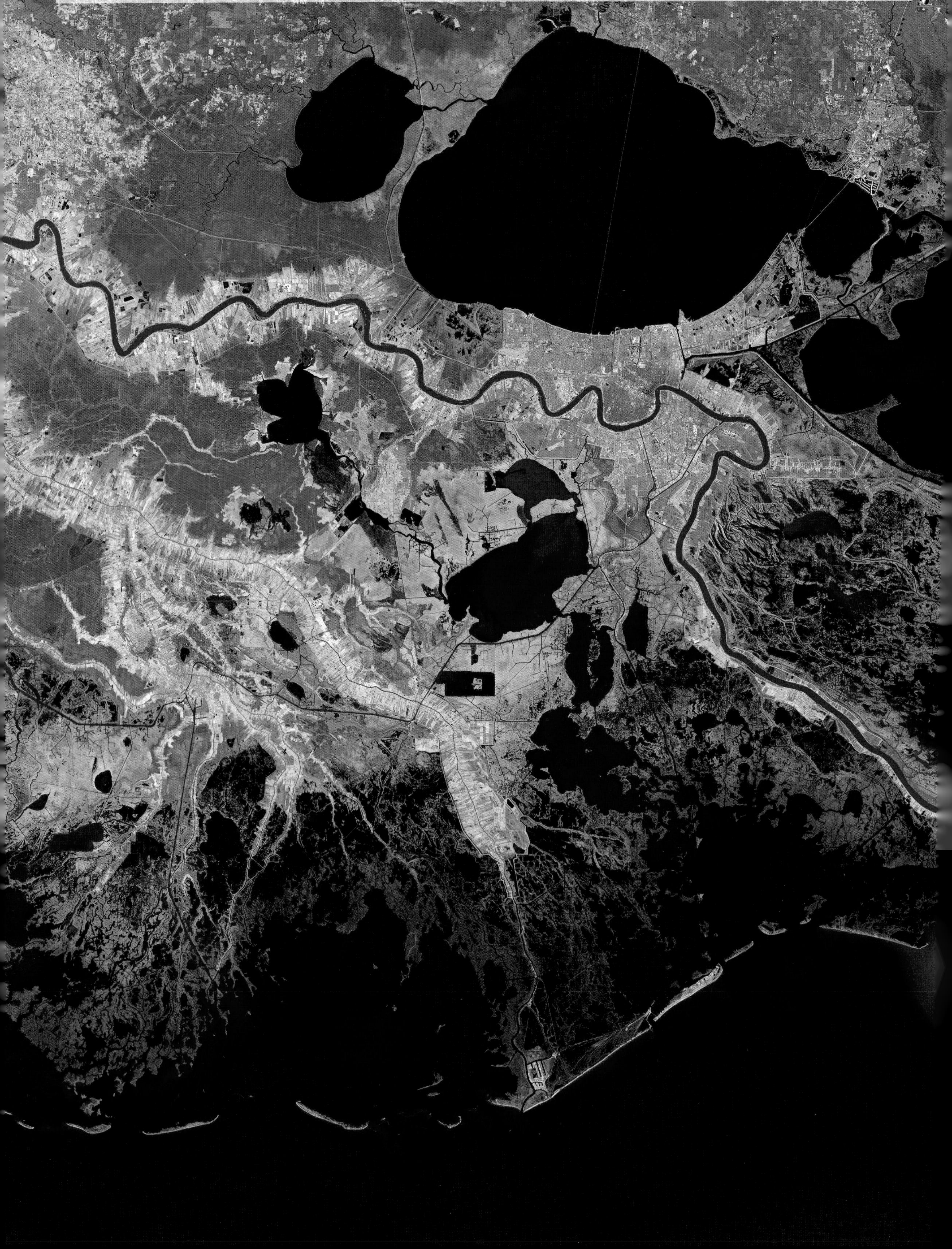

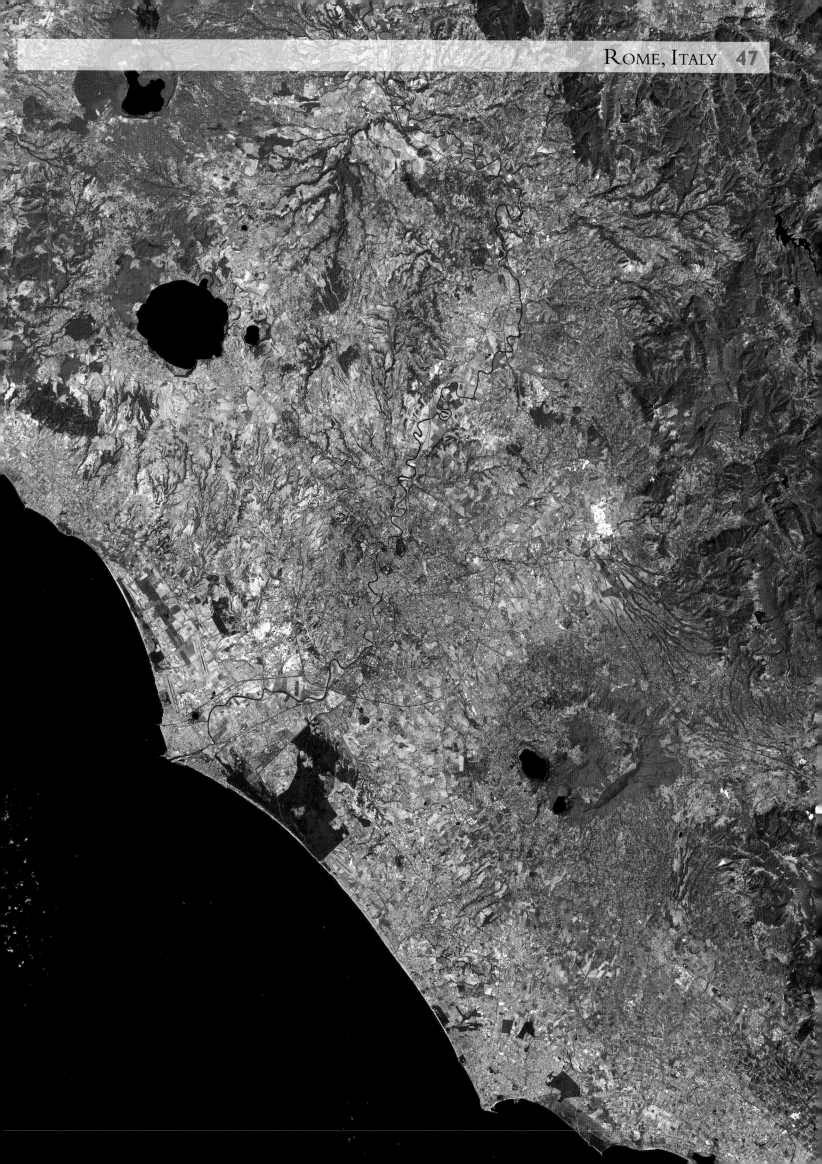

# WORLD MAPS

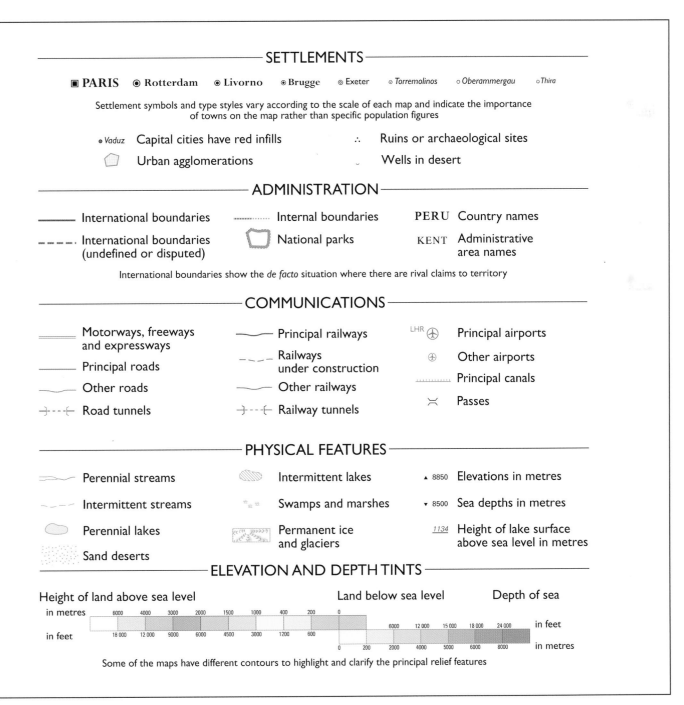

## SETTLEMENTS

■ **PARIS**  ◉ **Rotterdam**  ◉ **Livorno**  ◉ Brugge  ◎ Exeter  ○ *Torremolinos*  ○ *Oberammergau*  ○ *Thira*

Settlement symbols and type styles vary according to the scale of each map and indicate the importance of towns on the map rather than specific population figures

● *Vaduz*  Capital cities have red infills

∴  Ruins or archaeological sites

Urban agglomerations

⌣  Wells in desert

## ADMINISTRATION

—————  International boundaries

⋯⋯⋯  Internal boundaries

**PERU**  Country names

– – – –  International boundaries (undefined or disputed)

National parks

KENT  Administrative area names

International boundaries show the *de facto* situation where there are rival claims to territory

## COMMUNICATIONS

—————  Motorways, freeways and expressways

—————  Principal railways

LHR ✈  Principal airports

—————  Principal roads

– –  Railways under construction

⊕  Other airports

—————  Other roads

—————  Other railways

⋯⋯⋯  Principal canals

+ - - +  Road tunnels

+ - - +  Railway tunnels

⊱  Passes

## PHYSICAL FEATURES

∼∼  Perennial streams

Intermittent lakes

▲ 8850  Elevations in metres

– – –  Intermittent streams

Swamps and marshes

▼ 8500  Sea depths in metres

Perennial lakes

Permanent ice and glaciers

*1134*  Height of lake surface above sea level in metres

Sand deserts

## ELEVATION AND DEPTH TINTS

Height of land above sea level

Land below sea level

Depth of sea

| in metres | 6000 | 4000 | 3000 | 2000 | 1500 | 1000 | 400 | 200 | 0 |
| in feet | 18 000 | 12 000 | 9000 | 6000 | 4500 | 3000 | 1200 | 600 | |

| | 6000 | 12 000 | 15 000 | 18 000 | 24 000 | in feet |
| | 0 | 200 | 2000 | 4000 | 5000 | 6000 | 8000 | in metres |

Some of the maps have different contours to highlight and clarify the principal relief features

Equatorial Scale 1:95 000 000

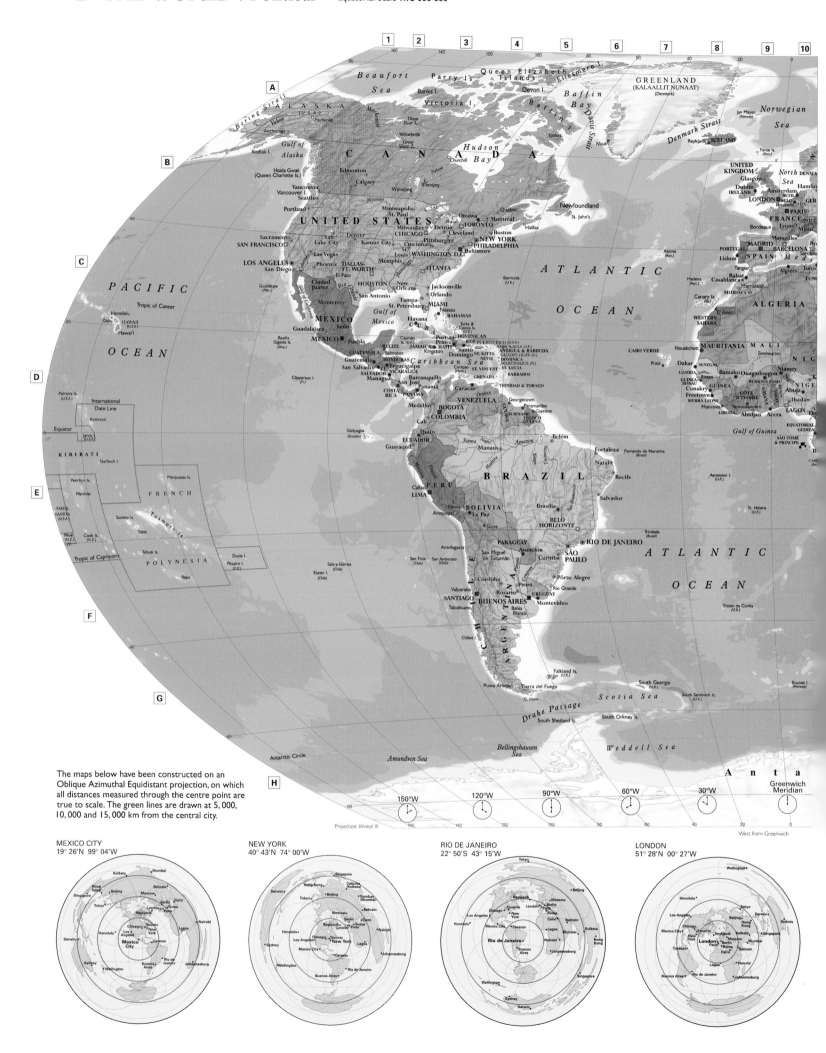

The maps below have been constructed on an Oblique Azimuthal Equidistant projection, on which all distances measured through the centre point are true to scale. The green lines are drawn at 5, 000, 10, 000 and 15, 000 km from the central city.

Projection: Winkel III

West from Greenwich

MEXICO CITY
19° 26'N 99° 04'W

NEW YORK
40° 43'N 74° 00'W

RIO DE JANEIRO
22° 50'S 43° 15'W

LONDON
51° 28'N 00° 27'W

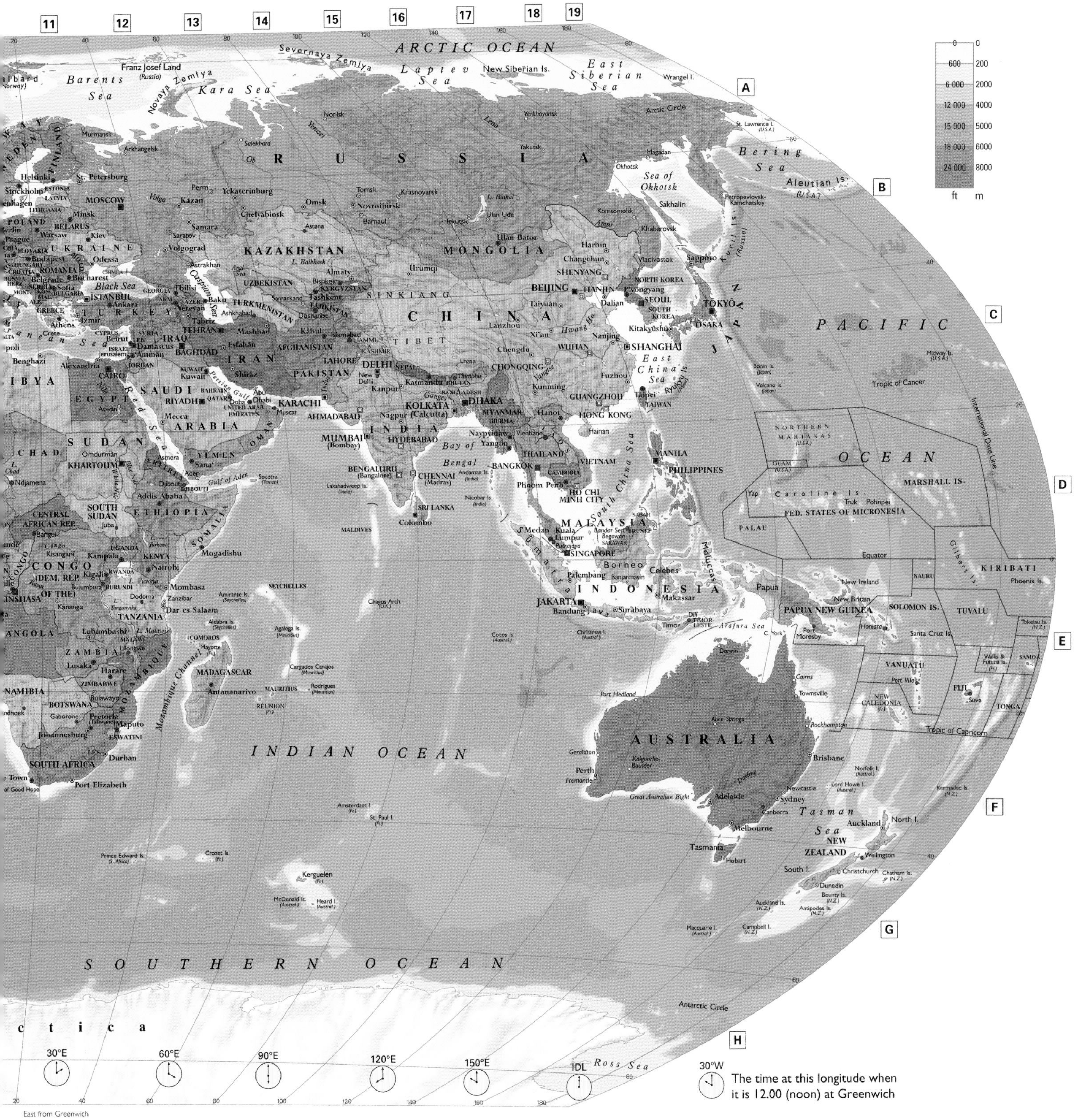

11   12   13   14   15   16   17   18   19

A
B
C
D
E
F
G
H

*(elevation legend)*

| ft | m |
|---|---|
| 0 | 0 |
| 600 | 200 |
| 6 000 | 2000 |
| 12 000 | 4000 |
| 15 000 | 5000 |
| 18 000 | 6000 |
| 24 000 | 8000 |

ARCTIC OCEAN

PACIFIC OCEAN

INDIAN OCEAN

SOUTHERN OCEAN

30°E   60°E   90°E   120°E   150°E   IDL   30°W

East from Greenwich

The time at this longitude when it is 12.00 (noon) at Greenwich

CAPE TOWN
33° 55'S  18° 35'E

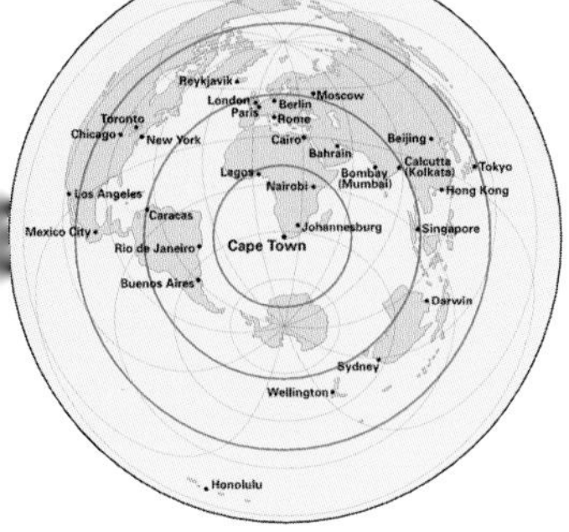

DELHI
28° 39'N  77° 13'E

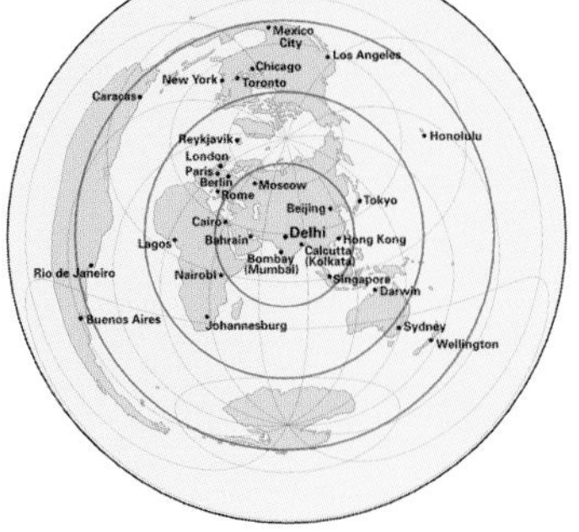

TOKYO
35° 33'N  139° 46'E

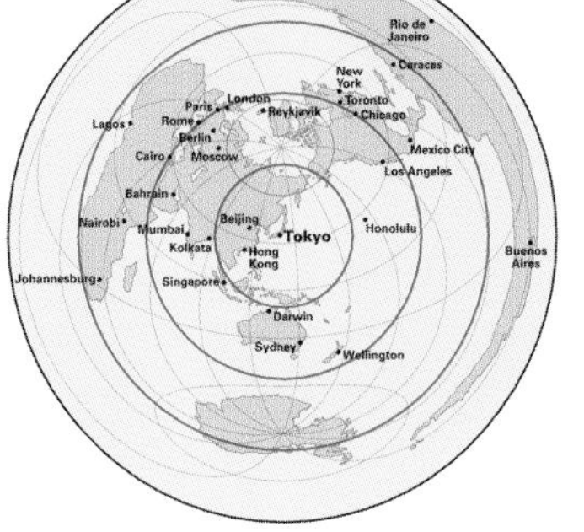

SYDNEY
33° 56'S  151° 10'E

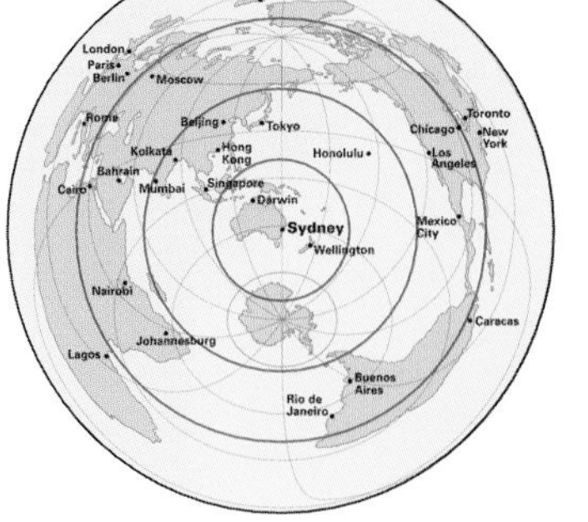

COPYRIGHT PHILIP'S

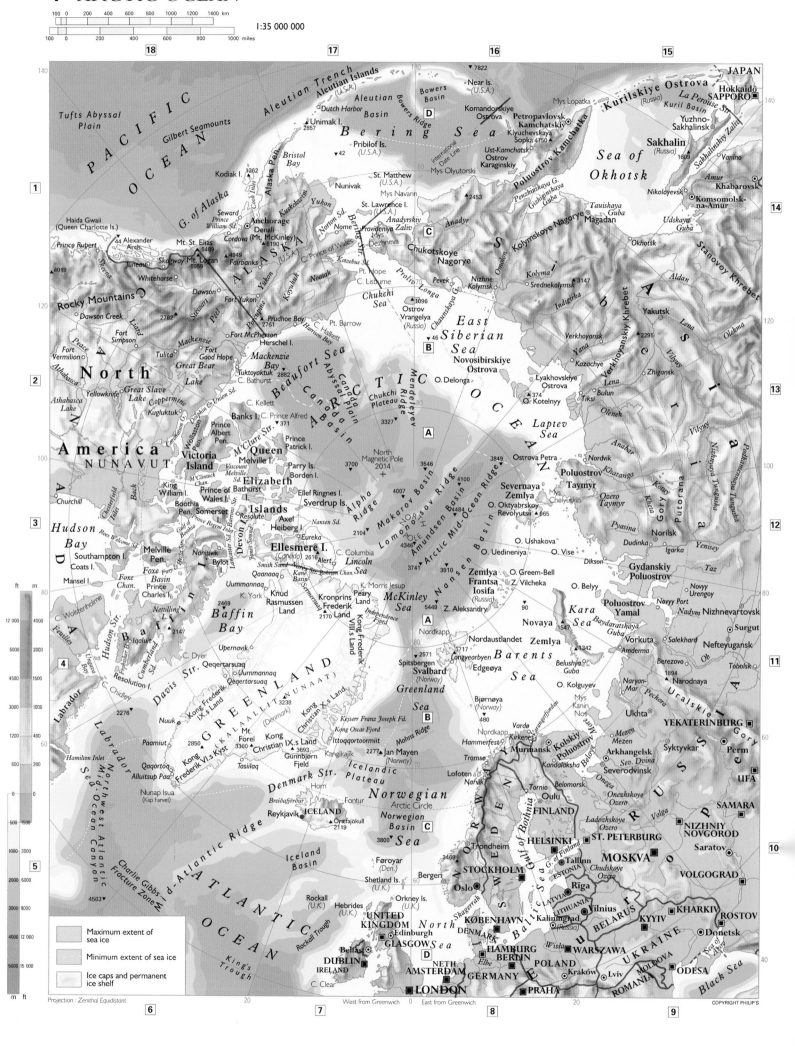

1:35 000 000

Maximum extent of sea ice

Minimum extent of sea ice

Ice caps and permanent ice shelf

Projection : Zenithal Equidistant

COPYRIGHT PHILIP'S

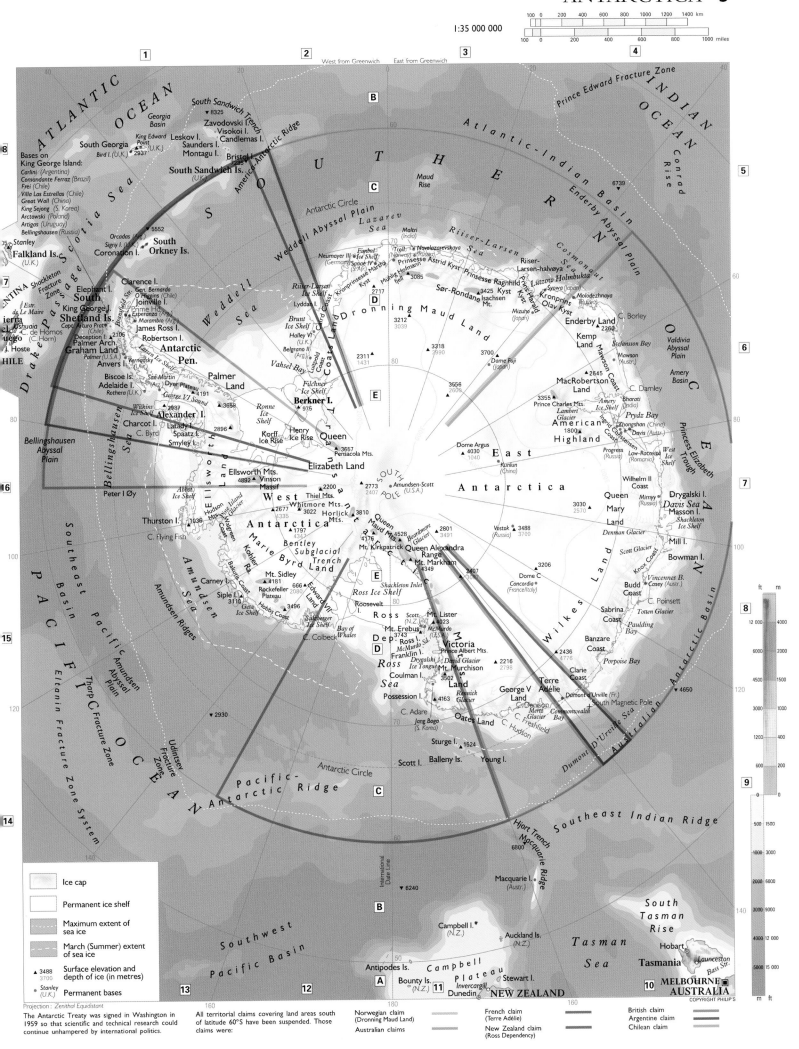

1:35 000 000

100 0 200 400 600 800 1000 1200 1400 km
100 0 200 400 600 800 1000 miles

Ice cap

Permanent ice shelf

Maximum extent of sea ice

March (Summer) extent of sea ice

▲ 3488
3700  Surface elevation and depth of ice (in metres)

• Stanley (U.K.)  Permanent bases

Projection: Zenithal Equidistant

The Antarctic Treaty was signed in Washington in 1959 so that scientific and technical research could continue unhampered by international politics.

All territorial claims covering land areas south of latitude 60°S have been suspended. Those claims were:

Norwegian claim (Dronning Maud Land)
Australian claims

French claim (Terre Adélie)
New Zealand claim (Ross Dependency)

British claim
Argentine claim
Chilean claim

COPYRIGHT PHILIP'S

1:20 000 000

1:20 000 000

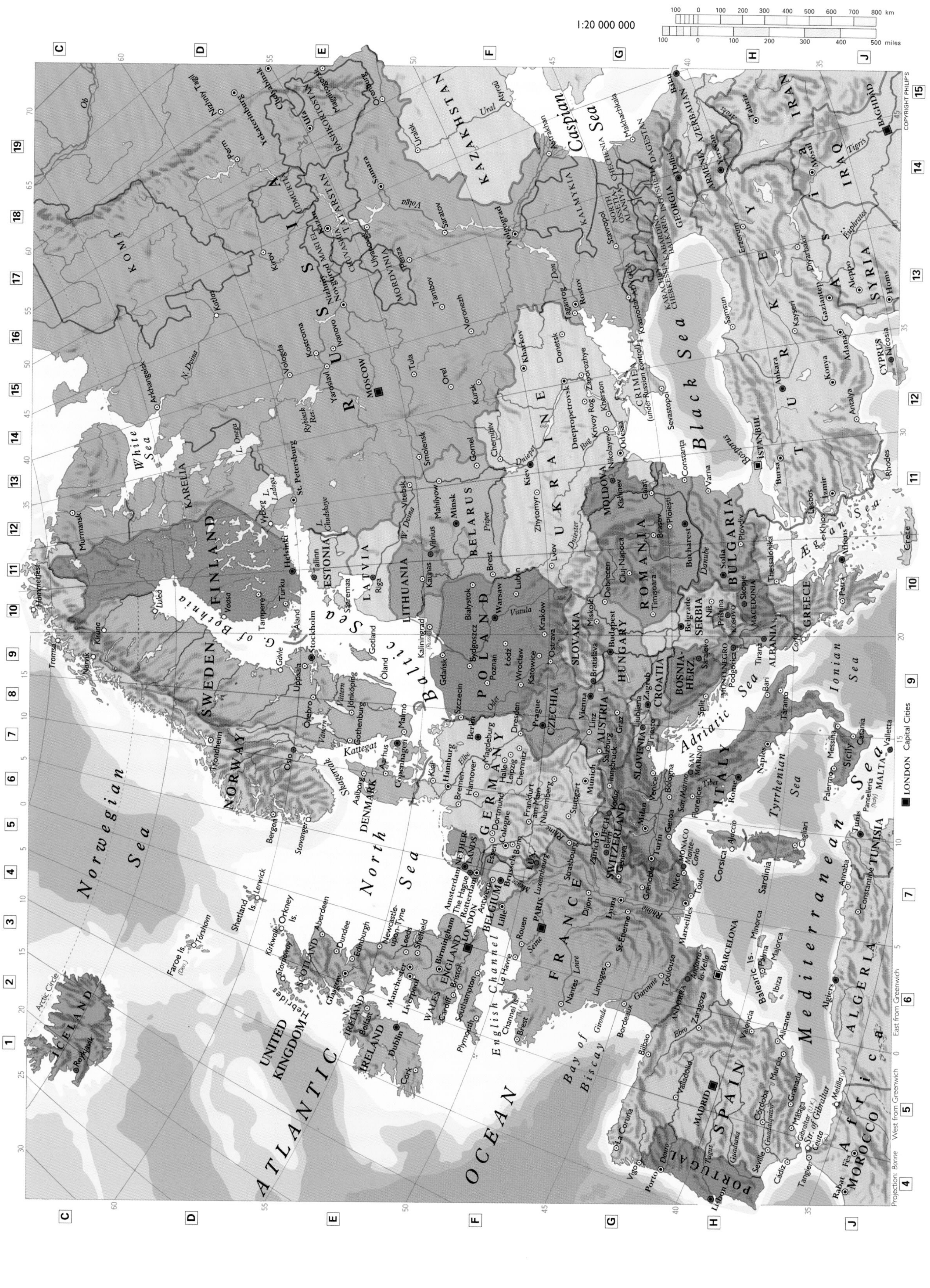

100 0 100 200 300 400 500 600 700 800 km
100 0 100 200 300 400 500 miles

COPYRIGHT PHILIP'S

■ LONDON Capital Cities

Projection: Bonne

East from Greenwich

West from Greenwich

**Seas and Oceans**

ATLANTIC OCEAN
Norwegian Sea
North Sea
White Sea
Baltic Sea
Gulf of Bothnia
Mediterranean Sea
Black Sea
Caspian Sea
Adriatic Sea
Tyrrhenian Sea
Ionian Sea
Aegean Sea
English Channel
Bay of Biscay
Kattegat

**Countries and Regions**

ICELAND
UNITED KINGDOM
SCOTLAND
ENGLAND
WALES
IRELAND
NORWAY
SWEDEN
FINLAND
DENMARK
NETHERLANDS
BELGIUM
LUXEMBOURG
FRANCE
SPAIN
PORTUGAL
GERMANY
SWITZERLAND
AUSTRIA
ITALY
MONACO
SAN MARINO
MALTA
POLAND
CZECHIA
SLOVAKIA
HUNGARY
SLOVENIA
CROATIA
BOSNIA-HERZ.
SERBIA
MONTENEGRO
MACEDONIA
ALBANIA
GREECE
BULGARIA
ROMANIA
MOLDOVA
UKRAINE
BELARUS
LITHUANIA
LATVIA
ESTONIA
RUSSIA
KAZAKHSTAN
GEORGIA
ARMENIA
AZERBAIJAN
TURKEY
CYPRUS
SYRIA
IRAQ
IRAN
MOROCCO
ALGERIA
TUNISIA
Africa
KOMI
KARELIA
BASHKORTOSTAN
TATARSTAN
MARI EL
MORDVINIA
UDMURTIA
CHUVASHIA
KALMYKIA
CRIMEA (under Russian control)
NORTH OSSETIA
CHECHENIA
DAGESTAN
KABARDINO-BALKARIA
KARACHAI-CHERKESSIA
INGUSHETIA
KOSOVO

**Cities**

Reykjavik, Lerwick, Kirkwall, Aberdeen, Dundee, Edinburgh, Glasgow, Newcastle-upon-Tyne, Leeds, Sheffield, Manchester, Liverpool, Birmingham, Bristol, Cardiff, London, Southampton, Plymouth, Belfast, Dublin, Cork, Torshavn

Tromsø, Narvik, Hammerfest, Kiruna, Luleå, Trondheim, Bergen, Stavanger, Oslo, Stockholm, Uppsala, Örebro, Göteborg, Malmö, Copenhagen, Aalborg, Aarhus, Kiel, Hamburg, Bremen, Hannover, Dortmund, Essen, Cologne, Bonn, Frankfurt am Main, Nuremberg, Stuttgart, Munich, Leipzig, Dresden, Chemnitz, Halle, Magdeburg, Berlin

Helsinki, Turku, Tampere, Vaasa, Murmansk, Arkhangelsk

Amsterdam, The Hague, Rotterdam, Antwerp, Brussels, Lille, Le Havre, Rouen, Paris, Strasbourg, Nancy, Dijon, Nantes, Tours, Limoges, Lyons, St-Étienne, Bordeaux, Toulouse, Montpellier, Marseilles, Toulon, Nice, Grenoble, Brest

Geneva, Zürich, Basle, Bern, Milan, Turin, Genoa, Venice, Bologna, Florence, Rome, Naples, Palermo, Messina, Catania, Cagliari, Ajaccio, Monte Carlo, Valletta

Lisbon, Porto, Vigo, La Coruña, Valladolid, Madrid, Barcelona, Zaragoza, Valencia, Alicante, Murcia, Granada, Málaga, Córdoba, Seville, Cádiz, Gibraltar, Ceuta, Melilla

St. Petersburg, Moscow, Vyborg, Petrozavodsk, Vologda, Kotlas, Syktyvkar, Kirov, Yaroslavl, Ivanovo, Nizhniy Novgorod, Kostroma, Kazan, Ulyanovsk, Samara, Saratov, Penza, Tambov, Tula, Orel, Kursk, Voronezh, Volgograd, Astrakhan, Rostov, Krasnodar, Stavropol, Makhachkala, Smolensk

Kaliningrad, Gdańsk, Szczecin, Bydgoszcz, Poznań, Warsaw, Łódź, Wrocław, Katowice, Kraków, Ostrava, Prague, Vienna, Bratislava, Budapest, Miskolc, Debrecen, Linz, Salzburg, Graz, Ljubljana, Zagreb, Trieste, Split, Sarajevo, Belgrade, Niš, Priština, Skopje, Tirana, Podgorica, Bari, Taranto

Tallinn, Riga, Vilnius, Kaunas, Minsk, Mahilyow, Vitebsk, Hrodna, Brest, Lublin, Białystok, Kiev, Zhytomyr, Lviv, Chernihiv, Gomel, Kharkiv, Donetsk, Dnepropetrovsk, Zaporozhye, Kryvyy Rog, Kherson, Mykolayiv, Odessa, Chişinău, Galaţi, Constanţa, Bucharest, Ploieşti, Braşov, Cluj-Napoca, Timişoara, Sofia, Plovdiv, Varna, Thessaloníki, Athens, Pátrai, Iráklion

Istanbul, Bursa, Ankara, Izmir, Konya, Adana, Antalya, Kayseri, Gaziantep, Erzurum, Diyarbakır, Mosul, Baghdad, Baku, Yerevan, Tbilisi, Nicosia, Aleppo, Homs, Tabriz

Rabat, Fès, Tangier, Oran, Algiers, Constantine, Annaba, Tunis, Tripoli

**Rivers and physical features**

Ob, Volga, Ural, Don, Dnieper, Danube, Rhine, Rhône, Loire, Seine, Garonne, Ebro, Tagus, Duero, Guadiana, Guadalquivir, Vistula, Oder, Elbe, Main, Tiber, Euphrates, Tigris, Arctic Circle, L. Ladoga, L. Onega, Rybinsk Res., L. Saimaa, Öland, Gotland, Crete, Rhodes, Lesbos, Cyprus, Sicily, Sardinia, Corsica, Balearic Is., Mallorca, Minorca, Ibiza, Shetland Is., Orkney Is., Faroe Is. (Den.), Hebrides, Channel Is.

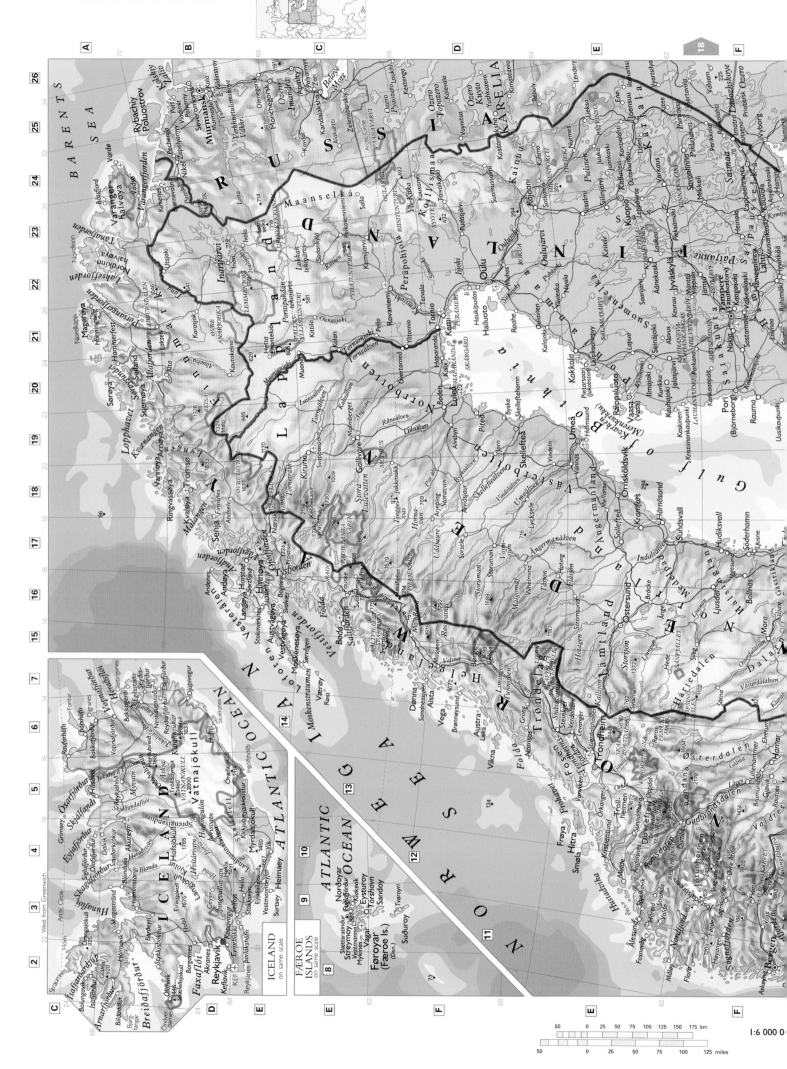

ICELAND
on same scale

FÆROE
ISLANDS
on same scale

50  0  25  50  75  100  125  150  175 km
50  0  25  50  75  100  125 miles

1:6 000 0

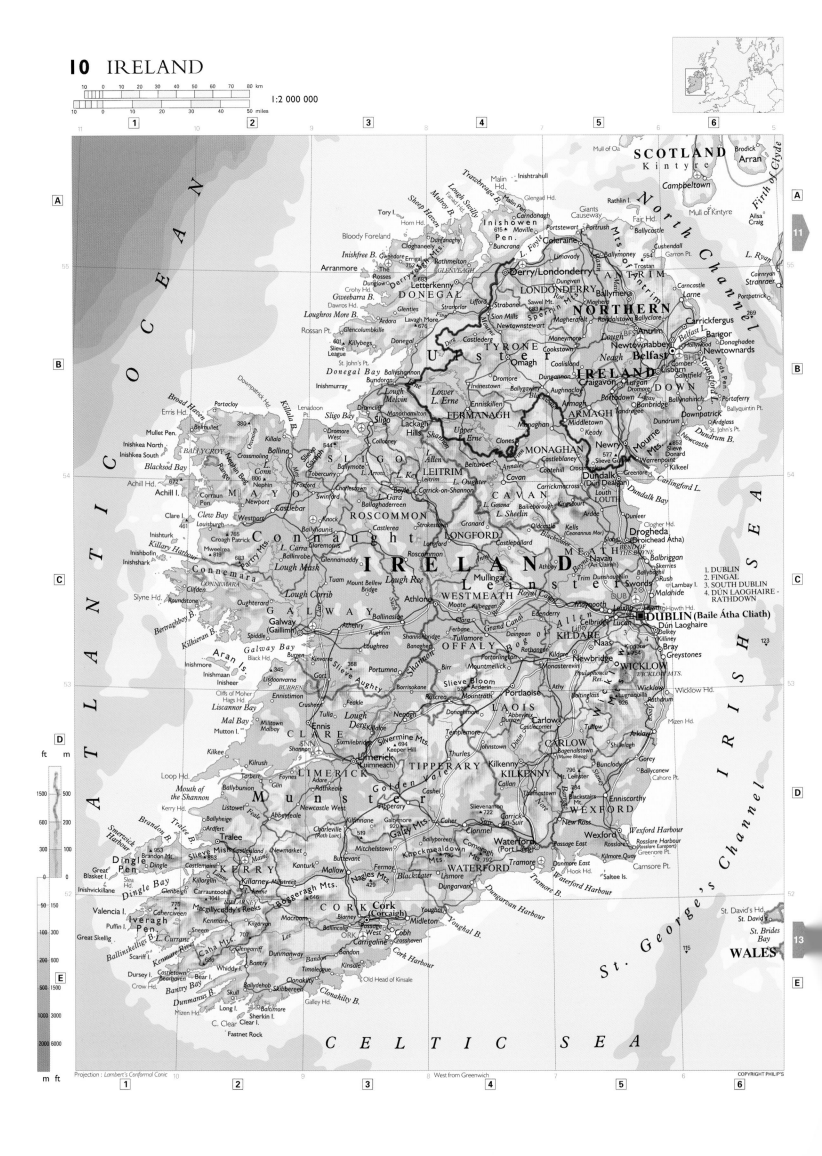

1:2 000 000

10  0  10  20  30  40  50  60  70  80 km
10  0  10  20  30  40  50 miles

Projection : Lambert's Conformal Conic

COPYRIGHT PHILIP'S

1. DUBLIN
2. FINGAL
3. SOUTH DUBLIN
4. DÚN LAOGHAIRE-RATHDOWN

1:2 000 000

**Key to Scottish unitary authorities on map**

| | |
|---|---|
| 1 ABERDEEN CITY | 8 EAST RENFREWSHIRE |
| 2 DUNDEE CITY | 9 NORTH LANARKSHIRE |
| 3 WEST DUNBARTONSHIRE | 10 FALKIRK |
| 4 EAST DUNBARTONSHIRE | 11 CLACKMANNANSHIRE |
| 5 GLASGOW CITY | 12 WEST LOTHIAN |
| 6 INVERCLYDE | 13 CITY OF EDINBURGH |
| 7 RENFREWSHIRE | 14 MIDLOTHIAN |

ORKNEY IS.
on same scale

SHETLAND IS.
on same scale

Projection : Lambert's Conformal Conic

West from Greenwich

COPYRIGHT PHILIP'S

1:2 000 000

10 0 10 20 30 40 50 60 70 80 km
10 0 10 20 30 40 50 miles

**Key to English unitary authorities on map**

25 HARTLEPOOL
26 DARLINGTON
27 STOCKTON-ON-TEES
28 MIDDLESBROUGH
29 REDCAR AND CLEVELAND
30 BLACKPOOL
31 BLACKBURN WITH DARWEN
32 HALTON
33 WARRINGTON
34 KINGSTON UPON HULL
35 NORTH EAST LINCOLNSHIRE
36 STOKE-ON-TRENT
37 TELFORD AND WREKIN
38 DERBY CITY
39 CITY OF NOTTINGHAM
40 LEICESTER CITY
41 RUTLAND
42 PETERBOROUGH
43 MILTON KEYNES
44 LUTON
45 NORTH SOMERSET
46 CITY OF BRISTOL
47 BATH AND NORTH EAST SOMERSET
48 SWINDON
49 READING
50 WOKINGHAM
51 WINDSOR AND MAIDENHEAD
52 SLOUGH
53 BRACKNELL FOREST
54 THURROCK
55 MEDWAY
56 SOUTHEND-ON-SEA
57 PLYMOUTH
58 TORBAY
59 POOLE
60 BOURNEMOUTH
61 SOUTHAMPTON
62 PORTSMOUTH
63 BRIGHTON AND HOVE
64 BEDFORD
65 CENTRAL BEDFORDSHIRE
66 CHESHIRE WEST AND CHESTER
67 CHESHIRE EAST

**Key to Welsh unitary authorities on map**

15 SWANSEA
16 NEATH PORT TALBOT
17 BRIDGEND
18 RHONDDA CYNON TAFF
19 MERTHYR TYDFIL
20 CAERPHILLY
21 BLAENAU GWENT
22 TORFAEN
23 CARDIFF
24 NEWPORT

N O R T H   S E A

S C O T L A N D

I R I S H   S E A

North Channel

NORTHERN IRELAND

ISLE OF MAN

Frith of Clyde

Solway Firth

LAKE DISTRICT

CUMBRIA

NORTHUMBERLAND

DURHAM

NORTH YORKSHIRE

LINCOLNSHIRE

LANCASHIRE

GWYNEDD

SNOWDONIA

The Wash

The Broads

GLASGOW
EDINBURGH
Newcastle-upon-Tyne
Sunderland
Middlesbrough
Hartlepool
York
Leeds
Bradford
MANCHESTER
LIVERPOOL
Sheffield
Nottingham
Derby
Stoke-on-Trent
Carlisle
Kingston upon Hull
Scarborough
Whitby

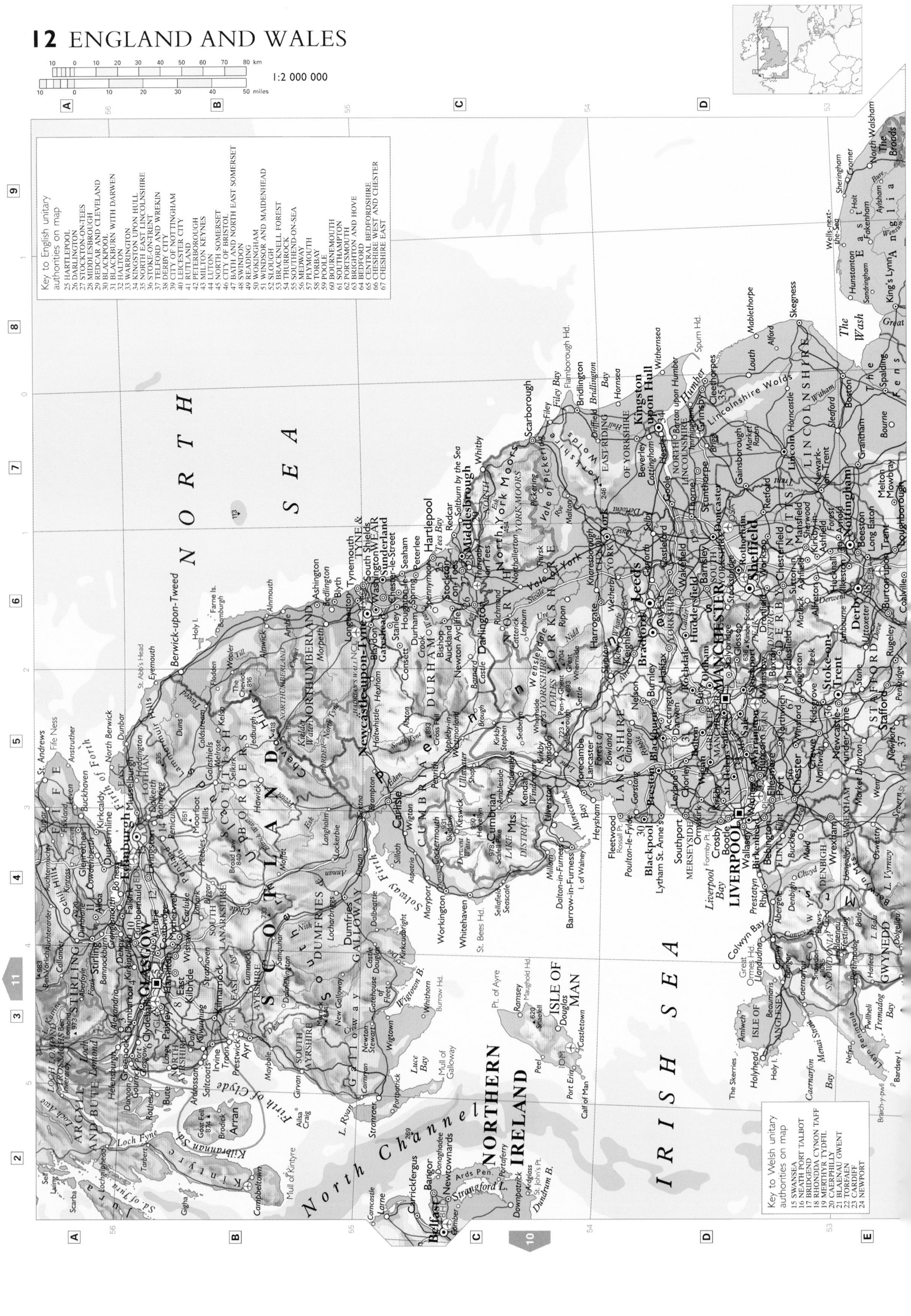

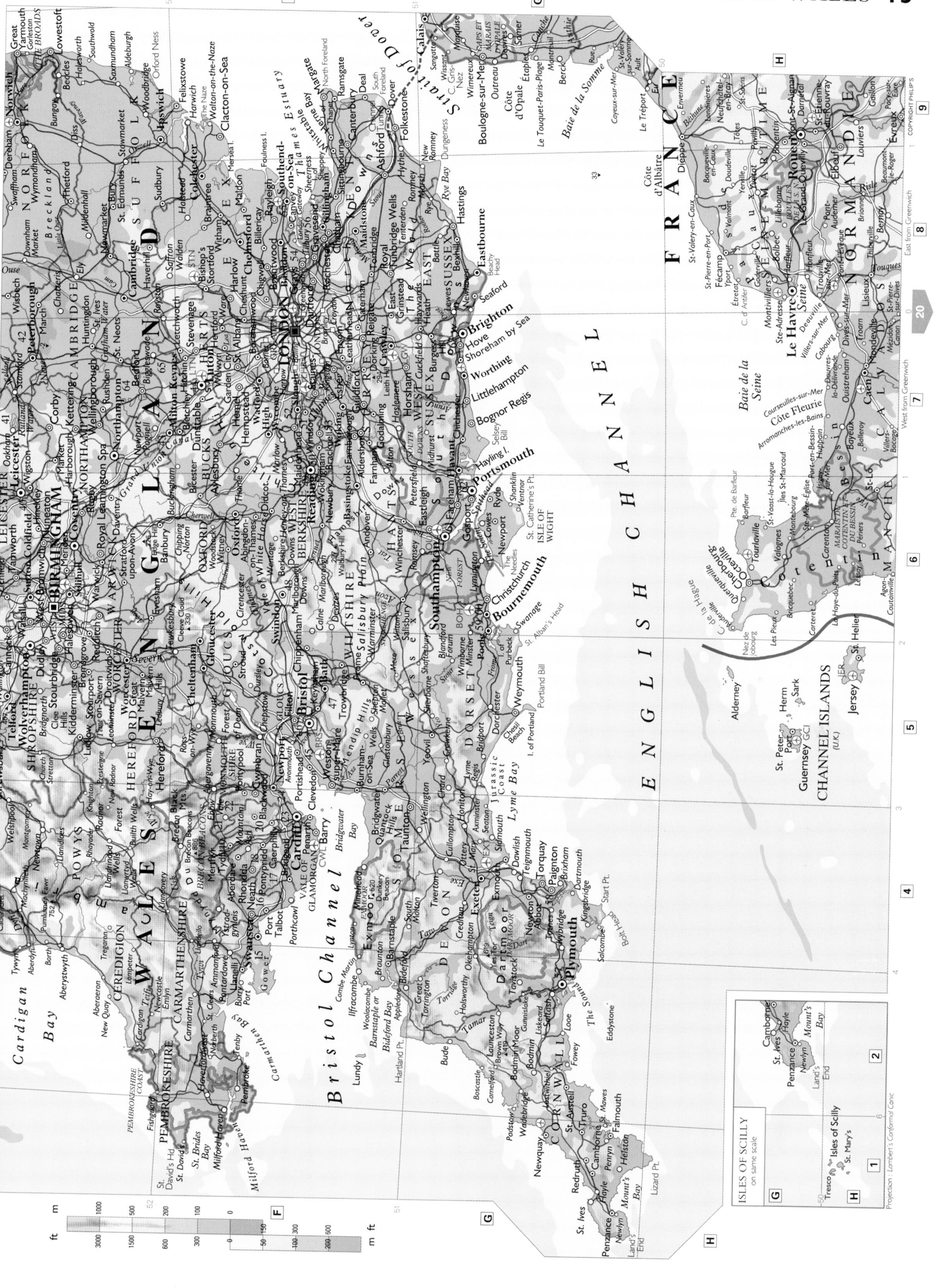

ENGLAND

WALES

FRANCE

NORMANDIE

SEINE-MARITIME

CALVADOS

MANCHE

ENGLISH CHANNEL

Bristol Channel

Cardigan Bay

Straits of Dover

Thames Estuary

LONDON

BIRMINGHAM

CHANNEL ISLANDS (U.K.)

ISLE OF WIGHT

ISLES OF SCILLY
on same scale

Projection: Lambert's Conformal Conic

COPYRIGHT PHILIP'S

East from Greenwich

West from Greenwich

1:5 000 000

A T L A N T I C   O C E A N

NORWAY

Bergen
Osøyro
Stord
Bømlo
Leirvik
Haugesund
Kopervik
Åkrahamn
Sandnes
Bryne
Stavanger
Nærbø

Shetland Is.
(U.K.)
Yell
Unst
Fetlar
Mainland
Lerwick
Foula
Fair Isle

N O R T H   S E A

Orkney Is.
Westray
Sanday
Stronsay
Mainland
Kirkwall
Hoy
South Ronaldsay

Pentland Firth

C. Wrath
Thurso
Wick
Helmsdale

North
Rona

Flannan Is.
Lewis
Stornoway
North Minch
Harris
St. Kilda
(U.K.)
North Uist
Benbecula
South Uist
Barra

Outer Hebrides

Sea of the Hebrides
Inner Hebrides

Skye
Portree
Rum
Eigg
Coll
Tiree
Tobermory
Mull
Iona
Colonsay
Jura
Islay

North West Highlands
Ullapool
Lairg
Golspie
Tain
Invergordon
Dingwall
Nairn
Elgin
Buckie
Banff
Fraserburgh
Peterhead
Inverness
Aviemore
CAIRNGORMS
Mts.
Huntly
Inverurie
Aberdeen
Glen Mor
L. Ness
Don
Dee
Ballater
Stonehaven

Moray Firth

SCOTLAND
Grampian Mts.
Ben Nevis
Fort William
Glencoe
Oban
L. Awe
L. Fyne
L. Lomond
L. Leven
TROSSACHS
Perth
Dundee
Arbroath
Montrose
Forfar
St. Andrews

Dumbarton
Greenock
Paisley
GLASGOW
Hamilton
East Kilbride
Irvine
Kilmarnock
Stirling
Dunfermline
Kirkcaldy
Glenrothes
EDINBURGH
Dunbar
Cumbernauld

Campbeltown
Arran
Ayr
Girvan
Southern Uplands
Jedburgh
Hawick
Cheviot Hills
Galashiels
Berwick-upon-Tweed
Alnwick

Firth of Clyde
North Channel
Mull of Galloway
Stranraer
Kirkcudbright
Dumfries
Annan
Carlisle
NORTHUMBERLAND
Hexham
Newcastle-upon-Tyne
South Shields
Gateshead
Sunderland
Durham
Hartlepool
Redcar
Middlesbrough
Stockton-on-Tees
Darlington
N. York Moors
Scarborough

Tory I.
Malin Hd.
Buncrana
Letterkenny
Derry/Londonderry
Coleraine
Ballymena
Larne
Bangor
Arranmore
GLENVEAGH
Lifford
Donegal
Omagh
Antrim
Lough Neagh
Belfast
Craigavon
Lisburn
Bundoran
Lower L. Erne
Enniskillen
Armagh
Newry
NORTHERN IRELAND
Ballina
Sligo
Leitrim
Clones
Castleblayney
Cookstown

Workington
Whitehaven
Cumbrian Mts.
LAKE DISTRICT
Keswick
Barrow-in-Furness
Pennines
YORKSHIRE DALES
Lancaster
Harrogate
York
Bridlington
Beverley
Kingston upon Hull

I. of Man
Douglas

UNITED KINGDOM

Castlebar
L. Conn
L. Mask
Westport
Roscommon
Longford
L. Ree
Mullingar
Athlone
Connemara
Galway B.
Galway
Aran Is.
BURREN
Lough Corrib
Ballinasloe
Tullamore
Birr
Kells
Drogheda
Boyne
Dundalk
IRELAND
Lough Derg
Ennis
Portlaoise
Athy
Carlow
Nenagh
Thurles
Tipperary
Kilkenny
Roscrea

Shannon
Tralee
Dingle
Carrauntoohil
Macgillycuddy's Reeks
Killarney
Mallow
Clonmel
Carrick-on-Suir
Valencia I.
C. Clear
Bantry
Bandon
Kinsale
Cobh
Cork
Youghal
Dungarvan
Waterford
Wexford
Rosslare

I R I S H   S E A

DUBLIN
Dun Laoghaire
Bray
Liffey
Wicklow Mts.
Arklow

Holyhead
Anglesey
Bangor
Colwyn Bay
Llandudno
Rhyl
Chester
Wrexham
Snowdon
SNOWDONIA
Cambrian Mts.
Pwllheli
Cardigan Bay
Aberystwyth
Welshpool
Shrewsbury
Telford

Blackpool
Preston
Blackburn
Burnley
Bolton
Bury
Southport
LIVERPOOL
Birkenhead
Warrington
St. Helens
Wigan
MANCHESTER
Stockport
Oldham
PEAK DISTRICT
Buxton
Crewe
Stoke-on-Trent
Stafford

Leeds
Bradford
Halifax
Huddersfield
Barnsley
Wakefield
Doncaster
Rotherham
SHEFFIELD
Chesterfield
Mansfield
Lincoln
Scunthorpe
Grimsby
Louth
Skegness
Boston
The Wash
King's Lynn

Cromer
Great Yarmouth
Lowestoft
THE BROADS
Norwich
Thetford
Bury St. Edmunds
Ipswich
Felixstowe
Harwich
Colchester
Clacton

ENGLAND

Derby
Nottingham
Trent
Granthem
Leicester
Nuneaton
Coventry
Rugby
BIRMINGHAM
Wolverhampton
Redditch
Worcester
Hereford
Royal Leamington Spa
Northampton
Bedford
Milton Keynes
Cambridge
Stevenage
Luton
Harlow

WALES
Merthyr Tydfil
BRECON BEACONS
Brecon
Carmarthen
Llanelli
Swansea
Neath
Port Talbot
Rhondda
Cwmbran
Newport
Cardiff
Barry
Bristol Channel
Gloucester
Cheltenham
Cotswold Hills
Cirencester
Oxford
High Wycombe
Hemel Hempstead
Watford
Slough
Reading
LONDON
Basildon
Southend-on-Sea
Chelmsford

EXMOOR
Barnstaple
Bideford
Taunton
Bridgwater
Weston-super-Mare
Bath
Bristol
Swindon
Newbury
Basingstoke
Guildford
Reigate
Crawley
Maidstone
Chatham
Canterbury
Margate
Dover
Folkestone
Ashford
Royal Tunbridge Wells

DARTMOOR
Newquay
Truro
St. Austell
Falmouth
Penzance
Land's End
Isles of Scilly
Bude
Exeter
Exmouth
Torbay
Plymouth
Torquay
Yeovil
Dorchester
Weymouth
Poole
Bournemouth
NEW FOREST
Southampton
Portsmouth
Havant
Fareham
Isle of Wight
Winchester
Salisbury
SOUTH DOWNS
Worthing
Brighton
Eastbourne
Hastings

C E L T I C   S E A

St. George's Channel
Fishguard
Haverfordwest
Milford Haven
PEMBROKESHIRE COAST

E N G L I S H   C H A N N E L

Str. of Dover
Gris Nez
Calais
Boulogne-sur-Mer
Le Touquet-Paris-Plage
Dunkerque
St-Omer
Béthune
Bruay-la-Buissière
Bruay-la-Bussière
LILLE
Roubaix
Tourcoing
Villeneuve d'Ascq
Valenciennes

BELGIUM
BRUSSELS
(Bruxelles)
Oostende
Zeebrugge
Brugge
Gent
Mechelen
Antwerpen

NETHERLANDS
Haarlem
's-Gravenhage
(Den Haag)
ROTTERDAM
Dordrecht
Zeeland
Vlissingen
Hoek van Holland
Texel
Den Helder
Alkmaar

FRANCE
Alderney
C. de la Hague
Pte. de Barfleur
Cherbourg-Octeville
Valognes
Guernsey
St. Peter Port
Sark
St. Helier
Jersey
Channel Is.
(U.K.)
Cotentin
Bayeux
Caen
Trouville-sur-Mer
Lisieux
Elbeuf
Seine
Rouen
Elbeuf
Fécamp
Le Havre
Bolbec
Yvetot
Pays de Caux
Le Tréport
Dieppe
Abbeville
Amiens
St-Quentin
Cambrai
Laon
PICARDIE

East from Greenwich
West from Greenwich

Projection: Conical with two standard parallels

COPYRIGHT PHILIP'S

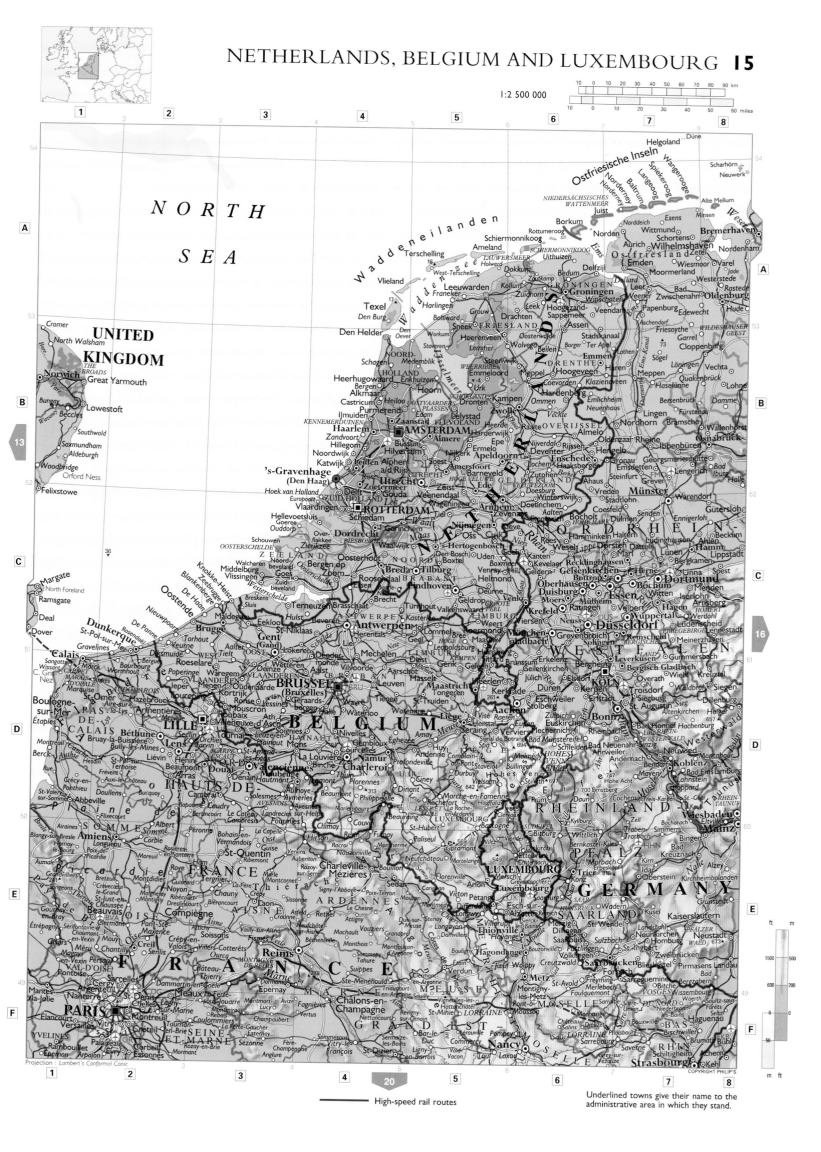

1:2 500 000

10  0  10  20  30  40  50  60  70  80  90 km
10  0  10  20  30  40  50 miles

**NORTH SEA**

**UNITED KINGDOM**

**NETHERLANDS**

**BELGIUM**

**FRANCE**

**GERMANY**

Projection : Lambert's Conformal Conic

COPYRIGHT PHILIP'S

—— High-speed rail routes

Underlined towns give their name to the administrative area in which they stand.

**1:5 000 000**

Projection: Conical with two standard parallels

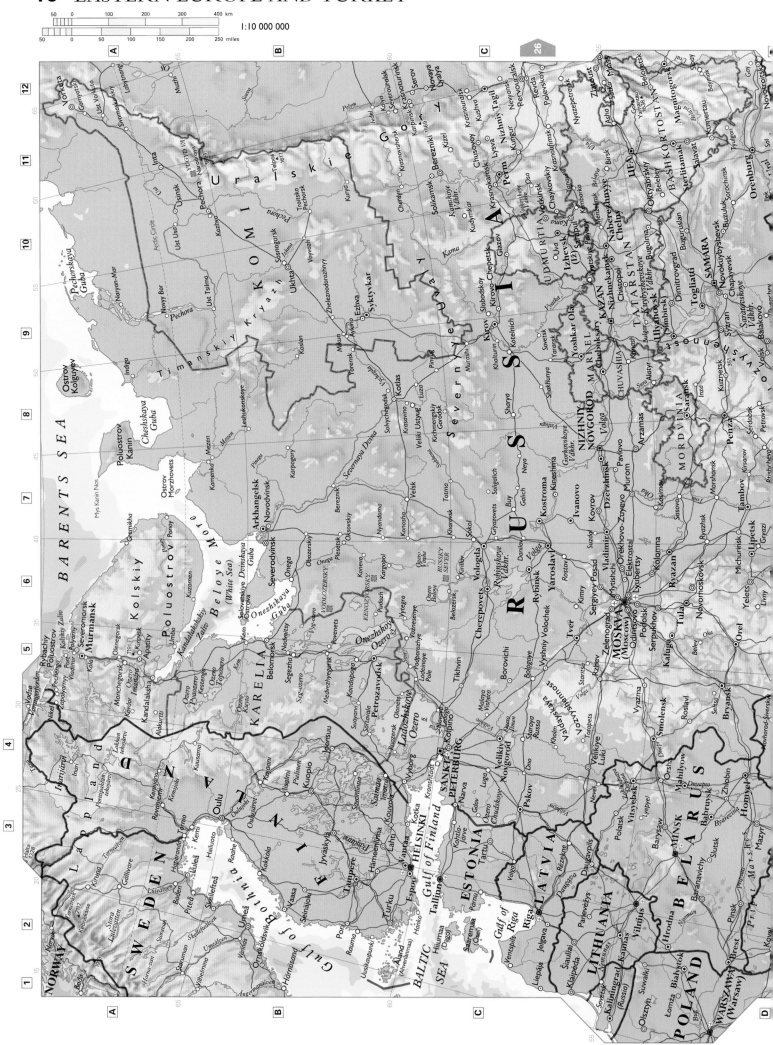

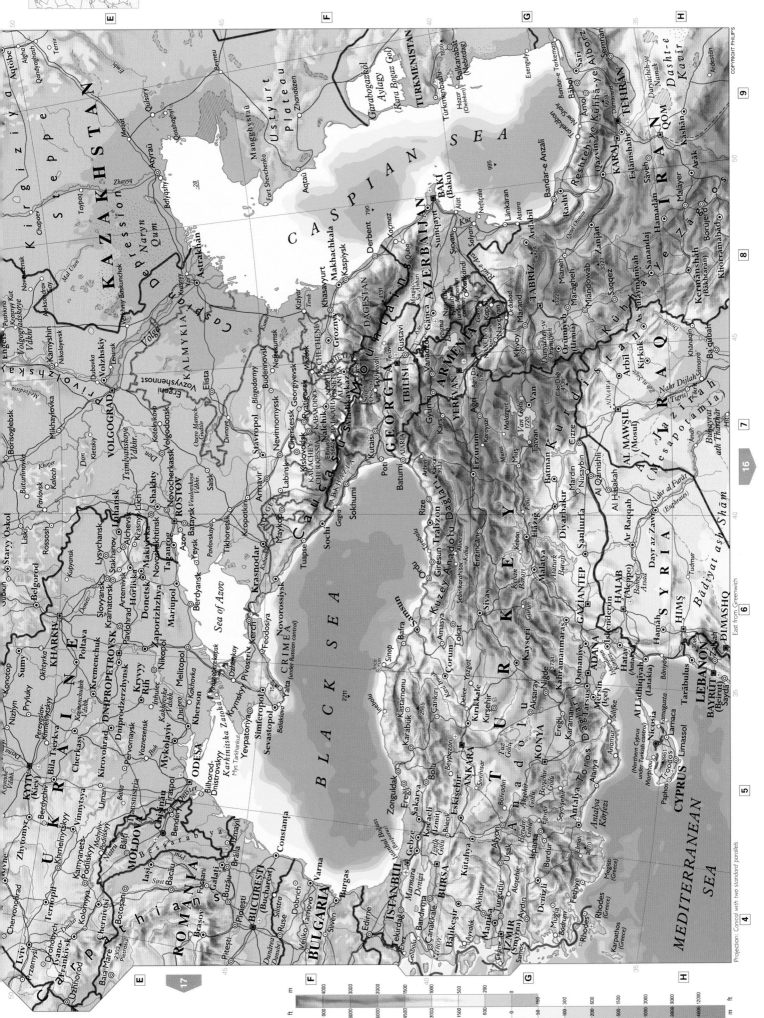

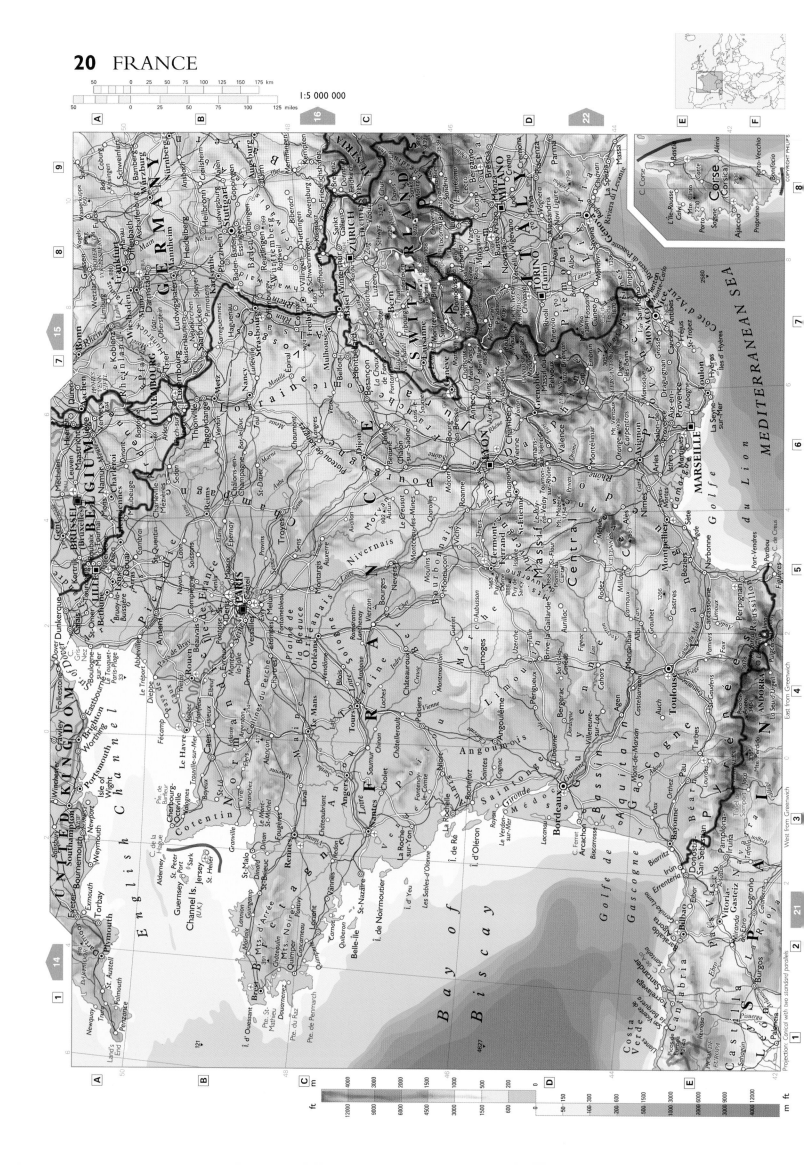

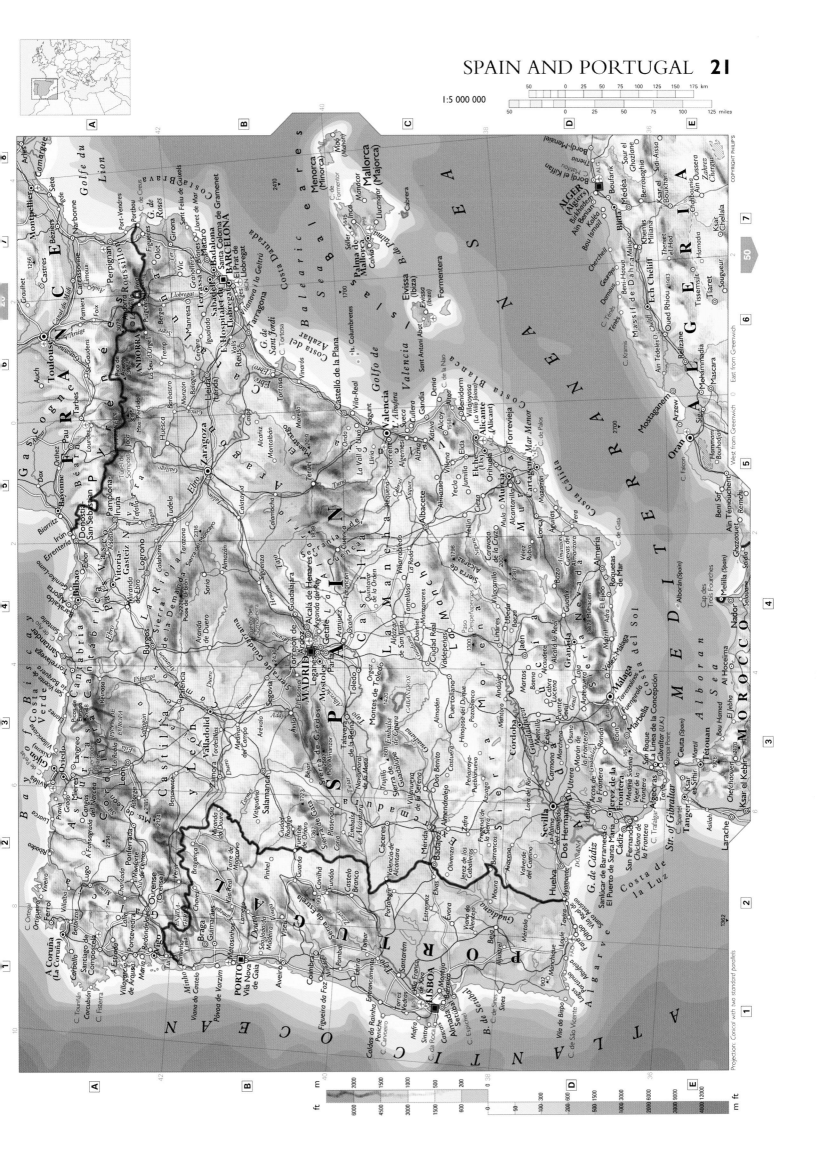

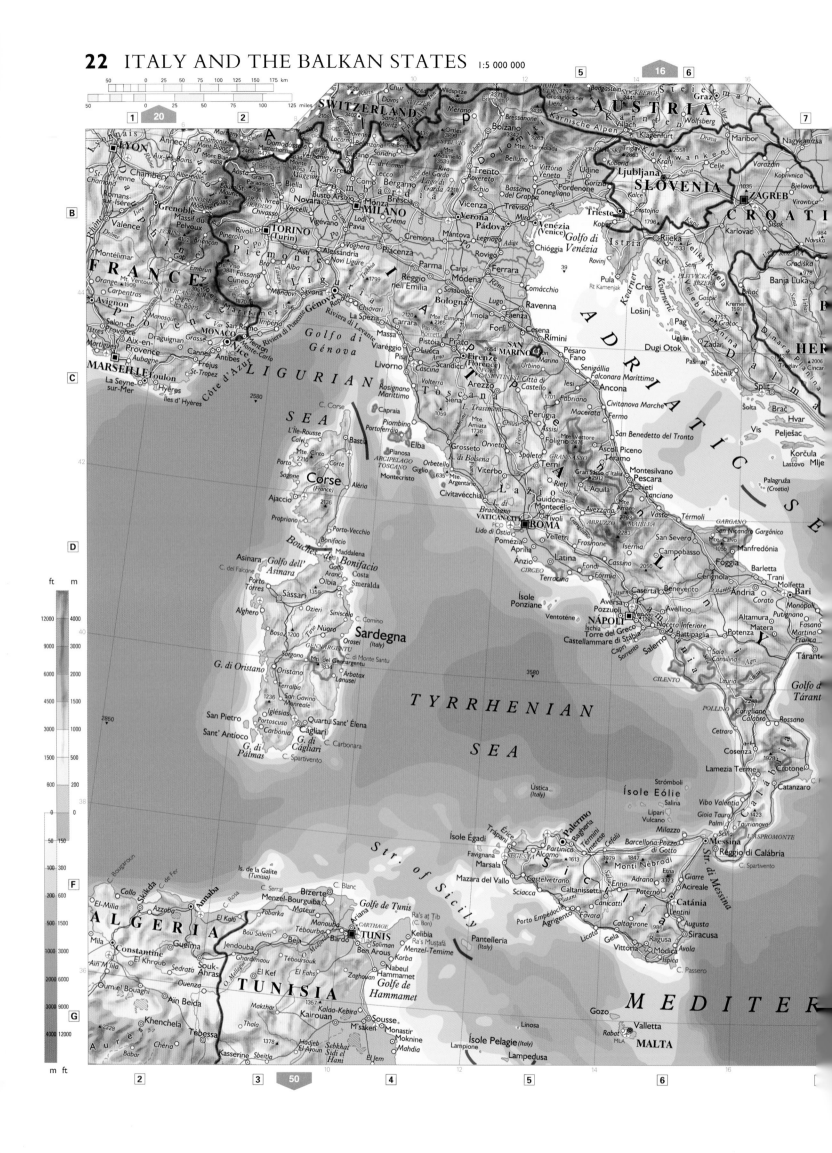

1:47 000 000

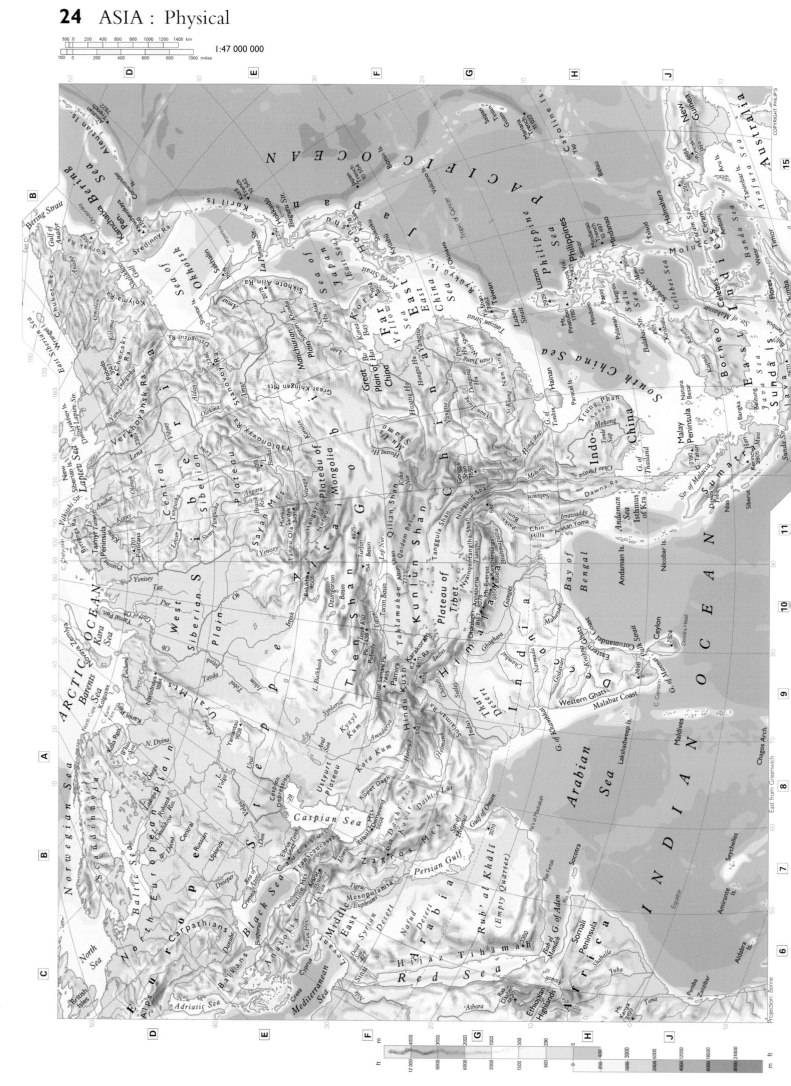

Projection: Bonne

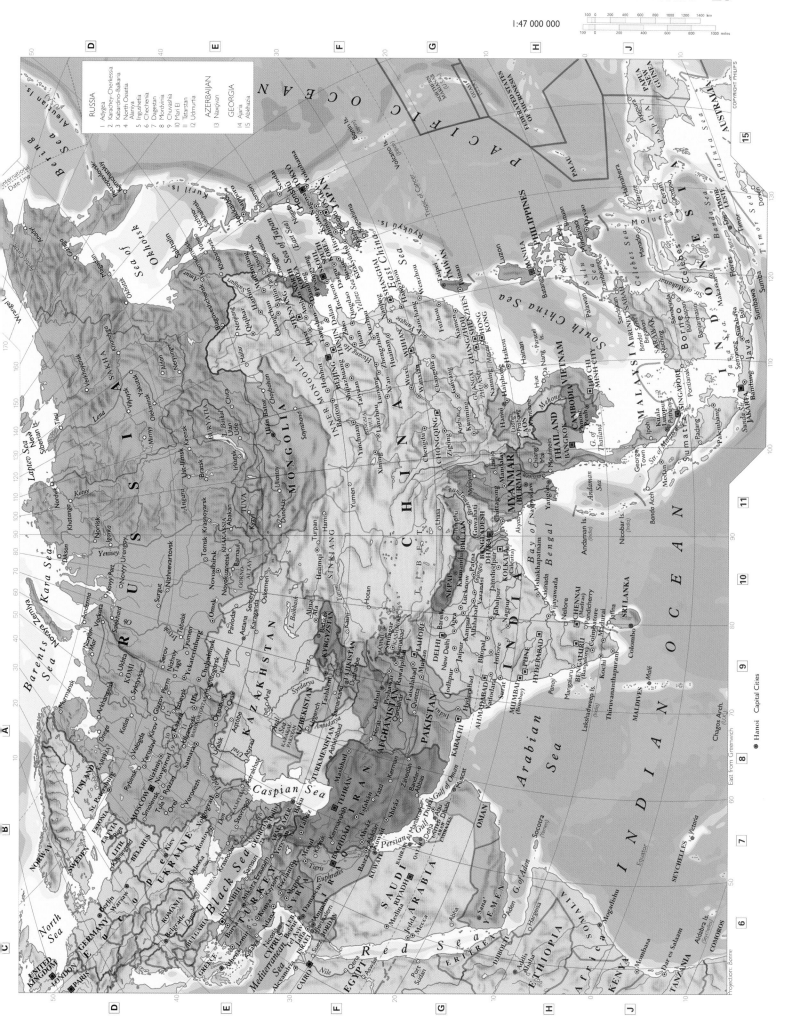

1:47 000 000

RUSSIA
1 Adygea
2 Karachey-Cherkessia
3 Kabardino-Balkaria
4 North Ossetia
  Alaniya
5 Ingushetia
6 Chechenia
7 Dagestan
8 Mordvinia
9 Chuvashia
10 Mari El
11 Tatarstan
12 Udmurtia

AZERBAIJAN
13 Naxçıvan

GEORGIA
14 Ajaria
15 Abkhazia

● Hanoi  Capital Cities

East from Greenwich

Projection: Bonne

1:20 000 000

RUSSIA
1 Adygea
2 Karachey-Cherkessia
3 Kabardino-Balkaria
4 North Ossetia-Alaniya
5 Ingushetia
6 Chechenia
7 Dagestan
8 Mordvinia
9 Chuvashia
10 Mari El
11 Tatarstan
12 Udmurtia
13 Khakassia
AZERBAIJAN
14 Naxçivan
GEORGIA
15 Ajaria
16 Abkhazia

Projection: Conical Orthomorphic with two standard parallels

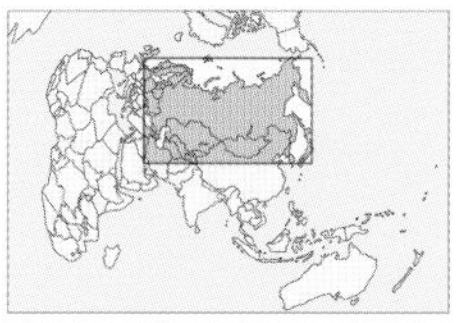

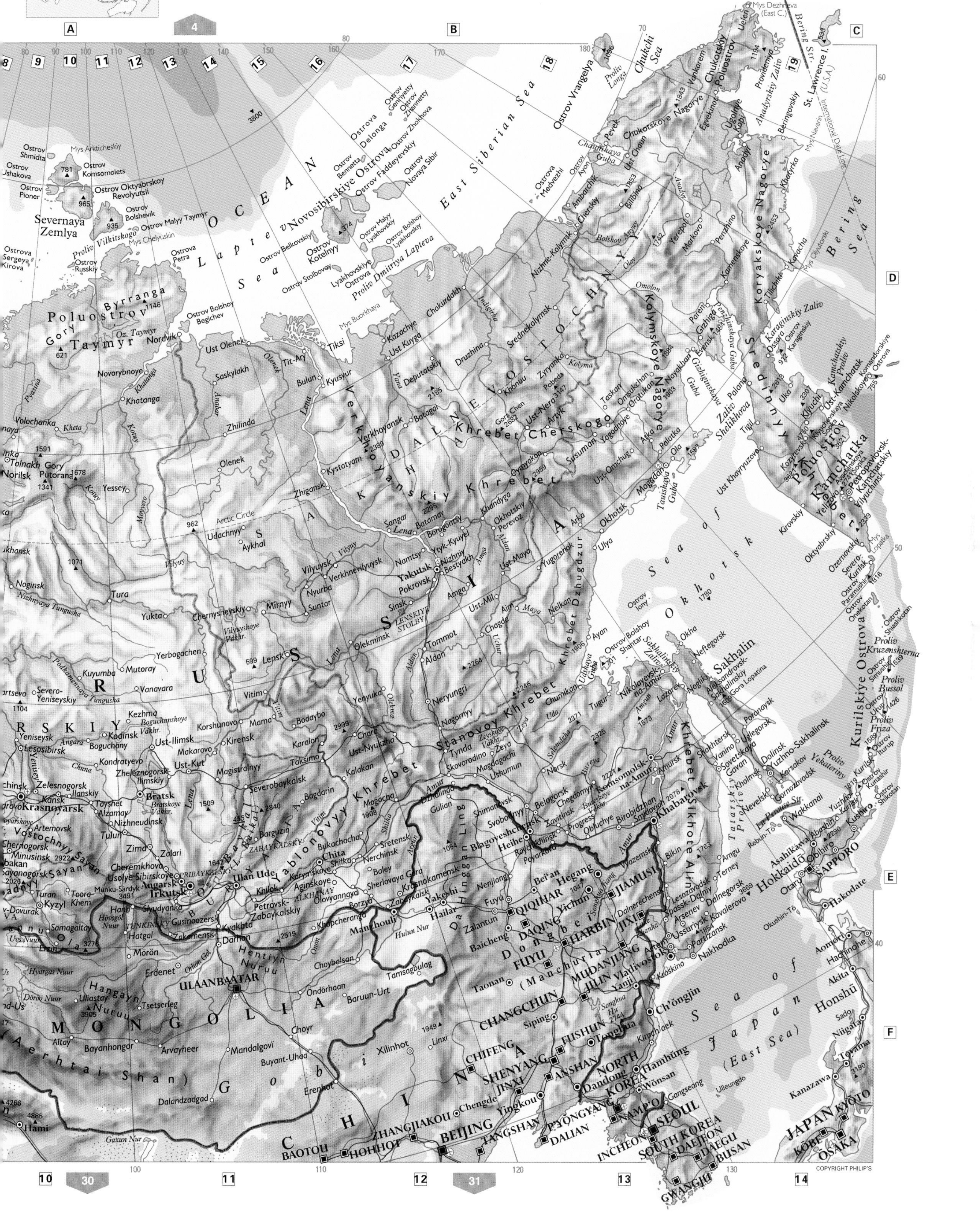

A 4 B C

Mys Dezhneva (East C.)

Chukchi Sea

**O C E A N**

**L a p t e v**

**Sea**

East Siberian Sea

Bering Str.

St. Lawrence I. (U.S.A.)

International Date Line

Ostrova Delonga
Ostrov Genyetty
Ostrov Zhinnetty
Ostrov Zhokhova

Ostrov Bennetta
Novosibirskiye Ostrova
Ostrov Faddeyevskiy
Ostrov Novaya Sibir

Ostrov Vrangelya
Proliv Longa

Chukotskoye Nagorye

Mys Arkticheskiy

Ostrov Shmidta
Ostrov Komsomolets
Ostrov Ushakova
Ostrov Pioner
Ostrov Oktyabrskoy Revolyutsii
Ostrov Bolshevik

Severnaya Zemlya

Ostrov Malyy Taymyr
Ostrov Russkiy
Ostrova Sergeya Kirova

Proliv Vilkitskogo
Mys Chelyuskin

Ostrov Bolshoy Begichev

Ostrov Kotelnyy
Lyakhovskiye Ostrova
Ostrov Bolshoy Lyakhovskiy

Proliv Dmitriya Lapteva

Ostrov Belkovskiy
Ostrov Stolbovoy

Ostrova Medvezhi

Ayon
Chaunskaya Guba

Bering Sea

Poluostrov Taymyr
Gory Byrranga

Koryakskoye Nagorye

Sredinnyy

Kamchatka

Poluostrov Kamchatka

Petropavlovsk-Kamchatskiy

Sea of Okhotsk

Sakhalin

Kurilskiye Ostrova

Severo-Kurilsk

Sea of Japan (East Sea)

Hokkaido
SAPPORO
Hakodate

Honshū

**MONGOLIA**

**ULAANBAATAR**

**C H I N A**

**(Manchuria)**

**HARBIN**
**CHANGCHUN**
**QIQIHAR**
**DAQING**
**JIAMUSI**
**JIXI**
**MUDANJIANG**
**JILIN**
**FUSHUN**
**SHENYANG**
**ANSHAN**
**FUYU**
**CHIFENG**
**BEIJING**
**TANGSHAN**
**BAOTOU**
**HOHHOT**
**ZHANGJIAKOU**
**DALIAN**

**NORTH KOREA**
**PYONGYANG**
**NAMPO**
**Hamhŭng**
**Wonsan**
**Chŏngjin**

**SOUTH KOREA**
**SEOUL**
**INCHEON**
**DAEJEON**
**DAEGU**
**BUSAN**
**GWANGJU**

**JAPAN**
**KYOTO**
**OSAKA**
**KOBE**

Bratsk
Irkutsk
Ulan Ude
Chita
Krasnoyarsk
Norilsk

Yakutsk
Verkhoyansk

Khrebet Cherskogo
Stanovoy Khrebet
Yablonovyy Khrebet

COPYRIGHT PHILIP'S

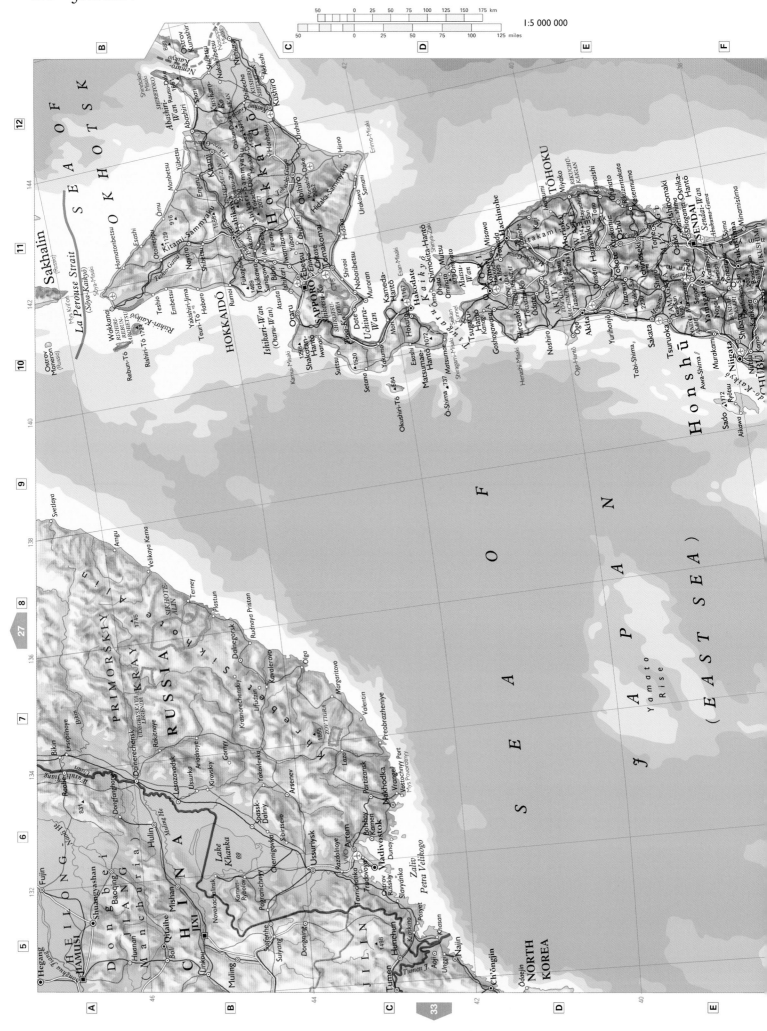

1:5 000 000

50    0   25  50  75  100  125 150  175 km
50       0      25    50     75    100   125 miles

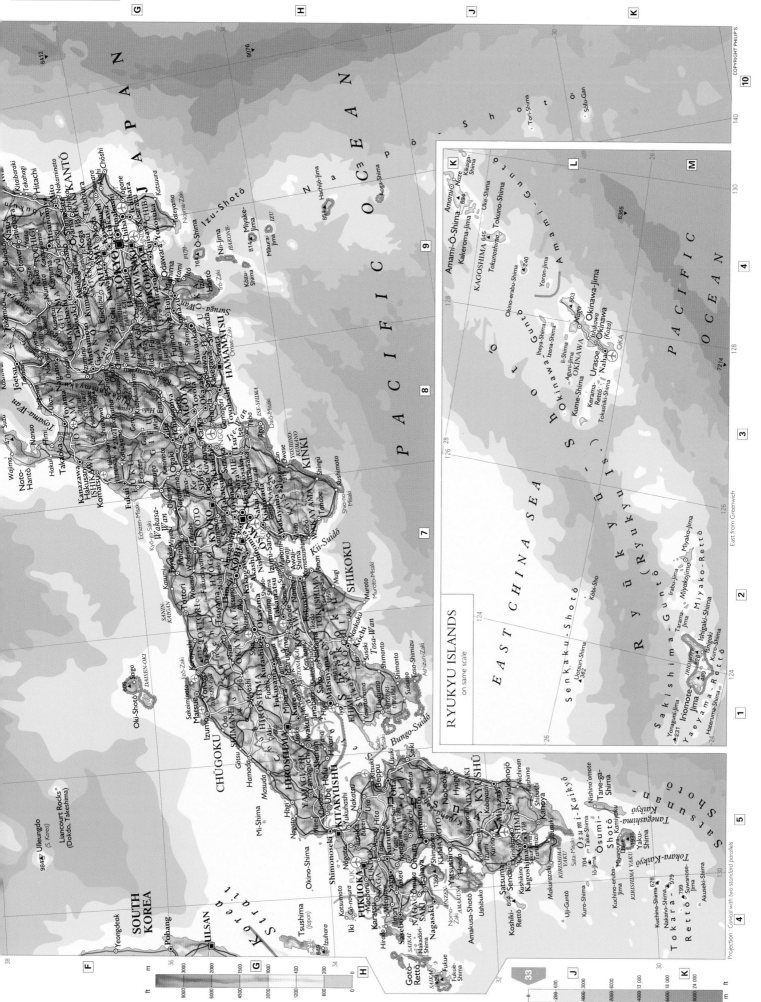

RYUKYU ISLANDS
on same scale

EAST CHINA SEA

PACIFIC OCEAN

PACIFIC OCEAN

SOUTH KOREA

JAPAN

Projection: Conical with two standard parallels

East from Greenwich

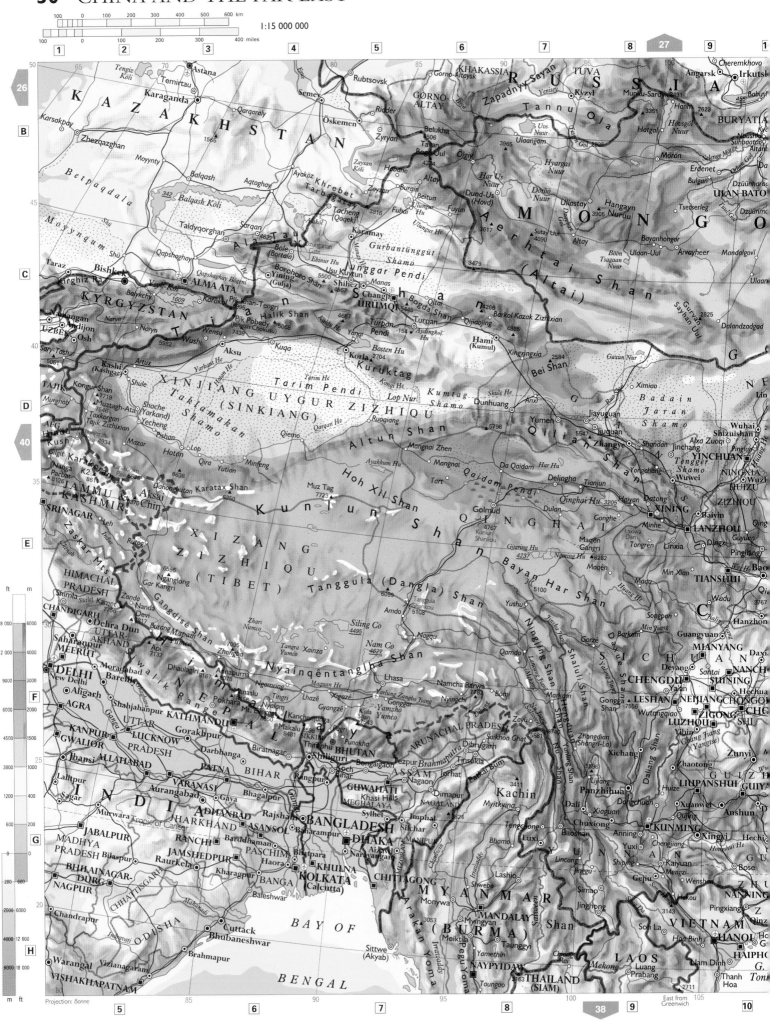

1:15 000 000

Projection: Bonne

East from Greenwich

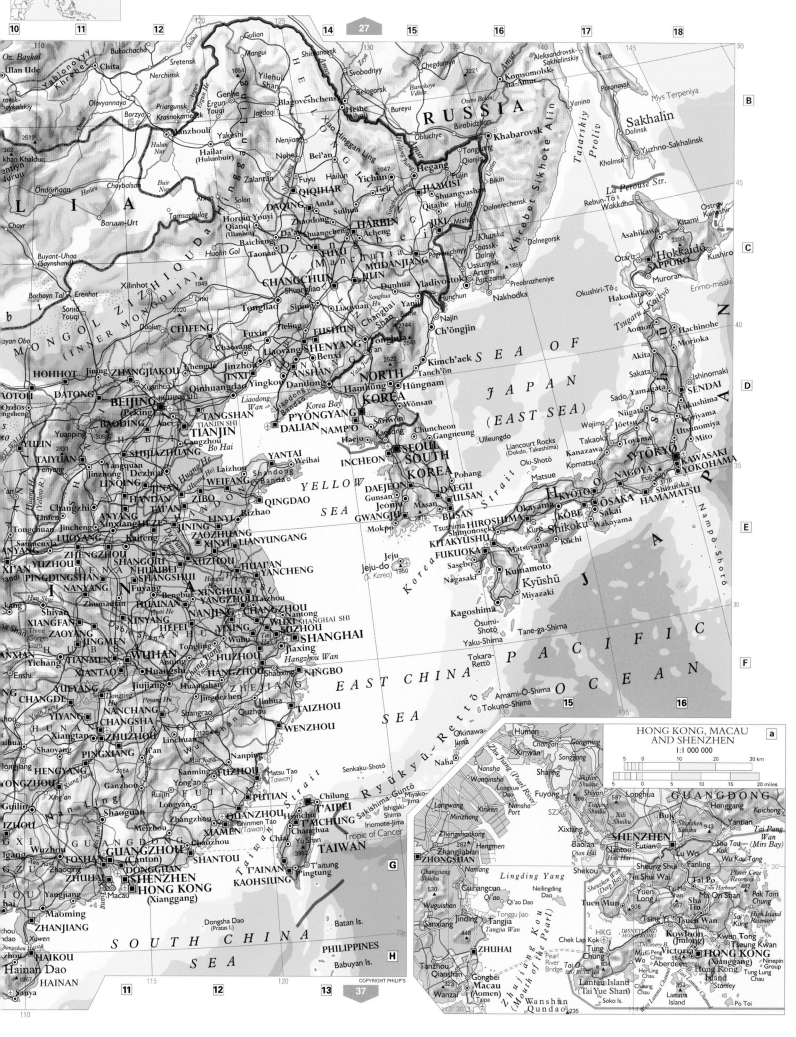

B

RUSSIA

C

Sakhalin

Z

Hokkaidō
SAPPORO

SEA OF

JAPAN
(EAST SEA)

D

NORTH
KOREA

P'YONGYANG

SEOUL
SOUTH
KOREA

TŌKYŌ
KAWASAKI
YOKOHAMA

E

YELLOW

SEA

H O N S H U

J A P A N

Nampō-Shotō

F

EAST CHINA

SEA

PACIFIC

OCEAN

Kyūshū

G

TAIWAN

Tropic of Cancer

Ryūkyū-Rettō

H

SOUTH CHINA

SEA

PHILIPPINES

Hainan Dao

HAINAN

COPYRIGHT PHILIP'S

### HONG KONG, MACAU AND SHENZHEN

1:1 000 000

GUANGDONG

SHENZHEN

ZHUHAI

Macau
(Aomen)

HONG KONG
(Xianggang)

Kowloon
(Julong)

Victoria

HONG KONG
(Xianggang)

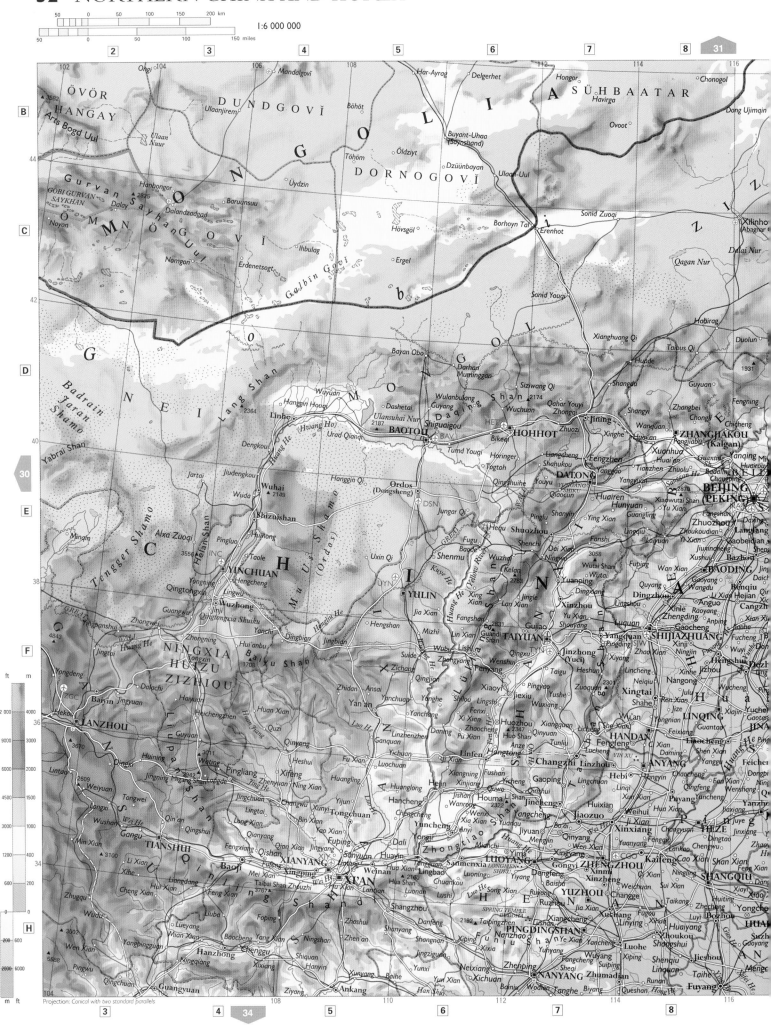

1:6 000 000

1:6 000 000

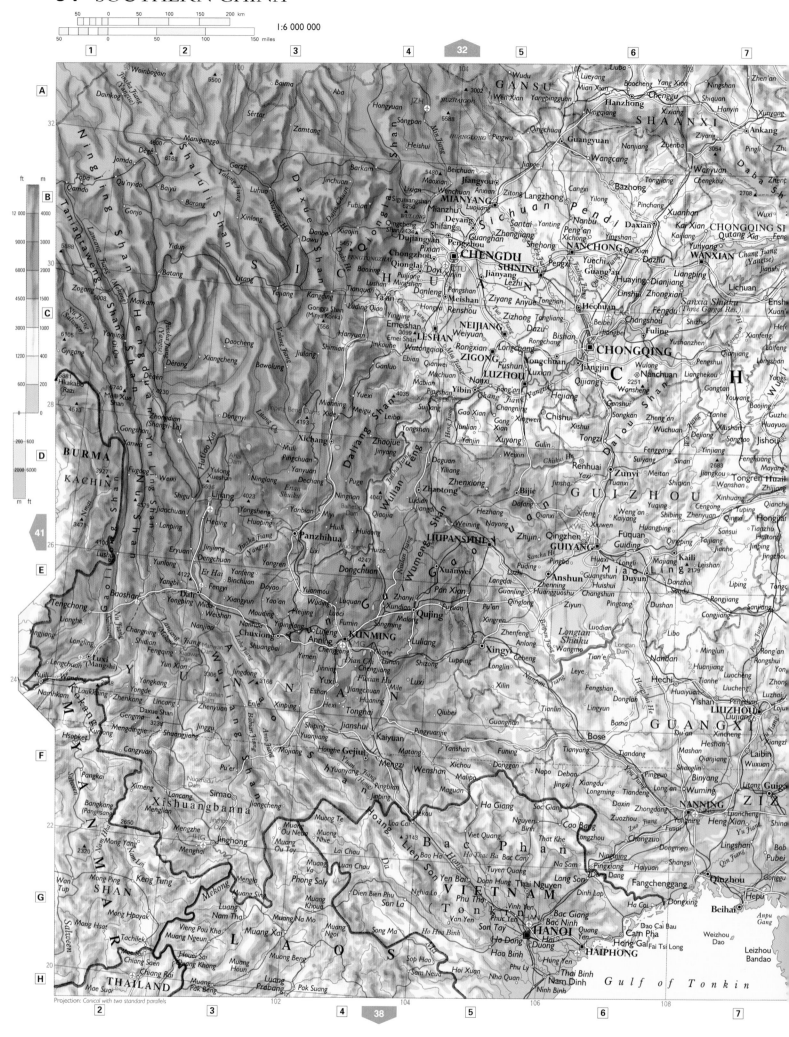

1:12 500 000

Projection: Mercator

East from Greenwich

## JAVA AND MADURA
1:7 500 000

50   0   50   100   150   200   250   300 km
50   0   50   100   150   200 miles

## BALI
1:2 000 000

10   0   10   20   30 km
10   0   10   20 miles

**Luzon**
Claveria, Babuyan Chan., C. Engaño
Bacarra, Laoag, Aparri, Tuguegarao
Vigan, Batac, Bangued, Tugo
Bontoc, Santiago, Palanan Pt., Palanan
San Fernando, Baguio, Bayombong, Casiguran
Bolinao, Lingayen, Cabanatuan, C. San Ildefonso
Dagupan, San Jose, Angeles, Mt. Pinatubo, Polillo Is.
Olongapo, San Fernando, Polillo Is.
Bataan, **MANILA**, Lamon Bay
Manila B., Cavite, Santa Cruz, Daet
Lubang, Batangas, Lucena, Calauag, Naga, Virac, Catanduanes
Calapan, Marinduque, Mayon Volcano, Legazpi, Lagonoy Gulf
Mamburao, Mindoro, Sibuyan, Tabaco, Burias, Sorsogon
Halcon, Romblon, Masbate, Bulan, Catarman, Samar
Tablas, Masbate, Oras, Taft

**Philippine Sea**

Sibuyan Sea, Visayan Sea, Borongan, General MacArthur, Guiuan
Kalibo, Pandan, Panay, Roxas, Leyte, Baybay, Tacloban
Iloilo, Pototan, Cadiz, San Carlos, Ormoc, Maasin
Bacolod, Guimaras, Bohol, Taliban, Dinagat, Siargao
Negros, Tanjay, Cebu, Mandaue, Surigao, Tandag
Dumaguete, Dipolog, Siquijor, Camiguin, L. Mainit, Cagayan
Puerto Princesa, Oroquieta, Cagayan de Oro, Butuan, Lianga
Iligan, Malaybalay, Cateel, Baganga
Ozamiz, Pagadian, Parang, Tagum
Zamboanga, Cotabato, Illang B., Talayan, Mt. Apo, **DAVAO**, Mati
Isabela, Lebak, Koronadal, Digos, Davao Gulf
Basilan, General Santos, Kiamba, Malita, C. San Agustin
Jolo, Samales Group, Sarangani B., Tinaca Pt., Kepulauan Nanusa

**SULU SEA**
**CELEBES SEA**

Tawi-tawi, Sibutu Passage, Sipadan, Tahuna
Pulau Sangihe, Salibabu, Kepulauan Talaud
Karakelong, Beo, Siau, Karakitang, Kepulauan Sangihe
Tahulandang, Biaro

**PACIFIC OCEAN**

Tobi (Palau), Helen Atoll (Palau), Merir (Palau)
Sopi, Berebere, Morotai, Galela, Tobelo
Bunaken, Manado, Kema, Tondano, Ibu, Akelamo, **Halmahera**
Amurang, Kotamobagu, Ternate, Tidore, Jailolo, Weda
**GORONTALO**, Tilamuta, Makian, Kayoa, Patani, Gebe
Gorontalo, Moutong, UTARA, Teluk Weda, Wosi, Umera, Waigeo
Togian, Poh, Peleng, Kepulauan Bacan, Mandioli, Gani
Palu, Parigi, Luwuk, Taliabu, Bisa, Obilatu, Kofiau, Salawati, Sorong
Poso, Tokala, Banggai, Mangole, Kawasi, Segel, Teminabuan
Kolonodale, Todeli, Kepulauan Sula, Obi, Sailolo, Inanwatan
Kendari, Buru, Namlea, Wamlan, Tifu, Namrole, Fluk, Misool, Bintuni
**Sulawesi (Celebes)**, Kolaka, Monse, Wowoni, Kayeli, Amahai, Tehoru, Waru
Watampone, Buton, Buton, Raha, Lawele, Ambon, **MALUKU**, Geser
Sinjai, Muna, Wangiwangi, Kepulauan Banda, Bandanaira, Manggawitu
Bulukumba, Baubau, Binongko, Tukangbesi, Kepulauan Watubela
Salayar, Benteng, Batuata, Kepulauan Kai
Tanahjampea, Kaloa, Bonerate, Gunungapi, Damar, Nila, Serua, Tual, Kai Besar
Kalaotoa, Wetar, Wasiri, Romang, Teun, Daya, Kai Kecil, Banda Elat, Doba
Huwati, Moa, Lakor, Babar, Wuliaru, Selu, Larat, Rebi, Trangan, Kepulauan Aru
Flores, Lorantuka, Adonara, Lomblen, Pantar, Alor, Atauro, Dili, Baucau, Leti, Sermata, Kepulauan Tanimbar, Saumlaki
**TIMOR-LESTE** (E. Timor), Viqueque, Eliase, Selaru, Tafermaar
**NUSA TENGGARA TIMUR**, Kefamenanu, Nikiniki, Tanjung Vals
Sumba, Waingapu, Waikabubak, Melolo, Baing, Sawu, Raijua, Dana, Rote, Selat Roti, Kupang
**SAWU SEA**, **ARAFURA SEA**

**BANDA SEA**, **FLORES SEA**

**IRIAN JAYA BARAT**, Sorong, Klamono, Teminabuan, Nabire, Pegunungan Sudirman, **Pegunungan Maoke**, Wamena, Timika, Tembagapura, Jayawijaya
**PAPUA NEW GUINEA**
Jayapura, Sarmi, Genyem, Krau
Pulau Dolak, Kimaam, Tanahmerah, Pirimapun, Muting, Okaba, Merauke, WASUR

**Java and Madura inset:**
Merak, Anyer, Serang, **JAKARTA**, Tangerang, Bekasi, Karawang, Pamanukan, Indramayu
Selat Sunda, Pulau Rakata, Labuhan, Rangkasbitung, **Bogor**, Purwakarta, Cirebon, Brebes, Tegal, Pekalongan, Kendal, Demak, Rembang, Tuban, **Madura**, Sumenep
**BANTEN**, Pelabuhanratu, Sukabumi, **BANDUNG**, Sumedang, Majalengka, Kuningan, Batang, **Semarang**, Pati, Blora, Bojonegoro, Bangkalan, Sampang, Pamekasan, Raas
Pangandaran, Tasikmalaya, Garut, Ciamis, Purwokerto, Purbalingga, Wonosobo, Magelang, Salatiga, Purwodadi, Ngawi, Mojokerto, **SURABAYA**, Sidoarjo, Gresik, Pasuruan, Situbondo
BARAT, TENGAH, Cilacap, Kebumen, Purworejo, Yogyakarta, Surakarta, Madiun, Kediri, Jombang, Pare, Malang, Probolinggo, Bondowoso, Jember, Banyuwangi
**TIMUR**, Pacitan, Trenggalek, Tulungagung, Blitar, Lumajang, Nusa Barung, Bali
**YOGYAKARTA**

**Bali inset:**
**BALI SEA**, Tanjung Batugondang, Singaraja, Kubutambahan, Tejakula
Gilimanuk, Gerokgak, Lovina, Seririt, Kintamani, Tianyar, Kubu
Banyuwangi, Glagah, Melaya, Gunung Batur, Songan, Amed
Negara, Mendoyo, Pupuan, Penelokan, Gunung Agung, Culik, Tirtagangga
Yehbuah, Belimbing, Bedugul, Karangasem (Amlapura), Saren
**Bali**, Tabanan, Bangli, Klungkung (Semarapura), Candi Dasa, **Lombok**
**Jawa**, Denpasar, Gianyar, Sukawati, Sanur, Kusamba, Padang Bai, Ampenan, Mataram
Legian, Kuta, Jimbaran, Nusa Dua, Nusa Lembongan, Nusa Penida, Gerung
Uluwatu, Tanjung Mebulu, Bukit Badung, **INDIAN OCEAN**, Teluk Terang, Blongas

**PACIFIC OCEAN**
**INDIAN OCEAN**

1:6 000 000

SOUTH CHINA SEA

Gulf of Thailand

Thailand

Kho Khot Kra (Isthmus of Kra)

ANDAMAN SEA

Straits of Malacca

MALAYSIA

PENINSULAR MALAYSIA

INDONESIA

SUMATERA

Kyunzu Myeik (Mergui Archipelago)

Gulf of Thailand

KO SAMUI 1:1 000 000

KO PHUKET 1:1 000 000

PINANG 1:1 000 000

Pulau Pinang

SINGAPORE 1:1 000 000

MALAYSIA

Straits of Singapore

INDONESIA

1:1 000 000

Projection: Conical with two standard parallels

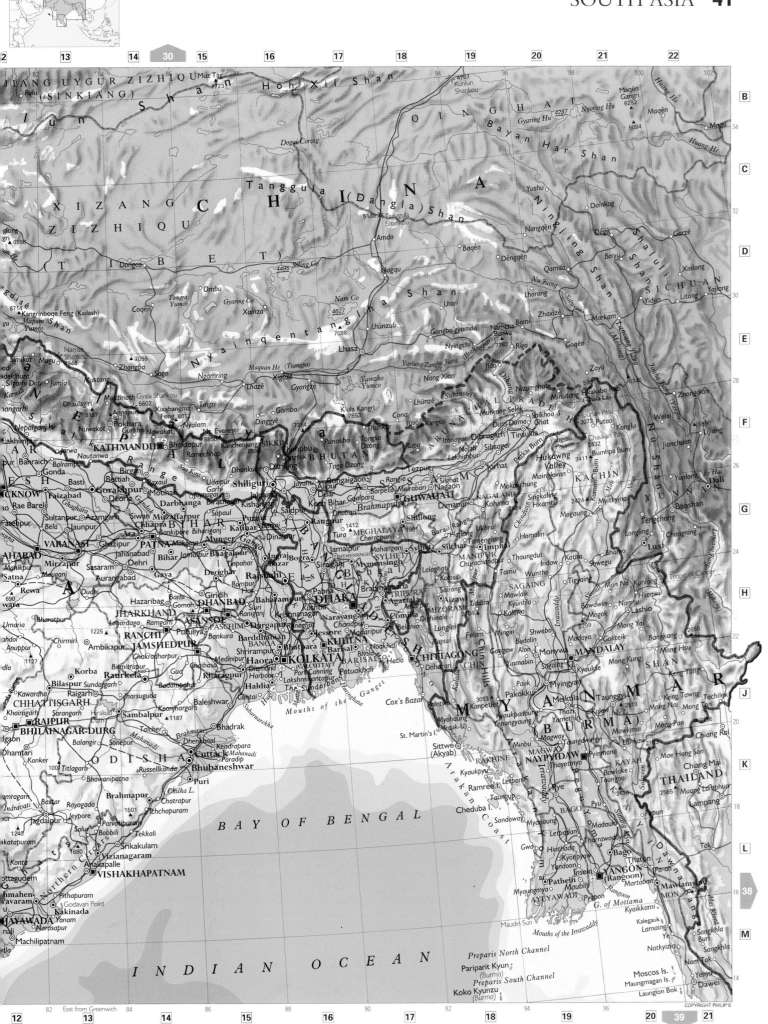

BAY OF BENGAL

INDIAN OCEAN

1:6 000 000

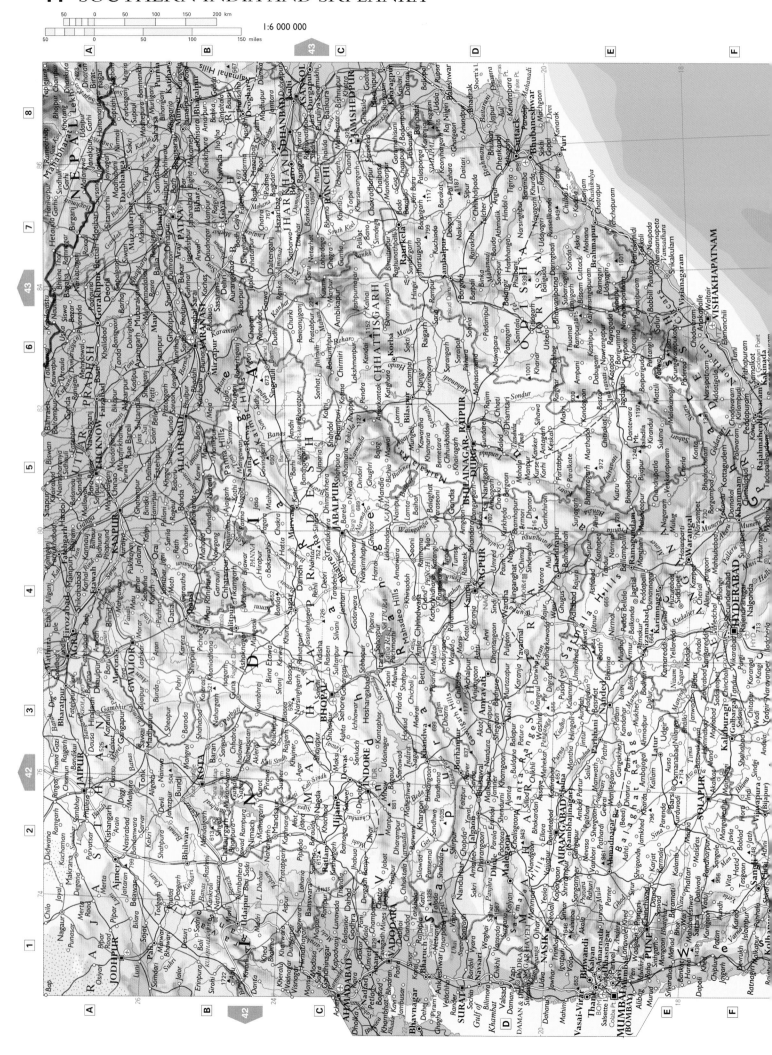

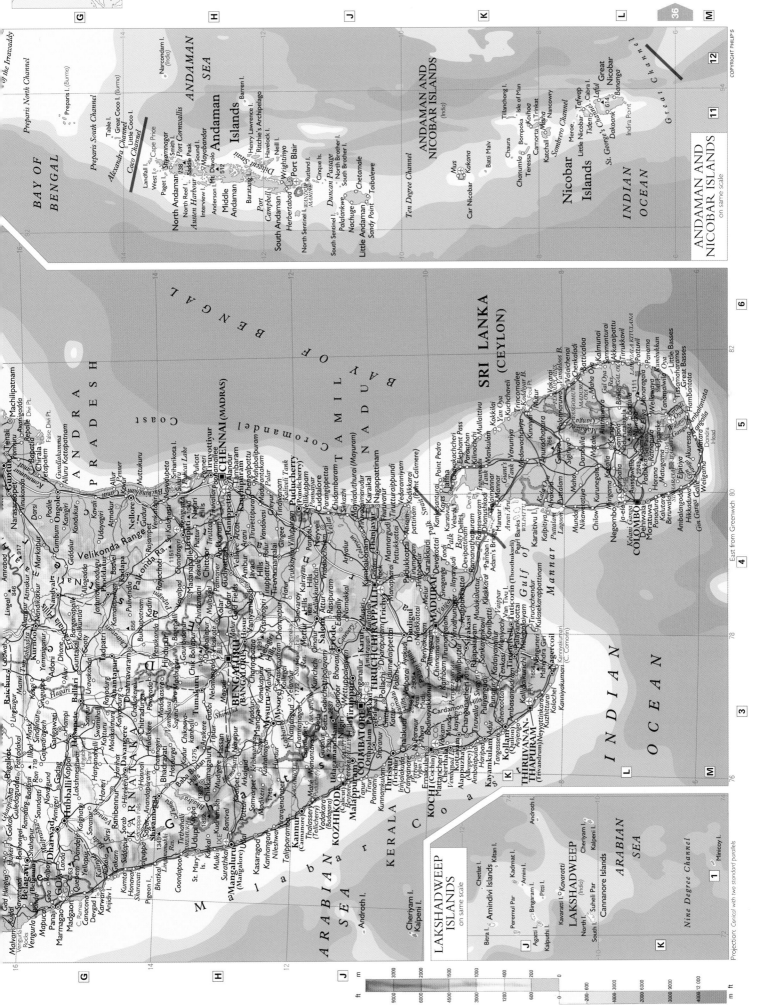

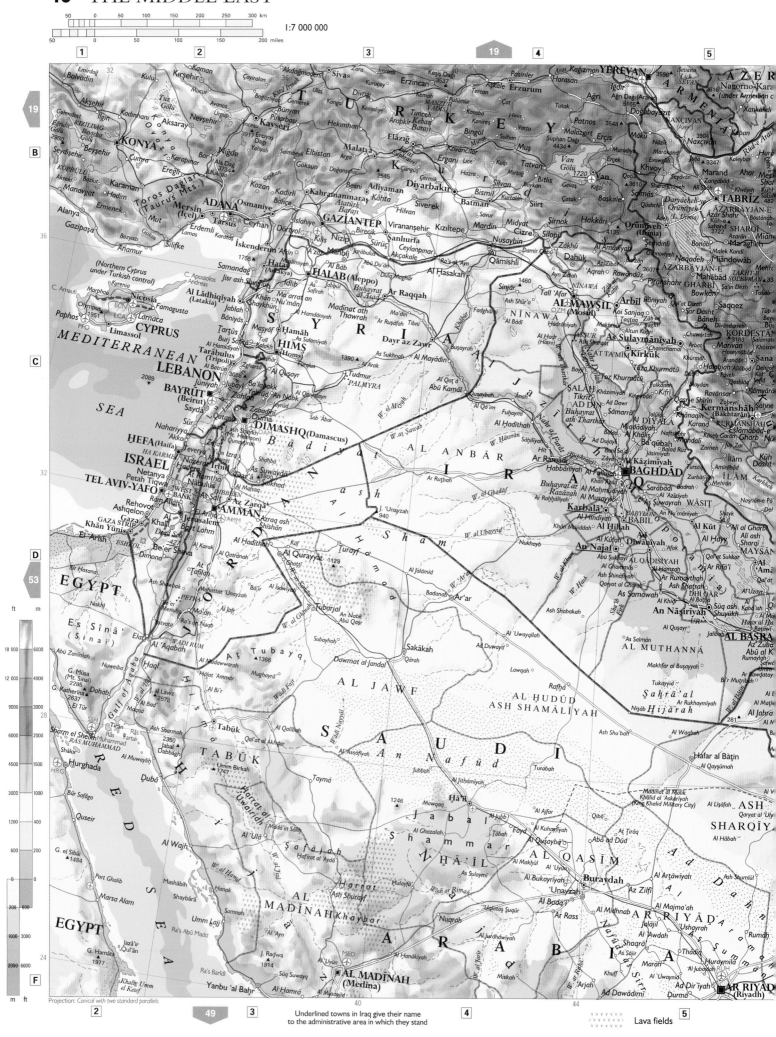

1:7 000 000

Projection: Conical with two standard parallels

Underlined towns in Iraq give their name
to the administrative area in which they stand

ⱽⱽⱽⱽⱽ
ⱽ ⱽ ⱽ ⱽ ⱽ   Lava fields

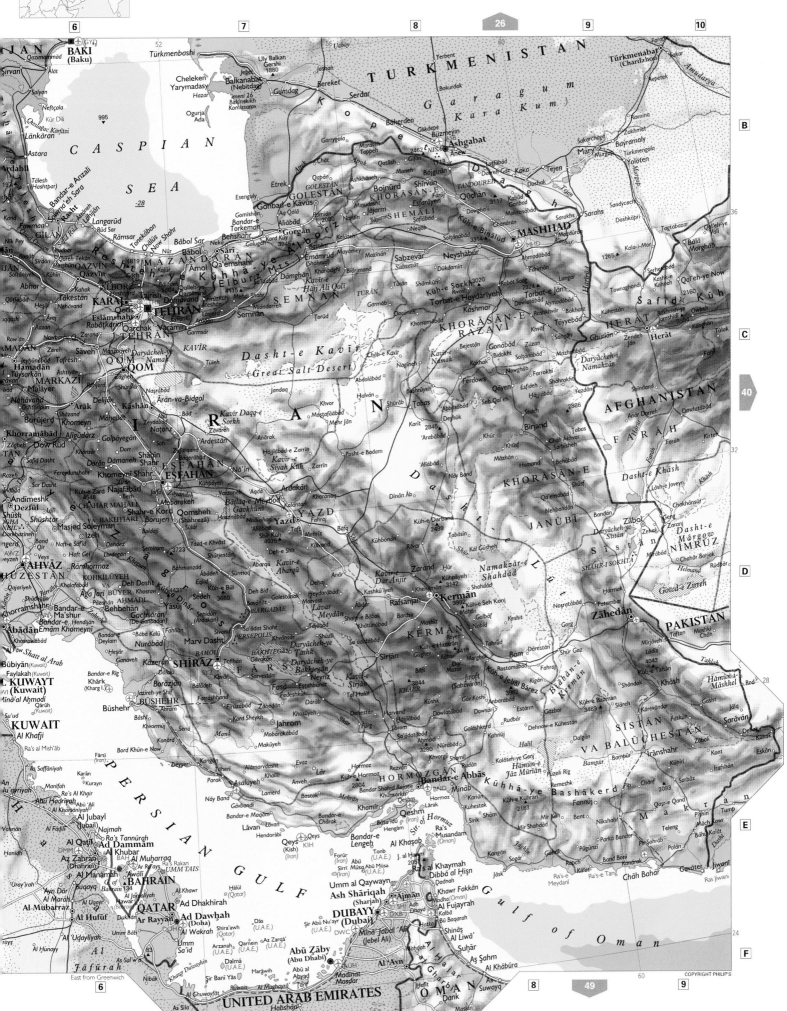

1:2 500 000

10 0 10 20 30 40 50 60 70 80 100 km
10 0 10 20 30 40 50 60 miles

| 1 | 2 | 3 | 4 | 46 5 | 6 |

**CYPRUS**

Paphos
PFO
Episkopi
Kividhes
Zyyi
Limassol
Akrotiri Bay
Episkopi Bay
C. Gata
▽ 2775

**M E D I T E R R A N E A N**

**S E A**

▽ 2089

Al Hamidiyah
HIMS
(Homs)
Kalakh
Shinshār
Furqlus

ASH SHAMĀL
Al Mīnā
**Tarābulus**
(Tripoli)
Zgharta
Qurnat as Sawdā ▲ 3088
Bsharri
Al Hirmil
Al Qusayr

**H I M Ş**

Al Batrūn
Qartaba
Jubayl
Ibrāhim
▲ 2464
Al Buráyj
Al Qaryatayn
Bi'r Ghadir

Al Labwah
2616

Jūniyah
Bikfayya
J. al Barūk

**BAYRŪT** (Beirut) BEY
Ash Shuwayfāt
Alayh
Zahlah
Singhaya
2628 J. Sannin
Ba'labakk
Yabrūd
An Nabk

**SYRIA**

Ad Dāmūr
JABAL LUBNĀN
Hawsh Mūssá
Az Zabadāni
Al Qutayfah
Khan Abū Shāmat

**LEBANON**
Saydā (Sidon)
Jazzīn
▲ 1942 J. al Barūk
Mt. Hermon 2814
Ash Shayk
Dūma
**DIMASHQ** (Damascus)
Darayya
DAM
Jaramānah
Qatana
Al Hājānah

An Nabatiyah at Tahta
Marj 'Uyun
Al Qunaytirah
Burāq
As Sanamayn

**AL JANŪB**
Sūr (Tyre)
Qiryat Shemona
Ash Shaykh
Al Khiyam
Q. Masada
A'war

D A R
D A R

Nahariyya
Hagalil (Galilee)
1208 Zefat
Yam Kinneret (Sea of Galilee)
Shaykh Miskin
As Suwaydā

'Akko (Acre)
Mifraz Hefa
Qiryat Karmi'el
Teverya (Tiberias)
▽ -210
Fiq
AL 'ASUWAYDĀ
Shahbā
▲ 1900

**HEFA** (Haifa)
Qiryat Ata
Har Ha Karmel 546
Nazerat (Nazareth)
Yarmūk
Sahem al Jawlān
Malah

HEFA KARMEL
TEL MEGIDDO
Afula
Taiyiba
Darā
Ar Ramthā

CAESAREA
Ummel Fahm
Bet She'an
**I R B I D**
Umm el Qittayn

Hadera
Jenin
Tirat Zevi
AJLŪN
Al Mafraq

Pardes Hanna-Karkur
**ISRAEL**
Shomron
SAMARIA
Tūbās
'Ajlūn
Jarash
**AL MAFRAQ**

Netanya
HAMERKAZ
Tulkarm
Nablus
N. az Zarqā
JARASH

Herzliyya
Ra'ananna
Kefar Sava
Al Balqā
Az Zarqā

Benē Beraq
**TEL AVIV-YAFO**
Petah Tiqwa
As Salt
Ar Ruşayfah

Ramat Gan
TLV
Jilā' al 'Ali
**AMMĀN**

Bat Yam
Holon
Lod
Rām Allāh (Ramallah)
Wādi as Sir
Al Quwaysimah

Rishon le Ziyyon
Yavne
Rehovot
El Arīhā (Jericho)
Na'ūr
AMM

Ashdod
Ramla
**WEST BANK**
Azraq ash Shishān

Qiryat Malakhi
Bet Shemesh
**Jerusalem** (Yerushalayim) (Al Quds)
Ma'daba
AZ ZARQĀ

Ashqelon
Qiryat Gat
Bayt Lāhm (Bethlehem)
MA'DABA

Beit Lāhiyā
Jabālyā
Al Khalīl (Hebron)
Dhibān

**GAZA STRIP**
Gaza
Sederot
Az Zāhiriyya
'En Gedi
UMM AR RASAS
AL Hadithah

Deir al Balah
Nuseirāt
Rahat
MASADA

Khān Yūnis
Rafah
Be'er Sheva (Beersheba)
En Boqeq
AL KARAK
Al Mazar

Arad
Sedom
1305
Al Karak

Būr Sa'īd (Port Said)
Būr Fu'ad
BŪR SA'ĪD
Khalig el Tina
Râs Burûn
Sabkhet el Bardawil
El Daheir
Bor Mashash
Dimona
-333
Al Qatrānah

Rāmāni
Bir el Abd
El 'Arîsh
Bir el Garārāt
Bir Lahfān
W. al Hasā

El Qantara
Bir Qatia
Bir el Duweidar
Bir Kaseiba
**SHAMĀL SÎNÎ**
Qezi'ot
Sedé Boqér
At Tafilah
Dana
J. ash Shawmari ▲ 1072

Wâhid
Bir Madkūr
892 ▲
Abu 'Aweigila
Birein
Mizpe Ramon
Nijil
Mahattat 'Unayzah

Ismâ'iliya
Talâta
Bir el Mâlhi
Bir Hasana
892
Hanegev (Negev Desert)
Rujm Talat al Jamālah
▲ 1736
PETRA
Al Jafr
Qa'el Jafr

**ISMĀ'ILÎYA**
Khamsa
El Buheirat el Murrat el Kubra (Great Bitter L.)
G. Yi 'Allaq ▲ 1094
Bir Beiqa
El Agrūd
El Quseima
N. Paran
Wādi Mūsá
Ma'ān

Gineifa
Bir el Thamāda
W. el Brūk
W. Cnatya
El Agrūd
**MA'ĀN**

**E G Y P T**
Mamarr Mitlā
Bir Gebel Hisn
W. Mahash'en
El Kuntilla
Yotvata
Ra's an Naqb
Mahattat ash Shidiyah

El Suweis (Suez)
Adabiya
Uyūn Mūsa
**S Î N Â' (Sinai)**
1592
1754
Râs Sudr
Nakhl
Ain Sudr
W. el Ruqa
El Thamad
Rum
WADI RUM
**S A U D I**

Râs Matarma
948 ▲ G. el Kabrit
Gebel el Tîh
Bi'r Abu Muhammad
'En Avrona
Ra's an Naqb ▲ 1435
Al Mudawwarah

Abu Şandūq ▲ 2272
**JANŪB SÎNÎ**
Bir el Biarât
Bi'r al Butayihāt
Bi'r al Qattār
**A R A B I A**

EL SUWEIS
Bir Wuseit
1165
Gulf of Aqaba
W. an Nahbri
El 'Aqaba
Ela
Al 'Aqaba
Haql
Batn al Ghul

**J O R D A N**
Al Heditha
Bā'ir

**AL 'ĀSIMAH**

**AL 'AQABAH**

**M A ' Ā N**

**At Tubayq**

⊏⊐⊏ 1974 Cease Fire Lines

ft m
9000 3000
6000 2000
4500 1500
3000 1000
1200 400
600 200
0 0
100
200 500
1000 3000
2000 6000
m ft

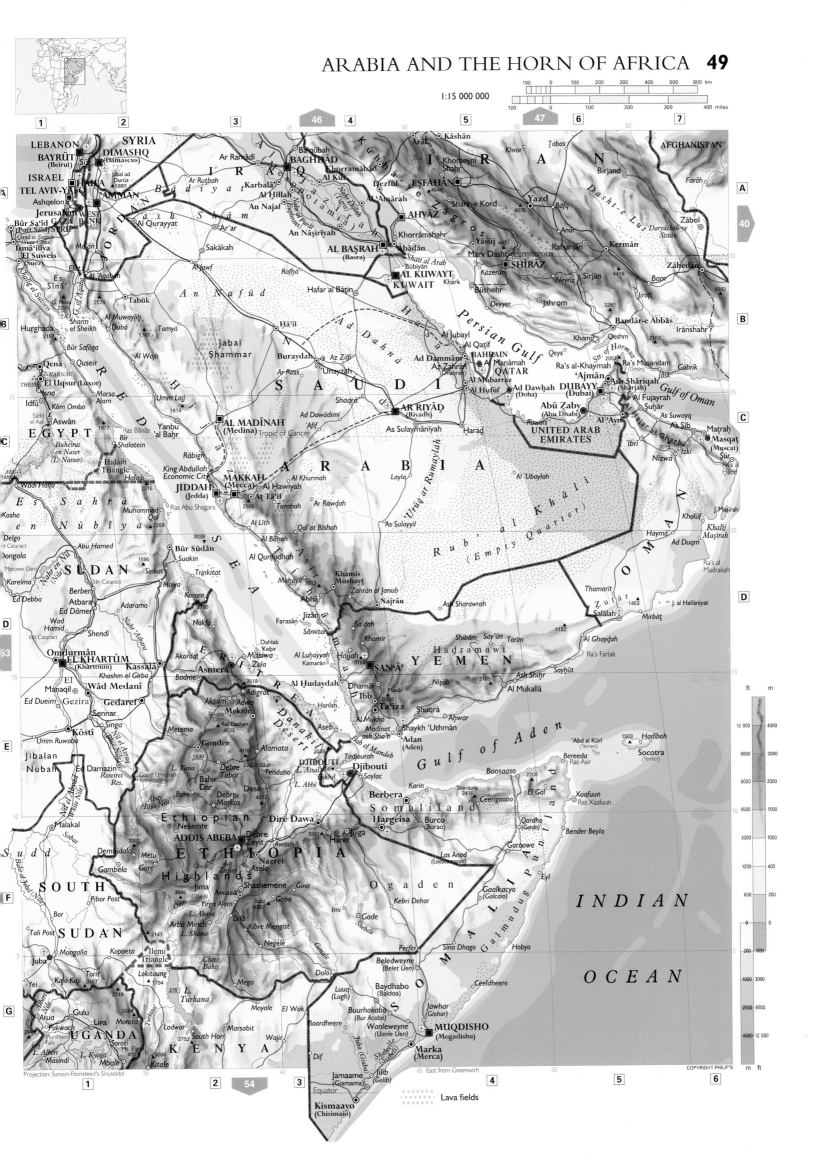

1:15 000 000

1:42 000 000

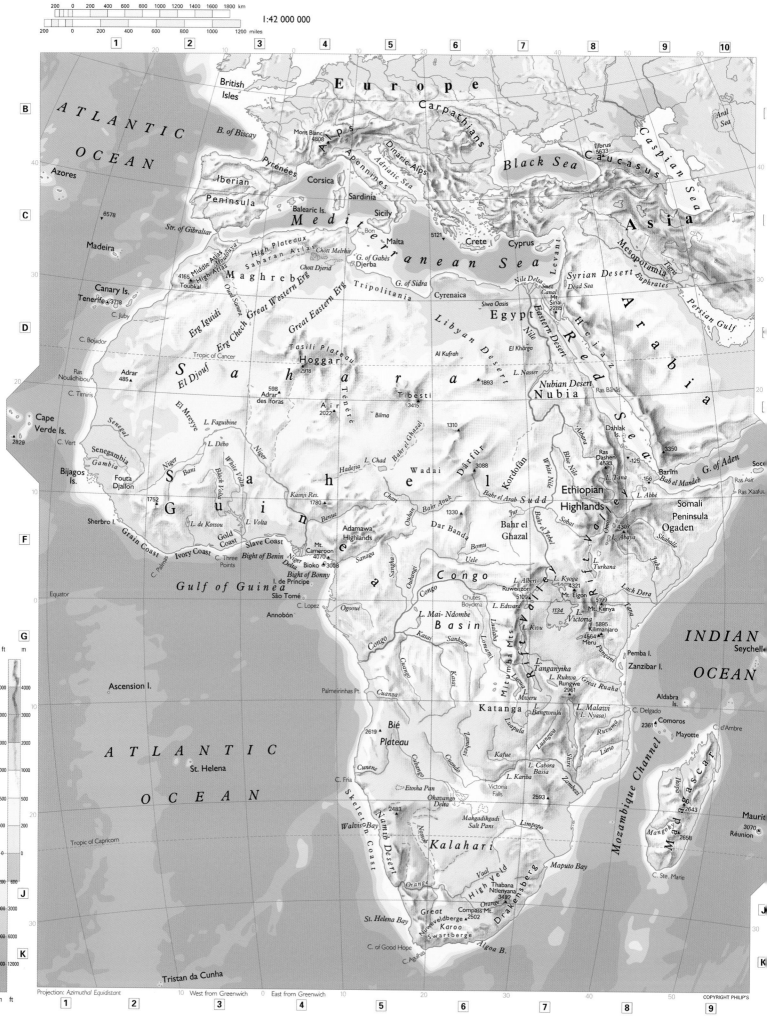

Projection: Azimuthal Equidistant

West from Greenwich    East from Greenwich

COPYRIGHT PHILIP'S

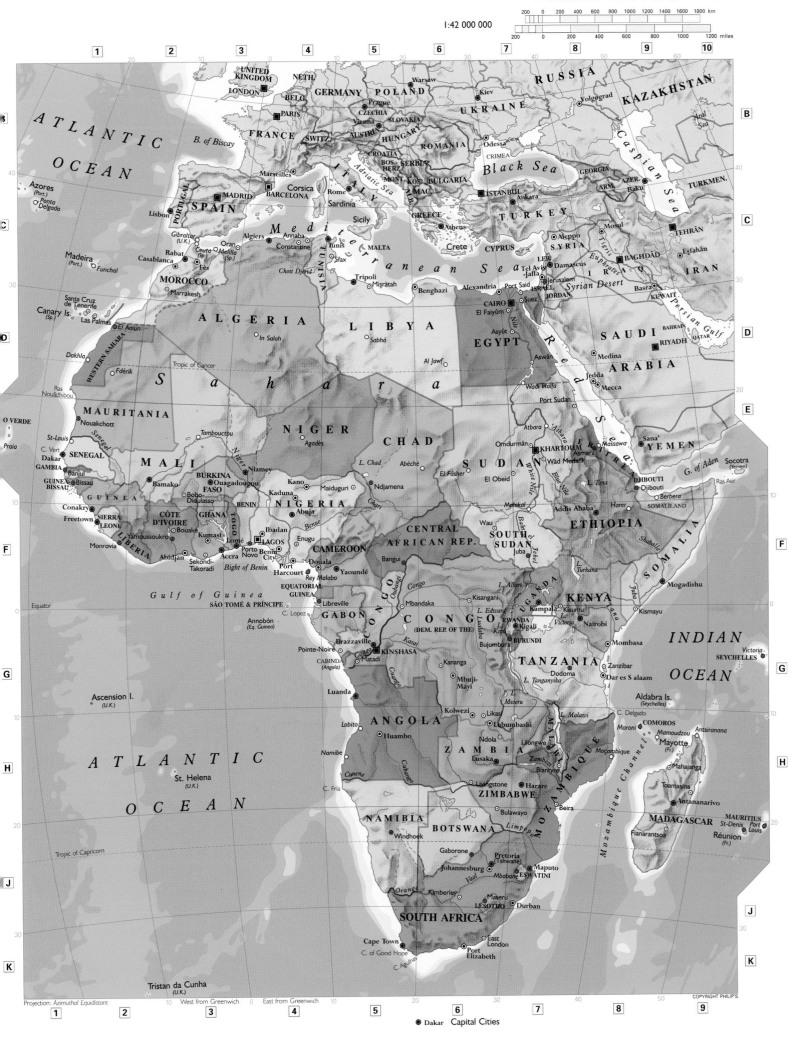

1:42 000 000

| 200 | 0 | 200 | 400 | 600 | 800 | 1000 | 1200 | 1400 | 1600 | 1800 km |
| 200 | 0 | 200 | 400 | 600 | 800 | 1000 | 1200 miles |

Projection: Azimuthal Equidistant

West from Greenwich    East from Greenwich

COPYRIGHT PHILIP'S

● Dakar  Capital Cities

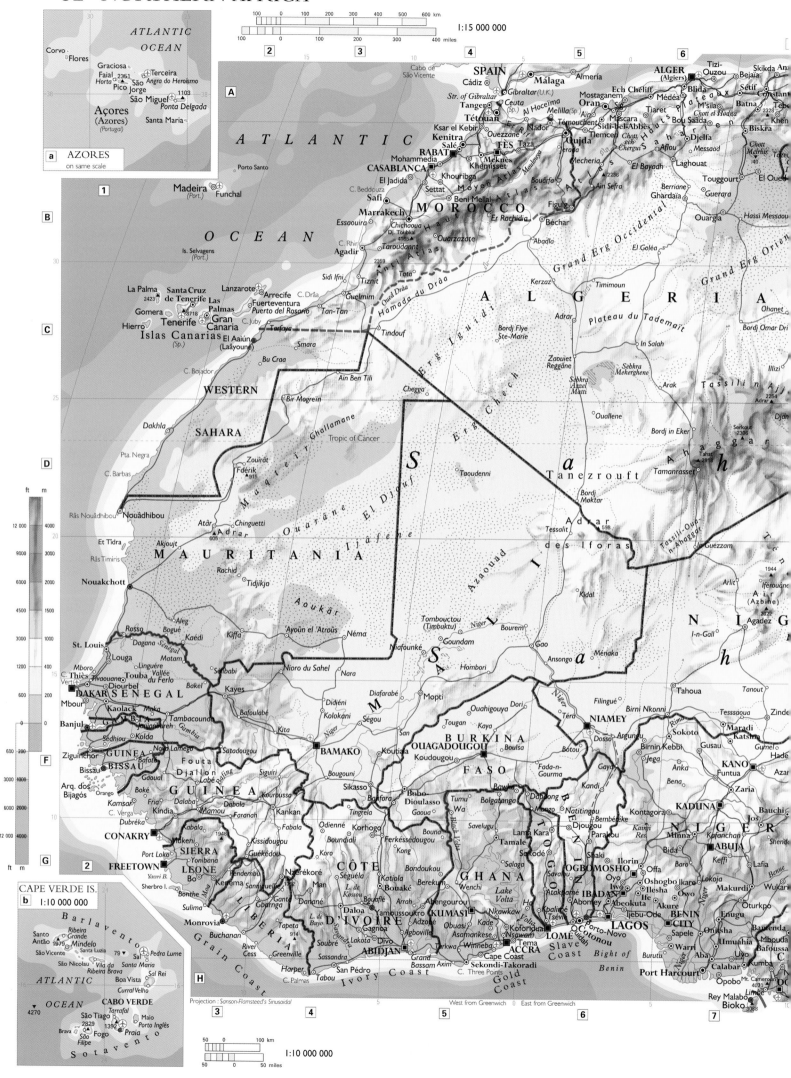

100 0 100 200 300 400 500 600 km

1:15 000 000

100 0 100 200 300 400 miles

**A**

ATLANTIC

OCEAN

Madeira (Port.) Funchal

Porto Santo

Is. Selvagens (Port.)

La Palma Santa Cruz Lanzarote
de Tenerife Arrecife C. Dráa
Gomera 2423 Las Fuerteventura
Tenerife Palmas Puerto del Rosario
Hierro Gran C. Juby
Islas Canarias Canaria
(Sp.) El Aaiún
(Laâyoune)

SPAIN
Cabo de São Vicente
Cádiz Málaga Almería ALGER (Algiers)
Str. of Gibraltar Tizi-Ouzou
Tanger Gibraltar (U.K.) Skikda Bejaïa
Ceuta (Sp.) Al Hoceima Constan
Tétouan Melilla (Sp.) Blida
Ksar el Kebir Nador Médéa Sétif
Kenitra Ouezzane Oujda Mascara Batna
RABAT Fès Taza Tiaret M'sila Biskra
Salé Meknès Sidi-bel-Abbès Aflou
CASABLANCA Khouribga Tlemcen Djelfa El
El Jadida Settat Beni Mellal Bou Saâda Laghouat
C. Beddouza Safi MOROCCO Figuig Ghardaïa Touggourt El Oued
Marrakech Er Rachidia Béchar El Goléa Ouargla
Essaouira Ouarzazate Abadla Grand Erg Occidental Hassi Messaoud
C. Rhir Agadir Anti Atlas Kerzaz Timimoun Grand Erg Orien
Sidi Ifni Tiznit Tata Ohanet
Guelmim Oued Dráa ALGERIA In Salah Plateau du Tademaït Bordj Omar Dri
Tan-Tan Hamada du Dráa Bordj Flye Ste-Marie Illizi
Tarfaya Tindouf Adrar Tassili n Ajj
Smara Erg Iguidi Zaouiet Sebkra 2254
Bu Craa Reggâne Mekerghene Adrar
WESTERN Chegga Sebkra Azzel Matti Arak
SAHARA Erg Chech Ouallene Bordj in Eker Serkout 2306
C. Bojador Maqteïr Ghallamane Ahaggar
Tropic of Cancer Tamanrasset
Zouîrât S a Tahat 2918 h
Fdérik Taoudenni Tanezrouft
915 Bordj Moktar
C. Barbas El Djouf Adrar Tassili-Oua
Râs Nouâdhibou Nouâdhibou Ouarâne Tessalit 598 n-Ahaggar
Atâr Chinguetti des Iforas In Guezzam
Et Tidra Adrar 605 Djan
Akjoujt 1944
MAURITANIA Kidal Iférouâne
Râs Timiris Rachid Air 2022
Nouakchott Tidjikja Azaouad (Azbine) Agadez
Aoukâr Arlit
Aleg Tombouctou Bourem I-n-Gall
Rosso Bogué Kaédi (Timbuktu) Gao N I G E
Dagana Kiffa 'Ayoûn el 'Atroûs Niger Ménaka Tahoua
St. Louis Sénégal Matam Néma Niafounké Tessaoua Zinde
Louga Linguère Nara Goundam Hombori Birni Nkonni Tanout
Mboro C. Thiès Diourbel Vallée Nioro du Sahel Ansongo Filingué Maradi
Verga Touba du Ferlo Kayes Tessalit Téra Katsina
DAKAR SENEGAL Bakel Diafarabé Dori NIAMEY Dosso Sokoto
Mbour Kaolack Tambacounda Didiéni Mopti Ouahigouya Argungu KANO
Banjul GAMBIA Kolda Kita Kolokani Ségou San Kaya BURKINA Botou Birnin Kebbi Funtua
Ziguinchor Sédhiou Bafoulabé BAMAKO Koutiala OUAGADOUGOU Fada-n-Gourma Jega Gusau
GUINEA Nova Lamego Satadougou Bougouni Koudougou FASO Kandi Zaria
BISSAU Bafatá Fouta Siguiri Sikasso Bobo- Tumu Bolgatanga Kontagora KADUNA
Bissau Djallon Labé Kankan Dioulasso Wa Pama Natitingou Minna
Arq. dos Boké Baling Dabola Banfora Gaoua Savelugu Bembéréké Bida ABUJA
Bijagós Kamsar Fria Kindia Dubréka Faranah Odienné Korhogo Tamale Sakodé Shaki NIGER
Dalaba Kabala Kissidougou Boundiali Ferkessédougou Kong Salaga Djougou OGBOMOSHO Ilorin Keffi
CONAKRY Mamou 1948 Fabala Bouna Parakou Oyo Offa Lafia
SIERRA Mokeni Nzérékoré Séguéla Katiola Bondoukou Lake Atakpamé Ife Oshogbo Lokoja
LEONE Yonibana Man Bouaké Berekum GHANA Volta Kpalimé Sévé Abeokuta Akure Wukari
FREETOWN Bo Danané Bouaflé Wenchi Nkawkaw Kade IBADAN Oturkpo
Sherbro I. Kenema Daloa Arrah Abengourou Obuasi LAGOS Porto- BENIN Enugu
Monrovia LIBERIA Tapeta 914 KUMASI Kumawu Asamankese LOMÉ Novo CITY Sapele
Buchanan D'IVOIRE Gagnoa Adzopé Koforidua ACCRA Cotonou Onitsha
Greenville Divo Abidjan Winneba Umuahia
CÔTE Sassandra Cape Coast Sekondi-Takoradi Slave Warri Aba
San Pédro Axim Bight of Port Harcourt Calabar
Tabou C. Three Points Gold Benin Bioko Mt. Cameroon
Harper Ivory Coast Coast Rey Malabo 4070 Limbé

Projection: Sanson-Flamsteed's Sinusoidal

West from Greenwich East from Greenwich

50 0 100 km
1:10 000 000
50 0 50 miles

Lava fields

1:15 000 000

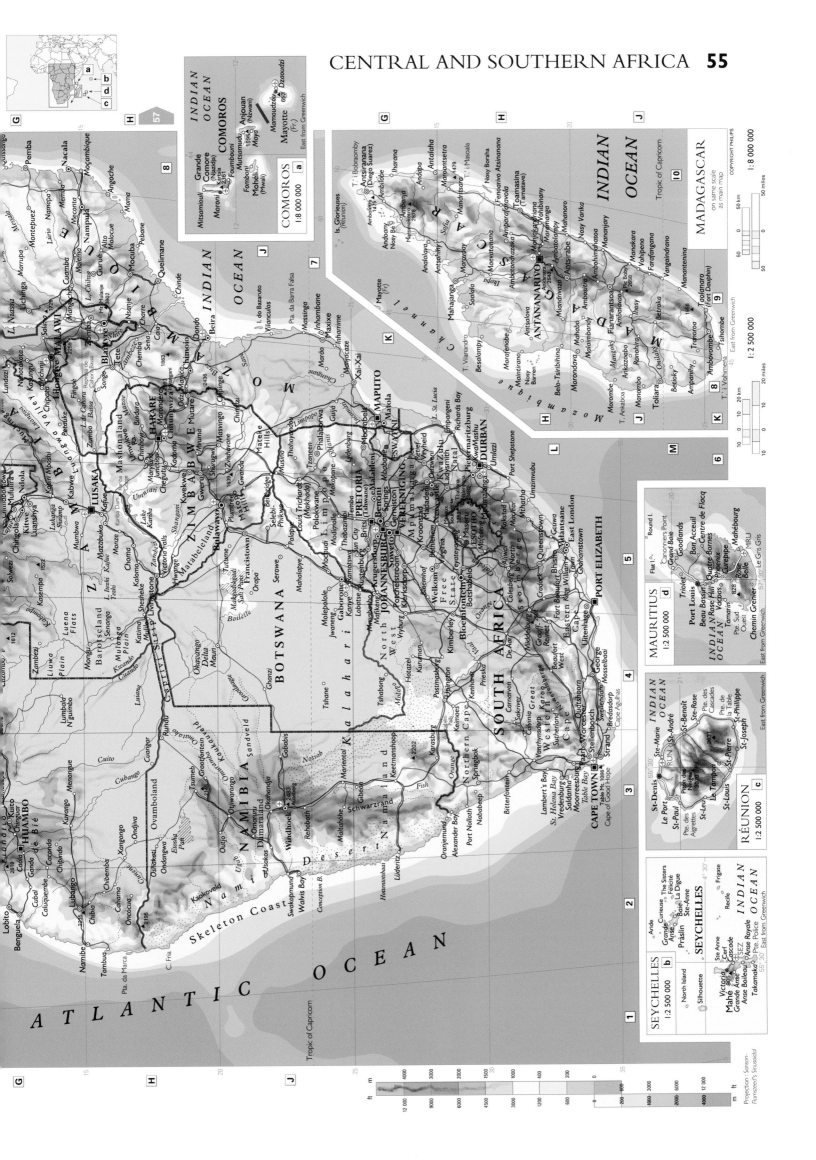

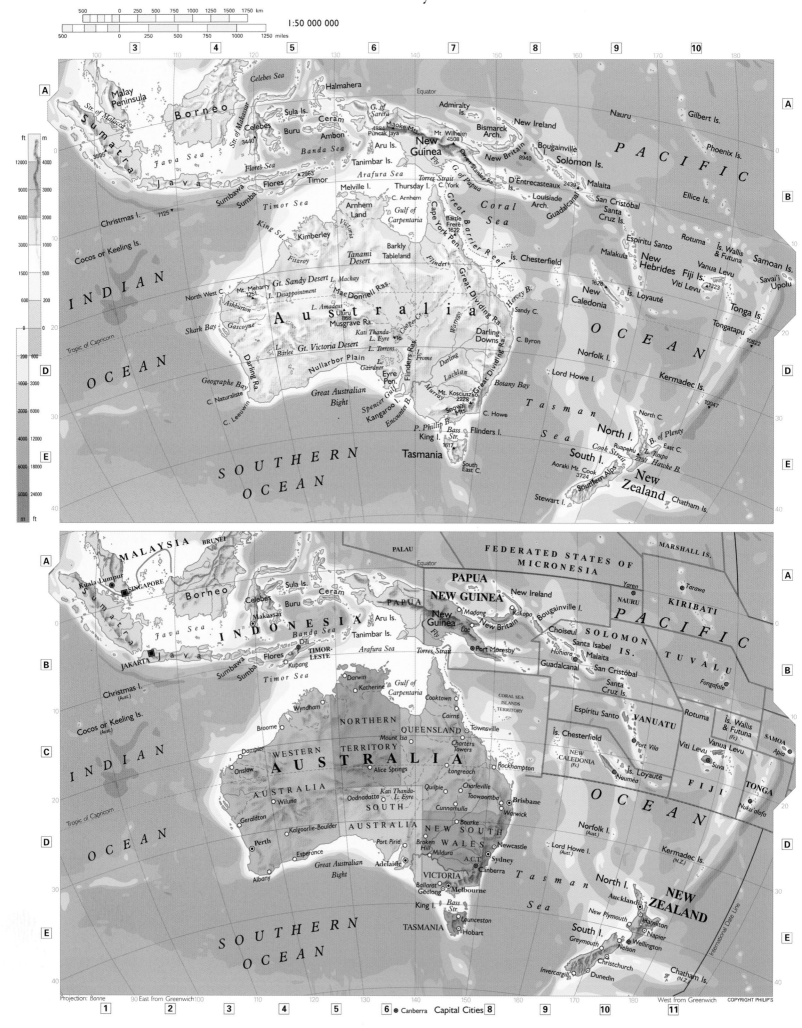

1:6 000 000

50    0    50    100    150    200 km
50    0    50    100    150 miles

FIJI
on same scale  [a]

PACIFIC OCEAN

Great Sea Reef    Kia    Udu Pt.    Ringgold Is.
Yaqaga    Labasa    Natewa Bay    Rabi
Yasawa Group    Yasawa    Yadua    Buca    Savusavu    Taveuni
Nacula    Nabouwalu    Somosomo    Naitaba
Viwa    Naviti    Somosomo    Namenalala    Cikobia
Waya    Vomo    Tavua    Rakiraki    Nasau    Koro    Vanua Balavu
Mamanuca Group    Mba    ▲1031    Makogai    Vatu    Vago    Northern Lau Group
Malolo    Navai ▲1323    Lawaki    Levuka    Wakaya    Vanua Vatu    Cicia
Lautoka    Nadi    Korovou    Ovalau    Batiki    Sawaleke    Lakeba    Tubou
Sigatoka    Koroleву    Vunidawa    Nairai    Moala    Moce
Yanuca    Beqa    Gau    Nayau    Lakeba Passage    Oneata    Southern Lau Group
Vatulele    Kadavu Passage    Suva    FIJI    Namuka-i-Lau    Yagasa Cluster
Kadavu    Ono    Vunisea    Matuku    Totoya    Fulaga    Ogea

KORO SEA
18 S

East from Greenwich    West from Greenwich    Ogea Driki

[2]    [3]

SAMOA
Asau    Safune    Pu'apu'a    PACIFIC OCEAN
Falelima    ▲1858    Salelologa
Savai'i    Taga    Mulifanua    Salelesi    Apia    Falefa    AMERICAN SAMOA (U.S.A.)
Manono    ▲818    Amaile    Ofu    Olosega
OLE PUPU PU'E    Falealupo    Safata Bay    'Upolu    Luma    Ta'u
14 S    Tutuila    Pago Pago    AMERICAN SAMOA    Manu'a Is.
Leone    Vaitogi

SAMOAN ISLANDS
on same scale  [b]

TONGA
on same scale  [c]

PACIFIC OCEAN

Fonualei    Toku
Vava'u    Neiafu
Late    Vava'u Group
Home Reef
Disney Reef
Ofolanga    Ha'ano
Tofua    Kao    Foa    Lifuka    Ha'apai Group
Kotu Group    Uiha
20 S    Fonuafo'ou    Nomuka    Oto Tolu Group
Hunga Ha'apai    Nomuka Group    Mango    Tonumea

TONGA
Nuku'alofa    Tongatapu
Tongatapu Group    Eua

West from Greenwich

[1]

NORTH ISLAND
(Te Ika-a-Māui)

C. Reinga    North C.
C. Maria van Diemen
Houhora Heads    Rangaunu B.
Ahipara B.    Kaitaia    C. Brett
Tauroa Pt.    Okaihau    Waitangi    B. of Islands
Rawene    Hikurangi    Whangarei
Hokianga Harbour    Kaikohe    Bream Hd.
Waipoua Forest    Whangarei Harb.
Dargaville    Waipu    Little Barrier I.    Great Barrier I.
Kaipara Harbour    Warkworth    C. Rodney    Cuvier I.
Helensville    C. Colville    Coromandel    Whitianga
Takapuna    Hauraki Gulf    Thames
AUCKLAND    Whangamata    Mayor I.
Manukau    Papakura    Pukekohe    Waihi    Tauranga Harb.
Waiuku    Mercer    Paeroa    Waihi    Whakatane (White I.)
Waikato    Huntly    Te Aroha    Tauranga    Bay of Plenty
Hamilton    Morrinsville    Te Puke    Opotiki    Runaway
Raglan    Cambridge    Whakatane    East C.
Te Awamutu    Rotorua    TE UREWERA    Waipiro
Kawhia Harbour    Putaruru    Murupara    Raukumara Ra.    Hikurangi ▲1753
North Taranaki Bight    Otorohanga    Tokoroa    Rotorua    Tolaga Bay
Waitomo Caves    Mangakino    Taupo    Ruatahuna    Gisborne
Mokau    Te Kuiti    Wairakei    Rotoiti    Waikaremoana    Poverty Bay
New Plymouth    Mokau    Ongarue    L. Taupo    Ormond
Waitara    WHANGANUI    Taumarunui    Turangi    Wairoa    Waikokopu
Mt. Taranaki or Mt. Egmont    Inglewood    Raetihi    Ruapehu ▲2797    Mahia Pen.
C. Egmont ▲2518    Stratford    Ohakune    TONGARIRO    Bay View
Opunake    Eltham    Waiouru    Rangitikei    Napier
Hawera    Taihape    C. Kidnappers    Hastings
South Taranaki Bight    Patea    Hunterville    Waipawa
Wanganui    Mangaweka    Waipukurau
Marton    Halcombe    Danevirke
Bulls    Feilding    Woodville
Foxton    Palmerston North    Pahiatua
Shannon    Levin    Eketahuna    C. Turnagain
Paraparaumu    Otaki    Masterton
Kapiti I.    Carterton
Upper Hutt    Featherston    Greytown
Pelorus    Petone    Martinborough
Lower Hutt    Wairarapa
Wellington    Cook Strait

SOUTH ISLAND
(Te Waipounamu)

TASMAN SEA

C. Farewell
Collingwood    Golden B.    D'Urville I.
Takaka    ABEL TASMAN
KAHURANGI    Tasman B.
Tasman Mts.    Motueka    Picton
Karamea    Nelson    Havelock    Blenheim
Karamea Bight    Richmond    Seddon
Seddonville    Wakefield    Ward
Granity    Murchison    NELSON LAKES
Westport    Lyell    Rotoiti    Tapuaenuku ▲2885    Clarence
Inangahua    Martins    Kekerengu
PAPAROA    Reefton    Spenser Mts.    Kaikoura
Punakaiki    Blackball    Hanmer Springs
Blackball    Runanga    Waiau
Greymouth    Stillwater    Kumara
Hokitika    L. Brunner    L. Jacksons    Kaikoura
Ross    ARTHUR'S PASS    Waipara    Pegasus Bay
Abut Hd.    Waikari    Rangiora    New Brighton
WESTLAND    Otira    Culverden    Oxford    Christchurch
TAI POUTINI    Arthur's P.    Springfield    Kaiapoi    Lyttelton
Aoraki    Coleridge    Darfield    Banks Pen.
Mt. Cook    Whitecliffs    Lincoln
Mt. Cook ▲3724    Methven    Riccarton    Little River
Mount Cook    Staveley    ORARI    Southbridge
ORAKI    Fairlie    Ashburton    Lake Ellesmere
Jackson B.    TE MOANA    Rangitata    Ellesmere
MOUNT ASPIRING    Tekapo    Temuka
Mt. Aspiring ▲3033    Ohau    Pukaki    Timaru
Milford Sd.    Lake    St. Andrews
Sutherland Falls    Earnslaw ▲2819    Twizel    Waimate
Bligh Sound    Milford    Wanaka    Kurow    Oamaru
George Sound    Sound    Arrowtown    Maheno
Secretary I.    Queenstown    Cromwell    Naseby    Hampden
Doubtful Sd.    Wakatipu    Clyde    OTAGO    Palmerston
FIORDLAND    Alexandra    Roxburgh    Waikouaiti
Resolution I.    Manapouri    Mts.    Dunback    Port Chalmers
Dusky Sd.    Te Anau    Ettrick    Waihola    Otago Harbour
Breaksea Sd.    Eyre Mts.    Lumsden    Mosgiel    Dunedin
Preservation Inlet    Mossburn    Edievale    Lawrence    Taieri
Chalky Inlet    Ohai    Nightcaps    Tapanui    Clinton    Balclutha
Te Waewae B.    Winton    Gore    Milton    Kaitangata
Solander I.    Orepuki    Riverton    Mataura    Nugget Pt.
Tuatapere    Hedgehope    Clinton    Owaka
Clifden    Wyndham    Tahakopa
Invercargill    Foveaux Str.    Bluff
RAKIURA    Ruapuke I.
Halfmoon Bay    South West C.
Stewart I. (Rakiura)    Port Pegasus

Projection: Conical with two standard parallels

PACIFIC OCEAN

TAHITI & MOOREA
1:1 000 000

Papetoai    Pte. Aroa
Paopao    Pte. Vénus    Mahina
B. de Matavai    Arue    Papenoo
Mt. Tohiea ▲1207    Papeete    Pirae    Tiarei
Moorea (France)    Faaa    Afareaitu    Tahiti (France)
Haapiti    Pte. Nuupere    Hitiaa
Mt. Aorai ▲2060    Mt. Orohena ▲2241
Punaauia    Mt. Terufaru ▲1799    Faaone
Maraa    Paea    Lac Vaihiria    Isthme de Taravao
Papara    Tautira    Afaahiti    Pte. Tautira
Atimaono    Mataiea    Vairao    Teahupoo    Mt. Rooniu ▲1332
Presqu'île de Taiarapu

West from Greenwich

COPYRIGHT PHILIP'S

ft    m
9000    3000
6000    2000
3000    1000
1200    400
600    200
0    0
200    600
2000    6000
4000    12000
6000    18000
m    ft

10    0    10 km
10    0    10 miles
1:1 000 000

1:8 000 000

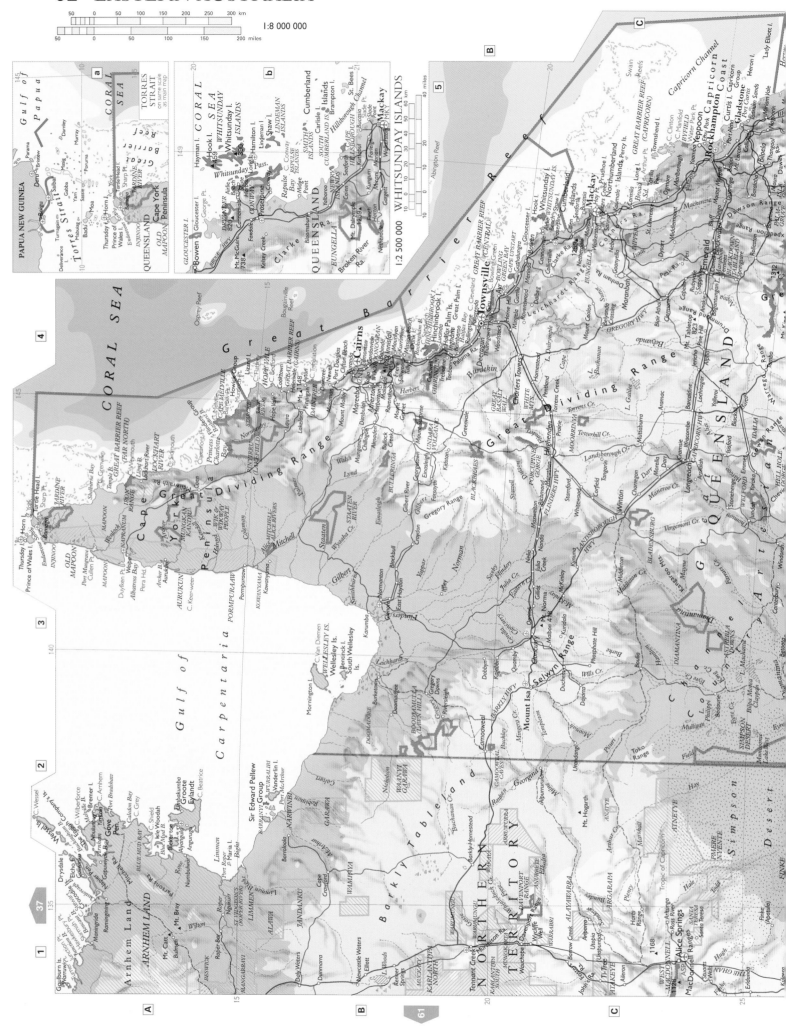

50   0   50   100   150   200   250   300 km

1:8 000 000

50   0   50   100   150   200 miles

**a**

PAPUA NEW GUINEA

Gulf of Papua

CORAL SEA

Torres Strait

TORRES STRAIT
on same scale
as main map

QUEENSLAND
Cape York Peninsula
OLD MAPOON

Great Barrier Reef

**b**

Gloucester I.
Bowen

CORAL SEA

WHITSUNDAY ISLANDS

Hayman I.
Hook I.
Whitsunday I.
Lindeman I.
Shaw I.

Cumberland
SMITH ISLANDS
Carlisle I.
Brampton I.

SOUTH CUMBERLAND IS.

REPULSE ISLANDS

Mackay

QUEENSLAND

EUNGELLA

WHITSUNDAY ISLANDS

1:2 500 000

CORAL SEA

GREAT BARRIER REEF

Townsville

Cairns

Cape Melville

HOPEVILLE

Cape York Peninsula

Great Dividing Range

Gulf of Carpentaria

ARNHEM LAND

NORTHERN TERRITORY

QUEENSLAND

Great Dividing Range

Mount Isa

Great Artesian Basin

Barkly Tableland

Simpson Desert

Alice Springs

Mackay

Rockhampton

Capricorn Coast

GREAT BARRIER REEF

Tropic of Capricorn

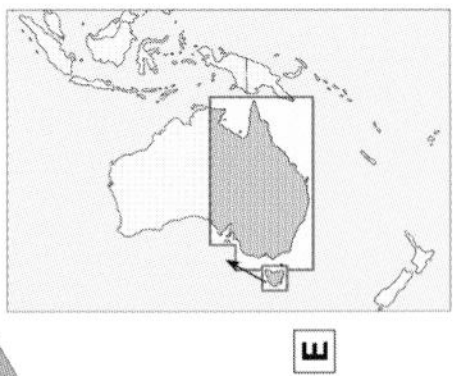

TASMAN SEA

QUEENSLAND

NEW SOUTH WALES

SOUTH AUSTRALIA

VICTORIA

TASMANIA

Great Dividing Range

Darling Downs

Bass Strait

Aboriginal lands

East from Greenwich

Projection: Bonne

on same scale

COPYRIGHT PHILIP'S

BRISBANE
SYDNEY
Canberra
MELBOURNE
ADELAIDE
Newcastle
Wollongong
Hobart

Equatorial Scale 1:54 000 000

RUSSIA
KAZAKHSTAN
MONGOLIA
CHINA
KYRGYZSTAN
TAJIKISTAN
AFGHANISTAN
PAKISTAN
XIZANG
NEPAL
INDIA
BANGLADESH
MYANMAR
LAOS
THAILAND
CAMBODIA
VIETNAM
MALAYSIA
BRUNEI
SINGAPORE
INDONESIA
PHILIPPINES
SRI LANKA
NORTH KOREA
SOUTH KOREA
JAPAN
TAIWAN
NORTHERN MARIANAS (U.S.A.)
GUAM (U.S.A.)
MARSHALL IS.
PALAU
FED. STATES OF MICRONESIA
PAPUA NEW GUINEA
NAURU
SOLOMON IS.
TUVALU
VANUATU
FIJI
NEW CALEDONIA (Fr.)
SAMOA
TONGA
AUSTRALIA
NEW ZEALAND
TIMOR-LESTE

Yekaterinburg
Moskva
Volga
Tomsk
Ob'
Novosibirsk
Irkutsk
Astana (Aqmola)
Semey
Lena
Chita
O. Baykal
Ulaanbaatar
Blagoveshchensk
Amur
Khabarovsk
Okhotsk
Sea of Okhotsk
Poluostrov Kamchatka
Komandorskiye Ostrova (Russia)
Near I. (U.S.A.)
Andreanof I.
Bering Sea
Aleutia
Aleutian Basin
Shirshov Ridge
Petropavlovsk-Kamchatskiy
7822
Sakhalin
Kuril'skiye Ostrova (Russia)
La Pérouse Str.
Kuril-Kamchatka Trench
10,542
Emperor Trough
Chinook Trough
Harbin
Changchun
Shenyang
Vladivostok
Sapporo
Hakodate
Northwest
Pacific
Basin
Almaty
Ürümqi
Toshkent
Aral Sea
Balqash Köl
Altay
Kunlun Shan
Kabul
Srinagar
Himalaya
Lahore
Delhi
Kanpur
Ganga
8850 Everest
Lhasa
Brahmaputra
Kolkata (Calcutta)
Dhaka
Irrawaddy
Mandalay
Hyderabad
Chennai (Madras)
Andaman Is. (India)
Yangôn
Bangkok
Phnom Penh
Bay of Bengal
Colombo
Nicobar Is. (India)
G. of Thailand
Andaman Is.
Beijing
Tianjin
Taiyuan
Huang He
Dalian
Qingdao
Lanzhou
Xi'an
Nanjing
Wuhan
Chongqing
Chang Jiang
Changsha
Hangzhou
Shanghai
East China Sea
Kunming
Fuzhou
Guangzhou
Macau
Hong Kong
Hainan
Hanoi
Thanh Pho Ho Chi Minh
South China Sea
Palawan
Kuala Lumpur
Singapore
Sumatera
Palembang
Jakarta
Jawa
Surabaya
Bali
Sumbawa
Sumba
Flores
Borneo
Makassar
Sulawesi
Flores Sea
Java Sea
Java Trench
Banda Sea
Timor
Dili
NORTH KOREA
SOUTH KOREA
Seoul
Nagoya
Kyoto
Osaka
Shikoku
Kyūshū
Sendai
Tōkyō
Yokohama
Kitakyūshū
Fuji-San 3776
Japan Trench
10,554
Sea of Japan
Yellow Sea
Okinawa
Ryūkyū-rettō
Taipei
TAIWAN
Iwo-Jima (Japan)
Ogasawara Gunto (Japan)
Kazan-Rettō (Japan)
Minami-Tori-Shima (Japan)
Wake I. (U.S.A.)
Shatsky Rise
Tamu Massif 1980
Pacific Basin
Midway Is. (U.S.A.)
Lisianski I. (U.S.A.)
International Date Line
Mid-Pacific Mountains
Philippine Sea
C. Engano
Luzon
Mindoro
Manila
Samar
10,497
Paracel Is.
Mindanao
Davao
Melekeok
Sulu Sea
Celebes Sea
4101
SABAH
SARAWAK
Halmahera
Buru
Seram
Maluku
Puncak Jaya 4884
PAPUA
New Guinea
Lae
Admiralty Is.
Bismarck Arch.
New Ireland
New Britain
Kokopo
8940
Bougainville
Port Moresby
Torres Strait
C. York
Louisiade Arch.
Arafura Sea
West Mariana Basin
Philippine Basin
NORTHERN MARIANAS (U.S.A.)
Tinian
Saipan
East Mariana Basin
Mariana Trench
Challenger 11,022 Deep
Yap
Caroline Is.
Chuuk
GUAM (U.S.A.)
Pohnpei
Palikir
FED. STATES OF MICRONESIA
East Caroline Basin
West Caroline Basin
Eauripik Rise
PALAU
Kyushu-Palau Ridge
Sitito-Ozima Ridge
MARSHALL IS.
Bikini Atoll
Enewetak Atoll
Kwajalein
Majuro
Jaluit I.
Ralik Chain
Ratak Chain
Micronesia
Melanesia
Solomon Rise
Melanesian Basin
Yaren
NAURU
Tarawa
Banaba
Butaritari
Gilbert Is.
Solomon Is.
Honiara
Guadalcanal
Santa Cruz Is. 9165
Wake I. (U.S.A.)
Howland I. (U.S.A.)
Baker I. (U.S.A.)
Phoenix Is.
Abariringa
Enderbury
KIRIBATI
PACIFIC
OCEAN
Central Pacific Basin
Fongafale
TUVALU
VANUATU
Espiritu Santo
Port Vila
Rotuma
Îs. Wallis & Futuna (Fr.)
SAMOA
Apia
Vanua Levu
Viti Levu
Suva
FIJI
West Fiji Basin
Nuku'alofa
TONGA
Tonga Trench
10,822
Îs. Chesterfield
Coral Sea Basin
Coral Sea
Great Barrier Reef
Cairns
Townsville
Rockhampton
Brisbane
Lord Howe Rise
Middleton Reef
NEW CALEDONIA (Fr.)
Nouméa
Îs. Loyauté
Norfolk I. (Austral.)
New Caledonia Trough
South Fiji Basin
Kermadec Trench 10,047
Kermadec Is. (N.Z.)
Tokelau I. (N.Z.)
Darwin
C. Arnhem
Gulf of Carpentaria
Mount Isa
North Australian Basin
Broome
North West C.
Exmouth Plateau
AUSTRALIA
Alice Springs
Kati Thanda-L. Eyre
Darling
Murray
Mt. Kosciuszko 2228
Great Dividing Ra.
Sydney
Canberra
Melbourne
Bass Str.
Tasmania
Hobart
East Tasman Plateau
South Tasman Rise
Tasman Sea
Tasman Basin
NEW ZEALAND
Auckland
Wellington
Christchurch
Dunedin
Invercargill
Cook Strait
Aoraki Mt. Cook 3724
Chatham I. (N.Z.)
Chatham Is. (N.Z.)
Chatham Rise
Bounty Trough
Bounty Is. (N.Z.)
Antipodes Is. (N.Z.)
Auckland Is. (N.Z.)
Campbell Plateau
Campbell I. (N.Z.)
Macquarie I. (Austral.)
Geraldton
Perth Basin
Perth
Naturaliste Plateau
Albany
Great Australian Bight
Adelaide
South Australian Basin
Wharton Basin
INDIAN OCEAN
Ninetyeast Ridge
Broken Ridge
Cocos Is. (Austral.)
Christmas I. (Austral.)
Sunda Trench
Mid-Indian Ridge
Nouvelle Amsterdam (Fr.)
Îs. St. Paul (Fr.)
Îs. Crozet (Fr.)
Kerguelen (Fr.)
Heard I. (Austral.)
SOUTHERN OCEAN
East Indian Ridge

East from Greenwich

ft m
12 000 4000
9000 3000
6000 2000
3000 1000
1500 500
600 200
0 0
200 600
1000 3000
2000 6000
4000 12 000
6000 18 000
8000 24 000
m ft

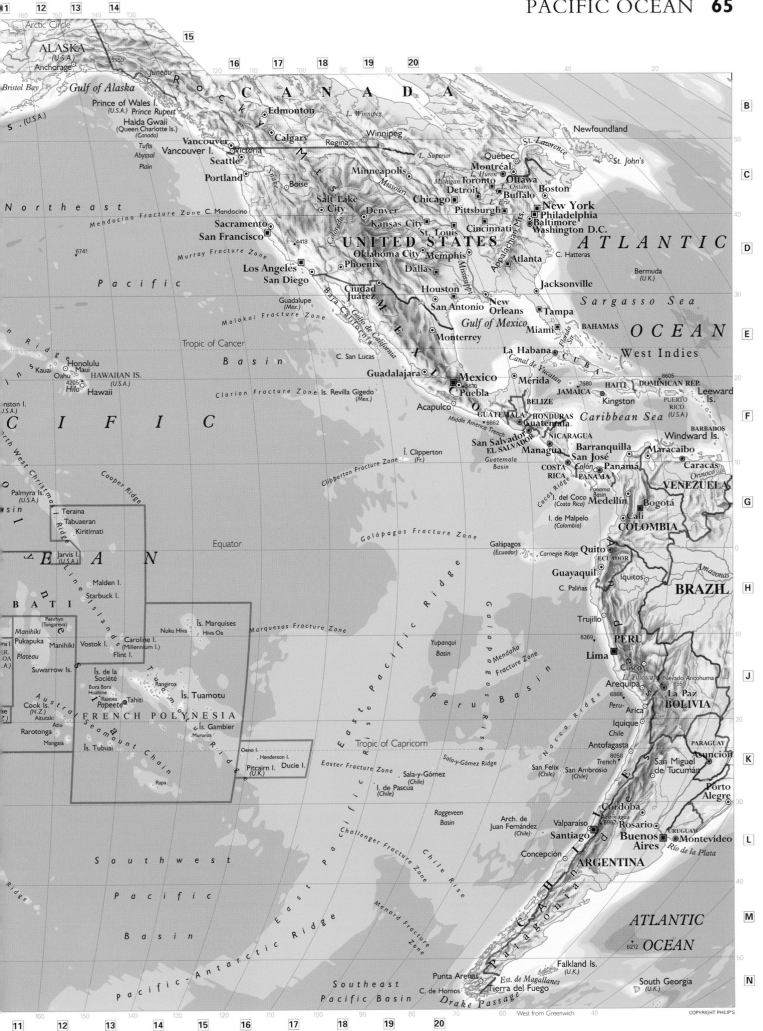

Arctic Circle
ALASKA
(U.S.A.)
Anchorage
6959
Bristol Bay
Gulf of Alaska
Juneau
Prince of Wales I.
(U.S.A.) Prince Rupert
Haida Gwaii
(Queen Charlotte Is.)
(Canada)
Tufts
Abyssal
Plain
CANADA
Edmonton
L. Winnipeg
Newfoundland
St. Lawrence
Vancouver
Vancouver I.
Victoria
Calgary
Regina
Winnipeg
Québec
St. John's
Seattle
L. Superior
Montréal
Portland
Boise
L. Huron
Toronto
Ottawa
Boston
Minneapolis
L. Michigan
Detroit
Buffalo
L. Ontario
L. Erie
Pittsburgh
New York
Philadelphia
Baltimore
Washington D.C.
Northeast
Mendocino Fracture Zone
C. Mendocino
Salt Lake
City
Denver
Chicago
St. Louis
Cincinnati
6741
Sacramento
Kansas City
4418
Pacific
San Francisco
Murray Fracture Zone
UNITED STATES
Oklahoma City
Memphis
Atlanta
ATLANTIC
C. Hatteras
Los Angeles
San Diego
Phoenix
Dallas
Bermuda
(U.K.)
Houston
Jacksonville
Ciudad
Juárez
San Antonio
New
Orleans
Sargasso Sea
OCEAN
Guadalupe
(Mex.)
Monterrey
Gulf of Mexico
Tampa
BAHAMAS
Molokai Fracture Zone
Miami
Tropic of Cancer
La Habana
West Indies
Basin
C. San Lucas
8605
Kauai
Honolulu
Maui
Guadalajara
Mexico
Mérida
JAMAICA
HAITI
DOMINICAN REP.
Oahu
HAWAIIAN IS.
4205
Puebla
7680
Leeward
Is.
Hilo
Hawaii
(U.S.A.)
Acapulco
BELIZE
Kingston
PUERTO
RICO
(U.S.A.)
Clarion Fracture Zone
Is. Revilla Gigedo
(Mex.)
GUATEMALA
5610
HONDURAS
Caribbean Sea
BARBADOS
Middle America Trench
6662
Guatemala
Windward Is.
San Salvador
NICARAGUA
CIFIC
Guatemala
Basin
EL SALVADOR
Managua
Barranquilla
Maracaibo
North West Christmas
Palmyra Is.
(U.S.A.)
Clipperton Fracture Zone
San José
Panamá
Caracas
COSTA
RICA
Colón
PANAMA
Orinoco
VENEZUELA
Teraina
Tabuaeran
Kiritimati
Cooper Ridge
I. del Coco
(Costa Rica)
Panama
Basin
Medellín
Bogotá
I. de Malpelo
(Colombia)
Cali
COLOMBIA
Equator
Jarvis I.
(U.S.A.)
Galápagos Fracture Zone
Galápagos
Quito
EN
Galápagos
(Ecuador)
Carnegie Ridge
ECUADOR
BATI
Malden I.
Guayaquil
Amazonas
Starbuck I.
C. Paliñas
Iquitos
BRAZIL
Penrhyn
(Tongareva)
Manihiki
Pukapuka
Manihiki
Îs. Marquises
Nuku Hiva
Hiva Oa
Marquesas Fracture Zone
Trujillo
Plateau
Vostok I.
Caroline I.
(Millennium I.)
6369
PERU
Suwarrow Is.
Flint I.
Yupanqui
Basin
Lima
Cusco
Îs. de la
Société
Rangiroa
Bora Bora
Huahine
Raiatea
Tahiti
Îs. Tuamotu
Peru Basin
L. Titicaca
Nevado Ancohuma
6550
Cook Is.
(N.Z.)
Papeete
Arequipa
La Paz
Aitutaki
Mendaña Fracture Zone
6866
Peru-
BOLIVIA
FRENCH POLYNESIA
Îs. Gambier
Iquique
Rarotonga
Atiu
Mururoa
Mangaia
Îs. Tubuai
Tropic of Capricorn
Antofagasta
PARAGUAY
Oeno I.
Henderson I.
Ducie I.
Sala-y-Gómez Ridge
San Felix
(Chile)
San Ambrosio
(Chile)
San Miguel
de Tucumán
Asunción
Pitcairn I.
(U.K.)
Easter Fracture Zone
Sala-y-Gómez
(Chile)
8050
Trench
Rapa
I. de Pascua
(Chile)
Porto
Alegre
Roggeveen
Basin
Córdoba
URUGUAY
Challenger Fracture Zone
Arch. de
Juan Fernández
(Chile)
Aconcagua
6962
Valparaíso
Rosario
Santiago
Buenos
Aires
Montevideo
Río de la Plata
Southwest
Concepción
ARGENTINA
Pacific
ATLANTIC
Menard Fracture Zone
Ridge
Basin
Pacific-Antarctic Ridge
6212
OCEAN
Falkland Is.
(U.K.)
Southeast
Punta Arenas
South Georgia
(U.K.)
C. de Hornos
Est. de Magallanes
Tierra del Fuego
Pacific Basin
Drake Passage
West from Greenwich

COPYRIGHT PHILIP'S

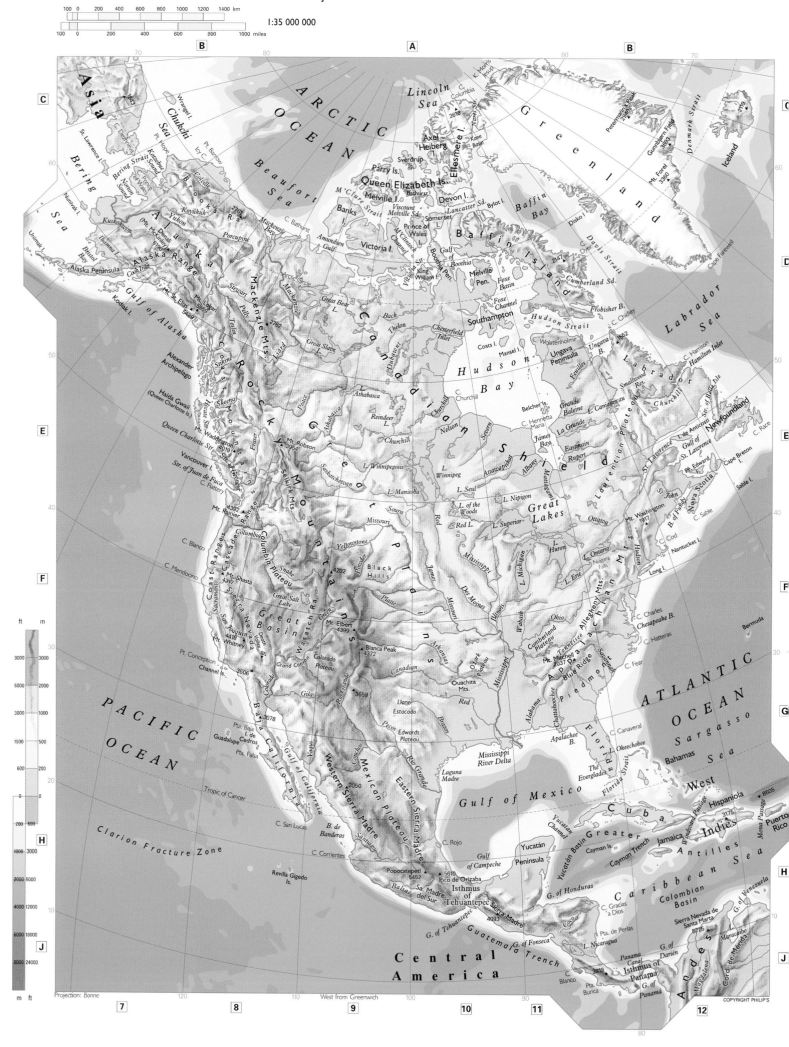

1:35 000 000

Projection: Bonne

West from Greenwich

COPYRIGHT PHILIP'S

1:35 000 000

| 100 | 0 | 200 | 400 | 600 | 800 | 1000 | 1200 | 1400 km |

| 100 | 0 | 200 | 400 | 600 | 800 | 1000 miles |

Projection: Bonne

West from Greenwich

COPYRIGHT PHILIP'S

**7** ■ MÉXICO Capital Cities **8**

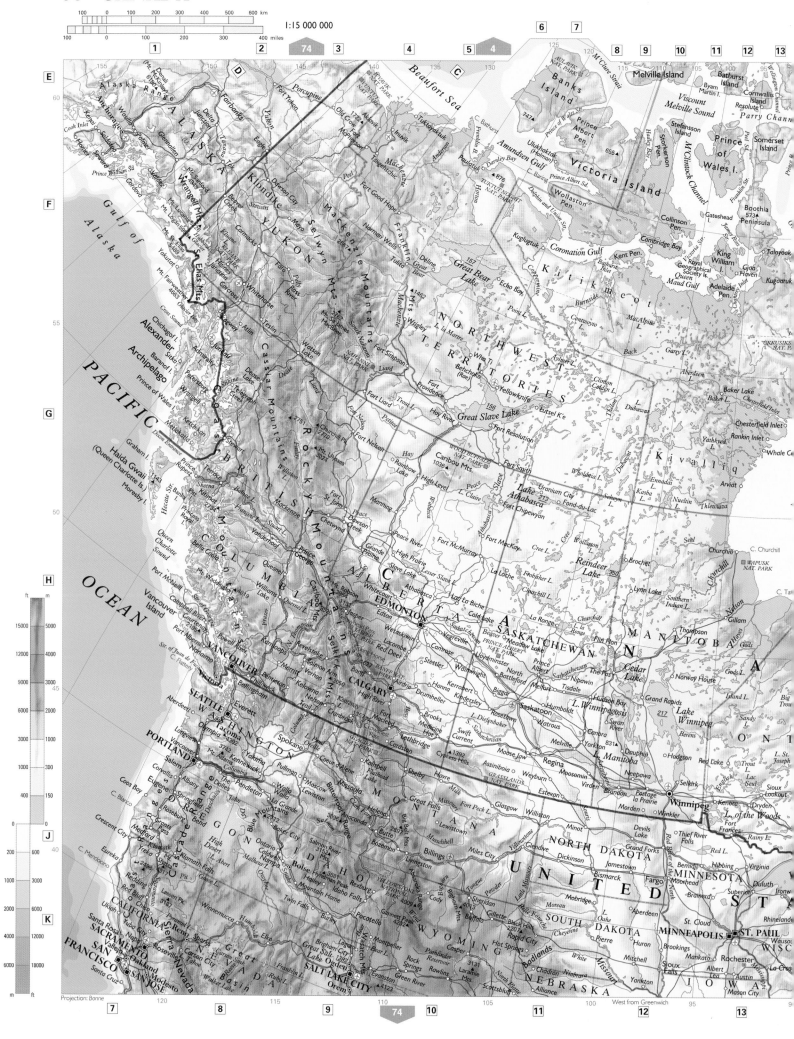

1:15 000 000

Projection: Bonne

## NORTHERN CANADA
continuation northwards on same scale as main map

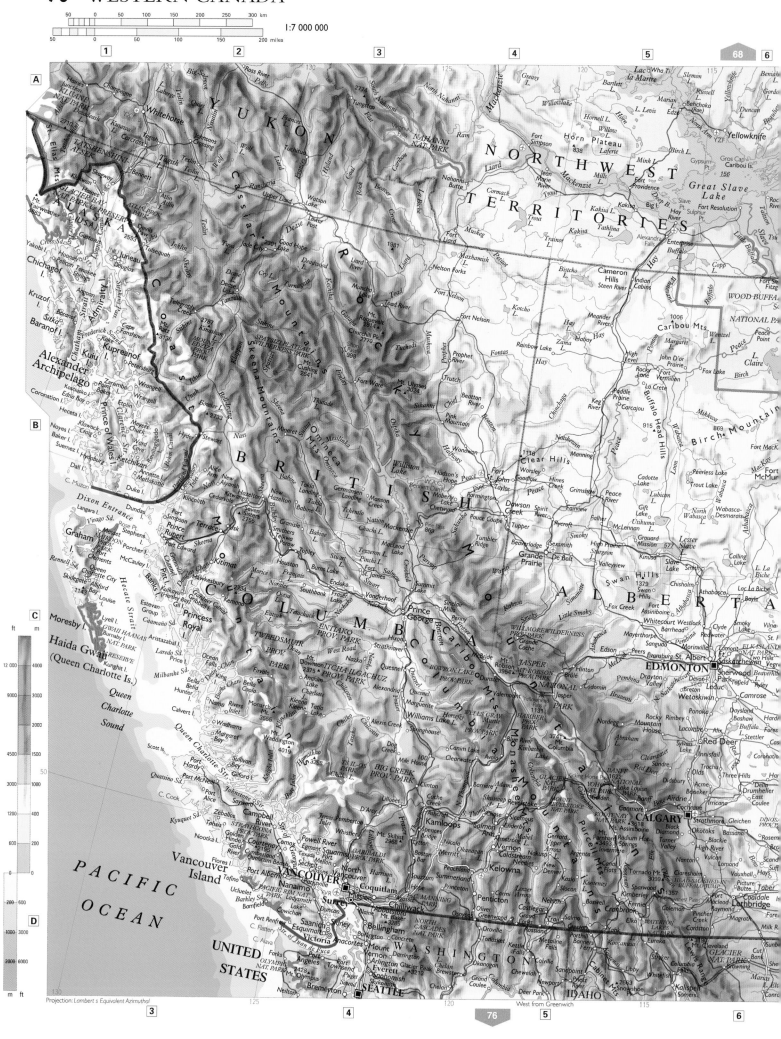

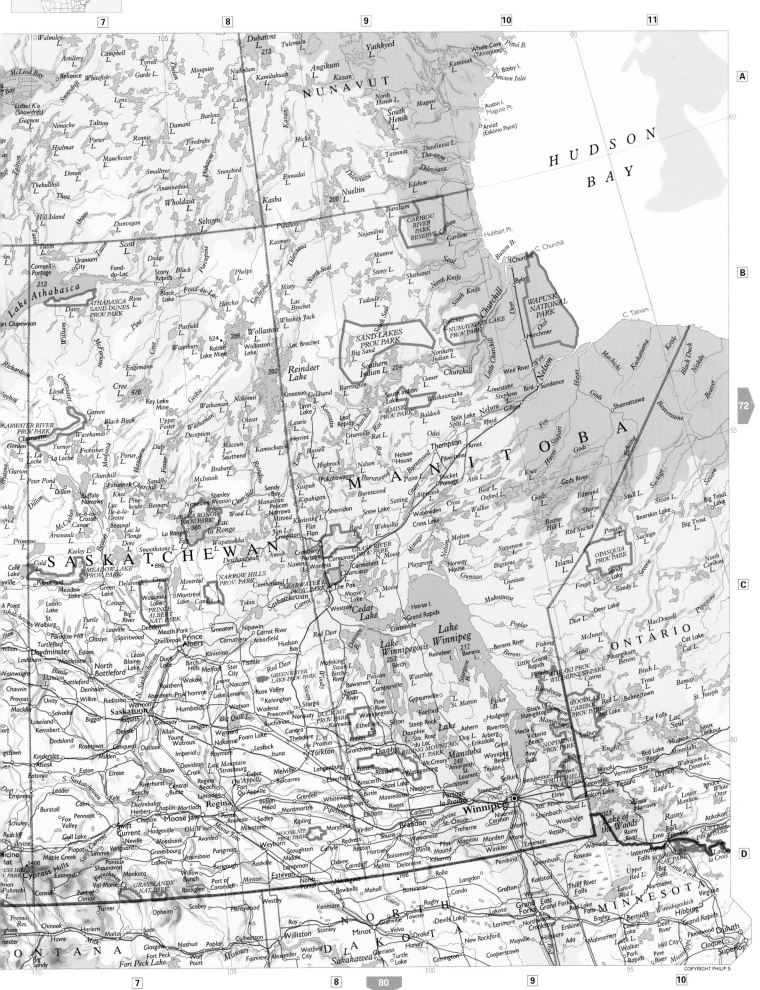

COPYRIGHT PHILIP'S

1:7 000 000

Projection: Lambert's Equivalent Azimuthal

LABRADOR SEA

Nunatsiavut

LABRADOR

NEWFOUNDLAND &

Labrador

Newfoundland

QUÉBEC

Smallwood Reservoir

Happy Valley-Goose Bay

Churchill Falls

Labrador City
Fermont
Wabush

Str. of Belle Isle

L'Anse aux Meadows
St. Anthony

GROS MORNE NAT. PARK

Long Range Mts.

Corner Brook

Grand Falls-Windsor

Gander

TERRA NOVA NAT. PARK

St. John's

Île d'Anticosti

Sept-Îles
Port-Cartier

Dét. de Jacques-Cartier

GULF OF
ST. LAWRENCE

Cabot Strait

ST-PIERRE-ET-MIQUELON (France)

Pén. de la Gaspésie
Mts. Chic-Chocs
Gaspé

Îs. de la Madeleine (Québec)

Cape Breton Island

CAPE BRETON HIGHLANDS NAT. PARK

Sydney

Chicoutimi
Jonquière
La Baie

Rimouski

Rivière-du-Loup

NEW BRUNSWICK

Bathurst

Campbellton

PRINCE EDWARD ISLAND

Charlottetown

Summerside

NOVA SCOTIA

Québec
Lévis

Fredericton

Moncton

Amherst

Truro

New Glasgow

BUNDY NAT. PARK

Saint John

MAINE

NEW HAMPSHIRE

Sherbrooke
Magog

Bangor

Augusta

Halifax
Dartmouth

ATLANTIC

Sable I. (Nova Scotia)

Portland

UNITED STATES

BOSTON

OCEAN

West from Greenwich

COPYRIGHT PHILIP'S

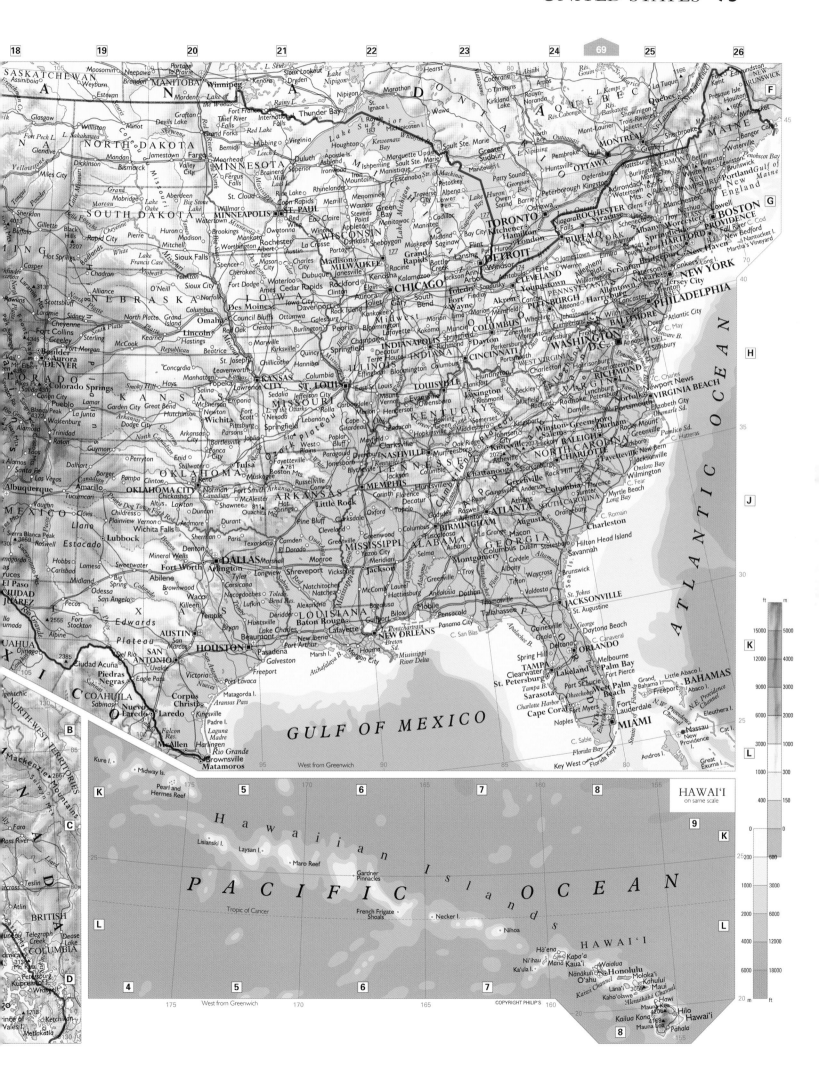

HAWAI'I
on same scale

COPYRIGHT PHILIP'S

1:6 700 000

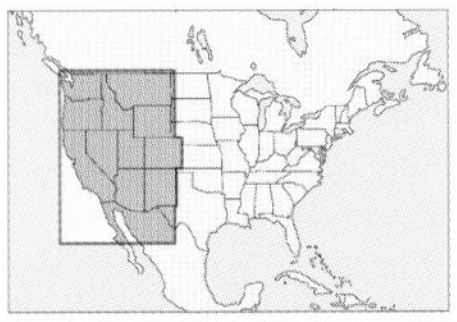

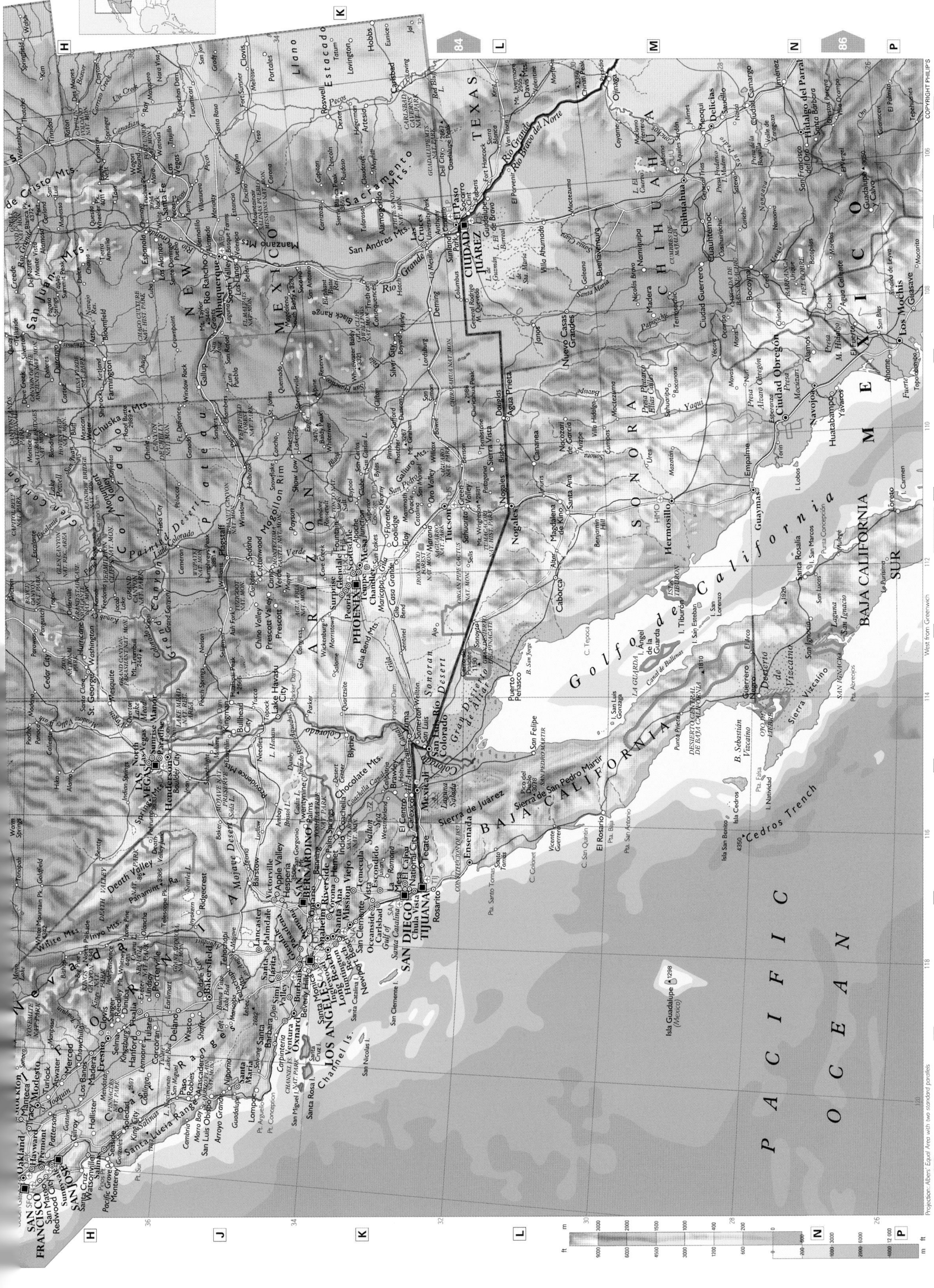

TEXAS

NEW MEXICO

ARIZONA

CALIFORNIA

NEVADA

CHIHUAHUA

SONORA

BAJA CALIFORNIA

BAJA CALIFORNIA SUR

M E X I C O

PACIFIC OCEAN

Golfo de California

Gran Desierto de Altar

Mojave Desert

Sonoran Desert

Painted Desert

Colorado Plateau

San Juan Mts.

Sacramento Mts.

SAN FRANCISCO

SAN JOSE

LOS ANGELES

SAN DIEGO

LAS VEGAS

PHOENIX

TUCSON

CIUDAD JUAREZ

El Paso

Hermosillo

Ciudad Obregón

Chihuahua

Tijuana

Mexicali

Nogales

Agua Prieta

Isla Guadalupe (Mexico) ▲1298

Cedros Trench

Lava fields

West from Greenwich

Projection: Albers' Equal Area with two standard parallels

COPYRIGHT PHILIP'S

1:2 500 000

km: 10 0 10 20 30 40 50 60 70 80 90 km
miles: 10 0 10 20 30 40 50 60 miles

WESTERN WASHINGTON REGION
on same scale

BRITISH COLUMBIA

Vancouver Island

Strait of Georgia

Strait of Juan de Fuca

PACIFIC RIM NATIONAL PARK RESERVE

OLYMPIC NATIONAL PARK

Olympic Mountains

Mt. Olympus 2428

WASHINGTON

OREGON

PORTLAND

MT. RAINIER NAT. PARK
Mt. Rainier 4392

MT. ST. HELENS NAT. VOLCANIC MONUMENT
Mt. St. Helens 2550

Mt. Adams 3742

VANCOUVER

Victoria

SEATTLE

Everett

Tacoma

Olympia

Aberdeen

PACIFIC OCEAN

Cascade Range

DEATH VALLEY

Pahute Mesa

Panamint

White Mts.

Inyo Mts.

Owens

Mono Lake

NEVADA

Reno

Sparks

Carson City

Lake Tahoe

Sierra Nevada

YOSEMITE NATIONAL PARK

KINGS CANYON NATIONAL PARK

SEQUOIA NATIONAL PARK

Mt. Whitney 4418

Sacramento Valley

SACRAMENTO

Stockton

Modesto

Fresno

Clovis

Visalia

Tulare

Porterville

San Joaquin Valley

Santa Clara Valley

SAN FRANCISCO

Oakland

Berkeley

SAN JOSE

Santa Cruz

Monterey Bay

Salinas Valley

Diablo Range

Santa Lucia Range

Napa

Santa Rosa

Chico

Yuba City

Russian

Morro Bay

Pt. Buchon

CALIFORNIA

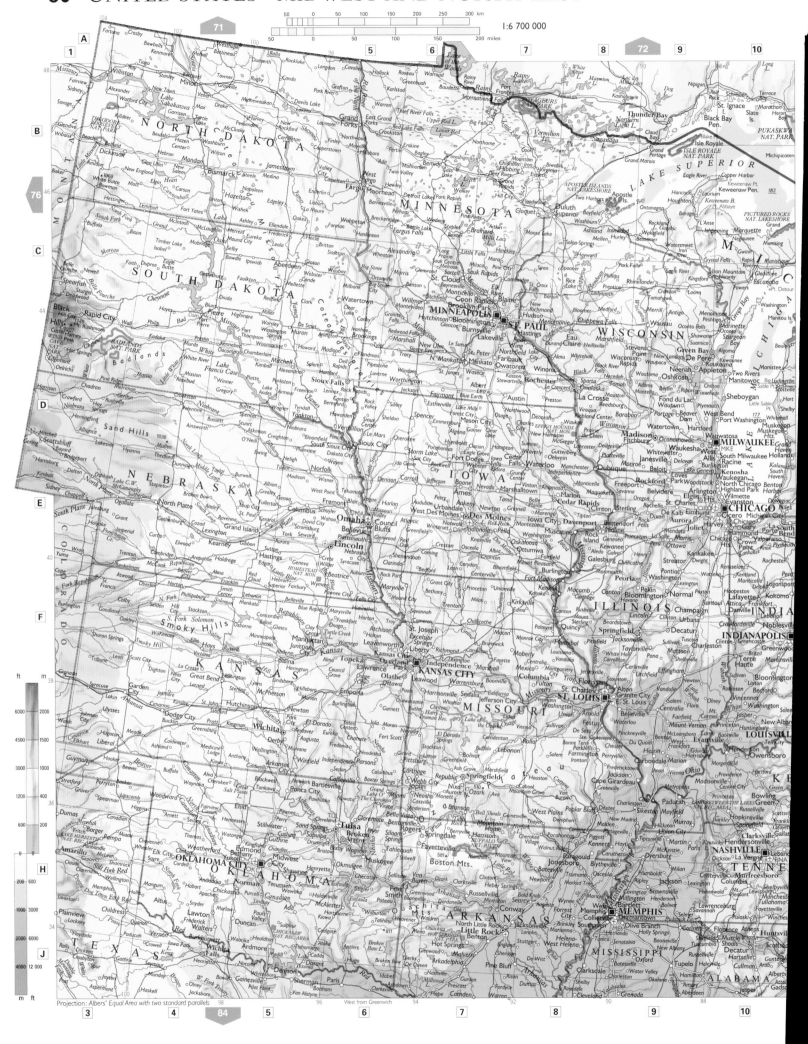

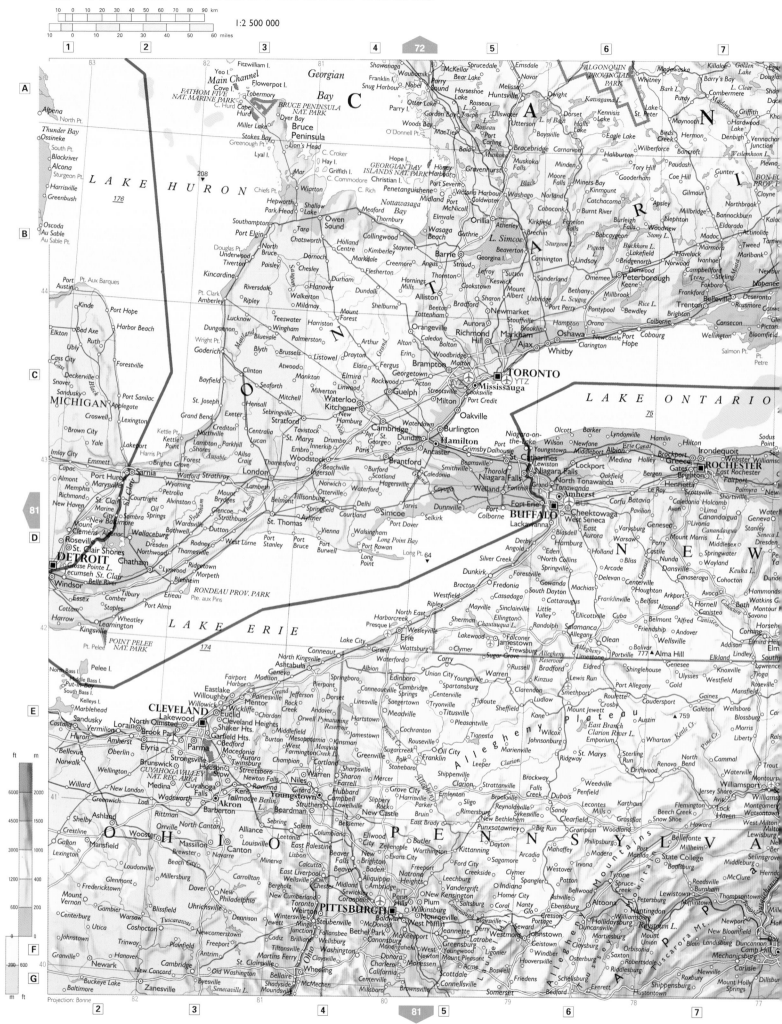

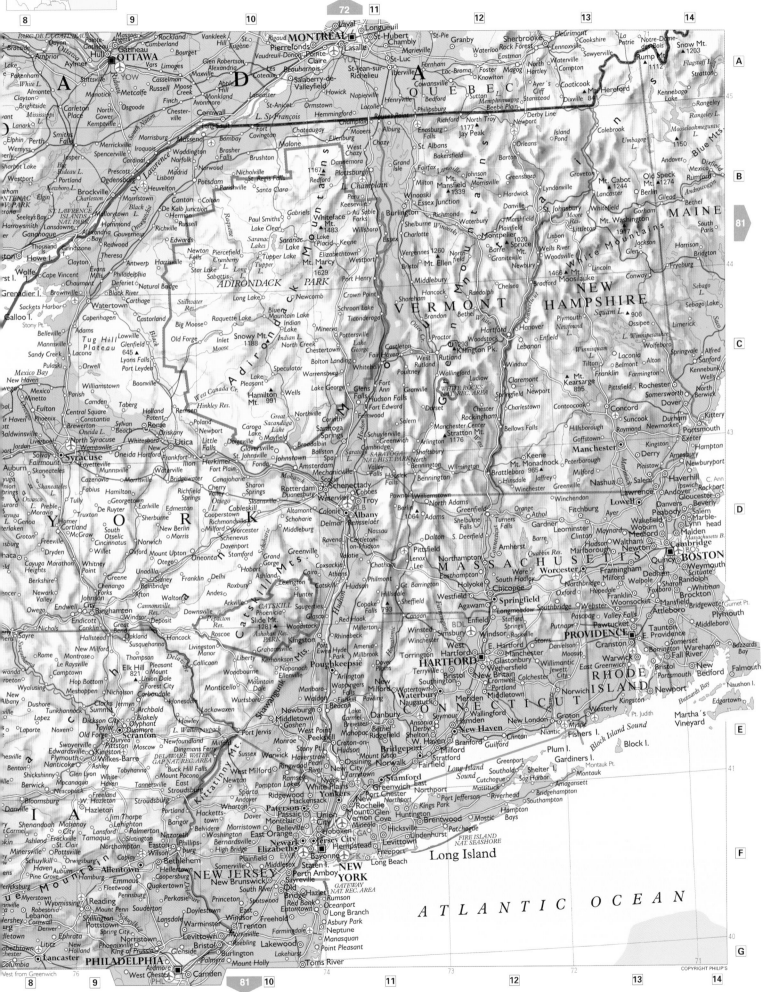

50   0   50   100   150   200   250   300 km
50   0   50   100   150   200 miles

1:8 000 000

Projection: Bi-polar oblique Conical Orthomorphic

West from Greenwich

State names in Central Mexico

1 DISTRITO FEDERAL   3 GUANAJUATO   5 MÉXICO   7 QUERÉTARO
2 AGUASCALIENTES   4 HIDALGO   6 MORELOS   8 TLAXCALA

**PUERTO RICO** d
1:3 000 000

**VIRGIN ISLANDS** e
1:2 000 000

**ST. LUCIA** f
1:1 000 000

**BARBADOS** g
1:1 000 000

ATLANTIC OCEAN

PUERTO RICO
(U.S.A.)

Pta. Aguijereada
Aguadilla
Isabela
Arecibo
Barceloneta
Manati
Vega Baja
Bayamón
SAN JUAN
SJU
Rio Grande
Carolina
Fajardo
Dewey
Culebra
Mayagüez
San Sebastian
Utuado
Adjuntas
Cordillera Central
1338 Cerro de Punta
Caguas
Cayey
Humacao
Naguabo
Vieques
Esperanza
San German
Yauco
Ponce
Coamo
Yabucoa
Pta. Aguila
Guanica
Guayama
I. Caja de Muertos

VIRGIN ISLANDS
(U.K.)

Rufling Pt.
The Settlement
Anegada
East Pt.
Virgin Is.
(U.S.A.)
Jost Van Dyke I.
Great Camanoe
Guana I.
521
Virgin Gorda
Spanish Town
Hans Lollik I.
Tortola
Beef I.
Road Town
Peter I.
Charlotte Amalie
St. John I.
Cruz Bay
St. Thomas I.

ST. LUCIA

Cap Point
Pte. Hardy
Esperance Bay
Gros Islet
Marquis
Castries
Girard
Anse la Raye
Dennery
Canaries
Millet
Trou Gras Pt.
Soufrière
Mt. Gimie
950
Micoud
Soufrière
Bay
750 Petit Piton
Vierge Pt.
Gros Piton Pt.
796 Gros Piton
UVF
Choiseul
ST. LUCIA
Laborie
Vieux Fort
C. Moule à Chique

BARBADOS

ATLANTIC OCEAN
Crab Hill
North Point
Spring Hall
Fustic
Boscobelle
Portland
245 Belleplaine
Speightstown
Bathsheba
BARBADOS
Westmoreland
440
Hillcrest
Alleynes Bay
Mt. Hillaby
Martin's Bay
Holetown
Massiah Street
Jackson
Bridgefield
Ragged Pt.
Black Rock
Ellerton
Six Cross Roads
Ivy
Edey
The Crane
Bridgetown
Oistins
St. Martins
Carlisle Bay
BGI
Worthing
Oistins Bay
Chancery Lane
South Point

ATLANTIC OCEAN

BAHAMAS

ur's Town
New Bight
Cat I.
an Salvador I.
Conception I.
Rum Cay
Long I.
Tropic of Cancer
Clarence Town
Samana Cay
Crooked I. Passage
Crooked I.
Plana Cays
Albert Town
Snug Corner
Acklins I.
Mira por vos Cay
Cay Verde
Hogsty Reef
Little Inagua I.
Mayaguana I.
Mayaguana Passage
Turks & Caicos Is.
(U.K.)
PLS
Caicos Is.
Cockburn Town
Turks Is.
Lake Rose
Great Inagua I.
Matthew Town
Caicos Passage
Turks Island Passage
Silver Bank Passage
Mouchoir Bank
Silver Bank
Navidad Bank

Santa mingo
Moa
ALEJANDRO DE HUMBOLDT
Baracoa
Pta. de Maisí
Î. de la Tortue
Monte Cristi
LA ISABELA POP
Cap-Haïtien
Santiago de los Caballeros
Puerto Plata
Cord.
La Vega
San Francisco de Macorís
Nagua
Samana
Sabana de la Mar
Puerto Rico Trench
Milwaukee Deep 8605

uantanamo
GUANTANAMO BAY (U.S.A.)
Jean Rabel
Port-de-Paix
Fort Liberté
Central
Hato Mayor
Higüey
C. Engaño
PUJ
Aguadilla
Arecibo
Bayamón
SAN JUAN
Carolina
St. John's
Virgin Gorda
Tortola
Anegada
Virgin Is.
(U.K.)
Sombrero (U.K.)
Cap-à-Foux
Gonaïves
St-Marc
Hinche
HAITI
DOMINICAN REP.
San Pedro de Macorís
La Romana
Fajardo
Road Town
Anguilla (U.K.)
Jérémie
AU-PRINCE
PORT-
PAP
L. Enriquillo
-40
Pico Duarte HAÏTISR
3087
SANTO DOMINGO
SDO
Ponce
Caguas
Charlotte Amalie
Culebra
Vieques
Virgin Is.
(U.S.A.)
SXM
St. Maarten (Neth.)
St-Martin (Fr.)
St.-Barthélemy (Fr.)
Saba (Neth.)
Cap-
Ste-
Dame Marie
Les Cayes
Massif de la Hotte
Aquin
Petit-Goâve
Jacmel
2680
SIERRA DE BAHORUCO
Barahona
San Cristóbal
Baní
B. de Yuma
I. Saona
Guayama
PUERTO RICO
(U.S.A.)
Frederiksted
St. Croix
Christiansted
St. Eustatius (Neth.)
1156
Mt. Liamuiga
St. KITTS & NEVIS
SKB
St. John's
ANU
Antigua
ANTIGUA & BARBUDA
Pointe-à-Gravois
Î. à Vache
Pedernales
Compostela
5500
Isla Mona
Mona Passage
Redonda
Nevis
Montserrat
(U.K.)
Soufrière
Hills
914
Guadeloupe Passage
Barbuda

Hispaniola

Muertas Trough

Antilles

4530

Venezuelan

SEA

Basin

5420

Le Moule
Ste-Rose
PTP
La Désirade
GUADELOUPE
(Fr.)
1467
Pointe-à-Pitre
Marie-Galante (Fr.)
Basse-Terre
Grand-Bourg
I. des Saintes
(Fr.)
Dominica Passage
Portsmouth
1447
DOMINICA
Diablotin
MORNE
DOM
Roseau
TROIS PITONS
Martinique Passage
Mt. Pelée
Ste-Marie
1397
Le Robert
Fort-de-France
FDF
Rivière-Pilote
MARTINIQUE
St. Lucia Channel (Fr.)
Castries
UVF
ST. LUCIA
Soufrière
950
St. Vincent Passage
Kingstown
St. Vincent
SVD
Soufrière 1234
340 BGI
Speightstown
Bequia
Bridgetown
BARBADOS
The Grenadines
ST. VINCENT & THE GRENADINES
Basin
Canouan
840
Carriacou
GRENADA
St. George's
GND

BEAN

Beata Ridge

ombian
asin

COLOMBIA

ABC Lesser Islands

Lesser

Antilles

Pta. Gallinas
Oranjestad
Aruba
(Neth.)
AUA
Curaçao
(Neth.)
Willemstad
CUR
Bonaire
(Neth.)
ARC. LOS ROQUES
I. Orchila
(Ven.)
I. Blanquilla (Ven.)
I. Los Hermanos
(Ven.)
I. Los Testigos
(Ven.)
Tobago
TAB
Scarborough
Windward Islands
Leeward Islands
Lesser Antilles
Grenada
Basin
Aves Ridge
Aves (Venezuela)
I. de Aves

GUAJIRA
Puerto Bolívar
Pen. de la Guajira
Pta. Espada
C. San Román
Pen. de Paraguaná
Ríohacha
Uribia
Maicao
Punto Fijo
Golfo de Venezuela
MÉDANOS DE CORO
Puerto Cumarebo
Is. Las Aves
(Ven.)
Is. Los Roques
(Ven.)
NUEVA ESPARTA
I. de Margarita
(Ven.)
CERRO EL COPEY
987
La Asunción
Porlamar
Tobago
Port of Spain
940
TRINIDAD & TOBAGO
Trinidad
POS
Rio Claro
Arima
Santa Marta
ISLA DE SALAMANCA
SA. NEVADA DE STA. MARTA
5775
Valledupar
CÉSAR
Villa del Rosario
Machiques
Ciudad Ojeda
Cabimas
MARACAIBO
MAR
Altagracia
La Concepción
Santa Rita
Mene de Mauroa
FALCÓN
Coro
La Vela
I. La Tortuga
(Ven.)
LAGUNA LA RESTINGO
PMV
Cumaná
SUCRE
Carúpano
Güiria
Pen. de Paria
San Fernando
Serpent's Mouth
MARIUSA
DELTA
Tucupita

BOLÍVAR
Ocaña
Cúcuta
TACHIRA
San Cristóbal
SANTANDER
NORTE DE
San Antonio
Mérida
MÉRIDA
SIERRA NEVADA
4981
ZULIA
Lago de Maracaibo
TRUJILLO
Valera
Trujillo
Betijoque
LARA
BARQUISIMETO
PORTUGUESA
El Guache
Guanare Portuguesa
COJEDES
El Baúl
San Carlos
Calabozo
GUÁRICO
Santa Maria de Ipire
ANZOÁTEGUI
Valle de la Pascua
Aragua de Barcelona
Cantaura
Anaco
Maturín
MONAGAS
AMACURO
Upata
El Tigre
Ciudad Guayana
Soledad
BARINAS
Barinas
Libertad
Ciudad Bolivia
Guanare de Nutrias
San Fernando de Apure
APURE
VENEZUELA
Orinoco
Caicara
BOLÍVAR
Ciudad Bolívar
Sierra Imataca
El Pao
Guasipati
El Callao
Tumeremo
Embalse de Guri

San Felipe
YARACUY
VALENCIA
MARACAY
CARABOBO
Maiquetía
La Guaira
VARGAS
CARACAS
MIRANDA
Los Teques
Ocumare del Tuy
San Juan de los Morros
Cúa
Puerto Cabello
Morón
Puerto La Cruz
Barcelona
Carúpano
Cariaco
Caripito

92

4000 3000 2000 1500 1000 400 200 0
600 6000 12 000 18 000 24 000 ft
12 000 9000 6000 4500 3000 1200 600
200 2000 4000 6000 8000 m

1:35 000 000

Projection: Lambert's Azimuthal Equal Area

COPYRIGHT PHILIP'S

1:35 000 000

100 0 200 400 600 800 1000 1200 1400 km
100 0 200 400 600 800 1000 miles

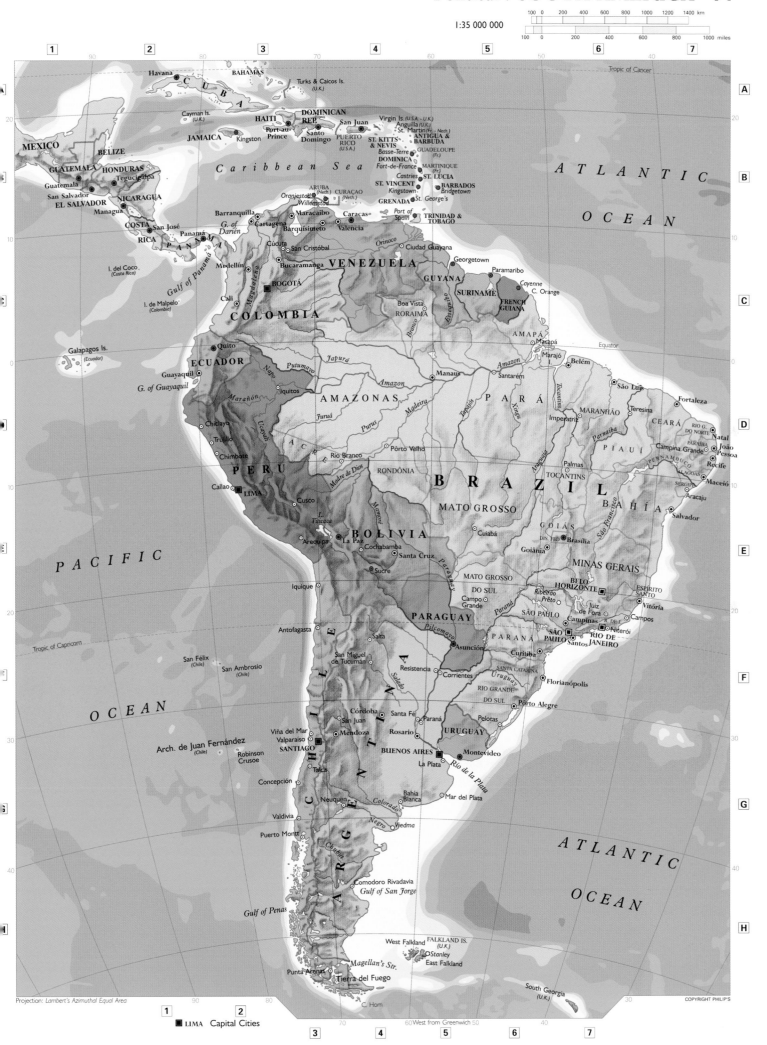

1 2 3 4 5 6 7

A

Havana
**C U B A**
BAHAMAS
Turks & Caicos Is.
(U.K.)
Tropic of Cancer

Cayman Is.
(U.K.)
HAITI
Port-au-
Prince
DOMINICAN
REP.
San Juan
Virgin Is. (U.S.A.-U.K.)
Anguilla (U.K.)
St. Martin (Fr.-Neth.)
**MEXICO**
**BELIZE**
JAMAICA
Kingston
Santo
Domingo
PUERTO
RICO
(U.S.A.)
ST. KITTS
& NEVIS
Basse-Terre
ANTIGUA &
BARBUDA
GUADELOUPE
(Fr.)
**GUATEMALA**
**HONDURAS**
Tegucigalpa
*Caribbean Sea*
DOMINICA
Fort-de-France
MARTINIQUE
(Fr.)
Guatemala
San Salvador
**EL SALVADOR**
NICARAGUA
Managua
Castries
ST. VINCENT
Kingstown
ST. LUCIA
BARBADOS
Bridgetown
ARUBA
(Neth.)
CURAÇAO
(Neth.)
GRENADA
St. George's
**COSTA**
**RICA**
San José
Panamá
Oranjestad
Willemstad
Port of
Spain
TRINIDAD &
TOBAGO
**PANAMA**
Barranquilla
Cartagena
Maracaibo
Caracas
I. del Coco
(Costa Rica)
G. of
Darién
Barquisimeto
Valencia
Cúcuta
San Cristóbal
Ciudad Guayana
*Orinoco*
Medellín
Bucaramanga
**VENEZUELA**
Georgetown
Paramaribo
Cayenne
C. Orange
I. de Malpelo
(Colombia)
Cali
**BOGOTÁ**
**GUYANA**
**SURINAME**
**FRENCH**
**GUIANA**
**COLOMBIA**
Boa Vista
RORAIMA
AMAPÁ
Macapá
Equator
Galapagos Is.
(Ecuador)
Quito
**ECUADOR**
*Putumayo*
*Japurá*
*Amazon*
Marajó
I.
Belém
Guayaquil
Iquitos
*Napo*
*Amazon*
Manaus
Santarém
São Luís
Fortaleza
G. of Guayaquil
**AMAZONAS**
*Madeira*
*Tapajós*
*Xingu*
**PARÁ**
**MARANHÃO**
Teresina
CEARÁ
RIO G.
DO NORTE
Natal
Chiclayo
*Furuá*
*Purus*
Imperatriz
*Parnaíba*
PIAUÍ
PARAÍBA
Campina Grande
João
Pessoa
Trujillo
ACRE
Rio Branco
Pôrto Velho
RONDÔNIA
*Araguaia*
TOCANTINS
Palmas
*São Francisco*
PERNAMBUCO
Recife
Chimbote
**PERU**
*Madre de Dios*
**B R A Z I L**
B A H Í A
ALAGOAS
Maceió
Callao
**LIMA**
Cusco
L.
Titicaca
*Mamoré*
MATO GROSSO
Cuiabá
GOIÁS
DIS. FED.
Brasília
Goiânia
SERGIPE
Aracaju
Salvador
Arequipa
**BOLIVIA**
La Paz
Cochabamba
Santa Cruz
Sucre
MATO GROSSO
DO SUL
Campo
Grande
Ribeirão
Prêto
**MINAS GERAIS**
BELO
HORIZONTE
ESPÍRITO
SANTO
Iquique
Vitória
**PACIFIC**
Antofagasta
**PARAGUAY**
*Paraná*
SÃO PAULO
Juiz
de Fora
Campos
Salta
*Pilcomayo*
**ASUNCIÓN**
PARANÁ
SÃO
PAULO
Campinas
R. DE J.
Niterói
RIO DE
JANEIRO
San Félix
(Chile)
San Ambrosio
(Chile)
San Miguel
de Tucumán
Santos
Curitiba
SANTA CATARINA
Florianópolis
Resistencia
Corrientes
*Uruguay*
RIO GRANDE
DO SUL
Córdoba
Santa Fé
Paraná
Pôrto Alegre
Arch. de Juan Fernández
(Chile)
San Juan
Rosario
Pelotas
**OCEAN**
Viña del Mar
Valparaíso
Mendoza
**URUGUAY**
Robinson
Crusoe
**SANTIAGO**
**BUENOS AIRES**
Montevideo
Talca
La Plata
*Río de la Plata*
Mar del Plata
Concepción
Neuquén
Bahía
Blanca
*Colorado*
Valdivia
*Negro*
Viedma
Puerto Montt
Comodoro Rivadavia
Gulf of San Jorge
**A R G E N T I N A**
*Chubut*
**C H I L E**
**ATLANTIC**
**OCEAN**
Gulf of Penas
West Falkland
FALKLAND IS.
(U.K.)
Magellan's Str.
Stanley
East Falkland
Punta Arenas
Tierra del Fuego
C. Horn
South Georgia
(U.K.)

*A T L A N T I C*

*O C E A N*

Tropic of Capricorn

Projection: Lambert's Azimuthal Equal Area

COPYRIGHT PHILIP'S

1 ■ LIMA 2 Capital Cities

60 West from Greenwich 50

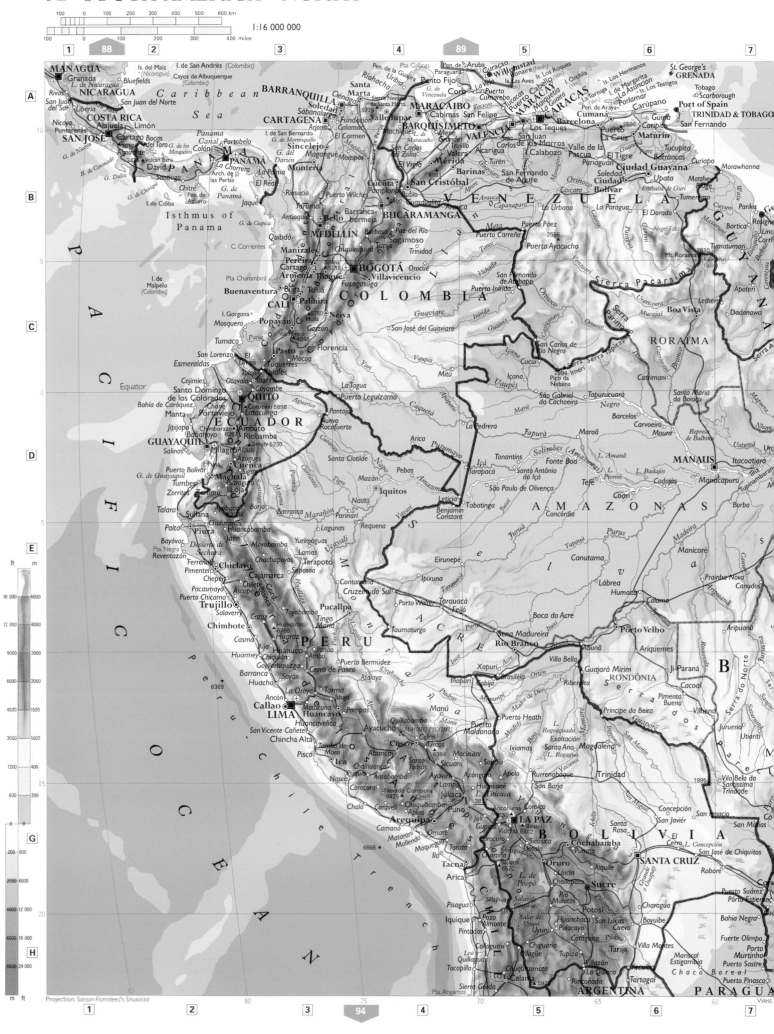

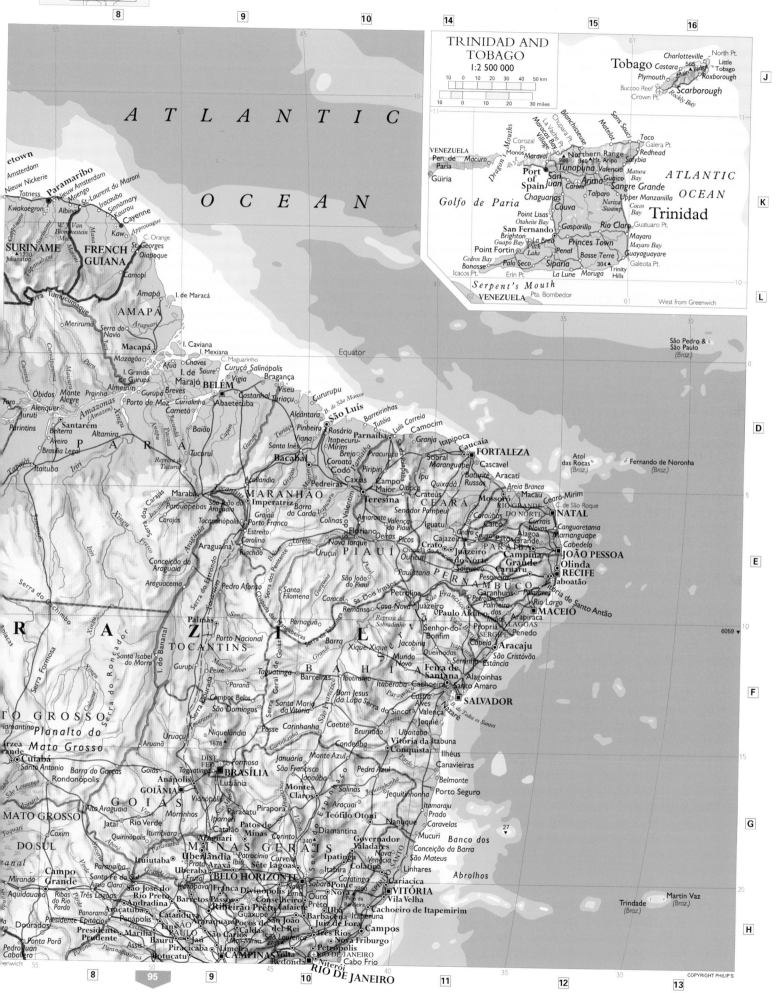

ATLANTIC

OCEAN

**TRINIDAD AND TOBAGO**
1:2 500 000

10 0 10 20 30 40 50 km

10 0 10 20 30 miles

Tobago
Charlotteville  North Pt.
Castara  565  Little
Plymouth  Main  Tobago
Buccoo Reef  Roxborough
Crown Pt.  Scarborough
Rockly Bay

VENEZUELA
Pen. de  Macuro
Paria  Maraval
Güiria  Monos I.
Blanchisseuse
La Vache Pt.  Chupara Pt.
Corozal  Sons Souci
Pt.  Maracas Bay  Toco  Redhead
Dragon's Mouths  Northern Range  Galera Pt.
936  340 Mt. Aripo  Matura
Port  Tunapuna  Valencia  Salybia
of Spain  San  Arima  Guaico  Matura
Juan  Caroni  Talparo  Sangre Grande  Bay
Chaguanas  Couva  Upper Manzanilla  ATLANTIC
Point Lisas  Narival  OCEAN
Otaheite Bay  Gasparillo  Rio Claro  Swamp  Cocos
San Fernando  La Brea  Princes Town  Mayaro  Bay
Brighton  Mayaro Bay  Trinidad
Point Fortin  Penal  Basse Terre  Guayaguayare
Cedros Bay  Pitch  Siparia  304  Galeota Pt.
Bonasse  Lake  La Lune  Moruga  Trinity
Icacos Pt.  Palo Seco  Hills
Erin Pt.  Pta. Bombedor
**VENEZUELA**  Serpent's Mouth  West from Greenwich
Golfo de Paria

ATLANTIC

OCEAN

São Pedro &
São Paulo
(Braz.)

Equator

SURINAME  FRENCH
Julianatop  GUIANA

Paramaribo
Nieuw Amsterdam
Moengo  St-Laurent du Maroni
Albina  Iracoubo
Sinnamary
Kourou
Cayenne
Kaw  Approuague
C. Orange
Sts Georges
Oiapoque

AMAPÁ
Macapá

Fernando de Noronha
(Braz.)

Atol
das Rocas
(Braz.)

FORTALEZA

6059

Martin Vaz
(Braz.)

Trindade
(Braz.)

27

BRAZIL

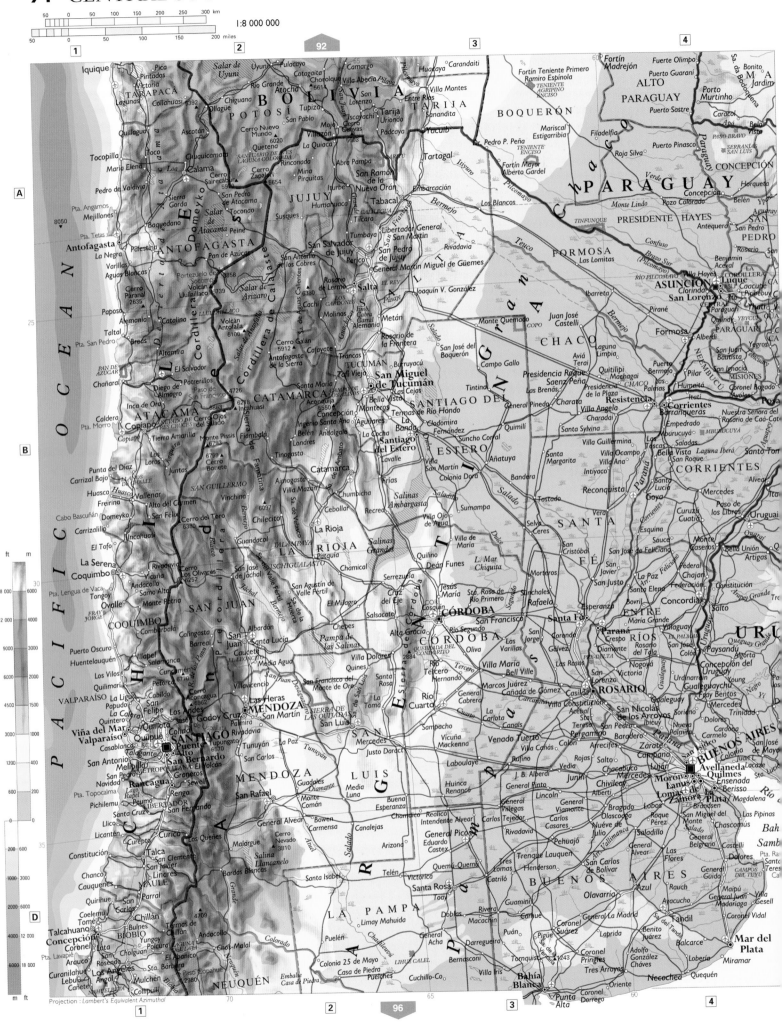

1:8 000 000

ATLANTIC

OCEAN

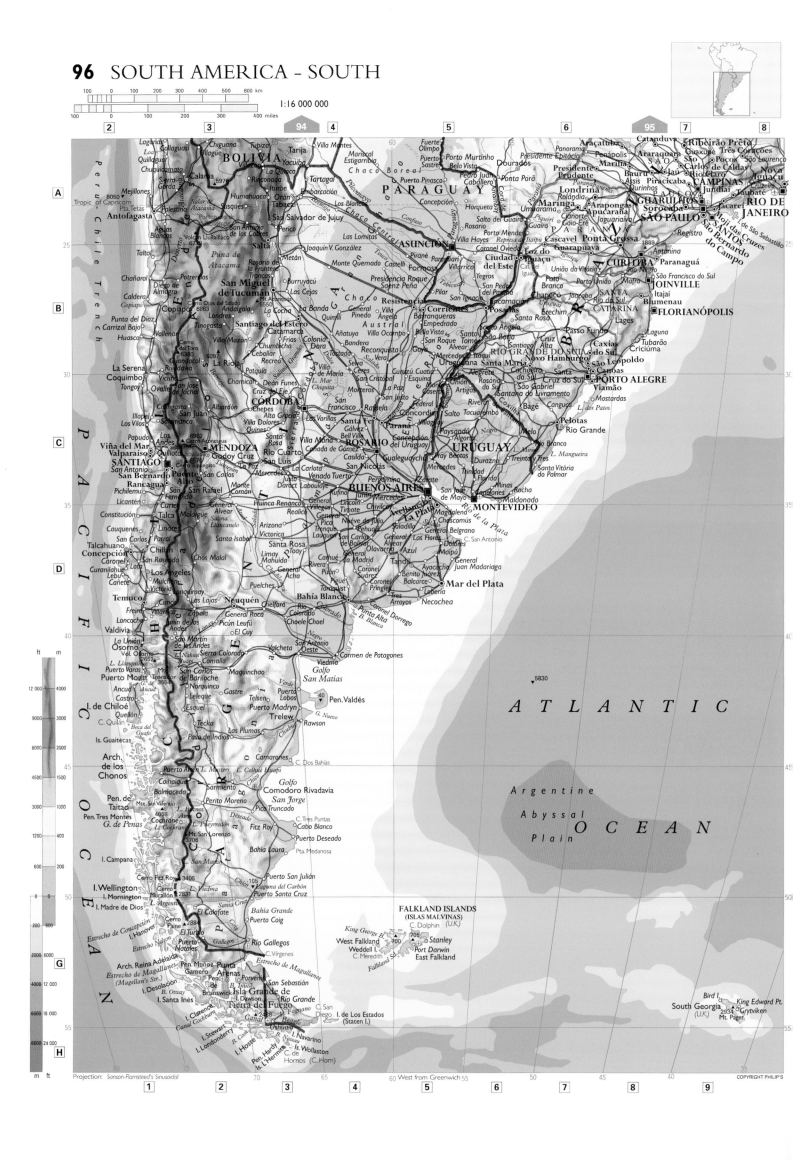

# INDEX TO WORLD MAPS

The index contains the names of all the principal places and features shown on the World Maps. Each name is followed by an additional entry in italics giving the country or region within which it is located. The alphabetical order of names composed of two or more words is governed primarily by the first word, then by the second, and then by the country or region name that follows. This is an example of the rule:

| | | |
|---|---|---|
| **Mīr Kūh** *Iran* | 26°22N 58°55E | **47** E8 |
| **Mīr Shahdād** *Iran* | 26°15N 58°29E | **47** E8 |
| **Mira** *Italy* | 45°26N 12°8E | **22** B5 |
| **Mira por vos Cay** *Bahamas* | 22°9N 74°30W | **89** B5 |

Physical features composed of a proper name (Erie) and a description (Lake) are positioned alphabetically by the proper name. The description is positioned after the proper name and is usually abbreviated:

| | | |
|---|---|---|
| **Erie, L.** *N. Amer.* | 42°15N 81°0W | **82** D4 |

Where a description forms part of a settlement or administrative name, however, it is always written in full and put in its true alphabetical position:

| | | |
|---|---|---|
| **Mount Morris** *U.S.A.* | 42°44N 77°52W | **82** D7 |

Names beginning with M' and Mc are indexed as if they were spelled Mac. Names beginning St. are alphabetized under Saint, but Sankt, Sint, Sant', Santa and San are all spelt in full and are alphabetized accordingly. If the same place name occurs two or more times in the index and all are in the same country, each is followed by the name of the administrative subdivision in which it is located.

The geographical co-ordinates which follow each name in the index give the latitude and longitude of each place. The first co-ordinate indicates latitude – the distance north or south of the Equator. The second co-ordinate indicates longitude – the distance east or west of the Greenwich Meridian. Both latitude and longitude are measured in degrees and minutes (there are 60 minutes in a degree).

The latitude is followed by N(orth) or S(outh) and the longitude by E(ast) or W(est).

The number in bold type which follows the geographical co-ordinates refers to the number of the map page where that feature or place will be found. This is usually the largest scale at which the place or feature appears.

The letter and figure that are immediately after the page number give the grid square on the map page, within which the feature is situated. The letter represents the latitude and the figure the longitude. A lower-case letter immediately after the page number refers to an inset map on that page.

In some cases the feature itself may fall within the specified square, while the name is outside. This is usually the case only with features that are larger than a grid square.

Rivers are indexed to their mouths or confluences, and carry the symbol ➔ after their names. The following symbols are also used in the index: ■ country, ☑ overseas territory or dependency, ☐ first-order administrative area, △ national park, ◠ other park (provincial park, nature reserve or game reserve), ✗ (LHR) principal airport (and location identifier), ◉ Australian aboriginal land.

## Abbreviations used in the index

*A.C.T.* – Australian Capital Territory
*A.R.* – Autonomous Region
*Afghan.* – Afghanistan
*Afr.* – Africa
*Ala.* – Alabama
*Alta.* – Alberta
*Amer.* – America(n)
*Ant.* – Antilles
*Arch.* – Archipelago
*Ariz.* – Arizona
*Ark.* – Arkansas
*Atl. Oc.* – Atlantic Ocean
*B.* – Baie, Bahía, Bay, Bucht, Bugt
*B.C.* – British Columbia
*Bangla.* – Bangladesh
*Barr.* – Barrage
*Bos.-H.* – Bosnia-Herzegovina
*C.* – Cabo, Cap, Cape, Coast
*C.A.R.* – Central African Republic
*C. Prov.* – Cape Province
*Calif.* – California
*Cat.* – Catarata
*Cent.* – Central
*Chan.* – Channel
*Colo.* – Colorado
*Conn.* – Connecticut
*Cord.* – Cordillera
*Cr.* – Creek
*D.C.* – District of Columbia
*Del.* – Delaware
*Dem.* – Democratic
*Dep.* – Dependency
*Des.* – Desert
*Dét.* – Détroit
*Dist.* – District
*Dj.* – Djebel
*Dom. Rep.* – Dominican Republic
*E.* – East

*El Salv.* – El Salvador
*Eq. Guin.* – Equatorial Guinea
*Est.* – Estrecho
*Falk. Is.* – Falkland Is.
*Fd.* – Fjord
*Fla.* – Florida
*Fr.* – French
*G.* – Golfe, Golfo, Gulf, Guba, Gebel
*Ga.* – Georgia
*Gt.* – Great, Greater
*Guinea-Biss.* – Guinea-Bissau
*H.K.* – Hong Kong
*H.P.* – Himachal Pradesh
*Hants.* – Hampshire
*Harb.* – Harbor, Harbour
*Hd.* – Head
*Hts.* – Heights
*I.(s).* – Île, Ilha, Insel, Isla, Island, Isle
*Ill.* – Illinois
*Ind.* – Indiana
*Ind. Oc.* – Indian Ocean
*J.* – Jabal, Jebel
*Jaz.* – Jazīrah
*Junc.* – Junction
*K.* – Kap, Kapp
*Kans.* – Kansas
*Kep.* – Kepulauan
*Ky.* – Kentucky
*L.* – Lac, Lacul, Lago, Lagoa, Lake, Limni, Loch, Lough
*La.* – Louisiana
*Ld.* – Land
*Liech.* – Liechtenstein
*Lux.* – Luxembourg
*Mad. P.* – Madhya Pradesh
*Madag.* – Madagascar
*Man.* – Manitoba
*Mass.* – Massachusetts
*Md.* – Maryland
*Me.* – Maine

*Medit. S.* – Mediterranean Sea
*Mich.* – Michigan
*Minn.* – Minnesota
*Miss.* – Mississippi
*Mo.* – Missouri
*Mont.* – Montana
*Mozam.* – Mozambique
*Mt.(s)* – Mont, Montaña, Mountain
*Mte.* – Monte
*Mti.* – Monti
*N.* – Nord, Norte, North, Northern, Nouveau, Nahal, Nahr
*N.B.* – New Brunswick
*N.C.* – North Carolina
*N. Cal.* – New Caledonia
*N. Dak.* – North Dakota
*N.H.* – New Hampshire
*N.I.* – North Island
*N.J.* – New Jersey
*N. Mex.* – New Mexico
*N.S.* – Nova Scotia
*N.S.W.* – New South Wales
*N.W.T.* – North West Territory
*N.Y.* – New York
*N.Z.* – New Zealand
*Nac.* – Nacional
*Nat.* – National
*Nebr.* – Nebraska
*Neths.* – Netherlands
*Nev.* – Nevada
*Nfld & L.* – Newfoundland and Labrador
*Nic.* – Nicaragua
*O.* – Oued, Ouadi
*Occ.* – Occidentale
*Okla.* – Oklahoma
*Ont.* – Ontario
*Or.* – Orientale
*Oreg.* – Oregon
*Os.* – Ostrov

*Oz.* – Ozero
*P.* – Pass, Passo, Pasul, Pulau
*P.E.I.* – Prince Edward Island
*Pa.* – Pennsylvania
*Pac. Oc.* – Pacific Ocean
*Papua N.G.* – Papua New Guinea
*Pass.* – Passage
*Peg.* – Pegunungan
*Pen.* – Peninsula, Péninsule
*Phil.* – Philippines
*Pk.* – Peak
*Plat.* – Plateau
*Prov.* – Province, Provincial
*Pt.* – Point
*Pta.* – Ponta, Punta
*Pte.* – Pointe
*Qué.* – Québec
*Queens.* – Queensland
*R.* – Rio, River
*R.I.* – Rhode Island
*Ra.* – Range
*Raj.* – Rajasthan
*Recr.* – Recreational, Récréatif
*Reg.* – Region
*Rep.* – Republic
*Res.* – Reserve, Reservoir
*Rhld-Pfz.* – Rheinland-Pfalz
*S.* – South, Southern, Sur
*Si. Arabia* – Saudi Arabia
*S.C.* – South Carolina
*S. Dak.* – South Dakota
*S.I.* – South Island
*S. Leone* – Sierra Leone
*Sa.* – Serra, Sierra
*Sask.* – Saskatchewan
*Scot.* – Scotland
*Sd.* – Sound
*Sev.* – Severnaya
*Sib.* – Siberia
*Sprs.* – Springs
*St.* – Saint

*Sta.* – Santa
*Ste.* – Sainte
*Sto.* – Santo
*Str.* – Strait, Stretto
*Switz.* – Switzerland
*Tas.* – Tasmania
*Tenn.* – Tennessee
*Terr.* – Territory, Territoire
*Tex.* – Texas
*Tg.* – Tanjung
*Trin. & Tob.* – Trinidad & Tobago
*U.A.E.* – United Arab Emirates
*U.K.* – United Kingdom
*U.S.A.* – United States of America
*Ut. P.* – Uttar Pradesh
*Va.* – Virginia
*Vdkhr.* – Vodokhranilishche
*Vdskh.* – Vodoskhovyshche
*Vf.* – Vírful
*Vic.* – Victoria
*Vol.* – Volcano
*Vt.* – Vermont
*W.* – Wadi, West
*W. Va.* – West Virginia
*Wall. & F. Is.* – Wallis and Futuna Is.
*Wash.* – Washington
*Wis.* – Wisconsin
*Wlkp.* – Wielkopolski
*Wyo.* – Wyoming
*Yorks.* – Yorkshire

## A


A Coruña *Spain* 43°20N 8°25W **21 A1**
A Estrada *Spain* 42°43N 8°27W **21 A1**
A Fonsagrada *Spain* 43°8N 7°4W **21 A2**
A Shau *Vietnam* 16°6N 107°22E **38 D6**
Aabenraa *Denmark* 55°3N 9°25E **9 J13**
Aachen *Germany* 50°45N 6°6E **16 C4**
Aalborg *Denmark* 57°2N 9°54E **9 H13**
Aalen *Germany* 48°51N 10°6E **16 D6**
Aalst *Belgium* 50°56N 4°2E **15 D4**
Aalten *Neths.* 51°56N 6°35E **15 C6**
Aalter *Belgium* 51°5N 3°28E **15 C3**
Äänekoski *Finland* 62°36N 25°44E **8 E21**
Aarau *Switz.* 47°23N 8°4E **20 C8**
Aare → *Switz.* 47°33N 8°14E **20 C8**
Aarhus *Denmark* 56°8N 10°11E **9 H14**
Aarschot *Belgium* 50°59N 4°49E **15 D4**
Aba *China* 32°59N 101°42E **34 A3**
Aba *Nigeria* 5°10N 7°19E **52 G7**
Abaco I. *Bahamas* 26°25N 77°10W **88 A4**
Ābādān *Iran* 30°22N 48°20E **47 D6**
Ābādeh *Iran* 31°8N 52°40E **47 D7**
Abadla *Algeria* 31°2N 2°45W **52 B5**
Abaetetuba *Brazil* 1°40S 48°50W **93 D9**
Abagnar Qi = Xilinhot *China* 43°52N 116°2E **32 C9**
Abah, Tanjung *Indonesia* 8°46S 115°38E **37 K18**
Abai *Paraguay* 25°58S 55°54W **95 B4**
Abakan *Russia* 53°40N 91°10E **27 D10**
Abancay *Peru* 13°35S 72°55W **92 F4**
Abang, Gunung *Indonesia* 8°16S 115°25E **37 J18**
Abariringa *Kiribati* 2°50S 171°40W **64 H10**
Abarqū *Iran* 31°10N 53°20E **47 D7**
Abashiri *Japan* 44°0N 144°15E **28 B12**
Abashiri-Wan *Japan* 44°0N 144°30E **28 C12**
Ābay = Nîl el Azraq → *Sudan* 15°38N 32°31E **53 E12**
Abay *Kazakhstan* 49°38N 72°53E **26 E8**
Abaya, L. *Ethiopia* 6°30N 37°50E **49 F2**
Abaza *Russia* 52°39N 90°6E **26 D10**
'Abbāsābād *Iran* 33°34N 58°23E **47 C8**
Abbay = Nîl el Azraq → *Sudan* 15°38N 32°31E **53 E12**
Abbaye, Pt. *U.S.A.* 46°58N 88°8W **80 B9**
Abbé, L. *Ethiopia* 11°8N 41°47E **49 E3**
Abbeville *France* 50°6N 1°49E **20 A4**
Abbeville *Ala., U.S.A.* 31°34N 85°15W **85 F12**
Abbeville *La., U.S.A.* 29°58N 92°8W **84 G8**
Abbeville *S.C., U.S.A.* 34°11N 82°23W **85 D13**
Abbeyfeale *Ireland* 52°23N 9°18W **10 D2**
Abbeyleix *Ireland* 52°54N 7°22W **10 D4**
Abbot Ice Shelf *Antarctica* 73°0S 92°0W **5 D16**
Abbotsford *Canada* 49°5N 122°20W **70 D4**
Abbottabad *Pakistan* 34°10N 73°15E **42 B5**
ABC Islands *W. Indies* 12°15N 69°0W **89 D6**
Abd al Kūrī *Yemen* 12°5N 52°20E **49 E5**
Ābdar *Iran* 30°16N 55°19E **47 D7**
'Abdolābād *Iran* 34°12N 56°30E **47 C8**
Abdulpur *Bangla.* 24°15N 88°59E **43 G13**
Abéché *Chad* 13°50N 20°35E **53 F10**
Abel Tasman △ *N.Z.* 40°59S 173°3E **59 D4**
Abengourou *Côte d'Ivoire* 6°42N 3°27W **52 G5**
Åbenrå = Aabenraa *Denmark* 55°3N 9°25E **9 J13**
Abeokuta *Nigeria* 7°3N 3°19E **52 G6**
Aberaeron *U.K.* 52°15N 4°15W **13 E3**
Aberayron = Aberaeron *U.K.* 52°15N 4°15W **13 E3**
Aberchirder *U.K.* 57°34N 2°37W **11 D6**
Abercorn *Australia* 25°12S 151°5E **63 D5**
Aberdare *U.K.* 51°43N 3°27W **13 F4**
Aberdaugleddau = Milford Haven *U.K.* 51°42N 5°7W **13 F2**
Aberdeen *Australia* 32°9S 150°56E **63 E5**
Aberdeen *Canada* 52°20N 106°8W **71 C7**
Aberdeen *S. Africa* 32°28S 24°2E **56 D3**
Aberdeen *U.K.* 57°9N 2°5W **11 D6**
Aberdeen *Idaho, U.S.A.* 42°57N 112°50W **76 E7**
Aberdeen *Md., U.S.A.* 39°31N 76°10W **81 F15**
Aberdeen *Miss., U.S.A.* 33°49N 88°33W **85 E10**
Aberdeen *S. Dak., U.S.A.* 45°28N 98°29W **80 C4**
Aberdeen *Wash., U.S.A.* 46°59N 123°50W **78 D3**
Aberdeen City ☐ *U.K.* 57°10N 2°10W **11 D6**
Aberdeen L. *Canada* 64°30N 99°0W **68 E12**
Aberdeenshire ☐ *U.K.* 57°17N 2°36W **11 D6**
Aberdovey = Aberdyfi *U.K.* 52°33N 4°3W **13 E3**
Aberdyfi *U.K.* 52°33N 4°3W **13 E3**
Aberfeldy *U.K.* 56°37N 3°51W **11 E5**
Aberfoyle *U.K.* 56°11N 4°23W **11 E4**
Abergavenny *U.K.* 51°49N 3°1W **13 F4**
Abergele *U.K.* 53°17N 3°35W **12 D4**
Abergwaun = Fishguard *U.K.* 52°0N 4°58W **13 E3**
Aberhonddu = Brecon *U.K.* 51°57N 3°23W **13 F4**
Abermaw = Barmouth *U.K.* 52°44N 4°4W **12 E3**
Abernathy *U.S.A.* 33°50N 101°51W **84 E4**
Aberpennar = Mountain Ash *U.K.* 51°40N 3°23W **13 F4**
Abert, L. *U.S.A.* 42°38N 120°14W **76 E3**
Abertawe = Swansea *U.K.* 51°37N 3°57W **13 F4**
Aberteifi = Cardigan *U.K.* 52°5N 4°40W **13 E3**
Aberystwyth *U.K.* 52°25N 4°5W **13 E3**
Abhā *Si. Arabia* 18°0N 42°34E **49 D3**
Abhar *Iran* 36°9N 49°13E **47 B6**
Abhayapuri *India* 26°24N 90°38E **43 F14**
Abidjan *Côte d'Ivoire* 5°26N 3°58W **52 G5**
Abilene *Kans., U.S.A.* 38°55N 97°13W **80 F5**
Abilene *Tex., U.S.A.* 32°28N 99°43W **84 E5**
Abingdon *U.S.A.* 36°43N 81°59W **81 G13**
Abingdon-on-Thames *U.K.* 51°40N 1°17W **13 F6**
Abington Reef *Australia* 18°0S 149°35E **62 B4**
Abisko △ *Sweden* 68°18N 18°44E **8 B18**
Abitau → *Canada* 59°53N 109°3W **71 B7**
Abitibi → *Canada* 51°3N 80°55W **72 B3**
Abitibi, L. *Canada* 48°40N 79°40W **72 C4**
Abkhaz Republic = Abkhazia ☐ *Georgia* 43°12N 41°5E **19 F7**
Abkhazia ☐ *Georgia* 43°12N 41°5E **19 F7**
Abminga *Australia* 26°8S 134°51E **63 D1**
Åbo = Turku *Finland* 60°30N 22°19E **9 F20**
Abohar *India* 30°10N 74°10E **42 D6**
Abomey *Benin* 7°10N 2°5E **52 G6**
Abong-Mbang *Cameroon* 4°0N 13°8E **54 D2**
Abou-Deïa *Chad* 11°20N 19°20E **53 F9**
Aboyne *U.K.* 57°4N 2°47W **11 D6**
Abra Pampa *Argentina* 22°43S 65°42W **94 A2**
Abraham L. *Canada* 52°15N 116°35W **70 C5**
Abreojos, Pta. *Mexico* 26°50N 113°40W **86 B2**
Abrolhos, Banco dos *Brazil* 18°0S 38°0W **90 E7**
Abrud *Romania* 46°19N 23°5E **17 E12**
Absaroka Range *U.S.A.* 44°45N 109°50W **76 D9**
Abu *India* 24°41N 72°50E **42 G5**
Abū al Abyad *U.A.E.* 24°11N 53°50E **47 E7**
Abū al Khaṣīb *Iraq* 30°25N 48°0E **46 D5**
Abū 'Alī *Si. Arabia* 27°20N 49°27E **47 E6**
Abū 'Alī → *Lebanon* 34°25N 35°50E **48 A4**
Abu Dhabi = Abū Ẓāby *U.A.E.* 24°28N 54°22E **47 E7**
Abū Du'ān *Syria* 36°25N 38°15E **46 B3**
Abu el Gaīn, W. → *Egypt* 29°35N 33°30E **48 F2**
Abu Ga'da, W. → *Egypt* 29°15N 32°53E **48 F1**
Abū Ḥadrīyah *Si. Arabia* 27°20N 48°58E **47 E6**
Abu Hamed *Sudan* 19°32N 33°13E **53 E12**
Abū Kamāl *Syria* 34°30N 41°0E **46 C4**
Abū Madd, Ra's *Si. Arabia* 24°50N 37°7E **46 E3**
Abū Mūsā *U.A.E.* 25°52N 55°3E **47 E7**
Abū Qaṣr *Si. Arabia* 30°21N 38°34E **46 D3**
Abu Shagara, Ras *Sudan* 21°4N 37°19E **53 D13**
Abu Simbel *Egypt* 22°18N 31°40E **53 D12**
Abū Şukhayr *Iraq* 31°54N 44°30E **46 D5**
Abu Zabad *Sudan* 12°25N 29°10E **53 F11**
Abū Ẓāby *U.A.E.* 24°28N 54°22E **47 E7**
Abū Zeydābād *Iran* 33°54N 51°45E **47 C6**
Abuja *Nigeria* 9°5N 7°32E **52 G7**
Abukuma-Gawa → *Japan* 38°6N 140°52E **28 E10**
Abukuma-Sammyaku *Japan* 37°30N 140°45E **28 F10**
Abunã *Brazil* 9°40S 65°20W **92 E5**
Abunã → *Brazil* 9°41S 65°20W **92 E5**
Abut Hd. *N.Z.* 43°7S 170°15E **59 E3**
Abyei ☒ *Sudan* 9°30N 28°30E **53 G11**
Ābyek *Iran* 36°4N 50°33E **47 B6**
Acadia △ *U.S.A.* 44°20N 68°13W **81 C19**
Açailândia *Brazil* 4°57S 47°30W **93 D9**
Acajutla *El Salv.* 13°36N 89°50W **88 D2**
Acámbaro *Mexico* 20°2N 100°44W **86 D4**
Acaponeta *Mexico* 22°30N 105°22W **86 C3**
Acapulco *Mexico* 16°51N 99°55W **87 D5**
Acapulco Trench *Pac. Oc.* 12°0N 88°0W **86 D4**
Acaraí, Serra *Brazil* 1°50N 57°50W **92 C7**
Acarai Mts. = Acaraí, Serra *Brazil* 1°50N 57°50W **92 C7**
Acarigua *Venezuela* 9°33N 69°12W **92 B5**
Acatlán *Mexico* 18°12N 98°3W **87 D5**
Acayucán *Mexico* 17°57N 94°55W **87 D6**
Accomac *U.S.A.* 37°43N 75°40W **81 G16**
Accra *Ghana* 5°35N 0°6W **52 G5**
Accrington *U.K.* 53°45N 2°22W **12 D5**
Acebal *Argentina* 33°20S 60°50W **94 C3**
Aceh ☐ *Indonesia* 4°15N 97°30E **36 D1**
Achalpur *India* 21°22N 77°32E **44 D3**
Acharnes *Greece* 38°5N 23°44E **23 E10**
Acheloos → *Greece* 38°19N 21°7E **23 E9**
Acheng *China* 45°30N 126°58E **33 B14**
Acher *India* 23°10N 72°32E **42 H5**
Achill Hd. *Ireland* 53°58N 10°15W **10 C1**
Achill I. *Ireland* 53°58N 10°1W **10 C1**
Achinsk *Russia* 56°20N 90°20E **27 D10**
Acireale *Italy* 37°37N 15°10E **22 F6**
Ackerman *U.S.A.* 33°19N 89°11W **85 E10**
Acklins I. *Bahamas* 22°30N 74°0W **89 B5**
Acme *Canada* 51°33N 113°30W **70 C6**
Acme *U.S.A.* 40°8N 79°26W **82 F5**
Aconcagua, Cerro *Argentina* 32°39S 70°0W **94 C2**
Aconquija, Mt. *Argentina* 27°0S 66°0W **94 B2**
Açores, Is. dos *Atl. Oc.* 38°0N 27°0W **52 a**
Acornhoek *S. Africa* 24°37S 31°2E **57 B5**
Acraman, L. *Australia* 32°2S 135°23E **63 E2**
Acre = 'Akko *Israel* 32°55N 35°4E **48 C4**
Acre ☐ *Brazil* 9°1S 71°0W **92 E4**
Acre → *Brazil* 8°45S 67°22W **92 E5**
Actinolite *Canada* 44°32N 77°19W **82 B7**
Acton *Canada* 43°38N 80°3W **82 C4**
Ad Dahnā *Si. Arabia* 24°30N 48°10E **49 C4**
Ad Dammām *Si. Arabia* 26°20N 50°5E **47 E6**
Ad Dāmūr *Lebanon* 33°43N 35°27E **48 B4**
Ad Dawādimī *Si. Arabia* 24°35N 44°15E **46 E5**
Ad Dawḥah *Qatar* 25°15N 51°35E **47 E6**
Ad Dawr *Iraq* 34°27N 43°47E **46 C4**
Ad Dhakhīrah *Qatar* 25°44N 51°33E **47 E6**
Ad Dir'īyah *Si. Arabia* 24°44N 46°35E **46 E5**
Ad Dīwānīyah *Iraq* 32°0N 45°0E **46 D5**
Ad Dujayl *Iraq* 33°51N 44°14E **46 C5**
Ad Duwayd *Si. Arabia* 30°15N 42°17E **46 D4**
Ada *Minn., U.S.A.* 47°18N 96°31W **80 B5**
Ada *Okla., U.S.A.* 34°46N 96°41W **84 D6**
Adabiya *Egypt* 29°53N 32°28E **48 F1**
Adair, C. *Canada* 71°30N 71°34W **69 C17**
Adaja → *Spain* 41°32N 4°52W **21 B3**
Adak *U.S.A.* 51°45N 176°45W **74 E4**
Adak I. *U.S.A.* 51°45N 176°45W **74 E4**
Adama = Nazret *Ethiopia* 8°32N 39°22E **49 F2**
Adamaoua, Massif de l' *Cameroon* 7°20N 12°20E **53 G8**
Adamawa Highlands = Adamaoua, Massif de l' *Cameroon* 7°20N 12°20E **53 G8**
Adamello, Mte. *Italy* 46°9N 10°30E **20 C9**
Adaminaby *Australia* 36°0S 148°45E **63 F4**
Adams *Mass., U.S.A.* 42°38N 73°7W **83 D11**
Adams *N.Y., U.S.A.* 43°49N 76°1W **83 C8**
Adams *Wis., U.S.A.* 43°57N 89°49W **80 D9**
Adams, Mt. *U.S.A.* 46°12N 121°30W **78 D5**
Adam's Bridge *Sri Lanka* 9°15N 79°40E **45 K4**
Adams L. *Canada* 51°10N 119°40W **70 C5**
Adam's Peak *Sri Lanka* 6°48N 80°30E **45 L5**
'Adan *Yemen* 12°45N 45°0E **49 E4**
Adana *Turkey* 37°0N 35°16E **46 B2**
Adang, Ko *Thailand* 6°33N 99°18E **39 J2**
Adapazarı = Sakarya *Turkey* 40°48N 30°25E **19 F5**
Adarama *Sudan* 17°10N 34°52E **53 E12**
Adare *Ireland* 52°34N 8°47W **10 D3**
Adare, C. *Antarctica* 71°0S 171°0E **5 D11**
Adaut *Indonesia* 8°8S 131°7E **37 F8**
Adavale *Australia* 25°52S 144°32E **63 D3**
Adda → *Italy* 45°8N 9°53E **20 D8**
Addatigala *India* 17°31N 82°3E **44 F6**
Addis Ababa = Addis Abeba *Ethiopia* 9°2N 38°42E **49 F2**
Addis Abeba *Ethiopia* 9°2N 38°42E **49 F2**
Addison *U.S.A.* 42°1N 77°14W **82 D7**
Addo *S. Africa* 33°32S 25°45E **56 D4**
Addo △ *S. Africa* 33°30S 25°50E **56 D4**
Ādeh *Iran* 37°42N 45°11E **46 B5**
Adel *U.S.A.* 31°8N 83°25W **85 F13**
Adelaide *Australia* 34°52S 138°30E **63 E2**
Adelaide *S. Africa* 32°42S 26°20E **56 D4**
Adelaide I. *Antarctica* 67°15S 68°30W **5 C17**
Adelaide Pen. *Canada* 68°15N 97°30W **68 D12**
Adelaide River *Australia* 13°15S 131°7E **60 B5**
Adelaide Village *Bahamas* 25°0N 77°31W **88 A4**
Adelanto *U.S.A.* 34°35N 117°22W **79 L9**
Adele I. *Australia* 15°32S 123°9E **60 C3**
Adélie, Terre *Antarctica* 68°0S 140°0E **5 C10**
Adelie Land = Adélie, Terre *Antarctica* 68°0S 140°0E **5 C10**
Aden = 'Adan *Yemen* 12°45N 45°0E **49 E4**
Aden, G. of *Ind. Oc.* 12°30N 47°30E **49 E4**
Adendorp *S. Africa* 32°15S 24°30E **56 D3**
Adh Dhayd *U.A.E.* 25°17N 55°53E **47 E7**
Adhoi *India* 23°26N 70°32E **42 H4**
Adi *Indonesia* 4°15S 133°30E **37 E8**
Adieu, C. *Australia* 32°0S 132°10E **61 F5**
Adieu Pt. *Australia* 15°14S 124°35E **60 C3**
Adige → *Italy* 45°9N 12°20E **22 B5**
Adigrat *Ethiopia* 14°20N 39°26E **49 E2**
Adilabad *India* 19°33N 78°20E **44 E4**
Adirondack △ *U.S.A.* 44°0N 74°20W **83 C10**
Adirondack Mts. *U.S.A.* 44°0N 74°0W **83 C10**
Adis Abeba = Addis Abeba *Ethiopia* 9°2N 38°42E **49 F2**
Adjuntas *Puerto Rico* 18°10N 66°43W **89 d**
Adlavik Is. *Canada* 55°0N 58°40W **73 B8**
Admiralty G. *Australia* 14°20S 125°55E **60 B4**
Admiralty Gulf ✪ *Australia* 14°16S 125°52E **60 B4**
Admiralty I. *U.S.A.* 57°30N 134°30W **70 B2**
Admiralty Inlet *Canada* 72°30N 86°0W **69 C14**
Admiralty Is. *Papua N. G.* 2°0S 147°0E **58 B7**
Adolfo González Chaves *Argentina* 38°2S 60°5W **94 D3**
Adolfo Ruiz Cortines, Presa *Mexico* 27°15N 109°6W **86 B3**
Adonara *Indonesia* 8°15S 123°5E **37 F6**
Adoni *India* 15°33N 77°18E **45 G3**
Adour → *France* 43°32N 1°32W **20 E3**
Adra *India* 23°30N 86°42E **43 H12**
Adra *Spain* 36°43N 3°3W **21 D4**
Adrano *Italy* 37°40N 14°50E **22 F6**
Adrar *Algeria* 27°51N 0°19W **52 C6**
Adrar *Mauritania* 20°30N 7°30W **52 D3**
Adrar des Iforas *Africa* 19°40N 1°40E **52 E6**
Adrian *Mich., U.S.A.* 41°54N 84°2W **81 E11**
Adrian *Tex., U.S.A.* 35°16N 102°40W **84 D3**
Adriatic Sea *Medit. S.* 43°0N 16°0E **22 C6**
Adua *Indonesia* 1°45S 129°50E **37 E7**
Adur *India* 9°8N 76°40E **45 K3**
Adwa *Ethiopia* 14°15N 38°52E **49 E2**
Adygea ☐ *Russia* 45°0N 40°0E **19 F7**
Adzhar Republic = Ajaria ☐ *Georgia* 41°30N 42°0E **19 F7**
Adzopé *Côte d'Ivoire* 6°7N 3°49W **52 G5**
Ægean Sea *Medit. S.* 38°30N 25°0E **23 E11**
Aerhtai Shan *Mongolia* 46°40N 92°45E **30 B7**
Afaahiti *Tahiti* 17°45S 149°17W **59 d**
'Afak *Iraq* 32°4N 45°15E **46 C5**
Afareaitu *Moorea* 17°33S 149°47W **59 d**
Afghanistan ■ *Asia* 33°0N 65°0E **40 C4**
Aflou *Algeria* 34°7N 2°3E **52 B6**
Afognak I. *U.S.A.* 58°15N 152°30W **74 D9**
Africa 10°0N 20°0E **50 E6**
'Afrīn *Syria* 36°32N 36°50E **46 B3**
Afton *N.Y., U.S.A.* 42°14N 75°32W **83 D9**
Afton *Wyo., U.S.A.* 42°44N 110°56W **76 E8**
Afuá *Brazil* 0°15S 50°20W **93 D8**
'Afula *Israel* 32°37N 35°17E **48 C4**
Afyon *Turkey* 38°45N 30°33E **19 G5**
Afyonkarahisar = Afyon *Turkey* 38°45N 30°33E **19 G5**
Āgā Jarī *Iran* 30°42N 49°50E **47 D6**
Agadés = Agadez *Niger* 16°58N 7°59E **52 E7**
Agadez *Niger* 16°58N 7°59E **52 E7**
Agadir *Morocco* 30°28N 9°55W **52 B4**
Agalega Is. *Mauritius* 11°0S 57°0E **3 E12**
Agar *India* 23°40N 76°2E **42 H7**
Agar → *India* 21°0N 82°57E **44 D6**
Agartala *India* 23°50N 91°23E **41 H17**
Agassiz *Canada* 49°14N 121°46W **70 D4**
Agassiz Icecap *Canada* 80°15N 76°0W **69 A16**
Agats *Indonesia* 5°33S 138°0E **37 F9**
Agatti I. *India* 10°50N 72°12E **45 J1**
Agattu I. *U.S.A.* 52°25N 173°35E **74 E2**
Agawam *U.S.A.* 42°5N 72°37W **83 D12**
Agboville *Côte d'Ivoire* 5°55N 4°15W **52 G5**
Ağdam *Azerbaijan* 40°0N 46°58E **46 B5**
Agde *France* 43°19N 3°28E **20 E5**
Agen *France* 44°12N 0°38E **20 D4**
Āgh Kand *Iran* 37°15N 48°4E **47 B6**
Aghios Efstratios *Greece* 39°34N 24°58E **23 E11**
Aghiou Orous, Kolpos *Greece* 40°6N 24°0E **23 D11**
Aginskoye *Russia* 51°6N 114°32E **27 D12**
Agnew *Australia* 28°1S 120°31E **61 E3**
Agori *India* 24°33N 82°57E **43 G10**
Agra *India* 27°17N 77°58E **42 F7**
Ağri *Turkey* 39°44N 43°3E **19 G7**
Agri → *Italy* 40°13N 16°44E **22 D7**
Ağrı Dağı *Turkey* 39°50N 44°15E **46 B5**
Ağri Karakose = Ağri *Turkey* 39°44N 43°3E **19 G7**
Agrigento *Italy* 37°19N 13°34E **22 F5**
Agrinio *Greece* 38°37N 21°27E **23 E9**
Agua Caliente *Mexico* 32°29N 116°59W **79 N10**
Agua Caliente Springs *U.S.A.* 32°56N 116°19W **79 N10**
Água Clara *Brazil* 20°25S 52°45W **93 H8**
Agua Fria ⌂ *U.S.A.* 34°14N 112°0W **77 J8**
Agua Hechicera *Mexico* 32°28N 116°15W **79 N10**
Agua Prieta *Mexico* 31°18N 109°34W **86 A3**
Aguadilla *Puerto Rico* 18°26N 67°10W **89 d**
Aguadulce *Panama* 8°15N 80°32W **88 E3**
Aguanga *U.S.A.* 33°27N 116°51W **79 M10**
Aguanish *Canada* 50°14N 62°2W **73 B7**
Aguanish → *Canada* 50°13N 62°5W **73 B7**
Aguapey → *Argentina* 29°7S 56°36W **94 B4**
Aguaray Guazú → *Paraguay* 24°47S 57°19W **94 A4**
Aguarico → *Ecuador* 0°59S 75°11W **92 D3**
Aguaro-Guariquito △ *Venezuela* 8°20N 66°35W **89 E6**
Aguas Blancas *Chile* 24°15S 69°55W **94 A2**
Aguas Calientes, Sierra de *Argentina* 25°26S 66°40W **94 B2**
Aguascalientes *Mexico* 21°53N 102°18W **86 C4**
Aguascalientes ☐ *Mexico* 22°0N 102°20W **86 C4**
Aguila, Punta *Puerto Rico* 17°57N 67°13W **89 d**
Aguilares *Argentina* 27°26S 65°35W **94 B2**
Águilas *Spain* 37°23N 1°35W **21 D5**
Aguja, C. de la *Colombia* 11°18N 74°12W **90 B3**
Agujereada, Pta. *Puerto Rico* 18°30N 67°8W **89 d**
Agulhas, C. *S. Africa* 34°52S 20°0E **56 D3**
Agung, Gunung *Indonesia* 8°20S 115°28E **37 J18**
Aguni-Jima *Japan* 26°30N 127°10E **29 L3**
Agusan → *Phil.* 9°0N 125°30E **37 C7**
Aha Mts. *Botswana* 19°45S 21°0E **56 A3**
Ahaggar *Algeria* 23°0N 6°30E **52 D7**
Ahai Dam *China* 27°21N 100°30E **34 D3**
Ahar *Iran* 38°35N 47°0E **46 B5**
Ahipara B. *N.Z.* 35°5S 173°5E **59 A4**
Ahiri *India* 19°30N 80°0E **44 E5**
Ahmad Wal *Pakistan* 29°18N 65°58E **42 E1**
Ahmadabad *India* 23°0N 72°40E **42 H5**
Aḥmadābād *Khorāsān, Iran* 35°3N 60°50E **47 C9**
Aḥmadābād *Khorāsān, Iran* 35°49N 59°42E **47 C8**
Aḥmadī *Iran* 27°56N 56°42E **47 E8**
Ahmadnagar *India* 19°7N 74°46E **44 E2**
Ahmadpur *India* 18°40N 76°57E **44 E3**
Ahmadpur East *Pakistan* 29°12N 71°10E **42 E4**
Ahmadpur Lamma *Pakistan* 28°19N 70°3E **42 E4**
Ahmedabad = Ahmadabad *India* 23°0N 72°40E **42 H5**
Ahmednagar = Ahmadnagar *India* 19°7N 74°46E **44 E2**
Ahome *Mexico* 25°55N 109°11W **86 B3**
Ahoskie *U.S.A.* 36°17N 76°59W **85 C16**
Ahram *Iran* 28°52N 51°16E **47 D6**
Ahuachapán *El Salv.* 13°54N 89°52W **88 D2**
Ahvāz *Iran* 31°20N 48°40E **47 D6**
Ahvenanmaa = Åland *Finland* 60°15N 20°0E **9 F19**
Aḥwar *Yemen* 13°30N 46°40E **49 E4**
Ai → *India* 26°26N 90°44E **43 F14**
Ai-Ais *Namibia* 27°54S 17°59E **56 C2**
Ai-Ais and Fish River Canyon △ *Namibia* 24°45S 17°15E **56 B2**
Aichi ☐ *Japan* 35°0N 137°15E **29 G8**
Aigrettes, Pte. des *Réunion* 21°3S 55°13E **55 c**
Aiguá *Uruguay* 34°13S 54°46W **95 C5**
Aigues-Mortes *France* 43°35N 4°12E **20 E6**
Aihui = Heihe *China* 50°10N 127°30E **31 A14**
Aija *Peru* 9°50S 77°45W **92 E3**
Aikawa *Japan* 38°2N 138°15E **28 E9**
Aiken *U.S.A.* 33°34N 81°43W **85 E14**
Ailao Shan *China* 24°0N 101°20E **34 F3**
Aileron *Australia* 22°39S 133°20E **62 C1**
Aillik *Canada* 55°11N 59°18W **73 A8**
Ailsa Craig *Canada* 43°8N 81°33W **82 C3**
Ailsa Craig *U.K.* 55°15N 5°6W **11 F3**
Aim *Russia* 59°0N 133°55E **27 D14**
Aimogasta *Argentina* 28°33S 66°50W **94 B2**
Aïn Ben Tili *Mauritania* 25°59N 9°27W **52 C4**
Aïn Sefra *Algeria* 32°47N 0°37W **52 B5**
Ain Sudr *Egypt* 29°50N 33°6E **48 F2**
Aïn Témouchent *Algeria* 35°16N 1°8W **52 A5**
Ainaži *Latvia* 57°50N 24°24E **9 H21**
Ainsworth *U.S.A.* 42°33N 99°52W **80 D4**
Aiquile *Bolivia* 18°10S 65°10W **92 G5**
Aïr *Niger* 18°30N 8°0E **52 E7**
Air Force I. *Canada* 67°58N 74°5W **69 D17**
Air Hitam *Malaysia* 1°55N 103°11E **39 M4**
Airdrie *Canada* 51°18N 114°2W **70 C6**
Airdrie *U.K.* 55°52N 3°57W **11 F5**
Aire → *U.K.* 53°43N 0°55W **12 D7**
Airlie Beach *Australia* 20°16S 148°43E **62 b**
Aisne → *France* 49°26N 2°50E **20 B5**
Ait *India* 25°54N 79°14E **43 G8**
Aitkin *U.S.A.* 46°32N 93°42W **80 B7**
Aitutaki *Cook Is.* 18°52S 159°45W **65 J12**
Aiud *Romania* 46°19N 23°44E **17 E12**
Aix-en-Provence *France* 43°32N 5°27E **20 E6**
Aix-la-Chapelle = Aachen *Germany* 50°45N 6°6E **16 C4**
Aix-les-Bains *France* 45°41N 5°53E **20 D6**
Aizawl *India* 23°40N 92°44E **41 H18**
Aizkraukle *Latvia* 56°36N 25°11E **9 H21**
Aizpute *Latvia* 56°43N 21°40E **9 H19**
Aizuwakamatsu *Japan* 37°30N 139°56E **28 F9**
Ajaccio *France* 41°55N 8°40E **20 F8**
Ajaigarh *India* 24°52N 80°16E **43 G9**
Ajalpan *Mexico* 18°22N 97°15W **87 D5**
Ajanta *India* 20°30N 75°48E **44 D2**
Ajanta Ra. *India* 20°28N 75°50E **44 D2**
Ajari Rep. = Ajaria ☐ *Georgia* 41°30N 42°0E **19 F7**
Ajaria ☐ *Georgia* 41°30N 42°0E **19 F7**
Ajax *Canada* 43°50N 79°1W **82 C5**
Ajdābiyā *Libya* 30°54N 20°4E **53 B10**
Ajitgarh *India* 30°47N 76°41E **42 D7**
Ajka *Hungary* 47°4N 17°31E **17 E9**
'Ajlūn *Jordan* 32°18N 35°47E **48 C4**
'Ajlūn ☐ *Jordan* 32°18N 35°47E **48 C4**
'Ajmān *U.A.E.* 25°25N 55°30E **47 E7**
Ajmer *India* 26°28N 74°37E **42 F6**
Ajnala *India* 31°50N 74°48E **42 D6**
Ajo *U.S.A.* 32°22N 112°52W **77 K7**
Ajo, C. de *Spain* 43°31N 3°35W **21 A4**
Akabira *Japan* 43°33N 142°5E **28 C11**
Akalkot *India* 17°32N 76°13E **44 F3**
Akan △ *Japan* 43°20N 144°20E **28 C12**
Akaroa *N.Z.* 43°49S 172°59E **59 E4**
Akashi *Japan* 34°45N 134°58E **29 G7**
Akbarpur *Bihar, India* 24°39N 83°58E **43 G10**
Akbarpur *Ut. P., India* 26°25N 82°32E **43 F10**
Akçakale *Turkey* 36°41N 38°56E **46 B3**
Akelamo *Indonesia* 1°35N 129°40E **37 D7**
Akeru → *India* 17°25N 80°5E **44 F5**
Aketi *Dem. Rep. of the Congo* 2°38N 23°47E **54 D4**
Akhisar *Turkey* 38°56N 27°48E **23 E12**
Akhnur *India* 32°52N 74°45E **43 C6**
Akhtyrka = Okhtyrka *Ukraine* 50°25N 35°0E **19 D5**
Aki *Japan* 33°30N 133°54E **29 H6**
Akimiski I. *Canada* 52°50N 81°30W **72 B3**
Akiōta *Japan* 34°36N 132°19E **29 G6**
Akita *Japan* 39°45N 140°7E **28 E10**
Akita ☐ *Japan* 39°40N 140°30E **28 E10**
Akjoujt *Mauritania* 19°45N 14°15W **52 E3**
Akkaraipattu *Sri Lanka* 7°13N 81°51E **45 L5**
Akkeshi *Japan* 43°2N 144°51E **28 C12**
'Akko *Israel* 32°55N 35°4E **48 C4**
Aklavik *Canada* 68°12N 135°0W **68 D4**
Aklera *India* 24°26N 76°32E **42 G7**
Akō *Japan* 34°45N 134°24E **29 G7**
Akola *Maharashtra, India* 20°42N 77°2E **44 D3**
Akola *Maharashtra, India* 19°32N 74°3E **44 E2**
Akordat *Eritrea* 15°30N 37°40E **49 D2**
Akot *India* 21°10N 77°10E **44 D3**
Akpatok I. *Canada* 60°25N 68°8W **69 E18**
Åkrahamn *Norway* 59°15N 5°10E **9 G11**
Akranes *Iceland* 64°19N 22°5W **8 D2**
Akron *Colo., U.S.A.* 40°10N 103°13W **76 F12**
Akron *Ohio, U.S.A.* 41°5N 81°31W **82 E3**
Aksai Chin *China* 35°15N 79°55E **43 B8**
Aksaray *Turkey* 38°25N 34°2E **46 B2**
Aksay = Aqsay *Kazakhstan* 51°11N 53°0E **19 D9**
Akşehir *Turkey* 38°18N 31°30E **46 B1**
Akşehir Gölü *Turkey* 38°30N 31°25E **19 G5**
Aksu *China* 41°5N 80°10E **30 C5**
Aksum *Ethiopia* 14°5N 38°40E **49 E2**
Aktsyabrski *Belarus* 52°38N 28°53E **17 B15**
Aktyubinsk = Aqtöbe *Kazakhstan* 50°17N 57°10E **19 D10**
Akure *Nigeria* 7°15N 5°5E **52 G7**
Akuressa *Sri Lanka* 6°5N 80°29E **45 L5**
Akureyri *Iceland* 65°40N 18°6W **8 D4**
Akuseki-Shima *Japan* 29°27N 129°37E **29 K4**
Akyab = Sittwe *Myanmar* 20°18N 92°45E **41 J18**
Al 'Adan = 'Adan *Yemen* 12°45N 45°0E **49 E4**
Al Aḥsā = Hasa *Si. Arabia* 25°50N 49°0E **47 E6**
Al Ajfar *Si. Arabia* 27°26N 43°0E **46 E4**
Al Amādīyah *Iraq* 37°5N 43°30E **46 B4**
Al 'Amārah *Iraq* 31°55N 47°15E **46 D5**
Al Anbār ☐ *Iraq* 33°25N 42°0E **46 C4**
Al 'Aqabah *Jordan* 29°31N 35°0E **48 F4**
Al 'Aqabah ☐ *Jordan* 29°30N 35°0E **48 F4**
Al Arak *Syria* 34°38N 38°35E **46 C3**
Al 'Aramah *Si. Arabia* 25°30N 46°0E **46 E5**
Al 'Arṭāwīyah *Si. Arabia* 26°31N 45°20E **46 E5**
Al 'Āṣimah ☐ *Jordan* 31°40N 36°30E **48 D5**
Al 'Assāfīyah *Si. Arabia* 28°17N 38°59E **46 D3**
Al 'Awdah *Si. Arabia* 25°32N 45°41E **46 E5**
Al 'Ayn *Si. Arabia* 25°4N 38°6E **46 E3**
Al 'Ayn *U.A.E.* 24°15N 55°45E **47 E7**
Al 'Azīzīyah *Iraq* 32°54N 45°4E **46 C5**
Al Bāb *Syria* 36°23N 37°29E **46 B3**
Al Bad' *Si. Arabia* 28°28N 35°1E **46 D2**
Al Bada'i' *Si. Arabia* 26°2N 43°33E **46 E4**
Al Bādī *Iraq* 35°56N 41°32E **46 C4**
Al Bāḥah *Si. Arabia* 20°1N 41°28E **49 C3**
Al Baḥrah *Kuwait* 29°40N 47°52E **46 D5**
Al Baḥral Mayyit = Dead Sea *Asia* 31°30N 35°30E **48 D4**
Al Balqā' ☐ *Jordan* 32°5N 35°45E **48 C4**
Al Bārūk, J. *Lebanon* 33°39N 35°40E **48 B4**
Al Başrah *Iraq* 30°30N 47°50E **46 D5**
Al Baṭḥā *Iraq* 31°6N 45°53E **46 D5**
Al Batrūn *Lebanon* 34°15N 35°40E **48 A4**
Al Bayḍā *Libya* 32°50N 21°44E **53 B10**
Al Biqā *Lebanon* 34°10N 36°10E **48 A5**
Al Bi'r *Si. Arabia* 28°51N 36°16E **46 D3**
Al Bukayrīyah *Si. Arabia* 26°9N 43°40E **46 E4**
Al Burayj *Syria* 34°15N 36°46E **48 A5**
Al Faḍilī *Si. Arabia* 26°58N 49°10E **47 E6**
Al Fallūjah *Iraq* 33°20N 43°55E **46 C4**
Al Fāw *Iraq* 30°0N 48°30E **47 D6**
Al Fujayrah *U.A.E.* 25°7N 56°18E **47 E8**
Al Ghadaf, W. → *Jordan* 31°26N 36°43E **48 D5**
Al Ghammās *Iraq* 31°45N 44°37E **46 D5**
Al Ghazālah *Si. Arabia* 26°48N 41°19E **46 E4**
Al Ghuwayfāt *U.A.E.* 24°10N 51°38E **47 E6**
Al Ḥadīthah *Iraq* 34°0N 41°13E **46 C4**
Al Ḥadīthah *Si. Arabia* 31°28N 37°8E **48 D6**
Al Ḥaḍr *Iraq* 35°35N 42°44E **46 C4**
Al Hājānah *Syria* 33°20N 36°33E **48 B5**

Al Ḩajar al Gharbī Oman 24°10N 56°15E 47 E8
Al Hāmad Si. Arabia 31°30N 39°30E 46 D3
Al Ḩamdānīyah Syria 35°25N 36°50E 46 C3
Al Ḩamīdīyah Syria 34°42N 35°57E 48 A4
Al Ḩammār Iraq 30°57N 46°51E 46 D5
Al Ḩamrā' Si. Arabia 24°2N 38°55E 46 E3
Al Ḩamzah Iraq 31°43N 44°58E 46 D5
Al Ḩanākīyah Si. Arabia 24°51N 40°31E 46 E4
Al Harūj al Aswad Libya 27°0N 17°10E 53 C9
Al Ḩasakah Syria 36°35N 40°45E 46 B4
Al Ḩayy Iraq 32°5N 46°5E 46 C5
Al Ḩillah Iraq 32°30N 44°25E 46 C5
Al Hindīyah Iraq 32°30N 44°10E 46 C5
Al Hirmil Lebanon 34°26N 36°24E 48 A5
Al Hoceïma Morocco 35°8N 3°58W 52 A5
Al Ḩudaydah Yemen 14°50N 43°0E 49 E3
Al Ḩudūd ash Shamālīyah □ Si. Arabia 29°10N 42°30E 46 D4
Al Hufūf Si. Arabia 25°25N 49°45E 47 E6
Al Ḩumayḑah Si. Arabia 29°14N 34°56E 46 D2
Al Ḩunayy Si. Arabia 25°58N 48°45E 47 E6
Al Īsāwīyah Si. Arabia 30°43N 37°59E 46 D3
Al Jafr Jordan 30°18N 36°14E 48 E5
Al Jāfūrah Si. Arabia 25°0N 50°15E 47 E7
Al Jaghbūb Libya 29°42N 24°38E 53 C10
Al Jahrah Kuwait 29°25N 47°40E 46 D5
Al Jalāmīd Si. Arabia 31°20N 40°6E 46 D3
Al Jamalīyah Qatar 25°37N 51°5E 47 E6
Al Janūb □ Lebanon 33°20N 35°20E 48 B4
Al Jawf Libya 24°10N 23°24E 53 D10
Al Jawf □ Si. Arabia 29°30N 39°30E 46 D3
Al Jazair = Algeria ■ Africa 28°30N 2°0E 52 C6
Al Jazirah Iraq 33°30N 44°0E 46 C5
Al Jithāmīyah Si. Arabia 27°41N 41°43E 46 E4
Al Jubayl Si. Arabia 27°0N 49°50E 47 E6
Al Jubaylah Si. Arabia 24°55N 46°25E 46 E5
Al Jubb Si. Arabia 27°11N 42°17E 46 E4
Al Junaynah Sudan 13°27N 22°45E 53 F10
Al Kabā'ish Iraq 30°58N 47°0E 46 D5
Al Karak Jordan 31°11N 35°42E 48 D4
Al Karak □ Jordan 31°0N 36°0E 48 E5
Al Kāẓimīyah Iraq 33°22N 44°18E 46 C5
Al Khābūrah Oman 23°57N 57°5E 47 F8
Al Khafji Si. Arabia 28°24N 48°29E 47 E6
Al Khalīl West Bank 31°32N 35°6E 48 D4
Al Khāliş Iraq 33°49N 44°32E 46 C5
Al Kharsānīyah Si. Arabia 27°13N 49°18E 47 E6
Al Khaşab Oman 26°14N 56°15E 47 E8
Al Khawr Qatar 25°41N 51°30E 47 E6
Al Khiḑr Iraq 31°12N 45°33E 46 D5
Al Khiyām Lebanon 33°20N 35°36E 48 B4
Al Khubar Si. Arabia 26°17N 50°12E 47 E6
Al Khums Libya 32°40N 14°17E 53 B8
Al Khurmah Si. Arabia 21°54N 42°3E 49 C3
Al Kiswah Syria 33°23N 36°14E 48 B5
Al Kūfah Iraq 32°2N 44°24E 46 C5
Al Kufrah Libya 24°17N 23°15E 53 D10
Al Kuhayfiyah Si. Arabia 27°12N 43°3E 46 E4
Al Kūt Iraq 32°30N 46°0E 46 C5
Al Kuwayt Kuwait 29°30N 48°0E 46 D5
Al Labwah Lebanon 34°11N 36°20E 48 A5
Al Lādhiqīyah Syria 35°30N 35°45E 46 C2
Al Līth Si. Arabia 20°9N 40°15E 49 C3
Al Liwā' Oman 24°31N 56°36E 47 E8
Al Luḩayyah Yemen 15°45N 42°40E 49 D3
Al Madīnah Iraq 30°57N 47°16E 46 D5
Al Madīnah Si. Arabia 24°35N 39°52E 46 E3
Al Mafraq Jordan 32°17N 36°14E 48 C5
Al Mafraq □ Jordan 32°17N 36°15E 48 C5
Al Maghreb = Morocco ■ N. Afr. 32°0N 5°50W 52 B4
Al Maḩmūdīyah Iraq 33°3N 44°21E 46 C5
Al Majma'ah Si. Arabia 25°57N 45°22E 46 E5
Al Makhruq, W. → Jordan 31°28N 37°0E 48 D6
Al Makḩūl Si. Arabia 26°37N 42°39E 46 E4
Al Manāmah Bahrain 26°10N 50°30E 47 E6
Al Maqwa' Kuwait 29°10N 47°59E 46 D5
Al Maraḩ Si. Arabia 25°35N 49°35E 47 E6
Al Marj Libya 32°25N 20°30E 53 B10
Al Maţlā Kuwait 29°24N 47°40E 46 D5
Al Mawşil Iraq 36°15N 43°5E 46 B4
Al Mayādin Syria 35°1N 40°27E 46 C4
Al Mazār Jordan 31°4N 35°41E 48 D4
Al Midhnab Si. Arabia 25°50N 44°18E 46 E5
Al Minā' Lebanon 34°24N 35°49E 48 A4
Al Miqdādīyah Iraq 34°0N 45°0E 46 C5
Al Mubarraz Si. Arabia 25°30N 49°40E 47 E6
Al Mudawwarah Jordan 29°19N 36°0E 48 F5
Al Mughayrā' U.A.E. 24°5N 53°32E 47 E7
Al Muḩarraq Bahrain 26°15N 50°40E 47 E6
Al Mukallā Yemen 14°33N 49°2E 49 E4
Al Mukhā Yemen 13°18N 43°15E 49 E3
Al Musayjīd Si. Arabia 24°5N 39°5E 46 E3
Al Musayyib Iraq 32°49N 44°20E 46 C5
Al Muthannā □ Iraq 30°30N 45°15E 46 D5
Al Muwayliḩ Si. Arabia 27°40N 35°30E 46 E2
Al Qādisīyah □ Iraq 32°0N 45°0E 46 D5
Al Qā'im Iraq 34°21N 41°7E 46 C4
Al Qalībah Si. Arabia 28°24N 37°42E 46 D3
Al Qāmishlī Syria 37°2N 41°14E 46 B4
Al Qaryatayn Syria 34°12N 37°13E 48 A6
Al Qaşīm □ Si. Arabia 26°0N 43°0E 46 E4
Al Qaţ'ā Syria 34°40N 40°48E 46 C4
Al Qaţīf Si. Arabia 26°35N 50°0E 47 E6
Al Qatrānah Jordan 31°12N 36°6E 48 D5
Al Qaţrūn Libya 24°56N 15°3E 53 D9
Al Qayşūmah Si. Arabia 28°20N 46°7E 46 D5
Al Qunayţirah Syria 33°5N 35°45E 48 B4
Al Qunfudhah Si. Arabia 19°3N 41°4E 49 D3
Al Qurayyāt Si. Arabia 31°20N 37°20E 46 D3
Al Qurnah Iraq 31°1N 47°25E 46 D5
Al Quşayr Iraq 30°39N 45°50E 46 D5
Al Quşayr Syria 34°31N 36°34E 48 A5
Al Quţayfah Syria 33°44N 36°36E 48 B5
Al Quwaysimah Jordan 31°55N 35°57E 48 D4
Al 'Ubaylah Si. Arabia 21°59N 50°57E 49 C5
Al 'Uḑaylīyah Si. Arabia 25°8N 49°18E 47 E6
Al 'Ulā Si. Arabia 26°35N 38°0E 46 E3
Al 'Uqayr Si. Arabia 25°40N 50°15E 47 E6
Al 'Uwaynid Si. Arabia 24°50N 46°0E 46 E5
Al 'Uwayqīlah Si. Arabia 30°30N 42°10E 46 D4
Al 'Uyūn Ḩijāz, Si. Arabia 24°33N 39°35E 46 E3
Al 'Uyūn Najd, Si. Arabia 26°30N 43°50E 46 E4
Al 'Uzayr Iraq 31°19N 47°25E 46 D5
Al Wajh Si. Arabia 26°10N 36°30E 46 E3
Al Wakrah Qatar 25°10N 51°40E 47 E6
Al Waqbah Si. Arabia 28°48N 45°33E 46 D5
Al Wari'āh Si. Arabia 27°51N 47°25E 46 E5
Al Yaman = Yemen ■ Asia 15°0N 44°0E 49 E3
Ala Dağ Turkey 37°44N 35°9E 46 B2
Ala Tau Asia 45°30N 80°40E 30 B5
Ala Tau Shankou = Dzungarian Gate Asia 45°10N 82°0E 30 B5
Alabama □ U.S.A. 33°0N 87°0W 85 E11
Alabama → U.S.A. 31°8N 87°57W 85 F11
Alabaster U.S.A. 33°15N 86°49W 85 E11
Alaçam Dağları Turkey 39°18N 28°49E 23 E13
Alacant = Alicante Spain 38°23N 0°30W 21 C5
Alachua U.S.A. 29°47N 82°30W 85 G13
Alagoa Grande Brazil 7°3S 35°35W 93 E11
Alagoas □ Brazil 9°0S 36°0W 93 E11
Alagoinhas Brazil 12°7S 38°20W 93 F11
Alaheaieatnu = Altaelva → Norway 69°54N 23°17E 8 B20
Alajuela Costa Rica 10°2N 84°8W 88 D3
Alaknanda → India 30°8N 78°36E 43 D8
Alakurtti Russia 66°58N 30°25E 8 C24
Alamarvdasht Iran 27°37N 52°59E 47 E7
Alameda U.S.A. 35°11N 106°37W 77 J10
Alamo U.S.A. 37°22N 115°10W 79 H11
Alamogordo U.S.A. 32°54N 105°57W 77 K11
Alamos Mexico 27°1N 108°56W 86 B3
Alamosa U.S.A. 37°28N 105°52W 77 H11
Alampur India 15°55N 78°6E 45 G4
Åland Finland 60°15N 20°0E 9 F19
Aland India 17°36N 76°35E 44 F3
Ålands hav Europe 60°0N 19°30E 9 G18
Alandur India 13°0N 80°15E 45 H5
Alaniya = North Ossetia-Alaniya □ Russia 43°30N 44°30E 19 F7
Alanya Turkey 36°38N 32°0E 46 B1
Alapayevsk Russia 57°52N 61°42E 26 D7
Alappuzha India 9°30N 76°28E 45 K3
Alaşehir Turkey 38°23N 28°30E 23 E13
Alaska □ U.S.A. 64°0N 154°0W 74 C9
Alaska, G. of Pac. Oc. 58°0N 145°0W 68 F3
Alaska Peninsula U.S.A. 56°0N 159°0W 74 D8
Alaska Range U.S.A. 62°50N 151°0W 68 E1
Älät Azerbaijan 39°58N 49°25E 47 B6
Alatau Shan = Ala Tau Asia 45°30N 80°40E 30 B5
Alatyr Russia 54°55N 46°35E 18 D8
Alausi Ecuador 2°0S 78°50W 92 D3
Alava, C. U.S.A. 48°10N 124°44W 78 B2
Alavo = Alavus Finland 62°35N 23°36E 8 E20
Alavus Finland 62°35N 23°36E 8 E20
Alawa ✪ Australia 15°42S 134°39E 62 B1
Alawoona Australia 34°45S 140°30E 63 E3
Alayawarra ✪ Australia 22°0S 134°30E 62 C1
'Alayh Lebanon 33°46N 35°33E 48 B4
Alba Italy 44°42N 8°2E 20 D8
Alba-Iulia Romania 46°8N 23°39E 17 E12
Albacete Spain 39°0N 1°50W 21 C5
Albacutya, L. Australia 35°45S 141°58E 63 F3
Albanel, L. Canada 50°55N 73°12W 72 B5
Albania ■ Europe 41°0N 20°0E 23 D9
Albany Australia 35°1S 117°58E 61 G2
Albany Ga., U.S.A. 31°35N 84°10W 85 F12
Albany N.Y., U.S.A. 42°39N 73°45W 83 D11
Albany Oreg., U.S.A. 44°38N 123°6W 76 D2
Albany Tex., U.S.A. 32°44N 99°18W 84 E5
Albany → Canada 52°17N 81°31W 72 B3
Albardón Argentina 31°20S 68°30W 94 C2
Albatross B. Australia 12°45S 141°30E 62 A3
Albemarle U.S.A. 35°21N 80°12W 85 D14
Albemarle Sd. U.S.A. 36°5N 76°0W 85 C16
Alberche → Spain 39°58N 4°46W 21 C3
Alberdi Paraguay 26°14S 58°20W 94 B4
Alberga → Australia 27°6S 135°33E 63 D2
Albert, L. Africa 1°30N 31°0E 54 D6
Albert, L. Australia 35°30S 139°10E 63 F2
Albert Edward Ra. Australia 18°17S 127°57E 60 C4
Albert Lea U.S.A. 43°39N 93°22W 80 D7
Albert Nile → Uganda 3°36N 32°2E 54 D6
Albert Town Bahamas 22°37N 74°33W 89 B5
Alberta □ Canada 54°40N 115°0W 70 C6
Alberti Argentina 35°1S 60°16W 94 D3
Albertinia S. Africa 34°11S 21°34E 56 D3
Alberton Canada 46°50N 64°0W 73 C7
Albertville France 45°40N 6°22E 20 D7
Albertville U.S.A. 34°16N 86°13W 85 D11
Albi France 43°56N 2°9E 20 E5
Albia U.S.A. 41°2N 92°48W 80 E7
Albina Suriname 5°37N 54°15W 93 B8
Albina, Ponta Angola 15°52S 11°44E 56 A1
Albion Mich., U.S.A. 42°15N 84°45W 81 D11
Albion Nebr., U.S.A. 41°42N 98°0W 80 E4
Albion Pa., U.S.A. 41°53N 80°22W 82 E4
Alborán Medit. S. 35°57N 3°0W 21 E4
Ålborg = Aalborg Denmark 57°2N 9°54E 9 H13
Alborz □ Iran 36°0N 50°50E 47 B6
Alborz, Reshteh-ye Kūhhā-ye Iran 36°0N 52°0E 47 C7
Albufeira Portugal 37°5N 8°15W 21 D1
Albuquerque U.S.A. 35°5N 106°39W 77 J10
Albuquerque, Cayos de Caribbean 12°10N 81°50W 88 D3
Alburg U.S.A. 44°59N 73°18W 83 B11
Albury Australia 36°3S 146°56E 63 F4
Alcalá de Henares Spain 40°28N 3°22W 21 B4
Alcalá la Real Spain 37°27N 3°57W 21 D4
Álcamo Italy 37°59N 12°55E 22 F5
Alcañiz Spain 41°2N 0°8W 21 B5
Alcântara Brazil 2°20S 44°30W 93 D10
Alcántara, Embalse de Spain 39°44N 6°50W 21 C2
Alcantarilla Spain 37°59N 1°12W 21 D5
Alcaraz, Sierra de Spain 38°40N 2°20W 21 C4
Alcaudete Spain 37°35N 4°5W 21 D3
Alcázar de San Juan Spain 39°24N 3°12W 21 C4
Alchevsk Ukraine 48°30N 38°45E 19 E6
Alcira = Alzira Spain 39°9N 0°30W 21 C5
Alcova U.S.A. 42°34N 106°43W 76 E10
Alcoy Spain 38°43N 0°30W 21 C5
Aldabra Is. Seychelles 9°22S 46°28E 51 G8
Aldama Mexico 22°55N 98°4W 87 C5
Aldan Russia 58°40N 125°30E 27 D13
Aldan → Russia 63°28N 129°35E 27 C13
Aldeburgh U.K. 52°10N 1°37E 13 E9
Alder Pk. U.S.A. 35°53N 121°22W 78 K5
Alderney U.K. 49°42N 2°11W 13 H5
Aldershot U.K. 51°15N 0°44W 13 F7
Aledo U.S.A. 41°12N 90°45W 80 E8
Aleg Mauritania 17°3N 13°55W 52 E3
Alegre Brazil 20°50S 41°30W 95 A7
Alegrete Brazil 29°40S 56°0W 95 B4
Aleksandriya = Oleksandriya Ukraine 50°37N 26°19E 17 C14
Aleksandrov Gay Russia 50°9N 48°34E 19 D8
Aleksandrovsk-Sakhalinskiy Russia 50°50N 142°20E 31 A17
Aleksandry, Zemlya Russia 80°25N 48°0E 26 A5
Além Paraíba Brazil 21°52S 42°41W 95 A7
Alemania Argentina 25°40S 65°30W 94 B2
Alemania Chile 25°10S 69°55W 94 B2
Alençon France 48°27N 0°4E 20 B4
Alenquer Brazil 1°56S 54°46W 93 D8
'Alenuihähä Channel U.S.A. 20°30N 156°0W 75 L8
Aleppo = Ḩalab Syria 36°10N 37°15E 46 B3
Aléria France 42°5N 9°26E 20 E9
Alert Canada 83°2N 60°0W 69 A20
Aleru India 17°39N 79°3E 44 F4
Alès France 44°9N 4°5E 20 D6
Alessándria Italy 44°54N 8°37E 20 D8
Ålesund Norway 62°28N 6°12E 8 E12
Aleutian Basin Pac. Oc. 57°0N 177°0E 64 B9
Aleutian Is. Pac. Oc. 52°0N 175°0W 64 B10
Aleutian Range U.S.A. 60°0N 154°0W 74 D9
Aleutian Trench Pac. Oc. 48°0N 180°0E 4 D17
Alexander U.S.A. 47°51N 103°39W 80 B2
Alexander, Mt. Australia 28°58S 120°16E 61 E3
Alexander Arch. U.S.A. 56°0N 136°0W 68 F4
Alexander Bay S. Africa 28°40S 16°30E 56 C2
Alexander City U.S.A. 32°56N 85°58W 85 E12
Alexander I. Antarctica 69°0S 70°0W 5 C17
Alexandra Australia 37°8S 145°40E 63 F4
Alexandra N.Z. 45°14S 169°25E 59 F2
Alexandra Channel Myanmar 14°7N 93°13E 45 G11
Alexandra Falls Canada 60°29N 116°18W 70 A5
Alexandria = El Iskandarîya Egypt 31°13N 29°58E 53 B11
Alexandria B.C., Canada 52°35N 122°27W 70 C4
Alexandria Ont., Canada 45°19N 74°38W 83 A10
Alexandria Romania 43°57N 25°24E 17 G13
Alexandria S. Africa 33°38S 26°28E 56 D4
Alexandria U.K. 55°59N 4°35W 11 F4
Alexandria La., U.S.A. 31°18N 92°27W 84 F8
Alexandria Minn., U.S.A. 45°53N 95°22W 80 C6
Alexandria S. Dak., U.S.A. 43°39N 97°47W 80 D5
Alexandria Bay U.S.A. 44°20N 75°55W 83 B9
Alexandrina, L. Australia 35°25S 139°10E 63 F2
Alexandroupoli Greece 40°50N 25°54E 23 D11
Alexis → Canada 52°33N 56°8W 73 B8
Alexis Creek Canada 52°10N 123°20W 70 C4
Aleysk Russia 52°40N 83°0E 26 D9
Alfenas Brazil 21°20S 46°10W 95 A6
Alford Aberds., U.K. 57°14N 2°41W 11 D6
Alford Lincs., U.K. 53°15N 0°10E 12 D8
Alfred Maine, U.S.A. 43°29N 70°43W 83 C14
Alfred N.Y., U.S.A. 42°16N 77°48W 82 D7
Alfreton U.K. 53°6N 1°24W 12 D6
Ålgård Norway 58°46N 5°53E 9 G11
Algarve Portugal 36°58N 8°20W 21 D1
Algeciras Spain 36°9N 5°28W 21 D3
Algemesí Spain 39°11N 0°27W 21 C5
Alger Algeria 36°42N 3°8E 52 A6
Algeria ■ Africa 28°30N 2°0E 52 C6
Algha Kazakhstan 49°53N 57°20E 19 E10
Alghero Italy 40°33N 8°19E 22 D3
Algiers = Alger Algeria 36°42N 3°8E 52 A6
Algoa B. S. Africa 33°50S 25°45E 56 D4
Algodones Dunes U.S.A. 32°50N 115°5W 79 N11
Algoma U.S.A. 44°36N 87°26W 80 C10
Algona U.S.A. 43°4N 94°14W 80 D6
Algonac U.S.A. 42°37N 82°32W 82 D2
Algonquin △ Canada 45°50N 78°30W 72 C4
Algorta Spain 43°21N 2°59W 21 A4
Algorta Uruguay 32°25S 57°24W 94 C4
Algorta Uruguay 32°25S 57°23W 96 C5
Alhucemas = Al Hoceïma Morocco 35°8N 3°58W 52 A5
'Alī al Gharbī Iraq 32°30N 46°45E 46 C5
'Alī ash Sharqī Iraq 32°7N 46°44E 46 C5
Äli Bayramlı = Şirvan Azerbaijan 39°59N 48°52E 47 B6
'Alī Khēl Afghan. 33°57N 69°43E 42 C3
Alī Shāh Iran 38°9N 45°50E 46 B5
'Alīābād Golestān, Iran 36°40N 54°33E 47 B7
'Alīābād Khorāsān, Iran 32°30N 57°30E 47 C8
'Alīābād Kordestān, Iran 35°4N 46°58E 46 C5
'Alīābād Yazd, Iran 31°41N 53°49E 47 D7
Aliağa Turkey 38°47N 26°59E 23 E12
Aliakmonas → Greece 40°30N 22°36E 23 D10
Alibag India 18°38N 72°56E 44 E1
Alicante Spain 38°23N 0°30W 21 C5
Alice S. Africa 32°48S 26°55E 56 D4
Alice U.S.A. 27°45N 98°5W 84 H5
Alice → Queens., Australia 24°2S 144°50E 62 C3
Alice → Queens., Australia 15°35S 142°20E 62 B3
Alice Arm Canada 55°29N 129°31W 70 B3
Alice Springs Australia 23°40S 133°50E 62 C1
Alicedale S. Africa 33°15S 26°4E 56 D4
Aliceville U.S.A. 33°8N 88°9W 85 E10
Aliganj India 27°30N 79°10E 43 F8
Aligarh Raj., India 25°55N 76°15E 42 G7
Aligarh Ut. P., India 27°55N 78°10E 42 F8
Alīgūdarz Iran 33°25N 49°45E 47 C6
Alingsås Sweden 57°56N 12°31E 9 H15
Alipur Pakistan 29°25N 70°55E 42 E4
Alipur Duar India 26°30N 89°35E 41 F16
Aliquippa U.S.A. 40°37N 80°15W 82 F4
Alishan Taiwan 23°31N 120°48E 35 F13
Alitus = Alytus Lithuania 54°24N 24°3E 9 J21
Aliwal North S. Africa 30°45S 26°45E 56 D4
Alix Canada 52°24N 113°11W 70 C6
Aljustrel Portugal 37°55N 8°10W 21 D1
Alkhanay △ Russia 51°0N 113°30E 27 D12
Alkmaar Neths. 52°37N 4°45E 15 B4
All American Canal U.S.A. 32°45N 115°15W 79 N11
Allagadda India 15°8N 78°30E 45 G4
Allagash → U.S.A. 47°5N 69°3W 81 B19
Allah Dad Pakistan 25°38N 67°34E 42 G2
Allahabad India 25°25N 81°58E 43 G9
Allan Canada 51°53N 106°4W 71 C7
Allanridge S. Africa 27°45S 26°40E 56 C4
Allegany U.S.A. 42°6N 78°30W 82 D6
Allegheny → U.S.A. 40°27N 80°1W 82 F5
Allegheny Mts. U.S.A. 38°15N 80°10W 81 F13
Allegheny Plateau U.S.A. 41°30N 78°30W 81 E14
Allegheny Res. U.S.A. 41°50N 79°0W 82 E6
Allègre, Pte. Guadeloupe 16°22N 61°46W 88 b
Allen, Bog of Ireland 53°15N 7°0W 10 C5
Allen, L. Ireland 54°8N 8°4W 10 B3
Allendale U.S.A. 33°1N 81°18W 85 E14
Allende Mexico 28°20N 100°51W 86 B4
Allentown U.S.A. 40°37N 75°29W 83 F9
Alleppey = Alappuzha India 9°30N 76°28E 45 K3
Aller → Germany 52°56N 9°12E 16 B5
Alleynes B. Barbados 13°13N 59°39W 89 g
Alliance Nebr., U.S.A. 42°6N 102°52W 80 D2
Alliance Ohio, U.S.A. 40°55N 81°6W 82 F3
Allier → France 46°57N 3°4E 20 C5
Alliford Bay Canada 53°12N 131°58W 70 C2
Alligator Pond Jamaica 17°52N 77°34W 88 a
Allinagaram India 10°2N 77°30E 45 J3
Alliston Canada 44°9N 79°52W 82 B5
Alloa U.K. 56°7N 3°47W 11 E5
Allora Australia 28°2S 152°0E 63 D5
Alluitsup Paa Greenland 60°30N 45°35W 4 C5
Allur India 14°40N 80°4E 45 G5
Alluru Kottapatnam India 15°24N 80°7E 45 G5
Alma Canada 48°35N 71°40W 73 C5
Alma Ga., U.S.A. 31°33N 82°28W 85 F13
Alma Kans., U.S.A. 39°1N 96°17W 80 F5
Alma Mich., U.S.A. 43°23N 84°39W 81 D11
Alma Nebr., U.S.A. 40°6N 99°22W 80 E4
Alma Wis., U.S.A. 44°20N 91°55W 80 C8
Alma Ata = Almaty Kazakhstan 43°15N 76°57E 30 C4
Alma Hill U.S.A. 42°2N 78°0W 82 D7
Almaden Australia 17°22S 144°40E 62 B3
Almadén Spain 38°49N 4°52W 21 C3
Almalyk = Olmaliq Uzbekistan 40°50N 69°35E 26 E7
Almanor, L. U.S.A. 40°14N 121°9W 76 F3
Almansa Spain 38°51N 1°5W 21 C5
Almanzor, Pico Spain 40°15N 5°18W 21 B3
Almanzora → Spain 37°14N 1°46W 21 D5
Almaty Kazakhstan 43°15N 76°57E 30 C4
Almazán Spain 41°30N 2°30W 21 B4
Almeirim Brazil 1°30S 52°34W 93 D8
Almelo Neths. 52°22N 6°42E 15 B6
Almendralejo Spain 38°41N 6°26W 21 C2
Almere Neths. 52°20N 5°15E 15 B5
Almería Spain 36°52N 2°27W 21 D4
Almirante Panama 9°10N 82°30W 88 E3
Almond U.S.A. 42°19N 77°44W 82 D7
Almont U.S.A. 42°55N 83°3W 82 D1
Almonte Canada 45°14N 76°12W 83 A8
Almora India 29°38N 79°40E 43 E8
Alness U.K. 57°41N 4°16W 11 D4
Alnmouth U.K. 55°24N 1°37W 12 B6
Alnwick U.K. 55°24N 1°42W 12 B6
Alon Myanmar 22°12N 95°5E 41 H19
Alor Indonesia 8°15S 124°30E 37 F6
Alor Setar Malaysia 6°7N 100°22E 39 J3
Alot India 23°56N 75°40E 42 H6
Aloysius, Mt. Australia 26°0S 128°38E 61 E4
Alpaugh U.S.A. 35°53N 119°29W 78 K7
Alpena U.S.A. 45°4N 83°27W 82 A1
Alpha Australia 23°39S 146°37E 62 C4
Alpha Ridge Arctic 84°0N 118°0W 4 A2
Alphen aan den Rijn Neths. 52°7N 4°40E 15 B4
Alpine Ariz., U.S.A. 33°51N 109°9W 77 K9
Alpine Calif., U.S.A. 32°50N 116°46W 79 N10
Alpine Tex., U.S.A. 30°22N 103°40W 84 F3
Alps Europe 46°30N 9°30E 16 E5
Alpurrulam Australia 20°59S 137°50E 62 C2
Alsace France 48°15N 7°25E 20 B7
Alsask Canada 51°21N 109°59W 71 C7
Alsasua Spain 42°54N 2°10W 21 A4
Alsek → U.S.A. 59°10N 138°12W 70 B1
Alsta Norway 65°58N 12°40E 8 D15
Alston U.K. 54°49N 2°25W 12 C5
Alta Norway 69°57N 23°10E 8 B20
Alta Gracia Argentina 31°40S 64°30W 94 C3
Alta Sierra U.S.A. 35°42N 118°33W 79 K8
Altaelva → Norway 69°54N 23°17E 8 B20
Altafjorden Norway 70°5N 23°5E 8 A20
Altai = Aerhtai Shan Mongolia 46°40N 92°45E 30 B7
Altai = Gorno-Altay □ Russia 51°0N 86°0E 26 D9
Altamaha → U.S.A. 31°20N 81°20W 85 F14
Altamira Brazil 3°12S 52°10W 93 D8
Altamira Chile 25°47S 69°51W 94 B2
Altamira Mexico 22°24N 97°55W 87 C5
Altamont U.S.A. 42°42N 74°2W 83 D10
Altamura Italy 40°49N 16°33E 22 D7
Altanbulag Mongolia 50°16N 106°30E 30 A10
Altar Mexico 30°43N 111°44W 86 A2
Altar, Gran Desierto de Mexico 31°50N 114°10W 86 B2
Altata Mexico 24°40N 107°55W 86 C3
Altavista U.S.A. 37°6N 79°17W 81 G14
Altay China 47°48N 88°10E 30 B6
Altay Mongolia 46°22N 96°15E 30 B8
Altea Spain 38°38N 0°2W 21 C5
Altiplano Bolivia 17°0S 68°0W 92 G5
Alto Araguaia Brazil 17°15S 53°20W 93 G8
Alto Cuchumatanes = Cuchumatanes, Sierra de los Guatemala 15°35N 91°25W 88 C1
Alto del Carmen Chile 28°46S 70°30W 94 B1
Alto Molocue Mozam. 15°50S 37°35E 55 H7
Alto Paraguay □ Paraguay 21°0S 58°30W 94 A4
Alto Paraná □ Paraguay 25°30S 54°50W 95 B5
Alton Canada 43°54N 80°5W 82 C4
Alton U.K. 51°9N 0°59W 13 F7
Alton Ill., U.S.A. 38°53N 90°11W 80 F8
Alton N.H., U.S.A. 43°27N 71°13W 83 C13
Altona Canada 49°6N 97°33W 71 D9
Altoona U.S.A. 40°31N 78°24W 82 F6
Altsasu = Alsasua Spain 42°54N 2°10W 21 A4
Altun Kupri Iraq 35°45N 44°9E 46 C5
Altun Shan China 38°30N 88°0E 30 D6
Alturas U.S.A. 41°29N 120°32W 76 F3
Altus U.S.A. 34°38N 99°20W 84 D5
Alucra Turkey 40°22N 38°47E 19 F6
Alūksne Latvia 57°24N 27°3E 9 H22
Alunite U.S.A. 35°59N 114°55W 79 K12
Alur India 15°24N 77°15E 45 E3
Alusi Indonesia 7°35S 131°40E 37 F8
Alutgama Sri Lanka 6°26N 79°59E 45 L4
Alutnuwara Sri Lanka 7°19N 80°59E 45 L5
Aluva India 10°8N 76°24E 45 J3
Alva U.S.A. 36°48N 98°40W 84 C5
Alvarado Mexico 18°46N 95°46W 87 D5
Alvarado U.S.A. 32°24N 97°13W 84 E6
Alvaro Obregón, Presa Mexico 27°52N 109°52W 86 B3
Alvear Argentina 29°5S 56°30W 94 B4
Alvesta Sweden 56°54N 14°35E 9 H16
Alvinston Canada 42°49N 81°52W 82 D3
Älvkarleby Sweden 60°34N 17°26E 9 F17
Alvord Desert U.S.A. 42°30N 118°25W 76 E4
Älvsbyn Sweden 65°40N 21°0E 8 D19
Alwar India 27°38N 76°34E 42 F7
Alwaye = Aluva India 10°8N 76°24E 45 J3
Alxa Zuoqi China 38°50N 105°40E 32 E3
Alyangula Australia 13°55S 136°30E 62 A2
Alyata = Älät Azerbaijan 39°58N 49°25E 47 B6
Alyth U.K. 56°38N 3°13W 11 E5
Alytus Lithuania 54°24N 24°3E 9 J21
Alzada U.S.A. 45°2N 104°25W 76 D11
Alzamay Russia 55°33N 98°39E 27 D10
Alzira Spain 39°9N 0°30W 21 C5
Am Timan Chad 11°0N 20°10E 53 F10
Amadeus, L. Australia 24°54S 131°0E 61 D5
Amadi South Sudan 5°29N 30°25E 53 G12
Amadjuak L. Canada 65°0N 71°8W 69 E17
Amagansett U.S.A. 40°59N 72°9W 83 F12
Amagi Japan 33°25N 130°39E 29 H5
Amahai Indonesia 3°20S 128°55E 37 E7
Amaile Samoa 13°59S 171°22W 59 b
Amakusa = Hondo Japan 32°27N 130°12E 29 H5
Amakusa-Shotō Japan 32°15N 130°10E 29 H5
Åmål Sweden 59°3N 12°42E 9 G15
Amalapuram India 16°35N 81°55E 45 F5
Amaliada Greece 37°47N 21°22E 23 F9
Amalner India 21°5N 75°5E 44 D2
Amamapare Indonesia 4°53S 136°38E 37 E9
Amambaí Brazil 23°5S 55°13W 95 A4
Amambaí → Brazil 23°22S 53°56W 95 A5
Amambay □ Paraguay 23°0S 56°0W 95 A4
Amambay, Cordillera de S. Amer. 23°0S 55°45W 95 A4
Amami Japan 28°22N 129°27E 29 K4
Amami-Guntō Japan 27°16N 129°21E 29 L4
Amami-Ō-Shima Japan 28°16N 129°21E 29 K4
Aman, Pulau Malaysia 5°16N 100°24E 39 c
Amanã, L. Brazil 2°35S 64°40W 92 D6
Amanat → India 24°7N 84°4E 43 G11
Amanda Park U.S.A. 47°28N 123°55W 78 C3
Amankeldi Kazakhstan 50°10N 65°10E 26 D7
Amapá Brazil 2°5N 50°50W 93 C8
Amapá □ Brazil 1°40N 52°0W 93 C8
Amarante Brazil 6°14S 42°50W 93 E10
Amaranth Canada 50°36N 98°43W 71 C9
Amaravati → India 11°0N 78°15E 45 J4
Amargosa → U.S.A. 36°14N 116°51W 79 J10
Amargosa Desert U.S.A. 36°40N 116°30W 79 J10
Amargosa Range U.S.A. 36°20N 116°45W 79 J10
Amarillo U.S.A. 35°13N 101°50W 84 D4
Amarkantak India 22°40N 81°45E 43 H9
Amarnath India 19°12N 73°22E 44 E1
Amaro, Mte. Italy 42°5N 14°5E 22 C6
Amarpur India 25°5N 87°0E 43 G12
Amarwara India 22°18N 79°10E 43 H8
Amasya Turkey 40°40N 35°50E 19 F6
Amata Australia 26°9S 131°9E 61 E5
Amatikulu S. Africa 29°3S 31°33E 57 C5
Amatitlán Guatemala 14°29N 90°38W 88 D1
Amay Belgium 50°33N 5°19E 15 D5
Amazon = Amazonas → S. Amer. 0°5S 50°0W 93 D8
Amazonas □ Brazil 5°0S 65°0W 92 E6
Amazonas → S. Amer. 0°5S 50°0W 93 D8
Ambad India 19°38N 75°50E 44 E2
Ambagarh Chowki India 20°47N 80°43E 44 D5
Ambah India 26°43N 78°13E 42 F8
Ambajogai India 18°44N 76°23E 44 E3
Ambala India 30°23N 76°56E 42 D7
Ambalangoda Sri Lanka 6°15N 80°5E 45 L5

Ambalantota Sri Lanka 6°27N 81°1E 45 L5
Ambalapulai India 9°25N 76°25E 45 K3
Ambalavao Madag. 21°50S 46°56E 55 J9
Ambanja Madag. 13°40S 48°27E 55 G9
Ambarchik Russia 69°40N 162°20E 27 C17
Ambasamudram India 8°43N 77°25E 45 K3
Ambato Ecuador 1°5S 78°42W 92 D3
Ambato, Sierra de Argentina 28°25S 66°10W 94 B2
Ambatolampy Madag. 19°20S 47°35E 55 H9
Ambatondrazaka Madag. 17°55S 48°28E 55 H9
Amberg Germany 49°26N 11°52E 16 D6
Ambergris Cay Belize 18°0N 87°55W 87 D7
Amberley Canada 44°2N 81°42W 82 B3
Amberley N.Z. 43°9S 172°44E 59 E4
Ambikapur India 23°15N 83°15E 43 H10
Ambilobé Madag. 13°10S 49°3E 55 G9
Amble U.K. 55°20N 1°36W 12 B6
Ambleside U.K. 54°26N 2°58W 12 C5
Ambo Peru 10°5S 76°10W 92 F3
Ambohitra Madag. 12°30S 49°10E 55 G9
Amboise France 47°24N 1°2E 20 C4
Ambon Indonesia 3°43S 128°12E 37 E7
Ambositra Madag. 20°31S 47°25E 55 J9
Ambovombe Madag. 25°11S 46°5E 55 K9
Amboy U.S.A. 34°33N 115°45W 79 L11
Amboyna Cay S. China Sea 7°50N 112°50E 36 C4
Ambridge U.S.A. 40°36N 80°14W 82 F4
Ambriz Angola 7°48S 13°8E 54 F2
Ambur India 12°48N 78°43E 45 H4
Amchitka I. U.S.A. 51°32N 179°0E 74 E3
Amderma Russia 69°45N 61°30E 26 C7
Amdhi India 23°51N 81°27E 43 H9
Amdo China 32°20N 91°40E 30 E7
Ameca Mexico 20°33N 104°2W 86 C4
Ameca → Mexico 20°41N 105°18W 86 C3
Amecameca de Juárez Mexico 19°8N 98°46W 87 D5
Amed Indonesia 8°19S 115°39E 37 J18
Ameland Neths. 53°27N 5°45E 15 A5
Amenia U.S.A. 41°51N 73°33W 83 E11
America-Antarctica Ridge S. Ocean 59°0S 16°0W 5 B2
American Falls U.S.A. 42°47N 112°51W 76 E7
American Falls Res. U.S.A. 42°47N 112°52W 76 E7
American Fork U.S.A. 40°23N 111°48W 76 F8
American Highland Antarctica 73°0S 75°0E 5 D6
American Samoa ⊘ Pac. Oc. 14°20S 170°0W 59 b
American Samoa △ Amer. Samoa 14°15S 170°28W 59 b
Americana Brazil 22°45S 47°20W 95 A6
Americus U.S.A. 32°4N 84°14W 85 E12
Amersfoort Neths. 52°9N 5°23E 15 B5
Amersfoort S. Africa 26°59S 29°53E 57 C4
Amery Basin S. Ocean 68°15S 74°30E 5 C6
Amery Ice Shelf Antarctica 69°30S 72°0E 5 C6
Ames U.S.A. 42°2N 93°37W 80 D7
Amesbury U.S.A. 42°51N 70°56W 83 D14
Amet India 25°18N 73°56E 42 G5
Amga Russia 60°50N 132°0E 27 C14
Amga → Russia 62°38N 134°32E 27 C14
Amgaon India 21°22N 80°22E 44 D5
Amgu Russia 45°45N 137°15E 28 B8
Amgun → Russia 52°56N 139°38E 27 D14
Amherst Canada 45°48N 64°8W 73 C7
Amherst Mass., U.S.A. 42°23N 72°31W 83 D12
Amherst N.Y., U.S.A. 42°59N 78°48W 82 D6
Amherst Ohio, U.S.A. 41°24N 82°14W 82 E2
Amherst I. Canada 44°8N 76°43W 83 B8
Amherstburg Canada 42°6N 83°6W 72 D3
Amiata, Mte. Italy 42°53N 11°37E 22 C4
Amidon U.S.A. 46°29N 103°19W 80 B2
Amiens France 49°54N 2°16E 20 B5
Amindivi Is. India 11°23N 72°23E 45 J1
Amini I. India 11°6N 72°45E 45 J1
Aminuis Namibia 23°43S 19°21E 56 B2
Amīrābād Iran 33°20N 46°16E 46 C5
Amirante Is. Seychelles 6°0S 53°0E 24 J7
Amisk ⌂ Canada 56°43N 98°0W 71 B9
Amisk L. Canada 54°35N 102°15W 71 C8
Amistad, Presa de la Mexico 29°26N 101°3W 86 B4
Amistad ⌂ U.S.A. 29°32N 101°12W 84 G4
Amite U.S.A. 30°44N 90°30W 85 F9
Amla India 21°56N 78°7E 42 J8
Amlapura Indonesia 8°27S 115°37E 37 J18
Amlia I. U.S.A. 52°4N 173°30W 74 E5
Amlwch U.K. 53°24N 4°20W 12 D3
'Ammān Jordan 31°57N 35°52E 48 D4
'Ammān ✕ (AMM) Jordan 31°45N 36°2E 48 D5
Ammanford U.K. 51°48N 3°59W 13 F4
Ammassalik = Tasiilaq Greenland 65°40N 37°20W 4 C6
Ammochostos = Famagusta Cyprus 35°8N 33°55E 46 C2
Ammon U.S.A. 43°28N 111°58W 76 E8
Amnat Charoen Thailand 15°51N 104°38E 38 E5
Amnura Bangla. 24°37N 88°25E 43 G13
Amo Jiang → China 23°0N 101°50E 34 F3
Āmol Iran 36°23N 52°20E 47 B7
Amorgos Greece 36°50N 25°57E 23 F11
Amory U.S.A. 33°59N 88°29W 85 E10
Amos Canada 48°35N 78°5W 72 C4
Åmot Norway 59°57N 9°54E 9 G13
Amoy = Xiamen China 24°25N 118°4E 35 E12
Ampang Malaysia 3°8N 101°45E 39 L3
Ampani India 19°35N 82°38E 44 E6
Ampanihy Madag. 24°40S 44°45E 55 J8
Ampenan Indonesia 8°34S 116°4E 37 K18
Amper → Germany 48°29N 11°55E 16 D6
Amphitrite Group S. China Sea 16°50N 112°20E 36 A4
Amphoe Kathu Thailand 7°55N 98°21E 39 a
Amphoe Thalang Thailand 8°1N 98°20E 39 a
Amqui Canada 48°28N 67°27W 73 C6
Amrabad India 16°23N 78°50E 45 F4
Amravati India 20°55N 77°45E 44 D3
Amreli India 21°35N 71°17E 42 J4
Amritsar India 31°35N 74°57E 42 D6
Amroha India 28°53N 78°30E 43 E8
Amsterdam U.S.A. 42°56N 74°11W 83 D10
Amsterdam I. = Nouvelle Amsterdam, Î. Ind. Oc. 38°30S 77°30E 3 F13
Amstetten Austria 48°7N 14°51E 16 D8
Amudarya → Uzbekistan 43°58N 59°34E 26 E6
Amukta Pass U.S.A. 52°0N 171°0W 74 E5
Amund Ringnes I. Canada 78°20N 96°25W 69 B12
Amundsen Abyssal Plain S. Ocean 65°0S 125°0W 5 C14
Amundsen Basin Arctic 87°30N 80°0E 4 A
Amundsen Gulf Canada 71°0N 124°0W 68 C7
Amundsen Ridges S. Ocean 69°15S 123°0W 5 C14
Amundsen-Scott Antarctica 90°0S 166°0E 5 E
Amundsen Sea Antarctica 72°0S 115°0W 5 D15
Amuntai Indonesia 2°28S 115°25E 36 E5
Amur → Russia 52°56N 141°10E 27 D15
Amurang Indonesia 1°5N 124°40E 37 D6
Amursk Russia 50°14N 136°54E 27 D14
Amyderya = Amudarya → Uzbekistan 43°58N 59°34E 26 E6
An Bang, Dao = Amboyna Cay S. China Sea 7°50N 112°50E 36 C4
An Bien Vietnam 9°45N 105°0E 39 H5
An Hoa Vietnam 15°40N 108°5E 38 E7
An Khe Vietnam 13°57N 108°51E 38 F7
An Nabatīyah at Tahta Lebanon 33°23N 35°27E 48 B4
An Nabk Syria 34°2N 36°44E 48 A5
An Nafūd Si. Arabia 28°15N 41°0E 46 D4
An Najaf Iraq 32°3N 44°15E 46 C5
An Nāşirīyah Iraq 31°0N 46°15E 46 D5
An Nhon = Binh Dinh Vietnam 13°55N 109°7E 38 F7
An Nu'ayrīyah Si. Arabia 27°30N 48°30E 47 E6
An Nu'mānīyah Iraq 32°32N 45°25E 46 C5
An Ros = Rush Ireland 53°31N 6°6W 10 C5
An Thoi, Quan Dao Vietnam 9°58N 104°0E 39 H5
Anabar → Russia 73°8N 113°36E 27 B12
Anaconda U.S.A. 46°8N 112°57W 76 C7
Anacortes U.S.A. 48°30N 122°37W 78 B4
Anadarko U.S.A. 35°4N 98°15W 84 D5
Anadolu Turkey 39°0N 30°0E 19 G5
Anadyr Russia 64°35N 177°20E 27 C18
Anadyr → Russia 64°55N 176°5E 27 C18
Anadyrskiy Zaliv Russia 64°0N 180°0E 27 C19
'Ānah Iraq 34°25N 42°0E 46 C4
Anaheim U.S.A. 33°50N 117°55W 79 M9
Anahim Lake Canada 52°28N 125°18W 70 C3
Anai Mudi India 10°12N 77°4E 45 J3
Anaimalai Hills India 10°20N 76°40E 45 J3
Anakapalle India 17°42N 83°6E 44 F6
Anakie Australia 23°32S 147°45E 62 C4
Analalava Madag. 14°35S 48°0E 55 G9
Anambar → Pakistan 30°15N 68°50E 42 D3
Anambas, Kepulauan Indonesia 3°20N 106°30E 36 D3
Anambas Is. = Anambas, Kepulauan Indonesia 3°20N 106°30E 36 D3
Anamosa U.S.A. 42°7N 91°17W 80 D8
Anamur Turkey 36°8N 32°58E 46 B2
Anan Japan 33°54N 134°40E 29 H7
Anand India 22°32N 72°59E 42 H5
Anandapuram India 14°5N 75°12E 45 G2
Anandpur India 21°16N 86°13E 44 D8
Anangu Pitjantjatjara ⊙ Australia 27°0S 132°0E 61 E5
Anantapur India 14°39N 77°42E 45 G3
Anantnag India 33°45N 75°10E 43 C6
Ananyiv Ukraine 47°44N 29°58E 17 E15
Anápolis Brazil 16°15S 48°50W 93 G9
Anapu → Brazil 1°53S 50°53W 93 D8
Anār Iran 30°55N 55°13E 47 D7
Anārak Iran 33°25N 53°40E 47 C7
Anas → India 23°26N 74°0E 42 H5
Anatolia = Anadolu Turkey 39°0N 30°0E 19 G5
Añatuya Argentina 28°20S 62°50W 94 B3
Anatye ⊙ Australia 22°29S 137°3E 62 C2
Anaunethad L. Canada 60°55N 104°25W 71 A8
Anbyŏn N. Korea 39°1N 127°35E 33 E14
Ancaster Canada 43°13N 79°59W 82 C5
Anchor Bay U.S.A. 38°48N 123°34W 78 G3
Anchorage U.S.A. 61°13N 149°54W 68 E2
Anchuthengu India 8°40N 76°46E 45 K3
Anci China 39°20N 116°40E 32 E9
Ancohuma, Nevado Bolivia 16°0S 68°50W 92 G5
Ancón Peru 11°50S 77°10W 92 F3
Ancona Italy 43°38N 13°30E 22 C5
Ancud Chile 42°0S 73°50W 96 E2
Ancud, G. de Chile 42°0S 73°0W 96 E2
Anda China 46°24N 125°19E 31 B14
Andacollo Argentina 37°10S 70°42W 94 D1
Andacollo Chile 30°14S 71°6W 94 C1
Andalgalá Argentina 27°40S 66°30W 94 B2
Åndalsnes Norway 62°35N 7°43E 8 E12
Andalucía □ Spain 37°35N 5°0W 21 D3
Andalusia = Andalucía □ Spain 37°35N 5°0W 21 D3
Andalusia U.S.A. 31°18N 86°29W 85 F11
Andaman & Nicobar Is. □ India 10°0N 93°0E 45 K11
Andaman Is. Ind. Oc. 12°30N 92°45E 45 H11
Andaman Sea Ind. Oc. 13°0N 96°0E 36 B1
Andamooka Australia 30°27S 137°9E 63 E2
Andapa Madag. 14°39S 49°39E 55 G9
Andara Namibia 18°2S 21°9E 56 A3
Andenes Norway 69°19N 16°18E 8 B17
Andenne Belgium 50°28N 5°5E 15 D5
Anderson Alaska, U.S.A. 64°25N 149°15W 74 C10
Anderson Calif., U.S.A. 40°27N 122°18W 76 F2
Anderson Ind., U.S.A. 40°10N 85°41W 81 E11
Anderson Mo., U.S.A. 36°39N 94°27W 80 G6
Anderson S.C., U.S.A. 34°31N 82°39W 85 D13
Anderson → Canada 69°42N 129°0W 68 D6
Anderson I. India 12°46N 92°43E 45 H11
Andes U.S.A. 42°12N 74°47W 83 D10
Andes, Cord. de los S. Amer. 20°0S 68°0W 92 H5
Andfjorden Norway 69°10N 16°20E 8 B17
Andhra, L. India 18°54N 73°32E 44 E1
Andhra Pradesh □ India 18°0N 79°0E 44 F4
Andijon Uzbekistan 41°10N 72°15E 30 C3
Andikíthira = Antikythira Greece 35°52N 23°15E 23 G10
Andīmeshk Iran 32°27N 48°21E 47 C6
Andizhan = Andijon Uzbekistan 41°10N 72°15E 30 C3
Andoany Madag. 13°25S 48°16E 55 G9
Andol India 17°51N 78°4E 44 F4
Andola India 16°57N 76°50E 44 F3
Andong S. Korea 36°40N 128°43E 33 F15
Andorra ◼ Europe 42°30N 1°30E 20 E4
Andorra La Vella Andorra 42°31N 1°32E 20 E4
Andover U.K. 51°12N 1°29W 13 F6
Andover Kans., U.S.A. 37°43N 97°7W 80 G5
Andover Maine, U.S.A. 44°38N 70°45W 83 B14
Andover Mass., U.S.A. 42°40N 71°8W 83 D13
Andover N.J., U.S.A. 40°59N 74°45W 83 F10
Andover N.Y., U.S.A. 42°10N 77°48W 82 D7
Andover Ohio, U.S.A. 41°36N 80°34W 82 E4
Andøya Norway 69°10N 15°50E 8 B16
Andradina Brazil 20°54S 51°23W 93 H8
Andreanof Is. U.S.A. 51°30N 176°0W 74 E4
Andrews S.C., U.S.A. 33°27N 79°34W 85 E15
Andrews Tex., U.S.A. 32°19N 102°33W 84 E3
Ándria Italy 41°13N 16°17E 22 D7
Andros Greece 37°50N 24°57E 23 F11
Andros I. Bahamas 24°30N 78°0W 88 B4
Andros Town Bahamas 24°43N 77°47W 88 B4
Androth I. India 10°50N 73°41E 45 J1
Andselv Norway 69°4N 18°34E 8 B18
Andújar Spain 38°3N 4°5W 21 C3
Andulo Angola 11°25S 16°45E 54 G3
Anegada Br. Virgin Is. 18°45N 64°20W 89 e
Anegada Passage W. Indies 18°15N 63°45W 89 C7
Aneto, Pico de Spain 42°37N 0°40E 21 A6
Anfu China 27°21N 114°40E 35 D10
Ang Thong Thailand 14°35N 100°31E 38 E3
Ang Thong, Ko Thailand 9°37N 99°41E 39 b
Ang Thong, Mu Ko △ Thailand 9°40N 99°43E 39 b
Angamos, Punta Chile 23°1S 70°32W 94 A1
Angara → Russia 58°5N 94°20E 27 D10
Angarsk Russia 52°30N 104°0E 30 A9
Angas Hills Australia 23°0S 127°50E 60 D4
Angaston Australia 34°30S 139°8E 63 E2
Ånge Sweden 62°31N 15°35E 8 E16
Ángel, Salto = Angel Falls Venezuela 5°57N 62°30W 92 B6
Ángel de la Guarda, I. Mexico 29°20N 113°25W 86 B2
Angel Falls Venezuela 5°57N 62°30W 92 B6
Angeles Phil. 15°9N 120°33E 37 A6
Ängelholm Sweden 56°15N 12°50E 9 H15
Angels Camp U.S.A. 38°4N 120°32W 78 G6
Ångermanälven → Sweden 63°0N 17°20E 8 E17
Ångermanland Sweden 63°36N 17°45E 8 E17
Angers Canada 45°31N 75°29W 83 A9
Angers France 47°30N 0°35W 20 C3
Ängesån → Sweden 66°16N 22°47E 8 C20
Angikuni L. Canada 62°12N 99°59W 71 A9
Angkor Cambodia 13°22N 103°50E 38 F4
Angledool Australia 29°5S 147°55E 63 D4
Anglesey U.K. 53°17N 4°20W 12 D3
Anglesey, Isle of □ U.K. 53°16N 4°18W 12 D3
Angleton U.S.A. 29°10N 95°26W 84 G7
Angmagssalik = Tasiilaq Greenland 65°40N 37°20W 4 C6
Ango Dem. Rep. of the Congo 4°10N 26°5E 54 D5
Angoche Mozam. 16°8S 39°55E 55 H7
Angol Chile 37°56S 72°45W 94 D1
Angola Ind., U.S.A. 41°38N 85°0W 81 E11
Angola N.Y., U.S.A. 42°38N 79°2W 82 D5
Angola ◼ Africa 12°0S 18°0E 55 G3
Angoulême France 45°39N 0°10E 20 D4
Angoumois France 45°50N 0°25E 20 D3
Angra do Heroísmo Azores 38°39N 27°13W 52 a
Angra dos Reis Brazil 23°0S 44°10W 95 A7
Angtassom Cambodia 11°1N 104°41E 39 G5
Anguang China 45°15N 123°45E 33 B12
Anguilla ⊘ W. Indies 18°14N 63°5W 89 C7
Angul India 20°51N 85°6E 44 D7
Anguo China 38°28N 115°15E 32 E8
Angurugu Australia 14°0S 136°25E 62 A2
Angus Canada 44°19N 79°53W 82 B5
Angus □ U.K. 56°46N 2°56W 11 E6
Angwa → Zimbabwe 16°0S 30°23E 57 A5
Anhanduí → Brazil 21°46S 52°9W 95 A5
Anholt Denmark 56°42N 11°33E 9 H14
Anhua China 28°23N 111°12E 35 C8
Anhui □ China 32°0N 117°0E 35 B11
Anhwei = Anhui □ China 32°0N 117°0E 35 B11
Anichab Namibia 21°0S 14°46E 56 B1
Animas → U.S.A. 36°43N 108°13W 77 H9
Anin Myanmar 15°36N 97°50E 38 E1
Anjalankoski Finland 60°45N 26°51E 8 F22
Anjangaon India 21°10N 77°20E 44 D3
Anjar = Hawsh Mūssá Lebanon 33°45N 35°55E 48 B4
Anjar India 23°6N 70°10E 42 H4
Anjengo = Anchuthengu India 8°40N 76°46E 45 K3
Anji China 30°46N 119°40E 35 B12
Anjidiv I. India 14°40N 74°10E 45 G2
Anjou France 47°20N 0°15W 20 C3
Anjouan Comoros Is. 12°15S 44°20E 55 a
Anju N. Korea 39°36N 125°40E 33 E13
Ankaboa, Tanjona Madag. 21°58S 43°20E 55 J8
Ankang China 32°40N 109°1E 32 H5
Ankara Turkey 39°57N 32°54E 19 G5
Ankaratra Madag. 19°25S 47°12E 55 H9
Ankazoabo Madag. 22°18S 44°31E 55 J8
Ankeny U.S.A. 41°44N 93°36W 80 E7
Ankleshwar India 21°38N 73°3E 44 D1
Ankola India 14°40N 74°18E 45 G2
Anlong China 25°2N 105°27E 34 E5
Anlong Veng Cambodia 14°14N 104°5E 38 E5
Anlu China 31°15N 113°45E 35 B9
Anmyeondo S. Korea 36°25N 126°25E 33 F14
Ann, C. U.S.A. 42°38N 70°35W 83 D14
Ann Arbor U.S.A. 42°17N 83°45W 81 D12
Anna U.S.A. 37°28N 89°15W 80 G9
Annaba Algeria 36°50N 7°46E 52 A7
Annalee → Ireland 54°2N 7°24W 10 B4
Annam = Trung Phan Vietnam 17°0N 109°0E 38 D6
Annamitique, Chaîne Asia 17°0N 106°40E 38 D6
Annan U.K. 54°59N 3°16W 11 G5
Annan → U.K. 54°58N 3°16W 11 G5
Annapolis U.S.A. 38°59N 76°30W 81 F15
Annapolis Royal Canada 44°44N 65°32W 73 D6
Annapurna Nepal 28°34N 83°50E 43 E10
Annean, L. Australia 26°54S 118°14E 61 E2
Annecy France 45°55N 6°8E 20 D7
Annette I. U.S.A. 55°9N 131°28W 70 B2
Annigeri India 15°26N 75°26E 45 G2
Anning China 24°55N 102°26E 34 E4
Anniston U.S.A. 33°39N 85°50W 85 E12
Annobón Atl. Oc. 1°25S 5°36E 51 G4
Annotto B. Jamaica 18°17N 76°45W 88 a
Annville U.S.A. 40°20N 76°31W 83 F8
Anping Hebei, China 38°15N 115°30E 32 E8
Anping Liaoning, China 41°5N 123°30E 33 D12
Anpu Gang China 21°25N 109°50E 34 G7
Anqing China 30°30N 117°3E 35 B11
Anqiu China 36°25N 119°10E 33 F10
Anren China 26°43N 113°18E 35 D9
Ansai China 36°50N 109°20E 32 F5
Ansan S. Korea 37°21N 126°52E 33 F14
Ansbach Germany 49°28N 10°34E 16 D6
Anse Boileau Seychelles 4°43S 55°29E 55 b
Anse la Raye St. Lucia 13°55N 61°3W 89 f
Anse Royale Seychelles 4°44S 55°31E 55 b
Anshan China 41°5N 122°58E 33 D12
Anshun China 26°18N 105°57E 34 D5
Ansley U.S.A. 41°18N 99°23W 80 E4
Anson U.S.A. 32°45N 99°54W 84 E5
Anson B. Australia 13°20S 130°6E 60 B5
Ansongo Mali 15°25N 0°35E 52 E6
Ansonia U.S.A. 41°21N 73°5W 83 E11
Anstruther U.K. 56°14N 2°41W 11 E6
Ansudu Indonesia 2°11S 139°22E 37 E9
Antabamba Peru 14°40S 73°0W 92 F4
Antagarh India 20°6N 81°9E 44 D5
Antakya = Hatay Turkey 36°14N 36°10E 46 B3
Antalaha Madag. 14°57S 50°20E 55 G10
Antalya Turkey 36°52N 30°45E 19 G5
Antalya Körfezi Turkey 36°15N 31°30E 19 G5
Antananarivo Madag. 18°55S 47°31E 55 H9
Antarctic Pen. Antarctica 67°0S 60°0W 5 C18
Antarctica 90°0S 0°0 5 E3
Antep = Gaziantep Turkey 37°6N 37°23E 46 B3
Antequera Paraguay 24°8S 57°7W 94 A4
Antequera Spain 37°5N 4°33W 21 D3
Antero, Mt. U.S.A. 38°41N 106°15W 76 G10
Anthony Kans., U.S.A. 37°9N 98°2W 80 G4
Anthony N. Mex., U.S.A. 32°0N 106°36W 77 K10
Anti Atlas Morocco 30°0N 8°30W 52 C4
Anti-Lebanon = Sharqi, Al Jabal ash Lebanon 33°40N 36°10E 48 B5
Antibes France 43°34N 7°6E 20 E7
Anticosti, Î. d' Canada 49°30N 63°0W 73 C7
Antigo U.S.A. 45°9N 89°9W 80 C9
Antigonish Canada 45°38N 61°58W 73 C7
Antigua Guatemala 14°34N 90°41W 88 D1
Antigua W. Indies 17°0N 61°50W 89 C7
Antigua & Barbuda ◼ W. Indies 17°20N 61°48W 89 C7
Antikythira Greece 35°52N 23°15E 23 G10
Antilla Cuba 20°40N 75°50W 88 B4
Antilles = West Indies Cent. Amer. 15°0N 65°0W 89 D7
Antioch U.S.A. 38°1N 121°48W 78 G5
Antioquia Colombia 6°40N 75°55W 92 B3
Antipodes Is. Pac. Oc. 49°45S 178°40E 64 M9
Antlers U.S.A. 34°14N 95°37W 84 D7
Antofagasta Chile 23°50S 70°30W 94 A1
Antofagasta □ Chile 24°0S 69°0W 94 A2
Antofagasta de la Sierra Argentina 26°5S 67°20W 94 B2
Antofalla Argentina 25°30S 68°5W 94 B2
Antofalla, Salar de Argentina 25°40S 67°45W 94 B2
Anton U.S.A. 33°49N 102°10W 84 E3
Antonina Brazil 25°26S 48°42W 95 B6
Antrim U.K. 54°43N 6°14W 10 B5
Antrim U.S.A. 40°7N 81°21W 82 F3
Antrim □ U.K. 54°56N 6°25W 10 B5
Antrim, Mts. of U.K. 55°3N 6°14W 10 A5
Antrim Plateau Australia 18°8S 128°20E 60 C4
Antsalova Madag. 18°40S 44°37E 55 H8
Antsirabe Madag. 19°55S 47°2E 55 H9
Antsiranana Madag. 12°25S 49°20E 55 G9
Antsohihy Madag. 14°50S 47°59E 55 G9
Antu China 42°30N 128°20E 33 C15
Antwerp = Antwerpen Belgium 51°13N 4°25E 15 C4
Antwerp U.S.A. 44°12N 75°37W 83 B9
Antwerpen Belgium 51°13N 4°25E 15 C4
Antwerpen □ Belgium 51°15N 4°40E 15 C4
Anupgarh India 29°10N 73°10E 42 E5
Anuppur India 23°6N 81°41E 43 H9
Anuradhapura Sri Lanka 8°22N 80°28E 45 K5
Anurrete ⊙ Australia 20°50S 135°38E 62 C2
Anveh Iran 27°23N 54°11E 47 E7
Anvers = Antwerpen Belgium 51°13N 4°25E 15 C4
Anvers I. Antarctica 64°30S 63°40W 5 C17
Anwen China 29°4N 120°26E 35 C13
Anxi Fujian, China 25°2N 118°12E 35 E12
Anxi Gansu, China 40°30N 95°43E 30 C8
Anxian China 31°40N 104°25E 34 B5
Anxiang China 29°27N 112°11E 35 C9
Anxious B. Australia 33°24S 134°45E 63 E1
Anyang China 36°5N 114°21E 32 F8
Anyang S. Korea 37°23N 126°55E 33 F14
Anyer Indonesia 6°4S 105°53E 37 G11
Anyi Jiangxi, China 28°49N 115°25E 35 C10
Anyi Shanxi, China 35°2N 111°2E 32 G6
Anyuan China 25°9N 115°21E 35 E10
Anyue China 30°9N 105°50E 34 B5
Anza U.S.A. 33°35N 116°39W 79 M10
Anze China 36°10N 112°12E 32 F7
Anzhero-Sudzhensk Russia 56°10N 86°0E 26 D9
Ánzio Italy 41°27N 12°37E 22 D5
Ao Makham Thailand 7°50N 98°24E 39 a
Ao Phangnga △ Thailand 8°10N 98°32E 39 a
Aoga-Shima Japan 32°28N 139°46E 29 H9
Aohan Qi China 43°18N 119°43E 33 C10
Aoji N. Korea 42°31N 130°23E 33 C16
Aomen = Macau China 22°12N 113°33E 35 F9
Aomori Japan 40°45N 140°45E 28 D10
Aomori □ Japan 40°45N 140°40E 28 D10
tAonach, An = Nenagh Ireland 52°52N 8°11W 10 D3
Aonla India 28°16N 79°11E 43 E8
Aorai, Mt. Tahiti 17°34S 149°30W 59 d
Aoraki Mount Cook N.Z. 43°36S 170°9E 59 E3
Aoral, Phnum Cambodia 12°0N 104°15E 39 G5
Aosta Italy 45°45N 7°20E 20 D7
Aotearoa = New Zealand ◼ Oceania 40°0S 176°0E 59 D6
Aoukâr Mauritania 17°40N 10°0W 52 E4
Aozou, Couloir d' Chad 22°0N 19°0E 53 D9
Apá → S. Amer. 22°6S 58°2W 94 A4
Apache U.S.A. 34°54N 98°22W 84 D5
Apache Junction U.S.A. 33°25N 111°33W 77 K8
Apalachee B. U.S.A. 30°0N 84°0W 85 G13
Apalachicola U.S.A. 29°43N 84°59W 85 G12
Apalachicola → U.S.A. 29°43N 84°58W 85 G12
Apaporis → Colombia 1°23S 69°25W 92 D5
Aparados da Serra △ Brazil 29°10S 50°8W 95 B5
Aparri Phil. 18°22N 121°38E 37 A6
Apatity Russia 67°34N 33°22E 8 C25
Apatula = Finke Australia 25°34S 134°35E 62 D1
Apatzingán Mexico 19°5N 102°21W 86 D4
Apeldoorn Neths. 52°13N 5°57E 15 B5
Apennines = Appennini Italy 44°30N 10°0E 22 B4
Api Nepal 30°0N 80°57E 30 F5
Apia Samoa 13°50S 171°50W 59 b
Apiacás, Serra dos Brazil 9°50S 57°0W 92 E7
Apies → S. Africa 25°15S 28°8E 57 C4
Apizaco Mexico 19°25N 98°8W 87 D5
Aplao Peru 16°0S 72°40W 92 G4
Apo, Mt. Phil. 6°53N 125°14E 37 C7
Apollonia = Sūsah Libya 32°52N 21°59E 53 B10
Apolo Bolivia 14°30S 68°30W 92 F5
Apopa El Salv. 13°48N 89°10W 88 D2
Aporé → Brazil 19°27S 50°57W 93 G8
Apostle Is. U.S.A. 47°0N 90°40W 80 B8
Apostle Islands ⌂ U.S.A. 46°55N 91°0W 80 B8
Apóstoles Argentina 28°0S 56°0W 95 B4
Apostolos Andreas, C. Cyprus 35°42N 34°35E 46 C2
Apoteri Guyana 4°2N 58°32W 92 C7
Appalachian Mts. U.S.A. 38°0N 80°0W 81 G14
Appennini Italy 44°30N 10°0E 22 B4
Apple Hill Canada 45°13N 74°46W 83 A10
Apple Valley U.S.A. 34°32N 117°14W 79 L9
Appleby-in-Westmorland U.K. 54°35N 2°29W 12 C5
Appledore U.K. 51°3N 4°13W 13 F3
Appleton U.S.A. 44°16N 88°25W 80 C9
Approuague → Fr. Guiana 4°30N 51°57W 93 C8
Aprília Italy 41°36N 12°39E 22 D5
Apsley Canada 44°45N 78°6W 82 B6
Apucarana Brazil 23°55S 51°33W 95 A5
Apure → Venezuela 7°37N 66°25W 92 B5
Apurímac → Peru 12°17S 73°56W 92 F4
Āq Qālā Iran 37°10N 54°30E 47 B7
Aqaba = Al 'Aqabah Jordan 29°31N 35°0E 48 F4
Aqaba, G. of Red Sea 29°0N 34°40E 46 D2
'Aqabah, Khalīj al = Aqaba, G. of Red Sea 29°0N 34°40E 46 D2
'Aqdā Iran 32°26N 53°37E 47 C7
'Aqrah Iraq 36°46N 43°45E 46 B4
Aqsay Kazakhstan 51°11N 53°0E 19 D9
Aqtaū Kazakhstan 43°39N 51°12E 19 F9
Aqtöbe Kazakhstan 50°17N 57°10E 19 D10
Aqtoghay Kazakhstan 46°57N 79°40E 26 E8
Aqua = Sokhumi Georgia 43°0N 41°0E 19 F7
Aquidauana Brazil 20°30S 55°50W 93 H7
Aquila Mexico 18°36N 103°30W 86 D4
Aquiles Serdán Mexico 28°36N 105°53W 86 B3
Aquin Haiti 18°16N 73°24W 89 C5
Aquitain, Bassin France 44°0N 0°30W 20 D3
Ar Horqin Qi China 43°45N 120°0E 33 C11
Ar Rafid Syria 32°57N 35°52E 48 C4
Ar Raḩḩālīyah Iraq 32°44N 43°23E 46 C4
Ar Ramādī Iraq 33°25N 43°20E 46 C4
Ar Ramthā Jordan 32°34N 36°0E 48 C5
Ar Raqqah Syria 35°59N 39°8E 46 C3
Ar Rashidiya = Er Rachidia Morocco 31°58N 4°20W 52 B5
Ar Rass Si. Arabia 25°50N 43°40E 46 E4
Ar Rawḑah Si. Arabia 21°16N 42°50E 49 C3
Ar Rayyan Qatar 25°17N 51°25E 47 E6
Ar Rifā'ī Iraq 31°50N 46°10E 46 D5

Ar Riyāḍ *Si. Arabia* 24°41N 46°42E **46** E5
Ar Ru'ays *Qatar* 26°8N 51°12E **47** E6
Ar Rukhaymīyah *Iraq* 29°22N 45°38E **46** D5
Ar Rumaythah *Iraq* 31°31N 45°12E **46** D5
Ar Ruṣāfah *Syria* 35°45N 38°49E **46** C3
Ar Ruṭbah *Iraq* 33°0N 40°15E **46** C4
Ara *India* 25°35N 84°32E **43** G11
Arab *U.S.A.* 34°19N 86°30W **85** D11
'Arab, Bahr el ⇥
  *South Sudan* 9°0N 29°30E **53** G11
Arab, Shatt al ⇥ *Asia* 29°57N 48°34E **47** D6
'Arabābād *Iran* 33°2N 57°41E **47** C8
Arabia *Asia* 25°0N 45°0E **24** F6
Arabian Desert = Sharqîya, Es
  Sahrâ esh *Egypt* 27°30N 32°30E **53** C12
Arabian Gulf = Persian Gulf
  *Asia* 27°0N 50°0E **47** E6
Arabian Sea *Ind. Oc.* 16°0N 65°0E **24** G8
Aracaju *Brazil* 10°55S 37°4W **93** F11
Aracati *Brazil* 4°30S 37°44W **93** D11
Araçatuba *Brazil* 21°10S 50°30W **95** A5
Aracena *Spain* 37°53N 6°38W **21** D2
Araçuaí *Brazil* 16°52S 42°4W **93** G10
'Arad *Israel* 31°15N 35°12E **48** D4
Arad *Romania* 46°10N 21°20E **17** E11
Arādān *Iran* 35°21N 52°30E **47** C7
Arafura Sea *E. Indies* 9°0S 135°0E **58** B6
Aragón □ *Spain* 41°25N 0°40W **21** B5
Aragón ⇥ *Spain* 42°13N 1°44W **21** A5
Araguacema *Brazil* 8°50S 49°20W **93** E9
Araguaia ⇥ *Brazil* 5°21S 48°41W **93** E9
Araguaína *Brazil* 7°12S 48°12W **93** E9
Araguari *Brazil* 18°38S 48°11W **93** G9
Araguari ⇥ *Brazil* 1°15N 49°55W **93** C9
Arain *India* 26°27N 75°2E **42** F6
Arak *Algeria* 25°20N 3°45E **52** C6
Arāk *Iran* 34°0N 49°40E **47** C6
Arakan = Rakhine □
  *Myanmar* 19°0N 94°15E **41** K18
Arakan Coast *Myanmar* 19°0N 94°0E **41** K19
Arakan Yoma *Myanmar* 20°0N 94°40E **41** K19
Arakkonam *India* 13°7N 79°43E **45** H4
Araks = Aras, Rūd-e ⇥
  *Asia* 40°5N 48°29E **46** B5
Aral *Kazakhstan* 46°41N 61°45E **26** E7
Aral Sea *Asia* 45°0N 58°20E **26** E7
Aral Tengizi = Aral Sea
  *Asia* 45°0N 58°20E **26** E7
Aralsk = Aral *Kazakhstan* 46°41N 61°45E **26** E7
Aralskoye More = Aral Sea
  *Asia* 45°0N 58°20E **26** E7
Aramac *Australia* 22°58S 145°14E **62** C4
Aran ⇥ *India* 19°55N 78°12E **44** E4
Aran I. = Arranmore
  *Ireland* 55°0N 8°30W **10** A3
Aran Is. *Ireland* 53°6N 9°38W **10** C2
Aranda de Duero *Spain* 41°39N 3°42W **21** B4
Arandān *Iran* 35°23N 46°55E **46** C5
Arani *India* 12°43N 79°19E **45** H4
Aranjuez *Spain* 40°1N 3°40W **21** B4
Aranos *Namibia* 24°9S 19°7E **56** B2
Aransas Pass *U.S.A.* 27°55N 97°9W **84** H6
Aranyaprathet *Thailand* 13°41N 102°30E **38** F4
Arapahoe *U.S.A.* 40°18N 99°54W **80** E4
Arapey Grande ⇥
  *Uruguay* 30°55S 57°49W **94** C4
Arapgir *Turkey* 39°5N 38°30E **46** B3
Arapiraca *Brazil* 9°45S 36°39W **93** E11
Arapongas *Brazil* 23°29S 51°28W **95** A5
Ar'ar *Si. Arabia* 30°59N 41°2E **46** D4
Araranguá *Brazil* 29°0S 49°30W **95** B6
Araraquara *Brazil* 21°50S 48°0W **93** H9
Ararás, Serra das *Brazil* 25°0S 53°10W **95** B5
Ararat *Australia* 37°16S 142°58E **63** F3
Ararat, Mt. = Ağrı Dağı
  *Turkey* 39°50N 44°15E **46** B5
Araria *India* 26°9N 87°33E **43** F12
Araripe, Chapada do
  *Brazil* 7°20S 40°0W **93** E11
Araruama, L. de *Brazil* 22°53S 42°12W **95** A7
Aras, Rūd-e ⇥ *Asia* 40°5N 48°29E **46** B5
Arauca *Colombia* 7°0N 70°40W **92** B4
Arauca ⇥ *Venezuela* 7°24N 66°35W **92** B5
Arauco *Chile* 37°16S 73°25W **94** D1
Aravalli Range *India* 25°0N 73°0E **42** G5
Araxá *Brazil* 19°35S 46°55W **93** G9
Araya, Pen. de *Venezuela* 10°40N 64°0W **92** A6
Arba Minch *Ethiopia* 6°0N 37°30E **49** F2
Arbat *Iraq* 35°25N 45°35E **46** C5
Árbatax *Italy* 39°56N 9°42E **22** E3
Arbîl *Iraq* 36°15N 44°5E **46** B5
Arborfield *Canada* 53°6N 103°39W **71** C8
Arborg *Canada* 50°54N 97°13W **71** C9
Arbroath *U.K.* 56°34N 2°35W **11** E6
Arbuckle *U.S.A.* 39°1N 122°3W **78** F4
Arcachon *France* 44°40N 1°10W **20** D3
Arcade *U.S.A.* 42°32N 78°25W **82** D6
Arcadia *Fla., U.S.A.* 27°13N 81°52W **85** H14
Arcadia *La., U.S.A.* 32°33N 92°55W **84** E8
Arcadia *Pa., U.S.A.* 40°47N 78°51W **82** F6
Arcata *U.S.A.* 40°52N 124°5W **76** F1
Archangel = Arkhangelsk
  *Russia* 64°38N 40°36E **18** B7
Archbald *U.S.A.* 41°30N 75°32W **83** E9
Archer ⇥ *Australia* 13°28S 141°41E **62** A3
Archer B. *Australia* 13°20S 141°30E **62** A3
Archer Bend = Mungkan
  Kandju △ *Australia* 13°35S 142°52E **62** A3
Arches △ *U.S.A.* 38°45N 109°25W **76** G9
Archipel-de-Mingan △
  *Canada* 50°13N 63°10W **73** B7
Archipiélago Los Roques △
  *Venezuela* 11°50N 66°44W **89** D6
Arckaringa Cr. ⇥
  *Australia* 28°10S 135°22E **63** D2
Arco *U.S.A.* 43°38N 113°18W **76** E7
Arcos de la Frontera
  *Spain* 36°45N 5°49W **21** D3
Arcot *India* 12°53N 79°20E **45** H4
Arctic Bay *Canada* 73°1N 85°7W **69** C14

Arctic Mid-Ocean Ridge
  *Arctic* 87°0N 90°0E **4** A
Arctic Ocean *Arctic* 78°0N 160°0W **4** B18
Arctic Red River = Tsiigehtchic
  *Canada* 67°15N 134°0W **68** D5
Arctowski *Antarctica* 62°30S 58°0W **5** C18
Arda ⇥ *Bulgaria* 41°40N 26°30E **23** D12
Ardabīl *Iran* 38°15N 48°18E **47** B6
Ardabīl □ *Iran* 38°15N 48°20E **47** B6
Ardakān = Sepīdān *Iran* 30°20N 52°5E **47** D7
Ardakān *Iran* 32°19N 53°59E **47** C7
Ardara *Ireland* 54°46N 8°25W **10** B3
Ardee *Ireland* 53°52N 6°33W **10** C5
Arden *Canada* 44°43N 76°56W **82** B8
Arden *Calif., U.S.A.* 38°36N 121°33W **78** G5
Arden *Nev., U.S.A.* 36°1N 115°14W **79** J11
Ardenne *Belgium* 49°50N 5°5E **15** E5
Ardennes = Ardenne
  *Belgium* 49°50N 5°5E **15** E5
Arderin *Ireland* 53°2N 7°39W **10** C4
Ardestān *Iran* 33°20N 52°25E **47** C7
Ardfert *Ireland* 52°20N 9°47W **10** D2
Ardglass *U.K.* 54°16N 5°36W **10** B6
Ardivachar Pt. *U.K.* 57°23N 7°26W **11** D1
Ardlethan *Australia* 34°22S 146°53E **63** E4
Ardmore *Okla., U.S.A.* 34°10N 97°8W **84** D6
Ardmore *Pa., U.S.A.* 40°2N 75°17W **83** F9
Ardnamurchan, Pt. of
  *U.K.* 56°43N 6°14W **11** E2
Ardnave Pt. *U.K.* 55°53N 6°20W **11** F2
Ardrossan *Australia* 34°26S 137°53E **63** E2
Ardrossan *U.K.* 55°39N 4°49W **11** F4
Ards Pen. *U.K.* 54°33N 5°34W **10** B6
Arecibo *Puerto Rico* 18°29N 66°43W **89** d
Areia Branca *Brazil* 5°0S 37°0W **93** E11
Arena, Pt. *U.S.A.* 38°57N 123°44W **78** G3
Arenal *Honduras* 15°21N 86°50W **88** C2
Arendal *Norway* 58°28N 8°46E **9** G13
Arequipa *Peru* 16°20S 71°30W **92** G4
Arévalo *Spain* 41°3N 4°43W **21** B3
Arga ⇥ *Turkey* 38°21N 37°59E **46** B3
Arganda del Rey *Spain* 40°19N 3°26W **21** B4
Argarapa ✪ *Australia* 22°20S 134°58E **62** C1
Argenta *Canada* 50°11N 116°56W **70** C5
Argentário, Mte. *Italy* 42°24N 11°9E **22** C4
Argentia *Canada* 47°18N 53°58W **73** C9
Argentina ■ *S. Amer.* 35°0S 66°0W **96** D3
Argentine Basin *Atl. Oc.* 45°0S 45°0W **96** H5
Argentino, L. *Argentina* 50°10S 73°0W **96** G2
Argeş ⇥ *Romania* 44°5N 26°38E **17** F14
Arghandab ⇥ *Afghan.* 31°30N 64°15E **42** D1
Argolikos Kolpos *Greece* 37°20N 22°52E **23** F10
Argos *Greece* 37°40N 22°43E **23** F10
Argostoli *Greece* 38°11N 20°29E **23** E9
Arguello, Pt. *U.S.A.* 34°35N 120°39W **79** L6
Argun ⇥ *Russia* 53°20N 121°28E **31** A13
Argungu *Nigeria* 12°40N 4°31E **52** F6
Argus Pk. *U.S.A.* 35°52N 117°26W **79** K9
Argyle, L. *Australia* 16°20S 128°40E **60** C4
Argyll & Bute □ *U.K.* 56°13N 5°28W **11** E3
Århus = Aarhus *Denmark* 56°8N 10°11E **9** H14
Ariadnoye *Russia* 45°8N 134°25E **28** B7
Ariamsvlei *Namibia* 28°9S 19°51E **56** C2
Ariana, L' *Tunisia* 36°52N 10°12E **53** A8
Arica *Chile* 18°32S 70°20W **92** G4
Arica *Colombia* 2°0S 71°50W **92** D4
Arid, C. *Australia* 34°1S 123°10E **61** F3
Arida *Japan* 34°5N 135°8E **29** G7
Aride *Seychelles* 4°13S 55°40E **55** b
Ariège ⇥ *France* 43°30N 1°25E **20** E4
Arima *Trin. & Tob.* 10°38N 61°17W **93** K15
Arinos ⇥ *Brazil* 10°25S 58°20W **92** F7
Ario de Rosales *Mexico* 19°12N 101°43W **86** D4
Aripo, Mt. *Trin. & Tob.* 10°45N 61°15W **93** K15
Aripuanã *Brazil* 9°25S 60°30W **92** E6
Aripuanã ⇥ *Brazil* 5°7S 60°25W **92** E6
Ariquemes *Brazil* 9°55S 63°6W **92** E6
Arisaig *U.K.* 56°55N 5°51W **11** E3
Aristazabal I. *Canada* 52°40N 129°10W **70** C3
Ariyalur *India* 11°8N 79°8E **45** J4
Arizaro, Salar de
  *Argentina* 24°40S 67°50W **94** A2
Arizona *Argentina* 35°45S 65°25W **94** D2
Arizona □ *U.S.A.* 34°0N 112°0W **77** J8
Arizpe *Mexico* 30°20N 110°10W **86** A2
'Arjah *Si. Arabia* 24°43N 44°17E **46** E5
Arjeplog *Sweden* 66°3N 17°54E **8** C17
Arjepluovve = Arjeplog
  *Sweden* 66°3N 17°54E **8** C17
Arjona *Colombia* 10°14N 75°22W **92** A3
Arjuna *Indonesia* 7°49S 112°34E **37** G15
Arka *Russia* 60°15N 142°0E **27** C15
Arkadelphia *U.S.A.* 34°7N 93°4W **84** D8
Arkaig, L. *U.K.* 56°59N 5°10W **11** E3
Arkalgud *India* 12°46N 76°3E **45** H3
Arkalyk = Arqalyk
  *Kazakhstan* 50°13N 66°50E **26** D7
Arkansas □ *U.S.A.* 35°0N 92°30W **84** D8
Arkansas ⇥ *U.S.A.* 33°47N 91°4W **84** E9
Arkansas City *U.S.A.* 37°4N 97°2W **80** G5
Arkhangelsk *Russia* 64°38N 40°36E **18** B7
Arki *India* 31°9N 76°58E **42** D7
Arkport *U.S.A.* 42°24N 77°42W **82** D7
Arkticheskiy, Mys *Russia* 81°10N 95°0E **27** A10
Arkville *U.S.A.* 42°9N 74°37W **83** D10
Arlanzón ⇥ *Spain* 42°3N 4°17W **21** A3
Arlbergpass *Austria* 47°9N 10°12E **16** E6
Arlbergtunnel *Austria* 47°9N 10°12E **16** E6
Arles *France* 43°41N 4°40E **20** E6
Arlington *S. Africa* 28°1S 27°53E **57** C4
Arlington *N.Y., U.S.A.* 41°42N 73°54W **83** E11
Arlington *Oreg., U.S.A.* 45°43N 120°12W **76** D3
Arlington *S. Dak., U.S.A.* 44°22N 97°8W **80** C5
Arlington *Vt., U.S.A.* 43°5N 73°9W **83** C11
Arlington *Wash., U.S.A.* 48°12N 122°8W **78** B4
Arlington Heights
  *U.S.A.* 42°5N 87°59W **80** D10

Arlit *Niger* 19°0N 7°38E **52** E7
Arlon *Belgium* 49°42N 5°49E **15** E5
Arlparra *Australia* 22°11S 134°30E **62** C1
Arltunga *Australia* 23°26S 134°41E **62** C1
Armadale *Australia* 32°9S 116°0E **61** F2
Armagh *U.K.* 54°21N 6°39W **10** B5
Armagh □ *U.K.* 54°18N 6°37W **10** B5
Armando Bermudez △
  *Dom. Rep.* 19°3N 71°0W **89** C5
Armavir *Russia* 45°2N 41°7E **19** E7
Armenia *Colombia* 4°35N 75°45W **92** C3
Armenia ■ *Asia* 40°20N 45°0E **19** F7
Armidale *Australia* 30°30S 151°40E **63** E5
Armori *India* 20°28N 79°59E **44** D4
Armour *U.S.A.* 43°19N 98°21W **80** D4
Armstrong *B.C., Canada* 50°25N 119°10W **70** C5
Armstrong *Ont., Canada* 50°18N 89°4W **72** B2
Armur *India* 18°48N 78°16E **44** E4
Arnarfjörður *Iceland* 65°48N 23°40W **8** D2
Arnaud ⇥ *Canada* 59°59N 69°46W **69** F18
Arnauti, C. *Cyprus* 35°6N 32°17E **46** C2
Arnett *U.S.A.* 36°8N 99°46W **84** C5
Arnhem *Neths.* 51°58N 5°55E **15** C5
Arnhem, C. *Australia* 12°20S 137°30E **62** A2
Arnhem B. *Australia* 12°20S 136°10E **62** A2
Arnhem Land *Australia* 13°10S 134°30E **62** A1
Arnhem Land ✪
  *Australia* 12°50S 134°50E **62** A1
Arno ⇥ *Italy* 43°41N 10°17E **22** C4
Arno Bay *Australia* 33°54S 136°34E **63** E2
Arnold *U.K.* 53°1N 1°7W **12** D6
Arnold *Calif., U.S.A.* 38°15N 120°21W **78** G6
Arnold *Mo., U.S.A.* 38°26N 90°23W **80** F8
Arnot *Canada* 55°56N 96°41W **71** B9
Arnøya *Norway* 70°9N 20°40E **8** A19
Arnprior *Canada* 45°26N 76°21W **83** A8
Arnsberg *Germany* 51°24N 8°5E **16** C5
Aroa, Pte. *Moorea* 17°28S 149°46W **59** d
Aroab *Namibia* 26°41S 19°39E **56** C2
Aron *India* 25°57N 77°56E **42** G6
Aros ⇥ *Mexico* 29°9N 107°57W **86** B3
Arqalyk *Kazakhstan* 50°13N 66°50E **26** D7
Arrah = Ara *India* 25°35N 84°32E **43** G11
Arrah *Côte d'Ivoire* 6°40N 3°58W **52** G5
Arran *U.K.* 55°34N 5°12W **11** F3
Arranmore *Ireland* 55°0N 8°30W **10** A3
Arras *France* 50°17N 2°46E **20** A5
Arrecife *Canary Is.* 28°57N 13°37W **52** C3
Arrecifes *Argentina* 34°6S 60°9W **94** C3
Arrée, Mts. d' *France* 48°26N 3°55W **20** B2
Arriaga *Mexico* 16°14N 93°54W **87** D6
Arrilalah *Australia* 23°43S 143°54E **62** C3
Arrino *Australia* 29°30S 115°40E **61** E2
Arrow, L. *Ireland* 54°3N 8°19W **10** B3
Arrowtown *N.Z.* 44°57S 168°50E **59** F2
Arroyo Grande *U.S.A.* 35°7N 120°35W **79** K6
Ars *Iran* 37°9N 47°46E **46** B5
Arsenault L. *Canada* 55°6N 108°32W **71** B7
Arsenev *Russia* 44°10N 133°15E **28** B6
Arsikere *India* 13°15N 76°15E **45** H3
Arta *Greece* 39°8N 21°2E **23** E9
Arteaga *Mexico* 18°28N 102°25W **86** D4
Artem *Russia* 43°22N 132°13E **28** C6
Artemivsk *Ukraine* 48°35N 38°0E **19** E6
Artemovsk *Russia* 54°45N 93°35E **27** D10
Artesia = Mosomane
  *Botswana* 24°2S 26°19E **56** B4
Artesia *U.S.A.* 32°51N 104°24W **77** K11
Arthur *Canada* 43°50N 80°32W **82** C4
Arthur ⇥ *Australia* 41°2S 144°40E **63** G3
Arthur Cr. ⇥ *Australia* 22°30S 136°25E **62** C2
Arthur Pt. *Australia* 22°7S 150°3E **62** C5
Arthur River *Australia* 33°20S 117°2E **61** F2
Arthur's Pass *N.Z.* 42°54S 171°35E **59** E3
Arthur's Pass △ *N.Z.* 42°53S 171°42E **59** E3
Arthur's Town *Bahamas* 24°38N 75°42W **89** B4
Artigas *Antarctica* 62°30S 58°0W **5** C18
Artigas *Uruguay* 30°20S 56°30W **94** C4
Artillery L. *Canada* 63°9N 107°52W **71** A7
Artois *France* 50°20N 2°30E **20** A5
Arts Bogd Uul *Mongolia* 44°40N 102°20E **32** B2
Artux *China* 39°40N 76°10E **32** C2
Artvin *Turkey* 41°14N 41°44E **19** F7
Artyk *Russia* 64°12N 145°6E **27** C15
Aru, Kepulauan *Indonesia* 6°0S 134°30E **37** F8
Aru Is. = Aru, Kepulauan
  *Indonesia* 6°0S 134°30E **37** F8
Arua *Uganda* 3°1N 30°58E **54** D6
Aruanã *Brazil* 14°54S 51°10W **93** F8
Aruba ☑ *W. Indies* 12°30N 70°0W **89** D6
Arué *Tahiti* 17°31S 149°30W **59** d
Arun ⇥ *Nepal* 26°55N 87°10E **43** F12
Arun ⇥ *U.K.* 50°49N 0°33W **13** G7
Arunachal Pradesh □
  *India* 28°0N 95°0E **41** F19
Arupukkottai *India* 9°31N 78°8E **45** K4
Arusha *Tanzania* 3°20S 36°40E **54** E7
Aruvi ⇥ *Sri Lanka* 8°48N 79°53E **45** K4
Aruwimi ⇥
  *Dem. Rep. of the Congo* 1°13N 23°36E **54** D4
Arvada *Colo., U.S.A.* 39°48N 105°5W **76** G11
Arvada *Wyo., U.S.A.* 44°39N 106°8W **76** D10
Arvakalu *Sri Lanka* 8°20N 79°58E **45** K4
Arvayheer *Mongolia* 46°15N 102°48E **30** B9
Arvi *India* 20°59N 78°16E **44** D4
Arviat *Canada* 61°6N 93°59W **71** A10
Arvidsjaur *Sweden* 65°35N 19°10E **8** D18
Arvika *Sweden* 59°40N 12°36E **9** G15
Arwal *India* 25°15N 84°41E **43** G11
Arxan *China* 47°11N 119°57E **31** B12
Arys *Kazakhstan* 42°26N 68°48E **26** E7
Arzamas *Russia* 55°27N 43°55E **18** C7
Arzanah *U.A.E.* 24°47N 52°34E **47** E7
As Saffānīyah *Si. Arabia* 27°55N 48°50E **47** E6
As Safirah *Syria* 36°5N 37°21E **46** B3
Aş Şahm *Oman* 24°10N 56°53E **47** E8
As Sājir *Si. Arabia* 25°11N 44°36E **46** E5

As Salamīyah *Syria* 35°1N 37°2E **46** C3
As Salmān *Iraq* 30°30N 44°32E **46** D5
As Salt *Jordan* 32°2N 35°43E **48** C4
As Sal'w'a *Qatar* 24°23N 50°50E **47** E6
As Samawah *Iraq* 31°15N 45°15E **46** D5
As Sanamayn *Syria* 33°3N 36°10E **48** B5
As Sila' *U.A.E.* 24°4N 51°45E **47** E6
As Sukhnah *Syria* 34°52N 38°52E **46** C3
As Sulaymānīyah *Iraq* 35°35N 45°29E **46** C5
As Sulayyil *Si. Arabia* 26°17N 41°21E **46** E4
As Summān *Si. Arabia* 25°0N 47°0E **46** E5
As Suwaydā' *Syria* 32°40N 36°30E **48** C5
As Suwaydā' □ *Syria* 32°45N 36°45E **48** C5
As Suwayq *Oman* 23°51N 57°26E **47** F8
Aş Şuwayrah *Iraq* 32°55N 45°0E **46** C5

Asab *Namibia* 25°30S 18°0E **56** C2
Asad, Buḩayrat al *Syria* 35°43N 38°15E **46** C3
Asahi *Japan* 35°43N 140°39E **29** E10
Asahi-Gawa ⇥ *Japan* 34°36N 133°58E **29** G6
Asahigawa = Asahikawa
  *Japan* 43°46N 142°22E **28** C11
Asahikawa *Japan* 43°46N 142°22E **28** C11
Asaluyeh *Iran* 27°29N 52°37E **47** E7
Asamankese *Ghana* 5°50N 0°40W **52** G5
Asan ⇥ *India* 26°37N 78°24E **43** F8
Asansol *India* 23°40N 87°1E **43** H12
Asau *Samoa* 13°27S 172°33W **59** b
Asbesberge *S. Africa* 29°0S 23°0E **56** D3
Asbestos *Canada* 45°47N 71°58W **73** C5
Asbury Park *U.S.A.* 40°13N 74°1W **83** F10
Ascensión *Mexico* 31°6N 107°59W **86** A3
Ascensión, B. de la
  *Mexico* 19°40N 87°30W **87** D7
Ascension I. *Atl. Oc.* 7°57S 14°23W **51** G2
Aschaffenburg *Germany* 49°58N 9°6E **16** D5
Aschersleben *Germany* 51°45N 11°29E **16** C6
Áscoli Piceno *Italy* 42°51N 13°34E **22** C5
Ascope *Peru* 7°46S 79°8W **92** E3
Ascotán *Chile* 21°45S 68°17W **94** A2
Aseb *Eritrea* 13°0N 42°40E **49** E3
Asela *Ethiopia* 8°0N 39°0E **49** F2
Asenovgrad *Bulgaria* 42°1N 24°51E **23** C11
Aşgabat = Ashgabat
  *Turkmenistan* 37°58N 58°24E **47** B8
Ash Fork *U.S.A.* 35°13N 112°29W **77** J7
Ash Grove *U.S.A.* 37°19N 93°35W **80** G7
Ash Shabakah *Iraq* 30°49N 43°39E **46** D4
Ash Shamāl □ *Lebanon* 34°25N 36°0E **48** A5
Ash Shāmīyah *Iraq* 31°55N 44°35E **46** D5
Ash Shāriqah *U.A.E.* 25°23N 55°26E **47** E7
Ash Sharmah *Si. Arabia* 28°1N 35°16E **46** D2
Ash Sharqāt *Iraq* 35°27N 43°16E **46** C4
Ash Shaṭrah *Iraq* 31°30N 46°10E **46** D5
Ash Shawbak *Jordan* 30°32N 35°34E **46** D2
Ash Shiḩr *Yemen* 14°45N 49°36E **49** E4
Ash Shināfiyah *Iraq* 31°35N 44°39E **46** D5
Ash Shu'bah *Si. Arabia* 28°54N 44°44E **46** D5
Ash Shumlūl *Si. Arabia* 26°31N 47°20E **46** E5
Ash Shūr'a *Iraq* 35°58N 43°13E **46** C4
Ash Shurayf *Si. Arabia* 25°43N 39°14E **46** E3
Ash Shuwayfāt *Lebanon* 33°45N 35°30E **48** B4
Asha *Russia* 55°0N 57°16E **18** D10
Ashbourne *U.K.* 53°2N 1°43W **12** D6
Ashburn *U.S.A.* 31°43N 83°39W **85** F13
Ashburton *N.Z.* 43°53S 171°48E **59** E3
Ashburton ⇥ *Australia* 21°40S 114°56E **60** D1
Ashcroft *Canada* 50°40N 121°20W **70** C4
Ashdod *Israel* 31°49N 34°35E **48** D3
Ashdown *U.S.A.* 33°40N 94°8W **84** E7
Asheboro *U.S.A.* 35°43N 79°49W **85** D15
Ashern *Canada* 51°11N 98°21W **71** C9
Asherton *U.S.A.* 28°27N 99°46W **84** G5
Asheville *U.S.A.* 35°36N 82°33W **85** D13
Ashewat *Pakistan* 31°22N 68°32E **42** D3
Asheweig ⇥ *Canada* 54°17N 87°12W **72** B2
Ashford *Australia* 29°15S 151°3E **63** D5
Ashford *U.K.* 51°8N 0°53E **13** F8
Ashgabat *Turkmenistan* 37°58N 58°24E **47** B8
Ashibetsu *Japan* 43°31N 142°11E **28** C11
Ashikaga *Japan* 36°28N 139°29E **29** F9
Ashington *U.K.* 55°11N 1°33W **12** B6
Ashizuri-Uwakai △
  *Japan* 32°56N 132°32E **29** H6
Ashizuri-Zaki *Japan* 32°44N 133°0E **29** H6
Ashkarkot *Afghan.* 33°3N 67°58E **42** C2
Ashkhabad = Ashgabat
  *Turkmenistan* 37°58N 58°24E **47** B8
Āshkhāneh *Iran* 37°26N 56°55E **47** B8
Ashland *Kans., U.S.A.* 37°11N 99°46W **80** G4
Ashland *Ky., U.S.A.* 38°28N 82°38W **81** F12
Ashland *Maine, U.S.A.* 46°38N 68°24W **81** B19
Ashland *Mont., U.S.A.* 45°36N 106°16W **76** D10
Ashland *Ohio, U.S.A.* 40°52N 82°19W **82** F2
Ashland *Oreg., U.S.A.* 42°12N 122°43W **76** E2
Ashland *Pa., U.S.A.* 40°45N 76°22W **83** F8
Ashland *Va., U.S.A.* 37°46N 77°29W **81** G15
Ashland *Wis., U.S.A.* 46°35N 90°53W **80** B8
Ashley *N. Dak., U.S.A.* 46°2N 99°22W **80** B4
Ashley *Pa., U.S.A.* 41°12N 75°55W **83** E9
Ashmore and Cartier Is.
  *Ind. Oc.* 12°14S 123°5E **60** B3
Ashmore Reef *Australia* 12°14S 123°5E **60** B3
Ashmyany *Belarus* 54°26N 25°52E **17** A13
Ashokan Res. *U.S.A.* 41°56N 74°13W **83** E10
Ashoknagar *India* 24°34N 77°43E **44** B3
Ashqelon *Israel* 31°42N 34°35E **48** D3
Ashta *India* 23°1N 76°43E **44** B3
Ashtabula *U.S.A.* 41°52N 80°47W **82** E4
Ashti *Maharashtra, India* 21°1N 78°11E **44** D4
Ashti *Maharashtra, India* 18°50N 75°15E **44** E2
Ashtiān *Iran* 34°31N 50°0E **47** C6
Ashton *S. Africa* 33°50S 20°5E **56** D3
Ashton *U.S.A.* 44°4N 111°27W **76** D8
Ashuanipi, L. *Canada* 52°45N 66°15W **73** B6
Ashuapmushuan ⇥
  *Canada* 48°37N 72°20W **72** C5
Ashur = Assur *Iraq* 35°27N 43°15E **46** C4
Ashville *U.S.A.* 40°34N 78°33W **82** F6

Asia *Asia* 45°0N 75°0E **24** E9

Asia, Kepulauan *Indonesia* 1°0N 131°13E **37** D8
Asifabad *India* 19°20N 79°24E **44** E4
Asinara *Italy* 41°4N 8°16E **22** D3
Asinara, G. dell' *Italy* 41°0N 8°30E **22** D3
Asino *Russia* 57°0N 86°0E **26** D9
Asipovichy *Belarus* 53°19N 28°33E **17** B15
'Asīr *Si. Arabia* 18°40N 42°30E **49** D3
Asir, Ras *Somalia* 11°55N 51°10E **49** E5
Aska *India* 19°2N 84°42E **44** K14
Askham *S. Africa* 26°59S 20°47E **56** C3
Askim *Norway* 59°35N 11°10E **9** G14
Askja *Iceland* 65°3N 16°48W **8** D5
Askøyna *Norway* 60°29N 5°10E **8** F11
Asmara = Asmera
  *Eritrea* 15°19N 38°55E **49** D2
Asmera *Eritrea* 15°19N 38°55E **49** D2
Åsnen *Sweden* 56°37N 14°45E **9** H16
Aso Kujū △ *Japan* 32°53N 131°6E **29** H5
Aspatria *U.K.* 54°47N 3°19W **12** C4
Aspen *U.S.A.* 39°11N 106°49W **76** G10
Aspermont *U.S.A.* 33°8N 100°14W **84** E4
Aspiring, Mt. *N.Z.* 44°23S 168°46E **59** F2
Aspur *India* 23°58N 74°7E **42** H6
Asquith *Canada* 52°8N 107°13W **71** C7
Assab = Aseb *Eritrea* 13°0N 42°40E **49** E3
Assal, L. *Djibouti* 11°40N 42°26E **49** E3
Assam □ *India* 26°0N 93°0E **41** G18
Assateague Island △
  *U.S.A.* 38°15N 75°10W **81** F16
Assaye *India* 20°15N 75°53E **44** D2
Asse *Belgium* 50°24N 4°10E **15** D4
Assen *Neths.* 53°0N 6°35E **15** A6
Assini boia *Canada* 49°40N 105°59W **71** D7
Assiniboine ⇥ *Canada* 49°53N 97°8W **71** D9
Assiniboine, Mt. *Canada* 50°52S 115°39W **70** C5
Assis *Brazil* 22°40S 50°20W **95** A5
Assisi *Italy* 43°4N 12°37E **22** C5
Assur *Iraq* 35°27N 43°15E **46** C4
Assynt, L. *U.K.* 58°10N 5°3W **11** C3
Astana *Kazakhstan* 51°10N 71°30E **30** A3
Āstāneh *Iran* 37°17N 49°59E **47** B6
Astara *Azerbaijan* 38°30N 48°50E **47** B6
Asterabad = Gorgān *Iran* 36°55N 54°30E **47** B7
Asti *Italy* 44°54N 8°12E **20** D8
Astipálaia *Greece* 36°32N 26°22E **23** F12
Astorga *Spain* 42°29N 6°8W **21** A2
Astoria *U.S.A.* 46°11N 123°50W **78** D3
Astrakhan *Russia* 46°25N 48°5E **19** E8
Astrebla Downs
  *Australia* 24°12S 140°34E **62** C3
Asturias □ *Spain* 43°15N 6°0W **21** A3
Asunción *Paraguay* 25°10S 57°30W **94** B4
Asunción Nochixtlán
  *Mexico* 17°28N 97°14W **87** D5
Aswân *Egypt* 24°4N 32°57E **53** D12
Aswan High Dam = Sadd el Aali
  *Egypt* 23°54N 32°54E **53** D12
Asyût *Egypt* 27°11N 31°4E **53** C12
At Ţafilah *Jordan* 30°45N 35°30E **48** E4
At Ţafilah □ *Jordan* 30°45N 35°30E **48** E4
Aţ Ţā'if *Si. Arabia* 21°5N 40°27E **49** C3
At Ta'mīm □ *Iraq* 35°30N 44°20E **46** C5
Aţ Ţirāq *Si. Arabia* 27°19N 44°33E **46** E5
Aţ Ţubayq *Si. Arabia* 29°30N 37°0E **46** D3
Aţ Ţunayb *Jordan* 31°48N 35°57E **48** D4
Atacama □ *Chile* 27°30S 70°0W **94** B2
Atacama, Desierto de
  *Chile* 24°0S 69°20W **94** A2
Atacama, Salar de *Chile* 23°30S 68°20W **94** A2
Atakeye ✪ *Australia* 22°30S 133°45E **60** D5
Atakpamé *Togo* 7°31N 1°13E **52** G6
Atalaya *Peru* 10°45S 73°50W **92** F4
Atami *Japan* 35°5N 139°4E **29** G9
Atamyrat *Turkmenistan* 37°50N 65°12E **26** F7
Atapupu *Indonesia* 9°0S 124°51E **37** F6
Atâr *Mauritania* 20°30N 13°5W **52** D3
Atari *Pakistan* 30°56N 74°2E **42** D6
Atascadero *U.S.A.* 35°29N 120°40W **78** K6
Atasū *Kazakhstan* 48°30N 71°0E **26** E8
Atatürk Barajı *Turkey* 37°28N 38°30E **19** G6
Atauro *Timor-Leste* 8°10S 125°30E **37** F7
Atbara *Sudan* 17°42N 33°59E **53** E12
'Atbara, Nahr ⇥ *Sudan* 17°40N 33°56E **53** E12
Atbasar *Kazakhstan* 51°48N 68°20E **26** D7
Atchafalaya B. *U.S.A.* 29°25N 91°25W **84** G9
Atchison *U.S.A.* 39°34N 95°7W **80** F6
Atebubu *Ghana* 7°47N 1°0W **52** G5
Ath *Belgium* 50°38N 3°47E **15** D3
Athabasca *Canada* 54°45N 113°20W **70** C6
Athabasca ⇥ *Canada* 58°40N 110°50W **71** B6
Athabasca, L. *Canada* 59°15N 109°15W **71** B7
Athabasca Sand Dunes △
  *Canada* 59°4N 108°43W **71** B7
Athagarh *India* 20°32N 85°37E **44** D7
Athboy *Ireland* 53°37N 6°56W **10** C5
Athenry *Ireland* 53°18N 8°44W **10** C3
Athens *Ala., U.S.A.* 34°48N 86°58W **85** D11
Athens *Ga., U.S.A.* 33°57N 83°23W **85** D13
Athens *N.Y., U.S.A.* 42°16N 73°49W **83** D11
Athens *Ohio, U.S.A.* 39°20N 82°6W **81** F12
Athens *Pa., U.S.A.* 41°57N 76°31W **83** E8
Athens *Tenn., U.S.A.* 35°27N 84°36W **85** D12
Athens *Tex., U.S.A.* 32°12N 95°51W **84** E7
Atherley *Canada* 44°37N 79°20W **82** B5
Atherton *Australia* 17°17S 145°30E **62** B4
Athlone *Ireland* 53°25N 7°56W **10** C4
Athmallik *India* 20°43N 84°32E **44** D7
Athni *India* 16°44N 75°6E **44** F2
Athol *U.S.A.* 42°36N 72°14W **83** D12
Atholl, Forest of *U.K.* 56°51N 3°50W **11** E5
Atholville *Canada* 47°59N 66°43W **73** C6
Athos *Greece* 40°9N 24°22E **23** D11
Athy *Ireland* 53°0N 7°0W **10** C5
Ati *Chad* 13°13N 18°20E **53** F9
Atik L. *Canada* 55°15N 96°0W **71** B9
Atikaki △ *Canada* 51°30N 95°31W **71** C9
Atikameg ⇥ *Canada* 52°30N 82°46W **72** B3
Atikokan *Canada* 48°45N 91°37W **72** C1
Atikonak L. *Canada* 52°40N 64°32W **73** B7
Atimaono *Tahiti* 17°46S 149°28W **59** d

102 Atirampattinam INDEX TO WORLD MAPS

Atirampattinam India 10°28N 79°20E 45 J4
Atiu Cook Is. 20°0S 158°10W 65 J12
Atka Russia 60°50N 151°48E 27 C16
Atka I. U.S.A. 52°7N 174°30W 74 E5
Atkinson U.S.A. 42°32N 98°59W 80 D4
Atlanta U.S.A. 33°7N 94°10W 84 E7
Atlantic U.S.A. 41°24N 95°1W 80 E6
Atlantic City U.S.A. 39°21N 74°27W 81 F16
Atlantic-Indian Basin Antarctica 60°0S 30°0E 5 B4
Atlantic Ocean 0°0 20°0W 2 D8
Atlantis S. Africa 33°34S 18°29E 56 D2
Atlas Mts. = Haut Atlas Morocco 32°30N 5°0W 52 B4
Atlin Canada 59°31N 133°41W 70 B2
Atlin, L. Canada 59°26N 133°45W 70 B2
Atlin △ Canada 59°10N 134°30W 70 B2
Atmakur Andhra Pradesh, India 14°37N 79°40E 45 G4
Atmakur Andhra Pradesh, India 15°53N 78°35E 45 G4
Atmakur Telangana, India 18°45N 78°39E 44 E4
Atmore U.S.A. 31°2N 87°29W 85 F11
Atoka U.S.A. 34°23N 96°8W 84 D6
Atolia U.S.A. 35°19N 117°37W 79 K9
Atqasuk U.S.A. 70°28N 157°24W 74 A8
Atrai → Bangla. 24°7N 89°22E 43 G13
Atrak = Atrek → Turkmenistan 37°35N 53°58E 47 B8
Atrauli India 28°2N 78°20E 42 E8
Atrek → Turkmenistan 37°35N 53°58E 47 B8
Atsuta Japan 43°24N 141°26E 28 C10
Attalla U.S.A. 34°1N 86°6W 85 D11
Attapeu Laos 14°48N 106°50E 38 E6
Attawapiskat Canada 52°56N 82°24W 72 B3
Attawapiskat → Canada 52°57N 82°18W 72 B3
Attawapiskat L. Canada 52°18N 87°54W 72 B2
Attica Ind., U.S.A. 40°18N 87°15W 80 E10
Attica Ohio, U.S.A. 41°4N 82°53W 82 E2
Attikamagen L. Canada 55°0N 66°30W 73 B6
Attleboro U.S.A. 41°57N 71°17W 83 E13
Attock Pakistan 33°52N 72°20E 42 C5
Attopu = Attapeu Laos 14°48N 106°50E 38 E6
Attu I. U.S.A. 52°55N 172°55E 74 E2
Attur India 11°35N 78°30E 45 J4
Atuel → Argentina 36°17S 66°50W 94 D2
Åtvidaberg Sweden 58°12N 16°0E 9 G17
Atwater U.S.A. 37°21N 120°37W 78 H6
Atwood Canada 43°40N 81°1W 82 C3
Atwood U.S.A. 39°48N 101°3W 80 F3
Atyraū Kazakhstan 47°5N 52°0E 19 E9
Au Sable U.S.A. 44°25N 83°20W 82 B1
Au Sable → U.S.A. 44°25N 83°20W 81 C12
Au Sable Forks U.S.A. 44°27N 73°41W 83 B11
Au Sable Pt. U.S.A. 44°20N 83°20W 82 B1
Auas Honduras 15°29N 84°20W 88 C3
Auasberg Namibia 22°37S 17°13E 56 B2
Aubagne France 43°17N 5°37E 20 E6
Aube → France 48°34N 3°43E 20 B5
Auberry U.S.A. 37°7N 119°29W 78 H7
Auburn Ala., U.S.A. 32°36N 85°29W 85 E12
Auburn Calif., U.S.A. 38°54N 121°4W 78 G5
Auburn Ind., U.S.A. 41°22N 85°4W 81 E11
Auburn Maine, U.S.A. 44°6N 70°14W 81 C18
Auburn N.Y., U.S.A. 42°56N 76°34W 83 D8
Auburn Nebr., U.S.A. 40°23N 95°51W 80 E6
Auburn Pa., U.S.A. 40°36N 76°6W 83 F8
Auburn Wash., U.S.A. 47°18N 122°14W 78 C4
Auburn Ra. Australia 25°15S 150°30E 63 D5
Auburndale U.S.A. 28°4N 81°48W 85 G14
Aubusson France 45°57N 2°11E 20 D5
Auch France 43°39N 0°36E 20 E4
Auchterarder U.K. 56°18N 3°41W 11 E5
Auchtermuchty U.K. 56°18N 3°13W 11 E5
Auckland N.Z. 36°52S 174°46E 59 B5
Auckland Is. Pac. Oc. 50°40S 166°5E 64 N8
Aude → France 43°13N 3°14E 20 E5
Auden Canada 50°14N 87°53W 72 B2
Audubon U.S.A. 41°43N 94°56W 80 E6
Augathella Australia 25°48S 146°35E 63 D4
Aughnacloy U.K. 54°25N 6°59W 10 B5
Aughrim Ireland 53°18N 8°19W 10 C3
Augrabies Falls S. Africa 28°35S 20°20E 56 C3
Augrabies Falls △ S. Africa 28°40S 20°22E 56 C3
Augsburg Germany 48°25N 10°52E 16 D6
Augusta Australia 34°19S 115°9E 61 F2
Augusta Italy 37°13N 15°13E 22 F6
Augusta Ark., U.S.A. 35°17N 91°22W 84 D9
Augusta Ga., U.S.A. 33°28N 81°58W 85 E14
Augusta Kans., U.S.A. 37°41N 96°59W 80 G5
Augusta Maine, U.S.A. 44°19N 69°47W 81 C19
Augusta Mont., U.S.A. 47°30N 112°24W 76 C7
Augustów Poland 53°51N 23°0E 17 B12
Augustus, Mt. Australia 24°20S 116°50E 61 D2
Augustus I. Australia 15°20S 124°30E 60 C3
Aujuittuq = Grise Fiord Canada 76°25N 82°57W 69 B15
Aukštaitija △ Lithuania 55°15N 26°0E 9 J22
Aukum U.S.A. 38°34N 120°43W 78 G6
Aul India 20°41N 86°39E 44 D8
Aulavik △ Canada 73°42N 119°55W 68 C8
Auld, L. Australia 22°25S 123°50E 60 D3
Ault U.S.A. 40°35N 104°44W 76 F11
Aundah India 19°32N 77°3E 44 E3
Aundh India 17°33N 74°23E 44 F2
Aunis France 46°5N 0°50W 20 C3
Aunu'u Amer. Samoa 14°20S 170°31W 59 b
Auponhia Indonesia 1°58S 125°27E 37 E7
Aur, Pulau Malaysia 2°35N 104°10E 39 L5
Auraiya India 26°28N 79°33E 43 F8
Aurangabad Bihar, India 24°45N 84°18E 43 G11
Aurangabad Maharashtra, India 19°50N 75°23E 44 E2
Aurich Germany 53°28N 7°28E 16 B4
Aurillac France 44°55N 2°26E 20 D5
Aurora Canada 44°0N 79°28W 82 C5
Aurora S. Africa 32°40S 18°29E 56 D2
Aurora Colo., U.S.A. 39°43N 104°49W 76 G11
Aurora Ill., U.S.A. 41°45N 88°19W 80 E9
Aurora Mo., U.S.A. 36°58N 93°43W 80 G7
Aurora N.Y., U.S.A. 42°45N 76°42W 83 D8
Aurora Nebr., U.S.A. 40°52N 98°0W 80 E5
Aurora Ohio, U.S.A. 41°21N 81°20W 82 E3
Aurukun Australia 13°20S 141°45E 62 A3
Aurukun ✪ Australia 13°36S 141°48E 62 A3
Aus Namibia 26°35S 16°12E 56 C2
Ausa India 18°15N 76°30E 44 E3
Ausable → Canada 43°19N 81°46W 82 C3
Auschwitz = Oświęcim Poland 50°2N 19°11E 17 C10
Auski Roadhouse Australia 22°22S 118°41E 60 D2
Austen Harbour India 12°55N 92°45E 45 H11
Austin Minn., U.S.A. 43°40N 92°58W 80 D7
Austin Nev., U.S.A. 39°30N 117°4W 76 G5
Austin Pa., U.S.A. 41°38N 78°6W 82 E6
Austin Tex., U.S.A. 30°17N 97°45W 84 F6
Austin, L. Australia 27°40S 118°0E 61 E2
Austin I. Canada 61°10N 94°0W 71 A10
Austra Norway 65°8N 11°55E 8 D14
Austral Is. = Tubuaï, Îs. French Polynesia 25°0S 150°0W 65 K13
Austral Seamount Chain Pac. Oc. 24°0S 150°0W 65 K13
Australia ■ Oceania 23°0S 135°0E 58 D6
Australian-Antarctic Basin S. Ocean 60°0S 120°0E 5 C9
Australian Capital Territory □ Australia 35°30S 149°0E 63 F4
Australind Australia 33°17S 115°42E 61 F2
Austria ■ Europe 47°0N 14°0E 16 E8
Austvågøya Norway 68°20N 14°40E 8 B16
Autlán de Navarro Mexico 19°46N 104°22W 86 D4
Autun France 46°58N 4°17E 20 C6
Auvergne France 45°20N 3°15E 20 D5
Auvergne, Mts. d' France 45°20N 2°55E 20 D5
Auxerre France 47°48N 3°32E 20 C5
Auyuittuq △ Canada 67°30N 66°0W 69 D18
Av-Dovurak Russia 51°17N 91°35E 27 D10
Ava U.S.A. 36°57N 92°40W 80 G7
Avachinskaya Sopka Russia 53°15N 158°50E 27 D16
Avallon France 47°30N 3°53E 20 C5
Avalon U.S.A. 33°21N 118°20W 79 M8
Avalon Pen. Canada 47°30N 53°20W 73 C9
Avanigadda India 16°0N 80°56E 45 G5
Avanos Turkey 38°43N 34°51E 46 B2
Avaré Brazil 23°4S 48°58W 95 A6
Avawatz Mts. U.S.A. 35°40N 116°30W 79 K10
Aveiro Brazil 3°10S 55°5W 93 D7
Aveiro Portugal 40°37N 8°38W 21 B1
Āvej Iran 35°40N 49°15E 47 C6
Avellino Italy 40°54N 14°47E 22 D6
Avenal U.S.A. 36°0N 120°8W 78 K6
Aversa Italy 40°58N 14°12E 22 D6
Avery U.S.A. 47°15N 115°49W 76 C6
Aves, I. de W. Indies 15°45N 63°55W 89 C7
Aves, Is. las Venezuela 12°0N 67°30W 89 D6
Avesta Sweden 60°9N 16°10E 9 F17
Aveyron → France 44°5N 1°16E 20 D4
Avezzano Italy 42°2N 13°25E 22 C5
Aviá Terai Argentina 26°45S 60°50W 94 B3
Aviemore U.K. 57°12N 3°50W 11 D5
Avignon France 43°57N 4°50E 20 E6
Ávila Spain 40°39N 4°43W 21 B3
Avila Beach U.S.A. 35°11N 120°44W 79 K6
Avilés Spain 43°35N 5°57W 21 A3
Avis U.S.A. 41°11N 77°19W 82 E7
Avissawella Sri Lanka 6°56N 80°11E 45 L5
Avoca U.S.A. 42°25N 77°25W 82 D7
Avoca → Australia 35°40S 143°43E 63 F3
Avoca → Ireland 52°48N 6°10W 10 D5
Avola Canada 51°45N 119°19W 70 C5
Avola Italy 36°56N 15°7E 22 F6
Avon U.S.A. 42°55N 77°45W 82 D7
Avon → Australia 31°40S 116°7E 61 F2
Avon → Bristol, U.K. 51°29N 2°41W 13 F5
Avon → Dorset, U.K. 50°44N 1°46W 13 G6
Avon → Warks., U.K. 52°0N 2°8W 13 E5
Avon Park U.S.A. 27°36N 81°31W 85 H14
Avonlea Canada 50°0N 105°0W 71 D8
Avonmore Canada 45°10N 74°58W 83 A10
Avonmouth U.K. 51°30N 2°42W 13 F5
Avranches France 48°40N 1°20W 20 B3
Awa-Shima Japan 38°27N 139°14E 28 E9
A'waj → Syria 33°23N 36°20E 48 B5
Awaji-Shima Japan 34°30N 134°50E 29 G7
'Awālī Bahrain 26°0N 50°30E 47 E6
Awantipur India 33°55N 75°3E 43 C6
Awarja → India 17°5N 76°15E 44 F3
Awasa Ethiopia 7°2N 38°28E 49 F2
Awash Ethiopia 9°1N 40°10E 49 F3
Awatere → N.Z. 41°37S 174°10E 59 D5
Awbārī Libya 26°46N 12°57E 53 C8
Awbārī, Idehan Libya 27°10N 11°30E 53 C8
Awe, L. U.K. 56°17N 5°16W 11 E3
Awjilah Libya 29°8N 21°7E 53 C10
Axe → U.K. 50°42N 3°4W 13 F5
Axel Heiberg I. Canada 80°0N 90°0W 69 B14
Axim Ghana 4°51N 2°15W 52 H5
Axios → Greece 40°57N 22°35E 23 D10
Axminster U.K. 50°46N 3°0W 13 G4
Ayabaca Peru 4°40S 79°53W 92 D3
Ayabe Japan 35°20N 135°20E 29 G7
Ayacucho Argentina 37°5S 58°20W 94 D4
Ayacucho Peru 13°0S 74°0W 92 F4
Ayaguz = Ayaköz Kazakhstan 48°10N 80°10E 30 B5
Ayakkum Hu China 37°30N 89°20E 30 D6
Ayaköz Kazakhstan 48°10N 80°10E 30 B5
Ayakudi India 10°28N 77°56E 45 J3
Ayamonte Spain 37°12N 7°24W 21 D2
Ayan Russia 56°30N 138°16E 27 D14
Ayaviri Peru 14°50S 70°35W 92 F4
Aydın Turkey 37°51N 27°51E 23 F12
Aydingkol Hu China 42°40N 89°15E 30 C6
Ayer U.S.A. 42°34N 71°35W 83 D13
Ayer Hitam Malaysia 5°24N 100°16E 39 c
Ayer's Cliff Canada 45°10N 72°3W 83 A12
Ayers Rock = Uluru Australia 25°23S 131°5E 61 E5
Ayeyarwady = Ayeyawadi → Myanmar 15°50N 95°6E 41 M19
Ayeyawadi → Myanmar 15°50N 95°6E 41 M19
Aykhal Russia 66°0N 111°30E 27 C12
Aykino Russia 62°15N 49°56E 18 B8
Aylesbury U.K. 51°49N 0°49W 13 F7
Aylmer Canada 42°46N 80°59W 82 D4
Aylmer, L. Canada 64°5N 108°30W 68 E10
Ayn Dār Si. Arabia 25°55N 49°10E 47 E7
Ayn Zālah Iraq 36°45N 42°35E 46 B4
Ayolas Paraguay 27°10S 56°59W 94 B4
Ayon, Ostrov Russia 69°50N 169°0E 27 C17
'Ayoûn el 'Atroûs Mauritania 16°38N 9°37W 52 E4
Ayr Australia 19°35S 147°25E 62 B4
Ayr Canada 43°17N 80°27W 82 C4
Ayr U.K. 55°28N 4°38W 11 F4
Ayr → U.K. 55°28N 4°38W 11 F4
Ayre, Pt. of I. of Man 54°25N 4°21W 12 C3
Ayteke Bi Kazakhstan 45°48N 62°6E 26 E7
Ayton Australia 15°56S 145°22E 62 B4
Aytos Bulgaria 42°42N 27°16E 23 C12
Ayu, Kepulauan Indonesia 0°35N 131°5E 37 D8
Ayutla Guatemala 14°40N 92°10W 88 D1
Ayutla de los Libres Mexico 16°54N 99°13W 87 D5
Ayutthaya = Phra Nakhon Si Ayutthaya Thailand 14°25N 100°30E 38 E3
Ayvacık Turkey 39°36N 26°24E 23 E12
Ayvalık Turkey 39°20N 26°46E 23 E12
Az Zabadānī Syria 33°43N 36°5E 48 B5
Az Zāhirīyah West Bank 31°25N 34°58E 48 D3
Az Zahrān Si. Arabia 26°10N 50°7E 47 E6
Az Zarqā Jordan 32°5N 36°4E 48 C5
Az Zarqā' U.A.E. 24°53N 53°4E 47 E7
Az Zarqā □ Jordan 32°5N 36°4E 48 C5
Az Zāwiyah Libya 32°52N 12°56E 53 B8
Az Zībār Iraq 36°52N 44°4E 46 B5
Az Zilfī Si. Arabia 26°12N 44°52E 46 E5
Az Zubayr Iraq 30°26N 47°40E 46 D5
Azad Kashmir □ Pakistan 33°50N 73°50E 43 C5
Azamgarh India 26°5N 83°13E 43 F10
Azangaro Peru 14°55S 70°13W 92 F4
Azaouad Mali 19°0N 3°0W 52 E5
Āzār Shahr Iran 37°45N 45°59E 46 B5
Azarān Iran 37°25N 47°16E 46 B5
Azärbayjan = Azerbaijan ■ Asia 40°20N 48°0E 19 F8
Āzarbāyjān-e Gharbī □ Iran 37°0N 44°30E 46 B5
Āzarbāyjān-e Sharqī □ Iran 37°20N 47°0E 46 B5
Azare Nigeria 11°55N 10°10E 52 F8
A'zāz Syria 36°36N 37°4E 46 B3
Azbine = Aïr Niger 18°30N 8°0E 52 E7
Azerbaijan ■ Asia 40°20N 48°0E 19 F8
Azogues Ecuador 2°35S 78°0W 92 D3
Azores = Açores, Is. dos Atl. Oc. 38°0N 27°0W 52 a
Azov Russia 47°3N 39°25E 19 E6
Azov, Sea of Europe 46°0N 36°30E 19 E6
Azovskoye More = Azov, Sea of Europe 46°0N 36°30E 19 E6
Azraq ash Shīshān Jordan 31°50N 36°49E 48 D5
Aztec U.S.A. 36°49N 107°59W 77 H10
Azua de Compostela Dom. Rep. 18°25N 70°44W 89 C5
Azuaga Spain 38°16N 5°39W 21 C3
Azuero, Pen. de Panama 7°30N 80°30W 88 E3
Azul Argentina 36°42S 59°43W 94 D4
Azumino Japan 36°20N 137°50E 29 F8
Azur, Côte d' France 43°25N 7°10E 20 E7
Azusa U.S.A. 34°8N 117°52W 79 L9
Azzel Matti, Sebkra Algeria 26°10N 0°43E 52 C6

## B

Ba Be △ Vietnam 22°25N 105°37E 38 A5
Ba Don Vietnam 17°45N 106°26E 38 D6
Ba Dong Vietnam 9°40N 106°33E 39 H6
Ba Ngoi Vietnam 11°54N 109°10E 39 G7
Ba Ria Vietnam 10°30N 107°10E 39 G6
Ba Tri Vietnam 10°2N 106°36E 39 G6
Ba Vi △ Vietnam 21°1N 105°22E 38 B5
Ba Xian = Bazhou China 39°8N 116°22E 32 E9
Baa Indonesia 10°50S 123°0E 60 B3
Baalbek = Ba'labakk Lebanon 34°0N 36°10E 48 B5
Baardheere Somalia 2°20N 42°27E 49 G3
Baarle-Nassau Belgium 51°27N 4°56E 15 C4
Bab el Mandeb Red Sea 12°35N 43°25E 49 E3
Bābā, Koh-i- Afghan. 34°30N 67°0E 40 B5
Baba Budan Hills India 13°30N 75°44E 45 H2
Baba Burnu Turkey 39°29N 26°2E 23 E12
Bābā Kalū Iran 30°7N 50°49E 47 D6
Babadag Romania 44°53N 28°44E 17 F15
Babaeski Turkey 41°26N 27°6E 23 D12
Babahoyo Ecuador 1°40S 79°30W 92 D3
Babai = Sarju → India 27°21N 81°23E 43 F9
Babai → Nepal 28°10N 82°21E 43 E10
Babar Indonesia 8°0S 129°30E 37 F7
Babar Pakistan 31°7N 69°32E 42 D3
Babarkach Pakistan 29°45N 68°0E 42 E3
Babb U.S.A. 48°51N 113°27W 76 B7
Baberu India 25°33N 80°43E 43 G9
Babi Besar, Pulau Malaysia 2°25N 103°59E 39 L4
Babian Jiang → China 22°55N 101°47E 34 F3
Bābil □ Iraq 32°30N 44°30E 46 C5
Babinda Australia 17°20S 145°56E 62 B4
Babine Canada 55°22N 126°37W 70 B3
Babine → Canada 55°45N 127°44W 70 B3
Babine L. Canada 54°48N 126°0W 70 C3
Babo Indonesia 2°30S 133°30E 37 E8
Bābol Iran 36°40N 52°50E 47 B7
Bābol Sar Iran 36°45N 52°45E 47 B7
Baboua C.A.R. 5°49N 14°58E 54 C2
Babruysk Belarus 53°10N 29°15E 17 B15
Babuhri India 26°49N 69°43E 42 F3
Babusar Pass Pakistan 35°12N 73°59E 43 B5
Babuyan Chan. Phil. 18°40N 121°30E 37 A6
Babylon Iraq 32°34N 44°22E 46 C5
Bac Can Vietnam 22°8N 105°49E 34 F5
Bac Giang Vietnam 21°16N 106°11E 34 G6
Bac Lieu Vietnam 9°17N 105°43E 39 H5
Bac Ninh Vietnam 21°13N 106°4E 34 G6
Bac Phan Vietnam 22°0N 105°0E 34 G5
Bacabal Brazil 4°15S 44°45W 93 D10
Bacalar Mexico 18°43N 88°27W 87 D7
Bacan, Kepulauan Indonesia 0°35S 127°30E 37 E7
Bacarra Phil. 18°15N 120°37E 37 A6
Bacău Romania 46°35N 26°55E 17 E14
Bacerac Mexico 30°18N 108°50W 86 A3
Bach Long Vi, Dao Vietnam 20°10N 107°40E 38 B6
Bach Ma △ Vietnam 16°11N 107°49E 38 D6
Bachhwara India 25°35N 85°54E 43 G11
Back → Canada 65°10N 104°0W 68 D11
Bacolod Phil. 10°40N 122°57E 37 B6
Bacuk Malaysia 6°4N 102°25E 39 J4
Bácum Mexico 27°33N 110°5W 86 B2
Bād Iran 33°41N 52°1E 47 C7
Bad → U.S.A. 44°21N 100°22W 80 C3
Bad Axe U.S.A. 43°48N 83°0W 82 C2
Bad Ischl Austria 47°44N 13°38E 16 E7
Bad Kissingen Germany 50°11N 10°4E 16 C6
Bada Barabil India 22°7N 85°24E 43 H11
Badagara = Vadakara India 11°35N 75°40E 45 J2
Badain Jaran Shamo China 40°23N 102°0E 30 C9
Badajós, L. Brazil 3°15S 62°50W 92 D6
Badajoz Spain 38°50N 6°59W 21 C2
Badakhshān □ Afghan. 36°30N 71°0E 40 A7
Badaling China 40°20N 116°0E 32 D9
Badalzai Afghan. 29°50N 65°35E 42 E1
Badami India 15°55N 75°41E 45 G2
Badampahar India 22°10N 86°10E 44 C8
Badanah Si. Arabia 30°58N 41°30E 46 D4
Badarinath India 30°45N 79°30E 43 D8
Badas, Kepulauan Indonesia 0°45N 107°5E 36 D3
Baddo → Pakistan 28°0N 64°20E 40 F4
Bade Indonesia 7°10S 139°35E 37 F9
Baden Austria 48°1N 16°13E 16 D9
Baden U.S.A. 40°38N 80°14W 82 F4
Baden-Baden Germany 48°44N 8°13E 16 D5
Baden-Württemberg □ Germany 48°20N 8°40E 16 D5
Badgam India 34°1N 74°45E 43 B6
Badgastein Austria 47°7N 13°9E 16 E7
Badger Canada 49°0N 56°4W 73 C8
Badger U.S.A. 36°38N 119°1W 78 J7
Bādghīs □ Afghan. 35°0N 63°0E 40 B3
Badgingarra △ Australia 30°23S 115°22E 61 F2
Badin Pakistan 24°38N 68°54E 42 G3
Badlands U.S.A. 43°55N 102°30W 80 D2
Badlands △ U.S.A. 43°38N 102°56W 80 D2
Badme Africa 14°43N 37°48E 49 E2
Badnera India 20°48N 77°44E 44 D3
Badrah Iraq 33°6N 45°58E 46 C5
Badrain Jaran Shamo China 40°40N 103°20E 32 D2
Badrinath India 30°44N 79°29E 43 D8
Badu Australia 10°7S 142°11E 62 a
Badulla Sri Lanka 7°1N 81°7E 45 L5
Badung, Bukit Indonesia 8°49S 115°10E 37 K18
Badung, Selat Indonesia 8°40S 115°22E 37 K18
Badvel India 14°45N 79°3E 45 G4
Baena Spain 37°37N 4°20W 21 D3
Baengnyeongdo S. Korea 37°57N 124°40E 33 F13
Baeza Spain 37°57N 3°25W 21 D4
Bafatá Guinea-Biss. 12°8N 14°40W 52 F3
Baffin B. N. Amer. 72°0N 64°0W 66 B13
Baffin I. Canada 68°0N 75°0W 69 D17
Bafing → Mali 13°49N 10°50W 52 F3
Bafliyūn Syria 36°37N 36°59E 46 B3
Bafoulabé Mali 13°50N 10°55W 52 F3
Bafoussam Cameroon 5°28N 10°25E 54 C2
Bāfq Iran 31°40N 55°25E 47 D7
Bafra Turkey 41°34N 35°54E 19 F6
Bāft Iran 29°15N 56°38E 47 D8
Bafwasende Dem. Rep. of the Congo 1°3N 27°5E 54 D5
Bagaha India 27°6N 84°5E 44 A7
Bagalkot India 16°10N 75°40E 45 F2
Bagamoyo Tanzania 6°28S 38°55E 54 F7
Bagan Datoh Malaysia 3°59N 100°47E 39 L3
Bagan Serai Malaysia 5°1N 100°32E 39 K3
Baganga Phil. 7°34N 126°33E 37 C7
Bagani Namibia 18°7S 21°41E 56 A3
Bagansiapiapi Indonesia 2°12N 100°50E 36 D2
Bagasra India 21°30N 71°0E 42 J4
Bagaud India 22°19N 75°53E 42 H6
Bagdad U.S.A. 34°35N 115°53W 79 L11
Bagdarin Russia 54°26N 113°36E 27 D12
Bagé Brazil 31°20S 54°15W 95 C5
Bagenalstown Ireland 52°42N 6°58W 10 D5
Bagepalli India 13°47N 77°47E 45 H3
Bageshwar India 29°51N 79°46E 43 E8
Bagevadi India 16°35N 75°58E 44 F2
Baggs U.S.A. 41°2N 107°39W 76 F10
Bagh Pakistan 33°59N 73°45E 43 C5
Baghain → India 25°32N 81°1E 43 G9
Bagheria Italy 38°5N 13°30E 22 E5
Baghlān Afghan. 32°12N 68°46E 40 A6
Baghlān □ Afghan. 36°0N 68°30E 40 B6
Bagley U.S.A. 47°32N 95°24W 80 B6
Baglung Nepal 28°16N 83°36E 43 E10
Bago Myanmar 17°20N 96°29E 41 L20
Bagodar India 24°5N 85°52E 43 G11
Bagrationovsk Russia 54°23N 20°39E 9 J19
Baguio Phil. 16°26N 120°34E 37 A6
Bahadurganj India 26°16N 87°49E 43 F12
Bahadurgarh India 28°40N 76°57E 42 E7
Bahama, Canal Viejo de W. Indies 22°10N 77°30W 88 B4
Bahamas ■ N. Amer. 24°0N 75°0W 89 B5
Bahār Iran 34°54N 48°26E 47 C6
Baharampur India 24°2N 88°27E 43 G13
Baharu Pandan = Pandan Malaysia 1°32N 103°46E 39 d
Bahawalnagar Pakistan 30°0N 73°15E 42 E5
Bahawalpur Pakistan 29°24N 71°40E 42 E4
Bäherden Turkmenistan 38°25N 57°26E 47 B8
Baheri India 28°45N 79°34E 43 E8
Bahgul → India 27°45N 79°36E 43 F8
Bahía = Salvador Brazil 13°0S 38°30W 93 F11
Bahía □ Brazil 12°0S 42°0W 93 F10
Bahía, Is. de la Honduras 16°45N 86°15W 88 C2
Bahía Blanca Argentina 38°35S 62°13W 94 D3
Bahía de Caráquez Ecuador 0°40S 80°27W 92 D2
Bahía de Los Angeles Mexico 28°56N 113°34W 86 B2
Bahía Honda Cuba 22°54N 83°10W 88 B3
Bahía Kino Mexico 28°47N 111°58W 86 B2
Bahía Laura Argentina 48°10S 66°30W 96 F3
Bahía Negra Paraguay 20°5S 58°5W 92 H7
Bahir Dar Ethiopia 11°37N 37°10E 49 E2
Bahmanzād Iran 31°15N 51°47E 47 D6
Bahraich India 27°38N 81°37E 43 F9
Bahrain ■ Asia 26°0N 50°35E 47 E6
Bahror India 27°51N 76°20E 42 F7
Bāhū Kalāt Iran 25°43N 61°25E 47 E9
Bai Bung, Mui = Ca Mau, Mui Vietnam 8°38N 104°44E 39 H5
Bai Thuong Vietnam 19°54N 105°23E 38 C5
Baia Mare Romania 47°40N 23°35E 17 E12
Baião Brazil 2°40S 49°40W 93 D9
Baïbokoum Chad 7°46N 15°43E 53 G9
Baicheng China 45°38N 122°42E 33 B12
Baidoa = Baydhabo Somalia 3°8N 43°30E 49 G3
Baie-Comeau Canada 49°12N 68°10W 73 C6
Baie-St-Paul Canada 47°28N 70°32W 73 C5
Baie Ste-Anne Seychelles 4°18S 55°45E 55 b
Baie-Trinité Canada 49°25N 67°20W 73 C6
Baie Verte Canada 49°55N 56°12W 73 C8
Baihar India 22°6N 80°33E 43 H9
Baihe Hubei, China 32°50N 110°5E 32 H6
Baihe Jilin, China 42°27N 128°9E 33 C15
Baihetan Dam China 27°11N 102°54E 34 D4
Ba'ījī Iraq 35°0N 43°30E 46 C4
Baijnath India 29°55N 79°37E 43 E8
Baikal, L. = Baykal, Oz. Russia 53°0N 108°0E 27 D11
Baikonur = Bayqonyr Kazakhstan 45°40N 63°20E 26 E7
Baikunthpur India 23°15N 82°33E 43 H10
Bailadila, Mt. India 18°43N 81°15E 44 E5
Baile Átha Cliath = Dublin Ireland 53°21N 6°15W 10 C5
Baile Átha Fhirdhia = Ardee Ireland 53°52N 6°33W 10 C5
Baile Átha Í = Athy Ireland 53°0N 7°0W 10 C5
Baile Átha Luain = Athlone Ireland 53°25N 7°56W 10 C4
Baile Átha Troim = Trim Ireland 53°33N 6°48W 10 C5
Baile Brigín = Balbriggan Ireland 53°37N 6°11W 10 C5
Baile Sear = Baleshare U.K. 57°31N 7°22W 11 D1
Băileşti Romania 44°1N 23°20E 17 F12
Bailhongal India 15°55N 74°53E 45 G2
Bailieborough Ireland 53°56N 6°59W 10 C5
Baima China 33°0N 100°26E 34 A3
Bainbridge Ga., U.S.A. 30°55N 84°35W 85 F12
Bainbridge N.Y., U.S.A. 42°18N 75°29W 83 D9
Bainbridge Island U.S.A. 47°38N 122°32W 78 C4
Baine China 42°0N 128°0E 31 C14
Baing Indonesia 10°14S 120°34E 37 F6
Bainiu China 32°50N 112°15E 32 H7
Bā'ir Jordan 30°45N 36°55E 48 E5
Baird Mts. U.S.A. 67°0N 160°0W 74 B8
Bairiki = Tarawa Kiribati 1°30N 173°0E 64 G9
Bairin Youqi China 43°30N 118°35E 33 C10
Bairin Zuoqi China 43°58N 119°15E 33 C10
Bairnsdale Australia 37°48S 147°36E 63 F4
Baisha China 34°20N 112°32E 32 G7
Baisha Li China 19°12N 109°20E 38 C7
Baishan = Hunjiang China 41°54N 126°26E 33 D14
Baishan China 42°43N 127°14E 33 C14
Baitadi Nepal 29°35N 80°25E 43 E9
Baitarani → India 20°45N 86°48E 44 D8
Baiyin China 36°45N 104°14E 32 F3
Baiyü China 31°16N 98°50E 34 B2
Baiyu Shan China 37°15N 107°30E 32 F4
Baj Baj India 22°30N 88°5E 43 H13
Baja Hungary 46°12N 18°59E 17 E10
Baja, Pta. Mexico 29°58N 115°49W 86 B1
Baja California Mexico 31°10N 115°12W 86 A1
Baja California □ Mexico 30°0N 115°0W 86 B2
Baja California Sur □ Mexico 25°50N 111°50W 86 B2
Bajag India 22°40N 81°21E 43 H9
Bajana India 23°7N 71°49E 42 H4
Bajatrejo Indonesia 8°29S 114°19E 37 J17
Bajawa Indonesia 8°47S 120°59E 37 F6
Bajera Indonesia 8°31S 115°2E 37 J18
Bājgīrān Iran 37°36N 58°24E 47 B8
Bajimba, Mt. Australia 29°17S 152°6E 63 D5
Bajo Boquete Panama 8°46N 82°27W 88 E3
Bajo Nuevo Caribbean 15°40N 78°50W 88 C4
Bajoga Nigeria 10°57N 11°20E 53 F8
Bajool Australia 23°40S 150°35E 62 C5
Bakel Senegal 14°56N 12°20W 52 F3
Baker Calif., U.S.A. 35°16N 116°4W 79 K10
Baker Mont., U.S.A. 46°22N 104°17W 76 C11
Baker, L. Canada 64°0N 96°0W 68 E12
Baker, Mt. U.S.A. 48°50N 121°49W 76 B3

Baker City U.S.A. 44°47N 117°50W **76 D5**
Baker I. Pac. Oc. 0°10N 176°35W **64 G10**
Baker I. U.S.A. 55°20N 133°40W **70 B2**
Baker I. Australia 26°54S 126°5E **61 E4**
Baker Lake Canada 64°20N 96°3W **68 E12**
Bakers Creek Australia 21°13S 149°7E **62 C4**
Bakers Dozen Is. Canada 56°45N 78°45W **72 A4**
Bakersfield Calif., U.S.A. 35°23N 119°1W **79 K8**
Bakersfield Vt., U.S.A. 44°45N 72°48W **83 B12**
Bakharden = Bäherden
  Turkmenistan 38°25N 57°26E **47 B8**
Bākhtarān = Kermānshāh
  Iran 34°23N 47°0E **46 C5**
Bākhtarān = Kermānshāh □
  Iran 34°30N 46°30E **46 C5**
Bakhtegān, Daryācheh-ye
  Iran 29°40N 53°50E **47 D7**
Bakhtegān △ Iran 29°51N 53°40E **47 D7**
Bakı Azerbaijan 40°29N 49°56E **47 A6**
Bakkafjörður Iceland 66°2N 14°48W **8 C6**
Bakkagerði Iceland 65°31N 13°49W **8 D7**
Bakony Hungary 47°10N 17°30E **17 E9**
Bakony Forest = Bakony
  Hungary 47°10N 17°30E **17 E9**
Bakouma C.A.R. 5°40N 22°56E **54 C4**
Bakswaho India 24°15N 79°18E **43 G8**
Bakutis Coast Antarctica 74°0S 120°0W **5 D15**
Baky = Bakı Azerbaijan 40°29N 49°56E **47 A6**
Bala Canada 45°1N 79°37W **82 A5**
Bala U.K. 52°54N 3°36W **12 E4**
Bala, L. U.K. 52°53N 3°37W **12 E4**
Balabac I. Phil. 8°0N 117°0E **36 C5**
Balabac Str. E. Indies 7°53N 117°5E **36 C5**
Balabagh Afghan. 34°25N 70°12E **42 B4**
Ba'labakk Lebanon 34°0N 36°10E **48 B5**
Balabalangan, Kepulauan
  Indonesia 2°20S 117°30E **36 E5**
Balad Iraq 34°0N 44°9E **46 C5**
Balad Rūz Iraq 33°42N 45°5E **46 C5**
Bālādeh Fārs, Iran 29°17N 51°56E **47 D6**
Bālādeh Māzandaran, Iran 36°12N 51°48E **47 B6**
Balaghat India 21°49N 80°12E **44 D5**
Balaghat Ra. India 18°50N 76°30E **44 E3**
Balaguer Spain 41°50N 0°50E **21 B6**
Balaklava Ukraine 44°30N 33°30E **19 F5**
Balakovo Russia 52°4N 47°55E **18 D8**
Balamau India 27°10N 80°21E **43 F9**
Balancán Mexico 17°48N 91°32W **87 D6**
Balangir India 20°43N 83°35E **44 D6**
Balapur India 20°40N 76°45E **44 D3**
Balashov Russia 51°30N 43°10E **19 D7**
Balasinor India 22°57N 73°23E **42 H5**
Balasore = Baleshwar
  India 21°35N 87°3E **44 G8**
Balaton Hungary 46°50N 17°40E **17 E9**
Balbina, Represa de Brazil 2°0S 59°30W **92 D7**
Balboa Panama 8°57N 79°34W **88 E4**
Balbriggan Ireland 53°37N 6°11W **10 C5**
Balcarce Argentina 38°0S 58°10W **94 D4**
Balcarres Canada 50°50N 103°35W **71 C8**
Balchik Bulgaria 43°28N 28°11E **23 C13**
Balclutha N.Z. 46°15S 169°45E **59 G2**
Balcones Escarpment
  U.S.A. 29°30N 99°15W **84 G5**
Bald I. Australia 34°57S 118°27E **61 F2**
Bald Knob U.S.A. 35°19N 91°34W **84 D9**
Baldock L. Canada 56°33N 97°57W **71 B9**
Baldwin Mich., U.S.A. 43°54N 85°51W **81 D11**
Baldwin Pa., U.S.A. 40°21N 79°58W **82 F5**
Baldwinsville U.S.A. 43°10N 76°20W **83 C8**
Baldy Peak U.S.A. 33°54N 109°34W **77 K9**
Baleares, Is. Spain 39°30N 3°0E **21 C7**
Baleares Is. = Baleares, Is.
  Spain 39°30N 3°0E **21 C7**
Balearic Sea Spain 40°0N 2°0E **21 B6**
Baleine → Canada 58°15N 67°40W **73 A6**
Baleine, Petite R. de la →
  Canada 56°0N 76°45W **72 A4**
Baler Phil. 15°46N 121°34E **37 A6**
Baleshare U.K. 57°31N 7°22W **11 D1**
Baleshwar India 21°35N 87°3E **44 G8**
Baley Russia 51°36N 116°37E **27 D12**
Balfate Honduras 15°48N 86°25W **88 C2**
Balgo Australia 20°9S 127°58E **60 D4**
Balharshah India 19°50N 79°23E **44 E4**
Bali India 25°11N 73°17E **42 G5**
Bali Indonesia 8°20S 115°0E **37 J18**
Bali □ Indonesia 8°20S 115°0E **37 J17**
Bali, Selat Indonesia 8°18S 114°25E **37 J17**
Bali Barat △ Indonesia 8°12S 114°35E **37 J17**
Bali Sea Indonesia 8°0S 115°0E **37 J17**
Baliapal India 21°40N 87°17E **43 J12**
Baliguda India 20°12N 83°55E **44 D6**
Balik Pulau Malaysia 5°21N 100°14E **39 c**
Balıkesir Turkey 39°39N 27°53E **23 E12**
Balikpapan Indonesia 1°10S 116°55E **36 E5**
Balimbing Malaysia 5°5N 119°58E **37 C5**
Baling Malaysia 5°41N 100°55E **39 K3**
Balkan Mts. = Stara Planina
  Bulgaria 43°15N 23°0E **23 C10**
Balkanabat Turkmenistan 39°30N 54°22E **47 B7**
Balkhash = Balqash
  Kazakhstan 46°50N 74°50E **26 E8**
Balkhash, Ozero = Balqash Köli
  Kazakhstan 46°0N 74°50E **30 B3**
Balkonda India 18°52N 78°21E **44 E4**
Ballachulish U.K. 56°41N 5°8W **11 E3**
Balladonia Australia 32°27S 123°51E **61 F3**
Ballaghadereen Ireland 53°55N 8°34W **10 C3**
Ballarat Australia 37°33S 143°50E **63 F3**
Ballard, L. Australia 29°20S 120°40E **61 E3**
Ballari India 15°10N 76°56E **45 G3**
Ballater U.K. 57°3N 3°3W **11 D5**
Ballenas, Canal de
  Mexico 29°10N 113°29W **86 B2**
Balleny Is. Antarctica 66°30S 163°0E **5 C11**
Ballia India 25°46N 84°12E **43 G11**
Ballina Australia 28°50S 153°31E **63 D5**
Ballina Ireland 54°7N 9°9W **10 B2**

Ballinasloe Ireland 53°20N 8°13W **10 C3**
Ballincollig Ireland 51°53N 8°33W **10 E3**
Ballinger U.S.A. 31°45N 99°57W **84 F5**
Ballinrobe Ireland 53°38N 9°13W **10 C2**
Ballinskelligs B. Ireland 51°48N 10°13W **10 E1**
Ballston Spa U.S.A. 43°0N 73°51W **83 D11**
Ballyboghil Ireland 53°32N 6°16W **10 C5**
Ballybunion Ireland 52°31N 9°40W **10 D2**
Ballycanew Ireland 52°37N 6°19W **10 D5**
Ballycastle U.K. 55°12N 6°15W **10 A5**
Ballyclare U.K. 54°46N 6°0W **10 B5**
Ballycroy △ Ireland 54°5N 9°50W **10 B2**
Ballydehob Ireland 51°34N 9°28W **10 E2**
Ballygawley U.K. 54°27N 7°2W **10 B4**
Ballyhaunis Ireland 53°46N 8°46W **10 C3**
Ballyheige Ireland 52°23N 9°49W **10 D2**
Ballymena U.K. 54°52N 6°17W **10 B5**
Ballymoney U.K. 55°5N 6°31W **10 A5**
Ballymote Ireland 54°5N 8°31W **10 B3**
Ballynahinch U.K. 54°24N 5°54W **10 B6**
Ballyporeen Ireland 52°16N 8°6W **10 D3**
Ballyquintin Pt. U.K. 54°20N 5°30W **10 B6**
Ballyshannon Ireland 54°30N 8°11W **10 B3**
Balmaceda Chile 46°0S 71°50W **96 F2**
Balmertown Canada 51°4N 93°41W **71 C10**
Balmoral Australia 37°15S 141°48E **63 F3**
Balmorhea U.S.A. 30°59N 103°45W **84 F3**
Balneário Camboriú
  Brazil 26°59S 48°38W **95 B6**
Balochistan = Baluchistan □
  Pakistan 27°30N 65°0E **40 F4**
Balod India 20°44N 81°13E **44 D5**
Balonne → Australia 28°47S 147°56E **63 D4**
Balotra India 25°50N 72°14E **42 G5**
Balqash Kazakhstan 46°50N 74°50E **26 E8**
Balqash Köli Kazakhstan 46°0N 74°50E **30 B3**
Balrampur India 27°30N 82°20E **43 F10**
Balranald Australia 34°38S 143°33E **63 E3**
Balsas → Brazil 7°15S 44°35W **93 E9**
Balsas → Mexico 17°55N 102°10W **86 D4**
Balsas del Norte Mexico 18°0N 99°46W **87 D5**
Balta Ukraine 47°56N 29°45E **17 D15**
Bălți Moldova 47°48N 27°58E **17 E14**
Baltic Sea Europe 57°0N 19°0E **9 H18**
Baltimore Ireland 51°29N 9°22W **10 E2**
Baltimore Md., U.S.A. 39°17N 76°36W **81 F15**
Baltimore Ohio, U.S.A. 39°51N 82°36W **82 G2**
Baltimore-Washington Int. ✈
  (BWI) U.S.A. 39°10N 76°40W **81 F15**
Baltinglass Ireland 52°56N 6°43W **10 D5**
Baltit Pakistan 36°15N 74°40E **43 A6**
Baltiysk Russia 54°41N 19°58E **9 J18**
Baluchistan □ Pakistan 27°30N 65°0E **40 F4**
Balurghat India 25°15N 88°44E **43 G13**
Balvi Latvia 57°8N 27°15E **9 H22**
Balya Turkey 39°44N 27°35E **23 E12**
Balykchy Kyrgyzstan 42°26N 76°12E **30 C4**
Balyqshy Kazakhstan 47°4N 51°52E **19 E9**
Bam Iran 29°7N 58°14E **47 D8**
Bama China 24°8N 107°12E **34 E6**
Bama Nigeria 11°33N 13°41E **53 F8**
Bamaga Australia 10°50S 142°25E **62 A3**
Bamaji L. Canada 51°9N 91°25W **72 B1**
Bamako Mali 12°34N 7°55W **52 F4**
Bambari C.A.R. 5°40N 20°35E **54 C4**
Bambaroo Australia 18°50S 146°10E **62 B4**
Bamberg Germany 49°54N 10°54E **16 D6**
Bamberg U.S.A. 33°18N 81°2W **85 E14**
Bamburgh U.K. 55°37N 1°43W **12 B6**
Bamenda Cameroon 5°57N 10°11E **54 C2**
Bamfield Canada 48°45N 125°10W **70 D3**
Bāmīān □ Afghan. 35°0N 67°0E **40 B5**
Bamiancheng China 43°15N 124°2E **33 C13**
Bamou △ Iran 29°45S 52°35E **47 D7**
Bampūr Iran 27°15N 60°21E **47 E9**
Bampūr → Iran 27°24N 59°0E **47 E8**
Ban Ao Tu Khun Thailand 8°9N 98°20E **39 a**
Ban Ban Laos 19°31N 103°30E **38 C4**
Ban Bang Hin Thailand 9°32N 98°35E **39 H2**
Ban Bang Khu Thailand 7°57N 98°23E **39 a**
Ban Bang Rong Thailand 8°3N 98°25E **39 a**
Ban Bo Phut Thailand 9°33N 100°2E **39 b**
Ban Chaweng Thailand 9°32N 100°3E **39 b**
Ban Chiang Thailand 17°30N 103°10E **38 D4**
Ban Chiang Klang
  Thailand 19°25N 100°55E **38 C3**
Ban Choho Thailand 15°2N 102°9E **38 E4**
Ban Dan Lan Hoi Thailand 17°0N 99°35E **38 D2**
Ban Don = Surat Thani
  Thailand 9°6N 99°20E **39 H2**
Ban Don Vietnam 12°53N 107°48E **38 F6**
Ban Dong Thailand 19°30N 100°59E **38 C3**
Ban Hong Thailand 18°18N 98°50E **38 C2**
Ban Hua Thanon Thailand 9°26N 100°1E **39 b**
Ban Kantang Thailand 7°25N 99°31E **39 J2**
Ban Karon Thailand 7°51N 98°18E **39 a**
Ban Kata Thailand 7°50N 98°18E **39 a**
Ban Keun Laos 18°22N 102°35E **38 C4**
Ban Khai Thailand 12°46N 101°18E **38 F3**
Ban Khuen Laos 20°13N 101°7E **38 B3**
Ban Khlong Khian Thailand 8°10N 98°26E **39 a**
Ban Khlong Kua Thailand 6°57N 100°8E **39 J3**
Ban Ko Yai Chim
  Thailand 11°17N 99°26E **39 G2**
Ban Laem Thailand 13°13N 99°59E **38 F2**
Ban Lamai Thailand 9°28N 100°3E **39 b**
Ban Lao Ngam Laos 15°28N 106°10E **38 E6**
Ban Le Kathe Thailand 15°49N 98°53E **38 E2**
Ban Lo Po Noi Thailand 8°1N 98°34E **39 a**
Ban Mae Chedi Thailand 19°11N 99°31E **38 C2**
Ban Mae Nam Thailand 9°34N 100°0E **39 b**
Ban Mae Sariang
  Thailand 18°10N 97°56E **38 C1**
Ban Mê Thuôt = Buon Ma Thuot
  Vietnam 12°40N 108°3E **38 F7**
Ban Mi Thailand 15°3N 100°32E **38 E3**
Ban Muang Mo Laos 19°4N 103°58E **38 C4**
Ban Na Bo Thailand 9°19N 99°41E **39 b**

Ban Na San Thailand 8°53N 99°52E **39 H2**
Ban Na Tong Laos 20°56N 101°47E **38 B3**
Ban Nam Bac Laos 20°38N 102°20E **38 B4**
Ban Nammi Laos 17°7N 105°40E **38 D5**
Ban Nong Bok Laos 16°51N 105°40E **38 D5**
Ban Nong Pling Thailand 15°40N 100°10E **38 E3**
Ban Pak Chan Thailand 10°32N 98°51E **39 G2**
Ban Patong Thailand 7°54N 98°18E **39 a**
Ban Phai Thailand 16°4N 102°44E **38 D4**
Ban Phak Chit Thailand 8°0N 98°24E **39 a**
Ban Pong Thailand 13°50N 99°55E **38 F2**
Ban Rawai Thailand 7°47N 98°20E **39 a**
Ban Ron Phibun Thailand 8°9N 99°51E **39 H2**
Ban Sakhu Thailand 8°4N 98°18E **39 a**
Ban Sanam Chai Thailand 7°33N 100°25E **39 a**
Ban Tak Thailand 17°2N 99°4E **38 D2**
Ban Tako Thailand 14°5N 102°40E **38 E4**
Ban Tha Nun Thailand 8°12N 98°18E **39 a**
Ban Tha Rua Thailand 7°59N 98°22E **39 a**
Ban Tha Yu Thailand 8°17N 98°22E **39 a**
Ban Thong Krut Thailand 9°25N 99°57E **39 b**
Ban Xien Kok Laos 20°54N 100°39E **38 B3**
Ban Yen Nhan Vietnam 20°57N 106°2E **38 B6**
Banaba Kiribati 0°45S 169°50E **64 H8**
Banagher Ireland 53°11N 7°59W **10 C3**
Banalia
  Dem. Rep. of the Congo 1°32N 25°5E **54 D5**
Banam Cambodia 11°20N 105°17E **39 G5**
Bananal, I. do Brazil 11°30S 50°30W **93 F8**
Bananga India 6°57N 93°54E **45 L11**
Banaras = Varanasi India 25°22N 83°0E **43 G10**
Banas → Gujarat, India 23°45N 71°25E **42 H4**
Banas → Mad. P., India 24°15N 81°30E **43 G9**
Bânâs, Ras Egypt 23°57N 35°59E **53 D13**
Banbridge U.K. 54°22N 6°16W **10 B5**
Banbury U.K. 52°4N 1°20W **13 E6**
Banchory U.K. 57°3N 2°29W **11 D6**
Bancroft Canada 45°3N 77°51W **82 A7**
Band Boni Iran 25°30N 59°33E **47 E8**
Band Qīr Iran 31°39N 48°53E **47 D6**
Banda Mad. P., India 24°3N 78°57E **43 G8**
Banda Maharashtra, India 15°49N 73°25E **45 G1**
Banda Ut. P., India 25°30N 80°26E **43 G9**
Banda, Kepulauan
  Indonesia 4°37S 129°50E **37 E7**
Banda Aceh Indonesia 5°35N 95°20E **36 C1**
Banda Banda, Mt.
  Australia 31°10S 152°28E **63 E5**
Banda Elat Indonesia 5°40S 133°5E **37 F8**
Banda Is. = Banda, Kepulauan
  Indonesia 4°37S 129°50E **37 E7**
Banda Sea Indonesia 6°0S 130°0E **37 F8**
Bandai-Asahi △ Japan 37°38N 140°5E **28 F10**
Bandai-San Japan 37°36N 140°4E **28 F10**
Bandān Iran 31°23N 60°44E **47 D9**
Bandanaira Indonesia 4°32S 129°54E **37 E7**
Bandanwara India 26°9N 74°38E **42 F6**
Bandar = Machilipatnam
  India 16°12N 81°8E **45 F5**
Bandar-e Abbās Iran 27°15N 56°15E **47 E8**
Bandar-e Anzalī Iran 37°30N 49°30E **47 B6**
Bandar-e Bushehr = Büshehr
  Iran 28°55N 50°55E **47 D6**
Bandar-e Chārak Iran 26°45N 54°20E **47 E7**
Bandar-e Deylam Iran 30°5N 50°10E **47 D6**
Bandar-e Emām Khomeynī
  Iran 30°30N 49°5E **47 D6**
Bandar-e Lengeh Iran 26°35N 54°58E **47 E7**
Bandar-e Maqām Iran 26°56N 53°29E **47 E7**
Bandar-e Ma'shur Iran 30°35N 49°10E **47 D6**
Bandar-e Rīg Iran 29°29N 50°38E **47 D6**
Bandar-e Torkeman Iran 37°0N 54°10E **47 B7**
Bandar Labuan Malaysia 5°20N 115°14E **36 C5**
Bandar Lampung
  Indonesia 5°20S 105°10E **36 F3**
Bandar Maharani = Muar
  Malaysia 2°3N 102°34E **39 L4**
Bandar Penggaram = Batu Pahat
  Malaysia 1°50N 102°56E **39 M4**
Bandar Seri Begawan
  Brunei 4°52N 115°0E **36 D5**
Bandar Shahid Rajaee Iran 27°7N 56°4E **47 E8**
Bandar Sri Aman
  Malaysia 1°15N 111°32E **36 D4**
Bandeira, Pico da Brazil 20°26S 41°47W **95 A7**
Bandera Argentina 28°55S 62°20W **94 B3**
Banderas, B. de Mexico 20°40N 105°25W **86 C3**
Bandhavgarh India 23°45N 81°10E **44 C5**
Bandhavgarh △ India 23°45N 81°0E **44 C5**
Bandi → India 26°12N 75°47E **42 F6**
Bandia → India 19°2N 80°28E **44 E5**
Bandikui India 27°3N 76°34E **42 F7**
Bandipur → India 11°35N 76°34E **45 J3**
Bandırma Turkey 40°20N 28°0E **23 D13**
Bandjarmasin = Banjarmasin
  Indonesia 3°20S 114°35E **36 E4**
Bandon Ireland 51°44N 8°44W **10 E3**
Bandon → Ireland 51°43N 8°37W **10 E3**
Bandundu
  Dem. Rep. of the Congo 3°15S 17°22E **54 E3**
Bandung Indonesia 6°54S 107°36E **37 G12**
Bāneh Iran 35°59N 45°53E **46 C5**
Banes Cuba 21°0N 75°42W **89 B4**
Banff Canada 51°10N 115°34W **70 C5**
Banff U.K. 57°40N 2°33W **11 D6**
Banff △ Canada 51°30N 116°15W **70 C5**
Bang Fai → Laos 16°57N 104°45E **38 D5**
Bang Hieng → Laos 16°10N 105°10E **38 D5**
Bang Krathum Thailand 16°34N 100°18E **38 D3**
Bang Lang △ Thailand 5°58N 101°9E **39 J3**
Bang Lang Res. Thailand 6°6N 101°17E **39 J3**
Bang Mun Nak Thailand 16°2N 100°23E **38 D3**
Bang Pa In Thailand 14°14N 100°35E **38 E3**
Bang Rakam Thailand 16°45N 100°7E **38 D3**
Bang Saphan Thailand 11°14N 99°28E **39 G2**
Bang Thao Thailand 7°59N 98°18E **39 a**
Banganapalle India 15°19N 78°14E **45 G4**

Banganga → India 27°6N 77°25E **42 F6**
Bangaon India 23°0N 88°47E **43 H13**
Bangassou C.A.R. 4°55N 23°7E **54 D4**
Banggai Indonesia 1°34S 123°30E **37 E6**
Banggai, Kepulauan
  Indonesia 1°40S 123°30E **37 E6**
Banggai Arch. = Banggai,
  Kepulauan Indonesia 1°40S 123°30E **37 E6**
Banggi, Pulau Malaysia 7°17N 117°12E **36 C5**
Banghāzī Libya 32°11N 20°3E **53 B10**
Bangka Sulawesi, Indonesia 1°50N 125°5E **37 D7**
Bangka Sumatera, Indonesia 2°0S 105°50E **36 E3**
Bangka, Selat Indonesia 2°30S 105°30E **36 E3**
Bangka-Belitung □
  Indonesia 2°30S 107°0E **36 E3**
Bangkalan Indonesia 7°2S 112°46E **37 G15**
Bangkang Myanmar 22°4N 99°1E **34 F2**
Bangkinang Indonesia 0°18N 101°5E **36 D2**
Bangko Indonesia 2°5S 102°9E **36 E2**
Bangkok, Bight of
  Thailand 12°55N 100°30E **38 F3**
Bangla = Paschimbanga □
  India 23°0N 88°0E **43 H13**
Bangladesh ■ Asia 24°0N 90°0E **41 H17**
Bangli Indonesia 8°27S 115°21E **37 J18**
Bangong Co China 33°45N 78°43E **43 C8**
Bangor Down, U.K. 54°40N 5°40W **10 B6**
Bangor Gwynedd, U.K. 53°14N 4°8W **12 D3**
Bangor Maine, U.S.A. 44°48N 68°46W **81 C19**
Bangor Pa., U.S.A. 40°52N 75°13W **83 F9**
Bangued Phil. 17°40N 120°37E **37 A6**
Bangui C.A.R. 4°23N 18°35E **54 D3**
Bangweulu, L. Zambia 11°0S 30°0E **54 G6**
Banhine △ Mozam. 22°49S 32°55E **57 B5**
Bani Dom. Rep. 18°16N 70°22W **89 C5**
Banī Sa'd Iraq 33°34N 44°32E **46 C5**
Banihal Pass India 33°30N 75°12E **43 C6**
Bāniyās Syria 35°10N 36°0E **46 C3**
Banja Luka Bos.-H. 44°49N 17°11E **22 B7**
Banjar India 31°38N 77°21E **42 D7**
Banjar → India 22°36N 80°22E **43 H9**
Banjarmasin Indonesia 3°20S 114°35E **36 E4**
Banjul Gambia 13°28N 16°40W **52 F2**
Banka India 24°53N 86°55E **43 G12**
Bankipore India 25°35N 85°10E **41 G14**
Bankot India 17°58N 73°2E **44 F1**
Banks I. = Moa Australia 10°11S 142°16E **62 a**
Banks I. B.C., Canada 53°20N 130°0W **70 C3**
Banks I. N.W.T., Canada 73°15N 121°30W **68 C7**
Banks Pen. N.Z. 43°45S 173°15E **59 E4**
Banks Str. Australia 40°40S 148°10E **63 G4**
Bankura India 23°11N 87°18E **43 H12**
Banmankhi India 25°53N 87°11E **43 G12**
Bann → Armagh, U.K. 54°30N 6°31W **10 B5**
Bann → L'derry., U.K. 55°8N 6°41W **10 A5**
Bannang Sata Thailand 6°16N 101°16E **39 J3**
Banning U.S.A. 33°56N 116°53W **79 M10**
Bannockburn Canada 44°39N 77°33W **82 B7**
Bannockburn U.K. 56°5N 3°55W **11 E5**
Bannu Pakistan 33°0N 70°18E **40 C7**
Bano India 22°40N 84°55E **43 H11**
Bansagar Dam India 24°11N 81°17E **44 B5**
Bansgaon India 26°33N 83°21E **43 F10**
Banská Bystrica
  Slovakia 48°46N 19°14E **17 D10**
Banswara India 23°32N 74°24E **42 H6**
Bantaeng Indonesia 5°32S 119°56E **37 F5**
Banteay Prei Nokor
  Cambodia 11°56N 105°40E **39 G5**
Banten □ Indonesia 6°30S 106°0E **37 G11**
Bantry Ireland 51°41N 9°27W **10 E2**
Bantry B. Ireland 51°37N 9°44W **10 E2**
Bantva India 21°29N 70°12E **42 J4**
Bantval India 12°55N 75°0E **45 H2**
Banyak, Kepulauan
  Indonesia 2°10N 97°10E **36 D1**
Banyo Cameroon 6°52N 11°45E **54 C2**
Banyuwangi Indonesia 8°13S 114°21E **37 J17**
Banzare Coast Antarctica 68°0S 125°0E **5 C9**
Bao Lac Vietnam 22°57N 105°40E **38 A5**
Bao Loc Vietnam 11°32N 107°48E **39 G6**
Bao'an China 22°34N 113°52E **31 a**
Baocheng China 33°12N 106°56E **34 A6**
Baode China 39°1N 111°5E **32 E6**
Baodi China 39°38N 117°20E **33 E9**
Baoding China 38°50N 115°28E **32 E8**
Baoji China 34°20N 107°5E **32 G4**
Baojing China 28°45N 109°41E **34 C7**
Baokang China 31°54N 111°12E **35 B8**
Baoshan China 25°10N 99°5E **34 E2**
Baotou China 40°32N 110°2E **32 D6**
Baoxing China 30°24N 102°50E **34 B4**
Baoying China 33°17N 119°20E **33 H10**
Baoyou = Ledong China 18°41N 109°5E **38 C7**
Bap India 27°23N 72°18E **42 F5**
Bapatla India 15°55N 80°30E **45 G5**
Bapaume France 50°7N 2°50E **20 A5**
Ba'qübah Iraq 33°45N 44°50E **46 C5**
Baquedano Chile 23°20S 69°52W **94 A2**
Bar Montenegro 42°8N 19°6E **23 C8**
Bar Ukraine 49°4N 27°40E **17 D14**
Bar Bigha India 25°21N 85°47E **43 G11**
Bar Harbor U.S.A. 44°23N 68°13W **81 C19**
Bara India 25°16N 81°43E **43 G9**
Bara Banki India 26°55N 81°12E **43 F9**
Barabai Indonesia 2°32S 115°34E **36 E5**
Baraboo U.S.A. 43°28N 89°45W **80 D9**
Baracoa Cuba 20°20N 74°30W **89 B5**
Baradā → Syria 33°33N 36°34E **48 B5**
Baradero Argentina 33°52S 59°29W **94 C4**
Baraga U.S.A. 46°47N 88°30W **80 B9**
Barah → India 27°42N 77°5E **42 F6**
Barahona Dom. Rep. 18°13N 71°7W **89 C5**
Barail Range India 25°15N 93°20E **41 G18**
Barakaldo Spain 43°18N 2°59W **21 A4**
Barakar → India 24°7N 86°14E **43 G12**
Barakot India 21°33N 84°59E **43 J11**
Baralaba Australia 24°13S 149°50E **62 C4**

Baralzon L. Canada 60°0N 98°3W **71 B9**
Baramati India 18°11N 74°33E **44 E2**
Baramba India 20°25N 85°23E **44 D7**
Baramula India 34°15N 74°20E **43 B6**
Baran India 25°9N 76°40E **42 G7**
Baran → Pakistan 25°13N 68°17E **42 G3**
Baranavichy Belarus 53°10N 26°0E **17 B14**
Baranof U.S.A. 57°5N 134°50W **70 B2**
Baranof I. U.S.A. 57°0N 135°0W **68 F4**
Barapasi Indonesia 2°15S 137°5E **37 E9**
Barasat India 22°46N 88°31E **43 H13**
Barat Daya, Kepulauan
  Indonesia 7°30S 128°0E **37 F7**
Baratang I. India 12°13N 92°45E **45 H11**
Barataria B. U.S.A. 29°20N 89°55W **85 G10**
Barauda India 23°33N 75°15E **42 H6**
Baraut India 29°13N 77°7E **42 E7**
Barbacena Brazil 21°15S 43°56W **95 A7**
Barbados ■ W. Indies 13°10N 59°30W **89 g**
Barbas, C. W. Sahara 22°20N 16°42W **52 D2**
Barbastro Spain 42°2N 0°5E **21 A6**
Barbeau Pk. Canada 81°54N 75°1W **69 A16**
Barberton S. Africa 25°42S 31°2E **57 C5**
Barberton U.S.A. 41°1N 81°39W **82 E3**
Barbosa Colombia 5°57N 73°37W **92 B4**
Barbourville U.S.A. 36°52N 83°53W **81 G12**
Barbuda W. Indies 17°30N 61°40W **89 C7**
Barcaldine Australia 23°43S 145°6E **62 C4**
Barcellona Pozzo di Gotto
  Italy 38°9N 15°13E **22 E6**
Barcelona Venezuela 10°10N 64°40W **92 A6**
Barceloneta Puerto Rico 18°27N 66°32W **89 d**
Barcelos Brazil 1°0S 63°0W **92 D6**
Barcoo → Australia 25°30S 142°50E **62 D3**
Bardaï Chad 21°25N 17°0E **53 D9**
Bardas Blancas Argentina 35°49S 69°45W **94 D2**
Bardawīl, Sabkhet el
  Egypt 31°10N 33°15E **48 D2**
Barddhaman India 23°14N 87°39E **43 H12**
Bardejov Slovakia 49°18N 21°15E **17 D11**
Bardera = Baardheere
  Somalia 2°20N 42°27E **49 G3**
Bardīyah Libya 31°45N 25°5E **53 B10**
Bardoli India 21°12N 73°5E **44 D1**
Bardsey I. U.K. 52°45N 4°47E **12 E3**
Bardstown U.S.A. 37°49N 85°28W **81 G11**
Bareilly India 28°22N 79°27E **43 E8**
Barela India 23°6N 80°3E **43 H9**
Barents Sea Arctic 73°0N 39°0E **4 B9**
Barfleur, Pte. de France 49°42N 1°16W **20 B3**
Bargara Australia 24°50S 152°25E **62 C5**
Bargarh India 21°20N 83°37E **44 D6**
Bargi Dam India 22°59N 80°0E **43 H8**
Barguzin Russia 53°37N 109°37E **27 D11**
Barh India 25°29N 85°46E **43 G11**
Barhaj India 26°18N 83°44E **43 F10**
Barharwa India 24°52N 87°47E **43 G12**
Barhi India 24°15N 85°25E **43 G11**
Bari India 26°39N 77°39E **42 F7**
Bari Italy 41°8N 16°51E **22 D7**
Bari Doab Pakistan 30°20N 73°0E **42 D5**
Bari Sadri India 24°28N 74°30E **42 G6**
Barīdī, Ra's Si. Arabia 24°17N 37°31E **46 E3**
Barīm Yemen 12°39N 43°25E **50 E8**
Barinas Venezuela 8°36N 70°15W **92 B4**
Baring, C. Canada 70°0N 117°30W **68 D8**
Baripada India 21°15N 86°45E **44 D8**
Barisal Bangla. 22°45N 90°20E **41 H17**
Barisal □ Bangla. 22°45N 90°20E **41 H17**
Barisan, Pegunungan
  Indonesia 3°30S 102°15E **36 E2**
Barito → Indonesia 4°0S 114°50E **36 E4**
Baritú △ Argentina 23°43S 64°40W **94 A3**
Barjüj, Wadi → Libya 25°26N 12°12E **53 C8**
Bark L. Canada 45°27N 77°51W **82 A7**
Barkakana India 23°37N 85°29E **43 H11**
Barkam China 31°51N 102°28E **34 B4**
Barker U.S.A. 43°20N 78°33W **82 C6**
Barkley, L. U.S.A. 37°1N 88°14W **85 C10**
Barkley Sound Canada 48°50N 125°10W **70 D3**
Barkly East S. Africa 30°58S 27°33E **56 E4**
Barkly Homestead
  Australia 19°52S 135°50E **62 B2**
Barkly Tableland
  Australia 17°50S 136°40E **62 B2**
Barkly West S. Africa 28°5S 24°31E **56 D3**
Barkol Kazak Zizhixian
  China 43°37N 93°2E **30 C7**
Bârlad Romania 46°15N 27°38E **17 E14**
Bârlad → Romania 45°38N 27°32E **17 F14**
Barlee, L. Australia 29°15S 119°30E **61 E2**
Barlee, Mt. Australia 24°38S 128°13E **61 D4**
Barletta Italy 41°19N 16°17E **22 D7**
Barlovento Cabo Verde 17°0N 25°0W **52 b**
Barlow L. Canada 62°0N 103°0W **71 A8**
Barmedman Australia 34°9S 147°21E **63 E4**
Barmer India 25°45N 71°20E **42 G4**
Barmera Australia 34°15S 140°28E **63 E3**
Barmouth U.K. 52°44N 4°4W **12 E3**
Barna → India 25°21N 83°3E **43 G10**
Barnagar India 23°7N 75°19E **42 H6**
Barnala India 30°23N 75°33E **42 D6**
Barnard Castle U.K. 54°33N 1°55W **12 C6**
Barnaul Russia 53°20N 83°40E **26 D9**
Barnesville Ga., U.S.A. 33°3N 84°9W **85 E12**
Barnesville Minn., U.S.A. 46°43N 96°28W **80 B5**
Barnet □ U.K. 51°38N 0°9W **13 F7**
Barneveld Neths. 52°7N 5°36E **15 B5**
Barnhart U.S.A. 31°8N 101°10W **84 F4**
Barnsley U.K. 53°34N 1°27W **12 D6**
Barnstable U.S.A. 41°42N 70°18W **81 E18**
Barnstaple U.K. 51°5N 4°4W **13 F3**
Barnstaple Bay = Bideford Bay
  U.K. 51°5N 4°20W **13 F3**
Barnwell U.S.A. 33°15N 81°23W **85 E14**
Baro Nigeria 8°35N 6°18E **52 G7**
Baro → Ethiopia 8°26N 33°13E **53 G12**
Baroda = Vadodara India 22°20N 73°10E **42 H5**
Baroda India 25°29N 76°35E **42 G7**
Baroe S. Africa 33°13S 24°33E **56 D3**
Baron Ra. Australia 23°30S 127°45E **60 D4**

Barong *China* 31°3N 99°20E **34** B2
Barotseland *Zambia* 15°0S 24°0E **55** H4
Barpali *India* 21°11N 83°35E **44** D6
Barpeta *India* 26°20N 91°10E **41** F17
Barqa *Libya* 27°0N 23°0E **53** C10
Barques, Pt. Aux *U.S.A.* 44°4N 82°58W **82** B2
Barquísimeto *Venezuela* 10°4N 69°19W **92** A5
Barr Smith Range
  *Australia* 27°4S 120°20E **61** E3
Barra *Brazil* 11°5S 43°10W **93** F10
Barra, Pta. *Mozam.* 57°0N 7°29W **11** E1
Barra, Sd. of *U.K.* 23°48S 35°32E **57** B6
Barra de Navidad 57°4N 7°25W **11** D1
  *Mexico* 19°12N 104°41W **86** D4
Barra do Corda *Brazil* 5°30S 45°10W **93** E9
Barra do Garças *Brazil* 15°54S 52°16W **93** G8
Barra do Pirai *Brazil* 22°30S 43°50W **95** A7
Barra Falsa, Pta. da
  *Mozam.* 22°58S 35°37E **57** B6
Barra Hd. *U.K.* 56°47N 7°40W **11** E1
Barra Mansa *Brazil* 22°35S 44°12W **95** A7
Barraba *Australia* 30°21S 150°35E **63** E5
Barranca *Lima, Peru* 10°45S 77°50W **92** F3
Barranca *Loreto, Peru* 4°50S 76°50W **92** D3
Barranca del Cobre △
  *Mexico* 27°18N 107°40W **86** B3
Barrancabermeja *Colombia* 7°0N 73°50W **92** B4
Barrancas *Venezuela* 8°55N 62°5W **92** B6
Barrancos *Portugal* 38°10N 6°58W **21** C2
Barranqueras *Argentina* 27°30S 59°0W **94** B4
Barranquilla *Colombia* 11°0N 74°50W **92** A4
Barraute *Canada* 48°26N 77°38W **72** C4
Barre, Mass., *U.S.A.* 42°25N 72°6W **83** D12
Barre *Vt., U.S.A.* 44°12N 72°30W **83** B12
Barreal *Argentina* 31°33S 69°28W **94** C2
Barreiras *Brazil* 12°8S 45°0W **93** F10
Barreirinhas *Brazil* 2°30S 42°50W **93** D10
Barren, Nosy *Madag.* 18°25S 43°40E **55** H8
Barren I. *India* 12°16N 93°51E **45** H11
Barretos *Brazil* 20°30S 48°35W **93** H9
Barrhead *Canada* 54°10N 114°24W **70** C6
Barrie *Canada* 44°24N 79°40W **82** B5
Barrier Ra. *Australia* 31°0S 141°30E **63** E3
Barrière *Canada* 51°12N 120°7W **70** C4
Barrington *U.S.A.* 41°44N 71°18W **83** E13
Barrington L. *Canada* 56°55N 100°15W **71** B8
Barrington Tops *Australia* 32°6S 151°28E **63** E5
Barringun *Australia* 29°1S 145°41E **63** D4
Barron *U.S.A.* 45°24N 91°51W **80** C8
Barrow *Ireland* 52°25N 6°58W **10** D5
Barrow, Pt. *U.S.A.* 71°23N 156°29W **74** A4
Barrow Creek *Australia* 21°30S 133°55E **62** C1
Barrow I. *Australia* 20°45S 115°20E **60** D2
Barrow-in-Furness *U.K.* 54°7N 3°14W **12** C4
Barrow Pt. *Australia* 14°20S 144°40E **62** A3
Barrow Ra. *Australia* 26°0S 127°40E **61** E4
Barrow Str. *Canada* 74°20N 95°0W **69** C13
Barry *U.K.* 51°24N 3°16W **13** F4
Barry's Bay *Canada* 45°29N 77°41W **82** A7
Barsat *Pakistan* 36°10N 72°45E **43** A5
Barsi *India* 18°10N 75°50E **44** E2
Barsoi *India* 25°48N 87°57E **41** G15
Barstow *U.S.A.* 34°54N 117°1W **79** L9
Bartica *Guyana* 6°25N 58°40W **92** B7
Bartle Frere *Australia* 17°27S 145°50E **62** B4
Bartlesville *U.S.A.* 36°45N 95°59W **84** C7
Bartlett, Calif., *U.S.A.* 36°29N 118°2W **78** J8
Bartlett *Tenn., U.S.A.* 35°12N 89°52W **85** D10
Bartlett, L. *Canada* 63°5N 118°20W **70** A5
Barton *U.S.A.* 44°45N 72°11W **83** B12
Barton-upon-Humber
  *U.K.* 53°41N 0°25W **12** D7
Bartow *U.S.A.* 27°54N 81°50W **85** H14
Barú, Volcan *Panama* 8°55N 82°35W **88** E3
Barung, Nusa *Indonesia* 8°30S 113°30E **37** H15
Baruunsuu *Mongolia* 43°43N 105°35E **32** C3
Barwani *India* 22°2N 74°57E **42** H6
Barysaw *Belarus* 54°17N 28°28E **17** A15
Barzán *Iraq* 36°55N 44°3E **46** B5
Bāsa'idū *Iran* 26°35N 55°20E **47** E7
Basal *Pakistan* 33°33N 72°13E **42** C5
Basankusu
  *Dem. Rep. of the Congo* 1°5N 19°50E **54** D3
Basarabeasca *Moldova* 46°21N 28°58E **17** E15
Basarabia = Bessarabiya
  *Moldova* 47°0N 28°10E **17** E15
Basavakalyan *India* 17°52N 76°57E **44** F3
Basawa *Afghan.* 34°15N 70°50E **42** B4
Bascuñán, C. *Chile* 28°52S 71°35W **94** B1
Basel *Switz.* 47°35N 7°35E **20** C7
Bashākerd, Kūhhā-ye
  *Iran* 26°42N 58°35E **47** E8
Bashaw *Canada* 52°35N 112°58W **70** C6
Bāshī *Iran* 28°41N 51°4E **47** D6
Bashkir Republic =
  Bashkortostan □
  *Russia* 54°0N 57°0E **18** D10
Bashkortostan □ *Russia* 54°0N 57°0E **18** D10
Basilan *Phil.* 6°35N 122°0E **37** C6
Basilan Str. *Phil.* 6°50N 122°0E **37** C6
Basildon *U.K.* 51°34N 0°28E **13** F8
Basim = Washim *India* 20°3N 77°0E **44** D3
Basin *U.S.A.* 44°23N 108°2W **76** D9
Basingstoke *U.K.* 51°15N 1°5W **13** F6
Baskatong, Rés. *Canada* 46°46N 75°50W **72** C4
Basle = Basel *Switz.* 47°35N 7°35E **20** C7
Basmat *India* 19°15N 77°12E **44** E3
Basoda *India* 23°52N 77°54E **42** H7
Basque Provinces = País Vasco □
  *Spain* 42°50N 2°45W **21** A4
Basra = Al Başrah *Iraq* 30°30N 47°50E **46** D5
Bass Str. *Australia* 39°15S 146°30E **63** F4
Bassano *Canada* 50°48N 112°20W **70** C6
Bassano del Grappa *Italy* 45°46N 11°44E **22** B4
Bassas da India *Ind. Oc.* 22°0S 39°0E **57** B6
Basse-Pointe *Martinique* 14°52N 61°8W **88** c
Basse-Terre *Guadeloupe* 16°0N 61°44W **88** b

Basse Terre *Trin. & Tob.* 10°7N 61°19W **93** K15
Bassein = Pathein
  *Myanmar* 16°45N 94°30E **41** L19
Basses, Pte. des *Guadeloupe* 15°52N 61°17W **88** b
Basseterre
  *St. Kitts & Nevis* 17°17N 62°43W **89** C7
Bassett *U.S.A.* 42°35N 99°32W **80** D4
Bassi *India* 30°44N 76°21E **42** D7
Bassett *U.S.A.* 42°35N 99°32W **80** D4
Bastak *Iran* 27°15N 54°25E **47** E7
Baştām *Iran* 36°29N 55°4E **47** B7
Bastar *India* 19°15N 81°40E **44** E5
Basti *India* 26°52N 82°55E **43** F10
Bastia *France* 42°40N 9°30E **20** E8
Bastogne *Belgium* 50°1N 5°43E **15** D5
Bastrop *La., U.S.A.* 32°47N 91°55W **84** E9
Bastrop *Tex., U.S.A.* 30°7N 97°19W **84** F6
Basuo = Dongfang
  *China* 18°50N 108°33E **38** C7
Bat Yam *Israel* 32°2N 34°44E **48** C3
Bata *Eq. Guin.* 1°57N 9°50E **54** D1
Bataan □ *Phil.* 14°40N 120°25E **37** B6
Batabanó *Cuba* 22°41N 82°18W **88** B3
Batabanó, G. de *Cuba* 22°30N 82°30W **88** B3
Batac *Phil.* 18°3N 120°34E **37** A6
Batagai *Russia* 67°38N 134°38E **27** C14
Batala *India* 31°48N 75°12E **42** D6
Batam *Indonesia* 1°10N 104°2E **39** d
Batamay *Russia* 63°30N 129°15E **27** C13
Batang *China* 30°1N 99°0E **34** B2
Batang *Indonesia* 6°55S 109°45E **37** G13
Batangafo *C.A.R.* 7°25N 18°20E **54** C3
Batangas *Phil.* 13°35N 121°10E **37** B6
Batanta *Indonesia* 0°55S 130°40E **37** E8
Batatais *Brazil* 20°54S 47°37W **95** A6
Batavia *U.S.A.* 43°0N 78°11W **82** D6
Batchelor *Australia* 13°4S 131°1E **60** B5
Batdambang *Cambodia* 13°7N 103°12E **38** F4
Batemans B. *Australia* 35°40S 150°12E **63** F5
Batemans Bay *Australia* 35°44S 150°11E **63** F5
Batesburg-Leesville
  *U.S.A.* 33°54N 81°33W **85** E14
Batesville *Ark., U.S.A.* 35°46N 91°39W **84** D9
Batesville *Miss., U.S.A.* 34°19N 89°57W **85** D10
Batesville *Tex., U.S.A.* 28°58N 99°37W **84** G5
Bath *Canada* 44°11N 76°47W **83** B8
Bath *Maine, U.S.A.* 43°55N 69°49W **81** D19
Bath *N.Y., U.S.A.* 42°20N 77°19W **82** D7
Bath & North East Somerset □
  *U.K.* 51°21N 2°27W **13** F5
Batheay *Cambodia* 11°59N 104°57E **39** G5
Bathsheba *Barbados* 13°13N 59°32W **89** g
Bathurst *Australia* 33°25S 149°31E **63** E4
Bathurst *Canada* 47°37N 65°43W **73** C6
Bathurst, C. *Canada* 70°34N 128°0W **68** C6
Bathurst B. *Australia* 14°16S 144°25E **62** A3
Bathurst Harb. *Australia* 43°15S 146°10E **63** G4
Bathurst I. *Australia* 11°30S 130°10E **60** B5
Bathurst I. *Canada* 76°0N 100°30W **69** B11
Bathurst Inlet *Canada* 66°50N 108°1W **68** D10
Batley *U.K.* 53°43N 1°38W **12** D6
Batlow *Australia* 35°31S 148°9E **63** F4
Batman *Turkey* 37°55N 41°5E **46** B4
Baţn al Ghūl *Jordan* 29°36N 35°56E **48** F4
Batna *Algeria* 35°34N 6°15E **52** A7
Baton Rouge *U.S.A.* 30°27N 91°11W **84** F9
Batong, Ko *Thailand* 6°32N 99°12E **39** J2
Batopilas *Mexico* 27°1N 107°44W **86** B3
Batouri *Cameroon* 4°30N 14°25E **54** D2
Båtsfjord *Norway* 70°38N 29°39E **8** A23
Battambang = Batdambang
  *Cambodia* 13°7N 103°12E **38** F4
Batti Malv *India* 8°50N 92°51E **45** K11
Batticaloa *Sri Lanka* 7°43N 81°45E **45** L5
Battipáglia *Italy* 40°37N 14°58E **22** D6
Battle *U.K.* 50°55N 0°30E **13** G8
Battle → *Canada* 52°43N 108°15W **71** C7
Battle Creek *U.S.A.* 42°19N 85°11W **81** D11
Battle Ground *U.S.A.* 45°47N 122°32W **78** E4
Battle Harbour *Canada* 52°16N 55°35W **73** B8
Battle Lake *U.S.A.* 46°17N 95°43W **80** B6
Battle Mountain *U.S.A.* 40°38N 116°56W **76** F5
Battleford *Canada* 52°45N 108°15W **71** C7
Batu *Ethiopia* 6°55N 39°45E **47** F2
Batu *Malaysia* 3°15N 101°40E **39** L3
Batu, Kepulauan *Indonesia* 0°30S 98°25E **36** E1
Batu Ferringhi *Malaysia* 5°28N 100°15E **39** c
Batu Gajah *Malaysia* 4°28N 101°3E **39** K3
Batu Is. = Batu, Kepulauan
  *Indonesia* 0°30S 98°25E **36** E1
Batu Pahat *Malaysia* 1°50N 102°56E **39** M4
Batu Puteh, Gunung
  *Malaysia* 4°15N 101°31E **39** K3
Batuata *Indonesia* 6°12S 122°42E **37** F6
Batugondang, Tanjung
  *Indonesia* 8°6S 114°29E **37** J17
Batukaru, Gunung
  *Indonesia* 8°20S 115°5E **37** J18
Batumi *Georgia* 41°39N 41°44E **19** F7
Batur, Gunung *Indonesia* 8°14S 115°23E **37** J18
Batura Sar *Pakistan* 36°30N 74°31E **43** A6
Baturaja *Indonesia* 4°11S 104°15E **36** E2
Baturité *Brazil* 4°28S 38°45W **93** D11
Baturiti *Indonesia* 8°19S 115°11E **37** J18
Bau *Malaysia* 1°25N 110°9E **36** D4
Baubau *Indonesia* 5°25S 122°38E **37** F6
Baucau *Timor-Leste* 8°27S 126°27E **37** F7
Bauchi *Nigeria* 10°22N 9°48E **52** F7
Bauda *India* 20°50N 84°25E **44** D7
Baudette *U.S.A.* 48°43N 94°36W **80** A6
Bauer, C. *Australia* 32°44S 134°4E **63** E1
Bauhinia *Australia* 24°35S 149°18E **62** C4
Baukau = Baucau
  *Timor-Leste* 8°27S 126°27E **37** F7
Bauld, C. *Canada* 51°38N 55°26W **69** G20
Bauru *Brazil* 22°10S 49°0W **95** A6
Bausi *India* 24°48N 87°1E **43** G12
Bauska *Latvia* 56°24N 24°15E **9** H21
Bautzen *Germany* 51°10N 14°26E **16** C8

Bavānāt *Iran* 30°28N 53°27E **47** D7
Bavaria = Bayern □
  *Germany* 48°50N 12°0E **16** D6
Bavispe → *Mexico* 29°15N 109°11W **86** B3
Bawdwin *Myanmar* 23°5N 97°20E **41** H20
Bawean *Indonesia* 5°46S 112°35E **36** F4
Bawku *Ghana* 11°3N 0°19W **52** F5
Bawlake *Myanmar* 19°11N 97°21E **41** K20
Bawolung *China* 28°50N 101°16E **34** C3
Baxley *U.S.A.* 31°47N 82°21W **85** F13
Baxter *U.S.A.* 46°21N 94°17W **80** B6
Baxter Springs *U.S.A.* 37°2N 94°44W **80** G6
Baxter State △ *U.S.A.* 46°5N 68°57W **81** B19
Bay City *Mich., U.S.A.* 43°36N 83°54W **81** D12
Bay City *Tex., U.S.A.* 28°59N 95°58W **84** G7
Bay Is. = Bahía, Is. de la
  *Honduras* 16°45N 86°15W **88** C2
Bay Minette *U.S.A.* 30°53N 87°46W **85** F11
Bay Roberts *Canada* 47°36N 53°16W **73** C9
Bay St. Louis *U.S.A.* 30°19N 89°20W **85** F10
Bay Springs *U.S.A.* 31°59N 89°17W **85** F10
Bay View *N.Z.* 39°25S 176°50E **59** C6
Bayamo *Cuba* 20°20N 76°40W **88** B4
Bayamón *Puerto Rico* 18°24N 66°9W **89** d
Bayan Har Shan *China* 34°0N 98°0E **30** E8
Bayan Hot = Alxa Zuoqi
  *China* 38°50N 105°40E **32** E3
Bayan Lepas *Malaysia* 5°17N 100°16E **39** c
Bayan Obo *China* 41°52N 109°59E **32** D5
Bayan-Ovoo = Erdenetsogt
  *Mongolia* 42°55N 106°5E **32** C4
Bayana *India* 26°55N 77°18E **42** F7
Bayanaŭyl *Kazakhstan* 50°45N 75°45E **26** D8
Bayanhongor *Mongolia* 46°8N 102°43E **30** B9
Bayard *N. Mex., U.S.A.* 32°46N 108°8W **77** K9
Bayard *Nebr., U.S.A.* 41°45N 103°20W **80** E2
Baybay *Phil.* 10°40N 124°55E **37** B6
Baydaratskaya Guba
  *Russia* 69°0N 67°30E **26** C7
Baydhabo *Somalia* 3°8N 43°30E **49** G3
Bayern □ *Germany* 48°50N 12°0E **16** D6
Bayeux *France* 49°17N 0°42W **20** B3
Bayfield *Canada* 43°34N 81°42W **82** C3
Bayfield *U.S.A.* 46°49N 90°49W **80** B8
Bayındır *Turkey* 38°13N 27°39E **23** E12
Baykal, Oz. *Russia* 53°0N 108°0E **27** D11
Baykan *Turkey* 38°7N 41°44E **46** B4
Baymak *Russia* 52°36N 58°19E **18** D10
Baynes Mts. *Namibia* 17°15S 13°0E **56** A1
Bayombong *Phil.* 16°30N 121°10E **37** A6
Bayonne *France* 43°30N 1°28W **20** E3
Bayovar *Peru* 5°50S 81°0W **92** E2
Bayqongyr *Kazakhstan* 45°40N 63°20E **26** E7
Bayram-Ali = Bayramaly
  *Turkmenistan* 37°37N 62°10E **47** B9
Bayramaly *Turkmenistan* 37°37N 62°10E **47** B9
Bayramiç *Turkey* 39°48N 26°36E **23** E12
Bayreuth *Germany* 49°56N 11°35E **16** D6
Bayrūt *Lebanon* 33°53N 35°31E **48** B4
Bays, L. of *Canada* 45°15N 79°4W **82** A5
Baysville *Canada* 45°9N 79°7W **82** A5
Baytown *U.S.A.* 29°43N 94°59W **84** G7
Bayquan *China* 40°16N 122°8E **33** D12
Baza *Spain* 37°30N 2°47W **21** D4
Bazaruto, I. do *Mozam.* 21°40S 35°28E **57** B6
Bazaruto △ *Mozam.* 21°42S 35°26E **57** B6
Bazhong *China* 31°52N 106°46E **34** B6
Bazhou *China* 39°8N 116°22E **32** E9
Bazmān, Kūh-e *Iran* 28°4N 60°1E **47** D9
Bé, Nosy *Madag.* 13°25S 48°15E **55** G9
Beach *U.S.A.* 46°58N 104°0W **80** B2
Beach City *U.S.A.* 40°39N 81°35W **82** F3
Beachport *Australia* 37°29S 140°0E **63** F3
Beachville *Canada* 43°5N 80°49W **82** C4
Beachy Hd. *U.K.* 50°44N 0°15E **13** G8
Beacon *Australia* 30°26S 117°52E **61** F2
Beacon *U.S.A.* 41°30N 73°58W **83** E11
Beaconsfield *Australia* 41°11S 146°48E **63** G4
Beagle, Canal *S. Amer.* 55°0S 68°30W **96** H3
Beagle Bay *Australia* 16°58S 122°40E **60** C3
Beagle Bay ○ *Australia* 16°53S 122°40E **60** C3
Beagle G. *Australia* 12°15S 130°25E **60** B5
Béal an Átha = Ballina
  *Ireland* 54°7N 9°9W **10** B2
Béal Átha na Sluaighe =
  Ballinasloe *Ireland* 53°20N 8°13W **10** C3
Beals Cr. → *U.S.A.* 32°10N 100°51W **84** E4
Beamsville *Canada* 43°12N 79°28W **82** C5
Bear → *Calif., U.S.A.* 38°56N 121°36W **78** G5
Bear → *Utah, U.S.A.* 41°30N 112°8W **74** G17
Bear I. = Bjørnøya *Arctic* 74°30N 19°0E **4** B8
Bear I. *Ireland* 51°38N 9°50W **10** E2
Bear L. *Canada* 55°8N 96°0W **71** B9
Bear L. *U.S.A.* 41°59N 111°21W **76** F8
Bear Lake *Canada* 45°27N 79°35W **82** A5
Beardmore *Canada* 49°36N 87°57W **72** C2
Beardmore Glacier
  *Antarctica* 84°30S 170°0E **5** E11
Beardstown *U.S.A.* 40°1N 90°26W **80** E8
Bearma → *India* 24°20N 79°51E **43** G8
Béarn *France* 43°20N 0°30W **20** E3
Bearpaw Mts. *U.S.A.* 48°12N 109°30W **76** B9
Bearskin Lake *Canada* 53°58N 91°2W **72** B1
Beas → *India* 31°10N 74°59E **42** D6
Beata, C. *Dom. Rep.* 17°40N 71°30W **89** C5
Beata, I. *Dom. Rep.* 17°34N 71°31W **89** C5
Beatrice *U.S.A.* 40°16N 96°45W **80** E6
Beatrice, C. *Australia* 14°20S 136°55E **62** A2
Beatton → *Canada* 56°15N 120°45W **70** B4
Beatton River *Canada* 57°26N 121°20W **70** B4
Beatty *U.S.A.* 36°54N 116°46W **78** J10
Beau Bassin *Mauritius* 20°13S 57°27E **55** d
Beauce, Plaine de la
  *France* 48°10N 1°45E **20** B4
Beauceville *Canada* 46°13N 70°46W **73** C5
Beaudesert *Australia* 27°59S 153°0E **63** D5
Beaufort *Malaysia* 5°30N 115°40E **36** C5
Beaufort *N.C., U.S.A.* 34°43N 76°40W **85** D16
Beaufort *S.C., U.S.A.* 32°26N 80°40W **85** E14
Beaufort Sea *Arctic* 72°0N 140°0W **66** B5

Beaufort West *S. Africa* 32°18S 22°36E **56** D3
Beauharnois *Canada* 45°20N 73°52W **83** A11
Beaulieu → *Canada* 62°3N 113°11W **70** A6
Beauly *U.K.* 57°30N 4°28W **11** D4
Beauly → *U.K.* 57°29N 4°27W **11** D4
Beaumaris *U.K.* 53°16N 4°6W **12** D3
Beaumont *Belgium* 50°15N 4°14E **15** D4
Beaumont *Calif., U.S.A.* 33°57N 116°59W **79** M9
Beaumont *Tex., U.S.A.* 30°5N 94°6W **84** F7
Beaune *France* 47°2N 4°50E **20** C6
Beaupré *Canada* 47°3N 70°54W **73** C5
Beauraing *Belgium* 50°7N 4°57E **15** D4
Beausejour *Canada* 50°5N 96°35W **71** C9
Beauvais *France* 49°25N 2°8E **20** B5
Beauval *Canada* 55°9N 107°37W **71** B7
Beaver *Okla., U.S.A.* 36°49N 100°31W **84** C4
Beaver *Pa., U.S.A.* 40°42N 80°19W **82** F4
Beaver *Utah, U.S.A.* 38°17N 112°38W **76** G7
Beaver → *B.C., Canada* 59°52N 124°20W **70** B4
Beaver → *Ont., Canada* 55°55N 87°48W **72** A2
Beaver → *Sask., Canada* 55°26N 107°45W **71** B7
Beaver → *U.S.A.* 36°35N 99°30W **84** C5
Beaver City *U.S.A.* 40°8N 99°50W **80** E4
Beaver Creek *Canada* 63°0N 141°0W **68** E3
Beaver Dam *U.S.A.* 43°28N 88°50W **80** D9
Beaver Falls *U.S.A.* 40°46N 80°20W **82** F4
Beaver Hill L. *Canada* 54°5N 94°50W **71** C10
Beaver I. *U.S.A.* 45°40N 85°33W **81** C11
Beavercreek *U.S.A.* 39°43N 84°11W **81** F11
Beaverhill L. *Canada* 53°27N 112°32W **70** C6
Beaverlodge *Canada* 55°11N 119°29W **70** B5
Beaverstone → *Canada* 54°59N 89°25W **72** B2
Beaverton *Canada* 44°26N 79°9W **82** B5
Beaverton *U.S.A.* 45°29N 122°48W **78** E4
Beawar *India* 26°3N 74°18E **42** F6
Bebedouro *Brazil* 21°0S 48°25W **95** A6
Bebera, Tanjung
  *Indonesia* 8°44S 115°51E **37** K18
Bebington *U.K.* 53°22N 3°0W **12** D4
Bécan *Mexico* 18°34N 89°31W **87** D7
Bécancour *Canada* 46°20N 72°26W **81** B17
Beccles *U.K.* 52°27N 1°35E **13** E9
Béchar *Algeria* 31°38N 2°18W **52** B5
Becharof L. *U.S.A.* 57°56N 156°23W **74** D8
Beckley *U.S.A.* 37°47N 81°11W **81** G13
Beddouza, C. *Morocco* 32°33N 9°9W **52** B4
Bedford *Canada* 45°7N 72°59W **83** A12
Bedford *S. Africa* 32°40S 26°10E **56** D4
Bedford *U.K.* 52°8N 0°28W **13** E7
Bedford *Ind., U.S.A.* 38°52N 86°29W **80** F10
Bedford *Iowa, U.S.A.* 40°40N 94°44W **80** E6
Bedford *Ohio, U.S.A.* 41°23N 81°32W **82** E3
Bedford *Pa., U.S.A.* 40°1N 78°30W **82** F6
Bedford *Va., U.S.A.* 37°20N 79°31W **81** G14
Bedford □ *U.K.* 52°4N 0°28W **13** E7
Bedford, C. *Australia* 15°14S 145°21E **62** B4
Bedourie *Australia* 24°30S 139°30E **62** C2
Bedti → *India* 14°50N 74°44E **45** M3
Bedugul *Indonesia* 8°17S 115°10E **37** J18
Bedum *Neths.* 53°18N 6°36E **15** A6
Beebe Plain *Canada* 45°1N 72°9W **83** A12
Beech Creek *U.S.A.* 41°5N 77°36W **82** E7
Beechy *Canada* 50°53N 107°24W **71** C7
Beed = Bir *India* 19°4N 75°46E **44** E2
Beef I. *Br. Virgin Is.* 18°26N 64°30W **89** e
Beenleigh *Australia* 27°43S 153°10E **63** D5
Be'er Sheva *Israel* 31°15N 34°48E **48** D3
Beersheba = Be'er Sheva
  *Israel* 31°15N 34°48E **48** D3
Beestekraal *S. Africa* 25°23S 27°38E **57** C4
Beeston *U.K.* 52°56N 1°14W **12** E6
Beeton *Canada* 44°5N 79°47W **82** B5
Beeville *U.S.A.* 28°24N 97°45W **84** G6
Befale
  *Dem. Rep. of the Congo* 0°25N 20°45E **54** D4
Bega *Australia* 36°41S 149°51E **63** F4
Begusarai *India* 25°24N 86°9E **43** G12
Behābād *Iran* 32°24N 59°47E **47** C8
Behbehān *Iran* 30°30N 50°15E **47** D6
Behchoko *Canada* 62°50N 116°3W **70** A5
Behm Canal *U.S.A.* 55°10N 131°0W **70** B2
Behshahr *Iran* 36°45N 53°35E **47** B7
Bei Jiang → *China* 23°2N 112°58E **35** F9
Bei Shan *China* 41°30N 96°0E **30** C8
Bei'an *China* 48°10N 126°20E **31** B14
Beibei *China* 29°47N 106°22E **34** C6
Beichuan *China* 31°55N 104°39E **34** B5
Beihai *China* 21°28N 109°6E **34** G7
Beijing *China* 39°55N 116°20E **32** E9
Beijing Capital Int. ✈ (PEK)
  *China* 40°5N 116°35E **32** D9
Beijing Shi □ *China* 39°55N 116°20E **32** E9
Beilen *Neths.* 52°52N 6°27E **15** B6
Beiliu *China* 22°41N 110°12E **35** F8
Beilpajah *Australia* 32°54S 143°52E **63** E3
Beinn na Faoghla = Benbecula
  *U.K.* 57°26N 7°21W **11** D1
Beipan Jiang → *China* 24°55N 106°5E **34** E6
Beipiao *China* 41°52N 120°32E **33** D11
Beira *Mozam.* 19°50S 34°52E **55** H6
Beirut = Bayrūt *Lebanon* 33°53N 35°31E **48** B4
Beiseker *Canada* 51°23N 113°32W **70** C6
Beit Lāhīyā *Gaza Strip* 31°33N 34°30E **48** D3
Beitaolaizhao *China* 44°58N 125°58E **33** B13
Beitbridge *Zimbabwe* 22°12S 30°0E **55** J6
Beizhen = Binzhou
  *China* 37°20N 118°2E **33** F10
Beizhen *China* 41°38N 121°54E **33** D11
Beizhengzhen *China* 44°31N 123°30E **33** B12
Beja *Portugal* 38°2N 7°53W **21** C2
Béja *Tunisia* 36°43N 9°12E **53** A7
Bejaïa *Algeria* 36°42N 5°2E **52** A7
Béjar *Spain* 40°23N 5°46W **21** B3
Bejestān *Iran* 34°30N 58°5E **47** C8
Bekaa Valley = Al Biqā
  *Lebanon* 34°10N 36°10E **48** A5
Bekasi *Indonesia* 6°14S 106°59E **37** G12
Békéscsaba *Hungary* 46°40N 21°5E **17** E11

Bekok *Malaysia* 2°20N 103°7E **39** L4
Bela *India* 25°50N 82°0E **43** G10
Bela *Pakistan* 26°12N 66°20E **42** F2
Bela Bela *S. Africa* 24°51S 28°19E **57** B4
Bela Crkva *Serbia* 44°55N 21°27E **23** B9
Bela Vista *Brazil* 22°12S 56°20W **94** A4
Bela Vista *Mozam.* 26°10S 32°44E **57** D5
Belagavi *India* 15°55N 74°35E **45** G2
Belan → *India* 24°2N 81°45E **43** G9
Belarus ■ *Europe* 53°30N 27°0E **17** B14
Belau = Palau ■ *Palau* 7°30N 134°30E **64** G5
Belawan *Indonesia* 3°33N 98°32E **36** D1
Belaya → *Russia* 54°40N 56°0E **18** C9
Belaya Tserkov = Bila Tserkva
  *Ukraine* 49°45N 30°10E **17** D16
Belaya Zemlya, Ostrova
  *Russia* 81°36N 62°18E **26** A7
Belcher Is. *Canada* 56°15N 78°45W **72** A3
Belden *U.S.A.* 40°2N 121°17W **78** E5
Belebey *Russia* 54°7N 54°7E **18** D9
Beledweyne *Somalia* 4°30N 45°5E **49** G4
Belém *Brazil* 1°20S 48°30W **93** D9
Belén *Argentina* 27°40S 67°5W **94** B2
Belén *Paraguay* 23°30S 57°6W **94** A4
Belen *U.S.A.* 34°40N 106°46W **77** J10
Belet Uen = Beledweyne
  *Somalia* 4°30N 45°5E **49** G4
Belev *Russia* 53°50N 36°5E **18** D6
Belfair *U.S.A.* 47°27N 122°50W **78** C4
Belfast = eMakhazeni
  *S. Africa* 25°42S 30°2E **57** C5
Belfast *U.K.* 54°37N 5°56W **10** B6
Belfast *Maine, U.S.A.* 44°26N 69°1W **81** C19
Belfast *N.Y., U.S.A.* 42°21N 78°7W **82** D6
Belfast, L. *U.K.* 54°40N 5°50W **10** B6
Belfield *U.S.A.* 46°53N 103°12W **80** B2
Belfort *France* 47°38N 6°50E **20** C7
Belfry *U.S.A.* 45°9N 109°1W **76** D9
Belgaum = Belagavi
  *India* 15°55N 74°35E **45** G2
Belgium ■ *Europe* 50°30N 5°0E **15** D4
Belgorod *Russia* 50°35N 36°35E **19** D6
Belgorod-Dnestrovskiy = Bilhorod-
  Dnistrovskyy *Ukraine* 46°11N 30°23E **19** E5
Belgrade = Beograd
  *Serbia* 44°50N 20°37E **23** B9
Belgrade *U.S.A.* 45°47N 111°11W **76** D8
Belgrano II *Antarctica* 77°52S 34°37W **5** D1
Belhaven *U.S.A.* 35°33N 76°37W **85** D16
Beli Drim → *Europe* 42°6N 20°25E **23** C9
Belimbing *Indonesia* 8°24S 115°2E **37** J18
Belinyu *Indonesia* 1°35S 105°50E **36** E3
Beliton Is. = Belitung
  *Indonesia* 3°10S 107°50E **36** E3
Belitung *Indonesia* 3°10S 107°50E **36** E3
Belize ■ *Cent. Amer.* 17°0N 88°30W **87** D7
Belize Barrier Reef *Belize* 17°9N 88°3W **87** D7
Belize City *Belize* 17°25N 88°10W **87** D7
Belkovskiy, Ostrov
  *Russia* 75°32N 135°44E **27** B14
Bell → *Canada* 49°48N 77°38W **72** C4
Bell I. *Canada* 50°46N 55°35W **73** B8
Bell-Irving → *Canada* 56°12N 129°5W **70** B3
Bell Peninsula *Canada* 63°50N 82°0W **69** E15
Bell Ville *Argentina* 32°40S 62°40W **94** C3
Bella Bella *Canada* 52°10N 128°10W **70** C3
Bella Coola *Canada* 52°25N 126°40W **70** C3
Bella Unión *Uruguay* 30°15S 57°40W **94** C4
Bella Vista *Corrientes,*
  *Argentina* 28°33S 59°0W **94** B4
Bella Vista *Tucuman,*
  *Argentina* 27°10S 65°25W **94** B2
Bella Vista *U.S.A.* 36°28N 94°16W **80** G6
Bellaire *U.S.A.* 40°1N 80°45W **82** F4
Bellata *Australia* 29°53S 149°46E **63** D4
Belle Fourche *U.S.A.* 44°40N 103°51W **80** C2
Belle Fourche → *U.S.A.* 44°26N 102°18W **80** C2
Belle Glade *U.S.A.* 26°41N 80°40W **85** H14
Belle-Île *France* 47°20N 3°10W **20** C2
Belle Isle *Canada* 51°57N 55°25W **73** B8
Belle Isle, Str. of *Canada* 51°30N 56°30W **73** B8
Belle Plaine *U.S.A.* 41°54N 92°17W **80** E7
Belle River *Canada* 42°18N 82°43W **82** D2
Bellefontaine *U.S.A.* 40°22N 83°46W **81** E12
Bellefonte *U.S.A.* 40°55N 77°47W **82** F7
Belleoram *Canada* 47°31N 55°25W **73** C8
Belleplaine *Barbados* 13°15N 59°34W **89** g
Belleville *Canada* 44°10N 77°23W **82** B7
Belleville *Ill., U.S.A.* 38°31N 89°59W **80** F9
Belleville *Kans., U.S.A.* 39°50N 97°38W **80** F5
Belleville *N.J., U.S.A.* 40°47N 74°9W **83** F10
Belleville *N.Y., U.S.A.* 43°46N 76°10W **83** C8
Bellevue *Idaho, U.S.A.* 43°28N 114°16W **76** E6
Bellevue *Nebr., U.S.A.* 41°9N 95°54W **80** E6
Bellevue *Ohio, U.S.A.* 41°17N 82°51W **82** E2
Bellevue *Wash., U.S.A.* 47°37N 122°12W **78** C4
Bellin = Kangirsuk
  *Canada* 60°0N 70°0W **69** F18
Bellingen *Australia* 30°25S 152°50E **63** E5
Bellingham *U.S.A.* 48°46N 122°29W **78** B4
Bellingshausen Abyssal Plain
  *S. Ocean* 64°0S 90°0W **5** C16
Bellingshausen Sea
  *Antarctica* 66°0S 80°0W **5** C17
Bellinzona *Switz.* 46°11N 9°1E **20** C8
Bello *Colombia* 6°20N 75°33W **92** B3
Bellows Falls *U.S.A.* 43°8N 72°27W **83** C12
Bellpat *Pakistan* 29°0N 68°5E **42** E3
Bellwood *U.S.A.* 40°36N 78°20W **82** F6
Belmont *Canada* 42°53N 81°5W **82** D3
Belmont *S. Africa* 29°28S 24°22E **56** D3
Belmont *U.S.A.* 42°14N 78°2W **82** D6
Belmonte *Brazil* 16°0S 39°0W **93** G11
Belmopan *Belize* 17°18N 88°30W **87** D7
Belmullet *Ireland* 54°14N 9°58W **10** B2
Belo Horizonte *Brazil* 19°55S 43°56W **93** G10
Belo-Tsiribihina *Madag.* 19°40S 44°30E **55** H8
Belogorsk *Russia* 51°0N 128°20E **27** D13
Beloit *Kans., U.S.A.* 39°28N 98°6W **80** F4

Beloit Wis., U.S.A. 42°31N 89°2W 80 D9
Belokorovichi Ukraine 51°7N 28°2E 17 C15
Belomorsk Russia 64°35N 34°54E 18 B5
Belonia India 23°15N 91°30E 41 H17
Beloretsk Russia 53°58N 58°24E 18 D10
Belorussia = Belarus ■
  Europe 53°30N 27°0E 17 B14
Belovo Russia 54°30N 86°0E 26 D9
Beloyarskiy Russia 63°42N 66°40E 26 C7
Beloye, Ozero Russia 60°10N 37°35E 18 B6
Beloye More Russia 66°30N 38°0E 18 A6
Belozersk Russia 60°1N 37°45E 18 B6
Belpre U.S.A. 39°17N 81°34W 81 F13
Belrain India 28°23N 80°55E 43 E9
Belt U.S.A. 47°23N 110°55W 76 C8
Beltana Australia 30°48S 138°25E 63 E2
Belterra Brazil 2°45S 55°0W 93 D8
Belton U.S.A. 31°3N 97°28W 84 F6
Belton L. U.S.A. 31°6N 97°28W 84 F6
Beltsy = Bălți Moldova 47°48N 27°58E 17 E14
Belturbet Ireland 54°6N 7°26W 10 B4
Belukha Russia 49°50N 86°50E 30 B6
Beluran Malaysia 5°48N 117°35E 36 C5
Belvidere Ill., U.S.A. 42°15N 88°50W 80 D9
Belvidere N.J., U.S.A. 40°50N 75°5W 83 F9
Belyando → Australia 21°38S 146°50E 62 C4
Belyando Crossing
  Australia 21°32S 146°51E 62 C4
Belyuen Australia 12°34S 130°42E 60 B5
Belyy, Ostrov Russia 73°30N 71°0E 26 B8
Belyy Yar Russia 58°26N 84°39E 26 D9
Belzoni U.S.A. 33°11N 90°29W 85 E9
Bembéréke Benin 10°11N 2°43E 52 F6
Bemetara India 21°42N 81°32E 43 J9
Bemidji U.S.A. 47°28N 94°53W 80 B6
Ben Iran 32°30N 50°45E 47 C6
Ben Cruachan U.K. 56°26N 5°8W 11 E3
Ben Dearg U.K. 57°47N 4°56W 11 D4
Ben En △ Vietnam 19°37N 105°30E 38 C5
Ben Gardane Tunisia 33°11N 11°11E 53 B8
Ben Hope U.K. 58°25N 4°36W 11 C4
Ben Lawers U.K. 56°32N 4°14W 11 E4
Ben Lomond N.S.W.,
  Australia 30°1S 151°43E 63 E5
Ben Lomond Tas.,
  Australia 41°38S 147°42E 63 G4
Ben Lomond U.K. 56°11N 4°38W 11 E4
Ben Lomond △ Australia 41°33S 147°39E 63 G4
Ben Luc Vietnam 10°39N 106°29E 39 G6
Ben Macdhui U.K. 57°4N 3°40W 11 D5
Ben Mhor U.K. 57°15N 7°18W 11 D1
Ben More Argyll & Bute,
  U.K. 56°26N 6°1W 11 E2
Ben More Stirling, U.K. 56°23N 4°32W 11 E4
Ben More Assynt U.K. 58°8N 4°52W 11 C4
Ben Nevis U.K. 56°48N 5°1W 11 E3
Ben Quang Vietnam 17°3N 106°55E 38 D6
Ben Tre Vietnam 10°14N 106°23E 39 G6
Ben Vorlich U.K. 56°21N 4°14W 11 E4
Ben Wyvis U.K. 57°40N 4°35W 11 D4
Bena Nigeria 11°20N 5°50E 52 F7
Benaco, L. di = Garda, L. di
  Italy 45°40N 10°41E 22 B4
Benalla Australia 36°30S 146°0E 63 F4
Benares = Varanasi India 25°22N 83°0E 43 G10
Benavente Spain 42°2N 5°43W 21 A3
Benavides U.S.A. 27°36N 98°25W 84 H5
Benbecula U.K. 57°26N 7°21W 11 D1
Benbonyathe Hill
  Australia 30°25S 139°11E 63 E2
Bend U.S.A. 44°4N 121°19W 76 D3
Bender Beyla Somalia 9°30N 50°48E 49 F5
Bendery Moldova 46°50N 29°30E 17 E15
Bendigo Australia 36°40S 144°15E 63 F3
Benê Beraq Israel 32°6N 34°51E 48 C3
Benevento Italy 41°8N 14°45E 22 D6
Beng Mealea Cambodia 13°28N 104°14E 38 F5
Bengal, Bay of Ind. Oc. 15°0N 90°0E 41 M17
Bengaluru India 12°59N 77°40E 45 H3
Bengbu China 32°58N 117°20E 33 H9
Benghazi = Banghāzī
  Libya 32°11N 20°3E 53 B10
Bengkalis Indonesia 1°30N 102°10E 39 M4
Bengkulu Indonesia 3°50S 102°12E 36 E2
Bengkulu □ Indonesia 3°48S 102°16E 36 E2
Bengough Canada 49°25N 105°10W 71 D7
Benguela Angola 12°37S 13°25E 55 G2
Benguérua, I. Mozam. 21°58S 35°28E 57 B6
Beni Dem. Rep. of the Congo 0°30N 29°27E 54 D5
Beni → Bolivia 10°23S 65°24W 92 F5
Beni Mellal Morocco 32°21N 6°21W 52 B4
Beni Suef Egypt 29°5N 31°6E 53 C12
Beniah L. Canada 63°23N 112°17W 70 A6
Benidorm Spain 38°33N 0°9W 21 C5
Benin ■ Africa 10°0N 2°0E 52 G6
Benin, Bight of W. Afr. 5°0N 3°0E 52 H6
Benin City Nigeria 6°20N 5°31E 52 G7
Benito Juárez Argentina 37°40S 59°43W 94 D4
Benjamin Aceval
  Paraguay 24°58S 57°34W 94 A4
Benjamin Constant Brazil 4°40S 70°15W 92 D4
Benjamin Hill Mexico 30°9N 111°7W 86 A2
Benkelman U.S.A. 40°3N 101°32W 80 E3
Bennett Canada 59°51N 135°0W 70 B2
Bennett, L. Australia 22°50S 131°2E 60 D5
Bennetta, Ostrov
  Russia 76°21N 148°56E 27 B15
Bennettsville U.S.A. 34°37N 79°41W 85 D15
Bennington N.H., U.S.A. 43°0N 71°55W 83 D11
Bennington Vt., U.S.A. 42°53N 73°12W 83 D11
Benom Malaysia 3°50N 102°6E 39 L4
Benoni S. Africa 26°11S 28°18E 57 C4
Benque Viejo del Carmen
  Belize 17°5N 89°8W 87 D7
Benson Ariz., U.S.A. 31°58N 110°18W 77 L8
Benson Minn., U.S.A. 45°19N 95°36W 80 C6
Bent Iran 26°20N 59°31E 47 E8
Benteng Indonesia 6°10S 120°30E 37 F6
Bentinck I. Australia 17°3S 139°35E 62 B2

Bentinck I. Myanmar 11°45N 98°3E 39 G2
Bentley Subglacial Trench
  Antarctica 80°0S 115°0W 5 E15
Bento Gonçalves Brazil 29°10S 51°31W 95 B5
Benton Ark., U.S.A. 34°34N 92°35W 84 D8
Benton Calif., U.S.A. 37°48N 118°32W 78 H8
Benton Ill., U.S.A. 38°0N 88°55W 80 F9
Benton Pa., U.S.A. 41°12N 76°23W 83 E8
Benton Harbor U.S.A. 42°6N 86°27W 80 D10
Bentong Malaysia 3°31N 101°55E 39 L3
Bentonville U.S.A. 36°22N 94°13W 84 C7
Benue → Nigeria 7°48N 6°46E 52 G7
Benxi China 41°20N 123°48E 33 D12
Beo Indonesia 4°25N 126°50E 37 D7
Beograd Serbia 44°50N 20°37E 23 B9
Beolgyo S. Korea 34°51N 127°21E 33 G14
Beppu Japan 33°15N 131°30E 29 H5
Beqa Fiji 18°23S 178°8E 59 a
Beqaa Valley = Al Biqā
  Lebanon 34°10N 36°10E 48 A5
Ber Mota India 23°27N 68°34E 42 H3
Bera, Tasik Malaysia 3°5N 102°38E 39 L4
Berach → India 25°15N 75°2E 42 G6
Berastagi Indonesia 3°11N 98°31E 39 L2
Berat Albania 40°43N 19°59E 23 D8
Berau = Tanjungredeb
  Indonesia 2°9N 117°29E 36 D5
Berau, Teluk Indonesia 2°30S 132°30E 37 E8
Berber Sudan 18°0N 34°0E 53 E12
Berbera Somalia 10°30N 45°2E 49 E4
Berbérati C.A.R. 4°15N 15°40E 54 D3
Berbice → Guyana 6°20N 57°32W 92 B7
Berdichev = Berdychiv
  Ukraine 49°57N 28°30E 17 D15
Berdsk Russia 54°47N 83°2E 26 D9
Berdyansk Ukraine 46°45N 36°50E 19 E6
Berdychiv Ukraine 49°57N 28°30E 17 D15
Berea U.S.A. 37°34N 84°17W 81 G11
Berebere Indonesia 2°25N 128°45E 37 D7
Bereeda Somalia 11°45N 51°0E 49 E5
Berehove Ukraine 48°15N 22°35E 17 D12
Bereket Turkmenistan 39°16N 55°32E 47 B7
Berekum Ghana 7°29N 2°34W 52 G5
Berens → Canada 52°25N 97°2W 71 C9
Berens I. Canada 52°18N 97°18W 71 C9
Berens River Canada 52°25N 97°0W 71 C9
Beresford Canada 43°5N 96°47W 80 D5
Berestechko Ukraine 50°22N 25°5E 17 C13
Bereza = Byaroza
  Belarus 52°31N 24°51E 17 B13
Berezhany Ukraine 49°26N 24°58E 17 D13
Berezina = Byarezina →
  Belarus 52°33N 30°14E 17 B16
Bereznik Russia 62°51N 42°40E 18 B7
Berezniki Russia 59°24N 56°46E 18 C10
Berezovo Russia 64°0N 65°0E 26 C7
Berga Spain 42°6N 1°48E 21 A6
Bergama Turkey 39°8N 27°11E 23 E12
Bérgamo Italy 45°41N 9°43E 20 D8
Bergaon India 20°41N 80°27E 44 D5
Bergen Neths. 52°40N 4°43E 15 B4
Bergen Norway 60°20N 5°20E 8 F11
Bergen U.S.A. 43°5N 77°57W 82 C7
Bergen op Zoom Neths. 51°28N 4°18E 15 C4
Bergerac France 44°51N 0°30E 20 D4
Bergholz U.S.A. 40°31N 80°53W 82 F4
Bergville S. Africa 28°52S 29°18E 57 C4
Berhala, Selat Indonesia 1°0S 104°15E 36 E2
Berhampore = Baharampur
  India 24°2N 88°27E 43 G13
Berhampur = Brahmapur
  India 19°15N 84°54E 44 E7
Bering Glacier U.S.A. 60°20N 143°30W 74 C11
Bering Sea Pac. Oc. 58°0N 171°0W 66 D2
Bering Strait Pac. Oc. 65°30N 169°0W 74 B6
Beringovskiy Russia 63°3N 179°19E 27 C18
Berisso Argentina 34°56S 57°50W 94 D4
Berja Spain 36°50N 2°56W 21 D4
Berkner I. Antarctica 79°30S 50°0W 5 D1
Berkshire U.S.A. 42°19N 76°11W 83 D8
Berkshire Downs U.K. 51°33N 1°29W 13 F6
Berlin Md., U.S.A. 38°20N 75°13W 81 F16
Berlin N.H., U.S.A. 44°28N 71°11W 83 B13
Berlin N.Y., U.S.A. 42°42N 73°23W 83 D11
Berlin Wis., U.S.A. 43°58N 88°57W 80 D9
Berlin L. U.S.A. 41°3N 81°0W 82 E4
Bermejo → Formosa,
  Argentina 26°51S 58°23W 94 B4
Bermejo → San Juan,
  Argentina 32°30S 67°30W 94 C2
Bermejo, Paso = Uspallata, P. de
  Argentina 32°37S 69°22W 94 C2
Bermen, L. Canada 53°35N 68°55W 73 B6
Bermuda ☑ Atl. Oc. 32°18N 64°45W 67 F13
Bernalillo U.S.A. 35°18N 106°33W 77 J10
Bernardo de Irigoyen
  Argentina 26°15S 53°40W 95 B5
Bernasconi Argentina 37°55S 63°44W 94 D3
Bernburg Germany 51°47N 11°44E 16 C6
Berne = Bern Switz. 46°57N 7°28E 20 C7
Berneray U.K. 57°43N 7°11W 11 D1
Bernier I. Australia 24°50S 113°12E 61 D1
Bernina, Piz Switz. 46°20N 9°54E 20 C8
Beroun Czechia 49°57N 14°5E 16 D8
Berri Australia 34°14S 140°35E 63 E3
Berriane Algeria 32°50N 3°46E 52 B6
Berry Australia 34°46S 150°43E 63 E5
Berry France 46°50N 2°0E 20 C5
Berry Is. Bahamas 25°40N 77°50W 88 A4
Berryessa, L. U.S.A. 38°31N 122°6W 78 G4
Berryville U.S.A. 36°22N 93°34W 84 C8
Berseba Namibia 26°0S 17°46E 56 C2
Bershad Ukraine 48°22N 29°31E 17 D15
Berthold U.S.A. 48°19N 101°44W 80 A3
Berthoud U.S.A. 40°19N 105°5W 76 F11
Bertoua Cameroon 4°30N 13°45E 54 D2
Bertraghboy B. Ireland 53°22N 9°54W 10 C2
Beruwala Sri Lanka 6°30N 80°0E 45 L4

Berwick U.S.A. 41°3N 76°14W 83 E8
Berwick-upon-Tweed U.K. 55°46N 2°0W 12 B6
Berwyn Mts. U.K. 52°54N 3°26W 12 E4
Besal Pakistan 35°4N 73°56E 43 B5
Besalampy Madag. 16°43S 44°29E 55 H8
Besançon France 47°15N 6°2E 20 C7
Besar Indonesia 2°40S 116°0E 36 E5
Besnard L. Canada 55°25N 106°0W 71 B7
Besni Turkey 37°41N 37°52E 46 B3
Besor, N. → Egypt 31°28N 34°22E 48 D3
Bessarabiya Moldova 47°0N 28°10E 17 E15
Bessarabka = Basarabeasca
  Moldova 46°21N 28°58E 17 E15
Bessemer Ala., U.S.A. 33°24N 86°58W 85 E11
Bessemer Mich., U.S.A. 46°29N 90°3W 80 B8
Bessemer Pa., U.S.A. 40°59N 80°30W 82 F4
Beswick Australia 14°34S 132°53E 60 B5
Beswick ◌ Australia 14°31S 132°51E 60 B5
Bet She'an Israel 32°30N 35°30E 48 C4
Bet Shemesh Israel 31°44N 35°0E 48 D4
Betanzos Spain 43°15N 8°12W 21 A1
Bétaré Oya Cameroon 5°40N 14°5E 54 C2
Bethal S. Africa 26°27S 29°28E 57 C4
Bethanien Namibia 26°31S 17°8E 56 C2
Bethany Canada 44°11N 78°34W 82 B6
Bethany Mo., U.S.A. 40°16N 94°2W 80 E6
Bethany Okla., U.S.A. 35°31N 97°38W 84 D6
Bethel Alaska, U.S.A. 60°48N 161°45W 74 C7
Bethel Conn., U.S.A. 41°22N 73°25W 83 E11
Bethel Maine, U.S.A. 44°25N 70°47W 83 B14
Bethel Vt., U.S.A. 43°50N 72°38W 83 C12
Bethel Park U.S.A. 40°19N 80°2W 82 F4
Bethlehem S. Africa 28°14S 28°18E 57 C4
Bethlehem U.S.A. 40°37N 75°23W 83 F9
Bethulie S. Africa 30°30S 25°59E 56 D4
Betioky Madag. 23°48S 44°20E 55 J8
Betong Malaysia 1°24N 111°31E 36 D4
Betong Thailand 5°45N 101°5E 39 K3
Betoota Australia 25°45S 140°42E 62 D3
Betpaqdala Kazakhstan 45°45N 70°30E 30 B3
Betroka Madag. 23°16S 46°0E 55 J9
Betsiamites Canada 48°56N 68°40W 73 C6
Betsiamites → Canada 48°56N 68°38W 73 C6
Bettendorf U.S.A. 41°32N 90°30W 80 E8
Bettiah India 26°48N 84°33E 43 F11
Betul India 21°58N 77°59E 44 D3
Betws-y-Coed U.K. 53°5N 3°48W 12 D4
Beulah Mich., U.S.A. 44°38N 86°6W 80 C10
Beulah N. Dak., U.S.A. 47°16N 101°47W 80 B3
Beveren Belgium 51°12N 4°16E 15 C4
Beverley Australia 32°9S 116°56E 61 F2
Beverley U.K. 53°51N 0°26W 12 D7
Beverly U.S.A. 42°33N 70°53W 83 D14
Beverly Hills U.S.A. 28°55N 82°28W 85 G13
Bewas → India 23°59N 79°21E 43 H8
Bewdley Canada 44°5N 78°19W 82 B6
Beyănlü Iran 36°0N 47°51E 46 C5
Beyneu Kazakhstan 45°18N 55°9E 19 E10
Beypazari Turkey 40°10N 31°56E 19 F5
Beypore → India 11°10N 75°47E 45 J2
Beyşehir Gölü Turkey 37°41N 31°33E 46 B1
Béziers France 43°20N 3°12E 20 E5
Bezwada = Vijayawada
  India 16°31N 80°39E 44 F5
Bhabua India 25°3N 83°37E 43 G10
Bhachau India 23°20N 70°16E 42 H4
Bhadar → Gujarat, India 22°17N 72°20E 42 H5
Bhadar → Gujarat, India 21°27N 69°47E 42 J3
Bhadarwah India 32°58N 75°46E 43 C6
Bhadgaon = Bhaktapur
  Nepal 27°38N 85°24E 43 F11
Bhadohi India 25°25N 82°34E 43 G10
Bhadra India 29°8N 75°14E 42 E6
Bhadra → India 14°0N 75°20E 45 H2
Bhadrachalam India 17°40N 80°53E 44 F5
Bhadrak India 21°10N 86°30E 44 D8
Bhadravati India 13°49N 75°40E 45 H2
Bhadran India 22°19N 72°6E 42 H5
Bhag Pakistan 29°2N 67°49E 42 E2
Bhagalpur India 25°10N 87°0E 43 G12
Bhagirathi → Paschimbanga,
  India 23°25N 88°23E 43 H13
Bhagirathi → Uttarakhand,
  India 30°8N 78°35E 43 D8
Bhainsa India 19°10N 77°58E 44 E3
Bhakkar Pakistan 31°40N 71°5E 42 D4
Bhakra Dam India 31°30N 76°45E 42 D7
Bhaktapur Nepal 27°38N 85°24E 43 F11
Bhalki India 18°2N 77°13E 44 E3
Bhamo Myanmar 24°15N 97°15E 41 G20
Bhamragarh India 19°30N 80°40E 44 E5
Bhandara India 21°5N 79°42E 44 D4
Bhanpura India 24°31N 75°44E 42 G6
Bhanrer Ra. India 23°40N 79°45E 43 H8
Bhaptiahi India 26°19N 86°44E 43 F12
Bharat = India ■ Asia 20°0N 78°0E 40 K11
Bharati Antarctica 69°24S 76°11E 5 C6
Bharatpur Chhattisgarh,
  India 23°44N 81°46E 43 H9
Bharatpur Raj., India 27°15N 77°30E 42 F7
Bharatpur Nepal 27°34N 84°10E 43 F11
Bharno India 23°14N 84°53E 43 H11
Bharraig = Barra U.K. 57°0N 7°29W 11 E1
Bharraig, Caolas = Barra, Sd. of
  U.K. 57°4N 7°25W 11 D1
Bharuch India 21°47N 73°0E 44 D1
Bhatarsaigh = Vatersay
  U.K. 56°55N 7°32W 11 E1
Bhatghar L. India 18°10N 73°48E 44 E1
Bhatinda India 30°15N 74°57E 42 D6
Bhatkal India 13°58N 74°35E 45 H2
Bhatpara India 22°50N 88°25E 43 H13
Bhattu India 29°36N 75°19E 42 E6
Bhaun Pakistan 32°55N 72°40E 42 C5
Bhaunagar = Bhavnagar
  India 21°45N 72°10E 44 D1
Bhavani India 11°27N 77°43E 45 J3
Bhavani → India 11°0N 78°15E 45 J3
Bhavnagar India 21°45N 72°10E 44 D1

Bhawanipatna India 19°55N 83°10E 44 E5
Bhawari India 25°42N 73°4E 42 G5
Bhayavadar India 21°51N 70°15E 42 J4
Bhearnaraigh = Berneray
  U.K. 57°43N 7°11W 11 D1
Bhera Pakistan 32°29N 72°57E 42 C5
Bheri → Nepal 28°47N 81°18E 43 E9
Bhikangaon India 21°52N 75°57E 42 J6
Bhilai = Bhilainagar-Durg
  India 21°13N 81°26E 44 D5
Bhilainagar-Durg India 21°13N 81°26E 44 D5
Bhilsa = Vidisha India 23°28N 77°53E 42 H7
Bhilwara India 25°25N 74°38E 42 G6
Bhima → India 16°25N 77°17E 44 F3
Bhimavaram India 16°30N 81°30E 45 F5
Bhimbar Pakistan 32°59N 74°3E 43 C6
Bhind India 26°30N 78°46E 43 F8
Bhinga India 27°43N 81°56E 43 F9
Bhinmal India 25°0N 72°15E 42 G5
Bhisho S. Africa 32°50S 27°23E 56 D4
Bhiwandi India 19°20N 73°0E 44 E1
Bhiwani India 28°50N 76°9E 42 E7
Bhogava → India 22°26N 72°20E 42 H5
Bhojpur Nepal 27°10N 87°3E 43 F12
Bhokardan India 20°16N 75°46E 44 D2
Bhola Bangla. 22°45N 90°35E 41 H17
Bholari Pakistan 25°19N 68°13E 42 G3
Bhongir India 17°30N 78°56E 44 F4
Bhopal India 23°20N 77°30E 42 H7
Bhopalpatnam India 18°52N 80°23E 44 E5
Bhor India 18°12N 73°53E 44 E1
Bhuban India 20°53N 85°50E 44 D7
Bhubaneshwar India 20°15N 85°50E 44 D7
Bhuj India 23°15N 69°49E 42 H3
Bhumiphol Res. Thailand 17°20N 98°40E 38 D2
Bhusawal India 21°3N 75°46E 44 D2
Bhutan ■ Asia 27°25N 90°30E 41 F17
Biafra, B. of = Bonny, Bight of
  Africa 3°30N 9°20E 54 D1
Biak Indonesia 1°10S 136°6E 37 E9
Biala Podlaska Poland 52°4N 23°6E 17 B12
Białogard Poland 54°2N 15°58E 16 A8
Biaora India 23°56N 76°56E 42 H7
Biārjmand Iran 36°6N 55°53E 47 B7
Biaro Indonesia 2°5N 125°26E 37 D7
Biarritz France 43°29N 1°33W 20 E3
Bibai Japan 43°19N 141°52E 28 C10
Bibby I. Canada 61°55N 93°0W 71 A10
Biberach Germany 48°5N 9°47E 16 D5
Bibile Sri Lanka 7°10N 81°25E 45 L5
Bicester U.K. 51°54N 1°9W 13 F6
Bicheno Australia 41°52S 148°18E 63 G4
Bichia India 22°27N 80°42E 43 H9
Bickerton I. Australia 13°45S 136°10E 62 A2
Bid = Bir India 19°4N 75°46E 44 E2
Bida Nigeria 9°3N 5°58E 52 G7
Bidar India 17°55N 77°35E 44 F3
Biddeford U.S.A. 43°30N 70°28W 81 D18
Bideford U.K. 51°1N 4°13W 13 F3
Bideford Bay U.K. 51°5N 4°20W 13 F3
Bidhuna India 26°49N 79°31E 43 F8
Bidokht Iran 34°20N 58°46E 47 C8
Bidor Malaysia 4°6N 101°15E 39 K3
Bidyadanga Australia 18°45S 121°43E 60 C3
Bié, Planalto de Angola 12°0S 16°0E 55 G3
Bieber U.S.A. 41°7N 121°8W 76 F3
Biel Switz. 47°8N 7°14E 20 C7
Bielefeld Germany 52°1N 8°33E 16 B5
Biella Italy 45°34N 8°3E 20 D8
Bielsk Podlaski Poland 52°47N 23°12E 17 B12
Bielsko-Biala Poland 49°50N 19°2E 17 D10
Bien Hoa Vietnam 10°57N 106°49E 39 G6
Bienne = Biel Switz. 47°8N 7°14E 20 C7
Bienville, L. Canada 55°5N 72°40W 72 A5
Biesbosch △ Neths. 51°45N 4°48E 15 C4
Biesiesfontein S. Africa 30°57S 17°58E 56 E2
Big → Canada 54°50N 58°55W 73 B8
Big B. Canada 55°43N 60°35W 73 A7
Big Bear City U.S.A. 34°16N 116°51W 79 L10
Big Bear Lake U.S.A. 34°15N 116°56W 79 L10
Big Belt Mts. U.S.A. 46°30N 111°25W 76 C8
Big Bend Eswatini 26°50S 31°58E 57 C5
Big Bend △ U.S.A. 29°20N 103°5W 84 G3
Big Black → U.S.A. 32°3N 91°4W 85 F9
Big Blue → U.S.A. 39°35N 96°34W 80 F5
Big Buddha
  Hong Kong, China 22°15N 113°54E 31 a
Big Creek U.S.A. 37°11N 119°14W 78 H7
Big Creek → U.S.A. 51°18N 123°10W 70 C4
Big Cypress △ U.S.A. 26°0N 81°10W 85 H14
Big Desert Australia 35°45S 141°10E 63 F3
Big Falls U.S.A. 48°12N 93°48W 80 A7
Big Fork → U.S.A. 48°31N 93°43W 80 A7
Big Horn Mts. = Bighorn Mts.
Big I. Canada 61°7N 116°45W 70 A5
Big Lake U.S.A. 31°12N 101°28W 84 F4
Big Moose U.S.A. 43°49N 74°58W 83 C10
Big Muddy Cr. →
  U.S.A. 48°8N 104°36W 76 B11
Big Pine U.S.A. 37°10N 118°17W 78 H8
Big Piney U.S.A. 42°32N 110°7W 76 E8
Big Quill L. Canada 51°55N 104°30W 71 C8
Big Rapids U.S.A. 43°42N 85°29W 81 D11
Big Rideau L. Canada 44°40N 76°15W 83 B8
Big River Canada 53°50N 107°0W 71 C7
Big Run U.S.A. 40°57N 78°55W 82 F6
Big Sable Pt. U.S.A. 44°3N 86°1W 80 C10
Big Salmon → Canada 61°52N 134°55W 70 A2
Big Sand L. Canada 57°45N 99°45W 71 B9
Big Sandy U.S.A. 48°11N 110°7W 76 B8
Big Sandy → U.S.A. 38°25N 82°36W 81 F12
Big Sandy Cr. = Sandy Cr. →
  U.S.A. 38°7N 102°29W 76 G12
Big Sandy Cr. → U.S.A. 38°7N 102°29W 76 G12
Big Sioux → U.S.A. 42°29N 96°27W 80 D5
Big South Fork △
  U.S.A. 36°27N 84°47W 85 G12
Big Spring U.S.A. 32°15N 101°28W 84 E4

Big Stone City U.S.A. 45°18N 96°28W 80 C5
Big Stone Gap U.S.A. 36°52N 82°47W 81 G12
Big Stone L. U.S.A. 45°18N 96°27W 80 C5
Big Sur U.S.A. 36°15N 121°48W 78 J5
Big Timber U.S.A. 45°50N 109°57W 76 D9
Big Trout L. Canada 53°40N 90°0W 72 B2
Big Trout Lake Canada 53°45N 90°0W 72 B2
Biğa Turkey 40°13N 27°14E 23 D12
Bigadiç Turkey 39°22N 28°7E 23 E13
Biggar Canada 52°4N 108°0W 71 C7
Biggar U.K. 55°38N 3°32W 11 F5
Bigge I. Australia 14°35S 125°10E 60 B4
Biggenden Australia 25°31S 152°4E 63 D5
Biggleswade U.K. 52°5N 0°14W 13 E7
Biggs U.S.A. 39°25N 121°43W 78 F5
Bighorn U.S.A. 46°10N 107°27W 76 C10
Bighorn → U.S.A. 46°10N 107°28W 76 C10
Bighorn Canyon △
  U.S.A. 45°10N 108°0W 76 D10
Bighorn L. U.S.A. 44°55N 108°15W 76 D10
Bighorn Mts. U.S.A. 44°25N 107°0W 76 D10
Bigstone L. Canada 53°42N 95°44W 71 C9
Bihać Bos.-H. 44°49N 15°57E 16 F8
Bihar India 25°5N 85°40E 43 G11
Bihar □ India 25°0N 86°0E 43 G12
Bihariganj India 25°44N 86°59E 43 G12
Bihor, Munţii Romania 46°29N 22°47E 17 E12
Bijagós, Arquipélago dos
  Guinea-Biss. 11°15N 16°10W 52 F2
Bijaipur India 26°2N 77°20E 42 F7
Bijapur = Vijayapura
  India 16°50N 75°55E 44 F2
Bijapur India 18°50N 80°50E 44 E5
Bījār Iran 35°52N 47°35E 46 C5
Bijauri Nepal 28°6N 82°20E 43 E10
Bijawar India 24°38N 79°30E 43 G8
Bijeljina Bos.-H. 44°46N 19°14E 23 B8
Bijie China 27°20N 105°16E 34 D5
Bijnor India 29°27N 78°11E 42 E8
Bikaner India 28°2N 73°18E 42 E5
Bikapur India 26°30N 82°7E 43 F10
Bikeqi China 40°43N 111°20E 32 D6
Bikfayyā Lebanon 33°55N 35°41E 48 B4
Bikin Russia 46°50N 134°20E 28 A7
Bikin → Russia 46°51N 134°2E 28 A7
Bikini Atoll Marshall Is. 12°0N 167°30E 64 F8
Bikita Zimbabwe 20°6S 31°41E 57 B5
Bikkū Bīttī Libya 22°0N 19°12E 53 D9
Bila Tserkva Ukraine 49°45N 30°10E 17 D16
Bilara India 26°14N 73°53E 42 F5
Bilaspur Chhattisgarh,
  India 22°2N 82°15E 43 H10
Bilaspur Punjab, India 31°19N 76°50E 42 D7
Bilauk Taungdan Thailand 13°0N 99°0E 38 F2
Bilauri Nepal 28°41N 80°21E 43 E9
Bilbao Spain 43°16N 2°56W 21 A4
Bilbo = Bilbao Spain 43°16N 2°56W 21 A4
Bildudalur Iceland 65°41N 23°36W 8 D2
Bílé Karpaty Europe 49°5N 18°0E 17 D9
Bilecik Turkey 40°5N 30°5E 19 F5
Bilgram India 27°11N 80°2E 43 F9
Bilhaur India 26°51N 80°5E 43 F9
Bilhorod-Dnistrovskyy
  Ukraine 46°11N 30°23E 19 E5
Bilibino Russia 68°3N 166°20E 27 C17
Bilimora India 20°45N 72°57E 44 D1
Bililuna Australia 19°37S 127°41E 60 C4
Billings U.S.A. 45°47N 108°30W 76 D9
Billiton Is. = Belitung
  Indonesia 3°10S 107°50E 36 E3
Bilma Niger 18°50N 13°30E 53 E8
Bilma, Grand Erg de Niger 18°30N 14°0E 53 E8
Biloela Australia 24°24S 150°31E 62 C5
Biloli India 18°46N 77°44E 44 E3
Biloxi U.S.A. 30°24N 88°53W 85 F10
Bilpa Morea Claypan
  Australia 25°0S 140°0E 62 D3
Biltine Chad 14°40N 20°50E 53 F10
Bim Son Vietnam 20°4N 105°51E 38 B5
Bima Indonesia 8°22S 118°49E 37 F5
Bimbo C.A.R. 4°15N 18°33E 54 D3
Bimini Is. Bahamas 25°42N 79°25W 88 A4
Bin Xian Heilongjiang,
  China 45°42N 127°32E 33 B14
Bin Xian Shaanxi, China 35°2N 108°4E 34 G5
Bina-Etawah India 24°13N 78°14E 42 G8
Binalong Australia 34°40S 148°39E 63 E4
Binalong, Kūh-e Iran 36°30N 58°30E 47 B8
Binatang = Bintangau
  Malaysia 2°10N 111°40E 36 D4
Binche Belgium 50°26N 4°10E 15 D4
Binchuan China 25°42N 100°38E 34 E3
Bindki India 26°2N 80°36E 43 F9
Bindura Zimbabwe 17°18S 31°18E 55 H6
Bingara Australia 29°52S 150°36E 63 D5
Bingaram I. India 10°56N 72°17E 45 J1
Bingham U.S.A. 45°3N 69°53W 81 C19
Binghamton U.S.A. 42°6N 75°55W 83 D9
Bingöl Turkey 38°53N 40°29E 46 B4
Binh Dinh Vietnam 13°55N 109°7E 38 F7
Binhai China 34°2N 119°49E 33 G10
Binjai Indonesia 3°20N 98°30E 36 D1
Binnaway Australia 31°28S 149°24E 63 E4
Binongko Indonesia 5°57S 124°2E 37 F6
Binscarth Canada 50°37N 101°17W 71 C8
Bintan Indonesia 1°0N 104°0E 36 D2
Bintulu Malaysia 3°10N 113°0E 36 D4
Binyang China 23°12N 108°47E 34 F7
Binzert = Bizerte Tunisia 37°15N 9°50E 53 A7
Binzhou China 37°20N 118°2E 33 F10
Biobío □ Chile 37°35S 72°30W 94 D1
Biobío → Chile 36°49S 73°10W 94 D1
Bioko Eq. Guin. 3°30N 8°40E 54 D1
Bīr India 19°4N 75°46E 44 E2
Bîr Abu Muḥammad
  Egypt 29°44N 34°14E 48 F3

Bi'r al Butayyihāt Jordan 29°47N 35°20E 48 F4
Bi'r al Mārī Jordan 30°4N 35°33E 48 E4
Bi'r al Qaṭṭār Jordan 29°47N 35°32E 48 F4
Bîr Atrun Sudan 18°15N 26°40E 53 E11
Bîr Beiḍa Egypt 30°25N 34°29E 48 E3
Bîr el 'Abd Egypt 31°2N 33°0E 48 D2
Bîr el Biarât Egypt 29°30N 34°43E 48 F3
Bîr el Duweidar Egypt 30°56N 32°32E 48 E1
Bîr el Garârât Egypt 31°3N 33°34E 48 D2
Bîr el Heisi Egypt 29°22N 34°36E 48 F3
Bîr el Jafir Egypt 30°50N 32°41E 48 E1
Bîr el Mâlḥi Egypt 30°38N 33°19E 48 E2
Bîr el Thamâda Egypt 30°12N 33°27E 48 E2
Bîr Gebeil Ḥiṣn Egypt 30°2N 33°18E 48 D2
Bi'r Ghaḍir Syria 34°6N 37°3E 48 A6
Bîr Ḥasana Egypt 30°29N 33°46E 48 E2
Bîr Kaseiba Egypt 31°0N 33°17E 48 E2
Bîr Lahfân Egypt 31°0N 33°51E 48 E2
Bîr Madkûr Egypt 30°44N 32°33E 48 E1
Bîr Mogreïn Mauritania 25°10N 11°25W 52 C3
Bi'r Muṭribah Kuwait 29°54N 47°17E 46 D5
Bîr Qaṭia Egypt 30°58N 32°45E 48 E1
Bîr Shalatein Egypt 23°5N 35°25E 53 D13
Birāk Libya 27°31N 14°20E 53 C8
Biratnagar Nepal 26°27N 87°17E 43 F12
Birch ~ Canada 58°28N 112°17W 70 B6
Birch Hills Canada 52°59N 105°25W 71 C7
Birch I. Canada 52°26N 99°54W 71 C9
Birch L. N.W.T., Canada 62°4N 116°33W 70 A5
Birch L. Ont., Canada 51°23N 92°18W 72 B1
Birch Mts. Canada 57°30N 113°10W 70 B6
Birch River Canada 52°24N 101°6W 71 C8
Birchip Australia 35°56S 142°55E 63 F3
Bird Canada 56°30N 94°13W 71 B10
Bird I. = Aves, I. de
  W. Indies 15°45N 63°55W 89 C7
Bird I. S. Georgia 54°0S 38°3W 96 G9
Birds Creek Canada 45°6N 77°52W 82 A7
Birdsville Australia 25°51S 139°20E 62 D2
Birdum Cr. ~ Australia 15°14S 133°0E 60 C5
Birecik Turkey 37°2N 38°0E 46 B3
Birein Israel 30°50N 34°28E 48 E3
Bireuen Indonesia 5°14N 96°39E 36 C1
Birganj Nepal 27°1N 84°52E 43 F11
Birigüi Brazil 21°18S 50°16W 95 A5
Bîrjand Iran 32°53N 59°13E 47 C8
Birkenhead U.K. 53°23N 3°2W 12 D4
Bîrlad = Bârlad Romania 46°15N 27°38E 17 E14
Birmingham U.K. 52°29N 1°52W 13 E6
Birmingham U.S.A. 33°31N 86°48W 85 E11
Birmingham Int. ✈ (BHX)
  U.K. 52°26N 1°45W 13 E6
Birmitrapur India 22°24N 84°46E 44 C7
Birni Nkonni Niger 13°55N 5°15E 52 F7
Birnin Kebbi Nigeria 12°32N 4°12E 52 F6
Birobidzhan Russia 48°50N 132°50E 31 B15
Birr Ireland 53°6N 7°54W 10 C4
Birrie ~ Australia 29°43S 146°37E 63 D4
Birsilpur India 28°11N 72°15E 42 E5
Birsk Russia 55°25N 55°30E 18 C10
Birtle Canada 50°30N 101°5W 71 C8
Birur India 13°30N 75°55E 40 N9
Birži Lithuania 56°11N 24°45E 9 H21
Bisa Indonesia 1°15S 127°28E 37 E7
Bisalpur India 28°14N 79°48E 43 E8
Bisbee U.S.A. 31°27N 109°55W 77 L9
Biscarrosse France 44°22N 1°20W 20 D3
Biscay, B. of Atl. Oc. 45°0N 2°0W 20 D1
Biscayne B. U.S.A. 25°40N 80°12W 85 J14
Biscoe Is. Antarctica 66°0S 67°0W 5 C17
Biscotasing Canada 47°18N 82°9W 72 C3
Bishan China 29°33N 106°12E 34 C6
Bishnupur India 23°8N 87°20E 43 H12
Bisho = Bhisho S. Africa 32°50S 27°23E 56 D4
Bishoftu = Debre Zeyit
  Ethiopia 8°50N 39°0E 49 F2
Bishop Calif., U.S.A. 37°22N 118°24W 78 H8
Bishop Tex., U.S.A. 27°35N 97°48W 84 H6
Bishop Auckland U.K. 54°39N 1°40W 12 C6
Bishop's Falls Canada 49°2N 55°30W 73 C8
Bishop's Stortford U.K. 51°52N 0°10E 13 F8
Biskra Algeria 34°50N 5°44E 52 B7
Bismarck U.S.A. 46°48N 100°47W 80 B3
Bismarck Arch.
  Papua N. G. 2°30S 150°0E 58 B7
Bison U.S.A. 45°31N 102°28W 80 C2
Bīsotūn Iran 34°23N 47°26E 46 C5
Bissagos = Bijagós, Arquipélago
  dos Guinea-Biss. 11°15N 16°10W 52 F2
Bissam Cuttack India 19°31N 83°31E 44 E6
Bissau Guinea-Biss. 11°45N 15°45W 52 F2
Bistcho L. Canada 59°45N 118°50W 70 B5
Bistriţa Romania 47°9N 24°35E 17 E13
Bistriţa ~ Romania 46°30N 26°57E 17 E14
Biswan India 27°29N 81°2E 43 F9
Bitam Gabon 2°5N 11°25E 54 D2
Bitkine Chad 11°59N 18°13E 53 F9
Bitlis Turkey 38°20N 42°3E 46 B4
Bitola Macedonia 41°1N 21°20E 23 D9
Bitolj = Bitola Macedonia 41°1N 21°20E 23 D9
Bitra I. India 11°33N 72°9E 45 J1
Bitter Creek U.S.A. 41°33N 108°33W 76 F9
Bitterfontein S. Africa 31°1S 18°32E 56 E2
Bitterroot ~ U.S.A. 46°52N 114°7W 76 C6
Bitterroot Range U.S.A. 46°0N 114°20W 76 D6
Bitterwater U.S.A. 36°23N 121°0W 78 J6
Biu Nigeria 10°40N 12°3E 53 F8
Biwa-Ko Japan 35°15N 136°10E 29 G8
Biwabik U.S.A. 47°32N 92°21W 80 B7
Bixby U.S.A. 35°57N 95°53W 84 D7
Biyang China 32°38N 113°21E 32 H7
Biysk Russia 52°40N 85°0E 26 D9
Bizana S. Africa 30°50S 29°52E 57 D4
Bizen Japan 34°43N 134°8E 29 G7
Bizerte Tunisia 37°15N 9°50E 53 A7
Bjargtangar Iceland 65°30N 24°30W 8 D1
Bjelovar Croatia 45°56N 16°49E 22 B7
Björneborg = Pori Finland 61°29N 21°48E 8 F19
Bjørnevatn Norway 69°40N 30°0E 8 B24

Bjørnøya Arctic 74°30N 19°0E 4 B8
Black = Da ~ Vietnam 21°15N 105°20E 34 G5
Black ~ Canada 44°42N 79°19W 82 B5
Black ~ Ariz., U.S.A. 33°44N 110°13W 77 K8
Black ~ Ark., U.S.A. 35°38N 91°20W 84 D9
Black ~ La., U.S.A. 31°16N 91°50W 84 F9
Black ~ Mich., U.S.A. 42°59N 82°27W 82 D2
Black ~ N.Y., U.S.A. 43°59N 76°4W 83 C8
Black ~ Wis., U.S.A. 43°57N 91°22W 80 D8
Black Bay Pen. Canada 48°38N 88°21W 72 C2
Black Birch L. Canada 56°53N 107°45W 71 B7
Black Canyon of the Gunnison △
  U.S.A. 38°40N 107°35W 76 G10
Black Diamond Canada 50°45N 114°14W 70 C6
Black Duck ~ Canada 56°51N 89°2W 72 A2
Black Forest = Schwarzwald
  Germany 48°30N 8°20E 16 D5
Black Forest U.S.A. 39°0N 104°43W 76 G11
Black Hd. Ireland 53°9N 9°16W 10 C2
Black Hills U.S.A. 44°0N 103°45W 80 D2
Black I. Canada 51°12N 96°30W 71 C9
Black L. Canada 59°12N 105°15W 71 B7
Black L. Mich., U.S.A. 45°28N 84°16W 81 C11
Black L. N.Y., U.S.A. 44°31N 75°36W 83 B9
Black Lake Canada 59°11N 105°20W 71 B7
Black Mesa U.S.A. 36°58N 102°58W 84 C3
Black Mt. = Mynydd Du
  U.K. 51°52N 3°50W 13 F4
Black Mts. U.K. 51°55N 3°7W 13 F4
Black Range U.S.A. 33°15N 107°50W 77 K10
Black River Jamaica 18°0N 77°50W 88 a
Black River U.S.A. 44°0N 75°47W 83 C9
Black River Falls U.S.A. 44°18N 90°51W 80 C8
Black Rock Barbados 13°7N 59°37W 89 g
Black Rock Desert
  U.S.A. 41°10N 118°50W 76 F4
Black Sea Eurasia 43°30N 35°0E 19 F6
Black Tickle Canada 53°28N 55°45W 73 B8
Black Volta ~ Africa 8°41N 1°33W 52 G5
Black Warrior ~
  U.S.A. 32°32N 87°51W 85 E11
Blackall Australia 24°25S 145°45E 62 C4
Blackball N.Z. 42°22S 171°26E 59 E3
Blackbraes △ Australia 19°10S 144°10E 62 B3
Blackbull Australia 17°55S 141°45E 62 B3
Blackburn U.K. 53°45N 2°29W 12 D5
Blackburn, Mt. U.S.A. 61°44N 143°26W 74 C11
Blackburn with Darwen □
  U.K. 53°45N 2°29W 12 D5
Blackdown Tableland △
  Australia 23°52S 149°8E 62 C4
Blackfoot U.S.A. 43°11N 112°21W 76 E7
Blackfoot ~ U.S.A. 46°52N 113°53W 76 C7
Blackfoot Res. U.S.A. 42°55N 111°39W 76 E8
Blackpool U.K. 53°49N 3°3W 12 D4
Blackpool □ U.K. 53°49N 3°3W 12 D4
Blackriver U.S.A. 44°46N 83°17W 82 B1
Blacks Harbour Canada 45°3N 66°49W 73 C6
Blacksburg U.S.A. 37°14N 80°25W 81 G13
Blacksod B. Ireland 54°6N 10°0W 10 B1
Blackstairs Mt. Ireland 52°33N 6°48W 10 D5
Blackstone U.S.A. 37°5N 78°0W 81 G14
Blackstone Ra. Australia 26°0S 128°30E 61 E4
Blackwater ~ Australia 23°35S 148°53E 62 C4
Blackwater → West Road ~
  Canada 53°18N 122°53W 70 C4
Blackwater Australia 23°35S 148°53E 62 C4
Blackwater ~ Meath,
  Ireland 53°39N 6°41W 10 C4
Blackwater → Waterford,
  Ireland 52°4N 7°52W 10 D4
Blackwater ~ U.K. 54°31N 6°35W 10 B5
Blackwell U.S.A. 36°48N 97°17W 84 C6
Blackwells Corner
  U.S.A. 35°37N 119°47W 79 K7
Blackwood U.K. 51°39N 3°12W 13 F4
Bladensburg △ Australia 22°30S 142°59E 62 C3
Blaenau Ffestiniog U.K. 53°0N 3°56W 12 E4
Blaenau Gwent □ U.K. 51°48N 3°12W 13 F4
Blåfjella-Skjækerfjella △
  Norway 64°15N 13°8E 8 D15
Blagodarnyy Russia 45°7N 43°37E 19 E7
Blagoevgrad Bulgaria 42°2N 23°5E 23 C10
Blagoveshchensk
  Russia 50°20N 127°30E 31 A14
Blahkiuh Indonesia 8°31S 115°12E 37 J18
Blain U.S.A. 40°20N 77°31W 82 F7
Blaine Minn., U.S.A. 45°10N 93°13W 80 C7
Blaine Wash., U.S.A. 48°59N 122°45W 78 B4
Blaine Lake Canada 52°51N 106°52W 71 C7
Blair U.S.A. 41°33N 96°8W 80 E5
Blair Athol Australia 22°42S 147°31E 62 C4
Blair Atholl U.K. 56°46N 3°50W 11 E5
Blairgowrie U.K. 56°35N 3°21W 11 E5
Blairsden U.S.A. 39°47N 120°37W 78 F6
Blairsville U.S.A. 40°26N 79°16W 82 F5
Blakang Mati, Pulau
  Singapore 1°15N 103°50E 39 d
Blake Pt. U.S.A. 48°11N 88°25W 80 A9
Blakely Ga., U.S.A. 31°23N 84°56W 85 F12
Blakely Pa., U.S.A. 41°28N 75°37W 83 E9
Blambangan, Semenanjung
  Indonesia 8°42S 114°29E 37 K17
Blanc, Mont Europe 45°48N 6°50E 20 D7
Blanca, B. Argentina 39°10S 61°30W 96 D4
Blanca, Cord. Peru 9°10S 77°35W 92 E3
Blanca, Costa Spain 38°25N 0°10W 21 C5
Blanca Peak U.S.A. 37°35N 105°29W 77 H11
Blanche, C. Australia 33°1S 134°9E 63 E1
Blanche, L. S. Austral.,
  Australia 29°15S 139°40E 63 D2
Blanche, L. W. Austral.,
  Australia 22°25S 123°17E 60 D3
Blanchisseuse
  Trin. & Tob. 10°48N 61°18W 93 K15
Blanco S. Africa 33°55S 22°23E 56 D3
Blanco U.S.A. 30°6N 98°25W 84 G5
Blanco, C. Costa Rica 9°34N 85°8W 88 E2
Blanco, C. U.S.A. 42°51N 124°34W 76 E1
Blanda ~ Iceland 65°37N 20°9W 8 D3

Blandford Forum U.K. 50°51N 2°9W 13 G5
Blanding U.S.A. 37°37N 109°29W 77 H9
Blanes Spain 41°40N 2°48E 21 B7
Blankenberge Belgium 51°20N 3°9E 15 C3
Blanquilla, I. Venezuela 11°51N 64°37W 89 D7
Blanquillo Uruguay 32°53S 55°37W 95 C4
Blantyre Malawi 15°45S 35°0E 55 H7
Blarney Ireland 51°56N 8°33W 10 E3
Blasdell U.S.A. 42°48N 78°50W 82 D6
Blåvands Huk Denmark 55°33N 8°4E 9 J13
Blaydon U.K. 54°58N 1°42W 12 C6
Blayney Australia 33°32S 149°14E 63 E4
Blaze, Pt. Australia 12°56S 130°11E 60 B5
Blekinge Sweden 56°25N 15°20E 9 H16
Blenheim Canada 42°20N 82°0W 82 D3
Blenheim N.Z. 41°38S 173°57E 59 D4
Bletchley U.K. 51°59N 0°44W 13 F7
Blida Algeria 36°30N 2°49E 52 A6
Bligh Sound N.Z. 44°47S 167°32E 59 F1
Bligh Water Fiji 17°0S 178°0E 59 a
Blind River Canada 46°10N 82°58W 72 C3
Bliss Idaho, U.S.A. 42°56N 114°57W 76 E6
Bliss N.Y., U.S.A. 42°34N 78°15W 82 D6
Blissfield U.S.A. 40°24N 81°58W 82 F3
Blitar Indonesia 8°5S 112°11E 37 H15
Block I. U.S.A. 41°11N 71°35W 83 E13
Block Island Sd. U.S.A. 41°15N 71°40W 83 E13
Bloemfontein S. Africa 29°6S 26°7E 56 C4
Bloemhof S. Africa 27°38S 25°32E 56 C4
Blois France 47°35N 1°20E 20 C4
Blönduós Iceland 65°40N 20°12W 8 D3
Blongas Indonesia 8°53S 116°2E 37 K19
Bloodvein ~ Canada 51°47N 96°43W 71 C9
Bloody Foreland Ireland 55°10N 8°17W 10 A3
Bloomer U.S.A. 45°6N 91°29W 80 C8
Bloomfield Canada 43°59N 77°14W 82 C7
Bloomfield Iowa, U.S.A. 40°45N 92°25W 80 E7
Bloomfield N. Mex.,
  U.S.A. 36°43N 107°59W 77 H10
Bloomfield Nebr., U.S.A. 42°36N 97°39W 80 D5
Bloomington Ill., U.S.A. 40°28N 89°0W 80 E9
Bloomington Ind.,
  U.S.A. 39°10N 86°32W 80 F10
Bloomington Minn.,
  U.S.A. 44°50N 93°17W 80 C7
Bloomsburg U.S.A. 41°0N 76°27W 83 F8
Bloomsbury Australia 20°48S 148°38E 62 b
Blora Indonesia 6°57S 111°25E 37 G14
Blossburg U.S.A. 41°41N 77°4W 82 E7
Blouberg S. Africa 23°8S 28°59E 57 B4
Blountstown U.S.A. 30°27N 85°3W 85 F12
Blue Earth U.S.A. 43°38N 94°6W 80 D6
Blue Hole △ Belize 17°9N 88°40W 88 C2
Blue Mesa Res. U.S.A. 38°28N 107°20W 76 G10
Blue Mountain Lake
  U.S.A. 43°51N 74°27W 83 C10
Blue Mountain Pk. Jamaica 18°3N 76°36W 88 a
Blue Mts. U.S.A. 40°30N 76°30W 83 F8
Blue Mts. Jamaica 18°3N 76°36W 88 a
Blue Mts. Maine, U.S.A. 44°50N 70°35W 83 B14
Blue Mts. Oreg., U.S.A. 45°0N 118°20W 76 D4
Blue Mud B. Australia 13°30S 136°0E 62 A2
Blue Nile = Nîl el Azraq ~
  Sudan 15°38N 32°31E 53 E12
Blue Rapids U.S.A. 39°41N 96°39W 80 F5
Blue Ridge U.S.A. 36°40N 80°50W 81 G13
Blue River Canada 52°6N 119°18W 70 C5
Bluefield U.S.A. 37°15N 81°17W 81 G13
Bluefields Nic. 12°20N 83°50W 88 D3
Bluevale Canada 43°51N 81°15W 82 C3
Bluff Australia 23°35S 149°4E 62 C4
Bluff N.Z. 46°37S 168°20E 59 G2
Bluff U.S.A. 37°17N 109°33W 77 H9
Bluff Knoll Australia 34°24S 118°15E 61 F2
Bluff Pt. Australia 27°50S 114°5E 61 E1
Bluffton Ind., U.S.A. 40°44N 85°11W 81 E11
Bluffton S.C., U.S.A. 32°14N 80°52W 85 E14
Blumenau Brazil 27°0S 49°0W 95 B6
Blunt U.S.A. 44°31N 99°59W 80 C4
Bly U.S.A. 42°24N 121°3W 76 E3
Blyde River Canyon △
  S. Africa 24°37S 31°2E 57 B5
Blyth Canada 43°44N 81°26W 82 C3
Blyth U.K. 55°8N 1°31W 12 B6
Blythe U.S.A. 33°37N 114°36W 79 M12
Blytheville U.S.A. 35°56N 89°55W 85 D10
Bo S. Leone 7°55N 11°50W 52 G3
Bo Duc Vietnam 11°58N 106°50E 39 G6
Bo Hai China 39°0N 119°0E 33 E10
Bo Hai Haixia Asia 38°25N 121°10E 33 E11
Bo Xian = Bozhou China 33°55N 115°41E 32 H8
Boa Vista Brazil 2°48N 60°30W 92 C6
Boa Vista Cabo Verde 16°0N 22°49W 52 b
Boaco Nic. 12°29N 85°35W 88 D2
Bo'ai China 35°10N 113°3E 32 G7
Boalsburg U.S.A. 40°47N 77°49W 82 F7
Boane Mozam. 26°6S 32°19E 57 C5
Boao China 19°8N 110°34E 38 C8
Boardman U.S.A. 41°2N 80°40W 82 E4
Bobadah Australia 32°19S 146°41E 63 E4
Bobai China 22°17N 109°59E 34 F7
Bobbili India 18°35N 83°30E 44 E6
Bobcaygeon Canada 44°33N 78°33W 82 B6
Boblad India 17°13N 75°26E 44 F2
Bobo-Dioulasso
  Burkina Faso 11°8N 4°13W 52 F5
Bobonong Botswana 21°58S 28°20E 57 B4
Bobraomby, Tanjon' i
  Madag. 12°40S 49°10E 55 G9
Bobruysk = Babruysk
  Belarus 53°10N 29°15E 17 B15
Boby, Pic Madag. 22°12S 46°55E 55 J9
Boca del Río Mexico 19°5N 96°4W 87 D5
Boca do Acre Brazil 8°50S 67°27W 92 E5
Boca Raton U.S.A. 26°21N 80°5W 85 H14
Bocas del Dragón = Dragon's
  Mouths Trin. & Tob. 11°0N 61°50W 93 K15

Bocas del Toro Panama 9°15N 82°20W 88 E3
Bochnia Poland 49°58N 20°27E 17 D11
Bochum = Senwabarana
  S. Africa 23°17S 29°7E 57 B4
Bochum Germany 51°28N 7°13E 16 C4
Bocoyna Mexico 27°52N 107°35W 86 B3
Bodaybo Russia 57°50N 114°0E 27 D12
Boddam U.K. 59°56N 1°17W 11 B7
Bodegraven Australia 32°50S 116°30E 61 F2
Bodega Bay U.S.A. 38°20N 123°3W 78 G3
Boden Sweden 65°50N 21°42E 8 D19
Bodensee Europe 47°35N 9°25E 20 C8
Bodh Gaya India 24°41N 84°59E 43 G11
Bodhan India 18°40N 77°44E 44 E3
Bodinayakkanur India 10°2N 77°10E 45 J3
Bodmin U.K. 50°28N 4°43W 13 G3
Bodmin Moor U.K. 50°33N 4°36W 13 G3
Bodø Norway 67°17N 14°24E 8 C16
Bodrog ~ Hungary 48°11N 21°22E 17 D11
Bodrum Turkey 37°3N 27°30E 23 F12
Boende
  Dem. Rep. of the Congo 0°24S 21°12E 54 E4
Boerne U.S.A. 29°47N 98°44W 84 G5
Boesmans ~ S. Africa 33°42S 26°39E 56 D4
Bogalusa U.S.A. 30°47N 89°52W 85 F10
Bogan ~ Australia 30°20S 146°55E 63 D4
Bogan Gate Australia 33°7S 147°49E 63 E4
Bogantungan Australia 23°41S 147°17E 62 C4
Bogata U.S.A. 33°28N 95°13W 84 E7
Bogda Shan China 43°35N 89°40E 30 C6
Boggabilla Australia 28°36S 150°24E 63 D5
Boggabri Australia 30°45S 150°5E 63 E5
Boggeragh Mts. Ireland 52°2N 8°55W 10 D3
Boglan = Solhan Turkey 38°57N 41°3E 46 B4
Bognes Norway 68°13N 16°5E 8 B17
Bognor Regis U.K. 50°47N 0°40W 13 G7
Bogo Phil. 11°3N 124°0E 37 B6
Bogong, Mt. Australia 36°47S 147°17E 63 F4
Bogor Indonesia 6°36S 106°48E 37 G12
Bogotá Colombia 4°34N 74°0W 92 C4
Bogotol Russia 56°15N 89°50E 26 D9
Bogra Bangla. 24°51N 89°22E 41 G16
Boguchanskoye Vdkhr.
  Russia 58°42N 99°9E 27 D10
Boguchany Russia 58°40N 97°30E 27 D10
Bogué Mauritania 16°45N 14°10W 52 E3
Bohemian Forest = Böhmerwald
  Germany 49°8N 13°14E 16 D7
Böhmerwald Germany 49°8N 13°14E 16 D7
Bohol □ Phil. 9°50N 124°10E 37 C6
Bohol Sea Phil. 9°0N 124°0E 37 C6
Bohorok Indonesia 3°30N 98°12E 39 L2
Böhöt Mongolia 45°13N 108°16E 32 B5
Bohuslän Sweden 58°25N 12°0E 9 G15
Boi, Pta. do Brazil 23°55S 45°15W 95 A6
Boiaçu Brazil 0°27S 61°46W 92 D6
Boigu Australia 9°16S 142°13E 62 a
Boileau, C. Australia 17°40S 122°7E 60 C3
Boipariguda India 18°46N 82°26E 44 E6
Boise U.S.A. 43°37N 116°13W 76 E5
Boise City U.S.A. 36°44N 102°31W 84 C3
Bojador C. W. Sahara 26°0N 14°30W 52 C3
Bojana ~ Albania 41°52N 19°22E 23 D8
Bojnūrd Iran 37°30N 57°20E 47 B8
Bojonegoro Indonesia 7°11S 111°54E 37 G14
Bokaro India 23°46N 85°55E 43 H11
Boké Guinea 10°56N 14°17W 52 F3
Bokhara ~ Australia 29°55S 146°42E 63 D4
Boknafjorden Norway 59°14N 5°40E 9 G11
Bokor △ Cambodia 10°50N 104°1E 39 G5
Bokoro Chad 12°25N 17°14E 53 F9
Bokpyin Myanmar 11°18N 98°42E 39 G2
Bokungu
  Dem. Rep. of the Congo 0°35S 22°50E 54 E4
Bolan ~ Pakistan 28°38N 67°42E 42 E2
Bolan Pass Pakistan 29°50N 67°20E 40 E5
Bolaños ~ Mexico 21°12N 104°5W 86 C4
Bolbec France 49°30N 0°30E 20 B4
Boldājī Iran 31°56N 51°3E 47 D6
Bole China 44°55N 81°37E 30 C5
Bolekhiv Ukraine 49°0N 23°57E 17 D12
Bolesławiec Poland 51°17N 15°37E 16 C8
Bolgatanga Ghana 10°44N 0°53W 52 F5
Bolgrad = Bolhrad
  Ukraine 45°40N 28°32E 17 F15
Bolhrad Ukraine 45°40N 28°32E 17 F15
Bolinao Phil. 16°23N 119°54E 37 A5
Bolivar Mo., U.S.A. 37°37N 93°25W 80 G7
Bolivar N.Y., U.S.A. 42°4N 78°10W 82 D6
Bolivar Tenn., U.S.A. 35°12N 89°0W 85 D10
Bolívar, Pico Venezuela 8°32N 71°2W 89 E5
Bolivia ■ S. Amer. 17°6S 64°0W 92 G6
Bolivian Plateau = Altiplano
  Bolivia 17°0S 68°0W 92 G5
Bollnäs Sweden 61°21N 16°24E 8 F17
Bollon Australia 28°2S 147°29E 63 D4
Bolmen Sweden 56°55N 13°40E 9 H15
Bolobo Dem. Rep. of the Congo 2°6S 16°20E 54 E3
Bologna Italy 44°29N 11°20E 22 B4
Bologoye Russia 57°55N 34°5E 18 C5
Bolomba
  Dem. Rep. of the Congo 0°35N 19°0E 54 D3
Bolonchén Mexico 20°1N 89°45W 87 D7
Boloven, Cao Nguyen
  Laos 15°10N 106°30E 38 E6
Bolpur India 23°40N 87°45E 43 H12
Bolsena, L. di Italy 42°36N 11°56E 22 C4
Bolshevik, Ostrov
  Russia 78°30N 102°0E 27 B11
Bolshoi Anyuy ~
  Russia 68°30N 160°49E 27 C17
Bolshoy Begichev, Ostrov
  Russia 74°20N 112°30E 27 B12
Bolshoy Kamen Russia 43°7N 132°19E 28 C6
Bolshoy Kavkaz = Caucasus
  Eurasia 42°50N 44°0E 19 F7
Bolshoy Lyakhovskiy, Ostrov
  Russia 73°35N 142°0E 27 B15
Bolshoy Tyuters, Ostrov
  Russia 59°51N 27°13E 9 G22

Bolsward Neths. 53°3N 5°32E 15 A5
Bolt Head U.K. 50°12N 3°48W 13 G4
Bolton Canada 43°54N 79°45W 82 C5
Bolton U.K. 53°35N 2°26W 12 D5
Bolton Landing U.S.A. 43°32N 73°35W 83 C11
Bolu Turkey 40°45N 31°35E 19 F5
Bolungavík Iceland 66°9N 23°15W 8 C2
Boluo China 23°3N 114°21E 35 F1
Bolvadin Turkey 38°45N 31°4E 46 B6
Bolzano Italy 46°31N 11°22E 22 A4
Bom Jesus da Lapa
  Brazil 13°15S 43°25W 93 F11
Boma Dem. Rep. of the Congo 5°50S 13°4E 54 F2
Bombala Australia 36°56S 149°15E 63 F4
Bombay = Mumbai India 18°56N 72°50E 44 E1
Bombedor, Pta. Venezuela 9°53N 61°37W 93 L1
Bomberai, Semenanjung
  Indonesia 3°0S 133°0E 37 E8
Bomboma
  Dem. Rep. of the Congo 2°25N 18°55E 54 D3
Bomi China 29°50N 95°45E 30 F7
Bømlo Norway 59°37N 5°13E 9 G11
Bompoka India 8°15N 93°13E 45 K1
Bomu ~ C.A.R. 4°40N 22°30E 54 D4
Bon, C. = Ra's aṭ Ṭib Tunisia 37°1N 11°2E 22 F7
Bon Accueil Mauritius 20°15S 57°40E 53 d
Bon Echo △ Canada 44°55N 77°16W 82 B
Bon Sar Pa Vietnam 12°24N 107°35E 38 F6
Bonāb Iran 36°35N 48°41E 47 B6
Bonaigarh India 21°50N 84°57E 43 J11
Bonaire W. Indies 12°10N 68°15W 89 D6
Bonampak Mexico 16°44N 91°5W 87 D6
Bonang Australia 37°11S 148°41E 63 F4
Bonanza Nic. 13°54N 84°35W 88 D3
Bonaparte Arch.
  Australia 14°0S 124°30E 60 B3
Bonar Bridge U.K. 57°54N 4°20W 11 D4
Bonasse Trin. & Tob. 10°5N 61°54W 93 K15
Bonaventure Canada 48°5N 65°32W 73 C6
Bonavista Canada 48°40N 53°5W 73 C9
Bonavista, C. Canada 48°42N 53°5W 73 C9
Bonavista B. Canada 48°45N 53°25W 73 C9
Bondo
  Dem. Rep. of the Congo 3°55N 23°53E 54 D4
Bondokodi Indonesia 9°33S 119°0E 60 A1
Bondoukou Côte d'Ivoire 8°2N 2°47W 52 G5
Bondowoso Indonesia 7°55S 113°49E 37 G15
Bonerate Indonesia 4°10S 120°50E 37 E6
Bonerate, Kepulauan
  Indonesia 6°30S 121°10E 37 F6
Bo'ness U.K. 56°1N 3°37W 11 E5
Bonete, Cerro Argentina 27°55S 68°40W 94 B3
Bong Son = Hoai Nhon
  Vietnam 14°28N 109°1E 38 E7
Bongaigaon India 26°28N 90°34E 30 F17
Bongandanga
  Dem. Rep. of the Congo 1°24N 21°3E 54 D4
Bongor Chad 10°35N 15°20E 53 F9
Bongos, Massif des C.A.R. 8°40N 22°25E 54 G4
Bonham U.S.A. 33°35N 96°11W 84 E6
Bonifacio France 41°24N 9°10E 20 F8
Bonifacio, Bouches de
  Medit. S. 41°12N 9°15E 22 D3
Bonin Is. = Ogasawara Gunto
  Pac. Oc. 27°0N 142°0E 64 E6
Bonn Germany 50°46N 7°6E 16 C4
Bonne Terre U.S.A. 37°55N 90°33W 80 G8
Bonners Ferry U.S.A. 48°42N 116°19W 76 B5
Bonney, L. Australia 37°50S 140°20E 63 F3
Bonnie Rock Australia 30°29S 118°22E 61 F2
Bonny, Bight of Africa 3°30N 9°20E 54 D1
Bonnyrigg U.K. 55°53N 3°6W 11 F5
Bonnyville Canada 54°20N 110°45W 71 C6
Bonoi Indonesia 1°45S 137°41E 37 E9
Bonsall U.S.A. 33°16N 117°14W 79 M9
Bontang Indonesia 0°10N 117°30E 36 D5
Bontebok △ S. Africa 34°5S 20°28E 56 D3
Bonthe S. Leone 7°30N 12°33W 52 G3
Bontoc Phil. 17°7N 120°58E 37 A6
Bonython Ra. Australia 23°40S 128°45E 60 D4
Boodjamulla △ Australia 18°15S 138°6E 62 B2
Bookabie Australia 31°50S 132°41E 61 F5
Booker U.S.A. 36°27N 100°32W 84 C4
Booligal Australia 33°58S 144°53E 63 E3
Böön Tsagaan Nuur
  Mongolia 45°35N 99°9E 30 B8
Boonah Australia 27°58S 152°41E 63 D5
Boone Iowa, U.S.A. 42°4N 93°53W 80 D7
Boone N.C., U.S.A. 36°13N 81°41W 85 C14
Booneville Ark., U.S.A. 35°8N 93°55W 84 D8
Booneville Miss., U.S.A. 34°39N 88°34W 85 D10
Boonville Calif., U.S.A. 39°1N 123°22W 78 F3
Boonville Ind., U.S.A. 38°3N 87°16W 80 F10
Boonville Mo., U.S.A. 38°58N 92°44W 80 F7
Boonville N.Y., U.S.A. 43°29N 75°20W 83 C9
Boorabbin △ Australia 31°30S 120°10E 61 F3
Boorindal Australia 30°22S 146°11E 63 E4
Boorowa Australia 34°28S 148°44E 63 E4
Boosaaso Somalia 11°12N 49°18E 49 E4
Boothia, Gulf of Canada 71°0N 90°0W 68 C14
Boothia Pen. Canada 71°0N 94°0W 68 C14
Bootle U.K. 53°28N 3°1W 12 D4
Bouaé Gabon 0°5S 11°55E 54 E2
Boquilla, Presa de la
  Mexico 27°31N 105°30W 86 B3
Boquillas del Carmen
  Mexico 29°11N 102°58W 86 B4
Bor Serbia 44°5N 22°7E 23 B10
Bor South Sudan 6°10N 31°40E 53 G12
Bor Mashash Israel 31°7N 34°50E 48 D3
Bora Bora
  French Polynesia 16°30S 151°45W 65 J12
Borah Peak U.S.A. 44°8N 113°47W 76 D7
Boraha, Nosy Madag. 16°50S 49°55E 55 H9
Borås Sweden 57°43N 12°56E 9 H15
Borāzjān Iran 29°22N 51°10E 47 D6
Borba Brazil 4°12S 59°34W 92 D7
Borborema, Planalto da
  Brazil 7°0S 37°0W 90 D7

Bord Khūn-e Now Iran 28°3N 51°28E 47 D6
Borda, C. Australia 35°45S 136°34E 63 F2
Bordeaux France 44°50N 0°36W 20 D3
Borden Australia 34°3S 118°12E 61 F2
Borden-Carleton Canada 46°18N 63°47W 73 C7
Borden Pen. Canada 73°0N 83°0W 69 C15
Borden I. Canada 78°30N 111°30W 69 B9
Border Ranges △ Australia 28°24S 152°56E 63 D5
Borders = Scottish Borders □ U.K. 55°35N 2°50W 11 F6
Bordertown Australia 36°19S 140°45E 63 F3
Borðeyri Iceland 65°12N 21°6W 8 D3
Bordj Flye Ste-Marie Algeria 27°19N 2°32W 52 C5
Bordj in Eker Algeria 24°9N 5°3E 52 D7
Bordj Mokhtar Algeria 21°20N 0°56E 52 D6
Bordj Omar Driss Algeria 28°10N 6°40E 52 C7
Borehamwood U.K. 51°40N 0°15W 13 F7
Borgampad India 17°39N 80°52E 44 F5
Borgarnes Iceland 64°32N 21°55W 8 D3
Børgefjellet Norway 65°20N 13°45E 8 D15
Borger Neths. 52°54N 6°44E 15 B6
Borger U.S.A. 35°39N 101°24W 84 D4
Borgholm Sweden 56°52N 16°39E 9 H17
Borhoyn Tal Mongolia 43°50N 111°58E 32 C6
Borigumma India 19°3N 82°33E 44 E6
Borikhane Laos 18°33N 103°43E 38 C4
Borisoglebsk Russia 51°27N 42°5E 19 D7
Borisov = Barysaw Belarus 54°17N 28°28E 17 A15
Borja Peru 4°20S 77°40W 92 D3
Borkou Chad 18°15N 18°50E 53 E9
Borkum Germany 53°34N 6°40E 16 B4
Borlänge Sweden 60°29N 15°26E 9 F16
Borley, C. Antarctica 66°15S 52°30E 5 C5
Borneo E. Indies 1°0N 115°0E 36 D5
Bornholm Denmark 55°10N 15°0E 9 J16
Borobudur △ Indonesia 7°36S 110°12E 37 G14
Borogontsy Russia 62°42N 131°8E 27 C14
Borohoro Shan China 44°6N 83°10E 30 C5
Boron U.S.A. 35°0N 117°39W 79 L9
Borongan Phil. 11°37N 125°26E 37 B7
Borovichi Russia 58°25N 33°55E 18 C5
Borrego Springs U.S.A. 33°15N 116°23W 79 M10
Borrisokane Ireland 53°0N 8°7W 10 D3
Borroloola Australia 16°4S 136°17E 62 B2
Borşa Romania 47°41N 24°50E 17 E13
Borsad India 22°25N 72°54E 42 H5
Bortala = Bole China 44°55N 81°37E 30 C5
Borth U.K. 52°29N 4°2W 13 E3
Borūjerd Iran 33°55N 48°50E 47 C6
Boryeong S. Korea 36°21N 126°36E 33 F14
Boryslav Ukraine 49°18N 23°28E 17 D12
Borzya Russia 50°24N 116°31E 31 A12
Bosa Italy 40°18N 8°30E 22 D3
Bosanska Gradiška = Gradiška Bos.-H. 45°10N 17°15E 22 B7
Boscastle U.K. 50°41N 4°42W 13 G3
Boscobelle Barbados 13°17N 59°35W 89 g
Bose China 23°53N 106°35E 34 F6
Boseong S. Korea 34°46N 127°5E 33 G14
Boshan China 36°28N 117°49E 33 F9
Boshof S. Africa 28°31S 25°13E 56 C4
Boshrūyeh Iran 33°50N 57°30E 47 C8
Bosna → Bos.-H. 45°4N 18°29E 23 B8
Bosna i Hercegovina = Bosnia-Herzegovina ■ Europe 44°0N 18°0E 22 B7
Bosnia-Herzegovina ■ Europe 44°0N 18°0E 22 B7
Bosnik Indonesia 1°5S 136°10E 37 E9
Bosobolo Dem. Rep. of the Congo 4°15N 19°50E 54 D3
Bosque Farms U.S.A. 35°51N 106°42W 77 J10
Bosra = Buşra ash Shām Syria 32°30N 36°25E 48 C5
Bossangoa C.A.R. 6°35N 17°30E 54 C3
Bossier City U.S.A. 32°31N 93°44W 84 E8
Bossiesvlei Namibia 25°1S 16°44E 56 C2
Bosso Niger 13°43N 13°19E 53 F8
Bostan Pakistan 30°26N 67°2E 42 D2
Bostānābād Iran 37°50N 46°50E 46 B5
Bosten Hu China 41°55N 87°40E 30 C6
Boston U.K. 52°59N 0°2W 12 E7
Boston Bar Canada 49°52N 121°30W 70 D4
Boston Mts. U.S.A. 35°42N 93°15W 84 D8
Boswell Canada 49°28N 116°45W 70 D5
Boswell U.S.A. 40°10N 79°2W 82 F5
Botad India 22°15N 71°40E 42 H4
Botene Laos 17°35N 101°12E 38 D3
Bothaville S. Africa 27°23S 26°34E 56 C4
Bothnia, G. of Europe 62°0N 20°0E 8 F19
Bothwell Australia 42°20S 147°1E 63 G4
Bothwell Canada 42°38N 81°52W 82 D3
Botletle → Botswana 20°10S 23°15E 56 B3
Botoşani Romania 47°42N 26°41E 17 E14
Botou Burkina Faso 12°42N 1°59E 52 F6
Botou China 38°4N 116°34E 32 E9
Botshabelo S. Africa 29°14S 26°44E 56 C4
Botswana ■ Africa 22°0S 24°0E 56 B3
Bottineau U.S.A. 48°50N 100°27W 80 A3
Botucatu Brazil 22°55S 48°30W 95 A6
Botum Sakor △ Cambodia 11°10N 103°15E 39 G4
Botwood Canada 49°6N 55°23W 73 C8
Bou Saâda Algeria 35°11N 4°9E 52 A6
Bouaflé Côte d'Ivoire 7°1N 5°47W 52 G4
Bouaké Côte d'Ivoire 7°40N 5°2W 52 G4
Bouar C.A.R. 6°0N 15°40E 54 C3
Bouârfa Morocco 32°32N 1°58W 52 B5
Boucaut B. Australia 12°0S 134°25E 62 A1
Bouctouche Canada 46°30N 64°45W 73 C7
Bougainville, C. Australia 13°57S 126°4E 60 B4
Bougainville I. Papua N. G. 6°0S 155°0E 58 B8
Bougainville Reef Australia 15°30S 147°5E 62 B4
Bougie = Bejaïa Algeria 36°42N 5°2E 52 A7
Bougouni Mali 11°30N 7°20W 52 F4
Bouillon Belgium 49°44N 5°3E 15 E5
Boulder Colo., U.S.A. 40°1N 105°17W 76 F11

Boulder Mont., U.S.A. 46°14N 112°7W 76 C7
Boulder City U.S.A. 35°58N 114°49W 79 K12
Boulder Creek U.S.A. 37°7N 122°7W 78 H4
Boulder Dam = Hoover Dam U.S.A. 36°1N 114°44W 79 K12
Boulia Australia 22°52S 139°51E 62 C2
Boulogne-sur-Mer France 50°42N 1°36E 20 A4
Boulsa Burkina Faso 12°39N 0°34W 52 F5
Boultoum Niger 14°45N 10°25E 53 F8
Bouma △ Fiji 16°50S 179°52W 59 a
Boun Neua Laos 21°38N 101°54E 38 B3
Boun Tai Laos 21°23N 101°58E 38 B3
Bouna Côte d'Ivoire 9°10N 3°0W 52 G5
Boundary Peak U.S.A. 37°51N 118°21W 78 H8
Boundiali Côte d'Ivoire 9°30N 6°20W 52 G4
Bountiful U.S.A. 40°53N 111°52W 76 F8
Bounty Is. Pac. Oc. 48°0S 178°30E 64 M9
Bounty Trough Pac. Oc. 46°0S 178°0E 64 M9
Bourbonnais France 46°28N 3°0E 20 C5
Bourdel L. Canada 56°43N 74°10W 72 A5
Bourem Mali 17°0N 0°24W 52 E5
Bourg-en-Bresse France 46°13N 5°12E 20 C6
Bourg-St-Maurice France 45°35N 6°46E 20 D7
Bourgas = Burgas Bulgaria 42°33N 27°29E 23 C12
Bourges France 47°9N 2°25E 20 C5
Bourget Canada 45°26N 75°9W 83 A9
Bourgogne France 47°0N 4°50E 20 C6
Bourke Australia 30°8S 145°55E 63 E4
Bourne U.K. 52°47N 0°22W 12 E7
Bournemouth U.K. 50°43N 1°52W 13 G6
Bournemouth □ U.K. 50°43N 1°52W 13 G6
Bouse U.S.A. 33°56N 114°0W 79 M13
Boussa Chad 10°34N 16°52E 53 F9
Bouvet I. = Bouvetøya Antarctica 54°26S 3°24E 2 G10
Bouvetøya Antarctica 54°26S 3°24E 2 G10
Bovanenkovo Russia 70°22N 68°40E 26 B7
Bovill U.S.A. 46°51N 116°24W 76 C5
Bovril Argentina 31°21S 59°26W 94 C4
Bow → Canada 49°57N 111°41W 70 C6
Bow Island Canada 49°50N 111°23W 70 C6
Bowbells U.S.A. 48°48N 102°15W 80 A2
Bowdle U.S.A. 45°27N 99°39W 80 C4
Bowelling Australia 33°25S 116°30E 61 F2
Bowen Argentina 35°0S 67°31W 94 D2
Bowen Australia 20°0S 148°16E 62 J4
Bowen Mts. Australia 37°0S 147°50E 63 F4
Bowers Basin Pac. Oc. 53°45N 176°0E 4 D16
Bowers Ridge Pac. Oc. 54°0N 180°0E 4 D17
Bowie Ariz., U.S.A. 32°19N 109°29W 77 K9
Bowie Tex., U.S.A. 33°34N 97°51W 84 E6
Bowkān Iran 36°31N 46°12E 46 B5
Bowland, Forest of U.K. 54°0N 2°30W 12 D5
Bowling Green Ky., U.S.A. 36°59N 86°27W 80 G10
Bowling Green Ohio, U.S.A. 41°23N 83°39W 81 E12
Bowling Green, C. Australia 19°19S 147°25E 62 B4
Bowling Green Bay △ Australia 19°26S 146°57E 62 B4
Bowman U.S.A. 46°11N 103°24W 80 B2
Bowman I. Antarctica 65°0S 104°0E 5 C8
Bowmanville = Clarington Canada 43°55N 78°41W 82 C6
Bowmore U.K. 55°45N 6°17W 11 F2
Bowral Australia 34°26S 150°27E 63 E5
Bowraville Australia 30°37S 152°52E 63 E5
Bowron → Canada 54°3N 121°50W 70 C4
Bowron Lake △ Canada 53°10N 121°5W 70 C4
Bowser L. Canada 56°30N 129°30W 70 B3
Bowsman Canada 52°14N 101°12W 71 C8
Box Cr. → Australia 34°10S 143°50E 63 E3
Boxmeer Neths. 51°38N 5°56E 15 C5
Boxtel Neths. 51°36N 5°20E 15 C5
Boyang China 29°0N 116°38E 35 C11
Boyce U.S.A. 31°23N 92°40W 84 F8
Boyd L. Canada 52°46N 76°42W 72 B4
Boyle Canada 54°35N 112°49W 70 C6
Boyle Ireland 53°59N 8°18W 10 C3
Boyne → Ireland 53°43N 6°15W 10 C5
Boyne, Bend of the Ireland 53°41N 6°27W 10 C5
Boyne City U.S.A. 45°13N 85°1W 81 C11
Boynton Beach U.S.A. 26°32N 80°4W 85 H14
Boyoma, Chutes Dem. Rep. of the Congo 0°35N 25°23E 50 F6
Boysen Res. U.S.A. 43°25N 108°11W 76 E9
Boyuibe Bolivia 20°25S 63°17W 92 G6
Boyup Brook Australia 33°50S 116°23E 61 F2
Boz Dağları Turkey 38°20N 28°0E 23 E13
Bozburun Turkey 36°43N 28°4E 23 F13
Bozcaada Turkey 39°49N 26°3E 23 E12
Bozdoğan Turkey 37°40N 28°17E 23 F13
Bozeman U.S.A. 45°41N 111°2W 76 D8
Bozen = Bolzano Italy 46°31N 11°22E 22 A4
Bozhou China 33°55N 115°41E 32 H8
Bozoum C.A.R. 6°25N 16°35E 54 C3
Bozyazı Turkey 36°N 33°0E 46 D2
Bra Italy 44°42N 7°51E 20 D7
Brabant □ Belgium 50°46N 4°30E 15 D4
Brabant L. Canada 55°58N 103°43W 71 B8
Brač Croatia 43°20N 16°40E 22 C7
Bracadale, L. U.K. 57°20N 6°30W 11 D2
Bracciano, L. di Italy 42°7N 12°14E 22 C5
Bracebridge Canada 45°2N 79°19W 82 A5
Bräcke Sweden 62°45N 15°26E 8 E16
Brackettville U.S.A. 29°19N 100°25W 84 G4
Bracknell U.K. 51°25N 0°43W 13 F7
Bracknell Forest □ U.K. 51°25N 0°44W 13 F7
Brad Romania 46°10N 22°50E 17 E12
Bradenton U.S.A. 27°30N 82°34W 85 H13
Bradford Canada 44°7N 79°34W 82 B5
Bradford U.K. 53°47N 1°45W 12 D6
Bradford Pa., U.S.A. 41°58N 78°38W 82 E6
Bradford Vt., U.S.A. 43°59N 72°9W 83 C12
Bradley Ark., U.S.A. 33°6N 93°39W 84 E8
Bradley Calif., U.S.A. 35°52N 120°48W 78 K6
Brady U.S.A. 31°9N 99°20W 84 F5
Braeside Canada 45°28N 76°24W 83 A8

Braga Portugal 41°35N 8°25W 21 B1
Bragado Argentina 35°2S 60°27W 94 D3
Bragança Brazil 1°0S 47°2W 93 D9
Bragança Portugal 41°48N 6°50W 21 B2
Bragança Paulista Brazil 22°55S 46°32W 95 A6
Brahestad = Raahe Finland 64°40N 24°28E 8 D21
Brahmanbaria Bangla. 23°58N 91°15E 41 H17
Brahmani → India 20°39N 86°46E 44 D8
Brahmapur India 19°15N 84°54E 44 E7
Brahmaputra → Asia 23°40N 90°35E 43 H13
Braich-y-pwll U.K. 52°47N 4°46W 12 E3
Braidwood Australia 35°27S 149°49E 63 F4
Brăila Romania 45°19N 27°59E 17 F14
Brainerd U.S.A. 46°22N 94°12W 80 B7
Braintree U.K. 51°53N 0°34E 13 F8
Braintree U.S.A. 42°13N 71°0W 83 D14
Brak → S. Africa 29°35S 22°55E 56 C3
Brakwater Namibia 22°28S 17°3E 56 B2
Bramhapuri India 20°36N 79°52E 44 D4
Brampton Canada 43°45N 79°45W 82 C5
Brampton U.K. 54°57N 2°44W 12 C5
Brampton I. Australia 20°49S 149°16E 62 b
Branco → Brazil 1°20S 61°50W 92 D6
Branco, C. Brazil 7°9S 34°47W 90 D7
Brandberg Namibia 21°10S 14°33E 56 B1
Brandberg △ Namibia 21°10S 14°30E 56 B1
Brandenburg = Neubrandenburg Germany 53°33N 13°15E 16 B7
Brandenburg Germany 52°25N 12°33E 16 B7
Brandenburg □ Germany 52°50N 13°0E 16 B6
Brandfort S. Africa 28°40S 26°30E 56 C4
Brandon Canada 49°50N 99°57W 71 D9
Brandon U.S.A. 43°48N 73°6W 83 C11
Brandon B. Ireland 52°17N 10°8W 10 D1
Brandon Mt. Ireland 52°15N 10°15W 10 D1
Brandsen Argentina 35°10S 58°15W 94 D4
Brandvlei S. Africa 30°25S 20°30E 56 D3
Branford U.S.A. 41°17N 72°49W 83 E12
Braniewo Poland 54°25N 19°50E 17 A10
Bransfield Str. Antarctica 63°0S 59°0W 5 C18
Branson U.S.A. 36°39N 93°13W 80 G7
Brantford Canada 43°10N 80°15W 82 C4
Bras d'Or L. Canada 45°50N 60°50W 73 C7
Brasher Falls U.S.A. 44°49N 74°47W 83 B10
Brasil = Brazil ■ S. Amer. 12°0S 50°0W 93 F9
Brasil, Planalto Brazil 18°0S 46°30W 90 E6
Brasiléia Brazil 11°0S 68°45W 92 F5
Brasília Brazil 15°47S 47°55W 93 G9
Brasília Legal Brazil 3°49S 55°36W 93 D7
Braslaw Belarus 55°38N 27°0E 9 J22
Braşov Romania 45°38N 25°35E 17 F13
Brasschaat Belgium 51°19N 4°27E 15 C4
Brassey, Banjaran Malaysia 5°0N 117°15E 36 D5
Brassey Ra. Australia 25°8S 122°15E 61 E3
Brasstown Bald U.S.A. 34°53N 83°49W 85 D13
Brastad Sweden 58°23N 11°30E 9 G14
Bratislava Slovakia 48°10N 17°7E 17 D9
Bratsk Russia 56°10N 101°30E 27 D11
Bratskoye Vdkhr. Russia 56°0N 101°40E 27 D11
Brattleboro U.S.A. 42°51N 72°34W 83 D12
Braunau am Inn Austria 48°15N 13°3E 16 D7
Braunschweig Germany 52°15N 10°31E 16 B6
Braunton U.K. 51°7N 4°10W 13 F3
Brava Cabo Verde 15°0N 24°40W 52 b
Brava, Costa Spain 41°30N 3°0E 21 B7
Bravo del Norte, Rio = Grande, Rio → N. Amer. 25°58N 97°9W 84 J6
Brawley U.S.A. 32°59N 115°31W 79 N11
Bray Ireland 53°13N 6°7W 10 C5
Bray, Mt. Australia 14°0S 134°30E 62 A1
Bray, Pays de France 49°46N 1°26E 20 B4
Brazeau → Canada 52°55N 115°14W 70 C5
Brazil U.S.A. 39°32N 87°8W 80 F10
Brazil ■ S. Amer. 12°0S 50°0W 93 F9
Brazilian Highlands = Brasil, Planalto Brazil 18°0S 46°30W 90 E6
Brazo Sur → S. Amer. 25°21S 57°42W 94 B4
Brazos → U.S.A. 28°53N 95°23W 84 G7
Brazzaville Congo 4°9S 15°12E 54 E3
Brčko Bos.-H. 44°54N 18°46E 23 B8
Bré = Bray Ireland 53°13N 6°7W 10 C5
Breaden, L. Australia 25°51S 125°28E 61 E4
Breaksea Sd. N.Z. 45°35S 166°35E 59 F1
Bream B. N.Z. 35°56S 174°28E 59 A5
Bream Hd. N.Z. 35°51S 174°36E 59 A5
Breas Chile 25°29S 70°24W 94 B1
Brebes Indonesia 6°52S 109°3E 37 G13
Brechin Canada 44°32N 79°10W 82 B5
Brechin U.K. 56°44N 2°39W 11 E6
Brecht Belgium 51°21N 4°38E 15 C4
Breckenridge Colo., U.S.A. 39°29N 106°3W 76 G10
Breckenridge Minn., U.S.A. 46°16N 96°35W 80 B5
Breckenridge Tex., U.S.A. 32°45N 98°54W 84 E5
Breckland U.K. 52°30N 0°40E 13 E8
Brecon U.K. 51°57N 3°23W 13 F4
Brecon Beacons U.K. 51°53N 3°26W 13 F4
Brecon Beacons △ U.K. 51°50N 3°30W 13 F4
Breda Neths. 51°35N 4°45E 15 C4
Bredasdorp S. Africa 34°33S 20°2E 56 E3
Bree Belgium 51°8N 5°35E 15 C5
Bregenz Austria 47°30N 9°45E 16 E5
Breiðafjörður Iceland 65°15N 23°15E 8 D2
Brejo Brazil 3°41S 42°47W 93 D10
Bremen Germany 53°4N 8°47E 16 B5
Bremer Bay Australia 34°21S 119°20E 61 F2
Bremer I. Australia 12°5S 136°45E 62 A2
Bremerhaven Germany 53°33N 8°36E 16 B5
Bremerton U.S.A. 47°34N 122°37W 78 C4
Brenham U.S.A. 30°10N 96°24W 84 F6
Brennerpass Austria 47°2N 11°30E 16 E6
Brent Canada 46°2N 78°29W 72 C4
Brentwood U.K. 51°37N 0°19E 13 F8
Brentwood Calif., U.S.A. 37°56N 121°42W 78 H5
Brentwood N.Y., U.S.A. 40°47N 73°15W 83 F11
Bréscia Italy 45°33N 10°15E 20 D9

Breskens Neths. 51°23N 3°33E 15 C3
Breslau = Wrocław Poland 51°5N 17°5E 17 C9
Bressanone Italy 46°43N 11°39E 22 A4
Bressay U.K. 60°9N 1°6W 11 A7
Brest Belarus 52°10N 23°40E 17 B12
Brest France 48°24N 4°31W 20 B1
Brest □ Belarus 52°30N 26°10E 17 B13
Brest-Litovsk = Brest Belarus 52°10N 23°40E 17 B12
Bretagne □ France 48°10N 3°0W 20 B2
Breton Canada 53°7N 114°28W 70 C6
Breton Sd. U.S.A. 29°35N 89°15W 85 G10
Brett, C. N.Z. 35°10S 174°20E 59 A5
Brevard U.S.A. 35°14N 82°44W 85 D13
Breves Brazil 1°40S 50°29W 93 D8
Brewarrina Australia 30°0S 146°51E 63 E4
Brewer U.S.A. 44°48N 68°46W 81 C19
Brewer, Mt. U.S.A. 36°44N 118°28W 78 J8
Brewster N.Y., U.S.A. 41°24N 73°36W 83 E11
Brewster Ohio, U.S.A. 40°43N 81°36W 82 F3
Brewster Wash., U.S.A. 48°6N 119°47W 76 B4
Brewster, Kap = Kangikajik Greenland 70°7N 22°0W 4 B6
Brewton U.S.A. 31°7N 87°4W 85 F11
Breyten S. Africa 26°16S 30°0E 57 C5
Bria C.A.R. 6°30N 21°58E 54 C4
Briançon France 44°54N 6°39E 20 D7
Bribie I. Australia 27°0S 153°10E 63 D5
Bribri Costa Rica 9°38N 82°50W 88 E3
Bridgefield Barbados 13°9N 59°36W 89 g
Bridgehampton U.S.A. 40°56N 72°19W 83 F12
Bridgend S. Africa 51°30N 3°34W 13 F4
Bridgend □ U.K. 51°36N 3°36W 13 F4
Bridgenorth Canada 44°23N 78°23W 82 B6
Bridgeport Calif., U.S.A. 38°15N 119°14W 78 G7
Bridgeport Conn., U.S.A. 41°11N 73°12W 83 E11
Bridgeport N.Y., U.S.A. 43°9N 75°58W 83 C9
Bridgeport Nebr., U.S.A. 41°40N 103°6W 80 E2
Bridgeport Tex., U.S.A. 33°13N 97°45W 84 E6
Bridger U.S.A. 45°18N 108°55W 76 D9
Bridgeton U.S.A. 39°26N 75°14W 81 F16
Bridgetown Australia 33°58S 116°7E 61 F2
Bridgetown Barbados 13°6N 59°37W 89 g
Bridgetown Canada 44°55N 65°18W 73 D6
Bridgewater Australia 42°44S 147°14E 63 G4
Bridgewater Canada 44°25N 64°31W 73 D7
Bridgewater Mass., U.S.A. 41°59N 70°58W 83 E14
Bridgewater N.Y., U.S.A. 42°53N 75°15W 83 D9
Bridgewater, C. Australia 38°23S 141°23E 63 F3
Bridgnorth U.K. 52°32N 2°25W 13 E5
Bridgton U.S.A. 44°3N 70°42W 83 B14
Bridgwater U.K. 51°8N 2°59W 13 F5
Bridgwater B. U.K. 51°15N 3°15W 13 F4
Bridlington U.K. 54°5N 0°12W 12 C7
Bridlington B. U.K. 54°4N 0°10W 12 C7
Bridport Australia 40°59S 147°23E 63 G4
Bridport U.K. 50°44N 2°45W 13 G5
Brig Switz. 46°18N 7°59E 20 C7
Brigham City U.S.A. 41°31N 112°1W 76 F7
Bright Australia 36°42S 146°56E 63 F4
Brighton Australia 35°5S 138°30E 63 F2
Brighton Canada 44°2N 77°44W 82 B7
Brighton Trin. & Tob. 10°15N 61°39W 93 K15
Brighton U.K. 50°49N 0°7W 13 G7
Brighton U.S.A. 43°8N 77°34W 82 C7
Brightside Canada 45°7N 76°29W 83 A8
Brilliant U.S.A. 40°15N 80°39W 82 F4
Brindisi Italy 40°39N 17°55E 23 D7
Brinkley U.S.A. 34°53N 91°12W 84 D9
Brinnon U.S.A. 47°41N 122°54W 78 C4
Brion, Î. Canada 47°46N 61°26W 73 C7
Brisay Canada 54°26N 70°31W 73 B5
Brisbane Australia 27°25S 153°2E 63 D5
Brisbane → Australia 27°24S 153°9E 63 D5
Brisbane ✈ (BNE) Australia 27°35S 153°7E 63 D5
Bristol U.K. 51°26N 2°35W 13 F5
Bristol Conn., U.S.A. 41°40N 72°57W 83 E12
Bristol Pa., U.S.A. 40°6N 74°51W 83 F10
Bristol R.I., U.S.A. 41°40N 71°16W 83 E13
Bristol Tenn., U.S.A. 36°36N 82°11W 85 C13
Bristol Vt., U.S.A. 44°8N 73°4W 83 B11
Bristol, City of □ U.K. 51°27N 2°36W 13 F5
Bristol B. Antarctica 58°0N 160°0W 74 D8
Bristol Channel U.K. 51°18N 4°30W 13 F3
Bristol I. Antarctica 58°45S 28°0W 5 B1
Bristol L. U.S.A. 34°28N 115°41W 79 L11
Bristow U.S.A. 35°50N 96°23W 84 D6
Britain = Great Britain Europe 54°0N 2°15W 6 E5
British Columbia □ Canada 55°0N 125°15W 70 C3
British Indian Ocean Terr. = Chagos Arch. ☑ Ind. Oc. 6°0S 72°0E 3 E13
British Isles Europe 54°0N 4°0W 14 D5
British Mts. N. Amer. 68°50N 140°0W 74 B12
British Virgin Is. ☑ W. Indies 18°30N 64°30W 89 e
Brits S. Africa 25°37S 27°48E 57 C4
Britstown S. Africa 30°37S 23°30E 56 D3
Britt Canada 45°46N 80°34W 72 C3
Brittany = Bretagne □ France 48°10N 3°0W 20 B2
Britton U.S.A. 45°48N 97°45W 80 C5
Brive-la-Gaillarde France 45°10N 1°32E 20 D4
Brixen = Bressanone Italy 46°43N 11°39E 22 A4
Brixham U.K. 50°23N 3°31W 13 G4
Brno Czechia 49°10N 16°35E 17 D9
Broach = Bharuch India 21°47N 73°0E 44 D1
Broad → U.S.A. 34°1N 81°4W 85 D14
Broad Arrow Australia 30°23S 121°15E 61 E3
Broad B. U.K. 58°14N 6°18W 11 C2
Broad Haven Ireland 54°20N 9°55W 10 B2
Broad Law U.K. 55°30N 3°21W 11 F5
Broad Pk. = Faichan Kangri India 35°48N 76°34E 43 B7
Broad Sd. Australia 22°0S 149°45E 62 C4

Broadalbin U.S.A. 43°4N 74°12W 83 C10
Broadback → Canada 51°21N 78°52W 72 B4
Broadhurst Ra. Australia 22°30S 122°30E 60 D3
Broads, The U.K. 52°45N 1°30E 12 E9
Broadus U.S.A. 45°27N 105°25W 76 D11
Brochet Canada 57°53N 101°40W 71 B8
Brochet, L. Canada 58°36N 101°35W 71 B8
Brock I. Canada 77°52N 114°19W 69 B9
Brocken Germany 51°47N 10°37E 16 C6
Brockport U.S.A. 43°13N 77°56W 82 C7
Brockton U.S.A. 42°5N 71°1W 83 D13
Brockville Canada 44°35N 75°41W 83 B9
Brockway Mont., U.S.A. 47°18N 105°45W 76 C11
Brockway Pa., U.S.A. 41°15N 78°47W 82 E6
Brocton U.S.A. 42°23N 79°26W 82 D5
Brodeur Pen. Canada 72°30N 88°10W 69 C14
Brodick U.K. 55°35N 5°9W 11 F3
Brodnica Poland 53°15N 19°25E 17 B10
Brody Ukraine 50°5N 25°10E 17 C13
Brogan U.S.A. 44°15N 117°31W 76 D5
Broken Arrow U.S.A. 36°3N 95°48W 84 C7
Broken Bow Nebr., U.S.A. 41°24N 99°38W 80 E4
Broken Bow Okla., U.S.A. 34°2N 94°44W 84 D7
Broken Bow Lake U.S.A. 34°9N 94°40W 84 D7
Broken Hill Australia 31°58S 141°29E 63 E3
Broken Ridge Ind. Oc. 30°0S 94°0E 64 L1
Broken River Ra. Australia 21°0S 148°22E 62 b
Bromo, Gunung Indonesia 7°56S 112°57E 37 H15
Bromo Tengger Semeru △ Indonesia 7°56S 112°57E 37 H15
Bromsgrove U.K. 52°21N 2°2W 13 E5
Brønderslev Denmark 57°16N 9°57E 9 H13
Bronkhorstspruit S. Africa 25°46S 28°45E 57 C4
Brønnøysund Norway 65°28N 12°14E 8 D15
Brook Park U.S.A. 41°23N 81°48W 82 E4
Brookhaven U.S.A. 31°35N 90°26W 85 F9
Brookings Oreg., U.S.A. 42°3N 124°17W 76 E1
Brookings S. Dak., U.S.A. 44°19N 96°48W 80 C5
Brooklin Canada 43°55N 78°55W 82 C6
Brooklyn Park U.S.A. 45°6N 93°23W 80 C7
Brooks Canada 50°35N 111°55W 70 C6
Brooks Range U.S.A. 68°0N 152°0W 74 B9
Brooksville U.S.A. 28°33N 82°23W 85 G13
Brookton Australia 32°22S 117°0E 61 F2
Brookville U.S.A. 41°10N 79°5W 82 E5
Broom, L. U.K. 57°55N 5°15W 11 D3
Broome Australia 18°0S 122°15E 60 C3
Brora U.K. 58°0N 3°52W 11 C5
Brora → U.K. 58°0N 3°51W 11 C5
Brosna → Ireland 53°14N 7°58W 10 C4
Brothers U.S.A. 43°49N 120°36W 76 E3
Brough U.K. 54°32N 2°18W 12 C5
Brough Hd. U.K. 59°8N 3°20W 11 B5
Broughton Island = Qikiqtarjuaq Canada 67°33N 63°0W 69 D19
Brown, L. Australia 31°5S 118°15E 61 F2
Brown, Pt. Australia 32°32S 133°50E 63 E1
Brown City U.S.A. 43°13N 82°59W 82 C2
Brown Willy U.K. 50°35N 4°37W 13 G3
Brownfield U.S.A. 33°11N 102°17W 84 E3
Browning U.S.A. 48°34N 113°1W 76 B7
Brownsville Oreg., U.S.A. 44°24N 122°59W 76 D2
Brownsville Pa., U.S.A. 40°1N 79°53W 82 F5
Brownsville Tenn., U.S.A. 35°36N 89°16W 85 D10
Brownsville Tex., U.S.A. 25°54N 97°30W 84 J6
Brownville U.S.A. 44°0N 75°59W 83 B9
Brownwood U.S.A. 31°43N 98°59W 84 F5
Browse I. Australia 14°7S 123°33E 60 B3
Bruas Malaysia 4°30N 100°47E 39 K3
Bruay-la-Buissière France 50°29N 2°33E 20 A5
Bruce, Mt. Australia 22°37S 118°8E 60 D2
Bruce Pen. Canada 45°0N 81°30W 82 A3
Bruce Peninsula △ Canada 45°14N 81°36W 82 A3
Bruce Rock Australia 31°52S 118°8E 61 F2
Bruck an der Leitha Austria 48°1N 16°47E 17 D9
Bruck an der Mur Austria 47°24N 15°16E 16 E8
Brue → U.K. 51°13N 2°59W 13 F5
Bruges = Brugge Belgium 51°13N 3°13E 15 C3
Brugge Belgium 51°13N 3°13E 15 C3
Brûk, W. el → Egypt 30°15N 33°50E 48 E2
Brûlé Canada 53°15N 117°58W 70 C5
Brûlé, L. Canada 53°35N 64°4W 73 B7
Brumado Brazil 14°14S 41°40W 93 F10
Brumunddal Norway 60°53N 10°56E 8 F14
Bruneau U.S.A. 42°53N 115°48W 76 E6
Bruneau → U.S.A. 42°56N 115°57W 76 E6
Brunei = Bandar Seri Begawan Brunei 4°52N 115°0E 36 D5
Brunei ■ Asia 4°50N 115°0E 36 D5
Brunette Downs Australia 18°40S 135°55E 62 B2
Brunssum Neths. 50°57N 5°59E 15 D5
Brunswick = Braunschweig Germany 52°15N 10°31E 16 B6
Brunswick Ga., U.S.A. 31°10N 81°30W 85 F14
Brunswick Maine, U.S.A. 43°55N 69°58W 81 D19
Brunswick Md., U.S.A. 39°19N 77°38W 81 F15
Brunswick Mo., U.S.A. 39°26N 93°8W 80 F7
Brunswick Ohio, U.S.A. 41°14N 81°51W 82 E3
Brunswick, Pen. de Chile 53°30S 71°30W 96 G2
Brunswick B. Australia 15°15S 124°50E 60 C3
Brunswick Junction Australia 33°15S 115°50E 61 F2
Brunt Ice Shelf Antarctica 75°30S 25°0W 5 D2
Brus Laguna Honduras 15°47N 84°35W 88 C3
Brush U.S.A. 40°15N 103°37W 76 F12
Brushton U.S.A. 44°50N 74°31W 83 B10
Brusque Brazil 27°5S 49°0W 95 B6
Brussels = Brussel Belgium 50°51N 4°21E 15 D4
Bruthen Australia 37°42S 147°50E 63 F4
Bryan Ohio, U.S.A. 41°28N 84°33W 81 E11

Bryan *Tex., U.S.A.* 30°40N 96°22W **84 F6**
Bryan, Mt. *Australia* 33°30S 139°5E **63 E2**
Bryansk *Russia* 53°13N 34°25E **18 D4**
Bryce Canyon △ *U.S.A.* 37°30N 112°10W **77 H7**
Bryne *Norway* 58°44N 5°38E **9 G11**
Bryson City *U.S.A.* 35°26N 83°27W **85 D13**
Bsharri *Lebanon* 34°15N 36°0E **48 A5**
Bū Baqarah *U.A.E.* 25°35N 56°25E **47 E8**
Bu Craa *W. Sahara* 26°45N 12°50W **52 C3**
Bū Ḥasā *U.A.E.* 23°30N 53°20E **47 F7**
Bua *Fiji* 16°48S 178°37E **59 a**
Bua Yai *Thailand* 15°33N 102°26E **38 E4**
Buan *S. Korea* 35°44N 126°44E **33 G14**
Buapinang *Indonesia* 4°40S 121°30E **37 E6**
Bubi → *Zimbabwe* 22°20S 31°7E **57 B5**
Būbiyān *Kuwait* 29°45N 48°15E **47 D6**
Buca *Fiji* 16°38S 179°52E **59 a**
Bucaramanga *Colombia* 7°0N 73°0W **92 B4**
Bucasia *Australia* 21°2S 149°10E **62 b**
Buccaneer Arch.
 *Australia* 16°7S 123°20E **60 C3**
Buccoo Reef *Trin. & Tob.* 11°10N 60°51W **93 J16**
Buchach *Ukraine* 49°5N 25°25E **17 D13**
Buchan *U.K.* 57°32N 2°21W **11 D6**
Buchan Ness *U.K.* 57°29N 1°46W **11 D7**
Buchanan *Canada* 51°40N 102°45W **71 C8**
Buchanan *Liberia* 5°57N 10°2W **52 G3**
Buchanan, L. *Queens.,*
 *Australia* 21°35S 145°52E **62 C4**
Buchanan, L. *W. Austral.,*
 *Australia* 25°33S 123°2E **61 E3**
Buchanan, L. *U.S.A.* 30°45N 98°25W **84 F5**
Buchanan Cr. →
 *Australia* 19°13S 136°33E **62 B2**
Buchans *Canada* 48°50N 56°52W **73 C8**
Bucharest = Bucureşti
 *Romania* 44°27N 26°10E **17 F14**
Bucheon *S. Korea* 37°28N 126°45E **33 F14**
Buchon, Pt. *U.S.A.* 35°15N 120°54W **78 K6**
Buck Hill Falls *U.S.A.* 41°11N 75°16W **83 E9**
Buckeye Lake *U.S.A.* 39°55N 82°29W **82 G2**
Buckhannon *U.S.A.* 39°0N 80°8W **81 F13**
Buckhaven *U.K.* 56°11N 3°3W **11 E5**
Buckhorn L. *Canada* 44°29N 78°23W **82 B6**
Buckie *U.K.* 57°41N 2°58W **11 D6**
Buckingham *Canada* 45°37N 75°24W **72 C4**
Buckingham *U.K.* 51°59N 0°57W **13 F7**
Buckingham B.
 *Australia* 12°10S 135°40E **62 A2**
Buckingham Canal *India* 14°0N 80°5E **45 H5**
Buckinghamshire □ *U.K.* 51°53N 0°55W **13 F7**
Buckle Hd. *Australia* 14°26S 127°52E **60 B4**
Buckleboo *Australia* 32°54S 136°12E **63 E2**
Buckley *U.K.* 53°10N 3°5W **12 D4**
Buckley → *Australia* 20°10S 138°49E **62 C2**
Bucklin *U.S.A.* 37°33N 99°38W **80 G4**
Bucks L. *U.S.A.* 39°54N 121°12W **78 F5**
Bucureşti *Romania* 44°27N 26°10E **17 F14**
Bucyrus *U.S.A.* 40°48N 82°59W **81 E12**
Budalin *Myanmar* 22°20N 95°10E **41 H19**
Budaun *India* 28°5N 79°10E **43 E8**
Budd Coast *Antarctica* 68°0S 112°0E **5 C8**
Bude *U.S.A.* 50°49N 4°34W **13 G3**
Budennovsk *Russia* 44°50N 44°10E **19 F7**
Budge Budge = Baj Baj
 *India* 22°30N 88°5E **43 H13**
Budgewoi *Australia* 33°13S 151°34E **63 E5**
Budjala
 *Dem. Rep. of the Congo* 2°50N 19°40E **54 D3**
Budo-Sungai Padi △
 *Thailand* 6°19N 101°42E **39 J3**
Buellton *U.S.A.* 34°37N 120°12W **79 L6**
Buena Esperanza
 *Argentina* 34°45S 65°15W **94 C2**
Buena Park *U.S.A.* 33°52N 117°59W **79 M9**
Buena Vista *Colo.,*
 *U.S.A.* 38°51N 106°8W **76 G10**
Buena Vista *Va., U.S.A.* 37°44N 79°21W **81 G14**
Buena Vista Lake Bed
 *U.S.A.* 35°12N 119°18W **79 K7**
Buenaventura *Colombia* 3°53N 77°4W **92 C3**
Buenaventura *Mexico* 29°51N 107°29W **86 B3**
Buenos Aires *Costa Rica* 9°10N 83°20W **88 E3**
Buenos Aires ♦ *Argentina* 36°30S 60°0W **94 D4**
Buenos Aires, L. = General
 Carrera, L. *S. Amer.* 46°35S 72°0W **96 F2**
Buffalo *Mo., U.S.A.* 37°39N 93°6W **80 G7**
Buffalo *N.Y., U.S.A.* 42°53N 78°53W **82 D6**
Buffalo *Okla., U.S.A.* 36°50N 99°38W **84 C5**
Buffalo *S. Dak., U.S.A.* 45°35N 103°33W **80 C2**
Buffalo *Wyo., U.S.A.* 44°21N 106°42W **76 D10**
Buffalo → *Canada* 60°5N 115°5W **70 A5**
Buffalo → *S. Africa* 28°43S 30°37E **57 C5**
Buffalo → *U.S.A.* 36°14N 92°36W **84 C8**
Buffalo Head Hills
 *Canada* 57°25N 115°55W **70 B5**
Buffalo L. *Alta., Canada* 52°27N 112°54W **70 C6**
Buffalo L. *N.W.T.,*
 *Canada* 60°12N 115°25W **70 A5**
Buffalo Narrows *Canada* 55°51N 108°29W **71 B7**
Buffels → *S. Africa* 29°36S 17°3E **56 C2**
Buford *U.S.A.* 34°7N 83°59W **85 D12**
Bug = Buh → *Ukraine* 46°59N 31°58E **19 E5**
Bug → *Poland* 52°31N 21°5E **17 B11**
Buga *Colombia* 4°0N 76°15W **92 C3**
Bugel, Tanjung *Indonesia* 6°26S 111°3E **37 G14**
Bugsuk I. *Phil.* 8°12N 117°18E **36 C5**
Bugulma *Russia* 54°33N 52°48E **18 D9**
Buguruslan *Russia* 53°39N 52°26E **18 D9**
Buh → *Ukraine* 46°59N 31°58E **19 E5**
Buhera *Zimbabwe* 19°18S 31°29E **57 A5**
Buhl *U.S.A.* 42°36N 114°46W **76 E6**
Builth Wells *U.K.* 52°9N 3°25E **13 E4**
Buir Nur *Mongolia* 47°50N 117°42E **31 B12**
Buji *China* 22°37N 114°5E **31 a**
Bujumbura *Burundi* 3°16S 29°18E **54 C2**
Bukachacha *Russia* 52°55N 116°50E **27 D12**
Bukavu
 *Dem. Rep. of the Congo* 2°20S 28°52E **54 C5**
Bukhara = Buxoro
 *Uzbekistan* 39°48N 64°25E **26 F7**

Bukhoro = Buxoro
 *Uzbekistan* 39°48N 64°25E **26 F7**
Bukhtarma Res. = Zaysan Köli
 *Kazakhstan* 48°0N 83°0E **26 E9**
Bukit Bendera *Malaysia* 5°25N 100°15E **39 c**
Bukit Mertajam *Malaysia* 5°22N 100°28E **39 c**
Bukit Nil *Malaysia* 1°22N 104°12E **39 d**
Bukit Tengah *Malaysia* 5°22N 100°28E **39 c**
Bukittinggi *Indonesia* 0°20S 100°20E **36 E2**
Bukkapatnam *India* 14°14N 77°46E **45 G3**
Bukoba *Tanzania* 1°20S 31°49E **54 E6**
Bukuru *Nigeria* 9°42N 8°48E **52 G7**
Bula *Indonesia* 3°6S 130°30E **37 E8**
Bulahdelah *Australia* 32°23S 152°13E **63 E5**
Bulan *Phil.* 12°40N 123°52E **37 B6**
Bulandshahr *India* 28°28N 77°51E **42 E7**
Bulawayo *Zimbabwe* 20°7S 28°32E **55 J5**
Buldan *Turkey* 38°2N 28°50E **23 E13**
Buldana *India* 20°30N 76°18E **44 D3**
Buldir I. *U.S.A.* 52°21N 175°56E **74 E3**
Bulgan *Mongolia* 48°45N 103°34E **30 B9**
Bulgar *Russia* 54°57N 49°4E **18 D8**
Bulgaria ■ *Europe* 42°35N 25°30E **23 C11**
Buli, Teluk *Indonesia* 0°48N 128°25E **37 D7**
Buliluyan, C. *Phil.* 8°20N 117°15E **36 C5**
Bulkley → *Canada* 55°15N 127°40W **70 B3**
Bull Shoals L. *U.S.A.* 36°22N 92°35W **84 C8**
Bullhead City *U.S.A.* 35°8N 114°32W **79 K12**
Büllingen *Belgium* 50°25N 6°16E **15 D6**
Bullock Creek *Australia* 17°43S 144°31E **62 B3**
Bulloo → *Australia* 28°43S 142°30E **63 D3**
Bulloo L. *Australia* 28°43S 142°25E **63 D3**
Bulls *N.Z.* 40°10S 175°24E **59 D5**
Bulman *Australia* 13°39S 134°20E **62 A1**
Bulnes *Chile* 36°42S 72°19W **94 D1**
Bulsar = Valsad *India* 20°40N 72°58E **44 D1**
Bultfontein *S. Africa* 28°18S 26°10E **56 C4**
Bulukumba *Indonesia* 5°33S 120°11E **37 F6**
Bulun *Russia* 70°37N 127°30E **27 B13**
Bumba
 *Dem. Rep. of the Congo* 2°13N 22°30E **54 D4**
Bumbah, Khalīj *Libya* 32°20N 23°15E **53 B10**
Bumhpa Bum *Myanmar* 26°51N 97°14E **41 F20**
Bunaken *Indonesia* 1°37N 124°46E **37 D6**
Bunbury *Australia* 33°20S 115°35E **61 F2**
Bunclody *Ireland* 52°39N 6°40W **10 D5**
Buncrana *Ireland* 55°8N 7°27W **10 A4**
Bundaberg *Australia* 24°54S 152°22E **63 C5**
Bundey → *Australia* 21°46S 135°37E **62 C2**
Bundi *India* 25°30N 75°35E **42 G6**
Bundjalung △ *Australia* 29°16S 153°21E **63 D5**
Bundoran *Ireland* 54°28N 8°18W **10 B3**
Bung Kan *Thailand* 18°23N 103°37E **38 C4**
Bungay *U.K.* 52°27N 1°28E **13 E9**
Bungil Cr. → *Australia* 27°5S 149°5E **63 D4**
Bungle Bungle = Purnululu △
 *Australia* 17°20S 128°20E **60 C4**
Bungo-Suidō *Japan* 33°0N 132°15E **29 H6**
Bungotakada *Japan* 33°35N 131°25E **29 H5**
Bunia
 *Dem. Rep. of the Congo* 1°35N 30°20E **54 D6**
Bunji *Pakistan* 35°45N 74°40E **43 B6**
Bunkie *U.S.A.* 30°57N 92°11W **84 F8**
Bunnell *U.S.A.* 29°28N 81°16W **85 G14**
Bunya Mts. △ *Australia* 26°51S 151°34E **63 D5**
Bunyu *Indonesia* 3°35N 117°50E **36 D5**
Buol *Indonesia* 1°15N 121°32E **37 D6**
Buon Brieng *Vietnam* 13°9N 108°12E **38 F7**
Buon Ho *Vietnam* 12°57N 108°18E **38 F7**
Buon Ma Thuot *Vietnam* 12°40N 108°3E **38 F7**
Buong Long *Cambodia* 13°44N 106°59E **38 F6**
Buorkhaya, Mys
 *Russia* 71°50N 132°40E **27 B14**
Buqayq *Si. Arabia* 26°0N 49°45E **47 E6**
Bur Acaba = Buurhakaba
 *Somalia* 3°12N 44°20E **49 G3**
Būr Safāga *Egypt* 26°43N 33°57E **46 C3**
Būr Sa'īd *Egypt* 31°16N 32°18E **53 B12**
Būr Sūdân *Sudan* 19°32N 37°9E **53 E13**
Burakin *Australia* 30°31S 117°10E **61 F2**
Burang *China* 30°15N 81°10E **30 E5**
Burao = Burco *Somalia* 9°32N 45°32E **49 F4**
Burāq *Syria* 33°11N 36°29E **48 B5**
Burathum *Nepal* 28°4N 84°50E **43 E11**
Buraydah *Si. Arabia* 26°20N 43°59E **46 E4**
Burco *Somalia* 9°32N 45°32E **49 F4**
Burda *India* 25°50N 77°35E **42 G7**
Burdekin → *Australia* 19°38S 147°25E **62 B4**
Burdur *Turkey* 37°45N 30°17E **19 G5**
Burdwan = Barddhaman
 *India* 23°14N 87°39E **43 H12**
Bure *Ethiopia* 10°40N 37°4E **49 E2**
Bure → *U.K.* 52°38N 1°43E **12 E9**
Bureskoye Vdkhr.
 *Russia* 50°16N 130°20E **27 D14**
Bureya → *Russia* 49°27N 129°30E **27 E13**
Burford *Canada* 43°7N 80°27W **82 C4**
Burgas *Bulgaria* 42°33N 27°29E **23 C12**
Burgeo *Canada* 47°37N 57°38W **73 C8**
Burgersdorp *S. Africa* 31°0S 26°20E **56 D4**
Burgess, Mt. *Australia* 30°50S 121°5E **61 F3**
Burghead *U.K.* 57°43N 3°30W **11 D5**
Burgos *Spain* 42°21N 3°41W **21 A4**
Burgsvik *Sweden* 57°3N 18°19E **9 H18**
Burgundy = Bourgogne
 *France* 47°0N 4°50E **20 C6**
Burhaniye *Turkey* 39°30N 26°58E **23 E12**
Burhanpur *India* 21°18N 76°14E **44 D3**
Burhi Gandak → *India* 25°20N 86°37E **43 G12**
Burhner → *India* 22°43N 80°31E **43 H9**
Burias I. *Phil.* 12°55N 123°5E **37 B6**
Burica, Pta. *Costa Rica* 8°3N 82°51W **88 E3**
Burien *U.S.A.* 47°28N 122°20W **78 C4**
Buriram *Thailand* 15°0N 103°0E **38 E4**
Burkburnett *U.S.A.* 34°6N 98°34W **84 D5**
Burke → *Australia* 23°12S 139°33E **62 C2**
Burke, Île de *Côte d'Ivoire* 6°16N 7°10W **52 G4**
Burketown *Australia* 17°45S 139°33E **62 B2**

Burkhan Khaldun
 *Mongolia* 48°45N 108°40E **31 B10**
Burkina Faso ■ *Africa* 12°0N 1°0W **52 F5**
Burk's Falls *Canada* 45°37N 79°24W **72 C4**
Burleigh Falls *Canada* 44°33N 78°12W **82 B6**
Burley *U.S.A.* 42°32N 113°48W **76 E7**
Burlingame *U.S.A.* 37°35N 122°21W **78 H4**
Burlington *Canada* 43°18N 79°45W **82 C5**
Burlington *Colo.,*
 *U.S.A.* 39°18N 102°16W **76 G12**
Burlington *Iowa, U.S.A.* 40°49N 91°14W **80 E8**
Burlington *Kans., U.S.A.* 38°12N 95°45W **80 F6**
Burlington *N.C., U.S.A.* 36°6N 79°26W **85 C15**
Burlington *N.J., U.S.A.* 40°4N 74°51W **83 F10**
Burlington *Vt., U.S.A.* 44°29N 73°12W **83 B11**
Burlington *Wash.,*
 *U.S.A.* 48°28N 122°20W **78 B4**
Burlington *Wis., U.S.A.* 42°41N 88°17W **80 D1**
Burma = Myanmar ■
 *Asia* 21°0N 96°30E **41 J20**
Burnaby I. *Canada* 52°25N 131°19W **70 C2**
Burnet *U.S.A.* 30°45N 98°14W **84 F5**
Burney *U.S.A.* 40°53N 121°40W **76 F3**
Burnham *U.S.A.* 40°38N 77°34W **82 F7**
Burnham-on-Sea *U.K.* 51°14N 3°0W **13 F5**
Burnie *Australia* 41°4S 145°56E **63 G4**
Burnley *U.K.* 53°47N 2°14W **12 D5**
Burns *U.S.A.* 43°35N 119°3W **76 E4**
Burns Junction *U.S.A.* 42°47N 117°51W **76 E5**
Burns Lake *Canada* 54°14N 125°45W **70 C3**
Burnside → *Canada* 66°51N 108°4W **68 D10**
Burnside, L. *Australia* 25°22S 123°0E **61 E3**
Burnsville *U.S.A.* 44°47N 93°17W **80 C7**
Burnt River *Canada* 44°41N 78°42W **82 B6**
Burntwood → *Canada* 56°8N 96°34W **71 B9**
Burntwood L. *Canada* 55°22N 100°26W **71 B8**
Burqān *Kuwait* 29°0N 47°57E **46 D5**
Burqin *China* 47°43N 87°0E **30 B6**
Burra *Australia* 33°40S 138°55E **63 E2**
Burray *U.K.* 58°51N 2°54W **11 C6**
Burren △ *Ireland* 53°9N 9°5W **10 C2**
Burren Junction *Australia* 30°7S 148°58E **63 E4**
Burrinjuck, L. *Australia* 35°0S 148°36E **63 F4**
Burro, Serranías del
 *Mexico* 28°56N 102°5W **86 B4**
Burrow Hd. *U.K.* 54°41N 4°24W **11 G4**
Burrum Coast △
 *Australia* 25°13S 152°36E **63 D5**
Burruyacú *Argentina* 26°30S 64°40W **94 B3**
Burry Port *U.K.* 51°41N 4°15W **13 F3**
Bursa *Turkey* 40°15N 29°5E **23 D13**
Burstall *Canada* 50°39N 109°54W **71 C7**
Burton *Ohio, U.S.A.* 41°28N 81°8W **82 E3**
Burton *S.C., U.S.A.* 32°26N 80°43W **85 E14**
Burton, L. *Canada* 54°45N 78°20W **72 B4**
Burton upon Trent *U.K.* 52°48N 1°38W **12 E6**
Buru *Indonesia* 3°30S 126°30E **37 E7**
Burûn, Râs *Egypt* 31°14N 33°7E **48 D2**
Burundi ■ *Africa* 3°15S 30°0E **54 E6**
Burutu *Nigeria* 5°20N 5°29E **52 G7**
Burwell *U.S.A.* 41°47N 99°8W **80 E4**
Burwick *U.K.* 58°45N 2°58W **11 C5**
Bury *U.K.* 53°35N 2°17W **12 D5**
Bury St. Edmunds *U.K.* 52°15N 0°43E **13 E8**
Buryatia □ *Russia* 53°0N 110°0E **27 D12**
Busan *S. Korea* 35°5N 129°0E **33 G15**
Busaso = Boosaaso
 *Somalia* 11°12N 49°18E **49 E4**
Buşayrah *Syria* 35°9N 40°26E **46 C4**
Büshehr *Iran* 28°55N 50°55E **47 D6**
Büshehr □ *Iran* 28°20N 51°45E **47 D6**
Bushire = Büshehr *Iran* 28°55N 50°55E **47 D6**
Businga
 *Dem. Rep. of the Congo* 3°16N 20°59E **54 D4**
Buşra ash Shām *Syria* 32°30N 36°25E **48 C5**
Busselton *Australia* 33°42S 115°15E **61 F2**
Bussol, Proliv *Russia* 46°30N 151°0E **27 E16**
Bussum *Neths.* 52°16N 5°10E **15 B5**
Busto Arsízio *Italy* 45°37N 8°51E **20 D8**
Busu Djanoa
 *Dem. Rep. of the Congo* 1°43N 21°23E **54 D4**
Busuanga I. *Phil.* 12°10N 120°0E **37 B6**
Busungbiu *Indonesia* 8°16S 114°58E **37 J17**
Buta *Dem. Rep. of the Congo* 2°50N 24°53E **54 D4**
Butare *Rwanda* 2°31S 29°52E **54 E5**
Butaritari *Kiribati* 3°30N 174°0E **64 G9**
Bute *U.K.* 55°48N 5°2W **11 F3**
Bute Inlet *Canada* 50°40N 124°53W **70 C4**
Butembo
 *Dem. Rep. of the Congo* 0°9N 29°18E **54 D5**
Butha-Buthe *Lesotho* 28°47S 28°14E **57 C4**
Butler *Mo., U.S.A.* 38°16N 94°20W **80 F6**
Butler *Pa., U.S.A.* 40°52N 79°54W **82 F5**
Buton *Indonesia* 5°0S 122°45E **37 E6**
Butte *Mont., U.S.A.* 46°0N 112°32W **76 C7**
Butte *Nebr., U.S.A.* 42°58N 98°51W **80 D4**
Butte Creek → *U.S.A.* 39°12N 121°56W **78 F5**
Butterworth = Gcuwa
 *S. Africa* 32°20S 28°11E **57 D4**
Butterworth *Malaysia* 5°24N 100°23E **39 c**
Buttfield, Mt. *Australia* 24°45S 128°9E **61 D4**
Button B. *Canada* 58°45N 94°23W **71 B10**
Buttonwillow *U.S.A.* 35°24N 119°28W **79 K7**
Butty Hd. *Australia* 33°54S 121°39E **61 F3**
Butuan *Phil.* 8°57N 125°33E **37 C7**
Butung = Buton *Indonesia* 5°0S 122°45E **37 E6**
Buturlinovka *Russia* 50°50N 40°35E **19 D7**
Butwal *Nepal* 27°33N 83°31E **43 F10**
Buurhakaba *Somalia* 3°12N 44°20E **49 G3**
Buxar *India* 25°34N 83°58E **43 G10**
Buxoro *Uzbekistan* 39°48N 64°25E **26 F7**
Buxtehude *Germany* 53°28N 9°39E **16 B5**
Buxton *U.K.* 53°16N 1°54W **12 D6**
Buy *Russia* 58°28N 41°28E **18 C7**
Buyant-Uhaa *Mongolia* 44°55N 110°11E **32 B6**
Buyo, Lac de *Côte d'Ivoire* 6°16N 7°0W **52 G4**
Büyük Menderes →
 *Turkey* 37°28N 27°11E **23 F12**

Büyükçekmece *Turkey* 41°2N 28°35E **23 D13**
Buyun Shan *China* 40°4N 122°43E **33 D12**
Buzău *Romania* 45°10N 26°50E **17 F14**
Buzău → *Romania* 45°26N 27°44E **17 F14**
Buzen *Japan* 33°35N 131°5E **29 H5**
Buzi → *Mozam.* 19°50S 34°43E **55 H6**
Büzmeýin *Turkmenistan* 38°3N 58°12E **47 B8**
Buzuluk *Russia* 52°48N 52°12E **18 D9**
Buzzards Bay *U.S.A.* 41°45N 70°37W **83 E14**
Byam Martin I. *Canada* 75°15N 104°15W **69 B11**
Byarezina → *Belarus* 52°33N 30°14E **17 B16**
Byaroza *Belarus* 52°31N 24°51E **17 B13**
Byblos = Jubayl *Lebanon* 34°5N 35°39E **48 A4**
Bydgoszcz *Poland* 53°10N 18°0E **17 B9**
Byelorussia = Belarus ■
 *Europe* 53°30N 27°0E **17 B14**
Byers *U.S.A.* 39°43N 104°14W **76 G11**
Byesville *U.S.A.* 39°58N 81°32W **82 G3**
Byfield △ *Australia* 22°52S 150°45E **62 C5**
Bykhaw *Belarus* 53°31N 30°14E **17 B16**
Bykhov = Bykhaw
 *Belarus* 53°31N 30°14E **17 B16**
Bylas *U.S.A.* 33°8N 110°7W **77 K8**
Bylderup *Denmark* 54°57N 9°6E **9 J13**
Bylot *Canada* 58°25N 94°8W **71 B10**
Bylot I. *Canada* 73°13N 78°34W **69 C16**
Byram *U.S.A.* 32°11N 90°15W **85 E9**
Byrd, C. *Antarctica* 69°38S 76°7W **5 C17**
Byrock *Australia* 30°40S 146°27E **63 E4**
Byron, C. *Australia* 28°43S 153°37E **63 D5**
Byron Bay *Australia* 28°43S 153°37E **63 D5**
Byrranga, Gory *Russia* 75°0N 100°0E **27 B11**
Byrranga Mts. = Byrranga, Gory
 *Russia* 75°0N 100°0E **27 B11**
Byske *Sweden* 64°57N 21°11E **8 D19**
Byskeälven → *Sweden* 64°57N 21°13E **8 D19**
Bytom *Poland* 50°25N 18°54E **17 C10**
Bytów *Poland* 54°10N 17°30E **17 A9**

## C

C.W. McConaughy, L.
 *U.S.A.* 41°14N 101°40W **80 E3**
Ca → *Vietnam* 18°45N 105°45E **38 C5**
Ca Mau *Vietnam* 9°7N 105°8E **39 H5**
Ca Mau, Mui *Vietnam* 8°38N 104°44E **39 H5**
Ca Na *Vietnam* 11°20N 108°54E **39 G7**
Caacupé *Paraguay* 25°23S 57°5W **94 B4**
Caaguazú ♦ *Paraguay* 26°5S 55°31W **95 B4**
Caála *Angola* 12°46S 15°30E **55 G3**
Caamaño Sd. *Canada* 52°55N 129°25W **70 C3**
Caazapá *Paraguay* 26°8S 56°19W **94 B4**
Caazapá □ *Paraguay* 26°10S 56°0W **95 B4**
Cabanatuan *Phil.* 15°30N 120°58E **37 A6**
Cabano *Canada* 47°40N 68°56W **73 C6**
Cabedelo *Brazil* 7°0S 34°50W **93 E12**
Cabhán, An = Cavan
 *Ireland* 54°0N 7°22W **10 B4**
Cabildo *Chile* 32°30S 71°5W **94 C1**
Cabimas *Venezuela* 10°23N 71°25W **92 A4**
Cabinda *Angola* 5°33S 12°11E **54 F2**
Cabinda □ *Angola* 5°0S 12°30E **54 F2**
Cabinet Mts. *U.S.A.* 48°10N 115°50W **76 B6**
Cabo Blanco *Argentina* 47°15S 65°47W **96 F3**
Cabo Frio *Brazil* 22°51S 42°3W **95 A7**
Cabo Pantoja *Peru* 1°0S 75°10W **92 D3**
Cabo Pulmo *Mexico* 23°20N 109°28E **86 C3**
Cabo San Lucas *Mexico* 22°53N 109°54W **86 C3**
Cabo Verde ■ *Atl. Oc.* 16°0N 24°0W **52 b**
Cabonga, Réservoir
 *Canada* 47°20N 76°40W **72 C4**
Cabool *U.S.A.* 37°7N 92°6W **80 G7**
Caboolture *Australia* 27°5S 152°58E **63 D5**
Cabora Bassa Dam = Cahora
 Bassa, Lago de *Mozam.* 15°20S 32°50E **55 H6**
Caborca *Mexico* 30°37N 112°6W **86 A2**
Cabot, Mt. *U.S.A.* 44°30N 71°25W **83 B13**
Cabot Hd. *Canada* 45°14N 81°17W **82 A3**
Cabot Str. *Canada* 47°15N 59°40W **73 C8**
Cabra *Spain* 37°30N 4°28W **21 D3**
Cabra I. *India* 7°18N 93°50E **45 L11**
Cabrera *Spain* 39°8N 2°57E **21 C7**
Cabri *Canada* 50°35N 108°25W **71 C7**
Cabriel → *Spain* 39°14N 1°3W **21 C5**
Caçador *Brazil* 26°47S 51°0W **95 B5**
Čačak *Serbia* 43°54N 20°20E **23 C9**
Caçapava do Sul *Brazil* 30°30S 53°30W **95 C5**
Cáceres *Brazil* 16°5S 57°40W **92 G7**
Cáceres *Spain* 39°26N 6°23W **21 C2**
Cache Bay *Canada* 46°22N 80°0W **72 C4**
Cache Cr. → *U.S.A.* 38°42N 121°42W **78 G5**
Cache Creek *Canada* 50°48N 121°19W **70 C4**
Cachi *Argentina* 25°5S 66°10W **94 B2**
Cachimbo, Serra do *Brazil* 9°30S 55°30W **93 E7**
Cachinal de la Sierra
 *Chile* 24°58S 69°32W **94 A2**
Cachoeira *Brazil* 12°30S 39°0W **93 F11**
Cachoeira do Sul *Brazil* 30°3S 52°53W **95 C5**
Cachoeiro de Itapemirim
 *Brazil* 20°51S 41°7W **95 A7**
Cacoal *Brazil* 11°32S 61°18W **92 F6**
Cacólo *Angola* 10°9S 19°21E **54 G3**
Caconda *Angola* 13°48S 15°8E **55 G3**
Caddo *U.S.A.* 34°7N 96°16W **84 D6**
Cader Idris *U.K.* 52°42N 3°53W **13 E4**
Cadereyta de Jiménez
 *Mexico* 25°36N 100°0W **86 B5**
Cadibarrawirracanna, L.
 *Australia* 28°52S 135°27E **63 D2**
Cadillac *U.S.A.* 44°15N 85°24W **81 C11**
Cádiz *Phil.* 10°57N 123°15E **37 B6**
Cádiz *Spain* 36°30N 6°20W **21 D2**
Cadiz *Calif., U.S.A.* 34°30N 115°29W **79 L11**
Cadiz *Ohio, U.S.A.* 40°22N 81°0W **82 F4**
Cádiz, G. de *Spain* 36°40N 7°0W **21 D2**
Cadiz L. *U.S.A.* 34°18N 115°24W **79 L11**
Cadney Park *Australia* 27°55S 134°3E **63 D1**
Cadomin *Canada* 53°2N 117°20W **70 C5**
Cadotte Lake *Canada* 56°26N 116°23W **70 B5**
Cadoux *Australia* 30°46S 117°7E **61 F2**

Caen *France* 49°10N 0°22W **20 B3**
Caerdydd = Cardiff *U.K.* 51°29N 3°10W **13 F4**
Caerfyrddin = Carmarthen
 *U.K.* 51°52N 4°19W **13 F3**
Caergybi = Holyhead
 *U.K.* 53°18N 4°38W **12 D3**
Caernarfon *U.K.* 53°8N 4°16W **12 D3**
Caernarfon B. *U.K.* 53°4N 4°40W **12 D3**
Caernarvon = Caernarfon
 *U.K.* 53°8N 4°16W **12 D3**
Caerphilly *U.K.* 51°35N 3°13W **13 F4**
Caerphilly □ *U.K.* 51°37N 3°12W **13 F4**
Caesarea *Israel* 32°30N 34°53E **48 C3**
Caetité *Brazil* 13°50S 42°32W **93 F10**
Cafayate *Argentina* 26°2S 66°0W **94 B2**
Cafu *Angola* 16°30S 15°8E **56 A2**
Cagayan de Oro *Phil.* 8°30N 124°40E **37 C6**
Cágliari *Italy* 39°13N 9°7E **22 E3**
Cágliari, G. di *Italy* 39°8N 9°11E **22 E3**
Caguán → *Colombia* 0°8S 74°18W **92 D4**
Caguas *Puerto Rico* 18°14N 66°2W **89 d**
Caha Mts. *Ireland* 51°45N 9°40W **10 E2**
Cahama *Angola* 16°17S 14°19E **56 A1**
Caherciveen *Ireland* 51°56N 10°14W **10 E1**
Cahir *Ireland* 52°22N 7°56W **10 D4**
Cahora Bassa, Lago de
 *Mozam.* 15°20S 32°50E **55 H6**
Cahore Pt. *Ireland* 52°33N 6°12W **10 D5**
Cahors *France* 44°27N 1°27E **20 D4**
Cahul *Moldova* 45°50N 28°15E **17 F15**
Cai Bau, Dao *Vietnam* 21°10N 107°27E **34 G6**
Cai Be *Vietnam* 10°20N 106°2E **39 G6**
Cai Nuoc *Vietnam* 8°56N 105°1E **39 H5**
Caia *Mozam.* 17°51S 35°24E **55 H7**
Caianda *Angola* 11°2S 23°31E **54 G4**
Caibarién *Cuba* 22°30N 79°30W **88 B4**
Caicara *Venezuela* 7°38N 66°10W **92 B5**
Caicó *Brazil* 6°20S 37°0W **93 E11**
Caicos Is. *Turks & Caicos* 21°40N 71°40W **89 B5**
Caicos Passage *W. Indies* 22°45N 72°45W **89 B5**
Caidian *China* 30°35N 114°2E **35 B10**
Caiguna *Australia* 32°16S 125°29E **61 F4**
Caird Coast *Antarctica* 75°0S 25°0W **5 D1**
Cairn Gorm *U.K.* 57°7N 3°39W **11 D5**
Cairngorm Mts. *U.K.* 57°6N 3°42W **11 D5**
Cairngorms △ *U.K.* 57°10N 3°50W **11 D5**
Cairnryan *U.K.* 54°59N 5°1W **11 G3**
Cairns *Australia* 16°57S 145°45E **62 B4**
Cairns L. *Canada* 51°42N 94°30W **71 C10**
Cairo = El Qâhira *Egypt* 30°2N 31°13E **53 B12**
Cairo *Ga., U.S.A.* 30°52N 84°13W **85 F12**
Cairo *Ill., U.S.A.* 37°0N 89°11W **80 G9**
Cairo *N.Y., U.S.A.* 42°18N 74°0W **83 D10**
Caiseal = Cashel *Ireland* 52°30N 7°53W **10 D4**
Caisleán an Bharraigh = Castlebar
 *Ireland* 53°52N 9°18W **10 C2**
Caithness *U.K.* 58°25N 3°35W **11 C5**
Caithness, Ord of *U.K.* 58°8N 3°36W **11 C5**
Caja de Muertos, I.
 *Puerto Rico* 17°54N 66°32W **89 d**
Cajamarca *Peru* 7°5S 78°28W **92 E3**
Cajàzeiras *Brazil* 6°52S 38°30W **93 E11**
Calabar *Nigeria* 4°57N 8°20E **52 H7**
Calabogie *Canada* 45°18N 76°43W **83 A8**
Calabozo *Venezuela* 9°0N 67°28W **92 B5**
Calábria □ *Italy* 39°0N 16°30E **22 E7**
Calahorra *Spain* 42°18N 1°59W **21 A5**
Calais *France* 50°57N 1°56E **20 A4**
Calais *U.S.A.* 45°11N 67°17W **81 C20**
Calakmul ⌂ *Mexico* 18°14N 89°48W **87 D7**
Calalaste, Cord. de
 *Argentina* 25°0S 67°0W **94 B2**
Calama *Brazil* 8°0S 62°50W **92 E6**
Calama *Chile* 22°30S 68°55W **94 A2**
Calamar *Colombia* 10°15N 74°55W **92 A4**
Calamian Group *Phil.* 11°50N 119°55E **37 B5**
Calamocha *Spain* 40°50N 1°17W **21 B5**
Calang *Indonesia* 4°37N 95°37E **36 D1**
Calanscio, Sarîr *Libya* 27°30N 22°30E **53 C10**
Calapan *Phil.* 13°25N 121°7E **37 B6**
Călăraşi *Romania* 44°12N 27°20E **17 F14**
Calatayud *Spain* 41°20N 1°40W **21 B5**
Calauag *Phil.* 13°55N 122°15E **37 B6**
Calavite, C. *Phil.* 13°26N 120°20E **37 B6**
Calbayog *Phil.* 12°4N 124°38E **37 B6**
Calca *Peru* 13°22S 72°0W **92 F4**
Calcasieu L. *U.S.A.* 29°55N 93°18W **84 G8**
Calcium *U.S.A.* 44°1N 75°50W **83 B9**
Calcutta *U.S.A.* 40°40N 80°34W **82 F4**
Caldas da Rainha *Portugal* 39°24N 9°8W **21 C1**
Calder → *U.K.* 53°44N 1°22W **12 D6**
Caldera *Chile* 27°5S 70°55W **94 B1**
Caldwell *Idaho, U.S.A.* 43°40N 116°41W **76 E5**
Caldwell *Kans., U.S.A.* 37°2N 97°37W **80 G5**
Caldwell *Tex., U.S.A.* 30°32N 96°42W **84 F6**
Caledon *Canada* 43°51N 79°51W **82 C5**
Caledon *S. Africa* 34°14S 19°26E **56 E2**
Caledon → *S. Africa* 30°31S 26°5E **56 D4**
Caledon B. *Australia* 12°45S 137°0E **62 A2**
Caledonia *Canada* 43°7N 79°58W **82 C5**
Caledonia *U.S.A.* 42°58N 77°51W **82 D7**
Calemba *Angola* 16°0S 15°44E **56 A2**
Caletones *Chile* 34°6S 70°27W **94 C1**
Calexico *U.S.A.* 32°40N 115°30W **79 N11**
Calf of Man *I. of Man* 54°3N 4°48W **12 C3**
Calgary *Canada* 51°0N 114°10W **70 C6**
Calhoun *U.S.A.* 34°30N 84°57W **85 D12**
Cali *Colombia* 3°25N 76°35W **92 C3**
Calicut = Kozhikode
 *India* 11°15N 75°43E **45 J2**
Cálida, Costa *Spain* 37°30N 1°30W **21 D5**
Caliente *U.S.A.* 37°37N 114°31W **77 H6**
California *Mo., U.S.A.* 38°38N 92°34W **80 F7**
California *Pa., U.S.A.* 40°4N 79°54W **82 F5**
California □ *U.S.A.* 37°30N 119°30W **78 H7**
California, Baja, T.N. = Baja
 California □ *Mexico* 30°0N 115°0W **86 B2**
California, Baja, T.S. = Baja
 California Sur □
 *Mexico* 25°50N 111°50W **86 B2**

California, G. de *Mexico* 27°N 111°0W **86** B2
California City *U.S.A.* 35°10N 117°55W **79** K9
California Hot Springs
  *U.S.A.* 35°51N 118°41W **79** K8
Calilegua △ *Argentina* 23°36S 64°50W **94** B3
Calingasta *Argentina* 31°15S 69°30W **94** C2
Calipatria *U.S.A.* 33°8N 115°31W **79** M11
Calistoga *U.S.A.* 38°35N 122°35W **78** G4
Calitzdorp *S. Africa* 33°33S 21°42E **56** D3
Callabonna, L. *Australia* 29°40S 140°5E **63** D3
Callan *Ireland* 52°32N 7°24W **10** D4
Callander *U.K.* 56°15N 4°13W **11** E4
Callao *Peru* 41°46N 75°3W **83** E9
Calling Lake *Canada* 55°15N 113°12W **70** B6
Calliope *Australia* 24°0S 151°16E **62** C5
Calne *U.K.* 51°26N 2°0W **13** F6
Calola *Angola* 16°25S 17°48E **56** A2
Caloundra *Australia* 26°45S 153°10E **63** D5
Calpella *U.S.A.* 39°14N 123°12W **78** F3
Calpine *U.S.A.* 39°40N 120°27W **78** F6
Calstock *Canada* 49°47N 84°9W **72** C3
Caltagirone *Italy* 37°14N 14°31E **22** F6
Caltanissetta *Italy* 37°29N 14°4E **22** F6
Calulo *Angola* 10°1S 14°56E **54** G2
Calvert → *Australia* 16°17S 137°44E **62** B2
Calvert I. *Canada* 51°30N 128°0W **70** C3
Calvert Ra. *Australia* 24°0S 122°30E **60** D3
Calvi *France* 42°34N 8°45E **20** E8
Calvià *Spain* 39°34N 2°31E **21** C7
Calvillo *Mexico* 21°51N 102°43W **86** C4
Calvinia *S. Africa* 31°28S 19°45E **56** E2
Calwa *U.S.A.* 36°42N 119°46W **78** J7
Cam → *U.K.* 52°21N 0°16E **13** E8
Cam Lam = Ba Ngoi
  *Vietnam* 11°54N 109°10E **39** G7
Cam Pha *Vietnam* 21°7N 107°18E **34** G6
Cam Ranh *Vietnam* 11°54N 109°12E **39** G7
Cam Xuyen *Vietnam* 18°15N 106°0E **38** C6
Camabatela *Angola* 8°20S 15°26E **54** F3
Camacupa *Angola* 11°58S 17°22E **55** G3
Camagüey *Cuba* 21°20N 77°55W **88** B4
Camaná *Peru* 16°30S 72°50W **92** G4
Camanche Res. *U.S.A.* 38°14N 121°1W **78** G6
Camaquã *Brazil* 30°51S 51°49W **95** C5
Camaquã → *Brazil* 31°17S 51°47W **95** C5
Camargo *Mexico* 26°19N 98°50W **87** B5
Camarillo *U.S.A.* 34°13N 119°2W **79** L7
Camarón, C. *Honduras* 16°0N 85°5W **88** C2
Camarones *Argentina* 44°50S 65°40W **96** E3
Camas *U.S.A.* 45°35N 122°24W **78** E4
Camas Valley *U.S.A.* 43°2N 123°40W **76** E2
Camballin *Australia* 17°59S 124°12E **60** C3
Cambará *Brazil* 23°2S 50°5W **95** A5
Cambay = Khambhat
  *India* 22°23N 72°33E **42** H5
Cambay, G. of = Khambhat, G. of
  *India* 20°45N 72°30E **40** J8
Cambodia ■ *Asia* 12°15N 105°0E **38** F5
Camborne *U.K.* 50°12N 5°19W **13** G2
Cambrai *France* 50°11N 3°14E **20** A5
Cambria *U.S.A.* 35°34N 121°5W **78** K5
Cambrian Mts. *U.K.* 52°3N 3°57W **13** E4
Cambridge *Canada* 43°23N 80°15W **82** C4
Cambridge *Jamaica* 18°18N 77°54W **88** a
Cambridge *N.Z.* 37°54S 175°29E **59** B5
Cambridge *U.K.* 52°12N 0°8E **13** E8
Cambridge *Minn., U.S.A.* 45°34N 93°13W **80** C7
Cambridge *Nebr., U.S.A.* 40°17N 100°10W **80** E3
Cambridge *N.Y., U.S.A.* 43°2N 73°22W **83** C11
Cambridge *Ohio, U.S.A.* 40°2N 81°35W **82** F3
Cambridge Bay *Canada* 69°10N 105°0W **68** D11
Cambridge G. *Australia* 14°55S 128°15E **60** B4
Cambridge Springs *U.S.A.* 41°48N 80°4W **82** E4
Cambridgeshire □ *U.K.* 52°25N 0°7W **13** E7
Cambuci *Brazil* 21°35S 41°55W **95** A7
Cambundi-Catembo
  *Angola* 10°10S 17°35E **54** G3
Camden *Australia* 32°28S 24°25E **56** D3
Camden *Australia* 34°1S 150°43E **63** B5
Camden *Ala., U.S.A.* 31°59N 87°17W **85** F11
Camden *Ark., U.S.A.* 33°35N 92°50W **84** E8
Camden *Maine, U.S.A.* 44°13N 69°4W **81** C19
Camden *N.J., U.S.A.* 39°55N 75°7W **83** G9
Camden *N.Y., U.S.A.* 43°20N 75°45W **83** C9
Camden *S.C., U.S.A.* 34°16N 80°36W **85** D14
Camden Sd. *Australia* 15°27S 124°25E **60** C3
Camdenton *U.S.A.* 38°1N 92°45W **80** F7
Camelford *U.K.* 50°37N 4°42W **13** G3
Cameron *Ariz., U.S.A.* 35°53N 111°25W **77** J8
Cameron *La., U.S.A.* 29°48N 93°20W **84** G8
Cameron *Mo., U.S.A.* 39°44N 94°14W **80** F7
Cameron *Tex., U.S.A.* 30°51N 96°59W **84** F6
Cameron Highlands
  *Malaysia* 4°27N 101°22E **39** K3
Cameron Hills *Canada* 59°48N 118°0W **70** B5
Cameroon ■ *Africa* 6°0N 12°30E **53** G7
Cameroun, Mt. *Cameroon* 4°13N 9°10E **54** D1
Cametá *Brazil* 2°12S 49°30W **93** D9
Camilla *U.S.A.* 31°14N 84°12W **85** F12
Caminha *Portugal* 41°50N 8°50W **21** B1
Camino *U.S.A.* 38°44N 120°41W **78** G6
Cammal *U.S.A.* 41°24N 77°28W **82** E7
Camocim *Brazil* 2°55S 40°50W **93** D10
Camooweal *Australia* 19°56S 138°7E **62** B2
Camooweal Caves △
  *Australia* 20°1S 138°11E **62** C2
Camopi *Fr. Guiana* 3°12N 52°17W **93** C8
Camorta *India* 8°8N 93°30E **45** K11
Camp Hill *U.S.A.* 40°14N 76°55W **82** F8
Camp Nelson *U.S.A.* 36°8N 118°39W **79** J8
Camp Pendleton *U.S.A.* 33°13N 117°24W **79** M9
Camp Verde *U.S.A.* 34°34N 111°51W **77** J8
Camp Wood *U.S.A.* 29°40N 100°1W **84** G4
Campana *Argentina* 34°10S 58°55W **94** C4
Campana, I. *Chile* 48°20S 75°20W **96** F1
Campánia □ *Italy* 41°0N 14°30E **22** D6
Campas del Tuyú △
  *Argentina* 36°17S 56°50W **94** D4
Campbell *S. Africa* 28°48S 23°44E **56** D3
Campbell *Calif., U.S.A.* 37°17N 121°57W **78** H5

Campbell *Ohio, U.S.A.* 41°5N 80°37W **82** E4
Campbell I. *Pac. Oc.* 52°30S 169°0E **64** N8
Campbell L. *Canada* 63°14N 106°55W **71** A7
Campbell Plateau *S. Ocean* 50°0S 170°0E **5** A11
Campbell River *Canada* 50°5N 125°20W **70** C3
Campbellford *Canada* 44°18N 77°48W **82** B7
Campbellpur *Pakistan* 33°46N 72°26E **42** C5
Campbellsville *U.S.A.* 37°21N 85°20W **81** G11
Campbellton *Canada* 47°57N 66°43W **73** C6
Campbelltown *Australia* 34°4S 150°49E **63** B5
Campbeltown *U.K.* 55°26N 5°36W **11** F3
Campeche *Mexico* 19°51N 90°32W **87** D6
Campeche □ *Mexico* 19°0N 90°30W **87** D6
Campeche, Banco *Mexico* 22°30N 88°0W **87** C7
Campeche, Golfo de
  *Mexico* 19°30N 93°0W **87** D6
Camperdown *Australia* 38°14S 143°9E **63** F3
Camperville *Canada* 51°59N 100°9W **71** C8
Câmpina *Romania* 45°10N 25°45E **17** F13
Campina Grande *Brazil* 7°20S 35°47W **93** E11
Campinas *Brazil* 22°50S 47°0W **95** A6
Campo de los Alisos △
  *Argentina* 27°15S 66°0W **94** B2
Campo Grande *Brazil* 20°25S 54°40W **93** H8
Campo Maíor *Brazil* 4°50S 42°12W **93** D10
Campo Mourão *Brazil* 24°3S 52°22W **95** A5
Campobasso *Italy* 41°34N 14°39E **22** D6
Campos *Brazil* 21°50S 41°20W **95** A7
Campos Belos *Brazil* 13°10S 47°3W **93** F9
Campos Novos *Brazil* 27°21S 51°50W **95** B5
Camptonville *U.S.A.* 39°27N 121°3W **78** F5
Camptown *U.S.A.* 41°44N 76°14W **83** E8
Camrose *Canada* 53°0N 112°50W **70** C6
Camsell Portage *Canada* 59°37N 109°15W **71** B7
Çan *Turkey* 40°2N 27°3E **23** D12
Can Gio *Vietnam* 10°25N 106°58E **39** G6
Can Tho *Vietnam* 10°2N 105°46E **39** G5
Canaan *U.S.A.* 42°2N 73°20W **83** D11
Canacona *India* 15°1N 74°4E **45** G2
Canada ■ *N. Amer.* 60°0N 100°0W **68** G11
Canada Abyssal Plain
  *Arctic* 80°0N 140°0W **4** B18
Canada Basin *Arctic* 75°0N 145°0W **4** B18
Cañada de Gómez
  *Argentina* 32°40S 61°30W **94** C3
Canadian *U.S.A.* 35°55N 100°23W **84** D4
Canadian → *U.S.A.* 35°28N 95°3W **84** D7
Canadian Shield *Canada* 53°0N 75°0W **66** D12
Canajoharie *U.S.A.* 42°54N 74°35W **83** D10
Çanakkale *Turkey* 40°8N 26°24E **23** D12
Çanakkale Boğazı
  *Turkey* 40°17N 26°32E **23** D12
Canal Flats *Canada* 50°10N 115°48W **70** C5
Canalejas *Argentina* 35°15S 66°34W **94** D2
Canals *Argentina* 33°35S 62°53W **94** C3
Canandaigua *U.S.A.* 42°54N 77°17W **82** D7
Canandaigua L. *U.S.A.* 42°47N 77°19W **82** D7
Cananea *Mexico* 31°0N 110°18W **86** A2
Canarias, Is. *Atl. Oc.* 28°30N 16°0W **52** C2
Canares *St. Lucia* 13°55N 61°4W **89** f
Canarreos, Arch. de los
  *Cuba* 21°35N 81°40W **88** B3
Canary Is. = Canarias, Is.
  *Atl. Oc.* 28°30N 16°0W **52** C2
Canaseraga *U.S.A.* 42°27N 77°45W **82** D7
Canatlán *Mexico* 24°31N 104°47W **86** C4
Canaveral, C. *U.S.A.* 28°27N 80°32W **85** G14
Canaveral △ *U.S.A.* 28°28N 80°34W **85** G14
Canavieiras *Brazil* 15°39S 39°0W **93** G11
Canberra *Australia* 35°15S 149°8E **63** F4
Canby *Calif., U.S.A.* 41°27N 120°52W **76** F3
Canby *Minn., U.S.A.* 44°43N 96°16W **80** C5
Canby *Oreg., U.S.A.* 45°16N 122°42W **78** E4
Cancún *Mexico* 21°8N 86°44W **87** C7
Candelaria *Argentina* 27°29S 55°44W **95** B4
Candelo *Australia* 36°47S 149°43E **63** F4
Candi Dasa *Indonesia* 8°30S 115°34E **37** J18
Candia = Iraklio *Greece* 35°20N 25°12E **23** G11
Candle L. *Canada* 53°50N 105°18W **71** C7
Candlemas I. *Antarctica* 57°3S 26°40W **5** B1
Cando *U.S.A.* 48°32N 99°12W **80** A4
Canea = Chania *Greece* 35°30N 24°4E **23** G11
Canelones *Uruguay* 34°32S 56°17W **95** C4
Cañete *Chile* 37°50S 73°30W **94** D1
Cangas del Narcea *Spain* 43°10N 6°32W **21** A2
Cangnan *China* 27°30N 120°23E **35** D13
Cangshan *China* 34°50N 118°2E **33** G10
Canguaretama *Brazil* 6°20S 35°5W **93** E11
Canguçu *Brazil* 31°22S 52°43W **95** C5
Canguçu, Serra do *Brazil* 31°20S 52°40W **95** C5
Cangxi *China* 31°47N 105°59E **34** B5
Cangyuan *China* 23°12N 99°14E **34** F2
Cangzhou *China* 38°19N 116°52E **32** E9
Caniapiscau → *Canada* 56°40N 69°30W **73** A6
Caniapiscau, L. *Canada* 54°10N 69°55W **73** B6
Canicattì *Italy* 37°21N 13°51E **22** F5
Canim Lake *Canada* 51°47N 120°54W **70** C4
Canindeyu □ *Paraguay* 24°10S 55°0W **95** A5
Canisteo *U.S.A.* 42°16N 77°36W **82** D7
Canisteo → *U.S.A.* 42°7N 77°8W **82** D7
Cañitas de Felipe Pescador
  *Mexico* 23°36N 102°43W **86** C4
Çankırı *Turkey* 40°40N 33°37E **19** F5
Cankuzo *Burundi* 3°10S 30°31E **54** E6
Canmore *Canada* 51°7N 115°18W **70** C5
Cann River *Australia* 37°35S 149°7E **63** F4
Canna *U.K.* 57°3N 6°33W **11** D2
Cannanore = Kannur
  *India* 11°53N 75°27E **45** J2
Cannanore Is. *India* 10°30N 72°30E **45** J1
Cannes *France* 43°32N 7°1E **20** E7
Canning Town = Port Canning
  *India* 22°23N 88°40E **43** H13
Cannington *Canada* 44°20N 79°2W **82** B5
Cannock *U.K.* 52°41N 2°1W **13** E5
Cannonball → *U.S.A.* 46°26N 100°38W **80** B3
Cannondale Mt.
  *Australia* 25°13S 148°57E **62** D4
Cannonsville Res. *U.S.A.* 42°4N 75°22W **83** D9
Cannonvale *Australia* 20°17S 148°43E **62** b

Canoas *Brazil* 29°56S 51°11W **95** B5
Canoe L. *Canada* 55°10N 108°15W **71** B7
Cañon City *U.S.A.* 38°27N 105°14W **76** G11
Cañón de Río Blanco △
  *Mexico* 18°43N 97°15W **87** D5
Canonniers Pt. *Mauritius* 20°2S 57°32E **55** d
Canora *Canada* 51°40N 102°30W **71** C8
Canowindra *Australia* 33°35S 148°38E **63** E4
Canso *Canada* 45°20N 61°0W **73** C7
Canso, Str. of *Canada* 45°37N 61°22W **73** C7
Cantabria □ *Spain* 43°10N 4°0W **21** A4
Cantabrian Mts. = Cantábrica,
  Cordillera *Spain* 43°0N 5°10W **21** A3
Cantábrica, Cordillera
  *Spain* 43°0N 5°10W **21** A3
Cantal, Plomb du *France* 45°3N 2°45E **20** D5
Canterbury *Australia* 25°23S 141°53E **62** D3
Canterbury *U.K.* 51°16N 1°6E **13** F9
Canterbury Bight *N.Z.* 44°16S 171°55E **59** F3
Canterbury Plains *N.Z.* 43°55S 171°22E **59** E3
Cantil *U.S.A.* 35°18N 117°58W **79** K9
Canton *Ga., U.S.A.* 34°14N 84°29W **85** D12
Canton *Ill., U.S.A.* 40°33N 90°2W **80** E8
Canton *Miss., U.S.A.* 32°37N 90°2W **85** E9
Canton *Mo., U.S.A.* 40°8N 91°32W **80** E8
Canton *N.Y., U.S.A.* 44°36N 75°10W **83** B9
Canton *Ohio, U.S.A.* 40°48N 81°23W **82** F3
Canton *Pa., U.S.A.* 41°39N 76°51W **82** E8
Canton *S. Dak., U.S.A.* 43°18N 96°35W **80** D5
Canton L. *U.S.A.* 36°6N 98°35W **84** C5
Canudos *Brazil* 7°13S 58°5W **92** E7
Canumã → *Brazil* 3°55S 59°10W **92** D7
Canutama *Brazil* 6°30S 64°20W **92** E6
Canutillo *U.S.A.* 31°55N 106°36W **84** F1
Canvey Island *U.K.* 51°31N 0°37E **13** F8
Canyon *U.S.A.* 34°59N 101°55W **84** D4
Canyon De Chelly △
  *U.S.A.* 36°10N 109°20W **77** H9
Canyonlands △ *U.S.A.* 38°15N 110°0W **77** G9
Canyons of the Ancients △
  *U.S.A.* 37°30N 108°55W **77** H9
Canyonville *U.S.A.* 42°56N 123°17W **76** E2
Cao Bang *Vietnam* 22°40N 106°15E **34** F6
Cao He → *China* 40°10N 124°32E **33** D13
Cao Lanh *Vietnam* 10°27N 105°38E **39** G5
Cao Xian *China* 34°50N 115°35E **32** G8
Caofeidian *China* 38°56N 118°32E **33** E10
Cap-aux-Meules *Canada* 47°23N 61°52W **73** C7
Cap-Chat *Canada* 49°6N 66°40W **73** C6
Cap-de-la-Madeleine
  *Canada* 46°22N 72°31W **72** C5
Cap-Haïtien *Haiti* 19°40N 72°20W **89** C5
Cap Pt. *St. Lucia* 14°7N 60°57W **89** f
Capac *U.S.A.* 43°1N 82°56W **82** D2
Capanaparo → *Venezuela* 7°1N 67°7W **92** B5
Cape → *Australia* 20°59S 146°51E **62** C4
Cape Arid △ *Australia* 33°58S 123°13E **61** F3
Cape Barren I. *Australia* 40°25S 148°15E **63** G4
Cape Breton Highlands △
  *Canada* 46°50N 60°40W **73** C7
Cape Breton I. *Canada* 46°0N 60°30W **73** C7
Cape Charles *U.S.A.* 37°16N 76°1W **81** G15
Cape Coast *Ghana* 5°5N 1°15W **52** G5
Cape Cod △ *U.S.A.* 41°56N 70°6W **81** E18
Cape Coral *U.S.A.* 26°33N 81°57W **85** H14
Cape Crawford *Australia* 16°41S 135°43E **62** B2
Cape Dorset = Kinngait
  *Canada* 64°14N 76°32W **69** E16
Cape Fear → *U.S.A.* 33°53N 78°1W **85** D15
Cape Girardeau *U.S.A.* 37°19N 89°32W **80** G9
Cape Hatteras △ *U.S.A.* 35°30N 75°28W **85** D17
Cape Hillsborough △
  *Australia* 20°54S 149°2E **62** b
Cape Lambert *Australia* 20°36S 117°11E **60** D2
Cape Le Grand △
  *Australia* 33°54S 122°26E **61** F3
Cape Lookout △ *U.S.A.* 35°45N 76°25W **85** D16
Cape May *U.S.A.* 38°56N 74°56W **81** F16
Cape May Point *U.S.A.* 38°56N 74°58W **81** F16
Cape Melville △
  *Australia* 14°26S 144°28E **62** A3
Cape Range △ *Australia* 22°3S 114°0E **60** D1
Cape St. George *Canada* 48°28N 59°14W **73** C8
Cape Tormentine *Canada* 46°8N 63°47W **73** C7
Cape Upstart △ *Australia* 19°45S 147°48E **62** B4
Cape Verde Is. = Cabo Verde ■
  *Atl. Oc.* 16°0N 24°0W **52** b
Cape Vincent *U.S.A.* 44°8N 76°20W **83** B8
Cape York Peninsula
  *Australia* 12°0S 142°30E **62** A3
Capela *Brazil* 10°30S 37°0W **93** E11
Capella *Australia* 23°2S 148°1E **62** C4
Capesterre-Belle-Eau
  *Guadeloupe* 16°4N 61°36W **88** b
Capesterre-de-Marie-Galante
  *Guadeloupe* 15°53N 61°14W **88** b
Capim → *Brazil* 1°40S 47°47W **93** D9
Capitan *U.S.A.* 33°35N 105°35W **77** K11
Capitán Arturo Prat
  *Antarctica* 63°0S 61°0W **5** C17
Capitol Reef △ *U.S.A.* 38°15N 111°10W **77** G8
Capitola *U.S.A.* 36°59N 121°57W **78** J5
Capodistria = Koper
  *Slovenia* 45°31N 13°44E **16** F7
Caporetto = Kobarid
  *Slovenia* 46°15N 13°30E **16** E7
Capraia *Italy* 43°2N 9°50E **20** E8
Capri *Italy* 40°33N 14°14E **22** D6
Capricorn Coast
  *Australia* 23°16S 150°49E **62** C5
Capricorn Group
  *Australia* 23°30S 151°55E **62** C5
Capricorn Ra. *Australia* 23°20S 116°50E **60** D2
Caprivi △ *Namibia* 17°55S 22°37E **56** A3
Caprivi Strip *Namibia* 18°0S 23°0E **56** A3
Captains Flat *Australia* 35°35S 149°27E **63** F4
Capulin Volcano △
  *U.S.A.* 36°47N 103°58W **84** C3
Caquetá → *Colombia* 1°15S 69°15W **92** D5

Caracal *Romania* 44°8N 24°22E **17** F13
Caracas *Venezuela* 10°30N 66°55W **92** A5
Caracol *Belize* 16°45N 89°6W **88** C2
Caracol *Mato Grosso do Sul,*
  *Brazil* 22°18S 57°1W **94** A4
Caracol *Piauí, Brazil* 9°15S 43°22W **93** E10
Carajas *Brazil* 6°5S 50°23W **93** E8
Carajás, Serra dos *Brazil* 6°0S 51°30W **93** E8
Carangola *Brazil* 20°44S 42°5W **95** A7
Caransebeş *Romania* 45°28N 22°18E **17** F12
Caraquet *Canada* 47°48N 64°57W **73** C6
Caratasca, L. de
  *Honduras* 15°20N 83°40W **88** C3
Caratinga *Brazil* 19°50S 42°10W **93** G10
Caraúbas *Brazil* 5°43S 37°33W **93** E11
Caravaca de la Cruz *Spain* 38°8N 1°52W **21** C5
Caravelas *Brazil* 17°45S 39°15W **93** G11
Caravelle, Presqu'île de la
  *Martinique* 14°46N 60°48W **88** c
Caraz *Peru* 9°3S 77°47W **92** E3
Carazinho *Brazil* 28°16S 52°46W **95** B5
Carballo *Spain* 43°13N 8°41W **21** A1
Carberry *Canada* 49°50N 99°25W **71** D9
Carbó *Mexico* 29°42N 110°58W **86** B2
Carbón, L. del *Argentina* 49°35S 68°21W **96** F3
Carbonara, C. *Italy* 39°6N 9°31E **22** E3
Carbondale *Colo.,*
  *U.S.A.* 39°24N 107°13W **76** G10
Carbondale *Ill., U.S.A.* 37°44N 89°13W **80** G9
Carbondale *Pa., U.S.A.* 41°35N 75°30W **83** E9
Carbonear *Canada* 47°42N 53°13W **73** C9
Carbónia *Italy* 39°10N 8°30E **22** E3
Carcajou *Canada* 57°47N 117°6W **70** B5
Carcarana → *Argentina* 32°27S 60°48W **94** C3
Carcasse, C. *Haiti* 18°30N 74°28W **89** C5
Carcassonne *France* 43°13N 2°20E **20** E5
Carcross *Canada* 60°13N 134°45W **70** A2
Cardamon Hills *India* 9°30N 77°15E **45** K3
Cardamon Mts. = Kravanh, Chuor
  Phnum *Cambodia* 12°0N 103°32E **39** G4
Cárdenas *Cuba* 23°0N 81°30W **88** B3
Cárdenas *San Luis Potosí,*
  *Mexico* 22°0N 99°38W **87** C5
Cárdenas *Tabasco, Mexico* 17°59N 93°22W **87** D6
Cardiff *U.K.* 51°29N 3°10W **13** F4
Cardiff □ *U.K.* 51°31N 3°12W **13** F4
Cardiff-by-the-Sea
  *U.S.A.* 33°1N 117°17W **79** M9
Cardigan *U.K.* 52°5N 4°40W **13** E3
Cardigan B. *U.K.* 52°30N 4°30W **13** E3
Cardinal *Canada* 44°47N 75°23W **83** B9
Cardona *Uruguay* 33°53S 57°18W **94** C4
Cardston *Canada* 49°15N 113°20W **70** D6
Cardwell *Australia* 18°14S 146°2E **62** B4
Careen L. *Canada* 57°0N 108°11W **71** B7
Carei *Romania* 47°40N 22°29E **17** E12
Carey *U.S.A.* 43°19N 113°57W **76** E7
Carey, L. *Australia* 29°0S 122°15E **61** E3
Carhué *Argentina* 37°10S 62°50W **94** D3
Caria *Turkey* 37°20N 28°10E **23** F13
Cariacica *Brazil* 20°16S 40°25W **93** H10
Caribbean Sea *W. Indies* 15°0N 75°0W **89** D5
Cariboo Mts. *Canada* 53°0N 121°0W **70** C4
Caribou *U.S.A.* 46°52N 68°1W **81** B19
Caribou → *Man.,*
  *Canada* 59°20N 94°44W **71** B10
Caribou → *N.W.T.,*
  *Canada* 61°27N 125°45W **70** A3
Caribou I. *Canada* 47°22N 85°49W **72** C2
Caribou Is. *Canada* 61°55N 113°15W **70** A6
Caribou L. *Man., Canada* 59°21N 96°10W **71** B9
Caribou L. *Ont., Canada* 50°25N 89°5W **72** B2
Caribou Mts. *Canada* 59°12N 115°40W **70** B5
Caribou River △ *Canada* 59°35N 96°35W **71** B9
Carichic *Mexico* 27°56N 107°3W **86** B3
Carinda *Australia* 30°28S 147°41E **63** E4
Carinhanha *Brazil* 14°15S 44°46W **93** F10
Carinhanha → *Brazil* 14°20S 43°47W **93** F10
Carinthia = Kärnten □
  *Austria* 46°52N 13°30E **16** E8
Caripito *Venezuela* 10°8N 63°6W **92** A6
Carleton, Mt. *Canada* 47°23N 66°53W **73** C6
Carleton Place *Canada* 45°8N 76°9W **83** A8
Carletonville *S. Africa* 26°23S 27°22E **56** C4
Carlin *U.S.A.* 40°43N 116°7W **76** F5
Carlingford L. *U.K.* 54°3N 6°9W **10** B5
Carlini Base *Antarctica* 62°30S 58°53W **5** C18
Carlinville *U.S.A.* 39°17N 89°53W **80** F9
Carlisle *U.K.* 54°54N 2°56W **12** C5
Carlisle *U.S.A.* 40°12N 77°12W **82** F7
Carlisle B. *Barbados* 13°5N 59°37W **89** g
Carlisle I. *Australia* 20°49S 149°18E **62** b
Carlos Casares *Argentina* 35°32S 61°20W **94** D3
Carlos Tejedor *Argentina* 35°25S 62°25W **94** D3
Carlow *Ireland* 52°50N 6°56W **10** D5
Carlow □ *Ireland* 52°43N 6°50W **10** D5
Carlsbad *Calif., U.S.A.* 33°10N 117°21W **79** M9
Carlsbad *N. Mex.,*
  *U.S.A.* 32°25N 104°14W **77** K11
Carlsbad Caverns △
  *U.S.A.* 32°10N 104°35W **77** K11
Carluke *U.K.* 55°45N 3°50W **11** F5
Carlyle *Canada* 49°40N 102°20W **71** D8
Carmacks *Canada* 62°5N 136°16W **68** E4
Carman *Canada* 49°30N 98°0W **71** D9
Carmarthen *U.K.* 51°52N 4°19W **13** F3
Carmarthen B. *U.K.* 51°40N 4°30W **13** F3
Carmarthenshire □ *U.K.* 51°55N 4°13W **13** F3
Carmaux *France* 44°3N 2°10E **20** D5
Carmel *U.S.A.* 41°26N 73°41W **83** E11
Carmel, Mt. = Ha Karmel, Har
  *Israel* 32°44N 35°3E **48** C4
Carmel-by-the-Sea
  *U.S.A.* 36°33N 121°55W **78** J5
Carmel Valley *U.S.A.* 36°29N 121°43W **78** J5
Carmelo *Uruguay* 34°0S 58°20W **94** C4
Carmen *Colombia* 9°43N 75°8W **92** B3
Carmen *Paraguay* 27°13S 56°12W **95** B4

Carmen, I. *Mexico* 25°57N 111°12W **86** B2
Carmen de Patagones
  *Argentina* 40°50S 63°0W **96** E4
Carmensa *Argentina* 35°15S 67°40W **94** D2
Carmi *Canada* 49°36N 119°8W **70** D5
Carmi *U.S.A.* 38°5N 88°10W **80** F9
Carmila *Australia* 21°55S 149°24E **62** C4
Carmona *Costa Rica* 10°0N 85°15W **88** E2
Carmona *Spain* 37°28N 5°42W **21** D3
Carn Ban *U.K.* 57°7N 4°15W **11** D4
Carn Eige *U.K.* 57°17N 5°8W **11** D3
Carnamah *Australia* 29°41S 115°53E **61** E2
Carnarvon *Australia* 24°51S 113°42E **61** D1
Carnarvon *Canada* 45°3N 78°41W **82** A6
Carnarvon *S. Africa* 30°56S 22°8E **56** E3
Carnarvon △ *Australia* 24°54S 148°2E **62** C4
Carnarvon Ra. *Queens.,*
  *Australia* 25°15S 148°30E **62** D4
Carnarvon Ra. *W. Austral.,*
  *Australia* 25°20S 120°45E **61** E3
Carnatic *India* 9°40N 77°50E **45** K3
Carnation *U.S.A.* 47°39N 121°55W **78** C5
Carncastle *U.K.* 54°54N 5°53W **10** B6
Carndonagh *Ireland* 55°16N 7°15W **10** A4
Carnduff *Canada* 49°10N 101°50W **71** D8
Carnegie *U.S.A.* 40°24N 80°5W **82** F4
Carnegie, L. *Australia* 26°5S 122°30E **61** E3
Carnegie Ridge *Pac. Oc.* 1°0S 87°0W **65** H19
Carney I. *Antarctica* 74°0S 121°0W **5** D14
Carnic Alps = Karnische Alpen
  *Europe* 46°36N 13°0E **16** E7
Carniche Alpi = Karnische Alpen
  *Europe* 46°36N 13°0E **16** E7
Carnot *C.A.R.* 4°59N 15°56E **54** D3
Carnot, C. *Australia* 34°57S 135°38E **63** E2
Carnoustie *U.K.* 56°30N 2°42W **11** E6
Carnsore Pt. *Ireland* 52°10N 6°22W **10** D5
Caro *U.S.A.* 43°29N 83°24W **81** D12
Caroga Lake *U.S.A.* 43°8N 74°28W **83** C10
Carolina *Brazil* 7°10S 47°30W **93** E9
Carolina *Puerto Rico* 18°23N 65°58W **89** d
Carolina *S. Africa* 26°5S 30°6E **57** C5
Caroline Is. *Kiribati* 9°58S 150°13W **65** H12
Caroline Is. *Micronesia* 8°0N 150°0E **64** G6
Caroni → *Venezuela* 8°21N 62°43W **92** B6
Caronie = Nébrodi, Monti
  *Italy* 37°54N 14°35E **22** F6
Caroona *Australia* 31°24S 150°26E **63** E5
Carpathians *Europe* 49°30N 21°0E **17** D11
Carpaţii Meridionali
  *Romania* 45°30N 25°0E **17** F13
Carpentaria, G. of *Australia* 14°0S 139°0E **62** A2
Carpentras *France* 44°3N 5°2E **20** D6
Carpi *Italy* 44°47N 10°53E **22** B4
Carpinteria *U.S.A.* 34°24N 119°31W **79** L7
Carr Boyd Ra. *Australia* 16°15S 128°35E **60** C4
Carra, L. *Ireland* 53°41N 9°14W **10** C2
Carrabelle *U.S.A.* 29°51N 84°40W **85** G12
Carraig Mhachaire Rois =
  Carrickmacross *Ireland* 53°59N 6°43W **10** C5
Carraig na Siúire =
  Carrick-on-Suir *Ireland* 52°21N 7°24W **10** D4
Carranya ○ *Australia* 19°13S 127°46E **60** C4
Carrara *Italy* 44°5N 10°6E **20** D9
Carrauntoohill *Ireland* 52°0N 9°45W **10** D2
Carrick-on-Shannon
  *Ireland* 53°57N 8°7W **10** C3
Carrick-on-Suir *Ireland* 52°21N 7°24W **10** D4
Carrickfergus *U.K.* 54°43N 5°49W **10** B6
Carrickmacross *Ireland* 53°59N 6°43W **10** C5
Carrieton *Australia* 32°25S 138°31E **63** E2
Carrigaline *Ireland* 51°48N 8°23W **10** E3
Carrillo *Mexico* 26°54N 103°55W **86** B4
Carrington *U.S.A.* 47°27N 99°8W **80** B4
Carrizal Bajo *Chile* 28°5S 71°20W **94** B1
Carrizalillo *Chile* 29°5S 71°30W **94** B1
Carrizo Cr. → *U.S.A.* 36°55N 103°55W **77** H12
Carrizo Plain △ *U.S.A.* 35°11N 119°47W **78** K7
Carrizo Springs *U.S.A.* 28°31N 99°52W **84** G5
Carrizozo *U.S.A.* 33°38N 105°53W **77** K11
Carroll *U.S.A.* 42°4N 94°52W **80** D6
Carrollton *Ga., U.S.A.* 33°35N 85°5W **85** E12
Carrollton *Ill., U.S.A.* 39°18N 90°24W **80** F8
Carrollton *Ky., U.S.A.* 38°41N 85°11W **81** F11
Carrollton *Mo., U.S.A.* 39°22N 93°30W **80** F7
Carrollton *Ohio, U.S.A.* 40°34N 81°5W **82** F3
Carron → *U.K.* 57°53N 4°22W **11** D4
Carron, L. *U.K.* 57°22N 5°35W **11** D3
Carrot → *Canada* 53°50N 101°17W **71** C8
Carrot River *Canada* 53°17N 103°35W **71** C8
Carruthers *Canada* 52°52N 109°16W **71** C7
Carson *Calif., U.S.A.* 33°49N 118°16W **79** M8
Carson *N. Dak., U.S.A.* 46°25N 101°34W **80** B3
Carson → *U.S.A.* 39°45N 118°40W **78** F8
Carson City *U.S.A.* 39°10N 119°46W **78** F7
Carson Sink *U.S.A.* 39°50N 118°25W **76** G4
Cartagena *Colombia* 10°25N 75°33W **92** A3
Cartagena *Spain* 37°38N 0°59W **21** D5
Cartago *Colombia* 4°45N 75°55W **92** C3
Cartago *Costa Rica* 9°50N 83°55W **88** E3
Carter Bar *U.K.* 55°21N 2°29W **11** F6
Cartersville *U.S.A.* 34°10N 84°48W **85** D12
Carterton *N.Z.* 41°2S 175°31E **59** D5
Carthage *Tunisia* 36°52N 10°20E **22** F4
Carthage *Ill., U.S.A.* 40°25N 91°8W **80** E8
Carthage *Mo., U.S.A.* 37°11N 94°19W **80** G6
Carthage *N.Y., U.S.A.* 43°59N 75°37W **83** C9
Carthage *Tex., U.S.A.* 32°9N 94°20W **84** E7
Cartier I. *Australia* 12°31S 123°29E **60** B3
Cartwright *Canada* 53°41N 56°58W **73** B8
Caruaru *Brazil* 8°15S 35°55W **93** E11
Carúpano *Venezuela* 10°39N 63°15W **92** A6
Caruthersville *U.S.A.* 36°11N 89°39W **80** G9
Carvoeiro *Brazil* 1°30S 61°59W **92** D6
Carvoeiro, C. *Portugal* 39°21N 9°24W **21** C1
Cary *U.S.A.* 35°47N 78°46W **85** D15
Cas-gwent = Chepstow
  *U.K.* 51°38N 2°41W **13** F5

Casa de Piedra *Argentina* 38°5S 67°28W 94 D2
Casa de Piedra, Embalse
  *Argentina* 38°5S 67°32W 94 D2
Casa Grande *U.S.A.* 32°53N 111°45W 77 K8
Casa Nova *Brazil* 9°25S 41°5W 93 E10
Casablanca *Chile* 33°20S 71°25W 94 C1
Casablanca *Morocco* 33°36N 7°36W 52 B4
Cascada de Basaseachic △
  *Mexico* 28°9N 108°15W 86 B3
Cascade *Seychelles* 4°39S 55°29E 55 b
Cascade *Idaho, U.S.A.* 44°31N 116°2W 76 D5
Cascade *Mont., U.S.A.* 47°16N 111°42W 76 C8
Cascade Locks *U.S.A.* 45°40N 121°54W 78 E5
Cascade Ra. *U.S.A.* 47°0N 121°30W 78 D5
Cascade Res. *U.S.A.* 44°32N 116°3W 76 D5
Cascades, Pte. des *Réunion* 21°9S 55°51E 55 c
Cascais *Portugal* 38°41N 9°25W 21 C1
Cascavel *Brazil* 24°57S 53°28W 95 A5
Cáscina *Italy* 43°41N 10°33E 22 C4
Casco B. *U.S.A.* 43°45N 70°0W 81 D19
Caserta *Italy* 41°4N 14°20E 22 D6
Casey *Antarctica* 66°0S 76°0E 5 C8
Caseyr, Raas = Asir, Ras
  *Somalia* 11°55N 51°10E 49 E5
Cashel *Ireland* 52°30N 7°53W 10 D4
Casiguran *Phil.* 16°22N 122°7E 37 A6
Casilda *Argentina* 33°10S 61°10W 94 C3
Casino *Australia* 28°52S 153°3E 63 D5
Casiquiare → *Venezuela* 2°1N 67°7W 92 C5
Casma *Peru* 9°30S 78°20W 92 E3
Casmalia *U.S.A.* 34°50N 120°32W 79 L6
Casnewydd = Newport
  *U.K.* 51°35N 3°0W 13 F5
Caspe *Spain* 41°14N 0°1W 21 B5
Casper *U.S.A.* 42°51N 106°19W 76 E10
Caspian Depression *Eurasia* 47°0N 48°0E 19 E8
Caspian Sea *Eurasia* 43°0N 50°0E 19 F9
Cass City *U.S.A.* 43°36N 83°10W 82 C1
Cass Lake *U.S.A.* 47°23N 94°37W 80 B6
Cassadaga *U.S.A.* 42°20N 79°19W 82 D5
Casselman *Canada* 45°19N 75°5W 83 A9
Casselton *U.S.A.* 46°54N 97°13W 80 B5
Cassiar Mts. *Canada* 59°30N 130°30W 70 B2
Cassino *Italy* 41°30N 13°49E 22 D5
Cassville *U.S.A.* 36°41N 93°52W 80 G7
Castaic *U.S.A.* 34°30N 118°38W 79 L8
Castalia *U.S.A.* 41°24N 82°49W 82 E2
Castanhal *Brazil* 1°18S 47°55W 93 D9
Castara *Trin. & Tob.* 11°17N 60°42W 93 J16
Casteddu = Cágliari *Italy* 39°13N 9°7E 22 E3
Castell-Nedd = Neath
  *U.K.* 51°39N 3°48W 13 F4
Castellammare di Stábia
  *Italy* 40°42N 14°29E 22 D6
Castelli *Argentina* 36°7S 57°47W 94 D4
Castelló de la Plana *Spain* 39°58N 0°3W 21 C5
Castelo *Brazil* 20°33S 41°14W 95 A7
Castelo Branco *Portugal* 39°50N 7°31W 21 C2
Castelsarrasin *France* 44°2N 1°7E 20 E4
Castelvetrano *Italy* 37°41N 12°47E 22 F5
Casterton *Australia* 37°30S 141°30E 63 F3
Castile *U.S.A.* 42°38N 78°3W 82 D6
Castilla-La Mancha □
  *Spain* 39°30N 3°30W 21 C4
Castilla y Leon □ *Spain* 42°0N 5°0W 21 B3
Castillos *Uruguay* 34°12S 53°52W 95 C5
Castle Dale *U.S.A.* 39°13N 111°1W 76 G8
Castle Douglas *U.K.* 54°56N 3°56W 11 G5
Castle Rock *Colo.,*
  *U.S.A.* 39°22N 104°51W 76 G11
Castle Rock *Wash.,*
  *U.S.A.* 46°17N 122°54W 78 D4
Castlebar *Ireland* 53°52N 9°18W 10 C2
Castlebay *U.K.* 56°57N 7°31W 11 E1
Castleblayney *Ireland* 54°7N 6°44W 10 B5
Castlecomer *Ireland* 52°48N 7°14W 10 D4
Castlederg *U.K.* 54°42N 7°36W 10 B4
Castleford *U.K.* 53°43N 1°21W 12 D6
Castlegar *Canada* 49°20N 117°40W 70 D5
Castleisland *Ireland* 52°14N 9°28W 10 D2
Castlemaine *Australia* 37°2S 144°12E 63 F3
Castlemaine *Ireland* 52°10N 9°42W 10 D2
Castlepollard *Ireland* 53°41N 7°19W 10 C4
Castlerea *Ireland* 53°46N 8°29W 10 C3
Castlereagh → *Australia* 30°12S 147°32E 63 E4
Castlereagh B. *Australia* 12°10S 135°10E 62 A2
Castleton *U.S.A.* 43°37N 73°11W 83 C11
Castleton-on-Hudson
  *U.S.A.* 42°31N 73°45W 83 D11
Castletown *I. of Man* 54°5N 4°38W 12 C3
Castletown Bearhaven
  *Ireland* 51°39N 9°55W 10 E2
Castor *Canada* 52°15N 111°50W 70 C6
Castor → *Canada* 53°24N 78°58W 72 B4
Castorland *U.S.A.* 43°53N 75°31W 83 C9
Castres *France* 43°37N 2°13E 20 E5
Castricum *Neths.* 52°33N 4°40E 15 B4
Castries *St. Lucia* 14°2N 60°58W 89 f
Castro *Brazil* 24°45S 50°0W 95 A6
Castro *Chile* 42°30S 73°50W 96 E2
Castro Alves *Brazil* 12°46S 39°33W 93 F11
Castro Valley *U.S.A.* 37°41N 122°5W 78 H4
Castroville *U.S.A.* 36°46N 121°45W 78 J5
Castuera *Spain* 38°43N 5°37W 21 C3
Cat Ba, Dao *Vietnam* 20°50N 107°0E 38 B6
Cat Ba △ *Vietnam* 20°47N 107°3E 38 B6
Cat I. *Bahamas* 24°30N 75°30W 89 B4
Cat L. *Canada* 51°40N 91°50W 72 B1
Cat Lake *Canada* 51°40N 91°50W 72 B1
Cat Tien △ *Vietnam* 11°25N 107°17E 39 G6
Catacamas *Honduras* 14°54N 85°56W 88 D2
Cataguases *Brazil* 21°23S 42°39W 95 A7
Catalão *Brazil* 18°10S 47°57W 93 G9
Çatalca *Turkey* 41°8N 28°27E 23 D13
Catalina *Canada* 48°31N 53°4W 73 C9
Catalina *Chile* 25°13S 69°43W 94 B2
Catalina *U.S.A.* 32°30N 110°50W 77 K8
Catalonia = Cataluña □
  *Spain* 41°40N 1°15E 21 B6
Cataluña □ *Spain* 41°40N 1°15E 21 B6

Catamarca *Argentina* 28°30S 65°50W 94 B2
Catamarca □ *Argentina* 27°0S 65°50W 94 B2
Catanduanes □ *Phil.* 13°50N 124°20E 37 B6
Catanduva *Brazil* 21°5S 48°58W 95 A6
Catánia *Italy* 37°30N 15°6E 22 F6
Catanzaro *Italy* 38°54N 16°35E 22 E7
Catarman *Phil.* 12°28N 124°35E 37 B6
Catatumbo-Bari △
  *Colombia* 9°3N 73°12W 89 E5
Catchacoma *Canada* 44°44N 78°19W 82 B6
Cateel *Phil.* 7°47N 126°24E 37 C7
Catembe *Mozam.* 26°0S 32°33E 57 C5
Caterham *U.K.* 51°15N 0°4W 13 F7
Cathair na Mart = Westport
  *Ireland* 53°48N 9°31W 10 C2
Cathcart *S. Africa* 32°18S 27°10E 56 D4
Cathedral City *U.S.A.* 33°47N 116°28W 79 M10
Cathlamet *U.S.A.* 46°12N 123°23W 78 D3
Catlettsburg *U.S.A.* 38°25N 82°36W 81 F12
Catoche, C. *Mexico* 21°35N 87°5W 87 C7
Catril→ *Argentina* 36°26S 63°24W 94 D3
Catrimani *Brazil* 0°27N 61°41W 92 C6
Catrimani → *Brazil* 0°28N 61°44W 92 C6
Catskill *U.S.A.* 42°14N 73°52W 83 D11
Catskill △ *U.S.A.* 42°8N 74°39W 83 D10
Catskill Mts. *U.S.A.* 42°10N 74°25W 83 D10
Catt, Mt. *Australia* 13°49S 134°23E 62 A1
Cattaraugus *U.S.A.* 42°20N 78°52W 82 D6
Catterick *U.K.* 54°23N 1°37W 12 C6
Catuala *Angola* 16°25S 19°2E 56 A2
Catuane *Mozam.* 26°48S 32°18E 57 C5
Cauca → *Colombia* 8°54N 74°28W 92 B4
Caucaia *Brazil* 3°40S 38°35W 93 D11
Caucasus Mountains
  *Eurasia* 42°50N 44°0E 19 F7
Caucete *Argentina* 31°38S 68°20W 94 C2
Caungula *Angola* 8°26S 18°38E 54 F3
Cauquenes *Chile* 36°0S 72°22W 94 D1
Caura → *Venezuela* 7°38N 64°53W 92 B6
Causapscal *Canada* 48°19N 67°12W 73 C6
Cauvery → *India* 11°9N 78°52E 45 J4
Caux, Pays de *France* 49°38N 0°35E 20 B4
Cavalier *U.S.A.* 48°48N 97°37W 80 A5
Cavan *Ireland* 54°0N 7°22W 10 B4
Cavan □ *Ireland* 54°1N 7°16W 10 C4
Cave Creek *U.S.A.* 33°50N 111°57W 77 K8
Cavenagh Ra. *Australia* 26°12S 127°55E 61 E4
Cavendish *Australia* 37°31S 142°2E 63 F3
Caviana, I. *Brazil* 0°10N 50°10W 93 C8
Cawndilla L. *Australia* 32°30S 142°15E 63 E3
Cawnpore = Kanpur
  *India* 26°28N 80°20E 43 F9
Caxias *Brazil* 4°55S 43°20W 93 D10
Caxias do Sul *Brazil* 29°10S 51°10W 95 B5
Cay Sal Bank *Bahamas* 23°45N 80°0W 88 B4
Cayambe *Ecuador* 0°3N 78°8W 92 C3
Cayenne *Fr. Guiana* 5°5N 52°18W 93 B8
Cayey *Puerto Rico* 18°7N 66°10W 89 d
Cayman Brac *Cayman Is.* 19°43N 79°49W 88 C4
Cayman Is. □ *W. Indies* 19°40N 80°30W 88 C3
Cayman Trench *Caribbean* 17°0N 83°0W 66 H11
Cayuga *Canada* 42°59N 79°50W 82 D5
Cayuga *U.S.A.* 42°54N 76°44W 83 D8
Cayuga Heights *U.S.A.* 42°27N 76°29W 83 D8
Cayuga L. *U.S.A.* 42°41N 76°41W 83 D8
Cazenovia *U.S.A.* 42°56N 75°51W 83 D9
Cazombo *Angola* 11°54S 22°56E 55 G4
Ceadîr-Lunga *Moldova* 46°3N 28°51E 17 E15
Ceanannus Mor = Kells
  *Ireland* 53°44N 6°53W 10 C5
Ceará = Fortaleza *Brazil* 3°45S 38°35W 93 D11
Ceará □ *Brazil* 5°0S 40°0W 93 E11
Ceará-Mirim *Brazil* 5°38S 35°25W 93 E11
Ceatharlach = Carlow
  *Ireland* 52°50N 6°56W 10 D5
Cébaco, I. de *Panama* 7°33N 81°9W 88 E3
Cebollar *Argentina* 29°10S 66°35W 94 B2
Cebu *Phil.* 10°18N 123°54E 37 B6
Cecil Plains *Australia* 27°30S 151°11E 63 D5
Cedar → *U.S.A.* 41°17N 91°21W 80 E8
Cedar City *U.S.A.* 37°41N 113°4W 77 H7
Cedar Creek Res. *U.S.A.* 32°11N 96°4W 84 E6
Cedar Falls, *Iowa, U.S.A.* 42°32N 92°27W 80 D7
Cedar Falls *Wash.,*
  *U.S.A.* 47°25N 121°45W 78 C5
Cedar Key *U.S.A.* 29°8N 83°2W 85 G13
Cedar L. *Canada* 53°10N 100°0W 71 C9
Cedar Park *U.S.A.* 30°30N 97°49W 84 F6
Cedar Rapids *U.S.A.* 41°59N 91°40W 80 E9
Cedartown *U.S.A.* 34°1N 85°15W 85 D12
Cedarvale *Canada* 55°1N 128°22W 70 B3
Cedarville *S. Africa* 30°23S 29°3E 57 D4
Cedral *Mexico* 23°50N 100°45W 86 C4
Cedro *Brazil* 6°34S 39°3W 93 E11
Cedros, I. *Mexico* 28°12N 115°15W 86 B1
Cedros B. *Trin. & Tob.* 10°16N 61°54W 93 K15
Ceduna *Australia* 32°7S 133°46E 63 E1
Ceel Gaal *Somalia* 10°58N 50°20E 49 E5
Ceel Waaq *Kenya* 2°49N 40°56E 54 D8
Ceeldheere *Somalia* 3°50N 47°8E 49 G4
Ceerigaabo *Somalia* 10°35N 47°20E 49 E4
Cefalù *Italy* 38°2N 14°1E 22 E6
Cegléd *Hungary* 47°11N 19°47E 17 E10
Ceheng *China* 24°58N 105°48E 34 E5
Cekik *Indonesia* 8°12S 114°27E 37 J17
Celaque △ *Honduras* 14°30N 88°43W 88 D2
Celaya *Mexico* 20°31N 100°37W 86 C4
Celbridge *Ireland* 53°20N 6°32W 10 C5
Celebes = Sulawesi
  *Indonesia* 2°0S 120°0E 37 E6
Celebes Sea *Indonesia* 3°0N 123°0E 37 D6
Celina *U.S.A.* 40°33N 84°35W 81 E11
Celje *Slovenia* 46°16N 15°18E 16 E8
Celle *Germany* 52°37N 10°4E 16 B6
Celtic Sea *Atl. Oc.* 50°9N 9°34W 14 F2
Cenderawasih, Teluk
  *Indonesia* 3°0S 135°20E 37 E9
Cengong *China* 27°13N 108°44E 34 D7

Centennial *U.S.A.* 39°34N 104°52W 76 G11
Center *N. Dak., U.S.A.* 47°7N 101°18W 80 B3
Center *Tex., U.S.A.* 31°48N 94°11W 84 F7
Centerville *Calif., U.S.A.* 36°44N 119°30W 78 J7
Centerville *Iowa, U.S.A.* 40°44N 92°52W 80 E7
Centerville *Pa., U.S.A.* 40°2N 79°59W 82 F5
Centerville *Tenn., U.S.A.* 35°47N 87°28W 85 D11
Centerville *Tex., U.S.A.* 31°16N 95°59W 84 F7
Central = Tsentralnyy □
  *Russia* 52°0N 40°0E 26 D4
Central □ *Botswana* 22°25S 26°30E 56 B4
Central, Cordillera *Colombia* 5°0N 75°0W 92 C4
Central, Cordillera
  *Costa Rica* 10°10N 84°5W 88 D3
Central, Cordillera
  *Dom. Rep.* 19°15N 71°0W 89 C5
Central, Cordillera
  *Puerto Rico* 18°8N 66°35W 89 d
Central African Rep. ■
  *Africa* 7°0N 20°0E 53 G9
Central America *America* 12°0N 85°0W 66 H11
Central Australia ◎
  *Australia* 22°30S 128°30E 60 D4
Central Bedfordshire □
  *U.K.* 52°5N 0°20W 13 E7
Central Butte *Canada* 50°48N 106°31W 71 C7
Central City *Colo.,*
  *U.S.A.* 39°48N 105°31W 76 G11
Central City *Ky., U.S.A.* 37°18N 87°7W 80 G10
Central City *Nebr., U.S.A.* 41°7N 98°0W 80 E4
Central Desert ◎
  *Australia* 19°56S 130°46E 60 C5
Central Japan Int. ✈ (NGO)
  *Japan* 34°53N 136°45E 29 G8
Central Kalahari □
  *Botswana* 22°36S 23°58E 56 B3
Central Makran Range
  *Pakistan* 26°30N 64°15E 40 F4
Central Pacific Basin
  *Pac. Oc.* 8°0N 175°0W 64 G10
Central Patricia *Canada* 51°30N 90°9W 72 B1
Central Point *U.S.A.* 42°23N 122°55W 76 E2
Central Russian Uplands
  *Europe* 54°0N 36°0E 6 E13
Central Siberian Plateau
  *Russia* 65°0N 105°0E 24 B12
Central Square *U.S.A.* 43°17N 76°9W 83 C8
Centralia *Canada* 43°17N 81°28W 82 C3
Centralia *Ill., U.S.A.* 38°32N 89°8W 80 F9
Centralia *Mo., U.S.A.* 39°13N 92°8W 80 F7
Centralia *Wash., U.S.A.* 46°43N 122°58W 78 D4
Centre de Flacq *Mauritius* 20°12S 57°43E 55 d
Centreville *N.Y., U.S.A.* 42°28N 78°14W 82 D6
Centreville *Pa., U.S.A.* 41°44N 79°45W 82 E5
Cenxi *China* 22°57N 110°57E 35 F8
Cephalonia = Kefalonia
  *Greece* 38°15N 20°30E 23 E9
Cepu *Indonesia* 7°9S 111°35E 37 G14
Ceram = Seram *Indonesia* 3°10S 129°0E 37 E7
Ceram Sea = Seram Sea
  *Indonesia* 2°30S 128°30E 37 E7
Ceredigion □ *U.K.* 52°16N 4°15W 13 E3
Ceres *Argentina* 29°55S 61°55W 94 B3
Ceres *S. Africa* 33°21S 19°18E 56 D2
Ceres *U.S.A.* 37°35N 120°57W 78 H6
Cerf *Seychelles* 4°38S 55°40E 55 b
Cerignola *Italy* 41°17N 15°53E 22 D6
Cerigo = Kythira *Greece* 36°8N 23°0E 23 F10
Çerkezköy *Turkey* 41°17N 28°0E 23 D12
Cerralvo, I. *Mexico* 24°15N 109°55W 86 C3
Cerritos *Mexico* 22°25N 100°16W 86 C4
Cerro Chato *Uruguay* 33°6S 55°8W 95 C4
Cerro Cofre de Perote △
  *Mexico* 19°29N 97°8W 87 D5
Cerro Corá △ *Paraguay* 22°35S 56°2W 95 A4
Cerro de Pasco *Peru* 10°45S 76°10W 92 F3
Cerro el Copey △
  *Venezuela* 10°59N 63°53W 89 D7
Cerro Hoya △ *Panama* 7°17N 80°45W 88 E3
Cerro Saroche △
  *Venezuela* 10°8N 69°38W 89 D6
Cerventes *Australia* 30°31S 115°3E 61 F2
Cervera *Spain* 41°40N 1°16E 21 B6
Cesena *Italy* 44°8N 12°15E 22 B5
Cēsis *Latvia* 57°18N 25°15E 9 H21
Česká Rep. = Czechia ■
  *Europe* 50°0N 15°0E 16 D8
České Budějovice *Czechia* 48°55N 14°25E 16 D8
Českomoravská Vrchovina
  *Czechia* 49°30N 15°40E 16 D8
Çeşme *Turkey* 38°20N 26°23E 23 E12
Cessnock *Australia* 32°50S 151°21E 63 E5
Cetinje *Montenegro* 42°23N 18°59E 23 C8
Cetraro *Italy* 39°31N 15°55E 22 E6
Ceuta *N. Afr.* 35°52N 5°18W 21 E3
Cévennes *France* 44°10N 3°50E 20 D5
Ceyhan *Turkey* 37°4N 35°47E 46 B2
Ceylanpınar *Turkey* 36°50N 40°2E 46 B4
Ceylon = Sri Lanka ■ *Asia* 7°30N 80°50E 45 L5
Cha-am *Thailand* 12°48N 99°58E 38 F2
Chacabuco *Argentina* 34°40S 60°27W 94 C3
Chachapoyas *Peru* 6°15S 77°50W 92 E3
Chachoengsao *Thailand* 13°42N 101°5E 38 F3
Chachro *Pakistan* 25°5N 70°15E 42 G4
Chaco □ *Argentina* 26°30S 61°0W 94 B3
Chaco □ *Paraguay* 26°0S 60°0W 94 B4
Chaco → *U.S.A.* 36°46N 108°39W 77 H9
Chaco △ *Argentina* 27°0S 59°30W 94 B4
Chaco Austral *S. Amer.* 27°0S 61°30W 96 B4
Chaco Boreal *S. Amer.* 22°0S 60°0W 92 H6
Chaco Central *S. Amer.* 24°0S 61°0W 96 A4
Chaco Culture △ *U.S.A.* 36°3N 107°58W 77 H10
Chacon, C. *U.S.A.* 54°42N 132°0W 70 C2
Chad ■ *Africa* 15°0N 17°15E 53 F8
Chad, L. = Tchad, L. *Chad* 13°30N 14°30E 53 F8
Chadileuvú → *Argentina* 37°46S 66°0W 94 D2
Chadron *U.S.A.* 42°50N 103°0W 80 D2
Chadyr-Lunga = Ceadîr-Lunga
  *Moldova* 46°3N 28°51E 17 E15

Chae Hom *Thailand* 18°43N 99°35E 38 C2
Chae Son △ *Thailand* 18°26N 99°26E 38 C2
Chaem → *Thailand* 18°11N 98°38E 38 C2
Chaeryŏng *N. Korea* 38°24N 125°36E 33 E13
Chagai Hills = Chāh Gay Hills
  *Afghan.* 29°30N 64°0E 40 E3
Chagda *Russia* 58°45N 130°38E 27 D14
Chaghcharān *Afghan.* 34°31N 65°15E 40 B4
Chagos Arch. ☑ *Ind. Oc.* 6°0S 72°0E 3 E13
Chagres → *Panama* 9°33N 79°37E 88 d
Chaguanas *Trin. & Tob.* 10°30N 61°26W 93 K15
Chāh Ākhvor *Iran* 32°41N 59°40E 47 C8
Chāh Bahar *Iran* 25°20N 60°40E 47 E9
Chāh Gay Hills *Afghan.* 29°30N 64°0E 40 E3
Chahār Borjak *Afghan.* 30°17N 62°3E 40 D3
Chahār Mahāll va Bakhtīarī □
  *Iran* 32°0N 49°0E 47 C6
Chai Badan *Thailand* 15°12N 101°8E 38 E3
Chaibasa *India* 22°42N 85°49E 43 H11
Chainat *Thailand* 15°11N 100°8E 38 E3
Chainpur *Nepal* 27°17N 87°19E 43 F12
Chaiya *Thailand* 9°23N 99°14E 39 H2
Chaiyaphum *Thailand* 15°48N 102°2E 38 E4
Chaj Doab *Pakistan* 32°15N 73°0E 42 C5
Chajari *Argentina* 30°42S 58°0W 94 C4
Chak Amru *Pakistan* 32°22N 75°11E 42 C6
Chakar → *Pakistan* 29°29N 68°2E 42 E3
Chakari *Zimbabwe* 18°5S 29°51E 57 A4
Chakhānsūr *Afghan.* 31°10N 62°0E 40 D3
Chakonipau, L. *Canada* 56°18N 68°30W 73 A6
Chakradharpur *India* 22°45N 85°40E 43 H11
Chakrata *India* 30°42N 77°51E 42 D7
Chakwal *Pakistan* 32°56N 72°53E 42 C5
Chala *Peru* 15°48S 74°20W 92 G4
Chalakudi *India* 10°18N 76°20E 45 J3
Chalchihuites *Mexico* 23°29N 103°53W 86 C4
Chalcis = Chalkida
  *Greece* 38°27N 23°42E 23 E10
Chaleur B. *Canada* 47°55N 65°30W 73 C6
Chalfant *U.S.A.* 37°32N 118°21W 78 H8
Chalhuanca *Peru* 14°15S 73°15W 92 F4
Chaling *China* 26°58N 113°30E 35 D9
Chalisgaon *India* 20°30N 75°10E 44 D2
Chalk River *Canada* 46°1N 77°27W 72 C4
Chalkida *Greece* 38°27N 23°42E 23 E10
Chalky Inlet *N.Z.* 46°3S 166°31E 59 G1
Challakere *India* 14°19N 76°39E 45 G3
Challapata *Bolivia* 18°53S 66°50W 92 G5
Challenger Deep *Pac. Oc.* 11°30N 142°0E 64 F6
Challenger Fracture Zone
  *Pac. Oc.* 35°0S 105°0W 65 L17
Challis *U.S.A.* 44°30N 114°14W 76 D6
Chalmette *U.S.A.* 29°56N 89°57W 85 G10
Chaloem Rattanakosin △
  *Thailand* 14°40N 99°17E 38 E2
Chalon-sur-Saône *France* 46°48N 4°50E 20 C6
Chalong *Thailand* 7°50N 98°22E 39 a
Châlons-en-Champagne
  *France* 48°58N 4°20E 20 B6
Chálten, Cerro = Fitz Roy, Cerro
  *Argentina* 49°17S 73°5W 96 F2
Chālūs *Iran* 36°38N 51°26E 47 B6
Cham, Cu Lao *Vietnam* 15°57N 108°30E 38 E7
Chama *U.S.A.* 36°54N 106°35W 77 H10
Chamaicó *Argentina* 35°3S 64°58W 94 D3
Chaman *Pakistan* 30°58N 66°25E 40 D5
Chamba *India* 32°35N 76°10E 42 C7
Chamba *Tanzania* 11°37S 37°0E 55 E4
Chambal → *India* 26°29N 79°15E 43 F8
Chamberlain *U.S.A.* 43°49N 99°20W 80 D4
Chamberlain →
  *Australia* 15°30S 127°54E 60 C4
Chamberlain L. *U.S.A.* 46°14N 69°19W 81 B19
Chambers *U.S.A.* 35°11N 109°26W 77 J9
Chambersburg *U.S.A.* 39°56N 77°40W 81 F15
Chambéry *France* 45°34N 5°55E 20 D6
Chambeshi → *Zambia* 11°53S 29°48E 54 G6
Chambly *Canada* 45°27N 73°17W 83 A11
Chambord *Canada* 48°25N 72°6W 73 C5
Chamchamal *Iraq* 35°32N 44°50E 46 C5
Chamela *Mexico* 19°32N 105°5W 86 D3
Chamical *Argentina* 30°22S 66°27W 94 C2
Chamkar Luong
  *Cambodia* 11°0N 103°45E 39 G4
Chamoli *India* 30°24N 79°21E 43 D8
Chamonix-Mont Blanc
  *France* 45°55N 6°51E 20 D7
Chamouchouane =
Ashuapmushuan →
  *Canada* 48°37N 72°20W 72 C5
Champa *India* 22°2N 82°43E 43 H10
Champagne *Canada* 60°49N 136°30W 70 A1
Champagne *France* 48°40N 4°20E 20 B6
Champaign *U.S.A.* 40°7N 88°15W 80 E9
Champaner *India* 22°29N 73°32E 42 H5
Champassak *Laos* 14°53N 105°52E 38 E5
Champawat *India* 29°20N 80°6E 43 E9
Champdoré, L. *Canada* 55°55N 65°49W 73 A6
Champion *U.S.A.* 41°19N 80°51W 82 E4
Champlain *U.S.A.* 44°59N 73°27W 83 B11
Champlain, L. *U.S.A.* 44°40N 73°20W 83 B11
Champotón *Mexico* 19°21N 90°43W 87 D6
Champua *India* 22°5N 85°40E 43 H11
Chamrajnagar *India* 11°52N 76°52E 45 J3
Chana *Thailand* 6°55N 100°44E 39 J3
Chañaral *Chile* 26°23S 70°40W 94 B1
Chanārān *Iran* 36°39N 59°6E 47 B8
Chanasma *India* 23°44N 72°5E 42 H5
Chancery Lane *Barbados* 13°3N 59°30W 89 g
Chanco *Chile* 35°44S 72°32W 94 D1
Chand *India* 21°57N 79°7E 43 J8
Chandan *India* 24°38N 86°40E 43 G12
Chandan Chauki *India* 28°33N 80°47E 43 E9
Chandannagar *India* 22°52N 88°24E 43 H13
Chandausi *India* 28°27N 78°49E 43 E8
Chandeleur Is. *U.S.A.* 29°55N 88°57W 85 G10
Chandeleur Sd. *U.S.A.* 29°55N 89°0W 85 G10
Chandigarh *India* 30°43N 76°47E 42 D7
Chandil *India* 22°58N 86°3E 43 H12
Chandler *Australia* 27°0S 133°19E 63 D1
Chandler *Canada* 48°18N 64°46W 73 C7

Chandler *Ariz., U.S.A.* 33°18N 111°50W 77 K7
Chandler *Okla., U.S.A.* 35°42N 96°53W 84 D6
Chandod *India* 21°59N 73°28E 42 J5
Chandpur *Bangla.* 23°8N 90°45E 41 H17
Chandragiri *India* 13°35N 79°19E 45 H4
Chandrapur *India* 19°57N 79°25E 44 E4
Chandrupatla *India* 18°33N 80°24E 44 E5
Chānf *Iran* 26°38N 60°29E 47 E9
Chang *Pakistan* 26°59N 68°30E 42 F7
Chang, Ko *Thailand* 12°0N 102°23E 39 G4
Chang, Ko *Thailand* 9°50N 98°27E 39 H
Ch'ang Chiang = Chang Jiang →
  *China* 31°48N 121°10E 35 B13
Chang Jiang → *China* 31°48N 121°10E 35 B13
Chang-won *S. Korea* 35°16N 128°37E 33 G15
Changan *China* 22°48N 113°48E 31
Changanacheri *India* 9°25N 76°31E 45 K3
Changanassery = Changanacheri
  *India* 9°25N 76°31E 45 K3
Changane → *Mozam.* 24°30S 33°30E 57 B5
Changbai *China* 41°25N 128°5E 33 D15
Changbai Shan *China* 42°20N 129°0E 33 C15
Changchiak'ou = Zhangjiakou
  *China* 40°48N 114°55E 32 D6
Ch'angchou = Changzhou
  *China* 31°47N 119°58E 35 B12
Changchun *China* 43°57N 125°17E 33 C13
Changchunling *China* 45°18N 125°27E 33 B13
Changde *China* 29°4N 111°35E 35 C8
Changdo-ri *N. Korea* 38°30N 127°40E 33 E14
Changfeng *China* 32°28N 117°10E 35 A11
Changge *China* 34°13N 113°46E 32 G7
Changhua *China* 30°12N 119°12E 35 B12
Changhua *Taiwan* 24°2N 120°30E 35 F13
Changhüngni *N. Korea* 40°24N 128°19E 33 D15
Changji *China* 44°1N 87°19E 30 C6
Changjiang *China* 19°20N 108°55E 38 C7
Changjiang Shuiku
  *China* 22°29N 113°27E 31
Changjin *N. Korea* 40°23N 127°15E 33 D14
Changjin-ho *N. Korea* 40°30N 127°15E 33 D14
Changle *China* 25°59N 119°27E 35 D12
Changli *China* 39°40N 119°13E 35 E10
Changling *China* 44°20N 123°58E 33 B12
Changlun *Malaysia* 6°25N 100°26E 39 J3
Changning *Hunan, China* 26°28N 112°22E 35 D9
Changning *Sichuan,*
  *China* 28°40N 104°56E 34 C5
Changning *Yunnan, China* 24°45N 99°30E 34 E2
Changping *China* 40°14N 116°12E 32 D9
Changsha *China* 28°12N 113°0E 35 C9
Changshan *China* 28°55N 118°27E 35 C12
Changshan Qundao
  *China* 39°11N 122°32E 33 E12
Changshou *China* 29°50N 107°4E 34 C6
Changshu *China* 31°38N 120°43E 35 B13
Changshun *China* 26°3N 106°25E 34 D6
Changtai *China* 24°35N 117°42E 35 E11
Changting *China* 26°3N 116°30E 35 D11
Changtu *China* 42°46N 124°6E 33 C13
Changuinola *Panama* 9°26N 82°31W 88 E3
Changwu *China* 23°25N 111°17E 35 F8
Changxing *China* 31°0N 119°55E 35 B12
Changyang *China* 30°30N 111°10E 35 B8
Changyi *China* 36°40N 119°30E 33 F10
Changyŏn *N. Korea* 38°15N 125°6E 33 E13
Changyuan *China* 35°15N 114°42E 32 G8
Changzhi *China* 36°10N 113°6E 32 F7
Changzhou *China* 31°47N 119°58E 35 B12
Chanhanga *Angola* 16°0S 14°8E 56 A1
Chania *Greece* 35°30N 24°4E 23 G11
Chanion, Kolpos *Greece* 35°33N 23°55E 23 G10
Channagiri *India* 14°2N 75°56E 45 G2
Channapatna *India* 12°40N 77°15E 45 H3
Channel Is. *U.K.* 49°19N 2°24W 13 H5
Channel Is. *U.S.A.* 33°40N 119°15W 79 M7
Channel Islands △
  *U.S.A.* 34°0N 119°24W 79 L7
Channel-Port aux Basques
  *Canada* 47°30N 59°9W 73 C8
Channel Tunnel *Europe* 51°0N 1°30E 13 F9
Channing *U.S.A.* 35°41N 102°20W 84 D3
Chantada *Spain* 42°36N 7°46W 21 A2
Chanthaburi *Thailand* 12°38N 102°12E 38 F4
Chantrey Inlet *Canada* 67°48N 96°20W 68 D12
Chanumla *India* 8°19N 93°5E 45 H11
Chanute *U.S.A.* 37°41N 95°27W 80 G6
Chao Hu *China* 31°30N 117°30E 35 B11
Chao Phraya →
  *Thailand* 13°40N 100°31E 38 F3
Chao Phraya Lowlands
  *Thailand* 15°30N 100°0E 38 E3
Chaocheng *China* 36°4N 115°37E 32 F8
Chaohu *China* 31°38N 117°50E 35 B11
Chaoyang *Guangdong,*
  *China* 23°17N 116°30E 35 F11
Chaoyang *Liaoning,*
  *China* 41°35N 120°22E 33 D11
Chaozhou *China* 23°42N 116°32E 35 F11
Chapais *Canada* 49°47N 74°51W 72 C5
Chapala, L. de *Mexico* 20°15N 103°0W 86 C4
Chapayevsk *Russia* 53°0N 49°40E 18 D9
Chapecó *Brazil* 27°14S 52°41W 95 B5
Chapel Hill *U.S.A.* 35°55N 79°4W 85 D15
Chapleau *Canada* 47°50N 83°24W 72 C3
Chaplin *Canada* 50°28N 106°40W 71 C7
Chaplin L. *Canada* 50°22N 106°36W 71 C7
Chappell *U.S.A.* 41°6N 102°28W 80 E2
Chapra = Chhapra *India* 25°48N 84°44E 43 G11
Chara *Russia* 56°54N 118°20E 27 D12
Charadai *Argentina* 27°35S 59°55W 94 B4
Charagua *Bolivia* 19°45S 63°10W 92 G6
Charambirá, Punta
  *Colombia* 4°16N 77°32W 92 C3
Charaña *Bolivia* 17°30S 69°25W 92 G5
Charanwala *India* 27°51N 72°10E 42 F5
Charata *Argentina* 27°13S 61°14W 94 B3

Charcas Mexico 23°8N 101°7W 86 C4
Charcot I. Antarctica 70°0S 70°0W 5 C17
Chard U.K. 50°52N 2°58W 13 G5
Chardon U.S.A. 41°35N 81°12W 82 E3
Chardzhou = Türkmenabat Turkmenistan 39°6N 63°34E 47 B9
Charente → France 45°57N 1°5W 20 D3
Chari → Chad 12°58N 14°31E 53 F8
Chārīkār Afghan. 35°0N 69°10E 40 B6
Chariton U.S.A. 41°1N 93°19W 80 E7
Chariton → U.S.A. 39°19N 92°58W 80 F7
Chärjew = Türkmenabat Turkmenistan 39°6N 63°34E 47 B9
Charkhari India 25°24N 79°45E 43 G8
Charkhi Dadri India 28°37N 76°17E 42 E7
Charleroi Belgium 50°24N 4°27E 15 D4
Charleroi U.S.A. 40°9N 79°57W 82 F5
Charles, C. U.S.A. 37°7N 75°58W 81 G16
Charles, Peak Australia 32°52S 121°11E 61 F3
Charles City U.S.A. 43°4N 92°41W 80 D7
Charles I. Canada 62°39N 74°15W 69 E17
Charles L. Canada 59°50N 110°33W 71 B6
Charles Town U.S.A. 39°17N 77°52W 81 F15
Charlesbourg Canada 46°51N 71°16W 81 B18
Charleston Ill., U.S.A. 39°30N 88°10W 80 F9
Charleston Miss., U.S.A. 34°1N 90°4W 85 D9
Charleston Mo., U.S.A. 36°55N 89°21W 80 G9
Charleston S.C., U.S.A. 32°46N 79°56W 85 E15
Charleston W. Va., U.S.A. 38°21N 81°38W 81 F13
Charleston L. Canada 44°32N 76°0W 83 B9
Charleston Peak U.S.A. 36°16N 115°42W 79 J11
Charlestown Ireland 53°58N 8°48W 10 C3
Charlestown S. Africa 27°26S 29°53E 57 C4
Charlestown Ind., U.S.A. 38°27N 85°40W 81 F11
Charlestown N.H., U.S.A. 43°14N 72°25W 83 C12
Charlestown of Aberlour U.K. 57°28N 3°14W 11 D5
Charleville Australia 26°24S 146°15E 63 D4
Charleville Ireland 52°21N 8°40W 10 D3
Charleville-Mézières France 49°44N 4°40E 20 B6
Charlevoix U.S.A. 45°19N 85°16W 81 C11
Charlotte Mich., U.S.A. 42°34N 84°50W 81 D11
Charlotte N.C., U.S.A. 35°13N 80°50W 85 D14
Charlotte Vt., U.S.A. 44°19N 73°16W 83 B11
Charlotte Amalie U.S. Virgin Is. 18°21N 64°56W 89 e
Charlotte-Douglas Int. ✈ (CLT) U.S.A. 35°12N 80°56W 85 D14
Charlotte Harbor U.S.A. 26°57N 82°4W 85 H13
Charlotte L. Canada 52°12N 125°19W 70 C3
Charlottesville U.S.A. 38°2N 78°30W 81 F14
Charlottetown Nfld. & L., Canada 52°46N 56°7W 73 B8
Charlottetown P.E.I., Canada 46°14N 63°8W 73 C7
Charlotteville Trin. & Tob. 11°20N 60°33W 93 J16
Charlton Australia 36°16S 143°24E 63 F3
Charlton I. Canada 52°0N 79°20W 72 B4
Charny Canada 46°43N 71°15W 73 C5
Charolles France 46°27N 4°16E 20 C6
Charre Mozam. 17°13S 35°10E 55 H7
Charsadda Pakistan 34°7N 71°45E 42 B4
Charters Towers Australia 20°5S 146°13E 62 C4
Chartres France 48°29N 1°30E 20 B4
Chascomús Argentina 35°30S 58°0W 94 D4
Chase Canada 50°50N 119°41W 70 C5
Chashma Barrage Pakistan 32°27N 71°20E 42 C4
Chāt Iran 37°59N 55°16E 47 B7
Châteaubriant France 47°43N 1°23W 20 C3
Chateaugay U.S.A. 44°56N 74°5W 83 B10
Châteauguay, L. Canada 56°26N 70°3W 73 A5
Châteaulin France 48°11N 4°8W 20 B1
Châteauroux France 46°50N 1°40E 20 C4
Châteaux, Pte. des Guadeloupe 16°15N 61°10W 88 b
Châtellerault France 46°50N 0°30E 20 C4
Chatham = Miramichi Canada 47°2N 65°28W 73 C6
Chatham Canada 42°24N 82°11W 82 D2
Chatham U.K. 51°22N 0°32E 13 F8
Chatham U.S.A. 42°21N 73°36W 83 D11
Chatham Is. Pac. Oc. 44°0S 176°40W 64 M10
Chatham Rise Pac. Oc. 43°30S 180°0E 64 M10
Chatmohar Bangla. 24°15N 89°15E 43 G13
Chatra India 24°12N 84°56E 43 G11
Chatrapur India 19°22N 85°2E 44 E7
Chats, L. des Canada 45°30N 76°20W 83 A8
Chatsu India 26°36N 75°57E 42 F6
Chatsworth Canada 44°27N 80°54W 82 B4
Chāttagâm = Chittagong Bangla. 22°19N 91°48E 41 H17
Chattahoochee U.S.A. 30°42N 84°51W 85 F12
Chattahoochee → U.S.A. 30°54N 84°57W 85 F12
Chattanooga U.S.A. 35°3N 85°19W 85 D12
Chatteris U.K. 52°28N 0°2E 13 E8
Chatturat Thailand 15°40N 101°51E 38 E3
Chau Doc Vietnam 10°42N 105°7E 39 G5
Chaukan Pass Myanmar 27°8N 97°10E 41 F20
Chaumont France 48°7N 5°8E 20 B6
Chaumont U.S.A. 44°4N 76°8W 83 B8
Chaunskaya G. Russia 69°0N 169°0E 27 C17
Chaura India 8°27N 93°2E 45 K11
Chautara Nepal 27°46N 85°42E 43 F11
Chautauqua L. U.S.A. 42°10N 79°24W 82 D5
Chauvin Canada 52°45N 110°10W 71 C6
Chavakachcheri Sri Lanka 9°39N 80°9E 45 K5
Chaves Brazil 0°15S 49°55W 93 D9
Chaves Portugal 41°45N 7°32W 21 B2
Chawang Thailand 8°25N 99°30E 39 H2
Chaykovskiy Russia 56°47N 54°9E 18 C9
Chazy U.S.A. 44°53N 73°26W 83 B11
Cheb Czechia 50°9N 12°28E 16 C7
Cheboksary Russia 56°8N 47°12E 18 C8
Cheboygan U.S.A. 45°39N 84°29W 81 C11
Chech, Erg Africa 25°0N 2°15W 52 D5
Chechenia □ Russia 43°30N 45°29E 19 F8
Checheno-Ingush Republic = Chechenia □ Russia 43°30N 45°29E 19 F8
Chechnya = Chechenia □ Russia 43°30N 45°29E 19 F8
Checotah U.S.A. 35°28N 95°31W 84 D7
Chedabucto B. Canada 45°25N 61°8W 73 C7
Cheduba I. Myanmar 18°45N 93°40E 41 K18
Cheektowaga U.S.A. 42°54N 78°45W 82 D6
Cheepie Australia 26°33S 145°0E 63 D4
Chegdomyn Russia 51°7N 133°1E 27 D14
Chegga Mauritania 25°27N 5°40W 52 C4
Chegutu Zimbabwe 18°10S 30°14E 55 H6
Chehalis U.S.A. 46°40N 122°58W 78 D4
Chehalis → U.S.A. 46°57N 123°50W 78 D3
Cheju = Jeju S. Korea 33°31N 126°32E 33 H14
Cheju-do = Jeju-do S. Korea 33°29N 126°34E 33 H14
Cheju Str. = Jeju Haehyop S. Korea 33°50N 126°30E 33 H14
Chekiang = Zhejiang □ China 29°0N 120°0E 35 C13
Chela, Sa. da Angola 16°20S 13°20E 56 A1
Chelan U.S.A. 47°51N 120°1W 76 C3
Chelan, L. U.S.A. 48°11N 120°30W 76 B3
Cheleken = Hazar Turkmenistan 39°34N 53°16E 19 G9
Cheleken Yarymadasy Turkmenistan 39°30N 53°15E 47 B7
Chelforó Argentina 39°0S 66°33W 96 D3
Chelkar = Shalqar Kazakhstan 47°48N 59°39E 26 E6
Chełm Poland 51°8N 23°30E 17 C12
Chełmno Poland 53°20N 18°30E 17 B10
Chelmsford U.K. 51°44N 0°29E 13 F8
Chelsea Australia 38°5S 145°8E 63 F4
Chelsea U.S.A. 43°59N 72°27W 83 C12
Cheltenham U.K. 51°54N 2°4W 13 F5
Chelyabinsk Russia 55°10N 61°24E 26 D7
Chelyuskin, C. = Chelyuskin, Mys Russia 77°30N 103°0E 27 B11
Chelyuskin, Mys Russia 77°30N 103°0E 27 B11
Chemainus Canada 48°55N 123°42W 78 B3
Chemba Mozam. 17°9S 34°53E 55 H6
Chemin Grenier Mauritius 20°29S 57°28E 55 d
Chemnitz Germany 50°51N 12°54E 16 C7
Chemult U.S.A. 43°14N 121°47W 76 E3
Chen, Gora Russia 65°16N 141°50E 27 C15
Chenab → Pakistan 30°23N 71°2E 42 D4
Chenab Nagar Pakistan 31°45N 72°55E 42 D5
Chenango Forks U.S.A. 42°15N 75°51W 83 D9
Chenchiang = Zhenjiang China 32°11N 119°26E 35 A12
Cheney U.S.A. 47°30N 117°35W 76 C5
Cheng Xian China 33°43N 105°42E 32 H3
Chengalpattu India 12°42N 79°58E 45 H4
Chengbu China 26°18N 110°16E 35 D8
Chengcheng China 35°8N 109°56E 32 G5
Chengchou = Zhengzhou China 34°45N 113°34E 32 G7
Chengde China 40°59N 117°58E 33 D9
Chengdong Hu China 32°15N 116°20E 35 A11
Chengdu China 30°38N 104°2E 34 B5
Chengdu Shuangliu Int. ✈ (CTU) China 30°35N 103°57E 34 B4
Chenggong China 24°52N 102°56E 34 E4
Chenggu China 33°10N 107°21E 34 A6
Chenghai China 23°30N 116°42E 35 F11
Chengjiang China 24°39N 103°0E 34 E4
Chengkou China 31°54N 108°31E 34 B7
Chengmai China 19°50N 109°58E 38 C7
Chengshan Jiao China 37°25N 122°44E 33 F12
Ch'engtu = Chengdu China 30°38N 104°2E 34 B5
Chengwu China 34°58N 115°50E 32 G8
Chengxi Hu China 32°15N 116°10E 35 A11
Chengyang China 36°18N 120°21E 33 F11
Chenjiagang China 34°23N 119°47E 33 G10
Chennakaladi Sri Lanka 7°47N 81°35E 45 L5
Chennai India 13°8N 80°19E 45 H5
Chenxi China 28°2N 110°12E 35 C8
Chenzhou China 25°47N 113°1E 35 E9
Cheò, Eilean a' = Skye U.K. 57°15N 6°10W 11 D2
Cheo Reo Vietnam 13°20N 108°25E 38 F7
Cheom Ksan Cambodia 14°13N 104°56E 38 E5
Cheonan S. Korea 36°48N 127°9E 33 F14
Cheongdo S. Korea 35°38N 128°42E 33 G15
Cheongju S. Korea 36°39N 127°27E 33 F14
Cheorwon S. Korea 38°15N 127°10E 33 E14
Chepén Peru 7°15S 79°23W 92 E3
Chepes Argentina 31°20S 66°35W 94 C2
Chepo Panama 9°10N 79°6W 88 E4
Chepstow U.K. 51°38N 2°41W 13 F5
Chequamegon B. U.S.A. 46°39N 90°51W 80 B8
Cher → France 47°21N 0°29E 20 C4
Cheraw U.S.A. 34°42N 79°53W 85 D15
Cherbourg-Octeville France 49°39N 1°40W 20 B3
Cherdyn Russia 60°24N 56°29E 18 B10
Cheremkhovo Russia 53°8N 103°1E 30 A9
Cherepovets Russia 59°5N 37°55E 18 C6
Chergui, Chott ech Algeria 34°21N 0°25E 52 B6
Cherial India 17°55N 78°59E 44 F4
Cherikov = Cherykaw Belarus 53°32N 31°20E 17 B16
Cheriyam I. India 10°9N 73°40E 45 J1
Cherkasy Ukraine 49°27N 32°4E 19 E5
Cherkessk Russia 44°15N 42°5E 19 F7
Cherla India 18°5N 80°49E 44 E5
Cherlak Russia 54°15N 74°55E 26 D8
Chernaya Russia 70°30N 89°10E 27 B9
Chernigov = Chernihiv Ukraine 51°28N 31°20E 18 D5
Chernigovka Russia 44°19N 132°34E 28 B6
Chernihiv Ukraine 51°28N 31°20E 18 D5
Chernivtsi Ukraine 48°15N 25°52E 17 D13
Chernobyl = Chornobyl Ukraine 51°20N 30°15E 17 C16
Chernogorsk Russia 53°49N 91°18E 27 D10
Chernovtsy = Chernivtsi Ukraine 48°15N 25°52E 17 D13
Chernyakhovsk Russia 54°36N 21°48E 9 J19
Chernysheyskiy Russia 63°0N 112°30E 27 C12
Cherokee Iowa, U.S.A. 42°45N 95°33W 80 D6
Cherokee Okla., U.S.A. 36°45N 98°21W 84 C5
Cherokee Village U.S.A. 36°18N 91°31W 84 C9
Cherokees, Grand Lake O' The U.S.A. 36°28N 94°55W 84 C7
Cherrapunji India 25°17N 91°47E 41 G17
Cherry Valley U.S.A. 42°48N 74°45W 83 D10
Cherskiy Russia 68°45N 161°18E 27 C17
Cherskogo Khrebet Russia 65°0N 143°0E 27 C15
Cherthala India 9°42N 76°20E 45 K3
Cherven Belarus 53°45N 28°28E 17 B15
Chervonohrad Ukraine 50°25N 24°10E 17 C13
Cherwell → U.K. 51°44N 1°14W 13 F6
Cherykaw Belarus 53°32N 31°20E 17 B16
Chesapeake U.S.A. 36°49N 76°16W 81 G15
Chesapeake B. U.S.A. 38°0N 76°10W 81 F14
Cheshire East □ U.K. 53°15N 2°15W 12 D5
Cheshire West and Chester □ U.K. 53°15N 2°40W 12 D5
Cheshskaya Guba Russia 67°20N 47°0E 18 A8
Cheshunt U.K. 51°43N 0°1W 13 F7
Chesil Beach U.K. 50°37N 2°33W 13 G5
Chesley Canada 44°17N 81°5W 82 B3
Chester U.K. 53°12N 2°53W 12 D5
Chester Calif., U.S.A. 40°19N 121°14W 76 F3
Chester Ill., U.S.A. 37°55N 89°49W 80 G9
Chester Mont., U.S.A. 48°31N 110°58W 76 B8
Chester Pa., U.S.A. 39°51N 75°22W 81 F16
Chester S.C., U.S.A. 34°43N 81°12W 85 D14
Chester Vt., U.S.A. 43°16N 72°36W 83 C12
Chester W. Va., U.S.A. 40°37N 80°34W 82 F4
Chester-le-Street U.K. 54°51N 1°34W 12 C6
Chesterfield U.K. 53°15N 1°25W 12 D6
Chesterfield, Îs. N. Cal. 19°52S 158°15E 58 C8
Chesterfield Inlet Canada 63°30N 90°45W 68 E13
Chesterton Ra. Australia 25°30S 147°27E 63 D4
Chesterton Range △ Australia 26°16S 147°22E 63 D4
Chestertown U.S.A. 43°40N 73°48W 83 C11
Chesterville Canada 45°6N 75°14W 83 A9
Chesuncook L. U.S.A. 46°0N 69°21W 81 C19
Chetamale India 10°43N 92°33E 45 J11
Chéticamp Canada 46°37N 60°59W 73 C7
Chetlat I. India 11°42N 72°42E 45 J1
Chetumal Mexico 18°30N 88°20W 87 D7
Chetumal, B. de Cent. Amer. 18°40N 88°10W 87 D7
Chetwynd Canada 55°45N 121°36W 70 B4
Cheviot, The U.K. 55°29N 2°9W 12 B5
Cheviot Hills U.K. 55°20N 2°30W 12 B5
Cheviot Ra. Australia 25°20S 143°45E 62 D3
Chew Bahir Ethiopia 4°40N 36°50E 49 G2
Chewelah U.S.A. 48°17N 117°43W 76 B5
Cheyenne Okla., U.S.A. 35°37N 99°40W 84 D5
Cheyenne Wyo., U.S.A. 41°8N 104°49W 76 F11
Cheyenne → U.S.A. 44°41N 101°18W 80 C3
Cheyenne Wells U.S.A. 38°49N 102°21W 76 G12
Cheyne B. Australia 34°35S 118°50E 61 F2
Cheyur India 12°21N 80°0E 45 H5
Chhabra India 24°40N 76°54E 42 G7
Chhaktala India 22°6N 74°11E 42 H6
Chhapra India 25°48N 84°44E 43 G11
Chhata India 27°42N 77°30E 42 F7
Chhatarpur Jharkhand, India 24°23N 84°11E 43 G11
Chhatarpur Mad. P., India 24°55N 79°35E 43 G8
Chhati India 20°47N 81°40E 44 D5
Chhattisgarh □ India 22°0N 82°0E 43 J10
Chhep Cambodia 13°45N 105°24E 38 F5
Chhindwara Mad. P., India 23°3N 79°29E 43 H8
Chhindwara Mad. P., India 22°2N 78°59E 43 H8
Chhinhdipada India 21°6N 84°52E 44 D7
Chhlong Cambodia 12°15N 105°58E 39 F5
Chhota Tawa → India 22°14N 76°36E 42 H7
Chhoti Kali Sindh → India 24°2N 75°31E 42 G6
Chhuikhadan India 21°32N 80°59E 43 J9
Chhuk Cambodia 10°46N 104°28E 39 G5
Chi → Thailand 15°11N 104°43E 38 E5
Chi Thanh Vietnam 13°17N 109°16E 38 F7
Chiai Taiwan 23°29N 120°25E 35 F13
Chiali Taiwan 23°9N 120°10E 35 F13
Chiang Dao Thailand 19°22N 98°58E 38 C2
Chiang Dao, Doi Thailand 19°23N 98°54E 38 C2
Chiang Kham Thailand 19°32N 100°18E 38 C3
Chiang Khan Thailand 17°52N 101°36E 38 D3
Chiang Khong Thailand 20°17N 100°24E 34 G3
Chiang Mai Thailand 18°47N 98°59E 38 C2
Chiang Rai Thailand 19°52N 99°50E 34 H2
Chiang Saen Thailand 20°16N 100°5E 34 G3
Chiapa de Corzo Mexico 16°42N 93°0W 87 D6
Chiapas □ Mexico 16°30N 92°30W 87 D6
Chiapas, Sa. Madre de Mexico 15°40N 93°0W 87 D6
Chiautla de Tapia Mexico 18°18N 98°36W 87 D5
Chiávari Italy 44°19N 9°19E 20 D8
Chiavenna Italy 46°19N 9°24E 20 C8
Chiba Japan 35°30N 140°7E 29 G10
Chiba □ Japan 35°30N 140°20E 29 G10
Chibabava Mozam. 20°17S 33°35E 57 B5
Chibemba Cunene, Angola 15°48S 14°8E 55 H2
Chibemba Huila, Angola 16°20S 15°20E 56 A2
Chibi Zimbabwe 20°18S 30°25E 57 B5
Chibia Angola 15°10S 13°42E 55 H2
Chibougamau Canada 49°56N 74°24W 72 C5
Chibougamau, L. Canada 49°50N 74°20W 72 C5
Chibuk Nigeria 10°52N 12°50E 53 F8
Chibuto Mozam. 24°40S 33°33E 57 B5
Chic-Chocs, Mts. Canada 48°55N 66°0W 73 C6
Chicacole = Srikakulam India 18°14N 83°58E 44 E6
Chicago Heights U.S.A. 41°30N 87°38W 80 E10
Chichagof I. U.S.A. 57°30N 135°30W 68 F4
Chichaoua Morocco 31°32N 8°44W 52 B4
Chichawatni Pakistan 30°32N 72°42E 42 D5
Chichén-Itzá Mexico 20°37N 88°35W 87 C7
Chicheng China 40°55N 115°55E 32 D8
Chichester U.K. 50°50N 0°47W 13 G7
Chichester Ra. Australia 22°12S 119°15E 60 D2
Chichibu Japan 35°59N 139°10E 29 F9
Chichibu-Tama-Kai △ Japan 35°52N 138°42E 29 G9
Ch'ich'ihaerh = Qiqihar China 47°26N 124°0E 31 B13
Chicholi India 22°1N 77°40E 42 H8
Chickasaw ⌂ U.S.A. 34°26N 97°0W 84 D6
Chickasha U.S.A. 35°3N 97°58W 84 D6
Chiclana de la Frontera Spain 36°26N 6°9W 21 D2
Chiclayo Peru 6°42S 79°50W 92 E3
Chico U.S.A. 39°44N 121°50W 78 F5
Chico → Chubut, Argentina 44°0S 67°0W 96 E3
Chico → Santa Cruz, Argentina 50°0S 68°30W 96 G3
Chicoa Mozam. 15°36S 32°20E 57 A5
Chicomo Mozam. 24°31S 34°6E 57 B5
Chicomostoc Mexico 22°28N 102°46W 86 C4
Chicontepec Mexico 20°58N 98°10W 87 C5
Chicopee U.S.A. 42°9N 72°37W 83 D12
Chicoutimi Canada 48°28N 71°5W 73 C5
Chicualacuala Mozam. 22°6S 31°42E 57 B5
Chidambaram India 11°20N 79°45E 45 J4
Chidenguele Mozam. 24°55S 34°11E 57 B5
Chidley, C. Canada 60°23N 64°26W 69 E19
Chiducuane Mozam. 24°35S 34°25E 57 B5
Chiede Angola 17°15S 16°22E 56 A2
Chiefs Pt. Canada 44°41N 81°18W 82 B3
Chiem Hoa Vietnam 22°12N 105°17E 38 A5
Chiemsee Germany 47°53N 12°28E 16 E7
Chiengmai = Chiang Mai Thailand 18°47N 98°59E 38 C2
Chiese → Italy 45°8N 10°25E 20 D9
Chieti Italy 42°21N 14°10E 22 C6
Chifeng China 42°18N 118°58E 33 C10
Chignecto B. Canada 45°30N 64°40W 73 C7
Chiguana Bolivia 21°0S 67°58W 94 A2
Chigwell U.K. 51°37N 0°6E 13 F8
Chihli, G. of = Bo Hai China 39°0N 119°0E 33 E10
Chihuahua Mexico 28°38N 106°5W 86 B3
Chihuahua □ Mexico 28°30N 106°0W 86 B3
Chiili = Shīeli Kazakhstan 44°20N 66°15E 26 E7
Chik Bollapur India 13°25N 77°45E 45 H3
Chikalda India 21°24N 77°19E 44 D3
Chikhli Ahmadabad, India 20°45N 73°4E 44 D1
Chikhli Maharashtra, India 20°20N 76°18E 44 D3
Chikkamagaluru India 13°15N 75°45E 45 H2
Chiknayakanhalli India 13°26N 76°37E 45 H3
Chikodi India 16°26N 74°38E 45 F2
Chilapa Mexico 17°36N 99°10W 87 D5
Chilas Pakistan 35°25N 74°5E 43 B6
Chilaw Sri Lanka 7°30N 79°50E 45 L4
Chilcotin → Canada 51°44N 122°23W 70 C4
Childers Australia 25°15S 152°17E 63 D5
Childress U.S.A. 34°25N 100°13W 84 D4
Chile ■ S. Amer. 35°0S 72°0W 96 D2
Chile Rise Pac. Oc. 38°0S 92°0W 65 L18
Chilecito Argentina 29°10S 67°30W 94 B2
Chilete Peru 7°10S 78°50W 92 E3
Chililabombwe Zambia 12°18S 27°43E 55 G5
Chilim Pakistan 35°5N 75°5E 43 B6
Chilin = Jilin China 43°44N 126°30E 33 C14
Chilka L. India 19°40N 85°25E 44 E7
Chilko → Canada 52°0N 123°40W 70 C4
Chilko L. Canada 51°20N 124°10W 70 C4
Chillagoe Australia 17°7S 144°33E 62 B3
Chillán Chile 36°40S 72°10W 94 D1
Chillicothe Ill., U.S.A. 40°55N 89°29W 80 E9
Chillicothe Mo., U.S.A. 39°48N 93°33W 80 F7
Chillicothe Ohio, U.S.A. 39°20N 82°59W 81 F12
Chilliwack Canada 49°10N 121°54W 70 D4
Chilo India 27°25N 73°32E 42 F5
Chiloane, I. Mozam. 20°40S 34°55E 57 B5
Chiloé, I. de Chile 42°30S 73°50W 96 E2
Chilpancingo Mexico 17°33N 99°30W 87 D5
Chiltern Hills U.K. 51°40N 0°53W 13 F7
Chilton U.S.A. 44°2N 88°10W 80 C9
Chilung Taiwan 25°3N 121°45E 35 E13
Chilwa, L. Malawi 15°15S 35°40E 55 H7
Chimaltitán Mexico 21°35N 103°50W 86 C4
Chimán Panama 8°45N 78°40W 88 E4
Chimanimani Zimbabwe 19°48S 32°52E 57 A5
Chimanimani △ Zimbabwe 19°48S 33°0E 57 A5
Chimay Belgium 50°3N 4°20E 15 D4
Chimayo U.S.A. 36°0N 105°56W 77 J11
Chimborazo Ecuador 1°29S 78°55W 92 D3
Chimbote Peru 9°0S 78°35W 92 E3
Chimboy Uzbekistan 42°57N 59°47E 26 E6
Chimkent = Shymkent Kazakhstan 42°18N 69°36E 26 E7
Chimoio Mozam. 19°4S 33°30E 55 H6
Chimur India 20°30N 79°23E 44 D4
Chin □ Myanmar 22°0N 93°0E 41 J18
Chin Hills Myanmar 22°30N 93°30E 41 H18
Chin Ling Shan = Qinling Shandi China 33°50N 108°10E 32 H5
China Mexico 25°42N 99°14W 87 B5
China ■ Asia 30°0N 110°0E 31 E11
China, Great Plain of Asia 35°0N 115°0E 24 E13
China Lake U.S.A. 35°44N 117°37W 79 K9
Chinan = Jinan China 36°38N 117°1E 32 F9
Chinandega Nic. 12°35N 87°12W 88 D2
Chinati Peak U.S.A. 29°57N 104°29W 84 G2
Chincha Alta Peru 13°25S 76°7W 92 F3
Chinchaga → Canada 58°53N 118°20W 70 B5
Chinchilla Australia 26°45S 150°38E 63 D5
Chincholi India 17°28N 77°26E 44 E3
Chinchorro, Banco Mexico 18°35N 87°22W 87 D7
Chinchou = Jinzhou China 41°5N 121°3E 33 D11
Chincoteague U.S.A. 37°56N 75°23W 81 G16
Chinde Mozam. 18°35S 36°30E 55 H7
Chindwin → Myanmar 21°26N 95°15E 41 J19
Chineni India 33°2N 75°15E 43 C6
Chingola Zambia 12°31S 27°53E 55 G5
Ch'ingtao = Qingdao China 36°5N 120°20E 33 F11
Chinguetti Mauritania 20°25N 12°24W 52 D3
Chingune Mozam. 20°33S 34°58E 57 B5
Chinhanguanine Mozam. 25°21S 32°30E 57 C5
Chinhoyi Zimbabwe 17°20S 30°8E 55 H6
Chiniot Pakistan 31°45N 73°0E 42 D5
Chínipas Mexico 27°23N 108°32W 86 B3
Chinji Pakistan 32°42N 72°22E 42 C5
Chinju = Jinju S. Korea 35°12N 128°2E 33 G15
Chinko → C.A.R. 4°50N 23°53E 54 D4
Chinle U.S.A. 36°9N 109°33W 77 H9
Chinmen Taiwan 24°26N 118°19E 35 E12
Chinmen Tao Taiwan 24°26N 118°22E 35 E12
Chinnamanur India 9°50N 77°24E 45 K3
Chinnampo = Namp'o N. Korea 38°52N 125°10E 33 E13
Chino Japan 35°59N 138°9E 29 G9
Chino U.S.A. 34°1N 117°41W 79 L9
Chino Valley U.S.A. 34°45N 112°27W 77 J7
Chinon France 47°10N 0°15E 20 C4
Chinook U.S.A. 48°35N 109°14W 76 B9
Chinook Trough Pac. Oc. 44°0N 175°0W 64 C10
Chinsura = Chunchura India 22°53N 88°27E 43 H13
Chintalapudi India 17°4N 80°59E 44 F5
Chintamani India 13°26N 78°3E 45 H4
Chióggia Italy 45°13N 12°17E 22 B5
Chíos Greece 38°27N 26°9E 23 E12
Chipata Zambia 13°38S 32°28E 55 G6
Chipindo Angola 13°49S 15°48E 55 G3
Chipinge Zimbabwe 20°13S 32°28E 55 J6
Chipley U.S.A. 30°47N 85°32W 85 F12
Chiplun India 17°31N 73°34E 44 F1
Chipman Canada 46°6N 65°53W 73 C6
Chippenham U.K. 51°27N 2°6W 13 F5
Chippewa → U.S.A. 44°25N 92°5W 80 C7
Chippewa Falls U.S.A. 44°56N 91°24W 80 C8
Chipping Norton U.K. 51°56N 1°32W 13 F6
Chiputneticook Lakes N. Amer. 45°35N 67°35W 81 C20
Chiquián Peru 10°10S 77°0W 92 F3
Chiquibul △ Belize 16°49N 88°52W 88 C2
Chiquimula Guatemala 14°51N 89°37W 88 D2
Chiquinquira Colombia 5°37N 73°50W 92 B4
Chirala India 15°50N 80°26E 45 G5
Chirawa India 28°14N 75°42E 42 E6
Chirchiq Uzbekistan 41°29N 69°35E 26 E7
Chiredzi Zimbabwe 21°0S 31°38E 57 B5
Chiricahua ⌂ U.S.A. 32°0N 109°20W 77 K9
Chiricahua Peak U.S.A. 31°51N 109°18W 77 L9
Chirikof I. U.S.A. 55°50N 155°40W 74 D8
Chiriquí, G. de Panama 8°0N 82°10W 88 E3
Chiriquí, L. de Panama 9°10N 82°0W 88 E3
Chirmiri India 23°15N 82°20E 43 H10
Chirripó Grande, Cerro Costa Rica 9°29N 83°29W 88 E3
Chirundu Zimbabwe 16°3S 28°50E 57 A4
Chisapani Nepal 28°37N 81°16E 43 E9
Chisasibi Canada 53°50N 79°0W 72 B4
Ch'ishan Taiwan 22°44N 120°31E 35 F13
Chisholm Canada 54°55N 114°10W 70 C6
Chisholm U.S.A. 47°29N 92°53W 80 B7
Chishtian Mandi Pakistan 29°50N 72°55E 42 E5
Chishui China 28°30N 105°42E 34 C5
Chishui He → China 28°49N 105°50E 34 C5
Chisimaio = Kismaayo Somalia 0°22S 42°32E 49 H3
Chişinău Moldova 47°2N 28°50E 17 E15
Chisos Mts. U.S.A. 29°5N 103°15W 84 G3
Chistopol Russia 55°25N 50°38E 18 C9
Chita Russia 52°0N 113°35E 31 A11
Chitapur India 17°10N 77°5E 44 F3
Chitose Japan 42°49N 141°39E 28 C10
Chitradurga India 14°14N 76°24E 45 G3
Chitrakot India 19°10N 81°40E 44 E5
Chitral Pakistan 35°50N 71°56E 40 B7
Chitravati → India 14°45N 78°15E 45 G4
Chitré Panama 7°59N 80°27W 88 E3
Chittagong Bangla. 22°19N 91°48E 41 H17
Chittagong □ Bangla. 24°5N 91°0E 41 G17
Chittaurgarh India 24°52N 74°38E 42 G6
Chittoor India 13°15N 79°5E 45 H4
Chittur India 10°40N 76°45E 45 J3
Chitungwiza Zimbabwe 18°0S 31°6E 55 H6
Chiusi Italy 43°1N 11°57E 22 C4
Chivasso Italy 45°11N 7°53E 20 D7
Chivilcoy Argentina 34°55S 60°0W 94 C4
Chixi China 22°0N 112°58E 35 G9
Chkalov = Orenburg Russia 51°45N 55°6E 18 D10
Chloride U.S.A. 35°25N 114°12W 79 K12
Cho-do N. Korea 38°30N 124°40E 33 E13
Cho Phuoc Hai Vietnam 10°26N 107°18E 39 G6
Chobe △ Botswana 18°37S 24°23E 56 A4
Chocolate Mts. U.S.A. 33°15N 115°15W 79 M11
Choctawhatchee → U.S.A. 30°25N 86°8W 85 F11
Chodavaram Andhra Pradesh, India 17°50N 82°57E 44 F6
Chodavaram Andhra Pradesh, India 17°27N 81°46E 44 F5
Choele Choel Argentina 39°11S 65°40W 96 D3
Choghā Zanbīl Iran 32°1N 48°32E 47 C6
Choiseul St. Lucia 13°47N 61°3W 89 f
Choiseul Solomon Is. 7°0S 156°40E 58 B8
Choix Mexico 26°43N 108°17W 86 B3
Chojnice Poland 53°42N 17°32E 17 B9
Chok Chai Thailand 14°44N 102°10E 38 E4
Chōkai-San Japan 39°6N 140°3E 28 E10
Choke Canyon Res. U.S.A. 28°30N 98°20W 84 G5
Chokurdakh Russia 70°38N 147°55E 27 B15

Chokwé Mozam. 24°32S 32°59E 57 B5
Cholame U.S.A. 35°44N 120°18W 78 K6
Cholet France 47°4N 0°52W 20 C3
Cholguan Chile 37°10S 72°3W 94 D1
Choloma Honduras 15°37N 87°57W 88 C2
Choluteca Honduras 13°20N 87°14W 88 D2
Choluteca → Honduras 13°0N 87°20W 88 D2
Chom Bung Thailand 13°37N 99°36E 38 F2
Chom Thong Thailand 18°25N 98°41E 38 C2
Choma Zambia 16°48S 26°59E 55 H5
Chomolungma = Everest, Mt.
  Nepal 28°5N 86°58E 43 E12
Chomun India 27°15N 75°40E 42 F6
Chomutov Czechia 50°28N 13°23E 16 C7
Chon Buri Thailand 13°21N 101°1E 38 F3
Chon Thanh Vietnam 11°24N 106°36E 39 G6
Chone Ecuador 0°40S 80°0W 92 D3
Chong Kai Cambodia 13°57N 103°35E 38 F4
Chong Mek Thailand 15°10N 105°27E 38 E5
Chong Phangan Thailand 9°39N 100°0E 39 b
Chong Samui Thailand 9°21N 99°50E 39 b
Chongde China 30°32N 120°26E 35 B13
Ch'ŏngjin N. Korea 41°47N 129°50E 33 D15
Chŏngju N. Korea 39°40N 125°5E 33 E13
Chongli China 40°58N 115°15E 32 D8
Chongming China 31°38N 121°23E 35 B13
Chongming Dao China 31°40N 121°32E 35 B13
Chŏngp'yŏng N. Korea 39°47N 127°23E 33 E14
Chongqing Chongqing,
  China 29°35N 106°25E 34 C6
Chongqing Sichuan,
  China 30°38N 103°40E 34 B4
Chongqing Jiangbei Int. ✈ (CKG)
  China 29°43N 106°38E 34 C6
Chongqing Shi □ China 30°0N 108°0E 34 C6
Chongren China 27°46N 116°3E 35 D11
Chonguene Mozam. 25°3S 33°49E 57 C5
Chongyi China 25°45N 114°29E 35 E10
Chongzuo China 22°23N 107°20E 34 C8
Chonogol Mongolia 45°54N 115°22E 32 B8
Chonos, Arch. de los Chile 45°0S 75°0W 96 F2
Chop Ukraine 48°26N 22°12E 17 D12
Chopda India 21°20N 75°15E 44 D2
Chopim → Brazil 25°35S 53°5W 95 B5
Chor Pakistan 25°31N 69°46E 42 G3
Chora Sfakion Greece 35°15N 24°9E 23 G11
Chorbat La India 34°42N 76°37E 43 B7
Chorley U.K. 53°39N 2°38W 12 D5
Chornobyl Ukraine 51°20N 30°15E 17 C16
Chorolque, Cerro Bolivia 20°59S 66°5W 94 A2
Chorregon Australia 22°40S 143°32E 62 C3
Chorro el Indio △
  Venezuela 7°43N 72°9W 89 E5
Chortkiv Ukraine 49°2N 25°46E 17 D13
Chorzów Poland 50°18N 18°57E 17 C10
Chos-Malal Argentina 37°20S 70°15W 94 D1
Ch'osan N. Korea 40°50N 125°47E 33 D13
Choszczno Poland 53°7N 15°25E 16 B8
Choteau U.S.A. 47°49N 112°11W 76 C7
Chotila India 22°23N 71°15E 42 H4
Chotta Udepur India 22°19N 74°1E 44 H6
Chowchilla U.S.A. 37°7N 120°16W 78 H6
Choybalsan Mongolia 48°4N 114°30E 31 B11
Choyr Mongolia 46°24N 108°30E 31 B10
Christchurch N.Z. 43°33S 172°47E 59 E4
Christchurch U.K. 50°44N 1°47W 13 G6
Christian I. Canada 44°50N 80°12W 82 B4
Christian Sd. U.S.A. 55°56N 134°40W 75 D13
Christiana S. Africa 27°52S 25°8E 56 C4
Christiansted
  U.S. Virgin Is. 17°45N 64°42W 89 C7
Christie B. Canada 62°32N 111°10W 71 A6
Christina → Canada 56°40N 111°3W 71 B6
Christmas Cr. →
  Australia 18°29S 125°23E 60 C4
Christmas I. = Kiritimati
  Kiribati 1°58N 157°27W 65 G12
Christmas I. Ind. Oc. 10°30S 105°40E 64 J2
Christopher, L. Australia 24°49S 127°42E 61 D4
Chū = Shū Kazakhstan 43°36N 73°42E 26 E8
Chu → Vietnam 19°53N 105°45E 38 C5
Chu Lai Vietnam 15°28N 108°45E 38 E7
Chu Mom Ray △
  Vietnam 14°29N 107°38E 38 E6
Chu Se Vietnam 13°40N 108°8E 38 F7
Chuadanga Bangla. 23°38N 88°51E 43 H13
Chuak, Ko Thailand 9°28N 99°41E 39 b
Ch'uanchou = Quanzhou
  China 24°55N 118°34E 35 E12
Chuankou China 34°20N 110°59E 32 G6
Chubbuck U.S.A. 42°55N 112°28W 76 E7
Chūbu □ Japan 36°45N 137°30E 29 F8
Chūbu-Sangaku △
  Japan 36°30N 137°40E 29 F8
Chubut → Argentina 43°20S 65°5W 96 E3
Chuçand = Khūjand
  Tajikistan 40°17N 69°37E 26 E7
Chuchi L. Canada 55°12N 124°30W 70 B4
Chuda India 22°29N 71°41E 42 H4
Chudskoye, Ozero Russia 58°13N 27°30E 9 G22
Chugach Mts. U.S.A. 60°45N 147°0W 74 C10
Chūgoku □ Japan 35°0N 133°0E 29 G6
Chūgoku-Sanchi Japan 35°0N 133°0E 29 G6
Chugwater U.S.A. 41°46N 104°50W 76 F11
Chukchi Plateau Arctic 78°0N 165°0W 4 B17
Chukchi Sea Russia 68°0N 175°0W 27 C19
Chukotskiy, Mys Russia 64°14N 173°8W 74 C5
Chukotskiy Poluostrov
  Russia 66°0N 174°0W 74 B5
Chukotskoye Nagorye
  Russia 68°0N 175°0E 27 C18
Chula Vista U.S.A. 32°38N 117°5W 79 N9
Chulband → India 20°40N 79°54E 44 D4
Chulucanas Peru 5°8S 80°10W 92 E2
Chulym → Russia 57°43N 83°51E 26 D9
Chum Phae Thailand 16°40N 102°6E 38 D4
Chum Saeng Thailand 15°55N 100°15E 38 E3
Chumar India 32°40N 78°35E 43 C8
Chumbicha Argentina 29°0S 66°10W 94 B2
Chumikan Russia 54°40N 135°10E 27 D14

Chumphon Thailand 10°35N 99°14E 39 G2
Chuna → Russia 57°47N 94°37E 27 D10
Chun'an China 29°35N 119°3E 35 C12
Chuncheon S. Korea 37°58N 127°44E 33 F14
Chunchura India 22°53N 88°27E 43 H13
Chunggang-ŭp
  N. Korea 41°48N 126°48E 33 D14
Chunghwa N. Korea 38°52N 125°47E 33 E13
Chungju S. Korea 36°58N 127°58E 33 F14
Chungking = Chongqing
  China 29°35N 106°25E 34 C6
Chungli Taiwan 24°57N 121°13E 35 E13
Chungt'iaoshan = Zhongtiao Shan
  China 35°0N 111°10E 32 G6
Chungyang Shanmo
  Taiwan 23°10N 121°0E 35 F13
Chunian Pakistan 30°57N 74°0E 42 D6
Chunya Tanzania 8°30S 33°27E 54 F6
Chunyang China 43°38N 129°23E 33 C15
Chupara Pt. Trin. & Tob. 10°49N 61°22W 93 K15
Chuquibamba Peru 15°47S 72°44W 92 G4
Chuquicamata Chile 22°15S 69°0W 94 A2
Chur Switz. 46°52N 9°32E 20 C8
Churachandpur India 24°20N 93°40E 41 G18
Church Stretton U.K. 52°32N 2°48W 13 E5
Churchill Canada 58°47N 94°11W 71 B10
Churchill → Man.,
  Canada 58°47N 94°12W 71 B10
Churchill → Nfld. & L.,
  Canada 53°19N 60°10W 73 B7
Churchill, C. Canada 58°46N 93°12W 71 B10
Churchill Falls Canada 53°36N 64°19W 73 B7
Churchill L. Canada 55°55N 108°20W 71 B7
Churchill Pk. Canada 58°10N 125°10W 70 B3
Churki India 23°50N 83°12E 43 H10
Churu India 28°20N 74°50E 42 E6
Churún Merú = Angel Falls
  Venezuela 5°57N 62°30W 92 B6
Chushal India 33°40N 78°40E 43 C8
Chuska Mts. U.S.A. 36°15N 108°50W 77 H9
Chusovoy Russia 58°22N 57°50E 18 C10
Chute-aux-Outardes
  Canada 49°7N 68°24W 73 C6
Chuuk = Truk Micronesia 7°25N 151°46E 64 G7
Chuvash Republic = Chuvashia □
  Russia 55°30N 47°0E 18 C8
Chuvashia □ Russia 55°30N 47°0E 18 C8
Chuwārtah Iraq 35°43N 45°34E 46 C5
Chuxiong China 25°2N 101°28E 34 E3
Chuy Uruguay 33°41S 53°27W 95 C5
Chuzhou China 32°19N 118°20E 35 A12
Ci Xian China 36°20N 114°25E 32 F8
Cianjur Indonesia 6°49S 107°8E 37 G12
Cianorte Brazil 23°37S 52°37W 95 A5
Cibola U.S.A. 33°17N 114°42W 79 M12
Cicia Fiji 17°45S 179°18W 59 a
Ciéagas del Cataumbo △
  Venezuela 9°25N 71°54W 89 E5
Ciechanów Poland 52°52N 20°38E 17 B11
Ciego de Ávila Cuba 21°50N 78°50W 88 B4
Ciénaga Colombia 11°1N 74°15W 92 A4
Cienfuegos Cuba 22°10N 80°30W 88 B3
Cieszyn Poland 49°45N 18°35E 17 D10
Cieza Spain 38°17N 1°23W 21 C5
Cihuatlán Mexico 19°14N 104°35W 86 D4
Cijara, Embalse de Spain 39°18N 4°52W 21 C3
Cijulang Indonesia 7°42S 108°27E 37 G13
Cilacap Indonesia 7°43S 109°0E 37 G13
Cili China 29°30N 111°8E 35 C8
Cill Airne = Killarney
  Ireland 52°4N 9°30W 10 D2
Cill Chainnigh = Kilkenny
  Ireland 52°39N 7°15W 10 D4
Cill Dara = Kildare Ireland 53°9N 6°55W 10 C5
Cill Droichid = Celbridge
  Ireland 53°20N 6°32W 10 C5
Cill Mhantáin = Wicklow
  Ireland 52°59N 6°3W 10 D5
Cilo Dağı Turkey 37°28N 43°55E 19 G7
Cima U.S.A. 35°14N 115°30W 79 K11
Cimarron Kans., U.S.A. 37°48N 100°21W 80 G3
Cimarron N. Mex.,
  U.S.A. 36°31N 104°55W 77 H11
Cimarron → U.S.A. 36°10N 96°16W 84 C6
Cimişlia Moldova 46°34N 28°44E 17 E15
Cimone, Mte. Italy 44°12N 10°42E 22 B4
Cîna → Spain 41°26N 0°21E 21 B6
Cincar Bos.-H. 43°55N 17°5E 22 C7
Cincinnati U.S.A. 39°9N 84°27W 81 F11
Cincinnatus U.S.A. 42°33N 75°54W 83 D9
Çine Turkey 37°37N 28°2E 23 F13
Ciney Belgium 50°18N 5°5E 15 D5
Cinque I. India 11°16N 92°42E 45 J11
Cinto, Mte. France 42°24N 8°54E 20 E8
Circle Alaska, U.S.A. 65°50N 144°4W 74 B11
Circle Mont., U.S.A. 47°25N 105°35W 76 C11
Circleville U.S.A. 39°36N 82°57W 81 F12
Cirebon Indonesia 6°45S 108°32E 37 G13
Cirencester U.K. 51°43N 1°57W 13 F6
Cisco U.S.A. 32°23N 98°59W 84 E5
Citlaltépetl = Orizaba, Pico de
  Mexico 18°58N 97°15W 87 D5
Citrus Heights U.S.A. 38°42N 121°17W 78 G5
Citrusdal S. Africa 32°35S 19°0E 56 E2
Città di Castello Italy 43°27N 12°14E 22 C5
Ciudad Acuña Mexico 29°18N 100°55W 86 B4
Ciudad Altamirano
  Mexico 18°20N 100°40W 86 D4
Ciudad Anáhuac Mexico 27°14N 100°7W 86 B4
Ciudad Bolívar Venezuela 8°5N 63°36W 92 B6
Ciudad Camargo
  Mexico 27°40N 105°10W 86 B3
Ciudad Cortés Costa Rica 8°55N 84°0W 88 E3
Ciudad del Carmen
  Mexico 18°38N 91°50W 87 D6
Ciudad del Este Paraguay 25°30S 54°50W 95 B5
Ciudad Delicias = Delicias
  Mexico 28°13N 105°28W 86 B3
Ciudad Frontera Mexico 26°56N 101°27W 86 B4

Ciudad Guayana Venezuela 8°0N 62°30W 92 B6
Ciudad Guerrero
  Mexico 28°33N 107°30W 86 B3
Ciudad Guzmán Mexico 19°41N 103°29W 86 D4
Ciudad Juárez Mexico 31°44N 106°29W 86 A3
Ciudad Lerdo Mexico 25°32N 103°32W 86 B4
Ciudad Madero Mexico 22°19N 97°50W 87 C5
Ciudad Mante Mexico 22°44N 98°59W 87 C5
Ciudad Obregón Mexico 27°29N 109°56W 86 B3
Ciudad Real Spain 38°59N 3°55W 21 C4
Ciudad Rodrigo Spain 40°35N 6°32W 21 B2
Ciudad Valles Mexico 21°59N 99°1W 87 C5
Ciudad Victoria Mexico 23°44N 99°8W 87 C5
Civitanova Marche Italy 43°18N 13°44E 22 C5
Civitavécchia Italy 42°6N 11°48E 22 C4
Cixi China 30°17N 121°9E 35 B13
Cizre Turkey 37°19N 42°10E 46 B4
Clackmannanshire □
  U.K. 56°10N 3°43W 11 E5
Clacton-on-Sea U.K. 51°47N 1°11E 13 F9
Claire, L. Canada 58°35N 112°5W 70 B6
Clairton U.S.A. 40°18N 79°53W 82 F5
Clallam Bay U.S.A. 48°15N 124°16W 78 B2
Clanton U.S.A. 32°51N 86°38W 85 E11
Clanwilliam S. Africa 32°11S 18°52E 56 E2
Clara Ireland 53°21N 7°37W 10 C4
Claraville U.S.A. 35°24N 118°20W 79 K8
Clare Australia 33°50S 138°37E 63 E2
Clare U.S.A. 43°49N 84°46W 81 D11
Clare □ Ireland 52°45N 9°0W 10 D3
Clare → Ireland 53°20N 9°2W 10 C2
Clare I. Ireland 53°47N 10°0W 10 C1
Claremont Calif., U.S.A. 34°6N 117°43W 79 L9
Claremont N.H., U.S.A. 43°23N 72°20W 83 C12
Claremont Pt. Australia 14°1S 143°41E 62 A3
Claremore U.S.A. 36°19N 95°36W 84 C7
Claremorris Ireland 53°45N 9°0W 10 C3
Clarence → Australia 29°25S 153°22E 63 D5
Clarence → N.Z. 42°10S 173°56E 59 E4
Clarence, I. Chile 54°0S 72°0W 96 G2
Clarence Str. Australia 12°0S 131°0E 60 B5
Clarence I. Antarctica 61°10S 54°0W 5 C18
Clarence Town Bahamas 23°6N 74°59W 89 B5
Clarendon Pa., U.S.A. 41°47N 79°6W 82 E5
Clarendon Tex., U.S.A. 34°56N 100°53W 84 D4
Clarenville Canada 48°10N 54°1W 73 C9
Claresholm Canada 50°2N 113°33W 70 D6
Clarie Coast Antarctica 68°0S 135°0E 5 C9
Clarinda U.S.A. 40°44N 95°2W 80 E6
Clarington Canada 43°55N 78°41W 82 C6
Clarion Iowa, U.S.A. 42°44N 93°44W 80 D7
Clarion Pa., U.S.A. 41°13N 79°23W 82 E5
Clarion → U.S.A. 41°7N 79°41W 82 E5
Clarion Fracture Zone
  Pac. Oc. 20°0N 120°0W 66 H7
Clark, Pt. Canada 44°4N 81°45W 82 B3
Clark Fork U.S.A. 48°9N 116°11W 76 B5
Clark Fork → U.S.A. 48°9N 116°15W 76 B5
Clarkdale U.S.A. 34°46N 112°3W 77 J7
Clarke City Canada 50°12N 66°38W 73 B6
Clarke I. Australia 40°32S 148°10E 63 G4
Clarks Fork Yellowstone →
  U.S.A. 45°32N 108°50W 76 D9
Clark's Harbour Canada 43°25N 65°38W 73 D6
Clarks Hill L. = J. Strom Thurmond
  L. U.S.A. 33°40N 82°12W 85 E13
Clarks Summit U.S.A. 41°30N 75°42W 83 E9
Clarksburg U.S.A. 39°17N 80°30W 81 F13
Clarksdale U.S.A. 34°12N 90°35W 85 D9
Clarkston U.S.A. 46°25N 117°3W 76 C5
Clarksville Ark., U.S.A. 35°28N 93°28W 84 D8
Clarksville Tenn., U.S.A. 36°32N 87°21W 85 C11
Clarksville Tex., U.S.A. 33°37N 95°3W 84 E7
Clatskanie U.S.A. 46°6N 123°12W 78 D3
Claude U.S.A. 35°7N 101°22W 84 D4
Claveria Phil. 18°37N 121°4E 37 A6
Clay U.S.A. 38°17N 121°10W 78 G5
Clay Center U.S.A. 39°23N 97°8W 80 F5
Claypool U.S.A. 33°25N 110°51W 77 K8
Claysburg U.S.A. 40°17N 78°27W 82 F6
Claysville U.S.A. 40°7N 80°25W 82 F4
Clayton Canada 45°11N 76°19W 83 A8
Clayton N. Mex., U.S.A. 36°27N 103°11W 77 H12
Clayton N.Y., U.S.A. 44°14N 76°5W 83 B8
Clear, C. Ireland 51°25N 9°32W 10 E2
Clear I. Ireland 51°26N 9°30W 10 E2
Clear L. U.S.A. 39°2N 122°47W 78 F4
Clear Lake Iowa, U.S.A. 43°8N 93°23W 80 D7
Clear Lake S. Dak., U.S.A. 44°45N 96°41W 80 C6
Clear Lake Res. U.S.A. 41°56N 121°5W 76 F3
Clearfield Pa., U.S.A. 41°2N 78°27W 82 E6
Clearfield Utah, U.S.A. 41°7N 112°2W 76 F7
Clearlake U.S.A. 38°57N 122°38W 78 G4
Clearwater Canada 51°38N 120°2W 70 C4
Clearwater → Alta.,
  Canada 52°22N 114°57W 70 C6
Clearwater → Alta.,
  Canada 56°44N 111°23W 71 B6
Clearwater L. Canada 53°34N 99°49W 71 C9
Clearwater Lake △
  Canada 54°0N 101°0W 71 C8
Clearwater Mts. U.S.A. 46°5N 115°20W 76 C6
Clearwater River △
  Canada 56°55N 109°10W 71 B7
Cleburne U.S.A. 32°21N 97°23W 84 E6
Clee Hills U.K. 52°26N 2°35W 13 E5
Cleethorpes U.K. 53°33N 0°3W 12 D7
Cleeve Cloud U.K. 51°56N 2°0W 13 F6
Clemson U.S.A. 34°41N 82°50W 85 D13
Clerke Reef Australia 17°22S 119°20E 60 C2
Clermont Australia 22°49S 147°39E 62 C4
Clermont U.S.A. 28°33N 81°46W 85 G14
Clermont-Ferrand France 45°46N 3°4E 20 D5
Clervaux Lux. 50°4N 6°2E 15 D6
Clevedon U.K. 51°26N 2°52W 13 F5

Cleveland Miss., U.S.A. 33°45N 90°43W 85 E9
Cleveland Ohio, U.S.A. 41°29N 81°41W 82 E3
Cleveland Okla., U.S.A. 36°19N 96°28W 84 C6
Cleveland Tenn., U.S.A. 35°10N 84°53W 85 D12
Cleveland Tex., U.S.A. 30°21N 95°5W 84 F7
Cleveland, Mt. U.S.A. 48°56N 113°51W 76 B7
Cleveland Heights U.S.A. 41°31N 81°33W 82 E3
Clevelândia Brazil 26°24S 52°23W 95 B5
Clew B. Ireland 53°50N 9°49W 10 C2
Clewiston U.S.A. 26°45N 80°56W 85 H14
Clifden Ireland 53°29N 10°1W 10 C1
Clifden N.Z. 46°1S 167°42E 59 G1
Cliffdell U.S.A. 46°56N 121°5W 78 D5
Cliffy Hd. Australia 35°1S 116°29E 61 G2
Clifton Australia 27°59S 151°53E 63 D5
Clifton Ariz., U.S.A. 33°3N 109°18W 77 K9
Clifton Colo., U.S.A. 39°7N 108°25W 76 G9
Clifton Tex., U.S.A. 31°47N 97°35W 84 F6
Clifton Beach Australia 16°46S 145°39E 62 B4
Clinch → U.S.A. 35°53N 84°29W 85 D12
Clingmans Dome
  U.S.A. 35°34N 83°30W 85 D13
Clint U.S.A. 31°35N 106°14W 84 F1
Clinton B.C., Canada 51°6N 121°35W 70 C4
Clinton Ont., Canada 43°37N 81°32W 82 C3
Clinton N.Z. 46°12S 169°23E 59 G2
Clinton Ark., U.S.A. 35°36N 92°28W 84 D8
Clinton Conn., U.S.A. 41°17N 72°32W 83 E12
Clinton Ill., U.S.A. 40°9N 88°57W 80 E9
Clinton Ind., U.S.A. 39°40N 87°24W 80 F10
Clinton Iowa, U.S.A. 41°51N 90°12W 80 E8
Clinton Mass., U.S.A. 42°25N 71°41W 83 D13
Clinton Miss., U.S.A. 32°20N 90°20W 85 E9
Clinton Mo., U.S.A. 38°22N 93°46W 80 F7
Clinton N.C., U.S.A. 35°0N 78°22W 85 D15
Clinton Okla., U.S.A. 35°31N 98°58W 84 D5
Clinton S.C., U.S.A. 34°29N 81°53W 85 D14
Clinton Tenn., U.S.A. 36°6N 84°8W 85 C12
Clinton Wash., U.S.A. 47°59N 122°21W 78 C4
Clinton, C. Australia 22°30S 150°45E 62 C5
Clinton Colden L.
  Canada 63°58N 107°27W 68 E10
Clipperton, Î. Pac. Oc. 10°18N 109°13W 65 F17
Clipperton Fracture Zone
  Pac. Oc. 19°0N 122°0W 65 G16
Clisham U.K. 57°58N 6°49W 11 D2
Clitheroe U.K. 53°53N 2°22W 12 D5
Clo-oose Canada 48°39N 124°49W 78 B2
Cloates, Pt. Australia 22°43S 113°40E 60 D1
Clocolan S. Africa 28°55S 27°34E 57 C4
Clodomira Argentina 27°35S 64°14W 94 B3
Cloghaneely Ireland 55°8N 8°14W 10 A3
Clogher Hd. Ireland 53°48N 6°14W 10 C5
Clonakilty Ireland 51°37N 8°53W 10 E3
Clonakilty B. Ireland 51°35N 8°51W 10 E3
Cloncurry Australia 20°40S 140°28E 62 C3
Cloncurry Ireland 53°26N 6°48W 10 C5
Cloncurry → Australia 18°37S 140°40E 62 B3
Clondalkin Ireland 53°19N 6°25W 10 C5
Clones Ireland 54°11N 7°15W 10 B4
Clonmel Ireland 52°21N 7°42W 10 D4
Cloquet U.S.A. 46°43N 92°28W 80 B7
Clorinda Argentina 25°16S 57°45W 94 B4
Cloud Peak U.S.A. 44°23N 107°11W 76 D10
Cloudcroft U.S.A. 32°58N 105°45W 77 K11
Cloverdale U.S.A. 38°48N 123°1W 78 G4
Clovis Calif., U.S.A. 36°49N 119°42W 78 J7
Clovis N. Mex., U.S.A. 34°24N 103°12W 77 J12
Cloyne Canada 44°49N 77°11W 82 B7
Cluain Meala = Clonmel
  Ireland 52°21N 7°42W 10 D4
Cluj-Napoca Romania 46°47N 23°38E 17 E12
Clunes Australia 37°20S 143°45E 63 F3
Clutha → N.Z. 46°20S 169°49E 59 G2
Clwyd → U.K. 53°19N 3°31W 12 D4
Clyde N.Z. 45°12S 169°20E 59 F2
Clyde U.S.A. 43°5N 76°52W 82 C8
Clyde → U.K. 55°55N 4°30W 11 F4
Clyde, Firth of U.K. 55°22N 5°1W 11 F3
Clyde River Canada 70°30N 68°30W 69 C18
Clydebank U.K. 55°54N 4°23W 11 F4
Clymer N.Y., U.S.A. 42°1N 79°37W 82 D5
Clymer Pa., U.S.A. 40°40N 79°1W 82 D5
Coachella U.S.A. 33°41N 116°10W 79 M10
Coachella Canal
  U.S.A. 32°43N 114°57W 79 N12
Coahoma U.S.A. 32°18N 101°18W 84 E4
Coahuayana → Mexico 18°41N 103°45W 86 D4
Coahuila □ Mexico 27°0N 103°0W 86 B4
Coal → Canada 59°39N 126°57W 70 B3
Coalcomán Mexico 18°46N 103°10W 86 D4
Coaldale Canada 49°45N 112°35W 70 D6
Coalgate U.S.A. 34°32N 96°13W 84 D6
Coalinga U.S.A. 36°9N 120°21W 78 J6
Coalisland U.K. 54°33N 6°42W 10 B5
Coalville U.K. 52°44N 1°23W 12 E6
Coalville U.S.A. 40°55N 111°24W 76 F8
Coamo Puerto Rico 18°5N 66°22W 89 d
Coari Brazil 4°8S 63°7W 92 D6
Coast □ Kenya 2°40S 39°45E 54 C4
Coast Mts. Canada 55°0N 129°20W 70 C3
Coast Ranges U.S.A. 39°0N 123°0W 78 G4
Coatbridge U.K. 55°52N 4°6W 11 F4
Coatepec Mexico 19°27N 96°58W 87 D5
Coatepeque Guatemala 14°46N 91°55W 88 D1
Coatesville U.S.A. 39°59N 75°50W 81 F16
Coaticook Canada 45°10N 71°46W 83 A13
Coats I. Canada 62°30N 83°0W 69 E15
Coats Land Antarctica 77°0S 25°0W 5 D1
Coatzacoalcos Mexico 18°7N 94°25W 87 D6
Cobá Mexico 20°31N 87°45W 87 C7
Cobalt Canada 47°25N 79°42W 72 C4
Cobar Australia 31°27S 145°48E 63 E4
Cobh Ireland 51°51N 8°17W 10 E3
Cóbh, An = Cobh Ireland 51°51N 8°17W 10 E3
Cobija Bolivia 11°0S 68°50W 92 F5
Cobleskill U.S.A. 42°41N 74°29W 83 D10
Coboconk Canada 44°39N 78°48W 82 B6

Cobourg Canada 43°58N 78°10W 82 C6
Cobourg Pen. Australia 11°20S 132°15E 60 B5
Cobram Australia 35°54S 145°40E 63 F4
Coburg Germany 50°15N 10°58E 16 C6
Coburg I. Canada 75°57N 79°26W 69 B16
Cocanada = Kakinada
  India 16°57N 82°11E 44 F6
Cochabamba Bolivia 17°26S 66°10W 92 G5
Cochin = Kochi India 9°58N 76°20E 45 K3
Cochin China = Nam Phan
  Vietnam 10°30N 106°0E 39 G6
Cochran U.S.A. 32°23N 83°21W 85 E13
Cochrane Alta., Canada 51°11N 114°30W 70 C6
Cochrane Ont., Canada 49°0N 81°0W 72 C3
Cochrane → Canada 59°0N 103°40W 71 B8
Cochrane, L. Chile 47°10S 72°0W 96 F2
Cochranton U.S.A. 41°31N 80°3W 82 E4
Cockburn Australia 32°5S 141°0E 63 E3
Cockburn, Canal Chile 54°30S 72°0W 96 G2
Cockburn I. Canada 45°55N 83°22W 72 C3
Cockburn Ra. Australia 15°46S 128°0E 60 C4
Cockermouth U.K. 54°40N 3°22E 12 C4
Cockpit Country, The
  Jamaica 18°15N 77°45W 88 a
Coco → Cent. Amer. 15°0N 83°8W 88 D3
Coco, I. del Pac. Oc. 5°25N 87°55W 65 G19
Coco Channel Asia 13°45N 93°10E 45 H11
Cocoa U.S.A. 28°21N 80°44W 85 G14
Cocobeach Gabon 0°59N 9°34E 54 D1
Cocos B. Trin. & Tob. 10°24N 61°2W 93 K15
Cocos I. = Coco, I. del
  Pac. Oc. 5°25N 87°55W 65 G19
Cocos Is. Ind. Oc. 12°10S 96°55E 64 J1
Cocos Ridge Pac. Oc. 4°0N 88°0W 65 G19
Cod, C. U.S.A. 42°5N 70°10W 81 D18
Codajás Brazil 3°55S 62°0W 92 D6
Codó Brazil 4°30S 43°55W 93 D10
Cody U.S.A. 44°32N 109°3W 76 D9
Coe Hill Canada 44°52N 77°50W 82 B7
Coelemu Chile 36°30S 72°48W 94 D1
Coen Australia 13°52S 143°12E 62 A3
Coevorden Neths. 52°40N 6°44E 15 B6
Coffeyville U.S.A. 37°2N 95°37W 80 G6
Coffin B. Australia 34°38S 135°28E 63 E2
Coffin Bay Australia 34°37S 135°19E 63 E2
Coffin Bay △ Australia 34°34S 135°19E 63 E2
Coffin Bay Peninsula
  Australia 34°32S 135°15E 63 E2
Coffs Harbour Australia 30°16S 153°5E 63 E5
Cognac France 45°41N 0°20W 20 D3
Cohocton U.S.A. 42°30N 77°30W 82 D7
Cohocton → U.S.A. 42°9N 77°6W 82 D7
Cohoes U.S.A. 42°46N 73°42W 83 D11
Cohuna Australia 35°45S 144°15E 63 F3
Coiba, I. de Panama 7°30N 81°40W 88 E3
Coig → Argentina 51°0S 69°10W 96 G3
Coigeach, Rubha U.K. 58°6N 5°26W 11 C3
Coihaique Chile 45°30S 71°45W 96 F2
Coimbatore India 11°2N 76°59E 45 J3
Coimbra Brazil 19°55S 57°48W 92 G7
Coimbra Portugal 40°15N 8°27W 21 B1
Coin Spain 36°40N 4°48W 21 D3
Coipasa, Salar de Bolivia 19°26S 68°9W 92 G5
Cojimies Ecuador 0°20N 80°0W 92 C3
Cojutepequé El Salv. 13°41N 88°54W 88 D2
Cokeville U.S.A. 42°5N 110°57W 76 E8
Colac Australia 38°21S 143°35E 63 F3
Colachel India 8°10N 77°15E 45 K3
Colatina Brazil 19°32S 40°37W 93 G10
Colbeck, C. Antarctica 77°6S 157°48W 5 D13
Colborne Canada 44°0N 77°53W 82 C7
Colby U.S.A. 39°24N 101°3W 80 F3
Colca → Peru 15°55S 72°43W 92 G4
Colchester U.K. 51°54N 0°55E 13 F8
Colchester U.S.A. 41°35N 72°20W 83 E12
Cold L. Canada 54°33N 110°5W 71 C7
Cold Lake Canada 54°27N 110°10W 71 C7
Coldstream Canada 50°13N 119°11W 70 C5
Coldstream U.K. 55°39N 2°15W 11 F6
Coldwater Canada 44°42N 79°40W 82 B5
Coldwater Kans., U.S.A. 37°16N 99°20W 80 G4
Coldwater Mich., U.S.A. 41°57N 85°0W 81 E11
Colebrook U.S.A. 44°54N 71°30W 83 B13
Coleman Canada 49°40N 114°30W 70 D6
Coleman U.S.A. 31°50N 99°26W 84 F5
Coleman → Australia 15°6S 141°38E 62 B3
Colenso S. Africa 28°44S 29°50E 57 D4
Coleraine Australia 37°36S 141°40E 63 F3
Coleraine U.K. 55°8N 6°41W 10 A5
Coleridge, L. N.Z. 43°17S 171°30E 59 E3
Coleroon → India 11°25N 79°50E 45 J4
Colesberg S. Africa 30°45S 25°5E 56 E4
Coleville U.S.A. 38°34N 119°30W 78 G7
Colfax Calif., U.S.A. 39°6N 120°57W 78 F6
Colfax La., U.S.A. 31°31N 92°42W 84 F8
Colfax Wash., U.S.A. 46°53N 117°22W 76 C5
Colhué Huapi, L.
  Argentina 45°30S 69°0W 96 F3
Coligny S. Africa 26°17S 26°15E 57 C4
Colima Mexico 19°14N 103°43W 86 D4
Colima □ Mexico 19°10N 104°0W 86 D4
Colima, Nevado de
  Mexico 19°33N 103°38W 86 D4
Colina Chile 33°13S 70°45W 94 C1
Colinas Brazil 6°0S 44°10W 93 E10
Coll U.K. 56°39N 6°34W 11 E2
Collaguasi Chile 21°5S 68°45W 94 A2
Collarenebri Australia 29°33S 148°34E 63 D4
College U.S.A. 64°52N 147°49W 74 C10
College Station U.S.A. 30°37N 96°21W 84 F6
Collie Australia 33°22S 116°8E 61 F2
Collier B. Australia 16°10S 124°15E 60 C3
Collier Ra. Australia 24°45S 119°10E 61 D2
Collier Range △ Australia 24°39S 119°7E 61 D2
Collierville U.S.A. 35°3N 89°40W 85 D10
Collina, Passo di Italy 44°2N 10°56E 22 B4

Collingwood Canada 44°29N 80°13W 82 B4
Collingwood N.Z. 40°41S 172°40E 59 D4
Collins Canada 50°17N 89°27W 72 B2
Collins Bay Canada 44°14N 76°36W 83 B8
Collinson Pen. Canada 69°58N 101°24W 68 D11
Collinsville Australia 20°30S 147°56E 62 C4
Collipulli Chile 37°55S 72°30W 94 D1
Collooney Ireland 54°11N 8°29W 10 B3
Colmar France 48°5N 7°20E 20 B7
Colo → Australia 33°25S 150°52E 63 E5
Cologne = Köln Germany 50°56N 6°57E 16 C4
Coloma U.S.A. 38°48N 120°53W 78 G6
Colomb-Béchar = Béchar Algeria 31°38N 2°18W 52 B5
Colombia ■ S. Amer. 3°45N 73°0W 92 C4
Colombian Basin Caribbean 14°0N 76°0W 88 D4
Colombo Sri Lanka 6°56N 79°58E 45 L4
Colón B. Aires, Argentina 33°53S 61°7W 94 C3
Colón Entre Ríos, Argentina 32°12S 58°10W 94 C4
Colón Cuba 22°42N 80°54W 88 B3
Colón Panama 9°20N 79°54W 88 E4
Colón, Arch. de Ecuador 0°0 91°0W 90 D1
Colonia del Sacramento Uruguay 34°25S 57°50W 94 C4
Colonia Dora Argentina 28°34S 62°59W 94 B3
Colonial Beach U.S.A. 38°15N 76°58W 81 F15
Colonie U.S.A. 42°43N 73°50W 83 D11
Colonsay Canada 51°59N 105°52W 71 C7
Colonsay U.K. 56°5N 6°12W 11 E2
Colorado □ U.S.A. 39°30N 105°30W 76 G11
Colorado → Argentina 39°50S 62°8W 96 D4
Colorado → N. Amer. 31°45N 114°40W 77 L6
Colorado → U.S.A. 28°36N 95°59W 84 G7
Colorado City U.S.A. 32°24N 100°52W 84 E4
Colorado Plateau U.S.A. 37°0N 111°0W 77 H8
Colorado River Aqueduct U.S.A. 33°50N 117°23W 79 L12
Colorado Springs U.S.A. 38°50N 104°49W 76 G11
Colotlán Mexico 22°6N 103°16W 86 C4
Colstrip U.S.A. 45°53N 106°38W 76 D10
Colton U.S.A. 44°33N 74°56W 83 B10
Columbia Ky., U.S.A. 37°6N 85°18W 81 G11
Columbia La., U.S.A. 32°6N 92°5W 84 E8
Columbia Miss., U.S.A. 31°15N 89°50W 85 F10
Columbia Mo., U.S.A. 38°57N 92°20W 80 F7
Columbia Pa., U.S.A. 40°2N 76°30W 83 F8
Columbia S.C., U.S.A. 34°0N 81°2W 85 D14
Columbia Tenn., U.S.A. 35°37N 87°2W 85 D11
Columbia → N. Amer. 46°15N 124°5W 78 D2
Columbia, C. Canada 83°6N 69°57W 69 A18
Columbia, District of □ U.S.A. 38°55N 77°0W 81 F15
Columbia, Mt. Canada 52°8N 117°20W 70 C5
Columbia Basin U.S.A. 46°45N 119°5W 76 C4
Columbia Falls U.S.A. 48°23N 114°11W 76 B6
Columbia Mts. Canada 52°0N 119°0W 70 C5
Columbia Plateau U.S.A. 44°0N 117°30W 76 E5
Columbiana U.S.A. 40°53N 80°42W 82 F4
Columbretes, Is. Spain 39°50N 0°50E 21 C6
Columbus Ga., U.S.A. 32°28N 84°59W 85 E12
Columbus Ind., U.S.A. 39°13N 85°55W 81 F11
Columbus Kans., U.S.A. 37°10N 94°50W 80 G6
Columbus Miss., U.S.A. 33°30N 88°25W 85 E10
Columbus Mont., U.S.A. 45°38N 109°15W 76 D9
Columbus N. Mex., U.S.A. 31°50N 107°38W 77 L10
Columbus Nebr., U.S.A. 41°26N 97°22W 80 E5
Columbus Ohio, U.S.A. 39°58N 83°0W 81 F12
Columbus Tex., U.S.A. 29°42N 96°33W 84 G6
Colusa U.S.A. 39°13N 122°1W 78 F4
Colville U.S.A. 48°33N 117°54W 76 B5
Colville → U.S.A. 70°25N 150°30W 74 A9
Colville, C. N.Z. 36°29S 175°21E 59 B5
Colwood Canada 48°26N 123°29W 78 B3
Colwyn Bay U.K. 53°18N 3°44W 12 D4
Comácchio Italy 44°42N 12°11E 22 B5
Comalcalco Mexico 18°16N 93°13W 87 D6
Comallo Argentina 41°0S 70°5W 96 E2
Comanche U.S.A. 31°54N 98°36W 84 F5
Comandante Ferraz Antarctica 62°30S 58°0W 5 C18
Comayagua Honduras 14°25N 87°37W 88 D2
Combahee → U.S.A. 32°31N 80°31W 85 E14
Combarbalá Chile 31°11S 71°2W 94 C1
Combe Martin U.K. 51°12N 4°3W 13 F3
Comber Canada 42°14N 82°33W 82 D2
Comber U.K. 54°33N 5°45W 10 B6
Combermere Canada 45°22N 77°37W 82 A7
Comblain-au-Pont Belgium 50°29N 5°35E 15 D5
Comeragh Mts. Ireland 52°18N 7°34W 10 D4
Comet Australia 23°36S 148°38E 62 C4
Comilla Bangla. 23°28N 91°10E 41 H17
Comino, C. Italy 40°32N 9°49E 22 D3
Comitán de Domínguez Mexico 16°15N 92°8W 87 D6
Commerce Ga., U.S.A. 34°12N 83°28W 85 D13
Commerce Tex., U.S.A. 33°15N 95°54W 84 E7
Committee B. Canada 68°30N 86°30W 69 D14
Commodore, C. Canada 44°47N 80°54W 82 B4
Commonwealth B. Antarctica 67°0S 144°0E 5 C10
Commoron Cr. → Australia 28°22S 150°8E 63 D5
Communism Pk. = imeni Ismail Samani, Pik Tajikistan 39°0N 72°2E 26 F8
Como Italy 45°47N 9°5E 20 D8
Como, L. di Italy 46°0N 9°11E 20 D8
Comodoro Rivadavia Argentina 45°50S 67°40W 96 F3
Comorin, C. = Kannyakumari India 8°3N 77°40E 45 K3
Comoros ■ Ind. Oc. 12°10S 44°15E 55 a
Comox Canada 49°42N 124°55W 70 D4
Compiègne France 49°24N 2°50E 20 B5
Compostela Mexico 21°14N 104°55W 86 C4
Comprida, I. Brazil 24°50S 47°42W 95 A6
Compton Canada 45°14N 71°49W 83 A13
Compton U.S.A. 33°53N 118°13W 79 M8
Comrat Moldova 46°18N 28°40E 17 E15
Con Cuong Vietnam 19°2N 104°54E 38 C5
Con Dao △ Vietnam 8°42N 106°35E 39 H6
Con Son, Dao Vietnam 8°41N 106°37E 39 H6
Conakry Guinea 9°29N 13°49W 52 G3
Conara Australia 41°50S 147°26E 63 G4
Concarneau France 47°52N 3°56W 20 C2
Conceição da Barra Brazil 18°35S 39°45W 93 G11
Conceição do Araguaia Brazil 8°0S 49°2W 93 E9
Concepción Argentina 27°20S 65°35W 94 B2
Concepción Bolivia 16°15S 62°8W 92 G6
Concepción Chile 36°50S 73°0W 94 D1
Concepción Paraguay 23°22S 57°26W 94 A4
Concepción □ Chile 37°0S 72°30W 94 D1
Concepción, Est. de Chile 50°30S 74°55W 96 G2
Concepción, L. Bolivia 17°20S 61°20W 92 G6
Concepción, Pta. Mexico 26°53N 111°50W 86 B2
Concepción del Oro Mexico 24°38N 101°25W 86 C4
Concepción del Uruguay Argentina 32°35S 58°20W 94 C4
Conception, Pt. U.S.A. 34°27N 120°28W 79 L6
Conception B. Canada 47°45N 53°0W 73 C9
Conception B. Namibia 23°55S 14°22E 56 B1
Conception I. Bahamas 23°52N 75°9W 89 B4
Conchas Dam U.S.A. 35°22N 104°11W 77 J11
Concho U.S.A. 34°28N 109°36W 77 J9
Concho → U.S.A. 31°34N 99°43W 84 F5
Conchos → Chihuahua, Mexico 29°35N 104°25W 86 B4
Conchos → Tamaulipas, Mexico 24°55N 97°38W 87 B5
Concord Calif., U.S.A. 37°59N 122°2W 78 H4
Concord N.C., U.S.A. 35°25N 80°35W 85 D14
Concord N.H., U.S.A. 43°12N 71°32W 83 C13
Concordia Antarctica 75°6S 123°23E 5 D9
Concordia Argentina 31°20S 58°2W 94 C4
Concórdia Amazonas, Brazil 4°36S 66°36W 92 D5
Concórdia Sta. Catarina, Brazil 27°14S 52°1W 95 B5
Concordia Mexico 23°17N 106°4W 86 C3
Concordia U.S.A. 39°34N 97°40W 80 F5
Concrete U.S.A. 48°32N 121°45W 76 B3
Condamine Australia 26°56S 150°9E 63 D5
Conde U.S.A. 45°9N 98°6W 80 C4
Condeúba Brazil 14°52S 42°0W 93 F10
Condobolin Australia 33°4S 147°6E 63 E4
Condon U.S.A. 45°14N 120°11W 76 D3
Conegliano Italy 45°53N 12°18E 22 B5
Conejos Mexico 26°14N 103°53W 86 B4
Conemaugh → U.S.A. 40°28N 79°19W 82 F5
Confuso → Paraguay 25°9S 57°34W 94 B4
Conghua China 23°36N 113°31E 35 F9
Congjiang China 25°43N 108°52E 34 E7
Congleton U.K. 53°10N 2°13W 12 D5
Congo (Brazzaville) = Congo ■ Africa 1°0S 16°0E 54 E3
Congo (Kinshasa) = Congo, Dem. Rep. of the ■ Africa 3°0S 23°0E 54 E4
Congo ■ Africa 1°0S 16°0E 54 E3
Congo → Africa 6°4S 12°24E 54 F2
Congo, Dem. Rep. of the ■ Africa 3°0S 23°0E 54 E4
Congo Basin Africa 0°10S 24°30E 54 E4
Congonhas Brazil 20°30S 43°52W 95 A7
Congress U.S.A. 34°9N 112°51W 77 J7
Coniston Canada 46°29N 80°51W 72 C3
Conjeeveram = Kanchipuram India 12°52N 79°45E 45 H4
Conklin Canada 55°38N 111°5W 71 B6
Conklin U.S.A. 42°2N 75°49W 83 D9
Conn, L. Ireland 54°3N 9°15W 10 B2
Connaught □ Ireland 53°43N 9°12W 10 C2
Conneaut U.S.A. 41°57N 80°34W 82 E4
Conneautville U.S.A. 41°45N 80°22W 82 E4
Connecticut □ U.S.A. 41°30N 72°45W 83 E12
Connecticut → U.S.A. 41°16N 72°20W 83 E12
Connell U.S.A. 46°40N 118°52W 76 C4
Connellsville U.S.A. 40°1N 79°35W 82 F5
Connemara Ireland 53°29N 9°45W 10 C2
Connemara △ Ireland 53°32N 9°52W 10 C2
Connersville U.S.A. 39°39N 85°8W 81 F11
Connors Ra. Australia 21°40S 149°10E 62 C4
Conquest Canada 51°32N 107°14W 71 C7
Conrad U.S.A. 48°10N 111°57W 76 B8
Conrad Rise S. Ocean 53°0S 41°0E 5 B5
Conran, C. Australia 37°49S 148°44E 63 F4
Conroe U.S.A. 30°19N 95°27W 84 F7
Consecon Canada 44°0N 77°31W 82 C7
Conselheiro Lafaiete Brazil 20°40S 43°48W 95 A7
Consett U.K. 54°51N 1°50W 12 C6
Consort Canada 52°1N 110°46W 71 C6
Constance = Konstanz Germany 47°40N 9°10E 16 E5
Constance, L. = Bodensee Europe 47°35N 9°25E 20 C8
Constanţa Romania 44°14N 28°38E 17 F15
Constantine Algeria 36°25N 6°42E 52 A7
Constitución Chile 35°20S 72°30W 94 D1
Constitución Uruguay 31°0S 57°50W 94 C4
Constitución de 1857 △ Mexico 32°4N 115°55W 86 A1
Consul Canada 49°20N 109°30W 71 D7
Contact U.S.A. 41°46N 114°45W 76 F6
Contai India 21°54N 87°46E 43 J12
Contamana Peru 7°19S 74°55W 92 E4
Contas → Brazil 14°17S 39°1W 93 F11
Contoocook U.S.A. 43°13N 71°45W 83 C13
Contra Costa Mozam. 25°9S 33°30E 57 C5
Contwoyto L. Canada 65°42N 110°50W 68 D9
Conway = Conwy U.K. 53°17N 3°50W 12 D4
Conway = Conwy → U.K. 53°17N 3°50W 12 D4
Conway Australia 20°24S 148°41E 62 b
Conway Canada 44°6N 76°54W 82 B8
Conway Ark., U.S.A. 35°5N 92°26W 84 D8
Conway N.H., U.S.A. 43°59N 71°7W 83 C13
Conway S.C., U.S.A. 33°51N 79°3W 85 E15
Conway, C. Australia 20°34S 148°46E 62 b
Conway, L. Australia 28°17S 135°35E 63 D2
Conwy U.K. 53°17N 3°50W 12 D4
Conwy □ U.K. 53°10N 3°44W 12 D4
Conwy → U.K. 53°17N 3°50W 12 D4
Coober Pedy Australia 29°1S 134°43E 63 D1
Cooch Behar = Koch Bihar India 26°22N 89°29E 41 F16
Cooinda Australia 13°15S 130°5E 60 B5
Cook Australia 30°37S 130°25E 61 F5
Cook U.S.A. 47°51N 92°41W 80 B7
Cook, B. Chile 55°10S 70°0W 96 H3
Cook, C. Canada 50°8N 127°55W 70 C3
Cook, Mt. = Aoraki Mount Cook N.Z. 43°36S 170°9E 59 E3
Cook Inlet U.S.A. 60°0N 152°0W 68 F1
Cook Is. ☒ Pac. Oc. 17°0S 160°0W 65 J12
Cook Strait N.Z. 41°15S 174°29E 59 D5
Cookeville U.S.A. 36°10N 85°30W 85 C12
Cookhouse S. Africa 32°44S 25°47E 56 D4
Cooks Harbour Canada 51°36N 55°52W 73 B8
Cookshire Canada 45°25N 71°38W 83 A13
Cookstown Canada 44°11N 79°42W 82 B5
Cookstown U.K. 54°38N 6°45W 10 B5
Cooktown Australia 15°30S 145°16E 62 B4
Coolabah Australia 31°1S 146°43E 63 E4
Cooladdi Australia 26°37S 145°23E 63 D4
Coolah Australia 31°48S 149°41E 63 E4
Coolamon Australia 34°46S 147°8E 63 E4
Coolgardie Australia 30°55S 121°8E 61 F3
Coolidge U.S.A. 32°59N 111°31W 77 K8
Coolidge Dam U.S.A. 33°10N 110°32W 77 K8
Cooma Australia 36°12S 149°8E 63 F4
Coon Rapids U.S.A. 45°9N 93°19W 80 C7
Coonabarabran Australia 31°14S 149°18E 63 E4
Coonamble Australia 30°56S 148°27E 63 E4
Coonana Australia 31°0S 123°0E 61 F3
Coonana ✪ Australia 30°51S 122°53E 61 F3
Coondapoor India 13°42N 74°40E 45 H2
Cooninnie, L. Australia 26°4S 139°59E 63 D2
Coonoor India 11°21N 76°45E 45 J3
Cooper U.S.A. 33°23N 95°42W 84 E7
Cooper Cr. → Australia 28°29S 137°46E 63 D2
Cooper Ridge Pac. Oc. 10°0N 150°30W 65 G12
Cooperstown N. Dak., U.S.A. 47°27N 98°8W 80 B4
Cooperstown N.Y., U.S.A. 42°42N 74°56W 83 D10
Coorabie Australia 31°54S 132°18E 61 F5
Coorong, The Australia 35°50S 139°20E 63 F2
Coorow Australia 29°53S 116°2E 61 E2
Cooroy Australia 26°22S 152°54E 63 D5
Coos Bay U.S.A. 43°22N 124°13W 76 E1
Coosa → U.S.A. 32°30N 86°16W 85 E11
Cootamundra Australia 34°36S 148°1E 63 E4
Cootehill Ireland 54°4N 7°5W 10 B4
Copahue Paso Argentina 37°49S 71°8W 94 D1
Copainalá Mexico 17°4N 93°18W 87 D6
Copake U.S.A. 42°7N 73°31W 83 D11
Copán Honduras 14°50N 89°9W 88 D2
Cope U.S.A. 39°40N 102°51W 76 G12
Copenhagen U.S.A. 43°54N 75°41W 83 C9
Copiapó Chile 27°30S 70°20W 94 B1
Copiapó → Chile 27°19S 70°56W 94 B1
Coplay U.S.A. 40°44N 75°29W 83 F9
Copo △ Argentina 25°53S 61°41W 94 B3
Copp L. Canada 60°14N 114°40W 70 A6
Coppename → Suriname 5°48N 55°55W 93 B7
Copper Canyon = Barranca del Cobre ⌂ Mexico 27°18N 107°40W 86 B3
Copper Center U.S.A. 61°58N 145°18W 74 C10
Copper Harbor U.S.A. 47°28N 87°53W 80 B10
Copperas Cove U.S.A. 31°8N 97°54W 84 F6
Coppermine = Kugluktuk Canada 67°50N 115°5W 68 D8
Coppermine → Canada 67°49N 116°4W 68 D8
Copperopolis U.S.A. 37°58N 120°38W 78 H6
Coquet → U.K. 55°20N 1°32W 12 B6
Coquille U.S.A. 43°11N 124°11W 76 E1
Coquimbo Chile 30°0S 71°20W 94 C1
Coquimbo □ Chile 31°0S 71°0W 94 C1
Coquitlam Canada 49°17N 122°45W 70 D4
Corabia Romania 43°48N 24°30E 17 G13
Coracora Peru 15°5S 73°45W 92 G4
Coraki Australia 28°59S 153°17E 63 D5
Coral U.S.A. 40°29N 79°10W 82 F5
Coral Bay Australia 23°8S 113°46E 60 D1
Coral Harbour Canada 64°8N 83°10W 69 E15
Coral Sea Pac. Oc. 15°0S 150°0E 58 C8
Coral Sea Basin Pac. Oc. 14°0S 152°0E 64 J7
Coral Sea Islands Terr. □ Australia 20°0S 155°0E 58 C8
Coral Springs U.S.A. 26°16N 80°16W 85 H14
Corantijn = Courantyne → S. Amer. 5°50N 57°8W 92 B7
Coraopolis U.S.A. 40°31N 80°10W 82 F4
Corato Italy 41°9N 16°25E 22 D7
Corbett △ India 29°20N 79°0E 43 E8
Corbin U.S.A. 36°57N 84°6W 81 G11
Corby U.K. 52°30N 0°41W 13 E7
Corcaigh = Cork Ireland 51°54N 8°29W 10 E3
Corcoran U.S.A. 36°6N 119°33W 78 J7
Corcovado △ Costa Rica 8°33N 83°35W 88 E3
Corcubión Spain 42°56N 9°12W 21 A1
Cordele U.S.A. 31°58N 83°47W 85 F13
Cordell U.S.A. 35°17N 98°59W 84 D5
Córdoba Argentina 31°20S 64°10W 94 C3
Córdoba Mexico 18°53N 96°56W 87 D5
Córdoba Spain 37°50N 4°50W 21 D3
Córdoba □ Argentina 31°22S 64°15W 94 C3
Córdoba, Sierra de Argentina 31°10S 64°25W 94 C3
Cordova U.S.A. 60°33N 145°45W 68 E2
Corella → Australia 19°34S 140°47E 62 B3
Corentyne = Courantyne → S. Amer. 5°50N 57°8W 92 B7
Corfield Australia 21°40S 143°21E 62 C3
Corfu = Kerkyra Greece 39°38N 19°50E 23 E8
Corfu U.S.A. 42°57N 78°24W 82 D6
Coria Spain 39°58N 6°33W 21 C2
Corigliano Cálabro Italy 39°36N 16°31E 22 E7
Coringa Is. Australia 16°58S 149°58E 62 B4
Corinth = Korinthos Greece 37°56N 22°55E 23 F10
Corinth Miss., U.S.A. 34°56N 88°31W 85 D10
Corinth N.Y., U.S.A. 43°15N 73°49W 83 C11
Corinth, G. of = Korinthiakos Kolpos Greece 38°16N 22°30E 23 E10
Corinto Brazil 18°20S 44°30W 93 G10
Corinto Nic. 12°30N 87°10W 88 D2
Cork Ireland 51°54N 8°29W 10 E3
Cork □ Ireland 51°57N 8°40W 10 E3
Cork Harbour Ireland 51°47N 8°16W 10 E3
Çorlu Turkey 41°11N 27°49E 23 D12
Cormack L. Canada 60°56N 121°37W 70 A4
Cormorant Canada 54°14N 100°35W 71 C8
Cormorant L. Canada 54°15N 100°50W 71 C8
Corn Is. = Maíz, Is. del Nic. 12°15N 83°4W 88 D3
Cornélio Procópio Brazil 23°7S 50°40W 95 A5
Corner Brook Canada 48°57N 57°58W 73 C8
Corneşti Moldova 47°21N 28°1E 17 E15
Corning Ark., U.S.A. 36°25N 90°35W 85 C9
Corning Calif., U.S.A. 39°56N 122°11W 76 G2
Corning Iowa, U.S.A. 40°59N 94°44W 80 E6
Corning N.Y., U.S.A. 42°9N 77°3W 82 D7
Cornwall Canada 45°2N 74°44W 83 A10
Cornwall U.S.A. 40°17N 76°25W 83 F8
Cornwall □ U.K. 50°26N 4°40W 13 G3
Cornwall I. Canada 77°37N 94°38W 69 B13
Cornwallis I. Canada 75°8N 95°0W 69 B13
Corny Pt. Australia 34°55S 137°0E 63 E2
Coro Venezuela 11°25N 69°41W 92 A5
Coroatá Brazil 4°8S 44°0W 93 D10
Corocoro Bolivia 17°15S 68°28W 92 G5
Coroico Bolivia 16°0S 67°50W 92 G5
Coromandel N.Z. 36°45S 175°31E 59 B5
Coromandel Coast India 12°30N 81°0E 45 H5
Corona Calif., U.S.A. 33°53N 117°34W 79 M9
Corona N. Mex., U.S.A. 34°15N 105°36W 77 J11
Coronado U.S.A. 32°41N 117°10W 79 N9
Coronado, B. de Costa Rica 9°0N 83°40W 88 E3
Coronados, Is. Los Mexico 32°26N 117°19W 79 N9
Coronation Canada 52°5N 111°27W 70 C6
Coronation Gulf Canada 68°25N 110°0W 68 D10
Coronation I. Antarctica 60°45S 46°0W 5 C18
Coronation Is. Australia 14°57S 124°55E 60 B3
Coronda Argentina 31°58S 60°56W 94 C3
Coronel Chile 37°0S 73°10W 94 D1
Coronel Bogado Paraguay 27°11S 56°18W 94 B4
Coronel Dorrego Argentina 38°40S 61°10W 94 D3
Coronel Oviedo Paraguay 25°24S 56°30W 94 B4
Coronel Pringles Argentina 38°0S 61°30W 94 D3
Coronel Suárez Argentina 37°30S 61°52W 94 D3
Coronel Vidal Argentina 37°28S 57°45W 94 D4
Coropuna, Nevado Peru 15°30S 72°41W 92 G4
Corowa Australia 35°58S 146°21E 63 F4
Corozal □ Belize 18°23N 88°23W 87 D7
Corozal Pt. Trin. & Tob. 10°45N 61°37W 93 K15
Corpus Argentina 27°10S 55°30W 95 B4
Corpus Christi U.S.A. 27°47N 97°24W 84 H6
Corpus Christi, L. U.S.A. 28°2N 97°52W 84 G6
Corraun Pen. Ireland 53°54N 9°54W 10 C2
Correntes, C. das Mozam. 24°6S 35°34E 57 B6
Corrib, L. Ireland 53°27N 9°16W 10 C2
Corrientes Argentina 27°30S 58°45W 94 B4
Corrientes □ Argentina 28°0S 57°0W 94 B4
Corrientes → Argentina 30°42S 59°38W 94 C4
Corrientes → Peru 3°43S 74°35W 92 D4
Corrientes, C. Colombia 5°30N 77°34W 92 B3
Corrientes, C. Cuba 21°43N 84°30W 88 B3
Corrientes, C. Mexico 20°25N 105°42W 86 C3
Corrigan U.S.A. 31°0N 94°52W 84 F7
Corrigin Australia 32°20S 117°53E 61 F2
Corriverton Guyana 5°55N 57°20W 92 B7
Corry U.S.A. 41°55N 79°39W 82 E5
Corse □ France 42°0N 9°0E 20 F8
Corse, C. France 43°1N 9°25E 20 E8
Corsica = Corse □ France 42°0N 9°0E 20 F8
Corsicana U.S.A. 32°6N 96°28W 84 E6
Corte France 42°19N 9°11E 20 E8
Cortés, Mar de = California, G. de Mexico 27°0N 111°0W 86 B2
Cortez U.S.A. 37°21N 108°35W 77 H9
Corthaidh, Inis = Enniscorthy Ireland 52°30N 6°34W 10 D5
Cortland N.Y., U.S.A. 42°36N 76°11W 83 D8
Cortland Ohio, U.S.A. 41°20N 80°44W 82 E4
Çorum Turkey 40°30N 34°57E 19 F5
Corumbá Brazil 19°0S 57°30W 92 G7
Corunna = A Coruña Spain 43°20N 8°25W 21 A1
Corvallis U.S.A. 44°34N 123°16W 76 D2
Corvette, L. de la Canada 53°25N 74°3W 72 B5
Corvo Azores 39°43N 31°8W 52 a
Corydon U.S.A. 40°46N 93°19W 80 E7
Cosalá Mexico 24°23N 106°41W 86 C3
Cosamaloapan de Carpio Mexico 18°22N 95°48W 87 D5
Cosenza Italy 39°18N 16°15E 22 E7
Coshocton U.S.A. 40°16N 81°51W 82 F3
Cosmo Newberry Australia 28°0S 122°54E 61 E3
Cosmo Newberry ✪ Australia 27°59S 122°53E 61 E3
Cosmonaut Sea S. Ocean 66°30S 40°0E 5 C5
Coso Junction U.S.A. 36°3N 117°57W 79 J9
Coso Pk. U.S.A. 36°13N 117°44W 79 J9
Cosquín Argentina 31°15S 64°30W 94 C3
Costa de la Luz Spain 36°15N 5°58W 21 D2
Costa del Azahar Spain 39°39N 0°13W 21 B6
Costa Mesa U.S.A. 33°38N 117°55W 79 M9
Costa Rica ■ Cent. Amer. 10°0N 84°0W 88 E3
Costa Verde Spain 43°22N 4°14W 21 A3
Cosumnes → U.S.A. 38°16N 121°26W 78 G5
Cotabato Phil. 7°14N 124°15E 37 C6
Cotagaita Bolivia 20°45S 65°40W 94 A2
Côte d'Ivoire ■ Africa 7°30N 5°0W 52 G4
Coteau des Prairies U.S.A. 45°20N 97°50W 80 C5
Coteau du Missouri U.S.A. 47°0N 100°0W 80 B4
Cotentin France 49°15N 1°30W 20 B3
Cotonou Benin 6°20N 2°25E 52 G6
Cotopaxi Ecuador 0°40S 78°30W 92 D3
Cotswold Hills U.K. 51°42N 2°10W 13 F5
Cottage Grove U.S.A. 43°48N 123°3W 76 E2
Cottam Canada 42°8N 82°45W 82 D2
Cottbus Germany 51°45N 14°20E 16 C8
Cottingham U.K. 53°48N 0°25W 12 D7
Cottonwood U.S.A. 34°45N 112°1W 77 J7
Cotulla U.S.A. 28°26N 99°14W 84 G5
Coudersport U.S.A. 41°46N 78°1W 82 E6
Couedic, C. du Australia 36°5S 136°40E 63 F2
Coulee City U.S.A. 47°37N 119°17W 76 C4
Coulee Dam Nat. Recr. Area = Lake Roosevelt ⌂ U.S.A. 48°5N 118°14W 76 B4
Coulman I. Antarctica 73°35S 170°0E 5 D11
Coulonge → Canada 45°52N 76°46W 72 C4
Coulterville U.S.A. 37°43N 120°12W 78 H6
Council Alaska, U.S.A. 64°53N 163°41W 74 C7
Council Idaho, U.S.A. 44°44N 116°26W 76 D5
Council Bluffs U.S.A. 41°16N 95°52W 80 E6
Council Grove U.S.A. 38°40N 96°29W 80 F5
Coupeville U.S.A. 48°13N 122°41W 78 B4
Courantyne → S. Amer. 5°50N 57°8W 92 B7
Courcelles Belgium 50°28N 4°22E 15 D4
Courtenay Canada 49°45N 125°0W 70 D4
Courtland Canada 42°51N 80°38W 82 D4
Courtland U.S.A. 38°20N 121°34W 78 G5
Courtrai = Kortrijk Belgium 50°50N 3°17E 15 D3
Courtright Canada 42°49N 82°28W 82 D2
Coushatta U.S.A. 32°1N 93°21W 84 E8
Coutts Crossing Australia 29°49S 152°55E 63 D5
Couva Trin. & Tob. 10°25N 61°27W 93 K15
Couvin Belgium 50°3N 4°29E 15 D4
Cove I. Canada 45°17N 81°44W 82 A3
Coventry U.K. 52°25N 1°28W 13 E6
Covilhã Portugal 40°17N 7°31W 21 B2
Covington Ga., U.S.A. 33°36N 83°51W 85 E13
Covington Ky., U.S.A. 39°5N 84°30W 81 F11
Covington Tenn., U.S.A. 35°34N 89°39W 85 D10
Covington Va., U.S.A. 37°47N 79°59W 81 G14
Cowal, L. Australia 33°40S 147°25E 63 E4
Cowan, L. Australia 31°45S 121°45E 61 F3
Cowan L. Canada 54°0N 107°15W 71 C7
Cowangie Australia 35°12S 141°26E 63 F3
Cowansville Canada 45°14N 72°46W 83 A12
Coward Springs Australia 29°24S 136°49E 63 D2
Cowcowing Lakes Australia 30°55S 117°20E 61 F2
Cowdenbeath U.K. 56°7N 3°21W 11 E5
Cowell Australia 33°39S 136°56E 63 E2
Cowes U.K. 50°45N 1°18W 13 G6
Cowichan L. Canada 48°53N 124°17W 78 B2
Cowlitz → U.S.A. 46°6N 122°55W 78 D4
Cowra Australia 33°49S 148°42E 63 E4
Coxilha Grande Brazil 28°18S 51°30W 95 B5
Coxim Brazil 18°30S 54°55W 93 G8
Cox's Bazar Bangla. 21°26N 91°59E 41 J17
Coyote Wells U.S.A. 32°44N 115°58W 79 N11
Coyuca de Benitez Mexico 17°2N 100°4W 87 D4
Coyuca de Catalán Mexico 18°20N 100°39W 86 D4
Cozad U.S.A. 40°52N 99°59W 80 E4
Cozumel Mexico 20°31N 86°55W 87 C7
Cozumel, Isla Mexico 20°30N 86°40W 87 C7
Crab Hill Barbados 13°19N 59°38W 89 g
Cracow = Kraków Poland 50°4N 19°57E 17 C10
Cracow Australia 25°17S 150°17E 63 D5
Cradle Mt.-Lake St. Clair △ Australia 41°49S 147°56E 63 G4
Cradock Australia 32°6S 138°31E 63 E2
Cradock S. Africa 32°8S 25°36E 56 D4
Craig U.S.A. 40°31N 107°33W 76 F10
Craigavon U.K. 54°27N 6°23W 10 B5
Craik Canada 51°3N 105°49W 71 C7
Crailsheim Germany 49°8N 10°5E 16 D6
Craiova Romania 44°21N 23°48E 17 F12
Cramsie Australia 23°20S 144°15E 62 C3
Cranberry L. U.S.A. 44°11N 74°50W 83 B10
Cranberry Portage Canada 54°35N 101°23W 71 C8
Cranbrook Australia 34°18S 117°33E 61 F2
Cranbrook Canada 49°30N 115°46W 70 D5
Crandon U.S.A. 45°34N 88°54W 80 C9
Crane Oreg., U.S.A. 43°25N 118°35W 76 E4
Crane Tex., U.S.A. 31°24N 102°21W 84 F3
Crane, The Barbados 13°6N 59°27W 89 g
Cranganore India 10°13N 76°13E 45 J3
Cranston U.S.A. 41°47N 71°26W 83 E13
Crater L. U.S.A. 42°56N 122°6W 76 E2
Crater Lake △ U.S.A. 42°55N 122°10W 76 E2
Craters of the Moon ⌂ U.S.A. 43°25N 113°30W 76 E7
Crateús Brazil 5°10S 40°39W 93 E10
Crato Brazil 7°10S 39°25W 93 E11
Craven, L. Canada 54°20N 76°56W 72 B4
Crawford U.S.A. 42°41N 103°25W 80 D2
Crawfordsville U.S.A. 40°2N 86°54W 80 E10
Crawley U.K. 51°7N 0°11W 13 F7
Crazy Mts. U.S.A. 46°12N 110°20W 76 C8
Crean L. Canada 54°5N 106°9W 71 C7
Crediton Canada 43°17N 81°33W 82 C3
Crediton U.K. 50°47N 3°40W 13 G4
Cree → Canada 58°57N 105°47W 71 B7
Cree → U.K. 54°55N 4°25W 11 G4

Cree L. *Canada* 57°30N 106°30W **71 B7**
Creede *U.S.A.* 37°51N 106°56W **77 H10**
Creekside *U.S.A.* 40°40N 79°11W **82 F5**
Creel *Mexico* 27°45N 107°38W **86 B3**
Creemore *Canada* 44°19N 80°6W **82 B4**
Creighton *Canada* 54°45N 101°54W **71 C8**
Creighton *U.S.A.* 42°28N 97°54W **80 D5**
Crema *Italy* 45°22N 9°41E **20 D8**
Cremona *Italy* 45°7N 10°2E **20 D9**
Cres *Croatia* 44°58N 14°25E **16 F8**
Crescent City *U.S.A.* 41°45N 124°12W **76 F1**
Crescent Group
  *S. China Sea* 16°30N 111°40E **36 A4**
Crespo *Argentina* 32°2S 60°19W **94 C3**
Cresson *U.S.A.* 40°28N 78°36W **82 F6**
Crestline *Calif., U.S.A.* 34°14N 117°18W **79 L9**
Crestline *Ohio, U.S.A.* 40°47N 82°44W **82 F2**
Creston *Canada* 49°10N 116°31W **70 D5**
Creston *Calif., U.S.A.* 35°32N 120°33W **78 K6**
Creston *Iowa, U.S.A.* 41°4N 94°22W **80 E7**
Crestview *Calif., U.S.A.* 37°46N 118°58W **78 H8**
Crestview *Fla., U.S.A.* 30°46N 86°34W **85 F11**
Crete = Kriti *Greece* 35°15N 25°0E **23 G11**
Crete *U.S.A.* 40°38N 96°58W **80 E5**
Creus, C. de *Spain* 42°20N 3°19E **21 A7**
Creuse → *France* 47°0N 0°34E **20 C4**
Crewe *U.K.* 53°6N 2°26W **12 D5**
Crewkerne *U.K.* 50°53N 2°48W **13 G5**
Crianlarich *U.K.* 56°24N 4°37W **11 E4**
Criciúma *Brazil* 28°40S 49°23W **95 B6**
Crieff *U.K.* 56°22N 3°50W **11 E5**
Crimea □ *Ukraine* 45°30N 33°10E **19 E5**
Crimean Pen. = Krymskyy
  Pivostriv *Ukraine* 45°0N 34°0E **19 F5**
Crişul Alb → *Romania* 46°42N 21°17E **17 E11**
Crişul Negru →
  *Romania* 46°42N 21°16E **17 E11**
Crna → *Macedonia* 41°33N 21°59E **23 D9**
Crna Gora = Montenegro ■
  *Europe* 42°40N 19°20E **23 C8**
Crna Gora *Macedonia* 42°10N 21°30E **23 C9**
Crna Reka = Crna →
  *Macedonia* 41°33N 21°59E **23 D9**
Croagh Patrick *Ireland* 53°46N 9°40W **10 C2**
Croatia ■ *Europe* 45°20N 16°0E **16 F9**
Crocker, Banjaran
  *Malaysia* 5°40N 116°30E **36 C5**
Crockett *U.S.A.* 31°19N 95°27W **84 F7**
Crocodile = Umgwenya →
  *Mozam.* 25°14S 32°18E **57 C5**
Crocodile → *S. Africa* 24°12S 26°53E **56 B4**
Crocodile Is. *Australia* 12°3S 134°58E **62 A1**
Crohy Hd. *Ireland* 54°55N 8°26W **10 B3**
Croix, L. la *Canada* 48°20N 92°15W **72 C1**
Croker, C. *Australia* 10°58S 132°35E **60 B5**
Croker, C. *Canada* 44°58N 80°59W **82 B4**
Croker I. *Australia* 11°12S 132°32E **60 B5**
Croker Islands Seas ◎
  *Australia* 11°20S 132°30E **60 B5**
Cromarty *U.K.* 57°40N 4°2W **11 D4**
Cromer *U.K.* 52°56N 1°17E **12 E9**
Cromwell *N.Z.* 45°3S 169°14E **59 F2**
Cromwell *U.S.A.* 41°36N 72°39W **83 E12**
Crook *U.K.* 54°43N 1°45W **12 C6**
Crooked → *Canada* 54°50N 122°54W **70 C4**
Crooked → *U.S.A.* 44°32N 121°16W **76 D3**
Crooked I. *Bahamas* 22°50N 74°10W **89 B5**
Crooked Island Passage
  *Bahamas* 22°55N 74°35W **89 B5**
Crookston *Minn., U.S.A.* 47°47N 96°37W **80 B5**
Crookston *Nebr., U.S.A.* 42°56N 100°45W **80 D3**
Crookwell *Australia* 34°28S 149°24E **63 E4**
Crosby *U.K.* 53°30N 3°3W **12 D4**
Crosby *N. Dak., U.S.A.* 48°55N 103°18W **80 A2**
Crosby *Pa., U.S.A.* 41°45N 78°23W **82 E6**
Crosbyton *U.S.A.* 33°40N 101°14W **84 E4**
Cross City *U.S.A.* 29°38N 83°7W **85 G13**
Cross Fell *U.K.* 54°43N 2°28W **12 C5**
Cross L. *Canada* 54°45N 97°30W **71 C9**
Cross Lake *Canada* 54°37N 97°47W **71 C9**
Cross Sound *U.S.A.* 58°0N 135°0W **68 F4**
Crossett *U.S.A.* 33°8N 91°58W **84 E9**
Crosshaven *Ireland* 51°47N 8°17W **10 E3**
Crossmaglen *U.K.* 54°5N 6°36W **10 B5**
Crossmolina *Ireland* 54°6N 9°20W **10 B2**
Crossville *U.S.A.* 35°57N 85°2W **85 D12**
Croswell *U.S.A.* 43°16N 82°37W **82 C2**
Croton-on-Hudson
  *U.S.A.* 41°12N 73°55W **83 E11**
Crotone *Italy* 39°5N 17°8E **22 E7**
Crow → *Canada* 59°41N 124°20W **70 B4**
Crow Agency *U.S.A.* 45°36N 107°28W **76 D10**
Crow Hd. *Ireland* 51°35N 10°9W **10 E1**
Crowell *U.S.A.* 33°59N 99°43W **84 E5**
Crowley *U.S.A.* 30°13N 92°22W **84 F8**
Crowley, L. *U.S.A.* 37°35N 118°42W **78 H8**
Crown Point *Ind., U.S.A.* 41°25N 87°22W **80 E10**
Crown Point *N.Y.,*
  *U.S.A.* 43°57N 73°26W **83 C11**
Crownpoint *U.S.A.* 35°41N 108°9W **77 J9**
Crows Landing *U.S.A.* 37°23N 121°6W **78 H5**
Crows Nest *Australia* 27°16S 152°4E **63 D5**
Crowsnest Pass *Canada* 49°40N 114°40W **70 D6**
Croydon *Australia* 18°13S 142°14E **62 B3**
Croydon □ *U.K.* 51°22N 0°5W **13 F7**
Crozet, Îs. *Ind. Oc.* 46°27S 52°0E **3 G12**
Crusheen *Ireland* 52°57N 8°53W **10 D3**
Cruz, C. *Cuba* 19°50N 77°50W **88 C4**
Cruz Alta *Brazil* 28°45S 53°40W **95 B5**
Cruz Bay *U.S. Virgin Is.* 18°20N 64°48W **89 e**
Cruz del Eje *Argentina* 30°45S 64°50W **94 C3**
Cruzeiro *Brazil* 22°33S 45°0W **95 A7**
Cruzeiro do Oeste *Brazil* 23°46S 53°4W **95 A5**
Cruzeiro do Sul *Brazil* 7°35S 72°35W **92 E4**
Cry L. *Canada* 58°45N 129°0W **70 B3**
Crystal Bay *U.S.A.* 39°15N 120°0W **78 F7**
Crystal Brook *Australia* 33°21S 138°12E **63 E2**
Crystal City *U.S.A.* 28°41N 99°50W **84 G5**
Crystal Falls *U.S.A.* 46°5N 88°20W **80 B9**

Crystal River *U.S.A.* 28°54N 82°35W **85 G13**
Crystal Springs *U.S.A.* 31°59N 90°21W **85 F9**
Csongrád *Hungary* 46°43N 20°12E **17 E11**
Cu Lao Hon *Vietnam* 10°54N 108°18E **39 G7**
Cua Rao *Vietnam* 19°16N 104°27E **38 C5**
Cuamato *Angola* 17°2S 15°7E **56 A2**
Cuamba *Mozam.* 14°45S 36°22E **55 E4**
Cuando → *Angola* 17°30S 23°15E **55 H4**
Cuangar *Angola* 17°36S 18°39E **56 A2**
Cuango = Kwango →
  *Dem. Rep. of the Congo* 3°14S 17°22E **54 E3**
Cuanza → *Angola* 9°21S 13°9E **54 F2**
Cuarto → *Argentina* 33°25S 63°2W **94 C3**
Cuatrociénegas *Mexico* 26°59N 102°5W **86 B4**
Cuauhtémoc *Mexico* 28°25N 106°52W **86 B3**
Cuba *N. Mex., U.S.A.* 36°1N 107°4W **77 H10**
Cuba *N.Y., U.S.A.* 42°13N 78°17W **82 D6**
Cuba ■ *W. Indies* 22°0N 79°0W **88 B4**
Cubango → *Africa* 18°50S 22°25E **56 A3**
Cuc Phuong △ *Vietnam* 20°17N 105°38E **38 B5**
Cuchumatanes, Sierra de los
  *Guatemala* 15°35N 91°25W **88 C1**
Cuckfield *U.K.* 51°1N 0°8W **13 F7**
Cucuí *Brazil* 1°12N 66°50W **92 C5**
Cucurpé *Mexico* 30°20N 110°43W **86 A2**
Cúcuta *Colombia* 7°54N 72°31W **92 B4**
Cuddalore *India* 11°46N 79°45E **45 J4**
Cuddapah = Kadapa
  *India* 14°30N 78°47E **45 G4**
Cuddapan, L. *Australia* 25°45S 141°26E **62 D3**
Cue *Australia* 27°25S 117°54E **61 E2**
Cuenca *Ecuador* 2°50S 79°9W **92 D3**
Cuenca *Spain* 40°5N 2°10W **21 B4**
Cuenca, Serranía de *Spain* 39°55N 1°50W **21 C5**
Cuernavaca *Mexico* 18°55N 99°15W **87 D5**
Cuero *U.S.A.* 29°6N 97°17W **84 G6**
Cueva de la Quebrada del Toro △
  *Venezuela* 10°46N 69°3W **89 D6**
Cuevas del Almanzora
  *Spain* 37°18N 1°58W **21 D5**
Cuevo *Bolivia* 20°15S 63°30W **92 H6**
Cuiabá *Brazil* 15°30S 56°0W **93 G7**
Cuiabá → *Brazil* 17°5S 56°36W **93 G7**
Cuihangcun *China* 22°27N 113°32E **31 a**
Cuijk *Neths.* 51°44N 5°50E **15 C5**
Cuilco *Guatemala* 15°24N 91°58W **88 C1**
Cuillin Hills *U.K.* 57°13N 6°15W **11 D2**
Cuillin Sd. *U.K.* 57°4N 6°20W **11 D2**
Cuilo = Kwilu →
  *Dem. Rep. of the Congo* 3°22S 17°22E **54 E3**
Cuito → *Angola* 18°1S 20°48E **56 A3**
Cuitzeo, L. de *Mexico* 19°55N 101°5W **86 D4**
Cukai *Malaysia* 4°13N 103°25E **39 K4**
Culbertson *U.S.A.* 48°9N 104°31W **76 B11**
Culcairn *Australia* 35°41S 147°3E **63 F4**
Culebra *Puerto Rico* 18°19N 65°18W **89 d**
Culgoa → *Australia* 29°56S 146°20E **63 D4**
Culgoa Flood Plain △
  *Australia* 28°58S 147°5E **63 D4**
Culiacán *Mexico* 24°50N 107°23W **86 C3**
Culiacán → *Mexico* 24°30N 107°42W **86 C3**
Culik *Indonesia* 8°21S 115°37E **37 J18**
Culion *Phil.* 11°54N 119°58E **37 B6**
Cullarin Ra. *Australia* 34°30S 149°30E **63 E4**
Cullen *U.K.* 57°42N 2°49W **11 D6**
Cullen Pt. *Australia* 11°57S 141°54E **62 A3**
Cullera *Spain* 39°9N 0°17W **21 C5**
Cullman *U.S.A.* 34°11N 86°51W **85 D11**
Cullompton *U.K.* 50°51N 3°24W **13 G4**
Culpeper *U.S.A.* 38°30N 78°0W **81 F14**
Culuene → *Brazil* 12°56S 52°51W **93 F8**
Culver, Pt. *Australia* 32°54S 124°43E **61 F3**
Culverden *N.Z.* 42°47S 172°49E **59 E4**
Cumaná *Venezuela* 10°30N 64°5W **92 A6**
Cumberland *B.C., Canada* 49°40N 125°0W **70 D4**
Cumberland *Ont., Canada* 45°29N 75°24W **83 A9**
Cumberland *U.S.A.* 39°39N 78°46W **81 F14**
Cumberland → *U.S.A.* 37°9N 88°25W **80 G9**
Cumberland, L. *U.S.A.* 36°52N 85°9W **81 G11**
Cumberland Gap △
  *U.S.A.* 36°36N 83°40W **81 G12**
Cumberland I. *U.S.A.* 30°50N 81°25W **85 F14**
Cumberland Is. *Australia* 20°35S 149°10E **62 b**
Cumberland Island △
  *U.S.A.* 30°12N 81°24W **85 F14**
Cumberland L. *Canada* 54°3N 102°18W **71 C8**
Cumberland Pen. *Canada* 67°0N 64°0W **69 D19**
Cumberland Plateau
  *U.S.A.* 36°0N 85°0W **85 D12**
Cumberland Sd. *Canada* 65°30N 66°0W **69 D18**
Cumbernauld *U.K.* 55°57N 3°58W **11 F5**
Cumborah *Australia* 29°40S 147°45E **63 D4**
Cumbres de Majalca △
  *Mexico* 28°48N 106°30W **86 B3**
Cumbres de Monterrey △
  *Mexico* 25°26N 100°25W **86 B4**
Cumbria □ *U.K.* 54°42N 2°52W **12 C5**
Cumbrian Mts. *U.K.* 54°30N 3°0W **12 C5**
Cumbum *India* 15°40N 79°10E **45 G4**
Cuminá → *Brazil* 1°30S 56°0W **93 D7**
Cummings Mt. *U.S.A.* 35°2N 118°34W **79 K8**
Cummins *Australia* 34°16S 135°43E **63 E2**
Cumnock *Australia* 32°59S 148°46E **63 E4**
Cumnock *U.K.* 55°28N 4°17W **11 F4**
Cumpas *Mexico* 30°2N 109°48W **86 B3**
Cunco *Chile* 38°55S 72°2W **96 D2**
Cumcumén *Chile* 31°53S 70°38W **94 C1**
Cundeelee ◎ *Australia* 30°43S 123°25E **61 F3**
Cunderdin *Australia* 31°37S 117°12E **61 F2**
Cunene → *Angola* 17°20S 11°50E **56 A1**
Cúneo *Italy* 44°23N 7°32E **20 D7**
Cung Son *Vietnam* 13°2N 108°58E **38 F7**
Cunnamulla *Australia* 28°2S 145°38E **63 D4**
Cupar *Canada* 50°57N 104°10W **71 C8**
Cupar *U.K.* 56°19N 3°1W **11 E5**
Cupertino *U.S.A.* 37°19N 122°2W **78 H4**
Cupica, G. de *Colombia* 6°25N 77°30W **92 B3**
Curaçao *W. Indies* 12°10N 69°0W **89 D6**
Curanilahue *Chile* 37°29S 73°28W **94 D1**

Curaray → *Peru* 2°20S 74°5W **92 D4**
Curepipe *Mauritius* 20°19S 57°31E **55 d**
Curepto *Chile* 35°8S 72°1W **94 D1**
Curiapo *Venezuela* 8°33N 61°5W **92 B6**
Curieuse *Seychelles* 4°15S 55°44E **55 b**
Curitiba *Brazil* 25°20S 49°10W **95 B6**
Curitibanos *Brazil* 27°18S 50°36W **95 B5**
Curonian Lagoon = Kurshskiy
  Zaliv *Russia* 55°9N 21°6E **9 J19**
Currabubula *Australia* 31°16S 150°44E **63 E5**
Currais Novos *Brazil* 6°13S 36°30W **93 E11**
Curral Velho *Cabo Verde* 16°8N 22°48W **52 b**
Curralinho *Brazil* 1°45S 49°46W **93 D9**
Currane, L. *Ireland* 51°49N 10°4W **10 E1**
Currant *U.S.A.* 38°44N 115°28W **76 G6**
Currawinya △ *Australia* 28°55S 144°27E **63 D3**
Current → *U.S.A.* 36°15N 90°55W **84 C9**
Currie *Australia* 39°56S 143°53E **63 F3**
Currie *U.S.A.* 40°16N 114°45W **76 F6**
Curtea de Argeş
  *Romania* 45°12N 24°42E **17 F13**
Curtin Springs *Australia* 25°20S 131°45E **61 E5**
Curtis *U.S.A.* 40°38N 100°31W **80 E3**
Curtis Group *Australia* 39°30S 146°37E **63 F4**
Curtis I. *Australia* 23°35S 151°10E **62 C5**
Curuápanema → *Brazil* 2°25S 55°2W **93 D7**
Curuçá *Brazil* 0°43S 47°50W **93 D9**
Curuguaty *Paraguay* 24°31S 55°42W **95 A4**
Çürüksu Çayi = Büyük
  Menderes → *Turkey* 37°28N 27°11E **23 F12**
Curup *Indonesia* 3°26S 102°13E **36 E2**
Cururupu *Brazil* 1°50S 44°50W **93 D10**
Curuzú Cuatiá *Argentina* 29°50S 58°5W **94 B4**
Curvelo *Brazil* 18°45S 44°27W **93 G10**
Cusco *Peru* 13°32S 72°0W **92 F4**
Cushendall *U.K.* 55°5N 6°4W **10 A5**
Cushing *U.S.A.* 35°59N 96°46W **84 D6**
Cushing, Mt. *Canada* 57°35N 126°57W **70 B3**
Cusihuiriáchic *Mexico* 28°14N 106°50W **86 B3**
Custer *U.S.A.* 43°46N 103°36W **80 D2**
Cut Bank *U.S.A.* 48°38N 112°20W **76 B7**
Cutchogue *U.S.A.* 41°1N 72°30W **83 E12**
Cuthbert *U.S.A.* 31°46N 84°48W **85 F12**
Cutler *U.S.A.* 36°31N 119°17W **78 J7**
Cuttaburra → *Australia* 29°43S 144°22E **63 D3**
Cuttack *India* 20°25N 85°57E **44 D7**
Cuvier, C. *Australia* 23°14S 113°22E **61 D1**
Cuvier I. *N.Z.* 36°27S 175°50E **59 B5**
Cuxhaven *Germany* 53°51N 8°41E **16 B5**
Cuyahoga Falls *U.S.A.* 41°8N 81°29W **82 E3**
Cuyahoga Valley △
  *U.S.A.* 41°24N 81°33W **82 E3**
Cuyo *Phil.* 10°51N 121°2E **37 B6**
Cuyuni → *Guyana* 6°23N 58°41W **92 B7**
Cuzco = Cusco *Peru* 13°32S 72°0W **92 F4**
Cuzco *Bolivia* 20°0S 66°50W **92 H5**
Cwmbran *U.K.* 51°39N 3°2W **13 F4**
Cyclades = Kyklades
  *Greece* 37°0N 24°30E **23 F11**
Cygnet *Australia* 43°8S 147°1E **63 G4**
Cynthiana *U.S.A.* 38°23N 84°18W **81 F11**
Cypress Hills *Canada* 49°40N 109°30W **71 D7**
Cypress Hills △ *Canada* 49°40N 109°30W **71 D7**
Cyprus ■ *Asia* 35°0N 33°0E **46 C2**
Cyrenaica = Barqa *Libya* 27°0N 23°0E **53 C10**
Cyrene *Libya* 32°53N 21°53E **53 B10**
Czar *Canada* 52°27N 110°50W **71 C6**
Czech Rep. = Czechia ■
  *Europe* 50°0N 15°0E **16 D8**
Czechia ■ *Europe* 50°0N 15°0E **16 D8**
Częstochowa *Poland* 50°49N 19°7E **17 C10**

# D

Da → *Vietnam* 21°15N 105°20E **34 G5**
Da Hinggan Ling *China* 48°0N 121°0E **31 B13**
Da Lat *Vietnam* 11°56N 108°25E **39 G7**
Da Nang *Vietnam* 16°4N 108°13E **38 D7**
Da Qaidam *China* 37°50N 95°15E **30 D8**
Da Yunhe → *Hopei,*
  *China* 39°10N 117°10E **33 E9**
Da Yunhe → *Jiangsu,*
  *China* 34°25N 120°5E **33 H10**
Da'an *China* 45°30N 124°7E **33 B13**
Daba Shan *China* 32°0N 109°0E **34 B7**
Dabbagh, Jabal *Si. Arabia* 27°52N 35°45E **46 E2**
Dabhoi *India* 22°10N 73°20E **42 H5**
Dabie Shan *China* 31°20N 115°20E **35 B10**
Dabola *Guinea* 10°50N 11°5W **52 F3**
Dabu *China* 24°22N 116°41E **35 E11**
Dabugam *India* 19°27N 82°26E **44 E6**
Dabung *Malaysia* 5°23N 102°1E **39 K4**
Dacca = Dhaka *Bangla.* 23°43N 90°26E **43 H14**
Dachang *China* 31°40N 115°58E **35 A12**
Dachaoshan Dam *China* 24°1N 100°22E **34 E3**
Dachigam △ *India* 34°10N 75°0E **42 B6**
Dacre *Canada* 45°22N 76°57W **82 A8**
Dadanawa *Guyana* 2°50N 59°30W **92 C7**
Dade City *U.S.A.* 28°22N 82°11W **85 G13**
Dadhar *Pakistan* 29°28N 67°39E **42 E2**
Dadnah *U.A.E.* 25°32N 56°22E **47 E8**
Dadra & Nagar Haveli □
  *India* 20°5N 73°0E **44 D1**
Dadri = Charkhi Dadri
  *India* 28°37N 76°17E **42 E7**
Dadu *Pakistan* 26°45N 67°45E **42 F2**
Dadu He → *China* 29°31N 103°44E **34 C5**
Daegu *S. Korea* 35°50N 128°37E **33 G15**
Daejeon *S. Korea* 36°20N 127°28E **33 F14**
Daejeong *S. Korea* 33°13N 126°15E **33 H14**
Daet *Phil.* 14°2N 122°55E **37 B6**
Dafang *China* 27°9N 105°39E **34 D5**
Dafeng *China* 33°12N 120°32E **35 H11**
Dagana *Senegal* 16°30N 15°35W **52 E2**
Dagestan □ *Russia* 42°30N 47°0E **19 F8**
Daggett *U.S.A.* 34°52N 116°52W **79 L10**
Daghestan Republic = Dagestan □
  *Russia* 42°30N 47°0E **19 F8**

Dağlıq Qarabağ = Nagorno-
  Karabakh □ *Azerbaijan* 39°55N 46°45E **46 B5**
Dağö = Hiiumaa *Estonia* 58°50N 22°45E **9 G20**
Dagu *China* 38°59N 117°40E **33 E9**
Daguan *China* 27°43N 103°56E **34 D4**
Dagupan *Phil.* 16°3N 120°20E **37 A6**
Daguragu *Australia* 17°33S 130°30E **60 C5**
Daguragu ◎ *Australia* 17°24S 130°48E **60 C5**
Dahab *Egypt* 28°31N 34°31E **46 D2**
Dahanu *India* 19°58N 72°44E **44 E1**
Dahivadi *India* 17°43N 74°33E **44 F2**
Dahlak Kebir *Eritrea* 15°50N 40°10E **49 D3**
Dahlonega *U.S.A.* 34°32N 83°59W **85 D13**
Dahod *India* 22°50N 74°15E **42 H6**
Dahong Shan *China* 31°25N 113°30E **35 B9**
Dahongliutan *China* 35°45N 79°20E **43 B8**
Dahra *Libya* 29°30N 17°50E **53 C9**
Dahūk *Iraq* 36°50N 43°1E **46 B3**
Dai Hao *Vietnam* 18°1N 106°25E **38 C6**
Dai-Sen *Japan* 35°22N 133°32E **29 G6**
Dai Shan *China* 30°25N 122°10E **35 B14**
Dai Xian *China* 39°4N 112°58E **32 E7**
Daicheng *China* 38°42N 116°38E **32 E9**
Daikondi = Dāykondī □
  *Afghan.* 34°0N 66°0E **40 C5**
Dailekh *Nepal* 28°50N 81°44E **43 E9**
Daingean *Ireland* 53°18N 7°17W **10 C4**
Daingean, An = Dingle
  *Ireland* 52°9N 10°17W **10 D1**
Dainkog *China* 32°30N 97°58E **34 A1**
Daintree *Australia* 16°20S 145°20E **62 B4**
Daintree △ *Australia* 16°8S 145°2E **62 B4**
Daiō-Misaki *Japan* 34°15N 136°45E **29 G8**
Daisen *Japan* 39°27N 140°29E **28 E10**
Daisen-Oki △ *Japan* 35°23N 133°34E **29 G6**
Daisetsu-Zan *Japan* 43°30N 142°57E **28 C11**
Daisetsu-Zan △ *Japan* 43°30N 142°55E **28 C11**
Daitari *India* 21°10N 85°46E **44 D7**
Daiyun Shan *China* 25°50N 118°15E **35 E12**
Dajarra *Australia* 21°42S 139°30E **62 C2**
Dajiawa *China* 37°9N 119°0E **33 F10**
Dajin Chuan → *China* 31°16N 101°59E **34 B3**
Dak Dam *Cambodia* 12°20N 107°21E **38 F6**
Dak Nhe *Vietnam* 15°4N 107°44E **38 E6**
Dak Pek *Vietnam* 15°4N 107°44E **38 E6**
Dak Song *Vietnam* 12°19N 107°35E **39 F6**
Dak Sui *Vietnam* 14°55N 107°43E **38 E6**
Dakar *Senegal* 14°34N 17°29W **52 F2**
Dakhla *W. Sahara* 23°50N 15°53W **52 D2**
Dakhla, El Wâhât el
  *Egypt* 25°30N 28°50E **53 C11**
Dakoank *India* 7°2N 93°43E **45 L11**
Dakor *India* 22°45N 73°11E **42 H5**
Dakota City *U.S.A.* 42°25N 96°25W **80 D5**
Đakovica = Gjakovë
  *Kosovo* 42°22N 20°26E **23 C9**
Dalachi *China* 36°48N 105°0E **32 F3**
Dalai Nur *China* 43°20N 116°45E **32 C9**
Dālakī *Iran* 29°26N 51°17E **47 D6**
Dalälven → *Sweden* 60°12N 16°43E **9 F17**
Dalaman → *Turkey* 36°41N 28°43E **23 F13**
Dalandzadgad *Mongolia* 43°27N 104°30E **32 C3**
Dalap-Uliga-Darrit = Majuro
  *Marshall Is.* 7°9N 171°12E **64 G9**
Dalarna *Sweden* 61°0N 14°0E **8 F16**
Dalay *Mongolia* 43°28N 103°30E **32 C2**
Dālbandīn *Pakistan* 29°0N 64°23E **40 E4**
Dalbeattie *U.K.* 54°56N 3°50W **11 G5**
Dalbeg *Australia* 20°16S 147°18E **62 C4**
Dalby *Australia* 27°10S 151°17E **63 D5**
Dale Hollow L. *U.S.A.* 36°32N 85°27W **85 C12**
Dalgān *Iran* 27°31N 59°19E **47 E8**
Dalhart *U.S.A.* 36°4N 102°31W **84 C3**
Dalhousie *Canada* 48°5N 66°26W **73 C6**
Dalhousie *India* 32°38N 75°58E **42 C6**
Dali *Shaanxi, China* 34°48N 109°58E **32 G5**
Dali *Yunnan, China* 25°40N 100°10E **34 E3**
Dalian *China* 38°50N 121°40E **33 E11**
Daliang Shan *China* 28°0N 102°45E **34 D4**
Daling He → *China* 40°55N 121°40E **33 D11**
Dâliyat el Karmel *Israel* 32°43N 35°2E **48 C4**
Dalkey *Ireland* 53°16N 6°6W **10 C5**
Dallas *U.S.A.* 44°55N 123°19W **76 D2**
Dallas-Fort Worth Int. ✈ (DFW)
  *U.S.A.* 32°54N 97°2W **84 E6**
Dalles, The *U.S.A.* 45°36N 121°10W **76 D3**
Dalmā *U.A.E.* 24°30N 52°20E **47 E7**
Dalmas, L. *Canada* 53°30N 71°50W **73 B5**
Dalmatia = Dalmacija
  *Croatia* 43°20N 17°0E **22 C7**
Dalmau *India* 26°4N 81°2E **43 F9**
Dalmellington *U.K.* 55°19N 4°23W **11 F4**
Dalnegorsk *Russia* 44°32N 135°33E **28 B7**
Dalnerechensk *Russia* 45°50N 133°40E **28 B6**
Dalnevostochnyy □
  *Russia* 67°0N 140°0E **27 C14**
Daloa *Côte d'Ivoire* 7°0N 6°30W **52 G4**
Dalou Shan *China* 28°15N 107°0E **34 C6**
Dalry *U.K.* 55°42N 4°43W **11 F4**
Dalrymple, L. *Australia* 20°40S 147°0E **62 C4**
Dalrymple, Mt. *Australia* 21°1S 148°39E **62 b**
Dalsland *Sweden* 58°50N 12°15E **9 G15**
Daltenganj *India* 24°0N 84°4E **43 H11**
Dalton *Ga., U.S.A.* 34°46N 84°58W **85 D12**
Dalton *Mass., U.S.A.* 42°28N 73°11W **83 D11**
Dalton *Nebr., U.S.A.* 41°25N 102°58W **80 E2**
Dalton-in-Furness *U.K.* 54°10N 3°11W **12 C4**
Dalvík *Iceland* 65°58N 18°32W **8 D4**
Dālvvadis = Jokkmokk
  *Sweden* 66°35N 19°50E **8 C18**
Dalwallinu *Australia* 30°17S 116°40E **61 F2**
Daly → *Australia* 13°35S 130°19E **60 B5**
Daly L. *Canada* 56°32N 105°39W **71 B7**
Daly River *Australia* 13°46S 130°42E **60 B5**
Daly River-Port Keats ◎
  *Australia* 14°13S 129°36E **60 B4**
Daly Waters *Australia* 16°15S 133°24E **62 B1**

Dam Ha *Vietnam* 21°21N 107°36E **38 B6**
Daman *India* 20°25N 72°57E **44 D1**
Daman & Diu □ *India* 20°25N 72°58E **44 D1**
Dāmaneh *Iran* 33°1N 50°29E **47 C6**
Damanganga → *India* 20°25N 72°58E **44 D1**
Damanhûr *Egypt* 31°0N 30°30E **53 B12**
Damant L. *Canada* 61°45N 105°5W **71 A7**
Damar *Indonesia* 7°7S 128°40E **37 F7**
Damara *C.A.R.* 4°58N 18°42E **54 D3**
Damaraland *Namibia* 20°0S 15°0E **56 B2**
Damascus = Dimashq
  *Syria* 33°30N 36°18E **48 B5**
Damaturu *Nigeria* 11°45N 11°55E **54 B2**
Dāmāvand *Iran* 35°57N 52°7E **47 C7**
Dāmāvand, Qolleh-ye
  *Iran* 35°57N 52°7E **47 C7**
Damba *Angola* 6°44S 15°20E **54 F3**
Dâmbovița → *Romania* 44°12N 26°26E **17 F14**
Dambulla *Sri Lanka* 7°51N 80°39E **45 L5**
Dame Marie *Haiti* 18°34N 74°26W **89 C5**
Dāmghān *Iran* 36°10N 54°17E **47 B7**
Damiel *Spain* 39°4N 3°37W **21 C4**
Damietta = Dumyât
  *Egypt* 31°24N 31°48E **53 B12**
Daming *China* 36°15N 115°6E **32 F8**
Damīr Qābū *Syria* 36°58N 41°51E **46 B4**
Dammam = Ad Dammām
  *Si. Arabia* 26°20N 50°5E **47 E6**
Damoh *India* 23°50N 79°28E **43 H8**
Dampier *Australia* 20°41S 116°42E **60 D2**
Dampier, Selat *Indonesia* 0°40S 131°0E **37 E8**
Dampier Arch. *Australia* 20°38S 116°32E **60 D2**
Damrei, Chuor Phnum
  *Cambodia* 11°30N 103°0E **39 G4**
Damyang *S. Korea* 35°19N 126°59E **33 G14**
Dana *Indonesia* 11°0S 121°15E **37 F6**
Dana *Jordan* 30°41N 35°37E **48 E4**
Dana *Nepal* 28°32N 83°37E **43 E10**
Dana, L. *Canada* 50°53N 77°20W **72 B4**
Dana, Mt. *U.S.A.* 37°54N 119°12W **78 H7**
Danakil Desert *Ethiopia* 12°45N 41°0E **49 E3**
Danané *Côte d'Ivoire* 7°16N 8°9W **52 G4**
Danba *China* 30°54N 101°48E **34 B3**
Danbury *U.S.A.* 41°24N 73°28W **83 E11**
Danby L. *U.S.A.* 34°13N 115°5W **79 L11**
Dand *Afghan.* 31°28N 65°32E **42 D1**
Dandeldhura *Nepal* 29°20N 80°35E **43 E9**
Dandeli *India* 15°5N 74°30E **45 G2**
Dandenong *Australia* 38°0S 145°15E **63 F4**
Dandong *China* 40°10N 124°20E **33 D13**
Danfeng *China* 33°45N 110°25E **32 H6**
Dangan Liedao *China* 22°2N 114°8E **35 F10**
Danger Is. = Pukapuka
  *Cook Is.* 10°53S 165°49W **65 J11**
Danger Pt. *S. Africa* 34°40S 19°17E **56 D2**
Dangla Shan = Tanggula Shan
  *China* 32°40N 92°10E **30 E7**
Dangrek, Mts. = Dangrek, Phnom
  *Thailand* 14°20N 104°0E **38 E5**
Dangrek, Phnom
  *Thailand* 14°20N 104°0E **38 E5**
Dangriga *Belize* 17°0N 88°13W **87 D7**
Dangshan *China* 34°27N 116°22E **32 G9**
Dangtu *China* 31°32N 118°25E **35 B12**
Dangyang *China* 30°52N 111°44E **35 B8**
Daniel *U.S.A.* 42°52N 110°4W **76 E8**
Daniel's Harbour *Canada* 50°13N 57°35W **73 B8**
Danielskuil *S. Africa* 28°11S 23°33E **56 C3**
Danielson *U.S.A.* 41°48N 71°53W **83 E13**
Danilov *Russia* 58°16N 40°13E **18 C7**
Daning *China* 36°28N 110°45E **32 F6**
Danjiangkou *China* 32°31N 111°30E **35 A8**
Danjiangkou Shuiku
  *China* 32°37N 111°30E **35 A8**
Dank *Oman* 23°33N 56°16E **47 F8**
Dankhar Gompa *India* 32°10N 78°10E **42 C8**
Danleng *China* 30°1N 103°31E **34 B4**
Danli *Honduras* 14°4N 86°35W **88 D2**
Danmark = Denmark ■
  *Europe* 55°45N 10°0E **9 J14**
Dannemora *U.S.A.* 44°43N 73°44W **83 B11**
Dannevirke *N.Z.* 40°12S 176°8E **59 D6**
Dannhauser *S. Africa* 28°0S 30°3E **57 C5**
Dansville *U.S.A.* 42°34N 77°42W **82 D7**
Danta *India* 24°11N 72°46E **42 G5**
Dantan *India* 21°57N 87°20E **43 J12**
Dante = Xaafuun *Somalia* 10°25N 51°16E **49 E5**
Dantewara *India* 18°54N 81°21E **44 E5**
Danube = Dunărea →
  *Europe* 45°20N 29°40E **17 F15**
Danville *Ill., U.S.A.* 40°8N 87°37W **80 E10**
Danville *Ky., U.S.A.* 37°39N 84°46W **81 G11**
Danville *Pa., U.S.A.* 40°58N 76°37W **83 F8**
Danville *Va., U.S.A.* 36°36N 79°23W **85 C15**
Danville *Vt., U.S.A.* 44°25N 72°9W **83 B12**
Danyang *China* 32°0N 119°31E **35 B12**
Danzhai *China* 26°11N 107°48E **34 D6**
Danzhou *China* 19°31N 109°33E **38 C7**
Danzig = Gdańsk *Poland* 54°22N 18°40E **17 A10**
Dao Xian *China* 25°36N 111°31E **35 E8**
Daocheng *China* 29°0N 100°10E **34 C3**
Daokou = Huaxian *China* 35°30N 114°30E **32 G8**
Daoukro *Côte d'Ivoire* 7°10N 3°58W **52 G5**
Dapaong *Togo* 10°55N 0°16E **52 F6**
Dapoli *India* 17°46N 73°11E **44 F1**
Daqing *China* 46°35N 125°0E **35 B13**
Daqing Shan *China* 40°40N 111°0E **32 D6**
Daqq-e Sorkh, Kavīr *Iran* 33°45N 52°50E **47 C7**
Daqu Shan *China* 30°25N 122°20E **35 B14**
Dar Banda *Africa* 8°0N 23°0E **50 F6**
Dar el Beida = Casablanca
  *Morocco* 33°36N 7°36W **52 B4**
Dar es Salaam *Tanzania* 6°50S 39°12E **54 F7**
Dar Mazār *Iran* 29°14N 57°20E **47 D8**
Dar'ā *Syria* 32°36N 36°7E **48 C5**
Dar'ā □ *Syria* 32°55N 36°10E **48 C5**
Dārāb *Iran* 28°50N 54°30E **47 D7**
Daraban *Pakistan* 31°44N 70°20E **42 D4**
Daraj *Libya* 30°10N 10°28E **53 B8**
Dārān *Iran* 32°59N 50°24E **47 C6**

Dārayyā Syria 33°28N 36°15E 48 B5
Darband Pakistan 34°20N 72°50E 42 B5
Darband, Kūh-e Iran 31°34N 57°8E 47 D8
D'Arcy Canada 50°33N 122°29W 70 C4
Dardanelle Ark., U.S.A. 35°13N 93°9W 84 D8
Dardanelle Calif., U.S.A. 38°20N 119°50W 78 G7
Dardanelles = Çanakkale Boğazı
Turkey 40°17N 26°32E 23 D12
Dārestān Iran 29°9N 58°42E 47 D8
Dārfūr Sudan 13°40N 24°0E 53 F10
Dargai Afghan. 34°25N 71°55E 42 B4
Dargaville N.Z. 35°57S 173°52E 59 A4
Darhan Mongolia 49°37N 106°21E 30 B10
Darhan Mumingan
China 41°40N 110°28E 32 D6
Darıca Turkey 40°45N 29°23E 23 D13
Darién, G. del Caribbean 9°0N 77°0W 92 E3
Darién △ Panama 7°36N 77°57W 88 E4
Dariganga = Ovoot
Mongolia 45°21N 113°45E 32 B7
Daringbadi India 19°54N 84°8E 44 E7
Darjeeling = Darjiling
India 27°3N 88°18E 43 F13
Darjiling India 27°3N 88°18E 43 F13
Darkan Australia 33°20S 116°43E 61 F2
Darkhana Pakistan 30°39N 72°11E 42 D5
Darkhazīneh Iran 31°54N 48°39E 47 D6
Darkot Pass Pakistan 36°45N 73°26E 43 A5
Darling → Australia 34°4S 141°54E 63 E3
Darling Downs Australia 27°30S 150°30E 63 D5
Darling Ra. Australia 32°30S 116°20E 61 F2
Darlington U.K. 54°32N 1°33W 12 C6
Darlington U.S.A. 34°18N 79°52W 85 D15
Darlington □ U.K. 54°32N 1°33W 12 C6
Darlington, L. S. Africa 33°10S 25°9E 56 D4
Darlot, L. Australia 27°48S 121°35E 61 E3
Darłowo Poland 54°25N 16°25E 16 A9
Darmstadt Germany 49°51N 8°39E 16 D5
Darnah Libya 32°45N 22°45E 53 B10
Darnall S. Africa 29°23S 31°18E 57 C5
Darnley Australia 9°35S 143°46E 62 a
Darnley, C. Antarctica 68°0S 69°0E 5 C6
Darnley B. Canada 69°30N 123°30W 68 D7
Darr → Australia 23°39S 143°50E 62 C3
Darra Pezu Pakistan 32°19N 70°44E 42 C4
Darrequeira Argentina 37°42S 63°10W 94 D3
Darrington U.S.A. 48°15N 121°36W 76 B3
Darsi India 15°46N 79°44E 45 G4
Dart → U.K. 50°24N 3°39W 13 G4
Dartmoor U.K. 50°38N 3°57W 13 G4
Dartmoor △ U.K. 50°37N 3°59W 13 G4
Dartmouth Canada 44°40N 63°30W 73 D7
Dartmouth U.K. 50°21N 3°36W 13 G4
Dartmouth, L. Australia 26°4S 145°18E 63 D4
Darvel, Teluk = Lahad Datu, Telok
Malaysia 4°50N 118°20E 37 D5
Darwen U.K. 53°42N 2°29W 12 D5
Darwendale Zimbabwe 17°41S 30°33E 57 A5
Darwha India 20°15N 77°45E 44 D3
Darwin Australia 12°25S 130°51E 60 B5
Darwin U.S.A. 36°15N 117°35W 79 J9
Darya Khan Pakistan 31°48N 71°6E 42 D4
Daryapur India 20°55N 77°20E 44 D3
Daryoi Amu = Amudarya →
Uzbekistan 43°58N 59°34E 28 E6
Dās U.A.E. 25°20N 53°30E 47 E7
Dashen, Ras Ethiopia 13°8N 38°26E 49 E2
Dashetai China 41°0N 109°5E 32 D5
Dashiqiao China 40°38N 122°30E 33 D12
Dashkōpri Turkmenistan 36°16N 62°8E 47 B9
Dasht → Pakistan 25°10N 61°40E 40 G2
Daska Pakistan 32°20N 74°20E 42 C6
Daşoguz Turkmenistan 41°49N 59°58E 26 E6
Dasuya India 31°49N 75°38E 42 D6
Datça Turkey 36°46N 27°40E 23 F12
Date Japan 42°28N 140°52E 28 F10
Datia India 25°39N 78°27E 43 G8
Datian China 25°40N 117°50E 35 E11
Datong Anhui, China 30°48N 117°44E 35 B11
Datong Qinghai, China 36°20N 102°50E 30 D9
Datong Shanxi, China 40°6N 113°18E 32 D7
Dattakhel Pakistan 32°54N 69°46E 42 C3
Dattapur = Dhamangaon
India 20°48N 78°9E 44 D4
Daventry U.K. 52°16N 1°10W 13 E6
David Panama 8°30N 82°30W 88 E3
David City U.S.A. 41°15N 97°8W 80 E5
David Glacier Antarctica 75°20S 162°0E 5 D11
David Gorodok = Davyd Haradok
Belarus 52°4N 27°8E 17 B14

Davidson Canada 51°16N 105°59W 71 C7
Davidson Mts. U.S.A. 68°41N 142°22W 74 B11
Davis Antarctica 68°34S 77°55E 5 C6
Davis U.S.A. 38°33N 121°44W 78 G5
Davis Dam U.S.A. 35°12N 114°34W 79 K12
Davis Mts. U.S.A. 30°50N 103°55W 84 F3
Davis Sea Antarctica 66°0S 92°0E 5 C7
Davis Str. N. Amer. 65°0N 58°0W 69 D19
Davos Switz. 46°48N 9°49E 20 C8
Davy L. Canada 58°53N 108°18W 71 B7
Davyd Haradok Belarus 52°4N 27°8E 17 B14
Dawei Myanmar 14°2N 98°12E 38 E2
Dawes Ra. Australia 24°40S 150°40E 62 C5
Dawmat al Jandal
Si. Arabia 29°55N 39°40E 46 D3
Dawna Ra. Myanmar 16°30N 98°30E 38 D2
Dawros Hd. Ireland 54°50N 8°33W 10 B3
Dawson U.S.A. 31°46N 84°27W 85 F12
Dawson, I. Chile 53°50S 70°50W 96 G2
Dawson B. Canada 52°53N 100°49W 71 C8
Dawson City Canada 64°10N 139°30W 68 E4
Dawson Creek Canada 55°45N 120°15W 70 B4
Dawson Inlet Canada 61°50N 93°25W 71 A10
Dawson Ra. Australia 24°30S 149°48E 62 C4
Dawu Hubei, China 31°34N 114°7E 35 B10
Dawu Sichuan, China 30°55N 101°10E 34 B3
Dax France 43°44N 1°3W 20 E3
Daxian China 31°15N 107°23E 34 B6
Daxindian China 37°30N 120°50E 33 F11
Daxinggou China 43°25N 129°40E 33 C15
Daxue Shan Sichuan,
China 30°30N 101°30E 34 B3
Daxue Shan Yunnan,
China 23°42N 99°48E 34 F2
Dayao China 25°43N 101°20E 34 E3
Daye China 30°6N 114°58E 35 B10
Dayi China 30°41N 103°29E 34 B4
Dāykondī □ Afghan. 34°0N 66°0E 40 C5
Daylesford Australia 37°21S 144°9E 63 F3
Dayong = Zhangjiajie
China 29°11N 110°30E 35 C8
Dayr az Zawr Syria 35°20N 40°5E 46 C4
Daysland Canada 52°50N 112°20W 70 C6
Dayton Nev., U.S.A. 39°14N 119°36W 78 F7
Dayton Ohio, U.S.A. 39°45N 84°12W 81 F11
Dayton Pa., U.S.A. 40°53N 79°15W 82 F5
Dayton Tenn., U.S.A. 35°30N 85°1W 85 D12
Dayton Wash., U.S.A. 46°19N 117°59W 76 C5
Dayton Wyo., U.S.A. 44°53N 107°16W 76 D10
Daytona Beach U.S.A. 29°13N 81°1W 85 G14
Dayu China 25°24N 114°22E 35 E10
Dayville U.S.A. 44°28N 119°32W 76 D4
Dazhu China 30°41N 107°15E 34 B6
Dazu China 29°40N 105°42E 34 C5
De Aar S. Africa 30°39S 24°0E 56 D3
De Funiak Springs
U.S.A. 30°43N 86°7W 85 F11
De Grey → Australia 20°12S 119°13E 60 D2
De Haan Belgium 51°16N 3°2E 15 C3
De Hoop △ S. Africa 34°30S 20°28E 56 D3
De Kalb Junction U.S.A. 44°30N 75°16W 83 B9
De Land U.S.A. 29°2N 81°18W 85 G14
De Leon U.S.A. 32°7N 98°32W 84 E5
De Long Mts. U.S.A. 68°10N 163°30W 74 B7
De Panne Belgium 51°6N 2°34E 15 C2
De Pere U.S.A. 44°27N 88°4W 80 C9
De Queen U.S.A. 34°2N 94°21W 84 D7
De Quincy U.S.A. 30°27N 93°26W 84 F8
De Ruyters U.S.A. 42°45N 75°53W 83 D9
De Smet U.S.A. 44°23N 97°33W 80 C5
De Soto U.S.A. 38°8N 90°34W 80 F8
De Tour Village U.S.A. 46°0N 83°56W 81 B12
De Witt U.S.A. 34°18N 91°20W 84 D9
Dead Sea Asia 31°30N 35°30E 48 D4
Deadwood U.S.A. 44°23N 103°44W 80 C2
Deadwood L. Canada 59°10N 128°30W 70 B3
Deal U.K. 51°13N 1°25E 13 F9
Deal I. Australia 39°30S 147°20E 63 F4
Dealesville S. Africa 28°41S 25°44E 56 C4
De'an China 29°21N 115°42E 35 C10
Dean → Canada 52°49N 126°58W 70 C3
Dean, Forest of U.K. 51°45N 2°33W 13 F5
Dean Chan. Canada 52°30N 127°15W 70 C3
Deán Funes Argentina 30°20S 64°20W 94 C3
Dease → Canada 59°56N 128°32W 70 B3
Dease L. Canada 58°40N 130°5W 70 B2
Dease Lake Canada 58°25N 130°6W 70 B2
Death Valley U.S.A. 36°15N 116°50W 79 J10
Death Valley △ U.S.A. 36°29N 117°6W 79 J9
Death Valley Junction
U.S.A. 36°20N 116°25W 79 J10
Deatnu = Tana →
Norway 70°30N 28°14E 8 A23
Debagram India 23°41N 88°18E 43 H13
Debao China 23°21N 106°46E 34 F6
Debar Macedonia 41°31N 20°30E 23 D9
Debden Canada 53°30N 106°50W 71 C7
Dębica Poland 50°2N 21°25E 17 C11
DeBolt Canada 55°12N 118°1W 70 B5
Deborah East, L.
Australia 30°45S 119°30E 61 F2
Deborah West, L.
Australia 30°45S 119°5E 61 F2
Debre Markos Ethiopia 10°20N 37°40E 49 E2
Debre Tabor Ethiopia 11°50N 38°26E 49 E2
Debre Zeyit Ethiopia 8°50N 39°0E 49 F2
Debrecen Hungary 47°33N 21°42E 17 E11
Decatur Ala., U.S.A. 34°36N 86°59W 85 D11
Decatur Ga., U.S.A. 33°47N 84°18W 85 D12
Decatur Ill., U.S.A. 39°51N 88°57W 80 F9
Decatur Ind., U.S.A. 40°50N 84°56W 81 E11
Decatur Tex., U.S.A. 33°14N 97°35W 84 E6
Deccan India 18°0N 79°0E 44 F4
Deception Bay Australia 27°10S 153°5E 63 D5
Deception I. Antarctica 63°0S 60°15W 5 C17
Deception L. Canada 56°33N 104°13W 71 B8
Dechang China 27°25N 102°11E 34 D4
Dechhu India 26°46N 72°20E 42 F5
Děčín Czechia 50°47N 14°12E 16 C8

Deckerville U.S.A. 43°32N 82°44W 82 C2
Decorah U.S.A. 43°18N 91°48W 80 D8
Dedéagach = Alexandroupoli
Greece 40°50N 25°54E 23 D11
Dee → Aberds., U.K. 57°9N 2°5W 11 D6
Dee → Dumf. & Gall., U.K. 54°51N 4°3W 11 G4
Dee → Wales, U.K. 53°22N 3°17W 12 D4
Deep B. Canada 61°15N 116°35W 70 A5
Deep Bay = Shenzhen Wan
China 22°27N 113°55E 31 a
Deepwater Australia 29°25S 151°51E 63 D5
Deer → Canada 58°23N 94°13W 71 B10
Deer L. Canada 52°40N 94°20W 71 C10
Deer Lake Nfld. & L.,
Canada 49°11N 57°27W 73 C8
Deer Lake Ont., Canada 52°36N 94°20W 71 C10
Deer Lodge U.S.A. 46°24N 112°44W 76 C7
Deer Park U.S.A. 47°57N 117°28W 76 C5
Deer River U.S.A. 47°20N 93°48W 80 B7
Deeragun Australia 19°16S 146°33E 62 B4
Defiance U.S.A. 41°17N 84°22W 81 E11
Degana India 26°50N 74°20E 42 F6
Dêgê China 31°44N 98°39E 34 B2
Dégelis Canada 47°30N 68°35W 73 C6
Deggendorf Germany 48°50N 12°57E 16 D7
Degh → Pakistan 31°3N 73°21E 42 D5
Deh Bīd Iran 30°39N 53°11E 47 D7
Deh Dasht Iran 30°47N 50°33E 47 D6
Deh-e Shīr Iran 31°29N 53°45E 47 D7
Dehaj Iran 30°42N 54°53E 47 D7
Dehak Iran 27°11N 62°37E 47 E9
Dehdez Iran 31°43N 50°17E 47 D6
Dehej India 21°44N 72°40E 42 J5
Dehestān Iran 28°30N 55°35E 47 D7
Dehgolān Iran 35°17N 47°25E 46 C5
Dehibat Tunisia 32°0N 10°47E 53 B8
Dehiwala Sri Lanka 6°50N 79°51E 45 L4
Dehlorān Iran 32°41N 47°16E 46 C5
Dehnow-e Kūhestān Iran 27°58N 58°32E 47 E8
Dehra Dun India 30°20N 78°4E 42 D8
Dehri India 24°50N 84°15E 43 G11
Dehua China 25°26N 118°14E 35 E12
Dehui China 44°30N 125°40E 33 B13
Deinze Belgium 50°59N 3°32E 15 D3
Deir al Balah Gaza Strip 31°25N 34°21E 48 D3
Dej Romania 47°10N 23°52E 17 E12
Dejiang China 28°18N 108°7E 34 C7
Deka → Zimbabwe 18°4S 26°42E 56 A4
DeKalb U.S.A. 41°56N 88°46W 80 E9
Dekese
Dem. Rep. of the Congo 3°24S 21°24E 54 E4
Del Mar U.S.A. 32°58N 117°16W 79 N9
Del Norte U.S.A. 37°41N 106°21W 77 H10
Del Rio U.S.A. 29°22N 100°54W 84 G4
Delambre I. Australia 20°26S 117°5E 60 D2
Delano U.S.A. 35°46N 119°15W 79 K7
Delano Peak U.S.A. 38°22N 112°22W 76 G7
Delareyville S. Africa 26°41S 25°26E 56 C4
Delaronde L. Canada 54°3N 107°3W 71 C7
Delavan U.S.A. 42°38N 88°39W 80 D9
Delaware U.S.A. 40°18N 83°4W 81 E12
Delaware □ U.S.A. 39°0N 75°20W 81 F16
Delaware B. U.S.A. 39°0N 75°10W 81 F16
Delaware Water Gap △
U.S.A. 41°10N 74°55W 83 E10
Delay → Canada 56°56N 71°28W 73 A5
Delegate Australia 37°4S 148°56E 63 F4
Delevan U.S.A. 42°29N 78°29W 82 D6
Delft Neths. 52°1N 4°22E 15 B4
Delft I. Sri Lanka 9°30N 79°40E 45 K4
Delfzijl Neths. 53°20N 6°55E 15 A6
Delgado, C. Mozam. 10°45S 40°40E 54 G8
Delgerhet Mongolia 45°50N 110°30E 32 B6
Delgo Sudan 20°6N 30°40E 53 D12
Delhi Canada 42°51N 80°30W 82 D4
Delhi India 28°38N 77°17E 42 E7
Delhi La., U.S.A. 32°28N 91°30W 84 E9
Delhi N.Y., U.S.A. 42°17N 74°55W 83 D10
Delia Canada 51°38N 112°23W 70 C6
Delice Turkey 39°54N 34°2E 19 G5
Delicias Mexico 28°13N 105°28W 86 B3
Delijān Iran 33°59N 50°40E 47 C6
Déline Canada 65°11N 123°25W 68 D7
Delingha China 37°23N 97°23E 30 D8
Delisle Canada 51°55N 107°8W 71 C7
Deliverance I. Australia 9°31S 141°34E 62 a
Dell City U.S.A. 31°56N 105°12W 84 F2
Dell Rapids U.S.A. 43°50N 96°43W 80 D5
Delmar U.S.A. 42°37N 73°47W 83 D11
Delmenhorst Germany 53°3N 8°37E 16 B5
Delonga, Ostrova
Russia 76°40N 149°20E 27 B15
Deloraine Australia 41°30S 146°40E 63 G4
Deloraine Canada 49°15N 100°29W 71 D8
Delphos U.S.A. 40°51N 84°21W 81 E11
Delportshoop S. Africa 28°22S 24°20E 56 C3
Delray Beach U.S.A. 26°28N 80°4W 85 H14
Delta Colo., U.S.A. 38°44N 108°4W 76 G9
Delta Utah, U.S.A. 39°21N 112°35W 76 G7
Delta Dunărea △
Romania 45°15N 29°23E 17 F15
Delta Junction U.S.A. 64°2N 145°44W 74 C10
Deltona U.S.A. 28°54N 81°16W 85 G14
Delungra Australia 29°39S 150°51E 63 D5
Delvada India 20°46N 71°2E 42 J4
Delvinë Albania 39°59N 20°6E 23 E9
Demak Indonesia 6°53S 110°38E 37 G14
Demanda, Sierra de la
Spain 42°15N 3°0W 21 A4
Dembidolo Ethiopia 8°34N 34°50E 47 G12
Demchok India 32°42N 79°29E 43 C8
Demer → Belgium 50°57N 4°42E 15 D4
Deming N. Mex.,
U.S.A. 32°16N 107°46W 77 K10
Deming Wash., U.S.A. 48°50N 122°13W 78 B4
Demini → Brazil 0°46S 62°56W 92 D6
Demirci Turkey 39°2N 28°38E 23 E13
Demopolis U.S.A. 32°31N 87°50W 85 E11
Dempo Indonesia 4°2S 103°15E 36 E2

Den Bosch = 's-Hertogenbosch
Neths. 51°42N 5°17E 15 C5
Den Burg Neths. 53°3N 4°47E 15 A4
Den Chai Thailand 17°59N 100°4E 38 D3
Den Haag = 's-Gravenhage
Neths. 52°7N 4°17E 15 B4
Den Helder Neths. 52°57N 4°45E 15 B4
Den Oever Neths. 52°56N 5°2E 15 B5
Denair U.S.A. 37°32N 120°48W 78 H6
Denali U.S.A. 63°4N 151°0W 68 E1
Denau = Denov
Uzbekistan 38°16N 67°54E 26 F7
Denbigh Canada 45°8N 77°15W 82 A7
Denbigh U.K. 53°12N 3°25W 12 D4
Denbighshire □ U.K. 53°8N 3°22W 12 D4
Dendang Indonesia 3°7S 107°56E 36 E3
Dendermonde Belgium 51°2N 4°5E 15 C4
Dengchuan China 25°59N 100°3E 34 E3
Dengfeng China 34°25N 113°2E 32 G7
Dengkou China 40°18N 106°55E 32 D4
Dengzhou China 32°34N 112°4E 35 A9
Denham Australia 25°56S 113°31E 61 E1
Denham, Mt. Jamaica 18°13N 77°32W 88 a
Denham Ra. Australia 21°55S 147°46E 62 C4
Denham Sd. Australia 25°45S 113°15E 61 E1
Denholm Canada 52°39N 108°1W 71 C7
Denia Spain 38°49N 0°8E 21 C6
Denial B. Australia 32°14S 133°32E 63 E1
Deniliquin Australia 35°30S 144°58E 63 F3
Denimoo = Fort Resolution
Canada 61°10N 113°40W 70 A6
Denison Iowa, U.S.A. 42°1N 95°21W 80 D6
Denison Tex., U.S.A. 33°45N 96°33W 84 E6
Denison, C. Antarctica 67°0S 142°40E 5 C10
Denison Plains Australia 18°35S 128°0E 60 C4
Deniyaya Sri Lanka 6°21N 80°33E 45 L5
Denizli Turkey 37°42N 29°2E 19 G4
Denman Glacier Antarctica 66°45S 100°0E 5 C8
Denmark Australia 34°59S 117°25E 61 F2
Denmark ■ Europe 55°45N 10°0E 9 J13
Denmark Str. Atl. Oc. 66°0N 30°0W 66 C17
Dennery St. Lucia 13°55N 60°54W 89 f
Dennison U.S.A. 40°24N 81°19W 82 F3
Denny U.K. 56°1N 3°55W 11 E5
Denov Uzbekistan 38°16N 67°54E 26 F7
Denpasar Indonesia 8°39S 115°13E 37 K18
Denpasar ✈ (DPS)
Indonesia 8°44S 115°10E 37 K18
Denton Mont., U.S.A. 47°19N 109°57W 76 C9
Denton Tex., U.S.A. 33°13N 97°8W 84 E6
D'Entrecasteaux, Pt.
Australia 34°50S 115°57E 61 F2
D'Entrecasteaux △
Australia 34°20S 115°33E 61 F2
D'Entrecasteaux Is.
Papua N. G. 9°0S 151°0E 58 B8
Denver Colo., U.S.A. 39°42N 104°59W 76 G11
Denver Pa., U.S.A. 40°14N 76°8W 83 F8
Denver City U.S.A. 32°58N 102°50W 84 E3
Denver Int. ✈ (DEN)
U.S.A. 39°52N 104°40W 76 G11
Deoband India 29°42N 77°43E 42 E7
Deobhog India 19°53N 82°44E 44 E6
Deodrug India 16°26N 76°55E 45 F3
Deogarh Odisha, India 21°32N 84°45E 44 D7
Deogarh Raj., India 25°32N 73°54E 42 G5
Deoghar India 24°30N 86°42E 43 G12
Deolali India 19°58N 73°50E 44 E8
Deoli = Devli India 25°50N 75°20E 42 G6
Deora India 26°22N 70°55E 42 F4
Deori India 23°24N 79°1E 43 H8
Deoria India 26°31N 83°48E 43 F10
Deosai Mts. Pakistan 35°40N 75°0E 43 B6
Deosri India 26°46N 90°29E 43 F14
Depalpur India 22°51N 75°33E 42 H6
Deposit U.S.A. 42°4N 75°25W 83 D9
Depuch I. Australia 20°37S 117°44E 60 D2
Deputatskiy Russia 69°18N 139°54E 27 C14
Dêqên China 28°34N 98°51E 34 C2
Deqing China 23°8N 111°42E 35 F8
Dera Ghazi Khan Pakistan 30°5N 70°43E 42 D4
Dera Ismail Khan
Pakistan 31°50N 70°50E 42 D4
Derabugti Pakistan 29°2N 69°9E 42 E3
Derawar Fort Pakistan 28°46N 71°20E 42 E4
Derbent Russia 42°5N 48°15E 19 F8
Derby Australia 17°18S 123°38E 60 C3
Derby U.K. 52°56N 1°28W 12 E6
Derby Conn., U.S.A. 41°19N 73°5W 83 E11
Derby Kans., U.S.A. 37°33N 97°16W 80 G5
Derby N.Y., U.S.A. 42°41N 78°58W 82 D6
Derby City □ U.K. 52°56N 1°28W 12 E6
Derby Line U.S.A. 45°0N 72°6W 83 B12
Derbyshire □ U.K. 53°11N 1°38W 12 E6
Dereham U.K. 52°41N 0°57E 13 E8
Derg → U.K. 54°44N 7°26W 10 B4
Derg, L. Ireland 53°0N 8°20W 10 D3
Deridder U.S.A. 30°51N 93°17W 84 F8
Dermott U.S.A. 33°32N 91°26W 84 E9
Dêrong China 28°44N 99°58E 34 C2
Derry = Londonderry U.K. 55°0N 7°20W 10 B4
Derry = Londonderry □
U.K. 55°0N 7°20W 10 B4
Derry N.H., U.S.A. 42°53N 71°19W 83 D13
Derry Pa., U.S.A. 40°20N 79°18W 82 F5
Derryveagh Mts. Ireland 54°56N 8°11W 10 B3
Derwent → Cumb., U.K. 54°39N 3°33W 12 C4
Derwent → Derby, U.K. 52°57N 1°28W 12 E6
Derwent → N. Yorks.,
U.K. 53°45N 0°58W 12 D7
Derwent Water U.K. 54°35N 3°9W 12 C4
Des Moines Iowa, U.S.A. 41°35N 93°37W 80 E7
Des Moines N. Mex.,
U.S.A. 36°46N 103°50W 77 H12
Des Moines Wash.,
U.S.A. 47°24N 122°19W 78 C4
Des Moines → U.S.A. 40°23N 91°25W 80 E8
Desaguadero →
Argentina 34°30S 66°46W 94 C2

Desaguadero → Bolivia 16°35S 69°5W 92 G5
Desaru Malaysia 1°31N 104°17E 39 d
Descanso, Pta. Mexico 32°21N 117°3W 79 N9
Deschaillons-sur-St-Laurent
Canada 46°32N 72°7W 73 C5
Deschambault L.
Canada 54°50N 103°30W 71 C8
Deschutes → U.S.A. 45°38N 120°55W 76 D3
Dese Ethiopia 11°5N 39°40E 49 E2
Deseado → Argentina 47°45S 65°54W 96 F3
Deseronto Canada 44°12N 77°3W 82 B7
Desert Center U.S.A. 33°43N 115°24W 79 M11
Desert Hot Springs
U.S.A. 33°58N 116°30W 79 M10
Deshnok India 27°48N 73°21E 42 F5
Desierto Central de Baja
California △ Mexico 29°40N 114°50W 86 B2
Desna → Ukraine 50°33N 30°32E 17 C16
Desolación, I. Chile 53°0S 74°0W 96 G2
Despeñaperros, Paso
Spain 38°24N 3°30W 21 C4
Dessau Germany 51°51N 12°14E 16 C7
Dessye = Dese Ethiopia 11°5N 39°40E 49 E2
D'Estrees B. Australia 35°55S 137°45E 63 F2
Desuri India 25°18N 73°35E 42 G5
Det Udom Thailand 14°54N 105°5E 38 E5
Dete Zimbabwe 18°38S 26°50E 56 A4
Detmold Germany 51°56N 8°52E 16 C5
Detour, Pt. U.S.A. 45°40N 86°40W 80 C10
Detroit U.S.A. 42°19N 83°12W 82 D1
Detroit Lakes U.S.A. 46°49N 95°51W 80 B6
Deua △ Australia 35°32S 149°46E 63 F4
Deurne Neths. 51°27N 5°49E 15 C5
Deutsche Bucht Germany 54°15N 8°0E 16 A5
Deutschland = Germany ■
Europe 51°0N 10°0E 16 C6
Deva Romania 45°53N 22°55E 17 F12
Devakottai India 9°55N 78°45E 45 K4
Devaprayag India 30°13N 78°35E 43 D8
Devarkonda India 16°42N 78°56E 44 F4
Deventer Neths. 52°15N 6°10E 15 B6
Deveron → U.K. 57°41N 2°32W 11 D6
Devgad I. India 14°48N 74°5E 45 G2
Devgadh Bariya India 22°40N 73°55E 42 H5
Devgarh India 16°23N 73°23E 45 F5
Devi → India 19°59N 86°24E 44 E8
Devikot India 26°42N 71°12E 42 F4
Devils Den U.S.A. 35°36N 119°58W 78 K7
Devils Hole = Death Valley △
U.S.A. 36°29N 117°6W 79 J9
Devils Lake U.S.A. 48°7N 98°52W 80 A4
Devils Paw Canada 58°47N 134°0W 70 B2
Devils Postpile △ U.S.A. 37°37N 119°5W 78 H7
Devil's Pt. Sri Lanka 9°26N 80°6E 45 K5
Devils Tower U.S.A. 44°35N 104°42W 76 D11
Devils Tower △ U.S.A. 44°48N 104°55W 76 D11
Devine U.S.A. 29°8N 98°54W 84 G5
Devipattinam India 9°29N 78°54E 45 K4
Devizes U.K. 51°22N 1°58W 13 F6
Devli India 25°50N 75°20E 42 G6
Devon Canada 53°24N 113°44W 70 C6
Devon U.K. 50°50N 3°40E 13 G4
Devon I. Canada 75°10N 85°0W 69 B15
Devonport Australia 41°10S 146°22E 63 G4
Devonport N.Z. 36°49S 174°49E 59 B5
Devrukh India 17°3N 73°37E 44 F1
Dewas India 22°59N 76°3E 42 H7
Dewetsdorp S. Africa 29°33S 26°39E 56 C4
Dewey Puerto Rico 18°18N 65°18W 89 d
Dexing China 28°46N 117°30E 35 C11
Dexter Maine, U.S.A. 45°1N 69°18W 81 C19
Dexter Mo., U.S.A. 36°48N 89°57W 80 G9
Dexter N. Mex., U.S.A. 33°12N 104°22W 77 K11
Dey-Dey, L. Australia 29°12S 131°4E 61 E5
Deyang China 31°3N 104°27E 34 B5
Deyhūk Iran 33°15N 57°30E 47 C8
Deyyer Iran 27°55N 51°55E 47 E6
Dez → Iran 31°39N 48°52E 47 D6
Dezadeash L. Canada 60°28N 136°58W 70 A1
Dezfūl Iran 32°20N 48°30E 47 C6
Dezhneva, Mys Russia 66°5N 169°40W 27 C19
Dezhou China 37°26N 116°18E 32 F9
Dhadhar → India 24°56N 85°24E 43 G11
Dhahiriya = Az Zāhirīyah
West Bank 31°25N 34°58E 48 D3
Dhahran = Az Zahrān
Si. Arabia 26°10N 50°7E 47 E6
Dhak Pakistan 32°25N 72°33E 42 C5
Dhaka Bangla. 23°43N 90°26E 43 H14
Dhaka □ Bangla. 23°30N 90°0E 43 H14
Dhamangaon India 20°48N 78°9E 44 D4
Dhamār Yemen 14°30N 44°20E 49 E3
Dhampur India 29°19N 78°33E 43 E8
Dhamra → India 20°47N 86°58E 44 D8
Dhamtari India 20°42N 81°35E 44 D5
Dhanbad India 23°50N 86°30E 43 H12
Dhangarhi Nepal 28°55N 80°40E 43 E9
Dhankuta Nepal 26°55N 87°40E 43 F12
Dhanora India 23°13N 81°30E 44 C5
Dhar India 22°35N 75°26E 42 H6
Dharampur India 22°13N 75°18E 42 H6
Dharamsala = Dharmsala
India 32°16N 76°23E 42 C7
Dharan Nepal 26°49N 87°17E 43 F12
Dharangaon India 21°1N 75°16E 44 D2
Dharapuram India 10°45N 77°34E 45 J3
Dhariwal India 31°57N 75°19E 42 D6
Dharla → Bangla. 25°46N 89°42E 43 G13
Dharmapuri India 12°10N 78°10E 45 H4
Dharmavaram India 14°29N 77°44E 45 G3
Dharmjaygarh India 22°28N 83°13E 43 H10
Dharmsala India 32°16N 76°23E 42 C7
Dharni India 21°33N 76°53E 42 J7
Dharwad India 15°30N 75°4E 45 G2
Dhasan → India 25°48N 79°24E 43 G8
Dhaulagiri Nepal 28°39N 83°28E 43 E10
Dhebar, L. India 24°10N 74°0E 42 G6

116 Dhenkanal INDEX TO WORLD MAPS


Dhenkanal India 20°45N 85°35E 44 D7
Dhī Qār □ Iraq 31°0N 46°15E 46 D5
Dhībān Jordan 31°30N 35°46E 48 D4
Dhilwan India 31°31N 75°21E 42 D6
Dhimarkhera India 23°28N 80°22E 43 H9
Dholka India 22°44N 72°29E 42 H5
Dhond = Daund India 18°26N 74°40E 44 E2
Dhone India 15°25N 77°53E 45 E3
Dhoraji India 21°45N 70°37E 42 J4
Dhorpatan Nepal 28°29N 83°4E 43 E10
Dhrangadhra India 22°59N 71°31E 42 H4
Dhrol India 22°33N 70°25E 42 H4
Dhuburi India 26°2N 89°59E 41 F16
Dhule India 20°58N 74°50E 44 D2
Di Linh Vietnam 11°35N 108°4E 39 G7
Di Linh, Cao Nguyen Vietnam 11°30N 108°0E 39 G7
Diablo Range U.S.A. 37°20N 121°25W 78 J5
Diafarabé Mali 14°9N 4°57W 52 F5
Diamante Argentina 32°5S 60°40W 94 C3
Diamante → Argentina 34°30S 66°46W 94 C2
Diamantina Brazil 18°17S 43°40W 93 G10
Diamantina → Australia 26°45S 139°10E 63 D2
Diamantina △ Australia 23°33S 141°23E 62 C3
Diamantino Brazil 14°30S 56°30W 93 F7
Diamond Bar U.S.A. 34°1N 117°48W 79 L9
Diamond Harbour India 22°11N 88°14E 43 H13
Diamond Is. Australia 17°25S 151°5E 62 B5
Diamond Mts. U.S.A. 39°40N 115°50W 76 G6
Diamond Springs U.S.A. 38°42N 120°49W 78 G6
Dian Chi China 24°50N 102°43E 34 E4
Dianbai China 21°33N 111°0E 35 G8
Diancheng China 21°30N 111°4E 35 G8
Dianjiang China 30°24N 107°20E 34 B6
Diaoyu Dao = Senkaku-Shotō E. China Sea 25°45N 123°30E 29 M1
Diaoyu Tai = Senkaku-Shotō E. China Sea 25°45N 123°30E 29 M1
Diavolo, Mt. India 12°40N 92°56E 45 H11
Diba = Dibbā al Ḩiṣn U.A.E. 25°45N 56°16E 47 E8
Dibai India 28°13N 78°15E 42 E8
Dibaya Dem. Rep. of the Congo 6°30S 22°57E 54 F4
Dibaya-Lubue Dem. Rep. of the Congo 4°12S 19°54E 54 E3
Dibbā al Ḩiṣn U.A.E. 25°45N 56°16E 47 E8
Dibbeen △ Jordan 32°20N 35°45E 48 C4
D'Iberville, Lac Canada 55°55N 73°15W 72 A5
Dibete Botswana 23°45S 26°32E 56 B4
Dibrugarh India 27°29N 94°55E 41 F19
Dickens U.S.A. 33°37N 100°50W 84 E4
Dickinson U.S.A. 46°53N 102°47W 80 B2
Dickson U.S.A. 36°5N 87°23W 85 C11
Dickson City U.S.A. 41°28N 75°36W 83 E9
Didiéni Mali 13°53N 8°6W 52 F4
Didsbury Canada 51°35N 114°10W 70 C6
Didwana India 27°23N 74°36E 42 F6
Diefenbaker, L. Canada 51°0N 106°55W 71 C7
Diego de Almagro Chile 26°22S 70°3W 94 B1
Diego Suarez = Antsiranana Madag. 12°25S 49°20E 55 G9
Diekirch Lux. 49°52N 6°10E 15 E6
Dien Ban Vietnam 15°53N 108°16E 38 E7
Dien Bien Phu Vietnam 21°20N 103°0E 34 G4
Dien Chau, Vinh Vietnam 19°0N 105°55E 38 C5
Dien Khanh Vietnam 12°15N 109°6E 39 F7
Dieppe France 49°54N 1°4E 20 B4
Dierks U.S.A. 34°7N 94°1W 84 D7
Diest Belgium 50°58N 5°4E 15 D5
Dif Somalia 0°59N 40°58E 49 G3
Differdange Lux. 49°31N 5°54E 15 E5
Dig India 27°28N 77°20E 42 F7
Digby Canada 44°38N 65°50W 73 D6
Digges Is. Canada 62°40N 77°50W 69 E16
Diggi India 26°22N 75°26E 42 F6
Dighinala Bangla. 23°15N 92°5E 41 H18
Dighton U.S.A. 38°29N 100°28W 80 F3
Diglur India 18°34N 77°33E 44 E3
Digne-les-Bains France 44°5N 6°12E 20 D7
Digos Phil. 6°45N 125°20E 37 C7
Digranes Iceland 66°4N 14°44W 8 C6
Digras India 20°6N 77°45E 44 D3
Digul → Indonesia 7°7S 138°42E 37 F9
Dihang = Brahmaputra → Asia 23°40N 90°35E 43 H13
Dijlah, Nahr → Asia 31°0N 47°25E 46 D5
Dijon France 47°20N 5°3E 20 C6
Dikhil Djibouti 11°8N 42°20E 49 E3
Diksmuide Belgium 51°2N 2°52E 15 C2
Dikson Russia 73°40N 80°5E 26 B9
Dikti Oros Greece 35°8N 25°30E 23 G11
Dila Ethiopia 6°21N 38°22E 49 F2
Dili Timor-Leste 8°39S 125°34E 37 F7
Diligent Strait India 12°11N 92°57E 45 H11
Dilley U.S.A. 28°40N 99°10W 84 G5
Dillingham U.S.A. 59°3N 158°28W 74 D8
Dillon Canada 55°56N 108°35W 71 B7
Dillon Mont., U.S.A. 45°13N 112°38W 76 D7
Dillon S.C., U.S.A. 34°25N 79°22W 85 D15
Dillon → Canada 55°56N 108°56W 71 B7
Dillsburg U.S.A. 40°7N 77°2W 82 F7
Dilolo Dem. Rep. of the Congo 10°28S 22°18E 54 G4
Dimapur India 25°54N 93°45E 30 F7
Dimas Mexico 23°43N 106°47W 86 C3
Dimashq Syria 33°30N 36°18E 48 B5
Dimashq □ Syria 33°30N 36°30E 48 B5
Dimbaza S. Africa 32°50S 27°14E 57 D4
Dimboola Australia 36°28S 142°7E 63 F3
Dîmboviţa = Dâmboviţa → Romania 44°12N 26°26E 17 F14
Dimbulah Australia 17°8S 145°4E 62 B4
Dimitrovgrad Bulgaria 42°5N 25°35E 23 C11
Dimitrovgrad Russia 54°14N 49°39E 18 D8
Dimitrovo = Pernik Bulgaria 42°35N 23°2E 23 C10
Dimmitt U.S.A. 34°33N 102°19W 84 D3
Dimona Israel 31°2N 35°1E 48 D4
Dinagat I. Phil. 10°10N 125°40E 37 B7
Dinajpur Bangla. 25°33N 88°43E 41 G16
Dinan France 48°28N 2°2W 20 B2
Dīnān Āb Iran 32°4N 56°49E 47 C8
Dinant Belgium 50°16N 4°55E 15 D4
Dinapur India 25°38N 85°5E 43 G11
Dīnār, Kūh-e Iran 30°42N 51°46E 47 D6
Dinara Planina Croatia 44°0N 16°30E 22 C7
Dinard France 48°38N 2°6W 20 B2
Dinaric Alps = Dinara Planina Croatia 44°0N 16°30E 22 C7
Dinbych-y-Pysgod = Tenby U.K. 51°40N 4°42W 13 F3
Dindi → India 16°24N 78°15E 45 F4
Dindigul India 10°25N 78°0E 45 J4
Dindori India 22°57N 81°5E 43 H9
Ding Xian = Dingzhou China 38°30N 114°59E 32 E8
Dinga Pakistan 25°26N 67°10E 42 G2
Ding'an China 19°42N 110°19E 38 C8
Dingbian China 37°35N 107°32E 32 F4
Dingle Ireland 52°9N 10°17W 10 D1
Dingle B. Ireland 52°3N 10°20W 10 D1
Dingle Pen. Ireland 52°12N 10°5W 10 D1
Dingmans Ferry U.S.A. 41°13N 74°55W 83 E10
Dingnan China 24°45N 115°0E 35 E10
Dingo Australia 23°38S 149°19E 62 C4
Dingtao China 35°5N 115°35E 32 G8
Dingwall U.K. 57°36N 4°26W 11 D4
Dingxi China 35°30N 104°33E 32 G3
Dingxiang China 38°30N 112°58E 32 E7
Dingyuan China 32°32N 117°41E 35 A11
Dingzhou China 38°30N 114°59E 32 E8
Dinh, Mui Vietnam 11°22N 109°1E 39 G7
Dinh Lap Vietnam 21°33N 107°6E 34 G6
Dinin → Ireland 52°43N 7°18W 10 D4
Dinira △ Venezuela 9°57N 70°6W 89 E6
Dinokwe Botswana 23°29S 26°37E 56 B4
Dinorwic Canada 49°41N 92°30W 71 D10
Dinosaur ⌂ Canada 50°47N 111°30W 70 C6
Dinosaur ⌂ U.S.A. 40°30N 108°45W 76 F9
Dinuba U.S.A. 36°32N 119°23W 78 J7
Diourbel Senegal 14°39N 16°12W 52 F2
Dipalpur Pakistan 30°40N 73°39E 42 D5
Diplo Pakistan 24°35N 69°35E 42 G3
Dipolog Phil. 8°36N 123°20E 37 C6
Dipperu △ Australia 21°56S 148°42E 62 C4
Dir Pakistan 35°8N 71°59E 40 B7
Dire Dawa Ethiopia 9°35N 41°45E 49 F3
Dirfis Oros Greece 38°40N 23°54E 23 E10
Diriamba Nic. 11°51N 86°19W 88 D2
Dirk Hartog I. Australia 25°50S 113°5E 61 E1
Dirranbandi Australia 28°33S 148°17E 63 D4
Disa India 24°18N 72°10E 42 G5
Disappointment, C. U.S.A. 46°18N 124°5W 78 D2
Disappointment, L. Australia 23°20S 122°40E 60 D3
Disaster B. Australia 37°15S 149°58E 63 F4
Discovery B. Australia 38°10S 140°40E 63 F3
Disko = Qeqertarsuaq Greenland 69°45N 53°30W 4 C5
Disney Reef Tonga 19°17S 174°7W 59 c
Diss U.K. 52°23N 1°7E 13 E9
Disteghil Sar Pakistan 36°20N 75°12E 43 A6
District of Columbia □ U.S.A. 38°55N 77°0W 81 F15
Distrito Federal □ Brazil 15°45S 47°45W 93 G9
Distrito Federal □ Mexico 19°15N 99°10W 87 D5
Diu India 20°45N 70°58E 42 J4
Dīvāndarreh Iran 35°55N 47°2E 46 C5
Divi Pt. India 15°59N 81°9E 45 G5
Divide U.S.A. 45°45N 112°45W 76 D7
Dividing Ra. Australia 27°45S 116°0E 61 E2
Divinópolis Brazil 20°10S 44°54W 93 H10
Divnoye Russia 45°55N 43°21E 19 E7
Divo Côte d'Ivoire 5°48N 5°15W 52 G4
Dīwāl Kol Afghan. 34°23N 67°52E 42 B2
Dixie Mt. U.S.A. 39°55N 120°16W 78 F6
Dixon Calif., U.S.A. 38°27N 121°49W 78 G5
Dixon Ill., U.S.A. 41°50N 89°29W 80 E9
Dixon Entrance U.S.A. 54°30N 132°0W 68 G5
Dixville Canada 45°4N 71°46W 83 A13
Diyālā □ Iraq 33°45N 44°50E 46 C5
Diyālā → Iraq 33°13N 44°30E 46 C5
Diyarbakır Turkey 37°55N 40°18E 46 B4
Diyodar India 24°8N 71°50E 42 G4
Djamba Angola 16°45S 13°58E 56 A1
Djambala Congo 2°32S 14°30E 54 E2
Djanet Algeria 24°35N 9°32E 52 D7
Djawa = Jawa Indonesia 7°0S 110°0E 36 F3
Djelfa Algeria 34°40N 3°15E 52 B6
Djerba, Î. de Tunisia 33°50N 10°48E 53 B8
Djerid, Chott Tunisia 33°42N 8°30E 52 B7
Djibouti Djibouti 11°30N 43°5E 49 E3
Djibouti ■ Africa 12°0N 43°0E 49 E3
Djolu Dem. Rep. of the Congo 0°35N 22°5E 54 D4
Djougou Benin 9°40N 1°45E 52 G6
Djoum Cameroon 2°41N 12°35E 54 D2
Djourab, Erg du Chad 16°40N 18°50E 53 E9
Djukbinj △ Australia 12°11S 131°2E 60 B5
Djúpivogur Iceland 64°39N 14°17W 8 D6
Dmitriya Lapteva, Proliv Russia 73°0N 140°0E 27 B15
Dnepr = Dnipro → Ukraine 46°30N 32°18E 19 E5
Dneprodzerzhinsk = Dniprodzerzhynsk Ukraine 48°32N 34°37E 19 E5
Dnepropetrovsk = Dnipropetrovsk Ukraine 48°30N 35°0E 19 E6
Dnestr = Dnister → Europe 46°18N 30°17E 17 E16
Dnieper = Dnipro → Ukraine 46°30N 32°18E 19 E5
Dniester = Dnister → Europe 46°18N 30°17E 17 E16
Dnipro → Ukraine 46°30N 32°18E 19 E5
Dniprodzerzhynsk Ukraine 48°32N 34°37E 19 E5
Dnipropetrovsk Ukraine 48°30N 35°0E 19 E6
Dnister → Europe 46°18N 30°17E 17 E16
Dno Russia 57°50N 29°58E 9 H23
Dnyapro = Dnipro → Ukraine 46°30N 32°18E 19 E5
Do Gonbadān = Gachsārān Iran 30°15N 50°45E 47 D6
Doaktown Canada 46°33N 66°8W 73 C6
Doan Hung Vietnam 21°30N 105°10E 34 G5
Doba Chad 8°40N 16°50E 53 G9
Dobandi Pakistan 31°13N 66°50E 42 D2
Dobbyn Australia 19°44S 140°2E 62 B3
Dobele Latvia 56°37N 23°16E 9 H20
Doberai, Jazirah Indonesia 1°25S 133°0E 37 E8
Doblas Argentina 37°5S 64°0W 94 D3
Dobo Indonesia 5°45S 134°15E 37 F8
Doboj Bos.-H. 44°46N 18°4E 23 B8
Dobrich Bulgaria 43°37N 27°49E 23 C12
Dobruja Europe 44°30N 28°15E 17 F15
Dobrush Belarus 52°25N 31°22E 17 B16
Doc, Mui Vietnam 17°58N 106°30E 38 D6
Docker River = Kaltukatjara Australia 24°52S 129°5E 61 D4
Doctor Arroyo Mexico 23°40N 100°11W 86 C4
Doctor Pedro P. Peña Paraguay 22°27S 62°21W 94 A3
Doda India 33°10N 75°34E 43 C6
Doda, L. Canada 49°25N 75°13W 72 C4
Doda Betta India 11°24N 76°44E 45 J3
Dodballapur India 13°18N 77°32E 45 H3
Dodecanese = Dodekanisa Greece 36°35N 27°0E 23 F12
Dodekanisa Greece 36°35N 27°0E 23 F12
Dodge City U.S.A. 37°45N 100°1W 80 G3
Dodge L. Canada 59°50N 105°36W 71 B7
Dodgeville U.S.A. 42°58N 90°8W 80 D8
Dodoma Tanzania 6°8S 35°45E 54 F7
Dodsland Canada 51°50N 108°45W 71 C7
Dodson U.S.A. 48°24N 108°15W 76 B9
Doesburg Neths. 52°1N 6°9E 15 B6
Doetinchem Neths. 51°59N 6°18E 15 C6
Dog Creek Canada 51°35N 122°14W 70 C4
Dog L. Man., Canada 51°2N 98°31W 71 C9
Dog L. Ont., Canada 48°48N 89°30W 72 C2
Dogran Pakistan 31°48N 73°35E 42 D5
Doğubayazıt Turkey 39°31N 44°5E 46 B5
Doha = Ad Dawḩah Qatar 25°15N 51°35E 47 E6
Doha Int. ✈ (DOH) Qatar 25°16N 51°34E 47 E6
Dohazari Bangla. 22°10N 92°5E 41 H18
Dohrighat India 26°16N 83°31E 43 F10
Doi Indonesia 2°14N 127°49E 37 D7
Doi Inthanon Thailand 18°35N 98°29E 38 C2
Doi Inthanon △ Thailand 18°33N 98°34E 38 C2
Doi Khuntan △ Thailand 18°33N 99°14E 38 C2
Doi Luang Thailand 18°30N 101°0E 38 C3
Doi Luang △ Thailand 19°22N 99°35E 38 C2
Doi Phukha △ Thailand 19°8N 101°9E 38 C3
Doi Saket Thailand 18°52N 99°9E 38 C2
Doi Suthep Pui △ Thailand 18°49N 98°53E 38 C2
Doi Toa Thailand 17°55N 98°30E 38 D2
Dois Irmãos, Sa. Brazil 9°0S 42°30W 93 E10
Dokdo = Liancourt Rocks Asia 37°15N 131°52E 29 F5
Dokkum Neths. 53°20N 5°59E 15 A5
Dokri Pakistan 27°25N 68°7E 42 F3
Dolak, Pulau Indonesia 8°0S 138°30E 37 F9
Dolbeau-Mistassini Canada 48°53N 72°14W 73 C5
Dole France 47°7N 5°31E 20 C6
Dolgellau U.K. 52°45N 3°53W 12 E4
Dolgelley = Dolgellau U.K. 52°45N 3°53W 12 E4
Dolinsk Russia 47°21N 142°48E 27 E15
Dollard Neths. 53°20N 7°10E 15 A7
Dolo Ethiopia 4°11N 42°3E 49 G3
Dolomites = Dolomiti Italy 46°23N 11°51E 22 A4
Dolomiti Italy 46°23N 11°51E 22 A4
Dolores Argentina 36°20S 57°40W 94 D4
Dolores Uruguay 33°34S 58°15W 94 C4
Dolores U.S.A. 37°28N 108°30W 77 H9
Dolores → U.S.A. 38°49N 109°17W 76 G9
Dolphin, C. Falk. Is. 51°10S 59°0W 96 G5
Dolphin and Union Str. Canada 69°5N 114°45W 68 D9
Dom Pedrito Brazil 31°0S 54°40W 95 C5
Domariaganj → India 26°17N 83°44E 43 F10
Dombarovskiy Russia 50°46N 59°32E 26 D6
Dombås Norway 62°4N 9°8E 8 E13
Dome Argus Antarctica 80°50S 76°30E 5 E6
Dome C. Antarctica 75°12S 123°37E 5 D9
Dome Fuji Antarctica 77°20S 39°45E 5 D5
Domel I. = Letsôk-aw Kyun Myanmar 11°30N 98°25E 39 G2
Domeyko Chile 29°0S 71°0W 94 B1
Domeyko, Cordillera Chile 24°30S 69°0W 94 A2
Dominador Chile 24°21S 69°20W 94 A2
Dominica ■ W. Indies 15°20N 61°20W 89 C7
Dominica Passage W. Indies 15°10N 61°20W 89 C7
Dominican Rep. ■ W. Indies 19°0N 70°30W 89 C5
Domodóssola Italy 46°7N 8°17E 20 C8
Domville, Mt. Australia 28°1S 151°15E 63 D5
Don → India 16°20N 76°15E 45 F3
Don → Russia 47°4N 39°18E 19 E6
Don → Aberds., U.K. 57°11N 2°5W 11 D6
Don → S. Yorks., U.K. 53°41N 0°52W 12 D7
Don, C. Australia 11°18S 131°46E 60 B5
Don Benito Spain 38°53N 5°51W 21 C3
Don Figuerera Mts. Jamaica 18°5N 77°36W 88 a
Don Sak Thailand 9°18N 99°41E 39 b
Donaghadee U.K. 54°39N 5°33W 10 B6
Donaghmore Ireland 52°52N 7°36W 10 D4
Donald Australia 36°23S 143°0E 63 F3
Donaldsonville U.S.A. 30°6N 90°59W 84 F9
Donalsonville U.S.A. 31°3N 84°53W 85 F12
Donau = Dunărea → Europe 45°20N 29°40E 17 F15
Donauwörth Germany 48°43N 10°47E 16 D6
Doncaster U.K. 53°32N 1°6W 12 D6
Dondo Angola 9°45S 14°25E 54 F2
Dondo, Teluk Indonesia 0°50N 120°30E 37 D6
Dondra Head Sri Lanka 5°55N 80°40E 45 M5
Donegal Ireland 54°39N 8°5W 10 B3
Donegal □ Ireland 54°53N 8°0W 10 B4
Donegal B. Ireland 54°31N 8°49W 10 B3
Donets → Russia 47°33N 40°55E 19 E7
Donets Basin Ukraine 49°0N 38°0E 6 F13
Donetsk Ukraine 48°0N 37°45E 19 E6
Dong Ba Thin Vietnam 12°8N 109°13E 39 F7
Dong Dang Vietnam 21°54N 106°42E 34 G6
Dong Giam Vietnam 19°25N 105°31E 38 C5
Dong Ha Vietnam 16°55N 107°8E 38 D6
Dong Hene Laos 16°40N 105°18E 38 D5
Dong Hoi Vietnam 17°29N 106°36E 38 D6
Dong Jiang → China 23°6N 114°0E 35 F10
Dong Khe Vietnam 22°26N 106°27E 38 A6
Dong Phayayen Thailand 14°20N 101°22E 38 E3
Dong Ujimqin Qi China 45°32N 116°55E 32 B9
Dong Van Vietnam 23°16N 105°22E 38 A5
Dong Xoai Vietnam 11°32N 106°55E 39 G6
Dong'an China 26°23N 111°12E 35 D8
Dongara Australia 29°14S 114°57E 61 E1
Dongargarh India 21°10N 80°40E 44 D5
Dongbei China 45°0N 125°0E 33 D13
Dongchuan China 26°8N 103°1E 34 D4
Dongfang China 18°50N 108°33E 38 C7
Dongfeng China 42°40N 125°34E 33 C13
Donggala Indonesia 0°30S 119°40E 37 E5
Donggan China 23°22N 105°9E 34 F5
Donggang China 39°52N 124°10E 33 E13
Dongguan China 22°58N 113°44E 35 F9
Dongguang China 37°50N 116°30E 32 F9
Donghae S. Korea 37°29N 129°7E 33 F15
Donghai Dao China 21°0N 110°15E 35 G8
Dongjingcheng China 44°5N 129°10E 33 B15
Dongkou China 27°6N 110°35E 35 D8
Donglan China 24°30N 107°21E 34 E6
Dongliao He → China 42°58N 123°32E 33 C12
Dongliu China 30°13N 116°55E 35 B11
Dongmen China 22°20N 107°48E 34 F6
Dongning China 44°2N 131°5E 33 B16
Dongnyi China 28°3N 100°15E 34 C3
Dongola Sudan 19°9N 30°22E 53 E12
Dongping China 35°55N 116°20E 32 G9
Dongsha Dao S. China Sea 20°45N 116°43E 35 G11
Dongshan China 23°43N 117°30E 35 F11
Dongsheng = Ordos China 39°50N 110°0E 32 E6
Dongtai China 32°51N 120°21E 33 H11
Dongting Hu China 29°18N 112°45E 35 C9
Dongtou China 27°51N 121°10E 35 D13
Dongxiang China 28°11N 116°34E 35 C11
Dongxing China 21°34N 108°0E 34 G7
Dongyang China 29°13N 120°15E 35 C13
Dongying China 37°37N 118°37E 33 F10
Dongyinggang China 37°55N 118°58E 33 F10
Dongzhi China 30°9N 117°0E 35 B11
Donington, C. Australia 34°45S 136°0E 63 E2
Doniphan U.S.A. 36°37N 90°50W 80 G8
Dønna Norway 66°6N 12°30E 8 C15
Donna U.S.A. 26°9N 98°4W 84 H5
Donnaconna Canada 46°41N 71°41W 73 C5
Donnelly's Crossing N.Z. 35°42S 173°38E 59 A4
Donner Pass U.S.A. 39°19N 120°20W 78 F6
Donnybrook Australia 33°34S 115°48E 61 F2
Donnybrook S. Africa 29°59S 29°48E 57 C4
Donora U.S.A. 40°11N 79°52W 82 F5
Donostia = Donostia-San Sebastián Spain 43°17N 1°58W 21 A5
Donostia-San Sebastián Spain 43°17N 1°58W 21 A5
Donwood Canada 44°19N 78°16W 82 B6
Doomadgee Australia 17°56S 138°49E 62 B2
Doomadgee ✪ Australia 17°56S 138°49E 62 B2
Doon → U.K. 55°27N 4°39W 11 F4
Doon Doon ✪ Australia 16°18S 128°14E 60 C4
Dora, L. Australia 22°0S 123°0E 60 D3
Dora Báltea → Italy 45°11N 8°3E 20 D8
Doran L. Canada 61°13N 108°6W 71 A7
Dorchester U.K. 50°42N 2°27W 13 G5
Dorchester, C. Canada 65°27N 77°27W 69 D16
Dordabis Namibia 22°52S 17°38E 56 B2
Dordogne → France 45°2N 0°36W 20 D3
Dordrecht Neths. 51°48N 4°39E 15 C4
Dordrecht S. Africa 31°20S 27°3E 56 D4
Doré L. Canada 54°46N 107°17W 71 C7
Dori Burkina Faso 14°3N 0°2W 52 F5
Doring → S. Africa 31°54S 18°39E 56 D2
Doringbos S. Africa 31°59S 19°16E 56 D2
Dorking U.K. 51°14N 0°19W 13 F7
Dornakal India 17°27N 80°10E 44 F5
Dornbirn Austria 47°25N 9°45E 16 E5
Dornie U.K. 57°17N 5°31W 11 D3
Dornoch Canada 44°18N 80°51W 82 B4
Dornoch U.K. 57°53N 4°2W 11 D4
Dornoch Firth U.K. 57°51N 4°4W 11 D4
Dornogovĭ □ Mongolia 44°0N 110°0E 32 C6
Doro, Kavo Greece 38°9N 24°38E 23 E11
Dorohoi Romania 47°56N 26°23E 17 E14
Döröö Nuur Mongolia 48°0N 93°0E 30 B7
Dorr Iran 33°17N 50°38E 47 C6
Dorre I. Australia 25°13S 113°12E 61 E1
Dorrigo Australia 30°20S 152°44E 63 E5
Dorris U.S.A. 41°58N 121°55W 76 F3
Dorset Canada 45°14N 78°54W 82 A6
Dorset Ohio, U.S.A. 41°40N 80°40W 82 E4
Dorset Vt., U.S.A. 43°15N 73°5W 83 C11
Dorset □ U.K. 50°45N 2°26W 13 G5
Dortmund Germany 51°30N 7°28E 16 C4
Dörtyol Turkey 36°50N 36°13E 46 B3
Dorūneh Iran 35°10N 57°18E 47 C8
Dos Bahías, C. Argentina 44°58S 65°32W 96 E3
Dos Hermanas Spain 37°16N 5°55W 21 D3
Dos Palos U.S.A. 36°59N 120°37W 78 J6
Dosso Niger 13°0N 3°13E 52 F6
Dothan U.S.A. 31°13N 85°24W 85 F12
Doty U.S.A. 46°38N 123°17W 78 D3
Douai France 50°21N 3°4E 20 A5
Douala Cameroon 4°0N 9°45E 54 D1
Douarnenez France 48°6N 4°21W 20 B1
Double Island Pt. Australia 25°56S 153°11E 63 D5
Double Mountain Fork → U.S.A. 33°16N 100°0W 84 E4
Doubs → France 46°53N 5°1E 20 C6
Doubtful Sd. N.Z. 45°20S 166°49E 59 F1
Doubtless B. N.Z. 34°55S 173°26E 59 A4
Douglas Canada 45°31N 76°56W 82 A8
Douglas I. of Man 54°10N 4°28W 12 C3
Douglas S. Africa 29°4S 23°46E 56 C3
Douglas Ariz., U.S.A. 31°21N 109°33W 77 L9
Douglas Ga., U.S.A. 31°31N 82°51W 85 F13
Douglas Wyo., U.S.A. 42°45N 105°24W 76 E11
Douglas Apsley △ Australia 41°45S 148°11E 63 G4
Douglas Chan. Canada 53°40N 129°20W 70 C3
Douglas Pt. Canada 44°19N 81°37W 82 B3
Douglasville U.S.A. 33°45N 84°45W 85 E12
Doumen China 22°10N 113°18E 35 F9
Dounreay U.K. 58°35N 3°44W 11 C5
Dourada, Serra Brazil 13°10S 48°45W 93 F9
Dourados Brazil 22°9S 54°50W 95 A5
Dourados → Brazil 21°58S 54°18W 95 A5
Dourados, Serra dos Brazil 23°30S 53°30W 95 A5
Douro → Europe 41°8N 8°40W 21 B1
Dove → U.K. 52°51N 1°36W 12 E6
Dove Creek U.S.A. 37°46N 108°54W 77 H9
Dover Australia 43°18S 147°2E 63 G4
Dover U.K. 51°7N 1°19E 13 F9
Dover Del., U.S.A. 39°10N 75°32W 81 F16
Dover N.H., U.S.A. 43°12N 70°56W 83 C14
Dover N.J., U.S.A. 40°53N 74°34W 83 F10
Dover Ohio, U.S.A. 40°32N 81°29W 82 F3
Dover, Pt. Australia 32°32S 125°32E 61 F4
Dover, Str. of Europe 51°0N 1°30E 13 G9
Dover-Foxcroft U.S.A. 45°11N 69°13W 81 C19
Dover Plains U.S.A. 41°43N 73°35W 83 E11
Dovey = Dyfi → U.K. 52°32N 4°3W 13 E3
Dovrefjell Norway 62°15N 9°33E 8 E13
Dovrefjell-Sunndalsfjella △ Norway 62°23N 9°11E 8 E13
Dow Rūd Iran 33°28N 49°4E 47 C6
Dowagiac U.S.A. 41°59N 86°6W 80 E10
Dowerin Australia 31°12S 117°2E 61 F2
Dowgha'i Iran 36°54N 58°32E 47 B8
Dowlatābād Kermān, Iran 28°20N 56°40E 47 D8
Dowlatābād Khorāsān, Iran 35°16N 59°29E 47 C8
Down □ U.K. 54°23N 6°2W 10 B5
Downey U.S.A. 42°26N 112°7W 76 E7
Downham Market U.K. 52°37N 0°23E 13 E8
Downieville U.S.A. 39°34N 120°50W 78 F6
Downpatrick U.K. 54°20N 5°43W 10 B6
Downpatrick Hd. Ireland 54°20N 9°21W 10 B2
Downsville U.S.A. 42°5N 75°0W 83 D10
Downton, Mt. Canada 52°42N 124°52W 70 C4
Dowsārī Iran 28°25N 57°59E 47 D8
Doyle U.S.A. 40°2N 120°6W 78 E6
Doylestown U.S.A. 40°21N 75°10W 83 F9
Dozois, Rés. Canada 47°30N 77°5W 72 C4
Dra Khel Pakistan 27°58N 66°45E 42 F2
Drâa, C. Morocco 28°47N 11°0W 52 C3
Drâa, Hamada du Algeria 28°0N 7°0W 52 C4
Drâa, Oued → Morocco 28°40N 11°10W 52 C3
Drachten Neths. 53°7N 6°5E 15 A6
Drăgăşani Romania 44°39N 24°17E 17 F13
Dragichyn Belarus 52°15N 25°8E 17 B13
Dragoman, Prokhod Bulgaria 42°58N 22°53E 23 C10
Dragon's Mouths Trin. & Tob. 11°0N 61°50W 93 K15
Draguignan France 43°32N 6°27E 20 E7
Drain U.S.A. 43°40N 123°19W 76 E2
Drake U.S.A. 47°55N 100°23W 80 B3
Drake Passage S. Ocean 58°0S 68°0W 5 B17
Drakensberg S. Africa 31°0S 28°0E 57 D4
Drama Greece 41°9N 24°10E 23 D11
Drammen Norway 59°42N 10°12E 9 G14
Drangajökull Iceland 66°9N 22°15W 8 C2
Dras India 34°25N 75°48E 43 B6
Drau = Drava → Croatia 45°33N 18°55E 23 B8
Drava → Croatia 45°33N 18°55E 23 B8
Drayton Canada 43°46N 80°40W 82 C4
Drayton Valley Canada 53°12N 114°58W 70 C6
Drenthe □ Neths. 52°52N 6°40E 15 B6
Dresden Canada 42°35N 82°11W 82 D2
Dresden Germany 51°3N 13°44E 16 C7
Dresden U.S.A. 42°41N 76°57W 82 D8
Dreux France 48°44N 1°23E 20 B4
Driffield U.K. 54°0N 0°26W 12 C7
Driftwood U.S.A. 41°20N 78°8W 82 E6
Driggs U.S.A. 43°44N 111°6W 76 E8
Drin → Albania 42°1N 19°38E 23 C8
Drina → Bos.-H. 44°53N 19°21E 23 B8
Drøbak Norway 59°39N 10°39E 9 G14
Drobeta-Turnu Severin Romania 44°39N 22°41E 17 F12
Drochia Moldova 48°2N 27°48E 17 D14
Drogheda Ireland 53°43N 6°22W 10 C5
Drogichin = Dragichyn Belarus 52°15N 25°8E 17 B13
Drogobych = Drohobych Ukraine 49°20N 23°30E 17 D12
Drohobych Ukraine 49°20N 23°30E 17 D12
Droichead Átha = Drogheda Ireland 53°43N 6°22W 10 C5
Droichead na Bandan = Bandon Ireland 51°44N 8°44W 10 E3

Droichead Nua = Newbridge
Ireland 53°11N 6°48W 10 C5
Droitwich U.K. 52°16N 2°8W 13 E5
Drôme → France 44°46N 4°46E 20 D6
Dromedary, C. Australia 36°17S 150°10E 63 F5
Dromore Down, U.K. 54°25N 6°9W 10 B5
Dromore Tyrone, U.K. 54°31N 7°28W 10 B4
Dromore West Ireland 54°15N 8°52W 10 B3
Dronfield U.K. 53°19N 1°27W 12 D6
Dronning Maud Land
Antarctica 72°30S 12°0E 5 D3
Dronten Neths. 52°32N 5°43E 15 B5
Druk Yul = Bhutan ■
Asia 27°25N 90°30E 41 F17
Drumbo Canada 43°16N 80°35W 82 C4
Drumcliff Ireland 54°20N 8°29W 10 B3
Drumheller Canada 51°25N 112°40W 70 C6
Drummond U.S.A. 46°40N 113°9W 76 C7
Drummond I. U.S.A. 46°1N 83°39W 81 B12
Drummond Pt. Australia 34°9S 135°16E 63 E2
Drummond Ra.
Australia 23°45S 147°10E 62 C4
Drummondville Canada 45°55N 72°25W 72 C5
Drumright U.S.A. 35°59N 96°36W 84 D6
Druskininkai Lithuania 54°3N 23°58E 9 J20
Drut → Belarus 53°8N 30°5E 17 B16
Druzhina Russia 68°14N 145°18E 27 C15
Dry Harbour Mts. Jamaica 18°19N 77°24W 88 a
Dry Tortugas U.S.A. 24°38N 82°55W 85 J13
Dryander △ Australia 20°13S 148°34E 62 b
Dryden Canada 49°47N 92°50W 71 D10
Dryden U.S.A. 42°30N 76°18W 83 D8
Drygalski I. Antarctica 66°0S 92°0E 5 C7
Drygalski Ice Tongue
Antarctica 75°24S 163°30E 5 D11
Drysdale → Australia 13°59S 126°51E 60 B4
Drysdale I. Australia 11°41S 136°0E 62 A2
Drysdale River △
Australia 14°56S 127°2E 60 B4
Du Gué → Canada 57°21N 70°45W 72 A5
Du He → China 32°48N 110°40E 35 A8
Du Quoin U.S.A. 38°1N 89°14W 80 G10
Du'an China 23°59N 108°3E 34 F7
Duanesburg U.S.A. 42°45N 74°11W 83 D10
Duaringa Australia 23°42S 149°42E 62 C4
Duarte, Pico Dom. Rep. 19°2N 70°59W 89 D5
Dubãsari Moldova 47°15N 29°10E 17 E15
Dubãsari Vdkhr. Moldova 47°30N 29°0E 17 E15
Dubawnt → Canada 64°33N 100°6W 71 A8
Dubawnt L. Canada 63°8N 101°28W 71 A8
Dubbo Australia 32°11S 148°35E 63 E4
Dublin Ireland 53°21N 6°15W 10 C5
Dublin Ga., U.S.A. 32°32N 82°54W 85 E13
Dublin Tex., U.S.A. 32°5N 98°21W 84 E5
Dublin □ Ireland 53°24N 6°20W 10 C5
Dublin ✈ (DUB) Ireland 53°26N 6°9W 10 C5
Dubno Ukraine 50°25N 25°45E 17 C13
Dubois Idaho, U.S.A. 44°10N 112°14W 76 D7
DuBois Pa., U.S.A. 41°7N 78°46W 82 E6
Dubossary = Dubãsari
Moldova 47°15N 29°10E 17 E15
Dubovka Russia 49°5N 44°50E 19 E7
Dubrajpur India 23°48N 87°25E 43 H12
Dubréka Guinea 9°46N 13°31W 52 G3
Dubrovitsa = Dubrovytsya
Ukraine 51°31N 26°35E 17 C14
Dubrovnik Croatia 42°39N 18°6E 23 C8
Dubrovytsya Ukraine 51°31N 26°35E 17 C14
Dubuque U.S.A. 42°30N 90°41W 80 D8
Duc Tho Vietnam 18°32N 105°35E 38 C5
Duchang China 29°18N 116°12E 35 C11
Duchesne U.S.A. 40°10N 110°24W 76 F8
Duchess Australia 21°20S 139°50E 62 C2
Ducie I. Pac. Oc. 24°40S 124°48W 65 K15
Duck → Canada 36°2N 87°52W 85 C11
Duck Cr. → Australia 22°37S 116°53E 60 D2
Duck Lake Canada 52°50N 106°16W 71 C7
Duck Mountain △
Canada 51°45N 101°0W 71 C8
Duckwall, Mt. U.S.A. 37°58N 120°7W 78 H6
Dudhi India 24°15N 83°10E 43 G10
Dudinka Russia 69°30N 86°13E 27 C9
Dudley U.K. 52°31N 2°5W 13 E5
Dudna → India 19°17N 76°54E 44 E3
Dudwa India 28°30N 80°41E 43 E9
Dudwa → India 28°30N 80°40E 43 E9
Duero = Douro → Europe 41°8N 8°40W 21 B1
Dufftown U.K. 57°27N 3°8W 11 D5
Dugi Otok Croatia 44°0N 15°3E 16 G8
Duisburg Germany 51°26N 6°45E 16 C4
Duiwelskloof = Modjadjiskloof
S. Africa 23°42S 30°10E 57 B5
Dujiangyan China 31°2N 103°38E 34 B4
Dūkdamīn Iran 35°59N 57°43E 47 C8
Dukelský Průsmyk
Slovakia 49°25N 21°42E 17 D11
Dukhān Qatar 25°25N 50°50E 47 E6
Duki Pakistan 30°14N 68°25E 40 D6
Duku Nigeria 10°43N 10°43E 53 F8
Dukuza = Stanger
S. Africa 29°27S 31°14E 57 C5
Dulan China 36°10N 98°0E 30 D8
Dulce U.S.A. 36°56N 107°0W 77 H10
Dulce → Argentina 30°32S 62°33W 94 C3
Dulce, G. Costa Rica 8°40N 83°20W 88 E3
Dulf Iraq 35°7N 45°51E 46 C5
Duliu China 39°2N 116°55E 32 E9
Dulles Int. ✈ (IAD)
U.S.A. 38°57N 77°27W 81 F15
Dullewala Pakistan 31°50N 71°25E 42 D4
Dullstroom S. Africa 25°27S 30°7E 57 C5
Dulq Maghār Syria 36°22N 38°39E 46 B3
Duluth U.S.A. 46°47N 92°6W 80 B7
Dum Duma India 27°40N 95°40E 41 F19
Dūmā Syria 33°34N 36°24E 48 B5
Dumaguete Phil. 9°17N 123°15E 37 C6
Dumai Indonesia 1°35N 101°28E 36 D2
Dumaran Phil. 10°33N 119°50E 37 B5
Dumas Ark., U.S.A. 33°53N 91°29W 84 E9
Dumas Tex., U.S.A. 35°52N 101°58W 84 D4

Dumayr Syria 33°39N 36°42E 48 B5
Dumbarton U.K. 55°57N 4°33W 11 F4
Dumbleyung Australia 33°17S 117°42E 61 F2
Dumfries U.K. 55°4N 3°37W 11 F5
Dumfries & Galloway □
U.K. 55°9N 3°58W 11 F5
Dumka India 24°12N 87°15E 43 G12
Dumoine → Canada 46°13N 77°51W 72 C4
Dumoine, L. Canada 46°55N 77°55W 72 C4
Dumont d'Urville
Antarctica 66°40S 140°0E 5 C10
Dumont d'Urville Sea
S. Ocean 63°30S 138°0E 5 C9
Dumyât Egypt 31°24N 31°48E 53 B12
Dún Dealgan = Dundalk
Ireland 54°1N 6°24W 10 B5
Dún Garbhán = Dungarvan
Ireland 52°5N 7°37W 10 D4
Dún Laoghaire Ireland 53°17N 6°8W 10 C5
Dún Laoghaire-Rathdown □
Ireland 53°14N 6°11W 10 C5
Duna = Dunãrea →
Europe 45°20N 29°40E 17 F15
Dunagiri India 30°31N 79°52E 43 D8
Dunaj = Dunãrea →
Europe 45°20N 29°40E 17 F15
Dunakeszi Hungary 47°37N 19°8E 17 E10
Dunãrea → Europe 45°20N 29°40E 17 F15
Dunaújváros Hungary 46°58N 18°57E 17 E10
Dunav = Dunãrea →
Europe 45°20N 29°40E 17 F15
Dunay Russia 42°52N 132°22E 28 C6
Dunback N.Z. 45°23S 170°36E 59 F3
Dunbar U.K. 56°0N 2°31W 11 E6
Dunblane U.K. 56°11N 3°58W 11 E5
Duncan Canada 48°45N 123°40W 78 B3
Duncan Ariz., U.S.A. 32°43N 109°6W 77 K9
Duncan Okla., U.S.A. 34°30N 97°57W 84 D6
Duncan, L. Canada 53°29N 77°58W 72 B4
Duncan L. Canada 62°51N 113°58W 70 A6
Duncan Passage India 11°0N 92°0E 45 J11
Duncan Town Bahamas 22°15N 75°45W 88 B4
Duncannon U.S.A. 40°23N 77°2W 82 F7
Duncansby Head U.K. 58°38N 3°1W 11 C5
Duncansville U.S.A. 40°25N 78°26W 82 F6
Dund-Us Mongolia 48°1N 91°38E 30 B7
Dundalk Canada 44°10N 80°24W 82 B4
Dundalk Ireland 54°1N 6°24W 10 B5
Dundalk U.S.A. 39°15N 76°31W 81 F15
Dundalk Bay Ireland 53°55N 6°15W 10 C5
Dundas = Uummannaq
Greenland 77°33N 68°52W 69 B18
Dundas Canada 43°17N 79°59W 82 D5
Dundas, L. Australia 32°35S 121°50E 61 F3
Dundas I. Canada 54°30N 130°50W 70 C2
Dundas Str. Australia 11°15S 131°35E 60 B5
Dundee S. Africa 28°11S 30°15E 57 C5
Dundee U.K. 56°28N 2°59W 11 E6
Dundee U.S.A. 42°32N 76°59W 82 D8
Dundee City □ U.K. 56°30N 2°58W 11 E6
Dundgovi □ Mongolia 45°10N 106°0E 32 B4
Dundrum U.K. 54°16N 5°52W 10 B6
Dundrum B. U.K. 54°13N 5°47W 10 B6
Dunedin N.Z. 45°50S 170°33E 59 F3
Dunedin U.S.A. 28°1N 82°46W 85 G13
Dunfanaghy Ireland 55°11N 7°58W 10 A4
Dunfermline U.K. 56°5N 3°27W 11 E5
Dungannon Canada 43°51N 81°36W 82 C3
Dungannon U.K. 54°31N 6°46W 10 B5
Dungarpur India 23°52N 73°45E 42 H5
Dungarvan Ireland 52°5N 7°37W 10 D4
Dungarvan Harbour
Ireland 52°4N 7°35W 10 D4
Dungeness U.K. 50°54N 0°59E 13 G8
Dungiven U.K. 54°56N 6°56W 10 B5
Dungloe Ireland 54°57N 8°21W 10 B3
Dungo, L. do Angola 17°15S 19°0E 56 A2
Dungog Australia 32°22S 151°46E 63 E5
Dungu
Dem. Rep. of the Congo 3°40N 28°32E 54 D5
Dungun Malaysia 4°45N 103°25E 39 K4
Dunhua China 43°20N 128°14E 33 C15
Dunhuang China 40°8N 94°36E 30 C7
Dunk I. Australia 17°59S 146°29E 62 B4
Dunkeld Australia 33°25S 149°29E 63 E4
Dunkeld U.K. 56°34N 3°35W 11 E5
Dunkerque France 51°2N 2°20E 20 A5
Dunkery Beacon U.K. 51°9N 3°36W 13 F4
Dunkirk = Dunkerque
France 51°2N 2°20E 20 A5
Dunkirk U.S.A. 42°29N 79°20W 82 D5
Dunleary = Dún Laoghaire
Ireland 53°17N 6°8W 10 C5
Dunleer Ireland 53°50N 6°24W 10 C5
Dunmanus B. Ireland 51°31N 9°50W 10 E2
Dunmanway Ireland 51°43N 9°6W 10 E2
Dunmarra Australia 16°42S 133°25E 62 B1
Dunmore U.S.A. 41°25N 75°38W 83 E9
Dunmore East Ireland 52°9N 7°0W 10 D5
Dunmore Town
Bahamas 25°30N 76°39W 88 A4
Dunn U.S.A. 35°19N 78°37W 85 D15
Dunnellon U.S.A. 29°3N 82°28W 85 G13
Dunnet Hd. U.K. 58°40N 3°21W 11 C5
Dunning U.S.A. 41°50N 100°6W 80 E3
Dunnolly Australia 36°51S 143°44E 63 F3
Dunoon U.K. 55°57N 4°56W 11 F4
Duns U.K. 55°47N 2°20W 11 F6
Dunseith U.S.A. 48°50N 100°3W 80 A3
Dunshaughlin Ireland 53°31N 6°33W 10 C5
Dunsmuir U.S.A. 41°13N 122°16W 76 F2
Dunstable U.K. 51°53N 0°32W 13 F7
Dunstan Mts. N.Z. 44°53S 169°35E 59 F2
Dunster Canada 53°8N 119°50W 70 C5
Dunvegan U.K. 57°27N 6°35W 11 D2
Dunvegan L. Canada 60°8N 107°10W 71 A7
Duolun China 42°12N 116°28E 32 D9
Duong Dong Vietnam 10°13N 103°58E 39 G4
Dupree U.S.A. 45°4N 101°35W 80 C3

Dupuyer U.S.A. 48°13N 112°30W 76 B7
Durack → Australia 15°33S 127°52E 60 C4
Durack Ra. Australia 16°50S 127°40E 60 C4
Durack River Australia 15°32S 127°39E 60 C4
Durance → France 43°55N 4°45E 20 E6
Durand U.S.A. 44°38N 91°58W 80 C8
Durango Mexico 24°3N 104°39W 86 C4
Durango □ Mexico 24°50N 105°20W 86 C4
Durango U.S.A. 37°16N 107°53W 77 H10
Durant Miss., U.S.A. 33°4N 89°51W 85 E10
Durant Okla., U.S.A. 33°59N 96°25W 84 E6
Durazno Uruguay 33°25S 56°31W 94 C4
Durazzo = Durrës
Albania 41°19N 19°28E 23 D8
Durban S. Africa 29°49S 31°1E 57 C5
Durban ✈ (DUR) S. Africa 29°37S 31°7E 57 C5
Durbuy Belgium 50°21N 5°28E 15 D5
Düren Germany 50°48N 6°29E 16 C4
Durg = Bhilainagar-Durg
India 21°13N 81°26E 44 D5
Durgapur India 23°30N 87°20E 43 H12
Durham Canada 44°10N 80°49W 82 B4
Durham U.K. 54°47N 1°34W 12 C6
Durham Calif., U.S.A. 39°39N 121°48W 78 F5
Durham N.C., U.S.A. 35°59N 78°54W 85 D15
Durham N.H., U.S.A. 43°8N 70°56W 83 C14
Durham □ U.K. 54°42N 1°45W 12 C6
Durlas = Thurles Ireland 52°41N 7°49W 10 D4
Durmã St. Arabia 24°37N 46°8E 46 E5
Durmitor Montenegro 43°10N 19°0E 23 C8
Durness U.K. 58°34N 4°45W 11 C4
Durrës Albania 41°19N 19°28E 23 D8
Durrow Ireland 52°51N 7°24W 10 D4
Dursey I. Ireland 51°36N 10°12W 10 E1
Dursley U.K. 51°40N 2°21W 13 F5
Dursunbey Turkey 39°35N 28°37E 23 E13
Durūz, Jabal ad Jordan 32°35N 36°40E 48 C5
D'Urville, Tanjung
Indonesia 1°28S 137°54E 37 E9
D'Urville I. N.Z. 40°50S 173°55E 59 D4
Duryea U.S.A. 41°20N 75°45W 83 E9
Dushak Turkmenistan 37°13N 60°1E 47 B9
Dushan China 25°48N 107°30E 34 E6
Dushanbe Tajikistan 38°33N 68°48E 26 F7
Dushore U.S.A. 41°31N 76°24W 83 E8
Dusky Sd. N.Z. 45°47S 166°30E 59 F1
Düsseldorf Germany 51°14N 6°47E 16 C4
Dutch Harbor U.S.A. 53°53N 166°32W 74 E6
Dutlwe Botswana 23°58S 23°46E 56 C3
Dutton Canada 42°39N 81°30W 82 D3
Dutton → Australia 20°44S 143°10E 62 C3
Dutywa S. Africa 32°8S 28°18E 57 D4
Duwayhin, Khawr
U.A.E. 24°20N 51°25E 47 E6
Duyfken Pt. Australia 12°33S 141°38E 62 A3
Duyun China 26°18N 107°29E 34 D6
Dvina, Severnaya →
Russia 64°32N 40°30E 18 B7
Dvinsk = Daugavpils
Latvia 55°53N 26°32E 9 J22
Dvinskaya Guba Russia 65°0N 39°0E 18 B6
Dwarka India 22°18N 69°8E 42 H3
Dwellingup Australia 32°43S 116°4E 61 F2
Dwight Canada 45°20N 79°1W 82 A5
Dwight U.S.A. 41°5N 88°26W 80 E9
Dyatlovo = Dzyatlava
Belarus 53°28N 25°28E 17 B13
Dyce U.K. 57°13N 2°12E 11 D6
Dyer, C. Canada 66°37N 61°16W 69 D19
Dyer Bay Canada 45°10N 81°20W 82 A3
Dyer Plateau Antarctica 70°45S 65°30W 5 D17
Dyersburg U.S.A. 36°3N 89°23W 85 C10
Dyfi → U.K. 52°32N 4°3W 13 E3
Dymer Ukraine 50°47N 30°18E 17 C16
Dysart Australia 22°32S 148°23E 62 C4
Dzaoudzi Mayotte 12°47S 45°16E 55 a
Dzavhan Gol →
Mongolia 48°54N 93°23E 30 B7
Dzerzhinsk Russia 56°14N 43°30E 18 C7
Dzhalinda Russia 53°26N 124°0E 27 D13
Dzhambul = Taraz
Kazakhstan 42°54N 71°22E 30 C3
Dzhankoy Ukraine 45°40N 34°20E 19 E5
Dzhezkazgan = Zhezqazghan
Kazakhstan 47°44N 67°40E 26 E7
Dzhizak = Jizzax
Uzbekistan 40°6N 67°50E 26 E7
Dzhugdzur, Khrebet
Russia 57°30N 138°0E 27 D14
Dzhungarskiye Vorota =
Dzungarian Gate Asia 45°10N 82°0E 30 B5
Działdowo Poland 53°15N 20°15E 17 B11
Dzibilchaltún Mexico 21°10N 89°35W 87 C7
Dzierżoniów Poland 50°45N 16°39E 17 C9
Dzilam de Bravo Mexico 21°24N 88°53W 87 C7
Dzükija △ Lithuania 54°10N 24°30E 9 J21
Dzungarian Basin = Junggar Pendi
China 44°30N 86°0E 30 C6
Dzungarian Gate Asia 45°10N 82°0E 30 B5
Dzuumod Mongolia 47°45N 106°58E 30 B10
Dzuunharaa Mongolia 48°52N 106°28E 30 B10
Dzuunmod Mongolia 47°45N 106°58E 30 B10
Dzyarzhynsk Belarus 53°40N 27°1E 17 B14
Dzyatlava Belarus 53°28N 25°28E 17 B13

E

E.C. Manning △ Canada 49°5N 120°45W 70 D4
Eabamet L. Canada 51°30N 87°46W 72 B2
Eabametoong Canada 51°30N 88°0W 72 B2
Éadan Doire = Edenderry
Ireland 53°21N 7°4W 10 C4
Eads U.S.A. 38°29N 102°47W 76 G12
Eagar U.S.A. 34°6N 109°17W 77 J9
Eagle Alaska, U.S.A. 64°47N 141°12W 68 E3
Eagle Colo., U.S.A. 39°39N 106°50W 76 G10
Eagle → Canada 53°36N 57°26W 73 B8
Eagle Butte U.S.A. 45°0N 101°10W 80 C3
Eagle Grove U.S.A. 42°40N 93°54W 80 D7

Eagle L. Canada 49°42N 93°13W 71 D10
Eagle L. Calif., U.S.A. 40°39N 120°45W 76 F3
Eagle L. Maine, U.S.A. 46°20N 69°22W 81 B19
Eagle Lake Canada 45°8N 78°29W 82 A6
Eagle Lake Maine, U.S.A. 47°3N 68°36W 81 B19
Eagle Lake Tex., U.S.A. 29°35N 96°20W 84 G6
Eagle Mountain
U.S.A. 33°49N 115°27W 79 M11
Eagle Nest U.S.A. 36°33N 105°16W 77 H11
Eagle Pass U.S.A. 28°43N 100°30W 84 G4
Eagle Pk. U.S.A. 38°10N 119°25W 78 G7
Eagle River Mich., U.S.A. 47°25N 88°18W 80 B9
Eagle River Wis., U.S.A. 45°55N 89°15W 80 C9
Eaglehawk Australia 36°44S 144°15E 63 F3
Eagles Mere U.S.A. 41°25N 76°33W 83 E8
Ear Falls Canada 50°38N 93°13W 71 C10
Earlimart U.S.A. 35°53N 119°16W 79 K7
Earlville U.S.A. 42°44N 75°32W 83 D9
Earn → U.K. 56°21N 3°18W 11 E5
Earn, L. U.K. 56°23N 4°13W 11 E4
Earnslaw, Mt. N.Z. 44°32S 168°27E 59 F2
Earth U.S.A. 34°14N 102°24W 84 D3
Easley U.S.A. 34°50N 82°36W 85 D13
East Anglia U.K. 52°50N 1°0E 12 E9
East Angus Canada 45°30N 71°40W 73 C5
East Antarctica Antarctica 80°0S 90°0E 5 D7
East Aurora U.S.A. 42°46N 78°37W 82 D6
East Ayrshire □ U.K. 55°26N 4°11W 11 F4
East Bengal Bangla. 24°0N 90°0E 41 G17
East Beskids = Vychodné Beskydy
Europe 49°20N 22°0E 17 D11
East Brady U.S.A. 40°59N 79°37W 82 F5
East Branch Clarion River L.
U.S.A. 41°35N 78°35W 82 E6
East C. = Dezhneva, Mys
Russia 66°5N 169°40W 27 C19
East C. N.Z. 37°42S 178°35E 59 B7
East Caroline Basin
Pac. Oc. 4°0N 146°45E 64 G6
East Chicago U.S.A. 41°38N 87°27W 80 E10
East China Sea Asia 30°0N 126°0E 31 F14
East Coulee Canada 51°23N 112°27W 70 C6
East Dereham = Dereham
U.K. 52°41N 0°57E 13 E8
East Dunbartonshire □
U.K. 55°57N 4°13W 11 F4
East Falkland Falk. Is. 51°30S 58°30W 96 G5
East Grand Forks U.S.A. 47°56N 97°1W 80 B5
East Greenwich U.S.A. 41°40N 71°27W 83 E13
East Grinstead U.K. 51°7N 0°0 13 F8
East Hartford U.S.A. 41°46N 72°39W 83 E12
East Haydon Australia 18°0S 141°30E 62 B3
East Helena U.S.A. 46°35N 111°56W 76 C8
East Indies Asia 0°0 120°0E 24 J14
East Kavango □ Namibia 18°0S 20°15E 56 A3
East Kilbride U.K. 55°47N 4°11W 11 F4
East Lansing U.S.A. 42°44N 84°29W 81 D11
East Liverpool U.S.A. 40°37N 80°35W 82 F4
East London S. Africa 33°0S 27°55E 57 E4
East Lothian □ U.K. 55°58N 2°44W 11 F6
East Main = Eastmain
Canada 52°10N 78°30W 72 B4
East Mariana Basin
Pac. Oc. 12°0N 153°0E 64 F7
East Northport U.S.A. 40°53N 73°19W 83 F11
East Orange U.S.A. 40°46N 74°12W 83 F10
East Pacific Rise Pac. Oc. 15°0S 110°0W 65 J17
East Palestine U.S.A. 40°50N 80°33W 82 F4
East Pine Canada 55°48N 120°12W 70 B4
East Providence U.S.A. 41°49N 71°23W 83 E13
East Pt. Br. Virgin Is. 18°40N 64°18W 89 e
East Pt. Canada 46°27N 61°58W 73 C7
East Renfrewshire □ U.K. 55°46N 4°21W 11 F4
East Retford = Retford
U.K. 53°19N 0°56W 12 D7
East Riding of Yorkshire □
U.K. 53°55N 0°30W 12 D7
East Rochester U.S.A. 43°7N 77°29W 82 C7
East St. Louis U.S.A. 38°37N 90°9W 80 F8
East Schelde = Oosterschelde →
Neths. 51°33N 4°0E 15 C4
East Sea = Japan, Sea of
Asia 40°0N 135°0E 28 E7
East Siberian Sea Russia 73°0N 160°0E 27 B17
East Stroudsburg U.S.A. 41°1N 75°11W 83 E9
East Sussex □ U.K. 50°56N 0°19E 13 G8
East Tasman Plateau
Pac. Oc. 43°30S 152°0E 64 M7
East Tawas U.S.A. 44°17N 83°29W 81 C12
East Timor = Timor-Leste ■
Asia 8°50S 126°0E 37 F7
East Toorale Australia 30°27S 145°28E 63 E4
East Walker → U.S.A. 38°52N 119°10W 78 G7
East Windsor U.S.A. 40°17N 74°34W 83 F10
Eastbourne N.Z. 41°19S 174°55E 59 D5
Eastbourne U.K. 50°46N 0°18E 13 G8
Eastend Canada 49°32N 108°50W 71 D7
Easter Fracture Zone
Pac. Oc. 25°0S 115°0W 65 K16
Easter I. = Pascua, I. de
Chile 27°7S 109°23W 65 K17
Eastern Cape □ S. Africa 32°0S 26°0E 56 E4
Eastern Cr. → Australia 20°40S 141°35E 62 C3
Eastern Desert = Sharqîya, Es
Sahrã esh Egypt 27°30N 32°30E 53 C12
Eastern Ghats India 14°0N 78°50E 45 H4
Eastern Group = Lau Group
Fiji 17°0S 178°30W 59 a
Eastern Guruma ◌
Australia 22°0S 117°30E 60 D2
Eastern Transvaal =
Mpumalanga □ S. Africa 26°0S 30°0E 57 C5
Easterville Canada 53°8N 99°49W 71 C9
Easthampton U.S.A. 42°16N 72°40W 83 D12
Eastlake U.S.A. 41°40N 81°26W 82 E3
Eastleigh U.K. 50°58N 1°21W 13 G6
Eastmain → Canada 52°10N 78°30W 72 B4

Eastmain → Canada 52°27N 78°26W 72 B4
Eastman Canada 45°18N 72°19W 83 A12
Eastman U.S.A. 32°12N 83°11W 85 E13
Easton Md., U.S.A. 38°47N 76°5W 81 F15
Easton Pa., U.S.A. 40°41N 75°13W 83 F9
Easton Wash., U.S.A. 47°14N 121°11W 78 C5
Eastport U.S.A. 44°56N 67°0W 81 C20
Eastsound U.S.A. 48°42N 122°55W 78 B4
Eaton U.S.A. 40°32N 104°42W 76 F11
Eatonia Canada 51°13N 109°25W 71 C7
Eatonton U.S.A. 33°20N 83°23W 85 E13
Eatontown U.S.A. 40°19N 74°4W 83 F10
Eatonville U.S.A. 46°52N 122°16W 78 D4
Eau Claire U.S.A. 44°49N 91°30W 80 C8
Eau Claire, L. à l' Canada 56°10N 74°25W 72 A5
Eauripik Rise Pac. Oc. 2°0N 142°0E 64 G6
Ebano Mexico 22°13N 98°24W 87 C5
Ebbw Vale U.K. 51°46N 3°12W 13 F4
Ebeltoft Denmark 56°12N 10°41E 9 H14
Ebensburg U.S.A. 40°29N 78°44W 82 F6
Eberswalde-Finow
Germany 52°50N 13°49E 16 B7
Ebetsu Japan 43°7N 141°34E 28 C10
Ebey's Landing △
U.S.A. 48°12N 122°41W 78 B4
Ebian China 29°11N 103°13E 34 C4
Ebinur Hu China 44°55N 82°55E 30 C5
Ebolowa Cameroon 2°55N 11°10E 54 D2
Ebonda
Dem. Rep. of the Congo 2°12N 22°21E 54 D4
Ebre = Ebro → Spain 40°43N 0°54E 21 B6
Ebro → Spain 40°43N 0°54E 21 B6
Ecatepec de Morelos
Mexico 19°36N 99°3W 87 D5
Ecbatana = Hamadãn
Iran 34°52N 48°32E 47 C6
Eceabat Turkey 40°11N 26°21E 23 D12
Ech Chéliff Algeria 36°10N 1°20E 52 A6
Echigo-Sammyaku
Japan 36°50N 139°50E 29 F9
Echizen Japan 35°50N 136°10E 29 G8
Echizen-Misaki Japan 35°59N 135°57E 29 G7
Echo Bay N.W.T., Canada 66°5N 117°55W 68 D8
Echo Bay Ont., Canada 46°29N 84°4W 72 C3
Echoing → Canada 55°51N 92°5W 72 B1
Echternach Lux. 49°49N 6°25E 15 E6
Echuca Australia 36°10S 144°45E 63 F3
Écija Spain 37°30N 5°10W 21 D3
Eclipse I. Australia 35°5S 117°58E 61 G2
Eclipse Is. Australia 13°54S 126°19E 60 B4
Eclipse Sd. Canada 72°38N 79°0W 69 C16
Ecuador ■ S. Amer. 2°0S 78°0W 92 D3
Ed Da'ein Sudan 11°26N 26°9E 54 B5
Ed Damazin Sudan 11°46N 34°21E 53 F12
Ed Dâmer Sudan 17°27N 34°0E 53 E12
Ed Dar el Beida = Casablanca
Morocco 33°36N 7°36W 52 B4
Ed Debba Sudan 18°0N 30°51E 53 E12
Ed Déffa Egypt 30°40N 26°30E 53 B11
Ed Dueim Sudan 14°0N 32°10E 53 F12
Edam Canada 53°11N 108°46W 71 C7
Edam Neths. 52°31N 5°3E 15 B5
Edapally India 11°19N 78°3E 45 J4
Eday U.K. 59°11N 2°47W 11 B6
Eddrachillis B. U.K. 58°17N 5°14W 11 C3
Eddystone U.K. 50°11N 4°16W 13 G3
Eddystone Pt. Australia 40°59S 148°20E 63 G4
Ede Neths. 52°4N 5°40E 15 B5
Edehon L. Canada 60°25N 97°15W 71 A9
Eden Australia 37°3S 149°55E 63 F4
Eden N.C., U.S.A. 36°29N 79°53W 85 C15
Eden N.Y., U.S.A. 42°39N 78°55W 82 D6
Eden Tex., U.S.A. 31°13N 99°51W 84 F5
Eden → U.K. 54°57N 3°1W 12 C4
Edenburg S. Africa 29°43S 25°58E 56 D4
Edendale S. Africa 29°39S 30°18E 57 C5
Edenderry Ireland 53°21N 7°4W 10 C4
Edenton U.S.A. 36°4N 76°39W 85 C16
Edenville S. Africa 27°37S 27°34E 57 D4
Eder → Germany 51°12N 9°28E 16 C5
Edfu = Idfû Egypt 24°55N 32°49E 53 D12
Edgar U.S.A. 40°22N 97°58W 80 E5
Edgartown U.S.A. 41°23N 70°31W 83 E14
Edge Hill U.K. 52°8N 1°26W 13 E6
Edgefield U.S.A. 33°47N 81°56W 85 E14
Edgeley U.S.A. 46°22N 98°43W 80 B4
Edgemont U.S.A. 43°18N 103°50W 80 D2
Edgeøya Svalbard 77°45N 22°30E 4 B9
Édhessa = Edessa Greece 40°48N 22°5E 23 D10
Edievale N.Z. 45°49S 169°22E 59 F2
Edina U.S.A. 40°10N 92°11W 80 E7
Edinboro U.S.A. 41°52N 80°8W 82 E4
Edinburg U.S.A. 26°18N 98°10W 84 H5
Edinburgh U.K. 55°57N 3°13W 11 F5
Edinburgh, City of □ U.K. 55°57N 3°17W 11 F5
Edineț Moldova 48°9N 27°18E 17 D14
Edirne Turkey 41°40N 26°34E 23 D12
Edison Australia 38°33N 122°27W 78 B4
Edithburgh Australia 35°5S 137°43E 63 F2
Edmeston U.S.A. 42°42N 75°15W 83 D9
Edmond U.S.A. 35°39N 97°29W 84 D6
Edmonton Australia 17°2S 145°46E 62 B4
Edmonton Canada 53°30N 113°30W 70 C6
Edmund L. Canada 54°45N 93°17W 72 B1
Edmundston Canada 47°23N 68°20W 73 C6
Edna U.S.A. 28°59N 96°39W 84 G6
Edremit Turkey 39°34N 27°0E 23 E12
Edson Canada 53°35N 116°28W 70 C5
Eduardo Castex
Argentina 35°50S 64°18W 94 D3
Eduardo Frei Montalva = Frei
Antarctica 62°30S 58°0W 5 C18
Edward → Australia 35°5S 143°30E 63 F3
Edward, L. Africa 0°25S 29°40E 54 E5
Edward VII Land
Antarctica 80°0S 150°0W 5 E13
Edwards Calif., U.S.A. 34°50N 117°40W 79 L9
Edwards N.Y., U.S.A. 44°20N 75°15W 83 B9

Edwards Plateau *U.S.A.* 30°45N 101°20W **84** F4
Edwardsville *U.S.A.* 41°15N 75°56W **83** E9
Edzná *Mexico* 19°39N 90°19W **87** D6
Edzo = Behchoko *Canada* 62°50N 116°3W **70** A5
Eeklo *Belgium* 51°11N 3°33E **15** C3
Eenhana *Namibia* 17°30S 16°23E **56** A2
Eesti = Estonia ■ *Europe* 58°30N 25°30E **9** G21
Effigy Mounds △ *U.S.A.* 43°5N 91°11W **80** D8
Effingham *U.S.A.* 39°7N 88°33W **80** F9
Égadi, Ísole *Italy* 37°55N 12°16E **22** F5
Egan Range *U.S.A.* 39°35N 114°55W **76** G6
Eganville *Canada* 45°32N 77°5W **82** A7
Eger = Cheb *Czechia* 50°9N 12°28E **16** C7
Eger *Hungary* 47°53N 20°27E **17** E11
Egersund *Norway* 58°26N 6°1E **9** G12
Egg L. *Canada* 55°5N 105°30W **71** B7
Éghezée *Belgium* 50°35N 4°55E **15** D4
Egilsstaðir *Iceland* 65°16N 14°25W **8** D6
Egio *Greece* 38°15N 22°5E **23** E10
Eglinton I. *Canada* 75°48N 118°30W **69** B8
Egmont *Canada* 49°45N 123°56W **70** D4
Egmont, C. *N.Z.* 39°16S 173°45E **59** C4
Egmont, Mt. = Taranaki, Mt.
  *N.Z.* 39°17S 174°5E **59** C5
Egmont △ *N.Z.* 39°17S 174°4E **59** C5
Egra *India* 21°54N 87°32E **43** J12
Eğridir *Turkey* 37°52N 30°51E **19** G5
Eğridir Gölü *Turkey* 37°53N 30°50E **46** B1
Egvekinot *Russia* 66°19N 179°50W **27** C19
Egypt ■ *Africa* 28°0N 31°0E **53** C12
Ehime □ *Japan* 33°30N 132°40E **29** H6
Ehrenberg *U.S.A.* 33°36N 114°31W **79** M12
Eibar *Spain* 43°11N 2°28W **21** A4
Eidsvold *Australia* 25°25S 151°12E **63** D5
Eidsvoll *Norway* 60°19N 11°14E **9** F14
Eielson *U.S.A.* 64°40N 147°4W **74** C10
Eifel *Germany* 50°15N 6°50E **16** C4
Eigg *U.K.* 56°54N 6°10W **11** E2
Eighty Mile Beach
  *Australia* 19°30S 120°40E **60** C3
Eil, L. *U.K.* 56°51N 5°16W **11** E3
Eilat = Elat *Israel* 29°30N 34°56E **48** F3
Eildon, L. *Australia* 37°10S 146°0E **63** F4
Eilean Siar □ *U.K.* 57°30N 7°10W **11** D1
Einasleigh *Australia* 18°32S 144°5E **62** B3
Einasleigh → *Australia* 17°30S 142°17E **62** B3
Eindhoven *Neths.* 51°26N 5°28E **15** C5
Eire = Ireland ■ *Europe* 53°50N 7°52W **10** C4
Eiríksjökull *Iceland* 64°46N 20°24W **8** D3
Eiriosgaigh = Eriskay *U.K.* 57°4N 7°18W **11** D1
Eirunepé *Brazil* 6°35S 69°53W **92** E5
Eiseb → *Namibia* 20°33S 20°59E **56** B2
Eisenach *Germany* 50°58N 10°19E **16** C6
Eisenerz *Austria* 47°32N 14°54E **16** E8
Eivissa *Spain* 38°54N 1°26E **21** C6
Ejutla *Mexico* 16°34N 96°44W **87** D5
Ekalaka *U.S.A.* 45°53N 104°33W **76** D11
Ekaterinburg = Yekaterinburg
  *Russia* 56°50N 60°30E **26** D7
Ekenäs = Raasepori
  *Finland* 60°0N 23°26E **9** G20
Eketahuna *N.Z.* 40°38S 175°43E **59** D5
Ekibastuz *Kazakhstan* 51°50N 75°10E **26** D8
Eksjö *Sweden* 57°40N 14°58E **9** H16
Ekuma → *Namibia* 18°40S 16°2E **56** A2
Ekwan → *Canada* 53°12N 82°15W **72** B3
Ekwan Pt. *Canada* 53°16N 82°7W **72** B3
El Aaiún *W. Sahara* 27°9N 13°12W **52** C3
El Abanico *Chile* 37°20S 71°31W **94** D1
El 'Agrûd *Egypt* 30°14N 34°24E **48** E3
El Alamein *Egypt* 30°48N 28°58E **53** B11
El 'Aqaba, W. → *Egypt* 30°7N 33°54E **48** E2
El Ariha *West Bank* 31°52N 35°27E **48** D4
El 'Arîsh *Egypt* 31°8N 33°50E **48** D2
El 'Arîsh, W. → *Egypt* 31°8N 33°47E **48** D2
El Asnam = Ech Chéliff
  *Algeria* 36°10N 1°20E **52** A6
El Bayadh *Algeria* 33°40N 1°1E **52** B6
El Bluff *Nic.* 11°59N 83°40W **88** D3
El Cajon *U.S.A.* 32°48N 116°58W **79** N10
El Calafate *Argentina* 50°19S 72°15W **96** G2
El Campo *U.S.A.* 29°12N 96°16W **84** G6
El Capitan *U.S.A.* 37°44N 119°38E **78** H7
El Carbón *Honduras* 15°25N 85°32W **88** C2
El Carmen *Colombia* 9°43N 75°8W **92** B3
El Centro *U.S.A.* 32°48N 115°34W **79** N11
El Cerro *Bolivia* 17°30S 61°40W **92** G6
El Compadre *Mexico* 32°20N 116°14W **79** N10
El Cuy *Argentina* 39°55S 68°25W **96** D3
El Cuyo *Mexico* 21°31N 87°41W **87** C7
El Daheir *Egypt* 31°13N 34°10E **48** D3
El Descanso *Mexico* 32°12N 116°58W **79** N10
El Desemboque *Mexico* 30°33N 113°1W **86** A2
El Diviso *Colombia* 1°22N 78°14W **92** C3
El Djouf *Mauritania* 21°25N 6°40W **50** D3
El Dorado *Mexico* 24°17N 107°21W **86** C3
El Dorado *Ark., U.S.A.* 33°12N 92°40W **84** E8
El Dorado *Kans., U.S.A.* 37°49N 96°52W **80** G5
El Dorado *Venezuela* 6°55N 61°37W **92** B6
El Dorado Springs *U.S.A.* 37°52N 94°1W **80** G6
El Escorial *Spain* 40°35N 4°7W **21** B3
El Faiyûm *Egypt* 29°19N 30°50E **53** C12
El Fâsher *Sudan* 13°33N 25°26E **53** F11
El Ferrol = Ferrol *Spain* 43°29N 8°15W **21** A1
El Fuerte *Mexico* 26°25N 108°39W **86** B3
El Geneina = Al Junaynah
  *Sudan* 13°27N 22°45E **53** F10
El Gezira □ *Sudan* 15°0N 33°0E **53** F12
El Gogorrón △ *Mexico* 21°49N 100°57W **86** C4
El Goléa *Algeria* 30°30N 2°50E **52** B6
El Guácharo △ *Venezuela* 10°8N 63°21W **89** D7
El Guache △ *Venezuela* 9°45N 69°30W **89** E6
El Iskandarîya *Egypt* 31°13N 29°58E **53** B11
El Istiwa'iya *Sudan* 5°0N 28°0E **53** G11
El Jadida *Morocco* 33°11N 8°17W **52** B4
El Jardal *Honduras* 14°54N 88°50W **88** D2
El Kef □ *Tunisia* 36°0N 9°0E **53** A7
El Khârga *Egypt* 25°30N 30°33E **53** C12
El Khartûm *Sudan* 15°31N 32°35E **53** E12
El Khartûm Bahrî *Sudan* 15°40N 32°31E **53** E12

El Kuntilla *Egypt* 30°1N 34°45E **48** E3
El Leoncito △ *Argentina* 31°58S 69°10W **94** C2
El Lucero *Mexico* 30°37N 106°31W **86** A3
El Maestrazgo *Spain* 40°30N 0°25W **21** B5
El Mahalla el Kubra *Egypt* 31°0N 31°0E **53** B12
El Malpais △ *U.S.A.* 34°53N 108°0W **77** J10
El Mansûra *Egypt* 31°0N 31°19E **53** B12
El Ménia = El Goléa
  *Algeria* 30°30N 2°50E **52** B6
El Milagro *Argentina* 30°59S 65°59W **94** C2
El Minyâ *Egypt* 28°7N 30°33E **53** C12
El Obeid *Sudan* 13°8N 30°10E **53** F12
El Odaiya *Sudan* 12°8N 28°12E **53** F11
El Oro *Mexico* 19°51N 100°7W **87** D4
El Oued *Algeria* 33°20N 6°58E **52** B7
El Palmar △ *Argentina* 32°10S 58°31W **94** C4
El Paso *U.S.A.* 31°45N 106°29W **84** F1
El Paso de Robles = Paso Robles
  *U.S.A.* 35°38N 120°41W **78** K6
El Pinacate y Gran Desierto de
  Altar = Gran Desierto del
  Pinacate △ *Mexico* 31°51N 113°32W **86** A2
El Portal *U.S.A.* 37°41N 119°47W **78** H7
El Porvenir *Mexico* 31°15N 105°51W **86** A3
El Progreso *Honduras* 15°26N 87°51W **88** C2
El Puerto de Santa María
  *Spain* 36°36N 6°13W **21** D2
El Qantara *Egypt* 30°51N 32°20E **48** E1
El Quseima *Egypt* 30°40N 34°15E **48** E3
El Real de Santa María
  *Panama* 8°0N 77°40W **92** B3
El Reno *U.S.A.* 35°32N 97°57W **75** H6
El Rey △ *Argentina* 24°40S 64°34W **94** A3
El Río *U.S.A.* 34°14N 119°10W **79** L7
El Rosario *Mexico* 30°1N 115°45W **86** A1
El Salto *Mexico* 23°47N 105°22W **86** C3
El Salvador ■ *Cent. Amer.* 13°50N 89°0W **88** D2
El Sauce *Nic.* 13°0N 86°40W **88** D2
El Suweis *Egypt* 29°58N 32°31E **53** C12
El Tamarani, W. → *Egypt* 30°7N 34°43E **48** E3
El Thamad *Egypt* 29°40N 34°28E **48** F3
El Tigre *Venezuela* 8°44N 64°15W **92** B6
El Tîh, Gebel *Egypt* 29°40N 33°50E **48** F2
El Tofo *Chile* 29°22S 71°18W **94** B1
El Tránsito *Chile* 28°52S 70°17W **94** B1
El Tûr *Egypt* 28°14N 33°36E **46** D2
El Turbio *Argentina* 51°45S 72°5W **96** G2
El Uqsur *Egypt* 25°41N 32°38E **53** C12
El Vergel *Mexico* 26°28N 106°22W **86** B3
El Vigía *Venezuela* 8°38N 71°39W **92** B4
El Wabeira *Egypt* 29°34N 33°6E **48** F2
El Wuz *Sudan* 15°5N 30°7E **53** E12
Elamanchili *India* 17°33N 82°50E **44** F6
Elat *Israel* 29°30N 34°56E **48** F3
Elâzığ *Turkey* 38°37N 39°14E **46** B3
Elba *Italy* 42°46N 10°17E **22** C4
Elba *U.S.A.* 31°25N 86°4W **85** F11
Elbasan *Albania* 41°9N 20°9E **23** D9
Elbe *U.S.A.* 46°45N 122°10W **78** D4
Elbe → *Europe* 53°50N 9°0E **16** B5
Elbert, Mt. *U.S.A.* 39°7N 106°27W **76** G10
Elberton *U.S.A.* 34°7N 82°52W **85** D13
Elbeuf *France* 49°17N 1°2E **20** B4
Elbing = Elbląg *Poland* 54°10N 19°25E **17** A10
Elbistan *Turkey* 38°13N 37°15E **46** B3
Elbląg *Poland* 54°10N 19°25E **17** A10
Elbow *Canada* 51°7N 106°35W **71** C7
Elbrus *Russia* 43°21N 42°30E **19** F7
Elburz Mts. = Alborz, Reshteh-ye
  Kūhhā-ye *Iran* 36°0N 52°0E **47** C7
Elche *Spain* 38°15N 0°42W **21** C5
Elcho I. *Australia* 11°55S 135°45E **62** A2
Elda *Spain* 38°29N 0°47W **21** C5
Elde → *Germany* 53°7N 11°15E **16** B6
Eldon *Mo., U.S.A.* 38°21N 92°35W **80** F7
Eldon *Wash., U.S.A.* 47°33N 123°3W **78** C3
Eldora *U.S.A.* 42°22N 93°5W **80** D7
Eldorado *Argentina* 26°28S 54°43W **95** B5
Eldorado *Canada* 44°35N 77°31W **82** B7
Eldorado *Ill., U.S.A.* 37°49N 88°26W **80** G9
Eldorado *Tex., U.S.A.* 30°52N 100°36W **84** F4
Eldoret *Kenya* 0°30N 35°17E **54** D7
Eldred *U.S.A.* 41°58N 78°23W **82** E6
Eleanora, Pk. *Australia* 32°57S 121°9E **61** F3
Elefantes → *Africa* 24°10S 32°40E **57** B5
Elektrostal *Russia* 55°41N 38°32E **18** C6
Elemi Triangle = Ilemi Triangle
  *Africa* 5°0N 35°20E **54** D7
Elephant Butte Res.
  *U.S.A.* 33°9N 107°11W **77** K10
Elephant I. *Antarctica* 61°0S 55°0W **5** C18
Elephant Pass *Sri Lanka* 9°35N 80°25E **45** K5
Eleuthera I. *Bahamas* 25°0N 76°20W **88** B4
Elgin *Canada* 44°36N 76°13W **83** B8
Elgin *U.K.* 57°39N 3°19W **11** D5
Elgin *Ill., U.S.A.* 42°2N 88°17W **80** D9
Elgin *N. Dak., U.S.A.* 46°24N 101°51W **80** B3
Elgin *Oreg., U.S.A.* 45°34N 117°55W **76** D5
Elgin *Tex., U.S.A.* 30°21N 97°22W **84** F6
Elgon, Mt. *Africa* 1°10N 34°30E **54** D6
Elhovo *Bulgaria* 42°10N 26°35E **23** C12
Eliase *Indonesia* 8°21S 130°48E **37** F8
Elim *Namibia* 17°48S 15°31E **56** A2
Elim *S. Africa* 34°35S 19°45E **56** E2
Elista *Russia* 46°16N 44°14E **19** E7
Elizabeth *Australia* 34°42S 138°41E **63** E2
Elizabeth *U.S.A.* 40°39N 74°13W **83** F10
Elizabeth City *U.S.A.* 36°18N 76°14W **85** C16
Elizabethton *U.S.A.* 36°21N 82°13W **85** C13
Elizabethtown *Ky..*
  *U.S.A.* 37°42N 85°52W **81** G11
Elizabethtown *N.Y.,*
  *U.S.A.* 44°13N 73°36W **83** B11
Elizabethtown *Pa., U.S.A.* 40°9N 76°36W **83** F8
Elk *Poland* 53°50N 22°21E **17** B12
Elk → *Canada* 49°11N 115°14W **70** D5
Elk → *U.S.A.* 34°46N 87°16W **85** D11
Elk City *U.S.A.* 35°25N 99°25W **84** D5
Elk Creek *U.S.A.* 39°36N 122°32W **78** F4
Elk Grove *U.S.A.* 38°25N 121°22W **78** G5

Elk Island △ *Canada* 53°35N 112°59W **70** C6
Elk Lake *Canada* 47°40N 80°25W **72** C3
Elk Point *Canada* 53°54N 110°55W **71** C6
Elk River *Idaho, U.S.A.* 46°47N 116°11W **76** C5
Elk River *Minn., U.S.A.* 45°18N 93°35W **80** C7
Elkedra → *Australia* 21°8S 136°22E **62** C2
Elkhart *Ind., U.S.A.* 41°41N 85°58W **81** E11
Elkhart *Kans., U.S.A.* 37°0N 101°54W **80** G3
Elkhorn *Canada* 49°59N 101°14W **71** D8
Elkhorn → *U.S.A.* 41°8N 96°19W **80** E6
Elkin *U.S.A.* 36°15N 80°51W **85** C14
Elkins *U.S.A.* 38°55N 79°51W **81** F14
Elkland *U.S.A.* 41°59N 77°19W **82** E7
Elko *Canada* 49°20N 115°10W **70** D5
Elko *U.S.A.* 40°50N 115°46W **76** F6
Elkton *U.S.A.* 43°49N 83°11W **82** C1
Ellas = Greece ■ *Europe* 40°0N 23°0E **23** E9
Ellef Ringnes I. *Canada* 78°30N 102°2W **69** B11
Ellen, Mt. *U.S.A.* 44°9N 72°56W **83** B12
Ellenburg *U.S.A.* 44°54N 73°48W **83** B11
Ellendale *U.S.A.* 46°0N 98°32W **80** B4
Ellensburg *U.S.A.* 46°59N 120°34W **76** C3
Ellenville *U.S.A.* 41°43N 74°24W **83** E10
Ellerton *Barbados* 13°7N 59°33W **89** g
Ellery, Mt. *Australia* 37°28S 148°47E **63** F4
Ellesmere, L. *N.Z.* 43°47S 172°28E **59** G4
Ellesmere I. *Canada* 79°30N 80°0W **69** B16
Ellesmere Port *U.K.* 53°17N 2°54W **12** D5
Ellice Is. = Tuvalu ■
  *Pac. Oc.* 8°0S 178°0E **58** B10
Ellicottville *U.S.A.* 42°17N 78°40W **82** D6
Ellington *U.S.A.* 42°13N 79°6W **82** D5
Elliot *Australia* 17°33S 133°32E **62** B1
Elliot *S. Africa* 31°22S 27°48E **57** D4
Elliot Lake *Canada* 46°25N 82°35W **72** C3
Elliotdale = Xhora
  *S. Africa* 31°55S 28°38E **57** D4
Ellis *U.S.A.* 38°56N 99°34W **80** F4
Elliston *Australia* 33°39S 134°53E **63** E1
Ellisville *U.S.A.* 31°36N 89°12W **85** F10
Ellon *U.K.* 57°22N 2°4W **11** D6
Ellora *India* 20°1N 75°10E **44** D2
Ellore = Eluru *India* 16°48N 81°8E **44** F5
Ellsworth *Kans., U.S.A.* 38°44N 98°14W **80** F4
Ellsworth *Maine, U.S.A.* 44°33N 68°25W **81** C19
Ellsworth Land *Antarctica* 76°0S 89°0W **5** D16
Ellsworth Mts. *Antarctica* 78°30S 85°0W **5** D16
Ellwood City *U.S.A.* 40°52N 80°17W **82** F4
Elma *Canada* 49°52N 95°55W **71** D9
Elma *U.S.A.* 47°0N 123°25W **78** D3
Elmali *Turkey* 36°44N 29°56E **19** G4
Elmhurst *U.S.A.* 41°53N 87°56W **80** E10
Elmira *Canada* 43°36N 80°33W **82** C4
Elmira *U.S.A.* 42°6N 76°48W **82** D8
Elmira Heights *U.S.A.* 42°8N 76°50W **82** D8
Elmore *Australia* 36°30S 144°37E **63** F3
Elmshorn *Germany* 53°43N 9°40E **16** B5
Elmvale *Canada* 44°35N 79°52W **82** B5
Elora *Canada* 43°41N 80°26W **82** C4
Eloy *U.S.A.* 32°45N 111°33W **77** K8
Elphin *Canada* 44°55N 76°37W **83** B8
Elpitiya *Sri Lanka* 6°17N 80°10E **45** L5
Elrose *Canada* 51°12N 108°0W **71** C7
Elsby △ *Australia* 14°55S 133°10E **60** B5
Elsie *U.S.A.* 45°52N 123°36W **78** E3
Elsinore = Helsingør
  *Denmark* 56°2N 12°35E **9** H15
Eltanin Fracture Zone System
  *S. Ocean* 54°0S 130°0W **5** B14
Eltham *N.Z.* 39°26S 174°19E **59** C5
Eluru *India* 16°48N 81°8E **44** F5
Elvas *Portugal* 38°50N 7°10W **21** C2
Elverum *Norway* 60°53N 11°34E **8** F14
Elvire → *Australia* 17°51S 128°11E **60** C4
Elvire, Mt. *Australia* 29°22S 119°36E **61** E2
Elwell, L. = Tiber Res.
  *U.S.A.* 48°19N 111°6W **76** B8
Elwood *Ind., U.S.A.* 40°17N 85°50W **81** E11
Elwood *Nebr., U.S.A.* 40°36N 99°52W **80** E4
Elx = Elche *Spain* 38°15N 0°42W **21** C5
Ely *U.K.* 52°24N 0°16E **13** E8
Ely *Minn., U.S.A.* 47°55N 91°51W **80** B8
Ely *Nev., U.S.A.* 39°15N 114°54W **76** G6
Elyria *U.S.A.* 41°22N 82°7W **82** E2
eMakhazeni *S. Africa* 25°42S 30°2E **57** C5
eMalahleni *S. Africa* 25°51S 29°14E **57** C4
Emāmrūd *Iran* 36°30N 55°0E **47** B7
eMbalenhle *S. Africa* 26°32S 29°4E **57** C4
Embarcación *Argentina* 23°10S 64°0W **94** A3
Embetsu *Japan* 44°44N 141°47E **28** B10
Embi *Kazakhstan* 48°50N 58°8E **26** E6
Embi → *Kazakhstan* 46°55N 53°28E **19** E9
Embro *Canada* 43°9N 80°54W **82** C4
Embrun *France* 44°34N 6°30E **20** D7
Emden *Germany* 53°21N 7°12E **16** B4
Emei Shan *China* 29°32N 103°46E **34** C4
Emeishan *China* 29°31N 103°23E **34** C4
Emerald *Australia* 23°32S 148°10E **62** C4
Emerald △ *U.S.A.* 76°48N 114°10W **81** F8
Emerson *Canada* 49°0N 97°10W **71** D9
Emet *Turkey* 39°20N 29°15E **23** E13
Emgwenya *S. Africa* 25°45S 30°18E **57** C5
Emi Koussi *Chad* 19°45N 18°55E **53** E9
Emine, Nos *Bulgaria* 42°2N 74°8E **42** C2
Emissi, Tarso *Chad* 21°27N 18°36E **53** D9
Emlenton *U.S.A.* 41°11N 79°43W **82** E5
Emmaus *U.S.A.* 40°32N 75°30W **83** F9
Emmeloord *Neths.* 52°44N 5°46E **15** B5
Emmen *Neths.* 52°48N 6°57E **15** B6
Emmet *Australia* 24°45S 144°30E **62** C3
Emmetsburg *U.S.A.* 43°7N 94°41W **80** D6
Emmett *Idaho, U.S.A.* 43°52N 116°30W **76** E5
Emmett *Mich., U.S.A.* 42°59N 82°46W **82** D2
Emmonak *U.S.A.* 62°47N 164°31W **74** C7

Emo *Canada* 48°38N 93°50W **71** D10
Empalme *Mexico* 27°58N 110°51W **86** B2
Empangeni *S. Africa* 28°50S 31°52E **57** C5
Empedrado *Argentina* 28°0S 58°46W **94** B4
Emperor Seamount Chain
  *Pac. Oc.* 40°0N 170°0E **64** D9
Emperor Trough *Pac. Oc.* 43°0N 175°30E **64** D9
Emporia *Kans., U.S.A.* 38°25N 96°11W **80** F5
Emporia *Va., U.S.A.* 36°42N 77°32W **81** G15
Emporium *U.S.A.* 41°31N 78°14W **82** E6
Empress *Canada* 50°57N 110°0W **71** C7
Empty Quarter = Rub' al Khālī
  *Si. Arabia* 19°0N 48°0E **49** D4
Ems → *Germany* 53°20N 7°12E **16** B4
Emsdale *Canada* 45°32N 79°19W **82** A5
Emu *China* 43°40N 128°6E **33** C15
Emu Park *Australia* 23°13S 150°50E **62** C5
'En 'Avrona *Israel* 29°43N 35°0E **48** F4
'En Bōqeq *Israel* 31°12N 35°21E **47** D4
'En Gedi *Israel* 31°28N 35°23E **47** D4
En Nahud *Sudan* 12°45N 28°25E **53** F11
Ena *Japan* 35°25N 137°25E **29** G8
Enard B. *U.K.* 58°5N 5°20W **11** C3
Enare träsk = Inarijärvi
  *Finland* 69°0N 28°0E **8** B23
Enarotali *Indonesia* 3°55S 136°21E **37** E9
Encampment *U.S.A.* 41°12N 106°47W **76** F10
Encantadas, Serra *Brazil* 30°40S 53°0W **95** C5
Encarnación *Paraguay* 27°15S 55°50W **95** B4
Encarnación de Díaz
  *Mexico* 21°31N 102°14W **86** C4
Encinitas *U.S.A.* 33°3N 117°17W **79** M9
Encino *U.S.A.* 34°39N 105°28W **77** J11
Encounter B. *Australia* 35°45S 138°45E **63** F2
Endako *Canada* 54°6N 125°2W **70** C3
Endau Rompin △
  *Malaysia* 2°27N 103°45E **39** L4
Ende *Indonesia* 8°45S 121°40E **37** F6
Endeavour Str. *Australia* 10°45S 142°0E **62** A3
Enderbury *Kiribati* 3°8S 171°5W **64** H10
Enderby *Canada* 50°35N 119°10W **70** C5
Enderby Abyssal Plain
  *S. Ocean* 60°0S 40°0E **5** C5
Enderby I. *Australia* 20°35S 116°30E **60** D2
Enderby Land *Antarctica* 66°0S 53°0E **5** C5
Enderlin *U.S.A.* 46°38N 97°36W **80** B5
Endicott *U.S.A.* 42°6N 76°4W **83** D8
Endicott Mts. *U.S.A.* 68°0N 152°0W **74** B9
Endwell *U.S.A.* 42°6N 76°2W **83** D8
Endyalgout I. *Australia* 11°40S 132°35E **60** B5
Eneabba *Australia* 29°49S 115°16E **61** E2
Enewetak Atoll
  *Marshall Is.* 11°30N 162°15E **64** F8
Enez *Turkey* 40°45N 26°5E **23** D12
Enfer, Pte. d' *Martinique* 14°22N 60°54W **88** c
Enfield *Canada* 44°56N 63°32W **73** D7
Enfield *Conn., U.S.A.* 41°58N 72°36W **83** E12
Enfield *N.C., U.S.A.* 36°11N 77°41W **85** C16
Enfield *N.H., U.S.A.* 43°39N 72°9W **83** C12
Engadin *Switz.* 46°45N 10°10E **20** C9
Engaño, C. *Dom. Rep.* 18°30N 68°20W **89** C6
Engaño, C. *Phil.* 18°35N 122°23E **37** A6
Engaru *Japan* 44°3N 143°31E **28** B11
Engcobo = Ngcobo
  *S. Africa* 31°37S 28°0E **57** D4
Engels *Russia* 51°28N 46°6E **19** D8
Engemann L. *Canada* 58°0N 106°55W **71** B7
Enggano *Indonesia* 5°20S 102°40E **36** F2
England *N.Z.* 34°33N 91°58W **84** D9
England □ *U.K.* 53°0N 2°0W **13** E5
Englee *Canada* 50°45N 56°5W **73** B8
Englehart *Canada* 47°49N 79°52W **72** C4
English → *Canada* 49°12N 91°5W **71** C10
English Bazar = Ingraj Bazar
  *India* 24°58N 88°10E **43** G13
English Channel *Europe* 50°0N 2°0W **13** G6
English Company's Is., The
  *Australia* 11°50S 136°32E **62** A2
English River *Canada* 49°14N 91°0W **72** C1
Enid *U.S.A.* 36°24N 97°53W **84** C6
Eniwa *Japan* 42°53N 141°35E **28** C10
Enkhuizen *Neths.* 52°42N 5°17E **15** B5
Enle *China* 24°0N 101°9E **34** F3
Enna *Italy* 37°34N 14°16E **22** F6
Ennadai L. *Canada* 60°58N 101°20W **71** A8
Ennedi *Chad* 17°15N 22°0E **53** E10
Enngonia *Australia* 29°21S 145°50E **63** D4
Ennis *Ireland* 52°51N 8°59W **10** D3
Ennis *Mont., U.S.A.* 45°21N 111°44W **76** D8
Ennis *Tex., U.S.A.* 32°20N 96°38W **84** E6
Enniscorthy *Ireland* 52°30N 6°34W **10** D5
Enniskillen *U.K.* 54°21N 7°39W **10** B4
Ennistymon *Ireland* 52°57N 9°17W **10** D2
Enns → *Austria* 48°14N 14°32E **16** D8
Eno *Finland* 62°47N 30°10E **8** E24
Enosburg Falls *U.S.A.* 44°55N 72°48W **83** B12
Enping *China* 22°16N 112°21E **35** F9
Enriquillo, L. *Dom. Rep.* 18°20N 71°40W **89** C5
Enschede *Neths.* 52°13N 6°53E **15** B6
Ensenada *Argentina* 34°55S 57°55W **94** C4
Ensenada *Mexico* 31°52N 116°37W **86** A1
Ensenada de los Muertos
  *Mexico* 23°59N 109°51W **86** C2
Enshi *China* 30°18N 109°29E **35** B8
Entebbe *Uganda* 0°4N 32°28E **54** D6
Enterprise *Canada* 60°47N 115°45W **70** A5
Enterprise *Ala., U.S.A.* 31°19N 85°51W **85** F12
Enterprise *Oreg., U.S.A.* 45°25N 117°17W **76** D5
Entiako △ *Canada* 53°28N 125°9W **70** C3
Entre Ríos *Bolivia* 21°30S 64°25W **94** A3
Entre Ríos □ *Argentina* 30°30S 58°30W **94** C4
Entroncamento *Portugal* 39°28N 8°28W **21** C1
Enugu *Nigeria* 6°30N 7°30E **52** G7
Enumclaw *U.S.A.* 47°12N 121°59W **78** C5
Eochaill = Youghal
  *Ireland* 51°56N 7°52W **10** E4
Éolie, Ís. *Italy* 38°30N 14°57E **22** E6
Epe *Neths.* 52°21N 5°59E **15** B5
Épernay *France* 49°3N 3°56E **20** B5

Ephesus *Turkey* 37°55N 27°22E **23** F12
Ephraim *U.S.A.* 39°22N 111°35W **76** G8
Ephrata *Pa., U.S.A.* 40°11N 76°11W **83** F8
Ephrata *Wash., U.S.A.* 47°19N 119°33W **76** C4
Epinal *France* 48°10N 6°27E **20** B7
Epsom *U.K.* 51°19N 0°16W **13** F7
Epukiro *Namibia* 21°40S 19°9E **56** B2
Equatoria = El Istiwa'iya
  *Sudan* 5°0N 28°0E **53** G11
Equatorial Guinea ■ *Africa* 2°0N 8°0E **54** D1
Er Hai *China* 25°48N 100°11E **34** E3
Er Rachidia *Morocco* 31°58N 4°20W **52** B5
Er Rahad *Sudan* 12°45N 30°32E **53** F12
Er Rif *Morocco* 35°1N 4°1W **52** A5
Erandol *India* 20°56N 75°20E **44** D2
Erāwadī Myit = Ayeyawadi →
  *Myanmar* 15°50N 95°6E **41** M19
Erāwadī Myitwanya = Irrawaddy,
  Mouths of the
  *Myanmar* 15°30N 95°0E **41** M19
Erawan △ *Thailand* 14°25N 98°58E **38** E2
Erçek *Turkey* 38°39N 43°36E **46** B4
Erciyaş Dağı *Turkey* 38°30N 35°30E **46** B2
Érd *Hungary* 47°22N 18°56E **17** E10
Erdao Jiang → *China* 42°37N 128°0E **33** C14
Erdek *Turkey* 40°23N 27°47E **23** D12
Erdene = Ulaan-Uul
  *Mongolia* 46°4N 100°49E **30** B9
Erdenet *Mongolia* 49°2N 104°5E **30** B9
Erdenetsogt *Mongolia* 42°55N 106°5E **32** C4
Erebus, Mt. *Antarctica* 77°35S 167°0E **5** D11
Erechim *Brazil* 27°35S 52°15W **95** B5
Ereğli *Konya, Turkey* 37°31N 34°4E **46** B2
Ereğli *Zonguldak, Turkey* 41°15N 31°24E **19** F5
Erenhot *China* 43°48N 112°2E **32** C7
Eresma → *Spain* 41°26N 4°45W **21** B3
Erfenisdam *S. Africa* 28°30S 26°50E **56** D4
Erfurt *Germany* 50°58N 11°2E **16** C6
Ergani *Turkey* 38°17N 39°49E **46** B3
Ergel *Mongolia* 43°8N 109°5E **32** C5
Ergeni Vozvyshennost
  *Russia* 47°0N 44°0E **19** E7
Ergli *Latvia* 56°54N 25°38E **9** H21
Ergun He = Argun →
  *Russia* 53°20N 121°28E **31** A13
Ergun Youqi *China* 50°15N 120°11E **31** A13
Erhlin *Taiwan* 23°54N 120°22E **35** F13
Eriboll, L. *U.K.* 58°30N 4°42W **11** C4
Érice *Italy* 38°2N 12°35E **22** E5
Erie *U.S.A.* 42°8N 80°5W **82** D4
Erie, L. *N. Amer.* 42°15N 81°0W **82** D4
Erie Canal *U.S.A.* 43°5N 78°43W **82** C7
Erieau *Canada* 42°16N 81°57W **82** D3
Erigavo = Ceerigaabo
  *Somalia* 10°35N 47°20E **49** E4
Eriksdale *Canada* 50°52N 98°7W **71** C9
Erimanthos *Greece* 37°57N 21°50E **23** F9
Erimo-Misaki *Japan* 41°50N 143°15E **28** D11
Erin *Canada* 43°45N 80°7W **82** C5
Erin Pt. *Trin. & Tob.* 10°3N 61°39W **93** K15
Erinpura *India* 25°9N 73°3E **42** G5
Eriskay *U.K.* 57°4N 7°18W **11** D1
Eritrea ■ *Africa* 14°0N 38°30E **49** E2
Erlangen *Germany* 49°36N 11°0E **16** D6
Erldunda *Australia* 25°14S 133°12E **62** D1
Ermelo *Neths.* 52°18N 5°35E **15** B5
Ermelo *S. Africa* 26°31S 29°59E **57** C4
Ermenek *Turkey* 36°38N 33°0E **46** B2
Ermoupoli *Greece* 37°28N 24°57E **23** F11
Ernakulam *India* 9°59N 76°22E **45** K3
Erne → *Ireland* 54°30N 8°16W **10** B3
Erne, Lower L. *U.K.* 54°28N 7°47W **10** B4
Erne, Upper L. *U.K.* 54°14N 7°32W **10** B4
Ernest Giles Ra. *Australia* 27°0S 123°45E **61** E3
Erode *India* 11°24N 77°45E **45** J3
Eromanga *Australia* 26°40S 143°11E **63** D3
Erongo *Namibia* 21°39S 15°58E **56** B2
Erongo □ *Namibia* 22°0S 15°0E **56** B2
Erramala Hills *India* 15°30N 78°15E **45** G4
Errenteria *Spain* 43°19N 1°54W **21** A5
Errigal *Ireland* 55°2N 8°6W **10** A3
Errinundra △ *Australia* 37°20S 148°47E **63** F4
Erris Hd. *Ireland* 54°17N 10°0W **10** B1
Erskine *U.S.A.* 47°40N 96°0W **80** B6
Ertan Shuiku *China* 27°5N 101°52E **34** D3
Ertis = Irtysh → *Russia* 61°4N 68°52E **26** C7
Erwin *U.S.A.* 36°9N 82°25W **85** C13
Eryuan *China* 26°7N 99°57E **34** D2
Erzgebirge *Germany* 50°27N 12°55E **16** C7
Erzin *Russia* 50°15N 95°10E **27** D10
Erzincan *Turkey* 39°46N 39°30E **46** B3
Erzurum *Turkey* 39°57N 41°15E **46** B4
Es Sînâ' *Egypt* 29°0N 34°0E **48** F2
Esan-Misaki *Japan* 41°40N 141°10E **28** D10
Esashi *Hokkaidō, Japan* 44°56N 142°35E **28** B11
Esashi *Hokkaidō, Japan* 41°52N 140°7E **28** D10
Esbjerg *Denmark* 55°29N 8°29E **9** J13
Esbo = Espoo *Finland* 60°12N 24°40E **9** F21
Escalante *U.S.A.* 37°47N 111°36W **77** H8
Escalante → *U.S.A.* 37°24N 110°57W **77** H8
Escalón *Mexico* 26°45N 104°20W **86** B4
Escanaba *U.S.A.* 45°45N 87°4W **80** C10
Escárcega *Mexico* 18°37N 90°43W **87** D6
Esch-sur-Alzette *Lux.* 49°32N 6°0E **15** E6
Escondido *U.S.A.* 33°7N 117°5W **79** M9
Escuinapa de Hidalgo
  *Mexico* 22°50N 105°50W **86** C3
Escuintla *Guatemala* 14°20N 90°48W **88** D1
Esenguly *Turkmenistan* 37°37N 53°59E **26** F6
Esfahān *Iran* 32°39N 51°43E **47** C6
Esfahān □ *Iran* 32°50N 51°50E **47** C6
Esfarāyen *Iran* 37°4N 57°30E **47** B8
Esfideh *Iran* 33°39N 59°46E **47** C8
Esh Sham = Dimashq
  *Syria* 33°30N 36°18E **48** B5
Esha Ness *U.K.* 60°29N 1°38W **11** A7
Eshan *China* 24°11N 102°24E **34** E4
Eshkol △ *Israel* 31°20N 34°30E **48** D3
Eshowe *S. Africa* 28°50S 31°30E **57** C5

INDEX TO WORLD MAPS
Filchner Ice Shelf 119

Esigodini *Zimbabwe* 20°18S 28°56E **57** B4
Esil = Ishim → *Russia* 57°45N 71°10E **26** D8
Esk → *Dumf. & Gall., U.K.* 54°58N 3°2W **11** G5
Esk → *N. Yorks., U.K.* 54°30N 0°37W **12** C7
Eskān *Iran* 26°48N 63°9E **47** E9
Esker Siding *Canada* 53°53N 66°25W **73** B6
Eskifjörður *Iceland* 65°3N 13°55W **8** D7
Eskilstuna *Sweden* 59°22N 16°32E **9** G17
Eskimo Point = Arviat *Canada* 61°6N 93°59W **71** A10
Eskişehir *Turkey* 39°50N 30°30E **19** G5
Esla → *Spain* 41°29N 6°3W **21** B2
Eslāmābād-e Gharb *Iran* 34°10N 46°30E **46** C5
Eslāmshahr *Iran* 35°40N 51°10E **47** C6
Eşme *Turkey* 38°23N 28°58E **23** E13
Esmeraldas *Ecuador* 1°0N 79°40W **92** C3
Esna = Isna *Egypt* 25°17N 32°30E **53** C12
Esnagi L. *Canada* 48°36N 84°33W **72** C3
España = Spain ■ *Europe* 39°0N 4°0W **21** B4
Espanola *Canada* 46°15N 81°46W **72** C3
Espanola *U.S.A.* 35°59N 106°5W **77** J10
Esparza *Costa Rica* 9°59N 84°40W **88** E3
Esperance *Australia* 33°45S 121°55E **61** F3
Esperance B. *Australia* 33°48S 121°55E **61** F3
Esperance Harbour *St. Lucia* 14°4N 60°55W **89** f
Esperanza *Antarctica* 65°0S 55°0W **5** C18
Esperanza *Argentina* 31°29S 61°3W **94** C3
Esperanza *Puerto Rico* 18°6N 65°28W **89** d
Espichel, C. *Portugal* 38°22N 9°16W **21** C1
Espigão, Serra do *Brazil* 26°35S 50°30W **95** B5
Espinazo, Sierra del = Espinhaço, Serra do *Brazil* 17°30S 43°30W **93** G10
Espinhaço, Serra do *Brazil* 17°30S 43°30W **93** G10
Espinilho, Serra do *Brazil* 28°30S 55°0W **95** B5
Espírito Santo □ *Brazil* 20°0S 40°45W **93** H10
Espírito Santo do Pinhal *Brazil* 22°10S 46°46W **95** A6
Espíritu Santo *Vanuatu* 15°15S 166°50E **58** C9
Espíritu Santo, B. del *Mexico* 19°20N 87°35W **87** D7
Espíritu Santo, I. *Mexico* 24°30N 110°22W **86** C2
Espita *Mexico* 21°1N 88°19W **87** C7
Espoo *Finland* 60°12N 24°40E **9** F21
Espungabera *Mozam.* 20°29S 32°45E **57** B5
Esquel *Argentina* 42°55S 71°20W **96** E2
Esquimalt *Canada* 48°26N 123°25W **78** B3
Esquina *Argentina* 30°0S 59°30W **94** C4
Essaouira *Morocco* 31°32N 9°42W **52** B4
Essen *Belgium* 51°28N 4°28E **15** C4
Essen *Germany* 51°28N 7°2E **16** C4
Essendon, Mt. *Australia* 25°0S 120°29E **61** E3
Essequibo → *Guyana* 6°50N 58°30W **92** B7
Essex *Canada* 42°10N 82°49W **82** D2
Essex *Calif., U.S.A.* 34°44N 115°15W **79** L11
Essex *N.Y., U.S.A.* 44°19N 73°21W **83** B11
Essex □ *U.K.* 51°54N 0°27E **13** F8
Essex Junction *U.S.A.* 44°29N 73°7W **83** B11
Esslingen *Germany* 48°44N 9°18E **16** D5
Estación Camacho *Mexico* 24°25N 102°18W **86** C4
Estación Simón *Mexico* 24°42N 102°35W **86** C4
Estados, I. de Los *Argentina* 54°40S 64°30W **96** G4
Eşţahbānāt *Iran* 29°8N 54°4E **47** D7
Estância *Brazil* 11°16S 37°26W **93** F11
Estancia *U.S.A.* 34°46N 106°4W **77** J10
Estārm *Iran* 28°21N 58°21E **47** D8
Estcourt *S. Africa* 29°0S 29°53E **57** C4
Este △ *Dom. Rep.* 18°14N 68°42W **89** C6
Estelí *Nic.* 13°9N 86°22W **88** D2
Esterhazy *Canada* 50°37N 102°5W **71** C8
Estevan *Canada* 49°10N 102°59W **71** D8
Estevan Group *Canada* 53°3N 129°38W **70** C3
Estherville *U.S.A.* 43°24N 94°50W **80** D6
Eston *Canada* 51°8N 108°40W **71** C7
Estonia ■ *Europe* 58°30N 25°30E **9** G21
Estreito *Brazil* 6°32S 47°25W **93** E9
Estrela, Serra da *Portugal* 40°10N 7°45W **21** B2
Estremoz *Portugal* 38°51N 7°39W **21** C2
Estrondo, Serra do *Brazil* 7°20S 48°0W **93** E9
Eswatini ■ *Africa* 26°30S 31°30E **57** C5
Esztergom *Hungary* 47°47N 18°44E **17** E10
Et Tîdra *Mauritania* 19°45N 16°20W **52** E2
Etah *India* 27°35N 78°40E **43** F8
Étampes *France* 48°26N 2°10E **20** B5
Etanga *Namibia* 17°55S 13°0E **56** A1
Etawah *India* 26°48N 79°6E **43** F8
Etawney L. *Canada* 57°50N 96°50W **71** B9
Etchojoa *Mexico* 26°55N 109°38W **86** B3
Etelä-Konneveden △ *Finland* 62°34N 26°39E **8** E22
eThekwini = Durban *S. Africa* 29°49S 31°1E **57** C5
Ethel *U.S.A.* 46°32N 122°46W **78** D4
Ethelbert *Canada* 51°32N 100°25W **71** C8
Ethiopia ■ *Africa* 8°0N 40°0E **49** F3
Ethiopian Highlands *Ethiopia* 10°0N 37°0E **49** F2
Etive, L. *U.K.* 56°29N 5°10W **11** E3
Etna *Italy* 37°50N 14°55E **22** F6
Etolin Strait *U.S.A.* 60°20N 165°15W **74** C6
Etosha △ *Namibia* 19°0S 16°0E **56** A2
Etosha Pan *Namibia* 18°40S 16°30E **56** A2
Etowah *U.S.A.* 35°20N 84°32W **85** D12
Etrek *Turkmenistan* 37°36N 54°46E **47** B7
Ettelbruck *Lux.* 49°51N 6°5E **15** E6
Ettrick Water → *U.K.* 55°31N 2°55W **11** F6
Etzná-Tixmucuy = Edzná *Mexico* 19°39N 90°19W **87** D6
Eua *Tonga* 21°22S 174°56W **59** c
Euboea = Evia *Greece* 38°30N 24°0E **23** E11
Eucla *Australia* 31°41S 128°52E **61** F4
Euclid *U.S.A.* 41°34N 81°32W **82** E3
Eucumbene, L. *Australia* 36°2S 148°40E **63** F4
Eudora *U.S.A.* 33°7N 91°16W **84** E9
Eufaula *Ala., U.S.A.* 31°54N 85°9W **85** F12
Eufaula *Okla., U.S.A.* 35°17N 95°35W **84** D7
Eufaula L. *U.S.A.* 35°18N 95°21W **84** D7
Eugene *U.S.A.* 44°5N 123°4W **76** D2
Eugowra *Australia* 33°22S 148°24E **63** E4
Eulo *Australia* 28°10S 145°3E **63** D4
Eungella △ *Australia* 20°57S 148°40E **62** b
Eunice *La., U.S.A.* 30°30N 92°25W **84** F8
Eunice *N. Mex., U.S.A.* 32°26N 103°10W **77** K12
Eupen *Belgium* 50°37N 6°3E **15** D6
Euphrates = Furāt, Nahr al → *Asia* 31°0N 47°25E **46** D5
Eureka *Canada* 80°0N 85°56W **69** B14
Eureka *Calif., U.S.A.* 40°47N 124°9W **76** F1
Eureka *Kans., U.S.A.* 37°49N 96°17W **80** G5
Eureka *Mont., U.S.A.* 48°53N 115°3W **76** B6
Eureka *Nev., U.S.A.* 39°31N 115°58W **76** G6
Eureka *S. Dak., U.S.A.* 45°46N 99°38W **80** C4
Eureka, Mt. *Australia* 26°35S 121°35E **61** E3
Eureka Sd. *Canada* 79°0N 85°0W **69** B15
Euroa *Australia* 36°44S 145°35E **63** F4
Europa, Île *Ind. Oc.* 22°20S 40°22E **57** B7
Europa, Picos de *Spain* 43°10N 4°49W **21** A3
Europa, Pt. *Gib.* 36°3N 5°21W **21** D3
Europe 50°0N 20°0E **6** E10
Europoort *Neths.* 51°57N 4°10E **15** C4
Euskadi = País Vasco □ *Spain* 42°50N 2°45W **21** A4
Eustis *U.S.A.* 28°51N 81°41W **85** G14
Eutsuk L. *Canada* 53°20N 126°45W **70** C3
Evale *Angola* 16°33S 15°44E **56** A2
Evans *U.S.A.* 40°23N 104°41W **76** F11
Evans, L. *Canada* 50°50N 77°0W **72** B4
Evans City *U.S.A.* 40°46N 80°4W **82** F4
Evans Head *Australia* 29°7S 153°27E **63** D5
Evansburg *Canada* 53°36N 114°59W **70** C5
Evanston *U.S.A.* 41°16N 110°58W **76** F8
Evansville *U.S.A.* 37°58N 87°35W **80** G10
Evaz *Iran* 27°46N 53°59E **47** E7
Eveleth *U.S.A.* 47°28N 92°32W **80** B7
Evensk *Russia* 62°12N 159°30E **27** C16
Everard, L. *Australia* 31°30S 135°0E **63** E2
Everard Ranges *Australia* 27°5S 132°28E **61** E5
Everest, Mt. *Nepal* 28°5N 86°58E **43** E12
Everett *Pa., U.S.A.* 40°1N 78°23W **82** F6
Everett *Wash., U.S.A.* 47°59N 122°12W **78** C4
Everglades, The *U.S.A.* 25°50N 81°0W **85** J14
Everglades △ *U.S.A.* 25°30N 81°0W **85** J14
Everglades City *U.S.A.* 25°52N 81°23W **85** J14
Evergreen *Ala., U.S.A.* 31°26N 86°57W **85** F11
Evergreen *Mont., U.S.A.* 48°14N 114°17W **76** B6
Evesham *U.K.* 52°6N 1°56W **13** E6
Evia *Greece* 38°30N 24°0E **23** E11
Evje *Norway* 58°36N 7°51E **9** G12
Évora *Portugal* 38°33N 7°57W **21** C2
Evowghlī *Iran* 38°43N 45°13E **46** B5
Évreux *France* 49°3N 1°8E **20** B4
Evros → *Greece* 41°40N 26°34E **23** D12
Évry *France* 48°38N 2°27E **20** B5
Évvoia = Evia *Greece* 38°30N 24°0E **23** E11
Ewe, L. *U.K.* 57°49N 5°38W **11** D3
Ewing *U.S.A.* 42°16N 98°21W **80** D4
Ewo *Congo* 0°48S 14°45E **54** E2
Exaltación *Bolivia* 13°10S 65°20W **92** F5
Excelsior Springs *U.S.A.* 39°20N 94°13W **80** F6
Exe → *U.K.* 50°41N 3°29W **13** G4
Exeter *Canada* 43°21N 81°29W **82** C3
Exeter *U.K.* 50°43N 3°31W **13** G4
Exeter *Calif., U.S.A.* 36°18N 119°9W **78** J7
Exeter *N.H., U.S.A.* 42°59N 70°57W **83** D14
Exmoor *U.K.* 51°12N 3°45W **13** F4
Exmoor △ *U.K.* 51°8N 3°42W **13** F4
Exmouth *Australia* 21°54S 114°10E **60** D1
Exmouth *U.K.* 50°37N 3°25W **13** G4
Exmouth G. *Australia* 22°15S 114°15E **60** D1
Exmouth Plateau *Ind. Oc.* 19°0S 114°0E **64** J3
Expedition △ *Australia* 25°41S 149°7E **63** D4
Expedition Ra. *Australia* 24°30S 149°12E **62** C4
Extremadura □ *Spain* 39°30N 6°5W **21** C2
Exuma Sound *Bahamas* 24°30N 76°20W **88** B4
Eyasi, L. *Tanzania* 3°30S 35°0E **54** E7
Eye Pen. *U.K.* 58°13N 6°10W **11** C2
Eyemouth *U.K.* 55°52N 2°5W **11** F6
Eyjafjallajökull *Iceland* 63°38N 19°36W **8** E4
Eyjafjörður *Iceland* 66°15N 18°30W **8** C4
Eyl *Somalia* 8°0N 49°50E **49** F4
Eyre, L. = Kati Thanda-Lake Eyre *Australia* 29°30S 137°26E **58** D6
Eyre Mts. *N.Z.* 45°25S 168°25E **59** F2
Eyre Pen. *Australia* 33°30S 136°17E **63** E2
Eysturoy *Færoe Is.* 62°13N 6°54W **8** E9
Eyvān = Jūy Zar *Iran* 33°50N 46°18E **46** C5
Eyvānkī *Iran* 35°24N 51°56E **47** C6
Ezhou *China* 30°23N 114°50E **35** B10
Ezhva *Russia* 61°48N 50°35E **18** B9
Ezine *Turkey* 39°48N 26°20E **23** E12

F

F.Y.R.O.M. = Macedonia ■ *Europe* 41°53N 21°40E **23** D9
Faaa *Tahiti* 17°34S 149°35W **59** d
Faaone *Tahiti* 17°40S 149°21W **59** d
Fabala *Guinea* 9°44N 9°5W **52** G4
Fabens *U.S.A.* 31°30N 106°10W **84** F1
Fabius *U.S.A.* 42°50N 75°59W **83** D9
Fabriano *Italy* 43°20N 12°54E **22** C5
Fachi *Niger* 18°6N 11°34E **53** E8
Fada *Chad* 17°13N 21°34E **53** E10
Fada-n-Gourma *Burkina Faso* 12°10N 0°30E **52** F6
Faddeyevskiy, Ostrov *Russia* 76°0N 144°0E **27** B15
Fadghāmī *Syria* 35°53N 40°52E **46** C4
Faenza *Italy* 44°17N 11°53E **22** B4
Færoe Is. = Føroyar ◩ *Atl. Oc.* 62°0N 7°0W **8** F9
Făgăraş *Romania* 45°48N 24°58E **17** F13
Fagersta *Sweden* 60°1N 15°46E **9** F16
Fagnano, L. *Argentina* 54°30S 68°0W **96** G3
Fahlīān *Iran* 30°11N 51°28E **47** D6
Fahraj *Kermān, Iran* 29°0N 59°0E **47** D8
Fahraj *Yazd, Iran* 31°46N 54°36E **47** D7
Fai Tsi Long *Vietnam* 21°0N 107°30E **34** G6
Faial *Azores* 38°34N 28°42W **52** a
Faichan Kangri *India* 35°48N 76°34E **43** B7
Fair Haven *N.Y., U.S.A.* 43°18N 76°42W **83** C8
Fair Haven *Vt., U.S.A.* 43°36N 73°16W **83** C11
Fair Hd. *U.K.* 55°14N 6°9W **10** A5
Fair Isle *U.K.* 59°32N 1°38W **14** B6
Fair Oaks *U.S.A.* 38°39N 121°16W **78** G5
Fairbanks *U.S.A.* 64°51N 147°43W **68** E2
Fairbury *U.S.A.* 40°8N 97°11W **80** E5
Fairfax *U.S.A.* 44°40N 73°1W **83** B11
Fairfield *Calif., U.S.A.* 38°15N 122°3W **78** G4
Fairfield *Conn., U.S.A.* 41°9N 73°16W **83** E11
Fairfield *Idaho, U.S.A.* 43°21N 114°44W **76** E6
Fairfield *Ill., U.S.A.* 38°23N 88°22W **80** F9
Fairfield *Iowa, U.S.A.* 40°56N 91°57W **80** E8
Fairfield *Tex., U.S.A.* 31°44N 96°10W **84** F6
Fairford *Canada* 51°37N 98°38W **71** C9
Fairhope *U.S.A.* 30°31N 87°54W **85** F11
Fairlie *N.Z.* 44°5S 170°49E **59** F3
Fairmead *U.S.A.* 37°5N 120°10W **78** H6
Fairmont *Minn., U.S.A.* 43°39N 94°28W **80** D6
Fairmont *W. Va., U.S.A.* 39°29N 80°9W **81** F13
Fairmount *Calif., U.S.A.* 34°45N 118°26W **79** L8
Fairmount *N.Y., U.S.A.* 43°5N 76°12W **83** C8
Fairplay *U.S.A.* 39°15N 106°2W **76** G10
Fairport *U.S.A.* 43°6N 77°27W **82** C7
Fairport Harbor *U.S.A.* 41°45N 81°17W **82** E3
Fairview *Canada* 56°5N 118°25W **70** B5
Fairview *Mont., U.S.A.* 47°51N 104°3W **76** C11
Fairview *Okla., U.S.A.* 36°16N 98°29W **84** C5
Fairweather, Mt. *U.S.A.* 58°55N 137°32W **70** B1
Faisalabad *Pakistan* 31°30N 73°5E **42** D5
Faith *U.S.A.* 45°2N 102°2W **80** C2
Faizabad *India* 26°45N 82°10E **43** F10
Faizpur *India* 21°14N 75°49E **44** D2
Fajardo *Puerto Rico* 18°20N 65°39W **89** d
Fajr, W. → *Si. Arabia* 29°10N 38°10E **46** D3
Fakenham *U.K.* 52°51N 0°51E **12** E8
Fakfak *Indonesia* 2°55S 132°18E **37** E8
Faku *China* 42°32N 123°21E **33** C12
Falaise *France* 48°54N 0°12W **20** B3
Falam *Myanmar* 23°0N 93°45E **41** H18
Falcón, Presa *Mexico* 26°35N 99°10W **87** B5
Falcon Lake *Canada* 49°42N 95°15W **71** D9
Falcon Res. *U.S.A.* 26°34N 99°10W **84** H5
Falconara Marittima *Italy* 43°37N 13°24E **22** C5
Falcone, C. del *Italy* 40°58N 8°12E **22** D3
Falconer *U.S.A.* 42°7N 79°12W **82** D5
Falefa *Samoa* 13°54S 171°31W **59** b
Falelatai *Samoa* 13°55S 171°59W **59** b
Falelima *Samoa* 13°32S 172°41W **59** b
Faleshty = Făleşti *Moldova* 47°32N 27°44E **17** E14
Făleşti *Moldova* 47°32N 27°44E **17** E14
Falfurrias *U.S.A.* 27°14N 98°9W **84** H5
Falher *Canada* 55°44N 117°15W **70** B5
Falkenberg *Sweden* 56°54N 12°30E **9** H15
Falkirk *U.K.* 56°0N 3°47W **11** F5
Falkirk □ *U.K.* 55°58N 3°49W **11** F5
Falkland *U.K.* 56°16N 3°12W **11** E5
Falkland Is. ◩ *Atl. Oc.* 51°30S 59°0W **96** G5
Falkland Sd. *Falk. Is.* 52°0S 60°0W **96** G5
Fall River *U.S.A.* 41°43N 71°10W **83** E13
Fallbrook *U.S.A.* 33°23N 117°15W **79** M9
Fallon *U.S.A.* 39°28N 118°47W **76** G4
Falls City *U.S.A.* 40°3N 95°36W **80** E6
Falls Creek *U.S.A.* 41°9N 78°48W **82** E6
Falmouth *Jamaica* 18°30N 77°40W **88** a
Falmouth *U.K.* 50°9N 5°5W **13** G2
Falmouth *U.S.A.* 41°33N 70°37W **83** E14
Falsa, Pta. *Mexico* 27°51N 115°3W **86** B1
False B. *S. Africa* 34°15S 18°40E **56** D2
False Divi Pt. *India* 15°43N 80°50E **45** G5
False Pt. *India* 20°18N 86°48E **44** D8
Falso, C. *Honduras* 15°12N 83°21W **88** C3
Falster *Denmark* 54°45N 11°55E **9** J14
Fălticeni *Romania* 47°21N 26°20E **17** E14
Falun *Sweden* 60°37N 15°37E **8** F16
Famagusta *Cyprus* 35°8N 33°55E **46** C2
Famatina, Sierra de *Argentina* 27°30S 68°0W **94** B2
Family L. *Canada* 51°54N 95°27W **71** C9
Famoso *U.S.A.* 35°37N 119°12W **79** K7
Fan Xian *China* 35°55N 115°38E **32** G8
Fanad Hd. *Ireland* 55°17N 7°38W **10** A4
Fang *Thailand* 19°55N 99°13E **38** C2
Fang Xian *China* 32°3N 110°40E **35** A8
Fangchang *China* 31°5N 118°4E **35** B12
Fangcheng *China* 33°18N 112°59E **32** H7
Fangchenggang *China* 21°42N 108°21E **34** G7
Fangliao *Taiwan* 22°22N 120°38E **35** F13
Fangshan *Beijing, China* 39°41N 116°0E **32** E9
Fangshan *Shanxi, China* 38°3N 111°25E **32** E6
Fangzi *China* 36°33N 119°10E **33** F10
Fanjiatun *China* 43°40N 125°15E **33** C13
Fanling *China* 22°30N 114°8E **31** a
Fannich, L. *U.K.* 57°38N 4°59W **11** D4
Fannūj *Iran* 26°35N 59°38E **47** E8
Fanø *Denmark* 55°25N 8°25E **9** J13
Fano *Italy* 43°50N 13°1E **22** C5
Fanshi *China* 39°12N 113°20E **32** E7
Fao = Al Fāw *Iraq* 30°0N 48°30E **47** D6
Faqirwali *Pakistan* 29°27N 73°0E **42** E5
Far East = Dalnevostochnyy □ *Russia* 67°0N 140°0E **27** C14
Far East *Asia* 40°0N 130°0E **24** E14
Faradje *Dem. Rep. of the Congo* 3°50N 29°45E **54** D5
Farafangana *Madag.* 22°49S 47°50E **55** J9
Farāh *Afghan.* 32°20N 62°7E **40** C3
Farāh □ *Afghan.* 32°25N 62°10E **40** C3
Faranah *Guinea* 10°3N 10°45W **52** F3
Farasān, Jazā'ir *Si. Arabia* 16°45N 41°55E **49** D3
Farasan Is. = Farasān, Jazā'ir *Si. Arabia* 16°45N 41°55E **49** D3
Fareham *U.K.* 50°51N 1°11W **13** G6
Farewell, C. = Nunap Isua *Greenland* 59°48N 43°55W **66** D15
Farewell, C. *N.Z.* 40°29S 172°43E **59** D4
Fargo *U.S.A.* 46°53N 96°48W **80** B5
Farg'ona *Uzbekistan* 40°23N 71°19E **26** E8
Fār'iah, W. al → *West Bank* 32°12N 35°27E **48** C4
Faribault *U.S.A.* 44°18N 93°16W **80** C7
Faridabad *India* 28°26N 77°19E **42** E6
Faridkot *India* 30°44N 74°45E **42** D6
Faridpur *Bangla.* 23°15N 89°55E **43** H13
Faridpur *India* 28°13N 79°33E **43** E8
Farīmān *Iran* 35°40N 59°49E **47** C8
Farleigh *Australia* 21°4S 149°8E **62** b
Farmerville *U.S.A.* 32°47N 92°24W **84** E8
Farmingdale *U.S.A.* 40°12N 74°10W **83** F10
Farmington *Canada* 55°54N 120°30W **70** B4
Farmington *Calif., U.S.A.* 37°55N 120°59W **78** H6
Farmington *Maine, U.S.A.* 44°40N 70°9W **81** C18
Farmington *Mo., U.S.A.* 37°47N 90°25W **80** G8
Farmington *N.H., U.S.A.* 43°24N 71°4W **83** C13
Farmington *N. Mex., U.S.A.* 36°44N 108°12W **77** H9
Farmington *Utah, U.S.A.* 40°59N 111°53W **76** F8
Farmington → *U.S.A.* 41°51N 72°38W **83** E12
Farmville *U.S.A.* 37°18N 78°24W **81** G14
Farne Is. *U.K.* 55°38N 1°37W **12** B6
Farnham *Canada* 45°17N 72°59W **83** A12
Farnham, Mt. *Canada* 50°29N 116°30W **70** C5
Faro *Brazil* 2°10S 56°39W **93** D7
Faro *Canada* 62°11N 133°22W **68** E5
Faro *Portugal* 37°2N 7°55W **21** D2
Fårö *Sweden* 57°55N 19°5E **9** H18
Farquhar, C. *Australia* 23°50S 113°36E **61** D1
Farrars Cr. → *Australia* 25°35S 140°43E **62** D3
Farrāshband *Iran* 28°57N 52°5E **47** D7
Farrell *U.S.A.* 41°13N 80°30W **82** E4
Farrokhī *Iran* 33°50N 59°31E **47** C8
Farrukhabad *India* 27°24N 79°34E **44** A4
Fārs □ *Iran* 29°30N 55°0E **47** D7
Farsala *Greece* 39°17N 22°23E **23** E10
Fārsī *Iran* 27°58N 50°11E **47** E6
Farson *U.S.A.* 42°7N 109°26W **76** E9
Farsund *Norway* 58°5N 6°55E **9** G12
Fartak, Râs *Si. Arabia* 28°5N 34°34E **46** D2
Fartak, Ra's *Yemen* 15°38N 52°15E **49** D5
Fartura, Serra da *Brazil* 26°21S 52°52W **95** B5
Fārūj *Iran* 37°14N 58°14E **47** B8
Farvel, Kap = Nunap Isua *Greenland* 59°48N 43°55W **66** D15
Farwell *U.S.A.* 34°23N 103°2W **84** D3
Fāryāb □ *Afghan.* 36°0N 65°0E **40** B4
Fasā *Iran* 29°0N 53°39E **47** D7
Fasano *Italy* 40°50N 17°22E **22** D7
Fastiv *Ukraine* 50°7N 29°57E **17** C15
Fastnet Rock *Ireland* 51°22N 9°37W **10** E2
Fastov = Fastiv *Ukraine* 50°7N 29°57E **17** C15
Fatagartuting, Tanjung *Indonesia* 2°46S 131°57E **37** E8
Fatehabad *Haryana, India* 29°31N 75°27E **42** E6
Fatehabad *Ut. P., India* 27°1N 78°19E **42** F8
Fatehgarh *India* 27°25N 79°35E **43** F8
Fatehpur *Bihar, India* 24°38N 85°14E **43** G11
Fatehpur *Raj., India* 28°0N 74°40E **42** F6
Fatehpur *Ut. P., India* 25°56N 81°13E **43** G9
Fatehpur *Ut. P., India* 27°10N 81°13E **43** F9
Fatehpur Sikri *India* 27°6N 77°40E **42** F6
Fathom Five ⌓ *Canada* 45°17N 81°40W **82** A3
Fatima *Canada* 47°24N 61°53W **73** C7
Faulkton *U.S.A.* 45°2N 99°8W **80** C4
Faure I. *Australia* 25°52S 113°50E **61** E1
Fauresmith *S. Africa* 29°44S 25°17E **56** C4
Fauske *Norway* 67°17N 15°25E **8** C16
Favara *Italy* 37°19N 13°39E **22** F5
Favignana *Italy* 37°56N 12°20E **22** F5
Fawcett, Pt. *Australia* 11°46S 130°2E **60** B5
Fawn → *Canada* 55°20N 87°35W **72** A2
Fawnskin *U.S.A.* 34°16N 116°56W **79** L10
Faxaflói *Iceland* 64°29N 23°0W **8** D2
Faya-Largeau *Chad* 17°58N 19°6E **53** E9
Fayd *Si. Arabia* 27°1N 42°52E **46** E4
Fayette *Ala., U.S.A.* 33°41N 87°50W **85** E11
Fayette *Mo., U.S.A.* 39°9N 92°41W **80** F7
Fayette *N.Y., U.S.A.* 42°48N 76°48W **83** D8
Fayetteville *Ark., U.S.A.* 36°4N 94°10W **84** C7
Fayetteville *N.C., U.S.A.* 35°3N 78°53W **85** D15
Fayetteville *N.Y., U.S.A.* 43°1N 76°0W **83** C9
Fayetteville *Tenn., U.S.A.* 35°9N 86°34W **85** D11
Faylakah *Kuwait* 29°27N 48°20E **47** D6
Fazilka *India* 30°27N 74°2E **42** D6
Fazilpur *Pakistan* 29°18N 70°29E **42** E4
Fdérik *Mauritania* 22°40N 12°45W **52** D3
Feakle *Ireland* 52°56N 8°40W **10** D3
Feale → *Ireland* 52°27N 9°37W **10** D2
Fear, C. *U.S.A.* 33°50N 77°58W **85** E16
Feather → *U.S.A.* 38°47N 121°36W **78** G5
Feather Falls *U.S.A.* 39°36N 121°16W **78** F5
Featherston *N.Z.* 41°6S 175°20E **59** D5
Fécamp *France* 49°45N 0°22E **20** B4
Fedala = Mohammedia *Morocco* 33°44N 7°21W **52** B4
Federación *Argentina* 31°0S 57°55W **94** C4
Féderal *Argentina* 30°57S 58°48W **94** C4
Federal *Argentina* 30°57S 58°48W **96** C5
Federal Way *U.S.A.* 47°18N 122°19W **78** C4
Fedeshkūh *Iran* 28°49N 53°50E **47** D7
Fehmarn *Germany* 54°27N 11°7E **16** A6
Fehmarn Bælt *Europe* 54°35N 11°20E **9** J14
Fehmarn Belt = Fehmarn Bælt *Europe* 54°35N 11°20E **9** J14
Fei Xian *China* 35°18N 117°59E **33** G9
Feicheng *China* 36°14N 116°45E **32** F9
Feidong *China* 32°0N 117°35E **35** B11
Feijó *Brazil* 8°9S 70°21W **92** E4
Feilding *N.Z.* 40°13S 175°35E **59** D5
Feira de Santana *Brazil* 12°15S 38°57W **93** F11
Feixi *China* 31°43N 117°59E **35** B11
Feixiang *China* 36°30N 114°45E **32** F8
Feldkirch *Austria* 47°15N 9°37E **16** E5
Félicité *Seychelles* 4°19S 55°52E **55** b
Felipe Carrillo Puerto *Mexico* 19°38N 88°3W **87** D7
Felixburg *Zimbabwe* 19°29S 30°51E **57** A5
Felixstowe *U.K.* 51°58N 1°23E **13** F9
Felton *U.S.A.* 37°3N 122°4W **78** H4
Femer Bælt = Fehmarn Bælt *Europe* 54°35N 11°20E **9** J14
Femunden *Norway* 62°10N 11°53E **8** E14
Femundsmarka △ *Norway* 62°18N 12°6E **8** E15
Fen He → *China* 35°36N 110°42E **32** G6
Fenelon Falls *Canada* 44°32N 78°45W **82** B6
Feng Xian *Jiangsu, China* 34°43N 116°35E **32** G9
Feng Xian *Shaanxi, China* 33°54N 106°40E **32** H4
Fengcheng *Jiangxi, China* 28°12N 115°48E **35** C10
Fengcheng *Liaoning, China* 40°28N 124°5E **33** D13
Fengdu *China* 29°55N 107°48E **34** C6
Fengfeng *China* 36°28N 114°8E **32** F8
Fenggang *China* 27°57N 107°47E **34** D6
Fenghua *China* 29°40N 121°25E **35** C13
Fenghuang *China* 27°57N 109°29E **34** D7
Fengjie *China* 31°3N 109°31E **34** B7
Fengkai *China* 23°24N 111°30E **35** F8
Fengkang *Taiwan* 22°12N 120°41E **35** F13
Fengle *China* 31°29N 112°29E **35** B9
Fenglin *Taiwan* 23°45N 121°26E **35** F13
Fengning *China* 41°10N 116°33E **32** D9
Fengqing *China* 24°38N 99°55E **34** E2
Fengqiu *China* 35°2N 114°25E **32** G8
Fengrun *China* 39°48N 118°8E **33** E10
Fengshan *Guangxi Zhuangzu, China* 24°39N 109°15E **34** E7
Fengshan *Guangxi Zhuangzu, China* 24°31N 107°3E **34** E6
Fengshan *Taiwan* 22°38N 120°21E **35** F13
Fengshun *China* 23°46N 116°10E **35** F11
Fengtai *China* 32°50N 116°40E **35** A11
Fengtongzhai △ *China* 30°32N 102°54E **34** B4
Fengxiang *China* 34°29N 107°25E **32** G4
Fengxin *China* 28°41N 115°18E **35** C10
Fengyang *China* 32°51N 117°29E **33** H9
Fengyi *China* 25°37N 100°20E **34** E3
Fengyüan *Taiwan* 24°15N 120°35E **35** E13
Fengzhen *China* 40°25N 113°2E **32** D7
Fenoarivo Atsinanana *Madag.* 17°22S 49°25E **55** H9
Fens, The *U.K.* 52°38N 0°2W **12** E7
Fenton *U.S.A.* 42°48N 83°42W **81** D12
Fenxi *China* 36°40N 111°31E **32** F6
Fenyang *China* 37°18N 111°48E **32** F6
Fenyi *China* 27°45N 114°47E **35** D10
Feodosiya *Ukraine* 45°2N 35°16E **19** E6
Ferbane *Ireland* 53°16N 7°50W **10** C4
Ferdows *Iran* 33°58N 58°2E **47** C8
Ferfer *Somalia* 5°4N 45°9E **49** F4
Fergana = Farg'ona *Uzbekistan* 40°23N 71°19E **26** E8
Fergus *Canada* 43°43N 80°24W **82** C4
Fergus Falls *U.S.A.* 46°17N 96°4W **80** B5
Ferizaj *Kosovo* 42°23N 21°10E **23** C9
Ferkéssédougou *Côte d'Ivoire* 9°35N 5°6W **52** G4
Ferland *Canada* 50°19N 88°27W **72** B2
Ferlo, Vallée du *Senegal* 15°15N 14°15W **52** E3
Fermanagh □ *U.K.* 54°21N 7°40W **10** B4
Fermo *Italy* 43°9N 13°43E **22** C5
Fermont *Canada* 52°47N 67°5W **73** B6
Fermoy *Ireland* 52°9N 8°16W **10** D3
Fernández *Argentina* 27°55S 63°50W **94** B3
Fernandina Beach *U.S.A.* 30°40N 81°27W **85** F14
Fernando de Noronha *Brazil* 4°0S 33°10W **93** D12
Fernando Póo = Bioko *Eq. Guin.* 3°30N 8°40E **54** D1
Ferndale *Canada* 44°58N 81°17W **82** B3
Ferndale *U.S.A.* 48°51N 122°36W **78** B4
Fernie *Canada* 49°30N 115°5W **70** D5
Fernlees *Australia* 23°51S 148°7E **62** C4
Fernley *U.S.A.* 39°36N 119°15W **76** G4
Fernwood *U.S.A.* 43°16N 73°38W **83** C11
Feroke *India* 11°9N 75°46E **45** J2
Ferozepore = Firozpur *India* 30°55N 74°40E **42** D6
Ferrara *Italy* 44°50N 11°35E **22** B4
Ferreñafe *Peru* 6°42S 79°50W **92** E3
Ferret, C. *France* 44°38N 1°15W **20** D3
Ferriday *U.S.A.* 31°38N 91°33W **84** F9
Ferrol *Spain* 43°29N 8°15W **21** A1
Ferron *U.S.A.* 39°5N 111°8W **76** G8
Ferryland *Canada* 47°2N 52°53W **73** C9
Fertile *U.S.A.* 47°32N 96°17W **80** B5
Fès *Morocco* 34°0N 5°0W **52** B5
Fessenden *U.S.A.* 47°39N 99°38W **80** B4
Festus *U.S.A.* 38°13N 90°24W **80** F8
Feteşti *Romania* 44°22N 27°51E **17** F14
Fethiye *Turkey* 36°36N 29°6E **19** G4
Fetlar *U.K.* 60°36N 0°52W **11** A8
Feuilles → *Canada* 58°47N 70°4W **69** F17
Fez = Fès *Morocco* 34°0N 5°0W **52** B5
Fezzan *Libya* 27°0N 13°0E **53** C8
Fiambalá *Argentina* 27°45S 67°37W **94** B2
Fianarantsoa *Madag.* 21°26S 47°5E **55** J9
Ficksburg *S. Africa* 28°51S 27°53E **57** C4
Field → *Australia* 23°48S 138°0E **62** C2
Field I. *Australia* 12°5S 132°23E **60** B5
Fier *Albania* 40°43N 19°33E **23** D8
Fife □ *U.K.* 56°16N 3°1W **11** E5
Fife Ness *U.K.* 56°17N 2°35W **11** E6
Fifth Cataract *Sudan* 18°22N 33°50E **53** E12
Figeac *France* 44°37N 2°2E **20** D5
Figueira da Foz *Portugal* 40°7N 8°54W **21** B1
Figueres *Spain* 42°18N 2°58E **21** A7
Figuig *Morocco* 32°5N 1°11W **52** B5
Fiji ■ *Pac. Oc.* 17°20S 179°0E **59** a
Filabus *Zimbabwe* 20°34S 29°20E **57** B4
Filadelfia *Paraguay* 22°21S 60°2W **94** A3
Filchner Ice Shelf *Antarctica* 79°0S 40°0W **5** D1

| | | |
|---|---|---|
| Filey *U.K.* | 54°12N 0°18W | **12** C7 |
| Filey B. *U.K.* | 54°12N 0°15W | **12** C7 |
| Filiatra *Greece* | 37°9N 21°35E | **23** F9 |
| Filingué *Niger* | 14°21N 3°22E | **52** F6 |
| Filipstad *Sweden* | 59°43N 14°9E | **9** G16 |
| Fillmore *Calif., U.S.A.* | 34°24N 118°55W | **79** L8 |
| Fillmore *Utah, U.S.A.* | 38°58N 112°20W | **76** G7 |
| Fimbul Ice Shelf *S. Ocean* | 69°30S 1°0W | **5** C2 |
| Finch *Canada* | 45°11N 75°7W | **83** A9 |
| Finch Hatton *Australia* | 20°25S 148°39E | **62** b |
| Findhorn → *U.K.* | 57°38N 3°38W | **11** D5 |
| Findlay *U.S.A.* | 41°2N 83°39W | **81** E12 |
| Fine *U.S.A.* | 44°14N 75°8W | **83** B9 |
| Fingal □ *Ireland* | 53°29N 6°14W | **10** C5 |
| Finger L. *Canada* | 53°33N 93°30W | **72** B1 |
| Finger Lakes *U.S.A.* | 42°40N 76°30W | **83** D8 |
| Fingoè *Mozam.* | 15°55S 31°50E | **55** G6 |
| Finisterre, C. = Fisterra, C. | | |
|   *Spain* | 42°50N 9°19W | **21** A1 |
| Finke *Australia* | 25°34S 134°35E | **62** D1 |
| Finke Gorge △ *Australia* | 24°8S 132°49E | **60** D5 |
| Finland ■ *Europe* | 63°0N 27°0E | **8** E22 |
| Finland, G. of *Europe* | 60°0N 26°0E | **9** G22 |
| Finlay → *Canada* | 57°0N 125°10W | **70** B3 |
| Finley *Australia* | 35°38S 145°35E | **63** F4 |
| Finley *U.S.A.* | 47°31N 97°50W | **80** B5 |
| Finn → *Ireland* | 54°51N 7°28W | **10** B4 |
| Finnigan, Mt. *Australia* | 15°49S 145°17E | **62** B4 |
| Finniss, C. *Australia* | 33°8S 134°51E | **63** E1 |
| Finnmark *Norway* | 69°37N 23°57E | **8** B20 |
| Finnsnes *Norway* | 69°14N 18°0E | **8** B18 |
| Finspång *Sweden* | 58°43N 15°47E | **9** G16 |
| Fiora → *Italy* | 42°20N 11°34E | **22** C4 |
| Fiordland △ *N.Z.* | 45°46S 167°0E | **59** F1 |
| Fiq *Syria* | 32°46N 35°41E | **48** C4 |
| Firat = Furāt, Nahr al → | | |
|   *Asia* | 31°0N 47°25E | **46** D5 |
| Fire Island △ *U.S.A.* | 40°38N 73°8W | **83** F11 |
| Firebag → *Canada* | 57°45N 111°21W | **71** B6 |
| Firebaugh *U.S.A.* | 36°52N 120°27W | **78** J6 |
| Firedrake L. *Canada* | 61°25N 104°30W | **71** A8 |
| Firenze *Italy* | 43°46N 11°15E | **22** C4 |
| Firk, Sha'ib → *Iraq* | 30°59N 44°34E | **46** D5 |
| Firozabad *India* | 27°10N 78°25E | **43** F8 |
| Firozpur *India* | 30°55N 74°40E | **42** D6 |
| Firozpur-Jhirka *India* | 27°48N 76°57E | **42** F7 |
| Fīrūzābād *Iran* | 28°52N 52°35E | **47** D7 |
| Fīrūzkūh *Iran* | 35°50N 52°50E | **47** C7 |
| Firvale *Canada* | 52°27N 126°13W | **70** C3 |
| Fish → *Namibia* | 28°7S 17°10E | **56** C2 |
| Fish → *S. Africa* | 31°30S 20°16E | **56** D3 |
| Fish River Canyon | | |
|   *Namibia* | 27°40S 17°35E | **56** C2 |
| Fisher B. *Canada* | 51°35N 97°13W | **71** C9 |
| Fishers I. *U.S.A.* | 41°15N 72°0W | **83** E13 |
| Fishguard *U.K.* | 52°0N 4°58W | **13** E3 |
| Fishing L. *Canada* | 52°10N 95°24W | **71** C9 |
| Fishkill *U.S.A.* | 41°32N 73°54W | **83** E11 |
| Fisterra, C. *Spain* | 42°50N 9°19W | **21** A1 |
| Fitchburg *Mass., U.S.A.* | 42°35N 71°48W | **83** D13 |
| Fitchburg *Wis., U.S.A.* | 42°58N 89°28W | **80** D9 |
| Fitz Roy *Argentina* | 47°0S 67°0W | **96** F3 |
| Fitz Roy, Cerro *Argentina* | 49°17S 73°5W | **96** F2 |
| Fitzgerald *Canada* | 59°51N 111°36W | **70** B6 |
| Fitzgerald *U.S.A.* | 31°43N 83°15W | **85** F13 |
| Fitzgerald River △ | | |
|   *Australia* | 33°53S 119°55E | **61** F3 |
| Fitzmaurice → *Australia* | 14°45S 130°5E | **60** B5 |
| Fitzroy → *Queens.,* | | |
|   *Australia* | 23°32S 150°52E | **62** C5 |
| Fitzroy → *W. Austral.,* | | |
|   *Australia* | 17°31S 123°35E | **60** C3 |
| Fitzroy Crossing *Australia* | 18°9S 125°38E | **60** C4 |
| Fitzwilliam I. *Canada* | 45°30N 81°45W | **82** A3 |
| Fiume = Rijeka *Croatia* | 45°20N 14°21E | **16** F8 |
| Five Points *U.S.A.* | 36°26N 120°6W | **78** J6 |
| Fizi *Dem. Rep. of the Congo* | 4°17S 28°55E | **54** E5 |
| Flagstaff *U.S.A.* | 35°12N 111°39W | **77** J8 |
| Flagstaff L. *U.S.A.* | 45°12N 70°18W | **83** A14 |
| Flaherty I. *Canada* | 56°15N 79°15W | **72** A4 |
| Flåm *Norway* | 60°50N 7°7E | **8** F12 |
| Flambeau → *U.S.A.* | 45°18N 91°14W | **80** C8 |
| Flamborough Hd. *U.K.* | 54°7N 0°5W | **12** C7 |
| Flaming Gorge △ | | |
|   *U.S.A.* | 41°10N 109°25W | **76** F9 |
| Flaming Gorge Res. | | |
|   *U.S.A.* | 41°10N 109°25W | **76** F9 |
| Flamingo, Teluk *Indonesia* | 5°30S 138°0E | **37** F9 |
| Flanders = Flandre *Europe* | 50°50N 2°30E | **15** B9 |
| Flandre *Europe* | 50°50N 2°30E | **15** B9 |
| Flandre-Occidentale = West- | | |
|   Vlaanderen □ *Belgium* | 51°0N 3°0E | **15** D2 |
| Flandre-Orientale = Oost- | | |
|   Vlaanderen □ *Belgium* | 51°5N 3°50E | **15** C3 |
| Flandreau *U.S.A.* | 44°3N 96°36W | **80** C5 |
| Flanigan *U.S.A.* | 40°10N 119°53W | **78** E7 |
| Flannan Is. *U.K.* | 58°17N 7°36W | **11** C1 |
| Flåsjön *Sweden* | 64°5N 15°40E | **8** D16 |
| Flat → *Canada* | 61°33N 125°18W | **70** A3 |
| Flat I. *Mauritius* | 19°53S 57°35E | **55** d |
| Flat I. *China Sea* | 10°49N 115°49E | **36** B5 |
| Flathead L. *U.S.A.* | 47°51N 114°8W | **76** C6 |
| Flattery, C. *Australia* | 14°58S 145°21E | **62** A4 |
| Flattery, C. *U.S.A.* | 48°23N 124°29W | **78** B2 |
| Flatwoods *U.S.A.* | 38°31N 82°43W | **81** F12 |
| Fleetwood *U.K.* | 53°55N 3°1W | **12** D4 |
| Fleetwood *U.S.A.* | 40°27N 75°49W | **83** F9 |
| Flekkefjord *Norway* | 58°18N 6°39E | **9** G12 |
| Flemington *U.S.A.* | 41°7N 77°28E | **82** F7 |
| Flensburg *Germany* | 54°47N 9°27E | **16** A5 |
| Flers *France* | 48°47N 0°33W | **20** B3 |
| Flesherton *Canada* | 44°16N 80°33W | **82** B4 |
| Flesko, Tanjung *Indonesia* | 0°29N 124°30E | **37** D6 |
| Fleurieu Pen. *Australia* | 35°40S 138°5E | **63** F2 |
| Flevoland □ *Neths.* | 52°30N 5°30E | **15** B5 |
| Flin Flon *Canada* | 54°46N 101°53W | **71** C8 |
| Flinders → *Australia* | 17°36S 140°36E | **62** B3 |
| Flinders B. *Australia* | 34°19S 115°19E | **61** F2 |
| Flinders Group *Australia* | 14°11S 144°15E | **62** A3 |
| Flinders I. *S. Austral.,* | | |
|   *Australia* | 33°44S 134°41E | **63** E1 |
| Flinders I. *Tas., Australia* | 40°0S 148°0E | **63** G4 |
| Flinders Ranges | | |
|   *Australia* | 31°30S 138°30E | **63** E2 |
| Flinders Reefs *Australia* | 17°37S 148°31E | **62** B4 |
| Flint *U.K.* | 53°15N 3°8W | **12** D4 |
| Flint *U.S.A.* | 43°1N 83°41W | **81** D12 |
| Flint → *U.S.A.* | 30°57N 84°34W | **85** F12 |
| Flint I. *Kiribati* | 11°26S 151°48W | **65** J12 |
| Flintshire □ *U.K.* | 53°17N 3°17W | **12** D4 |
| Flodden *U.K.* | 55°37N 2°8W | **12** B5 |
| Floodplains △ *Sri Lanka* | 8°10N 81°10E | **45** K5 |
| Floodwood *U.S.A.* | 46°56N 92°55W | **80** B7 |
| Flora *U.S.A.* | 38°40N 88°29W | **80** F9 |
| Florala *U.S.A.* | 31°0N 86°20W | **85** F11 |
| Florence = Firenze *Italy* | 43°46N 11°15E | **22** C4 |
| Florence *Ala., U.S.A.* | 34°48N 87°41W | **85** D11 |
| Florence *Ariz., U.S.A.* | 33°2N 111°23W | **77** K8 |
| Florence *Colo., U.S.A.* | 38°23N 105°8W | **76** G11 |
| Florence *Oreg., U.S.A.* | 43°58N 124°7W | **76** D1 |
| Florence *S.C., U.S.A.* | 34°12N 79°46W | **85** D15 |
| Florence, L. *Australia* | 28°53S 138°9E | **63** D2 |
| Florencia *Colombia* | 1°36N 75°36W | **92** C3 |
| Florennes *Belgium* | 50°15N 4°35E | **15** D4 |
| Florenville *Belgium* | 49°40N 5°19E | **15** E5 |
| Flores *Azores* | 39°26N 31°13W | **52** a |
| Flores *Guatemala* | 16°59N 89°50W | **88** C2 |
| Flores *Indonesia* | 8°35S 121°0E | **37** F6 |
| Flores I. *Canada* | 49°20N 126°10W | **70** D3 |
| Flores Sea *Indonesia* | 6°30S 120°0E | **37** F6 |
| Floreşti *Moldova* | 47°53N 28°17E | **17** E15 |
| Floresville *U.S.A.* | 29°8N 98°10W | **84** G5 |
| Floriano *Brazil* | 6°50S 43°0W | **93** E10 |
| Florianópolis *Brazil* | 27°30S 48°30W | **95** B6 |
| Florida *Cuba* | 21°32N 78°14W | **88** B4 |
| Florida *Uruguay* | 34°7S 56°10W | **95** C4 |
| Florida □ *U.S.A.* | 28°0N 82°0W | **85** G14 |
| Florida, Straits of *U.S.A.* | 25°0N 80°0W | **88** B4 |
| Florida B. *U.S.A.* | 25°0N 80°45W | **88** B3 |
| Florida Keys *U.S.A.* | 24°40N 81°0W | **85** J14 |
| Florin *U.S.A.* | 38°30N 121°24W | **78** G5 |
| Florina *Greece* | 40°48N 21°26E | **23** D9 |
| Florissant *U.S.A.* | 38°47N 90°19W | **80** F8 |
| Florø *Norway* | 61°35N 5°1E | **8** F11 |
| Flower Station *Canada* | 45°10N 76°41W | **83** A8 |
| Flowerpot I. *Canada* | 45°18N 81°38W | **82** A3 |
| Floydada *U.S.A.* | 33°59N 101°20W | **84** E4 |
| Fluk *Indonesia* | 1°42S 127°44E | **37** E7 |
| Flushing = Vlissingen | | |
|   *Neths.* | 51°26N 3°34E | **15** C3 |
| Fly → *Papua N. G.* | 8°25S 143°0E | **58** B7 |
| Flying Fish, C. *Antarctica* | 72°6S 102°29W | **5** D15 |
| Foa *Tonga* | 19°45S 174°18W | **59** c |
| Foam Lake *Canada* | 51°40N 103°32W | **71** C8 |
| Foça *Turkey* | 38°39N 26°46E | **23** E12 |
| Fochabers *U.K.* | 57°37N 3°6W | **11** D5 |
| Focşani *Romania* | 45°41N 27°15E | **17** F14 |
| Fogang *China* | 23°52N 113°30E | **35** F9 |
| Fóggia *Italy* | 41°27N 15°34E | **22** D6 |
| Fogo *Cabo Verde* | 15°5N 24°20W | **52** b |
| Fogo *Canada* | 49°43N 54°17W | **73** C9 |
| Fogo I. *Canada* | 49°40N 54°5W | **73** C9 |
| Föhr *Germany* | 54°43N 8°30E | **16** A5 |
| Foix *France* | 42°58N 1°38E | **20** E4 |
| Folda *Nord-Trøndelag,* | | |
|   *Norway* | 64°32N 10°30E | **8** D14 |
| Folda *Nordland, Norway* | 67°38N 14°50E | **8** C16 |
| Foley *Botswana* | 21°34S 27°21E | **56** B7 |
| Foley *U.S.A.* | 30°24N 87°41W | **85** F11 |
| Foleyet *Canada* | 48°15N 82°25W | **72** C3 |
| Folgefonna *Norway* | 60°3N 6°23E | **9** F12 |
| Foligno *Italy* | 42°57N 12°42E | **22** C5 |
| Folkestone *U.K.* | 51°5N 1°12E | **13** F9 |
| Folkston *U.S.A.* | 30°50N 82°0W | **85** F13 |
| Follansbee *U.S.A.* | 40°19N 80°35W | **82** F4 |
| Folsom *U.S.A.* | 38°40N 121°9W | **78** G5 |
| Folsom L. *U.S.A.* | 38°42N 121°9W | **78** G5 |
| Fomboni *Comoros Is.* | 12°18S 43°46E | **55** a |
| Fond-du-Lac *Canada* | 59°19N 107°12W | **71** B7 |
| Fond du Lac *U.S.A.* | 43°47N 88°27W | **80** D9 |
| Fond-du-Lac → *Canada* | 59°17N 106°0W | **71** B7 |
| Fonda *U.S.A.* | 42°57N 74°22W | **83** D10 |
| Fondi *Italy* | 41°21N 13°25E | **22** D5 |
| Fongafale *Tuvalu* | 8°31S 179°13E | **58** B10 |
| Fonsagrada = A Fonsagrada | | |
|   *Spain* | 43°8N 7°4W | **21** A2 |
| Fonseca, G. de | | |
|   *Cent. Amer.* | 13°10N 87°40W | **88** D2 |
| Fontainebleau *France* | 48°24N 2°40E | **20** B5 |
| Fontana *U.S.A.* | 34°6N 117°26W | **79** L9 |
| Fontas → *Canada* | 58°14N 121°48W | **70** B4 |
| Fonte Boa *Brazil* | 2°33S 66°0W | **92** D5 |
| Fontenay-le-Comte | | |
|   *France* | 46°28N 0°48W | **20** C3 |
| Fontenelle Res. *U.S.A.* | 42°1N 110°3W | **76** E8 |
| Fontur *Iceland* | 66°23N 14°32W | **8** C6 |
| Fonuafo'ou *Tonga* | 20°19S 175°25W | **59** c |
| Fonualei *Tonga* | 18°1S 174°19W | **59** c |
| Foochow = Fuzhou | | |
|   *China* | 26°5N 119°16E | **35** D12 |
| Foping *China* | 33°41N 108°0E | **32** H5 |
| Foraker, Mt. *U.S.A.* | 62°58N 151°24W | **74** C9 |
| Forbes *Australia* | 33°22S 148°5E | **63** E4 |
| Forbesganj *India* | 26°17N 87°18E | **43** F12 |
| Ford City *Calif., U.S.A.* | 35°9N 119°27W | **79** K7 |
| Ford City *Pa., U.S.A.* | 40°46N 79°32W | **82** F5 |
| Førde *Norway* | 61°27N 5°53E | **8** F11 |
| Fords Bridge *Australia* | 29°41S 145°29E | **63** D4 |
| Fordyce *U.S.A.* | 33°49N 92°25W | **84** E8 |
| Forel, Mt. *Greenland* | 66°52N 36°55W | **4** C6 |
| Foremost *Canada* | 49°26N 111°34W | **70** D6 |
| Forest *Canada* | 43°6N 82°0W | **82** C2 |
| Forest *U.S.A.* | 32°22N 89°29W | **85** E10 |
| Forest City *Iowa, U.S.A.* | 43°16N 93°39W | **80** D7 |
| Forest City *N.C., U.S.A.* | 35°20N 81°52W | **85** D14 |
| Forest City *Pa., U.S.A.* | 41°39N 75°28W | **83** E9 |
| Forest Grove *U.S.A.* | 45°31N 123°7W | **78** E3 |
| Forestburg *Canada* | 52°35N 112°1W | **70** C6 |
| Foresthill *U.S.A.* | 39°1N 120°49W | **78** F6 |
| Forestier Pen. *Australia* | 43°0S 148°0E | **63** G4 |
| Forestville *Canada* | 48°48N 69°2W | **73** C6 |
| Forestville *Calif., U.S.A.* | 38°28N 122°54W | **78** G4 |
| Forestville *N.Y., U.S.A.* | 42°28N 79°10W | **82** D5 |
| Forfar *U.K.* | 56°39N 2°53W | **11** E6 |
| Forillon △ *Canada* | 48°46N 64°12W | **73** C7 |
| Forks *U.S.A.* | 47°57N 124°23W | **78** C2 |
| Forksville *U.S.A.* | 41°29N 76°35W | **83** E8 |
| Forlì *Italy* | 44°13N 12°3E | **22** B5 |
| Forman *U.S.A.* | 46°7N 97°38W | **80** B5 |
| Formby Pt. *U.K.* | 53°33N 3°6W | **12** D4 |
| Formentera *Spain* | 38°43N 1°27E | **21** C6 |
| Formentor, C. de *Spain* | 39°58N 3°13E | **21** C7 |
| Former Yugoslav Republic of | | |
|   Macedonia = Macedonia ■ | | |
|   *Europe* | 41°53N 21°40E | **23** D9 |
| Fórmia *Italy* | 41°15N 13°37E | **22** D5 |
| Formosa = Taiwan ■ | | |
|   *Asia* | 23°30N 121°0E | **35** F13 |
| Formosa *Argentina* | 26°15S 58°10W | **94** B4 |
| Formosa *Brazil* | 15°32S 47°20W | **93** G9 |
| Formosa □ *Argentina* | 25°0S 60°0W | **94** B4 |
| Formosa, Serra *Brazil* | 12°0S 55°0W | **93** F8 |
| Forollhogna △ *Norway* | 62°39N 10°41E | **8** E14 |
| Føroyar ☐ *Atl. Oc.* | 62°0N 7°0W | **8** F9 |
| Forres *U.K.* | 57°37N 3°37W | **11** D5 |
| Forrest *Australia* | 30°51S 128°6E | **61** F4 |
| Forrest, Mt. *Australia* | 24°48S 127°45E | **61** D4 |
| Forrest City *U.S.A.* | 35°1N 90°47W | **85** D9 |
| Forsayth *Australia* | 18°33S 143°34E | **62** B3 |
| Forssa *Finland* | 60°49N 23°38E | **8** F20 |
| Forst *Germany* | 51°45N 14°37E | **16** C8 |
| Forster *Australia* | 32°12S 152°31E | **63** E5 |
| Forsyth *U.S.A.* | 46°16N 106°41W | **76** C10 |
| Fort Abbas *Pakistan* | 29°12N 72°52E | **42** E5 |
| Fort Albany *Canada* | 52°15N 81°35W | **72** B3 |
| Fort Assiniboine *Canada* | 54°20N 114°45W | **70** C6 |
| Fort Augustus *U.K.* | 57°9N 4°42W | **11** D4 |
| Fort Benton *U.S.A.* | 47°49N 110°40W | **76** C8 |
| Fort Bragg *U.S.A.* | 39°26N 123°48W | **76** G2 |
| Fort Bridger *U.S.A.* | 41°19N 110°23W | **76** F8 |
| Fort Chipewyan *Canada* | 58°42N 111°8W | **71** B6 |
| Fort Clatsop = Lewis and Clark △ | | |
|   *U.S.A.* | 46°8N 123°53W | **78** D3 |
| Fort Collins *U.S.A.* | 40°35N 105°5W | **76** F11 |
| Fort-Coulonge *Canada* | 45°50N 76°45W | **72** C4 |
| Fort Covington *U.S.A.* | 44°59N 74°29W | **83** B10 |
| Fort Dauphin = Taolanaro | | |
|   *Madag.* | 25°2S 47°0E | **55** K9 |
| Fort Davis *U.S.A.* | 30°35N 103°54W | **84** F3 |
| Fort-de-France *Martinique* | 14°36N 61°5W | **88** c |
| Fort Defiance *U.S.A.* | 35°45N 109°5W | **77** J9 |
| Fort Dodge *U.S.A.* | 42°30N 94°11W | **80** D6 |
| Fort Edward *U.S.A.* | 43°16N 73°35W | **83** C11 |
| Fort Erie *Canada* | 42°54N 78°56W | **82** D6 |
| Fort Fairfield *U.S.A.* | 46°46N 67°50W | **81** B20 |
| Fort Frances *Canada* | 48°36N 93°24W | **71** D10 |
| Fort Franklin = Déline | | |
|   *Canada* | 65°11N 123°25W | **68** D7 |
| Fort Garland *U.S.A.* | 37°26N 105°26W | **77** H11 |
| Fort George = Chisasibi | | |
|   *Canada* | 53°50N 79°0W | **72** B4 |
| Fort Good Hope *Canada* | 66°14N 128°40W | **68** D6 |
| Fort Hope = Eabametoong | | |
|   *Canada* | 51°30N 88°0W | **72** B2 |
| Fort Irwin *U.S.A.* | 35°16N 116°41W | **79** K10 |
| Fort Kent *U.S.A.* | 47°15N 68°36W | **81** B19 |
| Fort Klamath *U.S.A.* | 42°42N 122°0W | **76** D3 |
| Fort Laramie *U.S.A.* | 42°13N 104°31W | **76** E11 |
| Fort Liard *Canada* | 60°14N 123°30W | **70** A4 |
| Fort Liberté *Haiti* | 19°42N 71°51W | **89** C5 |
| Fort Lupton *U.S.A.* | 40°5N 104°49W | **76** F11 |
| Fort MacKay *Canada* | 57°12N 111°41W | **70** B6 |
| Fort Macleod *Canada* | 49°45N 113°30W | **70** D6 |
| Fort McMurray *Canada* | 56°44N 111°7W | **70** B6 |
| Fort McPherson *Canada* | 67°30N 134°55W | **68** D5 |
| Fort Madison *U.S.A.* | 40°38N 91°27W | **80** E8 |
| Fort Meade *U.S.A.* | 27°45N 81°48W | **85** H14 |
| Fort Morgan *U.S.A.* | 40°15N 103°48W | **76** F12 |
| Fort Myers *U.S.A.* | 26°39N 81°52W | **85** H14 |
| Fort Nelson *Canada* | 58°50N 122°44W | **70** B4 |
| Fort Nelson → *Canada* | 59°32N 124°0W | **70** B4 |
| Fort Norman = Tulita | | |
|   *Canada* | 64°57N 125°30W | **68** E6 |
| Fort Payne *U.S.A.* | 34°26N 85°43W | **85** D12 |
| Fort Peck *U.S.A.* | 48°1N 106°27W | **76** B10 |
| Fort Peck Dam *U.S.A.* | 48°0N 106°26W | **76** C10 |
| Fort Peck L. *U.S.A.* | 48°0N 106°26W | **76** C10 |
| Fort Pierce *U.S.A.* | 27°27N 80°20W | **85** H14 |
| Fort Pierre *U.S.A.* | 44°21N 100°22W | **80** C3 |
| Fort Plain *U.S.A.* | 42°56N 74°37W | **83** D10 |
| Fort Portal *Uganda* | 0°40N 30°20E | **54** D6 |
| Fort Providence *Canada* | 61°3N 117°40W | **70** A5 |
| Fort Qu'Appelle *Canada* | 50°45N 103°50W | **71** C8 |
| Fort Resolution *Canada* | 61°10N 113°40W | **70** A6 |
| Fort Ross *U.S.A.* | 38°32N 123°13W | **78** G3 |
| Fort Rupert = Waskaganish | | |
|   *Canada* | 51°30N 78°40W | **72** B4 |
| Fort St. James *Canada* | 54°30N 124°10W | **70** C4 |
| Fort St. John *Canada* | 56°15N 120°50W | **70** B4 |
| Fort Saskatchewan | | |
|   *Canada* | 53°40N 113°15W | **70** C6 |
| Fort Scott *U.S.A.* | 37°50N 94°42W | **80** G6 |
| Fort Severn *Canada* | 56°0N 87°40W | **72** A2 |
| Fort Shevchenko | | |
|   *Kazakhstan* | 44°35N 50°23E | **19** F9 |
| Fort Simpson *Canada* | 61°45N 121°15W | **70** A4 |
| Fort Smith *Canada* | 60°0N 111°51W | **70** B6 |
| Fort Smith *U.S.A.* | 35°23N 94°25W | **84** D7 |
| Fort Stockton *U.S.A.* | 30°53N 102°53W | **84** F3 |
| Fort Sumner *U.S.A.* | 34°28N 104°15W | **77** J11 |
| Fort Thompson *U.S.A.* | 44°3N 99°26W | **80** C4 |
| Fort Union △ *U.S.A.* | 35°54N 105°1W | **77** J11 |
| Fort Valley *U.S.A.* | 32°33N 83°53W | **85** E13 |
| Fort Vermilion *Canada* | 58°24N 116°0W | **70** B5 |
| Fort Walton Beach | | |
|   *U.S.A.* | 30°25N 86°36W | **85** F11 |
| Fort Ware *Canada* | 57°26N 125°41W | **70** B3 |
| Fort Wayne *U.S.A.* | 41°4N 85°9W | **81** E11 |
| Fort William *U.K.* | 56°49N 5°7W | **11** E3 |
| Fort Yates *U.S.A.* | 46°5N 100°38W | **80** B3 |
| Fort Yukon *U.S.A.* | 66°34N 145°16W | **68** D2 |
| Fortaleza *Brazil* | 3°45S 38°35W | **93** D11 |
| Forteau *Canada* | 51°28N 56°58W | **73** B8 |
| Fortescue → *Australia* | 21°0S 116°4E | **60** D2 |
| Fortescue River Roadhouse | | |
|   *Australia* | 21°17S 116°8E | **60** D2 |
| Forth → *U.K.* | 56°9N 3°50W | **11** E5 |
| Fortrose *U.K.* | 57°35N 4°9W | **11** D4 |
| Fortuna *Calif., U.S.A.* | 40°36N 124°9W | **76** F1 |
| Fortuna *N. Dak., U.S.A.* | 48°55N 103°47W | **80** A2 |
| Fortune *Canada* | 47°4N 55°50W | **73** C8 |
| Fortune B. *Canada* | 47°30N 55°22W | **73** C8 |
| Forūr *Iran* | 26°17N 54°32E | **47** E7 |
| Fosen *Norway* | 63°50N 10°20E | **8** E14 |
| Fosnavåg *Norway* | 62°22N 5°38E | **8** E11 |
| Fossano *Italy* | 44°33N 7°43E | **20** D7 |
| Fossil *U.S.A.* | 45°0N 120°9W | **76** D3 |
| Fossil Butte △ *U.S.A.* | 41°50N 110°27W | **76** F8 |
| Foster *Canada* | 45°17N 72°30W | **83** A12 |
| Foster → *Canada* | 55°47N 105°49W | **71** B7 |
| Fosters Ra. *Australia* | 21°35S 133°48E | **62** C1 |
| Fostoria *U.S.A.* | 41°10N 83°25W | **81** E12 |
| Fougères *France* | 48°21N 1°14W | **20** B3 |
| Foul Pt. *Sri Lanka* | 8°35N 81°18E | **45** K5 |
| Foula *U.K.* | 60°10N 2°5W | **11** A6 |
| Foulness I. *U.K.* | 51°36N 0°55E | **13** F8 |
| Foulpointe *Madag.* | 17°41S 49°31E | **55** B8 |
| Foumban *Cameroon* | 5°45N 10°50E | **54** C2 |
| Foumbouni *Comoros Is.* | 11°51S 43°29E | **55** a |
| Fountain *U.S.A.* | 38°41N 104°42W | **76** G11 |
| Fountain Hills *U.S.A.* | 33°37N 111°43W | **77** K8 |
| Fountain Springs | | |
|   *U.S.A.* | 35°54N 118°51W | **79** K8 |
| Four Mountains, Is. of | | |
|   *U.S.A.* | 53°0N 170°0W | **74** E5 |
| Fouriesburg *S. Africa* | 28°38S 28°14E | **57** D4 |
| Fourni *Greece* | 37°36N 26°32E | **23** F12 |
| Fourth Cataract *Sudan* | 18°47N 32°3E | **53** E12 |
| Fouta Djallon *Guinea* | 11°20N 12°10W | **52** F3 |
| Foux, Cap-à- *Haiti* | 19°43N 73°27W | **89** C5 |
| Foveaux Str. *N.Z.* | 46°42S 168°10E | **59** G2 |
| Fowey *U.K.* | 50°20N 4°39W | **13** G3 |
| Fowler *Calif., U.S.A.* | 36°38N 119°41W | **78** J7 |
| Fowler *Colo., U.S.A.* | 38°8N 104°2W | **76** G11 |
| Fowler, Pt. *Australia* | 32°2S 132°3E | **61** F5 |
| Fowlers B. *Australia* | 31°59S 132°34E | **61** F5 |
| Fowman *Iran* | 37°13N 49°19E | **47** B6 |
| Fox → *Canada* | 56°3N 93°18W | **71** B10 |
| Fox Creek *Canada* | 54°24N 116°48W | **70** C5 |
| Fox Is. *U.S.A.* | 53°0N 168°0W | **74** E6 |
| Fox Lake *Canada* | 58°28N 114°31W | **70** B6 |
| Fox Valley *Canada* | 50°30N 109°25W | **71** C7 |
| Foxboro *Canada* | 44°14N 77°26W | **82** B7 |
| Foxboro *U.S.A.* | 42°4N 71°16W | **83** D13 |
| Foxdale *Australia* | 20°22S 148°35E | **62** b |
| Foxe Basin *Canada* | 66°0N 77°0W | **69** D16 |
| Foxe Chan. *Canada* | 65°0N 80°0W | **69** E16 |
| Foxe Pen. *Canada* | 65°0N 76°0W | **69** E16 |
| Foxford *Ireland* | 53°59N 9°7W | **10** C2 |
| Foxton *N.Z.* | 40°29S 175°18E | **59** D5 |
| Foyle, Lough *U.K.* | 55°7N 7°4W | **10** A4 |
| Foynes *Ireland* | 52°37N 9°7W | **10** D2 |
| Foz do Cunene *Angola* | 17°15S 11°48E | **56** A1 |
| Foz do Iguaçu *Brazil* | 25°30S 54°30W | **95** B5 |
| Frackville *U.S.A.* | 40°47N 76°14W | **83** F8 |
| Fraile Muerto *Uruguay* | 32°31S 54°32W | **95** C5 |
| Framingham *U.S.A.* | 42°18N 71°24W | **83** D13 |
| Franca *Brazil* | 20°33S 47°30W | **93** H9 |
| Francavilla Fontana | | |
|   *Italy* | 40°32N 17°35E | **23** D7 |
| France ■ *Europe* | 47°0N 3°0E | **20** C5 |
| Frances → *Canada* | 36°41S 140°55E | **63** F3 |
| Frances → *Canada* | 60°16N 129°10W | **70** A3 |
| Frances L. *Canada* | 61°23N 129°30W | **70** A3 |
| Franceville *Gabon* | 1°40S 13°32E | **54** E2 |
| Franche-Comté *France* | 46°50N 5°55E | **20** C6 |
| Francis Case, L. *U.S.A.* | 43°4N 98°34W | **80** D4 |
| Francisco Beltrão *Brazil* | 26°5S 53°4W | **95** B5 |
| Francisco Ignacio Madero *Coahuila,* | | |
|   *Mexico* | 25°48N 103°18W | **86** B4 |
| Francisco Ignacio Madero *Durango,* | | |
|   *Mexico* | 24°26N 104°18W | **86** C4 |
| Francisco Ignacio Madero, Presa | | |
|   *Mexico* | 25°10N 105°37W | **86** B3 |
| Francistown *Botswana* | 21°7S 27°33E | **57** B4 |
| François *Canada* | 47°35N 56°45W | **73** C8 |
| François L. *Canada* | 54°0N 125°30W | **70** C3 |
| Francois Peron △ | | |
|   *Australia* | 25°42S 113°33E | **61** E1 |
| Franeker *Neths.* | 53°12N 5°33E | **15** A5 |
| Frank Hann △ *Australia* | 33°12S 120°19E | **61** F3 |
| Frankford *Canada* | 44°12N 77°36W | **82** B7 |
| Frankfort *S. Africa* | 27°17S 28°30E | **57** D4 |
| Frankfort *Ind., U.S.A.* | 40°17N 86°31W | **80** E10 |
| Frankfort *Kans., U.S.A.* | 39°42N 96°25W | **80** F5 |
| Frankfort *Ky., U.S.A.* | 38°12N 84°52W | **81** F11 |
| Frankfort *N.Y., U.S.A.* | 43°2N 75°4W | **83** C9 |
| Frankfurt *Brandenburg,* | | |
|   *Germany* | 52°20N 14°32E | **16** B8 |
| Frankfurt *Hessen, Germany* | 50°7N 8°41E | **16** C5 |
| Fränkische Alb *Germany* | 49°10N 11°23E | **16** D6 |
| Frankland → *Australia* | 35°0S 116°48E | **61** G2 |
| Franklin *Ky., U.S.A.* | 36°43N 86°35W | **80** G10 |
| Franklin *La., U.S.A.* | 29°48N 91°30W | **84** G9 |
| Franklin *Mass., U.S.A.* | 42°5N 71°24W | **83** D13 |
| Franklin *N.H., U.S.A.* | 43°27N 71°39W | **83** C13 |
| Franklin *N.Y., U.S.A.* | 42°20N 75°9W | **83** D9 |
| Franklin *Nebr., U.S.A.* | 40°6N 98°57W | **80** E4 |
| Franklin *Pa., U.S.A.* | 41°24N 79°50W | **82** E5 |
| Franklin *Va., U.S.A.* | 36°41N 76°56W | **81** G15 |
| Franklin *W. Va., U.S.A.* | 38°39N 79°20W | **81** F14 |
| Franklin B. *Canada* | 69°45N 126°0W | **68** D6 |
| Franklin D. Roosevelt L. | | |
|   *U.S.A.* | 48°18N 118°9W | **76** B4 |
| Franklin-Gordon Wild Rivers △ | | |
|   *Australia* | 42°19S 145°51E | **63** G4 |
| Franklin I. *Antarctica* | 76°10S 168°30E | **5** D11 |
| Franklin I. *Canada* | 45°24N 80°20W | **82** A4 |
| Franklin L. *U.S.A.* | 40°25N 115°22W | **76** F6 |
| Franklin Mts. *Canada* | 65°0N 125°0W | **68** C7 |
| Franklin Str. *Canada* | 72°0N 96°0W | **68** C12 |
| Franklinton *U.S.A.* | 30°51N 90°9W | **85** F9 |
| Franklinville *U.S.A.* | 42°20N 78°27W | **82** D6 |
| Frankston *Australia* | 38°8S 145°8E | **63** F4 |
| Fransfontein *Namibia* | 20°12S 15°1E | **56** C2 |
| Frantsa Iosifa, Zemlya | | |
|   *Arctic* | 82°0N 55°0E | **26** A6 |
| Franz *Canada* | 48°25N 84°30W | **72** C3 |
| Franz Josef Land = Frantsa Iosifa, | | |
|   Zemlya *Arctic* | 82°0N 55°0E | **26** A6 |
| Fraser → *B.C., Canada* | 49°7N 123°11W | **78** A3 |
| Fraser → *Nfld. & L.,* | | |
|   *Canada* | 56°39N 62°10W | **73** A7 |
| Fraser, Mt. *Australia* | 25°35S 118°20E | **61** E2 |
| Fraser I. *Australia* | 25°15S 153°10E | **63** D5 |
| Fraser Lake *Canada* | 54°0N 124°50W | **70** C4 |
| Fraserburg *S. Africa* | 31°55S 21°30E | **56** D3 |
| Fraserburgh *U.K.* | 57°42N 2°1W | **11** D6 |
| Fraserdale *Canada* | 49°55N 81°37W | **72** C3 |
| Fray Bentos *Uruguay* | 33°10S 58°15W | **94** C4 |
| Fray Jorge △ *Chile* | 30°42S 71°40W | **94** C1 |
| Frazier Downs ♦ | | |
|   *Australia* | 18°48S 121°42E | **60** C3 |
| Fredericia *Denmark* | 55°34N 9°45E | **9** J13 |
| Frederick *Md., U.S.A.* | 39°25N 77°25W | **81** F15 |
| Frederick *Okla., U.S.A.* | 34°23N 99°1W | **84** D5 |
| Frederick *S. Dak., U.S.A.* | 45°50N 98°31W | **80** C4 |
| Fredericksburg *Pa.,* | | |
|   *U.S.A.* | 40°27N 76°26W | **83** F8 |
| Fredericksburg *Tex.,* | | |
|   *U.S.A.* | 30°16N 98°52W | **84** F5 |
| Fredericksburg *Va.,* | | |
|   *U.S.A.* | 38°18N 77°28W | **81** F15 |
| Fredericktown *Mo.,* | | |
|   *U.S.A.* | 37°34N 90°18W | **80** G8 |
| Fredericktown *Ohio,* | | |
|   *U.S.A.* | 40°29N 82°33W | **82** F2 |
| Frederico Westphalen | | |
|   *Brazil* | 27°22S 53°24W | **95** B5 |
| Fredericton *Canada* | 45°57N 66°40W | **73** C6 |
| Fredericton Junction | | |
|   *Canada* | 45°41N 66°40W | **73** C6 |
| Frederikshåb = Paamiut | | |
|   *Greenland* | 62°0N 49°43W | **4** C5 |
| Frederikshamn = Hamina | | |
|   *Finland* | 60°34N 27°12E | **8** F22 |
| Frederikshavn *Denmark* | 57°28N 10°31E | **9** H14 |
| Frederiksted | | |
|   *U.S. Virgin Is.* | 17°43N 64°53W | **89** C7 |
| Fredonia *Ariz., U.S.A.* | 36°57N 112°32W | **77** H7 |
| Fredonia *Kans., U.S.A.* | 37°32N 95°49W | **80** G6 |
| Fredonia *N.Y., U.S.A.* | 42°26N 79°20W | **82** D5 |
| Fredrikstad *Norway* | 59°13N 10°57E | **9** G14 |
| Free State □ *S. Africa* | 28°30S 27°0E | **56** C4 |
| Freehold *U.S.A.* | 40°16N 74°17W | **83** F10 |
| Freeland *U.S.A.* | 41°1N 75°54W | **83** E9 |
| Freels, C. *Nfld. & L.,* | | |
|   *Canada* | 49°15N 53°30W | **73** C9 |
| Freels, C. *Nfld. & L.,* | | |
|   *Canada* | 46°37N 53°32W | **73** C9 |
| Freeman *Calif., U.S.A.* | 35°35N 117°53W | **79** K9 |
| Freeman *S. Dak., U.S.A.* | 43°21N 97°26W | **80** D5 |
| Freeport *Bahamas* | 26°30N 78°47W | **88** A4 |
| Freeport *Ill., U.S.A.* | 42°17N 89°36W | **80** D9 |
| Freeport *N.Y., U.S.A.* | 40°39N 73°35W | **83** F11 |
| Freeport *Ohio, U.S.A.* | 40°12N 81°15W | **82** F3 |
| Freeport *Pa., U.S.A.* | 40°41N 79°41W | **82** F5 |
| Freeport *Tex., U.S.A.* | 28°57N 95°21W | **84** G7 |
| Freetown *S. Leone* | 8°30N 13°17W | **52** G3 |
| Freeville *U.S.A.* | 42°30N 76°20W | **83** D8 |
| Frégate, L. de la *Canada* | 53°15N 74°45W | **72** B5 |
| Fregenal de la Sierra | | |
|   *Spain* | 38°10N 6°39W | **21** C2 |
| Fregon *Australia* | 26°45S 132°1E | **61** E5 |
| Frei *Antarctica* | 62°30S 58°0W | **5** C18 |
| Freibourg = Fribourg | | |
|   *Switz.* | 46°49N 7°9E | **20** C7 |
| Freiburg *Germany* | 47°59N 7°51E | **16** E4 |
| Freire *Chile* | 38°54S 72°38W | **96** D2 |
| Freirina *Chile* | 28°30S 71°10W | **94** B1 |
| Freising *Germany* | 48°24N 11°45E | **16** D6 |
| Freistadt *Austria* | 48°30N 14°30E | **16** D8 |
| Fréjus *France* | 43°25N 6°44E | **20** E7 |
| Fremantle *Australia* | 32°7S 115°47E | **61** F2 |
| Fremont *Calif., U.S.A.* | 37°32N 121°57W | **78** H4 |
| Fremont *Mich., U.S.A.* | 43°28N 85°57W | **81** D11 |
| Fremont *Nebr., U.S.A.* | 41°26N 96°30W | **80** E5 |
| Fremont *Ohio, U.S.A.* | 41°21N 83°7W | **81** E12 |
| Fremont → *U.S.A.* | 38°24N 110°42W | **76** G8 |
| French Camp *U.S.A.* | 37°53N 121°16W | **78** H5 |
| French Cays = Plana Cays | | |
|   *Bahamas* | 22°38N 73°30W | **89** B5 |
| French Creek → *U.S.A.* | 41°24N 79°50W | **82** E5 |
| French Frigate Shoals | | |
|   *U.S.A.* | 23°45N 166°10W | **75** L6 |
| French Guiana □ *S. Amer.* | 4°0N 53°0W | **93** C8 |
| French Polynesia □ | | |
|   *Pac. Oc.* | 20°0S 145°0W | **65** J13 |
| French Riviera = Azur, Côte d' | | |
|   *France* | 43°25N 7°10E | **20** E7 |
| Frenchman Cr. → | | |
|   *N. Amer.* | 48°31N 107°10W | **76** B10 |
| Frenchman Cr. → | | |
|   *U.S.A.* | 40°14N 100°50W | **80** E3 |
| Fresco → *Brazil* | 7°15S 51°30W | **93** E8 |
| Freshfield, C. *Antarctica* | 68°25S 151°10E | **5** C10 |
| Fresnillo *Mexico* | 23°10N 102°53W | **86** C4 |
| Fresno *U.S.A.* | 36°44N 119°47W | **78** J7 |
| Fresno Res. *U.S.A.* | 48°36N 109°57W | **76** B9 |
| Frew → *Australia* | 20°0S 135°38E | **62** C2 |
| Frewsburg *U.S.A.* | 42°3N 79°10W | **82** D5 |
| Freycinet △ *Australia* | 42°11S 148°19E | **63** G4 |
| Freycinet Pen. *Australia* | 42°10S 148°25E | **63** G4 |
| Fria *Guinea* | 10°27N 13°38W | **52** F3 |
| Fria, C. *Namibia* | 18°0S 12°0E | **56** A1 |
| Frías *Argentina* | 28°40S 65°5W | **94** B2 |
| Friant *U.S.A.* | 36°59N 119°43W | **78** J7 |
| Fribourg *Switz.* | 46°49N 7°9E | **20** C7 |

Friday Harbor *U.S.A.* 48°32N 123°1W **78 B3**
Friedens *U.S.A.* 40°3N 78°59W **82 F6**
Friedrichshafen *Germany* 47°39N 9°30E **16 E5**
Friendship *U.S.A.* 42°12N 78°58W **82 D6**
Friesland □ *Neths.* 53°5N 5°50E **15 A5**
Frigate *Seychelles* 4°35S 55°56E **55 b**
Frio → *U.S.A.* 28°26N 98°11W **84 G5**
Frio, C. *Brazil* 22°50S 41°50W **90 F6**
Friona *U.S.A.* 34°38N 102°43W **84 D3**
Frisco *U.S.A.* 39°38N 96°49W **84 E6**
Fritch *U.S.A.* 35°38N 101°36W **84 D4**
Friza, Proliv *Russia* 45°30N 149°0E **27 E15**
Frobisher B. *Canada* 62°30N 66°0W **69 E18**
Frobisher Bay = Iqaluit
  *Canada* 63°44N 68°31W **69 E18**
Frobisher L. *Canada* 56°20N 108°15W **71 B7**
Frohavet *Norway* 64°0N 9°30E **8 E13**
Frome *U.K.* 51°14N 2°19W **13 F5**
Frome, L. *Australia* 30°45S 139°45E **63 E2**
Front Range *U.S.A.* 40°25N 105°45W **76 F11**
Front Royal *U.S.A.* 38°55N 78°12W **81 F14**
Frontenac △ *Canada* 44°32N 76°30W **83 B8**
Frontera *Mexico* 18°32N 92°38W **87 D6**
Fronteras *Mexico* 30°56N 109°31W **86 A3**
Frosinone *Italy* 41°38N 13°19E **22 D5**
Frostburg *U.S.A.* 39°39N 78°56W **81 F14**
Frostisen *Norway* 68°14N 17°10E **8 B17**
Frøya *Norway* 63°43N 8°40E **8 E13**
Fruita *U.S.A.* 39°9N 108°44W **76 G9**
Frunze = Bishkek
  *Kyrgyzstan* 42°54N 74°46E **30 C3**
Frutal *Brazil* 20°0S 49°0W **93 H9**
Frýdek-Místek *Czechia* 49°40N 18°20E **17 D10**
Fryeburg *U.S.A.* 44°1N 70°59W **83 B14**
Fu Jiang → *China* 30°0N 106°16E **34 C6**
Fu Xian = Wafangdian
  *China* 39°38N 121°58E **33 E11**
Fu Xian *China* 36°0N 109°20E **32 G5**
Fu'an *China* 27°11N 119°36E **35 D12**
Fubian *China* 31°17N 102°22E **34 B4**
Fucheng *China* 37°50N 116°10E **32 F9**
Fuchuan *China* 24°50N 111°5E **35 E8**
Fuchun Jiang → *China* 30°5N 120°5E **35 B13**
Fuding *China* 27°20N 120°12E **35 D13**
Fuengirola *Spain* 36°32N 4°41W **21 D3**
Fuentes de Oñoro *Spain* 40°33N 6°52W **21 B2**
Fuerte → *Mexico* 25°54N 109°22W **86 B3**
Fuerte Olimpo *Paraguay* 21°0S 57°51W **94 A4**
Fuerteventura *Canary Is.* 28°30N 14°0W **52 C3**
Fufeng *China* 34°22N 108°0E **32 G5**
Fugong *China* 27°5N 98°47E **34 D2**
Fugou *China* 34°3N 114°25E **32 G8**
Fugu *China* 39°2N 111°3E **32 E6**
Fuhai *China* 47°2N 87°25E **30 B6**
Fuḥaymī *Iraq* 34°16N 42°10E **46 C4**
Fuidhaigh = Wiay *U.K.* 57°24N 7°13W **11 D1**
Fuji *Japan* 35°9N 138°39E **29 G9**
Fuji-Hakone-Izu △
  *Japan* 35°15N 138°45E **29 G9**
Fuji-San *Japan* 35°22N 138°44E **29 G9**
Fuji-Yoshida *Japan* 35°30N 138°46E **29 G9**
Fujian □ *China* 26°0N 118°0E **35 E12**
Fujin *China* 47°16N 132°1E **31 B15**
Fujinomiya *Japan* 35°10N 138°40E **29 G9**
Fujisawa *Japan* 35°22N 139°29E **29 G9**
Fujiyama, Mt. = Fuji-San
  *Japan* 35°22N 138°44E **29 G9**
Fukagawa *Japan* 43°43N 142°2E **28 C11**
Fukien = Fujian □ *China* 26°0N 118°0E **35 E12**
Fukuchiyama *Japan* 35°19N 135°9E **29 G7**
Fukue *Japan* 32°41N 128°51E **29 H4**
Fukue-Shima *Japan* 32°40N 128°45E **29 H4**
Fukui *Japan* 36°5N 136°10E **29 F8**
Fukui □ *Japan* 36°0N 136°12E **29 G8**
Fukuoka *Japan* 33°39N 130°21E **29 H5**
Fukuoka □ *Japan* 33°30N 131°0E **29 H5**
Fukushima *Japan* 37°44N 140°28E **28 F10**
Fukushima □ *Japan* 37°30N 140°15E **28 F10**
Fukuyama *Japan* 34°35N 133°20E **29 G6**
Fulaga *Fiji* 19°8S 178°33W **59 a**
Fulda *Germany* 50°32N 9°40E **16 C5**
Fulda → *Germany* 51°25N 9°39E **16 C5**
Fulford Harbour *Canada* 48°47N 123°27W **78 B3**
Fuliang *China* 29°23N 117°14E **35 C11**
Fuling *China* 29°39N 107°17E **34 C6**
Fullerton *Calif., U.S.A.* 33°53N 117°56W **79 M9**
Fullerton *Nebr., U.S.A.* 41°22N 97°58W **80 E5**
Fulongquan *China* 44°20N 124°42E **33 B13**
Fulton *Mo., U.S.A.* 38°52N 91°57W **80 F8**
Fulton *N.Y., U.S.A.* 43°19N 76°25W **83 C8**
Fumin *China* 25°10N 102°20E **34 E4**
Funabashi *Japan* 35°45N 140°0E **29 G10**
Funan *China* 32°39N 115°43E **35 A10**
Funchal *Madeira* 32°38N 16°54W **52 B2**
Fundación *Colombia* 10°31N 74°11W **92 A4**
Fundão *Portugal* 40°8N 7°30W **21 B2**
Fundy, B. of *Canada* 45°0N 66°0W **73 D6**
Fundy △ *Canada* 45°35N 65°10W **73 D6**
Funhalouro *Mozam.* 23°3S 34°25E **57 B5**
Funing *Hebei, China* 39°53N 119°12E **33 E10**
Funing *Jiangsu, China* 33°45N 119°50E **35 H10**
Funing *Yunnan, China* 23°35N 105°45E **34 F5**
Funtua *Nigeria* 11°30N 7°18E **52 F7**
Fuping *Hebei, China* 38°48N 114°12E **32 E8**
Fuping *Shaanxi, China* 34°42N 109°10E **32 G5**
Fuqing *China* 25°41N 119°21E **35 E12**
Fuquan *China* 26°40N 107°27E **34 D6**
Furano *Japan* 43°21N 142°23E **28 C11**
Furāt, Nahr al → *Asia* 31°0N 47°25E **46 D5**
Fürg *Iran* 28°18N 55°13E **47 D7**
Furnas, Represa de
  *Brazil* 20°50S 45°30W **95 A6**
Furneaux Group
  *Australia* 40°10S 147°50E **63 G4**
Furqlus *Syria* 34°36N 37°8E **48 A6**
Fürstenwalde *Germany* 52°22N 14°3E **16 B8**

Fürth *Germany* 49°28N 10°59E **16 D6**
Furukawa = Ōsaki
  *Japan* 38°34N 140°58E **28 E10**
Fury and Hecla Str.
  *Canada* 69°56N 84°0W **69 D15**
Fusagasugá *Colombia* 4°21N 74°22W **92 C4**
Fushan *Shandong, China* 37°30N 121°15E **33 F11**
Fushan *Shanxi, China* 35°58N 111°51E **32 G6**
Fushun *Liaoning, China* 41°50N 123°56E **33 D12**
Fushun *Sichuan, China* 29°13N 104°52E **34 C5**
Fusong *China* 42°20N 127°15E **33 C14**
Fustic *Barbados* 13°16N 59°38W **89 g**
Futian *China* 22°32N 114°4E **31 a**
Fuxian Hu *China* 24°30N 102°53E **34 E4**
Fuxin *China* 42°5N 121°48E **33 C11**
Fuyang *Anhui, China* 33°0N 115°48E **32 H8**
Fuyang *Zhejiang, China* 30°5N 119°57E **35 B12**
Fuyang He → *China* 38°12N 117°0E **32 E9**
Fuying Dao *China* 26°34N 120°9E **35 D13**
Fuyong *China* 22°40N 113°49E **31 a**
Fuyu *Heilongjiang, China* 47°49N 124°27E **31 B13**
Fuyu *Jilin, China* 45°12N 124°43E **33 B13**
Fuyuan *China* 25°40N 104°16E **34 E5**
Fuyun *China* 47°0N 89°28E **30 B6**
Fuzhou = Linchuan
  *China* 27°57N 116°15E **35 D11**
Fuzhou *China* 26°5N 119°16E **35 D12**
Fyn *Denmark* 55°20N 10°30E **9 J14**
Fyne, L. *U.K.* 55°59N 5°23W **11 F3**

# G

Gaalkacyo *Somalia* 6°30N 47°30E **49 F4**
Gabba *Australia* 9°45S 142°38E **62 a**
Gabela *Angola* 11°0S 14°24E **54 G2**
Gabès *Tunisia* 33°53N 10°2E **53 B8**
Gabès, G. de *Tunisia* 34°0N 10°30E **53 B8**
Gabon ■ *Africa* 0°10S 10°0E **54 E2**
Gaborone *Botswana* 24°45S 25°57E **56 C4**
Gabriels *U.S.A.* 44°26N 74°12W **83 B10**
Gäbrīk *Iran* 25°44N 58°28E **47 E8**
Gabrovo *Bulgaria* 42°52N 25°19E **23 C11**
Gāch Sār *Iran* 36°7N 51°19E **47 B6**
Gachsārān *Iran* 30°15N 50°45E **47 D6**
Gad Hinglaj *India* 16°14N 74°21E **45 F2**
Gadag *India* 15°30N 75°45E **45 G2**
Gadap *Pakistan* 25°5N 67°28E **42 G2**
Gadarwara *India* 22°50N 78°50E **43 H8**
Gadhada *India* 22°0N 71°35E **42 J4**
Gadra *Pakistan* 25°40N 70°38E **42 G4**
Gadsden *U.S.A.* 34°1N 86°1W **85 D11**
Gadwal *India* 16°10N 77°50E **45 F3**
Gaffney *U.S.A.* 35°5N 81°39W **85 D14**
Gafsa *Tunisia* 34°24N 8°43E **53 B7**
Gagaria *India* 25°43N 70°46E **42 G4**
Găgăuzia □ *Moldova* 46°10N 28°40E **17 E15**
Gagnoa *Côte d'Ivoire* 6°56N 6°16W **52 G4**
Gagnon *Canada* 51°50N 68°5W **73 B6**
Gagnon, L. *Canada* 62°3N 110°27W **71 A6**
Gahmar *India* 25°27N 83°49E **43 G10**
Gahnpa = Ganta *Liberia* 7°15N 8°59W **52 G4**
Gai Xian = Gaizhou
  *China* 40°22N 122°20E **33 D12**
Gail *U.S.A.* 32°46N 101°27W **84 E4**
Gaillimh = Galway *Ireland* 53°17N 9°3W **10 C2**
Gaines *U.S.A.* 41°46N 77°35W **82 E7**
Gainesville *Fla., U.S.A.* 29°40N 82°20W **85 G13**
Gainesville *Ga., U.S.A.* 34°18N 83°50W **85 D13**
Gainesville *Mo., U.S.A.* 36°36N 92°26W **80 G7**
Gainesville *Tex., U.S.A.* 33°38N 97°8W **84 E6**
Gainsborough *U.K.* 53°24N 0°46E **12 D7**
Gairdner, L. *Australia* 31°30S 136°0E **63 E2**
Gairloch *U.K.* 57°43N 5°41W **11 D3**
Gairloch, L. *U.K.* 57°43N 5°45W **11 D3**
Gaizhou *China* 40°22N 122°20E **33 D12**
Gaj → *Pakistan* 26°26N 67°21E **42 F2**
Gajendragarh *India* 15°44N 75°59E **45 G2**
Gakuch *Pakistan* 36°7N 73°45E **43 A5**
Gal Oya △ *Sri Lanka* 7°0N 81°20E **45 L5**
Gal Oya Res. *Sri Lanka* 7°5N 81°30E **45 L5**
Galán, Cerro *Argentina* 25°55S 66°52W **94 B2**
Galápagos = Colón, Arch. de
  *Ecuador* 0°0 91°0W **90 D1**
Galapagos Fracture Zone
  *Pac. Oc.* 3°0N 110°0W **65 G17**
Galapagos Rise *Pac. Oc.* 15°0S 95°0W **65 J18**
Galashiels *U.K.* 55°37N 2°49W **11 F6**
Galați *Romania* 45°27N 28°2E **17 F15**
Galatina *Italy* 40°10N 18°10E **23 D8**
Galax *U.S.A.* 36°40N 80°56W **81 G13**
Galbīn Govĭ *Mongolia* 43°0N 107°0E **32 C4**
Galcaio = Gaalkacyo
  *Somalia* 6°30N 47°30E **49 F4**
Galdhøpiggen *Norway* 61°38N 8°18E **8 F13**
Galeana *Chihuahua,
  Mexico* 30°7N 107°38W **86 A3**
Galeana *Nuevo León,
  Mexico* 24°50N 100°4W **86 A3**
Galela *Indonesia* 1°50N 127°49E **37 D7**
Galeota Pt. *Trin. & Tob.* 10°8N 60°59W **93 K16**
Galera Pt. *Trin. & Tob.* 10°49N 60°54W **93 K16**
Galesburg *U.S.A.* 40°57N 90°22W **80 E8**
Galeton *U.S.A.* 41°44N 77°39W **82 E7**
Galich *Russia* 58°22N 42°24E **18 C7**
Galicia □ *Spain* 42°43N 7°45W **21 A2**
Galilee = Hagalil *Israel* 32°53N 35°18E **48 C4**
Galilee, L. *Australia* 22°20S 145°50E **62 C4**
Galilee, Sea of = Yam Kinneret
  *Israel* 32°45N 35°35E **48 C4**
Galina Pt. *Jamaica* 18°24N 76°58W **88 a**
Galiuro Mts. *U.S.A.* 32°30N 110°20W **77 K8**
Galiwinku *Australia* 12°2S 135°34E **62 A2**
Gallan Hd. *U.K.* 58°15N 7°2W **11 C1**
Gállego → *Spain* 41°39N 0°51W **21 B5**
Gallegos → *Argentina* 51°35S 69°0W **96 G3**

Galley Hd. *Ireland* 51°32N 8°55W **10 E3**
Gallinas, Pta. *Colombia* 12°28N 71°40W **92 A4**
Gallipoli = Gelibolu
  *Turkey* 40°28N 26°43E **23 D12**
Gallipoli *Italy* 40°3N 17°58E **23 D8**
Gallipolis *U.S.A.* 38°49N 82°12W **81 F12**
Gällivare *Sweden* 67°9N 20°40E **8 C19**
Galloo I. *U.S.A.* 43°55N 76°25W **83 C8**
Galloway *U.K.* 55°1N 4°29W **11 F4**
Galloway, Mull of *U.K.* 54°39N 4°52W **11 G4**
Gallup *U.S.A.* 35°32N 108°45W **77 J9**
Galmudug *Somalia* 6°30N 48°0E **49 F4**
Galoya *Sri Lanka* 8°10N 80°55E **45 K5**
Galt *U.S.A.* 38°15N 121°18W **78 G5**
Galty Mts. *Ireland* 52°22N 8°10E **10 D3**
Galtymore *Ireland* 52°21N 8°11W **10 D3**
Galugāh *Iran* 36°43N 53°48E **47 B7**
Galva *U.S.A.* 41°10N 90°3W **80 E8**
Galveston *U.S.A.* 29°18N 94°48W **84 G7**
Galveston B. *U.S.A.* 29°36N 94°50W **84 G7**
Gálvez *Argentina* 32°0S 61°14W **94 C3**
Galway *Ireland* 53°17N 9°3W **10 C2**
Galway □ *Ireland* 53°22N 9°1W **10 C2**
Galway B. *Ireland* 53°13N 9°10W **10 C2**
Gam → *Vietnam* 21°55N 105°12E **38 B5**
Gamagōri *Japan* 34°50N 137°14E **29 G8**
Gambat *Pakistan* 27°17N 68°26E **42 F3**
Gambhir → *India* 26°58N 77°27E **42 F6**
Gambia ■ *W. Afr.* 13°25N 16°0W **52 F2**
Gambia → *W. Afr.* 13°28N 16°34W **52 F2**
Gambier *U.S.A.* 40°22N 82°23W **82 F2**
Gambier, C. *Australia* 11°56S 130°57E **60 B5**
Gambier, Îs.
  *French Polynesia* 23°8S 134°58W **65 K14**
Gambier Is. *Australia* 35°3S 136°30E **63 F2**
Gambo *Canada* 48°47N 54°13W **73 C9**
Gamboli *Pakistan* 29°53N 68°24E **42 E3**
Gamboma *Congo* 1°55S 15°52E **54 E3**
Gamka → *S. Africa* 33°18S 21°39E **56 E3**
Gamkab → *Namibia* 28°4S 17°54E **56 C2**
Gamlakarleby = Kokkola
  *Finland* 63°50N 23°8E **8 E20**
Gammon → *Canada* 51°24N 95°44W **71 C9**
Gammon Ranges △
  *Australia* 30°38S 139°8E **63 E2**
Gampaha *Sri Lanka* 7°5N 79°59E **45 L4**
Gampola *Sri Lanka* 7°10N 80°34E **45 L5**
Gamtoos → *S. Africa* 33°58S 25°1E **56 D4**
Gamzigrad-Romuliana
  *Serbia* 43°53N 22°11E **23 C10**
Gan Jiang → *China* 29°15N 116°0E **35 C11**
Ganado *U.S.A.* 35°43N 109°33W **77 J9**
Gananoque *Canada* 44°20N 76°10W **83 B8**
Ganāveh *Iran* 29°35N 50°35E **47 D6**
Gäncä *Azerbaijan* 40°45N 46°20E **19 F8**
Gancheng *China* 18°51N 108°37E **38 C7**
Gand = Gent *Belgium* 51°2N 3°42E **15 C3**
Ganda *Angola* 13°3S 14°35E **55 G2**
Gandajika
  *Dem. Rep. of the Congo* 6°46S 23°58E **54 F4**
Gandak → *India* 25°39N 85°13E **43 G11**
Gandava *Pakistan* 28°32N 67°32E **42 E2**
Gander *Canada* 48°58N 54°35W **73 C9**
Gander L. *Canada* 48°58N 54°35W **73 C9**
Gandhi Sagar *India* 24°40N 75°40E **42 G6**
Gandhinagar *India* 23°15N 72°45E **42 H5**
Gandia *Spain* 38°58N 0°9W **21 C5**
Ganedidalem = Gani
  *Indonesia* 0°48S 128°14E **37 E7**
Ganga → *India* 23°20N 90°30E **43 H14**
Ganga Sagar *India* 21°38N 88°5E **43 J13**
Gangakher *India* 18°57N 76°45E **44 E3**
Gangan → *India* 28°38N 78°58E **43 E8**
Ganganagar *India* 29°56N 73°56E **42 E5**
Gangapur *Maharashtra,
  India* 19°41N 75°1E **44 E2**
Gangapur *Raj., India* 26°32N 76°49E **42 F7**
Gangaw *Myanmar* 22°5N 94°5E **41 H19**
Gangawati *India* 15°30N 76°36E **45 G3**
Gangdisê Shan *China* 31°20N 81°0E **43 D9**
Ganges = Ganga →
  *India* 23°20N 90°30E **43 H14**
Ganges *Canada* 48°51N 123°31W **70 D4**
Ganges, Mouths of the
  *India* 21°30N 90°0E **43 J14**
Ganggyeong *S. Korea* 36°10N 127°0E **33 F14**
Gangneung *S. Korea* 37°45N 128°54E **33 F15**
Gangoh *India* 29°46N 77°18E **42 E7**
Gangotri *India* 30°50N 79°10E **43 D8**
Gangotri △ *India* 30°50N 79°10E **43 D8**
Gangseong *S. Korea* 38°24N 128°30E **33 E15**
Gangtok *India* 27°20N 88°37E **41 F16**
Gangu *China* 34°40N 105°15E **32 G3**
Gangyao *China* 44°12N 126°37E **33 B14**
Gani *Indonesia* 0°48S 128°14E **37 E7**
Ganj *India* 27°45N 78°57E **43 F8**
Ganjam *India* 19°23N 85°4E **44 K14**
Ganluo *China* 28°58N 102°59E **34 C4**
Ganquan *China* 36°20N 109°20E **32 F5**
Gansu □ *China* 36°0N 104°0E **32 G3**
Ganta *Liberia* 7°15N 8°59W **52 G4**
Gantheaume, C. *Australia* 36°4S 137°32E **63 F2**
Gantheaume B. *Australia* 27°40S 114°10E **61 E1**
Gantsevichi = Hantsavichy
  *Belarus* 52°49N 26°30E **17 B14**
Ganyem = Genyem
  *Indonesia* 2°46S 140°12E **37 E10**
Ganyu *China* 34°50N 119°8E **33 G10**
Ganzhou *China* 25°51N 114°56E **35 E10**
Gao *Mali* 16°15N 0°5W **52 E5**
Gao Xian *China* 28°21N 104°32E **34 C5**
Gao'an *China* 28°26N 115°17E **35 C10**
Gaobeidian *China* 39°19N 115°51E **32 E8**
Gaocheng *China* 38°2N 114°49E **32 E8**
Gaohebu *China* 30°43N 116°49E **35 B11**
Gaokeng *China* 27°40N 113°55E **35 D9**
Gaolan Dao *China* 21°55N 113°10E **35 G9**

Gaoligong Shan *China* 24°45N 98°45E **34 E2**
Gaomi *China* 36°20N 119°42E **33 F10**
Gaoping *China* 35°45N 112°55E **32 G7**
Gaotang *China* 36°50N 116°15E **32 F9**
Gaoua *Burkina Faso* 10°20N 3°8W **52 F5**
Gaoual *Guinea* 11°45N 13°25W **52 F3**
Gaoyang *China* 38°40N 115°45E **32 E8**
Gaoyao *China* 23°3N 112°27E **35 F9**
Gaoyou *China* 32°47N 119°26E **35 A12**
Gaoyou Hu *China* 32°45N 119°20E **33 H10**
Gaoyuan *China* 37°8N 117°58E **33 F9**
Gaozhou *China* 21°58N 110°50E **35 G8**
Gap *France* 44°33N 6°5E **20 D7**
Gapat → *India* 24°30N 82°28E **43 G10**
Gapuwiyak *Australia* 12°25S 135°43E **62 A2**
Gar *China* 32°10N 79°58E **30 E4**
Garabogazköl Aylagy
  *Turkmenistan* 41°0N 53°30E **19 F9**
Garachiné *Panama* 8°0N 78°12W **88 E4**
Garagum *Turkmenistan* 39°30N 60°0E **47 B8**
Garah *Australia* 29°5S 149°38E **63 D4**
Garanhuns *Brazil* 8°50S 36°30W **93 E11**
Garautha *India* 25°34N 79°18E **43 G8**
Garawa ◇ *Australia* 16°43S 136°51E **62 B2**
Garberville *U.S.A.* 40°6N 123°48W **76 F2**
Garbiyang *India* 30°8N 80°54E **43 D9**
Gard → *France* 43°51N 4°37E **20 E6**
Garda, L. di *Italy* 45°40N 10°41E **22 B4**
Garde L. *Canada* 62°50N 106°13W **71 A7**
Garden City *Ga., U.S.A.* 32°6N 81°9W **85 E14**
Garden City *Kans.,
  U.S.A.* 37°58N 100°53W **80 G3**
Garden City *Tex., U.S.A.* 31°52N 101°29W **84 F4**
Garden Grove *U.S.A.* 33°47N 117°55W **79 M9**
Gardēz *Afghan.* 33°37N 69°9E **42 C3**
Gardiner *Maine, U.S.A.* 44°14N 69°47W **81 C19**
Gardiner *Mont., U.S.A.* 45°2N 110°22W **76 D8**
Gardiners I. *U.S.A.* 41°6N 72°6W **83 E12**
Gardner *U.S.A.* 42°34N 71°59W **83 D13**
Gardner Canal *Canada* 53°27N 128°8W **70 C3**
Gardner Pinnacles
  *U.S.A.* 25°0N 167°55W **75 L6**
Gardnerville *U.S.A.* 38°56N 119°45W **78 G7**
Gardo = Qardho *Somalia* 9°30N 49°6E **49 F4**
Garey *U.S.A.* 34°53N 120°19W **79 L6**
Garfield *U.S.A.* 47°1N 117°9W **76 C5**
Garforth *U.K.* 53°47N 1°24W **12 D6**
Gargano, C. *Canada* 47°36N 85°2W **81 B11**
Gargett *Australia* 21°9S 148°46E **62 b**
Garhchiroli *India* 20°10N 80°0E **44 D5**
Garibaldi △ *Canada* 49°50N 122°40W **70 D4**
Gariep, L. *S. Africa* 30°40S 25°40E **56 E4**
Garies *S. Africa* 30°32S 17°59E **56 D2**
Garig Gunak Barlu △
  *Australia* 11°26S 131°58E **60 B5**
Garigliano → *Italy* 41°13N 13°45E **22 D5**
Garissa *Kenya* 0°25S 39°40E **54 E7**
Garland *U.S.A.* 41°45N 112°10W **76 F7**
Garmāb *Iran* 35°25N 56°45E **47 C8**
Garmisch-Partenkirchen
  *Germany* 47°30N 11°6E **16 E6**
Garmsār *Iran* 35°20N 52°25E **47 C7**
Garnett *U.S.A.* 38°17N 95°14W **80 F6**
Garo Hills *India* 25°30N 90°30E **43 G14**
Garoe = Garoowe *Somalia* 8°25N 48°33E **49 F4**
Garonne → *France* 45°2N 0°36W **20 D3**
Garoowe *Somalia* 8°25N 48°33E **49 F4**
Garot *India* 24°19N 75°41E **42 G6**
Garoua *Cameroon* 9°19N 13°21E **53 G8**
Garouaé = Garoua
  *Cameroon* 9°19N 13°21E **53 G8**
Garrauli *India* 25°5N 79°22E **43 G8**
Garrison *Mont., U.S.A.* 46°31N 112°49W **76 C7**
Garrison *N. Dak., U.S.A.* 47°40N 101°25W **80 B3**
Garrison Res. = Sakakawea, L.
  *U.S.A.* 47°30N 101°25W **80 B3**
Garron Pt. *U.K.* 55°3N 5°59W **10 A6**
Garry → *U.K.* 56°44N 3°47W **11 E5**
Garry, L. *Canada* 65°58N 100°18W **68 D11**
Garryaga *Turkmenistan* 39°5N 63°29E **47 B8**
Garson L. *Canada* 56°19N 110°2W **71 B6**
Garstang *U.K.* 53°55N 2°46W **12 D5**
Garu *India* 23°40N 84°14E **43 H11**
Garut *Indonesia* 7°14S 107°53E **37 G12**
Garvie Mts. *N.Z.* 45°30S 168°50E **59 F2**
Garwa = Garoua
  *Cameroon* 9°19N 13°21E **53 G8**
Garwa *India* 24°11N 83°47E **43 G10**
Gary *U.S.A.* 41°36N 87°20W **80 E10**
Garzê *China* 31°38N 100°1E **34 B3**
Garzón *Colombia* 2°10N 75°40W **92 C3**
Gas-San *Japan* 38°32N 140°1E **28 E10**
Gasan Kuli = Esenguly
  *Turkmenistan* 37°37N 53°59E **26 F6**
Gascogne *France* 43°45N 0°20E **20 E4**
Gascogne, G. de *Europe* 44°0N 2°0W **20 D2**
Gascony = Gascogne
  *France* 43°45N 0°20E **20 E4**
Gascoyne → *Australia* 24°52S 113°37E **61 D1**
Gascoyne Junction
  *Australia* 25°2S 115°17E **61 E2**
Gashaka *Nigeria* 7°20N 11°29E **53 G8**
Gashua *Nigeria* 12°54N 11°0E **53 F8**
Gaspar Str. = Gelasa, Selat
  *Indonesia* 2°50S 107°0E **36 E3**
Gasparillo *Trin. & Tob.* 10°18N 61°26W **93 K15**
Gaspé *Canada* 48°52N 64°30W **73 C7**
Gaspé, C. de *Canada* 48°48N 64°7W **73 C7**
Gaspé Pen. = Gaspésie, Pén. de la
  *Canada* 48°45N 65°40W **73 C6**
Gaspésie, Pén. de la
  *Canada* 48°45N 65°40W **73 C6**
Gaspésie △ *Canada* 48°55N 66°10W **73 C6**
Gasteiz = Vitoria-Gasteiz
  *Spain* 42°50N 2°41W **21 A4**
Gastonia *U.S.A.* 35°16N 81°11W **85 D14**
Gastre *Argentina* 42°20S 69°15W **96 E3**
Gata, C. de *Spain* 36°41N 2°13W **21 D4**

Gata, Sierra de *Spain* 40°20N 6°45W **21 B2**
Gataga → *Canada* 58°35N 126°59W **70 B3**
Gatchina *Russia* 59°35N 30°9E **9 G24**
Gatehouse of Fleet *U.K.* 54°53N 4°12W **11 G4**
Gates *U.S.A.* 43°9N 77°42W **82 C7**
Gateshead *U.K.* 54°57N 1°35W **12 C6**
Gateshead I. *Canada* 70°36N 100°26W **68 C11**
Gatesville *U.S.A.* 31°26N 97°45W **84 F6**
Gatineau *Canada* 45°29N 75°39W **83 A9**
Gatineau → *Canada* 45°27N 75°42W **72 C4**
Gatineau △ *Canada* 45°40N 76°0W **72 C4**
Gatton *Australia* 27°32S 152°17E **63 D5**
Gatún, L. *Panama* 9°7N 79°56W **88 E4**
Gatwick, London × (LGW)
  *U.K.* 51°10N 0°11W **13 F7**
Gatyana *S. Africa* 32°16S 28°31E **57 D4**
Gau *Fiji* 18°2S 179°18E **59 a**
Gauer L. *Canada* 57°0N 97°50W **71 B9**
Gauhati = Guwahati
  *India* 26°10N 91°45E **41 F17**
Gauja → *Latvia* 57°10N 24°16E **9 H21**
Gaujas △ *Latvia* 57°10N 24°50E **9 H21**
Gaula → *Norway* 63°21N 10°14E **8 E14**
Gauri Phanta *India* 28°41N 80°36E **43 E9**
Gauribidanur *India* 13°37N 77°32E **45 H3**
Gaustatoppen *Norway* 59°48N 8°40E **9 G13**
Gauteng □ *S. Africa* 26°0S 28°0E **57 C4**
Gāv Koshī *Iran* 28°38N 57°12E **47 D8**
Gāvakān *Iran* 29°37N 53°10E **47 D7**
Gäväter *Iran* 25°10N 61°31E **47 E9**
Gävbandī *Iran* 27°12N 53°4E **47 E7**
Gavdos *Greece* 34°50N 24°5E **23 G11**
Gaviota *U.S.A.* 34°29N 120°13W **79 L6**
Gawachab *Namibia* 27°4S 17°55E **56 C2**
Gawilgarh Hills *India* 21°15N 76°45E **44 D3**
Gawler *Australia* 34°30S 138°42E **63 E2**
Gawler Ranges *Australia* 32°30S 135°45E **63 E2**
Gaxun Nur *China* 42°22N 100°30E **30 C9**
Gay *Russia* 51°27N 58°27E **18 D10**
Gaya *India* 24°47N 85°4E **43 G11**
Gaya *Niger* 11°52N 3°28E **52 F6**
Gaylord *U.S.A.* 45°2N 84°41W **81 C11**
Gayndah *Australia* 25°35S 151°32E **63 D5**
Gaysin = Haysyn
  *Ukraine* 48°57N 29°25E **17 D15**
Gayvoron = Hayvoron
  *Ukraine* 48°22N 29°52E **17 D15**
Gaza *Gaza Strip* 31°30N 34°28E **48 D3**
Gaza □ *Mozam.* 23°10S 32°45E **57 C5**
Gaza Strip □ *Asia* 31°29N 34°25E **48 D3**
Gazanjyk = Bereket
  *Turkmenistan* 39°16N 55°32E **47 B7**
Gāzbor *Iran* 28°5N 58°51E **47 D8**
Gaziantep *Turkey* 37°6N 37°23E **46 B3**
Gāzīmağusa = Famagusta
  *Cyprus* 35°8N 33°55E **46 C2**
Gbadolite
  *Dem. Rep. of the Congo* 4°17N 21°1E **54 D4**
Gbarnga *Liberia* 7°19N 9°13W **52 G4**
Gcoverega *Botswana* 19°8S 24°18E **56 A3**
Gcuwa *S. Africa* 32°20S 28°11E **57 D4**
Gdańsk *Poland* 54°22N 18°40E **17 A10**
Gdansk B. = Gdańska, Zatoka
  *Poland* 54°30N 19°20E **17 A10**
Gdańska, Zatoka *Poland* 54°30N 19°20E **17 A10**
Gdov *Russia* 58°48N 27°55E **9 G22**
Gdynia *Poland* 54°35N 18°33E **17 A10**
Gebe *Indonesia* 0°5N 129°25E **37 D7**
Gebze *Turkey* 40°47N 29°25E **23 D13**
Gede, Tanjung *Indonesia* 6°46S 105°12E **37 G11**
Gediz → *Turkey* 38°35N 26°48E **23 E12**
Gedser *Denmark* 54°35N 11°55E **9 J14**
Gedung, Pulau *Malaysia* 5°17N 100°23E **39 c**
Geegully Cr. →
  *Australia* 18°32S 123°41E **60 C3**
Geel *Belgium* 51°10N 4°59E **15 C4**
Geelong *Australia* 38°10S 144°22E **63 F3**
Geelvink Chan. *Australia* 28°30S 114°0E **61 E1**
Geelvink B. = Cenderawasih,
  Teluk *Indonesia* 3°0S 135°20E **37 E9**
Geesthacht *Germany* 53°26N 10°22E **16 B6**
Geidam *Nigeria* 12°57N 11°57E **53 F8**
Geikie → *Canada* 57°45N 103°52W **71 B8**
Geikie Gorge △ *Australia* 18°11N 125°41E **60 C4**
Geistown *U.S.A.* 40°18N 78°52W **82 F6**
Gejiu *China* 23°20N 103°10E **34 F4**
Gel, Meydān-e *Iran* 29°4N 54°50E **47 D7**
Gela *Italy* 37°4N 14°15E **22 F6**
Gelang Patah *Malaysia* 1°27N 103°35E **39 d**
Gelasa, Selat *Indonesia* 2°50S 107°0E **36 E3**
Gelderland □ *Neths.* 52°5N 6°10E **15 B6**
Geldrop *Neths.* 51°25N 5°32E **15 C5**
Gelib = Jilib *Somalia* 0°29N 42°46E **49 G3**
Gelibolu *Turkey* 40°28N 26°43E **23 D12**
Gelsenkirchen *Germany* 51°32N 7°6E **16 C4**
Gelugur *Malaysia* 5°22N 100°18E **39 c**
Gemas *Malaysia* 2°37N 102°36E **39 L4**
Gembloux *Belgium* 50°34N 4°43E **15 D4**
Gemena
  *Dem. Rep. of the Congo* 3°13N 19°48E **54 D3**
Gemerek *Turkey* 39°15N 36°10E **46 B3**
Gemlik *Turkey* 40°26N 29°9E **23 D13**
Gemsbok △ *Botswana* 25°5S 21°1E **56 C3**
Genale → *Ethiopia* 6°2N 39°1E **49 F2**
General Acha *Argentina* 37°20S 64°38W **94 D3**
General Alvear *B. Aires,
  Argentina* 36°0S 60°0W **94 D4**
General Alvear *Mendoza,
  Argentina* 35°0S 67°40W **94 D2**
General Artigas
  *Paraguay* 26°52S 56°16W **94 B4**
General Belgrano
  *Argentina* 36°35S 58°47W **94 D4**
General Bernardo O'Higgins
  *Antarctica* 63°0S 58°3W **5 C18**
General Cabrera
  *Argentina* 32°53S 63°52W **94 C3**

General Carrera, L.
S. Amer. 46°35S 72°0W 96 F2
General Cepeda Mexico 25°21N 101°22W 86 B4
General Guido Argentina 36°40S 57°50W 94 D4
General Juan Madariaga
Argentina 37°0S 57°0W 94 D4
General La Madrid
Argentina 37°17S 61°20W 94 D3
General MacArthur
Phil. 11°18N 125°28E 37 B7
General Martin Miguel de Güemes
Argentina 24°50S 65°0W 94 A3
General Pico Argentina 35°45S 63°50W 94 D3
General Pinedo Argentina 27°15S 61°20W 94 B3
General Pinto Argentina 34°45S 61°50W 94 D3
General Roca Argentina 39°2S 67°35W 96 D3
General Santos Phil. 6°5N 125°14E 37 C7
General Treviño Mexico 26°14N 99°29W 87 B5
General Trías Mexico 28°21N 106°22W 86 B3
General Viamonte
Argentina 35°1S 61°39W 94 D3
General Villegas Argentina 35°5S 63°0W 94 D3
Genesee Idaho, U.S.A. 46°33N 116°56W 76 C5
Genesee Pa., U.S.A. 41°59N 77°54W 82 E7
→ U.S.A. 43°16N 77°36W 82 C7
Geneseo Ill., U.S.A. 41°27N 90°9W 80 E8
Geneseo N.Y., U.S.A. 42°48N 77°49W 82 D7
Geneva = Genève Switz. 46°12N 6°9E 20 C7
Geneva Ala., U.S.A. 31°2N 85°52W 85 F12
Geneva N.Y., U.S.A. 42°52N 76°59W 82 D8
Geneva Nebr., U.S.A. 40°32N 97°36W 80 E5
Geneva Ohio, U.S.A. 41°48N 80°57W 82 E4
Geneva, L. = Léman, L.
Europe 46°26N 6°30E 20 C7
Genève Switz. 46°12N 6°9E 20 C7
Gengma China 23°32N 99°20E 34 F2
Genhe China 50°47N 121°31E 31 A13
Genil → Spain 37°42N 5°19W 21 D3
Genk Belgium 50°58N 5°32E 15 D5
Gennargentu, Mti. del Italy 40°1N 9°19E 22 D3
Genoa = Génova Italy 44°25N 8°57E 20 D8
Genoa Australia 37°29S 149°35S 63 F4
Genoa N.Y., U.S.A. 42°40N 76°32W 83 D8
Genoa, Nebr., U.S.A. 41°27N 97°44W 80 E5
Genoa Nev., U.S.A. 39°2N 119°50W 78 F7
Génova Italy 44°25N 8°57E 20 D8
Génova, G. di Italy 44°0N 9°0E 22 C3
Genriyetty, Ostrov
Russia 77°6N 156°30E 27 B16
Gent Belgium 51°2N 3°42E 15 C3
Genteng Jawa Barat,
Indonesia 7°22S 106°24E 37 G12
Genteng Jawa Timur,
Indonesia 8°22S 114°9E 37 J17
Genyem Indonesia 2°46S 140°12E 37 E10
Geochang S. Korea 35°41N 127°55E 33 G14
Geographe B. Australia 33°30S 115°15E 61 F2
Geographe Chan.
Australia 24°30S 113°0E 61 D1
Geoje S. Korea 34°51N 128°35E 33 G15
Georga, Zemlya Russia 80°30N 49°0E 26 A5
George S. Africa 33°58S 22°29E 56 D3
George → Canada 58°49N 66°10W 73 A6
George, L. N.S.W.,
Australia 35°10S 149°25E 63 F4
George, L. S. Austral.,
Australia 37°25S 140°0E 63 F3
George, L. W. Austral.,
Australia 22°45S 123°40E 60 D3
George, L. Fla., U.S.A. 29°17N 81°36W 85 G14
George, L. N.Y., U.S.A. 43°37N 73°33W 83 C11
George Bush Intercontinental,
Houston ✈ (IAH)
U.S.A. 29°59N 95°20W 84 G7
George Gill Ra. Australia 24°22S 131°45E 60 D5
George Pt. Australia 20°6S 148°36E 62 b
George River = Kangiqsualujjuaq
Canada 58°30N 65°59W 69 F18
George Sound N.Z. 44°52S 167°25E 59 F1
George Town Australia 41°6S 146°49E 63 G4
George Town Bahamas 23°33S 75°47W 88 B4
George Town Cayman Is. 19°20N 81°24W 88 C3
George Town Malaysia 5°25N 100°20E 39 c
George V Land Antarctica 69°0S 148°0E 5 C10
George VI Sound Antarctica 71°0S 68°0W 5 D17
George West U.S.A. 28°20N 98°7W 84 G5
Georgetown = Janjanbureh
Gambia 13°30N 14°47W 52 F3
Georgetown Australia 18°17S 143°33E 62 B3
Georgetown Ont., Canada 43°40N 79°56W 82 C5
Georgetown P.E.I.,
Canada 46°13N 62°24W 73 C7
Georgetown Guyana 6°50N 58°12W 92 B7
Georgetown Calif.,
U.S.A. 38°54N 120°50W 78 G6
Georgetown Colo.,
U.S.A. 39°42N 105°42W 76 G11
Georgetown Ky., U.S.A. 38°13N 84°33W 81 F11
Georgetown N.Y., U.S.A. 42°46N 75°44W 83 D9
Georgetown Ohio,
U.S.A. 38°52N 83°54W 81 F12
Georgetown S.C., U.S.A. 33°23N 79°17W 85 E15
Georgetown Tex., U.S.A. 30°38N 97°41W 84 F6
Georgia □ U.S.A. 32°50N 83°15W 85 E13
Georgia ■ Asia 42°0N 43°0E 19 F7
Georgia, Str. of N. Amer. 49°25N 124°0W 78 A3
Georgia Basin S. Ocean 50°45S 35°30W 5 B1
Georgian B. Canada 45°15N 81°0W 82 A4
Georgian Bay Islands △
Canada 44°53N 79°52W 82 B5
Georgievka Kazakhstan 49°19N 84°34E 26 E9
Georgina → Australia 23°30S 139°47E 62 C2
Georgina I. Canada 44°22N 79°17W 82 B5
Georgiyevsk Russia 44°12N 43°28E 19 F7
Gera Germany 50°53N 12°4E 16 C7
Geraardsbergen Belgium 50°45N 3°53E 15 D3
Geral, Serra Brazil 26°25S 50°0W 95 B6
Geral de Goiás, Serra Brazil 12°0S 46°0W 93 F9
Geraldine U.S.A. 47°36N 110°16W 76 C8
Geraldton Australia 28°48S 114°32E 61 E1

Geraldton Canada 49°44N 87°10W 72 C2
Gerdine, Mt. U.S.A. 61°35N 152°27W 74 C9
Gereshk Afghan. 31°47N 64°35E 40 D4
Gerik Malaysia 5°50N 101°15E 39 K3
Gering U.S.A. 41°50N 103°40W 80 E2
Gerlach U.S.A. 40°39N 119°21W 76 F4
German Bight = Deutsche Bucht
Germany 54°15N 8°0E 16 A5
Germansen Landing
Canada 55°43N 124°40W 70 B4
Germantown U.S.A. 35°5N 89°49W 85 D10
Germany ■ Europe 51°0N 10°0E 16 C6
Germī Iran 39°1N 48°3E 47 B6
Gernika-Lumo Spain 43°19N 2°40W 21 A4
Gero Japan 35°48N 137°14E 29 G8
Gerokgak Indonesia 8°11S 114°27E 37 J17
Gerona = Girona Spain 41°58N 2°46E 21 B7
Gerrard Canada 50°30N 117°17W 70 C5
Gersoppa Falls India 14°12N 74°46E 45 G2
Gertak Sanggul Malaysia 5°17N 100°12E 39 c
Gertak Sanggul, Tanjung
Malaysia 5°16N 100°11E 39 c
Gerung Indonesia 8°43S 116°7E 37 K19
Geser Indonesia 3°50S 130°54E 37 E8
Gettysburg Pa., U.S.A. 39°50N 77°14W 81 F15
Gettysburg S. Dak., U.S.A. 45°1N 99°57W 80 C4
Getxo = Algorta Spain 43°21N 2°59W 21 A4
Getz Ice Shelf Antarctica 75°0S 130°0W 5 D14
Gevrai India 19°16N 75°45E 44 E2
Geyser U.S.A. 47°16N 110°30W 76 C8
Geyserville U.S.A. 38°42N 122°54W 78 G4
Gezhouba Dam China 30°40N 111°20E 35 B8
Ghadāf, W. al → Iraq 32°56N 43°30E 46 C4
Ghadāmis Libya 30°11N 9°29E 53 B8
Ghaggar → India 29°30N 74°53E 42 E6
Ghaghara → India 25°45N 84°40E 43 G11
Ghaghat → Bangla. 25°19N 89°38E 43 G13
Ghagra India 23°17N 84°33E 43 H11
Ghallamane Mauritania 23°15N 10°0E 52 D4
Ghana ■ W. Afr. 8°0N 1°0W 52 G5
Ghanpokhara Nepal 28°17N 84°14E 43 E11
Ghansor India 22°39N 80°1E 43 H9
Ghanzi Botswana 21°50S 21°34E 56 B3
Ghanzi □ Botswana 22°30S 22°30E 56 B3
Ghardaïa Algeria 32°20N 3°37E 52 B6
Gharm Tajikistan 39°0N 70°20E 26 F8
Gharyān Libya 32°10N 13°0E 53 B8
Ghāt Libya 24°59N 10°11E 53 D8
Ghatal India 22°40N 87°46E 43 H12
Ghatampur India 26°8N 80°13E 43 F9
Ghatgaon India 21°24N 85°53E 44 D7
Ghatprabha → India 16°15N 75°20E 45 F2
Ghats, Eastern India 14°0N 78°50E 45 H4
Ghats, Western India 14°0N 75°0E 45 H2
Ghatsila India 22°36N 86°29E 43 H12
Ghaṭṭī Si. Arabia 31°16N 37°31E 46 D3
Ghawdex = Gozo Malta 36°3N 14°15E 22 F6
Ghazal, Bahr el → Chad 13°0N 15°47E 53 F9
Ghazal, Bahr el →
South Sudan 9°31N 30°25E 53 G12
Ghaziabad India 28°42N 77°26E 42 E7
Ghazipur India 25°38N 83°35E 43 G10
Ghaznī Afghan. 33°30N 68°28E 42 C3
Ghaznī □ Afghan. 32°10N 68°20E 40 C6
Ghent = Gent Belgium 51°2N 3°42E 15 C3
Gheorghe Gheorghiu-Dej = Onești
Romania 46°17N 26°47E 17 E14
Ghīnah, Wādī al →
Si. Arabia 30°27N 38°14E 46 D3
Ghizar → Pakistan 36°15N 73°43E 43 A5
Ghod → India 18°30N 74°35E 44 E2
Ghogha India 21°40N 72°20E 44 D1
Ghotaru India 27°20N 70°1E 42 F4
Ghotki Pakistan 28°5N 69°21E 42 E3
Ghowr □ Afghan. 34°0N 64°20E 40 C4
Ghughri India 22°39N 80°41E 43 H9
Ghugus India 19°58N 79°12E 44 E4
Ghulam Mohammad Barrage
Pakistan 25°30N 68°20E 42 G3
Ghūrīān Afghan. 34°17N 61°25E 40 B2
Gia Dinh Vietnam 10°49N 106°42E 39 G6
Gia Lai = Plei Ku Vietnam 13°57N 108°0E 38 F7
Gia Nghia Vietnam 11°58N 107°42E 39 G6
Gia Ngoc Vietnam 14°50N 108°58E 38 E7
Gia Vuc Vietnam 14°42N 108°34E 38 E7
Giamama = Jamaame
Somalia 0°4N 42°44E 49 G3
Gianitsa Greece 40°46N 22°24E 23 D10
Giant Forest U.S.A. 36°36N 118°43W 78 J8
Giant Sequoia △ U.S.A. 36°10N 118°35W 78 K8
Giant's Causeway U.K. 55°16N 6°29W 10 A5
Giant's Tank Sri Lanka 8°51N 80°2E 45 K5
Gianyar Indonesia 8°32S 115°20E 37 K18
Giarabub = Al Jaghbūb
Libya 29°42N 24°38E 53 C10
Giarre Italy 37°43N 15°11E 22 F6
Gibara Cuba 21°9N 76°11W 88 B4
Gibb II Ethiopia 8°0N 37°30E 49 F2
Gibe II Ethiopia 8°0N 37°30E 49 F2
Gibe III Ethiopia 7°0N 37°30E 49 F2
Gibraltar ☑ Europe 36°7N 5°22W 21 D3
Gibraltar, Str. of Medit. S. 35°55N 5°40W 21 E3
Gibraltar Range △
Australia 29°31S 152°19E 63 D5
Gibson Desert Australia 24°0S 126°0E 60 D4
Gibsons Canada 49°24N 123°32W 70 D4
Gibsonville U.S.A. 39°46N 120°54W 78 F6
Giddalur India 15°20N 78°57E 45 G4
Giddings U.S.A. 30°11N 96°56W 84 F6
Giebnegáisi = Kebnekaise
Sweden 67°53N 18°33E 8 C18
Giessen Germany 50°34N 8°41E 16 C5
Gifan Iran 37°54N 57°28E 47 B8
Gift Lake Canada 55°53N 115°49W 70 B5
Gifu Japan 35°30N 136°45E 29 G8
Gifu □ Japan 35°40N 137°0E 29 G8
Giganta, Sa. de la Mexico 26°0N 111°39W 86 B2
Gigha U.K. 55°42N 5°44W 11 F3
Gíglio Italy 42°20N 10°52E 22 C4

Gijón Spain 43°32N 5°42W 21 A3
Gil I. Canada 53°12N 129°15W 70 C3
Gila → U.S.A. 32°43N 114°33W 77 K6
Gila Bend U.S.A. 32°57N 112°43W 77 K7
Gila Bend Mts. U.S.A. 33°10N 113°0W 77 K7
Gila Cliff Dwellings △
U.S.A. 33°12N 108°16W 77 K9
Gīlān □ Iran 37°0N 50°0E 47 B6
Gilbert → Australia 16°35S 141°15E 62 B3
Gilbert Is. Kiribati 1°0N 172°0E 58 A10
Gilbert River Australia 18°9S 142°52E 62 B3
Gilbert Seamounts
Pac. Oc. 52°50N 150°10W 4 D18
Gilead U.S.A. 44°24N 70°59W 83 B14
Gilf el Kebîr, Hadabat el
Egypt 23°50N 25°50E 53 D11
Gilford I. Canada 50°40N 126°30W 70 C3
Gilgandra Australia 31°43S 148°39E 63 E4
Gilgit India 35°50N 74°15E 43 B6
Gilgit → Pakistan 35°44N 74°37E 43 B6
Gilgit-Baltistan □ Pakistan 36°30N 73°0E 43 A5
Gilimanuk Indonesia 8°10S 114°26E 37 J17
Gillam Canada 56°20N 94°40W 71 B10
Gillen, L. Australia 26°11S 124°38E 61 E3
Gilles, L. Australia 32°50S 136°45E 63 E2
Gillette U.S.A. 44°18N 105°30W 76 D11
Gilliat Australia 20°40S 141°28E 62 C3
Gillingham U.K. 51°23N 0°33E 13 F8
Gilmer U.S.A. 32°44N 94°57W 84 E7
Gilmore, L. Australia 32°29S 121°37E 61 F3
Gilmour Canada 44°48N 77°37W 82 B7
Gilroy U.S.A. 37°1N 121°34W 78 H5
Gimcheon S. Korea 36°11N 128°4E 33 F15
Gimhae S. Korea 35°14N 128°53E 33 G15
Gimhwa S. Korea 38°17N 127°28E 33 E14
Gimie, Mt. St. Lucia 13°54N 61°0W 89 f
Gimje S. Korea 35°48N 126°45E 33 G14
Gimli Canada 50°40N 97°0W 71 C9
Gin → Sri Lanka 6°5N 80°7E 45 L5
Gin Gin Australia 25°0S 151°58E 63 D5
Gingee India 12°15N 79°25E 45 H4
Gingin Australia 31°22S 115°54E 61 F2
Gingindlovu S. Africa 29°2S 31°30E 57 C5
Ginir Ethiopia 7°6N 40°40E 49 F3
Giohar = Jawhar Somalia 2°48N 45°30E 49 G4
Giona, Oros Greece 38°38N 22°14E 23 E10
Gir → India 21°0N 71°0E 42 J4
Gir Hills India 21°0N 71°0E 42 J4
Girab India 26°2N 70°38E 42 F4
Girâfi, W. → Egypt 29°58N 34°39E 48 F3
Girard Kans., U.S.A. 37°31N 94°51W 80 G6
Girard Ohio, U.S.A. 41°9N 80°42W 82 E4
Girard Pa., U.S.A. 42°0N 80°19W 82 E4
Girdle Ness U.K. 57°9N 2°3W 11 D6
Giresun Turkey 40°55N 38°30E 19 F6
Girga Egypt 26°17N 31°55E 53 C12
Giri → India 30°28N 77°41E 42 D7
Giridih India 24°10N 86°21E 43 G12
Girne = Kyrenia Cyprus 35°20N 33°20E 46 C2
Giron = Kiruna Sweden 67°52N 20°15E 8 C19
Girona Spain 41°58N 2°46E 21 B7
Gironde → France 45°32N 1°7W 20 D3
Girraween △ Australia 28°46S 151°54E 63 D5
Girringun △ Australia 18°15S 145°32E 62 B4
Girvan U.K. 55°14N 4°51W 11 F4
Gisborne N.Z. 38°39S 178°5E 59 C7
Gisenyi Rwanda 1°41S 29°15E 54 E5
Gislaved Sweden 57°19N 13°32E 9 H15
Gitega Burundi 3°26S 29°56E 54 E5
Githio Greece 36°46N 22°34E 23 F10
Giuba = Juba → Somalia 1°30N 42°35E 49 G3
Giurgiu Romania 43°52N 25°57E 17 G13
Giyani S. Africa 23°19S 30°43E 57 B5
Gizab Afghan. 33°22N 66°17E 42 C1
Gizhiga Russia 62°3N 160°30E 27 C17
Gizhiginskaya Guba
Russia 61°0N 158°0E 27 C16
Gizo Solomon Is. 8°6S 156°51E 58 B8
Giżycko Poland 54°2N 21°48E 17 A11
Gjakovë Kosovo 42°22N 20°26E 23 C9
Gjirokastër Albania 40°7N 20°10E 23 D9
Gjoa Haven Canada 68°38N 95°53W 68 D12
Gjøvik Norway 60°47N 10°43E 8 F14
Glace Bay Canada 46°11N 59°58W 73 C8
Glacier △ Canada 51°15N 117°30W 70 C5
Glacier △ U.S.A. 48°42N 113°48W 76 B7
Glacier Bay U.S.A. 58°40N 136°0W 68 F4
Glacier Bay △ U.S.A. 58°45N 136°30W 70 B1
Glacier Peak U.S.A. 48°7N 121°7W 76 B3
Gladewater U.S.A. 32°33N 94°56W 84 E7
Gladstone Queens.,
Australia 23°52S 151°16E 62 C5
Gladstone S. Austral.,
Australia 33°15S 138°22E 63 E2
Gladstone Canada 50°13N 98°57W 71 C9
Gladstone U.S.A. 45°51N 87°1W 80 C10
Gladwin U.S.A. 43°59N 84°29W 81 D11
Glagah Indonesia 8°13S 114°18E 37 J17
Glâma = Glomma →
Norway 59°12N 10°57E 9 G14
Gláma Iceland 65°48N 23°0W 8 D2
Glamis U.S.A. 32°55N 115°5W 79 N11
Glamorgan, Vale of □
U.K. 51°28N 3°25W 13 F4
Glasco Kans., U.S.A. 39°22N 97°50W 80 F5
Glasco N.Y., U.S.A. 42°3N 73°57W 83 D11
Glasgow U.K. 55°51N 4°15W 11 F4
Glasgow Ky., U.S.A. 37°0N 85°55W 81 G11
Glasgow Mont., U.S.A. 48°12N 106°38W 76 B10
Glasgow City □ U.K. 55°51N 4°12W 11 F4
Glasgow Int. ✈ (GLA)
U.K. 55°51N 4°21W 11 F4
Glaslyn Canada 53°22N 108°21W 71 C7
Glastonbury U.K. 51°9N 2°43E 13 F5
Glastonbury U.S.A. 41°43N 72°37W 83 E12
Glazov Russia 58°9N 52°40E 18 C9
Gleichen Canada 50°52N 113°3W 70 C6
Gleiwitz = Gliwice
Poland 50°22N 18°41E 17 C10

Glen U.S.A. 44°7N 71°11W 83 B13
Glen Affric U.K. 57°17N 5°1W 11 D3
Glen Canyon U.S.A. 37°30N 110°40W 77 H8
Glen Canyon △ U.S.A. 37°15N 111°0W 77 H8
Glen Canyon Dam
U.S.A. 36°57N 111°29W 77 H8
Glen Coe U.K. 56°40N 5°0W 11 E3
Glen Cove U.S.A. 40°52N 73°38W 83 F11
Glen Garry U.K. 57°3N 5°7W 11 D3
Glen Innes Australia 29°44S 151°44E 63 D5
Glen Lyon U.S.A. 41°10N 76°5W 83 E8
Glen Mor U.K. 57°9N 4°37W 11 D4
Glen Moriston U.K. 57°11N 4°52W 11 D4
Glen Robertson Canada 45°22N 74°30W 83 A10
Glen Spean U.K. 56°53N 4°40W 11 E4
Glen Ullin U.S.A. 46°49N 101°50W 80 B3
Glenamaddy Ireland 53°37N 8°33W 10 C3
Glenbeigh Ireland 52°3N 9°58W 10 D2
Glencoe Canada 42°45N 81°43W 82 D3
Glencoe S. Africa 28°11S 30°11E 57 D5
Glencoe U.S.A. 44°46N 94°9W 80 C6
Glencolumbkille Ireland 54°43N 8°42W 10 B3
Glendale U.S.A. 33°32N 112°11W 77 K7
Glendive U.S.A. 47°7N 104°43W 76 C11
Glendo U.S.A. 42°30N 105°2W 76 E11
Glenelg → Australia 38°4S 140°59E 63 F3
Glenfield U.S.A. 43°43N 75°24W 83 C9
Glengad Hd. Ireland 55°20N 7°10W 10 A4
Glengarriff Ireland 51°45N 9°34W 10 E2
Glenmont U.S.A. 40°31N 82°6W 82 F2
Glenmorgan Australia 27°14S 149°42E 63 D4
Glenn U.S.A. 39°31N 122°1W 78 F4
Glennallen U.S.A. 62°7N 145°33W 68 E2
Glenns Ferry U.S.A. 42°57N 115°18W 76 E6
Glenora Canada 44°2N 77°3W 82 B7
Glenorchy Australia 42°49S 147°18E 63 G4
Glenore Australia 17°50S 141°12E 62 B3
Glenreagh Australia 30°2S 153°1E 63 E5
Glenrock U.S.A. 42°52N 105°52W 76 E11
Glenrothes U.K. 56°12N 3°10W 11 E5
Glens Falls U.S.A. 43°19N 73°39W 83 C11
Glenside U.S.A. 40°6N 75°9W 83 F9
Glenties Ireland 54°48N 8°17W 10 B3
Glenveagh △ Ireland 55°3N 8°1W 10 A3
Glenville U.S.A. 38°56N 80°50W 81 F13
Glenwood Canada 49°0N 54°58W 73 C9
Glenwood Ark., U.S.A. 34°20N 93°33W 84 D8
Glenwood Iowa, U.S.A. 41°3N 95°45W 80 E6
Glenwood Minn., U.S.A. 45°39N 95°23W 80 C6
Glenwood Wash., U.S.A. 46°1N 121°17W 78 D5
Glenwood Springs
U.S.A. 39°33N 107°19W 76 G10
Glettinganes Iceland 65°30N 13°37W 8 D7
Glin Ireland 52°34N 9°17W 10 D2
Gliwice Poland 50°22N 18°41E 17 C10
Globe U.S.A. 33°24N 110°47W 77 K8
Głogów Poland 51°37N 16°5E 16 C9
Glomma → Norway 59°12N 10°57E 9 G14
Glorieuses, Îs. Ind. Oc. 11°30S 47°20E 55 G9
Glossop U.K. 53°27N 1°56W 12 D6
Gloucester Australia 32°0S 151°59E 63 E5
Gloucester U.K. 51°53N 2°15W 13 F5
Gloucester U.S.A. 42°37N 70°40W 83 D14
Gloucester I. Australia 20°0S 148°30E 62 b
Gloucester Island △
Australia 20°0S 148°30E 62 b
Gloucester Point U.S.A. 37°15N 76°30W 81 G15
Gloucestershire □ U.K. 51°46N 2°15W 13 F5
Gloversville U.S.A. 43°3N 74°21W 83 C10
Glovertown Canada 48°40N 54°3W 73 C9
Glusk Belarus 52°53N 28°41E 17 B15
Glyn Ebwy = Ebbw Vale
U.K. 51°46N 3°12W 13 F4
Gmünd Austria 48°45N 15°0E 16 D8
Gmunden Austria 47°55N 13°48E 16 E7
Gniezno Poland 52°30N 17°35E 17 B9
Gnowangerup Australia 33°58S 117°59E 61 F2
Go Cong Vietnam 10°22N 106°40E 39 G6
Gö-no-ura Japan 33°44N 129°40E 29 H4
Goa India 15°33N 73°59E 45 G1
Goa □ India 15°33N 73°59E 45 G1
Goalen Hd. Australia 36°33S 150°4E 63 F5
Goalpara India 26°10N 90°40E 41 F17
Goaltor India 22°43N 87°10E 43 H12
Goalundo Ghat Bangla. 23°50N 89°47E 43 H13
Goat Fell U.K. 55°38N 5°11W 11 F3
Goba Ethiopia 7°1N 39°59E 49 F2
Goba Mozam. 26°15S 32°13E 57 D5
Gobabis Namibia 22°30S 19°0E 56 B2
Gobi Asia 44°0N 110°0E 32 C6
Gobi Gurvan Saykhan △
Mongolia 43°24N 101°24E 32 C2
Gobichettipalayam India 11°31N 77°21E 45 J3
Gobō Japan 33°53N 135°10E 29 H7
Gochas Namibia 24°59S 18°55E 56 B2
Godalming U.K. 51°11N 0°36W 13 F7
Godavari → India 16°25N 82°18E 44 F6
Godavari Pt. India 17°0N 82°20E 44 F6
Godbout Canada 49°20N 67°38W 73 C6
Godda India 24°50N 87°13E 43 G12
Goderich Canada 43°45N 81°41W 82 C3
Godfrey Ra. Australia 24°0S 117°0E 61 D2
Godhavn = Qeqertarsuaq
Greenland 69°15N 53°38W 4 C5
Godhra India 22°49N 73°40E 42 H5
Godoy Cruz Argentina 32°56S 68°52W 94 C2
Gods → Canada 56°22N 92°51W 72 A1
Gods L. Canada 54°40N 94°15W 72 B1
Gods River Canada 54°50N 94°5W 71 C10
Godthåb = Nuuk
Greenland 64°10N 51°35W 67 C14
Goeie Hoop, Kaap die = Good
Hope, C. of S. Africa 34°24S 18°30E 56 D2
Goéland, L. au Canada 49°50N 76°48W 72 C4
Goélands, L. aux Canada 55°27N 64°17W 73 A7
Goeree Neths. 51°50N 4°0E 15 C3
Goes Neths. 51°30N 3°55E 15 C3
Goffstown U.S.A. 43°1N 71°36W 83 C13
Gogama Canada 47°35N 81°43W 72 C3
Gogebic, L. U.S.A. 46°30N 89°35W 80 B9

Gogra = Ghaghara →
India 25°45N 84°40E 43 G11
Gogrial South Sudan 8°30N 28°8E 53 G11
Gohana India 29°8N 76°42E 42 E7
Goharganj India 23°1N 77°41E 42 H7
Goi → India 22°4N 74°46E 42 H6
Goiânia Brazil 16°43S 49°20W 93 G9
Goiás Brazil 15°55S 50°10W 93 G8
Goiás □ Brazil 12°10S 48°0W 93 F9
Goio-Erê Brazil 24°12S 53°1W 95 A5
Gojō Japan 34°21N 135°42E 29 G7
Gojra Pakistan 31°10N 72°40E 42 D5
Gokak India 16°11N 74°52E 45 F2
Gokarn India 14°33N 74°17E 45 G2
Gökçeada Turkey 40°10N 25°50E 23 D11
Gökova Körfezi Turkey 36°55N 27°50E 23 F12
Göksu → Turkey 36°19N 34°5E 46 B2
Gokteik Myanmar 22°26N 97°0E 41 H20
Gokurt Pakistan 29°40N 67°26E 42 E2
Gokwe Zimbabwe 18°7S 28°58E 57 A4
Gola India 28°3N 80°32E 43 E9
Golakganj India 26°8N 89°52E 43 F13
Golan Heights = Hagolan
Syria 33°0N 35°45E 48 C4
Goläshkerd Iran 27°59N 57°16E 47 E8
Golconda India 17°24N 78°23E 44 F4
Golconda U.S.A. 40°58N 117°30W 76 F5
Gold U.S.A. 41°52N 77°50W 82 E7
Gold Beach U.S.A. 42°25N 124°25W 76 E1
Gold Coast W. Afr. 4°0N 1°40W 52 H5
Gold Hill U.S.A. 42°26N 123°3W 76 E2
Gold River Canada 49°46N 126°3W 70 D3
Golden Canada 51°20N 116°59W 70 C5
Golden B. N.Z. 40°40S 172°50E 59 D4
Golden Gate Highlands △
S. Africa 28°40S 28°40E 57 C4
Golden Hinde Canada 49°40N 125°44W 70 D3
Golden Lake Canada 45°34N 77°21W 82 A7
Golden Rock India 10°45N 78°48E 45 J4
Golden Spike △ U.S.A. 41°37N 112°33W 76 F7
Golden Vale Ireland 52°33N 8°17W 10 D3
Goldendale U.S.A. 45°49N 120°50W 76 D3
Goldfield U.S.A. 37°42N 117°14W 77 H5
Goldsand L. Canada 57°2N 101°8W 71 B8
Goldsboro U.S.A. 35°23N 77°59W 85 D16
Goldsmith U.S.A. 31°59N 102°37W 84 F3
Goldthwaite U.S.A. 31°27N 98°34W 84 F5
Goleniów Poland 53°35N 14°50E 16 B8
Golestān □ Iran 37°20N 55°25E 47 B7
Golestānak Iran 30°36N 54°14E 47 D7
Goleta U.S.A. 34°27N 119°50W 79 L7
Golfito Costa Rica 8°41N 83°5W 88 E3
Golfo Aranci Italy 40°59N 9°38E 22 D3
Golfo de Santa Clara
Mexico 31°42N 114°30W 86 A2
Goliad U.S.A. 28°40N 97°23W 84 G6
Golmud China 36°25N 94°53E 30 D7
Golpäyegän Iran 33°27N 50°18E 47 C6
Golra Pakistan 33°37N 72°56E 42 C5
Golspie U.K. 57°58N 3°59W 11 D5
Goma Dem. Rep. of the Congo 1°37S 29°10E 54 E5
Gomal Pass Pakistan 31°56N 69°20E 42 D3
Gomati → India 25°32N 83°11E 43 G10
Gombe Nigeria 10°19N 11°2E 53 F8
Gomel = Homyel Belarus 52°28N 31°0E 17 B16
Gomera Canary Is. 28°7N 17°14W 52 C2
Gómez Palacio Mexico 25°34N 103°30W 86 B4
Gomīshān Iran 37°4N 54°6E 47 B7
Gomogomo Indonesia 6°39S 134°43E 37 F8
Gomoh India 23°52N 86°10E 43 H12
Gompa = Ganta Liberia 7°15N 8°59W 52 G4
Gonābād Iran 34°15N 58°45E 47 C8
Gonaïves Haiti 19°20N 72°42W 89 C5
Gonâve, G. de la Haiti 19°29N 72°42W 89 C5
Gonâve, Île de la Haiti 18°51N 73°3W 89 C5
Gonbad-e Kāvūs Iran 37°20N 55°25E 47 B7
Gonda India 27°9N 81°58E 43 F9
Gonder Ethiopia 12°39N 37°30E 49 E2
Gondia India 21°23N 80°10E 44 D5
Gönen Turkey 40°6N 27°39E 23 D12
Gong Xian China 28°23N 104°47E 34 C5
Gong'an China 30°7N 112°12E 35 B9
Gongbei China 22°12N 113°32E 31 a
Gongchangling China 41°7N 123°27E 33 D12
Gongcheng China 24°50N 110°49E 35 E8
Gongga Shan China 29°40N 101°55E 34 C3
Gonggar China 29°18N 90°37E 30 F7
Gongguan China 21°48N 109°36E 34 G7
Gonghe China 36°18N 100°32E 30 D7
Gongju S. Korea 36°27N 127°7E 33 F14
Gongming China 22°47N 113°33E 31 a
Gongolgon Australia 30°21S 146°54E 63 E4
Gongshan China 27°43N 98°39E 34 D2
Gongtan China 28°55N 108°20E 34 C7
Gongyi China 34°45N 112°58E 34 G7
Gongzhuling China 43°30N 124°40E 33 C13
Goniri Nigeria 11°30N 12°15E 53 F8
Gonjo China 30°50N 98°15E 34 B2
Gonzales Calif., U.S.A. 36°30N 121°26W 78 J5
Gonzales Tex., U.S.A. 29°30N 97°27W 84 G6
González Mexico 22°48N 98°25W 87 C5
Good Hope, C. of S. Africa 34°24S 18°30E 56 D2
Good Hope Lake Canada 59°16N 129°18W 70 B3
Gooderham Canada 44°54N 78°21W 82 B6
Goodhouse S. Africa 28°57S 18°13E 56 C2
Gooding U.S.A. 42°56N 114°43W 76 E6
Goodland U.S.A. 39°21N 101°43W 80 F3
Goodlands Mauritius 20°2S 57°39E 55 d
Goodlow Canada 56°20N 120°8W 70 B4
Goodooga Australia 29°3S 147°28E 63 D4
Goodsprings U.S.A. 35°49N 115°27W 79 K11
Goole U.K. 53°42N 0°53W 12 D7
Goolgowi Australia 33°58S 145°41E 63 E4
Goomalling Australia 31°15S 116°49E 61 F2
Goomeri Australia 26°12S 152°6E 63 D5
Goondiwindi Australia 28°30S 150°21E 63 D5
Goongarrie, L. Australia 30°3S 121°9E 61 F3
Goonyella Australia 21°47S 147°58E 62 C4

Goose → *Canada* 53°20N 60°35W **73** B7
Goose Creek *U.S.A.* 32°59N 80°2W **85** E14
Goose L. *U.S.A.* 41°56N 120°26W **76** F3
Gooty *India* 15°7N 77°41E **45** G3
Gop *India* 22°5N 69°50E **42** H3
Gopalganj *India* 26°28N 84°30E **43** F11
Göppingen *Germany* 48°42N 9°39E **16** D5
Gorakhpur *India* 26°47N 83°23E **43** F10
Goražde *Bos.-H.* 43°38N 18°58E **23** C8
Gorda, Pta. *Nic.* 14°20N 83°10W **88** D3
Gordan B. *Australia* 11°35S 130°10E **60** B5
Gordon *U.S.A.* 42°48N 102°12W **80** D2
Gordon → *Australia* 42°27S 145°30E **63** G4
Gordon Bay *Canada* 45°12N 79°47W **82** A5
Gordon L., *Alta., Canada* 56°30N 110°25W **71** B6
Gordon L. *N.W.T., Canada* 63°5N 113°11W **70** A6
Gordonvale *Australia* 17°5S 145°50E **62** B4
Goré *Chad* 7°59N 16°31E **53** G9
Gore *Ethiopia* 8°12N 35°32E **49** F2
Gore *N.Z.* 46°5S 168°58E **59** G2
Gore Bay *Canada* 45°57N 82°28W **72** C3
Gorey *Ireland* 52°41N 6°18W **10** D5
Gorg *Iran* 29°29N 59°43E **47** D8
Gorgān *Iran* 36°55N 54°30E **47** B7
Gorgona, I. *Colombia* 3°0N 78°10W **92** C3
Gorham *U.S.A.* 44°23N 71°10W **83** B13
Goribidnur = Gauribidanur
  *India* 13°37N 77°32E **45** H3
Goriganga → *India* 29°45N 80°23E **43** E9
Gorinchem *Neths.* 51°50N 4°59E **15** C4
Goris *Armenia* 39°31N 46°22E **19** G8
Gorízia *Italy* 45°56N 13°37E **22** B5
Gorkiy = Nizhniy Novgorod
  *Russia* 56°20N 44°0E **18** C7
Gorkovskoye Vdkhr.
  *Russia* 57°2N 43°4E **18** C7
Gorleston-on-Sea *U.K.* 52°35N 1°44E **13** E9
Görlitz *Germany* 51°9N 14°58E **16** C8
Gorlovka = Horlivka
  *Ukraine* 48°19N 38°5E **19** E6
Gorman *U.S.A.* 34°47N 118°51W **79** L8
Gorna Dzhumayo = Blagoevgrad
  *Bulgaria* 42°2N 23°5E **23** C10
Gorna Oryahovitsa
  *Bulgaria* 43°7N 25°40E **23** C11
Gorno-Altay □ *Russia* 51°0N 86°0E **26** D9
Gorno-Altaysk *Russia* 51°50N 86°5E **26** D9
Gornozavodsk *Russia* 46°33N 141°50E **27** E15
Gornyatski *Russia* 67°32N 64°3E **18** A11
Gornyy *Russia* 44°57N 133°59E **28** B6
Gorodenka = Horodenka
  *Ukraine* 48°41N 25°29E **17** D13
Gorodok = Horodok
  *Ukraine* 49°46N 23°32E **17** D12
Gorokhov = Horokhiv
  *Ukraine* 50°30N 24°45E **17** C13
Gorong, Kepulauan
  *Indonesia* 3°59S 131°25E **37** E8
Gorongose → *Mozam.* 20°30S 34°40E **57** B5
Gorongoza △ *Mozam.* 18°50S 34°29E **57** A5
Gorontalo *Indonesia* 0°35N 123°5E **37** D6
Gorontalo □ *Indonesia* 0°50N 122°20E **37** D6
Gort *Ireland* 53°3N 8°49W **10** C3
Gorumahisani *India* 22°20N 86°24E **44** C8
Goryeong *S. Korea* 35°44N 128°15E **33** G15
Gorzów Wielkopolski
  *Poland* 52°43N 15°15E **16** B8
Gosford *Australia* 33°23S 151°18E **63** E5
Goshen *Calif., U.S.A.* 36°21N 119°25W **78** J7
Goshen *Ind., U.S.A.* 41°35N 85°50W **81** E11
Goshen *N.Y., U.S.A.* 41°24N 74°20W **83** E10
Goshogawara *Japan* 40°48N 140°27E **28** D10
Goslar *Germany* 51°54N 10°25E **16** C6
Gospič *Croatia* 44°35N 15°23E **16** F8
Gosport *U.K.* 50°48N 1°9W **13** G6
Gosse → *Australia* 19°32S 134°37E **62** B1
Göta älv → *Sweden* 57°42N 11°54E **9** H14
Göta kanal *Sweden* 58°30N 15°58E **9** G16
Götaland *Sweden* 57°30N 14°30E **9** H16
Göteborg *Sweden* 57°43N 11°59E **9** H14
Gotha *Germany* 50°56N 10°42E **16** C6
Gothenburg = Göteborg
  *Sweden* 57°43N 11°59E **9** H14
Gothenburg *U.S.A.* 40°56N 100°10W **80** E3
Gotland *Sweden* 57°30N 18°33E **9** H18
Gotō = Fukue *Japan* 32°41N 128°51E **29** H4
Gotō-Rettō *Japan* 32°55N 129°5E **29** H4
Gotska Sandön *Sweden* 58°24N 19°15E **9** G18
Gōtsu *Japan* 35°0N 132°14E **29** G6
Göttingen *Germany* 51°31N 9°55E **16** C5
Gottwaldov = Zlín
  *Czechia* 49°14N 17°40E **17** D9
Goubangzi *China* 41°20N 121°52E **33** D11
Gouda *Neths.* 52°1N 4°42E **15** B4
Gouin, Rés. *Canada* 48°35N 74°40W **72** C5
Goulburn *Australia* 34°44S 149°44E **63** E4
Goulburn Is. *Australia* 11°40S 133°20E **62** A1
Goundam *Mali* 16°27N 3°40W **52** E5
Gourits → *S. Africa* 34°21S 21°52E **56** E3
Gourock *U.K.* 55°57N 4°49W **11** F4
Gouverneur *U.S.A.* 44°20N 75°28W **83** B9
Gove Peninsula
  *Australia* 12°17S 136°49E **62** A2
Governador Valadares
  *Brazil* 18°15S 41°57W **93** G10
Governor's Harbour
  *Bahamas* 25°10N 76°14W **88** A4
Govindgarh *India* 24°23N 81°18E **43** G9
Gowan Ra. *Australia* 25°0S 145°0E **62** D4
Gowanda *U.S.A.* 42°28N 78°56W **82** D6
Gower *U.K.* 51°35N 4°10W **13** F3
Gowna, L. *Ireland* 53°51N 7°34W **10** C4
Goya *Argentina* 29°10S 59°10W **94** B4
Goyder Lagoon *Australia* 27°3S 138°58E **63** D2
Goyllarisquizga *Peru* 10°31S 76°24W **92** F3
Goz Beïda *Chad* 12°10N 21°20E **53** F10
Gozo *Malta* 36°3N 14°15E **22** F6
Graaff-Reinet *S. Africa* 32°13S 24°32E **56** D3
Gračac *Croatia* 44°18N 15°57E **16** F8

Gracias a Dios, C.
  *Honduras* 15°0N 83°10W **88** D3
Graciosa *Azores* 39°4N 28°0W **52** a
Gradiška *Bos.-H.* 45°10N 17°15E **22** B7
Grado *Spain* 43°23N 6°4W **21** A2
Grady *U.S.A.* 34°49N 103°19W **77** J12
Grafham Water *U.K.* 52°19N 0°18W **13** E7
Grafton *Australia* 29°38S 152°58E **63** D5
Grafton *N. Dak., U.S.A.* 48°25N 97°25W **80** A5
Grafton *W. Va., U.S.A.* 39°21N 80°2W **81** F13
Graham *Canada* 49°20N 90°30W **72** C1
Graham *U.S.A.* 33°6N 98°35W **84** E5
Graham, Mt. *U.S.A.* 32°42N 109°52W **77** K9
Graham Bell, Ostrov = Greem-Bell,
  Ostrov *Russia* 81°0N 62°0E **26** A7
Graham I. *B.C., Canada* 53°40N 132°30W **70** C2
Graham I. *Nunavut,
  Canada* 77°25N 90°30W **69** B13
Graham Land *Antarctica* 65°0S 64°0W **5** C17
Grahamstown *S. Africa* 33°19S 26°31E **56** D4
Grahamsville *U.S.A.* 41°51N 74°33W **83** E10
Grain Coast *W. Afr.* 4°20N 10°0W **52** H3
Grajagan *Indonesia* 8°35S 114°13E **37** K17
Grajaú *Brazil* 5°50S 46°4W **93** E9
Grajaú → *Brazil* 3°41S 44°48W **93** D10
Grampian *U.S.A.* 40°58N 78°37W **82** F6
Grampian Highlands = Grampian
  Mts. *U.K.* 56°50N 4°0W **11** E5
Grampian Mts. *U.K.* 56°50N 4°0W **11** E5
Grampians, The
  *Australia* 37°15S 142°20E **63** F3
Gran Canaria *Canary Is.* 27°55N 15°35W **52** C2
Gran Chaco *S. Amer.* 25°0S 61°0W **94** B3
Gran Desierto del Pinacate △
  *Mexico* 31°51N 113°32W **86** A2
Gran Paradiso *Italy* 45°33N 7°17E **20** D7
Gran Sasso d'Itália *Italy* 42°27N 13°42E **22** C5
Granada *Nic.* 11°58N 86°0W **88** D2
Granada *Spain* 37°10N 3°35W **21** D4
Granada *U.S.A.* 38°4N 102°19W **76** G12
Granard *Ireland* 53°47N 7°30W **10** C4
Granbury *U.S.A.* 32°27N 97°47W **84** E6
Granby *Canada* 45°25N 72°45W **83** A12
Granby *U.S.A.* 40°5N 105°56W **76** F11
Grand → *Canada* 42°51N 79°34W **82** D5
Grand → *Mo., U.S.A.* 39°23N 93°7W **80** F7
Grand → *S. Dak., U.S.A.* 45°40N 100°45W **80** C3
Grand-Anse = Portsmouth
  *Dominica* 15°34N 61°27W **89** C7
Grand Bahama I.
  *Bahamas* 26°40N 78°30W **88** A4
Grand Baie *Mauritius* 20°0S 57°35E **55** d
Grand Bank *Canada* 47°6N 55°48W **73** C8
Grand Bassam *Côte d'Ivoire* 5°10N 3°49W **52** G5
Grand Bend *Canada* 43°18N 81°45W **82** C3
Grand-Bourg *Guadeloupe* 15°53N 61°19W **88** b
Grand Canal = Da Yunhe →
  *China* 34°25N 120°5E **33** H10
Grand Canyon *U.S.A.* 36°3N 112°9W **77** H7
Grand Canyon △
  *U.S.A.* 36°15N 112°30W **77** H7
Grand Canyon-Parashant △
  *U.S.A.* 36°30N 113°45W **77** H7
Grand Cayman
  *Cayman Is.* 19°20N 81°20W **88** C3
Grand Coulee *U.S.A.* 47°57N 119°0W **76** C4
Grand Coulee Dam
  *U.S.A.* 47°57N 118°59W **76** C4
Grand Falls *Canada* 47°3N 67°44W **73** C6
Grand Falls-Windsor
  *Canada* 48°56N 55°40W **73** C8
Grand Forks *Canada* 49°0N 118°30W **70** D5
Grand Forks *U.S.A.* 47°55N 97°3W **80** B5
Grand Gorge *U.S.A.* 42°21N 74°29W **83** D10
Grand Haven *U.S.A.* 43°4N 86°13W **80** D10
Grand I. *Mich., U.S.A.* 46°31N 86°40W **80** B10
Grand I. *N.Y., U.S.A.* 43°0N 78°58W **82** D6
Grand Island *U.S.A.* 40°55N 98°21W **80** E4
Grand Isle *La., U.S.A.* 29°14N 90°0W **85** G9
Grand Isle *Vt., U.S.A.* 44°43N 73°18W **83** B11
Grand Junction *U.S.A.* 39°4N 108°33W **76** G9
Grand L. *N.B., Canada* 45°57N 66°7W **73** C6
Grand L. *Nfld. & L., Canada* 49°0N 57°30W **73** C8
Grand L. *Nfld. & L.,
  Canada* 53°40N 60°30W **73** B7
Grand L. *U.S.A.* 29°55N 92°47W **84** G8
Grand Lake *U.S.A.* 40°15N 105°49W **76** F11
Grand Manan I. *Canada* 44°45N 66°52W **73** D6
Grand Marais *Mich.,
  U.S.A.* 46°40N 85°59W **81** B11
Grand Marais *Minn.,
  U.S.A.* 47°45N 90°25W **72** C1
Grand-Mère *Canada* 46°36N 72°40W **72** C5
Grand Portage *U.S.A.* 47°58N 89°41W **80** B9
Grand Rapids *Canada* 53°12N 99°19W **71** C9
Grand Rapids *Mich.,
  U.S.A.* 42°58N 85°40W **81** D11
Grand Rapids *Minn.,
  U.S.A.* 47°14N 93°31W **80** B7
Grand St-Bernard, Col du
  *Europe* 45°50N 7°10E **20** D7
Grand Staircase-Escalante △
  *U.S.A.* 37°25N 111°33W **77** H8
Grand Teton *U.S.A.* 43°54N 110°50W **76** E8
Grand Teton △ *U.S.A.* 43°50N 110°50W **76** E8
Grand Union Canal *U.K.* 52°7N 0°53W **13** E7
Grande → *Jujuy, Argentina* 24°20S 65°2W **94** A2
Grande → *Mendoza,
  Argentina* 36°52S 69°45W **94** D2
Grande → *Bolivia* 15°51S 64°39W **92** G6
Grande → *Bahia, Brazil* 11°30S 44°30W **93** F10
Grande → *Minas Gerais,
  Brazil* 20°6S 51°4W **93** H8
Grande, B. *Argentina* 50°30S 68°20W **96** G3
Grande, Rio → *N. Amer.* 25°58N 97°9W **84** J6
Grande Baleine →
  *Canada* 55°16N 77°47W **72** A4
Grande Cache *Canada* 53°53N 119°8W **70** C5
Grande Comore
  *Comoros Is.* 11°35S 43°20E **55** a

Grande-Entrée *Canada* 47°30N 61°40W **73** C7
Grande Prairie *Canada* 55°10N 118°50W **70** B5
Grande-Rivière *Canada* 48°26N 64°30W **73** C7
Grande-Terre *Guadeloupe* 16°20N 61°25W **88** b
Grande-Vallée *Canada* 49°14N 65°8W **73** C6
Grande Vigie, Pte. de la
  *Guadeloupe* 16°32N 61°27W **88** b
Grandfalls *U.S.A.* 31°20N 102°51W **84** F3
Grandview *Canada* 51°10N 100°42W **71** C8
Grandview *U.S.A.* 46°15N 119°54W **76** D4
Graneros *Chile* 34°5S 70°45W **94** C1
Grangemouth *U.K.* 56°1N 3°42W **11** E5
Granger *U.S.A.* 41°35N 109°58W **76** F9
Grangeville *U.S.A.* 45°56N 116°7W **76** D5
Granisle *Canada* 54°53N 126°13W **70** C3
Granite City *U.S.A.* 38°42N 90°8W **80** F8
Granite Falls *U.S.A.* 44°49N 95°33W **80** C6
Granite L. *Canada* 48°8N 57°5W **73** C8
Granite Mt. *U.S.A.* 33°5N 116°28W **79** M10
Granite Pk. *U.S.A.* 45°10N 109°48W **76** D9
Graniteville *U.S.A.* 44°8N 72°29W **83** B12
Granity *N.Z.* 41°39S 171°51E **59** D3
Granja *Brazil* 3°7S 40°50W **93** D10
Granollers *Spain* 41°39N 2°18E **21** B7
Grant *U.S.A.* 40°50N 101°43W **80** E3
Grant, Mt. *U.S.A.* 38°34N 118°48W **76** G4
Grant City *U.S.A.* 40°29N 94°25W **80** E6
Grant I. *Australia* 11°10S 132°52E **60** B5
Grant Range *U.S.A.* 38°30N 115°25W **76** G6
Grantham *U.K.* 52°55N 0°38W **12** E7
Grantown-on-Spey *U.K.* 57°20N 3°36W **11** D5
Grants *U.S.A.* 35°9N 107°52W **77** J10
Grants Pass *U.S.A.* 42°26N 123°19W **76** E2
Grantsville *U.S.A.* 40°36N 112°28W **76** F7
Granville *France* 48°50N 1°35W **20** B3
Granville *N. Dak., U.S.A.* 48°16N 100°47W **80** A3
Granville *N.Y., U.S.A.* 43°24N 73°16W **83** C11
Granville *Ohio, U.S.A.* 40°4N 82°31W **82** F2
Granville L. *Canada* 56°18N 100°30W **71** B8
Graskop *S. Africa* 24°56S 30°49E **57** B5
Grass → *Canada* 56°3N 96°33W **71** B9
Grass Range *U.S.A.* 47°2N 108°48W **76** C9
Grass River △ *Canada* 54°40N 100°50W **71** C8
Grass Valley *Calif., U.S.A.* 39°13N 121°4W **78** F6
Grass Valley *Oreg.,
  U.S.A.* 45°22N 120°47W **76** D3
Grasse *France* 43°38N 6°56E **20** E7
Grassflat *U.S.A.* 41°0N 78°6W **82** E6
Grasslands △ *Canada* 49°11N 107°38W **71** D7
Grassy *Australia* 40°3S 144°5E **63** G3
Graulhet *France* 43°45N 1°59E **20** E4
Gravelbourg *Canada* 49°50N 106°35W **71** D7
's-Gravenhage *Neths.* 52°7N 4°17E **15** B4
Gravenhurst *Canada* 44°52N 79°20W **82** B5
Gravesend *Australia* 29°35S 150°20E **63** D5
Gravesend *U.K.* 51°26N 0°22E **13** F8
Gravois, Pointe-à- *Haiti* 18°2N 73°56W **89** C5
Grayling *U.S.A.* 44°40N 84°43W **81** C11
Grays *U.K.* 51°28N 0°21E **13** F8
Grays Harbor *U.S.A.* 46°59N 124°1W **78** D2
Grays L. *U.S.A.* 43°4N 111°26W **76** E8
Grays River *U.S.A.* 46°21N 123°37W **78** D3
Graz *Austria* 47°4N 15°27E **16** E8
Greasy L. *Canada* 62°55N 122°12W **70** A4
Great Abaco I. = Abaco I.
  *Bahamas* 26°25N 77°10W **88** A4
Great Artesian Basin
  *Australia* 23°0S 144°0E **62** C3
Great Australian Bight
  *Australia* 33°30S 130°0E **61** F5
Great Bahama Bank
  *Bahamas* 23°15N 78°0W **88** B4
Great Barrier I. *N.Z.* 36°11S 175°25E **59** B5
Great Barrier Reef
  *Australia* 18°0S 146°50E **62** B4
Great Barrier Reef △
  *Australia* 20°0S 150°0E **62** B4
Great Barrington
  *U.S.A.* 42°12N 73°22W **83** D11
Great Basalt Wall △
  *Australia* 19°52S 145°43E **62** B4
Great Basin *U.S.A.* 40°0N 117°0W **76** G5
Great Basin △ *U.S.A.* 38°56N 114°15W **76** G6
Great Bear → *Canada* 65°0N 126°0W **68** B7
Great Bear L. *Canada* 65°30N 120°0W **68** B8
Great Belt = Store Bælt
  *Denmark* 55°20N 11°0E **9** J14
Great Bend *Kans., U.S.A.* 38°22N 98°46W **80** F4
Great Bend *Pa., U.S.A.* 41°58N 75°45W **83** E9
Great Blasket I. *Ireland* 52°6N 10°32W **10** D1
Great Britain *Europe* 54°0N 2°15W **6** E5
Great Camanoe
  *Br. Virgin Is.* 18°30N 64°35W **89** e
Great Channel *Asia* 6°0N 94°0E **45** L11
Great Coco I. = Koko Kyunzu
  *Myanmar* 14°7N 93°22E **45** G11
Great Codroy *Canada* 47°51N 59°16W **73** C8
Great Divide, The = Great Dividing
  Ra. *Australia* 23°0S 146°0E **62** C4
Great Divide Basin *U.S.A.* 42°0N 108°0W **76** E9
Great Dividing Ra.
  *Australia* 23°0S 146°0E **62** C4
Great Driffield = Driffield
  *U.K.* 54°0N 0°26W **12** C7
Great Exuma I. *Bahamas* 23°30N 75°50W **88** B4
Great Falls *U.S.A.* 47°30N 111°17W **76** C8
Great Fish = Groot-Vis →
  *S. Africa* 33°28S 27°5E **56** D4
Great Guana Cay
  *Bahamas* 24°0N 76°20W **88** B4
Great Himalayan △ *India* 31°30N 77°30E **42** D7
Great Inagua I. *Bahamas* 21°0N 73°20W **89** B5
Great Indian Desert = Thar Desert
  *India* 28°0N 72°0E **42** F5
Great Karoo *S. Africa* 31°55S 21°0E **56** D3
Great Khingan Mts. = Da Hinggan
  Ling *China* 48°0N 121°0E **31** B13

Great Lake *Australia* 41°50S 146°40E **63** G4
Great Lakes *N. Amer.* 46°0N 84°0W **66** E11
Great Limpopo Transfrontier △
  *Africa* 23°0S 31°45E **57** B5
Great Malvern *U.K.* 52°7N 2°18W **13** E5
Great Miami → *U.S.A.* 39°7N 84°49W **81** F11
Great Nicobar *India* 7°0N 93°50E **45** L11
Great Ormes Head *U.K.* 53°20N 3°52W **12** D4
Great Ouse → *U.K.* 52°48N 0°21E **12** E8
Great Palm I. *Australia* 18°45S 146°40E **62** B4
Great Pedro Bluff *Jamaica* 17°51N 77°44W **88** a
Great Pee Dee →
  *U.S.A.* 33°21N 79°10W **85** E15
Great Plains *N. Amer.* 47°0N 105°0W **66** E9
Great Ruaha → *Tanzania* 7°56S 37°52E **54** F7
Great Sacandaga L.
  *U.S.A.* 43°6N 74°16W **83** C10
Great Saint Bernard Pass = Grand
  St-Bernard, Col du
  *Europe* 45°50N 7°10E **20** D7
Great Salt Desert = Kavīr, Dasht-e
  *Iran* 34°30N 55°0E **47** C7
Great Salt L. *U.S.A.* 41°15N 112°40W **76** F7
Great Salt Lake Desert
  *U.S.A.* 40°50N 113°30W **76** F7
Great Salt Plains L. *U.S.A.* 36°45N 98°8W **84** C5
Great Sand Dunes △
  *U.S.A.* 37°48N 105°45W **77** H11
Great Sandy △ *Australia* 26°13S 153°2E **63** D5
Great Sandy Desert
  *Australia* 21°0S 124°0E **60** D3
Great Sangi = Sangihe, Pulau
  *Indonesia* 3°35N 125°30E **37** D7
Great Sea Reef *Fiji* 16°15S 179°0E **59** a
Great Sitkin I. *U.S.A.* 52°3N 176°6W **74** E4
Great Skellig *Ireland* 51°47N 10°33W **10** E1
Great Slave L. *Canada* 61°23N 115°38W **70** A5
Great Smoky Mts. △
  *U.S.A.* 35°40N 83°40W **85** D13
Great Stour = Stour →
  *U.K.* 51°18N 1°22E **13** F9
Great Victoria Desert
  *Australia* 29°30S 126°30E **61** E4
Great Wall *Antarctica* 62°30S 58°0W **5** C18
Great Wall *China* 38°30N 109°30E **32** E5
Great Whernside *U.K.* 54°10N 1°58W **12** C6
Great Yarmouth *U.K.* 52°37N 1°44E **13** E9
Great Zab = Zāb al Kabīr →
  *Iraq* 36°1N 43°24E **46** B4
Greater Antilles *W. Indies* 17°40N 74°0W **89** C5
Greater London □ *U.K.* 51°31N 0°6W **13** F7
Greater Manchester □
  *U.K.* 53°30N 2°15W **12** D5
Greater Sudbury *Canada* 46°30N 81°0W **72** C3
Greater Sunda Is. *Indonesia* 7°0S 112°0E **36** F4
Gredos, Sierra de *Spain* 40°20N 5°0W **21** B3
Greece *U.S.A.* 43°13N 77°41W **82** C7
Greece ■ *Europe* 40°0N 23°0E **23** E9
Greeley *Colo., U.S.A.* 40°25N 104°42W **76** F11
Greeley *Nebr., U.S.A.* 41°33N 98°32W **80** E4
Greely Fd. *Canada* 80°30N 85°0W **69** A15
Greem-Bell, Ostrov *Russia* 81°0N 62°0E **26** A7
Green → *Ky., U.S.A.* 37°54N 87°30W **80** G10
Green → *Utah, U.S.A.* 38°11N 109°53W **76** G9
Green B. *U.S.A.* 45°0N 87°30W **80** C10
Green Bay *U.S.A.* 44°31N 88°0W **80** C9
Green C. *Australia* 37°13S 150°1E **63** F5
Green Cove Springs
  *U.S.A.* 29°59N 81°42W **85** G14
Green I. = Lütao
  *Taiwan* 22°40N 121°30E **35** F13
Green Lake *Canada* 54°17N 107°47W **71** C7
Green Lake *U.S.A.* 43°45N 72°45W **83** C12
Green Mts. *U.S.A.* 43°45N 72°45W **83** C12
Green River *Utah,
  U.S.A.* 38°59N 110°10W **76** G8
Green River *Wyo.,
  U.S.A.* 41°32N 109°28W **76** F9
Green Valley *U.S.A.* 31°52N 110°56W **77** L8
Greenbank *U.S.A.* 48°6N 122°34W **78** B4
Greenbush *Mich., U.S.A.* 44°35N 83°19E **82** B1
Greenbush *Minn., U.S.A.* 48°42N 96°11W **80** A5
Greencastle *U.S.A.* 39°38N 86°52W **80** F10
Greene *U.S.A.* 42°20N 75°46W **83** D9
Greeneville *U.S.A.* 36°10N 82°50W **85** C13
Greenfield *Calif., U.S.A.* 36°19N 121°15W **78** J5
Greenfield *Calif., U.S.A.* 35°15N 119°0W **79** K8
Greenfield *Ind., U.S.A.* 39°47N 85°46W **81** F11
Greenfield *Iowa, U.S.A.* 41°18N 94°28W **80** E6
Greenfield *Mass., U.S.A.* 42°35N 72°36W **83** D12
Greenfield *Mo., U.S.A.* 37°25N 93°51W **80** G7
Greenland ☐ *N. Amer.* 66°0N 45°0W **67** C15
Greenland Sea *Arctic* 73°0N 10°0W **4** B7
Greenock *U.S.A.* 55°57N 4°46W **11** F4
Greenore *Ireland* 54°1N 6°9W **10** B5
Greenore Pt. *Ireland* 52°14N 6°19W **10** D5
Greenough *Australia* 28°58S 114°43E **61** E1
Greenough → *Australia* 28°51S 114°38E **61** E1
Greenough Pt. *Canada* 44°58N 81°26W **82** B3
Greenport *U.S.A.* 41°6N 72°22W **83** E12
Greensboro *Ga., U.S.A.* 33°35N 83°11W **85** E13
Greensboro *N.C., U.S.A.* 36°4N 79°48W **85** C15
Greensburg *Ind., U.S.A.* 39°20N 85°29W **81** F11
Greensburg *Kans., U.S.A.* 37°36N 99°18W **80** G4
Greensburg *Pa., U.S.A.* 40°18N 79°33W **82** F5
Greenstone = Geraldton
  *Canada* 49°44N 87°10W **72** C2
Greenstone Pt. *U.K.* 57°55N 5°37W **11** D3
Greenvale *Australia* 18°59S 145°7E **62** B4
Greenville *Liberia* 5°1N 9°6W **52** G4
Greenville *Ala., U.S.A.* 31°50N 86°38W **85** F11
Greenville *Calif., U.S.A.* 40°8N 120°57W **78** E6
Greenville *Maine, U.S.A.* 45°28N 69°35W **81** C19
Greenville *Mich., U.S.A.* 43°11N 85°15W **81** D11
Greenville *Miss., U.S.A.* 33°24N 91°4W **85** E9
Greenville *N.C., U.S.A.* 35°37N 77°23W **85** D16
Greenville *N.H., U.S.A.* 42°46N 71°49W **83** D13
Greenville *Ohio, U.S.A.* 40°6N 84°38W **81** E11

Greenville *Pa., U.S.A.* 41°24N 80°23W **82** E4
Greenville *S.C., U.S.A.* 34°51N 82°24W **85** D13
Greenville *Tex., U.S.A.* 33°8N 96°7W **84** E6
Greenwater Lake △
  *Canada* 52°32N 103°30W **71** C8
Greenwich *Conn., U.S.A.* 41°2N 73°38W **83** E11
Greenwich *N.Y., U.S.A.* 43°5N 73°30W **83** C11
Greenwich *Ohio, U.S.A.* 41°2N 82°31W **82** E2
Greenwood *Canada* 49°10N 118°40W **70** D5
Greenwood *Ark., U.S.A.* 35°13N 94°16W **84** D7
Greenwood *Ind., U.S.A.* 39°37N 86°7W **80** F10
Greenwood *Miss., U.S.A.* 33°31N 90°11W **85** E9
Greenwood *S.C., U.S.A.* 34°12N 82°10W **85** D13
Greenwood, Mt. *Australia* 13°48S 130°4E **60** B5
Gregory *U.S.A.* 43°14N 99°26W **80** D4
Gregory → *Australia* 17°53S 139°17E **62** B2
Gregory, L. *S. Austral.,
  Australia* 28°55S 139°0E **63** D2
Gregory, L. *W. Austral.,
  Australia* 20°0S 127°40E **60** D4
Gregory, L. *W. Austral.,
  Australia* 25°38S 119°58E **61** E2
Gregory △ *Australia* 15°38S 131°15E **60** C5
Gregory Downs
  *Australia* 18°35S 138°45E **62** B2
Gregory Ra. *Queens.,
  Australia* 19°30S 143°40E **62** B3
Gregory Ra. *W. Austral.,
  Australia* 21°20S 121°12E **60** D3
Greifswald *Germany* 54°5N 13°23E **16** A7
Greiz *Germany* 50°39N 12°10E **16** C7
Gremikha *Russia* 67°59N 39°47E **18** A6
Grenaa *Denmark* 56°25N 10°53E **9** H14
Grenada *U.S.A.* 33°47N 89°49W **85** E10
Grenada ■ *W. Indies* 12°10N 61°40W **89** D7
Grenadier I. *U.S.A.* 44°3N 76°22W **83** B8
Grenadines, The
  *St. Vincent* 12°40N 61°20W **89** D7
Grenen *Denmark* 57°44N 10°40E **9** H14
Grenfell *Australia* 33°52S 148°8E **63** E4
Grenfell *Canada* 50°30N 102°56W **71** C8
Grenoble *France* 45°12N 5°42E **20** D6
Grenville, C. *Australia* 12°0S 143°13E **62** A3
Grenville Chan. *Canada* 53°40N 129°46W **70** C3
Gresham *U.S.A.* 45°30N 122°25W **78** E4
Gresik *Indonesia* 7°13S 112°38E **37** G15
Gretna *U.K.* 55°0N 3°3W **11** F5
Grevenmacher *Lux.* 49°41N 6°26E **15** E6
Grey → *Canada* 47°34N 57°6W **73** C8
Grey → *N.Z.* 42°27S 171°12E **59** E3
Grey, C. *Australia* 13°0S 136°35E **62** A2
Grey Is. *Canada* 50°50N 55°35W **69** G20
Grey Ra. *Australia* 27°0S 143°30E **63** D3
Greybull *U.S.A.* 44°30N 108°3W **76** D9
Greymouth *N.Z.* 42°29S 171°13E **59** E3
Greystones *Ireland* 53°9N 6°5W **10** C5
Greytown *N.Z.* 41°5S 175°29E **59** D5
Greytown *S. Africa* 29°1S 30°36E **57** C5
Gribbell I. *Canada* 53°23N 129°0W **70** C3
Gridley *U.S.A.* 39°22N 121°42W **78** F5
Griekwastad *S. Africa* 28°49S 23°15E **56** D3
Griffin *U.S.A.* 33°15N 84°16W **85** E12
Griffith *Australia* 34°18S 146°2E **63** E4
Griffith *Canada* 45°15N 77°10W **82** A7
Griffith I. *Canada* 44°50N 80°55W **82** B4
Grimaylov = Hrymayliv
  *Ukraine* 49°20N 26°5E **17** D14
Grimes *U.S.A.* 39°4N 121°54W **78** F5
Grimsay *U.K.* 57°29N 7°14W **11** D1
Grimsby *Canada* 43°12N 79°34W **82** C5
Grimsby *U.K.* 53°34N 0°5W **12** D7
Grimsey *Iceland* 66°33N 17°58W **8** C5
Grimshaw *Canada* 56°10N 117°40W **70** B5
Grimstad *Norway* 58°20N 8°35E **9** G13
Grindstone I. *U.S.A.* 44°17N 76°27W **83** B8
Grinnell *U.S.A.* 41°45N 92°43W **80** E7
Grinnell Pen. *Canada* 76°40N 95°0W **69** B13
Griomasaigh = Grimsay
  *U.K.* 57°29N 7°14W **11** D1
Gris-Nez, C. *France* 50°52N 1°35E **20** A4
Grise Fiord *Canada* 76°25N 82°57W **69** B15
Groais I. *Canada* 50°55N 55°35W **73** B8
Groblersdal *S. Africa* 25°15S 29°25E **57** C4
Grodno = Hrodna
  *Belarus* 53°42N 23°52E **17** B12
Grodzyanka = Hrodzyanka
  *Belarus* 53°31N 28°42E **17** B15
Groesbeck *U.S.A.* 31°31N 96°32W **84** F6
Grójec *Poland* 51°50N 20°58E **17** C11
Grong *Norway* 64°25N 12°8E **8** D15
Groningen *Neths.* 53°15N 6°35E **15** A6
Groningen □ *Neths.* 53°16N 6°40E **15** A6
Groom *U.S.A.* 35°12N 101°6W **84** D4
Groot → *S. Africa* 33°45S 24°36E **56** D3
Groot-Berg → *S. Africa* 32°47S 18°8E **56** D2
Groot-Brakrivier *S. Africa* 34°2S 22°18E **56** D3
Groot Karasberge
  *Namibia* 27°20S 18°40E **56** D2
Groot-Kei → *S. Africa* 32°41S 28°22E **57** D4
Groot-Vis → *S. Africa* 33°28S 27°5E **56** D4
Grootdrink *S. Africa* 28°33S 21°42E **56** D3
Groote Eylandt *Australia* 14°0S 136°40E **62** A2
Groote Peel △ *Neths.* 51°22N 5°49E **15** C5
Grootfontein *Namibia* 19°31S 18°6E **56** A2
Grootlaagte → *Africa* 20°55S 21°27E **56** B3
Grootvloer → *S. Africa* 30°0S 20°40E **56** D3
Gros C. *Canada* 61°59N 113°32W **70** A6
Gros Islet *St. Lucia* 14°5N 60°58W **89** f
Gros Morne △ *Canada* 49°40N 57°50W **73** C8
Gros Piton *St. Lucia* 13°49N 61°5W **89** f
Gros Piton Pt. *St. Lucia* 13°49N 61°5W **89** f
Grosse Point *U.S.A.* 42°23N 82°54W **82** D2
Grosser Arber *Germany* 49°6N 13°8E **16** D7
Grosseto *Italy* 42°46N 11°8E **22** C4
Grossglockner *Austria* 47°5N 12°44E **16** E7
Groswater B. *Canada* 54°20N 57°40W **73** B8
Groton *Conn., U.S.A.* 41°21N 72°5W **83** E12
Groton *N.Y., U.S.A.* 42°36N 76°22W **83** D8
Groton *S. Dak., U.S.A.* 45°27N 98°6W **80** C4
Grouard Mission *Canada* 55°33N 116°9W **70** B5

**Groulx, Mts.** *Canada* 51°27N 68°41W **73** B6
**Groundhog** → *Canada* 48°45N 82°58W **72** C3
**Grouw** *Neths.* 53°5N 5°51E **15** A5
**Grove City** *U.S.A.* 41°10N 80°5W **82** E4
**Grove Hill** *U.S.A.* 31°42N 87°47W **85** F11
**Groveland** *U.S.A.* 37°50N 120°14W **78** H6
**Grover Beach** *U.S.A.* 35°7N 120°37W **79** K6
**Groves** *U.S.A.* 29°57N 93°54W **84** G8
**Groveton** *U.S.A.* 44°36N 71°31W **83** B13
**Grovetown** *U.S.A.* 33°27N 82°12W **85** E13
**Groznyy** *Russia* 43°20N 45°45E **19** F8
**Grudziądz** *Poland* 53°30N 18°47E **17** B10
**Gruinard B.** *U.K.* 57°56N 5°35W **11** D3
**Grundy Center** *U.S.A.* 42°22N 92°47W **80** D7
**Gruver** *U.S.A.* 36°16N 101°24W **84** C4
**Gryazi** *Russia* 52°30N 39°58E **18** D6
**Gryazovets** *Russia* 58°50N 40°10E **18** C7
**Grytviken** *S. Georgia* 54°19S 36°33W **96** G9
**Gua** *India* 22°18N 85°20E **43** H11
**Gua Musang** *Malaysia* 4°53N 101°58E **39** K3
**Guacanayabo, G. de** *Cuba* 20°40N 77°20W **88** B4
**Guachípas** → *Argentina* 25°40S 65°30W **94** B2
**Guadalajara** *Mexico* 20°40N 103°20W **86** C4
**Guadalajara** *Spain* 40°37N 3°12W **21** B4
**Guadalaviar = Turia** → *Spain* 39°27N 0°19W **21** C5
**Guadalcanal** *Solomon Is.* 9°32S 160°12E **58** B9
**Guadales** *Argentina* 34°30S 67°55W **94** C2
**Guadalete** → *Spain* 36°35N 6°13W **21** D2
**Guadalquivir** → *Spain* 36°47N 6°22W **21** D2
**Guadalupe = Guadeloupe** ☒ *W. Indies* 16°15N 61°40W **88** b
**Guadalupe** *Mexico* 22°45N 102°31W **86** C4
**Guadalupe** *U.S.A.* 34°58N 120°34W **79** L6
**Guadalupe** → *U.S.A.* 28°27N 96°47W **84** G6
**Guadalupe, Sierra de** *Spain* 39°28N 5°30W **21** C3
**Guadalupe de Bravo** *Mexico* 31°23N 106°7W **86** A3
**Guadalupe I.** *Pac. Oc.* 29°0N 118°50W **66** G8
**Guadalupe Mts.** △ *U.S.A.* 31°40N 104°30W **84** F2
**Guadalupe Peak** *U.S.A.* 31°50N 104°52W **84** F2
**Guadalupe y Calvo** *Mexico* 26°6N 106°58W **86** B3
**Guadarrama, Sierra de** *Spain* 41°0N 4°0W **21** B4
**Guadeloupe** ☒ *W. Indies* 16°15N 61°40W **88** b
**Guadeloupe** △ *Guadeloupe* 16°10N 61°40W **88** b
**Guadeloupe Passage** *W. Indies* 16°50N 62°15W **89** C7
**Guadiana** → *Portugal* 37°14N 7°22W **21** D2
**Guadix** *Spain* 37°18N 3°11W **21** D4
**Guafo, Boca del** *Chile* 43°35S 74°0W **96** E2
**Guåhån = Guam** ☒ *Pac. Oc.* 13°27N 144°45E **64** F6
**Guaico** *Trin. & Tob.* 10°35N 61°9W **93** K15
**Guainía** → *Colombia* 2°1N 67°7W **92** C5
**Guaíra** *Brazil* 24°5S 54°10W **95** A5
**Guaíra** □ *Paraguay* 25°45S 56°30W **94** B4
**Guaire = Gorey** *Ireland* 52°41N 6°18W **10** D5
**Guaitecas, Is.** *Chile* 44°0S 74°30W **96** E2
**Guajará-Mirim** *Brazil* 10°50S 65°20W **92** F5
**Guajira, Pen. de la** *Colombia* 12°0N 72°0W **92** A4
**Gualán** *Guatemala* 15°8N 89°22W **88** C2
**Gualeguay** *Argentina* 33°10S 59°14W **94** C4
**Gualeguaychú** *Argentina* 33°3S 59°31W **94** C4
**Gualequay** → *Argentina* 33°19S 59°39W **94** C4
**Guam** ☒ *Pac. Oc.* 13°27N 144°45E **64** F6
**Guaminí** *Argentina* 37°1S 62°28W **94** D3
**Guamúchil** *Mexico* 25°28N 108°6W **86** B3
**Guana I.** *Br. Virgin Is.* 18°30N 64°30W **89** e
**Guanabacoa** *Cuba* 23°8N 82°18W **88** B3
**Guanacaste, Cordillera de** *Costa Rica* 10°40N 85°4W **88** D2
**Guanacaste** △ *Costa Rica* 10°57N 85°30W **88** D2
**Guanaceví** *Mexico* 25°56N 105°57W **86** B3
**Guanahani = San Salvador I.** *Bahamas* 24°0N 74°30W **89** B5
**Guanaja** *Honduras* 16°30N 85°55W **88** C2
**Guanajay** *Cuba* 22°56N 82°42W **88** B3
**Guanajuato** *Mexico* 21°1N 101°15W **86** C4
**Guanajuato** □ *Mexico* 21°0N 101°0W **86** C4
**Guandacol** *Argentina* 29°30S 68°40W **94** B2
**Guandi Shan** *China* 37°53N 111°29E **32** F6
**Guane** *Cuba* 22°10N 84°7W **88** B3
**Guang'an** *China* 30°28N 106°35E **34** B6
**Guangchang** *China* 26°50N 116°21E **35** D11
**Guangde** *China* 30°54N 119°25E **35** B12
**Guangdong** □ *China* 23°0N 113°0E **35** F9
**Guangfeng** *China* 28°20N 118°15E **35** C12
**Guanghan** *China* 30°58N 104°17E **34** B5
**Guangling** *China* 39°47N 114°22E **32** E8
**Guangnan** *China* 24°5N 105°4E **34** E5
**Guangning** *China* 23°40N 112°22E **35** F9
**Guangrao** *China* 37°5N 118°25E **33** F10
**Guangshui** *China* 31°37N 114°0E **35** B10
**Guangshun** *China* 26°8N 106°21E **34** D6
**Guangwu** *China* 37°48N 105°57E **32** F3
**Guangxi Zhuangzu Zizhiqu** □ *China* 24°0N 109°0E **34** F7
**Guangyuan** *China* 32°26N 105°51E **32** H3
**Guangze** *China* 27°30N 117°12E **35** D11
**Guanica** *Puerto Rico* 17°58N 66°55W **89** d
**Guanipa** → *Venezuela* 9°56N 62°26W **92** B6
**Guanling** *China* 25°56N 105°35E **34** E5
**Guannan** *China* 34°8N 119°21E **33** G10
**Guantánamo** *Cuba* 20°10N 75°14W **89** B4
**Guantánamo B.** *Cuba* 19°59N 75°10W **89** C4
**Guantao** *China* 36°42N 115°25E **32** F8
**Guanting Shuiku** *China* 40°14N 115°35E **32** D8
**Guanyang** *China* 25°30N 111°8E **35** E8
**Guanyun** *China* 34°20N 119°18E **33** G10
**Guapay = Grande** → *Bolivia* 15°51S 64°39W **92** G6
**Guápiles** *Costa Rica* 10°10N 83°46W **88** D3
**Guapo B.** *Trin. & Tob.* 10°12N 61°41W **93** K15
**Guaporé** *Brazil* 28°51S 51°54W **95** B5
**Guaporé** → *Brazil* 11°55S 65°4W **92** F5
**Guaqui** *Bolivia* 16°41S 68°54W **92** G5
**Guaramacal** △ *Venezuela* 9°13N 70°12W **89** E5
**Guarapari** *Brazil* 20°40S 40°30W **95** A7
**Guarapuava** *Brazil* 25°20S 51°30W **95** B5
**Guaratinguetá** *Brazil* 22°49S 45°9W **95** A6
**Guaratuba** *Brazil* 25°53S 48°38W **95** B6
**Guarda** *Portugal* 40°32N 7°20W **21** B2
**Guardafui, C. = Asir, Ras** *Somalia* 11°55N 51°10E **49** E5
**Guárico** □ *Venezuela* 8°40N 66°35W **92** B5
**Guarujá** *Brazil* 24°2S 46°25W **95** A6
**Guarulhos** *Brazil* 23°29S 46°33W **95** A6
**Guasave** *Mexico* 25°34N 108°27W **86** B3
**Guasdualito** *Venezuela* 7°15N 70°44W **92** B4
**Guatemala** *Guatemala* 14°40N 90°22W **88** D1
**Guatemala** ■ *Cent. Amer.* 15°40N 90°30W **88** C1
**Guatemala Basin** *Pac. Oc.* 11°0N 95°0W **65** F18
**Guatemala Trench** *Pac. Oc.* 14°0N 95°0W **66** H10
**Guatopo** △ *Venezuela* 10°5N 66°30W **89** D6
**Guatuaro Pt.** *Trin. & Tob.* 10°19N 60°59W **93** K16
**Guaviare** → *Colombia* 4°3N 67°44W **92** C5
**Guaxupé** *Brazil* 21°10S 47°5W **95** A6
**Guayaguayare** *Trin. & Tob.* 10°8N 61°2W **93** K15
**Guayama** *Puerto Rico* 17°59N 66°7W **89** d
**Guayaquil** *Ecuador* 2°15S 79°52W **92** D3
**Guayaquil** *Mexico* 29°59N 115°4W **86** B1
**Guayaquil, G. de** *Ecuador* 3°10S 81°0W **92** D2
**Guaymas** *Mexico* 27°56N 110°54W **86** B2
**Gubbi** *India* 13°19N 76°56E **45** H3
**Gubkin** *Russia* 51°17N 37°32E **19** D6
**Gubkinskiy** *Russia* 64°27N 76°36E **26** C8
**Gucheng** *China* 32°20N 111°30E **35** A8
**Gudalur** *India* 11°30N 76°29E **45** J3
**Gudbrandsdalen** *Norway* 61°33N 10°10E **8** F14
**Guddu Barrage** *Pakistan* 28°30N 69°50E **42** E3
**Gudivada** *India* 16°30N 81°3E **45** F5
**Gudiyattam** *India* 12°57N 78°55E **45** H4
**Gudur** *India* 14°12N 79°55E **45** G4
**Guecho = Algorta** *Spain* 43°21N 2°59W **21** A4
**Guékédou** *Guinea* 8°40N 10°5W **52** G3
**Guelmim** *Morocco* 28°56N 10°0W **52** C3
**Guelph** *Canada* 43°35N 80°20W **82** C4
**Guéret** *France* 46°11N 1°51E **20** C4
**Guerneville** *U.S.A.* 38°30N 123°0W **78** G4
**Guernica = Gernika-Lumo** *Spain* 43°19N 2°40W **21** A4
**Guernsey** *U.K.* 49°26N 2°35W **13** H5
**Guernsey** *U.S.A.* 42°16N 104°45W **76** E11
**Guerrara** *Algeria* 32°51N 4°22E **52** B6
**Guerrero** □ *Mexico* 17°40N 100°0W **87** D5
**Gügher** *Iran* 29°28N 56°27E **47** D8
**Gui Jiang** → *China* 23°30N 111°15E **35** F8
**Guia Lopes da Laguna** *Brazil* 21°26S 56°7W **95** A4
**Guiana Highlands** *S. Amer.* 5°10N 60°40W **90** C4
**Guichi** *China* 30°39N 117°27E **35** B11
**Guiding** *China* 26°34N 107°11E **34** D6
**Guidong** *China* 26°7N 113°57E **35** D9
**Guidónia-Montecélio** *Italy* 42°1N 12°45E **22** C5
**Guigang** *China* 23°8N 109°35E **34** F7
**Guijá** *Mozam.* 24°27S 33°0E **57** B5
**Guildford** *U.K.* 51°14N 0°34W **13** F7
**Guilford** *U.S.A.* 41°17N 72°41W **83** E12
**Guilin** *China* 25°18N 110°15E **35** E8
**Guillaume-Delisle, L.** *Canada* 56°15N 76°17W **72** A4
**Guimarães** *Portugal* 41°28N 8°24W **21** B1
**Guimaras** □ *Phil.* 10°35N 122°37E **37** B6
**Guinda** *U.S.A.* 38°50N 122°12W **78** G4
**Guinea** *Africa* 8°0N 8°0E **50** F4
**Guinea** ■ *W. Afr.* 10°20N 11°30W **52** F3
**Guinea, Gulf of** *Atl. Oc.* 3°0N 2°30E **51** F4
**Guinea-Bissau** ■ *Africa* 12°0N 15°0W **52** F3
**Güines** *Cuba* 22°50N 82°0W **88** B3
**Guingamp** *France* 48°34N 3°10W **20** B2
**Guiping** *China* 23°21N 110°2E **35** F8
**Güiria** *Venezuela* 10°32N 62°18W **93** K14
**Guiuan** *Phil.* 11°5N 125°55E **37** B7
**Guixi** *China* 28°16N 117°15E **35** C11
**Guiyang** *Guizhou, China* 26°32N 106°40E **34** D6
**Guiyang** *Hunan, China* 25°46N 112°42E **35** E9
**Guizhou** □ *China* 27°0N 107°0E **34** D6
**Gujar Khan** *Pakistan* 33°16N 73°19E **42** C5
**Gujarat** □ *India* 23°20N 71°0E **42** H4
**Gujiang** *China* 27°11N 114°47E **35** D10
**Gujiao** *China* 37°54N 112°8E **32** F7
**Gujō** *Japan* 35°45N 136°57E **29** G8
**Gujranwala** *Pakistan* 32°10N 74°12E **42** C6
**Gujrat** *Pakistan* 32°40N 74°2E **42** C6
**Gulbarga = Kalaburagi** *India* 17°20N 76°50E **44** F3
**Gulbene** *Latvia* 57°8N 26°52E **9** H22
**Guledagudda** *India* 16°3N 75°48E **45** F2
**Gulf, The = Persian Gulf** *Asia* 27°0N 50°0E **47** E6
**Gulf Islands** ⌂ *U.S.A.* 30°10N 87°10W **85** F11
**Gulfport** *U.S.A.* 30°22N 89°6W **85** F10
**Gulgong** *Australia* 32°20S 149°49E **63** E4
**Gulin** *China* 28°1N 105°50E **34** C5
**Gulistan** *Pakistan* 30°30N 66°35E **42** D2
**Gulja = Yining** *China* 43°58N 81°10E **30** C5
**Gull Lake** *Canada* 50°10N 108°29W **71** C7
**Güllük** *Turkey* 37°14N 27°35E **23** F12
**Gulmarg** *India* 34°3N 74°25E **43** B6
**Gülshat** *Kazakhstan* 46°38N 74°21E **26** C8
**Gulu** *Uganda* 2°48N 32°17E **54** D6
**Gumal** → *Pakistan* 31°40N 71°50E **42** D4
**Gumbaz** *Pakistan* 30°2N 69°0E **42** D3
**Gumel** *Nigeria* 12°39N 9°22E **52** F7
**Gumi** *S. Korea* 36°10N 128°12E **33** F15
**Gumla** *India* 23°3N 84°33E **43** H11
**Gumlu** *Australia* 19°53S 147°41E **62** B4
**Gumzai** *Indonesia* 5°28S 134°42E **37** F8
**Guna** *India* 24°40N 77°19E **42** G7
**Gunbalanya** *Australia* 12°20S 133°4E **60** B5
**Gundabooka** △ *Australia* 30°30S 145°20E **63** E4
**Gundarehi** *India* 20°57N 81°17E **44** D5
**Gundlakamma** → *India* 15°30N 80°15E **45** G5
**Gundlupet** *India* 11°48N 76°41E **45** J3
**Gunisao** → *Canada* 53°56N 97°53W **71** C9
**Gunisao L.** *Canada* 53°33N 96°15W **71** C9
**Gunjyal** *Pakistan* 32°20N 71°55E **42** C4
**Gunma** □ *Japan* 36°30N 138°20E **29** F9
**Gunnbjørn Fjeld** *Greenland* 68°55N 29°47W **4** C6
**Gunnedah** *Australia* 30°59S 150°15E **63** E5
**Gunnewin** *Australia* 25°59S 148°33E **63** D4
**Gunningbar Cr.** → *Australia* 31°14S 147°6E **63** E4
**Gunnison** *Colo., U.S.A.* 38°33N 106°56W **76** G10
**Gunnison** *Utah, U.S.A.* 39°9N 111°49W **76** G8
**Gunnison** → *U.S.A.* 39°4N 108°35W **76** G9
**Gunsan** *S. Korea* 35°59N 126°45E **33** G14
**Guntakal** *India* 15°11N 77°27E **45** G3
**Gunter** *Canada* 44°52N 77°32W **82** B7
**Guntersville** *U.S.A.* 34°21N 86°18W **85** D11
**Guntong** *Malaysia* 4°36N 101°3E **39** K3
**Guntur** *India* 16°23N 80°30E **45** F5
**Gunung Ciremay** △ *Indonesia* 6°53S 108°24E **37** G13
**Gunungapi** *Indonesia* 6°45S 126°30E **37** F7
**Gunungsitoli** *Indonesia* 1°15N 97°30E **36** D1
**Gunupur** *India* 19°5N 83°50E **44** E6
**Gunza** *Angola* 10°50S 13°50E **54** G2
**Guo He** → *China* 32°59N 117°10E **33** H9
**Guoyang** *China* 33°32N 116°12E **32** H9
**Gupis** *Pakistan* 36°15N 73°20E **43** A5
**Gurbantünggüt Shamo** *China* 45°8N 87°20E **30** B6
**Gurdaspur** *India* 32°5N 75°31E **42** C6
**Gurdon** *U.S.A.* 33°55N 93°9W **84** E8
**Gurgaon = Gurugram** *India* 28°27N 77°1E **42** E7
**Gurgueia** → *Brazil* 6°50S 43°24W **93** E10
**Gurha** *India* 25°12N 71°39E **42** G4
**Guri, Embalse de** *Venezuela* 7°50N 62°52W **92** B6
**Gurkha** *Nepal* 28°5N 84°40E **43** E11
**Gurla Mandhata = Naimona'nyi Feng** *China* 30°26N 81°18E **43** D9
**Gurley** *Australia* 29°45S 149°48E **63** D4
**Gurnet Point** *U.S.A.* 42°1N 70°34W **83** D14
**Gurugram** *India* 28°27N 77°1E **42** E7
**Gurun** *Malaysia* 5°49N 100°27E **39** K3
**Gürün** *Turkey* 38°43N 37°15E **19** G6
**Gurupá** *Brazil* 1°25S 51°35W **93** D8
**Gurupá, I. Grande de** *Brazil* 1°25S 51°45W **93** D8
**Gurupi** *Brazil* 11°43S 49°4W **93** F9
**Gurupi** → *Brazil* 1°13S 46°6W **93** D9
**Guruwe** *Zimbabwe* 16°40S 30°42E **57** A5
**Gurvan Sayhan Uul** *Mongolia* 43°50N 104°0E **32** C3
**Guryev = Atyraū** *Kazakhstan* 47°5N 52°0E **19** E9
**Gusau** *Nigeria* 12°12N 6°40E **52** F7
**Gushan** *China* 39°50N 123°35E **33** E12
**Gushgy = Serhetabat** *Turkmenistan* 35°20N 62°18E **47** C9
**Gushi** *China* 32°11N 115°41E **35** A10
**Gusinoozersk** *Russia* 51°16N 106°27E **27** D11
**Gustavus** *U.S.A.* 58°25N 135°44W **70** B1
**Gustine** *U.S.A.* 37°16N 121°0W **78** H6
**Güstrow** *Germany* 53°47N 12°10E **16** B7
**Gütersloh** *Germany* 51°54N 8°24E **16** C5
**Gutha** *Australia* 28°58S 115°55E **61** E2
**Guthalungra** *Australia* 19°52S 147°50E **62** B4
**Guthrie** *Canada* 44°28N 79°32W **82** B5
**Guthrie** *Okla., U.S.A.* 35°53N 97°25W **84** D6
**Guthrie** *Tex., U.S.A.* 33°37N 100°19W **84** E4
**Gutian** *China* 26°32N 118°43E **35** D12
**Guttenberg** *U.S.A.* 42°47N 91°6W **80** D8
**Gutu** *Zimbabwe* 19°41S 31°9E **57** A5
**Guwahati** *India* 26°10N 91°45E **41** F17
**Guy Fawkes River** △ *Australia* 30°0S 152°20E **63** D5
**Guyana** ■ *S. Amer.* 5°0N 59°0W **92** C7
**Guyane française = French Guiana** ☒ *S. Amer.* 4°0N 53°0W **93** C8
**Guyang** *China* 41°0N 110°5E **32** D6
**Guyenne** *France* 44°30N 0°40E **20** D4
**Guymon** *U.S.A.* 36°41N 101°29W **84** C4
**Guyra** *Australia* 30°15S 151°40E **63** E5
**Guyuan** *Hebei, China* 41°37N 115°40E **32** D8
**Guyuan** *Ningxia Huizu, China* 36°0N 106°20E **32** F4
**Güzelyurt = Morphou** *Cyprus* 35°12N 32°59E **46** C2
**Guzhang** *China* 28°42N 109°58E **34** C7
**Guzhen** *China* 33°22N 117°18E **33** H9
**Guzmán, L. de** *Mexico* 31°20N 107°30W **86** A3
**Gwa** *Myanmar* 17°36N 94°34E **41** L19
**Gwabegar** *Australia* 30°37S 148°59E **63** E4
**Gwādar** *Pakistan* 25°10N 62°18E **40** G3
**Gwaii Haanas** △ *Canada* 52°21N 131°26W **70** C2
**Gwalior** *India* 26°12N 78°10E **42** F8
**Gwanda** *Zimbabwe* 20°55S 29°0E **55** J5
**Gwangju** *S. Korea* 35°9N 126°54E **33** G14
**Gwangyang** *S. Korea* 34°56N 127°41E **33** G14
**Gwanju = Gwangju** *S. Korea* 35°9N 126°54E **33** G14
**Gweebarra B.** *Ireland* 54°51N 8°23W **10** B3
**Gweedore** *Ireland* 55°3N 8°14W **10** A3
**Gweru** *Zimbabwe* 19°28S 29°45E **55** H5
**Gwinn** *U.S.A.* 46°19N 87°27W **80** B10
**Gwydir** → *Australia* 29°27S 149°48E **63** D4
**Gwynedd** □ *U.K.* 52°52N 4°10W **12** E3
**Gyandzha = Gäncä** *Azerbaijan* 40°45N 46°20E **19** F8
**Gyangzê** *China* 29°5N 89°47E **30** F6
**Gyaring Hu** *China* 34°50N 97°40E **30** E8
**Gydanskiy Poluostrov** *Russia* 70°0N 78°0E **26** C8
**Gyeonggi-man** *S. Korea* 37°0N 125°30E **33** F13
**Gyeongju** *S. Korea* 35°51N 129°14E **33** G15
**Gympie** *Australia* 26°11S 152°38E **63** D5
**Gyöngyös** *Hungary* 47°48N 19°56E **17** E10
**Győr** *Hungary* 47°41N 17°40E **17** E9
**Gypsum Pt.** *Canada* 61°53N 114°35W **70** A6
**Gypsumville** *Canada* 51°45N 98°40W **71** C9
**Gyula** *Hungary* 46°38N 21°17E **17** E11
**Gyumri** *Armenia* 40°47N 43°50E **19** F7
**Gyzylarbat = Serdar** *Turkmenistan* 39°4N 56°23E **47** B8
**Gyzyletrek = Etrek** *Turkmenistan* 37°36N 54°46E **47** B7

## H

**Ha 'Arava** → *Israel* 30°50N 35°20E **48** E4
**Ha Coi** *Vietnam* 21°26N 107°46E **34** G6
**Ha Dong** *Vietnam* 20°58N 105°46E **34** G5
**Ha Giang** *Vietnam* 22°50N 104°59E **34** F5
**Ha Karmel, Har** *Israel* 32°44N 35°3E **48** C4
**Ha Karmel** △ *Israel* 32°45N 35°5E **48** C4
**Ha Long = Hong Gai** *Vietnam* 20°57N 107°5E **34** G6
**Ha Long, Vinh** *Vietnam* 20°56N 107°3E **38** B6
**Ha Tien** *Vietnam* 10°23N 104°29E **39** G5
**Ha Tinh** *Vietnam* 18°20N 105°54E **38** C5
**Ha Trung** *Vietnam* 19°58N 105°50E **38** C5
**Haaksbergen** *Neths.* 52°9N 6°45E **15** B6
**Ha'ano** *Tonga* 19°41S 174°18W **59** c
**Ha'apai Group** *Tonga* 19°47S 174°27W **59** c
**Haapiti** *Moorea* 17°34S 149°52W **59** d
**Haapsalu** *Estonia* 58°56N 23°30E **9** G20
**Haarlem** *Neths.* 52°23N 4°39E **15** B4
**Haast** → *N.Z.* 43°50S 169°2E **59** E2
**Haasts Bluff** *Australia* 23°22S 132°0E **60** D5
**Haasts Bluff** ✪ *Australia* 23°39S 130°34E **60** D5
**Hab** → *Pakistan* 24°53N 66°41E **42** G3
**Hab Nadi Chauki** *Pakistan* 25°0N 66°50E **42** G2
**Habahe** *China* 48°3N 86°23E **30** B6
**Habay** *Canada* 58°50N 118°44W **70** B5
**Ḥabbānīyah** *Iraq* 33°17N 43°29E **46** C4
**Habirag** *China* 42°17N 115°42E **32** C8
**Haboro** *Japan* 44°22N 141°42E **28** B10
**Ḥabshān** *U.A.E.* 23°50N 53°37E **47** F7
**Hachijō-Jima** *Japan* 33°5N 139°45E **29** H9
**Hachiman = Gujō** *Japan* 35°45N 136°57E **29** G8
**Hachinohe** *Japan* 40°30N 141°29E **28** D10
**Hachiōji** *Japan* 35°40N 139°20E **29** G9
**Hackettstown** *U.S.A.* 40°51N 74°50W **83** F10
**Hadali** *Pakistan* 32°16N 72°11E **42** C5
**Hadarba, Ras** *Sudan* 22°4N 36°51E **53** D13
**Hadarom** □ *Israel* 31°0N 35°0E **48** E4
**Ḥadd, Ra's al** *Oman* 22°35N 59°50E **49** C6
**Haddington** *U.K.* 55°57N 2°47W **11** F6
**Hadejia** *Nigeria* 12°30N 10°5E **52** F7
**Ḥadera** *Israel* 32°27N 34°55E **48** C3
**Ḥadera, N.** → *Israel* 32°28N 34°52E **48** C3
**Haderslev** *Denmark* 55°15N 9°30E **9** J13
**Hadgaon** *India* 19°30N 77°40E **44** E3
**Hadhramaut = Ḥaḍramawt** □ *Yemen* 15°30N 49°30E **49** D4
**Hadīboh** *Yemen* 12°39N 54°2E **49** E5
**Hadley B.** *Canada* 72°31N 108°12W **68** C10
**Hadong** *S. Korea* 35°5N 127°44E **33** G14
**Ḥaḍramawt** □ *Yemen* 15°30N 49°30E **49** D4
**Ḥadrānīyah** *Iraq* 35°38N 43°14E **46** C4
**Hadrian's Wall** *U.K.* 55°0N 2°30W **12** B5
**Hae, Ko** *Thailand* 7°44N 98°22E **39** a
**Haeju** *N. Korea* 38°3N 125°45E **33** E13
**Hā'ena** *U.S.A.* 22°14N 159°34W **75** L8
**Haenam** *S. Korea* 34°34N 126°35E **33** G14
**Haenertsburg** *S. Africa* 24°0S 29°50E **57** B4
**Haerhpin = Harbin** *China* 45°48N 126°40E **33** B14
**Hafar al Bāṭin** *Si. Arabia* 28°32N 45°52E **46** D5
**Ḥafirat al 'Aydā** *Si. Arabia* 26°26N 39°12E **46** E3
**Ḥafit** *Oman* 23°59N 55°49E **47** F7
**Hafizabad** *Pakistan* 32°5N 73°40E **42** C5
**Haflong** *India* 25°10N 93°5E **41** G18
**Haft Gel** *Iran* 31°30N 49°32E **47** D6
**Hagalil** *Israel* 32°53N 35°18E **48** C4
**Hagari** → *India* 15°40N 77°0E **45** G3
**Hagemeister I.** *U.S.A.* 58°39N 160°54W **74** D7
**Hagen** *Germany* 51°21N 7°27E **16** C4
**Hagerman** *U.S.A.* 33°7N 104°20W **77** K11
**Hagerman Fossil Beds** ⌂ *U.S.A.* 42°48N 114°57W **76** E6
**Hagerstown** *U.S.A.* 39°39N 77°43W **81** F15
**Hagersville** *Canada* 42°58N 80°3W **82** D4
**Hagfors** *Sweden* 60°3N 13°45E **9** F15
**Hagi** *Japan* 34°30N 131°22E **29** G5
**Hagolan** *Syria* 33°0N 35°45E **48** C4
**Hagondange** *France* 49°16N 6°11E **20** B7
**Hags Hd.** *Ireland* 52°57N 9°28W **10** D2
**Hague, C. de la** *France* 49°44N 1°56W **20** B3
**Hague, The = 's-Gravenhage** *Neths.* 52°7N 4°17E **15** B4
**Haguenau** *France* 48°49N 7°47E **20** B7
**Hai Duong** *Vietnam* 20°56N 106°19E **34** G6
**Hai'an** *Guangdong, China* 20°18N 110°11E **35** G8
**Hai'an** *Jiangsu, China* 32°37N 120°27E **35** A13
**Haicheng** *China* 40°50N 122°45E **33** D12
**Haida Gwaii** *Canada* 53°20N 132°10W **70** C2
**Haidar Khel** *Afghan.* 33°58N 68°38E **42** C3
**Haidarâbâd = Hyderabad** *India* 17°22N 78°29E **44** F4
**Haidargarh** *India* 26°37N 81°22E **43** F9
**Haifa = Ḥefa** *Israel* 32°46N 35°0E **48** C4
**Haifeng** *China* 22°58N 115°10E **35** F10
**Haikou** *China* 20°1N 110°16E **38** B8
**Ḥā'il** *Si. Arabia* 27°28N 41°45E **46** E4
**Ḥā'il** □ *Si. Arabia* 26°40N 41°40E **46** E4
**Hailar** *China* 49°10N 119°38E **31** B12
**Hailey** *U.S.A.* 43°31N 114°19W **76** E6
**Haileybury** *Canada* 47°30N 79°38W **72** C4
**Hailin** *China* 44°37N 129°30E **33** B15
**Hailing Dao** *China* 21°35N 111°47E **35** G8
**Hailun** *China* 47°28N 126°50E **31** B14
**Hailuoto** *Finland* 65°3N 24°45E **8** D21
**Haimen** *Guangdong, China* 23°15N 116°38E **35** F11
**Haimen** *Jiangsu, China* 31°52N 121°10E **35** B13
**Hainan** □ *China* 19°0N 109°30E **38** C7
**Hainan Dao** *China* 19°0N 109°30E **38** C7
**Hainan Str. = Qiongzhou Haixia** *China* 20°10N 110°15E **38** B8
**Hainaut** □ *Belgium* 50°30N 4°0E **15** D4
**Haines** *Alaska, U.S.A.* 59°14N 135°26W **70** B1
**Haines** *Oreg., U.S.A.* 44°55N 117°56W **76** D5
**Haines City** *U.S.A.* 28°7N 81°38W **85** G14
**Haines Junction** *Canada* 60°45N 137°30W **70** A1
**Haining** *China* 30°28N 120°40E **35** B13
**Haiphong** *Vietnam* 20°47N 106°41E **34** G6
**Haitan Dao** *China* 25°30N 119°45E **35** E12
**Haiti** ■ *W. Indies* 19°0N 72°30W **89** C5
**Haiya** *Sudan* 18°20N 36°21E **53** E13
**Haiyan** *Qinghai, China* 36°53N 100°59E **30** D9
**Haiyan** *Zhejiang, China* 30°28N 120°58E **35** B13
**Haiyang** *China* 36°47N 121°9E **33** F11
**Haiyuan** *Guangxi Zhuangzu, China* 22°8N 107°35E **34** F6
**Haiyuan** *Ningxia Huizu, China* 36°35N 105°52E **32** F3
**Haizhou** *China* 34°37N 119°7E **33** G10
**Haizhou Wan** *China* 34°50N 119°20E **33** G10
**Hajdúböszörmény** *Hungary* 47°40N 21°30E **17** E11
**Haji Ibrahim** *Iraq* 36°40N 44°30E **46** B5
**Hajipur** *India* 25°45N 85°13E **43** G11
**Ḥājj Ali Qolī, Kavīr-e** *Iran* 35°55N 54°50E **47** C7
**Ḥajjah** *Yemen* 15°42N 43°36E **49** D3
**Ḥājjīābād** *Hormozgān, Iran* 28°19N 55°55E **47** D7
**Ḥājjīābād** *Khorāsān, Iran* 33°37N 60°0E **47** C9
**Ḥājjīābād-e Zarrīn** *Iran* 33°9N 54°51E **47** C7
**Hajnówka** *Poland* 52°47N 23°35E **17** B12
**Hakkâri** *Turkey* 37°34N 43°44E **46** B4
**Hakken-Zan** *Japan* 34°10N 135°54E **29** G7
**Hakkōda San** *Japan* 40°50N 141°0E **28** D10
**Hakodate** *Japan* 41°45N 140°44E **28** D10
**Hakos** *Namibia* 23°13S 16°21E **56** B2
**Hakskeenpan** *S. Africa* 26°48S 20°13E **56** C3
**Haku-San** *Japan* 36°9N 136°46E **29** F8
**Haku-San** △ *Japan* 36°15N 136°45E **29** F8
**Hakui** *Japan* 36°53N 136°47E **29** F8
**Hakusan** *Japan* 36°31N 136°34E **29** F8
**Hala** *Pakistan* 25°43N 68°20E **40** G6
**Ḥalab** *Syria* 36°10N 37°15E **46** B3
**Ḥalabjah** *Iraq* 35°10N 45°58E **46** C5
**Halaib** *Sudan* 22°12N 36°30E **53** D13
**Halaib Triangle** *Africa* 22°30N 35°20E **53** D13
**Ḥālat 'Ammār** *Si. Arabia* 29°10N 36°4E **46** D3
**Halbā** *Lebanon* 34°34N 36°6E **48** A5
**Halberstadt** *Germany* 51°54N 11°3E **16** C6
**Halcombe** *N.Z.* 40°8S 175°30E **59** D5
**Halcon, Mt.** *Phil.* 13°16N 121°0E **37** B6
**Halde Fjäll = Haltiatunturi** *Finland* 69°17N 21°18E **8** B19
**Halden** *Norway* 59°9N 11°23E **9** G14
**Haldia** *Bangla.* 22°1N 88°3E **43** H13
**Haldwani** *India* 29°31N 79°30E **43** E8
**Hale** → *Australia* 24°56S 135°53E **62** C2
**Halesowen** *U.K.* 52°27N 2°3W **13** E5
**Halesworth** *U.K.* 52°20N 1°31E **13** E9
**Haleyville** *U.S.A.* 34°14N 87°37W **85** D11
**Half Dome** *U.S.A.* 37°44N 119°32W **78** H7
**Halfmoon Bay** *N.Z.* 46°50S 168°5E **59** G2
**Halfway** → *Canada* 56°12N 121°32W **70** B4
**Halia** *India* 24°50N 82°19E **43** G10
**Haliburton** *Canada* 45°3N 78°30W **82** A6
**Halifax** *Australia* 18°32S 146°22E **62** B4
**Halifax** *Canada* 44°38N 63°35W **73** D7
**Halifax** *U.K.* 53°43N 1°52W **12** D6
**Halifax** *U.S.A.* 40°25N 76°55W **82** F8
**Halifax B.** *Australia* 18°50S 147°0E **62** B4
**Halifax I.** *Namibia* 26°38S 15°4E **56** C2
**Halik Shan** *China* 42°20N 81°22E **30** C5
**Halīl** → *Iran* 27°40N 58°30E **47** E8
**Halimun** △ *Indonesia* 6°42S 106°26E **37** G11
**Halkida = Chalkida** *Greece* 38°27N 23°42E **23** E10
**Halkirk** *U.K.* 58°30N 3°29W **11** C5
**Hall Beach** *Canada* 68°46N 81°12W **69** D15
**Hall Pen.** *Canada* 63°30N 66°0W **69** E18
**Hall Pt.** *Australia* 15°40S 124°23E **60** C3
**Halland** *Sweden* 57°8N 12°47E **9** H15
**Ḥallāniyat, Jazā'ir al** *Oman* 17°30N 55°58E **49** D6
**Hallasan** *S. Korea* 33°22N 126°32E **33** H14
**Halle** *Germany* 51°30N 11°56E **16** C6
**Hällefors** *Sweden* 59°47N 14°31E **9** G16
**Hallett** *Australia* 33°25S 138°55E **63** E2
**Hallettsville** *U.S.A.* 29°27N 96°57W **84** G6
**Halley** *Antarctica* 75°35S 26°39W **5** D1
**Hallia** → *India* 16°55N 79°20E **44** F4
**Hallim** *S. Korea* 33°24N 126°15E **33** H14
**Hallingdalselva** → *Norway* 60°23N 9°35E **8** F13
**Hallingskarvet** △ *Norway* 60°37N 7°45E **8** F12
**Hallock** *U.S.A.* 48°47N 96°57W **80** A5
**Halls Creek** *Australia* 18°16S 127°38E **60** C4
**Halls Gap** *Australia* 37°8S 142°34E **63** F3
**Halls Lake** *Canada* 45°7N 78°45W **82** A6
**Hallsberg** *Sweden* 59°5N 15°7E **9** G16
**Hallstead** *U.S.A.* 41°58N 75°45W **83** E9
**Halmahera** *Indonesia* 0°40N 128°0E **37** D7
**Halmahera Sea** *Indonesia* 2°0N 130°0E **37** D7
**Halmstad** *Sweden* 56°41N 12°52E **9** H15
**Halong Bay = Ha Long, Vinh** *Vietnam* 20°56N 107°3E **38** B6
**Hälsingborg = Helsingborg** *Sweden* 56°3N 12°42E **9** H15
**Hälsingland** *Sweden* 61°40N 16°5E **8** F17
**Halstead** *U.K.* 51°57N 0°40E **13** F8
**Haltiatunturi** *Finland* 69°17N 21°18E **8** B19
**Halton** □ *U.K.* 53°22N 2°45W **12** D5
**Haltwhistle** *U.K.* 54°58N 2°26W **12** C5
**Ḥālūl** *Qatar* 25°40N 52°40E **47** E7
**Halvad** *India* 23°1N 71°11E **42** H4

Halvän *Iran* 33°57N 56°15E **47 C8**
Hamab *Namibia* 28°7S 19°16E **56 C2**
Hamada *Japan* 34°56N 132°4E **29 G6**
Hamadān *Iran* 34°52N 48°32E **47 C6**
Hamadān □ *Iran* 35°0N 49°0E **47 C6**
Hamamatsu *Japan* 34°45N 137°45E **29 G8**
Hamar *Norway* 60°48N 11°7E **8 F14**
Hamâta, Gebel *Egypt* 24°5N 35°0E **46 E2**
Hamatonbetsu *Japan* 45°10N 142°20E **28 B11**
Hambantota *Sri Lanka* 6°10N 81°10E **45 L5**
Hamber △ *Canada* 52°20N 118°0W **70 C5**
Hamburg *Germany* 53°33N 9°59E **16 B5**
Hamburg *Ark., U.S.A.* 33°14N 91°48W **84 E9**
Hamburg *N.Y., U.S.A.* 42°43N 78°50W **82 D6**
Hamburg *Pa., U.S.A.* 40°33N 75°59W **83 F9**
Hamd, W. al → *Si. Arabia* 24°55N 36°20E **46 E3**
Hamden *U.S.A.* 41°23N 72°54W **83 E12**
Häme *Finland* 61°38N 25°10E **8 F21**
Hämeenlinna *Finland* 61°0N 24°28E **8 F21**
Hamelin Pool *Australia* 26°22S 114°20E **61 E1**
Hameln *Germany* 52°6N 9°21E **16 B5**
Hamerkaz □ *Israel* 32°15N 34°55E **48 C3**
Hamersley Ra. *Australia* 22°0S 117°45E **60 D2**
Hamhŭng *N. Korea* 39°54N 127°30E **33 E14**
Hami *China* 42°55N 93°25E **30 C7**
Hamilton *Australia* 37°45S 142°2E **63 F3**
Hamilton *Canada* 43°15N 79°50W **82 C5**
Hamilton *N.Z.* 37°47S 175°19E **59 B5**
Hamilton *U.K.* 55°46N 4°2W **11 F4**
Hamilton *Ala., U.S.A.* 34°9N 87°59W **85 D11**
Hamilton *Mont., U.S.A.* 46°15N 114°10W **76 C6**
Hamilton *N.Y., U.S.A.* 42°50N 75°33W **83 D9**
Hamilton *Ohio, U.S.A.* 39°24N 84°34W **81 F11**
Hamilton *Tex., U.S.A.* 31°42N 98°7W **84 F5**
Hamilton → *Queens.,*
  *Australia* 23°30S 139°47E **62 C2**
Hamilton → *S. Austral.,*
  *Australia* 26°40S 135°19E **63 D2**
Hamilton City *U.S.A.* 39°45N 122°1W **78 F4**
Hamilton I. *Australia* 20°21S 148°56E **62 b**
Hamilton Inlet *Canada* 54°0N 57°30W **73 B8**
Hamilton Mt. *U.S.A.* 43°25N 74°22W **83 C10**
Hamina *Finland* 60°34N 27°12E **8 F22**
Hamirpur *H.P., India* 31°41N 76°31E **42 D7**
Hamirpur *Ut. P., India* 25°57N 80°9E **43 G9**
Hamlet *U.S.A.* 34°53N 79°42W **85 D15**
Hamley Bridge *Australia* 34°17S 138°35E **63 E2**
Hamlin = Hameln *Germany* 52°6N 9°21E **16 B5**
Hamlin *N.Y., U.S.A.* 43°17N 77°55W **82 C7**
Hamlin *Tex., U.S.A.* 32°53N 100°8W **84 E4**
Hamm *Germany* 51°40N 7°50E **16 C4**
Hammär, Hawr al *Iraq* 30°50N 47°10E **46 D5**
Hammerfest *Norway* 70°39N 23°41E **8 A20**
Hammond *Ind., U.S.A.* 41°38N 87°30W **80 E10**
Hammond *La., U.S.A.* 30°30N 90°28W **85 F9**
Hammond *N.Y., U.S.A.* 44°27N 75°42W **83 B9**
Hammondsport *U.S.A.* 42°25N 77°13W **82 D7**
Hammonton *U.S.A.* 39°39N 74°48W **81 F16**
Hampden *N.Z.* 45°18S 170°50E **59 F3**
Hampi *India* 15°18N 76°28E **45 G3**
Hampshire □ *U.K.* 51°7N 1°23W **13 F6**
Hampshire Downs *U.K.* 51°15N 1°10W **13 F6**
Hampton *N.B., Canada* 45°32N 65°51W **73 C6**
Hampton *Ont., Canada* 43°58N 78°45W **82 C6**
Hampton *Ark., U.S.A.* 33°32N 92°28W **84 E8**
Hampton *Iowa, U.S.A.* 42°45N 93°13W **80 D7**
Hampton *N.H., U.S.A.* 42°57N 70°50W **83 D14**
Hampton *S.C., U.S.A.* 32°52N 81°7W **85 E14**
Hampton *Va., U.S.A.* 37°2N 76°21W **81 G15**
Hampton Bays *U.S.A.* 40°53N 72°30W **83 F12**
Hampton Tableland
  *Australia* 32°0S 127°0E **61 F4**
Hamyang *S. Korea* 35°32N 127°42E **33 G14**
Han = Hangang →
  *S. Korea* 37°50N 126°30E **33 F14**
Han Jiang → *China* 23°25S 116°40E **35 F11**
Han Pijesak *Bos.-H.* 44°5N 18°57E **23 B8**
Han Shui → *China* 30°34N 114°17E **35 B10**
Hanak *Si. Arabia* 25°32N 37°0E **46 E3**
Hanamaki *Japan* 39°23N 141°7E **28 E10**
Hanau *Germany* 50°7N 8°56E **16 C5**
Hanbogd = Ihbulag
  *Mongolia* 43°11N 107°10E **32 C4**
Hancheng *China* 35°31N 110°25E **32 G6**
Hanchuan *China* 30°40N 113°50E **35 B9**
Hancock *Mich., U.S.A.* 47°8N 88°35W **80 B9**
Hancock *N.Y., U.S.A.* 41°57N 75°17W **83 E9**
Hancock *Vt., U.S.A.* 43°55N 72°50W **83 C12**
Handa *Japan* 34°53N 136°55E **29 G8**
Handa I. *U.K.* 58°23N 5°11W **11 C3**
Handan *China* 36°35N 114°28E **32 F8**
Handwara *India* 34°21N 74°20E **43 B6**
Hanegev *Israel* 30°50N 35°0E **48 E4**
Hanford *U.S.A.* 36°20N 119°39W **78 J7**
Hanford Reach △
  *U.S.A.* 46°40N 119°30W **76 C4**
Hang Chat *Thailand* 18°20N 99°21E **38 C2**
Hangang → *S. Korea* 37°50N 126°30E **33 F14**
Hangayn Nuruu *Mongolia* 47°30N 99°0E **30 B8**
Hangchou = Hangzhou
  *China* 30°18N 120°11E **35 B13**
Hanggin Houqi *China* 40°58N 107°4E **32 D4**
Hanggin Qi *China* 39°52N 108°50E **32 E5**
Hangu *China* 39°18N 117°53E **33 E9**
Hangzhou *China* 30°18N 120°11E **35 B13**
Hangzhou Wan *China* 30°15N 120°45E **35 B13**
Hanh *Mongolia* 51°32N 100°35E **30 A9**
Hanhongor *Mongolia* 43°55N 104°28E **32 C3**
Hania = Chania *Greece* 35°30N 24°4E **25 G11**
Hanīdh *Si. Arabia* 26°35N 48°38E **47 E6**
Hanish *Yemen* 13°45N 42°46E **49 E3**
Hanjiang *China* 25°26N 119°6E **35 E12**
Hankinson *U.S.A.* 46°4N 96°54W **80 B5**
Hankö *Finland* 59°50N 22°57E **9 G20**
Hankou *China* 30°35N 114°30E **35 B10**
Hanle *India* 32°42N 79°4E **43 C8**
Hanmer Springs *N.Z.* 42°32S 172°50E **59 E4**
Hann → *Australia* 17°26S 126°17E **60 C4**

Hann, Mt. *Australia* 15°45S 126°0E **60 C4**
Hanna *Canada* 51°40N 111°54W **70 C6**
Hanna *U.S.A.* 41°52N 106°34W **76 F10**
Hannah B. *Canada* 51°40N 80°0W **72 B4**
Hannibal *Mo., U.S.A.* 39°42N 91°22W **80 F8**
Hannibal *N.Y., U.S.A.* 43°19N 76°35W **83 C8**
Hannover *Germany* 52°22N 9°46E **16 B5**
Hanoi *Vietnam* 21°5N 105°55E **34 G5**
Hanover = Hannover
  *Germany* 52°22N 9°46E **16 B5**
Hanover *Canada* 44°9N 81°2W **82 B3**
Hanover *S. Africa* 31°4S 24°29E **56 D3**
Hanover *N.H., U.S.A.* 43°42N 72°17W **83 C12**
Hanover *Ohio, U.S.A.* 40°4N 82°16W **82 F2**
Hanover *Pa., U.S.A.* 39°48N 76°59W **81 F15**
Hanover, I. *Chile* 51°0S 74°50W **96 G2**
Hans Lollik I.
  *U.S. Virgin Is.* 18°24N 64°53W **89 e**
Hansdiha *India* 24°36N 87°5E **43 G12**
Hanshou *China* 28°56N 111°50E **35 C8**
Hansi *H.P., India* 32°27N 77°50E **42 C7**
Hansi *Haryana, India* 29°10N 75°57E **42 E6**
Hanson, L. *Australia* 31°0S 136°15E **63 E2**
Hanting *China* 36°46N 119°12E **33 F10**
Hantsavichy *Belarus* 52°49N 26°30E **17 B14**
Hanumangarh *India* 29°35N 74°19E **42 E6**
Hanyin *China* 32°54N 108°28E **32 H5**
Hanyuan *China* 29°21N 102°40E **34 C4**
Hanzhong *China* 33°10N 107°1E **34 A6**
Hanzhuang *China* 34°33N 117°23E **33 G9**
Haoxue *China* 30°3N 112°2E **35 B9**
Haparanda *Sweden* 65°52N 24°8E **8 D21**
Haparanda Skärgård △
  *Sweden* 65°35N 23°44E **8 D20**
Happy *U.S.A.* 34°45N 101°52W **84 D4**
Happy Camp *U.S.A.* 41°48N 123°23W **76 F2**
Happy Valley-Goose Bay
  *Canada* 53°15N 60°20W **73 B7**
Hapsu *N. Korea* 41°13N 128°51E **33 D15**
Hapur *India* 28°45N 77°45E **42 E7**
Haql *Si. Arabia* 29°10N 34°58E **48 F3**
Har *Indonesia* 5°16S 133°14E **37 F8**
Har Hu *China* 38°20N 97°38E **30 D8**
Har Us Nuur *Mongolia* 48°0N 92°0E **30 B7**
Har Yehuda *Israel* 31°35N 34°57E **48 D3**
Haraḍ *Si. Arabia* 24°22N 49°0E **47 E6**
Haramosh *Pakistan* 35°50N 74°54E **43 B6**
Haranomachi = Minamisōma
  *Japan* 37°38N 140°58E **28 F10**
Harar = Harer *Ethiopia* 9°20N 42°8E **49 F3**
Harare *Zimbabwe* 17°43S 31°2E **55 H6**
Harazé *Chad* 9°57N 20°48E **53 G10**
Harbhanga *India* 20°38N 84°36E **44 D7**
Harbin *China* 45°48N 126°40E **33 B14**
Harbor Beach *U.S.A.* 43°51N 82°39W **82 C2**
Harborcreek *U.S.A.* 42°9N 79°57W **82 D5**
Harbour Breton *Canada* 47°29N 55°50W **73 C8**
Harbour Deep *Canada* 50°25N 56°32W **73 B8**
Harda *India* 22°27N 77°5E **42 H7**
Hardangerfjorden *Norway* 60°5N 6°0E **9 F12**
Hardangervidda *Norway* 60°7N 7°20E **9 F12**
Hardap □ *Namibia* 24°0S 17°0E **56 B2**
Hardap △ *Namibia* 24°29S 17°45E **56 B2**
Hardap Dam *Namibia* 24°32S 17°50E **56 B2**
Hardenberg *Neths.* 52°34N 6°37E **15 B6**
Harderwijk *Neths.* 52°21N 5°38E **15 B5**
Hardey → *Australia* 22°45S 116°8E **60 D2**
Hardin *U.S.A.* 45°44N 107°37W **76 D10**
Harding *S. Africa* 30°35S 29°55E **57 D4**
Harding Ra. *Australia* 16°17S 124°55E **60 C3**
Hardisty *Canada* 52°40N 111°18W **70 C6**
Hardoi *India* 27°26N 80°6E **43 F9**
Hardwar = Haridwar
  *India* 29°58N 78°9E **42 E8**
Hardwick *U.S.A.* 44°30N 72°22W **83 B12**
Hardwood Lake *Canada* 45°12N 77°26W **82 A7**
Hardy, Pen. *Chile* 55°30S 68°20W **96 H3**
Hardy, Pte. *St. Lucia* 14°6N 60°56W **89 f**
Hare B. *Canada* 51°15N 55°45W **73 B8**
Hareid *Norway* 62°22N 6°1E **8 E12**
Harer *Ethiopia* 9°20N 42°8E **49 F3**
Hargeisa *Somalia* 9°30N 44°2E **49 F3**
Hari → *Indonesia* 1°16S 104°5E **36 E2**
Haridwar *India* 29°58N 78°9E **42 E8**
Harihar *India* 14°32N 75°44E **45 G2**
Hariharpur Garhi *Nepal* 27°19N 85°29E **43 F11**
Harim, Jabal al *Oman* 25°58N 56°14E **47 E8**
Haringhata → *Bangla.* 22°0N 89°58E **41 J16**
Haripad *India* 9°14N 76°28E **45 K3**
Harirūd → *Asia* 37°24N 60°38E **47 B9**
Härjedalen *Sweden* 62°22N 13°5E **8 E15**
Harlan *Iowa, U.S.A.* 41°39N 95°19W **80 E6**
Harlan *Ky., U.S.A.* 36°51N 83°19W **81 G12**
Harlech *U.K.* 52°52N 4°6W **12 E3**
Harlem *U.S.A.* 48°32N 108°47W **76 B9**
Harlingen *Neths.* 53°11N 5°25E **15 A5**
Harlingen *U.S.A.* 26°12N 97°42W **84 H6**
Harlow *U.K.* 51°46N 0°8E **13 F8**
Harlowton *U.S.A.* 46°26N 109°50W **76 C9**
Harnai *India* 17°48N 73°6E **44 F1**
Harnai *Pakistan* 30°6N 67°56E **42 D2**
Harney Basin *U.S.A.* 43°0N 119°30W **76 E4**
Harney L. *U.S.A.* 43°14N 119°8W **76 E4**
Harney Peak *U.S.A.* 43°52N 103°32W **80 D2**
Härnösand *Sweden* 62°38N 17°55E **8 E17**
Haroldswick *U.K.* 60°48N 0°50W **11 A8**
Harp L. *Canada* 55°5N 61°50W **73 A7**
Harpanahalli *India* 14°47N 76°2E **45 G3**
Harper *Liberia* 4°25N 7°43W **52 H4**
Harper, Mt. *U.S.A.* 64°14N 143°51W **74 C11**
Harrai *India* 22°37N 79°13E **43 H8**
Harrand *Pakistan* 29°28N 70°3E **42 E4**
Harricana → *Canada* 50°56N 79°32W **72 B4**
Harriman *U.S.A.* 35°56N 84°33W **85 D12**
Harrington Harbour
  *Canada* 50°31N 59°30W **73 B8**
Harris *U.K.* 57°50N 6°55W **11 D2**
Harris, L. *Australia* 31°10S 135°10E **63 E2**

Harris, Sd. of *U.K.* 57°44N 7°6W **11 D1**
Harris Pt. *Canada* 43°6N 82°9W **82 C2**
Harrisburg *Ill., U.S.A.* 37°44N 88°32W **80 G9**
Harrisburg *Nebr., U.S.A.* 41°33N 103°44W **80 E2**
Harrisburg *Pa., U.S.A.* 40°16N 76°53W **82 F8**
Harrismith *S. Africa* 28°15S 29°8E **57 C4**
Harrison *Ark., U.S.A.* 36°14N 93°7W **84 C8**
Harrison *Maine, U.S.A.* 44°7N 70°39W **83 B14**
Harrison *Nebr., U.S.A.* 42°41N 103°53W **80 D2**
Harrison, C. *Canada* 54°55N 57°55W **73 B8**
Harrison Bay *U.S.A.* 70°40N 151°0W **74 A9**
Harrison L. *Canada* 49°33N 121°50W **70 D4**
Harrisonburg *U.S.A.* 38°27N 78°52W **81 F14**
Harrisonville *U.S.A.* 38°39N 94°21W **80 F6**
Harriston *Canada* 43°57N 80°53W **82 C4**
Harrisville *Mich., U.S.A.* 44°39N 83°17W **82 B1**
Harrisville *N.Y., U.S.A.* 44°9N 75°19W **83 B9**
Harrisville *Pa., U.S.A.* 41°8N 80°0W **82 E5**
Harrodsburg *U.S.A.* 37°46N 84°51W **81 G11**
Harrogate *U.K.* 54°0N 1°33W **12 C6**
Harrow *Canada* 42°2N 82°55W **82 D2**
Harrowsmith *Canada* 44°24N 76°40W **83 B8**
Harry S. Truman Res.
  *U.S.A.* 38°16N 93°24W **80 F7**
Harsīn *Iran* 34°18N 47°33E **46 C5**
Harstad *Norway* 68°48N 16°30E **8 B17**
Harsud *India* 22°6N 76°44E **42 H7**
Hart *U.S.A.* 43°42N 86°22W **80 D10**
Hart, L. *Australia* 31°10S 136°25E **63 E2**
Hartbees → *S. Africa* 28°45S 20°32E **56 C3**
Hartford *Conn., U.S.A.* 41°46N 72°41W **83 E12**
Hartford *Ky., U.S.A.* 37°27N 86°55W **80 G10**
Hartford *S. Dak., U.S.A.* 43°38N 96°57W **80 D5**
Hartford *Vt., U.S.A.* 43°40N 72°20W **83 C12**
Hartford *Wis., U.S.A.* 43°19N 88°22W **80 D9**
Hartford City *U.S.A.* 40°27N 85°22W **81 E11**
Hartland *Canada* 46°20N 67°32W **73 C6**
Hartland Pt. *U.K.* 51°1N 4°32W **13 F3**
Hartlepool *U.K.* 54°42N 1°13W **12 C6**
Hartlepool □ *U.K.* 54°42N 1°17W **12 C6**
Hartley Bay *Canada* 53°25N 129°15W **70 C3**
Hartmannberge *Namibia* 17°0S 13°0E **56 A1**
Hartney *Canada* 49°30N 100°35W **71 D8**
Harts → *S. Africa* 28°24S 24°17E **56 C3**
Harts Range *Australia* 23°6S 134°55E **62 C1**
Hartselle *U.S.A.* 34°27N 86°56W **85 D11**
Hartshorne *U.S.A.* 34°51N 95°34W **84 D7**
Hartstown *U.S.A.* 41°33N 80°23W **82 E4**
Hartsville *U.S.A.* 34°23N 80°4W **85 D14**
Hartswater *S. Africa* 27°34S 24°43E **56 C3**
Hartwell *U.S.A.* 34°21N 82°56W **85 D13**
Harvand *Iran* 28°25N 55°43E **47 D7**
Harvey *Australia* 33°5S 115°54E **61 F2**
Harvey *N. Dak., U.S.A.* 47°47N 99°56W **80 B4**
Harwich *U.K.* 51°56N 1°17E **13 F9**
Haryana □ *India* 29°0N 76°10E **42 E7**
Haryn → *Belarus* 52°7N 27°17E **17 B14**
Harz *Germany* 51°38N 10°44E **16 C6**
Hasa *Si. Arabia* 25°50N 49°0E **47 E6**
Ḥaṣā, W. al → *Jordan* 31°4N 35°29E **48 D4**
Ḥasanābād *Iran* 32°8N 52°44E **47 C7**
Hasanparti *India* 18°4N 79°32E **44 E4**
Ḥasb, W. → *Iraq* 31°45N 44°17E **46 D5**
Hasdo → *India* 21°44N 82°44E **43 J10**
Hashimoto *Japan* 34°19N 135°37E **29 G7**
Hashtjerd *Iran* 35°52N 50°40E **47 C6**
Hashtpur = Tālesh *Iran* 37°58N 48°58E **47 B6**
Haskell *U.S.A.* 33°10N 99°44W **84 E5**
Haskovo *Bulgaria* 41°56N 25°30E **23 D11**
Haslemere *U.K.* 51°5N 0°43W **13 F7**
Hasselt *Belgium* 50°56N 5°21E **15 D5**
Hassi Messaoud *Algeria* 31°51N 6°1E **52 B7**
Hässleholm *Sweden* 56°10N 13°46E **9 H15**
Hastings *N.Z.* 39°39S 176°52E **59 C6**
Hastings *U.K.* 50°51N 0°35E **13 G8**
Hastings *Mich., U.S.A.* 42°39N 85°17W **81 D11**
Hastings *Minn., U.S.A.* 44°44N 92°51W **80 C7**
Hastings *Nebr., U.S.A.* 40°35N 98°23W **80 E4**
Hastings Ra. *Australia* 31°15S 152°14E **63 E5**
Hat Lot *Vietnam* 21°5N 104°7E **38 B5**
Hat Yai *Thailand* 7°1N 100°27E **39 J3**
Hatanbulag = Ergel
  *Mongolia* 43°8N 109°5E **32 C5**
Hatay *Turkey* 36°14N 36°10E **46 B3**
Hatch *U.S.A.* 32°40N 107°9W **77 K10**
Hatchet L. *Canada* 58°36N 103°40W **71 B8**
Hateruma-Shima *Japan* 24°3N 123°47E **29 M1**
Hatfield *Australia* 33°54S 143°49E **63 E3**
Hatgal *Mongolia* 50°26N 100°9E **30 A9**
Hathras *India* 27°36N 78°6E **42 F8**
Hatia *Bangla.* 22°30N 91°5E **41 H17**
Hatia *Nepal* 27°43N 87°21E **43 F12**
Hatid *India* 17°17N 75°3E **44 F2**
Hato Mayor *Dom. Rep.* 18°46N 69°15W **89 C6**
Hatra = Al Ḥaḍr *Iraq* 35°35N 42°44E **46 C4**
Hatta *India* 24°7N 79°36E **43 G8**
Hatta *U.A.E.* 24°45N 56°4E **47 E8**
Hattah *Australia* 34°48S 142°17E **63 E3**
Hattah Kulkyne △
  *Australia* 34°16S 142°33E **63 E3**
Hatteras, C. *U.S.A.* 35°14N 75°32W **85 D17**
Hattiesburg *U.S.A.* 31°20N 89°17W **85 F10**
Hatvan *Hungary* 47°40N 19°45E **17 E10**
Hau → *Vietnam* 9°30N 106°13E **39 H6**
Haugesund *Norway* 59°23N 5°13E **9 G11**
Haukipudas *Finland* 65°12N 25°20E **8 D21**
Haultain → *Canada* 55°51N 106°46E **71 B7**
Hauraki G. *N.Z.* 36°35S 175°5E **59 B5**
Haut Atlas *Morocco* 32°30N 5°0W **52 B4**
Hautes-Fagnes = Hohes Venn
  *Belgium* 50°30N 6°5E **15 D6**
Hauts Plateaux *Algeria* 35°0N 1°0E **52 B6**
Havana = La Habana
  *Cuba* 23°8N 82°22W **88 B3**
Havana *U.S.A.* 40°18N 90°4W **80 E8**
Havant *U.K.* 50°51N 0°58W **13 G7**
Havasor = Kịzịn *Turkey* 38°18N 43°25E **46 B4**

Havasu, L. *U.S.A.* 34°18N 114°28W **79 L12**
Havelian *Pakistan* 34°2N 73°10E **42 B5**
Havelock *Canada* 44°26N 77°53W **82 B7**
Havelock *N.Z.* 41°17S 173°48E **59 D4**
Havelock *U.S.A.* 34°53N 76°54W **85 D16**
Havelock I. *India* 11°58N 93°0E **45 J11**
Haverfordwest *U.K.* 51°48N 4°58W **13 F3**
Haverhill *U.K.* 52°5N 0°28E **13 E8**
Haverstraw *U.S.A.* 41°12N 73°58W **83 E11**
Haveri *India* 14°53N 75°24E **45 G2**
Havering □ *U.K.* 51°34N 0°14E **13 F8**
Havirga *Mongolia* 45°41N 113°5E **32 B7**
Havířov *Czechia* 49°46N 18°20E **17 D10**
Havre *U.S.A.* 48°33N 109°41W **76 B9**
Havre-Aubert *Canada* 47°12N 61°56W **73 C7**
Havre-St.-Pierre *Canada* 50°18N 63°33W **73 B7**
Haw → *U.S.A.* 35°36N 79°3W **85 D15**
Hawai'i □ *U.S.A.* 19°30N 155°30W **75 M8**
Hawai'i *U.S.A.* 19°30N 155°30W **75 M8**
Hawaiian Is. *Pac. Oc.* 20°30N 156°0W **65 E12**
Hawaiian Ridge *Pac. Oc.* 24°0N 165°0W **65 E11**
Hawarden *U.S.A.* 43°0N 96°29W **80 D5**
Hawea, L. *N.Z.* 44°28S 169°19E **59 F2**
Hawera *N.Z.* 39°35S 174°19E **59 C5**
Hawi *U.S.A.* 20°14N 155°50W **75 L8**
Hawick *U.K.* 55°26N 2°47W **11 F6**
Hawk Junction *Canada* 48°5N 84°38W **72 C3**
Hawke B. *N.Z.* 39°25S 177°20E **59 C6**
Hawker *Australia* 31°59S 138°22E **63 E2**
Hawke's Bay *Canada* 50°36N 57°10W **73 B8**
Hawkesbury *Canada* 45°37N 74°37W **72 C5**
Hawkesbury I. *Canada* 53°37N 129°3W **70 C3**
Hawkesbury Pt. *Australia* 11°55S 134°5E **62 A1**
Hawkinsville *U.S.A.* 32°17N 83°28W **85 E13**
Hawley *Minn., U.S.A.* 46°53N 96°19W **80 B5**
Hawley *Pa., U.S.A.* 41°28N 75°11W **83 E9**
Hawrān, W. → *Iraq* 33°58N 42°34E **46 C4**
Hawsh Mūssá *Lebanon* 33°45N 35°55E **48 B4**
Hawthorne *U.S.A.* 38°32N 118°38W **76 G4**
Hay *Australia* 34°30S 144°51E **63 E3**
Hay → *Australia* 24°50S 138°0E **62 C2**
Hay → *Canada* 60°50N 116°26W **70 A5**
Hay, C. *Australia* 14°5S 129°29E **60 B4**
Hay I. *Canada* 44°53N 80°58W **82 B4**
Hay L. *Canada* 58°50N 118°50W **70 B5**
Hay-on-Wye *U.K.* 52°5N 3°8W **13 E4**
Hay Point *Australia* 21°18S 149°17E **62 C4**
Hay River *Canada* 60°51N 115°44W **70 A5**
Hay Springs *U.S.A.* 42°41N 102°41W **80 D3**
Hayachine-San *Japan* 39°34N 141°29E **28 E10**
Hayastan = Armenia ■
  *Asia* 40°20N 45°0E **19 F7**
Haydān, W. al → *Jordan* 31°29N 35°34E **48 D4**
Hayden *U.S.A.* 40°30N 107°16W **76 F10**
Haydon *U.S.A.* 44°23N 101°1W **80 C3**
Hayes *U.S.A.* 44°23N 101°1W **80 C3**
Hayes → *Canada* 57°3N 92°12W **72 A1**
Hayes, Mt. *U.S.A.* 63°37N 146°43W **74 C10**
Hayes Creek *Australia* 13°43S 131°22E **60 B5**
Hayle *U.K.* 50°11N 5°26W **13 G2**
Hayling I. *U.K.* 50°48N 0°59W **13 G7**
Hayman I. *Australia* 20°4S 148°53E **62 b**
Hayrabolu *Turkey* 41°12N 27°5E **23 D12**
Hays *Canada* 50°6N 111°48W **70 C6**
Hays *U.S.A.* 38°53N 99°20W **80 F4**
Haysyn *Ukraine* 48°57N 29°25E **17 D15**
Hayvoron *Ukraine* 48°22N 29°52E **17 D15**
Hayward *Calif., U.S.A.* 37°40N 122°4W **78 H4**
Hayward *Wis., U.S.A.* 46°1N 91°29W **80 B8**
Haywards Heath *U.K.* 51°0N 0°5W **13 G7**
Hazafon □ *Israel* 32°40N 35°20E **48 C4**
Hazar *Turkmenistan* 39°34N 53°16E **19 G9**
Hazārān, Kūh-e *Iran* 29°35N 57°20E **47 D8**
Hazaribag *India* 23°58N 85°26E **43 H11**
Hazaribag Road *India* 24°12N 85°57E **43 G11**
Hazelton *Canada* 55°20N 127°42W **70 B3**
Hazelton *U.S.A.* 46°29N 100°17W **80 B3**
Hazen *U.S.A.* 47°18N 101°38W **80 B3**
Hazen, L. *Canada* 81°47N 71°1W **69 A17**
Hazlehurst *Ga., U.S.A.* 31°52N 82°36W **85 F13**
Hazlehurst *Miss., U.S.A.* 31°52N 90°24W **85 F9**
Hazlet *U.S.A.* 40°25N 74°12W **83 F10**
Hazleton *U.S.A.* 40°57N 75°59W **83 F9**
Hazlett, L. *Australia* 21°30S 128°48E **60 D4**
Hazro *Turkey* 38°15N 40°47E **46 B4**
He Xian = Hezhou *China* 24°27N 111°30E **35 E8**
He Xian *China* 31°45N 118°0E **35 B12**
Head of Bight *Australia* 31°30S 131°25E **61 F5**
Head-Smashed-In Buffalo Jump
  *Canada* 49°44N 113°37W **70 D6**
Healdsburg *U.S.A.* 38°37N 122°52W **78 G4**
Healdton *U.S.A.* 34°14N 97°29W **84 D6**
Healesville *Australia* 37°35S 145°30E **63 F4**
Healy *U.S.A.* 63°52N 148°58W **74 C10**
Heany Junction *Zimbabwe* 20°6S 28°54E **57 B4**
Heard I. *Ind. Oc.* 53°6S 73°0E **3 G13**
Hearne *U.S.A.* 30°53N 96°36W **84 F6**
Hearst *Canada* 49°40N 83°41W **72 C3**
Heart → *U.S.A.* 46°46N 100°50W **80 B3**
Heart's Content *Canada* 47°54N 53°27W **73 C9**
Heath, Pte. *Canada* 49°8N 61°40W **73 C7**
Heavener *U.S.A.* 34°53N 94°36W **84 D7**
Hebbronville *U.S.A.* 27°18N 98°41W **84 H5**
Hebei □ *China* 39°0N 116°0E **32 E9**
Hebel *Australia* 28°58S 147°47E **63 D4**
Heber *U.S.A.* 34°30N 110°35W **77 J8**
Heber Springs *U.S.A.* 35°30N 92°2W **84 D8**
Hebgen L. *U.S.A.* 44°52N 111°20W **76 D8**
Hebi *China* 35°57N 114°7E **32 G8**
Hebrides, Sea of the *U.K.* 57°5N 7°0W **11 D2**
Hebron = Al Khalīl
  *West Bank* 31°32N 35°6E **48 D4**
Hebron *Canada* 58°5N 62°30W **69 F19**
Hebron *N. Dak., U.S.A.* 46°54N 102°3W **80 B2**
Hebron *Nebr., U.S.A.* 40°10N 97°35W **80 E5**
Hecate Str. *Canada* 53°10N 130°30W **70 C2**
Heceta I. *U.S.A.* 55°46N 133°40W **70 B2**
Hechi *China* 24°40N 108°2E **34 E7**

Hechuan *China* 30°2N 106°12E **34 B6**
Hecla *U.S.A.* 45°53N 98°9W **80 C4**
Hecla I. *Canada* 51°10N 96°43W **71 C9**
Hede *Sweden* 62°23N 13°30E **8 E15**
Hedemora *Sweden* 60°18N 15°58E **9 F16**
Heerde *Neths.* 52°24N 6°2E **15 B6**
Heerenveen *Neths.* 52°57N 5°55E **15 B5**
Heerhugowaard *Neths.* 52°40N 4°51E **15 B4**
Heerlen *Neths.* 50°55N 5°58E **15 D5**
Hefa *Israel* 32°46N 35°0E **48 C4**
Hefa □ *Israel* 32°40N 35°0E **48 C4**
Hefei *China* 31°52N 117°18E **35 B11**
Hefeng *China* 29°55N 109°52E **34 C7**
Hegang *China* 47°20N 130°19E **31 B15**
Heglig *Sudan* 10°0N 29°24E **53 G11**
Heichengzhen *China* 36°24N 106°3E **32 F4**
Heidelberg *Germany* 49°24N 8°42E **16 D5**
Heidelberg *S. Africa* 34°6S 20°59E **56 E3**
Heilbron *S. Africa* 27°16S 27°59E **57 C4**
Heilbronn *Germany* 49°9N 9°13E **16 D5**
Heilongjiang □ *China* 48°0N 126°0E **31 B14**
Heiloo *Neths.* 52°36N 4°42E **15 B4**
Heilunkiang = Heilongjiang □
  *China* 48°0N 126°0E **31 B14**
Heimaey *Iceland* 63°26N 20°17W **8 E3**
Heinola *Finland* 61°13N 26°2E **8 F22**
Heinze Chaung *Myanmar* 14°42N 97°52E **38 E1**
Heinze Kyun *Myanmar* 14°25N 97°45E **38 E1**
Heishan *China* 41°40N 122°5E **33 D12**
Heishui *Liaoning, China* 42°8N 119°30E **33 C10**
Heishui *Sichuan, China* 32°4N 103°2E **34 A4**
Hejaz = Ḥijāz *Si. Arabia* 24°0N 40°0E **46 E3**
Hejian *China* 38°25N 116°5E **32 E9**
Hejiang *China* 28°43N 105°46E **34 C5**
Hejin *China* 35°35N 110°42E **32 G6**
Hekimhan *Turkey* 38°50N 37°55E **46 B3**
Hekla *Iceland* 63°56N 19°35W **8 E4**
Hekou *Gansu, China* 36°10N 103°26E **32 F2**
Hekou *Guangdong, China* 23°13N 112°45E **35 F9**
Hekou *Yunnan, China* 22°30N 103°59E **34 F5**
Helan Shan *China* 38°30N 105°55E **32 E3**
Helen Atoll *Palau* 2°40N 132°0E **37 D8**
Helena *U.S.A.* 46°36N 112°2W **76 C7**
Helena -West Helena
  *U.S.A.* 34°32N 90°36W **85 D9**
Helendale *U.S.A.* 34°44N 117°19W **79 L9**
Helensburgh *U.K.* 56°1N 4°43W **11 E4**
Helensville *N.Z.* 36°41S 174°29E **59 B5**
Helenvale *Australia* 15°43S 145°14E **62 B4**
Helgeland *Norway* 66°7N 13°29E **8 C15**
Helgoland *Germany* 54°10N 7°53E **16 A4**
Heligoland = Helgoland
  *Germany* 54°10N 7°53E **16 A4**
Heligoland B. = Deutsche Bucht
  *Germany* 54°15N 8°0E **16 A5**
Hell Hole Gorge △
  *Australia* 25°35S 144°12E **62 D3**
Hella *Iceland* 63°50N 20°24W **8 E3**
Hellas = Greece ■ *Europe* 40°0N 23°0E **23 E9**
Hellertown *U.S.A.* 40°35N 75°21W **83 F9**
Hellespont = Çanakkale Boğazı
  *Turkey* 40°17N 26°32E **23 D12**
Hellevoetsluis *Neths.* 51°50N 4°8E **15 C4**
Hellín *Spain* 38°31N 1°40W **21 C5**
Hells Canyon △ *U.S.A.* 45°30N 117°45W **76 D5**
Helmand □ *Afghan.* 31°20N 64°0E **40 D4**
Helmand → *Afghan.* 31°12N 61°34E **40 D2**
Helmeringhausen
  *Namibia* 25°54S 16°57E **56 C2**
Helmond *Neths.* 51°29N 5°41E **15 C5**
Helmsdale *U.K.* 58°7N 3°39W **11 C5**
Helmsdale → *U.K.* 58°8N 3°43W **11 C5**
Helong *China* 42°40N 129°0E **33 C15**
Helper *U.S.A.* 39°41N 110°51W **76 G8**
Helsingborg *Sweden* 56°3N 12°42E **9 H15**
Helsingør *Denmark* 56°2N 12°35E **9 H15**
Helston *U.K.* 50°6N 5°17W **13 G2**
Helvellyn *U.K.* 54°32N 3°1W **12 C4**
Helvetinjärvi △ *Finland* 62°5S 23°47E **8 E20**
Helwân *Egypt* 29°50N 31°20E **53 C12**
Hemavati → *India* 12°30N 76°20E **45 H3**
Hemel Hempstead *U.K.* 51°44N 0°28W **13 F7**
Hemet *U.S.A.* 33°45N 116°58W **79 M10**
Hemingford *U.S.A.* 42°19N 103°4W **80 D2**
Hemis △ *India* 34°10N 77°15E **42 B7**
Hemmingford *Canada* 45°3N 73°35W **83 A11**
Hempstead *N.Y., U.S.A.* 40°42N 73°37W **83 F11**
Hempstead *Tex., U.S.A.* 30°6N 96°5W **84 F6**
Hemse *Sweden* 57°15N 18°22E **9 H18**
Henan □ *China* 34°0N 114°0E **32 H8**
Henares → *Spain* 40°24N 3°30W **21 B4**
Henashi-Misaki *Japan* 40°37N 139°51E **28 D9**
Henderson *Argentina* 36°18S 61°43W **94 D3**
Henderson *Ky., U.S.A.* 37°50N 87°35W **80 G10**
Henderson *N.C., U.S.A.* 36°20N 78°25W **85 C15**
Henderson *Nev., U.S.A.* 36°2N 114°59W **79 J12**
Henderson *Tenn., U.S.A.* 35°26N 88°38W **85 D10**
Henderson I. *Pac. Oc.* 24°22S 128°19W **65 K15**
Hendersonville *N.C.,*
  *U.S.A.* 35°19N 82°28W **85 D13**
Hendersonville *Tenn.,*
  *U.S.A.* 36°18N 86°37W **85 C11**
Hendijān *Iran* 30°14N 49°43E **47 D6**
Hendorābī *Iran* 26°40N 53°37E **47 E7**
Heng Jiang → *China* 28°40N 109°22E **34 C5**
Heng Xian *China* 22°40N 109°17E **34 F6**
Hengām *Iran* 26°38N 55°53E **47 E7**
Hengcheng *China* 38°18N 106°28E **32 E4**
Hēngch'un *Taiwan* 22°0N 120°44E **35 F13**
Hengdaohezi *China* 44°52N 129°0E **33 B15**
Hengduan Shan *China* 28°30N 98°50E **34 C2**
Hengelo *Neths.* 52°16N 6°48E **15 B6**
Henggang *China* 22°39N 114°12E **31 a**
Hengmen *China* 22°33N 113°35E **31 a**
Hengshan *Hunan, China* 27°16N 112°45E **35 D9**
Hengshan *Shaanxi, China* 37°58N 109°5E **32 F5**

Hengshui *China* 37°41N 115°40E **32 F8**
Hengyang *China* 26°59N 112°22E **35 D9**
Henley-on-Thames *U.K.* 51°32N 0°54W **13 F7**
Henlopen, C. *U.S.A.* 38°48N 75°6W **81 F16**
Hennenman *S. Africa* 27°59S 27°1E **56 C4**
Hennessey *U.S.A.* 36°6N 97°54W **84 C6**
Henri Pittier △ *Venezuela* 10°26N 67°37W **89 D6**
Henrietta, N.Y., U.S.A. 43°4N 77°37W **82 C7**
Henrietta *Tex., U.S.A.* 33°49N 98°12W **84 E5**
Henrietta, Ostrov = Genriyetty,
Ostrov *Russia* 77°6N 156°30E **27 B16**
Henrietta Maria, C.
*Canada* 55°9N 82°20W **72 A3**
Henry *U.S.A.* 41°7N 89°22W **80 E9**
Henry Ice Rise *Antarctica* 80°35S 62°0W **5 E17**
Henry Lawrence I. *India* 12°9N 93°5E **45 H11**
Henryetta *U.S.A.* 35°27N 95°59W **84 D7**
Henryville *Canada* 45°8N 73°11W **83 A11**
Hensall *Canada* 43°26N 81°30W **82 C3**
Hentiesbaai *Namibia* 22°8S 14°18E **56 B1**
Hentiyn Nuruu
*Mongolia* 48°30N 108°30E **31 B10**
Henty *Australia* 35°30S 147°3E **63 F4**
Henzada = Hinthada
*Myanmar* 17°38N 95°26E **41 L19**
Heping *China* 24°29N 115°0E **35 E10**
Heppner *U.S.A.* 45°21N 119°33W **76 D4**
Hepu *China* 21°40N 109°12E **34 G7**
Hepworth *Canada* 44°37N 81°9W **82 B3**
Heqing *China* 26°37N 100°11E **34 D3**
Hequ *China* 39°20N 111°15E **32 E6**
Héraðsflói *Iceland* 65°42N 14°12W **8 D6**
Héraðsvötn ⇀ *Iceland* 65°45N 19°25W **8 D4**
Heraklion = Iraklio
*Greece* 35°20N 25°12E **23 G11**
Herald Cays *Australia* 16°58S 149°9E **62 B4**
Herāt *Afghan.* 34°20N 62°7E **40 B3**
Herāt □ *Afghan.* 35°0N 62°0E **40 B3**
Herbert *Canada* 50°30N 107°10W **71 C7**
Herbert ⇀ *Australia* 18°31S 146°17E **62 B4**
Herberton *Australia* 17°20S 145°25E **62 B4**
Herbertsdale *S. Africa* 34°1S 21°46E **56 D3**
Herceg-Novi *Montenegro* 42°30N 18°33E **23 C8**
Herchmer *Canada* 57°22N 94°10W **71 B10**
Herðubreið *Iceland* 65°11N 16°21W **8 D5**
Hereford *U.K.* 52°4N 2°43W **13 E5**
Hereford *U.S.A.* 34°49N 102°24W **84 D3**
Herefordshire □ *U.K.* 52°8N 2°40W **13 E5**
Herentals *Belgium* 51°12N 4°51E **15 C4**
Herford *Germany* 52°7N 8°39E **16 B5**
Herington *U.S.A.* 38°40N 96°57W **80 F5**
Herkimer *U.S.A.* 43°2N 74°59W **83 D10**
Herlen ⇀ *Asia* 48°48N 117°0E **31 B12**
Herlong *U.S.A.* 40°8N 120°8W **78 F6**
Herm *U.K.* 49°30N 2°28W **13 H5**
Hermann *U.S.A.* 38°42N 91°27W **80 F8**
Hermannsburg *Australia* 23°57S 132°45E **60 D5**
Hermanus *S. Africa* 34°27S 19°12E **56 D2**
Hermidale *Australia* 31°30S 146°42E **63 E4**
Hermiston *U.S.A.* 45°51N 119°17W **76 D4**
Hermon *Canada* 45°6N 77°37W **82 A7**
Hermon *U.S.A.* 44°28N 75°14W **83 B9**
Hermon, Mt. = Shaykh, J. ash
*Lebanon* 33°25N 35°50E **48 B4**
Hermosillo *Mexico* 29°10N 111°0W **86 B2**
Hernád ⇀ *Hungary* 47°56N 21°8E **17 D11**
Hernandarias *Paraguay* 25°20S 54°40W **95 B5**
Hernandez *U.S.A.* 36°24N 120°46W **78 J6**
Hernando *Argentina* 32°28S 63°40W **94 C3**
Hernando *U.S.A.* 34°50N 90°0W **85 D10**
Herndon *U.S.A.* 40°43N 76°51W **82 F8**
Herne Bay *U.K.* 51°21N 1°8E **13 F9**
Herning *Denmark* 56°8N 8°58E **9 H13**
Heroica Caborca = Caborca
*Mexico* 30°37N 112°6W **86 A2**
Heroica Nogales = Nogales
*Mexico* 31°19N 110°56W **86 A2**
Heron Bay *Canada* 48°40N 86°25W **72 C2**
Heron I. *Australia* 23°27S 151°55E **62 C5**
Herreid *U.S.A.* 45°50N 100°4W **80 C3**
Herrin *U.S.A.* 37°48N 89°2W **80 G9**
Herriot *Canada* 56°22N 101°16W **71 B8**
Herschel I. *Canada* 69°35N 139°5W **4 C1**
Hershey *U.S.A.* 40°17N 76°39W **83 F8**
Herstal *Belgium* 50°40N 5°38E **15 D5**
Hertford *U.K.* 51°48N 0°4W **13 F7**
Hertfordshire □ *U.K.* 51°51N 0°5W **13 F7**
's-Hertogenbosch *Neths.* 51°42N 5°17E **15 C5**
Hertzogville *S. Africa* 28°9S 25°30E **56 C4**
Hervey B. *Australia* 25°0S 152°52E **62 C5**
Herzliyya *Israel* 32°10N 34°50E **48 C3**
Ḩeşār *Fārs, Iran* 29°52N 50°16E **47 D6**
Ḩeşār *Markazī, Iran* 35°50N 49°12E **47 C6**
Heshan *Guangdong, China* 22°34N 113°4E **35 F9**
Heshan *Guangxi Zhuangzu,
China* 23°50N 108°53E **34 F7**
Heshui *China* 35°48N 108°0E **32 G5**
Heshun *China* 37°22N 113°32E **32 F7**
Hesperia *U.S.A.* 34°25N 117°18W **79 L9**
Hesse = Hessen □ *Germany* 50°30N 9°0E **16 C5**
Hessen □ *Germany* 50°30N 9°0E **16 C5**
Hessle *U.K.* 53°44N 0°24W **12 D7**
Hetauda *Nepal* 27°25N 85°2E **43 F11**
Hetch Hetchy Aqueduct
*U.S.A.* 37°29N 122°19W **78 H5**
Hetta Enontekiö *Finland* 68°23N 23°37E **8 B20**
Hettinger *U.S.A.* 46°0N 102°42W **80 B2**
Heuksando *S. Korea* 34°40N 125°30E **33 G13**
Heunghae *S. Korea* 36°12N 129°21E **33 F15**
Heuvelton *U.S.A.* 44°37N 75°25W **83 B9**
Hewitt *U.S.A.* 31°28N 97°12W **84 F6**
Hexham *U.K.* 54°58N 2°4W **12 C5**
Hexi *Yunnan, China* 24°9N 102°38E **34 E4**
Hexi *Zhejiang, China* 27°58N 119°38E **35 D12**
Hexigten Qi *China* 43°18N 117°30E **33 C9**
Ḩeydarābād *Iran* 30°33N 55°38E **47 D7**
Heysham *U.K.* 54°3N 2°53W **12 C5**
Heyuan *China* 23°39N 114°40E **35 F10**
Heywood *Australia* 38°8S 141°37E **63 F3**

Heze *China* 35°14N 115°20E **32 G8**
Hezhang *China* 27°8N 104°41E **34 D5**
Hezhou *China* 24°27N 111°30E **35 E8**
Hi Vista *U.S.A.* 34°45N 117°46W **79 L9**
Hiawatha *U.S.A.* 39°51N 95°32W **80 F6**
Hibbing *U.S.A.* 47°25N 92°56W **80 B7**
Hibernia Reef *Australia* 12°0S 123°23E **60 B3**
Hickman *U.S.A.* 36°34N 89°11W **80 G9**
Hickory *U.S.A.* 35°44N 81°21W **85 D14**
Hicks, Pt. *Australia* 37°49S 149°17E **63 F4**
Hicks L. *Canada* 61°25N 100°0W **71 A9**
Hicksville *U.S.A.* 40°46N 73°32W **83 F11**
Hida-Gawa ⇀ *Japan* 35°26N 137°3E **29 G8**
Hida-Sammyaku *Japan* 36°30N 137°40E **29 F8**
Hidaka-Sammyaku
*Japan* 42°35N 142°45E **28 C11**
Hidalgo □ *Mexico* 20°30N 99°0W **87 C5**
Hidalgo del Parral
*Mexico* 26°56N 105°40W **86 B3**
Hierro *Canary Is.* 27°44N 18°0W **52 C2**
Higashiajima-San
*Japan* 37°40N 140°10E **28 F10**
Higashiōsaka *Japan* 34°39N 135°37E **29 G7**
Higgins *U.S.A.* 36°7N 100°2W **84 C4**
Higgins Corner *U.S.A.* 39°2N 121°5W **78 F5**
High Bridge *U.S.A.* 40°40N 74°54W **83 F10**
High Desert *U.S.A.* 43°40N 120°20W **76 E3**
High Island Res. *China* 22°22N 114°21E **31 a**
High Level *Canada* 58°31N 117°8W **70 B5**
High Point *U.S.A.* 35°57N 80°0W **85 D15**
High Prairie *Canada* 55°30N 116°30W **70 B5**
High River *Canada* 50°30N 113°50W **70 C6**
High Tatra = Tatry
*Slovakia* 49°20N 20°0E **17 D11**
High Veld *Africa* 27°0S 27°0E **50 J6**
High Wycombe *U.K.* 51°37N 0°45W **13 F7**
Highland □ *U.K.* 57°17N 4°21W **11 D4**
Highland Park *U.S.A.* 42°11N 87°48W **80 D10**
Highmore *U.S.A.* 44°31N 99°27W **80 C4**
Higüey *Dom. Rep.* 18°37N 68°42W **89 C6**
Hiidenportti △ *Finland* 63°53N 29°0E **8 E23**
Hiiumaa *Estonia* 58°50N 22°45E **9 G20**
Ḩijārah, Şaḩrā' al *Iraq* 30°25N 44°30E **46 D5**
Ḩijāz *Si. Arabia* 24°0N 40°0E **46 E3**
Hijo = Tagum *Phil.* 7°33N 125°53E **37 C7**
Hikari *Japan* 33°58N 131°58E **29 H5**
Hikkaduwa *Sri Lanka* 6°8N 80°6E **45 L5**
Hiko *U.S.A.* 37°32N 115°14W **78 H11**
Hikone *Japan* 35°15N 136°10E **29 G8**
Hikurangi *Gisborne, N.Z.* 37°55S 178°4E **59 C6**
Hikurangi *Northland,
N.Z.* 35°36S 174°17E **59 A5**
Hildesheim *Germany* 52°9N 9°56E **16 B5**
Hill ⇀ *Australia* 30°23S 115°3E **61 F2**
Hill City *Idaho, U.S.A.* 43°18N 115°3W **76 E6**
Hill City *Kans., U.S.A.* 39°22N 99°51W **80 F4**
Hill City *Minn., U.S.A.* 46°59N 93°36W **80 B7**
Hill City *S. Dak., U.S.A.* 43°56N 103°35W **80 D2**
Hill Island L. *Canada* 60°30N 109°50W **71 A7**
Hillaby, Mt. *Barbados* 13°12N 59°35W **89 g**
Hillcrest *Barbados* 13°13N 59°31W **89 g**
Hillegom *Neths.* 52°18N 4°35E **15 B4**
Hillsboro *Kans., U.S.A.* 38°21N 97°12W **80 F5**
Hillsboro *N. Dak., U.S.A.* 47°24N 97°3W **80 B6**
Hillsboro *Ohio, U.S.A.* 39°12N 83°37W **81 F12**
Hillsboro *Oreg., U.S.A.* 45°31N 122°59W **78 E4**
Hillsboro *Tex., U.S.A.* 32°1N 97°8W **84 E6**
Hillsborough *Grenada* 12°28N 61°28W **89 D7**
Hillsborough *U.S.A.* 43°7N 71°54W **83 C13**
Hillsborough Channel
*Australia* 20°56S 149°15E **62 b**
Hillsdale *Mich., U.S.A.* 41°56N 84°38W **81 E11**
Hillsdale *N.Y., U.S.A.* 42°11N 73°32W **83 D11**
Hillsport *Canada* 49°27N 85°34W **72 C2**
Hillston *Australia* 33°30S 145°31E **63 E4**
Hilo *U.S.A.* 19°44N 155°5W **75 M8**
Hilton *U.S.A.* 43°17N 77°48W **82 C7**
Hilton Head Island
*U.S.A.* 32°13N 80°45W **85 E14**
Hilversum *Neths.* 52°14N 5°10E **15 B5**
Himachal Pradesh □ *India* 31°30N 77°0E **42 D7**
Himalaya *Asia* 29°0N 84°0E **43 E11**
Himalchuli *Nepal* 28°27N 84°38E **43 E11**
Himatnagar *India* 23°37N 72°57E **42 H5**
Himeji *Japan* 34°50N 134°40E **29 G7**
Himi *Japan* 36°50N 136°55E **29 F8**
Ḩimş *Syria* 34°40N 36°45E **48 A5**
Ḩimş □ *Syria* 34°30N 37°0E **48 A6**
Hin Khom, Laem *Thailand* 9°25N 99°56E **39 b**
Hinche *Haiti* 19°9N 72°1W **89 C5**
Hinchinbrook I.
*Australia* 18°20S 146°15E **62 B4**
Hinchinbrook Island △
*Australia* 18°14S 146°6E **62 B4**
Hinckley *U.K.* 52°33N 1°22W **13 E6**
Hinckley *U.S.A.* 46°1N 92°56W **80 B7**
Hindaun *India* 26°44N 77°5E **42 F7**
Hindoli *India* 25°44N 75°32E **42 G6**
Hindu Bagh *Pakistan* 30°56N 67°50E **42 D2**
Hindu Kush *Asia* 36°0N 71°0E **40 B7**
Hindupur *India* 13°49N 77°32E **45 H10**
Hines Creek *Canada* 56°20N 118°40W **70 B5**
Hinesville *U.S.A.* 31°51N 81°36W **85 F14**
Hinganghat *India* 20°30N 78°52E **44 D4**
Hingir *India* 21°57N 83°41E **43 J10**
Hingoli *India* 19°41N 77°15E **44 E3**
Hinna = Imi *Ethiopia* 6°28N 42°10E **49 F3**
Hinnøya *Norway* 68°35N 15°50E **8 B16**
Hinojosa del Duque *Spain* 38°30N 5°9W **21 C3**
Hinsdale *U.S.A.* 42°47N 72°29W **83 D12**
Hinthada *Myanmar* 17°38N 95°26E **41 L19**
Hinton *Canada* 53°26N 117°34W **70 C5**
Hinton *U.S.A.* 37°40N 80°54W **81 G13**
Hios *Greece* 38°27N 26°9E **23 E12**
Hios = Chios *Greece* 38°27N 26°9E **23 E12**
Hirado *Japan* 33°22N 129°33E **29 H4**
Hirakud Dam *India* 21°32N 83°45E **44 D6**

Hiran ⇀ *India* 23°6N 79°21E **43 H8**
Hirapur *India* 24°22N 79°13E **43 G8**
Hirara = Miyakojima
*Japan* 24°48N 125°17E **29 M2**
Hiratsuka *Japan* 35°19N 139°21E **29 G9**
Hirekerur *India* 14°28N 75°23E **45 G2**
Hiroo *Japan* 42°17N 143°19E **28 C11**
Hirosaki *Japan* 40°34N 140°28E **28 D10**
Hiroshima *Japan* 34°24N 132°30E **29 G6**
Hiroshima □ *Japan* 34°50N 133°0E **29 G6**
Hisar *India* 29°12N 75°45E **42 E6**
Hisb, Sha'ib ⇀ = Ḩasb, W. ⇀
*Iraq* 31°45N 44°17E **46 D5**
Ḩismā *Si. Arabia* 28°30N 36°0E **46 D3**
Hispaniola *W. Indies* 19°0N 71°0W **89 C5**
Ḩīt *Iraq* 33°38N 42°49E **46 C4**
Hita *Japan* 33°20N 130°58E **29 H5**
Hitachi *Japan* 36°36N 140°39E **29 F10**
Hitchin *U.K.* 51°58N 0°16W **13 F7**
Hitiaa *Tahiti* 17°36S 149°18W **59 d**
Hitoyoshi *Japan* 32°13N 130°45E **29 H5**
Hitra *Norway* 63°30N 8°45E **8 E13**
Hiva Oa *French Polynesia* 9°45S 139°0W **65 H14**
Hixon *Canada* 53°25N 122°35W **70 C4**
Ḩiyyon, N. ⇀ *Israel* 30°25N 35°10E **48 E4**
Hjalmar L. *Canada* 61°33N 109°25W **71 A7**
Hjälmaren *Sweden* 59°18N 15°40E **9 G16**
Hjørring *Denmark* 57°29N 9°59E **9 H13**
Hjort Trench *S. Ocean* 58°0S 157°30E **5 B10**
Hkakabo Razi *Myanmar* 28°25N 97°23E **34 C1**
Hkamti *Myanmar* 26°0N 95°39E **41 G19**
Hlobane *S. Africa* 27°42S 31°0E **57 C5**
Hluhluwe *S. Africa* 28°1S 32°15E **57 C5**
Hluhluwe ≏ *S. Africa* 22°0S 32°5E **57 C5**
Hlyboka *Ukraine* 48°5N 25°56E **17 D13**
Ho *Ghana* 6°37N 0°27E **52 G6**
Ho Chi Minh City = Thanh Pho Ho
Chi Minh *Vietnam* 10°58N 106°40E **39 G6**
Ho Hoa Binh *Vietnam* 20°50N 105°0E **34 G5**
Ho Thac Ba *Vietnam* 21°42N 105°1E **38 A5**
Ho Thuong *Vietnam* 19°32N 105°48E **38 C5**
Hoa Binh *Vietnam* 20°50N 105°20E **34 G5**
Hoa Hiep *Vietnam* 11°34N 105°51E **39 G5**
Hoai Nhon *Vietnam* 14°28N 109°1E **38 E7**
Hoang Lien Son *Vietnam* 21°30N 105°32E **38 B5**
Hoang Lien Son *Vietnam* 22°0N 104°0E **34 F4**
Hoang Sa, Dao = Paracel Is.
*S. China Sea* 15°50N 112°0E **36 A4**
Hoanib ⇀ *Namibia* 19°27S 12°46E **56 A2**
Hoare B. *Canada* 65°17N 62°30W **69 D19**
Hoarusib ⇀ *Namibia* 19°3S 12°36E **56 A2**
Hobart *Australia* 42°50S 147°21E **63 G4**
Hobart *U.S.A.* 35°1N 99°6W **84 D5**
Hobbs *U.S.A.* 32°42N 103°8W **77 K12**
Hobbs Coast *Antarctica* 74°50S 131°0W **5 D14**
Hobe Sound *U.S.A.* 27°4N 80°8W **85 H14**
Hobro *Denmark* 56°39N 9°46E **9 H13**
Hoburgen *Sweden* 56°55N 18°7E **9 H18**
Hobyo *Somalia* 5°25N 48°30E **49 F4**
Hochfeld *Namibia* 21°28S 17°58E **56 B2**
Hodaka-Dake *Japan* 36°17N 137°39E **29 F8**
Hodeida = Al Ḩudaydah
*Yemen* 14°50N 43°0E **49 E3**
Hodgeville *Canada* 50°7N 106°58W **71 C7**
Hodgson *Canada* 51°13N 97°36W **71 C9**
Hódmezővásárhely
*Hungary* 46°28N 20°22E **17 E11**
Hodna, Chott el *Algeria* 35°26N 4°43E **52 A6**
Hodonín *Czechia* 48°50N 17°10E **17 D9**
Hoek van Holland *Neths.* 52°0N 4°7E **15 C4**
Hoengseong *S. Korea* 37°29N 127°59E **33 F14**
Hoeryong *N. Korea* 42°30N 129°45E **33 C15**
Hoeyang *N. Korea* 38°43N 127°36E **33 E14**
Hof *Germany* 50°19N 11°55E **16 C6**
Hofmeyr *S. Africa* 31°39S 25°50E **56 D4**
Höfn *Iceland* 64°15N 15°13W **8 D6**
Hofors *Sweden* 60°31N 16°15E **9 F17**
Hofsjökull *Iceland* 64°49N 18°48W **8 D4**
Hōfu *Japan* 34°3N 131°34E **29 G5**
Hogan Group *Australia* 39°13S 147°1E **63 F4**
Hogarth, Mt. *Australia* 21°48S 136°58E **62 C2**
Hoge Kempen △ *Belgium* 51°6N 5°35E **15 C5**
Hoge Veluwe ≏ *Neths.* 52°5N 5°46E **15 B5**
Hogenakai Falls *India* 12°6N 77°50E **45 H3**
Hoggar = Ahaggar *Algeria* 23°0N 6°30E **52 D7**
Hogsty Reef *Bahamas* 21°41N 73°48W **89 B5**
Hoh ⇀ *U.S.A.* 47°45N 124°29W **78 C2**
Hoh Xil Shan *China* 36°30N 89°0E **30 D6**
Hohenwald *U.S.A.* 35°33N 87°33W **85 D11**
Hoher Rhön = Rhön
*Germany* 50°24N 9°58E **16 C5**
Hohes Venn *Belgium* 50°30N 6°5E **15 D6**
Hohhot *China* 40°52N 111°40E **32 D6**
Hoi An *Vietnam* 15°53N 108°19E **38 E7**
Hoi Xuan *Vietnam* 20°25N 105°9E **34 G5**
Hoisington *U.S.A.* 38°31N 98°47W **80 F4**
Hōjō *Japan* 33°58N 132°46E **29 H6**
Hokianga Harbour *N.Z.* 35°31S 173°22E **59 A4**
Hokitika *N.Z.* 42°42S 171°0E **59 E3**
Hokkaidō □ *Japan* 43°30N 143°0E **28 C11**
Hokuto *Japan* 41°49N 140°39E **28 D10**
Holalkere *India* 14°0N 76°11E **45 G3**
Holbæk *Denmark* 55°40N 11°43E **9 J14**
Holbrook *Australia* 35°42S 147°18E **63 F4**
Holbrook *U.S.A.* 34°54N 110°10W **77 J8**
Holcomb *U.S.A.* 42°54N 77°25W **82 D7**
Holden *U.S.A.* 39°6N 112°16W **76 G7**
Holdenville *U.S.A.* 35°5N 96°24W **84 D6**
Holdrege *U.S.A.* 40°26N 99°23W **80 E4**
Hole-Narsipur *India* 12°48N 76°16E **45 H3**
Holetown *Barbados* 13°11N 59°38W **89 g**
Holguín *Cuba* 20°50N 76°20W **88 B4**
Hollams Bird I. *Namibia* 24°40S 14°30E **56 B1**
Holland = Netherlands ■
*Europe* 52°0N 5°30E **15 C5**
Holland *Mich., U.S.A.* 42°47N 86°7W **80 D10**
Holland *N.Y., U.S.A.* 42°38N 78°32W **82 D6**
Holland Centre *Canada* 44°23N 80°47W **82 B4**
Holland Patent *U.S.A.* 43°14N 75°16W **83 C9**
Hollandale *U.S.A.* 33°10N 90°51W **85 E9**
Holley *U.S.A.* 43°14N 78°2W **82 C6**

Hollidaysburg *U.S.A.* 40°26N 78°24W **82 F6**
Hollis *U.S.A.* 34°41N 99°55W **84 D5**
Hollister *Calif., U.S.A.* 36°51N 121°24W **78 J5**
Hollister *Idaho, U.S.A.* 42°21N 114°35W **76 E6**
Holly Hill *U.S.A.* 29°16N 81°3W **85 G14**
Holly Springs *U.S.A.* 34°46N 89°27W **85 D10**
Hollywood *U.S.A.* 33°6N 6°35W **10 B6**
Hollywood = Ulukhaktok
*Canada* 70°44N 117°44W **68 C8**
Hólmavík *Iceland* 65°42N 21°40W **8 D3**
Holmen *U.S.A.* 43°58N 91°15W **80 D8**
Holmes Reefs *Australia* 16°27S 148°0E **62 B4**
Holmsund *Sweden* 63°41N 20°20E **8 E19**
Holon *Israel* 32°0N 34°46E **48 C3**
Holroyd ⇀ *Australia* 14°10S 141°36E **62 A3**
Holstebro *Denmark* 56°22N 8°37E **9 H13**
Holsworthy *U.K.* 50°48N 4°22W **13 G3**
Holton *Canada* 54°31N 57°12W **73 B8**
Holton *U.S.A.* 39°28N 95°44W **80 F6**
Holtville *U.S.A.* 32°49N 115°23W **79 N11**
Holwerd *Neths.* 53°22N 5°54E **15 A5**
Holy Cross *U.S.A.* 62°12N 159°46W **74 C7**
Holy I., *Anglesey, U.K.* 53°17N 4°37W **12 D3**
Holy I., *Northumberland,
U.K.* 55°40N 1°47W **12 B6**
Holyhead *U.K.* 53°18N 4°38W **12 D3**
Holyoke *Colo., U.S.A.* 40°35N 102°18W **76 F12**
Holyoke *Mass., U.S.A.* 42°12N 72°37W **83 D12**
Holyrood *Canada* 47°27N 53°8W **73 C9**
Homalin *Myanmar* 24°55N 95°0E **41 G19**
Homand *Iran* 32°28N 59°37E **47 C8**
Homathko ⇀ *Canada* 51°0N 124°56W **70 C4**
Hombori *Mali* 15°20N 1°38W **52 E5**
Home B. *Canada* 68°40N 67°10W **69 D18**
Home Hill *Australia* 19°43S 147°25E **62 B4**
Home Reef *Tonga* 18°59S 174°47W **59 c**
Homedale *U.S.A.* 43°37N 116°56W **76 E5**
Homer *Alaska, U.S.A.* 59°39N 151°33W **68 F1**
Homer *La., U.S.A.* 32°48N 93°4W **84 E8**
Homer *N.Y., U.S.A.* 42°38N 76°10W **83 D8**
Homer City *U.S.A.* 40°32N 79°10W **82 F5**
Homestead *Australia* 20°20S 145°40E **62 C4**
Homestead △ *U.S.A.* 40°17N 96°50W **80 E5**
Homestead *U.S.A.* 25°28N 80°29W **85 J14**
Homnabad *India* 17°45N 77°11E **44 F3**
Homoine *Mozam.* 23°55S 35°8E **57 B6**
Homs = Ḩimş *Syria* 34°40N 36°45E **48 A5**
Homyel *Belarus* 52°28N 31°0E **17 B16**
Hon Chong *Vietnam* 10°25N 104°30E **39 G5**
Hon Hai *Vietnam* 10°0N 109°0E **39 H7**
Hon Me *Vietnam* 19°23N 105°56E **38 C5**
Honan = Henan □ *China* 34°0N 114°0E **32 H8**
Honavar *India* 14°17N 74°27E **45 G2**
Honbetsu *Japan* 43°7N 143°37E **28 C11**
Honcut *U.S.A.* 39°20N 121°32W **78 F5**
Hondeklipbaai *S. Africa* 30°19S 17°17E **56 D2**
Hondo *Japan* 32°27N 130°12E **29 H5**
Hondo *U.S.A.* 29°21N 99°9W **84 G5**
Hondo, Río ⇀ *Belize* 18°25N 88°21W **87 D7**
Honduras ■ *Cent. Amer.* 14°40N 86°30W **88 D2**
Honduras, G. de *Caribbean* 16°50N 87°0W **88 C2**
Hønefoss *Norway* 60°10N 10°18E **9 F14**
Honesdale *U.S.A.* 41°34N 75°16W **83 E9**
Honey Harbour *Canada* 44°52N 79°49W **82 B5**
Honey L. *U.S.A.* 40°15N 120°19W **78 E6**
Honfleur *France* 49°25N 0°13E **20 B4**
Hong ⇀ *Asia* 20°16N 106°34E **38 B5**
Hong Gai *Vietnam* 20°57N 107°5E **34 G6**
Hong He ⇀ *China* 32°25N 115°35E **32 H8**
Hong Hu *China* 29°54N 113°24E **35 C9**
Hong Kong □ *China* 22°11N 114°14E **31 a**
Hong'an *China* 31°20N 114°40E **35 B10**
Hongcheon *S. Korea* 37°44N 127°53E **33 F14**
Honghai Wan *China* 22°40N 115°0E **35 F10**
Honghe *China* 23°25N 102°25E **34 F4**
Honghu *China* 29°50N 113°30E **35 C9**
Hongjiang *China* 27°7N 109°59E **34 D7**
Hongliu He ⇀ *China* 38°0N 109°50E **32 F5**
Hongor *Mongolia* 45°45N 112°50E **32 B7**
Hongseong *S. Korea* 36°37N 126°38E **33 F14**
Hongshan *China* 36°38N 117°58E **33 F9**
Hongshui He ⇀ *China* 23°48N 109°30E **34 F7**
Hongtong *China* 36°16N 111°40E **32 F6**
Honguedo, Détroit d'
*Canada* 49°15N 64°0W **73 C7**
Hongwon *N. Korea* 40°0N 127°56E **33 E14**
Hongya *China* 29°57N 103°22E **34 C4**
Hongyuan *China* 32°51N 102°40E **34 B4**
Hongze Hu *China* 33°15N 118°35E **33 H10**
Honiara *Solomon Is.* 9°27S 159°57E **58 B8**
Honiton *U.K.* 50°47N 3°11W **13 G4**
Honjō = Yurihonjō
*Japan* 39°23N 140°3E **28 E10**
Honnali *India* 14°15N 75°40E **45 G2**
Honningsvåg *Norway* 70°59N 25°59E **8 A21**
Honolulu *U.S.A.* 21°19N 157°52W **75 L8**
Honshū *Japan* 36°0N 138°0E **29 F9**
Hood, Mt. *U.S.A.* 45°23N 121°42W **76 D3**
Hood, Pt. *Australia* 34°23S 119°34E **61 F2**
Hood River *U.S.A.* 45°43N 121°31W **76 D3**
Hoodsport *U.S.A.* 47°24N 123°9W **78 C3**
Hoogeveen *Neths.* 52°44N 6°28E **15 B6**
Hoogezand-Sappemeer
*Neths.* 53°9N 6°45E **15 A6**
Hooghly = Hugli ⇀ *India* 21°56N 88°4E **43 J13**
Hooghly-Chinsura = Chunchura
*India* 22°53N 88°27E **43 H13**
Hook Hd. *Ireland* 52°7N 6°56W **10 D5**
Hook I. *Australia* 20°4S 149°0E **62 b**
Hook of Holland = Hoek van
Holland *Neths.* 52°0N 4°7E **15 C4**
Hooker *U.S.A.* 36°52N 101°13W **84 C4**
Hooker Creek = Lajamanu
*Australia* 18°23S 130°38E **60 C5**
Hooker Creek ◌ *Australia* 18°6S 130°23E **60 C5**
Hoonah *U.S.A.* 58°7N 135°27W **70 B1**
Hooper Bay *U.S.A.* 61°32N 166°6W **74 C6**
Hoopeston *U.S.A.* 40°28N 87°40W **80 E10**
Hoopstad *S. Africa* 27°50S 25°55E **56 C4**
Hoorn *Neths.* 52°38N 5°4E **15 B5**

Hoover *U.S.A.* 33°24N 86°49W **85 E11**
Hoover Dam *U.S.A.* 36°1N 114°44W **79 K12**
Hooversville *U.S.A.* 40°9N 78°55W **82 F6**
Hop Bottom *U.S.A.* 41°42N 75°46W **83 E9**
Hope *Canada* 49°25N 121°25W **70 D4**
Hope *Ariz., U.S.A.* 33°43N 113°42W **79 M13**
Hope *Ark., U.S.A.* 33°40N 93°36W **84 E8**
Hope, L. *S. Austral.,
Australia* 28°24S 139°18E **63 D2**
Hope, L. *W. Austral.,
Australia* 32°35S 120°15E **61 F3**
Hope, Pt. *U.S.A.* 68°21N 166°47W **66 C3**
Hope I. *Canada* 44°55N 80°11W **82 B4**
Hope Town *Bahamas* 26°35N 76°57W **88 A4**
Hope Vale *Australia* 15°16S 145°20E **62 A4**
Hope Vale ◌ *Australia* 15°8S 145°15E **62 B4**
Hopedale *Canada* 55°28N 60°13W **73 A7**
Hopefield *S. Africa* 33°3S 18°22E **56 E2**
Hopei = Hebei □ *China* 39°0N 116°0E **32 E9**
Hopelchén *Mexico* 19°46N 89°51W **87 D7**
Hopetoun *Vic., Australia* 35°42S 142°22E **63 F3**
Hopetoun *W. Austral.,
Australia* 33°57S 120°7E **61 F3**
Hopetown *S. Africa* 29°34S 24°3E **56 C3**
Hopewell *U.S.A.* 37°18N 77°17W **81 G15**
Hopkins, L. *Australia* 24°15S 128°35E **60 D4**
Hopkinsville *U.S.A.* 36°52N 87°29W **80 G10**
Hopland *U.S.A.* 38°58N 123°7W **78 G3**
Hoquiam *U.S.A.* 46°59N 123°53W **78 D3**
Horana *Sri Lanka* 6°43N 80°4E **45 L5**
Hordern Hills *Australia* 20°15S 130°0E **60 D5**
Horinger *China* 40°28N 111°48E **32 D6**
Horizontina *Brazil* 27°37S 54°19W **95 B5**
Horlick Mts. *Antarctica* 84°0S 102°0W **5 E15**
Horlivka *Ukraine* 48°19N 38°5E **19 E6**
Hormak *Iran* 29°58N 60°51E **47 D9**
Hormoz *Iran* 27°35N 55°0E **47 E7**
Hormoz, Jaz.-ye *Iran* 27°8N 56°28E **47 E8**
Hormozgān □ *Iran* 27°30N 56°0E **47 E8**
Hormuz, Kūh-e *Iran* 27°27N 55°10E **47 E7**
Hormuz, Str. of *The Gulf* 26°30N 56°30E **47 E8**
Horn *Austria* 48°39N 15°40E **16 D8**
Horn ⇀ *Canada* 61°30N 118°1W **70 A5**
Horn, Cape = Hornos, C. de
*Chile* 55°50S 67°30W **96 H3**
Horn Head *Ireland* 55°14N 8°0W **10 A3**
Horn I. *Australia* 10°37S 142°17E **62 A3**
Horn Plateau *Canada* 62°15N 119°15W **70 A5**
Hornavan *Sweden* 66°15N 17°30E **8 C17**
Hornbeck *U.S.A.* 31°20N 93°24W **84 F8**
Hornbrook *U.S.A.* 41°55N 122°33W **76 F2**
Horncastle *U.K.* 53°13N 0°7W **12 D7**
Hornell *U.S.A.* 42°20N 77°40W **82 D7**
Hornell L. *Canada* 62°20N 119°25W **70 A5**
Hornepayne *Canada* 49°14N 84°48W **72 C3**
Hornings Mills *Canada* 44°9N 80°12W **82 B4**
Hornitos *U.S.A.* 37°30N 120°14W **78 H6**
Hornos, C. de *Chile* 55°50S 67°30W **96 H3**
Hornsby *Australia* 33°42S 151°2E **63 B5**
Hornsea *U.K.* 53°55N 0°11W **12 D7**
Horobetsu = Noboribetsu
*Japan* 42°24N 141°6E **28 C10**
Horodenka *Ukraine* 48°41N 25°29E **17 D13**
Horodok *Khmelnytskyy,
Ukraine* 49°10N 26°34E **17 D14**
Horodok *Lviv, Ukraine* 49°46N 23°32E **17 D12**
Horokhiv *Ukraine* 50°30N 24°45E **17 C13**
Horqin Youyi Qianqi
*China* 46°5N 122°3E **33 A12**
Horqin Zuoyi Zhongqi
*China* 44°8N 123°18E **33 B12**
Horqueta *Paraguay* 23°15S 56°55W **94 A4**
Horse Cr. ⇀ *U.S.A.* 41°57N 103°58W **76 F12**
Horse I. *Canada* 53°20N 99°6W **71 C9**
Horse Is. *Canada* 50°15N 55°50W **73 B8**
Horsefly L. *Canada* 52°25N 121°0W **70 C4**
Horseheads *U.S.A.* 42°10N 76°49W **82 D8**
Horsens *Denmark* 55°52N 9°51E **9 J13**
Horseshoe Lake *Canada* 44°59N 79°51W **82 A5**
Horsham *Australia* 36°44S 142°13E **63 F3**
Horsham *U.K.* 51°4N 0°20W **13 F7**
Horta *Azores* 38°32N 28°38W **52 a**
Horten *Norway* 59°25N 10°32E **9 G14**
Horti *India* 17°7N 75°47E **44 F2**
Horton *U.S.A.* 39°40N 95°32W **80 F6**
Horton ⇀ *Canada* 69°56N 126°52W **68 D6**
Horwood L. *Canada* 48°5N 82°20W **72 C3**
Hosadrug = Kanhangad
*India* 12°21N 74°58E **45 G2**
Hosdurga *India* 13°49N 76°17E **45 H3**
Ḩoseynābād *Khuzestān,
Iran* 32°45N 48°20E **47 C6**
Ḩoseynābād *Kordestān,
Iran* 35°33N 47°8E **46 C5**
Hoshangabad *India* 22°45N 77°45E **42 H7**
Hoshiarpur *India* 31°30N 75°58E **42 D6**
Hoskote *India* 13°4N 77°48E **45 H3**
Hospet = Hosapete *India* 15°15N 76°20E **45 G3**
Hoste, I. *Chile* 55°0S 69°0W **96 H3**
Hot *Thailand* 18°8N 98°29E **38 C2**
Hot Creek Range
*U.S.A.* 38°40N 116°20W **76 G5**
Hot Springs *Ark., U.S.A.* 34°31N 93°3W **84 D8**
Hot Springs *S. Dak.,
U.S.A.* 43°26N 103°29W **80 D2**
Hot Springs △ *U.S.A.* 34°31N 93°3W **84 D8**
Hotagen *Sweden* 63°59N 14°12E **8 E16**
Hotan *China* 37°25N 79°55E **30 D4**
Hotan He ⇀ *China* 40°22N 80°56E **30 C5**
Hotazel *S. Africa* 27°17S 22°58E **56 C3**
Hotchkiss *U.S.A.* 38°48N 107°43W **76 G10**
Hotham, C. *Australia* 12°2S 131°18E **60 B5**
Hoting *Sweden* 64°8N 16°15E **8 D17**
Hotte, Massif de la *Haiti* 18°30N 73°45W **89 C5**
Hottentotsbaai *Namibia* 26°8S 14°59E **56 D1**
Hou Hai *China* 22°32N 113°56E **31 a**
Houei Sai *Laos* 20°18N 100°26E **34 G3**

Houffalize *Belgium* 50°8N 5°48E **15** D5
Houghton *Mich., U.S.A.* 47°7N 88°34W **80** B9
Houghton *N.Y., U.S.A.* 42°25N 78°10W **82** D6
Houghton L. *U.S.A.* 44°21N 84°44W **81** C11
Houghton-le-Spring *U.K.* 54°51N 1°28W **12** C6
Houhora Heads *N.Z.* 34°49S 173°9E **59** A4
Houlton *U.S.A.* 46°8N 67°51W **81** B20
Houma *China* 35°36N 111°20E **32** G6
Houma *U.S.A.* 29°36N 90°43W **85** G9
Housatonic → *U.S.A.* 41°10N 73°7W **83** E11
Houston *Canada* 54°25N 126°39W **70** C3
Houston *Mo., U.S.A.* 37°22N 91°58W **80** G8
Houston *Tex., U.S.A.* 29°45N 95°21W **84** G7
Houston George Bush
  Intercontinental ✈ (IAH)
  *U.S.A.* 29°59N 95°20W **84** G7
Hout → Mogwadi →
  *S. Africa* 23°4S 29°36E **57** B4
Houtkraal *S. Africa* 30°23S 24°5E **56** D3
Houtman Abrolhos
  *Australia* 28°43S 113°48E **61** E1
Hovd = Dund-Us *Mongolia* 48°1N 91°38E **30** B7
Hove *U.K.* 50°50N 0°10W **13** G7
Hovenweep △ *U.S.A.* 37°20N 109°0W **77** H9
Hoveyzeh *Iran* 31°27N 48°4E **47** D6
Hövsgöl *Mongolia* 43°37N 109°39E **32** C5
Hövsgöl Nuur *Mongolia* 51°0N 100°30E **30** A9
Howar, Wadi → *Sudan* 17°30N 27°8E **53** E11
Howard *Australia* 25°16S 152°32E **63** D5
Howard *Pa., U.S.A.* 41°1N 77°40W **82** F7
Howard *S. Dak., U.S.A.* 44°1N 97°32W **80** C5
Howe *U.S.A.* 43°48N 113°0W **76** E7
Howe, C. *Australia* 37°30S 150°0E **63** F5
Howe, West Cape
  *Australia* 35°8S 117°36E **61** G2
Howe I. *U.S.A.* 44°16N 76°17W **83** B8
Howell *U.S.A.* 42°36N 83°56W **81** D12
Howick *Canada* 45°11N 73°51W **83** A11
Howick *S. Africa* 29°28S 30°14E **57** D5
Howick Group *Australia* 14°20S 145°30E **62** A4
Howitt, L. *Australia* 27°40S 138°40E **63** D2
Howland I. *Pac. Oc.* 0°48N 176°38W **64** G10
Howth *Ireland* 53°23N 6°7W **10** C5
Howth Hd. *Ireland* 53°22N 6°4W **10** C5
Höxter *Germany* 51°46N 9°22E **16** C5
Hoy *U.K.* 58°50N 3°15W **11** C5
Høyanger *Norway* 61°13N 6°4E **8** F12
Hoyerswerda *Germany* 51°26N 14°14E **16** C8
Hpa-an = Pa-an
  *Myanmar* 16°51N 97°40E **41** L20
Hpunan Pass *Asia* 27°30N 96°55E **41** F20
Hpyu = Pyu *Myanmar* 18°30N 96°28E **41** K20
Hradec Králové *Czechia* 50°15N 15°50E **16** C8
Hrodna *Belarus* 53°42N 23°52E **17** B12
Hrodzyanka *Belarus* 53°31N 28°42E **17** B15
Hron → *Slovakia* 47°49N 18°45E **17** E10
Hrvatska = Croatia ■
  *Europe* 45°20N 16°0E **16** F9
Hrymayliv *Ukraine* 49°20N 26°5E **17** D14
Hsenwi *Myanmar* 23°22N 97°55E **41** H20
Hsiamen = Xiamen
  *China* 24°25N 118°4E **35** E12
Hsian = Xi'an *China* 34°15N 109°0E **32** G5
Hsinchu *Taiwan* 24°48N 120°58E **35** E13
Hsinhailien = Lianyungang
  *China* 34°40N 119°11E **33** G10
Hsinkai = Bhamo
  *Myanmar* 24°15N 97°15E **41** G20
Hsinying *Taiwan* 23°21N 120°17E **35** F13
Hsopket *Myanmar* 23°11N 98°26E **34** F2
Hsüchou = Xuzhou
  *China* 34°18N 117°10E **33** G9
Htawei = Dawei *Myanmar* 14°2N 98°12E **38** E2
Hu Xian *China* 34°8N 108°42E **32** G5
Hua Hin *Thailand* 12°34N 99°58E **38** F2
Hua Muang *Laos* 20°13N 103°52E **38** B4
Hua Shan *China* 34°28N 110°4E **32** G6
Hua Xian *Henan, China* 35°30N 114°30E **32** G8
Hua Xian *Shaanxi, China* 34°30N 109°48E **32** G5
Hua'an *China* 25°1N 117°32E **35** E11
Huab → *Namibia* 20°52S 13°25E **56** A2
Huacheng *China* 24°4N 115°37E **35** E10
Huachinera *Mexico* 30°9N 108°55W **86** A3
Huacho *Peru* 11°10S 77°35W **92** F3
Huade *China* 41°55N 113°59E **32** D7
Huadian *China* 43°0N 126°40E **33** C14
Huadu *China* 23°22N 113°12E **35** F9
Huahine, Î.
  *French Polynesia* 16°46S 150°58W **65** J12
Huai Hat △ *Thailand* 16°52N 104°17E **38** D5
Huai He → *China* 33°0N 118°30E **35** A12
Huai Kha Khaeng △
  *Thailand* 15°20N 98°55E **38** E2
Huai Nam Dang △
  *Thailand* 19°30N 98°30E **38** C2
Huai Yot *Thailand* 7°45N 99°37E **39** J2
Huai'an *Hebei, China* 40°30N 114°20E **32** D8
Huai'an *Jiangsu, China* 33°30N 119°10E **33** H10
Huaibei *China* 34°0N 116°48E **32** G9
Huaibin *China* 32°32N 115°27E **35** A10
Huaide = Gongzhuling
  *China* 43°30N 124°40E **33** C13
Huaidezhen *China* 43°48N 124°50E **33** C13
Huaihua *China* 27°32N 109°57E **34** D6
Huaiji *China* 23°55N 112°12E **35** F9
Huainan *China* 32°38N 116°58E **35** A11
Huaining *China* 30°24N 116°40E **35** B11
Huairen *China* 39°48N 113°20E **32** E7
Huairou *China* 40°20N 116°35E **32** D9
Huaiyang *China* 33°40N 114°52E **32** H8
Huaiyin *China* 33°30N 119°2E **33** H10
Huaiyuan *Anhui, China* 32°55N 117°10E **33** H9
Huaiyuan *Guangxi Zhuangzu,
  China* 24°31N 108°22E **34** E7
Huajuapán de León
  *Mexico* 17°48N 97°46W **87** D5
Hualapai Peak *U.S.A.* 35°5N 113°54W **79** K13
Hualien *Taiwan* 23°59N 121°36E **35** F13
Huallaga → *Peru* 5°15S 75°30W **92** E3
Huambo *Angola* 12°42S 15°54E **55** G3

Huan Jiang → *China* 34°28N 109°0E **32** G5
Huan Xian *China* 36°33N 107°7E **32** F4
Huancabamba *Peru* 5°10S 79°15W **92** E3
Huancane *Peru* 15°10S 69°44W **92** G5
Huancavelica *Peru* 12°50S 75°5W **92** F3
Huancayo *Peru* 12°5S 75°12W **92** F3
Huanchaca *Bolivia* 20°15S 66°40W **92** H5
Huang Hai = Yellow Sea
  *China* 35°0N 123°0E **33** G12
Huang He → *China* 37°55N 118°50E **33** F10
Huang Xian *China* 37°38N 120°30E **33** F11
Huangchuan *China* 32°15N 115°10E **35** A10
Huangdao *China* 36°0N 120°7E **33** G11
Huanggang *China* 30°29N 114°52E **35** B10
Huangguoshu *China* 26°0N 105°40E **34** E5
Huanghua *China* 38°22N 117°20E **33** E9
Huanghuagang *China* 38°20N 117°54E **33** E9
Huangling *China* 35°34N 109°15E **32** G5
Huanglong *China* 35°30N 109°59E **32** G5
Huanglong △ *China* 32°44N 103°50E **34** A5
Huanglongtan *China* 32°40N 110°33E **35** A8
Huangmei *China* 30°5N 115°56E **35** B10
Huangpi *China* 30°50N 114°22E **35** B10
Huangping *China* 26°52N 107°54E **34** D6
Huangshan *Anhui, China* 30°8N 118°9E **35** B12
Huangshan *Anhui,
  China* 29°42N 118°25E **35** C12
Huangshi *China* 30°10N 115°3E **35** B10
Huangsongdian *China* 43°45N 127°25E **33** C14
Huangyan *China* 28°38N 121°19E **35** C13
Huangyangsi *China* 26°33N 111°39E **35** D8
Huaning *China* 24°17N 102°56E **34** E4
Huanren *China* 41°23N 125°20E **33** D13
Huantai *China* 36°58N 117°56E **33** F9
Huánuco *Peru* 9°55S 76°15W **92** E3
Huaping *China* 26°46N 101°25E **34** D3
Huaraz *Peru* 9°30S 77°32W **92** E3
Huarmey *Peru* 10°5S 78°5W **92** F3
Huarong *China* 29°29N 112°30E **35** C9
Huascarán, Nevado *Peru* 9°7S 77°37W **92** E3
Huasco *Chile* 28°30S 71°15W **94** B1
Huasco → *Chile* 28°27S 71°13W **94** B1
Huasna *U.S.A.* 35°6N 120°24W **79** K6
Huatabampo *Mexico* 26°50N 109°38W **86** B3
Huauchinango *Mexico* 20°12N 98°3W **87** C5
Huautla de Jiménez
  *Mexico* 18°8N 96°51W **87** D5
Huaxi *China* 26°25N 106°40E **34** D6
Huayin *China* 34°35N 110°5E **32** G6
Huaying *China* 30°8N 106°44E **34** B6
Huayuan *China* 28°37N 109°29E **34** C7
Huazhou *China* 21°33N 110°33E **35** G8
Hubbard *Ohio, U.S.A.* 41°9N 80°34W **82** E4
Hubbard *Tex., U.S.A.* 31°51N 96°48W **84** F6
Hubbard Glacier *Canada* 60°18N 139°22W **68** E4
Hubbart Pt. *Canada* 59°21N 94°41W **71** B10
Hubei □ *China* 31°0N 112°0E **35** B9
Hubli = Hubballi *India* 15°22N 75°15E **45** G2
Huch'ang *N. Korea* 41°25N 127°2E **33** D14
Hucknall *U.K.* 53°3N 1°13W **12** D6
Huddersfield *U.K.* 53°39N 1°47W **12** D6
Hudiksvall *Sweden* 61°43N 17°10E **8** F17
Hudson *Canada* 50°6N 92°9W **72** B1
Hudson *Mass., U.S.A.* 42°23N 71°34W **83** D13
Hudson *N.Y., U.S.A.* 42°15N 73°46W **83** D11
Hudson *Wis., U.S.A.* 44°58N 92°45W **80** C7
Hudson *Wyo., U.S.A.* 42°54N 108°35W **76** E9
Hudson → *U.S.A.* 40°42N 74°2W **83** F10
Hudson, C. *Antarctica* 68°21S 153°45E **5** C10
Hudson Bay *Nunavut,
  Canada* 60°0N 86°0W **69** F14
Hudson Bay *Sask.,
  Canada* 52°51N 102°23W **71** C8
Hudson Falls *U.S.A.* 43°18N 73°35W **83** C11
Hudson Mts. *Antarctica* 74°32S 99°20W **5** D16
Hudson Str. *Canada* 62°0N 70°0W **69** E18
Hudson's Hope *Canada* 56°0N 121°54W **70** B4
Hue *Vietnam* 16°30N 107°35E **38** D6
Huehuetenango
  *Guatemala* 15°20N 91°28W **88** C1
Huejúcar *Mexico* 22°21N 103°13W **86** C4
Huelva *Spain* 37°18N 6°57W **21** D2
Huentelauquén *Chile* 31°38S 71°33W **94** C1
Huerta, Sa. de la
  *Argentina* 31°10S 67°30W **94** C2
Huesca *Spain* 42°8N 0°25W **21** A5
Huetamo *Mexico* 18°35N 100°53W **86** D4
Hugh → *Australia* 25°1S 134°1E **62** D1
Hughenden *Australia* 20°52S 144°10E **62** C3
Hughesville *U.S.A.* 41°14N 76°44W **83** E8
Hugli → *India* 21°56N 88°4E **43** J13
Hugo *Colo., U.S.A.* 39°8N 103°28W **76** G12
Hugo *Okla., U.S.A.* 34°1N 95°31W **84** D7
Hugoton *U.S.A.* 37°11N 101°21W **80** G3
Hui Xian = Huixian
  *China* 35°27N 113°12E **32** G7
Hui Xian *China* 33°50N 106°4E **32** H4
Hui'an *China* 25°1N 118°43E **35** E12
Hui'anbu *China* 37°28N 106°38E **32** F4
Huichang *China* 25°32N 115°45E **35** E10
Huichapan *Mexico* 20°23N 99°39W **87** C5
Huichon *N. Korea* 40°10N 126°16E **33** D14
Huidong *Guangdong,
  China* 22°58N 114°43E **35** F10
Huidong *Sichuan, China* 26°34N 102°35E **34** D4
Huifa He → *China* 43°0N 127°50E **33** C14
Huila, Nevado del *Colombia* 3°0N 76°0W **92** C3
Huilai *China* 23°0N 116°18E **35** F11
Huili *China* 26°35N 102°17E **34** D4
Huimin *China* 37°27N 117°28E **33** F9
Huinan *China* 42°40N 126°2E **33** C14
Huinca Renancó
  *Argentina* 34°51S 64°22W **94** C3
Huining *China* 35°38N 105°0E **32** G3
Huinong *China* 39°5N 106°35E **32** E4
Huishui *China* 26°7N 106°38E **34** D6
Huiting *China* 34°5N 116°5E **32** G9
Huitong *China* 26°51N 109°45E **34** D7

Huixian *China* 35°27N 113°12E **32** G7
Huixtla *Mexico* 15°9N 92°28W **87** D6
Huize *China* 26°24N 103°15E **34** D4
Huizhou *China* 23°0N 114°23E **35** F10
Hukawng Valley
  *Myanmar* 26°30N 96°30E **41** F20
Hukeri *India* 16°14N 74°36E **45** F2
Hukou *China* 29°45N 116°21E **35** C11
Hukuntsi *Botswana* 23°58S 21°45E **56** C3
Ḩulayfā' *Si. Arabia* 25°58N 40°45E **46** E4
Hulin *China* 45°48N 132°59E **31** B15
Hulin He → *China* 45°0N 122°10E **33** B12
Hull = Kingston upon Hull
  *U.K.* 53°45N 0°21W **12** D7
Hull *Canada* 45°26N 75°43W **83** A9
Hull → *U.K.* 53°44N 0°20W **12** D7
Hulst *Neths.* 51°17N 4°2E **15** C4
Huludao *China* 40°45N 120°50E **33** D11
Hulun Nur *China* 49°0N 117°30E **31** B12
Hulunbuir = Hailar
  *China* 49°10N 119°38E **31** B11
Huma, Tanjung *Malaysia* 5°29N 100°16E **39** c
Humacao *Puerto Rico* 18°9N 65°50W **89** d
Humahuaca *Argentina* 23°10S 65°25W **94** A2
Humaitá *Brazil* 7°35S 63°1W **92** E6
Humaitá *Paraguay* 27°2S 58°31W **94** B4
Humansdorp *S. Africa* 34°2S 24°46E **56** D3
Humbe *Angola* 16°40S 14°55E **56** A1
Humber → *U.K.* 53°42N 0°27W **12** D7
Humboldt *Canada* 52°15N 105°9W **71** C7
Humboldt *Iowa, U.S.A.* 42°44N 94°13W **80** D6
Humboldt *Tenn., U.S.A.* 35°50N 88°55W **85** D10
Humboldt → *U.S.A.* 39°59N 118°36W **76** G4
Humboldt Gletscher = Sermersuaq
  *Greenland* 79°30N 62°0W **69** B19
Hume *Australia* 36°48N 118°54W **78** J8
Hume, L. *Australia* 36°0S 147°5E **63** F4
Humen *China* 22°50N 113°40E **31** a
Humenné *Slovakia* 48°55N 21°50E **17** D11
Humphreys, Mt. *U.S.A.* 37°17N 118°40W **78** H8
Humphreys Peak
  *U.S.A.* 35°21N 111°41W **77** J8
Humptulips *U.S.A.* 47°14N 123°57W **78** C3
Hūn *Libya* 29°2N 16°0E **53** C9
Hun Jiang → *China* 40°50N 125°38E **33** D13
Húnaflói *Iceland* 65°50N 20°50W **8** D3
Hunan □ *China* 27°30N 112°0E **35** D9
Hunchun *China* 42°52N 130°28E **33** C16
Hundewali *Pakistan* 31°55N 72°38E **42** D5
Hundred Mile House
  *Canada* 51°38N 121°18W **70** C4
Hunedoara *Romania* 45°40N 22°50E **17** F12
Hung Yen *Vietnam* 20°39N 106°4E **34** G6
Hunga Ha'apai *Tonga* 20°41S 175°7W **59** c
Hungary ■ *Europe* 47°20N 19°20E **17** E10
Hungary, Plain of *Europe* 47°0N 20°0E **6** F10
Hungerford *Australia* 28°58S 144°24E **63** D3
Húngnam *N. Korea* 39°49N 127°45E **33** E14
Hungt'ou Hsü = Lan Yü
  *Taiwan* 22°4N 121°25E **35** F13
Hunjiang *China* 41°54N 126°30E **33** D14
Hunsberge *Namibia* 27°45S 17°12E **56** C2
Hunsrück *Germany* 49°56N 7°27E **16** D4
Hunstanton *U.K.* 52°56N 0°29E **12** E8
Hunsur *India* 12°16N 76°16E **45** H3
Hunter *U.S.A.* 42°13N 74°13W **83** D10
Hunter I. *Australia* 40°30S 144°45E **63** G3
Hunter I. *Canada* 51°55N 128°0W **70** C3
Hunter Ra. *Australia* 32°45S 150°15E **63** E5
Hunterville *N.Z.* 39°56S 175°35E **59** C5
Huntingburg *U.S.A.* 38°18N 86°57W **80** F10
Huntingdon *Canada* 45°6N 74°10W **83** A10
Huntingdon *U.K.* 52°20N 0°11W **13** E7
Huntingdon *U.S.A.* 40°30N 78°1W **82** F6
Huntington *Ind., U.S.A.* 40°53N 85°30W **81** E11
Huntington *N.Y., U.S.A.* 40°52N 73°26W **83** F11
Huntington *Oreg.,
  U.S.A.* 44°21N 117°16W **76** D5
Huntington *Utah,
  U.S.A.* 39°20N 110°58W **76** G8
Huntington *W. Va.,
  U.S.A.* 38°25N 82°27W **81** F12
Huntington Beach
  *U.S.A.* 33°40N 118°5W **79** M9
Huntly *N.Z.* 37°34S 175°11E **59** B5
Huntly *U.K.* 57°27N 2°47W **11** D6
Huntsville *Canada* 45°20N 79°14W **82** A5
Huntsville *Ala., U.S.A.* 34°44N 86°35W **85** D11
Huntsville *Tex., U.S.A.* 30°43N 95°33W **84** F7
Hunyuan *China* 39°42N 113°42E **32** E7
Hunza → *India* 35°54N 74°20E **43** B6
Huo Shan *China* 36°26N 111°52E **32** F6
Huo Xian = Huozhou
  *China* 36°36N 111°42E **32** F6
Huolin Gol *China* 45°32N 119°38E **33** B10
Huonville *Australia* 43°0S 147°5E **63** G4
Huoqiu *China* 32°20N 116°12E **35** A11
Huoshan *China* 31°25N 116°20E **35** B11
Huoshao Dao = Lütao
  *Taiwan* 22°40N 121°30E **35** F13
Hupeh = Hubei □ *China* 31°0N 112°0E **35** B9
Hūr *Iran* 30°50N 57°7E **47** D8
Hurand *Iran* 38°51N 47°22E **46** B5
Ḩuraymīla *Si. Arabia* 25°8N 46°8E **46** E5
Hurd, C. *Canada* 45°13N 81°44W **82** A3
Hure Qi *China* 42°45N 121°45E **33** C11
Hurghada *Egypt* 27°15N 33°50E **53** C12
Hurley *N. Mex., U.S.A.* 32°42N 108°8W **77** K9
Hurley *Wis., U.S.A.* 46°27N 90°11W **80** B8
Huron *Calif., U.S.A.* 36°12N 120°6W **78** J6
Huron *Ohio, U.S.A.* 41°24N 82°33W **82** E2
Huron *S. Dak., U.S.A.* 44°22N 98°13W **80** C4
Huron, L. *U.S.A.* 44°30N 82°40W **82** B2
Huron East *Canada* 43°37N 81°30W **82** C3
Hurricane *U.S.A.* 37°11N 113°17W **77** H7
Hurunui → *N.Z.* 42°54S 173°18E **59** E4
Húsavík *Iceland* 66°3N 17°21W **8** C5
Huși *Romania* 46°41N 28°7E **17** E15
Hustadvika *Norway* 63°0N 7°0E **8** E12

Hustontown *U.S.A.* 40°3N 78°2W **82** F6
Hutchinson *Kans., U.S.A.* 38°5N 97°56W **80** F5
Hutchinson *Minn.,
  U.S.A.* 44°54N 94°22W **80** C6
Hutiao Xia *China* 27°13N 100°9E **34** D3
Hutte Sauvage, L. de la
  *Canada* 56°15N 64°45W **73** A7
Hutton, Mt. *Australia* 25°51S 148°20E **63** D4
Huwaki *Indonesia* 7°55S 126°30E **37** F7
Huy *Belgium* 50°31N 5°15E **15** D5
Huzhou *China* 30°51N 120°8E **35** B13
Huzurabad *India* 18°12N 79°25E **44** E4
Huzurnagar *India* 16°54N 79°53E **44** F4
Hvammstangi *Iceland* 65°24N 20°57W **8** D3
Hvar *Croatia* 43°11N 16°28E **22** C7
Hvítá → *Iceland* 64°30N 21°58W **8** D3
Hwacheon-Cheosuji
  *S. Korea* 38°5N 127°50E **33** E14
Hwang Ho = Huang He →
  *China* 37°55N 118°50E **33** F10
Hwange *Zimbabwe* 18°18S 26°30E **55** H5
Hwange △ *Zimbabwe* 19°0S 26°30E **56** A4
Hyannis *Mass., U.S.A.* 41°39N 70°17W **81** E18
Hyannis *Nebr., U.S.A.* 42°0N 101°46W **80** E3
Hyargas Nuur *Mongolia* 49°0N 93°0E **30** B7
Hydaburg *U.S.A.* 55°15N 132°50W **70** B2
Hyde Park *U.S.A.* 41°47N 73°56W **83** E11
Hyden *Australia* 32°24S 118°53E **61** F2
Hyderabad *India* 17°22N 78°29E **44** F4
Hyderabad *Pakistan* 25°23N 68°24E **42** G3
Hydra *Greece* 37°20N 23°28E **23** F10
Hyères *France* 43°8N 6°9E **20** E7
Hyères, Îs. d' *France* 43°0N 6°20E **20** E7
Hyesan *N. Korea* 41°20N 128°10E **33** D15
Hyland → *Canada* 59°52N 128°12W **70** B3
Hyndman Peak *U.S.A.* 43°45N 114°8W **76** E6
Hyōgo □ *Japan* 35°15N 134°50E **29** G7
Hyrum *U.S.A.* 41°38N 111°51W **76** F8
Hysham *U.S.A.* 46°18N 107°14W **76** C10
Hythe *U.K.* 51°4N 1°5E **13** F9
Hyūga *Japan* 32°25N 131°35E **29** H5
Hyvinge = Hyvinkää
  *Finland* 60°38N 24°50E **8** F21
Hyvinkää *Finland* 60°38N 24°50E **8** F21

## I

I-n-Gall *Niger* 16°51N 7°1E **52** E7
Iaco → *Brazil* 9°3S 68°34W **92** E5
Ialomița → *Romania* 44°42N 27°51E **17** F14
Iași *Romania* 47°10N 27°40E **17** E14
Ib → *India* 21°34N 83°48E **43** J10
Iba *Phil.* 15°22N 120°0E **37** A6
Ibadan *Nigeria* 7°22N 3°58E **52** G6
Ibagué *Colombia* 4°20N 75°20W **92** C3
Ibar → *Serbia* 43°43N 20°45E **23** C9
Ibaraki □ *Japan* 36°10N 140°10E **29** F10
Ibarra *Ecuador* 0°21N 78°7W **92** C3
Ibb *Yemen* 14°2N 44°10E **49** E3
Ibenga → *Congo* 2°19N 18°9E **54** D3
Ibera, L. *Argentina* 28°30S 57°9W **94** B4
Iberian Peninsula *Europe* 40°0N 5°0W **6** H5
Iberville *Canada* 45°19N 73°17W **83** A11
Iberville, Mt. d' *Canada* 58°50N 63°50W **69** F19
Ibiá *Brazil* 19°30S 46°30W **93** G9
Ibiapaba, Sa. da *Brazil* 4°0S 41°30W **93** D10
Ibicuí → *Brazil* 29°25S 56°47W **95** B4
Ibicuy *Argentina* 33°55S 59°10W **94** C4
Ibiza = Eivissa *Spain* 38°54N 1°26E **21** C6
Ibonma *Indonesia* 3°29S 133°31E **37** E8
Ibotirama *Brazil* 12°13S 43°12W **93** F10
Ibrāhīm → *Lebanon* 34°4N 35°38E **48** A4
'Ibrī *Oman* 23°14N 56°30E **49** C6
Ibu *Indonesia* 1°35N 127°33E **37** D7
Ibusuki *Japan* 31°12N 130°40E **29** J5
Ica *Peru* 14°0S 75°48W **92** F3
Içá → *Brazil* 2°55S 67°58W **92** D5
Icacos Pt. *Trin. & Tob.* 10°3N 61°57W **93** K15
Içana *Brazil* 0°21N 67°19W **92** C5
Içana → *Brazil* 0°26N 67°19W **92** C5
İçel = Mersin *Turkey* 36°51N 34°36E **46** B2
Iceland ■ *Europe* 64°45N 19°0W **8** D4
Iceland Basin *Atl. Oc.* 61°0N 19°0W **4** C7
Icelandic Plateau *Arctic* 64°0N 10°0W **4** C7
Ichalkaranji *India* 16°40N 74°33E **44** F2
Ich'ang = Yichang
  *China* 30°40N 111°20E **35** B8
Ichchapuram *India* 19°10N 84°40E **44** E7
Ichhawar *India* 23°1N 77°1E **42** H7
Ichihara *Japan* 35°28N 140°5E **29** G10
Ichikawa *Japan* 35°44N 139°55E **29** G9
Ichilo → *Bolivia* 15°57S 64°50W **92** G6
Ichinohe *Japan* 40°13N 141°17E **28** D10
Ichinomiya *Japan* 35°18N 136°48E **29** G8
Ichinoseki *Japan* 38°55N 141°8E **28** E10
Içoguz *Turkmenistan* 40°11N 58°24E **26** E6
Icy C. *U.S.A.* 70°20N 161°52W **66** B3
Ida Grove *U.S.A.* 42°21N 95°28W **80** D6
Idabel *U.S.A.* 33°54N 94°50W **84** E7
Idaho □ *U.S.A.* 45°0N 115°0W **76** D6
Idaho City *U.S.A.* 43°50N 115°50W **76** E6
Idaho Falls *U.S.A.* 43°30N 112°2W **76** E7
Idalia △ *Australia* 24°49S 144°36E **62** C3
Idar-Oberstein *Germany* 49°43N 7°16E **16** D4
Idensalmi = Iisalmi
  *Finland* 63°32N 27°10E **8** E22
Idfû *Egypt* 25°0N 32°49E **53** D12
Idi *Indonesia* 5°2N 97°37E **36** C1
Idi, Oros = Psiloritis, Oros
  *Greece* 35°15N 24°45E **23** G11
Idiofa *Dem. Rep. of the Congo* 4°55S 19°42E **54** E4
Idlib *Syria* 35°55N 36°36E **46** C3
Idra = Hydra *Greece* 37°20N 23°28E **23** F10
Idria *U.S.A.* 36°25N 120°41W **78** J6
Idutywa = Dutywa
  *S. Africa* 32°8S 28°18E **57** D4
Ieper *Belgium* 50°51N 2°53E **15** D2
Ierapetra *Greece* 35°1N 25°44E **23** G11

Iesi *Italy* 43°31N 13°14E **22** C5
Ifakara *Tanzania* 8°8S 36°41E **54** F7
'Ifāl, W. al → *Si. Arabia* 28°7N 35°3E **46** D2
Ife *Nigeria* 7°30N 4°31E **52** G6
Iffley *Australia* 18°53S 141°12E **62** B3
Iforas, Adrar des *Africa* 19°40N 1°40E **52** E6
Ifould L. *Australia* 30°52S 132°6E **61** F5
Igarapava *Brazil* 20°3S 47°47W **93** H9
Igarka *Russia* 67°30N 86°33E **26** C9
Igatpuri *India* 19°40N 73°35E **44** E1
Iggesund *Sweden* 61°39N 17°10E **8** F17
Iglésias *Italy* 39°19N 8°32E **22** E3
Igloolik = Iglulik
  *Canada* 69°20N 81°49W **69** D15
Igluligaarjuk = Chesterfield Inlet
  *Canada* 63°30N 90°45W **68** E13
Iglulik *Canada* 69°20N 81°49W **69** D15
İğneada Burnu *Turkey* 41°53N 28°2E **23** D13
Igoumenitsa *Greece* 39°32N 20°18E **23** E9
Igrim *Russia* 63°12N 64°30E **26** C7
Iguaçu → *Brazil* 25°36S 54°36W **95** B5
Iguaçu, Cat. del *Brazil* 25°41S 54°26W **95** B5
Iguaçu △ *Brazil* 25°30S 54°0W **95** B5
Iguaçu Falls = Iguaçu, Cat. del
  *Brazil* 25°41S 54°26W **95** B5
Iguala *Mexico* 18°21N 99°32W **87** D5
Igualada *Spain* 41°37N 1°37E **21** B6
Iguassu = Iguaçu →
  *Brazil* 25°36S 54°36W **95** B5
Iguatu *Brazil* 6°20S 39°18W **93** E11
Iguazú △ *Argentina* 25°42S 54°22W **95** B5
Iguidi, Erg *Africa* 27°0N 6°0W **52** C4
Iharana *Madag.* 13°25S 50°0E **55** G10
Ihbulag *Mongolia* 43°11N 107°10E **32** C4
Iheya-Shima *Japan* 27°4N 127°58E **29** L3
Ihosy *Madag.* 22°24S 46°8E **55** J9
Ii *Finland* 65°19N 25°22E **8** D21
Ii-Shima *Japan* 26°43N 127°47E **29** L3
Iida *Japan* 35°35N 137°50E **29** G8
Iijoki → *Finland* 65°20N 25°20E **8** D21
Iisalmi *Finland* 63°32N 27°10E **8** E22
Iiyama *Japan* 36°51N 138°22E **29** F9
Iizuka *Japan* 33°38N 130°42E **29** H5
Ijâfene *Mauritania* 20°40N 8°0W **52** D4
Ijebu-Ode *Nigeria* 6°47N 3°58E **52** G6
IJmuiden *Neths.* 52°28N 4°35E **15** B4
Ijo älv = Iijoki → *Finland* 65°20N 25°20E **8** D21
IJssel → *Neths.* 52°35N 5°50E **15** B5
IJsselmeer *Neths.* 52°45N 5°20E **15** B5
Ijuí *Brazil* 28°23S 53°55W **95** B5
Ijuí → *Brazil* 27°58S 55°20W **95** B4
Ikare *Nigeria* 7°32N 5°40E **52** G7
Ikaria *Greece* 37°35N 26°10E **23** F12
Ikeda *Japan* 34°1N 133°48E **29** G6
Ikela *Dem. Rep. of the Congo* 1°6S 23°6E **54** E4
Iki *Japan* 33°45N 129°42E **29** H4
Ikopa → *Madag.* 16°45S 46°40E **55** H9
Ikparjuk = Arctic Bay
  *Canada* 73°1N 85°7W **69** C14
Iksan *S. Korea* 35°59N 127°0E **33** G14
Ikuntji = Haasts Bluff
  *Australia* 23°22S 132°0E **60** D5
Ilagan *Phil.* 17°7N 121°53E **37** A6
Īlām *Iran* 33°36N 46°36E **46** C5
Ilam *Nepal* 26°58N 87°58E **43** F12
Īlām □ *Iran* 33°0N 47°0E **46** C5
Ilan *Taiwan* 24°45N 121°44E **35** E13
Ilanskiy *Russia* 56°14N 96°3E **27** D10
Iława *Poland* 53°36N 19°34E **17** B10
Ilayangudi *India* 9°34N 78°37E **45** K4
Ile → *Kazakhstan* 45°53N 77°10E **26** E8
Île-à-la-Crosse *Canada* 55°27N 107°53W **71** B7
Île-à-la-Crosse, Lac
  *Canada* 55°40N 107°45W **71** B7
Île-de-France □ *France* 49°0N 2°20E **20** B5
Ilebo *Dem. Rep. of the Congo* 4°17S 20°55E **54** E4
Ilek *Russia* 51°32N 53°21E **26** D6
Ilek → *Russia* 51°30N 53°22E **18** D9
Ilemi Triangle *Africa* 5°0N 35°30E **54** B4
Ilesha *Nigeria* 7°37N 4°40E **52** G6
Ilford *Canada* 56°4N 95°35W **71** B9
Ilfracombe *Australia* 23°30S 144°30E **62** C3
Ilfracombe *U.K.* 51°12N 4°8W **13** F3
Ilha Grande, Represa
  *Brazil* 23°10S 53°5W **95** A5
Ilha Grande △ *Brazil* 23°10S 53°20W **95** A5
Ilhéus *Brazil* 14°49S 39°2W **93** F11
Ili = Ile → *Kazakhstan* 45°53N 77°10E **26** E8
Iliamna L. *U.S.A.* 59°30N 155°0W **74** D8
Iligan *Phil.* 8°12N 124°13E **37** C6
Ilion *U.S.A.* 43°1N 75°2W **83** D9
Ilkal *India* 15°57N 76°8E **45** G3
Ilkeston *U.K.* 52°58N 1°19W **12** E6
Ilkley *U.K.* 53°56N 1°48W **12** D6
Illampu = Ancohuma, Nevado
  *Bolivia* 16°0S 68°50W **92** G5
Illana B. *Phil.* 7°35N 123°45E **37** C6
Illapel *Chile* 32°0S 71°10W **94** C1
Iller → *Germany* 48°23N 9°58E **16** D6
Illes Balears = Baleares, Is.
  *Spain* 39°30N 3°0E **21** C7
Illimani, Nevado *Bolivia* 16°30S 67°50W **92** G5
Illinois □ *U.S.A.* 38°58N 90°28W **80** F8
Illizi *Algeria* 26°31N 8°32E **52** C7
Ilma, L. *Australia* 29°13S 127°46E **61** E4
Ilmen, Ozero *Russia* 58°15N 31°10E **18** C5
Ilo *Peru* 17°40S 71°20W **92** G4
Iloilo *Phil.* 10°45N 122°33E **37** B6
Ilomantsi *Finland* 62°38N 30°57E **8** E24
Ilorin *Nigeria* 8°30N 4°35E **52** G6
Ilwaco *U.S.A.* 46°19N 124°3W **78** D2
Imabari *Japan* 34°4N 133°0E **29** G6
Imandra, Ozero *Russia* 67°30N 33°0E **8** C25
Imari *Japan* 33°15N 129°52E **29** H4
Imatra *Finland* 61°12N 28°48E **8** F23

imeni 26 Bakinskikh Komissarov
  = Neftçala *Azerbaijan* 39°19N 49°12E **47** B6

**imeni 26 Bakinskikh Komissarov**
*Turkmenistan* 39°22N 54°10E **47** B7
**imeni Ismail Samani, Pik**
*Tajikistan* 39°0N 72°2E **26** F8
**Imeri, Serra** *Brazil* 0°50N 65°25W **92** C5
**Imfolozi** △ *S. Africa* 28°18S 31°50E **57** C5
**Imi** *Ethiopia* 6°28N 42°10E **49** F3
**Imlay** *U.S.A.* 40°40N 118°9W **76** F4
**Imlay City** *U.S.A.* 43°2N 83°5W **82** D1
**Immingham** *U.K.* 53°37N 0°13W **12** D7
**Immokalee** *U.S.A.* 26°25N 81°25W **85** H14
**Imola** *Italy* 44°20N 11°42E **22** B4
**Imperatriz** *Brazil* 5°30S 47°29W **93** E9
**Impéria** *Italy* 43°53N 8°3E **20** D8
**Imperial** *Canada* 51°21N 105°28W **71** C7
**Imperial** *Calif., U.S.A.* 32°51N 115°34W **79** N11
**Imperial** *Nebr., U.S.A.* 40°31N 101°39W **80** E3
**Imperial Beach** *U.S.A.* 32°35N 117°6W **79** N9
**Imperial Dam** *U.S.A.* 32°55N 114°25W **79** N12
**Imperial Res.** *U.S.A.* 32°53N 114°28W **79** N12
**Imperial Valley** *U.S.A.* 33°0N 115°30W **79** N11
**Imperieuse Reef**
*Australia* 17°36S 118°50E **60** C2
**Impfondo** *Congo* 1°40N 18°0E **54** D3
**Imphal** *India* 24°48N 93°56E **41** G18
**İmroz = Gökçeada**
*Turkey* 40°10N 25°50E **23** D11
**Imuris** *Mexico* 30°47N 110°52W **86** A2
**Imuruan B.** *Phil.* 10°40N 119°10E **37** B5
**In Amenas** *Algeria* 28°5N 9°33E **53** C7
**In Guezzam** *Algeria* 19°37N 5°52E **52** E7
**In Salah** *Algeria* 27°10N 2°32E **52** C6
**Ina** *Japan* 35°50N 137°55E **29** G8
**Inagua** △ *Bahamas* 21°5N 73°24W **89** B5
**Inangahua** *N.Z.* 41°52S 171°59E **59** D3
**Inanwatan** *Indonesia* 2°8S 132°10E **37** E8
**Iñapari** *Peru* 11°0S 69°40W **92** F5
**Inari** *Finland* 68°54N 27°1E **8** B22
**Inarijärvi** *Finland* 69°0N 28°0E **8** B23
**Inawashiro-Ko** *Japan* 37°29N 140°6E **28** F10
**tInbhear Mór, An = Arklow**
*Ireland* 52°48N 6°10W **10** D5
**Inca** *Spain* 39°43N 2°54E **21** C7
**Inca de Oro** *Chile* 26°45S 69°54W **94** B2
**Incahuasi** *Argentina* 27°2S 68°18W **94** B2
**Incahuasi** *Chile* 29°12S 71°5W **94** B1
**İnce Burun** *Turkey* 42°7N 34°56E **19** F5
**İncesu** *Turkey* 38°38N 35°11E **46** B2
**Incheon** *S. Korea* 37°27N 126°40E **33** F14
**İncirliova** *Turkey* 37°50N 27°41E **23** F12
**Incline Village** *U.S.A.* 39°10N 119°58W **78** F7
**Incomáti** → *Mozam.* 25°46S 32°43E **57** C5
**Indalsälven** → *Sweden* 62°36N 17°30E **8** E17
**Indaw** *Myanmar* 24°15N 96°5E **41** G20
**Independence** *Calif., U.S.A.* 36°48N 118°12W **78** J8
**Independence** *Iowa, U.S.A.* 42°28N 91°54W **80** D8
**Independence** *Kans., U.S.A.* 37°14N 95°42W **80** G6
**Independence** *Ky., U.S.A.* 38°57N 84°33W **81** F11
**Independence** *Mo., U.S.A.* 39°6N 94°25W **80** F6
**Independence Fjord**
*Greenland* 82°10N 29°0W **4** A6
**Independence Mts.**
*U.S.A.* 41°20N 116°0W **76** F5
**Index** *U.S.A.* 47°50N 121°33W **78** C5
**Indi** *India* 17°10N 75°58E **44** F2
**India** ■ *Asia* 20°0N 78°0E **40** K11
**Indian** → *U.S.A.* 27°59N 80°34W **85** H14
**Indian Cabins** *Canada* 59°52N 117°40W **70** B5
**Indian Harbour** *Canada* 54°27N 57°13W **73** B8
**Indian Head** *Canada* 50°30N 103°41W **71** C8
**Indian L.** *U.S.A.* 43°46N 74°16W **83** C10
**Indian Lake** *U.S.A.* 43°47N 74°16W **83** C10
**Indian Springs** *U.S.A.* 36°35N 115°40W **79** J11
**Indiana** *U.S.A.* 40°37N 79°9W **82** F5
**Indiana** □ *U.S.A.* 40°0N 86°0W **81** F11
**Indianapolis** *U.S.A.* 39°46N 86°9W **80** F10
**Indianola** *Iowa, U.S.A.* 41°22N 93°34W **80** E7
**Indianola** *Miss., U.S.A.* 33°27N 90°39W **85** E9
**Indiga** *Russia* 67°38N 49°9E **18** A8
**Indigirka** → *Russia* 70°48N 148°54E **27** B15
**Indio** *U.S.A.* 33°43N 116°13W **79** M10
**Indira Gandhi Canal** *India* 28°0N 72°0E **42** F5
**Indira Pt.** *India* 6°44N 93°49E **45** L11
**Indira Sagar** *India* 22°15N 76°40E **42** H7
**Indo-China** *Asia* 15°0N 102°0E **24** G12
**Indonesia** ■ *Asia* 5°0S 115°0E **36** F5
**Indore** *India* 22°42N 75°53E **42** H6
**Indramayu** *Indonesia* 6°20S 108°19E **37** G13
**Indravati** → *India* 19°20N 80°20E **44** E5
**Indre** → *France* 47°16N 0°11E **20** C4
**Indulkana** *Australia* 26°58S 133°5E **63** D1
**Indus** → *Pakistan* 24°20N 67°47E **42** G2
**Indus, Mouths of the**
*Pakistan* 24°0N 68°0E **42** H3
**İnebolu** *Turkey* 41°55N 33°40E **19** F5
**Infiernillo, Presa del**
*Mexico* 18°35N 101°50W **86** D4
**Inga, Barrage d'**
*Dem. Rep. of the Congo* 5°39S 13°39E **54** F2
**Ingenio Santa Ana**
*Argentina* 27°25S 65°40W **94** B2
**Ingersoll** *Canada* 43°4N 80°55W **82** C4
**Ingham** *Australia* 18°43S 146°10E **62** B4
**Ingleborough** *U.K.* 54°10N 2°22E **12** C5
**Inglewood** *Queens., Australia* 28°25S 151°2E **63** D5
**Inglewood** *Vic., Australia* 36°29S 143°53E **63** F3
**Inglewood** *N.Z.* 39°9S 174°14E **59** C5
**Ingólfshöfði** *Iceland* 63°48N 16°39W **8** E5
**Ingolstadt** *Germany* 48°46N 11°26E **16** D6
**Ingomar** *U.S.A.* 46°35N 107°23W **76** C10
**Ingonish** *Canada* 46°42N 60°18W **73** C7
**Ingraj Bazar** *India* 24°58N 88°10E **43** G13
**Ingrid Christensen Coast**
*Antarctica* 69°30S 76°0E **5** C6
**Ingulec = Inhulec**
*Ukraine* 47°42N 33°14E **19** E5

**Ingushetia** □ *Russia* 43°20N 44°50E **19** F8
**Ingwavuma** *S. Africa* 27°9S 31°59E **57** C5
**Inhaca** *Mozam.* 26°1S 32°57E **57** C5
**Inhaca Pen.** *Mozam.* 26°13S 32°55E **57** C5
**Inhafenga** *Mozam.* 20°36S 33°53E **57** B5
**Inhambane** *Mozam.* 23°54S 35°30E **57** B6
**Inhambane** □ *Mozam.* 22°30S 34°20E **57** B5
**Inharrime** *Mozam.* 24°30S 35°0E **57** B6
**Inharrime** → *Mozam.* 24°30S 35°0E **57** B6
**Inhulec** *Ukraine* 47°42N 33°14E **19** E5
**Ining = Yining** *China* 43°58N 81°10E **30** C5
**Inírida** → *Colombia* 3°55N 67°52W **92** C5
**Inis = Ennis** *Ireland* 52°51N 8°59W **10** D3
**Inishbofin** *Ireland* 53°37N 10°13W **10** C1
**Inisheer** *Ireland* 53°3N 9°32W **10** C2
**Inishfree B.** *Ireland* 55°4N 8°23W **10** A3
**Inishkea North** *Ireland* 54°9N 10°11W **10** B1
**Inishkea South** *Ireland* 54°7N 10°12W **10** B1
**Inishmaan** *Ireland* 53°5N 9°35W **10** C2
**Inishmore** *Ireland* 53°8N 9°45W **10** C2
**Inishmurray** *Ireland* 54°26N 8°39W **10** B3
**Inishowen Pen.** *Ireland* 55°14N 7°15W **10** A4
**Inishshark** *Ireland* 53°37N 10°16W **10** C1
**Inishturk** *Ireland* 53°42N 10°7W **10** C1
**Inishvickillane** *Ireland* 52°3N 10°37W **10** D1
**Injinoo** ◎ *Australia* 10°56S 142°15E **62** A3
**Injune** *Australia* 25°53S 148°32E **63** D4
**Inklin** → *N. Amer.* 58°50N 133°10W **70** B2
**Inland Kaikoura Ra.**
*N.Z.* 41°59S 173°41E **59** D4
**Inland Sea = Setonaikai**
*Japan* 34°20N 133°30E **29** G6
**Inle L.** *Myanmar* 20°30N 96°58E **41** J20
**Inlet** *U.S.A.* 43°45N 74°48W **83** C10
**Inn** → *Austria* 48°35N 13°28E **16** D7
**Innamincka** *Australia* 27°44S 140°46E **63** D3
**Inner Hebrides** *U.K.* 57°0N 6°30W **11** E2
**Inner Mongolia = Nei Mongol**
**Zizhiqu** □ *China* 42°0N 112°0E **32** D7
**Inner Sound** *U.K.* 57°30N 5°55W **11** D3
**Innerkip** *Canada* 43°13N 80°42W **82** C4
**Innetalling I.** *Canada* 56°0N 79°0W **72** A4
**Innisfail** *Australia* 17°33S 146°5E **62** B4
**Innisfail** *Canada* 52°2N 113°57W **70** C6
**In'noshima** *Japan* 34°19N 133°10E **29** G6
**Innsbruck** *Austria* 47°16N 11°23E **16** E6
**Inny** → *Ireland* 53°32N 7°51W **10** C4
**Inongo**
*Dem. Rep. of the Congo* 1°55S 18°30E **54** E3
**Inouçdjouac = Inukjuak**
*Canada* 58°25N 78°15W **69** F16
**Inowrocław** *Poland* 52°50N 18°12E **17** B10
**Inscription, C.** *Australia* 25°29S 112°59E **61** E1
**Insein** *Myanmar* 16°50N 96°5E **41** L20
**Inta** *Russia* 66°5N 60°8E **18** A11
**Intendente Alvear**
*Argentina* 35°12S 63°32W **94** D3
**Interlaken** *Switz.* 46°41N 7°50E **20** C7
**Interlaken** *U.S.A.* 42°37N 76°44W **83** D8
**International Falls**
*U.S.A.* 48°36N 93°25W **80** A7
**Interview I.** *India* 12°55N 92°43E **45** H11
**Intiyaco** *Argentina* 28°43S 60°5W **94** B3
**Inukjuak** *Canada* 58°25N 78°15W **69** F16
**Inútil, B.** *Chile* 53°30S 70°15W **96** G2
**Inuvik** *Canada* 68°16N 133°40W **68** B6
**Inveraray** *U.K.* 56°14N 5°5W **11** E3
**Inverbervie** *U.K.* 56°51N 2°17W **11** E6
**Invercargill** *N.Z.* 46°24S 168°24E **59** G2
**Inverclyde** □ *U.K.* 55°54N 4°49W **11** F4
**Inverell** *Australia* 29°45S 151°8E **63** D5
**Invergordon** *U.K.* 57°41N 4°10W **11** D4
**Inverloch** *Australia* 38°38S 145°45E **63** F4
**Invermere** *Canada* 50°30N 116°2W **70** C5
**Inverness** *Canada* 46°15N 61°19W **73** C7
**Inverness** *U.K.* 57°29N 4°13W **11** D4
**Inverness** *U.S.A.* 28°50N 82°20W **85** G13
**Inverurie** *U.K.* 57°17N 2°23W **11** D6
**Investigator Group**
*Australia* 34°45S 134°20E **63** E1
**Investigator Str.** *Australia* 35°30S 137°0E **63** F2
**Inya** *Russia* 50°28N 86°37E **26** D9
**Inyangani** *Zimbabwe* 18°5S 32°50E **55** H6
**Inyantue** *Zimbabwe* 18°33S 26°39E **56** A4
**Inyo Mts.** *U.S.A.* 36°40N 118°0W **78** J9
**Inyokern** *U.S.A.* 35°39N 117°49W **79** K9
**Inza** *Russia* 53°55N 46°25E **18** D8
**Iō-Jima** *Japan* 30°48N 130°18E **29** J5
**Ioannina** *Greece* 39°42N 20°47E **23** E9
**Iola** *U.S.A.* 37°55N 95°24W **80** G6
**Iona** *U.K.* 56°20N 6°25W **11** E2
**Ione** *U.S.A.* 38°21N 120°56W **78** G6
**Ionia** *U.S.A.* 42°59N 85°4W **81** D11
**Ionian Is. = Ionioi Nisoi**
*Greece* 38°40N 20°0E **23** E9
**Ionian Sea** *Medit. S.* 37°30N 17°30E **23** E7
**Ionioi Nisoi** *Greece* 38°40N 20°0E **23** E9
**Iony, Ostrov** *Russia* 56°24N 143°22E **27** D15
**Ios** *Greece* 36°41N 25°20E **23** F11
**Iowa** □ *U.S.A.* 42°18N 93°30W **80** D7
**Iowa** → *U.S.A.* 41°10N 91°1W **80** E8
**Iowa City** *U.S.A.* 41°40N 91°32W **80** E8
**Iowa Falls** *U.S.A.* 42°31N 93°16W **80** D7
**Iowa Park** *U.S.A.* 33°57N 98°40W **84** E5
**Ipameri** *Brazil* 17°44S 48°9W **93** G9
**Ipatinga** *Brazil* 19°32S 42°30W **93** G10
**Ipiales** *Colombia* 0°50N 77°37W **92** C3
**Ipin = Yibin** *China* 28°45N 104°32E **34** C5
**Ipixuna** *Brazil* 7°0S 71°40W **92** E4
**Ipoh** *Malaysia* 4°35N 101°5E **39** K3
**Ippy** *C.A.R.* 6°5N 21°7E **54** C4
**İpsala** *Turkey* 40°55N 26°23E **23** D12
**Ipswich** *Australia* 27°35S 152°40E **63** D5
**Ipswich** *U.K.* 52°4N 1°10E **13** E9
**Ipswich** *Mass., U.S.A.* 42°41N 70°50W **83** D14
**Ipswich** *S. Dak., U.S.A.* 45°27N 99°2W **80** C4
**Ipu** *Brazil* 4°23S 40°44W **93** D10
**Iqaluit** *Canada* 63°44N 68°31W **69** E18
**Iqaluktuutiaq = Cambridge Bay**
*Canada* 69°10N 105°0W **68** D11

**Iquique** *Chile* 20°19S 70°5W **92** H4
**Iquitos** *Peru* 3°45S 73°10W **92** D4
**Irabu-Jima** *Japan* 24°50N 125°10E **29** M2
**Iracoubo** *Fr. Guiana* 5°30N 53°10W **93** B8
**Īrafshān** *Iran* 26°42N 61°56E **47** E9
**Iraklio** *Greece* 35°20N 25°12E **23** G11
**Iráklion = Iraklio** *Greece* 35°20N 25°12E **23** G11
**Irala** *Paraguay* 25°55S 54°35W **95** B5
**Iran** ■ *Asia* 33°0N 53°0E **47** C7
**Iran, Pegunungan**
*Malaysia* 2°20N 114°50E **36** D4
**Iran Ra. = Iran, Pegunungan**
*Malaysia* 2°20N 114°50E **36** D4
**Iranamadu Tank** *Sri Lanka* 9°23N 80°29E **45** K5
**Īrānshahr** *Iran* 27°15N 60°40E **47** E9
**Irapuato** *Mexico* 20°41N 101°28W **86** C4
**Iraq** ■ *Asia* 33°0N 44°0E **46** C5
**Irati** *Brazil* 25°25S 50°38W **95** B5
**Irazú, Volcan** *Costa Rica* 9°59N 83°51W **88** D3
**Irbid** *Jordan* 32°35N 35°48E **48** C4
**Irbid** □ *Jordan* 32°30N 35°50E **48** C5
**Irbil = Arbīl** *Iraq* 36°15N 44°5E **46** B5
**Irebu** *Dem. Rep. of the Congo* 0°40S 17°46E **54** E3
**Ireland** ■ *Europe* 53°50N 7°52W **10** C4
**Iri = Iksan** *S. Korea* 35°59N 127°0E **33** G14
**Irian Jaya = Papua** □
*Indonesia* 4°0S 137°0E **37** E9
**Irian Jaya Barat** □
*Indonesia* 2°5S 132°50E **37** E8
**Iringa** *Tanzania* 7°48S 35°43E **54** F7
**Irinjalakuda** *India* 10°21N 76°14E **45** J3
**Iriomote** △ *Japan* 24°29N 123°53E **29** M1
**Iriomote-Jima** *Japan* 24°19N 123°48E **29** M1
**Iriona** *Honduras* 15°57N 85°11W **88** C2
**Iriri** → *Brazil* 3°52S 52°37W **93** D8
**Irish Sea** *Europe* 53°38N 4°48W **12** D3
**Irkutsk** *Russia* 52°18N 104°20E **30** D9
**Irma** *Canada* 52°55N 111°14W **71** C6
**Irō-Zaki** *Japan* 34°36N 138°51E **29** G9
**Iron Baron** *Australia* 32°58S 137°11E **63** E2
**Iron Gate = Portile de Fier**
*Europe* 44°44N 22°30E **17** F12
**Iron Knob** *Australia* 32°46S 137°8E **63** E2
**Iron Mountain** *U.S.A.* 45°49N 88°4W **80** C9
**Iron Range** △ *Australia* 12°34S 143°18E **62** A3
**Iron River** *U.S.A.* 46°6N 88°39W **80** B9
**Irondequoit** *U.S.A.* 43°13N 77°35W **82** C7
**Ironton** *Mo., U.S.A.* 37°36N 90°38W **80** G8
**Ironton** *Ohio, U.S.A.* 38°32N 82°41W **81** F12
**Ironwood** *U.S.A.* 46°27N 90°9W **80** B8
**Ironwood Forest** ◌
*U.S.A.* 32°32N 111°28W **77** K8
**Iroquois** *Canada* 44°51N 75°19W **83** B9
**Iroquois Falls** *Canada* 48°46N 80°41W **72** C3
**Irpin** *Ukraine* 50°30N 30°15E **17** C16
**Irrara Cr.** → *Australia* 29°35S 145°31E **63** D4
**Irrawaddy = Ayeyarwady** →
*Myanmar* 15°50N 95°6E **41** M19
**Irrawaddy** □ *Myanmar* 17°0N 95°0E **41** L19
**Irrawaddy, Mouths of the**
*Myanmar* 15°30N 95°0E **41** M19
**Irricana** *Canada* 51°19N 113°37W **70** C6
**Irrunytju** *Australia* 26°3S 128°56E **61** E4
**Irtysh** → *Russia* 61°4N 68°52E **26** C7
**Irún** *Spain* 43°20N 1°52W **21** A5
**Irunea = Pamplona-Iruña**
*Spain* 42°48N 1°38W **21** A5
**Irvine** *Canada* 49°57N 110°16W **71** D6
**Irvine** *U.K.* 55°37N 4°41W **11** F4
**Irvine** *Calif., U.S.A.* 33°41N 117°46W **79** M9
**Irvine** *Ky., U.S.A.* 37°42N 83°58W **81** G12
**Irvinestown** *U.K.* 54°28N 7°39W **10** B4
**Irvona** *U.S.A.* 40°46N 78°33W **82** F6
**Irwin** → *Australia* 29°15S 114°54E **61** E1
**Irymple** *Australia* 34°14S 142°8E **63** E3
**Isa Khel** *Pakistan* 32°41N 71°17E **42** C4
**Isaac** → *Australia* 22°55S 149°20E **62** C4
**Isabel** *U.S.A.* 45°24N 101°26W **80** C3
**Isabel, I.** *Mexico* 21°51N 105°55W **86** C3
**Isabela** *Phil.* 6°40N 121°59E **37** C6
**Isabela** *Puerto Rico* 18°30N 67°2W **89** d
**Isabella, Cord.** *Nic.* 13°30N 85°25W **88** D2
**Isabella Ra.** *Australia* 21°0S 121°4E **60** D3
**Isachsen, C.** *Canada* 79°20N 105°28W **69** B10
**Isachsen Mt.** *Antarctica* 72°8S 26°5E **5** D4
**Īsafjarðardjúp** *Iceland* 66°10N 23°0W **8** C2
**Īsafjörður** *Iceland* 66°5N 23°9W **8** C2
**Isagarh** *India* 24°48N 77°51E **42** G7
**Isahaya** *Japan* 32°52N 130°2E **29** H5
**Isan** → *India* 26°51N 80°7E **43** F9
**Isana = Içana** → *Brazil* 0°26N 67°19W **92** C5
**Isar** → *Germany* 48°48N 12°57E **16** D7
**Íschia** *Italy* 40°44N 13°57E **22** D5
**Ischigualasto** △ *Argentina* 30°0S 68°0W **94** B2
**Isdell** → *Australia* 16°27S 124°51E **60** C3
**Ise** *Japan* 34°25N 136°45E **29** G8
**Ise-Shima** △ *Japan* 34°25N 136°48E **29** G8
**Ise-Wan** *Japan* 34°43N 136°43E **29** G8
**Isère** → *France* 44°59N 4°51E **20** D6
**Isérnia** *Italy* 41°36N 14°14E **22** D6
**Isfahan = Eşfahān** *Iran* 32°40N 51°38E **47** C6
**Ishigaki** *Japan* 24°26N 124°10E **29** M2
**Ishigaki-Shima** *Japan* 24°20N 124°10E **29** M2
**Ishikari-Gawa** →
*Japan* 43°15N 141°23E **28** C10
**Ishikari-Sammyaku**
*Japan* 43°30N 143°0E **28** C11
**Ishikari-Wan** *Japan* 43°25N 141°1E **28** C10
**Ishikawa** *Japan* 26°25N 127°49E **29** L3
**Ishikawa** □ *Japan* 36°30N 136°30E **29** F8
**Ishim** *Russia* 56°10N 69°30E **26** D7
**Ishim** → *Russia* 57°45N 71°10E **26** D8
**Ishinomaki** *Japan* 38°32N 141°20E **28** E10
**Ishioka** *Japan* 36°11N 140°16E **29** F10
**Ishkoman** *Pakistan* 36°30N 73°50E **43** A5
**Ishpeming** *U.S.A.* 46°29N 87°40W **80** B10
**Isil Kul** *Russia* 54°55N 71°16E **26** D8
**iSimangaliso** △ *S. Africa* 27°50S 32°32E **57** C5
**Isiro** *Dem. Rep. of the Congo* 2°53N 27°40E **54** D5

**Isisford** *Australia* 24°15S 144°21E **62** C3
**Iskar** → *Bulgaria* 43°45N 24°25E **23** C11
**İskenderun** *Turkey* 36°32N 36°10E **46** B3
**İskenderun Körfezi**
*Turkey* 36°40N 35°50E **19** G6
**Iskut** → *Canada* 56°45N 131°49W **70** B2
**Isla** → *U.K.* 56°32N 3°20W **11** E5
**Isla Coiba** △ *Panama* 7°33N 81°36W **88** E3
**Isla de Salamanca** △
*Colombia* 10°59N 74°40W **89** D5
**Isla Gorge** △ *Australia* 25°10S 149°57E **62** C4
**Isla Isabel** △ *Mexico* 21°54N 105°58W **86** C3
**Isla Tiburón y San Esteban** ◌
*Mexico* 29°0N 112°27W **86** B2
**Isla Vista** *U.S.A.* 34°25N 119°53W **79** L7
**Islam Headworks**
*Pakistan* 29°49N 72°33E **42** E5
**Islamabad** *Pakistan* 33°40N 73°10E **42** C5
**Islamgarh** *Pakistan* 27°51N 70°48E **42** F4
**Islamkot** *Pakistan* 24°42N 70°13E **42** G4
**Islampur** *Bihar, India* 25°9N 85°12E **43** G11
**Islampur** *Maharashtra, India* 17°2N 74°20E **44** F2
**Islampur** *Paschimbanga, India* 26°16N 88°12E **43** F13
**Island = Iceland** ■ *Europe* 64°45N 19°0W **8** D4
**Island L.** *Canada* 53°47N 94°25W **71** C10
**Island Lagoon** *Australia* 31°30S 136°40E **63** E2
**Island Pond** *U.S.A.* 44°49N 71°53W **83** B13
**Islands, B. of** *Canada* 49°11N 58°15W **73** C8
**Islands, B. of** *N.Z.* 35°15S 174°6E **59** A5
**Islay** *U.K.* 55°46N 6°10W **11** F2
**Isle** → *France* 44°55N 0°15W **20** D3
**Isle aux Morts** *Canada* 47°35N 59°0W **73** C8
**Isle of Wight** □ *U.K.* 50°41N 1°17W **13** G6
**Isle Royale** △ *U.S.A.* 48°0N 88°55W **80** B9
**Isleton** *U.S.A.* 38°10N 121°37W **78** G5
**Ismail = Izmayil** *Ukraine* 45°22N 28°46E **17** F15
**Ismâ'ilîya** *Egypt* 30°37N 32°18E **53** B12
**Isna** *Egypt* 25°17N 32°30E **53** C12
**Isojärvi** △ *Finland* 61°40N 25°0E **8** F21
**Isparta** *Turkey* 37°47N 30°30E **19** G5
**Íspica** *Italy* 36°47N 14°55E **22** F6
**Israel** ■ *Asia* 32°0N 34°50E **48** D3
**Issoire** *France* 45°32N 3°15E **20** D5
**Issyk-Kul = Balykchy**
*Kyrgyzstan* 42°26N 76°12E **30** C4
**Issyk-Kul, Ozero = Ysyk-Köl**
*Kyrgyzstan* 42°25N 77°15E **26** E8
**Istiea** *Greece* 38°57N 23°9E **23** E10
**Isto, Mt.** *U.S.A.* 69°12N 143°48W **74** B11
**Istokpoga, L.** *U.S.A.* 27°23N 81°17W **85** H14
**Istra** *Croatia* 45°10N 14°0E **16** F7
**İstres** *France* 43°31N 4°59E **20** E6
**Istria = Istra** *Croatia* 45°10N 14°0E **16** F7
**Itá** *Paraguay* 25°29S 57°21W **94** B4
**Itaberaba** *Brazil* 12°32S 40°18W **93** F10
**Itabira** *Brazil* 19°37S 43°13W **93** G10
**Itabirito** *Brazil* 20°15S 43°48W **95** A7
**Itabuna** *Brazil* 14°48S 39°16W **93** F11
**Itacaunas** → *Brazil* 5°21S 49°8W **93** E9
**Itacoatiara** *Brazil* 3°8S 58°25W **92** D7
**Itaguaí** *Brazil* 22°15S 43°46W **95** A7
**Itaipú, Represa de** *Brazil* 25°30S 54°30W **95** B5
**Itäisen Suomenlahti** △
*Finland* 60°25N 27°15E **8** F22
**Itaituba** *Brazil* 4°10S 55°50W **93** D7
**Itajaí** *Brazil* 27°50S 48°39W **95** B6
**Itajubá** *Brazil* 22°24S 45°30W **95** A6
**Italy** ■ *Europe* 42°0N 13°0E **22** C5
**Itamaraju** *Brazil* 17°4S 39°32W **93** G11
**Itapecuru Mirim** *Brazil* 3°24S 44°20W **93** D10
**Itaperuna** *Brazil* 21°10S 41°54W **95** A7
**Itapetininga** *Brazil* 23°36S 48°7W **95** A6
**Itapeva** *Brazil* 23°59S 48°59W **95** A6
**Itapicuru** → *Bahia, Brazil* 11°47S 37°32W **93** F11
**Itapicuru** → *Maranhão, Brazil* 2°52S 44°12W **93** D10
**Itapipoca** *Brazil* 3°30S 39°35W **93** D11
**Itapuá** □ *Paraguay* 26°40S 55°40W **95** B4
**Itaquí** *Brazil* 29°8S 56°30W **94** B4
**Itararé** *Brazil* 24°6S 49°23W **95** A6
**Itarsi** *India* 22°36N 77°51E **42** H7
**Itati** *Argentina* 27°16S 58°15W **94** B4
**Itatiaia** △ *Brazil* 22°25S 44°38W **95** A7
**Itchen** → *U.K.* 50°55N 1°22W **13** G6
**Itezhi Tezhi, L.** *Zambia* 15°30S 25°30E **55** H5
**Ithaca = Ithaki** *Greece* 38°25N 20°40E **23** E9
**Ithaca** *U.S.A.* 42°27N 76°30W **83** D8
**Ithaki** *Greece* 38°25N 20°40E **23** E9
**Itiquira** → *Brazil* 17°18S 56°44W **93** G7
**Itiyuro** → *Argentina* 22°40S 63°50W **94** A3
**Itō** *Japan* 34°58N 139°5E **29** G9
**Itoigawa** *Japan* 37°2N 137°51E **29** F8
**Itonamas** → *Bolivia* 12°28S 64°24W **92** F6
**Ittoqqortoormiit** *Greenland* 70°20N 23°0W **4** B6
**Itu** *Brazil* 23°17S 47°15W **95** A6
**Itu Aba I.** *S. China Sea* 10°23N 114°21E **36** B4
**Ituiutaba** *Brazil* 19°0S 49°25W **93** G9
**Itumbiara** *Brazil* 18°20S 49°10W **93** G9
**Iturbe** *Argentina* 23°0S 65°25W **94** A2
**Iturup, Ostrov** *Russia* 45°0N 148°0E **27** E15
**Ituxi** → *Brazil* 7°18S 64°51W **92** E6
**Itzehoe** *Germany* 53°55N 9°31E **16** B5
**Ivaí** → *Brazil* 23°18S 53°42W **95** A5
**Ivalo** *Finland* 68°38N 27°35E **8** B22
**Ivalojoki** → *Finland* 68°40N 27°40E **8** B22
**Ivanava** *Belarus* 52°7N 25°29E **17** B13
**Ivanhoe** *Australia* 32°56S 144°20E **63** E3
**Ivanhoe** *Canada* 44°23N 77°26W **82** B7
**Ivanhoe** *Calif., U.S.A.* 36°23N 119°13W **78** J7
**Ivanhoe** *Minn., U.S.A.* 44°28N 96°15W **80** C5
**Ivano-Frankivsk**
*Ukraine* 48°40N 24°40E **17** D13
**Ivanovo = Ivanava**
*Belarus* 52°7N 25°29E **17** B13

**Ivanovo** *Russia* 57°5N 41°0E **18** C7
**Ivatsevichy** *Belarus* 52°43N 25°21E **17** B13
**Ivdel** *Russia* 60°42N 60°24E **18** B11
**Iveragh Pen.** *Ireland* 51°52N 10°15W **10** E1
**Ivinheima** → *Brazil* 23°14S 53°42W **95** A5
**Ivinhema** *Brazil* 22°10S 53°37W **95** A5
**Ivory Coast = Côte d'Ivoire** ■
*Africa* 7°30N 5°0W **52** G4
**Ivory Coast** *W. Afr.* 4°20N 5°0W **52** H4
**Ivrea** *Italy* 45°28N 7°52E **20** D7
**Ivujivik** *Canada* 62°24N 77°55W **69** E16
**Ivvavik** △ *Canada* 69°6N 139°30W **68** D4
**Ivybridge** *U.K.* 50°23N 3°56W **13** G4
**Iwaizumi** *Japan* 39°50N 141°45E **28** E10
**Iwaki** *Japan* 37°3N 140°55E **29** F10
**Iwakuni** *Japan* 34°15N 132°8E **29** G6
**Iwamizawa** *Japan* 43°12N 141°46E **28** C10
**Iwanai** *Japan* 42°58N 140°30E **28** C10
**Iwata** *Japan* 34°42N 137°51E **29** G8
**Iwate** □ *Japan* 39°30N 141°30E **28** E10
**Iwate-San** *Japan* 39°51N 141°0E **28** E10
**Iwo** *Nigeria* 7°39N 4°9E **52** G6
**Ixiamas** *Bolivia* 13°50S 68°5W **92** F5
**Ixopo** *S. Africa* 30°11S 30°5E **57** D5
**Ixtepec** *Mexico* 16°34N 95°6W **87** D5
**Ixtlán del Río** *Mexico* 21°2N 104°22W **86** C4
**Iyo** *Japan* 33°45S 132°45E **29** H6
**Izabal, L. de** *Guatemala* 15°30N 89°10W **88** C2
**Izamal** *Mexico* 20°56N 89°1W **87** C7
**Izena-Shima** *Japan* 26°56N 127°56E **29** L3
**Izhevsk** *Russia* 56°51N 53°14E **18** C9
**Izhma** → *Russia* 65°19N 52°54E **18** A9
**Izmayil** *Ukraine* 45°22N 28°46E **17** F15
**İzmir** *Turkey* 38°25N 27°8E **23** E12
**İzmit = Kocaeli** *Turkey* 40°45N 29°50E **19** F4
**İznik Gölü** *Turkey* 40°27N 29°30E **23** D13
**Izra** *Syria* 32°51N 36°15E **48** C5
**Izu-Hantō** *Japan* 34°45N 139°0E **29** G9
**Izu-Shotō** *Japan* 34°30N 140°0E **29** G10
**Izúcar de Matamoros**
*Mexico* 18°36N 98°28W **87** D5
**Izumi** *Japan* 32°5N 130°22E **29** H5
**Izumi-Sano** *Japan* 34°23N 135°18E **29** G7
**Izumo** *Japan* 35°20N 132°46E **29** G6
**Izyaslav** *Ukraine* 50°5N 26°50E **17** C14**

**J**

**J.F.K. Int.** ✈ (JFK)
*U.S.A.* 40°38N 73°47W **83** F11
**J. Strom Thurmond L.**
*U.S.A.* 33°40N 82°12W **85** E13
**Ja-ela** *Sri Lanka* 7°5N 79°53E **45** L4
**Jabalpur** *India* 23°9N 79°58E **43** H8
**Jabālya** *Gaza Strip* 31°32N 34°29E **48** D3
**Jabbūl** *Syria* 36°4N 37°30E **46** B3
**Jabiru** *Australia* 12°40S 132°53E **60** B5
**Jablah** *Syria* 35°20N 36°0E **46** C3
**Jablonec nad Nisou**
*Czechia* 50°43N 15°10E **16** C8
**Jaboatão** *Brazil* 8°7S 35°1W **93** E11
**Jaboticabal** *Brazil* 21°15S 48°17W **95** A6
**Jaca** *Spain* 42°35N 0°33W **21** A5
**Jacareí** *Brazil* 23°20S 46°0W **95** A6
**Jacarèzinho** *Brazil* 23°5S 49°58W **95** A6
**Jack River** △ *Australia* 14°58S 144°19E **62** A3
**Jackman** *U.S.A.* 45°37N 70°15W **81** C18
**Jacksboro** *U.S.A.* 33°13N 98°10W **84** E5
**Jackson** *Barbados* 13°7N 59°36W **89** g
**Jackson** *Ala., U.S.A.* 31°31N 87°53W **85** F11
**Jackson** *Calif., U.S.A.* 38°21N 120°46W **78** G6
**Jackson** *Ky., U.S.A.* 37°33N 83°23W **81** G12
**Jackson** *Mich., U.S.A.* 42°15N 84°24W **81** D11
**Jackson** *Minn., U.S.A.* 43°37N 95°1W **80** D6
**Jackson** *Miss., U.S.A.* 32°18N 90°12W **85** E9
**Jackson** *Mo., U.S.A.* 37°23N 89°40W **80** G9
**Jackson** *N.H., U.S.A.* 44°10N 71°11W **83** B13
**Jackson** *Ohio, U.S.A.* 39°3N 82°39W **81** F12
**Jackson** *Tenn., U.S.A.* 35°37N 88°49W **85** D10
**Jackson** *Wyo., U.S.A.* 43°29N 110°46W **76** E8
**Jackson B.** *N.Z.* 43°58S 168°42E **59** E2
**Jackson L.** *U.S.A.* 43°52N 110°36W **76** E8
**Jacksons** *N.Z.* 42°46S 171°32E **59** E3
**Jackson's Arm** *Canada* 49°52N 56°47W **73** C8
**Jacksonville** *Ala., U.S.A.* 33°49N 85°46W **85** E12
**Jacksonville** *Calif., U.S.A.* 37°52N 120°24W **78** H6
**Jacksonville** *Fla., U.S.A.* 30°20N 81°39W **85** F14
**Jacksonville** *Ill., U.S.A.* 39°44N 90°14W **80** F8
**Jacksonville** *N.C., U.S.A.* 34°45N 77°26W **85** D16
**Jacksonville** *Tex., U.S.A.* 31°58N 95°17W **84** F7
**Jacksonville Beach**
*U.S.A.* 30°17N 81°24W **85** F14
**Jacmel** *Haiti* 18°14N 72°32W **89** C5
**Jacob Lake** *U.S.A.* 36°43N 112°13W **77** H7
**Jacobabad** *Pakistan* 28°20N 68°29E **42** E3
**Jacobina** *Brazil* 11°11S 40°30W **93** F10
**Jacques-Cartier, Dét. de**
*Canada* 50°0N 63°30W **73** C7
**Jacques-Cartier, Mt.**
*Canada* 48°57N 66°0W **73** C6
**Jacques-Cartier** →
*Canada* 47°15N 71°33W **73** C5
**Jacuí** → *Brazil* 30°2S 51°15W **95** C5
**Jacumba** *U.S.A.* 32°37N 116°11W **79** N10
**Jacundá** → *Brazil* 1°57S 50°26W **93** D8
**Jadcherla** *India* 16°45N 78°9E **44** F4
**Jade City** *Canada* 59°15N 129°37W **70** B3
**Jade Dragon Snow Mt. = Yulong**
**Xueshan** *China* 27°6N 100°10E **34** D3
**Jade Mt. = Yü Shan**
*Taiwan* 23°25N 120°52E **35** F13
**Jaén** *Peru* 5°25S 78°40W **92** E3
**Jaén** *Spain* 37°44N 3°43W **21** D4
**Jafarabad** *India* 20°52N 71°22E **42** J4
**Jaffa = Tel Aviv-Yafo**
*Israel* 32°4N 34°48E **48** C3

| | | |
|---|---|---|
| Jaffa, C. *Australia* | 36°58S 139°40E | 63 F2 |
| Jaffna *Sri Lanka* | 9°45N 80°2E | 45 K5 |
| Jaffrey *U.S.A.* | 42°49N 72°2W | 83 D12 |
| Jagadhri *India* | 30°10N 77°20E | 42 D7 |
| Jagadishpur *India* | 25°30N 84°21E | 43 G11 |
| Jagat *Nepal* | 28°19N 84°53E | 43 E11 |
| Jagdalpur *India* | 19°3N 82°0E | 44 E6 |
| Jagdaqi *China* | 50°25N 124°7E | 31 A13 |
| Jagersfontein *S. Africa* | 29°44S 25°27E | 56 C4 |
| Jaghīn → *Iran* | 27°17N 57°13E | 47 E8 |
| Jagodina *Serbia* | 44°5N 21°15E | 23 C9 |
| Jagraon *India* | 30°50N 75°25E | 42 D6 |
| Jagtial *India* | 18°50N 79°0E | 44 E4 |
| Jaguariaíva *Brazil* | 24°10S 49°50W | 95 A6 |
| Jaguaribe → *Brazil* | 4°25S 37°45W | 93 D11 |
| Jagüey Grande *Cuba* | 22°35N 81°7W | 88 B3 |
| Jahanabad *India* | 25°13N 84°59E | 43 G11 |
| Jahazpur *India* | 25°37N 75°17E | 42 G6 |
| Jahrom *Iran* | 28°30N 53°31E | 47 D7 |
| Jaigarh *India* | 17°17N 73°13E | 44 F1 |
| Jaijon *India* | 31°21N 76°9E | 42 D7 |
| Jailolo *Indonesia* | 1°5N 127°30E | 37 D7 |
| Jailolo, Selat *Indonesia* | 0°5N 129°5E | 37 D7 |
| Jaipur *India* | 27°0N 75°50E | 42 F6 |
| Jais *India* | 26°15N 81°32E | 43 F9 |
| Jaisalmer *India* | 26°55N 70°54E | 42 F4 |
| Jaisinghnagar *India* | 23°38N 78°34E | 43 H8 |
| Jaitaran *India* | 26°12N 73°56E | 42 G5 |
| Jaithari *India* | 23°14N 78°37E | 43 H8 |
| Jajarkot *Nepal* | 28°42N 82°14E | 43 E10 |
| Jājarm *Iran* | 36°58N 56°27E | 47 B8 |
| Jajpur *India* | 20°53N 86°22E | 44 D8 |
| Jakam → *India* | 23°54N 74°13E | 42 H6 |
| Jakarta Sukarno-Hatta Int. ✈ | | |
| (CGK) *Indonesia* | 6°7S 106°40E | 37 G12 |
| Jakhal *India* | 29°48N 75°50E | 42 E6 |
| Jakhau *India* | 23°13N 68°43E | 42 H3 |
| Jakobstad = Pietarsaari | | |
| *Finland* | 63°40N 22°43E | 8 E20 |
| Jal *U.S.A.* | 32°7N 103°12W | 77 K12 |
| Jalājil *Si. Arabia* | 25°40N 45°27E | 46 E5 |
| Jalālābād *Afghan.* | 34°30N 70°29E | 42 B4 |
| Jalalabad *India* | 27°41N 79°42E | 43 F8 |
| Jalalpur Jattan *Pakistan* | 32°38N 74°11E | 42 C6 |
| Jalama *U.S.A.* | 34°29N 120°29W | 79 L6 |
| Jalandhar *India* | 31°20N 75°40E | 42 D6 |
| Jalapa *Guatemala* | 14°39N 89°59W | 88 D2 |
| Jalapa Enríquez = Xalapa | | |
| *Mexico* | 19°32N 96°55W | 87 D5 |
| Jalasjärvi *Finland* | 62°29N 22°47E | 8 E20 |
| Jalaun *India* | 26°8N 79°25E | 43 F8 |
| Jaldhaka → *Bangla.* | 26°16N 89°16E | 43 F13 |
| Jalesar *India* | 27°29N 78°19E | 42 F8 |
| Jaleswar *Nepal* | 26°38N 85°48E | 43 F11 |
| Jalgaon *India* | 21°0N 75°42E | 44 D2 |
| Jalibah *Iraq* | 30°35N 46°32E | 46 D5 |
| Jalingo *Nigeria* | 8°55N 11°25E | 53 G8 |
| Jalisco □ *Mexico* | 20°20N 103°40W | 86 D4 |
| Jalkot *Pakistan* | 35°14N 73°24E | 43 B5 |
| Jalna *India* | 19°48N 75°38E | 44 E2 |
| Jalón → *Spain* | 41°47N 1°4W | 21 B5 |
| Jalor *India* | 25°21N 72°37E | 42 G5 |
| Jalpa *Mexico* | 21°38N 102°58W | 86 C4 |
| Jalpaiguri *India* | 26°32N 88°46E | 41 F16 |
| Jalpan *Mexico* | 21°14N 99°29W | 87 C5 |
| Jaluit I. *Marshall Is.* | 6°0N 169°30E | 64 G8 |
| Jalūlā *Iraq* | 34°16N 45°10E | 46 C5 |
| Jamaame *Somalia* | 0°4N 42°44E | 49 G3 |
| Jamaica ■ *W. Indies* | 18°10N 77°30W | 88 a |
| Jamalpur *Bangla.* | 24°52N 89°56E | 41 G16 |
| Jamalpur *India* | 25°18N 86°28E | 43 G12 |
| Jamalpurganj *India* | 23°2N 87°59E | 43 H13 |
| Jamanxim → *Brazil* | 4°43S 56°18W | 93 D7 |
| Jambewangi *Indonesia* | 8°11S 114°27E | 37 J17 |
| Jambi *Indonesia* | 1°38S 103°30E | 36 E2 |
| Jambi □ *Indonesia* | 1°30S 102°30E | 36 E2 |
| Jambongan, Pulau | | |
| *Malaysia* | 6°45N 117°20E | 36 C5 |
| Jambusar *India* | 22°3N 72°51E | 42 H5 |
| James → *S. Dak., U.S.A.* | 42°52N 97°18W | 80 D5 |
| James → *Va., U.S.A.* | 36°56N 76°27W | 81 G15 |
| James B. *Canada* | 54°0N 80°0W | 72 B3 |
| James Ranges *Australia* | 24°10S 132°30E | 60 D5 |
| James Ross I. *Antarctica* | 63°58S 57°50W | 5 C18 |
| James Ross Str. *Canada* | 69°40N 96°10W | 68 D12 |
| Jamesabad *India* | 25°17N 69°15E | 42 G3 |
| Jamestown *Australia* | 33°10S 138°32E | 63 E2 |
| Jamestown *S. Africa* | 31°6S 26°45E | 56 D4 |
| Jamestown *N. Dak.,* | | |
| *U.S.A.* | 46°54N 98°42W | 80 B4 |
| Jamestown *N.Y., U.S.A.* | 42°6N 79°14W | 82 D5 |
| Jamestown *Pa., U.S.A.* | 41°29N 80°27W | 82 E4 |
| Jamīlābād *Iran* | 34°24N 48°28E | 47 C6 |
| Jamira → *India* | 21°35N 88°28E | 43 J13 |
| Jamkhandi *India* | 16°30N 75°15E | 44 F2 |
| Jamkhed *India* | 18°43N 75°19E | 44 E2 |
| Jammalamadugu *India* | 14°51N 78°25E | 45 G4 |
| Jammu *India* | 32°43N 74°54E | 42 C6 |
| Jammu & Kashmir □ | | |
| *India* | 34°25N 77°0E | 43 B7 |
| Jamnagar *India* | 22°30N 70°6E | 42 H4 |
| Jamner *India* | 20°45N 75°52E | 44 D2 |
| Jamni → *India* | 25°13N 78°35E | 43 G8 |
| Jampur *Pakistan* | 29°39N 70°40E | 42 E4 |
| Jamrud *Pakistan* | 33°59N 71°24E | 42 C4 |
| Jämsä *Finland* | 61°53N 25°10E | 8 F21 |
| Jamshedpur *India* | 22°44N 86°12E | 43 H12 |
| Jamtara *India* | 23°59N 86°49E | 43 H12 |
| Jämtland *Sweden* | 63°31N 14°0E | 8 E16 |
| Jan L. *Canada* | 54°56N 102°55W | 71 C8 |
| Jan Mayen *Arctic* | 71°0N 9°0W | 4 B7 |
| Janakpur *Nepal* | 26°42N 85°55E | 43 F11 |
| Janaúba *Brazil* | 15°48S 43°19W | 93 G10 |
| Jand *Pakistan* | 33°30N 72°6E | 42 C5 |
| Jandanku ✈ *Australia* | 16°20S 135°45E | 62 B2 |
| Jandaq *Iran* | 34°3N 54°22E | 47 C7 |
| Jandola *Pakistan* | 32°20N 70°9E | 42 C4 |
| Jandowae *Australia* | 26°45S 151°7E | 63 D5 |
| Janesville *U.S.A.* | 42°41N 89°1W | 80 D9 |
| Jang Bogo *Antarctica* | 74°37S 164°12E | 5 D11 |

| | | |
|---|---|---|
| Jangamo *Mozam.* | 24°6S 35°21E | 57 B6 |
| Janghai *India* | 25°33N 82°19E | 43 G10 |
| Jangheung *S. Korea* | 34°41N 126°52E | 33 G14 |
| Jangipur *India* | 24°28N 88°4E | 43 G12 |
| Jangoon *India* | 17°44N 79°5E | 44 F4 |
| Janjanbureh *Gambia* | 13°30N 14°47W | 52 F3 |
| Janjgir *India* | 22°1N 82°34E | 43 J10 |
| Janos *Mexico* | 30°54N 108°10W | 86 A3 |
| Januária *Brazil* | 15°25S 44°25W | 93 G10 |
| Janub Sīnî □ *Egypt* | 29°30N 33°50E | 48 F2 |
| Janwada *India* | 18°0N 77°29E | 44 E3 |
| Jaora *India* | 23°40N 75°10E | 42 H6 |
| Japan ■ *Asia* | 36°0N 136°0E | 29 G8 |
| Japan, Sea of *Asia* | 40°0N 135°0E | 28 E7 |
| Japan Trench *Pac. Oc.* | 32°0N 142°0E | 64 D6 |
| Japen = Yapen *Indonesia* | 1°50S 136°0E | 37 E9 |
| Japla *India* | 24°33N 84°1E | 43 G11 |
| Japurá → *Brazil* | 3°8S 65°46W | 92 D5 |
| Jaquarão *Brazil* | 32°34S 53°23W | 95 C5 |
| Jaqué *Panama* | 7°27N 78°8W | 88 E4 |
| Jarābulus *Syria* | 36°49N 38°1E | 46 B3 |
| Jaraguá do Sul *Brazil* | 26°29S 49°4W | 95 B6 |
| Jarama → *Spain* | 40°24N 3°32W | 21 B4 |
| Jaranwala *Pakistan* | 31°15N 73°26E | 42 D5 |
| Jarash *Jordan* | 32°17N 35°54E | 48 C4 |
| Jarash □ *Jordan* | 32°17N 35°54E | 48 C4 |
| Jardim *Brazil* | 21°28S 56°2W | 94 A4 |
| Jardín América *Argentina* | 27°3S 55°14W | 95 B4 |
| Jardine River △ *Australia* | 11°9S 142°21E | 62 A3 |
| Jardines de la Reina, Arch. de los | | |
| *Cuba* | 20°50N 78°50W | 88 B4 |
| Jargalang *China* | 43°5N 122°55E | 33 C12 |
| Jari → *Brazil* | 1°9S 51°54W | 93 D8 |
| Jarīr, W. al → *Si. Arabia* | 25°38N 42°30E | 46 E4 |
| Jarosław *Poland* | 50°2N 22°42E | 17 C12 |
| Jarrahdale *Australia* | 32°24S 116°5E | 61 F2 |
| Jarrahi → *Iran* | 30°49N 48°48E | 47 D6 |
| Jartai *China* | 39°45N 105°48E | 32 E3 |
| Jarud Qi *China* | 44°28N 120°50E | 33 B11 |
| Järvenpää *Finland* | 60°29N 25°5E | 8 F21 |
| Jarvis *Canada* | 42°53N 80°6W | 82 D4 |
| Jarvis I. *Pac. Oc.* | 0°15S 160°5W | 65 H11 |
| Jarwa *India* | 27°38N 82°30E | 43 F10 |
| Jasdan *India* | 22°2N 71°12E | 42 H4 |
| Jashpurnagar *India* | 22°54N 84°9E | 43 H11 |
| Jasidih *India* | 24°31N 86°39E | 43 G12 |
| Jāsimīyah *Iraq* | 33°45N 44°41E | 46 C5 |
| Jasin *Malaysia* | 2°20N 102°26E | 39 L4 |
| Jāsk *Iran* | 25°38N 57°45E | 47 E8 |
| Jasło *Poland* | 49°45N 21°30E | 17 D11 |
| Jaso *India* | 24°30N 80°29E | 43 G9 |
| Jasper *Alta., Canada* | 52°55N 118°5W | 70 C5 |
| Jasper *Ont., Canada* | 44°52N 75°57W | 83 B9 |
| Jasper *Ala., U.S.A.* | 33°50N 87°17W | 85 E11 |
| Jasper *Fla., U.S.A.* | 30°31N 82°57W | 85 F13 |
| Jasper *Ind., U.S.A.* | 38°24N 86°56W | 80 F10 |
| Jasper *Tex., U.S.A.* | 30°56N 94°1W | 84 F7 |
| Jasper △ *Canada* | 52°50N 118°8W | 70 C5 |
| Jasrasar *India* | 27°43N 73°49E | 42 F5 |
| Jászberény *Hungary* | 47°30N 19°55E | 17 E10 |
| Jataí *Brazil* | 17°58S 51°48W | 93 G8 |
| Jath *India* | 17°3N 75°13E | 44 F2 |
| Jati *India* | 24°20N 68°19E | 42 G3 |
| Jatibarang *Indonesia* | 6°28S 108°18E | 37 G13 |
| Jatiluwih *Indonesia* | 8°23S 115°8E | 37 J18 |
| Játiva = Xátiva *Spain* | 38°59N 0°32W | 21 C5 |
| Jaú *Brazil* | 22°10S 48°30W | 95 A6 |
| Jauja *Peru* | 11°45S 75°15W | 92 F3 |
| Jaunpur *India* | 25°46N 82°44E | 43 G10 |
| Java = Jawa *Indonesia* | 7°0S 110°0E | 36 F3 |
| Java Sea *Indonesia* | 4°35S 107°15E | 36 E3 |
| Java Trench *Ind. Oc.* | 9°0S 105°0E | 36 F3 |
| Javadi Hills *India* | 12°40N 78°40E | 45 H4 |
| Javla *India* | 17°18N 75°9E | 44 F2 |
| Jawa *Indonesia* | 7°0S 110°0E | 36 F3 |
| Jawa Barat □ *Indonesia* | 7°0S 107°0E | 37 G12 |
| Jawa Tengah □ *Indonesia* | 7°0S 110°0E | 37 G14 |
| Jawa Timur □ *Indonesia* | 8°0S 113°0E | 37 G15 |
| Jawad *India* | 24°36N 74°51E | 42 G6 |
| Jawhar *India* | 19°55N 73°14E | 44 E1 |
| Jawhar *Somalia* | 2°48N 45°30E | 49 G4 |
| Jawoyn ✦ *Australia* | 14°16S 132°28E | 60 B5 |
| Jay Peak *U.S.A.* | 44°55N 72°32W | 83 B12 |
| Jaya, Puncak *Indonesia* | 3°57S 137°17E | 37 E9 |
| Jayanti *India* | 26°45N 89°40E | 41 F16 |
| Jayapura *Indonesia* | 2°28S 140°38E | 37 E10 |
| Jayawijaya, Pegunungan | | |
| *Indonesia* | 5°0S 139°0E | 37 F9 |
| Jaynagar *India* | 26°43N 86°9E | 43 F12 |
| Jaypur = Jeypore *India* | 18°50N 82°38E | 44 E6 |
| Jayrūd *Syria* | 33°49N 36°44E | 46 C3 |
| Jayton *U.S.A.* | 33°15N 100°34W | 84 E4 |
| Jāz Mūrīān, Hāmūn-e | | |
| *Iran* | 27°20N 58°55E | 47 E8 |
| Jazīreh-ye Shīf *Iran* | 29°4N 50°54E | 47 D6 |
| Jazminal *Mexico* | 24°52N 101°24W | 86 C4 |
| Jazzīn *Lebanon* | 33°31N 35°35E | 48 B4 |
| Jean *U.S.A.* | 35°47N 115°20W | 79 K11 |
| Jean Marie River | | |
| *Canada* | 61°32N 120°38W | 70 A4 |
| Jean-Rabel *Haiti* | 19°50N 73°5W | 89 C5 |
| Jeanerette *U.S.A.* | 29°55N 91°40W | 84 G9 |
| Jeanette, Ostrov = Zhannetty, | | |
| Ostrov *Russia* | 76°43N 158°0E | 27 B16 |
| Jeannette *U.S.A.* | 40°20N 79°36W | 82 F5 |
| Jebāl Bārez, Kūh-e *Iran* | 28°30N 58°20E | 47 D8 |
| Jebel, Bahr el → | | |
| *South Sudan* | 9°30N 30°25E | 53 G12 |
| Jebel Ali = Mina' Jabal 'Alī | | |
| *U.A.E.* | 25°2N 55°8E | 47 E7 |
| Jecheon *S. Korea* | 37°8N 128°12E | 33 F15 |
| Jedburgh *U.K.* | 55°29N 2°33W | 11 F6 |
| Jedda = Jiddah *Si. Arabia* | 21°29N 39°10E | 49 C2 |
| Jeddore L. *Canada* | 48°3N 55°55W | 73 C8 |
| Jędrzejów *Poland* | 50°35N 20°15E | 17 C11 |
| Jefferson *Iowa, U.S.A.* | 42°1N 94°23W | 80 D6 |
| Jefferson *Ohio, U.S.A.* | 41°44N 80°46W | 82 E4 |
| Jefferson *Tex., U.S.A.* | 32°46N 94°21W | 84 E7 |
| Jefferson, Mt. *Nev.,* | | |
| *U.S.A.* | 38°47N 116°56W | 76 G5 |

| | | |
|---|---|---|
| Jefferson, Mt. *Oreg.,* | | |
| *U.S.A.* | 44°41N 121°48W | 76 D3 |
| Jefferson City *Mo., U.S.A.* | 38°34N 92°10W | 80 F7 |
| Jefferson City *Tenn.,* | | |
| *U.S.A.* | 36°7N 83°30W | 85 C13 |
| Jeffersontown *U.S.A.* | 38°12N 85°35W | 81 F11 |
| Jeffersonville *U.S.A.* | 38°17N 85°44W | 81 F11 |
| Jeffrey City *U.S.A.* | 42°30N 107°49W | 76 E10 |
| Jega *Nigeria* | 12°15N 4°23E | 52 F6 |
| Jeju *S. Korea* | 33°31N 126°32E | 33 H14 |
| Jeju-do *S. Korea* | 33°29N 126°34E | 33 H14 |
| Jeju Haehyop *S. Korea* | 33°50N 126°30E | 33 H14 |
| Jēkabpils *Latvia* | 56°29N 25°57E | 9 H21 |
| Jekyll I. *U.S.A.* | 31°4N 81°25W | 85 F14 |
| Jelenia Góra *Poland* | 50°50N 15°45E | 16 C8 |
| Jelgava *Latvia* | 56°41N 23°49E | 9 H20 |
| Jemaluang *Malaysia* | 2°16N 103°52E | 39 L4 |
| Jember *Indonesia* | 8°11S 113°41E | 37 H15 |
| Jena *Germany* | 50°54N 11°35E | 16 C6 |
| Jena *U.S.A.* | 31°41N 92°8W | 84 F8 |
| Jengish Chokusu = Pobedy, Pik | | |
| *Asia* | 42°0N 79°58E | 30 C4 |
| Jenin *West Bank* | 32°28N 35°18E | 48 C4 |
| Jenkins *U.S.A.* | 37°10N 82°38W | 81 G12 |
| Jenner *U.S.A.* | 38°27N 123°7W | 78 G3 |
| Jennings *U.S.A.* | 30°13N 92°40W | 84 F8 |
| Jeong-eup *S. Korea* | 35°35N 126°50E | 33 G14 |
| Jeongseon *S. Korea* | 37°20N 128°45E | 33 F15 |
| Jeonju *S. Korea* | 35°50N 127°4E | 33 G14 |
| Jepara *Indonesia* | 7°40S 109°14E | 37 G14 |
| Jeparit *Australia* | 36°8S 142°1E | 63 F3 |
| Jequié *Brazil* | 13°51S 40°5W | 93 F10 |
| Jequitinhonha *Brazil* | 16°30S 41°0W | 93 G10 |
| Jequitinhonha → | | |
| *Brazil* | 15°51S 38°53W | 93 G11 |
| Jerada *Morocco* | 34°17N 2°10W | 52 B5 |
| Jerantut *Malaysia* | 3°56N 102°22E | 39 L4 |
| Jérémie *Haiti* | 18°40N 74°10W | 89 C5 |
| Jerez, Pta. *Mexico* | 22°58N 97°40W | 87 C5 |
| Jerez de García Salinas | | |
| *Mexico* | 22°39N 103°0W | 86 C4 |
| Jerez de la Frontera *Spain* | 36°41N 6°7W | 21 D2 |
| Jerez de los Caballeros | | |
| *Spain* | 38°20N 6°45W | 21 C2 |
| Jericho = El Arīḥā | | |
| *West Bank* | 31°52N 35°27E | 48 D4 |
| Jericho *Australia* | 23°38S 146°6E | 62 C4 |
| Jerid, Chott el = Djerid, Chott | | |
| *Tunisia* | 33°42N 8°30E | 52 B7 |
| Jerilderie *Australia* | 35°20S 145°41E | 63 F4 |
| Jermyn *U.S.A.* | 41°32N 75°33W | 83 E9 |
| Jerome *U.S.A.* | 42°44N 114°31W | 76 E6 |
| Jerramungup *Australia* | 33°55S 118°55E | 61 F2 |
| Jersey *U.K.* | 49°11N 2°7W | 13 H5 |
| Jersey Shore *U.S.A.* | 41°12N 77°15W | 82 E7 |
| Jerseyville *U.S.A.* | 39°7N 90°20W | 80 F8 |
| Jervis B. *Australia* | 35°8S 150°46E | 63 F5 |
| Jervis Inlet *Canada* | 50°0N 123°57W | 70 C4 |
| Jesi = Iesi *Italy* | 43°31N 13°14E | 22 C5 |
| Jessore *Bangla.* | 23°10N 89°10E | 41 H16 |
| Jesup *U.S.A.* | 31°36N 81°53W | 85 F14 |
| Jesús Carranza *Mexico* | 17°26N 95°2W | 87 D5 |
| Jesús María *Argentina* | 30°59S 64°5W | 94 C3 |
| Jetmore *U.S.A.* | 38°4N 99°54W | 80 F4 |
| Jetpur *India* | 21°45N 70°10E | 42 J4 |
| Jeumont *France* | 50°18N 4°7E | 15 D5 |
| Jevnaker *Norway* | 60°15N 10°26E | 9 F14 |
| Jewett *U.S.A.* | 40°22N 81°2W | 82 F3 |
| Jewett City *U.S.A.* | 41°36N 71°59W | 83 E13 |
| Jeyḥūnābād *Iran* | 34°58N 48°59E | 47 C6 |
| Jeypore *India* | 18°50N 82°38E | 44 E6 |
| Jha Jha *India* | 24°46N 86°22E | 43 G12 |
| Jhaarkand = Jharkhand □ | | |
| *India* | 24°0N 85°50E | 43 H11 |
| Jhabua *India* | 22°46N 74°36E | 42 H6 |
| Jhajjar *India* | 28°37N 76°42E | 42 E7 |
| Jhal *Pakistan* | 28°17N 67°27E | 42 E2 |
| Jhal Jhao *Pakistan* | 26°20N 65°35E | 40 F4 |
| Jhalawar *India* | 24°40N 76°10E | 42 G7 |
| Jhalida *India* | 23°22N 85°58E | 43 H11 |
| Jhalrapatan *India* | 24°33N 76°10E | 42 G7 |
| Jhang Maghiana | | |
| *Pakistan* | 31°15N 72°22E | 42 D5 |
| Jhang Sadr = Jhang Maghiana | | |
| *Pakistan* | 31°15N 72°22E | 42 D5 |
| Jhansi *India* | 25°30N 78°36E | 43 G8 |
| Jhargram *India* | 22°27N 86°59E | 43 H12 |
| Jharia *India* | 23°45N 86°26E | 43 H12 |
| Jharkhand □ *India* | 24°0N 85°50E | 43 H11 |
| Jharsuguda *India* | 21°56N 84°5E | 44 D7 |
| Jhelum *Pakistan* | 33°0N 73°45E | 42 C5 |
| Jhelum → *Pakistan* | 31°20N 72°10E | 42 D5 |
| Jhilmili *India* | 23°24N 82°51E | 43 H10 |
| Jhudo *Pakistan* | 24°58N 69°18E | 42 G3 |
| Jhunjhunun *India* | 28°10N 75°30E | 42 E6 |
| Ji-Paraná *Brazil* | 10°52S 62°57W | 92 F6 |
| Ji Xian *India* | 36°7N 110°40E | 32 F6 |
| Jia Xian *Henan, China* | 33°59N 113°12E | 32 H7 |
| Jia Xian *Shaanxi, China* | 38°12N 110°28E | 32 E6 |
| Jiahe *China* | 25°38N 112°19E | 35 E9 |
| Jiaji = Qionghai *China* | 19°15N 110°26E | 38 C8 |
| Jialing Jiang → *China* | 29°30N 106°20E | 34 C6 |
| Jiamusi *China* | 46°40N 130°26E | 31 B15 |
| Ji'an *Jilin, China* | 41°5N 126°10E | 33 D14 |
| Ji'an *Jiangxi, China* | 27°6N 114°59E | 35 D10 |
| Jianchang *China* | 40°55N 120°35E | 33 D11 |
| Jiande *China* | 29°23N 119°15E | 35 C12 |
| Jiang'an *China* | 28°40N 105°3E | 34 C5 |
| Jiangbei *China* | 29°40N 106°34E | 34 C6 |
| Jiangcheng *China* | 22°36N 101°52E | 34 F3 |
| Jiangchuan *China* | 24°8N 102°48E | 34 E4 |
| Jiangdi *China* | 26°57N 103°37E | 34 D4 |
| Jiangdu *China* | 32°27N 119°36E | 35 A12 |
| Jianghua *China* | 25°0N 111°47E | 35 E8 |
| Jiangjin *China* | 29°14N 106°14E | 34 C6 |
| Jiangkou *China* | 27°40N 108°49E | 34 D7 |
| Jiangle *China* | 26°42N 117°23E | 35 D11 |
| Jiangmen *China* | 22°32N 113°0E | 35 F9 |

| | | |
|---|---|---|
| Jiangning *China* | 31°55N 118°50E | 35 B12 |
| Jiangshan *China* | 28°40N 118°37E | 35 C12 |
| Jiangsu □ *China* | 33°0N 120°0E | 33 H11 |
| Jiangxi □ *China* | 27°30N 116°0E | 35 D11 |
| Jiangyan *China* | 32°30N 120°3E | 35 A13 |
| Jiangyin *China* | 31°54N 120°17E | 35 B13 |
| Jiangyong *China* | 25°20N 111°22E | 35 E8 |
| Jiangyuan *China* | 31°44N 104°43E | 34 B5 |
| Jiangyuan *China* | 42°2N 126°34E | 33 C14 |
| Jianhe *China* | 26°37N 108°31E | 34 D7 |
| Jianli *China* | 29°46N 112°56E | 35 C9 |
| Jianning *China* | 26°50N 116°50E | 35 D11 |
| Jian'ou *China* | 27°3N 118°17E | 35 D12 |
| Jianping *China* | 41°53N 119°42E | 33 D10 |
| Jianshi *China* | 30°37N 109°38E | 34 B7 |
| Jianshui *China* | 23°36N 102°43E | 34 F4 |
| Jianyang *Fujian, China* | 27°20N 118°5E | 35 D12 |
| Jianyang *Sichuan, China* | 30°24N 104°33E | 34 B5 |
| Jiao Xian = Jiaozhou | | |
| *China* | 36°18N 120°1E | 33 F11 |
| Jiaohe *Hebei, China* | 38°2N 116°20E | 32 E9 |
| Jiaohe *Jilin, China* | 43°40N 127°22E | 33 C14 |
| Jiaoling *China* | 24°41N 116°12E | 35 E11 |
| Jiaonan *China* | 35°52N 119°58E | 33 G10 |
| Jiaozhou *China* | 36°18N 120°1E | 33 F11 |
| Jiaozhou Wan *China* | 36°5N 120°10E | 33 F11 |
| Jiaozuo *China* | 35°16N 113°12E | 32 G7 |
| Jiawang *China* | 34°28N 117°26E | 33 G9 |
| Jiaxiang *China* | 35°25N 116°20E | 32 G9 |
| Jiaxing *China* | 30°49N 120°45E | 35 B13 |
| Jiayi = Chiai *Taiwan* | 23°29N 120°25E | 35 F13 |
| Jiayu *China* | 29°55N 113°55E | 35 C9 |
| Jiayuguan *China* | 39°49N 98°18E | 30 D8 |
| Jibuti = Djibouti ■ *Africa* | 12°0N 43°0E | 49 E3 |
| Jicarón, I. *Panama* | 7°10N 81°50W | 88 E3 |
| Jiddah *Si. Arabia* | 21°29N 39°10E | 49 C2 |
| Jido *India* | 29°2N 94°58E | 41 E19 |
| Jieshou *China* | 33°18N 115°22E | 32 H8 |
| Jiexiu *China* | 37°2N 111°55E | 32 F6 |
| Jieyang *China* | 23°35N 116°21E | 35 F11 |
| Jigalong *Australia* | 23°21S 120°47E | 60 D3 |
| Jigalong ✦ *Australia* | 23°21S 120°46E | 60 D3 |
| Jigni *China* | 25°45N 79°25E | 43 G8 |
| Jihlava *Czechia* | 49°28N 15°35E | 16 D8 |
| Jihlava → *Czechia* | 48°55N 16°36E | 17 D9 |
| Jijiga *Ethiopia* | 9°20N 42°50E | 49 F3 |
| Jilib *Somalia* | 0°29N 42°46E | 49 G3 |
| Jilin *China* | 43°44N 126°30E | 33 C14 |
| Jilin □ *China* | 44°0N 127°0E | 33 C14 |
| Jim Thorpe *U.S.A.* | 40°52N 75°44W | 83 F9 |
| Jima *Ethiopia* | 7°40N 36°47E | 49 F2 |
| Jimbaran, Teluk *Indonesia* | 8°46S 115°9E | 37 K18 |
| Jiménez *Mexico* | 27°8N 104°54W | 86 B4 |
| Jimeta *Nigeria* | 9°17N 12°28E | 54 C2 |
| Jimo *China* | 36°23N 120°30E | 33 F11 |
| Jin Xian = Jinzhou | | |
| *China* | 38°55N 121°42E | 33 E11 |
| Jinan *China* | 36°38N 117°1E | 32 F9 |
| Jinchang *China* | 38°30N 102°10E | 30 D9 |
| Jincheng *China* | 35°29N 112°50E | 32 G7 |
| Jinchuan *China* | 31°30N 102°3E | 34 B4 |
| Jind *India* | 29°19N 76°22E | 42 E7 |
| Jindabyne *Australia* | 36°25S 148°35E | 63 F4 |
| Jinding *China* | 22°22N 113°33E | 35 a |
| Jindo *S. Korea* | 34°28N 126°15E | 33 G14 |
| Jindřichův Hradec *Czechia* | 49°10N 15°2E | 16 D8 |
| Jing He → *China* | 31°20N 111°11E | 35 B8 |
| Jing Shan *China* | 31°20N 111°11E | 35 B8 |
| Jing Xian *China* | 38°25N 116°25E | 32 E9 |
| Jing'an *China* | 38°55N 115°17E | 32 C10 |
| Jingbian *China* | 37°20N 108°30E | 32 F5 |
| Jingchuan *China* | 35°20N 107°20E | 32 G4 |
| Jingde *China* | 30°15N 118°27E | 35 B12 |
| Jingdezhen *China* | 29°20N 117°11E | 35 C11 |
| Jingdong *China* | 24°23N 100°33E | 34 E3 |
| Jinggangshan *China* | 26°58N 114°15E | 35 D10 |
| Jinggu *China* | 23°35N 100°41E | 34 F3 |
| Jinghai *Guangdong,* | | |
| *China* | 22°59N 116°31E | 35 F11 |
| Jinghai *Tianjin, China* | 38°55N 116°55E | 32 E9 |
| Jinghong *China* | 22°0N 100°46E | 34 F3 |
| Jingjiang *China* | 32°2N 120°9E | 35 A13 |
| Jingle *China* | 38°20N 111°55E | 32 E6 |
| Jingmen *China* | 31°0N 112°10E | 35 B9 |
| Jingning *China* | 35°30N 105°43E | 32 G3 |
| Jingpo Hu *China* | 43°55N 128°55E | 33 C15 |
| Jingshan *China* | 31°1N 113°7E | 35 B9 |
| Jingtai *China* | 37°10N 104°6E | 32 F3 |
| Jingtang *China* | 39°10N 119°5E | 33 E10 |
| Jingxi *China* | 23°8N 106°27E | 34 F6 |
| Jingyang *China* | 34°30N 108°50E | 32 G5 |
| Jingyu *China* | 42°25N 126°45E | 33 C14 |
| Jingyuan *China* | 36°30N 104°40E | 32 F3 |
| Jingzhou *Hubei, China* | 30°21N 112°11E | 35 B9 |
| Jingzhou *Hunan, China* | 26°33N 109°40E | 34 D7 |
| Jingziguan *China* | 33°15N 111°0E | 32 H6 |
| Jinhua *China* | 29°8N 119°38E | 35 C12 |
| Jining *Nei Monggol Zizhiqu,* | | |
| *China* | 41°5N 113°0E | 32 D7 |
| Jining *Shandong, China* | 35°22N 116°34E | 32 G9 |
| Jinja *Uganda* | 0°25N 33°12E | 54 D6 |
| Jinjang *Malaysia* | 3°13N 101°39E | 39 L3 |
| Jinjiang *Fujian, China* | 24°43N 118°33E | 35 E12 |
| Jinjiang *Yunnan, China* | 26°14N 100°34E | 34 D3 |
| Jinkou *China* | 30°0N 114°8E | 35 B10 |
| Jinkouhe *China* | 29°30N 103°3E | 34 C4 |
| Jinmu Jiao *China* | 18°9N 109°34E | 38 C7 |
| Jinnah Barrage *Pakistan* | 32°58N 71°33E | 42 C4 |
| Jinotega *Nic.* | 13°6N 85°59W | 88 D2 |
| Jinotepe *Nic.* | 11°50N 86°10W | 88 D2 |
| Jinping *Guizhou, China* | 22°45N 112°11E | 35 C9 |
| Jinping *Yunnan, China* | 22°45N 103°18E | 34 F4 |
| Jinping Bend Dams *China* | 28°11N 101°39E | 34 C4 |
| Jinsha *China* | 27°30N 106°15E | 34 D6 |
| Jinsha Jiang → *China* | 28°50N 104°36E | 34 C5 |
| Jinshi *China* | 29°40N 111°50E | 35 C8 |

| | | |
|---|---|---|
| Jintan *China* | 31°42N 119°36E | 35 B12 |
| Jintur *India* | 19°37N 76°42E | 44 E3 |
| Jinxi *Jiangxi, China* | 27°56N 116°45E | 35 D11 |
| Jinxi *Liaoning, China* | 40°52N 120°50E | 33 D11 |
| Jinxian *China* | 28°26N 116°17E | 35 C11 |
| Jinxiang *China* | 35°5N 116°22E | 32 G9 |
| Jinyang *China* | 27°28N 103°5E | 34 D4 |
| Jinzhai *China* | 31°40N 115°53E | 35 B10 |
| Jinzhong *China* | 37°42N 112°46E | 32 F7 |
| Jinzhou *Liaoning, China* | 38°55N 121°42E | 33 E11 |
| Jinzhou *Liaoning, China* | 41°5N 121°3E | 33 D11 |
| Jiparaná → *Brazil* | 8°3S 62°52W | 92 E6 |
| Jipijapa *Ecuador* | 1°0S 80°40W | 92 D2 |
| Jiquilpan *Mexico* | 19°59N 102°43W | 86 D4 |
| Jirisan *S. Korea* | 35°20N 127°44E | 33 G14 |
| Jiroft *Iran* | 28°45N 57°50E | 47 D8 |
| Jishan *China* | 35°34N 110°58E | 32 G6 |
| Jishou *China* | 28°21N 109°43E | 34 C7 |
| Jishui *China* | 27°12N 115°8E | 35 D10 |
| Jisr ash Shughūr *Syria* | 35°49N 36°18E | 46 C4 |
| Jitarning *Australia* | 32°48S 117°57E | 61 F2 |
| Jitra *Malaysia* | 6°16N 100°25E | 39 J3 |
| Jiu → *Romania* | 43°47N 23°48E | 17 F12 |
| Jiudengkou *China* | 39°56N 106°40E | 32 E4 |
| Jiujiang *Guangdong, China* | 22°50N 113°0E | 35 F9 |
| Jiujiang *Jiangxi, China* | 29°42N 115°58E | 35 C10 |
| Jiuling Shan *China* | 28°40N 114°40E | 35 C10 |
| Jiulong *China* | 28°57N 101°31E | 34 C3 |
| Jiuquan *China* | 39°50N 98°20E | 30 D8 |
| Jiutai *China* | 44°10N 125°50E | 33 B13 |
| Jiuxincheng *China* | 39°17N 115°59E | 32 E8 |
| Jiuzhaigou △ *China* | 33°8N 103°52E | 34 A4 |
| Jiwani *Pakistan* | 25°1N 61°44E | 40 G2 |
| Jixi *Anhui, China* | 30°5N 118°34E | 35 B12 |
| Jixi *Heilongjiang, China* | 45°20N 130°50E | 33 B16 |
| Jiyang *China* | 37°0N 117°12E | 33 F9 |
| Jiyuan *China* | 35°7N 112°57E | 32 G7 |
| Jīzān *Si. Arabia* | 17°0N 42°20E | 49 D3 |
| Jize *China* | 36°54N 114°56E | 32 F8 |
| Jizhou *China* | 37°35N 115°30E | 32 F8 |
| Jizl, Wādī al → *Si. Arabia* | 25°39N 38°25E | 46 E3 |
| Jizō-Zaki *Japan* | 35°34N 133°20E | 29 G6 |
| Jizzax *Uzbekistan* | 40°6N 67°50E | 26 E7 |
| Joaçaba *Brazil* | 27°5S 51°31W | 95 B5 |
| João Pessoa *Brazil* | 7°10S 34°52W | 93 E12 |
| Joaquín V. González | | |
| *Argentina* | 25°10S 64°0W | 94 B3 |
| Jobat *India* | 22°25N 74°34E | 42 H6 |
| Jodhpur *India* | 26°23N 73°8E | 42 F5 |
| Jodiya *India* | 22°42N 70°18E | 42 H4 |
| Joensuu *Finland* | 62°37N 29°49E | 8 E23 |
| Jõetsu *Japan* | 37°12N 138°10E | 29 F9 |
| Jofane *Mozam.* | 21°15S 34°18E | 57 B5 |
| Jog Falls = Gersoppa Falls | | |
| *India* | 14°12N 74°46E | 45 G2 |
| Jogbani *India* | 26°25N 87°15E | 43 F12 |
| Jõgeva *Estonia* | 58°45N 26°24E | 9 G22 |
| Jogjakarta = Yogyakarta | | |
| *Indonesia* | 7°49S 110°22E | 37 G14 |
| Johannesburg *U.S.A.* | 35°22N 117°38W | 79 K9 |
| Johilla → *India* | 23°37N 81°14E | 43 H9 |
| John Crow Mts. *Jamaica* | 18°5N 76°25W | 88 a |
| John Day *U.S.A.* | 44°25N 118°57W | 76 D4 |
| John Day → *U.S.A.* | 45°44N 120°39W | 76 D3 |
| John Day Fossil Beds △ | | |
| *U.S.A.* | 44°33N 119°38W | 76 D4 |
| John D'or Prairie *Canada* | 58°30N 115°8W | 70 B5 |
| John H. Kerr Res. | | |
| *U.S.A.* | 36°36N 78°18W | 85 C15 |
| John o' Groats *U.K.* | 58°38N 3°4W | 11 C5 |
| Johnnie *U.S.A.* | 36°25N 116°5W | 79 J10 |
| John's Ra. *Australia* | 21°55S 133°23E | 62 C1 |
| Johnson *U.S.A.* | 44°38N 72°41W | 83 B12 |
| Johnson City *Kans.,* | | |
| *U.S.A.* | 37°34N 101°45W | 80 G3 |
| Johnson City *N.Y., U.S.A.* | 42°7N 75°58W | 83 D9 |
| Johnson City *Tenn.,* | | |
| *U.S.A.* | 36°19N 82°21W | 85 C13 |
| Johnson City *Tex., U.S.A.* | 30°17N 98°25W | 84 F5 |
| Johnsonburg *U.S.A.* | 41°29N 78°41W | 82 E6 |
| Johnsondale *U.S.A.* | 35°58N 118°32W | 79 K8 |
| Johnsons Crossing | | |
| *Canada* | 60°29N 133°18W | 70 A2 |
| Johnston, L. *Australia* | 32°25S 120°30E | 61 F3 |
| Johnston Atoll *Pac. Oc.* | 17°10N 169°8W | 65 F11 |
| Johnston Falls = Mambilima Falls | | |
| *Zambia* | 10°31S 28°45E | 54 G5 |
| Johnstone Str. *Canada* | 50°28N 126°0W | 70 C3 |
| Johnstown *Ireland* | 52°45N 7°33W | 10 D4 |
| Johnstown *N.Y., U.S.A.* | 43°0N 74°22W | 83 C10 |
| Johnstown *Ohio, U.S.A.* | 40°9N 82°41W | 82 F2 |
| Johnstown *Pa., U.S.A.* | 40°20N 78°55W | 82 F6 |
| Johor □ *Malaysia* | 2°5N 103°0E | 39 M4 |
| Johor, Selat *Asia* | 1°28N 103°47E | 39 d |
| Johor Bahru *Malaysia* | 1°28N 103°46E | 39 d |
| Johor Port *Malaysia* | 1°26N 103°53E | 39 d |
| Jõhvi *Estonia* | 59°22N 27°27E | 9 G22 |
| Joinville *Brazil* | 26°15S 48°55W | 95 B6 |
| Joinville I. *Antarctica* | 65°0S 55°30W | 5 C18 |
| Jojutla *Mexico* | 18°37N 99°11W | 87 D5 |
| Jokkmokk *Sweden* | 66°35N 19°50E | 8 C18 |
| Jökulsá á Bru → *Iceland* | 65°40N 14°16W | 8 D6 |
| Jökulsá á Fjöllum → | | |
| *Iceland* | 66°10N 16°30W | 8 C5 |
| Jolfā *Āzarbājān-e Sharqī,* | | |
| *Iran* | 38°57N 45°38E | 46 B5 |
| Jolfā *Eşfahan, Iran* | 32°58N 51°37E | 47 C6 |
| Joliet *U.S.A.* | 41°32N 88°5W | 80 E9 |
| Joliette *Canada* | 46°3N 73°24E | 72 C5 |
| Jolo *Phil.* | 6°0N 121°0E | 37 C6 |
| Jolon *U.S.A.* | 35°58N 121°9W | 78 K5 |
| Jombang *Indonesia* | 7°33S 112°14E | 37 G15 |
| Jomda *China* | 31°28N 98°12E | 34 B2 |
| Jonava *Lithuania* | 55°8N 24°12E | 9 J21 |
| Jones Sound *Canada* | 76°0N 85°0W | 69 B15 |
| Jonesboro *Ark., U.S.A.* | 35°50N 90°42W | 85 D9 |
| Jonesboro *La., U.S.A.* | 32°15N 92°43W | 84 E8 |
| Joniškis *Lithuania* | 56°13N 23°35E | 9 H20 |
| Jönköping *Sweden* | 57°45N 14°8E | 9 H16 |

Jonquière Canada 48°27N 71°14W **73** C5
Joplin U.S.A. 37°6N 94°31W **80** G6
Jora India 26°20N 77°49E **42** F6
Jordan Mont., U.S.A. 47°19N 106°55W **76** C10
Jordan N.Y., U.S.A. 43°4N 76°29W **83** C8
Jordan ■ Asia 31°0N 36°0E **48** E5
Jordan → Asia 31°48N 35°32E **48** D4
Jordan Valley U.S.A. 42°59N 117°3W **76** E5
Jorhat India 26°45N 94°12E **41** F19
Jörn Sweden 65°4N 20°1E **8** D19
Jorong Indonesia 3°58S 114°36E **36** E4
Jørpeland Norway 59°3N 6°1E **9** G12
Jorquera → Chile 28°3S 69°58W **94** B2
Jos Nigeria 9°53N 8°51E **52** G7
José Batlle y Ordóñez
　Uruguay 33°20S 55°10W **95** C4
Joseph, L. Canada 45°10N 79°44W **82** A5
Joseph Bonaparte G.
　Australia 14°35S 128°50E **60** B4
Joseph L. Canada 52°45N 65°18W **73** B6
Joshinath India 30°34N 79°34E **43** D8
Joshinetsu-Kōgen △
　Japan 36°42N 138°32E **29** F9
Joshua Tree U.S.A. 34°8N 116°19W **79** L10
Joshua Tree △ U.S.A. 33°55N 116°0W **79** M10
Jost Van Dyke I.
　Br. Virgin Is. 18°29N 64°47W **89** e
Jostedalsbreen Norway 61°40N 6°59E **8** F12
Jotunheimen Norway 61°35N 8°25E **8** F13
Joubertberge Namibia 18°30S 14°0E **56** B1
Jourdanton U.S.A. 28°55N 98°33W **84** G5
Jovellanos Cuba 22°40N 81°10W **88** B3
Ju Xian China 35°35N 118°20E **33** G10
Juan Aldama Mexico 24°19N 103°21W **86** C4
Juan Bautista Alberdi
　Argentina 34°26S 61°48W **94** C3
Juan de Fuca, Str of.
　N. Amer. 48°15N 124°0W **78** B3
Juan de Nova Ind. Oc. 17°3S 43°45E **57** A7
Juan Fernández, Arch. de
　Pac. Oc. 33°50S 80°0W **90** G2
Juan José Castelli
　Argentina 25°27S 60°57W **94** B3
Juan L. Lacaze Uruguay 34°26S 57°25W **94** C4
Juankoski Finland 63°3N 28°19E **8** E23
Juárez Mexico 27°37N 100°44W **86** B4
Juárez, Sa. de Mexico 32°0N 115°50W **86** A1
Juàzeiro Brazil 9°30S 40°30W **93** E10
Juàzeiro do Norte Brazil 7°10S 39°18W **93** E11
Juba South Sudan 4°50N 31°35E **53** H12
Juba → Somalia 1°30N 42°35E **49** G3
Jubail = Al Jubayl
　Si. Arabia 27°0N 49°50E **47** E6
Jubany = Carlini Base
　Antarctica 62°30S 58°0W **5** C18
Jubayl Lebanon 34°5N 35°39E **48** A4
Jubbah Si. Arabia 28°2N 40°56E **46** D4
Jubbal India 31°5N 77°40E **42** D7
Jubbulpore = Jabalpur
　India 23°9N 79°58E **43** H8
Jubilee L. Australia 29°0S 126°50E **61** E4
Juby, C. Morocco 28°0N 12°59W **52** C3
Júcar = Xúquer → Spain 39°5N 0°10W **21** C5
Júcaro Cuba 21°37N 78°51W **88** B4
Juchitán de Zaragoza
　Mexico 16°26N 95°1W **87** D5
Judea = Har Yehuda
　Israel 31°35N 34°57E **48** D3
Judith → U.S.A. 47°44N 109°39W **76** C9
Judith, Pt. U.S.A. 41°22N 71°29W **83** E13
Judith Gap U.S.A. 46°41N 109°45W **76** C9
Juigalpa Nic. 12°6N 85°26W **88** D2
Juist □ Myanmar 26°0N 97°30W **34** D1
Juiz de Fora Brazil 21°43S 43°19W **95** A7
Jujuy □ Argentina 23°20S 65°40W **94** A2
Julesburg U.S.A. 40°59N 102°16W **76** F12
Juli Peru 16°10S 69°25W **92** G5
Julia Cr. → Australia 20°0S 141°11E **62** C3
Julia Creek Australia 20°39S 141°44E **62** C3
Juliaca Peru 15°25S 70°10W **92** G4
Julian U.S.A. 33°4N 116°38W **79** M10
Julian, L. Canada 54°25N 77°57W **72** B4
Julianatop Suriname 3°40N 56°30W **93** C7
Julianehåb = Qaqortoq
　Greenland 60°43N 46°0W **4** C5
Julimes Mexico 28°25N 105°27W **86** B3
Jullundur = Jalandhar
　India 31°20N 75°40E **42** D6
Julu China 37°15N 115°2E **32** F8
Jumbo Pk. U.S.A. 36°12N 114°11W **79** J12
Jumentos Cays Bahamas 23°0N 75°40W **88** B4
Jumilla Spain 38°28N 1°19W **21** C5
Jumla Nepal 29°15N 82°13E **43** E10
Jumna = Yamuna →
　India 25°30N 81°53E **43** G9
Jumunjin S. Korea 37°55N 128°54E **33** F15
Junagadh India 21°30N 70°30E **42** J4
Junan China 35°12N 118°53E **33** G10
Junction Tex., U.S.A. 30°29N 99°46W **84** F5
Junction Utah, U.S.A. 38°14N 112°13W **77** G7
Junction B. Australia 11°52S 133°55E **62** A1
Junction City Kans., U.S.A. 39°2N 96°50W **80** F5
Junction City Oreg.,
　U.S.A. 44°13N 123°12W **76** D2
Junction Pt. Australia 11°45S 133°50E **62** A1
Jundah Australia 24°46S 143°2E **62** C3
Jundiaí Brazil 24°30S 47°0W **95** A6
Juneau U.S.A. 58°18N 134°25W **70** B2
Junee Australia 34°53S 147°35E **63** E4
Jungar Qi China 39°49N 110°57E **32** E6
Jungfrau Switz. 46°32N 7°58E **20** C7
Junggar Pendi China 44°30N 86°0E **30** C6
Jungshahi Pakistan 24°52N 67°44E **42** G2
Juniata → U.S.A. 40°24N 77°1W **82** F7
Junín Argentina 34°33S 60°57W **94** C3
Junín de los Andes
　Argentina 39°45S 71°0W **96** D2
Jûniyah Lebanon 33°59N 35°38E **48** B4
Junkerdal △ Norway 66°50N 15°50E **8** C16
Junlian China 28°8N 104°29E **34** C5
Junnar India 19°12N 73°58E **44** E1

Juntas Chile 28°24S 69°58W **94** B2
Juntura U.S.A. 43°45N 118°5W **76** E4
Jur → South Sudan 8°45N 29°15E **53** G11
Jura = Jura, Mts. du Europe 46°40N 6°5E **20** C7
Jura = Schwäbische Alb
　Germany 48°20N 9°30E **16** D5
Jura U.K. 56°0N 5°50W **11** F3
Jura, Mts. du Europe 46°40N 6°5E **20** C7
Jura, Sd. of U.K. 55°57N 5°45W **11** F3
Jurassic Coast U.K. 50°42N 2°50W **13** G5
Jurbarkas Lithuania 55°4N 22°46E **9** J20
Jurien Bay Australia 30°18S 115°2E **61** F2
Jūrmala Latvia 56°58N 23°34E **9** H20
Jurong China 31°57N 119°9E **35** B12
Juruá → Brazil 2°37S 65°44W **92** D5
Juruena Brazil 13°0S 58°10W **92** F7
Juruena → Brazil 7°20S 58°3W **92** E7
Juruti Brazil 2°9S 56°4W **93** D7
Justo Daract Argentina 33°52S 65°12W **94** C2
Jutaí → Brazil 2°43S 66°57W **92** D5
Juticalpa Honduras 14°40N 86°12W **88** D2
Jutland = Jylland Denmark 56°25N 9°30E **9** H13
Juuka Finland 63°13N 29°17E **8** E23
Juventud, I. de la Cuba 21°40N 82°40W **88** B3
Jūy Zar Iran 33°50N 46°18E **46** C5
Juye China 35°22N 116°5E **32** G9
Jwaneng Botswana 24°45S 24°50E **55** J4
Jylland Denmark 56°25N 9°30E **9** H13
Jyväskylä Finland 62°14N 25°50E **8** E21

# K

K2 Pakistan 35°58N 76°32E **43** B7
Kaakha = Kaka
　Turkmenistan 37°21N 59°36E **47** B8
Kaap Plateau S. Africa 28°30S 24°0E **56** C3
Kaapkruis Namibia 21°55S 13°57E **56** B1
Kabaena Indonesia 5°15S 122°0E **37** F6
Kabala S. Leone 9°38N 11°37W **52** G3
Kabale Uganda 1°15S 30°0E **54** E6
Kabalo Dem. Rep. of the Congo 6°0S 27°0E **54** F5
Kabambare
　Dem. Rep. of the Congo 4°41S 27°39E **54** E5
Kabanjahe Indonesia 3°6N 98°30E **36** D1
Kabankalan Phil. 9°59N 122°49E **37** C6
Kabara Fiji 18°59S 178°56W **59** a
Kabardino-Balkaria □
　Russia 43°30N 43°30E **19** F7
Kabarega Falls = Murchison Falls
　Uganda 2°15N 31°30E **54** D6
Kabasalan Phil. 7°47N 122°44E **37** C6
Kabat Indonesia 8°16S 114°19E **37** J17
Kabbani → India 12°13N 76°54E **45** H3
Kabin Buri Thailand 13°57N 101°43E **38** F3
Kabinakagami L. Canada 48°54N 84°25W **72** C3
Kabinda
　Dem. Rep. of the Congo 6°19S 24°20E **54** F4
Kabompo → Zambia 14°11S 23°11E **55** G4
Kabongo
　Dem. Rep. of the Congo 7°22S 25°33E **54** F5
Kabrît, G. el Egypt 29°42N 33°16E **48** F2
Kabūd Gonbad Iran 37°5N 59°45E **47** B8
Kābul Afghan. 34°28N 69°11E **42** B3
Kābul □ Afghan. 34°30N 69°0E **40** B6
Kābul → Pakistan 33°55N 72°14E **42** C5
Kaburuang Indonesia 3°50N 126°30E **37** D7
Kabwe Zambia 14°30S 28°29E **55** G5
Kachchh, Gulf of India 22°50N 69°15E **42** H3
Kachchh, Rann of India 24°0N 70°0E **42** H4
Kachchhidhana India 21°44N 78°46E **43** J8
Kachikau Botswana 18°8S 24°26E **56** A3
Kachin □ Myanmar 26°0N 97°30E **34** D1
Kachīry Kazakhstan 53°10N 75°50E **26** D8
Kachnara India 23°50N 75°6E **42** H6
Kachot Cambodia 11°30N 103°3E **39** G4
Kaçkar Turkey 40°45N 41°10E **19** F7
Kadaiyanallur India 9°3N 77°22E **45** K3
Kadan Kyun Myanmar 12°30N 98°20E **38** F2
Kadanai → Afghan. 31°22N 65°45E **42** D1
Kadapa India 14°30N 78°47E **45** M4
Kadavu Fiji 19°0S 178°15E **59** a
Kadavu Passage Fiji 18°45S 178°0E **59** a
Kade Ghana 6°7N 0°56W **52** G5
Kadhimain = Al Kāẕimīyah
　Iraq 33°22N 44°18E **46** C5
Kadi India 23°18N 72°23E **42** H5
Kadina Australia 33°55S 137°43E **63** E2
Kadipur India 26°10N 82°23E **43** F10
Kadirabad India 19°51N 75°54E **44** E2
Kadiri India 14°12N 78°13E **45** G4
Kadirli Turkey 37°23N 36°5E **46** B3
Kadiyevka = Stakhanov
　Ukraine 48°35N 38°40E **19** E6
Kadmat I. India 11°14N 72°47E **45** J1
Kadoka U.S.A. 43°50N 101°31W **80** D3
Kadoma Zimbabwe 18°20S 29°52E **55** F5
Kâdugli Sudan 11°0N 29°45E **53** F11
Kaduna Nigeria 10°30N 7°21E **52** F7
Kaduna → Nigeria 8°45N 5°48E **52** G7
Kaédi Mauritania 16°9N 13°28W **52** E3
Kaeng Khoi Thailand 14°35N 101°0E **38** E3
Kaeng Krachan △
　Thailand 12°57N 99°23E **38** F2
Kaeng Krung △ Thailand 9°30N 98°50E **39** H2
Kaeng Tana △ Thailand 15°25N 105°32E **38** E5
Kaesōng N. Korea 37°58N 126°35E **33** F14
Kāf Si. Arabia 31°25N 37°29E **46** D3
Kafan = Kapan Armenia 39°18N 46°27E **46** B5
Kafanchan Nigeria 9°40N 8°20E **52** G7
Kafinda Zambia 15°46S 28°9E **55** H5
Kafue → Zambia 15°30S 29°0E **55** H5
Kaga Japan 36°16N 136°15E **29** F8
Kaga Bandoro C.A.R. 7°0N 19°10E **54** C3
Kagawa □ Japan 34°15N 134°0E **29** G7
Kagera □ Uganda 0°57S 31°47E **54** E6
Kağızman Turkey 40°5N 43°10E **46** B4
Kagoshima Japan 31°35N 130°33E **29** J5
Kagoshima □ Japan 31°30N 130°30E **29** J5
Kagul = Cahul Moldova 45°50N 28°15E **17** F15
Kahak Iran 36°6N 49°46E **47** B6

Kahan Pakistan 29°18N 68°54E **42** E3
Kahang Malaysia 2°12N 103°32E **39** L4
Kahayan → Indonesia 3°40S 114°0E **36** E4
Kahemba
　Dem. Rep. of the Congo 7°18S 18°55E **54** F3
Kahnūj Iran 27°55N 57°40E **47** E8
Kahoka U.S.A. 40°25N 91°44W **80** E8
Kaho'olawe U.S.A. 20°33N 156°37W **75** L8
Kahramanmaraş Turkey 37°37N 36°53E **46** B3
Kâhta Turkey 37°46N 38°36E **46** B3
Kahului U.S.A. 20°54N 156°28W **75** L8
Kahurangi △ N.Z. 41°0S 172°32E **59** D4
Kahuta Pakistan 33°35N 73°24E **42** C5
Kai, Kepulauan Indonesia 5°55S 132°45E **37** F8
Kai Besar Indonesia 5°35S 133°0E **37** F8
Kai Is. = Kai, Kepulauan
　Indonesia 5°55S 132°45E **37** F8
Kai Kecil Indonesia 5°45S 132°40E **37** F8
Kai Xian China 31°11N 108°21E **34** B7
Kaiapoi N.Z. 43°24S 172°40E **59** E4
Kaidu He → China 41°46N 86°31E **30** C6
Kaieteur Falls Guyana 5°1N 59°10W **92** B7
Kaifeng China 34°48N 114°21E **32** G8
Kaihua China 29°12N 118°20E **35** C12
Kaikohe N.Z. 35°25S 173°49E **59** A4
Kaikoura N.Z. 42°25S 173°43E **59** E4
Kailash = Kangrinboqê Feng
　China 31°0N 81°25E **43** D9
Kaili China 26°33N 107°59E **34** D6
Kailu China 43°38N 121°18E **33** C11
Kailua Kona U.S.A. 19°39N 155°59W **75** M8
Kaimana Indonesia 3°39S 133°45E **37** E8
Kaimanawa Mts. N.Z. 39°15S 175°56E **59** C5
Kaimganj India 27°33N 79°24E **43** F8
Kaimur Hills India 24°30N 82°0E **43** G10
Kainab → Namibia 28°32S 19°34E **56** C2
Kainji Res. Nigeria 10°1N 4°40E **52** F6
Kainuu □ Finland 64°30N 29°7E **8** D23
Kaipara Harbour N.Z. 36°25S 174°14E **59** B5
Kaiping China 22°23N 112°42E **35** F9
Kaipokok B. Canada 54°54N 59°47W **73** B8
Kaira India 22°45N 72°50E **42** H5
Kairana India 29°24N 77°15E **42** E7
Kaironi Indonesia 0°47S 133°40E **37** E8
Kairouan Tunisia 35°45N 10°5E **53** A8
Kaiserslautern Germany 49°26N 7°45E **16** D4
Kaitaia N.Z. 35°8S 173°17E **59** A4
Kaitangata N.Z. 46°17S 169°51E **59** G2
Kaithal India 29°48N 76°26E **42** E7
Kaitu → Pakistan 33°10N 70°30E **42** C4
Kaiwi Channel U.S.A. 21°15N 157°30W **75** L8
Kaiyang China 27°4N 106°59E **34** D6
Kaiyuan Liaoning, China 42°28N 124°1E **33** C13
Kaiyuan Yunnan, China 23°40N 103°12E **34** F4
Kaiyuh Mts. U.S.A. 64°30N 158°0W **74** C8
Kajaani Finland 64°17N 27°46E **8** D22
Kajabbi Australia 20°0S 140°1E **62** C3
Kajana = Kajaani
　Finland 64°17N 27°46E **8** D22
Kajang Malaysia 2°59N 101°48E **39** L3
Kajo Kaji South Sudan 3°58N 31°40E **53** H12
Kaka Turkmenistan 37°21N 59°36E **47** B8
Kakabeka Falls Canada 48°24N 89°37W **72** C2
Kakadu △ Australia 12°0S 132°3E **60** B5
Kakamas S. Africa 28°45S 20°33E **56** D3
Kakamega Kenya 0°20N 34°46E **54** D6
Kakana India 9°7N 92°48E **45** K11
Kakanui Mts. N.Z. 45°10S 170°30E **59** F3
Kakdwip India 21°53N 88°11E **43** J13
Kake = Akiōta Japan 34°36N 132°19E **29** G6
Kake U.S.A. 56°59N 133°57W **70** B2
Kakegawa Japan 34°45N 138°1E **29** G9
Kakeroma-jima Japan 28°8N 129°14E **29** K4
Kākhak Iran 34°9N 58°38E **47** C8
Kakhovka Ukraine 46°45N 33°30E **19** E5
Kakhovske Vdskh. Ukraine 47°5N 34°0E **19** E5
Kakinada India 16°57N 82°11E **44** F6
Kakisa Canada 60°56N 117°25W **70** A5
Kakisa → Canada 61°3N 118°10W **70** A5
Kakisa L. Canada 60°56N 117°43W **70** A5
Kakogawa Japan 34°46N 134°51E **29** G7
Kakwa → Canada 54°37N 118°28W **70** C5
Kāl Gūsheh Iran 30°59N 58°12E **47** D8
Kal Sefid Iran 34°52N 47°23E **46** C5
Kala Oya → Sri Lanka 8°20N 79°45E **45** K4
Kalaallit Nunaat = Greenland ☑
　N. Amer. 66°0N 45°0W **67** C15
Kalabagh Pakistan 33°0N 71°28E **42** C4
Kalabahi Indonesia 8°13S 124°31E **37** F6
Kalaburagi India 17°20N 76°50E **44** F3
Kalach Russia 50°22N 41°0E **19** D7
Kaladan → Myanmar 20°20N 93°5E **41** J18
Kaladar Canada 44°37N 77°5W **82** B7
Kalahari Africa 24°0S 21°30E **56** B3
Kalahari Gemsbok △
　S. Africa 25°30S 20°30E **56** C3
Kalajoki Finland 64°12N 24°10E **8** D21
Kalakamati Botswana 20°40S 27°25E **57** C4
Kalakan Russia 55°15N 116°45E **27** D12
K'alak'unlun Shank'ou =
　Karakoram Pass Asia 35°33N 77°50E **43** B7
Kalam Pakistan 35°34N 72°30E **43** B5
Kalamata Greece 37°3N 22°10E **23** F10
Kalamazoo U.S.A. 42°17N 85°35W **81** D11
Kalamazoo → U.S.A. 42°40N 86°10W **80** D10
Kalamb India 18°43N 74°4E **44** E2
Kalamnuri India 19°40N 77°20E **44** E3
Kalan = Tunceli Turkey 39°6N 39°31E **46** B3
Kalannie Australia 30°22S 117°5E **61** F2
Kalāntarī Iran 32°10N 54°8E **47** C7
Kalao Indonesia 7°21S 121°0E **37** F6
Kalaotoa Indonesia 7°20S 121°50E **37** F6
Kālāt Iran 25°29N 59°22E **47** E9
Kalat Pakistan 29°8N 66°31E **40** E5
Kalāteh Iran 36°33N 55°41E **47** B7
Kalāteh-ye Ganj Iran 27°31N 57°55E **47** E8

Kalbarri Australia 27°40S 114°10E **61** E1
Kalbarri △ Australia 27°51S 114°30E **61** E1
Kalce Slovenia 45°54N 14°13E **16** F8
Kale Turkey 37°27N 28°49E **23** F13
Kalegauk Kyun
　Myanmar 15°33N 97°35E **38** E1
Kalemie
　Dem. Rep. of the Congo 5°55S 29°9E **54** F5
Kalewa Myanmar 23°10N 94°15E **41** H19
Kalgan → India 25°35N 86°36E **43** G12
Kalgoorlie-Boulder
　Australia 30°40S 121°22E **61** F3
Kali → India 27°6N 79°55E **43** F8
Kali Sindh → India 25°32N 76°17E **42** G6
Kaliakra, Nos Bulgaria 43°21N 28°30E **23** C13
Kalianda Indonesia 5°50S 105°45E **36** F3
Kalibo Phil. 11°43N 122°22E **37** B6
Kalimantan Indonesia 0°0 114°0E **36** E4
Kalimantan Barat □
　Indonesia 0°0 110°30E **36** E4
Kalimantan Selatan □
　Indonesia 2°30S 115°30E **36** E5
Kalimantan Tengah □
　Indonesia 2°0S 113°30E **36** E4
Kalimantan Timur □
　Indonesia 1°30N 116°30E **36** D5
Kálimnos Greece 37°0N 27°0E **23** F12
Kalimpong India 27°4N 88°35E **43** F13
Kalinadi → India 14°50N 74°7E **45** G2
Kaliningrad Russia 54°42N 20°32E **9** J19
Kalinkavichy Belarus 52°12N 29°20E **17** B15
Kalinkovichi = Kalinkavichy
　Belarus 52°12N 29°20E **17** B15
Kalispell U.S.A. 48°12N 114°19W **76** B6
Kalisz Poland 51°45N 18°8E **17** C10
Kaliveli Tank India 12°5N 79°50E **45** H4
Kalix Sweden 65°53N 23°12E **8** D20
Kalixälven → Sweden 65°50N 23°11E **8** D20
Kalka India 30°46N 76°57E **42** D7
Kalkarindji Australia 17°30S 130°47E **60** C5
Kalkaska U.S.A. 44°44N 85°11W **81** C11
Kalkfeld Namibia 20°57S 16°14E **56** B2
Kalkfontein Botswana 22°4S 20°57E **56** B3
Kalkrand Namibia 24°1S 17°35E **56** B2
Kallakkurichchi India 11°44N 79°1E **45** J4
Kallam India 18°36N 76°2E **44** E3
Kallavesi Finland 62°58N 27°30E **8** E22
Kallidaikurichi India 8°38N 77°31E **45** K3
Kallsjön Sweden 63°38N 13°0E **8** E15
Kalmar Sweden 56°40N 16°20E **9** H17
Kalmunai Sri Lanka 7°25N 81°49E **45** L5
Kalmykia □ Russia 46°5N 46°1E **19** E8
Kalna India 23°13N 88°25E **43** H13
Kalnai India 22°46N 83°30E **43** H10
Kalocsa Hungary 46°32N 19°0E **17** E10
Kalol Gujarat, India 22°37N 73°31E **42** H5
Kalol Gujarat, India 23°15N 72°33E **42** H5
Kalpeni I. India 10°5N 73°38E **45** J1
Kalpi India 26°8N 79°47E **43** F8
Kalpitiya Sri Lanka 8°14N 79°46E **45** K4
Kalputhi I. India 10°49N 72°10E **45** J1
Kalrayan Hills India 11°45N 78°40E **45** J4
Kalsubai India 19°35N 73°45E **44** E1
Kaltag U.S.A. 64°20N 158°43W **74** C8
Kaltukatjara Australia 24°52S 129°5E **61** D4
Kalu Pakistan 25°5N 67°39E **42** G2
Kaluga Russia 54°35N 36°10E **18** D6
Kalumburu Australia 13°55S 126°35E **60** B4
Kalumburu ◎ Australia 14°17S 126°38E **60** B4
Kalush Ukraine 49°3N 24°23E **17** D13
Kalutara Sri Lanka 6°35N 80°0E **45** L5
Kalwakurti India 16°41N 78°30E **44** F4
Kalya Russia 60°15N 59°59E **18** B10
Kalyan = Basavakalyan
　India 17°52N 76°57E **44** F3
Kalyan Maharashtra, India 20°30N 74°3E **44** D2
Kalyan Maharashtra, India 19°15N 73°9E **44** E1
Kalyandurg India 14°33N 77°21E **45** G3
Kalyansingapuram India 19°30N 83°19E **44** E6
Kama Japan 33°30N 130°49E **29** H5
Kama → Russia 55°45N 52°0E **18** C9
Kamaishi Japan 39°16N 141°53E **28** E10
Kamalapuram India 14°35N 78°39E **45** G4
Kamalia Pakistan 30°44N 72°42E **42** D5
Kaman India 27°39N 77°16E **42** F6
Kamanjab Namibia 19°35S 14°51E **56** A2
Kamarān Yemen 15°21N 42°35E **49** D3
Kamareddi India 18°19N 78°21E **44** E4
Kamativi Zimbabwe 18°20S 27°6E **56** A4
Kambalda West
　Australia 31°10S 121°37E **61** F3
Kambam India 9°45N 77°16E **45** K3
Kambangan, Nusa
　Indonesia 7°40S 108°10E **37** G13
Kambar Pakistan 27°37N 68°1E **42** F3
Kambarka Russia 56°15N 54°11E **18** C9
Kambove
　Dem. Rep. of the Congo 10°51S 26°33E **54** G5
Kamchatka, Poluostrov
　Russia 57°0N 160°0E **27** D17
Kamchatka Pen. = Kamchatka,
　Poluostrov Russia 57°0N 160°0E **27** D17
Kamchia → Bulgaria 43°4N 27°44E **23** C12
Kamen Russia 53°50N 81°30E **26** D9
Kamen-Rybolov Russia 44°46N 132°2E **28** B5
Kamenjak, Rt Croatia 44°47N 13°55E **16** F7
Kamenka Russia 65°58N 44°0E **18** A7
Kamensk Uralskiy Russia 56°25N 62°2E **26** D7
Kamenskoye Russia 62°45N 165°30E **27** C17
Kameoka Japan 35°0N 135°35E **29** G7
Kamet India 30°55N 79°35E **43** D8
Kamiah U.S.A. 46°14N 116°2W **76** C5
Kamieskroon S. Africa 30°9S 17°56E **56** E2
Kamilukuak L. Canada 62°22N 101°40E **71** A9
Kamin-Kashyrskyy
　Ukraine 51°39N 24°56E **17** C13

Kamina
　Dem. Rep. of the Congo 8°45S 25°0E **54** F5
Kaminak L. Canada 62°10N 95°0W **71** A10
Kaminoyama Japan 38°9N 140°17E **28** E10
Kamla → India 25°35N 86°36E **43** G12
Kamloops Canada 50°40N 120°20W **70** C4
Kamo Japan 37°39N 139°3E **28** F9
Kamoke Pakistan 32°4N 74°4E **42** C6
Kampala Uganda 0°20N 32°32E **54** D6
Kampar Malaysia 4°18N 101°9E **39** K3
Kampar → Indonesia 0°30N 103°8E **36** D2
Kampen Neths. 52°33N 5°53E **15** B5
Kampene
　Dem. Rep. of the Congo 3°36S 26°40E **54** E5
Kamphaeng Phet
　Thailand 16°28N 99°30E **38** D2
Kampong Cham
　Cambodia 12°0N 105°30E **39** G5
Kampong Chhnang
　Cambodia 12°20N 104°35E **39** F5
Kampong Pengerang
　Malaysia 1°22N 104°7E **39** d
Kampong Punggai
　Malaysia 1°27N 104°18E **39** d
Kampong Saom
　Cambodia 10°38N 103°30E **39** G4
Kampong Saom, Chaak
　Cambodia 10°50N 103°32E **39** G4
Kampong Tanjong Langsat
　Malaysia 1°28N 104°1E **39** d
Kampong Telok Ramunia
　Malaysia 1°22N 104°15E **39** d
Kampot Cambodia 10°36N 104°10E **39** G5
Kampuchea = Cambodia ■
　Asia 12°15N 105°0E **38** F5
Kampung Air Putih
　Malaysia 4°15N 103°10E **39** K4
Kampung Jerangau
　Malaysia 4°50N 103°10E **39** K4
Kampung Raja Malaysia 5°45N 102°35E **39** K4
Kampungbaru = Tolitoli
　Indonesia 1°5N 120°50E **37** D6
Kamrau, Teluk Indonesia 3°30S 133°36E **37** E8
Kamsack Canada 51°34N 101°54W **71** C8
Kamsar Guinea 10°40N 14°36W **52** F3
Kamskoye Vdkhr. Russia 58°41N 56°7E **18** C10
Kamthi India 21°9N 79°19E **44** D4
Kamuchawie L. Canada 56°18N 101°59W **71** B8
Kamui-Misaki Japan 43°20N 140°21E **28** C10
Kamyanets-Podilskyy
　Ukraine 48°45N 26°40E **17** D14
Kamyanka-Buzka
　Ukraine 50°8N 24°16E **17** C13
Kāmyārān Iran 34°47N 46°56E **46** C5
Kamyshin Russia 50°10N 45°24E **19** D8
Kanaaupscow → Canada 54°2N 76°30W **72** B4
Kanab U.S.A. 37°3N 112°32W **77** H7
Kanab Cr. → U.S.A. 36°24N 112°38W **77** H7
Kanacea Lau Group, Fiji 17°15S 179°6W **59** a
Kanacea Taveuni, Fiji 16°59S 179°56E **59** a
Kanaga I. U.S.A. 51°45N 177°22W **74** E4
Kanagi Japan 40°54N 140°27E **28** D10
Kanairiktok → Canada 55°2N 60°18W **73** A7
Kanakapura India 12°33N 77°28E **45** H3
Kananga
　Dem. Rep. of the Congo 5°55S 22°18E **54** F4
Kanash Russia 55°30N 47°32E **18** C8
Kanaskat U.S.A. 47°19N 121°54W **78** C5
Kanastraíon, Ákra = Paliouri,
　Akra Greece 39°57N 23°45E **23** E10
Kanawha → U.S.A. 38°50N 82°9W **81** F12
Kanazawa Japan 36°30N 136°38E **29** F8
Kanchanaburi Thailand 14°2N 99°31E **38** E2
Kanchenjunga Nepal 27°50N 88°10E **43** F13
Kanchipuram India 12°52N 79°45E **45** H4
Kandahar India 18°52N 77°12E **44** E3
Kandahār Afghan. 31°32N 65°43E **40** D4
Kandahār India 31°0N 65°0E **40** D4
Kandalaksha Russia 67°9N 32°30E **8** C25
Kandalakshskiy Zaliv
　Russia 66°0N 35°0E **18** A6
Kandangan Indonesia 2°50S 115°20E **36** E5
Kandavu = Kadavu Fiji 19°0S 178°15E **59** a
Kandavu Passage = Kadavu
　Passage Fiji 18°45S 178°0E **59** a
Kandhkot Pakistan 28°16N 69°8E **42** E3
Kandhla India 29°18N 77°19E **42** E7
Kandi Benin 11°7N 2°55E **52** F6
Kandi India 23°58N 88°5E **43** H13
Kandiaro Pakistan 27°4N 68°13E **42** F3
Kandla India 23°0N 70°10E **42** H4
Kandos Australia 32°45S 149°58E **63** E4
Kandy Sri Lanka 7°18N 80°43E **45** L5
Kane U.S.A. 41°40N 78°49W **82** E6
Kane Basin Greenland 79°1N 70°0W **69** B18
Kang Botswana 23°41S 22°50E **56** B3
Kangān Fārs, Iran 27°50N 52°3E **47** E7
Kangān Hormozgān, Iran 25°48N 57°28E **47** E8
Kangar Malaysia 6°27N 100°12E **39** J3
Kangaroo I. Australia 35°45S 137°0E **63** F2
Kangaroo Mts. Australia 23°29S 141°51E **62** C3
Kangasala Finland 61°28N 24°4E **8** F21
Kangāvar Iran 34°40N 48°0E **47** C6
Kangding China 30°2N 101°57E **34** B3
Kangdong N. Korea 39°9N 126°5E **33** E14
Kangean, Kepulauan
　Indonesia 6°55S 115°23E **36** F5
Kangean Is. = Kangean,
　Kepulauan Indonesia 6°55S 115°23E **36** F5
Kanggye N. Korea 41°0N 126°35E **33** D14
Kangikajik Greenland 70°7N 22°0W **4** B6
Kangiqliniq = Rankin Inlet
　Canada 62°30N 93°0W **68** E13
Kangiqsualujjuaq
　Canada 58°30N 65°59W **69** F18
Kangiqsujuaq Canada 61°30N 72°0W **69** E17
Kangiqtugaapik = Clyde River
　Canada 70°30N 68°30W **69** C18

Kangirsuk *Canada* 60°0N 70°0W **69** F18
Kangkar Chemaran
  *Malaysia* 1°34N 104°12E **39** d
Kangkar Sungai Tiram
  *Malaysia* 1°35N 103°55E **39** d
Kangkar Teberau
  *Malaysia* 1°32N 103°51E **39** d
Kangping *China* 42°43N 123°18E **33** C12
Kangra *India* 32°6N 76°16E **42** C7
Kangrinboqe Feng *China* 31°0N 81°25E **43** D9
Kangto *China* 27°50N 92°35E **41** F18
Kanha △ *India* 22°15N 80°40E **43** H9
Kanhan → *India* 21°4N 79°34E **44** D4
Kanhangad *India* 12°21N 74°58E **45** H2
Kanhar → *India* 24°28N 83°8E **43** G10
Kaniapiskau = Caniapiscau →
  *Canada* 56°40N 69°30W **73** A6
Kaniapiskau, L. = Caniapiscau, L.
  *Canada* 54°10N 69°55W **73** B6
Kanigiri *India* 15°24N 79°31E **45** G4
Kanin, Poluostrov *Russia* 68°0N 45°0E **18** A8
Kanin Nos, Mys *Russia* 68°39N 43°32E **18** A7
Kanin Pen. = Kanin, Poluostrov
  *Russia* 68°0N 45°0E **18** A8
Kaniva *Australia* 36°22S 141°18E **63** F3
Kanjut Sar *Pakistan* 36°7N 75°25E **43** A6
Kankaanpää *Finland* 61°44N 22°50E **8** F20
Kankakee *U.S.A.* 41°7N 87°52W **80** E2
Kankakee → *U.S.A.* 41°23N 88°15W **80** E9
Kankan *Guinea* 10°23N 9°15W **52** F4
Kankendy = Xankändi
  *Azerbaijan* 39°52N 46°49E **46** B5
Kanker *India* 20°10N 81°40E **44** D5
Kankesanturai *Sri Lanka* 9°49N 80°2E **45** K5
Kankroli *India* 25°4N 73°53E **42** G5
Kanmaw Kyun *Myanmar* 11°40N 98°28E **39** G2
Kannapolis *U.S.A.* 35°30N 80°37W **85** D14
Kannauj *India* 27°3N 79°56E **43** F8
Kanniyakumari *India* 8°5N 77°34E **45** K3
Kannod *India* 22°45N 76°40E **40** H10
Kannur *India* 11°53N 75°27E **45** J2
Kannyakumari *India* 8°3N 77°40E **45** K3
Kano *Nigeria* 12°2N 8°30E **52** F7
Kan'onji *Japan* 34°7N 133°39E **29** G6
Kanowit *Malaysia* 2°14N 112°20E **36** D4
Kanoya *Japan* 31°25N 130°50E **29** J5
Kanpetlet *Myanmar* 21°10N 93°59E **41** J18
Kanpur *India* 26°28N 80°20E **43** F9
Kansas □ *U.S.A.* 38°30N 99°0W **80** F4
Kansas → *U.S.A.* 39°7N 94°37W **80** F6
Kansas City *Kans., U.S.A.* 39°7N 94°38W **80** F6
Kansas City *Mo., U.S.A.* 39°6N 94°35W **80** F6
Kansk *Russia* 56°20N 95°37E **27** D10
Kansu = Gansu □ *China* 36°0N 104°0E **32** G3
Kantaphor *India* 22°35N 76°34E **42** H7
Kantharalak *Thailand* 14°39N 104°39E **38** E5
Kanthi = Contai *India* 21°54N 87°46E **43** J12
Kantli → *India* 28°20N 75°30E **42** E6
Kantō □ *Japan* 36°15N 139°30E **29** F9
Kantō-Sanchi *Japan* 35°59N 138°50E **29** G9
Kanturk *Ireland* 52°11N 8°54W **10** D3
Kanuma *Japan* 36°34N 139°42E **29** F9
Kanus *Namibia* 27°50S 18°39E **56** C2
Kanye *Botswana* 24°55S 25°28E **56** B4
Kao *Tonga* 19°40S 175°1W **59** c
Kao Phara *Thailand* 8°3N 98°22E **39** a
Kaohsiung *Taiwan* 22°35N 120°16E **35** F13
Kaokoveld *Namibia* 19°15S 14°30E **56** A1
Kaolack *Senegal* 14°5N 16°8W **52** F2
Kaoshan *China* 44°38N 124°50E **33** B13
Kapa'a *U.S.A.* 22°5N 159°19W **75** L8
Kapadvanj *India* 23°5N 73°0E **42** H5
Kapan *Armenia* 39°18N 46°27E **46** B5
Kapanga
  *Dem. Rep. of the Congo* 8°30S 22°40E **54** F4
Kapchagai = Qapshaghay
  *Kazakhstan* 43°51N 77°14E **26** E8
Kapela = Velika Kapela
  *Croatia* 45°10N 15°5E **16** F8
Kapfenberg *Austria* 47°26N 15°18E **16** E8
Kapiri Mposhi *Zambia* 13°59S 28°43E **55** G5
Kāpīsā □ *Afghan.* 35°0N 69°20E **40** B6
Kapiskau → *Canada* 52°47N 81°55W **72** B3
Kapit *Malaysia* 2°0N 112°55E **36** D4
Kapiti I. *N.Z.* 40°50S 174°56E **59** D5
Kaplan *U.S.A.* 30°0N 92°17W **84** F8
Kapoe *Thailand* 9°34N 98°32E **39** H2
Kapoeta *South Sudan* 4°50N 33°35E **53** H12
Kaposvár *Hungary* 46°25N 17°47E **17** E9
Kapowsin *U.S.A.* 46°59N 122°13W **78** D4
Kapps *Namibia* 22°32S 17°18E **56** B2
Kapsan *N. Korea* 41°4N 128°19E **33** D15
Kapsukas = Marijampolė
  *Lithuania* 54°33N 23°19E **9** J20
Kaptai L. *Bangla.* 22°40N 92°20E **41** H18
Kapuas → *Indonesia* 0°25S 109°20E **36** E3
Kapuas Hulu, Pegunungan
  *Malaysia* 1°30N 113°30E **36** D4
Kapuas Hulu Ra. = Kapuas Hulu,
  Pegunungan *Malaysia* 1°30N 113°30E **36** D4
Kapunda *Australia* 34°20S 138°56E **63** E2
Kapuni *N.Z.* 39°29S 174°8E **59** C5
Kapurthala *India* 31°23N 75°25E **42** D6
Kapuskasing → *Canada* 49°49N 82°0W **72** C3
Kapuskasing → *Canada* 49°49N 82°0W **72** C3
Kaputar, Mt. *Australia* 30°15S 150°10E **63** E5
Kara *Russia* 69°10N 65°0E **26** C7
Kara Bogaz Gol, Zaliv =
  Garabogazköl Aylagy
  *Turkmenistan* 41°0N 53°30E **19** F9
Kara Kala = Garrygala
  *Turkmenistan* 38°31N 56°29E **47** B8
Kara Kalpak Republic =
  Qoraqalpog'iston □
  *Uzbekistan* 43°0N 58°0E **26** E6
Kara Kum = Garagum
  *Turkmenistan* 39°30N 60°0E **47** B8
Kara Sea *Russia* 75°0N 70°0E **26** B8
Karabiǧa *Turkey* 40°23N 27°17E **23** D12
Karabük *Turkey* 41°12N 32°37E **19** F5

Karaburun *Turkey* 38°41N 26°28E **23** E12
Karabutak = Qarabutaq
  *Kazakhstan* 50°0N 60°14E **26** E7
Karacabey *Turkey* 40°12N 28°21E **23** D13
Karacasu *Turkey* 37°43N 28°35E **23** F13
Karachey-Cherkessia □
  *Russia* 43°40N 41°30E **19** F7
Karad *India* 17°15N 74°10E **44** F2
Karaganda = Qaraghandy
  *Kazakhstan* 49°50N 73°10E **30** B3
Karagayly = Qaraghayly
  *Kazakhstan* 49°26N 76°0E **26** E8
Karaginskiy, Ostrov
  *Russia* 58°45N 164°0E **27** D17
Karagiye, Vpadina
  *Kazakhstan* 43°27N 51°45E **19** F9
Karagiye Depression = Karagiye,
  Vpadina *Kazakhstan* 43°27N 51°45E **19** F9
Karagola Road *India* 25°29N 87°23E **43** G12
Karaikal *India* 10°59N 79°50E **45** J4
Karaikkudi *India* 10°5N 78°45E **45** J4
Karaj *Iran* 35°48N 51°0E **47** C6
Karajarri ⊙ *Australia* 19°0S 122°30E **60** C3
Karak *Malaysia* 3°25N 102°2E **39** L4
Karakalpakstan =
  Qoraqalpog'iston □
  *Uzbekistan* 43°0N 58°0E **26** E6
Karakelong *Indonesia* 4°35N 126°50E **37** D7
Karakitang *Indonesia* 3°14N 125°28E **37** D7
Karakol *Kyrgyzstan* 42°30N 78°20E **30** C4
Karakoram Pass *Asia* 35°33N 77°50E **43** B7
Karakoram Ra. *Pakistan* 35°30N 77°0E **43** B7
Karakuwisa *Namibia* 18°56S 19°40E **56** A2
Karalon *Russia* 57°5N 115°50E **27** D12
Karama *Jordan* 31°57N 35°35E **48** D4
Karaman *Turkey* 37°14N 33°13E **46** B2
Karambu *Indonesia* 3°53S 116°6E **36** E5
Karamea Bight *N.Z.* 41°22S 171°40E **59** D3
Karamnasa → *India* 25°31N 83°52E **43** G10
Karān *Si. Arabia* 27°43N 49°49E **47** E6
Karand *Iran* 34°16N 46°15E **46** C5
Karanganyar *Indonesia* 7°38S 109°37E **37** G13
Karangasem = Amlapura
  *Indonesia* 8°27S 115°37E **37** J18
Karanja *Maharashtra,*
  *India* 21°11N 78°24E **44** D4
Karanja *Maharashtra,*
  *India* 20°29N 77°31E **44** D3
Karanjia *India* 21°47N 85°58E **43** J11
Karas □ *Namibia* 27°0S 17°30E **56** C2
Karasburg *Namibia* 28°0S 18°44E **56** C2
Karasino *Russia* 66°50N 86°50E **26** C9
Karasjok *Norway* 69°27N 25°30E **8** B21
Karasuk *Russia* 53°44N 78°2E **26** D8
Karasuyama *Japan* 36°39N 140°9E **29** F10
Karatau, Khrebet = Qarataū
  *Kazakhstan* 43°30N 69°30E **26** E7
Karatax Shan *China* 35°57N 81°0E **30** D5
Karativu *Sri Lanka* 8°22N 79°47E **45** K4
Karatsu *Japan* 33°26N 129°58E **29** H5
Karaul *Russia* 70°6N 82°15E **26** B9
Karauli *India* 26°30N 77°4E **42** F7
Karawang *Indonesia* 6°30S 107°15E **37** G12
Karawanken *Europe* 46°30N 14°40E **16** E8
Karayazı *Turkey* 39°41N 42°9E **19** G7
Karazhal = Qarazhal
  *Kazakhstan* 48°2N 70°49E **26** E8
Karbalā' *Iraq* 32°36N 44°3E **46** C5
Karcag *Hungary* 47°19N 20°57E **17** E11
Karcha → *Pakistan* 34°45N 76°10E **43** B7
Karchana *India* 25°17N 81°56E **43** G9
Karditsa *Greece* 39°23N 21°54E **23** E9
Kärdla *Estonia* 59°0N 22°45E **9** G20
Kardzhali *Bulgaria* 41°38N 25°21E **23** D11
Kareeberge *S. Africa* 30°59S 21°50E **56** E3
Kareha → *India* 25°44N 86°21E **43** G12
Kareima *Sudan* 18°30N 31°49E **53** E12
Karelia □ *Russia* 65°30N 32°30E **18** A5
Karelian Republic = Karelia □
  *Russia* 65°30N 32°30E **18** A5
Karera *India* 25°32N 78°9E **42** G8
Kärevändar *Iran* 27°53N 60°44E **47** E9
Kargasok *Russia* 59°3N 80°53E **26** D9
Kargat *Russia* 55°10N 80°15E **26** D9
Kargil *India* 34°32N 76°12E **43** B7
Kargopol *Russia* 61°30N 38°58E **18** B6
Karīān *Iran* 26°57N 57°14E **47** E8
Kariba, L. *Zimbabwe* 16°40S 28°25E **55** H5
Kariba Dam *Zimbabwe* 16°30S 28°35E **55** H5
Kariba Gorge *Zambia* 16°30S 28°50E **55** H5
Karibib *Namibia* 22°0S 15°56E **56** B2
Karijini △ *Australia* 23°8S 118°15E **60** D2
Karimata, Kepulauan
  *Indonesia* 1°25S 109°0E **36** E3
Karimata, Selat *Indonesia* 2°0S 108°40E **36** E3
Karimata Is. = Karimata,
  Kepulauan *Indonesia* 1°25S 109°0E **36** E3
Karimnagar *India* 18°26N 79°10E **44** E4
Karimun, Pulau *Indonesia* 1°3N 103°22E **39** d
Karimun Kecil, Pulau
  *Indonesia* 1°8N 103°22E **39** d
Karimunjawa, Kepulauan
  *Indonesia* 5°50S 110°30E **36** F4
Karin *Somalia* 10°50N 45°52E **49** E4
Karīt *Iran* 33°29N 56°55E **47** C8
Kariya *Japan* 34°58N 137°1E **29** G8
Kariyangwe *Zimbabwe* 18°0S 27°38E **57** A4
Karjala *Finland* 62°0N 30°25E **8** F24
Karjat *India* 18°33N 75°0E **44** E2
Karkal *India* 13°15N 74°56E **45** H2
Karkaralinsk = Qarqaraly
  *Kazakhstan* 49°26N 75°30E **30** B4
Karkheh → *Iran* 31°2N 47°29E **46** D5
Karkinitska Zatoka
  *Ukraine* 45°56N 33°0E **19** E5
Karkinitskiy Zaliv = Karkinitska
  Zatoka *Ukraine* 45°56N 33°0E **19** E5
Karkuk = Kirkūk *Iraq* 35°30N 44°21E **46** C5

Karlantijpa North ⊙
  *Australia* 19°27S 133°33E **60** C5
Karlantijpa South ⊙
  *Australia* 20°31S 133°9E **60** D5
Karleby = Kokkola
  *Finland* 63°50N 23°8E **8** E20
Karlovac *Croatia* 45°31N 15°36E **16** F8
Karlovo *Bulgaria* 42°38N 24°47E **23** C11
Karlovy Vary *Czechia* 50°13N 12°51E **16** C7
Karlsbad = Karlovy Vary
  *Czechia* 50°13N 12°51E **16** C7
Karlsena, Mys *Russia* 77°0N 67°42E **26** B7
Karlshamn *Sweden* 56°10N 14°51E **9** H16
Karlskoga *Sweden* 59°28N 14°33E **9** G16
Karlskrona *Sweden* 56°10N 15°35E **9** H16
Karlsruhe *Germany* 49°0N 8°23E **16** D5
Karlstad *Sweden* 59°23N 13°30E **9** G15
Karlstad *U.S.A.* 48°35N 96°31W **80** A5
Karmala *India* 18°25N 75°12E **44** E2
Karmi'el *Israel* 32°55N 35°18E **48** C4
Karnak *Egypt* 25°43N 32°39E **53** C12
Karnal *India* 29°42N 77°2E **42** E7
Karnali = Ghaghara →
  *India* 25°45N 84°40E **43** G11
Karnali → *Nepal* 28°45N 81°16E **43** E9
Karnaphuli Res. = Kaptai L.
  *Bangla.* 22°40N 92°20E **41** H18
Karnaprayag *India* 30°16N 79°15E **43** D8
Karnataka □ *India* 13°15N 77°0E **45** H3
Karnes City *U.S.A.* 28°53N 97°54W **84** G6
Karnische Alpen *Europe* 46°36N 13°0E **16** E7
Kärnten □ *Austria* 46°52N 13°30E **16** E8
Karon, Ao *Thailand* 7°51N 98°17E **39** a
Karonga *Malawi* 9°57S 33°55E **54** F6
Karoo △ *S. Africa* 32°18S 22°27E **56** E3
Karoonda *Australia* 35°1S 139°59E **63** F2
Karor *Pakistan* 31°15N 70°59E **42** D4
Karora *Sudan* 17°44N 38°15E **53** E13
Karpathos *Greece* 35°37N 27°10E **23** G12
Karpinsk *Russia* 59°45N 60°1E **18** C11
Karpogory *Russia* 64°0N 44°27E **18** B7
Karpuz Burnu = Apostolos
  Andreas, C. *Cyprus* 35°42N 34°35E **46** C2
Karratha *Australia* 20°44S 116°52E **60** D2
Kars *Turkey* 40°40N 43°5E **19** F7
Karsakpay *Kazakhstan* 47°55N 66°40E **26** E7
Karshi = Qarshi
  *Uzbekistan* 38°53N 65°48E **26** F7
Karsiyang *India* 26°56N 88°18E **43** F13
Karsog *India* 31°23N 77°12E **42** D7
Kartala *Comoros Is.* 11°45S 43°21E **55** a
Kartaly *Russia* 53°3N 60°40E **26** D7
Kartapur *India* 31°27N 75°32E **42** D6
Karthaus *U.S.A.* 41°8N 78°9W **82** E6
Karufa *Indonesia* 3°50S 133°20E **37** E8
Karumba *Australia* 17°31S 140°50E **62** B3
Kārūn → *Iran* 30°26N 48°10E **47** D6
Karungu *Kenya* 0°50S 34°10E **54** E6
Karur *India* 10°59N 78°2E **45** J4
Karviná *Czechia* 49°53N 18°31E **17** D10
Karwan → *India* 27°26N 78°4E **42** F8
Karwar *India* 14°55N 74°13E **45** G2
Karwi *India* 25°12N 80°57E **43** G9
Karymskoye *Russia* 51°36N 114°21E **27** D12
Kasai →
  *Dem. Rep. of the Congo* 3°30S 16°10E **54** E3
Kasama *Zambia* 10°16S 31°9E **54** G6
Kasan-dong *N. Korea* 41°18N 126°55E **33** D14
Kasane *Namibia* 17°34S 24°50E **56** A3
Kasaragod *India* 12°30N 74°58E **45** H2
Kasba L. *Canada* 60°20N 102°10W **71** A8
Kāseh Garān *Iran* 34°5N 46°2E **46** C5
Kasempa *Zambia* 13°30S 25°44E **55** G5
Kasenga
  *Dem. Rep. of the Congo* 10°20S 28°45E **54** G5
Kasese *Uganda* 0°13N 30°3E **54** D6
Kasganj *India* 27°48N 78°42E **43** F8
Kashabowie *Canada* 48°40N 90°26W **72** C1
Kashaf *Iran* 35°58N 61°7E **47** C9
Kāshān *Iran* 34°5N 51°30E **47** C6
Kashechewan *Canada* 52°18N 81°37W **72** B3
Kashgar = Kashi *China* 39°30N 76°2E **30** D4
Kashi *China* 39°30N 76°2E **30** D4
Kashipur *Odisha, India* 19°16N 83°3E **44** E6
Kashipur *Uttarakhand,*
  *India* 29°15N 79°0E **43** E8
Kashiwazaki *Japan* 37°22N 138°33E **29** F9
Kashk-e Kohneh *Afghan.* 34°55N 62°30E **40** B3
Kashkū'īyeh *Iran* 30°31N 55°40E **47** D7
Kāshmar *Iran* 35°16N 58°26E **47** C8
Kashmir *Asia* 34°0N 76°0E **43** C7
Kashmor *Pakistan* 28°28N 69°32E **42** E3
Kashun Noerh = Gaxun Nur
  *China* 42°22N 100°30E **30** C9
Kasiari *India* 22°8N 87°14E **43** H12
Kasimov *Russia* 54°55N 41°20E **18** D7
Kasiruta *Indonesia* 0°25S 127°12E **37** E7
Kaskaskia → *U.S.A.* 37°58N 89°57W **80** G9
Kaskattama → *Canada* 57°3N 90°4W **71** B10
Kaskinen *Finland* 62°22N 21°15E **8** E19
Kaskö = Kaskinen
  *Finland* 62°22N 21°15E **8** E19
Kaslo *Canada* 49°55N 116°55W **70** D5
Kasmere L. *Canada* 59°34N 101°10W **71** B8
Kasongo
  *Dem. Rep. of the Congo* 4°30S 26°33E **54** E5
Kasongo Lunda
  *Dem. Rep. of the Congo* 6°35S 16°49E **54** F3
Kasos *Greece* 35°20N 26°55E **23** G12
Kassalâ *Sudan* 15°30N 36°0E **53** E13
Kassandra Kolpos *Greece* 40°5N 23°30E **23** D10
Kassel *Germany* 51°18N 9°26E **16** C5
Kasson *U.S.A.* 44°2N 92°45W **80** C7
Kastamonu *Turkey* 41°25N 33°43E **19** F5
Kasterlee *Belgium* 51°15N 4°59E **15** C4
Kastoria *Greece* 40°30N 21°19E **23** D9
Kastrom Mefa'a = Umm al Rasas
  *Jordan* 31°30N 35°55E **48** D5
Kasumi *Japan* 35°38N 134°38E **29** G7
Kasur *Pakistan* 31°5N 74°25E **42** D6

Kata, Ao *Thailand* 7°48N 98°18E **39** J2
Kata Tjuta *Australia* 25°20S 130°50E **61** E5
Kataka = Cuttack *India* 20°25N 85°57E **44** D7
Katanga
  *Dem. Rep. of the Congo* 8°0S 25°0E **54** F5
Katangi *India* 21°56N 79°50E **44** D4
Katanning *Australia* 33°40S 117°33E **61** F2
Katchall *India* 7°57N 93°22E **45** L11
Katerini *Greece* 40°18N 22°37E **23** D10
Katghora *India* 22°30N 82°33E **43** H10
Katha *Myanmar* 24°10N 96°30E **41** G20
Katherîna, Gebel *Egypt* 28°30N 33°57E **46** D2
Katherine *Australia* 14°27S 132°20E **60** B5
Katherine Gorge = Nitmiluk △
  *Australia* 14°6S 132°15E **60** B5
Kathi *India* 21°47N 74°3E **42** J6
Kathiawar *India* 22°20N 71°0E **42** H4
Kathmandu *Nepal* 27°45N 85°20E **43** F11
Kathua *India* 32°23N 75°34E **42** C6
Kati Thanda-Lake Eyre
  *Australia* 29°30S 137°26E **58** D6
Kati Thanda-Lake Eyre (North)
  *Australia* 28°30S 137°20E **63** D2
Kati Thanda-Lake Eyre (South)
  *Australia* 29°18S 137°25E **63** D2
Katihar *India* 25°34N 87°36E **43** G12
Katima Mulilo *Namibia* 17°28S 24°13E **56** A3
Katingan = Mendawai →
  *Indonesia* 3°30S 113°0E **36** E4
Katiola *Côte d'Ivoire* 8°10N 5°10W **52** G4
Katiti ⊙ *Australia* 25°1S 131°11E **61** E5
Katmandu = Kathmandu
  *Nepal* 27°45N 85°20E **43** F11
Katni *India* 23°51N 80°24E **43** H9
Katol *India* 21°17N 78°38E **44** D4
Katoomba *Australia* 33°41S 150°19E **63** E5
Katowice *Poland* 50°17N 19°5E **17** C10
Katrine, L. *U.K.* 56°15N 4°30W **11** E4
Katrineholm *Sweden* 59°9N 16°12E **9** G17
Katsina *Nigeria* 13°0N 7°32E **52** F7
Katsumoto *Japan* 33°51N 129°42E **29** H4
Katsuura *Japan* 35°10N 140°20E **29** G10
Katsuyama *Japan* 36°3N 136°30E **29** F8
Kattavia *Greece* 35°57N 27°46E **23** G12
Kattegat *Denmark* 56°40N 11°20E **9** H14
Katwa *India* 23°30N 88°5E **43** H13
Katwijk *Neths.* 52°12N 4°24E **15** B4
Kau-Ye Kyun *Myanmar* 11°1N 98°32E **39** G2
Kaua'i *U.S.A.* 22°3N 159°30W **75** L8
Kaudom △ *Namibia* 18°45S 20°51E **56** A3
Kaufman *U.S.A.* 32°35N 96°19W **84** E6
Kauhajoki *Finland* 62°25N 22°10E **8** E20
Kauhaneva-Pohjankangas △
  *Finland* 62°13N 22°20E **8** E20
Kaukauna *U.S.A.* 44°17N 88°17W **80** C9
Kaukauveld *Namibia* 20°0S 20°15E **56** B3
Ka'ula I. *U.S.A.* 21°40N 160°33W **75** L7
Kaunas *Lithuania* 54°54N 23°54E **9** J20
Kaunia *Bangla.* 25°46N 89°26E **43** G13
Kautokeino *Norway* 69°0N 23°4E **8** B20
Kauwapur *India* 27°31N 82°18E **43** F10
Kavacha *Russia* 60°16N 169°51E **27** C17
Kavala *Greece* 40°57N 24°28E **23** D11
Kavalerovo *Russia* 44°15N 135°4E **28** B7
Kavali *India* 14°55N 80°1E **45** G5
Kavango = Cubango →
  *Africa* 18°50S 22°25E **56** A3
Kavār *Iran* 29°11N 52°44E **47** D7
Kavaratti *India* 10°34N 72°37E **45** J1
Kavaratti I. *India* 10°33N 72°37E **45** J1
Kaveri = Cauvery → *India* 11°9N 78°52E **45** J4
Kavi *India* 22°12N 72°38E **42** H5
Kavimba *Botswana* 18°2S 24°38E **56** A3
Kavīr, Dasht-e *Iran* 34°30N 55°0E **47** C7
Kavīr △ *Iran* 34°40N 52°0E **47** C7
Kaw *Fr. Guiana* 4°30N 52°15W **93** C8
Kawagama L. *Canada* 45°18N 78°45W **82** A6
Kawagoe *Japan* 35°55N 139°29E **29** G9
Kawaguchi *Japan* 35°52N 139°45E **29** G9
Kawah Ijen △ *Indonesia* 8°3S 114°14E **37** H15
Kawanoe = Shikokuchūō
  *Japan* 34°1N 133°34E **29** G6
Kawardha *India* 22°0N 81°17E **43** J9
Kawasi *Indonesia* 1°38S 127°28E **37** E7
Kawawachikamach
  *Canada* 54°48N 66°50W **73** B6
Kawerau *N.Z.* 38°7S 176°42E **59** C6
Kawhia *N.Z.* 38°4S 174°49E **59** C5
Kawhia Harbour *N.Z.* 38°5S 174°51E **59** C5
Kawio, Kepulauan
  *Indonesia* 4°30N 125°30E **37** D7
Kawthaung *Myanmar* 10°5N 98°36E **39** H2
Kawthoolei = Kayin □
  *Myanmar* 18°0N 97°30E **41** L20
Kawthule = Kayin □
  *Myanmar* 18°0N 97°30E **41** L20
Kaya *Burkina Faso* 13°4N 1°10W **52** F5
Kayah □ *Myanmar* 19°15N 97°15E **41** K20
Kayan → *Indonesia* 2°55N 117°35E **36** D5
Kaycee *U.S.A.* 43°43N 106°38W **76** E10
Kayeli *Indonesia* 3°20S 127°10E **37** E7
Kayenta *U.S.A.* 36°44N 110°15W **77** H8
Kayes *Mali* 14°25N 11°30W **52** F3
Kayin □ *Myanmar* 18°0N 97°30E **41** L20
Kayoa *Indonesia* 0°1N 127°28E **37** D7
Kayseri *Turkey* 38°45N 35°30E **46** B2
Kaysville *U.S.A.* 41°2N 111°56W **76** F8
Kayts *Sri Lanka* 9°42N 79°51E **45** K4
Kazachye *Russia* 70°52N 135°58E **27** B14
Kazakhstan ■ *Asia* 50°0N 70°0E **26** E8
Kazan *Russia* 55°50N 49°10E **18** C8
Kazan → *Canada* 64°2N 95°29W **71** A9
Kazan-Rettō *Pac. Oc.* 25°0N 141°0E **64** E6
Kazanlak *Bulgaria* 42°38N 25°20E **23** C11
Kazatin = Kozyatyn
  *Ukraine* 49°45N 28°50E **17** D15
Kāzerūn *Iran* 29°38N 51°40E **47** D6
Kazi Magomed = Qazımämmäd
  *Azerbaijan* 40°3N 49°0E **47** A6

Kazipet *India* 17°58N 79°30E **44** F4
Kazuno *Japan* 40°10N 140°45E **28** D10
Kazym → *Russia* 63°54N 65°50E **26** C7
Kea *Greece* 37°35N 24°22E **23** F11
Keady *U.K.* 54°15N 6°42W **10** B5
Kearney *U.S.A.* 40°42N 99°5W **80** E4
Kearney ⊙ *Australia* 20°10S 128°4E **60** D4
Kearny *U.S.A.* 33°3N 110°55W **77** K8
Kearsarge *U.S.A.* 38°50N 38°50E **19** G6
Kearsarge, Mt. *U.S.A.* 43°22N 71°50W **83** C13
Keban *Turkey* 38°50N 38°50E **19** G6
Keban Baraji *Turkey* 38°41N 38°33E **46** B3
Kebnekaise *Sweden* 67°53N 18°33E **8** C18
Kebri Dehar *Ethiopia* 6°45N 44°17E **49** F3
Kebumen *Indonesia* 7°42S 109°40E **37** G13
Kechika → *Canada* 59°41N 127°12W **70** B3
Kecskemét *Hungary* 46°57N 19°42E **17** E10
Kedah □ *Malaysia* 5°50N 100°40E **39** K3
Kėdainiai *Lithuania* 55°15N 24°2E **9** J21
Kedarnath *India* 30°44N 79°4E **43** D8
Kedgwick *Canada* 47°40N 67°20W **73** C6
Kediri *Indonesia* 7°51S 112°1E **37** G15
Keeler *U.S.A.* 36°29N 117°52W **78** J9
Keeley L. *Canada* 54°54N 108°8W **71** C7
Keeling Is. = Cocos Is.
  *Ind. Oc.* 12°10S 96°55E **64** J1
Keelung = Chilung
  *Taiwan* 25°3N 121°45E **35** E13
Keene *Canada* 44°15N 78°10W **82** B6
Keene *Calif., U.S.A.* 35°13N 118°33W **79** K8
Keene *N.H., U.S.A.* 42°56N 72°17W **83** D12
Keene *N.Y., U.S.A.* 44°16N 73°46W **83** B11
Keep River → *Australia* 15°49S 129°18E **60** C4
Keeper Hill *Ireland* 52°45N 8°16W **10** D3
Keerweer, C. *Australia* 14°0S 141°32E **62** A3
Keeseville *U.S.A.* 44°29N 73°30W **83** B11
Keetmanshoop *Namibia* 26°35S 18°8E **56** C2
Keewatin *Canada* 49°46N 94°34W **71** D10
Keewatin → *Canada* 56°29N 100°46W **71** B8
Kefalonia *Greece* 38°15N 20°30E **23** E9
Kefamenanu *Indonesia* 9°28S 124°29E **37** F6
Kefar Sava *Israel* 32°11N 34°54E **48** C3
Keffi *Nigeria* 8°55N 7°43E **52** G7
Keflavík *Iceland* 64°2N 22°35W **8** D2
Keg River *Canada* 57°54N 117°55W **70** B5
Kegalla *Sri Lanka* 7°15N 80°21E **45** L5
Kegaska *Canada* 50°9N 61°18W **73** B7
Keighley *U.K.* 53°52N 1°54W **12** D6
Keila *Estonia* 59°18N 24°25E **9** G21
Keimoes *S. Africa* 28°41S 20°59E **56** D3
Keitele *Finland* 63°10N 26°20E **8** E22
Keith *Australia* 36°6S 140°20E **63** F3
Keith *U.K.* 57°32N 2°57W **11** D6
Keiyasi *Fiji* 17°53S 177°46E **59** a
Keizer *U.S.A.* 44°57N 123°1W **78** D2
Kejimkujik △ *Canada* 44°25N 65°25W **73** D6
Kejserr Franz Joseph Fd.
  *Greenland* 73°30N 24°30W **4** B6
Kekri *India* 26°0N 75°10E **42** G6
Kelan *China* 38°43N 111°31E **32** E6
Kelang = Klang *Malaysia* 3°2N 101°26E **39** L3
Kelani Ganga → *Sri Lanka* 6°58N 79°50E **45** L4
Kelantan □ *Malaysia* 5°10N 102°0E **39** K3
Kelantan → *Malaysia* 6°13N 102°14E **39** J4
Kelkit → *Turkey* 40°45N 36°32E **19** F6
Kellerberrin *Australia* 31°36S 117°38E **61** F2
Kellett, C. *Canada* 72°0N 126°0W **4** B1
Kelleys I. *U.S.A.* 41°36N 82°42W **82** E2
Kellogg *U.S.A.* 47°32N 116°7W **76** C5
Kells *Ireland* 53°44N 6°53W **10** C5
Kélo *Chad* 9°10N 15°45E **53** G9
Kelowna *Canada* 49°50N 119°25W **70** D5
Kelsey Creek *Australia* 20°26S 148°31E **62** b
Kelseyville *U.S.A.* 38°59N 122°50W **78** G4
Kelso *N.Z.* 45°54S 169°15E **59** F2
Kelso *U.K.* 55°36N 2°26W **11** F6
Kelso *U.S.A.* 46°9N 122°54W **78** D4
Keluang = Kluang
  *Malaysia* 2°3N 103°18E **39** L4
Kelud *Indonesia* 7°56N 112°18E **37** H15
Kelvington *Canada* 52°10N 103°30W **71** C8
Kem *Russia* 65°0N 34°38E **18** B5
Kem → *Russia* 64°57N 34°41E **18** B5
Kemah *Turkey* 39°32N 39°5E **46** B3
Kemaman *Malaysia* 4°12N 103°18E **39** K4
Kemano *Canada* 53°35N 128°0W **70** C3
Kemasik *Malaysia* 4°25N 103°27E **39** K4
Kemerovo *Russia* 55°20N 86°5E **26** D9
Kemi *Finland* 65°44N 24°34E **8** D21
Kemi älv = Kemijoki →
  *Finland* 65°47N 24°32E **8** D21
Kemi träsk = Kemijärvi
  *Finland* 66°43N 27°22E **8** C22
Kemijärvi *Finland* 66°43N 27°22E **8** C22
Kemijoki → *Finland* 65°47N 24°32E **8** D21
Kemmerer *U.S.A.* 41°48N 110°32W **76** F8
Kemp, L. *U.S.A.* 33°46N 99°9W **84** E5
Kemp Land *Antarctica* 69°0S 55°0E **5** C5
Kempas *Malaysia* 1°33N 103°42E **39** d
Kempsey *Australia* 31°1S 152°50E **63** E5
Kempt, L. *Canada* 47°25N 74°22W **72** C5
Kempten *Germany* 47°45N 10°17E **16** E6
Kempton *Australia* 42°31S 147°12E **63** G4
Kemptville *Canada* 45°0N 75°38W **83** B9
Ken → *India* 25°13N 80°27E **43** G9
Kenai *U.S.A.* 60°33N 151°16W **68** E1
Kenai Mts. *U.S.A.* 60°0N 150°0W **74** D9
Kendai *India* 22°45N 82°37E **43** H10
Kendal *Indonesia* 6°56S 110°14E **37** G14
Kendal *U.K.* 54°20N 2°44W **12** C5
Kendall *Australia* 31°35S 152°44E **63** E5
Kendall → *Australia* 14°4S 141°35E **62** A3
Kendallville *U.S.A.* 41°27N 85°16W **81** E11
Kendari *Indonesia* 3°50S 122°30E **37** E6
Kendawangan *Indonesia* 2°32S 110°17E **36** E4
Kendi, Pulau *Malaysia* 5°13N 100°11E **39** c
Kendrapara *India* 20°35N 86°30E **44** D8
Kendrew *S. Africa* 32°32S 24°30E **56** E3
Kene Thao *Laos* 17°44N 101°10E **38** D3
Kenedy *U.S.A.* 28°49N 97°51W **84** G6

Kenema *S. Leone* 7°50N 11°14W **52** G3
Keng Kok *Laos* 16°26N 105°12E **38** D5
Keng Tawng *Myanmar* 20°45N 98°18E **41** J21
Keng Tung *Myanmar* 21°18N 99°39E **38** B2
Kenhardt *S. Africa* 29°19S 21°12E **56** C3
Kenitra *Morocco* 34°15N 6°40W **52** B4
Kenli *China* 37°30N 118°20E **33** F10
Kenmare *Ireland* 51°53N 9°36W **10** E2
Kenmare *U.S.A.* 48°41N 102°5W **80** A2
Kenmare River → *Ireland* 51°48N 9°51W **10** E2
Kennebago Lake *U.S.A.* 45°4N 70°40W **83** A14
Kennebec *U.S.A.* 43°54N 99°52W **80** D4
Kennebec → *U.S.A.* 43°45N 69°46W **81** D19
Kennebunk *U.S.A.* 43°23N 70°33W **83** C14
Kennedy *Zimbabwe* 18°52S 27°10E **56** A4
Kennedy Channel *Arctic* 80°50N 66°0W **69** A18
Kennedy Ra. *Australia* 24°45S 115°10E **61** D2
Kennedy Range △
  *Australia* 24°34S 115°2E **61** D2
Kennemerduinen △
  *Neths.* 52°27N 4°33E **15** B4
Kennet → *U.K.* 51°27N 0°57W **13** F7
Kenneth Ra. *Australia* 23°50S 117°8E **61** D2
Kennett *U.S.A.* 36°14N 90°3W **80** G8
Kennewick *U.S.A.* 46°12N 119°7W **76** C4
Kennisis Lake *Canada* 45°13N 78°36W **82** A6
Kenogami → *Canada* 51°6N 84°28W **72** B3
Kenora *Canada* 49°47N 94°29W **71** D10
Kenosha *U.S.A.* 42°35N 87°49W **80** D10
Kenozersky △ *Russia* 62°5N 38°10E **26** C1
Kensington *Canada* 46°28N 63°34W **73** C7
Kent *Ohio, U.S.A.* 41°9N 81°22W **82** E3
Kent *Tex., U.S.A.* 31°4N 104°13W **84** F2
Kent *Wash., U.S.A.* 47°22N 122°14W **78** C4
Kent □ *U.K.* 51°12N 0°40E **13** F8
Kent Group *Australia* 39°30S 147°20E **63** F4
Kent Pen. *Canada* 68°30N 107°0W **68** D10
Kentaū *Kazakhstan* 43°32N 68°36E **26** E7
Kentland *U.S.A.* 40°46N 87°27W **80** E10
Kenton *U.S.A.* 40°39N 83°37W **81** E12
Kentucky □ *U.S.A.* 37°0N 84°0W **81** G11
Kentucky → *U.S.A.* 38°41N 85°11W **81** F11
Kentucky L. *U.S.A.* 37°1N 88°16W **80** G9
Kentville *Canada* 45°6N 64°29W **73** C7
Kentwood *U.S.A.* 30°56N 90°31W **85** F9
Kenya ■ *Africa* 1°0N 38°0E **54** D7
Kenya, Mt. *Kenya* 0°10S 37°18E **54** E7
Kenyir, Tasik *Malaysia* 5°1N 102°54E **39** K4
Keo Neua, Deo *Vietnam* 18°23N 105°10E **38** C5
Keokuk *U.S.A.* 40°24N 91°24W **80** E8
Keoladeo △ *India* 27°0N 77°20E **42** F7
Keonjhargarh *India* 21°28N 85°35E **43** J11
Kep *Cambodia* 10°29N 104°19E **39** G5
Kep *Vietnam* 21°24N 106°16E **38** B6
Kep △ *Cambodia* 10°30N 104°18E **39** G5
Kepala Batas *Malaysia* 5°31N 100°26E **39** c
Kepi *Indonesia* 6°32S 139°19E **37** F9
Kerala □ *India* 11°0N 76°15E **45** J3
Kerama-Rettō *Japan* 26°5N 127°15E **29** L3
Keran *India* 34°35N 73°59E **43** B5
Kerang *Australia* 35°40S 143°55E **63** F3
Keraudren, C. *Australia* 19°58S 119°45E **60** C2
Kerch *Ukraine* 45°20N 36°20E **19** E6
Kerepakupai-Meru = Angel Falls
  *Venezuela* 5°57N 62°30W **92** B6
Kerguelen *Ind. Oc.* 49°15S 69°10E **3** G13
Kerian, Kuala *Malaysia* 5°10N 100°25E **39** c
Kericho *Kenya* 0°22S 35°15E **54** E7
Kerinci *Indonesia* 1°40S 101°15E **36** E2
Kerki = Atamyrat
  *Turkmenistan* 37°50N 65°12E **26** F7
Kerkrade *Neths.* 50°53N 6°4E **15** D6
Kerkyra *Greece* 39°38N 19°50E **23** E8
Kermadec Is. *Pac. Oc.* 30°0S 178°15W **58** E11
Kermadec Trench
  *Pac. Oc.* 30°30S 176°0W **64** L10
Kermān *Iran* 30°15N 57°1E **47** D8
Kerman *U.S.A.* 36°43N 120°4W **78** J6
Kermān □ *Iran* 30°0N 57°0E **47** D8
Kermān, Bīābān-e *Iran* 28°45N 59°45E **47** D8
Kermānshāh *Iran* 34°23N 47°0E **46** C5
Kermānshāh □ *Iran* 34°0N 46°30E **46** C5
Kermit *U.S.A.* 31°52N 103°6W **84** F3
Kern → *U.S.A.* 35°16N 119°18W **79** K7
Kernow = Cornwall □
  *U.K.* 50°26N 4°40W **13** G3
Kernville *U.S.A.* 35°45N 118°26W **79** K8
Keroh *Malaysia* 5°43N 101°1E **39** K3
Kerrera *Malaysia* 56°24N 5°33W **11** E3
Kerrobert *Canada* 51°56N 109°8W **71** C7
Kerrville *U.S.A.* 30°3N 99°8W **84** F5
Kerry □ *Ireland* 52°7N 9°35W **10** D2
Kerry Hd. *Ireland* 52°25N 9°56W **10** D2
Kerulen = Herlen →
  *Asia* 48°48N 117°0E **31** B12
Kerzaz *Algeria* 29°29N 1°37W **52** C5
Kesagami → *Canada* 51°40N 79°45W **72** B4
Kesagami L. *Canada* 50°23N 80°15W **72** B3
Keşan *Turkey* 40°49N 26°38E **23** D12
Kesennuma *Japan* 38°54N 141°35E **28** E10
Keshit *Iran* 29°43N 58°17E **47** D8
Kesigi = Kosgi *India* 15°51N 77°16E **45** G3
Keskal *India* 20°5N 81°35E **44** D5
Kestenga *Russia* 65°50N 31°45E **8** D24
Keswick *U.K.* 54°36N 3°8W **12** C4
Ket → *Russia* 58°55N 81°32E **26** D9
Ketapang *Jawa Timur,*
  *Indonesia* 8°9S 114°23E **37** J17
Ketapang *Kalimantan Barat,*
  *Indonesia* 1°55S 110°0E **36** E4
Ketchikan *U.S.A.* 55°21N 131°39W **70** B2
Ketchum *U.S.A.* 43°41N 114°22W **76** E6
Keti Bandar *Pakistan* 24°8N 67°27E **42** G2
Ketri *India* 28°1N 75°50E **42** E6
Kętrzyn *Poland* 54°7N 21°22E **17** A11
Kettering *U.K.* 52°24N 0°43W **13** E7
Kettering *U.S.A.* 39°41N 84°10W **81** F11
Kettle → *Canada* 56°40N 89°34W **71** B11
Kettle Falls *U.S.A.* 48°37N 118°3W **76** B4
Kettle Point *Canada* 43°10N 82°1W **82** C2

Kettle Pt. *Canada* 43°13N 82°1W **82** C2
Kettleman City *U.S.A.* 36°1N 119°58W **78** J7
Keuka L. *U.S.A.* 42°30N 77°9W **82** D7
Keuruu *Finland* 62°16N 24°41E **8** E21
Kewanee *U.S.A.* 41°14N 89°56W **80** E9
Kewanee *Nepal* 27°57N 83°47E **43** F10
Kewaunee *U.S.A.* 44°27N 87°31W **80** C10
Keweenaw B. *U.S.A.* 47°0N 88°15W **80** B9
Keweenaw Pen. *U.S.A.* 47°15N 87°43W **80** B10
Keweenaw Pt. *U.S.A.* 47°25N 87°43W **80** B10
Key, L. *Ireland* 54°0N 8°15W **10** C3
Key Lake Mine *Canada* 57°5N 105°32W **71** B7
Key Largo *U.S.A.* 25°5N 80°27W **85** J14
Key West *U.S.A.* 24°33N 81°48W **88** B3
Keynsham *U.K.* 51°24N 2°29W **13** F5
Keyser *U.S.A.* 39°26N 78°59W **81** F14
Kezhma *Russia* 58°59N 101°9E **27** D11
Kezi *Zimbabwe* 20°58S 28°32E **57** B4
Kgalagadi □ *Botswana* 24°30S 22°0E **56** B3
Kgalagadi Transfrontier △
  *Africa* 25°10S 21°0E **56** C3
Khabarovsk *Russia* 48°30N 135°5E **31** B16
Khabr → *India* 28°51N 56°22E **47** D8
Khābūr → *Syria* 35°17N 40°35E **46** C4
Khachmas = Xaçmaz
  *Azerbaijan* 41°31N 48°42E **19** F8
Khachrod *India* 23°25N 75°20E **42** H6
Khadro *Pakistan* 26°11N 68°50E **42** F3
Khadzhilyangar = Dahongliutan
  *China* 35°45N 79°20E **43** B8
Khaga *India* 25°47N 81°7E **43** G9
Khagaria *India* 25°30N 86°32E **43** G12
Khaipur *Pakistan* 29°34N 72°17E **42** E5
Khair *India* 27°57N 77°46E **42** F7
Khairabad *India* 27°33N 80°47E **43** F9
Khairagarh *India* 21°27N 81°2E **43** J9
Khairpur *Pakistan* 27°32N 68°49E **42** F3
Khairpur Nathan Shah
  *Pakistan* 27°6N 67°44E **42** F2
Khairwara *India* 23°58N 73°38E **42** H5
Khaisor → *Pakistan* 31°17N 68°59E **42** D3
Khajuraho *India* 24°51N 79°55E **43** G8
Khajuri Kach *Pakistan* 32°4N 69°51E **42** C3
Khakassia □ *Russia* 53°0N 90°0E **26** D9
Khakhea *Botswana* 24°48S 23°22E **56** B3
Khalafābād *Iran* 30°54N 49°24E **47** D6
Khalilabad *India* 26°48N 83°5E **43** F10
Khalīlī *Iran* 27°38N 53°17E **47** E7
Khalkhāl *Iran* 37°37N 48°32E **47** B6
Khalkis = Chalkida
  *Greece* 38°27N 23°42E **23** E10
Khalmer Yu *Russia* 67°58N 65°1E **26** C7
Khalturin *Russia* 58°40N 49°0E **18** C8
Khalūf *Oman* 20°30N 58°13E **49** C6
Kham Keut *Laos* 18°15N 104°43E **38** C5
Khamaria *India* 23°5N 80°48E **43** H9
Khambhaliya *India* 22°14N 69°41E **42** H3
Khambhat *India* 22°23N 72°33E **42** H5
Khambhat, G. of *India* 20°45N 72°30E **40** J8
Khamgaon *India* 20°42N 76°37E **44** D3
Khamīr *Iran* 26°57N 55°36E **47** E7
Khamir *Yemen* 16°2N 44°0E **49** D3
Khamīs Mushayt
  *Si. Arabia* 18°18N 42°44E **49** D3
Khammam *India* 17°11N 80°6E **44** F5
Khamsa *Egypt* 30°27N 32°23E **48** E1
Khān Abū Shāmat *Syria* 33°39N 36°53E **48** B5
Khān Azād *Iraq* 33°7N 44°22E **46** C5
Khān Mujiddah *Iraq* 32°21N 43°48E **46** C4
Khān Shaykhūn *Syria* 35°26N 36°38E **46** C3
Khan Tengri, Pik *Asia* 42°12N 80°10E **30** C5
Khān Yūnis *Gaza Strip* 31°21N 34°18E **48** D3
Khanai *Pakistan* 30°30N 67°8E **42** D2
Khānaqīn *Iraq* 34°23N 45°25E **46** C5
Khānbāghī *Iran* 36°10N 55°25E **47** B7
Khandwa *India* 21°49N 76°22E **44** D3
Khandyga *Russia* 62°42N 135°35E **27** C14
Khanewal *Pakistan* 30°20N 71°55E **42** D4
Khangah Dogran
  *Pakistan* 31°50N 73°37E **42** D5
Khangchendzonga =
  Kanchenjunga △ *India* 27°42N 88°8E **43** F13
Khanh Duong *Vietnam* 12°44N 108°44E **38** F7
Khaniá = Chania *Greece* 35°30N 24°4E **23** G11
Khaniadhana *India* 25°1N 78°8E **42** G8
Khanka, L. *Asia* 45°0N 132°24E **28** B6
Khankendy = Xankändi
  *Azerbaijan* 39°52N 46°49E **46** B5
Khanna *India* 30°42N 76°16E **42** D7
Khanozai *Pakistan* 30°37N 67°19E **42** D2
Khanpur *Pakistan* 28°42N 70°35E **42** E4
Khanty-Mansiysk *Russia* 61°0N 69°0E **26** C7
Khao Khitchakut △
  *Thailand* 12°50N 102°10E **38** F4
Khao Laem △ *Thailand* 14°54N 98°31E **38** E2
Khao Laem Res. *Thailand* 14°50N 98°30E **38** E2
Khao Luak △ *Malaysia* 8°38N 98°18E **39** H2
Khao Luang △ *Thailand* 8°34N 99°42E **39** H2
Khao Nam Khang △
  *Thailand* 6°32N 100°35E **39** J3
Khao Phlu *Thailand* 9°29N 99°59E **39** b
Khao Pu -Khao Ya △
  *Thailand* 7°26N 99°57E **39** J2
Khao Sam Roi Yot △
  *Thailand* 12°13N 99°57E **39** F2
Khao Sok △ *Thailand* 8°55N 98°38E **39** H2
Khao Yai △ *Thailand* 14°21N 101°29E **38** E3
Khao Si Nakarin △
  *Thailand* 14°47N 99°0E **38** E2
Khapalu *Pakistan* 35°10N 76°20E **43** B7
Khapcheranga *Russia* 49°42N 112°24E **27** E12
Khaptao △ *Nepal* 29°20N 81°10E **43** E9
Kharaghoda *India* 23°11N 71°46E **42** H4
Kharagpur *India* 22°20N 87°25E **43** H12
Kharan Kalat *Pakistan* 28°34N 65°21E **40** E4
Kharānaq *Iran* 32°20N 54°45E **47** C7
Kharda *India* 18°40N 75°34E **44** E2
Khardung La *India* 34°20N 77°43E **43** B7
Kharg = Khārk, Jazīreh-ye
  *Iran* 29°15N 50°28E **47** D6

Khârga, El Wâhât el
  *Egypt* 25°10N 30°35E **53** C12
Khargon *India* 21°45N 75°40E **44** D2
Khari → *India* 25°54N 74°31E **42** G6
Kharian *Pakistan* 32°49N 73°52E **42** C5
Khariar *India* 20°17N 82°46E **44** D6
Khārk, Jazīreh-ye *Iran* 29°15N 50°28E **47** D6
Kharkiv *Ukraine* 49°58N 36°20E **19** E6
Kharkov = Kharkiv
  *Ukraine* 49°58N 36°20E **19** E6
Kharovsk *Russia* 59°56N 40°13E **18** C7
Kharsawangarh *India* 22°48N 85°50E **43** H11
Kharta *Turkey* 40°55N 29°7E **23** D13
Khartoum = El Khartûm
  *Sudan* 15°31N 32°35E **53** E12
Khartum *Canada* 45°15N 77°5W **82** A7
Khasan *Russia* 42°25N 130°40E **28** C5
Khāsh *Iran* 28°15N 61°15E **47** D9
Khashm el Girba *Sudan* 14°59N 35°58E **53** F13
Khat, Laem *Thailand* 8°6N 98°26E **39** a
Khatanga *Russia* 72°0N 102°20E **27** B11
Khatanga → *Russia* 72°55N 106°0E **27** B11
Khatauli *India* 29°17N 77°43E **42** E7
Khatra *India* 22°59N 86°51E **43** H12
Khātūnābād *Iran* 30°1N 55°25E **47** D7
Khatyrka *Russia* 62°3N 175°15E **27** C18
Khavda *India* 23°51N 69°43E **42** H3
Khawr Fakkān *U.A.E.* 25°21N 56°22E **47** E8
Khaybar, Ḥarrat
  *Si. Arabia* 25°30N 39°45E **46** E4
Khāzimiyah *Iraq* 34°46N 43°37E **46** C4
Khe Bo *Vietnam* 19°8N 104°41E **38** C5
Khe Long *Vietnam* 21°29N 104°46E **38** B5
Khe Sanh *Vietnam* 16°37N 106°45E **38** D6
Khed *Maharashtra, India* 17°43N 73°27E **44** F1
Khed *Maharashtra, India* 18°51N 73°56E **44** E1
Khed Brahma *India* 24°7N 73°5E **42** G5
Khekra *India* 28°52N 77°20E **42** E7
Khemarak Phouminville = Krong
  Kaoh Kong *Cambodia* 11°37N 102°59E **39** G4
Khemisset *Morocco* 33°50N 6°1W **52** B4
Khemmarat *Thailand* 16°10N 105°15E **38** D5
Khenāmān *Iran* 30°27N 56°29E **47** D8
Khenchela *Algeria* 35°28N 7°11E **52** A7
Khersān → *Iran* 31°33N 50°22E **47** D6
Kherson *Ukraine* 46°35N 32°35E **19** E5
Kheta → *Russia* 71°54N 102°6E **27** B11
Khewari *Pakistan* 26°36N 68°52E **42** F3
Khilchipur *India* 24°7N 76°34E **42** G7
Khilok *Russia* 51°30N 110°45E **27** D12
Khíos = Chios *Greece* 38°27N 26°9E **23** E12
Khirsadoh *India* 22°11N 78°47E **43** H8
Khiuma = Hiiumaa
  *Estonia* 58°50N 22°45E **9** G20
Khiva = Xiva *Uzbekistan* 41°30N 60°18E **26** E7
Khiwa = Xiva *Uzbekistan* 41°30N 60°18E **26** E7
Khlong Khlung *Thailand* 16°12N 99°43E **38** D2
Khlong Lan △ *Thailand* 16°12N 99°13E **38** D2
Khlong Phanom △
  *Thailand* 8°45N 98°38E **39** H2
Khmelnik *Ukraine* 49°33N 27°58E **17** D14
Khmelnytskyy *Ukraine* 49°23N 27°0E **17** D14
Khmelnytskyy □
  *Ukraine* 49°50N 26°40E **17** D14
Khmer Rep. = Cambodia ■
  *Asia* 12°15N 105°0E **38** F5
Khoai, Hon *Vietnam* 8°26N 104°50E **39** H5
Khobar = Al Khubar
  *Si. Arabia* 26°17N 50°12E **47** E6
Khodoriv *Ukraine* 49°24N 24°19E **17** D13
Khodzent = Khŭjand
  *Tajikistan* 40°17N 69°37E **26** E7
Khojak Pass *Afghan.* 30°51N 66°34E **42** D2
Khok Kloi *Thailand* 8°17N 98°19E **39** a
Khok Pho *Thailand* 6°43N 101°6E **39** J3
Khok Samrong *Thailand* 15°3N 100°43E **38** E3
Kholm *Russia* 57°10N 31°15E **18** C5
Kholmsk *Russia* 47°40N 142°5E **27** E15
Khomas □ *Namibia* 23°30S 17°0E **56** B2
Khomas Hochland
  *Namibia* 22°40S 16°0E **56** B2
Khomeyn *Iran* 33°40N 50°7E **47** C6
Khomeynī Shahr *Iran* 32°41N 51°31E **47** C6
Khomodino *Botswana* 22°46S 23°52E **56** B3
Khon Kaen *Thailand* 16°30N 102°47E **38** D4
Khong → *Cambodia* 13°32N 105°58E **38** F5
Khong Sedone *Laos* 15°34N 105°49E **38** E5
Khonuu *Russia* 66°30N 143°12E **27** C15
Khoper → *Russia* 49°30N 42°20E **19** E7
Khorāsān-e Janūb □ *Iran* 32°0N 59°0E **47** C8
Khorāsān-e Razavī □ *Iran* 35°0N 59°0E **47** C8
Khorāsān-e Shemālī □
  *Iran* 37°0N 57°0E **47** B8
Khorat = Nakhon Ratchasima
  *Thailand* 14°59N 102°12E **38** E4
Khorat, Cao Nguyen
  *Thailand* 15°30N 102°50E **38** E4
Khorixas *Namibia* 20°16S 14°59E **56** B1
Khorramābād *Khorāsān,*
  *Iran* 35°6N 57°57E **47** C8
Khorramābād *Lorestān,*
  *Iran* 33°30N 48°25E **47** C6
Khorramshahr *Iran* 30°29N 48°15E **47** D6
Khorugh *Tajikistan* 37°30N 71°36E **26** F8
Khosravī *Iran* 30°48N 51°28E **47** D6
Khosrowābād *Khuzestan,*
  *Iran* 30°10N 48°25E **47** D6
Khosrowābād *Kordestān,*
  *Iran* 35°31N 47°38E **46** C5
Khost *Pakistan* 30°13N 67°35E **42** D2
Khosūyeh *Iran* 28°32N 54°26E **47** D7
Khotang *Nepal* 27°1N 86°51E **43** F12
Khotyn *Ukraine* 48°31N 26°27E **17** D14
Khouribga *Morocco* 32°58N 6°57W **52** B4
Khowst *Afghan.* 33°22N 69°58E **42** C3
Khowst □ *Afghan.* 33°20N 70°0E **42** C3
Khoyniki *Belarus* 51°54N 29°55E **17** C15
Khram, Ko *Thailand* 12°42N 100°47E **38** F3
Khuan Na *Thailand* 7°53N 99°18E **39** a
Khudzhand = Khŭjand
  *Tajikistan* 40°17N 69°37E **26** E7

Khuff *Si. Arabia* 24°55N 44°53E **46** E5
Khŭgiānī *Afghan.* 31°34N 66°32E **42** D2
Khuis *Botswana* 26°40S 21°49E **56** C3
Khuiyala *India* 27°9N 70°25E **42** F4
Khŭjand *Tajikistan* 40°17N 69°37E **26** E7
Khujner *India* 23°47N 76°36E **42** H7
Khukhan *Thailand* 14°42N 104°12E **38** E5
Khulna *Bangla.* 22°45N 89°34E **41** H16
Khulna □ *Bangla.* 22°25N 89°35E **41** H16
Khumago *Botswana* 20°26S 24°32E **56** B3
Khunjerab △ *Pakistan* 36°40N 75°30E **43** A6
Khunjerab Pass = Kinjirap Daban
  *Asia* 36°40N 75°25E **40** A9
Khūnsorkh *Iran* 27°9N 56°7E **47** E8
Khunti *India* 23°5N 85°17E **43** H11
Khūr *Iran* 32°55N 58°18E **47** C8
Khurai *India* 24°3N 78°23E **42** G8
Khuraym *Si. Arabia* 25°6N 48°2E **47** E6
Khurda *India* 20°11N 85°37E **44** D7
Khurja *India* 28°15N 77°58E **42** E7
Khūrmāl *Iraq* 35°18N 46°2E **46** C5
Khurr, Wādī al *Iraq* 32°3N 43°52E **46** C4
Khūsf *Iran* 32°46N 58°53E **47** C8
Khushab *Pakistan* 32°20N 72°20E **42** C5
Khust *Ukraine* 48°10N 23°18E **17** D12
Khutse △ *Botswana* 23°31S 24°12E **56** B3
Khūzestān □ *Iran* 31°0N 49°0E **47** D6
Khvāf *Iran* 34°33N 60°8E **47** C9
Khvājeh *Iran* 38°9N 46°35E **46** B5
Khvānsār *Iran* 29°56N 54°8E **47** D7
Khvor *Iran* 33°45N 55°0E **47** C7
Khvorgū *Iran* 27°34N 56°27E **47** E8
Khvormūj *Iran* 28°40N 51°30E **47** D6
Khvoy *Iran* 38°35N 45°0E **46** B5
Khwae Noi → *Thailand* 14°1N 99°32E **38** E2
Khyber Pakhtunkhwa □
  *Pakistan* 34°0N 72°0E **42** C5
Khyber Pass *Afghan.* 34°10N 71°8E **42** B4
Kia *Fiji* 16°16S 179°8E **59** a
Kiadho → *India* 19°37N 77°40E **44** E3
Kiama *Australia* 34°40S 150°50E **63** E5
Kiamba *Phil.* 6°2N 124°46E **37** C6
Kiangsi = Jiangxi □
  *China* 27°30N 116°0E **35** D11
Kiangsu = Jiangsu □
  *China* 33°0N 120°0E **33** H11
Kibombo
  *Dem. Rep. of the Congo* 3°57S 25°53E **54** E5
Kibre Mengist *Ethiopia* 5°54N 38°59E **47** F2
Kibwezi *Kenya* 2°27S 37°57E **54** E7
Kichha *India* 28°41N 79°18E **43** E8
Kichmengskiy Gorodok
  *Russia* 59°59N 45°48E **18** B8
Kicking Horse Pass
  *Canada* 51°28N 116°16W **70** C5
Kidal *Mali* 18°26N 1°22E **52** E6
Kidderminster *U.K.* 52°24N 2°15W **13** E5
Kidnappers, C. *N.Z.* 39°38S 177°5E **59** C6
Kidsgrove *U.K.* 53°5N 2°14W **12** D5
Kidston *Australia* 18°52S 144°8E **62** B3
Kiel *Germany* 54°19N 10°8E **16** A6
Kiel Canal = Nord-Ostsee-Kanal
  *Germany* 54°12N 9°32E **16** A5
Kielce *Poland* 50°52N 20°42E **17** C11
Kielder Water *U.K.* 55°11N 2°31W **12** B5
Kieler Bucht *Germany* 54°35N 10°25E **16** A6
Kiev = Kyyiv *Ukraine* 50°30N 30°28E **17** C16
Kiffa *Mauritania* 16°37N 11°24W **52** E3
Kifrī *Iraq* 34°45N 45°0E **46** C5
Kigali *Rwanda* 1°59S 30°4E **54** E6
Kigoma-Ujiji *Tanzania* 4°55S 29°36E **54** E5
Kiğzı *Turkey* 38°18N 43°25E **46** B5
Kihnu *Estonia* 58°9N 24°1E **9** G21
Kii-Sanchi *Japan* 34°20N 136°0E **29** G8
Kii-Suidō *Japan* 33°40N 134°45E **29** H7
Kikaiga-Shima *Japan* 28°19N 129°59E **29** K4
Kikiak = Rigolet *Canada* 54°10N 58°23W **73** B8
Kikinda *Serbia* 45°50N 20°30E **23** B9
Kikládhes = Kyklades
  *Greece* 37°0N 24°30E **23** F11
Kikuchi *Japan* 32°59N 130°47E **29** H5
Kikwit *Dem. Rep. of the Congo* 5°0S 18°45E **54** F3
Kilakkarai *India* 9°12N 78°47E **45** K4
Kilar *India* 33°6N 76°25E **42** C7
Kilbeggan *Ireland* 53°22N 7°30W **10** C4
Kilbrannan Sd. *U.K.* 55°37N 5°26W **11** F3
Kilchu *N. Korea* 40°57N 129°25E **33** D15
Kilcoy *Australia* 26°59S 152°30E **63** D5
Kildare *Ireland* 53°9N 6°55W **10** C5
Kildare □ *Ireland* 53°10N 6°50W **10** C5
Kildinstroy *Russia* 68°48N 33°6E **8** B25
Kilfinnane *Ireland* 52°21N 8°28W **10** D3
Kilgarvan *Ireland* 51°54N 9°27W **10** E2
Kilgore *U.S.A.* 32°23N 94°53W **84** E7
Kilifi *Kenya* 3°40S 39°48E **54** E7
Kilimanjaro *Tanzania* 3°7S 37°20E **54** E7
Kilindini *Kenya* 4°4S 39°40E **54** E7
Kilinochchi *Sri Lanka* 9°24N 80°25E **45** K5
Kilis *Turkey* 36°42N 37°6E **46** B3
Kiliya *Ukraine* 45°28N 29°16E **17** F15
Kilkee *Ireland* 52°41N 9°39W **10** D2
Kilkeel *U.K.* 54°7N 5°55W **10** B5
Kilkenny *Ireland* 52°39N 7°15W **10** D4
Kilkenny □ *Ireland* 52°35N 7°15W **10** D4
Kilkieran B. *Ireland* 53°20N 9°41W **10** C2
Kilkis *Greece* 40°58N 22°57E **23** D10
Killala *Ireland* 54°13N 9°13W **10** B2
Killala B. *Ireland* 54°16N 9°8W **10** B2
Killaloe *Canada* 45°33N 77°25W **82** A7
Killaloe *Ireland* 52°48N 8°28W **10** D3
Killarney *Australia* 28°20S 152°18E **63** D5
Killarney *Canada* 45°55N 81°30W **72** C3
Killarney *Ireland* 52°4N 9°30W **10** D2
Killarney △ *Canada* 46°2N 81°35W **72** C3
Killary Harbour *Ireland* 53°38N 9°52W **10** C2
Killdeer *U.S.A.* 47°22N 102°45W **80** B2

Killeen *U.S.A.* 31°7N 97°44W **84** F6
Killin *U.K.* 56°28N 4°19W **11** E4
Killiney *Ireland* 53°15N 6°7W **10** C5
Killington Pk. *U.S.A.* 43°36N 72°49W **83** C12
Killini *Greece* 37°54N 22°25E **23** F10
Killiniq I. *Canada* 60°24N 64°37W **69** E19
Killorglin *Ireland* 52°6N 9°47W **10** D2
Killybegs *Ireland* 54°38N 8°26W **10** B3
Kilmarnock *U.K.* 55°37N 4°29W **11** F4
Kilmore *Australia* 37°25S 144°53E **63** F3
Kilmore Quay *Ireland* 52°10N 6°36W **10** D5
Kilosa *Tanzania* 6°48S 37°0E **54** F7
Kilrush *Ireland* 52°38N 9°29W **10** D2
Kiltan I. *India* 11°29N 73°0E **45** J1
Kilwa Kivinje *Tanzania* 8°45S 39°25E **54** F7
Kilwinning *U.K.* 55°39N 4°43W **11** F4
Kim *S. Africa* 37°15N 103°21W **77** H12
Kimaam *Indonesia* 7°58S 138°53E **37** F9
Kimba *Australia* 33°8S 136°23E **63** E2
Kimball *Nebr., U.S.A.* 41°14N 103°40W **80** E2
Kimball *S. Dak., U.S.A.* 43°45N 98°57W **80** D4
Kimberley *Australia* 16°20S 127°0E **60** C4
Kimberley *B.C., Canada* 49°40N 115°59W **70** D5
Kimberley *Ont., Canada* 44°23N 80°32W **82** B4
Kimberley *S. Africa* 28°43S 24°46E **56** D3
Kimberly *U.S.A.* 42°32N 114°22W **76** E6
Kimch'aek *N. Korea* 40°40N 129°10E **33** D15
Kimhae = Gimhae
  *S. Korea* 35°14N 128°53E **33** G15
Kimmirut *Canada* 62°50N 69°50W **69** E18
Kimpese
  *Dem. Rep. of the Congo* 5°33S 14°26E **54** F2
Kimry *Russia* 56°55N 37°15E **18** C6
Kinabalu, Gunung
  *Malaysia* 6°3N 116°14E **36** C5
Kinaskan L. *Canada* 57°38N 130°8W **70** B2
Kinbasket L. *Canada* 52°0N 118°10W **70** C5
Kincardine *Canada* 44°10N 81°40W **82** B3
Kincolith *Canada* 55°0N 129°57W **70** B3
Kinde *U.S.A.* 43°56N 83°0W **82** C2
Kinder Scout *U.K.* 53°24N 1°52W **12** D6
Kindersley *Canada* 51°30N 109°10W **71** C7
Kindia *Guinea* 10°0N 12°52W **52** F3
Kindu
  *Dem. Rep. of the Congo* 2°55S 25°50E **54** E5
Kineshma *Russia* 57°30N 42°5E **18** C7
Kinesi, L. *Canada* 33°10S 119°35E **82** C2
King, Mt. *Australia* 25°10S 147°30E **62** D4
King Abdullah Economic City
  *Si. Arabia* 22°24N 39°5E **49** C2
King Christian I.
  *Canada* 77°48N 101°40W **69** B11
King City *U.S.A.* 36°13N 121°8W **78** J5
King Cr. → *Australia* 24°35S 139°30E **62** C2
King Edward →
  *Australia* 14°14S 126°35E **60** B4
King Edward Point
  *S. Georgia* 54°17S 36°30W **96** G9
King Frederick VI Land = Kong
  Frederik VI.s Kyst
  *Greenland* 63°0N 43°0W **4** C5
King George B. *Falk. Is.* 51°30S 60°30W **96** G4
King George I. *Antarctica* 60°0S 60°0W **5** C18
King George Is. *Canada* 57°20N 80°30W **69** F15
King George Sd. *Australia* 35°5S 118°0E **61** G2
King I. = Kadan Kyun
  *Myanmar* 12°30N 98°20E **38** F2
King I. *Australia* 39°50S 144°0E **63** F3
King I. *Canada* 52°10N 127°40W **70** C3
King Khalid Int. ✈ (RUH)
  *Si. Arabia* 24°57N 46°42E **46** E4
King Khalid Military City =
  Madinat al Malik Khālid al
  Askariyah *Si. Arabia* 27°54N 45°31E **46** E5
King Leopold Ranges
  *Australia* 17°30S 125°45E **60** C4
King of Prussia *U.S.A.* 40°5N 75°23W **83** F9
King Sd. *Australia* 16°50S 123°20E **60** C3
King Sejong *Antarctica* 62°30S 58°0W **5** C18
King Shaka Int. ✈ (DUR)
  *S. Africa* 29°37S 31°7E **57** C5
King William I.
  *Canada* 69°10N 97°25W **68** D12
King William's Town
  *S. Africa* 32°51S 27°22E **56** D4
Kingaok = Bathurst Inlet
  *Canada* 66°50N 108°1W **68** D10
Kingaroy *Australia* 26°32S 151°51E **63** D5
Kingfisher *U.S.A.* 35°52N 97°56W **84** D6
Kingirbān *Iraq* 34°40N 44°54E **46** C5
Kingisepp = Kuressaare
  *Estonia* 58°15N 22°30E **9** G20
Kingisepp *Russia* 59°25N 28°40E **9** G23
Kingman *Ariz., U.S.A.* 35°12N 114°4W **79** K12
Kingman *Kans., U.S.A.* 37°39N 98°7W **80** G4
Kingoonya *Australia* 30°55S 135°19E **63** E2
Kingri *Pakistan* 30°27N 69°49E **42** D3
Kings → *U.S.A.* 36°3N 119°50W **78** J7
Kings Canyon *Australia* 24°15S 131°34E **60** D5
King's Lynn *U.K.* 52°45N 0°24E **12** E8
Kings Park *U.S.A.* 40°53N 73°16W **83** F11
Kings Peak *U.S.A.* 40°46N 110°23W **76** F8
Kingsbridge *U.K.* 50°17N 3°47W **13** G4
Kingscote *Australia* 35°40S 137°38E **63** F2
Kingscourt *Ireland* 53°54N 6°48W **10** C5
Kingsford *U.S.A.* 45°48N 88°4W **80** C9
Kingsland *U.S.A.* 30°48N 81°41W **85** F14
Kingsport *U.S.A.* 36°33N 82°33W **85** C13
Kingston *Canada* 44°14N 76°30W **83** B8
Kingston *Jamaica* 17°55N 76°50W **88** a
Kingston *N.Z.* 45°20S 168°43E **59** F2
Kingston *N.H., U.S.A.* 42°56N 71°3W **83** D13
Kingston *N.Y., U.S.A.* 41°56N 73°59W **83** E11
Kingston *Pa., U.S.A.* 41°16N 75°54W **83** E9
Kingston *R.I., U.S.A.* 41°29N 71°30W **83** E13
Kingston Pk. *U.S.A.* 35°44N 115°55W **79** K11
Kingston South East
  *Australia* 36°51S 139°55E **63** F2
Kingston upon Hull *U.K.* 53°45N 0°21W **12** D7

Kingston upon Hull □
  U.K.  53°45N 0°21W **12** D7
Kingstown St. Vincent 13°10N 61°10W **89** D7
Kingstree U.S.A. 33°40N 79°50W **85** E15
Kingsville Canada 42°2N 82°45W **82** D2
Kingsville U.S.A. 27°31N 97°52W **84** H6
Kingussie U.K. 57°6N 4°2W **11** D4
Kingwood U.S.A. 30°2N 95°16W **84** F7
Kınık Turkey 39°6N 27°24E **23** E12
Kinistino Canada 52°57N 105°2W **71** C7
Kinjirap Daban Asia 36°40N 75°25E **40** A9
Kinkala Congo 4°18S 14°49E **54** E2
Kinki □ Japan 33°45N 136°0E **29** H8
Kinleith N.Z. 38°20S 175°56E **59** C5
Kinlochleven U.K. 56°43N 5°0W **11** E4
Kinmount Canada 44°48N 78°45W **82** B6
Kinna Sweden 57°32N 12°42E **9** H15
Kinnairds Hd. U.K. 57°43N 2°1W **11** D6
Kinnarodden = Nordkinn
  Norway  71°8N 27°40E **8** A22
Kinngait Canada 64°14N 76°32W **69** E16
Kinniyai Sri Lanka 8°29N 81°11E **45** K5
Kino Nuevo Mexico 28°52N 112°33W **86** B2
Kinoje → Canada 52°8N 81°25W **72** B3
Kinomoto Japan 35°30N 136°13E **29** G8
Kinoosao Canada 57°5N 102°1W **71** B8
Kinross U.K. 56°13N 3°25W **11** E5
Kinsale Ireland 51°42N 8°31W **10** E3
Kinsale, Old Hd. of Ireland 51°37N 8°33W **10** E3
Kinsha = Chang Jiang →
  China  31°48N 121°10E **35** B13
Kinshasa
  Dem. Rep. of the Congo 4°20S 15°15E **54** E3
Kinsley U.S.A. 37°55N 99°25W **80** G4
Kinsman U.S.A. 41°26N 80°35W **82** E4
Kinston U.S.A. 35°16N 77°35W **85** D16
Kintamani Indonesia 8°14S 115°19E **37** J18
Kintore U.K. 57°14N 2°20W **11** D6
Kintore Ra. Australia 23°15S 128°47E **60** D4
Kintyre U.K. 55°30N 5°35W **11** F3
Kintyre, Mull of U.K. 55°17N 5°47W **11** F3
Kinushseo → Canada 55°15N 83°45W **72** A3
Kinuso Canada 55°20N 115°25W **70** B5
Kinvarra Ireland 53°8N 8°56W **10** C3
Kinwat India 19°38N 78°12E **44** E4
Kinzua U.S.A. 41°52N 78°58W **82** E6
Kiosk Canada 46°6N 78°53W **72** C4
Kiowa Kans., U.S.A. 37°1N 98°29W **80** G4
Kiowa Okla., U.S.A. 34°43N 95°54W **84** D7
Kipahigan L. Canada 55°20N 101°55W **71** B8
Kiparissia Greece 37°15N 21°40E **23** F9
Kiparissiakos Kolpos
  Greece  37°25N 21°25E **23** F9
Kipawa, L. Canada 46°50N 79°0W **72** C4
Kipling Canada 50°6N 102°38W **71** C8
Kippure Ireland 53°11N 6°21W **10** C5
Kipushi
  Dem. Rep. of the Congo 11°48S 27°12E **55** G5
Kirandul India 18°33N 81°10E **44** E5
Kirensk Russia 57°50N 107°55E **27** D11
Kirghiz Range Asia 42°40N 73°40E **30** C3
Kirghizia = Kyrgyzstan ■
  Asia  42°0N 75°0E **26** E8
Kirgiziya Steppe Eurasia 50°0N 55°0E **19** E10
Kiri Buru India 22°0N 85°0E **44** D7
Kiribati ■ Pac. Oc. 3°0S 180°0E **58** B10
Kırıkkale Turkey 39°51N 33°32E **19** G5
Kirillov Russia 59°49N 38°24E **18** C6
Kirin = Jilin China 43°44N 126°30E **33** C14
Kirindi Oya → Sri Lanka 6°15N 81°20E **45** L5
Kirinyaga = Kenya, Mt.
  Kenya  0°10S 37°18E **54** E7
Kirirom △ Cambodia 11°18N 104°5E **39** G5
Kirishima Japan 31°44N 130°46E **29** J5
Kirishima Yaku △ Japan 31°24N 130°50E **29** J5
Kiritimati Kiribati 1°58N 157°27W **65** G12
Kirkby U.K. 53°30N 2°54W **12** D5
Kirkby-in-Ashfield U.K. 53°6N 1°14W **12** D6
Kirkby Lonsdale U.K. 54°12N 2°36W **12** C5
Kirkby Stephen U.K. 54°29N 2°21W **12** C5
Kirkcaldy U.K. 56°7N 3°9W **11** E5
Kirkcudbright U.K. 54°50N 4°2W **11** G4
Kirkenes Norway 69°40N 30°5E **8** B24
Kirkfield Canada 44°34N 78°59W **82** B6
Kirkintilloch U.K. 55°56N 4°8W **11** F4
Kirkjubæjarklaustur
  Iceland  63°47N 18°4W **8** E4
Kirkkonummi Finland 60°8N 24°26E **9** F21
Kirkland U.S.A. 47°40N 122°12W **78** C4
Kirkland Lake Canada 48°9N 80°2W **72** C3
Kırklareli Turkey 41°44N 27°15E **23** D12
Kirkpatrick, Mt.
  Antarctica  84°20S 166°25E **5** E11
Kirksville U.S.A. 40°12N 92°35W **80** E7
Kirkūk Iraq 35°30N 44°21E **46** C5
Kirkwall U.K. 58°59N 2°58W **11** C6
Kirkwood S. Africa 33°22S 25°15E **56** D4
Kirlampudi India 17°12N 82°12E **44** F6
Kirov Russia 58°35N 49°40E **18** C8
Kirovabad = Gäncä
  Azerbaijan  40°45N 46°20E **19** F8
Kirovo-Chepetsk Russia 58°28N 50°0E **18** C9
Kirovograd = Kirovohrad
  Ukraine  48°35N 32°20E **19** E5
Kirovohrad Ukraine 48°35N 32°20E **19** E5
Kirovsk Russia 67°32N 33°41E **18** A5
Kirovskiy Kamchatka,
  Russia  54°27N 155°42E **27** D16
Kirovskiy Primorsk,
  Russia  45°7N 133°30E **28** B6
Kirriemuir U.K. 56°41N 3°1W **11** E5
Kirsanov Russia 52°35N 42°40E **18** D7
Kırşehir Turkey 39°14N 34°5E **46** B2
Kirthar △ Pakistan 25°45N 67°30E **42** F2
Kirthar Range Pakistan 27°0N 67°0E **42** F2
Kirtland U.S.A. 36°44N 108°21W **77** H9
Kiruna Sweden 67°52N 20°15E **8** C19
Kiryū Japan 36°24N 139°20E **29** F9
Kisangani
  Dem. Rep. of the Congo 0°35N 25°15E **54** D5

Kisar Indonesia 8°5S 127°10E **37** F7
Kisarazu Japan 35°23N 139°55E **29** G9
Kiselevsk Russia 54°5N 86°39E **26** D9
Kish = Qeys Iran 26°32N 53°58E **47** E7
Kishanganga → Pakistan 34°18N 73°28E **43** B5
Kishanganj India 26°3N 88°14E **43** F13
Kishangarh Raj., India 26°34N 74°52E **42** F6
Kishangarh Raj., India 27°50N 70°30E **42** F4
Kishinev = Chişinău
  Moldova  47°2N 28°50E **17** E15
Kishiwada Japan 34°28N 135°22E **29** G7
Kishtwar India 33°20N 75°48E **42** C6
Kisii Kenya 0°40S 34°45E **54** E6
Kiska I. U.S.A. 51°59N 177°30E **74** E3
Kiskörös Hungary 46°37N 19°20E **17** E10
Kiskunfélegyháza
  Hungary  46°42N 19°53E **17** E10
Kiskunhalas Hungary 46°28N 19°37E **17** E10
Kislovodsk Russia 43°50N 42°45E **19** F7
Kismaayo Somalia 0°22S 42°32E **49** H3
Kiso-Gawa → Japan 35°20N 136°45E **29** G8
Kiso-Sammyaku Japan 35°45N 137°45E **29** G8
Kisofukushima Japan 35°52N 137°43E **29** G8
Kissidougou Guinea 9°5N 10°5W **52** G3
Kissimmee U.S.A. 28°18N 81°24W **85** G14
Kissimmee → U.S.A. 27°9N 80°52W **85** H14
Kississing L. Canada 55°10N 101°20W **71** B8
Kisumu Kenya 0°3S 34°45E **54** E6
Kit Carson U.S.A. 38°46N 102°48W **76** G12
Kita Mali 13°5N 9°25W **52** F4
Kitaibaraki Japan 36°50N 140°45E **29** F10
Kitakami Japan 39°20N 141°10E **28** E10
Kitakami-Gawa →
  Japan  38°25N 141°19E **28** E10
Kitakami-Sammyaku
  Japan  39°30N 141°30E **28** E10
Kitakata Japan 37°39N 139°52E **28** F9
Kitakyūshū Japan 33°50N 130°50E **29** H5
Kitale Kenya 1°0N 35°0E **54** D7
Kitami Japan 43°48N 143°54E **28** C11
Kitami-Sammyaku
  Japan  44°22N 142°43E **28** B11
Kitchener Canada 43°27N 80°29W **82** C4
Kitee Finland 62°5N 30°8E **8** E24
Kitega = Gitega Burundi 3°26S 29°56E **54** E5
Kíthira = Kythira Greece 36°8N 23°0E **23** F10
Kíthnos = Kythnos
  Greece  37°26N 24°27E **23** F11
Kitikmeot Canada 67°0N 110°0W **68** D9
Kitimat Canada 54°3N 128°38W **70** C3
Kitinen → Finland 67°14N 27°27E **8** C22
Kitsuki Japan 33°25N 131°37E **29** H5
Kittakittaooloo, L.
  Australia  28°3S 138°14E **63** D2
Kittanning U.S.A. 40°49N 79°31W **82** F5
Kittatinny Mt. U.S.A. 41°19N 74°39W **83** F10
Kittery U.S.A. 43°5N 70°45W **83** C14
Kittilä Finland 67°40N 24°51E **8** C21
Kitui Kenya 1°17S 38°0E **54** E7
Kitwanga Canada 55°6N 128°4W **70** B3
Kitwe Zambia 12°54S 28°13E **55** G5
Kivalliq Canada 62°0N 97°30W **68** E12
Kivarli India 24°33N 72°46E **42** G5
Kivertsi Ukraine 50°50N 25°28E **17** C13
Kivu, L.
  Dem. Rep. of the Congo 1°48S 29°0E **54** E5
Kiwirrkurra Australia 22°49S 127°45E **60** D4
Kiwirrkurra ◉ Australia 22°49S 127°45E **60** D4
Kiyev = Kyyiv Ukraine 50°30N 30°28E **17** C16
Kiyevskoye Vdkhr. = Kyyivske
  Vdskh. Ukraine 51°0N 30°25E **17** C16
Kizel Russia 59°3N 57°40E **18** C10
Kızıl Irmak → Turkey 41°44N 35°58E **19** F6
Kizil Jilga China 35°26N 78°50E **43** B8
Kızıldağ △ Turkey 38°5N 31°20E **46** B1
Kızıltepe Turkey 37°12N 40°35E **46** B4
Kizlyar Russia 43°51N 46°40E **19** F8
Kizyl-Arvat = Serdar
  Turkmenistan  39°4N 56°23E **47** B8
Kjölur Iceland 64°50N 19°25E **8** D4
Kladno Czechia 50°10N 14°7E **16** C8
Klaeng Thailand 12°47N 101°39E **38** F3
Klagenfurt Austria 46°38N 14°20E **16** E8
Klaipėda Lithuania 55°43N 21°10E **9** J19
Klaksvík Færoe Is. 62°14N 6°35W **8** E9
Klamath → U.S.A. 41°33N 124°5W **76** F1
Klamath Falls U.S.A. 42°13N 121°46W **76** E3
Klamath Mts. U.S.A. 41°20N 123°0W **76** F2
Klamono Indonesia 1°8S 131°30E **37** E8
Klang Malaysia 3°2N 101°26E **39** L3
Klappan → Canada 58°0N 129°43W **70** B3
Klarälven → Sweden 59°23N 13°32E **9** G15
Klatovy Czechia 49°23N 13°18E **16** D7
Klawer S. Africa 31°44S 18°36E **56** D2
Klazienaveen Neths. 52°44N 7°0E **15** B6
Kleena Kleene Canada 52°0N 124°59W **70** C4
Klerksdorp S. Africa 26°53S 26°38E **56** D4
Klerkskraal S. Africa 26°13N 27°9E **57** D4
Kletsk = Klyetsk Belarus 53°5N 26°45E **17** B14
Kletskiy Russia 49°16N 43°11E **19** E7
Klickitat U.S.A. 45°49N 121°9W **78** E5
Klickitat → U.S.A. 45°42N 121°17W **78** E5
Klinaklini → Canada 51°21N 125°40W **70** C3
Klip → S. Africa 27°3S 29°3E **57** C4
Klipdale S. Africa 34°19S 19°57E **56** D2
Klipplaat S. Africa 33°1S 24°22E **56** D3
Kłodzko Poland 50°28N 16°38E **17** C9
Klondike Canada 64°0N 139°26W **68** E4
Klong Wang Chao △
  Thailand  16°20N 99°9E **38** D2
Kluane → Canada 60°45N 139°30W **70** A1
Kluane L. Canada 61°15N 138°40W **68** E4
Kluang Malaysia 2°3N 103°18E **39** L4
Kluczbork Poland 50°58N 18°12E **17** C10
Klukwan U.S.A. 59°24N 135°54W **70** B1
Klungkung Indonesia 8°32S 115°24E **37** K18
Klyetsk Belarus 53°5N 26°45E **17** B14
Klyuchevskaya, Sopka
  Russia  55°50N 160°30E **27** D17

Klyuchi Russia 56°18N 160°51E **27** D17
Knaresborough U.K. 54°1N 1°28W **12** C6
Knee L. Man., Canada 55°3N 94°45W **72** A1
Knee L. Sask., Canada 55°51N 107°0W **71** B7
Knight Inlet Canada 50°45N 125°40W **70** C3
Knighton U.K. 52°21N 3°3W **13** E4
Knights Ferry U.S.A. 37°50N 120°40W **78** H6
Knights Landing U.S.A. 38°48N 121°43W **78** G5
Knob, C. Australia 34°32S 119°16E **61** F2
Knock Ireland 53°48N 8°55W **10** C3
Knockmealdown Mts.
  Ireland  52°14N 7°56W **10** D4
Knokke-Heist Belgium 51°21N 3°17E **15** C3
Knossos Greece 35°16N 25°10E **23** G11
Knowlton Canada 45°13N 72°31W **83** A12
Knox U.S.A. 41°18N 86°37W **80** E10
Knoxville Iowa, U.S.A. 41°19N 93°6W **80** E7
Knoxville Pa., U.S.A. 41°57N 77°27W **82** E7
Knoxville Tenn., U.S.A. 35°58N 83°55W **85** D13
Knud Rasmussen Land
  Greenland  78°0N 60°0W **69** B20
Knysna S. Africa 34°2S 23°2E **56** D3
Ko Kha Thailand 18°11N 99°24E **38** C2
Ko Tarutao △ Thailand 6°31N 99°26E **39** J2
Ko Yao Thailand 8°7N 98°35E **39** a
Koartac = Quaqtaq
  Canada  60°55N 69°40W **69** E13
Koba Indonesia 6°37S 134°37E **37** F8
Kobarid Slovenia 46°15N 13°30E **16** E7
Kobayashi Japan 31°56N 130°59E **29** J5
Kōbe Japan 34°41N 135°13E **29** G7
Kōbi-Sho E. China Sea 25°56N 123°41E **29** M1
Koblenz Germany 50°21N 7°36E **16** C4
Kobryn Belarus 52°15N 24°22E **17** B13
Kobuk → U.S.A. 66°54N 160°38W **74** B7
Kocaeli Turkey 40°45N 29°50E **19** F4
Kočani Macedonia 41°55N 22°25E **23** D10
Koch Bihar India 26°22N 89°29E **41** F16
Kochas India 25°15N 83°56E **43** G10
Kochi India 9°58N 76°20E **45** K3
Kōchi Japan 33°30N 133°35E **29** H6
Kōchi □ Japan 33°40N 133°30E **29** H6
Kochiu = Gejiu China 23°20N 103°10E **34** D5
Kodala India 19°38N 84°57E **44** E7
Kodarma India 24°28N 85°36E **43** G11
Koddiyar B. Sri Lanka 8°33N 81°15E **45** K5
Kodiak U.S.A. 57°47N 152°24W **74** D9
Kodiak I. U.S.A. 57°30N 152°45W **74** D9
Kodikkarai = Point Calimere
  India  10°17N 79°49E **45** J4
Kodinar India 20°46N 70°46E **42** J4
Kodinsk Russia 58°40N 99°10E **27** D10
Kodlipet India 12°48N 75°53E **45** H2
Kodungallur = Cranganore
  India  10°13N 76°13E **45** J3
Koedoesberge S. Africa 32°40S 20°11E **56** D3
Koes Namibia 26°0S 19°15E **56** D2
Koffiefontein S. Africa 29°30S 25°0E **56** C4
Kofiau Indonesia 1°11S 129°50E **37** E7
Koforidua Ghana 6°3N 0°17W **52** G5
Kōfu Japan 35°40N 138°30E **29** G9
Koga Japan 36°11N 139°43E **29** F9
Kogaluc → Canada 56°12N 61°44W **73** A7
Køge Denmark 55°27N 12°11E **9** J15
Kogon Uzbekistan 39°43N 64°33E **26** F7
Koh-i-Khurd Afghan. 33°30N 65°59E **42** C1
Koh-i-Maran Pakistan 29°18N 66°50E **42** E2
Koh Ker Cambodia 13°47N 104°32E **38** F5
Koh Wai Thailand 11°54N 102°25E **39** H4
Kohat Pakistan 33°40N 71°29E **42** C4
Kohima India 25°35N 94°10E **41** G19
Kohkīlūyeh va Būyer Aḥmadī □
  Iran  31°30N 50°30E **47** D6
Kohler Ra. Antarctica 77°0S 110°0W **5** D15
Kohlu Pakistan 29°54N 69°15E **42** E3
Kohtla-Järve Estonia 59°20N 27°20E **9** G22
Koi Sanjaq Iraq 36°5N 44°38E **46** B5
Koihoa India 8°12N 93°29E **45** K11
Koilkuntla India 15°14N 78°19E **45** G4
Koillismaa Finland 65°44N 28°36E **8** D23
Koin N. Korea 40°28N 126°18E **33** D14
Kojǒ N. Korea 38°58N 127°58E **33** E14
Kojonup Australia 33°48S 117°10E **61** F2
Kojūr Iran 36°23N 51°43E **47** B6
Kokand = Qo'qon
  Uzbekistan  40°31N 70°56E **26** E8
Kokang Myanmar 23°45N 98°30E **34** F2
Kokas Indonesia 2°42S 132°26E **37** E8
Kokchetav = Kökshetaū
  Kazakhstan  53°20N 69°25E **26** D7
Kokemäenjoki →
  Finland  61°32N 21°44E **8** F19
Kokkilai Sri Lanka 9°0N 80°57E **45** K5
Kokkola Finland 63°50N 23°8E **8** E20
Koko Kyunzu Myanmar 14°7N 93°22E **45** G11
Koko Nur = Qinghai Hu
  China  36°40N 100°10E **30** D9
Kokomo U.S.A. 40°29N 86°8W **80** E10
Kokopo Papua N. G. 4°22S 152°19E **64** H7
Koksan N. Korea 38°46N 126°40E **33** E14
Kökshetaū Kazakhstan 53°20N 69°25E **26** D7
Koksoak → Canada 58°30N 68°10W **69** F18
Kokstad S. Africa 30°32S 29°29E **57** D4
Kokubu = Kirishima
  Japan  31°44N 130°46E **29** J5
Kola Indonesia 5°35S 134°30E **37** F8
Kola Russia 68°45N 33°8E **8** B25
Kola Pen. = Kolskiy Poluostrov
  Russia  67°30N 38°0E **18** A6
Kolachel India 8°10N 77°15E **45** K3
Kolachi → Pakistan 27°8N 67°2E **42** F2
Kolahoi India 34°12N 75°22E **43** B6
Kolaka Indonesia 4°3S 121°46E **37** E6
Kolar India 13°12N 78°15E **45** H4
Kolar Gold Fields India 12°58N 78°16E **45** H4
Kolaras India 25°14N 77°36E **42** G6
Kolari Finland 67°20N 23°48E **8** C20
Kolasib India 24°15N 92°45E **41** G18
Kolayat India 27°50N 72°50E **42** F5
Kolda Senegal 12°55N 14°57W **52** F3

Kolding Denmark 55°30N 9°29E **9** J13
Kolepom = Dolak, Pulau
  Indonesia  8°0S 138°30E **37** F9
Kolguyev, Ostrov Russia 69°20N 48°30E **18** A8
Kolhapur India 16°43N 74°15E **44** L9
Kolín Czechia 50°2N 15°9E **16** C8
Kolka rags Latvia 57°46N 22°37E **9** H20
Kollam India 8°50N 76°38E **45** K3
Kollegal India 12°9N 77°9E **45** H3
Kolleru L. India 16°40N 81°10E **44** L3
Kollum Neths. 53°17N 6°10E **15** A6
Kolmanskop Namibia 26°45S 15°14E **56** C2
Köln Germany 50°56N 6°57E **16** C4
Koło Poland 52°14N 18°40E **17** B10
Kołobrzeg Poland 54°10N 15°35E **16** A8
Kolokani Mali 13°35N 7°45W **52** F4
Kolomna Russia 55°8N 38°45E **18** C6
Kolomyya Ukraine 48°31N 25°2E **17** D13
Kolonodale Indonesia 2°0S 121°19E **37** E6
Kolpashevo Russia 58°20N 83°5E **26** D9
Kolpino Russia 59°44N 30°39E **18** C5
Kolskiy Poluostrov Russia 67°30N 38°0E **18** A6
Kolskiy Zaliv Russia 69°23N 34°0E **8** B26
Kolwezi
  Dem. Rep. of the Congo 10°40S 25°25E **54** G5
Kolyma → Russia 69°30N 161°0E **27** C17
Kolymskoye Nagorye
  Russia  63°0N 157°0E **27** C16
Kôm Ombo Egypt 24°25N 32°52E **53** D12
Komandorskiye Is. =
  Komandorskiye Ostrova
  Russia  55°0N 167°0E **27** D17
Komandorskiye Ostrova
  Russia  55°0N 167°0E **27** D17
Komárno Slovakia 47°49N 18°5E **17** E10
Komatipoort S. Africa 25°25S 31°55E **57** C5
Komatsu Japan 36°25N 136°30E **29** F8
Komatsushima Japan 34°0N 134°35E **29** H7
Komi □ Russia 64°0N 55°0E **18** B10
Kommamur Canal India 16°0N 80°25E **45** G5
Kommunarsk = Alchevsk
  Ukraine  48°30N 38°45E **19** E6
Kommunizma, Pik = imeni Ismail
  Samani, Pik Tajikistan 39°0N 72°2E **26** F8
Komodo Indonesia 8°37S 119°20E **37** F5
Komoran, Pulau
  Indonesia  8°18S 138°45E **37** F9
Komoro Japan 36°19N 138°26E **29** F9
Komotini Greece 41°9N 25°26E **23** D11
Kompasberg S. Africa 31°45S 24°32E **56** D3
Kompong Chhnang = Kampong
  Chhnang Cambodia 12°20N 104°35E **39** F5
Kompong Chikreng
  Cambodia  13°5N 104°18E **38** F5
Kompong Kleang
  Cambodia  13°6N 104°8E **38** F5
Kompong Luong
  Cambodia  11°49N 104°48E **39** G5
Kompong Pranak
  Cambodia  13°35N 104°55E **38** F5
Kompong Som = Kampong Saom
  Cambodia  10°38N 103°30E **39** G4
Kompong Som, Chhung =
  Kampong Saom, Chaak
  Cambodia  10°50N 103°32E **39** G4
Kompong Speu
  Cambodia  11°26N 104°32E **39** G5
Kompong Sralau
  Cambodia  14°5N 105°46E **38** E5
Kompong Thom
  Cambodia  12°35N 104°51E **38** F5
Kompong Trabeck
  Cambodia  13°6N 105°14E **38** F5
Kompong Trach
  Cambodia  11°25N 105°48E **39** G5
Kompong Tralach
  Cambodia  11°54N 104°47E **39** G5
Komrat = Comrat
  Moldova  46°18N 28°40E **17** E15
Komsberg S. Africa 32°40S 20°45E **56** D3
Komsomolets, Ostrov
  Russia  80°30N 95°0E **27** A10
Komsomolsk-na-Amur
  Russia  50°30N 137°0E **31** A16
Kon Ka Kinh △ Vietnam 14°19N 107°23E **38** E6
Kon Tum Vietnam 14°24N 108°0E **38** E7
Kon Tum, Plateau du
  Vietnam  14°30N 108°30E **38** E7
Konar □ Afghan. 34°30N 71°3E **40** B7
Konarak India 19°54N 86°7E **44** E8
Konawa U.S.A. 34°58N 96°45W **84** D6
Kondagaon India 19°35N 81°35E **44** E5
Kondinin Australia 32°34S 118°8E **61** F2
Kondoa Tanzania 4°55S 35°50E **54** E7
Kondopoga Russia 57°22N 34°11E **18** B8
Kondratyevo Russia 57°22N 98°15E **27** D10
Konduga Nigeria 11°35N 13°26E **53** F8
Könegürgench
  Turkmenistan  42°19N 59°10E **26** E6
Konevo Russia 62°8N 39°20E **18** B6
Kong Côte d'Ivoire 8°54N 4°36W **52** G5
Kong, Koh Cambodia 11°20N 103°0E **39** G4
Kong Christian IX.s Land
  Greenland  68°0N 36°0W **4** C6
Kong Christian X.s Land
  Greenland  74°0N 29°0W **4** B6
Kong Frederik IX.s Land
  Greenland  67°0N 52°0W **4** C5
Kong Frederik VI.s Kyst
  Greenland  63°0N 43°0W **4** C5
Kong Frederik VIII.s Land
  Greenland  78°30N 26°0W **4** B6
Kong Oscar Fjord
  Greenland  72°20N 24°0W **4** B6
Konglu Myanmar 27°13N 97°57E **41** F20
Kongola Namibia 17°45S 23°20E **56** A3

Kongolo
  Dem. Rep. of the Congo 5°22S 27°0E **54** F5
Kongsberg Norway 59°39N 9°39E **9** G13
Kongsvinger Norway 60°12N 12°2E **9** F15
Kongur Shan China 38°34N 75°18E **30** D4
Konin Poland 52°12N 18°15E **17** B10
Konjic Bos.-H. 43°42N 17°58E **23** C7
Konkiep Namibia 26°49S 17°15E **56** C2
Konnur India 16°14N 74°49E **45** F2
Konosha Russia 61°0N 40°5E **18** B7
Kōnosu Japan 36°3N 139°31E **29** F9
Konotop Ukraine 51°12N 33°7E **19** D5
Konqi He → China 40°45N 90°10E **30** C6
Końskie Poland 51°15N 20°23E **17** C11
Konstanz Germany 47°40N 9°10E **16** E5
Kont Iran 26°55N 61°50E **47** E9
Konta India 17°48N 81°23E **44** F5
Kontagora Nigeria 10°23N 5°27E **52** F7
Kontiolahti Finland 62°46N 29°50E **8** E23
Konya Turkey 37°52N 32°35E **46** B2
Koocanusa, L. Canada 49°20N 115°15W **76** B6
Kookynie Australia 29°17S 121°22E **61** E3
Koolyanobbing Australia 30°48S 119°36E **61** F2
Koonibba Australia 31°54S 133°25E **63** E1
Koorawatha Australia 34°2S 148°33E **63** E4
Koorda Australia 30°48S 117°35E **61** F2
Kooskia U.S.A. 46°9N 115°59W **76** C6
Kootenay → U.S.A. 49°19N 117°39W **70** D5
Kootenay △ Canada 51°0N 116°0W **70** C5
Kootenay L. Canada 49°45N 116°50W **76** B5
Kootjieskolk S. Africa 31°15S 20°21E **56** D3
Kopaonik Serbia 43°10N 20°50E **23** C9
Kopargaon India 19°51N 74°28E **44** E2
Kópavogur Iceland 64°6N 21°55W **8** D3
Koper Slovenia 45°31N 13°44E **16** F7
Kopervik Norway 59°17N 5°17E **9** G11
Kopet Dagh Asia 38°0N 58°0E **47** B8
Kopeysk Russia 55°7N 61°37E **26** D7
Kopi Australia 33°24S 135°40E **63** E2
Köping Sweden 59°31N 16°3E **9** G17
Koppa India 13°33N 75°21E **45** H2
Koppal India 15°23N 76°5E **45** G3
Koppeh Dāgh = Kopet Dagh
  Asia  38°0N 58°0E **47** B8
Koppies S. Africa 27°20S 27°30E **57** C4
Koprivnica Croatia 46°12N 16°45E **22** A7
Köprülü △ Turkey 37°20N 31°5E **46** B1
Kopychyntsi Ukraine 49°7N 25°58E **17** D13
Korab Macedonia 41°44N 20°40E **23** D9
Koral India 21°50N 73°12E **42** J5
Korangal India 17°6N 77°34E **44** E3
Koraput India 18°50N 82°40E **44** E6
Korba India 22°20N 82°45E **43** H10
Korbu, Gunung Malaysia 4°41N 101°18E **39** K3
Korçë Albania 40°37N 20°50E **23** D9
Korčula Croatia 42°56N 16°57E **22** C7
Kord Kūy Iran 36°48N 54°7E **47** B7
Kord Sheykh Iran 28°31N 52°53E **47** D7
Kordestān □ Iran 36°0N 47°0E **46** C5
Kordofân Sudan 13°0N 29°0E **53** F11
Korea, North ■ Asia 40°0N 127°0E **33** E14
Korea, South ■ Asia 36°0N 128°0E **33** G15
Korea Bay Korea 39°0N 124°0E **33** E13
Korea Strait Asia 34°0N 129°30E **33** H15
Koregaon India 17°40N 74°10E **44** F2
Korets Ukraine 50°40N 27°5E **17** C14
Korff Ice Rise Antarctica 79°0S 69°30W **5** D17
Korhogo Côte d'Ivoire 9°29N 5°28W **52** G4
Korinthiakos Kolpos
  Greece  38°16N 22°30E **23** E10
Korinthos Greece 37°56N 22°55E **23** F10
Kōriyama Japan 37°24N 140°23E **28** F10
Korla China 41°45N 86°4E **30** C6
Korneshty = Corneşti
  Moldova  47°21N 28°1E **17** E15
Koro Côte d'Ivoire 8°32N 7°30W **52** G4
Koro Fiji 17°19S 179°23E **59** a
Koro Sea Fiji 17°30S 179°45W **59** a
Korogwe Tanzania 5°5S 38°25E **54** F7
Korolevu Fiji 18°12S 177°46E **59** a
Koronadal Phil. 6°12N 124°51E **37** C6
Körös → Hungary 46°43N 20°12E **17** E11
Korosten Ukraine 50°54N 28°36E **17** C15
Korostyshev Ukraine 50°19N 29°4E **17** C15
Korovou Fiji 17°47S 178°32E **59** a
Koroyanitu △ Fiji 17°40S 177°35E **59** a
Korsakov Russia 46°36N 142°42E **27** E15
Korshunovo Russia 58°37N 110°10E **27** D12
Korsør Denmark 55°20N 11°9E **9** J14
Kortrijk Belgium 50°50N 3°17E **15** D3
Korwai India 24°7N 78°5E **42** G8
Koryakskoye Nagorye
  Russia  61°0N 171°0E **27** C18
Kos Greece 36°50N 27°15E **23** F12
Kosan N. Korea 38°52N 127°25E **33** E14
Kościan Poland 52°5N 16°40E **17** B9
Kosciusko U.S.A. 33°4N 89°35W **85** E10
Kosciuszko, Mt.
  Australia  36°27S 148°16E **63** F4
Kosgi Andhra Pradesh,
  India  16°58N 77°43E **44** F3
Kosgi Andhra Pradesh,
  India  15°51N 77°16E **45** G3
Kosha Sudan 20°50N 30°30E **53** D12
K'oshih = Kashi China 39°30N 76°2E **30** D4
Koshiki-Rettō Japan 31°45N 129°49E **29** J4
Kosi → India 27°48N 77°29E **42** F7
Kosi → India 28°41N 78°57E **43** E8
Košice Slovakia 48°42N 21°15E **17** D11
Kosŏng N. Korea 38°40N 128°22E **33** E15
Koslan Russia 63°34N 49°14E **18** B8
Kosovo ■ Europe 42°30N 21°0E **23** C9
Kosovska Mitrovica = Mitrovicë
  Kosovo  42°54N 20°52E **23** C9
Kossou, L. de Côte d'Ivoire 6°59N 5°31W **52** G4
Koster S. Africa 25°52S 26°54E **56** D4
Kŏstî Sudan 13°8N 32°43E **53** F12
Kostomuksha Russia 64°41N 30°49E **8** D24
Kostopil Ukraine 50°51N 26°22E **17** C14
Kostroma Russia 57°50N 40°58E **18** C7
Kostrzyn Poland 52°35N 14°39E **16** B8

Koszalin Poland 54°11N 16°8E 16 A9
Kot Addu Pakistan 30°30N 71°0E 42 D4
Kot Kapura India 30°35N 74°50E 42 D6
Kot Moman Pakistan 32°13N 73°0E 42 C5
Kot Sultan Pakistan 30°46N 70°56E 42 D4
Kota India 25°14N 75°49E 42 G6
Kota Barrage India 25°6N 75°51E 42 G6
Kota Belud Malaysia 6°21N 116°26E 36 C5
Kota Bharu Malaysia 6°7N 102°14E 39 J4
Kota I. = Loaita I.
S. China Sea 10°41N 114°25E 36 B4
Kota Kinabalu Malaysia 6°0N 116°4E 36 C5
Kota Tinggi Malaysia 1°44N 103°53E 39 M4
Kotaagung Indonesia 5°38S 104°29E 36 F2
Kotabaru Indonesia 3°20S 116°20E 36 E5
Kotabumi Indonesia 4°49S 104°54E 36 E2
Kotamobagu Indonesia 0°57N 124°31E 37 D6
Kotapad India 19°9N 82°21E 44 E6
Kotapinang Indonesia 1°53N 100°5E 39 M3
Kotcho L. Canada 59°7N 121°12W 70 B4
Kotdwara India 29°45N 78°32E 43 E8
Kotelnich Russia 58°22N 48°24E 18 C8
Kotelnikovo Russia 47°38N 43°8E 19 E7
Kotelnyy, Ostrov Russia 75°10N 139°0E 27 B14
Kothapet India 19°21N 79°28E 44 E4
Kothari → India 25°20N 75°4E 42 G6
Kothi Chhattisgarh, India 23°21N 82°3E 43 H10
Kothi Mad. P., India 24°45N 80°40E 43 G9
Kotiro Pakistan 26°17N 67°13E 42 F2
Kotka Finland 60°28N 26°58E 8 F22
Kotlas Russia 61°17N 46°43E 18 B8
Kotli Pakistan 33°30N 73°55E 42 C5
Kotlik U.S.A. 63°2N 163°33W 74 C7
Kotma India 23°12N 81°58E 43 H9
Kotor Montenegro 42°25N 18°47E 23 C8
Kotovsk Ukraine 47°45N 29°35E 17 E15
Kotputli India 27°43N 76°12E 42 F7
Kotri Pakistan 25°22N 68°22E 42 G3
Kotri → India 19°15N 80°35E 44 E5
Kottagudem India 17°30N 80°40E 44 F5
Kottayam India 9°35N 76°33E 45 K3
Kotto → C.A.R. 4°14N 22°2E 54 D4
Kottur India 10°34N 76°56E 45 J3
Kotturu India 14°45N 76°10E 45 G3
Kotu Group Tonga 20°0S 174°45W 59 c
Kotuy → Russia 71°54N 102°6E 27 B11
Kotzebue U.S.A. 66°53N 162°39W 74 B7
Kotzebue Sound U.S.A. 66°20N 163°0W 74 B7
Kouchibouguac △
Canada 46°50N 65°0W 73 C6
Koudougou Burkina Faso 12°10N 2°20W 52 F5
Kougaberge S. Africa 33°48S 23°50E 56 D3
Kouilou → Congo 4°10S 12°5E 54 E2
Koukdjuak → Canada 66°43N 73°0W 69 D17
Koula Moutou Gabon 1°15S 12°25E 54 E2
Koulen = Kulen
Cambodia 13°50N 104°40E 38 F5
Koumala Australia 21°38S 149°15E 62 C4
Koumra Chad 8°50N 17°35E 53 G9
Kountze U.S.A. 30°22N 94°19W 84 F7
Kourou Fr. Guiana 5°9N 52°39W 93 B8
Kouroussa Guinea 10°45N 9°45W 52 F4
Kousseri Cameroon 12°0N 14°55E 53 F8
Koutiala Mali 12°25N 5°23W 52 F4
Kouvola Finland 60°52N 26°43E 8 F22
Kovdor Russia 67°34N 30°24E 8 C24
Kovel Ukraine 51°11N 24°38E 17 C13
Kovilpatti India 9°10N 77°50E 45 K3
Kovrov Russia 56°25N 41°25E 18 C7
Kovur Andhra Pradesh, India 17°3N 81°39E 44 F5
Kovur Andhra Pradesh,
India 14°30N 80°1E 45 G5
Kowanyama Australia 15°29S 141°44E 62 B3
Kowanyama ⊙ Australia 15°20S 141°47E 62 B3
Kowŏn N. Korea 39°26N 127°14E 33 E14
Koyampattur = Coimbatore
India 11°2N 76°59E 45 J3
Köyceğiz Turkey 36°57N 28°40E 23 F13
Koyukuk → U.S.A. 64°55N 157°32W 74 C8
Koza = Okinawa Japan 26°19N 127°46E 29 L3
Kozan Turkey 37°26N 35°50E 46 B2
Kozani Greece 40°19N 21°47E 23 D9
Kozhikode India 11°15N 75°43E 45 J2
Kozhva Russia 65°10N 57°0E 18 A10
Kōzu-Shima Japan 34°13N 139°10E 29 G9
Kozyatyn Ukraine 49°45N 28°50E 17 D15
Kozyrevsk Russia 56°3N 159°51E 27 D16
Kpalimé Togo 6°57N 0°44E 52 G6
Kra, Isthmus of = Kra, Kho Khot
Thailand 10°15N 99°30E 39 G2
Kra, Kho Khot Thailand 10°15N 99°30E 39 G2
Kra Buri Thailand 10°22N 98°46E 39 G2
Kraai → S. Africa 30°40S 26°45E 56 D4
Krabi Thailand 8°4N 98°55E 39 H2
Kracheh = Kratie
Cambodia 12°32N 106°10E 38 F6
Kragan Indonesia 6°43S 111°38E 37 G14
Kragerø Norway 58°52N 9°25E 9 G13
Kragujevac Serbia 44°2N 20°56E 23 B9
Krakatau = Rakata, Pulau
Indonesia 6°10S 105°20E 37 G11
Krakatoa = Rakata, Pulau
Indonesia 6°10S 105°20E 37 G11
Krakor Cambodia 12°32N 104°12E 38 F5
Kraków Poland 50°4N 19°57E 17 C10
Kraksaan Indonesia 7°43S 113°23E 37 G16
Kralanh Cambodia 13°35N 103°25E 38 F4
Kraljevo Serbia 43°44N 20°41E 23 C9
Kramatorsk Ukraine 48°50N 37°30E 19 E6
Kramfors Sweden 62°55N 17°48E 8 E17
Kranj Slovenia 46°16N 14°22E 16 E8
Krankskop S. Africa 28°0S 30°47E 57 C5
Krasavino Russia 60°58N 46°29E 18 B8
Krasieo Res. Thailand 14°49N 99°30E 38 E2
Kraskino Russia 42°44N 130°48E 28 C5
Kraśnik Poland 50°55N 22°15E 17 C12
Krasnoarmeysk Russia 51°0N 45°42E 26 D5
Krasnodar Russia 45°5N 39°0E 19 E6
Krasnokamensk Russia 50°3N 118°0E 27 D12
Krasnokamsk Russia 58°4N 55°48E 18 C10
Krasnoperekopsk Ukraine 46°0N 33°54E 19 E5
Krasnorechenskiy
Russia 44°41N 135°14E 28 B7
Krasnoselkup Russia 65°20N 82°10E 26 C9
Krasnoturinsk Russia 59°46N 60°12E 18 C11
Krasnoufimsk Russia 56°36N 57°38E 18 C10
Krasnouralsk Russia 58°21N 60°3E 18 C11
Krasnovishersk Russia 60°23N 57°3E 18 B10
Krasnoyarsk Russia 56°8N 93°0E 27 D10
Krasnoyarskoye Vdkhr.
Russia 56°0N 92°30E 27 D10
Krasnyy Kut Russia 50°50N 47°0E 19 D8
Krasnyy Luch Ukraine 48°13N 39°0E 19 E6
Krasnyy Yar Russia 46°43N 48°23E 19 E8
Kratie Cambodia 12°32N 106°10E 38 F6
Krau Indonesia 3°19S 140°5E 37 E10
Kravanh, Chuor Phnum
Cambodia 12°0N 103°32E 39 G4
Krefeld Germany 51°20N 6°33E 16 C4
Kremen Croatia 44°28N 15°53E 16 F8
Kremenchuk Ukraine 49°5N 33°25E 19 E5
Kremenchuksk Vdskh.
Ukraine 49°20N 32°30E 19 E5
Kremenets Ukraine 50°8N 25°43E 17 C13
Kremmling U.S.A. 40°4N 106°24W 76 F10
Krems an der Donau
Austria 48°25N 15°36E 16 D8
Kretinga Lithuania 55°53N 21°15E 9 J19
Kribi Cameroon 2°57N 9°56E 54 D1
Krichev = Krychaw
Belarus 53°40N 31°41E 17 B16
Kril'on, Mys Russia 45°53N 142°5E 28 B11
Krishna → India 15°57N 80°59E 45 G5
Krishnagiri India 12°32N 78°16E 45 H4
Krishnanagar India 23°24N 88°33E 43 H13
Krishnaraja Sagar India 12°20N 76°30E 45 H3
Kristiansand Norway 58°8N 8°1E 9 G13
Kristianstad Sweden 56°2N 14°9E 9 H16
Kristiansund Norway 63°7N 7°45E 8 E12
Kristiinankaupunki
Finland 62°16N 21°21E 8 E19
Kristinehamn Sweden 59°18N 14°7E 9 G16
Kristinestad = Kristiinankaupunki
Finland 62°16N 21°21E 8 E19
Kriti Greece 35°15N 25°0E 23 G11
Krivoy Rog = Kryvyy Rih
Ukraine 47°51N 33°20E 19 E5
Krk Croatia 45°8N 14°40E 16 F8
Krokodil = Umgwenya →
Mozam. 25°14S 32°18E 57 C5
Krong Kaoh Kong
Cambodia 11°37N 102°59E 39 G4
Kronprins Frederik Land
Greenland 81°0N 45°0W 4 B5
Kronprins Olav Kyst
Antarctica 69°0S 42°0E 5 C5
Kronprinsesse Märtha Kyst
Antarctica 73°30S 10°0W 5 D2
Kronshtadt Russia 59°57N 29°51E 18 B4
Kroonstad S. Africa 27°43S 27°19E 56 C4
Kropotkin Russia 45°28N 40°28E 19 E7
Krosno Poland 49°42N 21°46E 17 D11
Krotoszyn Poland 51°42N 17°23E 17 C9
Kruger △ S. Africa 24°50S 26°10E 57 B4
Krugersdorp S. Africa 26°5S 27°46E 57 C4
Kruisfontein S. Africa 33°59S 24°43E 56 D3
Krupki Belarus 54°19N 29°8E 17 A15
Kruševac Serbia 43°35N 21°28E 23 C9
Kruzenshterna, Proliv
Russia 48°0N 154°0E 27 E16
Krychaw Belarus 53°40N 31°41E 17 B16
Krymskyy Poluostrov = Krymskyy
Pivostriv Ukraine 45°0N 34°0E 19 F5
Krymskyy Pivostriv
Ukraine 45°0N 34°0E 19 F5
Kryvyy Rih Ukraine 47°51N 33°20E 19 E5
Ksar el Kebir Morocco 35°0N 6°0W 52 B4
Ksar es Souk = Er Rachidia
Morocco 31°58N 4°20W 52 B5
Kuah Malaysia 6°19N 99°51E 39 J2
Kuala Belait Malaysia 4°35N 114°11E 36 D4
Kuala Berang Malaysia 5°5N 103°1E 39 K4
Kuala Dungun = Dungun
Malaysia 4°45N 103°25E 39 K4
Kuala Kangsar Malaysia 4°46N 100°56E 39 K3
Kuala Kelawang Malaysia 2°56N 102°5E 39 L4
Kuala Kerai Malaysia 5°30N 102°12E 39 K4
Kuala Kubu Bharu
Malaysia 3°34N 101°39E 39 L3
Kuala Lipis Malaysia 4°10N 102°3E 39 K4
Kuala Lumpur Malaysia 3°9N 101°41E 39 L3
Kuala Lumpur Int. ✕ (KUL)
Malaysia 2°44N 101°42E 39 L3
Kuala Nerang Malaysia 6°16N 100°37E 39 J3
Kuala Pilah Malaysia 2°45N 102°15E 39 L4
Kuala Rompin Malaysia 2°49N 103°29E 39 L4
Kuala Selangor Malaysia 3°20N 101°15E 39 L3
Kuala Sepetang Malaysia 4°49N 100°28E 39 K3
Kuala Terengganu
Malaysia 5°20N 103°8E 39 K4
Kualajelai Indonesia 2°58S 110°46E 36 E4
Kualakapuas Indonesia 2°55S 114°20E 36 E4
Kualakurun Indonesia 1°10S 113°50E 36 E4
Kualapembuang
Indonesia 3°14S 112°38E 36 E4
Kualasimpang Indonesia 4°17N 98°3E 36 D1
Kuancheng China 40°37N 118°30E 33 D10
Kuandang Indonesia 0°56N 123°1E 37 D6
Kuandian China 40°45N 124°45E 33 D13
Kuando Kubango □
Angola 16°25S 20°0E 56 A3
Kuanshan Taiwan 23°3N 121°9E 35 F13
Kuantan Malaysia 3°49N 103°20E 39 L4
Kuba = Quba Azerbaijan 41°21N 48°32E 19 F8
Kuban → Russia 45°20N 37°30E 19 E6
Kubokawa = Shimanto
Japan 33°12N 133°8E 29 H6
Kubu Indonesia 8°16S 115°35E 37 J18
Kubutambahan Indonesia 8°5S 115°10E 37 J18
Kucar, Tanjung
Indonesia 8°39S 114°34E 37 K18
Kuchaman India 27°13N 74°47E 42 F6
Kuchchaveli Sri Lanka 8°49N 81°6E 45 K5
Kuchinda India 21°44N 84°21E 43 J11
Kuching Malaysia 1°33N 110°25E 36 D4
Kuchino-eruba-Jima
Japan 30°28N 130°12E 29 J5
Kuchino-Shima Japan 29°57N 129°55E 29 K4
Kuchinotsu Japan 32°36N 130°11E 29 H5
Kucing = Kuching
Malaysia 1°33N 110°25E 36 D4
Kud → Pakistan 26°5N 66°20E 42 F2
Kuda India 23°10N 71°15E 42 H4
Kudal India 16°2N 73°41E 45 F1
Kudalier → India 18°35N 79°48E 44 E4
Kudat Malaysia 6°55N 116°55E 36 C5
Kudremukh India 13°15N 75°20E 45 H2
Kudus Indonesia 6°48S 110°51E 37 G14
Kudymkar Russia 59°1N 54°39E 18 C9
Kueiyang = Guiyang
China 26°32N 106°40E 34 D6
Kufra Oasis = Al Kufrah
Libya 24°17N 23°15E 53 D10
Kufstein Austria 47°35N 12°11E 16 E7
Kugaaruk = Pelly Bay
Canada 68°38N 89°50W 69 D14
Kugluktuk Canada 67°50N 115°5W 68 D8
Kugong I. Canada 56°18N 79°50W 72 A4
Kūh Dasht Iran 33°32N 47°36E 46 C5
Kūhak Iran 27°12N 63°10E 47 E9
Kuhan Pakistan 28°19N 67°14E 42 E2
Kūhbonān Iran 31°23N 56°19E 47 D8
Kūhestak Iran 26°47N 57°2E 47 E8
Kuhin Iran 36°22N 49°40E 47 B6
Kūhīrī Iran 26°55N 61°2E 47 E9
Kuhmo Finland 64°7N 29°31E 8 D23
Kuhn Chae △ Thailand 19°8N 99°24E 38 C2
Kūhpāyeh Eşfahan, Iran 32°44N 52°20E 47 C7
Kūhpāyeh Kermān, Iran 30°35N 57°15E 47 D8
Kūhrān, Kūh-e Iran 26°46N 58°12E 47 E8
Kui Buri Thailand 12°3N 99°52E 39 F2
Kuiburi △ Thailand 12°10N 99°37E 39 F2
Kuichong China 22°38N 114°25E 31 a
Kuiseb → Namibia 22°59S 14°31E 56 B1
Kuito Angola 12°22S 16°55E 55 G3
Kuiu I. U.S.A. 57°45N 134°10W 70 B2
Kujang N. Korea 39°57N 126°1E 33 E14
Kuji Japan 40°11N 141°46E 28 D10
Kujū-San Japan 33°5N 131°15E 29 H5
Kukës Albania 42°5N 20°27E 23 C9
Kukup Malaysia 1°20N 103°27E 39 d
Kukup, Pulau Malaysia 1°18N 103°25E 39 d
Kula Turkey 38°32N 28°40E 23 E13
K'ula Shan Bhutan 28°14N 90°36E 30 F7
Kulachi Pakistan 31°56N 70°27E 42 D4
Kulai Malaysia 1°44N 103°35E 39 M4
Kulasekarappattinam India 8°20N 78°5E 45 K4
Kuldīga Latvia 56°58N 21°59E 9 H19
Kulen Cambodia 13°50N 104°40E 38 F5
Kulgam India 33°36N 75°2E 43 C6
Kulgera Australia 25°50S 133°18E 62 D1
Kulim Malaysia 5°22N 100°34E 39 K3
Kulin Australia 32°40S 118°2E 61 F2
Kulittalai India 10°55N 78°25E 45 J4
Kulkayu = Hartley Bay
Canada 53°25N 129°15W 70 C3
Kullu India 31°58N 77°6E 42 D7
Kŭlob Tajikistan 37°55N 69°50E 26 F7
Kulsary = Qulsary
Kazakhstan 46°59N 54°1E 19 E9
Kulti India 23°43N 86°50E 43 H12
Kulunda Russia 52°35N 78°57E 26 D8
Kulungar Afghan. 34°0N 69°2E 42 C3
Kūlvand Iran 31°21N 54°35E 47 D7
Kulwin Australia 35°2S 142°42E 63 F3
Kulyab = Kŭlob Tajikistan 37°55N 69°50E 26 F7
Kuma → Russia 44°55N 47°0E 19 F8
Kumaganum Nigeria 13°8N 10°38E 53 F8
Kumagaya Japan 36°9N 139°22E 29 F9
Kumai Indonesia 2°44S 111°43E 36 E4
Kumamba, Kepulauan
Indonesia 1°36S 138°45E 37 E9
Kumamoto Japan 32°45N 130°45E 29 H5
Kumamoto □ Japan 32°55N 130°55E 29 H5
Kumanovo Macedonia 42°9N 21°42E 23 C9
Kumara N.Z. 42°37S 171°12E 59 E3
Kumarina Roadhouse
Australia 24°41S 119°32E 61 D2
Kumasi Ghana 6°41N 1°38W 52 G5
Kumba Cameroon 4°36N 9°24E 54 D1
Kumbakonam India 10°58N 79°25E 45 J4
Kumbarilla Australia 27°15S 150°55E 63 D5
Kumbhalgarh △ India 25°10N 73°35E 42 G5
Kumbhraj India 24°22N 77°3E 42 G7
Kumbia Australia 26°41S 151°39E 63 D5
Kumbukkan Oya →
Sri Lanka 6°35N 81°40E 45 L5
Kŭmch'ŏn N. Korea 38°10N 126°29E 33 E14
Kume-Shima Japan 26°20N 126°47E 29 L3
Kumertau Russia 52°45N 55°57E 18 D10
Kumharsain India 31°19N 77°27E 42 D7
Kumo Nigeria 10°1N 11°12E 53 F8
Kumo älv = Kokemäenjoki →
Finland 61°32N 21°44E 8 F19
Kumon Bum Myanmar 26°30N 97°15E 41 F20
Kumta India 14°29N 74°25E 45 G2
Kumtag Shamo China 39°40N 92°0E 30 D7
Kumul = Hami China 42°55N 93°25E 30 C7
Kuna U.S.A. 43°30N 116°25W 76 E5
Kunashir, Ostrov Russia 44°0N 146°0E 27 E15
Kunchha Nepal 28°8N 84°20E 43 E11
Kunda Estonia 59°30N 26°34E 9 G22
Kunda India 25°43N 81°31E 43 G9
Kundar → Pakistan 31°56N 69°19E 42 D3
Kundian Pakistan 32°27N 71°28E 42 C4
Kundla India 21°21N 71°25E 42 J4
Kunene □ Namibia 20°0S 14°0E 56 A1
Kung, Ao Thailand 8°5N 98°24E 39 a
Kunga → Bangla. 21°46N 89°30E 43 J13
Kunghit I. Canada 52°6N 131°3W 70 C2
Kungrad = Qŭnghirot
Uzbekistan 43°2N 58°50E 26 E6
Kungsbacka Sweden 57°30N 12°5E 9 H15
Kungur Russia 57°25N 56°57E 18 C10
Kungurri Australia 21°4S 148°45E 62 b
Kunhar → Pakistan 34°20N 73°30E 43 B5
Kuningan Indonesia 6°59S 108°29E 37 G13
Kunlong Myanmar 23°20N 98°50E 34 F2
Kunlun Antarctica 80°25S 77°7E 5 E6
Kunlun Shan Asia 36°0N 86°30E 30 D6
Kunlun Shankou China 35°38N 94°4E 30 D7
Kunming China 25°1N 102°41E 34 E4
Kunming Changshui Int. ✕ (KMG)
China 24°59N 102°45E 34 E4
Kunmunya ⊙ Australia 15°26S 124°42E 60 C3
Kunnamkulam India 10°38N 76°7E 45 J3
Kunshan China 31°22N 120°58E 35 B13
Kununurra Australia 15°40S 128°50E 60 C4
Kunwari → India 26°26N 79°11E 43 F8
Kunya-Urgench = Köneürgench
Turkmenistan 42°19N 59°10E 26 E6
Kuopio Finland 62°53N 27°35E 8 E22
Kupa → Croatia 45°28N 16°24E 16 F9
Kupang Indonesia 10°19S 123°39E 37 F6
Kupreanof I. U.S.A. 56°50N 133°30W 70 B2
Kupyansk-Uzlovoi
Ukraine 49°40N 37°43E 19 E6
Kuqa China 41°35N 82°30E 30 C5
Kür → Azerbaijan 39°29N 49°15E 19 G8
Kür Dili Azerbaijan 39°3N 49°13E 47 B6
Kura = Kür → Azerbaijan 39°29N 49°15E 19 G8
Kuranda Australia 16°48S 145°35E 62 B4
Kuranga India 22°4N 69°10E 42 H3
Kurashiki Japan 34°40N 133°50E 29 G6
Kurayn Si. Arabia 27°39N 49°50E 47 E6
Kurayoshi Japan 35°26N 133°50E 29 G6
Kŭrchatov Kazakhstan 50°45N 78°32E 26 D8
Kurduvadi India 18°8N 75°29E 44 E2
Kure Japan 34°14N 132°32E 29 G6
Kure I. U.S.A. 28°25N 178°25W 75 K4
Kuressaare Estonia 58°15N 22°30E 9 G20
Kurgan Russia 55°26N 65°18E 26 D7
Kuri India 26°37N 70°43E 42 F4
Kuria Maria Is. = Ḩallāniyat,
Jazā'ir al Oman 17°30N 55°58E 49 D6
Kurichchi India 11°36N 77°35E 45 J3
Kuridala Australia 21°16S 140°29E 62 C3
Kurigram Bangla. 25°49N 89°39E 41 G16
Kurikka Finland 62°36N 22°24E 8 E20
Kuril Basin Pac. Oc. 47°0N 150°0E 4 E15
Kuril Is. = Kurilskiye Ostrova
Russia 45°0N 150°0E 27 E16
Kuril-Kamchatka Trench
Pac. Oc. 44°0N 153°0E 64 C7
Kurilsk Russia 45°14N 147°53E 27 E15
Kurilskiye Ostrova
Russia 45°0N 150°0E 27 E16
Kurino Japan 31°57N 130°43E 29 J5
Kurinskaya Kosa = Kür Dili
Azerbaijan 39°3N 49°13E 47 B6
Kurkheda India 20°37N 80°12E 44 D5
Kurlkuta ⊙ Australia 24°0S 127°5E 60 D4
Kurnool India 15°45N 78°0E 45 G4
Kuro-Shima Kagoshima,
Japan 30°50N 129°57E 29 J4
Kuro-Shima Okinawa,
Japan 24°14N 124°1E 29 M2
Kurow N.Z. 44°44S 170°29E 59 F3
Kurram → Pakistan 32°36N 71°20E 42 C4
Kurri Kurri Australia 32°50S 151°28E 63 E5
Kurrimine Australia 17°47S 146°6E 62 B4
Kurse Korhi India 20°14N 80°46E 44 D5
Kurseong = Karsiyang
India 26°56N 88°18E 43 F13
Kurshskiy Zaliv Russia 55°9N 21°6E 9 J19
Kursk Russia 51°42N 36°11E 18 D6
Kuruçay Turkey 39°39N 38°29E 46 B3
Kurukshetra = Thanesar
India 30°1N 76°52E 42 D7
Kuruktag China 41°0N 89°0E 30 C6
Kuruman S. Africa 27°28S 23°28E 56 C3
Kuruman → S. Africa 26°56S 20°39E 56 C3
Kurume Japan 33°15N 130°30E 29 H5
Kurunegala Sri Lanka 7°30N 80°23E 45 L5
Kurya Russia 61°42N 57°9E 18 B10
Kus Gölü Turkey 40°10N 27°55E 23 D12
Kuşadası Turkey 37°52N 27°15E 23 F12
Kusamba Indonesia 8°34S 115°27E 37 K18
Kusatsu Japan 36°37N 138°36E 29 F9
Kusawa L. Canada 60°20N 136°13W 70 A1
Kushalgarh India 23°10N 74°27E 42 H6
Kushalnagar India 12°14N 75°57E 45 H2
Kushikino Japan 31°44N 130°16E 29 J5
Kushima Japan 31°29N 131°14E 29 J5
Kushimoto Japan 33°28N 135°47E 29 H7
Kushiro Japan 43°0N 144°25E 28 C12
Kushiro-Gawa →
Japan 42°59N 144°23E 28 C12
Kushiro Shitsugen △
Japan 43°9N 144°26E 28 C12
Kūshk Iran 28°46N 56°51E 47 D8
Kushka = Serhetabat
Turkmenistan 35°20N 62°18E 47 C9
Kushol India 33°40N 76°36E 43 C7
Kushtia Bangla. 23°55N 89°5E 41 H16
Kushva Russia 58°18N 59°45E 18 C10
Kuskokwim → U.S.A. 60°5N 162°25W 74 C7
Kuskokwim B. U.S.A. 59°45N 162°25W 74 D7
Kuskokwim Mts. U.S.A. 62°30N 156°0W 74 C8
Kusmi India 23°17N 83°55E 43 H10
Kusŏng N. Korea 39°59N 125°15E 33 E13
Kussharo-Ko Japan 43°38N 144°21E 28 C12
Kustanay = Qostanay
Kazakhstan 53°10N 63°35E 26 D7
Kut, Ko Thailand 11°40N 102°35E 39 G4
Kuta Indonesia 8°43S 115°11E 37 K18
Kütahya Turkey 39°30N 30°2E 19 G5
Kutaisi Georgia 42°19N 42°40E 19 F7
Kutaraja = Banda Aceh
Indonesia 5°35N 95°20E 36 C1
Kutch, Gulf of = Kachchh, Gulf of
India 22°50N 69°15E 42 H3
Kutch, Rann of = Kachchh, Rann
of India 24°0N 70°0E 42 H4
Kutiyana India 21°36N 70°2E 42 J4
Kutno Poland 52°15N 19°23E 17 B10
Kutru India 19°5N 80°46E 44 E5
Kutse Botswana 21°7S 22°16E 56 B3
Kuttabul Australia 21°1S 148°54E 62 b
Kutu Dem. Rep. of the Congo 2°40S 18°11E 54 E3
Kutum Sudan 14°10N 24°40E 53 F10
Kuujjuaq Canada 58°6N 68°15W 69 F18
Kuujjuarapik Canada 55°20N 77°35W 72 A4
Kuusamo Finland 65°57N 29°8E 8 D23
Kuusankoski Finland 60°55N 26°38E 8 F22
Kuwait = Al Kuwayt
Kuwait 29°30N 48°0E 46 D5
Kuwait ■ Asia 29°30N 47°30E 46 D5
Kuwana Japan 35°5N 136°43E 29 G8
Kuwana → India 26°25N 83°15E 43 F10
Kuybyshev = Samara
Russia 53°8N 50°6E 18 D9
Kuybyshev Russia 55°27N 78°19E 26 D8
Kuybyshevskoye Vdkhr.
Russia 55°2N 49°30E 18 C8
Kuye He → China 38°23N 110°46E 32 E6
Kūyeh Iran 38°45N 47°57E 46 B5
Kuyto, Ozero Russia 65°6N 31°20E 8 D24
Kuytun China 44°25N 85°0E 30 C6
Kuyumba Russia 60°58N 96°59E 27 C10
Kuzey Anadolu Dağları
Turkey 41°0N 36°45E 19 F6
Kuzhitturai India 8°18N 77°11E 45 K3
Kuznetsk Russia 53°12N 46°40E 18 D8
Kuzomen Russia 66°22N 36°50E 18 A6
Kvænangen Norway 70°5N 21°15E 8 A19
Kvaløya Norway 69°40N 18°30E 8 B18
Kvarner Croatia 44°50N 14°10E 16 F8
Kvarnerič Croatia 44°43N 14°37E 16 F8
Kwabhaca S. Africa 30°51S 29°0E 57 D4
Kwai = Khwae Noi →
Thailand 14°1N 99°32E 38 E2
Kwajalein Marshall Is. 9°5N 167°20E 64 G8
Kwakhanai Botswana 21°39S 21°16E 56 B3
Kwakoegron Suriname 5°12N 55°25W 93 B7
KwaMashu S. Africa 29°45S 30°58E 57 C5
Kwando → Africa 18°27S 23°32E 56 A3
Kwangdaeri N. Korea 40°34N 127°33E 33 D14
Kwango →
Dem. Rep. of the Congo 3°14S 17°22E 54 E3
Kwangsi-Chuang = Guangxi
Zhuangzu Zizhiqu □
China 24°0N 109°0E 34 F7
Kwangtung = Guangdong □
China 23°0N 113°0E 35 F9
Kwataboahegan →
Canada 51°9N 80°50W 72 B3
Kwatisore Indonesia 3°18S 134°50E 37 E8
KwaZulu Natal □ S. Africa 29°0S 30°0E 57 C5
Kweichow = Guizhou □
China 27°0N 107°0E 34 D6
Kwekwe Zimbabwe 18°58S 29°48E 55 H5
Kweneng □ Botswana 24°0S 25°0E 56 B3
Kwidzyn Poland 53°44N 18°55E 17 B10
Kwilu →
Dem. Rep. of the Congo 3°22S 17°22E 54 E3
Kwinana Australia 32°15S 115°47E 61 F2
Kwoka Indonesia 0°31S 132°27E 37 E8
Kyabra Cr. → Australia 25°36S 142°55E 63 D3
Kyabram Australia 36°19S 145°4E 63 F4
Kyaikto Myanmar 17°20N 97°3E 38 D1
Kyaing Tong = Keng Tung
Myanmar 21°18N 99°39E 38 B2
Kyakhta Russia 50°30N 106°25E 27 D11
Kyancutta Australia 33°8S 135°33E 63 E2
Kyaukpadaung Myanmar 20°52N 95°8E 41 J19
Kyaukpyu Myanmar 19°28N 93°30E 41 K18
Kyaukse Myanmar 21°36N 96°10E 41 J20
Kyburz U.S.A. 38°47N 120°18W 78 G6
Kyelang India 32°35N 77°2E 42 C7
Kyklades Greece 37°0N 24°30E 23 F11
Kyle Canada 50°50N 108°2W 71 C7
Kyle U.S.A. 29°59N 97°53W 84 F6
Kyle of Lochalsh U.K. 57°17N 5°44W 11 D3
Kymijoki → Finland 60°30N 26°55E 8 F22
Kymmene älv = Kymijoki →
Finland 60°30N 26°55E 8 F22
Kyneton Australia 37°10S 144°29E 63 F3
Kynuna Australia 21°37S 141°55E 62 C3
Kyō-ga-Saki Japan 35°45N 135°15E 29 G7
Kyoga, L. Uganda 1°35N 33°0E 54 D6
Kyogle Australia 28°40S 153°0E 63 D5
Kyŏngju = Gyeongju
S. Korea 35°51N 129°14E 33 G15
Kyŏngsŏng N. Korea 41°35N 129°36E 33 D15
Kyonpyaw Myanmar 17°12N 95°10E 41 L19
Kyōto Japan 35°0N 135°45E 29 G7
Kyōto □ Japan 35°15N 135°45E 29 G7
Kypros = Cyprus ■ Asia 35°0N 33°0E 46 C2
Kyrenia Cyprus 35°20N 33°20E 46 C2
Kyrgyzstan ■ Asia 42°0N 75°0E 26 E8
Kyro älv = Kyrönjoki →
Finland 63°14N 21°45E 8 E19
Kyrönjoki → Finland 63°14N 21°45E 8 E19
Kystatyam Russia 67°20N 123°10E 27 C13
Kythira Greece 36°8N 23°0E 23 F10
Kythnos Greece 37°26N 24°27E 23 F11
Kyunhla Myanmar 23°25N 95°15E 41 H19
Kyuquot Sound Canada 50°2N 127°22W 70 D3
Kyūshū Japan 33°0N 131°0E 29 H5
Kyūshū □ Japan 33°0N 131°0E 29 H5
Kyūshū-Palau Ridge
Pac. Oc. 20°0N 136°0E 64 E5
Kyūshū-Sanchi Japan 32°35N 131°17E 29 H5
Kyustendil Bulgaria 42°16N 22°41E 23 C10
Kyusyur Russia 70°19N 127°30E 27 B13
Kyyiv Ukraine 50°30N 30°28E 17 C16
Kyyivske Vdskh. Ukraine 51°0N 30°25E 17 C16
Kyzyl Russia 51°50N 94°30E 30 A7
Kyzyl Kum Uzbekistan 42°30N 65°0E 26 E7
Kyzyl-Kyya Kyrgyzstan 40°16N 72°8E 26 E8
Kyzyl Orda = Qyzylorda
Kazakhstan 44°48N 65°28E 26 E7

## L


La Alcarria Spain 40°31N 2°45W 21 B4
La Amistad △ Cent. Amer. 9°28N 83°18W 88 E3
La Asunción Venezuela 11°2N 63°51W 92 A6
La Baie Canada 48°19N 70°53W 73 C5
La Banda Argentina 27°45S 64°10W 94 B3
La Barca Mexico 20°17N 102°34W 86 C4
La Barge U.S.A. 42°16N 110°12W 76 E8
La Barra Nic. 12°54N 83°33W 88 D3
La Belle U.S.A. 26°46N 81°26W 85 H14
La Biche → Canada 59°57N 123°50W 70 B4
La Biche, L. Canada 54°50N 112°3W 70 C6
La Brea Trin. & Tob. 10°15N 61°37W 93 K15
La Calera Chile 32°50S 71°10W 94 C1
La Campana △ Chile 32°58S 71°14W 94 C1
La Carlota Argentina 33°30S 63°20W 94 C3
La Ceiba Honduras 15°40N 86°50W 88 C2
La Chaux-de-Fonds Switz. 47°7N 6°50E 20 C7
La Chorrera Panama 8°53N 79°47W 88 E4
La Cocha Argentina 27°50S 65°40W 94 B2
La Concepción Panama 8°31N 82°37W 88 E3
La Concordia Mexico 16°5N 92°38W 87 D6
La Coruña = A Coruña Spain 43°20N 8°25W 21 A1
La Crescent U.S.A. 43°50N 91°18W 80 D8
La Crete Canada 58°11N 116°24W 70 B5
La Crosse Kans., U.S.A. 38°32N 99°18W 80 F4
La Crosse Wis., U.S.A. 43°48N 91°15W 80 D8
La Cruz Costa Rica 11°4N 85°39W 88 D2
La Cruz Mexico 23°55N 106°54W 86 C3
La Désirade Guadeloupe 16°18N 61°3W 88 b
La Digue Seychelles 4°20S 55°51E 55 b
La Esperanza Cuba 22°46N 83°44W 88 B3
La Esperanza Honduras 14°15N 88°10W 88 D2
La Estrada = A Estrada Spain 42°43N 8°27W 21 A1
La Fayette U.S.A. 34°42N 85°17W 85 D12
La Fé Cuba 22°2N 84°15W 88 B3
La Follette U.S.A. 36°23N 84°7W 85 C12
La Gi Vietnam 10°40N 107°45E 39 G6
La Grande U.S.A. 45°20N 118°5W 76 D4
La Grande → Canada 53°50N 79°0W 72 B5
La Grande 3, Rés. Canada 53°40N 75°10W 72 B4
La Grande 4, Rés. Canada 54°0N 73°15W 72 B5
La Grange Calif., U.S.A. 37°42N 120°27W 78 H6
La Grange Ga., U.S.A. 33°2N 85°2W 85 E12
La Grange Ky., U.S.A. 38°24N 85°22W 81 F11
La Grange Tex., U.S.A. 29°54N 96°52W 84 G6
La Guaira Venezuela 10°36N 66°56W 92 A5
La Guarda △ Mexico 29°20N 113°27W 86 B2
La Habana Cuba 23°8N 82°22W 88 B3
La Independencia Mexico 16°15N 92°1W 87 D6
La Isabela Dom. Rep. 19°58N 71°2W 89 C5
La Junta U.S.A. 37°59N 103°33W 76 H12
La Libertad = Puerto Libertad Mexico 29°55N 112°43W 86 B2
La Libertad Guatemala 16°47N 90°7W 88 C1
La Ligua Chile 32°30S 71°16W 94 C1
La Línea de la Concepción Spain 36°15N 5°23W 21 D3
La Loche Canada 56°29N 109°26W 71 B7
La Louvière Belgium 50°27N 4°10E 15 D4
La Lune Trin. & Tob. 10°3N 61°22W 93 K15
La Malbaie Canada 47°40N 70°10W 73 C5
La Malinche △ Mexico 19°15N 98°3W 87 D5
La Mancha Spain 39°10N 2°54W 21 C4
La Martre, L. Canada 63°15N 117°55W 70 A5
La Mercy ✈ (DUR) S. Africa 29°37S 31°7E 57 C5
La Mesa Mexico 32°30N 116°57W 79 N10
La Mesa U.S.A. 32°46N 117°1W 79 N9
La Mesilla U.S.A. 32°16N 106°48W 77 K10
La Moure U.S.A. 46°21N 98°18W 80 B4
La Negra Chile 23°46S 70°18W 94 A1
La Oroya Peru 11°32S 75°54W 92 F3
La Palma Canary Is. 28°40N 17°50W 52 C2
La Palma Panama 8°15N 78°0W 88 E4
La Palma del Condado Spain 37°21N 6°38W 21 D2
La Paloma Chile 30°35S 71°0W 94 C1
La Pampa □ Argentina 36°50S 66°0W 94 D2
La Paragua Venezuela 6°50N 63°20W 92 B6
La Paz Entre Ríos, Argentina 30°50S 59°45W 94 C4
La Paz San Luis, Argentina 33°30S 67°20W 94 C2
La Paz Bolivia 16°20S 68°10W 92 G5
La Paz Honduras 14°20N 87°47W 88 D2
La Paz Mexico 24°10N 110°18W 86 C2
La Paz Centro Nic. 12°20N 86°41W 88 D2
La Pedrera Colombia 1°18S 69°43W 92 D5
La Pérade Canada 46°35N 72°12W 73 C5
La Perla Mexico 28°18N 104°32W 86 B4
La Perouse Str. Asia 45°40N 142°0E 28 B11
La Pesca Mexico 23°46N 97°47W 87 C5
La Piedad Mexico 20°21N 102°0W 86 C4
La Pine U.S.A. 43°40N 121°30W 76 E3
La Plata Argentina 35°0S 57°55W 94 C4
La Pocatière Canada 47°22N 70°2W 73 C5
La Porte U.S.A. 29°40N 95°1W 84 G7
La Purísima Mexico 26°10N 112°4W 86 B2
La Push U.S.A. 47°55N 124°38W 78 C2
La Quiaca Argentina 22°5S 65°35W 94 A2
La Rioja Argentina 29°20S 67°0W 94 B2
La Rioja □ Argentina 29°30S 67°0W 94 B2
La Rioja □ Spain 42°20N 2°20W 21 A4
La Robla Spain 42°50N 5°41W 21 A3
La Roche-en-Ardenne Belgium 50°11N 5°35E 15 D5
La Roche-sur-Yon France 46°40N 1°25W 20 C3
La Rochelle France 46°10N 1°9W 20 C3
La Roda Spain 39°13N 2°15W 21 C4
La Romaine Canada 50°13N 60°40W 73 B7
La Romana Dom. Rep. 18°27N 68°57W 89 C6
La Ronge Canada 55°5N 105°20W 71 B7
La Rumorosa Mexico 32°34N 116°6W 79 N10
La Salle U.S.A. 41°20N 89°6W 80 E9
La Sarre Canada 48°45N 79°15W 72 C4
La Scie Canada 49°57N 55°36W 73 C8
La Selva Beach U.S.A. 36°56N 121°51W 78 J5
La Serena Chile 29°55S 71°10W 94 B1
La Seu d'Urgell Spain 42°22N 1°23E 21 A6
La Seyne-sur-Mer France 43°7N 5°52E 20 E6
La Soufrière St. Vincent 13°20N 61°11W 89 D7
La Spézia Italy 44°7N 9°50E 20 D8
La Tagua Colombia 0°3N 74°40W 92 C4
La Tortuga, I. Venezuela 11°0N 65°22W 89 D6
La Trinité Martinique 14°45N 60°58W 88 c
La Tuque Canada 47°30N 72°50W 72 C5
La Unión Chile 40°10S 73°0W 96 E2
La Unión El Salv. 13°20N 87°50W 88 D2
La Unión Mexico 17°58N 101°49W 86 D4
La Urbana Venezuela 7°8N 66°56W 92 B5
La Vache Pt. Trin. & Tob. 10°47N 61°28W 93 K15
La Vall d'Uixó Spain 39°49N 0°15W 21 C5
La Vega Dom. Rep. 19°20N 70°30W 89 C5
La Vela de Coro Venezuela 11°27N 69°34W 92 A5
La Venta Mexico 18°5N 94°3W 87 D6
La Vergne U.S.A. 36°1N 86°35W 85 C11
La Villa Joiosa = Villajoyosa Spain 38°30N 0°12W 21 C5
Laascaanood = Las Anod Somalia 8°26N 47°19E 49 F4
Labasa Fiji 16°30S 179°27E 59 a
Labdah = Leptis Magna Libya 32°40N 14°12E 53 B8
Labe = Elbe → Europe 53°50N 9°0E 16 B5
Labé Guinea 11°24N 12°16W 52 F3
Laberge, L. Canada 61°11N 135°12W 70 A1
Labinsk Russia 44°40N 40°48E 19 F7
Labis Malaysia 2°22N 103°2E 39 L4
Laborie St. Lucia 13°45N 61°2W 89 f
Laboulaye Argentina 34°10S 63°30W 94 C3
Labrador Canada 53°20N 61°0W 73 B7
Labrador City Canada 52°57N 66°55W 73 B6
Labrador Sea Atl. Oc. 57°0N 54°0W 69 F21
Lábrea Brazil 7°15S 64°51W 92 E6
Labuan □ Malaysia 5°20N 115°12E 36 C4
Labuha Indonesia 0°30S 127°30E 37 E7
Labuhan Indonesia 6°22S 105°50E 37 G11
Labuhanbajo Indonesia 8°28S 119°54E 37 F6
Labuhanbilik Indonesia 2°31N 100°10E 39 L3
Labuk, Telok Malaysia 6°10N 117°50E 36 C5
Labyrinth, L. Australia 30°40S 135°11E 63 E2
Labytnangi Russia 66°39N 66°21E 18 A12
Lac-Bouchette Canada 48°16N 72°11W 73 C5
Lac-Édouard Canada 47°40N 72°16W 73 C5
Lac La Biche Canada 54°45N 111°58W 70 C6
Lac la Martre = Wha Ti Canada 63°8N 117°16W 68 E8
Lac La Ronge ⌓ Canada 55°9N 104°41W 71 B7
Lac-Mégantic Canada 45°35N 70°53W 73 C5
Lac Thien Vietnam 12°25N 108°11E 38 F7
Lacanau France 44°58N 1°5W 20 D3
Lacantún → Mexico 16°36N 90°39W 87 D6
Laccadive Is. = Lakshadweep Is. India 10°0N 72°30E 45 J1
Lacepede B. Australia 36°40S 139°40E 63 F2
Lacepede Is. Australia 16°55S 122°0E 60 C3
Lacey U.S.A. 47°7N 122°49W 78 C4
Lachhmangarh India 27°50N 75°4E 42 F6
Lachi Pakistan 33°25N 71°20E 42 C4
Lachlan → Australia 34°22S 143°55E 63 E3
Lachute Canada 45°39N 74°21W 72 C5
Lackagh Hills Ireland 54°16N 8°10W 10 B3
Lackawanna U.S.A. 42°50N 78°50W 82 D6
Lackawaxen U.S.A. 41°29N 74°59W 83 E10
Lacolle Canada 45°5N 73°22W 83 A11
Lacombe Canada 52°30N 113°44W 70 C6
Lacona U.S.A. 43°39N 76°10W 83 C8
Laconia U.S.A. 43°32N 71°28W 83 C13
Ladakh Ra. India 34°0N 78°0E 43 C8
Ladismith S. Africa 33°28S 21°15E 56 D3
Lādīz Iran 28°55N 61°15E 47 D9
Ladnun India 27°38N 74°25E 42 F6
Ladoga, L. = Ladozhskoye Ozero Russia 61°15N 30°30E 8 F24
Ladozhskoye Ozero Russia 61°15N 30°30E 8 F24
Lady Elliott I. Australia 24°7S 152°42E 62 C5
Lady Frere S. Africa 31°42S 27°14E 56 D4
Lady Grey S. Africa 30°43S 27°13E 56 D4
Ladybrand S. Africa 29°9S 27°29E 56 C4
Ladysmith Canada 49°0N 123°49W 78 B3
Ladysmith S. Africa 28°32S 29°46E 57 C4
Ladysmith U.S.A. 45°28N 91°12W 80 C8
Lae Papua N. G. 6°40S 147°2E 58 B7
Laem Chabang Thailand 13°5N 100°53E 38 F3
Laem Ngop Thailand 12°10N 102°26E 39 F4
Laem Son △ Thailand 9°29N 98°24E 39 H2
Læsø Denmark 57°15N 11°5E 9 H14
Lafayette Ind., U.S.A. 40°25N 86°54W 80 E10
Lafayette La., U.S.A. 30°14N 92°1W 84 F8
Lafayette Tenn., U.S.A. 36°31N 86°2W 85 C11
Laferte → Canada 61°53N 117°44W 70 A5
Lafia Nigeria 8°30N 8°34E 52 G7
Lafleche Canada 49°45N 106°40W 71 D7
Laful India 7°10N 93°52E 45 L11
Lagan → U.K. 54°36N 5°55W 10 B6
Lagarfljót → Iceland 65°40N 14°18W 8 D6
Lagdo, L. de Cameroon 8°40N 14°0E 53 G8
Lågen → Oppland, Norway 61°8N 10°25E 8 F14
Lågen → Vestfold, Norway 59°3N 10°3E 9 G14
Lages Brazil 27°48S 50°20W 95 B5
Laghouat Algeria 33°50N 2°59E 52 B6
Lagoa do Peixe △ Brazil 31°12S 50°55W 95 C5
Lagoa Vermelha Brazil 28°13S 51°32W 95 B5
Lagonoy G. Phil. 13°35N 123°50E 37 B6
Lagos Portugal 37°5N 8°41W 21 D1
Lagos de Moreno Mexico 21°21N 101°55W 86 C4
Lagrange = Bidyadanga Australia 18°45S 121°43E 60 C3
Lagrange B. Australia 18°38S 121°42E 60 C3
Laguna Brazil 28°30S 48°50W 95 B6
Laguna U.S.A. 35°2N 107°25W 77 J10
Laguna, Sa. de la Mexico 23°35N 109°55W 86 C3
Laguna Beach U.S.A. 33°33N 117°47W 79 M9
Laguna de la Restinga △ Venezuela 10°58N 64°0W 89 D6
Laguna de Lachuá △ Guatemala 15°55N 90°40W 88 C1
Laguna del Laja △ Chile 37°27S 71°20W 94 D1
Laguna del Tigre △ Guatemala 17°32N 90°56W 88 C1
Laguna Limpia Argentina 26°32S 59°45W 94 B4
Lagunas Chile 21°0S 69°45W 94 A2
Lagunas Peru 5°10S 75°35W 92 E3
Lagunas de Chacahua △ Mexico 16°0N 97°43W 87 D5
Lagunas de Montebello △ Mexico 16°4N 91°42W 87 D6
Lahad Datu Malaysia 5°0N 118°20E 37 D5
Lahad Datu, Telok Malaysia 4°50N 118°20E 37 D5
Lahan Sai Thailand 14°25N 102°52E 38 E4
Lahanam Laos 16°16N 105°16E 38 D5
Lahar India 26°12N 78°57E 43 F8
Laharpur India 27°43N 80°56E 43 F9
Lahat Indonesia 3°45S 103°30E 36 E2
Lahewa Indonesia 1°22N 97°12E 36 D1
Lāhījān Iran 37°10N 50°6E 47 B6
Lahn → Germany 50°19N 7°37E 16 C4
Laholm Sweden 56°30N 13°2E 9 H15
Lahore Pakistan 31°32N 74°22E 42 D6
Lahri Pakistan 29°11N 68°13E 42 E3
Lāhrūd Iran 38°30N 47°52E 46 B5
Lahti Finland 60°58N 25°40E 8 F21
Lahtis = Lahti Finland 60°58N 25°40E 8 F21
Lahugala Kitulana △ Sri Lanka 6°50N 81°40E 45 L5
Laï Chad 9°25N 16°18E 53 G9
Lai Chau Vietnam 22°5N 103°3E 34 F4
Lai'an China 32°28N 118°30E 35 A12
Laibin China 23°42N 109°14E 34 F7
Laifeng China 29°27N 109°20E 34 C7
Laila = Layla Si. Arabia 22°10N 46°40E 49 C4
Laingsburg S. Africa 33°9S 20°52E 56 D3
Lainioälven → Sweden 67°35N 22°40E 8 C20
Lairg U.K. 58°2N 4°24W 11 C4
Laiwu China 36°15N 117°40E 33 F9
Laixi China 36°50N 120°31E 33 F11
Laiyang China 36°59N 120°45E 33 F11
Laiyuan China 39°20N 114°40E 32 E8
Laizhou China 37°8N 119°57E 33 F10
Laizhou Wan China 37°30N 119°30E 33 F10
Lajamanu Australia 18°23S 130°38E 60 C5
Lak Sao Laos 18°11N 104°59E 38 C5
Lakaband Pakistan 31°2N 69°15E 42 D3
Lake U.S.A. 44°33N 110°24W 76 D8
Lake Alpine U.S.A. 38°29N 120°0W 78 G7
Lake Andes U.S.A. 43°9N 98°32W 80 D4
Lake Arthur U.S.A. 30°5N 92°41W 84 F8
Lake Bindegolly △ Australia 28°0S 144°12E 63 D3
Lake Cargelligo Australia 33°15S 146°22E 63 E4
Lake Charles U.S.A. 30°14N 93°13W 84 F8
Lake City Colo., U.S.A. 38°2N 107°19W 76 G10
Lake City Fla., U.S.A. 30°11N 82°38W 85 F13
Lake City Mich., U.S.A. 44°20N 85°13W 81 C11
Lake City Minn., U.S.A. 44°27N 92°16W 80 C7
Lake City Pa., U.S.A. 42°1N 80°21W 82 D4
Lake City S.C., U.S.A. 33°52N 79°45W 85 E15
Lake Cowichan Canada 48°49N 124°3W 70 D4
Lake District △ U.K. 54°30N 3°21W 12 C4
Lake Elsinore U.S.A. 33°38N 117°20W 79 M9
Lake Eyre △ Australia 28°40S 137°31E 63 D2
Lake Gairdner △ Australia 31°41S 135°51E 63 E2
Lake George U.S.A. 43°26N 73°43W 83 C11
Lake Grace Australia 33°7S 118°28E 61 F2
Lake Gregory ❂ Australia 20°12S 127°27E 60 D4
Lake Harbour = Kimmirut Canada 62°50N 69°50W 69 E18
Lake Havasu City U.S.A. 34°27N 114°22W 79 L12
Lake Hughes U.S.A. 34°41N 118°26W 79 L8
Lake Isabella U.S.A. 35°38N 118°28W 79 K8
Lake Jackson U.S.A. 29°3N 95°27W 84 G7
Lake King Australia 33°5S 119°45E 61 F2
Lake Lenore Canada 52°24N 104°59W 71 C8
Lake Louise Canada 51°30N 116°10W 70 C5
Lake Mackay ❂ Australia 21°48S 129°46E 60 D4
Lake Mead ⌓ U.S.A. 36°30N 114°22W 79 K12
Lake Meredith ⌓ U.S.A. 35°50N 101°50W 84 D4
Lake Mills U.S.A. 43°25N 93°32W 80 D7
Lake Placid U.S.A. 44°17N 73°59W 83 B11
Lake Pleasant U.S.A. 43°28N 74°25W 83 C10
Lake Providence U.S.A. 32°48N 91°10W 84 E9
Lake Roosevelt ⌓ U.S.A. 48°5N 118°14W 76 B4
Lake St. Peter Canada 45°18N 78°2W 82 A6
Lake Stevens U.S.A. 48°1N 122°4W 78 B4
Lake Superior ⌓ Canada 47°45N 84°45W 72 C3
Lake Torrens △ Australia 30°55S 137°40E 63 E2
Lake Village U.S.A. 33°20N 91°17W 84 E9
Lake Wales U.S.A. 27°54N 81°35W 85 H14
Lake Worth U.S.A. 26°37N 80°3W 85 H14
Lakeba Fiji 18°13S 178°47W 59 a
Lakeba Passage Fiji 18°0S 178°45W 59 a
Lakefield = Rinyirru △ Australia 15°24S 144°26E 62 B3
Lakefield Canada 44°25N 78°16W 82 B6
Lakehurst U.S.A. 40°1N 74°19W 83 F10
Lakeland Australia 15°49S 144°57E 62 B3
Lakeland U.S.A. 28°3N 81°57W 85 G14
Lakemba = Lakeba Fiji 18°13S 178°47W 59 a
Lakeport Calif., U.S.A. 39°3N 122°55W 78 F4
Lakeport Mich., U.S.A. 43°7N 82°30W 82 C2
Lakes Entrance Australia 37°50S 148°0E 63 F4
Lakeside Calif., U.S.A. 32°52N 116°55W 79 N10
Lakeside Nebr., U.S.A. 42°3N 102°26W 80 D2
Lakeside Ohio, U.S.A. 41°32N 82°46W 82 E2
Lakeview U.S.A. 42°11N 120°21W 76 E3
Lakeville U.S.A. 44°39N 93°14W 80 C7
Lakewood Colo., U.S.A. 39°42N 105°4W 76 G11
Lakewood N.J., U.S.A. 40°6N 74°13W 83 F10
Lakewood N.Y., U.S.A. 42°6N 79°19W 82 D5
Lakewood Ohio, U.S.A. 41°28N 81°47W 82 E3
Lakewood Wash., U.S.A. 47°11N 122°32W 78 C4
Lakha India 26°9N 70°54E 42 F4
Lakhimpur India 27°57N 80°46E 43 F9
Lakhisarai India 25°11N 86°5E 43 G12
Lakhnadon India 22°36N 79°36E 43 H8
Lakhnau = Lucknow India 26°50N 81°0E 43 F9
Lakhonpheng Laos 15°54N 105°34E 38 E5
Lakhpat India 23°48N 68°47E 42 H3
Lakin U.S.A. 37°57N 101°15W 80 G3
Lakitusaki → Canada 54°21N 82°25W 72 B3
Lakki Pakistan 32°36N 70°55E 42 C4
Lakonikos Kolpos Greece 36°40N 22°40E 23 F10
Lakor Indonesia 8°15S 128°17E 37 F7
Lakota Côte d'Ivoire 5°50N 5°30W 52 G4
Lakota U.S.A. 48°2N 98°21W 80 A4
Laksar India 29°46N 78°3E 42 E8
Laksefjorden Norway 70°45N 26°50E 8 A22
Lakselv Norway 70°2N 25°0E 8 A21
Laksettipet India 18°52N 79°13E 44 E4
Lakshadweep □ India 10°0N 72°30E 45 J1
Lakshadweep Is. India 10°0N 72°30E 45 J1
Lakshmanpur India 22°58N 83°3E 43 H10
Lakshmeshwar India 15°9N 75°28E 45 G2
Lakshmikantapur India 22°5N 88°20E 43 H13
Lala Musa Pakistan 32°40N 73°57E 42 C5
Lalaghat India 24°30N 92°40E 41 G18
L'Albufera Spain 39°20N 0°27W 21 C5
Lalganj India 25°52N 85°13E 43 G11
Lalgola India 24°25N 88°15E 43 G13
Lālī Iran 32°21N 49°6E 47 C6
Lalibela Ethiopia 12°3N 39°0E 49 E2
Lalin China 45°12N 127°0E 33 B14
Lalín Spain 42°40N 8°5W 21 A1
Lalin He → China 45°32N 125°40E 33 B13
Lalitpur India 24°42N 78°28E 43 G8
Lalitpur Nepal 27°40N 85°20E 43 F11
Lalkua India 29°5N 79°31E 43 E8
Lalsot India 26°34N 76°20E 42 F7
Lam Nam Nan △ Thailand 17°55N 100°28E 38 D3
Lam Pao Res. Thailand 16°50N 103°15E 38 D4
Lama Kara Togo 9°30N 1°15E 52 G6
Lamae Thailand 9°51N 99°5E 39 H2
Lamaing Myanmar 15°25N 97°53E 38 E1
Lamar Colo., U.S.A. 38°5N 102°37W 76 G12
Lamar Mo., U.S.A. 37°30N 94°16W 80 G6
Lamas Peru 6°28S 76°31W 92 E3
Lamayuru India 34°25N 76°56E 43 B7
Lambaréné Gabon 0°41S 10°12E 54 E2
Lambasa = Labasa Fiji 16°30S 179°27E 59 a
Lambay I. Ireland 53°29N 6°1W 10 C5
Lambert's Bay S. Africa 32°5S 18°17E 56 D2
Lambeth Canada 42°54N 81°18W 82 D3
Lame Deer U.S.A. 45°37N 106°40W 76 D10
Lamego Portugal 41°5N 7°52W 21 B2
Lamèque Canada 47°45N 64°38W 73 C7
Lameroo Australia 35°19S 140°33E 63 F3
Lamesa U.S.A. 32°44N 101°58W 84 E4
Lamia Greece 38°55N 22°26E 23 E10
Lamington △ Australia 28°13S 153°12E 63 D5
Lammermuir Hills U.K. 55°50N 2°40W 11 F6
Lamoille → U.S.A. 44°38N 73°13W 83 B11
Lamon B. Phil. 14°30N 122°20E 37 B6
Lamont Canada 53°46N 112°50W 70 C6
Lamont Calif., U.S.A. 35°15N 118°55W 79 K8
Lamont Wyo., U.S.A. 42°13N 107°29W 76 E10
Lampa Peru 15°22S 70°22W 92 G4
Lampang Thailand 18°16N 99°32E 38 C2
Lampasas U.S.A. 31°4N 98°11W 84 F5
Lampazos de Naranjo Mexico 27°1N 100°31W 86 B4
Lampedusa Medit. S. 35°36N 12°40E 22 G5
Lampeter U.K. 52°7N 4°4W 13 E3
Lamphun Thailand 18°40N 99°2E 38 C2
Lampione Medit. S. 35°33N 12°20E 22 G5
Lampman Canada 49°25N 102°50W 71 D8
Lampung □ Indonesia 5°30S 104°30E 36 F2
Lamta India 22°8N 80°7E 43 H9
Lamu Kenya 2°16S 40°55E 54 E8
Lamy U.S.A. 35°29N 105°53W 77 J11
Lan Xian China 38°15N 111°35E 32 E6
Lan Yü Taiwan 22°4N 121°25E 35 F13
Lāna'i U.S.A. 20°50N 156°55W 75 L8
Lanak La China 34°27N 79°32E 43 B8
Lanak'o Shank'ou = Lanak La China 34°27N 79°32E 43 B8
Lanark Canada 45°1N 76°22W 83 A8
Lanark U.K. 55°40N 3°47W 11 F5
Lanbi Kyun Myanmar 10°50N 98°20E 39 G2
Lancang China 22°36N 99°58E 34 F2
Lancang Jiang → China 21°40N 101°10E 34 G3
Lancashire □ U.K. 53°50N 2°48W 12 D5
Lancaster Canada 45°10N 74°30W 83 A10
Lancaster U.K. 54°3N 2°48W 12 C5
Lancaster Calif., U.S.A. 34°42N 118°8W 79 L8
Lancaster Ky., U.S.A. 37°37N 84°35W 81 G11
Lancaster N.H., U.S.A. 44°29N 71°34W 83 B13
Lancaster Ohio, U.S.A. 39°43N 82°36W 81 F12
Lancaster Pa., U.S.A. 40°2N 76°19W 83 F8
Lancaster S.C., U.S.A. 34°43N 80°46W 85 D14
Lancaster Wis., U.S.A. 42°51N 90°43W 80 D8
Lancaster Sd. Canada 74°13N 84°0W 69 C15
Lancelin Australia 31°0S 115°18E 61 F2
Lanchow = Lanzhou China 36°1N 103°52E 32 F2
Lanciano Italy 42°14N 14°23E 22 C6
Lancun China 36°25N 120°10E 33 F11
Land Between the Lakes ⌓ U.S.A. 36°25N 88°0W 85 C11
Landeck Austria 47°9N 10°34E 16 E6
Lander U.S.A. 42°50N 108°44W 76 E9
Lander → Australia 22°0S 132°0E 60 D5
Landes France 44°0N 1°0W 20 D3
Landfall I. India 13°40N 93°2E 45 H11
Landi Kotal Pakistan 34°7N 71°6E 42 B4
Landisburg U.S.A. 40°21N 77°19W 82 F7
Landmannalaugar Iceland 63°59N 19°4W 8 E4
Land's End U.K. 50°4N 5°44W 13 G2
Landsborough Cr. → Australia 22°28S 144°35E 62 C3
Landshut Germany 48°34N 12°8E 16 D7
Lanesboro U.S.A. 41°57N 75°34W 83 E9
Lanett U.S.A. 32°52N 85°12W 85 E12
Lang Shan China 41°0N 106°30E 32 D4
Lang Son Vietnam 21°52N 106°42E 34 G6
Lang Suan Thailand 9°57N 99°4E 39 H2
La'nga Co China 30°45N 81°15E 43 D9
Langar Iran 35°23N 60°25E 47 C9
Langara I. Canada 54°14N 133°1W 70 C2
Langarūd Iran 37°11N 50°8E 47 B6
Langdai China 26°6N 105°21E 34 D5
Langdon U.S.A. 48°45N 98°22W 80 A4
Langeberg S. Africa 33°55S 21°0E 56 D3
Langeberge S. Africa 28°15S 22°33E 56 C3
Langeland Denmark 54°56N 10°48E 9 J14
Langenburg Canada 50°51N 101°43W 71 C8
Langfang China 39°30N 116°41E 32 E9
Langholm U.K. 55°9N 3°0W 11 F5
Langjökull Iceland 64°39N 20°12W 8 D3
Langkawi, Pulau Malaysia 6°25N 99°45E 39 J2
Langklip S. Africa 28°12S 20°20E 56 C3
Langkon Malaysia 6°30N 116°40E 36 C5
Langley Canada 49°7N 122°39W 78 A4
Langøya Norway 68°45N 14°50E 8 B16
Langreo Spain 43°18N 5°40W 21 A3
Langres France 47°52N 5°20E 20 C6
Langres, Plateau de France 47°45N 5°3E 20 C6
Langsa Indonesia 4°30N 97°57E 36 D1
Langtang △ Nepal 28°10N 85°30E 43 E11
Langtou China 40°1N 124°19E 33 D13
Langtry U.S.A. 29°49N 101°34W 84 G4
Langu Thailand 6°53N 99°47E 39 J2
Languedoc France 43°58N 3°55E 20 E5
Langwang China 22°38N 113°27E 31 a
Langxi China 31°10N 119°12E 35 B12
Langzhong China 31°38N 105°58E 34 B5
Lanigan Canada 51°51N 105°2W 71 C7
Lanjigarh India 19°43N 83°23E 44 E6
Lankao China 34°48N 114°50E 32 G8
Länkäran Azerbaijan 38°48N 48°52E 47 B6
Lannion France 48°46N 3°29W 20 B2
L'Annonciation Canada 46°25N 74°55W 72 C5
Lanping China 26°28N 99°15E 34 D2
Lansang △ Thailand 16°45N 99°0E 38 D2
Lansdale U.S.A. 40°14N 75°17W 83 F9
Lansdowne Australia 31°48S 152°30E 63 E5
Lansdowne Canada 44°24N 76°1W 83 B8
Lansdowne India 29°50N 78°41E 43 E8
Lansdowne House = Neskantaga Canada 52°14N 87°53W 72 B2
L'Anse U.S.A. 46°45N 88°27W 80 B9
L'Anse au Loup Canada 51°32N 56°50W 73 B8
L'Anse aux Meadows Canada 51°36N 55°32W 73 B8
Lansford U.S.A. 40°50N 75°53W 83 F9
Lanshan China 25°24N 112°10E 35 E9
Lanshantou China 35°5N 119°20E 33 G10
Länsi-Turunmaa Finland 60°18N 22°18E 9 F20
Lansing U.S.A. 42°44N 84°33W 81 D11
Lanta, Ko Thailand 7°35N 99°3E 39 J2
Lantian China 34°11N 109°20E 32 G5
Lanusei Italy 39°52N 9°34E 22 E3
Lanxi China 29°13N 119°28E 35 C12
Lanzarote Canary Is. 29°0N 13°40W 52 C3
Lanzhou China 36°1N 103°52E 32 F2
Lao Cai Vietnam 22°30N 103°57E 34 F4
Laoag Phil. 18°7N 120°34E 37 A6
Laoang Phil. 12°32N 125°8E 37 B7
Laoha He → China 43°25N 120°35E 33 C11
Laohekou China 32°22N 111°38E 35 A8
Laois □ Ireland 52°57N 7°27W 10 D4
Laon France 49°33N 3°35E 20 B5
Laona U.S.A. 45°34N 88°40W 80 C9
Laos ■ Asia 17°45N 105°0E 38 D5
Lapa Brazil 25°46S 49°44W 95 B6
Lapeer U.S.A. 43°3N 83°19W 81 D12
Lapland = Lappland Europe 68°7N 24°0E 8 B21
LaPorte Ind., U.S.A. 41°36N 86°43W 80 E10
Laporte Pa., U.S.A. 41°25N 76°30W 83 E8
Lappeenranta Finland 61°3N 28°12E 8 F23
Lappland Europe 68°7N 24°0E 8 B21
Lappo = Lapua Finland 62°58N 23°0E 8 E20
Laprida Argentina 37°34S 60°45W 94 D3
Lâpseki Turkey 40°20N 26°41E 23 D12
Laptev Sea Russia 76°0N 125°0E 27 B13
Lapua Finland 62°58N 23°0E 8 E20
L'Àquila Italy 42°22N 13°22E 22 C5
Lār Iran 27°40N 54°14E 47 E7
Lārak Iran 26°51N 56°21E 47 E8
Laramie U.S.A. 41°19N 105°35W 76 F11
Laramie Mts. U.S.A. 42°0N 105°30W 76 F11
Laranda = Karaman Turkey 37°14N 33°13E 46 B2
Laranjeiras do Sul Brazil 25°23S 52°23W 95 B5
Larantuka Indonesia 8°21S 122°55E 37 F6
Larat Indonesia 7°0S 132°0E 37 F8
Larder Lake Canada 48°5N 79°40W 72 C4
Laredo U.S.A. 27°30N 99°30W 84 H5
Laredo Sd. Canada 52°30N 128°53W 70 C3
Largo U.S.A. 27°54N 82°47W 85 H13
Largs U.K. 55°47N 4°52W 11 F4
Lariang Indonesia 1°26S 119°17E 37 E5
Larimore U.S.A. 47°54N 97°38W 80 B5
Lario, Il = Como, L. di Italy 46°0N 9°11E 20 D8
Larisa Greece 39°36N 22°27E 23 E10
Larkana Pakistan 27°32N 68°18E 42 F3
Larnaca Cyprus 34°55N 33°38E 46 C2
Larne U.K. 54°51N 5°51W 10 B6
Larned U.S.A. 38°11N 99°6W 80 F4
Larose U.S.A. 29°34N 90°23W 85 G9
Larrimah Australia 15°35S 133°12E 60 C5
Larsen Ice Shelf Antarctica 67°0S 62°0W 5 C17
Larvik Norway 59°4N 10°2E 9 G14

Las Animas *U.S.A.* 38°4N 103°13W **76** G12
Las Anod *Somalia* 8°26N 47°19E **49** F4
Las Breñas *Argentina* 27°5S 61°7W **94** B3
Las Cejas *Argentina* 26°53S 64°44W **94** B3
Las Cejas *Argentina* 26°53S 64°44W **96** B4
Las Chimeneas *Mexico* 32°8N 116°5W **79** N10
Las Cruces *U.S.A.* 32°19N 106°47W **77** K10
Las Flores *Argentina* 36°10S 59°7W **94** D4
Las Heras *Argentina* 32°51S 68°49W **94** C2
Las Lajas *Argentina* 38°30S 70°25W **96** D2
Las Lomitas *Argentina* 24°43S 60°35W **94** A3
Las Palmas *Argentina* 27°8S 58°45W **94** B4
Las Palmas → *Mexico* 32°31N 116°58W **79** N10
Las Palmas de Gran Canaria
  *Canary Is.* 28°7N 15°26W **52** C2
Las Piedras *Uruguay* 34°44S 56°14W **95** C4
Las Pipinas *Argentina* 35°30S 57°19W **94** D4
Las Plumas *Argentina* 43°40S 67°15W **96** E3
Las Rosas *Argentina* 32°30S 61°35W **94** C3
Las Tablas *Panama* 7°49N 80°14W **88** E3
Las Toscas *Argentina* 28°21S 59°18W **94** B4
Las Tunas *Cuba* 20°58N 76°59W **88** B4
Las Varillas *Argentina* 31°50S 62°50W **94** C3
Las Vegas *U.S.A.* 35°36N 105°13W **77** J11
Lascano *Uruguay* 33°35S 54°12W **95** C5
Lash-e Joveyn *Afghan.* 31°45N 61°30E **40** D2
Lashburn *Canada* 53°10N 109°40W **71** C7
Lashio *Myanmar* 22°56N 97°45E **41** H20
Lashkar *India* 26°10N 78°10E **42** F8
Lāsjerd *Iran* 35°24N 53°4E **47** C7
Lassen Pk. *U.S.A.* 40°29N 121°30W **76** F3
Lassen Volcanic △
  *U.S.A.* 40°30N 121°20W **76** F3
Last Mountain L. *Canada* 51°5N 105°14W **71** C7
Lastchance Cr. →
  *U.S.A.* 40°2N 121°15W **78** F5
Lastoursville *Gabon* 0°55S 12°38E **54** E2
Lastovo *Croatia* 42°46N 16°55E **22** C7
Lat Yao *Thailand* 15°45N 99°48E **38** E2
Latacunga *Ecuador* 0°50S 78°35W **92** D3
Latady I. *Antarctica* 70°45S 74°35W **5** D17
Latakia = Al Lādhiqīyah
  *Syria* 35°30N 35°45E **46** C2
Latchford *Canada* 47°20N 79°50W **72** C4
Late *Tonga* 18°48S 174°39W **59** c
Latehar *India* 23°45N 84°30E **43** H11
Latham *Australia* 29°44S 116°20E **61** E2
Lathi *India* 27°43N 71°23E **42** F4
Lathrop Wells *U.S.A.* 36°39N 116°24W **79** J10
Latina *Italy* 41°28N 12°52E **22** D5
Latium = Lazio □ *Italy* 42°10N 12°30E **22** C5
Laton *U.S.A.* 36°26N 119°41W **78** J7
Latouche Treville, C.
  *Australia* 18°27S 121°49E **60** C3
Latrobe *Australia* 41°14S 146°30E **63** G4
Latrobe *U.S.A.* 40°19N 79°23W **82** F5
Latur *India* 18°25N 76°40E **44** E3
Latvia ■ *Europe* 56°50N 24°0E **9** H21
Lau Group *Fiji* 17°0S 178°30W **59** a
Lauchhammer *Germany* 51°29N 13°47E **16** C7
Lauge Koch Kyst
  *Greenland* 75°45N 57°45W **69** B20
Laughlin *U.S.A.* 35°10N 114°34W **79** K12
Lauhanvuori △ *Finland* 62°8N 22°4E **8** E20
Laukaa *Finland* 62°24N 25°56E **8** E21
Launceston *Australia* 41°24S 147°8E **63** G4
Launceston *U.K.* 50°38N 4°22W **13** G3
Laune → *Ireland* 52°7N 9°47W **10** D2
Launglon Bok *Myanmar* 13°50N 97°54E **38** F1
Laura *Australia* 15°32S 144°32E **62** B3
Laurel *Miss., U.S.A.* 31°41N 89°8W **85** F10
Laurel *Mont., U.S.A.* 45°40N 108°46W **76** D9
Laurel Hill *U.S.A.* 40°14N 79°6W **82** F5
Laurencekirk *U.K.* 56°50N 2°28W **11** E6
Laurens *U.S.A.* 34°30N 82°1W **85** D13
Laurentian Plateau *Canada* 52°0N 70°0W **73** B6
Lauria *Italy* 40°2N 15°50E **22** E6
Laurie L. *Canada* 56°35N 101°57W **71** B8
Laurinburg *U.S.A.* 34°47N 79°28W **85** D15
Laurium *U.S.A.* 47°14N 88°27W **80** B9
Lausanne *Switz.* 46°32N 6°38E **20** C7
Laut *Indonesia* 4°45N 108°0E **36** D3
Laut, Pulau *Indonesia* 3°40S 116°10E **36** E5
Laut Kecil, Kepulauan
  *Indonesia* 4°45S 115°40E **36** E5
Lautoka *Fiji* 17°37S 177°27E **59** a
Lauwersmeer △ *Neths.* 53°22N 6°11E **15** A6
Lava Beds △ *U.S.A.* 41°40N 121°30W **76** F3
Lavagh More *Ireland* 54°46N 8°6W **10** B3
Laval *France* 48°4N 0°48W **20** B3
Lavalle *Argentina* 28°15S 65°15W **94** B2
Lāvān *Iran* 26°48N 53°22E **47** E7
Lavant *Canada* 45°3N 76°42W **83** A8
Lāvar Meydān *Iran* 30°20N 54°30E **47** D7
Laverton *Australia* 28°44S 122°29E **61** E3
Lavras *Brazil* 21°20S 45°0W **95** A7
Lavrio *Greece* 37°40N 24°4E **23** F11
Lavumisa *Eswatini* 27°20S 31°55E **57** C5
Law-Racoviţă *Antarctica* 69°23S 76°23E **5** C6
Lawak I. = Nanshan I.
  *S. China Sea* 10°45N 115°49E **36** B5
Lawaki *Fiji* 17°40S 178°35E **59** a
Lawele *Indonesia* 5°13S 122°57E **37** F6
Lawn Hill = Boodjamulla △
  *Australia* 18°15S 138°6E **62** B2
Lawqah *Si. Arabia* 29°49N 42°45E **46** D4
Lawrence *N.Z.* 45°55S 169°41E **59** F2
Lawrence *Ind., U.S.A.* 39°50N 86°2W **80** F10
Lawrence *Kans., U.S.A.* 38°58N 95°14W **80** F6
Lawrence *Mass., U.S.A.* 42°43N 71°10W **83** D13
Lawrenceburg *Ind.,
  U.S.A.* 39°6N 84°52W **81** F11
Lawrenceburg *Tenn.,
  U.S.A.* 35°14N 87°20W **85** D11
Lawrenceville *Ga.,
  U.S.A.* 33°57N 83°59W **85** D13
Lawrenceville *Pa., U.S.A.* 41°59N 77°8W **82** E7
Laws *U.S.A.* 37°24N 118°20W **78** H8
Lawton *U.S.A.* 34°37N 98°25W **84** D5

Lawu *Indonesia* 7°40S 111°13E **37** G14
Laxford, L. *U.K.* 58°24N 5°6W **11** C3
Laxiwa Dam *China* 36°4N 101°11E **30** D9
Layla *Si. Arabia* 22°10N 46°40E **49** C4
Laylān *Iraq* 35°18N 44°31E **46** C5
Laysan I. *U.S.A.* 25°50N 171°50W **75** K5
Layton *U.S.A.* 41°4N 111°58W **76** F8
Laytonville *U.S.A.* 39°41N 123°29W **76** G2
Lazarev *Russia* 52°13N 141°30E **27** D15
Lazarev Sea *S. Ocean* 67°30S 3°0W **5** C2
Lázaro Cárdenas
  *Mexico* 17°55N 102°11W **86** D4
Lazio □ *Italy* 42°10N 12°30E **22** C5
Lazo *Russia* 43°25N 133°55E **28** C6
Le Bic *Canada* 48°20N 68°41W **73** C6
Le Creusot *France* 46°48N 4°24E **20** C6
Le François *Martinique* 14°38N 60°57W **88** c
Le Gosier *Guadeloupe* 16°14N 61°29W **88** b
Le Gris Gris *Mauritius* 20°31S 57°32E **55** d
Le Havre *France* 49°30N 0°5E **20** B4
Le Lamentin *Martinique* 14°35N 61°2W **88** c
Le Mans *France* 48°0N 0°10E **20** C4
Le Marin *Martinique* 14°27N 60°55W **88** c
Le Mars *U.S.A.* 42°47N 96°10W **80** D5
Le Mont-St-Michel *France* 48°40N 1°30W **20** B3
Le Moule *Guadeloupe* 16°20N 61°22W **88** b
Le Moyne, L. *Canada* 56°45N 68°47W **73** A6
Le Port *Réunion* 20°56S 55°18E **55** c
Le Prêcheur *Martinique* 14°50N 61°12W **88** c
Le Puy-en-Velay *France* 45°3N 3°52E **20** D5
Le Raysville *U.S.A.* 41°50N 76°10W **83** E8
Le Robert *Martinique* 14°40N 60°56W **88** c
Le Roy *U.S.A.* 42°58N 77°59W **82** D7
Le St-Esprit *Martinique* 14°34N 60°56W **88** c
Le Sueur *U.S.A.* 44°28N 93°55W **80** C7
Le Tampon *Réunion* 21°16S 55°32E **55** c
Le Thuy *Vietnam* 17°14N 106°49E **38** D6
Le Touquet-Paris-Plage
  *France* 50°30N 1°36E **20** A4
Le Tréport *France* 50°3N 1°20E **20** A4
Le Verdon-sur-Mer *France* 45°33N 1°4W **20** D3
Lea → *U.K.* 51°31N 0°1E **13** F8
Leach *Cambodia* 12°21N 103°46E **39** F4
Lead *U.S.A.* 44°21N 103°46W **80** C2
Leader *Canada* 50°50N 109°30W **71** C7
Leadville *U.S.A.* 39°15N 106°18W **76** G10
Leaf → *U.S.A.* 30°59N 88°44W **85** F10
Leaf Rapids *Canada* 56°30N 99°59W **71** B9
League City *U.S.A.* 29°31N 95°6W **84** C7
Leamington *Canada* 42°3N 82°36W **82** D2
Leamington *U.S.A.* 39°32N 112°17W **76** G7
Leamington Spa = Royal
  Leamington Spa *U.K.* 52°18N 1°31W **13** E6
Le'an *China* 27°22N 115°48E **35** D10
Leander *U.S.A.* 30°34N 97°52W **84** F5
Leandro Norte Alem
  *Argentina* 27°34S 55°15W **95** B4
Leane, L. *Ireland* 52°2N 9°32W **10** D2
Learmonth *Australia* 22°13S 114°10E **60** D1
Leask *Canada* 53°5N 106°45W **71** C7
Leatherhead *U.K.* 51°18N 0°20W **13** F7
Leavdnja = Lakselv *Norway* 70°2N 25°0E **8** A21
Leavenworth *Kans.,
  U.S.A.* 39°19N 94°55W **80** F6
Leavenworth *Wash.,
  U.S.A.* 47°36N 120°40W **76** C3
Leawood *U.S.A.* 38°58N 94°37W **80** F6
Lebak *Phil.* 6°32N 124°5E **37** C6
Lebam *U.S.A.* 46°34N 123°33W **78** D3
Lebanon *Ind., U.S.A.* 40°3N 86°28W **80** E10
Lebanon *Kans., U.S.A.* 39°49N 98°33W **80** F4
Lebanon *Ky., U.S.A.* 37°34N 85°15W **81** G11
Lebanon *Mo., U.S.A.* 37°41N 92°40W **80** G7
Lebanon *N.H., U.S.A.* 43°39N 72°15W **83** C12
Lebanon *Oreg., U.S.A.* 44°32N 122°55W **76** D2
Lebanon *Pa., U.S.A.* 40°20N 76°26W **83** F8
Lebanon *Tenn., U.S.A.* 36°12N 86°18W **85** C11
Lebanon ■ *Asia* 34°0N 36°0E **48** B5
Lebec *U.S.A.* 34°51N 118°52W **79** L8
Lebel-sur-Quévillon
  *Canada* 49°3N 76°59W **72** C4
Lebomboberge *S. Africa* 24°30S 32°0E **57** B5
Lebork *Poland* 54°33N 17°46E **17** A9
Lebowakgomo *S. Africa* 24°12S 29°30E **57** B4
Lebrija *Spain* 36°53N 6°5W **21** D2
Lebu *Chile* 37°40S 73°47W **94** D1
Lecce *Italy* 40°23N 18°11E **23** D8
Lecco *Italy* 45°51N 9°23E **20** D8
Lech → *Germany* 48°43N 10°56E **16** D6
Lechang *China* 25°10N 113°20E **35** E9
Lecontes Mills *U.S.A.* 41°5N 78°17W **82** E6
Łęczyca *Poland* 52°5N 19°15E **17** B10
Ledang, Gunung
  *Malaysia* 2°22N 102°37E **39** L4
Ledong *China* 18°41N 109°5E **38** C7
Leduc *Canada* 53°15N 113°30W **70** C6
Lee → *Ireland* 51°53N 8°56W **10** E3
Lee Vining *U.S.A.* 37°58N 119°7W **78** H7
Leech L. *U.S.A.* 47°10N 94°24W **80** B6
Leechburg *U.S.A.* 40°37N 79°36W **82** F5
Leeds *U.K.* 53°48N 1°33W **12** D6
Leeds *U.S.A.* 33°33N 86°33W **85** E11
Leek *Neths.* 53°10N 6°24E **15** A6
Leek *U.K.* 53°7N 2°1W **12** D5
Leeman *Australia* 29°57S 114°58E **61** E1
Leeper *U.S.A.* 41°22N 79°18W **82** E5
Leer *Germany* 53°13N 7°26E **16** B4
Leesburg *U.S.A.* 28°49N 81°53W **85** G14
Leesville *U.S.A.* 31°8N 93°16W **84** F8
Leeton *Australia* 34°33S 146°23E **63** E4
Leetonia *U.S.A.* 40°53N 80°45W **82** F4
Leeu Gamka *S. Africa* 32°47S 21°59E **56** D3
Leeuwarden *Neths.* 53°15N 5°48E **15** A5
Leeuwin, C. *Australia* 34°20S 115°9E **61** F2
Leeuwin Naturaliste △
  *Australia* 34°6S 115°3E **61** F2
Leeward Is. *Atl. Oc.* 16°30N 63°30W **89** C7
Lefkada *Greece* 38°40N 20°43E **23** E9
Lefkas = Lefkada *Greece* 38°40N 20°43E **23** E9
Lefkosia = Nicosia
  *Cyprus* 35°10N 33°25E **46** C2

Lefroy *Canada* 44°16N 79°34W **82** B5
Lefroy, L. *Australia* 31°21S 121°40E **61** F3
Legazpi *Phil.* 13°10N 123°45E **37** B6
Legendre I. *Australia* 20°22S 116°55E **60** D2
Leghorn = Livorno *Italy* 43°33N 10°19E **22** C4
Legian *Indonesia* 8°42S 115°10E **37** K18
Legionowo *Poland* 52°25N 20°50E **17** B11
Legnago *Italy* 45°11N 11°18E **22** B4
Legnica *Poland* 51°12N 16°10E **16** C9
Leh *India* 34°9N 77°35E **43** B7
Lehigh Acres *U.S.A.* 26°36N 81°39W **85** H14
Lehighton *U.S.A.* 40°50N 75°43W **83** F9
Lehututu *Botswana* 23°54S 21°55E **56** B3
Lei Shui → *China* 26°55N 112°35E **35** D9
Leiah *Pakistan* 30°58N 70°58E **42** D4
Leibo *China* 28°11N 103°34E **34** C4
Leicester *U.K.* 52°38N 1°8W **13** E6
Leicester City □ *U.K.* 52°38N 1°9W **13** E6
Leicestershire □ *U.K.* 52°41N 1°17W **13** E6
Leichhardt → *Australia* 17°35S 139°48E **62** B2
Leichhardt Ra. *Australia* 20°46S 147°40E **62** C4
Leiden *Neths.* 52°9N 4°30E **15** B4
Leie → *Belgium* 51°2N 3°45E **15** C3
Leimus *Nic.* 14°40N 84°3W **88** D3
Leine → *Germany* 52°43N 9°36E **16** B5
Leinster *Australia* 27°51S 120°36E **61** E3
Leinster □ *Ireland* 53°3N 7°8W **10** C4
Leinster, Mt. *Ireland* 52°37N 6°46W **10** D5
Leipzig *Germany* 51°18N 12°22E **16** C7
Leiria *Portugal* 39°46N 8°53W **21** C1
Leirvik *Norway* 59°47N 5°28E **9** G11
Leishan *China* 26°15N 108°20E **34** D7
Leisler, Mt. *Australia* 23°23S 129°20E **60** D4
Leith *U.K.* 55°59N 3°11W **11** F5
Leith Hill *U.K.* 51°11N 0°22W **13** F7
Leitir Ceanainn = Letterkenny
  *Ireland* 54°57N 7°45W **10** B4
Leitrim *Ireland* 54°8N 8°5W **10** B3
Leitrim □ *Ireland* 54°8N 8°0W **10** B3
Leixlip *Ireland* 53°22N 6°30W **10** C5
Leiyang *China* 26°27N 112°45E **35** D9
Leizhou *China* 20°52N 110°8E **35** G8
Leizhou Bandao *China* 21°0N 110°0E **34** G7
Leizhou Wan *China* 20°50N 110°20E **35** G8
Lek → *Neths.* 51°54N 4°35E **15** C4
Leka *Norway* 65°5N 11°35E **8** D14
Lek → *Neths.* 51°54N 4°35E **15** C4
Leland *Mich., U.S.A.* 45°1N 85°45W **81** C11
Leland *Miss., U.S.A.* 33°24N 90°54W **85** E9
Leleque *Argentina* 42°28S 71°0W **96** E2
Leling *China* 37°44N 117°13E **33** F9
Lelystad *Neths.* 52°30N 5°25E **15** B5
Léman, L. *Europe* 46°26N 6°30E **20** C7
Lembar *Indonesia* 8°45S 116°4E **37** K19
Lembongan, Nusa
  *Indonesia* 8°40S 115°27E **37** K18
Lembuak *Indonesia* 8°36S 116°11E **37** K19
Lemesós = Limassol
  *Cyprus* 34°42N 33°1E **46** C2
Lemhi Ra. *U.S.A.* 44°0N 113°0W **76** D7
Lemmenjoki △ *Finland* 68°40N 25°30E **8** B21
Lemmer *Neths.* 52°51N 5°43E **15** B5
Lemmon *U.S.A.* 45°57N 102°10W **80** C2
Lemon Grove *U.S.A.* 32°44N 117°1W **79** N9
Lemoore *U.S.A.* 36°18N 119°46W **78** J7
Lemvig *Denmark* 56°33N 8°20E **9** H13
Lena → *Russia* 72°52N 126°40E **27** B13
Lena Pillars = Lenskiy Stolby
  *Russia* 61°0N 127°0E **27** C13
Lenadoon Pt. *Ireland* 54°18N 9°3W **10** B2
Lengong *Malaysia* 5°6N 100°58E **39** K3
Lengshuijiang *China* 27°40N 111°26E **35** D8
Lengshuitan *China* 26°27N 111°35E **35** D8
Lengua de Vaca, Pta.
  *Chile* 30°14S 71°38W **94** C1
Leninogorsk = Ridder
  *Kazakhstan* 50°20N 83°30E **26** D9
Leninsk *Russia* 48°40N 45°15E **19** E8
Leninsk-Kuznetskiy
  *Russia* 54°44N 86°10E **26** D9
Lenkoran = Länkäran
  *Azerbaijan* 38°48N 48°52E **47** B6
Lenmalu *Indonesia* 1°45S 130°15E **37** E8
Lennox *U.S.A.* 43°21N 96°53W **80** D5
Lennoxville *Canada* 45°22N 71°51W **83** A13
Lenoir *U.S.A.* 35°55N 81°32W **85** D14
Lenoir City *U.S.A.* 35°48N 84°16W **85** D12
Lenore L. *Canada* 52°30N 104°59W **71** C8
Lenox *U.S.A.* 42°22N 73°17W **83** D11
Lens *France* 50°26N 2°50E **20** A5
Lensk *Russia* 60°48N 114°55E **27** C12
Lenskiy Stolby *Russia* 60°55N 126°0E **27** C13
Lentini *Italy* 37°17N 15°0E **22** F6
Lenwood *U.S.A.* 34°53N 117°7W **79** L9
Lenya *Myanmar* 11°33N 98°57E **39** G2
Leoben *Austria* 47°22N 15°5E **16** E8
Leodhais = Lewis *U.K.* 58°9N 6°40W **11** C2
Leola *U.S.A.* 45°43N 98°56W **80** C4
Leominster *U.K.* 52°14N 2°43W **13** E5
Leominster *U.S.A.* 42°32N 71°46W **83** D13
León *Mexico* 21°6N 101°41W **86** C4
León *Nic.* 12°27N 86°51W **88** D2
León *Spain* 42°38N 5°34W **21** A3
Leon → *U.S.A.* 31°14N 97°28W **84** F6
León, Montes de *Spain* 42°30N 6°18W **21** A2
Leonardtown *U.S.A.* 38°17N 76°38W **81** F15
Leonardville *Namibia* 23°29S 18°49E **56** B2
Leone *Amer. Samoa* 14°23S 170°48W **59** b
Leongatha *Australia* 38°30S 145°58E **63** F4
Leonora *Australia* 28°49S 121°19E **61** E3
Leopoldina *Brazil* 21°28S 42°40W **95** A7
Leopoldsburg *Belgium* 51°7N 5°13E **15** C5
Leoti *U.S.A.* 38°29N 101°21W **80** F3
Leova *Moldova* 46°28N 28°15E **17** E15
Leoville *Canada* 53°39N 107°33W **71** C7
Lepel = Lyepyel *Belarus* 54°50N 28°40E **9** J23
Leping *China* 28°47N 117°7E **35** C11
Lépo, L. do *Angola* 17°0S 19°0E **56** B2
Leppävirta *Finland* 62°29N 27°46E **8** E22
Leptis Magna *Libya* 32°40N 14°12E **53** B8
Leribe *Lesotho* 28°51S 28°3E **57** C4

Lérida = Lleida *Spain* 41°37N 0°39E **21** B6
Lerwick *U.K.* 60°9N 1°9W **11** A7
Les Cayes *Haiti* 18°15N 73°46W **89** C5
Les Coteaux *Canada* 45°15N 74°13W **83** A10
Les Escoumins *Canada* 48°21N 69°24W **73** C6
Les Sables-d'Olonne
  *France* 46°30N 1°45W **20** C3
Lesbos *Greece* 39°10N 26°20E **23** E12
Leshan *China* 29°33N 103°41E **34** C4
Leshukonskoye *Russia* 64°54N 45°46E **18** B8
Leskov I. *Antarctica* 56°0S 28°0W **5** B1
Leskovac *Serbia* 43°0N 21°58E **23** C9
Lesopilnoye *Russia* 46°44N 134°20E **28** A7
Lesotho ■ *Africa* 29°40S 28°0E **57** C4
Lesozavodsk *Russia* 45°30N 133°29E **28** B6
Lesse → *Belgium* 50°15N 4°54E **15** D4
Lesse et Lomme △ *Belgium* 50°8N 5°9E **15** D5
Lesser Antilles *W. Indies* 15°0N 61°0W **89** D7
Lesser Slave L. *Canada* 55°30N 115°25W **70** B5
Lesser Sunda Is. *Indonesia* 8°0S 120°0E **37** F6
Lessines *Belgium* 50°42N 3°50E **15** D3
Lestock *Canada* 51°19N 103°59W **71** C8
Lesueur △ *Australia* 30°11S 115°10E **61** F2
Lésvos = Lesbos *Greece* 39°10N 26°20E **23** E12
Leszno *Poland* 51°50N 16°30E **17** C9
Letaba *S. Africa* 23°59S 31°50E **57** B5
Letchworth Garden City
  *U.K.* 51°59N 0°13W **13** F7
Lethbridge *Canada* 49°45N 112°45W **70** D6
Lethem *Guyana* 3°20N 59°50W **92** C7
Leti, Kepulauan *Indonesia* 8°10S 128°0E **37** F7
Leti Is. = Leti, Kepulauan
  *Indonesia* 8°10S 128°0E **37** F7
Letiahau → *Botswana* 21°16S 24°0E **56** B3
Leticia *Colombia* 4°9S 70°0W **92** D5
Leting *China* 39°23N 118°55E **33** E10
Letjiesbos *S. Africa* 32°34S 22°16E **56** D3
Letlhakane *Botswana* 21°27S 25°30E **56** B4
Letlhakeng *Botswana* 24°0S 24°59E **56** B3
Letpadan *Myanmar* 17°45N 95°45E **41** L19
Letpan *Myanmar* 19°28N 94°10E **41** K19
Letsôk-aw Kyun
  *Myanmar* 11°30N 98°25E **39** G2
Letterkenny *Ireland* 54°57N 7°45W **10** B4
Leucadia *U.S.A.* 33°4N 117°18W **79** M9
Leuchars *U.K.* 56°24N 2°53W **11** E6
Leuser, Gunung *Indonesia* 3°46N 97°12E **36** D1
Leuven *Belgium* 50°52N 4°42E **15** D4
Leuze-en-Hainaut *Belgium* 50°36N 3°37E **15** D3
Levanger *Norway* 63°45N 11°19E **8** E14
Levelland *U.S.A.* 33°35N 102°23W **84** E3
Leven *U.K.* 56°12N 3°0W **11** E5
Leven, L. *U.K.* 56°12N 3°22W **11** E5
Leveque C. *Australia* 16°20S 123°0E **60** C3
Levice *Slovakia* 48°13N 18°35E **17** D10
Levin *N.Z.* 40°37S 175°18E **59** D5
Lévis *Canada* 46°48N 71°9W **73** C5
Levis, L. *Canada* 62°37N 117°58W **70** A5
Levittown *N.Y., U.S.A.* 40°44N 73°31W **83** F11
Levittown *Pa., U.S.A.* 40°9N 74°51W **83** F10
Levka Oros *Greece* 35°18N 24°3E **23** G11
Levkás = Lefkada *Greece* 38°40N 20°43E **23** E9
Levskigrad = Karlovo
  *Bulgaria* 42°38N 24°47E **23** C11
Levuka *Fiji* 17°34S 179°0E **59** a
Lewes *U.K.* 50°52N 0°1E **13** G8
Lewes *U.S.A.* 38°46N 75°9W **81** F16
Lewis → *U.K.* 58°9N 6°40W **11** C2
Lewis, Butt of *U.K.* 58°31N 6°16W **11** C2
Lewis → *U.S.A.* 45°51N 122°48W **78** E4
Lewis Ra. *Australia* 20°3S 128°50E **60** D4
Lewis Range *U.S.A.* 48°5N 113°5W **76** B7
Lewis Run *U.S.A.* 41°52N 78°40W **82** E6
Lewisburg *Pa., U.S.A.* 40°58N 76°54W **82** F8
Lewisburg *Tenn., U.S.A.* 35°27N 86°48W **85** D11
Lewisburg *W. Va.,
  U.S.A.* 37°48N 80°27W **81** G13
Lewisporte *Canada* 49°15N 55°3W **73** C8
Lewiston *Idaho, U.S.A.* 46°25N 117°1W **76** C5
Lewiston *Maine, U.S.A.* 44°6N 70°13W **81** C18
Lewiston *N.Y., U.S.A.* 43°11N 79°3W **82** C5
Lewistown *Mont., U.S.A.* 47°4N 109°26W **76** C9
Lewistown *Pa., U.S.A.* 40°36N 77°34W **82** F7
Lexington *Ill., U.S.A.* 40°39N 88°47W **80** E9
Lexington *Ky., U.S.A.* 38°3N 84°30W **81** F11
Lexington *Mich., U.S.A.* 43°16N 82°32W **82** C2
Lexington *Mo., U.S.A.* 39°11N 93°52W **80** F7
Lexington *N.C., U.S.A.* 35°49N 80°15W **85** D14
Lexington *Nebr., U.S.A.* 40°47N 99°45W **80** E4
Lexington *Ohio, U.S.A.* 40°41N 82°35W **82** F2
Lexington *S.C., U.S.A.* 33°59N 81°11W **85** E14
Lexington *Tenn., U.S.A.* 35°39N 88°24W **85** D10
Lexington *Va., U.S.A.* 37°47N 79°27W **81** G14
Lexington Park *U.S.A.* 38°16N 76°27W **81** F15
Leyburn *U.K.* 54°19N 1°48W **12** C6
Leyland *U.K.* 53°42N 2°43W **12** D5
Leye *China* 24°48N 106°29E **34** E6
Leyte □ *Phil.* 11°0N 125°0E **37** B7
Lezhë *Albania* 41°47N 19°39E **23** D8
Lezhi *China* 30°19N 104°58E **34** B5
Lhasa *China* 29°25N 90°58E **30** F7
Lhazê *China* 29°5N 87°38E **30** F6
L'Hermite, I. *Chile* 55°50S 68°0W **96** H3
Lhokkruet *Indonesia* 4°55N 95°24E **36** D1
Lhokseumawe *Indonesia* 5°10N 97°10E **36** C1
Li *Thailand* 17°48N 98°57E **38** D2
Li Jiang → *China* 24°40N 110°40E **35** E8
Li Jiang △ *China* 26°59N 100°10E **34** D3
Li Shan *China* 35°9N 111°56E **32** G6
Li Shui → *China* 29°24N 112°1E **35** C9
Li Xian *Hebei, China* 38°30N 115°35E **32** E8
Li Xian *Hunan, China* 29°36N 111°42E **35** C8
Liancheng *China* 25°42N 116°40E **35** E11
Liancourt Rocks *Asia* 37°15N 131°52E **29** F5
Lianga *Phil.* 8°38N 126°6E **37** C7

Liangcheng *Nei Monggol Zizhiqu,
  China* 40°28N 112°25E **32** D7
Liangcheng *Shandong,
  China* 35°32N 119°37E **33** G10
Liangdang *China* 33°56N 106°18E **32** H4
Lianghe *China* 24°50N 98°20E **34** E2
Lianghekou *China* 29°11N 108°44E **34** C7
Liangping *China* 30°38N 107°47E **34** B6
Liangpran *Indonesia* 1°4N 114°23E **36** D4
Lianhua *China* 27°3N 113°54E **35** D9
Lianhua Shan *China* 23°40N 115°48E **35** F10
Lianjiang *Fujian, China* 26°12N 119°27E **35** D12
Lianjiang *Guangdong,
  China* 21°40N 110°20E **35** G8
Lianping *China* 24°26N 114°30E **35** E10
Lianshan *China* 24°38N 112°8E **35** E9
Lianshanguan *China* 40°53N 123°43E **33** D12
Lianshui *China* 33°42N 119°20E **33** H10
Lianyuan *China* 27°40N 111°38E **35** D8
Lianyungang *China* 34°40N 119°11E **33** G10
Lianzhou *China* 24°51N 112°2E **35** E9
Liao He → *China* 41°0N 121°50E **33** D11
Liaocheng *China* 36°28N 115°58E **32** F8
Liaodong Bandao *China* 40°0N 122°30E **33** E12
Liaodong Wan *China* 40°20N 121°10E **33** D11
Liaotung, G. of = Liaodong Wan
  *China* 40°20N 121°10E **33** D11
Liaoyang *China* 41°15N 122°58E **33** D12
Liaoyuan *China* 42°58N 125°2E **33** C13
Liaozhong *China* 41°23N 122°50E **33** D12
Liard → *Canada* 61°51N 121°18W **70** A4
Liard River *Canada* 59°25N 126°5W **70** B3
Liari *Pakistan* 25°37N 66°30E **42** G2
Libanggaon *Nepal* 28°18N 82°38E **43** E10
Libau = Liepāja *Latvia* 56°30N 21°0E **9** H19
Libby *U.S.A.* 48°23N 115°33W **76** B6
Libenge
  *Dem. Rep. of the Congo* 3°40N 18°55E **54** D3
Liberal *U.S.A.* 37°3N 100°55W **80** G3
Liberec *Czechia* 50°47N 15°7E **16** C8
Liberia *Costa Rica* 10°40N 85°30W **88** D2
Liberia ■ *W. Afr.* 6°30N 9°30W **52** G4
Libertador □ *Chile* 34°15S 70°45W **94** C1
Liberty *Mo., U.S.A.* 39°15N 94°25W **80** F6
Liberty *N.Y., U.S.A.* 41°48N 74°45W **83** E10
Liberty *Pa., U.S.A.* 41°34N 77°6W **82** E7
Liberty *Tex., U.S.A.* 30°3N 94°48W **84** F7
Liberty-Newark Int. ✈ (EWR)
  *U.S.A.* 40°42N 74°10W **83** F10
Lībīya, Sahrā' *Africa* 25°0N 25°0E **53** C10
Libo *China* 25°22N 107°53E **34** E6
Libobo, Tanjung *Indonesia* 0°54S 128°28E **37** E7
Libode *S. Africa* 31°33S 29°2E **57** D4
Libong, Ko *Thailand* 7°15N 99°23E **39** J2
Libourne *France* 44°55N 0°14W **20** D3
Libramont *Belgium* 49°55N 5°23E **15** E5
Libreville *Gabon* 0°25N 9°26E **54** D1
Libya ■ *N. Afr.* 27°0N 17°0E **53** C9
Libyan Desert = Lībīya, Sahrā'
  *Africa* 25°0N 25°0E **53** C10
Libyan Plateau = Ed Déffa
  *Egypt* 30°40N 26°30E **53** B11
Licantén *Chile* 35°55S 72°0W **94** D1
Licata *Italy* 37°6N 13°56E **22** F5
Licheng *China* 36°28N 113°20E **32** F7
Lichfield *U.K.* 52°41N 1°49W **13** E6
Lichinga *Mozam.* 13°13S 35°11E **55** G7
Lichtenburg *S. Africa* 26°8S 26°8E **56** C4
Lichuan *Hubei, China* 30°18N 108°57E **34** B7
Lichuan *Jiangxi, China* 27°18N 116°55E **35** D11
Licking → *U.S.A.* 39°6N 84°30W **81** F11
Lida *Belarus* 53°53N 25°15E **17** B13
Lidköping *Sweden* 58°31N 13°7E **9** G15
Liebig, Mt. *Australia* 23°18S 131°22E **60** D5
Liechtenstein ■ *Europe* 47°8N 9°35E **20** C8
Liège *Belgium* 50°38N 5°35E **15** D5
Liège □ *Belgium* 50°32N 5°35E **15** D5
Liegnitz = Legnica *Poland* 51°12N 16°10E **16** C9
Lieksa *Finland* 63°18N 30°2E **8** E24
Lienyünchiangshih =
  Lianyungang *China* 34°40N 119°11E **33** G10
Lienz *Austria* 46°50N 12°46E **16** E7
Liepāja *Latvia* 56°30N 21°0E **9** H19
Lier *Belgium* 51°7N 4°34E **15** C4
Lierne △ *Norway* 64°20N 13°50E **8** D15
Lietuva = Lithuania ■
  *Europe* 55°30N 24°0E **9** J21
Lièvre → *Canada* 45°31N 75°26W **72** C4
Liffey → *Ireland* 53°21N 6°13W **10** C5
Lifford *Ireland* 54°51N 7°29W **10** B4
Lifudzin *Russia* 44°21N 134°58E **28** B7
Lightning Ridge *Australia* 29°22S 148°0E **63** D4
Lignières *France* 46°59N 2°10E **20** C5
Ligonier *U.S.A.* 40°15N 79°14W **82** F5
Liguria □ *Italy* 44°30N 8°50E **20** D8
Ligurian Sea *Medit. S.* 43°20N 9°0E **22** C3
Lihou Reefs and Cays
  *Australia* 17°25S 151°40E **62** B5
Lihué Calel △ *Argentina* 38°0S 65°10W **94** D2
Lik → *Laos* 18°31N 102°30E **38** C4
Likasi
  *Dem. Rep. of the Congo* 10°55S 26°48E **54** G5
L'Île-Rousse *France* 42°38N 8°57E **20** E8
Liling *China* 27°42N 113°29E **35** D9
Lille *France* 50°38N 3°3E **20** A5
Lille Bælt *Denmark* 55°20N 9°45E **9** J13
Lillehammer *Norway* 61°8N 10°30E **8** F14
Lillesand *Norway* 58°15N 8°23E **9** G13
Lillian Pt. *Australia* 27°40S 126°6E **61** E4
Lillooet *Canada* 50°44N 121°57W **70** C4
Lillooet → *Canada* 49°15N 121°57W **70** D4
Lilongwe *Malawi* 14°0S 33°48E **55** G6
Liloy *Phil.* 8°4N 122°39E **37** C6
Lim → *Europe* 43°45N 19°15E **23** C8
Lima *Indonesia* 3°39S 127°58E **37** E7
Lima *Mont., U.S.A.* 44°38N 112°36W **76** D7
Lima *N.Y., U.S.A.* 42°54N 77°37W **82** D7
Lima *Ohio, U.S.A.* 40°44N 84°6W **81** E11
Lima → *Portugal* 41°41N 8°50W **21** B1

Limassol *Cyprus* 34°42N 33°1E **46** C2
Limavady *U.K.* 55°3N 6°56W **10** A5
Limay → *Argentina* 39°0S 68°0W **96** D3
Limay Mahuida
 *Argentina* 37°10S 66°45W **94** D2
Limbang *Malaysia* 4°42N 115°6E **36** D5
Limbaži *Latvia* 57°31N 24°42E **9** H21
Limbdi *India* 22°34N 71°51E **42** H4
Limbe *Cameroon* 4°1N 9°10E **54** D1
Limburg *Germany* 50°22N 8°4E **16** C5
Limburg □ *Belgium* 51°2N 5°25E **15** C5
Limburg □ *Neths.* 51°20N 5°55E **15** C5
Limeira *Brazil* 22°35S 47°28W **95** A6
Limenas = Thasos
 *Greece* 40°40N 24°40E **23** D11
Limerick *Ireland* 52°40N 8°37W **10** D3
Limerick *U.S.A.* 43°41N 70°48W **83** C14
Limerick □ *Ireland* 52°30N 8°50W **10** D3
Limestone *U.S.A.* 42°2N 78°38W **82** D6
Limestone → *Canada* 56°31N 94°7W **71** B10
Limfjorden *Denmark* 56°55N 9°0E **9** H13
Limia = Lima → *Portugal* 41°41N 8°50W **21** B1
Limingen *Norway* 64°48N 13°35E **8** D15
Limmared *Sweden* 57°34N 13°20E **9** H15
Limmen ☉ *Australia* 15°15S 135°30E **62** B2
Limmen Bight *Australia* 14°40S 135°35E **62** A2
Limmen Bight →
 *Australia* 15°7S 135°44E **62** B2
Limnos *Greece* 39°50N 25°5E **23** E11
Limoges *Canada* 45°20N 75°16W **83** A9
Limoges *France* 45°50N 1°15E **20** D4
Limón *Costa Rica* 10°0N 83°2W **88** E3
Limon *U.S.A.* 39°16N 103°41W **76** G12
Limousin *France* 45°30N 1°30E **20** D4
Limoux *France* 43°4N 2°12E **20** E5
Limpopo □ *S. Africa* 24°5S 29°0E **57** B4
Limpopo → *Africa* 25°5S 33°30E **57** C5
Limuru *Kenya* 1°2S 36°35E **54** E7
Lin Xian *China* 37°57N 110°58E **32** F6
Lin'an *China* 30°15N 119°42E **35** B12
Linares *Chile* 35°50S 71°40W **94** D1
Linares *Mexico* 24°52N 99°34W **87** C5
Linares *Spain* 38°10N 3°40W **21** C4
Lincang *China* 23°58N 100°1E **34** F3
Lincheng *China* 37°25N 114°30E **32** F8
Linchuan *China* 27°57N 116°15E **35** D11
Lincoln = Beamsville
 *Canada* 43°12N 79°28W **82** C5
Lincoln *Argentina* 34°55S 61°30W **94** C3
Lincoln *N.Z.* 43°38S 172°30E **59** E4
Lincoln *U.K.* 53°14N 0°32W **12** D7
Lincoln *Calif., U.S.A.* 38°54N 121°17W **78** G5
Lincoln *Ill., U.S.A.* 40°9N 89°22W **80** E9
Lincoln *Kans., U.S.A.* 39°3N 98°9W **80** F4
Lincoln *Maine, U.S.A.* 45°22N 68°30W **81** C19
Lincoln *N.H., U.S.A.* 44°3N 71°40W **83** B13
Lincoln *N. Mex., U.S.A.* 33°30N 105°23W **77** K11
Lincoln *Nebr., U.S.A.* 40°49N 96°41W **80** E6
Lincoln City *U.S.A.* 44°57N 124°1W **76** D1
Lincoln Hav = Lincoln Sea
 *Arctic* 84°0N 55°0W **69** A21
Lincoln Sea *Arctic* 84°0N 55°0W **69** A21
Lincolnshire □ *U.K.* 53°14N 0°32W **12** D7
Lincolnshire Wolds *U.K.* 53°26N 0°13W **12** D7
Lincolnton *U.S.A.* 35°29N 81°16W **85** D5
Lind *U.S.A.* 46°58N 118°37W **76** C4
Linda *U.S.A.* 39°8N 121°34W **78** F5
Lindeman I. *Australia* 20°27S 149°3E **62** b
Lindeman Islands △
 *Australia* 20°28S 149°5E **62** b
Linden *Guyana* 6°0N 58°10W **92** B7
Linden *Ala., U.S.A.* 32°18N 87°48W **85** E11
Linden *Calif., U.S.A.* 38°1N 121°5W **78** G5
Linden *Tex., U.S.A.* 33°1N 94°22W **84** E7
Lindenhurst *U.S.A.* 40°41N 73°23W **83** F11
Lindesnes *Norway* 57°58N 7°3E **9** H12
Lindi *Tanzania* 9°58S 39°38E **54** F7
Lindi →
 *Dem. Rep. of the Congo* 0°33N 25°5E **54** D5
Lindley *U.S.A.* 42°1N 77°8W **82** D7
Lindos *Greece* 36°6N 28°4E **23** F13
Lindsay *Canada* 44°22N 78°43W **82** B6
Lindsay *Calif., U.S.A.* 36°12N 119°5W **78** J7
Lindsay *Okla., U.S.A.* 34°50N 97°38W **84** H6
Lindsborg *U.S.A.* 38°35N 97°40W **80** F5
Line Islands *Pac. Oc.* 7°0N 160°0W **65** H12
Linesville *U.S.A.* 41°39N 80°26W **82** E4
Linfen *China* 36°3N 111°30E **32** F6
Ling Xian *Hunan, China* 26°29N 113°48E **35** D9
Ling Xian *Shandong,*
 *China* 37°22N 116°30E **32** F9
Lingal *India* 16°17N 78°31E **45** F4
Linganamakki Res. *India* 14°6N 74°52E **45** G2
Lingao *China* 19°56N 109°42E **38** C7
Lingayen *Phil.* 16°1N 120°14E **37** A6
Lingayen G. *Phil.* 16°10N 120°15E **37** A6
Lingbao *China* 34°31N 110°51E **32** G6
Lingbi *China* 33°33N 117°33E **33** H9
Lingchuan *Guangxi Zhuangzu,*
 *China* 25°26N 110°21E **35** E8
Lingchuan *Shanxi, China* 35°45N 113°12E **32** G7
Lingding Yang *China* 22°25N 113°44E **31** a
Lingen *Germany* 52°31N 7°19E **16** B4
Lingga *Indonesia* 0°12S 104°37E **36** E2
Lingga, Kepulauan
 *Indonesia* 0°10S 104°30E **36** E2
Lingga Arch. = Lingga, Kepulauan
 *Indonesia* 0°10S 104°30E **36** E2
Linghai *China* 41°11N 121°22E **33** D11
Lingle *U.S.A.* 42°8N 104°21W **76** E11
Lingqiu *China* 39°28N 114°22E **32** E8
Lingshan *China* 22°25N 109°18E **34** F7
Lingshi *China* 36°48N 111°48E **32** F6
Lingshou *China* 38°20N 114°20E **32** E8
Lingshui *China* 18°27N 110°0E **38** C8
Lingsugur *India* 16°10N 76°31E **45** F3
Lingtai *China* 35°0N 107°40E **32** G4
Linguère *Senegal* 15°25N 15°5W **52** E2
Lingui *China* 25°12N 110°8E **35** E8
Lingwu *China* 38°6N 106°20E **32** E4
Lingyuan *China* 41°10N 119°15E **33** D10

Lingyun *China* 25°2N 106°35E **34** E6
Linhai *China* 28°50N 121°8E **35** C13
Linhares *Brazil* 19°25S 40°4W **93** G10
Linhe *China* 40°48N 107°20E **32** D4
Linjiang *China* 41°50N 127°0E **33** D14
Linköping *Sweden* 58°28N 15°36E **9** G16
Linkou *China* 45°15N 130°18E **33** B16
Linli *China* 29°27N 111°30E **35** C8
Linnansaari △ *Finland* 62°3N 28°40E **8** E23
Linnhe, L. *U.K.* 56°36N 5°25W **11** E3
Linosa *Medit. S.* 35°51N 12°50E **22** G5
Linqi *China* 35°45N 113°52E **32** G7
Linqing *China* 36°50N 115°42E **32** F8
Linqu *China* 36°25N 118°30E **33** F10
Linquan *China* 33°5N 115°17E **35** A10
Lins *Brazil* 21°40S 49°44W **95** A6
Linshu *China* 34°53N 118°38E **33** G10
Linshui *China* 30°21N 106°57E **34** B6
Lintao *China* 35°26N 103°58E **32** G2
Linton *Ind., U.S.A.* 39°2N 87°10W **80** F10
Linton *N. Dak., U.S.A.* 46°16N 100°14W **80** B3
Lintong *China* 34°20N 109°10E **32** G5
Linwood *Canada* 43°35N 80°43W **82** C4
Linwu *China* 25°19N 112°31E **35** E9
Linxi *Hebei, China* 39°42N 118°26E **33** E10
Linxi *Liaoning, China* 43°36N 118°2E **33** C10
Linxia *China* 35°36N 103°10E **30** D9
Linxiang *China* 29°28N 113°23E **35** C9
Linyanti → *Africa* 17°50S 25°5E **56** A4
Linyi *Shandong, China* 37°13N 116°54E **32** F9
Linyi *Shandong, China* 35°5N 118°21E **33** G10
Linying *China* 33°48N 113°56E **32** H7
Linz *Austria* 48°18N 14°18E **16** D8
Linzhenzhen *China* 36°30N 109°59E **32** F5
Linzhou *China* 36°4N 113°49E **32** F7
Linzi *China* 36°50N 118°20E **33** F10
Lion, G. du *France* 43°10N 4°0E **20** E6
Lions, G. of = Lion, G. du
 *France* 43°10N 4°0E **20** E6
Lion's Head *Canada* 44°58N 81°15W **82** B3
Lipa *Phil.* 13°57N 121°10E **37** B6
Lípari *Italy* 38°26N 14°58E **22** E6
Lípari, Is. = Eólie, Ís. *Italy* 38°30N 14°57E **22** E6
Lipcani *Moldova* 48°14N 26°48E **17** D14
Liperi *Finland* 62°31N 29°24E **8** E23
Lipetsk *Russia* 52°37N 39°35E **18** D6
Liping *China* 26°15N 109°7E **34** D7
Lipkany = Lipcani
 *Moldova* 48°14N 26°48E **17** D14
Lipovets *Ukraine* 49°12N 29°1E **17** D15
Lippe → *Germany* 51°39N 6°36E **16** C4
Lipscomb *U.S.A.* 36°14N 100°16W **84** C4
Liptrap, C. *Australia* 38°50S 145°55E **63** F4
Lipu *China* 24°30N 110°22E **35** E8
Lira *Uganda* 2°17N 32°57E **54** D6
Liria = Lliria *Spain* 39°37N 0°35W **21** C5
Lisala *Dem. Rep. of the Congo* 2°12N 21°38E **54** D4
Lisbon *N. Dak., U.S.A.* 46°27N 97°41W **80** B5
Lisbon *N.H., U.S.A.* 44°13N 71°55W **83** B13
Lisbon *N.Y., U.S.A.* 44°43N 75°19W **83** B9
Lisbon *Ohio, U.S.A.* 40°46N 80°46W **82** F4
Lisbon Falls *U.S.A.* 44°0N 70°4W **81** D18
Lisburn *U.K.* 54°31N 6°3W **10** B5
Lisburne, C. *U.S.A.* 68°53N 166°13W **74** B6
Liscannor B. *Ireland* 52°55N 9°24W **10** D2
Lisdoonvarna *Ireland* 53°2N 9°18W **10** C2
Lishe Jiang → *China* 24°15N 101°35E **34** E3
Lishi *China* 37°31N 111°8E **32** F6
Lishu *China* 43°20N 124°18E **33** C13
Lishui *Jiangsu, China* 31°38N 119°2E **35** B12
Lishui *Zhejiang, China* 28°28N 119°54E **35** C12
Lisianski I. *U.S.A.* 26°2N 174°0W **75** K5
Lisichansk = Lysychansk
 *Ukraine* 48°55N 38°30E **19** E6
Lisieux *France* 49°10N 0°12E **20** B4
Liski *Russia* 51°3N 39°30E **19** D6
Lismore *Australia* 28°44S 153°21E **63** D5
Lismore *Ireland* 52°8N 7°55W **10** D4
Lista *Norway* 58°7N 6°39E **9** G12
Lister, Mt. *Antarctica* 78°0S 162°0E **5** D11
Liston *Australia* 28°39S 152°6E **63** D5
Listowel *Canada* 43°44N 80°58W **82** C4
Listowel *Ireland* 52°27N 9°29W **10** D2
Litang *Guangxi Zhuangzu,*
 *China* 23°12N 109°8E **34** F7
Litang *Sichuan, China* 30°1N 100°17E **34** B3
Litang Qu → *China* 28°4N 101°32E **34** C3
Litani → *Lebanon* 33°20N 35°15E **48** B4
Litchfield *Calif., U.S.A.* 40°24N 120°23W **78** E6
Litchfield *Conn., U.S.A.* 41°45N 73°11W **83** E11
Litchfield *Ill., U.S.A.* 39°11N 89°39W **80** F9
Litchfield *Minn., U.S.A.* 45°8N 94°32W **80** C6
Litchfield △ *Australia* 13°14S 131°1E **60** B5
Lithgow *Australia* 33°25S 150°8E **63** E5
Lithino, Akra *Greece* 34°55N 24°44E **23** G11
Lithuania ■ *Europe* 55°30N 24°0E **9** J21
Lititz *U.S.A.* 40°9N 76°18W **83** F8
Litoměřice *Czechia* 50°33N 14°10E **16** C8
Little Abaco *Bahamas* 26°50N 77°30W **88** A4
Little Andaman I. *India* 10°45N 92°30E **45** J11
Little Barrier I. *N.Z.* 36°12S 175°8E **59** B5
Little Basses *Sri Lanka* 6°24N 81°43E **45** L5
Little Belt Mts. *U.S.A.* 46°40N 110°45W **76** C8
Little Bighorn Battlefield △
 *U.S.A.* 45°34N 107°25W **76** D10
Little Blue → *U.S.A.* 39°42N 96°41W **80** F6
Little Buffalo → *Canada* 61°0N 113°46W **70** A6
Little Cayman *Cayman Is.* 19°41N 80°3W **88** C3
Little Churchill →
 *Canada* 57°30N 95°22W **71** B9
Little Coco I. *Myanmar* 14°0N 93°13E **45** H11
Little Colorado →
 *U.S.A.* 36°12N 111°48W **77** H8
Little Current *Canada* 45°55N 81°57W **72** C3
Little Current → *Canada* 50°57N 84°36W **72** B3
Little Diomede I. *U.S.A.* 65°45N 168°56W **74** B6
Little Falls *Minn., U.S.A.* 45°59N 94°21W **80** C7
Little Falls *N.Y., U.S.A.* 43°3N 74°51W **83** C10
Little Fork → *U.S.A.* 48°31N 93°35W **80** A7

Little Grand Rapids
 *Canada* 52°0N 95°29W **71** C9
Little Humboldt →
 *U.S.A.* 41°1N 117°43W **76** F5
Little Inagua I. *Bahamas* 21°40N 73°50W **89** B5
Little Karoo *S. Africa* 33°45S 21°0E **56** E3
Little Khingan Mts. = Xiao
 Hinggan Ling *China* 49°0N 127°0E **31** B14
Little Lake *U.S.A.* 35°56N 117°55W **79** K9
Little Laut Is. = Laut Kecil,
 Kepulauan *Indonesia* 4°45S 115°40E **36** E5
Little Mecatina = Petit-
 Mécatina → *Canada* 50°40N 59°30W **73** B8
Little Minch *U.K.* 57°35N 6°45W **11** D2
Little Missouri →
 *U.S.A.* 47°36N 102°25W **80** B2
Little Nicobar *India* 7°20N 93°40E **45** L11
Little Ouse → *U.K.* 52°22N 1°12E **13** E9
Little Rann *India* 23°25N 71°25E **42** H4
Little Red → *U.S.A.* 35°11N 91°27W **84** D9
Little River *N.Z.* 43°45S 172°49E **59** E4
Little Rock *U.S.A.* 34°45N 92°17W **84** D8
Little Sable Pt. *U.S.A.* 43°38N 86°33W **80** D10
Little Sioux → *U.S.A.* 41°48N 96°4W **80** E5
Little Smoky → *Canada* 54°44N 117°11W **70** C5
Little Snake → *U.S.A.* 40°27N 108°26W **76** F9
Little Tobago
 *Trin. & Tob.* 11°18N 60°30W **93** J16
Little Valley *U.S.A.* 42°15N 78°48W **82** D6
Little Wabash → *U.S.A.* 37°55N 88°5W **80** G9
Little White → *U.S.A.* 43°40N 100°40W **80** D3
Little Zab = Zāb aş Şaghīr →
 *Iraq* 35°17N 43°29E **46** C4
Littlefield *U.S.A.* 33°55N 102°20W **84** E3
Littlehampton *U.K.* 50°49N 0°32W **13** G7
Littleton *U.S.A.* 44°18N 71°46W **83** B13
Liu He → *China* 40°55N 121°35E **33** D11
Liu Jiang → *China* 23°55N 109°30E **34** F7
Liuba *China* 33°38N 106°55E **34** A6
Liucheng *China* 24°38N 109°14E **34** E7
Liugou *China* 40°57N 118°15E **33** D10
Liuheng Dao *China* 29°40N 122°5E **35** C14
Liujiang *China* 24°26N 109°11E **34** E7
Liukang Tenggaja = Sabalana,
 Kepulauan *Indonesia* 6°45S 118°50E **37** F5
Liupan Shan *China* 35°39N 106°12E **32** G4
Liupanshui *China* 26°38N 104°48E **34** D5
Liuwa Plain *Zambia* 14°20S 22°30E **55** G4
Liuyang *China* 28°10N 113°37E **35** C9
Liuzhou *China* 24°22N 109°22E **34** E7
Liuzhuang *China* 33°12N 120°18E **33** H11
Livadia *Greece* 38°27N 22°54E **23** E10
Live Oak *Calif., U.S.A.* 39°17N 121°40W **78** F5
Live Oak *Fla., U.S.A.* 30°18N 82°59W **85** F13
Lively *Canada* 46°26N 81°9W **81** B13
Livermore *U.S.A.* 37°41N 121°47W **78** H5
Livermore, Mt. *U.S.A.* 30°38N 104°11W **84** F2
Livermore Falls *U.S.A.* 44°29N 70°11W **81** C18
Liverpool *Australia* 33°54S 150°58E **63** B5
Liverpool *Canada* 44°5N 64°41W **73** D7
Liverpool *U.K.* 53°25N 3°0W **12** D4
Liverpool *U.S.A.* 43°6N 76°13W **83** C8
Liverpool Ra. *Australia* 31°50S 150°30E **63** E5
Livingston *Guatemala* 15°50N 88°50W **88** C2
Livingston *U.K.* 55°54N 3°30W **11** F5
Livingston *Ala., U.S.A.* 32°35N 88°11W **85** E10
Livingston *Calif., U.S.A.* 37°23N 120°43W **78** H6
Livingston *Mont.,*
 *U.S.A.* 45°40N 110°34W **76** D8
Livingston *S.C., U.S.A.* 33°38N 81°7W **85** E14
Livingston *Tenn., U.S.A.* 36°23N 85°19W **85** C12
Livingston *Tex., U.S.A.* 30°43N 94°56W **84** F7
Livingston, L. *U.S.A.* 30°50N 95°10W **84** F7
Livingston Manor
 *U.S.A.* 41°54N 74°50W **83** E10
Livingstone *Zambia* 17°46S 25°52E **55** H5
Livingstonia *Malawi* 10°38S 34°5E **55** E6
Livny *Russia* 52°30N 37°30E **18** D6
Livonia *Mich., U.S.A.* 42°23N 83°23W **81** D12
Livonia *N.Y., U.S.A.* 42°49N 77°40W **82** D7
Livorno *Italy* 43°33N 10°19E **22** C4
Livramento *Brazil* 30°55S 55°30W **95** C4
Lixi *China* 26°23N 101°59E **34** D3
Lixian *China* 31°23N 103°13E **34** B4
Lixin *China* 33°8N 116°13E **35** A11
Liyang *China* 31°26N 119°28E **35** B12
Lizard I. *Australia* 14°42S 145°30E **62** A4
Lizard Pt. *U.K.* 49°57N 5°13W **13** H2
Ljubljana *Slovenia* 46°4N 14°33E **16** E8
Ljungan → *Sweden* 62°18N 17°23E **8** E17
Ljungby *Sweden* 56°49N 13°55E **9** H15
Ljusdal *Sweden* 61°46N 16°3E **8** F17
Ljusnan → *Sweden* 61°12N 17°8E **8** F17
Ljusne *Sweden* 61°13N 17°7E **8** F17
Llancanelo, Salina
 *Argentina* 35°40S 69°8W **94** D2
Llandeilo *U.K.* 51°53N 3°59W **13** F4
Llandovery *U.K.* 51°59N 3°48W **13** F4
Llandrindod Wells *U.K.* 52°14N 3°22W **13** E4
Llandudno *U.K.* 53°19N 3°50W **12** D4
Llanelli *U.K.* 51°41N 4°10W **13** F3
Llanes *Spain* 43°25N 4°50W **21** A3
Llanfair-ym-Muallt = Builth Wells
 *U.K.* 52°9N 3°25W **13** E4
Llangollen *U.K.* 52°58N 3°11W **12** E4
Llanidloes *U.K.* 52°27N 3°31W **13** E4
Llano *U.S.A.* 30°45N 98°41W **84** F5
Llano → *U.S.A.* 30°39N 98°26W **84** F5
Llano Estacado *U.S.A.* 33°30N 103°0W **84** E3
Llanos *S. Amer.* 5°0N 71°35W **92** C4
Llanos de Challe △ *Chile* 28°8S 71°1W **94** B1
Llanquihue, L. *Chile* 41°10S 72°50W **96** E1
Llanwrtyd Wells *U.K.* 52°7N 3°38W **13** E4
Lleida *Spain* 41°37N 0°39E **21** B6
Llera de Canales *Mexico* 23°19N 99°1W **87** C5
Lleyn Peninsula *U.K.* 52°51N 4°36W **12** E3
Llico *Chile* 34°46S 72°5W **94** C1
Lliria *Spain* 39°37N 0°35W **21** C5
Llobregat → *Spain* 41°19N 2°5E **21** B7

Lloret de Mar *Spain* 41°41N 2°53E **21** B7
Lloyd B. *Australia* 12°45S 143°27E **62** A3
Lloyd L. *Canada* 57°22N 108°57W **71** B7
Lloydminster *Canada* 53°17N 110°0W **71** C7
Llucmajor *Spain* 39°29N 2°53E **21** C7
Llullaillaco, Volcán
 *S. Amer.* 24°43S 68°30W **94** A2
Llullaillaco △ *Chile* 24°50S 68°51W **94** A2
Lo → *Vietnam* 21°18N 105°25E **38** B5
Loa *U.S.A.* 38°24N 111°39W **76** G8
Loa → *Chile* 21°26S 70°41W **94** A1
Loaita I. *S. China Sea* 10°41N 114°25E **36** B4
Loange →
 *Dem. Rep. of the Congo* 4°17S 20°2E **54** E4
Lobamba *Eswatini* 26°28S 31°12E **57** C5
Lobatse *Botswana* 25°12S 25°40E **56** C4
Lobería *Argentina* 38°10S 58°40W **94** D4
Lobito *Angola* 12°18S 13°35E **55** G2
Lobos *Argentina* 35°10S 59°0W **94** D4
Lobos, I. *Mexico* 27°20N 110°36W **86** B2
Loc Binh *Vietnam* 21°46N 106°54E **38** B6
Loc Ninh *Vietnam* 11°50N 106°34E **39** G6
Locarno *Switz.* 46°10N 8°47E **20** C8
Loch Garman = Wexford
 *Ireland* 52°20N 6°28W **10** D5
Loch Lomond and the Trossachs △
 *U.K.* 56°10N 4°40W **11** E4
Lochaber *U.K.* 56°59N 5°1W **11** E3
Locharbriggs *U.K.* 55°7N 3°35W **11** F5
Lochboisdale *U.K.* 57°9N 7°20W **11** D1
Loche, L. La *Canada* 56°30N 109°30W **71** B7
Lochem *Neths.* 52°9N 6°26E **15** B6
Loches *France* 47°7N 1°0E **20** C4
Lochgilphead *U.K.* 56°2N 5°26W **11** E3
Lochinver *U.K.* 58°9N 5°14W **11** C3
Lochmaddy *U.K.* 57°36N 7°10W **11** D1
Lochnagar *Australia* 23°33S 145°38E **62** C4
Lochnagar *U.K.* 56°57N 3°15W **11** E5
Lochy, L. *U.K.* 57°0N 4°53W **11** E4
Lock *Australia* 33°34S 135°46E **63** E2
Lock Haven *U.S.A.* 41°8N 77°28W **82** E7
Lockeford *U.S.A.* 38°10N 121°9W **78** G5
Lockeport *Canada* 43°47N 65°4W **73** D6
Lockerbie *U.K.* 55°7N 3°21W **11** F5
Lockhart *U.S.A.* 29°53N 97°40W **84** G6
Lockhart, L. *Australia* 33°15S 119°3E **61** F2
Lockhart River *Australia* 12°58S 143°30E **62** A3
Lockhart River ☉
 *Australia* 12°47S 143°20E **62** A3
Lockney *U.S.A.* 34°7N 101°27W **84** D4
Lockport *U.S.A.* 43°10N 78°42W **82** C6
Lod *Israel* 31°57N 34°54E **48** D3
Lodeinoye Pole *Russia* 60°44N 33°33E **18** B5
Lodge Bay *Canada* 52°14N 55°51W **73** B8
Lodge Grass *U.S.A.* 45°19N 107°22W **76** D10
Lodhran *Pakistan* 29°32N 71°30E **42** E4
Lodi *Italy* 45°19N 9°30E **20** D8
Lodi *Calif., U.S.A.* 38°8N 121°16W **78** G5
Lodi *Ohio, U.S.A.* 41°2N 82°1W **82** E3
Lodja *Dem. Rep. of the Congo* 3°30S 23°23E **54** E4
Lodwar *Kenya* 3°7N 35°36E **54** D7
Łódź *Poland* 51°45N 19°27E **17** C10
Loei *Thailand* 17°29N 101°35E **38** D3
Loeriesfontein *S. Africa* 31°0S 19°26E **56** D2
Lofa → *Liberia* 6°9N 11°7W **52** G3
Lofoten *Norway* 68°30N 13°59E **8** B16
Logan *Iowa, U.S.A.* 41°39N 95°47W **80** E6
Logan *Ohio, U.S.A.* 39°32N 82°25W **81** F12
Logan *Utah, U.S.A.* 41°44N 111°50W **76** F8
Logan *W. Va., U.S.A.* 37°51N 81°59W **81** G13
Logan, Mt. *Canada* 60°34N 140°23W **68** E3
Logandale *U.S.A.* 36°36N 114°29W **79** J12
Logansport *Ind., U.S.A.* 40°45N 86°22W **80** E10
Logansport *La., U.S.A.* 31°58N 94°0W **84** F8
Logone → *Chad* 12°6N 15°2E **53** F9
Logroño *Spain* 42°28N 2°27W **21** A4
Lohardaga *India* 23°27N 84°45E **43** H11
Loharia *India* 23°45N 74°14E **42** H6
Loharu *India* 28°27N 75°49E **42** E6
Lohri Wah → *Pakistan* 27°27N 67°37E **42** F2
Loikaw *Myanmar* 19°40N 97°17E **41** K20
Loimaa *Finland* 60°50N 23°5E **8** F20
Loir → *France* 47°33N 0°32W **20** C3
Loire → *France* 47°16N 2°10W **20** C2
Loja *Ecuador* 3°59S 79°16W **92** D3
Loja *Spain* 37°10N 4°10W **21** D3
Loji = Kawasi *Indonesia* 1°38S 127°28E **37** E7
Lojung *China* 24°20N 109°36E **34** E7
Lokeren *Belgium* 51°6N 3°59E **15** C3
Lokgwabe *Botswana* 24°10S 21°50E **56** C3
Lokitaung *Kenya* 4°12N 35°48E **54** D7
Lokkan tekojärvi *Finland* 67°55N 27°35E **8** C22
Lokoja *Nigeria* 7°47N 6°45E **52** G7
Lokolo →
 *Dem. Rep. of the Congo* 1°43S 18°23E **54** E3
Lolland *Denmark* 54°45N 11°30E **9** J14
Lolo *U.S.A.* 46°45N 114°5W **76** C6
Lom *Bulgaria* 43°48N 23°12E **23** C10
Lom Kao *Thailand* 16°53N 101°14E **38** D3
Lom Sak *Thailand* 16°47N 101°15E **38** D3
Loma *U.S.A.* 47°56N 110°30W **76** C8
Loma Linda *U.S.A.* 34°3N 117°16W **79** L9
Lomaloma *Fiji* 17°17S 178°59W **59** a
Lomami →
 *Dem. Rep. of the Congo* 0°46N 24°16E **54** D4
Lomas de Zamora
 *Argentina* 34°45S 58°24W **94** C4
Lombadina *Australia* 16°31S 122°54E **60** C3
Lombárdia □ *Italy* 45°40N 9°30E **20** D8
Lombardy = Lombárdia □
 *Italy* 45°40N 9°30E **20** D8
Lomblen *Indonesia* 8°30S 123°32E **37** F6
Lombok *Indonesia* 8°45S 116°30E **36** F5
Lombok, Selat *Indonesia* 8°30S 115°50E **37** K18
Lomé *Togo* 6°9N 1°20E **52** G6
Lomela
 *Dem. Rep. of the Congo* 2°19S 23°15E **54** E4
Lomela →
 *Dem. Rep. of the Congo* 0°15S 20°40E **54** E4
Lommel *Belgium* 51°14N 5°19E **15** C5

Lomond *Canada* 50°24N 112°36W **70** C6
Lomond, L. *U.K.* 56°8N 4°38W **11** E4
Lomonosov Ridge *Arctic* 88°0N 140°0E **4** A
Lomphat *Cambodia* 13°30N 106°59E **38** F6
Lompobatang *Indonesia* 5°24S 119°56E **37** F5
Lompoc *U.S.A.* 34°38N 120°28W **79** L6
Łomża *Poland* 53°10N 22°2E **17** B12
Lon, Ko *Thailand* 7°47N 98°23E **39** a
Lonavale *India* 18°46N 73°29E **44** E1
Loncoche *Chile* 39°20S 72°50W **96** D2
Londa *India* 15°30N 74°30E **45** G2
Londiani *Kenya* 0°10S 35°33E **54** E7
London *Canada* 42°59N 81°15W **82** D3
London *Ky., U.S.A.* 37°8N 84°5W **81** G11
London *Ohio, U.S.A.* 39°53N 83°27W **81** F12
London, Greater □ *U.K.* 51°36N 0°5W **13** F7
London Gateway *U.K.* 51°31N 0°29E **13** F8
London Gatwick ✈ (LGW)
 *U.K.* 51°10N 0°11W **13** F7
London Stansted ✈ (STN)
 *U.K.* 51°54N 0°14E **13** F8
Londonderry *U.K.* 55°0N 7°20W **10** B4
Londonderry □ *U.K.* 55°0N 7°20W **10** B4
Londonderry, C.
 *Australia* 13°45S 126°55E **60** B4
Londonderry, I. *Chile* 55°0S 71°0W **96** H2
Londres *Argentina* 27°46S 67°7W **94** B2
Londres *Argentina* 27°43S 67°7W **96** B3
Londrina *Brazil* 23°18S 51°10W **95** A5
Lone Pine *U.S.A.* 36°36N 118°4W **78** J8
Lonely Mine *Zimbabwe* 19°30S 28°49E **57** A4
Long B. *U.S.A.* 33°35N 78°45W **85** E15
Long Beach *Calif.,*
 *U.S.A.* 33°46N 118°11W **79** M8
Long Beach *N.Y., U.S.A.* 40°35N 73°39W **83** F11
Long Beach *Wash.,*
 *U.S.A.* 46°21N 124°3W **78** D2
Long Branch *U.S.A.* 40°18N 74°0W **83** F11
Long Creek *U.S.A.* 44°43N 119°6W **76** D4
Long Eaton *U.K.* 52°53N 1°15W **12** E6
Long I. *Australia* 20°22S 148°51E **62** b
Long I. *Bahamas* 23°20N 75°10W **89** B4
Long I. *Canada* 54°50N 79°20W **72** B4
Long I. *Ireland* 51°30N 9°34W **10** E2
Long I. *U.S.A.* 40°45N 73°30W **83** F11
Long Island Sd. *U.S.A.* 41°10N 73°0W **83** E12
Long L. *Canada* 49°30N 86°50W **72** C2
Long Lake *U.S.A.* 43°58N 74°25W **83** C10
Long Point *Canada* 42°34N 80°25W **82** D4
Long Point B. *Canada* 42°40N 80°10W **82** D4
Long Prairie *U.S.A.* 45°59N 94°52W **80** C6
Long Prairie → *U.S.A.* 46°20N 94°36W **80** B6
Long Pt. *Ont., Canada* 42°35N 80°2W **82** D4
Long Pt. *Ont., Canada* 43°56N 76°53W **83** C8
Long Range Mts. *Canada* 49°30N 57°30W **73** C8
Long Reef *Australia* 14°1S 125°48E **60** B4
Long Sault *Canada* 45°2N 74°53W **83** A10
Long Str. = Longa, Proliv
 *Russia* 70°0N 175°0E **27** C18
Long Thanh *Vietnam* 10°47N 106°57E **39** G6
Long Xian *China* 34°55N 106°55E **32** G4
Long Xuyen *Vietnam* 10°19N 105°28E **39** G5
Longa, Proliv *Russia* 70°0N 175°0E **27** C18
Long'an *China* 23°10N 107°40E **34** F6
Longbenton *U.K.* 55°1N 1°31W **12** B6
Longboat Key *U.S.A.* 27°23N 82°39W **85** H13
Longchang *China* 29°18N 105°15E **34** C5
Longchuan *Guangdong,*
 *China* 24°5N 115°17E **35** E10
Longchuan *Yunnan, China* 24°23N 97°58E **34** E1
Longde *China* 35°30N 106°20E **32** G4
Longford *Australia* 41°32S 147°3E **63** G4
Longford *Ireland* 53°43N 7°49W **10** C4
Longford □ *Ireland* 53°42N 7°45W **10** C4
Longhai *China* 24°25N 117°46E **35** E11
Longhua *Guangdong, China* 22°39N 114°0E **31** a
Longhua *Hebei, China* 41°18N 117°45E **33** D9
Longhui *China* 27°7N 111°2E **35** D8
Longiram *Indonesia* 0°5S 115°45E **36** E5
Longjing *China* 42°46N 129°25E **33** C15
Longjiang *Jiangxi, China* 26°8N 115°10E **35** D10
Longkou *Shandong,*
 *China* 37°40N 120°18E **33** F11
Longlac *Canada* 49°45N 86°25W **72** C2
Longli *China* 26°25N 106°58E **34** D6
Longlin *China* 24°47N 105°20E **34** E5
Longling *China* 24°37N 98°39E **34** E2
Longmeadow *U.S.A.* 42°3N 72°34W **83** D12
Longmen *China* 23°40N 114°18E **35** F10
Longmen Shiku *China* 34°28N 112°28E **32** G7
Longming *China* 22°59N 107°7E **34** F6
Longmont *U.S.A.* 40°10N 105°6W **76** F11
Longnan *China* 24°55N 114°47E **35** E10
Longnawan *Indonesia* 1°51N 114°55E **36** D4
Longquan *China* 28°7N 119°10E **35** C12
Longreach *Australia* 23°28S 144°14E **62** C3
Longshan *China* 29°29N 109°25E **34** C7
Longsheng *China* 25°48N 110°0E **35** E8
Longtan Dam *China* 24°37N 107°0E **34** E6
Longtan Shuiku *China* 24°37N 107°0E **34** E6
Longview *Tex., U.S.A.* 32°30N 94°44W **84** E7
Longview *Wash., U.S.A.* 46°8N 122°57W **78** D4
Longxi *China* 34°53N 104°40E **32** G3
Longxue Dao *China* 22°41N 113°38E **31** a
Longyan *China* 25°10N 117°0E **35** E11
Longyearbyen *Svalbard* 78°13N 15°40E **4** B8
Longyou *China* 29°1N 119°9E **35** C12
Longzhou *China* 22°22N 106°42E **34** F6
Lonoke *U.S.A.* 34°47N 91°54W **84** D9
Lonquimay *Chile* 38°26S 71°14W **96** D2
Lons-le-Saunier *France* 46°40N 5°31E **20** C6
Looe *U.K.* 50°22N 4°28W **13** G3
Lookout, C. *Canada* 55°18N 83°56W **72** A3
Lookout, C. *U.S.A.* 34°35N 76°32W **85** D16
Loon → *Alta., Canada* 57°8N 115°3W **70** B5
Loon → *Man., Canada* 55°53N 101°59W **71** B8
Loon Lake *Canada* 54°2N 109°10W **71** C7
Loongana *Australia* 30°52S 127°5E **61** F4

Loop Hd. Ireland 52°34N 9°56W 10 D2
Lop China 37°3N 80°11E 30 D5
Lop Nor = Lop Nur China 40°20N 90°10E 30 C7
Lop Nur China 40°20N 90°10E 30 C7
Lopatina, Gora Russia 50°47N 143°10E 27 D15
Lopatka, Mys Russia 50°52N 156°40E 27 D16
Lopburi Thailand 14°48N 100°37E 38 E3
Lopez U.S.A. 41°27N 76°20W 83 E8
Lopez, C. Gabon 0°47S 8°40E 54 E1
Lopphavet Norway 70°27N 21°15E 8 A19
Lora → Afghan. 31°35N 66°32E 40 D4
Lora, Hāmūn-i- Pakistan 29°38N 64°58E 40 E4
Lora Cr. → Australia 28°10S 135°22E 63 D2
Lora del Río Spain 37°39N 5°33W 21 D3
Lorain U.S.A. 41°28N 82°11W 82 E2
Loralai Pakistan 30°20N 68°41E 42 D3
Lorca Spain 37°41N 1°42W 21 D5
Lord Howe I. Pac. Oc. 31°33S 159°6E 58 E8
Lord Howe Rise Pac. Oc. 30°0S 162°30E 64 L8
Lord Loughborough I.
 Myanmar 10°25N 97°54E 39 G1
Lordsburg U.S.A. 32°21N 108°43W 77 K9
Lorestān □ Iran 33°30N 48°40E 47 C6
Loreto Brazil 7°5S 45°10W 93 E9
Loreto Mexico 26°0N 111°21W 86 B2
Lorient France 47°45N 3°23W 20 C2
Lormi India 22°17N 81°41E 43 H9
Lorn U.K. 56°26N 5°10W 11 E3
Lorn, Firth of U.K. 56°20N 5°40W 11 E3
Lorne Australia 38°33S 143°59E 63 F3
Lorraine France 48°53N 6°0E 20 B7
Los Alamos Calif., U.S.A. 34°44N 120°17W 79 L6
Los Alamos N. Mex.,
 U.S.A. 35°53N 106°19W 77 J10
Los Altos U.S.A. 37°23N 122°7W 78 H4
Los Andes Chile 32°50S 70°40W 94 C1
Los Angeles Chile 37°28S 72°23W 94 D1
Los Angeles U.S.A. 35°22N 118°5W 79 K9
Los Angeles Aqueduct
 U.S.A. 35°22N 118°5W 79 K9
Los Banos U.S.A. 37°4N 120°51W 78 H6
Los Blancos Argentina 23°40S 62°30W 94 A3
Los Cabos Int. ✈ (SJD)
 Mexico 23°9N 109°43W 86 C3
Los Cardones △ Argentina 25°8S 65°55W 94 B2
Los Chiles Costa Rica 11°2N 84°43W 88 D3
Los Gatos U.S.A. 37°14N 121°59W 78 H5
Los Haïtises △ Dom. Rep. 19°4N 69°36W 89 C6
Los Hermanos, Is.
 Venezuela 11°45N 64°25W 89 D7
Los Loros Chile 27°50S 70°6W 94 B1
Los Lunas U.S.A. 34°48N 106°44W 77 J10
Los Mochis Mexico 25°45N 108°57W 86 B3
Los Olivos U.S.A. 34°40N 120°7W 79 L6
Los Palacios Cuba 22°35N 83°15W 88 B3
Los Queñes Chile 35°1S 70°48W 94 D1
Los Reyes de Salgado
 Mexico 19°35N 102°29W 86 D4
Los Roques, Is. Venezuela 11°50N 66°45W 89 D6
Los Teques Venezuela 10°21N 67°2W 92 A5
Los Testigos, Is. Venezuela 11°23N 63°6W 89 D7
Los Vilos Chile 32°10S 71°30W 94 C1
Lošinj Croatia 44°30N 14°30E 16 F8
Loskop Dam S. Africa 25°23S 29°20E 57 C4
Lossiemouth U.K. 57°42N 3°17W 11 D5
Lostwithiel U.K. 50°24N 4°41W 13 G3
Lot → France 44°18N 0°20E 20 D4
Lota Chile 37°5S 73°10W 94 D1
Loţfābād Iran 37°32N 59°20E 47 B8
Lothair S. Africa 26°22S 30°27E 57 C5
Lotta → Europe 68°42N 31°6E 8 B24
Lotung Taiwan 24°41N 121°46E 35 E13
Loubomo Congo 4°9S 12°47E 54 E2
Loudi China 27°42N 111°59E 35 D8
Loudonville U.S.A. 40°38N 82°14W 82 F2
Louga Senegal 15°45N 16°5W 52 E2
Loughborough U.K. 52°47N 1°11W 12 E6
Loughrea Ireland 53°12N 8°33W 10 C3
Loughros More B. Ireland 54°48N 8°32W 10 B3
Louis Trichardt S. Africa 23°1S 29°43E 57 B4
Louis XIV, Pte. Canada 54°37N 79°45W 72 B4
Louisa U.S.A. 38°7N 82°36W 81 F12
Louisbourg Canada 45°55N 60°0W 73 C8
Louisburgh Ireland 53°46N 9°49W 10 C2
Louise I. Canada 52°55N 131°50W 70 C2
Louiseville Canada 46°20N 72°56W 72 C5
Louisiade Arch.
 Papua N. G. 11°10S 153°0E 58 C8
Louisiana U.S.A. 39°27N 91°3W 80 F8
Louisiana □ U.S.A. 30°50N 92°0W 84 F9
Louisville Ky., U.S.A. 38°15N 85°46W 81 F11
Louisville Miss., U.S.A. 33°7N 89°3W 85 E10
Louisville Ohio, U.S.A. 40°50N 81°16W 82 F3
Louisville Ridge Pac. Oc. 31°0S 172°30W 64 L10
Loulé Portugal 37°9N 8°0W 21 D1
Loup City U.S.A. 41°17N 98°58W 80 E4
Loups Marins, Lacs des
 Canada 56°30N 73°45W 72 A5
Lourdes France 43°6N 0°3W 20 E3
Lourdes-de-Blanc-Sablon
 Canada 51°24N 57°12W 73 B8
Louth Australia 30°30S 145°8E 63 E4
Louth Ireland 53°58N 6°32W 10 C5
Louth U.K. 53°22N 0°1W 12 D7
Louth □ Ireland 53°56N 6°34W 10 C5
Louvain = Leuven
 Belgium 50°52N 4°42E 15 D4
Louwsburg S. Africa 27°37S 31°7E 57 C5
Loveland U.S.A. 40°24N 105°5W 76 F11
Lovell U.S.A. 44°50N 108°24W 76 D9
Lovelock U.S.A. 40°11N 118°28W 76 F4
Loviisa Finland 60°28N 26°12E 8 F22
Lovina Indonesia 8°9S 115°1E 37 J18
Loving U.S.A. 32°17N 104°6W 77 K11
Lovington U.S.A. 32°57N 103°21W 77 K12
Lovisa = Loviisa Finland 60°28N 26°12E 8 F22
Low, L. Canada 52°29N 76°17W 72 B4
Low Pt. Australia 32°25S 127°25E 61 F4
Low Tatra = Nízké Tatry
 Slovakia 48°55N 19°30E 17 D10

Lowell U.S.A. 42°38N 71°19W 83 D13
Lowellville U.S.A. 41°2N 80°32W 82 E4
Löwen → Namibia 26°51S 18°17E 56 C2
Lower Alkali L. U.S.A. 41°16N 120°2W 76 F3
Lower Arrow L. Canada 49°40N 118°5W 70 D5
Lower California = Baja California
 Mexico 31°10N 115°12W 86 A1
Lower Hutt N.Z. 41°10S 174°55E 59 D5
Lower Lake U.S.A. 38°55N 122°37W 78 G4
Lower Manitou L.
 Canada 49°15N 93°0W 71 D10
Lower Post Canada 59°58N 128°30W 70 B3
Lower Red L. U.S.A. 47°58N 95°0W 80 B6
Lower Saxony = Niedersachsen □
 Germany 52°50N 9°0E 16 B5
Lower Tunguska = Tunguska,
 Nizhnyaya → Russia 65°48N 88°4E 27 C9
Lowestoft U.K. 52°29N 1°45E 13 E9
Lowgar □ Afghan. 34°0N 69°0E 40 B6
Łowicz Poland 52°6N 19°55E 17 B10
Lowther I. Canada 74°33N 97°30W 69 C12
Lowville U.S.A. 43°47N 75°29W 83 C9
Loxton Australia 34°28S 140°31E 63 E3
Loxton S. Africa 31°30S 22°22E 56 D3
Loyalton U.S.A. 39°41N 120°14W 78 F6
Loyalty Is. = Loyauté, Îs.
 N. Cal. 20°50S 166°30E 58 D9
Loyang = Luoyang
 China 34°40N 112°26E 32 G7
Loyauté, Îs. N. Cal. 20°50S 166°30E 58 D9
Loyev = Loyew Belarus 51°56N 30°46E 17 C16
Loyew Belarus 51°56N 30°46E 17 C16
Lü Shan China 29°30N 115°55E 35 C10
Lü Shan △ China 29°26N 115°52E 35 C10
Lu Wo China 22°33N 114°6E 31 a
Luachimo Angola 7°23S 20°48E 54 F4
Luajan → India 24°44N 85°1E 43 G11
Lualaba →
 Dem. Rep. of the Congo 0°26N 25°20E 54 D5
Lu'an China 31°45N 116°29E 35 B11
Luan Chau Vietnam 21°38N 103°24E 34 G4
Luan He → China 39°20N 119°5E 33 E10
Luan Xian China 39°40N 118°40E 33 E10
Luancheng Guangxi Zhuangzu,
 China 22°48N 108°55E 34 F7
Luancheng Hebei, China 37°53N 114°40E 32 F8
Luanda Angola 8°50S 13°15E 54 F2
Luang, Doi Thailand 18°30N 101°15E 38 C3
Luang, Thale Thailand 7°30N 100°15E 39 J3
Luang Nam Tha Laos 20°58N 101°30E 34 A3
Luang Prabang Laos 19°52N 102°10E 34 H4
Luangwa → Zambia 14°25S 30°25E 55 G6
Luangwa Valley Zambia 13°30S 31°30E 55 G6
Luangwe = Loange →
 Dem. Rep. of the Congo 4°17S 20°2E 54 E4
Luanne China 40°55N 117°40E 33 D9
Luanping China 40°53N 117°23E 33 D9
Luanshya Zambia 13°3S 28°28E 55 G5
Luapula → Africa 9°26S 28°33E 54 F5
Luarca Spain 43°32N 6°32W 21 A2
Luashi
 Dem. Rep. of the Congo 10°50S 23°36E 54 G4
Luau Angola 10°40S 22°10E 54 G4
Lubana, Ozero = Lubānas Ezers
 Latvia 56°45N 27°0E 9 H22
Lubānas Ezers Latvia 56°45N 27°0E 9 H22
Lubang Is. Phil. 13°50N 120°12E 37 B6
Lubango Angola 14°55S 13°30E 55 G2
Lubbock U.S.A. 33°35N 101°51W 84 E4
Lübeck Germany 53°52N 10°40E 16 B6
Lubero = Luofu
 Dem. Rep. of the Congo 0°10S 29°15E 54 E5
Lubicon L. Canada 56°23N 115°56W 70 B5
Lubilash →
 Dem. Rep. of the Congo 6°2S 23°45E 54 F4
Lubin Poland 51°24N 16°11E 16 C9
Lublin Poland 51°12N 22°38E 17 C12
Lubnān = Lebanon ■ Asia 34°0N 36°0E 48 B5
Lubnān, Jabal Lebanon 33°45N 35°40E 48 B4
Lubny Ukraine 50°3N 32°58E 26 D4
Lubudi
 Dem. Rep. of the Congo 9°57S 25°58E 54 F5
Lubuklinggau Indonesia 3°15S 102°55E 36 E2
Lubuksikaping Indonesia 0°10N 100°15E 36 D2
Lubumbashi
 Dem. Rep. of the Congo 11°40S 27°28E 55 G5
Lubutu
 Dem. Rep. of the Congo 0°45S 26°30E 54 E5
Lucan Canada 43°11N 81°24W 82 C3
Lucan Ireland 53°22N 6°28W 10 C5
Lucania, Mt. Canada 61°1N 140°27W 68 E3
Lucas Channel = Main Channel
 Canada 45°21N 81°45W 82 A3
Lucca Italy 43°50N 10°29E 22 C4
Luce Bay U.K. 54°45N 4°48W 11 G4
Lucea Jamaica 18°27N 78°10W 88 a
Lucedale U.S.A. 30°56N 88°35W 85 F10
Lucena Phil. 13°56N 121°37E 37 B6
Lucena Spain 37°27N 4°31W 21 D3
Lučenec Slovakia 48°18N 19°42E 17 D10
Lucerne = Luzern Switz. 47°3N 8°18E 20 C8
Lucerne U.S.A. 39°6N 122°48W 78 F4
Lucerne Valley U.S.A. 34°27N 116°57W 79 L10
Lucheng China 36°20N 113°11E 32 F7
Luchuan China 22°21N 110°12E 35 F8
Lucia U.S.A. 36°2N 121°33W 78 J5
Lucinda Australia 18°32S 146°20E 62 B4
Luckenwalde Germany 52°5N 13°10E 16 B7
Luckhoff S. Africa 29°44S 24°43E 56 D3
Lucknow Canada 43°57N 81°31W 82 C3
Lucknow India 26°50N 81°0E 43 F9
Lüda = Dalian China 38°50N 121°40E 33 E11
Lüderitz Namibia 26°41S 15°8E 56 D2
Lüderitzbaai Namibia 26°36S 15°8E 56 D2
Ludhiana India 30°57N 75°56E 42 D6
Ludian China 27°10N 103°33E 34 D4
Luding Qiao China 29°53N 102°12E 34 C4
Ludington U.S.A. 43°57N 86°27W 80 D10
Ludlow U.K. 52°22N 2°42W 13 E5

Ludlow Calif., U.S.A. 34°43N 116°10W 79 L10
Ludlow Pa., U.S.A. 41°43N 78°56W 82 E6
Ludlow Vt., U.S.A. 43°24N 72°42W 83 C12
Ludvika Sweden 60°8N 15°14E 9 F16
Ludwigsburg Germany 48°53N 9°11E 16 D5
Ludwigshafen Germany 49°29N 8°26E 16 D5
Luena Flats Zambia 14°47S 23°17E 55 G4
Luena Angola 11°45S 19°55E 55 G3
Lüeyang China 33°22N 106°10E 34 A5
Lufeng Guangdong,
 China 22°57N 115°38E 35 F10
Lufeng Yunnan, China 25°0N 102°5E 34 E4
Lufira →
 Dem. Rep. of the Congo 9°30S 27°0E 54 F5
Lufkin U.S.A. 31°21N 94°44W 84 F7
Luga Russia 58°40N 29°55E 9 G23
Lugano Switz. 46°1N 8°57E 20 C8
Lugansk = Luhansk
 Ukraine 48°38N 39°15E 19 E6
Lugenda → Mozam. 11°25S 38°33E 55 G7
Lugh = Luuq Somalia 3°48N 42°34E 49 G3
Lugnaquilla Ireland 52°58N 6°28W 10 D5
Lugo Italy 44°25N 11°54E 22 B4
Lugo Spain 43°2N 7°35W 21 A2
Lugoj Romania 45°42N 21°57E 17 F11
Lugovoy = Qulan
 Kazakhstan 42°55N 72°43E 26 E8
Luhansk Ukraine 48°38N 39°15E 19 E6
Luhuo China 31°21N 100°48E 34 B3
Lui → Angola 8°21S 17°33E 54 F3
Luiana Angola 17°25S 22°59E 56 B3
Luiana → Angola 17°24S 23°3E 55 H4
Luichow Pen. = Leizhou Bandao
 China 21°0N 110°0E 34 G7
Luimneach = Limerick
 Ireland 52°40N 8°37W 10 D3
Luing U.K. 56°14N 5°39W 11 E3
Luís Correia Brazil 3°0S 41°35W 93 D10
Luitpold Coast Antarctica 78°30S 32°0W 5 D1
Luiza Dem. Rep. of the Congo 7°40S 22°30E 54 F4
Luján Argentina 34°45S 59°5W 94 C4
Lukanga Swamp Zambia 14°30S 27°40E 55 G5
Lukenie →
 Dem. Rep. of the Congo 3°0S 18°50E 54 E3
Lukla Nepal 27°42N 86°43E 43 F12
Łuków Poland 51°55N 22°23E 17 C12
Lülang Shan China 38°0N 111°15E 32 F6
Luleå Sweden 65°35N 22°10E 8 D20
Luleälven → Sweden 65°35N 22°10E 8 D20
Lüleburgaz Turkey 41°23N 27°22E 23 D12
Luliang China 25°0N 103°40E 34 E4
Luling U.S.A. 29°41N 97°39W 84 G6
Lulong China 39°53N 118°51E 33 E10
Lulonga →
 Dem. Rep. of the Congo 1°0N 18°10E 54 D3
Lulua →
 Dem. Rep. of the Congo 4°30S 20°30E 54 E4
Luma Amer. Samoa 14°16S 169°33W 59 b
Lumajang Indonesia 8°8S 113°13E 37 H15
Lumbala N'guimbo
 Angola 14°18S 21°18E 55 G4
Lumberton N.C., U.S.A. 34°37N 79°0W 85 D15
Lumberton Tex., U.S.A. 30°16N 94°12W 84 F7
Lumsden Canada 50°39N 104°52W 71 C8
Lumsden N.Z. 45°44S 168°27E 59 F2
Lumut Malaysia 4°13N 100°37E 39 K3
Lumut, Tanjung Indonesia 3°50S 105°58E 36 E3
Luna India 23°43N 69°16E 42 H3
Lunan China 24°40N 103°18E 34 E4
Lunavada India 23°8N 73°37E 42 H5
Lund Sweden 55°44N 13°12E 9 J15
Lundazi Zambia 12°20S 33°7E 55 G6
Lundu Malaysia 1°40N 109°50E 36 D3
Lundy U.K. 51°10N 4°41W 13 F3
Lune → U.K. 54°0N 2°51W 12 C5
Lüneburg Germany 53°15N 10°24E 16 B6
Lüneburg Heath = Lüneburger
 Heide Germany 53°10N 10°12E 16 B6
Lüneburger Heide
 Germany 53°10N 10°12E 16 B6
Lunenburg Canada 44°22N 64°18W 73 D7
Lunéville France 48°36N 6°30E 20 B7
Lunglei India 22°55N 92°45E 41 H18
Luni India 26°0N 73°6E 42 G5
Luni → India 24°41N 71°14E 42 G4
Luninets = Luninyets
 Belarus 52°15N 26°50E 17 B14
Luning U.S.A. 38°30N 118°11W 76 G4
Luninyets Belarus 52°15N 26°50E 17 B14
Lunkaransar India 28°29N 73°44E 42 E5
Luo He → China 34°35N 110°20E 32 G6
Luocheng China 24°48N 108°53E 34 E7
Luochuan China 35°45N 109°26E 32 G5
Luoci China 25°30N 102°25E 34 E4
Luodian China 25°24N 106°43E 34 E6
Luoding China 22°45N 111°40E 35 F8
Luofu Dem. Rep. of the Congo 0°10S 29°15E 54 E5
Luohe China 33°32N 114°2E 32 H8
Luojiang China 31°18N 104°33E 34 B5
Luonan China 34°5N 110°10E 32 G6
Luoning China 34°35N 111°40E 32 G6
Luoshan China 32°13N 114°30E 35 A10
Luotian China 30°46N 115°22E 35 B10
Luoxiao Shan China 26°30N 114°1E 35 D10
Luoyang China 34°40N 112°26E 32 G7
Luoyuan China 26°28N 119°30E 35 D12
Luozigou China 43°42N 130°18E 33 C16
Luque Paraguay 25°19S 57°25W 94 B4
Luquillo, Sierra de
 Puerto Rico 18°20N 65°47W 89 d
Luray U.S.A. 38°40N 78°28W 81 F14
Lurgan U.K. 54°27N 6°20W 10 B5
Lusaka Zambia 15°28S 28°16E 55 H5
Lusambo
 Dem. Rep. of the Congo 4°58S 23°28E 54 E4

Luseland Canada 52°5N 109°24W 71 C7
Lushan Henan, China 33°45N 112°55E 32 H7
Lushan Sichuan, China 30°12N 102°52E 34 B4
Lushi China 34°3N 111°3E 32 G6
Lushnjë Albania 40°55N 19°41E 23 D8
Lüshun China 38°45N 121°15E 33 E11
Lusk U.S.A. 42°46N 104°27W 76 E11
Lūt, Dasht-e Iran 31°30N 58°0E 47 D8
Luta = Dalian China 38°50N 121°40E 33 E11
Lütao Taiwan 22°40N 121°30E 35 F13
Lutherstadt Wittenberg
 Germany 51°53N 12°39E 16 C7
Luton U.K. 51°53N 0°24W 13 F7
Luton □ U.K. 51°53N 0°24W 13 F7
Lutsel K'e Canada 62°24N 110°44W 71 A6
Lutsk Ukraine 50°50N 25°15E 17 C13
Lutto = Lotta → Europe 68°42N 31°6E 8 B24
Lützow Holmbukta
 Antarctica 69°10S 37°30E 5 C4
Lutzputs S. Africa 28°3S 20°40E 56 D3
Luuq Somalia 3°48N 42°34E 49 G3
Luverne Ala., U.S.A. 31°43N 86°16W 85 F11
Luverne Minn., U.S.A. 43°39N 96°13W 80 D5
Luvua →
 Dem. Rep. of the Congo 6°50S 27°30E 54 F5
Luvuvhu → S. Africa 22°25S 31°18E 57 B5
Luwuk Indonesia 0°56S 122°47E 37 E6
Luxembourg Lux. 49°37N 6°9E 15 E6
Luxembourg □ Belgium 49°58N 5°30E 15 E5
Luxembourg ■ Europe 49°45N 6°0E 15 E6
Luxembourg ✈ (LUX)
 Lux. 49°37N 6°10E 15 E6
Luxi Hunan, China 28°20N 110°7E 35 C8
Luxi Yunnan, China 24°40N 103°55E 34 E4
Luxi Yunnan, China 24°27N 98°36E 34 E2
Luxian China 29°9N 105°24E 34 C5
Luxor = El Uqsur Egypt 25°41N 32°38E 53 C12
Luyi China 33°50N 115°35E 32 H8
Luykau = Loikaw
 Myanmar 19°40N 97°17E 41 K20
Luza Russia 60°39N 47°10E 18 B8
Luzern Switz. 47°3N 8°18E 20 C8
Luzhai China 24°29N 109°42E 34 E7
Luzhi China 26°21N 105°19E 34 D5
Luzhou China 28°52N 105°20E 34 C5
Luziânia Brazil 16°20S 48°0W 93 G9
Luzon Phil. 16°0N 121°0E 37 A6
Luzon Strait Asia 21°0N 120°40E 35 G13
Lviv Ukraine 49°50N 24°0E 17 D13
Lviv □ Ukraine 49°30N 23°45E 17 D12
Lvov = Lviv Ukraine 49°50N 24°0E 17 D13
Lyakhavichy Belarus 53°2N 26°32E 17 B14
Lyakhovskiye, Ostrova
 Russia 73°40N 141°0E 27 B15
Lyal I. Canada 44°57N 81°24W 82 B3
Lybster U.K. 58°18N 3°15W 11 C5
Lycksele Sweden 64°38N 18°40E 8 D18
Lydda = Lod Israel 31°57N 34°54E 48 D3
Lyddan I. Antarctica 74°0S 21°0W 5 D2
Lydenburg S. Africa 25°10S 30°29E 57 C5
Lydia Turkey 38°48N 28°19E 23 E13
Lyell N.Z. 41°48S 172°4E 59 D4
Lyell I. Canada 52°40N 131°35W 70 C2
Lyepyel Belarus 54°50N 28°40E 9 J23
Lykens U.S.A. 40°34N 76°42W 83 F8
Lyman U.S.A. 41°20N 110°18W 76 F8
Lyme B. U.K. 50°42N 2°53W 13 G4
Lyme Regis U.K. 50°43N 2°57W 13 G5
Lymington U.K. 50°45N 1°32W 13 G6
Lynchburg U.S.A. 37°25N 79°9W 81 G14
Lynd → Australia 16°28S 143°18E 62 B3
Lynd Ra. Australia 25°30S 149°20E 63 D4
Lynden Canada 43°14N 80°9W 82 C4
Lynden U.S.A. 48°57N 122°27W 78 B4
Lyndhurst Australia 30°15S 138°18E 63 E2
Lyndon → Australia 23°29S 114°6E 61 D1
Lyndonville N.Y., U.S.A. 43°20N 78°23W 82 C6
Lyndonville Vt., U.S.A. 44°31N 72°1W 83 B12
Lyngen Norway 69°45N 20°30E 8 B19
Lynher Reef Australia 15°27S 121°55E 60 C3
Lynn U.S.A. 42°28N 70°57W 83 D14
Lynn Canal U.S.A. 58°50N 135°15W 74 D22
Lynn Haven U.S.A. 30°15N 85°39W 85 F12
Lynn Lake Canada 56°51N 101°3W 71 B8
Lynnwood U.S.A. 47°49N 122°18W 78 C4
Lynton U.K. 51°13N 3°50W 13 F4
Lyntupy Belarus 55°4N 26°23E 9 J22
Lynx L. Canada 62°25N 106°15W 71 A7
Lyon France 45°46N 4°50E 20 D6
Lyonnais France 45°45N 4°15E 20 D6
Lyons = Lyon France 45°46N 4°50E 20 D6
Lyons Ga., U.S.A. 32°12N 82°19W 85 E13
Lyons Kans., U.S.A. 38°21N 98°12W 80 F4
Lyons N.Y., U.S.A. 43°5N 77°0W 82 C8
Lyons → Australia 25°2S 115°9E 61 E2
Lyons Falls U.S.A. 43°37N 75°22W 83 C9
Lys = Leie → Belgium 51°2N 3°45E 15 C3
Lysva Russia 58°7N 57°49E 18 C10
Lysychansk Ukraine 48°55N 38°30E 19 E6
Lytham St. Anne's U.K. 53°45N 3°0W 12 D4
Lyttelton N.Z. 43°35S 172°44E 59 E4
Lytton Canada 50°13N 121°31W 70 C4
Lyubertsy Russia 55°39N 37°51E 18 C6
Lyuboml Ukraine 51°11N 24°4E 17 C13

# M

Ma → Vietnam 19°47N 105°56E 34 H5
Ma'adaba Jordan 31°43N 35°47E 48 D4
Ma'alot-Tarshiha Israel 33°1N 35°17E 48 B4
Maamba Zambia 17°17S 26°28E 56 A4
Ma'ān Jordan 30°12N 35°44E 48 E4
Ma'ān □ Jordan 30°0N 36°0E 48 F5
Maanselkä Finland 63°52N 28°23E 8 C23
Ma'anshan China 31°44N 118°29E 35 B12
Maarianhamina = Mariehamn
 Finland 60°5N 19°55E 9 F18
Ma'arrat an Nu'mān
 Syria 35°43N 36°43E 46 C3

Maas → Neths. 51°45N 4°32E 15 C4
Maaseik Belgium 51°6N 5°45E 15 C5
Maasin Phil. 10°8N 124°50E 37 B6
Maastricht Neths. 50°50N 5°40E 15 D5
Maave Mozam. 21°4S 34°47E 57 B5
Mababe Depression
 Botswana 18°50S 24°15E 56 A3
Mabalane Mozam. 23°37S 32°31E 57 B5
Mabel L. Canada 50°35N 118°43W 70 C5
Maberly Canada 44°50N 76°32W 83 B8
Mabian China 28°47N 103°37E 34 C4
Mabuasehube △ Botswana 25°5S 21°10E 56 C3
Mabuiag Australia 9°57S 142°11E 62 a
Mac Bac Vietnam 9°46N 106°7E 39 H6
Macachín Argentina 37°10S 63°43W 94 D3
Macaé Brazil 22°20S 41°43W 95 A7
McAlester U.S.A. 34°56N 95°46W 84 D7
McAllen U.S.A. 26°12N 98°14W 84 H5
Macamic Canada 48°45N 79°0W 72 C4
Macao = Macau China 22°12N 113°33E 35 F9
Macapá Brazil 0°5N 51°4W 93 C8
Macarao △ Venezuela 10°22N 67°7W 89 D6
McArthur → Australia 15°54S 136°40E 62 B2
McArthur, Port Australia 16°4S 136°23E 62 B2
Macau Brazil 5°15S 36°40W 93 E11
Macau China 22°12N 113°33E 35 F9
McBride Canada 53°20N 120°19W 70 C4
McCall U.S.A. 44°55N 116°6W 76 D5
McCamey U.S.A. 31°8N 102°14W 84 F2
McCammon U.S.A. 42°39N 112°12W 76 E7
McCauley I. Canada 53°40N 130°15W 70 C2
McCleary U.S.A. 47°3N 123°16W 78 C3
Macclenny U.S.A. 30°17N 82°7W 85 F13
Macclesfield U.K. 53°15N 2°8W 12 D5
Macclesfield Bank
 S. China Sea 16°0N 114°30E 36 A4
M'Clintock Chan.
 Canada 72°0N 102°0W 68 C12
McClintock Ra.
 Australia 18°44S 127°38E 60 C4
McCloud U.S.A. 41°15N 122°8W 76 F2
McCluer I. Australia 11°5S 133°0E 60 B5
McClure U.S.A. 40°42N 77°19W 82 F7
McClure, L. U.S.A. 37°35N 120°16W 78 H6
M'Clure Str. Canada 75°0N 119°0W 69 C8
McClusky U.S.A. 47°29N 100°27W 80 B3
McComb U.S.A. 31°15N 90°27W 85 F9
McCook U.S.A. 40°12N 100°38W 80 E3
McCreary Canada 50°47N 99°29W 71 C8
McCullough Mt.
 U.S.A. 35°35N 115°13W 79 K11
McCusker → Canada 55°32N 108°39W 71 B7
McDermitt U.S.A. 41°59N 117°43W 76 F5
McDonald U.S.A. 40°22N 80°14W 82 F4
McDonald Is. Ind. Oc. 53°0S 73°0E 3 G13
MacDonnell Ranges
 Australia 23°40S 133°0E 60 D5
McDouall Peak Australia 29°51S 134°55E 63 E1
McDowell L. Canada 52°15N 92°45W 72 B1
Macduff U.K. 57°40N 2°31W 11 D6
Macedonia U.S.A. 41°19N 81°31W 82 E3
Macedonia □ Greece 40°39N 22°0E 23 D10
Macedonia ■ Europe 41°53N 21°40E 23 D9
Maceió Brazil 9°40S 35°41W 93 E11
Macerata Italy 43°18N 13°27E 22 C5
McFarland U.S.A. 35°41N 119°14W 79 K7
McFarlane → Canada 59°12N 107°58W 71 B7
McFarlane, L. Australia 32°0S 136°40E 63 E2
McGehee U.S.A. 33°38N 91°24W 84 E9
McGill U.S.A. 39°23N 114°47W 76 G6
Macgillycuddy's Reeks
 Ireland 51°58N 9°45W 10 E2
McGraw U.S.A. 42°36N 76°8W 83 D8
McGregor U.S.A. 43°1N 91°11W 80 D8
McGregor Ra. Australia 27°0S 142°45E 63 D3
McGuire, Mt. Australia 20°18S 148°23E 62 b
Mach Pakistan 29°50N 67°20E 42 E2
Māch Kowr Iran 25°48N 61°28E 47 E9
Machado = Jiparaná →
 Brazil 8°3S 62°52W 92 E6
Machagai Argentina 26°56S 60°2W 94 B3
Machakos Kenya 1°30S 37°15E 54 E7
Machala Ecuador 3°20S 79°57W 92 D3
Machanga Mozam. 20°59S 35°0E 57 B6
Macheng China 31°12N 115°2E 35 B10
Macherla India 16°29N 79°26E 44 F4
Machgaon India 20°5N 86°17E 44 D8
Machhu → India 23°6N 70°46E 42 H4
Machiara △ Pakistan 34°40N 73°30E 42 B5
Machias Maine, U.S.A. 44°43N 67°28W 81 C20
Machias N.Y., U.S.A. 42°25N 78°29W 82 D6
Machichi → Canada 57°3N 92°6W 71 B10
Machilipatnam India 16°12N 81°8E 45 F5
Machiques Venezuela 10°4N 72°34W 92 A4
Machu Picchu Peru 13°8S 72°30W 92 F4
Machynlleth U.K. 52°35N 3°50W 13 E4
Macia Mozam. 25°2S 33°8E 57 C5
McIlwraith Ra. Australia 13°50S 143°20E 62 A3
McInnes L. Canada 52°13N 93°45W 72 B1
McIntosh U.S.A. 45°55N 101°21W 80 B3
Macintosh Ra. Australia 27°39S 125°32E 61 E4
Macintyre → Australia 28°37S 150°47E 63 D5
Mackay Australia 21°8S 149°11E 62 b
Mackay U.S.A. 43°55N 113°37W 76 E7
Mackay → Canada 57°10N 111°38W 70 B6
Mackay, L. Australia 22°30S 129°0E 60 D4
McKay Ra. Australia 23°0S 122°30E 60 D3
McKeesport U.S.A. 40°20N 79°51W 82 F5
McKellar Canada 45°30N 79°55W 82 A5
McKenna U.S.A. 46°56N 122°33W 78 D4
Mackenzie = Linden
 Guyana 6°0N 58°10W 92 B7
Mackenzie Canada 55°20N 123°5W 70 B4
McKenzie U.S.A. 36°8N 88°31W 85 C10

| | | |
|---|---|---|
| Mackenzie → *Australia* | 23°38S 149°46E | **62** C4 |
| Mackenzie → *Canada* | 69°10N 134°20W | **68** D5 |
| McKenzie → *U.S.A.* | 44°7N 123°6W | **76** D2 |
| Mackenzie Bay *Canada* | 69°0N 137°30W | **66** C6 |
| Mackenzie King I. | | |
| *Canada* | 77°45N 111°0W | **69** B9 |
| Mackenzie Mts. *Canada* | 64°0N 130°0W | **66** C6 |
| Mackinac, Straits of | | |
| *U.S.A.* | 45°50N 84°40W | **81** C11 |
| Mackinaw City *U.S.A.* | 45°47N 84°44W | **81** C11 |
| McKinlay *Australia* | 21°16S 141°18E | **62** C3 |
| McKinlay → *Australia* | 20°50S 141°28E | **62** C3 |
| McKinley, Mt. = Denali | | |
| *U.S.A.* | 63°4N 151°0W | **68** E1 |
| McKinley Sea *Arctic* | 82°0N 0°0 | **4** A7 |
| McKinney *U.S.A.* | 33°12N 96°37W | **84** E6 |
| McKittrick *U.S.A.* | 35°18N 119°37W | **79** K7 |
| Macklin *Canada* | 52°20N 109°56W | **71** C7 |
| Macksville *Australia* | 30°40S 152°56E | **63** E5 |
| McLaughlin *U.S.A.* | 45°49N 100°49W | **80** C3 |
| Maclean *Australia* | 29°26S 153°16E | **63** D5 |
| McLean *U.S.A.* | 35°14N 100°36W | **84** D4 |
| McLeansboro *U.S.A.* | 38°6N 88°32W | **80** F9 |
| Maclear *S. Africa* | 31°2S 28°23E | **57** D4 |
| Macleay → *Australia* | 30°56S 153°0E | **63** E5 |
| McLennan *Canada* | 55°42N 116°50W | **70** B5 |
| McLeod → *Canada* | 54°9N 115°44W | **70** C5 |
| MacLeod, L. *Australia* | 24°9S 113°47E | **61** D1 |
| MacLeod B. *Canada* | 62°53N 110°0W | **71** A7 |
| MacLeod Lake *Canada* | 54°58N 123°0W | **70** C4 |
| McLoughlin, Mt. *U.S.A.* | 42°27N 122°19W | **76** E2 |
| McMechen *U.S.A.* | 39°57N 80°44W | **82** G4 |
| McMinnville *Oreg.*, | | |
| *U.S.A.* | 45°13N 123°12W | **76** D2 |
| McMinnville *Tenn.*, | | |
| *U.S.A.* | 35°41N 85°46W | **85** D12 |
| McMurdo *Antarctica* | 77°51S 166°37E | **5** D11 |
| McMurdo Sd. *Antarctica* | 77°0S 170°0E | **5** D11 |
| McMurray = Fort McMurray | | |
| *Canada* | 56°44N 111°7W | **70** B6 |
| McMurray *U.S.A.* | 48°19N 122°14W | **78** B4 |
| Maçobere *Mozam.* | 21°13S 32°47E | **57** B5 |
| Macodoene *Mozam.* | 23°32S 35°5E | **57** B6 |
| Macomb *U.S.A.* | 40°27N 90°40W | **80** E8 |
| Mâcon *France* | 46°19N 4°50E | **20** C6 |
| Macon *Ga.*, *U.S.A.* | 32°51N 83°38W | **85** E13 |
| Macon *Miss.*, *U.S.A.* | 33°7N 88°34W | **85** E10 |
| Macon *Mo.*, *U.S.A.* | 39°44N 92°28W | **80** F7 |
| Macoun L. *Canada* | 56°32N 103°40W | **71** B8 |
| Macovane *Mozam.* | 21°30S 35°2E | **57** B6 |
| McPherson *U.S.A.* | 38°22N 97°40W | **80** F5 |
| McPherson Pk. *U.S.A.* | 34°53N 119°53W | **79** L7 |
| McPherson Ra. *Australia* | 28°15S 153°15E | **63** D5 |
| Macquarie → *Australia* | 30°7S 147°24E | **63** E4 |
| Macquarie Harbour | | |
| *Australia* | 42°15S 145°23E | **63** G4 |
| Macquarie I. *Pac. Oc.* | 54°36S 158°55E | **64** N7 |
| Macquarie Ridge *S. Ocean* | 57°0S 159°0E | **5** B10 |
| MacRobertson Land | | |
| *Antarctica* | 71°0S 64°0E | **5** D6 |
| Macroom *Ireland* | 51°54N 8°57W | **10** E3 |
| MacTier *Canada* | 45°8N 79°47W | **82** A5 |
| Macuira △ *Colombia* | 12°9N 71°21W | **89** D5 |
| Macumba → *Australia* | 27°52S 137°12E | **63** D2 |
| Macuro *Venezuela* | 10°42N 61°55W | **93** K15 |
| Macusani *Peru* | 14°4S 70°29W | **92** F4 |
| Macuspana *Mexico* | 17°46N 92°36W | **87** D6 |
| Macusse *Angola* | 17°48S 20°23E | **56** A3 |
| Ma'daba □ *Jordan* | 31°43N 35°47E | **48** D4 |
| Madadeni *S. Africa* | 27°43S 30°3E | **57** C5 |
| Madagascar ■ *Africa* | 20°0S 47°0E | **55** J9 |
| Madā'in Sālih *Si. Arabia* | 26°46N 37°57E | **46** E3 |
| Madakasira *India* | 13°56N 77°16E | **45** H3 |
| Madama *Niger* | 22°0N 13°40E | **53** D8 |
| Madame, I. *Canada* | 45°30N 60°58W | **73** C7 |
| Madanapalle *India* | 13°33N 78°28E | **45** H4 |
| Madang *Papua N. G.* | 5°12S 145°49E | **63** K3 |
| Madaripur *Bangla.* | 23°19N 90°15E | **41** H17 |
| Madauk *Myanmar* | 17°56N 96°52E | **41** L20 |
| Madawaska *Canada* | 45°30N 78°0W | **82** A7 |
| Madawaska → *Canada* | 45°27N 76°21W | **82** A7 |
| Madaya *Myanmar* | 22°12N 96°10E | **41** H20 |
| Maddalena *Italy* | 41°16N 9°23E | **22** D3 |
| Maddur *India* | 12°36N 77°4E | **45** H3 |
| Madeira *Atl. Oc.* | 32°50N 17°0W | **52** B2 |
| Madeira → *Brazil* | 3°22S 58°45W | **92** D7 |
| Madeleine, Îs. de la | | |
| *Canada* | 47°30N 61°40W | **73** C7 |
| Madera *Mexico* | 29°12N 108°7W | **86** B3 |
| Madera *Calif.*, *U.S.A.* | 36°57N 120°3W | **78** J6 |
| Madera *Pa.*, *U.S.A.* | 40°49N 78°26W | **82** F6 |
| Madgaon *India* | 15°12N 73°58E | **45** G1 |
| Madha *India* | 18°0N 75°30E | **44** L9 |
| Madhavpur *India* | 21°15N 69°58E | **42** J3 |
| Madhepura *India* | 26°11N 86°23E | **43** F12 |
| Madhira *India* | 16°55N 80°22E | **44** L5 |
| Madhubani *India* | 26°21N 86°7E | **43** F12 |
| Madhugiri *India* | 13°40N 77°12E | **45** H3 |
| Madhupur *India* | 24°16N 86°39E | **43** G12 |
| Madhya Pradesh □ *India* | 22°50N 78°0E | **42** J8 |
| Madidi → *Bolivia* | 12°32S 66°52W | **92** F5 |
| Madikeri *India* | 12°30N 75°45E | **45** H2 |
| Madill *U.S.A.* | 34°6N 96°46W | **84** D6 |
| Madimba | | |
| *Dem. Rep. of the Congo* | 4°58S 15°5E | **54** E3 |
| Ma'din *Syria* | 35°45N 39°36E | **46** C3 |
| Madinat al Malik Khālid al | | |
| Askarīyah *Si. Arabia* | 27°54N 45°31E | **46** E5 |
| Madinat Masdar *U.A.E.* | 24°34N 54°37E | **47** E7 |
| Madingou *Congo* | 4°10S 13°33E | **54** E2 |
| Madison *Calif.*, *U.S.A.* | 38°41N 121°59W | **78** G5 |
| Madison *Fla.*, *U.S.A.* | 30°28N 83°25W | **85** F13 |
| Madison *Ind.*, *U.S.A.* | 38°44N 85°23W | **81** F11 |
| Madison *Nebr.*, *U.S.A.* | 41°50N 97°27W | **80** E6 |
| Madison *Ohio*, *U.S.A.* | 41°46N 81°3W | **82** E3 |
| Madison *S. Dak.*, *U.S.A.* | 44°0N 97°7W | **80** C5 |
| Madison *Wis.*, *U.S.A.* | 43°4N 89°24W | **80** D9 |
| Madison → *U.S.A.* | 45°56N 111°31W | **76** D8 |
| Madison Heights *U.S.A.* | 37°25N 79°8W | **81** G14 |

| | | |
|---|---|---|
| Madisonville *Ky.*, | | |
| *U.S.A.* | 37°20N 87°30W | **80** G10 |
| Madisonville *Tex.*, *U.S.A.* | 30°57N 95°55W | **84** F7 |
| Madista *Botswana* | 21°15S 25°6E | **56** B4 |
| Madiun *Indonesia* | 7°38S 111°32E | **37** G14 |
| Madoc *Canada* | 44°30N 77°28W | **82** B7 |
| Madoi *China* | 34°46N 98°18E | **30** E8 |
| Madona *Latvia* | 56°53N 26°5E | **9** H22 |
| Madrakah, Ra's al *Oman* | 19°0N 57°50E | **49** D6 |
| Madras = Chennai *India* | 13°8N 80°19E | **45** H5 |
| Madras = Tamil Nadu □ | | |
| *India* | 11°0N 77°0E | **45** J3 |
| Madras *U.S.A.* | 44°38N 121°8W | **76** D3 |
| Madre, L. *U.S.A.* | 26°50N 97°30W | **84** J6 |
| Madre, Sierra *Phil.* | 17°0N 122°0E | **37** A6 |
| Madre de Dios → *Bolivia* | 10°59S 66°8W | **92** F5 |
| Madre de Dios, I. *Chile* | 50°20S 75°10W | **96** G1 |
| Madre del Sur, Sierra | | |
| *Mexico* | 17°30N 100°0W | **87** D5 |
| Madre Occidental, Sierra | | |
| *Mexico* | 27°0N 107°0W | **86** B3 |
| Madre Oriental, Sierra | | |
| *Mexico* | 25°0N 100°0W | **86** C5 |
| Madri *India* | 24°16N 73°32E | **42** G5 |
| Madrid *U.S.A.* | 44°45N 75°8W | **83** B9 |
| Madura *Australia* | 31°55S 127°0E | **61** F4 |
| Madura *Indonesia* | 7°30S 114°0E | **37** G15 |
| Madura, Selat *Indonesia* | 7°30S 113°20E | **37** G15 |
| Madura Oya △ *Sri Lanka* | 7°20N 81°10E | **45** L5 |
| Madurai *India* | 9°55N 78°10E | **45** K4 |
| Madurantakam *India* | 12°30N 79°50E | **45** H4 |
| Mae Chan *Thailand* | 20°9N 99°52E | **38** B2 |
| Mae Charim △ *Thailand* | 18°17N 100°59E | **38** C3 |
| Mae Hong Son *Thailand* | 19°16N 97°56E | **38** C2 |
| Mae Khlong → *Thailand* | 13°24N 100°0E | **38** F3 |
| Mae Moei △ *Thailand* | 17°26N 98°7E | **38** D2 |
| Mae Phang △ *Thailand* | 19°7N 99°13E | **38** C2 |
| Mae Phrik △ *Thailand* | 17°27N 99°7E | **38** D2 |
| Mae Ping △ *Thailand* | 17°37N 98°51E | **38** D2 |
| Mae Ramat *Thailand* | 16°58N 98°31E | **38** D2 |
| Mae Rim *Thailand* | 18°54N 98°57E | **38** C2 |
| Mae Sai *Thailand* | 20°20N 99°55E | **34** G2 |
| Mae Sot *Thailand* | 16°43N 98°34E | **38** D2 |
| Mae Suai *Thailand* | 19°39N 99°33E | **34** H2 |
| Mae Tha *Thailand* | 18°28N 99°8E | **38** C2 |
| Mae Tup Res. *Thailand* | 17°52N 98°45E | **38** D2 |
| Mae Wa △ *Thailand* | 17°23N 99°16E | **38** D2 |
| Mae Wong △ *Thailand* | 15°54N 99°12E | **38** E2 |
| Mae Yom △ *Thailand* | 18°43N 100°15E | **38** C3 |
| Maebaru *Japan* | 33°33N 130°12E | **29** H5 |
| Maebashi *Japan* | 36°24N 139°4E | **29** F9 |
| Maelpaeg, L. *Canada* | 48°20N 56°30W | **73** C8 |
| Maestra, Sierra *Cuba* | 20°15N 77°0W | **88** B4 |
| Maevatanana *Madag.* | 16°56S 46°49E | **55** H9 |
| Mafadi △ *S. Africa* | 29°12S 29°21E | **57** C4 |
| Mafeking = Mafikeng | | |
| *S. Africa* | 25°50S 25°38E | **56** C4 |
| Mafeking *Canada* | 52°40N 101°10W | **71** C8 |
| Mafeteng *Lesotho* | 29°51S 27°15E | **56** C4 |
| Maffra *Australia* | 37°53S 146°58E | **63** F4 |
| Mafia I. *Tanzania* | 7°45S 39°50E | **54** F7 |
| Mafikeng *S. Africa* | 25°50S 25°38E | **56** C4 |
| Mafra *Brazil* | 26°10S 49°55W | **95** B6 |
| Mafra *Portugal* | 38°55N 9°20W | **21** C1 |
| Magadan *Russia* | 59°38N 150°50E | **27** D16 |
| Magadi *India* | 12°58N 77°14E | **45** H3 |
| Magaliesburg *S. Africa* | 26°0S 27°32E | **57** C4 |
| Magallanes, Estrecho de | | |
| *Chile* | 52°30S 75°0W | **96** G2 |
| Magangué *Colombia* | 9°14N 74°45W | **92** B4 |
| Magdagachi *Russia* | 53°27N 125°48E | **27** D13 |
| Magdalen Is. = Madeleine, Îs. de la | | |
| *Canada* | 47°30N 61°40W | **73** C7 |
| Magdalena *Argentina* | 35°5S 57°30W | **94** D4 |
| Magdalena *Bolivia* | 13°13S 63°57W | **92** F6 |
| Magdalena → *Colombia* | 11°6N 74°51W | **92** A4 |
| Magdalena *U.S.A.* | 34°7N 107°15W | **77** J10 |
| Magdalena, B. *Mexico* | 24°35N 112°0W | **86** C2 |
| Magdalena, I. *Mexico* | 24°40N 112°15W | **86** C2 |
| Magdalena, Llano de | | |
| *Mexico* | 25°0N 111°25W | **86** C2 |
| Magdalena de Kino | | |
| *Mexico* | 30°38N 110°57W | **86** A2 |
| Magdeburg *Germany* | 52°7N 11°38E | **16** B6 |
| Magdelaine Cays | | |
| *Australia* | 16°33S 150°18E | **62** B5 |
| Magee *U.S.A.* | 31°52N 89°44W | **85** F10 |
| Magelang *Indonesia* | 7°29S 110°13E | **37** G14 |
| Magellan's Str. = Magallanes, | | |
| Estrecho de *Chile* | 52°30S 75°0W | **96** G2 |
| Magenta, L. *Australia* | 33°30S 119°2E | **61** F2 |
| Mageroya *Norway* | 71°3N 25°40E | **8** A21 |
| Maggiore, L. *Italy* | 45°57N 8°39E | **20** D8 |
| Maggotty *Jamaica* | 18°9N 77°46W | **88** a |
| Maghâgha *Egypt* | 28°38N 30°50E | **53** C12 |
| Maghera *U.K.* | 54°51N 6°41W | **10** B5 |
| Magherafelt *U.K.* | 54°45N 6°37W | **10** B5 |
| Maghreb *N. Afr.* | 32°0N 4°0W | **50** C3 |
| Magnetic Pole (North) | | |
| *Arctic* | 85°9N 149°0W | **4** A1 |
| Magnetic Pole (South) | | |
| *Antarctica* | 64°8S 138°8E | **5** C9 |
| Magnitogorsk *Russia* | 53°27N 59°4E | **18** D10 |
| Magnolia *Ark.*, *U.S.A.* | 33°16N 93°14W | **84** E8 |
| Magnolia *Miss.*, *U.S.A.* | 31°9N 90°28W | **85** F9 |
| Mago *Fiji* | 17°26S 179°8W | **59** a |
| Magog *Canada* | 45°18N 72°9W | **83** A12 |
| Magpie, L. *Canada* | 51°0N 64°41W | **73** B7 |
| Maguan *China* | 23°0N 104°21E | **34** F5 |
| Maguarinho, C. *Brazil* | 0°15S 48°30W | **93** D9 |
| Magude *Mozam.* | 25°2S 32°40E | **57** C5 |
| Maguse L. *Canada* | 61°37N 95°10W | **71** A9 |
| Maguse Pt. *Canada* | 61°20N 93°50W | **71** A10 |
| Magvana *India* | 23°13N 69°22E | **42** H3 |
| Magway *Myanmar* | 20°10N 95°0E | **41** J19 |
| Magyarország = Hungary ■ | | |
| *Europe* | 47°20N 19°20E | **17** E10 |

| | | |
|---|---|---|
| Maha Oya *Sri Lanka* | 7°31N 81°22E | **45** L5 |
| Maha Sarakham | | |
| *Thailand* | 16°12N 103°16E | **38** D4 |
| Mahābād *Iran* | 36°50N 45°45E | **46** B5 |
| Mahabaleshwar *India* | 17°58N 73°43E | **44** F1 |
| Mahabalipuram *India* | 12°37N 80°11E | **45** H5 |
| Mahabharat Lekh *Nepal* | 28°30N 82°0E | **43** E10 |
| Mahabo *Madag.* | 20°23S 44°40E | **55** J8 |
| Mahad *India* | 18°6N 73°29E | **44** F1 |
| Mahadeo Hills *India* | 22°20N 78°30E | **43** H8 |
| Mahadeopur *India* | 18°48N 80°0E | **44** E5 |
| Mahaffey *U.S.A.* | 40°53N 78°44W | **82** F6 |
| Mahajan *India* | 28°48N 73°56E | **42** E5 |
| Mahajanga *Madag.* | 15°40S 46°25E | **55** H9 |
| Mahakam → *Indonesia* | 0°35S 117°17E | **36** E5 |
| Mahalapye *Botswana* | 23°1S 26°51E | **56** B4 |
| Mahale Mts. *Tanzania* | 6°20S 30°0E | **54** F6 |
| Mahallāt *Iran* | 33°55N 50°30E | **47** C6 |
| Mahan *Iran* | 23°30N 82°50E | **43** H10 |
| Mahanadi → *India* | 20°20N 86°25E | **44** D8 |
| Mahananda → *India* | 25°12N 87°52E | **43** G12 |
| Mahanoro *Madag.* | 19°54S 48°48E | **55** H9 |
| Mahanoy City *U.S.A.* | 40°49N 76°9W | **83** F8 |
| Maharashtra □ *India* | 20°30N 75°30E | **44** D2 |
| Mahasamund *India* | 21°6N 82°6E | **44** D6 |
| Mahasham, W. → *Egypt* | 30°15N 34°10E | **48** E3 |
| Mahattat ash Shīdīyah | | |
| *Jordan* | 29°55N 35°55E | **48** F4 |
| Mahattat 'Unayzah | | |
| *Jordan* | 30°30N 35°47E | **48** E4 |
| Mahaweli Ganga → | | |
| *Sri Lanka* | 8°27N 81°13E | **45** K5 |
| Mahaxay *Laos* | 17°22N 105°12E | **38** D5 |
| Mahbubabad *India* | 17°42N 80°2E | **44** F5 |
| Mahbubnagar *India* | 16°45N 77°59E | **44** F3 |
| Mahda *U.A.E.* | 25°20N 56°15E | **47** E8 |
| Mahdah *Oman* | 24°24N 55°59E | **47** E7 |
| Mahdia *Tunisia* | 35°28N 11°0E | **53** A8 |
| Mahe *Jammu & Kashmir*, | | |
| *India* | 33°10N 78°32E | **43** C8 |
| Mahé *Puducherry*, *India* | 11°42N 75°34E | **45** J2 |
| Mahé *Seychelles* | 5°0S 55°30E | **55** b |
| Mahébourg *Mauritius* | 20°24S 57°42E | **55** d |
| Mahendra Giri *India* | 8°20N 77°30E | **45** K3 |
| Mahendragarh *India* | 28°17N 76°14E | **42** E7 |
| Mahendranagar *Nepal* | 28°55N 80°20E | **43** E9 |
| Mahenge *Tanzania* | 8°45S 36°41E | **54** F7 |
| Maheno *N.Z.* | 45°10S 170°50E | **59** F3 |
| Mahesana *India* | 23°39N 72°26E | **42** H5 |
| Maheshwar *India* | 22°11N 75°35E | **42** H6 |
| Mahgawan *India* | 26°29N 78°37E | **43** F8 |
| Mahi → *India* | 22°15N 72°55E | **42** H5 |
| Mahia Pen. *N.Z.* | 39°9S 177°55E | **59** C6 |
| Mahikeng = Mafikeng | | |
| *S. Africa* | 25°50S 25°38E | **56** C4 |
| Mahilyow *Belarus* | 53°55N 30°18E | **17** B16 |
| Mahim *India* | 19°39N 72°44E | **44** E1 |
| Mahina *Tahiti* | 17°30S 149°27W | **59** d |
| Mahinerangi, L. *N.Z.* | 45°50S 169°56E | **59** F2 |
| Mahmud Kot *Pakistan* | 30°16N 71°0E | **42** D4 |
| Mahnomen *U.S.A.* | 47°19N 95°58W | **80** B6 |
| Maho *Sri Lanka* | 7°49N 80°16E | **45** L5 |
| Mahoba *India* | 25°15N 79°55E | **43** G8 |
| Mahón = Maó *Spain* | 39°53N 4°16E | **21** C8 |
| Mahone Bay *Canada* | 44°27N 64°23W | **73** D7 |
| Mahongo △ *Namibia* | 18°0S 23°15E | **56** B3 |
| Mahopac *U.S.A.* | 41°22N 73°45W | **83** E11 |
| Mahuva *India* | 21°5N 71°48E | **42** J4 |
| Mai-Ndombe, L. | | |
| *Dem. Rep. of the Congo* | 2°0S 18°20E | **54** E3 |
| Mai Thon, Ko *Thailand* | 7°40N 98°28E | **39** a |
| Maicuru → *Brazil* | 2°14S 54°17W | **93** D8 |
| Maidan Khula *Afghan.* | 33°36N 69°50E | **42** C3 |
| Maidenhead *U.K.* | 51°31N 0°42W | **13** F7 |
| Maidstone *Canada* | 53°5N 109°20W | **71** C7 |
| Maidstone *U.K.* | 51°16N 0°32E | **13** F8 |
| Maiduguri *Nigeria* | 12°0N 13°20E | **53** F8 |
| Maigh Nuad = Maynooth | | |
| *Ireland* | 53°23N 6°34W | **10** C5 |
| Maihar *India* | 24°16N 80°45E | **43** G9 |
| Maikala Ra. *India* | 22°0N 81°0E | **44** D5 |
| Mailani *India* | 28°17N 80°21E | **43** E9 |
| Mailsi *Pakistan* | 29°48N 72°15E | **42** E5 |
| Main → *Germany* | 50°0N 8°18E | **16** C5 |
| Main → *U.K.* | 54°48N 6°18W | **10** B5 |
| Main Channel *Canada* | 45°21N 81°45E | **82** A3 |
| Main Range △ *Australia* | 28°11S 152°27E | **63** D5 |
| Main Ridge *Trin. & Tob.* | 11°16N 60°40W | **93** J16 |
| Maindargi *India* | 17°28N 76°18E | **44** F3 |
| Maine *France* | 48°20N 0°15W | **20** C3 |
| Maine □ *U.S.A.* | 45°20N 69°0W | **81** C19 |
| Maine → *Ireland* | 52°9N 9°45W | **10** D2 |
| Maine, G. of *U.S.A.* | 43°0N 68°30W | **75** G26 |
| Maingkwan *Myanmar* | 26°15N 96°37E | **41** F20 |
| Mainistir na Corann = Midleton | | |
| *Ireland* | 51°55N 8°10W | **10** E3 |
| Mainit, L. *Phil.* | 9°31N 125°30E | **37** C7 |
| Mainland *Orkney*, *U.K.* | 58°59N 3°8W | **11** C5 |
| Mainland *Shet.*, *U.K.* | 60°15N 1°22W | **11** A7 |
| Mainpuri *India* | 27°18N 79°4E | **43** F8 |
| Maintirano *Madag.* | 18°3S 44°1E | **55** H8 |
| Mainz *Germany* | 50°1N 8°14E | **16** C5 |
| Maio *Cabo Verde* | 15°10N 23°10W | **52** b |
| Maipú *Argentina* | 36°52S 57°50W | **94** D4 |
| Maiquetía *Venezuela* | 10°36N 66°57W | **92** A5 |
| Mairabari *India* | 26°30N 92°22E | **41** F18 |
| Maisí *Cuba* | 20°17N 74°9W | **89** B5 |
| Maisí, Pta. de *Cuba* | 20°10N 74°10W | **89** B5 |
| Maitland *N.S.W.*, | | |
| *Australia* | 32°33S 151°36E | **63** E5 |
| Maitland *S. Austral.*, | | |
| *Australia* | 34°23S 137°40E | **63** E2 |
| Maitland → *Canada* | 43°45N 81°43W | **82** C3 |
| Maitri *Antarctica* | 70°0S 3°0W | **5** D3 |
| Maiyuan *China* | 25°34N 117°28E | **35** E11 |
| Maiz, Is. del *Nic.* | 12°15N 83°4W | **88** D3 |
| Maizuru *Japan* | 35°25N 135°22E | **29** G7 |
| Majalengka *Indonesia* | 6°50S 108°13E | **37** G13 |

| | | |
|---|---|---|
| Majene *Indonesia* | 3°38S 118°57E | **37** E5 |
| Majiang *China* | 26°28N 107°32E | **34** D6 |
| Majorca = Mallorca *Spain* | 39°30N 3°0E | **21** C7 |
| Majuro *Marshall Is.* | 7°9N 171°12E | **64** G9 |
| Mak, Ko *Thailand* | 11°49N 102°29E | **39** G4 |
| Maka *Senegal* | 13°40N 14°10W | **52** F3 |
| Makalamabedi *Botswana* | 20°19S 23°51E | **56** B3 |
| Makale *Indonesia* | 3°6S 119°51E | **37** E5 |
| Makalu *Nepal* | 27°55N 87°8E | **43** F12 |
| Makalu-Barun △ *Nepal* | 27°45N 87°10E | **43** F12 |
| Makarikari = Makgadikgadi Salt | | |
| Pans *Botswana* | 20°40S 25°45E | **56** B4 |
| Makarov Basin *Arctic* | 87°0N 150°0W | **4** A |
| Makarovo *Russia* | 57°40N 107°45E | **27** D11 |
| Makassar *Indonesia* | 5°10S 119°20E | **37** F5 |
| Makassar, Selat *Indonesia* | 1°0S 118°20E | **37** E5 |
| Makassar, Str. of = Makassar, | | |
| Selat *Indonesia* | 1°0S 118°20E | **37** E5 |
| Makat = Maqat | | |
| *Kazakhstan* | 47°39N 53°19E | **19** E9 |
| Makedonija = Macedonia ■ | | |
| *Europe* | 41°53N 21°40E | **23** D9 |
| Makeni *S. Leone* | 8°55N 12°5W | **52** G3 |
| Makeyevka = Makiyivka | | |
| *Ukraine* | 48°0N 38°0E | **19** E6 |
| Makgadikgadi △ | | |
| *Botswana* | 20°27S 24°47E | **56** B3 |
| Makgadikgadi Salt Pans | | |
| *Botswana* | 20°40S 25°45E | **56** B4 |
| Makhachkala *Russia* | 43°0N 47°30E | **19** F8 |
| Makhado = Louis Trichardt | | |
| *S. Africa* | 23°1S 29°43E | **57** B4 |
| Makham, Ao *Thailand* | 7°51N 98°25E | **39** a |
| Makhfar al Buşayyah *Iraq* | 30°0N 46°10E | **46** D5 |
| Makhmūr *Iraq* | 35°46N 43°35E | **46** C4 |
| Makhtal *India* | 16°30N 77°31E | **45** E3 |
| Makian *Indonesia* | 0°20N 127°20E | **37** D7 |
| Makinsk *Kazakhstan* | 52°37N 70°26E | **26** D8 |
| Makira = San Cristóbal | | |
| *Solomon Is.* | 10°30S 161°0E | **58** C9 |
| Makiyivka *Ukraine* | 48°0N 38°0E | **19** E6 |
| Makkah *Si. Arabia* | 21°30N 39°54E | **49** C2 |
| Makkovik *Canada* | 55°10N 59°10W | **73** A8 |
| Makó *Hungary* | 46°14N 20°33E | **17** E11 |
| Makogai *Fiji* | 17°28S 179°0E | **59** a |
| Makokou *Gabon* | 0°40N 12°50E | **54** D2 |
| Makrai *India* | 22°2N 77°0E | **42** H7 |
| Makran Coast Range | | |
| *Pakistan* | 25°40N 64°0E | **40** G4 |
| Makrana *India* | 27°2N 74°46E | **42** F6 |
| Makri *India* | 19°46N 81°55E | **44** E5 |
| Mākū *Iran* | 39°15N 44°31E | **46** B5 |
| Makunda *Botswana* | 22°30S 20°7E | **56** B3 |
| Makung *Taiwan* | 23°34N 119°34E | **35** F12 |
| Makurazaki *Japan* | 31°15N 130°20E | **29** J5 |
| Makurdi *Nigeria* | 7°43N 8°35E | **52** G7 |
| Makushin Volcano | | |
| *U.S.A.* | 53°53N 166°55W | **74** E6 |
| Makūyeh *Iran* | 28°7N 53°9E | **47** D7 |
| Makwassie *S. Africa* | 27°17S 26°0E | **56** D4 |
| Makwiro *Zimbabwe* | 17°58S 30°25E | **57** A5 |
| Mal B. *Ireland* | 52°50N 9°30W | **10** D2 |
| Mala = Mallow *Ireland* | 52°8N 8°39W | **10** D3 |
| Mala ◊ *Australia* | 21°39S 130°45E | **60** D5 |
| Mala, Pta. *Panama* | 7°28N 80°0W | **88** E3 |
| Malabar Coast *India* | 11°0N 75°0E | **45** J2 |
| Malacca, Straits of *Indonesia* | 3°0N 101°0E | **39** L3 |
| Malad City *U.S.A.* | 42°12N 112°15W | **76** E7 |
| Maladzyechna *Belarus* | 54°20N 26°50E | **17** A14 |
| Málaga *Spain* | 36°43N 4°23W | **21** D3 |
| Malagasy Rep. = Madagascar ■ | | |
| *Africa* | 20°0S 47°0E | **55** J9 |
| Malahide *Ireland* | 53°26N 6°9W | **10** C5 |
| Malaimbandy *Madag.* | 20°20S 45°36E | **55** J9 |
| Malaita *Solomon Is.* | 9°0S 161°0E | **58** B9 |
| Malakal *South Sudan* | 9°33N 31°40E | **53** G12 |
| Malakanagiri *India* | 18°21N 81°54E | **44** E5 |
| Malakand *Pakistan* | 34°40N 71°55E | **42** B4 |
| Malakula *Vanuatu* | 16°15S 167°30E | **58** C9 |
| Malakwal *Pakistan* | 32°34N 73°13E | **42** C5 |
| Malamala *Indonesia* | 3°21S 120°55E | **37** E6 |
| Malanda *Australia* | 17°22S 145°35E | **62** B4 |
| Malang *Indonesia* | 7°59S 112°45E | **37** G15 |
| Malangen *Norway* | 69°24N 18°37E | **8** B18 |
| Malangwa *Nepal* | 26°52N 85°34E | **43** F11 |
| Malanje *Angola* | 9°36S 16°17E | **54** F3 |
| Mälappuram *India* | 11°7N 76°11E | **45** J3 |
| Malargüe *Argentina* | 35°32S 69°30W | **94** D2 |
| Malartic *Canada* | 48°9N 78°9W | **72** C4 |
| Malaryta *Belarus* | 51°50N 24°3E | **17** C13 |
| Malaspina Glacier | | |
| *U.S.A.* | 59°50N 140°30W | **74** D11 |
| Malatya *Turkey* | 38°25N 38°20E | **46** B3 |
| Malawi ■ *Africa* | 11°55S 34°0E | **55** E6 |
| Malawi, L. *Africa* | 12°30S 34°30E | **55** G6 |
| Malay Pen. *Asia* | 7°25N 100°0E | **39** J3 |
| Malaya Vishera *Russia* | 58°55N 32°25E | **18** C5 |
| Malayer *Iran* | 34°19N 48°51E | **47** C6 |
| Malaysia ■ *Asia* | 5°0N 110°0E | **36** D4 |
| Malazgirt *Turkey* | 39°10N 42°33E | **46** B4 |
| Malbon *Australia* | 21°5S 140°17E | **62** C3 |
| Malbooma *Australia* | 30°41S 134°11E | **63** E1 |
| Malbork *Poland* | 54°3N 19°1E | **17** B10 |
| Malcolm *Australia* | 28°51S 121°25E | **61** E3 |
| Malcolm, Pt. *Australia* | 33°48S 123°45E | **61** F3 |
| Maldah *India* | 25°2N 88°9E | **43** G13 |
| Maldegem *Belgium* | 51°14N 3°26E | **15** C3 |
| Malden *U.S.A.* | 36°34N 89°57W | **80** G9 |
| Malden I. *Kiribati* | 4°3S 155°1W | **65** H12 |
| Maldives ■ *Ind. Oc.* | 5°0N 73°0E | **26** H9 |
| Maldon *U.K.* | 51°44N 0°42E | **13** F8 |
| Maldonado *Uruguay* | 34°59S 55°0W | **95** C5 |
| Maldonado, Pta. *Mexico* | 16°20N 98°33W | **87** D5 |
| Malé *Maldives* | 4°0N 73°28E | **26** H9 |
| Malé Karpaty *Slovakia* | 48°30N 17°20E | **17** D9 |
| Maleas, Akra *Greece* | 36°28N 23°7E | **23** F10 |
| Malebo, Pool *Africa* | 4°17S 15°20E | **54** E3 |
| Malegaon *India* | 20°30N 74°38E | **44** D2 |

| | | |
|---|---|---|
| Malek Kandī *Iran* | 37°9N 46°6E | **46** B5 |
| Malema *Mozam.* | 14°57S 37°20E | **55** G7 |
| Maler Kotla *India* | 30°32N 75°58E | **42** D6 |
| Malgomaj *Sweden* | 64°40N 16°30E | **8** D17 |
| Malha *Sudan* | 15°8N 25°10E | **53** E11 |
| Malhargarh *India* | 24°17N 74°59E | **42** G6 |
| Malheur → *U.S.A.* | 44°4N 116°59W | **76** D5 |
| Malheur L. *U.S.A.* | 43°20N 118°48W | **76** E4 |
| Mali ■ *Africa* | 17°0N 3°0W | **52** E5 |
| Mali → *Myanmar* | 25°42N 97°30E | **41** G20 |
| Mali Kyun *Myanmar* | 13°0N 98°20E | **38** F2 |
| Malibu *U.S.A.* | 34°2N 118°41W | **79** L8 |
| Maliku = Minicoy I. *India* | 8°17N 73°2E | **45** K1 |
| Maliku *Indonesia* | 0°39S 123°16E | **37** E6 |
| Malili *Indonesia* | 2°42S 121°6E | **37** E6 |
| Malimba, Mts. | | |
| *Dem. Rep. of the Congo* | 7°30S 29°30E | **54** F5 |
| Malin Hd. *Ireland* | 55°23N 7°23W | **10** A4 |
| Malin Pen. *Ireland* | 55°20N 7°17W | **10** A4 |
| Malindi *Kenya* | 3°12S 40°5E | **54** E8 |
| Malines = Mechelen | | |
| *Belgium* | 51°2N 4°29E | **15** C4 |
| Malino *Indonesia* | 1°0N 121°0E | **37** D6 |
| Malipo *China* | 23°7N 104°42E | **34** F5 |
| Malita *Phil.* | 6°19N 125°39E | **37** C7 |
| Maliwun *Myanmar* | 10°17N 98°40E | **39** G2 |
| Maliya *India* | 23°5N 70°46E | **42** H4 |
| Malkapur *India* | 20°53N 76°12E | **44** D3 |
| Malkara *Turkey* | 40°53N 26°53E | **23** D12 |
| Malkangiri = Malakanagiri | | |
| *India* | 18°21N 81°54E | **44** E5 |
| Mallacoota Inlet | | |
| *Australia* | 37°34S 149°40E | **63** F4 |
| Mallaig *U.K.* | 57°0N 5°50W | **11** D3 |
| Mallawan *India* | 27°4N 80°12E | **43** F9 |
| Mallawi *Egypt* | 27°44N 30°44E | **53** C12 |
| Mallicolo = Malakula | | |
| *Vanuatu* | 16°15S 167°30E | **58** C9 |
| Mallorca *Spain* | 39°30N 3°0E | **21** C7 |
| Mallorytown *Canada* | 44°29N 75°53W | **83** B9 |
| Mallow *Ireland* | 52°8N 8°39W | **10** D3 |
| Malmberget *Sweden* | 67°11N 20°40E | **8** C19 |
| Malmédy *Belgium* | 50°25N 6°2E | **15** D6 |
| Malmesbury *S. Africa* | 33°28S 18°41E | **56** D2 |
| Malmivaara = Malmberget | | |
| *Sweden* | 67°11N 20°40E | **8** C19 |
| Malmö *Sweden* | 55°36N 12°59E | **9** J15 |
| Malolo *Fiji* | 17°45S 177°11E | **59** a |
| Malolos *Phil.* | 14°50N 120°49E | **37** B6 |
| Malolotja △ *Eswatini* | 26°3S 31°6E | **57** C5 |
| Malone *U.S.A.* | 44°51N 74°18W | **83** B10 |
| Malong *China* | 25°24N 103°34E | **34** E4 |
| Maloti Mts. = Drakensberg | | |
| *S. Africa* | 31°0S 28°0E | **57** D4 |
| Måløy *Norway* | 61°57N 5°6E | **8** F11 |
| Malpaso, Presa = Netzahualcóyotl, | | |
| Presa *Mexico* | 17°8N 93°35W | **87** D6 |
| Malpelo, I. de *Colombia* | 4°3N 81°35W | **92** C2 |
| Malprabha → *India* | 16°20N 76°5E | **45** F3 |
| Malpur *India* | 23°21N 73°27E | **42** H5 |
| Malpura *India* | 26°17N 75°23E | **42** F6 |
| Malsiras *India* | 17°52N 74°55E | **44** F2 |
| Malta *Idaho*, *U.S.A.* | 42°18N 113°22W | **76** E7 |
| Malta *Mont.*, *U.S.A.* | 48°21N 107°52W | **76** B10 |
| Malta ■ *Europe* | 35°55N 14°26E | **22** G6 |
| Malta Freeport *Malta* | 35°49N 14°32E | **22** a |
| Maltahöhe *Namibia* | 24°55S 17°0E | **56** B2 |
| Malton *U.K.* | 54°8N 0°49W | **12** C7 |
| Maluku *Indonesia* | 1°0S 127°0E | **37** E7 |
| Maluku □ *Indonesia* | 3°0S 128°0E | **37** E7 |
| Maluku Sea = Molucca Sea | | |
| *Indonesia* | 0°0 125°0E | **37** E6 |
| Malur *India* | 13°0N 77°55E | **45** H3 |
| Malvalli *India* | 12°28N 77°8E | **45** H3 |
| Malvan *India* | 16°2N 73°30E | **45** F1 |
| Malvern *U.S.A.* | 34°22N 92°49W | **84** D8 |
| Malvern Hills *U.K.* | 52°0N 2°19W | **13** E5 |
| Malvinas, Is. = Falkland Is. ☑ | | |
| *Atl. Oc.* | 51°30S 59°0W | **96** G5 |
| Malyn *Ukraine* | 50°46N 29°3E | **17** C15 |
| Malyy Lyakhovskiy, Ostrov | | |
| *Russia* | 74°7N 140°36E | **27** B15 |
| Malyy Taymyr, Ostrov | | |
| *Russia* | 78°6N 107°15E | **27** B11 |
| Mama *Russia* | 58°18N 112°54E | **27** D12 |
| Mamanguape *Brazil* | 6°50S 35°4W | **93** E11 |
| Mamanuca Group *Fiji* | 17°35S 177°5E | **59** a |
| Mamarr Mitla *Egypt* | 30°2N 32°54E | **48** E1 |
| Mamasa *Indonesia* | 2°55S 119°20E | **37** E5 |
| Mamberamo → *Indonesia* | 2°0S 137°50E | **37** E9 |
| Mambilima Falls *Zambia* | 10°31S 28°45E | **54** G5 |
| Mamburao *Phil.* | 13°13N 120°39E | **37** B6 |
| Mameigwess L. *Canada* | 52°35N 87°50W | **72** B2 |
| Mamers *France* | 48°21N 0°22E | **20** B4 |
| Mammoth *U.S.A.* | 32°43N 110°39W | **77** K8 |
| Mammoth Cave △ | | |
| *U.S.A.* | 37°8N 86°13W | **80** G10 |
| Mammoth Lakes | | |
| *U.S.A.* | 37°39N 118°59W | **78** H8 |
| Mamoré → *Bolivia* | 10°23S 65°53W | **92** F5 |
| Mamou *Guinea* | 10°15N 12°0W | **52** F3 |
| Mamoudzou *Mayotte* | 12°48S 45°14E | **55** a |
| Mamuno *Botswana* | 22°16S 20°1E | **56** C3 |
| Mamuju *Indonesia* | 2°41S 118°50E | **37** E5 |
| Man *Côte d'Ivoire* | 7°30N 7°40W | **52** G4 |
| Man → *India* | 17°31N 75°32E | **44** F2 |
| Man, I. of *India* | 28°8N 93°36E | **45** K1 |
| Man, I. of *U.K.* | 54°15N 4°30W | **12** C3 |
| Man-Bazar *India* | 23°4N 86°39E | **43** H12 |
| Man Na *Myanmar* | 23°27N 97°19E | **41** H20 |
| Mänä *U.S.A.* | 22°2N 159°47W | **75** L8 |
| Mana → *Fr. Guiana* | 5°45N 53°55W | **93** B8 |
| Manaar, G. of = Mannar, G. of | | |
| *Asia* | 8°30N 79°0E | **45** K4 |
| Manacapuru *Brazil* | 3°16S 60°37W | **92** D6 |
| Manacor *Spain* | 39°34N 3°13E | **21** C7 |
| Manado *Indonesia* | 1°29N 124°51E | **37** D6 |
| Managua *Nic.* | 12°6N 86°20W | **88** D2 |
| Managua, L. de *Nic.* | 12°20N 86°30W | **88** D2 |
| Manakara *Madag.* | 22°8S 48°1E | **55** J9 |

Manali India 32°16N 77°10E 42 C7
Manama = Al Manāmah Bahrain 26°10N 50°30E 47 E6
Mananjary Madag. 21°13S 48°20E 55 J9
Manantavadi India 11°49N 76°1E 45 J3
Manantenina Madag. 24°17S 47°19E 55 J9
Manaos = Manaus Brazil 3°0S 60°0W 92 D7
Manapire → Venezuela 7°42N 66°7W 92 B5
Manapouri N.Z. 45°34S 167°39E 59 F1
Manapouri, L. N.Z. 45°32S 167°32E 59 F1
Manapparai India 10°36N 78°25E 45 J4
Manar → India 18°50N 77°20E 44 E3
Manār, Jabal Yemen 14°2N 44°17E 49 E3
Manas China 44°17N 86°10E 30 C6
Manas → India 26°12N 90°40E 41 F17
Manas He → China 45°38N 85°12E 30 B6
Manaslu Nepal 28°33N 84°33E 43 E11
Manasquan U.S.A. 40°8N 74°3W 83 F10
Manassa U.S.A. 37°11N 105°56W 77 H11
Manatí Puerto Rico 18°26N 66°29W 89 d
Manaus Brazil 3°0S 60°0W 92 D7
Manawan L. Canada 55°24N 103°14W 71 B8
Manbij Syria 36°31N 37°57E 46 B3
Manchegorsk Russia 67°54N 32°58E 26 C4
Manchester U.K. 53°29N 2°12W 12 D5
Manchester Calif., U.S.A. 38°58N 123°41W 78 G3
Manchester Conn., U.S.A. 41°47N 72°31W 83 E12
Manchester Ga., U.S.A. 32°51N 84°37W 85 E12
Manchester Iowa, U.S.A. 42°29N 91°27W 80 D8
Manchester Ky., U.S.A. 37°9N 83°46W 81 G12
Manchester N.H., U.S.A. 42°59N 71°28W 83 D13
Manchester N.Y., U.S.A. 42°56N 77°16W 82 D7
Manchester Pa., U.S.A. 40°4N 76°43W 83 F8
Manchester Tenn., U.S.A. 35°29N 86°5W 85 D11
Manchester Vt., U.S.A. 43°10N 73°5W 83 C11
Manchester Int. ✈ (MAN) U.K. 53°21N 2°17W 12 D5
Manchester L. Canada 61°28N 107°29W 71 A7
Manchhar L. Pakistan 26°25N 67°39E 42 F2
Manchuria = Dongbei China 45°0N 125°0E 33 D13
Manchurian Plain China 47°0N 124°0E 24 D14
Mand → India 21°42N 83°15E 43 J10
Mand → Iran 28°20N 52°30E 47 D7
Mandaguari Brazil 23°32S 51°42W 95 A5
Mandah = Töhöm Mongolia 44°27N 108°2E 32 B5
Mandal Norway 58°2N 7°25E 9 G12
Mandala, Puncak Indonesia 4°44S 140°20E 37 E10
Mandalay Myanmar 22°0N 96°4E 41 J20
Mandale = Mandalay Myanmar 22°0N 96°4E 41 J20
Mandalgarh India 25°12N 75°6E 42 G6
Mandalgovĭ Mongolia 45°45N 106°10E 32 B4
Mandalī Iraq 33°43N 45°28E 46 C5
Mandan U.S.A. 46°50N 100°54W 80 B3
Mandar, Teluk Indonesia 3°32S 119°21E 37 E5
Mandaue Phil. 10°20N 123°56E 37 B6
Mandeville Jamaica 18°2N 77°31W 88 a
Mandi India 31°39N 76°58E 42 D7
Mandi Burewala Pakistan 30°9N 72°41E 42 D5
Mandi Dabwali India 29°58N 74°42E 42 E6
Mandimba Mozam. 14°20S 35°40E 55 G7
Mandioli Indonesia 0°40S 127°20E 37 E7
Mandla India 22°39N 80°30E 43 H9
Mandorah Australia 12°32S 130°42E 60 B5
Mandra Pakistan 33°23N 73°12E 42 C5
Mandritsara Madag. 15°50S 48°49E 55 H9
Mandsaur India 24°3N 75°8E 42 G6
Mandurah Australia 32°36S 115°48E 61 F2
Mandvi India 22°51N 69°22E 42 H3
Mandya India 12°30N 77°0E 45 H3
Mandzai Pakistan 30°55N 67°6E 42 D2
Maneh Iran 37°39N 57°7E 47 B8
Maner → India 18°30N 79°40E 44 E4
Maneroo Cr. → Australia 23°21S 143°53E 62 C3
Manfalût Egypt 27°20N 30°52E 53 C12
Manfredónia Italy 41°38N 15°55E 22 D6
Mangabeiras, Chapada das Brazil 10°0S 46°30W 93 F9
Mangaia Cook Is. 21°55S 157°55W 65 K12
Mangalagiri India 16°26N 80°36E 45 F5
Mangalia Romania 43°50N 28°35E 17 G15
Mangalore = Mangaluru India 12°55N 74°47E 45 H2
Mangaluru India 12°55N 74°47E 45 H2
Mangalvedha India 17°31N 75°28E 44 F2
Mangan India 27°31N 88°32E 43 F13
Mangaon India 18°15N 73°20E 44 E1
Mangarrayi ✪ Australia 15°5S 133°10E 62 B1
Mangawan India 24°41N 81°33E 43 G9
Mangaweka N.Z. 39°48S 175°47E 59 C5
Mangetti △ Namibia 18°43S 19°8E 56 A2
Manggar Indonesia 2°50S 108°10E 36 E3
Manggawitu Indonesia 4°8S 133°32E 37 E8
Mangghystaū Tübegi Kazakhstan 44°30N 52°30E 26 E6
Manggis Indonesia 8°29S 115°31E 37 J18
Mangkalihat, Tanjung Indonesia 1°2N 118°59E 37 D5
Mangkururrpa ✪ Australia 20°35S 129°43E 60 D4
Mangla Pakistan 33°7N 73°39E 42 C5
Mangla Dam Pakistan 33°9N 73°44E 43 C5
Manglaur India 29°44N 77°49E 42 E7
Mangnai China 37°52N 91°43E 30 D7
Mangnai Zhen China 38°24N 90°14E 30 D7
Mango Togo 10°20N 0°30E 52 F6
Mango Tonga 20°17S 174°29W 59 c
Mangoche Malawi 14°25S 35°16E 55 G7
Mangoky → Madag. 21°29S 43°41E 55 J8
Mangole Indonesia 1°50S 125°55E 37 E6
Mangonui N.Z. 35°1S 173°32E 59 A4
Mangrol Mad. P., India 21°7N 70°7E 42 J4
Mangrol Raj., India 25°20N 76°31E 42 G6
Mangrul Pir India 20°19N 77°21E 44 D3
Mangshi = Luxi China 24°27N 98°36E 34 E2
Mangueira, L. da Brazil 33°0S 52°50W 95 C5
Mangui China 52°3N 122°3E 31 A13
Mangum U.S.A. 34°53N 99°30W 84 D5
Manguri Australia 28°58S 134°22E 63 A1
Mangyshlak, Poluostrov = Mangghystaū Tübegi Kazakhstan 44°30N 52°30E 26 E6
Manhattan U.S.A. 39°11N 96°35W 80 F5
Manhiça Mozam. 25°23S 32°49E 57 C5
Manica Mozam. 18°58S 32°59E 57 A5
Manica □ Mozam. 19°10S 33°45E 57 A5
Manicoré Brazil 5°48S 61°16W 92 E6
Manicouagan → Canada 49°30N 68°30W 73 C6
Manicouagan, Rés. Canada 51°5N 68°40W 73 B6
Manīfah Si. Arabia 27°44N 49°0E 47 E6
Manifold, C. Australia 22°41S 150°50E 62 C5
Maniganggo China 31°56N 99°10E 34 B2
Manigotagan Canada 51°6N 96°18W 71 C9
Manigotagan → Canada 51°7N 96°20W 71 C9
Manihari India 25°21N 87°38E 43 G12
Manihiki Cook Is. 10°24S 161°1W 65 J11
Manihiki Plateau Pac. Oc. 11°0S 164°0W 65 J11
Manikpur India 25°4N 81°7E 43 G9
Manila U.S.A. 40°59N 109°43W 76 F9
Manila B. Phil. 14°40N 120°35E 37 B6
Manilla Australia 30°45S 150°43E 63 E5
Maningrida Australia 12°3S 134°13E 62 A1
Manipa, Selat Indonesia 3°20S 127°25E 37 E7
Manipur □ India 25°0N 94°0E 41 G19
Manipur → Myanmar 23°45N 94°20E 41 H19
Manisa Turkey 38°38N 27°30E 23 E12
Manistee U.S.A. 44°15N 86°19W 80 C10
Manistee → U.S.A. 44°15N 86°21W 80 C10
Manistique U.S.A. 45°57N 86°15W 80 C10
Manitoba □ Canada 53°30N 97°0W 71 B9
Manitoba, L. Canada 51°0N 98°45W 71 C9
Manitou Canada 49°15N 98°32W 71 D9
Manitou, L. Canada 50°55N 65°17W 73 B6
Manitou Is. U.S.A. 45°8N 86°0W 80 C10
Manitou L. Canada 52°43N 109°43W 71 C7
Manitou Springs U.S.A. 38°52N 104°55W 76 G11
Manitoulin I. Canada 45°40N 82°30W 72 C3
Manitouwadge Canada 49°8N 85°48W 72 C2
Manitowoc U.S.A. 44°5N 87°40W 80 C10
Maniyachi India 8°51N 77°55E 45 K3
Manizales Colombia 5°5N 75°32W 92 B3
Manjacaze Mozam. 24°45S 34°0E 57 B5
Manjakandriana Madag. 18°55S 47°47E 55 H9
Manjhand Pakistan 25°50N 68°10E 42 G3
Manjimup Australia 34°15S 116°6E 61 F2
Manjlegaon India 19°9N 76°14E 44 E3
Manjra → India 18°49N 77°52E 44 E3
Mankato Kans., U.S.A. 39°47N 98°13W 80 F4
Mankato Minn., U.S.A. 44°10N 94°0W 80 C6
Mankayane Eswatini 26°40S 31°4E 57 C5
Mankera Pakistan 31°23N 71°26E 42 D4
Mankota Canada 49°25N 107°5W 71 D7
Mankulam Sri Lanka 9°8N 80°26E 45 K5
Manlay = Üydzin Mongolia 44°9N 107°0E 32 B4
Manmad India 20°18N 74°28E 44 D2
Mann Ranges Australia 26°6S 130°5E 61 E5
Manna Indonesia 4°25S 102°55E 36 E2
Mannahill Australia 32°25S 140°0E 63 E3
Mannar Sri Lanka 9°1N 79°54E 45 K4
Mannar, G. of Asia 8°30N 79°0E 45 K4
Mannar I. Sri Lanka 9°5N 79°45E 45 K4
Mannargudi India 10°45N 79°51E 45 J4
Mannheim Germany 49°29N 8°29E 16 D5
Manning Canada 56°53N 117°39W 70 B5
Manning Oreg., U.S.A. 45°45N 123°13W 78 E3
Manning S.C., U.S.A. 33°42N 80°13W 85 E14
Mannum Australia 34°50S 139°20E 63 E2
Manoharpur India 22°23N 85°12E 43 H11
Manokwari Indonesia 0°54S 134°0E 37 E8
Manombo Madag. 22°57S 43°28E 55 J8
Manono Dem. Rep. of the Congo 7°15S 27°25E 54 F5
Manono Samoa 13°50S 172°5W 59 b
Manorhamilton Ireland 54°18N 8°11W 10 B3
Manosque France 43°49N 5°47E 20 E6
Manotick Canada 45°13N 75°41W 83 A9
Manouane → Canada 49°30N 71°10W 73 C5
Manouane, L. Canada 50°45N 70°45W 73 B5
Manp'o N. Korea 41°6N 126°24E 33 D14
Manpojin = Manp'o N. Korea 41°6N 126°24E 33 D14
Manpur Chhattisgarh, India 23°17N 83°35E 43 H10
Manpur Chhattisgarh, India 20°22N 80°43E 44 D5
Manpur Mad. P., India 22°26N 75°37E 42 H6
Manresa Spain 41°48N 1°50E 21 B6
Mansa Gujarat, India 23°27N 72°45E 42 H5
Mansa Punjab, India 30°0N 75°27E 42 E6
Mansa Zambia 11°13S 28°55E 54 G5
Mansehra Pakistan 34°20N 73°15E 42 B5
Mansel I. Canada 62°0N 80°0W 69 E15
Mansfield Australia 37°4S 146°6E 63 F4
Mansfield U.K. 53°9N 1°11W 12 D6
Mansfield La., U.S.A. 32°2N 93°43W 84 E8
Mansfield Mass., U.S.A. 42°2N 71°13W 83 D13
Mansfield Ohio, U.S.A. 40°45N 82°31W 82 F2
Mansfield Pa., U.S.A. 41°48N 77°5W 82 E7
Mansfield, Mt. U.S.A. 44°33N 72°49W 83 B12
Manson Creek Canada 55°37N 124°32W 70 B4
Manta Ecuador 1°0S 80°40W 92 D2
Mantalingajan, Mt. Phil. 8°55N 117°45E 36 C5
Manteca U.S.A. 37°48N 121°13W 78 H5
Manteo U.S.A. 35°55N 75°40W 85 D17
Mantes-la-Jolie France 48°58N 1°41E 20 B4
Mantha India 19°40N 76°23E 44 E3
Manthani India 18°40N 79°35E 44 E4
Manti U.S.A. 39°16N 111°38W 76 G8
Mantiqueira, Serra da Brazil 22°0S 44°0W 95 A7
Manton U.S.A. 44°25N 85°24W 81 C11
Mántova Italy 45°9N 10°48E 22 B4
Mänttä Vilppula Finland 62°3N 24°40E 8 E21
Mantua = Mántova Italy 45°9N 10°48E 22 B4
Manuae Cook Is. 19°30S 159°0W 65 J12
Manuae Indonesia 2°10N 118°35E 37 D5
Manú Peru 12°10S 70°51W 92 F4
Manú → Peru 12°16S 70°55W 92 F4
Manu'a Is. Amer. Samoa 14°13S 169°35W 59 b
Manuel Alves → Brazil 11°19S 48°28W 93 F9
Manui Indonesia 3°35S 123°5E 37 E6
Manukau N.Z. 37°0S 174°52E 59 B5
Manuripi → Bolivia 11°6S 67°36W 92 F5
Manvi India 15°57N 76°59E 45 G3
Manwan Dam China 24°44N 100°20E 34 E3
Manwath India 19°19N 76°32E 44 E3
Many U.S.A. 31°34N 93°29W 84 F8
Manyallaluk ✪ Australia 14°16S 132°49E 60 B5
Manych-Gudilo, Ozero Russia 46°24N 42°38E 19 E7
Manyoni Tanzania 5°45S 34°55E 54 F6
Manzai Pakistan 32°12N 70°15E 42 C4
Manzanar ⌂ U.S.A. 36°44N 118°9W 78 J7
Manzanares Spain 39°2N 3°22W 21 C4
Manzanillo Cuba 20°20N 77°31W 88 B4
Manzanillo Mexico 19°3N 104°20W 86 D4
Manzanillo, Pta. Panama 9°30N 79°40W 88 E4
Manzano Mts. U.S.A. 34°40N 106°20W 77 J10
Manzarīyeh Iran 34°53N 50°50E 47 C6
Manzhouli China 49°35N 117°25E 31 B12
Manzini Eswatini 26°30S 31°25E 57 C5
Manzouli = Manzhouli China 49°35N 117°25E 31 B12
Manzur Vadisi △ Turkey 39°10N 39°30E 46 B3
Mao Chad 14°4N 15°19E 53 F9
Maó Spain 39°53N 4°16E 21 C8
Maoke, Pegunungan Indonesia 3°40S 137°30E 37 E9
Maolin China 43°58N 123°30E 33 C12
Maoming China 21°50N 110°54E 35 G8
Maopi T'ou China 21°56N 120°43E 35 G13
Maoxian China 31°41N 103°49E 34 B4
Maoxing China 45°28N 124°40E 33 B13
Mapam Yumco China 30°45N 81°28E 43 D9
Mapastepec Mexico 15°26N 92°54W 87 D6
Maphrao, Ko Thailand 7°56N 98°26E 39 a
Mapia, Kepulauan Indonesia 0°50N 134°20E 37 D8
Mapimí Mexico 25°49N 103°51W 86 B4
Mapimí, Bolsón de Mexico 27°0N 104°15W 86 B4
Maping China 31°34N 113°32E 35 B9
Mapinhane Mozam. 22°20S 35°0E 57 B6
Maple Creek Canada 49°55N 109°29W 71 D7
Maple Valley U.S.A. 47°25N 122°3W 78 C4
Mapleton U.S.A. 44°2N 123°52W 76 D2
Mapoon ✪ Australia 11°44S 142°8E 62 A3
Mapuca India 15°36N 73°46E 45 G1
Mapuera → Brazil 1°5S 57°2W 92 D7
Mapulanguene Mozam. 24°29S 32°6E 57 B5
Mapungubwe △ S. Africa 22°12S 29°22E 57 B4
Maputo Mozam. 25°58S 32°32E 57 C5
Maputo □ Mozam. 26°0S 32°25E 57 C5
Maputo, B. de Mozam. 25°50S 32°45E 57 C5
Maputo ⌂ Mozam. 26°23S 32°48E 57 C5
Maqat Kazakhstan 47°39N 53°19E 19 E9
Maqên China 34°24N 100°6E 30 E9
Maqên Gangri China 34°55N 99°18E 30 E8
Maqiaohe China 44°40N 130°30E 33 B16
Maqnā Si. Arabia 28°25N 34°50E 46 D2
Maqteïr Mauritania 21°50N 11°40W 52 D3
Maqu China 33°52N 101°42E 30 E9
Maquan He = Brahmaputra → Asia 23°40N 90°35E 43 H13
Maquela do Zombo Angola 6°0S 15°15E 54 F3
Maquinchao Argentina 41°15S 68°50W 96 E3
Maquoketa U.S.A. 42°4N 90°40W 80 D8
Mar Canada 44°49N 81°12W 82 B3
Mar, Serra do Brazil 25°30S 49°0W 95 B6
Mar Chiquita, L. Argentina 30°40S 62°50W 94 C3
Mar del Plata Argentina 38°0S 57°30W 94 D4
Mar Menor Spain 37°40N 0°45W 21 D5
Mara Indonesia 1°52S 65°25W 92 D5
Maraã Brazil 1°52S 65°25W 92 D5
Maraa Tahiti 17°46S 149°34W 59 d
Marabá Brazil 5°20S 49°5W 93 E9
Maraboon, L. Australia 23°41S 148°0E 62 C4
Maracá, I. de Brazil 2°10N 50°30W 93 C8
Maracaibo Venezuela 10°40N 71°37W 92 A4
Maracaibo, L. de Venezuela 9°40N 71°30W 92 B4
Maracaju Brazil 21°38S 55°9W 95 A4
Maracas Bay Village Trin. & Tob. 10°46N 61°28W 93 K15
Maracay Venezuela 10°15N 67°28W 92 A5
Marādah Libya 29°15N 19°15E 53 C9
Maradi Niger 13°29N 7°20E 52 F7
Marāgheh Iran 37°30N 46°12E 46 B5
Marāh Si. Arabia 25°0N 45°35E 46 E5
Marajo, I. de Brazil 1°0S 49°30W 93 D9
Marākand Iran 38°51N 45°16E 46 B5
Marakele △ S. Africa 24°30S 25°30E 57 D4
Maralinga Australia 30°13S 131°32E 61 F5
Maralinga Tjarutja ✪ Australia 29°30S 131°0E 61 E5
Marambio Antarctica 64°0S 56°0W 5 C18
Maran Malaysia 3°35N 102°45E 39 L4
Marana U.S.A. 32°27N 111°13W 77 K8
Maranboy Australia 14°40S 132°39E 60 B5
Marand Iran 38°30N 45°45E 46 B5
Marang Malaysia 5°12N 103°13E 39 K4
Maranguape Brazil 3°55S 38°50W 93 D11
Maranhão = São Luís Brazil 2°39S 44°15W 93 D10
Maranhão □ Brazil 5°0S 46°0W 93 E9
Maranoa → Australia 27°50S 148°37E 63 D4
Marañón → Peru 4°30S 73°35W 92 D4
Marão Mozam. 24°18S 34°2E 57 B5
Maraş = Kahramanmaraş Turkey 37°37N 36°53E 46 B3
Marathon Australia 20°51S 143°32E 62 C3
Marathon Canada 48°44N 86°23W 72 C2
Marathon N.Y., U.S.A. 42°27N 76°2W 83 D8
Marathon Tex., U.S.A. 30°12N 103°15W 84 F3
Maratua Indonesia 2°10N 118°35E 37 D5
Maraval Trin. & Tob. 10°42N 61°31W 93 K15
Maravatío Mexico 19°54N 100°27W 86 D4
Marāwih U.A.E. 24°18N 53°18E 47 E7
Marbella Spain 36°30N 4°57W 21 D3
Marble Bar Australia 21°9S 119°44E 60 D2
Marblehead Mass., U.S.A. 42°29N 70°51W 83 D14
Marblehead Ohio, U.S.A. 41°32N 82°44W 82 E2
Marburg Germany 50°47N 8°46E 16 C5
Marca, Pta. do Angola 16°31S 11°43E 55 H2
March U.K. 52°33N 0°5E 13 E8
Marche France 46°5N 1°20E 20 C4
Marche-en-Famenne Belgium 50°14N 5°19E 15 D5
Marchena Spain 37°18N 5°23W 21 D3
Marco Island U.S.A. 25°58N 81°44W 85 J14
Marcos Juárez Argentina 32°42S 62°5W 94 C3
Marcus Baker, Mt. U.S.A. 61°26N 147°45W 74 C10
Marcus I. = Minami-Tori-Shima Pac. Oc. 24°20N 153°58E 64 E7
Marcy, Mt. U.S.A. 44°7N 73°56W 83 B11
Mardan Pakistan 34°20N 72°0E 42 B5
Mardie Australia 21°12S 115°59E 60 D2
Mardin Turkey 37°20N 40°43E 46 B4
Maree, L. U.K. 57°40N 5°26W 11 D3
Mareeba Australia 16°59S 145°28E 62 B4
Mareetsane S. Africa 26°9S 25°25E 56 C4
Marek = Stanke Dimitrov Bulgaria 42°17N 23°9E 23 C10
Marengo U.S.A. 41°48N 92°4W 80 E7
Marfa U.S.A. 30°19N 104°1W 84 F2
Margao = Madgaon India 15°12N 73°58E 45 G1
Margaret → Australia 18°9S 125°41E 60 C4
Margaret Bay Canada 51°20N 127°35W 70 C3
Margaret L. Canada 58°56N 115°25W 70 B5
Margaret River Australia 33°57S 115°4E 61 F2
Margarita, I. de Venezuela 11°0N 64°0W 92 A6
Margaritovo Russia 43°25N 134°45E 28 C7
Margate S. Africa 30°50S 30°20E 57 D5
Margate U.K. 51°23N 1°23E 13 F9
Marg'ilon Uzbekistan 40°27N 71°42E 26 E8
Mārgow, Dasht-e Afghan. 30°40N 62°30E 40 D3
Marguerite Canada 52°30N 122°25W 70 C4
Mari El □ Russia 56°30N 48°0E 18 C8
Mari Indus Pakistan 32°57N 71°34E 42 C4
Mari Republic = Mari El □ Russia 56°30N 48°0E 18 C8
María Elena Chile 22°18S 69°40W 94 A2
María Grande Argentina 31°45S 59°55W 94 C4
Maria I. N. Terr., Australia 14°52S 135°45E 62 A2
Maria I. Tas., Australia 42°35S 148°0E 63 G4
Maria Island △ Australia 42°38S 148°5E 63 G4
Maria van Diemen, C. N.Z. 34°29S 172°40E 59 A4
Mariala △ Australia 25°57S 145°2E 63 D4
Marian Australia 21°9S 148°57E 62 b
Marian L. Canada 63°0N 116°15W 70 A5
Mariana Trench Pac. Oc. 13°0N 145°0E 64 F6
Marianna Ark., U.S.A. 34°46N 90°46W 85 D9
Marianna Fla., U.S.A. 30°46N 85°14W 85 F12
Marias → U.S.A. 47°56N 110°30W 76 C8
Marías, Is. Mexico 21°25N 106°28W 86 C3
Mariato, Punta Panama 7°12N 80°52W 88 E3
Maribor Slovenia 46°36N 15°40E 16 E8
Marico → Africa 23°35S 26°57E 56 B4
Maricopa Ariz., U.S.A. 33°4N 112°3W 77 K7
Maricopa Calif., U.S.A. 35°4N 119°24W 79 K7
Marié → Brazil 0°27S 66°26W 92 D5
Marie Byrd Land Antarctica 79°30S 125°0W 5 D14
Marie-Galante Guadeloupe 15°56N 61°16W 88 b
Mariecourt = Kangiqsujuaq Canada 61°30N 72°0W 69 E17
Mariehamn Finland 60°5N 19°55E 9 F18
Mariembourg Belgium 50°6N 4°31E 15 D4
Mariental Namibia 24°36S 18°0E 56 B2
Marienville U.S.A. 41°28N 79°8W 82 E5
Mariestad Sweden 58°43N 13°50E 9 G15
Marietta Ga., U.S.A. 33°57N 84°33W 85 E12
Marietta Ohio, U.S.A. 39°25N 81°27W 81 F13
Marieville Canada 45°26N 73°10W 83 A11
Mariinsk Russia 56°10N 87°20E 26 D9
Marijampolė Lithuania 54°33N 23°19E 9 J20
Marília Brazil 22°13S 50°0W 95 A6
Marín Spain 42°23N 8°42W 21 A1
Marina U.S.A. 36°41N 121°48W 78 J5
Marinduque Phil. 13°25N 122°0E 37 B6
Marine City U.S.A. 42°43N 82°30W 82 D2
Marinette U.S.A. 45°6N 87°38W 80 C10
Maringá Brazil 23°26S 52°2W 95 A5
Marion Ala., U.S.A. 32°38N 87°19W 85 E11
Marion Ark., U.S.A. 35°13N 90°12W 80 H8
Marion Ill., U.S.A. 37°44N 88°56W 80 G9
Marion Ind., U.S.A. 40°32N 85°40W 81 E11
Marion Iowa, U.S.A. 42°2N 91°36W 80 D8
Marion Kans., U.S.A. 38°21N 97°1W 80 F5
Marion N.C., U.S.A. 35°41N 82°1W 85 D13
Marion Ohio, U.S.A. 40°35N 83°8W 81 E12
Marion S.C., U.S.A. 34°11N 79°24W 85 D15
Marion Va., U.S.A. 36°50N 81°31W 81 G13
Marion, L. U.S.A. 33°28N 80°10W 85 E14
Mariposa U.S.A. 37°29N 119°58W 78 H7
Mariscal Estigarribia Paraguay 22°3S 60°40W 94 A3
Maritime Alps = Maritimes, Alpes Europe 44°10N 7°10E 20 D7
Maritimes, Alpes Europe 44°10N 7°10E 20 D7
Maritsa = Evros → Greece 41°40N 26°34E 23 D12
Mariupol Ukraine 47°5N 37°31E 19 E6
Mariusa △ Venezuela 9°24N 61°27W 89 E7
Marīvān Iran 35°30N 46°25E 46 C5
Marj 'Uyūn Lebanon 33°21N 35°34E 48 B4
Marka Somalia 1°48N 44°50E 49 G3
Markam China 29°42N 98°38E 34 C2
Markapur India 15°44N 79°19E 45 G4
Markazī □ Iran 34°0N 49°30E 47 C6
Markdale Canada 44°19N 80°39W 82 B4
Marked Tree U.S.A. 35°32N 90°25W 85 D9
Market Drayton U.K. 52°54N 2°29W 12 E5
Market Harborough U.K. 52°29N 0°55W 13 E7
Market Rasen U.K. 53°24N 0°20W 12 D7
Markham, Mt. Antarctica 83°0S 164°0E 5 E11
Markleeville U.S.A. 38°42N 119°47W 78 G7
Markovo Russia 64°40N 170°24E 27 C17
Marks Russia 51°45N 46°50E 18 D8
Marksville U.S.A. 31°8N 92°4W 84 F8
Marla Australia 27°19S 133°33E 63 D1
Marlbank Canada 44°26N 77°6W 82 B7
Marlboro U.S.A. 41°36N 73°59W 83 E11
Marlborough Australia 22°46S 149°52E 62 C4
Marlborough U.K. 51°25N 1°43W 13 F6
Marlborough U.S.A. 42°21N 71°33W 83 D13
Marlborough Downs U.K. 51°27N 1°53W 13 F6
Marlin U.S.A. 31°18N 96°54W 84 F6
Marlow U.K. 51°34N 0°46W 13 F7
Marlow U.S.A. 34°39N 97°58W 84 D6
Marmagao India 15°25N 73°56E 45 G1
Marmara Turkey 40°35N 27°34E 23 D12
Marmara, Sea of = Marmara Denizi Turkey 40°45N 28°15E 23 D13
Marmara Denizi Turkey 40°45N 28°15E 23 D13
Marmaris Turkey 36°50N 28°14E 23 F13
Marmion, Mt. Australia 29°16S 119°50E 61 E2
Marmion L. Canada 48°55N 91°20W 72 C1
Marmolada, Mte. Italy 46°26N 11°51E 22 A4
Marmora Canada 44°28N 77°41W 82 B7
Marne → France 48°47N 2°29E 20 B5
Maro Reef U.S.A. 25°25N 170°35W 75 K5
Maroantsetra Madag. 15°26S 49°44E 55 H9
Maroelaboom Namibia 19°15S 18°53E 56 A2
Marondera Zimbabwe 18°5S 31°42E 55 H6
Maroni → Fr. Guiana 5°30N 54°0W 93 B8
Maroochydore Australia 26°29S 153°5E 63 D5
Maroona Australia 37°27S 142°54E 63 F3
Maroua Cameroon 10°40N 14°20E 53 F8
Marovoay Madag. 16°6S 46°39E 55 H9
Marquard S. Africa 28°40S 27°28E 56 C4
Marquesas Fracture Zone Pac. Oc. 9°0S 125°0W 65 H15
Marquesas Is. = Marquises, Îs. French Polynesia 9°30S 140°0W 65 H14
Marquette U.S.A. 46°33N 87°24W 80 B10
Marquis St. Lucia 14°2N 60°54W 89 f
Marquises, Îs. French Polynesia 9°30S 140°0W 65 H14
Marra, Djebel Sudan 13°10N 24°22E 53 F10
Marracuene Mozam. 25°45S 32°35E 57 C5
Marrakech Morocco 31°9N 8°0W 52 B4
Marrawah Australia 40°55S 144°42E 63 G3
Marree Australia 29°39S 138°1E 63 D2
Marrimane Mozam. 22°58S 33°34E 57 B5
Marromeu Mozam. 18°15S 36°25E 57 A6
Marromeu ⌂ Mozam. 19°0S 36°0E 57 A6
Marrowie Cr. → Australia 33°23S 145°40E 63 E4
Marrupa Mozam. 13°8S 37°30E 55 G7
Mars Hill U.S.A. 46°31N 67°52W 81 B20
Marsá 'Alam Egypt 25°5N 34°54E 49 B1
Marsá Matrûh Egypt 31°19N 27°9E 53 B11
Marsabit Kenya 2°18N 38°0E 54 D7
Marsala Italy 37°48N 12°26E 22 F5
Marsden Australia 33°47S 147°32E 63 E4
Marseille France 43°18N 5°23E 20 E6
Marseilles = Marseille France 43°18N 5°23E 20 E6
Marsh I. U.S.A. 29°34N 91°53W 84 G9
Marshall Ark., U.S.A. 35°55N 92°38W 84 D8
Marshall Mich., U.S.A. 42°16N 84°58W 81 D11
Marshall Minn., U.S.A. 44°27N 95°47W 80 C6
Marshall Mo., U.S.A. 39°7N 93°12W 80 F7
Marshall Tex., U.S.A. 32°33N 94°23W 84 E7
Marshall → Australia 22°59S 136°59E 62 C2
Marshall Is. ■ Pac. Oc. 9°0N 171°0E 64 G9
Marshalltown U.S.A. 42°3N 92°55W 80 D7
Marshbrook Zimbabwe 18°33S 31°9E 57 A5
Marshfield Mo., U.S.A. 37°15N 92°54W 80 G7
Marshfield Vt., U.S.A. 44°20N 72°20W 83 B12
Marshfield Wis., U.S.A. 44°40N 90°10W 80 C8
Marshūn Iran 36°19N 49°23E 47 B6
Märsta Sweden 59°37N 17°52E 9 G17
Mart U.S.A. 31°33N 96°50W 84 F6
Martaban Myanmar 16°30N 97°35E 41 L20
Martaban, G. of = Mottama, G. of Myanmar 16°5N 96°30E 41 L20
Martapura Kalimantan Selatan, Indonesia 3°22S 114°47E 36 E4
Martapura Sumatera Selatan, Indonesia 4°19S 104°22E 36 E2
Marte R. Gómez, Presa Mexico 26°10N 99°0W 87 B5
Martelange Belgium 49°49N 5°43E 15 E5
Marthapal India 19°24N 81°37E 44 E5
Martha's Vineyard U.S.A. 41°25N 70°38W 83 E14
Martigny Switz. 46°6N 7°3E 20 C7
Martigues France 43°24N 5°4E 20 E6
Martin Slovakia 49°6N 18°58E 17 D10
Martin S. Dak., U.S.A. 43°11N 101°44W 80 D3
Martin Tenn., U.S.A. 36°21N 88°51W 85 C10
Martin L. U.S.A. 32°41N 85°55W 85 E12
Martina Franca Italy 40°42N 17°20E 22 D7
Martinborough N.Z. 41°14S 175°29E 59 D5
Martinez Calif., U.S.A. 38°1N 122°8W 78 G4
Martinez Ga., U.S.A. 33°31N 82°5W 85 E13
Martinique ☒ W. Indies 14°40N 61°0W 88 c
Martinique Passage W. Indies 15°15N 61°0W 89 C7
Martinópolis Brazil 22°11S 51°12W 95 A5
Martins Bay Barbados 13°12N 59°29W 89 g
Martins Ferry U.S.A. 40°6N 80°44W 82 F4
Martinsburg Pa., U.S.A. 40°19N 78°20W 82 F6

Martinsburg W. Va., U.S.A. 39°27N 77°58W 81 F15
Martinsville Ind., U.S.A. 39°26N 86°25W 80 F10
Martinsville Va., U.S.A. 36°41N 79°52W 81 G14
Marton N.Z. 40°4S 175°23E 59 D5
Martos Spain 37°44N 3°58W 21 D4
Martu ○ Australia 22°30S 122°30E 60 D3
Marudi Malaysia 4°11N 114°19E 36 D4
Maruf Afghan. 31°30N 67°6E 40 D5
Marugame Japan 34°15N 133°40E 29 G6
Marunga Angola 17°28S 20°2E 56 A3
Maruwa ○ Australia 22°30S 127°30E 60 D4
Marv Dasht Iran 29°50N 52°40E 47 D7
Marvast Iran 30°30N 54°15E 47 D7
Marvel Loch Australia 31°28S 119°29E 61 F2
Marwar India 25°43N 73°45E 42 G5
Mary Turkmenistan 37°40N 61°50E 47 B9
Maryborough = Portlaoise Ireland 53°2N 7°18W 10 C4
Maryborough Queens., Australia 25°31S 152°37E 63 D5
Maryborough Vic., Australia 37°3S 143°44E 63 F3
Maryfield Canada 49°50N 101°35W 71 D8
Maryland □ U.S.A. 39°0N 76°30W 81 F15
Maryland Junction Zimbabwe 17°45S 30°31E 55 H6
Maryport U.K. 54°44N 3°28W 12 C4
Mary's Harbour Canada 52°18N 55°51W 73 B8
Marystown Canada 47°10N 55°10W 73 C8
Marysville Calif., U.S.A. 39°9N 121°35W 78 F5
Marysville Kans., U.S.A. 39°51N 96°39W 80 F5
Marysville Mich., U.S.A. 42°54N 82°29W 82 D2
Marysville Ohio, U.S.A. 40°14N 83°22W 81 E12
Maryville Mo., U.S.A. 40°21N 94°52W 80 E6
Maryville Tenn., U.S.A. 35°46N 83°58W 85 D13
Masada Israel 31°18N 35°21E 48 D4
Masai Malaysia 1°29N 103°55E 39 d
Masai Steppe Tanzania 4°30S 36°30E 54 E7
Masaka Uganda 0°21S 31°45E 54 E6
Masalembo, Kepulauan Indonesia 5°35S 114°30E 36 F4
Masalima, Kepulauan Indonesia 5°4S 117°5E 36 F5
Masamba Indonesia 2°30S 120°15E 37 E6
Masan S. Korea 35°11N 128°32E 33 G15
Masandam, Ra's Oman 26°30N 56°30E 47 E8
Masasi Tanzania 10°45S 38°52E 54 G7
Masaya Nic. 12°0N 86°7W 88 D2
Masbate Phil. 12°21N 123°36E 37 B6
Mascara Algeria 35°26N 0°6E 52 A5
Mascarene Is. Ind. Oc. 22°0S 55°0E 50 J9
Mascota Mexico 20°32N 104°49W 86 C4
Masdar City = Madīnat Masdar U.A.E. 24°26N 54°37E 47 E7
Masela Indonesia 8°9S 129°51E 37 F7
Maseru Lesotho 29°18S 27°30E 56 C4
Mashābih Si. Arabia 25°35N 36°30E 46 E3
Mashan China 23°40N 108°11E 34 F7
Mashang China 36°48N 117°57E 33 F9
Mashatu ○ Botswana 22°45S 29°5E 57 D4
Masherbrum Pakistan 35°38N 76°18E 43 B7
Mashhad Iran 36°20N 59°35E 47 B8
Mashīz Iran 29°56N 56°37E 47 D8
Māshkel, Hāmūn-i- Pakistan 28°20N 62°56E 47 D9
Mashki Chāh Pakistan 29°5N 62°30E 40 E3
Mashonaland Zimbabwe 16°30S 31°0E 55 H6
Mashonaland Central □ Zimbabwe 17°30S 31°0E 57 A5
Mashonaland East □ Zimbabwe 18°0S 32°0E 57 A5
Mashonaland West □ Zimbabwe 17°30S 29°30E 57 A4
Mashrakh India 26°7N 84°48E 43 F11
Masi Manimba Dem. Rep. of the Congo 4°40S 17°54E 54 E3
Masig Australia 9°45S 143°24E 62 a
Masindi Uganda 1°40N 31°43E 54 D6
Maşīrah, Jazīrat Oman 21°0N 58°50E 49 C6
Maşīrah, Khalīj Oman 20°10N 58°10E 49 C6
Masisi Dem. Rep. of the Congo 1°23S 28°49E 54 E5
Masjed Soleyman Iran 31°55N 49°18E 47 D6
Mask, L. Ireland 53°36N 9°22W 10 C2
Maski India 15°56N 76°46E 45 G3
Maskin Oman 23°44N 56°52E 47 F8
Masoala, Tanjon' i Madag. 15°59S 50°13E 55 H10
Masohi = Amahai Indonesia 3°20S 128°55E 37 E7
Mason Nev., U.S.A. 38°56N 119°8W 78 G7
Mason Tex., U.S.A. 30°45N 99°14W 84 F5
Mason City U.S.A. 43°9N 93°12W 80 D7
Masqaţ Oman 23°37N 58°36E 49 C6
Massa Italy 44°1N 10°9E 20 D9
Massachusetts □ U.S.A. 42°30N 72°0W 83 D13
Massachusetts B. U.S.A. 42°25N 70°50W 83 D14
Massakory Chad 13°0N 15°49E 53 F9
Massangena Mozam. 21°34S 33°0E 57 B5
Massango Angola 8°2S 16°21E 54 F3
Massawa = Mitsiwa Eritrea 15°35N 39°25E 49 D2
Massena U.S.A. 44°56N 74°54W 83 B10
Massenya Chad 11°21N 16°9E 53 F9
Masset Canada 54°2N 132°10W 70 C2
Massiah Street Barbados 13°9N 59°29W 89 g
Massif Central France 44°55N 3°0E 20 D5
Massillon U.S.A. 40°48N 81°32W 82 F3
Massinga Mozam. 23°15S 35°22E 57 B6
Massingir Mozam. 23°51S 32°4E 57 B5
Masson-Angers Canada 45°32N 75°25W 83 A9
Masson I. Antarctica 66°10S 93°20E 5 C7
Mastani = Momchilgrad Bulgaria 41°33N 25°23E 23 D11
Masterton N.Z. 40°56S 175°39E 59 D5
Mastic U.S.A. 40°47N 72°54W 83 F12
Mastuj Pakistan 36°20N 72°36E 43 A5

Mastung Pakistan 29°50N 66°56E 40 E5
Masty Belarus 53°27N 24°38E 17 B13
Masuda Japan 34°40N 131°51E 29 G5
Masuku = Franceville Gabon 1°40S 13°32E 54 E2
Masurian Lakes = Mazurski, Pojezierze Poland 53°50N 21°0E 17 B11
Masvingo Zimbabwe 20°8S 30°49E 55 J6
Maşyāf Syria 35°4N 36°20E 46 C3
Mata-au = Clutha → N.Z. 46°20S 169°49E 59 G2
Matabeleland Zimbabwe 18°0S 27°0E 55 H5
Matachewan Canada 47°56N 80°39W 72 C3
Matadi Dem. Rep. of the Congo 5°52S 13°31E 54 F2
Matagalpa Nic. 13°0N 85°58W 88 D2
Matagami Canada 49°45N 77°34W 72 C4
Matagami, L. Canada 49°50N 77°40W 72 C4
Matagorda B. U.S.A. 28°40N 96°12W 84 G6
Matagorda I. U.S.A. 28°15N 96°30W 84 G6
Mataiea Tahiti 17°46S 149°25W 59 d
Matak Indonesia 3°18N 106°16E 36 D3
Matam Sri Lanka 7°30N 80°37E 45 L5
Matam Senegal 15°34N 13°17W 52 E3
Matamoros Coahuila, Mexico 25°32N 103°15W 86 B4
Matamoros Tamaulipas, Mexico 25°53N 97°30W 87 B5
Ma'ţan as Sarra Libya 21°45N 22°0E 53 D10
Matane Canada 48°50N 67°33W 73 C6
Matang China 23°30N 104°7E 34 F5
Matanomadh India 23°33N 68°57E 42 H3
Matanzas Cuba 23°0N 81°40W 88 B3
Matapa Botswana 23°11S 24°39E 56 B3
Matapan, C. = Tenaro, Akra Greece 36°22N 22°27E 23 F10
Matapédia Canada 48°0N 66°59W 73 C6
Matara Sri Lanka 5°58N 80°30E 45 M5
Mataram Indonesia 8°35S 116°7E 37 K19
Matarani Peru 17°0S 72°10W 92 G4
Mataranka Australia 14°55S 133°4E 60 B5
Matarma, Râs Egypt 30°27N 32°44E 48 E1
Mataró Spain 41°32N 2°29E 21 B7
Matatiele S. Africa 30°20S 28°49E 57 D4
Matatila Dam India 25°0N 78°22E 44 B4
Mataura N.Z. 46°11S 168°51E 59 G2
Matavai, B. de Tahiti 17°30S 149°23W 59 d
Matehuala Mexico 23°39N 100°39W 86 C4
Mateke Hills Zimbabwe ¡ 21°48S 31°0E 55 J6
Matelot Trin. & Tob. 10°50N 61°7W 93 K15
Matera Italy 40°40N 16°36E 22 D7
Mathis U.S.A. 28°6N 97°50W 84 G6
Mathraki Greece 39°48N 19°31E 23 E8
Mathura India 27°30N 77°40E 42 F7
Mati Phil. 6°55N 126°15E 37 C7
Matiali India 26°56N 88°49E 43 F13
Matías Romero Mexico 16°53N 95°2W 87 D5
Matiri Ra. N.Z. 41°38S 172°20E 59 D4
Matjiesfontein S. Africa 33°14S 20°35E 56 D3
Matla → India 21°40N 88°40E 43 J13
Matlamanyane Botswana 19°33S 25°57E 56 A4
Matli Pakistan 25°2N 68°39E 42 G3
Matlock U.K. 53°9N 1°33W 12 D6
Mato Grosso □ Brazil 14°0S 55°0W 93 F8
Mato Grosso, Planalto do Brazil 15°0S 55°0W 93 G8
Mato Grosso do Sul □ Brazil 18°0S 55°0W 93 G8
Matochkin Shar, Proliv Russia 73°23N 55°12E 26 B6
Matola Mozam. 25°57S 32°27E 57 C5
Matopo Hills Zimbabwe 20°36S 28°20E 55 J5
Matosinhos Portugal 41°11N 8°42W 21 B1
Matroosberg S. Africa 33°23S 19°40E 56 D2
Maţruħ Oman 23°37N 58°30E 49 C6
Matsu Tao Taiwan 26°8N 119°56E 35 D12
Matsue Japan 35°25N 133°10E 29 G6
Matsum, Ko Thailand 9°22N 99°59E 39 b
Matsumae Japan 41°26N 140°7E 28 D10
Matsumae-Hantō Japan 41°30N 140°15E 28 D10
Matsumoto Japan 36°15N 138°0E 29 F9
Matsusaka Japan 34°34N 136°32E 29 G8
Matsushima Japan 38°20N 141°10E 28 E10
Matsuura Japan 33°20N 129°49E 29 H4
Matsuyama Japan 33°45N 132°45E 29 H6
Mattagami → Canada 50°43N 81°29W 72 B3
Mattancheri India 9°50N 76°15E 45 K3
Mattawa Canada 46°20N 78°45W 72 C4
Matterhorn Switz. 45°58N 7°39E 20 D7
Matthew Town Bahamas 20°57N 73°40W 89 B5
Matthews Ridge Guyana 7°37N 60°10W 92 B6
Mattice Canada 49°40N 83°20W 72 C3
Mattili India 18°33N 82°12E 44 E6
Mattituck U.S.A. 40°59N 72°32W 83 F12
Mattō = Hakusan Japan 36°31N 136°34E 29 F8
Mattoon U.S.A. 39°29N 88°23W 80 F1
Matuba Mozam. 24°28S 32°49E 57 B5
Matucana Peru 11°55S 76°25W 92 F3
Matugama Sri Lanka 6°31N 80°7E 45 L5
Matuku Fiji 19°10S 179°44E 59 a
Matún = Khowst Afghan. 33°22N 69°58E 42 C3
Matura B. Trin. & Tob. 10°39N 61°1W 93 K15
Maturín Venezuela 9°45N 63°11W 92 B6
Mau Mad. P., India 26°17N 78°41E 43 F8
Mau Ut. P., India 25°56N 83°33E 43 G10
Mau Ut. P., India 25°17N 81°23E 43 G9
Mau Ranipur India 25°16N 79°8E 43 G8
Maubeuge France 50°17N 3°57E 20 A6
Maubin Myanmar 16°44N 95°39E 41 L19
Maud, Pt. Australia 23°6S 113°45E 60 D1
Maud Rise S. Ocean 66°0S 3°0E 5 C3
Maude Australia 34°29S 144°18E 63 E3
Maudin Sun Myanmar 16°0N 94°30E 41 M19
Maués Brazil 3°20S 57°45W 92 D7
Mauganj India 24°50N 81°55E 43 G9
Maughold Hd. I. of Man 54°18N 4°18W 12 C3
Maula Pakistan 27°20N 72°36E 43 A5
Maulamyaing = Mawlamyine Myanmar 16°30N 97°40E 41 L20

Maule □ Chile 36°5S 72°30W 94 D1
Maumee U.S.A. 41°34N 83°39W 81 E12
Maumee → U.S.A. 41°42N 83°28W 81 E12
Maumere Indonesia 8°38S 122°13E 37 F6
Maun Botswana 20°0S 23°26E 56 B3
Mauna Kea U.S.A. 19°50N 155°28W 75 M8
Mauna Loa U.S.A. 19°30N 155°35W 75 M8
Maunath Bhanjan = Mau India 25°56N 83°33E 43 G10
Maungmagan Kyunzu Myanmar 14°0N 97°48E 38 E1
Maupin U.S.A. 45°11N 121°5W 76 D3
Maurepas, L. U.S.A. 30°15N 90°30W 85 F9
Maurice, L. Australia 29°30S 131°0E 61 E5
Mauricie △ Canada 46°45N 73°0W 72 C5
Mauritania ■ Africa 20°50N 10°0W 52 E3
Mauritius ■ Ind. Oc. 20°0S 57°0E 53 d
Mauston U.S.A. 43°48N 90°5W 80 D8
Mavli India 24°45N 73°55E 42 G5
Mawai India 22°30N 81°4E 43 H9
Mawana India 29°6N 77°58E 42 E7
Mawand Pakistan 29°33N 68°38E 42 E3
Mawjib, W. al → Jordan 31°28N 35°36E 48 D4
Mawkmai Myanmar 20°14N 97°37E 41 J20
Mawlaik Myanmar 23°40N 94°26E 41 H19
Mawlamyine Myanmar 16°30N 97°40E 41 L20
Mawqaq Si. Arabia 27°25N 41°8E 46 E4
Mawson Antarctica 67°30S 62°53E 5 C6
Mawson Coast Antarctica 68°30S 63°0E 5 C6
Max U.S.A. 47°49N 101°18W 80 B3
Maxcanú Mexico 20°35N 90°0W 87 C6
Maxesibeni S. Africa 30°49S 29°23E 57 D4
Maxhamish L. Canada 59°50N 123°17W 70 B4
Maxixe Mozam. 23°54S 35°17E 57 B6
Maxville Canada 45°17N 74°51W 83 A10
Maxwell U.S.A. 39°17N 122°11W 78 F4
Maxwelton Australia 20°43S 142°41E 62 C3
May, C. U.S.A. 38°56N 74°58W 81 F16
May Pen Jamaica 17°58N 77°15W 88 a
Maya → Russia 60°28N 134°28E 27 D14
Maya, Costa Mexico 18°44N 87°42W 87 D7
Maya Mts. Belize 16°30N 89°0W 87 D7
Mayabandar India 12°56N 92°56E 45 H11
Mayaguana I. Bahamas 22°30N 72°44W 89 B5
Mayaguana Passage Bahamas 22°32N 73°15W 89 B5
Mayagüez Puerto Rico 18°12N 67°9W 89 d
Mayāmey Iran 36°24N 55°42E 47 B7
Mayang China 27°53N 109°49E 34 D7
Mayanup Australia 33°57S 116°27E 61 F2
Mayapán Mexico 20°29N 89°11W 87 C7
Mayarí Cuba 20°40N 75°41W 89 B4
Mayaro Trin. & Tob. 10°17N 61°1W 93 K16
Mayaro B. Trin. & Tob. 10°14N 60°59W 93 K16
Mayavaram = Mayiladuthurai India 11°3N 79°42E 45 J4
Maybell U.S.A. 40°31N 108°5W 76 F9
Maybole U.K. 55°21N 4°42W 11 F4
Maydān Iraq 34°55N 45°37E 46 C5
Mayenne → France 47°30N 0°32W 20 C3
Mayer U.S.A. 34°24N 112°14W 77 J7
Mayerthorpe Canada 53°57N 115°8W 70 C5
Mayfield Ky., U.S.A. 36°44N 88°38W 80 G3
Mayfield N.Y., U.S.A. 43°6N 74°16W 83 C10
Mayhill U.S.A. 32°53N 105°29W 77 K11
Mayiladuthurai India 11°3N 79°42E 45 J4
Maykop Russia 44°35N 40°10E 19 F7
Maymyo = Pyin-U-Lwin Myanmar 22°2N 96°28E 38 A1
Maynard Mass., U.S.A. 42°26N 71°27W 83 D13
Maynard Wash., U.S.A. 47°59N 122°55W 78 C4
Maynard Hills Australia 28°28S 119°49E 61 E2
Mayne → Australia 23°40S 141°55E 62 C3
Maynooth Canada 45°13N 77°56W 82 A7
Maynooth Ireland 53°23N 6°34W 10 C5
Mayo Canada 63°38N 135°57W 68 E4
Mayo → Ireland 53°53N 9°3W 10 C2
Mayon Volcano Phil. 13°15N 123°41E 37 B6
Mayor I. N.Z. 37°16S 176°17E 59 B6
Mayotte ☑ Ind. Oc. 12°50S 45°10E 55 a
Maysān □ Iraq 31°55N 47°15E 46 D5
Maysville U.S.A. 38°39N 83°46W 81 F12
Mayu Indonesia 1°30N 126°30E 37 D7
Mayuram = Mayiladuthurai India 11°3N 79°42E 45 J4
Mayville N. Dak., U.S.A. 47°30N 97°20W 80 B5
Mayville N.Y., U.S.A. 42°15N 79°30W 82 D5
Mazabuka Zambia 15°52S 27°44E 55 H5
Mazagán = El Jadida Morocco 33°11N 8°17W 52 B4
Mazagão Brazil 0°7S 51°16W 93 D8
Mazán Peru 3°30S 73°0W 92 D4
Māzandarān □ Iran 36°30N 52°0E 47 B7
Mazapil Mexico 24°39N 101°34W 86 C4
Mazar China 36°32N 77°1E 30 D4
Mazara del Vallo Italy 37°39N 12°35E 22 F5
Mazarrón Spain 37°38N 1°19W 21 D5
Mazaruni → Guyana 6°25N 58°35W 92 B7
Mazatán Mexico 29°0N 110°8W 86 B2
Mazatenango Guatemala 14°35N 91°30W 88 D1
Mazatlán Mexico 23°13N 106°25W 86 C3
Mažeikiai Lithuania 56°20N 22°20E 9 H20
Māzhān Iran 32°30N 59°0E 47 C8
Mazīnān Iran 36°19N 56°56E 47 B8
Mazoe → Mozam. 16°20S 33°30E 55 H6
Mazurski, Pojezierze Poland 53°50N 21°0E 17 B11
Mazyr Belarus 51°59N 29°15E 17 B15
Mba Fiji 17°33S 177°41E 59 a
Mbabane Eswatini 26°18S 31°6E 57 D5
Mbaïki C.A.R. 3°53N 18°1E 54 D3
Mbala Zambia 8°46S 31°24E 54 F6
Mbale Uganda 1°8N 34°12E 54 D6
Mbalmayo Cameroon 3°33N 11°33E 54 D2
Mbamba Bay Tanzania 11°13S 34°49E 55 E3
Mbandaka Dem. Rep. of the Congo 0°1N 18°18E 54 D3
Mbanza Congo Angola 6°18S 14°16E 54 F2
Mbanza Ngungu Dem. Rep. of the Congo 5°12S 14°53E 54 F2

Mbarara Uganda 0°35S 30°40E 54 E6
Mbengga = Beqa Fiji 18°23S 178°8E 59 a
Mbeya Tanzania 8°54S 33°29E 54 F6
Mbhashe → S. Africa 32°15S 28°54E 57 D4
Mbini = Río Muni □ Eq. Guin. 1°30N 10°0E 54 D2
Mbizi Zimbabwe 21°23S 31°1E 57 B5
Mbombela S. Africa 25°29S 30°59E 57 C5
Mbomou = Bomu → C.A.R. 4°40N 22°30E 54 D4
Mbouda Cameroon 5°38N 10°15E 52 G8
M'boukou, L. de Cameroon 6°23N 12°50E 54 D7
Mbour Senegal 14°22N 16°54W 52 F2
Mbuji-Mayi Dem. Rep. of the Congo 6°9S 23°40E 54 F4
Mbulu Tanzania 3°45S 35°30E 54 E7
Mburucuyá Argentina 28°1S 58°14W 94 B4
Mburucuyá △ Argentina 28°1S 58°12W 94 B4
Mchinji Malawi 13°47S 32°58E 55 E3
Mdantsane S. Africa 32°56S 27°46E 57 D4
Mead, L. U.S.A. 36°0N 114°44W 79 J12
Meade U.S.A. 37°17N 100°20W 80 G3
Meade River = Atqasuk U.S.A. 70°28N 157°24W 74 A8
Meadow Lake Canada 54°10N 108°26W 71 C7
Meadow Lake △ Canada 54°27N 109°0W 71 C7
Meadow Valley Wash → U.S.A. 36°40N 114°34W 79 J12
Meadville U.S.A. 41°39N 80°9W 82 E4
Meaford Canada 44°36N 80°35W 82 B4
Meakan Dake Japan 43°15N 144°0E 28 C11
Mealy Mts. Canada 53°10N 58°0W 73 B8
Meander River Canada 59°2N 117°42W 70 B5
Meares, C. U.S.A. 45°37N 124°0W 76 D1
Meath □ Ireland 53°40N 6°57W 10 C5
Meath Park Canada 53°27N 105°22W 71 C7
Meaux France 48°58N 2°50E 20 B5
Mebechi-Gawa → Japan 40°31N 141°31E 28 D10
Mebulu, Tanjung Indonesia 8°50S 115°5E 37 K18
Mecca = Makkah Si. Arabia 21°30N 39°54E 49 C2
Mecca U.S.A. 33°34N 116°5W 79 M10
Mechanicsburg U.S.A. 40°13N 77°1W 82 F8
Mechanicville U.S.A. 42°54N 73°41W 83 D11
Mechelen Belgium 51°2N 4°29E 15 C4
Mecheria Algeria 33°35N 0°18W 52 B5
Mecklenburg Germany 53°33N 11°40E 16 B7
Mecklenburger Bucht Germany 54°20N 11°40E 16 A7
Meconta Mozam. 14°59S 39°50E 55 G7
Medan Indonesia 3°40N 98°38E 36 D1
Médanos de Coro △ Venezuela 11°35N 69°44W 89 D6
Medanosa, Pta. Argentina 48°8S 66°0W 96 F3
Medawachchiya Sri Lanka 8°30N 80°30E 45 K5
Medchal India 17°37N 78°29E 44 F4
Médéa Algeria 36°12N 2°50E 52 A6
Medellín Colombia 6°15N 75°35W 92 B3
Medelpad Sweden 62°33N 16°30E 8 E17
Medemblik Neths. 52°46N 5°8E 15 B5
Medford Oreg., U.S.A. 42°19N 122°52W 76 E2
Medford Wis., U.S.A. 45°9N 90°20W 80 C8
Medgidia Romania 44°15N 28°19E 17 F15
Media Agua Argentina 31°58S 68°25W 94 C2
Media Luna Argentina 34°45S 66°44W 94 C2
Medianeira Brazil 25°17S 54°5W 95 B5
Medias Romania 46°9N 24°22E 17 E13
Medicine Bow U.S.A. 41°54N 106°12W 76 F10
Medicine Bow Mts. U.S.A. 40°40N 106°0W 76 F10
Medicine Hat Canada 50°0N 110°45W 71 D6
Medicine Lake U.S.A. 48°30N 104°30W 76 B11
Medicine Lodge U.S.A. 37°17N 98°35W 80 G4
Medina = Al Madīnah Si. Arabia 24°35N 39°52E 46 E3
Medina N. Dak., U.S.A. 46°54N 99°18W 80 B4
Medina N.Y., U.S.A. 43°13N 78°23W 82 C6
Medina Ohio, U.S.A. 41°8N 81°52W 82 E3
Medina → U.S.A. 29°16N 98°29W 84 G5
Medina del Campo Spain 41°18N 4°55W 21 B3
Medina L. U.S.A. 29°32N 98°56W 84 G5
Medina Sidonia Spain 36°28N 5°57W 21 D3
Medinipur India 22°25N 87°21E 43 H12
Mediterranean Sea Europe 35°0N 15°0E 6 H7
Médoc France 45°10N 0°50W 20 D3
Medveditsa → Russia 49°35N 42°41E 19 E7
Medvezhi, Ostrava Russia 71°0N 161°0E 27 B17
Medvezhyegorsk Russia 63°0N 34°25E 18 B5
Medway □ U.K. 51°25N 0°32E 13 F8
Medway → U.K. 51°27N 0°46E 13 F8
Meekatharra Australia 26°32S 118°29E 61 E2
Meeker U.S.A. 40°2N 107°55W 76 F10
Meerut India 29°1N 77°42E 42 E7
Meeteetse U.S.A. 44°9N 108°52W 76 D9
Mega Ethiopia 3°57N 38°19E 49 G2
Megara Greece 37°58N 23°22E 23 F10
Megasini India 21°38N 86°21E 43 J12
Meghalaya □ India 25°50N 91°0E 41 G17
Meghna → Bangla. 22°50N 90°50E 41 H17
Mégiscane, L. Canada 48°35N 75°55W 72 C4
Meharry, Mt. Australia 22°59S 118°35E 60 D2
Mehekar India 20°9N 76°34E 44 D3
Mehlville U.S.A. 38°31N 90°19W 80 F8
Mehndawal India 26°58N 83°5E 43 F10
Mehr Jān Iran 33°50N 55°6E 47 C7
Mehr Iran 37°46N 10°6E 46 C5
Mehrābād Iran 36°53N 47°55E 46 B5
Mehrān Iran 33°7N 46°10E 46 C5
Mehrān → Iran 26°45N 55°26E 47 E7
Mehrgarh Pakistan 29°30N 67°30E 42 E2
Mehriz Iran 31°35N 54°28E 47 D7
Mei Jiang → China 24°25N 116°35E 35 E11
Mei Xian China 34°18N 107°55E 32 G4
Meicheng China 29°28N 119°0E 35 C12
Meichengzhen China 28°9N 111°40E 35 C8
Meichuan China 30°8N 115°31E 35 B10

Meighen I. Canada 80°0N 99°30W 69 B12
Meigu China 28°16N 103°20E 34 C4
Meihekou China 42°32N 125°40E 33 C13
Meiktila Myanmar 20°53N 95°54E 41 J19
Meili Xue Shan China 28°30N 98°39E 34 C2
Meimyu = Pyin-U-Lwin Myanmar 22°2N 96°28E 38 A1
Meishan China 30°3N 103°23E 34 B4
Meissen Germany 51°9N 13°29E 16 C7
Meitan China 27°45N 107°29E 34 C6
Meizhou China 24°16N 116°6E 35 E11
Meja India 25°9N 82°7E 43 G10
Mejillones Chile 23°10S 70°30W 94 A1
Mekele Ethiopia 13°33N 39°30E 49 E2
Mekerghene, Sebkra Algeria 26°21N 1°30E 52 C6
Mekhtar Pakistan 30°30N 69°15E 40 D6
Meknès Morocco 33°57N 5°33W 52 B4
Mekong → Asia 9°30N 106°15E 39 H6
Mekvari = Kür → Azerbaijan 39°29N 49°15E 19 G8
Melagiri Hills India 12°20N 77°30E 45 H3
Melaka Malaysia 2°15N 102°15E 39 L4
Melaka □ Malaysia 2°15N 102°15E 39 L4
Melanesia Pac. Oc. 4°0S 155°0E 64 H7
Melanesian Basin Pac. Oc. 0°5N 160°35E 64 G8
Melapalaiyam India 8°39N 77°44E 45 K3
Melaya Indonesia 8°17S 114°30E 37 J17
Melbourne U.S.A. 28°5N 80°37W 85 G14
Melchor Múzquiz Mexico 27°53N 101°31W 86 B4
Melchor Ocampo Mexico 24°51N 101°39W 86 C4
Melekeok Palau 7°27N 134°38E 64 G5
Mélèzes → Canada 57°40N 69°29W 72 A5
Melfort Canada 52°50N 104°37W 71 C8
Melhus Norway 63°17N 10°18E 8 E14
Melilla N. Afr. 35°21N 2°57W 21 E4
Melipilla Chile 33°42S 71°15W 94 C1
Melissa Canada 45°24N 79°14W 82 A5
Melita Canada 49°15N 101°0W 71 D8
Melitopol Ukraine 46°50N 35°22E 19 E6
Melk Austria 48°13N 15°20E 16 D8
Mellansel Sweden 63°26N 18°19E 8 E18
Mellen U.S.A. 46°20N 90°40W 80 B8
Mellerud Sweden 58°41N 12°28E 9 G15
Mellette U.S.A. 45°9N 98°30W 80 C4
Melo Uruguay 32°20S 54°10W 95 C5
Melolo Indonesia 9°53S 120°40E 37 F6
Melouprey Cambodia 13°48N 105°16E 38 F5
Melrhir, Chott Algeria 34°13N 6°30E 52 B7
Melrose Australia 32°42S 146°57E 63 E4
Melrose U.K. 55°36N 2°43W 11 F6
Melrose Minn., U.S.A. 45°40N 94°49W 80 C6
Melrose N. Mex., U.S.A. 34°26N 103°38W 77 J12
Melstone U.S.A. 46°36N 107°52W 76 C10
Melton Mowbray U.K. 52°47N 0°54W 12 E7
Melun France 48°32N 2°39E 20 B5
Melung Nepal 27°31N 86°3E 43 F12
Melur India 10°2N 78°23E 45 J4
Melville Canada 50°55N 102°50W 71 C8
Melville, C. Australia 14°11S 144°30E 62 A3
Melville, L. Canada 53°30N 60°0W 73 B8
Melville B. Australia 12°0S 136°45E 62 A2
Melville B. Greenland 75°30N 63°0W 69 B19
Melville I. Australia 11°30S 131°0E 60 B5
Melville I. Canada 75°30N 112°0W 69 B9
Melville Pen. Canada 68°0N 84°0W 69 D15
Melvin, Lough Ireland 54°26N 8°10W 10 B3
Memba Mozam. 14°11S 40°30E 55 G8
Memboro Indonesia 9°30S 119°30E 60 A2
Memel = Klaipėda Lithuania 55°43N 21°10E 9 J19
Memel S. Africa 27°38S 29°36E 57 C4
Memmingen Germany 47°58N 10°10E 16 E6
Mempawah Indonesia 0°30N 109°5E 36 D3
Memphis Mich., U.S.A. 42°54N 82°46W 82 D2
Memphis Tenn., U.S.A. 35°8N 90°2W 85 D9
Memphis Tex., U.S.A. 34°44N 100°33W 84 D4
Memphrémagog, L. N. Amer. 45°8N 72°17W 83 B12
Mena U.S.A. 34°35N 94°15W 84 D7
Menado = Manado Indonesia 1°29N 124°51E 37 D6
Menai Strait U.K. 53°11N 4°13W 12 D3
Ménaka Mali 15°59N 2°18E 52 E6
Menan = Chao Phraya → Thailand 13°40N 100°31E 38 F3
Menard U.S.A. 30°55N 99°47W 84 F5
Menard Fracture Zone Pac. Oc. 43°0S 97°0W 65 M18
Mendaña Fracture Zone Pac. Oc. 16°0S 91°0W 65 J18
Mendawai → Indonesia 3°30S 113°0E 36 E4
Mende France 44°31N 3°30E 20 D5
Mendeleyev Ridge Arctic 80°0N 178°0W 4 B17
Mendhar India 33°35N 74°10E 43 C6
Mendip Hills U.K. 51°17N 2°40W 13 F5
Mendocino, C. U.S.A. 40°26N 124°25W 76 F1
Mendocino Fracture Zone Pac. Oc. 40°0N 142°0W 65 D13
Mendota Calif., U.S.A. 36°45N 120°23W 78 J6
Mendota Ill., U.S.A. 41°33N 89°7W 80 E9
Mendoyo Indonesia 8°23S 114°42E 37 J17
Mendoza Argentina 32°50S 68°52W 94 C2
Mendoza □ Argentina 33°0S 69°0W 94 C2
Mene Grande Venezuela 9°49N 70°56W 92 B4
Menemen Turkey 38°34N 27°3E 23 E12
Menen Belgium 50°47N 3°7E 15 D3
Mengcheng China 33°12N 116°36E 32 H9
Mengdingjie China 23°33N 99°5E 34 F2
Menggala Indonesia 4°30S 105°15E 36 E3
Mengjin China 34°55N 112°45E 32 G7
Mengla China 21°20N 101°25E 34 G3
Mengliang China 35°5N 117°40E 33 G9
Mengshan China 24°14N 110°55E 35 E8
Mengyin China 35°40N 117°58E 33 G9

Mengzhe *China* 22°2N 100°15E **34** F3
Mengzi *China* 23°20N 103°22E **34** F4
Menifee *U.S.A.* 33°41N 117°10W **79** M9
Menihek *Canada* 54°28N 56°36W **73** B6
Menihek L. *Canada* 54°0N 67°0W **73** B6
Menin = Menen *Belgium* 50°47N 3°7E **15** D3
Menindee *Australia* 32°20S 142°25E **63** E3
Menindee L. *Australia* 32°20S 142°25E **63** E3
Meningie *Australia* 35°50S 139°18E **63** F2
Menjangan, Pulau *Indonesia* 8°7S 114°31E **37** J17
Menlo Park *U.S.A.* 37°27N 122°12W **78** H4
Menngen ⚙ *Australia* 15°21S 131°16E **60** C5
Menominee *U.S.A.* 45°6N 87°37W **80** C10
Menominee → *U.S.A.* 45°6N 87°35W **80** C10
Menomonie *U.S.A.* 44°53N 91°55W **80** C8
Menongue *Angola* 14°48S 17°52E **55** G3
Menorca *Spain* 40°0N 4°0E **21** C8
Mentakab *Malaysia* 3°29N 102°21E **39** L4
Mentawai, Kepulauan *Indonesia* 2°0S 99°0E **36** E1
Menton *France* 43°50N 7°29E **20** E7
Mentor *U.S.A.* 41°40N 81°21W **82** E3
Menzelinsk *Russia* 55°47N 53°11E **18** C9
Menzies *Australia* 29°40S 121°2E **61** E3
Meob B. *Namibia* 24°25S 14°34E **56** B1
Meoqui *Mexico* 28°17N 105°29W **86** B3
Meppel *Neths.* 52°42N 6°12E **15** B6
Merak *Indonesia* 6°10N 106°26E **37** F12
Meramangye, L. *Australia* 28°25S 132°13E **61** E5
Meran = Merano *Italy* 46°40N 11°9E **22** A4
Merano *Italy* 46°40N 11°9E **22** A4
Merauke *Indonesia* 8°29S 140°24E **37** F10
Merbein *Australia* 34°10S 142°2E **63** E3
Merca = Marka *Somalia* 1°48N 44°50E **49** G3
Merced *U.S.A.* 37°18N 120°29W **78** H6
Merced → *U.S.A.* 37°21N 120°59W **78** H6
Merced Pk. *U.S.A.* 37°36N 119°24W **78** H7
Mercedes *B. Aires, Argentina* 34°40S 59°30W **94** C4
Mercedes *Corrientes, Argentina* 29°10S 58°5W **94** B4
Mercedes *San Luis, Argentina* 33°40S 65°21W **94** C2
Mercedes *Uruguay* 33°12S 58°0W **94** C4
Merceditas *Chile* 28°20S 70°35W **94** B1
Mercer *N.Z.* 37°16S 175°5E **59** B5
Mercer *U.S.A.* 41°14N 80°15W **82** E4
Mercer Island *U.S.A.* 47°34N 122°13W **78** C4
Mercury *U.S.A.* 36°40N 115°59W **79** J11
Mercy, C. *Canada* 65°0N 63°30W **69** E19
Mere *U.K.* 51°6N 2°16W **13** F5
Merebuk, Gunung *Indonesia* 8°13S 114°39E **37** J17
Meredith, C. *Falk. Is.* 52°15S 60°40W **96** G4
Meredith, L. *U.S.A.* 35°43N 101°33W **84** D4
Mergui *Myanmar* 12°26N 98°34E **38** F2
Mergui Arch. = Myeik Kyunzu *Myanmar* 11°30N 97°30E **39** G1
Mérida *Mexico* 20°58N 89°37W **87** C7
Mérida *Spain* 38°55N 6°25W **21** C2
Mérida *Venezuela* 8°24N 71°8W **92** B4
Mérida, Cord. de *Venezuela* 9°0N 71°0W **92** B4
Meriden *U.K.* 52°26N 1°38W **13** E6
Meriden *U.S.A.* 41°32N 72°48W **83** E12
Meridian *Calif., U.S.A.* 39°9N 121°55W **78** F5
Meridian *Idaho, U.S.A.* 43°37N 116°24W **76** E5
Meridian *Miss., U.S.A.* 32°22N 88°42W **85** E10
Merinda *Australia* 20°2S 148°11E **62** C4
Merir *Palau* 4°10N 132°30E **37** D8
Merirumã *Brazil* 1°15N 54°50W **93** C8
Merkel *U.S.A.* 32°28N 100°1W **84** E4
Mermaid Reef *Australia* 17°6S 119°36E **60** C2
Meroe *India* 7°33N 93°33E **45** L11
Merowe Dam *Sudan* 18°35N 31°56E **53** E12
Merredin *Australia* 31°28S 118°18E **61** F2
Merrick *U.K.* 55°8N 4°28W **11** F4
Merrickville *Canada* 44°55N 75°50W **83** B9
Merrill *Oreg., U.S.A.* 42°1N 121°36W **76** E3
Merrill *Wis., U.S.A.* 45°11N 89°41W **80** C9
Merrimack → *U.S.A.* 42°49N 70°49W **83** D14
Merriman *U.S.A.* 42°55N 101°42W **80** D3
Merritt *Canada* 50°10N 120°45W **70** C4
Merritt Island *U.S.A.* 28°21N 80°42W **85** G14
Merriwa *Australia* 32°6S 150°22E **63** E5
Merry I. *Canada* 55°29N 77°31W **72** A4
Merryville *U.S.A.* 30°45N 93°33W **84** F8
Mersch *Lux.* 49°44N 6°7E **15** E6
Mersea I. *U.K.* 51°47N 0°58E **13** F8
Merseburg *Germany* 51°22N 11°59E **16** C6
Mersey → *U.K.* 53°25N 3°1W **12** D4
Merseyside □ *U.K.* 53°31N 3°2W **12** D4
Mersin *Turkey* 36°51N 34°36E **46** B2
Mersing *Malaysia* 2°25N 103°50E **39** L4
Merta *India* 26°39N 74°4E **42** F6
Merta Road *India* 26°43N 73°55E **42** F5
Merthyr Tydfil *U.K.* 51°45N 3°22W **13** F4
Merthyr Tydfil □ *U.K.* 51°46N 3°21W **13** F4
Mértola *Portugal* 37°40N 7°40W **21** D2
Mertz Glacier *Antarctica* 67°30S 144°45E **5** C10
Mertzon *U.S.A.* 31°16N 100°49W **84** F4
Meru *Kenya* 0°3N 37°40E **54** D7
Meru *Tanzania* 3°15S 36°46E **54** E7
Meru Betiri △ *Indonesia* 8°27S 113°51E **37** H15
Mesa *U.S.A.* 33°25N 111°50W **77** K8
Mesa Verde △ *U.S.A.* 37°11N 108°29W **77** H9
Mesada = Masada *Israel* 31°18N 35°21E **48** D4
Mesgouez, L. *Canada* 51°20N 75°0W **72** B5
Meshed = Mashhad *Iran* 36°20N 59°35E **47** B8
Meshgīn Shahr *Iran* 38°30N 47°45E **46** B5
Meshoppen *U.S.A.* 41°36N 76°3W **83** E8
Mesilinka → *Canada* 56°6N 124°30W **70** B4
Mesolongi *Greece* 38°21N 21°28E **23** E9
Mesopotamia = Al Jazirah *Iraq* 33°30N 44°0E **46** C5
Mesopotamia *U.S.A.* 41°27N 80°57W **82** E4
Mesquite *Nev., U.S.A.* 36°48N 114°4W **77** H6
Mesquite *Tex., U.S.A.* 32°47N 96°36W **84** E6
Messaad *Algeria* 34°8N 3°30E **52** B6
Messalo → *Mozam.* 12°25S 39°15E **55** G7
Messene *Greece* 37°4N 22°1E **23** F10
Messina = Musina *S. Africa* 22°20S 30°5E **57** B5
Messina *Italy* 38°11N 15°34E **22** E6
Messina, Str. di *Italy* 38°15N 15°35E **22** F6
Messiniakos Kolpos *Greece* 36°45N 22°5E **23** F10
Mesta = Nestos → *Europe* 40°54N 24°49E **23** D11
Meta → *S. Amer.* 6°12N 67°28W **92** B5
Meta Incognita Pen. *Canada* 62°45N 68°30W **69** E18
Metabetchouan *Canada* 48°26N 71°52W **73** C5
Metaline Falls *U.S.A.* 48°52N 117°22W **76** B5
Metán *Argentina* 25°30S 65°0W **94** B3
Metcalfe *Canada* 45°14N 75°28W **83** A9
Metema *Ethiopia* 12°58N 36°12E **49** E2
Methven *N.Z.* 43°38S 171°40E **59** E3
Metlakatla *U.S.A.* 55°8N 131°35W **68** F5
Metropolis *U.S.A.* 37°9N 88°44W **80** G9
Metropolitana □ *Chile* 33°30S 70°50W **94** C1
Mettuppalaiyam *India* 11°18N 76°59E **45** J3
Mettur *India* 11°48N 77°47E **45** J3
Metu *Ethiopia* 8°18N 35°35E **49** F2
Metz *France* 49°8N 6°10E **20** B7
Meulaboh *Indonesia* 4°11N 96°3E **36** D1
Meureudu *Indonesia* 5°19N 96°10E **36** C1
Meuse → *Europe* 50°45N 5°41E **15** D5
Mexia *U.S.A.* 31°41N 96°29W **84** F6
Mexiana, I. *Brazil* 0°0 49°30W **93** D9
Mexicali *Mexico* 32°40N 115°30W **79** N11
Mexican Plateau *Mexico* 25°0N 104°0W **66** G9
Mexican Water *U.S.A.* 36°57N 109°32W **77** H9
Mexico *Maine, U.S.A.* 44°34N 70°33W **83** B14
Mexico *Mo., U.S.A.* 39°10N 91°53W **80** F8
Mexico *N.Y., U.S.A.* 43°28N 76°14W **83** C8
México □ *Mexico* 19°20N 99°30W **87** D5
Mexico ■ *Cent. Amer.* 25°0N 105°0W **86** C4
Mexico, G. of *Cent. Amer.* 25°0N 90°0W **87** C7
Mexico B. *U.S.A.* 43°35N 76°20W **83** C8
Meydān-e Naftūn *Iran* 31°56N 49°18E **47** D6
Meydani, Ra's-e *Iran* 25°24N 59°6E **47** E8
Meyers Chuck *U.S.A.* 55°45N 132°15W **70** B2
Meymaneh *Afghan.* 35°53N 64°38E **40** B4
Mezen *Russia* 65°50N 44°20E **18** A7
Mezen → *Russia* 65°44N 44°22E **18** A7
Mézenc, Mt. *France* 44°54N 4°11E **20** D6
Mezhdurechensk *Russia* 53°41N 88°3E **26** D9
Mezhdurechenskiy *Russia* 59°36N 65°56E **26** D7
Mezőkövesd *Hungary* 47°49N 20°35E **17** E11
Mezőtúr *Hungary* 47°1N 20°41E **17** E11
Mezquital *Mexico* 23°29N 104°23W **86** C4
Mfolozi → *S. Africa* 28°25S 32°26E **57** C5
Mhow *India* 22°33N 75°50E **42** H6
Miahuatlán *Mexico* 16°20N 96°36W **87** D5
Miami *Fla., U.S.A.* 25°46N 80°11W **85** J14
Miami *Okla., U.S.A.* 36°53N 94°53W **84** C7
Miami *Tex., U.S.A.* 35°42N 100°38W **84** D4
Mian Xian *China* 33°10N 106°32E **34** A6
Mianchi *China* 34°48N 111°48E **32** G6
Mīāndarreh *Iran* 35°37N 53°39E **47** C7
Mīāndowāb *Iran* 37°0N 46°5E **46** B5
Miandrivazo *Madag.* 19°31S 45°29E **55** H9
Mīāneh *Iran* 37°30N 47°40E **46** B5
Mianning *China* 28°32N 102°9E **34** C4
Mianwali *Pakistan* 32°38N 71°28E **42** C4
Mianyang *China* 31°22N 104°47E **34** B5
Mianzhu *China* 31°22N 104°7E **34** B5
Miao Ling *China* 26°5N 107°30E **34** D6
Miaodao Qundao *China* 38°10N 120°45E **33** E11
Miaoli *Taiwan* 24°37N 120°49E **35** E13
Miass *Russia* 54°59N 60°6E **18** D11
Mica *S. Africa* 24°10S 30°48E **57** B5
Michalovce *Slovakia* 48°47N 21°58E **17** D11
Michigan □ *U.S.A.* 44°0N 85°0W **81** C11
Michigan, L. *U.S.A.* 44°0N 87°0W **80** D10
Michigan City *U.S.A.* 41°43N 86°54W **80** E10
Michipicoten I. *Canada* 47°40N 85°40W **72** C2
Michoacán □ *Mexico* 19°10N 101°50W **86** D4
Michurin *Bulgaria* 42°9N 27°51E **23** C12
Michurinsk *Russia* 52°58N 40°27E **18** D7
Micoud *St. Lucia* 13°49N 60°54W **89** f
Micronesia *Pac. Oc.* 11°0N 160°0E **64** G7
Micronesia, Federated States of ■ *Pac. Oc.* 9°0N 150°0E **64** G7
Mid-Indian Ridge *Ind. Oc.* 30°0S 75°0E **64** M1
Mid-Oceanic Ridge *Ind. Oc.* 42°0S 90°0E **64** M1
Mid-Pacific Seamounts *Pac. Oc.* 18°0N 177°0W **64** F10
Midai *Indonesia* 3°0N 107°47E **36** D3
Midale *Canada* 49°25N 103°20W **71** D8
Middelburg *Neths.* 51°30N 3°36E **15** C3
Middelburg *Eastern Cape, S. Africa* 31°30S 25°0E **56** D4
Middelburg *Mpumalanga, S. Africa* 25°49S 29°28E **57** C4
Middelpos *S. Africa* 31°55S 20°13E **56** D3
Middelwit *S. Africa* 24°51S 27°3E **56** B4
Middle Alkali L. *U.S.A.* 41°27N 120°5W **76** F3
Middle America Trench = Guatemala Trench *Pac. Oc.* 14°0N 95°0W **66** H10
Middle Andaman I. *India* 12°30N 92°50E **45** H11
Middle Bass I. *U.S.A.* 41°41N 82°48W **82** E2
Middle East *Asia* 35°0N 40°0E **24** E5
Middle Fork Feather → *U.S.A.* 38°33N 121°30W **78** F5
Middle I. *Australia* 34°6S 123°11E **61** F3
Middle Loup → *U.S.A.* 41°17N 98°24W **80** E4
Middleboro *U.S.A.* 41°54N 70°55W **83** E14
Middleburg *Fla., U.S.A.* 30°4N 81°52W **85** F14
Middleburg *Pa., U.S.A.* 40°47N 77°3W **82** F7
Middleburgh *U.S.A.* 42°36N 74°20W **83** D10
Middlebury *U.S.A.* 44°1N 73°10W **83** B11
Middlefield *U.S.A.* 41°27N 81°4W **82** E3
Middlemount *Australia* 22°50S 148°40E **62** C4
Middleport *N.Y., U.S.A.* 43°13N 78°29W **82** C6
Middleport *Ohio, U.S.A.* 39°0N 82°3W **81** F12
Middlesboro *U.S.A.* 36°36N 83°43W **81** G12
Middlesbrough *U.K.* 54°35N 1°13W **12** C6
Middlesbrough □ *U.K.* 54°28N 1°13W **12** C6
Middlesex *Belize* 17°2N 88°31W **88** C2
Middlesex *N.J., U.S.A.* 40°36N 74°30W **83** F10
Middlesex *N.Y., U.S.A.* 42°42N 77°16W **82** D7
Middleton *Australia* 22°22S 141°32E **62** C3
Middleton *Canada* 44°57N 65°4W **73** D6
Middleton Cr. → *Australia* 22°35S 141°51E **62** C3
Middleton I. *U.S.A.* 59°26N 146°20W **74** D10
Middletown *U.K.* 54°17N 6°51W **10** B5
Middletown *Calif., U.S.A.* 38°45N 122°37W **78** G4
Middletown *Conn., U.S.A.* 41°34N 72°39W **83** E12
Middletown *N.Y., U.S.A.* 41°27N 74°25W **83** E10
Middletown *Ohio, U.S.A.* 39°31N 84°24W **81** F11
Middletown *Pa., U.S.A.* 40°12N 76°44W **83** F8
Midge Point *Australia* 20°39S 148°43E **62** b
Midhurst *Canada* 44°26N 79°43W **82** B5
Midhurst *U.K.* 50°59N 0°44W **13** G7
Midi, Canal du → *France* 43°45N 1°21E **20** E4
Midland *Australia* 31°54S 116°1E **61** F2
Midland *Canada* 44°45N 79°50W **82** B5
Midland *Calif., U.S.A.* 33°52N 114°48W **79** M12
Midland *Mich., U.S.A.* 43°37N 84°14W **81** D11
Midland *Pa., U.S.A.* 40°39N 80°27W **82** F4
Midland *Tex., U.S.A.* 32°0N 102°3W **84** F3
Midleton *Ireland* 51°55N 8°10W **10** E3
Midlothian □ *U.K.* 55°51N 3°5W **11** F5
Midnapore = Medinipur *India* 22°25N 87°21E **43** H12
Midu *China* 25°18N 100°30E **34** E3
Midway Is. *Pac. Oc.* 28°13N 177°22W **75** K4
Midway Wells *U.S.A.* 32°41N 115°7W **79** N11
Midwest *U.S.A.* 42°0N 90°0W **75** G22
Midwest *Wyo., U.S.A.* 43°25N 106°16W **76** E10
Midwest City *U.S.A.* 35°27N 97°24W **84** D6
Midyat *Turkey* 37°25N 41°23E **46** B4
Midžor *Bulgaria* 43°24N 22°40E **23** C10
Mie □ *Japan* 34°30N 136°10E **29** G8
Międzychód *Poland* 52°35N 15°53E **16** B8
Międzyrzec Podlaski *Poland* 51°58N 22°45E **17** C12
Mielec *Poland* 50°15N 21°25E **17** C11
Mienga *Angola* 17°12S 19°48E **56** A2
Miercurea-Ciuc *Romania* 46°21N 25°48E **17** E13
Mieres *Spain* 43°18N 5°48W **21** A3
Mifflintown *U.S.A.* 40°34N 77°24W **82** F7
Mifraz Ḥefa *Israel* 32°52N 35°0E **48** C4
Migang Shan *China* 35°32N 106°13E **32** G4
Miguasha △ *Canada* 48°5N 66°26W **73** C6
Miguel Alemán, Presa *Mexico* 18°15N 96°32W **87** D5
Miguel Hidalgo, Presa *Mexico* 26°30N 108°34W **86** B3
Mihara *Japan* 34°24N 133°5E **29** G6
Mikhaylovgrad = Montana *Bulgaria* 43°27N 23°16E **23** C10
Mikhaylovka *Russia* 50°3N 43°5E **19** D7
Mikkeli *Finland* 61°43N 27°15E **8** F22
Mikkwa → *Canada* 58°25N 114°46W **70** B6
Míkonos = Mykonos *Greece* 37°30N 25°25E **23** F11
Mikun *Russia* 62°20N 50°0E **18** B9
Milaca *U.S.A.* 45°45N 93°39W **80** C7
Milagro *Ecuador* 2°11S 79°36W **92** D3
Milan = Milano *Italy* 45°28N 9°10E **20** D8
Milan *Mo., U.S.A.* 40°12N 93°7W **80** E7
Milan *Tenn., U.S.A.* 35°55N 88°46W **85** D10
Milâs *Turkey* 37°20N 27°50E **23** F12
Milazzo *Italy* 38°13N 15°15E **22** E6
Milbank *U.S.A.* 45°13N 96°38W **80** C5
Milbanke Sd. *Canada* 52°19N 128°33W **70** C3
Milden *Canada* 51°29N 107°32W **71** C7
Mildenhall *U.K.* 52°21N 0°32E **13** E8
Mildmay *Canada* 44°3N 81°7W **82** B3
Mildura *Australia* 34°13S 142°9E **63** E3
Mile *China* 24°28N 103°20E **34** E4
Miles *Australia* 26°40S 150°9E **63** D5
Miles City *U.S.A.* 46°25N 105°51W **76** C11
Milestone *Canada* 49°59N 104°31W **71** D8
Miletus *Turkey* 37°30N 27°18E **23** F12
Milford *Calif., U.S.A.* 40°10N 120°22W **78** E6
Milford *Conn., U.S.A.* 41°14N 73°3W **83** E11
Milford *Del., U.S.A.* 38°55N 75°26W **81** F16
Milford *Mass., U.S.A.* 42°8N 71°31W **83** D13
Milford *N.H., U.S.A.* 42°50N 71°39W **83** D13
Milford *N.Y., U.S.A.* 42°35N 74°56W **83** D10
Milford *Pa., U.S.A.* 41°19N 74°48W **83** E10
Milford *Utah, U.S.A.* 38°24N 113°1W **76** G7
Milford Haven *U.K.* 51°42N 5°7W **13** F2
Milford Sd. *N.Z.* 44°41S 167°47E **59** F1
Milford Sound *N.Z.* 44°41S 167°55E **59** F1
Milḥ, Baḥr al = Razāzah, Buḥayrat ar *Iraq* 32°40N 43°35E **46** C4
Milikapiti *Australia* 11°26S 130°40E **60** B5
Miling *Australia* 30°30S 116°17E **61** F2
Milk River *Canada* 49°10N 112°5W **70** D6
Mill → *U.S.A.* 42°57N 83°23W **82** D1
Mill I. *Antarctica* 66°0S 101°30E **5** C8
Mill I. *Canada* 63°58N 77°47W **69** E16
Mill Valley *U.S.A.* 37°54N 122°32W **78** H4
Millau *France* 44°8N 3°4E **20** D5
Millbridge *Canada* 44°41N 77°36W **82** B7
Millbrook *Canada* 44°10N 78°29W **82** B6
Millbrook *Ala., U.S.A.* 32°29N 86°22W **85** E11
Millbrook *N.Y., U.S.A.* 41°47N 73°42W **83** E11
Mille Lacs, L. des *Canada* 48°45N 90°35W **72** C1
Mille Lacs L. *U.S.A.* 46°15N 93°39W **80** B7
Milledgeville *U.S.A.* 33°5N 83°14W **85** E13
Millen *U.S.A.* 32°48N 81°57W **85** E14
Millennium I. = Caroline I. *Kiribati* 9°58S 150°13W **65** H12
Miller *U.S.A.* 44°31N 98°59W **80** C4
Miller Lake *Canada* 45°6N 81°26W **82** A3
Millersburg *Ohio, U.S.A.* 40°33N 81°55W **82** F3
Millersburg *Pa., U.S.A.* 40°32N 76°58W **82** F8
Millerton *U.S.A.* 41°57N 73°31W **83** E11
Millerton L. *U.S.A.* 37°1N 119°41W **78** J7
Millet *St. Lucia* 13°55N 60°59W **89** f
Millheim *U.S.A.* 40°54N 77°29W **82** F7
Millicent *Australia* 37°34S 140°21E **63** F3
Millington *U.S.A.* 35°20N 89°53W **85** D10
Millinocket *U.S.A.* 45°39N 68°43W **81** C19
Millmerran *Australia* 27°53S 151°16E **63** D5
Millom *U.K.* 54°13N 3°16W **12** C4
Mills L. *Canada* 61°30N 118°20W **70** A5
Millsboro *U.S.A.* 40°0N 80°0W **82** G5
Millstream Chichester △ *Australia* 21°35S 117°6E **60** D2
Millstreet *Ireland* 52°4N 9°4W **10** D2
Millville *N.J., U.S.A.* 39°24N 75°2W **81** F16
Millville *Pa., U.S.A.* 41°7N 76°32W **83** E8
Millwood L. *U.S.A.* 33°42N 93°58W **84** E8
Milne → *Australia* 21°10S 137°33E **62** C2
Milo *U.S.A.* 45°15N 68°59W **81** C19
Milos *Greece* 36°44N 24°25E **23** F11
Milparinka *Australia* 29°46S 141°57E **63** D3
Milpitas *U.S.A.* 37°26N 121°55W **78** H5
Milton *N.S., Canada* 44°4N 64°45W **73** D7
Milton *Ont., Canada* 43°31N 79°53W **82** C5
Milton *N.Z.* 46°7S 169°59E **59** G2
Milton *Calif., U.S.A.* 38°3N 120°51W **78** G6
Milton *Fla., U.S.A.* 30°38N 87°3W **85** F11
Milton *Pa., U.S.A.* 41°1N 76°51W **82** F8
Milton *Vt., U.S.A.* 44°38N 73°7W **83** B11
Milton-Freewater *U.S.A.* 45°56N 118°23W **76** D4
Milton Keynes *U.K.* 52°1N 0°44W **13** E7
Milton Keynes □ *U.K.* 52°1N 0°44W **13** E7
Miltown Malbay *Ireland* 52°52N 9°24W **10** D2
Miluo *China* 29°0N 112°59E **35** C9
Milverton *Canada* 43°34N 80°55W **82** C4
Milwaukee *U.S.A.* 43°2N 87°54W **80** D10
Milwaukee Deep *Atl. Oc.* 19°50N 68°0W **89** C6
Milwaukie *U.S.A.* 45°26N 122°38W **78** E4
Mimili *Australia* 27°0S 132°42E **61** E5
Min Jiang → *Fujian, China* 26°0N 119°35E **35** E12
Min Jiang → *Sichuan, China* 28°45N 104°40E **34** C5
Min Xian *China* 34°25N 104°5E **32** G3
Mīnā' al Aḥmadī *Kuwait* 29°5N 48°10E **47** D6
Mīnā' Jabal 'Alī *U.A.E.* 25°2N 55°8E **47** E7
Mina Pirquitas *Argentina* 22°40S 66°30W **94** A2
Mīnā Su'ud *Si. Arabia* 28°45N 48°28E **47** D6
Minago → *Canada* 54°33N 98°59W **71** C9
Minaki *Canada* 49°59N 94°40W **71** D10
Minamata *Japan* 32°10N 130°30E **29** H5
Minami-Arapusa △ *Japan* 35°30N 138°9E **29** G9
Minami-Tori-Shima *Pac. Oc.* 24°20N 153°58E **64** E7
Minamiaizu *Japan* 37°12N 139°46E **29** F9
Minamiawaji *Japan* 34°10N 134°42E **29** G7
Minamisōma *Japan* 37°38N 140°58E **28** F10
Minas *Uruguay* 34°20S 55°10W **95** C4
Minas, Sierra de las *Guatemala* 15°9N 89°31W **88** C2
Minas Basin *Canada* 45°20N 64°12W **73** C7
Minas Gerais □ *Brazil* 18°50S 46°0W **93** G9
Minatitlán *Mexico* 17°59N 94°31W **87** D6
Minbu *Myanmar* 20°10N 94°52E **41** J19
Minchinabad *Pakistan* 30°10N 73°34E **42** D5
Mindanao *Phil.* 8°0N 125°0E **37** C7
Mindanao Sea = Bohol Sea *Phil.* 9°0N 124°0E **37** C6
Mindanao Trench *Pac. Oc.* 12°0N 126°6E **37** B7
Mindelo *Cabo Verde* 16°24N 25°0W **52** b
Minden *Canada* 44°55N 78°43W **82** B6
Minden *Germany* 52°17N 8°55E **16** B5
Minden *La., U.S.A.* 32°37N 93°17W **84** E8
Minden *Nev., U.S.A.* 38°57N 119°46W **78** G7
Mindibungu = Billiluna *Australia* 19°37S 127°41E **60** C4
Mindiptana *Indonesia* 5°55S 140°22E **37** F10
Mindoro *Phil.* 13°0N 121°0E **37** B6
Mindoro Str. *Phil.* 12°30N 120°30E **37** B6
Mine *Japan* 34°12N 131°7E **29** G5
Minehead *U.K.* 51°12N 3°29W **13** F4
Mineola *N.Y., U.S.A.* 40°44N 73°38W **83** F11
Mineola *Tex., U.S.A.* 32°40N 95°29W **84** E7
Mineral King *U.S.A.* 36°27N 118°36W **78** J8
Mineral Wells *U.S.A.* 32°48N 98°7W **84** E5
Miners Bay *Canada* 44°49N 78°46W **82** B6
Minersville *U.S.A.* 40°41N 76°16W **83** F8
Minerva *N.Y., U.S.A.* 43°47N 73°59W **83** C11
Minerva *Ohio, U.S.A.* 40°44N 81°6W **82** F3
Minetto *U.S.A.* 43°24N 76°28W **83** C8
Minfeng *China* 37°4N 82°46E **30** D5
Mingäçevir Su Anbarı *Azerbaijan* 40°57N 46°50E **19** F8
Mingan *Canada* 50°20N 64°0W **73** B7
Mingechaurskoye Vdkhr. = Mingäçevir Su Anbarı *Azerbaijan* 40°57N 46°50E **19** F8
Mingela *Australia* 19°52S 146°38E **62** B4
Mingenew *Australia* 29°12S 115°21E **61** E2
Mingera Cr. → *Australia* 20°38S 137°45E **62** C2
Minggang *China* 32°24N 114°3E **35** A10
Mingguang *China* 32°46N 117°59E **35** A11
Mingin *Myanmar* 22°50N 94°30E **41** H19
Minglun *China* 25°10N 108°21E **34** E7
Mingo Junction *U.S.A.* 40°19N 80°37W **82** F4
Mingora *Pakistan* 34°48N 72°22E **43** B5
Mingshan *China* 29°55N 103°10E **34** B4
Mingteke Daban = Mintaka Pass *Pakistan* 37°0N 74°58E **43** A6
Mingxi *China* 26°18N 117°12E **35** D11
Mingyuegue *China* 43°2N 128°50E **33** C15
Minhe *China* 36°9N 102°45E **30** D9
Minho = Miño → *Spain* 41°52N 8°40W **21** A2
Minho *Portugal* 41°25N 8°20W **21** B1
Minhou *China* 26°0N 119°15E **35** E12
Minicoy I. *India* 8°17N 73°2E **45** K1
Minidoka *U.S.A.* 42°45N 113°29W **76** E7
Minigwal, L. *Australia* 29°31S 123°14E **61** E3
Minilya → *Australia* 23°45S 114°0E **61** D1
Minilya Roadhouse *Australia* 23°55S 114°0E **61** D1
Minipi L. *Canada* 52°25N 60°45W **73** B7
Minjilang *Australia* 11°8S 132°33E **60** B5
Mink L. *Canada* 61°54N 117°40W **70** A5
Minna *Nigeria* 9°37N 6°30E **52** G7
Minneapolis *Kans., U.S.A.* 39°8N 97°42W **80** F5
Minneapolis *Minn., U.S.A.* 44°57N 93°16W **80** C7
Minneapolis-St. Paul Int. ✖ (MSP) *U.S.A.* 44°53N 93°13W **80** C7
Minnedosa *Canada* 50°14N 99°50W **71** C9
Minnesota □ *U.S.A.* 46°0N 94°15W **80** B6
Minnesota → *U.S.A.* 44°54N 93°9W **80** C7
Minnewaukan *U.S.A.* 48°4N 99°15W **80** A4
Minnipa *Australia* 32°51S 135°9E **63** E2
Minnitaki L. *Canada* 49°57N 92°10W **72** C1
Mino *Japan* 35°32N 136°55E **29** G8
Miño → *Spain* 41°52N 8°40W **21** A2
Minorca = Menorca *Spain* 40°0N 4°0E **21** C8
Minot *U.S.A.* 48°14N 101°18W **80** A3
Minqin *China* 38°38N 103°20E **32** E2
Minqing *China* 26°15N 118°50E **35** D12
Minsk *Belarus* 53°52N 27°30E **17** B14
Mińsk Mazowiecki *Poland* 52°10N 21°33E **17** B11
Mintabie *Australia* 27°15S 133°7E **63** D1
Mintaka Pass *Pakistan* 37°0N 74°58E **43** A6
Minto *Canada* 46°5N 66°5W **73** C6
Minto, L. *Canada* 57°13N 75°0W **72** A5
Minton *Canada* 49°10N 104°35W **71** D8
Minturn *U.S.A.* 39°35N 106°26W **76** G10
Minudasht *Iran* 37°17N 56°7E **47** B8
Minusinsk *Russia* 53°43N 91°20E **27** D10
Minutang *India* 28°15N 96°30E **41** E20
Minvoul *Gabon* 2°9N 12°8E **54** D2
Minya Konka = Gongga Shan *China* 29°40N 101°55E **34** C3
Minzhong *China* 22°37N 113°30E **31** a
Miquelon *Canada* 49°25N 76°27W **72** C4
Miquelon *St-P. & M.* 47°8N 56°22W **73** C8
Mir *Belarus* 53°27N 26°28E **17** B14
Mīr Kūh *Iran* 26°22N 58°55E **47** E8
Mīr Shahdād *Iran* 26°15N 58°29E **47** E8
Mira *Italy* 45°26N 12°8E **22** B5
Mira por vos Cay *Bahamas* 22°9N 74°30W **89** B5
Mirabello, Kolpos *Greece* 35°10N 25°50E **23** G11
Mirador-Río Azul △ *Guatemala* 17°45N 89°50W **88** C2
Miraj *India* 16°50N 74°45E **44** F2
Miram Shah *Pakistan* 33°0N 70°2E **42** C4
Miramar *Argentina* 38°15S 57°50W **94** D4
Miramar *Mozam.* 23°50S 35°35E **57** B6
Miramichi *Canada* 47°2N 65°28W **73** C6
Miramichi B. *Canada* 47°15N 65°0W **73** C7
Miranda *Brazil* 20°10S 56°15W **93** H7
Miranda → *Brazil* 19°25S 57°20W **92** G7
Miranda de Ebro *Spain* 42°41N 2°57W **21** A4
Miranda do Douro *Portugal* 41°30N 6°16W **21** B2
Mirandópolis *Brazil* 21°9S 51°6W **95** A5
Mirani *Australia* 21°8S 148°53E **62** b
Mirassol *Brazil* 20°46S 49°28W **95** A6
Mirbāṭ *Oman* 17°0N 54°45E **49** D5
Miri *Malaysia* 4°23N 113°59E **36** D4
Mirialguda *India* 16°52N 79°35E **44** F4
Miriam Vale *Australia* 24°20S 151°33E **62** C5
Mirigama *Sri Lanka* 7°15N 80°8E **45** L5
Mirim, L. *S. Amer.* 32°45S 52°50W **95** C5
Miriuwung Gajerrong ⚙ *Australia* 15°0S 128°45E **60** C4
Mīrjāveh *Iran* 29°1N 61°30E **47** D9
Mirnyy *Antarctica* 66°50S 92°30E **5** C14
Mirnyy *Russia* 62°33N 113°53E **27** C12
Mirokhan *Pakistan* 27°46N 68°6E **42** F3
Mirond L. *Canada* 55°6N 102°47W **71** B8
Mirpur *Pakistan* 33°32N 73°56E **43** C5
Mirpur Batoro *Pakistan* 24°44N 68°16E **42** G3
Mirpur Bibiwari *Pakistan* 28°33N 67°44E **42** E2
Mirpur Khas *Pakistan* 25°30N 69°0E **42** G3
Mirpur Sakro *Pakistan* 24°33N 67°41E **42** G2
Mirs Bay = Tai Pang Wan *China* 22°33N 114°24E **31** a
Mirtağ *Turkey* 38°23N 41°56E **46** B4
Mirtoo Sea *Greece* 37°0N 23°20E **23** F10
Miryang *S. Korea* 35°31N 128°44E **33** G15
Mirzapur *India* 25°10N 82°34E **43** G10
Mirzapur-cum-Vindhyachal = Mirzapur *India* 25°10N 82°34E **43** G10
Misantla *Mexico* 19°56N 96°50W **87** D5
Misawa *Japan* 40°41N 141°24E **28** D10
Miscou I. *Canada* 47°57N 64°31W **73** C7
Misha *India* 7°59N 93°20E **45** L10
Mish'āb, Ra's al *Si. Arabia* 28°15N 48°43E **47** D6
Mishan *China* 45°37N 131°48E **28** B5
Mishawaka *U.S.A.* 41°40N 86°11W **80** E10
Mishima *Japan* 35°10N 138°52E **29** G9
Misión *Mexico* 32°6N 116°53W **79** N10
Misiones □ *Argentina* 27°0S 55°0W **95** B5
Misiones □ *Paraguay* 27°0S 56°0W **94** B4
Miskah *Si. Arabia* 24°49N 42°56E **46** E4
Miskitos, Cayos *Nic.* 14°26N 82°50W **88** D3
Miskolc *Hungary* 48°7N 20°50E **17** D11
Misool *Indonesia* 1°52S 130°10E **37** E8
Mişr = Egypt ■ *Africa* 28°0N 31°0E **53** C12
Mişrātah *Libya* 32°24N 15°3E **53** B9
Missanabie *Canada* 48°20N 84°6W **72** C3
Missinaibi → *Canada* 50°43N 81°29W **72** B3
Missinaibi L. *Canada* 48°23N 83°40W **72** C3
Mission *Canada* 49°10N 122°15W **70** D4
Mission *S. Dak., U.S.A.* 43°18N 100°39W **80** D3
Mission *Tex., U.S.A.* 26°13N 98°20W **84** H5
Mission Beach *Australia* 17°53S 146°6E **62** B4
Mission Viejo *U.S.A.* 33°36N 117°40W **79** M9
Missisa L. *Canada* 52°20N 85°7W **72** B2
Missisicabi → *Canada* 51°14N 79°31W **72** B4

…i → Canada 46°15N 83°9W 72 C3
…ppi □ U.S.A. 33°0N 90°0W 85 E10
…ppi → U.S.A. 29°9N 89°15W 85 G10
…ppi L. Canada 45°5N 76°10W 83 A8
…sippi River Delta
…A. 29°10N 89°15W 85 G10
…sissippi Sd. U.S.A. 30°20N 89°0W 85 F10
…ssoula U.S.A. 46°52N 114°1W 76 C6
…ssouri □ U.S.A. 38°25N 92°30W 80 F7
…issouri → U.S.A. 38°49N 90°7W 80 F8
…issouri City U.S.A. 29°37N 95°32W 84 G7
…ssouri Valley U.S.A. 41°34N 95°53W 80 E6
…ist U.S.A. 45°59N 123°15W 78 E3
…istassibi → Canada 48°53N 72°13W 73 B5
Mistassini Canada 48°53N 72°12W 73 C5
Mistassini → Canada 48°42N 72°20W 73 C5
Mistassini, L. Canada 51°0N 73°30W 72 B5
Mistastin L. Canada 55°57N 63°20W 73 A7
Mistinibi, L. Canada 55°56N 64°17W 73 A7
Mistissini Canada 48°53N 72°12W 73 C5
Misty L. Canada 58°53N 101°40W 71 B8
Misurata = Mişrātah
Libya 32°24N 15°3E 53 B9
Mitchell Australia 26°29S 147°58E 63 D4
Mitchell Canada 43°28N 81°12W 82 C3
Mitchell Nebr., U.S.A. 41°57N 103°49W 80 E2
Mitchell Oreg., U.S.A. 44°34N 120°9W 76 D3
Mitchell S. Dak., U.S.A. 43°43N 98°2W 80 D4
Mitchell → Australia 15°12S 141°35E 62 B3
Mitchell, Mt. U.S.A. 35°46N 82°16W 85 D13
Mitchell-Alice Rivers △
Australia 15°28S 142°5E 62 B3
Mitchell Ra. Australia 12°49S 135°36E 62 A2
Mitchelstown Ireland 52°15N 8°16W 10 D3
Mitha Tiwana Pakistan 32°13N 72°6E 42 C5
Mithi Pakistan 24°44N 69°48E 42 G3
Mithrao Pakistan 27°28N 69°40E 42 F3
Mitilini Greece 39°6N 26°35E 23 E12
Mitla Pass = Mamarr Mitlā
Egypt 30°2N 32°54E 48 E1
Mito Japan 36°20N 140°30E 29 F10
Mitrovicë Kosovo 42°54N 20°52E 23 C9
Mitsamiouli Comoros Is. 11°20S 43°16E 55 a
Mitsiwa Eritrea 15°35N 39°25E 49 D2
Mitsukaidō Japan 36°1N 139°59E 29 F9
Mittagong Australia 34°28S 150°29E 63 E5
Mittimatalik = Pond Inlet
Canada 72°40N 77°0W 69 C16
Mitú Colombia 1°15N 70°13W 92 C4
Mitumba, Mts.
Dem. Rep. of the Congo 7°0S 27°30E 54 F5
Mitwaba
Dem. Rep. of the Congo 8°2S 27°17E 54 F5
Mixteco → Mexico 18°11N 98°30W 87 D5
Miyagi □ Japan 38°15N 140°45E 28 E10
Miyāh, W. el → Syria 34°44N 39°57E 46 C3
Miyake-Jima Japan 34°5N 139°30E 29 G9
Miyako Japan 39°40N 141°59E 28 E10
Miyako-Jima Japan 24°45N 125°20E 29 M2
Miyako-Rettō Japan 24°24N 125°0E 29 M2
Miyakojima Japan 24°48N 125°17E 29 M2
Miyakonojō Japan 31°40N 131°5E 29 J5
Miyani India 21°50N 69°26E 42 J3
Miyanoura-Dake Japan 30°20N 130°31E 29 J5
Miyazaki Japan 31°56N 131°30E 29 J5
Miyazaki □ Japan 32°30N 131°30E 29 H5
Miyazu Japan 35°35N 135°10E 29 G7
Miyet, Bahr el = Dead Sea
Asia 31°30N 35°30E 48 D4
Miyi China 26°47N 102°9E 34 D4
Miyoshi Japan 34°48N 132°51E 29 G6
Miyun China 40°28N 116°50E 32 D9
Miyun Shuiku China 40°30N 117°0E 33 D9
Mizdah Libya 31°30N 13°0E 53 B8
Mizen Hd. Cork, Ireland 51°27N 9°50W 10 E2
Mizen Hd. Wicklow, Ireland 52°51N 6°4W 10 D5
Mizhi China 37°47N 110°12E 32 F6
Mizoram □ India 23°30N 92°40E 41 H18
Mizpe Ramon Israel 30°34N 34°49E 48 E3
Mizuho Antarctica 70°30S 41°0E 5 D5
Mizusawa = Ōshū Japan 39°8N 141°8E 28 E10
Mjölby Sweden 58°20N 15°10E 9 G16
Mjøsa Norway 60°40N 11°0E 8 F14
Mkhaya ⌂ Eswatini 26°34S 31°45E 57 C5
Mkhuze ⌂ S. Africa 29°27S 29°30E 57 C4
Mkomazi → S. Africa 30°12S 30°50E 57 D5
Mkuze S. Africa 27°10S 32°0E 57 C5
Mladá Boleslav Czechia 50°27N 14°53E 16 C8
Mlange = Mulanje, Mt.
Malawi 16°2S 35°33E 55 H7
Mława Poland 53°9N 20°25E 17 B11
Mlawula ⌂ Eswatini 26°12S 32°2E 57 C5
Mljet Croatia 42°43N 17°30E 22 C7
Mmabatho S. Africa 25°49S 25°30E 56 C4
Mo i Rana Norway 66°20N 14°7E 8 C16
Moa Australia 10°11S 142°16E 62 a
Moa Cuba 20°40N 74°56W 89 B4
Moa Indonesia 8°0S 128°0E 37 F7
Moa → S. Leone 6°59N 11°36W 52 G3
Moab U.S.A. 38°35N 109°33W 76 G9
Moala Fiji 18°36S 179°53E 59 a
Moama Australia 36°7S 144°46E 63 F3
Moamba Mozam. 25°36S 32°15E 57 C5
Moapa U.S.A. 36°40N 114°37W 79 J12
Moate Ireland 53°24N 7°44W 10 C4
Mobārakābād Iran 28°24N 53°20E 47 D7
Mobaye C.A.R. 4°25N 21°5E 54 D4
Moberly U.S.A. 39°25N 92°26W 80 F7
Moberly Lake Canada 55°50N 121°44W 70 B4
Mobile U.S.A. 30°41N 88°3W 85 F10
Mobile B. U.S.A. 30°30N 88°0W 85 F11
Mobridge U.S.A. 45°32N 100°26W 80 C3
Moc Chau Vietnam 20°50N 104°38E 38 B5
Moc Hoa Vietnam 10°46N 105°56E 39 G5
Moçambique = Mozambique ■
Africa 19°0S 35°0E 55 H7
Moçambique Mozam. 15°3S 40°42E 55 H8
Mocanaqua U.S.A. 41°9N 76°8W 83 E8
Moce Fiji 18°40S 178°29W 59 a
Mochima △ Venezuela 10°30N 64°5W 89 D7
Mochudi Botswana 24°27S 26°7E 56 B4
Mocimboa da Praia
Mozam. 11°25S 40°20E 54 G8
Moclips U.S.A. 47°14N 124°13W 78 C2
Mocoa Colombia 1°7N 76°35W 92 C3
Mococa Brazil 21°28S 47°0W 95 A6
Mocorito Mexico 25°29N 107°55W 86 B3
Moctezuma Mexico 29°48N 109°42W 86 B3
Moctezuma → Mexico 21°59N 98°34W 87 C5
Mocuba Mozam. 16°54S 36°57E 55 H7
Modane France 45°12N 6°40E 20 D7
Modasa India 23°30N 73°21E 42 H5
Modder → S. Africa 29°2S 24°37E 56 C3
Modderrivier S. Africa 29°2S 24°38E 56 C3
Módena Italy 44°40N 10°55E 22 B4
Modena U.S.A. 37°48N 113°56W 77 H7
Modesto U.S.A. 37°39N 121°0W 78 H6
Módica Italy 36°52N 14°46E 22 F6
Modimolle S. Africa 24°42S 28°22E 57 B4
Modjadjiskloof S. Africa 23°42S 30°10E 57 B5
Moe Australia 38°12S 146°19E 63 F4
Moengo Suriname 5°45N 54°20W 93 B8
Moenjodaro = Mohenjodaro
Pakistan 27°19N 68°7E 42 F3
Moffat U.K. 55°21N 3°27W 11 F5
Moga India 30°48N 75°8E 42 D6
Mogadishu = Muqdisho
Somalia 2°2N 45°25E 49 G4
Mogador = Essaouira
Morocco 31°32N 9°42W 52 B4
Mogalakwena →
S. Africa 22°38S 28°40E 57 B4
Mogami-Gawa → Japan 38°45N 140°0E 28 E10
Mogaung Myanmar 25°20N 97°0E 41 G20
Mogi-Mirim Brazil 22°29S 47°0W 93 H9
Mogilev = Mahilyow
Belarus 53°55N 30°18E 17 B16
Mogilev-Podilskiy = Mohyliv-
Podilskyy Ukraine 48°26N 27°48E 17 D14
Mogocha Russia 53°40N 119°50E 27 D12
Mogoditshane Botswana 24°37S 25°51E 56 B4
Mogok Myanmar 23°0N 96°40E 41 H20
Mogollon Rim U.S.A. 34°10N 110°50W 77 J8
Mogumber Australia 31°2S 116°3E 61 F2
Mogwadi → S. Africa 23°4S 29°36E 57 B4
Mohács Hungary 45°58N 18°41E 17 F10
Mohala India 20°35N 80°44E 44 D5
Mohales Hoek Lesotho 30°7S 27°26E 56 D4
Mohali = Ajitgarh India 30°47N 76°41E 42 D7
Mohall U.S.A. 48°46N 101°31W 80 A3
Moḥammadābād Iran 37°52N 59°5E 47 B8
Mohammedia Morocco 33°44N 7°21W 52 B4
Mohana India 19°27N 84°16E 44 E7
Mohana → India 24°43N 85°0E 43 G11
Mohanlalganj India 26°41N 80°58E 43 F9
Mohave, L. U.S.A. 35°12N 114°34W 79 K12
Mohawk → U.S.A. 42°47N 73°41W 83 D11
Mohéli Comoros Is. 12°20S 43°40E 55 a
Mohenjodaro Pakistan 27°19N 68°7E 42 F3
Moher, Cliffs of Ireland 52°58N 9°27W 10 D2
Mohicanville Res. U.S.A. 40°45N 82°9W 82 F2
Mohns Ridge Arctic 72°30N 5°0W 4 B7
Mohsenābād Iran 36°40N 59°35E 47 B8
Mohyliv-Podilskyy
Ukraine 48°26N 27°48E 17 D14
Moidart, L. U.K. 56°47N 5°52W 11 E3
Moinabad India 17°44N 77°16E 44 F3
Moira → Canada 44°21N 77°24W 82 B7
Moisaküla Estonia 58°3N 25°12E 9 G21
Moisie Canada 50°12N 66°1W 73 B6
Moisie → Canada 50°14N 66°5W 73 B6
Mojave U.S.A. 35°3N 118°10W 79 K8
Mojave ⌂ U.S.A. 35°7N 115°32W 79 K11
Mojave Desert U.S.A. 35°0N 116°30W 79 L10
Moji das Cruzes Brazil 23°31S 46°11W 95 A6
Moji-Guaçu → Brazil 20°53S 48°10W 95 A6
Mojiang China 23°37N 101°35E 34 F3
Mojo Bolivia 21°48S 65°33W 94 A2
Mojokerto Indonesia 7°28S 112°26E 37 G15
Mokai N.Z. 38°32S 175°56E 59 C5
Mokala △ S. Africa 29°10S 24°10E 56 C3
Mokameh India 25°24N 85°55E 43 G11
Mokau N.Z. 38°42S 174°39E 59 C5
Mokelumne → U.S.A. 38°13N 121°28W 78 G5
Mokelumne Hill U.S.A. 38°18N 120°43W 78 G6
Mokhotlong Lesotho 29°22S 29°2E 57 C4
Mokoan, L. Australia 36°27S 146°5E 63 C4
Mokokchung India 26°15N 94°30E 41 F19
Mokolo → S. Africa 23°14S 27°43E 57 B4
Mokopane S. Africa 24°10S 28°55E 57 B4
Mokpo S. Korea 34°50N 126°25E 33 G14
Mokra Gora Europe 42°50N 20°30E 23 C9
Mol Belgium 51°11N 5°5E 15 C5
Molakalmuru India 14°55N 76°50E 45 G3
Molchanovo Russia 57°40N 83°50E 26 D9
Mold U.K. 53°9N 3°8W 12 D4
Moldavia = Moldova ■
Europe 47°0N 28°0E 17 E15
Moldavia Romania 46°30N 27°0E 17 E14
Molde Norway 62°45N 7°9E 8 E12
Moldova ■ Europe 47°0N 28°0E 17 E15
Moldoveanu, Vf.
Romania 45°36N 24°45E 17 F13
Mole → U.K. 51°24N 0°21W 13 F7
Molepolole Botswana 24°28S 25°28E 56 B4
Molfetta Italy 41°12N 16°36E 22 D7
Moline U.S.A. 41°30N 90°31W 80 E8
Molinos Argentina 25°28S 66°15W 94 B2
Mollendo Peru 17°0S 72°0W 92 G4
Mollerin, L. Australia 30°30S 117°35E 61 F2
Molodechno = Maladzyechna
Belarus 54°20N 26°50E 17 A14
Molodezhnaya Antarctica 67°40S 45°51E 5 C9
Moloka'i U.S.A. 21°8N 157°0W 75 L8
Molokai Fracture Zone
Pac. Oc. 28°0N 125°0W 65 E15
Molong Australia 33°5S 148°54E 63 E4
Molopo → Africa 27°30S 20°12E 56 C3
Molson L. Canada 54°22N 96°40W 71 C9
Molteno S. Africa 31°22S 26°22E 56 D4
Molu Indonesia 6°45S 131°40E 37 F8
Molucca Sea Indonesia 0°0 125°0E 37 E6
Moluccas = Maluku
Indonesia 1°0S 127°0E 37 E7
Moma Mozam. 16°47S 39°4E 55 H7
Mombasa Kenya 4°3S 39°40E 54 E7
Mombetsu Japan 44°21N 143°22E 28 B11
Momchilgrad Bulgaria 41°33N 25°23E 23 D11
Mompós Colombia 9°14N 74°26W 92 B4
Møn Denmark 54°57N 12°20E 9 J15
Mon □ Myanmar 16°0N 97°30E 41 L20
Mona, Canal de la = Mona
Passage W. Indies 18°30N 67°45W 89 C6
Mona, Isla Puerto Rico 18°5N 67°54W 89 C6
Mona, Pta. Costa Rica 9°37N 82°36W 88 E3
Mona Passage W. Indies 18°30N 67°45W 89 C6
Monaca U.S.A. 40°41N 80°17W 82 F4
Monaco ■ Europe 43°46N 7°23E 20 E7
Monadhliath Mts. U.K. 57°10N 4°4W 11 D4
Monadnock, Mt. U.S.A. 42°52N 72°7W 83 D12
Monaghan Ireland 54°15N 6°57W 10 B5
Monaghan □ Ireland 54°11N 6°56W 10 B5
Monahans U.S.A. 31°36N 102°54W 84 F3
Monar, L. U.K. 57°26N 5°8W 11 D3
Monaragala Sri Lanka 6°52N 81°22E 45 L5
Monarch Mt. Canada 51°55N 125°57W 70 C3
Monashee Mts. Canada 51°0N 118°43W 70 C5
Monasterevin Ireland 53°8N 7°4W 10 C4
Monastir = Bitola
Macedonia 41°1N 21°20E 23 D9
Monastir Tunisia 35°50N 10°49E 53 A8
Monbetsu = Hidaka
Japan 42°30N 142°10E 28 C11
Moncayo, Sierra del Spain 41°48N 1°50W 21 B5
Monchegorsk Russia 67°54N 32°58E 8 C25
Mönchengladbach
Germany 51°11N 6°27E 16 C4
Monchique Portugal 37°19N 8°38W 21 D1
Moncks Corner U.S.A. 33°12N 80°1W 85 E14
Monclova Mexico 26°54N 101°25W 86 B4
Moncton Canada 46°7N 64°51W 73 C7
Mondego → Portugal 40°9N 8°52W 21 B1
Mondeodo Indonesia 3°34S 122°9E 37 E6
Mondlo S. Africa 27°59S 30°43E 57 C5
Mondovì Italy 44°23N 7°49E 20 D7
Mondrain I. Australia 34°9S 122°14E 61 F3
Moneague Jamaica 18°16N 77°7W 88 a
Moneron, Ostrov
Russia 46°15N 141°16E 28 A10
Monessen U.S.A. 40°9N 79°54W 82 F5
Monett U.S.A. 36°55N 93°55W 80 G7
Moneymore U.K. 54°41N 6°40W 10 B5
Monforte de Lemos Spain 42°31N 7°33W 21 A2
Mong Hpayak Myanmar 20°52N 99°55E 38 B2
Mong Hsat Shan,
Myanmar 21°54N 98°30E 34 G2
Mong Hsat Shan,
Myanmar 20°31N 99°15E 38 B2
Mong Kung Myanmar 21°35N 97°35E 41 J20
Mong Nai Myanmar 20°32N 97°46E 41 J20
Mong Ping Myanmar 21°22N 99°2E 34 G2
Mong Tai = Shan □
Myanmar 21°30N 98°30E 41 J21
Mong Ton Myanmar 20°17N 98°45E 41 J21
Mong Yai Myanmar 22°21N 98°3E 41 H21
Mong Yang Myanmar 21°50N 99°41E 38 B2
Mongalla South Sudan 5°8N 31°42E 53 G12
Mongers, L. Australia 29°25S 117°5E 61 E2
Monghyr = Munger
India 25°23N 86°30E 43 G12
Mongibello = Etna Italy 37°50N 14°55E 22 F6
Mongo Chad 12°14N 18°43E 53 F9
Mongolia ■ Asia 47°0N 103°0E 30 B9
Mongolia, Plateau of
Asia 45°0N 105°0E 24 D12
Mongu Zambia 15°16S 23°12E 55 H4
Môngua Angola 16°43S 15°20E 56 A2
Monifieth U.K. 56°30N 2°48W 11 E6
Monkey Mia Australia 25°48S 113°43E 61 E1
Monkey River Belize 16°22N 88°29W 87 D7
Monkland Canada 45°11N 74°52W 83 A10
Monkoto
Dem. Rep. of the Congo 1°38S 20°35E 54 E4
Monkton Canada 43°35N 81°5W 82 C3
Monmouth U.K. 51°48N 2°42W 13 F5
Monmouth Ill., U.S.A. 40°55N 90°39W 80 E8
Monmouth Oreg.,
U.S.A. 44°51N 123°14W 76 D2
Monmouthshire □ U.K. 51°48N 2°54W 13 F5
Mono, Pta. Nic. 12°0N 83°30W 88 D3
Mono L. U.S.A. 38°1N 119°1W 78 H7
Monolith U.S.A. 35°7N 118°22W 79 K8
Monongahela U.S.A. 40°12N 79°56W 82 F5
Monópoli Italy 40°57N 17°18E 22 D7
Monos I. Trin. & Tob. 10°42N 61°44W 93 K15
Monroe Ga., U.S.A. 33°47N 83°43W 85 E13
Monroe La., U.S.A. 32°30N 92°7W 84 E8
Monroe Mich., U.S.A. 41°55N 83°24W 81 E12
Monroe N.C., U.S.A. 34°59N 80°33W 85 D14
Monroe N.Y., U.S.A. 41°20N 74°11W 83 E10
Monroe Utah, U.S.A. 38°38N 112°7W 76 G7
Monroe Wash., U.S.A. 47°51N 121°58W 78 C5
Monroe Wis., U.S.A. 42°36N 89°38W 80 D9
Monroe City U.S.A. 39°39N 91°44W 80 F8
Monroeton U.S.A. 41°43N 76°29W 83 E8
Monroeville Ala., U.S.A. 31°31N 87°20W 85 F11
Monroeville Pa., U.S.A. 40°26N 79°45W 82 F5
Monrovia Liberia 6°18N 10°47W 52 G3
Mons Belgium 50°27N 3°58E 15 D3
Monse Indonesia 4°7S 123°15E 37 E6
Mont-de-Marsan France 43°54N 0°31W 20 E3
Mont-Joli Canada 48°37N 68°10W 73 C6
Mont-Laurier Canada 46°35N 75°30W 72 C4
Mont-Louis Canada 49°15N 65°44W 73 C6
Mont-St-Michel, Le
France 48°40N 1°30W 20 B3
Mont-Tremblant ⌂
Canada 46°30N 74°30W 72 C5
Montagu S. Africa 33°45S 20°8E 56 D3
Montagu I. Antarctica 58°25S 26°20W 5 B1
Montague Canada 46°10N 62°39W 73 C7
Montague, I. Mexico 31°45N 114°48W 86 A2
Montague I. U.S.A. 60°0N 147°30W 74 D10
Montague Ra. Australia 27°15S 119°30E 61 E2
Montague Sd. Australia 14°28S 125°20E 60 B4
Montalbán Spain 40°50N 0°45W 21 B5
Montalvo U.S.A. 34°15N 119°12W 79 L7
Montana Bulgaria 43°27N 23°16E 23 C10
Montaña Peru 6°0S 73°0W 92 E4
Montana □ U.S.A. 47°0N 110°0W 76 C9
Montargis France 47°59N 2°43E 20 C5
Montauban France 44°2N 1°21E 20 D4
Montauk U.S.A. 41°3N 71°57W 83 E13
Montauk Pt. U.S.A. 41°4N 71°51W 83 E13
Montbéliard France 47°31N 6°48E 20 C7
Montceau-les-Mines
France 46°40N 4°23E 20 C6
Montclair U.S.A. 40°49N 74°12W 83 F10
Monte Albán Mexico 17°2N 96°46W 87 D5
Monte Alegre Brazil 2°0S 54°0W 93 D8
Monte Azul Brazil 15°9S 42°53W 93 G10
Monte-Carlo Monaco 43°44N 7°25E 20 E7
Monte Caseros Argentina 30°10S 57°50W 94 C4
Monte Comán Argentina 34°40S 67°53W 94 C2
Monte Cristi Dom. Rep. 19°52N 71°39W 89 C5
Monte Lindo →
Paraguay 23°56S 57°12W 94 A4
Monte Patria Chile 30°42S 70°58W 94 C1
Monte Quemado
Argentina 25°53S 62°41W 94 B3
Monte Rio U.S.A. 38°28N 123°0W 78 G4
Monte Santu, C. di Italy 40°5N 9°44E 22 D3
Monte Vista U.S.A. 37°35N 106°9W 77 H10
Monteagudo Argentina 27°14S 54°8W 95 B5
Montebello Canada 45°40N 74°55W 72 C5
Montebello Is. Australia 20°30S 115°45E 60 D2
Montecarlo Argentina 26°34S 54°47W 95 B5
Montecito U.S.A. 34°26N 119°40W 79 L7
Montecristo Italy 42°20N 10°19E 22 C4
Montego Bay Jamaica 18°28N 77°55W 88 a
Montélimar France 44°33N 4°45E 20 D6
Montello U.S.A. 43°48N 89°20W 80 D9
Montemorelos Mexico 25°12N 99°49W 87 B5
Montenegro Brazil 29°39S 51°29W 95 B5
Montenegro ■ Europe 42°40N 19°20E 23 C8
Montepuez Mozam. 13°8S 38°59E 55 G7
Monterey U.S.A. 36°37N 121°55W 78 J5
Monterey B. U.S.A. 36°45N 122°0W 78 J5
Montería Colombia 8°46N 75°53W 92 B3
Monteros Argentina 27°11S 65°30W 94 B2
Monterrey Mexico 25°40N 100°19W 86 B4
Montes Azules ⌂ Mexico 16°21N 91°3W 87 D6
Montes Claros Brazil 16°30S 43°50W 93 G10
Montesano U.S.A. 46°59N 123°36W 78 D3
Montesilvano Italy 42°29N 14°8E 22 C6
Montevideo Uruguay 34°50S 56°11W 95 C4
Montevideo U.S.A. 44°57N 95°43W 80 C6
Montezuma U.S.A. 41°35N 92°32W 80 E7
Montezuma Castle ⌂
U.S.A. 34°39N 111°45W 77 J8
Montgomery U.K. 52°34N 3°8W 13 E4
Montgomery Ala.,
U.S.A. 32°23N 86°19W 85 E11
Montgomery Pa., U.S.A. 41°10N 76°53W 82 E8
Montgomery W. Va.,
U.S.A. 38°11N 81°19W 81 F13
Montgomery City U.S.A. 38°59N 91°30W 80 F8
Monticello Ark., U.S.A. 33°38N 91°47W 84 E9
Monticello Fla., U.S.A. 30°33N 83°52W 85 F13
Monticello Ind., U.S.A. 40°45N 86°46W 80 E10
Monticello Iowa, U.S.A. 42°15N 91°12W 80 D8
Monticello Ky., U.S.A. 36°50N 84°51W 81 G11
Monticello Minn., U.S.A. 45°18N 93°48W 80 C7
Monticello Miss., U.S.A. 31°33N 90°7W 85 F9
Monticello N.Y., U.S.A. 41°39N 74°42W 83 E10
Monticello Utah, U.S.A. 37°52N 109°21W 77 H9
Montijo Portugal 38°41N 8°54W 21 C1
Montilla Spain 37°36N 4°40W 21 D3
Montluçon France 46°22N 2°36E 20 C5
Montmagny Canada 46°58N 70°34W 73 C5
Montmartre Canada 50°14N 103°27W 71 C8
Montmorillon France 46°26N 0°50E 20 C4
Monto Australia 24°52S 151°6E 62 C5
Montongbuwoh Indonesia 8°33S 116°4E 37 K19
Montoro Spain 38°1N 4°27W 21 C3
Montour Falls U.S.A. 42°21N 76°51W 82 D8
Montoursville U.S.A. 41°15N 76°55W 82 E8
Montpelier Idaho, U.S.A. 42°19N 111°18W 76 E8
Montpelier Vt., U.S.A. 44°16N 72°35W 83 B12
Montpellier France 43°37N 3°52E 20 E5
Montreal → Canada 47°14N 84°39W 72 C3
Montréal L. Canada 54°20N 105°45W 71 C7
Montreal Lake Canada 54°3N 105°46W 71 C7
Montreux Switz. 46°26N 6°55E 20 C7
Montrose U.K. 56°44N 2°27W 11 E6
Montrose Colo., U.S.A. 38°29N 107°53W 76 G10
Montrose Pa., U.S.A. 41°50N 75°53W 83 E9
Monts, Pte. des Canada 49°20N 67°12W 73 C6
Montserrat ☒ W. Indies 16°40N 62°10W 89 C7
Monywa Myanmar 22°7N 95°11E 41 H19
Monze Zambia 16°17S 27°29E 55 H5
Monze, C. Pakistan 24°47N 66°37E 42 G2
Monzón Spain 41°52N 0°10E 21 B6
Mooers U.S.A. 44°58N 73°35W 83 B11
Mooi → S. Africa 28°45S 30°34E 57 C5
Mooi River S. Africa 29°13S 29°50E 57 C4
Mookgopong S. Africa 24°31S 28°44E 57 B4
Moomba Australia 28°6S 140°12E 63 A3
Moonah → Australia 22°3S 138°33E 62 C2
Moonda, L. Australia 25°52S 140°25E 62 D3
Moonie Australia 27°46S 150°20E 63 D5
Moonie → Australia 29°19S 148°43E 63 D4
Moonta Australia 34°6S 137°32E 63 E2
Moora Australia 30°37S 115°58E 61 F2
Moorcroft U.S.A. 44°16N 104°57W 76 D11
Moore → Australia 31°22S 115°30E 61 F2
Moore, L. Australia 29°50S 117°35E 61 E2
Moore Falls Canada 44°48N 78°48W 82 B6
Moore Park Australia 24°43S 152°17E 62 C5
Moore Res. U.S.A. 44°20N 71°53W 83 B13
Moore River △ Australia 31°7S 115°39E 61 F2
Moorea French Polynesia 17°30S 149°50W 59 d
Moorefield U.S.A. 39°4N 78°58W 81 F14
Moorfoot Hills U.K. 55°44N 3°8W 11 F5
Moorhead U.S.A. 46°53N 96°45W 80 B5
Moorpark U.S.A. 34°17N 118°53W 79 L8
Moorreesburg S. Africa 33°6S 18°38E 56 D2
Moorrinya △ Australia 21°42S 144°58E 62 C3
Moose → Canada 51°20N 80°25W 72 B3
Moose → U.S.A. 43°38N 75°24W 83 C9
Moose Creek Canada 45°15N 74°58W 83 A10
Moose Factory Canada 51°16N 80°32W 72 B3
Moose Jaw Canada 50°24N 105°30W 71 C7
Moose Jaw → Canada 50°34N 105°18W 71 C7
Moose Lake Canada 53°46N 100°8W 71 C8
Moose Lake U.S.A. 46°27N 92°46W 80 B7
Moose Mountain ⌂
Canada 49°48N 102°25W 71 D8
Moosehead L. U.S.A. 45°38N 69°40W 81 C19
Mooselookmeguntic L.
U.S.A. 44°55N 70°49W 83 B14
Moosilauke, Mt. U.S.A. 44°3N 71°40W 83 B13
Moosomin Canada 50°9N 101°40W 71 C8
Moosonee Canada 51°17N 80°39W 72 B3
Moosup U.S.A. 41°43N 71°53W 83 E13
Mopane S. Africa 22°37S 29°52E 57 B4
Mopipi Botswana 21°6S 24°55E 56 B3
Mopti Mali 14°30N 4°0W 52 F5
Moqor Afghan. 32°50N 67°42E 42 C2
Moquegua Peru 17°15S 70°46W 92 G4
Mora Sweden 61°2N 14°38E 8 F16
Mora Minn., U.S.A. 45°53N 93°18W 80 C7
Mora N. Mex., U.S.A. 35°58N 105°20W 77 J11
Moradabad India 28°50N 78°50E 43 E8
Morafenobe Madag. 17°50S 44°53E 55 H8
Moramanga Madag. 18°56S 48°12E 55 H9
Moran Kans., U.S.A. 37°55N 95°10W 80 G6
Moran Wyo., U.S.A. 43°50N 110°31W 76 E8
Moranbah Australia 22°1S 148°6E 62 C4
Morang = Biratnagar
Nepal 26°27N 87°17E 43 F12
Morant Bay Jamaica 17°53N 76°25W 88 a
Morant Cays Jamaica 17°22N 76°0W 88 C4
Morant Pt. Jamaica 17°55N 76°12W 88 a
Morar India 26°14N 78°14E 42 F8
Morar, L. U.K. 56°57N 5°40W 11 E3
Moratuwa Sri Lanka 6°45N 79°55E 45 L4
Morava → Serbia 44°36N 21°4E 23 B9
Morava → Slovakia 48°10N 16°59E 17 D9
Moravia U.S.A. 42°43N 76°25W 83 D8
Moravian Hts. = Českomoravská
Vrchovina Czechia 49°30N 15°40E 16 D8
Morawa Australia 29°13S 116°0E 61 E2
Morawhanna Guyana 8°30N 59°40W 92 B7
Moray □ U.K. 57°31N 3°18W 11 D5
Moray Firth U.K. 57°40N 3°52W 11 D5
Morbi India 22°50N 70°42E 42 H4
Morden Canada 49°15N 98°10W 71 D9
Mordovian Republic =
Mordvinia □ Russia 54°20N 44°30E 18 D7
Mordvinia □ Russia 54°20N 44°30E 18 D7
Moreau → U.S.A. 45°18N 100°43W 80 C3
Morebeng S. Africa 23°30S 29°55E 57 B4
Morecambe U.K. 54°5N 2°52W 12 C5
Morecambe B. U.K. 54°7N 3°0W 12 C5
Moree Australia 29°28S 149°54E 63 D4
Morehead U.S.A. 38°11N 83°26W 81 F12
Morehead City U.S.A. 34°43N 76°43W 85 D16
Morel → India 26°13N 76°36E 42 F7
Morelia Mexico 19°42N 101°7W 86 D4
Morella Australia 23°0S 143°52E 62 C3
Morella Spain 40°35N 0°5W 21 B5
Morelos Mexico 26°42N 107°40W 86 B3
Morelos □ Mexico 18°45N 99°0W 87 D5
Moremi ⌂ Botswana 19°18S 23°10E 56 A3
Morena India 26°30N 78°4E 42 F8
Morena, Sierra Spain 38°20N 4°0W 21 C3
Moreno Valley U.S.A. 33°56N 117°14W 79 M10
Moresby I. Canada 52°30N 131°40W 70 C2
Moreton I. Australia 27°10S 153°25E 63 D5
Moreton Island △
Australia 27°2S 153°24E 63 D5
Morgan U.S.A. 41°2N 111°41W 76 F8
Morgan City U.S.A. 29°42N 91°12W 84 G9
Morgan Hill U.S.A. 37°8N 121°39W 78 H5
Morganfield U.S.A. 37°41N 87°55W 80 G10
Morgan's Port U.S.A. 29°40N 95°0W 84 G7
Morganton U.S.A. 35°45N 81°41W 85 D14
Morgantown U.S.A. 39°38N 79°57W 81 F14
Morgenzon S. Africa 26°45S 29°36E 57 C4
Morghak Iran 29°7N 57°54E 47 D8
Morhar → India 25°29N 85°11E 43 G11
Mori Japan 42°6N 140°35E 28 C10
Moriarty U.S.A. 34°59N 106°3W 77 J10
Morice L. Canada 53°50N 127°40W 70 C3
Morinville Canada 53°49N 113°41W 70 C6
Morioka Japan 39°45N 141°8E 28 E10
Moris Mexico 28°10N 108°32W 86 B3
Morlaix France 48°36N 3°52W 20 B2
Mormugao = Marmagao
India 15°25N 73°56E 45 G1
Mornington Australia 38°15S 145°5E 63 F4
Mornington, I. Chile 49°50S 75°30W 96 F1
Mornington I. Australia 16°30S 139°30E 62 B2
Moro Pakistan 26°40N 68°0E 42 F2
Moro → Pakistan 29°42N 67°22E 42 E2
Moro G. Phil. 6°30N 123°0E 37 C6
Morocco ■ N. Afr. 32°0N 5°50W 52 B4
Morogoro Tanzania 6°50S 37°40E 54 F7
Moroleón Mexico 20°8N 101°12W 86 C4
Morombe Madag. 21°45S 43°22E 55 J8
Moron Argentina 34°39S 58°37W 94 C4
Morón Cuba 22°8N 78°39W 88 B4
Mörön Mongolia 49°38N 100°9E 30 B9
Morón de la Frontera
Spain 37°6N 5°28W 21 D3
Morona → Peru 4°40S 77°10W 92 D3
Morondava Madag. 20°17S 44°17E 55 J8
Morongo Valley U.S.A. 34°3N 116°37W 79 L10
Moroni Comoros Is. 11°40S 43°16E 55 a

**Moroni** *U.S.A.* 39°32N 111°35W **76** G8
**Morotai** *Indonesia* 2°10N 128°30E **37** D7
**Moroto** *Uganda* 2°28N 34°42E **54** D6
**Morpeth** *Canada* 42°23N 81°50W **82** D3
**Morpeth** *U.K.* 55°10N 1°41W **12** B6
**Morphou** *Cyprus* 35°12N 32°59E **46** C2
**Morrilton** *U.S.A.* 35°9N 92°44W **84** D8
**Morrinhos** *Brazil* 17°45S 49°10W **93** G9
**Morrinsville** *N.Z.* 37°40S 175°32E **59** B5
**Morris** *Canada* 49°25N 97°22W **71** D9
**Morris** *Ill., U.S.A.* 41°22N 88°26W **80** E9
**Morris** *Minn., U.S.A.* 45°35N 95°55W **80** C6
**Morris** *N.Y., U.S.A.* 42°33N 75°15W **83** D9
**Morris** *Pa., U.S.A.* 41°35N 77°17W **82** E7
**Morris, Mt.** *Australia* 26°9S 131°4E **61** E5
**Morris Jesup, Kap** *Greenland* 83°40N 34°0W **66** A16
**Morrisburg** *Canada* 44°55N 75°7W **83** B9
**Morristown** *Ariz., U.S.A.* 33°51N 112°37W **77** K7
**Morristown** *N.J., U.S.A.* 40°48N 74°29W **83** F10
**Morristown** *N.Y., U.S.A.* 44°35N 75°39W **83** B9
**Morristown** *Tenn., U.S.A.* 36°13N 83°18W **85** C13
**Morrisville** *N.Y., U.S.A.* 42°53N 75°35W **83** D9
**Morrisville** *Pa., U.S.A.* 40°13N 74°47W **83** F10
**Morrisville** *Vt., U.S.A.* 44°34N 72°36W **83** B12
**Morro, Pta.** *Chile* 27°6S 71°0W **94** B1
**Morro Bay** *U.S.A.* 35°22N 120°51W **78** K6
**Morrocoy △** *Venezuela* 10°48N 68°13W **89** D6
**Morrosquillo, G. de** *Colombia* 9°35N 75°40W **88** E4
**Morrumbene** *Mozam.* 23°31S 35°16E **57** B6
**Morshansk** *Russia* 53°28N 41°50E **18** D7
**Morsi** *India* 21°21N 78°0E **44** D4
**Morteros** *Argentina* 30°50S 62°0W **94** C3
**Mortlach** *Canada* 50°27N 106°4W **71** C7
**Mortlake** *Australia* 38°5S 142°50E **63** F3
**Morton** *Tex., U.S.A.* 33°44N 102°46W **84** E3
**Morton** *Wash., U.S.A.* 46°34N 122°17W **78** D4
**Moruga** *Trin. & Tob.* 10°4N 61°16W **93** K15
**Morundah** *Australia* 34°57S 146°19E **63** E4
**Moruya** *Australia* 35°58S 150°3E **63** F5
**Morvan** *France* 47°5N 4°3E **20** C6
**Morven** *Australia* 26°22S 147°5E **63** D4
**Morvern** *U.K.* 56°38N 5°44W **11** E3
**Morwell** *Australia* 38°10S 146°22E **63** F4
**Morzhovets, Ostrov** *Russia* 66°44N 42°35E **18** A7
**Mosakahiken = Moose Lake** *Canada* 53°46N 100°8W **71** C8
**Moscos Is.** *Myanmar* 14°0N 97°30E **38** F1
**Moscow** *Idaho, U.S.A.* 46°44N 117°0W **76** C5
**Moscow** *Pa., U.S.A.* 41°20N 75°31W **83** E9
**Mosel →** *Europe* 50°22N 7°36E **20** A7
**Moselle = Mosel →** *Europe* 50°22N 7°36E **20** A7
**Moses Lake** *U.S.A.* 47°8N 119°17W **76** C4
**Mosgiel** *N.Z.* 45°53S 170°21E **59** F3
**Moshaweng →** *S. Africa* 26°35S 22°50E **56** C3
**Moshchnyy, Ostrov** *Russia* 60°1N 27°50E **9** F22
**Moshi** *Tanzania* 3°22S 37°18E **54** E7
**Moshupa** *Botswana* 24°46S 25°29E **56** B4
**Mosi-oa-Tunya = Victoria Falls** *Zimbabwe* 17°58S 25°52E **55** H5
**Mosjøen** *Norway* 65°51N 13°12E **8** D15
**Moskenesøya** *Norway* 67°58N 13°0E **8** C15
**Moskenstraumen** *Norway* 67°47N 12°45E **8** C15
**Mosomane** *Botswana* 24°2S 26°19E **56** B4
**Mosonmagyaróvár** *Hungary* 47°52N 17°18E **17** E9
**Mosquera** *Colombia* 2°35N 78°24W **92** C3
**Mosquero** *U.S.A.* 35°47N 103°58W **77** J12
**Mosquitia** *Honduras* 15°20N 84°10W **88** C3
**Mosquito Creek L.** *U.S.A.* 41°18N 80°46W **82** E4
**Mosquito L.** *Canada* 62°35N 103°20W **71** A8
**Mosquitos, G. de los** *Panama* 9°15N 81°10W **88** E3
**Moss** *Norway* 59°27N 10°40E **9** G14
**Moss Vale** *Australia* 34°32S 150°25E **63** E5
**Mossaka** *Congo* 1°15S 16°45E **54** E3
**Mossbank** *Canada* 49°56N 105°56W **71** D7
**Mossburn** *N.Z.* 45°41S 168°15E **59** F2
**Mosselbaai** *S. Africa* 34°11S 22°8E **56** D3
**Mossendjo** *Congo* 2°55S 12°42E **54** E2
**Mossgiel** *Australia* 33°15S 144°5E **63** E3
**Mossman** *Australia* 16°21S 145°15E **62** B4
**Mossoró** *Brazil* 5°10S 37°15W **93** E11
**Most** *Czechia* 50°31N 13°38E **16** C7
**Mostaganem** *Algeria* 35°54N 0°5E **52** A6
**Mostar** *Bos.-H.* 43°22N 17°50E **23** C7
**Mostardas** *Brazil* 31°2S 50°51W **95** C5
**Mostiska = Mostyska** *Ukraine* 49°48N 23°4E **17** D12
**Mosty = Masty** *Belarus* 53°27N 24°38E **17** B13
**Mostyska** *Ukraine* 49°48N 23°4E **17** D12
**Mosul = Al Mawşil** *Iraq* 36°15N 43°5E **46** B4
**Motagua →** *Guatemala* 15°44N 88°14W **88** C2
**Motala** *Sweden* 58°32N 15°1E **9** G16
**Motaze** *Mozam.* 24°48S 32°52E **57** B5
**Moth** *India* 25°43N 78°57E **43** G8
**Motherwell** *U.K.* 55°47N 3°58W **11** F5
**Motihari** *India* 26°30N 84°55E **43** F11
**Motozintla de Mendoza** *Mexico* 15°22N 92°14W **87** D6
**Motril** *Spain* 36°31N 3°37W **21** D4
**Mott** *U.S.A.* 46°23N 102°20W **80** B2
**Mottama, G. of** *Myanmar* 16°5N 96°30E **41** L20
**Motueka** *N.Z.* 41°7S 173°1E **59** D4
**Motueka →** *N.Z.* 41°5S 173°1E **59** D4
**Motul** *Mexico* 21°6N 89°17W **87** C7
**Mouchalagane →** *Canada* 50°56N 68°41W **73** B6
**Mouding** *China* 25°20N 101°28E **34** E3
**Moudros** *Greece* 39°50N 25°18E **23** E11
**Mouhoun = Black Volta →** *Africa* 8°41N 1°33W **52** G5
**Mouila** *Gabon* 1°50S 11°0E **54** E2
**Moulamein** *Australia* 35°3S 144°1E **63** F3
**Moule à Chique, C.** *St. Lucia* 13°43N 60°57W **89** f
**Moulins** *France* 46°35N 3°19E **20** C5
**Moulmein = Mawlamyine** *Myanmar* 16°30N 97°40E **41** L20
**Moulouya, O. →** *Morocco* 35°5N 2°25W **52** B5
**Moultrie** *U.S.A.* 31°11N 83°47W **85** F13
**Moultrie, L.** *U.S.A.* 33°20N 80°5W **85** E14
**Mound City** *Mo., U.S.A.* 40°7N 95°14W **80** E6
**Mound City** *S. Dak., U.S.A.* 45°44N 100°4W **80** C3
**Moundou** *Chad* 8°40N 16°10E **53** G9
**Moundsville** *U.S.A.* 39°55N 80°44W **82** G4
**Moung** *Cambodia* 12°46N 103°27E **38** F4
**Mount Airy** *U.S.A.* 36°31N 80°37W **85** C14
**Mount Albert** *Canada* 44°8N 79°19W **82** B5
**Mount Aspiring △** *N.Z.* 44°19S 168°47E **59** F2
**Mount Barker** *S. Austral., Australia* 35°5S 138°52E **63** F2
**Mount Barker** *W. Austral., Australia* 34°38S 117°40E **61** F2
**Mount Barnett Roadhouse** *Australia* 16°39S 125°57E **60** C4
**Mount Brydges** *Canada* 42°54N 81°29W **82** D3
**Mount Burr** *Australia* 37°34S 140°26E **63** F3
**Mount Carleton ⌂** *Canada* 47°25N 66°55W **73** C6
**Mount Carmel = Ha Karmel △** *Israel* 32°45N 35°5E **48** C4
**Mount Carmel** *Ill., U.S.A.* 38°25N 87°46W **80** F10
**Mount Carmel** *Pa., U.S.A.* 40°47N 76°26W **83** F8
**Mount Clemens** *U.S.A.* 42°35N 82°53W **82** D2
**Mount Coolon** *Australia* 21°25S 147°25E **62** C4
**Mount Desert I.** *U.S.A.* 44°21N 68°20W **81** C19
**Mount Dora** *U.S.A.* 28°48N 81°38W **85** G14
**Mount Ebenezer** *Australia* 25°6S 132°34E **61** E5
**Mount Edziza ⌂** *Canada* 57°30N 130°45W **70** B2
**Mount Field △** *Australia* 42°39S 146°35E **63** G4
**Mount Fletcher** *S. Africa* 30°40S 28°30E **57** D4
**Mount Forest** *Canada* 43°59N 80°43W **82** C4
**Mount Frankland △** *Australia* 31°47S 116°37E **61** F2
**Mount Frederick ☼** *Australia* 19°39S 129°18E **60** C4
**Mount Gambier** *Australia* 37°50S 140°46E **63** F3
**Mount Garnet** *Australia* 17°37S 145°6E **62** B4
**Mount Holly** *U.S.A.* 39°59N 74°47W **83** G10
**Mount Holly Springs** *U.S.A.* 40°7N 77°12W **82** F7
**Mount Hope** *N.S.W., Australia* 32°51S 145°51E **63** E4
**Mount Hope** *S. Austral., Australia* 34°7S 135°23E **63** E2
**Mount Isa** *Australia* 20°42S 139°26E **62** C2
**Mount James ☼** *Australia* 24°51S 116°54E **61** D2
**Mount Jewett** *U.S.A.* 41°44N 78°39W **82** E6
**Mount Kaputar △** *Australia* 30°16S 150°10E **63** E5
**Mount Kisco** *U.S.A.* 41°12N 73°44W **83** E11
**Mount Laguna** *U.S.A.* 32°52N 116°25W **79** N10
**Mount Larcom** *Australia* 23°48S 150°59E **62** C5
**Mount Lofty Ranges** *Australia* 34°35S 139°5E **63** E2
**Mount Magnet** *Australia* 28°2S 117°47E **61** E2
**Mount Maunganui** *N.Z.* 37°40S 176°14E **59** B6
**Mount Molloy** *Australia* 16°42S 145°20E **62** B4
**Mount Morgan** *Australia* 23°40S 150°25E **62** C5
**Mount Morris** *U.S.A.* 42°44N 77°52W **82** D7
**Mount Pearl** *Canada* 47°31N 52°47W **73** C9
**Mount Penn** *U.S.A.* 40°20N 75°54W **83** F9
**Mount Perry** *Australia* 25°13S 151°42E **63** D5
**Mount Pleasant** *Iowa, U.S.A.* 40°58N 91°33W **80** E8
**Mount Pleasant** *Mich., U.S.A.* 43°36N 84°46W **81** D11
**Mount Pleasant** *Pa., U.S.A.* 40°9N 79°33W **82** F5
**Mount Pleasant** *S.C., U.S.A.* 32°47N 79°52W **85** E15
**Mount Pleasant** *Tenn., U.S.A.* 35°32N 87°12W **85** D11
**Mount Pleasant** *Tex., U.S.A.* 33°9N 94°58W **84** E7
**Mount Pleasant** *Utah, U.S.A.* 39°33N 111°27W **76** G8
**Mount Pocono** *U.S.A.* 41°7N 75°22W **83** E9
**Mount Rainier △** *U.S.A.* 46°55N 121°50W **78** D5
**Mount Revelstoke △** *Canada* 51°5N 118°30W **70** C5
**Mount Robson ⌂** *Canada* 53°0N 119°0W **70** C5
**Mount St. Helens ⌂** *U.S.A.* 46°14N 122°11W **78** D4
**Mount Selinda** *Zimbabwe* 20°24S 32°43E **57** B5
**Mount Shasta** *U.S.A.* 41°19N 122°19W **76** F2
**Mount Signal** *U.S.A.* 32°39N 115°37W **79** N11
**Mount Sterling** *Ill., U.S.A.* 39°59N 90°45W **80** F8
**Mount Sterling** *Ky., U.S.A.* 38°4N 83°56W **81** F12
**Mount Surprise** *Australia* 18°10S 144°17E **62** B3
**Mount Union** *U.S.A.* 40°23N 77°53W **82** F7
**Mount Upton** *U.S.A.* 42°26N 75°23W **83** D9
**Mount Vernon** *Ill., U.S.A.* 38°19N 88°55W **80** F9
**Mount Vernon** *Ind., U.S.A.* 37°56N 87°54W **75** H22
**Mount Vernon** *Ohio, U.S.A.* 40°23N 82°29W **82** F2
**Mount Vernon** *Wash., U.S.A.* 48°25N 122°20W **78** B4
**Mount William △** *Australia* 40°56S 148°14E **63** G4
**Mountain Ash** *U.K.* 51°40N 3°23W **13** F4
**Mountain Center** *U.S.A.* 33°42N 116°44W **79** M10
**Mountain City** *Nev., U.S.A.* 41°50N 115°58W **76** F6
**Mountain City** *Tenn., U.S.A.* 36°29N 81°48W **85** C14
**Mountain Dale** *U.S.A.* 41°41N 74°32W **83** E10
**Mountain Grove** *U.S.A.* 37°8N 92°16W **80** G7
**Mountain Home** *Ark., U.S.A.* 36°20N 92°23W **84** C8
**Mountain Home** *Idaho, U.S.A.* 43°8N 115°41W **76** E6
**Mountain Iron** *U.S.A.* 47°32N 92°37W **80** B7
**Mountain Pass** *U.S.A.* 35°29N 115°35W **79** K11
**Mountain View** *Ark., U.S.A.* 35°52N 92°7W **84** D8
**Mountain View** *Calif., U.S.A.* 37°23N 122°5W **78** H4
**Mountain Zebra △** *S. Africa* 32°14S 25°27E **56** D4
**Mountainair** *U.S.A.* 34°31N 106°15W **77** J10
**Mountbellew** *Ireland* 53°28N 8°31W **10** C3
**Mountlake Terrace** *U.S.A.* 47°47N 122°18W **78** C4
**Mountmellick** *Ireland* 53°7N 7°20W **10** C4
**Mountrath** *Ireland* 53°0N 7°28W **10** D4
**Moura** *Australia* 24°35S 149°58E **62** C4
**Moura** *Brazil* 1°32S 61°38W **92** D6
**Moura** *Portugal* 38°7N 7°30W **21** C2
**Mourdi, Dépression du** *Chad* 18°10N 23°0E **53** E10
**Mourilyan** *Australia* 17°35S 146°3E **62** B4
**Mourne →** *U.K.* 54°52N 7°26W **10** B4
**Mourne Mts.** *U.K.* 54°10N 6°0W **10** B5
**Mouscron** *Belgium* 50°45N 3°12E **15** D3
**Moussoro** *Chad* 13°41N 16°35E **53** F9
**Moutong** *Indonesia* 0°28N 121°13E **37** D6
**Movas** *Mexico* 28°10N 109°25W **86** B3
**Moville** *Ireland* 55°11N 7°3W **10** A4
**Mowandjum** *Australia* 17°22S 123°40E **60** C3
**Moy →** *Ireland* 54°8N 9°8W **10** B2
**Moya** *Comoros Is.* 12°18S 44°18E **55** a
**Moyale** *Kenya* 3°30N 39°4E **54** D7
**Moyen Atlas** *Morocco* 33°0N 5°0W **52** B4
**Moyo** *Indonesia* 8°10S 117°40E **36** F5
**Moyobamba** *Peru* 6°0S 77°0W **92** E3
**Møysalen △** *Norway* 68°32N 15°29E **8** B16
**Moyyero →** *Russia* 68°44N 103°42E **27** C11
**Moyynqum** *Kazakhstan* 44°12N 71°0E **30** C3
**Moyynty** *Kazakhstan* 47°10N 73°18E **26** E8
**Mozambique = Moçambique** *Mozam.* 15°3S 40°42E **55** H8
**Mozambique ■** *Africa* 19°0S 35°0E **55** H7
**Mozambique Chan.** *Africa* 17°30S 42°30E **57** A7
**Mozdok** *Russia* 43°45N 44°48E **19** F7
**Mozdūrān** *Iran* 36°9N 60°35E **47** B9
**Mozhnābād** *Iran* 34°7N 60°6E **47** C9
**Mozyr = Mazyr** *Belarus* 51°59N 29°15E **17** B15
**Mpanda** *Tanzania* 6°23S 31°1E **54** F6
**Mphoeng** *Zimbabwe* 21°10S 27°51E **57** B4
**Mpika** *Zambia* 11°51S 31°25E **55** G6
**Mpumalanga** *S. Africa* 29°50S 30°33E **57** C5
**Mpumalanga □** *S. Africa* 26°0S 30°0E **57** C5
**Mpwapwa** *Tanzania* 6°23S 36°30E **54** F7
**Mqanduli** *S. Africa* 31°49S 28°45E **57** D4
**Msaken** *Tunisia* 35°49N 10°33E **53** A8
**M'sila** *Algeria* 35°46N 4°30E **52** A6
**Mstislavl = Mstsislaw** *Belarus* 54°0N 31°50E **17** A16
**Mstsislaw** *Belarus* 54°0N 31°50E **17** A16
**Mtamvuna = Mthamvuna →** *S. Africa* 31°6S 30°12E **57** D5
**Mthamvuna →** *S. Africa* 31°6S 30°12E **57** D5
**Mthatha** *S. Africa* 31°36S 28°49E **57** D4
**Mtubatuba** *S. Africa* 28°30S 32°8E **57** C5
**Mtwalume** *S. Africa* 30°30S 30°38E **57** D5
**Mtwara-Mikindani** *Tanzania* 10°20S 40°20E **54** G8
**Mu Gia, Deo** *Vietnam* 17°40N 105°47E **38** D5
**Mu Ko Chang △** *Thailand* 11°59N 102°22E **39** G4
**Mu Ko Surin** *Thailand* 9°30N 97°55E **39** H1
**Mu Us Shamo** *China* 39°0N 109°0E **32** E5
**Muang Beng** *Laos* 20°23N 101°46E **34** G3
**Muang Chiang Rai = Chiang Rai** *Thailand* 19°52N 99°50E **34** H2
**Muang Et** *Laos* 20°49N 104°1E **38** B5
**Muang Hiam** *Laos* 20°5N 103°22E **38** B4
**Muang Hongsa** *Laos* 19°43N 101°20E **38** C3
**Muang Houn** *Laos* 20°8N 101°23E **34** G3
**Muang Kau** *Laos* 15°6N 105°47E **38** E5
**Muang Khao** *Laos* 19°38N 103°32E **38** C4
**Muang Khong** *Laos* 14°7N 105°51E **38** E5
**Muang Khoua** *Laos* 21°5N 102°31E **34** G4
**Muang Liap** *Laos* 18°29N 101°40E **38** C3
**Muang Mai** *Thailand* 8°5N 98°21E **39** a
**Muang May** *Laos* 14°49N 106°56E **38** E6
**Muang Na Mo** *Laos* 21°3N 101°49E **34** G3
**Muang Ngeun** *Laos* 20°36N 101°3E **34** G3
**Muang Ngoi** *Laos* 20°43N 102°41E **34** G4
**Muang Nong** *Laos* 16°22N 106°30E **38** D6
**Muang Ou Neua** *Laos* 22°18N 101°48E **34** F3
**Muang Ou Tay** *Laos* 22°7N 101°48E **34** F3
**Muang Pak Beng** *Laos* 19°54N 101°8E **34** H3
**Muang Phalane** *Laos* 16°39N 105°34E **38** D5
**Muang Phiang** *Laos* 19°6N 101°32E **38** C3
**Muang Phine** *Laos* 16°32N 106°2E **38** D6
**Muang Phonhong** *Laos* 18°30N 102°25E **38** C4
**Muang Saiapoun** *Laos* 18°24N 101°31E **38** C3
**Muang Sing** *Laos* 21°11N 101°9E **34** G3
**Muang Son** *Laos* 20°27N 103°19E **38** B4
**Muang Soui** *Laos* 19°33N 102°52E **38** C4
**Muang Va** *Laos* 21°53N 102°19E **34** G4
**Muang Va** *Laos* 18°18N 101°20E **38** C3
**Muang Xai** *Laos* 20°42N 101°59E **34** G3
**Muang Xamteu** *Laos* 19°59N 104°38E **38** C5
**Muar** *Malaysia* 2°3N 102°34E **39** L4
**Muarabungo** *Indonesia* 1°28S 102°52E **36** E2
**Muaraenim** *Indonesia* 3°40S 103°50E **36** E2
**Muarajuloi** *Indonesia* 0°12S 114°3E **36** E4
**Muarakaman** *Indonesia* 0°2S 116°45E **36** E5
**Muaratebo** *Indonesia* 1°30S 102°26E **36** E2
**Muaratembesi** *Indonesia* 1°42S 103°8E **36** E2
**Muarateweh** *Indonesia* 0°58S 114°52E **36** E4
**Mubarakpur** *India* 26°6N 83°18E **43** F10
**Mubarraz = Al Mubarraz** *Si. Arabia* 25°30N 49°40E **47** E6
**Mubi** *Nigeria* 10°18N 13°16E **53** F8
**Mucajaí →** *Brazil* 2°25N 60°52W **92** C6
**Muchinga Mts.** *Zambia* 11°30S 31°30E **55** G6
**Muchuan** *China* 28°57N 103°55E **34** C5
**Muck** *U.K.* 56°50N 6°15W **11** E2
**Muckadilla** *Australia* 26°35S 148°23E **63** D4
**Muckaty ☼** *Australia* 18°37S 133°52E **62** B1
**Muckle Flugga** *U.K.* 60°51N 0°54W **11** A8
**Mucuri** *Brazil* 18°0S 39°36W **93** G11
**Mucusso** *Angola* 18°1S 21°25E **56** A3
**Mudanjiang** *China* 44°38N 129°30E **33** B15
**Mudanya** *Turkey* 40°25N 28°50E **23** D13
**Muddebihal** *India* 16°20N 76°8E **45** F3
**Muddus △** *Sweden* 66°58N 20°15E **8** C19
**Muddy Cr. →** *U.S.A.* 38°24N 110°42W **76** G8
**Mudgee** *Australia* 32°32S 149°31E **63** E4
**Mudhol** *Karnataka, India* 16°21N 75°17E **45** F2
**Mudhol** *Telangana, India* 18°58N 77°55E **44** E3
**Mudigere** *India* 13°8N 75°38E **45** H2
**Mudjatik →** *Canada* 56°1N 107°36W **71** B7
**Mudukulattur** *India* 9°21N 78°31E **45** K4
**Mudumu △** *Namibia* 18°5S 23°29E **56** A3
**Mueller Ranges** *Australia* 18°18S 126°46E **60** C4
**Muerto, Mar** *Mexico* 16°10N 94°10W **87** D6
**Mufu Shan** *China* 29°20N 114°30E **35** C10
**Mufulira** *Zambia* 12°32S 28°15E **55** G5
**Mughal Sarai** *India* 25°18N 83°7E **43** G10
**Mughayrā'** *Si. Arabia* 29°17N 37°41E **46** D3
**Mugi** *Japan* 33°40N 134°25E **29** H7
**Muğla** *Turkey* 37°15N 28°22E **23** F13
**Mugu** *Nepal* 29°45N 82°30E **43** E10
**Mugu Karnali →** *Nepal* 29°38N 81°51E **43** E9
**Muhammad, Râs** *Egypt* 27°44N 34°16E **46** E2
**Muhammad Qol** *Sudan* 20°53N 37°9E **53** D13
**Muhammadabad** *India* 26°4N 83°25E **43** F10
**Muḩāyil** *Si. Arabia* 18°33N 42°3E **49** D3
**Mühlhausen** *Germany* 51°12N 10°27E **16** C6
**Mühlig Hofmann fjell** *Antarctica* 72°30S 5°0E **5** D3
**Muhos** *Finland* 64°47N 25°59E **8** D21
**Muhu** *Estonia* 58°36N 23°11E **9** G20
**Muileanri gCearr, An = Mullingar** *Ireland* 53°31N 7°21W **10** C4
**Muine Bheag = Bagenalstown** *Ireland* 52°42N 6°58W **10** D5
**Muineachán = Monaghan** *Ireland* 54°15N 6°57W **10** B5
**Muir, L.** *Australia* 34°30S 116°40E **61** F2
**Muir of Ord** *U.K.* 57°32N 4°28W **11** D4
**Mujeres, I.** *Mexico* 21°13N 86°43W **88** B2
**Muka, Tanjung** *Malaysia* 5°28N 100°11E **39** c
**Mukacheve** *Ukraine* 48°27N 22°45E **17** D12
**Mukachevo = Mukacheve** *Ukraine* 48°27N 22°45E **17** D12
**Mukah** *Malaysia* 2°55N 112°5E **36** D4
**Mukandwara** *India* 24°49N 75°59E **42** G6
**Mukdahan** *Thailand* 16°32N 104°43E **38** D5
**Mukdahan △** *Thailand* 16°26N 104°45E **38** D5
**Mukden = Shenyang** *China* 41°48N 123°27E **33** D12
**Mukerian** *India* 31°57N 75°37E **42** D6
**Mukher** *India* 18°42N 77°22E **44** E3
**Mukinbudin** *Australia* 30°55S 118°5E **61** F2
**Muko Phetra △** *Thailand* 6°57N 99°33E **39** J2
**Mukomuko** *Indonesia* 2°30S 101°10E **36** E2
**Muktinath** *Nepal* 28°49N 83°53E **43** E10
**Muktsar** *India* 30°30N 74°30E **42** D6
**Mukur = Moqor** *Afghan.* 32°50N 67°42E **42** C2
**Mukutuwa →** *Canada* 53°10N 97°24W **71** C9
**Mul** *India* 20°4N 79°40E **44** D4
**Mula** *Spain* 38°3N 1°33W **21** C5
**Mula →** *India* 18°34N 74°21E **44** E2
**Mula →** *Pakistan* 27°57N 67°36E **42** F2
**Mulanje, Mt.** *Malawi* 16°2S 35°33E **55** H7
**Mulbagal** *India* 13°10N 78°24E **45** H4
**Mulchatna →** *U.S.A.* 59°40N 157°7W **74** D8
**Mulchén** *Chile* 37°45S 72°20W **94** D1
**Mulde →** *Germany* 51°53N 12°15E **16** C7
**Mule Creek Junction** *U.S.A.* 43°23N 104°13W **76** E11
**Mulegé** *Mexico* 26°53N 111°59W **86** B2
**Muleshoe** *U.S.A.* 34°13N 102°43W **84** D3
**Mulgrave** *Canada* 45°38N 61°31W **73** C7
**Mulgrave I. = Badu** *Australia* 10°7S 142°11E **62** a
**Mulhacén** *Spain* 37°4N 3°20W **21** D4
**Mulhouse** *France* 47°40N 7°20E **20** C7
**Muli** *China* 27°52N 101°8E **34** D3
**Mulifanua** *Samoa* 13°50S 171°59W **59** b
**Muling** *China* 44°35N 130°10E **33** B16
**Mulki** *India* 13°6N 74°48E **45** H2
**Mull** *U.K.* 56°25N 5°56W **11** E3
**Mull, Sound of** *U.K.* 56°30N 5°50W **11** E3
**Mullach Íde = Malahide** *Ireland* 53°26N 6°9W **10** C5
**Mullaittivu** *Sri Lanka* 9°15N 80°49E **45** K5
**Mullen** *U.S.A.* 42°3N 101°1W **80** D3
**Mullengudgery** *Australia* 31°43S 147°23E **63** B4
**Mullens** *U.S.A.* 37°35N 81°23W **81** G13
**Muller, Pegunungan** *Indonesia* 0°30N 113°30E **36** D4
**Mullet Pen.** *Ireland* 54°13N 10°2W **10** B1
**Mullewa** *Australia* 28°29S 115°30E **61** E2
**Mulligan →** *Australia* 25°0S 139°0E **62** D2
**Mullingar** *Ireland* 53°31N 7°21W **10** C4
**Mullins** *U.S.A.* 34°12N 79°15W **85** D15
**Mullumbimby** *Australia* 28°30S 153°30E **63** D5
**Mulonga Plain** *Zambia* 16°20S 22°40E **55** H4
**Mulroy B.** *Ireland* 55°15N 7°46W **10** A4
**Mulshi L.** *India* 18°30N 73°48E **44** E1
**Multai** *India* 21°50N 78°21...
**Multan** *Pakistan* 30°15N 71°36E...
**Mulug** *India* 18°11N 79°57E...
**Mulvane** *U.S.A.* 37°29N 97°15W...
**Mulwala, L.** *Australia* 35°59S 146°1E **63**...
**Mun →** *Thailand* 15°19N 105°30E **38** E5
**Muna** *Indonesia* 5°0S 122°30E **37** F6
**Munabao** *India* 25°45N 70°17E **42** G4
**Munamagi** *Estonia* 57°43N 27°4E **9** H22
**Munaung** *Myanmar* 18°45N 93°40E **41** K18
**Munaung I. = Cheduba I.** *Myanmar* 18°45N 93°40E **41** K18
**Muncan** *Indonesia* 8°34S 115°11E **37** K18
**Muncar** *Indonesia* 8°26S 114°20E **37** J17
**Munchen-Gladbach = Mönchengladbach** *Germany* 51°11N 6°27E **16** C4
**Muncho Lake** *Canada* 59°0N 125°50W **70** B3
**Munch'ŏn** *N. Korea* 39°14N 127°19E **33** E14
**Muncie** *U.S.A.* 40°12N 85°23W **81** E11
**Muncoonie L. West** *Australia* 25°12S 138°40E **62** D2
**Mundabbera** *Australia* 25°36S 151°18E **63** D5
**Mundakayam** *India* 9°30N 76°50E **45** K3
**Mundal** *Sri Lanka* 7°48N 79°48E **45** L4
**Munday** *U.S.A.* 33°27N 99°38W **84** E5
**Münden** *Germany* 51°25N 9°38E **16** C5
**Mundiwindi** *Australia* 23°47S 120°9E **60** D3
**Mundo Novo** *Brazil* 11°50S 40°29W **93** F10
**Mundra** *India* 22°54N 69°48E **42** H3
**Mundrabilla** *Australia* 31°52S 127°51E **61** F4
**Muneru →** *India* 16°45N 80°3E **44** F5
**Mungallala** *Australia* 26°28S 147°34E **63** D4
**Mungallala Cr. →** *Australia* 28°53S 147°5E **63** D4
**Mungana** *Australia* 17°8S 144°27E **62** B3
**Mungaoli** *India* 24°24N 78°7E **42** G8
**Mungbere** *Dem. Rep. of the Congo* 2°36N 28°28E **54** D5
**Mungeli** *India* 22°4N 81°41E **43** H9
**Munger** *India* 25°23N 86°30E **43** G12
**Mungerannie** *Australia* 28°1S 138°39E **63** A2
**Mungilli ☼** *Australia* 25°14S 124°17E **61** E3
**Mungkan Kandju △** *Australia* 13°35S 142°52E **62** A3
**Mungkarta ☼** *Australia* 20°22S 134°2E **62** C1
**Munising** *U.S.A.* 46°25N 86°40W **80** B10
**Munku-Sardyk** *Russia* 51°45N 100°20E **27** D11
**Munnsville** *U.S.A.* 42°58N 75°35W **83** D9
**Muñoz Gamero, Pen.** *Chile* 52°30S 73°5W **96** G2
**Munroe L.** *Canada* 59°13N 98°35W **71** B9
**Munsan** *S. Korea* 37°51N 126°48E **33** F14
**Münster** *Germany* 51°58N 7°37E **16** C4
**Munster □** *Ireland* 52°18N 8°44W **10** D3
**Muntadgin** *Australia* 31°45S 118°33E **61** F2
**Muntok** *Indonesia* 2°5S 105°10E **36** E3
**Muong Nhie** *Vietnam* 22°12N 102°28E **34** F4
**Muong Sen** *Vietnam* 19°24N 104°8E **38** C5
**Muong Te** *Vietnam* 22°24N 102°49E **34** F4
**Muong Xia** *Vietnam* 20°19N 104°50E **38** B5
**Muonio** *Finland* 67°57N 23°40E **8** C20
**Muonio älv = Muonionjoki →** *Finland* 67°11N 23°34E **8** C20
**Muonioälven = Muonionjoki →** *Finland* 67°11N 23°34E **8** C20
**Muonionjoki →** *Finland* 67°11N 23°34E **8** C20
**Mupa →** *Mozam.* 18°58S 35°54E **57** A6
**Muping** *China* 37°22N 121°36E **33** F11
**Muqdisho** *Somalia* 2°2N 45°25E **49** G4
**Mur →** *Austria* 47°18N 16°52E **17** E9
**Murakami** *Japan* 38°14N 139°29E **28** E9
**Muralag = Prince of Wales I.** *Australia* 10°40S 142°10E **62** A3
**Murallón, Cerro** *Chile* 49°48S 73°30W **96** F2
**Murang'a** *Kenya* 0°45S 37°9E **54** E7
**Murashi** *Russia* 59°30N 49°0E **18** C8
**Murat →** *Turkey* 38°46N 40°0E **19** G7
**Muratlı** *Turkey* 41°10N 27°29E **23** D12
**Murayama** *Japan* 38°30N 140°25E **28** E10
**Murchison →** *Australia* 27°45S 114°0E **61** E1
**Murchison, Mt.** *Antarctica* 73°25S 166°20E **5** D11
**Murchison Falls** *Uganda* 2°15N 31°30E **54** D6
**Murchison Ra.** *Australia* 20°0S 134°10E **62** C1
**Murchison Roadhouse** *Australia* 27°39S 116°14E **61** E2
**Murcia** *Spain* 38°5N 1°10W **21** D5
**Murcia □** *Spain* 37°50N 1°30W **21** D5
**Murdo** *U.S.A.* 43°53N 100°43W **80** D3
**Murdoch Pt.** *Australia* 14°37S 144°55E **62** A3
**Mureş →** *Romania* 46°15N 20°13E **17** E11
**Mureşul = Mureş →** *Romania* 46°15N 20°13E **17** E11
**Murewa** *Zimbabwe* 17°39S 31°47E **57** A5
**Murfreesboro** *N.C., U.S.A.* 36°27N 77°6W **85** C16
**Murfreesboro** *Tenn., U.S.A.* 35°51N 86°24W **85** D11
**Murgap** *Tajikistan* 38°10N 74°2E **26** F8
**Murgap →** *Turkmenistan* 38°18N 61°12E **47** B9
**Murgenella** *Australia* 11°34S 132°56E **60** B5
**Murgha Kibzai** *Pakistan* 30°44N 69°25E **42** D3
**Murghob = Murgap** *Tajikistan* 38°10N 74°2E **26** F8
**Murgon** *Australia* 26°15S 151°54E **63** D5
**Muri** *India* 23°22N 85°52E **43** H11
**Muria** *Indonesia* 6°36S 110°53E **37** G14
**Muriaé** *Brazil* 21°8S 42°23W **95** A7
**Müritz** *Germany* 53°25N 12°42E **16** B7
**Murliganj** *India* 25°54N 86°59E **43** G12
**Murmansk** *Russia* 68°57N 33°10E **8** B25
**Murmashi** *Russia* 68°47N 32°42E **8** B25
**Murom** *Russia* 55°35N 42°3E **18** C7
**Muroran** *Japan* 42°25N 141°0E **28** C10
**Muroto** *Japan* 33°18N 134°9E **29** H7
**Muroto-Misaki** *Japan* 33°15N 134°10E **29** H7
**Murphy** *U.S.A.* 43°13N 116°33W **76** E5
**Murphys** *U.S.A.* 38°8N 120°28W **78** G6
**Murray** *Australia* 9°56S 144°2E **62** a

Murray Ky., U.S.A. 36°37N 88°19W 80 G9
Murray Utah, U.S.A. 40°40N 111°53W 76 F8
Murray → Australia 35°20S 139°22E 63 F2
Murray, L. U.S.A. 34°3N 81°13W 85 D14
Murray Bridge Australia 35°6S 139°14E 63 F2
Murray Fracture Zone Pac. Oc. 35°0N 130°0W 65 D14
Murray Harbour Canada 46°0N 62°28W 73 C7
Murray River △ Australia 34°23S 140°32E 63 E3
Murraysburg S. Africa 31°58S 23°47E 56 D3
Murree Pakistan 33°56N 73°28E 42 C5
Murrieta U.S.A. 33°33N 117°13W 79 M9
Murrumbidgee → Australia 34°43S 143°12E 63 E3
Murrumburrah Australia 34°32S 148°22E 63 E4
Murrurundi Australia 31°42S 150°51E 63 E5
Murshidabad India 24°11N 88°19E 43 G13
Murtazapur India 20°40N 77°25E 44 D3
Murtle L. Canada 52°8N 119°38W 70 C5
Murtoa Australia 36°35S 142°28E 63 F3
Murud India 18°19N 72°58E 44 E1
Mururoa French Polynesia 21°52S 138°55W 65 K14
Murwara India 23°46N 80°28E 43 H9
Murwillumbah Australia 28°18S 153°27E 63 D5
Murzūq Libya 25°53N 13°57E 53 C8
Murzūq, Idehān Libya 24°50N 13°51E 53 D8
Mürzzuschlag Austria 47°36N 15°41E 16 E8
Mus India 9°14N 92°47E 45 K11
Muş Turkey 38°45N 41°30E 46 B4
Mûsa, Gebel Egypt 28°33N 33°59E 46 D2
Musa Khel Pakistan 30°59N 69°52E 42 D3
Mūsa Qal'eh Afghan. 32°20N 64°50E 40 C4
Musafirkhana India 26°22N 81°48E 43 F9
Musala Bulgaria 42°13N 23°37E 23 C10
Musala Indonesia 1°41N 98°28E 36 D1
Musan N. Korea 42°12N 129°12E 33 C15
Muscat = Masqat Oman 23°37N 58°36E 49 C6
Muscatine U.S.A. 41°25N 91°3W 80 E8
Muscle Shoals U.S.A. 34°45N 87°40W 85 D11
Musgrave Harbour Canada 49°27N 53°58W 73 C9
Musgrave Ranges Australia 26°0S 132°0E 61 E5
Mushie Dem. Rep. of the Congo 2°56S 16°55E 54 E3
Musi → India 16°41N 79°40E 44 F4
Musi → Indonesia 2°20S 104°56E 36 E2
Musina S. Africa 22°20S 30°5E 57 B5
Musiri India 10°56N 78°27E 45 J4
Muskeg → Canada 60°20N 123°20W 70 A4
Muskegon U.S.A. 43°14N 86°16W 80 D10
Muskegon → U.S.A. 43°14N 86°21W 80 D10
Muskegon Heights U.S.A. 43°12N 86°16W 80 D10
Muskogee U.S.A. 35°45N 95°22W 84 D7
Muskoka, L. Canada 45°0N 79°25W 82 B5
Muskoka Falls Canada 44°59N 79°17W 82 B5
Muskwa → Canada 58°47N 122°48W 70 B4
Muslīmiyah Syria 36°19N 37°12E 46 B3
Musoma Tanzania 1°30S 33°48E 54 E6
Musquaro, L. Canada 50°38N 61°5W 73 B7
Musquodoboit Harbour Canada 44°50N 63°9W 73 D7
Musselburgh U.K. 55°57N 3°2W 11 F5
Musselshell → U.S.A. 47°21N 107°57W 76 C10
Mussende Angola 10°32S 16°5E 54 G3
Mussoorie India 30°27N 78°6E 42 D8
Mussuco Angola 17°2S 19°3E 56 A2
Mustafakemalpaşa Turkey 40°2N 28°24E 23 D13
Mustang Nepal 29°10N 83°55E 43 E10
Musters, L. Argentina 45°20S 69°25W 96 F3
Musudan N. Korea 40°50N 129°43E 33 D15
Muswellbrook Australia 32°16S 150°56E 63 E5
Mût Egypt 25°28N 28°58E 53 C11
Mut Turkey 36°40N 33°28E 46 B2
Mutanda Mozam. 21°0S 33°34E 57 B5
Mutare Zimbabwe 18°58S 32°38E 55 H6
Mutawintji △ Australia 31°10S 142°30E 63 E3
Muting Indonesia 7°23S 140°20E 37 F10
Mutki = Mirtağ Turkey 38°23N 41°56E 46 B4
Mutoko Zimbabwe 17°24S 32°13E 57 A5
Mutoray Russia 60°56N 101°0E 27 C11
Mutsamudu Comoros Is. 12°10S 44°25E 55 a
Mutsu Japan 41°5N 140°55E 28 D10
Mutsu-Wan Japan 41°5N 140°55E 28 D10
Muttaburra Australia 22°38S 144°29E 62 C3
Mutton I. Ireland 52°49N 9°32W 10 D2
Muttukuru India 14°16N 80°6E 45 G5
Mutur Sri Lanka 8°27N 81°16E 45 K5
Muweilih Egypt 30°42N 34°19E 48 E3
Muy Muy Nic. 12°39N 85°36W 88 D2
Mŭynoq Uzbekistan 43°44N 59°10E 26 E6
Muyunkum, Peski = Moyynqum Kazakhstan 44°12N 71°0E 30 C3
Muz Tag China 36°25N 87°25E 30 D6
Muzaffarabad Pakistan 34°25N 73°30E 43 B5
Muzaffargarh Pakistan 30°5N 71°14E 42 D4
Muzaffarnagar India 29°26N 77°40E 42 E7
Muzaffarpur India 26°7N 85°23E 43 F11
Muzafirpur Pakistan 30°58N 69°9E 42 D3
Muzhi Russia 65°25N 64°40E 18 A11
Muztagh-Ata China 38°17N 75°7E 30 D4
Mvuma Zimbabwe 19°16S 30°30E 55 H6
Mwali = Mohéli Comoros Is. 12°20S 43°40E 55 a
Mwanza Dem. Rep. of the Congo 7°55S 26°43E 54 F5
Mwanza Tanzania 2°30S 32°58E 54 E6
Mweelrea Ireland 53°39N 9°49W 10 C2
Mweka Dem. Rep. of the Congo 4°50S 21°34E 54 E4
Mwene-Ditu Dem. Rep. of the Congo 6°35S 22°27E 54 F4
Mwenga Dem. Rep. of the Congo 3°1S 28°28E 54 E5
Mweru, L. Zambia 9°0S 28°40E 54 F5
Mwinilunga Zambia 11°43S 24°25E 55 G4
My Son Vietnam 15°48N 108°7E 38 E7
My Tho Vietnam 10°29N 106°23E 39 G6
Myajlar India 26°15N 70°20E 42 F4
Myanaung Myanmar 18°18N 95°22E 41 K19
Myanmar ■ Asia 21°0N 96°30E 41 J20
Myaungmya Myanmar 16°30N 94°40E 41 L19
Mycenæ = Mykenes Greece 37°43N 22°46E 23 F10
Myeik = Mergui Myanmar 12°26N 98°34E 38 F2
Myeik Kyunzu Myanmar 11°30N 97°30E 39 G1
Myerstown U.S.A. 40°22N 76°19W 83 F8
Myingyan Myanmar 21°30N 95°20E 41 J19
Myitkyina Myanmar 25°24N 97°26E 41 G20
Mykenes Greece 37°43N 22°46E 23 F10
Mykines Færoe Is. 62°7N 7°35W 8 E9
Mykolayiv Ukraine 46°58N 32°0E 19 E5
Mykonos Greece 37°30N 25°25E 23 F11
Mymensingh Bangla. 24°45N 90°24E 41 G17
Mynydd Du U.K. 51°52N 3°50W 13 F4
Mýrdalsjökull Iceland 63°40N 19°6W 8 E4
Myrtle Beach U.S.A. 33°42N 78°53W 85 E15
Myrtle Creek U.S.A. 43°1N 123°17W 76 E2
Myrtle Point U.S.A. 43°4N 124°8W 76 E1
Myrtoan Sea = Mirtoo Sea Greece 37°0N 23°20E 23 F10
Mysia Turkey 39°50N 27°0E 23 E12
Mysore = Karnataka □ India 13°15N 77°0E 45 H3
Mysore = Mysuru India 12°17N 76°41E 45 H3
Mystic U.S.A. 41°21N 71°58W 83 E13
Mysuru India 12°17N 76°41E 45 H3
Myszków Poland 50°45N 19°22E 17 C10
Mytilene = Mitilini Greece 39°6N 26°35E 23 E12
Mytishchi Russia 55°50N 37°50E 18 C6
Mývatn Iceland 65°36N 17°0W 8 D5
Mzimkulu → S. Africa 30°44S 30°28E 57 D5
Mzimvubu → S. Africa 31°38S 29°33E 57 D4
Mzuzu Malawi 11°30S 33°55E 54 G6

## N

Na Clocha Liatha = Greystones Ireland 53°9N 6°5W 10 C5
Na Haeo △ Thailand 17°31N 100°58E 38 D3
Na Hearadh = Harris U.K. 57°50N 6°55W 11 D2
Na Hearadh, Caolas = Harris, Sd. of U.K. 57°44N 7°6W 11 D1
Na Noi Thailand 18°19N 100°43E 38 C3
Na Phao Laos 17°35N 105°44E 38 D5
Na Sam Vietnam 22°3N 106°37E 34 F6
Na Sceirí = Skerries Ireland 53°35N 6°8W 10 C5
Na Thon Thailand 9°32N 99°56E 39 b
Naab → Germany 49°1N 12°2E 16 D6
Naantali Finland 60°29N 22°2E 9 F20
Naas Ireland 53°12N 6°40W 10 C5
Nababeep S. Africa 29°36S 17°46E 56 C2
Nabadwip = Navadwip India 23°34N 88°20E 43 H13
Nabawa Australia 28°30S 114°48E 61 E1
Nabberu, L. Australia 25°50S 120°30E 61 E3
Naberezhnyye Chelny Russia 55°42N 52°19E 18 C9
Nabeul Tunisia 36°30N 10°44E 53 A8
Nabha India 30°26N 76°14E 42 D7
Nabīd Iran 29°40N 57°38E 47 D8
Nabire Indonesia 3°15S 135°26E 37 E9
Nabisar Pakistan 25°8N 69°40E 42 G3
Nabisipi → Canada 50°14N 62°13W 73 B7
Nāblus = Nābulus West Bank 32°14N 35°15E 48 C4
Naboomspruit S. Africa 24°32S 28°40E 57 B4
Nabouwalu Fiji 17°0S 178°45E 59 a
Nābulus West Bank 32°14N 35°15E 48 C4
Nacala Mozam. 14°32S 40°34E 55 G8
Nacaome Honduras 13°31N 87°30W 88 D2
Naches U.S.A. 46°44N 120°42W 76 C3
Naches → U.S.A. 46°38N 120°31W 78 D6
Nachicapau, L. Canada 56°40N 68°5W 73 A6
Nachingwea Tanzania 10°23S 38°49E 54 G7
Nachna India 27°34N 71°41E 42 F4
Nachuge India 10°47N 92°21E 45 J11
Nacimiento, L. U.S.A. 35°46N 120°53W 78 K6
Naco Mexico 31°19N 109°56W 86 A3
Nacogdoches U.S.A. 31°36N 94°39W 84 F7
Nácori Chico Mexico 29°40N 108°57W 86 B3
Nacozari de García Mexico 30°25N 109°38W 86 A3
Nacula Fiji 16°54S 177°27E 59 a
Nada = Danzhou China 19°31N 109°33E 38 C7
Nådendal = Naantali Finland 60°29N 22°2E 9 F20
Nadi Fiji 17°42S 177°20E 59 a
Nadiad India 22°41N 72°56E 42 H5
Nador Morocco 35°14N 2°58W 52 B5
Nadūshan Iran 32°2N 53°35E 47 C7
Nadvirna Ukraine 48°37N 24°30E 17 D13
Nadvoitsy Russia 63°52N 34°14E 18 B5
Nadvornaya = Nadvirna Ukraine 48°37N 24°30E 17 D13
Nadym Russia 65°35N 72°42E 26 C8
Nadym → Russia 66°12N 72°0E 26 C8
Nærbø Norway 58°40N 5°39E 9 G11
Næstved Denmark 55°13N 11°44E 9 J14
Nafarroa = Navarra □ Spain 42°40N 1°40W 21 A5
Nafpaktos Greece 38°24N 21°50E 23 E9
Nafplio Greece 37°33N 22°50E 23 F10
Naft-e Safīd Iran 31°40N 49°17E 47 D6
Naftshahr Iran 34°0N 45°30E 46 C5
Nafud Desert = An Nafūd Si. Arabia 28°15N 41°0E 46 D4
Naga Phil. 13°38N 123°15E 37 B6
Nagagami Canada 50°23N 84°20W 72 B3
Nagahama Japan 35°23N 136°16E 29 G8
Nagai Japan 38°6N 140°2E 28 E10
Nagaland □ India 26°0N 94°30E 41 G19
Nagano Japan 36°40N 138°10E 29 F9
Nagano □ Japan 36°15N 138°0E 29 F9
Nagaoka Japan 37°27N 138°51E 29 F9
Nagaon India 26°20N 92°50E 41 F18
Nagappattinam India 10°46N 79°51E 45 J4
Nagar → Bangla. 24°27N 89°12E 43 G13
Nagar Karnul India 16°29N 78°20E 45 F4
Nagar Parkar Pakistan 24°28N 70°46E 42 G4
Nagaram India 18°21N 80°26E 44 E5
Nagarhole △ India 12°0N 76°10E 45 J3
Nagari Hills India 13°3N 79°45E 45 H4
Nagarjuna Sagar India 16°30N 79°13E 45 F4
Nagasaki Japan 32°47N 129°50E 29 H4
Nagasaki □ Japan 32°50N 129°40E 29 H4
Nagato Japan 34°19N 131°5E 29 G5
Nagaur India 27°15N 73°45E 42 F5
Nagbhir India 20°34N 79°55E 44 D4
Nagda India 23°27N 75°25E 42 H6
Nagercoil India 8°12N 77°26E 45 K3
Nagina India 29°30N 78°30E 43 E8
Nagīneh Iran 34°20N 57°15E 47 C8
Nagir Pakistan 36°12N 74°42E 43 A6
Nagles Mts. Ireland 52°8N 8°30W 10 D3
Nagod India 24°34N 80°36E 43 G9
Nagoorin Australia 24°17S 151°15E 62 C5
Nagorno-Karabakh □ Azerbaijan 39°55N 46°45E 46 B5
Nagornyy Russia 55°58N 124°57E 27 D13
Nagoya Japan 35°10N 136°50E 29 G8
Nagoya ✈ (NGO) Japan 34°53N 136°45E 29 G8
Nagpur India 21°8N 79°10E 44 D4
Nagqu China 31°29N 92°3E 30 E7
Nagua Dom. Rep. 19°23N 69°50W 89 C6
Naguabo Puerto Rico 18°13N 65°44W 89 d
Nagurunguru ✪ Australia 16°45S 129°45E 60 C4
Nagykanizsa Hungary 46°28N 17°0E 17 E9
Nagykőrös Hungary 47°5N 19°48E 17 E10
Naha Japan 26°13N 127°42E 29 L3
Nahan India 30°33N 77°18E 42 D7
Nahanni △ Canada 61°36N 125°41W 70 A4
Nahanni Butte Canada 61°2N 123°31W 70 A4
Nahargarh Mad. P., India 24°10N 75°14E 42 G6
Nahargarh Raj., India 24°55N 75°50E 42 G7
Nahariyya Israel 33°1N 35°5E 46 C2
Nahāvand Iran 34°10N 48°22E 47 C6
Nahuel Huapi, L. Argentina 41°0S 71°32W 96 E2
Nahuelbuta △ Chile 37°44S 72°57W 94 D1
Nai Yong Thailand 8°14N 98°22E 39 a
Naicá Mexico 27°53N 105°31W 86 B3
Naicam Canada 52°30N 104°30W 71 C8
Naikoon ⌂ Canada 53°55N 131°55W 70 C2
Naikul India 21°20N 84°58E 44 D7
Naimisharanya India 27°21N 80°30E 43 F9
Naimona'nyi Feng China 30°26N 81°18E 43 D9
Nain Canada 56°34N 61°40W 73 A7
Nā'īn Iran 32°54N 53°0E 47 C7
Naini Tal India 29°30N 79°30E 43 E8
Nainpur India 22°30N 80°10E 43 H9
Nainwa India 25°46N 75°51E 42 G6
Nairai Fiji 17°49S 179°15E 59 a
Nairn U.K. 57°35N 3°53W 11 D5
Nairobi Kenya 1°17S 36°48E 54 E7
Naissaar Estonia 59°34N 24°29E 9 G21
Naitaba Fiji 17°0S 179°16W 59 a
Naivasha Kenya 0°40S 36°30E 54 E7
Najaf = An Najaf Iraq 32°3N 44°15E 46 C5
Najafābād Iran 32°40N 51°15E 47 C6
Najd Si. Arabia 26°30N 42°0E 49 B3
Najibabad India 29°40N 78°20E 42 E8
Najin N. Korea 42°12N 130°15E 33 C16
Najmah Si. Arabia 26°42N 50°6E 47 E6
Najrān Si. Arabia 17°34N 44°18E 49 D3
Naju S. Korea 35°3N 126°43E 33 G14
Nakadōri-Shima Japan 32°57N 129°4E 29 H4
Nakaminato Japan 36°21N 140°36E 29 F10
Nakamura = Shimanto Japan 32°59N 132°56E 29 H6
Nakano Japan 36°45N 138°22E 29 F9
Nakano-Shima Japan 29°51N 129°52E 29 K4
Nakashibetsu Japan 43°33N 144°59E 28 C12
Nakfa Eritrea 16°40N 38°32E 49 D2
Nakha Yai, Ko Thailand 8°3N 98°28E 39 a
Nakhichevan = Naxçıvan Azerbaijan 39°12N 45°15E 46 B5
Nakhichevan Rep. = Naxçıvan □ Azerbaijan 39°25N 45°26E 46 B5
Nakhl Egypt 29°55N 33°43E 48 F2
Nakhl-e Taqī Iran 27°28N 52°36E 47 E7
Nakhodka Russia 42°53N 132°54E 28 C6
Nakhon Nayok Thailand 14°12N 101°13E 38 E3
Nakhon Pathom Thailand 13°49N 100°3E 38 F3
Nakhon Phanom Thailand 17°23N 104°43E 38 D5
Nakhon Ratchasima Thailand 14°59N 102°12E 38 E4
Nakhon Sawan Thailand 15°35N 100°10E 38 E3
Nakhon Si Thammarat Thailand 8°29N 100°0E 39 H3
Nakhon Thai Thailand 17°5N 100°44E 38 D3
Nakhtarana India 23°20N 69°15E 42 H3
Nakina Canada 50°10N 86°40W 72 B2
Nakodar India 31°8N 75°31E 42 D6
Naktong → S. Korea 35°7N 128°57E 33 G15
Nakuru Kenya 0°15S 36°4E 54 E7
Nakusp Canada 50°20N 117°45W 70 C5
Nal Pakistan 27°40N 66°12E 42 F2
Nal → Pakistan 25°20N 65°30E 42 G1
Nalázi Mozam. 24°3S 33°20E 57 B5
Nalchik Russia 43°30N 43°33E 19 F7
Nalgonda India 17°6N 79°15E 44 F4
Nalhati India 24°17N 87°52E 43 G12
Naliya India 23°16N 68°50E 42 H3
Nallamalai Hills India 15°30N 78°50E 45 G4
Nam Can Vietnam 8°46N 104°59E 39 H5
Nam-ch'on N. Korea 38°15N 126°26E 33 E14
Nam Co China 30°30N 90°45E 30 E7
Nam Dinh Vietnam 20°25N 106°5E 34 G6
Nam Du, Quan Dao Vietnam 9°41N 104°21E 39 H5
Nam Hka → Myanmar 21°34N 95°41E 34 G2
Nam Loi → Myanmar 21°3N 98°27E 34 G3
Nam Nao △ Thailand 16°44N 101°32E 38 D3
Nam Ngum Res. Laos 18°35N 102°34E 38 C4
Nam Phan Vietnam 10°30N 106°0E 39 G6
Nam Phong Thailand 16°42N 102°52E 38 D4
Nam Theun Res. Laos 17°51N 105°3E 38 D5
Nam Tok Thailand 14°21N 99°4E 38 E2
Nam Un Res. Thailand 17°13N 103°44E 38 D4
Namacunde Angola 17°18S 15°50E 56 A2
Namacurra Mozam. 17°30S 36°50E 57 A6
Namak, Daryācheh-ye Iran 34°30N 52°0E 47 C7
Namak, Kavir-e Iran 34°30N 57°30E 47 C8
Namakkal India 11°13N 78°13E 45 J4
Namakzār, Daryācheh-ye Iran 34°0N 60°30E 47 C9
Namaland Namibia 26°0S 17°0E 56 B2
Namangan Uzbekistan 41°0N 71°40E 30 C3
Namapa Mozam. 13°43S 39°50E 55 G7
Namaqua △ S. Africa 30°0S 17°30E 56 D2
Namaqualand S. Africa 30°0S 17°25E 56 D2
Namber Indonesia 1°2S 134°49E 37 E8
Nambour Australia 26°32S 152°58E 63 D5
Nambouwalu = Nabouwalu Fiji 17°0S 178°45E 59 a
Nambucca Heads Australia 30°37S 153°0E 63 E5
Nambung △ Australia 30°30S 115°5E 61 F2
Namcha Barwa China 29°40N 95°10E 30 F8
Namche Bazar Nepal 27°51N 86°47E 43 F12
Namchonjŏm = Nam-ch'on N. Korea 38°15N 126°26E 33 E14
Namenalala Fiji 17°8S 179°9E 59 a
Namew L. Canada 54°14N 101°56W 71 C8
Namgia India 31°48N 78°40E 43 D8
Namhkam Myanmar 23°50N 97°41E 34 E1
Namib Desert Namibia 22°30S 15°0E 56 B2
Namib-Naukluft ⌂ Namibia 24°40S 15°16E 56 B2
Namibe Angola 15°7S 12°11E 55 H2
Namibe □ Angola 16°35S 12°30E 56 A1
Namibia ■ Africa 22°0S 18°9E 56 B2
Namibwoestyn = Namib Desert Namibia 22°30S 15°0E 56 B2
Namīnūs = Lubango Angola 14°55S 13°30E 55 G2
Namīnūs = Lüderitz Namibia 26°41S 15°8E 56 C2
Namjeju S. Korea 33°14N 126°33E 33 H14
Namlea Indonesia 3°18S 127°5E 37 E7
Namoi → Australia 30°12S 149°30E 63 E4
Nampa U.S.A. 43°34N 116°34W 76 E5
Namp'o N. Korea 38°52N 125°10E 33 E13
Nampō-Shotō Japan 32°0N 140°0E 29 J10
Nampula Mozam. 15°6S 39°15E 55 H7
Namrole Indonesia 3°46S 126°46E 37 E7
Namse Shankou China 30°0N 82°25E 43 E10
Namsen → Norway 64°28N 11°37E 8 D14
Namsos Norway 64°29N 11°30E 8 D14
Namtok Chat Trakan △ Thailand 17°17N 100°40E 38 D3
Namtok Huay Yang △ Thailand 11°35N 99°30E 39 G2
Namtok Mae Surin △ Thailand 18°55N 98°2E 38 C2
Namtok Ngao △ Thailand 9°58N 98°46E 39 H2
Namtok Phlew △ Thailand 12°32N 102°13E 38 F4
Namtok Yong △ Thailand 8°15N 98°45E 39 H2
Namtsy Russia 62°43N 129°37E 27 C13
Namtu Myanmar 23°5N 97°28E 41 H20
Namu Canada 51°52N 127°50W 70 C3
Namuka-i-Lau Fiji 18°53S 178°37W 59 a
Namur Belgium 50°27N 4°52E 15 D4
Namur □ Belgium 50°17N 5°0E 15 D4
Namutoni Namibia 18°49S 16°55E 56 A2
Namwon S. Korea 35°23N 127°23E 33 G14
Namyang N. Korea 42°57N 129°52E 33 C15
Namyit I. S. China Sea 10°11N 114°22E 36 C4
Nan Thailand 18°48N 100°46E 38 C3
Nan → Thailand 15°42N 100°9E 38 E3
Nan Ling China 25°0N 112°30E 35 E9
Nan Xian China 29°20N 112°22E 35 C9
Nanaimo Canada 49°10N 124°0W 70 D4
Nānākuli U.S.A. 21°24N 158°9W 75 L8
Nanam N. Korea 41°44N 129°40E 33 D15
Nan'an China 24°59N 118°21E 35 E12
Nanango Australia 26°40S 152°0E 63 D5
Nan'ao China 23°28N 117°5E 35 F11
Nanao Japan 37°0N 137°0E 29 F8
Nanbu China 31°18N 106°3E 34 B6
Nanchang China 28°42N 115°55E 35 C10
Nancheng China 27°33N 116°35E 35 D11
Nanching = Nanjing China 32°2N 118°47E 35 A12
Nanchong China 30°43N 106°2E 34 B6
Nanchuan China 29°9N 107°6E 34 C6
Nancowry India 7°59N 93°32E 45 L11
Nancy France 48°42N 6°12E 20 B7
Nanda Devi India 30°23N 79°59E 43 D8
Nanda Devi △ India 30°30N 79°50E 43 D8
Nanda Kot India 30°17N 80°5E 43 D9
Nandan = Minamiawaji Japan 34°10N 134°42E 29 G7
Nandan China 24°58N 107°29E 34 E6
Nanded India 19°10N 77°20E 44 E3
Nandewar Ra. Australia 30°15S 150°35E 63 E5
Nandgaon India 20°19N 74°39E 44 D2
Nandi = Nadi Fiji 17°42S 177°20E 59 a
Nandi Zimbabwe 20°58S 31°44E 57 B5
Nandigama India 16°47N 80°18E 44 F5
Nandigram India 22°1N 87°58E 43 H12
Nandikotkur India 15°52N 78°18E 45 G4
Nandura India 20°52N 76°25E 44 D3
Nandurbar India 21°20N 74°15E 44 D2
Nandyal India 15°30N 78°30E 45 G4
Nanfeng Guangdong, China 23°45N 111°47E 35 F8
Nanfeng Jiangxi, China 27°12N 116°28E 35 D11
Nang Rong Thailand 14°38N 102°48E 38 E4
Nanga-Eboko Cameroon 4°41N 12°22E 54 D2
Nanga Parbat Pakistan 35°10N 74°35E 43 B6
Nangapinoh Indonesia 0°20S 111°44E 36 E4
Nangarhār □ Afghan. 34°20N 70°0E 40 B7
Nangatayap Indonesia 1°32S 110°34E 36 E4
Nangong China 37°23N 115°22E 32 F8
Nanguneri India 8°29N 77°40E 45 K3
Nanhua China 25°13N 101°21E 34 E3
Nanhuang China 36°58N 121°48E 33 F11
Nanhui China 31°5N 121°44E 35 B13
Nanisivik Canada 73°2N 84°33W 69 C15
Nanjangud India 12°6N 76°43E 45 H3
Nanji Shan China 27°27N 121°4E 35 D13
Nanjian China 25°2N 100°25E 34 E3
Nanjiang China 32°28N 106°51E 34 A6
Nanjing Fujian, China 24°25N 117°20E 35 E11
Nanjing Jiangsu, China 32°2N 118°47E 35 A12
Nankana Sahib Pakistan 31°27N 73°38E 42 D5
Nankang China 25°40N 114°45E 35 E10
Nanking = Nanjing China 32°2N 118°47E 35 A12
Nankoku Japan 33°39N 133°44E 29 H6
Nanlang China 22°30N 113°32E 31 a
Nanling China 30°55N 118°20E 35 B12
Nannial India 19°4N 79°38E 44 E4
Nanning China 22°48N 108°20E 34 F7
Nannup Australia 33°59S 115°48E 61 F2
Nanpan Jiang → China 25°10N 106°5E 34 E6
Nanpara India 27°52N 81°33E 43 F9
Nanping Fujian, China 26°38N 118°10E 35 D12
Nanping Henan, China 29°55N 112°3E 35 C9
Nanri Dao China 25°15N 119°25E 35 E12
Nansei-Shotō = Ryūkyū-Rettō Japan 26°0N 126°0E 29 M3
Nansen Basin Arctic 84°0N 50°0E 4 A10
Nansen Sd. Canada 81°0N 91°0W 69 A13
Nansha China 22°45N 113°34E 31 a
Nansha Port China 22°40N 113°40E 31 a
Nanshan China 18°19N 109°10E 38 C7
Nanshan I. S. China Sea 10°45N 115°49E 36 B5
Nantawarrinna ✪ Australia 30°49S 138°58E 63 B2
Nantes France 47°12N 1°33W 20 C3
Nanticoke U.S.A. 41°12N 76°0W 83 E8
Nanton Canada 50°21N 113°46W 70 C6
Nantong China 32°1N 120°52E 35 A13
Nantou China 22°32N 113°55E 31 a
Nant'ou Taiwan 23°55N 120°41E 35 F13
Nantucket U.S.A. 41°17N 70°6W 81 E18
Nantucket I. U.S.A. 41°16N 70°5W 81 E18
Nantwich U.K. 53°4N 2°31W 12 D5
Nanty Glo U.S.A. 40°28N 78°50W 82 F6
Nanuku Passage Fiji 16°45S 179°15W 59 a
Nanuque Brazil 17°50S 40°21W 93 G10
Nanusa, Kepulauan Indonesia 4°45N 127°1E 37 D7
Nanutarra Roadhouse Australia 22°32S 115°30E 60 D2
Nanxi China 28°54N 104°59E 34 C5
Nanxiong China 25°6N 114°15E 35 E10
Nanyang China 33°11N 112°30E 32 H7
Nanyi Hu China 31°5N 119°0E 35 B12
Nanyuan China 39°47N 116°24E 32 E9
Nanyuki Kenya 0°2N 37°4E 54 D7
Nanzhang China 31°45N 111°50E 35 B8
Nanzhao China 33°30N 112°20E 32 H7
Nao, C. de la Spain 38°44N 0°14E 21 C6
Naococane, L. Canada 52°50N 70°45W 73 B5
Naozhou Dao China 20°55N 110°20E 38 B8
Napa U.S.A. 38°18N 122°17W 78 G4
Napa → U.S.A. 38°10N 122°19W 78 G4
Napanee Canada 44°15N 77°0W 82 B8
Napanoch U.S.A. 41°44N 74°22W 83 E10
Nape Laos 18°18N 105°6E 38 C5
Nape Pass = Keo Neua, Deo Vietnam 18°23N 105°10E 38 C5
Napier N.Z. 39°30S 176°56E 59 C6
Napier Broome B. Australia 14°2S 126°37E 60 B4
Napier Pen. Australia 12°4S 135°43E 62 A2
Napierville Canada 45°11N 73°25W 83 A11
Naples = Nápoli Italy 40°50N 14°15E 22 D6
Naples U.S.A. 26°8N 81°48W 85 H14
Napo China 23°22N 105°50E 34 F5
Napo → Peru 3°20S 72°40W 92 D4
Napoleon N. Dak., U.S.A. 46°30N 99°46W 80 B4
Napoleon Ohio, U.S.A. 41°23N 84°8W 81 E11
Nápoli Italy 40°50N 14°15E 22 D6
Naqadeh Iran 36°57N 45°23E 46 B5
Naqb, Ra's an Jordan 29°48N 35°44E 48 F4
Naqqāsh Iran 35°40N 49°6E 47 C6
Nara Japan 34°40N 135°49E 29 G7
Nara Mali 15°10N 7°20W 52 E4
Nara □ Japan 34°30N 136°0E 29 G8
Nara Canal Pakistan 24°30N 69°20E 42 G3
Nara Visa U.S.A. 35°37N 103°6W 77 J12
Naracoorte Australia 36°58S 140°45E 63 F3
Naradhan Australia 33°34S 146°17E 63 E4
Naraini India 25°11N 80°29E 43 G9
Naranjos Mexico 21°21N 97°41W 87 C5
Narasannapeta India 18°25N 84°3E 44 E7
Narasapur India 16°26N 81°40E 45 F5
Narasaraopet India 16°14N 80°4E 45 F5
Narathiwat Thailand 6°30N 101°48E 39 J3
Narayanapatnam India 18°53N 83°10E 44 E6
Narayangadh = Bharatpur Nepal 27°34N 84°10E 43 F11
Narayanganj Bangla. 23°40N 90°33E 41 H17
Narayanpet India 16°45N 77°30E 44 F3
Narberth U.K. 51°47N 4°44W 13 F3
Narbonne France 43°11N 3°0E 20 E5
Narcondam I. India 13°20N 94°16E 45 H12
Nardīn Iran 37°3N 55°59E 47 B7
Nardò Italy 40°11N 18°2E 23 D8
Narembeen Australia 32°7S 118°24E 61 F2
Nares Str. Arctic 80°0N 70°0W 69 B18
Naretha Australia 31°0S 124°45E 61 F3
Narew → Poland 52°26N 20°41E 17 B11
Nari → Pakistan 28°0N 67°40E 42 F2

Narin *Afghan.* 36°5N 69°0E **40** A6
Narita *Japan* 35°47N 140°19E **29** G10
Nariva Swamp
  *Trin. & Tob.* 10°26N 61°4W **93** K15
Narmada → *India* 21°38N 72°36E **42** J5
Narmada Canal *India* 22°20N 73°45E **44** C1
Narnaul *India* 28°5N 76°11E **42** E7
Narodnaya *Russia* 65°5N 59°58E **18** A10
Narooma *Australia* 36°14S 150°4E **63** F5
Narowal *Pakistan* 32°6N 74°52E **42** C6
Narrabri *Australia* 30°19S 149°46E **63** E4
Narran → *Australia* 28°37S 148°12E **63** D4
Narrandera *Australia* 34°42S 146°31E **63** E4
Narrogin *Australia* 32°58S 117°14E **61** F2
Narromine *Australia* 32°12S 148°12E **63** E4
Narrow Hills △ *Canada* 54°0N 104°37W **71** C8
Narsampet *India* 17°57N 79°58E **44** F4
Narsimhapur *India* 22°54N 79°14E **43** H8
Narsinghgarh *India* 23°45N 76°40E **42** H7
Narsinghpur *India* 20°28N 85°5E **44** D7
Narsipatnam *India* 17°40N 82°37E **44** F6
Narutō = Sanmu *Japan* 34°11N 134°37E **29** G7
Narva *Estonia* 59°23N 28°12E **9** G4
Narva → *Russia* 59°27N 28°2E **9** G23
Narva Bay = Narva Laht
  *Estonia* 59°35N 27°35E **9** G22
Narva Laht *Estonia* 59°35N 27°35E **9** G22
Narvik *Norway* 68°28N 17°26E **8** B17
Narwana *India* 29°39N 76°6E **42** E7
Narwinbi ☉ *Australia* 16°7S 136°17E **62** B2
Naryan-Mar *Russia* 67°42N 53°12E **18** A9
Narym *Russia* 59°0N 81°30E **26** D9
Naryn *Kyrgyzstan* 41°26N 75°58E **30** C4
Naryn Qum *Kazakhstan* 47°30N 49°0E **26** E5
Nás, An = Naas *Ireland* 53°12N 6°40W **10** C5
Nasa *Norway* 66°29N 15°23E **8** C16
Nasau *Fiji* 17°19S 179°27E **59** a
Nasca *Peru* 14°50S 74°57W **92** F4
Nasca Ridge *Pac. Oc.* 20°0S 80°0W **65** K19
Naseby *N.Z.* 45°1S 170°10E **59** F3
Naselle *U.S.A.* 46°22N 123°49W **78** D3
Naser, Buheirat en *Egypt* 23°0N 32°30E **53** D12
Nashik = Nasik *India* 19°58N 73°50E **44** E1
Nashua *Mont., U.S.A.* 48°8N 106°22W **76** B10
Nashua *N.H., U.S.A.* 42°45N 71°28W **83** D13
Nashville *Ark., U.S.A.* 33°57N 93°51W **84** E8
Nashville *Ga., U.S.A.* 31°12N 83°15W **85** F13
Nashville *Tenn., U.S.A.* 36°10N 86°47W **85** C11
Nasik *India* 19°58N 73°50E **44** E1
Nasirabad *India* 26°15N 74°45E **42** F6
Nasirabad *Pakistan* 28°23N 68°24E **42** E3
Nasiri = Ahvāz *Iran* 31°20N 48°40E **47** D6
Nasiriyah = An Nāşiriyah
  *Iraq* 31°0N 46°15E **46** D5
Naskaupi → *Canada* 53°47N 60°51W **73** B7
Naşrābād *Iran* 34°8N 51°26E **47** C6
Naşrīān-e Pā'īn *Iran* 32°52N 46°52E **46** C5
Nass → *Canada* 55°0N 129°40W **70** C3
Nassau *Bahamas* 25°5N 77°20W **88** A4
Nassau *U.S.A.* 42°31N 73°37W **83** D11
Nassau, B. *Chile* 55°20S 68°0W **96** H3
Nasser, L. = Naser, Buheirat en
  *Egypt* 23°0N 32°30E **53** D12
Nässjö *Sweden* 57°39N 14°42E **9** H16
Nastapoka → *Canada* 56°55N 76°33W **72** A4
Nastapoka, Is. *Canada* 56°55N 76°50W **72** A4
Nasushiobara *Japan* 36°58N 140°3E **29** F10
Nata *Botswana* 20°12S 26°12E **56** B4
Nata → *Botswana* 20°14S 26°10E **56** B4
Natal *Brazil* 5°47S 35°13W **93** E11
Natal *Indonesia* 0°35N 99°7E **36** D1
Natal Drakensberg = uKhahlamba Drakensberg △
  *S. Africa* 29°27S 29°30E **57** C4
Naţanz *Iran* 33°30N 51°55E **47** C6
Natashquan *Canada* 50°14N 61°46W **73** B7
Natashquan → *Canada* 50°7N 61°50W **73** B7
Natchez *U.S.A.* 31°34N 91°24W **84** F9
Natchitoches *U.S.A.* 31°46N 93°5W **84** F8
Natewa B. *Fiji* 16°35S 179°40E **59** a
Nathalia *Australia* 36°1S 145°13E **63** F4
Nathdwara *India* 24°55N 73°50E **42** G5
Natimuk *Australia* 36°42S 142°0E **63** F3
Nation → *Canada* 55°30N 123°32W **70** B4
National City *U.S.A.* 32°40N 117°5W **79** N9
Natitingou *Benin* 10°20N 1°26E **52** F6
Natividad, I. *Mexico* 27°52N 115°11W **86** B1
Natkyizin *Myanmar* 14°57N 97°59E **38** E1
Natron, L. *Tanzania* 2°20S 36°0E **54** E7
Natrona Heights *U.S.A.* 40°37N 79°44W **82** F5
Natuashish *Canada* 55°55N 61°8W **73** A7
Natukanaoka Pan
  *Namibia* 18°40S 15°45E **56** A2
Natuna Besar, Kepulauan
  *Indonesia* 4°0N 108°15E **36** D3
Natuna Is. = Natuna Besar, Kepulauan *Indonesia* 4°0N 108°15E **36** D3
Natuna Selatan, Kepulauan
  *Indonesia* 2°45N 109°0E **36** D3
Natural Bridge *U.S.A.* 44°5N 75°30W **83** B9
Natural Bridges △
  *U.S.A.* 37°36N 110°0W **77** H9
Naturaliste, C. *Tas., Australia* 40°50S 148°15E **63** G4
Naturaliste, C. *W. Austral., Australia* 33°32S 115°0E **61** F2
Naturaliste Plateau
  *Ind. Oc.* 34°0S 112°0E **64** L3
Nau Qala *Afghan.* 34°5N 68°5E **42** B3
Naugatuck *U.S.A.* 41°30N 73°3W **83** E11
Naujaat = Repulse Bay
  *Canada* 66°30N 86°30W **69** D14
Naumburg *Germany* 51°9N 11°47E **16** C6
Naupada *India* 18°34N 84°18E **44** E7
Nauru ■ *Pac. Oc.* 1°0S 166°0E **58** B9
Naushahra = Nowshera
  *Pakistan* 34°0N 72°0E **40** C8
Naushahro *Pakistan* 26°50N 68°7E **42** F3
Naushon I. *U.S.A.* 41°29N 70°45W **83** E14
Nausori *Fiji* 18°2S 178°32E **59** a

Nauta *Peru* 4°31S 73°35W **92** D4
Nautanwa *India* 27°20N 83°25E **43** F10
Naute △ *Namibia* 26°55S 17°57E **56** C2
Nautla *Mexico* 20°13N 96°47W **87** C5
Nava *Mexico* 28°25N 100°45W **86** B4
Navadwip *India* 23°34N 88°20E **43** H13
Navahrudak *Belarus* 53°40N 25°50E **17** B13
Navajo Res. *U.S.A.* 36°48N 107°36W **77** H10
Navalgund *India* 15°34N 75°22E **45** G2
Navalmoral de la Mata
  *Spain* 39°52N 5°33W **21** C3
Navan *Ireland* 53°39N 6°41W **10** C5
Navarin, Mys *Russia* 62°15N 179°5E **27** C18
Navarino, I. *Chile* 55°0S 67°40W **96** H3
Navarra □ *Spain* 42°40N 1°40W **21** A5
Navarre *U.S.A.* 40°43N 81°31W **82** F3
Navarro → *U.S.A.* 39°11N 123°45W **78** F3
Navasota *U.S.A.* 30°23N 96°5W **84** F6
Navassa I. *W. Indies* 18°30N 75°0W **89** C5
Naver → *U.K.* 58°32N 4°14W **11** C4
Navibandar *India* 21°26N 69°48E **42** J3
Navidad *Chile* 33°57S 71°50W **94** C1
Navirai *Brazil* 23°8S 54°13W **95** A5
Naviti *Fiji* 17°7S 177°15E **59** a
Navlakhi *India* 22°58N 70°28E **42** H4
Năvodari *Romania* 44°19N 28°36E **17** F15
Navoiy *Uzbekistan* 40°9N 65°22E **26** E7
Navojoa *Mexico* 27°6N 109°26W **86** B3
Navolato *Mexico* 24°47N 107°42W **86** C3
Navsari *India* 20°57N 72°59E **44** D1
Navua *Fiji* 18°12S 178°11E **59** a
Nawa Kot *Pakistan* 28°21N 71°24E **42** E4
Nawab Khan *Pakistan* 30°17N 69°12E **42** D3
Nawabganj *Ut. P., India* 26°56N 81°14E **43** F9
Nawabganj *Ut. P., India* 28°32N 79°40E **43** E8
Nawabshah *Pakistan* 26°15N 68°25E **42** F3
Nawada *India* 24°50N 85°33E **43** G11
Nawakot *Nepal* 27°55N 85°10E **43** F11
Nawalgarh *India* 27°50N 75°15E **42** F6
Nawanshahr *India* 32°33N 74°48E **43** C6
Nawapara *India* 20°46N 82°33E **44** D6
Nawar, Dasht-i- *Afghan.* 33°52N 68°0E **42** C3
Nawoiy = Navoiy
  *Uzbekistan* 40°9N 65°22E **26** E7
Naxçıvan *Azerbaijan* 39°12N 45°15E **46** B5
Naxçıvan □ *Azerbaijan* 39°25N 45°26E **46** B5
Naxos *Greece* 37°8N 25°25E **23** F11
Nay, Mui *Vietnam* 12°54N 109°26E **38** F7
Năy Band *Būshehr, Iran* 27°20N 52°40E **47** E7
Năy Band *Khorāsān, Iran* 32°20N 57°34E **47** C8
Nay Pyi Taw = Naypyidaw
  *Myanmar* 19°44N 96°12E **30** H8
Nayagarh *India* 20°8N 85°6E **44** D7
Nayakhan *Russia* 61°56N 159°0E **27** C16
Nayarit □ *Mexico* 22°0N 105°0W **86** C4
Nayau *Fiji* 18°6S 178°10E **59** a
Nayong *China* 26°50N 105°20E **34** D5
Nayoro *Japan* 44°21N 142°28E **28** B11
Naypyidaw *Myanmar* 19°44N 96°12E **30** H8
Nayudupeta *India* 13°54N 79°54E **45** H4
Nayyāl, W. → *Si. Arabia* 28°35N 39°4E **46** D3
Nazaré *Brazil* 13°2S 39°0W **93** F11
Nazareth = Nazerat *Israel* 32°42N 35°17E **48** C4
Nazareth *U.S.A.* 40°44N 75°19W **83** F9
Nazarovo *Russia* 57°2N 90°40E **27** D10
Nazas *Mexico* 25°14N 104°8W **86** B4
Nazas → *Mexico* 25°12N 104°12W **86** B4
Nazca = Nasca *Peru* 14°50S 74°57W **92** F4
Naze, The *U.K.* 51°53N 1°18E **13** F9
Nazerat *Israel* 32°42N 35°17E **48** C4
Nazik *Iran* 39°1N 45°4E **46** B5
Nazilli *Turkey* 37°55N 28°15E **23** F13
Nazko *Canada* 53°1N 123°37W **70** C4
Nazko → *Canada* 53°7N 123°34W **70** C4
Nazret *Ethiopia* 8°32N 39°22E **49** F2
Ndalatando *Angola* 9°12S 14°48E **54** F2
Ndélé *C.A.R.* 8°25N 20°36E **54** C4
Ndjamena *Chad* 12°10N 15°0E **53** F8
Ndola *Zambia* 13°0S 28°34E **55** G5
Ndomo → *S. Africa* 26°52S 32°15E **57** C5
Ndoto Mts. *Kenya* 2°0N 37°0E **54** D7
Neagh, Lough *U.K.* 54°37N 6°25W **10** B5
Neah Bay *U.S.A.* 48°22N 124°37W **78** B2
Neale, L. *Australia* 24°15S 130°0E **60** D5
Neales → *Australia* 28°8S 136°47E **63** D2
Near Is. *U.S.A.* 52°30N 174°0E **74** E2
Neath *U.K.* 51°39N 3°48W **13** F4
Neath Port Talbot □ *U.K.* 51°42N 3°45W **13** F4
Nebine Cr. → *Australia* 29°27S 146°56E **63** D4
Nebitdag = Balkanabat
  *Turkmenistan* 39°30N 54°22E **47** B7
Nebo *Australia* 21°42S 148°42E **62** C4
Nebraska □ *U.S.A.* 41°30N 99°30W **80** E4
Nebraska City *U.S.A.* 40°41N 95°52W **80** E6
Nébrodi, Monti *Italy* 37°54N 14°35E **22** F6
Necedah *U.S.A.* 44°2N 90°4W **80** C8
Nechako → *Canada* 53°55N 122°40W **70** C4
Neches → *U.S.A.* 29°58N 93°51W **84** G8
Neckar → *Germany* 49°27N 8°29E **16** D5
Necker I. *U.S.A.* 23°35N 164°42W **75** L7
Necochea *Argentina* 38°30S 58°50W **94** D4
Nederland = Netherlands ■
  *Europe* 52°0N 5°30E **15** C5
Needles *Canada* 49°53N 118°7W **70** D5
Needles *U.S.A.* 34°51N 114°37W **79** L12
Needles, The *U.K.* 50°39N 1°35W **13** G6
Neembucú □ *Paraguay* 27°0S 58°0W **94** B4
Neemuch = Nimach
  *India* 24°30N 74°56E **42** G6
Neenah *U.S.A.* 44°11N 88°28W **80** C9
Neepawa *Canada* 50°15N 99°30W **71** C9
Neftçala *Azerbaijan* 39°19N 49°12E **47** C6
Neftegorsk *Russia* 53°1N 142°58E **27** D15
Neftekumsk *Russia* 44°46N 44°50E **19** F7
Neftyugansk *Russia* 61°5N 72°42E **26** C8
Nefyn *U.K.* 52°56N 4°31W **12** E3
Negapatam = Nagappattinam
  *India* 10°46N 79°51E **45** J4
Negara *Indonesia* 8°22S 114°37E **37** J17

Negaunee *U.S.A.* 46°30N 87°36W **80** B10
Negele *Ethiopia* 5°20N 39°36E **49** F2
Negeri Sembilan □
  *Malaysia* 2°45N 102°10E **39** L4
Negev Desert = Hanegev
  *Israel* 30°50N 35°0E **48** E4
Negombo *Sri Lanka* 7°12N 79°50E **45** L4
Negotin *Serbia* 44°16N 22°37E **23** B10
Negra, Pta. *Mauritania* 22°54N 16°18W **52** D2
Negra, Pta. *Peru* 6°6S 81°10W **92** E2
Negrais, C. = Maudin Sun
  *Myanmar* 16°0N 94°30E **41** M19
Negril *Jamaica* 18°22N 78°20W **88** a
Negro → *Argentina* 41°2S 62°47W **96** E4
Negro → *Brazil* 3°0S 60°0W **92** D7
Negro → *Uruguay* 33°24S 58°22W **94** C4
Negros *Phil.* 9°30N 122°40E **37** C6
Neguac *Canada* 47°15N 65°5W **73** C6
Nehalem → *U.S.A.* 45°40N 123°56W **78** E3
Nehāvand *Iran* 35°56N 49°31E **47** C6
Nehbandān *Iran* 31°35N 60°5E **47** D9
Nehe *China* 48°29N 124°50E **31** B13
Nei Mongol Zizhiqu □
  *China* 42°0N 112°0E **32** D7
Neiafu *Tonga* 18°39S 173°59W **59** c
Neijiang *China* 29°35N 104°55E **34** C5
Neilingding Dao *China* 22°25N 113°48E **31** a
Neill I. *India* 11°50N 93°3E **45** J11
Neillsville *U.S.A.* 44°34N 90°36W **80** C8
Neiqiu *China* 37°15N 114°30E **32** F8
Neiva *Colombia* 2°56N 75°18W **92** C3
Neixiang *China* 33°10N 111°52E **32** H6
Nejanilini L. *Canada* 59°33N 97°48W **71** B9
Nejd = Najd *Si. Arabia* 26°30N 42°0E **49** B3
Nekā *Iran* 36°39N 53°19E **47** B7
Nekemte *Ethiopia* 9°4N 36°30E **49** F2
Neksø *Denmark* 55°4N 15°8E **9** J16
Nelamangala *India* 13°6N 77°24E **45** H3
Nelia *Australia* 20°39S 142°12E **62** C3
Neligh *U.S.A.* 42°8N 98°2W **80** D4
Nelkan *Russia* 57°40N 136°4E **27** D14
Nellikuppam *India* 11°46N 79°43E **45** J4
Nellore *India* 14°27N 79°59E **45** G4
Nelson *Canada* 49°30N 117°20W **70** D5
Nelson *N.Z.* 41°18S 173°16E **59** D4
Nelson *U.K.* 53°50N 2°13W **12** D5
Nelson *Ariz., U.S.A.* 35°31N 113°19W **77** J7
Nelson *Nev., U.S.A.* 35°42N 114°49W **79** K12
Nelson → *Canada* 54°33N 98°2W **71** C9
Nelson, C. *Australia* 38°26S 141°32E **63** F3
Nelson, Estrecho *Chile* 51°30S 75°0W **96** G2
Nelson Forks *Canada* 59°30N 124°0W **70** B4
Nelson House *Canada* 55°47N 98°51W **71** B9
Nelson Lakes △ *N.Z.* 41°55S 172°44E **59** D4
Nelspoort *S. Africa* 32°7S 23°0E **56** E3
Nelspruit = Mbombela
  *S. Africa* 25°29S 30°59E **57** C5
Néma *Mauritania* 16°40N 7°15W **52** E4
Neman = Nemunas →
  *Lithuania* 55°25N 21°10E **9** J19
Nembrala *Indonesia* 10°53S 122°50E **60** B3
Nemeiben L. *Canada* 55°20N 105°20W **71** B7
Nemiscau *Canada* 51°18N 76°54W **72** B4
Nemiscau, L. *Canada* 51°25N 76°40W **72** B4
Nemunas → *Lithuania* 55°25N 21°10E **9** J19
Nemuro *Japan* 43°20N 145°35E **28** C12
Nemuro-Kaikyō *Japan* 43°30N 145°30E **28** C12
Nen Jiang → *China* 45°28N 124°30E **33** B13
Nenagh *Ireland* 52°52N 8°11W **10** D3
Nenana *U.S.A.* 64°34N 149°5W **74** C10
Nenasi *Malaysia* 3°9N 103°23E **39** L4
Nene → *U.K.* 52°49N 0°11E **13** E8
Nenjiang *China* 49°10N 125°10E **31** B14
Neodesha *U.S.A.* 37°25N 95°41W **80** G6
Neora Valley △ *India* 27°0N 88°45E **43** F13
Neosho *U.S.A.* 36°52N 94°22W **80** G6
Neosho → *U.S.A.* 36°48N 95°18W **84** C7
Nepal ■ *Asia* 28°0N 84°30E **43** F11
Nepalganj *Nepal* 28°5N 81°40E **43** E9
Nepalganj Road *India* 28°1N 81°41E **43** E9
Nephi *U.S.A.* 39°43N 111°50W **76** G8
Nephin *Ireland* 54°1N 9°22W **10** B2
Nephin Beg Range *Ireland* 54°0N 9°40W **10** C2
Neptune *U.S.A.* 40°13N 74°2W **83** F10
Neqāb *Iran* 36°57N 57°25E **47** B8
Nerang *Australia* 27°58S 153°20E **63** D5
Nerchinsk *Russia* 52°0N 116°39E **27** D12
Néret, L. *Canada* 54°45N 70°44W **73** B5
Neretva → *Croatia* 43°1N 17°27E **23** C7
Neringa *Lithuania* 55°20N 21°5E **9** J19
Neris → *Lithuania* 55°8N 24°16E **9** J21
Neryungri *Russia* 57°38N 124°28E **27** D13
Nescopeck *U.S.A.* 41°3N 76°12W **83** E8
Neskantaga *Canada* 52°14N 87°53W **72** B2
Ness, L. *U.K.* 57°15N 4°32W **11** D4
Ness City *U.S.A.* 38°27N 99°54W **80** F4
Nesterov = Zhovkva
  *Ukraine* 50°4N 23°58E **17** C12
Nestos → *Europe* 40°54N 24°49E **23** D11
Nesvizh = Nyasvizh
  *Belarus* 53°14N 26°38E **17** B14
Netanya *Israel* 32°20N 34°51E **48** C3
Netarhat *India* 23°29N 84°16E **43** H11
Nete → *Belgium* 51°7N 4°14E **15** C4
Netherdale *Australia* 21°10S 148°33E **62** b
Netherlands ■ *Europe* 52°0N 5°30E **15** C5
Netherlands Antilles = ABC
  Islands *W. Indies* 12°15N 69°0W **89** D6
Netrang *India* 21°39N 73°21E **42** J5
Nettilling L. *Canada* 66°30N 71°0W **69** D17
Netzahualcóyotl, Presa
  *Mexico* 17°8N 93°35W **87** D6
Neubrandenburg
  *Germany* 53°33N 13°15E **16** B7
Neuchâtel *Switz.* 47°0N 6°55E **20** C7
Neuchâtel, Lac de *Switz.* 46°53N 6°50E **20** C7

Neufchâteau *Belgium* 49°50N 5°25E **15** E5
Neumayer III *Antarctica* 71°0S 68°30W **5** D2
Neumünster *Germany* 54°4N 9°58E **16** A5
Neunkirchen *Germany* 49°20N 7°9E **16** D4
Neuquén *Argentina* 38°55S 68°0W **96** D3
Neuquén □ *Argentina* 38°0S 69°50W **94** D2
Neuruppin *Germany* 52°55N 12°48E **16** B7
Neuse → *U.S.A.* 35°6N 76°29W **85** D16
Neusiedler See *Austria* 47°50N 16°47E **17** E9
Neustrelitz *Germany* 53°21N 13°4E **16** B7
Neva → *Russia* 59°56N 30°20E **18** C5
Nevada *Iowa, U.S.A.* 42°1N 93°27W **80** D7
Nevada *Mo., U.S.A.* 37°51N 94°22W **80** G6
Nevada □ *U.S.A.* 39°0N 117°0W **76** G5
Nevada City *U.S.A.* 39°16N 121°1W **78** F6
Nevado, Cerro *Argentina* 35°30S 68°32W **94** D2
Nevado de Colima = Volcán de
  Colima △ *Mexico* 19°30N 103°40W **86** D4
Nevado de Tres Cruces △
  *Chile* 27°13S 69°5W **94** B2
Nevasa *India* 19°34N 75°0E **44** E2
Nevel *Russia* 56°0N 29°55E **18** C4
Nevelsk *Russia* 46°40N 141°51E **27** E15
Nevers *France* 47°0N 3°9E **20** C5
Nevertire *Australia* 31°50S 147°44E **63** E4
Neville *Canada* 49°58N 107°39W **71** D7
Nevinnomyssk *Russia* 44°40N 42°0E **19** F7
Nevis *St. Kitts & Nevis* 17°0N 62°30W **89** C7
Nevşehir *Turkey* 38°33N 34°40E **46** B2
Nevyansk *Russia* 57°30N 60°13E **18** C11
New → *U.S.A.* 38°10N 81°12W **81** F13
New Aiyansh *Canada* 55°12N 129°4W **70** B3
New Albany *Ind., U.S.A.* 38°18N 85°49W **81** F11
New Albany *Miss., U.S.A.* 34°29N 89°0W **85** D10
New Albany *Pa., U.S.A.* 41°36N 76°27W **83** E8
New Amsterdam *Guyana* 6°15N 57°36W **92** B7
New Baltimore *U.S.A.* 42°41N 82°44W **82** D2
New Bedford *U.S.A.* 41°38N 70°56W **83** E14
New Berlin *N.Y., U.S.A.* 42°37N 75°20W **83** D9
New Berlin *Pa., U.S.A.* 40°50N 76°57W **82** F8
New Bern *U.S.A.* 35°7N 77°3W **85** D16
New Bethlehem *U.S.A.* 41°0N 79°20W **82** F5
New Bight *Bahamas* 24°19N 75°24W **89** B4
New Bloomfield *U.S.A.* 40°25N 77°11W **82** F7
New Boston *U.S.A.* 33°28N 94°25W **84** E7
New Braunfels *U.S.A.* 29°42N 98°8W **84** G5
New Brighton *N.Z.* 43°29S 172°43E **59** E4
New Brighton *U.S.A.* 40°42N 80°19W **82** F4
New Britain *Papua N. G.* 5°50S 150°20E **58** B8
New Britain *U.S.A.* 41°40N 72°47W **83** E12
New Brunswick *U.S.A.* 40°30N 74°27W **83** F10
New Brunswick □
  *Canada* 46°50N 66°30W **73** C6
New Caledonia ☑ *Pac. Oc.* 21°0S 165°0E **58** D9
New Caledonia Trough
  *Pac. Oc.* 30°0S 165°0E **64** L8
New Castle = Castilla-La
  Mancha □ *Spain* 39°30N 3°30W **21** C4
New Castle *Ind., U.S.A.* 39°55N 85°22W **81** F11
New Castle *Pa., U.S.A.* 41°0N 80°21W **82** F4
New Chitose ✈ (CTS)
  *Japan* 42°46N 141°41E **28** C10
New City *U.S.A.* 41°9N 73°59W **83** E11
New Concord *U.S.A.* 39°59N 81°54W **82** G3
New Cumberland *U.S.A.* 40°30N 80°36W **82** F4
New Cuyama *U.S.A.* 34°57N 119°38W **79** L7
New Denver *Canada* 50°0N 117°25W **70** D5
New Don Pedro Res.
  *U.S.A.* 37°43N 120°24W **78** H6
New England *U.S.A.* 43°0N 71°0W **75** G25
New England *N. Dak., U.S.A.* 46°32N 102°52W **80** B2
New England Ra.
  *Australia* 30°20S 151°45E **63** E5
New Forest △ *U.K.* 50°53N 1°34W **13** G6
New Galloway *U.K.* 55°5N 4°9W **11** F4
New Glasgow *Canada* 45°35N 62°36W **73** C7
New Guinea *Oceania* 4°0S 136°0E **58** B6
New Hamburg *Canada* 43°23N 80°42W **82** C4
New Hampshire □
  *U.S.A.* 44°0N 71°30W **83** C13
New Hampton *U.S.A.* 43°3N 92°19W **80** D7
New Hanover *S. Africa* 29°22S 30°31E **57** C5
New Hartford *U.S.A.* 43°4N 75°18W **83** C9
New Haven *Conn., U.S.A.* 41°18N 72°55W **83** E12
New Haven *Mich., U.S.A.* 42°44N 82°48W **82** D2
New Haven *N.Y., U.S.A.* 43°28N 76°18W **83** C8
New Hazelton *Canada* 55°20N 127°30W **70** B3
New Hebrides = Vanuatu ■
  *Pac. Oc.* 15°0S 168°0E **58** C9
New Holland *U.S.A.* 40°6N 76°5W **83** F8
New Iberia *U.S.A.* 30°1N 91°49W **84** F9
New Ireland *Papua N. G.* 3°20S 151°50E **58** B8
New Jersey □ *U.S.A.* 40°0N 74°30W **81** F16
New Kensington *U.S.A.* 40°34N 79°46W **82** F5
New Lexington *U.S.A.* 39°43N 82°13W **81** F12
New Liskeard *Canada* 47°31N 79°41W **72** C4
New London *Conn., U.S.A.* 41°22N 72°6W **83** E12
New London *Ohio, U.S.A.* 41°5N 82°24W **82** E2
New London *Wis., U.S.A.* 44°23N 88°45W **80** C9
New Madrid *U.S.A.* 36°36N 89°32W **80** G9
New Martinsville
  *U.S.A.* 39°39N 80°52W **81** F13
New Meadows *U.S.A.* 44°58N 116°18W **76** D5
New Melones L. *U.S.A.* 37°57N 120°31W **78** H6
New Mexico □ *U.S.A.* 34°30N 106°0W **77** J11
New Milford *Conn., U.S.A.* 41°35N 73°25W **83** E11
New Milford *Pa., U.S.A.* 41°52N 75°44W **83** E9
New Norcia *Australia* 30°57S 116°13E **61** F2
New Norfolk *Australia* 42°46S 147°2E **63** G4
New Orleans *U.S.A.* 29°57N 90°4W **85** G9
New Philadelphia *U.S.A.* 40°30N 81°27W **82** F3
New Plymouth *N.Z.* 39°4S 174°5E **59** C5
New Plymouth *U.S.A.* 43°58N 116°49W **76** E5
New Port Richey *U.S.A.* 28°16N 82°43W **85** G13
New Providence
  *Bahamas* 25°25N 77°35W **88** A4

New Quay *U.K.* 52°13N 4°21W **13** E3
New Radnor *U.K.* 52°15N 3°9W **13** E4
New Richmond *Canada* 48°15N 65°45W **73** C6
New Richmond *U.S.A.* 45°7N 92°32W **80** C7
New River Gorge △
  *U.S.A.* 37°53N 81°5W **81** G13
New Roads *U.S.A.* 30°42N 91°26W **84** F9
New Rochelle *U.S.A.* 40°55N 73°46W **83** F11
New Rockford *U.S.A.* 47°41N 99°8W **80** B4
New Romney *U.K.* 50°59N 0°57E **13** G8
New Ross *Ireland* 52°23N 6°57W **10** D5
New Salem *U.S.A.* 46°51N 101°25W **80** B4
New Scone = Scone *U.K.* 56°25N 3°24W **11** E5
New Siberian I. = Novaya Sibir,
  Ostrov *Russia* 75°10N 150°0E **27** B16
New Siberian Is. = Novosibirskiye
  Ostrova *Russia* 75°0N 142°0E **27** B15
New Smyrna Beach
  *U.S.A.* 29°1N 80°56W **85** G14
New South Wales □
  *Australia* 33°0S 146°0E **63** E4
New Tecumseth = Alliston
  *Canada* 44°9N 79°52W **82** B5
New Town *U.S.A.* 47°59N 102°30W **80** B2
New Ulm *U.S.A.* 44°19N 94°28W **80** C6
New Waterford *Canada* 46°13N 60°4W **73** C7
New Westminster
  *Canada* 49°13N 122°55W **78** A4
New York □ *U.S.A.* 43°0N 75°0W **83** D9
New York J.F. Kennedy Int. ✈
  (JFK) *U.S.A.* 40°38N 73°47W **83** F11
New Zealand ■ *Oceania* 40°0S 176°0E **59** D6
Newaj → *India* 24°24N 76°49E **42** G7
Newark *Del., U.S.A.* 39°41N 75°46W **81** F16
Newark *N.J., U.S.A.* 40°44N 74°10W **83** F10
Newark *N.Y., U.S.A.* 43°3N 77°6W **82** C7
Newark *Ohio, U.S.A.* 40°3N 82°24W **82** F2
Newark Liberty Int. ✈ (EWR)
  *U.S.A.* 40°42N 74°10W **83** F10
Newark-on-Trent *U.K.* 53°5N 0°48W **12** D7
Newark Valley *U.S.A.* 42°14N 76°11W **83** D8
Newberg *U.S.A.* 45°18N 122°58W **76** D2
Newberry *Mich., U.S.A.* 46°21N 85°30W **81** B11
Newberry *S.C., U.S.A.* 34°17N 81°37W **85** D14
Newberry Springs
  *U.S.A.* 34°50N 116°41W **79** L10
Newboro L. *Canada* 44°38N 76°20W **83** B8
Newbridge *Ireland* 53°11N 6°48W **10** C5
Newburgh *Canada* 44°19N 76°52W **82** B8
Newburgh *U.S.A.* 41°30N 74°1W **83** E10
Newbury *U.K.* 51°24N 1°20W **13** F6
Newbury *N.H., U.S.A.* 43°19N 72°3W **83** B12
Newbury *Vt., U.S.A.* 44°5N 72°4W **83** B12
Newburyport *U.S.A.* 42°49N 70°53W **83** D14
Newcastle *Australia* 33°0S 151°46E **63** E5
Newcastle *N.B., Canada* 47°1N 65°38W **73** C6
Newcastle *Ont., Canada* 43°55N 78°35W **72** D4
Newcastle *Ireland* 52°27N 9°3E **10** D2
Newcastle *S. Africa* 27°45S 29°58E **57** C4
Newcastle *U.K.* 54°13N 5°54W **10** B6
Newcastle *Calif., U.S.A.* 38°53N 121°8W **78** G5
Newcastle *Wyo.,*
  *U.S.A.* 43°50N 104°11W **76** E11
Newcastle Emlyn *U.K.* 52°2N 4°28W **13** E3
Newcastle Ra. *Australia* 15°45S 130°15E **60** C5
Newcastle-under-Lyme
  *U.K.* 53°1N 2°14W **12** D5
Newcastle-upon-Tyne
  *U.K.* 54°58N 1°36W **12** C6
Newcastle Waters
  *Australia* 17°30S 133°28E **62** B1
Newcomb *U.S.A.* 43°58N 74°10W **83** C10
Newcomerstown *U.S.A.* 40°16N 81°36W **82** F3
Newdegate *Australia* 33°6S 119°0E **61** F2
Newell *Australia* 16°20S 145°16E **62** B4
Newell *U.S.A.* 44°43N 103°25W **80** C2
Newenham, C. *U.S.A.* 58°39N 162°11W **74** D7
Newfane *U.S.A.* 43°17N 78°43W **82** C6
Newfield *U.S.A.* 42°18N 76°33W **83** D8
Newfound L. *U.S.A.* 43°40N 71°47W **83** C13
Newfoundland *Canada* 49°0N 55°0W **73** C8
Newfoundland *U.S.A.* 41°18N 75°19W **83** E9
Newfoundland & Labrador □
  *Canada* 52°0N 58°0W **73** B8
Newhaven *U.K.* 50°47N 0°3E **13** G8
Newkirk *U.S.A.* 36°53N 97°3W **84** C6
Newlyn *U.K.* 50°6N 5°34W **13** G2
Newman *Australia* 23°18S 119°45E **60** D2
Newman *U.S.A.* 37°19N 121°1W **78** H5
Newmarket *Canada* 44°3N 79°28W **82** B5
Newmarket *Ireland* 52°13N 9°0W **10** D2
Newmarket *U.K.* 52°15N 0°25E **13** E8
Newmarket *U.S.A.* 43°5N 70°56W **83** C14
Newnan *U.S.A.* 33°23N 84°48W **85** E12
Newport *Ireland* 53°53N 9°33W **10** C2
Newport *I. of W., U.K.* 50°42N 1°17W **13** G6
Newport *Newport, U.K.* 51°35N 3°0W **13** F5
Newport *Ark., U.S.A.* 35°37N 91°16W **84** D9
Newport *Ky., U.S.A.* 39°5N 84°29W **81** F11
Newport *N.H., U.S.A.* 43°22N 72°10W **83** C12
Newport *N.Y., U.S.A.* 43°11N 75°1W **83** C9
Newport *Oreg., U.S.A.* 44°39N 124°3W **76** D1
Newport *Pa., U.S.A.* 40°29N 77°8W **82** F7
Newport *R.I., U.S.A.* 41°29N 71°19W **83** E13
Newport *Tenn., U.S.A.* 35°58N 83°11W **85** D13
Newport *Vt., U.S.A.* 44°56N 72°13W **83** B12
Newport *Wash., U.S.A.* 48°11N 117°3W **76** B5
Newport □ *U.K.* 51°33N 3°1W **13** F4
Newport Beach *U.S.A.* 33°37N 117°56W **79** M9
Newport News *U.S.A.* 36°58N 76°25W **81** G15
Newport Pagnell *U.K.* 52°5N 0°43W **13** E7
Newquay *U.K.* 50°25N 5°6W **13** G2
Newry *U.K.* 54°11N 6°21W **10** B5
Newry Islands △
  *Australia* 20°51S 148°56E **62** b
Newton *Ill., U.S.A.* 38°59N 88°10W **80** F9
Newton *Iowa, U.S.A.* 41°42N 93°3W **80** E7
Newton *Kans., U.S.A.* 38°3N 97°21W **80** F5
Newton *Miss., U.S.A.* 32°19N 89°10W **85** E10
Newton *N.C., U.S.A.* 35°40N 81°13W **85** D14

Newton *N.J., U.S.A.* 41°3N 74°45W **83** E10
Newton *Tex., U.S.A.* 30°51N 93°46W **84** F8
Newton Abbot *U.K.* 50°32N 3°37W **13** G4
Newton Aycliffe *U.K.* 54°37N 1°34W **12** C6
Newton Falls *N.Y., U.S.A.* 44°12N 74°59W **83** B10
Newton Falls *Ohio, U.S.A.* 41°11N 80°59W **82** E4
Newton Stewart *U.K.* 54°57N 4°30W **11** G4
Newtonmore *U.K.* 57°4N 4°8W **11** D4
Newtown *U.K.* 52°31N 3°19W **13** E4
Newtownabbey *U.K.* 54°40N 5°56W **10** B6
Newtownards *U.K.* 54°36N 5°42W **10** B6
Newtownbarry = Bunclody
  *Ireland* 52°39N 6°40W **10** D5
Newtownstewart *U.K.* 54°43N 7°23W **10** B4
Newville *U.S.A.* 40°10N 77°24W **82** F7
Neya *Russia* 58°21N 43°49E **18** C7
Neyrīz *Iran* 29°15N 54°19E **47** D7
Neyshābūr *Iran* 36°10N 58°50E **47** B8
Neyveli *India* 11°32N 79°29E **45** J4
Neyyattinkara *India* 8°26N 77°5E **45** K3
Nezhin = Nizhyn *Ukraine* 51°5N 31°55E **19** D5
Nezperce *U.S.A.* 46°14N 116°14W **76** C5
Nga, Laem *Thailand* 7°55N 98°27E **39** a
Ngaanyatjarra ◎
  *Australia* 22°40S 127°0E **60** D4
Ngabang *Indonesia* 0°23N 109°55E **36** D3
Ngabordamlu, Tanjung
  *Indonesia* 6°56S 134°11E **37** F8
N'Gage *Angola* 7°46S 15°15E **54** F3
Ngaliwurru Nungali ◎
  *Australia* 15°42S 130°4E **60** C5
Ngalurrtju ◎ *Australia* 22°44S 132°5E **60** D5
Ngami Depression
  *Botswana* 20°30S 22°46E **56** B3
Ngamring *China* 29°14N 87°10E **30** F6
Nganglong Kangri *China* 33°0N 81°0E **43** C9
Ngao *Thailand* 18°46N 99°59E **38** C2
Ngaoundéré *Cameroon* 7°15N 13°35E **54** C2
Ngapara *N.Z.* 44°57S 170°46E **59** F3
Ngaruma ◎ *Australia* 21°30S 118°30E **60** D2
Ngawi *Indonesia* 7°24S 111°26E **37** G14
Ngcobo *S. Africa* 31°37S 28°0E **57** D4
Ngerulmud = Melekeok
  *Palau* 7°27N 134°38E **64** G5
Nghia Lo *Vietnam* 21°33N 104°28E **34** G5
Ngoring Hu *China* 34°55N 97°5E **30** E8
Ngorongoro *Tanzania* 3°11S 35°32E **54** E7
Nguigmi *Niger* 14°20N 13°20E **53** F8
Nguiu *Australia* 11°46S 130°38E **60** B5
Ngukurr *Australia* 14°44S 134°44E **62** A1
Ngum → *Laos* 18°31N 102°32E **38** C4
Ngundu *Zimbabwe* 18°11S 31°15E **57** A5
Nguru *Nigeria* 12°56N 10°29E **53** F8
Nguyen Binh *Vietnam* 22°39N 105°56E **34** F5
Ngwaketse ◎ *Botswana* 25°0S 25°0E **56** C3
Nha Bang *Vietnam* 10°37N 105°0E **39** G5
Nha Trang *Vietnam* 12°16N 109°10E **39** F7
Nhacoongo *Mozam.* 24°18S 35°14E **57** B6
Nhamundá → *Brazil* 2°12S 56°41W **93** D7
Nhangulaze, L. *Mozam.* 24°0S 34°30E **57** B5
Nharnuwangga, Wajarri and
  Ngarlawangga ◎
  *Australia* 24°50S·118°0E **61** D2
Nhill *Australia* 36°18S 141°40E **63** F3
Nho Quan *Vietnam* 20°18N 105°45E **34** G5
Nhulunbuy *Australia* 12°10S 137°20E **62** A2
Niafounké *Mali* 16°0N 4°5W **52** E5
Niagara Falls *Canada* 43°7N 79°5W **82** C5
Niagara Falls *U.S.A.* 43°5N 79°4W **82** C6
Niagara-on-the-Lake
  *Canada* 43°15N 79°4W **82** C5
Niah *Malaysia* 3°58N 113°46E **36** D4
Niamey *Niger* 13°27N 2°6E **52** F6
Niangara
  *Dem. Rep. of the Congo* 3°42N 27°50E **54** D5
Niantic *U.S.A.* 41°20N 72°11W **83** E12
Nias *Indonesia* 1°0N 97°30E **36** D1
Niassa, L. = Malawi, L.
  *Africa* 12°30S 34°30E **55** G6
Nibāk *Si. Arabia* 24°25N 50°50E **47** E7
Nicaragua ■ *Cent. Amer.* 11°40N 85°30W **88** D2
Nicaragua, L. de *Nic.* 12°0N 85°30W **88** D2
Nicastro *Italy* 38°59N 16°19E **22** E7
Nice *France* 43°42N 7°14E **20** E7
Niceville *U.S.A.* 30°31N 86°30W **85** F11
Nichicun, L. *Canada* 53°5N 71°0W **73** B5
Nichinan *Japan* 31°38N 131°23E **29** J5
Nicholás, Canal *Caribbean* 23°30N 80°5W **88** B3
Nicholas Channel = Nicholás,
  Canal *Caribbean* 23°30N 80°5W **88** B3
Nicholasville *U.S.A.* 37°53N 84°34W **81** G11
Nichols *U.S.A.* 42°1N 76°22W **83** D8
Nicholson *Australia* 18°2S 128°54E **60** C4
Nicholson *U.S.A.* 41°37N 75°47W **83** E9
Nicholson → *Australia* 17°31S 139°36E **62** B2
Nicholson L. *Canada* 62°40N 102°40W **71** A8
Nicholson Ra. *Australia* 27°15S 116°45E **61** E2
Nicholville *U.S.A.* 44°41N 74°39W **83** B10
Nicobar Is. *Ind. Oc.* 8°0N 93°30E **45** L11
Nicola *Canada* 50°12N 120°40W **70** C4
Nicolls Town *Bahamas* 25°8N 78°0W **88** A4
Nicosia *Cyprus* 35°10N 33°25E **46** C2
Nicoya *Costa Rica* 10°9N 85°27W **88** D2
Nicoya, G. de *Costa Rica* 10°0N 85°0W **88** E3
Nicoya, Pen. de *Costa Rica* 9°45N 85°40W **88** E2
Nidd → *U.K.* 53°59N 1°23W **12** D6
Niedersachsen □ *Germany* 52°50N 9°0E **16** B5
Niekerkshoop *S. Africa* 29°19S 22°51E **56** C3
Niemen = Nemunas →
  *Lithuania* 55°25N 21°10E **9** J19
Nienburg *Germany* 52°39N 9°13E **16** B5
Nieu Bethesda *S. Africa* 31°51S 24°34E **56** D3
Nieuw Amsterdam
  *Suriname* 5°53N 55°5W **93** B7
Nieuw Nickerie *Suriname* 6°0N 56°59W **93** B7
Nieuwoudtville *S. Africa* 31°23S 19°7E **56** E2
Nieuwpoort *Belgium* 51°8N 2°45E **15** C2
Niğde *Turkey* 37°58N 34°40E **46** B2

Nigel *S. Africa* 26°27S 28°25E **57** C4
Niger ■ *W. Afr.* 17°30N 10°0E **52** E7
Niger → *W. Afr.* 5°33N 6°33E **52** G7
Nigeria ■ *W. Afr.* 8°30N 8°0E **52** G7
Nighasin *India* 28°14N 80°52E **43** E9
Nightcaps *N.Z.* 45°57S 168°2E **59** F2
Nihoa *U.S.A.* 23°6N 161°58W **75** L7
Nihon = Japan ■ *Asia* 36°0N 136°0E **29** G8
Nii-Jima *Japan* 34°20N 139°15E **29** G9
Niigata *Japan* 37°58N 139°0E **28** F9
Niigata □ *Japan* 37°15N 138°45E **29** F9
Niihama *Japan* 33°55N 133°16E **29** H6
Ni'ihau *U.S.A.* 21°54N 160°9W **75** L7
Niimi *Japan* 34°59N 133°28E **29** G6
Niitsu *Japan* 37°48N 139°7E **28** F9
Nijil *Jordan* 30°32N 35°33E **48** E4
Nijkerk *Neths.* 52°13N 5°30E **15** B5
Nijmegen *Neths.* 51°50N 5°52E **15** C5
Nijverdal *Neths.* 52°22N 6°28E **15** B6
Nīk Pey *Iran* 36°50N 48°10E **47** B6
Nikawaratiya *Sri Lanka* 7°45N 80°7E **45** L5
Nikel *Russia* 69°24N 30°13E **8** B24
Nikiniki *Indonesia* 9°49S 124°30E **60** A3
Nikkō *Japan* 36°45N 139°35E **29** F9
Nikkō △ *Japan* 36°56N 139°37E **29** F9
Nikolayev = Mykolayiv
  *Ukraine* 46°58N 32°0E **19** E5
Nikolayevsk *Russia* 50°0N 45°35E **19** E8
Nikolayevsk-na-Amur
  *Russia* 53°8N 140°44E **27** D15
Nikolskoye *Russia* 55°12N 166°0E **27** D17
Nikopol *Ukraine* 47°35N 34°25E **19** E5
Nikshahr *Iran* 26°15N 60°10E **47** E9
Nikšić *Montenegro* 42°50N 18°57E **23** C8
Nîl, Nahr en → *Africa* 30°10N 31°6E **53** B12
Nîl el Abyad → *Sudan* 15°38N 32°31E **53** E12
Nîl el Azraq → *Sudan* 15°38N 32°31E **53** E12
Nila *Indonesia* 6°44S 129°31E **37** F7
Nilakkottai *India* 10°10N 77°52E **45** J3
Niland *U.S.A.* 33°14N 115°31W **79** M11
Nilanga *India* 18°6N 76°46E **44** E3
Nile = Nîl, Nahr en →
  *Africa* 30°10N 31°6E **53** B12
Niles *Mich., U.S.A.* 41°50N 86°15W **80** E10
Niles *Ohio, U.S.A.* 41°11N 80°46W **82** E4
Nileshwar *India* 12°15N 75°6E **45** H2
Nilgiri Hills *India* 11°30N 76°30E **45** J3
Nim Ka Thana *India* 27°44N 75°48E **42** F6
Nimach *India* 24°30N 74°56E **42** G6
Nimbahera *India* 24°37N 74°45E **42** G6
Nîmes *France* 43°50N 4°23E **20** E6
Nimfaíon, Ákra = Pines, Akra
  *Greece* 40°5N 24°20E **23** D11
Nimmitabel *Australia* 36°29S 149°15E **63** F4
Nīnawá *Iraq* 36°25N 43°10E **46** B4
Nīnawá □ *Iraq* 36°15N 43°0E **46** B4
Nindigully *Australia* 28°21S 148°50E **63** D4
Nine Degree Channel *India* 9°0N 73°0E **45** K1
Ninepin Group *China* 22°16N 114°21E **31** a
Nineveh = Nīnawá *Iraq* 36°25N 43°10E **46** B4
Ning Xian *China* 35°30N 107°58E **32** G4
Ningaloo Marine △
  *Australia* 22°23S 113°32E **60** D1
Ning'an *China* 44°22N 129°20E **33** B15
Ningbo *China* 29°51N 121°28E **35** C13
Ningcheng *China* 41°32N 119°53E **33** D10
Ningde *China* 26°38N 119°23E **35** D12
Ningdu *China* 26°25N 115°59E **35** D10
Ninggang *China* 26°42N 113°55E **35** D9
Ningguo *China* 30°35N 119°0E **35** B12
Ninghai *China* 29°15N 121°27E **35** C13
Ninghua *China* 26°14N 116°45E **35** D11
Ningjin *China* 37°35N 114°57E **32** F8
Ningjing Shan *China* 31°0N 98°20E **34** C2
Ninglang *China* 27°0N 100°55E **34** D3
Ningling *China* 34°25N 115°22E **32** G8
Ningming *China* 22°8N 107°4E **34** F6
Ningnan *China* 27°5N 102°36E **34** D4
Ningpo = Ningbo
  *China* 29°51N 121°28E **35** C13
Ningqiang *China* 32°47N 106°15E **32** H4
Ningshan *China* 33°21N 108°21E **34** A7
Ningsia Hui A.R. = Ningxia Huizu
  Zizhiqu □ *China* 38°0N 106°0E **32** F4
Ningwu *China* 39°0N 112°18E **32** E7
Ningxia Huizu Zizhiqu □
  *China* 38°0N 106°0E **32** F4
Ningxiang *China* 28°15N 112°30E **35** C9
Ningyang *China* 35°47N 116°45E **32** G9
Ningyuan *China* 25°37N 111°57E **35** E8
Ninh Binh *Vietnam* 20°15N 105°55E **34** G5
Ninh Giang *Vietnam* 20°44N 106°24E **38** B6
Ninh Hoa *Vietnam* 12°30N 109°7E **38** F7
Ninh Ma *Vietnam* 12°48N 109°21E **38** F7
Ninove *Belgium* 50°51N 4°2E **15** D4
Nioaque *Brazil* 21°5S 55°50W **95** A4
Niobrara *U.S.A.* 42°45N 98°2W **80** D4
Niobrara → *U.S.A.* 42°46N 98°3W **80** D4
Nioro du Sahel *Mali* 15°15N 9°30W **52** E4
Niort *France* 46°19N 0°29W **20** C3
Nipani *India* 16°20N 74°25E **45** F2
Nipawin *Canada* 53°20N 104°0W **71** C8
Nipigon *Canada* 49°0N 88°17W **72** C2
Nipigon, L. *Canada* 49°50N 88°30W **72** C2
Nipishish L. *Canada* 54°12N 60°45W **73** B7
Nipissing, L. *Canada* 46°20N 80°0W **72** C4
Nipomo *U.S.A.* 35°3N 120°29W **79** K6
Nippon = Japan ■ *Asia* 36°0N 136°0E **29** G8
Nipton *U.S.A.* 35°28N 115°16W **79** K11
Niquelândia *Brazil* 14°33S 48°23W **93** F9
Nīr *Iran* 38°2N 47°59E **46** B5
Nira → *India* 17°58N 75°8E **44** F2
Nirasaki *Japan* 35°42N 138°27E **29** G9
Nirmal *India* 19°3N 78°20E **44** E4
Nirmali *India* 26°20N 86°35E **43** F12
Niš *Serbia* 43°19N 21°58E **23** C9
Nisa *Turkmenistan* 37°59N 58°11E **47** B8
Nişāb *Si. Arabia* 29°11N 44°43E **46** D5
Nişāb *Yemen* 14°25N 46°29E **49** E4
Nishino'omote *Japan* 30°43N 130°59E **29** J5

Nishiwaki *Japan* 34°59N 134°58E **29** G7
Niskibi → *Canada* 56°29N 88°9W **72** A2
Nisqually → *U.S.A.* 47°7N 122°42W **78** C4
Nissum Bredning *Denmark* 56°40N 8°20E **9** H13
Nistru = Dnister →
  *Europe* 46°18N 30°17E **17** E16
Nisutlin → *Canada* 60°14N 132°34W **70** A2
Nitchequon *Canada* 53°10N 70°58W **73** B5
Nith → *Canada* 43°12N 80°23W **82** C4
Nith → *U.K.* 55°14N 3°33W **11** F5
Nitmiluk △ *Australia* 14°6S 132°15E **60** B5
Nitra *Slovakia* 48°19N 18°4E **17** D10
Nitra → *Slovakia* 47°46N 18°10E **17** E10
Niue ☑ *Pac. Oc.* 19°2S 169°54W **65** J11
Niulan Jiang → *China* 27°30N 103°5E **34** D4
Niut *Indonesia* 0°55N 109°54E **36** D4
Niutou Shan *China* 29°5N 121°59E **35** C13
Niuzhuang *China* 40°58N 122°28E **33** D12
Nivala *Finland* 63°56N 24°57E **8** E21
Nivelles *Belgium* 50°35N 4°20E **15** D4
Nivernais *France* 47°15N 3°30E **20** C5
Niverville *Canada* 49°36N 97°3W **71** D9
Niwas *India* 23°3N 80°26E **43** H9
Nixa *U.S.A.* 37°3N 93°18W **80** G7
Nixon *U.S.A.* 29°16N 97°46W **84** G6
Nizam Sagar *India* 18°10N 77°58E **44** E3
Nizamabad *India* 18°45N 78°7E **44** E4
Nizamghat *India* 28°20N 95°45E **41** E19
Nizhne-Kolymsk
  *Russia* 68°34N 160°55E **27** C17
Nizhnekamsk *Russia* 55°38N 51°49E **18** C9
Nizhneudinsk *Russia* 54°54N 99°3E **27** D10
Nizhnevartovsk *Russia* 60°56N 76°38E **26** C8
Nizhniy Bestyakh
  *Russia* 61°57N 129°54E **27** C13
Nizhniy Novgorod *Russia* 56°20N 44°0E **18** C7
Nizhniy Tagil *Russia* 57°55N 59°57E **18** C10
Nizhyn *Ukraine* 51°5N 31°55E **19** D5
Nizip *Turkey* 37°5N 37°50E **46** B3
Nízké Tatry *Slovakia* 48°55N 19°30E **17** D10
Nizwá *Oman* 22°56N 57°32E **49** C6
Njazidja = Grande Comore
  *Comoros Is.* 11°35S 43°20E **55** a
Njombe *Tanzania* 9°20S 34°50E **54** F6
Nkandla *S. Africa* 28°37S 31°5E **57** C5
Nkawkaw *Ghana* 6°36N 0°49W **52** G5
Nkhotakota *Malawi* 12°56S 34°15E **55** G6
Nkongsamba *Cameroon* 4°55N 9°55E **54** D1
Nkurenkuru *Namibia* 17°42S 18°32E **56** A2
Nmai → *Myanmar* 25°30N 97°25E **34** F2
Noakhali *Bangla.* 22°48N 91°10E **41** H17
Nobel *Canada* 45°25N 80°6W **82** A4
Nobeoka *Japan* 32°36N 131°41E **29** H5
Noblesville *U.S.A.* 40°3N 86°1W **80** E10
Noboribetsu *Japan* 42°24N 141°6E **28** C10
Noccundra *Australia* 27°50S 142°36E **63** D3
Nocera Inferiore *Italy* 40°44N 14°38E **22** D6
Nocona *U.S.A.* 33°47N 97°44W **84** E6
Noda *Japan* 35°56N 139°52E **29** G9
Nogales *Mexico* 31°19N 110°56W **86** A2
Nogales *U.S.A.* 31°21N 110°56W **77** L8
Nōgata *Japan* 33°48N 130°44E **29** H5
Noggerup *Australia* 33°32S 116°5E **61** F2
Noginsk *Russia* 64°30N 90°50E **27** C10
Nogliki *Russia* 51°50N 143°10E **27** D15
Nogoa → *Australia* 23°40S 147°55E **62** C4
Nogoyá *Argentina* 32°24S 59°48W **94** C4
Nohar *India* 29°11N 74°49E **42** E6
Nohta *India* 23°40N 79°34E **43** H8
Noires, Mts. *France* 48°11N 3°40W **20** B2
Noirmoutier, Î. de *France* 46°58N 2°10W **20** C2
Nojane *Botswana* 23°15S 20°14E **56** B3
Nojima-Zaki *Japan* 34°54N 139°53E **29** G9
Nok Kundi *Pakistan* 28°50N 62°45E **40** E3
Nok Ta Phao, Ko *Thailand* 9°23N 99°40E **39** b
Nokaneng *Botswana* 19°40S 22°17E **56** B3
Nokia *Finland* 61°30N 23°30E **8** F20
Nokomis *Canada* 51°35N 105°0W **71** C8
Nokomis L. *Canada* 57°0N 103°0W **71** B8
Nola *C.A.R.* 3°35N 16°4E **54** D3
Noma Omuramba →
  *Namibia* 18°52S 20°53E **56** A3
Nombre de Dios *Panama* 9°34N 79°28E **88** E4
Nome *U.S.A.* 64°30N 165°25W **74** C6
Nomgon *Mongolia* 42°50N 105°8E **32** C3
Nomo-Zaki *Japan* 32°35N 129°44E **29** H4
Nomuka *Tonga* 20°17S 174°48W **59** c
Nomuka Group *Tonga* 20°20S 174°48W **59** c
Nonacho L. *Canada* 61°42N 109°40W **71** A7
Nonda *Australia* 20°40S 142°28E **62** C3
Nong Chang *Thailand* 15°23N 99°51E **38** E2
Nong Han Res. *Thailand* 17°11N 104°9E **38** D5
Nong Het *Laos* 19°29N 103°59E **38** C4
Nong Khai *Thailand* 17°50N 102°46E **38** D4
Nong'an *China* 44°25N 125°5E **33** B13
Nongoma *S. Africa* 27°58S 31°35E **57** C5
Nongsa *Indonesia* 1°11N 104°8E **39** d
Nonoava *Mexico* 27°28N 106°44W **86** B3
Nonsan *S. Korea* 36°12N 127°5E **33** F14
Noonamah *Australia* 12°40S 131°4E **60** B5
Noondie, L. *Australia* 28°30S 119°30E **61** E2
Noonkanbah ◎
  *Australia* 18°30S 124°50E **60** C3
Noord Brabant □ *Neths.* 51°40N 5°0E **15** C5
Noord Holland □ *Neths.* 52°30N 4°45E **15** B5
Noordbeveland *Neths.* 51°35N 3°50E **15** C3
Noordoostpolder *Neths.* 52°45N 5°45E **15** B5
Noordwijk *Neths.* 52°14N 4°26E **15** B4
Noosa Heads *Australia* 26°25S 153°6E **63** D5
Nootka I. *Canada* 49°32N 126°42W **70** D3
Nopiming △ *Canada* 50°30N 95°37W **71** C9
Noralee *Canada* 53°59N 126°26W **70** C3
Noranda = Rouyn-Noranda
  *Canada* 48°20N 79°0W **72** C4
Norco *U.S.A.* 33°56N 117°33W **79** M9
Nord-Ostsee-Kanal
  *Germany* 54°12N 9°32E **16** A5
Nordaustlandet *Svalbard* 79°14N 23°0E **4** B9
Nordegg *Canada* 52°29N 116°5W **70** C5
Norderney *Germany* 53°42N 7°9E **16** B4

Norderstedt *Germany* 53°42N 10°1E **16** B5
Nordfjord *Norway* 61°55N 5°30E **8** F11
Nordfriesische Inseln
  *Germany* 54°40N 8°20E **16** A5
Nordhausen *Germany* 51°30N 10°47E **16** C6
Norðoyar *Faroe Is.* 62°17N 6°35W **8** E9
Nordkapp *Norway* 71°10N 25°50E **8** A21
Nordkapp *Svalbard* 80°31N 20°0E **4** A9
Nordkinn *Norway* 71°8N 27°40E **8** A22
Nordkinnhalvøya
  *Norway* 70°55N 27°40E **8** A22
Nordrhein-Westfalen □
  *Germany* 51°45N 7°30E **16** C4
Nordvik *Russia* 74°2N 111°32E **27** B12
Nore → *Ireland* 52°25N 6°58W **10** D4
Noreland *Canada* 44°43N 78°48W **82** B6
Norfolk = Simcoe
  *Canada* 42°50N 80°23W **82** D4
Norfolk *N.Y., U.S.A.* 44°48N 74°59W **83** B10
Norfolk *Nebr., U.S.A.* 42°2N 97°25W **80** D5
Norfolk *Va., U.S.A.* 36°50N 76°17W **81** G15
Norfolk □ *U.K.* 52°39N 0°54E **13** E8
Norfolk Broads △ *U.K.* 52°45N 1°30E **13** E9
Norfolk I. *Pac. Oc.* 28°58S 168°3E **58** D9
Norfolk Ridge *Pac. Oc.* 29°0S 168°0E **64** K8
Norfork L. *U.S.A.* 36°15N 92°14W **84** C8
Norge = Norway ■ *Europe* 63°0N 11°0E **8** E14
Norilsk *Russia* 69°20N 88°6E **27** C9
Norma, Mt. *Australia* 20°55S 140°42E **62** C3
Normal *U.S.A.* 40°31N 88°59W **80** E9
Norman *U.S.A.* 35°13N 97°26W **84** D6
Norman → *Australia* 19°18S 141°51E **62** B3
Norman Wells *Canada* 65°17N 126°51W **68** D6
Normanby → *Australia* 14°23S 144°10E **62** A3
Normandie *France* 48°45N 0°10E **20** B4
Normandin *Canada* 48°49N 72°31W **72** C5
Normandy = Normandie
  *France* 48°45N 0°10E **20** B4
Normanhurst, Mt.
  *Australia* 25°4S 122°30E **61** E3
Normanton *Australia* 17°40S 141°10E **62** B3
Normétal *Canada* 49°0N 79°22W **72** C4
Norquay *Canada* 51°53N 102°5W **71** C8
Norquinco *Argentina* 41°51S 70°55W **96** E2
Norrbottens län □ *Sweden* 66°50N 20°0E **8** C19
Norris Point *Canada* 49°31N 57°53E **73** C8
Norristown *U.S.A.* 40°7N 75°21W **83** F9
Norrköping *Sweden* 58°37N 16°11E **9** G17
Norrland *Sweden* 62°15N 15°45E **8** E16
Norrtälje *Sweden* 59°46N 18°42E **9** G18
Norseman *Australia* 32°8S 121°43E **61** F3
Norsk *Russia* 52°30N 130°5E **27** D14
Norte, Serra do *Brazil* 11°20S 59°0W **92** F7
North, C. *Canada* 47°2N 60°20W **73** C7
North Adams *U.S.A.* 42°42N 73°7W **83** D11
North America 40°0N 100°0W **66** F10
North Andaman I. *India* 13°15N 92°55E **45** H11
North Arm *Canada* 62°0N 114°30W **70** A5
North Augusta *U.S.A.* 33°30N 81°59W **85** E14
North Australian Basin
  *Ind. Oc.* 14°30S 116°30E **64** J3
North Ayrshire □ *U.K.* 55°45N 4°44W **11** F4
North Bass I. *U.S.A.* 41°40N 82°56W **82** E2
North Battleford *Canada* 52°50N 108°17W **71** C7
North Bay *Canada* 46°20N 79°30W **72** C4
North Belcher Is. *Canada* 56°50N 79°50W **72** A4
North Bend *Oreg.,*
  *U.S.A.* 43°24N 124°14W **76** E1
North Bend *Pa., U.S.A.* 41°20N 77°42W **82** E7
North Bend *Wash.,*
  *U.S.A.* 47°30N 121°47W **78** C5
North Bennington
  *U.S.A.* 42°56N 73°15W **83** D11
North Berwick *U.K.* 56°4N 2°42W **11** E6
North Berwick *U.S.A.* 43°18N 70°44W **83** C14
North Brother I. *India* 10°59N 92°40E **45** J11
North Bruce *Canada* 44°22N 81°26W **82** B3
North C. *Canada* 47°5N 64°0W **73** C7
North C. *N.Z.* 34°23S 173°4E **59** A4
North Canadian →
  *U.S.A.* 35°22N 95°37W **84** D7
North Canton *U.S.A.* 40°53N 81°24W **82** F3
North Cape = Nordkapp
  *Norway* 71°10N 25°50E **8** A21
North Caribou L. *Canada* 52°50N 90°40W **72** B1
North Carolina □ *U.S.A.* 35°30N 80°0W **85** H5
North Cascades △
  *U.S.A.* 48°45N 121°10W **76** B3
North Channel *Canada* 46°0N 83°0W **72** C3
North Channel *U.K.* 55°13N 5°52W **11** F3
North Charleston
  *U.S.A.* 32°53N 79°58W **85** E15
North Chicago *U.S.A.* 42°19N 87°51W **80** D10
North Collins *U.S.A.* 42°35N 78°56W **82** D6
North Creek *U.S.A.* 43°42N 73°59W **83** C11
North Dakota □ *U.S.A.* 47°30N 100°15W **80** B3
North Downs *U.K.* 51°19N 0°21E **13** F8
North East *U.S.A.* 42°13N 79°50W **82** D5
North East □ *Botswana* 20°45S 27°30E **57** B4
North East Frontier Agency =
  Arunachal Pradesh □
  *India* 28°0N 95°0E **41** F19
North East Lincolnshire □
  *U.K.* 53°34N 0°2W **12** D7
North Esk → *U.K.* 56°46N 2°24W **11** E6
North European Plain
  *Europe* 55°0N 25°0E **6** E10
North Foreland *U.K.* 51°22N 1°28E **13** F9
North Fork *U.S.A.* 37°14N 119°21W **78** H7
North Fork American →
  *U.S.A.* 38°57N 120°59W **78** G5
North Fork Feather →
  *U.S.A.* 38°33N 121°30W **78** F5
North Fork Grand →
  *U.S.A.* 45°47N 102°16W **80** C2
North Fork Red →

Norderstedt *Germany* 53°42N 10°1E **16** B5
North Hd. *Australia* 30°14S 114°59E **61** F1
North Henik L. *Canada* 61°45N 97°40W **71** A9
North Highlands *U.S.A.* 38°40N 121°23W **78** G5
North I. *India* 10°8N 72°20E **45** J1
North I. *N.Z.* 38°0S 175°0E **59** C5
North I. *Seychelles* 4°25S 55°13E **55** b
North Kingsville *U.S.A.* 41°54N 80°42W **82** E4
North Knife → *Canada* 58°53N 94°45W **71** B10
North Koel → *India* 24°45N 83°50E **43** G10
North Korea ■ *Asia* 40°0N 127°0E **33** E14
North Lakhimpur *India* 27°14N 94°7E **41** F19
North Lanarkshire □
  *U.K.* 55°52N 3°56W **11** F5
North Lincolnshire □
  *U.K.* 53°36N 0°30W **12** D7
North Little Rock *U.S.A.* 34°45N 92°16W **84** D8
North Loup → *U.S.A.* 41°17N 98°24W **80** E4
North Magnetic Pole
  *Arctic* 85°9N 149°0W **4** A1
North Mankato *U.S.A.* 44°10N 94°2W **80** C6
North Minch *U.K.* 58°5N 5°55W **11** C3
North Moose L. *Canada* 54°4N 100°12W **71** C8
North Myrtle Beach
  *U.S.A.* 33°48N 78°42W **85** E15
North Nahanni →
  *Canada* 62°15N 123°20W **70** A4
North Olmsted *U.S.A.* 41°25N 81°56W **82** E3
North Ossetia-Alaniya □
  *Russia* 43°30N 44°30E **19** F7
North Pagai, I. = Pagai Utara,
  Pulau *Indonesia* 2°35S 100°0E **36** E2
North Palisade *U.S.A.* 37°6N 118°31W **78** H8
North Paravar *India* 10°13N 76°14E **45** J3
North Platte *U.S.A.* 41°8N 100°46W **80** E3
North Platte → *U.S.A.* 41°7N 100°42W **80** E3
North Pole *Arctic* 90°0N 0°0 **4** A
North Portal *Canada* 49°0N 102°33W **71** D8
North Powder *U.S.A.* 45°2N 117°55W **76** D5
North Pt. *Barbados* 13°20N 59°37W **89** g
North Pt. *Trin. & Tob.* 11°21N 60°31W **93** J16
North Pt. *U.S.A.* 45°2N 83°16W **82** A1
North Reef I. *India* 13°5N 92°43E **45** H11
North Rhine Westphalia =
  Nordrhein-Westfalen □
  *Germany* 51°45N 7°30E **16** C4
North River *Canada* 53°49N 57°6W **73** B8
North Rona *Atl. Oc.* 59°7N 5°49W **14** B4
North Ronaldsay *U.K.* 59°22N 2°26W **11** B6
North Saskatchewan →
  *Canada* 53°15N 105°5W **71** C7
North Sea *Europe* 56°0N 4°0E **6** D6
North Seal → *Canada* 58°50N 98°7W **71** B9
North Sentinel I. *India* 11°33N 92°15E **45** J11
North Slope ☆ *U.S.A.* 69°15N 152°0W **74** B9
North Somerset □ *U.K.* 51°24N 2°45W **13** F5
North Sydney *Canada* 46°12N 60°15W **73** C7
North Syracuse *U.S.A.* 43°8N 76°7W **83** C8
North Taranaki Bight
  *N.Z.* 38°50S 174°15E **59** C5
North Thompson →
  *Canada* 50°40N 120°20W **70** C4
North Tonawanda *U.S.A.* 43°2N 78°53W **82** C6
North Troy *U.S.A.* 45°0N 72°24W **83** B12
North Twin I. *Canada* 53°20N 80°0W **72** B4
North Tyne → *U.K.* 55°0N 2°8W **12** B5
North Uist *U.K.* 57°40N 7°15W **11** D1
North Vancouver *Canada* 49°19N 123°4W **78** A3
North Vernon *U.S.A.* 39°0N 85°38W **81** F11
North Wabasca L.
  *Canada* 56°0N 113°55W **70** B6
North Walsham *U.K.* 52°50N 1°22E **12** E9
North West = Severo-Zapadnyy □
  *Russia* 65°0N 40°0E **26** C4
North West □ *Botswana* 19°0S 22°30E **56** A3
North-West □ *S. Africa* 27°0S 25°0E **56** C4
North West C. *Australia* 21°45S 114°9E **60** D1
North West Christmas I. Ridge
  *Pac. Oc.* 6°30N 165°0W **65** F11
North West Frontier = Khyber
  Pakhtunkhwa □
  *Pakistan* 34°0N 72°0E **42** C5
North West Highlands
  *U.K.* 57°33N 4°58W **11** D4
North West River *Canada* 53°30N 60°10W **73** B7
North Wildwood *U.S.A.* 39°0N 74°48W **81** F16
North York Moors *U.K.* 54°23N 0°53W **12** C7
North York Moors △
  *U.K.* 54°27N 0°51W **12** C7
North Yorkshire □ *U.K.* 54°15N 1°25W **12** C6
Northallerton *U.K.* 54°20N 1°26W **12** C6
Northam *Australia* 31°35S 116°42E **61** F2
Northam *S. Africa* 24°56S 27°18E **56** C4
Northampton *Australia* 28°27S 114°33E **61** E1
Northampton *U.K.* 52°15N 0°53W **13** E7
Northampton *Mass.,*
  *U.S.A.* 42°19N 72°38W **83** D12
Northampton *Pa., U.S.A.* 40°41N 75°30W **83** F9
Northamptonshire □
  *U.K.* 52°16N 0°55W **13** E7
Northbridge *U.S.A.* 42°9N 71°39W **83** D13
Northbrook *Canada* 44°44N 77°9W **82** B7
Northcliffe *Australia* 34°39S 116°7E **61** F2
Northeast Pacific Basin
  *Pac. Oc.* 32°0N 145°0W **65** D13
Northeast Providence Channel
  *W. Indies* 26°0N 76°0W **88** A4
Northern = Limpopo □
  *S. Africa* 24°5S 29°0E **57** B4
Northern Areas = Gilgit-
  Baltistan □ *Pakistan* 36°30N 73°0E **43** A5
Northern Cape □ *S. Africa* 30°0S 20°0E **56** C3
Northern Circars *India* 17°30N 82°30E **44** F6
Northern Dvina = Dvina,
  Severnaya → *Russia* 64°32N 40°30E **18** B7
Northern Indian L.
  *Canada* 57°20N 97°20W **71** B9
Northern Ireland □ *U.K.* 54°45N 7°0W **10** B5
Northern Lau Group *Fiji* 17°30S 178°59W **59** a
Northern Light L. *Canada* 48°15N 90°39W **72** C1
Northern Marianas ☑
  *Pac. Oc.* 17°0N 145°0E **64** F6

148 Northern Province INDEX TO WORLD MAPS


**Northern Province** □ *S. Africa* 24°0S 29°0E **57** B4
**Northern Range** *Trin. & Tob.* 10°46N 61°15W **93** K15
**Northern Sporades = Voreios Sporades** *Greece* 39°15N 23°30E **23** E10
**Northern Territory** □ *Australia* 20°0S 133°0E **60** D5
**Northfield** *Minn., U.S.A.* 44°27N 93°9W **80** C7
**Northfield** *Vt., U.S.A.* 44°9N 72°40W **83** B12
**Northgate** *Canada* 49°0N 102°16W **71** D8
**Northland** □ *N.Z.* 35°30S 173°30E **59** A4
**Northome** *U.S.A.* 47°52N 94°17W **80** B6
**Northport** *Ala., U.S.A.* 33°14N 87°35W **85** E11
**Northport** *N.Y., U.S.A.* 40°54N 73°21W **83** F11
**Northport** *Wash., U.S.A.* 48°55N 117°48W **76** B5
**Northumberland** □ *U.K.* 55°12N 2°0W **12** B6
**Northumberland, C.** *Australia* 38°5S 140°40E **63** F3
**Northumberland Is.** *Australia* 21°30S 149°50E **62** C4
**Northumberland Str.** *Canada* 46°20N 64°0W **73** C7
**Northville** *Canada* 43°10N 81°56W **82** C3
**Northville** *U.S.A.* 43°13N 74°11W **83** C10
**Northwest Pacific Basin** *Pac. Oc.* 32°0N 165°0E **64** D8
**Northwest Providence Channel** *W. Indies* 26°0N 78°0W **88** A4
**Northwest Territories** □ *Canada* 63°0N 118°0W **68** E8
**Northwich** *U.K.* 53°15N 2°31W **12** D5
**Northwood** *Iowa, U.S.A.* 43°27N 93°13W **80** D7
**Northwood** *N. Dak., U.S.A.* 47°44N 97°34W **80** B5
**Norton** *U.S.A.* 39°50N 99°53W **80** F4
**Norton Sd.** *U.S.A.* 63°50N 164°0W **74** C7
**Norwalk** *Calif., U.S.A.* 33°54N 118°4W **79** M8
**Norwalk** *Conn., U.S.A.* 41°7N 73°22W **83** E11
**Norwalk** *Iowa, U.S.A.* 41°29N 93°41W **80** E7
**Norwalk** *Ohio, U.S.A.* 41°15N 82°37W **82** E2
**Norway** *Maine, U.S.A.* 44°13N 70°32W **81** C18
**Norway** *Mich., U.S.A.* 45°47N 87°55W **80** C10
**Norway** ■ *Europe* 63°0N 11°0E **8** E14
**Norway House** *Canada* 53°59N 97°50W **71** C9
**Norwegian B.** *Canada* 77°30N 90°0W **69** B14
**Norwegian Basin** *Atl. Oc.* 68°0N 2°0W **4** C7
**Norwegian Sea** *Atl. Oc.* 66°0N 1°0E **6** B6
**Norwich** *Canada* 42°59N 80°36W **82** D4
**Norwich** *U.K.* 52°38N 1°18E **13** E9
**Norwich** *Conn., U.S.A.* 41°31N 72°5W **83** E12
**Norwich** *N.Y., U.S.A.* 42°32N 75°32W **83** D9
**Norwood** *Canada* 44°23N 77°59W **82** B7
**Norwood** *U.S.A.* 44°45N 75°0W **83** B10
**Nosappu-Misaki** *Japan* 45°26N 141°39E **28** C12
**Noshiro** *Japan* 40°12N 140°0E **28** D10
**Noşratābād** *Iran* 29°55N 60°0E **47** D8
**Noss Hd.** *U.K.* 58°28N 3°3W **11** C5
**Nossob** → *S. Africa* 26°55S 20°45E **56** C3
**Nosy Varika** *Madag.* 20°35S 48°32E **55** J9
**Noteć** → *Poland* 52°44N 15°26E **16** B8
**Notikewin** → *Canada* 57°2N 117°38W **70** B5
**Noto-Hantō** *Japan* 37°15N 136°40E **29** F8
**Notodden** *Norway* 59°35N 9°17E **9** G13
**Notre Dame B.** *Canada* 49°45N 55°30W **73** C8
**Notre-Dame-de-Koartac = Quaqtaq** *Canada* 60°55N 69°40W **69** E18
**Notre-Dame-des-Bois** *Canada* 45°24N 71°4W **83** A13
**Notre-Dame-d'Ivugivic = Ivujivik** *Canada* 62°24N 77°55W **69** E16
**Notre-Dame-du-Nord** *Canada* 47°36N 79°30W **72** C4
**Nottawasaga B.** *Canada* 44°35N 80°15W **82** B4
**Nottaway** → *Canada* 51°22N 78°55W **72** B4
**Nottingham** *U.K.* 52°58N 1°10W **12** E6
**Nottingham, City of** □ *U.K.* 52°58N 1°10W **12** E6
**Nottingham I.** *Canada* 63°20N 77°55W **69** E16
**Nottinghamshire** □ *U.K.* 53°10N 1°3W **12** D6
**Nottoway** → *U.S.A.* 36°33N 76°55W **81** G15
**Notwane** → *Botswana* 23°35S 26°58E **56** B4
**Nouâdhibou** *Mauritania* 20°54N 17°0W **52** D2
**Nouâdhibou, Râs** *Mauritania* 20°50N 17°0W **52** D2
**Nouakchott** *Mauritania* 18°9N 15°58W **52** E2
**Nouméa** *N. Cal.* 22°17S 166°30E **58** D9
**Noupoort** *S. Africa* 31°10S 24°57E **56** D3
**Nouveau Comptoir = Wemindji** *Canada* 53°0N 78°49W **72** B4
**Nouvelle Amsterdam, Î.** *Ind. Oc.* 38°30S 77°30E **3** F13
**Nouvelle-Calédonie = New Caledonia** ☑ *Pac. Oc.* 21°0S 165°0E **58** D9
**Nova Esperança** *Brazil* 23°8S 52°24W **95** A5
**Nova Friburgo** *Brazil* 22°16S 42°30W **95** A7
**Nova Iguaçu** *Brazil* 22°45S 43°28W **95** A7
**Nova Iorque** *Brazil* 7°0S 44°5W **93** E10
**Nova Lamego** *Guinea-Biss.* 12°19N 14°11W **52** F3
**Nova Mambone** *Mozam.* 21°0S 35°3E **57** B6
**Nova Scotia** □ *Canada* 45°10N 63°0W **73** C7
**Nova Sofala** *Mozam.* 20°7S 34°42E **57** B5
**Nova Venécia** *Brazil* 18°45S 40°24W **93** G10
**Nova Zagora** *Bulgaria* 42°32N 26°1E **23** C11
**Novar** *Canada* 45°27N 79°15W **82** A5
**Novara** *Italy* 45°28N 8°38E **20** D8
**Novato** *U.S.A.* 38°6N 122°35W **78** G4
**Novaya Ladoga** *Russia* 60°7N 32°16E **18** B5
**Novaya Lyalya** *Russia* 59°4N 60°45E **18** C11
**Novaya Sibir, Ostrov** *Russia* 75°10N 150°0E **27** B16
**Novaya Zemlya** *Russia* 75°0N 56°0E **26** B6
**Nové Zámky** *Slovakia* 48°2N 18°8E **17** D10
**Novgorod = Velikiy Novgorod** *Russia* 58°30N 31°25E **18** C5
**Novgorod-Severskiy = Novhorod-Siverskyy** *Ukraine* 52°2N 33°10E **18** D5
**Novhorod-Siverskyy** *Ukraine* 52°2N 33°10E **18** D5
**Novi Lígure** *Italy* 44°46N 8°47E **20** D8
**Novi Pazar** *Serbia* 43°12N 20°28E **23** C9
**Novi Sad** *Serbia* 45°18N 19°52E **23** B8
**Novo Hamburgo** *Brazil* 29°37S 51°7W **95** B5
**Novo Mesto** *Slovenia* 45°47N 15°12E **22** B6
**Novoaltaysk** *Russia* 53°30N 84°0E **26** D9
**Novocherkassk** *Russia* 47°27N 40°15E **19** E7
**Novodvinsk** *Russia* 64°25N 40°42E **18** B7
**Novogrudok = Navahrudak** *Belarus* 53°40N 25°50E **17** B13
**Novohrad-Volynskyy** *Ukraine* 50°34N 27°35E **17** C14
**Novokachalinsk** *Russia* 45°5N 132°0E **28** B5
**Novokuybyshevsk** *Russia* 53°7N 49°58E **18** D8
**Novokuznetsk** *Russia* 53°45N 87°10E **26** D9
**Novolazarevskaya** *Antarctica* 71°0S 12°0E **5** D3
**Novomoskovsk** *Russia* 54°5N 38°15E **18** D6
**Novorossiysk** *Russia* 44°43N 37°46E **19** F6
**Novorybnoye** *Russia* 72°50N 105°50E **27** B11
**Novoselytsya** *Ukraine* 48°14N 26°15E **17** D14
**Novoshakhtinsk** *Russia* 47°46N 39°58E **19** E6
**Novosibirsk** *Russia* 55°0N 83°5E **26** D9
**Novosibirskiye Ostrova** *Russia* 75°0N 142°0E **27** B15
**Novotroitsk** *Russia* 51°10N 58°15E **18** D10
**Novouzensk** *Russia* 50°32N 48°17E **19** D8
**Novovolynsk** *Ukraine* 50°45N 24°4E **17** C13
**Novska** *Croatia* 45°19N 17°0E **22** B7
**Novyy Bor** *Russia* 66°43N 52°19E **18** A9
**Novyy Port** *Russia* 67°40N 72°30E **26** C8
**Novyy Urengoy** *Russia* 65°48N 76°52E **26** C8
**Nowa Sól** *Poland* 51°48N 15°44E **16** C8
**Nowata** *U.S.A.* 36°42N 95°38W **84** C7
**Nowbarān** *Iran* 35°8N 49°42E **47** C6
**Nowghāb** *Iran* 33°53N 59°4E **47** C8
**Nowgong = Nagaon** *India* 26°20N 92°50E **41** F18
**Nowgong** *India* 25°4N 79°27E **43** G8
**Nowra** *Australia* 34°53S 150°35E **63** E5
**Nowrangapur** *India* 19°14N 82°33E **44** E6
**Nowshera** *Pakistan* 34°0N 72°0E **40** C8
**Nowy Sącz** *Poland* 49°40N 20°41E **17** D11
**Nowy Targ** *Poland* 49°29N 20°2E **17** D11
**Nowy Tomyśl** *Poland* 52°19N 16°10E **16** B9
**Noxen** *U.S.A.* 41°25N 76°4W **83** E8
**Noyabr'sk** *Russia* 64°34N 76°21E **26** C8
**Noyon** *France* 49°34N 2°59E **20** B5
**Noyon** *Mongolia* 43°2N 102°4E **32** C2
**Nqutu** *S. Africa* 28°13S 30°32E **57** C5
**Nsanje** *Malawi* 16°55S 35°12E **55** H7
**Nsawam** *Ghana* 5°50N 0°24W **52** G5
**Ntaria** ✪ *Australia* 24°0S 132°41E **60** D5
**Nu Jiang** → *China* 29°58N 97°25E **34** E2
**Nu Shan** *China* 26°0N 99°20E **34** E2
**Nuba Mts. = Nubah, Jibalan** *Sudan* 12°0N 31°0E **53** F12
**Nubah, Jibalan** *Sudan* 12°0N 31°0E **53** F12
**Nubia** *Africa* 21°0N 32°0E **50** D7
**Nubian Desert = Nûbîya, Es Sahrâ en** *Sudan* 21°30N 33°30E **53** D12
**Nûbîya, Es Sahrâ en** *Sudan* 21°30N 33°30E **53** D12
**Nuboai** *Indonesia* 2°10S 136°30E **37** E9
**Nubra** → *India* 34°35N 77°35E **43** B7
**Nueces** → *U.S.A.* 27°51N 97°30W **84** H6
**Nueltin L.** *Canada* 60°30N 99°30W **71** A9
**Nuestra Señora del Rosario de Caá-Catí** *Argentina* 27°45S 57°36W **94** B4
**Nueva Ciudad Guerrero** *Mexico* 26°34N 99°12W **87** B5
**Nueva Gerona** *Cuba* 21°53N 82°49W **88** B3
**Nueva Palmira** *Uruguay* 33°52S 58°20W **94** C4
**Nueva Rosita** *Mexico* 27°57N 101°13W **86** B4
**Nueva San Salvador** *El Salv.* 13°40N 89°18W **88** D2
**Nuéve de Julio** *Argentina* 35°30S 61°0W **94** D3
**Nuevitas** *Cuba* 21°30N 77°20W **88** B4
**Nuevo, G.** *Argentina* 43°0S 64°30W **96** E4
**Nuevo Casas Grandes** *Mexico* 30°25N 107°55W **86** A3
**Nuevo Laredo** *Mexico* 27°30N 99°31W **87** B5
**Nuevo León** □ *Mexico* 25°20N 100°0W **86** C5
**Nuevo Rocafuerte** *Ecuador* 0°55S 75°27W **92** D3
**Nugget Pt.** *N.Z.* 46°27S 169°50E **59** G2
**Nuhaka** *N.Z.* 39°3S 177°45E **59** C6
**Nukey Bluff** *Australia* 32°26S 135°29E **63** E2
**Nukhayb** *Iraq* 32°4N 42°3E **46** C4
**Nuku Hiva** *French Polynesia* 8°54S 140°6W **65** H13
**Nuku'alofa** *Tonga* 21°10S 175°12W **59** c
**Nukus** *Uzbekistan* 42°27N 59°41E **26** E6
**Nulato** *U.S.A.* 64°43N 158°6W **74** C8
**Nullagine** *Australia* 21°53S 120°7E **60** D3
**Nullagine** → *Australia* 21°20S 120°20E **60** D3
**Nullarbor** *Australia* 31°28S 130°55E **61** F5
**Nullarbor** △ *Australia* 32°39S 130°0E **61** F4
**Nullarbor Plain** *Australia* 31°10S 129°0E **61** F4
**Numalla, L.** *Australia* 28°43S 144°20E **63** D3
**Numan** *Nigeria* 9°29N 12°3E **53** G8
**Numata** *Japan* 36°45N 139°4E **29** F9
**Numaykoos Lake** ⌂ *Canada* 57°52N 95°58W **71** B9
**Numazu** *Japan* 35°7N 138°51E **29** G9
**Numbulwar** *Australia* 14°15S 135°45E **62** A2
**Numfoor** *Indonesia* 1°0S 134°50E **37** E8
**Numurkah** *Australia* 36°5S 145°26E **63** F4
**Nunaksaluk I.** *Canada* 55°49N 60°20W **73** A7
**Nunap Isua** *Greenland* 59°48N 43°55W **66** D15
**Nunatsiavut** *Canada* 55°30N 62°0W **73** A7
**Nunavik** *Canada* 56°30N 71°0W **69** F17
**Nunavik** *Greenland* 71°50N 54°25W **69** C21
**Nunavut** □ *Canada* 66°0N 85°0W **69** D15
**Nunda** *U.S.A.* 42°35N 77°56W **82** D7
**Nuneaton** *U.K.* 52°32N 1°27W **13** E6
**Nungarin** *Australia* 31°12S 118°6E **61** F2
**Nunivak I.** *U.S.A.* 60°10N 166°30W **74** C6
**Nunkun** *India* 33°57N 76°2E **43** C7
**Núoro** *Italy* 40°20N 9°20E **22** D3
**Nuozhadu Dam** *China* 22°39N 100°25E **34** F3
**Nūr** *Iran* 36°33N 52°1E **47** B7
**Nūrābād** *Hormozgān, Iran* 27°47N 57°12E **47** E8
**Nūrābād** *Lorestān, Iran* 34°4N 47°58E **46** C5
**Nuremberg = Nürnberg** *Germany* 49°27N 11°3E **16** D6
**Nuri** *Mexico* 28°5N 109°22W **86** B3
**Nuriootpa** *Australia* 34°27S 139°0E **63** E2
**Nuristān** □ *Afghan.* 35°20N 71°0E **40** B7
**Nurmes** *Finland* 63°33N 29°10E **8** E23
**Nürnberg** *Germany* 49°27N 11°3E **16** D6
**Nurpur** *Pakistan* 31°53N 71°54E **42** D4
**Nurran, L. = Terewah, L.** *Australia* 29°52S 147°35E **63** D4
**Nurrari Lakes** *Australia* 29°1S 130°5E **61** E5
**Nusa Dua** *Indonesia* 8°48S 115°14E **37** K18
**Nusa Tenggara Barat** □ *Indonesia* 8°50S 117°30E **36** F5
**Nusa Tenggara Timur** □ *Indonesia* 9°30S 122°0E **37** F6
**Nusaybin** *Turkey* 37°3N 41°10E **19** G7
**Nuşeirat** *Gaza Strip* 31°27N 34°24E **48** D3
**Nushki** *Pakistan* 29°35N 66°0E **42** E2
**Nuuk** *Greenland* 64°10N 51°35W **67** C14
**Nuupere, Pte.** *Moorea* 17°36S 149°47W **59** d
**Nuwakot** *Nepal* 28°10N 83°55E **43** E10
**Nuwara Eliya** *Sri Lanka* 6°58N 80°48E **45** L5
**Nuwayb'ī, W. an** → *Si. Arabia* 29°18N 34°57E **48** F3
**Nuweiba'** *Egypt* 28°59N 34°39E **46** D2
**Nuwerus** *S. Africa* 31°8S 18°24E **56** D2
**Nuweveldberge** *S. Africa* 32°10S 21°45E **56** D3
**Nuyts, Pt.** *Australia* 35°4S 116°38E **61** G2
**Nuyts Arch.** *Australia* 32°35S 133°20E **63** E1
**Nxai Pan** △ *Botswana* 19°50S 24°46E **56** A3
**Nxaunxau** *Botswana* 18°57S 21°4E **56** A3
**Nyabing** *Australia* 33°33S 118°9E **61** F2
**Nyack** *U.S.A.* 41°5N 73°55W **83** E11
**Nyagan** *Russia* 62°30N 65°38E **26** C7
**Nyahururu** *Kenya* 0°2N 36°27E **54** D7
**Nyainqêntanglha Shan** *China* 30°0N 90°0E **30** F7
**Nyâlâ** *Sudan* 12°2N 24°58E **53** F10
**Nyalam** *China* 28°32N 86°4E **30** F6
**Nyandoma** *Russia* 61°40N 40°12E **18** B7
**Nyangana** *Namibia* 18°0S 20°40E **56** A3
**Nyasa, L. = Malawi, L.** *Africa* 12°30S 34°30E **55** G6
**Nyasvizh** *Belarus* 53°14N 26°38E **17** B14
**Nyaungdon = Yandoon** *Myanmar* 17°0N 95°40E **41** L19
**Nyazepetrovsk** *Russia* 56°3N 59°36E **18** C10
**Nybro** *Sweden* 56°44N 15°55E **9** H16
**Nyda** *Russia* 66°40N 72°58E **26** C8
**Nyeboe Land** *Greenland* 82°0N 57°0W **69** A20
**Nyingchi** *China* 29°32N 94°25E **30** F7
**Nyíregyháza** *Hungary* 47°58N 21°47E **17** E11
**Nykarleby = Uusikaarlepyy** *Finland* 63°32N 22°31E **8** E20
**Nykøbing** *Nordjylland, Denmark* 56°48N 8°51E **9** H13
**Nykøbing** *Sjælland, Denmark* 54°56N 11°52E **9** J14
**Nykøbing** *Sjælland, Denmark* 55°55N 11°40E **9** J14
**Nyköping** *Sweden* 58°45N 17°1E **9** G17
**Nylstroom = Modimolle** *S. Africa* 24°42S 28°22E **57** B4
**Nymagee** *Australia* 32°7S 146°20E **63** E4
**Nymboida** △ *Australia* 29°38S 152°26E **63** D5
**Nynäshamn** *Sweden* 58°54N 17°57E **9** G17
**Nyngan** *Australia* 31°30S 147°8E **63** E4
**Nyoma Rap** *India* 33°10N 78°40E **43** C8
**Nyoman = Nemunas** → *Lithuania* 55°25N 21°10E **9** J19
**Nysa** *Poland* 50°30N 17°22E **17** C9
**Nysa** → *Europe* 52°4N 14°46E **16** B8
**Nyslott = Savonlinna** *Finland* 61°52N 28°53E **8** F23
**Nyssa** *U.S.A.* 43°53N 117°0W **76** E5
**Nystad = Uusikaupunki** *Finland* 60°47N 21°25E **8** F19
**Nyunzu** *Dem. Rep. of the Congo* 5°57S 27°58E **54** F5
**Nyurba** *Russia* 63°17N 118°28E **27** C12
**Nzega** *Tanzania* 4°10S 33°12E **54** E6
**Nzérékoré** *Guinea* 7°49N 8°48W **52** G4
**Nzeto** *Angola* 7°10S 12°52E **54** F2
**Nzwani = Anjouan** *Comoros Is.* 12°15S 44°20E **55** a


## O


**O Le Pupū Pu'e** △ *Samoa* 13°59S 171°43W **59** b
**Ō-Shima** *Hokkaidō, Japan* 41°30N 139°22E **28** D9
**Ō-Shima** *Shizuoka, Japan* 34°44N 139°24E **29** G9
**O.R. Tambo Int.** ✕ **(JNB)** *S. Africa* 26°8S 28°15E **57** C4
**Oa, Mull of** *U.K.* 55°35N 6°20W **11** F2
**Oacoma** *U.S.A.* 43°48N 99°24W **80** D4
**Oahe, L.** *U.S.A.* 44°27N 100°24W **80** C3
**Oahe Dam** *U.S.A.* 44°27N 100°24W **80** C3
**O'ahu** *U.S.A.* 21°28N 157°58W **75** L8
**Oak Harbor** *U.S.A.* 48°18N 122°39W **78** B4
**Oak Hill** *U.S.A.* 37°59N 81°9W **81** G13
**Oak Island** *U.S.A.* 33°55N 78°10W **85** E15
**Oak Ridge** *U.S.A.* 36°1N 84°16W **85** C12
**Oak View** *U.S.A.* 34°24N 119°18W **79** L7
**Oakan-Dake** *Japan* 43°27N 144°10E **28** C12
**Oakdale** *Calif., U.S.A.* 37°46N 120°51W **78** H6
**Oakdale** *La., U.S.A.* 30°49N 92°40W **84** F8
**Oakes** *U.S.A.* 46°8N 98°6W **80** B4
**Oakesdale** *U.S.A.* 47°8N 117°15W **76** C5
**Oakey** *Australia* 27°25S 151°43E **63** D5
**Oakfield** *U.S.A.* 43°4N 78°16W **82** C6
**Oakham** *U.K.* 52°40N 0°43W **13** E7
**Oakhurst** *U.S.A.* 37°19N 119°40W **78** H7
**Oakland** *U.S.A.* 41°57N 75°36W **83** E9
**Oakley** *Idaho, U.S.A.* 42°15N 113°53W **76** E7
**Oakley** *Kans., U.S.A.* 39°8N 100°51W **80** F3
**Oakover** → *Australia* 21°0S 120°40E **60** D3
**Oakridge** *U.S.A.* 43°45N 122°28W **76** E2
**Oakville** *Canada* 43°27N 79°41W **82** C5
**Oakville** *U.S.A.* 46°51N 123°14W **78** D3
**Oamaru** *N.Z.* 45°5S 170°59E **59** F3
**Oasis** *Calif., U.S.A.* 37°29N 117°55W **78** H9
**Oasis** *Calif., U.S.A.* 33°28N 116°6W **79** M10
**Oates Land** *Antarctica* 69°0S 160°0E **5** C11
**Oatman** *U.S.A.* 35°1N 114°19W **79** K12
**Oaxaca** *Mexico* 17°3N 96°43W **87** D5
**Oaxaca** □ *Mexico* 17°0N 96°30W **87** D5
**Ob** → *Russia* 66°45N 69°30E **26** C7
**Oba** *Canada* 49°4N 84°7W **72** C3
**Obama** *Japan* 35°30N 135°45E **29** G7
**Oban** *U.K.* 56°25N 5°29W **11** E3
**Obbia = Hobyo** *Somalia* 5°25N 48°30E **49** F4
**Oberá** *Argentina* 27°21S 55°2W **95** B4
**Oberhausen** *Germany* 51°28N 6°51E **16** C4
**Oberlin** *Kans., U.S.A.* 39°49N 100°32W **80** F3
**Oberlin** *La., U.S.A.* 30°37N 92°46W **84** F8
**Oberlin** *Ohio, U.S.A.* 41°18N 82°13W **82** E2
**Oberon** *Australia* 33°45S 149°52E **63** E4
**Obi, Kepulauan** *Indonesia* 1°23S 127°45E **37** E7
**Óbidos** *Brazil* 1°50S 55°30W **93** D7
**Obihiro** *Japan* 42°56N 143°12E **28** C11
**Obilatu** *Indonesia* 1°25S 127°20E **37** E7
**Obluchye** *Russia* 49°1N 131°4E **27** E14
**Obo** *C.A.R.* 5°20N 26°32E **54** C5
**Oboyan** *Russia* 51°15N 36°21E **26** D4
**Obozerskaya = Obozerskiy** *Russia* 63°34N 40°21E **18** B7
**Obozerskiy** *Russia* 63°34N 40°21E **18** B7
**Observatory Inlet** *Canada* 55°10N 129°54W **70** B3
**Obshchi Syrt** *Russia* 52°0N 53°0E **6** E16
**Obskaya Guba** *Russia* 69°0N 73°0E **26** C8
**Obuasi** *Ghana* 6°17N 1°40W **52** G5
**Ocala** *U.S.A.* 29°11N 82°8W **85** G13
**Ocampo** *Chihuahua, Mexico* 28°11N 108°23W **86** B3
**Ocampo** *Tamaulipas, Mexico* 22°50N 99°20W **87** C5
**Ocaña** *Spain* 39°55N 3°30W **21** C4
**Occidental, Cordillera** *Colombia* 5°0N 76°0W **92** C3
**Occidental, Grand Erg** *Algeria* 30°20N 1°0E **52** B6
**Ocean City** *Md., U.S.A.* 38°20N 75°5W **81** F16
**Ocean City** *N.J., U.S.A.* 39°17N 74°35W **81** F16
**Ocean City** *Wash., U.S.A.* 47°4N 124°10W **78** C2
**Ocean Falls** *Canada* 52°18N 127°48W **70** C3
**Ocean I. = Banaba** *Kiribati* 0°45S 169°50E **64** H8
**Ocean Park** *U.S.A.* 46°30N 124°3W **78** D2
**Oceano** *U.S.A.* 35°6N 120°37W **79** K6
**Oceanport** *U.S.A.* 40°19N 74°3W **83** F10
**Oceanside** *U.S.A.* 33°12N 117°23W **79** M9
**Ochil Hills** *U.K.* 56°14N 3°40W **11** E5
**Ocho Rios** *Jamaica* 18°24N 77°6W **88** a
**Ocilla** *U.S.A.* 31°36N 83°15W **85** F13
**Ocmulgee** → *U.S.A.* 31°58N 82°33W **85** F13
**Ocnița** *Moldova* 48°25N 27°30E **17** D14
**Oconee** → *U.S.A.* 31°58N 82°33W **85** F13
**Oconomowoc** *U.S.A.* 43°7N 88°30W **80** D9
**Oconto** *U.S.A.* 44°53N 87°52W **80** C10
**Oconto Falls** *U.S.A.* 44°52N 88°9W **80** C9
**Ocosingo** *Mexico* 16°53N 92°6W **87** D6
**Ocotal** *Nic.* 13°41N 86°31W **88** D2
**Ocotlán** *Jalisco, Mexico* 20°21N 102°46W **86** C4
**Ocotlán** *Oaxaca, Mexico* 16°48N 96°40W **87** D5
**Ōda** *Japan* 35°11N 132°30E **29** G6
**Ódáðahraun** *Iceland* 65°5N 17°0W **8** D5
**Ŏdaejin** *N. Korea* 41°34N 129°40E **28** D4
**Odate** *Japan* 40°16N 140°34E **28** D10
**Odawara** *Japan* 35°20N 139°6E **29** G9
**Odda** *Norway* 60°3N 6°35E **9** F12
**Odei** → *Canada* 56°6N 96°54W **71** B9
**Ödemiş** *Turkey* 38°15N 28°0E **23** E13
**Odendaalsrus** *S. Africa* 27°48S 26°45E **56** C4
**Odense** *Denmark* 55°22N 10°23E **9** J14
**Oder** → *Europe* 53°33N 14°38E **16** B8
**Odesa** *Ukraine* 46°30N 30°45E **19** E5
**Odessa = Odesa** *Ukraine* 46°30N 30°45E **19** E5
**Odessa** *Canada* 44°17N 76°43W **83** B8
**Odessa** *Tex., U.S.A.* 31°52N 102°23W **84** F3
**Odessa** *Wash., U.S.A.* 47°20N 118°41W **76** C4
**Odiakwe** *Botswana* 20°12S 25°17E **56** B4
**Odienné** *Côte d'Ivoire* 9°30N 7°34W **52** G4
**Odintsovo** *Russia* 55°40N 37°16E **18** C6
**Odisha** □ *India* 20°0N 84°0E **44** E7
**O'Donnell** *U.S.A.* 32°58N 101°50W **84** E4
**O'Donnell Pt.** *Canada* 45°5N 80°5W **82** A4
**Odorheiu Secuiesc** *Romania* 46°21N 25°21E **17** E13
**Odra = Oder** → *Europe* 53°33N 14°38E **16** B8
**Odzi** *Zimbabwe* 19°0S 32°20E **57** A5
**Odzi** → *Zimbabwe* 19°45S 32°23E **57** A5
**Oecussi = Pante Macassar** *Timor-Leste* 9°30S 123°58E **37** F6
**Oeiras** *Brazil* 7°0S 42°8W **93** E10
**Oelrichs** *U.S.A.* 43°11N 103°14W **80** D2
**Oelwein** *U.S.A.* 42°41N 91°55W **80** D8
**Oeno I.** *Pac. Oc.* 24°0S 131°0W **65** K14
**Oenpelli = Gunbalanya** *Australia* 12°20S 133°4E **60** B5
**Ofanto** → *Italy* 41°22N 16°13E **22** D7
**Offa** *Nigeria* 8°13N 4°42E **52** G6
**Offaly** □ *Ireland* 53°15N 7°30W **10** C4
**Offenbach** *Germany* 50°6N 8°44E **16** C5
**Offenburg** *Germany* 48°28N 7°56E **16** D4
**Officer Cr.** → *Australia* 27°46S 132°30E **61** E5
**Ofolanga** *Tonga* 19°38S 174°27W **59** c
**Ofotfjorden** *Norway* 68°27N 17°0E **8** B17
**Ofu** *Amer. Samoa* 14°11S 169°41W **59** b
**Ōfunato** *Japan* 39°4N 141°43E **28** E10
**Oga** *Japan* 39°55N 139°50E **28** E9
**Oga-Hantō** *Japan* 39°58N 139°47E **28** E9
**Ogaden** *Ethiopia* 7°30N 45°30E **49** F3
**Ōgaki** *Japan* 35°21N 136°37E **29** G8
**Ogallala** *U.S.A.* 41°8N 101°43W **80** E3
**Ogasawara Gunto** *Pac. Oc.* 27°0N 142°0E **64** E6
**Ogbomosho** *Nigeria* 8°1N 4°11E **52** G6
**Ogden** *U.S.A.* 41°13N 111°58W **76** F8
**Ogdensburg** *U.S.A.* 44°42N 75°30W **83** B9
**Ogea Driki** *Fiji* 19°12S 178°27W **59** a
**Ogea Levu** *Fiji* 19°8S 178°24W **59** a
**Ogeechee** → *U.S.A.* 31°50N 81°3W **85** F14
**Ogilby** *U.S.A.* 32°49N 114°50W **79** N12
**Óglio** → *Italy* 45°2N 10°39E **22** B4
**Ogmore** *Australia* 22°37S 149°35E **62** C4
**Ogoki** *Canada* 51°38N 85°58W **72** B2
**Ogoki** → *Canada* 51°38N 85°57W **72** B2
**Ogoki L.** *Canada* 50°50N 87°10W **72** B2
**Ogoki Res.** *Canada* 50°45N 88°15W **72** B2
**Ogooué** → *Gabon* 1°0S 9°0E **54** E1
**Ogowe = Ogooué** → *Gabon* 1°0S 9°0E **54** E1
**Ogre** *Latvia* 56°49N 24°36E **9** H21
**Ogurja Ada** *Turkmenistan* 38°55N 53°2E **47** B7
**Ohai** *N.Z.* 45°55S 168°0E **59** F2
**Ohakune** *N.Z.* 39°24S 175°24E **59** C5
**Ohangwena** □ *Namibia* 17°30S 17°0E **56** A2
**Ohata** *Japan* 41°24N 141°10E **28** D10
**Ohau, L.** *N.Z.* 44°15S 169°53E **59** F2
**Ohio** □ *U.S.A.* 40°15N 82°45W **82** F2
**Ohio** → *U.S.A.* 36°59N 89°8W **80** G9
**Ohře** → *Czechia* 50°30N 14°10E **16** C8
**Ohrid** *Macedonia* 41°8N 20°52E **23** D9
**Ohridsko Jezero** *Macedonia* 41°8N 20°52E **23** D9
**Ohrigstad** *S. Africa* 24°39S 30°36E **57** B5
**Oi Qu** → *China* 28°37N 98°16E **34** C2
**Oiapoque** *Brazil* 3°50N 51°50W **93** C8
**Oikou** *China* 38°35N 117°42E **33** E9
**Oil City** *U.S.A.* 41°26N 79°42W **82** E5
**Oil Springs** *Canada* 42°47N 82°7W **82** D2
**Oildale** *U.S.A.* 35°25N 119°1W **79** K7
**Oise** → *France* 49°0N 2°4E **20** B5
**Oistins** *Barbados* 13°4N 59°33W **89** g
**Oistins B.** *Barbados* 13°4N 59°33W **89** g
**Ōita** *Japan* 33°14N 131°36E **29** H5
**Ōita** □ *Japan* 33°15N 131°30E **29** H5
**Oiticica** *Brazil* 5°3S 41°5W **93** E10
**Ojai** *U.S.A.* 34°27N 119°15W **79** L7
**Ojhar** *India* 20°6N 73°56E **44** D1
**Ojinaga** *Mexico* 29°34N 104°25W **86** B4
**Ojiya** *Japan* 37°18N 138°48E **29** F9
**Ojo Caliente** *Mexico* 22°34N 102°15W **86** C4
**Ojo de Liebre, L.** *Mexico* 27°45N 114°15W **86** B2
**Ojos del Salado, Cerro** *Argentina* 27°0S 68°40W **94** B2
**Oka** → *Russia* 56°20N 43°59E **18** C7
**Okaba** *Indonesia* 8°6S 139°42E **37** F9
**Okahandja** *Namibia* 22°0S 16°59E **56** B2
**Okakarara** *Namibia* 20°35S 17°27E **56** B2
**Okanagan L.** *Canada* 50°0N 119°30W **70** D5
**Okandja** *Gabon* 0°35S 13°45E **54** E2
**Okanogan** *U.S.A.* 48°22N 119°35W **76** B4
**Okanogan** → *U.S.A.* 48°6N 119°44W **76** B4
**Okanogan Range** *N. Amer.* 49°0N 119°55W **70** D5
**Okaputa** *Namibia* 20°5S 17°0E **56** B2
**Okara** *Pakistan* 30°50N 73°31E **42** D5
**Okarukambe = Steinhausen** *Namibia* 21°49S 18°20E **56** B2
**Okaukuejo** *Namibia* 19°10S 16°0E **56** A2
**Okavango = Cubango** → *Africa* 18°50S 22°25E **56** A3
**Okavango Delta** *Botswana* 18°45S 22°45E **56** A3
**Okavango Swamp = Okavango Delta** *Botswana* 18°45S 22°45E **56** A3
**Okaya** *Japan* 36°5N 138°10E **29** F9
**Okayama** *Japan* 34°40N 133°54E **29** G6
**Okayama** □ *Japan* 35°0N 133°50E **29** G6
**Okazaki** *Japan* 34°57N 137°10E **29** G8
**Okeechobee** *U.S.A.* 27°15N 80°50W **85** H14
**Okeechobee, L.** *U.S.A.* 27°0N 80°50W **85** H14
**Okefenokee** ⌂ *U.S.A.* 30°45N 82°18W **85** F13
**Okefenokee Swamp** *U.S.A.* 30°40N 82°20W **85** F13
**Okehampton** *U.K.* 50°44N 4°0W **13** G4
**Okha** *India* 22°27N 69°4E **42** H3
**Okha** *Russia* 53°40N 143°0E **27** D15
**Okhotsk** *Russia* 59°20N 143°10E **27** D15
**Okhotsk, Sea of** *Asia* 55°0N 145°0E **27** D15
**Okhotskiy Perevoz** *Russia* 61°52N 135°35E **27** C14
**Okhtyrka** *Ukraine* 50°25N 35°0E **19** D5
**Oki-Shotō** *Japan* 36°5N 133°15E **29** F6
**Okiep** *S. Africa* 29°39S 17°53E **56** C2
**Okinawa** *Japan* 26°19N 127°46E **29** L3
**Okinawa** □ *Japan* 26°40N 128°0E **29** L4
**Okinawa-Guntō** *Japan* 26°40N 128°0E **29** L4
**Okinawa-Jima** *Japan* 26°32N 128°0E **29** L4
**Okino-erabu-Shima** *Japan* 27°21N 128°33E **29** L4
**Oklahoma** □ *U.S.A.* 35°20N 97°30W **84** D6
**Oklahoma City** *U.S.A.* 35°30N 97°30W **84** D6
**Okmulgee** *U.S.A.* 35°37N 95°58W **84** D7
**Oknitsa = Ocnița** *Moldova* 48°25N 27°30E **17** D14
**Okolona** *U.S.A.* 34°0N 88°45W **85** E10
**Okombahe** *Namibia* 21°23S 15°22E **56** B2
**Okotoks** *Canada* 50°43N 113°58W **70** C6
**Oksovskiy** *Russia* 62°33N 39°57E **18** B6
**Oktyabrsk = Qandyaghash** *Kazakhstan* 49°28N 57°25E **19** E10
**Oktyabrskiy = Aktsyabrski** *Belarus* 52°38N 28°53E **17** B15
**Oktyabrskiy** *Bashkortostan, Russia* 54°28N 53°28E **18** D9
**Oktyabrskiy** *Kamchatka, Russia* 52°39N 156°14E **27** D16
**Oktyabrskoy Revolyutsii, Ostrov** *Russia* 79°30N 97°0E **27** B10
**Okuru** *N.Z.* 43°55S 168°55E **59** E2
**Okushiri-Tō** *Japan* 42°15N 139°30E **28** C9
**Okwa** → *Botswana* 22°30S 23°0E **56** B3
**Ola** *Russia* 59°35N 151°17E **27** D16
**Ola** *U.S.A.* 35°2N 93°13W **84** D8
**Ólafsfjörður** *Iceland* 66°4N 18°39W **8** C4
**Ólafsvík** *Iceland* 64°53N 23°43W **8** D2

Olancha *U.S.A.* 36°17N 118°1W **79** J8
Olancha Pk. *U.S.A.* 36°16N 118°7W **79** J8
Olanchito *Honduras* 15°30N 86°30W **88** C2
Öland *Sweden* 56°45N 16°38E **9** H17
Olary *Australia* 32°18S 140°19E **63** E3
Olascoaga *Argentina* 35°15S 60°39W **94** D3
Olathe *U.S.A.* 38°53N 94°49W **80** F6
Olavarría *Argentina* 36°55S 60°20W **94** D3
Oława *Poland* 50°57N 17°20E **17** C9
Ólbia *Italy* 40°55N 9°31E **22** D3
Olcott *U.S.A.* 43°20N 78°42W **82** C6
Old Bahama Chan. = Bahama,
Canal Viejo de
*W. Indies* 22°10N 77°30W **88** B4
Old Baldy Pk. = San Antonio, Mt.
*U.S.A.* 34°17N 117°38W **79** L9
Old Bridge *U.S.A.* 40°25N 74°22W **83** F10
Old Castile = Castilla y Leon □
*Spain* 42°0N 5°0W **21** B3
Old Crow *Canada* 67°30N 139°55W **68** D4
Old Dale *U.S.A.* 34°8N 115°47W **79** L11
Old Forge *N.Y., U.S.A.* 43°43N 74°58W **83** C10
Old Forge *Pa., U.S.A.* 41°22N 75°45W **83** E9
Old Mapoon ⊙ *Australia* 11°5S 142°22E **62** A3
Old Perlican *Canada* 48°5N 53°1W **73** C9
Old Speck Mt. *U.S.A.* 44°34N 70°57W **83** B14
Old Town *U.S.A.* 44°56N 68°39W **81** C19
Old Wives L. *Canada* 50°5N 106°0W **71** C7
Oldbury *U.K.* 51°38N 2°33W **13** F5
Oldcastle *Ireland* 53°46N 7°10W **10** C4
Oldenburg *Germany* 53°9N 8°13E **16** B5
Oldenzaal *Neths.* 52°19N 6°53E **15** B6
Oldham *U.K.* 53°33N 2°7W **12** D5
Oldman → *Canada* 49°57N 111°42W **70** D6
Oldmeldrum *U.K.* 57°20N 2°19W **11** D6
Olds *Canada* 51°50N 114°10W **70** C6
Öldziyt *Mongolia* 44°40N 109°1E **32** B5
Olean *U.S.A.* 42°5N 78°26W **82** D6
Olekma → *Russia* 60°22N 120°42E **27** C13
Olekminsk *Russia* 60°25N 120°30E **27** C13
Oleksandriya *Ukraine* 50°37N 26°19E **17** C14
Olema *U.S.A.* 38°3N 122°47W **78** G4
Olenegorsk *Russia* 68°9N 33°18E **8** B25
Olenek *Russia* 68°28N 112°18E **27** C12
Olenek → *Russia* 73°0N 120°10E **27** B13
Oléron, Î. d' *France* 45°55N 1°15W **20** D3
Oleśnica *Poland* 51°13N 17°22E **17** C9
Olevsk *Ukraine* 51°12N 27°39E **17** C14
Olga, L. *Canada* 49°47N 77°15W **72** C4
Olgas, The = Kata Tjuta
*Australia* 25°20S 130°50E **61** E5
Ölgiy *Mongolia* 48°56N 89°57E **30** B4
Olhão *Portugal* 37°3N 7°48W **21** D2
Olifants = Elefantes →
*Africa* 24°10S 32°40E **57** B5
Olifants → *Namibia* 25°30S 19°30E **56** B2
Olifantshoek *S. Africa* 27°57S 22°42E **56** C3
Ólimbos, Óros = Olymbos Oros
*Greece* 40°6N 22°23E **23** D10
Olímpia *Brazil* 20°44S 48°54W **95** A6
Olinda *Brazil* 8°1S 34°51W **93** E12
Oliva *Argentina* 32°0S 63°38W **94** C3
Olivares, Cerro los
*Argentina* 30°18S 69°55W **94** C2
Olive Branch *U.S.A.* 34°57N 89°49W **85** D10
Olivehurst *U.S.A.* 39°6N 121°34W **78** F5
Olivenza *Spain* 38°41N 7°9W **21** C2
Oliver *Canada* 49°13N 119°37W **70** D5
Oliver L. *Canada* 56°56N 103°22W **71** B8
Ollagüe *Chile* 21°15S 68°10W **94** A2
Olmaliq *Uzbekistan* 40°50N 69°35E **26** E7
Olney *Ill., U.S.A.* 38°44N 88°5W **80** F9
Olney *Tex., U.S.A.* 33°22N 98°45W **84** E5
Olomane → *Canada* 50°14N 60°37W **73** B7
Olomouc *Czechia* 49°38N 17°12E **17** D9
Olonets *Russia* 61°0N 32°54E **18** B5
Olongapo *Phil.* 14°50N 120°18E **37** B6
Olosega *Amer. Samoa* 14°10S 169°37W **59** b
Olosenga = Swains I.
*Amer. Samoa* 11°11S 171°4W **65** J11
Olot *Spain* 42°11N 2°30E **21** A7
Olovyannaya *Russia* 50°58N 115°35E **27** D12
Oloy → *Russia* 66°29N 159°29E **27** C16
Olsztyn *Poland* 53°48N 20°29E **17** B11
Olt → *Romania* 43°43N 24°51E **17** G13
Olteniţa *Romania* 44°7N 26°42E **17** F14
Olton *U.S.A.* 34°11N 102°8W **84** D3
Oluan Pi *Taiwan* 21°53N 120°51E **35** G13
Olymbos Oros *Greece* 40°6N 22°23E **23** D10
Olympia *Greece* 37°39N 21°39E **23** F9
Olympia *U.S.A.* 47°3N 122°53W **78** D4
Olympic △ *U.S.A.* 47°45N 123°43W **78** C3
Olympic Dam *Australia* 30°30S 136°55E **63** E2
Olympic Mts. *U.S.A.* 47°55N 123°45W **78** C3
Olyphant *U.S.A.* 41°27N 75°36W **83** E9
Olyutorskiy, Mys
*Russia* 59°55N 170°27E **27** D18
Om → *Russia* 54°59N 73°22E **26** D8
Om Koi *Thailand* 17°48N 98°22E **38** D2
Ōma *Japan* 41°45N 141°5E **28** D10
Ōmachi *Japan* 36°30N 137°50E **28** E9
Omae-Zaki *Japan* 34°36N 138°14E **29** G9
Ōmagari = Daisen
*Japan* 39°27N 140°29E **28** E10
Omagh *U.K.* 54°36N 7°19W **10** B4
Omagh □ *U.K.* 54°35N 7°15W **10** B4
Omaha *U.S.A.* 41°17N 95°58W **80** E6
Omaheke □ *Namibia* 21°30S 19°0E **56** B2
Oman ■ *Asia* 23°0N 58°0E **49** C6
Oman, G. of *Asia* 24°30N 58°30E **47** E8
Omaruru *Namibia* 21°26S 16°0E **56** B2

Omaruru → *Namibia* 22°7S 14°15E **56** B1
Omate *Peru* 16°45S 71°0W **92** G4
Ombai, Selat *Indonesia* 8°30S 124°50E **37** F6
Omboué *Gabon* 1°35S 9°15E **54** E1
Ombrone → *Italy* 42°42N 11°5E **22** C4
Omdurmân *Sudan* 15°40N 32°28E **53** E12
Omemee *Canada* 44°18N 78°33W **82** B6
Ometepe, I. de *Nic.* 11°32N 85°35W **88** D2
Ometepec *Mexico* 16°41N 98°25W **87** D5
Ominato *Japan* 41°17N 141°10E **28** D10
Omineca → *Canada* 56°3N 124°16W **70** B4
Omineca Mts. *Canada* 56°30N 125°30W **70** B3
Omitara *Namibia* 22°16S 18°2E **56** B2
Ōmiya = Saitama *Japan* 35°54N 139°38E **29** G9
Ommen *Neths.* 52°31N 6°26E **15** B6
Ömnögovi □ *Mongolia* 43°15N 104°0E **32** C3
Omo → *Ethiopia* 6°25N 36°10E **49** F2
Omolon → *Russia* 68°42N 158°36E **27** C16
Omono-Gawa → *Japan* 39°46N 140°3E **28** E10
Ompha *Canada* 45°0N 76°50W **83** B8
Omsk *Russia* 55°0N 73°12E **26** D8
Omsukchan *Russia* 62°32N 155°48E **27** C16
Ōmu *Japan* 44°34N 142°58E **28** B11
Omul, Vf. *Romania* 45°27N 25°29E **17** F13
Ōmura *Japan* 32°56N 129°57E **29** H4
Omuramba Omatako →
*Namibia* 17°45S 20°25E **56** A2
Omuramba Ovambo →
*Namibia* 18°45S 16°59E **56** A2
Omusati □ *Namibia* 18°30S 15°0E **56** A1
Ōmuta *Japan* 33°5N 130°26E **29** H5
Omuthiya *Namibia* 17°43S 16°13E **56** A2
Onaga *U.S.A.* 39°29N 96°10W **80** F5
Onalaska *U.S.A.* 43°53N 91°14W **80** D8
Onancock *U.S.A.* 37°43N 75°45W **81** G16
Onang → *Gabon* 0°57S 10°4E **54** E2
Onaping L. *Canada* 47°3N 81°30W **72** C3
Onavas *Mexico* 28°31N 109°35W **86** B3
Onawa *U.S.A.* 42°2N 96°6W **80** D5
Oncócua *Angola* 16°30S 13°25E **56** A1
Onda *Spain* 39°55N 0°17W **21** C5
Ondangwa *Namibia* 17°57S 16°4E **56** A2
Ondjiva *Angola* 16°48S 15°50E **56** A2
Öndörhaan *Mongolia* 47°19N 110°39E **31** B11
Öndverðarnes *Iceland* 64°52N 24°0W **8** D2
One Arm Point *Australia* 16°26S 123°3E **60** C3
One Arm Point ⊙
*Australia* 16°31S 122°53E **60** C3
One Tree *Australia* 34°11S 144°43E **63** E3
Oneata *Fiji* 18°26S 178°25W **59** a
Onega *Russia* 64°0N 38°10E **18** B6
Onega → *Russia* 63°58N 38°2E **18** B6
Onega, G. of = Onezhskaya Guba
*Russia* 64°24N 36°38E **18** B6
Onega, L. = Onezhskoye Ozero
*Russia* 61°44N 35°22E **18** B6
Oneida *U.S.A.* 43°6N 75°39W **83** C9
Oneida L. *U.S.A.* 43°12N 75°54W **83** C9
O'Neill *U.S.A.* 42°27N 98°39W **80** D4
Onekotan, Ostrov
*Russia* 49°25N 154°45E **27** E16
Oneonta *U.S.A.* 42°27N 75°4W **83** D9
Oneşti *Romania* 46°17N 26°47E **17** E14
Onezhskaya Guba *Russia* 64°24N 36°38E **18** B6
Onezhskoye Ozero *Russia* 61°44N 35°22E **18** B6
Ongarue *N.Z.* 38°42S 175°19E **59** C5
Ongea Levu = Ogea Levu
*Fiji* 19°8S 178°24W **59** a
Ongers → *S. Africa* 31°4S 23°13E **56** D3
Ongerup *Australia* 33°58S 118°28E **61** F2
Ongi *Mongolia* 45°27N 103°54E **32** B2
Ongjin *N. Korea* 37°56N 125°21E **33** F13
Ongkharak *Thailand* 14°8N 101°1E **38** E3
Ongniud Qi *China* 43°0N 118°38E **33** C10
Ongole *India* 15°33N 80°2E **45** G5
Ongon = Havirga
*Mongolia* 45°41N 113°5E **32** B7
Ongwediva *Namibia* 17°47S 15°46E **56** A2
Onida *U.S.A.* 44°42N 100°4W **80** C3
Onilahy → *Madag.* 23°34S 43°45E **55** J8
Onitsha *Nigeria* 6°6N 6°42E **52** G7
Onoda *Japan* 33°59N 131°11E **29** G5
Ono *Fiji* 18°55S 178°29E **59** a
Onslow *Australia* 21°40S 115°12E **60** D2
Onslow B. *U.S.A.* 34°20N 77°15W **85** D16
Ontake-San *Japan* 35°53N 137°29E **29** G8
Ontario *Calif., U.S.A.* 34°4N 117°39W **79** L9
Ontario *Oreg., U.S.A.* 44°2N 116°58W **76** D5
Ontario □ *Canada* 48°0N 83°0W **72** B2
Ontario, L. *N. Amer.* 43°20N 78°0W **82** C7
Ontonagon *U.S.A.* 46°52N 89°19W **80** B9
Onyx *U.S.A.* 35°41N 118°14W **79** K8
Oodnadatta *Australia* 27°33S 135°30E **63** D2
Ooldea *Australia* 30°27S 131°50E **61** F5
Oombulgurri *Australia* 15°15S 127°45E **60** C4
Oombulgurri ⊙
*Australia* 15°10S 127°50E **60** C4
Oorindi *Australia* 20°40S 141°1E **62** C3
Oost-Vlaanderen □
*Belgium* 51°5N 3°50E **15** C3
Oostende *Belgium* 51°15N 2°54E **15** C2
Oosterhout *Neths.* 51°39N 4°47E **15** C4
Oosterschelde → *Neths.* 51°33N 4°0E **15** C4
Oosterwolde *Neths.* 53°0N 6°17E **15** B6
Oosterschelde □ *Neths.* 51°40N 3°40E **15** C3
Oostvaardersplassen △
*Neths.* 52°27N 5°22E **15** B5
Ootacamund = Udagamandalam
*India* 11°30N 76°44E **45** J3
Ootsa L. *Canada* 53°50N 126°2W **70** C3
Ooty = Udagamandalam
*India* 11°30N 76°44E **45** J3
Op Luang △ *Thailand* 18°12S 98°32E **38** C2
Opala *Dem. Rep. of the Congo* 0°40S 24°20E **54** E4
Opanake *Sri Lanka* 6°35N 80°40E **45** L5
Opasatika *Canada* 49°30N 82°50W **72** C3
Opasquia △ *Canada* 53°33N 93°5W **72** B1
Opava *Czechia* 49°57N 17°58E **17** D9
Opelika *U.S.A.* 32°39N 85°23W **85** E12
Opelousas *U.S.A.* 30°32N 92°5W **84** F8

Opémisca, L. *Canada* 49°56N 74°52W **72** C5
Opheim *U.S.A.* 48°51N 106°24W **76** B10
Ophthalmia Ra.
*Australia* 23°15S 119°30E **60** D2
Opinaca → *Canada* 52°15N 78°2W **72** B4
Opinaca, Rés. *Canada* 52°39N 76°20W **72** B4
Opinnagau → *Canada* 54°12N 82°25W **72** B3
Opiscotéo, L. *Canada* 53°10N 68°10W **73** B6
Opobo *Nigeria* 4°35N 7°34E **52** H7
Opole *Poland* 50°42N 17°58E **17** C9
Oponono L. *Namibia* 18°8S 15°45E **56** A2
Oporto = Porto *Portugal* 41°8N 8°40W **21** B1
Opotiki *N.Z.* 38°1S 177°19E **59** C6
Opp *U.S.A.* 31°17N 86°16W **85** F11
Oppdal *Norway* 62°35N 9°41E **8** E13
Opportunity *U.S.A.* 47°39N 117°15W **76** C5
Opua *N.Z.* 35°19S 174°9E **59** A5
Opunake *N.Z.* 39°26S 173°52E **59** C4
Opuwo *Namibia* 18°3S 13°45E **56** A1
Oracle *U.S.A.* 32°37N 110°46W **77** K8
Oradea *Romania* 47°2N 21°58E **17** E11
Örefajökull *Iceland* 64°2N 16°39W **8** D5
Orai *India* 25°58N 79°30E **43** G8
Oral = Zhayyq →
*Kazakhstan* 47°0N 51°48E **19** E9
Oral *Kazakhstan* 51°20N 51°20E **19** D9
Oran *Algeria* 35°45N 0°39W **52** A5
Orange *Australia* 33°15S 149°7E **63** E4
Orange *France* 44°8N 4°47E **20** D6
Orange *Calif., U.S.A.* 33°47N 117°51W **79** M9
Orange *Mass., U.S.A.* 42°35N 72°19W **83** D12
Orange *Tex., U.S.A.* 30°6N 93°44W **84** F8
Orange *Va., U.S.A.* 38°15N 78°7W **81** F14
Orange → *S. Africa* 28°41S 16°28E **56** C2
Orange, C. *Brazil* 4°20N 51°30W **93** C8
Orange Cove *U.S.A.* 36°38N 119°19W **78** J7
Orange Free State = Free State □
*S. Africa* 28°30S 27°0E **56** C4
Orange Grove *U.S.A.* 27°58N 97°56W **84** H6
Orange Walk *Belize* 18°6N 88°33W **87** D7
Orangeburg *U.S.A.* 33°30N 80°52W **85** E14
Orangeville *Canada* 43°55N 80°5W **82** C4
Orango *Guinea-Biss.* 11°5N 16°0W **52** F2
Oranienburg *Germany* 52°45N 13°14E **16** B7
Oranje = Orange →
*S. Africa* 28°41S 16°28E **56** C2
Oranjemund *Namibia* 28°38S 16°29E **56** C2
Oranjerivier *S. Africa* 29°40S 24°12E **56** C3
Oranjestad *Aruba* 12°32N 70°2W **89** D5
Orapa *Botswana* 21°15S 25°30E **55** J5
Oras *Phil.* 12°9N 125°28E **37** B7
Orbetello *Italy* 42°27N 11°13E **22** C4
Orbisonia *U.S.A.* 40°15N 77°54W **82** F7
Orbost *Australia* 37°40S 148°29E **63** F4
Orcadas *Antarctica* 60°44S 44°37W **5** C18
Orcas I. *U.S.A.* 48°42N 122°56W **78** B4
Orchard City *U.S.A.* 38°50N 107°58W **76** G10
Orchard Homes *U.S.A.* 46°55N 114°4W **76** C6
Orchid I. = Lan Yü
*Taiwan* 22°4N 121°25E **35** F13
Orchila, I. *Venezuela* 11°48N 66°10W **89** D6
Orcutt *U.S.A.* 34°52N 120°27W **79** L6
Ord *U.S.A.* 41°36N 98°56W **80** E4
Ord → *Australia* 15°33S 128°15E **60** C4
Ord, Mt. *Australia* 17°20S 125°34E **60** C4
Ord Mts. *U.S.A.* 34°39N 116°45W **79** L10
Orderville *U.S.A.* 37°17N 112°38W **77** H7
Ordos = Mu Us Shamo
*China* 39°0N 109°0E **32** E5
Ordos *China* 39°50N 110°0E **32** E5
Ordu *Turkey* 40°55N 37°53E **19** F6
Ordway *U.S.A.* 38°13N 103°46W **76** G12
Ore Mts. = Erzgebirge
*Germany* 50°27N 12°55E **16** C7
Örebro *Sweden* 59°20N 15°18E **9** G16
Oregon *U.S.A.* 42°1N 89°20W **80** D9
Oregon □ *U.S.A.* 44°0N 121°0W **76** E3
Oregon City *U.S.A.* 45°21N 122°36W **78** E4
Oregon Dunes △ *U.S.A.* 43°40N 124°10W **76** E1
Orekhovo-Zuyevo *Russia* 55°50N 38°55E **18** C6
Orel *Russia* 52°57N 36°3E **18** D6
Orem *U.S.A.* 40°19N 111°42W **76** F8
Ören *Turkey* 37°3N 27°57E **23** F12
Orenburg *Russia* 51°45N 55°6E **18** D10
Orense = Ourense *Spain* 42°19N 7°55W **21** A2
Orepuki *N.Z.* 46°19S 167°46E **59** G1
Orestes Pereyra *Mexico* 26°30N 105°39W **86** B3
Orestiada *Greece* 41°30N 26°33E **23** D12
Orfanos Kolpos *Greece* 40°33N 24°0E **23** D11
Orford Ness *U.K.* 52°5N 1°35E **13** E9
Organ Pipe Cactus △
*U.S.A.* 32°0N 112°52W **77** K7
Orgaz *Spain* 39°39N 3°53W **21** C4
Orgeyev = Orhei
*Moldova* 47°24N 28°50E **17** E15
Orhaneli *Turkey* 39°54N 28°59E **23** E13
Orhangazi *Turkey* 40°29N 29°18E **23** D13
Orhei *Moldova* 47°24N 28°50E **17** E15
Orhon Gol → *Mongolia* 50°21N 106°0E **30** A10
Oriental, Cordillera
*Colombia* 6°0N 73°0W **92** B4
Oriental, Grand Erg *Algeria* 30°0N 6°30E **52** B7
Oriente *Argentina* 38°44S 60°37W **94** D3
Orihuela *Spain* 38°7N 0°55W **21** C5
Orillia *Canada* 44°40N 79°24W **82** B5
Orinoco → *Venezuela* 9°15N 61°30W **92** B6
Orion *Canada* 49°27N 110°49W **71** D6
Oriskany *U.S.A.* 43°10N 75°20W **83** C9
Orissa = Odisha □ *India* 20°0N 84°0E **44** E7
Orissaare *Estonia* 58°34N 23°5E **9** G20
Oristano *Italy* 39°54N 8°36E **22** E3
Oristano, G. di *Italy* 39°50N 8°29E **22** E3
Orizaba *Mexico* 18°51N 97°6W **87** D5
Orizaba, Pico de *Mexico* 18°58N 97°15W **87** D5
Orkanger *Norway* 63°18N 9°52E **8** E13
Orkhon = Orhon Gol →
*Mongolia* 50°21N 106°0E **30** A10
Orkla → *Norway* 63°18N 9°51E **8** E13
Orkney *S. Africa* 26°58S 26°40E **56** C4
Orkney □ *U.K.* 59°2N 3°13W **11** B5

Orkney Is. *U.K.* 59°0N 3°0W **11** B6
Orland *U.S.A.* 39°45N 122°12W **78** F4
Orléanais *France* 48°0N 2°0E **20** C5
Orléans *France* 47°54N 1°52E **20** C4
Orleans *U.S.A.* 44°49N 72°12W **83** B12
Orléans, Î. d' *Canada* 46°54N 70°58W **73** C5
Ormara *Pakistan* 25°16N 64°33E **40** G4
Ormoc *Phil.* 11°0N 124°37E **37** B6
Ormond *N.Z.* 38°33S 177°56E **59** C6
Ormond Beach *U.S.A.* 29°17N 81°3W **85** G14
Ormskirk *U.K.* 53°35N 2°54W **12** D5
Ormstown *Canada* 45°8N 74°0W **83** A11
Örnsköldsvik *Sweden* 63°17N 18°40E **8** E18
Oro *N. Korea* 40°1N 127°27E **33** D14
Oro → *Mexico* 25°35N 105°2W **86** B3
Oro Grande *U.S.A.* 34°36N 117°20W **79** L9
Oro Valley *U.S.A.* 32°26N 110°58W **77** K8
Orocué *Colombia* 4°48N 71°20W **92** C4
Orofino *U.S.A.* 46°29N 116°15W **76** C5
Orohena, Mt. *Tahiti* 17°37S 149°28W **59** d
Orol Dengizi = Aral Sea
*Asia* 45°0N 58°20E **26** E7
Oromocto *Canada* 45°54N 66°29W **73** C6
Orono *Canada* 43°59N 78°37W **82** C6
Orono *U.S.A.* 44°53N 68°40W **81** C19
Oronsay *U.K.* 56°1N 6°15W **11** E2
Oroquieta *Phil.* 8°32N 123°44E **37** C6
Orosei *Italy* 40°23N 9°42E **22** D3
Orosháza *Hungary* 46°32N 20°42E **17** E11
Orotukan *Russia* 62°16N 151°42E **27** C16
Oroville *Calif., U.S.A.* 39°31N 121°33W **78** F5
Oroville *Wash., U.S.A.* 48°56N 119°26W **76** B4
Oroville, L. *U.S.A.* 39°33N 121°29W **78** F5
Orroroo *Australia* 32°43S 138°38E **63** E2
Orrville *U.S.A.* 40°50N 81°46W **82** F3
Orsha *Belarus* 54°30N 30°25E **18** D5
Orsk *Russia* 51°12N 58°34E **26** D6
Orşova *Romania* 44°41N 22°25E **17** F12
Ortaca *Turkey* 36°49N 28°45E **23** F13
Ortegal, C. *Spain* 43°43N 7°52W **21** A2
Orthez *France* 43°29N 0°48W **20** E3
Ortigueira *Spain* 43°40N 7°50W **21** A2
Orting *U.S.A.* 47°6N 122°12W **78** C4
Ortles *Italy* 46°31N 10°33E **20** C9
Ortón → *Bolivia* 10°50S 67°0W **92** F5
Ortonville *U.S.A.* 45°19N 96°27W **80** C5
Orūmīyeh *Iran* 37°40N 45°0E **46** B5
Orūmīyeh, Daryācheh-ye
*Iran* 37°50N 45°30E **46** B5
Oruro *Bolivia* 18°0S 67°9W **92** G5
Orust *Sweden* 58°10N 11°40E **9** G14
Oruzgān □ *Afghan.* 33°0N 66°0E **40** C5
Orvieto *Italy* 42°43N 12°7E **22** C5
Orwell *N.Y., U.S.A.* 43°35N 75°50W **83** C9
Orwell *Ohio, U.S.A.* 41°32N 80°52W **82** E4
Orwell → *U.K.* 51°59N 1°18E **13** F9
Orwigsburg *U.S.A.* 40°38N 76°6W **83** F8
Oryakhovo *Bulgaria* 43°40N 23°57E **23** C10
Oryol = Orel *Russia* 52°57N 36°3E **18** D6
Osa *Russia* 57°17N 55°26E **18** C10
Osa, Pen. de *Costa Rica* 8°0N 84°0W **88** E3
Osage *U.S.A.* 43°17N 92°49W **80** D7
Osage → *U.S.A.* 38°36N 91°57W **80** F8
Osage City *U.S.A.* 38°38N 95°50W **80** F6
Ōsaki *Japan* 38°34N 140°58E **28** E10
Osawatomie *U.S.A.* 38°31N 94°57W **80** F6
Osborne *U.S.A.* 39°26N 98°42W **80** F5
Osceola *Ark., U.S.A.* 35°42N 89°58W **85** D10
Osceola *Iowa, U.S.A.* 41°2N 93°46W **80** E7
Oscoda *U.S.A.* 44°26N 83°20W **82** B1
Ösel = Saaremaa *Estonia* 58°30N 22°30E **9** G20
Osgoode *Canada* 45°8N 75°36W **83** A9
Osh *Kyrgyzstan* 40°37N 72°49E **30** C3
Oshakati *Namibia* 17°45S 15°40E **55** H3
Oshana □ *Namibia* 17°50S 15°40E **56** A2
Oshawa *Canada* 43°50N 78°50W **82** C6
Oshigambo *Namibia* 17°45S 16°5E **56** A2
Oshika-Hantō *Japan* 38°20N 141°32E **28** E10
Oshikoto □ *Namibia* 18°30S 17°0E **56** A2
Oshivelo *Namibia* 18°37S 17°10E **56** A2
Oshkosh *Nebr., U.S.A.* 41°24N 102°21W **80** E2
Oshkosh *Wis., U.S.A.* 44°1N 88°33W **80** C9
Oshmyany = Ashmyany
*Belarus* 54°26N 25°52E **17** A13
Oshnovīyeh *Iran* 37°2N 45°6E **46** B5
Oshogbo *Nigeria* 7°48N 4°37E **52** G6
Oshtorīnān *Iran* 34°1N 48°38E **47** C6
Ōshū *Japan* 39°8N 141°8E **28** E10
Oshwe
*Dem. Rep. of the Congo* 3°25S 19°28E **54** E3
Osijek *Croatia* 45°34N 18°41E **23** B8
Osipenko = Berdyansk
*Ukraine* — 
Osipovichi = Asipovichy
*Belarus* 53°19N 28°33E **17** B15
Osiyan *India* 26°43N 72°55E **42** F5
Osizweni *S. Africa* 27°49S 30°7E **57** C5
Oskaloosa *U.S.A.* 41°18N 92°39W **80** E7
Oskarshamn *Sweden* 57°15N 16°27E **9** H17
Oskélanéo *Canada* 48°5N 75°15W **72** C4
Öskemen *Kazakhstan* 50°0N 82°36E **26** D9
Öskjöfjorden *Norway* 59°45N 9°14E **9** G14
Osmanabad *India* 18°5N 76°10E **44** E3
Osmaniye *Turkey* 37°5N 36°10E **46** C3
Osmannagar *India* 18°30N 79°20E **44** E4
Osnabrück *Germany* 52°17N 8°3E **16** B5
Osogbo = Oshogbo *Nigeria* 7°48N 4°37E **52** G6
Osório *Brazil* 29°53S 50°17W **95** B5
Osorno *Chile* 40°25S 73°0W **96** E2
Osorno, Vol. *Chile* 41°0S 72°30W **96** D1
Osoyoos *Canada* 49°0N 119°30W **70** D5
Osøyro *Norway* 60°9N 5°30E **8** F11
Ospika → *Canada* 56°20N 124°0W **70** B4
Osprey Reef *Australia* 13°52S 146°36E **62** A4
Oss *Neths.* 51°46N 5°32E **15** C5
Ossa, Mt. *Australia* 41°52S 146°3E **63** G4
Ossa, Óros *Greece* 39°47N 22°42E **23** E10
Ossabaw I. *U.S.A.* 31°50N 81°5W **85** F14
Ossining *U.S.A.* 41°10N 73°55W **83** E11
Ossipee *U.S.A.* 43°41N 71°7W **83** C13
Ossokmanuan L. *Canada* 53°25N 65°0W **73** B7
Ossora *Russia* 59°20N 163°13E **27** D17

Ostend = Oostende
*Belgium* 51°15N 2°54E **15** C2
Oster *Ukraine* 50°57N 30°53E **17** C16
Österbotten = Pohjanmaa ◇
*Finland* 62°58N 22°50E **8** E20
Osterburg *U.S.A.* 40°16N 78°31W **82** F6
Österdalälven → *Sweden* 60°30N 15°7E **8** F15
Østerdalen *Norway* 61°40N 10°50E **8** F14
Östermyra = Seinäjoki
*Finland* 62°40N 22°51E **8** E20
Österreich = Austria ■
*Europe* 47°0N 14°0E **16** E8
Östersund *Sweden* 63°10N 14°38E **8** E16
Ostfriesische Inseln
*Germany* 53°42N 7°0E **16** B4
Ostrava *Czechia* 49°51N 18°18E **17** D10
Ostróda *Poland* 53°42N 19°58E **17** B10
Ostroh *Ukraine* 50°20N 26°30E **17** C14
Ostrołęka *Poland* 53°4N 21°32E **17** B11
Ostrów Mazowiecka
*Poland* 52°50N 21°51E **17** B11
Ostrów Wielkopolski
*Poland* 51°36N 17°44E **17** C9
Ostrowiec-Świętokrzyski
*Poland* 50°55N 21°22E **17** C11
Ostuni *Italy* 40°44N 17°35E **23** D7
Ōsumi-Kaikyō *Japan* 30°55N 131°0E **29** J5
Ōsumi-Shotō *Japan* 30°30N 130°0E **29** J5
Osuna *Spain* 37°14N 5°8W **21** D3
Oswegatchie → *U.S.A.* 44°42N 75°30W **83** B9
Oswego *U.S.A.* 43°27N 76°31W **83** C8
Oswego → *U.S.A.* 43°27N 76°30W **83** C8
Oswestry *U.K.* 52°52N 3°3W **12** E4
Oświęcim *Poland* 50°2N 19°11E **17** C10
Otago □ *N.Z.* 45°15S 170°0E **59** F2
Otago Harbour *N.Z.* 45°47S 170°42E **59** F3
Otaheite B. *Trin. & Tob.* 10°15N 61°30W **93** K15
Ōtake *Japan* 34°12N 132°13E **29** G6
Ōtaki *N.Z.* 40°45S 175°10E **59** D5
Otaru *Japan* 43°10N 141°0E **28** C10
Otaru-Wan = Ishikari-Wan
*Japan* 43°25N 141°1E **28** C10
Otavalo *Ecuador* 0°13N 78°20W **92** C3
Otavi *Namibia* 19°40S 17°24E **56** A2
Ōtawara *Japan* 36°50N 140°5E **29** F10
Otchinjau *Angola* 16°30S 13°56E **56** A1
Otego *U.S.A.* 42°23N 75°10W **83** D9
Otelnuk, L. *Canada* 56°9N 68°12W **73** A6
Othello *U.S.A.* 46°50N 119°10W **76** C4
Otish, Mts. *Canada* 52°22N 70°30W **73** B5
Otjinene *Namibia* 21°8S 18°45E **56** B2
Otjiwarongo *Namibia* 20°30S 16°33E **56** B2
Otjozondjupa □ *Namibia* 21°0S 17°0E **56** B2
Oto Tolu Group *Tonga* 20°21S 174°32W **59** c
Otoineppu *Japan* 44°44N 142°16E **28** B11
Otorohanga *N.Z.* 38°12S 175°14E **59** C5
Otoskwin → *Canada* 52°13N 88°6W **72** B2
Otra → *Norway* 58°9N 8°1E **9** G13
Otranto *Italy* 40°9N 18°28E **23** D8
Otranto, C. d' *Italy* 40°7N 18°30E **23** D8
Otranto, Str. of *Italy* 40°15N 18°40E **23** D8
Otse *S. Africa* 25°2S 25°45E **56** C4
Otsego L. *U.S.A.* 42°45N 74°53W **83** D10
Ōtsu *Japan* 35°0N 135°50E **29** G7
Ōtsuki *Japan* 35°36N 138°57E **29** G9
Ottapalam *India* 10°46N 76°23E **45** J3
Ottawa = Outaouais →
*Canada* 45°27N 74°8W **72** C5
Ottawa *Canada* 45°26N 75°42W **83** A9
Ottawa *Ill., U.S.A.* 41°21N 88°51W **80** E9
Ottawa *Kans., U.S.A.* 38°37N 95°16W **80** F6
Ottawa Is. *Canada* 59°35N 80°10W **69** F15
Otter Cr. → *U.S.A.* 44°13N 73°17W **83** B11
Otter Lake *Canada* 45°17N 79°56W **82** A5
Otterville *Canada* 42°55N 80°36W **82** D4
Ottery St. Mary *U.K.* 50°44N 3°17W **13** G4
Ottosdal *S. Africa* 26°46S 25°59E **56** C4
Ottumwa *U.S.A.* 41°1N 92°25W **80** E8
Oturkpo *Nigeria* 7°16N 8°8E **52** G7
Otway, B. *Chile* 53°30S 74°0W **96** G2
Otway, C. *Australia* 38°52S 143°30E **63** F3
Otwock *Poland* 52°5N 21°20E **17** B11
Ou → *Laos* 20°4N 102°13E **38** B4
Ou-Sammyaku *Japan* 39°20N 140°35E **28** E10
Ouachita → *U.S.A.* 31°38N 91°49W **84** F9
Ouachita, L. *U.S.A.* 34°34N 93°12W **84** D8
Ouachita Mts. *U.S.A.* 34°30N 94°30W **84** D7
Ouagadougou
*Burkina Faso* 12°25N 1°30W **52** F5
Ouahigouya *Burkina Faso* 13°31N 2°25W **52** F5
Ouahran = Oran *Algeria* 35°45N 0°39W **52** A5
Ouallene *Algeria* 24°41N 1°11E **52** D6
Ouarâne *Mauritania* 21°0N 10°30W **52** D3
Ouargla *Algeria* 31°59N 5°16E **52** B7
Ouarra → *C.A.R.* 5°5N 24°26E **54** C4
Ouarzazate *Morocco* 30°55N 6°50W **52** B4
Oubangi →
*Dem. Rep. of the Congo* 0°30S 17°50E **54** E3
Ouddorp *Neths.* 51°50N 3°57E **15** C3
Oude Rijn → *Neths.* 52°12N 4°24E **15** B4
Oudenaarde *Belgium* 50°50N 3°37E **15** D3
Oudtshoorn *S. Africa* 33°35S 22°14E **56** E3
Ouessant, Î. d' *France* 48°28N 5°6W **20** B1
Ouesso *Congo* 1°37N 16°5E **54** D3
Ouest, Pte. de l' *Canada* 49°52N 64°40W **73** C7
Ouezzane *Morocco* 34°51N 5°35W **52** B4
Oughter, L. *Ireland* 54°1N 7°28W **10** B4
Oughterard *Ireland* 53°26N 9°18W **10** C2
Ouidah *Benin* 6°25N 2°0E **52** G6
Oujda *Morocco* 34°41N 1°55W **52** B5
Oulainen *Finland* 64°17N 24°47E **8** D21
Oulanka △ *Finland* 66°26N 29°25E **8** C23
Oulujärvi *Finland* 64°25N 27°15E **8** D22
Oulujoki → *Finland* 65°1N 25°30E **8** D21
Oulu *Finland* 65°1N 25°29E **8** D21
Oum Chalouba *Chad* 15°48N 20°46E **53** E10
Oum Hadjer *Chad* 13°18N 19°41E **53** F9
Ounasjoki → *Finland* 66°31N 25°40E **8** C21
Ounguati *Namibia* 22°0S 15°46E **56** B2
Ounianga Kébir *Chad* 19°4N 20°29E **53** E10

Our → Lux. 49°55N 6°5E **15 E6**
Ouray U.S.A. 38°1N 107°40W **77 G10**
Ourense Spain 42°19N 7°55W **21 A2**
Ouricuri Brazil 7°53S 40°5W **93 E10**
Ourinhos Brazil 23°0S 49°54W **95 A6**
Ouro Fino Brazil 22°16S 46°25W **95 A6**
Ouro Prêto Brazil 20°20S 43°30W **95 A7**
Ourthe → Belgium 50°29N 5°35E **15 D5**
Ouse → E. Sussex, U.K. 50°47N 0°4E **13 G8**
Ouse → N. Yorks., U.K. 53°44N 0°55W **12 D7**
Outaouais → Canada 45°27N 74°8W **72 C5**
Outapi Namibia 17°30S 15°0E **56 A2**
Outardes → Canada 49°24N 69°30W **73 C6**
Outer Hebrides U.K. 57°30N 7°15W **11 D1**
Outjo Namibia 20°5S 16°7E **56 B2**
Outlook Canada 51°30N 107°0W **71 C7**
Outokumpu Finland 62°43N 29°1E **8 E23**
Ouyen Australia 35°1S 142°22E **63 F3**
Ovalau Fiji 17°40S 178°48E **59 a**
Ovalle Chile 30°33S 71°18W **94 C1**
Ovamboland Namibia 18°30S 16°0E **56 A2**
Overflakkee Neths. 51°44N 4°10E **15 C4**
Overijssel □ Neths. 52°25N 6°35E **15 B6**
Overland Park U.S.A. 38°58N 94°40W **80 F6**
Overlander Roadhouse
  Australia 26°19S 114°28E **61 E1**
Overton U.S.A. 36°33N 114°27W **79 J12**
Övertorneå Sweden 66°23N 23°38E **8 C20**
Ovid U.S.A. 42°41N 76°49W **83 D8**
Oviedo Spain 43°25N 5°50W **21 A3**
Ovišrags Latvia 57°33N 21°44E **9 H19**
Ovoot Mongolia 45°21N 113°45E **32 B7**
Övör Hangay □ Mongolia 45°0N 102°30E **32 B2**
Øvre Anárjohka △
  Norway 68°30N 24°40E **8 B21**
Øvre Årdal Norway 61°19N 7°48E **8 F12**
Øvre Dividal △ Norway 68°43N 19°50E **8 B18**
Øvre Pasvik △ Norway 69°6N 28°54E **8 B23**
Ovruch Ukraine 51°25N 28°45E **17 C15**
Owaka N.Z. 46°27S 169°40E **59 G2**
Owambo = Ovamboland
  Namibia 18°30S 16°0E **56 A2**
Owasco L. U.S.A. 42°50N 76°31W **83 D8**
Owase Japan 34°7N 136°12E **29 G8**
Owatonna U.S.A. 44°5N 93°14W **80 C7**
Owbeh Afghan. 34°28N 63°10E **40 B3**
Owego U.S.A. 42°6N 76°16W **83 D8**
Owen Sound Canada 44°35N 80°55W **82 B4**
Owen Stanley Ra.
  Papua N. G. 8°30S 147°0E **58 B7**
Oweniny → Ireland 54°8N 9°34W **10 B2**
Owens → U.S.A. 36°32N 117°59W **78 J9**
Owens L. U.S.A. 36°26N 117°57W **79 J9**
Owensboro U.S.A. 37°46N 87°7W **80 G10**
Owl → Canada 57°51N 92°44W **71 B10**
Owo Nigeria 7°10N 5°39E **52 G7**
Owosso U.S.A. 43°0N 84°10W **81 D11**
Owyhee U.S.A. 41°57N 116°6W **76 F5**
Owyhee → U.S.A. 43°49N 117°2W **76 E5**
Owyhee, L. U.S.A. 43°38N 117°14W **76 E5**
Ox Mts. = Slieve Gamph
  Ireland 54°6N 9°0W **10 B3**
Öxarfjörður Iceland 66°15N 16°45W **8 C5**
Oxbow Canada 49°14N 102°10W **71 D8**
Oxelösund Sweden 58°43N 17°5E **9 G17**
Oxford N.Z. 43°18S 172°11E **59 E4**
Oxford U.K. 51°46N 1°15W **13 F6**
Oxford Mass., U.S.A. 42°7N 71°52W **83 D13**
Oxford Miss., U.S.A. 34°22N 89°31W **85 D10**
Oxford N.C., U.S.A. 36°19N 78°35W **85 C15**
Oxford N.Y., U.S.A. 42°27N 75°36W **83 D9**
Oxford Ohio, U.S.A. 39°31N 84°45W **81 F11**
Oxford L. Canada 54°51N 95°37W **71 C9**
Oxfordshire □ U.K. 51°48N 1°16W **13 F6**
Oxnard U.S.A. 34°12N 119°11W **79 L7**
Oxus = Amudarya →
  Uzbekistan 43°58N 59°34E **26 E6**
Oya Malaysia 2°55N 111°55E **36 D4**
Oyama Japan 36°18N 139°48E **29 F9**
Oyem Gabon 1°34N 11°31E **54 D2**
Oyen Canada 51°22N 110°28W **71 C6**
Oykel → U.K. 57°56N 4°26W **11 D4**
Oymyakon Russia 63°25N 142°44E **27 C15**
Oyo Nigeria 7°46N 3°56E **52 G6**
Õyûbari Japan 43°1N 142°5E **28 C11**
Ozamiz Phil. 8°15N 123°50E **37 C6**
Ozar = Ojhar India 20°6N 73°56E **44 D1**
Ozark Ala., U.S.A. 31°28N 85°39W **85 F12**
Ozark Ark., U.S.A. 35°29N 93°50W **84 D8**
Ozark Mo., U.S.A. 37°1N 93°12W **80 G7**
Ozark Plateau U.S.A. 37°20N 91°40W **80 G9**
Ozarks, L. of the U.S.A. 38°12N 92°38W **80 F7**
Ózd Hungary 48°14N 20°15E **17 D11**
Ozernovskiy Russia 51°30N 156°31E **27 D16**
Ozette L. U.S.A. 48°6N 124°38W **78 B2**
Ozieri Italy 40°35N 9°0E **22 D3**
Ozona U.S.A. 30°43N 101°12W **84 F4**
Ozuluama Mexico 21°40N 97°51W **87 C5**

**P**

Pa-an Myanmar 16°51N 97°40E **41 L20**
Pa Mong Dam Thailand 18°0N 102°22E **38 D4**
Pa Sak → Thailand 15°30N 101°0E **38 E3**
Paamiut Greenland 62°0N 49°43W **4 C5**
Paanayarvi △ Russia 66°16N 30°10E **8 C24**
Paarl S. Africa 33°45S 18°56E **56 D2**
Pab Hills Pakistan 26°30N 66°45E **42 F2**
Pabaidh = Pabbay U.K. 57°46N 7°14W **11 D1**
Pabbay U.K. 57°46N 7°14W **11 D1**
Pabianice Poland 51°40N 19°20E **17 C10**
Pabna Bangla. 24°1N 89°18E **41 G16**
Pacaja → Brazil 1°56S 50°50W **93 D8**
Pacaraima, Sa. S. Amer. 4°0N 62°30W **92 C6**
Pacasmayo Peru 7°20S 79°35W **92 E3**
Pachitea → Peru 8°46S 74°33W **92 E4**
Pachmarhi India 22°28N 78°26E **43 H8**
Pachora India 20°38N 75°29E **44 D2**
Pachpadra India 25°58N 72°10E **42 G5**
Pachuca Mexico 20°7N 98°44W **87 C5**

Pacific Antarctic Ridge
  Pac. Oc. 43°0S 115°0W **5 B13**
Pacific Grove U.S.A. 36°38N 121°56W **78 J5**
Pacific Ocean 10°0N 140°0W **65 G14**
Pacific Rim △ Canada 48°40N 124°45W **78 B2**
Pacitan Indonesia 8°12S 111°7E **37 H14**
Packwood U.S.A. 46°36N 121°40W **78 D5**
Padaido, Kepulauan
  Indonesia 1°15S 136°30E **37 E9**
Padampur India 20°59N 83°4E **44 J6**
Padang Riau, Indonesia 1°30N 102°30E **39 M4**
Padang Sumatera Barat,
  Indonesia 1°0S 100°20E **36 E2**
Padang Endau Malaysia 2°40N 103°38E **39 L4**
Padangpanjang Indonesia 0°40S 100°20E **36 E2**
Padangsidempuan
  Indonesia 1°30N 99°15E **36 D1**
Paddle Prairie Canada 57°57N 117°29W **70 B5**
Paderborn Germany 51°42N 8°45E **16 C5**
Paderoo India 18°5N 82°40E **44 E6**
Padjelanta △ Sweden 67°20N 16°35E **8 C17**
Padma → India 24°12N 85°22E **43 G11**
Pádova Italy 45°25N 11°53E **22 B4**
Padra India 22°15N 73°7E **42 H5**
Padrauna India 26°54N 83°59E **43 F10**
Padre I. U.S.A. 27°10N 97°25W **84 H6**
Padre Island △ U.S.A. 27°0N 97°25W **84 H6**
Padstow U.K. 50°33N 4°58W **13 G3**
Padua = Pádova Italy 45°25N 11°53E **22 B4**
Paducah Ky., U.S.A. 37°5N 88°37W **80 G9**
Paducah Tex., U.S.A. 34°1N 100°18W **84 D4**
Padukka Sri Lanka 6°50N 80°6E **45 L5**
Padwa India 18°27N 82°47E **44 E6**
Paea Tahiti 17°41S 149°35W **59 d**
Paektu-san N. Korea 41°59N 128°4E **33 D15**
Paeroa N.Z. 37°23S 175°41E **59 B5**
Pafúri Mozam. 22°28S 31°17E **57 B5**
Pag Croatia 44°25N 15°3E **16 F8**
Pagadian Phil. 7°55N 123°30E **37 C6**
Pagai Selatan, Pulau
  Indonesia 3°0S 100°15E **36 E2**
Pagai Utara, Pulau
  Indonesia 2°35S 100°0E **36 E2**
Pagalu = Annobón Atl. Oc. 1°25S 5°36E **51 G4**
Pagara India 24°22N 80°1E **43 G9**
Pagasas I. = Thitu I.
  S. China Sea 11°3N 114°17E **36 B4**
Pagastikos Kolpos Greece 39°15N 23°0E **23 E10**
Pagatan Indonesia 3°33S 115°59E **36 E5**
Page U.S.A. 36°57N 111°27W **77 H8**
Paget, Mt. S. Georgia 54°26S 36°31W **96 G9**
Paget I. India 13°26N 92°50E **45 H11**
Pago Pago Amer. Samoa 14°16S 170°43W **59 b**
Pagosa Springs U.S.A. 37°16N 107°1W **77 H10**
Pagri China 27°45N 89°10E **30 F6**
Pagwa River Canada 50°2N 85°14W **72 B2**
Pāhala U.S.A. 19°12N 155°29W **75 M8**
Pahang □ Malaysia 3°30N 102°45E **39 L4**
Pahang → Malaysia 3°30N 103°9E **39 L4**
Pahiatua N.Z. 40°27S 175°50E **59 D5**
Pahokee U.S.A. 26°50N 80°40W **85 H14**
Pahrump U.S.A. 36°12N 115°59W **79 J11**
Pahute Mesa U.S.A. 37°20N 116°45W **78 H10**
Pai Thailand 19°19N 98°27E **38 C2**
Paicines U.S.A. 36°44N 121°17W **78 J5**
Paide Estonia 58°53N 25°33E **9 G21**
Paignton U.K. 50°26N 3°35W **13 G4**
Paiho Taiwan 23°21N 120°25E **35 F13**
Päijänne Finland 61°30N 25°30E **8 F21**
Pailani India 25°45N 80°26E **43 G9**
Pailin Cambodia 12°46N 102°36E **38 F4**
Painan Indonesia 1°21S 100°34E **36 E2**
Painesville U.S.A. 41°43N 81°15W **82 E3**
Paint Hills = Wemindji
  Canada 53°0N 78°49W **72 B4**
Paint L. Canada 55°28N 97°57W **71 B9**
Painted Desert U.S.A. 36°0N 111°0W **77 H8**
Paintsville U.S.A. 37°49N 82°48W **81 G12**
País Vasco □ Spain 42°50N 2°45W **21 A4**
Paisley Canada 44°18N 81°16W **82 B3**
Paisley U.K. 55°50N 4°25W **11 F4**
Paisley U.S.A. 42°42N 120°32W **76 E3**
Paita Peru 5°11S 81°9W **92 E2**
Paithan India 19°29N 75°23E **44 E2**
Paizhou China 30°12N 113°55E **35 B9**
Pajares, Puerto de Spain 42°58N 5°46W **21 A3**
Pak Lay Laos 18°15N 101°27E **38 C3**
Pak Ou Laos 20°3N 102°12E **38 B4**
Pak Phanang Thailand 8°21N 100°12E **39 H3**
Pak Sane Laos 18°22N 103°39E **38 C4**
Pak Song Laos 15°11N 106°14E **38 E6**
Pak Suang Laos 19°58N 102°15E **34 H4**
Pak Tam Chung China 22°24N 114°19E **31 a**
Pak Thong Chai Thailand 14°43N 102°1E **38 E4**
Pakala India 13°29N 79°8E **45 H4**
Pakaur India 24°38N 87°51E **43 G12**
Pakch'ŏn N. Korea 39°44N 125°33E **33 E13**
Pakenham Canada 45°18N 76°18W **83 A8**
Pakhuis S. Africa 32°9S 19°5E **56 D2**
Pakistan ■ Asia 30°0N 70°0E **42 E4**
Pakkading Laos 18°19N 103°59E **38 C4**
Pakkōku Myanmar 21°20N 95°0E **41 J19**
Pakowki L. Canada 49°20N 111°0W **71 D6**
Pakpattan Pakistan 30°25N 73°27E **42 D5**
Pakse Laos 15°5N 105°52E **38 E5**
Pal Lahara India 21°27N 85°11E **43 J11**
Pala Chad 9°25N 15°5E **53 G9**
Pala India 33°22N 117°5W **79 M9**
Palacios U.S.A. 28°42N 96°13W **84 G6**
Palagruža Croatia 42°24N 16°15E **22 C7**
Palakkad India 10°46N 76°42E **45 J3**
Palakol India 16°31N 81°46E **45 F5**
Palalankwe India 10°52N 92°29E **45 J11**
Palam India 19°0N 77°0E **44 E3**
Palampur India 32°10N 76°30E **42 C7**
Palana Australia 39°45S 147°55E **63 F4**
Palana Russia 59°10N 159°59E **27 D16**

Palanan Phil. 17°8N 122°29E **37 A6**
Palanan Pt. Phil. 17°17N 122°30E **37 A6**
Palandri Pakistan 33°42N 73°40E **43 C5**
Palanga Lithuania 55°58N 21°3E **9 J19**
Palangkaraya Indonesia 2°16S 113°56E **36 E4**
Palani India 10°30N 77°33E **45 J3**
Palani Hills India 10°14N 77°33E **45 J3**
Palanpur India 24°10N 72°25E **42 G5**
Palapye Botswana 22°30S 27°7E **56 B4**
Palar → India 12°27N 80°13E **45 H5**
Palas Pakistan 35°4N 73°14E **43 B5**
Palasponga India 21°47N 85°34E **43 J11**
Palatka Russia 60°6N 150°54E **27 C16**
Palatka U.S.A. 29°39N 81°38W **85 G14**
Palau ■ Palau 7°30N 134°30E **64 G5**
Palauk Myanmar 13°10N 98°40E **38 F2**
Palawan Phil. 9°30N 118°30E **36 C5**
Palayankottai India 8°45N 77°45E **45 K3**
Paldiski Estonia 59°23N 24°9E **9 G21**
Paleleh Indonesia 1°10N 121°50E **37 D6**
Palembang Indonesia 3°0S 104°50E **36 E2**
Palencia Spain 42°1N 4°34W **21 A3**
Palenque Mexico 17°29N 92°1W **87 D6**
Palermo Italy 38°7N 13°22E **22 E5**
Palermo U.S.A. 39°26N 121°33W **78 F5**
Palestina Chile 23°50S 69°47W **94 A2**
Palestina Chile 23°50S 69°47W **96 A3**
Palestine Asia 32°0N 35°0E **48 D4**
Palestine U.S.A. 31°46N 95°38W **84 F7**
Paletwa Myanmar 21°10N 92°50E **41 J18**
Palghat = Palakkad India 10°46N 76°42E **45 J3**
Palgrave, Mt. Australia 23°22S 115°58E **60 D2**
Palhoça Brazil 27°38S 48°40W **95 B6**
Pali India 25°50N 73°20E **42 G5**
Palikir Micronesia 6°55N 158°9E **64 G7**
Paliouri, Akra Greece 39°57N 23°45E **23 E10**
Palisades Res. U.S.A. 43°20N 111°12W **76 E8**
Paliseul Belgium 49°54N 5°8E **15 E5**
Palitana India 21°32N 71°49E **42 J4**
Palizada Mexico 18°15N 92°5W **87 D6**
Palk Bay Asia 9°30N 79°15E **45 K4**
Palk Strait Asia 10°0N 79°45E **45 K4**
Palkānah Iraq 35°49N 44°26E **46 C5**
Palkonda India 18°36N 83°48E **44 E6**
Palkonda Ra. India 13°50N 79°20E **45 H4**
Palkot India 22°53N 84°39E **43 H11**
Pallanza = Verbánia Italy 45°56N 8°33E **20 D8**
Pallarenda Australia 19°12S 146°46E **62 B4**
Pallas-Yllästunturi △
  Finland 68°8N 24°15E **8 B21**
Palleru → India 16°45N 80°2E **44 F5**
Pallinup → Australia 34°27S 118°50E **61 F2**
Pallu India 28°59N 74°14E **42 E6**
Palm Bay U.S.A. 28°2N 80°35W **85 G14**
Palm Beach U.S.A. 26°43N 80°2W **85 H14**
Palm Coast U.S.A. 29°35N 81°12W **85 G14**
Palm Desert U.S.A. 33°43N 116°22W **79 M10**
Palm-Grove △ Australia 24°57S 149°21E **62 C4**
Palm Is. Australia 18°40S 146°35E **62 B4**
Palm Springs U.S.A. 33°50N 116°33W **79 M10**
Palma, B. de Spain 39°30N 2°39E **21 C7**
Palma de Mallorca Spain 39°35N 2°39E **21 C7**
Palma Soriano Cuba 20°15N 76°0W **88 B4**
Palmaner India 13°12N 78°45E **45 H4**
Palmares Brazil 8°41S 35°28W **93 E11**
Palmas Brazil 26°29S 52°0W **95 B5**
Palmas, C. Liberia 4°27N 7°46W **52 H4**
Pálmas, G. di Italy 39°0N 8°30E **22 E3**
Palmdale U.S.A. 34°35N 118°7W **79 L8**
Palmeira das Missões
  Brazil 27°55S 53°17W **95 B5**
Palmeira dos Índios
  Brazil 9°25S 36°37W **93 E11**
Palmer Antarctica 64°35S 65°0W **5 C17**
Palmer U.S.A. 61°36N 149°7W **68 E2**
Palmer → Australia 16°0S 142°26E **62 B3**
Palmer Arch. Antarctica 64°15S 65°0W **5 C17**
Palmer Lake U.S.A. 39°7N 104°55W **76 G11**
Palmer Land Antarctica 73°0S 63°0W **5 D18**
Palmerston Australia 12°31S 130°59E **60 B5**
Palmerston Canada 43°50N 80°51W **82 C4**
Palmerston N.Z. 45°29S 170°43E **59 F3**
Palmerston North N.Z. 40°21S 175°39E **59 D5**
Palmerton U.S.A. 40°48N 75°37W **83 F9**
Palmetto U.S.A. 27°31N 82°34W **85 H13**
Palmi Italy 38°21N 15°51E **22 E6**
Palmira Argentina 32°59S 68°34W **94 C2**
Palmira Colombia 3°32N 76°16W **92 C3**
Palmyra = Tudmur Syria 34°36N 38°15E **46 C3**
Palmyra N.J., U.S.A. 39°48N 91°32W **80 F8**
Palmyra N.J., U.S.A. 40°0N 75°1W **83 F9**
Palmyra N.Y., U.S.A. 43°5N 77°18W **82 C7**
Palmyra Pa., U.S.A. 40°18N 76°36W **83 F8**
Palmyra Is. Pac. Oc. 5°52N 162°5W **65 G11**
Palmyras Pt. India 20°46N 87°1E **44 D8**
Palo Alto U.S.A. 37°27N 122°10W **78 H4**
Palo Seco Trin. & Tob. 10°4N 61°36W **93 K15**
Palo Verde U.S.A. 26°36N 114°44W **79 M12**
Palo Verde △ Costa Rica 10°21N 85°21W **88 D2**
Palopo Indonesia 3°0S 120°16E **37 E6**
Palos, C. de Spain 37°38N 0°40W **21 D5**
Palos Verdes, Pt. U.S.A. 33°46N 118°25W **79 M8**
Palos Verdes Estates
  U.S.A. 33°48N 118°23W **79 M8**
Palu Indonesia 1°0S 119°52E **37 E5**
Palu Turkey 38°45N 40°0E **46 B3**
Paluma Ra. Australia 19°9S 146°22E **62 B4**
Palwal India 28°8N 77°19E **42 E7**
Pamanukan Indonesia 6°16S 107°49E **37 G12**
Pamban I. India 9°15N 79°20E **45 K4**
Pamekasan Indonesia 7°10S 113°28E **37 G15**
Pamenang Indonesia 8°24S 116°6E **37 J19**
Pamiers France 43°7N 1°39E **20 E4**
Pamir Tajikistan 37°40N 73°0E **26 F8**
Pamlico → U.S.A. 35°20N 76°28E **85 H7**
Pamlico Sd. U.S.A. 35°20N 76°0W **85 H8**
Pampa U.S.A. 35°32N 100°58W **84 D4**
Pampa de las Salinas
  Argentina 32°1S 66°58W **94 C2**

Pampanua Indonesia 4°16S 120°8E **37 E6**
Pampas Argentina 35°0S 63°0W **94 D3**
Pampas Peru 12°20S 74°50W **92 F4**
Pamplona Colombia 7°23N 72°39W **92 B4**
Pamplona-Iruña Spain 42°48N 1°38W **21 A5**
Pan de Azúcar Chile 24°55S 68°10W **94 A2**
Pan de Azúcar △ Chile 26°0S 70°40W **94 B1**
Pan Xian China 25°46N 104°38E **34 E5**
Pana U.S.A. 39°23N 89°5W **80 F10**
Panaca U.S.A. 37°47N 114°23W **77 H6**
Panadura Sri Lanka 6°47N 79°53E **45 L4**
Panaitan Indonesia 6°36S 105°12E **37 G11**
Panaji India 15°25N 73°50E **45 G1**
Panamá Panama 9°0N 79°25E **88 E4**
Panama Sri Lanka 6°45N 81°48E **45 L5**
Panama ■ Cent. Amer. 8°48N 79°55W **88 E4**
Panamá, G. de Panama 8°4N 79°20W **88 E4**
Panama, Isthmus of
  Cent. Amer. 9°0N 79°0W **88 E4**
Panama Basin Pac. Oc. 5°0N 83°30W **65 G19**
Panama Canal Panama 9°10N 79°37W **88 E4**
Panama City U.S.A. 30°10N 85°40W **85 F12**
Panamint Range U.S.A. 36°20N 117°20W **79 J9**
Panamint Springs
  U.S.A. 36°20N 117°28W **79 J9**
Panão Peru 9°55S 75°55W **92 E3**
Panare Thailand 6°51N 101°30E **39 J3**
Panay Phil. 11°10N 122°30E **37 B6**
Panay G. Phil. 11°0N 122°30E **37 B6**
Pančevo Serbia 44°52N 20°41E **23 B9**
Panch'iao Taiwan 25°1N 121°27E **35 E13**
Panda Mozam. 24°2S 34°45E **57 B5**
Pandan Malaysia 1°32N 103°46E **39 d**
Pandan Phil. 11°45N 122°10E **37 B6**
Pandan Tampoi = Tampoi
  Malaysia 1°30N 103°39E **39 d**
Pandegelang Indonesia 6°25S 106°5E **37 G12**
Pandhana India 21°42N 76°13E **42 J7**
Pandharkawada India 20°1N 78°32E **44 D4**
Pandharpur India 17°41N 75°20E **44 F2**
Pandhurna India 21°36N 78°35E **44 D4**
Pando Uruguay 34°44S 56°0W **95 C4**
Pando, L. = Hope, L.
  Australia 28°24S 139°18E **63 D2**
Pandora Costa Rica 9°43N 83°3W **88 E3**
Panevėžys Lithuania 55°42N 24°25E **9 J21**
Pang Sida = Thailand 14°5N 102°17E **38 E4**
Pangandaran Indonesia 7°40S 108°39E **37 G13**
Pangandaran △
  Indonesia 7°43S 108°42E **37 G13**
Pangani Tanzania 5°25S 38°58E **54 F7**
Pangfou = Bengbu
  China 32°58N 117°20E **33 H9**
Pangga, Tanjung
  Indonesia 8°54S 116°2E **37 K19**
Panghsang = Bangkang
  Myanmar 22°4N 99°1E **34 F2**
Pangjiabu China 40°38N 115°26E **32 D8**
Pangkah, Tanjung
  Indonesia 6°51S 112°33E **37 G15**
Pangkai Myanmar 22°49N 98°39E **34 F2**
Pangkajene Indonesia 4°46S 119°34E **37 E5**
Pangkalanbrandan
  Indonesia 4°1N 98°20E **36 D1**
Pangkalanbuun Indonesia 2°41S 111°37E **36 E4**
Pangkalpinang Indonesia 2°10S 106°10E **36 E3**
Pangkor, Pulau Malaysia 4°13N 100°34E **39 K3**
Pangniqtuuq = Pangnirtung
  Canada 66°8N 65°43W **69 D18**
Pangnirtung Canada 66°8N 65°43W **69 D18**
Pangody Russia 65°52N 74°27E **26 C8**
Pangong Tso = Bangong Co
  China 33°45N 78°43E **43 C8**
Panguitch U.S.A. 37°50N 112°26W **77 H7**
Pangutaran Group Phil. 6°18N 120°34E **37 C6**
Panhala India 16°49N 74°7E **44 F2**
Panhandle U.S.A. 35°21N 101°23W **84 D4**
Pani Mines India 22°29N 73°50E **42 H5**
Panikota I. India 20°46N 71°21E **42 J4**
Panipat India 29°25N 77°2E **42 E7**
Panjal Range = Pir Panjal Range
  India 32°30N 76°50E **42 C7**
Panjgur Pakistan 27°0N 64°5E **40 F4**
Panjhra → India 21°13N 74°57E **44 D2**
Panjim = Panaji India 15°25N 73°50E **45 G1**
Panjin China 41°3N 122°2E **33 D12**
Panjnad → Pakistan 28°57N 70°30E **42 E4**
Panjnad Barrage Pakistan 29°22N 71°15E **42 E4**
Panjwai Afghan. 31°26N 65°27E **42 D1**
Panmunjŏm N. Korea 37°59N 126°38E **33 F14**
Panna India 24°40N 80°15E **43 G9**
Panna △ India 24°40N 80°0E **43 G8**
Panna Hills India 24°40N 81°15E **43 G9**
Pannawonica Australia 21°39S 116°19E **60 D2**
Pano Akil Pakistan 27°51N 69°7E **42 F3**
Panorama Brazil 21°21S 51°51W **95 A5**
Panruti India 11°46N 79°35E **45 J4**
Pansemal India 21°39N 74°42E **42 J6**
Panshan = Panjin China 41°3N 122°2E **33 D12**
Panshi China 42°58N 126°5E **33 C14**
Pantanal Brazil 17°30S 57°40W **92 H7**
Pantanos de Centla △
  Mexico 18°25N 92°25W **87 D6**
Pantar Indonesia 8°28S 124°10E **37 F6**
Pante Macassar
  Timor-Leste 9°30S 123°58E **37 F6**
Pantelleria Italy 36°50N 11°57E **22 F4**
Pánuco Mexico 22°3N 98°10W **87 C5**
Panvel India 18°59N 73°4E **44 F1**
Panzhihua China 26°33N 101°44E **34 D3**
Paola U.S.A. 38°35N 94°53W **80 F6**
Paonia U.S.A. 38°52N 107°36W **76 G10**
Paopao Moorea 17°30S 149°49W **59 d**
Paoting = Baoding
  China 38°50N 115°28E **32 E8**
Paot'ou = Baotou China 40°32N 110°2E **32 D6**
Paoua C.A.R. 7°9N 16°20E **54 C3**
Pápa Hungary 47°22N 17°30E **17 E9**
Papa Stour U.K. 60°20N 1°42W **11 A7**

Papa Westray U.K. 59°20N 2°55W **11 B6**
Papagayo → Mexico 16°46N 99°43W **87 D5**
Papagayo, G. de
  Costa Rica 10°30N 85°50W **88 D2**
Papagni → India 15°35N 77°45E **45 G3**
Papakura N.Z. 37°4S 174°59E **59 B5**
Papantla Mexico 20°27N 97°19E **87 C5**
Papar Malaysia 5°45N 116°0E **36 C5**
Papara Tahiti 17°43S 149°31W **59 d**
Paparoa △ N.Z. 42°7S 171°26E **59 E3**
Papeete Tahiti 17°32S 149°34W **59 d**
Papenoo Tahiti 17°30S 149°25W **59 d**
Papenoo → Tahiti 17°30S 149°25W **59 d**
Papetoai Moorea 17°29S 149°52W **59 d**
Paposo Chile 25°0S 70°30W **94 B1**
Papua □ Indonesia 4°0S 137°0E **37 E9**
Papua, G. of Papua N. G. 9°0S 144°50E **58 B7**
Papua New Guinea ■
  Oceania 8°0S 145°0E **58 B7**
Papudo Chile 32°29S 71°27E **94 C1**
Papun Myanmar 18°2N 97°30E **41 K20**
Pará = Belém Brazil 1°20S 48°30W **93 D9**
Pará □ Brazil 3°20S 52°0W **93 D8**
Paraburdoo Australia 23°14S 117°32E **60 D2**
Paracatu Brazil 17°10S 46°50W **93 G9**
Paracel Is. S. China Sea 15°50N 112°0E **36 A4**
Parachilna Australia 31°10S 138°21E **63 E2**
Parachinar Pakistan 33°55N 70°5E **42 C4**
Paradip India 20°15N 86°35E **44 D8**
Paradise U.S.A. 39°46N 121°37W **78 F5**
Paradise → Canada 53°27N 57°19W **73 B8**
Paradise Hill Canada 53°32N 109°28W **71 C7**
Paradise River Canada 53°27N 57°17W **73 B8**
Paradise Valley U.S.A. 41°30N 117°32W **76 F5**
Paragould U.S.A. 36°3N 90°29W **85 C9**
Paragua → Venezuela 6°55N 62°55W **92 B6**
Paraguaçu → Brazil 12°45S 38°54W **93 F11**
Paraguaçu Paulista
  Brazil 22°22S 50°35W **95 A5**
Paraguaná, Pen. de
  Venezuela 12°0N 70°0W **92 A5**
Paraguarí Paraguay 25°36S 57°0W **94 B4**
Paraguarí □ Paraguay 26°0S 57°10W **94 B4**
Paraguay ■ S. Amer. 23°0S 57°0W **94 A4**
Paraguay → Paraguay 27°18S 58°38W **94 B4**
Paraíba = João Pessoa
  Brazil 7°10S 34°52W **93 E12**
Paraíba □ Brazil 7°0S 36°0W **93 E11**
Paraíba do Sul → Brazil 21°37S 41°3W **95 A7**
Paraíso Mexico 18°24N 93°14W **87 D6**
Parak Iran 27°38N 52°25E **47 E7**
Parakou Benin 9°25N 2°40E **52 G6**
Paralkote India 19°47N 80°41E **44 E5**
Paramaribo Suriname 5°50N 55°10W **93 B7**
Páramos del Batallón y La Negra △
  Venezuela 8°2N 71°55W **89 E5**
Paramushir, Ostrov
  Russia 50°24N 156°0E **27 D16**
Paran → Israel 30°20N 35°10E **48 E4**
Paraná Argentina 31°45S 60°30W **94 C3**
Paraná Brazil 12°30S 47°48W **93 F9**
Paraná □ Brazil 24°30S 51°0W **95 A5**
Paraná → Argentina 33°43S 59°15W **94 C4**
Paranaguá Brazil 25°30S 48°30W **95 B6**
Paranaíba Brazil 19°40S 51°11W **93 G8**
Paranaíba → Brazil 20°6S 51°4W **93 H8**
Paranal, Cerro Chile 24°38S 70°24W **94 A1**
Paranapanema → Brazil 22°40S 53°9W **95 A5**
Paranapiacaba, Serra do
  Brazil 24°31S 48°35W **95 A6**
Paranavaí Brazil 23°4S 52°56W **95 A5**
Parang Maguindanao, Phil. 7°23N 124°16E **37 C6**
Parang Sulu, Phil. 5°55N 120°54E **37 C6**
Parângippettai India 11°30N 79°38E **45 J4**
Parângul Mare, Vf.
  Romania 45°20N 23°37E **17 F12**
Paranthan Sri Lanka 9°26N 80°24E **45 K5**
Paraparaumu N.Z. 40°57S 175°3E **59 D5**
Parauapebas Brazil 6°4S 49°54W **93 E9**
Parbati → Mad. P., India 25°50N 76°30E **42 G7**
Parbati → Raj., India 26°54N 77°53E **42 F7**
Parbhani India 19°8N 76°52E **44 E3**
Parchim Germany 53°26N 11°52E **16 B6**
Pardes Hanna-Karkur
  Israel 32°28N 34°57E **48 C3**
Pardo → Bahia, Brazil 15°40S 39°0W **93 G11**
Pardo → Mato Grosso,
  Brazil 21°46S 52°9W **95 A5**
Pardoo Roadhouse
  Australia 20°6S 119°3E **60 D2**
Pardubice Czechia 50°3N 15°45E **16 C8**
Pare Indonesia 7°43S 112°12E **37 G15**
Parecis, Serra dos Brazil 13°0S 60°0W **92 F7**
Paren Russia 62°30N 163°15E **27 C17**
Parenda India 18°16N 75°28E **44 E2**
Parent Canada 47°55N 74°35W **72 C5**
Parent, L. Canada 48°31N 77°1W **72 C4**
Parepare Indonesia 4°0S 119°40E **37 E5**
Parga Greece 39°15N 20°29E **23 E9**
Pargas = Länsi-Turunmaa
  Finland 60°18N 22°18E **9 F20**
Pargi India 17°11N 77°53E **44 E3**
Parham Canada 44°39N 76°43W **83 B8**
Paria → U.S.A. 36°52N 111°36W **77 H8**
Paria, G. de Venezuela 10°30N 61°40W **93 K14**
Pariaguán Venezuela 8°51N 64°34W **92 B6**
Paricutín, Cerro Mexico 19°28N 102°15W **86 D4**
Parigi Indonesia 0°50S 120°5E **37 E6**
Parika Guyana 6°50N 58°20W **92 B7**
Parikkala Finland 61°33N 29°31E **8 F23**
Parima, Serra Brazil 2°30N 64°0W **92 C6**
Parinari Peru 4°35S 74°25W **92 D4**
Pariñas, Pta. Peru 4°30S 82°0W **90 D2**
Parintins Brazil 2°40S 56°50W **93 D7**
Pariparit Kyun
  Myanmar 14°52N 93°41E **45 G11**
Paris France 48°50N 2°20E **20 B5**
Paris Idaho, U.S.A. 42°14N 111°24W **76 E8**
Paris Ky., U.S.A. 38°13N 84°15W **81 F11**

Paris Tenn., U.S.A. 36°18N 88°19W 85 C10
Paris Tex., U.S.A. 33°40N 95°33W 84 E7
Parish U.S.A. 43°25N 76°8W 83 C8
Parishville U.S.A. 44°38N 74°49W 83 B10
Pariti Indonesia 10°1S 123°45E 60 B3
Park U.S.A. 48°45N 122°18W 78 B4
Park City U.S.A. 37°48N 97°20W 80 G5
Park Falls U.S.A. 45°56N 90°27W 80 C8
Park Head Canada 44°36N 81°9W 82 B3
Park Hills U.S.A. 37°51N 90°51W 80 G8
Park Range U.S.A. 40°41N 106°41W 76 F10
Park Rapids U.S.A. 46°55N 95°4W 80 B6
Park River U.S.A. 48°24N 97°45W 80 A5
Park Rynie S. Africa 30°25S 30°45E 57 D5
Parkā Bandar Iran 25°55N 59°35E 47 E8
Parkano Finland 62°1N 23°0E 8 E20
Parker Ariz., U.S.A. 34°9N 114°17W 79 L12
Parker Pa., U.S.A. 41°5N 79°41W 82 E5
Parker Dam U.S.A. 34°18N 114°8W 79 L12
Parkersburg U.S.A. 39°16N 81°34W 81 F13
Parkes Australia 33°9S 148°11E 63 E4
Parkfield U.S.A. 35°54N 120°26W 78 K6
Parkhill Canada 43°15N 81°38W 82 C3
Parkland U.S.A. 47°9N 122°26W 78 C4
Parkston U.S.A. 43°24N 97°59W 80 D5
Parksville Canada 49°20N 124°21W 70 D4
Parkway U.S.A. 38°32N 121°26W 78 G5
Parla Spain 40°14N 3°46W 21 B4
Parlakimidi India 18°45N 84°5E 44 E7
Parli India 18°50N 76°35E 44 E3
Parma Italy 44°48N 10°20E 20 D9
Parma Idaho, U.S.A. 43°47N 116°57W 76 E5
Parma Ohio, U.S.A. 41°24N 81°43W 82 E3
Parnaguá Brazil 10°10S 44°38W 93 F10
Parnaíba Brazil 2°54S 41°47W 93 D10
Parnaíba → Brazil 3°0S 41°50W 93 D10
Parnassos Greece 38°35N 22°30E 23 E10
Parner India 19°0N 74°26E 44 E2
Pärnu Estonia 58°28N 24°33E 9 G21
Paro Dzong Bhutan 27°32N 89°53E 43 F13
Parola India 20°47N 75°7E 44 D2
Paroo → Australia 31°28S 143°32E 63 E3
Paros Greece 37°5N 25°12E 23 F11
Parowan U.S.A. 37°51N 112°50W 77 H7
Parral Chile 36°10S 71°52W 94 D1
Parramatta Australia 33°48S 151°1E 63 B5
Parras Mexico 25°25N 102°11W 86 B4
Parrett → U.K. 51°12N 3°1W 13 F4
Parris I. U.S.A. 32°20N 80°41W 85 E14
Parrsboro Canada 45°30N 64°25W 73 C7
Parry Channel Canada 74°15N 94°0W 69 C13
Parry I. Canada 45°18N 80°10W 82 A4
Parry Is. Canada 77°0N 110°0W 69 B10
Parry Sound Canada 45°20N 80°0W 82 A5
Parsnip → Canada 55°10N 123°2W 70 B4
Parsons U.S.A. 37°20N 95°16W 80 G6
Parsons Ra. Australia 13°30S 135°15E 62 A2
Partabpur India 20°0N 80°42E 44 E5
Partinico Italy 38°3N 13°7E 22 E5
Partizansk Russia 43°8N 133°9E 27 E14
Partridge I. Canada 55°59N 87°37W 72 A2
Partry Mts. Ireland 53°40N 9°28W 10 C2
Partur India 19°40N 76°14E 44 E3
Paru → Brazil 1°33S 52°38W 93 D8
Parur = North Paravar India 10°13N 76°14E 45 J3
Parvān □ Afghan. 35°0N 69°0E 40 B6
Parvatipuram India 18°50N 83°25E 44 E6
Parvatsar India 26°52N 74°49E 42 F6
Parys S. Africa 26°52S 27°29E 56 C4
Pas, The Canada 53°45N 101°15W 71 C8
Pasadena Canada 49°1N 57°36W 73 C8
Pasadena U.S.A. 29°43N 95°13W 84 G7
Pasaje → Argentina 25°39S 63°56W 94 B3
Pasar Indonesia 8°27S 114°54E 37 J17
Pasargadae Iran 30°11N 53°10E 47 D7
Pascagoula U.S.A. 30°21N 88°33W 85 F10
Pascagoula → U.S.A. 30°23N 88°37W 85 F10
Paşcani Romania 47°14N 26°45E 17 E14
Paschimbanga □ India 23°0N 88°0E 43 H13
Pasco U.S.A. 46°14N 119°6W 76 C4
Pasco I. Australia 20°57S 115°20E 60 D2
Pascoag U.S.A. 41°57N 71°42W 83 E13
Pascua, I. de Chile 27°7S 109°23W 65 K17
Pasfield L. Canada 58°24N 105°20W 71 B7
Pasir Mas Malaysia 6°2N 102°8E 39 J4
Pasir Putih Malaysia 5°50N 102°24E 39 K4
Paskūh Iran 27°34N 61°39E 47 E9
Pasley, C. Australia 33°52S 123°35E 61 F3
Pašman Croatia 43°58N 15°20E 16 G8
Pasni Pakistan 25°15N 63°27E 40 G3
Paso Bravo △ Paraguay 22°32S 57°5W 94 A4
Paso Cantinela Mexico 32°33N 115°47W 79 N11
Paso de Indios Argentina 43°55S 69°0W 96 E3
Paso de los Libres Argentina 29°44S 57°10W 94 B4
Paso de los Toros Uruguay 32°45S 56°30W 94 C4
Paso Robles U.S.A. 35°38N 120°41W 78 K6
Paspébiac Canada 48°3N 65°17W 73 C6
Pasrur Pakistan 32°16N 74°43E 42 C6
Passage East Ireland 52°14N 7°0W 10 D5
Passage West Ireland 51°52N 8°21W 10 E3
Passau Germany 48°34N 13°28E 16 D7
Passero, C. Italy 36°41N 15°10E 22 F6
Passo Fundo Brazil 28°10S 52°20W 95 B5
Passos Brazil 20°45S 46°37W 93 H9
Pastavy Belarus 55°4N 26°50E 9 J22
Pastaza → Peru 4°50S 76°52W 92 D3
Pasto Colombia 1°13N 77°17W 92 C3
Pasuruan Indonesia 7°40S 112°44E 37 G15
Patag I. = Flat I. S. China Sea 10°49N 115°49E 36 B5
Patagonia Argentina 45°0S 69°0W 96 F3
Patagonia U.S.A. 31°33N 110°45W 77 L8
Patambar Iran 29°45N 60°17E 47 D9
Patan = Lalitpur Nepal 27°40N 85°20E 43 F11
Patan = Somnath India 20°53N 70°22E 42 J4
Patan Gujarat, India 23°54N 72°14E 42 H5
Patan Maharashtra, India 17°22N 73°57E 44 F1
Patani Indonesia 0°20N 128°50E 37 D7
Pataudi India 28°18N 76°48E 42 E7
Patchewollock Australia 35°22S 142°12E 63 F3
Patchogue U.S.A. 40°46N 73°1W 83 F11
Patea N.Z. 39°45S 174°30E 59 C5
Patensie S. Africa 33°46S 24°49E 56 D3
Paternò Italy 37°34N 14°54E 22 F6
Pateros U.S.A. 48°3N 119°54W 76 B4
Paterson U.S.A. 40°54N 74°9W 83 F10
Paterson Ra. Australia 21°45S 122°10E 60 D3
Pathankot India 32°18N 75°45E 42 C6
Pathardi India 19°10N 75°11E 44 E2
Pathein Myanmar 16°45N 94°30E 41 L19
Pathfinder Res. U.S.A. 42°28N 106°51W 76 E10
Pathiu Thailand 10°42N 99°19E 39 G2
Pathri India 19°15N 76°27E 44 E3
Pathum Thani Thailand 14°1N 100°32E 38 E3
Pati Indonesia 6°45S 111°1E 37 G14
Patía → Colombia 2°13N 78°40W 92 C3
Patiala Punjab, India 30°23N 76°26E 42 D7
Patiala Ut. P., India 27°43N 79°1E 43 F8
Patkai Bum India 27°0N 95°30E 41 F19
Patmos Greece 37°21N 26°36E 23 F12
Patna India 25°35N 85°12E 43 G11
Patnagarh India 20°43N 83°9E 44 D6
Pato Branco Brazil 26°13S 52°40W 95 B5
Patong, Ao Thailand 7°54N 98°17E 39 a
Patos Brazil 6°55S 37°16W 93 E11
Patos, L. dos Brazil 31°20S 51°0W 95 C5
Patos, Río de los → Argentina 31°18S 69°25W 94 C2
Patos de Minas Brazil 18°35S 46°32W 93 G9
Patquía Argentina 30°2S 66°55W 94 C2
Patra Greece 38°14N 21°47E 23 E9
Patraikos Kolpos Greece 38°17N 21°30E 23 E9
Patras = Patra Greece 38°14N 21°47E 23 E9
Patrocínio Brazil 18°57S 47°0W 93 G9
Pattadakal India 16°1N 75°42E 45 F2
Pattani Thailand 6°48N 101°15E 39 J3
Pattaya Thailand 12°52N 100°55E 38 F3
Patten U.S.A. 46°0N 68°38W 81 B19
Patterson Calif., U.S.A. 37°28N 121°8W 78 H5
Patterson La., U.S.A. 29°42N 91°18W 84 G9
Patterson, Mt. U.S.A. 38°29N 119°20W 78 G7
Patti Punjab, India 31°17N 74°54E 42 D6
Patti Ut. P., India 25°55N 82°12E 43 G10
Pattoki Pakistan 31°5N 73°52E 42 D5
Patton U.S.A. 40°38N 78°39W 82 F6
Pattukkattai India 10°25N 79°20E 45 J4
Patuakhali Bangla. 22°20N 90°25E 41 H17
Patuanak Canada 55°55N 107°43W 71 B7
Patuca → Honduras 15°50N 84°18W 88 C3
Patuca, Punta Honduras 15°49N 84°14W 88 C3
Patuca △ Honduras 14°30N 85°30W 88 D2
Patur India 20°27N 76°56E 44 D3
Patvinsuo △ Finland 63°7N 30°45E 8 E24
Pátzcuaro Mexico 19°31N 101°38W 86 D4
Pau France 43°19N 0°25W 20 E3
Paudash Canada 44°59N 77°58W 82 B7
Pauk Myanmar 21°27N 94°30E 41 J19
Paul I. Canada 56°30N 61°20W 73 A7
Paul Smiths U.S.A. 44°26N 74°15W 83 B10
Paulatuk Canada 69°25N 124°0W 68 D7
Paulding Bay S. Ocean 66°0S 118°0E 5 C8
Paulistana Brazil 8°9S 41°9W 93 E10
Paulo Afonso Brazil 9°21S 38°15W 93 E11
Paulpietersburg S. Africa 27°23S 30°50E 57 C5
Pauls Valley U.S.A. 34°44N 97°13W 84 D6
Pauma Valley U.S.A. 33°16N 116°58W 79 M10
Pauni India 20°48N 79°40E 44 D4
Pauri India 30°9N 78°47E 43 D8
Pavagada India 14°6N 77°16E 45 G3
Pāveh Iran 35°3N 46°22E 46 C5
Pavia Italy 45°7N 9°8E 20 D8
Pavilion U.S.A. 42°52N 78°1W 82 D6
Pāvilosta Latvia 56°53N 21°14E 9 H19
Pavlodar Kazakhstan 52°33N 77°0E 26 D8
Pavlograd = Pavlohrad Ukraine 48°30N 35°52E 19 E6
Pavlohrad Ukraine 48°30N 35°52E 19 E6
Pavlovo Russia 55°58N 43°5E 18 C7
Pavlovsk Russia 50°26N 40°5E 19 D7
Pavlovskaya Russia 46°17N 39°47E 19 E6
Pawai, Pulau Singapore 1°11N 103°44E 39 d
Pawayan India 28°4N 80°6E 43 E9
Pawhuska U.S.A. 36°40N 96°20W 84 C6
Pawling U.S.A. 41°34N 73°36W 83 E11
Pawnee U.S.A. 36°20N 96°48W 84 C6
Pawnee City U.S.A. 40°7N 96°9W 80 E5
Pawtucket U.S.A. 41°53N 71°23W 83 E13
Paxi Greece 39°14N 20°12E 23 E9
Paxton U.S.A. 40°27N 88°6W 80 E9
Payakumbuh Indonesia 0°20S 100°35E 36 E2
Payette U.S.A. 44°5N 116°56W 76 D5
Payne Bay = Kangirsuk Canada 60°0N 70°0W 69 F18
Payne L. Canada 59°30N 74°30W 69 F17
Paynes Find Australia 29°15S 117°42E 61 E2
Paynesville U.S.A. 45°23N 94°43W 80 C6
Paysandú Uruguay 32°19S 58°8W 94 C4
Payson Ariz., U.S.A. 34°14N 111°20W 77 J8
Payson Utah, U.S.A. 40°3N 111°44W 76 F8
Paz → Guatemala 13°44N 90°10W 88 D1
Paz, B. de la Mexico 24°9N 110°25W 86 C2
Pāzanān Iran 30°35N 49°59E 47 D6
Pazardzhik Bulgaria 42°12N 24°20E 23 C11
Pe Ell U.S.A. 46°34N 123°18W 78 D3
Peabody U.S.A. 42°31N 70°56W 83 D14
Peace → Canada 59°0N 111°25W 70 B6
Peace Point Canada 59°7N 112°27W 70 B6
Peace River Canada 56°15N 117°18W 70 B5
Peach Springs U.S.A. 35°32N 113°25W 77 J7
Peachland Canada 49°47N 119°45W 70 D5
Peachtree City U.S.A. 33°25N 84°35W 85 E12
Peak, The = Kinder Scout U.K. 53°24N 1°52W 12 D6
Peak Charles △ Australia 32°42S 121°10E 61 F3
Peak District △ U.K. 53°24N 1°46W 12 D6
Peak Hill Australia 32°47S 148°11E 63 E4
Peak Ra. Australia 22°50S 148°20E 62 C4
Peake Cr. → Australia 28°2S 136°7E 63 D2
Peale, Mt. U.S.A. 38°26N 109°14W 76 G9
Pearblossom U.S.A. 34°30N 117°55W 79 L9
Pearl → U.S.A. 30°11N 89°32W 85 F10
Pearl and Hermes Reef U.S.A. 27°55N 175°45W 75 K4
Pearl Banks Sri Lanka 8°45N 79°45E 45 K4
Pearl River = Zhu Jiang → China 22°45N 113°37E 35 F9
Pearl River U.S.A. 41°4N 74°2W 83 E10
Pearl River Bridge China 22°15N 113°48E 31 a
Pearsall U.S.A. 28°54N 99°6W 84 G5
Peary Chan. Canada 79°40N 101°30W 69 B11
Peary Land Greenland 82°40N 33°0W 4 A6
Pease → U.S.A. 34°12N 99°2W 84 D5
Peawanuck Canada 55°15N 85°12W 72 A2
Pebane Mozam. 17°10S 38°8E 55 H7
Pebas Peru 3°10S 71°46W 92 D4
Pebble Beach U.S.A. 36°34N 121°57W 78 J5
Peć = Pejë Kosovo 42°40N 20°17E 23 C9
Pechenga Russia 69°29N 31°4E 8 B24
Pechenizhyn Ukraine 48°30N 24°48E 17 D13
Pechora Russia 65°10N 57°11E 18 A10
Pechora → Russia 68°13N 54°15E 18 A9
Pechorskaya Guba Russia 68°40N 54°0E 18 A9
Pechory Russia 57°48N 27°40E 9 H22
Pecos N. Mex., U.S.A. 35°35N 105°41W 77 J11
Pecos Tex., U.S.A. 31°26N 103°30W 84 F3
Pecos → U.S.A. 29°42N 101°22W 84 G4
Pécs Hungary 46°5N 18°15E 17 E10
Pedasí Panama 7°32N 80°2W 88 E3
Pedda Bellala India 19°4N 78°49E 44 E4
Peddapalli India 18°40N 79°24E 44 E4
Peddapuram India 17°6N 82°8E 44 F6
Pedder, L. Australia 42°55S 146°10E 63 G4
Peddie S. Africa 33°14S 27°7E 57 D4
Pedernales Dom. Rep. 18°2N 71°44W 89 C5
Pedirka Desert Australia 26°47S 134°11E 63 A1
Pedra Azul Brazil 16°2S 41°17W 93 G10
Pedra Lume Cabo Verde 16°40N 22°52W 52 b
Pedreiras Brazil 4°32S 44°40W 93 D10
Pedro Afonso Brazil 9°0S 48°10W 93 E9
Pedro Cays Jamaica 17°5N 77°48W 88 C4
Pedro de Valdivia Chile 22°55S 69°38W 94 A2
Pedro Juan Caballero Paraguay 22°30S 55°40W 95 A4
Pee Dee = Great Pee Dee → U.S.A. 33°21N 79°10W 85 E15
Peebinga Australia 34°52S 140°57E 63 E3
Peebles U.K. 55°40N 3°11W 11 F5
Peekskill U.S.A. 41°17N 73°55W 83 E11
Peel I. of Man 54°13N 4°40W 12 C3
Peel → Australia 30°50S 150°29E 63 E5
Peel → Canada 67°0N 135°0W 68 D5
Peel Sd. Canada 73°0N 96°0W 68 C12
Peera Peera Poolanna L. Australia 26°30S 138°0E 63 D2
Peerless Lake Canada 56°37N 114°40W 70 B6
Peers Canada 53°40N 116°0W 70 C5
Pegasus Bay N.Z. 43°20S 173°10E 59 E4
Pegu = Bago Myanmar 17°20N 96°29E 41 L20
Pegu Yoma Myanmar 19°0N 96°0E 41 K20
Pehuajó Argentina 35°45S 62°0W 94 D3
Pei Xian China 34°44N 116°55E 32 G9
Peikang Taiwan 23°34N 120°18E 35 F13
Peine Chile 23°45S 68°8W 94 A2
Peine Germany 52°19N 10°14E 16 B6
Peipus, L. = Chudskoye, Ozero Russia 58°13N 27°30E 9 G22
Peixe Brazil 12°0S 48°40W 93 F9
Peixe → Brazil 21°31S 51°58W 93 H8
Pejë Kosovo 42°40N 20°17E 23 C9
Pekalongan Indonesia 6°53S 109°40E 37 G13
Pekan Malaysia 3°30N 103°25E 39 L4
Pekan Nenas Malaysia 1°31N 103°31E 39 d
Pekanbaru Indonesia 0°30N 101°15E 36 D2
Pekin U.S.A. 40°35N 89°40W 80 E9
Pekutatan Indonesia 8°25S 114°49E 37 J17
Pelabuhan Ratu, Teluk Indonesia 7°5S 106°30E 37 G12
Pelagie, Is. Italy 35°39N 12°33E 22 G5
Pelaihari Indonesia 3°55S 114°45E 36 E4
Peleaga, Vf. Romania 45°22N 22°55E 17 F12
Pelée, Mt. Martinique 14°48N 61°10W 88 c
Pelee, Pt. Canada 41°54N 82°31W 72 D3
Pelee I. Canada 41°47N 82°40W 82 E2
Peleng Indonesia 1°20S 123°30E 37 E6
Pelentong Malaysia 1°32N 103°49E 39 d
Pelican U.S.A. 57°58N 136°14W 70 B1
Pelican L. Canada 52°28N 100°20W 71 C8
Pelican Narrows Canada 55°10N 102°56W 71 B8
Pelješac Croatia 42°55N 17°25E 22 C7
Pelkosenniemi Finland 67°6N 27°28E 8 C22
Pella S. Africa 29°1S 19°6E 56 C2
Pella U.S.A. 41°25N 92°55W 80 E7
Pello Finland 66°47N 23°59E 8 C20
Pelly → Canada 62°47N 137°19W 70 A1
Pelly Bay Canada 68°38N 89°50W 69 D14
Peloponnesos □ Greece 37°10N 22°0E 23 F10
Pelorus Sd. N.Z. 40°59S 173°59E 59 D4
Pelotas Brazil 31°42S 52°23W 95 C5
Pelotas → Brazil 27°28S 51°55W 95 B5
Pelvoux, Massif du France 44°52N 6°20E 20 D7
Pemalang Indonesia 6°53S 109°23E 37 G13
Pemanggil, Pulau Malaysia 2°37N 104°21E 39 L5
Pematangsiantar Indonesia 2°57N 99°5E 36 D1
Pemba Mozam. 12°58S 40°30E 55 G8
Pemba I. Tanzania 5°0S 39°45E 54 F7
Pemberton Australia 34°30S 116°0E 61 F2
Pemberton Canada 50°25N 122°50W 70 C4
Pembina → Canada 54°45N 114°17W 70 C6
Pembroke Canada 45°50N 77°7W 72 C4
Pembroke U.K. 51°41N 4°55W 13 F3
Pembrokeshire □ U.K. 51°52N 4°56W 13 F3
Pembrokeshire Coast △ U.K. 51°50N 5°2W 13 F2
Pen India 18°45N 73°5E 44 E1
Pen-y-bont ar Ogwr = Bridgend U.K. 51°30N 3°34W 13 F4
Pen-y-Ghent U.K. 54°10N 2°14W 12 C5
Penal Trin. & Tob. 10°9N 61°29W 93 K15
Penang = Pinang Malaysia 5°25N 100°15E 39 c
Penápolis Brazil 21°30S 50°0W 95 A6
Peñarroya-Pueblonuevo Spain 38°19N 5°16W 21 C3
Penarth U.K. 51°26N 3°11W 13 F4
Peñas, C. de Spain 43°42N 5°52W 21 A3
Peñas, G. de Chile 47°0S 75°0W 96 F2
Pench → India 21°17N 79°10E 44 D4
Pench △ India 21°45N 79°20E 43 J8
Pench'i = Benxi China 41°20N 123°48E 33 D12
Pend Oreille → U.S.A. 49°4N 117°37W 76 B5
Pend Oreille, L. U.S.A. 48°10N 116°21W 76 B5
Pendembu S. Leone 9°7N 11°14W 52 G3
Pender B. Australia 16°45S 122°42E 60 C3
Pendleton U.S.A. 45°40N 118°47W 76 D4
Pendra India 22°46N 81°57E 43 H9
Penedo Brazil 10°15S 36°36W 93 F11
Penelokan Indonesia 8°17S 115°22E 37 J18
Penetanguishene Canada 44°50N 79°55W 82 B5
Penfield U.S.A. 41°13N 78°35W 82 E6
Penfro = Pembroke U.K. 51°41N 4°55W 13 F3
Peng'an China 31°2N 106°22E 34 B6
Penganga → India 19°53N 79°9E 44 E4
P'enghu Ch'üntou Taiwan 23°34N 119°30E 35 F12
Penglai China 37°48N 120°42E 33 F11
Pengshan China 30°14N 103°58E 34 B4
Pengshui China 29°17N 108°12E 34 C7
Penguin Australia 41°8S 146°6E 63 G4
Pengxi China 30°44N 105°45E 34 B5
Pengze China 29°52N 116°32E 35 C11
Pengzhou China 31°4N 103°32E 34 B4
Peniche Portugal 39°19N 9°22W 21 C1
Penida, Nusa Indonesia 8°45S 115°30E 37 K18
Peninsular Malaysia □ Malaysia 4°0N 102°0E 39 L4
Penitente, Serra do Brazil 8°45S 46°20W 93 E9
Penkridge U.K. 52°44N 2°6W 12 E5
Penmarch, Pte. de France 47°48N 4°22W 20 C1
Penn Hills U.S.A. 40°28N 79°52W 82 F5
Penn Yan U.S.A. 42°40N 77°3W 82 D7
Pennant Canada 50°32N 108°14W 71 C7
Penner → India 14°35N 80°10E 45 G5
Pennines U.K. 54°45N 2°27W 12 C5
Pennington U.S.A. 39°15N 121°47W 78 F5
Pennsburg U.S.A. 40°23N 75°29W 83 F9
Pennsylvania □ U.S.A. 40°45N 77°30W 81 E15
Penny Canada 53°51N 121°20W 70 C4
Penobscot → U.S.A. 44°30N 68°48W 81 C19
Penobscot B. U.S.A. 44°35N 68°50W 81 C19
Penola Australia 37°25S 140°48E 63 F3
Penong Australia 31°56S 133°1E 61 F5
Penonomé Panama 8°31N 80°21W 88 E3
Penrhyn Cook Is. 9°0S 158°0W 65 H12
Penrith Australia 33°43S 150°38E 63 E5
Penrith U.K. 54°40N 2°45W 12 C5
Penryn U.K. 50°9N 5°7W 13 G2
Pensacola U.S.A. 30°25N 87°13W 85 F11
Pensacola Mts. Antarctica 84°0S 40°0W 5 E1
Pense Canada 50°25N 104°59W 71 C8
Penshurst Australia 37°49S 142°20E 63 F3
Penticton Canada 49°30N 119°38W 70 D5
Pentland Australia 20°32S 145°25E 62 C4
Pentland Firth U.K. 58°43N 3°10W 11 C5
Pentland Hills U.K. 55°48N 3°25W 11 F5
Penukonda India 14°5N 77°38E 45 G3
Penza Russia 53°15N 45°5E 18 D8
Penzance U.K. 50°7N 5°33W 13 G2
Penzhino Russia 63°30N 167°55E 27 C17
Penzhinskaya Guba Russia 61°30N 163°0E 27 C17
Peoria Ariz., U.S.A. 33°43N 112°14W 77 K7
Peoria Ill., U.S.A. 40°42N 89°36W 80 E9
Pepacton Res. U.S.A. 42°5N 74°58W 83 D10
Pepani → S. Africa 25°49S 22°47E 56 C3
Pera Hd. Australia 12°55S 141°37E 62 A3
Perabumulih Indonesia 3°27S 104°15E 36 E2
Perak □ Malaysia 5°0N 101°0E 39 K3
Perak → Malaysia 4°0N 100°50E 39 K3
Perämeri △ Finland 65°35N 24°22E 8 D21
Perancak Indonesia 8°24S 114°37E 37 J17
Peräpohjola Finland 66°16N 26°10E 8 C22
Percé Canada 48°31N 64°13W 73 C7
Perche, Collines du France 48°30N 0°40E 20 B4
Percival Lakes Australia 21°25S 125°0E 60 D4
Percy Is. Australia 21°39S 150°16E 62 C5
Perdido, Mte. Spain 42°40N 0°5E 21 A6
Perdu, Mt. = Perdido, Mte. Spain 42°40N 0°5E 21 A6
Pereira Colombia 4°49N 75°43W 92 C3
Peremul Par India 11°10N 72°4E 45 J1
Perenjori Australia 29°26S 116°16E 61 E2
Pereyaslav-Khmelnytskyy Ukraine 50°3N 31°28E 19 D5
Pérez, I. Mexico 22°24N 89°42W 87 C7
Pergamino Argentina 33°52S 60°30W 94 C3
Pergau → Malaysia 5°23N 102°2E 39 K3
Perham U.S.A. 46°36N 95°34W 80 B6
Perhentian, Kepulauan Malaysia 5°54N 102°42E 39 K4
Péribonka → Canada 48°45N 72°5W 73 C5
Péribonka, L. Canada 50°1N 71°10W 73 B5
Péribonka, La Centrale de Canada 49°30N 71°10W 73 C5
Perico Argentina 24°20S 65°5W 94 A2
Pericos Mexico 25°3N 107°42W 86 B3
Périgueux France 45°10N 0°42E 20 D4
Perijá, Sierra de Colombia 9°30N 73°3W 92 B4
Perijá △ Venezuela 9°30N 72°55W 89 E5
Peringat Malaysia 6°2N 102°17E 39 J4
Perito Moreno Argentina 46°36S 70°56W 96 F2
Periyakulam India 10°5N 77°30E 45 J3
Periyar → India 10°15N 76°10E 45 J3
Periyar, L. India 9°25N 77°10E 45 K3
Periyar △ India 9°25N 77°10E 45 K3
Perkasie U.S.A. 40°22N 75°18W 83 F9
Perlas, Arch. de las Panama 8°41N 79°7W 88 E4
Perlas, Punta de Nic. 12°30N 83°30W 88 D3
Perlis □ Malaysia 6°30N 100°15E 39 J2
Perm Russia 58°0N 56°10E 18 C10
Pernambuco = Recife Brazil 8°0S 35°0W 93 E12
Pernambuco □ Brazil 8°0S 37°0W 93 E11
Pernatty Lagoon Australia 31°30S 137°12E 63 E2
Pernik Bulgaria 42°35N 23°2E 23 C10
Peron Is. Australia 13°9S 130°4E 60 B5
Peron Pen. Australia 26°0S 113°10E 61 E1
Perow Canada 54°35N 126°10W 70 C3
Perpignan France 42°42N 2°53E 20 E5
Perris U.S.A. 33°47N 117°14W 79 M9
Perry Fla., U.S.A. 30°7N 83°35W 85 F13
Perry Ga., U.S.A. 32°28N 83°44W 85 E13
Perry Iowa, U.S.A. 41°51N 94°6W 80 E6
Perry N.Y., U.S.A. 42°42N 78°0W 82 D7
Perry Okla., U.S.A. 36°17N 97°14W 84 C6
Perryton U.S.A. 36°24N 100°48W 84 C4
Perryville U.S.A. 37°43N 89°52W 80 G9
Persepolis Iran 29°55N 52°50E 47 D7
Pershotravensk Ukraine 50°13N 27°40E 17 C14
Persia = Iran ■ Asia 33°0N 53°0E 47 C7
Persian Gulf Asia 27°0N 50°0E 47 E6
Perth Australia 31°57S 115°52E 61 F2
Perth Canada 44°55N 76°15W 83 B8
Perth U.K. 56°24N 3°26W 11 E5
Perth & Kinross □ U.K. 56°45N 3°55W 11 E5
Perth Amboy U.S.A. 40°30N 74°15W 83 F10
Perth-Andover Canada 46°44N 67°42W 73 C6
Perth Basin Ind. Oc. 30°0S 108°0E 64 L2
Peru Ind., U.S.A. 40°45N 86°4W 80 E10
Peru N.Y., U.S.A. 44°35N 73°32W 83 B11
Peru ■ S. Amer. 4°0S 75°0W 92 D4
Peru Basin Pac. Oc. 20°0S 95°0W 65 J18
Peru-Chile Trench Pac. Oc. 20°0S 72°0W 92 G3
Perugia Italy 43°7N 12°23E 22 C5
Pervomaysk Ukraine 48°10N 30°46E 19 E5
Pervouralsk Russia 56°59N 59°59E 18 C10
Pésaro Italy 43°54N 12°55E 22 C5
Pescadores = P'enghu Ch'üntou Taiwan 23°34N 119°30E 35 F12
Pescara Italy 42°28N 14°13E 22 C6
Peshawar Pakistan 34°2N 71°37E 42 B4
Peshkopi Albania 41°41N 20°25E 23 D9
Peshtigo U.S.A. 45°3N 87°45W 80 C10
Pesqueira Brazil 8°20S 36°42W 93 E11
Petah Tiqwa Israel 32°6N 34°53E 48 C3
Petaling Jaya Malaysia 3°4N 101°42E 39 L3
Petaluma U.S.A. 38°14N 122°39W 78 G4
Pétange Lux. 49°33N 5°55E 15 E5
Petaro Pakistan 25°31N 68°18E 42 G3
Petatlán Mexico 17°31N 101°16W 86 D4
Petauke Zambia 14°14S 31°20E 55 G6
Petawawa Canada 45°54N 77°17W 72 C4
Petén Itzá, L. Guatemala 16°58N 89°50W 88 C2
Peter I. Br. Virgin Is. 18°22N 64°35W 89 e
Peter I. Øy Antarctica 69°0S 91°0W 5 C16
Peter Pond L. Canada 55°55N 108°44W 71 B7
Peterbell Canada 48°36N 83°21W 72 C3
Peterborough Australia 32°58S 138°51E 63 E2
Peterborough Canada 44°20N 78°20W 82 B6
Peterborough U.K. 52°35N 0°15W 13 E7
Peterborough U.S.A. 42°53N 71°57W 83 D13
Peterborough □ U.K. 52°35N 0°15W 13 E7
Peterculter U.K. 57°6N 2°16W 11 D6
Peterhead U.K. 57°31N 1°48W 11 D7
Peterlee U.K. 54°47N 1°20W 12 C6
Petermann ✡ Australia 24°58S 130°0E 61 E4
Petermann Gletscher Greenland 80°30N 60°0W 69 A20
Petermann Ranges Australia 26°0S 130°0E 61 E5
Petersburg Alaska, U.S.A. 56°48N 132°58W 68 F5
Petersburg Pa., U.S.A. 40°34N 78°3W 82 F6
Petersburg Va., U.S.A. 37°14N 77°24W 81 G15
Petersburg W. Va., U.S.A. 39°1N 79°5W 81 F14
Petersfield U.K. 51°1N 0°56W 13 F7
Petit-Canal Guadeloupe 16°25N 61°31W 88 b
Petit-Goâve Haiti 18°27N 72°51W 89 C5
Petit Lac Manicouagan Canada 51°25N 67°40W 73 B6
Petit-Mécatina → Canada 50°40N 59°30W 73 B8
Petit-Mécatina, Î. du Canada 50°30N 59°25W 73 B8
Petit Piton St. Lucia 13°51N 61°5W 89 f
Petit-Saguenay Canada 48°15N 70°4W 73 C5
Petitcodiac Canada 45°57N 65°11W 73 C6
Petite Terre, Îles de la Guadeloupe 16°13N 61°9W 88 b
Petitot → Canada 60°14N 123°29W 70 A4
Petitsikapau L. Canada 54°37N 66°25W 73 B6
Petlad India 22°30N 72°45E 42 H5
Peto Mexico 20°8N 88°55W 87 C7
Petone N.Z. 41°13S 174°53E 59 D5
Petorca Chile 32°15S 70°56W 94 C1
Petoskey U.S.A. 45°22N 84°57W 81 C11
Petra Jordan 30°20N 35°22E 48 E4
Petra, Ostrov Russia 76°15N 118°30E 27 B12
Petra Velikogo, Zaliv Russia 42°40N 132°0E 28 C6
Petre, Pt. Canada 43°50N 77°9W 82 C7
Petrich Bulgaria 41°24N 23°13E 23 D10
Petrified Forest △ U.S.A. 35°0N 109°30W 77 J9
Petrikov = Pyetrikaw Belarus 52°11N 28°29E 17 B15
Petrolândia Brazil 9°5S 38°20W 93 E11
Petrolia Canada 42°54N 82°9W 82 D2
Petrolina Brazil 9°24S 40°30W 93 E10
Petropavl Kazakhstan 54°53N 69°13E 26 D7
Petropavlovsk = Petropavl Kazakhstan 54°53N 69°13E 26 D7
Petropavlovsk-Kamchatskiy Russia 53°3N 158°43E 27 D16
Petrópolis Brazil 22°33S 43°9W 95 A7
Petroşani Romania 45°28N 23°20E 17 F12
Petrovaradin Serbia 45°16N 19°55E 23 B8

Petrovsk *Russia* 52°22N 45°19E **18 D8**
Petrovsk-Zabaykalskiy *Russia* 51°20N 108°55E **27 D11**
Petrozavodsk *Russia* 61°41N 34°20E **18 B5**
Petrus Steyn *S. Africa* 27°38S 28°8E **57 C4**
Petrusburg *S. Africa* 29°4S 25°26E **56 C4**
Peumo *Chile* 34°21S 71°12W **94 C1**
Peureulak *Indonesia* 4°48N 97°45E **36 D1**
Pevek *Russia* 69°41N 171°19E **27 C18**
Pforzheim *Germany* 48°52N 8°41E **16 D5**
Pha Taem △ *Thailand* 15°32N 105°30E **38 E5**
Phagwara *India* 31°10N 75°40E **42 D6**
Phala *Botswana* 23°45S 26°50E **56 B4**
Phalaborwa *S. Africa* 23°57S 31°7E **57 B5**
Phalera = Phulera *India* 26°52N 75°16E **42 F6**
Phalodi *India* 27°12N 72°24E **42 F5**
Phaltan *India* 17°59N 74°26E **44 F2**
Phaluai, Ko *Thailand* 9°32N 99°41E **39 b**
Phan *Thailand* 19°28N 99°43E **38 C2**
Phan Rang -Thap Cham *Vietnam* 11°34N 109°0E **39 G7**
Phan Ri Cua *Vietnam* 11°16N 108°40E **39 G7**
Phan Si Pan *Vietnam* 22°18N 103°46E **38 A4**
Phan Thiet *Vietnam* 11°1N 108°9E **39 G7**
Phan Thiet, Vinh *Vietnam* 10°53N 108°5E **39 G7**
Phan Wa, Laem *Thailand* 7°47N 98°25E **39 a**
Phanat Nikhom *Thailand* 13°27N 101°11E **38 F3**
Phangan, Ko *Thailand* 9°45N 100°0E **39 H3**
Phangnga *Thailand* 8°28N 98°30E **39 H2**
Phangnga, Ao *Thailand* 8°16N 98°33E **39 a**
Phanom Sarakham *Thailand* 13°45N 101°21E **38 F3**
Phaphund *India* 26°36N 79°28E **43 F8**
Pharenda *India* 27°5N 83°17E **43 F10**
Pharr *India* 26°12N 98°11W **84 H5**
Phatthalung *Thailand* 7°39N 100°6E **39 J3**
Phayam, Ko *Thailand* 9°44N 98°25E **39 H2**
Phayao *Thailand* 19°11N 99°55E **38 C2**
Phelps *U.S.A.* 42°58N 77°3W **82 D7**
Phelps L. *Canada* 59°15N 103°15W **71 B8**
Phenix City *U.S.A.* 32°28N 85°1W **85 E12**
Phet Buri = Phetchaburi *Thailand* 13°1N 99°55E **38 F2**
Phetchabun *Thailand* 16°25N 101°8E **38 D3**
Phetchabun, Thiu Khao *Thailand* 16°0N 101°20E **38 E3**
Phetchaburi *Thailand* 13°1N 99°55E **38 F2**
Phi Phi, Ko *Thailand* 7°45N 98°46E **39 J2**
Phiafay *Laos* 14°48N 106°0E **38 E6**
Phibun Mangsahan *Thailand* 15°14N 105°14E **38 E5**
Phichai *Thailand* 17°22N 100°10E **38 D3**
Phichit *Thailand* 16°26N 100°22E **38 D3**
Philadelphia *Miss., U.S.A.* 32°46N 89°7W **85 E10**
Philadelphia *N.Y., U.S.A.* 44°9N 75°43W **83 B9**
Philadelphia *Pa., U.S.A.* 39°57N 75°9W **83 G9**
Philadelphia Int. ✕ (PHL) *U.S.A.* 39°51N 75°18W **83 G9**
Philip *U.S.A.* 44°2N 101°40W **80 C3**
Philip Smith Mts. *U.S.A.* 68°0N 148°0W **74 B10**
Philippeville *Belgium* 50°12N 4°33E **15 D4**
Philippi *U.S.A.* 39°9N 80°3W **81 F13**
Philippi L. *Australia* 24°20S 138°55E **62 C2**
Philippine Basin *Pac. Oc.* 17°0N 132°0E **64 F5**
Philippine Sea *Pac. Oc.* 18°0N 125°0E **64 F4**
Philippine Trench = Mindanao Trench *Pac. Oc.* 12°0N 126°6E **37 B7**
Philippines ■ *Asia* 12°0N 123°0E **37 B6**
Philippolis *S. Africa* 30°15S 25°16E **56 D4**
Philippopolis = Plovdiv *Bulgaria* 42°8N 24°44E **23 C11**
Philipsburg *Canada* 45°2N 73°5N **83 A11**
Philipsburg *Mont., U.S.A.* 46°20N 113°18W **76 C7**
Philipsburg *Pa., U.S.A.* 40°54N 78°13W **82 F6**
Philipstown = Daingean *Ireland* 53°18N 7°17W **10 C4**
Philipstown *S. Africa* 30°28S 24°30E **56 D3**
Phillip I. *Australia* 38°30S 145°12E **63 F4**
Phillips *U.S.A.* 45°42N 90°24W **80 C8**
Phillipsburg *Kans., U.S.A.* 39°45N 99°19W **80 F4**
Phillipsburg *N.J., U.S.A.* 40°42N 75°12W **83 F9**
Philmont *U.S.A.* 42°15N 73°39W **83 D11**
Philomath *U.S.A.* 44°32N 123°22W **76 D2**
Phimai *Thailand* 15°13N 102°30E **38 E4**
Phitsanulok *Thailand* 16°50N 100°12E **38 D3**
Phnom Kulen △ *Cambodia* 13°38N 104°15E **38 F5**
Phnom Penh *Cambodia* 11°33N 104°55E **39 G5**
Phnum Penh = Phnom Penh *Cambodia* 11°33N 104°55E **39 G5**
Pho, Laem *Thailand* 6°55N 101°19E **39 J3**
Phoenicia *U.S.A.* 42°5N 74°14W **83 D10**
Phoenix *Mauritius* 20°17S 57°30E **55 d**
Phoenix *Ariz., U.S.A.* 33°26N 112°4W **77 K7**
Phoenix *N.Y., U.S.A.* 43°14N 76°18W **83 C8**
Phoenix Is. *Kiribati* 3°30S 172°0W **64 H10**
Phoenix Sky Harbour Int. ✕ (PHX) *U.S.A.* 33°26N 112°1W **77 K7**
Phoenixville *U.S.A.* 40°8N 75°31W **83 F9**
Phon *Thailand* 15°49N 102°36E **38 E4**
Phong → *Thailand* 16°23N 102°56E **38 D4**
Phong Nha -Ke Bang △ *Vietnam* 17°30N 106°10E **38 D6**
Phong Saly *Laos* 21°42N 102°9E **34 G4**
Phong Tho *Vietnam* 22°32N 103°21E **38 A4**
Phonsavan *Laos* 19°27N 103°10E **38 C4**
Phonum *Thailand* 8°49N 98°48E **39 H2**
Phosphate Hill *Australia* 21°53S 139°58E **62 C2**
Phothaem *Thailand* 13°41N 99°51E **38 F2**
Phra Nakhon Si Ayutthaya *Thailand* 14°25N 100°30E **38 E3**
Phra Thong, Ko *Thailand* 9°5N 98°17E **39 H2**
Phrae *Thailand* 18°7N 100°9E **38 C3**
Phrom Phiram *Thailand* 17°2N 100°11E **38 D3**
Phrom Thep, Laem *Thailand* 7°45N 98°19E **39 a**
Phu Bia *Laos* 19°10N 103°0E **38 C4**

Phu Chong -Na Yoi △ *Thailand* 14°25N 105°30E **38 E5**
Phu Hin Rong Kla △ *Thailand* 17°0N 100°59E **38 D3**
Phu Kao -Phu Phan Kham △ *Thailand* 16°53N 102°31E **38 D4**
Phu Kradung △ *Thailand* 17°2N 101°44E **38 D3**
Phu Loi *Laos* 20°14N 103°14E **38 B4**
Phu Luang △ *Thailand* 17°15N 101°29E **38 D3**
Phu Ly *Vietnam* 20°35N 105°50E **34 G5**
Phu My *Vietnam* 14°15N 109°5E **38 E7**
Phu Pha Man △ *Thailand* 16°44N 101°50E **38 D3**
Phu Phan △ *Thailand* 17°0N 103°56E **38 D4**
Phu Quoc, Dao *Vietnam* 10°20N 104°0E **39 G4**
Phu Sa Dok Bua △ *Thailand* 16°11N 104°45E **38 D5**
Phu Sang △ *Thailand* 19°35N 100°19E **38 C3**
Phu Tho *Vietnam* 21°24N 105°13E **34 G5**
Phu Wiang △ *Thailand* 16°39N 102°23E **38 D4**
Phuc Yen *Vietnam* 21°16N 105°45E **34 G5**
Phuket *Thailand* 7°53N 98°24E **39 a**
Phuket, Ko *Thailand* 8°0N 98°22E **39 a**
Phul *India* 30°19N 75°14E **42 D6**
Phulad *India* 25°38N 73°49E **42 G5**
Phulbani *India* 20°28N 84°14E **44 D7**
Phulchari *Bangla.* 25°11N 89°37E **43 G13**
Phulera *India* 26°52N 75°16E **42 F6**
Phulpur *India* 25°31N 82°49E **43 G10**
Phunphin *Thailand* 9°7N 99°12E **39 H2**
Phuntsholing *Bhutan* 26°51N 89°23E **43 F13**
Phuphrabat *Thailand* 17°40N 100°54E **38 D4**
Phuthaditjhaba *S. Africa* 28°29S 28°48E **57 C4**
Phyu = Pyu *Myanmar* 18°22N 96°28E **41 K20**
Pia ✪ *Australia* 27°7S 116°23E **61 E2**
Piacenza *Italy* 45°1N 9°40E **20 D8**
Piai, Tanjung *Malaysia* 1°17N 103°30E **39 d**
Pian Cr. → *Australia* 30°2S 148°12E **63 E4**
Pianosa *Italy* 42°35N 10°5E **22 C4**
Piao'ertun *China* 41°50N 123°47E **33 D12**
Piapot *Canada* 49°59N 109°8W **71 D7**
Piatra Neamţ *Romania* 46°56N 26°21E **17 E14**
Piauí □ *Brazil* 7°0S 43°0W **93 E10**
Piauí → *Brazil* 6°38S 42°42W **93 E10**
Piave → *Italy* 45°32N 12°44E **22 B5**
Pibor Post *South Sudan* 6°47N 33°3E **53 G12**
Picardie *France* 49°50N 3°0E **20 B5**
Picardy = Picardie *France* 49°50N 3°0E **20 B5**
Picayune *U.S.A.* 30°32N 89°41W **85 F10**
Pichhor *India* 25°58N 78°20E **43 G8**
Pichilemu *Chile* 34°22S 72°0W **94 C1**
Pichor *India* 25°11N 78°11E **42 G8**
Pickerel L. *Canada* 48°40N 91°25W **72 C1**
Pickering *U.K.* 54°15N 0°46W **12 C7**
Pickering, Vale of *U.K.* 54°14N 0°45W **12 C7**
Pickle Lake *Canada* 51°30N 90°12W **72 B1**
Pickwick L. *U.S.A.* 35°4N 88°15W **85 D10**
Pico *Azores* 38°28N 28°20W **52 a**
Pico Bonito △ *Honduras* 15°34N 86°48W **88 C2**
Pico Truncado *Argentina* 46°40S 68°0W **96 F3**
Picos *Brazil* 7°5S 41°28W **93 E10**
Picton *Canada* 44°1N 77°9W **82 B7**
Picton *N.Z.* 41°18S 174°3E **59 D5**
Pictou *Canada* 45°41N 62°42W **73 C7**
Picture Butte *Canada* 49°55N 112°45W **70 D6**
Pictured Rocks △ *U.S.A.* 46°30N 86°30W **80 B10**
Picún Leufú *Argentina* 39°30S 69°5W **96 D3**
Pidurutalagala *Sri Lanka* 7°10N 80°50E **45 L5**
Piedmont = Piemonte □ *Italy* 45°0N 8°0E **20 D7**
Piedmont *Ala., U.S.A.* 33°55N 85°37W **85 E12**
Piedmont *S.C., U.S.A.* 34°42N 82°28W **66 F11**
Piedras Negras *Mexico* 28°42N 100°31W **86 B4**
Pieksämäki *Finland* 62°18N 27°10E **8 E22**
Pielinen *Finland* 63°15N 29°40E **8 E23**
Pieljekaise △ *Sweden* 66°20N 16°45E **8 C17**
Piemonte □ *Italy* 45°0N 8°0E **20 D7**
Pienaarsrivier *S. Africa* 25°15S 28°18E **57 C4**
Piercefield *U.S.A.* 44°13N 74°35W **83 B10**
Pierceland *Canada* 54°20N 109°46W **71 C7**
Pierpont *U.S.A.* 41°45N 80°34W **82 E4**
Pierre *U.S.A.* 44°22N 100°21W **80 C4**
Pierrefonds *Canada* 45°29N 73°51W **83 A11**
Piet Retief *S. Africa* 27°1S 30°50E **57 C5**
Pietarsaari *Finland* 63°40N 22°43E **8 E20**
Pietermaritzburg *S. Africa* 29°35S 30°25E **57 C5**
Pietersburg = Polokwane *S. Africa* 23°54S 29°25E **57 B4**
Pietrosul, Vf. *Maramureş, Romania* 47°35N 24°43E **17 E13**
Pietrosul, Vf. *Suceava, Romania* 47°12N 25°18E **17 E13**
Pigeon I. *India* 14°2N 74°20E **45 G2**
Pigeon L. *Canada* 44°27N 78°30W **82 B6**
Piggott *U.S.A.* 36°23N 90°11W **85 C9**
Pigüe *Argentina* 37°36S 62°25W **94 D3**
Pihani *India* 27°36N 80°15E **43 F9**
Pihlajavesi *Finland* 61°45N 28°45E **8 F23**
Pijijiapan *Mexico* 15°42N 93°14W **87 D6**
Pikangikum *Canada* 51°49N 94°0W **71 C10**
Pikes Peak *U.S.A.* 38°50N 105°3W **76 G11**
Piketberg *S. Africa* 32°55S 18°40E **56 D2**
Pikou *China* 39°18N 122°22E **33 E12**
Pikwitonei *Canada* 55°35N 97°9W **71 B9**
Piła *Poland* 53°10N 16°48E **17 B9**
Pilanesberg △ *S. Africa* 25°15S 27°4E **56 C4**
Pilani *India* 28°22N 75°33E **42 E6**
Pilar *Paraguay* 26°50S 58°20W **94 B4**
Pilaya → *Bolivia* 20°55S 64°4W **92 H6**
Pilbara *Australia* 21°15S 118°16E **60 D2**
Pilcomayo → *Paraguay* 25°21S 57°42W **94 B4**
Pilgrim's Rest *S. Africa* 24°55S 30°44E **57 B5**
Pilibhit *India* 28°40N 79°50E **43 E8**
Pilica → *Poland* 51°52N 21°17E **17 C11**
Pilipinas = Philippines ■ *Asia* 12°0N 123°0E **37 B6**
Pilkhawa *India* 28°43N 77°42E **42 E7**
Pilliga *Australia* 30°21S 148°54E **63 E4**

Pilos *Greece* 36°55N 21°42E **23 F9**
Pilot Mound *Canada* 49°15N 98°54W **71 D9**
Pilot Point *U.S.A.* 33°24N 96°58W **84 E6**
Pilot Rock *U.S.A.* 45°29N 118°50W **76 D4**
Pima *U.S.A.* 32°54N 109°50W **77 K9**
Pimba *Australia* 31°18S 136°46E **63 E2**
Pimenta Bueno *Brazil* 11°35S 61°10W **92 F6**
Pimentel *Peru* 6°45S 79°55W **92 E3**
Pimpri Chinchwad *India* 18°37N 73°47E **44 E1**
Pin Valley △ *India* 31°50N 77°50E **42 D7**
Pinang *Malaysia* 5°25N 100°15E **39 c**
Pinang *Malaysia* 5°20N 100°20E **39 K3**
Pinar del Río *Cuba* 22°26N 83°40W **88 B3**
Pinarhisar *Turkey* 41°37N 27°30E **23 D12**
Pinatubo, Mt. *Phil.* 15°8N 120°21E **37 A6**
Pinawa *Canada* 50°9N 95°50W **71 C9**
Pinchang *China* 31°36N 107°3E **34 B6**
Pincher Creek *Canada* 49°30N 113°57W **70 D6**
Pinchi L. *Canada* 54°38N 124°30W **70 C4**
Pinckneyville *U.S.A.* 38°5N 89°23W **80 F9**
Pińczów *Poland* 50°32N 20°32E **17 C11**
Pindar *Australia* 28°30S 115°47E **61 E2**
Pindera Downs ✪ *Australia* 29°24S 142°37E **63 A3**
Pindi Gheb *Pakistan* 33°14N 72°21E **42 C5**
Pindos Oros *Greece* 40°0N 21°0E **23 E9**
Pindus Mts. = Pindos Oros *Greece* 40°0N 21°0E **23 E9**
Pine → *B.C., Canada* 56°8N 120°43W **70 B4**
Pine → *Sask., Canada* 58°50N 105°38W **71 B7**
Pine Bluff *U.S.A.* 34°13N 92°1W **84 D8**
Pine Bluffs *U.S.A.* 41°11N 104°4W **76 F11**
Pine City *U.S.A.* 45°50N 92°59W **80 C7**
Pine Cr. → *U.S.A.* 41°10N 77°16W **82 E7**
Pine Creek *Australia* 13°50S 131°50E **60 B5**
Pine Falls *Canada* 50°34N 96°11W **71 C9**
Pine Flat L. *U.S.A.* 36°50N 119°20W **78 J7**
Pine Grove *U.S.A.* 40°33N 76°23W **83 F8**
Pine Hill *Australia* 23°38S 146°57E **62 C4**
Pine Island Glacier *Antarctica* 76°0S 100°0W **5 D15**
Pine Pass *Canada* 55°25N 122°42W **70 B4**
Pine Ridge *U.S.A.* 43°2N 102°33W **80 D2**
Pine River *Canada* 51°45N 100°30W **71 C8**
Pine River *U.S.A.* 46°43N 94°24W **80 B6**
Pine Valley *U.S.A.* 32°50N 116°32W **79 N10**
Pinecrest *U.S.A.* 38°12N 120°1W **78 G6**
Pinedale *Calif., U.S.A.* 36°50N 119°48W **78 J7**
Pinedale *Wyo., U.S.A.* 42°52N 109°52W **76 E9**
Pinega → *Russia* 64°30N 44°19E **18 B8**
Pinehouse L. *Canada* 55°32N 106°35W **71 B7**
Pineimuta → *Canada* 52°8N 88°33W **72 B1**
Pinerolo *Italy* 44°53N 7°21E **20 D7**
Pines, Akra *Greece* 40°5N 24°20E **23 D11**
Pinetop-Lakeside *U.S.A.* 34°9N 109°58W **77 J9**
Pinetown *S. Africa* 29°48S 30°54E **57 C5**
Pineville *U.S.A.* 31°19N 92°26W **84 F8**
Ping → *Thailand* 15°42N 100°9E **38 E3**
Pingaring *Australia* 32°40S 118°32E **61 F2**
Pingba *China* 26°23N 106°12E **34 D6**
Pingbian *China* 23°0N 103°45E **34 F4**
Pingchuan *China* 27°35N 101°55E **34 D3**
Pingding *China* 37°47N 113°38E **32 F7**
Pingdingshan *China* 33°43N 113°27E **34 H7**
Pingdu *China* 36°42N 119°59E **33 F10**
Pingelly *Australia* 32°32S 117°5E **61 F2**
Pingguo *China* 23°19N 107°36E **34 F6**
Pinghe *China* 24°17N 117°21E **35 E11**
Pinghu *China* 30°40N 121°2E **35 B13**
Pingjiang *China* 28°45N 113°36E **35 C9**
Pingli *China* 32°27N 109°22E **34 A7**
Pingliang *China* 35°35N 106°31E **32 G4**
Pinglu *China* 39°31N 112°30E **32 E7**
Pingluo *China* 38°52N 106°30E **32 E4**
Pingnan *Fujian, China* 26°55N 119°0E **35 D12**
Pingnan *Guangxi Zhuangzu, China* 23°33N 110°22E **35 F8**
Pingquan *China* 41°1N 118°37E **33 D10**
Pingrup *Australia* 33°32S 118°29E **61 F2**
Pingshan *China* 28°39N 104°3E **34 C5**
Pingtan *China* 25°31N 119°47E **35 E12**
Pingtang *China* 25°49N 107°17E **34 E6**
P'ingtung *Taiwan* 22°38N 120°30E **35 F13**
Pingwu *China* 32°25N 104°30E **34 H3**
Pixian *China* 30°48N 103°52E **34 B4**
Pingxiang *Guangxi Zhuangzu, China* 22°6N 106°46E **34 F6**
Pingxiang *Jiangxi, China* 27°43N 113°48E **35 D9**
Pingyao *China* 37°12N 112°10E **32 F7**
Pingyi *China* 35°30N 117°35E **33 G9**
Pingyin *China* 36°20N 116°25E **32 F9**
Pingyuan *Guangdong, China* 24°37N 115°57E **35 E10**
Pingyuan *Shandong, China* 37°10N 116°22E **32 F9**
Pingyuanjie *China* 23°45N 103°48E **34 F4**
Pinheiro *Brazil* 2°31S 45°5W **93 D9**
Pinheiro Machado *Brazil* 31°34S 53°23W **95 C5**
Pinhel *Portugal* 40°50N 7°1W **21 B2**
Pini *Indonesia* 0°10N 98°40E **36 D1**
Pinios → *Greece* 39°55N 22°41E **23 E10**
Pinjarra *Australia* 32°37S 115°52E **61 F2**
Pink Mountain *Canada* 57°3N 122°52W **70 B4**
Pinnacle Is. = Senkaku-Shotō *E. China Sea* 25°30N 123°30E **29 M1**
Pinnacles △ *U.S.A.* 36°25N 121°12W **78 J5**
Pinnaroo *Australia* 35°17S 140°53E **63 F3**
Pinon Hills *U.S.A.* 34°26N 117°39W **79 L9**
Pinos *Mexico* 22°18N 101°34W **86 C4**
Pinos, Mt. *U.S.A.* 34°49N 119°8W **79 L7**
Pinos Pt. *U.S.A.* 36°38N 121°57W **77 H3**
Pinrang *Indonesia* 3°46S 119°41E **37 E5**
Pins, Pte. aux *Canada* 42°15N 81°51W **82 D3**
Pinsk *Belarus* 52°10N 26°1E **17 B14**
Pintados *Chile* 20°35S 69°40W **92 H5**
Pinyang *China* 27°42N 120°31E **35 D13**
Pinyug *Russia* 60°5N 48°0E **18 B8**
Pioche *U.S.A.* 37°56N 114°27W **77 H6**
Piombino *Italy* 42°55N 10°32E **22 C4**
Pioner, Ostrov *Russia* 79°50N 92°0E **27 B10**

Piopiotaki = Milford Sd. *N.Z.* 44°41S 167°47E **59 F1**
Piorini, L. *Brazil* 3°15S 62°35W **92 D6**
Piotrków Trybunalski *Poland* 51°23N 19°43E **17 C10**
Pīp *Iran* 26°45N 60°10E **47 E9**
Pipar *India* 26°25N 73°31E **42 F5**
Pipar Road *India* 26°27N 73°27E **42 F5**
Piparia *Mad. P., India* 22°45N 78°23E **42 H8**
Piparia *Mad. P., India* 21°49N 77°37E **42 J7**
Pipestone *U.S.A.* 44°0N 96°19W **80 D5**
Pipestone → *Canada* 52°53N 89°23W **72 B2**
Pipestone Cr. → *Canada* 49°38N 100°15W **71 D8**
Piplan *Pakistan* 32°17N 71°21E **42 C4**
Piploda *India* 23°37N 74°56E **42 H6**
Pipmuacan, Rés. *Canada* 49°45N 70°30W **73 C5**
Pippingarra *Australia* 20°27S 118°42E **60 D2**
Piqua *U.S.A.* 40°9N 84°15W **81 E11**
Piquiri → *Brazil* 24°3S 54°14W **95 A5**
Pir Panjal Range *India* 32°30N 76°50E **42 C7**
Pīr Sohrāb *Iran* 25°44N 60°54E **47 E9**
Piracicaba *Brazil* 22°45S 47°40W **95 A6**
Piracuruca *Brazil* 3°50S 41°50W **93 D10**
Pirae *Tahiti* 17°31S 149°32W **59 d**
Pirajuí *Brazil* 21°59S 49°29W **95 A6**
Piram I. *India* 21°36N 72°21E **42 J5**
Pirané *Argentina* 25°42S 59°6W **94 B4**
Pirapora *Brazil* 17°20S 44°56W **93 G10**
Pirawa *India* 24°10N 76°2E **42 G7**
Pirgos *Greece* 37°40N 21°27E **23 F9**
Piribebuy *Paraguay* 25°26S 57°2W **94 B4**
Pirimapun *Indonesia* 6°20S 138°24E **37 F9**
Pirin Planina *Bulgaria* 41°40N 23°30E **23 D10**
Pirineos = Pyrénées *Europe* 42°45N 0°18E **20 E4**
Piripiri *Brazil* 4°15S 41°46W **93 D10**
Pirlangimpi *Australia* 11°24S 130°26E **60 B5**
Pirmasens *Germany* 49°12N 7°36E **16 D4**
Pirot *Serbia* 43°9N 22°33E **23 C10**
Piru *Indonesia* 3°4S 128°12E **37 E7**
Piru *U.S.A.* 34°25N 118°48W **79 L8**
Pisa *Italy* 43°43N 10°23E **22 C4**
Pisagua *Chile* 19°40S 70°15W **92 G4**
Pisco *Peru* 13°50S 76°12W **92 F3**
Pisek *Czechia* 49°19N 14°10E **16 D8**
Pishan *China* 37°30N 78°33E **30 D4**
Pishin *Iran* 26°6N 61°47E **47 E9**
Pishin *Pakistan* 30°35N 67°0E **42 D2**
Pishin Lora → *Pakistan* 29°9N 64°5E **42 E1**
Pising *Indonesia* 5°8S 121°53E **37 F6**
Pismo Beach *U.S.A.* 35°9N 120°38W **79 K6**
Pissis, Cerro *Argentina* 27°45S 68°48W **94 B2**
Pissouri *Italy* 43°55N 10°54E **22 C4**
Pistol B. *Canada* 62°25N 92°37W **71 A10**
Pisuerga → *Spain* 41°33N 4°52W **21 B3**
Pit → *U.S.A.* 40°47N 122°6W **76 F2**
Pitarpunga L. *Australia* 34°24S 143°30E **63 E3**
Pitcairn I. *Pac. Oc.* 25°5S 130°5W **65 K14**
Pitch L. *Trin. & Tob.* 10°14N 61°39W **93 K15**
Piteå *Sweden* 65°20N 21°25E **8 D19**
Piteålven → *Sweden* 65°20N 21°25E **8 D19**
Piteşti *Romania* 44°52N 24°54E **17 F13**
Pithapuram *India* 17°10N 82°15E **44 F6**
Pithara *Australia* 30°20S 116°35E **61 F2**
Pithora *India* 21°16N 82°31E **44 D6**
Pithoragarh *India* 29°35N 80°13E **43 E9**
Pithoro *Pakistan* 25°31N 69°23E **42 G3**
Pitlochry *U.K.* 56°42N 3°44W **11 E5**
Pitt I. *Canada* 53°30N 129°50W **70 C3**
Pitti I. *India* 10°50N 72°38E **45 J1**
Pittsburg *Calif., U.S.A.* 38°2N 121°53W **78 G5**
Pittsburg *Kans., U.S.A.* 37°25N 94°42W **80 G6**
Pittsburg *Tex., U.S.A.* 33°0N 94°59W **84 E7**
Pittsburgh *U.S.A.* 40°26N 79°58W **82 F5**
Pittsfield *Ill., U.S.A.* 39°36N 90°49W **80 F8**
Pittsfield *Maine, U.S.A.* 44°47N 69°23W **81 C19**
Pittsfield *Mass., U.S.A.* 42°27N 73°15W **83 D11**
Pittsfield *N.H., U.S.A.* 43°18N 71°20E **83 C13**
Pittston *U.S.A.* 41°19N 75°47W **83 E9**
Pittsworth *Australia* 27°41S 151°37E **63 D5**
Pituri → *Australia* 22°35S 138°30E **62 C2**
Piura *Peru* 5°15S 80°38W **92 E2**
Piuthan *Nepal* 28°7N 82°52E **43 E10**
Pixian *China* 30°48N 103°52E **34 B4**
Pixley *U.S.A.* 35°58N 119°18W **78 K7**
Pizhou = Pei Xian *China* 34°44N 116°55E **32 G9**
Pizhou *China* 34°18N 117°57E **33 G9**
Placentia *Canada* 47°20N 54°0W **73 C9**
Placentia B. *Canada* 47°0N 54°40W **73 C9**
Placerville *U.S.A.* 38°44N 120°48W **78 G6**
Placetas *Cuba* 22°15N 79°44W **88 B4**
Plaine des Jarres *Laos* 19°27N 103°10E **38 C4**
Plainfield *N.J., U.S.A.* 40°37N 74°25W **83 F10**
Plainfield *Ohio, U.S.A.* 40°13N 81°43W **82 F3**
Plainfield *Vt., U.S.A.* 44°17N 72°26W **83 B12**
Plains *Mont., U.S.A.* 47°28N 114°53W **76 C6**
Plains *Tex., U.S.A.* 33°11N 102°50W **84 E3**
Plainview *Nebr., U.S.A.* 42°21N 97°47W **80 D5**
Plainview *Tex., U.S.A.* 34°11N 101°43W **84 D4**
Plainwell *U.S.A.* 42°27N 85°38W **81 D11**
Plaistow *U.S.A.* 42°50N 71°6W **83 D13**
Plaka, Akra *Greece* 35°11N 26°19E **23 D8**
Plana Cays *Bahamas* 22°38N 73°30E **89 B5**
Planada *U.S.A.* 37°16N 120°19W **78 H6**
Plano *U.S.A.* 33°1N 96°42W **84 E6**
Plant City *U.S.A.* 28°1N 82°7W **85 G13**
Plaquemine *U.S.A.* 30°17N 91°14W **84 F9**
Plasencia *Spain* 40°3N 6°8W **21 B2**
Plaster City *U.S.A.* 32°47N 115°51W **79 N11**
Plaster Rock *Canada* 46°53N 67°22E **73 C6**
Plastun *Russia* 44°45N 136°19E **28 B8**
Plata, Río de la → *S. Amer.* 34°45S 57°30W **94 C4**
Plátani → *Italy* 37°23N 13°16E **22 F5**
Platte → *Mo., U.S.A.* 39°16N 94°50W **80 F6**
Platte → *Nebr., U.S.A.* 41°4N 95°53W **80 E6**
Platte *U.S.A.* 43°23N 98°51W **80 D4**
Platteville *U.S.A.* 42°44N 90°29W **80 D8**

Plattsburgh *U.S.A.* 44°42N 73°28W **83 B11**
Plattsmouth *U.S.A.* 41°1N 95°53W **80 E6**
Plauen *Germany* 50°30N 12°8E **16 C7**
Plavinas *Latvia* 56°35N 25°46E **9 H21**
Playa del Carmen *Mexico* 20°37N 87°4W **87 C7**
Playgreen L. *Canada* 54°0N 98°15W **71 C9**
Pleasant Bay *Canada* 46°51N 60°48W **73 C7**
Pleasant Hill *U.S.A.* 37°57N 122°4W **78 H4**
Pleasant Mount *U.S.A.* 41°44N 75°26W **83 E9**
Pleasanton *Calif., U.S.A.* 37°39N 121°52W **78 H5**
Pleasanton *Tex., U.S.A.* 28°58N 98°29W **84 G5**
Pleasantville *N.J., U.S.A.* 39°24N 74°32W **81 F16**
Pleasantville *Pa., U.S.A.* 41°35N 79°34W **82 E5**
Plei Ku *Vietnam* 13°57N 108°0E **38 F7**
Plenty → *Australia* 23°25S 136°31E **62 C2**
Plenty, B. of *N.Z.* 37°45S 177°0E **59 B6**
Plesetsk *Russia* 62°43N 40°20E **18 B7**
Plessisville *Canada* 46°14N 71°47W **73 C5**
Plétipi, L. *Canada* 51°44N 70°6W **73 B5**
Pleven *Bulgaria* 43°26N 24°37E **23 C11**
Plevna *Canada* 44°58N 76°59W **82 B8**
Pljevlja *Montenegro* 43°21N 19°21E **23 C8**
Plock *Poland* 52°32N 19°40E **17 B10**
Plöckenstein *Germany* 48°46N 13°51E **16 D7**
Ploieşti *Romania* 44°57N 26°5E **17 F14**
Plonge, Lac la *Canada* 55°8N 107°20W **71 B7**
Plovdiv *Bulgaria* 42°8N 24°44E **23 C11**
Plover Cove Res. *China* 22°28N 114°15E **31 a**
Plum *U.S.A.* 40°29N 79°47W **82 F5**
Plum I. *U.S.A.* 41°11N 72°12W **83 E12**
Plumas *U.S.A.* 39°45N 120°4W **78 F6**
Plummer *U.S.A.* 47°20N 116°53W **76 C5**
Plumridge Lakes *Australia* 29°26S 125°16E **61 E4**
Plumtree *Zimbabwe* 20°27S 27°55E **55 J5**
Plunge *Lithuania* 55°53N 21°59E **9 J19**
Plymouth *Trin. & Tob.* 11°14N 60°48W **93 J16**
Plymouth *U.K.* 50°22N 4°10W **13 G3**
Plymouth *Calif., U.S.A.* 38°29N 120°51W **78 G6**
Plymouth *Ind., U.S.A.* 41°21N 86°19W **80 E10**
Plymouth *Mass., U.S.A.* 41°57N 70°40W **83 E14**
Plymouth *N.C., U.S.A.* 35°52N 76°43W **85 D16**
Plymouth *N.H., U.S.A.* 43°45N 71°41W **83 C13**
Plymouth *Pa., U.S.A.* 41°14N 75°57W **83 E9**
Plymouth *Wis., U.S.A.* 43°45N 87°59W **80 D10**
Plympton-Wyoming = Wyoming *Canada* 42°57N 82°7W **82 D2**
Plynlimon = Pumlumon Fawr *U.K.* 52°28N 3°46W **13 E4**
Plyusa *Russia* 58°28N 29°27E **9 G23**
Plzeň *Czechia* 49°45N 13°22E **16 D7**
Pmere Nyente ✪ *Australia* 24°15S 136°10E **62 C2**
Po → *Italy* 44°57N 12°4E **22 B5**
Po Hai = Bo Hai *China* 39°0N 119°0E **33 E10**
Po Toi *China* 22°10N 114°16E **31 b**
Pobeda *Russia* 65°12N 146°12E **27 C15**
Pobedy, Pik *Asia* 42°0N 79°58E **30 C4**
Pocahontas *Ark., U.S.A.* 36°16N 90°58W **85 C9**
Pocahontas *Iowa, U.S.A.* 42°44N 94°40W **80 D6**
Pocatello *U.S.A.* 42°52N 112°27W **76 E7**
Pocomoke City *U.S.A.* 38°5N 75°34W **81 F16**
Poços de Caldas *Brazil* 21°50S 46°33W **95 A6**
Podgorica *Montenegro* 42°30N 19°19E **23 C8**
Podile *India* 15°37N 79°37E **45 G4**
Podilska Vysochyna *Ukraine* 49°0N 28°0E **17 D14**
Podolsk *Russia* 55°25N 37°30E **18 C6**
Podporozhye *Russia* 60°55N 34°2E **18 B5**
Pofadder *S. Africa* 29°10S 19°22E **56 D2**
Pogranichnyy *Russia* 44°25N 131°24E **28 B5**
Poh *Indonesia* 0°46S 122°51E **37 E6**
Pohang *S. Korea* 36°1N 129°23E **33 F15**
Pohjanmaa □ *Finland* 62°58N 22°50E **8 E20**
Pohnpei *Micronesia* 6°55S 158°10E **64 G7**
Pohri *India* 25°32N 77°22E **42 G6**
Poinsett, C. *Antarctica* 65°42S 113°18E **5 C8**
Point Arena *U.S.A.* 38°55N 123°41W **78 G3**
Point Baker *U.S.A.* 56°21N 133°37W **70 B2**
Point Calimere *India* 10°17N 79°49E **45 J4**
Point Fortin *Trin. & Tob.* 10°10N 61°42W **93 K15**
Point Hope *U.S.A.* 68°21N 166°47W **74 B6**
Point L. *Canada* 65°15N 113°4W **68 B9**
Point Lisas *Trin. & Tob.* 10°24N 61°29W **93 K15**
Point Pedro *Sri Lanka* 9°50N 80°15E **45 K5**
Point Pelee △ *Canada* 41°57N 82°31W **82 E2**
Point Pleasant *N.J., U.S.A.* 40°5N 74°4W **83 F10**
Point Pleasant *W. Va., U.S.A.* 38°51N 82°8W **81 F12**
Point Reyes △ *U.S.A.* 38°10N 122°55W **78 G2**
Pointe-à-Pitre *Guadeloupe* 16°15N 61°32W **88 b**
Pointe-au-Pic = La Malbaie *Canada* 47°40N 70°10W **73 C5**
Pointe-Claire *Canada* 45°27N 73°50W **83 A11**
Pointe-Gatineau *Canada* 45°27N 75°41W **83 A9**
Pointe-Noire *Congo* 4°48S 11°53E **54 E2**
Pointe-Noire *Guadeloupe* 16°14N 61°47W **88 b**
Poipet *Cambodia* 13°39N 102°33E **38 F4**
Poisonbush Ra. *Australia* 22°30S 121°30E **60 D3**
Poissonnier Pt. *Australia* 19°57S 119°10E **60 C2**
Poitiers *France* 46°35N 0°20E **20 C4**
Poitou *France* 46°40N 0°10W **20 C3**
Pojoaque *U.S.A.* 35°54N 106°1W **77 J10**
Pokaran *India* 27°0N 71°50E **42 F4**
Pokataroo *Australia* 29°30S 148°36E **63 D4**
Pokhara *Nepal* 28°14N 83°58E **43 E10**
Poko *Dem. Rep. of the Congo* 3°7N 26°52E **54 D5**
Pokrovsk *Russia* 61°29N 129°0E **27 C13**
Pola = Pula *Croatia* 44°54N 13°57E **16 F7**
Polacca *U.S.A.* 35°50N 110°23W **77 J8**
Polan *Iran* 25°30N 61°10E **47 E9**
Poland ■ *Europe* 52°0N 20°0E **17 C10**
Polar Bear △ *Canada* 55°0N 83°45W **72 A2**
Polatsk *Belarus* 55°30N 28°50E **9 J23**
Polavaram *India* 17°15N 81°38E **44 F5**
Polcura *Chile* 37°17S 71°43W **94 D1**

INDEX TO WORLD MAPS Princess Elizabeth Trough 153

Polesye = Pripet Marshes
Europe 52°10N 27°10E 17 B15
Polevskoy Russia 56°26N 60°11E 18 C11
Police Poland 53°33N 14°33E 16 B8
Police, Pte. Seychelles 4°51S 55°32E 55 b
Poligiros Greece 40°23N 23°25E 23 D10
Polillo Is. Phil. 14°56N 122°0E 37 B6
Polk U.S.A. 41°22N 79°56W 82 E5
Pollachi India 10°35N 77°0E 45 J3
Polnovat Russia 63°50N 65°54E 26 C7
Polokwane S. Africa 23°54S 29°25E 57 B4
Polokwane → S. Africa 22°25S 30°5E 57 B5
Polonnaruwa Sri Lanka 7°56N 81°0E 45 L5
Polonne Ukraine 50°6N 27°30E 17 C14
Polonnoye = Polonne
Ukraine 50°6N 27°30E 17 C14
Polson U.S.A. 47°41N 114°9W 76 C6
Poltava Ukraine 49°35N 34°35E 19 E5
Põltsamaa Estonia 58°39N 25°58E 9 G21
Polunochnoye Russia 60°52N 60°25E 26 C7
Polur India 12°32N 79°11E 45 H4
Põlva Estonia 58°3N 27°3E 9 G22
Polyarny Russia 69°8N 33°20E 8 B25
Polyarnyye Zori Russia 67°22N 32°30E 8 C25
Polynesia Pac. Oc. 10°0S 162°0W 65 F11
Polynésie française = French
Polynesia ☒ Pac. Oc. 20°0S 145°0W 65 J13
Pombal Portugal 39°55N 8°40W 21 C1
Pomene Mozam. 22°53S 35°33E 57 B6
Pomeroy Ohio, U.S.A. 39°2N 82°2W 81 F12
Pomeroy Wash., U.S.A. 46°28N 117°36W 76 C5
Pomézia Italy 41°40N 12°30E 22 D5
Pomona Australia 26°22S 152°52E 63 D5
Pomona U.S.A. 34°4N 117°45W 79 L9
Pomorskie, Pojezierze
Poland 53°40N 16°37E 17 B9
Pompeys Pillar U.S.A. 45°59N 107°57W 76 D10
Pompeys Pillar ⌂ U.S.A. 46°0N 108°0W 76 D10
Pompton Lakes U.S.A. 41°0N 74°17W 83 F10
Ponape = Pohnpei
Micronesia 6°55N 158°10E 64 G7
Ponask L. Canada 54°0N 92°41W 72 B1
Ponca U.S.A. 42°34N 96°43W 80 D5
Ponca City U.S.A. 36°42N 97°5W 84 C6
Ponce Puerto Rico 18°1N 66°37W 89 d
Ponchatoula U.S.A. 30°26N 90°26W 85 F9
Poncheville, L. Canada 50°10N 76°55W 72 B4
Pond U.S.A. 35°43N 119°20W 79 K7
Pond Inlet Canada 72°40N 77°0W 69 C16
Pondicherry = Puducherry
India 11°59N 79°50E 45 J4
Ponds, I. of Canada 53°27N 55°52W 73 B8
Ponferrada Spain 42°32N 6°35W 21 A2
Ponnaiyar → India 11°50N 79°45E 45 J4
Ponnani India 10°45N 75°59E 45 J2
Ponneri India 13°20N 80°15E 45 H5
Ponnuru India 16°5N 80°34E 45 F5
Ponoka Canada 52°42N 113°40W 70 C6
Ponorogo Indonesia 7°52S 111°27E 37 G14
Ponoy Russia 67°0N 41°13E 18 A7
Ponoy → Russia 66°59N 41°17E 18 A7
Ponta Delgada Azores 37°44N 25°40W 52 a
Ponta Grossa Brazil 25°7S 50°10W 95 B5
Ponta Porã Brazil 22°20S 55°35W 95 A4
Pontardawe U.K. 51°43N 3°51W 13 F3
Pontarlier France 46°54N 6°20E 20 C7
Pontchartrain, L. U.S.A. 30°5N 90°5W 85 F9
Ponte Nova Brazil 20°25S 42°54W 95 A7
Ponteix Canada 49°46N 107°29W 71 D7
Pontevedra Spain 42°26N 8°40W 21 A1
Pontiac Ill., U.S.A. 40°53N 88°38W 80 E9
Pontiac Mich., U.S.A. 42°38N 83°18W 81 D12
Pontian Kechil Malaysia 1°29N 103°23E 39 d
Pontianak Indonesia 0°3S 109°15E 36 E3
Pontine Is. = Ponziane, Ísole
Italy 40°55N 12°57E 22 D5
Pontine Mts. = Kuzey Anadolu
Dağları Turkey 41°0N 36°45E 19 F6
Pontivy France 48°5N 2°58W 20 B2
Pontoise France 49°3N 2°5E 20 B5
Ponton → Canada 58°27N 116°11W 70 B5
Pontypool Canada 44°6N 78°38W 82 B6
Pontypool U.K. 51°42N 3°2W 13 F4
Pontypridd U.K. 51°36N 3°20W 13 F4
Ponziane, Ísole Italy 40°55N 12°57E 22 D5
Poochera Australia 32°43S 134°51E 63 E1
Poole U.K. 50°43N 1°59W 13 G6
Poole ☐ U.K. 50°43N 1°59W 13 G6
Poona = Pune India 18°29N 73°57E 44 E1
Poonamallee India 13°3N 80°10E 45 H5
Pooncarie Australia 33°22S 142°31E 63 E3
Poopelloe L. Australia 31°40S 144°0E 63 E3
Poopó, L. de Bolivia 18°30S 67°35W 92 G5
Popayán Colombia 2°27N 76°36W 92 C3
Poperinge Belgium 50°51N 2°42E 15 D2
Popilta L. Australia 33°10S 141°42E 63 E3
Popio L. Australia 33°10S 141°52E 63 E3
Poplar U.S.A. 48°7N 105°12W 76 B11
Poplar → Canada 53°0N 97°19W 71 C9
Poplar Bluff U.S.A. 36°46N 90°24W 80 G8
Poplarville U.S.A. 30°51N 89°32W 85 F10
Popocatépetl, Volcán
Mexico 19°2N 98°38W 87 D5
Popokabaka
Dem. Rep. of the Congo 5°41S 16°40E 54 F3
Poprad Slovakia 49°3N 20°18E 17 D11
Porali → Pakistan 25°58N 66°26E 42 G2
Porbandar India 21°44N 69°43E 42 J3
Porcher I. Canada 53°50N 130°30W 70 C2
Porcupine → Canada 59°11N 104°46W 71 B8
Porcupine → U.S.A. 66°34N 145°19W 68 D2
Porcupine Gorge △
Australia 20°22S 144°26E 62 C3
Pordenone Italy 45°57N 12°39E 22 B5
Pori Finland 61°29N 21°48E 8 F19
Porkhov Russia 57°45N 29°38E 9 H23
Porlamar Venezuela 10°57N 63°51W 92 A6
Pormpuraaw Australia 14°59S 141°26E 62 A3
Pormpuraaw ✪
Australia 14°55S 141°47E 62 A3
Poronaysk Russia 49°13N 143°0E 31 B17
Poroshiri-Dake Japan 42°41N 142°52E 28 C11
Porpoise B. Antarctica 66°0S 127°0E 5 C9
Porsangerfjorden Norway 70°40N 25°40E 8 A21
Porsgrunn Norway 59°10N 9°40E 9 G13
Port Alberni Canada 49°14N 124°50W 70 D4
Port Alfred S. Africa 33°36S 26°55E 56 D4
Port Alice Canada 50°20N 127°25W 70 C3
Port Allegany U.S.A. 41°48N 78°17W 82 E6
Port Allen U.S.A. 30°27N 91°12W 84 F9
Port Alma Australia 23°38S 150°53E 62 C5
Port Alma Canada 42°10N 82°14W 82 D2
Port Angeles U.S.A. 48°7N 123°27W 78 B3
Port Antonio Jamaica 18°10N 76°26W 88 a
Port Aransas U.S.A. 27°50N 97°4W 84 H6
Port Arthur Australia 43°7S 147°50E 63 G4
Port Arthur U.S.A. 29°54N 93°56W 84 G8
Port au Choix Canada 50°43N 57°22W 73 B8
Port au Port B. Canada 48°40N 58°50W 73 C8
Port-au-Prince Haiti 18°40N 72°20W 89 C5
Port Augusta Australia 32°30S 137°50E 63 E2
Port Austin U.S.A. 44°3N 83°1W 82 B2
Port Blair India 11°40N 92°45E 45 J11
Port Blandford Canada 48°20N 54°10W 73 C9
Port Bradshaw Australia 12°30S 137°20E 62 A2
Port Broughton
Australia 33°37S 137°56E 63 E2
Port Bruce Canada 42°39N 81°0W 82 D4
Port Burwell Canada 42°40N 80°48W 82 D4
Port Campbell India 11°56N 92°37E 45 J11
Port Canning India 22°23N 88°40E 43 H13
Port Carling Canada 45°7N 79°35W 82 A5
Port-Cartier Canada 50°2N 66°50W 73 B6
Port Chalmers N.Z. 45°49S 170°30E 59 F3
Port Charlotte U.S.A. 26°59N 82°6W 85 H13
Port Chester U.S.A. 41°0N 73°40W 83 F11
Port Clements Canada 53°40N 132°10W 70 C2
Port Clinton U.S.A. 41°31N 82°56W 81 E12
Port Colborne Canada 42°50N 79°10W 82 D5
Port Coquitlam Canada 49°15N 122°45W 78 A4
Port Cornwallis India 13°17N 93°5E 45 H11
Port Credit Canada 43°33N 79°35W 82 C5
Port Curtis Australia 23°57S 151°20E 62 C5
Port Dalhousie Canada 43°13N 79°16W 82 C5
Port Darwin Australia 12°24S 130°45E 60 B5
Port Darwin Falk. Is. 51°50S 59°0W 96 G5
Port Davey Australia 43°16S 145°55E 63 G4
Port-de-Paix Haiti 19°50N 72°50W 89 C5
Port Dickson Malaysia 2°30N 101°49E 39 L3
Port Douglas Australia 16°30S 145°30E 62 B4
Port Dover Canada 42°47N 80°12W 82 D4
Port Edward Canada 54°12N 130°10W 70 C2
Port Elgin Canada 44°25N 81°25W 82 B3
Port Elizabeth S. Africa 33°58S 25°40E 56 D4
Port Ellen U.K. 55°38N 6°11W 11 F2
Port Erin I. of Man 54°5N 4°45W 12 C3
Port Essington Australia 11°15S 132°10E 60 B5
Port Ewen U.S.A. 41°54N 73°59W 83 E11
Port Fairy Australia 38°22S 142°12E 63 F3
Port Gamble U.S.A. 47°51N 122°34W 78 C4
Port-Gentil Gabon 0°40S 8°50E 54 E1
Port Germein Australia 33°1S 138°1E 63 E2
Port Ghalib Egypt 25°20N 34°50E 46 E2
Port Gibson U.S.A. 31°58N 90°59W 84 F9
Port Glasgow U.K. 55°56N 4°41W 11 F4
Port Harcourt Nigeria 4°40N 7°10E 52 H7
Port Hardy Canada 50°41N 127°30W 70 C3
Port Harrison = Inukjuak
Canada 58°25N 78°15W 69 F16
Port Hawkesbury
Canada 45°36N 61°22W 73 C7
Port Hedland Australia 20°25S 118°35E 60 D2
Port Henry U.S.A. 44°3N 73°28W 83 B11
Port Hood Canada 46°0N 61°32W 73 C7
Port Hope Canada 43°56N 78°20W 82 C6
Port Hope U.S.A. 43°57N 82°43W 82 C2
Port Hope Simpson
Canada 52°33N 56°18W 73 B8
Port Hueneme U.S.A. 34°7N 119°12W 79 L7
Port Huron U.S.A. 42°58N 82°26W 82 D2
Port Jefferson U.S.A. 40°57N 73°3W 83 F11
Port Jervis U.S.A. 41°22N 74°41W 83 E10
Port Kenny Australia 33°10S 134°41E 63 E1
Port Klang Malaysia 3°0N 101°35E 39 L3
Port Láirge = Waterford
Ireland 52°15N 7°8W 10 D4
Port Lavaca U.S.A. 28°37N 96°38W 84 G6
Port Leyden U.S.A. 43°35N 75°21W 83 C9
Port Lincoln Australia 34°42S 135°52E 63 E2
Port Loko S. Leone 8°48N 12°46W 52 G3
Port-Louis Guadeloupe 16°28N 61°32W 88 b
Port Louis Mauritius 20°10S 57°30E 55 d
Port MacDonnell
Australia 38°5S 140°48E 63 F3
Port McNeill Canada 50°35N 127°6W 70 C3
Port Macquarie
Australia 31°25S 152°25E 63 E5
Port Maria Jamaica 18°22N 76°54W 88 a
Port Matilda U.S.A. 40°48N 78°3W 82 F6
Port McNicoll Canada 44°44N 79°48W 82 B5
Port Mellon Canada 49°32N 123°31W 70 D4
Port-Menier Canada 49°51N 64°15W 73 C7
Port Moody Canada 49°17N 122°51W 78 A4
Port Morant Jamaica 17°54N 76°19W 88 a
Port Moresby Papua N. G. 9°24S 147°8E 58 B7
Port Muhammed Bin Qasim = Port
Qasim Pakistan 24°46N 67°20E 42 G2
Port Musgrave Australia 11°55S 141°50E 62 A3
Port Neches U.S.A. 30°0N 93°59W 84 G8
Port Nolloth S. Africa 29°17S 16°52E 56 C2
Port Nouveau-Québec =
Kangiqsualujjuaq
Canada 58°30N 65°59W 69 F18
Port of Climax Canada 49°10N 108°20W 71 D7
Port of Coronach Canada 49°7N 105°31W 71 D7
Port of Spain
Trin. & Tob. 10°40N 61°31W 93 K15
Port Orange U.S.A. 29°9N 80°59W 85 G14
Port Orchard U.S.A. 47°32N 122°38W 78 C4
Port Orford U.S.A. 42°45N 124°30W 76 E1
Port Pegasus N.Z. 47°12S 167°41E 59 G1
Port Perry Canada 44°6N 78°56W 82 B6
Port Phillip B. Australia 38°10S 144°50E 63 F3
Port Pirie Australia 33°10S 138°1E 63 E2
Port Qasim Pakistan 24°46N 67°20E 42 G2
Port Renfrew Canada 48°30N 124°20W 78 B2
Port Roper Australia 14°45S 135°25E 62 A2
Port Rowan Canada 42°40N 80°30W 82 D4
Port Safaga = Bûr Safâga
Egypt 26°43N 33°57E 46 E2
Port Said = Bûr Sa'îd
Egypt 31°16N 32°18E 53 B12
Port St. Joe U.S.A. 29°49N 85°18W 85 G12
Port St. Johns = Umzimvubu
S. Africa 31°38S 29°33E 57 D4
Port St. Lucie U.S.A. 27°18N 80°21W 85 H14
Port Sanilac U.S.A. 43°26N 82°33W 82 C2
Port Severn Canada 44°48N 79°43W 82 B5
Port Shepstone S. Africa 30°44S 30°28E 57 D5
Port Simpson Canada 54°30N 130°20W 70 C2
Port Stanley = Stanley
Falk. Is. 51°40S 59°51W 96 G5
Port Stanley Canada 42°40N 81°10W 82 D3
Port Sudan = Bûr Sûdân
Sudan 19°32N 37°9E 53 E13
Port Sulphur U.S.A. 29°29N 89°42W 85 G10
Port Talbot U.K. 51°35N 3°47W 13 F4
Port Townsend U.S.A. 48°7N 122°45W 78 B4
Port-Vendres France 42°32N 3°8E 20 E5
Port Vila Vanuatu 17°45S 168°18E 58 C9
Port Vladimir Russia 69°25N 33°6E 8 B25
Port Wakefield Australia 34°12S 138°10E 63 E2
Port Washington
U.S.A. 43°23N 87°53W 80 D10
Porta Orientalis Romania 45°6N 22°18E 17 F12
Portacloy Ireland 54°20N 9°46W 10 B2
Portadown U.K. 54°25N 6°27W 10 B5
Portaferry U.K. 54°23N 5°33W 10 B6
Portage Pa., U.S.A. 40°23N 78°41W 82 F6
Portage Wis., U.S.A. 43°33N 89°28W 80 D9
Portage la Prairie
Canada 49°58N 98°18W 71 D9
Portageville U.S.A. 36°26N 89°42W 80 G9
Portalegre Portugal 39°19N 7°25W 21 C2
Portales U.S.A. 34°11N 103°20W 77 J12
Portarlington Ireland 53°9N 7°14W 10 C4
Portbou Spain 42°25N 3°9E 21 A7
Porter L. N.W.T., Canada 61°41N 108°5W 71 A7
Porter L. Sask., Canada 56°20N 107°20W 71 B7
Porterville S. Africa 33°0S 19°0E 56 D2
Porterville U.S.A. 36°4N 119°1W 78 J8
Porth Tywyn = Burry Port
U.K. 51°41N 4°15W 13 F3
Porthcawl U.K. 51°29N 3°42W 13 F4
Porthill U.S.A. 48°59N 116°30W 76 B5
Porthmadog U.K. 52°55N 4°8W 12 E3
Portile de Fier Europe 44°44N 22°30E 17 F12
Portimão Portugal 37°8N 8°32W 21 D1
Portishead U.K. 51°29N 2°46W 13 F5
Portknockie U.K. 57°42N 2°51W 11 D6
Portland N.S.W., Australia 33°20S 150°0E 63 E5
Portland Vic., Australia 38°20S 141°35E 63 F3
Portland Canada 44°42N 76°12W 83 B8
Portland Conn., U.S.A. 41°34N 72°38W 83 E12
Portland Maine, U.S.A. 43°39N 70°16W 81 D18
Portland Mich., U.S.A. 42°52N 84°54W 81 D11
Portland Oreg., U.S.A. 45°32N 122°37W 78 E4
Portland Pa., U.S.A. 40°55N 75°6W 83 F9
Portland Tex., U.S.A. 27°53N 97°20W 84 H6
Portland, I. of U.K. 50°33N 2°26W 13 G5
Portland B. Australia 38°15S 141°45E 63 F3
Portland Bight Jamaica 17°52N 77°5W 88 a
Portland Bill U.K. 50°31N 2°28W 13 G5
Portland Canal U.S.A. 55°56N 130°0W 70 B2
Portland Int. ✈ (PDX)
U.S.A. 45°35N 122°36W 78 E4
Portland Pt. Jamaica 17°42N 77°11W 88 a
Portlaoise Ireland 53°2N 7°18W 10 C4
Portmadoc = Porthmadog
U.K. 52°55N 4°8W 12 E3
Portmore Jamaica 17°53N 76°53W 88 a
Porto France 42°16N 8°42E 20 E8
Porto Portugal 41°8N 8°40W 21 B1
Pôrto Alegre Brazil 30°5S 51°10W 95 C5
Porto de Moz Brazil 1°41S 52°13W 93 D8
Porto Empédocle Italy 37°17N 13°32E 22 F5
Porto Esperança Brazil 19°37S 57°29W 92 G7
Porto Franco Brazil 6°20S 47°24W 93 E9
Porto Inglês = Vila do Maio
Cabo Verde 15°21N 23°10W 52 b
Porto Mendes Brazil 24°30S 54°15W 95 A5
Porto Murtinho Brazil 21°45S 57°55W 92 H7
Porto Nacional Brazil 10°40S 48°30W 93 F9
Porto-Novo Benin 6°23N 2°42E 52 G6
Porto Primavera, Represa
Brazil 22°10S 52°45W 95 A5
Porto Santo, I. de
Madeira 33°45N 16°25W 52 B2
Porto São José Brazil 22°43S 53°10W 95 A5
Porto Seguro Brazil 16°26S 39°5W 93 G11
Porto Tórres Italy 40°50N 8°24E 22 D3
Porto União Brazil 26°10S 51°10W 95 B5
Porto-Vecchio France 41°35N 9°16E 20 F8
Porto Velho Brazil 8°46S 63°54W 92 E6
Porto Walter Brazil 8°15S 72°40W 92 E4
Portobelo Panama 9°35N 79°42W 88 E4
Portoferráio Italy 42°48N 10°20E 22 C4
Portola U.S.A. 39°49N 120°28W 78 F6
Portoscuso Italy 39°12N 8°24E 22 E3
Portoviejo Ecuador 1°7S 80°28W 92 D2
Portpatrick U.K. 54°51N 5°7W 11 G3
Portree U.K. 57°25N 6°12W 11 D2
Portrush U.K. 55°12N 6°40W 10 A5
Portsmouth Dominica 15°34N 61°27W 89 C7
Portsmouth U.K. 50°48N 1°6W 13 G6
Portsmouth N.H., U.S.A. 43°5N 70°45W 83 C14
Portsmouth Ohio, U.S.A. 38°44N 82°57W 81 F12
Portsmouth R.I., U.S.A. 41°36N 71°15W 83 E13
Portsmouth Va., U.S.A. 36°58N 76°23W 81 G15
Portsmouth ☐ U.K. 50°48N 1°6W 13 G6
Portsoy U.K. 57°41N 2°41W 11 D6
Portstewart U.K. 55°11N 6°43W 10 A5
Porttipahdan tekojärvi
Finland 68°5N 26°40E 8 B22
Portugal ■ Europe 40°0N 8°0W 21 C1
Portumna Ireland 53°6N 8°14W 10 C3
Portville U.S.A. 42°3N 78°20W 82 D6
Poruma Australia 10°2S 143°4E 62 a
Porvenir Chile 53°10S 70°16W 96 G2
Posadas Argentina 27°30S 55°50W 95 B4
Posht-e Badam Iran 33°2N 55°23E 47 C7
Poso Indonesia 1°20S 120°55E 37 E6
Poso, Danau Indonesia 1°52S 120°35E 37 E6
Posse Brazil 14°4S 46°18W 93 F9
Possession I. Antarctica 72°4S 172°0E 5 D11
Possum Kingdom L.
U.S.A. 32°52N 98°26W 84 E5
Post U.S.A. 33°12N 101°23W 84 E4
Post Falls U.S.A. 47°43N 116°57W 76 C5
Postavy = Pastavy Belarus 55°4N 26°50E 9 J22
Poste-de-la-Baleine =
Kuujjuarapik Canada 55°20N 77°35W 72 A4
Postmasburg S. Africa 28°18S 23°5E 56 C3
Postojna Slovenia 45°46N 14°12E 16 F8
Poston U.S.A. 34°0N 114°24W 79 M12
Postville Canada 54°54N 59°47W 73 B8
Posyet Russia 42°39N 130°48E 28 C5
Potchefstroom S. Africa 26°41S 27°7E 56 C4
Poteau U.S.A. 35°3N 94°37W 84 D7
Poteet U.S.A. 29°2N 98°35W 84 G5
Potenza Italy 40°38N 15°48E 22 D6
Poteriteri, L. N.Z. 46°5S 167°10E 59 G1
Potgietersrus = Mokopane
S. Africa 24°10S 28°55E 57 B4
Poti Georgia 42°10N 41°38E 19 F7
Potiskum Nigeria 11°39N 11°2E 53 F8
Potomac → U.S.A. 38°0N 76°23W 81 F14
Potosí Bolivia 19°38S 65°50W 92 G5
Potosi Mt. U.S.A. 35°57N 115°29W 79 K11
Pototan Phil. 10°54N 122°38E 37 B6
Potrerillos Chile 26°30S 69°30W 94 B2
Potsdam U.S.A. 44°40N 74°59W 83 B10
Pottangi India 18°34N 82°58E 44 E6
Pottersville U.S.A. 43°43N 73°50W 83 C11
Pottstown U.S.A. 40°15N 75°39W 83 F9
Pottsville U.S.A. 40°41N 76°12W 83 F8
Pottuvil Sri Lanka 6°55N 81°50E 45 L5
P'otzu Taiwan 23°28N 120°15E 35 F13
Pouce Coupé Canada 55°40N 120°10W 70 B4
Poughkeepsie U.S.A. 41°42N 73°56W 83 E11
Poulaphouca Res. Ireland 53°8N 6°30W 10 C5
Poulsbo U.S.A. 47°44N 122°38W 78 C4
Poultney U.S.A. 43°31N 73°14W 83 C11
Poulton-le-Fylde U.K. 53°51N 2°58W 12 D5
Pouso Alegre Brazil 22°14S 45°57W 95 A6
Pouthisat Cambodia 12°34N 103°50E 38 F4
Považská Bystrica
Slovakia 49°8N 18°27E 17 D10
Povenets Russia 62°50N 34°50E 18 B5
Poverty B. N.Z. 38°43S 178°2E 59 C7
Poverty Point Nat. Monument ⌂
U.S.A. 32°39N 91°24W 84 E9
Póvoa de Varzim Portugal 41°25N 8°46W 21 B1
Povorotnyy, Mys Russia 42°40N 133°2E 28 C6
Povungnituk = Puvirnituq
Canada 60°2N 77°10W 69 E16
Powassan Canada 46°5N 79°25W 72 C4
Poway U.S.A. 32°58N 117°2W 79 N9
Powder → U.S.A. 46°45N 105°26W 76 C11
Powder River U.S.A. 43°2N 106°59W 76 E10
Powell U.S.A. 44°45N 108°46W 76 D9
Powell, L. U.S.A. 36°57N 111°29W 77 H8
Powell River Canada 49°50N 124°35W 70 D4
Powers U.S.A. 45°41N 87°32W 80 C10
Pownal U.S.A. 42°45N 73°14W 83 D11
Powys ☐ U.K. 52°20N 3°20W 13 E4
Poyang Hu China 29°5N 116°20E 35 C11
Poyarkovo Russia 49°36N 128°41E 27 E13
Poza Rica Mexico 20°33N 97°27W 87 C5
Požarevac Serbia 44°35N 21°18E 23 B9
Poznań Poland 52°25N 16°55E 17 B9
Pozo U.S.A. 35°20N 120°24W 79 K6
Pozo Almonte Chile 20°10S 69°50W 92 H5
Pozo Colorado Paraguay 23°30S 58°45W 94 A4
Pozoblanco Spain 38°23N 4°51W 21 C3
Pozzuoli Italy 40°49N 14°7E 22 D6
Prachin Buri Thailand 14°0N 101°25E 38 F3
Prachuap Khirikhan
Thailand 11°49N 99°48E 39 G2
Prado Brazil 17°20S 39°13W 93 G11
Prahita → India 19°0N 79°55E 44 E4
Praia Cabo Verde 15°2N 23°34W 52 b
Prainha Brazil 1°45S 53°30W 93 D8
Prainha Nova Brazil 7°10S 60°30W 92 E6
Prairie Australia 20°50S 144°35E 62 C3
Prairie City U.S.A. 44°28N 118°43W 76 D4
Prairie Dog Town Fork Red →
U.S.A. 34°34N 99°58W 84 D5
Prairie du Chien U.S.A. 43°3N 91°9W 80 D8
Prairies, L. of the
Canada 51°16N 101°32W 71 C8
Prambanan △ Indonesia 7°45S 110°28E 37 G14
Pran Buri Thailand 12°23N 99°55E 38 F2
Prapat Indonesia 2°41N 98°58E 36 D1
Praslin Seychelles 4°18S 55°45E 55 b
Prata Brazil 19°25S 48°54W 93 G9
Pratabpur India 23°28N 83°15E 43 H10
Pratapgarh Raj., India 24°2N 74°40E 42 G6
Pratapgarh Ut. P., India 25°56N 81°59E 43 G9
Pratas I. = Dongsha Dao
S. China Sea 20°45N 116°43E 35 G11
Prato Italy 43°53N 11°6E 22 C4
Pratt U.S.A. 37°39N 98°44W 80 G4
Prattville U.S.A. 32°28N 86°29W 85 E11
Pravara → India 19°35N 74°45E 44 E2
Pravia Spain 43°30N 6°12W 21 A2
Praya Indonesia 8°39S 116°17E 36 F5
Prayag = Allahabad
India 25°25N 81°58E 43 G9
Pre-delta △ Argentina 32°10S 60°40W 94 C3
Preah Seihanu = Kampong Saom
Cambodia 10°38N 103°30E 39 G4
Preah Vihear Cambodia 14°23N 104°41E 38 E5
Preble U.S.A. 42°44N 76°8W 83 D8
Precipice △ Australia 25°18S 150°5E 63 D5
Precordillera Argentina 30°0S 69°1W 94 C2
Preeceville Canada 51°57N 102°40W 71 C8
Preiļi Latvia 56°18N 26°43E 9 H22
Premont U.S.A. 27°22N 98°7W 84 H5
Prentice U.S.A. 45°33N 90°17W 80 C8
Preobrazheniye Russia 42°54N 133°54E 28 C6
Preparis I. = Pariparit Kyun
Myanmar 14°52N 93°41E 45 G11
Preparis North Channel
Ind. Oc. 15°27N 94°5E 45 G11
Preparis South Channel
Ind. Oc. 14°33N 93°30E 45 G11
Přerov Czechia 49°28N 17°27E 17 D9
Prescott Canada 44°45N 75°30W 83 B9
Prescott Ariz., U.S.A. 34°33N 112°28W 77 J7
Prescott Ark., U.S.A. 33°48N 93°23W 84 E8
Prescott Valley U.S.A. 34°40N 112°18W 77 J7
Preservation Inlet N.Z. 46°8S 166°35E 59 G1
Presho U.S.A. 43°54N 100°3W 80 D3
Presidencia de la Plaza
Argentina 27°0S 59°50W 94 B4
Presidencia Roque Saenz Peña
Argentina 26°45S 60°30W 94 B3
Presidente Epitácio Brazil 21°56S 52°6W 93 H8
Presidente Hayes ☐
Paraguay 24°0S 59°0W 94 A4
Presidente Prudente
Brazil 22°5S 51°25W 95 A5
Presidio U.S.A. 29°34N 104°22W 84 G2
Prešov Slovakia 49°0N 21°15E 17 D11
Prespa, L. = Prespansko Jezero
Macedonia 40°55N 21°0E 23 D9
Prespansko Jezero
Macedonia 40°55N 21°0E 23 D9
Presque I. U.S.A. 42°10N 80°6W 82 D4
Presque Isle U.S.A. 46°41N 68°1W 81 B19
Prestatyn U.K. 53°20N 3°24W 12 D4
Presteigne U.K. 52°17N 3°0W 13 E5
Preston Canada 43°23N 80°21W 82 C4
Preston U.K. 53°46N 2°42W 12 D5
Preston Idaho, U.S.A. 42°6N 111°53W 76 E8
Preston Minn., U.S.A. 43°40N 92°5W 80 D7
Preston, C. Australia 20°51S 116°12E 60 D2
Prestonsburg U.S.A. 37°40N 82°47W 81 G12
Prestwick U.K. 55°29N 4°37W 11 F4
Pretoria S. Africa 25°44S 28°12E 57 C4
Preveza Greece 38°57N 20°45E 23 E9
Prey Veng Cambodia 11°35N 105°29E 39 G5
Pribaykalsky △ Russia 52°30N 106°0E 27 D11
Pribilof Is. U.S.A. 57°0N 170°0W 74 D6
Příbram Czechia 49°41N 14°2E 16 D8
Price U.S.A. 39°36N 110°49W 76 G8
Price, C. India 13°34N 93°3E 45 H11
Price I. Canada 52°23N 128°41W 70 C3
Prichard U.S.A. 30°44N 88°5W 85 F10
Priekule Latvia 56°26N 21°35E 9 H19
Prienai Lithuania 54°38N 23°57E 9 J20
Prieska S. Africa 29°40S 22°42E 56 C3
Priest L. U.S.A. 48°35N 116°52W 76 B5
Priest River U.S.A. 48°11N 116°55W 76 B5
Priest Valley U.S.A. 36°10N 120°39W 78 J6
Prievidza Slovakia 48°46N 18°36E 17 D10
Prikaspiyskaya Nizmennost =
Caspian Depression
Eurasia 47°0N 48°0E 19 E8
Prilep Macedonia 41°21N 21°32E 23 D9
Priluki = Pryluky
Ukraine 50°30N 32°24E 19 D5
Prime Hd. Antarctica 63°12S 48°57W 5 C18
Prime Seal I. Australia 40°3S 147°43E 63 G4
Primo Tapia Mexico 32°16N 116°54W 79 N10
Primorskiy Kray ☐ Russia 45°0N 135°0E 28 B7
Primrose L. Canada 54°55N 109°45W 71 C7
Prince Albert Canada 53°15N 105°50W 71 C7
Prince Albert S. Africa 33°12S 22°2E 56 D3
Prince Albert △ Canada 54°0N 106°25W 71 C7
Prince Albert Mts.
Antarctica 76°0S 161°30E 5 D11
Prince Albert Pen.
Canada 72°30N 116°0W 68 C8
Prince Albert Sd. Canada 70°25N 115°0W 68 C9
Prince Alfred, C. Canada 74°20N 124°40W 4 B1
Prince Charles I.
Canada 67°47N 76°12W 69 D16
Prince Charles Mts.
Antarctica 72°0S 67°0E 5 D6
Prince Edward Fracture Zone
Ind. Oc. 46°0S 35°0E 5 A4
Prince Edward I. ☐
Canada 46°20N 63°20W 73 C7
Prince Edward Is. Ind. Oc. 46°35S 38°0E 3 G11
Prince George Canada 53°55N 122°50W 70 C4
Prince of Wales, C.
U.S.A. 65°36N 168°5W 74 B6
Prince of Wales I.
Australia 10°40S 142°10E 62 A3
Prince of Wales I. Canada 73°0N 99°0W 68 C12
Prince of Wales I.
U.S.A. 55°47N 132°50W 68 F5
Prince of Wales Icefield
Canada 78°15N 79°0W 69 B16
Prince of Wales Str.
Canada 73°0N 117°0W 68 C8
Prince Patrick I. Canada 77°0N 120°0W 69 B8
Prince Regent Inlet
Canada 73°0N 90°0W 69 C14
Prince Rupert Canada 54°20N 130°20W 70 C2
Prince William Sd.
U.S.A. 60°40N 147°0W 68 E2
Princes Town
Trin. & Tob. 10°16N 61°23W 93 K15
Princess Charlotte B.
Australia 14°25S 144°0E 62 A3
Princess Elizabeth Trough
S. Ocean 64°10S 83°0E 5 C7

154 Princess May Ranges
INDEX TO WORLD MAPS

Princess May Ranges Australia 15°30S 125°30E 60 C4
Princess Royal I. Canada 53°0N 128°40W 70 C3
Princeton Canada 49°27N 120°30W 70 D4
Princeton Calif., U.S.A. 39°24N 122°1W 78 F4
Princeton Ill., U.S.A. 41°23N 89°28W 80 E9
Princeton Ind., U.S.A. 38°21N 87°34W 80 F10
Princeton Ky., U.S.A. 37°7N 87°53W 80 G10
Princeton Mo., U.S.A. 40°24N 93°35W 80 E7
Princeton N.J., U.S.A. 40°21N 74°39W 83 F10
Princeton W. Va., U.S.A. 37°22N 81°6W 81 G13
Príncipe São Tomé & Príncipe 1°37N 7°25E 50 F4
Principe da Beira Brazil 12°20S 64°30W 92 F6
Prineville U.S.A. 44°18N 120°51W 76 D3
Prins Harald Kyst Antarctica 70°0S 35°1E 5 D4
Prinsesse Astrid Kyst Antarctica 70°45S 12°30E 5 D3
Prinsesse Ragnhild Kyst Antarctica 70°15S 27°30E 5 D4
Prinzapolca Nic. 13°20N 83°35W 88 D3
Priozersk Russia 61°2N 30°7E 8 F24
Pripet = Prypyat → Europe 51°20N 30°15E 17 C16
Pripet Marshes Europe 52°10N 27°10E 17 B15
Pripyat Marshes = Pripet Marshes Europe 52°10N 27°10E 17 B15
Pripyats = Prypyat → Europe 51°20N 30°15E 17 C16
Prishtinë Kosovo 42°40N 21°13E 23 C9
Priština = Prishtinë Kosovo 42°40N 21°13E 23 C9
Privas France 44°45N 4°37E 20 D6
Privolzhskaya Vozvyshennost Russia 51°0N 46°0E 19 D8
Privolzhskiy □ Russia 56°0N 50°0E 26 D6
Prizren Kosovo 42°13N 20°45E 23 C9
Probolinggo Indonesia 7°46S 113°13E 37 G15
Proctor U.S.A. 43°40N 73°2W 83 C11
Proddatur India 14°45N 78°30E 45 G4
Profondeville Belgium 50°23N 4°52E 15 D4
Progreso Coahuila, Mexico 27°28N 100°59W 86 B4
Progreso Yucatán, Mexico 21°20N 89°40W 87 C7
Progress Antarctica 66°22S 76°22E 5 C12
Progress Russia 49°45N 129°37E 27 E13
Prokopyevsk Russia 54°0N 86°45E 26 D9
Prokuplje Serbia 43°16N 21°36E 23 C9
Prome = Pye Myanmar 18°49N 95°13E 41 K19
Prophet → Canada 58°48N 122°40W 70 B4
Prophet River Canada 58°6N 122°43W 70 B4
Propriá Brazil 10°13S 36°51W 93 F11
Propriano France 41°41N 8°52E 20 F8
Proserpine Australia 20°21S 148°36E 62 b
Prosna → Poland 52°6N 17°44E 17 B9
Prospect U.S.A. 43°18N 75°9W 83 C9
Prosser U.S.A. 46°12N 119°46W 76 C4
Prostějov Czechia 49°30N 17°9E 17 D9
Proston Australia 26°8S 151°32E 63 D5
Provence France 43°40N 5°46E 20 E6
Providence Ky., U.S.A. 37°24N 87°46W 80 G10
Providence R.I., U.S.A. 41°49N 71°24W 83 E13
Providence Bay Canada 45°41N 82°15W 72 C3
Providence Mts. U.S.A. 35°10N 115°15W 79 K11
Providencia, I. de Caribbean 13°25N 81°26W 88 D3
Provideniya Russia 64°23N 173°18W 27 C19
Provincetown U.S.A. 42°3N 70°11W 81 D18
Provins France 48°33N 3°15E 20 B5
Provo U.S.A. 40°14N 111°39W 76 F8
Provost Canada 52°25N 110°20W 71 C6
Prudhoe Bay U.S.A. 70°18N 148°22W 74 A10
Prudhoe I. Australia 21°19S 149°41E 62 C4
Prud'homme Canada 52°20N 105°54W 71 C7
Pruszków Poland 52°9N 20°49E 17 B11
Prut → Romania 45°28N 28°10E 17 F15
Pruzhany Belarus 52°33N 24°28E 17 B13
Prydz B. Antarctica 69°0S 74°0E 5 C6
Pryluky Ukraine 50°30N 32°24E 19 D5
Pryor U.S.A. 36°19N 95°19W 84 C7
Prypyat → Europe 51°20N 30°15E 17 C16
Prypyatsky △ Belarus 52°0N 28°0E 17 C14
Przemyśl Poland 49°50N 22°45E 17 D12
Przhevalsk = Karakol Kyrgyzstan 42°30N 78°20E 30 C4
Psara Greece 38°37N 25°38E 23 E11
Psiloritis, Oros Greece 35°15N 24°45E 23 G11
Pskov Russia 57°50N 28°25E 9 H23
Ptich = Ptsich → Belarus 52°9N 28°52E 17 B15
Ptolemaida Greece 40°30N 21°43E 23 D9
Ptsich → Belarus 52°9N 28°52E 17 B15
Pu Xian China 36°24N 111°6E 32 F6
Pua Thailand 19°11N 100°55E 38 C3
Puán Argentina 37°30S 62°45W 94 D3
Pu'an China 25°46N 104°57E 34 E5
Pu'apu'a Samoa 13°34S 172°9W 59 b
Pubei China 22°16N 109°31E 34 F7
Pucallpa Peru 8°25S 74°30W 92 E4
Pucheng China 27°59N 118°31E 35 D12
Puch'on = Bucheon S. Korea 37°28N 126°45E 33 F14
Pudasjärvi Finland 65°23N 26°53E 8 D22
Puding China 26°18N 105°44E 34 D5
Pudozh Russia 61°48N 36°32E 18 B6
Pudu = Suizhou China 31°42N 113°24E 35 B9
Puducherry India 11°59N 79°50E 45 J4
Pudukkottai India 10°28N 78°47E 45 J4
Puebla Mexico 19°3N 98°12W 87 D5
Puebla □ Mexico 18°50N 98°0W 87 D5
Pueblo U.S.A. 38°16N 104°37W 76 G11
Puelches Argentina 38°5S 65°51W 94 D2
Puelén Argentina 37°32S 67°38W 94 D2
Puente Alto Chile 33°32S 70°35W 94 C1
Puente-Genil Spain 37°22N 4°47W 21 D3
Pu'er China 23°0N 101°15E 34 F3
Puerca, Pta. Puerto Rico 18°13N 65°36W 89 d
Puerco → U.S.A. 34°22N 107°50W 77 J10
Puerto Aisén Chile 45°27S 73°0W 96 F2
Puerto Ángel Mexico 15°40N 96°29W 87 D5
Puerto Arista Mexico 15°56N 93°48W 87 D6
Puerto Armuelles Panama 8°20N 82°51W 88 E3
Puerto Ayacucho Venezuela 5°40N 67°35W 92 B5
Puerto Barrios Guatemala 15°40N 88°32W 88 C2
Puerto Bermejo Argentina 26°55S 58°34W 94 B4
Puerto Bermúdez Peru 10°20S 74°58W 92 F4
Puerto Bolívar Ecuador 3°19S 79°55W 92 D3
Puerto Cabello Venezuela 10°28N 68°1W 92 A5
Puerto Cabezas Nic. 14°0N 83°30W 88 D3
Puerto Cabo Gracias á Dios Nic. 15°0N 83°10W 88 D3
Puerto Carreño Colombia 6°12N 67°22W 92 B5
Puerto Castilla Honduras 16°0N 86°0W 88 C2
Puerto Chicama Peru 7°45S 79°20W 92 E3
Puerto Coig Argentina 50°54S 69°15W 96 G3
Puerto Cortés Honduras 15°51N 88°0W 88 C2
Puerto Cumarebo Venezuela 11°29N 69°30W 92 A5
Puerto de los Angeles ⌂ Mexico 23°39N 105°45W 86 C3
Puerto del Rosario Canary Is. 28°30N 13°52W 52 C3
Puerto Deseado Argentina 47°55S 66°0W 96 F3
Puerto Escondido Mexico 15°50N 97°3W 87 D5
Puerto Heath Bolivia 12°34S 68°39W 92 F5
Puerto Inírida Colombia 3°53N 67°52W 92 C5
Puerto Juárez Mexico 21°11N 86°49W 87 C7
Puerto La Cruz Venezuela 10°13N 64°38W 92 A6
Puerto Leguízamo Colombia 0°12S 74°46W 92 D4
Puerto Lempira Honduras 15°16N 83°46W 88 C3
Puerto Libertad Mexico 29°55N 112°43W 86 B2
Puerto Limón Colombia 3°23N 73°30W 92 C4
Puerto Lobos Argentina 42°0S 65°3W 96 E3
Puerto Madryn Argentina 42°48S 65°4W 96 E3
Puerto Maldonado Peru 12°30S 69°10W 92 F5
Puerto Manatí Cuba 21°22N 76°50W 88 B4
Puerto Montt Chile 41°28S 73°0W 96 E2
Puerto Morazán Nic. 12°51N 87°11W 88 D2
Puerto Morelos Mexico 20°50N 86°52W 87 C7
Puerto Natales Chile 51°45S 72°15W 96 G2
Puerto Oscuro Chile 31°24S 71°35W 94 C1
Puerto Padre Cuba 21°13N 76°35W 88 B4
Puerto Páez Venezuela 6°13N 67°28W 92 B5
Puerto Peñasco Mexico 31°20N 113°33W 86 A2
Puerto Pinasco Paraguay 22°36S 57°50W 94 A4
Puerto Plata Dom. Rep. 19°48N 70°45W 89 C5
Puerto Princesa Phil. 9°46N 118°45E 37 C5
Puerto Quepos Costa Rica 9°29N 84°6W 88 E3
Puerto Rico ☒ W. Indies 18°15N 66°45W 89 d
Puerto Rico Trench Atl. Oc. 19°50N 66°0W 89 C6
Puerto San Julián Argentina 49°18S 67°43W 96 F3
Puerto Santa Cruz Argentina 50°0S 68°32W 96 G3
Puerto Sastre Paraguay 22°2S 57°55W 94 A4
Puerto Suárez Bolivia 18°58S 57°52W 92 G7
Puerto Vallarta Mexico 20°37N 105°15W 86 C3
Puerto Varas Chile 41°19S 72°59W 96 E2
Puerto Wilches Colombia 7°21N 73°54W 92 B4
Puertollano Spain 38°43N 4°7W 21 C3
Pueu Tahiti 17°44S 149°13W 59 d
Pueyrredón, L. Argentina 47°20S 72°0W 96 F2
Puffin I. Ireland 51°50N 10°24W 10 E1
Pugachev Russia 52°0N 48°49E 18 D8
Pugal India 28°30N 72°48E 42 E5
Puge China 27°20N 102°31E 34 D4
Puget Sound U.S.A. 47°50N 122°30W 78 C4
Pugŏdong N. Korea 42°5N 130°0E 33 C16
Pūgūnzī Iran 25°49N 59°10E 47 E8
Puigcerdà Spain 42°24N 1°50E 21 A6
Puijiang China 30°14N 103°30E 34 B4
Pujiang China 29°29N 119°54E 35 C12
Pujon-ho N. Korea 40°35N 127°35E 33 D14
Pukaki, L. N.Z. 44°4S 170°1E 59 F3
Pukapuka Cook Is. 10°53S 165°49W 65 J11
Pukaskwa △ Canada 48°20N 86°0W 72 C2
Pukatawagan Canada 55°45N 101°20W 71 B8
Pukchin N. Korea 40°12N 125°45E 33 D13
Pukch'ŏng N. Korea 40°14N 128°19E 33 D15
Pukekohe N.Z. 37°12S 174°55E 59 B5
Pukhrayan India 26°14N 79°51E 43 F8
Puksubaek-san N. Korea 40°42N 127°45E 33 D14
Pula Croatia 44°54N 13°57E 16 F7
Pulacayo Bolivia 20°25S 66°41W 92 H5
Pulandian China 39°25N 121°58E 33 E11
Pulaski N.Y., U.S.A. 43°34N 76°8W 83 C8
Pulaski Tenn., U.S.A. 35°12N 87°2W 85 D11
Pulaski Va., U.S.A. 37°3N 80°47W 81 G13
Pulau → Indonesia 5°50S 138°15E 37 F9
Pulau Gili Indonesia 8°21S 116°1E 37 J19
Puławy Poland 51°23N 21°59E 17 C11
Pulga U.S.A. 39°48N 121°29W 78 F5
Pulgaon India 20°44N 78°21E 44 D4
Pulicat India 13°25N 80°19E 45 H5
Pulicat L. India 13°40N 80°15E 45 H5
Pulivendla India 14°25N 78°14E 45 G4
Puliyangudi India 9°11N 77°24E 45 K3
Pullman U.S.A. 46°44N 117°10W 76 C5
Pulog, Mt. Phil. 16°40N 120°50E 37 A6
Pułtusk Poland 52°43N 21°6E 17 B11
Pumlumon Fawr U.K. 52°28N 3°46W 13 E4
Puná, I. Ecuador 2°55S 80°5W 92 D2
Punaauia Tahiti 17°37S 149°34W 59 d
Punakaiki N.Z. 42°7S 171°20E 59 E3
Punakha Dzong Bhutan 27°42N 89°52E 41 F16
Punalur India 9°0N 76°56E 45 K3
Punasar India 27°6N 73°6E 42 F5
Punata Bolivia 17°32S 65°50W 92 G5
Punch India 33°48N 74°4E 43 C6
Punch → Pakistan 33°12N 73°40E 42 C5
Punda Maria S. Africa 22°40S 31°5E 57 B5
Pune India 18°29N 73°57E 44 E1
P'ungsan N. Korea 40°50N 128°9E 33 D15
Puning China 23°20N 116°12E 35 F11
Punjab □ India 31°0N 76°0E 42 D7
Punjab □ Pakistan 32°0N 72°30E 42 E6
Puno Peru 15°55S 70°3W 92 G4
Punpun → India 25°31N 85°18E 43 G11
Punta, Cerro de Puerto Rico 18°10N 66°37W 89 d
Punta Alta Argentina 38°53S 62°4W 96 D4
Punta Arenas Chile 53°10S 71°0W 96 G2
Punta del Díaz Chile 28°0S 70°45W 94 B1
Punta Gorda Belize 16°10N 88°45W 87 D7
Punta Gorda U.S.A. 26°56N 82°3W 85 H13
Punta Prieta Mexico 28°58N 114°17W 86 B2
Puntarenas Costa Rica 10°0N 84°50W 88 E3
Puntland Somalia 9°0N 50°0E 49 F4
Punto Fijo Venezuela 11°50N 70°13W 92 A4
Punxsutawney U.S.A. 40°57N 78°59W 82 F6
Pupuan Indonesia 8°19S 115°0E 37 J18
Puqi China 29°40N 113°50E 35 C9
Puquio Peru 14°45S 74°10W 92 F4
Pur → Russia 67°31N 77°55E 26 C8
Puracé, Vol. Colombia 2°21N 76°23W 92 C3
Puralia = Puruliya India 23°17N 86°24E 43 H12
Puranpur India 28°31N 80°9E 43 E9
Purbalingga Indonesia 7°23S 109°21E 37 G13
Purbeck, Isle of U.K. 50°39N 1°59W 13 G5
Purcell U.S.A. 35°1N 97°22W 84 D6
Purcell Mts. Canada 49°55N 116°15W 70 D5
Purdy Canada 45°19N 77°44W 82 A7
Puri India 19°50N 85°58E 44 E7
Purmerend Neths. 52°32N 4°58E 15 B4
Purna → India 19°6N 77°2E 44 E3
Purnia India 25°45N 87°31E 43 G12
Purnululu △ Australia 17°20S 128°20E 60 C4
Pursat = Pouthisat Cambodia 12°34N 103°50E 38 F4
Purukcahu Indonesia 0°35S 114°35E 36 E4
Puruliya India 23°17N 86°24E 43 H12
Purus → Brazil 3°42S 61°28W 92 D6
Puruvesi Finland 61°50N 29°30E 8 F23
Purvis U.S.A. 31°9N 89°25W 85 F10
Purwa India 26°28N 80°47E 43 F9
Purwakarta Indonesia 6°35S 107°29E 37 G12
Purwo, Tanjung Indonesia 8°44S 114°21E 37 K18
Purwodadi Indonesia 7°7S 110°55E 37 G14
Purwokerto Indonesia 7°25S 109°14E 37 G13
Puryŏng N. Korea 42°5N 129°43E 33 C15
Pus → India 19°55N 77°55E 44 E3
Pusa India 25°59N 85°41E 43 G11
Pusad India 19°56N 77°36E 44 E3
Pusan = Busan S. Korea 35°5N 129°0E 33 G15
Pushkin Russia 59°45N 30°25E 9 G24
Pushkino Russia 51°16N 47°0E 19 D8
Put-in-Bay U.S.A. 41°39N 82°49W 82 E2
Putahow L. Canada 59°54N 100°40W 71 B8
Putao Myanmar 27°28N 97°30E 41 F20
Putaruru N.Z. 38°2S 175°50E 59 C5
Puteran Indonesia 7°5S 114°0E 37 G15
Putian China 25°23N 119°0E 35 E12
Putignano Italy 40°51N 17°7E 22 D7
Puting, Tanjung Indonesia 3°31S 111°46E 36 E4
Putnam U.S.A. 41°55N 71°55W 83 E13
Putorana, Gory Russia 69°0N 95°0E 27 C10
Putrajaya Malaysia 2°55N 101°40E 39 L3
Puttalam Sri Lanka 8°1N 79°55E 45 K5
Puttalam Lagoon Sri Lanka 8°15N 79°45E 45 K4
Puttgarden Germany 54°30N 11°10E 16 A6
Puttur Andhra Pradesh, India 13°27N 79°33E 45 H4
Puttur Karnataka, India 12°46N 75°12E 45 H2
Putumayo → S. Amer. 3°7S 67°58W 92 D5
Putuo China 29°56N 122°20E 35 C14
Putussibau Indonesia 0°50N 112°56E 36 D4
Puvirnituq Canada 60°2N 77°10W 69 E16
Puy-de-Dôme France 45°46N 2°57E 20 D5
Puyallup U.S.A. 47°12N 122°18W 78 C4
Puyang China 35°40N 115°1E 32 G8
Pūzeh Rīg Iran 27°20N 58°40E 47 E8
Pweto Dem. Rep. of the Congo 8°25S 28°51E 54 F5
Pwllheli U.K. 52°53N 4°25W 12 E3
Pyaozero, Ozero Russia 66°5N 30°58E 8 C24
Pyapon Myanmar 16°20N 95°40E 41 L19
Pyasina → Russia 73°30N 87°0E 27 B9
Pyatigorsk Russia 44°2N 43°6E 19 F7
Pyay = Pye Myanmar 18°49N 95°13E 41 K19
Pye Myanmar 18°49N 95°13E 41 K19
Pyeongtaek S. Korea 37°1N 127°4E 33 F14
Pyetrikaw Belarus 52°11N 28°29E 17 B15
Pyhäjoki → Finland 64°28N 24°14E 8 D21
Pyhätunturi △ Finland 66°58N 27°5E 8 C22
Pyin-U-Lwin Myanmar 22°2N 96°28E 38 A1
Pyinmana Myanmar 19°45N 96°12E 41 K20
Pymatuning Res. U.S.A. 41°30N 80°28W 82 E4
Pyŏktong N. Korea 40°50N 125°50E 33 D13
P'yŏnggang N. Korea 38°24N 127°17E 33 E14
P'yŏngsong N. Korea 39°14N 125°52E 33 E13
P'yŏngyang N. Korea 39°0N 125°30E 33 E13
Pyote U.S.A. 31°32N 103°8W 84 F3
Pyramid L. U.S.A. 40°1N 119°35W 76 F4
Pyramid Pk. U.S.A. 36°25N 116°37W 79 J10
Pyrénées Europe 42°45N 0°18E 20 E4
Pyu Myanmar 18°30N 96°28E 41 K20

Q

Qaanaaq Greenland 77°30N 69°10W 69 B18
Qachasnek S. Africa 30°6S 28°42E 57 D4
Qa'el Jafr Jordan 30°20N 36°25E 48 E5
Qa'emābād Iran 31°44N 60°2E 47 D9
Qā'emshahr Iran 36°30N 52°53E 47 B7
Qagan Nur Jilin, China 45°15N 124°18E 33 B13
Qagan Nur Nei Monggol Zizhiqu, China 43°30N 114°55E 32 C8
Qahar Youyi Zhongqi China 41°12N 112°40E 32 D7
Qahremānshahr = Kermānshāh Iran 34°23N 47°0E 46 C5
Qaidam Pendi China 37°0N 95°0E 30 D8
Qajarīyeh Iran 31°1N 48°22E 47 D6
Qala-i-Jadid = Spīn Būldak Afghan. 31°1N 66°25E 42 D2
Qala Viala Pakistan 30°49N 67°17E 42 D2
Qala Yangi Afghan. 34°20N 66°30E 42 B2
Qal'at al Akhḑar Si. Arabia 28°4N 37°9E 46 E3
Qal'at Dīzah Iraq 36°11N 45°7E 46 B5
Qal'at Şāliḩ Iraq 31°31N 47°16E 46 D5
Qal'at Sukkar Iraq 31°51N 46°5E 46 D5
Qamani'tuaq = Baker Lake Canada 64°20N 96°3W 68 E12
Qamdo China 31°15N 97°6E 34 B1
Qamea Fiji 16°45S 179°45W 59 a
Qamruddin Karez Pakistan 31°45N 68°20E 42 D3
Qandahār = Kandahār Afghan. 31°32N 65°43E 40 D4
Qandahār = Kandahār □ Afghan. 31°0N 65°0E 40 D4
Qandyaghash Kazakhstan 49°28N 57°25E 19 E10
Qapān Iran 37°40N 55°47E 47 B7
Qapshaghay Kazakhstan 43°51N 77°14E 26 E8
Qaqortoq Greenland 60°43N 46°0W 4 C5
Qara Qash → China 35°0N 78°30E 43 B8
Qarabutaq Kazakhstan 50°0N 60°14E 26 E7
Qaraghandy Kazakhstan 49°50N 73°10E 30 B3
Qaraghayly Kazakhstan 49°26N 76°0E 26 E8
Qārah Si. Arabia 29°55N 40°3E 46 D4
Qarataū Ongtüstik Qazaqstan, Kazakhstan 43°30N 69°30E 26 E7
Qarataū Zhambyl, Kazakhstan 43°10N 70°28E 26 E8
Qarazhal Kazakhstan 48°2N 70°49E 26 E8
Qarchak Iran 35°25N 51°34E 47 C6
Qardho Somalia 9°30N 49°6E 49 F4
Qareh → Iran 39°25N 47°22E 46 B5
Qareh Tekān Iran 36°38N 49°29E 47 B6
Qarnein U.A.E. 24°56N 52°52E 47 E7
Qarqan He → China 39°30N 88°30E 30 D6
Qarqaraly Kazakhstan 49°26N 75°30E 30 B4
Qarshi Uzbekistan 38°53N 65°48E 26 F7
Qartabā Lebanon 34°4N 35°50E 48 A4
Qārūh Kuwait 28°49N 48°46E 47 D6
Qaryat al Gharab Iraq 31°27N 44°48E 46 D5
Qaryat al 'Ulyā Si. Arabia 27°33N 47°42E 46 E5
Qasr 'Amra Jordan 31°48N 36°35E 46 D3
Qaşr-e Qand Iran 26°15N 60°45E 47 E9
Qaşr-e Shīrīn Iran 34°31N 45°35E 46 C5
Qasr Farâfra Egypt 27°0N 28°1E 53 C11
Qasuittuq = Resolute Canada 74°42N 94°54W 69 C13
Qatanā Syria 33°26N 36°4E 48 B5
Qatar ■ Asia 25°30N 51°15E 47 E6
Qatlīsh Iran 37°50N 57°19E 47 B8
Qattâra, Munkhafed el Egypt 29°30N 27°30E 53 C11
Qattâra Depression = Qattâra, Munkhafed el Egypt 29°30N 27°30E 53 C11
Qausuittuq △ Canada 76°0N 101°0W 69 B11
Qawām al Ḩamzah = Al Ḩamzah Iraq 31°43N 44°58E 46 D5
Qāyen Iran 33°40N 59°10E 47 C8
Qazaqstan = Kazakhstan ■ Asia 50°0N 70°0E 26 E8
Qazımämmäd Azerbaijan 40°3N 49°0E 47 A6
Qazvīn Iran 36°15N 50°0E 47 B6
Qazvīn □ Iran 36°20N 50°0E 47 B6
Qena Egypt 26°10N 32°43E 53 C12
Qeqertarsuaq Qaasuitsup, Greenland 69°45N 53°30W 4 C5
Qeqertarsuaq Qaasuitsup, Greenland 69°15N 53°38W 4 C5
Qeshlāq Iran 34°55N 46°28E 46 C5
Qeshm Iran 26°55N 56°10E 47 E8
Qeys Iran 26°32N 53°58E 47 E7
Qezel Owzen → Iran 36°45N 49°22E 47 B6
Qezi'ot Israel 30°52N 34°26E 48 E3
Qi Xian China 34°40N 114°48E 32 G8
Qian Gorlos China 45°5N 124°42E 33 B13
Qian Hai China 22°32N 113°54E 31 a
Qian Xian China 34°31N 108°15E 32 G5
Qian'an China 40°0N 118°41E 33 E10
Qiancheng China 27°12N 109°50E 34 D7
Qianjiang Guangxi Zhuangzu, China 23°38N 108°58E 34 F7
Qianjiang Hubei, China 30°24N 112°55E 35 B9
Qianjiang Sichuan, China 29°33N 108°47E 34 C7
Qianjin China 47°34N 133°4E 31 B15
Qianshan Anhui, China 30°37N 116°35E 35 B11
Qianshan Guangdong, China 22°15N 113°31E 31 a
Qianwei China 29°13N 103°56E 34 C4
Qianxi China 27°3N 106°3E 34 D6
Qianyang Hunan, China 27°18N 110°10E 35 D8
Qianyang Shaanxi, China 34°40N 107°8E 32 G4
Qianyang Zhejiang, China 30°11N 119°25E 35 B12
Qi'ao China 22°25N 113°39E 31 a
Qi'ao Dao China 22°25N 113°38E 31 a
Qiaocun China 39°56N 112°55E 32 E7
Qiaojia China 26°56N 102°58E 34 D4
Qichun China 30°18N 115°25E 35 B10
Qidong Hunan, China 26°49N 112°7E 35 D9
Qidong Jiangsu, China 31°48N 121°38E 35 B13
Qiemo China 38°8N 85°32E 30 D6
Qijiang China 28°57N 106°35E 34 C6
Qijiaojing China 43°28N 91°36E 30 C7
Qikiqtaaluk = Baffin I. Canada 68°0N 75°0W 69 D17
Qikiqtarjuaq Canada 67°33N 63°0W 69 D19
Qila Saifullāh Pakistan 30°45N 68°17E 42 D3
Qilian Shan China 38°30N 96°0E 30 D8
Qimen China 29°50N 117°42E 35 C11
Qin He → China 35°1N 113°22E 32 G7
Qin Jiang → Guangxi Zhuangzu, China 21°53N 108°35E 34 F7
Qin Jiang → Jiangxi, China 26°15N 115°55E 35 D10
Qin Ling = Qinling Shandi China 33°50N 108°10E 32 H5
Qin'an China 34°48N 105°40E 32 G3
Qing Xian China 38°35N 116°45E 32 E9
Qingcheng China 37°15N 117°40E 33 F9
Qingcheng Shan China 30°58N 103°31E 34 B4
Qingchuan China 32°36N 105°9E 32 H3
Qingdao China 36°5N 120°20E 33 F11
Qingfeng China 35°52N 115°8E 32 G8
Qinghai □ China 36°0N 98°0E 30 D8
Qinghai Hu China 36°40N 100°10E 30 D9
Qinghecheng China 41°28N 124°15E 33 D13
Qinghemen China 41°48N 121°25E 33 D11
Qingjian China 37°8N 110°8E 32 F6
Qingjiang = Huaiyin China 33°30N 119°2E 33 H10
Qingliu China 26°11N 116°48E 35 D11
Qinglong China 25°49N 105°12E 34 E5
Qingping China 26°39N 107°47E 34 D6
Qingshui China 34°48N 106°8E 32 G4
Qingshuihe China 39°55N 111°35E 32 E6
Qingtian China 28°12N 120°15E 35 C13
Qingtongxia China 38°2N 106°3E 32 E4
Qingtongxia Shuiku China 37°50N 105°58E 32 F3
Qingxi China 27°8N 108°43E 34 D7
Qingxu China 37°34N 112°22E 32 F7
Qingyang Anhui, China 30°38N 117°50E 35 B11
Qingyang Gansu, China 36°2N 107°55E 32 F4
Qingyi Jiang → China 29°32N 103°44E 34 C4
Qingyuan Guangdong, China 23°40N 112°59E 35 F9
Qingyuan Liaoning, China 42°10N 124°55E 33 C13
Qingyuan Zhejiang, China 27°36N 119°3E 35 D12
Qingyun China 37°45N 117°20E 33 F9
Qingzhen China 26°31N 106°25E 34 D6
Qinhuangdao China 39°56N 119°30E 33 E10
Qinling Shandi China 33°50N 108°10E 32 H5
Qinshui China 35°40N 112°8E 32 G7
Qinyang = Jiyuan China 35°7N 112°57E 32 G7
Qinyang China 35°12N 112°56E 32 G7
Qinyuan China 36°29N 112°20E 32 F7
Qinzhou China 21°58N 108°38E 34 G7
Qionghai China 19°15N 110°26E 38 C8
Qionglai China 30°25N 103°31E 34 B4
Qionglai Shan China 31°0N 102°30E 34 B4
Qiongshan China 19°51N 110°26E 38 C8
Qiongzhou Haixia China 20°10N 110°15E 38 B8
Qiqihar China 47°26N 124°0E 31 B13
Qira China 37°0N 80°48E 30 D5
Qiraîya, W. → Egypt 30°27N 34°0E 48 E3
Qiryat Ata Israel 32°47N 35°6E 48 C4
Qiryat Gat Israel 31°32N 34°46E 48 D3
Qiryat Mal'akhi Israel 31°44N 34°44E 48 D3
Qiryat Shemona Israel 33°13N 35°35E 48 B4
Qiryat Yam Israel 32°51N 35°4E 48 C4
Qishan China 34°25N 107°38E 32 G4
Qitai China 44°2N 89°35E 30 C6
Qitaihe China 45°48N 130°51E 28 B5
Qiubei China 24°2N 104°12E 34 E5
Qixia China 37°17N 120°52E 33 F11
Qiyang China 26°35N 111°50E 35 D8
Qızılağac Körfäzi Azerbaijan 39°9N 49°0E 47 B6
Qods Iran 35°45N 51°15E 47 C6
Qojūr Iran 36°12N 47°55E 46 B5
Qom Iran 34°40N 51°0E 47 C6
Qom □ Iran 34°40N 51°0E 47 C6
Qomolangma Feng = Everest, Mt. Nepal 28°5N 86°58E 43 E12
Qomsheh Iran 32°0N 51°55E 47 D6
Qoqek = Tacheng China 46°40N 82°58E 30 B5
Qoqon = Qo'qon Uzbekistan 40°31N 70°56E 26 E8
Qo'qon Uzbekistan 40°31N 70°56E 26 E8
Qoraqalpog'istan □ Uzbekistan 43°0N 58°0E 26 E6
Qorveh Iran 35°10N 47°48E 46 C5
Qosshaghyl Kazakhstan 46°40N 54°0E 19 E9
Qostanay Kazakhstan 53°10N 63°35E 26 D7
Qu Jiang → China 30°1N 106°24E 34 B6
Qu Xian China 30°48N 106°58E 34 B6
Quabbin Res. U.S.A. 42°20N 72°20W 83 D12
Quairading Australia 32°0S 117°21E 61 F2
Quakertown U.S.A. 40°26N 75°21W 83 F9
Qualicum Beach Canada 49°22N 124°26W 70 D4
Quambatook Australia 35°49S 143°34E 63 F3
Quambone Australia 30°57S 147°53E 63 E4
Quamby Australia 20°22S 140°17E 62 C3
Quan Long = Ca Mau Vietnam 9°7N 105°8E 39 H5
Quanah U.S.A. 34°18N 99°44W 84 D5
Quang Ngai Vietnam 15°13N 108°58E 38 E7
Quang Tri Vietnam 16°45N 107°13E 38 D6
Quang Yen Vietnam 20°56N 106°52E 34 G6
Quannan China 24°45N 114°33E 35 E10
Quantock Hills U.K. 51°8N 3°10W 13 F4
Quanyang China 42°21N 127°32E 33 C14
Quanzhou Fujian, China 24°55N 118°34E 35 E12
Quanzhou Guangxi Zhuangzu, China 25°57N 111°5E 35 E8
Qu'Appelle → Canada 50°33N 103°53W 71 C8
Quaqtaq Canada 60°55N 69°40W 69 E18
Quaraí Brazil 30°15S 56°20W 94 C4
Quartu Sant'Élena Italy 39°15N 9°10E 22 E3
Quartzsite U.S.A. 33°40N 114°13W 79 M12
Quatre Bornes Mauritius 20°15S 57°28E 55 d
Quatsino Sd. Canada 50°25N 127°58W 70 C3
Quba Azerbaijan 41°21N 48°32E 19 F8
Qūchān Iran 37°10N 58°27E 47 B8
Queanbeyan Australia 35°17S 149°14E 63 F4
Québec Canada 46°52N 71°13W 73 C5
Québec □ Canada 48°0N 74°0W 72 B6
Quebrada del Condorito △ Argentina 31°49S 64°40W 94 C3
Queen Alexandra Ra. Antarctica 85°0S 170°0E 5 E11
Queen Charlotte City Canada 53°15N 132°2W 70 C2
Queen Charlotte Is. = Haida Gwaii Canada 53°20N 132°10W 70 C2

Queen Charlotte Sd.
  Canada                    51°0N 128°0W 70 C3
Queen Charlotte Strait
  Canada                    50°45N 127°10W 70 C3
Queen Elizabeth Is.
  Canada                    76°0N 95°0W 69 B13
Queen Elizabeth Land
  Antarctica                85°0S 60°0W 5 E17
Queen Mary Land Antarctica 70°0S 95°0E 5 D7
Queen Maud G.
  Canada                    68°15N 102°30W 68 D11
Queen Maud Land = Dronning
  Maud Land Antarctica      72°30S 12°0E 5 D3
Queen Maud Mts.
  Antarctica                86°0S 160°0W 5 E12
Queens Channel Australia    15°0S 129°30E 60 C4
Queenscliff Australia       38°16S 144°39E 63 F3
Queensland □ Australia      22°0S 142°0E 62 C3
Queenstown Australia        42°4S 145°35E 63 G4
Queenstown N.Z.             45°1S 168°40E 59 F2
Queenstown S. Africa        31°52S 26°52E 56 D4
Queets U.S.A.               47°32N 124°19W 78 C2
Queguay Grande →
  Uruguay                   32°9S 58°9W 94 C4
Queimadas Brazil            11°0S 39°38W 93 F11
Quelimane Mozam.            17°53S 36°58E 55 H7
Quellón Chile               43°7S 73°37W 96 E2
Quelpart = Jeju-do
  S. Korea                  33°29N 126°34E 33 H14
Quemado N. Mex.,
  U.S.A.                    34°20N 108°30W 77 J9
Quemado Tex., U.S.A.        28°56N 100°37W 84 G4
Quemoy = Chinmen
  Taiwan                    24°26N 118°19E 35 E12
Quemú-Quemú Argentina       36°3S 63°36W 94 D3
Quepem India                15°13N 74°3E 45 G2
Quequén Argentina           38°30S 58°30W 94 D4
Querétaro Mexico            20°36N 100°23W 86 C4
Querétaro □ Mexico          21°0N 99°55W 86 C5
Queshan China               32°55N 114°2E 35 A10
Quesnel Canada              53°0N 122°30W 70 C4
Quesnel → Canada            52°58N 122°29W 70 C4
Quesnel L. Canada           52°30N 121°20W 70 C4
Questa U.S.A.               36°42N 105°36W 77 H11
Quetico △ Canada            48°30N 91°45W 72 C1
Quetta Pakistan             30°15N 66°55E 42 D2
Quetzaltenango
  Guatemala                 14°50N 91°30W 88 D1
Qufar Si. Arabia            27°26N 41°37E 46 E4
Qufu China                  35°36N 116°58E 32 G9
Qui Nhon Vietnam            13°40N 109°13E 38 F7
Quibala Angola              10°46S 14°59E 54 G2
Quibaxe Angola              8°24S 14°27E 54 F2
Quibdó Colombia             5°42N 76°40W 92 B3
Quiberon France             47°29N 3°9W 20 C2
Quiet L. Canada             61°5N 133°5W 70 A2
Quiindy Paraguay            25°58S 57°14W 94 B4
Quilá Mexico                24°23N 107°13W 86 C3
Quilán, C. Chile            43°15S 74°30W 96 E2
Quilcene U.S.A.             47°49N 122°53W 78 C4
Quilimarí Chile             32°5S 71°30W 94 C1
Quilino Argentina           30°14S 64°29W 94 C3
Quillabamba Peru            12°50S 72°50W 92 F4
Quillagua Chile             21°40S 69°40W 94 A2
Quillota Chile              32°54S 71°16W 94 C1
Quilmes Argentina           34°43S 58°15W 94 C4
Quilon = Kollam India       8°50N 76°38E 45 K3
Quilpie Australia           26°35S 144°11E 63 D3
Quilpué Chile               33°5S 71°33W 94 C1
Quimilí Argentina           27°40S 62°30W 94 B3
Quimper France              48°0N 4°9W 20 B1
Quimperlé France            47°53N 3°33W 20 C2
Quinault → U.S.A.           47°21N 124°18W 78 C2
Quincy Calif., U.S.A.       39°56N 120°57W 78 F6
Quincy Fla., U.S.A.         30°35N 84°34W 85 F12
Quincy Ill., U.S.A.         39°56N 91°23W 80 F8
Quincy Wash., U.S.A.        47°14N 119°51W 76 C4
Quines Argentina            32°13S 65°48W 94 C2
Quintana Roo □ Mexico       19°40N 88°30W 87 D7
Quintana Roo △ Quintana Roo,
  Mexico                    20°15N 87°45W 87 C7
Quintanar de la Orden
  Spain                     39°36N 3°5W 21 C4
Quintero Chile              32°45S 71°30W 94 C1
Quirihue Chile              36°15S 72°35W 94 D1
Quirindi Australia          31°28S 150°40E 63 E5
Quirinópolis Brazil         18°32S 50°30W 93 G8
Quissanga Mozam.            12°24S 40°28E 55 G8
Quissico Mozam.             24°42S 34°44E 57 B5
Quitilipi Argentina         26°50S 60°13W 94 B3
Quitman U.S.A.              30°47N 83°34W 85 F13
Quito Ecuador               0°15S 78°35W 92 D3
Quixadá Brazil              4°55S 39°0W 93 D11
Qujing China                25°32N 103°41E 34 E5
Qulan Kazakhstan            42°55N 72°43E 26 E8
Qul'an, Jazā'ir Egypt       24°22N 35°31E 46 E2
Qulsary Kazakhstan          46°59N 54°1E 19 E9
Qumbu S. Africa             31°10S 28°48E 57 D4
Quneitra = Al Qunayţirah
  Syria                     33°5N 35°45E 48 B4
Qünghirot Uzbekistan        43°2N 58°50E 26 E6
Qu'nyido China              31°15N 98°8E 34 B2
Quoin I. Australia          14°54S 129°32E 60 B4
Quoin Pt. S. Africa         34°46S 19°37E 56 E2
Quorn Australia             32°25S 138°5E 63 E2
Qurnat as Sawdā' Lebanon    34°18N 36°6E 48 A5
Quşaybā' Si. Arabia         26°53N 43°35E 46 E4
Qusaybah Iraq               34°24N 40°59E 46 C4
Quseir Egypt                26°7N 34°16E 46 E2
Quseir Amra = Qasr 'Amra
  Jordan                    31°48N 36°35E 46 D3
Qūshchī Iran                37°59N 45°3E 46 B5
Qutang Gorge = Qutang Xia
  China                     31°0N 109°40E 34 B7
Qutang Xia China            31°0N 109°40E 34 B7
Quthing Lesotho             30°25S 27°36E 57 D4
Qūţīābād Iran               35°47N 48°30E 47 C6
Quttinirpaaq = Ellesmere I.
  Canada                    79°30N 80°0W 69 B16
Quttinirpaaq △ Canada       82°13N 72°13W 69 A17

Quwo China                  35°38N 111°25E 32 G6
Quyang China                38°35N 114°40E 32 E8
Quynh Nhai Vietnam          21°49N 103°33E 38 B4
Quyon Canada                45°31N 76°14W 83 A8
Quzhou China                28°57N 118°54E 35 C12
Quzi China                  36°20N 107°20E 32 F4
Qyzylorda Kazakhstan        44°48N 65°28E 26 E7

# R

Ra, Ko Thailand             9°13N 98°16E 39 H2
Raahe Finland               64°40N 24°28E 8 D21
Raalte Neths.               52°23N 6°16E 15 B6
Raas Indonesia              7°8S 114°33E 37 G16
Raasay U.K.                 57°25N 6°4W 11 D2
Raasay, Sd. of U.K.         57°30N 6°8W 11 D2
Raasepori Finland           60°0N 23°26E 9 G20
Rába → Hungary              47°38N 17°38E 17 E9
Rabat Malta                 35°53N 14°24E 22 G6
Rabat Morocco               34°2N 6°48W 52 B4
Rabaul Papua N. G.          4°24S 152°18E 58 B8
Rabbit Flat Australia       20°11S 130°1E 60 D5
Rabbit Lake Mine Canada     58°4N 104°5W 71 B8
Rabi Fiji                   16°30S 179°59W 59 a
Rābigh Si. Arabia           22°50N 39°5E 49 C2
Râbniţa = Rîbniţa
  Moldova                   47°45N 29°0E 17 E15
Rābor Iran                  29°17N 56°55E 47 D8
Rabwah = Chenab Nagar
  Pakistan                  31°45N 72°55E 42 D5
Race, C. Canada             46°40N 53°5W 73 C9
Rach Gia Vietnam            10°5N 105°5E 39 G5
Rach Soi Vietnam            9°57N 105°7E 39 H5
Racha Noi, Ko Thailand      7°30N 98°19E 39 J2
Racha Yai, Ko Thailand      7°36N 98°21E 39 J2
Rachid Mauritania           18°45N 11°35W 52 E3
Racibórz Poland             50°7N 18°18E 17 C10
Racine U.S.A.               42°44N 87°47W 80 D10
Rackerby U.S.A.             39°26N 121°22W 78 F5
Rădăuţi Romania             47°50N 25°59E 17 E13
Radcliff U.S.A.             37°51N 85°57W 81 G11
Radekhiv Ukraine            50°25N 24°32E 17 C13
Radekhov = Radekhiv
  Ukraine                   50°25N 24°32E 17 C13
Radford U.S.A.              37°8N 80°34W 81 G13
Radhanpur India             23°50N 71°38E 42 H4
Radhwa, Jabal Si. Arabia    24°34N 38°18E 46 E3
Radisson Qué., Canada       53°47N 77°37W 72 B4
Radisson Sask., Canada      52°30N 107°20W 71 C7
Radium Hot Springs
  Canada                    50°35N 116°2W 70 C5
Radnor Forest U.K.          52°17N 3°10W 13 E4
Radom Poland                51°23N 21°12E 17 C11
Radomsko Poland             51°5N 19°28E 17 C10
Radomyshl Ukraine           50°30N 29°12E 17 C15
Radstock, C. Australia      33°12S 134°20E 63 E1
Raduzhnyy Russia            62°5N 77°28E 26 C8
Radville Canada             49°30N 104°15W 71 D8
Rae = Behchoko Canada       62°50N 116°3W 70 A5
Rae Bareli India            26°18N 81°20E 43 F9
Rae Isthmus Canada          66°40N 87°30W 69 D14
Raeren Belgium              50°41N 6°7E 15 D6
Raeside, L. Australia       29°20S 122°0E 61 E3
Raetihi N.Z.                39°25S 175°17E 59 C5
Rafaela Argentina           31°10S 61°30W 94 C3
Rafah Gaza Strip            31°18N 34°14E 48 D3
Rafhā Si. Arabia            29°35N 43°35E 46 D4
Rafsanjān Iran              30°30N 56°5E 47 D8
Raft Pt. Australia          16°4S 124°26E 60 C3
Raga South Sudan            8°28N 25°41E 53 G11
Ragachow Belarus            53°8N 30°5E 17 B16
Ragama Sri Lanka            7°0N 79°50E 40 R11
Raghunathpalli India        22°14N 84°48E 43 H11
Raghunathpur India          23°33N 86°40E 43 H12
Ragusa Italy                36°55N 14°44E 22 F6
Raha Indonesia              4°55S 123°0E 37 E6
Rahaeng = Tak Thailand      16°52N 99°8E 38 D2
Rahat Israel                31°24N 34°45E 48 D3
Rahatgarh India             23°47N 78°22E 43 H8
Rahimyar Khan Pakistan      28°30N 70°25E 42 E4
Rāhjerd Iran                35°22N 50°22E 47 C6
Rahon India                 31°3N 76°7E 42 D7
Rahuri India                19°23N 74°39E 44 E2
Rai, Hon Vietnam            9°48N 104°38E 39 H5
Raiatéa, Î.
  French Polynesia          16°50S 151°25W 65 J12
Raichur India               16°10N 77°20E 45 F3
Raiganj India               25°37N 88°10E 43 G13
Raigarh India               21°56N 83°25E 44 D6
Raighar India               19°51N 82°6E 44 E6
Raijua Indonesia            10°37S 121°36E 37 F6
Raikot India                30°41N 75°42E 42 D6
Railton Australia           41°25S 146°28E 63 G4
Rainbow Bridge △
  U.S.A.                    37°5N 110°58W 77 H8
Rainbow Lake Canada         58°30N 119°23W 70 B5
Rainier U.S.A.              46°53N 122°41W 78 D4
Rainier, Mt. U.S.A.         46°52N 121°46W 78 D5
Rainy L. Canada             48°42N 93°10W 71 D10
Rainy River Canada          48°43N 94°29W 71 D10
Raippaluoto Finland         63°13N 21°14E 8 E19
Raipur India                21°17N 81°45E 44 D5
Rairakhol India             21°4N 84°21E 44 D7
Raisen India                23°20N 77°48E 42 H8
Raisio Finland              60°28N 22°11E 9 F20
Raj Nandgaon India          21°5N 81°5E 44 D6
Raj Nilgiri India           21°28N 86°46E 43 J12
Raja, Ujung Indonesia       3°40N 96°25E 36 D1
Raja Ampat, Kepulauan
  Indonesia                 0°30S 130°0E 37 E8
Rajahmahendravaram
  India                     17°1N 81°48E 44 F5
Rajahmundry =
  Rajahmahendravaram
  India                     17°1N 81°48E 44 F5
Rajaji △ India              30°10N 78°20E 42 D8

Rajampet India              14°11N 79°10E 45 G4
Rajang → Malaysia           2°30N 112°0E 36 D4
Rajanpur Pakistan           29°6N 70°19E 42 E4
Rajapalaiyam India          9°25N 77°35E 45 K3
Rajapur India               16°40N 73°31E 44 F1
Rajasthan □ India           26°45N 73°30E 42 F5
Rajasthan Canal = Indira Gandhi
  Canal India               28°0N 72°0E 42 F5
Rajauri India               33°25N 74°21E 43 C6
Rajendranagar India         17°16N 78°27E 44 F4
Rajgarh Mad. P., India      24°2N 76°45E 42 G7
Rajgarh Raj., India         27°14N 76°38E 42 F7
Rajgarh Raj., India         28°40N 75°25E 42 E6
Rajghat Dam India           24°45N 78°20E 44 B4
Rajgir India                25°2N 85°25E 43 G11
Rajim India                 20°58N 81°53E 44 D5
Rajkot India                22°15N 70°56E 42 H4
Rajmahal Hills India        24°30N 87°30E 43 G12
Rajpipla India              21°50N 73°30E 44 D1
Rajpur India                22°18N 74°21E 42 H6
Rajpura India               30°25N 76°32E 42 D7
Rajsamand = Kankroli
  India                     25°4N 73°53E 42 G5
Rajshahi Bangla.            24°22N 88°39E 41 G16
Rajshahi □ Bangla.          25°0N 89°0E 43 G13
Rajula India                21°3N 71°26E 42 J4
Rajur India                 20°7N 78°55E 44 D4
Rajura India                19°47N 79°22E 44 E4
Rakaia N.Z.                 43°45S 172°1E 59 E4
Rakaia → N.Z.               43°36S 172°15E 59 E4
Rakan, Ra's Qatar           26°10N 51°20E 47 E6
Rakaposhi Pakistan          36°10N 74°25E 43 A6
Rakata, Pulau Indonesia     6°10S 105°20E 37 G11
Rakhine □ Myanmar           19°0N 94°15E 41 K18
Rakhiv Ukraine              48°3N 24°12E 17 D13
Rakhni Pakistan             30°4N 69°56E 42 D3
Rakhni → Pakistan           29°31N 69°36E 42 E3
Rakiraki Fiji               17°22S 178°11E 59 a
Rakitnoye Russia            45°36N 134°17E 28 B7
Rakiura = Stewart I.
  N.Z.                      46°58S 167°54E 59 G1
Rakiura △ N.Z.              47°0S 167°50E 59 G1
Rakops Botswana             21°1S 24°28E 56 B3
Rakvere Estonia             59°20N 26°25E 9 G22
Raleigh U.S.A.              35°47N 78°39W 85 D15
Ralik Chain Pac. Oc.        8°0N 168°0E 64 G8
Ralls U.S.A.                33°41N 101°24W 84 E4
Ralston U.S.A.              41°30N 76°57W 82 E8
Ram → Canada                62°1N 123°41W 70 A4
Rama Nic.                   12°9N 84°15W 88 D3
Ramachandrapuram India      16°50N 82°4E 44 F6
Ramagiri Udayagiri India    19°5N 84°18E 44 E7
Ramagundam India            18°55N 79°15E 44 E4
Ramakona India              21°43N 78°50E 43 J8
Raman Thailand              6°29N 101°18E 39 J3
Ramanathapuram India        9°25N 78°55E 45 K4
Ramanujganj India           23°48N 83°42E 43 H10
Ramas C. India              15°5N 73°55E 45 G1
Ramat Gan Israel            32°4N 34°48E 48 C3
Ramatlhabama S. Africa      25°37S 25°33E 56 C4
Ramban India                33°14N 75°12E 43 C6
Rambi = Rabi Fiji           16°30S 179°59W 59 a
Rambipuji Indonesia         8°12S 113°37E 37 H15
Ramdurg India               15°58N 75°22E 45 G2
Rame Hd. Australia          37°47S 149°30E 63 F4
Ramechhap Nepal             27°25N 86°10E 43 F12
Ramelton Ireland            55°2N 7°39W 10 A4
Rameswaram India            9°17N 79°18E 45 K4
Ramganga → India            27°5N 79°58E 43 F8
Ramgarh Jharkhand,
  India                     23°40N 85°35E 43 H11
Ramgarh Raj., India         27°16N 75°14E 42 F6
Ramgarh Raj., India         27°30N 70°36E 42 F4
Rāmhormoz Iran              31°15N 49°35E 47 D6
Ramīān Iran                 37°3N 55°16E 47 B7
Ramingining Australia       12°19S 135°3E 62 A2
Ramla Israel                31°55N 34°52E 48 D3
Ramm = Rum Jordan           29°35N 35°24E 48 F4
Ramm, Jabal Jordan          29°35N 35°24E 48 F4
Ramnad = Ramanathapuram
  India                     9°25N 78°55E 45 K4
Ramnagar Jammu & Kashmir,
  India                     32°47N 75°18E 43 C6
Ramnagar Uttarakhand,
  India                     29°24N 79°7E 43 E8
Râmnicu Sărat Romania       45°26N 27°3E 17 F14
Râmnicu Vâlcea Romania      45°9N 24°21E 17 F13
Ramona U.S.A.               33°2N 116°52W 79 M10
Ramore Canada               48°30N 80°25W 72 C3
Ramotswa Botswana           24°50S 25°52E 56 B4
Rampur H.P., India          31°26N 77°43E 42 D7
Rampur Mad. P., India       23°25N 73°53E 42 H5
Rampur Odisha, India        21°48N 83°58E 44 D6
Rampur Uttar P., India      28°50N 79°5E 43 E8
Rampur Hat India            24°10N 87°50E 43 G12
Rampura India               24°30N 75°27E 42 G6
Ramrama Tola India          21°52N 79°55E 43 J8
Ramree I. Myanmar           19°0N 93°40E 41 K19
Ramsar Iran                 36°53N 50°41E 47 B6
Ramsey I. of Man            54°20N 4°22W 12 C3
Ramsey U.S.A.               41°4N 74°9W 83 E10
Ramsey L. Canada            47°13N 82°15W 72 C3
Ramsgate U.K.               51°20N 1°25E 13 F9
Ramtek India                21°20N 79°15E 44 D4
Rana Pratap Sagar Dam
  India                     24°58N 75°38E 42 G6
Ranaghat India              23°15N 88°35E 43 H13
Ranahu Pakistan             25°55N 69°45E 42 G3
Ranau Malaysia              6°2N 116°40E 36 C5
Rancagua Chile              34°10S 70°50W 94 C1
Rancheria → Canada          60°13N 129°7W 70 A3
Ranchester U.S.A.           44°54N 107°10W 76 D10
Ranchi India                23°19N 85°27E 43 H11
Rancho Cordova U.S.A.       38°36N 121°18W 78 G5
Rancho Cucamonga
  U.S.A.                    34°10N 117°30W 79 L9
Randalstown U.K.            54°45N 6°19W 10 B5
Randers Denmark             56°29N 10°1E 9 H14
Randfontein S. Africa       26°8S 27°45E 57 C4

Randle U.S.A.               46°32N 121°57W 78 D5
Randolph Mass., U.S.A.      42°10N 71°2W 83 D13
Randolph N.Y., U.S.A.       42°10N 78°59W 82 D6
Randolph Utah, U.S.A.       41°40N 111°11W 76 F8
Randolph Vt., U.S.A.        43°55N 72°40W 83 C12
Råneälven → Sweden          65°50N 22°20E 8 D20
Rangae Thailand             6°19N 101°44E 39 J3
Rangaunu B. N.Z.            34°51S 173°15E 59 A4
Rangeley U.S.A.             44°58N 70°39W 83 B14
Rangeley L. U.S.A.          44°55N 70°43W 83 B14
Rangely U.S.A.              40°5N 108°48W 76 F9
Ranger U.S.A.               32°28N 98°41W 84 E5
Rangia India                26°28N 91°38E 41 F17
Rangiora N.Z.               43°19S 172°36E 59 E4
Rangitaiki → N.Z.           37°54S 176°49E 59 B6
Rangitata → N.Z.            43°45S 171°15E 59 E3
Rangitoto ke te tonga = D'Urville I.
  N.Z.                      40°50S 173°55E 59 D4
Rangkasbitung
  Indonesia                 6°21S 106°15E 37 G12
Rangoon = Yangôn
  Myanmar                   16°45N 96°20E 41 L20
Rangpur Bangla.             25°42N 89°22E 41 G16
Rangsang Indonesia          1°20N 103°5E 39 M4
Rani-ki-Vav India           23°51N 72°6E 42 H4
Ranibennur India            14°35N 75°30E 45 G2
Raniganj Paschimbanga,
  India                     23°40N 87°5E 41 H15
Raniganj Ut. P., India      27°3N 82°13E 43 F9
Ranikhet India              29°39N 79°25E 43 E8
Ranippettai India           12°56N 79°23E 45 H4
Raniwara India              24°50N 72°10E 42 G5
Rāniyah Iraq                36°15N 44°53E 46 B5
Ranka India                 23°59N 83°47E 43 H10
Ranken → Australia          20°31S 137°36E 62 C2
Rankin U.S.A.               31°13N 101°56W 84 F4
Rankin Inlet Canada         62°30N 93°0W 68 E13
Rankins Springs
  Australia                 33°49S 146°14E 63 E4
Rannoch, L. U.K.            56°41N 4°20W 11 E4
Rannoch Moor U.K.           56°38N 4°48W 11 E4
Ranohira Madag.             22°29S 45°24E 55 J9
Ranong Thailand             9°56N 98°40E 39 H2
Ranpur India                20°5N 85°20E 44 D7
Rānsa Iran                  33°39N 48°18E 47 C6
Ransiki Indonesia           1°30S 134°10E 37 E8
Rantau Abang Malaysia       4°52N 103°24E 39 K4
Rantauprapat Indonesia      2°15N 99°50E 36 D1
Rantemario Indonesia        3°15S 119°57E 37 E5
Rantoul U.S.A.              40°19N 88°9W 80 E9
Raoche China                46°47N 134°0E 28 A7
Raoyang China               38°15N 115°45E 32 E8
Rapa French Polynesia       27°35S 144°20W 65 K13
Rap, Ko Thailand            9°19N 99°58E 39 b
Rapallo Italy               44°21N 9°14E 20 D8
Rapar India                 23°34N 70°38E 42 H4
Rapel, Lago Chile           34°20S 71°14W 94 C1
Raper, C. Canada            69°44N 67°6W 69 D18
Rapid City U.S.A.           44°5N 103°14W 80 C2
Rapid River U.S.A.          45°55N 86°58W 80 C10
Rapla Estonia               59°1N 24°52E 9 G21
Rapti → India               26°18N 83°41E 43 F10
Raquette → U.S.A.           45°0N 74°42W 83 B10
Raquette Lake U.S.A.        43°49N 74°40W 83 C10
Rara △ Nepal                29°30N 82°10E 43 E10
Rarotonga Cook Is.         21°30S 160°0W 65 K12
Ra's al 'Ayn Syria          36°45N 40°12E 46 B4
Ra's Al Khair Si. Arabia    27°27N 49°18E 47 E6
Ra's al Khaymah U.A.E.      25°50N 55°59E 47 E7
Ra's aţ Ţīb Tunisia         37°1N 11°2E 22 F4
Rasa, Pta. Argentina        36°20S 56°41W 94 D4
Raseiniai Lithuania         55°25N 23°5E 9 J20
Rashmi India                25°4N 74°22E 42 G6
Rasht Iran                  37°20N 49°40E 47 B6
Rasi Salai Thailand         15°20N 104°9E 38 E5
Rasipuram India             11°30N 78°15E 45 J4
Raskot Nepal                29°14N 81°39E 43 E9
Rason L. Australia          28°45S 124°25E 61 E3
Rasra India                 25°50N 83°50E 43 G10
Rasua Garhi Nepal           28°17N 85°23E 43 E11
Rasul Pakistan              32°42N 73°34E 42 C5
Rat → Canada                49°35N 97°10W 71 D9
Rat Buri = Ratchaburi
  Thailand                  13°30N 99°54E 38 F2
Rat Islands U.S.A.          52°0N 178°0E 74 E3
Rat L. Canada               56°10N 99°40W 71 B9
Ratak Chain Pac. Oc.        1°0N 170°0E 64 G8
Ratangarh India             28°5N 74°35E 42 E6
Rath India                  25°36N 79°37E 43 G8
Rath Luirc = Charleville
  Ireland                   52°21N 8°40W 10 D3
Rathangan Ireland           53°14N 7°0W 10 C4
Rathdrum Ireland            52°56N 6°14W 10 D5
Rathenow Germany            52°37N 12°19E 16 B7
Rathkeale Ireland           52°32N 8°56W 10 D3
Rathlin I. U.K.             55°18N 6°14W 10 A5
Ratibor = Racibórz
  Poland                    50°7N 18°18E 17 C10
Ratlam India                23°20N 75°0E 42 H6
Ratmanova, Ostrov
  Russia                    65°46N 169°6W 74 B6
Ratnagiri India             16°57N 73°18E 44 F1
Ratnapura Sri Lanka         6°40N 80°20E 45 L5
Ratodero Pakistan           27°48N 68°18E 42 F3
Raton U.S.A.                36°54N 104°24W 77 H11
Rattaphum Thailand          7°8N 100°16E 39 J3
Rattray Hd. U.K.            57°38N 1°50W 11 D7
Raudales Mexico             17°27N 93°39W 87 D6
Raufarhöfn Iceland          66°27N 15°57W 8 C6

Raufoss Norway              60°44N 10°37E 8 F14
Raukumara Ra. N.Z.          38°5S 177°55E 59 C6
Rauma Finland               61°10N 21°30E 8 F19
Raumo = Rauma Finland       61°10N 21°30E 8 F19
Raung, Gunung Indonesia     8°8S 114°3E 37 J17
Raurkela India              22°14N 84°50E 43 H11
Rausu-Dake Japan            44°4N 145°7E 28 B12
Rava-Ruska Ukraine          50°15N 23°42E 17 C12
Rava Russkaya = Rava-Ruska
  Ukraine                   50°15N 23°42E 17 C12
Ravalli U.S.A.              47°17N 114°11W 76 C6
Ravānsar Iran               34°43N 46°40E 46 C5
Rāvar Iran                  31°20N 56°51E 47 D8
Ravena U.S.A.               42°28N 73°49W 83 D11
Ravenna Italy               44°25N 12°12E 22 B5
Ravenna Nebr., U.S.A.       41°1N 98°55W 80 E4
Ravenna Ohio, U.S.A.        41°9N 81°15W 82 E3
Ravensburg Germany          47°46N 9°36E 16 E5
Ravenshoe Australia         17°37S 145°29E 62 B4
Ravensthorpe Australia      33°35S 120°2E 61 F3
Ravenswood Australia        20°6S 146°54E 62 C4
Ravenswood U.S.A.           38°57N 81°46W 81 F13
Raver India                 21°15N 76°2E 44 D3
Ravi → Pakistan             30°35N 71°49E 42 D4
Rawalpindi Pakistan         33°38N 73°8E 42 C5
Rawang Malaysia             3°20N 101°35E 39 L3
Rawene N.Z.                 35°25S 173°32E 59 A4
Rawi, Ko Thailand           6°33N 99°14E 39 J2
Rawlinna Australia          30°58S 125°28E 61 F4
Rawlins U.S.A.              41°47N 107°14W 76 F10
Rawlinson Ra. Australia     24°40S 128°30E 61 D4
Rawson Argentina            43°15S 65°5W 96 E3
Raxaul India                26°59N 84°51E 43 F11
Ray U.S.A.                  48°21N 103°10W 80 A2
Ray, C. Canada              47°33N 59°15W 73 C8
Ray Mts. U.S.A.             66°0N 152°0W 74 B9
Raya Ring, Ko Thailand      8°18N 98°29E 39 a
Rayachoti India             14°4N 78°50E 45 G4
Rayadurg India              14°40N 76°50E 45 G3
Rayagada India              19°15N 83°20E 44 E6
Raychikhinsk Russia         49°46N 129°25E 27 E13
Räyen Iran                  29°34N 57°26E 47 D8
Rayleigh U.K.               51°36N 0°37E 13 F8
Raymond Canada              49°30N 112°35W 70 D6
Raymond Calif., U.S.A.      37°13N 119°54W 78 H7
Raymond N.H., U.S.A.        43°2N 71°11W 83 C13
Raymond Wash., U.S.A.       46°41N 123°44W 78 D3
Raymondville U.S.A.         26°29N 97°47W 84 H6
Raymore Canada              51°25N 104°31W 71 C8
Rayón Mexico                29°43N 110°35W 86 B2
Rayong Thailand             12°40N 101°20E 38 F3
Raystown L. U.S.A.          40°25N 78°5W 82 F6
Raz, Pte. du France         48°2N 4°47W 20 C1
Razan Iran                  35°23N 49°2E 47 C6
Razāzah, Buḩayrat ar
  Iraq                      32°40N 43°35E 46 C4
Razdel'naya = Rozdilna
  Ukraine                   46°50N 30°2E 17 E16
Razdolnoye Russia           43°30N 131°52E 28 C5
Razeh Iran                  32°47N 48°9E 47 C6
Razgrad Bulgaria            43°33N 26°34E 23 C12
Razim, Lacul Romania        44°50N 29°0E 17 F15
Razmak Pakistan             32°45N 69°50E 42 C3
Razzaza, L. = Razāzah, Buḩayrat
  ar Iraq                   32°40N 43°35E 46 C4
Re, Cu Lao Vietnam          15°22N 109°8E 38 E7
Ré, Î. de France            46°12N 1°30W 20 C3
Reading U.K.                51°27N 0°58W 13 F7
Reading □ U.K.              51°27N 0°58W 13 F7
Reading U.S.A.              40°20N 75°56W 83 F9
Realicó Argentina           35°0S 64°15W 94 D3
Ream Cambodia               10°34N 103°39E 39 G4
Ream △ Cambodia             10°30N 103°45E 39 G4
Reay Forest U.K.            58°22N 4°55W 11 C4
Rebecca, L. Australia       30°0S 122°15E 61 F3
Rebi Indonesia              6°23S 134°7E 37 F8
Rebiana, Sahrâ' Libya       24°30N 21°0E 53 D10
Reboly Russia               63°49N 30°47E 8 E24
Rebun-Tō Japan              45°23N 141°2E 28 B10
Recherche, Arch. of the
  Australia                 34°15S 122°50E 61 F3
Rechna Doab Pakistan        31°35N 73°30E 42 D5
Rechytsa Belarus            52°21N 30°24E 17 B16
Recife Brazil               8°0S 35°0W 93 E12
Recife Seychelles           4°36S 55°42E 55 b
Reckong Peo India           31°32N 78°16E 42 D8
Reconquista Argentina       29°10S 59°45W 94 B4
Recreo Argentina            29°25S 65°10W 94 B2
Red = Hong → Asia           20°16N 106°34E 38 B5
Red → U.S.A.                31°1N 91°45W 84 F9
Red Bank U.S.A.             40°21N 74°5W 83 F10
Red Bay Canada              51°44N 56°25W 73 B8
Red Bluff U.S.A.            40°11N 122°15W 76 F2
Red Bluff Res. U.S.A.       31°54N 103°55W 77 L12
Red Cliffs Australia        34°19S 142°11E 63 E3
Red Cloud U.S.A.            40°5N 98°32W 80 E4
Red Creek U.S.A.            43°14N 76°45W 83 C8
Red Deer Canada             52°20N 113°50W 70 C6
Red Deer → Alta.,
  Canada                    50°58N 110°0W 71 C7
Red Deer → Man.,
  Canada                    52°53N 101°1W 71 C8
Red Deer L. Canada          52°55N 101°20W 71 C8
Red Hook U.S.A.             41°55N 73°53W 83 E11
Red Indian L. Canada        48°35N 57°0W 73 C8
Red L. Canada               51°3N 93°49W 71 C10
Red Lake Canada             51°3N 93°49W 71 C10
Red Lake Falls U.S.A.       47°53N 96°16W 80 B5
Red Lake Road Canada        49°59N 93°25W 71 C10
Red Lodge U.S.A.            45°11N 109°15W 76 D9
Red Mountain U.S.A.         35°37N 117°38W 79 K9
Red Oak U.S.A.              41°1N 95°14W 80 E6
Red River of the North →
  N. Amer.                  49°0N 97°15W 80 A5
Red Rock Canada             48°55N 88°15W 72 C2
Red Rock, L. U.S.A.         41°22N 92°59W 80 E7
Red Rocks Pt. Australia     32°13S 127°32E 61 F4
Red Sea Asia                25°0N 36°0E 49 C2
Red Slate Mt. U.S.A.        37°31N 118°52W 78 H8

Red Sucker L. Canada 54°9N 93°40W 72 B1
Red Tower Pass = Turnu Roşu, P.
  Romania 45°33N 24°17E 17 F13
Red Wing U.S.A. 44°34N 92°31W 80 C7
Redang, Pulau Malaysia 5°49N 103°2E 39 K4
Redcar U.K. 54°37N 1°4W 12 C6
Redcar & Cleveland □
  U.K. 54°29N 1°0W 12 C6
Redcliff Canada 50°10N 110°50W 76 A8
Redcliffe Australia 27°12S 153°6E 63 D5
Redcliffe, Mt. Australia 28°30S 121°30E 61 E3
Reddersburg S. Africa 29°41S 26°10E 56 C4
Redding U.S.A. 40°35N 122°24W 76 F2
Redditch U.K. 52°18N 1°55W 13 E6
Redfield U.S.A. 44°53N 98°31W 80 C4
Redford U.S.A. 44°38N 73°48W 83 B11
Redhead Trin. & Tob. 10°44N 60°58W 93 K16
Redlands U.S.A. 34°4N 117°11W 79 M9
Redmond Oreg., U.S.A. 44°17N 121°11W 76 D3
Redmond Wash., U.S.A. 47°40N 122°7W 78 C4
Redon France 47°40N 2°6W 20 C2
Redonda Antigua & B. 16°58N 62°19W 89 C7
Redondela Spain 42°15N 8°38W 21 A1
Redondo Beach U.S.A. 33°50N 118°23W 79 M8
Redoubt Volcano
  U.S.A. 60°29N 152°45W 74 C9
Redruth U.K. 50°14N 5°14W 13 G2
Redvers Canada 49°35N 101°40W 71 D8
Redwater Canada 53°55N 113°6W 70 C6
Redwood U.S.A. 44°18N 75°48W 83 B9
Redwood △ U.S.A. 41°40N 124°5W 76 F1
Redwood City U.S.A. 37°30N 122°15W 78 H4
Redwood Falls U.S.A. 44°32N 95°7W 80 C7
Ree, L. Ireland 53°35N 8°0W 10 C3
Reed City U.S.A. 43°53N 85°31W 81 D11
Reed L. Canada 54°38N 100°30W 71 C8
Reedley U.S.A. 36°36N 119°27W 78 J7
Reedsburg U.S.A. 43°32N 90°0W 80 D8
Reedsport U.S.A. 43°42N 124°6W 76 E1
Reedsville U.S.A. 40°39N 77°35W 82 F7
Reefton N.Z. 42°6S 171°51E 59 E3
Reese → U.S.A. 40°48N 117°4W 76 F5
Refugio U.S.A. 28°18N 97°17W 84 G6
Regensburg Germany 49°1N 12°6E 16 D7
Reggâne = Zaouiet Reggâne
  Algeria 26°32N 0°3E 52 C6
Réggio di Calábria Italy 38°6N 15°39E 22 E6
Réggio nell'Emília Italy 44°43N 10°36E 22 B4
Reghin Romania 46°46N 24°42E 17 E13
Regina Canada 50°27N 104°35W 71 C8
Regina Beach Canada 50°47N 105°0W 71 C8
Registro Brazil 24°29S 47°49W 95 A6
Rehar → India 23°55N 82°40E 43 H10
Rehli India 23°38N 79°5E 43 H8
Rehoboth Namibia 23°15S 17°4E 56 B2
Rehovot Israel 31°54N 34°48E 48 D3
Reichenbach Germany 50°37N 12°17E 16 C7
Reid Australia 30°49S 128°26E 61 F4
Reidsville U.S.A. 36°21N 79°40W 85 C15
Reigate U.K. 51°14N 0°12W 13 F7
Reims France 49°15N 4°1E 20 B6
Reina Adelaida, Arch.
  Chile 52°20S 74°0W 96 G2
Reindeer → Canada 55°36N 103°11W 71 B8
Reindeer I. Canada 52°30N 98°0W 71 C9
Reindeer L. Canada 57°15N 102°15W 71 B8
Reinga, C. N.Z. 34°25S 172°43E 59 A4
Reinheimen △ Norway 62°10N 7°45E 8 E12
Reinosa Spain 43°2N 4°15W 21 A3
Reitz S. Africa 27°48S 28°29E 57 C4
Reivilo S. Africa 27°36S 24°8E 56 C3
Reliance Canada 63°0N 109°20W 71 A7
Remanso Brazil 9°41S 42°4W 93 E10
Remarkable, Mt.
  Australia 32°48S 138°10E 63 E2
Rembang Indonesia 6°42S 111°21E 37 G14
Remedios Panama 8°15N 81°50W 88 E3
Remeshk Iran 26°55N 58°50E 47 E8
Remich Lux. 49°32N 6°22E 15 E6
Ren Xian China 37°8N 114°40E 32 F8
Rendang Indonesia 8°26S 115°25E 37 J18
Rendsburg Germany 54°17N 9°39E 16 A5
René-Levasseur, Î.
  Canada 51°20N 68°40W 73 B6
Renfrew Canada 45°30N 76°40W 83 A8
Renfrewshire □ U.K. 55°49N 4°38W 11 F4
Rengat Indonesia 0°30S 102°45E 36 E2
Rengo Chile 34°24S 70°50W 94 C1
Renhua China 25°5N 113°40E 35 E9
Renhuai China 27°48N 106°24E 34 D6
Reni = Taranagar India 28°43N 74°50E 42 E6
Reni Ukraine 45°28N 28°15E 17 F15
Renigunta India 13°38N 79°30E 45 H4
Renmark Australia 34°11S 140°43E 63 E3
Rennell Sd. Canada 53°23N 132°35W 70 C2
Renner Springs Australia 18°20S 133°47E 62 B1
Rennes France 48°7N 1°41W 20 B3
Rennick Glacier
  Antarctica 70°30S 161°45E 5 D11
Rennie L. Canada 61°32N 105°35W 71 A7
Reno U.S.A. 39°31N 119°48W 78 F7
Reno → Italy 44°38N 12°16E 22 B5
Renovo U.S.A. 41°20N 77°45W 82 E7
Renqiu China 38°43N 116°5E 32 E9
Renshou China 29°59N 104°9E 34 C5
Rensselaer Ind., U.S.A. 40°57N 87°9W 80 E10
Rensselaer N.Y., U.S.A. 42°38N 73°45W 83 D11
Renton U.S.A. 47°28N 122°12W 78 C4
Renukoot India 24°12N 83°2E 43 G10
Reotipur India 25°33N 83°45E 43 G10
Repalle India 16°2N 80°45E 45 F5
Republic Mo., U.S.A. 37°7N 93°29W 80 G7
Republic Wash., U.S.A. 48°39N 118°44W 76 B4
Republican → U.S.A. 39°4N 96°48W 80 F5
Repulse B. Australia 20°35S 148°46E 62 b
Repulse Bay Canada 66°32N 86°30W 69 D14
Requena Peru 5°5S 73°52W 92 E4
Requena Spain 39°30N 1°4W 21 C5
Reserve U.S.A. 33°43N 108°45W 77 K9

Resht = Rasht Iran 37°20N 49°40E 47 B6
Resistencia Argentina 27°30S 59°0W 94 B4
Reşiţa Romania 45°18N 21°53E 17 F11
Reso = Raisio Finland 60°28N 22°11E 9 F20
Resolute Canada 74°42N 94°54W 69 C13
Resolution I. Canada 61°30N 65°0W 69 E19
Resolution I. N.Z. 45°40S 166°40E 59 F1
Ressano Garcia Mozam. 25°25S 32°0E 57 C5
Reston Canada 49°33N 101°6W 71 D8
Retalhuleu Guatemala 14°33N 91°46W 88 D1
Retford U.K. 53°19N 0°56W 12 D7
Rethímno Greece 35°18N 24°30E 23 G11
Reti Pakistan 28°5N 69°48E 42 E3
Réunion ☑ Ind. Oc. 21°0S 56°0E 55 c
Reus Spain 41°10N 1°5E 21 B6
Reutlingen Germany 48°29N 9°12E 16 D5
Reval = Tallinn Estonia 59°22N 24°48E 9 G21
Revda Russia 56°48N 59°57E 18 C10
Revelganj India 25°50N 84°40E 43 G11
Revelstoke Canada 51°0N 118°10W 70 C5
Reventazón Peru 6°10S 80°58W 92 E2
Revillagigedo, Is. de
  Pac. Oc. 18°40N 112°0W 86 D2
Revillagigedo Archipelago △
  Mexico 19°0N 112°30W 86 D2
Rewa → India 24°33N 81°25E 43 G9
Rewa India 24°33N 81°25E 43 G9
Rewari India 28°15N 76°40E 42 E7
Rexburg U.S.A. 43°49N 111°47W 76 E8
Rey, I. del Panama 8°20N 78°30W 88 E4
Rey, L. del Mexico 27°1N 103°26W 86 B4
Rey Malabo Eq. Guin. 3°45N 8°50E 54 D1
Reyes, Pt. U.S.A. 38°0N 123°0W 78 H3
Reykjahlíð Iceland 65°40N 16°55W 8 D5
Reykjanes Iceland 63°48N 22°40W 8 E2
Reykjavík Iceland 64°10N 21°57W 8 D3
Reynolds Ra. Australia 22°30S 133°0E 60 D5
Reynoldsville U.S.A. 41°6N 78°53W 82 E6
Reynosa Mexico 26°7N 98°18W 87 B5
Rēzekne Latvia 56°30N 27°17E 9 H22
Rezvān Iran 27°34N 56°6E 47 E8
Rhayader U.K. 52°18N 3°29W 13 E4
Rhein → Europe 51°52N 6°2E 15 C6
Rhein-Main-Donau-Kanal
  Germany 49°1N 11°27E 16 D6
Rheine Germany 52°17N 7°26E 16 B4
Rheinland-Pfalz □ Germany 50°0N 7°0E 16 C4
Rhin = Rhein → Europe 51°52N 6°2E 15 C6
Rhine = Rhein → Europe 51°52N 6°2E 15 C6
Rhinebeck U.S.A. 41°56N 73°55W 83 E11
Rhineland-Palatinate =
  Rheinland-Pfalz □
  Germany 50°0N 7°0E 16 C4
Rhinelander U.S.A. 45°38N 89°25W 80 C9
Rhinns Pt. U.K. 55°40N 6°29W 11 F2
Rhir, Cap Morocco 30°38N 9°54W 52 B4
Rhode Island □ U.S.A. 41°40N 71°30W 83 E13
Rhodes Greece 36°15N 28°10E 23 F13
Rhodope Mts. = Rodopi Planina
  Bulgaria 41°40N 24°20E 23 D11
Rhön Germany 50°24N 9°58E 16 C5
Rhondda U.K. 51°39N 3°31W 13 F4
Rhondda Cynon Taff □
  U.K. 51°42N 3°27W 13 F4
Rhône → France 43°28N 4°42E 20 E6
Rhum = Rùm U.K. 57°0N 6°20W 11 E2
Rhydaman = Ammanford
  U.K. 51°48N 3°59W 13 F4
Rhyl U.K. 53°20N 3°29W 12 D4
Riachão Brazil 7°20S 46°37W 93 E9
Riang, Laem Thailand 8°7N 98°27E 39 a
Riasi India 33°10N 74°50E 43 C6
Riau □ Indonesia 0°0 102°35E 36 E2
Riau, Kepulauan □
  Indonesia 0°30N 104°20E 36 D2
Riau Arch. = Riau, Kepulauan □
  Indonesia 0°30N 104°20E 36 D2
Ribadeo Spain 43°35N 7°5W 21 A2
Ribas do Rio Pardo
  Brazil 20°27S 53°46W 93 H8
Ribble → U.K. 53°52N 2°25W 12 D5
Ribe Denmark 55°19N 8°44E 9 J13
Ribeira Grande Cabo Verde 17°0N 25°4W 52 b
Ribeirão Prêto Brazil 21°10S 47°50W 95 A6
Riberalta Bolivia 11°0S 66°0W 92 F5
Ribnița Moldova 47°45N 29°0E 17 E15
Riccarton N.Z. 43°32S 172°37E 59 E4
Rice U.S.A. 34°5N 114°51W 79 L12
Rice L. Canada 44°12N 78°10W 82 B6
Rice Lake U.S.A. 45°30N 91°44W 80 C8
Rich, C. Canada 44°43N 80°38W 82 B4
Richards Bay S. Africa 28°48S 32°6E 57 C5
Richardson → Canada 58°25N 111°14W 71 B6
Richardson Lakes
  U.S.A. 44°46N 70°58W 81 C18
Richardson Springs
  U.S.A. 39°51N 121°46W 78 F5
Riche, C. Australia 34°36S 118°47E 61 F2
Richey U.S.A. 47°39N 105°4W 76 C11
Richfield U.S.A. 38°46N 112°5W 76 G7
Richfield Springs U.S.A. 42°51N 74°59W 83 D10
Richford U.S.A. 45°0N 72°40W 83 B12
Richibucto Canada 46°42N 64°54W 73 C7
Richland Ga., U.S.A. 32°5N 84°40W 85 E12
Richland Wash., U.S.A. 46°17N 119°18W 76 C4
Richland Center U.S.A. 43°21N 90°23W 80 D8
Richlands U.S.A. 37°6N 81°48W 81 G13
Richmond Australia 20°43S 143°8E 62 C3
Richmond N.Z. 41°20S 173°12E 59 D4
Richmond U.K. 54°25N 1°43W 12 C6
Richmond Calif., U.S.A. 37°56N 122°21W 78 H4
Richmond Ind., U.S.A. 39°50N 84°53W 81 F11
Richmond Ky., U.S.A. 37°45N 84°18W 81 G11
Richmond Mich., U.S.A. 42°49N 82°45W 82 D2
Richmond Mo., U.S.A. 39°17N 93°58W 80 F7
Richmond Tex., U.S.A. 29°35N 95°46W 84 G7
Richmond Utah, U.S.A. 41°56N 111°48W 76 F8
Richmond Va., U.S.A. 37°33N 77°27W 81 G15
Richmond Hill Canada 43°52N 79°27W 82 C5

Richmond Ra. Australia 29°0S 152°45E 63 D5
Richmondville U.S.A. 42°38N 74°33W 83 D10
Richtersveld △ S. Africa 28°15S 17°10E 56 C2
Richville U.S.A. 44°25N 75°23W 83 B9
Richwood U.S.A. 38°14N 80°32W 81 F13
Ridder Kazakhstan 50°20N 83°30E 26 D9
Riddlesburg U.S.A. 40°9N 78°15W 82 F6
Rideau → Canada 45°27N 75°42W 83 A9
Ridgecrest U.S.A. 35°38N 117°40W 79 K9
Ridgefield Conn., U.S.A. 41°17N 73°30W 83 E11
Ridgefield Wash., U.S.A. 45°49N 122°45W 78 E4
Ridgeland Miss., U.S.A. 32°26N 90°8W 85 E9
Ridgeland S.C., U.S.A. 32°29N 80°59W 85 E14
Ridgetown Canada 42°26N 81°52W 82 D3
Ridgewood U.S.A. 40°59N 74°7W 83 F10
Ridgway U.S.A. 41°25N 78°44W 82 E6
Riding Mountain △
  Canada 50°50N 100°0W 71 C9
Ridley, Mt. Australia 33°12S 122°7E 61 F3
Riebeek-Oos S. Africa 33°10S 26°10E 56 D4
Ried Austria 48°14N 13°30E 16 D7
Riesa Germany 51°17N 13°17E 16 C7
Riet → S. Africa 29°0S 23°54E 56 C3
Rietbron S. Africa 32°54S 23°10E 56 D3
Rietfontein Namibia 21°58S 20°58E 56 B3
Rieti Italy 42°24N 12°51E 22 C5
Rif = Er Rif Morocco 35°1N 4°1W 52 A5
Riffe L. U.S.A. 46°32N 122°26W 78 D4
Rifle U.S.A. 39°32N 107°47W 76 G10
Rift Valley Africa 7°0N 30°0E 50 G7
Riga Latvia 56°53N 24°8E 9 H21
Riga, G. of Latvia 57°40N 23°45E 9 H20
Rīgān Iran 28°37N 58°58E 47 D8
Rīgas Jūras Līcis = Riga, G. of
  Latvia 57°40N 23°45E 9 H20
Rigaud Canada 45°29N 74°18W 83 A10
Rigby U.S.A. 43°40N 111°55W 76 E8
Rīgestān Afghan. 30°15N 65°0E 40 D4
Riggins U.S.A. 45°25N 116°19W 76 D5
Rigolet Canada 54°10N 58°23W 73 B8
Rihand Dam India 24°9N 83°2E 43 G10
Riihimäki Finland 60°45N 24°48E 8 F21
Riiser-Larsen-halvøya
  Antarctica 68°0S 35°0E 5 C4
Riiser-Larsen Ice Shelf
  S. Ocean 74°0S 19°0W 5 D2
Riiser-Larsen Sea S. Ocean 67°30S 22°0E 5 C4
Riisitunturi △ Finland 66°27N 28°27E 8 C23
Rijeka Croatia 45°20N 14°21E 16 F8
Rijssen Neths. 52°19N 6°31E 15 B6
Rikuchū-Kaigan △
  Japan 39°20N 142°0E 28 E11
Rikuzentakata Japan 39°0N 141°40E 28 E10
Riley U.S.A. 43°32N 119°28W 76 E4
Rima → Nigeria 13°4N 5°10E 52 F7
Rimah, Wadi ar →
  Si. Arabia 26°5N 41°30E 46 E4
Rimau, Pulau Malaysia 5°15N 100°16E 39 c
Rimbey Canada 52°35N 114°15W 70 C6
Rimersburg U.S.A. 41°3N 79°30W 82 E5
Rímini Italy 44°3N 12°33E 22 B5
Rimouski Canada 48°27N 68°30W 73 C6
Rimrock U.S.A. 46°40N 121°7W 78 D5
Rinca Indonesia 8°45S 119°35E 37 F5
Rincón de Romos
  Mexico 22°14N 102°18W 86 C4
Rinconada Argentina 22°26S 66°10W 94 A2
Rind → India 25°53N 80°33E 43 G9
Ringas India 27°21N 75°34E 42 F6
Ringgold Is. Fiji 16°15S 179°25W 59 a
Ringkøbing Denmark 56°5N 8°15E 9 H13
Ringvassøya Norway 69°56N 19°15E 8 B18
Ringwood U.S.A. 41°7N 74°15W 83 E10
Rinjani, Gunung
  Indonesia 8°24S 116°28E 36 F5
Rinyirru △ Australia 15°24S 144°26E 62 B3
Río Branco Brazil 9°58S 67°49W 92 E5
Río Branco Uruguay 32°40S 53°40W 95 C5
Río Bravo Mexico 25°59N 98°6W 87 B5
Río Bravo → N. Amer. 25°57N 97°9W 87 B5
Río Bravo del Norte →
  Mexico 25°57N 97°9W 87 B5
Río Brilhante Brazil 21°48S 54°33W 95 A5
Río Claro Brazil 22°19S 47°35W 95 A6
Río Claro Trin. & Tob. 10°20N 61°10W 93 K15
Río Colorado Argentina 39°0S 64°0W 96 D4
Río Cuarto Argentina 33°10S 64°25W 94 C3
Río de Janeiro Brazil 22°50S 43°0W 95 A7
Río do Sul Brazil 27°13S 49°37W 95 B6
Río Dulce △ Guatemala 15°43N 88°50W 88 C2
Río Gallegos Argentina 51°35S 69°15W 96 G3
Río Grande Argentina 53°50S 67°45W 96 G3
Río Grande Brazil 32°0S 52°20W 95 C5
Río Grande Mexico 23°50N 103°2W 86 C4
Río Grande Puerto Rico 18°23N 65°50W 89 d
Río Grande → N. Amer. 25°58N 97°9W 84 J6
Río Grande City U.S.A. 26°23N 98°49W 84 H5
Río Grande de Santiago →
  Mexico 21°36N 105°26W 86 C3
Río Grande do Norte □
  Brazil 5°40S 36°0W 93 E11
Río Grande do Sul □ Brazil 30°0S 53°0W 95 C5
Río Hato Panama 8°22N 80°10W 88 E3
Río Lagartos Mexico 21°36N 88°10W 87 C7
Río Largo Brazil 9°28S 35°50W 93 E11
Río Mulatos Bolivia 19°40S 66°50W 92 G5
Río Muni □ Eq. Guin. 1°30N 10°0E 54 D2
Río Negro Brazil 26°0S 49°55W 95 B6
Río Pardo Brazil 30°0S 52°30W 95 C5
Río Pilcomayo △ Argentina 25°5S 58°5W 94 B4
Río Plátano △ Honduras 15°45N 85°0W 88 C3
Río Rancho U.S.A. 35°14N 106°41W 77 J10
Río Segundo Argentina 31°40S 63°59W 94 C3
Río Tercero Argentina 32°15S 64°8W 94 C3
Río Verde Brazil 17°50S 51°0W 93 G8
Río Verde Mexico 21°56N 99°59W 87 C5
Río Vista U.S.A. 38°10N 121°42W 78 G5
Ríobamba Ecuador 1°50S 78°45W 92 D3
Ríohacha Colombia 11°33N 72°55W 92 A4

Ríosucio Colombia 7°27N 77°7W 92 B3
Riou L. Canada 59°7N 106°25W 71 B7
Ripley Canada 44°4N 81°35W 82 B3
Ripley U.S.A. 33°32N 114°39W 79 M12
Ripley N.Y., U.S.A. 42°16N 79°43W 82 D5
Ripley Tenn., U.S.A. 35°45N 89°32W 85 D10
Ripley W. Va., U.S.A. 38°49N 81°43W 81 F13
Ripon U.K. 54°9N 1°31W 12 C6
Ripon Calif., U.S.A. 37°44N 121°7W 78 H5
Ripon Wis., U.S.A. 43°51N 88°50W 80 D9
Rishā', W. ar → Si. Arabia 25°33N 44°5E 46 E5
Rishikesh India 30°7N 78°19E 42 D8
Rishiri-Rebun-Sarobetsu △
  Japan 45°26N 141°30E 28 B10
Rishiri-Tō Japan 45°11N 141°15E 28 B10
Rishon le Ziyyon Israel 31°58N 34°48E 48 D3
Rison U.S.A. 33°58N 92°11W 84 E8
Risør Norway 58°43N 9°13E 9 G13
Rita Blanca Cr. →
  U.S.A. 35°40N 102°29W 84 D3
Ritchie's Arch. India 12°14N 93°10E 45 H11
Ritter, Mt. U.S.A. 37°41N 119°12W 78 H7
Rittman U.S.A. 40°58N 81°47W 82 F3
Ritzville U.S.A. 47°8N 118°23W 76 C4
Riva del Garda Italy 45°53N 10°50E 22 B4
Rivadavia B. Aires,
  Argentina 35°29S 62°59W 94 D3
Rivadavia Mendoza,
  Argentina 33°13S 68°30W 94 C2
Rivadavia Salta, Argentina 24°5S 62°54W 94 A3
Rivadavia Chile 29°57S 70°35W 94 B1
Rivas Nic. 11°30N 85°50W 88 D2
Rivera Argentina 37°12S 63°14W 94 D3
Rivera Uruguay 31°0S 55°50W 95 C4
Riverbank U.S.A. 37°44N 120°56W 78 H6
Riverdale U.S.A. 36°26N 119°52W 78 J7
Riverhead U.S.A. 40°55N 72°40W 83 F12
Riverhurst Canada 50°55N 106°50W 71 C7
Rivers Canada 50°2N 100°14W 71 C8
Rivers Inlet Canada 51°42N 127°15W 70 C3
Riversdale Canada 44°5N 81°20W 82 B3
Riversdale S. Africa 34°7S 21°15E 56 D3
Riverside U.S.A. 33°59N 117°22W 79 M9
Riversleigh Australia 19°5S 138°40E 62 B2
Riverton Australia 34°10S 138°46E 63 E2
Riverton Canada 51°1N 97°0W 71 C9
Riverton N.Z. 46°21S 168°0E 59 G2
Riverton U.S.A. 43°2N 108°23W 76 E9
Riviera = Azur, Côte d'
  France 43°25N 7°10E 20 E7
Riviera U.S.A. 35°4N 114°35W 79 K12
Riviera di Levante Italy 44°15N 9°30E 20 D8
Riviera di Ponente Italy 44°10N 8°20E 20 D8
Rivière-au-Renard
  Canada 48°59N 64°23W 73 C7
Rivière-du-Loup Canada 47°50N 69°30W 73 C6
Rivière-Pentecôte Canada 49°57N 67°1W 73 C6
Rivière-Pilote Martinique 14°26N 60°53W 88 c
Rivière St-Paul Canada 51°28N 57°45W 73 B8
Rivière-Salée Martinique 14°31N 61°0W 88 c
Rivne Ukraine 50°40N 26°10E 17 C14
Rivne □ Ukraine 51°15N 26°30E 17 C14
Rívoli Italy 45°3N 7°31E 20 D7
Rívoli B. Australia 37°32S 140°3E 63 F3
Riyadh = Ar Riyāḍ
  Si. Arabia 24°41N 46°42E 46 E5
Rize Turkey 41°0N 40°30E 19 F7
Rizhao China 35°25N 119°30E 33 G10
Rizzuto, C. Italy 38°53N 17°5E 22 E7
Rjukan Norway 59°54N 8°33E 9 G13
Road Town Br. Virgin Is. 18°27N 64°37W 89 e
Roan Plateau U.S.A. 39°20N 109°20W 76 G9
Roanne France 46°3N 4°4E 20 C6
Roanoke Ala., U.S.A. 33°9N 85°22W 85 E12
Roanoke Va., U.S.A. 37°16N 79°56W 81 G14
Roanoke → U.S.A. 35°57N 76°42W 85 D17
Roanoke I. U.S.A. 35°53N 75°39W 85 D17
Roanoke Rapids U.S.A. 36°28N 77°40W 85 C16
Roatán Honduras 16°18N 86°35W 88 C2
Robāṭ Sang Iran 35°35N 59°10E 47 C8
Robāṭkarīm Iran 35°25N 50°59E 47 C6
Robben I. S. Africa 33°48S 18°22E 56 D2
Robbins I. Australia 40°42S 145°0E 63 G4
Robe → Australia 21°42S 116°15E 60 D2
Robert Bourassa, Rés.
  Canada 53°40N 76°55W 72 B4
Robert Lee U.S.A. 31°54N 100°29W 84 F4
Robertsdale U.S.A. 40°11N 78°6W 82 F6
Robertsganj India 24°44N 83°4E 43 G10
Robertson S. Africa 33°46N 19°50E 56 D2
Robertson I. Antarctica 65°15S 59°30S 5 C18
Robertson Ra. Australia 23°15S 121°0E 60 D3
Robertstown Australia 33°58S 139°5E 63 E2
Roberval Canada 48°32N 72°15W 73 C5
Robeson Chan. N. Amer. 82°0N 61°30W 69 A19
Robesonia U.S.A. 40°21N 76°8W 83 F8
Robinson → Australia 16°3S 137°16E 62 B2
Robinson Crusoe I.
  Pac. Oc. 33°38S 78°52W 90 F2
Robinson Ra. Australia 25°40S 119°0E 61 E2
Robinvale Australia 34°40S 142°45E 63 E3
Roblin Canada 51°14N 101°21W 71 C8
Roboré Bolivia 18°10S 59°45W 92 G7
Robson, Mt. Canada 53°10N 119°10W 70 C5
Robstown U.S.A. 27°47N 97°40W 84 H6
Roca, C. da Portugal 38°40N 9°31W 21 C1
Roca Partida, I. Mexico 19°1N 112°2W 86 D2
Rocas, Atol das Brazil 4°0S 34°1W 93 D12
Rocha Uruguay 34°30S 54°25W 95 C5
Rochdale U.K. 53°38N 2°9W 12 D5
Rochefort Belgium 50°9N 5°12E 15 D5
Rochefort France 45°56N 0°57W 20 D3
Rochelle U.S.A. 41°56N 89°4W 80 E9
Rocher River Canada 61°23N 112°44W 70 A6
Rochester U.K. 51°23N 0°31E 13 F8
Rochester Ind., U.S.A. 41°4N 86°13W 80 E10

Rochester Minn., U.S.A. 44°1N 92°28W 80 C7
Rochester N.H., U.S.A. 43°18N 70°59W 83 C14
Rochester N.Y., U.S.A. 43°10N 77°37W 82 C7
Rock → Canada 60°7N 127°7W 70 A3
Rock, The Australia 35°15S 147°2E 63 F4
Rock Creek U.S.A. 41°40N 80°52W 82 E4
Rock Falls U.S.A. 41°47N 89°41W 80 E9
Rock Hill U.S.A. 34°56N 81°1W 85 D14
Rock Island U.S.A. 41°30N 90°34W 80 E8
Rock Port U.S.A. 40°25N 95°31W 80 E6
Rock Rapids U.S.A. 43°26N 96°10W 80 D5
Rock Sound Bahamas 24°54N 76°12W 88 B4
Rock Springs Mont.,
  U.S.A. 46°49N 106°15W 76 C10
Rock Springs Wyo.,
  U.S.A. 41°35N 109°14W 76 F9
Rock Valley U.S.A. 43°12N 96°18W 80 D5
Rockall Atl. Oc. 57°37N 13°42W 6 D3
Rockdale Tex., U.S.A. 30°39N 97°0W 84 F6
Rockdale Wash., U.S.A. 47°22N 121°28W 78 C5
Rockeby = Mungkan Kandju △
  Australia 13°35S 142°52E 62 A3
Rockefeller Plateau
  Antarctica 76°0S 130°0W 5 E14
Rockford U.S.A. 42°16N 89°6W 80 D9
Rockglen Canada 49°11N 105°57W 71 D7
Rockhampton Australia 23°22S 150°32E 62 C5
Rockingham Australia 32°15S 115°38E 61 F2
Rockingham N.C.,
  U.S.A. 34°57N 79°46W 85 D15
Rockingham Vt., U.S.A. 43°11N 72°29W 83 C12
Rockingham B. Australia 18°5S 146°10E 62 B4
Rocklake U.S.A. 48°47N 99°15W 80 A4
Rockland Canada 45°33N 75°17W 83 A9
Rockland Idaho, U.S.A. 42°34N 112°53W 76 E7
Rockland Maine, U.S.A. 44°6N 69°7W 81 C19
Rockland Mich., U.S.A. 46°44N 89°11W 80 B9
Rocklin U.S.A. 38°48N 121°14W 78 G5
Rockly B. Trin. & Tob. 11°9N 60°46W 93 K16
Rockmart U.S.A. 34°0N 85°3W 85 D12
Rockport Mass., U.S.A. 42°39N 70°37W 83 D14
Rockport Tex., U.S.A. 28°2N 97°3W 84 G6
Rocksprings U.S.A. 30°1N 100°13W 84 F4
Rockville Conn., U.S.A. 41°52N 72°28W 83 E12
Rockville Md., U.S.A. 39°5N 77°9W 81 F15
Rockwall U.S.A. 32°56N 96°28W 84 E6
Rockwell City U.S.A. 42°24N 94°38W 80 D6
Rockwood Canada 43°37N 80°8W 82 C4
Rockwood Maine,
  U.S.A. 45°41N 69°45W 81 C19
Rockwood Tenn., U.S.A. 35°52N 84°41W 85 D12
Rocky Ford U.S.A. 38°3N 103°43W 76 G12
Rocky Gully Australia 34°30S 116°57E 61 F2
Rocky Harbour Canada 49°36N 57°55W 73 C8
Rocky Island L. Canada 46°55N 83°0W 72 C3
Rocky Lane Canada 58°31N 116°22W 70 B5
Rocky Mount U.S.A. 35°57N 77°48W 85 D16
Rocky Mountain △
  U.S.A. 40°25N 105°45W 76 F11
Rocky Mountain House
  Canada 52°22N 114°55W 70 C6
Rocky Mts. N. Amer. 49°0N 115°0W 76 B6
Rocky Point Namibia 19°3S 12°30E 56 A2
Rod Pakistan 28°10N 63°5E 40 E3
Rødbyhavn Denmark 54°39N 11°22E 9 J14
Roddickton Canada 50°51N 56°8W 73 B8
Rodez France 44°21N 2°33E 20 D5
Ródhos = Rhodes Greece 36°15N 28°10E 23 F13
Rodna ◇ Australia 23°45S 132°4E 60 D5
Rodney C. N.Z. 36°17S 174°50E 59 B5
Rodney, C. N.Z. 36°17S 174°50E 59 B5
Rodopi Planina Bulgaria 41°40N 24°20E 23 D11
Rodrigues Ind. Oc. 19°45S 63°20E 3 E13
Roe → U.K. 55°6N 6°59W 10 A5
Roebling U.S.A. 40°7N 74°47W 83 F10
Roebourne Australia 20°44S 117°9E 60 D2
Roebuck B. Australia 18°5S 122°20E 60 C3
Roebuck Roadhouse
  Australia 17°59S 122°36E 60 C3
Roermond Neths. 51°12N 6°0E 15 C6
Roes Welcome Sd. Canada 65°0N 87°0W 69 E14
Roeselare Belgium 50°57N 3°7E 15 D3
Rogachev = Ragachow
  Belarus 53°8N 30°5E 17 B16
Rogagua, L. Bolivia 13°43S 66°50W 92 F5
Rogatyn Ukraine 49°24N 24°36E 17 D13
Rogers U.S.A. 36°20N 94°7W 84 C7
Rogers City U.S.A. 45°25N 83°49W 81 C12
Rogersville Canada 46°44N 65°26W 73 C6
Roggan → Canada 54°24N 79°25W 72 B4
Roggan L. Canada 54°8N 77°50W 72 B4
Roggeveen Basin
  Pac. Oc. 31°30S 95°30W 65 L18
Roggeveldberge S. Africa 32°10S 20°10E 56 D3
Rogoaguado, L. Bolivia 13°0S 65°30W 92 F5
Rogojampi Indonesia 8°19S 114°17E 37 J17
Rogue → U.S.A. 42°26N 124°26W 76 E1
Roha India 18°26N 73°7E 44 E1
Rohnert Park U.S.A. 38°16N 122°40W 78 G4
Rohri Pakistan 27°45N 68°51E 42 F3
Rohri Canal Pakistan 26°15N 68°27E 42 F3
Rohtak India 28°55N 76°43E 42 E7
Roi Et Thailand 16°4N 103°40E 38 D4
Roja Latvia 57°29N 22°43E 9 H20
Rojas Argentina 34°10S 60°45W 94 C3
Rojo, C. Mexico 21°33N 97°20W 87 C5
Rokan → Indonesia 2°0N 100°50E 36 D2
Rokiškis Lithuania 55°55N 25°35E 9 J21
Rokua △ Finland 64°30N 26°15E 8 D22
Rolândia Brazil 23°18S 51°23W 95 A5
Rolla Mo., U.S.A. 37°57N 91°46W 80 G8
Rolla N. Dak., U.S.A. 48°52N 99°37W 80 A4
Rolleston Australia 24°28S 148°35E 62 C4
Rollingstone Australia 19°2S 146°24E 62 B4
Roma Australia 26°32S 148°49E 63 D4
Roma Sweden 57°32N 18°26E 9 H18
Roma-Los Saenz U.S.A. 26°24N 99°1W 84 H5

Romang *Indonesia* 7°30S 127°20E **37** F7
Români *Egypt* 30°59N 32°38E **48** E1
Romania ■ *Europe* 46°0N 25°0E **17** F12
Romano, Cayo *Cuba* 22°0N 77°30W **88** B4
Romans-sur-Isère *France* 45°3N 5°3E **20** D6
Romanzof C. *U.S.A.* 61°49N 166°6W **74** C6
Romblon *Phil.* 12°33N 122°17E **37** B6
Rome *Ga., U.S.A.* 34°15N 85°10W **85** D12
Rome *N.Y., U.S.A.* 43°13N 75°27W **83** C9
Rome *Pa., U.S.A.* 41°51N 76°21W **83** E8
Romney *U.S.A.* 39°21N 78°45W **81** F14
Romney Marsh *U.K.* 51°2N 0°54E **13** F8
Rømø *Denmark* 55°10N 8°30E **9** J13
Romorantin-Lanthenay
 *France* 47°21N 1°45E **20** C4
Rompin → *Malaysia* 2°49N 103°29E **39** L4
Romsdalen *Norway* 62°25N 7°52E **8** E12
Romsey *U.K.* 51°0N 1°29W **13** G6
Ron *India* 15°40N 75°44E **45** G2
Ron *Vietnam* 17°53N 106°27E **38** D6
Rona *U.K.* 57°34N 5°59W **11** D3
Ronan *U.S.A.* 47°32N 114°6W **76** C6
Roncador, Cayos
 *Caribbean* 13°32N 80°4W **88** D3
Roncador, Serra do
 *Brazil* 12°30S 52°30W **93** F8
Ronda *Spain* 36°46N 5°12W **21** D3
Rondane *Norway* 61°57N 9°50E **8** F13
Rondônia □ *Brazil* 11°0S 63°0W **92** F6
Rondonópolis *Brazil* 16°28S 54°38W **93** G8
Rondu *Pakistan* 35°32N 75°10E **43** B6
Rong, Koh *Cambodia* 10°45N 103°15E **39** G4
Rong Jiang → *China* 24°35N 109°20E **34** E7
Rong Xian *China* 22°50N 110°31E **35** F8
Rong'an *China* 25°14N 109°22E **34** E7
Rongcang *China* 29°20N 105°32E **34** C5
Rongcheng *China* 37°9N 122°23E **33** F12
Ronge, L. la *Canada* 55°6N 105°17W **71** B7
Rongjiang *China* 25°57N 108°28E **34** E7
Rongshui *China* 25°5N 109°12E **34** E7
Rongxian *China* 29°23N 104°22E **34** C5
Rønne *Denmark* 55°6N 14°43E **9** J16
Ronne Ice Shelf *Antarctica* 77°30S 60°0W **5** D18
Ronsard, C. *Australia* 24°46S 113°10E **61** D1
Ronse *Belgium* 50°45N 3°35E **15** D3
Roodepoort *S. Africa* 26°11S 27°54E **57** C4
Roof Butte *U.S.A.* 36°28N 109°5W **77** H9
Rooiboklaagte → *Namibia* 20°50S 21°0E **56** B3
Rooniu, Mt. *Tahiti* 17°49S 149°12W **59** d
Roorkee *India* 29°52N 77°59E **42** E7
Roosendaal *Neths.* 51°32N 4°29E **15** C4
Roosevelt *U.S.A.* 40°18N 109°59W **76** F9
Roosevelt → *Brazil* 7°35S 60°20W **92** E6
Roosevelt, Mt. *Canada* 58°26N 125°20W **70** B3
Roosevelt I. *Antarctica* 79°30S 162°0W **5** D12
Roper → *Australia* 14°43S 135°27E **62** A2
Roper Bar *Australia* 14°44S 134°44E **62** A1
Roper River = St. Vidgeon's ✪
 *Australia* 14°47S 134°53E **62** A1
Roque Pérez *Argentina* 35°25S 59°24W **94** D4
Roquetas de Mar *Spain* 36°46N 2°36W **21** D4
Roraima □ *Brazil* 2°0N 61°30W **92** C6
Roraima, Mt. *Venezuela* 5°10N 60°40W **92** B6
Røros *Norway* 62°35N 11°23E **8** E14
Ros Comáin = Roscommon
 *Ireland* 53°38N 8°11W **10** C3
Ros Mhic Thriúin = New Ross
 *Ireland* 52°23N 6°57W **10** D5
Rosa, Monte *Europe* 45°57N 7°53E **20** D7
Rosalia *U.S.A.* 47°14N 117°22W **76** C5
Rosamond *U.S.A.* 34°52N 118°10W **79** L8
Rosario *Argentina* 33°0S 60°40W **94** C3
Rosário *Brazil* 3°0S 44°15W **93** D10
Rosario *Mexico* 22°58N 105°53W **86** C3
Rosario *Paraguay* 24°30S 57°35W **94** A4
Rosario de la Frontera
 *Argentina* 25°50S 65°0W **94** B3
Rosario de Lerma
 *Argentina* 24°59S 65°35W **94** A2
Rosario del Tala
 *Argentina* 32°20S 59°10W **94** C4
Rosário do Sul *Brazil* 30°15S 54°55W **95** C5
Rosarito *Baja Calif.,*
 *Mexico* 32°20N 117°2W **79** N9
Rosarito *Baja Calif.,*
 *Mexico* 28°38N 114°1W **86** B2
Roscoe *U.S.A.* 41°56N 74°55W **83** E10
Roscommon *Ireland* 53°38N 8°11W **10** C3
Roscommon □ *Ireland* 53°49N 8°23W **10** C3
Roscrea *Ireland* 52°57N 7°49W **10** D4
Rose → *Australia* 14°16S 135°45E **62** A2
Rose, L. *Bahamas* 21°0N 73°30W **89** B5
Rose Belle *Mauritius* 20°24S 57°36E **55** d
Rose Blanche *Canada* 47°38S 58°45W **73** C8
Rose Hill *Mauritius* 20°14S 57°27E **55** d
Rose Pt. *Canada* 54°11N 131°39W **70** C2
Rose Valley *Canada* 52°19N 103°49W **71** C8
Roseau *Dominica* 15°17N 61°24W **89** C7
Roseau *U.S.A.* 48°51N 95°46W **80** A6
Rosebery *Australia* 41°46S 145°33E **63** G4
Rosebud *S. Dak., U.S.A.* 43°14N 100°51W **80** D3
Rosebud *Tex., U.S.A.* 31°4N 96°59W **84** F6
Roseburg *U.S.A.* 43°13N 123°20W **76** E2
Rosedale *U.S.A.* 33°51N 91°2W **85** E9
Rosehearty *U.K.* 57°42N 2°7W **11** D6
Roseland *U.S.A.* 38°25N 122°43W **78** G4
Rosemary *Canada* 50°46N 112°5W **70** C6
Rosenberg *U.S.A.* 29°34N 95°49W **84** G7
Rosenheim *Germany* 47°51N 12°7E **16** E7
Roses, G. de *Spain* 42°10N 3°15E **21** A7
Rosetown *Canada* 51°35N 107°59W **71** C7
Roseville *Calif., U.S.A.* 38°45N 121°17W **78** G5
Roseville *Mich., U.S.A.* 42°30N 82°56W **82** D2
Roseville *Pa., U.S.A.* 41°51N 76°57W **83** E8
Rosewood *Australia* 27°38S 152°36E **63** D5
Roshkhvār *Iran* 34°58N 59°37E **47** C8
Rosignano Maríttimo
 *Italy* 43°24N 10°28E **22** C4
Rosignol *Guyana* 6°15N 57°30W **92** B7

Roșiori de Vede *Romania* 44°9N 25°0E **17** F13
Roskilde *Denmark* 55°38N 12°3E **9** J15
Roslavl *Russia* 53°57N 32°55E **18** D5
Roslyn *Australia* 34°29S 149°37E **63** E4
Rosmead *S. Africa* 31°29S 25°8E **56** D4
Ross *Australia* 42°2S 147°30E **63** G4
Ross *N.Z.* 42°53S 170°49E **59** E3
Ross Dependency
 *Antarctica* 76°0S 170°0W **5** D12
Ross I. *Antarctica* 77°30S 168°0E **5** D11
Ross Ice Shelf *Antarctica* 80°0S 180°0E **5** E12
Ross L. *U.S.A.* 48°44N 121°4W **76** B3
Ross-on-Wye *U.K.* 51°54N 2°34W **13** F5
Ross River *Australia* 23°44S 134°30E **62** C1
Ross River *Canada* 62°30N 131°30W **70** A2
Ross Sea *Antarctica* 74°0S 178°0E **5** D11
Rossall Pt. *U.K.* 53°55N 3°3W **12** D4
Rossan Pt. *Ireland* 54°42N 8°47W **10** B3
Rossano *Italy* 39°36N 16°39E **22** E7
Rossburn *Canada* 50°40N 100°49W **71** C8
Rosseau *Canada* 45°16N 79°39W **82** A5
Rosseau, L. *Canada* 45°10N 79°35W **82** A5
Rosses, The *Ireland* 55°2N 8°20W **10** A3
Rossignol, L. *Canada* 52°43N 73°40W **72** B5
Rossignol L. *Canada* 44°12N 65°10W **73** D6
Rossiya = Russia ■
 *Eurasia* 62°0N 105°0E **27** C11
Rossland *Canada* 49°6N 117°50W **70** D5
Rosslare *Ireland* 52°17N 6°24W **10** D5
Rosslare Europort = Rosslare
 Harbour *Ireland* 52°15N 6°20W **10** D5
Rosslare Harbour *Ireland* 52°15N 6°20W **10** D5
Rossmore *Canada* 44°8N 77°23W **82** B7
Rosso *Mauritania* 16°40N 15°45W **52** E2
Rossosh *Russia* 50°15N 39°28E **19** D6
Røssvatnet *Norway* 65°45N 14°5E **8** D16
Røst *Norway* 67°32N 12°10E **8** C15
Rosthern *Canada* 52°40N 106°20W **71** C7
Rostock *Germany* 54°5N 12°8E **16** A7
Rostov *Don, Russia* 47°15N 39°45E **19** E6
Rostov *Yaroslavl, Russia* 57°14N 39°25E **18** C6
Roswell *Ga., U.S.A.* 34°2N 84°22W **85** D12
Roswell *N. Mex., U.S.A.* 33°24N 104°32W **77** K11
Rotan *U.S.A.* 32°51N 100°28W **84** E4
Rote *Indonesia* 10°50S 123°0E **37** F6
Rother → *U.K.* 50°59N 0°45E **13** G8
Rothera *Antarctica* 67°34S 68°8W **5** C17
Rotherham *U.K.* 53°26N 1°20W **12** D6
Rothes *U.K.* 57°32N 3°13W **11** D5
Rothesay *Canada* 45°23N 66°0W **73** C6
Rothesay *U.K.* 55°50N 5°3W **11** F3
Roti = Rote *Indonesia* 10°50S 123°0E **37** F6
Roto *Australia* 33°0S 145°30E **63** E4
Rotondo, Mte. *France* 42°14N 9°8E **20** E8
Rotoroa, L. *N.Z.* 41°55S 172°39E **59** D4
Rotorua *N.Z.* 38°9S 176°16E **59** C6
Rotorua, L. *N.Z.* 38°5S 176°18E **59** C6
Rotterdam *Neths.* 51°55N 4°30E **15** C4
Rotterdam *U.S.A.* 42°48N 74°1W **83** D10
Rottnest I. *Australia* 32°0S 115°27E **61** F2
Rottumeroog *Neths.* 53°33N 6°34E **15** A6
Rottweil *Germany* 48°9N 8°37E **16** D5
Rotuma *Fiji* 12°25S 177°5E **58** C10
Roubaix *France* 50°40N 3°10E **20** A5
Rouen *France* 49°27N 1°4E **20** B4
Rouleau *Canada* 50°10N 104°56W **71** C8
Roulpmaulpma ✪
 *Australia* 23°52S 133°0E **60** D5
Round I. *Mauritius* 19°51S 57°45E **55** d
Round Mountain *U.S.A.* 38°43N 117°4W **76** G5
Round Rock *U.S.A.* 30°26S 152°16E **63** E5
Round Rock *U.S.A.* 30°31N 97°41W **84** F6
Roundup *U.S.A.* 46°27N 108°33W **76** C9
Rousay *U.K.* 59°10N 3°2W **11** B5
Rouses Point *U.S.A.* 44°59N 73°22W **83** B11
Rouseville *U.S.A.* 41°28N 79°42W **82** E5
Rousillon *France* 42°30N 2°35E **20** E5
Rousse = Ruse *Bulgaria* 43°48N 25°59E **23** C12
Roussillon *France* 42°30N 2°35E **20** E5
Rouxville *S. Africa* 30°25S 26°50E **56** E4
Rouyn-Noranda *Canada* 48°20N 79°0W **72** C4
Rovaniemi *Finland* 66°29N 25°41E **8** C21
Rovereto *Italy* 45°53N 11°3E **22** B4
Rovigo *Italy* 45°4N 11°47E **22** B4
Rovinj *Croatia* 45°5N 13°40E **16** F7
Rovno = Rivne *Ukraine* 50°40N 26°10E **17** C14
Rovuma = Ruvuma →
 *Tanzania* 10°29S 40°28E **54** G8
Row'ān *Iran* 35°8N 48°51E **47** C6
Rowena *Australia* 29°48S 148°55E **63** D4
Rowley I. *Canada* 69°6N 77°52W **69** D16
Rowley Shoals *Australia* 17°30S 119°0E **60** C2
Roxas *Phil.* 11°36N 122°49E **37** B6
Roxboro *U.S.A.* 36°24N 78°59W **85** C15
Roxborough *Trin. & Tob.* 11°15N 60°35W **93** J16
Roxburgh *N.Z.* 45°33S 169°19E **59** F2
Roxbury *N.Y., U.S.A.* 42°17N 74°33W **83** D10
Roxbury *Pa., U.S.A.* 40°6N 77°39W **82** F7
Roxby Downs *Australia* 30°43S 136°46E **63** E2
Roy *Mont., U.S.A.* 47°20N 108°58W **76** C9
Roy *N. Mex., U.S.A.* 35°57N 104°12W **77** J11
Roy *Utah, U.S.A.* 41°10N 112°2W **76** F7
Roy Hill *Australia* 22°41S 119°57E **60** D3
Royal Bardia △ *Nepal* 28°20N 81°20E **43** E9
Royal Canal *Ireland* 53°30N 7°13W **10** C4
Royal Chitawan △
 *Nepal* 26°30N 84°30E **43** F11
Royal Geographical Society Is.
 *Canada* 68°56N 100°15W **68** D11
Royal Leamington Spa
 *U.K.* 52°18N 1°31W **13** E6
Royal Natal △ *S. Africa* 28°43S 28°51E **57** C4
Royal Tunbridge Wells
 *U.K.* 51°7N 0°16E **13** F8
Royale, Isle *U.S.A.* 48°0N 88°54W **80** B9
Royan *France* 45°37N 1°2W **20** D3
Royston *U.K.* 52°3N 0°0 **13** E7
Rozdilna *Ukraine* 46°50N 30°2E **17** E16
Rozhyshche *Ukraine* 50°54N 25°15E **17** C13
Rtishchevo *Russia* 52°18N 43°46E **18** D7
Ruacaná *Namibia* 17°27S 14°21E **56** A1
Ruahine Ra. *N.Z.* 39°55S 176°2E **59** C6

Ruapehu *N.Z.* 39°17S 175°35E **59** C5
Ruapuke I. *N.Z.* 46°46S 168°31E **59** G2
Ruâq, W. → *Egypt* 30°0N 33°49E **48** F2
Rub' al Khālī *Si. Arabia* 19°0N 48°0E **49** D4
Rubh a' Mhail *U.K.* 55°56N 6°8W **11** F2
Rubha Hunish *U.K.* 57°42N 6°20W **11** D2
Rubha Robhanais = Lewis, Butt of
 *U.K.* 58°31N 6°16W **11** C2
Rubicon → *U.S.A.* 38°53N 121°4W **78** G5
Rubio *Venezuela* 7°43N 72°22W **92** B4
Rubtsovsk *Russia* 51°30N 81°10E **30** A5
Ruby L. *U.S.A.* 40°10N 115°28W **76** F6
Ruby Mts. *U.S.A.* 40°30N 115°20W **76** F6
Rubyvale *Australia* 23°25S 147°42E **62** C4
Rucheng *China* 25°33N 113°38E **35** E9
Rūd Sar *Iran* 37°8N 50°18E **47** B6
Rudall *Australia* 33°43S 136°17E **63** E2
Rudall → *Australia* 22°34S 122°13E **60** D3
Rudall River △ *Australia* 22°38S 122°30E **60** D3
Rudbar *Iran* 36°48N 49°23E **47** B6
Rudnyy *Kazakhstan* 52°57N 63°7E **26** D7
Rudong *China* 32°20N 121°12E **35** A13
Rudrapur *India* 28°59N 79°24E **43** E8
Rudyard *U.S.A.* 46°14N 84°36W **81** B11
Ruffling Pt. *Br. Virgin Is.* 18°44N 64°27W **89** e
Rufiji → *Tanzania* 7°50S 39°15E **54** F7
Rufino *Argentina* 34°20S 62°50W **94** C3
Rugao *China* 32°23N 120°31E **35** A13
Rugby *U.K.* 52°23N 1°16W **13** E6
Rugby *U.S.A.* 48°22N 100°0W **80** A4
Rügen *Germany* 54°22N 13°24E **16** A7
Ruhnu *Estonia* 57°48N 23°15E **9** H20
Ruhr → *Germany* 51°27N 6°43E **16** C4
Rui'an *China* 27°47N 120°40E **35** D13
Ruichang *China* 29°40N 115°39E **35** C10
Ruidoso *U.S.A.* 33°20N 105°41W **77** K11
Ruijin *China* 25°48N 116°0E **35** E10
Ruili *China* 24°6N 97°46E **34** E1
Rujm Tal'at al Jamā'ah
 *Jordan* 30°24N 35°30E **48** E4
Ruk *Pakistan* 27°50N 68°42E **42** F3
Rukhla *Pakistan* 32°27N 71°57E **42** C4
Ruki →
 *Dem. Rep. of the Congo* 0°5N 18°17E **54** E3
Rukumkot *Nepal* 28°37N 82°37E **43** E10
Rukwa □ *Tanzania* 8°0S 32°20E **54** F6
Rulhieres, C. *Australia* 13°56S 127°22E **60** B4
Rum *Jordan* 29°39N 35°26E **48** F4
Rùm *U.K.* 57°0N 6°20W **11** E2
Rum Cay *Bahamas* 23°40N 74°58W **89** B5
Rum Jungle *Australia* 13°0S 130°59E **60** B5
Rumāḥ *Si. Arabia* 25°29N 47°10E **44** E5
Rumania = Romania ■
 *Europe* 46°0N 25°0E **17** F12
Rumaylah *Iraq* 30°47N 47°37E **46** D5
Rumaylah, 'Urūq ar
 *Si. Arabia* 22°0N 48°30E **49** C4
Rumbek *South Sudan* 6°54N 29°37E **53** G11
Rumford *U.S.A.* 44°33N 70°33W **83** B14
Rumia *Poland* 54°37N 18°25E **17** A10
Rumoi *Japan* 43°56N 141°39E **28** C10
Rumson *U.S.A.* 40°23N 74°0W **83** F11
Runan *China* 33°0N 114°30E **32** H8
Runanga *N.Z.* 42°25S 171°15E **59** E3
Runaway, C. *N.Z.* 37°32S 177°59E **59** B6
Runaway Bay *Jamaica* 18°27N 77°20W **88** a
Runcorn *U.K.* 53°21N 2°44W **12** D5
Rundu *Namibia* 17°52S 19°43E **56** B2
Rungwa *Tanzania* 9°11S 33°32E **54** F6
Rungwe *Tanzania* 9°8S 33°40E **54** F6
Rungwe, Mt. *Tanzania* 9°8S 33°40E **54** F6
Runton Ra. *Australia* 23°31S 123°6E **60** D3
Ruo Shui → *China* 41°0N 100°16E **30** C9
Ruokolahti *Finland* 61°17N 28°50E **8** F23
Ruoqiang *China* 38°55N 88°10E **30** D6
Rupa *India* 27°15N 92°21E **41** F18
Rupar = Rupnagar *India* 31°2N 76°38E **42** D7
Rupat *Indonesia* 1°45N 101°40E **36** D2
Rupen → *India* 23°28N 71°31E **42** H4
Rupert *U.S.A.* 42°37N 113°41W **76** E7
Rupert → *Canada* 51°29N 78°45W **72** B4
Rupert B. *Canada* 51°35N 79°0W **72** B4
Rupert House = Waskaganish
 *Canada* 51°30N 78°40W **72** B4
Rupnagar *India* 31°2N 76°38E **42** D7
Rupsa *India* 21°37N 87°1E **43** J12
Rurrenabaque *Bolivia* 14°30S 67°32W **92** F5
Ruschuk = Ruse
 *Bulgaria* 43°48N 25°59E **23** C12
Ruse *Bulgaria* 43°48N 25°59E **23** C12
Rush *Ireland* 53°31N 6°6W **10** C5
Rushan *China* 36°56N 121°30E **33** F11
Rushden *U.K.* 52°18N 0°35W **13** E7
Rushikulya → *India* 19°23N 85°5E **44** E7
Rushmore, Mt. *U.S.A.* 43°53N 103°28W **80** D2
Rushville *Ill., U.S.A.* 40°7N 90°34W **80** E8
Rushville *Ind., U.S.A.* 39°37N 85°27W **81** F11
Rushville *Nebr., U.S.A.* 42°43N 102°28W **80** D2
Russas *Brazil* 4°55S 37°50W **93** D11
Russell *Canada* 50°50N 101°20W **71** C8
Russell *N.Z.* 35°16S 174°10E **59** A5
Russell *U.S.A.* 38°54N 98°52W **80** F4
Russell L. *Man., Canada* 56°15N 101°30W **71** B8
Russell L. *N.W.T., Canada* 63°5N 115°44W **70** A5
Russellkonda *India* 19°57N 84°42E **44** E7
Russellville *Ala., U.S.A.* 34°30N 87°44W **85** D11
Russellville *Ark., U.S.A.* 35°17N 93°8W **84** D8
Russellville *Ky., U.S.A.* 36°51N 86°53W **80** G10
Russia ■ *Eurasia* 62°0N 105°0E **27** C11
Russian → *U.S.A.* 38°27N 123°8W **78** G3
Russkaya Arktika △
 *Russia* 73°40N 55°55E **26** B6
Russkiy, Ostrov *Russia* 73°0N 131°50E **27** B12
Rustam Shahr *Pakistan* 26°58N 66°6E **42** F2
Rustavi *Georgia* 41°30N 45°0E **19** F8
Rustenburg *S. Africa* 25°41S 27°14E **56** D4
Ruston *U.S.A.* 32°32N 92°38W **84** E8
Ruteng *Indonesia* 8°35S 120°30E **37** F6

Rutenga *Zimbabwe* 21°15S 30°44E **57** B5
Ruth *U.S.A.* 43°42N 82°45W **82** C2
Rutherford *U.S.A.* 38°26N 122°24W **78** G4
Rutland □ *U.K.* 52°38N 0°40W **13** E7
Rutland I. *India* 11°25N 92°10E **45** J11
Rutland Water □ *U.K.* 52°39N 0°38W **13** E7
Rutledge → *Canada* 61°4N 112°0W **71** A6
Rutledge L. *Canada* 61°33N 110°47W **71** A6
Rutog *China* 33°27N 79°42E **30** E4
Rutshuru
 *Dem. Rep. of the Congo* 1°13S 29°25E **54** E5
Ruvuma → *Tanzania* 10°29S 40°28E **54** G8
Ruwais *U.A.E.* 24°5N 52°50E **47** E7
Ruwenzori *Africa* 0°30N 29°55E **54** D5
Ruya → *Zimbabwe* 16°27S 32°5E **57** A5
Ruyang *China* 34°9N 112°27E **32** G7
Ruyuan *China* 24°46N 113°16E **35** E9
Ruzhou *China* 34°11N 112°52E **32** G7
Ružomberok *Slovakia* 49°3N 19°17E **17** D10
Rwanda ■ *Africa* 2°0S 30°0E **54** E5
Ryan, L. *U.K.* 55°0N 5°2W **11** G3
Ryazan *Russia* 54°40N 39°40E **18** D6
Ryazhsk *Russia* 53°45N 40°3E **18** D7
Rybachiy Poluostrov
 *Russia* 69°43N 32°0E **8** B25
Rybachye = Balykchy
 *Kyrgyzstan* 42°26N 76°12E **30** C4
Rybinsk *Russia* 58°5N 38°50E **18** C6
Rybinskoye Vdkhr.
 *Russia* 58°30N 38°25E **18** C6
Rybnitsa = Rîbnița
 *Moldova* 47°45N 29°0E **17** E15
Rycroft *Canada* 55°45N 118°40W **70** B5
Ryde *U.K.* 50°43N 1°9W **13** G6
Ryderwood *U.S.A.* 46°23N 123°3W **78** D3
Rye *U.K.* 50°57N 0°45E **13** G8
Rye → *U.K.* 54°11N 0°44W **12** C7
Rye Bay *U.K.* 50°52N 0°49E **13** G8
Rye Patch Res. *U.S.A.* 40°28N 118°19W **76** F4
Ryegate *U.S.A.* 46°18N 109°15W **76** C9
Ryley *Canada* 53°17N 112°26W **70** C6
Rylstone *Australia* 32°46S 149°58E **63** E4
Ryn Peski = Naryn Qum
 *Kazakhstan* 47°30N 49°0E **26** E5
Ryōtsu *Japan* 38°5N 138°26E **28** E9
Rypin *Poland* 53°3N 19°25E **17** B10
Ryūgasaki *Japan* 35°54N 140°11E **29** G10
Ryukyu Is. = Ryūkyū-Rettō
 *Japan* 26°0N 126°0E **29** M3
Ryūkyū-Rettō *Japan* 26°0N 126°0E **29** M3
Rzeszów *Poland* 50°5N 21°58E **17** C11
Rzhev *Russia* 56°20N 34°20E **18** C5

## S

Sa Dec *Vietnam* 10°20N 105°46E **39** G5
Sa Kaeo *Thailand* 13°49N 102°4E **38** F4
Sa Pa *Vietnam* 22°20N 103°47E **38** A4
Sa'ādah Shahr *Iran* 30°10N 53°5E **47** D7
Sa'ādatābād *Hormozgān,*
 *Iran* 28°3N 55°53E **47** D7
Sa'ādatābād *Kermān, Iran* 29°40N 55°51E **47** D7
Saale → *Germany* 51°56N 11°54E **16** C6
Saalfeld *Germany* 50°38N 11°21E **16** C6
Saanich *Canada* 48°29N 123°26W **78** B3
Saar → *Europe* 49°41N 6°32E **15** E6
Saarbrücken *Germany* 49°14N 6°59E **16** D4
Saaremaa *Estonia* 58°30N 22°30E **9** G20
Saarijärvi *Finland* 62°43N 25°16E **8** E21
Sab 'Ābar *Syria* 33°46N 37°41E **46** C3
Saba *W. Indies* 17°38N 63°14W **89** C7
Šabac *Serbia* 44°48N 19°42E **23** B8
Sabadell *Spain* 41°28N 2°7E **21** B7
Sabah □ *Malaysia* 6°0N 117°0E **36** C5
Sabak Bernam *Malaysia* 3°46N 100°58E **39** L3
Sabalān, Kūhhā-ye *Iran* 38°15N 47°45E **46** B5
Sabalana, Kepulauan
 *Indonesia* 6°45S 118°50E **37** F5
Sabana de la Mar
 *Dom. Rep.* 19°7N 69°24W **89** C6
Sábanalarga *Colombia* 10°38N 74°55W **92** A4
Sabang *Indonesia* 5°50N 95°15E **36** C1
Sabari → *India* 17°35N 81°16E **44** F5
Sabarmati → *India* 22°18N 72°22E **42** H5
Sabattis *U.S.A.* 44°6N 74°40W **83** B10
Saberania *Indonesia* 2°5S 138°18E **37** E9
Sabhā *Libya* 27°9N 14°29E **53** C8
Sabi → *India* 28°29N 76°44E **42** E7
Sabie *S. Africa* 25°10S 30°48E **57** C5
Sabinas *Mexico* 27°51N 101°7W **86** B4
Sabinas → *Mexico* 27°37N 100°42W **86** B4
Sabinas Hidalgo *Mexico* 26°30N 100°10W **86** B4
Sabine → *U.S.A.* 29°59N 93°47W **84** G8
Sabine L. *U.S.A.* 29°53N 93°51W **84** G8
Sabine Pass *U.S.A.* 29°44N 93°54W **84** H8
Sablayan *Phil.* 12°50N 120°50E **37** B6
Sable *C. Canada* 55°30N 68°21W **73** A6
Sable, C. *Canada* 43°29N 65°38W **73** E6
Sable, C. *U.S.A.* 25°9N 81°8W **88** A3
Sable I. *Canada* 44°0N 60°0W **73** D8
Sabrina Coast *Antarctica* 68°0S 120°0E **5** C9
Sabulubek *Indonesia* 1°36S 98°40E **36** E1
Sabzevār *Iran* 36°15N 57°40E **47** B8
Sabzvārān = Jiroft *Iran* 28°45N 57°50E **47** D8
Sac City *U.S.A.* 42°25N 95°0W **80** D6
Săcele *Romania* 45°37N 25°41E **17** F13
Sacheon *S. Korea* 35°0N 128°6E **33** G15
Sachigo → *Canada* 55°6N 88°58W **72** A2
Sachigo, L. *Canada* 53°50N 92°12W **72** B1
Sachin *India* 21°5N 72°53E **44** D1
Sachsen □ *Germany* 50°55N 13°10E **16** C7
Sachsen-Anhalt □
 *Germany* 52°0N 12°0E **16** C7
Sackets Harbor *U.S.A.* 43°57N 76°7W **83** C8
Sackville *Canada* 45°54N 64°22W **73** C7
Saco *Maine, U.S.A.* 43°30N 70°27W **83** C14
Saco *Mont., U.S.A.* 48°28N 107°21W **76** B10

Sacramento *U.S.A.* 38°35N 121°29W **78** G5
Sacramento → *U.S.A.* 38°3N 121°56W **78** G5
Sacramento Mts.
 *U.S.A.* 32°30N 105°30W **77** K11
Sacramento Valley
 *U.S.A.* 39°30N 122°0W **78** G5
Sada-Misaki *Japan* 33°20N 132°5E **29** H6
Sadabad *India* 27°27N 78°3E **42** F8
Ṣa'dah *Yemen* 16°15N 43°37E **49** D3
Sadao *Thailand* 6°38N 100°26E **39** J3
Sadaseopet *India* 17°38N 77°59E **44** F3
Sadd el Aali *Egypt* 23°54N 32°54E **53** D12
Saddle Mt. *U.S.A.* 45°58N 123°41W **78** E3
Saddle Pk. *India* 13°9N 93°1E **45** H11
Sado *Japan* 38°0N 138°25E **28** E9
Sadra *India* 23°21N 72°43E **42** H5
Sadri *India* 25°11N 73°26E **42** G5
Sæby *Denmark* 57°21N 10°30E **9** H14
Saegertown *U.S.A.* 41°43N 80°9W **82** E4
Ṣafājah *S. Arabia* 26°25N 39°0E **44** E3
Safata B. *Samoa* 14°0S 171°50W **59** b
Säffle *Sweden* 59°8N 12°55E **9** G15
Safford *U.S.A.* 32°50N 109°43W **77** K9
Saffron Walden *U.K.* 52°1N 0°16E **13** E8
Safi *Morocco* 32°18N 9°20W **52** B4
Ṣafīābād *Iran* 36°45N 57°58E **47** B8
Safid Dasht *Iran* 33°27N 48°11E **47** C6
Safid Kūh *Afghan.* 34°45N 63°0E **40** B3
Safid Rūd → *Iran* 37°23N 50°11E **47** B6
Safipur *India* 26°44N 80°21E **43** F9
Ṣāfītā *Syria* 34°48N 36°7E **46** C4
Safune *Samoa* 13°25S 172°21W **59** b
Ṣafwān *Iraq* 30°7N 47°43E **46** D5
Sag Harbor *U.S.A.* 41°0N 72°18W **83** F12
Saga *Japan* 33°15N 130°16E **29** H5
Saga □ *Japan* 33°15N 130°20E **29** H5
Sagae *Japan* 38°22N 140°17E **28** E10
Sagaing *Myanmar* 21°52N 95°59E **41** J19
Sagamore *U.S.A.* 40°46N 79°14W **82** F5
Saganaga L. *Canada* 48°14N 90°52W **80** A8
Saganthit Kyun
 *Myanmar* 11°56N 98°29E **39** G2
Sagar *Karnataka, India* 16°38N 76°48E **44** F3
Sagar *Karnataka, India* 14°14N 75°6E **45** G2
Sagar *Mad. P., India* 23°50N 78°44E **43** H8
Sagarmatha = Everest, Mt.
 *Nepal* 28°5N 86°58E **43** E12
Sagarmatha △ *Nepal* 27°55N 86°45E **43** F12
Saginaw *U.S.A.* 43°26N 83°56W **81** D12
Saginaw B. *U.S.A.* 43°50N 83°40W **81** D12
Saglouc = Salluit
 *Canada* 62°14N 75°38W **69** E16
Sagone *France* 42°7N 8°42E **20** E8
Sagua la Grande *Cuba* 22°50N 80°10W **88** B3
Saguache *U.S.A.* 38°5N 106°8W **76** G10
Saguaro △ *U.S.A.* 32°12N 110°38W **77** K8
Saguenay → *Canada* 48°22N 71°0W **73** C5
Sagunt *Spain* 39°42N 0°18W **21** C5
Sagunto = Sagunt *Spain* 39°42N 0°18W **21** C5
Sagwara *India* 23°41N 74°1E **42** H6
Sahagún *Spain* 42°18N 5°2W **21** A3
Saham al Jawlān *Syria* 32°45N 35°55E **48** C4
Sahand, Kūh-e *Iran* 37°44N 46°27E **46** B5
Sahara *Africa* 23°0N 5°0E **52** D6
Saharan Atlas = Saharien, Atlas
 *Algeria* 33°30N 1°0E **52** B6
Saharanpur *India* 29°58N 77°33E **42** E7
Saharien, Atlas *Algeria* 33°30N 1°0E **52** B6
Saharsa *India* 25°53N 86°36E **43** G12
Sahaswan *India* 28°5N 78°45E **43** E8
Saheira, W. el → *Egypt* 30°5N 33°25E **48** E2
Sahel *Africa* 16°0N 5°0E **52** E5
Sahibganj *India* 25°12N 87°40E **43** G12
Sāḥilīyah *Iraq* 33°43N 42°42E **46** C4
Sahiwal *Pakistan* 30°45N 73°8E **42** D5
Ṣaḥneh *Iran* 34°29N 47°41E **46** C5
Sahrawi = Western Sahara ■
 *Africa* 25°0N 13°0W **52** D3
Sahuaripa *Mexico* 29°3N 109°14W **86** B3
Sahuarita *U.S.A.* 31°57N 110°58W **77** L8
Sahuayo de Díaz *Mexico* 20°4N 102°43W **86** C4
Sai → *India* 25°39N 82°47E **43** G10
Sai Buri *Thailand* 6°43N 101°45E **39** J3
Sai Thong △ *Thailand* 15°56N 101°10E **38** E3
Sai Yok △ *Thailand* 14°25N 98°40E **38** E2
Saibai I. *Australia* 9°25S 142°40E **62** a
Sa'id Bundas *South Sudan* 8°24N 24°48E **53** G10
Sa'īdābād = Sīrjān *Iran* 29°30N 55°45E **47** D7
Sa'īdābād *Iran* 36°8N 54°11E **47** B7
Saidpur *Bangla.* 25°48N 89°0E **41** G16
Saidpur *India* 25°33N 83°11E **43** G10
Saidu Sharif *Pakistan* 34°43N 72°24E **43** B5
Saigō *Japan* 36°12N 133°20E **29** F6
Saigon = Thanh Pho Ho Chi Minh
 *Vietnam* 10°58N 106°40E **39** G6
Saijō *Japan* 33°55N 133°11E **29** H6
Saikai △ *Japan* 33°12N 129°35E **29** H4
Saikhoa Ghat *India* 27°50N 95°40E **41** F19
Saiki *Japan* 32°58N 131°51E **29** H5
Sailana *India* 23°28N 74°55E **42** H6
Sailolof *Indonesia* 1°15S 130°46E **37** E8
Sailu *India* 19°28N 76°28E **44** E3
Saimaa *Finland* 61°15N 28°15E **8** F23
Saimen = Saimaa *Finland* 61°15N 28°15E **8** F23
Ṣa'in Dezh *Iran* 36°40N 46°25E **46** B5
St. Abb's Head *U.K.* 55°55N 2°8W **11** F6
St. Alban's *Canada* 47°51N 55°50W **73** C8
St. Albans *U.K.* 51°45N 0°19W **13** F7
St. Albans *Vt., U.S.A.* 44°49N 73°5W **83** B11
St. Albans *W. Va.,*
 *U.S.A.* 38°23N 81°50W **81** F13
St. Alban's Head *U.K.* 50°34N 2°4W **13** G5
St. Albert *Canada* 53°37N 113°32W **70** C6
St-André *Réunion* 20°57S 55°39E **55** c
St. Andrew's *Canada* 47°45N 59°15W **73** C8
St. Andrews *U.K.* 56°20N 2°47W **11** E6
St-Anicet *Canada* 45°8N 74°22W **83** A10
St. Anne *U.K.* 49°43N 2°11W **13** H5
St. Annes *Canada* 49°40N 96°39W **71** D9
St. Anns B. *Canada* 46°22N 60°25W **73** C7
St. Ann's Bay *Jamaica* 18°26N 77°12W **88** a

St. Anthony Canada 51°22N 55°35W 73 B8
St. Anthony U.S.A. 43°58N 111°41W 76 E8
St-Antoine Canada 46°22N 64°45W 73 C7
St. Arnaud Australia 36°40S 143°16E 63 F3
St-Augustin Canada 51°13N 58°38W 73 B8
St-Augustin → Canada 51°16N 58°40W 73 B8
St. Augustine U.S.A. 29°54N 81°19W 85 G14
St. Austell U.K. 50°20N 4°47W 13 G3
St. Barbe Canada 51°12N 56°46W 73 B8
St-Barthélemy ☑ W. Indies 17°50N 62°50W 89 C7
St. Barts = St-Barthélemy ☑ W. Indies 17°50N 62°50W 89 C7
St. Bees Hd. U.K. 54°31N 3°38W 12 C4
St. Bees I. Australia 20°56S 149°26E 62 b
St-Benoît Réunion 21°2S 55°43E 55 c
St. Bride's Canada 46°56N 54°10W 73 C9
St. Brides B. U.K. 51°49N 5°9W 13 F2
St-Brieuc France 48°30N 2°46W 20 B2
St. Catharines Canada 43°10N 79°15W 82 C5
St. Catherines I. U.S.A. 31°40N 81°10W 85 F14
St. Catherine's Pt. U.K. 50°34N 1°18W 13 G6
St-Chamond France 45°28N 4°31E 20 D6
St. Charles Ill., U.S.A. 41°54N 88°19W 80 E9
St. Charles Md., U.S.A. 38°36N 76°56W 81 F15
St. Charles Mo., U.S.A. 38°47N 90°29W 80 F8
St. Charles Va., U.S.A. 36°48N 83°4W 81 G12
St. Christopher-Nevis = St. Kitts & Nevis ■ W. Indies 17°20N 62°40W 89 C7
St. Clair Mich., U.S.A. 42°50N 82°30W 82 D2
St. Clair Pa., U.S.A. 40°43N 76°12W 83 F8
St. Clair → U.S.A. 42°38N 82°31W 82 D2
St. Clair, L. N. Amer. 42°27N 82°39W 82 D2
St. Clairsville U.S.A. 40°5N 80°54W 82 F4
St. Claude Canada 49°40N 98°20W 71 D9
St. Clears U.K. 51°49N 4°31W 13 F3
St-Clet Canada 45°21N 74°13W 83 A10
St. Cloud Fla., U.S.A. 28°15N 81°17W 85 G14
St. Cloud Minn., U.S.A. 45°34N 94°10W 80 C6
St. Cricq, C. Australia 25°17S 113°6E 61 E1
St. Croix U.S. Virgin Is. 17°45N 64°45W 89 C7
St. Croix → U.S.A. 44°45N 92°48W 80 C7
St. Croix Falls U.S.A. 45°24N 92°38W 80 C7
St. David's Canada 48°12N 58°52W 73 C8
St. David's U.K. 51°53N 5°16W 13 F2
St. David's Head U.K. 51°54N 5°19W 13 F2
St-Denis Réunion 20°52S 55°27E 55 c
St-Denis ✈ (RUN) Réunion 20°53S 55°32E 55 c
St-Dizier France 48°38N 4°56E 20 B6
St. Elias, Mt. U.S.A. 60°18N 140°56W 68 E3
St. Elias Mts. N. Amer. 60°33N 139°28W 70 A1
St-Étienne France 45°27N 4°22E 20 D6
St. Eugène Canada 45°30N 74°28W 83 A10
St. Eustatius W. Indies 17°20N 63°0W 89 C7
St-Félicien Canada 48°40N 72°25W 72 C5
St-Flour France 45°2N 3°6E 20 D5
St. Francis U.S.A. 39°47N 101°48W 80 F3
St. Francis → U.S.A. 34°38N 90°36W 85 D9
St. Francis, C. S. Africa 34°14S 24°49E 56 D3
St. Francisville U.S.A. 30°47N 91°23W 84 F9
St-François, L. Canada 45°10N 74°22W 83 A10
St-Gabriel Canada 46°17N 73°24W 72 C5
St. Gallen = Sankt Gallen Switz. 47°26N 9°22E 20 C8
St-Gaudens France 43°6N 0°44E 20 E4
St. George Australia 28°1S 148°30E 63 D4
St. George N.B., Canada 45°11N 66°50W 73 C6
St. George Ont., Canada 43°15N 80°15W 82 C4
St. George S.C., U.S.A. 33°11N 80°35W 85 E14
St. George Utah, U.S.A. 37°6N 113°35W 77 H7
St. George, C. Canada 48°30N 59°16W 73 C8
St. George, C. U.S.A. 29°40N 85°5W 85 G12
St. George I. U.S.A. 56°35N 169°35W 74 D6
St. George Ra. Australia 18°40S 125°0E 60 C4
St. George's Canada 48°26N 58°31W 73 C8
St-Georges Canada 46°8N 70°40W 73 C5
St. George's Grenada 12°5N 61°43W 89 D7
St. George's B. Canada 48°24N 58°53W 73 C8
St. Georges Basin N.S.W., Australia 35°7S 150°36E 63 F5
St. Georges Basin W. Austral., Australia 15°23S 125°2E 60 C4
St. George's Channel Europe 52°0N 6°0W 10 E6
St. George's Channel India 7°15N 93°43E 45 L11
St. Georges Hd. Australia 35°12S 150°42E 63 F5
St. Gotthard P. = San Gottardo, P. del Switz. 46°33N 8°33E 20 C8
St. Helena Atl. Oc. 15°58S 5°42W 50 H3
St. Helena U.S.A. 38°30N 122°28W 78 G4
St. Helena, Mt. U.S.A. 38°40N 122°36W 78 G4
St. Helena B. S. Africa 32°40S 18°10E 56 D2
St. Helens Australia 41°20S 148°15E 63 G4
St. Helens U.K. 53°27N 2°44W 12 D5
St. Helens U.S.A. 45°52N 122°48W 78 E4
St. Helens, Mt. U.S.A. 46°12N 122°12W 78 D4
St. Helier U.K. 49°10N 2°7W 13 H5
St-Hyacinthe Canada 45°40N 72°58W 72 C5
St. Ignace U.S.A. 45°52N 84°44W 81 C11
St. Ignace I. Canada 48°45N 88°0W 72 C2
St. Ignatius U.S.A. 47°19N 114°6W 76 C6
St. Ives Cambs., U.K. 52°20N 0°4W 13 E7
St. Ives Corn., U.K. 50°12N 5°30W 13 G2
St. James U.S.A. 43°59N 94°38W 80 D6
St-Jean → Canada 50°17N 64°20W 73 B7
St-Jean, L. Canada 48°40N 72°0W 73 C5
St-Jean-Port-Joli Canada 47°15N 70°13W 73 C5
St-Jean-sur-Richelieu Canada 45°20N 73°20W 83 A11
St-Jérôme Canada 45°47N 74°0W 72 C5
St. John Canada 45°20N 66°8W 73 C6
St. John U.S.A. 38°0N 98°46W 80 F4
St. John → N. Amer. 45°12N 66°5W 81 C20
St. John, C. Canada 50°0N 55°32W 73 C8
St. John I. U.S. Virgin Is. 18°20N 64°42W 89 e
St. John's Antigua & B. 17°6N 61°51W 89 C7
St. John's Canada 47°35N 52°40W 73 C9
St. Johns Ariz., U.S.A. 34°30N 109°22W 77 J9
St. Johns Mich., U.S.A. 43°0N 84°33W 81 D11
St. Johns → U.S.A. 30°24N 81°24W 85 F14
St. John's Pt. Ireland 54°34N 8°27W 10 B3
St. Johnsbury U.S.A. 44°25N 72°1W 83 B12
St. Johnsville U.S.A. 43°0N 74°43W 83 C10
St. Joseph Canada 43°24N 81°42W 82 C3
St-Joseph Martinique 14°39N 61°4W 88 c
St-Joseph Réunion 21°22S 55°37E 55 c
St. Joseph La., U.S.A. 31°55N 91°14W 84 F9
St. Joseph Mo., U.S.A. 39°46N 94°50W 80 F6
St. Joseph → U.S.A. 42°7N 86°29W 80 D10
St. Joseph, I. Canada 46°12N 83°58W 72 C3
St. Joseph, L. Canada 51°10N 90°35W 72 B1
St. Kilda U.K. 57°49N 8°34W 14 C2
St. Kitts & Nevis ■ W. Indies 17°20N 62°40W 89 C7
St. Laurent Canada 50°25N 97°58W 71 C9
St. Lawrence Australia 22°16S 149°31E 62 C4
St. Lawrence Canada 46°54N 55°23W 73 C8
St. Lawrence → Canada 49°30N 66°0W 73 C6
St. Lawrence, Gulf of Canada 48°25N 62°0W 73 C7
St. Lawrence I. U.S.A. 63°30N 170°30W 74 C5
St. Lawrence Islands △ Canada 44°27N 75°52W 83 B9
St. Léonard Canada 47°12N 67°58W 73 C6
St-Leu Réunion 21°9S 55°18E 55 c
St. Lewis → Canada 52°26N 56°11W 73 B8
St-Lô France 49°7N 1°5W 20 B3
St-Louis Guadeloupe 15°56N 61°19W 88 b
St-Louis Réunion 21°16S 55°25E 55 c
St-Louis Senegal 16°8N 16°27W 52 E2
St. Louis U.S.A. 38°37N 90°11W 80 F8
St. Louis → U.S.A. 46°44N 92°9W 80 B7
St-Luc Canada 45°22N 73°18W 83 A11
St. Lucia ■ W. Indies 14°0N 60°57W 89 f
St. Lucia, L. S. Africa 28°5S 32°30E 57 C5
St. Lucia ⌂ S. Africa 28°6S 32°27E 57 C5
St. Lucia Channel W. Indies 14°15N 61°0W 89 D7
St. Maarten ☑ W. Indies 18°2N 63°5W 89 C7
St. Magnus B. U.K. 60°25N 1°35W 11 A7
St-Malo France 48°39N 2°1W 20 B2
St-Marc Haiti 19°10N 72°41W 89 C5
St. Maries U.S.A. 47°19N 116°35W 76 C5
St-Martin ☑ W. Indies 18°5N 63°5W 89 C7
St-Martin, C. Martinique 14°52N 61°14W 88 c
St. Martin, L. Canada 51°40N 98°30W 71 C9
St. Martins Barbados 13°5N 59°28W 89 g
St. Mary Is. India 13°20N 74°35E 45 H2
St. Mary Pk. Australia 31°32S 138°34E 63 E2
St. Marys Australia 41°35S 148°11E 63 G4
St. Marys Canada 43°20N 81°10W 82 C3
St. Mary's Corn., U.K. 49°55N 6°18W 13 H1
St. Mary's Orkney, U.K. 58°54N 2°54W 11 C6
St. Marys Ga., U.S.A. 30°44N 81°33W 85 F14
St. Marys Pa., U.S.A. 41°26N 78°34W 82 E6
St. Mary's, C. Canada 46°50N 54°12W 73 C9
St. Mary's B. Canada 46°50N 53°50W 73 C9
St. Mary's Bay Canada 44°25N 66°10W 73 D6
St-Mathieu, Pte. France 48°20N 4°45W 20 B1
St. Matthew I. U.S.A. 60°24N 172°42W 74 C5
St-Maurice → Canada 46°21N 72°31W 72 C5
St. Mawes U.K. 50°10N 5°2W 13 G2
St-Nazaire France 47°17N 2°12W 20 C2
St. Neots U.K. 52°14N 0°15W 13 E7
St-Omer France 50°45N 2°15E 20 A5
St-Pamphile Canada 46°58N 69°48W 73 C6
St-Pascal Canada 47°32N 69°48W 73 C6
St. Paul Canada 54°0N 111°17W 70 C6
St-Paul Réunion 20°59S 55°17E 55 c
St. Paul Minn., U.S.A. 44°56N 93°5W 80 C7
St. Paul Nebr., U.S.A. 41°13N 98°27W 80 E4
St-Paul → Canada 51°27N 57°42W 73 B8
St. Paul, Î. Ind. Oc. 38°55S 77°34E 3 F13
St. Paul I. Canada 47°12N 60°9W 73 C7
St. Paul I. U.S.A. 57°10N 170°15W 74 D5
St. Peter U.S.A. 44°20N 93°57W 80 C7
St. Peter Port U.K. 49°26N 2°33W 13 H5
St. Peters N.S., Canada 45°40N 60°53W 73 C7
St. Peters P.E.I., Canada 46°25N 62°35W 73 C7
St. Petersburg U.S.A. 27°46N 82°40W 85 H13
St-Phillippe Réunion 21°21S 55°44E 55 c
St-Pie Canada 45°30N 72°54W 83 A12
St-Pierre Martinique 14°45N 61°10W 88 c
St-Pierre Réunion 21°19S 55°28E 55 c
St-Pierre St-P. & M. 46°46N 56°12W 73 C8
St-Pierre, L. Canada 46°12N 72°52W 72 C5
St-Pierre-et-Miquelon ☑ N. Amer. 46°55N 56°10W 73 C8
St-Quentin Canada 47°30N 67°23W 73 C6
St-Quentin France 49°50N 3°16E 20 B5
St. Regis U.S.A. 47°18N 115°6W 76 C6
St. Regis Falls U.S.A. 44°40N 74°32W 83 B10
St-Siméon Canada 47°51N 69°54W 73 C6
St. Simons I. U.S.A. 31°12N 81°15W 85 F14
St. Simons Island U.S.A. 31°9N 81°22W 85 F14
St. Stephen Canada 45°16N 67°17W 73 C6
St. Thomas Canada 42°45N 81°10W 82 D3
St. Thomas I. U.S. Virgin Is. 18°20N 64°55W 89 e
St-Tite Canada 46°45N 72°34W 72 C5
St-Trond = Sint-Truiden Belgium 50°48N 5°10E 15 D5
St-Tropez France 43°17N 6°38E 20 E7
St. Vidgeon's ✪ Australia 14°47S 134°53E 62 A1
St. Vincent = São Vicente Cabo Verde 17°0N 25°0W 52 b
St. Vincent, G. Australia 35°0S 138°0E 63 F2
St. Vincent & the Grenadines ■ W. Indies 13°0N 61°10W 89 D7
St. Vincent Passage W. Indies 13°30N 61°0W 89 D7
St-Vith Belgium 50°17N 6°9E 15 D6
St. Walburg Canada 53°39N 109°12W 71 C7
Saintala India 20°26N 83°20E 44 D6
Ste-Agathe-des-Monts Canada 46°3N 74°17W 72 C5
Ste-Anne Guadeloupe 16°13N 61°24W 88 b
Ste-Anne Seychelles 4°36S 55°31E 55 b
Ste-Anne, L. Canada 50°0N 67°42W 73 B6
Ste-Anne-des-Monts Canada 49°8N 66°30W 73 C6
Ste. Genevieve U.S.A. 37°59N 90°2W 80 G8
Ste-Marguerite → Canada 50°9N 66°36W 73 B6
Ste-Marie Canada 46°26N 71°0W 73 C5
Ste-Marie Martinique 14°48N 61°1W 88 c
Ste-Marie Réunion 20°53S 55°33E 55 c
Ste-Marie, Ile = Boraha, Nosy Madag. 16°50S 49°55E 55 H9
Ste-Rose Guadeloupe 16°20N 61°45W 88 b
Ste-Rose Réunion 21°8S 55°45E 55 c
Ste. Rose du Lac Canada 51°4N 99°30W 71 C9
Saintes France 45°45N 0°37W 20 D3
Saintes, Îs. des Guadeloupe 15°50N 61°35W 88 b
Saintfield U.K. 54°28N 5°49W 10 B6
Saintonge France 45°40N 0°50W 20 D3
Saipal Nepal 29°50N 81°40E 43 E9
Saipan N. Marianas 15°12N 145°45E 64 F6
Sairang India 23°50N 92°45E 41 H18
Sairecábur, Cerro Bolivia 22°43S 67°54W 94 A2
Sāitah Si. Arabia 16°36N 42°56E 49 D3
Saitama Japan 35°54N 139°38E 29 G9
Saitama □ Japan 36°25N 139°30E 29 F9
Saiyid Pakistan 33°7N 73°2E 42 C5
Sajama Bolivia 18°7S 69°0W 92 G5
Sajószentpéter Hungary 48°12N 20°44E 17 D11
Sajum India 33°20N 79°0E 43 C8
Sak → S. Africa 30°52S 20°25E 56 D3
Sakaide Japan 34°19N 133°50E 29 G6
Sakaiminato Japan 35°38N 133°11E 29 G6
Sakākah Si. Arabia 30°0N 40°8E 46 D4
Sakakawea, L. U.S.A. 47°30N 101°25W 80 B3
Sakami → Canada 53°40N 76°40W 72 B4
Sakami, L. Canada 53°15N 77°0W 72 B4
Sakartvelo = Georgia ■ Asia 42°0N 43°0E 19 F7
Sakarya Turkey 40°48N 30°25E 19 F5
Sakashima-Guntō Japan 24°46N 124°0E 29 M2
Sakata Japan 38°55N 139°50E 28 E9
Sakchu N. Korea 40°23N 125°2E 33 D13
Sakha □ Russia 66°0N 130°0E 27 C14
Sakhalin Russia 51°0N 143°0E 27 D15
Sakhalinskiy Zaliv Russia 54°0N 141°0E 27 D15
Sakhi Gopal India 19°58N 85°50E 44 E7
Šakiai Lithuania 54°59N 23°2E 9 J20
Sakoli India 21°5N 79°59E 44 D4
Sakon Nakhon Thailand 17°10N 104°9E 38 D5
Sakrand Pakistan 26°10N 68°15E 42 F3
Sakri Maharashtra, India 26°13N 86°5E 43 F12
Sakri Maharashtra, India 21°2N 74°20E 44 D2
Sakrivier S. Africa 30°54S 20°28E 56 D3
Sakti India 22°2N 82°58E 43 H10
Sakuma Japan 35°3N 137°49E 29 G8
Sakurai Japan 34°30N 135°51E 29 G7
Sal Cabo Verde 16°45N 22°55W 52 b
Sal Rei Cabo Verde 16°11N 22°53W 52 b
Sala Sweden 59°58N 16°35E 9 G17
Sala Consilina Italy 40°23N 15°36E 22 D6
Sala-y-Gómez Pac. Oc. 26°28S 105°28W 65 K17
Sala-y-Gómez Ridge Pac. Oc. 25°0S 98°0W 65 K18
Salaberry-de-Valleyfield Canada 45°15N 74°8W 83 A10
Salada, L. Mexico 32°20N 115°40W 77 K6
Saladas Argentina 28°15S 58°40W 94 B4
Saladillo Argentina 35°40S 59°55W 94 D4
Salado → B. Aires, Argentina 35°44S 57°22W 94 D4
Salado → La Pampa, Argentina 37°30S 67°0W 96 D3
Salado → Santa Fe, Argentina 31°40S 60°41W 94 C3
Salado → Mexico 26°52N 99°19W 84 H5
Salaga Ghana 8°31N 0°31W 52 G5
Sālah Syria 32°40N 36°45E 48 C5
Şalāḩ ad Dīn □ Iraq 34°35N 43°35E 46 C4
Salālah Oman 16°56N 53°59E 49 D5
Salamajärvi △ Finland 63°12N 24°50E 8 E21
Salamanca Chile 31°46S 70°59W 94 C1
Salamanca Spain 40°58N 5°39W 21 B3
Salamanca U.S.A. 42°10N 78°43W 82 D6
Salāmatābād Iran 35°39N 47°50E 46 C5
Salamina Greece 37°56N 23°30E 23 F10
Salar de Atacama Chile 23°30S 68°25W 94 A2
Salar de Uyuni Bolivia 20°30S 67°45W 92 H5
Salatiga Indonesia 7°19S 110°30E 37 G14
Salavat Russia 53°21N 55°55E 18 D10
Salaverry Peru 8°15S 79°0W 92 E3
Salawati Indonesia 1°7S 130°52E 37 E8
Salawin △ Thailand 18°18N 97°40E 38 C1
Salaya India 22°19N 69°35E 42 H3
Salayar Indonesia 6°7S 120°30E 37 F6
Salcombe U.K. 50°14N 3°47W 13 G4
Saldanha S. Africa 33°0S 17°58E 56 D2
Saldanha B. S. Africa 33°6S 18°0E 56 D2
Saldus Latvia 56°38N 22°30E 9 H20
Sale Australia 38°6S 147°6E 63 F4
Salé Morocco 34°3N 6°48W 52 B4
Sale U.K. 53°26N 2°19W 12 D5
Salekhard Russia 66°30N 66°35E 26 C7
Salelologa Samoa 13°41S 172°11W 59 b
Salem India 11°40N 78°11E 45 J4
Salem Ill., U.S.A. 38°38N 88°57W 80 F9
Salem Ind., U.S.A. 38°36N 86°6W 80 F10
Salem Mass., U.S.A. 42°31N 70°53W 83 D14
Salem Mo., U.S.A. 37°39N 91°32W 80 G8
Salem N.H., U.S.A. 42°45N 71°12W 83 D13
Salem N.J., U.S.A. 39°34N 75°28W 81 F16
Salem N.Y., U.S.A. 43°10N 73°20W 83 C11
Salem Ohio, U.S.A. 40°54N 80°52W 82 F4
Salem Oreg., U.S.A. 44°56N 123°2W 76 D2
Salem S. Dak., U.S.A. 43°44N 97°23W 80 D5
Salem Va., U.S.A. 37°18N 80°3W 81 G13
Salerno Italy 40°41N 14°47E 22 D6
Salford U.K. 53°30N 2°18W 12 D5
Salgótarján Hungary 48°5N 19°47E 17 D10
Salgueiro Brazil 8°4S 39°6W 93 E11
Salher India 20°40N 73°55E 44 D1
Salibabu Indonesia 3°51N 126°40E 37 D7
Salibea = Salybia Trin. & Tob. 10°43N 61°2W 93 K15
Salida U.S.A. 38°32N 106°0W 76 G11
Salihli Turkey 38°28N 28°8E 23 E13
Salihorsk Belarus 52°51N 27°27E 17 B14
Salima Malawi 13°47S 34°28E 55 G6
Salina Italy 38°34N 14°50E 22 E6
Salina Kans., U.S.A. 38°50N 97°37W 80 F5
Salina Utah, U.S.A. 38°58N 111°51W 76 G8
Salina Cruz Mexico 16°10N 95°12W 87 D5
Salinas Brazil 16°10S 42°10W 93 G10
Salinas Ecuador 2°10S 80°58W 92 D2
Salinas U.S.A. 36°40N 121°39W 78 J5
Salinas → Guatemala 16°28N 90°31W 87 D6
Salinas → U.S.A. 36°45N 121°48W 78 J5
Salinas, B. de Nic. 11°4N 85°45W 88 D2
Salinas, Pampa de las Argentina 31°58S 66°42W 94 C2
Salinas Ambargasta Argentina 29°0S 65°0W 94 B3
Salinas de Hidalgo Mexico 22°38N 101°43W 86 C4
Salinas Grandes Argentina 30°0S 65°0W 94 C3
Salinas Pueblo Missions ⌂ U.S.A. 34°6N 106°4W 77 J10
Salinas Valley U.S.A. 36°15N 121°15W 78 J5
Saline → Ark., U.S.A. 33°10N 92°8W 84 E8
Saline → Kans., U.S.A. 38°52N 97°30W 80 F5
Salinópolis Brazil 0°40S 47°20W 93 D9
Salisbury Australia 34°46S 138°38E 63 E2
Salisbury U.K. 51°4N 1°47W 13 F6
Salisbury Md., U.S.A. 38°22N 75°36W 81 F16
Salisbury N.C., U.S.A. 35°40N 80°29W 85 D14
Salisbury I. Canada 63°30N 77°0W 69 E16
Salisbury Plain U.K. 51°14N 1°55W 13 F6
Şalkhad Syria 32°29N 36°43E 48 C5
Salla Finland 66°50N 28°49E 8 C23
Salliq = Coral Harbour Canada 64°8N 83°10W 69 E15
Sallisaw U.S.A. 35°28N 94°47W 84 D7
Salluit Canada 62°14N 75°38W 69 E16
Sallyana Nepal 28°22N 82°10E 43 E10
Salmās Iran 38°11N 44°47E 46 B5
Salmo Canada 49°10N 117°20W 70 D5
Salmon U.S.A. 45°11N 113°54W 76 D7
Salmon → Canada 54°3N 122°40W 70 C4
Salmon → U.S.A. 45°51N 116°47W 76 D5
Salmon Arm Canada 50°40N 119°15W 70 C5
Salmon Gums Australia 32°59S 121°38E 61 F3
Salmon Pt. Canada 43°52N 77°15W 82 C7
Salmon River Mts. U.S.A. 44°50N 115°30W 76 D6
Salmon River Res. U.S.A. 43°32N 75°55W 83 C9
Salo Finland 60°22N 23°10E 9 F20
Salome U.S.A. 33°47N 113°37W 79 M13
Salon India 26°2N 81°27E 43 F9
Salon-de-Provence France 43°39N 5°6E 20 E6
Salonica = Thessaloniki Greece 40°38N 22°58E 23 D10
Salonta Romania 46°49N 21°42E 17 E11
Salpausselkä Finland 61°3N 26°15E 8 F22
Salsacate Argentina 31°20S 65°5W 94 C2
Salsk Russia 46°28N 41°30E 19 E7
Salso → Italy 37°6N 13°57E 22 F5
Salt → Canada 60°0N 112°25W 70 B6
Salt → U.S.A. 33°23N 112°19W 77 K7
Salt Fork Red → U.S.A. 34°27N 99°21W 84 D5
Salt L. Australia 30°6S 142°8E 63 E3
Salt Lake City U.S.A. 40°45N 111°53W 76 F8
Salt Lake City Int. ✈ (SLC) U.S.A. 40°47N 111°58W 76 F7
Salt Range Pakistan 32°30N 72°25E 42 C5
Salta Argentina 24°57S 65°25W 94 A2
Salta □ Argentina 24°48S 65°30W 94 A2
Saltash U.K. 50°24N 4°14W 13 G3
Saltburn-by-the-Sea U.K. 54°35N 0°58W 12 C7
Saltcoats U.K. 55°38N 4°47W 11 F4
Saltee Is. Ireland 52°7N 6°37W 10 D5
Saltfjellet Norway 66°40N 15°15E 8 C16
Saltfjellet-Svartisen △ Norway 66°45N 15°10E 8 C16
Saltfjorden Norway 67°15N 14°10E 8 C16
Saltillo Mexico 25°25N 101°0W 86 B4
Salto Argentina 34°20S 60°15W 94 C3
Salto Uruguay 31°27S 57°50W 94 C4
Salto → Italy 42°26N 12°25E 22 C5
Salto del Guaíra Paraguay 24°3S 54°17W 95 A5
Salton City U.S.A. 33°18N 115°57W 79 M11
Salton Sea U.S.A. 33°15N 115°45W 79 M11
Saltsburg U.S.A. 40°29N 79°27W 82 F5
Saluda → U.S.A. 34°1N 81°4W 85 D14
Salue Timpaus, Selat Indonesia 1°50S 123°50E 37 E6
Salûm Egypt 31°31N 25°7E 53 B11
Salur India 18°27N 83°18E 44 E6
Salvador Brazil 13°0S 38°30W 93 F11
Salvador Canada 52°10N 109°32W 71 C7
Salvador, El ■ Cent. Amer. 13°50N 89°0W 88 D2
Salvador, L. U.S.A. 29°43N 90°15W 85 G9
Salween → Myanmar 16°31N 97°37E 41 L20
Salyan Azerbaijan 39°33N 48°59E 47 B6
Salybia Trin. & Tob. 10°43N 61°2W 93 K15
Salzach → Austria 48°12N 12°56E 16 D7
Salzburg Austria 47°48N 13°2E 16 E7
Salzgitter Germany 52°9N 10°19E 16 B6
Salzwedel Germany 52°52N 11°10E 16 B6
Sam India 26°50N 70°31E 42 F4
Sam Neua Laos 20°29N 104°5E 34 G5
Sam Ngao Thailand 17°18N 99°0E 38 D2
Sam Rayburn Res. U.S.A. 31°4N 94°5W 84 F7
Sam Rong, Laem Thailand 9°35N 100°4E 39 b
Sam Son Vietnam 19°44N 105°54E 38 C5
Sama de Langreo = Langreo Spain 43°18N 5°40W 21 A3
Samagaltay Russia 50°36N 95°3E 27 D10
Samales Group Phil. 6°0N 122°0E 37 C6
Samalga Pass U.S.A. 52°50N 169°0W 74 E6
Samalkot India 17°3N 82°13E 44 F6
Samana India 30°10N 76°13E 42 D7
Samana Cays Bahamas 23°3N 73°45W 89 B5
Samangān □ Afghan. 36°15N 68°3E 40 B5
Samani Japan 42°7N 142°56E 28 C11
Samar Phil. 12°0N 125°0E 37 B7
Samara Russia 53°8N 50°6E 18 D9
Samarinda Indonesia 0°30S 117°9E 36 E5
Samarkand = Samarqand Uzbekistan 39°40N 66°55E 26 F7
Samarqand Uzbekistan 39°40N 66°55E 26 F7
Sāmarrā' Iraq 34°12N 43°52E 46 C4
Samastipur India 25°50N 85°50E 43 G11
Samba India 32°32N 75°10E 43 C6
Sambalpur India 21°28N 84°4E 44 D7
Sambar, Tanjung Indonesia 2°59S 110°19E 36 E4
Sambas Indonesia 1°20N 109°20E 36 D3
Sambhajinagar = Aurangabad India 19°50N 75°23E 44 E2
Sambhal India 28°35N 78°37E 43 E8
Sambhar India 26°52N 75°6E 42 F6
Sambhar L. India 26°55N 75°12E 42 F6
Sambir Ukraine 49°30N 23°10E 17 D12
Sambor Cambodia 12°46N 106°0E 38 F6
Sambor Prei Kuk Cambodia 12°46N 105°58E 38 F5
Samborombón, B. Argentina 36°5S 57°20W 94 D4
Samcheok S. Korea 37°26N 129°10E 33 F15
Samet, Ko Thailand 12°34N 101°27E 38 F3
Sammanturai Sri Lanka 7°36N 81°39E 45 L5
Samnah Si. Arabia 25°10N 37°15E 46 E3
Samo Alto Chile 30°22S 71°0W 94 C1
Samoa ■ Pac. Oc. 14°0S 172°0W 59 b
Samoan Is. Pac. Oc. 14°0S 171°0W 59 b
Samokov Bulgaria 42°18N 23°35E 23 C10
Samos Greece 37°45N 26°50E 23 F12
Samothráki = Mathraki Greece 39°48N 19°31E 23 E8
Samothraki Greece 40°28N 25°28E 23 D11
Sampacho Argentina 33°20S 64°50W 94 C3
Sampalan Indonesia 8°41S 115°34E 37 K18
Sampang Indonesia 7°11S 113°13E 37 G15
Sampit Indonesia 2°34S 113°0E 36 E4
Sampit, Teluk Indonesia 3°5S 113°3E 36 E4
Samrong Cambodia 14°15N 103°30E 38 E4
Samsø Denmark 55°50N 10°35E 9 J14
Samsun Turkey 41°15N 36°22E 19 F6
Samui, Ko Thailand 9°30N 100°0E 39 b
Samut Sakhon Thailand 13°32N 100°17E 38 F3
Samut Songkhram Thailand 13°24N 100°1E 38 F3
Samwari Pakistan 28°30N 66°46E 42 E2
San Mali 13°15N 4°57W 52 F5
San → Cambodia 13°32N 105°57E 38 F5
San → Poland 50°45N 21°51E 17 C11
San Agustin, C. Phil. 6°20N 126°13E 37 C7
San Agustín de Valle Fértil Argentina 30°35S 67°30W 94 C2
San Ambrosio Pac. Oc. 26°28S 79°53W 90 F3
San Andreas U.S.A. 38°12N 120°41W 78 G6
San Andrés, I. de Caribbean 12°42N 81°46W 88 D3
San Andres Mts. U.S.A. 33°0N 106°30W 77 K10
San Andrés Tuxtla Mexico 18°27N 95°13W 87 D5
San Angelo U.S.A. 31°28N 100°26W 84 F4
San Anselmo U.S.A. 37°59N 122°34W 78 H4
San Antonio Belize 16°15N 89°2W 87 D7
San Antonio Chile 33°40S 71°40W 94 C1
San Antonio N. Mex., U.S.A. 33°55N 106°52W 77 K10
San Antonio Tex., U.S.A. 29°25N 98°29W 84 G5
San Antonio → U.S.A. 28°30N 96°54W 84 G6
San Antonio, C. Argentina 36°15S 56°40W 94 D4
San Antonio, C. de Cuba 21°50N 84°57W 88 B3
San Antonio, Mt. U.S.A. 34°17N 117°38W 79 L9
San Antonio de los Baños Cuba 22°54N 82°31W 88 B3
San Antonio de los Cobres Argentina 24°10S 66°17W 94 A2
San Antonio Oeste Argentina 40°40S 65°0W 96 E4
San Ardo U.S.A. 36°1N 120°54W 78 J6
San Augustine U.S.A. 31°32N 94°7W 84 F7
San Benedetto del Tronto Italy 42°57N 13°53E 22 C5
San Benedicto, I. Mexico 19°18N 110°49W 86 D2
San Benito U.S.A. 26°8N 97°38W 84 H6
San Benito → U.S.A. 36°53N 121°34W 78 J5
San Benito Mt. U.S.A. 36°22N 120°37W 78 J6
San Bernardino U.S.A. 34°7N 117°19W 79 L9
San Bernardino Mts. U.S.A. 34°10N 116°45W 79 L10
San Bernardino Str. Phil. 12°30N 124°10E 37 B7
San Bernardo Chile 33°40S 70°50W 94 C1
San Bernardo, I. de Colombia 9°45N 75°50W 92 B3
San Blas Mexico 26°5N 108°46W 86 B3
San Blas, Arch. de Panama 9°50N 78°31W 88 E4
San Blas, C. U.S.A. 29°40N 85°21W 85 G12
San Borja Bolivia 14°50S 66°52W 92 F5
San Buenaventura = Ventura U.S.A. 34°17N 119°18W 79 L7
San Buenaventura Mexico 27°5N 101°32W 86 B4
San Carlos Argentina 33°50S 69°0W 94 C2
San Carlos Chile 36°10S 72°0W 94 D1
San Carlos Baja Calif. S., Mexico 24°47N 112°7W 86 C2
San Carlos Coahuila, Mexico 29°1N 100°51W 86 B4
San Carlos Nic. 11°12N 84°50W 88 D3
San Carlos Phil. 10°29N 123°25E 37 B6
San Carlos Uruguay 34°46S 54°58W 95 C5
San Carlos U.S.A. 33°21N 110°27W 77 K8
San Carlos Venezuela 9°40N 68°36W 92 B5
San Carlos de Bariloche Argentina 41°10S 71°25W 96 E2

San Carlos de Bolívar
  *Argentina*                    36°15S 61°6W **94** D3
San Carlos del Zulia
  *Venezuela*                     9°1N 71°55W **92** B4
San Carlos L. *U.S.A.*        33°11N 110°32W **77** K8
San Clemente *Chile*         35°30S 71°29W **94** D1
San Clemente *U.S.A.*      33°26N 117°37W **79** N9
San Clemente I. *U.S.A.*  32°53N 118°29W **79** N8
San Cristóbal *Argentina*  30°20S 61°10W **94** C3
San Cristóbal *Dom. Rep.*  18°25N 70°6W **89** C5
San Cristóbal *Solomon Is.* 10°30S 161°0E **58** C9
San Cristóbal *Venezuela*   7°46N 72°14W **92** B4
San Cristóbal de las Casas
  *Mexico*                    16°45N 92°38W **87** D6
San Diego *Calif., U.S.A.*  32°42N 117°9W **79** N9
San Diego *Tex., U.S.A.*    27°46N 98°14W **84** H5
San Diego, C. *Argentina*   54°40S 65°10W **96** G3
San Diego de la Unión
  *Mexico*                    21°28N 100°52W **86** C4
San Diego Int. ✈ (SAN)
  *U.S.A.*                    32°44N 117°11W **79** N9
San Estanislao *Paraguay*  24°39S 56°26W **94** A4
San Felipe *Chile*          32°43S 70°42W **94** C1
San Felipe *Mexico*         31°1N 114°52W **86** A2
San Felipe *Venezuela*      10°20N 68°44W **92** A5
San Felipe ➝ *U.S.A.*    33°10N 115°49W **79** M11
San Félix *Chile*           28°56S 70°28W **94** B1
San Félix *Pac. Oc.*        26°23S 80°0W **90** F2
San Fernando *Chile*        34°30S 71°0W **94** C1
San Fernando *Mexico*       24°51N 98°10W **87** C5
San Fernando *La Union,
  Phil.*                      16°40N 120°23E **37** A6
San Fernando *Pampanga,
  Phil.*                      15°5N 120°37E **37** A6
San Fernando *Spain*        36°28N 6°17W **21** D2
San Fernando
  *Trin. & Tob.*             10°16N 61°28W **93** K15
San Fernando *U.S.A.*       34°17N 118°26W **79** L8
San Fernando de Apure
  *Venezuela*                  7°54N 67°15W **92** B5
San Fernando de Atabapo
  *Venezuela*                  4°3N 67°42W **92** C5
San Francisco *Argentina*  31°30S 62°5W **94** C3
San Francisco ➝
  *U.S.A.*                    32°59N 109°22W **77** K9
San Francisco, C. de
  *Colombia*                   6°18N 77°29W **90** C3
San Francisco, Paso de
  *S. Amer.*                  27°0S 68°0W **94** B2
San Francisco de Macorís
  *Dom. Rep.*                19°19N 70°15W **89** C5
San Francisco del Monte de Oro
  *Argentina*                32°36S 66°8W **94** C2
San Francisco del Oro
  *Mexico*                    26°52N 105°51W **86** B3
San Francisco Int. ✈ (SFO)
  *U.S.A.*                    37°37N 122°22W **78** H4
San Gabriel *Chile*         33°47S 70°15W **94** C1
San Gabriel Chilac
  *Mexico*                    18°19N 97°21W **87** D5
San Gabriel Mts. *U.S.A.*  34°17N 117°38W **79** L9
San Gavino Monreale
  *Italy*                     39°33N 8°47E **22** E3
San German *Puerto Rico*   18°4N 67°4W **89** d
San Gorgonio Mt.
  *U.S.A.*                    34°6N 116°50W **79** L10
San Gottardo, P. del *Switz.* 46°33N 8°33E **20** C8
San Gregorio *Uruguay*     32°37S 55°40W **95** C4
San Gregorio *U.S.A.*      37°20N 122°23W **78** H4
San Guillermo △
  *Argentina*                27°50S 69°45W **94** B2
San Ignacio *Belize*       17°10N 89°5W **87** D7
San Ignacio *Bolivia*      16°20S 60°55W **92** G6
San Ignacio *Mexico*       27°27N 112°51W **86** B2
San Ignacio *Paraguay*     26°52S 57°3W **94** B4
San Ignacio, L. *Mexico*  26°54N 113°13W **86** B2
San Ildefonso, C. *Phil.*  16°0N 122°1E **37** A6
San Isidro *Argentina*     34°29S 58°31W **94** C4
San Jacinto *U.S.A.*       33°47N 116°57W **79** M10
San Javier *Misiones,
  Argentina*                 27°55S 55°5W **95** B4
San Javier *Santa Fe,
  Argentina*                 30°40S 59°55W **94** C4
San Javier *Bolivia*       16°18S 62°30W **92** G6
San Javier *Chile*         35°40S 71°45W **94** D1
San Jerónimo Taviche
  *Mexico*                    16°44N 96°35W **87** D5
San Joaquin *U.S.A.*       36°36N 120°11W **78** J6
San Joaquin ➝ *U.S.A.*   38°4N 121°51W **78** G5
San Joaquin Valley
  *U.S.A.*                    37°20N 121°0W **78** J6
San Jon *U.S.A.*           35°6N 103°20W **77** J12
San Jorge *Argentina*      31°54S 61°50W **94** C3
San Jorge, B. *Mexico*    31°20N 113°20W **86** A2
San Jorge, G. *Argentina*  46°0S 66°0W **96** F3
San José *Argentina*       32°12S 58°15W **94** C2
San José *Costa Rica*       9°55N 84°2W **88** E3
San José *Guatemala*       14°0N 90°50W **88** D1
San José *Mind. Occ., Phil.* 12°27N 121°4E **37** B6
San Jose *Nueva Ecija,
  Phil.*                     15°45N 120°55E **37** A6
San Jose *U.S.A.*          37°20N 121°53W **78** H5
San Jose ➝ *U.S.A.*      34°25N 106°45W **77** J10
San Jose I. *Mexico*       25°0N 110°38W **86** C2
San Jose de Buenavista
  *Phil.*                    10°45N 121°56E **37** B6
San José de Chiquitos
  *Bolivia*                  17°53S 60°50W **92** G6
San José de Feliciano
  *Argentina*                30°26S 58°46W **94** C4
San José de Jáchal
  *Argentina*                30°15S 68°46W **94** C2
San José de Mayo
  *Uruguay*                  34°27S 56°40W **94** C4
San José del Cabo *Mexico* 23°3N 109°41W **86** C3
San José del Guaviare
  *Colombia*                  2°35N 72°38W **92** C4
San Juan *Argentina*       31°30S 68°30W **94** C2
San Juan *Puerto Rico*     18°28N 66°7W **89** d
San Juan *Trin. & Tob.*    10°39N 61°29W **93** K15

San Juan □ *Argentina*     31°9S 69°0W **94** C2
San Juan ➝ *Argentina*   32°20S 67°25W **94** C2
San Juan ➝ *Nic.*        10°56N 83°42W **88** D3
San Juan ➝ *U.S.A.*      37°16N 110°26W **77** H8
San Juan Bautista
  *Paraguay*                 26°37S 57°6W **94** B4
San Juan Bautista
  *U.S.A.*                   36°51N 121°32W **78** J5
San Juan Capistrano
  *U.S.A.*                   33°30N 117°40W **79** M9
San Juan Cr. ➝ *U.S.A.*  35°40N 120°22W **78** J5
San Juan de Guadalupe
  *Mexico*                   24°38N 102°44W **86** C4
San Juan de la Costa
  *Mexico*                   24°20N 110°41W **86** C2
San Juan de los Lagos
  *Mexico*                   21°15N 102°18W **86** C4
San Juan de los Morros
  *Venezuela*                 9°55N 67°21W **92** B5
San Juan del Norte *Nic.*  10°58N 83°40W **88** D3
San Juan del Norte, B. de
  *Nic.*                     11°0N 83°40W **88** D3
San Juan del Río *Mexico*  20°23N 100°0W **87** C5
San Juan del Sur *Nic.*    11°20N 85°51W **88** D2
San Juan I. *U.S.A.*       48°32N 123°5W **78** B3
San Juan Island △
  *U.S.A.*                   48°35N 123°8W **78** B4
San Juan Mts. *U.S.A.*    37°30N 107°0W **77** H10
San Justo *Argentina*      30°47S 60°30W **94** C3
San Kamphaeng *Thailand*  18°45N 99°8E **38** C2
San Lázaro, C. *Mexico*   24°50N 112°18W **86** C2
San Leandro *U.S.A.*       37°42N 122°9W **78** H4
San Lorenzo *Argentina*    32°45S 60°45W **94** C3
San Lorenzo *Ecuador*       1°15N 78°50W **92** C3
San Lorenzo *Paraguay*     25°20S 57°32W **94** B4
San Lorenzo ➝ *Mexico*   24°15N 107°24W **86** C3
San Lorenzo, I. *Mexico*  28°38N 112°51W **86** B2
San Lorenzo, Mte.
  *Argentina*                47°40S 72°20W **96** F2
San Lucas = Cabo San Lucas
  *Mexico*                   22°53N 109°54W **86** C3
San Lucas *Bolivia*        20°5S 65°7W **92** H5
San Lucas *Mexico*         27°10N 112°14W **86** B2
San Lucas *U.S.A.*         36°8N 121°1W **78** J5
San Lucas, C. *Mexico*    22°52N 109°53W **86** C3
San Luis *Argentina*       33°20S 66°20W **94** C2
San Luis *Cuba*            22°17N 83°46W **88** B3
San Luis *Guatemala*       16°14N 89°27W **88** C2
San Luis *Ariz., U.S.A.*  32°29N 114°47W **77** K6
San Luis *Colo., U.S.A.*  37°12N 105°25W **77** H11
San Luis □ *Argentina*    34°0S 66°0W **94** C2
San Luis, I. *Mexico*     29°58N 114°26W **86** B2
San Luis, Sierra de
  *Argentina*                32°30S 66°10W **94** C2
San Luis de la Paz
  *Mexico*                   21°18N 100°31W **86** C4
San Luis Obispo *U.S.A.*  35°17N 120°40W **79** K6
San Luis Potosí *Mexico*  22°9N 100°59W **86** C4
San Luis Potosí □ *Mexico* 23°0N 101°0W **86** C4
San Luis Res. *U.S.A.*    37°4N 121°5W **78** H5
San Luis Río Colorado
  *Mexico*                   32°29N 114°58W **86** A2
San Manuel *U.S.A.*        32°36N 110°38W **77** K8
San Marcos *Calif., U.S.A.* 33°9N 117°10W **79** M9
San Marcos *Tex., U.S.A.*  29°53N 97°56W **84** G6
San Marcos, I. *Mexico*   27°13N 112°6W **86** B2
San Marino *San Marino*   43°55N 12°30E **16** G7
San Marino ■ *Europe*     43°56N 12°25E **22** C5
San Martín *Antarctica*   68°11S 67°0W **5** C17
San Martín *Argentina*    33°5S 68°28W **94** C2
San Martín ➝ *Bolivia*   13°8S 63°43W **92** F6
San Martín, L. *Argentina* 48°50S 72°50W **96** F2
San Martín de los Andes
  *Argentina*                40°10S 71°20W **96** E2
San Mateo *U.S.A.*         37°34N 122°19W **78** H4
San Matías *Bolivia*       16°25S 58°20W **92** G7
San Matías, G. *Argentina* 41°30S 64°0W **96** E4
San Miguel *Brazil*        33°30N 88°12W **88** D2
San Miguel *El Salv.*      13°30N 88°12W **88** D2
San Miguel *Panama*         8°27N 78°55W **88** E4
San Miguel ➝ *U.S.A.*    35°45N 120°42W **78** K6
San Miguel ➝ *Bolivia*   13°52S 63°56W **92** F6
San Miguel de Tucumán
  *Argentina*                26°50S 65°20W **94** B2
San Miguel del Monte
  *Argentina*                35°23S 58°50W **94** D4
San Miguel I. *U.S.A.*    34°2N 120°23W **79** L6
San Nicandro Gargánico
  *Italy*                    41°50N 15°34E **22** D6
San Nicolás de los Arroyos
  *Argentina*                33°25S 60°10W **94** C3
San Nicolas I. *U.S.A.*   33°15N 119°30W **79** M7
San Onofre *U.S.A.*        33°22N 117°34W **79** M9
San Pablo *Bolivia*        21°43S 66°38W **94** A2
San Pablo *U.S.A.*         37°58N 122°21W **78** H4
San Pedro *B. Aires,
  Argentina*                33°40S 59°40W **94** C4
San Pedro *Misiones,
  Argentina*                26°30S 54°10W **95** B5
San Pedro *Chile*          33°54S 71°28W **94** C1
San Pedro *Côte d'Ivoire*   4°50N 6°33W **52** H4
San Pedro ➝ *Nayarit,
  Mexico*                   21°45N 105°30W **86** C3
San Pedro ➝ *Chihuahua,
  Mexico*                   28°21N 105°25W **86** B3
San Pedro ➝ *U.S.A.*     32°59N 110°47W **77** K8
San Pedro Channel
  *U.S.A.*                   33°30N 118°25W **79** M8
San Pedro de Atacama
  *Chile*                    22°55S 68°15W **94** A2
San Pedro de Jujuy
  *Argentina*                24°12S 64°55W **94** A3
San Pedro de las Colonias
  *Mexico*                   25°45N 102°59W **86** B4
San Pedro de Macorís
  *Dom. Rep.*               18°30N 69°18W **89** C6
San Pedro del Norte *Nic.* 13°4N 84°33W **88** D3

San Pedro del Paraná
  *Paraguay*                 26°43S 56°13W **94** B4
San Pedro Mártir, Sa. de
  *Mexico*                   30°45N 115°13W **86** A1
San Pedro Ocampo = Melchor
  Ocampo *Mexico*          24°51N 101°39W **86** C4
San Pedro Pochutla
  *Mexico*                   15°44N 96°28W **87** D5
San Pedro Sula *Honduras*  15°30N 88°0W **88** C2
San Pedro Tututepec
  *Mexico*                   16°9N 97°38W **87** D5
San Pietro *Italy*         39°8N 8°17E **22** E3
San Rafael *Argentina*     34°40S 68°21W **94** C2
San Rafael *Calif., U.S.A.* 37°58N 122°32W **78** H4
San Rafael *N. Mex.,
  U.S.A.*                    35°7N 107°53W **77** J10
San Rafael Mt. *U.S.A.*   34°41N 119°52W **79** L7
San Rafael Mts. *U.S.A.*  34°40N 119°50W **79** L7
San Ramón de la Nueva Orán
  *Argentina*                23°10S 64°20W **94** A3
San Remo *Italy*           43°49N 7°46E **20** E7
San Roque *Argentina*      28°25S 58°45W **94** B4
San Roque *Spain*          36°17N 5°21W **21** D3
San Rosendo *Chile*        37°16S 72°43W **94** D1
San Salvador *El Salv.*    13°40N 89°10W **88** D2
San Salvador de Jujuy
  *Argentina*                24°10S 64°48W **94** A3
San Salvador I. *Bahamas*  24°0N 74°30W **89** B5
San Sebastián = Donostia-San
  Sebastián *Spain*         43°17N 1°58W **21** A5
San Sebastián *Argentina*  53°10S 68°30W **96** G3
San Sebastián *Puerto Rico* 18°20N 66°59W **89** d
San Severo *Italy*         41°41N 15°23E **22** D6
San Simeon *U.S.A.*        35°39N 121°11W **78** K5
San Simon *U.S.A.*         32°16N 109°14W **77** K9
San Telmo *Mexico*         30°58N 116°6W **86** A1
San Tiburcio *Mexico*      24°8N 101°32W **86** C4
San Valentin, Mte. *Chile* 46°30S 73°30W **96** F2
San Vicente de Cañete
  *Peru*                     13°8S 76°30W **92** F3
San Vicente de la Barquera
  *Spain*                    43°23N 4°29W **21** A3
San Vito *Costa Rica*       8°50N 82°58W **88** E3
Sana' = Şan'ā' *Yemen*    15°27N 44°12E **49** D3
Şan'ā' *Yemen*            15°27N 44°12E **49** D3
Sana ➝ *Bos.-H.*         45°3N 16°23E **16** F9
Sanaa = Şan'ā' *Yemen*    15°27N 44°12E **49** D3
Sanae IV *Antarctica*      70°20S 9°0W **5** D2
Sanaga ➝ *Cameroon*       3°35N 9°38E **54** D1
Sanak I. *U.S.A.*          54°25N 162°40W **74** E7
Sanalona, Presa *Mexico*  24°49N 107°7W **86** C3
Sanana *Indonesia*          2°4S 125°58E **37** E7
Sanand *India*             22°59N 72°25E **42** H5
Sanandaj *Iran*            35°18N 47°1E **46** C5
Sanandita *Bolivia*        21°40S 63°45W **94** A3
Sanawad *India*            22°11N 76°5E **42** H7
Sancha *India*             26°48N 106°7E **34** D6
Sanchahe *China*           44°50N 126°2E **33** B14
Sánchez *Dom. Rep.*        19°15N 69°36W **89** C6
Sanchi *India*             23°28N 77°44E **42** H7
Sanchor *India*            24°45N 71°55E **42** G4
Sancti Spíritus *Cuba*     21°52N 79°33W **88** B4
Sancy, Puy de *France*     45°32N 2°50E **20** D5
Sand = Polokwane ➝
  *S. Africa*               22°25S 30°5E **57** B5
Sand Hills *U.S.A.*        42°10N 101°30W **80** D3
Sand Lakes △ *Canada*     57°51N 98°32W **71** B9
Sand Springs *U.S.A.*      36°9N 96°7W **84** C6
Sanda *Japan*              34°53N 135°14E **29** G7
Sandakan *Malaysia*         5°53N 118°4E **36** C5
Sandan = Sambor
  *Cambodia*                12°46N 106°0E **38** F6
Sandanski *Bulgaria*       41°35N 23°16E **23** D10
Sanday *U.K.*              59°16N 2°31W **11** B6
Sandefjord *Norway*        59°10N 10°15E **9** G14
Sanders *U.S.A.*           35°13N 109°20W **77** J9
Sanderson *U.S.A.*         30°9N 102°24W **84** F3
Sandersville *U.S.A.*      32°59N 82°48W **85** E13
Sandfire Roadhouse
  *Australia*               19°45S 121°15E **60** C3
Sandfly L. *Canada*        55°43N 106°6W **71** B7
Sandfontein *Namibia*      23°48S 19°1E **56** B2
Sandheads, The *India*     21°10N 88°20E **43** J13
Sandia *Peru*              14°10S 69°30W **92** F5
Sandila *India*            27°5N 80°31E **43** F9
Sandnes *Norway*           58°50N 5°45E **9** G11
Sandnessjøen *Norway*      66°2N 12°38E **8** C15
Sandoa
  *Dem. Rep. of the Congo*   9°41S 23°0E **54** F4
Sandomierz *Poland*        50°40N 21°43E **17** C11
Sandover ➝ *Australia*    21°43S 136°32E **62** C2
Sandoway = Thandwe
  *Myanmar*                 18°20N 94°30E **41** K19
Sandoy *Færoe Is.*         61°52N 6°46W **8** F9
Sandpoint *U.S.A.*         48°17N 116°33W **76** B5
Sandray *U.K.*             56°53N 7°31W **11** E1
Sandringham *U.K.*         52°51N 0°31E **12** E8
Sandstone *Australia*      27°59S 119°16E **61** E2
Sandu *China*             26°0N 107°52E **34** D6
Sandur *India*            15°5N 76°40E **45** F3
Sandusky *Mich., U.S.A.*  43°25N 82°50W **82** C2
Sandusky *Ohio, U.S.A.*   41°27N 82°42W **82** E2
Sandveld *Namibia*         21°25S 20°0E **56** B3
Sandviken *Sweden*         60°38N 16°46E **8** F17
Sandwich, C. *Australia*   18°14S 146°18E **62** B4
Sandwich B. *Canada*       53°40N 57°15W **73** B8
Sandwich B. *Namibia*      23°25S 14°20E **56** B1
Sandy *Oreg., U.S.A.*     45°24N 122°16W **78** E4
Sandy *Pa., U.S.A.*       41°6N 78°46W **82** E6
Sandy *Utah, U.S.A.*      40°32N 111°50W **76** F8
Sandy Bay *Canada*         55°31N 102°19W **71** B8
Sandy Bight *Australia*    33°50S 123°20E **61** F3
Sandy C. *Queens.,
  Australia*                24°42S 153°15E **62** C5
Sandy C. *Tas., Australia* 41°25S 144°45E **63** G3
Sandy Cay *Bahamas*        23°13N 75°18W **89** B4
Sandy Cr. ➝ *Australia*   31°54S 145°18E **63** E4
Sandy Cr. ➝ *U.S.A.*     41°51N 109°47W **76** F9
Sandy Creek *U.S.A.*       43°38N 76°5W **83** C8

Sandy L. *Canada*          53°2N 93°0W **72** B1
Sandy Lake *Canada*        53°0N 93°15W **72** B1
Sandy Point *India*        10°32N 92°22E **45** J11
Sandy Valley *U.S.A.*      35°49N 115°38W **79** K11
Sånfjället △ *Sweden*     62°17N 13°35E **8** E15
Sanford *Fla., U.S.A.*    28°48N 81°16W **85** G14
Sanford *Maine, U.S.A.*   43°27N 70°47W **83** C14
Sanford *N.C., U.S.A.*    35°29N 79°10W **85** D15
Sanford ➝ *Australia*    27°22S 115°53E **61** E2
Sanford, Mt. *U.S.A.*     62°13N 144°8W **68** E3
Sang-i-Masha *Afghan.*    33°8N 67°27E **42** C2
Sanga ➝ *Congo*           1°5S 17°0E **54** E3
Sangamner *India*          19°37N 74°15E **44** E2
Sangān *Iran*             34°23N 60°15E **47** C9
Sangar *Afghan.*           32°56N 65°30E **42** C1
Sangar *Russia*            64°2N 127°31E **27** C13
Sangareddi *India*         17°38N 78°7E **44** F4
Sangarh ➝ *Pakistan*     30°43N 70°44E **42** D4
Sangay *Ecuador*            2°0S 78°20W **92** D3
Sangeang *Indonesia*        8°12S 119°6E **37** F5
Sanger *U.S.A.*           36°42N 119°33W **78** J7
Sangerhausen *Germany*    51°28N 11°18E **16** C6
Sanggan He ➝ *China*     38°12N 117°15E **32** E9
Sanggau *Indonesia*         0°5N 110°30E **36** D4
Sanghar *Pakistan*        26°2N 68°57E **42** F3
Sangihe, Kepulauan
  *Indonesia*                3°0N 125°30E **37** D7
Sangihe, Pulau *Indonesia* 3°35N 125°30E **37** D7
Sangiran △ *Indonesia*    7°27S 110°50E **37** G14
Sangju *S. Korea*         36°25N 128°10E **33** F15
Sangkapura *Indonesia*     5°52S 112°40E **36** F4
Sangkha *Thailand*        14°37N 103°52E **38** E4
Sangkhla Buri *Thailand*  14°57N 98°28E **38** E2
Sangkulirang *Indonesia*   0°59N 117°58E **36** D5
Sangla *Pakistan*         31°43N 73°23E **42** D5
Sangli *India*            16°55N 74°33E **44** F2
Sangmélima *Cameroon*      2°57N 12°1E **54** D2
Sango *Zimbabwe*          18°44S 31°44E **57** A5
Sangod *India*            24°55N 76°17E **42** G7
Sangole *India*           17°26N 75°12E **44** F2
Sangre de Cristo Mts.
  *U.S.A.*                  37°30N 105°20W **77** H11
Sangre Grande
  *Trin. & Tob.*           10°35N 61°8W **93** K15
Sangrur *India*           30°14N 75°50E **42** D6
Sangudo *Canada*          53°50N 114°54W **70** C6
Sangue ➝ *Brazil*        11°1S 58°39W **92** F7
Sangzhi *China*           29°25N 110°12E **35** C8
Sanibel *U.S.A.*          26°27N 82°1W **85** H13
Sanikluaq *Canada*        56°32N 79°14W **72** A4
Sanin-Kaigan △ *Japan*   35°39N 134°37E **29** G7
Sanirajak = Hall Beach
  *Canada*                 68°46N 81°12W **69** D15
Sanjawi *Pakistan*        30°17N 68°21E **42** D3
Sanjiang *China*          25°48N 109°37E **34** E7
Sanjo *Japan*             37°37N 138°57E **28** F9
Sankarankovil *India*     9°10N 77°35E **45** K3
Sankeshwar *India*        16°23N 74°32E **45** F2
Sankh ➝ *India*          22°15N 84°48E **43** H11
Sankt Gallen *Switz.*     47°26N 9°22E **20** C8
Sankt Michel = Mikkeli
  *Finland*                61°43N 27°15E **8** F22
Sankt Moritz *Switz.*     46°30N 9°51E **20** C8
Sankt Pölten *Austria*    48°12N 15°38E **16** D8
Sankuru ➝
  *Dem. Rep. of the Congo*   4°17S 20°25E **54** E4
Sanlıurfa *Turkey*        37°12N 38°50E **46** B3
Sanlúcar de Barrameda
  *Spain*                   36°46N 6°21W **21** D2
Sanmen *China*            29°5N 121°35E **35** C13
Sanmenxia *China*         34°47N 111°12E **32** G6
Sanming *China*           26°15N 117°40E **35** D11
Sanmu *Japan*             34°11N 134°37E **29** G7
Sanndraigh = Sandray
  *U.K.*                   56°53N 7°31W **11** E1
Sânnicolau Mare
  *Romania*                46°5N 20°39E **17** E11
Sannieshof *S. Africa*    26°30S 25°47E **56** D4
Sannīn, J. *Lebanon*     33°57N 35°52E **48** B4
Sanniquellie *Liberia*     7°19N 8°38E **52** G4
Sano *Japan*             36°19N 139°35E **29** F9
Sanok *Poland*            49°35N 22°10E **17** D12
Sanquhar *U.K.*           55°22N 3°54W **11** F5
Sanremo = San Remo
  *Italy*                   43°49N 7°46E **20** E7
Sans Souci *Trin. & Tob.* 10°50N 61°0W **93** K16
Sansha *China*            26°58N 120°58E **35** D13
Sanshui *China*           23°10N 112°56E **35** F9
Sansui *China*            26°58N 108°39E **34** D7
Sant Antoni de Portmany
  *Spain*                   38°59N 1°19E **21** C6
Sant Feliu de Guíxols *Spain* 41°45N 3°1E **21** B7
Sant Jordi, G. de *Spain*  40°53N 1°2E **21** B6
Santa Ana *Bolivia*       13°50S 65°40W **92** F5
Santa Ana *El Salv.*      14°0N 89°31W **88** D2
Santa Ana *Mexico*        30°33N 111°7W **86** A2
Santa Ana *U.S.A.*        33°46N 117°52W **79** M9
Santa Ana de los Ríos de Cuenca =
  Cuenca *Ecuador*          2°50S 79°9W **92** D3
Santa Bárbara *Chile*     37°40S 72°1W **94** D1
Santa Bárbara *Honduras*  14°53N 88°14W **88** D2
Santa Bárbara *Mexico*    26°48N 105°49W **86** B3
Santa Barbara *U.S.A.*    34°25N 119°42W **79** L7
Santa Barbara Channel
  *U.S.A.*                  34°15N 120°0W **79** L7
Santa Barbara I. *U.S.A.* 33°29N 119°2W **79** M7
Santa Catalina, Gulf of
  *U.S.A.*                  33°10N 117°50W **79** N9
Santa Catalina, I.
  *Mexico*                  25°40N 110°47W **86** B2
Santa Catalina I.
  *U.S.A.*                  33°23N 118°25W **79** M8
Santa Catarina □ *Brazil* 27°25S 48°30W **95** B6
Santa Catarina, I. de
  *Brazil*                  27°30S 48°40W **95** B6
Santa Cecília *Brazil*    26°56S 50°18W **95** B5
Santa Clara *Cuba*        22°20N 80°0W **88** B4
Santa Clara *Calif.,
  U.S.A.*                   37°21N 121°57W **78** H5

Santa Clara *N.Y., U.S.A.* 44°38N 74°27W **83** B10
Santa Clara *Utah, U.S.A.* 37°8N 113°39W **77** H7
Santa Clara ➝ *Mexico*   29°51N 107°6W **86** A3
Santa Clara de Olimar
  *Uruguay*                 32°50S 54°54W **95** C5
Santa Clara Valley
  *U.S.A.*                  36°50N 121°30W **78** J5
Santa Clarita *U.S.A.*    34°24N 118°33W **79** L8
Santa Clotilde *Peru*      2°33S 73°45W **92** D4
Santa Cruz *Bolivia*      17°43S 63°10W **92** G6
Santa Cruz *Chile*        34°38S 71°27W **94** C1
Santa Cruz *Costa Rica*   10°15N 85°35W **88** D2
Santa Cruz *Phil.*        14°20N 121°24E **37** B6
Santa Cruz *U.S.A.*       36°58N 122°1W **78** J4
Santa Cruz ➝ *Argentina* 50°10S 68°20W **96** G3
Santa Cruz de Mompox = Mompós
  *Colombia*                9°14N 74°26W **92** B4
Santa Cruz de Tenerife
  *Canary Is.*             28°28N 16°15W **52** C2
Santa Cruz del Norte
  *Cuba*                   23°9N 81°55W **88** B3
Santa Cruz del Sur *Cuba* 20°44N 78°0W **88** B4
Santa Cruz do Rio Pardo
  *Brazil*                 22°54S 49°37W **95** A6
Santa Cruz do Sul *Brazil* 29°42S 52°25W **95** B5
Santa Cruz I. *U.S.A.*    34°1N 119°43W **79** M7
Santa Cruz Is. *Solomon Is.* 10°30S 166°0E **58** C9
Santa Cruz Mts. *Jamaica* 17°58N 77°43W **88** a
Santa Elena *Argentina*   30°58S 59°47W **94** C4
Santa Elena, C.
  *Costa Rica*             10°54N 85°56W **88** D2
Santa Fé *Argentina*      31°35S 60°41W **94** C3
Santa Fe *U.S.A.*         35°41N 105°57W **77** J11
Santa Fé □ *Argentina*   31°50S 60°55W **94** C3
Santa Fé do Sul *Brazil*  20°13S 50°56W **93** H8
Santa Filomena *Brazil*    9°6S 45°50W **93** E9
Santa Inês *Brazil*       13°17S 39°48W **93** F11
Santa Inés, I. *Chile*    54°0S 73°0W **96** G2
Santa Isabel *Argentina*  36°10S 66°54W **94** D2
Santa Isabel do Morro
  *Brazil*                 11°34S 50°40W **93** F8
Santa Lucía *Corrientes,
  Argentina*                28°58S 59°5W **94** B4
Santa Lucía *San Juan,
  Argentina*                31°30S 68°30W **94** C2
Santa Lucía *Uruguay*     34°27S 56°24W **94** C4
Santa Lucia Range
  *U.S.A.*                  36°0N 121°20W **78** K5
Santa Luzia *Cabo Verde*  16°50N 24°35W **52** b
Santa Margarita
  *Argentina*              38°28S 61°35W **94** D3
Santa Margarita *U.S.A.*  35°23N 120°37W **78** K6
Santa Margarita ➝
  *U.S.A.*                  33°13N 117°23W **79** M9
Santa Margarita, I.
  *Mexico*                  24°27N 111°50W **86** C2
Santa María *Argentina*   26°40S 66°0W **94** B2
Santa Maria *Azores*      36°58N 25°6W **52** a
Santa Maria *Brazil*      29°40S 53°48W **95** B5
Santa Maria *Cabo Verde*  16°31N 22°53W **52** b
Santa Maria *U.S.A.*      34°57N 120°26W **79** L6
Santa María ➝ *Mexico*   31°0N 107°14W **86** A3
Santa María, B. de *Mexico* 25°4N 108°6W **86** B3
Santa María, Vol.
  *Guatemala*              14°45N 91°33W **88** D1
Santa Maria da Vitória
  *Brazil*                 13°24S 44°12W **93** F10
Santa Maria di Léuca, C.
  *Italy*                   39°47N 18°22E **23** E8
Santa Marta *Colombia*    11°15N 74°13W **92** A4
Santa Marta, Sierra Nevada de
  *Colombia*                10°55N 73°50W **92** A4
Santa Marta Grande, C.
  *Brazil*                 28°43S 48°50W **95** B6
Santa Maura = Lefkada
  *Greece*                 38°40N 20°43E **23** E9
Santa Monica Mts. △
  *U.S.A.*                  34°4N 118°44W **79** L8
Santa Paula *U.S.A.*      34°21N 119°4W **79** L7
Santa Rosa *La Pampa,
  Argentina*                36°40S 64°17W **94** D3
Santa Rosa *San Luis,
  Argentina*                32°21S 65°10W **94** C2
Santa Rosa *Brazil*       27°52S 54°29W **95** B5
Santa Rosa *Calif., U.S.A.* 38°26N 122°43W **78** G4
Santa Rosa *N. Mex.,
  U.S.A.*                   34°57N 104°41W **77** J11
Santa Rosa and San Jacinto Mts. △
  *U.S.A.*                  33°28N 116°20W **79** M10
Santa Rosa de Copán
  *Honduras*               14°47N 88°46W **88** D2
Santa Rosa de Río Primero
  *Argentina*              31°8S 63°20W **94** C3
Santa Rosa del Sara
  *Bolivia*                17°7S 63°35W **92** G6
Santa Rosa I. *Calif.,
  U.S.A.*                   33°58N 120°6W **79** M6
Santa Rosa I. *Fla.,
  U.S.A.*                   30°20N 86°50W **85** F11
Santa Rosa Range
  *U.S.A.*                  41°45N 117°40W **76** F5
Santa Rosalía *Mexico*    27°19N 112°17W **86** B2
Santa Sylvina *Argentina* 27°50S 61°10W **94** B3
Santa Tecla = Nueva San Salvador
  *El Salv.*               13°40N 89°18W **88** D2
Santa Teresa *Argentina*  33°25S 60°47W **94** C3
Santa Teresa *Australia*  24°8S 134°22E **62** C1
Santa Teresa *Mexico*     25°17N 97°51W **87** B5
Santa Teresa △ *Uruguay* 33°57S 53°31W **95** C5
Santa Teresita *Mexico*   36°32S 56°41W **94** D4
Santa Vitória do Palmar
  *Brazil*                 33°32S 53°25W **95** C5
Santa Ynez ➝ *U.S.A.*   34°41N 120°36W **79** L6
Santa Ynez Mts. *U.S.A.*  34°30N 120°0W **79** L6
Santa Ysabel *U.S.A.*     33°7N 116°40W **79** M10
Santai *China*           31°5N 104°58E **34** B5
Santana, Coxilha de
  *Brazil*                 30°50S 55°35W **95** C4
Santana do Livramento
  *Brazil*                 30°55S 55°30W **95** C4

Santander *Spain* 43°27N 3°51W **21** A4
Santander Jiménez
　*Mexico* 24°13N 98°28W **87** C5
Santanilla, Is. *Honduras* 17°22N 83°57W **88** C3
Santaquin *U.S.A.* 39°59N 111°47W **76** G8
Santarém *Brazil* 2°25S 54°42W **93** D8
Santarém *Portugal* 39°12N 8°42W **21** C1
Santaren Channel
　*W. Indies* 24°0N 79°30W **88** B4
Santee *U.S.A.* 32°50N 116°58W **79** N10
Santee ~ *U.S.A.* 33°7N 79°17W **85** E15
Santiago = Río Grande de
　Santiago ~ *Mexico* 21°36N 105°26W **86** C3
Santiago = São Tiago
　*Cabo Verde* 15°0N 23°40W **52** b
Santiago *Brazil* 29°11S 54°52W **95** B5
Santiago *Panama* 8°0N 81°0W **88** E3
Santiago *Phil.* 16°41N 121°33E **37** A6
Santiago ~ *Peru* 4°27S 77°38W **92** D3
Santiago de Compostela
　*Spain* 42°52N 8°37W **21** A1
Santiago de Cuba *Cuba* 20°0N 75°49W **88** C4
Santiago de los Caballeros
　*Dom. Rep.* 19°30N 70°40W **89** C5
Santiago del Estero
　*Argentina* 27°50S 64°15W **94** B3
Santiago del Estero □
　*Argentina* 27°40S 63°15W **94** B3
Santiago Ixcuintla
　*Mexico* 21°49N 105°13W **86** C3
Santiago Jamiltepec
　*Mexico* 16°17N 97°49W **87** D5
Santiago Papasquiaro
　*Mexico* 25°3N 105°25W **86** C3
Santiago Pinotepa Nacional
　*Mexico* 16°19N 98°1W **87** D5
Santiaguillo, L. de
　*Mexico* 24°48N 104°48W **86** C4
Santo Amaro *Brazil* 12°30S 38°43W **93** F11
Santo Anastácio *Brazil* 21°58S 51°39W **95** A5
Santo André *Brazil* 23°39S 46°29W **95** A6
Santo Ângelo *Brazil* 28°15S 54°15W **95** B5
Santo Antão *Cabo Verde* 16°52N 25°10W **52** b
Sant' Antíoco *Italy* 39°4N 8°27E **22** E3
Santo Antônio do Içá
　*Brazil* 3°5S 67°57W **92** D5
Santo Antônio do Leverger
　*Brazil* 15°52S 56°5W **93** G7
Santo Domingo
　*Dom. Rep.* 18°30N 69°59W **89** C6
Santo Domingo *Mexico* 25°29N 111°55W **86** B2
Santo Domingo *Nic.* 12°14N 84°59W **88** D3
Santo Domingo, Cay
　*Bahamas* 21°25N 75°45W **88** B4
Santo Domingo de los Colorados
　*Ecuador* 0°15S 79°9W **92** D3
Santo Domingo Pueblo
　*U.S.A.* 35°31N 106°22W **77** J10
Santo Domingo Tehuantepec =
　Tehuantepec *Mexico* 16°21N 95°13W **87** D5
Santo Tomás *Mexico* 31°33N 116°24W **86** A1
Santo Tomás *Peru* 14°26S 72°8W **92** F4
Santo Tomé *Argentina* 28°40S 56°5W **95** B4
Santo Tomé de Guayana = Ciudad
　Guayana *Venezuela* 8°0N 62°30W **92** B6
Santoña *Spain* 43°29N 3°27W **21** A4
Santorini *Greece* 36°23N 25°27E **23** F11
Santos *Brazil* 24°0S 46°20W **95** A6
Santos Dumont *Brazil* 22°55S 43°10W **95** A7
Santuario de Aves Laguna
　Colorada △ *Bolivia* 22°10S 67°45W **94** A2
Sanuki *Japan* 34°19N 134°10E **29** G7
Sanur *Indonesia* 8°41S 115°15E **37** K18
Sanwer *India* 22°59N 75°50E **42** H6
Sanxia Shuiku *China* 30°3N 107°58E **34** B6
Sanxiang *China* 22°21N 113°25E **31** a
Sanya *China* 18°14N 109°29E **38** C7
Sanyuan *China* 34°35N 108°58E **32** G5
São Bernardo do Campo
　*Brazil* 23°45S 46°34W **95** A6
São Borja *Brazil* 28°39S 56°0W **95** B4
São Carlos *Brazil* 22°0S 47°50W **95** A6
São Cristóvão *Brazil* 11°1S 37°15W **93** F11
São Domingos *Brazil* 13°25S 46°19W **93** F9
São Filipe *Cabo Verde* 15°2N 24°30W **52** b
São Francisco *Brazil* 16°0S 44°50W **93** G10
São Francisco ~ *Brazil* 10°30S 36°24W **93** F11
São Francisco do Sul
　*Brazil* 26°15S 48°36W **95** B6
São Gabriel *Brazil* 30°20S 54°20W **95** C5
São Gonçalo *Brazil* 22°48S 43°5W **95** A7
São João da Boa Vista
　*Brazil* 22°0S 46°52W **95** A6
São João da Madeira
　*Portugal* 40°54N 8°30W **21** B1
São João del Rei *Brazil* 21°8S 44°15W **95** A7
São João do Araguaia
　*Brazil* 5°23S 48°46W **93** E9
São João do Piauí *Brazil* 8°21S 42°15W **93** E10
São Joaquim *Brazil* 28°18S 49°56W **95** B6
São Joaquim △ *Brazil* 28°12S 49°37W **95** B6
São Jorge *Azores* 38°38N 28°3W **52** a
São José *Brazil* 27°38S 48°39W **95** B6
São José do Norte *Brazil* 32°1S 52°3W **95** C5
São José do Rio Preto
　*Brazil* 20°50S 49°20W **95** A6
São José dos Campos
　*Brazil* 23°7S 45°52W **95** A6
São Leopoldo *Brazil* 29°50S 51°10W **95** B5
São Lourenço *Brazil* 22°7S 45°3W **95** A6
São Lourenço ~ *Brazil* 17°53S 57°27W **93** G7
São Lourenço do Sul
　*Brazil* 31°22S 51°58W **95** C5
São Luís *Brazil* 2°39S 44°15W **93** D10
São Luís Gonzaga *Brazil* 28°25S 55°0W **95** B5
São Marcos ~ *Brazil* 18°15S 47°37W **93** G9
São Marcos, B. de *Brazil* 2°0S 44°0W **93** D10
São Mateus *Brazil* 18°44S 39°50W **93** G11
São Mateus do Sul *Brazil* 25°52S 50°23W **95** B5
São Miguel *Azores* 37°47N 25°30W **52** a

São Miguel do Oeste
　*Brazil* 26°45S 53°34W **95** B5
São Nicolau *Cabo Verde* 16°20N 24°20W **52** b
São Paulo □ *Brazil* 22°0S 49°0W **95** A6
São Paulo de Olivença
　*Brazil* 3°27S 68°48W **92** D5
São Roque, C. de *Brazil* 5°30S 35°16W **93** E11
São Sebastião, I. de
　*Brazil* 23°50S 45°18W **95** A6
São Sebastião do Paraíso
　*Brazil* 20°54S 46°59W **95** A6
São Tiago *Cabo Verde* 15°0N 23°40W **52** b
São Tomé
　*São Tomé & Príncipe* 0°10N 6°39E **50** F4
São Tomé, C. de *Brazil* 22°0S 40°59W **95** A7
São Tomé & Príncipe ■
　*Africa* 0°12N 6°39E **51** F4
São Vicente *Brazil* 23°57S 46°23W **95** A6
São Vicente *Cabo Verde* 17°0N 25°0W **52** b
São Vicente, C. de *Portugal* 37°0N 9°0W **21** D1
Saona, I. *Dom. Rep.* 18°10N 68°40W **89** C6
Saône ~ *France* 45°44N 4°50E **20** D6
Saonek *Indonesia* 0°22S 130°55E **37** E8
Sapam, Ao *Thailand* 8°0N 98°26E **39** a
Saparua *Indonesia* 3°33S 128°40E **37** E7
Sape *Indonesia* 8°34S 118°59E **37** F5
Sapele *Nigeria* 5°50N 5°40E **52** G7
Sapelo I. *U.S.A.* 31°25N 81°12W **85** F14
Saposoa *Peru* 6°55S 76°45W **92** E3
Sapphire *Australia* 23°28S 147°43E **62** C4
Sappho *U.S.A.* 48°4N 124°16W **78** B2
Sapporo *Japan* 43°0N 141°21E **28** C10
Sapporo New Chitose ✈ (CTS)
　*Japan* 42°46N 141°41E **28** C10
Sapt Kosi ~ *Nepal* 26°32N 86°56E **43** F12
Sapudi *Indonesia* 7°6S 114°20E **37** G16
Sapulpa *U.S.A.* 35°59N 96°5W **84** D6
Saqqez *Iran* 36°15N 46°20E **46** B5
Sar Dasht *Āzarbāyjān-e Gharbī,*
　*Iran* 36°9N 45°28E **46** B5
Sar Dasht *Khuzestān, Iran* 32°32N 48°52E **47** C6
Sar-e Pol □ *Afghan.* 36°20N 65°50E **40** B4
Sar Gachīneh = Yāsūj
　*Iran* 30°31N 51°31E **47** D6
Sar Planina *Macedonia* 42°0N 21°0E **23** C9
Sara Buri = Saraburi
　*Thailand* 14°30N 100°55E **38** E3
Sarāb *Iran* 37°55N 47°40E **46** B5
Sarābādī *Iraq* 33°1N 44°48E **46** C5
Saraburi *Thailand* 14°30N 100°55E **38** E3
Saradiya *India* 21°34N 70°2E **42** J4
Saragossa = Zaragoza
　*Spain* 41°39N 0°53W **21** B5
Saraguro *Ecuador* 3°35S 79°16W **92** D3
Sarahs *Turkmenistan* 36°32N 61°13E **47** B9
Sarai Naurang *Pakistan* 32°50N 70°47E **42** C4
Saraikela *India* 22°42N 85°56E **43** H11
Saraipali *India* 21°20N 82°59E **44** D6
Sarajevo *Bos.-H.* 43°52N 18°26E **23** C8
Sarakhs = Sarahs
　*Turkmenistan* 36°32N 61°13E **47** B9
Saran, Gunung *Indonesia* 0°30S 111°25E **36** E4
Saranac Lake *U.S.A.* 44°20N 74°10W **83** B10
Saranac Lakes *U.S.A.* 44°20N 74°28W **83** B10
Sarandí del Yí *Uruguay* 33°18S 55°38W **95** C4
Sarandí Grande *Uruguay* 33°44S 56°20W **94** C4
Sarangani B. *Phil.* 6°0N 125°13E **37** C7
Sarangani Is. *Phil.* 5°25N 125°25E **37** C7
Sarangarh *India* 21°30N 83°5E **44** D6
Saransk *Russia* 54°10N 45°10E **18** D8
Sarapul *Russia* 56°28N 53°48E **18** C9
Sarasota *U.S.A.* 27°20N 82°32W **85** H13
Saratoga *Calif., U.S.A.* 37°16N 122°2W **78** H4
Saratoga *Wyo., U.S.A.* 41°27N 106°49W **76** F10
Saratoga △ *U.S.A.* 43°0N 73°50W **83** D11
Saratoga L. *U.S.A.* 43°1N 73°44W **83** C11
Saratoga Springs *U.S.A.* 43°5N 73°47W **83** C11
Saratok *Malaysia* 1°55N 111°17E **36** D4
Saratov *Russia* 51°30N 46°2E **19** D8
Saravan *Iran* 27°25N 62°15E **47** E9
Saravane *Laos* 15°43N 106°25E **38** E6
Sarawak □ *Malaysia* 2°0N 113°0E **36** D4
Saray *Turkey* 41°26N 27°55E **23** D12
Sarayköy *Turkey* 37°55N 28°54E **23** F13
Sarbāz *Iran* 26°38N 61°19E **47** E9
Sarbīsheh *Iran* 32°30N 59°40E **47** C8
Sarda ~ *India* 27°21N 81°23E **43** F9
Sardar Sarovar Dam
　*India* 21°50N 73°50E **44** D1
Sardarshahr *India* 28°30N 74°29E **42** E6
Sardegna □ *Italy* 40°0N 9°0E **22** D3
Sardhana *India* 29°9N 77°39E **42** E7
Sardinia = Sardegna □ *Italy* 40°0N 9°0E **22** D3
Sardis *Turkey* 38°28N 27°58E **23** E12
Sārdūīyeh = Dar Mazār
　*Iran* 29°14N 57°20E **47** D8
Sarek △ *Sweden* 67°22N 17°35E **8** C17
Saren *Indonesia* 8°26S 115°34E **37** J18
Sarera, G. of *Indonesia* 2°0S 135°0E **58** B6
Sargasso Sea *Atl. Oc.* 27°0N 72°0W **66** G13
Sargodha *Pakistan* 32°10N 72°40E **42** C5
Sarh *Chad* 9°5N 18°23E **53** G9
Sārī *Iran* 36°30N 53°4E **47** B7
Saria *India* 21°21N 71°25E **42** J4
Sariab *Pakistan* 30°6N 66°59E **42** D2
Sarıgöl *Turkey* 38°14N 28°41E **23** E13
Sarikei *Malaysia* 2°8N 111°30E **36** D4
Sarila *India* 25°46N 79°41E **43** G8
Sarina *Australia* 21°22S 149°13E **62** C4
Sarita *U.S.A.* 27°13N 97°47W **84** H6
Sariwŏn *N. Korea* 38°31N 125°46E **33** E13
Sarju ~ *India* 27°21N 81°23E **43** F9
Sark *U.K.* 49°25N 2°22W **13** H5
Sarkari Tala *India* 27°39N 70°52E **42** F4
Şarköy *Turkey* 40°36N 27°6E **23** D12
Sarlat-la-Canéda *France* 44°54N 1°13E **20** D4
Sarmi *Indonesia* 1°49S 138°44E **37** E9
Sarmiento *Argentina* 45°35S 69°5W **96** F3
Särna *Sweden* 61°41N 13°8E **8** F15
Sarnia *Canada* 42°58N 82°23W **82** D2

Sarolangun *Indonesia* 2°19S 102°42E **36** E2
Saronikos Kolpos *Greece* 37°45N 23°45E **23** F10
Saros Körfezi *Turkey* 40°30N 26°15E **23** D12
Sarpsborg *Norway* 59°16N 11°7E **9** G14
Sarqan *Kazakhstan* 45°24N 79°55E **30** B4
Sarre = Saar ~ *Europe* 49°41N 6°32E **15** E6
Sarreguemines *France* 49°5N 7°4E **20** B7
Sartell *U.S.A.* 45°37N 94°12W **80** C6
Sarthe □ *France* 47°33N 0°31W **20** C3
Saruna ~ *Pakistan* 26°31N 67°7E **42** F2
Sarvar *India* 26°4N 75°0E **42** F6
Sarvestān *Iran* 29°20N 53°10E **47** D7
Sary-Tash *Kyrgyzstan* 39°44N 73°15E **26** F8
Saryshaghan *Kazakhstan* 46°12N 73°38E **26** E8
Sasan Gir *India* 21°10N 70°36E **42** J4
Sasaram *India* 24°57N 84°5E **43** G11
Sasebo *Japan* 33°10N 129°43E **29** H4
Saser Kangri *India* 34°50N 77°50E **43** B7
Saskatchewan □ *Canada* 54°40N 106°0W **71** C7
Saskatchewan ~
　*Canada* 53°37N 100°40W **71** C8
Saskatoon *Canada* 52°10N 106°38W **71** C7
Saskylakh *Russia* 71°55N 114°1E **27** B12
Saslaya △ *Nic.* 13°45N 85°4W **88** D2
Sasolburg *S. Africa* 26°46S 27°49E **57** C4
Sasovo *Russia* 54°25N 41°55E **18** D7
Sassandra *Côte d'Ivoire* 4°55N 6°8W **52** H4
Sassandra ~ *Côte d'Ivoire* 4°58N 6°5W **52** H4
Sássari *Italy* 40°43N 8°34E **22** D3
Sassie *Australia* 10°2S 142°51E **62** a
Sassnitz *Germany* 54°29N 13°39E **16** A7
Sassuolo *Italy* 44°33N 10°47E **22** B4
Sastamala *Finland* 61°20N 22°54E **8** F20
Sasvad *India* 18°20N 74°2E **44** E2
Sasyk, Ozero *Ukraine* 45°45N 29°40E **17** F15
Sata-Misaki *Japan* 31°0N 130°40E **29** J5
Satadougou *Mali* 12°25N 11°25W **52** F3
Satakunta □ *Finland* 61°45N 23°0E **8** F20
Satara *India* 17°44N 73°58E **44** F1
Satara *S. Africa* 24°29S 31°47E **57** B5
Satarwa *India* 23°55N 84°16E **43** H11
Satevó *Mexico* 27°57N 106°7W **86** B3
Satilla ~ *U.S.A.* 30°59N 81°29W **85** F14
Satka *Russia* 55°3N 59°1E **18** C10
Satluj = Sutlej ~ *Pakistan* 29°23N 71°3E **42** E4
Satmala Hills *Maharashtra,*
　*India* 20°15N 74°40E **44** D2
Satmala Hills *Telangana,*
　*India* 19°45N 78°45E **44** E4
Satna *India* 24°35N 80°50E **43** G9
Sátoraljaújhely *Hungary* 48°25N 21°41E **17** D11
Satpura △ *India* 22°40N 78°15E **42** H8
Satpura Ra. *India* 21°25N 76°10E **44** D3
Satsuma-Sendai *Japan* 31°50N 130°20E **29** J5
Satsunan-Shotō *Japan* 30°0N 130°0E **29** K5
Sattahip *Thailand* 12°41N 100°54E **38** F3
Sattenapalle *India* 16°25N 80°6E **45** F5
Satu Mare *Romania* 47°46N 22°55E **17** E12
Satui *Indonesia* 3°50S 115°27E **36** E5
Satun *Thailand* 6°43N 100°2E **39** J3
Saturn'itea *Samoa* 13°45S 172°18W **59** b
Saturnina ~ *Brazil* 12°15S 58°10W **92** F7
Sauce *Argentina* 30°5S 58°46W **94** C4
Sauceda *Mexico* 25°46N 101°19W **86** B4
Saucillo *Mexico* 28°1N 105°17W **86** B3
Sauda *Norway* 59°40N 6°20E **9** G12
Sauðarkrókur *Iceland* 65°45N 19°40W **8** D4
Saudi Arabia ■ *Asia* 26°0N 44°0E **46** B3
Sauerland *Germany* 51°12N 7°59E **16** C4
Saugeen ~ *Canada* 44°30N 81°22W **82** B3
Saugerties *U.S.A.* 42°5N 73°57W **83** D11
Saugus *U.S.A.* 34°25N 118°32W **79** L8
Sauk Centre *U.S.A.* 45°44N 94°57W **80** C6
Sauk Rapids *U.S.A.* 45°35N 94°10W **80** C6
Sault Ste. Marie *Canada* 46°30N 84°20W **72** C3
Sault Ste. Marie *U.S.A.* 46°30N 84°21W **81** B11
Saumlaki *Indonesia* 7°55S 131°20E **37** F8
Saumur *France* 47°15N 0°5W **20** C3
Saundatti *India* 15°47N 75°7E **45** G2
Saunders, C. *N.Z.* 45°53S 170°45E **59** F4
Saunders I. *Antarctica* 57°48S 26°28W **5** B1
Saunders Pt. *Australia* 27°52S 125°38E **61** E4
Saurimo *Angola* 9°40S 20°12E **54** F4
Savá *Honduras* 15°32N 86°15W **88** C2
Sava ~ *Serbia* 44°50N 20°26E **23** B9
Savage *U.S.A.* 47°27N 104°21W **76** C11
Savage I. = Niue ☑
　*Pac. Oc.* 19°2S 169°54W **65** J11
Savage River *Australia* 41°31S 145°14E **63** G4
Savai'i *Samoa* 13°28S 172°24W **59** b
Savalou *Benin* 7°57N 1°58E **52** G6
Savanna *U.S.A.* 42°5N 90°8W **80** D8
Savanna-la-Mar *Jamaica* 18°10N 78°10W **88** a
Savannah *Ga., U.S.A.* 32°5N 81°6W **85** E14
Savannah *Mo., U.S.A.* 39°56N 94°50W **80** F6
Savannah *Tenn., U.S.A.* 35°14N 88°15W **85** D10
Savannah ~ *U.S.A.* 32°2N 80°53W **85** E14
Savannakhet *Laos* 16°30N 104°49E **38** D5
Savant L. *Canada* 50°16N 90°44W **72** B1
Savant Lake *Canada* 50°14N 90°40W **72** B1
Savanur *India* 14°59N 75°21E **45** G2
Savarkundla = Kundla
　*India* 21°21N 71°25E **42** J4
Savda *India* 21°9N 75°56E **44** D2
Save ~ *Mozam.* 21°16S 34°0E **57** B5
Sāveh *Iran* 35°2N 50°20E **47** C6
Savelugu *Ghana* 9°38N 0°54W **52** G5
Savo *Finland* 62°45N 27°30E **8** E22
Savoie □ *France* 45°26N 6°25E **20** D7
Savolax = Savo *Finland* 62°45N 27°30E **8** E22
Savona *Italy* 44°17N 8°30E **20** D8
Savonlinna *Finland* 61°52N 28°53E **8** F23
Savoy = Savoie □ *France* 45°26N 6°25E **20** D7
Savur *Turkey* 37°34N 40°53E **46** B4
Savusavu *Fiji* 16°34S 179°15E **59** a
Savusavu B. *Fiji* 16°45S 179°0E **59** a
Savuti *Botswana* 18°37S 24°15E **56** A3
Sawahlunto *Indonesia* 0°40S 100°52E **36** E2

Sawai *Indonesia* 3°0S 129°5E **37** E7
Sawai Madhopur *India* 26°0N 76°25E **42** G7
Sawaleke *Fiji* 17°59S 179°18E **59** a
Sawang Daen Din
　*Thailand* 17°28N 103°28E **38** D4
Sawankhalok *Thailand* 17°19N 99°50E **38** D2
Sawara *Japan* 35°55N 140°30E **29** G10
Sawatch Range *U.S.A.* 39°0N 106°30W **76** G10
Sawel Mt. *U.K.* 54°50N 7°2W **10** B4
Sawi *Thailand* 10°14N 99°5E **39** G2
Sawmills *Zimbabwe* 19°30S 28°2E **55** H5
Sawtooth △ *U.S.A.* 44°0N 114°50W **76** D6
Sawtooth Range *U.S.A.* 44°3N 114°58W **76** D6
Sawu *Indonesia* 10°35S 121°50E **37** F6
Sawu Sea *Indonesia* 9°30S 121°50E **37** F6
Saxby ~ *Australia* 18°25S 140°53E **62** B3
Saxmundham *U.K.* 52°13N 1°30E **13** E9
Saxony = Sachsen □
　*Germany* 50°55N 13°10E **16** C7
Saxony, Lower = Niedersachsen □
　*Germany* 52°50N 9°0E **16** B5
Saxton *U.S.A.* 40°13N 78°15W **82** F6
Sayabec *Canada* 48°35N 67°41W **73** C6
Sayaboury *Laos* 19°15N 101°45E **38** C3
Sayán *Peru* 11°8S 77°12W **92** F3
Sayan, Vostochnyy *Russia* 54°0N 96°0E **27** D10
Sayan, Zapadnyy *Russia* 52°30N 94°0E **30** A7
Sayanogorsk *Russia* 53°5N 91°23E **27** D10
Saydā *Lebanon* 33°35N 35°25E **48** B4
Sayhandulaan = Öldziyt
　*Mongolia* 44°40N 109°1E **32** B5
Sayhūt *Yemen* 15°12N 51°10E **49** D5
Saylac *Somalia* 11°21N 43°30E **49** E3
Saynshand = Buyant-Uhaa
　*Mongolia* 44°55N 110°11E **32** B6
Sayre *Okla., U.S.A.* 35°18N 99°38W **84** D5
Sayre *Pa., U.S.A.* 41°59N 76°32W **83** E8
Sayreville *U.S.A.* 40°28N 74°22W **83** F10
Sayula *Mexico* 19°52N 103°36W **86** D4
Say'ūn *Yemen* 15°56N 48°47E **49** D4
Sayward *Canada* 50°21N 125°55W **70** C3
Sazanit *Albania* 40°30N 19°20E **23** D8
Sázava ~ *Czechia* 49°53N 14°24E **16** D8
Sazin *Pakistan* 35°35N 73°30E **43** B5
Scafell Pike *U.K.* 54°27N 3°14W **12** C4
Scalloway *U.K.* 60°9N 1°17W **11** A7
Scalpay *U.K.* 57°18N 6°0W **11** D3
Scandia *Canada* 50°20N 112°2W **70** C6
Scandicci *Italy* 43°45N 11°11E **22** C4
Scandinavia *Europe* 64°0N 12°0E **8** E15
Scapa Flow *U.K.* 58°53N 3°3W **11** C5
Scappoose *U.S.A.* 45°45N 122°53W **78** E4
Scarba *U.K.* 56°11N 5°43W **11** E3
Scarborough
　*Trin. & Tob.* 11°11N 60°42W **93** J16
Scarborough *U.K.* 54°17N 0°24W **12** C7
Scariff I. *Ireland* 51°44N 10°15W **10** E1
Scarp *U.K.* 58°1N 7°8W **11** C1
Scebeli = Shabeelle ~
　*Somalia* 2°0N 44°0E **49** G3
Schaffhausen *Switz.* 47°42N 8°39E **20** C8
Schagen *Neths.* 52°49N 4°48E **15** B4
Schaghticoke *U.S.A.* 42°54N 73°35W **83** D11
Schefferville *Canada* 54°48N 66°50W **73** B6
Schelde ~ *Belgium* 51°15N 4°16E **15** C4
Schell Creek Ra. *U.S.A.* 39°25N 114°40W **76** G6
Schellsburg *U.S.A.* 40°3N 78°39W **82** F6
Schenectady *U.S.A.* 42°49N 73°57W **83** D11
Schenevus *U.S.A.* 42°33N 74°50W **83** D10
Schiedam *Neths.* 51°55N 4°25E **15** C4
Schiermonnikoog *Neths.* 53°30N 6°15E **15** A6
Schiermonnikoog △
　*Neths.* 53°30N 6°15E **15** A6
Schio *Italy* 45°43N 11°21E **22** B4
Schleswig *Germany* 54°31N 9°34E **16** A5
Schleswig-Holstein □
　*Germany* 54°30N 9°30E **16** A5
Schœlcher *Martinique* 14°36N 61°7W **88** c
Schoharie *U.S.A.* 42°40N 74°19W **83** D10
Schoharie Cr. ~
　*U.S.A.* 42°57N 74°18W **83** D10
Schokland *Neths.* 52°38N 5°46E **15** B5
Scholls *U.S.A.* 45°24N 122°56W **78** E4
Schouten I. *Australia* 42°20S 148°20E **63** G4
Schouten Is. = Supiori
　*Indonesia* 1°0S 136°0E **37** E9
Schouwen *Neths.* 51°43N 3°45E **15** C3
Schreiber *Canada* 48°45N 87°20W **72** C2
Schroffenstein *Namibia* 27°11S 18°42E **56** C2
Schroon Lake *U.S.A.* 43°50N 73°46W **83** C11
Schuler *Canada* 50°20N 110°6W **71** C6
Schumacher *Canada* 48°30N 81°16W **72** C3
Schurz *U.S.A.* 38°57N 118°49W **76** G4
Schuyler *U.S.A.* 41°27N 97°4W **80** E5
Schuylerville *U.S.A.* 43°6N 73°35W **83** C11
Schuylkill ~ *U.S.A.* 39°53N 75°12W **83** G9
Schuylkill Haven *U.S.A.* 40°37N 76°11W **83** F8
Schwäbische Alb *Germany* 48°20N 9°30E **16** D5
Schwaner, Pegunungan
　*Indonesia* 1°0S 112°30E **36** E4
Schwarzrand *Namibia* 25°37S 16°50E **56** C2
Schwarzwald *Germany* 48°30N 8°20E **16** D5
Schwatka Mts. *U.S.A.* 67°0N 156°30W **74** B8
Schweinfurt *Germany* 50°3N 10°14E **16** C6
Schweiz = Switzerland ■
　*Europe* 46°30N 8°0E **20** C8
Schweizer-Reneke
　*S. Africa* 27°11S 25°18E **56** C4
Schwenningen = Villingen-
　Schwenningen *Germany* 48°3N 8°26E **16** D5
Schwerin *Germany* 53°36N 11°22E **16** B6
Schwyz *Switz.* 47°2N 8°39E **20** C8
Sciacca *Italy* 37°31N 13°3E **22** F5
Scilla *Italy* 38°15N 15°43E **22** E6
Scilly, Isles of *U.K.* 49°56N 6°22W **13** H1
Scioto ~ *U.S.A.* 38°44N 83°1W **81** F12
Scobey *U.S.A.* 48°47N 105°25W **76** B11
Scone *Australia* 32°5S 150°52E **63** E5
Scone *U.K.* 56°25N 3°24W **11** E5

Scoresbysund = Ittoqqortoormiit
　*Greenland* 70°20N 23°0W **4** B6
Scotia *Calif., U.S.A.* 40°29N 124°6W **76** F1
Scotia *N.Y., U.S.A.* 42°50N 73°58W **83** D11
Scotia Sea *Antarctica* 56°5S 56°0W **5** B18
Scotland *Canada* 43°1N 80°22W **82** C4
Scotland □ *U.K.* 57°0N 4°0W **11** E5
Scott *Antarctica* 77°0S 166°0E **5** D11
Scott, C. *Australia* 13°30S 129°49E **60** B4
Scott City *U.S.A.* 38°29N 100°54W **80** F4
Scott Glacier *Antarctica* 66°15S 100°5E **5** C8
Scott I. *Antarctica* 67°0S 179°0E **5** C11
Scott Is. *Canada* 50°48N 128°40W **70** C3
Scott L. *Canada* 59°55N 106°18W **71** B7
Scott Reef *Australia* 14°0S 121°50E **60** B3
Scottburgh *S. Africa* 30°15S 30°47E **57** D5
Scottdale *U.S.A.* 40°6N 79°35W **82** F5
Scottish Borders □ *U.K.* 55°35N 2°50W **11** F6
Scotts Valley *U.S.A.* 37°3N 122°1W **78** H4
Scottsbluff *U.S.A.* 41°52N 103°40W **80** E2
Scottsboro *U.S.A.* 34°40N 86°2W **85** D11
Scottsburg *U.S.A.* 38°41N 85°47W **81** F11
Scottsdale *Australia* 41°9S 147°31E **63** G4
Scottsdale *U.S.A.* 33°40N 111°53W **77** K8
Scottsville *Ky., U.S.A.* 36°45N 86°11W **80** G10
Scottsville *N.Y., U.S.A.* 43°2N 77°47W **82** C7
Scottville *U.S.A.* 43°58N 86°17W **80** D10
Scranton *U.S.A.* 41°25N 75°40W **83** E9
Scugog, L. *Canada* 44°10N 78°55W **82** B6
Scunthorpe *U.K.* 53°36N 0°39W **12** D7
Scutari = Shkodër *Albania* 42°4N 19°32E **23** C8
Sea Is. *U.S.A.* 31°30N 81°7W **85** F14
Seabrook, L. *Australia* 30°55S 119°40E **61** F2
Seaford *U.K.* 50°47N 0°7E **13** G8
Seaford *U.S.A.* 38°39N 75°37W **81** F16
Seaforth *Australia* 20°55S 148°57E **62** b
Seaforth *Canada* 43°35N 81°25W **82** C3
Seaforth, L. *U.K.* 57°52N 6°36W **11** D2
Seagraves *U.S.A.* 32°57N 102°34W **84** E3
Seaham *U.K.* 54°50N 1°20W **12** C6
Seal ~ *Canada* 59°4N 94°48W **71** B10
Seal L. *Canada* 54°20N 61°30W **73** B7
Sealy *U.S.A.* 29°47N 96°9W **84** G6
Searchlight *U.S.A.* 35°28N 114°55W **79** K12
Searcy *U.S.A.* 35°15N 91°44W **84** D9
Searles L. *U.S.A.* 35°44N 117°21W **79** K9
Seascale *U.K.* 54°24N 3°29W **12** C4
Seaside *Calif., U.S.A.* 36°37N 121°50W **78** J5
Seaside *Oreg., U.S.A.* 46°0N 123°56W **78** E3
Seaspray *Australia* 38°25S 147°15E **63** F4
Seattle *U.S.A.* 47°36N 122°19W **78** C4
Seattle-Tacoma Int. ✈ (SEA)
　*U.S.A.* 47°27N 122°18W **78** C4
Seba *Indonesia* 10°29S 121°50E **60** B3
Sebago L. *U.S.A.* 43°52N 70°34W **83** C14
Sebago Lake *U.S.A.* 43°51N 70°34W **83** C14
Sebastián Vizcaíno, B.
　*Mexico* 28°0N 114°30W **86** B2
Sebastopol = Sevastopol
　*Ukraine* 44°35N 33°30E **19** F5
Sebastopol *U.S.A.* 38°24N 122°49W **78** G4
Sebewaing *U.S.A.* 43°44N 83°27W **81** D12
Sebha = Sabhā *Libya* 27°9N 14°29E **53** C8
Şebinkarahisar *Turkey* 40°22N 38°28E **19** F6
Sebring *Fla., U.S.A.* 27°30N 81°27W **85** H14
Sebring *Ohio, U.S.A.* 40°55N 81°2W **82** F3
Sebringville *Canada* 43°24N 81°4W **82** C3
Sebta = Ceuta *N. Afr.* 35°52N 5°18W **21** E3
Sebuku *Indonesia* 3°30S 116°25E **36** E5
Sechelt *Canada* 49°25N 123°42W **70** D4
Sechura, Desierto de *Peru* 6°0S 80°30W **92** E2
Secretary I. *N.Z.* 45°15S 166°56E **59** F1
Secunderabad *India* 17°28N 78°30E **44** F4
Security *U.S.A.* 38°45N 104°45W **76** G11
Sedalia *U.S.A.* 38°42N 93°14W **80** F7
Sedam *India* 17°11N 77°17E **44** F3
Sedan *France* 49°43N 4°57E **20** B6
Sedan *U.S.A.* 37°8N 96°11W **80** G5
Sedbergh *U.K.* 54°20N 2°31W **12** C5
Seddon *N.Z.* 41°40S 174°7E **59** D5
Seddonville *N.Z.* 41°33S 172°1E **59** D4
Sedé Boqér *Israel* 30°52N 34°47E **48** E3
Sedeh *Fārs, Iran* 30°45N 52°11E **47** D7
Sedeh *Khorāsān, Iran* 33°20N 59°14E **47** C8
Sederot *Israel* 31°32N 34°37E **48** D3
Sédhiou *Senegal* 12°44N 15°30W **52** F2
Sedley *Canada* 50°10N 104°0W **71** C8
Sedona *U.S.A.* 34°52N 111°46W **77** J8
Sedova, Pik *Russia* 73°29N 54°58E **26** B6
Sedro-Woolley *U.S.A.* 48°30N 122°14W **78** B4
Seeheim *Namibia* 26°50S 17°45E **56** D2
Seeis *Namibia* 22°29S 17°39E **56** B2
Seekoei ~ *S. Africa* 30°18S 25°1E **56** E4
Seeley's Bay *Canada* 44°29N 76°14W **83** B8
Seemandhra = Andhra Pradesh □
　*India* 18°0N 79°0E **44** F4
Seferihisar *Turkey* 38°10N 26°50E **23** E12
Sefophe *Botswana* 22°11S 27°58E **57** B4
Seg-ozero *Russia* 63°20N 33°46E **18** B5
Segamat *Malaysia* 2°30N 102°50E **39** L4
Segesta *Italy* 37°56N 12°50E **22** F5
Segezha *Russia* 63°44N 34°19E **18** B5
Ségou *Mali* 13°30N 6°16W **52** F4
Segovia = Coco ~
　*Cent. Amer.* 15°0N 83°8W **88** D3
Segovia *Spain* 40°57N 4°10W **21** B3
Segre ~ *Spain* 41°40N 0°43E **21** B6
Seguam I. *U.S.A.* 52°19N 172°30W **74** E5
Séguéla *Côte d'Ivoire* 7°55N 6°40W **52** G4
Seguin *U.S.A.* 29°34N 97°58W **84** G6
Segundo ~ *Argentina* 30°53S 62°44W **94** C3
Segura ~ *Spain* 38°3N 0°44W **21** C5
Seh Konj, Kūh-e *Iran* 30°6N 57°30E **47** D8
Seh Qal'eh *Iran* 33°40N 58°24E **47** C8
Sehitwa *Botswana* 20°30S 22°30E **56** B3
Sehlabathebe △ *Lesotho* 29°53S 29°7E **57** C4
Sehore *India* 23°10N 77°5E **42** H7
Sehwan *Pakistan* 26°28N 67°53E **42** F2

Seil U.K. 56°18N 5°38W **11** E3
Seiland Norway 70°25N 23°15E **8** A20
Seiling U.S.A. 36°9N 98°56W **84** C5
Seinäjoki Finland 62°40N 22°51E **8** E20
Seine → France 49°26N 0°26E **20** B4
Seistan = Sīstān Asia 30°50N 61°0E **47** D9
Seistan, Daryācheh-ye = Sīstān, Daryācheh-ye Iran 31°0N 61°0E **47** D9
Seitseminen △ Finland 61°55N 23°25E **8** F20
Sekayu Indonesia 2°51S 103°51E **36** E2
Sekondi-Takoradi Ghana 4°58N 1°45W **52** H5
Sekudai Malaysia 1°32N 103°39E **39** d
Sekuma Botswana 24°36S 23°50E **56** B3
Selah U.S.A. 46°39N 120°32W **76** C3
Selama Malaysia 5°12N 100°42E **39** K3
Selangor □ Malaysia 3°10N 101°30E **39** L3
Selaru Indonesia 8°9S 131°0E **37** F8
Selatan, Selat Malaysia 5°15N 100°20E **39** c
Selawik L. U.S.A. 66°30N 160°45W **74** B7
Selby U.K. 53°47N 1°5W **12** D6
Selby U.S.A. 45°31N 100°2W **80** C3
Selçuk Turkey 37°56N 27°22E **23** F12
Selden U.S.A. 39°33N 100°34W **80** F4
Sele → Italy 40°29N 14°56E **22** D6
Selebi-Phikwe Botswana 21°58S 27°48E **57** B4
Selemdzha → Russia 51°42N 128°53E **27** D13
Selenga = Selenge Mörön → Asia 52°16N 106°16E **30** A10
Selenge Mörön → Asia 52°16N 106°16E **30** A10
Seletan, Tanjung Indonesia 4°10S 114°40E **36** E4
Seligman U.S.A. 35°20N 112°53W **77** J7
Selîma Sudan 21°22N 29°19E **53** D11
Selinda Spillway → Botswana 18°35S 23°10E **56** A3
Selinsgrove U.S.A. 40°48N 76°52W **82** F8
Selkirk Man., Canada 50°10N 96°55W **71** C9
Selkirk Ont., Canada 42°49N 79°56W **82** D5
Selkirk U.K. 55°33N 2°50W **11** F6
Selkirk I. = Horse I. Canada 53°20N 99°6W **71** C9
Selkirk Mts. Canada 51°15N 117°40W **68** G8
Sellafield U.K. 54°25N 3°29W **12** C4
Sells U.S.A. 31°55N 111°53W **77** L8
Selma Ala., U.S.A. 32°25N 87°1W **85** E11
Selma Calif., U.S.A. 36°34N 119°37W **78** J7
Selma N.C., U.S.A. 35°32N 78°17W **85** D15
Selmer U.S.A. 35°10N 88°36W **85** D10
Selpele Indonesia 0°1S 130°5E **37** E8
Selsey Bill U.K. 50°43N 0°47W **13** G7
Seltso Russia 53°22N 34°4E **18** D5
Selu Indonesia 7°32S 130°55E **37** F8
Selva Argentina 29°50S 62°0W **94** B3
Selva Lancandona = Montes Azules △ Mexico 16°21N 91°3W **87** D6
Selvagens, Ilhas Madeira 30°5N 15°55W **52** B2
Selvas Brazil 6°30S 67°0W **92** E5
Selwyn L. Canada 60°0N 104°30W **71** B8
Selwyn Mts. Canada 63°0N 130°0W **68** E5
Selwyn Ra. Australia 21°10S 140°0E **62** C3
Seman → Albania 40°47N 19°30E **23** D8
Semarang Indonesia 7°0S 110°26E **37** G14
Semarapura = Klungkung Indonesia 8°32S 115°24E **37** K18
Sembung Indonesia 8°28S 115°11E **37** J18
Semeru Indonesia 8°4S 112°55E **37** H15
Semey Kazakhstan 50°30N 80°10E **30** A5
Seminoe Res. U.S.A. 42°9N 106°55W **76** E10
Seminole Okla., U.S.A. 35°14N 96°41W **84** D6
Seminole Tex., U.S.A. 32°43N 102°39W **84** E3
Seminole Draw → U.S.A. 32°27N 102°20W **84** E3
Semipalatinsk = Semey Kazakhstan 50°30N 80°10E **30** A5
Semirara Is. Phil. 12°0N 121°20E **37** B6
Semisopochnoi I. U.S.A. 51°55N 179°36E **74** E3
Semitau Indonesia 0°29N 111°57E **36** D4
Semmering P. Austria 47°41N 15°45E **16** E8
Semnān Iran 35°40N 53°23E **47** C7
Semnān □ Iran 36°0N 54°0E **47** C7
Semporna Malaysia 4°30N 118°33E **37** D5
Semuda Indonesia 2°51S 112°58E **36** E4
Sen → Cambodia 12°32N 104°28E **38** F5
Sena Iran 28°27N 51°36E **47** D6
Sena Madureira Brazil 9°5S 68°45W **92** E5
Senador Pompeu Brazil 5°40S 39°20W **93** E11
Senang, Pulau Singapore 1°11N 103°52E **39** d
Senanga Zambia 16°7S 23°16E **55** H4
Senatobia U.S.A. 34°37N 89°58W **85** D10
Sendai = Satsuma-Sendai Japan 31°50N 130°20E **29** J5
Sendai Japan 38°15N 140°53E **28** E10
Sendai-Wan Japan 38°15N 141°0E **28** E10
Sendhwa India 21°41N 75°6E **42** J6
Sendurjana India 21°32N 78°17E **44** D4
Seneca U.S.A. 34°41N 82°57W **85** D13
Seneca Falls U.S.A. 42°55N 76°48W **83** D8
Seneca L. U.S.A. 42°40N 76°54W **82** D8
Senecaville L. U.S.A. 39°55N 81°25W **82** G3
Senegal ■ W. Afr. 14°30N 14°30W **52** F3
Sénégal → W. Afr. 15°48N 16°32W **52** E2
Senegambia Africa 12°45N 12°0W **50** E2
Senekal S. Africa 28°20S 27°36E **57** C4
Senge Khambab = Indus → Pakistan 24°20N 67°47E **42** G2
Senggigi Indonesia 8°29S 116°2E **37** J19
Senhor-do-Bonfim Brazil 10°30S 40°10W **93** F10
Senigállia Italy 43°43N 13°13E **22** C5
Senj Croatia 45°0N 14°58E **16** F8
Senja Norway 69°25N 17°30E **8** B17
Senkaku-Shotō E. China Sea 25°45N 123°30E **29** M1
Senlis France 49°13N 2°35E **20** B5
Senmonorom Cambodia 12°27N 107°12E **38** F6
Senneterre Canada 48°25N 77°15W **72** C4
Seno Laos 16°35N 104°50E **38** D5
Senqu → = Orange → S. Africa 28°41S 16°28E **56** C2

Sens France 48°11N 3°15E **20** B5
Senta Serbia 45°55N 20°3E **23** B9
Sentinel U.S.A. 32°52N 113°13W **77** K7
Senwabarana S. Africa 23°17S 29°7E **57** B4
Seo de Urgel = La Seu d'Urgell Spain 42°22N 1°23E **21** A6
Seogwipo S. Korea 33°13N 126°34E **33** H14
Seohara India 29°15N 78°33E **43** E8
Seondha India 26°9N 78°48E **43** G8
Seongnam S. Korea 37°26N 127°8E **33** F14
Seoni India 22°5N 79°30E **43** H8
Seoni Malwa India 22°27N 77°28E **42** H8
Seonsan S. Korea 36°14N 128°17E **33** F15
Seoriuarayan India 21°45N 82°34E **44** D6
Seosan S. Korea 36°47N 126°27E **33** F14
Sepang Malaysia 2°49N 101°44E **39** L3
Sepīdān Iran 30°20N 52°5E **47** D7
Sepo-ri N. Korea 38°57N 127°25E **33** E14
Sepone Laos 16°45N 106°13E **38** D6
Sept-Îles Canada 50°13N 66°22W **73** B6
Sequim U.S.A. 48°5N 123°6W **78** B3
Sequoia △ U.S.A. 36°30N 118°30W **78** J8
Seraing Belgium 50°35N 5°32E **15** D5
Seram Indonesia 3°10S 129°0E **37** E7
Seram Sea Indonesia 2°30S 128°30E **37** E7
Serampore = Shrirampur India 22°44N 88°21E **43** H13
Serang Indonesia 6°8S 106°10E **37** G12
Serasan Indonesia 2°29N 109°4E **36** D3
Serbia ■ Europe 43°20N 20°0E **23** B9
Serdar Turkmenistan 39°4N 56°23E **47** B8
Serdobsk Russia 52°28N 44°10E **18** D7
Seremban Malaysia 2°43N 101°53E **39** L3
Serengeti Plain Tanzania 2°40S 35°0E **54** E7
Sereth = Siret → Romania 45°24N 28°1E **17** F14
Sergeya Kirova, Ostrova Russia 77°30N 89°0E **27** B10
Sergino Russia 62°25N 65°12E **26** C7
Sergipe □ Brazil 10°30S 37°30W **93** F11
Sergiyev Posad Russia 56°20N 38°10E **18** C6
Serhetabat Turkmenistan 35°20N 62°18E **47** C9
Seria Brunei 4°37N 114°23E **36** D4
Serian Malaysia 1°10N 110°31E **36** D4
Sérifos Greece 37°9N 24°30E **23** F11
Sérigny → Canada 56°47N 66°0W **73** A6
Seringapatam Reef Australia 13°38S 122°5E **60** B3
Seririt Indonesia 8°12S 114°56E **37** J17
Serkout Algeria 23°56N 6°47E **52** D7
Sermata Indonesia 8°15S 128°50E **37** F7
Sermersuaq Greenland 79°30N 62°0W **69** B19
Serov Russia 59°29N 60°35E **18** C11
Serowe Botswana 22°25S 26°43E **56** B4
Serpentine Lakes Australia 28°30S 129°10E **61** E4
Serpent's Mouth = Sierpe, Bocas de la Venezuela 10°0N 61°30W **93** L15
Serpukhov Russia 54°55N 37°28E **18** D6
Serra do Navio Brazil 0°59N 52°3W **93** C8
Serranía San Luís △ Paraguay 22°35S 57°22W **94** A4
Serranía San Rafael △ Paraguay 26°30S 56°0W **95** B4
Serres Greece 41°5N 23°31E **23** D10
Serrezuela Argentina 30°40S 65°20W **94** C2
Serrinha Brazil 11°39S 39°0W **93** F11
Sertanópolis Brazil 23°4S 51°2W **95** A5
Sêrtar China 32°20N 100°41E **34** A3
Serua Indonesia 6°18S 130°1E **37** F8
Serui Indonesia 1°53S 136°10E **37** E9
Serule Botswana 21°57S 27°20E **56** B4
Sesepe Indonesia 1°30S 127°59E **37** E7
Sesfontein Namibia 19°7S 13°39E **56** A1
Sesheke Zambia 17°29S 24°13E **56** A3
Setana Japan 42°26N 139°51E **28** C9
Sète France 43°25N 3°42E **20** E5
Sete Lagoas Brazil 19°27S 44°16W **93** G10
Seti → Nepal 28°59N 81°8E **43** E9
Sétif Algeria 36°9N 5°26E **52** A7
Seto Japan 35°14N 137°6E **29** G8
Setonaikai Japan 34°20N 133°30E **29** G6
Setonaikai △ Japan 34°15N 133°15E **29** G6
Settat Morocco 33°0N 7°40W **52** B4
Setting L. Canada 55°0N 98°38W **71** C9
Settle U.K. 54°5N 2°16W **12** C5
Settlement, The Br. Virgin Is. 18°43N 64°22W **89** e
Settlers S. Africa 25°2S 28°30E **57** C4
Setúbal Portugal 38°30N 8°58W **21** C1
Setúbal, B. de Portugal 38°40N 8°56W **21** C1
Seul, Lac Canada 50°20N 92°30W **72** B1
Sevan, Ozero = Sevana Lich Armenia 40°30N 45°20E **46** A5
Sevana Lich Armenia 40°30N 45°20E **46** A5
Sevastopol Ukraine 44°35N 33°30E **19** F5
Seven Sisters Canada 54°56N 128°10W **70** C3
Severn → Canada 56°2N 87°36W **72** A2
Severn → U.K. 51°35N 2°40W **13** F5
Severnaya Zemlya Russia 79°0N 100°0E **27** B11
Severnyye Uvaly Russia 60°0N 50°0E **18** C8
Severo-Kurilsk Russia 50°40N 156°8E **27** D16
Severo-Yeniseyskiy Russia 60°22N 93°1E **27** C10
Severo-Zapadnyy □ Russia 65°0N 40°0E **26** C4
Severobaykalsk Russia 55°39N 109°19E **27** D11
Severodvinsk Russia 64°27N 39°58E **18** B6
Severomorsk Russia 69°5N 33°27E **8** B25
Severouralsk Russia 60°9N 59°57E **18** B10
Seversk Russia 56°36N 84°49E **26** D9
Sevier → U.S.A. 39°4N 113°6W **76** G7
Sevier Desert U.S.A. 39°40N 112°45W **76** G7
Sevier L. U.S.A. 38°54N 113°9W **76** G7
Sevilla Spain 37°23N 5°58W **21** D2
Seville = Sevilla Spain 37°23N 5°58W **21** D2
Sevlievo Bulgaria 43°2N 25°6E **23** C11
Sewani India 28°58N 75°39E **42** E6
Seward Alaska, U.S.A. 60°7N 149°27W **68** E2
Seward Nebr., U.S.A. 40°55N 97°6W **80** E5

Seward Pa., U.S.A. 40°25N 79°1W **82** F5
Seward Peninsula U.S.A. 65°30N 166°0W **74** B6
Sewell Chile 34°10S 70°23W **94** C1
Sewer Indonesia 5°53S 134°40E **37** F8
Sewickley U.S.A. 40°32N 80°12W **82** F4
Seychelles ■ Ind. Oc. 5°0S 56°0E **55** b
Seyðisfjörður Iceland 65°16N 13°57W **8** D7
Seydişehir Turkey 37°25N 31°51E **19** G5
Seydvān Iran 38°34N 45°2E **46** B5
Seyhan → Turkey 36°43N 34°53E **46** B2
Seym → Ukraine 51°27N 32°34E **19** D5
Seymour Australia 37°2S 145°10E **63** F4
Seymour S. Africa 32°33S 26°46E **57** D4
Seymour Conn., U.S.A. 41°24N 73°4W **83** E11
Seymour Ind., U.S.A. 38°58N 85°53W **81** F11
Seymour Tex., U.S.A. 33°35N 99°16W **84** E5
Sfântu Gheorghe Romania 45°52N 25°48E **17** F13
Sfax Tunisia 34°49N 10°48E **53** B8
Sha Tau Kok China 22°33N 114°13E **31** a
Sha Xi → China 26°35N 118°0E **35** D12
Sha Xian China 26°23N 117°45E **35** D11
Shaanxi □ China 35°0N 109°0E **32** G5
Shaba = Katanga Dem. Rep. of the Congo 8°0S 25°0E **54** F5
Shabeelle → Somalia 2°0N 44°0E **49** G3
Shabogamo L. Canada 53°15N 66°30W **73** B6
Shabunda Dem. Rep. of the Congo 2°40S 27°16E **54** E5
Shache China 38°20N 77°10E **30** D4
Shackleton Fracture Zone S. Ocean 60°0S 60°0W **5** B18
Shackleton Ice Shelf Antarctica 66°0S 100°0E **5** C8
Shackleton Inlet Antarctica 83°0S 160°0E **5** E11
Shādegān Iran 30°40N 48°38E **47** D6
Shadi China 26°7N 114°47E **35** D10
Shadi India 33°24N 77°14E **43** C7
Shadrinsk Russia 56°5N 63°32E **26** D7
Shadyside U.S.A. 39°58N 80°45W **82** G4
Shafter U.S.A. 35°30N 119°16W **79** K7
Shaftesbury U.K. 51°0N 2°11W **13** F5
Shagram Pakistan 36°24N 72°20E **43** A5
Shah Alam Malaysia 3°5N 101°32E **39** L3
Shah Alizai Pakistan 29°25N 66°33E **42** E2
Shah Bunder Pakistan 24°13N 67°56E **42** G2
Shahabad Karnataka, India 17°10N 76°54E **44** F3
Shahabad Punjab, India 30°10N 76°55E **42** D7
Shahabad Raj., India 25°15N 77°11E **42** G7
Shahabad Ut. P., India 27°36N 79°56E **43** F8
Shahada India 21°33N 74°30E **44** D2
Shahadpur Pakistan 25°55N 68°35E **42** G3
Shahapur India 15°50N 74°34E **45** G2
Shahbā' Syria 32°52N 36°38E **48** C5
Shahdād Iran 30°30N 57°40E **47** D8
Shahdād, Namakzār-e Iran 30°20N 58°20E **47** D8
Shahdadkot Pakistan 27°50N 67°55E **42** F2
Shahdol India 23°19N 81°26E **43** H9
Shahe China 37°0N 114°32E **32** F8
Shahganj India 26°3N 82°44E **43** F10
Shahgarh India 27°15N 69°50E **42** F3
Shahid Rajaee Port = Bandar Shahid Rajaee Iran 27°7N 56°4E **47** E8
Shāhīn Shahr Iran 32°49N 51°32E **47** C6
Shahjahanpur India 27°54N 79°57E **43** F8
Shahpur = Salmās Iran 38°11N 44°47E **46** B5
Shahpur Karnataka, India 16°40N 76°48E **44** F3
Shahpur Mad. P., India 22°12N 77°58E **42** H7
Shahpur Baluchistan, Pakistan 28°46N 68°27E **42** E3
Shahpur Punjab, Pakistan 32°17N 72°26E **42** C5
Shahpur Chakar Pakistan 26°9N 68°39E **42** F3
Shahpura Mad. P., India 23°10N 80°45E **43** H9
Shahpura Raj., India 25°38N 74°56E **42** G6
Shahr-e Bābak Iran 30°7N 55°9E **47** D7
Shahr-e Kord Iran 32°15N 50°55E **47** C6
Shahr-I Sokhta Iran 30°34N 61°21E **47** D9
Shahrakht Iran 33°38N 60°16E **47** C9
Shāhrezā = Qomsheh Iran 32°0N 51°55E **47** C6
Shahrig Pakistan 30°15N 67°40E **42** D2
Shāhrūd = Emāmrūd Iran 36°30N 55°0E **47** B7
Shahukou China 40°20N 112°18E **32** D7
Shaikhabad Afghan. 34°2N 68°45E **42** B3
Shajapur India 23°27N 76°21E **42** H7
Shajing China 22°44N 113°48E **31** a
Shakargarh Pakistan 32°17N 75°10E **42** C6
Shakawe Botswana 18°28S 21°49E **56** A3
Shaker Heights U.S.A. 41°28N 81°32W **82** E3
Shakhtersk Russia 49°10N 142°8E **27** E15
Shakhty Russia 47°40N 40°16E **19** E7
Shakhunya Russia 57°40N 46°46E **18** C8
Shaki Nigeria 8°41N 3°21E **52** G6
Shakotan-Hantō Japan 43°10N 140°30E **28** C10
Shaksgam Valley Asia 36°0N 76°20E **43** A7
Shallow Lake Canada 44°36N 81°5W **82** B3
Shalqar Kazakhstan 47°48N 59°39E **26** E6
Shaluli Shan China 30°40N 99°55E **34** B2
Shām Iran 26°39N 57°21E **47** E8
Shām, Bādiyat ash Asia 32°0N 40°0E **46** D4
Shamattawa Canada 55°1N 85°23W **72** A2
Shamīl Iran 27°30N 56°55E **47** E8
Shāmkūh Iran 35°47N 57°50E **47** C8
Shamli India 29°32N 77°18E **42** E7
Shammar, Jabal Si. Arabia 27°40N 41°0E **46** E4
Shamo = Gobi Asia 44°0N 110°0E **32** C6
Shamo, L. Ethiopia 5°45N 37°30E **49** F2
Shamokin U.S.A. 40°47N 76°34W **83** F8
Shamrock Canada 46°14N 64°32W **73** C7
Shamrock U.S.A. 35°13N 100°15W **84** D4
Shan □ Myanmar 21°30N 98°30E **41** J21
Shan Xian China 34°50N 116°5E **34** G9
Shanchengzhen China 42°20N 125°20E **33** C13
Shāndak Iran 28°28N 60°27E **47** D9
Shandan China 38°45N 101°15E **30** D9
Shandon U.S.A. 35°39N 120°23W **78** K6
Shandong □ China 36°0N 118°0E **33** G10
Shandong Bandao China 37°0N 121°0E **33** F11
Shandur Pass Pakistan 36°4N 72°31E **43** A5
Shang Xian = Shangzhou China 33°50N 109°58E **32** H5
Shangani Zimbabwe 19°41S 29°20E **57** A4
Shangani → Zimbabwe 18°41S 27°10E **55** H5
Shangbancheng China 40°50N 118°1E **33** D10
Shangcheng China 31°47N 115°26E **35** B10
Shangchuan Dao China 21°40N 112°50E **35** G9
Shangdu China 41°30N 113°30E **32** D7
Shanggao China 28°17N 114°55E **35** C10
Shanghai Shi □ China 31°0N 121°30E **35** B13
Shanghang China 25°2N 116°23E **35** E11
Shanghe China 37°20N 117°10E **33** F9
Shanglin China 23°27N 108°33E **34** F7
Shangnan China 33°32N 110°50E **32** H6
Shangqiu China 34°26N 115°36E **32** G8
Shangrao China 28°25N 117°59E **35** C11
Shangri-La = Zhongdian China 27°48N 99°42E **34** D2
Shangshui China 33°42N 114°35E **32** H8
Shangsi China 22°8N 107°58E **34** F6
Shangyi China 41°4N 113°57E **32** D7
Shangyou China 25°48N 114°32E **35** E10
Shangyu China 30°0N 120°52E **35** B13
Shangzhi China 45°22N 127°56E **33** B14
Shangzhou China 33°50N 109°58E **32** H5
Shanhetun China 44°33N 127°15E **33** B14
Shanklin U.K. 50°38N 1°11W **13** G6
Shannon N.Z. 40°33S 175°25E **59** D5
Shannon → Ireland 52°35N 9°30W **10** D2
Shannon ✈ (SNN) Ireland 52°42N 8°57W **10** D3
Shannon, Mouth of the Ireland 52°30N 9°55W **10** D2
Shannon △ Australia 34°35S 116°25E **61** F2
Shannonbridge Ireland 53°17N 8°3W **10** C3
Shansi = Shanxi □ China 37°0N 112°0E **32** F7
Shantar, Ostrov Bolshoy Russia 55°9N 137°40E **27** D14
Shantipur India 23°17N 88°25E **43** H13
Shantou China 23°18N 116°40E **35** F11
Shantung = Shandong □ China 36°0N 118°0E **33** G10
Shanwei China 22°48N 115°22E **35** F10
Shanxi □ China 37°0N 112°0E **32** F7
Shanyang China 33°31N 109°55E **32** H5
Shanyin China 39°25N 112°56E **32** E7
Shaodong China 27°15N 111°43E **35** D8
Shaoguan China 24°48N 113°35E **35** E9
Shaoshan China 27°55N 112°33E **35** D9
Shaowu China 27°22N 117°28E **35** D11
Shaoxing China ~30°0N 120°35E **35** C13
Shaoyang China 27°14N 111°25E **35** D8
Shap U.K. 54°32N 2°40W **12** C5
Shapinsay U.K. 59°3N 2°51W **11** B6
Shaqra' Si. Arabia 25°15N 45°16E **46** E5
Sharafkhāneh Iran 38°11N 45°29E **46** B5
Sharavati → India 14°20N 74°25E **45** G2
Sharbot Lake Canada 44°46N 76°41W **83** B8
Shari Japan 43°55N 144°40E **28** C12
Sharjah = Ash Shāriqah U.A.E. 25°23N 55°26E **47** E7
Shark B. Australia 25°30S 113°32E **61** E1
Shark Bay △ Australia 25°30S 113°30E **61** E1
Sharm el Sheikh Egypt 27°53N 34°18E **53** C12
Sharon Canada 44°6N 79°26W **82** B5
Sharon Mass., U.S.A. 42°7N 71°11W **83** D13
Sharon Pa., U.S.A. 41°14N 80°31W **82** E4
Sharon Springs Kans., U.S.A. 38°54N 101°45W **80** F3
Sharon Springs N.Y., U.S.A. 42°48N 74°37W **83** D10
Sharp Pt. Australia 10°58S 142°43E **62** A3
Sharpe L. Canada 54°24N 93°40W **72** B1
Sharpsville U.S.A. 41°15N 80°29W **82** E4
Sharqi, Al Jabal ash Lebanon 33°40N 36°10E **48** B5
Sharqīya, Es Sahrâ esh Egypt 27°30N 32°30E **53** C12
Sharya Russia 58°22N 45°20E **18** C8
Shashemene Ethiopia 7°13N 38°33E **49** F2
Shashi Botswana 21°15S 27°27E **57** B4
Shashi → Africa 21°14S 29°20E **55** J5
Shasta, Mt. U.S.A. 41°25N 122°12W **76** F2
Shasta L. U.S.A. 40°43N 122°25W **76** F2
Shatsky Rise Pac. Oc. 34°0N 157°0E **64** D7
Shatt al Arab Asia 29°57N 48°34E **47** D6
Shaunavon Canada 49°35N 108°25W **71** D7
Shaver L. U.S.A. 37°9N 119°18W **78** H7
Shaw → Australia 20°21S 119°17E **60** D2
Shaw I. Australia 20°30S 149°2E **62** b
Shawanaga Canada 45°31N 80°17W **82** A4
Shawangunk Mts. U.S.A. 41°35N 74°30W **83** E10
Shawano U.S.A. 44°47N 88°36W **80** C9
Shawinigan Canada 46°35N 72°50W **72** C5
Shawmari, J. ash Jordan 30°35N 36°35E **48** E5
Shawnee U.S.A. 35°20N 96°55W **84** D6
Shay Gap Australia 20°35S 120°10E **60** D3
Shayang China 30°42N 112°29E **35** B9
Shaybārā Si. Arabia 25°26N 36°47E **46** E3
Shaykh, Jabal ash Lebanon 33°25N 35°50E **48** B4
Shaykh Miskīn Syria 32°49N 36°9E **48** C5
Shaykh Sa'd Iraq 32°34N 46°17E **46** C5
Shaykh 'Uthmān Yemen 12°52N 44°59E **49** E3
Shāzand Iran 33°56N 49°24E **47** C6
Shchūchīnsk Kazakhstan 52°56N 70°12E **26** D8
She Xian Hebei, China 36°30N 113°40E **32** F7
Shebele = Shabeelle → Somalia 2°0N 44°0E **49** G3
Sheboygan U.S.A. 43°46N 87°45W **80** D10
Shediac Canada 46°14N 64°32W **73** C7
Sheelin, L. Ireland 53°48N 7°20W **10** C4
Sheenjek → U.S.A. 66°45N 144°33W **74** B11
Sheep Haven Ireland 55°11N 7°52W **10** A4
Sheep Range U.S.A. 36°35N 115°15W **79** J11
Sheerness U.K. 51°26N 0°47E **13** F8
Sheet Harbour Canada 44°56N 62°31W **73** D7
Sheffield U.K. 53°23N 1°28W **12** D6

Sheffield Ala., U.S.A. 34°46N 87°41W **85** D11
Sheffield Mass., U.S.A. 42°5N 73°21W **83** D11
Sheffield Pa., U.S.A. 41°42N 79°3W **82** E5
Shegaon India 20°48N 76°47E **44** D3
Shehong China 30°54N 105°18E **34** B5
Sheikhpura India 25°9N 85°53E **43** G11
Shekhupura Pakistan 31°42N 73°58E **42** D5
Shekou China 22°30N 113°55E **31** a
Shelburne N.S., Canada 43°47N 65°20W **73** D6
Shelburne Ont., Canada 44°4N 80°15W **82** B4
Shelburne U.S.A. 44°23N 73°14W **83** B11
Shelburne B. Australia 11°50S 142°50E **62** A3
Shelburne Falls U.S.A. 42°36N 72°45W **83** D12
Shelby Mich., U.S.A. 43°37N 86°22W **80** D10
Shelby Miss., U.S.A. 33°57N 90°46W **85** E9
Shelby Mont., U.S.A. 48°30N 111°51W **76** B8
Shelby N.C., U.S.A. 35°17N 81°32W **85** D14
Shelby Ohio, U.S.A. 40°53N 82°40W **82** F2
Shelbyville Ill., U.S.A. 39°24N 88°48W **80** F7
Shelbyville Ind., U.S.A. 39°31N 85°47W **81** F11
Shelbyville Ky., U.S.A. 38°13N 85°14W **81** F11
Shelbyville Tenn., U.S.A. 35°29N 86°28W **85** D11
Sheldon U.S.A. 43°11N 95°51W **80** D6
Sheldrake Canada 50°20N 64°51W **73** B7
Shelikhova, Zaliv Russia 59°30N 157°0E **27** D16
Shelikof Strait U.S.A. 57°30N 155°0W **74** D9
Shell Lakes Australia 29°20S 127°30E **61** E4
Shellbrook Canada 53°13N 106°24W **71** C7
Shellharbour Australia 34°31S 150°51E **63** E5
Shelter I. U.S.A. 41°4N 72°20W **83** E12
Shelton Conn., U.S.A. 41°19N 73°5W **83** E11
Shelton Wash., U.S.A. 47°13N 123°6W **78** C3
Shen Xian China 36°15N 115°40E **32** F8
Shenandoah Iowa, U.S.A. 40°46N 95°22W **80** E6
Shenandoah Pa., U.S.A. 40°49N 76°12W **83** F8
Shenandoah Va., U.S.A. 38°29N 78°37W **81** F14
Shenandoah → U.S.A. 39°19N 77°44W **81** F15
Shenandoah △ U.S.A. 38°35N 78°22W **81** F14
Shenchi China 39°8N 112°10E **32** E7
Shencottah India 8°59N 77°18E **45** K3
Shendam Nigeria 8°49N 9°30E **52** G7
Shendî Sudan 16°46N 33°22E **53** E12
Shengfang China 39°3N 116°42E **32** E9
Shengzhou China 29°35N 120°50E **35** C13
Shenjingzi China 44°40N 124°30E **33** B13
Shenmu China 38°50N 110°29E **32** E6
Shennongjia China 31°43N 110°44E **35** B8
Shenqiu China 33°25N 115°5E **32** H8
Shensi = Shaanxi □ China 35°0N 109°0E **32** G5
Shenyang China 41°48N 123°27E **33** D12
Shenzhen China 22°32N 114°5E **35** F10
Shenzhen Bao'an Int. ✈ (SZX) China 22°41N 113°49E **31** a
Shenzhen Shuiku China 22°34N 114°8E **31** a
Shenzhen Wan China 22°27N 113°55E **31** a
Sheo India 26°11N 71°15E **42** F4
Sheopur Kalan India 25°40N 76°40E **42** G7
Shepetivka Ukraine 50°10N 27°10E **17** C14
Shepparton Australia 36°23S 145°26E **63** F4
Sheppey, I. of U.K. 51°25N 0°48E **13** F8
Shepton Mallet U.K. 51°11N 2°33W **13** F5
Sheqi China 33°12N 112°57E **32** H7
Sher Qila Pakistan 36°7N 74°2E **43** A6
Sherborne U.K. 50°57N 2°31W **13** G5
Sherbro I. S. Leone 7°30N 12°40W **52** G3
Sherbrooke N.S., Canada 45°8N 61°59W **73** C7
Sherbrooke Qué., Canada 45°28N 71°57W **83** A13
Sherburne U.S.A. 42°41N 75°30W **83** D9
Shergarh India 26°20N 72°18E **42** F5
Sherghati India 24°34N 84°47E **43** G11
Sheridan Ark., U.S.A. 34°19N 92°24W **84** D8
Sheridan Wyo., U.S.A. 44°48N 106°58W **76** D10
Sheringham U.K. 52°56N 1°13E **12** E9
Sherkin I. Ireland 51°28N 9°26W **10** E2
Sherkot India 29°22N 78°35E **43** E8
Sherlovaya Gora Russia 50°34N 116°15E **27** D12
Sherman N.Y., U.S.A. 42°9N 79°35W **82** D5
Sherman Tex., U.S.A. 33°38N 96°36W **84** E6
Sherpur India 25°34N 83°47E **43** G10
Sherridon Canada 55°8N 101°5W **71** B8
Shertallai = Cherthala India 9°42N 76°20E **45** K3
Sherwood Forest U.K. 53°6N 1°7W **12** D6
Sherwood Park Canada 53°31N 113°19W **70** C6
Sheslay → Canada 58°48N 132°5W **70** B2
Shethanei L. Canada 58°48N 97°50W **71** B9
Shetland □ U.K. 60°30N 1°30W **11** A7
Shetland Is. U.K. 60°30N 1°30W **11** A7
Shetrunji → India 21°19N 72°7E **42** J5
Sheung Shui China 22°31N 114°7E **31** a
Shevaroy Hills India 11°58N 78°12E **45** J4
Shevgaon India 19°21N 75°14E **44** E2
Shey-Phoksundo △ Nepal 29°30N 82°45E **43** E10
Sheyang China 33°48N 120°29E **33** H11
Sheyenne → U.S.A. 47°2N 96°50W **80** B5
Shiashkotan, Ostrov Russia 48°49N 154°6E **27** E16
Shibām Yemen 15°59N 48°36E **49** D4
Shibata Japan 37°57N 139°20E **28** F9
Shibecha Japan 43°17N 144°36E **28** C12
Shibetsu Hokkaidō, Japan 43°30N 145°10E **28** C12
Shibetsu Hokkaidō, Japan 44°10N 142°23E **28** B11
Shibing China 27°2N 108°7E **34** D7
Shibogama L. Canada 53°35N 88°15W **72** B2
Shibushi Japan 31°25N 131°8E **29** J5
Shicheng China 26°22N 116°6E **35** D11
Shickshinny U.S.A. 41°9N 76°9W **83** E8
Shickshock Mts. = Chic-Chocs, Mts. Canada 48°55N 66°0W **73** C6
Shidao China 36°50N 122°25E **33** F12
Shidian China 24°40N 99°55E **34** E2
Shido = Sanuki Japan 34°19N 134°10E **29** G7
Shiel, L. U.K. 56°48N 5°34W **11** E3
Shield, C. Australia 13°20S 136°20E **62** A2

Shīeli Kazakhstan 44°20N 66°15E 26 E7
Shifang China 31°8N 104°10E 34 B5
Shiga □ Japan 35°20N 136°0E 29 G8
Shigu China 26°51N 99°56E 34 D2
Shiguaigou China 40°52N 110°15E 32 D6
Shihchiachuangi = Shijiazhuang China 38°2N 114°28E 32 E8
Shihezi China 44°15N 86°2E 30 C6
Shijiazhuang China 38°2N 114°28E 32 E8
Shijiu Hu China 31°25N 118°50E 35 B12
Shikarpur India 28°17N 78°7E 42 E8
Shikarpur Pakistan 27°57N 68°39E 42 F3
Shikohabad India 27°6N 78°36E 43 F8
Shikokochūō Japan 34°1N 133°34E 29 G6
Shikoku □ Japan 33°30N 133°30E 29 H6
Shikoku-Sanchi Japan 33°30N 133°30E 29 H6
Shikotan, Ostrov Asia 43°47N 146°44E 27 E15
Shikotsu-Ko Japan 42°45N 141°25E 28 C10
Shikotsu-Tōya △ Japan 44°4N 145°8E 28 C10
Shiliguri India 26°45N 88°25E 41 F16
Shiliu = Changjiang China 19°20N 108°55E 38 C7
Shilka Russia 52°0N 115°55E 27 D12
Shilka → Russia 53°20N 121°26E 27 D13
Shillelagh Ireland 52°45N 6°32W 10 D5
Shillington U.S.A. 40°18N 75°58W 83 F9
Shillong India 25°35N 91°53E 41 G17
Shilo West Bank 32°4N 35°18E 48 C4
Shilong China 23°5N 113°52E 35 F9
Shilou China 37°0N 110°48E 32 F6
Shimabara Japan 32°48N 130°20E 29 H5
Shimada Japan 34°49N 138°10E 29 G9
Shimane □ Japan 35°0N 132°30E 29 G6
Shimanovsk Russia 52°15N 127°30E 27 D13
Shimanto Kōchi, Japan 33°12N 133°8E 29 H6
Shimanto Kōchi, Japan 32°59N 132°56E 29 H6
Shimbiris Somalia 10°44N 47°14E 49 E4
Shimen China 29°35N 111°20E 35 C8
Shimenjie China 29°29N 116°48E 35 C11
Shimian China 29°17N 102°23E 34 C4
Shimizu Japan 35°0N 138°30E 29 G9
Shimla India 31°2N 77°9E 42 D7
Shimodate Japan 36°20N 139°55E 29 F9
Shimoga = Shivamogga India 13°57N 75°32E 45 H2
Shimokita-Hantō Japan 41°20N 141°0E 28 D10
Shimonoseki Japan 33°58N 130°55E 29 H5
Shimpuru Rapids Namibia 17°45S 19°55E 56 A2
Shimsha → India 13°15N 77°10E 45 H3
Shin, L. U.K. 58°5N 4°30W 11 C4
Shinan China 22°44N 109°53E 34 F7
Shinano-Gawa → Japan 36°50N 138°30E 29 F9
Shināş Oman 24°46N 56°28E 47 E8
Shīndand Afghan. 33°12N 62°8E 40 C3
Shinglehouse U.S.A. 41°58N 78°12W 82 E6
Shingū Japan 33°40N 135°55E 29 H7
Shingwidzi S. Africa 23°5S 31°25E 57 B5
Shinjō Japan 38°46N 140°18E 28 E10
Shinkolobwe Dem. Rep. of the Congo 11°10S 26°40E 54 G5
Shinshār Syria 34°36N 36°43E 48 A5
Shinyanga Tanzania 3°45S 33°27E 54 E6
Shio-no-Misaki Japan 33°25N 135°45E 29 H7
Shiogama Japan 38°19N 141°1E 28 E10
Shiojiri Japan 36°6N 137°58E 29 F8
Shipchenski Prokhod Bulgaria 42°45N 25°15E 23 C11
Shiphoirt, L. = Seaforth, L. U.K. 57°52N 6°36W 11 D2
Shiping China 23°45N 102°23E 34 F4
Shippagan Canada 47°45N 64°45W 73 C7
Shippensburg U.S.A. 40°3N 77°31W 82 F7
Shippenville U.S.A. 41°15N 79°28W 82 E5
Shiprock U.S.A. 36°47N 108°41W 77 H9
Shiqian China 27°32N 108°13E 34 D7
Shiqma, N. → Israel 31°37N 34°30E 48 D3
Shiquan China 33°5N 108°15E 34 A7
Shiquan He = Indus → Pakistan 24°20N 67°47E 42 G2
Shīr Kūh Iran 31°39N 54°3E 47 D7
Shira'awh Qatar 25°2N 52°14E 47 E7
Shiragami-Misaki Japan 41°24N 140°12E 28 D10
Shirakawa Fukushima, Japan 37°7N 140°13E 29 F10
Shirakawa Gifu, Japan 36°17N 136°56E 29 F8
Shirane-San Gumma, Japan 36°48N 139°22E 29 F9
Shirane-San Yamanashi, Japan 35°42N 138°9E 29 G9
Shiraoi Japan 42°33N 141°21E 28 C10
Shīrāz Iran 29°42N 52°30E 47 D7
Shire → Africa 17°42S 35°19E 55 H7
Shiren China 41°57N 126°34E 33 D14
Shiretoko △ Japan 44°15N 145°15E 28 B12
Shiretoko-Misaki Japan 44°21N 145°20E 28 B12
Shirinab → Pakistan 30°15N 66°28E 42 D2
Shiriya-Zaki Japan 41°25N 141°30E 28 D10
Shiroishi Japan 38°0N 140°37E 28 F10
Shirol India 16°47N 74°41E 44 F2
Shirpur India 21°21N 74°57E 44 D2
Shirshov Ridge Pac. Oc. 58°0N 170°0E 64 B8
Shīrvān Iran 37°30N 57°50E 47 B8
Shirwa, L. = Chilwa, L. Malawi 15°15S 35°40E 55 H7
Shishaldin Volcano U.S.A. 54°45N 163°58W 74 E7
Shishi China 24°44N 118°37E 35 E12
Shishou China 29°38N 112°22E 35 C9
Shitai China 30°12N 117°25E 35 B11
Shivamogga India 13°57N 75°32E 45 H2
Shivpuri India 25°26N 77°42E 42 G7
Shixian China 43°5N 129°50E 33 C15
Shixing China 24°46N 114°5E 35 E10
Shiyan Guangdong, China 22°42N 113°56E 31 a
Shiyan Hubei, China 32°35N 110°45E 35 A8
Shiyan Shuiku China 22°42N 113°54E 31 a
Shizhu China 29°58N 108°7E 34 C7
Shizong China 24°50N 104°0E 34 E5
Shizuishan China 39°15N 106°50E 32 E4
Shizuoka Japan 34°57N 138°24E 29 G9
Shizuoka □ Japan 35°15N 138°40E 29 G9
Shklov = Shklow Belarus 54°16N 30°15E 17 A16
Shklow Belarus 54°16N 30°15E 17 A16
Shkodër Albania 42°4N 19°32E 23 C8
Shkumbini → Albania 41°2N 19°31E 23 D8
Shmidta, Ostrov Russia 81°0N 91°0E 27 A10
Shō-Gawa → Japan 36°47N 137°4E 29 F8
Shoal L. Canada 49°33N 95°1W 71 D9
Shoal Lake Canada 50°30N 100°35W 71 C8
Shōdo-Shima Japan 34°30N 134°15E 29 G7
Sholapur = Solapur India 17°43N 75°56E 44 F2
Shōmrōn West Bank 32°15N 35°13E 48 C4
Shoranur India 10°46N 76°19E 45 J3
Shorapur India 16°31N 76°48E 45 F3
Shoreham U.S.A. 43°53N 73°18W 83 C11
Shoreham-by-Sea U.K. 50°50N 0°16W 13 G7
Shori → Pakistan 28°29N 69°44E 42 E3
Shorkot Pakistan 30°50N 72°0E 42 D4
Shorkot Road Pakistan 30°47N 72°15E 42 D5
Shortt's I. India 20°47N 87°4E 44 D8
Shoshone Calif., U.S.A. 35°58N 116°16W 79 K10
Shoshone Idaho, U.S.A. 42°56N 114°25W 76 E6
Shoshone L. U.S.A. 44°22N 110°43W 76 D8
Shoshone Mts. U.S.A. 39°20N 117°25W 76 G5
Shoshong Botswana 22°56S 26°31E 56 B4
Shoshoni U.S.A. 43°14N 108°7W 76 E9
Shou Xian China 32°37N 116°42E 35 A11
Shouchang China 29°18N 119°12E 35 C12
Shouguang China 37°52N 118°45E 33 F10
Shouning China 27°27N 119°31E 35 D12
Shouyang China 37°54N 113°8E 32 F7
Show Low U.S.A. 34°15N 110°2W 77 J8
Shqipëria = Albania ■ Europe 41°0N 20°0E 23 D9
Shreveport U.S.A. 32°31N 93°45W 84 E8
Shrewsbury U.K. 52°43N 2°45W 13 E5
Shri Mohangarh India 27°17N 71°18E 42 F4
Shrigonda India 18°37N 74°41E 44 E2
Shrirampur India 22°44N 88°21E 43 H13
Shropshire □ U.K. 52°36N 2°45W 13 E5
Shū Kazakhstan 43°36N 73°42E 26 E8
Shuangbai China 24°42N 101°38E 34 E3
Shuangcheng China 45°20N 126°15E 33 B14
Shuangfeng China 27°29N 112°11E 35 D9
Shuanggou China 34°2N 117°30E 33 G9
Shuangjiang China 23°26N 99°58E 34 F2
Shuangliao China 43°29N 123°30E 33 C12
Shuangshanzi China 40°20N 119°8E 33 D10
Shuangyang China 43°28N 125°40E 33 C13
Shuangyashan China 46°28N 131°5E 31 B15
Shucheng China 31°28N 116°57E 35 B11
Shuiji China 27°13N 118°20E 35 D12
Shujalpur India 23°18N 76°46E 42 H7
Shukpa Kunzang India 34°22N 78°22E 43 B8
Shulan China 44°28N 127°0E 33 B14
Shule China 39°25N 76°3E 30 D4
Shule He → China 40°20N 92°50E 30 C7
Shumagin Is. U.S.A. 55°7N 160°30W 74 D7
Shumen Bulgaria 43°18N 26°55E 23 C12
Shumikha Russia 55°10N 63°15E 26 D7
Shunān Japan 34°3N 131°50E 29 G5
Shunchang China 26°54N 117°48E 35 D11
Shunde China 22°42N 113°14E 35 F9
Shungnak U.S.A. 66°52N 157°9W 74 B8
Shuo Xian = Shuozhou China 39°20N 112°33E 32 E7
Shuozhou China 39°20N 112°33E 32 E7
Shuqrā' Yemen 13°22N 45°44E 49 E4
Shūr → Fārs, Iran 28°30N 55°0E 47 D7
Shūr → Kermān, Iran 30°52N 57°37E 47 D8
Shūr → Yazd, Iran 31°45N 55°15E 47 D7
Shūr Āb Iran 34°23N 51°11E 47 C6
Shūr Gaz Iran 29°10N 59°20E 47 D8
Shūrāb Iran 33°43N 56°29E 47 C8
Shūrjestān Iran 31°24N 52°25E 47 D7
Shurugwi Zimbabwe 19°40S 30°0E 55 H6
Shūsf Iran 31°50N 60°5E 47 D9
Shūshtar Iran 32°0N 48°50E 47 D6
Shuswap L. Canada 50°55N 119°3W 70 C5
Shute Harbour △ Australia 20°17S 148°47E 62 b
Shuyang China 34°10N 118°42E 33 G10
Shūzū Iran 29°52N 54°30E 47 D7
Shwebo Myanmar 22°30N 95°45E 41 H19
Shwegu Myanmar 24°15N 96°26E 41 G20
Shweli → Myanmar 23°45N 96°45E 41 H20
Shyamnagar India 13°21N 92°57E 45 H11
Shymkent Kazakhstan 42°18N 69°36E 26 E7
Shyok India 34°13N 78°12E 43 B8
Shyok → Pakistan 35°13N 75°53E 43 B6
Si Kiang = Xi Jiang → China 22°5N 113°20E 35 F9
Si Lanna △ Thailand 19°17N 99°12E 38 C2
Si Nakarin Res. Thailand 14°35N 99°0E 38 E2
Si-ngan = Xi'an China 34°15N 109°0E 32 G5
Si Phangnga Thailand 9°8N 98°29E 39 H2
Si Prachan Thailand 14°37N 100°9E 38 E3
Si Racha Thailand 13°10N 100°48E 38 F3
Si Sa Ket Thailand 15°8N 104°23E 38 E5
Siachen Glacier Asia 35°20N 77°30E 43 B7
Siahaf → Pakistan 29°3N 68°57E 42 E3
Siahan Range Pakistan 27°30N 64°40E 40 F4
Siak Sri Indrapura Indonesia 0°51N 102°0E 36 D2
Sialkot Pakistan 32°32N 74°30E 42 C6
Siam = Thailand ■ Asia 16°0N 102°0E 38 E4
Sian = Xi'an China 34°15N 109°0E 32 G5
Sian Ka'an ⌓ Mexico 19°35N 87°40W 87 D7
Siantan Indonesia 3°10N 106°15E 36 D3
Sīāreh Iran 28°5N 60°14E 47 D9
Siargao I. Phil. 9°52N 126°3E 37 C7
Siasi Phil. 5°34N 120°50E 37 C6
Siau Indonesia 2°50N 125°25E 37 D7
Šiauliai Lithuania 55°56N 23°15E 9 J20
Siavonga Zambia 16°33S 28°42E 57 A4
Sibâi, Gebel el Egypt 25°45N 34°10E 46 E2
Sibang Indonesia 8°34S 115°13E 37 K18
Sibay Russia 52°42N 58°39E 18 D10
Sibayi, L. S. Africa 27°20S 32°45E 57 C5
Šibenik Croatia 43°48N 15°54E 22 C6
Siberia = Sibirskiy □ Russia 58°0N 90°0E 27 D10
Siberia Russia 60°0N 100°0E 24 B12
Siberut Indonesia 1°30S 99°0E 36 E1
Sibi Pakistan 29°30N 67°54E 42 E2
Sibirskiy □ Russia 58°0N 90°0E 27 D10
Sibirtsevo Russia 44°12N 132°26E 28 B5
Sibiti Congo 3°38S 13°19E 54 E2
Sibiu Romania 45°45N 24°9E 17 F13
Sibley U.S.A. 43°24N 95°45W 80 D6
Sibolga Indonesia 1°42N 98°45E 36 D1
Siborongborong Indonesia 2°13N 98°58E 39 L2
Sibsagar = Sivasagar India 27°0N 94°36E 41 F19
Sibu Malaysia 2°18N 111°49E 36 D4
Sibuco Phil. 7°20N 122°10E 37 C6
Sibuguey B. Phil. 7°50N 122°45E 37 C6
Sibut C.A.R. 5°46N 19°10E 54 C3
Sibutu Phil. 4°45N 119°30E 37 D5
Sibutu Passage E. Indies 4°50N 120°0E 37 D6
Sibuyan I. Phil. 12°25N 122°40E 37 B6
Sibuyan Sea Phil. 12°30N 122°20E 37 B6
Sicamous Canada 50°49N 119°0W 70 C5
Siccus → Australia 31°55S 139°17E 63 E2
Sichon Thailand 9°0N 99°54E 39 H2
Sichuan □ China 30°30N 103°0E 34 B5
Sichuan Pendi China 31°0N 105°0E 34 B5
Sicilia Italy 37°30N 14°30E 22 F6
Sicily = Sicilia Italy 37°30N 14°30E 22 F6
Sicily, Str. of Medit. S. 37°35N 11°56E 22 F4
Sico → Honduras 15°58N 84°58W 88 C3
Sicuani Peru 14°21S 71°10W 92 F4
Siddapur India 14°20N 74°53E 45 G2
Siddhapur India 23°56N 72°25E 42 H5
Siddipet India 18°5N 78°51E 44 E4
Sidhauli India 27°17N 80°50E 43 F9
Sidhi India 24°25N 81°53E 43 G9
Sidi-bel-Abbès Algeria 35°13N 0°39W 52 A5
Sidi Ifni Morocco 29°29N 10°12W 52 C3
Sidikalang Indonesia 2°45N 98°19E 39 L2
Sidlaw Hills U.K. 56°32N 3°2W 11 E5
Sidley, Mt. Antarctica 77°2S 126°2W 5 D14
Sidmouth U.K. 50°40N 3°15W 13 G4
Sidmouth, C. Australia 13°25S 143°36E 62 A3
Sidney Canada 48°39N 123°24W 78 B3
Sidney Mont., U.S.A. 47°43N 104°9W 76 C11
Sidney N.Y., U.S.A. 42°19N 75°24W 83 D9
Sidney Nebr., U.S.A. 41°8N 102°59W 80 E2
Sidney Ohio, U.S.A. 40°17N 84°9W 81 E11
Sidney Lanier, L. U.S.A. 34°10N 84°4W 85 D12
Sidoarjo Indonesia 7°27S 112°43E 37 G15
Sidon = Saydā Lebanon 33°35N 35°25E 48 B4
Sidra = Surt Libya 31°11N 16°39E 53 B9
Sidra, G. of = Surt, Khalīj Libya 31°40N 18°30E 53 B9
Siedlce Poland 52°10N 22°20E 17 B12
Sieg → Germany 50°46N 7°6E 16 C4
Siegen Germany 50°51N 8°0E 16 C5
Siem Pang Cambodia 14°7N 106°23E 38 E6
Siem Reap = Siemreab Cambodia 13°20N 103°52E 38 F4
Siemreab Cambodia 13°20N 103°52E 38 F4
Siena Italy 43°19N 11°21E 22 C4
Sieradz Poland 51°37N 18°41E 17 C10
Sierpe, Bocas de la Venezuela 10°0N 61°30W 93 L15
Sierra Blanca U.S.A. 31°11N 105°22W 84 F2
Sierra Blanca Peak U.S.A. 33°23N 105°49W 77 K11
Sierra City U.S.A. 39°34N 120°38W 78 F6
Sierra Colorada Argentina 40°35S 67°50W 96 E3
Sierra de Agalta △ Honduras 15°1N 85°48W 88 C2
Sierra de Bahoruco △ Dom. Rep. 18°10N 71°25W 89 C5
Sierra de La Culata △ Venezuela 8°45N 71°10W 89 E5
Sierra de Lancandón △ Guatemala 16°59N 90°23W 88 C1
Sierra de las Quijadas △ Argentina 32°29S 67°5W 94 C2
Sierra de San Luis △ Venezuela 11°20N 69°43W 89 D6
Sierra de San Pedro Mártir △ Mexico 31°10N 115°30W 86 A1
Sierra Gorda Chile 22°50S 69°15W 94 A2
Sierra Leone ■ W. Afr. 9°0N 12°0W 52 G3
Sierra Madre Mexico 16°0N 93°0W 87 D6
Sierra Madre Occidental Mexico 27°0N 107°0W 86 B3
Sierra Madre Oriental Mexico 25°0N 100°0W 86 C5
Sierra Mojada Mexico 27°18N 103°41W 86 B4
Sierra Nevada Spain 37°3N 3°15W 21 D4
Sierra Nevada U.S.A. 39°0N 120°30W 78 H8
Sierra Nevada △ Venezuela 8°35N 70°45W 89 E5
Sierra Nevada de Santa Marta △ Colombia 10°56N 73°36W 89 D5
Sierra Vista U.S.A. 31°33N 110°18W 77 L8
Sierraville U.S.A. 39°36N 120°22W 78 F6
Sifnos Greece 37°0N 24°45E 23 F11
Sifton Canada 51°21N 100°8W 71 C8
Sifton Pass Canada 57°52N 126°15W 70 B3
Sig Algeria 35°32N 0°12W 52 A5
Sigatoka Fiji 18°8S 177°32E 59 a
Sighetu-Marmaţiei Romania 47°57N 23°52E 17 E12
Sighişoara Romania 46°12N 24°50E 17 E13
Sigiriya Sri Lanka 7°57N 80°45E 45 L5
Sigli Indonesia 5°25N 96°0E 36 C1
Siglufjörður Iceland 66°12N 18°55W 8 C4
Signal de Botrang Belgium 50°29N 6°4E 15 D6
Signal Pk. U.S.A. 33°20N 114°2W 79 M12
Signy I. Antarctica 60°43S 45°36W 5 C18
Sígsig Ecuador 3°0S 78°50W 92 D3
Sigüenza Spain 41°3N 2°40W 21 B4
Siguiri Guinea 11°31N 9°10W 52 F4
Sigulda Latvia 57°10N 24°55E 9 H21
Siguniangshan China 31°15N 103°10E 34 B4
Sihawa India 20°19N 81°55E 44 D5
Sihong China 33°27N 118°16E 33 H10
Sihora India 23°29N 80°6E 43 H9
Sihui China 23°20N 112°40E 35 F9
Siikajoki → Finland 64°50N 24°43E 8 D21
Siilinjärvi Finland 63°4N 27°39E 8 E22
Sika India 22°26N 69°47E 42 H3
Sikanni Chief → Canada 57°47N 122°15W 70 B4
Sikao Thailand 7°34N 99°21E 39 J2
Sikar India 27°33N 75°10E 42 F6
Sikasso Mali 11°18N 5°35W 52 F4
Sikeston U.S.A. 36°53N 89°35W 80 G9
Sikhote Alin, Khrebet Russia 45°0N 136°0E 28 B8
Sikhote Alin Ra. = Sikhote Alin, Khrebet Russia 45°0N 136°0E 28 B8
Sikinos Greece 36°40N 25°8E 23 F11
Sikkim □ India 27°50N 88°30E 41 F16
Sil → Spain 42°27N 7°43W 21 A2
Silacayoapan Mexico 17°30N 98°9W 87 D5
Silawad India 21°54N 74°54E 42 J6
Silchar India 24°49N 92°48E 41 G18
Silent Valley △ India 11°10N 76°20E 45 J3
Siler City U.S.A. 35°44N 79°28W 85 D15
Sileru → India 17°49N 81°24E 44 F5
Silesia = Śląsk Poland 51°0N 16°30E 16 C9
Silgarhi Doti Nepal 29°15N 81°0E 43 E9
Silghat India 26°35N 93°0E 41 F18
Silhouette Seychelles 4°29S 55°12E 55 b
Silicon Valley = Santa Clara Valley U.S.A. 36°50N 121°30W 78 J5
Silifke Turkey 36°22N 33°58E 46 B2
Siliguri = Shiliguri India 26°45N 88°25E 41 F16
Siling Co China 31°50N 89°20E 30 E6
Silistra Bulgaria 44°6N 27°19E 23 B12
Silivri Turkey 41°4N 28°14E 23 D13
Siljan Sweden 60°55N 14°45E 8 F16
Silkeborg Denmark 56°10N 9°32E 9 H13
Silkwood Australia 17°45S 146°2E 62 B4
Sillajhuay, Cordillera Chile 19°46S 68°40W 92 G5
Sillamäe Estonia 59°24N 27°45E 9 G22
Sillod India 20°18N 75°39E 44 D2
Silloth U.K. 54°52N 3°23W 12 C4
Siloam Springs U.S.A. 36°11N 94°32W 84 C7
Silopi Turkey 37°15N 42°27E 46 B4
Šilutė Lithuania 55°21N 21°33E 9 J19
Silvan Turkey 38°7N 41°2E 46 B4
Silvani India 23°18N 78°25E 43 H8
Silvassa India 20°16N 73°1E 44 D1
Silver City U.S.A. 32°46N 108°17W 77 K9
Silver Cr. → U.S.A. 43°16N 119°13W 76 E4
Silver Creek U.S.A. 42°33N 79°10W 82 D5
Silver L. U.S.A. 38°39N 120°6W 78 G6
Silver Lake Calif., U.S.A. 35°21N 116°7W 79 K10
Silver Lake Oreg., U.S.A. 43°8N 121°3W 76 E3
Silvermine Mts. Ireland 52°47N 8°15W 10 D3
Silverton Colo., U.S.A. 37°49N 107°40W 77 H10
Silverton Tex., U.S.A. 34°28N 101°19W 84 D4
Silvies → U.S.A. 43°34N 119°2W 76 E4
Simaltala India 24°43N 86°33E 43 G12
Simanggang = Bandar Sri Aman Malaysia 1°15N 111°32E 36 D4
Simao China 22°47N 101°5E 34 F3
Simard, L. Canada 47°40N 78°40W 72 C4
Simav Turkey 39°4N 28°58E 23 E13
Simbirsk = Ulyanovsk Russia 54°20N 48°25E 18 D8
Simcoe Canada 42°50N 80°23W 82 D4
Simcoe, L. Canada 44°25N 79°20W 82 B5
Simdega India 22°37N 84°31E 43 H11
Simeria Romania 45°51N 23°1E 17 F12
Simeulue Indonesia 2°45N 95°45E 36 D1
Simferopol Ukraine 44°55N 34°3E 19 F5
Simi Greece 36°35N 27°50E 23 F12
Simi Valley U.S.A. 34°16N 118°47W 79 L8
Simikot Nepal 30°0N 81°50E 43 E9
Simla = Shimla India 31°2N 77°9E 42 D7
Simlipal △ India 21°45N 86°30E 43 J12
Simmie Canada 49°56N 108°6W 71 D7
Simmler U.S.A. 35°21N 119°59W 79 K7
Simo älv = Simojoki → Finland 65°35N 25°1E 8 D21
Simojoki → Finland 65°35N 25°1E 8 D21
Simojovel Mexico 17°12N 92°38W 87 D6
Simonette → Canada 55°9N 118°15W 70 B5
Simonstown S. Africa 34°14S 18°26E 56 D2
Simpang Empat Malaysia 5°27N 100°29E 39 c
Simplonpass Switz. 46°15N 8°3E 20 C8
Simpson Desert Australia 25°0S 137°0E 62 D2
Simpson Desert △ Australia 24°59S 138°21E 62 C2
Simpson Pen. Canada 68°34N 88°45W 69 D14
Simrishamn Sweden 55°33N 14°22E 9 J16
Simsbury U.S.A. 41°53N 72°48W 83 E12
Simushir, Ostrov Russia 46°50N 152°30E 27 E16
Sin Cowe I. S. China Sea 9°53N 114°19E 36 C4
Sina → India 17°30N 75°55E 44 F2
Sina Dhago Somalia 5°50N 47°0E 49 F4
Sinabang Indonesia 2°30N 96°24E 36 D1
Sinai = Es Sînâ' Egypt 29°0N 34°0E 48 F2
Sinai, Mt. = Mûsa, Gebel Egypt 28°33N 33°59E 46 D2
Sinaloa □ Mexico 25°0N 107°30W 86 C3
Sinaloa de Leyva Mexico 25°50N 108°14W 86 B3
Sinan China 27°56N 108°13E 34 D7
Sincelejo Colombia 9°18N 75°24W 92 B3
Sinch'ang N. Korea 40°7N 128°28E 33 D15
Sinch'ŏn N. Korea 38°17N 125°21E 33 E13
Sinclair U.S.A. 41°47N 107°7W 76 F10
Sinclair Mills Canada 54°5N 121°40W 70 C4
Sinclair's B. U.K. 58°31N 3°5W 11 C5
Sinclairville U.S.A. 42°16N 79°16W 82 D5
Sincorá, Serra do Brazil 13°10S 41°20W 93 F10
Sind = Sindh □ Pakistan 26°0N 69°0E 42 G3
Sind → Jammu & Kashmir, India 34°18N 74°45E 43 B6
Sind → Mad. P., India 26°26N 79°13E 43 F8
Sind Sagar Doab Pakistan 32°0N 71°30E 42 D4
Sindangan Phil. 8°10N 123°5E 37 C6
Sindangbarang Indonesia 7°27S 107°1E 37 G12
Sindewahi India 20°17N 79°39E 44 D4
Sindgi India 16°55N 76°14E 44 F3
Sindh = Indus → Pakistan 24°20N 67°47E 42 G2
Sindh □ Pakistan 26°0N 69°0E 42 G3
Sindhnur India 15°47N 76°46E 45 F3
Sindhuli Garhi Nepal 27°16N 85°58E 43 F11
Sindi India 20°48N 78°52E 44 D4
Sindri India 23°45N 86°42E 43 H12
Sines Portugal 37°56N 8°51W 21 D1
Sines, C. de Portugal 37°58N 8°53W 21 D1
Sing Buri Thailand 14°53N 100°25E 38 E3
Singa Sudan 13°10N 33°57E 53 F12
Singalila △ India 27°10N 88°5E 43 F13
Singanallur India 11°2N 77°1E 45 J3
Singapore, Straits of Asia 1°15N 104°0E 39 d
Singaraja Indonesia 8°7S 115°6E 37 J18
Singatoka = Sigatoka Fiji 18°8S 177°32E 59 a
Singida Tanzania 4°49S 34°48E 54 E6
Singkang Indonesia 4°8S 120°1E 37 E6
Singkawang Indonesia 1°0N 108°57E 36 D3
Singkep Indonesia 0°30S 104°25E 36 E2
Singkil Indonesia 2°17N 97°49E 39 L1
Singkuang Indonesia 1°3N 98°55E 39 L2
Singleton Australia 32°33S 151°10E 63 E5
Singleton, Mt. N. Terr., Australia 22°0S 130°46E 60 D5
Singleton, Mt. W. Austral., Australia 29°27S 117°15E 61 E2
Singoli India 25°0N 75°22E 42 G6
Singora = Songkhla Thailand 7°13N 100°37E 39 J3
Singrauli India 24°7N 82°23E 43 G10
Sinh Ton, Dao = Sin Cowe I. S. China Sea 9°53N 114°19E 36 C4
Sinharaja Sri Lanka 6°25N 80°30E 45 L5
Sinhgarh India 18°22N 73°45E 44 E1
Sinhŭng N. Korea 40°11N 127°34E 33 D14
Siniscóla Italy 40°34N 9°41E 22 D3
Sinjai Indonesia 5°7S 120°20E 37 F6
Sinjār Iraq 36°19N 41°52E 46 B4
Sinkat Sudan 18°55N 36°49E 53 E13
Sinkiang = Xinjiang Uygur Zizhiqu □ China 42°0N 86°0E 30 C6
Sinmak N. Korea 38°25N 126°14E 33 E14
Sinmi-do N. Korea 39°33N 124°53E 33 E13
Sinnamary Fr. Guiana 5°25N 53°0W 93 B8
Sinnar India 19°48N 74°0E 44 E2
Sinni → Italy 40°8N 16°41E 22 D7
Sinop Turkey 42°1N 35°11E 19 F6
Sinor India 21°55N 73°20E 42 J5
Sinp'o N. Korea 40°0N 128°13E 33 E15
Sinsk Russia 61°8N 126°48E 27 C13
Sint-Hubert Belgium 50°2N 5°23E 15 D5
Sint-Niklaas Belgium 51°10N 4°8E 15 C4
Sint-Truiden Belgium 50°48N 5°10E 15 D5
Sintang Indonesia 0°5N 111°35E 36 D4
Sinton U.S.A. 28°2N 97°31W 84 G6
Sintra Portugal 38°47N 9°25W 21 C1
Sinŭiju N. Korea 40°5N 124°24E 33 D13
Siocon Phil. 7°40N 122°10E 37 C6
Siófok Hungary 46°54N 18°3E 17 E10
Sion Switz. 46°14N 7°20E 20 C7
Sion Mills U.K. 54°48N 7°29W 10 B4
tSionainn, An = Shannon → Ireland 52°35N 9°30W 10 D2
Sioux Center U.S.A. 43°5N 96°11W 80 D5
Sioux City U.S.A. 42°30N 96°24W 80 D5
Sioux Falls U.S.A. 43°33N 96°44W 80 D5
Sioux Lookout Canada 50°10N 91°50W 72 B1
Sioux Narrows Canada 49°25N 94°10W 71 D10
Sipadan Malaysia 4°6N 118°38E 37 D5
Siparia Trin. & Tob. 10°8N 61°31W 93 K15
Siping China 43°8N 124°21E 33 C13
Sipiwesk L. Canada 55°5N 97°35W 71 B9
Siple I. Antarctica 73°40S 125°10W 5 D14
Sipra → India 23°55N 75°28E 42 H6
Sipsongpanna = Xishuangbanna China 22°5N 101°1E 34 F3
Sipur India 21°11N 85°9E 44 D7
Sipura Indonesia 2°18S 99°40E 36 E1
Siquia → Nic. 12°10N 84°20W 88 D3
Siquijor Phil. 9°12N 123°35E 37 C6
Siquirres Costa Rica 10°6N 83°30W 88 D3
Şīr Abu Nu'ayr U.A.E. 25°20N 54°20E 47 E7
Şīr Banī Yās U.A.E. 24°19N 52°37E 47 E7
Sir Edward Pellew Group Australia 15°40S 137°10E 62 B2
Sir Graham Moore Is. Australia 13°53S 126°34E 60 B4
Sir James MacBrien, Mt. Canada 62°7N 127°41W 68 E6
Sira India 13°41N 76°49E 45 H3
Sira → Norway 58°23N 6°34E 9 G12
Siracusa Italy 37°4N 15°17E 22 F6
Sirajganj Bangla. 24°25N 89°47E 43 G13
Sirathu India 25°39N 81°19E 43 G9
Sīrdān Iran 36°39N 49°12E 47 B6
Siren U.S.A. 45°47N 92°24W 80 C7
Siret → Romania 45°24N 28°1E 17 F14
Sirghāyā Syria 33°51N 36°8E 48 B5
Sirikit Res. Thailand 17°45N 100°34E 38 C3
Sirinat △ Thailand 8°6N 98°17E 39 a
Sīrjān Iran 29°30N 55°45E 47 D7
Sirkali = Sirkazhi India 11°15N 79°41E 45 J4
Sirkazhi India 11°15N 79°41E 45 J4
Sirmaur India 24°51N 81°23E 43 G9
Sirmilik △ Canada 72°50N 80°35W 69 C15
Sirohi India 24°52N 72°53E 42 G5
Sironj India 24°5N 77°39E 42 G7
Síros = Ermoupoli Greece 37°28N 24°57E 23 F11
Sirpur India 19°29N 79°36E 44 E4
Sirr, Nafud as Si. Arabia 25°33N 44°35E 46 E5
Sirretta Pk. U.S.A. 35°56N 118°19W 79 K8
Sīrrī Iran 25°55N 54°32E 47 E7
Sirsa India 29°33N 75°4E 42 E6
Sirsa → India 26°51N 79°4E 43 F8

Sirsi *India* 14°40N 74°49E **45** G2
Sirsilla *India* 18°23N 78°50E **44** E4
Sirte = Surt *Libya* 31°11N 16°39E **53** B9
Siruguppa *India* 15°38N 76°54E **45** F3
Sirur *India* 18°50N 74°23E **44** E2
Şirvan *Azerbaijan* 39°59N 48°52E **47** B6
Sisak *Croatia* 45°30N 16°21E **16** F9
Sishen *S. Africa* 27°47S 22°59E **56** C3
Sishui *China* 35°42N 117°18E **33** G9
Sisipuk L. *Canada* 55°45N 101°50W **71** B8
Sisophon *Cambodia* 13°38N 102°59E **38** F4
Sisseton *U.S.A.* 45°40N 97°3W **80** C5
Sīstān *Asia* 30°50N 61°0E **47** D9
Sīstān, Daryācheh-ye *Iran* 31°0N 61°0E **47** D9
Sīstān va Balūchestān □
    *Iran* 27°0N 62°0E **47** E9
Sisters *U.S.A.* 44°18N 121°33W **76** D3
Sisters, The *Seychelles* 4°16S 55°52E **55** b
Siswa Bazar *India* 27°9N 83°46E **43** F10
Sitamarhi *India* 26°37N 85°30E **43** F11
Sitapur *India* 27°38N 80°45E **43** F9
Siteki *Eswatini* 26°32S 31°58E **57** C5
Sitges *Spain* 41°17N 1°47E **21** B6
Sitia *Greece* 35°13N 26°6E **23** G12
Sitito-Ozima Ridge *Pac. Oc.* 23°0N 143°0E **64** E6
Sitka *U.S.A.* 57°3N 135°20W **70** B1
Sitkaing = Sagaing
    *Myanmar* 21°52N 95°59E **41** J19
Sitoti *Botswana* 23°15S 23°40E **56** B3
Sittang Myit →
    *Myanmar* 17°20N 96°45E **41** L20
Sittard *Neths.* 51°0N 5°52E **15** C5
Sittingbourne *U.K.* 51°21N 0°45E **13** F8
Sittoung = Sittang Myit →
    *Myanmar* 17°20N 96°45E **41** L20
Sittwe *Myanmar* 20°18N 92°45E **41** J18
Situbondo *Indonesia* 7°42S 113°56E **37** G16
Si'umu *Samoa* 14°1S 171°48W **59** b
Siuna *Nic.* 13°37N 84°45W **88** D3
Siuri *India* 23°50N 87°34E **43** H12
Sivaganga *India* 9°50N 78°28E **45** K4
Sivagiri *India* 9°16N 77°26E **45** K3
Sivakasi *India* 9°24N 77°47E **45** K3
Sīvand *Iran* 30°5N 52°55E **47** D7
Sivas *Turkey* 39°43N 36°58E **46** B3
Sivasagar *India* 27°0N 94°36E **41** F19
Sivasamudram *India* 12°16N 77°10E **45** H3
Siverek *Turkey* 37°50N 39°19E **46** B3
Sivomaskinskiy *Russia* 66°40N 62°35E **18** A11
Sivrihisar *Turkey* 39°30N 31°35E **19** G5
Sîwa *Egypt* 29°11N 25°31E **53** C11
Sîwa, El Wâhât es *Egypt* 29°10N 25°30E **50** D6
Siwa Oasis = Sîwa, El Wâhât es
    *Egypt* 29°10N 25°30E **50** D6
Siwalik Range *Nepal* 28°0N 83°0E **43** F10
Siwan *India* 26°13N 84°21E **43** F11
Siwana *India* 25°38N 72°25E **42** G5
Six Cross Roads *Barbados* 13°7N 59°28E **89** g
Sixian *China* 33°30N 117°50E **33** H9
Sixmilebridge *Ireland* 52°44N 8°46W **10** D3
Sixth Cataract *Sudan* 16°20N 32°42E **53** E12
Siyabuswa *S. Africa* 25°7S 29°3E **57** C4
Siyah Kuh, Kavīr-e *Iran* 32°55N 53°55E **47** C7
Siyang *China* 33°42N 118°40E **33** H10
Siziwang Qi *China* 41°25N 111°40E **32** D6
Sjælland *Denmark* 55°30N 11°30E **9** J14
Sjumen = Shumen
    *Bulgaria* 43°18N 26°55E **23** C12
Skadarsko Jezero *Europe* 42°10N 19°20E **23** C8
Skaftafell *Iceland* 64°1N 17°0W **8** D5
Skagafjörður *Iceland* 65°54N 19°35W **8** D4
Skagastølstindane *Norway* 61°28N 7°52E **8** F12
Skagaströnd *Iceland* 65°50N 20°19W **8** D3
Skagen *Denmark* 57°43N 10°35E **9** H14
Skagerrak *Denmark* 57°30N 9°0E **9** H13
Skagit → *U.S.A.* 48°23N 122°22W **78** B4
Skagway *U.S.A.* 59°28N 135°19W **68** F4
Skala-Podilska *Ukraine* 48°50N 26°15E **17** D14
Skalat *Ukraine* 49°23N 25°55E **17** D13
Skåne *Sweden* 55°59N 13°30E **9** J15
Skaneateles *U.S.A.* 42°57N 76°26W **83** D8
Skaneateles L. *U.S.A.* 42°51N 76°22W **83** D8
Skardu *Pakistan* 35°20N 75°44E **43** B6
Skarvan og Roltdalen △
    *Norway* 63°16N 11°31E **8** E14
Skarżysko-Kamienna
    *Poland* 51°7N 20°52E **17** C11
Skeena → *Canada* 54°9N 130°5W **70** C2
Skeena Mts. *Canada* 56°40N 128°30W **70** B3
Skegness *U.K.* 53°9N 0°20E **12** D8
Skeleton Coast *Namibia* 20°0S 13°0E **55** J2
Skeleton Coast △ *Namibia* 20°0S 13°20E **56** B1
Skellefteå *Sweden* 64°45N 20°50E **8** D19
Skellefteälven → *Sweden* 64°45N 21°10E **8** D19
Skelleftehamn *Sweden* 64°40N 21°9E **8** D19
Skellig Michael = Great Skellig
    *Ireland* 51°47N 10°33W **10** E1
Skerries *Ireland* 53°35N 6°8W **10** C5
Skerries, The *U.K.* 53°25N 4°36W **12** D3
Ski *Norway* 59°43N 10°52E **9** G14
Skiathos *Greece* 39°12N 23°30E **23** E10
Skibbereen *Ireland* 51°33N 9°16W **10** E2
Skiddaw *U.K.* 54°39N 3°9W **12** C4
Skidegate *Canada* 53°15N 132°1W **70** C2
Skien *Norway* 59°12N 9°35E **9** G13
Skierniewice *Poland* 51°58N 20°10E **17** C11
Skihist, Mt. *Canada* 50°12N 121°54W **70** C4
Skikda *Algeria* 36°50N 6°58E **52** A7
Skipton *U.K.* 53°58N 2°3W **12** D5
Skirmish Pt. *Australia* 11°59S 134°17E **62** A1
Skíros = Skyros *Greece* 38°55N 24°34E **23** E11
Skive *Denmark* 56°33N 9°2E **9** H13
Skjálfandafljót → *Iceland* 65°59N 17°25W **8** D5
Skjálfandi *Iceland* 66°5N 17°30W **8** C5
Skole *Ukraine* 49°3N 23°30E **17** D12
Skopelos *Greece* 39°9N 23°47E **23** E10
Skopje *Macedonia* 42°1N 21°26E **23** C9
Skövde *Sweden* 58°24N 13°50E **9** G15
Skovorodino *Russia* 54°0N 124°0E **27** D13
Skowhegan *U.S.A.* 44°46N 69°43W **81** C19
Skull *Ireland* 51°32N 9°34W **10** E2

Skunk → *U.S.A.* 40°42N 91°7W **80** E8
Skuodas *Lithuania* 56°16N 21°33E **9** H19
Skvyra *Ukraine* 49°44N 29°40E **17** D15
Sky Harbour Int., Phoenix ✈
    (PHX) *U.S.A.* 33°26N 112°5W **77** K7
Skye *U.K.* 57°15N 6°10W **11** D2
Skykomish *U.S.A.* 47°42N 121°22W **76** C3
Skyros *Greece* 38°55N 24°34E **23** E11
Slade Point *Australia* 21°4S 149°13E **62** b
Slade Pt. *Australia* 21°5S 149°13E **62** b
Slættaratindur *Færoe Is.* 62°18N 7°1W **8** E9
Slagelse *Denmark* 55°23N 11°19E **9** J14
Slamet *Indonesia* 7°16S 109°8E **37** G13
Slane *Ireland* 53°42N 6°33W **10** C5
Slaney → *Ireland* 52°26N 6°33W **10** D5
Slangberge *S. Africa* 31°32S 20°48E **56** D3
Śląsk *Poland* 51°0N 16°30E **16** C9
Slate Is. *Canada* 48°40N 87°0W **72** C2
Slatina *Romania* 44°28N 24°22E **17** F13
Slatington *U.S.A.* 40°45N 75°37W **83** F9
Slaton *U.S.A.* 33°26N 101°39W **84** E4
Slave → *Canada* 61°18N 113°39W **70** A6
Slave Coast *W. Afr.* 6°0N 2°30E **52** G6
Slave Lake *Canada* 55°17N 114°43W **70** B6
Slave Pt. *Canada* 61°11N 115°56W **70** A5
Slavgorod *Russia* 53°1N 78°37E **26** D8
Slavonski Brod *Croatia* 45°11N 18°1E **23** B8
Slavuta *Ukraine* 50°15N 27°2E **17** C14
Slavyanka *Russia* 42°53N 131°21E **28** C5
Slavyansk = Slovyansk
    *Ukraine* 48°55N 37°36E **19** E6
Slawharad *Belarus* 53°27N 31°0E **17** B16
Slea Hd. *Ireland* 52°6N 10°27W **10** D1
Sleaford *U.K.* 53°0N 0°24W **12** D7
Sleaford B. *Australia* 34°55S 135°45E **63** E2
Sleat, Sd. of *U.K.* 57°5N 5°47W **11** D3
Sleeper Is. *Canada* 58°30N 81°0W **69** F15
Sleeping Bear Dunes △
    *U.S.A.* 44°50N 86°5W **80** C10
Sleepy Eye *U.S.A.* 44°18N 94°43W **80** C6
Slemon L. *Canada* 63°13N 116°4W **70** A5
Slide Mt. *U.S.A.* 42°0N 74°25W **83** E10
Slidell *U.S.A.* 30°17N 89°47W **85** F10
Slieve Aughty *Ireland* 53°4N 8°30W **10** C3
Slieve Bloom *Ireland* 53°4N 7°40W **10** C4
Slieve Donard *U.K.* 54°11N 5°55W **10** B6
Slieve Gamph *Ireland* 54°6N 9°0W **10** B3
Slieve Gullion *U.K.* 54°7N 6°26W **10** B5
Slieve League *Ireland* 54°40N 8°42W **10** B3
Slieve Mish *Ireland* 52°12N 9°50W **10** D2
Slievenamon *Ireland* 52°25N 7°34W **10** D4
Sligeach = Sligo *Ireland* 54°16N 8°28W **10** B3
Sligo *Ireland* 54°16N 8°28W **10** B3
Sligo *U.S.A.* 41°6N 79°29W **82** E5
Sligo □ *Ireland* 54°8N 8°42W **10** B3
Sligo B. *Ireland* 54°18N 8°40W **10** B3
Slippery Rock *U.S.A.* 41°4N 80°3W **82** E4
Slite *Sweden* 57°42N 18°48E **9** H18
Sliven *Bulgaria* 42°42N 26°19E **23** C12
Sloan *U.S.A.* 35°57N 115°13W **79** K11
Sloansville *U.S.A.* 42°45N 74°22W **83** D10
Slobodskoy *Russia* 58°40N 50°6E **18** C9
Slobozia *Romania* 44°34N 27°23E **17** F14
Slocan *Canada* 49°48N 117°28W **70** D5
Slonim *Belarus* 53°4N 25°19E **17** B13
Slough *U.K.* 51°30N 0°36W **13** F7
Slough □ *U.K.* 51°30N 0°36W **13** F7
Sloughhouse *U.S.A.* 38°26N 121°12W **78** G5
Slovak Rep. = Slovakia ■
    *Europe* 48°30N 20°0E **17** D10
Slovakia ■ *Europe* 48°30N 20°0E **17** D10
Slovakian Ore Mts. = Slovenské
    Rudohorie *Slovakia* 48°45N 20°0E **17** D10
Slovenia ■ *Europe* 45°58N 14°30E **16** F8
Slovenija = Slovenia ■
    *Europe* 45°58N 14°30E **16** F8
Slovenská = Slovakia ■
    *Europe* 48°30N 20°0E **17** D10
Slovenské Rudohorie
    *Slovakia* 48°45N 20°0E **17** D10
Slovyansk *Ukraine* 48°55N 37°36E **19** E6
Sluch → *Ukraine* 51°37N 26°38E **17** C14
Sluis *Neths.* 51°18N 3°23E **15** C3
Słupsk *Poland* 54°30N 17°3E **17** A9
Slurry *S. Africa* 25°49S 25°42E **56** C4
Slutsk *Belarus* 53°2N 27°31E **17** B14
Slyne Hd. *Ireland* 53°25N 10°10W **10** C1
Slyudyanka *Russia* 51°40N 103°40E **27** D11
Småland *Sweden* 57°15N 15°25E **9** H16
Smalltree L. *Canada* 61°0N 105°0W **71** A8
Smallwood Res. *Canada* 54°5N 64°30W **73** B7
Smarhon *Belarus* 54°20N 26°24E **17** A14
Smartt Syndicate Dam
    *S. Africa* 30°45S 23°10E **56** D3
Smartville *U.S.A.* 39°13N 121°18W **78** F5
Smeaton *Canada* 53°30N 104°49W **71** C8
Smederevo *Serbia* 44°40N 20°57E **23** B9
Smeralda, Costa *Italy* 41°5N 9°35E **22** D3
Smerwick Harbour
    *Ireland* 52°12N 10°23W **10** D1
Smethport *U.S.A.* 41°49N 78°27W **82** E6
Smidovich *Russia* 48°36N 133°49E **27** E14
Smith *Canada* 55°10N 114°0W **70** B6
Smith Center *U.S.A.* 39°47N 98°47W **80** F4
Smith I. *Canada* 60°45N 78°25W **69** E16
Smith I. *U.S.A.* 38°0N 75°45E **44** H11
Smith Islands △ *Australia* 20°40S 149°9E **62** b
Smith River → *U.S.A.* 41°55N 124°0W **76** F2
Smith Sd. *N. Amer.* 78°30N 74°0W **69** B17
Smithburne → *Australia* 17°3S 140°57E **62** B3
Smithers *Canada* 54°45N 127°10W **70** C3
Smithfield *S. Africa* 30°9S 26°30E **57** D4
Smithfield *N.C., U.S.A.* 35°31N 78°21W **85** D15
Smithfield *Utah, U.S.A.* 41°50N 111°50W **76** F8
Smiths Falls *Canada* 44°55N 76°0W **83** B9
Smithton *Australia* 40°53S 145°6E **63** G4
Smithville *Canada* 43°6N 79°33W **82** C5
Smithville *U.S.A.* 30°1N 97°10W **84** F6
Smoke Creek Desert
    *U.S.A.* 40°30N 119°40W **76** F4
Smoky → *Canada* 56°10N 117°21W **70** B5

Smoky Bay *Australia* 32°22S 134°13E **63** E1
Smoky Hill → *U.S.A.* 39°4N 96°48W **80** F6
Smoky Hills *U.S.A.* 39°15N 99°30W **80** F4
Smoky Lake *Canada* 54°10N 112°30W **70** C6
Smøla *Norway* 63°23N 8°3E **8** E13
Smolensk *Russia* 54°45N 32°5E **18** D5
Smolikas, Oros *Greece* 40°9N 20°58E **23** D9
Smolyan *Bulgaria* 41°36N 24°38E **23** D11
Smooth Rock Falls
    *Canada* 49°17N 81°37W **72** C3
Smoothstone L. *Canada* 54°40N 106°50W **71** C7
Smorgon = Smarhon
    *Belarus* 54°20N 26°24E **17** A14
Smyley I. *Antarctica* 72°55S 78°0W **5** D17
Smyrna = İzmir *Turkey* 38°25N 27°8E **23** E12
Smyrna *U.S.A.* 39°18N 75°36W **81** F16
Snæfell *Iceland* 64°48N 15°34W **8** D6
Snaefell *I. of Man* 54°16N 4°27W **12** C3
Snæfellsjökull *Iceland* 64°49N 23°46W **8** D2
Snake → *U.S.A.* 46°12N 119°2W **76** C4
Snake I. *Australia* 38°47S 146°33E **63** F4
Snake Range *U.S.A.* 39°0N 114°20W **76** G6
Snake River Plain *U.S.A.* 42°50N 114°0W **76** E7
Snåsavatnet *Norway* 64°12N 12°0E **8** D15
Sneek *Neths.* 53°2N 5°40E **15** A5
Sneem *Ireland* 51°50N 9°54W **10** E2
Sneeuberge *S. Africa* 31°46S 24°20E **56** D3
Snelling *U.S.A.* 37°31N 120°26W **78** H6
Snežka *Europe* 50°41N 15°50E **16** C8
Snizort, L. *U.K.* 57°33N 6°28W **11** D2
Snøhetta *Norway* 62°19N 9°16E **8** E13
Snohomish *U.S.A.* 47°55N 122°6W **78** C4
Snoqualmie *U.S.A.* 47°31N 121°49W **78** C5
Snoqualmie Pass *U.S.A.* 47°25N 121°25W **78** C5
Snoul *Cambodia* 12°4N 106°26E **39** F6
Snover *U.S.A.* 43°27N 82°58W **82** C2
Snow Hill *U.S.A.* 38°11N 75°24W **81** F16
Snow Lake *Canada* 54°52N 100°3W **71** C8
Snow Mt. *Calif., U.S.A.* 39°23N 122°45W **78** F4
Snow Mt. *Maine, U.S.A.* 45°18N 70°48W **83** A14
Snow Shoe *U.S.A.* 41°2N 77°57W **82** E7
Snowbird L. *Canada* 60°45N 103°0W **71** A8
Snowdon *U.K.* 53°4N 4°5W **12** D3
Snowdonia △ *U.K.* 53°7N 3°59W **12** D4
Snowdrift = Lutsel K'e
    *Canada* 62°24N 110°44W **71** A6
Snowdrift → *Canada* 62°24N 110°44W **71** A6
Snowflake *U.S.A.* 34°30N 110°5W **77** J8
Snowshoe Pk. *U.S.A.* 48°13N 115°41W **76** B6
Snowtown *Australia* 33°46S 138°14E **63** E2
Snowville *U.S.A.* 41°58N 112°43W **76** F7
Snowy → *Australia* 37°46S 148°30E **63** F4
Snowy Mt. *U.S.A.* 43°42N 74°23W **83** C10
Snowy Mts. *Australia* 36°30S 148°20E **63** F4
Snug Corner *Bahamas* 22°33S 72°52W **89** B5
Snug Harbour *Canada* 45°22N 80°17W **82** A4
Snyatyn *Ukraine* 48°27N 25°38E **17** D13
Snyder *Okla., U.S.A.* 34°40N 98°57W **84** D5
Snyder *Tex., U.S.A.* 32°44N 100°55W **84** E4
Soalala *Madag.* 16°6S 45°20E **55** H9
Soan → *Pakistan* 33°1N 71°44E **42** C4
Sobat → *South Sudan* 9°22N 31°33E **53** G12
Sobhapur *India* 22°47N 78°17E **42** H8
Sobradinho, Represa de
    *Brazil* 9°30S 42°0W **93** E10
Sobral *Brazil* 3°50S 40°20W **93** D10
Soc Giang *Vietnam* 22°54N 106°1E **34** F6
Soc Trang *Vietnam* 9°37N 105°50E **39** H5
Socastee *U.S.A.* 33°41N 78°59W **85** D15
Soch'e = Shache *China* 38°20N 77°10E **30** D4
Sochi *Russia* 43°35N 39°40E **19** F6
Société, Îs. de la
    *French Polynesia* 17°0S 151°0W **65** J12
Society Is. = Société, Îs. de la
    *French Polynesia* 17°0S 151°0W **65** J12
Socompa, Portezuelo de
    *Chile* 24°27S 68°18W **94** A2
Socorro *N. Mex., U.S.A.* 34°4N 106°54W **77** J10
Socorro *Tex., U.S.A.* 31°39N 106°18W **84** F1
Socorro, I. *Mexico* 18°45N 110°58W **86** D2
Socotra *Yemen* 12°30N 54°0E **49** E5
Soda L. *U.S.A.* 35°10N 116°4W **79** K10
Soda Plains *India* 35°30N 79°0E **43** B8
Soda Springs *U.S.A.* 42°39N 111°36W **76** E8
Sodankylä *Finland* 67°29N 26°40E **8** C22
Soddy-Daisy *U.S.A.* 35°17N 85°10W **85** D12
Söderhamn *Sweden* 61°18N 17°10E **8** F17
Söderköping *Sweden* 58°31N 16°20E **9** G17
Södermanland *Sweden* 58°56N 16°55E **9** G17
Södertälje *Sweden* 59°12N 17°39E **9** G17
Sodiri *Sudan* 14°27N 29°0E **53** F11
Sodus *U.S.A.* 43°14N 77°4W **82** C7
Sodwana Bay △ *S. Africa* 27°35S 32°43E **57** C5
Soe *Indonesia* 9°52S 124°17E **60** A3
Soekmekaar = Morebeng
    *S. Africa* 23°30S 29°55E **57** B4
Soest *Neths.* 52°9N 5°19E **15** B5
Sofala □ *Mozam.* 19°30S 34°30E **57** B5
Sofia *Bulgaria* 42°45N 23°20E **23** C10
Sofia → *Madag.* 15°27S 47°23E **55** H9
Sofiya = Sofia *Bulgaria* 42°45N 23°20E **23** C10
Sôfu-Gan *Japan* 29°49N 140°21E **29** K10
Sogamoso *Colombia* 5°43N 72°56W **92** B4
Sogār *Iran* 25°53N 58°6E **47** E8
Sogndalsfjøra *Norway* 61°14N 7°5E **8** F12
Søgne *Norway* 58°5N 7°48E **9** G12
Sognefjorden *Norway* 61°10N 5°50E **8** F11
Soh *Iran* 33°26N 51°27E **47** C6
Sohâg *Egypt* 26°33N 31°43E **53** C12
Sohagpur *India* 22°42N 78°12E **42** H8
Sohar = Şuḩār *Oman* 24°20N 56°40E **47** E8
Sohela *India* 21°18N 83°24E **44** D6
Soheuksando *S. Korea* 34°4N 125°7E **33** G13
Soignies *Belgium* 50°35N 4°5E **15** D4
Soissons *France* 49°25N 3°19E **20** B5
Sōja *Japan* 34°40N 133°45E **29** G6
Sojat *India* 25°55N 73°45E **42** G5
Sokal *Ukraine* 50°31N 24°15E **17** C13
Sokcho *S. Korea* 38°12N 128°36E **33** E15
Söke *Turkey* 37°48N 27°28E **23** F12
Sokhumi *Georgia* 43°0N 41°0E **19** F7

Sokodé *Togo* 9°0N 1°11E **52** G6
Sokol *Russia* 59°30N 40°5E **18** C7
Sokółka *Poland* 53°25N 23°30E **17** B12
Sokołów Podlaski
    *Poland* 52°25N 22°15E **17** B12
Sokoto *Nigeria* 13°2N 5°16E **52** F7
Sol, Costa del *Spain* 36°30N 4°30W **21** D3
Sol Iletsk *Russia* 51°10N 55°0E **18** D10
Solan *India* 30°55N 77°7E **42** D7
Solana Beach *U.S.A.* 32°58N 117°16W **79** N9
Solander I. *N.Z.* 46°34S 166°54E **59** G1
Solapur *India* 17°43N 75°56E **44** F2
Soldotna *U.S.A.* 60°29N 151°3W **68** E1
Soledad *Colombia* 10°55N 74°46W **92** A4
Soledad *U.S.A.* 36°26N 121°20W **78** J5
Soledad *Venezuela* 8°10N 63°34W **92** B6
Solent, The *U.K.* 50°45N 1°25W **13** G6
Solfonntaggen *Norway* 60°2N 6°57E **9** F12
Solhan *Turkey* 38°57N 41°3E **46** B4
Soligalich *Russia* 59°5N 42°10E **18** C7
Soligorsk = Salihorsk
    *Belarus* 52°51N 27°27E **17** B14
Solihull *U.K.* 52°26N 1°47W **13** E6
Solikamsk *Russia* 59°38N 56°50E **18** C10
Solimões = Amazonas →
    *S. Amer.* 0°5S 50°0W **93** D8
Solingen *Germany* 51°10N 7°5E **16** C4
Sollefteå *Sweden* 63°12N 17°20E **8** E17
Sóller *Spain* 39°46N 2°43E **21** C7
Solo → *Indonesia* 6°47S 112°22E **37** G15
Sologne *France* 47°40N 1°45E **20** C4
Solok *Indonesia* 0°45S 100°40E **36** E2
Solola *Guatemala* 14°49N 91°10W **88** D1
Solomon, N. Fork →
    *U.S.A.* 39°29N 98°26W **80** F4
Solomon, S. Fork →
    *U.S.A.* 39°25N 99°12W **80** F4
Solomon Is. ■ *Pac. Oc.* 6°0S 155°0E **58** B8
Solomon Rise *Pac. Oc.* 1°0N 157°0E **64** G7
Solon *China* 46°32N 121°10E **31** B13
Solon Springs *U.S.A.* 46°22N 91°49W **80** B8
Solor *Indonesia* 8°27S 123°0E **37** F6
Solothurn *Switz.* 47°13N 7°32E **20** C7
Solovetskiye Ostrova
    *Russia* 65°5N 35°40E **18** B6
Šolta *Croatia* 43°24N 16°15E **22** C7
Solţānābād *Khorāsān, Iran* 34°13N 59°58E **47** C8
Solţānābād *Khorāsān, Iran* 36°29N 58°5E **47** B8
Solţānīyeh *Iran* 36°26N 48°47E **47** B6
Solunska Glava
    *Macedonia* 41°44N 21°31E **23** D9
Solvang *U.S.A.* 34°36N 120°8W **79** L6
Solvay *U.S.A.* 43°3N 76°13W **83** D8
Sölvesborg *Sweden* 56°5N 14°35E **9** H16
Solvychegodsk *Russia* 61°21N 46°56E **18** B8
Solway Firth *U.K.* 54°49N 3°35W **12** C4
Solwezi *Zambia* 12°11S 26°21E **55** G5
Sōma *Japan* 37°40N 140°50E **28** F10
Soma *Turkey* 39°10N 27°35E **23** E12
Somabhula *Zimbabwe* 19°42S 29°40E **57** A4
Somali Pen. *Africa* 7°0N 46°0E **50** F8
Somalia ■ *Africa* 7°0N 47°0E **49** F4
Somaliland □ *Somalia* 10°0N 46°0E **49** F4
Sombor *Serbia* 45°46N 19°9E **23** B8
Sombra *Canada* 42°43N 82°29W **82** D2
Sombrerete *Mexico* 23°38N 103°39W **86** C4
Sombrero *Anguilla* 18°37N 63°30W **89** C7
Sombrero Channel *India* 7°41N 93°35E **45** L11
Somdari *India* 25°47N 72°38E **42** G5
Somers *U.S.A.* 48°5N 114°13W **76** B6
Somerset *Ky., U.S.A.* 37°5N 84°36W **81** G11
Somerset *Mass., U.S.A.* 41°47N 71°8W **83** E13
Somerset *Pa., U.S.A.* 40°1N 79°5W **82** F5
Somerset □ *U.K.* 51°9N 3°0W **13** F5
Somerset East *S. Africa* 32°42S 25°35E **56** D4
Somerset I. *Canada* 73°30N 93°0W **68** C13
Somerset West *S. Africa* 34°8S 18°50E **56** D2
Somersworth *U.S.A.* 43°16N 70°52W **83** C14
Somerton *U.S.A.* 32°36N 114°43W **77** K6
Somerville *U.S.A.* 40°35N 74°38W **83** F10
Someş → *Romania* 47°49N 22°43E **17** D12
Somme → *France* 50°11N 1°38E **20** A4
Somnath *India* 20°53N 70°22E **42** J4
Somosierra, Puerto de
    *Spain* 41°4N 3°35W **21** B4
Somosomo *Fiji* 16°47S 179°58W **59** a
Somosomo Str. *Fiji* 16°0S 180°0E **59** a
Somoto *Nic.* 13°28N 86°37W **88** D2
Somport, Túnel de *Spain* 42°48N 0°31W **20** E3
Somvarpet *India* 12°36N 75°52E **45** H2
Son → *India* 25°42N 84°52E **43** G11
Son, Laem *Thailand* 7°59N 98°16E **39** a
Son Ha *Vietnam* 15°3N 108°34E **38** E7
Son La *Vietnam* 21°20N 103°50E **34** G4
Son Tay *Vietnam* 21°8N 105°30E **34** G5
Son Tinh *Vietnam* 15°10N 108°40E **38** E7
Soná *Panama* 8°0N 81°20W **88** E3
Sonamarg *India* 34°18N 75°21E **43** B6
Sonamukhi *India* 23°18N 87°27E **43** H12
Sonar → *India* 24°24N 79°56E **43** G8
Sönch'ön *N. Korea* 39°48N 124°55E **33** E13
Sondags → *S. Africa* 33°44S 25°51E **56** D4
Sóndrio *Italy* 46°10N 9°52E **20** C8
Sonepur *India* 20°55N 83°50E **44** D6
Sonepur *India* 20°55N 83°50E **44** D6
Song *Thailand* 18°28N 100°11E **38** C3
Song Cau *Vietnam* 13°27N 109°18E **38** F7
Song Ma *Vietnam* 20°56N 103°53E **34** G4
Song Xian *China* 34°12N 112°8E **32** G7
Songadh *India* 21°9N 73°33E **44** D1
Songan *Indonesia* 8°13S 115°24E **37** J18
Songanga *S. Africa* 26°8S 29°27E **57** D4
Songcheng = Xiapu *China* 26°54N 120°5E **35** D12
Songea *Tanzania* 10°40S 35°40E **54** G7
Songgang *China* 22°46N 113°50E **31** a
Songhua Hu *China* 43°35N 126°50E **33** C14
Songhua Jiang →
    *China* 47°45N 132°30E **31** B15
Songjianghe *China* 42°10N 127°29E **33** C14

Sŏngjin = Kimch'aek
    *N. Korea* 40°40N 129°10E **33** D15
Songkan *China* 28°35N 106°52E **34** C6
Songkhla *Thailand* 7°13N 100°37E **39** J3
Songming *China* 25°12N 103°2E **34** E4
Songnim *N. Korea* 38°45N 125°39E **33** E13
Songo *Mozam.* 15°34S 32°38E **57** A5
Songpan *China* 32°40N 103°30E **34** A4
Songtao *China* 28°11N 109°10E **34** C7
Songxi *China* 27°31N 118°44E **35** D12
Songzi *China* 30°12N 111°45E **35** B8
Sonhat *India* 23°29N 82°31E **43** H10
Sonid Youqi *China* 42°45N 112°48E **32** C7
Sonid Zuoqi *China* 43°50N 113°42E **32** C7
Sonipat *India* 29°0N 77°5E **42** E7
Sonkach *India* 22°59N 76°21E **42** H7
Sonmiani *Pakistan* 25°25N 66°40E **42** G2
Sonmiani B. *Pakistan* 25°15N 66°30E **42** G2
Sono → *Brazil* 9°58S 48°11W **93** E9
Sonoma *U.S.A.* 38°18N 122°28W **78** G4
Sonora *Calif., U.S.A.* 37°59N 120°23W **78** H6
Sonora *Tex., U.S.A.* 30°34N 100°39W **84** F4
Sonora □ *Mexico* 29°20N 110°40W **86** B2
Sonora → *Mexico* 29°5N 110°55W **86** B2
Sonoran Desert *U.S.A.* 33°40N 113°30W **79** L12
Sonoyta *Mexico* 31°51N 112°50W **86** A2
Sonsonate *El Salv.* 13°43N 89°44W **88** D2
Soochow = Suzhou
    *China* 31°19N 120°38E **35** B13
Sooke *Canada* 48°13N 123°43W **78** B3
Soomaaliya = Somalia ■
    *Africa* 7°0N 47°0E **49** F4
Sop Hao *Laos* 20°33N 104°27E **34** G5
Sop Prap *Thailand* 17°53N 99°20E **38** D2
Sopi *Indonesia* 2°34N 128°28E **37** D7
Sopot *Poland* 54°27N 18°31E **17** A10
Sopron *Hungary* 47°45N 16°32E **17** E9
Sopur *India* 34°18N 74°27E **43** B6
Sør-Rondane *Antarctica* 72°0S 25°0E **5** D4
Sorab *India* 14°23N 75°6E **45** G2
Sorada *India* 19°45N 84°26E **44** E7
Sorah *Pakistan* 27°13N 68°56E **42** F3
Soraon *India* 25°37N 81°51E **43** G9
Sord = Swords *Ireland* 53°28N 6°13W **10** C5
Sorel-Tracy *Canada* 46°0N 73°10W **72** C5
Sórgono *Italy* 40°1N 9°6E **22** D3
Soria *Spain* 41°43N 2°32W **21** B4
Soriano *Uruguay* 33°24S 58°19W **94** C4
Sorkh, Kuh-e *Iran* 35°40N 58°30E **47** C8
Soroca *Moldova* 48°8N 28°12E **17** D15
Sorocaba *Brazil* 23°31S 47°27W **95** A6
Sorochinsk *Russia* 52°26N 53°10E **18** D9
Soroki = Soroca *Moldova* 48°8N 28°12E **17** D15
Sorong *Indonesia* 0°55S 131°15E **37** E8
Soroti *Uganda* 1°43N 33°35E **54** D6
Sørøya *Norway* 70°40N 22°30E **8** A20
Sørøysundet *Norway* 70°25N 23°0E **8** A20
Sorrell *Australia* 42°47S 147°34E **63** G4
Sorrento *Italy* 40°37N 14°22E **22** D6
Sorsele *Sweden* 65°31N 17°30E **8** D17
Sorsogon *Phil.* 13°0N 124°0E **37** B6
Sortavala *Russia* 61°42N 30°41E **8** F24
Sortland *Norway* 68°42N 15°25E **8** B16
Sørvågen *Norway* 67°53N 13°1E **8** C15
Soscumica, L. *Canada* 50°15N 77°27W **72** B4
Sosnogorsk *Russia* 63°37N 53°51E **18** B9
Sosnowiec *Poland* 50°20N 19°10E **17** C10
Sossus Vlei *Namibia* 24°40S 15°23E **56** B2
Sôsura *N. Korea* 42°16N 130°36E **33** C16
Sot → *India* 27°27N 79°37E **43** F8
Sotavento *Cabo Verde* 15°0N 24°0W **52** b
Sotkamo *Finland* 64°8N 28°23E **8** D23
Soto la Marina *Mexico* 23°46N 98°13W **87** C5
Soto la Marina →
    *Mexico* 23°45N 97°45W **87** C5
Sotuta *Mexico* 20°36N 89°1W **87** C7
Souanké *Congo* 2°10N 14°3E **54** D2
Soudas, Ormos *Greece* 35°25N 24°10E **23** G11
Souderton *U.S.A.* 40°19N 75°19W **83** F9
Soufrière *Guadeloupe* 16°5N 61°40W **88** b
Soufrière *St. Lucia* 13°51N 61°3W **89** f
Soufrière Bay *Dominica* 15°13N 61°22W **89** f
Soukhouma *Laos* 14°38N 105°48E **38** E5
Sound, The *U.K.* 50°20N 4°10W **13** G3
Sound I. *India* 12°58N 92°59E **45** H11
Sources, Mt. aux *Lesotho* 28°45S 28°50E **57** C4
Soure *Brazil* 0°35S 48°30W **93** D9
Souris *Man., Canada* 49°40N 100°20W **71** D8
Souris *P.E.I., Canada* 46°21N 62°15W **73** C7
Souris → *N. Amer.* 49°40N 99°34W **80** A4
Sousa *Brazil* 6°45S 38°10W **93** E11
Sousse *Tunisia* 35°50N 10°38E **53** A8
Sout → *S. Africa* 31°35S 18°24E **56** D2
South Africa ■ *Africa* 32°0S 23°0E **56** D3
South America 10°0S 60°0W **90** E5
South Andaman *India* 11°45N 92°10E **45** J11
South Aulatsivik I.
    *Canada* 56°45N 61°30W **73** A7
South Australia □
    *Australia* 32°0S 139°0E **63** E2
South Australian Basin
    *Ind. Oc.* 38°0S 126°0E **64** L4
South Ayrshire □ *U.K.* 55°18N 4°41W **11** F4
South Baldy Pk. *U.S.A.* 34°6N 107°11W **77** J10
South Bass I. *U.S.A.* 41°39N 82°49W **82** E2
South Bend *Ind., U.S.A.* 41°41N 86°15W **80** E10
South Bend *Wash.,
    U.S.A.* 46°40N 123°48W **78** D3
South Boston *U.S.A.* 36°42N 78°54W **81** G14
South Branch *Canada* 47°55N 59°2W **73** C8
South Brook *Canada* 49°26N 56°5W **73** C8
South Brother I. *India* 10°56N 92°37E **45** J11
South Bruny I. *Australia* 43°20S 147°15E **63** G4
South Carolina □ *U.S.A.* 34°0N 81°0W **85** E14
South Charleston
    *U.S.A.* 38°22N 81°44W **81** F13
South China Sea *Asia* 10°0N 113°0E **36** C4
South Cumberland Is. △
    *Australia* 20°42S 149°11E **62** b
South Dakota □ *U.S.A.* 44°15N 100°0W **80** C4
South Dayton *U.S.A.* 42°21N 79°3W **82** D5

South Deerfield *U.S.A.* 42°29N 72°37W **83 D12**
South Downs *U.K.* 50°52N 0°25W **13 G7**
South Downs △ *U.K.* 50°50N 0°50W **13 G7**
South Dublin □ *Ireland* 53°16N 6°24W **10 C5**
South East □ *Botswana* 24°17S 123°30E **61 F3**
South East C. *Australia* 43°40S 146°50E **63 G4**
South East Is. *Australia* 34°17S 123°30E **61 F3**
South Esk → *U.K.* 56°43N 2°31W **11 E6**
South Fiji Basin *Pac. Oc.* 26°0S 175°0E **64 K9**
South Foreland *U.K.* 51°8N 1°24E **13 F9**
South Fork American →
  *U.S.A.* 38°57N 120°59W **78 G5**
South Fork Feather →
  *U.S.A.* 39°17N 121°36W **78 F5**
South Fork Grand →
  *U.S.A.* 45°43N 102°17W **80 C2**
South Fork Milk →
  *U.S.A.* 48°4N 106°19W **76 B10**
South Fork Republican →
  *U.S.A.* 40°3N 101°31W **80 E3**
South Georgia *Antarctica* 54°30S 37°0W **96 G9**
South Gloucestershire □
  *U.K.* 51°32N 2°28W **13 F5**
South Hadley *U.S.A.* 42°16N 72°35W **83 D12**
South Haven *U.S.A.* 42°24N 86°16W **80 D10**
South Henik L. *Canada* 61°30N 97°20W **71 A9**
South Horr *Kenya* 2°12N 36°56E **54 D7**
South I. *India* 10°3N 72°17E **45 J1**
South I. *N.Z.* 44°0S 170°0E **59 F3**
South Indian Lake
  *Canada* 56°47N 98°56W **71 B9**
South Invercargill *N.Z.* 46°26S 168°23E **59 G2**
South Knife → *Canada* 58°55N 94°37W **71 B10**
South Koel → *India* 22°32N 85°14E **43 H11**
South Korea ■ *Asia* 36°0N 128°0E **33 G15**
South Lake Tahoe
  *U.S.A.* 38°57N 119°59W **78 G6**
South Lanarkshire □
  *U.K.* 55°37N 3°53W **11 F5**
South Loup → *U.S.A.* 41°4N 98°39W **80 E4**
South Magnetic Pole
  *Antarctica* 64°8S 138°8E **5 C9**
South Milwaukee
  *U.S.A.* 42°55N 87°52W **80 D10**
South Molton *U.K.* 51°1N 3°51W **13 F4**
South Moose L. *Canada* 53°49N 100°1W **71 C8**
South Nahanni →
  *Canada* 61°3N 123°21W **70 A4**
South Nation → *Canada* 45°34N 75°6W **83 A9**
South Natuna Is. = Natuna
  Selatan, Kepulauan
  *Indonesia* 2°45N 109°0E **36 D3**
South Negril Pt. *Jamaica* 18°16N 78°22W **88 a**
South Orkney Is. *Antarctica* 63°0S 45°0W **5 C18**
South Ossetia □ *Georgia* 42°21N 44°2E **19 F7**
South Otselic *U.S.A.* 42°38N 75°46W **83 D9**
South Pagai, I. = Pagai Selatan,
  Pulau *Indonesia* 3°0S 100°15E **36 E2**
South Paris *U.S.A.* 44°14N 70°31W **83 B14**
South Pittsburg *U.S.A.* 35°1N 85°42W **85 D12**
South Platte → *U.S.A.* 41°7N 100°42W **80 E4**
South Pole *Antarctica* 90°0S 0°0 **5 E**
South Porcupine *Canada* 48°30N 81°12W **72 C3**
South Portland *U.S.A.* 43°38N 70°15W **81 D18**
South Pt. *Barbados* 13°2N 59°32W **89 g**
South Pt. *U.S.A.* 44°52N 83°19W **82 B1**
South River *Canada* 45°52N 79°23W **82 A5**
South River *U.S.A.* 40°27N 74°23W **83 F10**
South Ronaldsay *U.K.* 58°48N 2°58W **11 C6**
South Sandwich Is.
  *Antarctica* 57°0S 27°0W **5 B1**
South Sandwich Trench
  *Atl. Oc.* 56°0S 24°0W **5 B1**
South Saskatchewan →
  *Canada* 53°15N 105°5W **71 C7**
South Seal → *Canada* 58°48N 98°8W **71 B9**
South Sentinel I. *India* 10°59N 92°14E **45 J11**
South Shetland Is.
  *Antarctica* 62°0S 59°0W **5 C18**
South Shields *U.K.* 55°0N 1°25W **12 C6**
South Sioux City *U.S.A.* 42°28N 96°24W **80 D5**
South Sister *U.S.A.* 44°4N 121°51W **76 D3**
South Sudan ■ *Africa* 8°0N 30°0E **53 G11**
South Taranaki Bight
  *N.Z.* 39°40S 174°5E **59 C5**
South Tasman Rise
  *S. Ocean* 48°0S 146°0E **5 A10**
South Thompson →
  *Canada* 50°40N 120°20W **70 C4**
South Twin I. *Canada* 53°7N 79°52W **72 B4**
South Tyne → *U.K.* 54°59N 2°8W **12 C5**
South Uist *U.K.* 57°20N 7°15W **11 D1**
South Valley *U.S.A.* 35°1N 106°41W **77 J10**
South Wellesley Is.
  *Australia* 16°58S 139°17E **62 B2**
South West C. *Australia* 43°34S 146°3E **63 G4**
South West C. *N.Z.* 47°17S 167°28E **59 G1**
South Williamsport
  *U.S.A.* 41°13N 77°0W **82 E8**
South Yorkshire □ *U.K.* 53°27N 1°36W **12 D6**
Southampton *Canada* 44°30N 81°25W **82 B3**
Southampton *U.K.* 50°54N 1°23W **13 G6**
Southampton □ *U.K.* 40°53N 72°23W **83 F12**
Southampton *U.S.A.* 50°54N 1°23W **13 G6**
Southampton I. *Canada* 64°30N 84°0W **69 E15**
Southaven *U.S.A.* 34°59N 90°8W **85 D9**
Southbank *Canada* 54°2N 125°46W **70 C3**
Southbridge *N.Z.* 43°48S 172°16E **59 E4**
Southbridge *U.S.A.* 42°5N 72°2W **83 D12**
Southend *Canada* 56°19N 103°22W **71 B8**
Southend-on-Sea *U.K.* 51°32N 0°44E **13 F8**
Southend-on-Sea □ *U.K.* 51°32N 0°44E **13 F8**
Southern = Yuzhnyy □
  *Russia* 44°0N 40°0E **26 E5**
Southern Alps *N.Z.* 43°41S 170°11E **59 E3**
Southern Cross *Australia* 31°12S 119°15E **61 F2**
Southern Indian L.
  *Canada* 57°10N 98°30W **71 B9**
Southern Lau Group *Fiji* 18°40S 178°40W **59 a**
Southern Ocean 62°0S 60°0E **5 C6**
Southern Pines *U.S.A.* 35°11N 79°24W **85 D15**

Southern Uplands *U.K.* 55°28N 3°52W **11 F5**
Southington *U.S.A.* 41°36N 72°53W **83 E12**
Southland □ *N.Z.* 45°30S 168°0E **59 F1**
Southold *U.S.A.* 41°4N 72°26W **83 E12**
Southport *Australia* 27°58S 153°25E **63 D5**
Southport *U.K.* 53°39N 3°0W **12 D4**
Southport *U.S.A.* 42°3N 76°49W **82 D8**
Southwest △ *Australia* 43°8S 146°5E **63 G4**
Southwest Pacific Basin
  *Pac. Oc.* 40°0S 140°0W **5 A12**
Southwold *U.K.* 52°20N 1°41E **13 E9**
Southwood △ *Australia* 27°48S 150°8E **63 D5**
Soutpansberg *S. Africa* 23°0S 29°30E **57 B4**
Sovetsk *Kaliningrad, Russia* 55°6N 21°50E **9 J19**
Sovetsk *Kirov, Russia* 57°38N 48°53E **18 C8**
Sovetskaya Gavan
  *Russia* 48°58N 140°18E **27 E15**
Sowma'eh Sarā *Iran* 37°17N 49°18E **47 B6**
Sōya-Kaikyō = La Perouse Str.
  *Asia* 45°40N 142°0E **28 B11**
Sōya-Misaki *Japan* 45°30N 141°55E **28 B10**
Soyo *Angola* 6°13S 12°20E **54 F2**
Sozh → *Belarus* 51°57N 30°48E **17 B16**
Spa *Belgium* 50°29N 5°53E **15 D5**
Spaatz I. *Antarctica* 73°10S 75°0W **5 D17**
Spain ■ *Europe* 39°0N 4°0W **21 B4**
Spalding *Australia* 33°30S 138°37E **63 E2**
Spalding *U.K.* 52°48N 0°9W **12 E7**
Spanaway *U.S.A.* 47°6N 122°26W **78 C4**
Spangler *U.S.A.* 40°39N 78°48W **82 F6**
Spanish *Canada* 46°12N 82°20W **72 C3**
Spanish Fork *U.S.A.* 40°7N 111°39W **76 F8**
Spanish Town
  *Br. Virgin Is.* 18°26N 64°26W **89 e**
Spanish Town *Jamaica* 18°0N 76°57W **88 a**
Sparks *U.S.A.* 39°32N 119°45W **78 F7**
Sparta = Sparti *Greece* 37°5N 22°25E **23 F10**
Sparta *Mich., U.S.A.* 43°10N 85°42W **81 D11**
Sparta *N.J., U.S.A.* 41°2N 74°38W **83 E10**
Sparta *Wis., U.S.A.* 43°56N 90°49W **80 D8**
Sparti *Greece* 37°5N 22°25E **23 F10**
Spartanburg *U.S.A.* 34°56N 81°57W **85 D14**
Spartivento, C. *Calabria,*
  *Italy* 37°55N 16°4E **22 F7**
Spartivento, C. *Sard., Italy* 38°53N 8°50E **22 E3**
Sparwood *Canada* 49°44N 114°53W **70 D6**
Spassk-Dalniy *Russia* 44°40N 132°48E **28 B6**
Spatha, Akra *Greece* 35°42N 23°43E **23 G10**
Spatsizi → *Canada* 57°42N 128°7W **70 B3**
Spatsizi Plateau Wilderness △
  *Canada* 57°40N 128°0W **70 B3**
Spean → *U.K.* 56°55N 4°59W **11 E4**
Spearfish *U.S.A.* 44°30N 103°52W **80 C2**
Spearman *U.S.A.* 36°12N 101°12W **84 C4**
Speculator *U.S.A.* 43°30N 74°22W **83 C10**
Speightstown *Barbados* 13°15N 59°39W **89 g**
Spence Bay = Taloyoak
  *Canada* 69°32N 93°32W **68 D13**
Spencer *Idaho, U.S.A.* 44°22N 112°11W **76 D7**
Spencer *Iowa, U.S.A.* 43°9N 95°9W **80 D6**
Spencer *N.Y., U.S.A.* 42°13N 76°30W **83 D8**
Spencer *Nebr., U.S.A.* 42°53N 98°42W **80 D4**
Spencer, C. *Australia* 35°20S 136°53E **63 F2**
Spencer B. *Namibia* 25°30S 14°47E **56 C1**
Spencer G. *Australia* 34°0S 137°20E **63 E2**
Spencerville *Canada* 44°51N 75°33W **83 B9**
Spences Bridge *Canada* 50°25N 121°20W **70 C4**
Spennymoor *U.K.* 54°42N 1°36W **12 C6**
Spenser Mts. *N.Z.* 42°15S 172°45E **59 E4**
Sperrgebiet △ *Namibia* 27°38S 15°56E **56 C2**
Sperrin Mts. *U.K.* 54°50N 7°0W **10 B5**
Spey → *U.K.* 57°40N 3°6W **11 D5**
Speyer *Germany* 49°29N 8°25E **16 D5**
Spezand *Pakistan* 29°59N 67°0E **42 E2**
Spiddal *Ireland* 53°15N 9°18W **10 C2**
Spin Būldak *Afghan.* 31°1N 66°25E **42 D2**
Spinifex ◎ *Australia* 28°30S 128°30E **61 E4**
Spirit Lake *U.S.A.* 46°15N 122°9W **78 D4**
Spirit River *Canada* 55°45N 118°50W **70 B5**
Spiritwood *Canada* 53°24N 107°33W **71 C7**
Spithead *U.K.* 50°45N 1°10W **13 G6**
Spitsbergen = Svalbard
  *Arctic* 78°0N 17°0E **4 B8**
Spjelkavik *Norway* 62°28N 6°22E **8 E12**
Split *Croatia* 43°31N 16°26E **22 C7**
Split L. *Canada* 56°8N 96°15W **71 B9**
Split Lake *Canada* 56°8N 96°15W **71 B9**
Spofford *U.S.A.* 29°10N 100°25W **84 G4**
Spokane *U.S.A.* 47°40N 117°24W **76 C5**
Spoleto *Italy* 42°44N 12°44E **22 C5**
Spooner *U.S.A.* 45°50N 91°53W **80 C8**
Sporyy Navolok, Mys
  *Russia* 75°50N 68°40E **26 B7**
Sprague *U.S.A.* 47°18N 117°59W **76 C5**
Spratly I. *S. China Sea* 8°38N 111°55E **36 C4**
Spratly Is. *S. China Sea* 8°20N 112°0E **36 C4**
Spray *U.S.A.* 44°50N 119°48W **76 D4**
Spree → *Germany* 52°32N 13°12E **16 B7**
Sprengisandur *Iceland* 64°52N 18°7W **8 D5**
Spring City *U.S.A.* 40°11N 75°33W **83 F9**
Spring Creek *U.S.A.* 40°44N 115°35W **76 F6**
Spring Garden *U.S.A.* 39°52N 120°47W **78 F6**
Spring Hall *Barbados* 13°18N 59°36W **89 g**
Spring Hill *U.S.A.* 28°27N 82°41W **85 G13**
Spring Mts. *U.S.A.* 36°0N 115°45W **79 J11**
Spring Temple Buddha
  *China* 33°46N 112°27E **32 H7**
Spring Valley *U.S.A.* 32°44N 116°59W **79 N10**
Springbok *S. Africa* 29°42S 17°54E **56 C2**
Springboro *U.S.A.* 41°48N 80°22W **82 E4**
Springdale *Canada* 49°30N 56°6W **73 C8**
Springdale *U.S.A.* 36°11N 94°8W **84 C7**
Springer *U.S.A.* 36°22N 104°36W **77 H11**
Springerville *U.S.A.* 34°8N 109°17W **77 J9**
Springfield *Canada* 42°50N 80°56W **82 D4**
Springfield *N.Z.* 43°19S 171°56E **59 E3**
Springfield *Colo.,*
  *U.S.A.* 37°24N 102°37W **77 H12**
Springfield *Ill., U.S.A.* 39°48N 89°39W **80 F10**
Springfield *Mass., U.S.A.* 42°6N 72°35W **83 D12**
Springfield *Mo., U.S.A.* 37°13N 93°17W **80 G7**

Springfield *Ohio, U.S.A.* 39°55N 83°49W **81 F12**
Springfield *Oreg., U.S.A.* 44°3N 123°1W **76 D2**
Springfield *Tenn., U.S.A.* 36°31N 86°53W **85 C11**
Springfield *Vt., U.S.A.* 43°18N 72°29W **83 C12**
Springfontein *S. Africa* 30°15S 25°40E **56 D4**
Springhill *Canada* 45°40N 64°4W **73 C7**
Springhill *U.S.A.* 33°0N 93°28W **84 E8**
Springhouse *Canada* 51°56N 122°7W **70 C4**
Springlands = Corriverton
  *Guyana* 5°55N 57°20W **92 B7**
Springs *S. Africa* 26°13S 28°25E **57 C4**
Springsure *Australia* 24°8S 148°6E **62 C4**
Springvale *Australia* 43°28N 70°48W **83 C14**
Springville *Calif., U.S.A.* 36°8N 118°49W **78 J8**
Springville *N.Y., U.S.A.* 42°31N 78°40W **82 D6**
Springville *Utah, U.S.A.* 40°10N 111°37W **76 F8**
Springwater *U.S.A.* 42°38N 77°35W **82 D7**
Spruce-Creek *U.S.A.* 40°36N 78°9W **82 F6**
Spruce Knob-Seneca Rocks △
  *U.S.A.* 38°50N 79°30W **81 F14**
Spruce Mt. *U.S.A.* 44°12N 72°19W **83 B12**
Sprucedale *Canada* 45°29N 79°28W **82 A5**
Spur *U.S.A.* 33°28N 100°52W **84 E4**
Spurn Hd. *U.K.* 53°35N 0°8E **12 D8**
Spuzzum *Canada* 49°37N 121°23W **70 D4**
Squam L. *U.S.A.* 43°45N 71°32W **83 C13**
Squamish *Canada* 49°45N 123°10W **70 D4**
Square Islands *Canada* 52°47N 55°47W **73 B8**
Squires, Mt. *Australia* 26°14S 127°28E **61 E4**
Srbija = Serbia ■ *Europe* 43°20N 20°0E **23 B9**
Sre Ambel *Cambodia* 11°8N 103°46E **39 G4**
Sre Khtum *Cambodia* 12°10N 106°52E **39 F6**
Sre Umbell = Sre Ambel
  *Cambodia* 11°8N 103°46E **39 G4**
Srebrenica *Bos.-H.* 44°6N 19°18E **23 B8**
Sredinnyy Khrebet
  *Russia* 57°0N 160°0E **27 D17**
Sredinnyy Ra. = Sredinnyy
  Khrebet *Russia* 57°0N 160°0E **27 D17**
Srednekolymsk *Russia* 67°27N 153°40E **27 C16**
Sredniy Khrebet *Russia* 42°35N 118°40W **76 E4**
Śrem *Poland* 52°6N 17°2E **17 B9**
Sremska Mitrovica *Serbia* 44°59N 19°38E **23 B8**
Srepok → *Cambodia* 13°33N 106°16E **38 F6**
Sretensk *Russia* 52°10N 117°40E **27 D12**
Sri Aman = Bandar Sri Aman
  *Malaysia* 1°15N 111°32E **36 D4**
Sri Kalahasti *India* 13°45N 79°44E **45 H4**
Sri Lanka ■ *Asia* 7°30N 80°50E **45 L5**
Sri Pada = Adam's Peak
  *Sri Lanka* 6°48N 80°30E **45 L5**
Sriharikota I. *India* 13°40N 80°20E **45 H5**
Srikakulam *India* 18°14N 83°58E **44 E6**
Srinagar *India* 34°5N 74°50E **43 B6**
Srivardhan *India* 18°4N 73°3E **44 E1**
Srivilliputtur *India* 9°31N 77°40E **45 K3**
Srono *Indonesia* 8°24S 114°16E **37 J17**
Srungavarapukota *India* 18°7N 83°10E **44 E6**
Staaten → *Australia* 16°24S 141°17E **62 B3**
Staaten River △
  *Australia* 16°15S 142°40E **62 B3**
Stabbursdalen △ *Norway* 70°5N 24°15E **8 A21**
Stade *Germany* 53°35N 9°29E **16 B5**
Stadskanaal *Neths.* 53°4N 6°55E **15 A6**
Staffa *U.K.* 56°27N 6°21W **11 E2**
Stafford *U.K.* 52°49N 2°7W **12 E5**
Stafford *U.S.A.* 37°58N 98°36W **80 G4**
Stafford Springs *U.S.A.* 41°57N 72°18W **83 E12**
Staffordshire □ *U.K.* 52°53N 2°10W **12 E5**
Staines-upon-Thames
  *U.K.* 51°26N 0°29W **13 F7**
Stakhanov *Ukraine* 48°35N 38°40E **19 E6**
Stalowa Wola *Poland* 50°34N 22°3E **17 C12**
Stalybridge *U.K.* 53°28N 2°3W **12 D5**
Stamford *Australia* 21°15S 143°46E **62 C3**
Stamford *U.K.* 52°39N 0°29W **13 E7**
Stamford *Conn., U.S.A.* 41°3N 73°32W **83 E11**
Stamford *N.Y., U.S.A.* 42°25N 74°38W **83 D10**
Stamford *Tex., U.S.A.* 32°57N 99°48W **84 E5**
Stampriet *Namibia* 24°20S 18°28E **56 B2**
Stamps *U.S.A.* 33°22N 93°30W **84 E8**
Standerton *S. Africa* 26°55S 29°7E **57 C4**
Standish *U.S.A.* 43°59N 83°57W **81 D12**
Stanford *S. Africa* 34°26S 19°29E **56 D2**
Stanford *U.S.A.* 47°9N 110°13W **76 C8**
Stanger *S. Africa* 29°27S 31°14E **57 C5**
Stanislaus → *U.S.A.* 37°40N 121°14W **78 H5**
Stanke Dimitrov *Bulgaria* 42°17N 23°9E **23 C10**
Stanley *Australia* 40°46S 145°19E **63 G4**
Stanley *Falk. Is.* 51°40S 59°51W **96 G5**
Stanley *U.K.* 54°53N 1°41W **12 C6**
Stanley *Idaho, U.S.A.* 44°13N 114°56W **76 D6**
Stanley *N. Dak., U.S.A.* 48°19N 102°23W **80 A2**
Stanley *N.Y., U.S.A.* 42°48N 77°6W **82 D7**
Stanley Mission *Canada* 55°25N 104°33W **71 B8**
Stanley Res. *India* 11°50N 77°40E **45 J3**
Stanovoy Khrebet *Russia* 55°0N 130°0E **27 D14**
Stanovoy Ra. = Stanovoy Khrebet
  *Russia* 55°0N 130°0E **27 D14**
Stansmore Ra. *Australia* 21°23S 128°33E **60 D4**
Stansted, London ✈ (STN)
  *U.K.* 51°54N 0°14E **13 F8**
Stanthorpe *Australia* 28°36S 151°59E **63 D5**
Stanton *U.S.A.* 32°8N 101°48W **84 E4**
Stanwood *U.S.A.* 48°15N 122°23W **78 B4**
Staples *Canada* 42°10N 82°35W **82 D2**
Stapleton *U.S.A.* 41°29N 100°31W **80 E3**
Star City *Canada* 52°50N 104°20W **71 C8**
Star Lake *U.S.A.* 44°10N 75°2W **83 B9**
Stara Planina *Bulgaria* 43°15N 23°0E **23 C10**
Stara Zagora *Bulgaria* 42°26N 25°39E **23 C11**
Starachowice *Poland* 51°3N 21°2E **17 C11**
Staraya Russa *Russia* 57°58N 31°23E **18 C5**
Starbuck I. *Kiribati* 5°37S 155°55W **65 H12**
Starcke △ *Australia* 14°56S 145°2E **62 A4**
Stargard Szczeciński
  *Poland* 53°20N 15°0E **16 B8**
Staritsa *Russia* 56°33N 34°55E **18 C5**

Starke *U.S.A.* 29°57N 82°7W **85 G13**
Starkville *U.S.A.* 33°28N 88°49W **85 E10**
Starogard Gdański
  *Poland* 53°59N 18°30E **17 B10**
Starokonstantinov =
  Starokonstyantyniv
  *Ukraine* 49°48N 27°10E **17 D14**
Starokonstyantyniv
  *Ukraine* 49°48N 27°10E **17 D14**
Start B. *U.K.* 50°13N 3°39W **13 G4**
Staryy Chartoryysk
  *Ukraine* 51°15N 25°54E **17 C13**
Staryy Oskol *Russia* 51°19N 37°55E **19 D6**
State College *U.S.A.* 40°48N 77°52W **82 F7**
Stateline *U.S.A.* 38°57N 119°56W **78 G7**
Staten, I. = Estados, I. de Los
  *Argentina* 54°40S 64°30W **96 G4**
Staten I. *U.S.A.* 40°35N 74°9W **83 F10**
Statesboro *U.S.A.* 32°27N 81°47W **85 E14**
Statesville *U.S.A.* 35°47N 80°53W **85 D14**
Statia = St. Eustatius
  *W. Indies* 17°20N 63°0W **89 C7**
Stauffer *U.S.A.* 34°45N 119°3W **79 L7**
Staunton *Ill., U.S.A.* 39°1N 89°47W **80 F9**
Staunton *Va., U.S.A.* 38°9N 79°4W **81 F14**
Stavanger *Norway* 58°57N 5°40E **9 G11**
Staveley *N.Z.* 43°40S 171°32E **59 E3**
Stavelot *Belgium* 50°23N 5°55E **15 D5**
Stavern *Norway* 59°0N 10°1E **9 G14**
Staveren *Neths.* 52°53N 5°22E **15 B5**
Stavropol *Russia* 45°5N 42°0E **19 E7**
Stawell *Australia* 37°5S 142°47E **63 F3**
Stawell → *Australia* 20°20S 142°55E **62 C3**
Stayner *Canada* 44°25N 80°5W **82 B4**
Stayton *U.S.A.* 44°48N 122°48W **76 D2**
Steamboat Springs
  *U.S.A.* 40°29N 106°50W **76 F10**
Steele *U.S.A.* 46°51N 99°55W **80 B4**
Steelton *U.S.A.* 40°14N 76°50W **82 F8**
Steen River *Canada* 59°40N 117°12W **70 B5**
Steens Mt. *U.S.A.* 42°35N 118°40W **76 E4**
Steenwijk *Neths.* 52°47N 6°7E **15 B6**
Steep Pt. *Australia* 26°8S 113°8E **61 E1**
Steep Rock *Canada* 51°30N 98°48W **71 C9**
Stefanie L. = Chew Bahir
  *Ethiopia* 4°40N 36°50E **49 G2**
Stefansson Bay *Antarctica* 67°20S 59°8E **5 C5**
Stefansson I. *Canada* 73°20N 105°45W **69 C10**
Steiermark □ *Austria* 47°26N 15°0E **16 E8**
Steilacoom *U.S.A.* 47°10N 122°36W **78 C4**
Steilrandberge *Namibia* 17°45S 13°20E **56 A1**
Steinbach *Canada* 49°32N 96°40W **71 D9**
Steinhausen *Namibia* 21°49S 18°20E **56 B2**
Steinkjer *Norway* 64°1N 11°31E **8 D14**
Steinkopf *S. Africa* 29°18S 17°43E **56 C2**
Stellarton *Canada* 45°32N 62°30W **73 C7**
Stellenbosch *S. Africa* 33°58S 18°50E **56 D2**
Stendal *Germany* 52°36N 11°53E **16 B6**
Steornabhaigh = Stornoway
  *U.K.* 58°13N 6°23W **11 C2**
Stepanakert = Xankändi
  *Azerbaijan* 39°52N 46°49E **46 B5**
Stephens Creek *Australia* 31°50S 141°30E **63 E3**
Stephens I. *Canada* 54°10N 130°45W **70 C2**
Stephens L. *Canada* 56°32N 95°0W **71 B9**
Stephenville *Canada* 48°31N 58°35W **73 C8**
Stephenville *U.S.A.* 32°13N 98°12W **84 E5**
Steppe *Asia* 50°0N 50°0E **24 C7**
Sterkstroom *S. Africa* 31°32S 26°32E **56 D4**
Sterling *Colo., U.S.A.* 40°37N 103°13W **76 F12**
Sterling *Ill., U.S.A.* 41°48N 89°42W **80 E9**
Sterling *Kans., U.S.A.* 38°13N 98°12W **80 F4**
Sterling City *U.S.A.* 31°51N 101°0W **84 F4**
Sterling Heights *U.S.A.* 42°35N 83°2W **81 D12**
Sterling Run *U.S.A.* 41°25N 78°12W **82 E6**
Sterlitamak *Russia* 53°40N 56°0E **18 D10**
Stettin = Szczecin *Poland* 53°27N 14°27E **16 B8**
Stettiner Haff *Germany* 53°47N 14°15E **16 B8**
Stettler *Canada* 52°19N 112°40W **70 C6**
Steubenville *U.S.A.* 40°22N 80°37W **82 F4**
Stevenage *U.K.* 51°55N 0°13W **13 F7**
Stevens Point *U.S.A.* 44°31N 89°34W **80 C9**
Stevenson → *Australia* 27°6S 135°33E **63 D2**
Stevenson L. *Canada* 53°55N 96°0W **71 C9**
Stevensville *U.S.A.* 46°30N 114°5W **76 C6**
Stewart *Canada* 55°56N 129°57W **70 B3**
Stewart *U.S.A.* 39°5N 119°46W **78 F7**
Stewart → *Canada* 63°19N 139°26W **68 E4**
Stewart, I. *Chile* 54°50S 71°15W **96 G2**
Stewart, I. *N.Z.* 46°58S 167°54E **59 G1**
Stewarts Point *U.S.A.* 38°39N 123°24W **78 G3**
Stewartville *U.S.A.* 43°51N 92°29W **80 D7**
Stewiacke *Canada* 45°9N 63°22W **73 C7**
Steynsburg *S. Africa* 31°15S 25°49E **56 D4**
Steyr *Austria* 48°3N 14°25E **16 D8**
Steytlerville *S. Africa* 33°17S 24°19E **56 D3**
Stigler *U.S.A.* 35°15N 95°8W **84 D7**
Stikine → *Canada* 56°40N 132°30W **70 B2**
Stilfontein *S. Africa* 26°51S 26°50E **56 D4**
Stillwater *N.Z.* 42°27S 171°20E **59 E3**
Stillwater *N.Y., U.S.A.* 42°55N 73°41W **83 D11**
Stillwater *Okla., U.S.A.* 36°7N 97°4W **84 C6**
Stillwater Range *U.S.A.* 39°50N 118°5W **76 G4**
Stillwater Res. *U.S.A.* 43°54N 75°3W **83 C9**
Stilwell *U.S.A.* 35°49N 94°38W **84 D7**
Stînga Nistrului = Transnistria □
  *Moldova* 47°20N 29°15E **17 E15**
Ştip *Macedonia* 41°42N 22°10E **23 D10**
Stirling *Canada* 44°18N 77°33W **82 B7**
Stirling *U.K.* 56°8N 3°57W **11 E5**
Stirling □ *U.K.* 56°12N 4°18W **11 E4**
Stirling Ra. *Australia* 34°23S 118°0E **61 F2**
Stirling Range △
  *Australia* 34°26S 118°20E **61 F2**
Stittsville *Canada* 45°15N 75°55W **83 A9**
Stjernøya *Norway* 70°20N 22°40E **8 A20**
Stjørdalshalsen *Norway* 63°29N 10°51E **8 E14**
Stockerau *Austria* 48°24N 16°12E **16 D9**
Stockport *U.K.* 53°25N 2°9W **12 D5**

Stocksbridge *U.K.* 53°29N 1°35W **12 D6**
Stockton *Calif., U.S.A.* 37°58N 121°17W **78 H5**
Stockton *Kans., U.S.A.* 39°26N 99°16W **80 F4**
Stockton *Mo., U.S.A.* 37°42N 93°48W **80 G7**
Stockton-on-Tees *U.K.* 54°35N 1°19W **12 C6**
Stockton-on-Tees □ *U.K.* 54°35N 1°19W **12 C6**
Stockton Plateau
  *U.S.A.* 30°30N 102°30W **84 F3**
Stoeng Treng *Cambodia* 13°31N 105°58E **38 F5**
Stoer, Pt. of *U.K.* 58°16N 5°23W **11 C3**
Stoke-on-Trent *U.K.* 53°1N 2°11W **12 D5**
Stoke-on-Trent □ *U.K.* 53°1N 2°11W **12 D5**
Stokes △ *Australia* 33°45S 121°11E **61 F3**
Stokes Bay *Canada* 45°0N 81°28W **82 B3**
Stokes Pt. *Australia* 40°10S 143°56E **63 G3**
Stokes Ra. *Australia* 15°50S 130°50E **60 C5**
Stokksnes *Iceland* 64°14N 14°58W **8 D6**
Stokmarknes *Norway* 68°34N 14°54E **8 B16**
Stolac *Bos.-H.* 43°5N 17°59E **23 C7**
Stolbovoy, Ostrov
  *Russia* 74°44N 135°14E **27 B14**
Stolbtsy = Stowbtsy
  *Belarus* 53°30N 26°43E **17 B14**
Stolin *Belarus* 51°53N 26°50E **17 C14**
Stone *U.K.* 52°55N 2°9W **12 E5**
Stoneboro *U.S.A.* 41°20N 80°7W **82 E4**
Stonehaven *U.K.* 56°59N 2°12W **11 E6**
Stonehenge *Australia* 24°22S 143°17E **62 C3**
Stonehenge *U.K.* 51°9N 1°45W **13 F6**
Stonewall *Canada* 50°10N 97°19W **71 C9**
Stony L. *Man., Canada* 58°51N 98°40W **71 B9**
Stony L. *Ont., Canada* 44°30N 78°5W **82 B6**
Stony Point *U.S.A.* 41°14N 73°59W **83 E11**
Stony Pt. *U.S.A.* 43°50N 76°18W **83 C8**
Stony Rapids *Canada* 59°16N 105°50W **71 B7**
Stony Tunguska = Tunguska,
  Podkamennaya →
  *Russia* 61°50N 90°13E **27 C10**
Stonyford *U.S.A.* 39°23N 122°33W **78 F4**
Stora Lulevatten *Sweden* 67°10N 19°30E **8 C18**
Stora Sjöfallet △ *Sweden* 67°36N 17°45E **8 C17**
Storavan *Sweden* 65°45N 18°10E **8 D18**
Stord *Norway* 59°52N 5°23E **9 G11**
Store Bælt *Denmark* 55°20N 11°0E **9 J14**
Storkerson Pen.
  *Canada* 72°30N 106°30W **68 C10**
Storm B. *Australia* 43°10S 147°30E **63 G4**
Storm Lake *U.S.A.* 42°39N 95°13W **80 D6**
Stormberge *S. Africa* 31°16S 26°17E **56 D4**
Stormsrivier *S. Africa* 33°59S 23°52E **56 D3**
Stornoway *U.K.* 58°13N 6°23W **11 C2**
Storozhinets = Storozhynets
  *Ukraine* 48°14N 25°45E **17 D13**
Storozhynets *Ukraine* 48°14N 25°45E **17 D13**
Storrs *U.S.A.* 41°49N 72°15W **83 E12**
Storsjön *Sweden* 63°9N 14°30E **8 E16**
Storuman *Sweden* 65°5N 17°10E **8 D17**
Storuman, L. *Sweden* 65°13N 16°50E **8 D17**
Stouffville *Canada* 43°58N 79°15W **82 C5**
Stoughton *Canada* 49°40N 103°0W **71 D8**
Stour → *Dorset, U.K.* 50°43N 1°47W **13 G6**
Stour → *Kent, U.K.* 51°18N 1°22E **13 F9**
Stour → *Suffolk, U.K.* 51°57N 1°4E **13 F9**
Stourbridge *U.K.* 52°28N 2°8W **13 E5**
Stout L. *Canada* 52°0N 94°40W **71 C10**
Stove Pipe Wells Village
  *U.S.A.* 36°35N 117°11W **79 J9**
Stow *U.S.A.* 41°10N 81°27W **82 E3**
Stowbtsy *Belarus* 53°30N 26°43E **17 B14**
Stowmarket *U.K.* 52°12N 1°0E **13 E9**
Strabane *U.K.* 54°50N 7°27W **10 B4**
Strahan *Australia* 42°9S 145°20E **63 G4**
Stralsund *Germany* 54°18N 13°4E **16 A7**
Strand *S. Africa* 34°9S 18°48E **56 D2**
Stranda *Møre og Romsdal,*
  *Norway* 62°19N 6°58E **8 E12**
Stranda *Nord-Trøndelag,*
  *Norway* 63°33N 10°14E **8 E14**
Strangford L. *U.K.* 54°30N 5°37W **10 B6**
Stranorlar *Ireland* 54°48N 7°46W **10 B4**
Stranraer *U.K.* 54°54N 5°1W **11 G3**
Strasbourg *Canada* 51°4N 104°55W **71 C8**
Strasbourg *France* 48°35N 7°42E **20 B7**
Stratford *Canada* 43°23N 81°0W **82 C4**
Stratford *N.Z.* 39°20S 174°19E **59 C5**
Stratford *Calif., U.S.A.* 36°11N 119°49W **78 J7**
Stratford *Conn., U.S.A.* 41°12N 73°8W **83 E11**
Stratford *Tex., U.S.A.* 36°20N 102°4W **84 C3**
Stratford-upon-Avon
  *U.K.* 52°12N 1°42W **13 E6**
Strath Spey *U.K.* 57°9N 3°49W **11 D5**
Strathalbyn *Australia* 35°13S 138°53E **63 F2**
Strathaven *U.K.* 55°40N 4°5W **11 F4**
Strathcona △ *Canada* 49°38N 125°40W **70 D3**
Strathmore *Canada* 51°5N 113°18W **70 C6**
Strathmore *U.K.* 56°37N 3°7W **11 E5**
Strathmore *U.S.A.* 36°9N 119°4W **78 J7**
Strathnaver *Canada* 53°20N 122°33W **70 C4**
Strathpeffer *U.K.* 57°35N 4°32W **11 D4**
Strathroy *Canada* 42°58N 81°38W **82 D3**
Strathy Pt. *U.K.* 58°36N 4°1W **11 C4**
Strattanville *U.S.A.* 41°12N 79°19W **82 E5**
Stratton *U.S.A.* 45°8N 70°26W **83 A14**
Stratton Mt. *U.S.A.* 43°4N 72°55W **83 C12**
Straubing *Germany* 48°52N 12°34E **16 D7**
Straumnes *Iceland* 66°26N 23°8W **8 C2**
Strawberry → *U.S.A.* 40°10N 110°24W **76 F8**
Strawberry *U.S.A.* 32°48S 134°13E **63 E1**
Streaky Bay *Australia* 32°51S 134°18E **63 E1**
Streator *U.S.A.* 41°8N 88°50W **80 E9**
Streetsboro *U.S.A.* 41°14N 81°21W **82 E3**
Streetsville *Canada* 43°35N 79°42W **82 C5**
Streng → *Cambodia* 13°12N 103°37E **38 F4**
Streymoy *Færoe Is.* 62°8N 7°5W **8 E9**
Strezhevoy *Russia* 60°42N 77°34E **26 C8**
Strimonas → *Greece* 40°46N 23°51E **23 D10**
Strokestown *Ireland* 53°47N 8°5W **10 C3**
Stroma *U.K.* 58°41N 3°7W **11 C5**
Strómboli *Italy* 38°47N 15°13E **22 E6**
Stromeferry *U.K.* 57°21N 5°33W **11 D3**

Stromness U.K. 58°58N 3°17W 11 C5
Stromsberg U.S.A. 41°7N 97°36W 80 E5
Strömstad Sweden 58°56N 11°10E 9 G14
Strongsville U.S.A. 41°19N 81°50W 82 E3
Stronsay U.K. 59°7N 2°35W 11 B6
Stroud U.K. 51°45N 2°13W 13 F5
Stroud Road Australia 32°18S 151°57E 63 E5
Stroudsburg U.S.A. 40°59N 75°12W 83 F9
Struer Denmark 56°30N 8°35E 9 H13
Strugi Krasnyye Russia 58°21N 29°1E 9 G23
Strumica Macedonia 41°28N 22°41E 23 D10
Struthers U.S.A. 41°4N 80°39W 82 E4
Stryker U.S.A. 48°41N 114°46W 76 B6
Stryy Ukraine 49°16N 23°48E 17 D12
Strzelecki Cr. → Australia 29°37S 139°59E 63 D2
Strzelecki Desert Australia 29°30S 140°0E 63 D3
Stuart Fla., U.S.A. 27°12N 80°15W 85 H14
Stuart Nebr., U.S.A. 42°36N 99°8W 80 D4
Stuart → Canada 54°0N 123°35W 70 C4
Stuart Bluff Ra. Australia 22°50S 131°52E 60 D5
Stuart I. U.S.A. 63°35N 162°30W 74 C7
Stuart L. Canada 54°30N 124°30W 70 C4
Stuart Ra. Australia 29°10S 134°56E 63 D1
Stull L. Canada 54°24N 92°34W 72 B1
Stung Treng = Stoeng Treng Cambodia 13°31N 105°58E 38 F5
Stupart → Canada 56°0N 93°25W 72 A1
Sturge I. Antarctica 67°26S 164°47E 5 C11
Sturgeon B. Canada 52°0N 97°50W 71 C9
Sturgeon Bay U.S.A. 44°50N 87°23W 80 C1
Sturgeon Falls Canada 46°25N 79°57W 72 C4
Sturgeon L. Alta., Canada 55°6N 117°32W 70 B5
Sturgeon L. Ont., Canada 50°0N 90°45W 72 C1
Sturgeon L. Ont., Canada 44°28N 78°43W 82 B6
Sturgis Canada 51°56N 102°36W 71 C8
Sturgis Mich., U.S.A. 41°48N 85°25W 81 E11
Sturgis S. Dak., U.S.A. 44°25N 103°31W 80 C2
Sturt △ Australia 27°17S 141°37E 63 D3
Sturt Cr. → Australia 19°8S 127°50E 60 C4
Sturt Stony Desert Australia 28°30S 141°0E 63 D3
Stutterheim S. Africa 32°33S 27°28E 56 D4
Stuttgart Germany 48°48N 9°11E 16 D5
Stuttgart U.S.A. 34°30N 91°33W 84 D9
Stuyvesant U.S.A. 42°23N 73°45W 83 D11
Stykkishólmur Iceland 65°2N 22°40W 8 D2
Styria = Steiermark □ Austria 47°26N 15°0E 16 E8
Su Xian = Suzhou China 33°41N 116°59E 32 H9
Suakin Sudan 19°8N 37°20E 53 E13
Suamico U.S.A. 44°38N 88°2W 80 C9
Suan N. Korea 38°42N 126°22E 33 E14
Suana Indonesia 8°44S 115°36E 37 K18
Suar India 29°2N 79°3E 43 E8
Şuḃa Si. Arabia 27°10N 35°40E 46 E2
Subang Indonesia 6°34S 107°45E 37 G12
Subansiri → India 26°48N 93°50E 41 F18
Subarnagiri India 19°50N 83°54E 44 E6
Subarnarekha → India 22°34N 87°24E 43 H12
Subayhah Si. Arabia 30°2N 38°50E 46 D3
Subi Indonesia 2°58N 108°50E 36 D3
Subotica Serbia 46°6N 19°39E 23 A8
Suceava Romania 47°38N 26°16E 17 E14
Suchan = Partizansk Russia 43°8N 133°9E 27 E14
Suchil Mexico 23°39N 103°54W 86 C4
Suchou = Suzhou China 31°19N 120°38E 35 B13
Süchow = Xuzhou China 34°18N 117°10E 33 G9
Suck → Ireland 53°17N 8°3W 10 C3
Sucre Bolivia 19°0S 65°15W 92 G5
Sucuriú → Brazil 20°47S 51°38W 93 H8
Sud, Pte. du Canada 49°3N 62°14W 73 C7
Sud-Ouest, Pte. Canada 49°23N 63°36W 73 C7
Sud Ouest, Pte. Mauritius 20°28S 57°18E 55 d
Sudan U.S.A. 34°4N 102°31W 84 D3
Sudan ■ Africa 15°0N 30°0E 53 E11
Sudbury Canada 46°30N 81°0W 72 C3
Sudbury U.K. 52°2N 0°45E 13 E8
Sudd South Sudan 8°20N 30°0E 53 G12
Sudeten Mts. = Sudety Europe 50°20N 16°45E 17 C9
Sudety Europe 50°20N 16°45E 17 C9
Suðuroy Færoe Is. 61°32N 6°50W 8 F9
Sudirman, Pegunungan Indonesia 4°30S 137°0E 37 E9
Sudong, Pulau Singapore 1°13N 103°44E 39 d
Sueca Spain 39°12N 0°21W 21 C5
Suemez I. U.S.A. 55°15N 133°20W 70 B2
Suez = El Suweis Egypt 29°58N 32°31E 53 C12
Suez, G. of = Suweis, Khalîg el Egypt 28°40N 33°0E 53 C12
Suez Canal = Suweis, Qanâ es Egypt 31°0N 32°20E 53 B12
Suffield Canada 50°12N 111°10W 70 C6
Suffolk U.S.A. 36°44N 76°35W 81 G15
Suffolk □ U.K. 52°16N 1°0E 13 E9
Sugag = Sagaing Myanmar 21°52N 95°59E 41 J19
Sugar Grove U.S.A. 41°59N 79°20W 82 E5
Sugarcreek U.S.A. 41°25N 79°52W 82 E5
Sugarive → India 26°16N 86°24E 43 F12
Sugluk = Salluit Canada 62°14N 75°38W 69 E16
Şuḩār Oman 24°20N 56°40E 47 E8
Sühbaatar Mongolia 50°17N 106°10E 30 A10
Sühbaatar □ Mongolia 45°30N 114°0E 32 B8
Suheli Par India 10°5N 72°17E 45 J1
Suhl Germany 50°36N 10°42E 16 C6
Sui Pakistan 28°37N 69°19E 42 E3
Sui Xian China 34°25N 115°2E 32 G8
Suichang China 28°29N 119°15E 35 C12
Suichuan China 26°20N 114°32E 35 D10
Suide China 37°30N 110°12E 32 F6
Suifenhe China 44°25N 131°10E 33 B16
Suihua China 46°32N 126°55E 31 B14
Suijiang China 28°40N 103°59E 34 C4
Suining Hunan, China 26°35N 110°10E 35 D8
Suining Jiangsu, China 33°56N 117°58E 33 H9
Suining Sichuan, China 30°26N 105°35E 34 B5
Suiping China 33°10N 113°59E 32 H7
Suir → Ireland 52°16N 7°9W 10 D4
Suisse = Switzerland ■ Europe 46°30N 8°0E 20 C8
Suisun City U.S.A. 38°15N 122°2W 78 G4
Suixi China 30°10N 118°18E 35 B12
Suiyang Guizhou, China 27°58N 107°18E 34 D6
Suiyang Heilongjiang, China 44°30N 130°56E 33 B16
Suizhong China 40°21N 120°20E 33 D11
Suizhou China 31°42N 113°24E 35 B9
Sujangarh India 27°42N 74°31E 42 F6
Sujiatun China 41°39N 123°20E 33 D12
Sukabumi Indonesia 6°56S 106°50E 37 G12
Sukadana Indonesia 1°10S 110°0E 36 E4
Sukagawa Japan 37°17N 140°23E 29 F10
Sukamade Indonesia 8°30S 113°52E 37 H15
Sukaraja Indonesia 2°28S 110°25E 36 E4
Sukarno-Hatta Int., Jakarta ✈ (CGK) Indonesia 6°7S 106°40E 37 G12
Sukawati Indonesia 8°35S 115°17E 37 K18
Sukch'ŏn N. Korea 39°22N 125°35E 33 E13
Sukhona → Russia 61°15N 46°39E 18 C6
Sukhothai Thailand 17°1N 99°49E 38 D2
Sukhumi = Sokhumi Georgia 43°0N 41°0E 19 F7
Sukkur Pakistan 27°42N 68°54E 42 F3
Sukkur Barrage Pakistan 27°40N 68°50E 42 F3
Sukma India 18°24N 81°45E 44 E5
Sukri → India 25°4N 71°43E 42 G4
Sukumo Japan 32°56N 132°44E 29 H6
Sukunka → Canada 55°45N 121°15W 70 B4
Sula, Kepulauan Indonesia 1°45S 125°0E 37 E7
Sulaco → Honduras 15°2N 87°44W 88 C2
Sulaiman Range Pakistan 30°30N 69°50E 42 D3
Sülär Iran 31°53N 51°54E 47 D6
Sulawesi Indonesia 2°0S 120°0E 37 E6
Sulawesi Barat □ Indonesia 3°0S 119°0E 37 E5
Sulawesi Sea = Celebes Sea Indonesia 3°0N 123°0E 37 D6
Sulawesi Selatan □ Indonesia 2°30S 120°0E 37 E6
Sulawesi Tengah □ Indonesia 1°30S 121°0E 37 E6
Sulawesi Tenggara □ Indonesia 3°50S 122°0E 37 E6
Sulawesi Utara □ Indonesia 1°0N 124°0E 37 D6
Sulima S. Leone 6°58N 11°32W 52 G3
Sulina Romania 45°10N 29°40E 17 F15
Sulitjelma Norway 67°9N 16°3E 8 C17
Sullana Peru 4°52S 80°39W 92 D2
Sullivan Ill., U.S.A. 39°36N 88°37W 80 F9
Sullivan Ind., U.S.A. 39°6N 87°24W 80 F10
Sullivan Mo., U.S.A. 38°13N 91°10W 80 F8
Sullivan Bay Canada 50°55N 126°50W 70 C3
Sullivan I. = Lanbi Kyun Myanmar 10°50N 98°20E 39 G2
Sullom Voe U.K. 60°27N 1°20W 11 A7
Sulphur La., U.S.A. 30°14N 93°23W 84 F8
Sulphur Okla., U.S.A. 34°31N 96°58W 84 D6
Sulphur Pt. Canada 60°56N 114°48W 70 A6
Sulphur Springs U.S.A. 33°8N 95°36W 84 E7
Sultan Canada 47°36N 82°47W 72 C3
Sultan U.S.A. 47°52N 121°49W 78 C5
Sultanabad = Arāk Iran 34°0N 49°40E 47 C6
Sultanpur Mad. P., India 23°9N 77°56E 42 H8
Sultanpur Punjab, India 31°13N 75°11E 42 D6
Sultanpur Ut. P., India 26°18N 82°4E 43 F10
Sulu Arch. Phil. 6°0N 121°0E 37 C6
Sulu Sea E. Indies 8°0N 120°0E 37 C6
Suluq Libya 31°44N 20°14E 53 B10
Suluru India 13°42N 80°1E 45 H5
Sulzberger Ice Shelf Antarctica 78°0S 150°0W 5 E13
Sumalata Indonesia 1°0N 122°31E 37 D6
Sumampa Argentina 29°25S 63°29W 94 B3
Sumatera Indonesia 0°40N 100°20E 36 D2
Sumatera Barat □ Indonesia 1°0S 101°0E 36 E2
Sumatera Selatan □ Indonesia 3°0S 104°0E 36 E2
Sumatera Utara □ Indonesia 2°30N 98°0E 36 D1
Sumatra = Sumatera Indonesia 0°40N 100°20E 36 D2
Sumba Indonesia 9°45S 119°35E 37 F5
Sumba, Selat Indonesia 9°0S 118°40E 37 F5
Sumbawa Indonesia 8°26S 117°30E 36 F5
Sumbawa Besar Indonesia 8°30S 117°26E 36 F5
Sumbawanga □ Tanzania 8°0S 31°30E 54 F6
Sumbe Angola 11°10S 13°48E 54 G2
Sumburgh Hd. U.K. 59°52N 1°17W 11 B7
Sumdeo India 31°26N 78°44E 43 D8
Sumdo China 35°6N 78°41E 43 B8
Sumedang Indonesia 6°52S 107°55E 37 G12
Šumen = Shumen Bulgaria 43°18N 26°55E 23 C12
Sumenep Indonesia 7°1S 113°52E 37 G15
Sumgait = Sumqayıt Azerbaijan 40°34N 49°38E 19 F8
Summer L. U.S.A. 42°50N 120°45W 76 E3
Summerland Canada 49°32N 119°41W 70 D5
Summerside Canada 46°24N 63°47W 73 C7
Summersville U.S.A. 38°17N 80°51W 81 F13
Summerville Ga., U.S.A. 34°29N 85°21W 85 D12
Summerville S.C., U.S.A. 33°1N 80°11W 85 E14
Summit Lake Canada 54°20N 122°40W 70 C4
Summit Peak U.S.A. 37°21N 106°42W 77 H10
Sumner Iowa, U.S.A. 42°51N 92°6W 80 D7
Sumner Wash., U.S.A. 47°12N 122°14W 78 C4
Sumoto Japan 34°21N 134°54E 29 G7
Šumperk Czechia 49°59N 16°59E 17 D9
Sumqayıt Azerbaijan 40°34N 49°38E 19 F8
Sumter U.S.A. 33°55N 80°21W 85 E14
Sumy Ukraine 50°57N 34°50E 19 D5
Sun City S. Africa 25°17S 27°3E 56 C4
Sun City U.S.A. 33°42N 112°17W 77 K7
Sun City Center U.S.A. 27°43N 82°18W 85 H13
Sun Kosi → Nepal 26°55N 87°9E 43 F12
Sun Lakes U.S.A. 33°10N 111°52W 77 K8
Sun Valley U.S.A. 43°42N 114°21W 76 E6
Sunagawa Japan 43°29N 141°55E 28 C10
Sunan N. Korea 39°15N 125°40E 33 E13
Sunart, L. U.K. 56°42N 5°43W 11 E3
Sunburst U.S.A. 48°53N 111°55W 76 B8
Sunbury Australia 37°35S 144°44E 63 F3
Sunbury U.S.A. 40°52N 76°48W 83 F8
Sunchales Argentina 30°58S 61°35W 94 C3
Suncheon S. Korea 34°52N 127°31E 33 G14
Suncho Corral Argentina 27°55S 63°27W 94 B3
Sunch'ŏn N. Korea 39°25N 125°56E 33 E13
Suncook U.S.A. 43°8N 71°27W 83 C13
Sunda, Selat Indonesia 6°20S 105°30E 36 F3
Sunda Is. Indonesia 5°0S 105°0E 64 H2
Sunda Str. = Sunda, Selat Indonesia 6°20S 105°30E 36 F3
Sunda Trench = Java Trench Ind. Oc. 9°0S 105°0E 36 F3
Sundance Canada 56°32N 94°4W 71 B10
Sundance U.S.A. 44°24N 104°23W 76 D11
Sundar Nagar India 31°32N 76°53E 42 D7
Sundarbans Asia 22°0N 89°0E 41 J16
Sundarbans S. Asia 22°0N 88°45E 43 J13
Sundargarh India 22°4N 84°5E 44 C7
Sundays → S. Africa 33°44S 25°51E 56 D4
Sunderland Canada 44°16N 79°4W 82 B5
Sunderland U.K. 54°55N 1°23W 12 C6
Sundown △ Australia 28°49S 151°38E 63 D5
Sundre Canada 51°49N 114°38W 70 C6
Sundsvall Sweden 62°23N 17°17E 8 E17
Sungai Acheh Malaysia 5°8N 100°30E 39 c
Sungai Kolok Thailand 6°2N 101°58E 39 J3
Sungai Lembing Malaysia 3°55N 103°3E 39 L4
Sungai Petani Malaysia 5°37N 100°30E 39 K3
Sungaigerong Indonesia 2°59S 104°52E 36 E2
Sungailiat Indonesia 1°51S 106°8E 36 E3
Sungaipenuh Indonesia 2°1S 101°20E 36 E2
Sungari = Songhua Jiang → China 47°45N 132°30E 31 B15
Sunghua Chiang = Songhua Jiang → China 47°45N 132°30E 31 B15
Sunland Park U.S.A. 31°50N 106°40W 77 L10
Sunndalsøra Norway 62°40N 8°33E 8 E13
Sunnyside U.S.A. 46°20N 120°0W 76 C4
Sunnyvale U.S.A. 37°23N 122°2W 78 H4
Suntar Russia 62°15N 117°30E 27 C12
Suomenselkä Finland 62°52N 24°0E 8 E21
Suomi = Finland ■ Europe 63°0N 27°0E 8 E22
Suomussalmi Finland 64°54N 29°10E 8 D23
Suoyarvi Russia 62°3N 32°20E 18 B5
Supai U.S.A. 36°15N 112°41W 77 H7
Supaul India 26°10N 86°40E 43 F12
Superior Ariz., U.S.A. 33°18N 111°6W 77 K8
Superior Mont., U.S.A. 47°12N 114°53W 76 C6
Superior Nebr., U.S.A. 40°1N 98°4W 80 E4
Superior Wis., U.S.A. 46°44N 92°6W 80 B7
Superior, L. N. Amer. 47°0N 87°0W 72 C2
Suphan Buri Thailand 14°14N 100°10E 38 E3
Suphan Dağı Turkey 38°54N 42°48E 46 B4
Supiori Indonesia 1°0S 136°0E 37 E9
Supung Shuiku China 40°35N 124°50E 33 D13
Sûq ash Shuyūkh Iraq 30°53N 46°28E 46 D5
Sûq Suwayq Si. Arabia 24°23N 38°27E 46 E3
Suqian China 33°54N 118°8E 33 H10
Suquţra = Socotra Yemen 12°30N 54°0E 49 E5
Şûr Lebanon 33°19N 35°16E 48 B4
Şür Oman 22°34N 59°32E 49 C6
Sur, Pt. U.S.A. 36°18N 121°54W 78 J5
Sura → Russia 56°6N 46°0E 18 C8
Surab Pakistan 28°25N 66°15E 42 E2
Surabaja = Surabaya Indonesia 7°17S 112°45E 37 G15
Surabaya Indonesia 7°17S 112°45E 37 G15
Surakarta Indonesia 7°35S 110°48E 37 G14
Surat Australia 27°10S 149°6E 63 D4
Surat India 21°12N 72°55E 44 D1
Surat Thani Thailand 9°6N 99°20E 39 H2
Suratgarh India 29°18N 73°55E 42 E5
Surathkal India 12°58N 74°48E 45 H2
Surendranagar India 22°45N 71°40E 42 H4
Surf U.S.A. 34°41N 120°36W 79 L6
Surfers Paradise Australia 28°0S 153°25E 63 D5
Surgana India 20°34N 73°37E 44 D1
Surgut Russia 61°14N 73°20E 26 C8
Suriapet India 17°10N 79°40E 44 F4
Surigao Phil. 9°47N 125°29E 37 C7
Surin Thailand 14°50N 103°34E 38 E4
Surinam = Suriname ■ S. Amer. 4°0N 56°0W 93 C7
Suriname ■ S. Amer. 4°0N 56°0W 93 C7
Suriname → Suriname 5°50N 55°15W 93 B7
Surjagarh India 19°36N 80°25E 44 E5
Sürmaq Iran 31°3N 52°48E 47 D7
Surprise U.S.A. 33°38N 112°19W 77 K7
Surrey Canada 49°7N 122°45W 78 A4
Surrey □ U.K. 51°15N 0°31W 13 F7
Sursand India 26°39N 85°43E 43 F11
Sursar → India 26°14N 87°3E 43 F12
Surt Libya 31°11N 16°39E 53 B9
Surt, Khalīj Libya 31°40N 18°30E 53 B9
Surtanaha Pakistan 26°22N 70°0E 42 F4
Surtsey Iceland 63°20N 20°30W 8 E3
Suruga-Wan Japan 34°45N 138°30E 29 G9
Susaki Japan 33°22N 133°17E 29 H6
Süsangerd Iran 31°35N 48°6E 47 D6
Susanville U.S.A. 40°25N 120°39W 76 F3
Susner India 23°57N 76°5E 42 H7
Susong China 30°10N 116°5E 35 B11
Susquehanna U.S.A. 41°57N 75°36W 83 E9
Susquehanna → U.S.A. 39°33N 76°5W 83 G8
Susques Argentina 23°35S 66°25W 94 A2
Sussex Canada 45°45N 65°37W 73 C6
Sussex U.S.A. 41°13N 74°37W 83 E10
Sussex, East □ U.K. 51°0N 0°20E 13 G8
Sussex, West □ U.K. 51°0N 0°30W 13 G7
Sustut → Canada 56°20N 127°30W 70 B3
Susuman Russia 62°47N 148°10E 27 C15
Susunu Indonesia 3°7S 133°39E 37 E8
Susurluk Turkey 39°54N 28°8E 23 E13
Sutay Uul Asia 46°35N 93°38E 30 B7
Sutherland S. Africa 32°24S 20°40E 56 D3
Sutherland U.K. 58°12N 4°50W 11 C4
Sutherland U.S.A. 41°10N 101°8W 80 E3
Sutherland Falls N.Z. 44°48S 167°46E 59 F1
Sutherlin U.S.A. 43°23N 123°19W 76 E2
Suthri India 23°3N 68°55E 42 H3
Sutlej → Pakistan 29°23N 71°3E 42 E4
Sutter U.S.A. 39°10N 121°45W 78 F5
Sutter Buttes U.S.A. 39°12N 121°49W 78 F5
Sutter Creek U.S.A. 38°24N 120°48W 78 G6
Sutton Canada 45°6N 72°37W 83 A12
Sutton Nebr., U.S.A. 40°36N 97°52W 80 E5
Sutton W. Va., U.S.A. 38°40N 80°43W 81 F13
Sutton → Canada 55°15N 83°45W 72 A3
Sutton Coldfield U.K. 52°35N 1°49W 13 E6
Sutton in Ashfield U.K. 53°8N 1°16W 12 D6
Sutton L. Canada 54°15N 84°42W 72 B3
Suttor → Australia 21°36S 147°2E 62 C4
Suttsu Japan 42°48N 140°14E 28 C10
Sutwik I. U.S.A. 56°34N 157°12W 74 D8
Suva Fiji 18°6S 178°30E 59 a
Suva Planina Serbia 43°10N 22°5E 23 C10
Suvorov Is. = Suwarrow Is. Cook Is. 13°15S 163°5W 65 J11
Suwałki Poland 54°8N 22°59E 17 A12
Suwannaphum Thailand 15°33N 103°47E 38 E4
Suwannee → U.S.A. 29°17N 83°10W 85 G13
Suwanose-Jima Japan 29°38N 129°43E 29 K4
Suwarrow Is. Cook Is. 13°15S 163°5W 65 J11
Suweis, Khalîg el Egypt 28°40N 33°0E 53 C12
Suweis, Qanâ es Egypt 31°0N 32°20E 53 B12
Suwŏn S. Korea 37°17N 127°1E 33 F14
Suzdal Russia 56°29N 40°26E 18 C7
Suzhou Anhui, China 33°41N 116°59E 32 H9
Suzhou Jiangsu, China 31°19N 120°38E 35 B13
Suzu Japan 37°25N 137°17E 29 F8
Suzu-Misaki Japan 37°31N 137°21E 29 F8
Suzuka Japan 34°55N 136°36E 29 G8
Svalbard Arctic 78°0N 17°0E 4 B8
Svalbard Radio = Longyearbyen Svalbard 78°13N 15°40E 4 B8
Svappavaara Sweden 67°40N 21°3E 8 C19
Svartisen Norway 66°40N 13°59E 8 C15
Svay Chek Cambodia 13°48N 102°58E 38 F4
Svay Rieng Cambodia 11°9N 105°45E 39 G5
Sveelanda Sweden 60°20N 15°0E 9 F16
Sveg Sweden 62°2N 14°21E 8 E16
Svendborg Denmark 55°4N 10°35E 9 J14
Sverdrup Chan. Canada 79°56N 96°25W 69 B12
Sverdrup Is. Canada 79°0N 97°0W 66 B10
Sverige = Sweden ■ Europe 57°0N 15°0E 9 H16
Svetlaya Russia 46°33N 138°18E 28 A9
Svetlogorsk = Svyetlahorsk Belarus 52°38N 29°46E 17 B15
Svir → Russia 60°30N 32°48E 18 B5
Svishtov Bulgaria 43°36N 25°23E 23 C11
Svislach Belarus 53°3N 24°2E 17 B13
Svizzera = Switzerland ■ Europe 46°30N 8°0E 20 C8
Svobodnyy Russia 51°20N 128°0E 27 D13
Svolvær Norway 68°15N 14°34E 8 B16
Svyetlahorsk Belarus 52°38N 29°46E 17 B15
Swabian Alps = Schwäbische Alb Germany 48°20N 9°30E 16 D5
Swaffham U.K. 52°39N 0°42E 13 E8
Swains I. Amer. Samoa 11°11S 171°4W 65 J11
Swainsboro U.S.A. 32°36N 82°20W 85 E13
Swakop → Namibia 22°38S 14°36E 56 C2
Swakopmund Namibia 22°37S 14°30E 56 C1
Swale → U.K. 54°5N 1°20W 12 C6
Swamihalli India 14°52N 76°38E 45 G3
Swan → Australia 32°3S 115°45E 61 F2
Swan → Canada 52°30N 100°45W 71 C8
Swan Hill Australia 35°20S 143°33E 63 F3
Swan Hills Canada 54°43N 115°24W 70 C5
Swan Is. = Santanilla, Is. Honduras 17°22N 83°57W 88 C3
Swan L. Man., Canada 52°30N 100°40W 71 C8
Swan L. Ont., Canada 54°16N 91°11W 72 B1
Swan Ra. U.S.A. 48°0N 113°45W 76 C7
Swan River Canada 52°10N 101°16W 71 C8
Swanage U.K. 50°36N 1°58E 13 G6
Swansea Australia 42°8S 148°4E 63 G4
Swansea U.K. 51°37N 3°57W 13 F4
Swansea □ U.K. 51°38N 4°3W 13 F3
Swartberge S. Africa 33°20S 22°0E 56 D3
Swartmodder S. Africa 28°1S 20°32E 56 D3
Swartnossob → Namibia 23°8S 18°42E 56 B2
Swartruggens S. Africa 25°39S 26°42E 56 C4
Swastika Canada 48°7N 80°6W 72 C3
Swat → Pakistan 34°40N 72°5E 43 B5
Swatow = Shantou China 23°18N 116°40E 35 F11
Swaziland = Eswatini ■ Africa 26°30S 31°30E 57 C5
Sweden ■ Europe 57°0N 15°0E 9 H16
Sweet Grass U.S.A. 48°59N 111°58W 76 B8
Sweet Home U.S.A. 44°24N 122°44W 76 D2
Sweetwater Nev., U.S.A. 38°27N 119°9W 78 G7
Sweetwater Tenn., U.S.A. 35°36N 84°28W 85 D12
Sweetwater Tex., U.S.A. 32°28N 100°25W 84 E4
Sweetwater → U.S.A. 42°31N 107°2W 76 E9
Swellendam S. Africa 34°1S 20°26E 56 D3
Świdnica Poland 50°50N 16°30E 17 C9
Świdnik Poland 51°13N 22°39E 17 C12
Świebodzin Poland 52°15N 15°31E 16 B8
Świecie Poland 53°25N 18°30E 17 B10
Swift Current Canada 50°20N 107°45W 71 C7
Swift Current → Canada 50°38N 107°44W 71 C7
Swilly, L. Ireland 55°12N 7°33W 10 A4
Swindon U.K. 51°34N 1°46W 13 F6
Swindon □ U.K. 51°34N 1°46W 13 F6
Swinemünde = Świnoujście Poland 53°54N 14°16E 16 B8
Świnoujście Poland 53°54N 14°16E 16 B8
Switzerland ■ Europe 46°30N 8°0E 20 C8
Swords Ireland 53°28N 6°13W 10 C5
Swoyerville U.S.A. 41°18N 75°53W 83 E9

Sydenham → Canada 42°33N 82°25W 82 D2
Sydney Canada 46°7N 60°7W 73 C7
Sydney L. Canada 50°41N 94°25W 71 C10
Sydney Mines Canada 46°18N 60°15W 73 C7
Sydprøven = Alluitsup Paa Greenland 60°30N 45°35W 4 C5
Sydra, G. of = Surt, Khalīj Libya 31°40N 18°30E 53 B9
Sykesville U.S.A. 41°3N 78°50W 82 E6
Syktyvkar Russia 61°45N 50°40E 18 B9
Sylacauga U.S.A. 33°10N 86°15W 85 E11
Sylarna Sweden 63°2N 12°13E 8 E15
Sylhet Bangla. 24°54N 91°52E 41 E17
Sylhet □ Bangla. 24°50N 91°50E 41 G17
Sylt Germany 54°54N 8°22E 16 A5
Sylvan Beach U.S.A. 43°12N 75°44W 83 C9
Sylvan Lake Canada 52°20N 114°3W 70 C6
Sylvania Ga., U.S.A. 32°45N 81°38W 85 E14
Sylvania Ohio, U.S.A. 41°43N 83°42W 81 E12
Sylvester U.S.A. 31°32N 83°50W 85 F13
Sym Russia 60°20N 88°18E 26 C9
Synnot Ra. Australia 16°30S 125°20E 60 C4
Syôte △ Finland 65°44N 27°58E 8 D22
Syowa Antarctica 68°50S 12°0E 5 C5
Syracuse Kans., U.S.A. 37°59N 101°45W 80 G3
Syracuse N.Y., U.S.A. 43°3N 76°9W 83 C8
Syracuse Nebr., U.S.A. 40°39N 96°11W 80 E5
Syrdarya → Kazakhstan 46°3N 61°0E 26 E7
Syria ■ Asia 35°0N 38°0E 46 C3
Syrian Desert = Shām, Bādiyat ash Asia 32°0N 40°0E 46 C3
Syros = Ermoupoli Greece 37°28N 24°57E 23 F11
Syzran Russia 53°12N 48°30E 18 D8
Szczecin Poland 53°27N 14°27E 16 B8
Szczecinek Poland 53°43N 16°41E 17 B9
Szczeciński, Zalew = Stettiner Haff Germany 53°47N 14°15E 16 B8
Szczytno Poland 53°33N 21°0E 17 B11
Szechuan = Sichuan □ China 30°30N 103°0E 34 B5
Szechwan = Sichuan □ China 30°30N 103°0E 34 B5
Szechuan Basin = Sichuan Pendi China 31°0N 105°0E 34 B5
Szeged Hungary 46°16N 20°10E 17 E11
Székesfehérvár Hungary 47°15N 18°25E 17 E10
Szekszárd Hungary 46°22N 18°42E 17 E10
Szentes Hungary 46°39N 20°21E 17 E11
Szolnok Hungary 47°10N 20°15E 17 E11
Szombathely Hungary 47°14N 16°38E 17 E9

**T**

Ta Khli Thailand 15°15N 100°21E 38 E3
Ta Lai Vietnam 11°24N 107°23E 39 G6
Ta Phraya △ Thailand 14°1N 102°49E 38 E4
Taal Volcano Phil. 14°7N 120°59E 37 B6
Taamisaari = Raasepori Finland 60°0N 23°26E 9 G20
Tabacal Argentina 23°15S 64°15W 94 A3
Tabaco Phil. 13°22N 123°44E 37 B6
Ṭābah Si. Arabia 26°55N 42°38E 46 E4
Tabanan Indonesia 8°32S 115°8E 37 K18
Ṭabas Khorāsān, Iran 32°48N 60°12E 47 C9
Ṭabas Yazd, Iran 33°35N 56°55E 47 C8
Tabasará, Serranía de Panama 8°35N 81°40W 88 E3
Tabasco □ Mexico 18°0N 92°40W 87 D6
Ṭabāsīn Iran 31°12N 57°54E 47 D8
Tabatinga Brazil 4°16S 69°56W 92 D5
Tabatinga, Serra da Brazil 10°30S 44°0W 93 F10
Taber Canada 49°47N 112°8W 70 D6
Tablas I. Phil. 12°25N 122°2E 37 B6
Table, Pte. de la Réunion 21°14S 55°48E 55 c
Table B. Canada 53°40N 56°25W 73 B8
Table I. Myanmar 14°12N 93°22E 45 G11
Table Rock L. U.S.A. 36°36N 93°19W 80 G7
Tabletop, Mt. Australia 23°24S 147°11E 62 C4
Tábor Czechia 49°25N 14°39E 16 D8
Tabora Tanzania 5°2S 32°50E 54 F6
Tabou Côte d'Ivoire 4°30N 7°20W 52 H4
Tabrīz Iran 38°7N 46°20E 46 B5
Tabuaeran Kiribati 3°51N 159°22W 65 G12
Tabūk Si. Arabia 28°23N 36°36E 46 D3
Tabūk □ Si. Arabia 27°40N 36°50E 46 E3
Tacámbaro de Codallos Mexico 19°14N 101°28W 86 D4
Tacheng China 46°40N 82°58E 30 B5
Tach'i Taiwan 24°53N 121°17E 35 E13
Tachia Taiwan 24°25N 120°28E 35 E13
Tachilek Myanmar 20°29N 99°57E 38 B2
Tach'ing Shan = Daqing Shan China 40°40N 111°0E 32 D6
Tacloban Phil. 11°15N 124°58E 37 B6
Tacna Peru 18°0S 70°20W 92 G4
Tacuarembó Uruguay 31°45S 56°0W 95 C4
Tademaït, Plateau du Algeria 28°30N 2°30E 52 C6
Tādepallegudem India 16°50N 81°30E 44 F5
Tadjourah Djibouti 11°50N 42°55E 47 E3
Tadmor N.Z. 41°27S 172°45E 59 D4
Tadoba △ India 20°30N 79°20E 44 D4
Tadoussac Canada 48°11N 69°42W 73 C6
Tadpatri India 14°55N 78°1E 45 G4
Tadzhikistan = Tajikistan ■ Asia 38°30N 70°0E 26 F8
Taegu = Daegu S. Korea 35°50N 128°37E 33 G15
Taegwan N. Korea 40°13N 125°12E 33 D13
Taejŏn = Daejeon S. Korea 36°20N 127°28E 33 F14
Taen, Ko Thailand 9°22N 99°57E 39 b
Tafalla Spain 42°30N 1°41W 21 A5
Tafermaar Indonesia 6°47S 134°10E 37 F8
Tafi Viejo Argentina 26°43S 65°17W 94 B2
Tafihān Iran 29°25N 52°39E 47 D7
Tafresh Iran 34°45N 49°57E 47 C6
Taft Iran 31°45N 54°14E 47 D7
Taft Phil. 11°57N 125°30E 37 B7

Taft U.S.A. 35°8N 119°28W **79** K7
Taftan Pakistan 29°0N 61°30E **40** E2
Taftān, Kūh-e Iran 28°40N 61°0E **47** D9
Tafwap India 7°23N 93°43E **45** L11
Taga Samoa 13°46S 172°28W **59** b
Taga Dzong Bhutan 27°5N 89°55E **41** F16
Tagbilaran Phil. 9°39N 123°51E **37** C6
Tagish Canada 60°19N 134°16W **70** A2
Tagish L. Canada 60°10N 134°20W **70** A2
Tagliamento → Italy 45°38N 13°6E **22** B5
Taguatinga Brazil 12°27S 46°22W **93** F10
Tagum Phil. 7°33N 125°53E **37** C7
Tagus = Tejo → Europe 38°40N 9°24W **21** C1
Tahakopa N.Z. 46°30S 169°23E **59** G2
Tahan, Gunung Malaysia 4°34N 102°17E **39** K4
Tahat Algeria 23°18N 5°33E **52** D7
Tāherī Iran 27°43N 52°20E **47** E7
Tahiti French Polynesia 17°37S 149°27W **59** d
Tahiti, I. Tahiti 17°37S 149°27W **59** d
Tahlequah U.S.A. 35°55N 94°58W **84** D7
Tahoe, L. U.S.A. 39°6N 120°2W **78** G6
Tahoe City U.S.A. 39°10N 120°9W **78** F6
Tahoka U.S.A. 33°10N 101°48W **84** E4
Taholah U.S.A. 47°21N 124°17W **78** C2
Tahoua Niger 14°57N 5°16E **52** F7
Tahrūd Iran 29°26N 57°49E **47** D8
Tahsis Canada 49°55N 126°40W **70** D3
Tahta Egypt 26°44N 31°32E **53** C12
Tahulandang Indonesia 2°27N 125°23E **37** D7
Tahuna Indonesia 3°38N 125°30E **37** D7
Tai Hu China 31°5N 120°10E **35** B13
Tai Pang Wan China 22°33N 114°24E **31** a
Tai Po China 22°27N 114°10E **31** a
Tai Rom Yen △ Thailand 8°45N 99°30E **39** H2
Tai Shan China 36°25N 117°20E **33** F9
Tai'an China 36°12N 117°8E **33** F9
Taiarapu, Presqu'île de Tahiti 17°47S 149°14W **59** d
Taibai Shan China 33°57N 107°45E **32** H4
Taibus Qi China 41°54N 115°22E **32** D8
Taicang China 31°30N 121°5E **35** B13
T'aichung Taiwan 24°9N 120°37E **35** E13
Taieri → N.Z. 46°3S 170°12E **59** G3
Taigu China 37°28N 112°30E **32** F7
Taihang Shan China 36°0N 113°30E **32** G7
Taihape N.Z. 39°41S 175°48E **59** C5
Taihe Anhui, China 33°20N 115°42E **32** H8
Taihe Jiangxi, China 26°47N 114°52E **35** D10
Taihu China 30°22N 116°20E **35** B11
Taijiang China 26°39N 108°21E **34** D7
Taikang China 34°5N 114°50E **32** G8
Tailem Bend Australia 35°12S 139°29E **63** F2
T'ailuo Taiwan 24°9N 121°37E **35** E13
Taimyr Peninsula = Taymyr, Poluostrov Russia 75°0N 100°0E **27** B11
Tain U.K. 57°49N 4°4W **11** D4
T'ainan Taiwan 23°0N 120°10E **35** F13
Taining China 26°54N 117°9E **35** D11
Taipa China 22°10N 113°35E **31** a
T'aipei Taiwan 25°4N 121°29E **35** E13
Taiping China 30°15N 118°6E **35** B12
Taiping Malaysia 4°51N 100°44E **39** K3
Taiping Dao = Itu Aba I. S. China Sea 10°23N 114°21E **36** B4
Taipingchuan China 44°23N 123°11E **33** B12
Taipingzhen China 33°35N 111°42E **32** H6
Taishan China 22°14N 112°41E **35** F9
Taishun China 27°30N 119°42E **35** D12
Taitao, Pen. de Chile 46°30S 75°0W **96** F2
T'aitung Taiwan 22°43N 121°4E **35** F13
Taivalkoski Finland 65°33N 28°12E **8** D23
Taiwan ■ Asia 23°30N 121°0E **35** F13
Taiwan Strait Asia 24°40N 120°0E **35** E12
Taixing China 32°11N 120°0E **35** A13
Taiyiba Israel 32°36N 35°27E **48** C4
Taiyuan China 37°52N 112°33E **32** F7
Taizhou Jiangsu, China 32°28N 119°55E **35** A12
Taizhou Zhejiang, China 28°40N 121°24E **35** C13
Taizhou Liedao China 28°30N 121°55E **35** C13
Ta'izz Yemen 13°35N 44°2E **49** E3
Taj Mahal India 27°10N 78°2E **42** F8
Tājābād Iran 30°2N 54°24E **47** D7
Tajikistan ■ Asia 38°30N 70°0E **26** F8
Tajima = Minamiaizu Japan 37°12N 139°46E **29** F9
Tajo = Tejo → Europe 38°40N 9°24W **21** C1
Tak Thailand 16°52N 99°8E **38** D2
Takāb Iran 36°24N 47°7E **46** B5
Takachiho Japan 32°42N 131°18E **29** H5
Takachu Botswana 22°37S 21°58E **56** B3
Takada Japan 37°7N 138°15E **29** F9
Takahagi Japan 36°43N 140°45E **29** F10
Takaka N.Z. 40°51S 172°50E **59** D4
Takamaka Seychelles 4°50S 55°30E **55** b
Takamatsu Japan 34°20N 134°5E **29** G7
Takaoka Japan 36°47N 137°0E **29** F8
Takapuna N.Z. 36°47S 174°47E **59** B5
Takasaki Japan 36°20N 139°0E **29** F9
Takatsuki Japan 34°51N 135°37E **29** G7
Takayama Japan 36°18N 137°11E **29** F8
Take-Shima Japan 30°49N 130°26E **29** J5
Takefu = Echizen Japan 35°50N 136°10E **29** G8
Takengon Indonesia 4°45N 96°50E **36** D1
Takeo Cambodia 10°59N 104°47E **39** G5
Takeo Japan 33°12N 130°1E **29** H5
Takeshima = Liancourt Rocks Asia 37°15N 131°52E **29** F5
Tākestān Iran 36°0N 49°40E **47** C6
Taketa Japan 32°58N 131°24E **29** H5
Takh India 33°6N 77°32E **43** C7
Takhmau Cambodia 11°29N 104°57E **39** G5
Takht-e Soleymān Iran 36°36N 47°14E **46** B5
Takht-Sulaiman Pakistan 31°40N 69°58E **42** D3
Takikawa Japan 43°33N 141°54E **28** C10
Takla L. Canada 55°15N 125°45W **70** B3
Takla Landing Canada 55°30N 125°50W **70** B3
Taklamakan China 38°0N 83°0E **30** D5
Taklamakan Shamo = Taklamakan China 38°0N 83°0E **30** D5
Taksimo Russia 56°20N 114°52E **27** D12

Taku → Canada 58°30N 133°50W **70** B2
Takua Thung Thailand 8°24N 98°27E **39** a
Tal Halāl Iran 28°54N 55°1E **47** D7
Tala Uruguay 34°21S 55°46W **95** C4
Talagang Pakistan 32°55N 72°25E **42** C5
Talagante Chile 33°40S 70°50W **94** C1
Talaimannar Sri Lanka 9°6N 79°43E **45** K4
Talamanca, Cordillera de Cent. Amer. 9°20N 83°20W **88** E3
Talampaya △ Argentina 29°43S 67°42W **94** B2
Talara Peru 4°38S 81°18W **92** D2
Talas Kyrgyzstan 42°30N 72°13E **26** E8
Talāta Egypt 30°36N 32°20E **48** E1
Talaud, Kepulauan Indonesia 4°30N 126°50E **37** D7
Talaud Is. = Talaud, Kepulauan Indonesia 4°30N 126°50E **37** D7
Talavera de la Reina Spain 39°55N 4°46W **21** C3
Talayan Phil. 6°52N 124°24E **37** C6
Talbandh India 22°3N 86°20E **43** H12
Talbot, C. Australia 13°48S 126°43E **60** B4
Talbragar → Australia 32°12S 148°37E **63** E4
Talca Chile 35°28S 71°40W **94** D1
Talcahuano Chile 36°40S 73°10W **94** D1
Talcher India 21°0N 85°18E **44** D7
Taldy Kurgan = Taldyqorghan Kazakhstan 45°10N 78°45E **30** B4
Taldyqorghan Kazakhstan 45°10N 78°45E **30** B4
Tālesh Iran 37°58N 48°58E **47** B6
Tālesh, Kūhhā-ye Iran 37°42N 48°55E **47** B6
Talguppa India 14°13N 74°56E **45** G2
Tali Post South Sudan 5°55N 30°44E **53** G12
Taliabu Indonesia 1°50S 125°0E **37** E6
Talibon Phil. 10°9N 124°20E **37** B6
Talihina U.S.A. 34°45N 95°3W **84** D7
Talikota India 16°29N 76°17E **45** F3
Talipparamba India 12°3N 75°21E **45** H2
Taliwang Indonesia 8°50S 116°55E **36** F5
Talkot Nepal 29°37N 81°19E **43** E9
Tall 'Afar Iraq 36°22N 42°27E **46** B4
Tall Kalakh Syria 34°41N 36°15E **48** A5
Talladega U.S.A. 33°26N 86°6W **85** E11
Tallahassee U.S.A. 30°27N 84°17W **85** F12
Tallangatta Australia 36°15S 147°19E **63** F4
Tallering Pk. Australia 28°6S 115°37E **61** E2
Talli Pakistan 29°32N 68°8E **42** E3
Tallinn Estonia 59°22N 24°48E **9** G21
Tallmadge U.S.A. 41°6N 81°27W **82** E3
Tallulah U.S.A. 32°25N 91°11W **84** E9
Talnakh Russia 69°29N 88°22E **27** C9
Taloda India 21°34N 74°11E **44** D2
Taloyoak Canada 69°32N 93°32W **68** D13
Talpa de Allende Mexico 20°23N 104°51W **86** C4
Talparo Trin. & Tob. 10°30N 61°17W **93** K15
Talsi Latvia 57°10N 22°30E **9** H20
Taltal Chile 25°23S 70°33W **94** B1
Taltson → Canada 61°24N 112°46W **70** A6
Talwood Australia 28°29S 149°29E **63** D4
Talyawalka Cr. → Australia 32°28S 142°22E **63** E3
Tam Dao → Vietnam 21°45N 105°45E **38** B5
Tam Ky Vietnam 15°34N 108°29E **38** E7
Tam Quan Vietnam 14°35N 109°3E **38** E7
Tama U.S.A. 41°58N 92°35W **80** E7
Tama Abu, Banjaran Malaysia 3°50N 115°5E **36** D5
Tamale Ghana 9°22N 0°50W **52** G5
Taman Negara △ Malaysia 4°38N 102°26E **39** K4
Tamano Japan 34°29N 133°59E **29** G6
Tamanrasset Algeria 22°50N 5°30E **52** D7
Tamaqua U.S.A. 40°48N 75°58W **83** F9
Tamar → U.K. 50°27N 4°15W **13** G3
Tamarin Mauritius 20°19S 57°20E **55** d
Tamashima Japan 34°32N 133°40E **29** G6
Tamatave = Toamasina Madag. 18°10S 49°25E **55** H9
Tamaulipas □ Mexico 24°0N 98°45W **87** C5
Tamaulipas, Sierra de Mexico 23°30N 98°20W **87** C5
Tamazula Mexico 24°57N 106°57W **86** C3
Tamazunchale Mexico 21°16N 98°47W **87** C5
Tambacounda Senegal 13°45N 13°40W **52** F3
Tambaram India 12°55N 80°7E **45** H5
Tambelan, Kepulauan Indonesia 1°0N 107°30E **36** D3
Tambellup Australia 34°4S 117°37E **61** F2
Tambo Australia 24°54S 146°14E **62** C4
Tambo de Mora Peru 13°30S 76°8W **92** F3
Tambora Indonesia 8°12S 118°5E **36** F5
Tambov Russia 52°45N 41°28E **18** D7
Tambuku Indonesia 7°8S 113°40E **37** G15
Tâmega → Portugal 41°5N 8°21W **21** B1
Tamenglong India 25°0N 93°35E **41** G18
Tamiahua, L. de Mexico 21°35N 97°35W **87** C5
Tamil Nadu □ India 11°0N 77°0E **45** J3
Tamluk India 22°18N 87°58E **43** H12
Tammerfors = Tampere Finland 61°30N 23°50E **8** F20
Tampa U.S.A. 27°56N 82°27W **85** H13
Tampa, Tanjung Indonesia 8°55S 116°12E **37** K19
Tampa B. U.S.A. 27°50N 82°30W **85** H13
Tampere Finland 61°30N 23°50E **8** F20
Tampico Mexico 22°13N 97°51W **87** C5
Tampin Malaysia 2°28N 102°13E **39** L4
Tampoi Indonesia 10°30S 103°39E **39** d
Tamsagbulag Mongolia 47°14N 117°21E **31** B12
Tamu Myanmar 24°13N 94°12E **41** G19
Tamworth Australia 31°7S 150°58E **63** E5
Tamworth Canada 44°29N 77°0W **82** B8
Tamworth U.K. 52°39N 1°41W **13** E6
Tan An Vietnam 10°32N 106°25E **39** G6
Tan Chau Vietnam 10°48N 105°12E **39** G5
Tan Hiep Vietnam 10°27N 106°21E **39** G6
Tan-Tan Morocco 28°29N 11°1W **52** C3
Tan Yen Vietnam 22°4N 105°3E **38** A5
Tana → Kenya 2°32S 40°31E **54** E8
Tana → Norway 70°30N 28°14E **8** A23

Tana, L. Ethiopia 13°5N 37°30E **49** E2
Tanabe Japan 33°44N 135°22E **29** H7
Tanafjorden Norway 70°45N 28°25E **8** A23
Tanah Merah Malaysia 5°48N 102°9E **39** K4
Tanahbala Indonesia 0°30S 98°30E **36** E1
Tanahgrogot Indonesia 1°55S 116°15E **36** E5
Tanahjampea Indonesia 7°10S 120°35E **37** F6
Tanahmasa Indonesia 0°12S 98°39E **36** E1
Tanahmerah Indonesia 6°5S 140°16E **37** F10
Tanakpur India 29°5N 80°7E **43** E9
Tanami Desert Australia 18°50S 132°0E **60** C5
Tanana U.S.A. 65°10N 152°4W **74** B9
Tanana → U.S.A. 65°10N 151°58W **68** D1
Tananarive = Antananarivo Madag. 18°55S 47°31E **55** H9
Tánaro → Italy 44°55N 8°40E **20** D8
Tancheng China 34°25N 118°20E **33** G10
Tanch'ŏn N. Korea 40°27N 128°54E **33** D15
Tanda Ut. P., India 26°33N 82°35E **43** F10
Tanda Ut. P., India 28°57N 78°56E **43** E8
Tandag Phil. 9°4N 126°9E **37** C7
Tandaué Angola 16°58S 18°5E **56** A2
Tandil Argentina 37°15S 59°6W **94** D4
Tandil, Sa. del Argentina 37°30S 59°0W **94** D4
Tandlianwala Pakistan 31°3N 73°9E **42** D5
Tando Adam Pakistan 25°45N 68°40E **42** G3
Tando Allahyar Pakistan 25°28N 68°43E **42** G3
Tando Bago Pakistan 24°47N 68°58E **42** G3
Tando Mohommed Khan Pakistan 25°8N 68°32E **42** G3
Tandou L. Australia 32°40S 142°5E **63** E3
Tandoureh △ Iran 37°50N 59°0E **47** B8
Tandragee U.K. 54°21N 6°24W **10** B5
Tandula → India 21°6N 81°14E **44** D5
Tandula Tank India 20°40N 81°12E **44** D5
Tandur Telangana, India 19°11N 79°30E **44** E4
Tandur Telangana, India 17°14N 77°35E **44** F3
Tane-ga-Shima Japan 30°30N 131°0E **29** J5
Taneatua N.Z. 38°4S 177°1E **59** C6
Tanen Tong Dan = Dawna Ra. Myanmar 16°30N 98°30E **38** D2
Tanezrouft Algeria 23°9N 0°11E **52** D6
Tang, Koh Cambodia 10°16N 103°7E **39** G4
Tang, Ra's-e Iran 25°21N 59°52E **47** E8
Tang Krasang Cambodia 12°34N 105°3E **38** F5
Tanga Tanzania 5°5S 39°2E **54** F7
Tangalla Sri Lanka 6°1N 80°48E **45** L5
Tanganyika, L. Africa 6°40S 30°0E **54** F6
Tangasseri India 8°53N 76°35E **45** K3
Tanger Morocco 35°50N 5°49W **52** A4
Tangerang Indonesia 6°11S 106°37E **37** G12
Tanggu China 39°2N 117°40E **33** E9
Tanggula Shan China 32°40N 92°10E **30** E7
Tanggula Shankou China 32°42N 92°27E **30** E7
Tanghe China 32°47N 112°50E **32** H7
Tanghla Range = Tanggula Shan China 32°40N 92°10E **30** E7
Tangi India 19°56N 85°24E **44** E7
Tangier = Tanger Morocco 35°50N 5°49W **52** A4
Tangjia China 22°22N 113°35E **31** a
Tangjia Wan China 22°21N 113°36E **31** a
Tangorin Australia 21°47S 144°12E **62** C3
Tangra Yumco China 31°0N 86°38E **30** E6
Tangshan China 39°38N 118°10E **33** E10
Tangtou China 35°28N 118°30E **33** G10
Tangxi China 29°3N 119°25E **35** C12
Tangyan He → China 28°54N 108°19E **34** C7
Tangyin China 35°54N 114°21E **32** G8
Taniantaweng Shan China 31°20N 98°0E **34** B2
Tanimbar, Kepulauan Indonesia 7°30S 131°30E **37** F8
Tanimbar Is. = Tanimbar, Kepulauan Indonesia 7°30S 131°30E **37** F8
Tanintharyi = Taninthayi Myanmar 12°6N 99°3E **39** F2
Taninthayi Myanmar 12°6N 99°3E **39** F2
Tanjay Phil. 9°30N 123°5E **37** C6
Tanjore = Thanjavur India 10°48N 79°12E **45** J4
Tanjung Kalimantan Selatan, Indonesia 2°10S 115°25E **36** E5
Tanjung Nusa Tenggara Barat, Indonesia 8°21S 116°9E **37** J19
Tanjung Malim Malaysia 3°42N 101°31E **39** L3
Tanjung Pelepas Malaysia 1°21N 103°33E **39** d
Tanjung Tokong Malaysia 5°28N 100°18E **39** c
Tanjungbalai Indonesia 2°55N 99°44E **36** D1
Tanjungbatu Indonesia 2°23N 118°3E **36** D5
Tanjungkarang Telukbetung = Bandar Lampung Indonesia 5°20S 105°10E **36** F3
Tanjungpandan Indonesia 2°43S 107°38E **36** E3
Tanjungpinang Indonesia 1°5N 104°30E **36** D2
Tanjungredeb Indonesia 2°9N 117°29E **36** D5
Tanjungselor Indonesia 2°55N 117°25E **36** D5
Tank Pakistan 32°14N 70°25E **42** C4
Tankhala India 21°58N 73°47E **42** J5
Tannersville U.S.A. 41°3N 75°18W **83** E9
Tannu Ola Asia 51°0N 94°0E **30** A7
Tannum Sands Australia 23°57S 151°22E **62** C5
Tanout Niger 14°50N 8°55E **52** F7
Tanshui Taiwan 25°10N 121°28E **35** E13
Tansing Nepal 27°52N 83°33E **43** F10
Tanta Egypt 30°45N 30°57E **53** B12
Tantoyuca Mexico 21°21N 98°14W **87** C5
Tantung = Dandong China 40°10N 124°20E **33** D13
Tanuku India 16°45N 81°44E **44** F5
Tanunda Australia 34°30S 139°0E **63** E2
Tanur India 11°1N 75°52E **45** J2
Tanzania ■ Africa 6°0S 34°0E **54** F6
Tanzilla → Canada 58°8N 130°43W **70** B2
Tao, Ko Thailand 10°5N 99°52E **39** G2

Tao'an = Taonan China 45°22N 122°40E **33** B12
Tao'er He → China 45°45N 124°5E **33** B13
Taohua Dao China 29°50N 122°20E **35** C14
Taolanaro Madag. 25°2S 47°0E **55** K9
Taole China 38°48N 106°40E **32** E4
Taonan China 45°22N 122°40E **33** B12
Taos U.S.A. 36°24N 105°35W **77** H11
Taoudenni Mali 22°40N 3°55W **52** D5
Taourirt Morocco 34°25N 2°53W **52** B5
T'aoyüan Taiwan 25°0N 121°4E **35** E13
Tapa Estonia 59°15N 25°50E **9** G21
Tapa Shan = Daba Shan China 32°0N 109°0E **34** B7
Tapachula Mexico 14°54N 92°17W **87** E6
Tapah Malaysia 4°12N 101°15E **39** K3
Tapajós → Brazil 2°24S 54°41W **93** D8
Tapaktuan Indonesia 3°15N 97°10E **36** D1
Tapanahoni → Suriname 4°20N 54°25W **93** C8
Tapanui N.Z. 45°56S 169°18E **59** F2
Tapauá → Brazil 5°40S 64°21W **92** E6
Tapes Brazil 30°40S 51°23W **95** C5
Tapeta Liberia 6°29N 8°52W **52** G4
Taphan Hin Thailand 16°13N 100°26E **38** D3
Tapirapecó, Serra Venezuela 1°10N 65°0W **92** C6
Taplejung Nepal 27°1N 86°16E **43** F12
Tapo-Capara △ Venezuela 7°55N 71°15W **89** E5
Tapti → India 21°8N 72°41E **44** D1
Tapuae-o-Uenuku N.Z. 42°0S 173°39E **59** E4
Tapul Group Phil. 5°35N 120°50E **37** C6
Tapurucuará Brazil 0°24S 65°2W **92** D5
Taquara Brazil 29°36S 50°46W **95** B5
Taquari → Brazil 19°15S 57°17W **92** G7
Tara Australia 27°17S 150°31E **63** D5
Tara Canada 44°28N 81°9W **82** B3
Tara Russia 56°55N 74°24E **26** D8
Tara → Montenegro 43°21N 18°51E **23** C8
Tarābulus Lebanon 34°31N 35°50E **48** A4
Tarābulus Libya 32°49N 13°7E **53** B8
Tarābulus Libya 31°0N 13°0E **53** B8
Taradehi India 23°18N 79°21E **43** H8
Tarakan Indonesia 3°20N 117°35E **36** D5
Tarama-Jima Japan 24°39N 124°42E **29** M2
Taran, Mys Russia 54°56N 19°59E **9** J18
Taranagar India 28°43N 74°50E **42** E6
Taranaki □ N.Z. 39°25S 174°30E **59** C5
Tarancón Spain 40°1N 3°1W **21** B4
Taransay U.K. 57°54N 7°0W **11** D1
Táranto Italy 40°28N 17°14E **22** D7
Táranto, G. di Italy 40°8N 17°20E **22** D7
Tarapacá Colombia 2°56S 69°46W **92** D5
Tarapacá □ Chile 20°45S 69°30W **94** A2
Tarapoto Peru 6°30S 76°20W **92** E3
Tararua Ra. N.Z. 40°45S 175°25E **59** D5
Tarasaigh = Taransay U.K. 57°54N 7°0W **11** D1
Tarashcha Ukraine 49°30N 30°31E **17** D16
Tarauacá Brazil 8°6S 70°48W **92** E4
Tarauacá → Brazil 6°42S 69°48W **92** E5
Taravao Tahiti 17°43S 149°18W **59** d
Taravao, Isthme de Tahiti 17°43S 149°19W **59** d
Tarawa Kiribati 1°30N 173°0E **64** G9
Tarawera N.Z. 39°2S 176°36E **59** C6
Tarawera, L. N.Z. 38°13S 176°27E **59** C6
Taraz Kazakhstan 42°54N 71°22E **30** C3
Tarazona Spain 41°55N 1°43W **21** B5
Tarbagatay, Khrebet Kazakhstan 48°0N 83°0E **30** B5
Tarbat Ness U.K. 57°52N 3°47W **11** D5
Tarbela Dam Pakistan 34°8N 72°52E **42** B5
Tarbert Ireland 52°34N 9°22W **10** D2
Tarbert Argyll & Bute, U.K. 55°52N 5°25W **11** F3
Tarbert W. Isles, U.K. 57°54N 6°49E **11** D2
Tarbes France 43°15N 0°3E **20** E4
Tarboro U.S.A. 35°54N 77°32W **85** D16
Tarcoola Australia 30°44S 134°36E **63** E1
Tarcoon Australia 30°15S 146°43E **63** E4
Taree Australia 31°50S 152°30E **63** E5
Tarfaya Morocco 27°55N 12°55W **52** C3
Targovishte Bulgaria 43°17N 26°38E **23** C12
Târgovişte Romania 44°55N 25°27E **17** F13
Târgu Jiu Romania 45°5N 23°19E **17** F12
Târgu Mureş Romania 46°31N 24°38E **17** E13
Ţarif U.A.E. 24°3N 53°46E **47** E7
Tarifa Spain 36°1N 5°36W **21** D3
Tarija Bolivia 21°30S 64°40W **94** A3
Tarija □ Bolivia 21°30S 63°30W **94** A3
Tariku → Indonesia 2°55S 138°26E **37** E9
Tarīm Yemen 16°3N 49°0E **49** D4
Tarim Basin = Tarim Pendi China 40°0N 84°0E **30** C5
Tarim He → China 39°30N 88°30E **30** D6
Tarim Pendi China 40°0N 84°0E **30** C5
Taritatu → Indonesia 2°54S 138°27E **37** E9
Tarka → S. Africa 32°10S 26°0E **56** D4
Tarka La Bhutan 27°12N 89°44E **43** F13
Tarkastad S. Africa 32°0S 26°16E **56** D4
Tarkhankut, Mys Ukraine 45°25N 32°30E **19** E5
Tarko Sale Russia 64°55N 77°50E **26** C8
Tarkwa Ghana 5°20N 2°0W **52** G5
Tarlac Phil. 15°29N 120°35E **37** A6
Tarma Peru 11°25S 75°45W **92** F3
Tarn → France 44°5N 1°6E **20** E4
Târnăveni Romania 46°19N 24°13E **17** E13
Tarnobrzeg Poland 50°35N 21°41E **17** C11
Tarnów Poland 50°3N 21°0E **17** C11
Tarnowskie Góry Poland 50°27N 18°54E **17** C10
Ţārom Iran 28°11N 55°46E **47** D7
Taroom Australia 25°36S 149°48E **63** D4
Taroudannt Morocco 30°30N 8°52W **52** B4
Tarpon Springs U.S.A. 28°9N 82°45W **85** G13
Tarrafal Cabo Verde 15°18N 23°39W **52** b
Tarragona Spain 41°5N 1°17E **21** B6
Tarraleah Australia 42°17S 146°26E **63** G4
Tarrasa = Terrassa Spain 41°34N 2°1E **21** B7
Tarrytown U.S.A. 41°4N 73°52W **83** E11

Tarsus Turkey 36°58N 34°55E **46** B2
Tartagal Argentina 22°30S 63°50W **94** A3
Tartu Estonia 58°20N 26°44E **9** G22
Ţarţūs Syria 34°55N 35°55E **46** C2
Tarumizu Japan 31°29N 130°42E **29** J5
Tarutao = Ko Tarutao △ Thailand 6°31N 99°26E **39** J2
Tarutao, Ko Thailand 6°33N 99°40E **39** J2
Tarutung Indonesia 2°0N 98°54E **36** D1
Taseko → Canada 52°8N 123°45W **70** C4
Tasgaon India 17°2N 74°39E **44** F2
Tash-Kömür Kyrgyzstan 41°40N 72°10E **26** E8
Tashauz = Daşoguz Turkmenistan 41°49N 59°58E **26** E6
Tashi Chho Dzong = Thimphu Bhutan 27°31N 89°45E **41** F16
Tashk, Daryācheh-ye Iran 29°45N 53°35E **47** D7
Tashkent = Toshkent Uzbekistan 41°20N 69°10E **26** E7
Tashtagol Russia 52°47N 87°53E **26** D9
Tasiilaq Greenland 65°40N 37°20W **4** C6
Tasikmalaya Indonesia 7°18S 108°12E **37** G13
Tåsjön Sweden 64°15N 15°40E **8** D16
Taskan Russia 62°59N 150°20E **27** C16
Tasman B. N.Z. 40°59S 173°25E **59** D4
Tasman Basin Pac. Oc. 46°0S 158°0E **64** M7
Tasman Mts. N.Z. 41°3S 172°25E **59** D4
Tasman Pen. Australia 43°10S 148°0E **63** G4
Tasman Sea Pac. Oc. 36°0S 160°0E **58** E9
Tasmania □ Australia 42°0S 146°30E **63** G4
Tasmanian Wilderness World Heritage Area △ Australia 43°0S 146°0E **63** G4
Tassili n'Ajjer Algeria 25°47N 8°1E **52** C7
Tassili-oua-n-Ahaggar Algeria 20°41N 5°30E **52** D7
Tata Hungary 47°32N 18°25E **17** E10
Tata Morocco 29°46N 7°56W **52** C4
Tatabánya Hungary 47°32N 18°25E **17** E10
Tataouine Tunisia 32°57N 10°29E **53** B8
Tatar Republic = Tatarstan □ Russia 55°30N 51°30E **18** C9
Tatarbunary Ukraine 45°50N 29°39E **17** F15
Tatarsk Russia 55°14N 76°0E **26** D8
Tatarskiy Proliv Russia 50°0N 141°0E **27** E15
Tatarstan □ Russia 55°30N 51°30E **18** C9
Tatatua, Pte. Tahiti 17°44S 149°8W **59** d
Tateyama Japan 35°0N 139°50E **29** G9
Tathlina L. Canada 60°33N 117°39W **70** A5
Tathra Australia 36°44S 149°59E **63** F4
Tatinnai L. Canada 60°55N 97°40W **71** A9
Tatla Lake Canada 52°0N 124°20W **70** C4
Tatnam, C. Canada 57°16N 91°0W **71** B10
Tatra = Tatry Slovakia 49°20N 20°0E **17** D11
Tatry Slovakia 49°20N 20°0E **17** D11
Tatshenshini → Canada 59°28N 137°45W **70** B1
Tatshenshini-Alsek △ Canada 59°55N 137°45W **70** B1
Tatsuno Japan 34°52N 134°33E **29** G7
Tatta = Thatta Pakistan 24°42N 67°55E **42** G2
Tatuï Brazil 23°25S 47°53W **95** A6
Tatum U.S.A. 33°16N 103°19W **77** K12
Tat'ung = Datong China 40°6N 113°18E **32** D7
Tatvan Turkey 38°31N 42°15E **46** B4
Ta'ū Amer. Samoa 14°15S 169°30W **59** b
Taubaté Brazil 23°0S 45°36W **95** A6
Tauern Austria 47°15N 12°40E **16** E7
Taumarunui N.Z. 38°53S 175°15E **59** C5
Taumaturgo Brazil 8°54S 72°51W **92** E4
Taung S. Africa 27°33S 24°47E **56** C3
Taungdwingyi Myanmar 20°1N 95°40E **41** J19
Taunggyi Myanmar 20°50N 97°0E **41** J20
Taungoo = Tounggoo Myanmar 19°0N 96°30E **41** K20
Taungup Pakistan 30°42N 70°39E **42** D4
Taunsa Pakistan 30°42N 70°39E **42** D4
Taunsa Barrage Pakistan 30°42N 70°50E **42** D4
Taunton U.K. 51°1N 3°5W **13** F4
Taunton U.S.A. 41°54N 71°6W **83** E13
Taunus Germany 50°13N 8°34E **16** C5
Taupo N.Z. 38°41S 176°7E **59** C6
Taupo, L. N.Z. 38°46S 175°55E **59** C5
Tauragė Lithuania 55°14N 22°16E **9** J20
Tauranga N.Z. 37°42S 176°11E **59** B6
Tauranga Harb. N.Z. 37°30S 176°5E **59** B6
Taureau, Rés. Canada 46°46N 73°50W **72** C5
Taurianova Italy 38°21N 16°1E **22** E7
Taurus Mts. = Toros Dağları Turkey 37°0N 32°30E **46** B2
Tautira Tahiti 17°44S 149°9W **59** d
Tauyskaya Guba Russia 59°20N 150°20E **27** D16
Tavan Bogd Uul Mongolia 49°10N 87°49E **30** B6
Tavastehus = Hämeenlinna Finland 61°0N 24°28E **8** F21
Tavda Russia 58°7N 65°8E **26** D7
Tavda → Russia 57°47N 67°18E **26** D7
Taverner B. Canada 67°12N 72°25W **69** D17
Taveuni Fiji 16°51S 179°58W **59** a
Tavira Portugal 37°8N 7°40W **21** D2
Tavistock Canada 43°19N 80°50W **82** C4
Tavistock U.K. 50°33N 4°9W **13** G3
Tavoy = Dawei Myanmar 14°2N 98°12E **38** E2
Tavoy Pt. Myanmar 13°32N 98°10E **38** E2
Tavrichanka Russia 43°18N 131°55E **28** C5
Tavua Fiji 17°37S 177°5E **59** a
Tavuki Fiji 19°7S 178°8E **59** a
Taw → U.K. 51°4N 4°4W **13** F3
Tawa → India 22°48N 77°48E **42** H8
Tawas City U.S.A. 44°16N 83°31W **81** C12
Tawau Malaysia 4°20N 117°55E **36** D5
Tawi-tawi I. Phil. 5°10N 120°15E **37** C6
Tawu Taiwan 22°21N 120°54E **35** F13
Taxco Mexico 18°33N 99°36W **87** D5
Taxila Pakistan 33°42N 72°52E **42** C5
Taxkorgan Tajik Zizhixian China 37°49N 75°14E **30** D4
Tay → U.K. 56°37N 3°38W **11** E5

Tay, Firth of *U.K.* 56°25N 3°8W **11** E5
Tay, L. *Australia* 32°55S 120°48E **61** F3
Tay, L. *U.K.* 56°32N 4°8W **11** E4
Tay △ *U.K.* 56°43N 3°59W **11** E5
Tay Ninh *Vietnam* 11°20N 106°5E **39** G6
Tayabamba *Peru* 8°15S 77°16W **92** E3
Taygetos Oros *Greece* 37°0N 22°23E **23** F10
Taylakova *Russia* 59°13N 74°0E **26** D8
Taylor *Canada* 56°13N 120°40W **70** B4
Taylor, Nebr., *U.S.A.* 41°46N 99°23W **80** E4
Taylor, Pa., *U.S.A.* 41°23N 75°43W **83** E9
Taylor, Tex., *U.S.A.* 30°34N 97°25W **84** F6
Taylor, Mt. *U.S.A.* 35°14N 107°37W **77** J10
Taylorville *U.S.A.* 39°33N 89°18W **80** F9
Taymā *Si. Arabia* 27°35N 38°45E **46** E3
Taymyr, Oz. *Russia* 74°20N 102°0E **27** B11
Taymyr, Poluostrov
    *Russia* 75°0N 100°0E **27** B11
Taypaq *Kazakhstan* 49°0N 51°47E **19** E9
Tayport *U.K.* 56°27N 2°52W **11** E6
Tayrona △ *Colombia* 11°20N 74°2W **89** D5
Tayshet *Russia* 55°58N 98°1E **27** D10
Taytay *Phil.* 10°45N 119°30E **37** B6
Ṭayyebād *Iran* 34°45N 60°45E **47** C9
Ṭāyyebād □ *Iran* 34°44N 60°45E **47** C9
Taz → *Russia* 67°32N 78°40E **26** C8
Taza *Morocco* 34°16N 4°6W **52** B5
Tāza Khurmātū *Iraq* 35°18N 44°20E **46** C5
Tazawa-Ko *Japan* 39°43N 140°40E **28** E10
Tazerbo *Libya* 25°45N 21°0E **53** C10
Tazin → *Canada* 59°48N 109°55W **71** B7
Tazin L. *Canada* 59°44N 108°42W **71** B7
Tazovskiy *Russia* 67°30N 78°44E **26** C8
Tbilisi *Georgia* 41°43N 44°50E **19** F7
Tchad = Chad ■ *Africa* 15°0N 17°15E **53** F8
Tchad, L. *Chad* 13°30N 14°30E **53** F8
Tch'eng-tou = Chengdu
    *China* 30°38N 104°2E **34** B5
Tchentlo L. *Canada* 55°15N 125°0W **70** B4
Tchibanga *Gabon* 2°45S 11°0E **54** E2
Tchogha Zanbil = Choghā Zanbil
    *Iran* 32°1N 48°32E **47** C6
Tch'ong-k'ing = Chongqing
    *China* 29°35N 106°25E **34** C6
Tczew *Poland* 54°8N 18°50E **17** A10
Te Anau, L. *N.Z.* 45°15S 167°45E **59** F1
Te Aroha *N.Z.* 37°32S 175°44E **59** B5
Te Awamutu *N.Z.* 38°1S 175°20E **59** C5
Te Ika-a-Māui = North I.
    *N.Z.* 38°0S 175°0E **59** C5
Te Kuiti *N.Z.* 38°20S 175°11E **59** C5
Te Puke *N.Z.* 37°46S 176°22E **59** B6
Te Waewae B. *N.Z.* 46°13S 167°33E **59** G1
Te Waipounamu = South I.
    *N.Z.* 44°0S 170°0E **59** F3
Teague *U.S.A.* 31°38N 96°17W **84** F6
Teahupoo *Tahiti* 17°50S 149°16W **59** d
Teapa *Mexico* 17°33N 92°57W **87** D6
Tebakang *Malaysia* 1°6N 110°30E **36** D4
Teberau → *Malaysia* 1°30N 103°42E **39** d
Tébessa *Algeria* 35°22N 8°8E **52** A7
Tebicuary → *Paraguay* 26°36S 58°16W **94** B4
Tebingtinggi *Riau,*
    *Indonesia* 1°0N 102°45E **36** E2
Tebingtinggi *Sumatera Utara,*
    *Indonesia* 3°20N 99°9E **36** D1
Tecate *Mexico* 32°34N 116°38W **79** N10
Tecka *Argentina* 43°29S 70°48W **96** E2
Tecomán *Mexico* 18°55N 103°53W **86** D4
Tecopa *U.S.A.* 35°51N 116°13W **79** K10
Tecoripa *Mexico* 28°37N 109°57W **86** B3
Tecuala *Mexico* 22°23N 105°27W **86** C3
Tecuci *Romania* 45°51N 27°27E **17** F14
Tecumseh *Canada* 42°19N 82°54W **82** D2
Tecumseh *Mich., U.S.A.* 42°0N 83°57W **81** D12
Tecumseh *Okla., U.S.A.* 35°15N 96°56W **84** D6
Tedzhen = Tejen
    *Turkmenistan* 37°23N 60°31E **26** F7
Tees → *U.K.* 54°37N 1°10W **12** C6
Tees B. *U.K.* 54°40N 1°9W **12** C6
Teeswater *Canada* 43°59N 81°17W **82** C3
Tefé *Brazil* 3°25S 64°50W **92** D6
Tegal *Indonesia* 6°52S 109°8E **37** G13
Tegallalang *Indonesia* 8°27S 115°17E **37** J18
Tegalsari *Indonesia* 8°25S 114°8E **37** J17
Tegid, L. = Bala, L. *U.K.* 52°53N 3°37W **12** E4
Tegucigalpa *Honduras* 14°5N 87°14W **88** D2
Tehachapi *U.S.A.* 35°8N 118°27W **79** K8
Tehachapi Mts. *U.S.A.* 35°0N 118°30W **79** L8
Tehoru *Indonesia* 3°23S 129°30E **37** E7
Tehrān □ *Iran* 35°30N 51°30E **47** C6
Tehri *India* 30°23N 78°29E **43** D8
Tehuacán *Mexico* 18°27N 97°23W **87** D5
Tehuantepec *Mexico* 16°21N 95°13W **87** D5
Tehuantepec, G. de
    *Mexico* 15°50N 95°12W **87** D5
Tehuantepec, Istmo de
    *Mexico* 17°15N 94°30W **87** D6
Teifi → *U.K.* 52°5N 4°41W **13** E3
Teign → *U.K.* 50°32N 3°32W **13** G4
Teignmouth *U.K.* 50°33N 3°31W **13** G4
Teinainano = Tarawa
    *Kiribati* 1°30N 173°0E **64** G9
Tejakula *Indonesia* 8°8S 115°20E **37** J18
Tejen *Turkmenistan* 37°23N 60°31E **26** F7
Tejen → *Turkmenistan* 37°24N 60°38E **47** B9
Tejo → *Europe* 38°40N 9°24W **21** C1
Tejon Pass *U.S.A.* 34°49N 118°53W **79** L8
Tekamah *U.S.A.* 41°47N 96°13W **80** E6
Tekapo, L. *N.Z.* 43°53S 170°33E **59** E3
Tekax *Mexico* 20°12N 89°17W **87** C7
Tekeli *Kazakhstan* 44°50N 79°0E **26** E8
Tekeze Dam *Ethiopia* 14°7N 39°4E **49** E2
Tekirdağ *Turkey* 40°58N 27°30E **23** D12
Tekkali *India* 18°37N 84°15E **44** E7
Tekoa *U.S.A.* 47°14N 117°4W **76** C5
Tekong Besar, Pulau
    *Singapore* 1°25N 104°3E **39** d
Tel → *India* 20°50N 83°54E **44** D6
Tel Aviv ✈ (TLV) *Israel* 32°5N 34°49E **48** C3
Tel Aviv-Yafo *Israel* 32°4N 34°48E **48** C3

Tel Lakhish *Israel* 31°34N 34°51E **48** D3
Tel Megiddo *Israel* 32°35N 35°11E **48** C4
Tela *Honduras* 15°40N 87°28W **88** C2
Telanaipura = Jambi
    *Indonesia* 1°38S 103°30E **36** E2
Telangana □ *India* 17°30N 78°30E **44** F4
Telavi *Georgia* 42°0N 45°30E **19** F8
Telegraph Creek *Canada* 58°0N 131°10W **70** B2
Telekhany = Tsyelyakhany
    *Belarus* 52°30N 25°46E **17** B13
Telemark *Norway* 59°15N 7°40E **9** G12
Telén *Argentina* 36°15S 65°31W **94** D2
Teleng *Iran* 25°47N 61°3E **47** E9
Teles Pires → *Brazil* 7°21S 58°3W **92** E7
Telescope Pk. *U.S.A.* 36°10N 117°5W **79** J9
Telford *U.K.* 52°40N 2°27W **13** E5
Telford and Wrekin □
    *U.K.* 52°45N 2°27W **12** E5
Telkwa *Canada* 54°41N 127°5W **70** C3
Tell City *U.S.A.* 37°57N 86°46W **80** G10
Teller *U.S.A.* 65°16N 166°22W **74** B6
Tellicherry = Thalassery
    *India* 11°45N 75°30E **45** J2
Telluride *U.S.A.* 37°56N 107°49W **77** H10
Teloloapán *Mexico* 18°21N 99°51W **87** D5
Telpos Iz *Russia* 63°16N 59°13E **18** B10
Teluk Anson = Teluk Intan
    *Malaysia* 4°3N 101°0E **39** K3
Teluk Bahang *Malaysia* 5°28N 100°13E **39** c
Teluk Betung = Bandar Lampung
    *Indonesia* 5°20S 105°10E **36** F3
Teluk Intan *Malaysia* 4°3N 101°0E **39** K3
Teluk Kumbar *Malaysia* 5°18N 100°14E **39** c
Telukbutun *Indonesia* 4°13N 108°12E **36** D3
Telukdalam *Indonesia* 0°33N 97°50E **36** D1
Tema *Ghana* 5°41N 0°0 **52** G5
Temagami, L. *Canada* 47°0N 80°10W **72** C3
Temax *Mexico* 21°9N 88°56W **87** C7
Temba △ *S. Africa* 25°20S 28°17E **57** C4
Tembagapura *Indonesia* 4°20S 137°0E **37** E9
Temblor Range *U.S.A.* 35°20N 119°50W **79** K7
Teme → *U.K.* 52°11N 2°13W **13** E5
Temecula *U.S.A.* 33°30N 117°9W **79** M9
Temengor, Tasik
    *Malaysia* 5°24N 101°18E **39** K3
Temerloh *Malaysia* 3°27N 102°25E **39** L4
Teminabuan *Indonesia* 1°26S 132°1E **37** E8
Temir *Kazakhstan* 49°1N 57°14E **19** E10
Temirtau *Kazakhstan* 50°5N 72°56E **30** A3
Témiscamie → *Canada* 50°59N 73°5W **73** B5
Témiscaming *Canada* 46°44N 79°5W **72** C4
Témiscamingue, L.
    *Canada* 47°10N 79°25W **72** C4
Temosachic *Mexico* 28°57N 107°51W **86** B3
Tempe *U.S.A.* 33°24N 111°54W **77** K8
Tempiute *U.S.A.* 37°39N 115°38W **78** H11
Temple *U.S.A.* 31°6N 97°21W **84** F6
Temple B. *Australia* 12°15S 143°3E **62** A3
Templemore *Ireland* 52°47N 7°51W **10** D4
Templeton *U.S.A.* 35°33N 120°42W **78** K6
Templeton → *Australia* 21°0S 138°40E **62** C2
Tempoal de Sánchez
    *Mexico* 21°31N 98°23W **87** C5
Temuco *Chile* 38°45S 72°40W **96** D2
Temuka *N.Z.* 44°14S 171°17E **59** F3
Ten Degree Channel
    *India* 10°0N 92°30E **45** K11
Tenabo *Mexico* 20°3N 90°14W **87** C6
Tenaha *U.S.A.* 31°57N 94°15W **84** F7
Tenakee Springs *U.S.A.* 57°47N 135°13W **70** D1
Tenali *India* 16°15N 80°35E **45** F5
Tenancingo *Mexico* 18°58N 99°38W **87** D5
Tenango del Valle *Mexico* 19°7N 99°33W **87** D5
Tenaro, Akra *Greece* 36°22N 22°27E **23** F10
Tenasserim = Taninthayi
    *Myanmar* 12°6N 99°3E **39** F2
Tenasserim □ *Myanmar* 14°0N 98°30E **38** F2
Tenasserim → *Myanmar* 12°24N 98°37E **38** F2
Tenby *U.K.* 51°40N 4°42W **13** F3
Tenda, Colle di *France* 44°7N 7°36E **20** D7
Tendaho *Ethiopia* 11°48N 40°54E **49** E3
Tendō *Japan* 38°20N 140°30E **28** E10
Tendukhera *India* 23°24N 79°33E **43** H8
Ténéré, Erg du *Niger* 17°35N 10°55E **53** E8
Tenerife *Canary Is.* 28°15N 16°35W **52** C2
Teng Xian *Guangxi Zhuangzu,*
    *China* 23°21N 110°56E **35** F8
Teng Xian *Shandong,*
    *China* 35°5N 117°10E **33** G9
Tengah, Kepulauan
    *Indonesia* 7°5S 118°15E **36** F5
Tengchong *China* 25°0N 98°28E **34** C2
Tengchowfu = Penglai
    *China* 37°48N 120°42E **33** F11
Tenggarong *Indonesia* 0°24S 116°58E **36** E5
Tengger Shamo *China* 38°0N 104°10E **32** F3
Tenggol, Pulau *Malaysia* 4°48N 103°41E **39** K4
Tengiz Köli *Kazakhstan* 50°30N 69°0E **30** A2
Tengzhou *China* 35°4N 117°9E **33** G9
Teniente Enciso △
    *Paraguay* 21°5S 61°8W **94** A3
Tenino *U.S.A.* 46°51N 122°51W **78** D4
Tenkasi *India* 8°55N 77°20E **45** K3
Tennant Creek *Australia* 19°30S 134°15E **62** B1
Tennessee □ *U.S.A.* 36°0N 86°30W **85** D11
Tennessee → *U.S.A.* 37°4N 88°34W **85** C10
Tenojoki = Tana →
    *Norway* 70°30N 28°14E **8** A23
Tenom *Malaysia* 5°4N 115°57E **36** C5
Tenosique *Mexico* 17°29N 91°26W **87** D6
Tenryū-Gawa → *Japan* 35°39N 137°48E **29** G8
Tenterden *U.K.* 51°4N 0°42E **13** F8
Tenterfield *Australia* 29°0S 152°0E **63** D5
Teófilo Otoni *Brazil* 17°50S 41°30W **93** G10
Tepa *Indonesia* 7°52S 129°31E **37** F7
Tepalcatepec → *Mexico* 18°35N 101°59W **86** D4
Tepehuanes *Mexico* 25°21N 105°44W **86** B3
Tepetongo *Mexico* 22°28N 103°9W **86** C4

Tepic *Mexico* 21°30N 104°54W **86** C4
Teplice *Czechia* 50°40N 13°48E **16** C7
Tequila *Mexico* 20°54N 103°47W **86** C4
Ter → *Spain* 42°2N 3°12E **21** A7
Ter Apel *Neths.* 52°53N 7°5E **15** B7
Téra *Niger* 14°0N 0°45E **52** F6
Teraina *Kiribati* 4°43N 160°25E **65** G12
Téramo *Italy* 42°39N 13°42E **22** C5
Terang *Australia* 38°15S 142°55E **63** F3
Terang, Teluk *Indonesia* 8°44S 116°0E **37** K19
Terceira *Azores* 38°43N 27°13W **52** a
Tercero → *Argentina* 32°58S 61°47W **94** C3
Terdal *India* 16°33N 75°3E **44** F2
Terebovlya *Ukraine* 49°18N 25°44E **17** D13
Terek → *Russia* 44°0N 47°30E **19** F8
Terengganu □ *Malaysia* 4°55N 103°0E **39** K4
Terepaima △ *Venezuela* 9°58N 69°17W **89** E6
Teresina *Brazil* 5°9S 42°45W **93** E10
Teressa *India* 8°15N 93°10E **45** K11
Terewah, L. *Australia* 29°52S 147°35E **63** D4
Teridgerie Cr. →
    *Australia* 30°25S 148°50E **63** E4
Termas de Río Hondo
    *Argentina* 27°29S 64°52W **94** B3
Términi Imerese *Italy* 37°59N 13°42E **22** F5
Términos, L. de *Mexico* 18°37N 91°33W **87** D6
Termiz *Uzbekistan* 37°15N 67°15E **26** F7
Térmoli *Italy* 42°0N 15°0E **22** C6
Ternate *Indonesia* 0°45N 127°25E **37** D7
Terneuzen *Neths.* 51°20N 3°50E **15** C3
Terney *Russia* 45°3N 136°37E **28** B8
Terni *Italy* 42°34N 12°37E **22** C5
Ternopil *Ukraine* 49°30N 25°40E **17** D13
Ternopil □ *Ukraine* 48°10N 25°10E **17** D13
Ternopol = Ternopil
    *Ukraine* 49°30N 25°40E **17** D13
Terowie *Australia* 33°8S 138°55E **63** E2
Terra Bella *U.S.A.* 35°58N 119°3W **79** K7
Terra Nova △ *Canada* 48°33S 53°55W **73** C9
Terrace *Canada* 54°30N 128°35W **70** C3
Terrace Bay *Canada* 48°47N 87°5W **72** C2
Terracina *Italy* 41°17N 13°15E **22** D5
Terralba *Italy* 39°43N 8°39E **22** E3
Terrassa *Spain* 41°34N 2°1E **21** B7
Terre Haute *U.S.A.* 39°28N 87°25W **80** F10
Terrebonne B. *U.S.A.* 29°5N 90°35W **85** G9
Terrenceville *Canada* 47°40N 54°44W **73** C9
Terry *U.S.A.* 46°47N 105°19W **76** C11
Terryville *U.S.A.* 41°41N 73°3W **83** E11
Terschelling *Neths.* 53°25N 5°20E **15** A5
Teruel *Spain* 40°22N 1°8W **21** B5
Tervola *Finland* 66°6N 24°49E **8** C21
Teryaweynya L.
    *Australia* 32°18S 143°22E **63** E3
Teshio *Japan* 44°53N 141°44E **28** B10
Teshio-Gawa → *Japan* 44°53N 141°45E **28** B10
Tesiyn Gol → *Mongolia* 50°40N 93°20E **30** A7
Teslin *Canada* 60°10N 132°43W **70** A2
Teslin → *Canada* 61°34N 134°35W **70** A2
Teslin L. *Canada* 60°15N 132°57W **70** A2
Tessalit *Mali* 20°12N 1°0E **52** D6
Tessaoua *Niger* 13°47N 7°56E **52** F7
Test → *U.K.* 50°56N 1°29W **13** G6
Testigos, Is. Los *Venezuela* 11°23N 63°7W **89** D7
Tetachuck L. *Canada* 53°18N 125°55W **70** C3
Tetas, Pta. *Chile* 23°31S 70°38W **94** A1
Tete *Mozam.* 16°13S 33°33E **55** H6
Teterev → *Ukraine* 51°1N 30°5E **17** C16
Teteven *Bulgaria* 42°58N 24°17E **23** C11
Tethul → *Canada* 60°35N 112°12W **70** A6
Tetiyev *Ukraine* 49°22N 29°38E **17** D15
Tetlit Zheh = Fort McPherson
    *Canada* 67°30N 134°55W **68** D5
Teton → *U.S.A.* 47°56N 110°31W **76** C8
Tétouan *Morocco* 35°35N 5°21W **52** A4
Tetovo *Macedonia* 42°1N 20°58E **23** C9
Tetufera, Mt. *Tahiti* 17°40S 149°26W **59** d
Teuco → *Argentina* 25°35S 60°11W **94** B3
Teulon *Canada* 50°23N 97°16W **71** C9
Teun *Indonesia* 6°59S 129°8E **37** F7
Teuri-Tō *Japan* 44°26N 141°19E **28** B10
Teutoburger Wald *Germany* 52°5N 8°22E **16** B5
Tevere → *Italy* 41°44N 12°14E **22** D5
Teverya *Israel* 32°47N 35°32E **48** C4
Teviot → *U.K.* 55°29N 2°38W **11** F6
Tewantin *Australia* 26°27S 153°3E **63** D5
Tewkesbury *U.K.* 51°59N 2°9W **13** F5
Texada I. *Canada* 49°40N 124°25W **70** D4
Texarkana *Ark., U.S.A.* 33°26N 94°2W **84** E7
Texarkana *Tex., U.S.A.* 33°26N 94°3W **84** E7
Texas *Australia* 28°49S 151°9E **63** D5
Texas □ *U.S.A.* 31°40N 98°30W **84** F5
Texas City *U.S.A.* 29°24N 94°54W **84** G7
Texel *Neths.* 53°5N 4°50E **15** A4
Texline *U.S.A.* 36°23N 103°2W **84** G3
Texoma, L. *U.S.A.* 33°50N 96°34W **84** E6
Teyateyaneng *Lesotho* 29°7S 27°34E **56** D4
Tezin *Afghan.* 34°24N 69°30E **42** B3
Teziutlán *Mexico* 19°49N 97°21W **87** D5
Tezpur *India* 26°40N 92°45E **41** F18
Tezzeron L. *Canada* 54°43N 124°30W **70** C4
Tha-anne → *Canada* 60°31N 94°37W **71** A10
Tha Deua *Laos* 17°57N 102°53E **38** D4
Tha Deua *Laos* 19°26N 101°50E **38** C3
Tha Li *Thailand* 17°37N 101°25E **38** D3
Tha Pla *Thailand* 17°48N 100°32E **38** D3
Tha Rua *Thailand* 14°34N 100°44E **38** E3
Tha Sala *Thailand* 8°40N 99°56E **39** H2
Tha Song Yang *Thailand* 17°34N 97°55E **38** D1
Thaba Putsoa *Lesotho* 29°45S 28°0E **57** D4
Thaba-Tseka *Lesotho* 29°32S 28°36E **57** D4
Thabana Ntlenyana
    *Lesotho* 29°30S 29°16E **57** D4
Thabazimbi *S. Africa* 24°40S 27°21E **57** B4
Thādiq *Si. Arabia* 25°18N 45°52E **46** E5
Thai Binh *Vietnam* 20°35N 106°1E **34** G6
Thai Muang *Thailand* 8°24N 98°16E **39** H2
Thai Nguyen *Vietnam* 21°35N 105°55E **34** G5
Thailand ■ *Asia* 16°0N 102°0E **38** E4
Thailand, G. of *Asia* 11°30N 101°0E **39** G3
Thakhek *Laos* 17°25N 104°45E **38** D5

Thal *Pakistan* 33°28N 70°33E **42** C4
Thal Desert *Pakistan* 31°10N 71°30E **42** D4
Thala La = Hkakabo Razi
    *Myanmar* 28°25N 97°23E **34** C1
Thalabarivat *Cambodia* 13°33N 105°57E **38** F5
Thalang = Amphoe Thalang
    *Thailand* 8°1N 98°20E **39** a
Thalara *Nepal* 29°20N 80°59E **43** E9
Thalassery *India* 11°45N 75°30E **45** J2
Thale Sap Songkhla
    *Thailand* 7°12N 100°28E **39** J3
Thallon *Australia* 28°39S 148°49E **63** D4
Thalu, Ko *Thailand* 9°26N 99°54E **39** b
Tham Lot *Thailand* 19°34N 98°16E **38** C2
Thamarit *Oman* 17°39N 54°2E **49** D5
Thames *N.Z.* 37°7S 175°34E **59** B5
Thames → *Canada* 42°20N 82°25W **82** D2
Thames → *U.K.* 51°29N 0°34E **13** F8
Thames → *U.S.A.* 41°18N 72°5W **83** E12
Thames Estuary *U.K.* 51°29N 0°52E **13** F8
Thamesford *Canada* 43°4N 81°0W **82** C4
Thamesville *Canada* 42°33N 81°59W **82** D3
Than *India* 22°34N 71°11E **42** H4
Than Kyun *Myanmar* 9°49N 98°4E **39** H1
Than Uyen *Vietnam* 22°0N 103°54E **38** B4
Thana Gazi *India* 27°25N 76°19E **42** F7
Thandla *India* 23°0N 74°34E **42** H6
Thandwe *Myanmar* 18°20N 94°30E **41** K19
Thane *India* 19°12N 72°59E **44** E1
Thanesar *India* 30°1N 76°52E **42** D7
Thanet, I. of *U.K.* 51°21N 1°20E **13** F9
Thangool *Australia* 24°38S 150°42E **62** C5
Thanh Hoa *Vietnam* 19°48N 105°46E **38** C5
Thanh Hung *Vietnam* 9°55N 105°43E **39** H5
Thanh Pho Ho Chi Minh
    *Vietnam* 10°58N 106°40E **39** G6
Thanh Thuy *Vietnam* 22°55N 104°51E **38** A5
Thanjavur *India* 10°48N 79°12E **45** J4
Thanlwin = Salween →
    *Myanmar* 16°31N 97°37E **41** L20
Thano Bula Khan
    *Pakistan* 25°22N 67°50E **42** G2
Thanya Buri *Thailand* 14°1N 100°45E **38** E3
Thaoge → *Botswana* 20°27S 22°36E **56** B3
Thaolintoa L. *Canada* 61°30N 96°25W **71** A9
Thap Lan △ *Thailand* 14°15N 102°16E **38** E4
Thap Sakae *Thailand* 11°30N 99°37E **39** G2
Thap Than *Thailand* 15°27N 99°54E **38** E2
Thar Desert *India* 28°0N 72°0E **42** F5
Tharad *India* 24°30N 71°44E **42** G4
Thargomindah *Australia* 27°58S 143°46E **63** D3
Tharp Fracture Zone
    *S. Ocean* 54°0S 135°0W **5** B14
Tharrawaddy *Myanmar* 17°38N 95°48E **41** L19
Tharthār, Buḩayrat ath
    *Iraq* 34°0N 43°15E **46** C4
Tharthar, L. = Tharthār, Buḩayrat
    ath *Iraq* 34°0N 43°15E **46** C4
Tharthar, W. ath → *Iraq* 34°32N 43°4E **46** C4
Thasos *Greece* 40°40N 24°40E **23** D11
That Khe *Vietnam* 22°16N 106°28E **34** F6
Thatcher *Ariz., U.S.A.* 32°51N 109°46W **77** K9
Thatcher *Colo., U.S.A.* 37°33N 104°7W **77** H11
Thaton *Myanmar* 16°55N 97°22E **41** L20
Thatta *Pakistan* 24°42N 67°55E **42** G2
Thaungdut *Myanmar* 24°30N 94°40E **41** G19
Thayawthadangy Kyun
    *Myanmar* 12°19N 98°0E **38** F1
Thayer *U.S.A.* 36°31N 91°33W **80** G8
Thayetmyo *Myanmar* 19°20N 95°10E **41** K19
Thazi *Myanmar* 21°0N 96°5E **41** J20
Thbeng Meanchey
    *Cambodia* 13°49N 104°58E **38** F5
The Bahamas ■ *N. Amer.* 24°0N 75°0W **89** B5
The Broads *U.K.* 52°45N 1°30E **12** E9
The Everglades *U.S.A.* 25°50N 81°0W **85** J14
The Gambia ■ *W. Afr.* 13°25N 16°0W **52** F2
The Gulf = Persian Gulf
    *Asia* 27°0N 50°0E **47** E6
The Hague = 's-Gravenhage
    *Neths.* 52°7N 4°17E **15** B4
The Pas *Canada* 53°45N 101°15W **71** C8
The Wash *U.K.* 52°58N 0°20E **12** E8
The Weald *U.K.* 51°4N 0°20E **13** F8
Thebes = Thiva *Greece* 38°19N 23°19E **23** E10
Thebes *Egypt* 25°40N 32°35E **53** C12
Thedford *U.S.A.* 41°59N 100°35W **80** E3
Theebine *Australia* 25°57S 152°34E **63** D5
Thekulthili L. *Canada* 61°3N 110°0W **71** A7
Thelon → *Canada* 64°16N 96°4W **71** A8
Theodore *Australia* 24°55S 150°3E **62** C5
Theodore *Canada* 51°26N 102°55W **71** C8
Theodore *U.S.A.* 30°33N 88°10W **85** K10
Theodore Roosevelt △
    *U.S.A.* 47°0N 103°25W **80** B2
Theodore Roosevelt L.
    *U.S.A.* 33°40N 111°10W **77** K8
Thepha *Thailand* 6°52N 100°58E **39** J3
Theresa *U.S.A.* 44°13N 75°48W **83** B9
Thermaïkos Kolpos
    *Greece* 40°15N 22°45E **23** D10
Thermopolis *U.S.A.* 43°39N 108°13W **76** E9
Thermopylæ *Greece* 38°48N 22°35E **23** E10
Thessalon *Canada* 46°20N 83°30W **72** C3
Thessalonica, Gulf of =
    Thermaïkos Kolpos
    *Greece* 40°15N 22°45E **23** D10
Thessaloníki *Greece* 40°38N 22°58E **23** D10
Thetford *U.K.* 52°25N 0°45E **13** E8
Thetford Mines *Canada* 46°8N 71°18W **73** C5
Theun → *Laos* 18°19N 104°0E **38** C5
Theunissen *S. Africa* 28°26S 26°43E **56** D4
Thevenard *Australia* 32°9S 133°38E **63** E1
Thibodaux *U.S.A.* 29°48N 90°49W **85** G9
Thicket Portage *Canada* 55°19N 97°42W **71** B9
Thief River Falls *U.S.A.* 48°7N 96°10W **80** A5
Thiel Mts. *Antarctica* 85°15S 91°0W **5** E16
Thiers *France* 45°52N 3°33E **20** D5
Thiès *Senegal* 14°50N 16°51W **52** F2
Thika *Kenya* 1°1S 37°5E **54** E7
Thimphu *Bhutan* 27°31N 89°45E **41** F16

Thina → *S. Africa* 31°18S 29°13E **57** D4
Þingvallavatn *Iceland* 64°11N 21°9W **8** D3
Thionville *France* 49°20N 6°10E **20** B7
Thira = Santorini *Greece* 36°23N 25°27E **23** F11
Third Cataract *Sudan* 19°42N 30°20E **53** E12
Thirsk *U.K.* 54°14N 1°19W **12** C6
Thiruvananthapuram
    *India* 8°41N 77°0E **45** K3
Thiruvarur *India* 10°46N 79°38E **45** J4
Thisted *Denmark* 56°58N 8°40E **9** H13
Thistle I. *Australia* 35°0S 136°8E **63** F2
Thithia = Cicia *Fiji* 17°45S 179°18W **59** a
Thitu I. *S. China Sea* 11°3N 114°17E **36** B4
Thiva *Greece* 38°19N 23°19E **23** E10
Þjórsá → *Iceland* 63°47N 20°48E **8** E4
Thlewiaza → *Canada* 60°29N 94°40W **71** A10
Thmar Puok *Cambodia* 13°57N 103°4E **38** F4
Tho Chu, Dao *Vietnam* 9°20N 103°28E **39** H4
Tho Vinh *Vietnam* 19°16N 105°42E **38** C5
Thoa → *Canada* 60°31N 109°47W **71** A7
Thoen *Thailand* 17°43N 99°12E **38** D2
Thoeng *Thailand* 19°41N 100°12E **38** C3
Thohoyandou *S. Africa* 22°58S 30°29E **55** J6
Thomas *U.S.A.* 35°45N 98°45W **84** D5
Thomas, L. *Australia* 26°4S 137°58E **63** D2
Thomas Hubbard, C.
    *Canada* 82°0N 94°25W **69** A13
Thomaston *U.S.A.* 32°53N 84°20W **85** E12
Thomasville *Ala., U.S.A.* 31°55N 87°44W **85** F11
Thomasville *Ga., U.S.A.* 30°50N 83°59W **85** F13
Thomasville *N.C., U.S.A.* 35°53N 80°5W **85** H5
Thompson *Canada* 55°45N 97°52W **71** B9
Thompson *U.S.A.* 41°52N 75°31W **83** E9
Thompson → *Canada* 50°15N 121°24W **70** C4
Thompson → *U.S.A.* 39°46N 93°37W **80** F7
Thompson Falls *U.S.A.* 47°36N 115°21W **76** C6
Thompson Pk. *U.S.A.* 41°0N 123°2W **76** F2
Thompson Springs
    *U.S.A.* 38°58N 109°43W **76** G9
Thompsontown *U.S.A.* 40°33N 77°14W **82** F7
Thomson *U.S.A.* 33°28N 82°30W **85** E13
Thomson → *Australia* 25°11S 142°53E **62** C3
Thong Yang *Thailand* 9°28N 99°56E **39** b
Thoothukudi = Tuticorin
    *India* 8°50N 78°12E **45** K4
Þórisvatn *Iceland* 64°20N 18°55W **8** D4
Thornaby on Tees *U.K.* 54°33N 1°18W **12** C6
Thornbury *Canada* 44°34N 80°26W **82** B4
Thorne *U.K.* 53°37N 0°57W **12** D7
Thornton *Canada* 44°34N 79°43W **82** B5
Thornton *U.S.A.* 39°52N 104°58W **76** G11
Thorold *Canada* 43°7N 79°12W **82** C5
Þórshöfn *Iceland* 66°12N 15°20W **8** C6
Thouin, C. *Australia* 20°20S 118°10E **60** D2
Thousand Islands *Canada* 44°20N 76°0W **83** B9
Thousand Oaks *U.S.A.* 34°10N 118°50W **79** L8
Thrace *Europe* 41°0N 27°0E **23** D12
Three Forks *U.S.A.* 45°54N 111°33W **76** D8
Three Gorges Dam
    *China* 30°45N 111°15E **35** B8
Three Gorges Res. = Sanxia
    Shuiku *China* 30°30N 107°58E **34** B6
Three Hills *Canada* 51°43N 113°15W **70** C6
Three Hummock I.
    *Australia* 40°25S 144°55E **63** G3
Three Pagodas Pass *Asia* 15°20N 98°30E **38** E2
Three Points, C. *Ghana* 4°42N 2°6W **52** H5
Three Rivers *Calif.,
    U.S.A.* 36°26N 118°54W **78** J8
Three Rivers *Tex., U.S.A.* 28°28N 98°11W **84** G5
Three Springs *Australia* 29°32S 115°45E **61** E2
Thrissur *India* 10°30N 76°18E **45** J3
Throssell, L. *Australia* 27°33S 124°10E **61** E3
Throssell Ra. *Australia* 22°3S 121°43E **60** D3
Thrushton △ *Australia* 27°47S 147°40E **63** D4
Thu Dau Mot *Vietnam* 10°58N 106°39E **39** G6
Thua → *Kenya* 1°31S 39°30E **54** E7
Thuamal Rampur *India* 19°23N 82°56E **44** E6
Thuan Hoa *Vietnam* 8°58N 105°30E **39** H5
Thubun Lakes *Canada* 61°30N 112°0W **71** A6
Thuin *Belgium* 50°20N 4°17E **15** D4
Thule = Qaanaaq
    *Greenland* 77°30N 69°10W **69** B18
Thule Air Base = Uummannaq
    *Greenland* 77°33N 68°52W **69** B18
Thun *Switz.* 46°45N 7°38E **20** C7
Thunder B. *U.S.A.* 45°0N 83°20W **82** B1
Thunder Bay *Canada* 48°20N 89°15W **72** C2
Thung Salaeng Luang △
    *Thailand* 16°43N 100°50E **38** D3
Thung Song *Thailand* 8°10N 99°40E **39** H2
Thungyai △ *Thailand* 15°20N 98°55E **38** E2
Thunkar *Bhutan* 27°55N 91°0E **41** F17
Thuong Tra *Vietnam* 16°2N 107°42E **38** D6
Thüringer Wald *Germany* 50°35N 11°0E **16** C6
Thuringowa △ *Australia* 19°18S 146°43E **62** B4
Thurles *Ireland* 52°41N 7°49W **10** D4
Thurrock □ *U.K.* 51°31N 0°23E **13** F8
Thursday I. *Australia* 10°30S 142°3E **62** A3
Thurso *Canada* 45°36N 75°15W **72** C4
Thurso *U.K.* 58°36N 3°32W **11** C5
Thurso → *U.K.* 58°36N 3°32W **11** C5
Thutade L. *Canada* 57°0N 126°55W **70** B3
Ti-Tree *Australia* 22°5S 133°22E **62** C1
Tian Shan *Asia* 40°30N 76°0E **30** C4
Tianchang *China* 32°40N 119°0E **35** A12
Tiandeng *China* 23°6N 107°7E **34** F6
Tiandong *China* 23°36N 107°8E **34** F6
Tian'e *China* 25°1N 107°9E **34** E6
Tianhe *China* 24°48N 108°40E **34** E7
Tianjin *China* 39°7N 117°12E **33** E9
Tianjin Shi □ *China* 39°7N 117°12E **33** E9
Tianjun *China* 37°0N 98°55E **32** C2
Tianlin *China* 24°21N 106°12E **34** E6
Tianmen *China* 30°39N 113°9E **35** B9
Tianquan *China* 30°7N 102°43E **34** B4
Tianshifu *China* 41°7N 124°22E **33** D13
Tiantai *China* 29°10N 121°2E **35** C13
Tianya *China* 18°18N 109°20E **38** C7

Tianyang *China* 23°42N 106°53E **34** F6
Tianyar *Indonesia* 8°12S 115°30E **37** J18
Tianzhen *China* 40°24N 114°5E **32** D8
Tianzhu *China* 26°54N 109°11E **34** D7
Tianzhuangtai *China* 40°43N 122°5E **33** D12
Tiarei *Tahiti* 17°32S 149°20W **59** d
Tiaret *Algeria* 35°20N 1°21E **52** A6
Tibagi *Brazil* 24°30S 50°24W **95** A5
Tibagi → *Brazil* 22°47S 51°1W **95** A5
Tibastī, Sarīr *Libya* 22°50N 18°30E **53** D9
Tibati *Cameroon* 6°22N 12°30E **54** C2
Tiber = Tevere → *Italy* 41°44N 12°14E **22** D5
Tiber Res. *U.S.A.* 48°19N 111°6W **76** B8
Tiberias = Teverya *Israel* 32°47N 35°32E **48** C4
Tiberias, L. = Yam Kinneret *Israel* 32°45N 35°35E **48** C4
Tibesti *Chad* 21°0N 17°30E **53** D9
Tibet = Xizang Zizhiqu □ *China* 32°0N 88°0E **30** E6
Tibet, Plateau of *Asia* 32°0N 86°0E **24** E10
Tibnī *Syria* 35°36N 39°50E **46** C3
Tibooburra *Australia* 29°26S 142°1E **63** D3
Tibrikot *Nepal* 29°3N 82°48E **43** E10
Tiburón, I. *Mexico* 29°0N 112°25W **86** B2
Ticino → *Italy* 45°9N 9°14E **20** D8
Ticonderoga *U.S.A.* 43°51N 73°26W **83** C11
Ticul *Mexico* 20°24N 89°32W **87** C7
Tidaholm *Sweden* 58°12N 13°58E **9** G15
Tiddim *Myanmar* 23°28N 93°45E **41** H18
Tiden *India* 7°15N 93°33E **45** L11
Tidioute *U.S.A.* 41°41N 79°24W **82** E5
Tidjikja *Mauritania* 18°29N 11°35W **52** E3
Tidore *Indonesia* 0°40N 127°25E **37** D7
Tiefa *China* 42°28N 123°26E **33** C12
Tiegang Shuiku *China* 22°37N 113°53E **31** a
Tiel *Neths.* 51°53N 5°26E **15** C5
Tieli *China* 46°57N 128°3E **31** B14
Tieling *China* 42°20N 123°55E **33** C12
Tielt *Belgium* 51°0N 3°20E **15** C3
Tien Shan = Tian Shan *Asia* 40°30N 76°0E **30** C4
Tien-tsin = Tianjin *China* 39°7N 117°12E **33** E9
Tien Yen *Vietnam* 21°20N 107°24E **38** B6
T'ienching = Tianjin *China* 39°7N 117°12E **33** E9
Tienen *Belgium* 50°48N 4°57E **15** D4
Tientsin = Tianjin *China* 39°7N 117°12E **33** E9
Tieri *Australia* 23°2S 148°21E **62** C4
Tierra Amarilla *Chile* 27°28S 70°18W **94** B1
Tierra Amarilla *U.S.A.* 36°42N 106°33W **77** H10
Tierra Colorada *Mexico* 17°11N 99°32W **87** D5
Tierra de Campos *Spain* 42°10N 4°50W **21** A3
Tierra del Fuego, I. Grande de *Argentina* 54°0S 69°0W **96** G3
Tiétar → *Spain* 39°50N 6°1W **21** C3
Tietê → *Brazil* 20°40S 51°35W **95** A5
Tiffin *U.S.A.* 41°7N 83°11W **81** E12
Tifton *U.S.A.* 31°27N 83°31W **85** F13
Tifu *Indonesia* 3°39S 126°24E **37** E7
Tiger Leaping Gorge = Hutiao Xia *China* 27°13N 100°9E **34** D3
Tighina = Bendery *Moldova* 46°50N 29°30E **17** E15
Tigil *Russia* 57°49N 158°40E **27** D16
Tigiria *India* 20°29N 85°31E **44** D7
Tignish *Canada* 46°58N 64°2W **73** C7
Tigre → *Peru* 4°30S 74°10W **92** D4
Tigre → *Venezuela* 9°20N 62°30W **92** B6
Tigris = Dijlah, Nahr → *Asia* 31°0N 47°25E **46** D5
Tigyaing *Myanmar* 23°45N 96°10E **41** H20
Tihāmah *Asia* 15°3N 41°55E **49** D3
Tiilikka △ *Finland* 63°40N 28°15E **8** E23
Tijara *India* 27°56N 76°31E **42** F7
Tijuana *Mexico* 32°32N 117°1W **79** N9
Tikal *Guatemala* 17°13N 89°24W **88** C2
Tikal △ *Guatemala* 17°23N 89°33W **88** C2
Tikamgarh *India* 24°44N 78°50E **43** G8
Tikchik Lakes *U.S.A.* 60°0N 159°0W **74** D8
Tikhoretsk *Russia* 45°56N 40°5E **19** E7
Tikhvin *Russia* 59°35N 33°30E **18** C5
Tikirarjuaq = Whale Cove *Canada* 62°10N 92°34W **71** A10
Tikrīt *Iraq* 34°35N 43°37E **46** C4
Tiksi *Russia* 71°40N 128°45E **27** B13
Tilā' al 'Alī *Jordan* 32°0N 35°52E **48** D4
Tilamuta *Indonesia* 0°32N 122°37E **37** D6
Tilburg *Neths.* 51°31N 5°6E **15** C5
Tilbury *Canada* 42°17N 82°23W **82** D2
Tilbury *U.K.* 51°27N 0°22E **13** F8
Tilcara *Argentina* 23°36S 65°23W **94** A2
Tilden *U.S.A.* 42°3N 97°50W **80** D5
Tilhar *India* 28°0N 79°45E **43** F8
Tilichiki *Russia* 60°27N 166°5E **27** C17
Till → *U.K.* 55°41N 2°13W **12** B5
Tillamook *U.S.A.* 45°27N 123°51W **76** D2
Tillanchong I. *India* 8°30N 93°37E **45** K11
Tillsonburg *Canada* 42°53N 80°44W **82** D4
Tilos *Greece* 36°27N 27°27E **23** F12
Tilpa *Australia* 30°57S 144°24E **63** E3
Tilt → *U.K.* 56°46N 3°51W **11** E5
Tilton *U.S.A.* 43°27N 71°36W **83** C13
Tiltonsville *U.S.A.* 40°10N 80°41W **82** F4
Timanskiy Kryazh *Russia* 65°58N 50°5E **18** A9
Timaru *N.Z.* 44°23S 171°14E **59** F3
Timber Creek *Australia* 15°40S 130°29E **60** C5
Timber Lake *U.S.A.* 45°26N 101°5W **80** C3
Timber Mt. *U.S.A.* 37°6N 116°28W **78** H10
Timbué, Ponta *Mozam.* 18°47S 36°22E **57** A6
Timbuktu = Tombouctou *Mali* 16°50N 3°0W **52** E5
Timika *Indonesia* 4°47S 136°32E **37** E9
Timimoun *Algeria* 29°14N 0°16E **52** C6
Timiris, Râs *Mauritania* 19°21N 16°30W **52** E2
Timiskaming, L. = Témiscamingue, L. *Canada* 47°10N 79°25W **72** C4
Timișoara *Romania* 45°43N 21°15E **17** F11
Timmins *Canada* 48°28N 81°25W **72** C3
Timok → *Serbia* 44°10N 22°40E **23** B10
Timoleague *Ireland* 51°39N 8°46W **10** E3

Timor *Asia* 9°0S 125°0E **37** F7
Timor-Leste ■ *Asia* 8°50S 126°0E **37** F7
Timor Sea *Ind. Oc.* 12°0S 127°0E **60** B4
Tin Can Bay *Australia* 25°56S 153°0E **63** D5
Tin Mt. *U.S.A.* 36°50N 117°10W **78** J10
Tin Shui Wai *China* 22°28N 114°0E **31** a
Tina = Thina → *S. Africa* 31°18S 29°13E **57** D4
Tîna, Khalîg el *Egypt* 31°10N 32°40E **48** D1
Tinaca Pt. *Phil.* 5°30N 125°25E **37** C7
Tindal *Australia* 14°31S 132°22E **60** B5
Tindivanam *India* 12°15N 79°41E **45** H4
Tindouf *Algeria* 27°42N 8°10W **52** C4
Tinfunque △ *Paraguay* 23°55S 60°17W **94** A3
Ting Jiang → *China* 24°45N 116°35E **35** E11
Tinggi, Pulau *Malaysia* 2°18N 104°7E **39** L5
Tingo María *Peru* 9°10S 75°54W **92** E3
Tingrela *Côte d'Ivoire* 10°27N 6°25W **52** F4
Tingri *China* 28°34N 86°38E **30** F6
Tinh Bien *Vietnam* 10°36N 104°57E **39** G5
Tinian *N. Marianas* 15°0N 145°38E **64** F6
Tinnevelly = Tirunelveli *India* 8°45N 77°45E **45** K3
Tinogasta *Argentina* 28°5S 67°32W **94** B2
Tinos *Greece* 37°33N 25°8E **23** F11
Tinpahar *India* 24°59N 87°44E **43** G12
Tintina *Argentina* 27°2S 62°45W **94** B3
Tintinara *Australia* 35°48S 140°2E **63** F3
Tiobraid Árann = Tipperary *Ireland* 52°28N 8°10W **10** D3
Tioga *N. Dak., U.S.A.* 48°24N 102°56W **80** A2
Tioga *Pa., U.S.A.* 41°55N 77°8W **82** E7
Tioman, Pulau *Malaysia* 2°50N 104°10E **39** L5
Tionesta *U.S.A.* 41°30N 79°28W **82** E5
Tipperary *Ireland* 52°28N 8°10W **10** D3
Tipperary □ *Ireland* 52°37N 7°55W **10** D4
Tipton *Calif., U.S.A.* 36°4N 119°19W **78** J7
Tipton *Iowa, U.S.A.* 41°46N 91°8W **80** E8
Tipton Mt. *U.S.A.* 35°32N 114°12W **79** K12
Tiptonville *U.S.A.* 36°23N 89°29W **85** C10
Tiptur *India* 13°15N 76°26E **45** H3
Tīrān *Iran* 32°45N 51°8E **47** C6
Tiranë *Albania* 41°18N 19°49E **23** D8
Tirari Desert *Australia* 28°22S 138°7E **63** D2
Tiraspol *Moldova* 46°55N 29°35E **17** E15
Tire *Turkey* 38°5N 27°45E **23** E12
Tirebolu *Turkey* 40°58N 38°45E **19** F6
Tiree *U.K.* 56°31N 6°55W **11** E2
Tiree, Passage of *U.K.* 56°30N 6°30W **11** E2
Tîrgovişte = Târgovişte *Romania* 44°55N 25°27E **17** F13
Tîrgu Jiu = Târgu Jiu *Romania* 45°5N 23°19E **17** F12
Tîrgu Mureş = Târgu Mureş *Romania* 46°31N 24°38E **17** E13
Tirich Mir *Pakistan* 36°15N 71°55E **40** A7
Tiritiri o te Moana = Southern Alps *N.Z.* 43°41S 170°11E **59** E3
Tirna → *India* 18°4N 76°57E **44** E3
Tirnavos *Greece* 39°45N 22°18E **23** E10
Tirodi *India* 21°40N 79°44E **44** J4
Tirol □ *Austria* 47°3N 10°43E **16** E6
Tirrukkovil *Sri Lanka* 7°7N 81°51E **45** L5
Tirso → *Italy* 39°53N 8°32E **22** E3
Tirtagangga *Indonesia* 8°24S 115°35E **37** J18
Tirthahalli *India* 13°42N 75°14E **45** H2
Tiruchchendur *India* 8°30N 78°11E **45** K4
Tiruchchirappalli *India* 10°45N 78°45E **45** J4
Tirukkoyilur *India* 11°57N 79°12E **45** J4
Tirumangalam *India* 9°49N 77°58E **45** K3
Tirumayam *India* 10°14N 78°45E **45** J4
Tirunelveli *India* 8°45N 77°45E **45** K3
Tirupati *India* 13°39N 79°25E **45** H4
Tiruppattur *Tamil Nadu, India* 10°8N 78°37E **45** J4
Tiruppattur *Tamil Nadu, India* 12°30N 78°30E **45** H4
Tiruppur *India* 11°5N 77°22E **45** J3
Tirur *India* 10°54N 75°55E **45** J2
Tiruttani *India* 13°11N 79°58E **45** H4
Tirutturaippundi *India* 10°32N 79°41E **45** J4
Tiruvalla *India* 9°23N 76°34E **45** K3
Tiruvallar *India* 13°9N 79°57E **45** H4
Tiruvannamalai *India* 12°15N 79°5E **45** H4
Tiruvettipuram *India* 12°39N 79°33E **45** H4
Tiruvottiyur *India* 13°10N 80°22E **45** H5
Tisa *India* 32°50N 76°9E **42** C7
Tisa → *Serbia* 45°15N 20°17E **23** B9
Tisdale *Canada* 52°50N 104°0W **71** C8
Tishomingo *U.S.A.* 34°14N 96°41W **84** D6
Tisza = Tisa → *Serbia* 45°15N 20°17E **23** B9
Tit-Ary *Russia* 71°55N 127°2E **27** B13
Tithwal *Pakistan* 34°21N 73°50E **43** B5
Titicaca, L. *S. Amer.* 15°30S 69°30W **92** G5
Titiwa *Nigeria* 12°14N 12°53E **53** F8
Titlagarh *India* 20°15N 83°11E **44** D6
Titule *Dem. Rep. of the Congo* 3°15N 25°31E **54** D5
Titusville *Fla., U.S.A.* 28°37N 80°49W **85** G14
Titusville *Pa., U.S.A.* 41°38N 79°41W **82** E5
Tivaouane *Senegal* 14°56N 16°45W **52** F2
Tiverton *Canada* 44°16N 81°32W **82** B3
Tiverton *U.K.* 50°54N 3°29W **13** G4
Tivoli *Italy* 41°58N 12°45E **22** D5
Tiwi *Australia* 11°33S 130°42E **60** B5
Tizi-Ouzou *Algeria* 36°42N 4°3E **52** A6
Tizimín *Mexico* 21°9N 88°9W **87** C7
Tiznit *Morocco* 29°48N 9°45W **52** C4
Tjeggelvas *Sweden* 66°37N 17°45E **8** C17
Tjeggelvas = Tjeggelvas *Sweden* 66°37N 17°45E **8** C17
Tjirebon = Cirebon *Indonesia* 6°45S 108°32E **37** G13
Tjirrkarli ⊙ *Australia* 26°0S 125°28E **61** E4
Tjluring *Indonesia* 8°25S 114°13E **37** J17
Tjörn *Sweden* 58°0N 11°35E **9** H14
Tjukayirla Roadhouse *Australia* 27°10S 124°34E **61** E3
Tjurabalan ⊙ *Australia* 19°50S 128°0E **60** C4
Tlacotalpan *Mexico* 18°37N 95°40W **87** D5

Tlahualilo de Zaragoza *Mexico* 26°7N 103°27W **86** B4
Tlaquepaque *Mexico* 20°39N 103°19W **86** C4
Tlaxcala *Mexico* 19°19N 98°14W **87** D5
Tlaxcala □ *Mexico* 19°25N 98°10W **87** D5
Tlaxiaco *Mexico* 17°25N 97°35W **87** D5
Tlemcen *Algeria* 34°52N 1°21W **52** B5
Tlokweng *Botswana* 24°40S 25°58E **56** B4
To Bong *Vietnam* 12°45N 109°16E **38** F7
Toad → *Canada* 59°25N 124°57W **70** B4
Toad River *Canada* 58°51N 125°14W **70** B3
Toamasina *Madag.* 18°10S 49°25E **55** H9
Toay *Argentina* 36°43S 64°38W **94** D3
Toba *China* 31°19N 97°42E **34** B1
Toba *Japan* 34°30N 136°51E **29** G8
Toba, Danau *Indonesia* 2°30N 98°30E **36** D1
Toba Kakar *Pakistan* 31°30N 69°0E **42** D3
Toba Tek Singh *Pakistan* 30°55N 72°25E **42** D5
Tobago *Trin. & Tob.* 11°10N 60°30W **93** J16
Tobelo *Indonesia* 1°45N 127°56E **37** D7
Tobermory *Canada* 45°12N 81°40W **82** A3
Tobermory *U.K.* 56°38N 6°5W **11** E2
Tobi *Palau* 2°40N 131°10E **37** D8
Tobi-Shima *Japan* 41°12N 139°34E **28** D9
Tobin, L. *Australia* 21°45S 125°49E **60** D4
Tobin L. *Canada* 53°35N 103°30W **71** C8
Toboali *Indonesia* 3°0S 106°25E **36** E3
Tobol → *Russia* 58°10N 68°12E **26** D7
Toboli *Indonesia* 0°38S 120°5E **37** E6
Tobolsk *Russia* 58°15N 68°10E **26** D7
Tobruk = Tubruq *Libya* 32°7N 23°55E **53** B10
Tobyhanna *U.S.A.* 41°11N 75°25W **83** E9
Tobyl = Tobol → *Russia* 58°10N 68°12E **26** D7
Tocantinópolis *Brazil* 6°20S 47°25W **93** E9
Tocantins □ *Brazil* 10°0S 48°0W **93** F9
Tocantins → *Brazil* 1°45S 49°10W **93** D9
Toccoa *U.S.A.* 34°35N 83°19W **85** D13
Tochi → *Pakistan* 32°49N 70°41E **42** C4
Tochigi *Japan* 36°25N 139°45E **29** F9
Tochigi □ *Japan* 36°45N 139°45E **29** F9
Toco *Trin. & Tob.* 10°49N 60°57W **93** K16
Toconao *Chile* 23°11S 68°1W **94** A2
Tocopilla *Chile* 22°5S 70°10W **94** A1
Tocumwal *Australia* 35°51S 145°31E **63** F4
Tocuyo → *Venezuela* 11°3N 68°23W **92** A5
Todd → *Australia* 24°52S 135°48E **62** C2
Todeli *Indonesia* 1°40S 124°29E **37** E6
Todgarh *India* 25°42N 73°58E **42** G5
Todos os Santos, B. de *Brazil* 12°48S 38°38W **93** F11
Todos Santos *Mexico* 23°26N 110°13W **86** C2
Toe Hd. *U.K.* 57°50N 7°8W **11** D1
Tofield *Canada* 53°25N 112°40W **70** C6
Tofino *Canada* 49°11N 125°55W **70** D3
Töfsingdalen △ *Sweden* 62°10N 12°28E **8** E15
Tofua *Tonga* 19°45S 175°5W **59** c
Tōgane *Japan* 35°33N 140°22E **29** G10
Togian, Kepulauan *Indonesia* 0°20S 121°50E **37** E6
Togliatti *Russia* 53°32N 49°24E **18** D8
Togo ■ *W. Afr.* 8°30N 1°35E **52** G6
Togtoh *China* 40°15N 111°10E **32** D6
Tohiea, Mt. *Moorea* 17°33S 149°49W **59** d
Tōhoku □ *Japan* 39°50N 141°45E **28** E10
Tōhöm *Mongolia* 44°27N 108°2E **32** B5
Toibalewe *India* 10°32N 92°30E **45** J11
Toinya *South Sudan* 6°17N 29°46E **53** G11
Toiyabe Range *U.S.A.* 39°30N 117°0W **76** G5
Tojikiston = Tajikistan ■ *Asia* 38°30N 70°0E **26** F8
Tōjō *Japan* 34°53N 133°16E **29** G6
Tok *U.S.A.* 63°20N 142°59W **68** E3
Tokachi-Dake *Japan* 43°17N 142°5E **28** C11
Tokachi-Gawa → *Japan* 42°44N 143°42E **28** C11
Tokala *Indonesia* 1°30S 121°40E **37** E6
Tōkamachi *Japan* 37°8N 138°43E **29** F9
Tokanui *N.Z.* 46°34S 168°56E **59** G2
Tokara-Rettō *Japan* 29°37N 129°43E **29** K4
Tokarahi *N.Z.* 44°56S 170°39E **59** F3
Tokashiki-Shima *Japan* 26°11N 127°21E **29** L3
Tokat *Turkey* 40°22N 36°35E **19** F6
Tŏkch'ŏn *N. Korea* 39°45N 126°18E **33** E14
Tokdo = Liancourt Rocks *Asia* 37°15N 131°52E **29** F5
Tokeland *U.S.A.* 46°42N 123°59W **78** D3
Tokelau Is. ☑ *Pac. Oc.* 9°0S 171°45W **64** H10
Tokmak *Kyrgyzstan* 42°49N 75°15E **26** E8
Toko Ra. *Australia* 23°5S 138°20E **62** C2
Tokoro-Gawa → *Japan* 44°7N 144°5E **28** B12
Toku *Tonga* 18°10S 174°11W **59** c
Tokuno-Shima *Japan* 27°56N 128°55E **29** L4
Tokushima *Japan* 34°4N 134°34E **29** G7
Tokushima □ *Japan* 33°55N 134°0E **29** H7
Tokuyama = Shunan *Japan* 34°3N 131°50E **29** G5
Tokyo *Japan* 35°43N 139°45E **29** G9
Tolaga Bay *N.Z.* 38°21S 178°20E **59** C7
Tolbukhin = Dobrich *Bulgaria* 43°37N 27°49E **23** C12
Toledo *Brazil* 24°44S 53°45W **95** A5
Toledo *Spain* 39°50N 4°2W **21** C3
Toledo *Ohio, U.S.A.* 41°39N 83°33W **81** E12
Toledo *Oreg., U.S.A.* 44°37N 123°56W **76** D2
Toledo *Wash., U.S.A.* 46°26N 122°51W **78** D4
Toledo, Montes de *Spain* 39°33N 4°20E **21** C3
Toledo Bend Res. *U.S.A.* 31°11N 93°34W **84** F8
Tolga *Algeria* 17°15S 145°29E **52** B7
Toliara *Madag.* 23°21S 43°40E **55** J8
Tolima *Colombia* 4°40N 75°19W **92** C3
Tolitoli *Indonesia* 1°5N 120°50E **37** D6
Tollhouse *U.S.A.* 37°1N 119°24W **78** H7
Tolmachevo *Russia* 58°56N 29°51E **9** G23
Tolo, Teluk *Indonesia* 2°20S 122°10E **37** E6
Toluca *Mexico* 19°17N 99°40W **87** D5
Tolyatti = Togliatti *Russia* 53°32N 49°24E **18** D8
Tom Burke *S. Africa* 23°5S 28°0E **57** B4
Tom Price *Australia* 22°40S 117°48E **60** D2
Tomah *U.S.A.* 43°59N 90°30W **80** D8
Tomahawk *U.S.A.* 45°28N 89°44W **80** C9

Tomakomai *Japan* 42°38N 141°36E **28** C10
Tomales *U.S.A.* 38°15N 122°53W **78** G4
Tomales B. *U.S.A.* 38°15N 123°58W **78** G3
Tomanivi *Fiji* 17°37S 178°1E **59** a
Tomar *Portugal* 39°36N 8°25W **21** C1
Tomatlán *Mexico* 19°56N 105°15W **86** D3
Tombador, Serra do *Brazil* 12°0S 58°0W **92** F7
Tombigbee → *U.S.A.* 31°8N 87°57W **85** F11
Tombouctou *Mali* 16°50N 3°0W **52** E5
Tombstone *U.S.A.* 31°43N 110°4W **77** L8
Tombua *Angola* 15°55S 11°55E **56** A1
Tomé *Chile* 36°36S 72°57W **94** D1
Tome *Japan* 38°40N 141°20E **28** E10
Tomelloso *Spain* 39°10N 3°2W **21** C4
Tomini *Indonesia* 0°30N 120°30E **37** D6
Tomini, Teluk *Indonesia* 0°10S 121°0E **37** E6
Tomintoul *U.K.* 57°15N 3°23W **11** D5
Tomkinson Ranges *Australia* 26°11S 129°5E **61** E4
Tommot *Russia* 59°4N 126°20E **27** D13
Tomnop Ta Suos *Cambodia* 11°20N 104°15E **39** G5
Tomo → *Colombia* 5°20N 67°48W **92** B5
Toms Place *U.S.A.* 37°34N 118°41W **78** H8
Toms River *U.S.A.* 39°58N 74°12W **83** G10
Tomsk *Russia* 56°30N 85°5E **26** D9
Tomür Feng = Pobedy, Pik *Asia* 42°0N 79°58E **30** C4
Tonalá *Chiapas, Mexico* 16°4N 93°45W **87** D6
Tonalá *Jalisco, Mexico* 20°37N 103°14W **86** C4
Tonantins *Brazil* 2°45S 67°45W **92** D5
Tonasket *U.S.A.* 48°42N 119°26W **76** B4
Tonawanda *U.S.A.* 43°1N 78°53W **82** D6
Tonb = Tunb *U.A.E.* 26°15N 55°15E **47** E7
Tonbridge *U.K.* 51°11N 0°17E **13** F8
Tondano *Indonesia* 1°35N 124°54E **37** D6
Tondi *India* 9°45N 79°4E **45** K4
Tondoro *Namibia* 17°45S 18°50E **56** A2
Tone → *Australia* 34°25S 116°25E **61** F2
Tone-Gawa → *Japan* 35°44N 140°51E **29** F9
Tonekābon *Iran* 36°45N 51°12E **47** B6
Tong Xian *China* 39°55N 116°35E **32** E9
Tong-yeong *S. Korea* 34°50N 128°20E **33** G15
Tonga ■ *Pac. Oc.* 19°50S 174°30W **59** c
Tonga Trench *Pac. Oc.* 18°0S 173°0W **64** J10
Tongaat *S. Africa* 29°33S 31°9E **57** D5
Tong'an *China* 24°37N 118°8E **35** E12
Tongareva = Penrhyn *Cook Is.* 9°0S 158°0W **65** H12
Tongariro △ *N.Z.* 39°8S 175°33E **59** C6
Tongatapu *Tonga* 21°10S 175°10W **59** c
Tongatapu Group *Tonga* 21°0S 175°0W **59** c
Tongbai *China* 32°25N 113°35E **35** A9
Tongcheng *Anhui, China* 31°4N 116°56E **35** B11
Tongcheng *Hubei, China* 29°15N 113°50E **35** C9
Tongchuan *China* 35°6N 109°3E **32** G5
Tongdao *China* 26°10N 109°42E **34** D7
Tongeren *Belgium* 50°47N 5°28E **15** D5
Tonggu *China* 28°31N 114°20E **35** C10
Tonggu Jiao *China* 22°22N 113°37E **31** a
Tongguan *China* 34°40N 110°25E **32** G6
Tonghai *China* 24°10N 102°53E **34** E4
Tonghua *China* 41°42N 125°58E **33** D13
Tongjiang *Heilongjiang, China* 47°40N 132°27E **31** B15
Tongjiang *Sichuan, China* 31°58N 107°11E **34** B6
Tongjosŏn-man *N. Korea* 39°30N 128°0E **33** E15
Tongking, G. of = Tonkin, G. of *Asia* 20°0N 108°0E **38** C7
Tongliang *China* 29°50N 106°3E **34** C6
Tongliao *China* 43°38N 122°18E **33** C12
Tongling *China* 30°55N 117°48E **35** B11
Tonglu *China* 29°45N 119°37E **35** C12
Tongnan = Anyue *China* 30°9N 105°50E **34** B5
Tongoy *Chile* 30°16S 71°31W **94** C1
Tongren *Guizhou, China* 27°43N 109°11E **34** D7
Tongren *Qinghai, China* 35°25N 102°5W **34** D9
Tongres = Tongeren *Belgium* 50°47N 5°28E **15** D5
Tongsa Dzong *Bhutan* 27°31N 90°31E **41** F17
Tongshi *China* 18°50N 109°20E **38** C7
Tongue *U.K.* 58°29N 4°25W **11** C4
Tongue → *U.S.A.* 46°25N 105°52W **76** C11
Tongwei *China* 35°0N 105°5E **32** G3
Tongxin *China* 36°59N 105°58E **32** F3
Tongyang *N. Korea* 39°9N 126°53W **33** E14
Tongyu *China* 44°45N 123°4E **33** B12
Tongzhou *China* 32°12N 121°2E **35** A13
Tongzi *China* 28°9N 106°49E **34** C6
Tonj *South Sudan* 7°20N 28°44E **53** G11
Tonk *India* 26°6N 75°54E **42** F6
Tonkawa *U.S.A.* 36°41N 97°18W **84** C6
Tonkin = Bac Phan *Vietnam* 22°0N 105°0E **34** G5
Tonkin, G. of *Asia* 20°0N 108°0E **38** C7
Tonlé Sap *Cambodia* 13°0N 104°0E **38** F5
Tono *Japan* 39°19N 141°32E **28** E10
Tonopah *U.S.A.* 38°4N 117°14W **77** G5
Tonosí *Panama* 7°20N 80°20W **88** E3
Tons → *Haryana, India* 30°30N 77°39E **42** D7
Tons → *Ut. P., India* 26°1N 83°33E **43** F10
Tønsberg *Norway* 59°19N 10°25E **9** G14
Tonto △ *U.S.A.* 33°39N 111°7W **77** K8
Tonumea *Tonga* 20°30S 174°30W **59** c
Toobanna *Australia* 18°42S 146°9E **62** B4
Toodyay *Australia* 31°34S 116°28E **61** F2
Tooele *U.S.A.* 40°32N 112°18W **76** F7
Toompine *Australia* 27°15S 144°19E **63** D3
Toora *Australia* 38°39S 146°23E **63** F4
Toora-Khem *Russia* 52°28N 96°17E **27** D10
Toowoomba *Australia* 27°32S 151°56E **63** D5
Top Springs *Australia* 16°37S 131°51E **60** C5
Topaz *U.S.A.* 38°41N 119°30E **78** G7
Topley *Canada* 54°49N 126°30W **70** C3
Topocalma, Pta. *Chile* 34°10S 72°2W **94** C1
Topock *U.S.A.* 34°46N 114°29W **79** L12

Topol'čany *Slovakia* 48°35N 18°12E **17** D10
Topolobampo *Mexico* 25°36N 109°3W **86** B3
Topozero, Ozero *Russia* 65°35N 32°0E **8** D25
Toppenish *U.S.A.* 46°23N 120°19W **76** C3
Torata *Peru* 17°23S 70°1W **92** G4
Torbalı *Turkey* 38°10N 27°21E **23** E12
Torbat-e Heydārīyeh *Iran* 35°15N 59°12E **47** C8
Torbat-e Jām *Iran* 35°16N 60°35E **47** C9
Torbay *Canada* 47°40N 52°42W **73** C9
Torbay □ *U.K.* 50°26N 3°31W **13** G4
Tordesillas *Spain* 41°30N 5°0W **21** B3
Torfaen □ *U.K.* 51°43N 3°3W **13** F4
Torgau *Germany* 51°34N 13°0E **16** C7
Torhout *Belgium* 51°5N 3°7E **15** C3
Tori-Shima *Japan* 30°29N 140°19E **29** J10
Torilla Pen. *Australia* 22°29S 150°5E **62** C5
Torino *Italy* 45°3N 7°40E **20** D7
Torit *South Sudan* 4°27N 32°31E **53** H12
Torkamān *Iran* 37°35N 47°23E **46** B5
Tormes → *Spain* 41°18N 6°29W **21** B2
Tornado Mt. *Canada* 49°55N 114°40W **70** D6
Torneå = Tornio *Finland* 65°50N 24°12E **8** D21
Torneälven → *Europe* 65°50N 24°12E **8** D21
Torneträsk *Sweden* 68°24N 19°15E **8** B18
Torngat Mountains Nat. Park △ *Canada* 59°0N 63°40W **69** F19
Torngat Mts. *Canada* 59°0N 63°40W **69** F19
Tornio *Finland* 65°50N 24°12E **8** D21
Tornionjoki = Torneälven → *Europe* 65°50N 24°12E **8** D21
Tornquist *Argentina* 38°8S 62°15W **94** D3
Toro, Cerro del *Chile* 29°10S 69°50W **94** B2
Toro Pk. *U.S.A.* 33°34N 116°24W **79** M10
Toronto *Canada* 43°39N 79°20W **82** C5
Toronto *U.S.A.* 40°28N 80°36W **82** F4
Toropets *Russia* 56°30N 31°40E **18** C5
Tororo *Uganda* 0°45N 34°12E **54** D6
Toros Dağları *Turkey* 37°0N 32°30E **46** B2
Torpa *India* 22°57N 85°6E **43** H11
Torquay *U.K.* 50°27N 3°32W **13** G4
Torrance *U.S.A.* 33°50N 118°20W **79** M8
Torre de Moncorvo *Portugal* 41°12N 7°8W **21** B2
Torre del Greco *Italy* 40°47N 14°22E **22** D6
Torrejón de Ardoz *Spain* 40°27N 3°29W **21** B4
Torrelavega *Spain* 43°20N 4°5W **21** A3
Torremolinos *Spain* 36°38N 4°30W **21** D3
Torrens, L. *Australia* 31°0S 137°50E **63** E2
Torrens Cr. → *Australia* 22°23S 145°9E **62** C4
Torrens Creek *Australia* 20°48S 145°3E **62** C4
Torrent *Spain* 39°27N 0°28W **21** C5
Torreón *Mexico* 25°33N 103°26W **86** B4
Torres *Brazil* 29°21S 49°44W **95** B5
Torres *Mexico* 28°46N 110°47W **86** B2
Torres Strait *Australia* 9°50S 142°20E **62** a
Torres Vedras *Portugal* 39°5N 9°15W **21** C1
Torrevieja *Spain* 37°59N 0°42W **21** D5
Torrey *U.S.A.* 38°18N 111°25W **76** G8
Torridge → *U.K.* 51°0N 4°13W **13** G3
Torridon, L. *U.K.* 57°35N 5°50W **11** D3
Torrington *Conn., U.S.A.* 41°48N 73°7W **83** E11
Torrington *Wyo., U.S.A.* 42°4N 104°11W **76** E11
Tórshavn *Færoe Is.* 62°5N 6°56W **8** E9
Tortola *Br. Virgin Is.* 18°19N 64°45W **89** e
Tortosa *Spain* 40°49N 0°31E **21** B6
Tortosa, C. *Spain* 40°41N 0°52E **21** B6
Tortue, Î. de la *Haiti* 20°5N 72°57W **89** B5
Tortuguero △ *Costa Rica* 10°31N 83°29W **88** D3
Ţorūd *Iran* 35°25N 55°5E **47** C7
Toruń *Poland* 53°2N 18°39E **17** B10
Tory Hill *Canada* 44°58N 78°16W **82** B6
Tory I. *Ireland* 55°16N 8°13W **10** A3
Tosa *Japan* 33°24N 133°23E **29** H6
Tosa-Shimizu *Japan* 32°52N 132°58E **29** H6
Tosa-Wan *Japan* 33°15N 133°30E **29** H6
Toscana □ *Italy* 43°25N 11°0E **22** C4
Toshka, Buheirat en *Egypt* 22°50N 31°0E **53** D12
Toshkent *Uzbekistan* 41°20N 69°10E **26** E7
Tostado *Argentina* 29°15S 61°50W **94** B3
Tosu *Japan* 33°22N 130°31E **29** H5
Toteng *Botswana* 20°22S 22°58E **56** B3
Totma *Russia* 60°0N 42°40E **18** C7
Totnes *U.K.* 50°26N 3°42W **13** G4
Totness *Suriname* 5°53N 56°19W **93** B7
Totonicapán *Guatemala* 14°58N 91°12W **88** D1
Totten Glacier *Antarctica* 66°45S 116°10E **5** C8
Tottenham *Australia* 32°14S 147°21E **63** E4
Tottenham *Canada* 44°1N 79°49W **82** B5
Tottori *Japan* 35°30N 134°15E **29** G7
Tottori □ *Japan* 35°30N 134°12E **29** G7
Toubkal, Djebel *Morocco* 31°0N 8°0W **52** B4
Tougan *Burkina Faso* 13°11N 2°58W **52** F5
Touggourt *Algeria* 33°6N 6°4E **52** B7
Toul *France* 48°40N 5°53E **20** B6
Touliu *Taiwan* 23°42N 120°31E **35** F13
Toulon *France* 43°10N 5°55E **20** E6
Toulouse *France* 43°37N 1°27E **20** E4
Toummo *Niger* 22°45N 14°8E **53** D8
Tounan *Taiwan* 23°41N 120°28E **35** F13
Tounggoo *Myanmar* 19°0N 96°30E **41** K20
Touraine *France* 47°20N 0°30E **20** C4
Tourcoing *France* 50°42N 3°10E **20** A5
Touriñán, C. *Spain* 43°3N 9°18W **21** A1
Tournai *Belgium* 50°35N 3°25E **15** D3
Tournon-sur-Rhône *France* 45°4N 4°50E **20** D6
Tours *France* 47°22N 0°40E **20** C4
Toussoro, Mt. *C.A.R.* 9°7N 23°14E **54** C4
Touws → *S. Africa* 33°45S 21°11E **56** D3
Touwsrivier *S. Africa* 33°20S 20°2E **56** D3
Towada *Japan* 40°37N 141°13E **28** D10
Towada-Hachimantai △ *Japan* 40°20N 140°55E **28** D10
Towada-Ko *Japan* 40°28N 140°55E **28** D10
Tower *U.S.A.* 47°48N 92°17W **80** B7
Towerhill Cr. → *Australia* 22°28S 144°35E **62** C3
Towner *U.S.A.* 48°21N 100°25W **80** A3
Townsend *U.S.A.* 46°19N 111°31W **76** C8

Townshend I. Australia 22°10S 150°31E 62 C5
Townsville Australia 19°15S 146°45E 62 B4
Towraghondī Afghan. 35°13N 62°16E 40 B3
Towson U.S.A. 39°24N 76°36W 81 F15
Towuti, Danau Indonesia 2°45S 121°32E 37 E6
Tōya-Ko Japan 42°35N 140°51E 28 C10
Toyama Japan 36°40N 137°15E 29 F8
Toyama □ Japan 36°45N 137°30E 29 F8
Toyama-Wan Japan 37°0N 137°30E 29 F8
Toyapakeh Indonesia 8°41S 115°29E 37 K18
Toyohashi Japan 34°45N 137°25E 29 G8
Toyokawa Japan 34°48N 137°27E 29 G8
Toyooka Japan 35°35N 134°48E 29 G7
Toyota Japan 35°3N 137°7E 29 G8
Tozeur Tunisia 33°56N 8°8E 52 B7
Trá Li = Tralee Ireland 52°16N 9°42W 10 D2
Trá Mhór = Tramore
  Ireland 52°10N 7°10W 10 D4
Tra On Vietnam 9°58N 105°55E 39 H5
Tra Vinh Vietnam 9°50N 106°15E 39 H6
Trabzon Turkey 41°0N 39°45E 19 F6
Tracadie Canada 47°30N 64°55W 73 C7
Tracy Canada 46°1N 73°9W 72 C5
Tracy Calif., U.S.A. 37°44N 121°26W 78 H5
Tracy Minn., U.S.A. 44°14N 95°37W 80 C6
Trafalgar, C. Spain 36°10N 6°2W 21 D2
Trail Canada 49°5N 117°40W 70 D5
Trainor L. Canada 60°24N 120°17W 70 A4
Trakai △ Lithuania 54°30N 25°10E 9 J21
Tralee Ireland 52°16N 9°42W 10 D2
Tralee B. Ireland 52°17N 9°55W 10 D2
Tram Chim △ Vietnam 10°43N 105°31E 39 G5
Tramore Ireland 52°10N 7°10W 10 D4
Tramore B. Ireland 52°9N 7°10W 10 D4
Tran Ninh, Cao Nguyen
  Laos 19°30N 103°10E 38 C4
Tranås Sweden 58°3N 14°59E 9 G16
Trancas Argentina 26°11S 65°20W 94 B2
Trang Thailand 7°33N 99°38E 39 J2
Trangan Indonesia 6°40S 134°20E 37 F8
Trangie Australia 32°4S 148°0E 63 E4
Trani Italy 41°17N 16°25E 22 D7
Tranoroa Madag. 24°42S 45°4E 55 J9
Tranqueras Uruguay 31°13S 55°45W 95 C4
Transantarctic Mts.
  Antarctica 85°0S 170°0W 5 E12
Transilvania Romania 46°30N 24°0E 17 E12
Transilvanian Alps = Carpaţii
  Meridionali Romania 45°30N 25°0E 17 F13
Transnistria □ Moldova 47°0N 29°15E 17 E15
Transylvania = Transilvania
  Romania 46°30N 24°0E 17 E12
Trápani Italy 38°1N 12°29E 22 E5
Trapper Pk. U.S.A. 45°54N 114°18W 76 D6
Traralgon Australia 38°12S 146°34E 63 F4
Trasimeno, L. Italy 43°8N 12°6E 22 C5
Trat Thailand 12°14N 102°33E 39 F4
Tratani → Pakistan 29°19N 68°20E 42 E3
Traun Austria 48°14N 14°15E 16 D8
Travellers L. Australia 33°20S 142°0E 63 E3
Travemünde Germany 53°57N 10°52E 16 B6
Travers, Mt. N.Z. 42°1S 172°45E 59 E4
Traverse City U.S.A. 44°46N 85°38W 81 C11
Travis, L. U.S.A. 30°24N 97°55W 84 F6
Travnik Bos.-H. 44°17N 17°39E 23 B7
Trawbreaga B. Ireland 55°20N 7°25W 10 A4
Trébbia → Italy 45°4N 9°41E 20 D8
Třebíč Czechia 49°14N 15°55E 16 D8
Trebinje Bos.-H. 42°44N 18°22E 23 C8
Trebonne Australia 18°37S 146°5E 62 B4
Trefaldwyn = Montgomery
  U.K. 52°34N 3°8W 13 E4
Trefynwy = Monmouth
  U.K. 51°48N 2°42W 13 F5
Tregaron U.K. 52°14N 3°56W 13 E4
Tregrosse Is. Australia 17°41S 150°43E 62 B5
Treherne Canada 49°38N 98°42W 71 D9
Treinta y Tres Uruguay 33°16S 54°17W 95 C5
Trelawney Zimbabwe 17°30S 30°30E 57 A5
Trelew Argentina 43°10S 65°20W 96 E3
Trelleborg Sweden 55°20N 13°10E 9 J15
Tremadog Bay U.K. 52°51N 4°18W 12 E3
Tremonton U.S.A. 41°43N 112°10W 76 F7
Tremp Spain 42°10N 0°52E 21 A6
Trenche → Canada 47°46N 72°53W 72 C5
Trenčín Slovakia 48°52N 18°4E 17 D10
Trenggalek Indonesia 8°3S 111°43E 37 H14
Trenque Lauquen
  Argentina 36°5S 62°45W 94 D3
Trent → Canada 44°6N 77°34W 82 B7
Trent → U.K. 53°41N 0°42W 12 D7
Trento Italy 46°4N 11°8E 22 A4
Trenton Canada 44°10N 77°34W 82 B7
Trenton Mo., U.S.A. 40°5N 93°37W 80 E7
Trenton N.J., U.S.A. 40°14N 74°46W 83 F10
Trenton Nebr., U.S.A. 40°11N 101°1W 80 E3
Trepassey Canada 46°43N 53°25W 73 C9
Tres Arroyos Argentina 38°26S 60°20W 94 D3
Três Corações Brazil 21°44S 45°15W 95 A6
Três Lagoas Brazil 20°50S 51°43W 93 H8
Tres Lomas Argentina 36°27S 62°51W 94 D3
Tres Montes, C. Chile 46°50S 75°30W 96 F1
Tres Pinos U.S.A. 36°48N 121°19W 78 J5
Três Pontas Brazil 21°23S 45°29W 95 A6
Tres Puentes Chile 27°50S 70°15W 94 B1
Tres Puntas, C. Argentina 47°0S 66°0W 96 F3
Três Rios Brazil 22°20S 43°30W 95 A7
Tres Valles Mexico 18°15N 96°8W 87 D5
Tresco U.K. 49°57N 6°20W 13 H1
Treviso Italy 45°40N 12°15E 22 B5
Triabunna Australia 42°30S 147°55E 63 G4
Triangle Zimbabwe 21°2S 31°28E 57 B5
Tribal Areas □ Pakistan 33°0N 70°0E 42 C4
Tribulation, C. Australia 16°5S 145°29E 62 B4
Tribune U.S.A. 38°28N 101°45W 80 F3
Trichinopoly = Tiruchirappalli
  India 10°45N 78°45E 45 J4
Trichur = Thrissur India 10°30N 76°18E 45 J3
Trichy = Tiruchirappalli
  India 10°45N 78°45E 45 J4
Trida Australia 33°1S 145°1E 63 E4

Trier Germany 49°45N 6°38E 16 D4
Trieste Italy 45°40N 13°46E 22 B5
Triglav Slovenia 46°21N 13°50E 16 E7
Trikala Greece 39°34N 21°47E 23 E9
Trikora, Puncak
  Indonesia 4°15S 138°45E 37 E9
Trim Ireland 53°33N 6°48W 10 C5
Trimbak India 19°56N 73°33E 44 K1
Trimmu Dam Pakistan 31°10N 72°8E 42 D5
Trincomalee Sri Lanka 8°38N 81°15E 45 K5
Trindade Atl. Oc. 20°20S 29°50W 2 F8
Trindade Brazil 16°40S 49°30W 93 G9
Trinidad Bolivia 14°46S 64°50W 92 F6
Trinidad Cuba 21°48N 80°0W 88 B4
Trinidad Paraguay 27°7S 55°47W 95 B4
Trinidad Trin. & Tob. 10°30N 61°15W 93 K15
Trinidad Uruguay 33°30S 56°50W 94 C4
Trinidad U.S.A. 37°10N 104°31W 77 H11
Trinidad & Tobago ■
  W. Indies 10°30N 61°20W 93 K15
Trinity Canada 48°59N 53°55W 73 C9
Trinity U.S.A. 30°57N 95°22W 84 F7
Trinity → Calif., U.S.A. 41°11N 123°42W 76 F2
Trinity → Tex., U.S.A. 29°45N 94°43W 84 G7
Trinity B. Canada 48°20N 53°10W 73 C9
Trinity Hills Trin. & Tob. 10°7N 61°7W 93 K15
Trinity Is. U.S.A. 56°33N 154°25W 74 D9
Trinity Range U.S.A. 40°10N 118°40W 76 F4
Trinkat India 8°5N 93°30E 45 K11
Trinkitat Sudan 18°45N 37°51E 53 E13
Trinway U.S.A. 40°9N 82°1E 82 F2
Triolet Mauritius 20°4S 57°32E 55 d
Tripoli = Tarābulus
  Lebanon 34°31N 35°50E 48 A4
Tripoli = Tarābulus Libya 32°49N 13°7E 53 B8
Tripoli Greece 37°31N 22°25E 23 F10
Tripolitania = Tarābulus
  Libya 31°0N 13°0E 53 B8
Tripura □ India 24°0N 92°0E 41 H18
Tristan da Cunha Atl. Oc. 37°6S 12°20W 51 K2
Trisul India 30°19N 79°47E 43 D8
Triton I. S. China Sea 15°47N 111°12E 36 A4
Trivandrum =
  Thiruvananthapuram
  India 8°41N 77°0E 45 K3
Trnava Slovakia 48°23N 17°35E 17 D9
Trochu Canada 51°50N 113°13W 70 C6
Trodely I. Canada 52°15N 79°26W 72 B4
Troglav Croatia 43°56N 16°36E 22 C7
Troilus, L. Canada 50°50N 74°35W 72 B5
Trois-Pistoles Canada 48°5N 69°10W 73 C6
Trois-Rivières Canada 46°25N 72°34W 72 C5
Trois-Rivières Guadeloupe 15°57N 61°40W 88 b
Troitsk Russia 54°10N 61°35E 26 D7
Troitsko Pechorsk
  Russia 62°40N 56°10E 18 B10
Troll Antarctica 72°0S 2°30E 5 D3
Trölladyngja Iceland 64°54N 17°16W 8 D5
Trollhättan Sweden 58°17N 12°20E 9 G15
Trollheimen Norway 62°46N 9°1E 8 E13
Trombetas → Brazil 1°55S 55°35W 93 D7
Tromsø Norway 69°40N 18°56E 8 B18
Tron Thailand 17°28N 100°7E 38 D3
Trona U.S.A. 35°46N 117°23W 79 K9
Tronador, Mte. Argentina 41°10S 71°50W 96 E2
Trondelag Norway 64°17N 11°50E 8 D14
Trondheim Norway 63°36N 10°25E 8 E14
Trondheimsfjorden
  Norway 63°35N 10°30E 8 E14
Troon U.K. 55°33N 4°39W 11 F4
Tropic U.S.A. 37°37N 112°5W 77 H7
Trostan U.K. 55°3N 6°10W 10 A5
Trou Gras Pt. St. Lucia 13°51N 60°53W 89 f
Trout → Canada 61°19N 119°51W 70 A5
Trout L. N.W.T., Canada 60°40N 121°14W 70 A4
Trout L. Ont., Canada 51°20N 93°15W 71 C10
Trout Lake Canada 56°30N 114°32W 70 B6
Trout Lake U.S.A. 46°0N 121°32W 78 E5
Trout River Canada 49°29N 58°8W 73 C8
Trout Run U.S.A. 41°23N 77°3W 82 E7
Trouville-sur-Mer France 49°21N 0°5E 20 B4
Trowbridge U.K. 51°18N 2°12W 13 F5
Troy Turkey 39°57N 26°12E 23 E12
Troy Ala., U.S.A. 31°48N 85°58W 85 F12
Troy Kans., U.S.A. 39°47N 95°5W 80 F6
Troy Mo., U.S.A. 38°59N 90°59W 80 F8
Troy Mont., U.S.A. 48°28N 115°53W 76 B6
Troy N.Y., U.S.A. 42°44N 73°41W 83 D11
Troy Ohio, U.S.A. 40°2N 84°12W 81 E11
Troy Pa., U.S.A. 41°47N 76°47W 83 E8
Troyes France 48°19N 4°3E 20 B6
Truchas Pk. U.S.A. 35°58N 105°39W 77 J11
Trucial States = United Arab
  Emirates ■ Asia 23°50N 54°0E 47 F7
Truckee U.S.A. 39°20N 120°11W 78 F6
Trudovoye Russia 43°17N 132°5E 28 C6
Trujillo Honduras 16°0N 86°0W 88 C2
Trujillo Peru 8°6S 79°0W 92 E3
Trujillo Spain 39°28N 5°55E 21 C3
Trujillo U.S.A. 35°32N 104°42W 77 J11
Trujillo Venezuela 9°22N 70°38W 92 B4
Truk Micronesia 7°25N 151°46E 64 G7
Trumann U.S.A. 35°41N 90°31W 85 D9
Trumansburg U.S.A. 42°33N 76°40W 83 D8
Trumbull, Mt. U.S.A. 36°25N 113°19W 77 H7
Trundle Australia 32°53S 147°35E 63 E4
Trung Lon, Hon Vietnam 8°36N 106°8E 39 H6
Trung Phan Vietnam 17°0N 109°0E 38 D6
Truong Sa, Dao = Spratly I.
  S. China Sea 8°38N 111°55E 36 C4
Truro Canada 45°21N 63°14W 73 C7
Truro U.K. 50°16N 5°4W 13 G2
Truskavets Ukraine 49°17N 23°30E 17 D12
Trutch Canada 57°44N 122°57W 70 B4
Truth or Consequences
  U.S.A. 33°8N 107°15W 77 K10
Trutnov Czechia 50°37N 15°54E 16 C8
Tryonville U.S.A. 41°42N 79°48W 82 E5
Tsaratanana Madag. 16°47S 47°39E 55 B8
Tsau Botswana 20°8S 22°22E 56 B3

Tsavo Kenya 2°59S 38°28E 54 E7
Tsentralnyy □ Russia 52°0N 40°0E 26 D4
Tses Namibia 25°58S 18°8E 56 C2
Tsetserleg Mongolia 47°36N 101°32E 30 B9
Tsévié Togo 6°25N 1°20E 52 G6
Tshabong Botswana 26°2S 22°29E 56 C3
Tshane Botswana 24°5S 21°54E 56 C3
Tshela Dem. Rep. of the Congo 4°57S 13°4E 54 E2
Tshesebe Botswana 21°51S 27°32E 57 B4
Tshikapa
  Dem. Rep. of the Congo 6°28S 20°48E 54 F4
Tshwane = Pretoria
  S. Africa 25°44S 28°12E 57 C4
Tshwane Botswana 22°24S 22°1E 56 B3
Tsigara Botswana 20°22S 25°54E 56 B4
Tsihombe Madag. 25°10S 45°41E 55 K9
Tsiigehtchic Canada 67°15N 134°0W 68 D5
Tsimlyansk Res. = Tsimlyanskoye
  Vdkhr. Russia 48°0N 43°0E 19 E7
Tsimlyanskoye Vdkhr.
  Russia 48°0N 43°0E 19 E7
Tsinan = Jinan China 36°38N 117°1E 32 F9
Tsineng S. Africa 27°5S 23°5E 56 D3
Tsinghai = Qinghai □
  China 36°0N 98°0E 30 D8
Tsingtao = Qingdao
  China 36°5N 120°20E 33 F11
Tsirigo = Kythira Greece 36°8N 23°0E 23 F10
Tsitsikamma △ S. Africa 34°3S 23°40E 56 D3
Tskhinvali Georgia 42°14N 44°1E 19 F7
Tsna → Russia 54°55N 41°58E 18 D7
Tsobis Namibia 19°27S 17°30E 56 A2
Tsodilo Hills Botswana 18°49S 21°43E 56 A3
Tsogttsetsiy = Baruunsuu
  Mongolia 43°43N 105°35E 32 C3
Tsolo S. Africa 31°18S 28°37E 57 D4
Tsomo S. Africa 32°0S 27°42E 57 D4
Tsu Japan 34°45N 136°25E 29 G8
Tsu L. Canada 60°40N 111°52W 70 A6
Tsuchiura Japan 36°5N 140°15E 29 F10
Tsugaru-Hantō Japan 41°0N 140°30E 28 D10
Tsugaru-Kaikyō Japan 41°35N 141°0E 28 D10
Tsumeb Namibia 19°9S 17°44E 56 A2
Tsumis Namibia 23°39S 17°29E 56 B2
Tsuruga Japan 35°45N 136°2E 29 G8
Tsurugi-San Japan 33°51N 134°6E 29 H7
Tsuruoka Japan 38°44N 139°50E 28 E9
Tsushima Gifu, Japan 35°10N 136°43E 29 G8
Tsushima Nagasaki,
  Japan 34°20N 129°20E 29 G4
Tsuyama Japan 35°3N 134°0E 29 G7
Tsyelyakhany Belarus 52°30N 25°46E 17 B13
Tuam = Tuam Ireland 53°31N 8°51W 10 C3
Tuamotu, Îs.
  French Polynesia 17°0S 144°0W 65 J13
Tuamotu Arch. = Tuamotu, Îs.
  French Polynesia 17°0S 144°0W 65 J13
Tuamotu Ridge Pac. Oc. 20°0S 138°0W 65 K14
Tuan Giao Vietnam 21°35N 103°25E 38 B4
Tuanfeng China 30°38N 114°52E 35 B10
Tuanxi China 27°28N 107°8E 34 D6
Tuao Phil. 17°45N 121°22E 37 A6
Tuapse Russia 44°5N 39°10E 19 F6
Tuatapere N.Z. 46°8S 167°41E 59 G1
Tuba City U.S.A. 36°8N 111°14W 77 H8
Tuban Indonesia 6°54S 112°3E 37 G15
Tubani Botswana 24°46S 24°18E 56 B3
Tubarão Brazil 28°30S 49°0W 95 B6
Tūbās West Bank 32°20N 35°22E 48 C4
Tubas → Namibia 22°54S 14°35E 56 B2
Tübingen Germany 48°31N 9°4E 16 D5
Tubou Fiji 18°13S 178°48W 59 a
Tubruq Libya 32°7N 23°55E 53 B10
Tubuaï, Îs.
  French Polynesia 25°0S 150°0W 65 K13
Tuc Trung Vietnam 11°1N 107°12E 39 G6
Tucacas Venezuela 10°48N 68°19W 92 A5
T'uch'ang Taiwan 24°35N 121°29E 35 E13
Tuchitua Canada 60°55N 129°13W 70 A3
Tuchodi → Canada 58°17N 123°42W 70 B4
Tucson U.S.A. 32°13N 110°58W 77 K8
Tucumán □ Argentina 26°48S 66°2W 94 B2
Tucumcari U.S.A. 35°10N 103°44W 77 J12
Tucupita Venezuela 9°2N 62°3W 92 B6
Tucuruí Brazil 3°42S 49°44W 93 D9
Tucuruí, Represa de Brazil 4°0S 49°30W 93 D9
Tudela Spain 42°4N 1°39W 21 A5
Tudmur Syria 34°36N 38°15E 46 C3
Tudor, L. Canada 55°50N 65°25W 73 A6
Tug Hill Plateau U.S.A. 43°45N 75°50W 83 C9
Tugela → S. Africa 29°14S 31°30E 57 C5
Tugela Falls S. Africa 28°42S 29°51E 57 C4
Tuguegarao Phil. 17°35N 121°42E 37 A6
Tugur Russia 53°44N 136°45E 27 D14
Tui Spain 42°3N 8°39W 21 A1
Tukangbesi, Kepulauan
  Indonesia 6°0S 124°0E 37 F6
Tukarak I. Canada 56°15N 78°45W 72 A4
Tukayyid Iraq 29°47N 45°36E 46 D5
Tuktoyaktuk Canada 69°27N 133°2W 68 D6
Tuktut Nogait △ Canada 69°15N 122°0W 68 D7
Tukums Latvia 56°58N 23°10E 9 H20
Tukuyu Tanzania 9°17S 33°35E 54 F6
Tula Hidalgo, Mexico 20°3N 99°21W 87 C5
Tula Tamaulipas, Mexico 23°0N 99°40W 87 C5
Tula Russia 54°13N 37°38E 18 D6

Tulchyn Ukraine 48°41N 28°49E 17 D15
Tüleh Iran 34°35N 52°33E 47 C7
Tulemalu L. Canada 62°58N 99°25W 71 A9
Tulia U.S.A. 34°32N 101°46W 84 D4
Tulita Canada 64°57N 125°30W 68 E6
Tullahoma U.S.A. 35°22N 86°13W 85 D11
Tulla Ireland 52°53N 8°46W 10 D3
Tülkarm West Bank 32°19N 35°2E 48 C4
Tullamore Australia 32°39S 147°36E 63 E4
Tullamore Ireland 53°16N 7°31W 10 C4
Tulle France 45°16N 1°46E 20 D4
Tullow Ireland 52°49N 6°45W 10 D5
Tully Australia 17°56S 145°55E 62 B4
Tully U.S.A. 42°48N 76°7W 83 D8
Tulsa U.S.A. 36°10N 95°55W 84 C7
Tulsequah Canada 58°39N 133°35W 70 B2
Tuluá Colombia 4°6N 76°11W 92 C3
Tulum Mexico 20°13N 87°28W 87 C7
Tulun Russia 54°32N 100°35E 27 D11
Tulungagung Indonesia 8°5S 111°54E 37 H14
Tuma → Nic. 13°6N 84°35W 88 D3
Tumacacori △ U.S.A. 31°35N 111°6W 77 L8
Tumaco Colombia 1°50N 78°45W 92 C3
Tumakuru India 13°18N 77°6E 45 H3
Tumatumari Guyana 5°20N 58°55W 92 B7
Tumba Sweden 59°12N 17°48E 9 G17
Tumba, L.
  Dem. Rep. of the Congo 0°50S 18°0E 54 E3
Tumbarumba Australia 35°44S 148°0E 63 F4
Tumbaya Argentina 23°50S 65°26W 94 A2
Tumbes Peru 3°37S 80°27W 92 D2
Tumbler Ridge Canada 55°8N 121°0W 70 B4
Tumby Bay Australia 34°21S 136°8E 63 E2
Tumd Youqi China 40°30N 110°30E 32 D6
Tumen China 43°0N 129°50E 28 C4
Tumen Jiang → China 42°20N 130°35E 33 C16
Tumeremo Venezuela 7°18N 61°30W 92 B6
Tumkur = Tumakuru
  India 13°18N 77°6E 45 H3
Tump Pakistan 26°7N 62°16E 40 F3
Tumpat Malaysia 6°11N 102°10E 39 J4
Tumsar India 21°26N 79°45E 44 J4
Tumu Ghana 10°56N 1°56W 52 F5
Tumucumaque, Serra
  Brazil 2°0N 55°0W 93 C8
Tumut Australia 35°16S 148°13E 63 F4
Tumwater U.S.A. 47°1N 122°54W 78 C4
Tuna India 22°59N 70°5E 42 H4
Tunapuna Trin. & Tob. 10°38N 61°24W 93 K15
Tunas de Zaza Cuba 21°39N 79°34W 88 B4
Tunbridge Wells = Royal
  Tunbridge Wells U.K. 51°7N 0°10E 13 F8
Tunceli Turkey 39°6N 39°31E 46 B3
Tunchang China 19°21N 110°5E 38 C8
Tuncurry Australia 32°17S 152°29E 63 E5
Tundla India 27°12N 78°17E 42 F8
Tundzha → Bulgaria 41°40N 26°35E 23 C11
Tunga → India 15°57N 78°15E 45 G4
Tungabhadra → India 15°57N 78°15E 45 G4
Tungabhadra Dam India 15°0N 75°50E 45 G2
Tungla Nic. 13°24N 84°21W 88 D3
Tungsha Tao = Dongsha Dao
  S. China Sea 20°45N 116°43E 35 G11
Tungshih Taiwan 24°12N 120°43E 35 E13
Tungsten Canada 61°57N 128°16W 70 A3
Tunguska, Nizhnyaya →
  Russia 65°48N 88°4E 27 C9
Tunguska, Podkamennaya →
  Russia 61°50N 90°13E 27 C10
Tuni India 17°22N 82°36E 44 F6
Tunica U.S.A. 34°41N 90°23W 85 D9
Tunis Tunisia 36°50N 10°11E 53 A8
Tunja Colombia 5°33N 73°25W 92 B4
Tunkhannock U.S.A. 41°32N 75°57W 83 E9
Tunkinsky △ Russia 51°30N 102°0E 27 D11
Tunliu China 36°13N 112°52E 32 F7
Tunnel Creek △
  Australia 17°41S 125°18E 60 C4
Tunnsjøen Norway 64°45N 13°25E 8 D15
Tunungayualok I. Canada 56°0N 61°0W 73 A7
Tunuyán Argentina 33°35S 69°0W 94 C2
Tunuyán → Argentina 33°33S 67°30W 94 C2
Tunxi = Huangshan
  China 29°42N 118°25E 35 C12
Tuo Jiang → China 28°50N 105°35E 34 C5
Tuolumne U.S.A. 37°58N 120°15W 78 H6
Tuolumne → U.S.A. 37°36N 121°13W 78 H5
Tūp Āghāj Iran 36°3N 47°50E 46 B5
Tupã Brazil 21°57S 50°28W 95 A5
Tupelo U.S.A. 34°16N 88°43W 85 D10
Tupinambarana, I. Brazil 3°0S 58°0W 92 D7
Tupiza Bolivia 21°30S 65°40W 94 A2
Tupman U.S.A. 35°18N 119°21W 79 K7
Tupper Canada 55°32N 120°1W 70 B4
Tupper L. U.S.A. 44°10N 74°32W 83 B10
Tupper Lake U.S.A. 44°14N 74°28W 83 B10
Tupungato, Cerro
  S. Amer. 33°15S 69°50W 94 C2
Tuquan China 45°18N 121°38E 33 B11
Túquerres Colombia 1°5N 77°37W 92 C3
Tura Russia 64°20N 100°17E 27 C11
Turabah Si. Arabia 28°20N 43°15E 46 D5
Tūrān Iran 35°39N 56°42E 47 C8
Turan Russia 51°55N 94°0E 27 D10
Turayf Si. Arabia 31°41N 38°39E 46 D3
Turda Romania 46°34N 23°47E 17 E12
Turek Poland 52°3N 18°30E 17 B10
Turén Venezuela 9°17N 69°6W 92 B5
Turfan = Turpan China 42°40N 89°25E 30 C6
Turfan Basin = Turpan Pendi
  China 42°40N 89°25E 30 C6
Turfan Depression = Turpan Pendi
  China 42°40N 89°25E 30 C6
Turgeon → Canada 50°0N 78°56W 72 C4
Turgutlu Turkey 38°30N 27°43E 23 E12
Turgwe → Zimbabwe 21°31S 32°15E 57 B5
Turia → Spain 39°27N 0°19W 21 C5
Turiaçu Brazil 1°40S 45°19W 93 D9
Turiaçu → Brazil 1°36S 45°19W 93 D9

Turin = Torino Italy 45°3N 7°40E 20 D7
Turkana, L. Africa 3°30N 36°5E 54 D7
Turkestan = Türkistan
  Kazakhstan 43°17N 68°16E 26 E7
Turkey Creek = Warmun
  Australia 17°2S 128°12E 60 C4
Turkey ■ Eurasia 39°0N 36°0E 19 G6
Türkistan Kazakhstan 43°17N 68°16E 26 E7
Türkmenabat
  Turkmenistan 39°6N 63°34E 47 B9
Türkmenbashi
  Turkmenistan 40°5N 53°5E 47 A7
Turkmenistan ■ Asia 39°0N 59°0E 26 F6
Turks & Caicos Is. ☑
  W. Indies 21°20N 71°20W 89 B5
Turks Island Passage
  Turks & Caicos 21°25N 71°19W 89 B5
Turku Finland 60°30N 22°19E 9 F20
Turkwel → Kenya 3°6N 36°6E 54 D7
Turlock U.S.A. 37°30N 120°51W 78 H6
Turnagain Australia 9°34S 142°17E 62 a
Turnagain → Canada 59°12N 127°35W 70 B3
Turneffe Is. Belize 17°20N 87°50W 87 D7
Turner U.S.A. 48°51N 108°24W 76 B9
Turner Pt. Australia 11°47S 133°32E 62 A1
Turner Valley Canada 50°40N 114°17W 70 C6
Turners Falls U.S.A. 42°36N 72°33W 83 D12
Turnhout Belgium 51°19N 4°57E 15 C4
Turnor L. Canada 56°35N 108°35W 71 B7
Tŭrnovo = Veliko Tarnovo
  Bulgaria 43°5N 25°41E 23 C11
Turnu Măgurele
  Romania 43°46N 24°56E 17 G13
Turnu Roşu, P. Romania 45°33N 24°17E 17 F13
Turpan China 43°58N 89°10E 30 C6
Turpan Pendi China 42°40N 89°25E 30 C6
Turriff U.K. 57°32N 2°27W 11 D6
Tursāq Iraq 33°27N 45°47E 46 C5
Turtle Head I. Australia 10°56S 142°37E 62 A3
Turtle L. Canada 53°36N 108°38W 71 C7
Turtle Lake U.S.A. 47°31N 100°53W 80 B3
Turtleford Canada 53°23N 108°57W 71 C7
Turuépano △ Venezuela 10°34N 62°43W 89 D7
Turukhansk Russia 65°21N 88°5E 27 C9
Tuscaloosa U.S.A. 33°12N 87°34W 85 E11
Tuscany = Toscana □
  Italy 43°25N 11°0E 22 C4
Tuscarawas → U.S.A. 40°24N 81°25W 82 F3
Tuscarora Mt. U.S.A. 40°55N 77°55W 82 F7
Tuscola Ill., U.S.A. 39°48N 88°17W 80 F9
Tuscola Tex., U.S.A. 32°12N 99°48W 84 E5
Tuscumbia U.S.A. 34°44N 87°42W 85 D11
Tuskegee U.S.A. 32°25N 85°42W 85 E12
Tuticorin India 8°50N 78°12E 45 K4
Tutóia Brazil 2°45S 42°20W 93 D10
Tutong Brunei 4°47N 114°40E 36 D4
Tutrakan Bulgaria 44°2N 26°40E 23 B12
Tuttle Creek L. U.S.A. 39°15N 96°36W 80 F5
Tuttlingen Germany 47°58N 8°48E 16 E5
Tutuala Timor-Leste 8°25S 127°15E 37 F7
Tutuila Amer. Samoa 14°19S 170°50W 59 b
Tuva □ Russia 51°30N 95°0E 27 D10
Tuvalu ■ Pac. Oc. 8°0S 178°0E 58 B10
Tuvuca Fiji 17°40S 178°48W 59 a
Tuxpan Mexico 20°57N 97°24W 87 C5
Tuxtla Gutiérrez Mexico 16°45N 93°7W 87 D6
Tuy = Tui Spain 42°3N 8°39W 21 A1
Tuy Duc Vietnam 12°15N 107°27E 39 F6
Tuy Phong Vietnam 11°14N 108°43E 39 G7
Tuya L. Canada 59°7N 130°35W 70 B2
Tuyen Hoa Vietnam 17°50N 106°10E 38 D6
Tuyen Quang Vietnam 21°50N 105°10E 34 G5
Tüysarkān Iran 34°33N 48°27E 47 C6
Tuz Gölü Turkey 38°42N 33°18E 19 G5
Tūz Khurmātū Iraq 34°56N 44°38E 46 C5
Tuzigoot △ U.S.A. 34°46N 112°2W 77 J7
Tuzla Bos.-H. 44°34N 18°41E 23 B8
Tver Russia 56°55N 35°59E 18 C6
Twain U.S.A. 40°1N 121°3W 78 E5
Twain Harte U.S.A. 38°2N 120°14W 78 G6
Twee River Namibia 25°27S 19°27E 56 C2
Tweed Canada 44°29N 77°19W 82 B7
Tweed → U.K. 55°45N 2°0W 11 F6
Tweed Heads Australia 28°10S 153°31E 63 D5
Tweedsmuir △ Canada 53°0N 126°20W 70 C3
Twentynine Palms
  U.S.A. 34°8N 116°3W 79 L10
Twillingate Canada 49°42N 54°45W 73 C9
Twin Bridges U.S.A. 45°33N 112°20W 76 D7
Twin Falls Canada 53°30N 64°32W 73 B7
Twin Falls U.S.A. 42°34N 114°28W 76 E6
Twin Valley U.S.A. 47°16N 96°16W 80 B5
Twinsburg U.S.A. 41°19N 81°26W 82 E3
Twitchell Res. U.S.A. 34°59N 120°19W 79 L6
Two Harbors U.S.A. 47°2N 91°40W 80 B8
Two Hills Canada 53°43N 111°52W 70 C6
Two Rivers U.S.A. 44°9N 87°34W 80 C10
Two Rocks Australia 31°30S 115°35E 61 F2
Twofold B. Australia 37°8S 149°59E 63 F4
Twyfelfontein Namibia 20°34S 14°27E 56 B1
Tyachiv Ukraine 48°1N 23°35E 17 D12
Tychy Poland 50°9N 18°59E 17 C10
Tyler Minn., U.S.A. 44°17N 96°8W 80 C5
Tyler Tex., U.S.A. 32°21N 95°18W 84 E7
Tynda Russia 55°10N 124°43E 27 D13
Tyndall U.S.A. 43°0N 97°50W 80 D5
Tyne → U.K. 54°59N 1°32W 12 C6
Tyne & Wear □ U.K. 55°6N 1°17W 12 B6
Tynemouth U.K. 55°1N 1°26W 12 B6
Tyre = Şūr Lebanon 33°19N 35°16E 48 B4
Tyrifjorden Norway 60°2N 10°8E 9 F14
Tyrol = Tirol □ Austria 47°3N 10°43E 16 E6
Tyrone U.S.A. 40°40N 78°14W 82 F6
Tyrone □ U.K. 54°38N 7°11W 10 B4
Tyrrell → Australia 35°26S 142°51E 63 F3
Tyrrell, L. Australia 35°20S 142°50E 63 F3
Tyrrell L. Canada 63°7N 105°27W 71 A7
Tyrrhenian Sea Medit. S. 40°0N 12°30E 22 E5

Tysfjorden Norway 68°7N 16°25E 8 B17
Tyulgan Russia 52°22N 56°12E 18 D10
Tyumen Russia 57°11N 65°29E 26 D7
Tywi → U.K. 51°48N 4°21W 13 F3
Tywyn U.K. 52°35N 4°5W 13 E3
Tzaneen S. Africa 23°47S 30°9E 57 B5
Tzukong = Zigong
China 29°15N 104°48E 34 C5

## U

U.S.A. = United States of
America ■ N. Amer. 37°0N 96°0W 75 H20
U.S. Virgin Is. ☑ W. Indies 18°20N 65°0W 89 e
Uaimh, An = Navan
Ireland 53°39N 6°41W 10 C5
Uanle Uen = Wanleweyne
Somalia 2°37N 44°54E 49 G3
Uatumã → Brazil 2°26S 57°37W 92 D7
Uaupés Brazil 0°8S 67°5W 92 D5
Uaupés → Brazil 0°2N 67°16W 92 D5
Uaxactún Guatemala 17°25N 89°29W 88 C2
Ubá Brazil 21°8S 43°0W 95 A7
Ubaitaba Brazil 14°18S 39°20W 93 F11
Ubangi = Oubangi →
Dem. Rep. of the Congo 0°30S 17°50E 54 E3
Ubauro Pakistan 28°15N 69°45E 42 E3
Ubayyiḍ, W. al → Iraq 32°34N 43°48E 46 C4
Ube Japan 33°56N 131°15E 29 H5
Úbeda Spain 38°3N 3°23W 21 C4
Uberaba Brazil 19°50S 47°55W 93 G9
Uberlândia Brazil 19°0S 48°20W 93 G9
Ubly U.S.A. 43°42N 82°55W 82 C2
Ubolratna Res. Thailand 16°45N 102°30E 38 D4
Ubombo S. Africa 27°31S 32°4E 57 C5
Ubon Ratchathani
Thailand 15°15N 104°50E 38 E5
Ubort → Belarus 52°6N 28°30E 17 B15
Ubud Indonesia 8°30S 115°16E 37 J18
Ubundu
Dem. Rep. of the Congo 0°22S 25°30E 54 E5
Ucayali → Peru 4°30S 73°30W 92 D4
Uchab Namibia 19°47S 17°42E 56 A2
Uchiura-Wan Japan 42°25N 140°40E 28 C10
Uchquduq Uzbekistan 41°50N 62°50E 26 E7
Uchur → Russia 58°48N 130°35E 27 D14
Ucluelet Canada 48°57N 125°32W 70 D3
Uda → Russia 54°42N 135°14E 27 D14
Uda Walawe △ Sri Lanka 6°20N 81°0E 45 L5
Udachnyy Russia 66°25N 112°24E 27 C12
Udagamandalam India 11°30N 76°44E 45 J3
Udainagar India 22°33N 76°13E 42 H7
Udaipur India 24°36N 73°44E 42 G5
Udaipur Garhi Nepal 27°0N 86°35E 43 F12
Udala India 21°35N 86°34E 43 J12
Udayagiri Andhra Pradesh,
India 14°52N 79°19E 45 G4
Udayagiri Odisha, India 20°8N 84°23E 44 D7
Uddevalla Sweden 58°21N 11°55E 9 G14
Uddjaure Sweden 65°56N 17°49E 8 D17
Udegeyskaya Legenda △
Russia 45°45N 135°30E 28 B7
Uden Neths. 51°40N 5°37E 15 C5
Udgir India 18°25N 77°5E 44 E3
Udhampur India 33°0N 75°5E 43 C6
Údine Italy 46°3N 13°14E 22 A5
Udintsev Fracture Zone
S. Ocean 57°0S 145°0W 5 B13
Udmurtia ☐ Russia 57°30N 52°30E 18 C9
Udon Thani Thailand 17°29N 102°46E 38 D4
Udong Cambodia 11°48N 104°45E 38 F5
Udskaya Guba Russia 54°50N 135°45E 27 D14
Udu Pt. Fiji 16°9S 179°57W 59 a
Udumalaippettai India 10°35N 77°15E 45 J3
Udupi India 13°25N 74°42E 45 H2
Udva India 20°5N 73°0E 44 D1
Udzungwa Range Tanzania 9°30S 35°10E 54 F7
Ueda Japan 36°24N 138°16E 29 F9
Uedineniya, Os. Russia 78°0N 85°0E 4 B12
Uele →
Dem. Rep. of the Congo 3°45N 24°45E 54 D4
Uelen Russia 66°10N 170°0W 27 C19
Uelzen Germany 52°57N 10°32E 16 B6
Ufa Russia 54°45N 55°55E 18 D10
Ufa → Russia 54°40N 56°0E 18 D10
Ugab → Namibia 20°55S 13°30E 56 B1
Ugalla → Tanzania 5°8S 30°42E 54 F6
Uganda ■ Africa 2°0N 32°0E 54 D6
Ugie S. Africa 31°10S 28°13E 57 D4
Uglegorsk Russia 49°5N 142°2E 27 E15
Ugljan Croatia 44°12N 15°10E 16 F8
Ugolnye Kopi Russia 64°44N 177°42E 27 C18
Uhlenhorst Namibia 23°45S 17°55E 56 B2
Uhrichsville U.S.A. 40°24N 81°21W 82 F3
Uibhist a Deas = South Uist
U.K. 57°20N 7°15W 11 D1
Uibhist a Tuath = North Uist
U.K. 57°40N 7°15W 11 D1
Uig U.K. 57°35N 6°21W 11 D2
Uíge Angola 7°30S 14°40E 54 F2
Uiha Tonga 19°54S 174°25W 59 c
Uijeongbu S. Korea 37°44N 127°2E 33 F14
Úiju N. Korea 40°15N 124°35E 33 D13
Uinta Mts. U.S.A. 40°45N 110°30W 76 F8
Uis Namibia 21°8S 14°49E 56 B1
Uiseong S. Korea 36°21N 128°45E 33 F15
Uitenhage S. Africa 33°40S 25°28E 56 D4
Uithuizen Neths. 53°24N 6°41E 15 A6
Ujh → India 32°10N 75°18E 42 C6
Ujhani India 28°0N 79°6E 43 F8
Uji-guntō Japan 31°15N 129°25E 29 J4
Ujjain India 23°9N 75°43E 42 H6
Ujung Kulon △
Indonesia 6°46S 105°19E 37 G11
Ujung Pandang = Makassar
Indonesia 5°10S 119°20E 37 F5
Uka Russia 57°50N 162°0E 27 D17
Ukai Sagar India 21°20N 73°43E 44 D1
Uke-Shima Japan 28°12N 129°14E 29 K4
uKhahlamba Drakensberg △
S. Africa 29°27S 29°30E 57 C4

Ukhrul India 25°10N 94°25E 41 G19
Ukhta Russia 63°34N 53°41E 18 B9
Ukiah U.S.A. 39°9N 123°13W 78 F3
Ukkusiksalik △ Canada 65°20N 89°30W 68 D14
Ukmergė Lithuania 55°15N 24°45E 9 J21
Ukraine ■ Europe 49°0N 32°0E 19 E5
Ukwi Botswana 23°29S 20°30E 56 B3
Ulaan Nuur Mongolia 44°30N 103°40E 32 B2
Ulaan-Uul Mongolia 46°4N 100°49E 32 B5
Ulaanbaatar Mongolia 47°55N 106°53E 30 B10
Ulaangom Mongolia 50°5N 92°10E 30 A7
Ulaanjirem Mongolia 45°5N 105°30E 32 B3
Ulak I. U.S.A. 51°22N 178°57W 74 E4
Ulan Bator = Ulaanbaatar
Mongolia 47°55N 106°53E 30 B10
Ulan Ude Russia 51°45N 107°40E 31 A10
Ulanhad = Chifeng
China 42°18N 118°58E 33 C10
Ulansuhai Nur China 40°53N 108°51E 32 D5
Ulcinj Montenegro 41°58N 19°10E 23 D8
Ule älv = Oulujoki →
Finland 65°1N 25°30E 8 D21
Ule träsk = Oulujärvi
Finland 64°25N 27°15E 8 D22
Uleåborg = Oulu Finland 65°1N 25°29E 8 D21
Ulefoss Norway 59°17N 9°16E 9 G13
Ulhasnagar India 19°15N 73°10E 44 E1
Uliastay Mongolia 47°56N 97°28E 30 B8
Uljin S. Korea 36°59N 129°24E 33 F15
Ulladulla Australia 35°21S 150°29E 63 F5
Ullal India 12°48N 74°51E 45 H2
Ulleungdo S. Korea 37°30N 130°30E 29 F5
Ullswater Canada 45°12N 79°29W 82 A5
Ullswater U.K. 54°34N 2°52W 12 C5
Ulm Germany 48°23N 9°58E 16 D5
Ulmarra Australia 29°37S 153°4E 63 D5
Ulricehamn Sweden 57°46N 13°26E 9 H15
Ulsan S. Korea 35°20N 129°15E 33 G15
Ulsta U.K. 60°30N 1°9W 11 A7
Ulster ☐ U.K. 54°35N 6°30W 10 B5
Ulubat Gölü Turkey 40°9N 28°35E 23 D13
Uludağ Turkey 40°4N 29°13E 23 D13
Ulukhaktok Canada 70°44N 117°44W 68 C8
Ulundi S. Africa 28°20S 31°25E 57 C5
Ulungur He → China 47°1N 87°24E 30 B6
Ulungur Hu China 47°20N 87°10E 30 B6
Uluru Australia 25°23S 131°5E 61 E5
Uluru-Kata Tjuta △
Australia 25°19S 131°1E 61 E5
Uluwatu Indonesia 8°50S 115°5E 37 K18
Ulva U.K. 56°29N 6°13W 11 E2
Ulverston U.K. 54°13N 3°5W 12 C4
Ulverstone Australia 41°11S 146°11E 63 G4
Ulya Russia 59°10N 142°0E 27 D15
Ulyanovsk Russia 54°20N 48°25E 18 D8
Ulyasutay = Uliastay
Mongolia 47°56N 97°28E 30 B8
Ulysses Kans., U.S.A. 37°35N 101°22W 80 G3
Ulysses Pa., U.S.A. 41°54N 77°46W 82 E7
Ulysses, Mt. Canada 57°20N 124°5W 70 B4
Ulytau Kazakhstan 48°39N 67°1E 26 E7
Umala Bolivia 17°25S 68°5W 92 G5
'Umān = Oman ■ Asia 23°0N 58°0E 49 C6
Uman Ukraine 48°40N 30°12E 17 D16
Umaria India 23°35N 80°50E 43 H9
Umarkhed India 19°37N 77°46E 44 E3
Umarkot Pakistan 25°15N 69°40E 42 G3
Umarpada India 21°27N 73°30E 42 J5
Umatilla U.S.A. 45°55N 119°21W 76 D4
Umba Russia 66°42N 34°11E 18 A5
Umbagog L. U.S.A. 44°46N 71°3W 83 B13
Umbakumba Australia 13°47S 136°50E 62 A2
Umbrella Mts. N.Z. 45°35S 169°5E 59 F2
Umeå Sweden 63°45N 20°20E 8 E19
Umeälven → Sweden 63°45N 20°20E 8 E19
Umera Indonesia 0°12S 129°37E 37 E7
Umgwenya → Mozam. 25°14S 32°18E 57 D5
Umiujaq Canada 56°33N 76°33W 72 A4
Umkomaas S. Africa 30°13S 30°48E 57 D5
Umlazi S. Africa 29°59S 30°54E 56 L6
Umm ad Daraj, J. Jordan 32°18N 35°48E 48 C4
Umm al Qaywayn U.A.E. 25°30N 55°35E 47 E7
Umm al Qittayn Jordan 32°18N 36°40E 48 C5
Umm al Rasas Jordan 31°30N 35°55E 48 D4
Umm Bāb Qatar 25°12N 50°48E 47 E6
Umm Durman = Omdurmân
Sudan 15°40N 32°28E 53 E12
Umm el Fahm Israel 32°31N 35°9E 48 C4
Umm el Ketef, Khalig
Egypt 23°40N 35°35E 46 F2
Umm Keddada Sudan 13°33N 26°35E 53 F11
Umm Lajj Si. Arabia 25°0N 37°23E 46 E3
Umm Qasr Iraq 30°1N 47°58E 46 D5
Umm Ruwaba Sudan 12°50N 31°20E 53 F12
Umm Sa'id Qatar 25°0N 51°33E 47 E6
Umm Tais △ Qatar 26°7N 51°15E 47 E6
Umnak I. U.S.A. 53°15N 168°20W 74 E6
Umniati → Zimbabwe 16°49S 28°45E 55 H5
Umpang → U.S.A. 43°40N 124°12W 76 E1
Umred India 20°51N 79°18E 44 D4
Umreth India 22°41N 73°4E 42 H5
Umri India 19°2N 77°54E 44 E3
Umtata = Mthatha
S. Africa 31°36S 28°49E 57 D4
Umuarama Brazil 23°45S 53°20W 95 A5
Umvukwe Ra. Zimbabwe 16°45S 30°45E 55 H6
Umzimvubu S. Africa 31°38S 29°33E 57 D4
Umzinto = eMuziwezinto
S. Africa 30°15S 30°45E 57 D5
Una India 20°46N 71°8E 42 J4
Una → Bos.-H. 45°0N 16°20E 16 F9
Unadilla U.S.A. 42°20N 75°19W 83 D9
Unalakleet U.S.A. 63°52N 160°47W 74 C7
Unalaska U.S.A. 53°53N 166°32W 74 E6
Unalaska I. U.S.A. 53°35N 166°50W 74 E6
'Unayzah Si. Arabia 26°6N 43°58E 46 E4
'Unayzah, J. Asia 32°12N 39°18E 46 C3

Uncía Bolivia 18°25S 66°40W 92 G5
Uncompahgre Peak
U.S.A. 38°4N 107°28W 76 G10
Uncompahgre Plateau
U.S.A. 38°20N 108°15W 76 G9
Undara Volcanic △
Australia 18°14S 144°41E 62 B3
Underbool Australia 35°10S 141°51E 63 F3
Underwood Canada 44°18N 81°29W 82 B3
Ungarie Australia 33°38S 146°56E 63 E4
Ungarra Australia 34°12S 136°2E 63 E2
Ungava, Pén. d' Canada 60°0N 74°0W 69 F17
Ungava B. Canada 59°30N 67°30W 69 F18
Ungeny = Ungheni
Moldova 47°11N 27°51E 17 E14
Unggi N. Korea 42°16N 130°28E 33 C16
Ungheni Moldova 47°11N 27°51E 17 E14
Unguja = Zanzibar
Tanzania 6°12S 39°12E 54 F7
União da Vitória Brazil 26°13S 51°5W 95 B5
Unimak I. U.S.A. 54°45N 164°0W 74 E7
Unimak Pass. U.S.A. 54°15N 164°30W 74 E7
Union Miss., U.S.A. 32°34N 89°7W 85 E10
Union Mo., U.S.A. 38°27N 91°0W 80 F8
Union S.C., U.S.A. 34°43N 81°37W 85 D14
Union City Calif., U.S.A. 37°36N 122°1W 78 H4
Union City Pa., U.S.A. 41°54N 79°51W 82 E5
Union City Tenn., U.S.A. 36°26N 89°3W 85 C10
Union Dale U.S.A. 41°43N 75°29W 83 E9
Union Gap U.S.A. 46°33N 120°28W 76 C3
Union Springs Ala.,
U.S.A. 32°9N 85°43W 85 E12
Union Springs N.Y.,
U.S.A. 42°50N 76°41W 83 D8
Uniondale S. Africa 33°39S 23°7E 56 D3
Uniontown U.S.A. 39°54N 79°44W 81 F5
Unionville U.S.A. 40°29N 93°1W 80 E7
United Arab Emirates ■
Asia 23°50N 54°0E 47 F7
United Kingdom ■ Europe 53°0N 2°0W 14 E6
United States of America ■
N. Amer. 37°0N 96°0W 75 H20
Unity Canada 52°30N 109°5W 71 C7
University Park U.S.A. 32°17N 106°45W 77 K10
University Place U.S.A. 47°14N 122°33W 78 C4
Unjha India 23°46N 72°24E 42 H5
Unnao India 26°35N 80°30E 43 F9
Unst U.K. 60°44N 0°53W 11 A8
Unuk → Canada 56°5N 131°3W 70 B2
Unzen-Amakusa △
Japan 32°15N 130°10E 29 H5
Uong Bi Vietnam 21°2N 106°47E 38 B6
Uotsuri-Shima
E. China Sea 25°45N 123°29E 29 M1
Uozu Japan 36°48N 137°24E 29 F8
Upata Venezuela 8°1N 62°24W 92 B6
Upemba, L.
Dem. Rep. of the Congo 8°30S 26°20E 54 F5
Upernavik Greenland 72°49N 56°20W 4 B5
Upington S. Africa 28°25S 21°15E 56 D3
Upleta India 21°46N 70°16E 42 J4
'Upolu Samoa 13°58S 172°0W 59 b
Upper Alkali L. U.S.A. 41°47N 120°8W 76 F3
Upper Arrow L. Canada 50°30N 117°50W 70 C5
Upper Daly ☉ Australia 14°26S 131°3E 60 B5
Upper Darby U.S.A. 39°55N 75°16W 81 F16
Upper Foster L. Canada 56°47N 105°20W 71 B7
Upper Hutt N.Z. 41°8S 175°5E 59 D5
Upper Klamath L.
U.S.A. 42°25N 121°55W 76 E3
Upper Lake U.S.A. 39°10N 122°54W 78 F4
Upper Liard Canada 60°3N 128°54W 70 A3
Upper Manzanilla
Trin. & Tob. 10°31N 61°4W 93 K15
Upper Missouri Breaks △
U.S.A. 47°53N 109°55W 76 C9
Upper Musquodoboit
Canada 45°10N 62°58W 73 C7
Upper Red L. U.S.A. 48°8N 94°45W 80 A6
Upper Sandusky U.S.A. 40°50N 83°17W 81 E12
Upper Volta = Burkina Faso ■
Africa 12°0N 1°0W 52 F5
Uppland Sweden 59°59N 17°48E 9 G17
Uppsala Sweden 59°53N 17°38E 9 G17
Upshi India 33°48N 77°52E 43 C7
Upton U.S.A. 44°6N 104°38W 76 D11
Uqsuqtuuq = Gjoa Haven
Canada 68°38N 95°53W 68 D12
Ur Iraq 30°55N 46°25E 46 D5
Urad Qianqi China 40°40N 108°30E 32 D5
Uraho Japan 42°50N 143°40E 28 C11
Urakawa Japan 42°9N 142°47E 28 C11
Ural = Uralskiy ☐ Russia 64°0N 70°0E 26 C7
Ural = Zhayyq →
Kazakhstan 47°0N 51°48E 19 E9
Ural Australia 33°21S 146°12E 63 E4
Ural Mts. = Uralskie Gory
Eurasia 60°0N 59°0E 18 C10
Uralla Australia 30°37S 151°29E 63 E5
Uralsk = Oral Kazakhstan 51°20N 51°20E 19 D9
Uralskie Gory Eurasia 60°0N 59°0E 18 C10
Uralskiy ☐ Russia 64°0N 70°0E 26 C7
Urambo Tanzania 5°4S 32°0E 54 F6
Urandangi Australia 21°32S 138°14E 62 C2
Uranium City Canada 59°34N 108°37W 71 B7
Urapuntja = Utopia
Australia 22°14S 134°33E 62 C1
Uraricoera → Brazil 3°2N 60°30W 92 C6
Urasoe Japan 26°15N 127°43E 29 L3
Uravakonda India 14°57N 77°12E 45 G3
Urawa = Saitama Japan 35°54N 139°38E 29 G9
Uray Russia 60°5N 65°15E 26 C7
'Uray'irah Si. Arabia 25°57N 48°53E 47 E6
Urbana Ill., U.S.A. 40°7N 88°12W 80 E9
Urbana Ohio, U.S.A. 40°7N 83°45W 81 E12
Urbandale U.S.A. 41°38N 93°43W 80 E7
Urbino Italy 43°43N 12°38E 22 C5
Urbión, Picos de Spain 42°1N 2°52W 21 A4
Urcos Peru 13°40S 71°38W 92 F4
Urdinarrain Argentina 32°37S 58°52W 94 C4
Ure → U.K. 54°5N 1°20W 12 C6

Urengoy Russia 65°58N 78°22E 26 C8
Ures Mexico 29°26N 110°24W 86 B2
Urewera △ N.Z. 38°29S 177°7E 59 C6
Urfa = Sanliurfa Turkey 37°12N 38°50E 46 B3
Urganch Uzbekistan 41°40N 60°41E 26 E7
Urgench = Urganch
Uzbekistan 41°40N 60°41E 26 E7
Ürgüp Turkey 38°38N 34°56E 46 B2
Urho Kekkonen △
Finland 68°20N 27°40E 8 B22
Uri India 34°8N 74°2E 43 B6
Uribia Colombia 11°43N 72°16W 92 A4
Urique Mexico 27°13N 107°55W 86 B3
Urique → Mexico 26°29N 107°58W 86 B3
Urk Neths. 52°39N 5°36E 15 B5
Urla Turkey 38°20N 26°47E 23 E12
Urmia = Orūmīyeh Iran 37°40N 45°0E 46 B5
Uroševac = Ferizaj
Kosovo 42°23N 21°10E 23 C9
Uroyan, Montanas de
Puerto Rico 18°12N 66°50W 89 d
Urrampinyi Iltjiltarri ☉
Australia 24°20S 132°10E 60 D5
Uruaçu Brazil 14°30S 49°10W 93 F9
Uruapan Mexico 19°24N 102°3W 86 D4
Urubamba → Peru 10°43S 73°48W 92 F4
Urucará Brazil 2°32S 57°45W 92 D7
Uruçuí Brazil 7°20S 44°28W 93 E10
Uruguai → Brazil 26°0S 53°30W 95 B5
Uruguaiana Brazil 29°50S 57°0W 94 B4
Uruguay ■ S. Amer. 32°30S 56°30W 94 C4
Uruguay → S. Amer. 34°12S 58°18W 94 C4
Urumchi = Ürümqi China 43°45N 87°45E 30 C6
Ürümqi China 43°45N 87°45E 30 C6
Uruna ☉ Australia 24°3S 133°1E 60 D5
Urup, Ostrov Russia 46°0N 151°0E 27 E16
Usa → Russia 66°16N 59°49E 18 A10
Uşak Turkey 38°43N 29°28E 19 G4
Usakos Namibia 21°54S 15°31E 56 B2
Usedom Germany 53°55N 14°2E 16 B8
Useless Loop Australia 26°8S 113°23E 61 E1
Ushakova, Ostrov Russia 82°0N 80°0E 27 A8
Ushant = Ouessant, Î. d'
France 48°28N 5°6W 20 B1
'Ushayrah Si. Arabia 25°35N 45°47E 46 E5
Ushibuka Japan 32°11N 130°1E 29 H5
Üshtöbe Kazakhstan 45°16N 78°0E 26 E8
Ushuaia Argentina 54°50S 68°23W 96 G3
Ushumun Russia 52°47N 126°32E 27 D13
Usinsk Russia 65°57N 57°27E 18 A10
Usk Canada 54°38N 128°26W 70 C3
Usk → U.K. 51°33N 2°58W 13 F5
Usk → U.K. 51°33N 2°58W 13 F5
Usman Russia 52°5N 39°48E 18 D6
Usolye-Sibirskoye
Russia 52°48N 103°40E 27 D11
Uspallata, P. de Argentina 32°37S 69°22W 94 C2
Ussuriysk Russia 43°48N 131°59E 28 C5
Ussurka Russia 45°12N 133°31E 28 B6
Ust-Chaun Russia 68°47N 170°30E 27 C18
Ust-Ilimsk Russia 58°3N 102°39E 27 D11
Ust-Ishim Russia 57°45N 71°10E 26 D8
Ust-Kamchatsk Russia 56°10N 162°28E 27 D17
Ust-Kamenogorsk = Öskemen
Kazakhstan 50°0N 82°36E 26 D9
Ust-Khayryuzovo
Russia 57°15N 156°45E 27 D16
Ust-Kut Russia 56°50N 105°42E 27 D11
Ust-Kuyga Russia 70°1N 135°43E 27 B14
Ust-Maya Russia 60°30N 134°28E 27 C14
Ust-Mil Russia 59°40N 133°11E 27 D14
Ust-Nera Russia 64°35N 143°15E 27 C15
Ust-Nyukzha Russia 56°34N 121°37E 27 D13
Ust-Olenek Russia 73°0N 120°5E 27 B12
Ust-Omchug Russia 61°9N 149°38E 27 C15
Ust-Port Russia 69°40N 84°26E 26 C9
Ust' Shchugor Russia 64°16N 57°36E 18 B10
Ust-Tsilma Russia 65°28N 52°11E 18 A9
Ust-Urt = Ustyurt Plateau
Asia 44°0N 55°0E 26 E6
Ust-Usa Russia 66°2N 56°57E 18 A10
Ust-Vorkuta Russia 67°24N 64°0E 18 A11
Ústí nad Labem Czechia 50°41N 14°3E 16 C8
Ustinov = Izhevsk Russia 56°51N 53°14E 18 C9
Ustyurt Plateau Asia 44°0N 55°0E 26 E6
Usu China 44°27N 84°40E 30 C5
Usuki Japan 33°8N 131°49E 29 H5
Usulután El Salv. 13°25N 88°28W 88 D2
Usumacinta → Mexico 18°24N 92°38W 87 D6
Usumbura = Bujumbura
Burundi 3°16S 29°18E 54 E5
Usutuo → Mozam. 26°48S 32°7E 57 D5
Uta Indonesia 4°33S 136°0E 37 E9
Utah ☐ U.S.A. 39°20N 111°30W 76 G8
Utah L. U.S.A. 40°12N 111°48W 76 F8
Utara, Selat Malaysia 5°28N 100°20E 39 c
Utarni India 26°5N 71°58E 42 F4
Utatlan Guatemala 15°2N 91°11W 88 C1
Ute Creek → U.S.A. 35°21N 103°50W 77 J12
Utena Lithuania 55°27N 25°40E 9 J22
Uthai Thani Thailand 15°22N 100°3E 38 E3
Uthal Pakistan 25°44N 66°40E 42 G2
Utiariti Brazil 13°0S 58°10W 92 F7
Utica N.Y., U.S.A. 43°6N 75°14W 83 C9
Utica Ohio, U.S.A. 40°14N 82°27W 82 F2
Utikuma L. Canada 55°50N 115°30W 70 B5
Utila Honduras 16°6N 86°56W 88 C2
Utkela India 20°9N 83°28E 44 D6
Utmuru India 19°22N 78°46E 44 E4
Utopia Australia 22°14S 134°33E 62 C1
Utraula India 27°19N 82°25E 43 F10
Utrecht Neths. 52°5N 5°8E 15 B5
Utrecht S. Africa 27°38S 30°20E 57 C5
Utrecht ☐ Neths. 52°6N 5°7E 15 B5
Utrera Spain 37°12N 5°48W 21 D3
Utsjoki → Finland 69°51N 26°59E 8 B22
Utsunomiya Japan 36°30N 139°50E 29 F9
Uttar Pradesh ☐ India 27°0N 80°0E 43 F9

Uttaradit Thailand 17°36N 100°5E 38 D3
Uttarakhand ☐ India 30°0N 79°30E 43 D8
Utterson Canada 45°12N 79°19W 82 A5
Uttoxeter U.K. 52°54N 1°52W 12 E6
Utuado Puerto Rico 18°16N 66°42W 89 d
Uummannaq Qaasuitsup,
Greenland 70°58N 52°17W 4 B5
Uummannaq Qaasuitsup,
Greenland 77°33N 68°52W 69 B18
Uummannarsuaq = Nunap Isua
Greenland 59°48N 43°55W 66 D15
Uusikaarlepyy Finland 63°32N 22°31E 8 E20
Uusikaupunki Finland 60°47N 21°25E 8 F19
Uva Russia 56°59N 52°13E 18 C9
Uvalde U.S.A. 29°13N 99°47W 84 G5
Uvat Russia 59°5N 68°50E 26 D7
Uvinza Tanzania 5°5S 30°24E 54 F6
Uvira Dem. Rep. of the Congo 3°22S 29°3E 54 E5
Uvs Nuur Mongolia 50°20N 92°30E 30 A4
'Uwairidh, Ḥarrat al
Si. Arabia 26°50N 38°0E 46 E3
Uwajima Japan 33°10N 132°35E 29 H6
Uweinat, Jebel Sudan 21°54N 24°58E 53 D10
Uxbridge Canada 44°6N 79°7W 82 B5
Uxin Qi China 38°50N 109°5E 32 E5
Uxmal Mexico 20°22N 89°46W 87 C7
Üydzin Mongolia 44°9N 107°0E 32 B4
Uyo Nigeria 5°1N 7°53E 52 G7
Uyûn Mûsa Egypt 29°53N 32°40E 48 F1
Uyuni Bolivia 20°28S 66°47W 92 H5
Uzbekistan ■ Asia 41°30N 65°0E 26 E7
Uzboy → Turkmenistan 39°30N 55°0E 47 B7
Uzen, Mal → Kazakhstan 49°4N 49°44E 19 E8
Uzerche France 45°25N 1°34E 20 D4
Uzh → Ukraine 51°15N 30°12E 17 C16
Uzhgorod = Uzhhorod
Ukraine 48°36N 22°18E 17 D12
Uzhhorod Ukraine 48°36N 22°18E 17 D12
Užice Serbia 43°55N 19°50E 23 C8
Uzunköprü Turkey 41°16N 26°43E 23 D12

## V

Vaal → S. Africa 29°4S 23°38E 56 C3
Vaal Dam S. Africa 27°0S 28°14E 57 C4
Vaalwater S. Africa 24°15S 28°8E 57 B4
Vaasa Finland 63°6N 21°38E 8 E19
Vác Hungary 47°49N 19°10E 17 E10
Vacaria Brazil 28°31S 50°52W 95 B5
Vach = Vakh → Russia 60°45N 76°45E 26 C8
Vache, Î. à Haiti 18°2N 73°35W 89 C5
Vacoas Mauritius 20°18S 57°29E 55 e
Vada India 19°39N 73°8E 44 E1
Vadakara India 11°35N 75°40E 45 J2
Vadnagar India 23°47N 72°40E 42 H5
Vadodara India 22°20N 73°10E 42 H5
Vadsø Norway 70°3N 29°50E 8 A23
Vaduj India 17°36N 74°27E 44 F2
Vaduz Liech. 47°8N 9°31E 20 C8
Vadvetjåkka △ Sweden 68°30N 18°28E 8 B18
Værøy Norway 67°40N 12°40E 8 C15
Vágar Faroe Is. 62°5N 7°15W 8 E9
Vågsfjorden Norway 68°50N 16°50E 8 B17
Váh → Slovakia 47°43N 18°7E 17 D9
Vahsel B. Antarctica 75°0S 35°0W 5 D1
Váhtjer = Gällivare
Sweden 67°9N 20°40E 8 C19
Vaiaku = Fongafale
Tuvalu 8°31S 179°13E 58 B10
Vaigai → India 9°15N 79°10E 45 K4
Vaihiria, L. Tahiti 17°40S 149°25W 59 d
Vaijapur India 19°58N 74°45E 44 E2
Vaikam India 9°45N 76°25E 45 K3
Vail U.S.A. 39°40N 106°20W 76 G10
Vaippar → India 9°0N 78°25E 45 K4
Vairao Tahiti 17°47S 149°17W 59 d
Vaisali → India 26°28N 78°53E 43 F8
Vaitogi Amer. Samoa 14°24S 170°44W 59 b
Vajpur India 21°24N 73°17E 44 D1
Vakarai Sri Lanka 8°8N 81°26E 45 K5
Vakh → Russia 60°45N 76°45E 26 C8
Val-d'Or Canada 48°7N 77°47W 72 C4
Val Marie Canada 49°15N 107°45W 71 D7
Valaam Russia 61°22N 30°57E 8 F24
Valahia Romania 44°35N 25°0E 17 F13
Valaichenai Sri Lanka 7°54N 81°32E 45 L5
Valandovo Macedonia 41°19N 22°34E 23 D10
Valatie U.S.A. 42°24N 73°40W 83 D11
Valcheta Argentina 40°40S 66°8W 96 E3
Valdai Hills = Valdayskaya
Vozvyshennost Russia 57°0N 33°30E 18 C5
Valdayskaya Vozvyshennost
Russia 57°0N 33°30E 18 C5
Valdepeñas Spain 38°43N 3°25W 21 C4
Valdés, Pen. Argentina 42°30S 63°45W 96 E4
Valdez U.S.A. 61°7N 146°16W 68 E2
Valdivia Chile 39°50S 73°14W 96 D2
Valdivia Abyssal Plain
S. Ocean 62°30S 70°0E 5 D6
Valdosta U.S.A. 30°50N 83°17W 85 F13
Valdres Norway 61°5N 9°5E 8 F13
Vale of Glamorgan ☐
U.K. 51°28N 3°25W 13 F4
Valemount Canada 52°50N 119°15W 70 C5
Valença Brazil 13°20S 39°5W 93 F11
Valença do Piauí Brazil 6°20S 41°45W 93 E10
Valence France 44°57N 4°54E 20 D6
Valencia Spain 39°27N 0°23W 21 C5
Valencia Trin. & Tob. 10°37N 61°11W 93 K15
Valencia Venezuela 10°11N 68°0W 92 A5
Valencia ☐ Spain 39°20N 0°40W 21 C5
Valencia, G. de Spain 39°30N 0°20E 21 C6
Valencia de Alcántara
Spain 39°25N 7°14W 21 C2
Valencia I. Ireland 51°54N 10°22W 10 E1
Valenciennes France 50°20N 3°34E 20 A5
Valentim, Sa. do Brazil 6°0S 43°30W 93 E10
Valentin Russia 43°8N 134°17E 28 C7

Valentine *Nebr., U.S.A.* 42°52N 100°33W **80** D3
Valentine *Tex., U.S.A.* 30°35N 104°30W **84** F2
Valera *Venezuela* 9°19N 70°37W **92** B4
Valga *Estonia* 57°47N 26°2E **9** H22
Valier *U.S.A.* 48°18N 112°16W **76** B7
Valjevo *Serbia* 44°18N 19°53E **23** B8
Valka *Latvia* 57°46N 26°3E **9** H22
Valkeakoski *Finland* 61°16N 24°2E **8** F21
Valkenswaard *Neths.* 51°21N 5°29E **15** C5
Vall de Uxó = La Vall d'Uixó
  *Spain* 39°49N 0°15W **21** C5
Valladolid *Mexico* 20°41N 88°12W **87** C7
Valladolid *Spain* 41°38N 4°43W **21** B3
Valle de la Pascua
  *Venezuela* 9°13N 66°0W **92** B5
Valle de las Palmas
  *Mexico* 32°20N 116°43W **79** N10
Valle de Santiago
  *Mexico* 20°23N 101°12W **86** C4
Valle de Zaragoza
  *Mexico* 27°25N 105°50W **86** B3
Valle Fértil, Sierra del
  *Argentina* 30°20S 68°0W **94** C2
Valle Hermoso *Mexico* 25°35N 97°40W **87** B5
Valle Nacional *Mexico* 17°47N 96°18W **87** D5
Valledupar *Colombia* 10°29N 73°15W **92** A4
Vallejo *U.S.A.* 38°7N 122°14W **78** G4
Vallenar *Chile* 28°30S 70°50W **94** B1
Valletta *Malta* 35°54N 14°31E **22** G6
Valley Center *U.S.A.* 33°13N 117°2W **79** M9
Valley City *U.S.A.* 46°55N 98°0W **80** B5
Valley Falls *Oreg., U.S.A.* 42°29N 120°17W **76** E3
Valley Falls *R.I., U.S.A.* 41°54N 71°24W **83** E13
Valley of Flowers △ *India* 30°50N 79°40E **43** D8
Valley Springs *U.S.A.* 38°12N 120°50W **78** G6
Valley View *U.S.A.* 40°39N 76°33W **83** F8
Valley Wells *U.S.A.* 35°27N 115°46W **79** K11
Valleyview *Canada* 55°5N 117°17W **70** B5
Vallimanca, Arroyo
  *Argentina* 35°40S 59°10W **94** D4
Valls *Spain* 41°18N 1°15E **21** B6
Valmiera *Latvia* 57°37N 25°29E **9** H21
Valognes *France* 49°30N 1°28W **20** B3
Valona = Vlorë *Albania* 40°32N 19°28E **23** D8
Valozhyn *Belarus* 54°3N 26°30E **17** A14
Valparai *India* 10°22N 76°58E **45** J3
Valparaíso *Chile* 33°2S 71°40W **94** C1
Valparaíso *Mexico* 22°46N 103°34W **86** C4
Valparaíso *U.S.A.* 41°28N 87°4W **80** E10
Valparaíso □ *Chile* 33°2S 71°40W **94** C1
Valpoy *India* 15°32N 74°8E **45** G2
Vals → *S. Africa* 27°23S 26°30E **56** C4
Vals, Tanjung *Indonesia* 8°26S 137°25E **37** F9
Valsad *India* 20°40N 72°58E **44** D1
Valverde del Camino
  *Spain* 37°35N 6°47W **21** D2
Vambori *India* 19°17N 74°44E **44** E2
Vammala = Sastamala
  *Finland* 61°20N 22°54E **8** F20
Vamsadhara → *India* 18°21N 84°8E **44** E7
Van *Turkey* 38°30N 43°0E **46** B4
Van, L. = Van Gölü *Turkey* 38°30N 43°0E **46** B4
Van Alstyne *U.S.A.* 33°25N 96°35W **84** E6
Van Blommestein Meer
  *Suriname* 4°45N 55°5W **93** C7
Van Buren *Canada* 47°10N 67°55W **73** C6
Van Buren *Ark., U.S.A.* 35°26N 94°21W **84** D7
Van Buren *Maine,*
  *U.S.A.* 47°10N 67°58W **81** B20
Van Buren *Mo., U.S.A.* 37°0N 91°1W **80** G8
Van Canh *Vietnam* 13°37N 109°0E **38** F7
Van Diemen, C. *N. Terr.,*
  *Australia* 11°9S 130°24E **60** B5
Van Diemen, C. *Queens.,*
  *Australia* 16°30S 139°46E **62** B2
Van Diemen G. *Australia* 11°45S 132°0E **60** B5
Van Gölü *Turkey* 38°30N 43°0E **46** B4
Van Horn *U.S.A.* 31°3N 104°50W **84** F2
Van Ninh *Vietnam* 12°42N 109°14E **38** F7
Van Rees, Pegunungan
  *Indonesia* 2°35S 138°15E **37** E9
Van Tivu *India* 8°51N 78°15E **45** K4
Van Wert *U.S.A.* 40°52N 84°35W **81** E11
Van Yen *Vietnam* 21°4N 104°42E **34** G5
Van Zylsrus *S. Africa* 26°52S 22°4E **56** C3
Vanadzor *Armenia* 40°48N 44°30E **19** F7
Vanavara *Russia* 60°22N 102°16E **27** C11
Vancouver *Canada* 49°15N 123°7W **78** A3
Vancouver *U.S.A.* 45°38N 122°40W **78** E4
Vancouver, C. *Australia* 35°2S 118°11E **61** G2
Vancouver I. *Canada* 49°50N 126°0W **78** B2
Vancouver Int. ✈ (YVR)
  *Canada* 49°10N 123°10W **78** A3
Vandalia *Ill., U.S.A.* 38°58N 89°6W **80** F9
Vandalia *Mo., U.S.A.* 39°19N 91°29W **80** F8
Vandavasi *India* 12°30N 79°30E **45** H4
Vandeloos B. *Sri Lanka* 8°0N 81°45E **45** L5
Vandenberg Village
  *U.S.A.* 34°43N 120°28W **79** L6
Vanderbijlpark *S. Africa* 26°42S 27°54E **57** C4
Vandergrift *U.S.A.* 40°36N 79°34W **82** F5
Vanderhoof *Canada* 54°0N 124°0W **70** C4
Vanderkloof Dam *S. Africa* 30°4S 24°40E **56** D3
Vanderlin I. *Australia* 15°44S 137°2E **62** B2
Vänern *Sweden* 58°47N 13°30E **9** G15
Vänersborg *Sweden* 58°26N 12°19E **9** G15
Vang Vieng *Laos* 18°58S 102°32E **38** C4
Vangaindrano *Madag.* 23°21S 47°36E **55** J9
Vanguard *Canada* 49°55N 107°20W **71** D7
Vanino *Russia* 48°50N 140°5E **27** E15
Vanivilasa Sagara *India* 13°45N 76°30E **45** H3
Vaniyambadi *India* 12°46N 78°44E **45** H4
Vankleek Hill *Canada* 45°32N 74°40W **83** A10
Vännäs *Sweden* 63°58N 19°48E **8** E18
Vannes *France* 47°40N 2°47W **20** C2
Vannoya *Norway* 70°6N 19°50E **8** A18
Vanrhynsdorp *S. Africa* 31°36S 18°44E **56** D2
Vansada *India* 20°47N 73°25E **44** D1
Vansbro *Sweden* 60°32N 14°15E **9** F16
Vansittart B. *Australia* 14°3S 126°17E **60** B4
Vansittart I. *Canada* 65°50N 84°0W **69** D15

Vanua Balavu *Fiji* 17°12S 178°55W **59** a
Vanua Levu *Fiji* 16°33S 179°15E **59** a
Vanua Vatu *Fiji* 18°22S 179°15W **59** a
Vanuatu ■ *Pac. Oc.* 15°0S 168°0E **58** C9
Vanwyksvlei *S. Africa* 30°18S 21°49E **56** D3
Vapi *India* 20°22N 72°54E **44** D1
Vapnyarka *Ukraine* 48°32N 28°45E **17** D15
Var → *France* 43°39N 7°12E **20** E7
Varada → *India* 15°0N 75°40E **45** G2
Varāmīn *Iran* 35°20N 51°39E **47** C6
Varāmīn □ *Iran* 35°18N 51°35E **47** B6
Varanasi *India* 25°22N 83°0E **43** G10
Varangerfjorden *Norway* 70°3N 29°25E **8** A23
Varangerhalvøya
  *Norway* 70°25N 29°30E **8** A23
Varaždin *Croatia* 46°20N 16°20E **16** E9
Varberg *Sweden* 57°6N 12°20E **9** H15
Vardak □ *Afghan.* 34°0N 68°0E **40** B6
Vardar = Axios →
  *Greece* 40°57N 22°35E **23** D10
Varde *Denmark* 55°38N 8°29E **9** J13
Vardø *Norway* 70°23N 31°5E **8** A24
Varella, Mui = Nay, Mui
  *Vietnam* 12°54N 109°26E **38** F7
Varèna *Lithuania* 54°12N 24°30E **9** J21
Varese *Italy* 45°48N 8°50E **20** D8
Varginha *Brazil* 21°33S 45°25W **95** A6
Varillas *Chile* 24°0S 70°10W **94** A1
Varkaus *Finland* 62°19N 27°50E **8** E22
Varna *Bulgaria* 43°13N 27°56E **23** C12
Varna → *India* 16°48N 74°32E **44** F2
Värnamo *Sweden* 57°10N 14°3E **9** H16
Várnjárga = Varangerhalvøya
  *Norway* 70°25N 29°30E **8** A23
Vars *Canada* 45°21N 75°21W **83** A9
Varysburg *U.S.A.* 42°46N 78°19W **82** D6
Varzaneh *Iran* 32°25N 52°40E **47** C7
Vasa = Vaasa *Finland* 63°6N 21°38E **8** E19
Vasa Barris → *Brazil* 11°10S 37°10W **93** F11
Vasai-Virar *India* 19°28N 72°48E **44** E1
Vascongadas = País Vasco □
  *Spain* 42°50N 2°45W **21** A4
Vasht = Khāsh *Iran* 28°15N 61°15E **47** D9
Vasilkov = Vasylkiv
  *Ukraine* 50°7N 30°15E **17** C16
Vaslui *Romania* 46°38N 27°42E **17** E14
Vassar *Canada* 49°10N 95°55W **71** D9
Vassar *U.S.A.* 43°22N 83°35W **81** D12
Västerås *Sweden* 59°37N 16°38E **9** G17
Västerbotten *Sweden* 64°36N 20°4E **8** D19
Västerdalälven → *Sweden* 60°30N 15°7E **8** F16
Västervik *Sweden* 57°43N 16°33E **9** H17
Västmanland *Sweden* 59°45N 16°20E **9** G17
Vasto *Italy* 42°8N 14°40E **22** C6
Vasylkiv *Ukraine* 50°7N 30°15E **17** C16
Vat Phou *Laos* 14°51N 105°49E **38** E5
Vatersay *U.K.* 56°55N 7°32W **11** E1
Vatiu = Atiu *Cook Is.* 20°0S 158°10W **65** J12
Vatnajökull *Iceland* 64°30N 16°48W **8** D5
Vatnajökull △ *Iceland* 64°24N 16°48W **8** D5
Vatra-Dornei *Romania* 47°22N 25°22E **17** E13
Vatrak → *India* 23°9N 73°2E **42** H5
Vatu Vara *Fiji* 17°26S 179°31W **59** a
Vatulele *Fiji* 18°33S 177°37E **59** a
Vaudreuil-Dorion
  *Canada* 45°23N 74°3W **83** A10
Vaughn *Mont., U.S.A.* 47°33N 111°33W **76** C8
Vaughn *N. Mex.,*
  *U.S.A.* 34°36N 105°13W **77** J11
Vaujours L. *Canada* 55°27N 74°15W **72** A5
Vaupés = Uaupés →
  *Brazil* 0°2N 67°16W **92** C5
Vaupés □ *Colombia* 1°0N 71°0W **92** C4
Vauxhall *Canada* 50°5N 112°9W **70** C6
Vav *India* 24°22N 71°31E **42** G4
Vava'u *Tonga* 18°36S 174°0W **59** c
Vava'u Group *Tonga* 18°40S 174°0W **59** c
Vavuniya *Sri Lanka* 8°45N 80°30E **45** K5
Vawkavysk *Belarus* 53°9N 24°30E **17** B13
Växjö *Sweden* 56°52N 14°50E **9** H16
Vayalpad *India* 13°39N 78°38E **45** H4
Vaygach, Ostrov *Russia* 70°0N 60°0E **26** C7
Veaikevárri = Svappavaara
  *Sweden* 67°40N 21°3E **8** C19
Vechte → *Neths.* 52°34N 6°6E **15** B6
Vedaranniyam *India* 10°25N 79°50E **45** J4
Vedea → *Romania* 43°42N 25°41E **17** G13
Vedia *Argentina* 34°30S 61°31W **94** C3
Veendam *Neths.* 53°5N 6°52E **15** A6
Veenendaal *Neths.* 52°2N 5°34E **15** B5
Vefsna → *Norway* 65°48N 13°10E **8** D15
Vega *Norway* 65°40N 11°55E **8** D14
Vega *U.S.A.* 35°15N 102°26W **84** D3
Vega Baja *Puerto Rico* 18°27N 66°23W **89** d
Vegreville *Canada* 53°30N 112°5W **70** C6
Vejer de la Frontera *Spain* 36°15N 5°59W **21** D3
Vejle *Denmark* 55°43N 9°30E **9** J13
Velachha *India* 21°26N 73°1E **44** D1
Velanai I. *Sri Lanka* 9°45N 79°45E **45** K4
Velas, C. *Costa Rica* 10°21N 85°52W **88** D2
Velasco, Sierra de
  *Argentina* 29°20S 67°10W **94** B2
Velddrif *S. Africa* 32°42S 18°11E **56** E2
Velebit Planina *Croatia* 44°50N 15°20E **16** F8
Veles *Macedonia* 41°46N 21°47E **23** D9
Vélez Rubio *Spain* 37°41N 2°5W **21** D4
Vélez-Málaga *Spain* 36°48N 4°5W **21** D3
Velhas → *Brazil* 17°13S 44°49W **93** G10
Velika Kapela *Croatia* 45°10N 15°5E **16** F8
Velikaya → *Russia* 57°48N 28°10E **18** C4
Velikaya Kema *Russia* 45°30N 137°12E **28** B8
Velikiy Ustyug *Russia* 60°47N 46°20E **18** B8
Velikiye Luki *Russia* 56°25N 30°32E **18** C5
Veliko Tarnovo *Bulgaria* 43°5N 25°41E **23** C11
Velikonda Range *India* 14°45N 79°10E **45** G4
Velletri → *India* 11°30N 79°9E **45** J4
Velletri *Italy* 41°41N 12°47E **22** D5
Vellore *India* 12°57N 79°10E **45** H4

Velsk *Russia* 61°10N 42°0E **18** B7
Veluwezoom △ *Neths.* 52°5N 6°0E **15** B6
Velva *U.S.A.* 48°4N 100°56W **80** A3
Vembanad L. *India* 9°36N 76°15E **45** K3
Venado *Mexico* 22°56N 101°6W **86** C4
Venado Tuerto *Argentina* 33°50S 62°0W **94** C3
Vendée □ *France* 46°50N 1°35W **20** C3
Vendôme *France* 47°47N 1°3E **20** C4
Vi Thanh *Vietnam* 9°42N 105°26E **39** H5
Venézia *Italy* 45°27N 12°21E **22** B5
Venézia, G. di *Italy* 45°15N 13°0E **22** B5
Venezuela ■ *S. Amer.* 8°0N 66°0W **92** B5
Venezuela, G. de
  *Venezuela* 11°30N 71°0W **92** A4
Vengurla *India* 15°53N 73°45E **45** G1
Vengurla Rocks *India* 15°55N 73°22E **45** G1
Venice = Venézia *Italy* 45°27N 12°21E **22** B5
Venice *U.S.A.* 27°6N 82°27W **85** H13
Venkatagiri *India* 14°0N 79°35E **45** H4
Venkatapuram *India* 18°20N 80°30E **44** E5
Venlo *Neths.* 51°22N 6°11E **15** C6
Vennachar Junction
  *Canada* 45°5N 77°14W **82** A7
Vennesla *Norway* 58°15N 7°59E **9** G12
Venray *Neths.* 51°31N 6°0E **15** C6
Ventana, Sa. de la
  *Argentina* 38°0S 62°30W **94** D3
Ventersburg *S. Africa* 28°7S 27°9E **56** D4
Venterstad *S. Africa* 30°47S 25°48E **56** D4
Ventnor *U.K.* 50°36N 1°12W **13** G6
Ventoténe *Italy* 40°47N 13°25E **22** D5
Ventoux, Mt. *France* 44°10N 5°17E **20** D6
Ventspils *Latvia* 57°25N 21°32E **9** H19
Ventuarí → *Venezuela* 3°58N 67°2W **92** C5
Ventucopa *U.S.A.* 34°50N 119°29W **79** L7
Ventura *U.S.A.* 34°17N 119°18W **79** L7
Venus B. *Australia* 38°40S 145°42E **63** F4
Venustiano Carranza
  *Mexico* 30°25N 115°53W **86** A1
Venustiano Carranza, Presa
  *Mexico* 27°30N 100°37W **86** B4
Vera *Argentina* 29°30S 60°20W **94** B3
Vera *Spain* 37°15N 1°51W **21** D5
Veracruz *Mexico* 19°11N 96°8W **87** D5
Veracruz □ *Mexico* 19°0N 96°15W **87** D5
Veraval *India* 20°53N 70°27E **42** J4
Verbánia *Italy* 45°56N 8°33E **20** D8
Verbano, L. di = Maggiore, L.
  *Italy* 45°57N 8°39E **20** D8
Vercelli *Italy* 45°19N 8°25E **20** D8
Verdalsøra *Norway* 63°48N 11°30E **8** E14
Verde → *Goiás, Brazil* 18°1S 50°14W **93** G8
Verde → *Mato Grosso do Sul,*
  *Brazil* 21°25S 52°20W **93** H8
Verde → *Chihuahua,*
  *Mexico* 26°39N 107°11W **86** B3
Verde → *Jalisco, Mexico* 20°42N 103°14W **86** C4
Verde → *Oaxaca, Mexico* 15°59N 97°50W **87** D5
Verde → *Paraguay* 23°9S 57°37W **94** A4
Verde → *U.S.A.* 33°33N 111°40W **77** K8
Verde, Cay *Bahamas* 23°0N 75°5W **88** B4
Verden *Germany* 52°55N 9°14E **16** B5
Verdi *U.S.A.* 39°31N 119°59W **78** F7
Verdun *France* 49°9N 5°24E **20** B6
Vereeniging *S. Africa* 26°38S 27°57E **57** C4
Verga, C. *Guinea* 10°30N 14°10W **52** F3
Vergara *Uruguay* 32°56S 53°57W **95** C5
Vergemont Cr. →
  *Australia* 24°16S 143°16E **62** C3
Vergennes *U.S.A.* 44°10N 73°15W **83** B11
Veria *Greece* 40°34N 22°12E **23** D10
Verín *Spain* 41°57N 7°27W **21** B2
Verkhnetulomskoye Vdkhr.
  *Russia* 68°36N 31°12E **8** B24
Verkhnevilyuysk
  *Russia* 63°27N 120°18E **27** C13
Verkhniy Baskunchak
  *Russia* 48°14N 46°44E **19** E8
Verkhoyansk *Russia* 67°35N 133°25E **27** C14
Verkhoyansk Ra. =
  Verkhoyanskiy Khrebet
  *Russia* 66°0N 129°0E **27** C13
Verkhoyanskiy Khrebet
  *Russia* 66°0N 129°0E **27** C13
Vermilion *Canada* 53°20N 110°50W **71** C6
Vermilion *U.S.A.* 41°25N 82°22W **82** E2
Vermilion → *Canada* 53°22N 110°51W **71** C6
Vermilion B. *Canada* 29°42N 92°0W **84** G9
Vermilion Bay *Canada* 49°51N 93°34W **71** D10
Vermilion Cliffs Nat. Monument △
  *U.S.A.* 36°54N 112°5W **77** H8
Vermilion L. *U.S.A.* 47°53N 92°26W **80** B7
Vermillion *U.S.A.* 42°47N 96°56W **80** D5
Vermillion → *Canada* 47°38N 72°56W **72** C5
Vermont □ *U.S.A.* 44°0N 73°0W **83** C12
Vernadsky *Antarctica* 65°0S 64°0W **5** C17
Vernal *U.S.A.* 40°27N 109°32W **76** F9
Vernalis *U.S.A.* 37°36N 121°17W **78** H5
Verner *Canada* 46°25N 80°8W **72** C3
Verneukpan *S. Africa* 30°0S 21°0E **56** D3
Vernon *Canada* 50°20N 119°15W **70** C5
Vernon *U.S.A.* 34°9N 99°17W **84** D5
Vernonia *U.S.A.* 45°52N 123°11W **78** E3
Vero Beach *U.S.A.* 27°38N 80°24W **85** H14
Véroia = Veria *Greece* 40°34N 22°12E **23** D10
Verona *Canada* 44°29N 76°42W **83** B8
Verona *Italy* 45°27N 10°59E **22** B4
Vert, C. *Senegal* 14°45N 17°30W **52** F2
Verulam *S. Africa* 29°38S 31°2E **57** C5
Verviers *Belgium* 50°37N 5°52E **15** D5
Vila Bela da Santissima Trindade
  *Brazil* 15°0S 59°57W **92** G7
Vila da Ribeira Brava
  *Cabo Verde* 16°32N 24°25W **52** b
Vila do Bispo *Portugal* 37°5N 8°53W **21** D1
Vila do Maio *Cabo Verde* 15°10N 23°10W **52** b
Vila Franca de Xira
  *Portugal* 38°57N 8°59W **21** C1
Vila Gomes da Costa
  *Mozam.* 24°20S 33°37E **57** B5
Vila Nova de Gaia *Portugal* 41°4N 8°40W **21** B1
Vila Real *Portugal* 41°17N 7°48W **21** B2
Vila-Real *Spain* 39°55N 0°3W **21** C5

Vila Real de Santo António
  *Portugal* 37°10N 7°28W **21** D2
Vila Velha *Brazil* 20°20S 40°17W **95** A7
Vilagarcía de Arousa
  *Spain* 42°34N 8°46W **21** A1
Vilaine → *France* 47°30N 2°27W **20** C2
Vilanandro, Tanjona
  *Madag.* 16°11S 44°27E **55** H8
Vilanculos *Mozam.* 22°1S 35°17E **57** B6
Vilanova i la Geltrú *Spain* 41°13N 1°40E **21** B6
Vilcheka, Ostrov *Russia* 80°0N 58°31E **26** B6
Vilcheka, Zemlya *Russia* 80°0N 55°0E **4** A11
Vileyka *Belarus* 54°30N 26°53E **17** A14
Vilhelmina *Sweden* 64°35N 16°39E **8** D17
Vilhena *Brazil* 12°40S 60°5W **92** F6
Viliya = Neris → *Lithuania* 55°8N 24°16E **9** J21
Viliya *Estonia* 58°28N 25°30E **9** G21
Vilkitskogo, Proliv
  *Russia* 78°0N 103°0E **27** B11
Vilkovo = Vylkove
  *Ukraine* 45°28N 29°32E **17** F15
Villa Abecia *Bolivia* 21°0S 68°18W **94** A2
Villa Ana *Argentina* 28°28S 59°40W **94** B4
Villa Ángela *Argentina* 27°34S 60°45W **94** B3
Villa Bella *Bolivia* 10°25S 65°22W **92** F5
Villa Cañás *Argentina* 34°0S 61°35W **94** C3
Villa Constitución
  *Argentina* 33°15S 60°20W **94** C3
Villa de Arriaga *Mexico* 21°56N 101°20W **86** C4
Villa de María *Argentina* 29°55S 63°43W **94** B3
Villa de Méndez *Mexico* 25°7N 98°34W **87** B5
Villa Dolores *Argentina* 31°58S 65°15W **94** C2
Villa Gesell *Argentina* 37°15S 56°55W **94** D4
Villa Guillermina
  *Argentina* 28°15S 59°29W **94** B4
Villa Hayes *Paraguay* 25°5S 57°20W **94** B4
Villa Hidalgo *Mexico* 24°15N 99°26W **87** C5
Villa Iris *Argentina* 38°12S 63°12W **94** D3
Villa Las Estrellas = Frei
  *Antarctica* 62°30S 58°0W **5** C18
Villa María *Argentina* 32°20S 63°10W **94** C3
Villa Mazán *Argentina* 28°40S 66°30W **94** B2
Villa Montes *Bolivia* 21°10S 63°30W **94** A3
Villa Ocampo *Argentina* 28°30S 59°20W **94** B4
Villa Ocampo *Mexico* 26°27N 105°31W **86** B3
Villa Ojo de Agua
  *Argentina* 29°30S 63°44W **94** B3
Villa San Martín
  *Argentina* 28°15S 64°9W **94** B3
Villa Unión *Mexico* 23°12N 106°14W **86** C3
Villacarrillo *Spain* 38°7N 3°3W **21** C4
Villach *Austria* 46°37N 13°51E **16** E7
Villagrán *Mexico* 24°29N 99°29W **87** C5
Villaguay *Argentina* 32°0S 59°0W **94** C4
Villahermosa *Mexico* 17°59N 92°55W **87** D6
Villajoyosa *Spain* 38°30N 0°12W **21** C5
Villalba *Spain* 43°26N 7°40W **21** A2
Villanueva *U.S.A.* 35°16N 105°22W **77** J11
Villanueva de la Serena
  *Spain* 38°59N 5°50W **21** C3
Villanueva y Geltrú = Vilanova i la
  Geltrú *Spain* 41°13N 1°40E **21** B6
Villarreal = Vila-Real
  *Spain* 39°55N 0°3W **21** C5
Villarrica *Chile* 39°15S 72°15W **96** D2
Villarrica *Paraguay* 25°40S 56°30W **94** B4
Villarrobledo *Spain* 39°18N 2°36W **21** C4
Villavicencio *Argentina* 32°28S 69°0W **94** C2
Villavicencio *Colombia* 4°9N 73°37W **92** C4
Villaviciosa *Spain* 43°32N 5°27W **21** A3
Villazón *Bolivia* 22°0S 65°35W **94** A2
Ville-Marie *Canada* 47°20N 79°30W **72** C4
Ville Platte *U.S.A.* 30°41N 92°17W **84** F8
Villena *Spain* 38°39N 0°52W **21** C5
Villeneuve-d'Ascq *France* 50°38N 3°9E **20** A5
Villeneuve-sur-Lot *France* 44°24N 0°42E **20** D4
Villiers *S. Africa* 27°2S 28°36E **57** C4
Villingen-Schwenningen
  *Germany* 48°3N 8°26E **16** D5
Villmanstrand = Lappeenranta
  *Finland* 61°3N 28°12E **8** F23
Villupuram *India* 11°59N 79°31E **45** J4
Vilna *Canada* 54°7N 111°55W **70** C6
Vilnius *Lithuania* 54°38N 25°19E **9** J21
Vilyuchinsk *Russia* 52°55N 158°24E **27** D16
Vilyuy → *Russia* 64°24N 126°26E **27** C13
Vilyuysk *Russia* 63°40N 121°35E **27** C13
Vilyuyskoye Vdkhr.
  *Russia* 63°0N 112°0E **27** C12
Viña del Mar *Chile* 33°0S 71°30W **94** C1
Vinaròs *Spain* 40°30N 0°27E **21** B6
Vincennes *U.S.A.* 38°41N 87°32W **80** F10
Vincennes Bay *S. Ocean* 66°0S 109°0E **5** C8
Vincent *U.S.A.* 34°33N 118°11W **79** L8
Vinchina *Argentina* 28°45S 68°15W **94** B2
Vindelälven → *Sweden* 63°55N 19°50E **8** E18
Vindeln *Sweden* 64°12N 19°43E **8** D18
Vindhya Ra. *India* 22°50N 77°0E **42** H7
Vineland *U.S.A.* 39°29N 75°2W **81** F16
Vinh *Vietnam* 18°45N 105°38E **38** C5
Vinh Long *Vietnam* 10°16N 105°57E **39** G5
Vinh Moc *Vietnam* 17°5N 107°3E **38** D6
Vinh Yen *Vietnam* 21°21N 105°35E **38** B5
Vinita *U.S.A.* 36°39N 95°9W **84** C7
Vinkovci *Croatia* 45°19N 18°48E **23** B8
Vinnitsa = Vinnytsya
  *Ukraine* 49°15N 28°30E **17** D15
Vinnytsya *Ukraine* 49°15N 28°30E **17** D15
Vinton *Calif., U.S.A.* 39°48N 120°10W **78** F6
Vinton *Iowa, U.S.A.* 42°10N 92°1W **80** D7
Vinton *La., U.S.A.* 30°11N 93°35W **84** F8
Vinukonda *India* 16°5N 79°45E **45** F4
Violet Valley ◎ *Australia* 17°10S 127°55E **60** C4
Vioolsdrif *S. Africa* 28°26S 17°42E **56** D2
Viqueque *Timor-Leste* 8°52S 126°23E **37** F7
Virac *Phil.* 13°30N 124°20E **37** B6
Virachey △ *Cambodia* 14°14N 106°55E **38** E6
Virago Sd. *Canada* 54°0N 132°30W **70** C2

172 Virajpet INDEX TO WORLD MAPS


Virajpet = Virarajendrapet India 12°10N 75°50E 45 H2
Viramgam India 23°5N 72°0E 42 H5
Viranşehir Turkey 37°13N 39°45E 46 B3
Virarajendrapet India 12°10N 75°50E 45 H2
Virawah Pakistan 24°31N 70°46E 42 G4
Virden Canada 49°50N 100°56W 71 D8
Vire France 48°50N 0°53W 20 B3
Vírgenes, C. Argentina 52°19S 68°21W 96 G3
Virgin → U.S.A. 36°28N 114°21W 77 H6
Virgin Gorda Br. Virgin Is. 18°30N 64°26W 89 e
Virgin Is. (British) ⊠ W. Indies 18°30N 64°30W 89 e
Virgin Is. (U.S.) ⊠ W. Indies 18°20N 65°0W 89 e
Virgin Islands △ U.S. Virgin Is. 18°21N 64°43W 89 C7
Virginia S. Africa 28°8S 26°55E 56 C4
Virginia U.S.A. 47°31N 92°32W 80 B7
Virginia □ U.S.A. 37°30N 78°45W 81 G14
Virginia Beach U.S.A. 36°49N 76°9W 81 F16
Virginia City Mont., U.S.A. 45°18N 111°56W 76 D8
Virginia City Nev., U.S.A. 39°19N 119°39W 78 F7
Virginia Falls Canada 61°38N 125°42W 70 A3
Virginiatown Canada 48°9N 79°36W 72 C4
Viroqua U.S.A. 43°34N 90°53W 80 D8
Virovitica Croatia 45°51N 17°21E 22 B7
Virpur India 21°51N 70°42E 42 J4
Virton Belgium 49°35N 5°32E 15 E5
Virudhunagar India 9°30N 77°58E 45 K3
Vis Croatia 43°4N 16°10E 22 C7
Visalia U.S.A. 36°20N 119°18W 78 J7
Visayan Sea Phil. 11°30N 123°30E 37 B6
Visby Sweden 57°37N 18°18E 9 H18
Viscount Melville Sd. Canada 74°10N 108°0W 69 C10
Visé Belgium 50°44N 5°41E 15 D5
Vise, Ostrov Russia 79°33N 76°50E 26 B8
Višegrad Bos.-H. 43°47N 19°17E 23 C8
Viseu Brazil 1°10S 46°5W 93 D9
Viseu Portugal 40°40N 7°55W 21 B2
Vishakhapatnam India 17°45N 83°20E 44 F6
Visnagar India 23°45N 72°32E 42 H5
Viso, Mte. Italy 44°38N 7°5E 20 D7
Visokoi I. Antarctica 56°43S 27°15W 5 B1
Vista U.S.A. 33°12N 117°14W 79 M9
Vistula = Wisła → Poland 54°22N 18°55E 17 A10
Vita India 17°17N 74°33E 44 F2
Vitebsk = Vitsyebsk Belarus 55°10N 30°15E 18 C5
Viterbo Italy 42°25N 12°6E 22 C5
Viti Levu Fiji 17°30S 177°30E 59 a
Vitigudino Spain 41°1N 6°26W 21 B2
Vitim Russia 59°28N 112°35E 27 D12
Vitim → Russia 59°26N 112°34E 27 D12
Vitória Brazil 20°20S 40°22W 93 H10
Vitória da Conquista Brazil 14°51S 40°51W 93 F10
Vitória de Santo Antão Brazil 8°10S 35°20W 93 E11
Vitoria-Gasteiz Spain 42°50N 2°41W 21 A4
Vitsyebsk Belarus 55°10N 30°15E 18 C5
Vittória Italy 36°57N 14°32E 22 F6
Vittório Véneto Italy 45°59N 12°18E 22 B5
Viveiro Spain 43°39N 7°38W 21 A2
Vivian U.S.A. 32°53N 93°59W 84 E8
Viwa Fiji 17°10S 177°58E 59 a
Vizcaíno, Desierto de Mexico 27°30N 113°45W 86 B2
Vizcaíno, Sierra Mexico 27°30N 114°0W 86 B2
Vize Turkey 41°34N 27°45E 23 D12
Vizianagaram India 18°6N 83°30E 44 E6
Vlaardingen Neths. 51°55N 4°21E 15 C4
Vladikavkaz Russia 43°0N 44°35E 19 F7
Vladimir Russia 56°15N 40°30E 18 C7
Vladimir Volynskiy = Volodymyr-Volynskyy Ukraine 50°50N 24°18E 17 C13
Vladivostok Russia 43°10N 131°53E 28 C5
Vlieland Neths. 53°16N 4°55E 15 A4
Vlissingen Neths. 51°26N 3°34E 15 C3
Vlorë Albania 40°32N 19°28E 23 D8
Vltava → Czechia 50°21N 14°30E 16 D8
Vo Dat Vietnam 11°9N 107°31E 39 G6
Vodlozersky △ Russia 62°40N 37°5E 26 C1
Voe U.K. 60°21N 1°16W 11 A7
Vogelkop = Doberai, Jazirah Indonesia 1°25S 133°0E 37 E8
Vogelsberg Germany 50°31N 9°12E 16 C5
Voghera Italy 44°59N 9°1E 20 D8
Vohibinany Madag. 18°49S 49°4E 55 H9
Vohimarina = Iharana Madag. 13°25S 50°0E 55 G10
Vohimena, Tanjon' i Madag. 25°36S 45°8E 55 K9
Vohipeno Madag. 22°22S 47°51E 55 J9
Voi Kenya 3°25S 38°32E 54 E7
Voiron France 45°22N 5°35E 20 D6
Voisey B. Canada 56°15N 61°50W 73 A7
Vojmsjön Sweden 65°0N 16°24E 8 D17
Vojvodina □ Serbia 45°20N 20°0E 23 B9
Volborg U.S.A. 45°51N 105°41W 76 D11
Volcán de Colima △ Mexico 19°30N 103°40W 86 D4
Volcano Is. = Kazan-Rettō Pac. Oc. 25°0N 141°0E 64 E6
Volda Norway 62°9N 6°5E 8 E12
Volga = Privolzhskiy □ Russia 56°0N 50°0E 26 D6
Volga → Russia 46°0N 48°30E 19 E8
Volga Hts. = Privolzhskaya Vozvyshennost Russia 51°0N 46°0E 19 D8
Volgodonsk Russia 47°33N 42°5E 19 E7
Volgograd Russia 48°40N 44°25E 19 E7
Volgogradskoye Vdkhr. Russia 50°0N 45°20E 19 D8
Volkhov → Russia 60°8N 32°20E 18 B5
Volkovysk = Vawkavysk Belarus 53°9N 24°30E 17 B13
Volksrust S. Africa 27°24S 29°53E 57 C4
Volochanka Russia 71°0N 94°28E 27 B10
Volodymyr-Volynskyy Ukraine 50°50N 24°18E 17 C13
Vologda Russia 59°10N 39°45E 18 C6
Volos Greece 39°24N 22°59E 23 E10
Volosovo Russia 59°27N 29°32E 9 G23
Volovets Ukraine 48°43N 23°11E 17 D12
Volozhin = Valozhyn Belarus 54°3N 26°30E 17 A14
Volsk Russia 52°5N 47°22E 18 D8
Volta → Ghana 5°46N 0°41E 50 F4
Volta, L. Ghana 7°30N 0°0 52 G6
Volta Redonda Brazil 22°31S 44°5W 95 A7
Voltaire, C. Australia 14°16S 125°35E 60 B4
Volterra Italy 43°24N 10°51E 22 C4
Volturno → Italy 41°1N 13°55E 22 D5
Volyn □ Ukraine 51°15N 24°30E 17 C13
Volzhskiy Russia 48°56N 44°46E 19 E7
Vomo Fiji 17°30S 177°15E 59 a
Vopnafjörður Iceland 65°45N 14°50W 8 D6
Voreios Sporades Greece 39°15N 23°30E 23 E10
Vorkuta Russia 67°48N 64°20E 18 A11
Vormsi Estonia 59°1N 23°13E 9 G20
Voronezh Russia 51°40N 39°10E 19 D6
Võrts järv Estonia 58°16N 26°3E 9 G22
Võru Estonia 57°48N 26°54E 9 H22
Vosges France 48°20N 7°10E 20 B7
Voss Norway 60°38N 6°26E 8 F12
Vostochnyy Port Russia 42°44N 133°4E 28 C6
Vostok Antarctica 78°30S 106°50E 5 D8
Vostok I. Kiribati 10°5S 152°23W 65 J12
Votkinsk Russia 57°0N 53°55E 18 C9
Votkinskoye Vdkhr. Russia 57°22N 55°12E 18 C10
Vouga → Portugal 40°41N 8°40W 21 B1
Voyageurs △ U.S.A. 48°32N 93°0W 80 A7
Voynitsa Russia 65°10N 30°20E 8 D24
Voyvozh Russia 62°56N 54°56E 18 B9
Vozhe, Ozero Russia 60°45N 39°0E 18 B6
Voznesensk Ukraine 47°35N 31°21E 19 E5
Voznesenye Russia 61°0N 35°28E 18 B6
Vrangel Russia 42°43N 133°5E 28 C6
Vrangelya, Ostrov Russia 71°0N 180°0E 27 B18
Vranje Serbia 42°34N 21°54E 23 C9
Vratsa Bulgaria 43°15N 23°30E 23 C10
Vrbas → Bos.-H. 45°8N 17°29E 22 B7
Vrede S. Africa 27°24S 29°6E 57 C4
Vredefort S. Africa 27°0S 27°22E 56 C4
Vredenburg S. Africa 32°56S 18°0E 56 D2
Vredendal S. Africa 31°41S 18°35E 56 D2
Vriddhachalam India 11°30N 79°20E 45 J4
Vrindavan India 27°37N 77°40E 42 F7
Vršac Serbia 45°8N 21°20E 23 B9
Vryburg S. Africa 26°55S 24°45E 56 C3
Vryheid S. Africa 27°45S 30°47E 57 C5
Vu Liet Vietnam 18°43N 105°23E 38 C5
Vukovar Croatia 45°21N 18°59E 23 B8
Vuktyl Russia 63°52N 57°20E 26 C6
Vulcan Canada 50°25N 113°15W 70 C6
Vulcan Romania 45°23N 23°17E 17 F12
Vulcăneşti Moldova 45°41N 28°18E 17 F15
Vulcano Italy 38°24N 14°58E 22 E6
Vulkaneshty = Vulcăneşti Moldova 45°41N 28°18E 17 F15
Vung Tau Vietnam 10°21N 107°4E 39 G6
Vunidawa Fiji 17°50S 178°21E 59 a
Vunisea Fiji 19°3S 178°10E 59 a
Vuntut △ Canada 68°25N 139°41W 68 D4
Vyara India 21°8N 73°28E 44 D1
Vyartsilya Russia 62°8N 30°45E 8 E24
Vyatka = Kirov Russia 58°35N 49°40E 18 C8
Vyatka → Russia 55°37N 51°28E 18 C9
Vyatskiye Polyany Russia 56°14N 51°5E 18 C9
Vyazemskiy Russia 47°32N 134°45E 27 E14
Vyazma Russia 55°10N 34°15E 18 C5
Vyborg Russia 60°43N 28°47E 8 F23
Vychegda → Russia 61°18N 46°36E 18 B8
Vychodné Beskydy Europe 49°20N 22°0E 17 D11
Vyg-ozero Russia 63°47N 34°29E 18 B5
Vylkove Ukraine 45°28N 29°32E 17 F15
Vynohradiv Ukraine 48°9N 23°2E 17 D12
Vypin India 10°10N 76°15E 45 J3
Vyrnwy, L. U.K. 52°48N 3°31W 12 E4
Vyshniy Volochek Russia 57°30N 34°30E 18 C5
Vyshzha = imeni 26 Bakinskikh Komissarov Turkmenistan 39°22N 54°10E 47 B7
Vyškov Czechia 49°17N 17°0E 17 D9
Vytegra Russia 61°0N 36°27E 18 B6


## W


W.A.C. Bennett Dam Canada 56°2N 122°6W 70 B4
Wa Ghana 10°7N 2°25W 52 F5
Waal → Neths. 51°37N 5°0E 15 C5
Waalwijk Neths. 51°42N 5°4E 15 C5
Waanyi-Garawa ✪ Australia 18°2S 137°33E 62 B2
Wabakimi △ Canada 50°43N 89°29W 72 B2
Wabana Canada 47°40N 53°0W 73 C9
Wabasca → Canada 58°22N 115°20W 70 B5
Wabasca-Desmarais Canada 55°57N 113°56W 70 B6
Wabash U.S.A. 40°48N 85°49W 81 E11
Wabash → U.S.A. 37°48N 88°2W 80 G9
Wabigoon L. Canada 49°44N 92°44W 71 D10
Wabowden Canada 54°55N 98°38W 71 C9
Wabu Hu China 32°20N 116°50E 35 A11
Wabuk Pt. Canada 55°20N 85°5W 72 A2
Wabush Canada 52°55N 66°52W 73 B6
Waco U.S.A. 31°33N 97°9W 84 F6
Waconichi, L. Canada 50°8N 74°0W 72 B5
Wad Hamid Sudan 16°30N 32°45E 53 E12
Wad Medanî Sudan 14°28N 33°30E 53 F12
Wad Thana Pakistan 27°22N 66°23E 42 F2
Wadayama Japan 35°19N 134°52E 29 G7
Waddeneilanden Neths. 53°25N 5°10E 15 A5
Waddenzee Neths. 53°6N 5°10E 15 A5
Waddington U.S.A. 44°52N 75°12W 83 B9
Waddington, Mt. Canada 51°23N 125°15W 70 C3
Waddy Pt. Australia 24°58S 153°21E 63 C5
Wadebridge U.K. 50°31N 4°51W 13 G3
Wadena Canada 51°57N 103°47W 71 C8
Wadena U.S.A. 46°26N 95°8W 80 B6
Wadeye Australia 14°28S 129°52E 60 B4
Wadgaon India 18°44N 73°39E 44 E1
Wadhams Canada 51°30N 127°30W 70 C3
Wadhwan India 22°42N 71°41E 42 H4
Wadi India 17°4N 76°59E 44 F3
Wādī as Sīr Jordan 31°56N 35°49E 48 D4
Wadi Halfa Sudan 21°53N 31°19E 53 D12
Wādī Rum △ Jordan 29°30N 35°20E 48 F4
Wadian China 32°42N 112°29E 35 A9
Wadsworth Nev., U.S.A. 39°38N 119°17W 76 G4
Wadsworth Ohio, U.S.A. 41°2N 81°44W 82 E3
Waegwan S. Korea 35°59N 128°23E 33 G15
Wafangdian China 39°38N 121°58E 33 E11
Wafrah Kuwait 28°33N 47°56E 46 D5
Wagait ✪ Australia 13°1S 130°5E 60 B5
Wageningen Neths. 51°58N 5°40E 15 C5
Wager B. Canada 65°26N 88°40W 69 D14
Wagga Wagga Australia 35°7S 147°24E 63 F4
Waghai India 20°46N 73°29E 44 D1
Waghete Indonesia 4°10S 135°50E 37 E9
Wagin Australia 33°17S 117°25E 61 F2
Wagner U.S.A. 43°5N 98°18W 80 D4
Wagon Mound U.S.A. 36°1N 104°42W 77 H11
Wagoner U.S.A. 35°58N 95°22W 84 D7
Wah Pakistan 33°45N 72°40E 42 C5
Wahai Indonesia 2°48S 129°35E 37 E7
Wâḥid Egypt 30°48N 32°21E 48 E1
Wahnai Afghan. 32°40N 65°50E 42 C1
Wahoo U.S.A. 41°13N 96°37W 80 E5
Wahpeton U.S.A. 46°16N 96°36W 80 B5
Wai India 17°56N 73°57E 44 F1
Waialua U.S.A. 21°34N 158°8W 75 L8
Waiau → N.Z. 42°47S 173°22E 59 E4
Waiawe Ganga → Sri Lanka 6°15N 81°0E 45 L5
Waibeem Indonesia 0°30S 132°59E 37 E8
Waigeo Indonesia 0°20S 130°40E 37 E8
Waihi N.Z. 37°23S 175°52E 59 B5
Waihou → N.Z. 37°15S 175°40E 59 B5
Waikabubak Indonesia 9°45S 119°25E 37 F5
Waikaremoana, L. N.Z. 38°49S 177°9E 59 C6
Waikari N.Z. 42°58S 172°41E 59 E4
Waikato → N.Z. 37°23S 174°43E 59 B5
Waikelo Indonesia 9°24S 119°19E 60 A2
Waikerie Australia 34°9S 140°0E 63 E3
Waikokopu N.Z. 39°3S 177°52E 59 C6
Waikouaiti N.Z. 45°36S 170°41E 59 F3
Waimakariri → N.Z. 43°24S 172°42E 59 E4
Waimate N.Z. 44°45S 171°3E 59 F3
Wainganga → India 18°50N 79°55E 44 E4
Waingapu Indonesia 9°35S 120°11E 37 F6
Waini → Guyana 8°20N 59°50W 92 B7
Wainwright Canada 52°50N 110°50W 71 C6
Wainwright U.S.A. 70°38N 160°2W 74 A7
Waiouru N.Z. 39°28S 175°41E 59 C5
Waipara N.Z. 43°3S 172°46E 59 E4
Waipawa N.Z. 39°56S 176°38E 59 C6
Waipiro N.Z. 38°2S 178°22E 59 C7
Waipoua Forest N.Z. 35°39S 173°33E 59 A4
Waipu N.Z. 35°59S 174°29E 59 A5
Waipukurau N.Z. 40°1S 176°33E 59 D6
Wairakei N.Z. 38°37S 176°6E 59 C6
Wairarapa, L. N.Z. 41°14S 175°15E 59 D5
Wairoa N.Z. 39°3S 177°25E 59 C6
Waitaki → N.Z. 44°56S 171°7E 59 F3
Waitangi N.Z. 35°16S 174°5E 59 A5
Waitara N.Z. 38°59S 174°15E 59 C5
Waitomo Caves N.Z. 38°16S 175°7E 59 C5
Waitsburg U.S.A. 46°16N 118°9W 76 C4
Waiuku N.Z. 37°15S 174°45E 59 B5
Wajima Japan 37°30N 137°0E 29 F8
Wajir Kenya 1°42N 40°5E 54 D8
Wakasa Japan 35°20N 134°24E 29 G7
Wakasa-Wan Japan 35°40N 135°30E 29 G7
Wakatipu, L. N.Z. 45°5S 168°33E 59 F2
Wakaw Canada 52°39N 105°44W 71 C7
Wakaya Fiji 17°37S 179°0E 59 a
Wakayama Japan 34°15N 135°15E 29 G7
Wakayama □ Japan 33°50N 135°30E 29 H7
Wake Forest U.S.A. 35°59N 78°30W 85 D15
Wake I. Pac. Oc. 19°18N 166°36E 64 F8
WaKeeney U.S.A. 39°1N 99°53W 80 F4
Wakefield Jamaica 18°26N 77°42W 88 a
Wakefield N.Z. 41°24S 173°5E 59 D4
Wakefield U.K. 53°41N 1°29W 12 D6
Wakefield U.S.A. 46°29N 89°56W 80 B9
Wakkanai Japan 45°28N 141°35E 28 B10
Wakkerstroom S. Africa 27°24S 30°10E 57 C5
Wakool Australia 35°28S 144°23E 63 F3
Wakool → Australia 35°5S 143°33E 63 F3
Wakre Indonesia 0°19S 131°5E 37 E8
Wakuach, L. Canada 55°34N 67°32W 73 A6
Walagunya ✪ Australia 23°10S 120°50E 60 D3
Wałbrzych Poland 50°45N 16°18E 16 C9
Walbury Hill U.K. 51°21N 1°28W 13 F6
Walcha Australia 30°55S 151°31E 63 E5
Walcheren Neths. 51°30N 3°35E 15 C3
Walcott U.S.A. 41°46N 106°51W 76 F10
Wałcz Poland 53°17N 16°27E 16 B9
Waldburg Ra. Australia 24°40S 117°35E 61 D2
Walden Colo., U.S.A. 40°44N 106°17W 76 F10
Walden N.Y., U.S.A. 41°34N 74°11W 83 E10
Waldport U.S.A. 44°26N 124°4W 76 D1
Waldron U.S.A. 34°54N 94°5W 84 D7
Walebing Australia 30°41S 116°13E 61 F2
Wales □ U.K. 52°19N 4°43W 13 E3
Wales I. Canada 68°1N 86°40W 69 D14
Walgett Australia 30°0S 148°5E 63 E4
Walgreen Coast Antarctica 75°15S 105°0W 5 D15
Walker U.S.A. 47°6N 94°35W 80 B6
Walker, L. Canada 50°20N 67°11W 73 B6
Walker L. Canada 54°42N 95°57W 71 C9
Walker L. U.S.A. 38°42N 118°43W 76 G4
Walkerston Australia 21°11S 149°8E 62 b
Walkerton Canada 44°10N 81°10W 82 B3
Wall U.S.A. 44°0N 102°8W 80 C2
Walla Walla U.S.A. 46°4N 118°20W 76 C4
Wallace Idaho, U.S.A. 47°28N 115°56W 76 C6
Wallace N.C., U.S.A. 34°44N 77°59W 85 D16
Wallaceburg Canada 42°34N 82°23W 82 D2
Wallachia = Valahia Romania 44°35N 25°0E 17 F13
Wallal Australia 26°32S 146°7E 63 D4
Wallam Cr. → Australia 28°40S 147°20E 63 D4
Wallambin, L. Australia 30°57S 117°35E 61 F2
Wallangarra Australia 28°56S 151°58E 63 D5
Wallaroo Australia 33°56S 137°39E 63 E2
Wallasey U.K. 53°25N 3°2W 12 D4
Wallenpaupack, L. U.S.A. 41°25N 75°15W 83 E9
Wallingford Conn., U.S.A. 41°27N 72°50W 83 E12
Wallingford Vt., U.S.A. 43°28N 72°58W 83 C12
Wallis & Futuna, Îs. ⊠ Pac. Oc. 13°18S 176°10W 58 C11
Wallowa U.S.A. 45°34N 117°32W 76 D5
Wallowa Mts. U.S.A. 45°20N 117°30W 76 D5
Walls U.K. 60°14N 1°33W 11 A7
Walls of Jerusalem △ Australia 41°56S 146°15E 63 G4
Wallula U.S.A. 46°5N 118°54W 76 C4
Wallumbilla Australia 26°33S 149°9E 63 D4
Walmsley L. Canada 63°25N 108°36W 71 A7
Walney, I. of U.K. 54°6N 3°15W 12 C4
Walnut Canyon ⌂ U.S.A. 35°15N 111°20W 77 J8
Walnut Creek U.S.A. 37°54N 122°4W 78 H4
Walnut Ridge U.S.A. 36°4N 90°57W 85 C9
Walpole Australia 34°58S 116°44E 61 F2
Walpole U.S.A. 42°9N 71°15W 83 D13
Walpole-Nornalup △ Australia 35°0S 116°45E 61 G2
Walsall U.K. 52°35N 1°58W 13 E6
Walsenburg U.S.A. 37°38N 104°47W 77 H11
Walsh U.S.A. 37°23N 102°17W 77 H12
Walsh → Australia 16°31S 143°42E 62 B3
Walsingham Canada 42°40N 80°31W 82 D4
Waltair India 17°44N 83°23E 44 F6
Walter F. George Res. U.S.A. 31°38N 85°4W 85 F12
Walterboro U.S.A. 32°55N 80°40W 85 E14
Walters U.S.A. 34°22N 98°19W 84 D5
Waltman U.S.A. 43°4N 107°12W 76 E10
Walton U.S.A. 42°10N 75°8W 83 D9
Walton-on-the-Naze U.K. 51°51N 1°17E 13 F9
Walvis Bay Namibia 23°0S 14°28E 56 B1
Walvisbaai = Walvis Bay Namibia 23°0S 14°28E 56 B1
Wamba Dem. Rep. of the Congo 2°10N 27°57E 54 D5
Wambardi ✪ Australia 16°2S 130°55E 60 C5
Wamego U.S.A. 39°12N 96°18W 80 F5
Wamena Indonesia 4°4S 138°57E 37 E9
Wampana Karlantijpa ✪ Australia 17°45S 132°10E 60 C5
Wampaya ✪ Australia 17°20S 135°0E 62 B2
Wampsville U.S.A. 43°4N 75°42W 83 C9
Wamsutter U.S.A. 41°40N 107°58W 76 F10
Wamulan Indonesia 3°27S 126°7E 37 E7
Wan Tup Myanmar 21°13N 98°42E 34 G2
Wan Xian China 38°47N 115°7E 32 E8
Wana Pakistan 32°20N 69°32E 42 C3
Wanaaring Australia 29°38S 144°9E 63 D3
Wanaka N.Z. 44°42S 169°9E 59 F2
Wanaka, L. N.Z. 44°33S 169°7E 59 F2
Wan'an China 26°26N 114°49E 35 D10
Wanapitei L. Canada 46°45N 80°40W 72 C3
Wandel Sea = McKinley Sea Arctic 82°0N 0°0 4 A7
Wandhari Pakistan 27°42N 66°48E 42 F2
Wanding China 24°5N 98°4E 34 E2
Wandoan Australia 26°5S 149°55E 63 D4
Wandur Marine △ India 11°30N 92°30E 45 J11
Wanfu China 40°8N 122°38E 33 D12
Wang → Thailand 17°8N 99°2E 38 D2
Wang Noi Thailand 14°13N 100°44E 38 E3
Wang Saphung Thailand 17°18N 101°46E 38 D3
Wang Thong Thailand 16°50N 100°26E 38 D3
Wanganella Australia 35°6S 144°49E 63 F3
Wanganui N.Z. 39°56S 175°3E 59 C5
Wangaratta Australia 36°21S 146°19E 63 F4
Wangary Australia 34°35S 135°29E 63 E2
Wangcang China 32°18N 106°20E 34 A6
Wangcheng China 28°22N 112°49E 35 C9
Wangcun China 36°41N 117°41E 33 F9
Wangdu China 38°40N 115°7E 32 E8
Wangerooge Germany 53°47N 7°54E 16 B4
Wangiwangi Indonesia 5°22S 123°37E 37 F6
Wangjiang China 30°10N 116°42E 35 B11
Wangmo China 25°11N 106°5E 34 E6
Wangqing China 43°12N 129°42E 33 C15
Wani India 20°5N 78°55E 44 D4
Wanimiyn ✪ Australia 15°55S 130°49E 60 C5
Wanjina Wunggurr Wilinggin ✪ Australia 16°0S 127°0E 60 C4
Wankaner India 22°35N 71°0E 42 H4
Wanless Canada 54°11N 101°21W 71 C8
Wanleweyne Somalia 2°37N 44°54E 49 G3
Wanneroo Australia 31°42S 115°46E 61 F2
Wannian China 28°42N 117°4E 35 C11
Wanning China 18°48N 110°22E 38 C8
Wannoo Billabong Roadhouse Australia 27°25S 115°49E 61 E2
Wanon Niwat Thailand 17°38N 103°46E 38 D4
Wanqinsha China 22°43N 113°33E 31 a
Wanquan China 40°50N 114°40E 32 D8
Wanrong China 35°25N 110°50E 32 G6
Wanshan China 27°30N 109°12E 34 D7
Wanshan Qundao China 21°57N 113°45E 31 a
Wansheng China 28°57N 106°53E 34 C6
Wantage U.K. 51°35N 1°25W 13 F6
Wanxian China 30°42N 108°20E 34 B7
Wanyuan China 32°4N 108°3E 34 A7
Wanzai Guangdong, China 22°12N 113°31E 31 a
Wanzai Jiangxi, China 28°7N 114°30E 35 C10
Wapakoneta U.S.A. 40°34N 84°12W 81 E11
Wapato U.S.A. 46°27N 120°25W 76 C3
Wapawekka L. Canada 54°55N 104°40W 71 C8
Wapikopa L. Canada 52°56N 87°53W 72 B2
Wapiti → Canada 55°5N 118°18W 70 B5
Wappingers Falls U.S.A. 41°36N 73°55W 83 E11
Wapsipinicon → U.S.A. 41°44N 90°19W 80 E8
Wapusk △ Canada 57°46N 93°22W 71 B10
Warakurna Australia 24°59S 128°17E 61 D4
Warangal India 17°58N 79°35E 44 F4
Waraseoni India 21°45N 80°2E 43 J9
Waratah Australia 41°30S 145°30E 63 G4
Waratah B. Australia 38°54S 146°5E 63 F4
Warburton Vic., Australia 37°47S 145°42E 63 F4
Warburton W. Austral., Australia 26°8S 126°35E 61 E4
Warburton ✪ Australia 26°7S 126°34E 61 E4
Warburton → Australia 28°4S 137°28E 63 D2
Warburton Groove Australia 28°18S 137°8E 63 A2
Warburton Ra. Australia 25°55S 126°28E 61 E4
Ward N.Z. 41°49S 174°11E 59 D5
Ward → Australia 26°28S 146°6E 63 D4
Ward Mt. U.S.A. 37°12N 118°54W 78 H8
Warden S. Africa 27°50S 29°0E 57 C4
Wardha India 20°45N 78°39E 44 D4
Wardha → India 19°57N 79°11E 44 E4
Wardsville Canada 42°39N 81°45W 82 D3
Ware U.K. 51°49N 0°0 13 F8
Ware U.S.A. 42°16N 72°14W 83 D12
Waregem Belgium 50°53N 3°27E 15 D3
Wareham U.S.A. 41°46N 70°43W 83 E14
Waremme Belgium 50°43N 5°15E 15 D5
Warialda Australia 29°29S 150°33E 63 D5
Warin Chamrap Thailand 15°12N 104°53E 38 E5
Warkopi Indonesia 1°12S 134°9E 37 E8
Warm Springs U.S.A. 38°10N 116°20W 77 G5
Warman Canada 52°19N 106°30W 71 C7
Warmbad = Bela Bela S. Africa 24°51S 28°19E 57 B4
Warmbad Namibia 28°25S 18°42E 56 C2
Warminster U.K. 51°12N 2°10W 13 F5
Warminster U.S.A. 40°12N 75°6W 83 F9
Warmun Australia 17°2S 128°12E 60 C4
Warner Mts. U.S.A. 41°40N 120°15W 76 F3
Warner Robins U.S.A. 32°37N 83°36W 85 E13
Waroona Australia 32°50S 115°58E 61 F2
Warora India 20°14N 79°1E 44 D4
Warrabri ✪ Australia 21°1S 134°19E 62 C1
Warracknabeal Australia 36°9S 142°26E 63 F3
Warragul Australia 38°10S 145°58E 63 F4
Warrego → Australia 30°24S 145°21E 63 E4
Warrego Ra. Australia 24°58S 146°0E 62 C4
Warren Australia 31°42S 147°51E 63 E4
Warren Ark., U.S.A. 33°37N 92°4W 84 E8
Warren Mich., U.S.A. 42°28N 83°1W 81 D12
Warren Minn., U.S.A. 48°12N 96°46W 80 A5
Warren Ohio, U.S.A. 41°14N 80°49W 82 E4
Warren Pa., U.S.A. 41°51N 79°9W 82 E5
Warrenpoint U.K. 54°6N 6°15W 10 B5
Warrensburg Mo., U.S.A. 38°46N 93°44W 80 F7
Warrensburg N.Y., U.S.A. 43°29N 73°46W 83 C11
Warrenton S. Africa 28°9S 24°47E 56 C3
Warrenton U.S.A. 46°10N 123°56W 78 D3
Warri Nigeria 5°30N 5°41E 52 G7
Warrington U.K. 53°24N 2°35W 12 D5
Warrington U.S.A. 30°23N 87°17W 85 F11
Warrington □ U.K. 53°24N 2°35W 12 D5
Warrnambool Australia 38°25S 142°30E 63 F3
Warroad U.S.A. 48°54N 95°19W 80 A6
Warruwi Australia 11°36S 133°20E 62 A1
Warsak Dam Pakistan 34°11N 71°19E 42 B4
Warsaw Ind., U.S.A. 41°14N 85°51W 81 E11
Warsaw N.Y., U.S.A. 42°45N 78°8W 82 D6
Warsaw Ohio, U.S.A. 40°20N 82°0W 82 F3
Warta → Poland 52°35N 14°39E 16 B8
Warthe = Warta → Poland 52°35N 14°39E 16 B8
Waru Indonesia 3°30S 130°36E 37 E8
Warud India 21°30N 78°16E 44 D4
Warumungu ✪ Australia 19°15S 134°44E 62 B1
Warwick Australia 28°10S 152°1E 63 D5
Warwick U.K. 52°18N 1°35W 13 E6
Warwick N.Y., U.S.A. 41°16N 74°22W 83 E10
Warwick R.I., U.S.A. 41°42N 71°28W 83 E13
Warwickshire □ U.K. 52°14N 1°38W 13 E6
Wasaga Beach Canada 44°31N 80°1W 82 B4
Wasagaming Canada 50°39N 99°58W 71 C9
Wasatch Ra. U.S.A. 40°0N 111°30W 76 F8
Wasbank S. Africa 28°15S 30°9E 57 C5
Wasco Calif., U.S.A. 35°36N 119°20W 79 K7
Wasco Oreg., U.S.A. 45°36N 120°42W 76 D3
Waseca U.S.A. 44°5N 93°30W 80 C7
Wasekamio L. Canada 56°45N 108°45W 71 B7
Wasgomuwa △ Sri Lanka 7°45N 81°0E 45 L5
Wash, The U.K. 52°58N 0°20E 12 E8
Washago Canada 44°45N 79°20W 82 B5
Washburn N. Dak., U.S.A. 47°17N 101°2W 80 B3
Washburn Wis., U.S.A. 46°40N 90°54W 80 B8
Washim India 20°3N 77°0E 44 D3
Washington U.K. 54°55N 1°30W 12 C6
Washington Ga., U.S.A. 33°44N 82°44W 85 E13
Washington Ind., U.S.A. 38°40N 87°10W 80 F10
Washington Iowa, U.S.A. 41°18N 91°42W 80 E8
Washington Mo., U.S.A. 38°33N 91°1W 80 F8
Washington N.C., U.S.A. 35°33N 77°3W 85 D16
Washington N.J., U.S.A. 40°46N 74°59W 83 F10
Washington Pa., U.S.A. 40°10N 80°15W 82 F4
Washington Utah, U.S.A. 37°8N 113°31W 77 H7
Washington □ U.S.A. 47°30N 120°30W 76 C3
Washington, Mt. U.S.A. 44°16N 71°18W 83 B13
Washington Court House U.S.A. 39°32N 83°26W 81 F12

Washington Dulles Int. ✈ (IAD)
  U.S.A.                    38°57N 77°27W **81** F15
Washington I. *U.S.A.*     45°23N 86°54W **80** C10
Washougal *U.S.A.*         45°35N 122°21W **78** E4
Washpool △ *Australia*     29°22S 152°20E **63** D5
Wasian *Indonesia*         1°47S 133°19E **37** E8
Wasilla *U.S.A.*           61°35N 149°26W **68** E2
Wasior *Indonesia*         2°43S 134°30E **37** E8
Wasiri *Indonesia*         7°30S 126°30E **37** F7
Wāsiṭ □ *Iraq*             32°50N 45°50E **46** C5
Waskaganish *Canada*       51°30N 78°40W **72** B4
Waskaiowaka L. *Canada*    56°33N 96°23W **71** B9
Waskesiu Lake *Canada*     53°55N 106°5W **71** C7
Wasserkuppe *Germany*      50°29N 9°55E **16** C5
Wasur △ *Indonesia*        8°41S 140°44E **37** F10
Waswanipi *Canada*         49°40N 76°29W **72** C4
Waswanipi, L. *Canada*     49°35N 76°40W **72** C4
Watampone *Indonesia*      4°29S 120°25E **37** E6
Watarrka △ *Australia*     24°20S 131°30E **60** D5
Water Park Pt. *Australia* 22°56S 150°47E **62** C5
Water Valley *U.S.A.*      34°10N 89°38W **85** D10
Waterberg Plateau △
  *Namibia*                20°25S 17°18E **56** B2
Waterberge *S. Africa*     24°10S 28°0E **57** B4
Waterbury *Conn., U.S.A.*  41°33N 73°3W **83** E11
Waterbury *Vt., U.S.A.*    44°20N 72°46W **83** B12
Waterbury L. *Canada*      58°10N 104°22W **71** B8
Waterdown *Canada*         43°20N 79°53W **82** C5
Waterford *Canada*         42°56N 80°17W **82** D4
Waterford *Ireland*        52°15N 7°8W **10** D4
Waterford *Calif., U.S.A.* 37°38N 120°46W **78** H6
Waterford *Pa., U.S.A.*    41°57N 79°59W **82** E5
Waterford □ *Ireland*      52°10N 7°40W **10** D4
Waterford Harbour *Ireland* 52°8N 6°58W **10** D5
Waterhen L. *Canada*       52°10N 99°40W **71** C9
Waterloo *Ont., Canada*    43°30N 80°32W **82** C4
Waterloo *Qué., Canada*    45°22N 72°32W **83** A12
Waterloo *Ill., U.S.A.*    38°20N 90°9W **80** F8
Waterloo *Iowa, U.S.A.*    42°30N 92°21W **80** D7
Waterloo *N.Y., U.S.A.*    42°54N 76°52W **82** D8
Watersmeet *U.S.A.*        46°16N 89°11W **80** B9
Waterton Lakes △
  *Canada*                 48°45N 115°0W **70** D6
Watertown *Conn., U.S.A.*  41°36N 73°7W **83** E11
Watertown *N.Y., U.S.A.*   43°59N 75°55W **83** C9
Watertown *S. Dak., U.S.A.* 44°54N 97°7W **80** C5
Watertown *Wis., U.S.A.*   43°12N 88°43W **80** D9
Waterval-Boven = Emgwenya
  *S. Africa*               25°40S 30°18E **57** C5
Waterville *Canada*        45°16N 71°54W **83** A13
Waterville *Maine, U.S.A.* 44°33N 69°38W **81** C19
Waterville *N.Y., U.S.A.*  42°56N 75°23W **83** D9
Waterville *Pa., U.S.A.*   41°19N 77°21W **82** E7
Waterville *Wash., U.S.A.* 47°39N 120°4W **76** C3
Watervliet *U.S.A.*        42°44N 73°42W **83** D11
Wates *Indonesia*          7°51S 110°10E **37** G14
Watford *Canada*           42°57N 81°53W **82** D3
Watford *U.K.*             51°40N 0°24W **13** F7
Watford City *U.S.A.*      47°48N 103°17W **80** B2
Wathaman → *Canada*        57°16N 102°59W **71** B8
Wathaman L. *Canada*       56°58N 103°44W **71** B8
Watheroo *Australia*       30°15S 116°5E **61** F2
Watheroo △ *Australia*     30°19S 115°48E **61** F2
Wating *China*             35°40N 106°38E **32** G4
Watkins Glen *U.S.A.*      42°23N 76°52W **82** D8
Watling I. = San Salvador I.
  *Bahamas*                24°0N 74°30W **89** B5
Watonga *U.S.A.*           35°51N 98°25W **84** D5
Watrous *Canada*           51°40N 105°25W **71** C7
Watrous *U.S.A.*           35°48N 104°59W **77** J11
Watsa *Dem. Rep. of the Congo* 3°4N 29°30E **54** D5
Watseka *U.S.A.*           40°47N 87°44W **80** E10
Watson *Canada*            52°10N 104°30W **71** C8
Watson Lake *Canada*       60°6N 128°49W **70** A3
Watsontown *U.S.A.*        41°5N 76°52W **82** E8
Watsonville *U.S.A.*       36°55N 121°45W **78** J5
Wattiwarriganna Cr. →
  *Australia*              28°57S 136°10E **63** D2
Watuata = Batuata
  *Indonesia*              6°12S 122°42E **37** F6
Watubela, Kepulauan
  *Indonesia*              4°28S 131°35E **37** E8
Watubela Is. = Watubela,
  Kepulauan *Indonesia*    4°28S 131°35E **37** E8
Wau *South Sudan*         7°45N 28°1E **53** G11
Waubamik *Canada*          45°27N 80°1W **82** A4
Waubay *U.S.A.*            45°20N 97°18W **80** C5
Wauchope *N.S.W.,
  Australia*               31°28S 152°45E **63** E5
Wauchope *N. Terr.,
  Australia*               20°36S 134°15E **62** C1
Wauchula *U.S.A.*          27°33N 81°49W **85** H14
Waukarlycarly, L.
  *Australia*              21°18S 121°56E **60** D3
Waukegan *U.S.A.*          42°22N 87°50W **80** D10
Waukesha *U.S.A.*          43°1N 88°14W **80** D9
Waukon *U.S.A.*            43°16N 91°29W **80** D8
Waupaca *U.S.A.*           · 44°21N 89°5W **80** C9
Waupun *U.S.A.*            43°38N 88°44W **80** D9
Waurika *U.S.A.*           34°10N 98°0W **84** D6
Wausau *U.S.A.*            44°58N 89°38W **80** C9
Wautoma *U.S.A.*           44°4N 89°18W **80** C9
Wauwatosa *U.S.A.*         43°2N 88°0W **80** D9
Wave Hill = Kalkarindji
  *Australia*              17°30S 130°47E **60** C5
Wave Rock △ *Australia*    32°26S 118°53E **61** F2
Waveney → *U.K.*           52°35N 1°39E **13** E9
Waverley *N.Z.*            39°46S 174°37E **59** C5
Waverly *Iowa, U.S.A.*     42°44N 92°29W **80** D7
Waverly *N.Y., U.S.A.*     42°1N 76°32W **83** E8
Wavre *Belgium*            50°43N 4°38E **15** D4
Wâw = Wau *South Sudan*    7°45N 28°1E **53** G11
Wâw al Kabīr *Libya*       25°20N 16°43E **53** C9
Wawa *Canada*              47°59N 84°47W **72** C3
Wawanesa *Canada*          49°36N 99°40W **71** D9
Wawona *U.S.A.*            37°32N 119°39W **78** H7
Waxahachie *U.S.A.*        32°24N 96°51W **84** E6
Way, L. *Australia*        26°45S 120°16E **61** E3
Waya *Fiji*                17°19S 177°10E **59** a
Waycross *U.S.A.*          31°13N 82°21W **85** F13
Wayland *U.S.A.*           42°34N 77°35W **82** D7

Wayne *Nebr., U.S.A.*      42°14N 97°1W **80** D5
Wayne *W. Va., U.S.A.*     38°13N 82°27W **81** F12
Waynesboro *Ga., U.S.A.*   33°6N 82°1W **85** E13
Waynesboro *Miss.,
  U.S.A.*                  31°40N 88°39W **85** F10
Waynesboro *Pa., U.S.A.*   39°45N 77°35W **81** F15
Waynesboro *Va., U.S.A.*   38°4N 78°53W **81** F14
Waynesburg *U.S.A.*        39°54N 80°11W **81** F13
Waynesville *U.S.A.*       35°28N 82°58W **85** D13
Waynoka *U.S.A.*           36°35N 98°53W **84** C5
Wazirabad *Pakistan*       32°30N 74°8E **42** C6
Waziristan *Pakistan*      33°0N 70°0E **42** C4
We *Indonesia*             5°51N 95°18E **36** C1
Weald, The *U.K.*          51°4N 0°20E **13** F8
Wear → *U.K.*              54°55N 1°23W **12** C6
Weatherford *Okla.,
  U.S.A.*                  35°32N 98°43W **84** D5
Weatherford *Tex., U.S.A.* 32°46N 97°48W **84** E6
Weaverville *U.S.A.*       40°44N 122°56W **76** F2
Webb City *U.S.A.*         37°9N 94°28W **80** G6
Webequie *Canada*          52°59N 87°21W **72** B2
Webster *Mass., U.S.A.*    42°3N 71°53W **83** D13
Webster *N.Y., U.S.A.*     43°13N 77°26W **82** C7
Webster *S. Dak., U.S.A.*  45°20N 97°31W **80** C5
Webster City *U.S.A.*      42°28N 93°49W **80** D7
Webster Springs *U.S.A.*   38°29N 80°25W **81** F13
Weda *Indonesia*           0°21N 127°50E **37** D7
Weda, Teluk *Indonesia*    0°20N 128°0E **37** D7
Weddell Abyssal Plain
  *S. Ocean*               65°0S 20°0W **5** C2
Weddell I. *Falk. Is.*     51°50S 61°0W **96** G4
Weddell Sea *Antarctica*   72°30S 40°0W **5** D1
Wedderburn *Australia*     36°26S 143°33E **63** F3
Wedgeport *Canada*         43°44N 65°59W **73** D6
Wee Waa *Australia*        30°11S 149°26E **63** E4
Weed *U.S.A.*              41°25N 122°23W **76** F2
Weed Heights *U.S.A.*      38°59N 119°13W **78** G7
Weedsport *U.S.A.*         43°2N 76°33W **83** C8
Weedville *U.S.A.*         41°17N 78°30W **82** E6
Weenen *S. Africa*         28°48S 30°7E **57** C5
Weert *Neths.*             51°15N 5°43E **15** C5
Wei He → *Hebei, China*    36°10N 115°45E **32** F8
Wei He → *Shaanxi,
  China*                   34°38N 110°15E **32** G6
Weichang *China*           41°58N 117°49E **33** D9
Weichuan *China*           34°20N 113°59E **32** G7
Weiden *Germany*           49°41N 12°10E **16** D7
Weifang *China*            36°44N 119°7E **33** F10
Weihai *China*             37°30N 122°6E **33** F12
Weihui *China*             35°25N 114°3E **32** G8
Weimar *Germany*           50°58N 11°19E **16** C6
Weinan *China*             34°31N 109°29E **32** G5
Weining *China*            26°50N 104°17E **34** D5
Weipa *Australia*          12°40S 141°50E **62** A3
Weir → *Australia*         28°20S 149°50E **63** D4
Weir → *Canada*            56°54N 93°21W **71** B10
Weir River *Canada*        56°49N 94°6W **71** B10
Weirton *U.S.A.*           40°24N 80°35W **82** F4
Weiser *U.S.A.*            44°15N 116°58W **76** D5
Weishan *Shandong, China*  34°47N 117°5E **33** G9
Weishan *Yunnan, China*    25°12N 100°20E **34** E3
Weishan Hu *China*         34°35N 117°14E **33** G9
Weixi *China*              27°10N 99°10E **34** D2
Weixin *China*             27°48N 105°3E **34** D5
Weiyuan *Gansu, China*     35°7N 104°10E **32** G3
Weiyuan *Sichuan, China*   29°35N 104°36E **34** C5
Weizhou Dao *China*        21°0N 109°5E **34** G7
Wejherowo *Poland*         54°35N 18°12E **17** A10
Wekusko L. *Canada*        54°30N 99°50W **71** C9
Welch *U.S.A.*             37°26N 81°35W **81** G13
Welford △ *Australia*      25°5S 143°16E **62** D3
Weligama *Sri Lanka*       5°58N 80°25E **45** M5
Welkom *S. Africa*         28°0S 26°46E **56** C4
Welland *Canada*           43°0N 79°15W **82** D5
Welland → *U.K.*           52°51N 0°5W **13** E7
Wellawaya *Sri Lanka*      6°44N 81°6E **45** L5
Wellesley Is. *Australia*  16°42S 139°30E **62** B2
Wellesley Islands ○
  *Australia*              16°32S 139°23E **62** B2
Wellingborough *U.K.*      52°19N 0°41W **13** E7
Wellington *Australia*     32°35S 148°59E **63** E4
Wellington *Canada*        43°57N 77°20W **82** C7
Wellington *N.Z.*          41°19S 174°46E **59** D5
Wellington *S. Africa*     33°38S 19°1E **56** D2
Wellington *Somst., U.K.*  50°58N 3°13W **13** G4
Wellington *Telford & Wrekin,
  U.K.*                    52°42N 2°30W **13** E5
Wellington *Colo., U.S.A.* 40°42N 105°0W **76** F11
Wellington *Kans., U.S.A.* 37°16N 97°24W **80** G5
Wellington *Nev., U.S.A.*  38°45N 119°23W **78** G7
Wellington *Ohio, U.S.A.*  41°10N 82°13W **82** E2
Wellington *Tex., U.S.A.*  34°51N 100°13W **84** D4
Wellington, I. *Chile*     49°30S 75°0W **96** F2
Wellington, L. *Australia* 38°6S 147°20E **63** F4
Wellington Chan. *Canada*  75°0N 93°0W **69** C13
Wells *U.K.*               51°13N 2°39W **13** F5
Wells *Maine, U.S.A.*      43°20N 70°35W **83** C14
Wells *N.Y., U.S.A.*       43°24N 74°17W **83** C10
Wells *Nev., U.S.A.*       41°7N 114°58W **76** F6
Wells, L. *Australia*      26°44S 123°15E **61** E3
Wells, Mt. *Australia*     17°25S 127°8E **60** C4
Wells Gray △ *Canada*      52°30N 120°15W **70** C4
Wells-next-the-Sea *U.K.*  52°57N 0°51E **12** E8
Wells River *U.S.A.*       44°9N 72°4W **83** B12
Wellsboro *U.S.A.*         41°45N 77°18W **82** E7
Wellsburg *U.S.A.*         40°16N 80°37W **82** F4
Wellsville *N.Y., U.S.A.*  42°7N 77°57W **82** D7
Wellsville *Ohio, U.S.A.*  40°36N 80°39W **82** F4
Wellsville *Utah, U.S.A.*  41°38N 111°56W **76** F8
Wellton *U.S.A.*           32°40N 114°8W **77** K6
Welshpool *U.K.*           52°39N 3°8W **13** E4
Welwyn Garden City *U.K.*  51°48N 0°12W **13** F7
Wem *U.K.*                 52°52N 2°44W **13** E5
Wemindji *Canada*          53°0N 78°49W **72** B4
Wemyss *Canada*            44°52N 76°23W **83** B8
Wen Xian *Gansu, China*    32°43N 104°36E **32** H3
Wen Xian *Henan, China*    34°55N 113°5E **32** G7
Wenatchee *U.S.A.*         47°25N 120°19W **76** C3
Wenchang *China*           19°38N 110°42E **38** C8

Wencheng *China*           27°46N 120°4E **35** D13
Wenchi *Ghana*             7°46N 2°8W **52** G5
Wenchow = Wenzhou
  *China*                  28°0N 120°38E **35** D13
Wenchuan *China*           31°22N 103°35E **34** B4
Wenden *U.S.A.*            33°49N 113°33W **79** M13
Wendeng *China*            37°15N 122°5E **33** F12
Wendover *U.S.A.*          40°44N 114°2W **76** F6
Weng'an *China*            27°5N 107°25E **34** D6
Wengcheng *China*          24°22N 113°50E **35** E9
Wengyuan *China*           24°20N 114°9E **35** E10
Wenling *China*            28°21N 121°20E **35** C13
Wenlock → *Australia*      12°2S 141°55E **62** A3
Wenshan *China*            23°20N 104°18E **34** F5
Wenshang *China*           35°45N 116°30E **32** G9
Wenshui *China*            37°26N 112°1E **32** F7
Wensleydale *U.K.*         54°17N 2°0W **12** C6
Wensu *China*              41°15N 80°10E **30** C5
Wensum → *U.K.*            52°40N 1°15E **12** E8
Wentworth *Australia*      34°2S 141°54E **63** E3
Wentzel L. *Canada*        59°2N 114°28W **70** B6
Wenut *Indonesia*          3°11S 133°19E **37** E8
Wenxi *China*              35°20N 111°10E **32** G6
Wenzhou *China*            28°0N 120°38E **35** D13
Weott *U.S.A.*             40°20N 123°55W **76** F2
Wepener *S. Africa*        29°42S 27°3E **56** C4
Werda *Botswana*           25°24S 23°15E **56** C3
Weri *Indonesia*           3°10S 132°38E **37** E8
Werra → *Germany*          51°24N 9°39E **16** C5
Werrimull *Australia*      34°25S 141°38E **63** E3
Werris Creek *Australia*   31°18S 150°38E **63** E5
Weser → *Germany*          53°36N 8°28E **16** B5
Weslaco *U.S.A.*           26°10N 97°58W **84** H6
Weslemkoon L. *Canada*     45°2N 77°25W **82** A7
Wesleyville *Canada*       49°9N 53°33W **73** C9
Wesleyville *U.S.A.*       42°9N 80°1W **82** D4
Wessel, C. *Australia*     10°59S 136°46E **62** A2
Wessel Is. *Australia*     11°10S 136°45E **62** A2
Wessex *U.K.*              51°0N 2°0W **13** F5
Wessington Springs
  *U.S.A.*                 44°5N 98°34W **80** C4
West *U.S.A.*              31°48N 97°6W **84** F6
West → *U.S.A.*            42°52N 72°33W **83** D12
West Allis *U.S.A.*        43°1N 88°0W **80** D9
West Antarctica *Antarctica* 80°0S 90°0W **5** D15
West Baines →
  *Australia*              15°38S 129°59E **60** C4
West Bank □ *Asia*         32°6N 35°13E **48** C4
West Bend *U.S.A.*         43°25N 88°11W **80** D9
West Bengal = Paschimbanga □
  *India*                  23°0N 88°0E **43** H13
West Berkshire □ *U.K.*    51°25N 1°17W **13** F6
West Beskids = Západné Beskydy
  *Europe*                 49°30N 19°0E **17** D10
West Branch *U.S.A.*       44°17N 84°14W **81** C11
West Branch Susquehanna →
  *U.S.A.*                 40°53N 76°48W **83** F8
West Bromwich *U.K.*       52°32N 1°59W **13** E6
West Burra *U.K.*          60°5N 1°21W **11** A7
West Canada Cr. →
  *U.S.A.*                 43°1N 74°58W **83** C10
West Caroline Basin
  *Pac. Oc.*               4°0N 138°0E **64** G5
West Chazy *U.S.A.*        44°49N 73°28W **83** B11
West Chester *U.S.A.*      39°58N 75°36W **83** G9
West Coast □ *Namibia*     21°53S 14°14E **56** B1
West Coast △ *S. Africa*   33°13S 18°0E **56** D2
West Columbia *U.S.A.*     29°9N 95°39W **84** G7
West Covina *U.S.A.*       34°4N 117°54W **79** L9
West Des Moines *U.S.A.*   41°35N 93°43W **80** E7
West Dunbartonshire □
  *U.K.*                   55°59N 4°30W **11** F4
West End *Bahamas*         26°41N 78°58W **88** A4
West Falkland *Falk. Is.*  51°40S 60°0W **96** G4
West Fargo *U.S.A.*        46°52N 96°54W **80** B5
West Fiji Basin *Pac. Oc.* 17°0S 173°0E **64** J9
West Fjord = Vestfjorden
  *Norway*                 67°55N 14°0E **8** C16
West Fork Trinity →
  *U.S.A.*                 32°48N 96°54W **84** E6
West Frankfort *U.S.A.*    37°54N 88°55W **80** G9
West Grand L. *U.S.A.*     45°14N 67°51W **81** C20
West Hartford *U.S.A.*     41°45N 72°44W **83** E12
West Haven *U.S.A.*        41°17N 72°57W **83** E12
West Hazleton *U.S.A.*     40°58N 76°0W **83** F9
West Hurley *U.S.A.*       41°59N 74°7W **83** E10
West I. *India*            13°35N 92°54E **45** H11
West Ice Shelf *Antarctica* 67°0S 85°0E **5** C7
West Indies *Cent. Amer.*  15°0N 65°0W **89** D7
West Jordan *U.S.A.*       40°36N 111°56W **76** F8
West Kavango □ *Namibia*   18°0S 18°30E **56** B2
West Linn *U.S.A.*         45°21N 122°36W **78** E4
West Lorne *Canada*        42°36N 81°36W **82** D3
West Lothian □ *U.K.*      55°54N 3°36W **11** F5
West MacDonnell △
  *Australia*              23°38S 132°59E **60** D5
West Mariana Basin
  *Pac. Oc.*               15°0N 137°0E **64** F5
West Memphis *U.S.A.*      35°8N 90°10W **85** D9
West Midlands □ *U.K.*     52°26N 2°0W **13** E6
West Mifflin *U.S.A.*      40°21N 79°52W **82** F5
West Milford *U.S.A.*      41°8N 74°22W **83** E10
West Milton *U.S.A.*       41°1N 76°50W **82** E8
West Monroe *U.S.A.*       32°31N 92°9W **84** E8
West Newton *U.S.A.*       40°14N 79°46W **82** F5
West Odessa *U.S.A.*       31°50N 102°30W **84** F3
West Palm Beach *U.S.A.*   26°43N 80°3W **85** H14
West Plains *U.S.A.*       36°44N 91°51W **80** G8
West Point *Miss., U.S.A.* 33°36N 88°39W **85** E10
West Point *Nebr., U.S.A.* 41°51N 96°43W **80** E5
West Point *N.Y., U.S.A.*  41°24N 73°58W **83** E11
West Point *Va., U.S.A.*   37°32N 76°48W **81** G15
West Point L. *U.S.A.*     33°8N 85°0W **85** E12
West Pt. = Ouest, Pte. de l'
  *Canada*                 49°52N 64°40W **73** C7
West Pt. *Australia*       35°1S 135°56E **63** F2
West Road → *Canada*       53°18N 122°53W **70** C4
West Rutland *U.S.A.*      43°36N 73°3W **83** C11
West Schelde = Westerschelde →
  *Neths.*                 51°25N 3°25E **15** C3

West Seneca *U.S.A.*       42°51N 78°48W **82** D6
West Siberian Plain *Russia* 62°0N 75°0E **24** B9
West Sussex □ *U.K.*       50°55N 0°30W **13** G7
West-Terschelling *Neths.* 53°22N 5°13E **15** A5
West Valley City *U.S.A.*  40°42N 111°58W **76** F8
West Virginia □ *U.S.A.*   38°45N 80°30W **81** F13
West-Vlaanderen □ *Belgium* 51°0N 3°0E **15** D2
West Walker → *U.S.A.*     38°54N 119°9W **78** G7
West Wyalong *Australia*   33°56S 147°10E **63** E4
West Yellowstone *U.S.A.*  44°40N 111°6W **76** D8
West Yorkshire □ *U.K.*    53°45N 1°40W **12** D6
Westall, Pt. *Australia*   32°55S 134°4E **63** E1
Westbrook *U.S.A.*         43°41N 70°22W **81** D18
Westbury *Australia*       41°30S 146°51E **63** G4
Westby *U.S.A.*            48°52N 104°3W **76** B11
Westend *U.S.A.*           35°42N 117°24W **79** K9
Westerland *Germany*       54°54N 8°17E **16** A5
Westerly *U.S.A.*          41°22N 71°50W **83** E13
Western Australia □
  *Australia*              25°0S 118°0E **61** E2
Western Cape □ *S. Africa* 34°0S 20°0E **56** D3
Western Dvina = Daugava →
  *Latvia*                 57°4N 24°3E **9** H21
Western Ghats *India*      14°0N 75°0E **45** H2
Western Isles = Eilean Siar □
  *U.K.*                   57°30N 7°10W **11** D1
Western Sahara ■ *Africa*  25°0N 13°0W **52** D3
Western Samoa = Samoa ■
  *Pac. Oc.*               14°0S 172°0W **59** b
Western Sierra Madre = Madre
  Occidental, Sierra
  *Mexico*                 27°0N 107°0W **86** B3
Westernport *U.S.A.*       39°29N 79°3W **81** F14
Westerschelde → *Neths.*   51°25N 3°25E **15** C3
Westerwald *Germany*       50°38N 7°56E **16** C4
Westfield *Mass., U.S.A.*  42°7N 72°45W **83** D12
Westfield *N.Y., U.S.A.*   42°20N 79°35W **82** D5
Westfield *Pa., U.S.A.*    41°55N 77°32W **82** E7
Westhill *U.K.*            57°9N 2°19W **11** D6
Westhope *U.S.A.*          48°55N 101°1W **80** A3
Westland Bight *N.Z.*      42°55S 170°5E **59** E3
Westland Tai Poutini △
  *N.Z.*                   43°16S 170°16E **59** E2
Westlock *Canada*          54°9N 113°55W **70** C6
Westmar *Australia*        27°55S 149°44E **63** D4
Westmeath □ *Ireland*      53°33N 7°34W **10** C4
Westminster *Calif.,
  U.S.A.*                  33°45N 118°0W **79** M8
Westminster *Colo.,
  U.S.A.*                  39°50N 105°2W **76** G11
Westminster *Md.,
  U.S.A.*                  39°34N 76°59W **81** F15
Westmont *U.S.A.*          40°19N 78°58W **82** F6
Westmoreland *Barbados*    13°13N 59°37W **89** g
Westmorland *U.S.A.*       33°2N 115°37W **79** M11
Weston *Oreg., U.S.A.*     45°49N 118°26W **76** D4
Weston *W. Va., U.S.A.*    39°2N 80°28W **81** F13
Weston I. *Canada*         52°33N 79°36W **72** B4
Weston-super-Mare *U.K.*   51°21N 2°58W **13** F5
Westover *U.S.A.*          40°45N 78°40W **82** F6
Westport *Canada*          44°40N 76°25W **83** B8
Westport *Ireland*         53°48N 9°31W **10** C2
Westport *N.Z.*            41°46S 171°37E **59** D3
Westport *N.Y., U.S.A.*    44°11N 73°26W **83** B11
Westport *Oreg., U.S.A.*   46°8N 123°23W **78** D3
Westport *Wash., U.S.A.*   46°53N 124°6W **78** D2
Westray *Canada*           53°36N 101°24W **71** C8
Westray *U.K.*             59°18N 3°0W **11** B5
Westree *Canada*           47°26N 81°34W **72** C3
Westville *U.S.A.*         39°8N 120°42W **78** F6
Westwood *U.S.A.*          40°18N 121°0W **76** F3
Wetar *Indonesia*          7°48S 126°30E **37** F7
Wetaskiwin *Canada*        52°55N 113°24W **70** C6
Wete *Tanzania*            5°4S 39°43E **54** F7
Wetherby *U.K.*            53°56N 1°23W **12** D6
Wethersfield *U.S.A.*      41°42N 72°40W **83** E12
Wetteren *Belgium*         51°0N 3°53E **15** D3
Wetzlar *Germany*          50°32N 8°31E **16** C5
Wewoka *U.S.A.*            35°9N 96°30W **84** D6
Wexford *Ireland*          52°20N 6°28W **10** D5
Wexford □ *Ireland*        52°20N 6°25W **10** D5
Wexford Harbour *Ireland*  52°20N 6°25W **10** D5
Weyburn *Canada*           49°40N 103°50W **71** D8
Weymouth *Canada*          44°30N 66°1W **73** D6
Weymouth *U.K.*            50°37N 2°28W **13** G5
Weymouth *U.S.A.*          42°13N 70°58W **83** D14
Weymouth, C. *Australia*   12°37S 143°27E **62** A3
Wha Ti *Canada*            63°8N 117°16W **68** B8
Whakaari *N.Z.*            37°30S 177°13E **59** B6
Whakatane *N.Z.*           37°57S 177°1E **59** B6
Whale = Baleine →
  *Canada*                 58°15N 67°40W **73** A6
Whale B. *Myanmar*         11°37N 98°38E **39** G2
Whale Cove *Canada*        62°10N 92°34W **71** A10
Whales, B. of *Antarctica* 78°0S 160°0W **5** D12
Whalsay *U.K.*             60°22N 0°59W **11** A8
Whangamata *N.Z.*          37°12S 175°53E **59** B5
Whangamomona *N.Z.*        39°8S 174°44E **59** C5
Whanganui □ *N.Z.*         39°17S 174°53E **59** C5
Whangarei *N.Z.*           35°43S 174°21E **59** A5
Whangarei Harb. *N.Z.*     35°45S 174°28E **59** A5
Wharekauri = Chatham Is.
  *Pac. Oc.*               44°0S 176°40W **64** M10
Wharfe → *U.K.*            53°51N 1°9W **12** D6
Wharfedale *U.K.*          54°6N 2°1W **12** C5
Wharton *N.J., U.S.A.*     40°54N 74°35W **83** F10
Wharton *Pa., U.S.A.*      41°31N 78°1W **82** E6
Wharton *Tex., U.S.A.*     29°19N 96°6W **84** G6
Wharton Basin *Ind. Oc.*   20°0S 102°0E **64** K1
Wheatland *Calif., U.S.A.* 39°1N 121°25W **78** F5
Wheatland *Wyo., U.S.A.*   42°3N 104°58W **76** E11
Wheatley *Canada*          42°6N 82°27W **82** D2
Wheaton *Md., U.S.A.*      39°3N 77°3W **81** F15
Wheaton *Minn., U.S.A.*    45°48N 96°30W **80** C5
Wheelbarrow Pk.
  *U.S.A.*                 37°26N 116°5W **78** H10
Wheeler *Oreg., U.S.A.*    45°41N 123°53W **76** D2
Wheeler *Tex., U.S.A.*     35°27N 100°16W **84** D4
Wheeler → *Canada*         57°2N 67°13W **73** A6
Wheeler L. *U.S.A.*        34°48N 87°23W **85** D11

Wheeler Pk. *N. Mex.,
  U.S.A.*                  36°34N 105°25W **77** H11
Wheeler Pk. *Nev.,
  U.S.A.*                  38°57N 114°15W **76** G6
Wheeler Ridge *U.S.A.*     35°0N 118°57W **79** L8
Wheelersburg *U.S.A.*      38°44N 82°51W **81** F12
Wheeling *U.S.A.*          40°4N 80°43W **82** F4
Whernside *U.K.*           54°14N 2°24W **12** C5
Whiddy I. *Ireland*        51°41N 9°31W **10** E2
Whim Creek *Australia*     20°50S 117°49E **60** D2
Whiskey Jack L. *Canada*   58°23N 101°55W **71** B8
Whiskeytown-Shasta-Trinity △
  *U.S.A.*                 40°45N 122°15W **76** F2
Whistleduck Cr. →
  *Australia*              20°15S 135°18E **62** C2
Whistler *Canada*          50°7N 122°58W **70** C4
Whitby *Canada*            43°52N 78°56W **82** C6
Whitby *U.K.*              54°29N 0°37W **12** C7
White → *Ark., U.S.A.*     33°57N 91°5W **84** E9
White → *Ind., U.S.A.*     38°25N 87°45W **80** F10
White → *S. Dak., U.S.A.*  43°42N 99°27W **80** D4
White → *Tex., U.S.A.*     33°14N 100°56W **84** E4
White → *Utah, U.S.A.*     40°4N 109°41W **76** F9
White → *Vt., U.S.A.*      43°37N 72°20W **83** C12
White → *Wash., U.S.A.*    47°12N 122°15W **78** C4
White, L. *Australia*      21°9S 128°56E **60** D4
White B. *Canada*          50°0N 56°35W **73** C8
White Bird *U.S.A.*        45°46N 116°18W **76** D5
White Butte *U.S.A.*       46°23N 103°18W **80** B2
White City *U.S.A.*        42°26N 122°51W **76** E2
White Cliffs *Australia*   30°50S 143°10E **63** E3
White Hall *U.S.A.*        39°26N 90°24W **80** F8
White Haven *U.S.A.*       41°4N 75°47W **83** E9
White Horse, Vale of *U.K.* 51°37N 1°30W **13** F6
White I. = Whakaari
  *N.Z.*                   37°30S 177°13E **59** B6
White L. *Canada*          45°18N 76°31W **83** A8
White L. *U.S.A.*          29°44N 92°30W **84** G8
White Lake *Canada*        45°21N 76°29W **83** A8
White Mountain Peak
  *U.S.A.*                 37°38N 118°15W **78** H8
White Mts. *Calif., U.S.A.* 37°30N 118°15W **78** H8
White Mts. *N.H., U.S.A.*  44°15N 71°15W **83** B13
White Mts. △ *Australia*   20°43S 145°12E **62** C4
White Nile = Nil el Abyad →
  *Sudan*                  15°38N 32°31E **53** E12
White Otter L. *Canada*    49°5N 91°55W **72** C1
White Pass *U.S.A.*        46°38N 121°24W **78** D5
White Plains *U.S.A.*      41°2N 73°46W **83** E11
White River *Canada*       48°35N 85°20W **72** C2
White River *U.S.A.*       43°34N 100°45W **80** D3
White Rock *Canada*        49°2N 122°48W **78** A4
White Rock *U.S.A.*        35°50N 106°12W **77** J10
White Rocks Nat. Recr. Area △
  *U.S.A.*                 43°22N 72°55W **83** C12
White Russia = Belarus ■
  *Europe*                 53°30N 27°0E **17** B14
White Sands △ *U.S.A.*     32°46N 106°20W **77** K10
White Sea = Beloye More
  *Russia*                 66°30N 38°0E **18** A6
White Sulphur Springs *Mont.,
  U.S.A.*                  46°33N 110°54W **76** C8
White Sulphur Springs *W. Va.,
  U.S.A.*                  37°48N 80°18W **81** G13
White Swan *U.S.A.*        46°23N 120°44W **78** D6
Whitecliffs *N.Z.*         43°26S 171°55E **59** E3
Whitecourt *Canada*        54°10N 115°45W **70** C5
Whiteface Mt. *U.S.A.*     44°22N 73°54W **83** B11
Whitefield *U.S.A.*        44°23N 71°37W **83** B13
Whitefish *U.S.A.*         48°25N 114°20W **76** B6
Whitefish B. *U.S.A.*      46°40N 84°55W **72** C3
Whitefish L. *Canada*      62°41N 106°48W **71** A7
Whitefish Pt. *U.S.A.*     46°45N 84°59W **81** B11
Whitegull, L. = Goélands, L. aux
  *Canada*                 55°27N 64°17W **73** A7
Whitehall *Mich., U.S.A.*  43°24N 86°21W **80** D10
Whitehall *Mont., U.S.A.*  45°52N 112°6W **76** D7
Whitehall *N.Y., U.S.A.*   43°33N 73°24W **83** C11
Whitehall *Wis., U.S.A.*   44°22N 91°19W **80** C8
Whitehaven *U.K.*          54°33N 3°35W **12** C4
Whitehorse *Canada*        60°43N 135°3W **70** A1
Whitemark *Australia*      40°7S 148°3E **63** G4
Whiteriver *U.S.A.*        33°50N 109°58W **77** K9
Whitesand → *Canada*       60°9N 115°45W **70** A5
Whitesands *S. Africa*     34°23S 20°50E **56** D3
Whitesboro *N.Y., U.S.A.*  43°7N 75°18W **83** C9
Whitesboro *Tex., U.S.A.*  33°39N 96°54W **84** E6
Whiteshell △ *Canada*      50°0N 95°40W **71** D9
Whiteville *U.S.A.*        34°20N 78°42W **85** D15
Whitewater *U.S.A.*        42°50N 88°44W **80** D9
Whitewater Baldy
  *U.S.A.*                 33°20N 108°39W **77** K9
Whitewater L. *Canada*     50°50N 89°10W **72** B2
Whitewood *Australia*      21°28S 143°30E **62** C3
Whitewood *Canada*         50°20N 102°20W **71** C8
Whithorn *U.K.*            54°44N 4°26W **11** G4
Whitianga *N.Z.*           36°47S 175°41E **59** B5
Whitman *U.S.A.*           42°5N 70°56W **83** D14
Whitney *Canada*           45°31N 78°14W **82** A6
Whitney, Mt. *U.S.A.*      36°35N 118°18W **78** J8
Whitney Point *U.S.A.*     42°20N 75°58W **83** D9
Whitstable *U.K.*          51°21N 1°3E **13** F9
Whitsunday I. *Australia*  20°15S 149°4E **62** b
Whitsunday Islands △
  *Australia*              20°15S 149°0E **62** b
Whittier *U.S.A.*          60°47N 148°41W **74** C10
Whittlesea *Australia*     37°27S 145°9E **63** F4
Wholdaia L. *Canada*       60°43N 104°20W **71** A8
Whyalla *Australia*        33°2S 137°30E **63** E2
Wiang Kosai △ *Thailand*   17°54N 99°29E **38** D2
Wiang Sa *Thailand*        18°34N 100°45E **38** C3
Wiarton *Canada*           44°40N 81°10W **82** B3
Wibaux *U.S.A.*            46°59N 104°11W **76** C11
Wichian Buri *Thailand*    15°39N 101°7E **38** E3
Wichita *U.S.A.*           37°42N 97°20W **80** G5
Wichita Falls *U.S.A.*     33°54N 98°30W **84** E5
Wick *U.K.*                58°26N 3°5W **11** C5
Wickenburg *U.S.A.*        33°58N 112°44W **77** K7

Wickepin Australia 32°50S 117°30E 61 F2
Wickham Australia 20°42S 117°11E 60 D2
Wickham, C. Australia 39°35S 143°57E 63 F3
Wickliffe U.S.A. 41°36N 81°28W 82 E3
Wicklow Ireland 52°59N 6°3W 10 D5
Wicklow ☐ Ireland 52°57N 6°25W 10 D5
Wicklow Hd. Ireland 52°58N 6°0W 10 D6
Wicklow Mts. Ireland 52°58N 6°26W 10 C5
Wicklow Mts. △ Ireland 53°6N 6°21W 10 C5
Widgeegoara Cr. ⇢
  Australia 28°51S 146°34E 63 D4
Widgiemooltha Australia 31°30S 121°34E 61 F3
Widnes U.K. 53°23N 2°45W 12 D5
Wieluń Poland 51°15N 18°34E 17 C10
Wiener Neustadt Austria 47°49N 16°16E 16 E9
Wiesbaden Germany 50°4N 8°14E 16 C5
Wigan U.K. 53°33N 2°38W 12 D5
Wiggins Colo., U.S.A. 40°14N 104°4W 76 F11
Wiggins Miss., U.S.A. 30°51N 89°8W 85 F10
Wight, I. of U.K. 50°41N 1°17W 13 G6
Wigston U.K. 52°35N 1°6W 13 E6
Wigton U.K. 54°50N 3°10W 12 C4
Wigtown U.K. 54°53N 4°27W 11 G4
Wigtown B. U.K. 54°46N 4°15W 11 G4
Wik and Wikway People ♦
  Australia 13°55S 142°28E 62 A3
Wilber U.S.A. 40°29N 96°58W 80 E5
Wilberforce Canada 45°2N 78°13W 82 A6
Wilberforce, C. Australia 11°54S 136°35E 62 A2
Wilburton U.S.A. 34°55N 95°19W 84 D7
Wilcannia Australia 31°30S 143°26E 63 E3
Wilcox U.S.A. 41°35N 78°41W 82 E6
Wildomar U.S.A. 33°36N 117°16W 79 M9
Wildrose U.S.A. 36°14N 117°11W 79 J9
Wildspitze Austria 46°53N 10°53E 16 E6
Wilge ⇢ S. Africa 27°3S 28°20E 57 C4
Wilhelm II Coast Antarctica 68°0S 90°0E 5 C7
Wilhelmshaven Germany 53°31N 8°7E 16 B5
Wilhelmstal Namibia 21°58S 16°21E 56 B2
Wilis Indonesia 7°51S 111°48E 37 G15
Wilkes-Barre U.S.A. 41°15N 75°53W 83 E9
Wilkes Land Antarctica 69°0S 120°0E 5 D9
Wilkie Canada 52°27N 108°42W 71 C7
Wilkins Ice Shelf
  Antarctica 70°30S 72°0W 5 C17
Wilkinsburg U.S.A. 40°26N 79°52W 82 F5
Wilkinson Lakes
  Australia 29°40S 132°39E 61 E5
Willandra Creek ⇢
  Australia 33°22S 145°52E 63 E4
Willapa B. U.S.A. 46°40N 124°0W 78 D3
Willapa Hills U.S.A. 46°35N 123°25W 78 D3
Willard U.S.A. 41°3N 82°44W 82 E2
Willare Bridge Roadhouse
  Australia 17°43S 123°38E 60 C3
Willcox U.S.A. 32°15N 109°50W 77 K9
Willemstad Curaçao 12°5N 68°55W 89 D6
William ⇢ Canada 59°8N 109°19W 71 B7
William 'Bill' Dannelly Res.
  U.S.A. 32°6N 87°24W 85 E11
William Creek Australia 28°58S 136°22E 63 D2
Williams Australia 33°2S 116°52E 61 F2
Williams Ariz., U.S.A. 35°15N 112°11W 77 J7
Williams Calif., U.S.A. 39°9N 122°9W 78 F4
Williams Harbour
  Canada 52°33N 55°47W 73 B8
Williams Lake Canada 52°10N 122°10W 70 C4
Williamsburg Ky.,
  U.S.A. 36°44N 84°10W 81 G11
Williamsburg Pa., U.S.A. 40°28N 78°12W 82 F6
Williamsburg Va.,
  U.S.A. 37°16N 76°43W 81 G15
Williamson N.Y., U.S.A. 43°14N 77°11W 82 C7
Williamson W. Va.,
  U.S.A. 37°41N 82°17W 81 G12
Williamsport U.S.A. 41°15N 77°1W 82 E7
Williamston U.S.A. 35°51N 77°4W 85 D16
Williamstown Ky.,
  U.S.A. 38°38N 84°34W 81 F11
Williamstown Mass.,
  U.S.A. 42°43N 73°12W 83 D11
Williamstown N.Y.,
  U.S.A. 43°26N 75°53W 83 C9
Willimantic U.S.A. 41°43N 72°13W 83 E12
Willingboro U.S.A. 40°3N 74°54W 81 E16
Williston S. Africa 31°20S 20°53E 56 D3
Williston Fla., U.S.A. 29°23N 82°27W 85 G13
Williston N. Dak., U.S.A. 48°9N 103°37W 80 A2
Williston L. Canada 56°0N 124°0W 70 B4
Willits U.S.A. 39°25N 123°21W 78 G2
Willmar U.S.A. 45°7N 95°3W 80 C6
Willmore Wilderness ◯
  Canada 53°45N 119°30W 70 C5
Willoughby U.S.A. 41°39N 81°24W 82 E3
Willow Bunch Canada 49°20N 105°35W 71 D7
Willow L. Canada 62°10N 119°8W 70 A5
Willow Wall, The China 42°10N 122°0E 33 C12
Willowick U.S.A. 41°38N 81°28W 82 E3
Willowlake ⇢ Canada 62°42N 123°8W 70 A4
Willowmore S. Africa 33°15S 23°30E 56 D3
Willows U.S.A. 39°31N 122°12W 78 F4
Willowvale = Gatyana
  S. Africa 32°16S 28°31E 57 D4
Wills, L. Australia 21°25S 128°51E 60 D4
Wills Cr. ⇢ Australia 22°43S 140°2E 62 C3
Willsboro U.S.A. 44°21N 73°24W 83 B11
Willunga Australia 35°15S 138°30E 63 F2
Wilmington Australia 32°39S 138°7E 63 E2
Wilmington Del., U.S.A. 39°45N 75°33W 81 F16
Wilmington N.C.,
  U.S.A. 34°14N 77°55W 85 D16
Wilmington Ohio,
  U.S.A. 39°27N 83°50W 81 F12
Wilmington Vt., U.S.A. 42°52N 72°52W 83 D12
Wilmslow U.K. 53°19N 2°13W 12 D5
Wilpattu △ Sri Lanka 8°20N 79°50E 45 K4
Wilpena Cr. ⇢ Australia 31°25S 139°29E 63 E2
Wilsall U.S.A. 45°59N 110°38W 76 D8
Wilson N.C., U.S.A. 35°44N 77°55W 85 D16
Wilson N.Y., U.S.A. 43°19N 78°50W 82 C6
Wilson Pa., U.S.A. 40°41N 75°15W 83 F9

Wilson ⇢ Australia 16°48S 128°16E 60 C4
Wilson Bluff Australia 31°41S 129°0E 61 F4
Wilson Inlet Australia 35°0S 117°22E 61 G2
Wilsons Promontory
  Australia 38°59S 146°23E 63 F4
Wilton U.S.A. 47°10N 100°47W 80 B3
Wilton ⇢ Australia 14°45S 134°33E 62 A1
Wiltshire ☐ U.K. 51°18N 1°53W 13 F6
Wiltz Lux. 49°57N 5°55E 15 E5
Wiluna Australia 26°36S 120°14E 61 E3
Wimborne Minster U.K. 50°48N 1°59W 13 G6
Wimmera ⇢ Australia 36°8S 141°56E 63 F3
Winburg S. Africa 28°30S 27°2E 56 C4
Winchendon U.S.A. 42°41N 72°3W 83 D12
Winchester U.K. 51°4N 1°18W 13 F6
Winchester Idaho,
  U.S.A. 46°14N 116°38W 76 C5
Winchester Ind., U.S.A. 40°10N 84°59W 81 E11
Winchester Ky., U.S.A. 37°59N 84°11W 81 G11
Winchester N.H., U.S.A. 42°46N 72°23W 83 D12
Winchester Tenn., U.S.A. 35°11N 86°7W 85 D11
Winchester Va., U.S.A. 39°11N 78°10W 81 F14
Wind ⇢ U.S.A. 43°12N 108°12W 76 E9
Wind Cave △ U.S.A. 43°32N 103°17W 80 D2
Wind River Range
  U.S.A. 43°0N 109°30W 76 E9
Windamere, L. Australia 32°48S 149°51E 63 B4
Windau = Ventspils
  Latvia 57°25N 21°32E 9 H19
Windber U.S.A. 40°14N 78°50W 82 F6
Winder U.S.A. 34°0N 83°45W 85 D13
Windermere U.K. 54°23N 2°55W 12 C5
Windhoek Namibia 22°35S 17°4E 56 B2
Windidda ◯ Australia 26°23S 122°12E 61 E3
Windjana Gorge △
  Australia 17°51S 125°0E 60 C3
Windom U.S.A. 43°52N 95°7W 80 D7
Windorah Australia 25°24S 142°36E 62 D3
Window Rock U.S.A. 35°41N 109°3W 77 J9
Windrush ⇢ U.K. 51°43N 1°24W 13 F6
Windsor Australia 33°37S 150°50E 63 E5
Windsor N.S., Canada 44°59N 64°5W 73 D7
Windsor Ont., Canada 42°18N 83°0W 82 D2
Windsor U.K. 51°29N 0°36W 13 F7
Windsor Calif., U.S.A. 38°33N 122°49W 78 G4
Windsor Colo., U.S.A. 40°29N 104°54W 76 F11
Windsor Conn., U.S.A. 41°50N 72°39W 83 E12
Windsor Mo., U.S.A. 38°32N 93°31W 80 F7
Windsor N.Y., U.S.A. 42°5N 75°37W 83 D9
Windsor & Maidenhead ☐
  U.K. 51°29N 0°40W 13 F7
Windsorton S. Africa 28°16S 24°44E 56 C4
Windward Is. W. Indies 13°0N 61°0W 89 D7
Windward Passage = Vientos,
  Paso de los Caribbean 20°0N 74°0W 89 C5
Winefred L. Canada 55°30N 110°30W 71 B6
Winfield U.S.A. 37°15N 96°59W 80 G5
Wingate Mts. Australia 14°25S 130°40E 60 B5
Wingellina = Irruntyju
  Australia 26°3S 128°56E 61 E4
Wingham Australia 31°48S 152°22E 63 E5
Wingham Canada 43°55N 81°20W 82 C3
Winisk ⇢ Canada 55°17N 85°5W 72 A2
Winisk L. Canada 52°55N 87°22W 72 B2
Wink U.S.A. 31°45N 103°9W 84 F3
Winkler Canada 49°10N 97°56W 71 D9
Winlock U.S.A. 46°30N 122°56W 78 D4
Winneba Ghana 5°25N 0°36W 52 G5
Winnebago, L. U.S.A. 44°0N 88°26W 80 D9
Winnecke Cr. ⇢
  Australia 18°35S 131°34E 60 C5
Winnemucca U.S.A. 40°58N 117°44W 76 F5
Winnemucca L. U.S.A. 40°7N 119°21W 76 F4
Winner U.S.A. 43°22N 99°52W 80 D4
Winnett U.S.A. 47°0N 108°21W 76 C9
Winfield U.S.A. 31°56N 92°38W 84 F8
Winnibigoshish, L.
  U.S.A. 47°27N 94°13W 80 B7
Winnipeg Canada 49°54N 97°9W 71 D9
Winnipeg ⇢ Canada 50°38N 96°19W 71 C9
Winnipeg, L. Canada 52°0N 97°0W 71 C9
Winnipeg Beach Canada 50°30N 96°58W 71 C9
Winnipegosis Canada 51°39N 99°55W 71 C9
Winnipegosis L. Canada 52°30N 100°0W 71 C9
Winnipesaukee, L.
  U.S.A. 43°38N 71°21W 83 C13
Winnisquam L. U.S.A. 43°33N 71°31W 83 C13
Winnsboro La., U.S.A. 32°10N 91°43W 84 E9
Winnsboro S.C., U.S.A. 34°23N 81°5W 85 D14
Winnsboro Tex., U.S.A. 32°58N 95°17W 84 E7
Winokapau, L. Canada 53°15N 62°50W 73 B7
Winona Minn., U.S.A. 44°3N 91°39W 80 C8
Winona Miss., U.S.A. 33°29N 89°44W 85 E10
Winooski U.S.A. 44°29N 73°11W 83 B11
Winooski ⇢ U.S.A. 44°32N 73°17W 83 B11
Winschoten Neths. 53°9N 7°3E 15 A7
Winsford U.K. 53°12N 2°31W 12 D5
Winslow = Bainbridge Island
  U.S.A. 38°31N 122°32W 78 C4
Winslow U.S.A. 35°2N 110°42W 77 J8
Winsted U.S.A. 41°55N 73°4W 83 E11
Winston-Salem U.S.A. 36°6N 80°15W 85 C14
Winter Garden U.S.A. 28°34N 81°35W 85 G14
Winter Haven U.S.A. 28°1N 81°44W 85 G14
Winter Park U.S.A. 28°36N 81°20W 85 G14
Winterhaven U.S.A. 32°44N 114°38W 79 N12
Winters U.S.A. 38°32N 121°58W 78 G5
Winterset U.S.A. 41°20N 94°1W 80 E6
Wintersville U.S.A. 40°23N 80°42W 82 F4
Winterswijk Neths. 51°58N 6°43E 15 C6
Winterthur Switz. 47°30N 8°44E 20 C8
Winthrop U.S.A. 48°28N 120°10W 76 B3
Winton Australia 22°24S 143°3E 62 C3
Winton N.Z. 46°8S 168°20E 59 G2
Wirlyajarrayi ◯
  Australia 21°45S 132°35E 60 D5
Wirrulla Australia 32°24S 134°31E 63 E1
Wisbech U.K. 52°41N 0°9E 13 E8
Wisconsin ☐ U.S.A. 44°45N 89°30W 80 C9

Wisconsin ⇢ U.S.A. 43°0N 91°15W 80 D8
Wisconsin Rapids U.S.A. 44°23N 89°49W 80 C9
Wisdom U.S.A. 45°37N 113°27W 76 D7
Wiseman U.S.A. 67°25N 150°6W 74 B9
Wishaw U.K. 55°46N 3°54W 11 F5
Wishek U.S.A. 46°16N 99°33W 80 B4
Wisła ⇢ Poland 54°22N 18°55E 17 A10
Wislany, Zalew Poland 54°20N 19°50E 17 A10
Wismar Germany 53°54N 11°29E 16 B6
Wisner U.S.A. 41°59N 96°55W 80 E5
Witbank = eMalahleni
  S. Africa 25°51S 29°14E 57 C4
Witches Gorge = Wu Xia
  China 31°2N 110°10E 35 B8
Witdraai S. Africa 26°58S 20°48E 56 C3
Witham U.K. 51°48N 0°40E 13 F8
Witham ⇢ U.K. 52°59N 0°2W 12 E7
Withernsea U.K. 53°44N 0°1E 12 D8
Witjira △ Australia 26°22S 135°37E 63 D2
Witless Bay Canada 47°17N 52°50W 73 C9
Witney U.K. 51°48N 1°28W 13 F6
Witnossob ⇢ Namibia 23°55S 18°45E 56 C3
Witriver S. Africa 25°20S 31°0E 57 C5
Wittenberge Germany 53°0N 11°45E 16 B6
Wittenoom Australia 22°15S 118°20E 60 D2
Witvlei Namibia 22°23S 18°32E 56 B2
Wiwon N. Korea 40°54N 126°3E 33 D14
Wkra ⇢ Poland 52°27N 20°44E 17 B11
Wlingi Indonesia 8°5S 112°25E 37 H15
Włocławek Poland 52°40N 19°3E 17 B10
Włodawa Poland 51°33N 23°31E 17 C12
Wodian China 32°50N 112°35E 32 H7
Wodonga Australia 36°5S 146°50E 63 F4
Woinbogoin China 32°51N 98°39E 34 A2
Wokam Indonesia 5°45S 134°28E 37 F8
Woking U.K. 51°19N 0°34W 13 F7
Wokingham U.K. 51°24N 0°49W 13 F7
Wokingham ☐ U.K. 51°25N 0°51W 13 F7
Wolf ⇢ Canada 60°17N 132°33W 70 A2
Wolf Creek U.S.A. 47°0N 112°4W 76 C7
Wolf L. Canada 60°24N 131°40W 70 A2
Wolf Point U.S.A. 48°5N 105°39W 76 B11
Wolfe Creek Crater △
  Australia 19°10S 127°47E 60 C4
Wolfe I. Canada 44°7N 76°20W 83 B8
Wolfeboro U.S.A. 43°35N 71°13W 83 C13
Wolfsberg Austria 46°50N 14°52E 16 E8
Wolfsburg Germany 52°25N 10°48E 16 B6
Wolin Poland 53°50N 14°37E 16 B8
Wollaston, Is. Chile 55°40S 67°30W 96 H3
Wollaston L. Canada 58°7N 103°10W 71 B8
Wollaston Lake Canada 58°3N 103°33W 71 B8
Wollaston Pen. Canada 69°30N 115°0W 68 D7
Wollongong Australia 34°25S 150°54E 63 E5
Wolmaransstad S. Africa 27°12S 25°59E 56 C4
Wolseley S. Africa 33°26S 19°7E 56 D2
Wolsey U.S.A. 44°25N 98°28W 80 C4
Wolstenholme, C.
  Canada 62°35N 77°30W 66 C12
Wolvega Neths. 52°52N 6°0E 15 B6
Wolverhampton U.K. 52°35N 2°7W 13 E5
Wondai Australia 26°20S 151°49E 63 D5
Wongalarroo L. Australia 31°32S 144°0E 63 E3
Wongan Hills Australia 30°51S 116°37E 61 F2
Wonju S. Korea 37°22N 127°58E 33 F14
Wonosari Indonesia 7°58S 110°38E 37 G14
Wonosobo Indonesia 7°22S 109°54E 37 G13
Wonowon Canada 56°44N 121°48W 70 B4
Wonsan N. Korea 39°11N 127°27E 33 E14
Wonthaggi Australia 38°37S 145°37E 63 F4
Wood Buffalo △ Canada 59°0N 113°41W 70 B6
Wood Is. Australia 16°24S 123°19E 60 C3
Wood L. Canada 55°17N 103°17W 71 B8
Woodah, I. Australia 13°27S 136°10E 62 A2
Woodbourne U.S.A. 41°46N 74°36W 83 E10
Woodbridge U.K. 52°6N 1°20E 13 E9
Woodburn Australia 29°6S 153°23E 63 D5
Woodburn U.S.A. 45°9N 122°51W 76 D2
Woodenbong Australia 28°24S 152°39E 63 D5
Woodend Australia 37°20S 144°33E 63 F3
Woodford Australia 26°58S 152°47E 63 D5
Woodfords U.S.A. 38°47N 119°50W 78 G7
Woodlake U.S.A. 36°25N 119°6W 78 J7
Woodland Calif., U.S.A. 38°41N 121°46W 78 G5
Woodland Maine, U.S.A. 45°9N 67°25W 81 C20
Woodland Pa., U.S.A. 41°0N 78°21W 82 F6
Woodland Wash., U.S.A. 45°54N 122°45W 78 E4
Woodland Caribou △
  Canada 51°0N 94°45W 71 C10
Woodlands, The U.S.A. 30°9N 95°29W 84 F7
Woodonga Australia 36°10S 146°50E 63 F4
Woodridge Canada 49°20N 96°9W 71 D9
Woodroffe, Mt. Australia 26°58S 131°49E 61 E5
Woods, L. Australia 17°50S 133°30E 62 B1
Woods, L. of the
  N. Amer. 49°15N 94°45W 71 D10
Woods Bay Canada 45°8N 79°59W 82 A5
Woodstock Australia 19°35S 146°50E 62 B4
Woodstock N.B., Canada 46°11N 67°37W 73 C6
Woodstock Ont., Canada 43°10N 80°45W 82 C4
Woodstock U.K. 51°51N 1°20W 13 F6
Woodstock Ill., U.S.A. 42°19N 88°27W 80 D9
Woodstock N.Y., U.S.A. 42°2N 74°7W 83 D10
Woodstock Vt., U.S.A. 43°37N 72°31W 83 C12
Woodsville U.S.A. 44°9N 72°2W 83 B13
Woodville N.Z. 40°20S 175°53E 59 D5
Woodville Miss., U.S.A. 31°6N 91°18W 84 F9
Woodville Tex., U.S.A. 30°47N 94°25W 84 F7
Woodward U.S.A. 36°26N 99°24W 84 C5
Woody U.S.A. 35°42N 118°50W 79 K8
Woody I. S. China Sea 16°50N 112°20E 36 A4
Woolacombe U.K. 51°10N 4°13W 13 F3
Woolamai, C. Australia 38°30S 145°23E 63 F4
Wooler U.K. 55°33N 2°1W 12 B5
Woolgoolga Australia 30°6S 153°11E 63 E5
Woomera Australia 31°5S 136°50E 63 E2
Woonsocket R.I., U.S.A. 42°0N 71°31W 83 E13
Woonsocket S. Dak.,
  U.S.A. 44°3N 98°17W 80 C4

Wooramel ⇢ Australia 25°47S 114°10E 61 E1
Wooramel Roadhouse
  Australia 25°45S 114°17E 61 E1
Wooroonooran △
  Australia 16°25S 146°1E 62 B4
Wooster U.S.A. 40°48N 81°56W 82 F3
Worcester S. Africa 33°39S 19°27E 56 D2
Worcester U.K. 52°11N 2°12W 13 E5
Worcester Mass., U.S.A. 42°16N 71°48W 83 D13
Worcester N.Y., U.S.A. 42°36N 74°45W 83 D10
Worcestershire ☐ U.K. 52°13N 2°10W 13 E5
Workington U.K. 54°39N 3°33W 12 C4
Worksop U.K. 53°18N 1°7W 12 D6
Workum Neths. 52°59N 5°26E 15 B5
Worland U.S.A. 44°1N 107°57W 76 D10
Worms Germany 49°37N 8°21E 16 D5
Worsley Canada 56°31N 119°8W 70 B5
Wortham U.S.A. 31°47N 96°28W 84 F6
Worthing Barbados 13°5N 59°35W 89 g
Worthing U.K. 50°49N 0°21W 13 G7
Worthington Minn.,
  U.S.A. 43°37N 95°36W 80 D6
Worthington Pa., U.S.A. 40°50N 79°38W 82 F5
Wosi Indonesia 0°15S 128°0E 37 E7
Wotjalum ◯ Australia 16°30S 123°45E 60 C3
Wotjobaluk ◯ Australia 37°0S 142°0E 63 C3
Wou-han = Wuhan
  China 30°31N 114°18E 35 B10
Wousi = Wuxi China 31°33N 120°18E 35 B13
Wowoni Indonesia 4°5S 123°5E 37 E6
Wrangel I. = Vrangelya, Ostrov
  Russia 71°0N 180°0E 27 B18
Wrangell U.S.A. 56°28N 132°23W 70 B2
Wrangell Mts. U.S.A. 61°30N 142°0W 68 E3
Wrath, C. U.K. 58°38N 5°1W 11 C3
Wray U.S.A. 40°5N 102°13W 76 F12
Wrekin, The U.K. 52°41N 2°32W 13 E5
Wrens U.S.A. 33°12N 82°23W 85 E13
Wrexham U.K. 53°3N 3°0W 12 D4
Wrexham ☐ U.K. 53°1N 2°58W 12 D5
Wright Fla., U.S.A. 30°27N 86°38W 85 F11
Wright Wyo., U.S.A. 43°45N 105°28W 76 E11
Wright Pt. Canada 43°48N 81°44W 82 C3
Wrightmyo India 11°47N 92°43E 45 J11
Wrightson, Mt. U.S.A. 31°42N 110°51W 77 L8
Wrightwood U.S.A. 34°22N 117°38W 79 L9
Wrigley Canada 63°16N 123°37W 68 E7
Wrocław Poland 51°5N 17°5E 17 C9
Września Poland 52°21N 17°36E 17 B9
Wu Jiang ⇢ China 29°40N 107°20E 34 C6
Wu Kau Tang China 22°30N 114°14E 31 a
Wu Xia China 31°2N 110°10E 35 B8
Wu'an China 36°40N 114°15E 32 F8
Wubalawun ◯ Australia 15°28S 133°1E 60 B5
Wubin Australia 30°6S 116°37E 61 F2
Wubu China 37°28N 110°42E 32 F6
Wuchang China 44°55N 127°5E 33 B14
Wucheng China 37°12N 116°20E 32 F9
Wuchuan Guangdong,
  China 21°33N 110°43E 35 G8
Wuchuan Guizhou, China 28°25N 108°3E 34 C7
Wuchuan Nei Monggol Zizhiqu,
  China 41°5N 111°28E 32 D6
Wuda China 39°29N 106°42E 32 E4
Wudang Shan China 32°23N 111°2E 35 A8
Wudi China 37°40N 117°35E 33 F9
Wuding China 25°24N 102°12E 34 E4
Wuding He ⇢ China 37°2N 110°23E 32 F6
Wudinna Australia 33°0S 135°22E 63 E2
Wudongde Dam China 26°20N 102°15E 34 D4
Wudu China 33°22N 104°54E 32 H3
Wufeng China 30°12N 110°42E 35 B8
Wugang China 26°44N 110°35E 35 D8
Wugong Shan China 27°30N 114°0E 35 D10
Wuguishan China 22°25N 113°25E 31 a
Wugullar = Beswick
  Australia 14°34S 132°53E 60 B5
Wuhai China 39°39N 106°48E 32 E4
Wuhan China 30°31N 114°18E 35 B10
Wuhe China 33°10N 117°50E 35 H9
Wuhsi = Wuxi China 31°33N 120°18E 35 B13
Wuhu China 31°22N 118°21E 35 B12
Wujiang China 31°10N 120°38E 35 B13
Wukari Nigeria 7°51N 9°42E 52 G7
Wulajie China 44°6N 126°33E 33 B14
Wulanbulang China 41°5N 110°55E 32 D6
Wular L. India 34°20N 74°30E 43 B6
Wulian China 35°40N 119°12E 33 G10
Wulian Feng China 27°48N 103°36E 34 D4
Wuliang Shan China 24°30N 100°40E 34 E3
Wuliaru Indonesia 7°27S 131°0E 37 F8
Wuling Shan China 30°0N 110°0E 34 C7
Wulingyuan △ China 29°20N 110°30E 35 C8
Wulong China 29°22N 107°43E 34 C6
Wulong ⇢ China 31°8N 103°5E 34 B4
Wulumuchi = Ürümqi
  China 43°45N 87°45E 30 C6
Wumeng Shan China 26°48N 104°0E 34 D5
Wuming China 23°12N 108°18E 34 F7
Wuning China 29°17N 115°5E 35 C10
Wunna ⇢ India 20°18N 78°48E 44 D4
Wunnummin L. Canada 52°55N 89°10W 72 B2
Wuntho Myanmar 23°55N 95°45E 41 H19
Wupatki △ U.S.A. 35°35N 111°20W 77 J8
Wuping China 25°5N 116°5E 35 E11
Wuppertal Germany 51°16N 7°12E 16 C4
Wuppertal S. Africa 32°13S 19°12E 56 D2
Wuqing China 39°23N 117°4E 33 E9
Wurralibi ◯ Australia 15°43S 137°1E 62 B2
Wurtsboro U.S.A. 41°35N 74°29W 83 E10
Würzburg Germany 49°46N 9°55E 16 D5
Wushan China 34°43N 104°53E 32 G3
Wushi China 41°9N 79°13E 30 C4
Wutai China 38°40N 113°12E 32 E8
Wutai Shan China 39°3N 113°32E 32 E7
Wuting = Huimin China 37°27N 117°28E 33 F9
Wutong China 25°24N 110°4E 35 E8
Wutonghaolai China 42°50N 120°5E 33 C11
Wutongqiao China 29°22N 103°50E 34 C4
Wuwei Anhui, China 31°18N 117°54E 35 B11
Wuwei Gansu, China 37°57N 102°34E 30 D9

Wuxi Jiangsu, China 31°33N 120°18E 35 B13
Wuxi Sichuan, China 31°23N 109°35E 34 B7
Wuxiang China 36°49N 112°50E 32 F7
Wuxuan China 23°34N 109°38E 34 F7
Wuxue China 29°52N 115°33E 35 C10
Wuyang China 33°25N 113°35E 32 H7
Wuyi Hebei, China 37°46N 115°56E 32 F8
Wuyi Zhejiang, China 28°52N 119°50E 35 C12
Wuyi Shan China 27°0N 117°0E 35 D11
Wuyishan China 27°45N 118°0E 35 D12
Wuyishan △ China 27°55N 117°54E 35 D11
Wuyuan Jiangxi, China 29°15N 117°50E 35 C11
Wuyuan Nei Monggol Zizhiqu,
  China 41°2N 108°20E 32 D5
Wuzhai China 38°54N 111°48E 32 E6
Wuzhi Shan China 18°45N 109°30E 38 C7
Wuzhishan = Tongshi
  China 18°50N 109°20E 38 C7
Wuzhong China 38°2N 106°12E 32 E4
Wuzhou China 23°30N 111°18E 35 F8
Wyaaba Cr. ⇢ Australia 16°27S 141°35E 62 B3
Wyalkatchem Australia 31°8S 117°22E 61 F2
Wyalusing U.S.A. 41°40N 76°16W 83 E8
Wyandotte U.S.A. 42°12N 83°9W 81 D12
Wyandra Australia 27°12S 145°56E 63 D4
Wyangala, L. Australia 33°54S 149°0E 63 E4
Wyara, L. Australia 28°42S 144°14E 63 D3
Wycheproof Australia 36°5S 143°17E 63 F3
Wycliffe Well Australia 20°48S 134°14E 62 C1
Wye ⇢ U.K. 51°38N 2°40W 13 F5
Wyemandoo Australia 28°28S 118°29E 61 E2
Wymondham U.K. 52°35N 1°7E 13 E9
Wymore U.S.A. 40°7N 96°40W 80 E6
Wyndham Australia 15°33S 128°3E 60 C4
Wyndham N.Z. 46°20S 168°51E 59 G2
Wynne U.S.A. 35°14N 90°47W 85 D9
Wynyard Australia 41°5S 145°44E 63 G4
Wynyard Canada 51°45N 104°10W 71 C8
Wyola L. Australia 29°8S 130°17E 61 E5
Wyoming Canada 42°57N 82°7W 82 D2
Wyoming ☐ U.S.A. 43°0N 107°30W 76 E10
Wyomissing U.S.A. 40°20N 75°59W 83 F9
Wyong Australia 33°14S 151°24E 63 E5
Wytheville U.S.A. 36°57N 81°5W 81 G13

## X

Xaafuun Somalia 10°25N 51°16E 49 E5
Xaafuun, Ras Somalia 10°27N 51°24E 49 E5
Xaçmaz Azerbaijan 41°31N 48°42E 19 F8
Xai-Xai Mozam. 25°6S 33°31E 57 C5
Xaignabouri = Sayaboury
  Laos 19°15N 101°45E 38 C3
Xainza China 30°58N 88°35E 30 E6
Xalapa Mexico 19°32N 96°55W 87 D5
Xangongo Angola 16°45S 15°5E 56 B2
Xankändi Azerbaijan 39°52N 46°49E 46 B5
Xanthi Greece 41°10N 24°58E 23 D11
Xanxerê Brazil 26°53S 52°23W 95 B5
Xapuri Brazil 10°35S 68°35W 92 F5
Xar Moron He ⇢
  China 43°25N 120°35E 33 C11
Xátiva Spain 38°59N 0°32W 21 C5
Xau, L. Botswana 21°15S 24°44E 56 B3
Xavantina Brazil 21°15S 52°48W 95 A5
Xebert China 44°2N 122°0E 33 B12
Xenia U.S.A. 39°41N 83°56W 81 F12
Xhora S. Africa 31°55S 28°38E 57 D4
Xhumo Botswana 21°7S 24°35E 56 B3
Xi Jiang ⇢ China 22°5N 113°20E 35 F9
Xi Ujimqin Qi China 44°32N 117°40E 33 B9
Xi Xian Henan, China 32°20N 114°43E 35 A10
Xi Xian Shanxi, China 36°41N 110°58E 32 F6
Xia Xian China 35°8N 111°12E 32 G6
Xiachengzi China 44°40N 130°18E 33 B16
Xiaguan China 25°32N 100°16E 30 F9
Xiajiang China 27°30N 115°10E 35 D10
Xiajin China 36°56N 116°0E 32 F9
Xiamen China 24°25N 118°4E 35 E12
Xi'an China 34°15N 109°0E 32 G5
Xian Xian China 38°12N 116°6E 32 E9
Xian Xianyang Int. ✈ (XIY)
  China 34°27N 108°45E 32 G5
Xianfeng China 29°40N 109°8E 34 C7
Xiang Jiang ⇢ China 28°55N 112°50E 35 C9
Xiang Khouang Laos 19°17N 103°25E 38 C4
Xiangcheng Henan,
  China 33°50N 113°27E 32 H7
Xiangcheng Sichuan,
  China 28°53N 99°47E 34 C2
Xiangdu China 23°13N 106°58E 34 F6
Xiangfan China 32°2N 112°8E 35 A9
Xianggang = Hong Kong ☐
  China 22°11N 114°14E 31 a
Xianghuang Qi China 42°2N 113°50E 32 C7
Xiangjiaba Dam China 28°37N 104°17E 34 C5
Xiangning China 35°58N 110°50E 32 G6
Xiangquan China 36°30N 113°1E 32 F7
Xiangquan He = Sutlej ⇢
  Pakistan 29°23N 71°3E 42 E4
Xiangshan China 29°29N 121°51E 35 C13
Xiangshui China 34°12N 119°33E 33 G10
Xiangtan China 27°51N 112°54E 35 D9
Xiangxiang China 27°43N 112°28E 35 D9
Xiangyin China 28°38N 112°54E 35 C9
Xiangyun China 25°34N 100°35E 34 E3
Xiangzhou China 23°58N 109°40E 34 F7
Xianju China 28°51N 120°44E 35 C13
Xianning China 29°51N 114°16E 35 C10
Xianshui He ⇢ China 30°10N 100°59E 34 B3
Xiantao China 30°25N 113°25E 35 B9
Xianyang China 34°20N 108°40E 32 G5
Xianyou China 25°22N 118°38E 35 E12
Xiao Hinggan Ling China 49°0N 127°0E 31 B14
Xiao Xian China 34°15N 116°55E 32 G9
Xiaofeng China 30°35N 119°32E 35 B12
Xiaogan China 30°52N 113°55E 35 B9
Xiaojin China 31°0N 102°21E 34 B4
Xiaolan China 22°38N 113°13E 35 F9
Xiaoshan China 30°12N 120°18E 35 B13